The Guide

to

United States

Popular Culture

The Guide
to
United States
Popular Culture

edited by

Ray B. Browne

and

Pat Browne

Bowling Green State University Popular Press
Bowling Green, OH 43403

A
PCA/ACA
ENDOWMENT
SPECIAL IMPRINT
BOOK

Library of Congress Cataloging-in-Publication Data
The guide to United States popular culture / edited by Ray B. Browne and Pat Browne.
    p.   cm.
  Includes bibliographical references and index.
  ISBN 0-87972-821-3
  1. Popular culture--United States--History--20th century--Dictionaries. 2. Popular
culture--United States--Dictionaries. 3. United States--Civilization--20th
century--Dictionaries. 4. United States--Civilizations--Dictionaries. I. Browne, Ray
Broadus. II. Browne, Pat.

E169.1 D399 2000
306'.0973'03--dc21   00-057211

Cover design by Dumm Art

Contents

Advisory Editors

Liahna Babener
Central Washington Univ.

Literature

Peter Rollins
Oklahoma State Univ.

Electronic Media

Kristin Congdon
Univ. of Central Florida

Art, Arts, Comic

Fred Schroeder
Univ. of Minnesota-Duluth (Retired)

Material Culture

Doug Noverr and Larry Ziewacz
Michigan State Univ.

Sports

Ingrid Shafer
Univ. of Science
and Arts of Oklahoma

Heroes, Rituals, Religions,
Outdoor Entertainments

Sub-Editors

Robert Baird
Univ. of Illinois, Champaign–Urbana

Film

Dan Jones
Univ. of Houston/Downtown

Nonfiction Genres

Richard Bartone
Bronx, New York

Television

Doug Noverr
Michigan State Univ.

Sports Literature

Elizabeth Bird
Univ. of South Florida

Tabloids

William Reynolds
Hope College

Mystery & Detective Fiction

William Brigman
Univ. of Houston/Downtown

Erotica/Pornography

Garyn Roberts
Northwestern Michigan College

Western, Science
Fiction, etc.

Frank Chorba
Washburn Univ.

Radio

M. K. Schoenecke
Texas Tech Univ.

Music

Carl D. Esbjornson
Bozeman, Montana

Nature Writing

Elizabeth Trembley
Davenport College

Mystery & Detective Fiction

Bruce Goebel
Univ. of Utah

Children's Literature

Melody Zajdel
Montana State Univ.

Romance

Gary Hoppenstand
Michigan State Univ.

Western, Horror, Gothic, etc.

Contributors

Ed Adams
Daniel P. Agatino
Henry B. Aldridge
Angela Aleiss
Richard J. Allen
Adelaide P. Amore
Barbara Anderson
Janice Walker Anderson
Linda Anderson
Ted Anton
Mary Welek Atwell
Liahna Babener
Don Bacigalupi
Robert Baird
John Baky
Susan J. Bandy
S. K. Bane
Cryder Bankes
Ray Barfield
Lynn Bartholome
Matthew Bashore
Scott Logan Baugh
Peter L. Bayers
Theodore S. Beardsley, Jr.
Sue Bridwell Beckham
Dorothy Behling
Carole Bender
Michael G. Bennett
Marvin R. Bensman
Arthur Asa Berger
Marion Bermondy
Aimee Bernd
Gordon Berry
Deborah Bice
Kenneth G. Bielen
Ted Billy
S. Elizabeth Bird
Thomas A. Birk
Patrick Bjork
Kristine L. Blair
Doug Blandy
Richard Bleiler
Marilyn Lawrence Boemer
William C. Boles
Sue Boonstra
Susan Boot
Rob Bowman
John M. Bozeman
Jerry C. Brigham
William E. Brigman
Douglas Brown

Ray B. Browne
Jeffrey M. Brumley
Margaret Bruzelius
Paul T. Bryant
Harriette C. Buchanan
Charlene E. Bunnell
Justin J. Burke
Ken Burke
Gary Burns
Linda Lattin Burns
Geoffrey S. Cahn
Sheri Carder
Robert L. Carringer
Carole L. Carroll
Charles E. Case
Donna R. Casella
Roger N. Casey
Mary Cassata
Robert Michael Cerello
Rafael Chabrán
Kathleen Chamberlain
Robert Chamberlain
William Chamberlain
Angela E. Chamblee
Jean C. Chance
Lynnea Chapman King
Yong Peng Chen
Stephen Chenault
Brent Chesley
Linda Christian-Smith
Mary Clark-Upchurch
Daryl R. Coats
David Cody
Michael Cohen
Linda Collette
Kristin G. Congdon
Steve Connelly
Charles Conrad
Marguerite Cotto
Brian Cowlishaw
J. Randolph Cox
Jane Cramer
Iain Crawford
Scott A. G. M. Crawford
Don Cusic
Douglass K. Daniel
Sammy R. Danna
Lynn Darroch
Solomon Davidoff
Steven L. Davis
Ellen Day

Ann de Onis
Michael Delahoyde
Mary Jean DeMarr
Corley F. Dennison, III
Cheryl Desforges
Howard A. DeWitt
Mary Dezelski
John Dizer
John J. Doherty
Katherine Doman
Joseph Dorinson
Johanna L. Draper
Kenneth Dvorak
Gary Edgerton
Harry Eiss
Eric Alden Eliason
Allen Ellis
Reuben Ellis
Leonard Engel
Jonathon S. Epstein
Su Epstein
John H. Esperian
Michael Espinosa
Linda F. Ettinger
Kathy Evans
Deborah Fant
Anita Clair Fellman
Jim Ferreira
Frank Ferriano
Lawrence W. Fielding
John E. Findling
Stephen Finley
Craig Fischer
Roger Fischer
L. Fischman
Kathleen Brosnahan Fish
George V. Flannery
Don Florence
Jody L. Flynn
Philip K. Flynn
Hugh Foley
Chris Foran
Susan Allen Ford
Linda Foss
Robert Foulke
Elizabeth Foxwell
June M. Frazer
Thomas B. Frazier
James A. Freeman
John Freeman
Mary P. Freier

William F. Fry
Mark K. Fulk
Daniel J. Fuller
Kathryn H. Fuller
Steven H. Gale
Charles F. Ganzert
Elizabeth Garber
Greg Garrett
W. Anthony Gengarelly
Owen W. Gilman, Jr.
Theresa L. Glavin
Cheryll Glotfelty
Bruce Goebel
Michael Goldberg
Billy Golden
Richard M. Goldstein
Douglas Gomery
Michael W. Gos
Angela Graham
Barry Keith Grant
Joseph Greco
Roberta F. Green
Barbara Gregorich
Larry D. Griffin
John L. Griffith
Kate Grilley
Fred Guida
Larry Gunter
Glenn Gutmacher
William M. Hagen
Maryellen Hains
Drew Philip Halevy
James P. Hanlan
John Hanners
Mary Anne Hansen
Donna Waller Harper
Mark Harrison
Stanley D. Harrison
Denise Hartsough
Susan Harum
Philip J. Harwood
Zia Hasan
Khwaja Moinul Hassan
Alan Havig
Barrie Hayne
John Hayward
Harry Hellenbrand
Cyndy Hendershot
Bruce Henderson
Wayne E. Hensley
Dawn Henwood

Irene Heskes
Linda R. Hill
Michael L. Hilt
Lynn Hinds
John E. Hirsch
John L. Hochheimer
Jack Hodgson
Elizabeth Hoffman
Morris B. Holbrook
Harry Hollenbrand
Teresa Hollingsworth
Peter C. Holloran
Carl Holmberg
Jason Holz
Michael Hoover
Gary Hoppenstand
Jay R. Howard
W. A. Kelly Huff
E. D. Huntley
Katie Hutchinson
Cecil Kirk Hutson
Saundra Hybels
Jana L. Hyde
Allen E. Hye
James F. Iaccino
Barbara J. Irwin
Fred Isaac
Kathy Merlock Jackson
Michael Jackson
Jeanne M. Jacobson
Dean James
Arthur R. Jarvis, Jr.
David K. Jeffrey
Richard Jensen
MaryAnn Johanson
Carla Johnson
Deidre Johnson
Frank W. Johnson, Jr.
Gary Johnson
Phylis Johnson
Robert C. Johnson
Beverly J. Jones
Louise Conley Jones
Myra Hunter Jones
Steve Jones
William M. Jones
Patricia W. Julius
Anne R. Kaler
Martin R. Kalfatovic
Mary C. Kalfatovic
Michael B. Kassel

Peter Katopes
Susan Kattwinkel
B. Kaufman
Richard S. Kaufman
Heather Kavan
Alan Kelly
Ernece B. Kelly
W. P. Kenney
Cynthia S. Kerchmar
Janet Kilbride
John A. Kinch
Margaret J. King
Timothy K. Kinsella
Kathleen Gregory Klein
William R. Klink
Marty S. Knepper
Claire Koegler
Karen Koegler
Paul R. Kohl
Richele Kortering
Joan G. Kotker
John Kramer
Don H. Krug
Yasue Kuwahara
Douglas R. Laird
Kimberly J. Laird
Mary E. Beardsley Land
Jason Landrum
Sydney Langdon
John S. Lawrence
Judith Yaross Lee
Mary Beth Leidman
Cameron Lenahan
John A. Lent
Cristine Levenduski
Fred Lifton
Lori Liggett
Lucy A. Liggett
Steve Lipkin
Jeremy Harris Lipschultz
Steven Liu
Robert H. Lochte
Craig A. Lockard
Deborah Weber Long
Kristi S. Long
Devoney Looser
Delano Lopez
Carolyn Lott
Ramona Lucius
Barbara Lupack
Andrew Macdonald
Gina Macdonald
David MacGregor
Jennifer A. Machiorlatti
Susan P. Madigan

Mark Madrigan
Chris J. Magoc
Bill Mansfield
Eileen Margerum
Scott M. Martin
Elena J. P. Marts
Robert Mastrangelo
John Matviko
D. Ann Maukonen
Jeffrey Mayer
Robert McColley
Jack W. McCullough
Mark R. McDermott
Eric McDowell
Barbara Basore McIver
William McKeen
Margo B. Mead
Greg Metcalf
Richard E. Meyer
R. D. Michael
Lori K. Miller
Doug A. Mishler
Bill Mistichelli
Bruce M. Mitchell
Debby L. Mitchell
John F. Moe
Lewis D. Moore
Cathy Mullen
Kenneth M. Nagelberg
Frank Nevius
Robert Niemi
Alleen Pace Nilsen
Don L. F. Nilsen
David Norton
Douglas A. Noverr
Laura Apol Obbink
Linda Obbink
Gerry O'Connor
John E. O'Connor
Robert M. Ogles
Anthony Oldknow
Catherine Olson
Patrice A. Oppliger
Tim Orwig
J. Roger Osterholm
Eric Pakula
Daniel A. Panici
David Ray Papke
Lee Ann Paradise-Schober
Carole D. Parnes
Timothy L. Parrish
Mitali R. Pati
Roy Pearson
Rick Perlstein

Susan L. Peters
David R. Peterson
Mona Phillips
George Plasketes
Linda Pohly
Richard L. Poole
David L. Porter
Carol Poster
Lynn A. Powers
James Prest
William Prior
June Michele Pulliam
James Rachels
Gary P. Radford
Pat Rafferty
Nicholas Ranson
Peggy Stevenson Ratliff
Helaine Razovsky
Rusty Reed
Diana C. Reep
Ronald Reichertz
Jacqueline Reid-Walsh
William Reynolds
Alex Richardson
Betty Richardson
Granetta L. Richardson
Stephanie A. Richardson
Edward J. Rielly
Dale Rigby
Jeff Ritter
A. R. Riverol
Garyn G. Roberts
Virginia Woods Roberts
John Rogers
Peter C. Rollins
Susan Rollins
Deane L. Root
Bruce A. Rubenstein
Janet A. Rudolph
G. Albert Ruesga
Sharon Russell
Frank A. Salamone
Clinton R. Sanders
Steve Sanders
Kevin S. Sandler
David Sanjek
Jack Santino
Samuel J. Sauls
Jennifer Scanlon
Nancy Schaefer
George L. Scheper
Michael Brian Schiffer
Thomas J. Schlereth
Phyllis Schmidt

Elizabeth W. B. Schmitt
Milton Welsh Schober
Michael Schoenecke
Ann Schoonmaker
M. Therese Schramm
Fred E. H. Schroeder
Raymond Schuck
Ginny Schwartz
Wayne H. Scott
April Selley
Keith Semmel
Michael Sevastakis
Ed Shane
William F. Shea
Steven O. Shields
James Shokoff
Janet P. Sholty
Brant Short
Curtis Shumaker
Mary Ann Simet
Philip Simpson
Suzie Sims-Fletcher
James Sirotzki
Christopher Slogar
J. Steven Smethers
Bruce L. Smith
Maureen Smith
Janice Snapp
Vivian Sobchack
Stephen Soitos
David M. Sokol
Albert Solomon
Kerry D. Soper
Kevin D. Soper
Susan Eike Spalding
Lynn C. Spangler
William David Spencer
Robert Sprich
Nicole St. John
Pamela Steinle
Lisa Odham Stokes
Melissa Stout
Marion Barber Stowell
Thomas Strychacz
William E. Studwell
Mary Siobhan Sullivan
Joel Super
Frederic Joseph Svoboda
Jean Swanson
Sylvia Tag
Jill Talbot
Martha A. Tanner
Ron Tanner
Rhonda Harris Taylor

Richard L. Testa, Jr.
Joe Thomas
Robert J. Thompson
Mary Timmons
Bonnie Elgin Todd
Kathleen D. Toerpe
Lori Tomlinson
Albert Tonik
Grant Tracey
Elizabeth A. Trembley
Vitus Tsang
Pat Tyrer
Rebecca A. Umland
Samuel J. Umland
Benjamin K. Urish
Janet Valade
J. K. Van Dover
Peter Vandenberg
Scott D. Vander Ploeg
Richard Veteikes
Anita M. Vickers
Cynthia J. Wachter
David C. Wallace
Carol M. Ward
A. Washington
Michael Washington
Mary Ann Watson
Robert G. Weiner
Susan Weiner
David Weinstein
Robert Weir
Linda S. Welker
Michael Wentworth
Jan Whitaker
Fred D. White
Christine Whittington
Mel R. Wilhoit
Carol Traynor Williams
Erik Williams
Tony Williams
April D. Wilson
Tamra Mabe Wilson
Connie Wineland
John D. Wineland
Ian Wojcik-Andrews
Richard Wolff
Kenneth Womack
Eugene F. Wong
Jerry Jaye Wright
Jean Anne Yackshaw
Gary A. Yoggy
Melody M. Zajdel
Lawrence E. Ziewacz
Mark Zust

Introduction

Accompanying *The Guide to United States Popular Culture* should be a strong effort to clarify the various meanings people have associated with popular culture through the years; otherwise misunderstandings and frustrations might result. A clear and precise definition is necessary.

Such a definition is particularly difficult for popular culture because of its nature. The term *popular culture* as used today is relatively new, though its subject matter is as old as human society. Defining the term is a difficult effort because it has a double barrier to overcome: to melt the prejudice against it and to reshape the various definitions that people have about it. These two prejudices can be summarized in the statement, "I know what it is and I state publicly that I don't like it."

Yet every academic field has had to cope with popular culture to one degree or another, especially lately. Such fields as anthropology, sociology, religion, communications, theater, and, to a lesser degree, history, literature, and psychology, have had to work to some extent in the broad fields of the everyday culture of people. Each has developed its own definition. Generally the definition has been associated with entertainment and leisure time activities, and usually with a negative connotation.

With the explosion of democracy in education since World War II has come a firm insistence on the inclusion without prejudice of democratic aspects of life. This changing attitude has brought a new attitude toward this inclusion and new fields and new seriousness and dignity toward those fields.

At first the new attitude and the resulting new subjects were treated with fear and derision, fear that the old canon and its shibboleths would be destroyed and replaced, and derision as a weapon to fight for retention of the old. Linguistically, in the fight to keep popular cultures out of academia, the terms of derision were "pop culture," "mass culture," and "cheap trash." Some academics and the general public—speaking through the media—seized on the term *pop culture* because it was short, quotable, convenient and because it set apart and cheapened the culture it named. This downputting continued for at least a decade.

But familiarity, though it breeds contempt, can also foster respect. So it was with the recognition of the place popular culture—read everyday cultures in the plural—has played in the emergence of the United States as one of the leading nations in the world for democracy. Academia and the public at large—except for a conservative group who think in terms of yesteryear's clichés—have dignified the field by calling it *popular culture* and recognizing that in a democracy the proper studies are of democratic institutions. Democracy demands an understanding of its strengths and weaknesses if it is to survive. A case can be made that demo-cratic life poses greater possible triumphs and more potential threats. Thrones and empires topple when ruled by people who forget or ignore the culture of their power bases. A case could be made that Rome fell because the rulers forgot the popular cultures which created and supported it for a thousand years. Crime novelist John Maddox Roberts, in *Saturnalia* (1999), writing of the Rome of Caesar, reveals a mountainous knowledge of details of daily life in Rome at that time but criticizes the aristocrats in power for having forgotten their folk roots. Perhaps their greater flaw was in despising and never trying to benefit from the cultures of their conquered people.

Other nations have likewise stumbled. Hitler's Third Reich that was destined to last a thousand years died early because its popular culture powerbase crumbled. And Communism's Berlin Wall toppled because the leaders did not understand the will and power of the masses they claimed to serve. Popular culture levels up, and as a hurricane gains strength from the warm waters at its base, generates irresistible power. Not to recognize this potential and to keep it struggling as an undesired, outside alien invites destruction. The fighting chant "power to the people" really means "power to the people's cultures." That power is becoming more and more powerful—and needs to have its base and dynamics understood.

Along with the public's—and media's—recognition of the power and importance of everyday culture has come the realization in academia of the importance of everyday cultures of the present and the past in the understanding of the world around us. There has not yet been an enthusiastic open-armed embrace by all academics, but demands are marching around the walls of the Ivory Tower as though they enclosed Jericho, and if the walls haven't yet come tumbling down, cracks are evident, and many people are coming out of the city to see what the action is, and even to join in on the call for a more open academic awareness and approach to education and the things that are important in education and life.

What then is a proper and workable definition of popular culture? We have said already that it is far more than entertainment and leisure time activities. It is the bone and flesh of a society from which the spirit emanates and soars—or falls.

Popular culture is the way of life in which and by which most people in any society live. In a democracy like the United States, it is the voice of the people—their practices, likes, and dislikes—the lifeblood of their daily existence, a way of life. The popular culture is the voice of democracy, speaking and acting, the seedbed in which democracy grows. Popular culture in all cultures—from the most authoritarian to the most democratic—democratizes society and makes democracy truly democratic. It is the everyday world around

1

us: the mass media, entertainments, diversions; it is our heroes, icons, rituals, everyday actions, psychology, and religion—our total life pictures. It is the way of life we inherit, practice, modify as we please and then pass on to our descendants. It is what we do while we are awake and how we do it; it is the dreams we dream while asleep, as well as where and how we sleep, as well as how long.

Obviously, then, since there are many manifestations of people's behavior dictated by race, history, custom, gender, age, locality, and group-size conditions, popular culture actually consists of many overlapping and interworking cultures, like scales on a fish. The only way to talk of a singular popular culture is to realize that it is a mixture of many small and large cultures which are controlled by elements smaller than and different from the large national picture, the living fish.

The many ethnicities of people and their histories and cultures from around the world who have poured into the United States over the past two centuries have brought their many elements of cultures and added them to the dominant Protestant Western European base. So the culture of the United States today is a broader stirring, both vertically and laterally, of all the people who make up our society. It would have been completely different if this continent had been discovered, colonized, and developed west to east instead of east to west, by Asians instead of Europeans; or south to north instead of north to south, by Catholics instead of predominantly Protestants. The same basic human needs would have been present, but their traditional and current development would have been entirely different in expression and degree. Culture developments are driven by and develop within the needs and constraints of a people. They extend in directions and to degrees allowed by the physical, mental, and emotional attitudes.

Popular culture has nothing to do with popularity in the sense of number of people engaged in it. That kind of popularity has only to do with how widely something is used. It also has nothing to do with quality, though at times we might wish it did. Popular culture is the lifestyle and lifeblood of groups—large or small—of people.

In 2000—popularly (if not mathematically) considered the beginning of a new millennium—an estimated 327 languages and dialects are spoken in the United States. The smallest ethnic and nationalist, cultish, religious, or political group using one of those languages or dialects lives in and by their everyday culture. That culture identifies the people and makes them cohere as a part of the larger culture of the United States. The dominant popular culture is like a patchwork quilt made up of many patches. This large quilt then covers the many smaller groups. In such societies, citizens must speak several cultural languages, those of their own—and similar—group, and that of the dominant culture. As the peoples of the earth necessarily become more and more mixed, any and all cultures will become more complex.

One indication of the complexity of a national culture can be seen in just one manifestation—geographical—by looking at it as an inverted pyramid. The United States as a nation has many cultures. So, too, in a kind of shrinkage to an American region, does the U.S. "South." So does a state

in the South, say Alabama, and a region in that state. For example, during the Civil War, Winston County, Alabama, opposed secession and threatened to set up an independent state; surely in many ways Winston County differed from the surrounding counties and still does. Still reducing the size of a geographical unit, we recognize that a city or town in Alabama differs from the others and from the South in general. So, too, does a family and even an individual. Though a family's culture usually reflects that of the community, sometimes it differs so much that it is looked upon as eccentric or even dangerous. But such a culture is a living entity.

Further, popular culture has nothing to do with so-called quality, with the "good and beautiful" in life as distinguished from those elements which are considered neither good nor beautiful. Some aspects of culture are positive, some negative, some beneficial, some detrimental. Popular culture, especially in a country like the United States, is the total of all ways and means of life, for better or worse, desired or undesired.

Popular culture in many instances is distributed by the mass media, but other, more old-fashioned, media like habit, the "grapevine," gossip, imitation, observation, and indifference are much more powerful controls. In popular culture, though at times we feel it is dictated by powerful forces beyond our control, eventually the people control it. Though a movie, for example, may get strong official approval or condemnation, it is word-of-mouth reviews that make or break it. The approving or disapproving glance and its supporting verbal comments control our culture. We vote at the ballot box but also with our feet and pocketbook, and when we walk away from or fail to support an element of our popular culture, sooner or later it will become inconsequential or disappear. The complexity of popular culture can be illustrated in the accompanying diagram.

It is in this context of easy fluid movement and mixing of cultures, then, that we talk of the popular culture—singular—of the United States. The degree of comprehensiveness and complexity of this culture is demonstrated by the con-

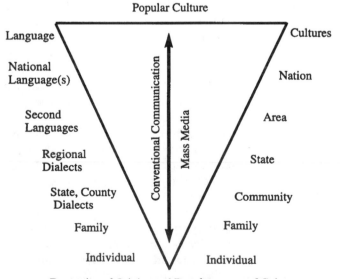

Dynamics of Origins and Developments of Culture

2

tents of this volume, which is about the popular culture of the United States, not of America.

In a capitalistic democracy, taxpayers and voters pay the piper and consequently call the tune. In the sea of culture, in President John Kennedy's words, the tide eventually floats all boats at the same level. In the present-day outbursts of democratic culture, you can hardly identify the cultural status of a boat owner by where he or she docks the craft. The demands of ethnopietistic, nationalistic, cultist, religious, political, economic, and gender groups display varied flags on their crafts and create many eddies of water movement. But all float on a common body of United States—mixed with those from around the globe—popular culture.

Though all people throughout the world have many aspects of popular culture in common, citizens of the United States possess and treasure many which mark them uniquely "American." Our popular culture is the cause and result of our democracy. Without it, our democratic culture as we know it would not exist. After Columbus in 1492 Europeans looked at a new world that seemed to be a new Garden of Eden, a freshly created Paradise, and a new start for humankind. Shakespeare called it a "brave new world." Through the centuries it continued to dazzle world eyes.

The French philosopher Jean de Crèvecoeur in 1782 asked "What is an American?" and "What is America?" and "Why is America?" The cultural historian Jacques Barzun once said that to know America one must understand baseball. That may have been correct when he said it and might even be useful today, but it is not sufficient. There are thousands of aspects of American life that all of us must comprehend in order to understand the United States and ourselves.

Today the answers to the questions "What is America?" and "What is an American?", given by ourselves generally with pride though sometimes with fear and horror, define what democratic capitalism in a new and rich land has done and can do. So the answers lie in the generalization "Both are the result of the nation's everyday culture." Our popular culture is the United States. Its impact directs the development of the United States and, because of its strength and worldwide distribution, is shaping the everyday culture around the globe.

As the voice of the people, popular culture makes up another philosophical aspect of society, the humanities, and should properly be called the New Humanities. Historically, people who treasure the humanities have insisted that they teach us how to live life most fully. The humanities are those attitudes and actions that seem to make us different from other animals and superior to them in our love for and treatment of other animals and human beings in compassion and empathy. Often traditional humanists have treated the humanities as though they were to be denied to the ordinary taxpayer as being above his or understanding and appreciation or not possibly a part of his nature. But the New Humanists believe that this traditional elitist point of view is tunnel-visioned and short-sighted and not acceptable in a democracy. In a democratic culture, one cannot assume that only a few elements, those historically accepted by a fraction of the population, make up the potential of the humanities and their enrichment of the human race. The humanities and human potential are much more complicated.

In studying and trying to understand a culture—drawing forth its humanities—one must mine all fields of human experience, especially the popular culture. Many aspects of that popular culture may not be pleasing, to be sure. But neither are many elements of so-called elite culture, especially until age and customs have made them familiar and valuable. They have then become popular culture, and are doing the job of perpetuating all culture, not a section of it. In fact, the popular humanities do most of the job of carrying on a culture. The very elitist poet T. S. Eliot years ago recognized the heavy duty of popular culture in perpetuating culture when he cried out against popular books, in his time a major force in dispensing popular culture, in his book *Essays Ancient and Modern*: "I incline to come to the alarming conclusion that it is just the literature [nowadays read entertainment] that we read for 'amusement' or 'purely for pleasure' that may have the greatest...least suspected...earliest...influence upon us." It is both ironic and somehow satisfying that, like Shakespeare the icon of elitists, Eliot in the electronic age has come to be known and appreciated most widely by the people he feared and despised in the stage production of *Cats*, a popular rendition of his power on the subject collectively called *Old Possum's Book of Practical Cats*.

Actually, in what seems to be a gap between what might be called elite and popular humanities, there is no break whatsoever, as Robert Coles, psychologist and Pulitzer Prize winner, recognizes: "The Humanities," he says, "belong to no one kind of person; they are part of the lives of ordinary people, who have their own various ways of struggling for coherence, for a compelling faith, for social vision, for an ethical position, for a sense of historical perspective," for, in other words, a meaning of life.

The popular culture in and of the United States obviously has meaning to its citizens, their way of existence, and the continuation of "the American way of life." It *is* that way of life. It is the humanities and at times the inhumanities. It is the good and the bad, the satisfying and the dissatisfying. To paraphrase what someone has said in another connection, "We have seen our popular culture and it is us." United States popular culture is ourselves and our country, and we, for better or worse, are our popular culture.

Clearly, we must understand what popular culture is, accept it as such, and study it in all its various expressions if we are to comprehend democracy and our humanities and ourselves. This understanding will not come easily. In the first place, understanding the concept of cultures and their aggregate culture is for some of us not easy. The difficulty probably comes from the engrained, constantly repeated, and virtually written-in-stone concept that culture has something to do with uplift, with improvement, with our better selves. Such an attitude is too narrow and exclusive. Popular culture is all those things and more. It is more than the sum of its parts and its participants. Recognizing this demands a step into the metaphysical world around us, a combination of the physical-social-spiritual existence which makes up our world.

Second, we must respect our popular culture. For some, this may not be easy. Most of us honor the concept of democracy while tending to avoid at least some of its practical applications. Indeed, we try to prove that some of us are more equal than others, and using our popular culture as the down side of that proof is sometimes convenient. It is easy to make a scapegoat of elements of our popular culture and the people who participate in it.

The main trouble in understanding popular culture is that the differences among the elements seem to be slight. But that sameness is only seeming. The very essence of humanity is based on the democratic assumption that all individuals may be nearly alike to the casual observer and have equality of opportunity, but in fact have differences that are profound. So, too, with popular culture. The differences between elements may seem to be negligible but are in fact deep. For example, anyone who says that all rock 'n' roll music is alike simply has an undistinguishing tin ear. Anyone who says that all popular fiction is alike does not understand popular fiction. And so on. In the final analysis, anyone who says that all fast food hamburgers are alike has a palate trained to detect and appreciate only major differences in food, which means that the gourmet tongue cannot differentiate between subtle differences.

As long as these deficiencies persist in observers of popular culture, we will be unable to understand fully and appreciate that popular culture. In many ways, one of our first tasks is to appreciate the subtleties of popular culture and through that appreciation come to understand it.

Take two examples from the world of rock music which to the outsider may appear to be only differences of the same activity. Moshing and surfing are two concert activities that grew in popularity in the 1990s. The former has been around since the '70s, the latter in some ways perhaps longer. In moshing, the concertgoers grind and bang into one another with as much force as space and strength allow. Resulting injuries usually are confined to twisted ankles and wrists, bruises, and an occasional broken bone. Surfing consists of being raised above the crowd on everybody's hands and being passed to the front of the group in order to get better positioning for the concert. Sometimes the body is carelessly or jokingly dropped, with resulting injuries.

In these two activities the broken bones may be the same, but the activities which cause them have different drives, at times glaringly dissimilar and at times subtly similar. All make up the popular culture of the United States.

This collection of some 1600 entries demonstrates just how widespread, varied, and complex the popular culture of the United States is. Some 500 people familiar with all aspects of this culture helped make the choices for inclusion. These choices sometimes may seem to have been personal and arbitrary. Though at times an individual reader may not find some item he or she considers important, on the whole the sketches included are a consensus and represent mainstream U.S. popular culture.

The aim of the editors in commissioning and choosing entries was twofold: They want to use the selections to demonstrate the peripheries and content of popular culture, the many kinds of culture which must be included if the full dimensions and power of popular culture are to be recognized. The editors felt that the cultural geography, philosophy, and dynamics of popular culture need to be established. Thus, the name of the book, *The Guide to United States Popular Culture* rather than *Encyclopedia*....

Second, in order to keep this book within convenient bounds, the editors had to look upon the collection as a kind of mosaic of representative parts, not all parts. As demonstrated by the numerous encyclopedias of various segments of popular culture around us—folklore, sports, etc.—including all parts would have resulted in at least ten volumes. So the more *representative* collection.

Within the selection of included material, more decisions had to be made about representation, since obviously readers are going to open the book with different alphabetical expectations. To satisfy the various expectations we have included some general essays on topics such as museums, sports, pageantry, quilts, golf. But some general topics are simply too long and varied to be included in a single essay. Crime fiction, for example, is discussed in 30+ entries, our feeling being that people interested in crime fiction would not want to read what would amount to a short book about all kinds in order to get finally to their specific concern.

In many more particular instances, the user of this guide will be looking for individuals, specific groups, particular items. Many will be found here, though we had to make representative choices. Many not individualized will be discussed in the general essays or may be found in the suggestions for further reading at the end of the entry.

Altogether the entries constitute a mosaic background of the popular culture of the United States, standing out from which will be the clear lettering "Life in the United States," which moves toward answering the questions: "What is the U.S.?" and "What is a U.S. citizen?"

Reading through or browsing in the entries will at times be a step into the safe country of nostalgia, or, at other times, a daring venture into a virtually unknown country. But mainly it will be a trip in our world. It will be like holding up a giant mirror before ourselves and seeing in that reflection a whole society with ourselves at the center. Sometimes the view may be frightening, but it will always be educational. It's our world, so let's understand it.

Welcome to a great adventure of discovery, recognition, and enjoyment...

Ray B. Browne
Pat Browne

Abbey, Edward (1927-1989), is perhaps best known for his boisterous 1975 novel, *The Monkey Wrench Gang,* which inspired the radical environmental organization Earth First! whose activities have ranged from sabotaging logging operations to unrolling an immense plastic "crack" down the face of Glen Canyon dam.

Abbey's writings are diverse and influential, encompassing various genres, from Westerns to cultural criticism. His second novel, a Western parable entitled *The Brave Cowboy* (1956), was filmed as *Lonely Are the Brave* in 1962, starring Kirk Douglas and Walter Matthau. But it was the publication of *Desert Solitaire* in 1968, a collection of essays tracing a season he spent as a park ranger at Arches National Park in southern Utah, that brought him a mass readership. The essays bring together landscape meditations and a wry critique of American industry; frequently reprinted, their enduring appeal has helped to build popular appreciation of the desert Southwest.

Abbey wrote 23 books, including eight novels and a book of poetry. When he died in 1989, friends cached his body (illegally) somewhere deep in the Southwestern desert.

Bibliography

Hepworth, James, and Gregory McNamee, eds. *Resist Much, Obey Little: Some Notes on Edward Abbey.* Salt Lake City: Dream Garden, 1985.

McCann, Garth. *Edward Abbey.* Boise: Boise State UP, 1977.

Ronald, Ann. *The New West of Edward Abbey.* Albuquerque: U of New Mexico P, 1982.

Fred Lifton

ABC Television Network, The, was begun, not by creative entrepreneurship, but by government order. In 1943, as a result of several investigations, the U.S. government forced NBC to sell one of its two radio networks. Edward J. Noble, famous as the father of Life Savers candy, purchased NBC Blue, the weaker of NBC's station lineups, for $8 million. In 1945 he formally changed the name to the American Broadcasting Company (ABC).

From this radio base came the ABC television network. NBC and CBS had already lined up the strongest television stations. Having fewer affiliates, ABC-TV started from a base of a smaller potential audience and was thus perpetually at the short end. Indeed, as television began to expand, popular radio and movie stars naturally gravitated to CBS or NBC. Program packagers developed shows for NBC and CBS, rarely risking investments in third-place ABC-TV.

Through the late 1940s and early 1950s ABC-TV had to make do with low-cost programs such as featuring roller derby and professional wrestling. As late as 1954 ABC had affiliations with but 40 stations of the then more than 300 television stations on the air. ABC-TV might have gone out of business, as rival DuMont did, had it not been for Leonard Goldenson and his United Paramount Theaters. In 1948 the U.S. Supreme Court ruled that Hollywood's Paramount Pictures studio had to sell its chain of movie theaters. Goldenson took charge of the new theater company, and in 1952 merged with ABC.

Thereafter Goldenson and his able assistants looked for niche audiences not served by his two far larger network rivals. For the next 20 years, in particular, ABC-TV sought out and cornered the youth market with such shows as *American Bandstand, Maverick,* and *The Mickey Mouse Club.* ABC-TV stars were Edd "Kookie" Byrnes and Ricky Nelson, both 1950s teen heart-throbs. Goldenson pioneered by striking deals with major Hollywood studios and, with help from Warner Bros., ABC-TV aired *Cheyenne, 77 Sunset Strip, Surfside 6,* and *Hawaiian Eye.* But success hardly came overnight; it was not until the mid-1970s that ABC-TV would finally rank with NBC and CBS.

Through the 1950s and 1960s Goldenson and his staff constantly experimented. They ran a newscast on Sunday nights against Ed Sullivan's highly popular *Toast of the Town.* They boldly telecast—live—the highly controversial Army-McCarthy hearings. They presented non-traditional sports, such as rodeo and college baseball, with slow-motion instant replays.

The successes, particularly in prime time in the early days, were few and far between. In the early 1960s the top-rated ABC-TV shows were *My Three Sons, The Real McCoys,* and *The Flintstones,* the first animated prime-time television series. In the more turbulent late '60s, ABC-TV mixed the traditional (*The F.B.I.* and *Marcus Welby, M.D.*) with the more adventuresome (*Mod Squad* and *Bewitched*). It was not until the 1976-77 season that ABC-TV finally rose to the top of the network ratings; its prime-time hits that season were *Happy Days, Laverne and Shirley,* and *Monday Night Football.*

Indeed, in sports telecasting ABC-TV was always a leader and true pioneer. It led the way with *ABC Wide World of Sports, Monday Night Football,* and notable coverage of both the summer and winter Olympics. But there also were hit entertainment shows such as *The Six Million Dollar Man* and *Welcome Back, Kotter.* In particular, the miniseries *Roots* set ratings records and won numerous awards. The made-for-TV movie was also innovated at ABC-TV, which presented *Brian's Song, The Thorn Birds,* and *The Winds of War* (see Television Movies).

By the late 1970s, under Fred Silverman, ABC-TV had ceased to be thought of as a network stepchild, and was for several years atop the ratings race. But the 1980s brought fewer hits. These included *Dynasty, Moonlighting, Roseanne,* and *The Wonder Years.*

In 1986 Capital Cities, Inc., owner of some of the most profitable television stations in the U.S., bought ABC for

$3.5 billion, then the largest purchase in mass media history. In turn, Capital Cities/ABC was in 1996 acquired by the Disney Company (see Walt Disney Television). As part of Disney, the ABC Television Network now owns eight of the most profitable television stations in the U.S., and has some 200 affiliates.

Bibliography

Bergreen, Laurence. *Look Now, Pay Later: The Rise of Network Broadcasting.* New York: Doubleday, 1980.
Goldenson, Leonard H. *Beating the Odds: The Untold Story behind the Rise of ABC.* New York: Scribner's, 1991.
Quinlan, Sterling. *Inside ABC: American Broadcasting Company's Rise to Power.* New York: Hastings, 1979.
Williams, Huntington. *Beyond Control: ABC and the Fate of the Networks.* New York: Atheneum, 1989.

Douglas Gomery

Abshire, Nathan (1915-1981), Cajun singer and accordionist, was born near Bayou Queue de Tortue in South Louisiana. Though he never learned to read music and claimed he could not even sign his name, he became one of the greatest Cajun music makers of the 20th century. Like the zydeco king Clifton Chenier, Abshire, though white, credited Amédé Ardoin, the black Creole musician whose legend inspired the Lafayette festival, as his artistic muse.

Abshire was born just in time to ride the first wave of popularity of Cajun music, though few outside of Louisiana ever heard about it; *fais dodo*, or country dancing, was a Cajun family affair. Then from the mid-1930s until the 1950s, Cajun music went underground even in Louisiana, as many preferred assimilation to ethnic diversity. But Abshire just kept playing and was poised for fame when the revival began in the 1960s with the popularity of the Balfa Brothers. While much Cajun music has been influenced by country, blues, and rock, Abshire has remained close to his roots, and his sound is pure Cajun.

Illiterate in both English and French, Abshire spoke English with difficulty, but he communicated through his accordion and the high-pitched Louisiana French that characterizes Cajun music. Louisiana folklorist Barry Jean Ancelet calls his style "bluesy" and "emotional," his music "soulful pathos" and "exuberant joy." His recordings include "Good Times Are Killing Me" and "Pine Grove Blues," done with the Balfa Brothers; his "Alligator Stomp," "Cajun Social Music," "Le Gran Mamou," and "J'ai été au Bal" appear in anthologies under a variety of labels: Rounder, Swallow, Maison de Soul, Mardi Gras, and Arhoolie.

Bibliography

Ancelet, Barry Jean. *Cajun Music: Its Origins and Development.* Lafayette: Center for Louisiana Studies, 1989.
——. *The Makers of Cajun Music.* Canada: PU du Québec, 1984.
Broven, John. *South to Louisiana: The Music of the Cajun Bayous.* Gretna: Pelican, 1983.
Lichtenstein, Grace, and Laura Dankner. *Musical Gumbo: The Music of New Orleans.* New York: Norton, 1993.
Rodenbeck, Arlene, and Suzanne Farrer. *A Brief Bibliography on Cajun Music.* Washington, DC: Library of Congress, 1981.
Savoy, Ann Allen. *Cajun Music: A Reflection of a People.* Eunice: Bluebird, 1984.

Bonnie Elgin Todd

See also
Zydeco

Academic Mystery is a recognized subgenre of mystery and detective fiction. Set mainly in colleges, such mysteries center on the manners and morals of faculty and administrators; students may appear at the stories' margins, but they are rare as central characters. College mysteries are most often cozy mysteries (see entry) with action taking a definite second place to talk. In most, murder temporarily disrupts the official business of the institution in question. The miscreant is then found out, and is ultimately expunged from the campus. As the detection proceeds, readers ordinarily meet a host of collegiate suspects burdened with eccentricities or guilty secrets. Through such characters, college mysteries often direct satire at the world of higher education.

The first college mysteries, which began appearing early in this century, were usually simple puzzlers composed by journeymen writers. The form did not come to full flower until the 1930s, when real-life academics began to write on-campus detective novels with complex structures and more incisive treatments of the higher-education environment. The outstanding academic mysteries of the 1930s were British, in particular John Masterman's *An Oxford Tragedy* (1933), Dorothy L. Sayers's *Gaudy Night* (1935), and Michael Innes's *Death at the President's Lodging* (1936).

Since the 1930s, academic mysteries have appeared at the rate of five or six each year, and their cumulative number now exceeds 400. Most are set at American colleges and universities. Four of the more noteworthy are Amanda Cross's *Death in a Tenured Position* (1981), Helen Eustis's *The Horizontal Man* (1946), Hilary Waugh's *Last Seen Wearing* (1952), and Robert B. Parker's *The Godwulf Manuscript* (1974).

Set at Harvard, *Death in a Tenured Position* is part of a series in which English professor Kate Fansler serves as detective. Something approaching half of all campus mysteries feature professors as detectives, and Professor Fansler—the creation of Carolyn Heilbrun—is undoubtedly the best known of mystery fiction's legion of professor-sleuths, the heroine of a vibrant ongoing series. *The Horizontal Man*, set at a fictionalized version of Smith College, the author's alma mater, is significant for featuring a heavy psychological component. Conventional sleuthing is downplayed in favor of a focus on the teacher-villain's disturbed mental condition.

Last Seen Wearing, generally considered a police procedural exemplar, takes its police detectives to the campus of a small New England college for women where they investigate the disappearance of a student. And *The Godwulf Manuscript* features Spenser, Robert B. Parker's popular private detective, in his first adventure, amidst free-loving coeds and corrupt professors at a university in Boston. Academic mysteries represent an increasingly popular trend in the world of detection.

Bibliography
Kramer, John. *College Mystery Novels: An Annotated Bibliography*. New York: Garland, 1983.

John Kramer

See also
Golden Age of Detective Fiction

Academy of Television Arts & Sciences (ATAS), The (1946–), a nonprofit trade organization, has a current membership of over 7,500 members. The Academy is most widely recognized for its sponsorship and presentation of the prime-time Emmy Awards. In addition, the Academy annually honors outstanding contributions to the television industry with its Television Hall of Fame. It also sponsors and services a wide variety of educational and research activities, under the auspices of its companion organization, the Television Academy foundation. These, along with many other of the Academy's programs and activities, are designed specifically to promote the advancement of television's arts and sciences, and to encourage creative leadership within the television industry.

Academy membership is divided into four classifications: National Active, National Associate, Los Angeles Area, and Student. All national members of the Academy belong to one of 24 branches of membership. In keeping with the Academy's overall agenda, each branch is related to either an artistic, technical, or business area of the television industry. The branches are Animation, Art Directors, Casting Executives, Children's Programming, Cinematographers, Commercials, Costume Designers/Supervisors, Daytime Programming, Directors/Choreographers, Electronic Production, Informational Programming, Music, Makeup Artists/Hairstylists, Members at Large, Performers, Producers, Production Executives, Public Relations, Sound, Sound Editors, Television Executives, Television Motion Picture Editors, Title & Graphic Design, and Writers.

The Academy was originally organized in response to the advent of network television. In 1946, the New York-based American Television Society denied a request by Los Angeles television columnist Syd Cassyd to start a Los Angeles branch. In an effort to begin a West Coast–based television alliance, Cassyd in October 1946 brought together six individuals who discussed the development of an academy that would study the development of television, and determine how this new medium would best serve the public interest. In Cassyd's vision, membership in the academy would be "an honor conferred on those whose knowledge makes them worthy of it," and the primary purpose of the organization would be educational. Cassyd and his associates also acknowledged that at some point, the academy might begin to regularly present awards for excellence in television programming.

The ATAS, however, did not achieve national attention until it selected its first president. Edgar Bergen (see entry), the extremely popular radio and film star, known internationally for his ventriloquist act featuring a "dummy" named Charlie McCarthy, took office in January 1947. Besides lending the Academy immediate credibility, Bergen shared Cassyd's serious concern about the development of television.

Over the ensuing decade, the Academy continued to grow under the leadership of many celebrities. In the 1950s, national presidents of the Academy included film mogul Hal Roach, Jr., actor Don DeFore, composer Johnny Mercer, and the popular and powerful columnist and variety show host Ed Sullivan.

In 1957, the Academy was reshaped in an effort to accommodate the demands of the New Yorkers. The organization was renamed the National Academy of Television Arts and Sciences (NATAS), with Los Angeles and New York sharing the responsibilities as founding chapters.

The next few years saw significant growth and development in the Academy. By 1961 the NATAS had chapters in eight cities, including Chicago, Baltimore, and Washington, DC. The Emmy Awards programs were being telecast nationally each year on network television. And in 1962 the Academy published its first issue of *Television Quarterly: The Journal of the National Academy of Television Arts and Sciences*. The journal was, and continues to be, a publication that strives to look at the popular medium of television from a scholarly, critical, and historical perspective.

But despite the continued growth and expansion of the Academy, the tensions and problems between the New York and Los Angeles branches remained and escalated. After a number of ineffective attempts at compromise, these differences led to a series of lawsuits. In July 1977 a separation agreement was reached. All lawsuits were dropped as the New York chapter remained known as NATAS, maintaining the rights to *Television Quarterly*. NATAS also kept control of the daytime, sports, and news Emmy Awards. The Hollywood branch reclaimed the name American Academy of Television Arts and Sciences, and was given the right to present the prime-time Emmy Awards. The ATAS also created *Emmy*, now a bimonthly entertainment magazine targeted to those working in the television industry.

Since the separation, the ATAS has continued to present the prime-time Emmys, now broadcast annually on alternating networks. It has also instituted the Television Hall of Fame and the Academy Foundation. Among the foundation's most influential projects is its internship program, which introduces college students to the world of professional television.

The prime-time Emmy Awards were first presented in 1949. The statue was named "Emmy" at the suggestion of the ATAS's third president, Harry C. Lubcke. The name was inspired by the term *Immy*, after the nickname for the image orthicon camera tube, which was instrumental in the technical development of television.

The first Emmy Awards were limited to programs produced in Los Angeles, as national linkage of broadcast signals was not available until 1951. Thus, Shirley Dinsdale, a young ventriloquist with a popular Los Angeles puppet show, received the first Emmy Award ever presented. Within a year, the rules were broadened, and national stars such as Milton Berle and Ed Wynn were among the winners. The awards ceremony has been broadcast nationally since 1955, and nearly 5,000 Emmy Awards have been presented.

The Television Academy Hall of Fame was conceived in 1981 by John Mitchell, then the Academy president. It was meant to honor the performers, directors, executives, scientists, writers, and sponsors who have made lasting and significant contributions to television. The first inductees, announced in 1984, were Lucille Ball, Norman Lear, Milton Berle, William S. Paley, Edward R. Murrow, Paddy Chayefsky, and David Sarnoff (the last three were honored posthumously). In the years since, inductees have included George Burns and Gracie Allen, Steve Allen, Walter Cronkite, Carol Burnett, Ed Sullivan, Rod Serling, Norman Lear, and Bob Hope.

The Academy of Television Arts and Sciences moved to its permanent international headquarters in North Hollywood, CA, in 1991.

Bibliography

——. Academy of Television Arts & Sciences. *About the Academy.* Los Angeles, 1993.
Academy of Television Arts & Sciences. *Membership Requirements.* Los Angeles, 1993.
Hicks, Price. "From the Director's Chair." *Debut: The Educational Programs and Services Newsletter* Winter 1994: 2.
Link, Tom. "Dreams and Dissent: The Television Academy's Forty Years." *Emmy* Sept./Oct. 1988: 32-57.
Polevoi, Gail. "Three Years for the Hall of Fame." *Emmy* Mar./Apr. 1986: 16-20.

Richard J. Allen

Acid Rock, also known as psychedelic rock, is a type of rock music closely associated with the use of LSD or other hallucinogenic drugs (peyote, mescaline, etc.) by the performers, the audience, or both. Acid rock began in California, particularly the San Francisco Bay area, in 1965 and quickly spread before fading out at the end of the decade.

The Grateful Dead were among the first musicians to experiment with LSD, joining writer Ken Kesey (*One Flew over the Cuckoo's Nest*) and his Merry Pranksters in parties known as acid tests. These were documented by author Tom Wolfe in his book *The Electric Kool-Aid Acid Test* (1968). The developing music scene centered around the Haight-Ashbury District of San Francisco. The Grateful Dead, led by lead guitarist Jerry "Captain Trips" Garcia, played frequently at the Avalon Ballroom and the Fillmore Auditorium, later joined by Quicksilver Messenger Service and the Jefferson Airplane. Bands in the rest of the country also took up acid rock, such as the 13th Floor Elevators, based in Austin, TX, who recorded *Psychedelic Sounds* in 1967.

The first successful acid rock song on the popular music charts was "Psychotic Reaction," recorded by San Jose's Count Five. The song took a traditional rock music lyrical theme, unrequited love, to its extreme: having a psychotic reaction to being spurned by a lover. The most characteristic element of this and other early acid rock music was the replacement of the melodic electric guitar of earlier rock with howling feedback and distortion. Acid rock was characterized by long solos on the electric guitar (as in the Grateful Dead's concert recording of "Dark Star") or organ (as in the Doors' "Light My Fire").

Acid rock songs frequently made reference to drugs, as in the Jefferson Airplane's "White Rabbit" ("One pill makes you larger/And one pill makes you small") and Jimi Hendrix's "Purple Haze" (a type of LSD). Songs were also misinterpreted, and critics complained that Peter, Paul and Mary's "Puff, the Magic Dragon" and the Association's "Along Comes Mary" were about smoking marijuana.

Heavy metal music had its origins in the acid rock groups that sacrificed meaningful lyrics for extremely loud, repetitive music. Steppenwolf's "Magic Carpet Ride" and Ted Nugent and the Amboy Dukes' "Journey to the Center of Your Mind" had references to drug use, but it was the sheer volume of the music that attracted audiences.

Acid rock was often blended with other musical styles. The Grateful Dead's first album featured rhythm and blues standards like "Sittin' on Top of the World," and Tracy Nelson (with Mother Earth) also incorporated blues into her performances. The New Riders of the Purple Sage toured with the Grateful Dead, sharing musicians with the Dead as they played country and western and bluegrass music. Dan Hicks and His Hot Licks had a nostalgic jazz sound borrowed from the big band era. Lead guitarist Carlos Santana and his group, Santana, used Latin rhythms as the basis for their psychedelic music.

Although acid rock started in the United States, the Beatles' *Sgt. Pepper's Lonely Hearts Club Band* album had a major influence on American acid rock groups. The use of sophisticated electronic and multitrack recording techniques drove many groups into the recording studio. The Beach Boys recorded two albums with complex recording techniques, *Sunflower* and *Surf's Up*, while the Grateful Dead mixed electronic instruments and used sophisticated tape editing in *Anthem of the Sun* and *Aoxamoxoa*.

Acid rock was glamorized by the 1969 motion picture *Easy Rider*. Among other songs on its soundtrack was Steppenwolf's "Born to Be Wild." But acid rock turned tragic after Hell's Angels security guards stomped a man to death during the Rolling Stones' concert at Altamont racetrack in December 1969 (see Altamont). Then drug overdoses took the lives of some of acid rock's fixtures—Jimi Hendrix (September 1970), the Doors' Jim Morrison (July 1971), and Janis Joplin (October 1970), who was associated with acid rock through her band, Big Brother and the Holding Company.

Psychedelic music was kept alive for a short while by British groups like Pink Floyd, King Crimson, Yes, and Emerson, Lake, and Palmer. But those groups quickly moved away from drug-themed music to experiments in electronics and in using classical themes in rock music.

Bibliography

Johnson, Vernon. *The Acid Trip: A Complete Guide to Psychedelic Music.* Todmorden, U.K.: Babylon, 1984.
Sculatti, Gene. *San Francisco Nights: The Psychedelic Music Trip, 1965-68.* New York: St. Martin's, 1985.

Kenneth M. Nagelberg

Acuff, Roy (1903-1992). Recognized as the most influential figure in the history of country music, Roy Acuff, the "Grand-dad of the Grand Ole Opry," was the Opry's first solo star and

Roy Acuff. Photo courtesy of Sound Recording Archives, Bowling Green State University, Bowling Green, OH.

remained its enduring human symbol throughout his life. He is best known for "Wabash Cannonball" and "The Great Speckled Bird," which he performed during his debut appearance at the Opry in 1938. Acuff continued to perform every Saturday night at the Opry up to a month before his death.

Roy Claxton Acuff was born near Maynardsville in the Smoky Mountains of eastern Tennessee. His father, Neill Acuff, was a Baptist preacher, and while growing up Roy sang during his church services. When his family moved to Knoxville, Acuff at 16 became a star athlete at Central High School, excelling in baseball. The New York Yankees even offered him a contract, but a severe and recurring case of sunstroke ended his baseball career. He taught himself to play the fiddle by listening to his father's records, Gid Tanner and the Skillet Lickers, and Fiddlin' John Carson. Acuff started touring the mountains of Tennessee and Virginia with Doc Hower's Medicine Show, where he learned how to sing out loud enough for a large crowd to hear him without a microphone. Soon after, Acuff and his band, the Crazy Tennesseans, began performing on WNOX, a radio station in Knoxville. The name of the band was changed to the Smoky Mountain Boys, for fear the original name was derogatory to the state. In 1936, Acuff was discovered by agent Arthur Satherly, who signed him to Columbia Records. Acuff and the Smoky Mountain Boys moved into the Opry in 1938, and the NBC radio network began broadcasting the show in 1939.

Acuff expanded his career in 1942 when he joined with songwriter Fred Rose to start the Acuff-Rose publishing company, the first one based in Nashville. The two became millionaires by publishing the writing of Hank Williams, the Louvin Brothers, Don Gibson, Redd Stewart, Roy Orbison, and many others. Acuff also stepped out of the world of country music and into the world of Hollywood when he starred in the 1940 movie *The Grand Ole Opry*. After appearing in seven more films, Acuff was asked to remain in Hollywood to portray the "singing cowboy," but refused and returned to recording, singing, and performing.

Acuff is best known best for songs like "Wabash Cannonball," "The Great Speckled Bird," "The Precious Jewel," "Wreck on the Highway," and "All the World Is Lonely Now." His high, heart-piercing mountain vocals echoed in the Grand Ole Opry for over 50 years, bringing dignity to the music that created a legend.

Bibliography

Gates, David. "I'm Able to Reach the People." *Newsweek* 7 Dec. 1992: 83.

Hurst, Jack. "Roy Acuff, One of a Kind." *Chicago Tribune* 3 Dec. 1992: 5, 10.

Rosen, Craig. "Country Patriarch Roy Acuff Dies." *Billboard* 5 Dec. 1992: 3.

"Roy Acuff." *Current Biography Yearbook.* Ed. Charles Moritz. New York: Wilson, 1976.

Jill Talbot

See also

Grand Ole Opry

Adler, Richard, and Jerry Ross, a songwriting team, composed the scores to just two musicals, but those two rank among the most popular musicals in the history of Broadway—*The Pajama Game* and *Damn Yankees*. The music and lyrics of Adler (1921-) and Ross (1926-1955), though usually cheerful and catchy, had a hard-edged, cynical tone similar to that of Frank Loesser. Loesser was, perhaps not coincidentally, an early promoter of Adler and Ross.

Richard Adler was born in New York City. Though his father was the well-known pianist Clarence Adler, Richard Adler had no formal musical training and his degree from the University of North Carolina, from which he graduated in 1943, was in literature. After serving in the U.S. Navy during World War II, Adler returned to New York and took a job in the public relations department of a textile manufacturer. Eventually he began writing songs in his spare time. In 1950, Adler was introduced to songwriter Jerry Ross as they both stood outside the Brill Building, the unofficial headquarters of the music publishing business. The two young songwriters immediately decided to team up. The team had no division of labor and both partners worked on music and lyrics.

Jerry Ross was born Jerold Rosenberg to a working-class Russian-Jewish immigrant family. As a child, Ross acted in the Yiddish language theater. He later studied music at New York University but never received a degree. In 1951 Adler and Ross were signed to a contract by Frank Loesser, the Broadway composer who was starting up a music publishing company. Two years later an Adler and Ross song, "Rags to Riches," was a chart-topping hit for singer Tony Bennett. Adler and Ross also contributed several songs to the Broadway revue *John Murray Anderson's Almanac*, most notably "Acorn in the Meadow," which was sung in the show by Harry Belafonte.

At the recommendation of Frank Loesser, producers Frederick Brisson, Robert Griffiths, and Harold Prince, who had recently scored a big success with the Bernstein/Comden/Green musical *Wonderful Town*, hired the untested Adler and Ross to write the score to *The Pajama Game*, a musical version of Richard Bissell's novel *7 1/2 Cents. The*

Pajama Game opened at the St. James Theater in New York on May 13, 1954, very late in the theatrical season and was quickly hailed as the finest musical of the season. The show's romantic ballad "Hey There" became a No. 1 hit for singer Rosemary Clooney later in the year. *The Pajama Game* won the Tony Award for best musical and ran for 1,061 performances.

Soon after the successful launching of *The Pajama Game* producers Brisson, Griffiths, and Prince put Adler and Ross to work on *Damn Yankees*, a lighthearted variation on the Faust legend. The musical was based on the novel *The Year the Yankees Lost the Pennant* by Douglass Wallop (who wrote the musical's libretto). *Damn Yankees* opened at the 46th St. Theater on May 5, 1955, to reviews not as enthusiastic as those accorded *The Pajama Game*. Nevertheless, *Damn Yankees* also won the Tony Award for best musical and enjoyed a remarkably long run (1,019 performances). Popular songs from the show were "You Gotta Have Heart" (a hit for both Eddie Fisher and the Four Aces in 1955) and "Whatever Lola Wants Lola Gets." *Damn Yankees* established Gwen Verdon, a dancer who had gained attention two years earlier in a supporting role in Cole Porter's *Can-Can*, as a major star of the musical theater.

The lucky partnership of Richard Adler and Jerry Ross ended on November 11, 1955, when Ross died at age 29 of a lung ailment from which he had suffered since childhood. Richard Adler enjoyed no further success on Broadway after Ross's death. His first solo effort was *Kwamina* (1961), a musical about an interracial romance in Africa and featuring Adler's then-wife, Sally Ann Howes. *Kwamina* lasted only 32 performances. In 1968, Adler's *A Mother's Kisses*, starring Beatrice Arthur, closed before reaching New York. A third Adler show, *Music Is*, a musical reworking of Shakespeare's *Twelfth Night*, lasted only eight performances in December 1976. In the same year Adler served as producer for the ill-fated Richard Rodgers-Sheldon Harnick collaboration *Rex*.

Adler had better luck with activities away from Broadway. In 1958 Doris Day's recording of "Everybody Loves a Lover," with lyrics by Adler and music by Robert Allen, was a major hit. Adler produced John F. Kennedy's glittering birthday celebration at Madison Square Garden in 1962 and also produced several extravaganzas for the Johnson administration. A many-times-married "bon vivant," Adler published a name-dropping autobiography in 1990.

Bibliography

Adler, Richard, with Lee Davis. *You Gotta Have Heart: An Autobiography.* New York: Fine, 1990.

Millstein, Gilbert. "Upbeat for a Song-Writing Duo." *New York Times Magazine* 19 June 1955: 20, 30-31.

"The Show's the Thing." *Time* 19 July 1954 : 32.

"This Is Adrenalin." *Newsweek* 7 June 1954: 82.

Who's Who in the Theater. Vol. 1. 17th ed. Detroit: Gale, 1981.

Mary C. Kalfatovic

Adolescent Mystery is a unique—and major—American contribution to the mystery genre, popular in the United

Popular adolescent mysteries. Photo courtesy of Popular Culture Library, Bowling Green State University, Bowling Green, OH.

States and beyond. When created by masters of the craft, mysteries for young adults can achieve genuine literary worth—though recognition of that stature has been a long time coming. The genre burst into print at the end of the period between the wars (1918-39), when American lifestyles, values, and characteristic faith in progress were in a state of flux.

With the exception of occasional books like Louisa May Alcott's *Little Women* (1868), few works for adolescent readers were written before the 20th century. Young people craving thrills on the printed page had to find them in adult fiction, including the lurid tales serialized in newspapers and magazines or published in cheap "penny-dreadful" or "yellow book" editions. In the 1920s, the works of authors like Agatha Christie and Mary Roberts Rinehart with their adult and mostly male detectives were discovered by a teen readership.

In 1904, the birth of the Stratemeyer Syndicate (see entry) revolutionized the mystery market for young people. Edward Stratemeyer, who used anonymous contract writers for his various series, had enormous early success with the *Bobbsey Twins* (begun in 1904) and *Tom Swift* (begun in 1910), among others. In 1927 he produced *The Hardy Boys* mystery series for boys and soon after created a similar series for girls.

Stratemeyer, father of two daughters, came up with the kind of heroine every early-adolescent girl longed to be: thoroughly modern, independent, intelligent, fun-loving, kind, and popular with everyone. She was close to a father who had considerable power and respected her, and had no mother saying "be careful" or "girls don't do that." *Nancy Drew* (see entry; written over time by several hands under the pen name Carolyn Keene) changed the course of mystery-writing history, launched the adolescent mystery as a major genre, served as a role model for generations of young girls, and inspired numerous women mystery writers. All that has followed in adolescent mystery has either been "like Nancy Drew" or "not like Nancy Drew."

The various series books in the same vein (such as Judy Bolton, the Dana Girls, Trixie Belden, and others) ran to many volumes. With the advent of the original paperback, the 1980s paperback publishers experimented with mystery miniseries of three to six books each. In the 1990s, especially in hardcover, emphasis has been on the individual volume of literary merit and paperback potential.

Mysteries published as adolescent fiction usually have mid-to-late-adolescent protagonists. Subgenres encompass the wide range found in the adult field: suspense, crime, supernatural, gothic, humorous, teen-in-jeopardy, high tech/cyberspace, and international intrigue. The one form not generally written for a young adult readership is the hard-boiled mystery, although some authors are beginning to push this boundary also.

Adolescent mysteries provide their readers with a feeling of empowerment. The secret strength in these works is often the same as in the enduringly popular "women's mysteries" of the golden age and beyond: the power of the nonentity who is overlooked and underestimated by the dominant culture or power structure, and who uses that misreading to gain the invisibility from which to operate undercover. Like the little old ladies with steel-trap minds who populate the mysteries of Agatha Christie and others, adolescents who behave as if they know their place may use their unobtrusive position to see freshly what adults fail to notice.

The authors of young adult mysteries have created admirable protagonists and memorable stories. Distinctive and popular titles include E. L. Koenigsburg's *From the Mixed-Up Files of Mrs. Basil E. Frankweiler* (1967), about two runaway children who hide out in a museum and uncover the secrets of one of its statues; Ellen Raskin's puzzle-mystery, *The Westing Game* (1978), about a young girl who pieces together the identity of a man's killer from clues planted in his will; Virginia Hamilton's *The House of Dies Drear* (1968), in which an African-American family discovers its hidden heritage in an old house; Rumer Godden's *The Rocking Horse Secret* (1978) and Eleanor Clymer's *The Horse in the Attic* (1983), both of which feature valuables concealed in an attic and young heroines who discover their worth when adults fail to recognize it; and Eve Bunting's *Is Anybody There?* (1988), which blends domestic drama and suspense as young Marcus investigates his widowed mother's new friend Nick.

Bibliography

Billman, Carol. *The Secret of the Stratemeyer Syndicate: Nancy Drew, the Hardy Boys, and the Million Dollar Fiction Factory.* New York: Ungar, 1986.
Dyer, Carolyn Stewart, and Nancy Tillman Romalov. *Rediscovering Nancy Drew.* Iowa City: U of Iowa P, 1955.
Johnson, Deidre. *Edward Stratemeyer and the Stratemeyer Syndicate.* New York: Twayne, 1993.

Nicole St. John

See also
Children's Literature
Ethnic Mysteries

Adolescent Romance Fiction is as popular as ever among its predominately female audience, ages 12 to 15, despite earlier predictions of waning readership. Translated into 15 languages, Bantam's Sweet Valley High romance series has over 40 million books in print. Shortly after the series became the first young adult novel on the *New York Times* paperback best-seller list. These formulaic novels of first love have antecedents in adolescent fiction by Maureen Daly and Betty Cavanna in the 1940s and 1950s. Teen romance novels reappeared in 1980 as a response to the findings from a study conducted by Scholastic Books showing a demand for such material by young women's school book clubs. Scholastic's romance line, Wildfire, incorporated the series format and the multimedia advertising campaigns used to promote adult romance fiction. Wildfire's first-year sales of over 2.25 million prompted the creation of Bantam's Sweet Dreams division, Dell's Young Love, and Simon & Schuster's First Love sequences.

These romance series were immediately condemned by some reviewers and critics for their gender, class, and racial stereotypes. Linda Christian-Smith's school study of young women as reluctant readers of romances draws parallels between the traditional views of femininity that such novels tend to advance and the rise of conservative political interests in America since 1980. Historically, romance reading for teenage girls has provided an escape from school and home problems, tutored readers about boys and romantic relationships, and afforded a means for reflecting on developing desires and feminine identity; hence they can be powerful tools of ideological reinforcement. In romances currently popular, school achievement and careers uneasily coexist with heart and hearth as young women's destinies.

Bibliography

Christian-Smith, Linda. *Becoming a Woman through Romance.* New York: Routledge, 1990.
——. *Text of Desire: Essays on Fiction, Femininity and Schooling.* London: Falmor, 1993.
Huntwork, Mary. "Why Girls Flock to Sweet Valley High." *School Library Journal* 1990.

Linda Christian-Smith

Adventure Comics (1938-1983) capitalized on earlier pulp magazine successes like *Adventure* (1929) and its later continuance, *New Adventure* (1937). From the start, *Adventure Comics* was a vehicle for introducing a variety of superheroes, some of whom were later given their own comic book. It is perhaps best known for highlighting Superboy since 1946, along with various other hallmarks. April 1958 brought Cosmic Boy, Saturn Girl, and then-named Lightning Boy as representatives of the Legion of Super Heroes, a group from Superboy's future—thus initiating regular time travel. Later, in September 1958, red kryptonite was revealed for the first time. Later hallmarks included tales of the Bizarro World and the replacement of Superboy by Supergirl in 1969.

Earlier heroes hit upon a diversity of powers. Sandman, Hourman, and Starman were stars of the early 1940s, having mystical, cosmic powers. Congo Bill was a hunter-adventurer who got in many a jam. Similarly, Roy Raymond, TV detective, used his smarts and fists to solve mysteries. They starred in the aftermath of World War II when superheroes—except for Superboy—were temporarily out of favor. Yet Johnny Quick, whose scientific formula endowed him with super speed, was joined by Green Arrow, Aquaman, and

Adventure Comics. Photo courtesy of Popular Culture Library, Bowling Green State University, Bowling Green, OH.

Robotman. Of particular interest is the appearance of Black Orchid, a woman with a secret identity which was kept secret, even from the readers. Spectre, a golden age hero, made his reappearance, followed by J'Onn J'Onzz, the Martian Manhunter, whose major weakness was fire.

Bibliography

Benton, Mike. *Superhero Comics of the Silver Age.* Dallas: Taylor, 1991.

Daniels, Les. *DC Comics: Sixty Years of the World's Favorite Comic Book Heroes.* Boston: Little, Brown, 1995.

Carl Holmberg

Adventure Fiction, a very popular form of fiction today, is one of the easiest narrative formulas to recognize and one of the hardest to define specifically. The reason for this seeming contradiction is that so many other genres of popular fiction emphasize adventure as an important dimension of their formulas. Nevertheless, the adventure story does possess a handful of readily identifiable characteristics that should be collectively present to be classified as a discrete literary type.

The most important quality is adventure. The adventure story de-emphasizes such things as characterization in favor of narrative action. It also features larger-than-life-heroes as its central protagonists. The single defining element of all the great adventure heroes—from Sir H. Rider Haggard's Allan Quatermain to Tom Clancy's Jack Ryan—is their ability to conquer their adversaries or prevail over a hostile environment. This is why the dramatic conflict in many adventure stories is structured as a series of traps and escapes, a literary convention that allows the hero to demonstrate great strength, courage, and intelligence by escaping an otherwise inevitable destruction. At a larger, thematic level, the adventure hero's triumph over imminent death becomes a symbolic conquest of human mortality. Finally, the adventure story tends to reinforce certain imperialistic ideas or beliefs. A number of the various types of popular fiction that can be collected under the general heading of the adventure story are set in foreign lands or exotic locales. The heroes of these stories, as part of the author's intended construction of dramatic conflict, often engage in hostilities with the native peoples of these foreign lands, frequently either subjugating them or killing them.

The origins of the adventure story may be located in the novels of British authors Daniel Defoe and Sir Walter Scott. Defoe, an important innovator of the novel, helped to establish a number of the conventions found in the adventure story—as perhaps best illustrated in such works as *Robinson Crusoe* (1719) and *Adventures of Captain Singleton* (1720). Defoe was one of the first authors of fiction to use descriptive action as a crucial narrative device in the structuring of a story's plot. In addition, Defoe was among the earliest writers to feature an adventure hero who facilitates or manages a story's narrative pace.

Sir Walter Scott expanded on Defoe's earlier efforts by combining historical fact with the writing of adventure fiction. Considered to be the creator of the historical romance, Scott's body of fiction, including *Waverley* (1814), *Rob Roy* (1817), and *Ivanhoe* (1819), established a fundamentally ideological understanding of heroism and the hero's obligations to a chivalric code. Scott's historical fiction influenced a considerable number of important 19th-century novelists.

In France, for example, Alexandre Dumas's massive novels—*The Three Musketeers* (1844), *The Count of Monte Cristo* (1844-45), and *The Man in the Iron Mask* (1848-50)—revived the slumping popularity of the historical romance in both Europe and America. In Great Britain, Robert Louis Stevenson's *Treasure Island* (1883) and *Kidnapped* (1886) attracted an adolescent readership to the historical romance, as did Sir Arthur Conan Doyle's *The White Company* (1891). In America, James Fenimore Cooper (see entry), in his Leatherstocking series, transplanted Scott's historical romance to the New World frontier. Cooper's five novels featuring the exploits of the backwoodsman Natty Bumppo—*The Pioneers* (1823), *The Last of the Mohicans* (1826), *The Prairie* (1827), *The Pathfinder* (1840), and *The Deerslayer* (1841)—transformed Scott's European aristocratic adventure hero into a more democratized protagonist, in the process defining nobility as a virtue the hero achieves rather than a quality the hero is born with. Cooper's frontier adventure story became a major source of inspiration for the modern American Western. For example, Cooper's work helped to influence Owen Wister's *The Virginian* (1902), a novel regarded as one of the first popular Westerns.

A sampling of classic, swashbuckling, historical adventures published during the early decades of the 20th century includes Baroness Orczy's *The Scarlet Pimpernel* (1905), Johnston McCulley's *The Mark of Zorro* (published in serial form in 1919 as *The Curse of Capistrano*), and Rafael Sabatini's *Captain Blood: His Odyssey* (1922).

Collectively, all the stories that can be defined as popular adventure fiction have descended from these two basic narrative traditions: Scott's "historical" adventure story and Defoe's "contemporary" adventure story. Perhaps the strongest proponent of the Defoe variant of the contemporary adventure story during the late 19th century was the popular British author Sir H. Rider Haggard. Haggard's essay "About Fiction," published in the February 1887 issue of *The Contemporary Review*, created a stir among literary critics because of its advocacy of the imaginative "romance" and its attack against the "naturalistic" school of fiction.

The contemporary adventure story (as popular fiction) begins with H. Rider Haggard's publication of *King Solomon's Mines* (1885; see Haggard entry). This exotic tale of three intrepid adventurers—including the African hunter Allan Quatermain—who explore the proverbial "heart" of Africa and discover the legendary diamond mines of King Solomon, enjoyed tremendous commercial success in late Victorian England. Along with *King Solomon's Mines*, Haggard's other great adventure romance, *She* (1886-87), inspired an entire generation of "lost world" fiction, from Edgar Rice Burroughs's Tarzan series, to Sir Arthur Conan Doyle's *The Lost World* (1912), to the wondrous tales of the American fantasist A. Merritt. In addition, Haggard's African settings for his adventure novels may be seen as influencing the best-selling fiction of Wilbur Smith (see entry), who also specializes in employing African settings in his several epic, multigenerational adventure series.

India-born British author Rudyard Kipling was Haggard's friend and his equal in popularity, but whereas Haggard wrote primarily novel-length fiction, Kipling's forte was the short story. Kipling's best work includes his series of military adventure stories featuring the notorious "soldiers three" (Learoyd, Mulvaney, and Ortheris of the British Army serving in India), some 18 tales anthologized in five collections, *Plain Tales from the Hills* (1888), *Soldiers Three* (1890), *Life's Handicap* (1891), *Many Inventions* (1893), and *Actions and Reactions* (1909). Kipling's work influenced many other writers of war tales, such as P. C. Wren, author of the classic French Foreign Legion novel *Beau Geste* (1924), Alistair MacLean, author of the World War II novels *H.M.S. Ulysses* (1955) and *Where Eagles Dare* (1967), and Bernard Cornwell, author of *Sharpe's Rifles* (1988), the first of a series of military adventures set during the Napoleonic Wars. Among Kipling's handful of novels, *Captains Courageous* (1897) and *Kim* (1901) have become adventure classics. Kipling was also quite adept at writing adventure fiction for children, his most notable efforts in this area being his two Jungle Book anthologies, *The Jungle Book* (1894) and *The Second Jungle Book* (1895). Edgar Rice Burroughs, in his popular Tarzan stories, borrowed from and elaborated upon Kipling's depiction of the feral child protagonist, Mowgli, in the Jungle Books.

As the adventure story moved from the 19th to the 20th century, several American authors began to dominate the genre. The foremost of these was Jack London (see entry), who, like Stevenson and Kipling, attracted both adolescent and adult readers with his adventure stories, the most popular of which include *The Call of the Wild* (1903), *The Sea Wolf* (1904), and *White Fang* (1906).

At the same time that London was discovering the lucrative serial magazine and hardcover book markets, a number of American authors were establishing a reputation in the pulp magazines (see entry). Although narrative elements of adventure frequently appeared in the American dime novels and British "penny dreadfuls" of the 19th century, the adventure story, as a distinct literary genre, became firmly established in the pulps. Early general fiction pulp magazines published Edgar Rice Burroughs's initial literary efforts, including *A Princess of Mars* (first appearing in the pulp *Argosy* in 1911 with the title *Under the Moons of Mars*), which introduced the archetypal swashbuckling fantasy hero John Carter of Mars, and *Tarzan of the Apes* (first appearing in the pulp *All-Story* in 1912), which introduced perhaps the world's most recognizable adventure hero. Burroughs also developed several other classic adventure-oriented series, including the Pellucidar and Carson of Venus stories, eventually becoming one of the most popular and influential authors of adventure and science fiction in the 20th century.

During those decades between the two world wars, a number of important adventure heroes were introduced to an avid reading public. In England, the Bulldog Drummond stories by "Sapper" (pseudonym of Herman Cyril McNeile) and the Fu Manchu tales by Sax Rohmer helped to define the formula of the modern adventure "thriller" (see The Thriller).

In recent years, the "techno-thriller" has come to dominate the adventure genre, and three best-selling authors, Michael Crichton, Clive Cussler, and Tom Clancy (see entries), have come to dominate the techno-thriller. Crichton helped to design the techno-thriller in novels like *The Andromeda Strain* (1969), *The Terminal Man* (1972), and *Congo* (1980), and perfected the formula in *Sphere* (1987), *Jurassic Park* (1993) and its sequel *The Lost World* (1997), *Rising Sun* (1992), and *Disclosure* (1993). Both Cussler and Clancy created popular techno-thriller series featuring James Bond-like protagonists who are well-versed in the application of technology in combating evil. Cussler introduced deep-sea expert Dirk Pitt's first adventure in *Pacific Vortex* (1982), while Clancy introduced CIA intelligence specialist Jack Ryan's in *The Hunt for Red October* (1984).

In its many guises, the adventure story continues to prosper. Authors like Michael Crichton and Wilbur Smith succeed in placing their latest efforts squarely at the top of the international best-seller lists. The adventure story also continues to evolve. Subsequent generations of adventure writers craft their work to meet the particular needs and expectations of a popular readership. Best-selling writers like Don Pendleton, author of *War against the Mafia* (1969) and master of the vigilante thriller; Robin Cook, author of *Coma* (1977) and master of the medical thriller; Jack Higgins, author of *Storm Warning* (1976) and master of the World War II political thriller; and John Grisham, author of *The Firm* (1991) and master of the legal thriller, have successfully explored new literary avenues in which to take the tale of adventure. With such talented writers making their unique contributions to the genre, the adventure story will remain for years to come one of popular fiction's most commercially successful formula types.

Bibliography

Cawelti, John G. *Adventure, Mystery, and Romance: Formula Stories as Art and Popular Culture.* Chicago: U of Chicago P, 1976.

Hoppenstand, Gary. *In Search of the Paper Tiger: A Sociological Perspective of Myth, Formula and the Mystery Genre* in the Entertainment Print Mass Medium. Bowling Green, OH: Bowling Green State U Popular P, 1987.

Jones, Robert Kenneth. *The Lure of Adventure*. Mercer Island: Starmont House, 1989.

Rovin, Jeff. *Adventure Heroes: Legendary Characters from Odysseus to James Bond*. New York: Facts on File, 1994.

Sampson, Robert. *Deadly Excitements: Shadows and Phantoms*. Bowling Green, OH: Bowling Green State U Popular P, 1989.

Gary Hoppenstand

Advertising and Popular Culture are as compatible as fish and water. Through the years, advertising has attempted to keep up with the most appealing trends, customs, and fashions in American culture. It is truly a part of our communication system, drawing from, as well as adding to, our significant icons and symbols. In various ways, advertising advises, informs, directs, and persuades, in harmony with our values and our picture of the good life.

In 1976, *Life* magazine published a special issue, relating to significant, impressionable events of the previous century. An advertising ploy then is now a classic popular culture icon: the Uneeda Biscuit boy, dressed in a bulky, bright yellow raincoat and hat. He is carrying a box of Uneeda Biscuits, made by the National Biscuit Company—now Nabisco.

According to some historians, truly modern, national advertising has existed only about 100 years. Numerous factors—all generally coming together in the 1890s—were necessary. These included sufficient national marketing of brand-name products and a national transportation system (primarily railroads); adequate major media (newspapers and magazines); and practical, high-speed printing means (linotype typesetters and rotary presses).

It was not until 1928 that radio, a major new medium, would become a national advertising force (see Radio Advertising). Its electronic counterpart, television, attained a comparable position by 1948 (see next entry). Direct marketing grew tremendously between 1955 and 1975, including not only direct mail but also television, magazines and newspapers, billboards, and yellow pages as direct sales forms of conventional media. In addition, non-conventional or alternative ad forms have grown significantly. These often include posters, handbills, numerous in-store varieties, A-frame signs, and mobile billboards (see Billboard/Poster Art and Advertising). Alternative formats include public-

address-type audio and closed-circuit TV commercials (including interactive video), various signs, as well as flashing lights on automatic coupon dispensers. TV monitor ads find their way to numerous public places such as subway platforms. Finally, poster or handbill ads have even appeared on restroom walls and doors—the new graffiti of corporate America inundating our private moments.

14

While most industry and business leaders feel advertising is a necessary part of most marketing efforts, occasionally strong criticisms arise from this practice. Since 1914, the Federal Trade Commission (FTC) has led government oversight of advertising. False and misleading claims are investigated and appropriate action recommended.

There was a time, especially around the turn of the century, when there arose a public as well as industry outcry against advertising. Blatant medical and patent medicine advertisements—many of which were considered outrageously false, misleading, and dangerous—provided protest groups sufficient ammunition. This helped prompt creation of the Food and Drug Administration (FDA) in 1906. During the 1920s, a decade when advertising became ever more pervasive in American life, social critic Stuart Chase formulated an analysis of this institution. He noted that advertising went beyond earlier concerns about dishonesty and deception. Chase examined advertising's role in facilitating waste and in furnishing fantasies for the masses.

Numerous false and misleading ads continue to be reported to and investigated by the FTC. Today, there are very loud cries against cigarette advertising of any kind. Especially significant are those ads likely to appeal to children and younger adults. Consider, for instance, Joe Camel, the cartoon character. Concern over his appeal to children led to his retirement in 1997.

The 1980s and 1990s have been classified as times of rapid advancement of new technologies such as satellite and cable TV communication. In addition, audience fragmentation, consolidation of ad agencies, and the formation of fewer powerful media entities have complicated the advertising industry. Examples of advertising clutter exist not only in TV, but also other media such as magazines.

Certainly, advertisements can mislead, annoy, and even disgust consumers. They constantly tell us that we are a little inadequate, that we need to buy-buy-buy in order to become happy, healthy, and whole. However, advertising and popular culture continue to complement each other as ads proceed to inform, persuade, and stimulate potential customers.

Bibliography

Danna, Sammy. *Advertising and Popular Culture: Studies in Variety and Versatility*. Bowling Green, OH: Bowling Green State U Popular P, 1992.

Goodrum, Charles, and Helen Dalrymple. *Advertising in America: The First 200 Years*. New York: Abrams, 1990.

Holme, Bryan. *Advertising: Reflections of a Century*. New York: Viking, 1982.

O'Barr, William M. *Culture and the Ad*. Boulder: Westview, 1994.

Russell, J. Thomas, and W. Ronald Lane. *Kleppner's Advertising Procedure*. 12th ed. Englewood Cliffs: Prentice-Hall, 1993.

Sammy R. Danna

Advertising and TV are so integral to each other in the minds of Americans that no one finds it odd when *Sesame Street*, a noncommercial children's educational program, features individual numbers and letters as "sponsors" of each episode.

Ads have been on television since summer 1939, when NBC included them in the first experimental broadcast of a major league baseball game. The first authorized ad was a brief "Time Check" by the Bulova Watch Company aired on July 1, 1941, during a baseball game on WNBT, the NBC station in New York.

National links came gradually. In 1955, a coaxial cable linked New York and Chicago; in 1962, it finally reached San Francisco. During what is now called the golden age of television, most dramatic or variety shows were produced live in New York by advertising agencies and included the sponsor's name in their title: *Armstrong Circle Theater, U.S. Steel Hour, Kraft Television Theater, Colgate Comedy Hour*. Kinescopes, film records of the flickering images that appeared on the TV picture tubes, were made for later rebroadcast. Milton Berle, TV's first superstar, began in 1947 as featured performer on *The Texaco Star Theater;* later he starred on the *Buick Berle Show*.

There were few ways to produce ads. On variety shows, the host/star read the commercial or introduced the actors who did. Arthur Godfrey, transplanted radio star, seemed to ad lib commercials for Lipton soups or tea while consuming the product on-camera. The ensemble troupe on *The Garry Moore Show* transformed product messages into comedy skits and song parodies. From 1949 to 1960, Betty Furness did live weekly demonstrations of Westinghouse electrical products during *Studio One* intermissions, becoming one of the first celebrities created by television. Furness's credibility was so high that she later served as consumer affairs advisor in the Johnson administration.

During the late 1950s, the major networks struggled to wrest control of production from corporate sponsors and their advertising agencies. By 1961, all corporate-sponsored weekly programs had succumbed to increasing production costs and steeply higher rates for network time.

Networks offered 60-second spots in network-produced programs with content unrelated to the sponsor. With 12 60-second slots in any program hour, advertisers vied to get viewers' attention. Magazine format shows, of which pioneer NBC's *Today Show* and *Tonight Show* still remain, were deliberately segmented to allow commercial inserts.

Many advertising practitioners consider the 1960s to be the golden age of TV advertising. In 1959, the American TV Commercials Festival began; it awarded the first Clios in 1962. The pressure to create ads that viewers would recognize and remember resulted in a creative explosion. Among the 1960s classics in *Advertising Age*'s 50 Best are the Marlboro man series, Noxema shaving cream's "Take it off" ads, Hertz's "Puts you in the driver's seat" ads showing people floating into a convertible, and Alka-Seltzer's multiple jokes on heartburn, including "Mama Mia, atsa some spicy meatball." All influenced popular thinking by adding phrases or ideas to the language.

The most talked-about ad of the 1960s, considered a seminal political commercial, was "Daisy" (1964). Melding from a little girl plucking daisy petals into a nuclear countdown and ultimate explosion, the ad worked on voters' fears about GOP presidential candidate Barry Goldwater's nuclear policy without mentioning his name. The Johnson campaign pulled the ad after one showing, but more people saw the ad when it was rerun on TV news and commentary programs than when it originally aired.

In 1971, when TV networks voluntarily banned cigarette advertising, they compensated for lost revenues by raising ad slot prices and offered 15- and 30-second slots in prime time. As ad clutter grew, the pressure for memorable ads increased. The results were as gentle as Anheuser-Busch's still-used Christmas ad for Budweiser, with Clydesdales strutting through a snowy landscape, and as enigmatic as Chanel's new wave "Share the fantasy" ad.

The ad "1984," introduced Macintosh computers during that year's Super Bowl, is called "the greatest commercial ever" by *Advertising Age*. Juxtaposing Orwellian nightmare with Olympic hope, it has dramatic wordless action. Like "Daisy," it contains an implication (IBM is like Big Brother) and was often repeated on news and commentary shows.

But TV advertising's future is not assured. During the 1980s, networks' share of viewership began shrinking as niche-oriented cable channels proliferated. Target audiences fragmented. The advent of home-buying and pay-per-view channels disconnected the link between advertising and entertainment. Videocassettes, CD-ROM players, and interactive games provided new on-demand forms of entertainment. Congress passed the Children's Television Act of 1990, limiting ads on children's programming to 10.5 minutes per hour on weekends and 12 minutes on weekdays. Old Milwaukee Beer's popular "Swedish Bikini Team" ads, which Stroh Brewery claimed were spoofs of typical beer-and-babes ads, were cited in sexual harrassment suits by eight Stroh workers in 1991. In a 1994 viewership poll, 74 percent said they switched channels to avoid commercials (a process called "zapping"; see entry) and 50 percent occasionally muted the message.

Bibliography

Diamant, Lincoln. *Television's Classic Commercials: The Golden Years, 1948-1958*. New York: Hastings, 1971.

"Fifty Years of TV Advertising." *Advertising Age*. Special Collector's Edition, Spring 1995.

Greenfield, Jeff. *Television: The First Fifty Years*. New York: Abrams, 1977.

Hall, Jim. *Mighty Minutes: An Illustrated History of Television's Best Commercials*. New York: Harmony, 1984.

Spigel, Lynn. *Make Room for TV: Television and the Family Ideal in Postwar America*. Chicago: U of Chicago P, 1992.

Eileen Margerum

Advice Columns are forums, in almost every national periodical, through which research-oriented mediators dispense guidance and information to questioning readers. The range of concerns addressed in a contemporary advice column is typically defined by the interests of the publication in which it appears. However, topic-specific advice forums, such as "The *Playboy* Advisor" or Judith Martin's "Miss Manners," have their archetype in the general, nationally syndicated columns that appear in hundreds of daily newspapers.

Frequently referred to as "mirrors of America," twin sisters Esther Friedman Lederer (Ann Landers) and Pauline Friedman Phillips (Abigail Van Buren) write the country's longest-running advice columns. The name Ann Landers originated at the Chicago *Sun-Times*, where Lederer replaced the first Ann Landers upon her death. She celebrated 40 years as Ann Landers in 1995 after joining her sister (who writes "Dear Abby") at the Chicago *Tribune* in 1987; together, their columns appear worldwide in more than 2,400 newspapers.

Both Ann Landers and "Dear Abby" have been credited with remodeling the advice column genre from its early role as moral standard-bearer into a location for information exchange. Unlike their predecessors in the Miss Lonelyhearts tradition, such as "Dear Beatrice Fairfax" and Dorothy Dix, contemporary advice columnists function less like a prim aunt and more like a reference librarian, matching inquiring readers with the work of degreed professionals in an attempt to dispel misinformation and myth with contemporary science and scholarship.

Ann Landers's movement from advisor to mediator demonstrates the advice columnist as a strong antecedent for other relatively recent popular cultural opinion exchanges with a strong emphasis on the personal—talk radio and TV talk shows. For some 80 million daily readers, the columns function as a kind of fossil record of the changing face of American popular culture. "I don't need a Gallup poll to give me the pulse of America," says Jeffrey Zaslow, who writes "All That Zazz" for the Chicago *Sun-Times*. "All I have to do is ask my readers."

Bibliography

McNulty, Henry. "Dear Ann Landers, How You've Changed ..." *Quill* 74 (1986): 22-23.

Olson, Lynne. "Dear Beatrice Fairfax..." *American Heritage* May/June 1992: 90-97.

Pottker, Jan, and Bob Speziale. *Dear Ann, Dear Abby: The Unauthorized Biography of Ann Landers and Abigail Van Buren*. New York: Dodd, 1987.

Rottenberg, Dan. "Ann and Abby's Lessons for Journalists." *Quill* 72 (1984): 20-24.

Zaslow, Jeffrey. *Tell Me All about It*. New York: Morrow, 1990.

Peter Vandenberg

Aerobics, formerly known as aerobic dance, is thought to be the most common fitness activity in the U.S. These activities performed to music are usually in the form of calisthenics, which may include a combination of stepping, walking, jogging, skipping, kicking, and arm-swinging movements.

The aerobics concept was initially developed in the early 1970s by Jacki Sorensen as a fitness program for Air Force wives in Puerto Rico. At approximately the same time, Judy Missett, the founder of Jazzercise, was incorporating jazz dance into fitness routines. Jazzercise is a nationally known fitness program incorporating choreographed routines with classes held all over the world. At first considered a fad, aerobics is now a legitimate fitness activity with more than 20 million participants of all ages. Aerobics became the hook to get people moving. Aerobics are now part of school curricula, health clubs, and recreational facilities.

During the last 25 years the number of people participating in physical fitness programs has increased tremendously. The increase in the number of fitness participants is attributed primarily to scientific evidence linking vigorous exercise and positive lifestyle habits to better overall health, cardiovascular endurance, and improved quality of life.

Among the fun aspects of aerobic exercise are the many different choices of activities that promote cardiovascular development. Undeniably, aerobic dance exercise classes have diversified to the point of including practically everyone, no matter what their limitations might be. In addition to "regular" aerobic classes, there are classes for children, mothers-to-be, older adults, and people with disabilities. The format of these classes is equally as varied, to include water aerobics, dance, high impact, moderate impact, low impact, nonimpact, resistance aerobics that utilize rubber bands and/or light, free, or attached weights, step aerobics, slide, box aerobics, plyometrics, and aerobic interval training.

As aerobic dance became more popular so did the need for highly trained instructors. Certifications became required so professionals could stay updated on the latest information on safety, technique, and fitness research. Certifications at first were general but eventually became very specific for each type of aerobic activity. Requirements include not only credible certifications from organizations such as ACE (American Council on Exercise), ACSM (American Council of Sports Medicine), and AFFA (Aerobics and Fitness Association of America), but also a yearly CPR certification.

Many participants find an aerobic class to be a very social experience and will bond with each other and the instructor. Some participants prefer to work out and exercise undisturbed, in their own personal space, and find they can in the context of the aerobic class. From the initial fad, fitness programs have become a trend that is now very much a part of the American way of life.

Bibliography

Dintman, George B., Robert G. Davis, and Jude C. Pennington. *Discovering Lifetime Fitness: Concepts of Exercise and Weight Control.* St. Paul: West, 1989.

Hoeger, Werner W. K., and Sharon A. Hoeger. *Fitness and Wellness.* Englewood: Morton, 1993.

Personal Trainer Manual: The Resource for Fitness Instructors. San Diego: American Council on Exercise, 1991.

Debby L. Mitchell

African Americans and Entertainment TV have had, at best, an uneasy relationship. While white Americans reveled in the golden age of television, African Americans found it a period marked by either deplorable stereotypes or blatant exclusion. Although today's programming features more African-American programs, many of the images continue to cater to entrenched societal stereotypes. Ironically, while African-American purchasing power continues to rise, equitable treatment in the media remains an uphill battle.

Many of the stereotypes existing today are based on the characters created by minstrel shows, which made their appearance in the 1840s. While emancipation brought freedom, African Americans remained enslaved in the minstrel show stereotype, which painted them as ignorant and lazy buffoons with exaggerated dialects and facial features.

The minstrel show had almost vanished by the time radio took hold. Nevertheless, the misconceptions and stereotypes regarding African Americans remained. This was clearly demonstrated by the debut of America's first sitcom, *Sam 'n' Henry*, which became the infamous *Amos 'n' Andy* when it moved to WGN radio in 1926. *Amos 'n' Andy* (see entry) was the creation of two southern whites, Freeman Gosden and Charles Correll. It became one of the most popular programs, dominating radio and television airwaves for nearly 50 years. In the audio arena, Gosden and Correll replaced burnt cork with exaggerated dialects as their portrayal of *Amos 'n' Andy* became one of the few happy memories for mainstream Depression-era Americans. In some communities, movie theaters would stop their films to pipe in *Amos 'n' Andy* broadcasts.

Amos 'n' Andy became a particular problem for the National Association for the Advancement of Colored People (NAACP), which was beginning to increase its efforts towards civil rights. This posed a particular problem in the South, where news of civil rights activities was censored by southern network affiliates. Thus, after southern blacks were preached civil rights, they went home to the minstrel-show-influenced images of *Amos 'n' Andy*. If justice was ever to be achieved, reasoned the NAACP leadership, the images perpetuated by *Amos 'n' Andy* would have to go.

Mounting a 12-point attack on the series, the NAACP eventually brought pressure to bear on the program's sponsor, Blatz beer, which eventually pulled its sponsorship. In 1953, CBS, claiming it had "bowed to the change in national thinking," removed the show from first-run programming. However, the 78 episodes already filmed continued to be shown in syndication. Meanwhile, the sitcom *Beulah*, which featured Louise Beavers in the title role as a black maid, also went off the air in 1953 when Beavers decided to leave the show; the series had also been targeted by the NAACP. In 1955, when Roy Wilkins became president of the NAACP, more emphasis was placed on civil rights actions than television images, and *Amos 'n' Andy* continued in syndication.

The end of first-run programs such as *Amos 'n' Andy* and *Beulah* lead to a dearth of new African-American images on television. While *Amos 'n' Andy* had allowed for the portrayal of some blacks in professional roles, dramatic portrayals of doctors, lawyers, and Western heroes were still reserved for white actors only.

There were a few exceptions in which African Americans appeared. Variety programs, a popular format of the 1950s and 1960s, often featured such performers as Sammy Davis, Jr., Lena Horne, and Louis Armstrong. Nat King Cole, who had crossed racial boundaries by having four No. 1 hits in *Billboard* magazine in 1956, became the first African American to host his own variety show, which debuted that same year. Despite poor ratings, NBC attempted a number of schedule changes to help the show survive. By 1957, however, the series was canceled. According to Cole, the program's sponsors felt uncomfortable with their products being associated with an African American.

One of the only programs during the early 1960s to present African Americans in nonstereotypical roles was *The Dick Van Dyke Show*, created by Carl Reiner and produced by Sheldon Leonard. The most significant of these was the flashback episode "That's My Boy?" in which Rob Petrie (Van Dyke) recounts the time his son was born. Through a series of mishaps, Rob comes to think that the hospital has switched his son with a baby born on the same day to a Mr. and Mrs. Peters. The episode reaches a hilarious climax when Rob confronts Mr. Peters, an African American played by Richard Morris.

This rare moment, one of the longest recorded laughs in sitcom history, was significant for three reasons. First and foremost, it cast the white character, Rob, as the buffoon. Second, it portrayed Morris as a well-dressed, well-mannered professional. Finally, because these two images were so inconsistent with previous TV portrayals, the incongruence created an incredibly humorous situation. In 1965, another *Dick Van Dyke* episode featured Rob accepting an award from a committee for racial understanding, and in 1966 the series featured Godfrey Cambridge as an FBI agent. Unfortunately, *The Dick Van Dyke Show* was the only "equal opportunity" program of its day.

To correct some of the imbalance, the NAACP increased its pressure on sponsors and networks. In 1964, an NAACP boycott of Lever Brothers products led to the first commercial to use an African-American actor. Two years later, the NAACP proved instrumental in finally pulling the plug on the syndicated version of *Amos 'n' Andy*, which has never again been publicly broadcast. Videos of episodes from the series have since become popular rentals in video stores.

After African Americans and concerned mainstream citizens—encouraged by such influential leaders as Dr. Martin Luther King, Jr.—fought and died for the cause of civil rights, television finally began to introduce a small number of programs that featured African Americans in a positive light. The first was the 1965 dramatic series *I Spy* (see entry), starring Robert Culp and Bill Cosby. Sheldon Leonard, the courageous producer who brought positive black images to *The Dick Van Dyke Show*, did not write the series for an African-American character; however, after seeing Cosby on a variety show, Leonard became convinced Cosby was the best man for the job.

Cosby, as Alexander Scott, portrayed a humorous, personable character in a responsible, professional position working as a spy for American intelligence. Unlike previous African-American comics, Cosby's humor did not come at a sacrifice to his dignity. A year later, actor Greg Morris was featured in a similar yet more serious role in *Mission: Impossible*, another spy drama. Morris, as electronics expert Barney Collier, helped further the positive African-American image pioneered by Cosby.

Such contributions were seen as important by Don Mitchell, who in 1967 won the supporting *Ironside* role of Mark Sanger, a reformed delinquent who became an assistant to the wheelchair-bound police chief. Mitchell proved a marvelous role model; during the run of the popular series, his character attended and graduated from law school. Also important in Mitchell's character—unlike those of Cosby or Morris—was how racial injustice played a role in Mitchell's character development. Thus, *Ironside* successfully walked the fine line between mainstreaming and recognizing cultural diversity.

Although 82 percent of the television series during the 1967-68 season were still devoid of black characters, those programs that featured blacks did so in a careful and tasteful manner. Ratings data for such shows as *The Mod Squad* (1968) and *I Spy* indicated that mainstream America was willing to accept these images; however, the shows were still written and produced by whites.

Between 1966 and 1970, more sitcoms, dramas, and variety programs began to feature African Americans in either recurring or starring roles. Nichelle Nichols in *Star Trek* (1966), Hari Rhodes in *Daktari* (1966), Gail Fisher in *Mannix* (1968), Leslie Uggams in *The Leslie Uggams Show* (1969), and Clarence Williams III in *The Mod Squad* were among them.

Perhaps the most important shows of the period, however, were two half-hour shows, *Julia* and *Room 222*, which debuted in 1969. Although NBC was quick to tout its virtues in bringing *Julia* to television, the network almost backed out on the series when it discovered the serious tone its $200,000 pilot had taken. Diahann Carroll starred in the title role as a widowed nurse trying to raise her son. To make the series even more contemporary, Julia had lost her husband in Vietnam.

Julia's debut was met with a hail of hype and publicity, and NBC was keenly aware of its public relations value in response to the NAACP's concern with the depiction of African Americans. Building upon the work of Cosby, Morris, and Mitchell, Carroll gave viewers an articulate professional African-American woman who was about as far from the stereotypical characters of *Amos 'n' Andy* as one could get. However, many African Americans were upset that *Julia* had become too mainstreamed to be representative of the African-American community.

Lloyd Haynes played a similar role as teacher Pete Dixon in ABC's *Room 222*. The series also starred Denise Nicholas as guidance counselor Liz McIntyre, and Heshimu as Jason Allen, one of Dixon's students. Within the confines of his social studies class in Los Angeles High's Room 222, Dixon and his students discussed the important issues of the day, with Dixon often leaving the decisions to the kids. Although ABC kept the series on the air for five years, it did not meet with much ratings success.

Surprisingly, one of the most controversial series regarding black issues was one in which blacks served only in recurring roles. *All in the Family* (see entry), a Norman Lear and Bud Yorkin adaptation of the British series *Till Death Do Us Part*, starred Carroll O'Connor as blue-collar bigot Archie Bunker.

Part of CBS's shift toward removing its rural programming in favor of more contemporary and sophisticated programs, *All in the Family* is credited for both positive and negative effects on African Americans. On the one hand, the series featured bigoted Bunker as a narrow-minded anachronism who was often shown up by his liberal son-in-law, Mike, and liberated daughter, Gloria. On the other hand, Archie Bunker surprisingly became a lovable character, providing many Americans with a level of understanding for such bigots. Many African Americans also complained about the series' language—Archie would use *coon* and *spade* as liberally as he would use *heeb, chink, spic,* and *mic*. Nevertheless, Archie's use of such language was clearly depicted as deplorable and, although it got laughs, it also raised consciousness.

Some of *All in the Family*'s brightest moments came from Archie's confrontations with neighbor Lionel Jefferson, played by Mike Evans. Lionel was a hard-working, industrious African American whom Archie would often refer to as "one of the good ones." While Lionel would feed Archie the lines he knew the bigot wanted to hear, Lionel always got his own point across, forcing Archie to show himself as a big white buffoon.

Lionel, as well as his father, George, and mother, Louise, eventually got their own series, *The Jeffersons*, in 1975. Ultimately, *All in the Family* led to three successful spinoffs. The first, *Maude* (1972), starred Beatrice Arthur as a true anti-Archie—Maude was an ardent defender of civil rights, but in an interesting twist, the producers showed that Maude was subject to stereotypes and prejudice herself. Whereas Archie Bunker would not choose to live next to a black family, Maude, always eager to prove her egalitarianism, would kill for the chance.

Maude's maid, Florida Evans (Esther Rolle), received her own show, *Good Times*, in 1974. While originally a well-defined series that explored African Americans living in the Chicago projects, the series quickly deteriorated to little more than a vehicle for comic Jimmie Walker, who played Florida's son. Walker's stereotypical arm flailing and rhythmic phrases (remember "Dy-no-Mite"?) launched Walker to brief stardom as a standup comic, yet detracted from the important message of the series.

The Jeffersons, starring Sherman Helmsley and Isabel Sanford, featured a successful black family that left "Bunkerville" to "move on up" to New York's East Side. While the premise was interesting, the series was prone to stereotypical strutting and jiving that often angered many African Americans. While a few episodes focused on issues important to African Americans, *The Jeffersons* was basically a white sitcom with black actors.

Sanford and Son (1972), also produced by Lear and Yorkin, was somewhat better received, if only because of the wonderful interplay between veteran comic Redd Foxx and actor Demond Wilson, who played father and son Fred and Lamont Sanford, owners of a near-bankrupt L.A. junkyard. Fred's scheming and bigotry was well balanced by Lamont's political correctness. Like many of Lear and Yorkin's programs, however, stereotypical behavior formed part of the humor.

Ironically, during the period dubbed the Great Age of TV Relevance, the strides blacks had made in the 1960s were giving way to stereotypical treatment under the guise of promoting racial understanding. The Lear and Yorkin programs were fostered by the producers' desire to do something positive. *All in the Family* and *Maude*—and, to a lesser extent, *Good Times* and *The Jeffersons*—were well-written shows that made a significant impact on the television industry.

Two important shows from 1978 were *WKRP in Cincinnati* and *The White Shadow* (see entries), both produced by Mary Tyler Moore Enterprises. *The White Shadow* featured Ken Howard as the white coach of a predominately black inner-city high school basketball team. Honest in its portrayal of teens in general, and blacks in particular, the show was well received by African Americans. *WKRP in Cincinnati*'s Tim Reid, while originally presented as a jive-talking, slick-dressing DJ, evolved into a proud African American who questioned his role in both the black and mainstream communities. Several episodes—including those written by Reid—investigated not just overt racism but also the tacit racism that exists among co-workers and friends.

Then came *The Cosby Show* (1984; see entry). In a period where the sitcom itself was being seen as a fading genre, *Cosby* revitalized the format, NBC, and most important, the positive black image. As Dr. Heathcliff Huxtable, Bill Cosby used his low-key humor and cross-cultural appeal to captivate American viewers as he and his wife, Clair, guided their children toward leading productive and responsible lives. As married professionals, the Huxtables represented a family that had risen to the apex of society without sacrificing their cultural dignity or heritage.

In 1987, Tim Reid starred in another of the most significant African-American sitcoms to date—*Frank's Place*. The critically acclaimed series, set in a predominately black section of New Orleans, often approached the quality of a one-act play. Unlike *Cosby*, the characters of *Frank's Place* represented a wide diversity of socioeconomic backgrounds. Nevertheless, the realistic African-American images failed to score with either white or black viewers.

Perhaps this explains why modern programs continue to fall short of providing positive or accurate depictions. While networks will point with pride to the number of African Americans in today's sitcoms and dramas, quantity does not substitute for quality. Such fare as *Fresh Prince of Bel Air* (1990), *Hangin' with Mr. Cooper* (1992), *Martin* (1992), and *Sinbad* (1993), as well as the family-oriented sitcom *Family Matters* (1989), are either devoid of cultural significance or filled with stereotypical actions that date back to *Amos 'n' Andy*. Three exceptions—*In Living Color* (1990), *Roc* (1991), and *South Central* (1993)—have featured African-American characters who are more concerned with their cultural heritage. Nevertheless, only the hip comedy series *In Living Color* has been able to pass the acid test of successful ratings. While Nielsen Media Research claims its ratings data depicts a true reflection of national diversity, there have been frequent complaints that African Americans are not counted on a truly representative basis.

Bibliography
Andrews, Bart, and Ahrgus Julliard. *Holy Mackerel: The Amos 'n' Andy Story.* New York: Dutton, 1986.
Brooks, Tim, and Earle Marsh. *The Complete Directory to Prime Time Network TV Shows, 1946-Present.* New York: Ballantine, 1992.
Null, Gary. *Black Hollywood.* New York: Citadel, 1993.
Sackett, Susan. *Prime Time Hits.* New York: Billboard, 1993.
Watson, Mary Ann. *The Expanding Vista.* Durham: Duke UP, 1994.

Michael B. Kassel

Airbrush Painting, popular throughout the United States, is by no means a new art form. Between the years 1836 and 1940, a series of discoveries in Western Europe revealed a unique artistic legacy. Some 35,000 years prior, Aurignacian peoples had used hollow reeds or bones and powdered red ochre to paint a vast series of murals on cavern walls throughout Western Europe. The murals discovered at Lascaux and Peche-merle, France, are the earliest known examples of what is often considered to be a quintessentially modern medium—airbrush, the applying of paint by means of a fine spray. It was not until the 17th century in Japan that spray was used again, and modern airbrush did not evolve until the late 19th century and the advent of compressed air.

The development of the modern airbrush is commonly credited to an American, Charles Burdick. In 1893, he patented the device and set up a manufacturing company in London. It is believed that Burdick developed the airbrush in his search for a method of layering one watercolor on top of another without disturbing the bottom color.

The first broadly used application of airbrush was photo tinting. Color was not reproduced effectively in photography until the early 20th century, but the public wanted color photographs. Since around 1860 black-and-white photos had been hand tinted. The airbrush made tinting easier and much more effective and left no visible brush strokes. With masking, it achieved a level of precision that had been previously impossible. The airbrush was also used to touch up any embarrassing physical flaws that might appear in photographic portraiture.

When the first issue of *Esquire* appeared in 1933, it included a cartoon pinup girl by George Petty. Petty, a former photo retoucher, had taken his skills of blemish removal one step further. He had created the "perfect" woman out of thin air. *Esquire* continued to publish Petty's pinups throughout the 1930s. In 1940, also in *Esquire*, the first of Antonio Vargas's pinups appeared. Vargas's name has become synonymous with the airbrush pinup. In 1943, 1 million orders were received for his calendar. With the creation of the pinup girl, Petty and Vargas had created a style that would become one of the hallmarks of airbrush artistry. Their pinups presented a plastic reality that achieved levels of perfection unattainable in everyday life. These idealized (and objectified) images of women constituted a kind of super-reality, an unapproachable beauty.

From the postwar years into the late 1950s, airbrush was largely absent from commercial art. In the 1960s, however, with the resurgence of poster art and the advent of Pop Art and advertising in mass culture, airbrush made a major comeback. The sense of unapproachable perfection developed by Petty and Vargas readily lent itself to advertising.

In the mid-seventies, the rapidly increasing popularity of science fiction and fantasy created a whole new market for commercial airbrush work. The super-real look of airbrush made it the ideal medium for rendering alien landscapes and heavily muscled barbarian warriors. In addition to appearing on book covers and in illustrated science fiction and fantasy magazines such as *Heavy Metal*, these illustrations also found their way onto the sides of a multitude of vans.

This van art (see entry) was the outgrowth of an earlier marriage of airbursh and auto. In the '50s, a young Southern Californian revolutionized the business of car painting. Known as Von Dutch, Kenneth Robert Howard invented custom pin-striping. Through his use of airbrush-based auto customizing, he introduced a whole new level to the American obsession with the automobile.

Currently, airbrush is commonly used in conjunction with photography to create slick images for advertising, as well as in science fiction and fantasy art and general graphic design. One of airbrush's more popular uses is in customizing jackets and T-shirts. Whatever its use, airbrush has left an indelible mark on American popular culture.

Bibliography
Kraft, Charles. "Mechanical Dreams, Von Dutch and Kustom Kulture." *Art Forum* 32.3 (1993): 93-97.
Rubelman, Steve. *Encyclopedia of the Airbrush.* New York: Art Directions, 1981.
Tombs, Curtis, Seng-Gye, and Christopher Hunt. *The Airbrush Book.* New York: Van Nostrand, 1980.

Mark Harrison

Aircraft and activities associated with flying, especially in movies, represent the very spirit of popular entertainment. Flying represents heroism, villainy, glory, peril, advanced technology, freedom, adventure, mysticism, and passionate love. Amusement parks and arcades would be deficient without imaginary flying and air combat. Fighter aces, like commercial pilots, have been popular heroes since World War I, as depicted in *The Dawn Patrol* (1930, remade 1938) and *The Blue Max* (1966). Early hot-air and gas balloons and dirigibles are depicted in *Madam Satan* (1930), *Here Comes the Navy* (1934), *Around the World in Eighty Days* (1956), and *Five Weeks in a Balloon* (1962).

Wings (1927, silent) was the first film to win the Academy Award. Aviation films of the 1930s include *Hell's Angels*, *Things to Come*, and *Five Came Back*. Some, like *Christopher Strong* (1933) and *Without Orders* (1936), stress the capabilities of female pilots. Even before 1942, aviation films included comedies with Laurel and Hardy and Abbott and Costello. The airplane films during and about World War II helped secure the unheralded genre of aviation films, both romantic and realistic. *Airplane!* (1980, a parody of *Zero Hour* of 1957 and its 1971 TV version *Terror in the Sky*) and the sequel are postmodern plots of discontinuity.

In films the flier is often an independent braggart who becomes sensitive. Early commercial service is reflected in *Air Mail* (1932), *Central Airport* (1933), and *Only Angels Have Wings* (1939). *Flying Down to Rio* (1933) applies innovative techniques to show an aerial chorus line. Technical advances are featured in *Ceiling Zero* (1935), *Test Pilot* (1938), and *X-15* (1961). Rocket packs strapped to the back are depicted in the serial *King of the Rocket Men* (1949) and the feature *The Rocketeer* (1991). Fanciful achievements occur in *Raiders of the Lost Ark* (1981) and clever aircraft appear in many James Bond films beginning in the 1960s. The desire to fly is the focus of Frank Capra's *Flight* (1929), *The Lost Squadron* (1932), *Men with Wings* (1938), *I Wanted Wings* (1941), and others. Fated barnstormers of the 1920s and 1930s are portrayed in *The Tarnished Angels* (1958, from William Faulkner's 1935 novel *Pylon*), *The Gypsy Moths* (1969), and *The Great Waldo Pepper* (1975).

Lighted airways and audible radio navigation aids, which gave us the phrase "on the beam," appeared by 1930. The appeal of airships ended when the German *Hindenburg* crashed in 1937, depicted in a 1975 film. Flying across the oceans and around the world increased from 1919 to May 1927, when Charles A. Lindbergh (1902-1974), in the *Spirit of St. Louis*, achieved a solo flight from New York to Paris in 33:29 hours to enhance internationalism, the subject of a 1957 film. Later Amelia Earhart (1898-1937), Wiley Post (1900-1935), Howard Hughes (1905-1976), and others made distance and speed records in famous aircraft. Douglas "Wrong Way" Corrigan, who appears in *The Flying Irishman* (1939), ordered in 1938 not to fly transatlantic, landed at Dublin in 28:13 hours.

The National Air Races (the Thompson Trophy), now held at Reno, NV, began in the mid-1920s in Cleveland; the first women's race occurred in 1929. Today aviation shows are regional with aerobatics and displays, and the best is staged by the Experimental Aircraft Association at an annual fly-in convention at Oshkosh, WI.

Exceeding the sound barrier, achieved in 1947, is misrepresented in *Breaking the Sound Barrier* (British, 1952) but accurate in *Toward the Unknown* (1956), *On the Threshold of Space* (1956), and *Bailout at 43,000 Feet* (1957). It is documented in *The Right Stuff* (1983, based on Tom Wolfe's 1979 book). A female pilot is the topic of *Pancho Barnes* (TV, 1988), about a friend of Chuck Yeager (1923-), who first flew the Bell X-1 beyond Mach 1, the speed of sound.

Belying the eminent safety of commercial flying since 1950, films of peril in the air continued, like *The High and the Mighty* (1954), *Julie* (1956), *Jet over the Atlantic* (1960), the *Airport* series (1970-79), and *Passenger 57* (1992). The "ordinary" side of aviation appears in *Come Fly with Me* (1963) and *If It's Tuesday, This Must Be Belgium* (1969). Transatlantic flights produced jet lag while improving international relations, and airports contributed to the decline of city centers. In 1971, America rejected a Boeing Supersonic Transport, which could fly at 1,000 m.p.h. as noisy and harmful to the ozone layer.

General (business and private) and sport planes round out aircraft types that appear in films. Sport flying includes glid-ers, motorized ultralights, and the *Gossamer Condor*, which achieved human-powered flight in 1977. The dream is for a National Aero-Space Plane (the X-30) that was depicted in *Starflight: The Plane That Couldn't Land* (TV, 1983).

The most important writers on aviation include William Faulkner, especially in his early novels and many stories; Frank "Spig" Wead, a film writer and subject of *The Wings of Eagles* (1957); Ernest K. Gann; Arthur Hailey; Martin Caidin; mystic Richard D. Bach; and Joseph Heller (*Catch-22*, 1961, film 1970).

Bibliography

Bilstein, Roger E. *Flight in America: From the Wrights to the Astronauts*. Baltimore: Johns Hopkins UP, 1984.

Boyne, Walter J. *The Smithsonian Book of Flight*. New York: Orion, 1987.

Jablonsky, Edward. *Airwar*. 4 vols. Garden City: Doubleday, 1971.

Taylor, Michael J. H., ed. *Jane's Encyclopedia of Aviation*. New York: Portland, 1989.

Walkers, John, ed. "Airplanes." *Halliwell's Filmgoer's and Video Viewer's Companion*. 10th ed. New York: HarperCollins, 1993.

Roger Osterholm

See also

Space Exploration

Alcott, Louisa May (1832-1888), is one of America's most famous 19th-century authors, having written *Little Women* (1868-69), perhaps the most significant didactic novel for young girls written in America before the modern era, and

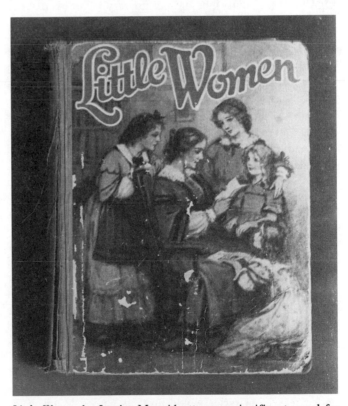

Little Women by Louisa May Alcott was a significant novel for young girls. Photo courtesy of Popular Culture Library, Bowling Green State University, Bowling Green, OH.

one that has remained continuously in print since its publication. *Little Women* is the story of four sisters, Meg, Jo, Beth, and Amy, growing up in New England in the shadow of the Civil War. Although sentimental by today's standards, the book questions gender roles and gives girls a tomboy heroine to identify with, Jo, who overcomes social restraints to become a writer. Alcott herself was the model for Jo, although unlike her protagonist, she never married.

Although Alcott's career began with melodramatic potboilers (now being rediscovered), she remains known for children's books. *Little Women* has seen four film versions, one as recent as 1994. Alcott wrote three sequels to *Little Women*: *Good Wives* (1869), *Little Men* (1871), and *Jo's Boys* (1886), but her first book remains the most important. Long considered a minor writer, Alcott is currently being reevaluated by scholars.

Bibliography

Stern, Madeleine B., ed. *Critical Essays on Louisa May Alcott.* Boston: Hall, 1984.

Myra Hunter Jones

Alda, Alan (1936-), TV superstar with an offbeat approach, was born in New York City. His father, Robert Alda, whose real name was Alphonso Giuseppe Giovanni Roberto D'Abruzzo, was a vaudeville entertainer and stage/ film actor. He created his stage name from the first two letters of both Alphonso and D'Abruzzo, a change Alan chose to retain. In spite of his own career choice, Robert wanted his son to be a doctor. While Alan was later to become a superstar playing Doctor Benjamin Franklin "Hawkeye" Pierce on *M*A*S*H* (see entry), he did not go very far in his real-life attempt to become a physician.

In the time-honored tradition of ex-pre-med students, Alda abandoned becoming a doctor after failing a chemistry final exam. Switching majors to English literature, he graduated from Fordham University in 1956, and he then studied acting at the Cleveland Playhouse. Little known at the time he was offered the role of Hawkeye in *M*A*S*H* in 1972, he had nevertheless appeared in a number of TV, off-Broadway, Broadway, and movie productions. Television appearances included a regular role in 1964 on *That Was the Week That Was*, American television's first effort at political and news satire. Alda had also worked on several movies, all unsuccessful, including *The Extraordinary Seaman* (1969), *The Moonshine War* (1970), *Jenny* (1970), and *The Mephisto Waltz* (1971).

Alda's best early film role was as a professor jailed for murder in *The Glass House* (1972), a CBS TV movie based on Truman Capote's condemnation of the treatment of inmates in American prisons. On Broadway, Alda was well received in *The Owl and the Pussy Cat* and the musical *The Apple Tree*, for which he received a Tony Award nomination.

There were spells before *M*A*S*H* when Alda supplemented his income with odd jobs like cab driving and performing as a gas station clown. He was not eager, however, to accept a role in *M*A*S*H*, believing that involvement in a failed television series would hurt his career. Many in the industry did expect a sitcom set in a battlefield MASH (Mobile Army Surgical Hospital) unit near the front lines of the Korean War to fail. Furthermore, the tensions of the day over the Vietnam War, one similar in many ways to the Korean conflict, made the series' demise seem even more inevitable.

The series aired from September 17, 1972, to September 19, 1983, long outlasting the end of the Vietnam War, whose parallels the show relied on in part for its satire of war. It was the quality of the characterization that kept audiences tuning in years after the U.S. withdrew from Vietnam and in spite of some half-dozen shifts in air time made by CBS.

Like other entertainers who have become exceptionally well liked for TV roles, and on whom the public has been reluctant to bestow the same popularity for new roles, Alda has had difficulty finding a different niche for himself. Even before the end of *M*A*S*H*, Alda tried his hand at writing in 1975, creating the short-lived series *We'll Get By*, which focused on the problems of a suburban New Jersey family and the importance of communication and family love.

Alda also wrote the script for and directed the movie *The Four Seasons* during the *M*A*S*H* years. This 1981 movie, a comedy about the friendship of three couples who learn that their friendship is one of the most satisfying ingredients in their lives, starred Alda, Carol Burnett, and Sandy Dennis.

Alda has appeared in other movies, such as Woody Allen's *Crimes and Misdemeanors* (1989), and *Manhattan Murder Mystery* (1993). In 1993 he also appeared in the TV movie *And the Band Played On*, about the AIDS epidemic. Further movie appearances include: *Mad City* (1997), *Object of My Affection* (1998), and *Keepers of the Frame* (1999). In spite of his numerous movie efforts, his most significant contribution to modern American popular culture continues to be his writing, directing, and acting for *M*A*S*H*.

Bibliography

Brooks, Tim, and Earle Marsh. *The Complete Directory to Prime Time Network TV Shows, 1946-Present.* 4th ed. New York: Ballantine, 1992.

Kalter, Suzy. *The Complete Book of* M*A*S*H. New York: Abrams, 1988.

Katz, Ephraim. *The Film Encyclopedia.* New York: Harper-Collins, 1994.

Reiss, David S. M*A*S*H: *The Exclusive Inside Story of TV's Most Popular Show.* Foreword by Alan Alda. Mt. Pleasant: Flying Eagle, 1980.

Strait, Raymond. *Alan Alda: A Biography.* New York: St. Martins, 1983.

Alan Kelly

Aldrich Family, The (1939-1953). The 20th century may not have invented teenagers, but it supplied the most memorable examples. In radio's *The Aldrich Family*, teen Henry Aldrich and his imitators defined the standard crises, all poignant yet laughable. Although his origin was unpromising, he carried on the Tom Sawyer/Penrod Schofield character of unintentional mischief maker. Clifford Goldsmith's 1937 play *What a Life!* plunked Henry in the principal's office, accused of stealing band instruments when he had only cheated on a test in order to attend the dance. Henry's world grew when Rudy Vallee and Kate Smith commissioned sketches for their shows. By 1939, the vignettes expanded to a 30-minute show on NBC's Blue radio network.

Although *The Aldrich Family* provided lasting memories, the cast changed frequently. Only Jackie Kelk remained throughout as Henry's pal Homer. House Jameson, barely in charge as lawyer Sam, had more authority as Renfrew of the Mounted. Ezra Stone was the best-known Henry—his reedy voice captured the nearly out-of-control mood that characterized each program. Even Clifford Goldsmith relied on other writers, but his vision still dictated their versions. Several shows copied the Aldrich formula: *Archie Andrews* and *That Brewster Boy* echoed the male adolescent's turmoil; *A Date with Judy, Maudie's Diary,* and *Meet Corliss Archer* presented the female version.

Bibliography
Dunning, John. *Tune in Yesterday: The Ultimate Encyclopedia of Old-Time Radio, 1925-1976.* Englewood Cliffs: Prentice-Hall, 1976.
Harmon, Jim. *The Great Radio Comedians.* Garden City: Doubleday, 1970.
"Radio Oddities" [Clifford Goldsmith]. *Tune In* 4 (Aug. 1946): 43.
Witham, W. Tasker. *The Adolescent in the American Novel 1920-1960.* New York: Ungar, 1964.

James A. Freeman

Alger, Horatio, Jr. (1832-1899), wrote approximately 120 boys' books in the period from 1864 to 1897. He is associated today with the "strive and succeed" or "rags to riches" attitudes of the last century. Alger was the son of a Unitarian minister and came from a distinguished Massachusetts family. He graduated Phi Beta Kappa from Harvard in 1852, taught school, and wrote for newspapers before graduating from Cambridge Divinity School in 1860. *Frank's Campaign*, his first juvenile book, was published in 1864; following a brief stint as a minister, Alger moved to New York City in 1866 and concentrated on writing for boys.

His books were favorably reviewed for many years, although his reputation had declined by the end of his life. Alger's most popular juvenile book was *Ragged Dick*, a story of street life in the city, published in 1868. In many of his later books he wrote about the homeless children in New York, as well as the newsboys and bootblacks. His dominant plot was of a poor boy who rose to respectability through hard work and thrift, usually with an element of luck. Alger's prose style was pedestrian and his books were repetitious, but they were enormously popular, selling an estimated total of 17 million copies and published well into the 1920s. His writings exemplified the American Dream and he is considered a major influence on the development of American culture.

Bibliography
Bennett, Bob. *Horatio Alger, Jr.: A Comprehensive Bibliography.* Mt. Pleasant: Flying Eagle, 1980.
Dizer, John. *Tom Swift and Company.* Jefferson: McFarland, 1982.
Gardner, Ralph. *Horatio Alger, or The American Hero Era.* Mendota: Wayside, 1964.

Scharnhorst, Gary, and Jack Bales. *The Lost Life of Horatio Alger, Jr.* Bloomington: Indiana UP, 1985.

John Dizer

Ali, Muhammad (1942-), born Cassius Marcellus Clay in Louisville, KY, became a boxing legend and revolutionized the heavyweight division. His interest in boxing began when his bicycle was stolen and he reported it to the police. The officer who took the report, Joe Elsby Martin, was also the director of boxing at a local recreation center. He saw some potential for talent and extended an invitation to young Cassius, who quickly demonstrated his potential.

As an amateur, Clay triumphed in 100 of 108 contests and won six Kentucky Golden Gloves championships. In 1960, he won the U.S. Olympic boxing trials in the heavyweight division and captured the heavyweight Olympic Gold Medal in Rome.

He soon turned professional and claimed his first professional victory on October 29, 1960, beating Tunney Hunsaker in six rounds. His victory string continued; in 1964 he defeated the current heavyweight champion, Sonny Liston. In the bout he demonstrated his footwork and his fighting philosophy of "floating like a butterfly and stinging like a bee." He also developed the habit of self-aggrandizement, calling himself "the Greatest," and recited poetry that boasted of his next conquest. He was cocky and arrogant, but he possessed all the skills, speed, and agility to deliver on his boasts.

Soon afterwards, Clay joined the Nation of Islam, a controversial and militant black Muslim group, and changed his name to Muhammad Ali. This created a public relations backlash, which intensified dramatically in 1967 when he refused to be inducted into the Armed Services after he was drafted. He was found guilty of violating the Selective Service Act, was stripped of his title, and barred from boxing. Ali's stand against the Vietnam War was not mere publicity posturing based on the tenets of his Muslim religion, it cost him his boxing title and his livelihood.

After Ali's conviction was reversed by the Supreme Court in 1970, he resumed his boxing career. Four years later he regained his heavyweight crown by knocking out George Foreman in eight rounds in 1974.

Ali lost his title to Joe Frazier on March 8, 1971, in fifteen rounds in a close but unanimous decision. He vowed to fight on, but in 1972 had his jaw broken in a close loss to Ken Norton. He beat Norton in a rematch and, in a much awaited rematch, edged Joe Frazier in a close decision. However, Frazier had previously lost the crown to George Foreman, so it was not a championship bout.

Ali fought Foreman in the so-called "Rumble in the Jungle" in Kenya on October 30, 1974. Using what he termed "rope a dope techniques," Ali allowed Foreman to exhaust himself throwing punches, and then knocked Foreman out with two seconds left in the eighth round. He made the heavyweight championship bout a premier international event and in his career would eventually earn over $60 million for his 61 professional fights.

Ali then battled Joe Frazier in the "Thrilla in Manila" on September 30, 1975. In a grueling contest, Frazier did not leave his stool for the bell in the fifteenth round and Ali collapsed from exhaustion after the fight. Both boxers were hospitalized after the grueling battle in heat over a hundred degrees.

Ali successfully defended his title six times before being beaten by Leon Spinks on February 15, 1978. Seven months later he defeated Spinks and became the first boxer to capture the heavyweight crown three times.

Ali announced his retirement in 1979 and his record was 56-3. He returned to fight Larry Holmes in 1980 and Trevor Berbick in 1981 but lost both fights.

In 1984, Ali was diagnosed as suffering from "punch drunk syndrome," which resembles Parkinson's disease. Although his speech is slurred and almost inaudible and he has mobility problems, he has achieved an incredible dignity of presence and the demeanor of a peaceful and graceful man.

Bibliography

Diamond, Arthur. *Muhammad Ali.* San Diego: Lucent, 1995.

Hauser, Thomas. *Muhammad Ali: His Life and Times.* New York: Simon & Schuster, 1991.

Pacheco, Ferdie. *Muhammad Ali: A View from the Corner.* New York: Carol Pub. Group, 1992.

Lawrence E. Ziewacz

All in the Family (1971-1979) was the most popular television series of the 1970s, as well as the most influential situation comedy of the past 25 years, before spending its last years as *Archie Bunker's Place.* In that time, it was the No. 1-rated show on television for five consecutive seasons, 1971-72 to 1975-76.

All in the Family's significance, however, extends far beyond its popularity. Upon its debut at 9:30 on Tuesday night, January 12, 1971, *All in the Family* immediately shattered the parameters of the situation comedy in terms of language, content, and tone (see Sitcom). Social, political, and sexual manners and mores of all kinds were open targets for discussion among the politically and generationally polarized main characters.

All in the Family was created by Norman Lear and Alan "Bud" Yorkin, who had the concept ready as early as 1969. Lear based the show on a British series, *Till Death Do Us Part,* created by Johnny Speight, the story of a British family of modest means with a bigoted father and live-in son-in-law. Lear took his concept to ABC, the No. 3 network at the time, believing they would be most likely to take a chance on a risky concept. The network financed a pilot, titled *Those Were the Days,* but even after a second pilot, ABC let its option lapse, worried that audience tests had not been positive. CBS picked up the series and added it as a replacement for *To Rome with Love* starring John Forsythe.

All in the Family starred Carroll O'Connor as Archie Bunker, a loading-dock foreman and conservative bigot, and Jean Stapleton as Edith, his good-natured but simple wife. The couple lived a quiet, lower-middle-class existence at 704 Hauser Street in Queens, a quiet that was quickly interrupted by the arrival of their daughter, Gloria (Sally Struthers), and her new husband, Mike Stivic (Rob Reiner), a Polish-American graduate student in sociology. Politically, Mike and Gloria were 180 degrees from Archie, but family ties pre-vailed and the Bunkers let the Stivics live under their roof, rent-free, while Mike finished his degree. The political and generational gap between the Bunkers and the Stivics allowed for the airing of controversial issues that had seldom, if ever, disrupted the airwaves of network television, and it is this aspect of *All in the Family* that makes it the most influential situation comedy since *I Love Lucy.*

All in the Family also introduced new words and phrases to the English language, such as *meathead,* Archie's put-down for Mike, *dingbat,* his term of endearment for Edith, and *stifle yourself,* Archie's command to Edith when he had heard enough from her. Schoolteachers requested study guides to the program so that topics could be discussed with students. As a final testament to the show's impact on Americana, the set was eventually placed on permanent display at the Smithsonian Institution.

All in the Family certainly had the respect of its peers, winning the Emmy Award for best comedy series four times, in 1971, 1972, 1973, and 1978. O'Connor won four Emmys for playing Archie. Stapleton and Reiner each won two for their roles, and Struthers won one. The show also won numerous writing and directing Emmys.

All in the Family didn't simply open the doors to new language and subject matter for television comedy; it blasted them down. Its closest popular culture analog may be Bob Dylan, who changed the face of pop music by introducing poetic language and topicality that had never before been attempted. The words of Archie Bunker may not have had the poetic resonance of Dylan's, but their impact in changing the face of television was no less powerful.

Bibliography

Gitlin, Todd. *Inside Prime Time.* New York: Pantheon, 1985.

Jones, Gerard. *Honey, I'm Home! Sitcoms: Selling the American Dream.* New York: Grove, 1992.

Marc, David. *Comic Visions: Television Comedy and American Culture.* Boston: Unwin, 1989.

McNeil, Alex. *Total Television: A Comprehensive Guide to Programming from 1948 to the Present.* 3d ed. New York, 1991.

Mitz, Rick. *The Great TV Sitcom Book.* New York: Perigee, 1983.

Paul R. Kohl

All My Children (1970-), created by Agnes Nixon (see entry), made its television debut January 5, 1970, on ABC, and continues to be one of the most popular daytime dramas in the U.S. today. Originally a half hour show, *All My Children* (*AMC*) expanded to hour-long broadcasts in the spring of 1977.

AMC's storylines focus on domestic problems, and it has often broken new ground in daytime and in television in general with its storylines that deal with current social and medical issues. Erica Kane had television's first abortion, Devon McFadden was daytime's first lesbian, and Phil Brent was daytime's first contact with the war in Vietnam when, after being drafted, he became an MIA for a period; even Phoebe Tyler spoke sympathetically of the peace movement. *AMC* has also dealt with such issues as domestic violence, child sexual abuse, racism, drunken driving, sexual harassment, interracial marriage, drug abuse, and alcoholism. Medical subjects treated by *AMC* include diabetes, AIDS, organ donation, and leukemia. During *AMC*'s leukemia storyline, First Lady Barbara Bush made a special appearance in which she asked viewers to register as bone-marrow donors.

Among daytime dramas, *AMC* has probably the most supportive attitude toward its female characters. While many other soaps still present storylines where marriages break up because a woman puts a great deal of energy into her career, *AMC* presents women's working outside the home as the norm, and even shows female characters, most notably Brooke English, who can be happy without a man in their lives. And while it is a rarity to see anyone doing mundane tasks in daytime, on *AMC* one often sees men taking care of their children. Consistently among television's top-rated soap operas, *AMC* has endured as ABC's most popular show in the genre.

Bibliography

Buckman, Peter. *All for Love: A Study in Soap Opera.* Salem: Salem, 1985.

Warner, Gary. *All My Children.* Los Angeles: General, 1994.

June Michele Pulliam

See also

Soap Opera

All-American Girls Professional Baseball League, The (1943-1954), became popular evidence that women can play sports. The release of Penny Marshall's 1992 film, *A League of Their Own,* popularized the fact that women once played professional baseball. The film itself was inspired by the 1987 documentary of the same title, written and produced by Kelly Candaele, one of the five sons of Helen Callaghan, who in 1945 won the AAGPBL batting championship with a .299 average. Prior to the release of Marshall's film, the AAGPBL Players Association helped bring the league story to the public. The association was largely responsible for the opening of the 1988 exhibit dedicated to the history of women in baseball in the National Baseball Hall of Fame in Cooperstown, NY.

The Players Association held its first meeting in 1987 after several years of groundwork that began when June Peppas, a former player, published a newsletter in 1980. Of the approximately 560 women who had played in the league, most had lost touch with the others. Not until the AAGPBL's first reunion, held in Chicago in 1982, did players see teammates they had not seen in almost 30 years. From that reunion came the founding of the Players Association to disseminate the story of the AAGPBL.

The All-American Girls Professional Baseball League had its origin in World War II. Chicago Cubs owner Phillip K. Wrigley feared that because major leaguers were going to war, attendance at ballgames would decrease. Thus Wrigley proposed having women play softball in major league stadiums; during the winter baseball meetings of 1942, he tried to convince other owners to open their stadiums to female ballplayers.

Striking out with his peers, Wrigley employed his own baseball scouts to recruit women for a new league. Tryouts were held in 1943 in Wrigley Field. From more than 200 women, a total of 60 were chosen for four teams: the Racine (WI) Belles; the Kenosha (WI) Comets; the Rockford (IL) Peaches; and the South Bend (IN) Blue Sox. In 1944, the Milwaukee Chicks and the Minneapolis Millerettes were added; in 1945 both expansion teams moved, the Chicks to Grand Rapids (MI) and the Millerettes to Fort Wayne (IN), where they became the Daisies.

During the height of AAGPBL popularity in 1948, ten teams competed in a two-division league: the Peoria (IL) Redwings, Muskegon (MI) Lassies, Springfield (IL) Sallies, and Chicago Colleens completed the membership. Total attendance that year reached the one million mark, but thereafter attendance fell rapidly as the postwar economy led to the baby boom as well as increased housing construction, college attendance, and spending. The construction of highways and the popularity of television turned people away from local team sports and toward televised major league games. In 1954, the AAGPBL played its last season, often to crowds of only 300 to 400 per game. The minor leagues and Negro leagues were similarly affected.

The game the women played started out as softball, with a 12-inch ball, a mound 40 feet from the plate, and basepaths 65 feet long. Pitching was underhand. The major difference between League ball and softball was that the AAGPBL permitted base stealing. This decreased the dominance of the (softball) pitcher and led to a more exciting game. Instead of playing in silken shorts, as did women's softball players, or in flannel uniforms, as did male baseball players, league women played in a one-piece tunic and knee socks. At all times, both on and off the field, League players were required to follow a "feminine" dress code.

Each year, changes were made in the size of the ball and the length of the basepaths until, by 1948, pitching was overhand and the game was hardball. As it progressed from softball to baseball, the League underwent various name changes, starting out as the All-American Girls Softball League in 1943 and ending up as the American Girls Baseball League in 1954.

During the war years and after, the AAGPBL provided female athletes with an opportunity to play a team sport on a professional level. It provided fans with the opportunity to see women play the national pastime. Even 40 years after its demise, the AAGPBL lives in the hearts of its fans.

Bibliography

"All-American Girls Baseball League." *Major League Baseball* (yearly editions, 1944-1949). Ed. H. G. Salsinger, Harry G. Heilmann, Don H. Black. New York: Dell, 1947.

Fidler, Merrie A. "The Development and Decline of the All-American Girls Baseball League, 1943-54." Master's thesis. U of Massachusetts, 1976.

Gregorich, Barbara. *Women at Play: The Story of Women in Baseball.* San Diego: Harcourt, 1993.

Johnson, Susan E. *When Women Played Hardball.* Seattle: Seal, 1994.

Roepke, Sharon L. *Diamond Gals.* Michigan: AAGL Cards, 1986.

Barbara Gregorich

See also

Women in Baseball

Allen, Fred (1894-1956), vaudeville and radio superstar, was born John Florence Sullivan in Somerville, MA, and raised in a poor Irish-Catholic family. His earnings from a variety of jobs helped to support the family while he completed a commercial course at the Boston High School of Commerce. But it was vaudeville that fascinated Johnny Sullivan, and in 1911 he began performing at amateur nights as a comic juggler. In 1914, now a 20-year-old professional, he moved to vaudeville's capital, New York. Until he left the stage for radio in 1932, Fred Allen (he adopted the name in 1918) became an accomplished "single" in small-time vaudeville, and a successful monologist in a succession of Broadway revues.

Seeking employment in radio when the Depression devastated stage entertainment, Allen debuted in the Linit Bath Club Revue on October 23, 1932. Teamed with wife Portland Hoffa, Allen was a headline comedian in seven different program series, and was on the air almost continuously until his last show aired on June 26, 1949. The best known of his series included *Town Hall Tonight* (July 1934-June 1939), featuring hour-long comedy shows in which Allen drew heavily on the news for comedy and presented a weekly skit featuring the Mighty Allen Art Players. On the *Texaco Star Theater* (October 1940-June 1944) and the *Fred Allen Show* (October 1945-June 1949), he developed the feature for which he is best known: Allen's Alley. During weekly strolls down this fictive lane, Allen met and interviewed characters like Mrs. Pansy Nussbaum, Fallstaff Openshaw, and Titus Moody. Allen's scripts—he was the chief author of his programs' dialogue—and the skilled voice acting of performers like Minerva Pious (Mrs. Nussbaum), Kenny Delmar (Senator Claghorn), and Alan Reed (Fallstaff Openshaw), made these invisible, imaginary characters come alive for millions of loyal listeners. Allen's manufactured-for-laughs feud with Jack Benny, which began on *Town Hall Tonight* in 1937, continued to the end of his radio career, appearing even on the last program in 1949.

Fred Allen is notable for three achievements. First, he created some of radio comedy's best-known features and unforgettable characters; Allen's Alley and its residents are an example. Second, although he served his apprenticeship on the stage, where sight was more important than sound, Allen became skilled at creating an audible comedy most appropriate to radio, a medium that had to communicate through sound. Finally, Allen served American radio as a "critic from within." In 1954, Allen published his radio memoirs, *Treadmill to Oblivion*. Fred Allen died on March 17, 1956, in New York City, while in the process of writing his second volume of memoirs. They were published after his death as *Much Ado about Me* (1956).

Bibliography

Havig, Alan. *Fred Allen's Radio Comedy.* Philadelphia: Temple UP, 1990.

Taylor, Robert. *Fred Allen: His Life and Wit.* Boston: Little, Brown, 1989.

Weeks, Edward. "Fred Allen." *Dictionary of American Biography.* Supplement 6 (1956-60). Ed. John A. Garraty. New York: Scribner, 1980. 12-13.

Alan Havig

Allen, Steve (1921-2000), born Stephen Valentine Patrick William Allen in New York City, has had a remarkable show business career. Among his many achievements are hosting the first *Tonight Show* on NBC, having a successful variety show that competed with Ed Sullivan for three seasons, and being a better-than-average pianist, composer, fiction writer, radio host, and political activist, among other accomplishments.

On July 27, 1953, Allen, already a show business veteran though barely in his thirties, began a late-night program on a local New York City station. On September 27, 1954, it became *The Tonight Show* on NBC. Allen stayed with the program until January 25, 1957, when he left to concentrate on his Sunday evening variety show.

Many of his regulars went on to forge respectable show business careers of their own. These included Steve Lawrence, Eydie Gorme, Don Knotts, Bill Dana, Andy Williams, and Skitch Henderson, the show's musical director. The show was a mixture of conversation, sketches, and performance. Allen featured many jazz artists on this and his other programs, often joining them and displaying his own talents in that area.

His wife, Jayne Meadows, joined him on *The Steve Allen Show*, and it survived from June 24, 1956, to May 3, 1959, in spite of being opposite the unbeatable *Ed Sullivan Show*. Allen had his regulars, many from the late-night program, and kept a steady pace, filled with jazz guests. The show appealed to the hip but finally had to yield.

There were attempts to revive the program and various other programs over the years. Notable among Allen's programs was a 1977 PBS show, *Meeting of the Minds,* in which historical characters from different eras met to discuss important topics. The words were their own, spoken through fine actors, including Allen and Meadows. It survives in syndication and is often used in classrooms. In 1986, Allen was named to the Television Hall of Fame.

Bibliography

Brown, Les. *Encyclopedia of Television.* Detroit: Gale, 1992.

Terrace, Vincent. *Encyclopedia of Television Series, Pilots and Specials: 1937-1973.* Vol. 1. New York: Zoetrope, 1985.

——. *Encyclopedia of Television Series, Pilots and Specials: 1974-1984.* Vol. 2. New York: Zoetrope, 1985.

——. *Fifty Years of Television.* New York: Cornwall, 1991.

Frank A. Salamone

Allen, Woody (1935-), one of America's more successful, and controversial, movie producers, directors, and stars, was born Allen Stewart Konigsberg, in Brooklyn, NY, and as Woody Allen is synonymous with New York City. Allen's cinematic art is as diverse as New York culture, as in his black and white experiments, ranging from the sharpness of imagery in *Manhattan* (1979) to the smoky interiors of New York nightclubs sporting Tony Bennett–type lounge singers in *Broadway Danny Rose* (1984).

A review of Woody Allen's cinematic achievements over the past 30 years reveals a virtually comprehensive gallery of styles and movements that reflect the diversity of modern art. His work is a symbolic representation of the eclectic nature of the Big Apple and both embraces the uncertainties of living in a contemporary culture and reflects movements of current and past cinematic efforts. The panorama ranges from the murky look of *Shadows and Fog* (1991) with its hazy textures of light and shadow, resembling Orson Welles's best efforts or the qualities of German expressionism, to his experimentation with fluid, free-roaming camera techniques with zoom-lens shots that capture quick closeups in *Husbands and Wives* (1992), to the combination of humor and paranoia that captures the dizzying pace of New York in *Manhattan Murder Mystery* (1993). Allen's *Annie Hall* (1977), with Diane Keaton as the ditzy title character, was his most popular film, making the neurotic character he often plays familiar to general audiences and winning Oscars for best actress, director (Allen), best picture, and writing.

Allen's influence on contemporary filmmakers is most notably perhaps in *Forrest Gump* (1994). That film's method of blending images of the main character into film footage of such notables as John F. Kennedy directly mirrors Allen's efforts in *Zelig* (1983), a film about a human "chameleon man" who curiously takes on the look and personality of whomever he happens to associate with.

Allen's personal life in the 1990s also affected contemporary culture, and his 1980 film *Stardust Memories* was prophetic in depicting a filmmaker's adoring public being curious to the point of obsession with not only his art but his private life as well. The dark side of that idea was seen in Allen himself during the summer of 1992, when his long-term companion and leading actress, Mia Farrow, accused him of the alleged sexual abuse of their adopted daughter, Soon-Y Previn (Woody and Soon-Yi later married and now have a child). Media exposure was instantaneous and frequent.

Over the years, Allen has stimulated viewers to laugh at the plight of his now-classic comic persona—the insecure, tortured "little guy," overwhelmed by life, love, and sexual relationships—but more significantly to look inside themselves for a deeper response to the variety of images and ideas he presents in his films, which are always provocative for the range of cinematic styles and themes, and curious for the nuances that characterize relationships.

Bibliography:
Hirsch, Foster. *Love, Sex, Death and the Meaning of Life: The Films of Woody Allen.* New York: Limelight, 1991.
McCann, Graham. *Woody Allen: New Yorker.* Cambridge: Polity, 1991.

Eric McDowell

Allman Brothers, The, formed in Macon, GA, in 1969, became the quintessential southern rock band. Prior to 1969, brothers Gregg Allman, keyboards and vocals (1947-), and Duane Allman, guitars (1946-1971), played in a number of bands including the Allman Joys, Almanac, and Hour Glass. Duane's performances with Hour Glass, which recorded and toured, led to his becoming a sought-after session musician who eventually contributed to recordings by Wilson Pickett, King Curtis, and Aretha Franklin. In 1969, the Allmans were joined by Dickey Betts, guitars (1943-); Berry Oakley, bass

(1948-72); Jai Jai Johanson, drums (1944-); and Butch Trucks, drums, to form the first of many incarnations of the Allman Brothers Band.

The group's debut album, *Allman Brothers Band*, was released in 1970 on the Atco label but failed to do well on the charts. In 1970, Duane also performed with Eric Clapton on Derek and the Dominos' *Layla* album; the guitar duet on the title track is one of the most famous in the history of popular music.

The Allman Brothers Band's second album, *Idlewild South*, was released toward the end of 1970 and charted at #38. However, the band began to find a following for its live shows, which won audiences over with their southern-flavored rock and blues sound and extended guitar-powered jamming. In 1971, the band released the live *At the Fillmore* (#13), which became the band's first gold album, but in October of that year, Duane Allman was killed in a motorcycle accident. In 1972, another live album, *Eat a Peach* (#4), which contains some of Duane's last recordings, was released. This album is their most successful. Also that year, a collection of outtakes, *Duane and Gregg Allman*, was released and went gold. However, tragedy struck again when bassist Berry Oakley died in a motorcycle accident just three blocks from the site of Duane's death in Macon, GA.

In 1973, the band released two albums, *Brother and Sisters* (#1) (dedicated to Oakley), and the gold album, *Win Lose or Draw* (#5). The same year, Gregg Allman released his first solo album, *Laid Back*. In July 1973, the Allman Brothers performed with the Grateful Dead and the Band at Watkins Glen Raceway in upstate New York, before a crowd of 600,000 in the biggest rock festival ever staged. Then in October 1973, the band scored a #2 hit on the singles chart with "Ramblin' Man."

In 1974, two members of the band released albums: Betts's *Highway Call* and Allman's *Gregg Allman Tour*. In 1975, Allman was called to testify against his former road manager and bodyguard for drug trafficking, and later that year, he married television star Cher, with whom he released *Allman and Woman* in 1976 (the two divorced in 1978). The band broke up in 1976, and a greatest hits package, *Road Goes on Forever*, was released. The rest of the seventies saw Allman and Betts releasing various solo records, while several other former band members performed as the group Sea Level.

The Allman Brothers Band re-formed in 1978, and released *Enlightened Rogues* in 1979 (#9), featuring the #29 single "Crazy Love." During 1980 and 1981, the band released *Reach for the Sky* (#27) and *Brothers of the Road* (#44), but split up again in 1981. In 1987, Gregg Allman's solo, "I'm No Angel" (#30), from the album with the same title, became a hit on rock radio, and reached #49 on the pop charts. In 1989, the band again re-formed, adding Johnny Neel (keyboards), Warren Hayes (guitars), and Allen Woody (bass) and released the four-CD boxed set *Dreams* (#103).

Seven Turns (#53), the band's first studio album in nine years, was released in 1990. *Shades of Two Worlds* (#85) was released in 1991, and Allman starred in the movie *Rush*. In

1992, the live set *An Evening with the Allman Brothers* (#80), was produced by the band's original producer, Tom Dowd, and later that year, three years after its release, *Dreams* went gold. In 1993, the band performed at President Clinton's inauguration festivities.

The band released *Where It All Began* (#45) in 1994 and also headlined the HORDE rock festival. In 1995, the Allman Brothers Band was inducted into the Rock and Roll Hall of Fame, and released *2nd Set* (#88). The band's trademark instrumental, "Jessica," won the 1996 Grammy for Best Rock Instrumental Performance, and in 1997, Grateful Dead Records released the mail-order *Allman Brothers 2/11-12 1970,* to much critical acclaim. Hayes and Woody left the band to form the group Gov't Mule; they were replaced by Jack Pearson (guitar) and Oteil Burbridge. The Allman Brothers Band continues to perform and define southern rock, a sound straight from America's heartland.

Bibliography

Freeman, Scott. *Midnight Riders: The Story of the Allman Brothers.* Boston: Little, Brown, 1996.

Nolan, Tom. *The Allman Brothers Band.* Ed. Greg Shaw. New York: Barnes & Noble, 1976.

Rees, Dafydd, and Luke Crampton. *Encyclopedia of Rock Stars.* New York: D. K. Publishing, 1996.

Robert G. Weiner

Almanac Singers, The, was a folk group of the early 1940s that specialized in topical and political material and became a model for later such groups. The group arose out of the Depression years and the hothouse atmosphere of New York City, where many folk musicians and political radicals had settled. While traveling the country collecting songs and experiences, folksinger Pete Seeger (see entry) met Lee Hays, a former Arkansas union organizer, and Millard Lampell, a writer. Reuniting in New York in 1940, they formed the Almanac Singers, taking their name from the *Farmer's Almanac*, according to Hays one of the two books (along with the Bible) owned by most farm families. In 1941, Woody Guthrie (see entry), the Dust Bowl balladeer and seminal folk musician of the era, joined the group. All of these men held progressive political views and an interest in using song in support of activist causes (see Protest Music). Indeed, Guthrie was a model for the political uses of folk music. The group hoped to promote and popularize populist songs, some of which they wrote, and well understood the power of group singing. They recorded a series of thematic albums with songs extolling peace, labor unions, and the working class. In a beat-up Buick they traveled the country, singing for college students, union meetings, factory workers, migrant camps, antifascist rallies, and on street corners. Their standard repertoire included songs like "Talking Union," "Which Side Are You On?" (composed by Florence Reece in 1932 for striking Kentucky coalminers), "Union Maid" (written by Guthrie), "Hold the Fort" (a venerable labor anthem from the 1880s), "Union Train" (a product of the Southern Tenant Farmers' Union), and "Solidarity Forever" (a staple of the International Workers of the World), as well as antiwar songs and traditional folk material. The Almanacs spread many labor songs that previously had a mostly local or regional audience.

In late 1941, the Almanacs returned to New York City and established Almanac House, a co-op apartment in Greenwich Village where they lived communally. Here they held weekly "hootenannies," a term adapted by Guthrie and Seeger from the gatherings of leftwing clubs in Seattle. The Almanac "hoots" provided work for New York–based folksingers (such as Appalachian exile Aunt Molly Jackson), attracted many to folk music, more closely integrated folk music with radical politics, and inspired the hootenanny craze of the late 1950s and early 1960s. The Almanacs had a fluctuating membership that also included at various times Agnes "Sis" Cunningham, Gordon Friesen, Butch and Bess (Lomax) Hawes, Cisco Houston, Burl Ives, Brownie McGhee, Earl Robinson, Arthur Stern, Sonny Terry, and Josh White. Seeger and Guthrie were the constant core, the latter writing much of his autobiography, *Bound for Glory*, while living in Almanac House. There was an unrehearsed quality to their performances; Guthrie once observed ruefully that the Almanacs were the only group to rehearse on stage.

Initially the Almanacs were deeply involved in the peace movement that opposed U.S. intervention in World War II. The militant left favored strict neutrality. In 1941, they recorded an album for the American Peace Mobilization (*Songs for John Doe*). Among their better known antiwar songs were "The Ballad of October 16" (which opposed the first peacetime draft in U.S. history), "C for Conscription," "Plow Under" (which opposed militarism as a strategy to generate prosperity), and "The Strange Death of John Doe" (which emphasized the senseless waste of human life in war).

After the war, many Almanac alumni remained active in folk music. Guthrie and Seeger were both instrumental in the founding of People's Songs, a left-oriented organization to promote folk and topical music. People's Songs served as a booking agency and also published the first magazine devoted exclusively to folk music, but it ran afoul of McCarthyism and Cold War–driven anticommunist paranoia, closing down in 1949. Nonetheless, Guthrie pursued his successful solo career, recording several important albums (some with a clear political focus) until he was hospitalized with the Huntington's disease that would eventually kill him. Guthrie's significance in American music history was great; he not only spawned many folksingers who emulated him (Seeger dubbed them "Woody's Children") such as Ramblin' Jack Elliott, Bob Dylan, Joan Baez, Phil Ochs, and Tom Paxton, but also influenced later rock singers like Bruce Springsteen and John Cougar Mellencamp. Hays and Seeger formed the Weavers in 1949, a group clearly based on the Almanacs but with a more polished act and mainstream appeal. The Weavers became one of the most popular folk groups in history. Seeger, both as a Weavers member and later as a solo act, was instrumental to the folk music revival of the later 1950s and early 1960s. Lampell wrote books and collaborated with Earl Robinson on his folk cantata "The Lonesome Train." McGhee and Terry became a noted folk blues duo while Houston, Ives, and White established successful folk music careers. In the later 1940s, folk music began to enter the pop mainstream, with folk festivals, hootenannies, radio programs and folk concerts at colleges, summer camps, coffee houses, and nightclubs. Folk music expanded beyond the political left, becoming a commercial commodity. Later, in the 1960s, folk or folk-flavored groups like the New Christy Minstrels adopted a singing style based on the Almanac model.

The Almanacs as a group, not to mention the individual members, would be an important part of the popularization of this very American musical style and served as a bridge between rural and labor folk traditions on the one hand and a mass audience on the other.

Bibliography

Denisoff, R. Serge. *Great Day Coming: Folk Music and the American Left*. Urbana: U of Illinois P, 1971.

Dunaway, David King. *How Can I Keep from Singing: Pete Seeger*. New York: McGraw-Hill, 1981.

Klein, Joe. *Woody Guthrie: A Life*. New York: Ballantine, 1980.

Lieberman, Robbie. *"My Song Is My Weapon": People's Songs, American Communism, and the Politics of Culture, 1930-1950*. Urbana: U of Illinois P, 1989.

Willens, Doris. *Lonesome Traveller: The Life of Lee Hays*. New York: Norton, 1988.

Craig Lockard

Alpert, Herb (1935-), leader of the popular musical group the Tijuana Brass, was born in Los Angeles, CA. His family was musically oriented, with every member playing an instrument: dad on mandolin, mom on violin, sister on piano, and brother on drums. When he was eight, Alpert took up the trumpet.

By the early 1960s, Alpert was making enough money from his music to support his wife and baby boy, yet he had not made a name for himself. He went out to his garage one day to play "Twinkle Star," written by his friend, Sol Lake. After much experimentation, he recorded an arrangement that closely resembled Mexican mariachi music. He asked another friend, Jerry Moss, to listen to his recording. Moss liked it and they agreed to split the cost of a studio recording session.

They changed the title to "The Lonely Bull" and prepared a song called "Acapulco 1922" for the flip side. After deciding that the studio version needed something extra, they motored off to the Tijuana, Mexico, bullring with a sound engineer to record the sounds of the bullfights. These sounds were dubbed into the final mix of "The Lonely Bull." Because of the influence of Tijuana in Alpert's life, the record was distributed under the group name of the Tijuana Brass. Also, a new record company joined the industry, A&M. Alpert and Moss could have easily failed, as the odds were against such an independent venture. The record, released in August 1962, made it onto the charts and in December they released an album by the same name.

Alpert's second LP, *Marching through Madrid* (1963), never made the Top 40 and distributors told him that he had a "regional sound." He countered that it was lack of exposure that was hurting sales. The third album, *Herb Alpert's Tijuana Brass* (1963), and fourth, *South of the Border* (1964),

did better. "Mexican Shuffle," a single from the fourth album, was Alpert's real breakthrough. The Clark Teaberry Gum Company bought the rights to it for a national ad campaign and changed the title to "The Teaberry Shuffle." Alpert's unique sound became known throughout the U.S.

With this exposure, distributors began to support Alpert and the Brass, and his albums moved right up the charts. Soon after its release, his fifth album, *Whipped Cream and Other Delights*, moved to the No. 1 spot. "A Taste of Honey," from this album, raced to the seventh spot on *Billboard*'s Hot 100 in 1965. This led Alpert to form his first touring band. The albums were done with pickup bands at the studio. The band set attendance records at concerts and appeared on television. This exposure also pushed A&M Records into the limelight. By now, A&M had attracted other feature acts, including Burt Bacharach. Alpert was named *Billboard*'s Record Man of the Year in 1966.

A&M's success meant that Alpert had to devote more of his time to running the record company. Although he rarely performed, Alpert made it back onto the charts with his albums *Summertime* in 1971 and *Solid Brass* in 1972 and the single "Jerusalem." By the early 1970s, A&M had become one of the Top 10 U.S. record companies.

In 1979, Alpert returned to the studio and recorded *Rise*, written by his nephew, Randy Badazz, and Andy Armer. The title song rose to No. 1 the week of October 20 and stayed there for another week. By 1982, he had recorded three more albums and booked numerous concert dates. In 1984, he put together a new Tijuana Brass to play several shows in connection with the summer Olympics. Along with this, Alpert wrote and co-produced a new album, *Bullish* (1984). He subsequently recorded several more albums: *Wild Romance* (1985), *Keep Your Eye on Me* (1987), *Under a Spanish Moon* (1988), *My Abstract Heart* (1989), *North on South Street* (1991), *Midnight Sun* (1992), and *Second Wind* (1996).

Bibliography

Larkin, Colin, ed. *The Guinness Encyclopedia of Popular Music*. Vol. 1. Middlesex, U.K.: Guinness, 1995.

Stambler, Irwin. "Herb Alpert." *The Encyclopedia of Pop, Rock, and Soul*. New York: St. Martin's, 1989.

Milton Welsh Schober
Lee Ann Paradise-Schober

Altamont, a rock concert, took place on December 6, 1969, at the Altamont Speedway, Livermore, CA, 50 miles southeast of San Francisco. Originally intended to be a free outdoor concert in the spirit of Woodstock (see entry) and of the Hyde Park concert in London earlier that same year, Altamont turned out differently. Staged only four months after Woodstock, at which peace and calm prevailed, the Altamont show resulted in at least one death and hundreds of injuries. Taking place literally at the end of the 1960s, it also wound up representing the spiritual death of the decade. No longer could anyone assume that the behavior of a large gathering of Age of Aquarius devotees would represent the collective, nonviolent values that had been so convincingly modeled at Woodstock.

The free concert idea was meant to represent a gesture of generosity on the part of the main performing group at Altamont, the Rolling Stones, who at the time were finishing up a lucrative 14-city U.S. tour. The other groups scheduled for the bill were the Bay Area bands the Flying Burrito Brothers, Jefferson Airplane, the Grateful Dead, and Crosby, Stills, Nash and Young.

An unfortunate decision was to hire the Hell's Angels Motorcycle Club as security. For the Stones' Hyde Park appearance their British counterparts had been successfully used, but they represented style more than substance, often riding around on mopeds. Payment for the American outlaw gang was a truckload of beer, and plenty of red wine, and large amounts of LSD were also at their disposal. The size of the crowd was estimated at 400 thousand. Forty miles of traffic jams resulted, largely because of a late change of venue.

As the film documentary *Gimme Shelter* shows, Angels, fans, and even the occasional dog roamed across the stage during the concert. The Angels abused, spat upon, and clubbed spectators. The Jefferson Airplane's set came to an abrupt end when the Angels knocked lead singer Marty Balin unconscious. Some rode their motorcycles through the crowd. Crosby, Stills, Nash and Young fled after giving half of their scheduled performance. The Grateful Dead, after hearing about the violence, refused to play altogether.

The climax of violence came during the Stones' performance of their song "Sympathy for the Devil," when an 18-year-old black man named Meredith Hunter waved a pistol 20 feet from the stage. One Angel stabbed him repeatedly, and he was beaten by others and later died. The Stones, after calling for an ambulance, played on and finished the show.

Rock promoter Bill Graham described some years later the lasting effects of this event: "Altamont. The word conjures up an event which was more costly to rock and roll than any single day in the history of entertainment.... It will always be something for the critics of rock and roll to use. You can't let all these people gather *here* for a concert. They may hurt each other. Look at *Altamont*."

Bibliography

Gimme Shelter. Dir. David and Albert Maysles and Charlotte Zwerin. Maysles Films, 1970.

Gitlin, Todd. *The Sixties: Years of Hope, Days of Rage.* New York: Bantam, 1987.

Graham, Bill, and Robert Greenfield. *Bill Graham Presents.* New York: Dell, 1992.

Sanford, Christopher. *Mick Jagger, Primitive Cool.* New York: St. Martin's, 1993.

Bruce Henderson

Alternative Contemporary Christian Music (CCM) artists tend to represent the progressive end of the musical spectrum, with styles that range from new wave (e.g., Undercover) to heavy metal (e.g., REZ) to folk-rock (e.g., Mark Heard). But it is primarily the lyrical content of their music that defines this face of CCM (see Christian Radio Music Formats). Alternative CCM artists tend to think of themselves as artists rather than as ministers. They view their music as a reflection of the creative image of God found in all humans. By reflecting that divine image in their music, they consider their music to be worthwhile, without feeling the need to make it a vehicle for evangelism or exhortation.

As in crossover CCM, the lyrics of alternative CCM artists often lack overtly religious references. However, rather than removing religious references in order to facilitate crossover success, alternative artists do so in an attempt to communicate more honestly and effectively. These artists are often frustrated by the "Christianese" clichés that are found in much of CCM and by the lack of relevance of the music (and lyrics) beyond the CCM subculture. Alternative artists note that an abundance of religious-sounding terminology does not necessarily make the lyrics spiritually substantial and deep. Instead, this approach may mislead the listener into believing the Christian life is a uniformly positive experience.

CCM audiences have frequently resisted artist attempts to expand the range of their subject matter beyond the simple presentation of the gospel message itself. Leslie Phillips found these demands intolerable, "quitting" the CCM industry after recording three very successful pop-rock albums, explaining to *Newsweek,* "The audience was demanding propaganda.... People would say you're a heretic if you asked questions, and didn't give them the fundamentalist line." Steve Taylor, who took a prolonged vacation from CCM, suggests in *True Tunes News* that "a lot of [CCM] music is just telling people what they want to hear."

Alternative CCM artists offer a critique of both society and the church. Sarcasm, a self-reflective cynicism, and a raw, often painful look at the world dominate the lyrics of bands such as Daniel Amos (see entry), the Resurrection Band (aka REZ), Steve Taylor, and Mark Heard. The tensions between an audience and industry that often wants music filled with religious truisms and artists who want to fashion an honest reflection of life's struggles leaves alternative CCM artists seeking a niche in the highly censoring world of the church, Christian radio, and the retail world.

Bibliography

Eischer, Mark. "Evolution and the Ascent of REZ." *Harvest Rock Syndicate* Spring 1986: 10-11.

Giles, Jeff. "She's Stirred, Not Shaken." *Newsweek* 4 April 1994: 60.

Southern, Mike. "When the Dancer Becomes the Dance: The Power of Incarnation in Life and Art." *Contemporary Christian Magazine* April 1986: 28-29.

Thompson, John J. "Steve Taylor on Staring into the Sun: Squint or You'll Miss It." *True Tunes News* 5.9 (1993): 45.

Jay Howard

Alternative Music is popular music dedicated to alternative lifestyle and goals. Although widely used in the 1980s to describe music outside the corporate music industry and commercial media's narrow definition of rock 'n' roll, by the 1990s alternative was an industry marketing term to designate a style of music best described as grown-up punk and used to draw consumers' attention to clothing, beer, retail outlets, and television shows. Of course, the grab bag of alternative music is hard to categorize, yet is largely based on the traditional elements of rock 'n' roll, as well as punk and new wave music. The benefit of the term is that music heretofore unrecognized by the music industry and mainstream media now has a legitimate category in which to flourish by virtue of at least three reasons: *Billboard* magazine, the radio and record industry trade magazine, started its modern rock chart in 1988 to gauge the airplay of alternative music on commercial and noncommercial radio stations; in 1990, the Grammy Awards, the music industry's Oscar, announced its best alternative music recording category for its annual awards; and according to *Billboard*, modern rock was the 12th most programmed music in the U.S. on commercial radio in 1993, having increased more than any other format that year.

The term "alternative" in this sense is rooted in the counterculture of the 1960s, when any alternative to the establishment was the accepted course of action among many young people. Alternative music's roots are those of rock 'n' roll. In the 1950s, the energetic, raucous and sexual music of Elvis Presley, Little Richard, Jerry Lee Lewis, and Chuck Berry was an alternative to the homogenized pop of the time and spoke directly to teenagers in their language. The era was over by 1959, replaced by a variety of smoothed-over singers who became proponents of a watered-down version of the style.

By 1963, the British Invasion reinvigorated popular music, causing countless unknowns all over the country to pick up guitars and start forming garage bands, in what was generally known as the proto-punk era. As the schism in American society widened between youth and the establishment as a result of the Vietnam War and the civil rights movement, rock music became the voice of that generation. Just as its college radio counterpart would help bring alternative music to listeners in the 1980s, FM radio became the alternative to Top 40 programming in the mid-1960s. The avant-garde styles of Captain Beefheart via Frank Zappa, the arty Velvet Underground, and the emergence of Detroit's Stooges featuring Iggy Pop laid the foundation for the alternative movement of the 1980s.

By the early 1970s, rock split into a number of factions: heavy metal, southern rock, glam, country rock, funk rock, the beginnings of new wave via Jonathan Richman, and punk in the form of the New York Dolls. As Ira Robbins writes in *The Trouser Press Record Guide*, the New York Dolls' 1973 self-titled album "single-handedly began the local New York scene that later spawned the Ramones, Blondie, Television, Talking Heads, and others." In 1976-77, these groups were a reaction to the prevalence of disco and arena rock. Punk rock (see entry) was the alternative to both, enabling anyone with an instrument and an attitude to start a band and take the stage regardless of skill or singing abilities. The record industry decided *new wave* would be a more marketable term for groups with punk roots, however, and what was left of the New York underground, along with newer groups like Devo, the B-52s, the Cars, and others, lined up under that banner. At a time when the Eagles and the Bee Gees topped the U.S. charts, new wave provided an alternative for young music fans eager to hear witty, danceable songs performed by anybody but hippies or disco groups.

Around 1980, the beginnings of an organized alternative underground began to take shape. On the West Coast, Black Flag pioneered the form called hardcore, since their songs were "bluntly anthemic," the opposite of new wave and thereby a direct link to the sloganeering punk rock of the 1970s. Black Flag went on to blaze a trail around the U.S. finding all clubs that would book them, and other bands followed, creating an alternative network and laying the groundwork for a nationwide scene. The list of bands that made this period pivotal in the development of alternative music is well chronicled in *The Trouser Press Record Guide*. While hardcore flourished on the West Coast, groups also came out of Minneapolis, New York, Boston, San Francisco, Austin, Washington, DC, and, perhaps most important, the college town of Athens, GA, which provided R.E.M.

In 1991, the genre was crowned by a No. 1 album, *Nevermind*, by Nirvana (see entry), the power punk trio from Aberdeen, WA. Although R.E.M. had major successes with their albums in the 1980s and 1990s, Nirvana's brash guitars and urgent vocals required the pop world and rapidly graying classic rock radio, of which R.E.M was then a member, however unwittingly, to play music with direct links to punk and youth culture. The next generation of rock music had arrived, but it had been tagged as alternative and many critics felt the term had little value outside of marketing and could be compared to the way blues records were once called race records; therefore the categorization amounted to a modern-day musical segregation. Critics also differ on whether or not the signing of underground bands to million-dollar contracts, creating a realistic possibility of cult and college radio bands "making it," will stultify the progression of the music in hopes of commercial potential. By 1995, the term alternative was given mock funerals and generally despised by the underground music community from which it came. Also in 1995, a new radio format called Adult Album Alternative took the term a step further and was called by some industry people the "alternative to alternative," thus furthering the emptiness of the original term for music that is essentially rock 'n' roll to which no one in the mainstream is paying any substantial attention.

Bibliography

Arnold, Gina. *Route 666: On the Road to Nirvana*. New York: St. Martin's, 1993.

Miller, Jim, ed. *The Rolling Stone Illustrated History of Rock & Roll*. New York: Random House, 1980.

Robbins, Ira. *The Trouser Press Record Guide*. New York: Collier, 1991.

Hugh Foley

Amazing Stories (1926-) was a very influential pilot publication in science fiction. Hugo Gernsback (1884-1967) and his Experimenter Publishing Company published the first issue of *Amazing Stories* in early 1926. (The magazine was dated April 1926.) Originally, *Amazing Stories* was an oversized (bedsheet-formatted) "pulp" magazine, and was for some time subtitled "The Magazine of Scientifiction." While literary and other narrative elements of science fiction have existed almost as long as people have, it was Gernsback and *Amazing Stories* that were ultimately responsible for identifying and celebrating these elements (e.g., regarding speculations about the nature of the universe and its inhabitants, space travel, scientific inventions and advances) that characterize and make unique the term and genre Gernsback and his magazine deemed science fiction.

In February 1904, Hugo Gernsback, a native of Luxembourg, left for the U.S. to market his newly invented form of battery. During the next several years, Gernsback, now a resident of New York City, increased his talents as scientist, writer, and marketer. He soon discovered fiction grounded in sound, up-to-date scientific fact and theory, and published it in catalogs and magazines advertising his products, which increased sales of these products. Ultimately, Gernsback was responsible for a score of science fact and science fiction–related magazine series. The most famous, though not his first, was *Amazing Stories.*

Through the years, the pages of *Amazing Stories* have featured an array of famous and not so famous authors. Early issues showcased reprinted stories of Edgar Allan Poe, Jules Verne, and H. G. Wells; they also featured a range of already established and new authors of the day—included in the former group were A(braham) Merritt and Murray Leinster; in the latter, Dr. David H. Keller and Jack Williamson. Landmark *Amazing Stories* authors, stories and serials that debuted in *Amazing Stories* during the next few years included Edgar Rice Burroughs's *The Master Mind of Mars* (the sixth John Carter of Mars novel—1927), E. E. "Doc" Smith's *The Skylark of Space* (1928), Philip Francis Nowlan's *Armageddon 2419 A.D.* (the first Buck Rogers story, 1928), Edmond Hamilton's *The Universe Wreckers* (1930), and Jack Williamson's *The Green Girl* (1930).

Frank R. Paul (1884-1963) did many of the colorful, imaginative, detailed, larger-than-life paintings that graced the covers of *Amazing Stories* during its early years. Paul's portrayals of magazine storylines that featured speculations about futuristic technologies, alien races, space travel, monsters, and more were highlights for readers of Hugo Gernsback's brainchild.

In the 1930s, *Astounding Stories* pulp magazine proved *Amazing*'s chief competitor. (John W. Campbell [1910-1971], famed science fiction writer, served as editor of *Astounding* from 1937 until his death.) *Amazing Stories*, having gone through several editorial and ownership and format changes, is published today as a pulp digest much like *Ellery Queen's Mystery Magazine* and *The Magazine of Fantasy and Science Fiction.*

Bibliography

Asimov, Isaac, and Martin H. Greenberg, eds. *Amazing Stories: 60 Years of the Best Science Fiction.* Lake Geneva: TSR, 1985.
Gernsback, Hugo. *Ralph 124C 41+.* Boston: Stratford, 1925.
Moskowitz, Sam. *Explorers of the Infinite.* Cleveland: World, 1960.
Pratt, Fletcher. Foreword. *Ralph 124C 41+.* By Hugo Gernsback. New York: Fawcett/Crest, 1958.
Roberts, Garyn G. "Hugo Gernsback." *Dictionary of Literary Biography 137: American Magazine Journalists, 1900-1960.* Second Series. Ed. Sam G. Riley. Columbia: Bruccoli, 1994. 96-103.

Garyn G. Roberts

Amblinmation is a form of animation created by Steven Spielberg through his Amblin Entertainment company. Spielberg began to indulge in his love of animation when he "executive produced" Donald Bluth's 1986 release, *An American Tail.* Spielberg also produced Tim Burton's cartoon, *The Family Dog,* as an episode of the *Amazing Stories* TV show in 1986. A *Family Dog* series was started as a collaboration between Amblin Entertainment, Burton, Universal Studios, and Warner Brothers, but the series wasn't the equal of Burton's one-shot special. Six poorly reviewed episodes were aired during the summer of 1993. The same combination produced the 1994 holiday special *A Wish for Wings that Work*, starring Berke Breathed's Opus the Penguin and Bill the Cat.

Amblin Entertainment set up its own studio in London to produce *Who Framed Roger Rabbit?* When the movie became the box-office smash of 1988, the studio was kept together to produce *An American Tail II: Fievel Goes West*, followed by the 1993 dinosaur tale, *We're Back!*

Spielberg collaborated with Warner Brothers as the driving force behind television's *Tiny Toon Adventures* and *Animaniacs!* He also contracted for Saturday morning cartoons of his *Back to the Future* and *Fievel's American Tales.* The studio, now christened Amblinmation, has moved its facilities from London to Universal Studios in Hollywood. Other productions include *Balto* (1995), from the true story of a dog who saved Nome, AK, from an outbreak of diptheria; animated effects for the live-action *Casper* (1995); *Lost World* (1997), and *The Mask of Zorro* (1998).

Mark McDermott

American Culture Association (1978-), the leading academic association dedicated to the study of all aspects of American culture, was founded by several academics who, although already active in furthering the Popular Culture Association (see entry), felt that another dimension in academic study of American culture would be useful. Instrumental in starting and nurturing the American Culture Association (ACA) were Ray B. Browne, Marshall W. Fishwick, and Russel B. Nye. The ACA has had a great impact on studies in American culture by broadening and enriching the fields of teaching and researching the phenomenon of America. The ACA has always been housed at Bowling Green State University, Bowling Green, OH. It publishes the *Journal of American Culture* (see entry).

Bibliography

Browne, Ray. *Against Academia.* Bowling Green, OH: Bowling Green State U Popular P, 1989.

Peter Rollins

American Graffiti (1973) was George Lucas's second feature film. His first, *THX-1138* (1971), depicted a drab futuristic society not unlike that of George Orwell's *1984*. *American Graffiti* covers one 12-hour period in the lives of four teenagers: Curt (Richard Dreyfuss), Steve (Ron Howard), Terry (Charles Martin Smith), and John (Paul LeMat). Curt and Steve have reached a major decisional point: they have graduated from high school and been accepted to a college "in the East." They are scheduled to leave their generic California town (resembling Modesto, where George Lucas grew up) the next morning; but both are feeling somewhat ambivalent.

American Graffiti is set in a simpler era than ours: the Age of Camelot, the Kennedy presidency, when JFK had challenged young people to follow their dreams and to ask what they could do for their country. In such a context, the major decision one had to make was whether to be adventurous and leave home or to stay, get a job, and vegetate.

Since *American Graffiti* is so much concerned with cars, it is appropriate that the film concludes with a drag race at dawn (a "duel in the sun"?), followed by a departure on the aptly named Magic Carpet Airlines. In one night, each of the four main characters has gained significant insights about himself, and the viewers have been transported back to the early 1960s. The continued popularity of *American Graffiti* results not only, as Roger Ebert has said, from its having shown us "exactly how it was to be alive at that cultural instant," but also from the fact that it captures an archetypal aspect of adolescent development to which people of any age can relate.

The sequel, *More American Graffiti* (1979), was disappointing; but several other films have dealt successfully with similar themes, including *Breaking Away* (1979), *The Breakfast Club* (1985), and *Dazed and Confused* (1993).

Bibliography

Magill, Frank N., ed. *Magill's American Film Guide*. Vol. 1. Englewood Cliffs: Salem, 1983.

Pollock, Dale. *Skywalking: The Life and Films of George Lucas*. Hollywood: French, 1990.

Robert Sprich

American Magazines have developed in and become the voice of American culture. The first American magazines followed close upon the first English ones, Defoe's *Review* (1704), Addison and Steele's *Tatler* (1709) and *Spectator* (1711), and, most notably, the *Gentleman's Magazine* (1731), which was the first to call itself a magazine. Though not the first American magazine, Benjamin Franklin's *General Magazine and Historical Chronicle* (1741) was the most influential, addressing an audience on both sides of the Atlantic as the War of Independence approached. As in England, the 18th-century American magazines were both polemical and presided over by major literary figures: Tom Paine (*Pennsylvania Magazine*), Noah Webster (the *American Magazine*), and Charles Brockden Brown, who edited the *Monthly Magazine and American Review* (1799-1802) and the *Literary Magazine and American Register* (1803-10), the former out of New York, and the latter out of Philadelphia, which in these early years was the principal center of magazine production. A little later, Washington Irving edited for two years the *Analectic Review* (1813-21), and later still Edgar Allan Poe filled editorial positions on a number of publications, most notably the *Southern Literary Messenger* (1834-64), in Richmond, and *Graham's Magazine* (1826-58), in Philadelphia. Aptly, as he wrote in his *Marginalia*, "The whole tendency of the age is Magazineward."

The contribution of all these writers marks the turn of interest in the American magazine toward literary production rather than primarily political issues. One magazine that took up this interest was the *Saturday Evening Post* (see entry), first issued in 1821. The *Post*, one of the most beloved of American publications, though often derided by the intelligentsia (the "Saturday Evening Pest"), was *not* founded by Benjamin Franklin, but for at least a century it was "the reflection of a nation," and its publisher, the Curtis company, which also produced the *Ladies' Home Journal* (1883), was the leading magazine house. The *Post* lasted until 1968 (though still publishing sporadically today), when its values of a kinder, gentler America had lost their former power.

As the 19th century advanced, the aims of the American magazine became more discernible. The *Knickerbocker Magazine* (1833-65), out of New York, and the *North American Review* (1815-1939), out of Boston, but greatly altered after its move to New York in the 1870s, were both literary-nationalistic, though the *NAR* veered more often in the direction of historical writing; Henry Adams was one of its notable contributors. In the middle of the century, two of the most popular magazines, less intellectual than the *Knickerbocker* or the *NAR*, were (and still are) *Harper's* (1850) and the *Atlantic* (1857). The former, from New York, was at first less concerned with literary nationalism and profited much from reprinting such writers as Dickens, Thackeray, and Trollope. Later, under the long reign of Henry M. Alden (1869-1919), it became more nationalistic, the change symbolized especially by W. D. Howells's occupancy of the "Easy Chair" for the last 20 years of his life. The *Atlantic*, however, bore from the beginning the marks of Yankee Brahmanism, edited by James Russell Lowell, and with Emerson, Holmes, Longfellow, Whittier, and H. B. Stowe as frequent contributors. Howells came to edit it as well, at which point it became less parochial and more—if possible—messianically American. Almost as important as these two publications was *Putnam's Magazine* (1853-57 in its first and most important incarnation). It, too, was dedicated to American literature, and published several of Herman Melville's pieces.

From 1860 to 1900, as James Playsted Wood points out, the number of monthly magazines went from 280 to over 1,800. In 1879, facilitating such an increase, Congress allowed second-class postal privileges to magazines "published for the dissemination of information of a public character, or devoted to literature, the sciences, arts, or some special industry." The rest of the century saw the advent of such major periodicals as the *Century* (1881-1930), evolving out of *Scribner's Monthly*, and *Scribner's Magazine* (1887-1939). Of lesser circulation, but of greater literary cachet, was the *Galaxy* (1866-78), founded in New York as a counterweight to Boston and the *Atlantic*, and publishing both Mark Twain, who was an assistant editor, and the young Henry James. In this golden age of magazine publishing, the periodicals that began long runs included *McCall's* (1870), *Cosmopolitan* (1886), and the *National Geographic* (1888). The period was also the threshold of magazine illustration. The *Illustrated London News* had set an example as early as the 1840s, with its steel engravings, and *Harper's* soon followed suit. The *Atlantic* was resolutely unillustrated, as was the *Galaxy*, but the *Century* and *Scribner's* moved closer to photography, and by the turn of the century many magazines regularly used the camera image.

Another kind of graphic introduces us to another kind of magazine, where illustration came even earlier—the "woman's magazine." This type, with its fashion plates, perhaps reached its apogee with *Ladies' Home Journal* (see entry), but had certainly found an earlier bright star in *Godey's Lady's Book* (1830-98), which interpolated American writers among its patterns; *Woman's Home Companion* (1873) provided more of an outlet for women writers, including Willa Cather and Zona Gale; and *Good Housekeeping* in 1885 and *Vogue* in 1892 began long terms of catering to a predominantly female audience. Another kind of graphic ushered in the "man's magazine," though not until much later, at least in a form normally preserved in libraries. The most important of these was *Esquire* (1933)—"Man at his best"—semi-risqué in its day, but later quite outstripped by *Playboy* (1953); both published or republished stories and articles by distinguished authors, larded with a strong tincture of sexual titillation, a tincture more pungent by 1973 than in 1933.

These "gender-specific" magazines tended—with the exception of *Esquire*—to be rather solemn, but there was no shortage of magazines of humor. By the end of the 19th century there were *Puck* (1877-1918), which, under the long editorship of H. C. Bunner, was both Democratic and anti-Tammany, and *Judge*, which was founded by secession from *Puck* in 1881, the *soi-disant* "world's wittiest weekly," sophisticatedly Republican. Both *Puck* and *Judge* were weeklies, and both featured copious illustration, the former after the school of Thomas Nast, the latter more in the style the *New Yorker* (1925; see entry) would later adopt. Both ran on into the new century, as did *Life* (1883-1936; see entry), of distinctively Harvardian stamp, which early on featured the illustrations of E. W. Kemble and Charles Dana Gibson. The most sophisticated humorous magazine of its day, *Life* was eventually eclipsed by the *New Yorker*, and its name bought by Henry Luce for his own purpose.

Matching the grin at the turn of the century was the frown of the muck-raking magazines, which sought out the abuses in a society idealistically moving towards equality. The most notable of these was *McClure's* magazine (1893-1933), but there were many, several of which had begun under different banners, such as *Cosmopolitan* and *Munsey's* (1889-1929).

It was in the 20th century, and especially in the 1920s that magazines went mass market. That decade saw the first publication of *Reader's Digest* (1922), *Time* (1923), and the *New Yorker*, all still thriving more than 70 years later. While *Reader's Digest* had its predecessors in such magazines as the *Literary Digest* (1890-1938), and the *New Yorker* built upon the past, as we have seen, *Time* (see entry) was virtually without precedent, inventing the digest of news, little different from a weekly newspaper, which spawned such other long-lived newsmagazines as *Newsweek* (1933) and *U.S. News and World Report* (1948). With the coming of television, *TV Guide* (1953) joined and eventually overtook the high-circulation magazines, and for more than a decade has disputed back and forth the top position with *Reader's Digest*. But the appeal to the widest audience inevitably produced a pandering to the lowest common denominator. Such was *Liberty* (1924-50), which purveyed cheap fiction and simple-minded journalism (with a suggested time for reading its articles); 50 years later, such is *People* (1974; see entry), with its sometimes scandalous revelations of the rich and famous. Even further pandering occurs at the level of the supermarket checkout counter (see Tabloid Newspapers).

Throughout the last 70 years, the literary and intellectual strain in magazine publication has continued to flow in such magazines as *The Nation*, first published in 1865, and always identified with the social underdog; *The New Republic*, founded in 1914, with Walter Lippmann on its editorial board; the *Saturday Review* (1924-86), and the *Reporter* (1949-68). The emphasis in all these publications was or is on informed commentary and, in most cases, scholarly criticism of the arts. While such magazines took political stances, these were rarely biased, and absolute political commitment, solemnly held to ("My party right or wrong"), is largely a product of more recent years. William Buckley's *National Review* (1955) and *Mother Jones* (1976) may be taken as representative of this contemporary (and often uncivil) polarity. As American society has become less monolithic, a number of magazines have arisen to fill the needs or aspirations of minority groups. Among the best of these are *Commonwealth* (1924), with a Catholic point of view, *Commentary* (1945), published by the American Jewish Committee, and *Ebony* (1945), aimed at a primarily African-American readership.

In a not dissimilar category from these, though really *sui generis*, was the *American Mercury*, founded in 1924 by H. L. Mencken, and very much an expression of his antipathy for the mass mind. Mencken had earlier been editor of the *Smart Set* (1890-1930), which had begun as a journal of wit and sophistication, especially under Willard Huntington Wright's editorship, before it too joined the attack on the "booboisie." The acquisition in 1913 by Condé Nast of *Vanity Fair* turned it into a competitor for the *Smart Set*, though both were eventually eclipsed by the *New Yorker*, and *Vanity Fair* (which would be resurrected 50 years later) was folded into *Vogue* in 1936.

At the other extreme from the mass market, more akin to these magazines for the intelligentsia, are the "little magazines"—the university reviews (from *Daedalus*, a Harvard organ first appearing in 1846, to the *Kenyon Review*, the sometimes platform of the Southern agrarians, founded in 1939) in particular. Others without university affiliation include *Poetry* (1912), Harriet Monroe's famous hospice for the 20th-century poetic; *Partisan Review* (1934), which began as a partisan for Communism, a god that soon failed it; and *Hound and Horn* (1927-34), guided by R. P. Blackmur and Yvor Winters, and important not least for its part in the revival of Henry James.

Among the more specialized magazines of the 20th century, most of which announce their province in their titles, and many of which sell by subscription rather than on the newsstands, are *Business Week* (1929) and *Fortune* (1930), yet another Luce publication; *Scientific American* (1945); *Better Homes and Gardens* (1922) and *Harrowsmith* (1976); *Sports Illustrated* (1954); and the *Old Farmer's Almanac*; see also Nature Magazines and Children's Magazines. All these publications have been of great value to their targeted audiences, though the *Old Farmer's Almanac* knows no boundaries in its readership. Founded in 1793, while Washington was still president, it continues to be both a practical guide to the seasons and the weather, and a window of insight into New England manners and mindsets.

Thus, the American magazine has a proud and distinguished history of interpreting American life and letters, of spurring the country to action or inaction, or merely of advertising what commerce has to offer. Its two golden ages, the decades after the Civil War, and the second quarter of the 20th century, produced publications of the highest literary and intellectual quality that, taken together, give a comprehensive view of what America was doing and saying and thinking—to be found nowhere else. To read these magazines is to know America.

Bibliography

Mott, Frank Luther. *A History of American Magazines*. Vols. 1-5. Cambridge: Harvard UP, 1930-68.

Peterson, Theodore. *Magazines in the Twentieth Century*. Urbana: U of Illinois P, 1964.

Wood, James Playsted. *Magazines in the United States*. 3d ed. New York: Ronald, 1971.

Barrie Hayne

See also
Underground Press, The

American Musical Theater has triumphed and become distinctive in a tradition that has been in existence since the ancient Greek era, when all drama was accompanied by music, and many of the choral passages were actually songs. In the 18th and 19th centuries popular theater in France put words to well-known tunes in order to bypass the strict rules of the upper-class theaters. This form of the musical continued into England and the U.S. as music hall, cabaret, and variety theater, but American writers created and developed the musical that is so popular today the world over with such hits as *Phantom of the Opera, Cats, The Fantasticks, A Chorus Line,* and *Into the Woods.*

Although this style of drama has no written rules, and evolved slowly, the musical comedy *The Black Crook*, written by Charles M. Barras in 1863 and produced at Niblo's Garden in New York in 1866, is generally considered the first American musical comedy. With a highly sketchy plot, fantastic scenery, and special effects, the play was mostly an excuse to show off dancing girls in skin-colored bodysuits. Essentially "a lavishly produced girlie show," once called immoral by many critics, *The Black Crook* got back its investment times seven within the first year and ran almost continuously throughout the country until the end of the century.

In the early 1900s, various forms of musicals were extremely popular among the theater-going audience. In the 1920s and 1930s musical revues, especially those of the Ziegfeld Follies, were among the most popular theatrical forms (see Revue). These revues were composed of a series of skits and musical numbers unconnected by plot or throughline, but offering spectacular costumes and sets as well as singing and dancing. Musical revues were larger, more elaborate versions of the skits produced on the vaudeville stage. It was in these latter performances that George M. Cohan began his career, eventually creating full-length musicals such as *Little Johnny Jones* (1904) and *Forty-five Minutes from Broadway* (1906). Another precursor to the modern American musical was *Show Boat*, written in 1927 by Oscar Hammerstein II and Jerome Kern. In this show the performers for the first time sang songs that were appropriate to their characters, although they did not forward the plot.

The modern American musical took full form in the 1940s and 1950s. In *Oklahoma!*, written in 1943 by Richard Rodgers and Oscar Hammerstein, the chorus line was omitted, making everyone on stage a more fully developed character. Choreography was taken seriously, with Agnes de Mille integrating narrative, dramatic ballet into the story. Called at the time an operetta, *Oklahoma!* established a vogue for historical settings in musicals, and its popularity demanded that it be distinguished from its Italian namesake, so the term "musical play" was brought into use to apply to productions in which the music and dance is an integral part of the plot. *Oklahoma!* continues to be extremely popular, enjoying dozens of productions a year in community, regional and education theaters across the country.

Two other often-revived musicals from this time period are *Carousel* (1945) and *West Side Story* (1957), both more accurately called "musical plays" than "musical comedies" because of their unhappy endings. In the first, a Richard Rodgers and Oscar Hammerstein II retelling of the play *Liliom,* a man is given a chance to return to earth to redeem his crimes, but errs and must return to purgatory, leaving his widow and daughter to find their own way in the world. The second, a modern version of the Romeo and Juliet story, by Arthur Laurents and Leonard Bernstein, leaves another woman alone after the death of her lover to contemplate the violence of gang warfare.

Today it is the American musical that is keeping the Broadway theater scene alive. Although writers like Andrew Lloyd Webber (see entry; *Phantom of the Opera, Cats, Jesus Christ Superstar, Evita*) have moved some of the focus to British writers, others like Stephen Sondheim (see entry;

Passion, Into the Woods, Sunday in the Park with George, Company, Sweeney Todd) have ensured the continued presence of American writers in this Broadway mainstay. It was Sondheim who determined the path that the musical would take in the 1970s and after. His musical *Company* (1970) was a concept musical, which explored the ideas surrounding marriage without a strongly developed storyline. Other writers followed his lead, most specifically Michael Bennett, James Kirkwood, and others with their 1970 production of *A Chorus Line,* a concept musical about auditioning for a Broadway musical. *A Chorus Line* ran for 6,147 performances and became the longest-running show in Broadway history. It closed on April 28, 1990, after a 15-year run, taking in over $277.5 million, employing over 500 performers on Broadway, and touring to 104 U.S. cities.

The American musical is without a doubt the most popular form of theater in the U.S. today. Many people who do not regularly attend the theater will buy tickets to a Broadway musical while on vacation there, or will go to local productions of popular musicals such as *Oklahoma!, Anything Goes!, Nunsense,* or *Carousel.* While the American theater establishment continues to worry about the decline of Broadway and theater in general, the American musical consistently draws in huge crowds, whether the productions are new or old. Revivals have become increasingly popular in both musicals and straight plays, and in 1994, the American Theatre Wing introduced two new categories to their annual Tony Awards—best revival of a play and best revival of a musical. The first award for best revival of a musical went to a new production of *Carousel.*

Bibliography

Bordman, Gerald, ed. *The Concise Oxford Companion to American Theatre.* New York: Oxford UP, 1987.

Brockett, Oscar G. *Century of Innovation.* Boston: Allyn, 1991.

Kuritz, Paul. *The Making of Theatre History.* Englewood Cliffs: Prentice-Hall, 1988.

Mandelbaum, Ken. *A Chorus Line and the Musicals of Michael Bennett.* New York: St. Martin's, 1989.

Matlaw, Myron, ed. The Black Crook *and Other Nineteenth-Century American Plays.* New York: Dutton, 1967.

Susan Kattwinkel

See also
Musical Films
Theater (20th Century)

America's Most Wanted (1988-) a successful TV show dedicated to aiding the law in the capture of lawbreakers. David James Roberts was the first fugitive profiled and apprehended by the Fox Broadcasting Company network series; he was arrested by FBI agents in Staten Island, New York, only four days after the premier episode of the series. Though a Top 10 FBI fugitive, Roberts was running a homeless shelter and was recognized by several friends and fellow workers after his crimes were reenacted on *America's Most Wanted.* He had escaped from the Indiana State Prison, where he was serving six life sentences for murder, arson, rape, and kidnapping.

Roberts is one of hundreds of fugitives captured after their crimes were featured on the show. The series first aired in February 11, 1988, on the Fox-owned-and-operated stations and was carried nationwide by its affiliates in April of that same year. A typical episode of *America's Most Wanted* re-creates several crimes. These dramatizations are reenacted at the actual locations of the events being reconstructed and frequently include "actual participants in the events—the victim's last companions, for example, or police officers who discovered the victim's body. When actors are used, they typically bear a striking resemblance to the persons being portrayed," as noted in *ABA Journal.* The segments also include interviews with witnesses and police officers, as well as photographs, descriptions, and psychological profiles of the criminals. Each week, several thousand viewers call in with leads and tips on a toll-free hotline: 1-800-CRIME-TV. On hand in the studio are police officers and federal agents involved with the cases reenacted that night. When one of the operators gets a good tip demonstrating special knowledge about the case, an officer intercedes.

In essence, the series uses a simple two-step technique: capturing viewer's attention with reenactments and then flashing an indelible image of the suspect's face on the screen. Much of the show's credibility, as well as its popularity, derives from its host, John Walsh. His previous experience before cameras came in 1981, following the disappearance of his six-year-old son, Adam. According to *ABA Journal,* Walsh found the police "unable or unwilling to help search for the boy. Desperate, he turned to the media. Two weeks later a volunteer search party found Adam's body. He had been brutally murdered." The tragedy turned Walsh, a former Florida hotel developer, into a passionate crusader on behalf of missing and exploited children. He and his wife, Reve, have testified before Congress and the legislatures of most states. They were instrumental in the passage of legislation to coordinate information regarding missing youths. NBC made a TV movie about the Walshes' work, *Adam* (1983), and a sequel *Adam: His Song Continues* (1986). Daniel Travanti, who portrayed Walsh in those movies, became a close friend and together they hosted a critically acclaimed HBO documentary, *How to Raise a Street-Smart Child.*

Tapping into the tremendous amount of frustration with crime in the U.S., *America's Most Wanted* has continued in popularity. Although concerned with criticism from the legal community (i.e., concerns for the rights of those profiled, prejudicial pretrial publicity), the five federal agencies cooperating with *America's Most Wanted*—the FBI, the Bureau of Alcohol, Tobacco, and Firearms, the Drug Enforcement Administration, the U.S. Customs Service, and the U.S. Marshal Service—view the show as serving the purpose of law enforcement. *America's Most Wanted* reaches an estimated audience of 20 million, and calls to the toll-free number average 2,000 on most nights of airing and 3,500 by the end of the week. On July 16, 1989, *America's Most Wanted* was the first Fox program to rank first in its time slot.

Bibliography

Bartley, D. "John Walsh: Fighting Back." *Saturday Evening Post* Apr. 1990: 44-47.

Breslin, Jack. *America's Most Wanted: How Television Catches Crooks*. New York: Harper, 1990.

Jacoby, T. "Murder, They Broadcast: *America's Most Wanted* Solves a Gory Mystery." *Newsweek* 12 June 1989: 58.

White, D. *"America's Most Wanted." ABA Journal* 75 (Oct. 1989): 92-96.

Daniel A. Panici

Amos 'n' Andy (1928-1960), one of radio's most successful shows, as well as a TV series (1951-53), has always been two-faced in American entertainment (see African Americans and Entertainment TV). Before *Julia* and *I Spy*, before *Good Times* and *The Jeffersons*, before *The Cosby Show* and Black Entertainment Television, there was Amos 'n' Andy. From a civil-rights perspective, it has always been an issue whether *Amos 'n' Andy* was part of the solution or the problem. Especially in its radio version, *Amos 'n' Andy* grew from morally questionable traditions of blackface and minstrel shows.

Amos 'n' Andy began as a radio comedy series in 1928. The show was created by two white men, Freeman Fisher Gosden and Charles J. Correll, and was a copy of their earlier series *Sam 'n' Henry* (1926-28, WGN-Chicago). *Amos 'n' Andy* told the story of two black men who experience culture shock upon moving from Georgia to Chicago. Much of the humor in the show was based on the stereotypical stupidity and shiftlessness of the title characters, played by Gosden and Correll.

Amos 'n' Andy originated at WMAQ-Chicago and was picked up by the NBC Blue network for national distribution in 1929. The show was a 15-minute daily serial. Production moved to Los Angeles in 1937 and to CBS in 1939, then back to NBC in 1943. With this move to NBC, *Amos 'n' Andy* switched to a weekly, half-hour, episodic format. It was back to CBS in 1948, and at this point CBS bought ownership rights to Gosden and Correll's creation. In the mid 1950s, the radio version of *Amos 'n' Andy* changed to a pseudo-variety format consisting of recorded music and comedic, disc-jockey-type routines. The radio series ended in 1960, having run longer than any other radio comedy.

Meanwhile, *The Amos 'n' Andy Show*, a half-hour episodic series, debuted on CBS-TV in 1951 and ran until 1953, with syndicated reruns continuing until 1966. The TV series was set in Harlem rather than Chicago and starred black actors instead of Gosden and Correll. Alvin Childress played Amos, and Spencer Williams, Jr., played Andy, but the real star of the show was Tim Moore as George "Kingfish" Stevens. Kingfish was a sly good-for-nothing who, week after week, swindled his lodge brother Andy and involved him in various get-rich-quick schemes and familial intrigues.

Amos and Andy were an early case of what we would today call a "franchise." In addition to radio and TV series, the franchise included a feature film, a newspaper comic strip, a short animated film, sound recordings, at least two books, and personal appearances by Gosden and Correll in blackface. For almost 40 years, Amos and Andy were a multimedia phenomenon and enormously popular.

However, both the radio and TV versions of *Amos 'n' Andy* also elicited numerous protests. The sponsor of the TV series, Blatz beer, was the target of an informal boycott encouraged by the National Association for the Advancement of Colored People (NAACP) in 1951. Although the effect on beer sales was minimal, the controversy surrounding the TV series both echoed earlier campaigns against the radio program and established issues that continue to be debated in discussions of TV's depiction of African Americans.

Critics of *Amos 'n' Andy* argue that the main characters in the series present a negative image of African Americans, perpetuating many of the worst stereotypes left over from the minstrel-show era. Males are often lazy, stupid, or dishonest. Females are shrewish. The issue of image was especially salient in the early 1950s, when *The Amos 'n' Andy Show* was practically the only picture of black life available on American television. The only African Americans who had any role in creating this picture were the actors, who were of course under the direction of white men. In later years, *The Amos 'n' Andy Show* has often been seen as an unwanted reminder of old wounds. Even the theme music, "The Perfect Song," used in both the radio and TV series, has a racist connotation in that it was drawn from the score of D. W. Griffith's 1915 film *The Birth of a Nation*, which celebrated the rise of the Ku Klux Klan.

A number of points may be raised in defense of Amos and Andy, starting with the fact that many African Americans liked them. The NAACP's long-standing opposition to the TV series has not been unanimous, even among the organization's own leaders. The black actors employed in the series generally defended it, as have numerous other black performers. *The Amos 'n' Andy Show* was the first TV series to have an all-black cast and at the time was practically the only TV series to employ black actors. To some extent, it paved the way for future generations of African-American TV performers. In addition to the positive role of Amos, *The Amos 'n' Andy Show* routinely showed blacks as doctors, judges, and business owners, and in many other respectable positions. This was something of a breakthrough from earlier Hollywood stereotypes of African Americans.

There is no definitive explanation as to why CBS canceled the TV series in 1953 or why it has withheld the show from syndication since 1966. The program's controversial reputation must surely be a factor. Similarly, the ongoing objections to *The Amos 'n' Andy Show* during its syndication may have been seen by the networks as a good reason not to develop new series with black actors. In fact, it was not until *I Spy* in 1965 that the next starring role materialized for a black actor in a network dramatic series. Amos and Andy themselves remain out of circulation on American television. Now more than ever, they are "invisible men."

Bibliography

Andrews, Bart, and Ahrgus Juilliard. *Holy Mackerel! The Amos 'n' Andy Story*. New York: Dutton, 1986.

Correll, Charles J. *All about Amos 'n' Andy and Their Creators Correll and Gosden*. New York: Rand McNally, 1929.

Cripps, Thomas. "*Amos 'n' Andy* and the Debate over American Racial Integration." *American History/American Television: Interpreting the Video Past.* Ed. John E. O'Connor. New York: Ungar, 1983. 33-54.

Ely, Melvin Patrick. *The Adventures of Amos 'n' Andy: A Social History of an American Phenomenon.* New York: Free, 1991.

Hilmes, Michele. "Invisible Men: *Amos 'n' Andy* and the Roots of Broadcast Discourse." *Critical Studies in Mass Communication* 10 (1993): 301-21.

Gary Burns

Andersonville Trial, The (1970), a live television performance (3 acts; 150 minutes) of Saul Levitt's 1959 Broadway play of the same name, presented the post–Civil War trial of Henry Wirz, commandant of the infamous Andersonville (Georgia) prisoner-of-war camp, replaying in chilling, vivid dialogue the circumstances by which 14,000 Union soldiers lost their lives as a consequence of their mistreatment and neglect. The play, produced by KCET-Los Angeles and Lewis Freedman, was aired in 1970 over NET to mark the debut of *Hollywood Television Theater*, a dramatic anthology program funded by the Ford Foundation. The television version of Levitt's play was written for the screen by the playwright himself and directed by George C. Scott, who had starred in its Broadway run. *The Andersonville Trial* starred Richard Basehart as Wirz, William Shatner as the judge advocate, and Jack Cassidy as the defense attorney. The cast also included Martin Sheen, Buddy Ebsen, Cameron Mitchell, John Anderson, Harry Townes, Michael Burns, Albert Salmi, Whit Bissell, and Lou Frizzell. Levitt's play about a military court-martial presented moral responsibility vs. military obligation utilizing one set (the courtroom). It was interrupted only three times for commercials. *The Andersonville Trial* won a Peabody that year as well as two Emmys awarded for outstanding writing achievement in drama, adaptation (Saul Levitt) and technical achievement (Tom Ancell, Rick Bennewitz, Larry Bentley, and Jack Reader); Jack Cassidy was nominated for outstanding single performance by an actor in a leading role.

Bibliography
O'Neil, Thomas. *The Emmys.* New York: Penguin, 1992.

Susan P. Madigan

Andy Griffith Show, The (1960-1968), a perennial Top 10 hit for the CBS television network, has in syndication consistently maintained a large, loyal following. The show's premise, main character, and setting were introduced in an episode of *The Danny Thomas Show* (see Thomas, Danny) in which Thomas's character was stopped for speeding by Sheriff Andy Taylor of Mayberry, NC.

Fictional Mayberry provided the backdrop for the program, but contrary to popular myth Griffith did not model it after his hometown of Mount Airy, NC. Perhaps no other situation comedy in television history was as well cast as *The Andy Griffith Show*. Griffith's Sheriff Taylor, a widower raising a small boy named Opie (Ron Howard), was the strong central figure. His sidekick was his deputy and cousin Barney Fife, played to perfection by Don Knotts. (Knotts

was not originally intended to be a regular performer, but Barney Fife was such a hit that he became a mainstay for five years (1960-65). (Knotts, who won five Emmys for his work, would have continued the role. However, Griffith had always contended that he would end the show after five years, and even into the fifth year he had not recanted. Knotts, uncertain of the show's future, signed a movie deal that prevented him from remaining as a regular.) In addition to Barney Fife, a cast of unique supporting characters was introduced and developed over the eight-year run. Among the more prevalent and notable of these characters were Andy's Aunt Bee (Frances Bavier), barber Floyd Lawson (Howard McNear), filling station attendant Gomer Pyle (Jim Nabors), town clerk Howard Sprague (Jack Dodson), Opie's teacher and Andy's girlfriend Helen Crump (Aneta Corsaut), Barney's girlfriend Thelma Lou (Betty Lynn), town drunk Otis Campbell (Hal Smith), and George Lindsey as Goober Pyle. Gomer was introduced in 1963, and remained on the show into the 1964 season when the character was spun off into his own series, *Gomer Pyle, U.S.M.C.* (1964-70; see entry).

In its last year *The Andy Griffith Show* was the No. 1 program of the year. Unlike the much-ballyhooed finales of other popular shows, such as *Cheers* and *M*A*S*H*, *The Andy Griffith Show* ended its eight-year run by becoming *Mayberry, R.F.D.* Some of the original characters stayed on, such as Aunt Bee, Goober Pyle, Howard Sprague, and Sam Jones (Ken Berry), but most left the show. Berry, playing a farmer and city councilman, joined the cast in the show's last year. With the transition to *Mayberry, R.F.D.*, Berry's character replaced Sheriff Andy Taylor as the main character. *The Andy Griffith Show* has been one of the more successful shows ever put into syndication. Over the past few years, a number of television specials have capitalized on the popularity. *The Andy Griffith Show* has given its fans a legacy that will continue to last for a long time to come. Mayberry and its townspeople offer fans an excellent means of escape from the harried pace of their own reality.

Bibliography
Beck, Ken, and Jim Clark. *The Andy Griffith Show Book.* New York: St. Martin's, 1985.

Kelly, Richard. *The Andy Griffith Show.* Winston-Salem: Blair, 1981.

McNeil, Alex. *Total Television: A Comprehensive Guide to Programming from 1948 to the Present.* New York: Penguin, 1991.

Pfeiffer, Lee. *The Official Andy Griffith Show Scrapbook.* New York: Citadel, 1994.

W. A. Kelly Huff

Animal Detectives have long played important roles in mystery fiction, providing clues and serving as murder weapons, but seldom becoming central characters. Recently, however, animals, especially pet dogs and cats, have taken on more active roles in finding resolutions. While some animals become assistants to human investigators, others actually engage in detection, providing answers that would not be possible without their intervention.

Animals' sleuthing is primarily limited by their inability to communicate with people, but their animal attributes allow them access to information unavailable to humans. Susan Conant's dogs (introduced in *New Leash on Death,* 1990) sniff out evidence because they are real Malamutes. Some animal investigators display strongly anthropomorphic traits. Koko, the cat who stars in Lilian Jackson Braun's books (such as *The Cat Who Moved a Mountain,* 1979), demonstrates a level of extrasensory perception even his owner finds amazing. Midnight Louie, a cat in Carole Nelson Douglas's fiction (for example *Pussyfoot,* 1993), adds his own voice to the third-person narratives of his fictional owner's investigations. Sneaky Pie Brown claims authorship of her novels, including *Murder at Monticello: Or, Old Sins* (1995), in which several animals work together to solve crimes and protect and inform humans. In such cases, the animals' physical actions usually remain realistic, but their mental activity becomes part of a fantasy indulged in by their owners who are close to their pets and imagine them partners in the crime-solving venture.

Bibliography

Klein, Kathleen Gregory. *Great Women Mystery Writers: Classic to Contemporary.* Westport: Greenwood, 1994.

Ward, Carol M. *Rita Mae Brown.* New York: Twayne, 1993.

Sharon Russell

Animal Stories for Children have been consistently popular with American children during the past century. They generally fall into two categories: animal fantasy and animal realism. Young boys and girls, up to age eight or nine, are fascinated with the magic of fantasy tales in which authors present animals such as rabbits, monkeys, bears, mice, and elephants with child-like thoughts and emotions. Beatrix Potter's *The Tale of Peter Rabbit* (1902) is the best-selling children's book of all time. Many of these fantasies portray animals who are nearly human in every respect but appearance. In Kenneth Grahame's *The Wind in the Willows* (1908), Toad, Badger, and Mole live in houses, attend parties, and go on adventures together. The little bunny in Margaret Wise Brown's *Goodnight Moon* (1947) reflects the bedtime behavior of children by saying goodnight to a multitude of household pets and items in an effort to delay the moment of sleep, and the titular character in Dr. Seuss's *The Cat in the Hat* (1957) juggles, performs magic, and talks to entertain two bored children.

In recent years, the didactic Berenstain Bears series has proved immensely popular among parents and children, offering stories about first visits to the dentist, keeping one's room clean, practicing good manners, and anticipating the arrival of a new baby. Other fantasies portray animals more closely to their natural characteristics, but with human-like feelings. Robert McCloskey's *Make Way for Ducklings* (1941) illustrates the worries two ducks share as they try to find a suitable nesting spot in Boston. The monkey in H. A. Rey's Curious George stories stays within the realm of animal behavior while accidentally calling the fire department, letting a farmer's animals loose, stealing a kite, and other such debacles, all the while being chased by the man in the yellow hat. Some animal stories create whole communities of creatures that mimic human worlds. Laurent de Brunhoff's Babar stories depict an elephant society in a mythical kingdom in Africa with all the virtues and foibles of human culture. Many of Bill Peet's stories introduce contemporary issues through animal behaviors, such as *Farewell to Shady Glade* (1966) addressing environmentalism, and *Kermit the Hermit* (1965), about isolation from the community. And E. B. White's *Charlotte's Web* (1952), about Charlotte the spider's attempts to save Wilbur the pig from the butcher block, has touched the hearts of millions of American children.

More realistic stories of animals hold an appeal for older children. With a few notable exceptions (such as Rudyard Kipling's *Jungle* books [1894-95]), realistic animal stories focus on dogs and horses and their relationships with people. Jack London's *White Fang* (1906) and *Call of the Wild* (1903) explore the lives of dogs and their role in human survival in the frozen wilderness of Alaska. Both *Lassie Come-Home* (1940), by Eric Knight, and *The Incredible Journey* (1961), by Sheila Burnford, chronicle the struggles that dogs (and a cat) undergo in returning home to their masters. And Wilson Rawls's *Where the Red Fern Grows* (1974) reveals the depths of love a young boy can feel for his dogs and the agony of loss when they die. Such fictions as *Black Beauty* (1877) by Anna Sewell, *Misty of Chincoteague* (1947) by Marguerite Henry, and *My Friend Flicka* (1941) by Mary O'Hara reveal the imagined lives of horses in and out of relationships with human beings.

Bibliography

Cullinan, Bernice. *Literature and the Child.* San Diego: Harcourt, 1989.

Huck, Charlotte, Susan Hepler, and Janet Hickman. *Children's Literature in the Elementary School.* New York: Henry, 1989.

Bruce Goebel

Animation (Early). Always one of the most popular forms of entertainment, animation began as simple films exploiting the illusion of moving drawings. J. Stuart Blackton's *Humorous Phases of Funny Faces* (1906), in which a series of cartoon faces drawn on a blackboard seemed to change expression, is a generally conceded starting point.

The first major artist in American animation was Winsor McCay (1867?-1934), already renowned for his classic newspaper strips *Little Nemo in Slumberland* and *Dream of the Rarebit Fiend.* Working laboriously and with little or no assistance, McCay translated the elaborately detailed style and fantastic imagination of his newspaper work to the screen. His first film, *Little Nemo,* appeared in 1911. Probably his most famous film was *Gertie the Dinosaur* (1914), which McCay used as part of his vaudeville act. In it a marvelously lifelike diplodocus responded to McCay's commands from the stage. Later McCay films included the propaganda effort *The Sinking of the Lusitania* (1918), a hauntingly beautiful film despite its subject, and *The Pet* (1921), in which a small, cuddly house pet gradually grew to gargantuan proportions.

McCay's early films inspired a generation of animators, but John R. Bray (1879-1978) was perhaps even more influential. Bray introduced a variety of labor-saving devices, and simplified the production of his films so that they could be turned out as quickly and cheaply as possible. The resulting films had a plain, no-frills look, but they could be produced on a regular schedule for theatrical distribution. Bray's first series of films concerned a character named Colonel Heeza Liar, a good-natured parody of Teddy Roosevelt. In December 1914, he established Bray Studios, hiring a staff of artists to help him. One of the most important was Earl Hurd (1880-1940), who had patented a major labor-saving device of his own: the practice of animating the moving figures on transparent sheets of celluloid (later called "cels"), so that the stationary background behind them need only be drawn or painted once. The pooling of Bray's and Hurd's technological devices resulted in the Bray-Hurd Process Company, which controlled a group of key patents vital to the budding animation industry.

Two important pre-1920 animation studios were Hearst International Film Service, which produced films based on strips in the Hearst newspapers—George Herriman's *Krazy Kat,* Frederick Opper's *Happy Hooligan,* Rudolf Dirks's *Katzenjammer Kids*—and the Raoul Barré (1874-1932) studio, with a series based on Bud Fisher's *Mutt and Jeff.* Typically, the artist who had originated the strip would be associated with the related films in name only. The crude *Krazy Kat* of the screen, for example, bore little relation to the sophisticated, cerebral humor of Herriman's strip.

The 1920s brought a number of animated characters who could and did stand on their own, and the most successful of these was Felix the Cat. The Felix films were nominally produced by Pat Sullivan, but the anonymous artist who actually created them was Otto Messmer (1892-1983). Felix caught the imagination of audiences because of his impish, resourceful personality. He used gags that fully exploited the medium; often his tail would detach itself and form a question mark over his head, or become a baseball bat or some other useful implement. The original Felix cartoons are still fresh and delightful today, far superior to the lackluster television series of later years.

Another successful series of the 1920s was *Out of the Inkwell,* created by Bray Studios alumnus Max Fleischer (1883-1972). This series, which initially owed much to a Fleischer invention called the rotoscope, centered on a character named Koko the Clown. The series displayed an uncommon level of wit and invention, producing such outstanding entries as *Bedtime* (1923) and *Koko the Kop* (1927). Behind the camera Fleischer was assisted by his brothers, notably Dave Fleischer (1894-1979), generally credited as director of the studio's films. In 1924, the Fleischers inaugurated a successful series of singalong shorts, in which the now-familiar bouncing ball followed the lyrics of popular songs.

Of course, there were many other successful animators working in American films during the 1920s. Paul Terry (1887-1971), another former Bray artist, produced a series of *Aesop's Fables.* These little films had nothing to do with Aesop or his fables, but were merely haphazard collections of gags, often featuring Terry's character Farmer Al Falfa. And an unknown young artist named Walt Disney (1901-1966), after a failed attempt to establish an animation studio

in Kansas City, set up shop in Hollywood. There he enjoyed a modest success with two series: Alice Comedies—featuring a little girl, filmed in live action, inhabiting a cartoon world—and, subsequently, the all-animated Oswald the Lucky Rabbit.

It was with his entry into sound films that Disney really hit his stride in the animation business. His landmark film *Steamboat Willie* (1928) was not, as has so often been claimed, the first cartoon with synchronized sound; but it exploited the novelty of sound so cleverly, with gags so intrinsically based on music and sound effects, that it created a sensation.

The impact of Disney's and Mickey Mouse's success on the animation industry in 1929-30 cannot be overstated. Overnight, nearly every animation studio was scrambling to produce its own Mickey clone. The influence of Disney's Silly Symphonies can be seen in the subsequent offerings of rival studios: Looney Tunes, Merrie Melodies, Happy Harmonies, Color Rhapsodies.

Most of the prominent animation studios of the 1930s had roots in the silent era. The Fleischer studio continued to prosper, but in its films Koko the Clown was superseded by a new character named Betty Boop (see entry). Betty was a baby-faced, jazz-age flapper whose appeal was mildly risqué —until the establishment of the Production Code Administration in the mid-1930s, when her costumes and behavior became more circumspect. Beginning in 1933, the studio produced perhaps the most successful of all comic-strip adaptations: a series starring E. C. Segar's Popeye the Sailor. And the bouncing-ball singalong films continued, the addition of sound making it possible to add performances of the songs by well-known singers.

Walter Lantz (1900-1993), another silent-era veteran who had stayed with the Bray Studios until 1927, landed a contract with Universal Pictures to produce a series of sound cartoons featuring Oswald the Rabbit, Disney's former silent character. Lantz's version of Oswald was pleasant but undistinguished, and was phased out in 1938 to make room for Andy Panda. Lantz ultimately enjoyed a long career in animation; his greatest success would arrive in the 1940s with Woody Woodpecker. Paul Terry likewise continued production into the sound era (using the series title Terrytoons), and he, too, is best remembered for a 1940s creation, Mighty Mouse.

In 1930, Hugh Harman (1908-1982) and Rudolf Ising (1903-1992), two veterans of Disney's silent films, established (under producer Leon Schlesinger) the Warner Bros. cartoon studio. Their initial efforts, featuring a nondescript character called Bosko, were derivative and undistinguished, and the studio remained stuck in the Disney-imitation rut for several years. It was only after a personnel turnover in the mid-1930s that the real explosion in Warners' cartoons would take place (see Warner Brothers Cartoons). MGM entered the cartoon business in 1931 by releasing the films of Ub Iwerks (1901-1971), formerly Disney's leading animator. Neither of his characters, Flip the Frog nor Willie Whopper (a boy who told tall tales), was successful, and by the end of the decade Iwerks was back at the Disney studio. Beginning in 1934, MGM released a series of films by Harman and Ising, produced with a beauty and lavishness that rivaled the Disney cartoons. But by the early 1940s Harman and Ising would be supplanted at MGM by other directors.

Bibliography

Canemaker, John. *Felix: The Twisted Tale of the World's Most Famous Cat.* New York: Pantheon, 1991.

——. *Winsor McCay: His Life and Art.* New York: Abbeville, 1987.

Crafton, Donald. *Before Mickey: The Animated Film 1898-1928.* Cambridge: MIT P, 1982.

Maltin, Leonard. *Of Mice and Magic.* New York: McGraw-Hill, 1980.

Peary, Gerald, and Danny Peary. *The American Animated Cartoon: A Critical Anthology.* New York: Dutton, 1980.

B. Kaufman

See also
Amblinmation
Cartoons: Theatrical and Television
Stop-Motion Animation

Anne of Green Gables (1908) mothered a series of successful novels. Her Canadian author, Lucy Maud Montgomery, first envisioned Anne as the heroine of a Sunday School serial, but the intriguing character and immense popularity of *Anne of Green Gables* led to a sequence of eight books, following Anne from a young girl to a mature woman with a family. The story begins when an aging brother and sister, Matthew and Marilla Cuthbert of Prince Edward Island, seek a boy orphan to help out with farm chores, and Anne, a scrawny, loquacious, red-haired girl, arrives instead. Although their initial impulse is to send her back, Anne brings color and warmth into their lives and eventually to everyone in the community. Her character is a classic of children's literature, with her unflinching honesty, optimism, and sense of expectancy about life. Anne is driven by an ambition to learn, enhanced by her rivalry with Gilbert Blythe, a rivalry destined eventually to become partnership in love and marriage.

By the end of *Anne of Green Gables* Anne encounters real sorrow (Matthew's death) and disappointment (postponing college). Both Anne's red hair and her temper have lost some of their fire. In the subsequent books, Anne works as a teacher, attends college, marries Gilbert Blythe, raises a family, and endures separation and death during World War I. Anne's abiding popularity stems from her spunk and imagination, as well as her all-too-human tendency to make mistakes.

Bibliography

Reimer, Mavis, ed. *Such a Simple Little Tale: Critical Responses to L. M. Montgomery's* Anne of Green Gables. Metuchen: Scarecrow, 1992.

Mary Welek Atwell

Anthony Adverse (1933) is an epic historical novel that gripped the popular imagination in an age before such fiction was an established genre. The first novel of Hervey Allen (1880-1949), an American author who went on to write five other novels, none of which is as widely read as the first, *Anthony Adverse* chronicles the episodic adventures of its title character.

A grand and sweeping story, *Anthony Adverse* is an American *Tom Jones* (Henry Fielding's 1749 novel of an English foundling that is the prototype for the picaresque adventure novel). Allen also wrote one of the most colorful and engaging biographies of Edgar Allan Poe, *Israfel* (1926).

Bibliography

Knee, Stuart E. *Hervey Allen: A Literary Historian in America.* Lewiston: Mellen, 1988.

Liahna Babener

Anthony, Piers (1934-), born in England, came to the United States in 1940, where he has established a career as a leading author of fantasy and science fiction. His first novel, *Chthon* (1967), set forth the characteristic patterns of his work: action that takes place in an extraterrestrial world whose features partake of elements of folklore and classical, Norse, and biblical mythology; a drama that is centered around the conflicts between various kinds of intelligence, such as mechanical and organic; dilemmas that reflect an interest in psychology and psychoanalysis; and larger themes that address the ethical and ecological fate of humankind. Anthony is known for his agile wordplay and his clever use of fantastical elements, not merely dragons, centaurs, and other magical beings, but also imaginative fusions of the organic and the inanimate, such as shoe-trees that produce shoe offspring.

In addition to a number of discrete novels, Anthony's writings have been grouped into several series: the Incarnations of Immortality series that successfully integrates magic and science in a universe where common people can achieve Godhood; the Bio of a Space Tyrant books that tell the story of a drifter who achieves intergalactic fame; the Apprentice Adept, Battle Circle, Jason Striker, and Omnivore series; and the best-known, the Magic of Xanthe group, stories that take place in a magical world built on puns. There are now over 18 books in the Xanthe sequence.

Recently, Anthony has expanded his repertoire to include historical fiction and horror. While he has been criticized for sexist attitudes within his works, he has also been praised for the imaginative worlds he has created.

Bibliography

Anthony, Piers. *Piers, Bio of an Ogre: The Autobiography of Piers Anthony to Age 50.* New York: Ace, 1988.

Collings, Michael. *Piers Anthony.* Mercer Island: Starmont, 1983.

Platt, Charles. *Dream Makers Volume II: The Uncommon Men and Women Who Write Science Fiction.* New York: Berkley, 1983.

Solomon Davidoff

Anything But Love (1989-1992), a half-hour situation comedy on ABC, which was indicative of a more liberal television industry, revolved around the relationship of Hannah Miller and Marty Gold, employees of a Chicago magazine. Hannah was played by Jamie Lee Curtis, fresh from her success in the movie comedy *A Fish Called Wanda.* Marty was played by Richard Lewis, yet another standup comic attempting to follow the sitcom success of Bill Cosby and Roseanne.

Created by Wendy Kout and developed by Dennis Koenig, Peter Noah (see entry) replaced them after the first six episodes as co-developer, co-executive producer and head writer.

The show was canceled by ABC, but critical acclaim, a boost in ratings from the last episode, and popular comedian John Ritter (*Three's Company, Hooperman*) as a guest star worked together to convince the network to return *Anything But Love* in February 1991. Ritter's character served as a foil for Hannah and Marty's relationship for three episodes, but by the fourth one the couple were not only in bed, but they stayed there, discussing the strength of their orgasms. ABC gave executive producer Noah no trouble over this episode, but the show was to last only another year.

Bibliography

Brooks, Tim, and Earle Marsh. *The Complete Directory to Prime Time Network TV Shows, 1946-Present.* 5th ed. New York: Ballantine, 1992.

Noah, Peter. Personal interview, 17 April 1991.

Terrace, Vincent. *Television Character and Story Facts.* Jefferson: McFarland, 1993.

Lynn C. Spangler

Apocalypse Now (1979), Francis Ford Coppola's film, loosely based on Joseph Conrad's *Heart of Darkness*, has a unique place among Vietnam films, if not the larger genre of war films. While not acclaimed as an "epic" in all respects, the film was acknowledged as a powerful spectacle, especially in its 70 mm version with six-track Dolby sound. The editing, its Oscar-winning cinematography and sound, particularly in the helicopter assault and other action/detonation sequences, made it an instant "study text" for would-be filmmakers. The acting, the screenplay, and its episodic plot have not fared as well in the short or long runs of commentary, but, as a whole, it is still the best expression of the surreal side of America's Vietnam experience—if not the way it was for the combatants, at least the way it *seemed* to many who watched it unfold on television.

The various phases of writing and production, in combination with Coppola's habit of in-process structuring, led to a film with strong scenic values, but somewhat contradictory plot and thematic tendencies. In his initial screenplay, John Milius kept the basic thrust of Conrad's novel while radically changing the treatment and outcome of the journey. The Marlow figure (eventually Willard, played by Martin Sheen) is supposed to find Colonel Kurtz (Marlon Brando) in the middle of a thick jungle, the object being (as in Conrad) more a matter of ending his independent brutalities than rescuing or bringing him to trial. The colonel is perceived as an outstanding soldier who has gone mad, and in going toward him through the wilderness, the main character is drawn to him. The madness in Milius's (and Coppola's) treatment is the Vietnam War itself, with Kurtz representing, somehow, a more authentic form of it.

That *Apocalypse Now* continues to fascinate scholars, students, and fans has partially to do with a characteristic of great art, even if Coppola's film has hardly ensured its status. Due to the process of its creation, the mixed motives of its

Apocalypse Now is a Francis Ford Coppola war film. Photo courtesy of Popular Culture Library, Bowling Green State University, Bowling Green, OH.

creator, and America's continuing struggle with its abortive involvement in Vietnam, *Apocalypse Now* has an ambiguity of impact, a depth of layers, a density of texts and archetypes.

Bibliography

Anderegg, Michael, ed. *Inventing Vietnam.* Philadelphia: Temple UP, 1991.

Apocalypse Now Sessions. Liner notes. Passport Records.

Conradiana 13.1 (1981).

Rollins, Peter, ed. *Hollywood as Historian.* Lexington: UP of Kentucky, 1983.

William M. Hagen

See also

Vietnam Films and Documentaries

Arden, Eve (1907-1990), is considered by many observers to be one of this century's most beautiful and talented comedic specialists. She, Billie Burke, and Carmen Miranda were those who had types of roles named after them in Hollywood despite their being confined largely to supporting roles in feature films. Before she undertook television roles, Arden had appeared in 50 feature films. She evolved a style of delivering lines that earned her the title Queen of the

Caustic Crack. She never took her beauty seriously and regarded her important career as secondary to her roles as wife and mother. Yet she became a sensation in her one nightclub appearance. She wrote articles and triumphed in feature movies, in series leads on television, in guest-starring assignments, and on radio and on the stage.

Eve Arden was born Eunice Quedens in Mill Valley, CA. She entered show business early and performed in the Ziegfeld Follies, appeared for Cole Porter and other creators of musicals, then entered Hollywood's world while maintaining her theatrical career. Her most acclaimed film roles included *Stage Door* (1937), *Cover Girl* (1944), *The Dough-girls* (1944), *We're Not Married* (1952), and *Anatomy of a Murder* (1959).

After several years, Eve Arden took her highly popular radio show, *Our Miss Brooks* (see entry), to television in 1952. Viewers forgave the CBS entry its excessive parody elements to cheer for the irrepressible Connie Brooks as she pursued Philip Boynton, a shy, sexually obtuse biology teacher, while avoiding the volcanic wrath of her principal, Osgood Conklin. She won an Emmy for the role in 1953. Her second series, *The Eve Arden Show*, was based upon Emily Kimbrough's life as writer and mother; it lasted only one season (1956-57). Another pilot film starring Arden failed to sell to the networks; but the next, *The Mothers in Law*, became a popular success in 1967-69. Arden and a talented cast made this show about determinedly helpful parents of newlyweds a delight. It was inexplicably canceled after two seasons.

Thereafter, Arden played Auntie Mame and many other roles, many of them opposite her actor husband Brooks West in regional theaters. At the same time, she played roles in such television series as *Bewitched, Run for Your Life, The Man from U.N.C.L.E.*, and many more. She played important roles in feature films such as *Grease* (1976) and made-for-television films, and participated in television specials.
Bibliography
Arden, Eve. *Three Phases of Eve: An Autobiography.* New York: St. Martin's, 1985.

Robert Michael Cerello

Arlen, Harold (1905-1986), famed American composer, was born Hyman Arluck in Buffalo, NY, into a cantorial family. His grandfather, Moses Arluck (Erlich), had emigrated from Vilna in Eastern Europe to serve as cantor at a congregation in Louisville, KY, and his father, Samuel Arluck, held cantorial positions in Buffalo and then in Syracuse, NY. Both men were officiants at what is known as traditional (Orthodox) Jewish ritual services.

By the age of seven, Harold Arlen was singing in the liturgical choir directed by his father. Arlen had a highly productive songwriting career, composing many lyrical ballads as well as "peppy tunes" for Broadway and touring stage productions and then for films. Over the years, he wrote special numbers for such leading performers as Jack Benny, Ray Bolger, Eddie Cantor, Al Jolson, Bert Lahr, Beatrice Lillie, Ethel Merman, Frank Sinatra, and Rudy Vallee. Arlen began his theatrical work as rehearsal pianist, arranger, and

then composer in shows along with George and Ira Gershwin, Vernon Duke, and Vincent Youmans. His music was featured in the popular "varieties" revues of Earl Carroll and George White, and particularly at the Harlem Cotton Club. In 1932, Arlen, with Billy Rose and E. Y. Harburg, created the song "It's Only a Paper Moon," and the following year, he wrote "Stormy Weather" for singer Ethel Waters.

By the late 1930s, Arlen was also shaping tunes for Hollywood movies, and in 1938, he wrote the music for *The Wizard of Oz*. Over the decades, his songs were performed and recorded by such film stars as Judy Garland, Bob Hope, Lena Horne, Danny Kaye, and Dinah Shore. Arlen's notable lyricist collaborators were Ira Gershwin, E. Y. "Yip" Harburg, and in particular the gifted Johnny Mercer, who partnered Arlen in crafting some wonderful "classic" selections.
Bibliography

Ferriano, Frank. "Did He Write That? America's Great Unknown Songwriter Harold Arlen." *Trackings: Popular Music Studies* 3.1 (1990): 8-17.
Jablonski, Edward. *Harold Arlen: Happy with the Blues.* Garden City: Doubleday, 1961 and New York: Da Capo, 1985.
——. *Harold Arlen: Rhythm, Rainbows, and Blues.* Boston: Northeastern UP, 1996.

Irene Heskes

Armstrong, Edwin Howard (1890-1954), invented an array of radio improvements such as FM radio, superheterodyne, and regenerative or feedback system. The latter two basically contribute to radio amplification, while the former constitutes broadcasting by frequency modulation (FM).

Born in New York City, Armstrong lived during much of his childhood in Yonkers. In 1913, he received his engineering degree from Columbia University. Early in 1912, his laboratory investigations led him to the conclusion that the audion (three-element vacuum tube) was essentially a device relaying electrons able to generate radio waves as well as detect and amplify them.

Armstrong's regenerative discovery took place during his undergraduate years at Columbia. This feedback circuit greatly increased the value of the audion, unshackling its potential. Therefore, Armstrong showed that part of the received current could be fed back through the audion to reinforce itself many times.

Although Armstrong patented his feedback system in 1914, his triumph would be marred by a more than 14-year litigation with Lee DeForest (see entry), who claimed he actually invented the circuit prior to Armstrong. The eventual U.S. Supreme Court decision against Armstrong is called a "judicial misunderstanding" of the nature of the invention, and most scientists have credited Armstrong as the true feedback inventor.

The feedback circuit became a stepping-stone for Armstrong's next great invention, the superheterodyne circuit. In 1918, he developed and later patented it while serving as a World War I major in the Signal Corps in France. The invention greatly exceeded amplification capabilities of the regenerative system. After the war, Armstrong returned to his radio experiments in the laboratory at Columbia University.

During the late 1920s, Armstrong began working full time on the basic principles of FM transmitting and receiving. At last, he was ready to file for his first basic FM patents in 1930. In 1933, he secured four additional patents on advanced circuits, finally solving this last basic FM problem. Also that year, Armstrong demonstrated his work to RCA, hoping to impress its head, David Sarnoff. Conclusive field tests took place during 1934. Unfortunately, Sarnoff and his scientists were far more interested in perfecting television than static-free, high fidelity FM radio.

In March 1934, the inventor installed an experimental FM transmitter atop New York's Empire State Building. The first public demonstration of FM's broadcast capabilities took place in November 1935, via 100-watt W2AG, Yonkers. In 1936, the Federal Communications Commission (FCC) issued Armstrong an experimental FM station permit. Thus, 50,000-watt FM station W2XMN went on the air in 1938, and by July 1939 offered a regular program schedule.

Finally, in 1940, the first FM and AM-FM combination receivers became available to the general public. Commericial FM broadcasting began January 1, 1941, increasing interest and subsequent applications for stations. However, the advent of World War II stopped progress of the new radio medium. Only about 50 commercial FM stations remained on the air during the war, while more than 400 applications were on file with the FCC.

In June 1945, the FCC moved the FM band from 42-50 mhz to its present 88-108 MHz location. This meant that all FM receivers became obsolete, causing a major, though temporary setback for the young medium. In addition, changes in transmitting equipment were needed. This blow especially troubled and depressed Armstrong, but FM continued its slow progress. Television entered the scene in full force between 1948 and 1952, offering more reasons to retard FM's growth. It would not be until the 1970s that FM would truly triumph, overtaking AM radio's leadership.

Bibliography

Barnouw, Erik. *The Golden Web: A History of Broadcasting in the United States*. Vol. 2. 1933-1963. New York: Oxford UP, 1968.

Dunlap, Orrin E., Jr. *Radio's 100 Men of Science*. New York: Harper, 1944.

Erickson, Don V. *Armstrong's Fight for FM Broadcasting: One Man vs. Big Business and Bureaucracy*. Tuscaloosa: U of Alabama P, 1973.

Lessing, Lawrence P. *Man of High Fidelity*. New York: Bantam, 1969.

Lewis, Tom. *Empire of the Air*. New York: HarperCollins, 1991.

Sammy R. Danna

Armstrong, Louis Daniel (1901-1971), is a name synonymous with jazz. Certainly, there is ample reason for that identification. Armstrong was not only the first major popularizer of the idiom, he was also its first major innovator. He was a man of myth.

The myth of his July 4th birth has been recently corrected (to August 4). But the myth was fitting to a man who

A young Louis Armstrong. Photo courtesy of Sound Recording Archives, Bowling Green State University, Bowling Green, OH.

so well represented the best in America that he could release an album entitled *Ambassador Satch* with no further explanation required. The album title referred to his participation in the cultural exchange program in which jazz played so prominent a role, but it could also refer to his overall embodiment of the American success story. ("Satch" was one of his nicknames [also "Pops"], for "Satchelmouth"—a reference to his generous mouth.)

Armstrong's father abandoned the family at Louis's birth. By all accounts, Louis was a spirited young man who basically ran the streets of New Orleans, singing on corners and finding other ways to survive. His African-born grandmother tried to keep him in tow, but even then Armstrong was a master at charming people to get his way. Eventually, when he was about 12 years old Armstrong was placed in the New Orleans Coloured Waif's Home (1913-14) after firing a gun to celebrate New Year's Eve.

Music became his way out of the hunger and poverty that attended his youth. In the Coloured Waif's Home he began to play music and eventually learned to play the cornet, an instrument on which he eventually made his first recordings in 1923. Long before then, he played numerous gigs on borrowed cornets and employed a bravura style filled with precision that he quite plausibly learned in the Waif's Home. This style distinguished him from earlier jazz trumpet players and remained with him throughout his career.

In common with many other jazz musicians, Armstrong served an apprenticeship with an older musician. In his case, it was one with Joe "King" Oliver (see entry). "Pampa Joe" Oliver used Armstrong as a second cornetist in his band and eventually took him to Chicago in 1922, where they made a number of classic recordings with an all-star band, including Johnny and Baby Dodds and Kid Ory. Armstrong had been a member of Kid Ory's band in 1918, his first important band job.

The pianist in Pampa Joe Oliver's Chicago band was Lil Hardin, who urged Armstrong to quit the band and go out on his own. In 1924, they married and Armstrong left Oliver to join Fletcher Henderson in New York. This move was important both for Armstrong and jazz. Armstrong virtually single-handedly taught the big band to swing. He did some arranging with Henderson, and in turn, Henderson and his men improved Armstrong's reading and aided his own sense of musical discipline.

In 1925, he moved back to Chicago to join his wife's band. Lil Armstrong featured him as the "world's greatest trumpeter," anticipating the way in which his later manager, Joe Glaser, would also present him with bands that were not really his own. Soon after, in 1927 and 1928, Armstrong recorded his Hot Five and Hot Seven sides. About the same time, Armstrong recorded with a series of female blues singers named Smith: Bessie, Trixie, and Clara. For many, these late 1920s recordings mark the high point of his creative achievement.

In 1932, he took the first of many trips to Europe, where he was a huge success. In 1938, he divorced Lil Hardin Armstrong and married Alpha Smith. That marriage also ended, and in 1942, he married Lucille Wilson, who survived him.

From time to time, Armstrong appeared in feature films, recording with Ellington, Basie, and other major stars. He lends great presence to the film *High Society*, the remake of *The Philadelphia Story* set at the Newport Jazz Festival. Armstrong was often featured on television, and there exists a memorable tape of Satchmo playing with his old friendly rival, Dizzy Gillespie.

Armstrong made many overseas trips for the State Department's Cultural Exchange Program. Perhaps the most exciting was his 1956-57 tour, his first overseas tour since 1936. He played in the Gold Coast, soon to be Ghana, Britain, and the West Indies. He then returned to play at Newport and almost immediately left for Latin America. A movie, *Satchmo the Great*, narrated by Edward R. Murrow, captures some of the excitement of this period.

In 1957, he released a four-volume Columbia anthology that presented new recordings and commentary on his old hits. His career sagged again in the early 1960s, but the hit song and movie *Hello, Dolly!* bolstered it once more and it never faltered again. Satch even appeared in the movie version of the play. He died secure in the knowledge that he was still popular and that his contributions would outlive him.

Mark Gridley notes among Armstrong's significant contributions his foremost role of the jazz soloist, his virtual invention of swing rhythm, his sense of form and drama in solo construction, his repertory of jazz phrases which even the most "modern" soloists borrow, the invention of new melody lines played over the chord changes of the original melody, his trumpet tone and technique, the virtual invention of scat singing, and the great influence he has had on vocalists over the years.

Bibliography

Balliett, Whitney. *Night Creature*. New York: Oxford UP, 1981.

Collier, Lincoln. *The Making of Jazz*. Boston: Houghton, 1978.

Feather, Leonard. *Encyclopedia of Jazz*. New York: Da Capo, 1984.

——. *The New Yearbook of Jazz*. New York: Horizon, 1958.

Gridley, Mark. *Jazz Styles*. Englewood Cliffs: Prentice-Hall, 1994.

Frank A. Salamone

Arness, James (1923-), represents for television the Western heroes portrayed by John Wayne in film, men who were fair dealers and straight shooters with enough conviction to challenge an erring community when necessary. In both cases the actors spent many years cultivating personae which became indistinguishable from the men themselves.

Arness was born in Minneapolis, MN. After being discharged from military service in North Africa and Italy, Arness moved to California, where after an apprentice period in community theater, he signed a contract with MGM in 1948. In a role with no lines but with a dramatic appearance, he played the strange magnetic monster in *The Thing* (1951). Of more importance for his later career were the films made with John Wayne, *Big Jim McLain* (1952) and *Hondo* (1953). When the successful radio Western *Gunsmoke* (1952-55) was developed for television, the role of Matt Dillon was offered to John Wayne. Wayne did not want to make an extended commitment to television, but he recommended Arness, who was eventually signed for the part. Beginning as a half-hour series in 1955, *Gunsmoke* (see entry) was extended to an hour format in 1962 and to color in 1967. When it was canceled in 1976, it had long since become the longest-running series in television history.

After *Gunsmoke* was canceled, Arness made a television film, *The Macahans* (1976), and a miniseries, *How the West Was Won* (1977), later developed into a series (1977-79). In this venue he played Zeb Macahan, a mountain man and family patriarch. This character was much less restricted by considerations of law and order than the marshal had been.

Arness also was featured in the series *McClain's Law* (1981-82) and in five television film sequels to *Gunsmoke* (1987-94). His career is remarkable for the character he created, which, while conforming in many ways to Western stereotype, nevertheless was played with sensitivity and intelligence.

Bibliography

Barabas, SuzAnne. *Gunsmoke: A Complete History and Analysis of the Legendary Broadcast Series with a Comprehensive Episode-by-Episode Guide to Both Radio and Television Programs*. Jefferson: McFarland, 1990.

Brooks, Tim. *The Complete Directory to Prime Time TV Stars, 1946-Present*. New York: Ballantine, 1987.

CBS News Release, July 1964.

Current Biography 1973: 15-17.
Lindsey, Robert. Personal interview with James Arness. Dallas Times Herald 15 Sept. 1977: C-4.
Miller, Lee D. The Great Cowboy Stars of Movies and Television. Westport: Arlington, 1979.

Janet P. Sholty

Arzner, Dorothy (1900-1979), was a Hollywood director who profoundly influenced the movies of her day. During the 1970s, the women's movement "rediscovered" director Dorothy Arzner, reevaluating her films and their importance to women in particular and to filmgoers in general (see Women in Film). Dorothy Arzner was among only a small handful of women directors active in Hollywood under the studio system and was certainly the only woman director then to establish a coherent body of work, including *Fashions for Women* (1927), *Christopher Strong* (1933), starring Katharine Hepburn, *Craig's Wife* (1936), and *Dance, Girl, Dance* (1940). However, after directing nearly 20 films and riding to significant wealth and stature in Hollywood, Arzner left the industry permanently in 1943. For the last year before her departure, Arzner battled a respiratory ailment that made it virtually impossible for her to work. After that time, and until her death in 1979, Arzner lived near Palm Desert, CA.

While her films are "women's pictures," Arzner went past presenting the world from a woman's point of view to question the dominant order she found around her. Arzner's films present a series of women who discover their own identity through social transgression of and desires that often find their objects beyond the masculine reality of their worlds. That is, Arzner's women characters (often flashy, always independent) do not achieve their freedom by avoiding masculine society, but rather by confronting it directly, whether through career or through obsessive behavior or through other attempts at independence.

Bibliography
Cook, Pam. "Approaching the World of Dorothy Arzner." *Feminism and Film Theory*. Ed. Constance Penley. New York: Routledge, 1988.
Heck-Rabi, Louise. *Women Filmmakers: A Critical Reception*. Metuchen: Scarecrow, 1984.
Kay, Karyn, and Gerald Peary. *Women and the Cinema: A Critical Anthology*. New York: Dutton, 1977.
Johnston, Claire. "Dorothy Arzner: Critical Strategies." *Feminism and Film Theory*. Ed. Constance Penley. New York: Routledge, 1988.
——, ed. *The Work of Dorothy Arzner: Towards a Feminist Cinema*. London: British Film Institute, 1975.

Roberta F. Green

As the World Turns (1956-), one of the longest-running and most traditional of television's soap operas, premiered on CBS. Creators Irna Phillips and Ted Corday set out to develop a soap opera that was innovative, and *As the World Turns* was the result. It was the first soap opera to begin on television, as a 30-minute show. It was taking a risk by not having the benefit of a radio audience to carry over to televi-sion; and it differed from other soap operas in its concentration on multidimensional characters rather than characters easily identified as "good" or bad." Irna Phillips and Agnes Nixon teamed up to write the Procter and Gamble serial, and Ted Corday served as director. The program had a low rating and showed little growth during its first year. Irna Phillips had, however, insisted on a clause in her contract that protected the show from cancellation for one year, even if the ratings were poor. After two years on the air, *As the World Turns* was rated higher than any other soap opera, a position that the serial would maintain for an unprecedented 13 years. During the height of its popularity, *As the World Turns* became the first soap opera to spin off another series, *Our Private World* (1965), a prime-time serial that CBS hoped would compete with ABC's *Peyton Place*. Starring Eileen Fulton, the serial dramatized the adventures of Lisa Miller Hughes but ran in prime time for only four months.

In 1970, Irna Phillips left *As the World Turns*, reportedly for health reasons, although it was widely suspected that her primary reason for leaving was to work with her daughter, Katherine Phillips, to develop another soap opera, *A World Apart*, for ABC. *A World Apart* was canceled after 15 months. After two years without Irna, the ratings for *As the World Turns* had slipped, and Irna returned. However, the ratings failed to improve, and in 1973 she was fired by Procter and Gamble, who brought in Robert Soderberg and Edith Sommer, a husband-and-wife team who had been writing for *The Guiding Light*. The show continued its slow pace and traditional, conservative nature, and expanded to one hour on December 1, 1975. During the late 1970s, *As the World Turns* lost its direction, with long-running characters being written out, and new characters being brought on. Longer scenes were replaced with shorter clips, and bedroom scenes multiplied. Audiences continued to tune out. In the 1980s and '90s, the addition of younger characters, a stepped-up pace, updated production values, and contemporary plot twists blended with traditional values kept the show alive despite the program's aging audience and a general decline in soap watching (see Soap Opera).

Bibliography
LaGuardia, Robert. *Soap World*. New York: Arbor House, 1983.
Schemering, Christopher. *The Soap Opera Encyclopedia*. New York: Ballantine, 1987.

Barbara J. Irwin

Asimov, Isaac (1920-1992), the author of over 400 books, influenced science fiction greatly through his stories about robots and his future history, the Foundation series. The robot stories began with "Robbie" (originally entitled "Strange Playfellow"), which appeared in Frederik Pohl's *Super Science Stories* (September 1940). These stories eventually filled five anthologies: *I, Robot* (1950), *The Rest of the Robots* (1964), *The Complete Robot* (1982), *Robot Dreams* (1986), and *Robot Visions* (1990).

In an effort to counter the image of robots as life-threatening monsters, Asimov devised his Three Laws of Robotics, which appeared in *I, Robot*: "1.) A robot may not injure a human being, or, through inaction, allow a human being to come to harm, 2.) A robot must obey the orders given it by human beings except where such orders would conflict with the First Law, and 3.) A robot must protect its own existence as long as such protection does not conflict with the First or Second Law." Many of the robot stories involve problems that robots and humans have interpreting these laws. Asimov also wrote four robot novels. In the first three—*Caves of Steel* (1954), *The Naked Sun* (1957), and *The Robots of Dawn* (1983)—Asimov pairs a human detective with a robot partner to investigate various murders. The fourth novel, *Robots and Empire* (1985), connects all of Asimov's robot fiction with his Foundation series. Asimov's sweeping future history began with the publication of the short story "Foundation" in John W. Campbell's *Astounding* (May 1942).

Many stories followed, as Asimov created a history of a galactic empire far more sophisticated than those which had appeared earlier in popular culture. Central to the series is Asimov's invented science of psychohistory, which reveals the laws that govern the development of societies. Using psychohistory, the characters attempt to guide events in order to avoid cultural setbacks. The Foundation short stories were anthologized in *Foundation* (1951), *Foundation and Empire* (1952), and *Second Foundation* (1954). Asimov later wrote two more Foundation novels set after the time of *Second Foundation—Foundation's Edge* (1982) and *Foundation and Earth* (1987)—and a third, *Prelude to Foundation* (1988), which involves the development of psychohistory. In addition to his robot and Foundation tales, Asimov created "Nightfall" (1941), which many science fiction authors consider the best short story in the genre. "Nightfall" occurs on a world that experiences night only once every 2,000 years, and on which, for reasons no one has recorded, civilizations never outlive that span of time. When night arrives and people see a dark sky lit by stars, they begin to burn everything they can to create light. In addition to his science fiction, Asimov wrote mysteries, literary guides, and popularizations of science.

Asimov was born in Russia but moved with his family to Brooklyn in 1923. He discovered science fiction at the age of nine by reading magazines sold in his father's candy store. He attended Columbia University and eventually earned a Ph.D. in chemistry. In 1949, he accepted a position as an instructor of biochemistry at the Boston University School of Medicine. In 1958, he became a full-time writer.

Bibliography

Asimov, Isaac. *Asimov on Science Fiction*. New York: Doubleday, 1981.

——. *I, Robot*. New York: Gnome, 1951.

James, Edward. *Science Fiction in the 20th Century*. Oxford: Oxford UP, 1994.

Platt, Charles. *Dream Makers*. New York: Berkley, 1980.

Touponce, William. *Isaac Asimov*. Boston: Hall, 1991.

Brent Chesley

Asner, Edward (1929-), accomplished actor and labor leader, was born in Kansas City. Despite an everyman's appearance that threatened to typecast him, Asner enriched television in the 1970s with versatile performances. Appearing in influential comedy, drama, and miniseries programming, he earned critical praise and became a highly popular performer. Controversy over his politics and leadership of the Screen Actors Guild stifled his career during the 1980s.

A stocky build, thinning hair, and gruff countenance made Asner credible as a tough guy, whether as a blue-collar worker, policeman, or menacing villain. He played such parts in episodes of *The Fugitive* (ABC, 1963-67), *Mission: Impossible* (CBS, 1966-73), and more than 15 other series as well as in films like *The Slender Thread* (1965) with Anne Bancroft and Sidney Poitier and *El Dorado* (1967) with John Wayne and Robert Mitchum. His only regular role was that of a political reporter in the drama series *Slattery's People* (CBS, 1964-65).

As a journeyman actor with little comedy experience, Asner seemed an odd choice for the role of the television newsroom boss Lou Grant in the situation comedy *The Mary Tyler Moore Show* (CBS, 1970-77; see entry). Lou Grant was a comic showcase, capable of blustery anger at one turn and endearing sentiment at another. Asner brought excellent timing and unusual range to a flawless ensemble cast guided by fine scripts and direction. The series settled in for seven years as a ratings hit that garnered 27 Emmy Awards, including three for Asner as supporting actor in a comedy (1971, 1972, 1975).

Asner used his growing stature as a comic actor to build his dramatic career. He appeared in several films and television movies, including leading roles in a Huey Long biography and a Christmas story, *The Gathering* (1977), about a dying father coming to terms with his estranged family. However, no other dramatic roles matched the impact of his supporting work in the decade's two top miniseries. As a bitter father in *Rich Man, Poor Man* (1976) and a slave ship captain in *Roots* (1977), Asner shook off his comic persona to reveal the darker and more compelling side of his talents. He also won two more Emmy Awards.

The Mary Tyler Moore Show left the air in 1977 while still popular. Asner then starred in his own series, *Lou Grant* (CBS, 1977-82; see entry). The actor's task was monumental: to transfer a comic character filmed with three cameras before a live audience to a one-camera drama striving for realism. As the city editor of a metropolitan newspaper, Lou Grant was no longer the humorous figure that reached for a bottle in his desk. He was the paper's conscience, a strong voice for press fairness and a humane perspective of social issues. Critics hailed *Lou Grant* as one of television's few intelligent and thoughtful series. Two Emmys as outstanding actor (1978, 1980) raised Asner's total to seven.

Off the screen, Asner was a longtime supporter of humanitarian and liberal causes, particularly labor. In 1980, he emerged as a spokesman for striking actors, winning the first of two terms as Screen Actors Guild president the following year. He strengthened its bargaining power and negotiated better contracts during his four-year tenure, but opponents contended he made SAG more militant and political.

Asner returned to series television but had trouble finding a vehicle that supported both his talents and an audience.

He played a garment-factory owner in the comedy *Off the Rack* (ABC, 1985) and a tough inner-city high school principal in the drama *The Bronx Zoo* (NBC, 1987-88). He earned supporting roles in the drama *The Trials of Rosie O'Neill* (CBS, 1990-91) and in the comedy *Hearts Afire* (CBS, 1992-93). He was back in a starring role in the sitcom *Thunder Alley* (ABC, 1994-95), playing a crusty grandfather and auto shop owner. His occasional work in feature films was highlighted by a role as a conspirator in *JFK* (1991).

Bibliography

Alley, Robert S. *Love Is All Around: The Making of the Mary Tyler Moore Show.* New York: Delta, 1989.

Daniel, Douglass K. *Lou Grant: The Making of TV's Top Newspaper Drama.* Foreword by Ed Asner. Syracuse: Syracuse UP, 1996.

Douglass K. Daniel

Astaire, Fred, and Ginger Rogers each had successful careers both before and after their partnership in a series of nine films for RKO Picture Corporation, but it was in their famous partnership that they truly captured the public's imagination. They were individuals, of course, and the stars of their films, but their myth, their cachet, their look, and their style—everything the public responded to—came as a package: Astaire and Rogers. The lasting attraction of that package was (and is) its complexity. It is an attraction based on oppositions. The supreme elegance of their physical persons combined with the average-Joe characters they often played; the corny, generally formulaic plots staged on the highly artificial, fantastical Big White Sets; the light romantic comedy played against the suave, eclectic dance routines—these components were combined by Astaire, Rogers, and the RKO studio staff into a highly profitable and enduring American myth.

Both Astaire and Rogers started out their careers as children. Astaire (1899-1987), born in Omaha, attended dancing school in New York with his sister Adele, and began touring with her on the vaudeville circuit at age seven. Fred and Adele dissolved their act in 1932 so she could marry Lord Charles Cavendish. Thereafter, Astaire continued with his stage career, until he agreed to a brief appearance in *Dancing Lady* (1933) with Joan Crawford and then began shooting *Flying Down to Rio* (1933). These films launched his motion picture career.

Rogers (1911-1995) had a happy but much less ideal childhood, being raised by her mother and grandparents after her parents' divorce. Ginger Rogers began her professional career at age five, appearing in a locally produced commercial in Kansas City. Her dramatic stage debut came in a high school play her mother wrote; her dancing debut came filling in for a dancer in Eddie Foy's vaudeville troupe during its stay in Fort Worth. Winning a Charleston contest at age 14 set her firmly on her course and from 1925 to 1928, she toured with a vaudeville trio act, then with her own solo song-and-dance act. She married her first husband, Jack Culpepper, in 1929 and toured with him briefly. While still working in vaudeville, she started her movie career in the short film *Campus Sweethearts* and then graduated to Broadway in late 1929 with a supporting role in *Top Speed.* Her

first role in a feature-length film came in *Young Man of Manhattan* (1930) at Paramount's New York studios.

After the pair's well-received appearance in *Flying Down to Rio* in 1933, the producer Pandro S. Berman decided to pair Astaire and Rogers in a film adaptation of *The Gay Divorcee*, which Astaire had been doing in London. The partnership was born, and soon became a cultural institution.

Reviews of the Astaire-Rogers films chronicle a rapid change in the critics' assessment of their work from "pleasant entertainment" to "American institution." Thus, in their first film, *Flying Down to Rio*, he is a "nimble-toed" and she a "charming" supporting player. By their third film two years later—*Roberta* (1935)—they've created a "bright and shimmering pleasure dome" whose opening the audience greeted with cheers. With *Top Hat* in the late summer of the same year, Astaire and Rogers are "the best of the current cinema teams," "providing the most urbane fun that you will find anywhere on the screen." By the release of their sixth film, *Swing Time,* Frank Nugent's review affirms their popularity by noting: "That was no riot outside the Music Hall yesterday; it was merely the populace storming the Rockefeller's cinema citadel." And fan disappointment at the dissolution of the Astaire/Rogers partnership following *The Story of Vernon and Irene Castle* (1939) can be gauged by the review greeting their return in *The Barkleys of Broadway* (1949), which opined: "Next to the patching of relations between Russia and the United States, there is probably no rapprochement that has been more universally desired than the bringing back together of Ginger Rogers and Fred Astaire."

Behind this cultural institution worked a fairly consistent team of art director, dance director, and costume designer at RKO. Together they created much of the visual style and panache that made the dance team so popular. Van Nest Polglase receives screen credit for art direction on all nine RKO films, and Carroll Clark worked as associate art director on eight of them. Together, they established the streamlined, geometric, largely white look, in everything from table lamps to stair banisters, the furniture to the famous shiny Bakelite floors, that came to embody a film starring Astaire and Rogers.

Most writers agree that the Astaire/Rogers partnership was a Pygmalion/Galatea one, where he took a modest dancer and molded her into the perfect partner for him—one with a grace and elegance of movement to match his, yet with comic timing and irreverence to leaven the mix. Astaire's dancing style—and thus, his choreography for their dances together—has been described as an "outlaw" or eclectic one. It fused elements from ballroom, tap, and even ballet into a personal style in service of twin goals: entertaining with the dances and supporting the story. He is known both for his insistence on originality of steps and routines from film to film, always trying to introduce something new, and his preference for single-shot takes to capture the dance as an artistic whole. His constant innovations and inventiveness seem to spring from the wealth of experience his years in vaudeville and the musical theater provided. Among these inventive contributions to screen dancing, says Arlene Croce, was the notion that screen choreography could consist of a man dancing alone in his living room, as in the "Needle in a Haystack" (*The Gay Divorcee*) and "No Strings" (*Top Hat*) numbers. The appeal of the Astaire/Rogers dances, and the films functioning as their vehicles, seems to lie in the juxtaposition of seriously played dances of seduction and courtship ("Let's Face the Music and Dance," "Cheek to Cheek") to specialty/comic dances ("Pick Yourself Up," "Let's Call the Whole Thing Off") which recast the varied pleasures of vaudeville in a unified form for a national audience.

Bibliography

Astaire, Fred. *Steps in Time*. 1959.

Croce, Arlene. *The Fred Astaire and Ginger Rogers Book*, New York: Vintage, 1972.

Delamater, Jerome. *Dance in the Hollywood Musical*. Ann Arbor: UMI Research, 1981.

Rogers, Ginger. *Ginger: My Story*. New York: Harper-Collins, 1991.

Joel Super

Atkins, (Chester) "Chet" (1924-), played a crucial role in shaping the sound and direction of country music from the early 1950s to the mid-1970s. The accommodation that he engineered between traditional country and pop styles—known as the Nashville sound—helped country music move from a rural, largely regional style to a nationwide product consumed by urban middle classes. That more sophisticated sound also contributed to the proliferation of all-country radio formats during the late 1950s and 1960s, and it helped make country music more acceptable to urban middle-class TV audiences in the late 1960s. Atkins guided the careers of many musicians who recorded for RCA Records in Nashville, whose records often crossed over from country to pop music hits.

Due in part to the vision and efforts of Atkins, the country music industry assumed a prominent place in mainstream American culture in the 1970s and 1980s, but his impact was not limited to the role of producer. The finger style approach to guitar which Atkins developed influenced several generations of guitarists in and outside the country field. And it was his musicianship, first of all, that gained Atkins opportunities in the record business.

Born on a farm in Luttrell, TN, into a long line of country fiddlers, Atkins rose from rural poverty to a powerful position in an industry that was shaping American taste, as detailed in his autobiography, *Country Gentleman*. His father's formal musical training gave Atkins the technical background to accompany the concentration on music and guitar performance he developed during childhood. That background and his personal drive for perfection helped Atkins move steadily up the career ladder, where he worked as a sideman for top touring artists and as a radio studio musician on the best-known country radio show in the nation during the late 1940s.

Because New York-based record producers were not constantly on the scene in Nashville in the early 1950s, they needed a reliable local contact to arrange and lead recording sessions as well as perform as a sideman. When Atkins moved to Nashville in 1950, he was well prepared to fill that influential role. He became repertory assistant for RCA Records in 1952 and started producing sessions himself. When he was named manager of RCA's newly constructed Nashville studio in 1955, his influence increased, especially after assisting new star Elvis Presley on the recording of "Heartbreak Hotel."

Atkins was responsible for a number of major country singers who developed into country pop stars. He also cultivated important songwriters, including Don Gibson ("I Can't Stop Loving You"). Atkins dates his 1958 sessions with Gibson ("Oh Lonesome Me") as the beginning of his efforts to consciously adapt country to the pop category, and the years from 1957 to 1962 are known as Nashville's golden age, when 17 country hits reached No. 1 on the pop charts.

Atkins added new sophistication to existing country finger-style guitar by playing bass and melody lines as well as chords with his right hand and incorporating jazz touches with a clean, fast technique. An early advocate of the electric guitar in the country field, since the 1960s he also performed classical guitar repertoire. Atkins has been honored for his broad knowledge and taste in a field where the folk elements once dominated. That knowledge enabled him to create the sophisticated arrangements and polished productions that made the Nashville sound appealing to an urban audience.

To create that sound, Atkins moved away from the honky-tonk and southwest dance-hall styles (represented by Hank Williams and Bob Wills, respectively) that dominated the post–World War II years. He was the first to use the techniques of popular music, including background string and horn sections, on country recordings to create a sweeter, more laid-back and intimate style that was still country-sounding enough to be played on rural jukeboxes.

Bibliography

Atkins, Chet, with Bill Neely. *Country Gentleman*. Chicago: Regnery, 1974.

Ivey, William. "Chet Atkins." *Stars of Country Music*. Ed. Bill C. Malone and Judith McCulloh. Urbana: U of Illinois P, 1975.

Malone, Bill C. *Country Music U.S.A.: A Fifty-Year History*. Austin: U of Texas P, 1985.

Lynn Darroch

Atlas, Charles (1893-1972), an early example of how bodybuilding leads to success and happiness and of how advertising can create an icon, began in a real incident. One summer day in 1909, a 15-year-old, skinny Italian immigrant boy took his girlfriend to the Coney Island beach. Suddenly, a big, muscular lifeguard kicked sand in his face. The youth felt helpless to react, and his girlfriend appeared somewhat disturbed and embarrassed. This youngster was Angelo Siciliano, who later would become Charles Atlas, one of the most famous bodybuilders of the last two centuries.

In countless comic book and magazine advertisements for Charles Atlas's exercise courses, this bully experience would be recounted with virtually the same theme. These multiframe comic book ads became one of the longest-run-

Charles Atlas. Photo courtesy of Popular Culture Library, Bowling Green State University, Bowling Green, OH.

ning, best-remembered, and most successful sales-producing ad campaigns in American marketing history.

This painful experience so strongly impressed the sensitive youth that he swore nothing like this would ever again happen to him. In essence, however, he got quite a different type of revenge—that of really "looking good" after he had vigorously worked out and changed his skinny 97-pound weakling image to one of mass and muscle.

Charles Atlas, as he became known, soon was making $100 per week as New York's most coveted male model. In 1921, Atlas got his first big break in bodybuilding, winning a major national contest. The rather faddish fitness enthusiast Bernarr MacFadden, through his fitness magazine, *Physical Culture,* held a bodybuilder contest to find the "World's Most Beautiful Man." Charles Atlas won not only in 1921 but also in 1922, when the title was "America's Most Perfectly Developed Man." Atlas went on to become a model and then opened a gym and offered an exercise course, featuring the "Dynamic-Tension" method of muscle development, with marketer Charles P. Roman. Atlas became an advertising and public relations figure, not only touting his "Dynamic-Tension" courses, but also physical fitness in general. In his familiar pose in bikini-type shorts, legs planted apart, standing on white-hot sand, Atlas asked the underde-

veloped male to give him five days to turn the youth into towering strength. In 1990, over 12,000 exercise courses were still being sold. It is likely that Charles Atlas had more of a profound effect in inspiring youth to physical fitness than anyone in history.

Bibliography

Bushyeager, Peter. "The World of Atlas," *Men's Health* Oct. 1991: 56-61.

"Charles Atlas, the Body-Builder and Weightlifter, Is Dead at 79." *New York Times* 24 Dec. 1972: 40, Sect. 4.

Gaines, Charles, George Butler, and Charles P. Roman. *Yours in Perfect Manhood, Charles Atlas.* New York: Fireside, 1982.

Gaustaitis, Joseph. "Charles Atlas: 'The World's Most Perfectly Developed Man.'" *American History Illustrated* Sept. 1986: 16-17.

Webster, David. *Bodybuilding: An Illustrated History.* New York: Arco, 1982.

Sammy R. Danna

See also
Bodybuilding

Audio-Cassette Tapes, or, more commonly, simply the cassette, one of sound recording's success stories, were introduced by the Philips Company in 1963. Although recording cartridges had been developed as early as the 1930s to make threading tape recorders less difficult, the need to keep their size small meant that little tape could fit in them and, thus, a tradeoff had to be made between length of recording time and audio quality. This problem was ultimately solved by incorporating a noise reduction system (most often a variation of the one created by Dolby Labs) in cassette decks to encode and decode tapes and effectively keep unwanted noise to a minimum. By the 1970s, the cassette's audio quality was good enough for cassette decks to be considered standard components of high-fidelity audio systems, and penetration of cassette decks into households, autos, offices, etc., rivaled that of the television. But the development of the compact disk began to erode the cassette's popularity in the 1990s.

Bibliography

Baert, Luc, et al. *Digital Audio and Compact Disc Technology.* Oxford, U.K.: Focal, 1995.

Banerjee, Sumanta. *Audio Cassettes: The User Medium.* Paris: Unesco, 1977.

Hickling, Mark. "Prerecorded Cassette Sales Boom." *Rolling Stone* 26 Nov. 1981.

Kirkeby, Mark. "The Decline of the LP." *Rolling Stone* 25 June 1981.

Miller, Debby. "Cassettes Outsell LPs in So-So Year." *Rolling Stone* 5 July 1984.

Steve Jones

Automobiles (passenger cars, trucks, buses) were central to popular culture throughout the 20th century as objects in themselves, as influences in the development of other aspects of American culture, and as subjects in the popular media. Although there was considerable interest in the early inventions of the last decades of the 19th century, automobiles became truly popular with endurance racing, especially the 1905 transcontinental race from New York to Portland, OR. The public was entranced with twin Oldsmobiles that completed the race in 44 days and were immortalized in the same year by the best-selling song "In My Merry Oldsmobile" by Gus Edwards (1879-1945). The "merry Oldsmobiles" were stock cars, which Ransom E. Olds (1864-1950) was selling for as low as $650. These horseless carriages can be called the first mass-produced cars, with 425 coming off the line in 1901. How much the song, which remained popular for at least two decades, had to do with the longevity of the Oldsmobile name is hard to say, but of the over 3,000 makes of cars and trucks in U.S. automotive history, this is the only one to be in continuous existence since the Gay Nineties (1896).

Another great race was in 1908 from Times Square to Paris via California, Siberia, and Europe. This served as a theme for the 1965 epic comedy-chase film *The Great Race*, with Tony Curtis's "Leslie Special" closely resembling the winning "Thomas Flyer." In several other respects 1908 was a milestone year: General Motors Corporation was formed, combining the Oldsmobile, Buick, and Oakland lines, while Henry Ford rolled out 800 of the first Model T. In 1908, there were more than 250 makes of automobiles produced in some two dozen states, but for the next three decades manufacturing centralized into the Midwest, especially the Detroit area. By 1929, about 80 percent of the production was controlled by Ford, General Motors, and the relative newcomer Chrysler Corporation (1925). Of the several thousand defunct makes, a few have retained a place in popular culture. Jack Benny's radio car (sound effects by Mel Blanc) gave rather unfair immortality to the Maxwell name, while the Stanley Steamer came to stand for technological absurdity (although a Stanley was the first car to exceed two miles per minute and had been in production from 1897 to 1924). Similarly, Ford's ill-fated Edsel (1957-59) lives on as a design and publicity fiasco. Other extinct cars never ridiculed are the prematurely streamlined DeSoto and Chrysler Airflo of 1934.

More commonly, the popularity persists for legendary great luxury models of the past, such as the Stutz Bearcat (1921), the front-wheel drive Cord (1930), and the richly customized Duesenbergs of the 1930s, whose elegance introduced a new aesthetic superlative into the popular tongue: "It's a *doozy!*" Other models are famous for their revolutionary influence on popular design, such as the 1946 Studebaker, that replaced the small rear window with all glass (and prompted radio comics to joke about not being able to tell which way it was going) and the 1948 Cadillac that introduced tailfins and led to what Stephen Sears called "Detroit's age of the baroque." In a class by itself is the Tucker Torpedo (1947) because of Francis Ford Coppola's 1988 film *Tucker: The Man and His Dream*, possibly the only movie devoted to the industry itself.

Without question the greatest popularity goes to the Ford Model T (15 million produced 1908-27), for the "tin lizzie" put car culture within reach of almost all America with low prices, minimal options, and virtually unchanged design. This was reflected in the song "You Can't Afford to Marry If You Can't Afford a Ford." A first car for millions of families (who usually "traded up," thus contributing to the decline of Model A "flivver" sales), the lizzies were affectionately demolished in countless silent comedies of Mack Sennett and Laurel and Hardy. Possibly the only rivals to the T are the Jeep (1941-) and the Beetle (1937-). The Jeep (from GP, short for General Purpose vehicle, combined with Jeep, an extraordinary creature from the *Popeye* comic strip) was so popular with GIs that its manufacturer, Willys (now Daimler-Chrysler), continued it as a civilian model, and despite gentrification beginning with the Jeepster, Jeeps retain the boxy styling and four-wheel drive-tough image. The Volkswagen Beetle was conceived by Adolf Hitler on the model of Henry Ford's mass-produced cheap and simple "people's car." Jeeps are ubiquitous in war films; but in Sydney Pollack's 1969 *Castle Keep*, American soldiers encounter an indestructible Nazi Beetle. They may have been German cars, but they quickly became part of U.S. popular culture, the theme of a Volkswagen with a mind of its own being carried further also in 1969 in Disney's *The Love Bug*, followed by three more films starring Herbie the VW in the next decade. Jokes about the rear engine ("I've got a spare motor in the trunk") and student contests to see how many people could be stuffed into a VW were but two aspects of Beetle folklore. In 1999, Volkswagen introduced a new model.

Fortunately, historic cars are preserved in many private and public collections found in most states. The largest is Harrah's Automobile Collection in Reno, also a major auction site for antique car collectors. The Henry Ford Museum in Dearborn, MI, is one of the best and most comprehensive collections, while there are many specialized museums, like the Auto Racing Hall of Fame in Speedway, IN, and Chevyland U.S.A. in Elm Creek, NE. The Chicago Historical Antique Automobile Museum has a Cars of the Stars exhibit including the Batmobile, Green Hornet, Bonnie and Clyde Death Car, and Elvis Presley's 24 Karat Gold Continental. Movie World in Buena Park, CA, has the Leslie Special, Fatty Arbuckle's custom-built Pierce-Arrow Phaeton, and a 1949 Daimler convertible built for Queen Elizabeth.

Outside of museums, there are many antique car buffs who participate in parades, rallies, and meets. Separate from the restoration and preservation groups are the rod and custom enthusiasts who personalize cars from the chassis, bodies, and parts of cars of various types and vintage, celebrated in the Beach Boys' "My Little Deuce Coupe." Less drastic are those who add to their stock models popular accessories and ornaments such as wheel covers, spotlights, special paint jobs, fur dice, bumper stickers, and vanity license plates. Such a host of automotive social groups demands a network of suppliers of materials and information. Among these are the J. C. Whitney mail-order catalog and such national auto parts chains as NAPA and Crown. Interstate truck plazas are major retailers of automotive pop paraphernalia. Periodicals serving automotive popular culture include *Car and Driver, Road and Track, Rod and Custom,* and *Auto Weekly,* with many specialized newsletters for antiques, memorabilia, and car clubs. In the 1990s, National Public Radio's weekly series "Car Talk" presented Boston auto-mechanics Tom and Ray Magliozzi (the "Tappet brothers") trading quips and auto folklore while dispensing practical advice to distraught owners of lemons and geriatric cars. Cars figure in many urban legends such as "The Death Car," "The Cheap Jeep," and "Hook Man."

Automobiles are so pervasive in popular entertainment that it is difficult to select a few examples of films and music. Sears states that there were over 120 pieces of "motoring music" from 1905 to 1907 alone, and E. L. Widmer in *Roadside America* lists many automotive blues from the mid-1920s on, such as "Sports Model Mama" and "Terraplane Blues," and one of the earliest modern rock tunes celebrating the flashy new Olds in the 1951 "Rocket 88." Two classic films that explore the interactions of cars and culture are *The Grapes of Wrath* (1940) and *Rebel without a Cause* (1955). Car chases figure in both film and music. Police cars were essential losers from the Keystone Kops on, but some unusual vehicles include semi-trailer trucks in *Smokey and the Bandit* (1977) and sequels, a full-ladder fire rig in *A View to a Kill* (1985)—only one of the thrilling James Bond travelogue chases—and a bus in *Speed* (1994). A few songs in the chase mode are the Playmates' "Beep Beep" (where a Nash Rambler beats a Cadillac), the Beach Boys' "She's Real Fine My 409," Jan and Dean's "Dead Man's Curve," Chuck Berry's "Maybellene," and Bruce Springsteen's "Racing in the Streets."

The effects of automobiles on many other aspects of American popular culture have been far reaching. Leisure activities such as "going out for a spin" with the family on a Sunday afternoon contributed to the development of state and national highway systems. With longer distance travel on highways, roadside accommodations developed, with names and amenities advancing from tourist camps to tourist courts, from motor hotels to motels, both mom-and-pop and mass-market chains like Motel 6 and the more elegant Holiday Inns. Frank Capra's 1934 *It Happened One Night* preserves the Depression tourist camp (along with early interurban bus transportation). By the 1980s, luxury high-rise hotels at cloverleaf intersections of major highways joined the motel network. Automobile camping appeared as an outdoor sport very early; the 1910 Abercrombie & Fitch mail order catalog offered complete outfits. From such rugged outfitting there has been a continuous growth in camping vehicles and services. By 1936, the National Automobile Show displayed house trailers along with new car models. The Airstream was proudly touted by owners as "the Cadillac of trailers." Non-trailer rolling homes began modestly with homemade conversions of buses and panel trucks pre–World War II; in the postwar years these grew into luxurious RVs (recreational vehicles) led by the Winnebago line. Sociologically, these came to represent a subculture of nomadic retirees, many of whom sold their homes to travel throughout North America, often pulling compact-size cars behind, with motorcycles strapped in front and a boat on top. The camping and nomadic lives spurred the development of national and state parks, as well as commercial chains like KOA (Kampgrounds of America) that emphasized hook-ups to electricity, water, and sewers rather than the natural settings of parks.

The automobile also changed courtship patterns in many ways, not only making it easy to escape the watchful eyes of parents and neighbors but, within closed cars, providing a convenient if not very comfortable room for heavy petting and intercourse. During and after Prohibition, roadhouses located beyond restrictive city and county jurisdictions were accessible only by automobile, variously providing illegal hooch, beer, gambling, and sex. Drive-ins first appeared in the early 1930s, notable among the early ones, the A&W Rootbeer stands in bright orange and black with curbside service by carhops. In addition to such drive-in restaurants (which, along with the urban White Castles contributed to later fast-food chains with inside, outside, and in-transit eating), *Roadside America* examines these and other types of popular architecture that developed from auto culture such as service stations, garages, movie theaters, car dealerships, commercial strips, and highway signage.

Writers often refer to Americans' "love affair" with the automobile. The figure is apt in several ways. In *Roadside America*, E. L. Widmer shows how song lyrics about cars are often sexual ("I've Got Ford Engine Movements in My Hips," "I'm Your Vehicle, Baby"). In the same book, James E. Paster analyzes snapshots for the expressed relationships between people and their cars. The affection for Tin Lizzies was expressed in joke books as early as 1915, and Sears lists some of the quips painted on "flivvers" such as "Capacity 5 Gals," "Chicken, Here's Your Roost," "Girls Wanted: Apply at Side Door," and "The Tin You Love to Touch." In the late 1960s, Volkswagen commissioned outstanding cartoonists and humorists such as Charles Addams, Virgil Partch, H. Allen Smith, and Jean Sheperd to *Think Small* in a book distributed to loving Beetle owners. At the other end of the scale, the affection for American power and individualism was chronicled by Tom Wolfe in *The Kandy-Kolored Tangerine-Flake Streamline Baby* about California rod-and-custom youth and "The Last American Hero" about the southeastern stock-car good ol' boys.

As auto advertisements throughout the century indicate, Americans did not look on their cars as transportation but as status symbols, as objects of pride, as keys to personal freedom, as expressions of identity, or simply as close members of the family. An advertising jingle captured the essence well: "Baseball, Hot Dogs, Apple Pie, and Chevrolet."

Bibliography

Flink, James J. *The Car Culture*. Cambridge: MIT P, 1975.

Motor Vehicle Manufacturers Association of the United States, Inc. *Automobiles of America*. 4th ed. Detroit: Wayne State UP, 1974.

Roadside America: The Automobile in Design and Culture. Ed. Jan Jennings. Ames: Iowa State UP, 1990.

Sears, Stephen W. *The American Heritage History of the Automobile in America*. New York: American Heritage, 1977.

Fred E. H. Schroeder

Axis Radio Personalities were one of Nazi Germany's many efforts to control the culture of an enemy nation. These foreign nationals were hired to broadcast propaganda to their respective countries. This practice enabled a number of Americans to serve as broadcasters for German radio. A few others worked in a similar capacity for Italy and Japan.

Known as "Axis Sally," Mildred Gillars was born in Maine in 1900. Her wartime broadcasts to Allied soldiers on German radio attempted to intensify their feelings of loneliness, fatigue, and the futility of continued fighting. Their morale seemingly unaffected, they liked the current American music she featured.

William Joyce—known to his listeners as "Lord Haw Haw"—was born in Brooklyn, NY, in 1906, the son of an immigrant Irish father and an English mother. He was educated in Ireland and ended up in England. As a wartime broadcaster for German radio, he attacked the British government, tried to frighten the British citizenry, and urged British soldiers to desert their country.

Douglas Chandler, known on German radio as "Paul Revere," was born in Chicago on May 26, 1889. By training a journalist, Chandler began broadcasting for German radio in late April 1941. He attacked what he perceived to be a government in Washington that was orchestrated by Jewish advisers. He attempted to alienate the American general public from the Roosevelt administration by habitually promoting American isolationism and defeatism while alluding to racism and class bias.

Other Americans who worked as broadcasters for the Axis powers include Jane Anderson, Max Otto Koischwitz, Robert Best, Donald Day, Ezra Pound, and Iva Toguri D'Aquino.

A Georgian, Jane Anderson was born in 1893. She was a correspondent for the London *Daily Mail* both during World War I and the Spanish Civil War. Captured by government forces in the latter, she languished in captivity until October 1936. As a broadcaster for German radio, her *Georgia Peach* program first aired in April 1941. Interviews were her forte, but some of her broadcasts sought to comment on the eco-nomic well-being of Germany despite its wartime commitments.

Max Otto Koischwitz, born in Silesia in 1902, immigrated to the United States in 1924. Returning to Germany in 1939, he began broadcasting for German radio in early 1940, first as "Mr. O.K." and then as host of his own *College Hour* program. He attempted to drive a wedge between U.S.-British friendship and spoke convincingly of the invincibility of the Axis.

Robert Best was born in 1896 and called Pacolet, SC, his hometown. From his first broadcast on German radio on April 10, 1942, when he coyly identified himself as "Mr. Guess Who," to those that followed on what eventually became *Best's Berlin Broadcasts,* his primary targets were President Roosevelt, the Jews, and the Soviet Union.

Donald Day, a long-time correspondent for the Chicago *Tribune*, was known as the last recruit for the U.S.A. Zone of the Reichsrundfunk. Born in Brooklyn, NY, in 1895, Day eventually became a European correspondent for the *Tribune*. Gradually falling under the Nazi influence, Best began his career for German radio on September 1944. He lashed out at Roosevelt and bolshevism.

Ezra Pound, the American poet, was charged with, but never tried for, treason as a result of making anti-American broadcasts from Rome during World War II. He died in 1972.

Iva Toguri D'Aquino, a Japanese-American commonly held to be "Tokyo Rose" after the war, broadcast a program of recorded music to American troops in the South Pacific. She identified herself as "Orphan Ann" on the air. Apparently, "Tokyo Rose" was the composite name given to numerous women who broadcast for Japan during the war.

Bibliography

Cole, L. A. *Lord Haw-Haw and William Joyce: The Full Story.* New York: Farrar, 1964.

Edwards, John C. *Berlin Calling: Americans Broadcasting in Service to the Third Reich.* New York: Praeger, 1991.

Selwyn, Francis. *Hitler's Englishman: The Crime of Lord Haw Haw.* London: Penguin, 1993.

West, Rebecca. *The New Meaning of Treason.* New York: Viking, 1964.

Zeman, Z. A. B. *Nazi Propaganda.* London: Oxford UP, 1964.

Philip J. Harwood

B

B Movie, The. The institutional origins of the B movie lie in the Depression. Declining box-office receipts led Hollywood to inaugurate the practice of double features in 1935 as a means of enticing the public to return to movie theaters. Between 1930 and 1933 weekly attendance dropped from 110 million to 60 million, and many executives felt that offering two films for the price of one might turn the tide. The RKO and Loew's chains, the latter owned by MGM interests, began the practice in 1935. A year later, 85 percent of the nation's theaters had followed suit. For the next dozen years, the B movie flourished until the government, as part of the 1947 "Paramount Decision," forced the major studios to divest themselves of theater ownership so as to end the vertical integration of the means of both production and distribution. Those studios that owned theaters prior to governmental divestment profited directly from the rental of Bs, for the exhibitors fees returned to the company coffers. Many of the smaller firms, however, operated by means of a "states rights" system, through which films were rented out to individual theaters on a regional basis with the ticket sales split between the exhibitor, distributor, and production company. Such a system dominated in the South, where B films often were not, as in other portions of the country, subordinated to a major studio feature but constituted the whole bill. Nonetheless, whatever region one examines, a voracious public was willing to consume any form of visual entertainment, and Hollywood fed their desires until television provided an alternate and eventually dominant form of stimulation.

Each of the major studios included a B movie division, while the second tier companies specialized in the field. At the majors the B unit traditionally was headed by a single executive, including Bryan Foy (Warner Brothers), Sol C. Siegal (Paramount), and Sol Wurtzel (20th Century-Fox), who inspired the pun "from bad to Wurtzel." In other cases, a producer or set of producers associated solely with Bs affiliated with a major studio and a particular genre: William H. Pine and William B. Thomas (known to Hollywood for their frugality as the "two dollar Bills") assembled action features, often starring Richard Arlen, for Paramount, while Val Lewton assembled a series of high-class horror features for RKO—two of the most successful being *Cat People* (1942) and *I Walked with a Zombie* (1943)—that some consider among the best Bs of all time. Producing B movies permitted the major studios simultaneously to fulfill a number of goals. They provided a training ground for young untested performers; allowed inexperienced directors the chance to hone their craft; absorbed fiscal overhead by reaping maximal profits from minimal investments; permitted executives the opportuniity to chastise recalcitrant stars by forcing them to appear in work they considered beneath them; and offered aging actors a chance to keep themselves before the public eye.

While B storylines often were drawn from preexistent materials—either remakes of earlier films or adaptations of well-known narratives in the public domain—many more constituted entries in periodic series that featured recurring characters, a number of whom figured in popular fiction, comic strips, or radio programs. Some series, *Charlie Chan* and *Tarzan* come to mind, passed from studio to studio, in the former case from 20th Century-Fox to Monogram and in the latter from MGM to RKO. Others remained affiliated with a single organization: Columbia carried *Boston Blackie*, *Blondie,* and *Jungle Jim*; MGM *Dr. Kildare, Maisie,* and *Andy Hardy*; 20th Century-Fox *Mr. Moto, Mike Shayne,* and the *Cisco Kid*; and RKO *The Mexican Spitfire*, *The Falcon*, and *Dick Tracy*. Predecessors in narrative form to contemporary episodic television, the series film delivered a balance of repetition leavened with variation. Some series ran for as long as two decades, while others constitute just a handful of episodes. So well-oiled were the formats that when a principal actor died, as in the case of Warner Oland, who first played Charlie Chan, he was easily replaced without upsetting the audience's consciousness or the films' continuity.

The budgets for Bs varied more broadly than the designation "Poverty Row" implies, as did the profits accrued from them. Some cost as little as $20,000, the amount expended on Edgar G. Ulmer's classic film noir *Detour* (1945), while others might require nearly half a million dollars. Monogram, one of the principal B studios, released over 400 films during the 1940s and averaged nearly $2,000 profit on each of them. Annual gross rentals for the company over that period amounted to nearly $10 million and as little as $2 million, while net profits ran the gamut from slightly over $1 million to as little as $11,000. The largest, most stable, and consistently successful of the B studios, Republic, operated on the basis of four budgetary categories: the "Jubilee" film, typically a Western shot on a seven-day schedule for around $50,000; the "Anniversary" film, shot over 14-16 days for $175,000 to $250,000; the "Deluxe" film, often helmed by the company's top contract director, Joseph Kane, who was given a 22-day schedule at a cost of around $500,000; and the top-of-the-line "Premiere" release, Republic's attempt to compete in quality and talent with the major studios, which could cost over a million dollars. This last category included work the studio commissioned from the likes of John Ford, Fritz Land, and Orson Welles. However, the "Jubilee" and "Anniversary" formats kept the company afloat, bringing in an average of $500,000 in profit for each category.

The auteur theory profitably enables one to separate the wheat from the chaff amongst B movies and their creators. Directors in the field, aside from the plethora of hacks, can be categorized in any number of ways. Many were silent film veterans on their way down, their sound work a pale reflection of earlier triumphs; they include Monta Bell, Herbert Brennan, James Cruze, William K. Howard, Malcolm St. Clair, and, most telling of all, the expatriate German expressionist E. A. Dupont, who went from producing the groundbreaking *Variety* (1925) to the execrable *The Neanderthal Man* (1953). Some began in the B field only to rise amongst the ranks to A material, even if their earlier films pale before their later efforts, as is arguably the case with Edward Dmytryk, Richard Fleisher, Mark Robson, John Sturges (see entry), and Robert Wise. Some produced creditable work in both the A and B categories: Anthony Mann, Don Siegel, Robert Siodmak (see entry), Douglas Sirk, and Jacques Tourneur to name a few. Some few truly managed to break the stigma of the B label attached to them but are amongst the shining lights of the form: Robert Florey, Sam Fuller, Phil Karlson, Joseph H. Lewis, Gerd Oswald, and Edgar G. Ulmer. Finally, others began in the days before sound and achieved if not celebrity at least longevity, amongst them Christy Cabane, Elmer Clifton, and William Beaudine. One of the most prolific directors in film history, Beaudine apparently accepted any offer of work and therefore can be credited during his more than 50-year and several-hundred-film career with such heights as the Mary Pickford features *Little Annie Rooney* (1925) and *Sparrows* (1926) and lows as *Bela Lugosi Meets a Brooklyn Gorilla* and his final feature, *Billy the Kid vs. Dracula* (1966).

The demise of the studio system in the 1950s and increasing competition from television brought about the end of a number of B firms, but others rose in their wake. American-International Pictures, the most successful of them, discerned a bankable marketplace in the burgeoning teenage audience and the institution of the drive-in. Presently, the B movie exists (although the term is no longer applicable) as a phenomenon of the video store in the guise of the direct-to-video motion picture released by such studios as Full Moon, Concorde, and others. They illustrate that as long as an audience exists and a bottom line can be met, the B movie will survive.

Bibliography

Cross, Robin. *The Big Book of B Movies, Or, How Low Was My Budget.* New York: St. Martin's, 1981.

McClelland, Doug. *The Golden Age of "B" Movies.* New York: Bonanza, 1981.

Miller, Don. *"B" Movies: An Informal Survey of the American Low-Budget Film, 1933-1945.* New York: Curtis, 1973.

David Sanjek

Back to the Future (1985) was the highest grossing film of 1985 and the eighth most popular film of the 1980s (earning over $350 million by the end of the decade). With its two sequels, the *Back to the Future* trilogy joined a spate of 1980s time-travel films.

The three Universal films were directed by Robert Zemeckis (*Romancing the Stone, Who Framed Roger Rabbit?*) and produced by Bob Gale and Neil Canton from the Zemeckis and Gale screenplays, with special effects by Industrial Light & Magic. Steven Spielberg's credit as executive producer primarily served box-office purposes. The first film, set in fictional (and paradoxical) Hill Valley, 1985,

introduces the McFly family: burnt-out mother Lorraine (Lea Thompson), geeky father George (Crispin Glover), two worthless siblings, and 17-year-old Marty (played by 24-year-old Michael J. Fox of TV's *Family Ties* after the producers' dissatisfaction with Eric Stoltz five weeks and $4 million into the filming). Marty assists crackpot inventor Dr. ("Doc") Emmett Brown (Christopher Lloyd from TV's *Taxi*), who experiments with time-travel in a DeLorean car powered by stolen plutonium. He ends up traveling back to 1955, when he interrupts his parents' first meeting. Thus, he must unite his future parents or jeopardize his own existence.

The film proved the best of the trilogy because of its gentle nostalgia and irony: the town's 1985 porno-theater ran in 1955 a Ronald Reagan movie, *Cattle Queen of Montana* (1954); the dealership selling Toyotas in 1985 sold Studebakers in 1955; the aerobics center was once the small-town drugstore. Despite the cartoonishness and a trivialization of the Oedipal dilemma, many critics praised Fox's timing and the film's sweet nature. Self-serving and typically Spielbergian product placement, however, was universally denounced.

Containing too much sequel material for a single film, *Back to the Future Part II* (1989) and *Part III* (1990) were shot at the same time but released six months apart. In *Part II*, Marty and his girlfriend travel with Doc to 2015 where, among levitating skateboards, *Jaws XIX*, hydrating pizzas, and 1980s nostalgia, Marty must save his future son from Griff Tannen, descendent of his father's old rival Biff. In the process, Doc helps Marty return to 1955, where, though successful, Marty is left stranded when Doc is transported to the Old West of 1885. The trailer for the next film, included before the credits, was booed by audiences, but the film still earned over $300 million. In the last part, Marty retrieves the DeLorean to save Doc from being shot in 1885.

The *Back to the Future* trilogy is among a group of self-reflexive, metahistorical 1980s films like *The Terminator, Somewhere in Time, Star Trek IV,* and *Peggy Sue Got Married,* in which reshaping the past alters subsequent history and time-travel provides solutions to future problems.

Bibliography

Bell-Metereau, Rebecca. "Back to the Future II." *Magill's Cinema Annual 1990*: 36-39.

Lucas, Blake. "Back to the Future." *Magill's Cinema Annual 1986*: 65-74.

Palmer, William J. *The Films of the Eighties: A Social History.* Carbondale: Southern Illinois UP, 1993.

Pulleine, Tim. "Back to the Future." *The Film Year Book 1987*. Ed. Al Clark. New York: St. Martin's, 1987. 102-3.

Michael Delahoyde

Backwording. The advent of sound recording created unprecedented opportunities for the manipulation of sound. One such manipulation quickly seized by avant-garde composers was the "reversal" of sound by means of playing a record or tape backwards. That technique, applied to vocal recording, results in backwording, or backward masking, a process by which the words that are recorded backwards can sound like other words when they are played forwards.

Though painstaking if properly done, more often than not simply recording a sentence backwards results in what is perceived to be a coherent set of words when played forward. Backwording was used most prominently by the Beatles and other rock groups, though examples of it can be found in a variety of audio media including prominent use in segments of David Lynch's *Twin Peaks* TV series (see entry) and in the allegation that one can hear satanic messages when playing the theme from the TV series *Mr. Ed* backwards.

Bibliography

Aranza, Jacob. *More Rock, Country, and Backward Masking Unmasked.* Shreveport: Huntington, 1985.

Lawhead, Steve. *Rock of This Age: The Real and Imagined Dangers of Rock Music.* Donner's Grove: Inter Varsity, 1987.

Steve Jones

Baez, Joan (1941-), is often called the queen of contemporary folk music, the female counterpart to the king, Bob Dylan. She has had a successful recording career and appeared at numerous folk festivals, political rallies, and benefits in the 1960s, 1970s, and 1980s.

Baez is a native of New York City's Staten Island, the daughter of a Mexican-born father and a Scottish-Irish mother. She faced discrimination there and later, when her parents moved to the small New York town of Clarence Center, because of her dark skin. She became interested in politics while attending Boston University.

Baez made her public debut as a folk singer at the 1959 Newport Folk Festival, performing a repertoire of primarily traditional folk songs. Vanguard Records signed her to a recording contract in 1960, and released her first album, *Joan Baez*, that year. In 1961, her career took off as *Joan Baez, Vol. 2* reached No. 13 on the charts.

The live recording *Joan Baez in Concert* was released in 1962 and climbed to No. 10 on the charts. Baez's early albums were characterized by her clear voice and simple accompaniment (often just her own acoustic guitar playing). Many of the songs were traditional folk ballads like "Matty Groves," "Barbara Allen," and "Kumbaya," although she also recorded more contemporary folk songs like Malvina Reynolds's "What Have They Done to the Rain."

Baez was the headline act for the first Monterey Folk Festival in May 1963, sharing the top bill with Bob Dylan. The performance was the beginning of a close personal and professional relationship between Baez and Dylan for the next two years. Baez helped popularize Dylan's music by recording many of his songs in the mid-1960s. Baez also introduced Dylan at the 1963 Newport Folk Festival, the first one held since her appearance there in 1959.

Baez's first single was the civil rights protest song "We Shall Overcome." The recording was made at a concert in Birmingham, AL. It became the anthem of the civil rights movement in the 1960s, despite only modest commercial success (it peaked at No. 90 in November 1963). Two more concert recordings were released as albums in December 1963, *The Best of Joan Baez* (from the 1959 Newport concert) and *Joan Baez in Concert, Part 2*.

In 1964, the album *Joan Baez 5* was released, reaching No. 12 on the U.S. charts in early 1965. Her recordings of Dylan songs like "It's All Over Now Baby Blue" and "Farewell Angelina" helped buoy the success of her albums. Baez devoted an increasing part of her time to political activities, and in 1965 she founded the Institute for the Study of Non-Violence in Carmel, CA. But Dylan and Baez grew apart as he shied away from politics and shifted his songwriting focus to personal issues.

Baez married antiwar protest leader David Harris in 1968. She also recorded an LP of the songs of Bob Dylan, *Any Day Now*, which reached No. 30 on the U.S. charts. The single "Love Is Just a Four Letter Word" was a moderate success. When Harris was jailed for draft evasion in 1969, Baez increased the intensity of protest sentiments in her music, recording *David's Album* (dedicated to Harris) and *One Day at a Time*. Baez also gave birth to a child, Gabriel.

As the 1970s began, Baez used more rock instrumentation and backup vocalists, and her voice was deeper and stronger than in her earlier folk recordings. The biggest hit of her career was a cover version of Robbie Robertson's "The Night They Drove Old Dixie Down," a million-seller that reached the No. 3 position. The song was included on the 1971 album *Blessed Are*, which also included a cover version of the Beatles' "Let It Be."

Baez left Vanguard Records in 1972 and released her first album on A&M Records, *Come from the Shadows*. The only single from the LP was her sister Mimi Farina's tribute to Janis Joplin, "In the Quiet Morning." Baez continued her antiwar activism despite the U.S. pullout from Vietnam, devoting one side of the 1973 album *Where Are You Now, My Son* to a documentary account of a bombing raid on Hanoi. She also became involved in South American politics, joining those opposed to the overthrow of Chilean president Allende.

Baez released two albums in 1975, *Blue Sky* and *Diamonds and Rust*. The title track from the latter album was an autobiographical account of her relationship with Bob Dylan. She toured with Dylan's Rolling Thunder Revue in October 1975. Baez recorded two more albums for A&M Records, the live LP *From Every Stage* and *Gulf Winds*, both released in 1976.

Baez left A&M Records in 1977, signing with Portrait Records. *Blowin' Away* reached No. 54 on the U.S. charts in 1977, and A&M Records released a compilation of recordings from her albums on that label in 1978. That same year, she appeared with Bob Dylan in his autobiographical film, *Renaldo and Clara*. While her recording career was waning, Baez continued her involvement in social causes in the 1980s. She toured South America in the summer of 1981 on behalf of human rights issues. In June 1982, she performed before one million people at a peace rally in Central Park. In 1987, Baez published her autobiography, *And a Voice to Sing With*.

Bibliography

Baez, Joan. *And a Voice to Sing With: A Memoir.* New York: Summit, 1987.

Swanekamp, Joan. *Diamonds and Rust: A Bibliography and Discography on Joan Baez.* Ann Arbor: Pierian, 1980.

Ken Nagelberg

Baker, (Chesney Henry) "Chet" (1929-1988), leading trumpet player, was born in Yale, OK, and moved at age 11 to Glendale, CA, where he studied music in high school, playing mostly by ear and trying to emulate the trumpet sound of Harry James. Further musical training occurred during Baker's tours of duty in the army (1946-48, 1950-51), when he played in various military big bands and began listening to the current crop of bebop trumpeters like Dizzy Gillespie, Miles Davis, and Red Rodney. After his service in the armed forces, which ended when he went AWOL and got a psychiatric discharge, Baker settled in Southern California, began playing gigs in the Los Angeles area, and caught the attention of the visiting Charlie "Bird" Parker. As heard on some recordings that he cut with Parker at about this time, Baker was an energetic but somewhat clumsy improviser with a sound reminiscent of Miles Davis.

Baker joined with Gerry Mulligan to form the first incarnation of the Gerry Mulligan Quartet (1952-53), often credited as the first small group without a piano or other chording instrument to make a name for itself in jazz. While playing in this group, Baker won popularity with "My Funny Valentine," which became his "trademark." Later, Baker formed his own quartet with Russ Freeman on piano. The Baker-Freeman Quartet specialized in hard-swinging performances with the crackling precision and vital energy displayed, for example, on their lightning-fast version of "Love Nest."

The quartet with Russ Freeman built a solid body of vibrant jazz recordings and captured an expanded national audience when Baker began to sing and to record vocal albums. Following his first success with haunting vocal renditions of songs like "I Fall in Love Too Easily" and "Look for the Silver Lining," Baker turned increasingly to work that featured his melancholy singing.

Baker passed briefly through New York in 1958-59 and recorded some music that received scathing reviews from jazz critics alienated by his *enfant terrible* image. Continuing his odyssey, Baker ended up in Italy (1959-61), where he found that even the relatively lenient Italian law enforcers would not stand for such shenanigans as succumbing to his drug habit and camping out in a gas-station lavatory. From the early 1960s on, Baker dodged the law by moving from Italy to Germany to Switzerland to Paris to England to Spain and back again. Deported from Germany in 1963, he briefly passed through Boston, playing masterfully but looking deeply damaged. After returning to California and doing a series of execrable pop-oriented albums featuring Top 40 songs with a woeful group called the Mariachi Brass, Baker reached his nadir in 1968 when some thugs whom he had antagonized in San Francisco beat him up and knocked out most of his teeth—a blow from which most trumpet players would never have recovered.

But armed with his survival instincts and what appears to have been an indomitable spirit, phoenix-like, Baker did reascend from the ashes of his career. In New York over the next few years, he made some top-notch recordings in the company of such jazz masters as Paul Desmond on alto saxophone (*She Was Too Good to Me*; *You Can't Go Home Again*) and Jim Hall on guitar (*Concierto*; *Studio Trieste*). Returning to Europe in 1975, Baker began a series of recordings that eventually resurrected his reputation as a jazz improviser of high repute. Particularly fruitful were his albums for the Danish Steeple Chase label, many of which featured the brilliant bassist Niels-Henning Orsted Pederson (*The Touch of Your Lips*; *No Problem*; *Daybreak*; *This Is Always*; *Someday My Prince Will Come*; *Diane*; *When Sunny Gets Blue*). Homeless, ceaselessly traveling, and always quixotic, Baker toured everywhere on the Continent and recorded some of his most beautiful work during his later years in England, France, Germany, Brussels, Holland, Norway, Sweden, and Italy. European jazz fans idolized Baker, but the noted fashion photographer Bruce Weber featured Baker as a sort of aging *bête noire* in a thoroughly depressing documentary (*Let's Get Lost*), wherein he emerges as a tragic figure with little self-understanding who has disappointed even his own mother.

Bibliography

Carr, Roy, Brian Case, and Fred Dellar. *The Hip: Hipsters, Jazz, and the Beat Generation.* London: Faber, 1986.

Gioia, Ted. *West Coast Jazz: Modern Jazz in California, 1945-1960.* New York: Oxford UP, 1992.

Gordon, Robert E. *Jazz West Coast: The Los Angeles Jazz Scene of the 1950s.* London: Quartet, 1986.

Lerfeldt, Hans Henrik, and Thorbjorn Sjogren. *Chet: The Discography of Chesney Henry Baker.* Copenhagen: Tiderne Skifter, 1985.

Wulff, Ingo. *Chet Baker in Europe.* Kiel: Nieswand Verlag, 1993.

Morris B. Holbrook

Bakker, (James Orsen) "Jim" (1940-), televangelist, founded the PTL broadcasting network (initially "Praise the Lord" later "People That Love"). Bakker was born in Michigan, the son of a factory worker. In his youth Bakker had a crisis experience in which he ran over a child while driving his father's car. The child recovered completely but the shock led Bakker to commit his life to God and fully embrace his parents' Assemblies of God (AG) religion. After graduating from high school in 1959, he attended the AG North Central Bible College (NCBC).

In 1961, Bakker and fellow Bible College student Tammy Faye La Valley decided to marry. Consequently he and Tammy were expelled from NCBC. They spent the next five years as itinerant evangelists specializing in puppet shows for children. In 1964 Jim was ordained by the AG, and the following year the couple signed up with Christian Broadcasting Network (CBN) to do a children's radio/TV show called *The Jim and Tammy Show*. In 1973, after leaving CBN, Jim became co-founder of the Trinity Broadcasting Network. In 1974 he started the *PTL Club*, a daily talk and variety show in North Carolina, which he co-hosted with Tammy. This developed into the PTL television network.

The PTL network became highly successful, and by 1987 Jim and Tammy had established a $172 million religious enterprise that included Heritage USA, a theme park in North Carolina. Bakker preached prosperity, maintaining that God would bless believers materially as well as spiritually. Nevertheless, PTL had a history of financial crises and mismanagement and was parodied by a Charlottesville radio station as the "Pass the Loot Club."

In 1987, Tammy was admitted into a Carolina clinic suffering from dependency on a prescription tranquilizer. Then, amid rumors that televangelist Jimmy Swaggart was plotting to take over the PTL, Bakker resigned as chairman and as an AG minister and asked Baptist fundamentalist preacher Jerry Falwell to rescue the ministry.

Meanwhile, scandals in the PTL hit the headlines. Bakker admitted to having a sexual encounter with church secretary Jessica Hahn and paying her $265,000 in hush money. Falwell's auditors revealed that Bakker's salary and bonuses for 1986-87 totaled $1.6 million and that the PTL had amassed $70 million in debt. Falwell further claimed to have heard taped testimony that Bakker had made homosexual advances. Bakker denied accusations of homosexuality, noting that one case involved an alleged "homosexual look," and demanded Falwell return his ministry. Falwell refused. The conflict, described by the press as a "holy war," widened the historical schism between fundamentalists, now represented by Falwell, and Pentecostals such as Bakker.

In 1988, Bakker was charged with 24 counts of fraud and conspiracy. In the following year he was convicted of bilking his followers out of $158 million, allegedly lavished on expensive homes, cars, jewelry, and an air-conditioned dog house. He was sentenced to 45 years in prison. Bakker's sentence was later reduced twice, first to 18 years and then to eight. With the PTL club bankrupt and the money apparently frittered away, the victims received no restitution. While Bakker was in prison, Tammy divorced him and married his friend Roe Messner. Bakker served four and a half years in prison, a month in a halfway house, and four months under house arrest.

Bibliography

Hadden, Jeffrey K., and Charles E. Swann. *Prime Time Preachers*. Reading: Addison-Wesley, 1981.

Mitchell, Louis D. "Blessed Be the Poor: American Evangelists in Trouble." *The Month* Aug./Sept. 1987.

Ostling, Richard M. "Jim Bakker's Crumbling World." *Time* 19 Dec. 1988.

——. "Of God and Greed." *Time* 8 June 1987.

Heather Kavan

See also
Televangelists

Ball, Lucille (1911-1989), wife of Desi Arnaz and Gary Morton, mother of Lucie Arnaz Luckinbill and Desi Arnaz, Jr., consummate actress and comedienne extraordinaire, five-time Emmy winner, zany redhead, and perhaps the most intergenerationally loved entertainer of the 20th century. She was born to Henry and Desiree ("DeDe") Hunt Ball in Jamestown, NY. When her father died in 1915, she and her mother moved to her grandfather's home in Celeron, NY.

Lucy was always determined to "act" and started performing locally at a very early age before she left for New York City at 15 (with $50 sewn in her underwear). In 1933, she was approached in front of the Palace Theater and asked if she would be willing to go to Hollywood as a Goldwyn Girl and contract player (for more than $100 a week). She agreed, and her first film was an Eddie Cantor project, *Roman Scandals*. She would do seven RKO films then sign with MGM in 1942. Lucy reigned as queen of the B movie for 15 years. She recalls: "I never cared whether I was A pictures, B, pictures, C, D, or F ones as long as I was working."

While still with RKO, in 1940, Lucy the redhead met the Cuban band leader Desi Arnaz (Desiderio Alberto Arnaz y de Acha III, 1917-1986) during the RKO production of *Too Many Girls*. They were married six months later, on November 30, 1940. Their marriage began to dissolve quickly (Lucy first filed for divorced in 1944), and in an effort to save her failing marriage to Arnaz, she insisted Desi play her husband when *My Favorite Husband* was being loosely adapted from radio to television in 1948. The Arnazes won, and *I Love Lucy* was born (see entry). The popular program aired from 1951 to 1957 with 179 half-hour episodes. The "Lucy" format was then expanded into 13 one-hour segments (*Desilu Theater* and *The Lucy Desi Comedy Hour*) featuring the original cast and celebrity guests (1957-60).

Their 20-year marriage produced two children, Lucie (July 17, 1951) and Desi, Jr. (January 19, 1953). After the divorce in 1960, Lucy returned to the stage in the Broadway production of *Wildcat* at the Alvin Theater. After a theater performance, she met the temperate, suave Gary Morton. They were married November 19, 1961, and it was Morton who convinced Lucy to return to television. But it was Desi who initially produced *The Lucy Show* until 1962, when Lucy bought out Desi's share of Desilu Productions.

The Lucy Show reunited Lucy (as Lucy) and Vivian Vance (as Vivian) and ran from 1962 to 1968 with 156 episodes. She formed Lucille Productions in 1968 and began her third sitcom, *Here's Lucy*, which starred Gale Gordon and her children. It ran from 1968 to 1974 with 144 episodes.

Offscreen, in her later years, she devoted much of her time to teaching acting workshops and working with apprentice actors (funded by Desilu), to benefiting children's humanitarian causes, and especially to grandparenting Simon and Joseph Luckinbill. As long as we have reruns, we will always have her talent, but when Lucille Ball's heart died on April 26, 1989, in Cedars-Sinai Hospital, she clearly took a little bit of ours with her.

Bibliography

Brady, Kathleen. *Lucille: The Life of Lucille Ball*. New York: Hyperion, 1994.

Brochu, James. *Lucy in the Afternoon*. New York: Pocket, 1991.

Sanders, Coyne Steven, and Tim Gilbert. *Desilu: The Story of Lucille Ball and Desi Arnaz*. New York: Morrow, 1993.

Deborah Bice

See also
Sitcom

Ballroom Dancing has been and remains a staple of American dancing. *The Scent of a Woman* (1992), *Dirty Dancing* (1987), and other movies, like the Fred Astaire and Ginger Rogers movies of the 1930s, testify to the current popularity of ballroom dancing. Many major universities offer ballroom dance classes and competitions. Public television broadcasts the Ohio Star Ball (a competition), while state and local fairs offer nonprofessional dance demonstrations. Although never reaching the popularity that it did in 1940, ballroom dancing is an established part of American society today.

Traditional closed-couple dance began in the U.S. after 1860, when young people moved from rural environments to cities looking for employment. Alone for the first time, many young adults sought public meeting and dancing places. Because the newer dances like the waltz (Viennese) and the Polka (Czech) allowed closer than usual contact between partners, large segments of the public condemned this behavior. Closed-couple dancing became acceptable only after 1912, when the dance team of Vernon and Irene Castle began performing the waltz, the one-step (a dance using the beat of ragtime music), the tango (Spanish), and a few other dances to audiences across the country.

Through their performances and as dance instructors, the Castles also influenced hair and dress styles. Irene Castle wore the latest bobbed hairstyle and marketed a special elastic corset giving women more mobility to dance. Among the Castles' many pupils was a young entrepreneur named Arthur Murray, who in 1920 marketed dance lessons through the mail, which made dance both affordable and standardized.

Another major influence on social dance was ragtime, a new style of music emphasizing syncopation in the melody line. These early jazz sounds originated as a result of the fusion of Irish and African-American music forms. Around 1912, vaudeville actor Harry Fox fashioned a dance called the fox trot after the 19th-century African-American ragtime dances, the turkey trot and the cake walk. The fox trot soon became popular among Anglo-American audiences across the country.

One of the largest and most popular ballrooms in the U.S., the Savoy, opened in March 1926. Because of its large size and double raised bandstand, it attracted the best dancers in the New York area, including African Americans. Eventually the music the African-American patrons danced to became known as swing jazz and their acrobatic dance style was called the lindy hop. By the end of 1936, this dance (also called jitterbug, jive, and swing) was popular throughout the U.S. Because of increased tourism to Latin America, the rumba (Cuban) and the samba (Brazilian) also became fashionable.

During the wartime years of the 1940s, the size of the ballroom bands continued to expand. At the same time, musicians were harder to find and they required higher salaries. Coupled with newly imposed federal ballroom taxes, the cost of operating bands eventually became impracticable. When the war ended, young adults began spending their money on tangible items instead of on entertainment. Many ballrooms closed.

The next generation of dancers chose rock and roll music requiring smaller bands and dance floors. The teenagers of the late 1950s began dancing separately with simple movements. With the exception of an interest in a Cuban dance, the cha-cha, ballroom dancing declined and reached its lowest point in popularity in the late 1960s. To distinguish current dance styles from those of the previous generation, ballroom dancing became identified as the earlier closed-couple dances.

Since that time, ballroom dancing's popularity has depended on the trends and influences of other pastimes. For example, in the 1970s, the hustle, a disco dance originating in Manhattan and fashioned after the lindy, sparked a renewed interest in couple dancing. Today, ballroom dancing is promoted through an abundance of instructional videos as well as cruises and resorts, which feature this activity. Popular magazines with readership totaling over 20,000 have also contributed to the popularization of dancing. In the late 1990s, swing dancing (and music) became popular once more.

The widespread attraction of ballroom dancing lies in its ability to satisfy several needs in our society today: the formal costumes worn by many dancers appeal to the sense of elegance otherwise missing from these casual times; dancers look and feel confident while socially interacting; ballroom dancing fosters grace; and with today's emphasis on fitness many find this dancing style an enjoyable alternative to other exercise routines.

Bibliography

Stephenson, Richard, and Joseph Iaccareno. *The Complete Book of Ballroom Dancing*. Garden City: Doubleday, 1980.

Cynthia S. Kerchmar

Bar Code VCR Programming. Programming the video cassette recorder to record off-air broadcasts has baffled owners of VCRs since their introduction to the home market in the early 1980s. Early units required owners to activate a complicated series of small buttons. Based on the number of jokes, cartoons, satirical articles, and consultants devoted to VCR programming difficulties, few VCR owners have mastered this high-tech skill. In 1987 a new VCR feature was introduced to simplify the lives of VCR owners—bar code programming.

Using a pen-shaped wand or remote control, VCR users scan over four bar codes to program the date, start time, stop time, and channel, then push a button to transfer the information to the VCR. VCR bar codes look like the universal bar codes printed on most supermarket and retail merchandise scanned at the checkout counter.

Bar codes for time, channel, and date come on a card supplied with the machine. The bar code card was intended to be superfluous when codes became available in newspaper TV listings and in *TV Guide*. Printing bar codes with TV listings never caught on, however, due in large part to the space required for printing. A *TV Guide* issue including bar codes would be three times its current size. Additionally, few newspapers regularly print bar codes in TV listings. In 1990 bar code programming took a back seat to VCR Plus+. In contrast to bar codes, the 4-8 digit numerical codes used to program with VCR Plus+ are printed in most newspapers and *TV Guide*.

Bibliography
Lenk, John D. *VCR Troubleshooting and Repair.* Englewood Cliffs: Prentice-Hall, 1989.

Cynthia J. Wachter

Barber, (Walter Lanier) "Red" (1908-1992), one of America's most famous sports announcers, was born in Columbus, MS, of an extroverted, story-telling engineer-father and a scholarly, church-going schoolteacher-mother who read Greek and Roman mythology to her children. It was this background that nurtured Barber's language—a mixture of scholarly and country talk.

Barber began his broadcasting career while attending the University of Florida. He worked at a radio station delivering the news, farm reports, and features, played records and did play-by-play recounting of University of Florida football games. Barber began his baseball announcing career with the Cincinnati Reds in 1934, but it was when he joined the Brooklyn Dodgers in 1939 that the love affair between Red and his radio audience flourished.

The man who became known as the "Voice of Baseball" brought a style to announcing games that had not been heard before. His ease of delivery and down-home style attracted fans for the Dodgers, and for the sport. His southern accent and funny expressions, such as "rhubarb" (for a fight or argument), "catbird seat" (for being in an enviable position), and "tearing up the pea patch" (a rally in progress), were credited with bringing Dodger fans back to Ebbetts Field. Barber was also a reporter. He was allowed to analyze the team rather than be a public relations mouthpiece. For that reason, Brooklyn fans were called the most knowledgeable baseball fans that ever were.

Barber called himself "a child of radio," and spent 62 years in broadcasting. Besides the Reds and Dodgers, Barber spent 13 seasons broadcasting New York Yankee games. For the 12 years prior to his death he contributed weekly commentaries on National Public Radio's *Morning Edition.*

Broadcasting magazine called Barber, at the time of his death, part of "baseball and broadcast history." His career included numerous firsts, including broadcasting play-by-play of Major League Baseball's first night game, the first televised baseball game, and Jackie Robinson's breaking of the color barrier. In 1978, Red Barber, along with longtime New York Yankee announcer Mel Allen, became the first broadcasters inducted into the Major League Baseball Hall of Fame. He was one of the charter honorees of the *Broadcasting* magazine Hall of Fame in 1991.

Bibliography
Edwards, Bob. *Fridays with Red: A Radio Friendship.* New York: Simon & Schuster, 1993.
Golenbock, Peter. *Bums: An Oral History of the Brooklyn Dodgers.* New York: Putnam, 1984.

Michael L. Hilt

Barbie, known in the toy industry as "the Queen," is the best-selling doll in history. She is the creation of Ruth Handler, who, along with her husband, Elliot, and a friend, Harold Mattson, founded Mattel in 1945. Mattson left the company after a few years because of ill health, leaving Elliot as creator of new toys and Ruth as chief marketer.

Handler noticed that her daughter Barbie preferred playing with paper fashion dolls rather than with the baby dolls that dominated the doll market. Interested in creating a teenage fashion doll with an exciting wardrobe, Handler bought the rights to a German doll named Lilli. From this model, Mattel created the Barbie doll, named after the Handlers' daughter. Priced at $3, Barbie sported a black and white striped jersey bathing suit, designed to accentuate her well-developed breasts and trim waist; on her face she wore heavy makeup and an aloof expression.

From the beginning, Barbie's clothes—not the doll—were the focus. Marketed as a teenage fashion model, Barbie was only part of a toy line that included elaborate outfits, accompanied by accessories such as sunglasses, hats, earrings, handbags, and shoes. When Mattel unveiled Barbie at the New York Toy Show of 1959, she was not a hit among the predominantly male toy buyers. However, once Barbie dolls hit the toy-store shelves, they became an instant success with young girls. Just as Ruth Handler predicted, Barbie's wardrobe—designed not by a toy maker but by a fashion designer committed to seeing that Barbie's apparel had the same authentic details as women's clothes—was the key to her appeal. A three-page color spread in the August 23, 1963, issue of *Life*, dubbing Barbie as "the most popular doll in town" and picturing her complete 64-outfit wardrobe valued at $136, pegged her as "the despair of nine million fathers who now find that Barbie has to be clothed just like their wives and daughters."

Among the most popular—and, at $5, the most expensive—of Barbie's early outfits was a bridal gown, which necessitated the need for another doll to be her groom. Thus, in 1960, Mattel added Barbie's boyfriend Ken, named after the Handlers' son. Gradually, an entire entourage followed, including Barbie's best friend, Midge; younger sister, Skipper; sibling twins Todd and Tutti; and several other friends. Over the years, Barbie became the ultimate materialist: she acquired a dream house, Ferrari, sauna, boat, horse, and ice cream parlor, all woven into girls' fantasy play with the doll.

Barbie's popularity and longevity are legendary. Since 1959, Mattel, targeting girls between the ages of four and eight, has sold over 500 million Barbies. Each year, the company sells approximately 20 million dolls and also produces just as many outfits, making Mattel one of the largest manufacturers, per unit, of women's wear in the world. In 1987, a typical year, the doll's product line generated $360 million in sales, over 90 percent of its product category. Mattel estimates that 98 percent of U.S. girls have Barbie dolls.

The key to Barbie's success seems to be her ability to remain constant while also changing with the times, thus making the doll an important reflector of cultural trends. The Barbie doll, for example, demonstrates advances in doll making. In 1965, Barbie acquired blinking eyes, in 1966 bendable legs, in 1967 a "twist 'n' turn" waist, and in the 1970 Living Barbie, fully bendable joints. Nevertheless, she was always anatomically "incorrect," until the addition of a belly button in 2000.

In 1967, the first black doll, Francie, appeared in the Barbie line, followed the next year by another black doll, Talking Christie, both reflective of Americans' growing attention toward issues of race and civil rights. In subsequent years, Mattel proved to be one of the few major dollmakers to market black and Hispanic dolls, although it did not offer a multiracial Barbie series until the 1980s.

Barbie's clothes provided a running showcase of American fashion and lifestyles. Over the years, Barbie outfitted herself as a fashion model, student, nightclub singer, airline attendant, doctor, nurse, ballerina, hippie, astronaut, and executive (the last, albeit, with a hot pink suit and briefcase).

Bibliography

Boy, Billy. *Barbie! Her Life and Times and the New Theater of Fashion*. New York: Crown, 1987.

DeWein, Sibyl, and Joan Ashabraner. *The Encyclopedia of Barbie Dolls and Collectibles*. Paducah: Collector, 1977.

Lord, M. G. *Forever Barbie*. New York: Morrow, 1994.

Motz, Marilyn Ferris. "'Seen through Rose-Tinted Glasses': The Barbie Doll in American Society." *Popular Culture: An Introductory Text*. Ed. Jack Nachbar and Kevin Lause. Bowling Green, OH: Bowling Green State U Popular P, 1992.

Robins, Cynthia. *Barbie: Thirty Years of America's Doll*. Chicago: Contemporary, 1989.

Kathy Merlock Jackson

Barker, Clive (1952-), along with Stephen King, Anne Rice, and Dean Koontz, is a member of an elite handful of contemporary best-selling authors of dark fantasy and horror fiction, but his achievements extend beyond popular writing to a variety of creative arts. Early in his career, he worked with the live theater in England, composing and acting in avant-garde plays. He is now a successful motion picture screenwriter, director, and producer, and his graphic art has been published to great critical acclaim.

Barker's fiction has been equally profitable. Each of his epic-length fantasy novels has appeared on the international best-seller lists. He started his literary career writing unorthodox, nightmarish horror stories eventually collected between 1984 and 1985 in a six-volume anthology entitled *Clive Barker's Books of Blood*. Barker's inventive reinterpretation of the horror tale heralded the advent of "splatterpunk," a category of horror fiction featuring explicit depictions of sex and mayhem in order to elicit shock value, though Barker himself would deny this categorization of his work. "Rawhead Rex" (1984), for example, features a child murderer who dines on his victim. Titles from the *Books of Blood* group are revealing: "The Midnight Meat Train," "The Skins of the Fathers," "Confessions of a Pornographer's Shroud," "Human Remains," "The Life of Death," and other grisly allusions.

In recent years, Barker has turned to writing massive fantasy novels, including *The Damnation Game* (1985), about larger-than-life rival villains whose enmity stretches across years and continents; *Weaveworld* (1987), a romance about a people with magic powers who conceal their secrets in a tapestry; and others, including *Imajica* (1991) and *Everville* (1994). His fiction (what he would term the "fantastique") covers the entire spectrum of fantasy, from horror to high fantasy.

Bibliography

Brown, Michael. *Pandemonium*. Staten Island: Eclipse, 1991.

Hoppenstand, Gary. *Clive Barker's Short Stories*. Jefferson: McFarland, 1994.

Jones, Stephen, ed. *Clive Barker's Shadows in Eden*. Lancaster: Underwood-Miller, 1991.

Gary Hoppenstand

Barks, Carl (1901-2000), premier creator of animal cartoons and comic books, was born on a ranch near Merrill, OR, and actually trying his own hand at farming may have contributed to Barks's later ability to see the human characteristics in his famous animal characters. His ability to see the "perversity" of animals as well as the talent to translate that perversity into believable storylines is part of what made his cartoon creations legendary and earned him the nickname of "Duckman."

Barks became interested in cartooning at an early age and signed up for a correspondence course when he was 15. While he dropped the course after only a few lessons, he never forgot the dream of selling his drawings. Throughout various manual labor jobs, Barks continued to take samples of his work to newspapers and magazines with no success until 1928, when he began selling gag cartoons to the *Calgary Eye-Opener*. However, it was the fact that he lost his job in a box factory as a result of the Depression that forced him to become a full-time cartoonist. In 1935, after four years of working for the *Eye-Opener*, Barks sent some of his cartoons to Walt Disney, who replied, telling Barks to come out for a trial period during which he, along with other potential employees, would attend a Disney art class, observe Disney animation, and work on some simple material. They liked his work, so at the age of 34, Barks got his big break.

His first challenge was "Modern Inventions" (1937). Walt Disney was Donald Duck's biggest fan and he gave Donald's cartoons his personal attention. With Barks and the "Duck unit" in charge, they had one cartoon hit after another. "Good Scouts" (1938) and "Truant Officer Donald" (1941) were nominated for Academy Awards.

In 1942, Barks left the Disney Studios and went to work for Western publishing, where he would spend the next 23 years creating comic books. Carl Barks is associated primarily with the Disney Ducks, but from 1944 to 1947 he drew stories with Barney Bear and Benny Burro as well as Happy Hound (Droopy). None of these characters allowed him the depth that Donald did, however. So as the years went by, Barks was to develop the character of Donald more fully, along with creating new characters to plague the temperamental duck, such as Uncle Scrooge and Gladstone Gander. The addition of these characters as well as the Beagle Boys, Magica de Spell, Gyro Gearloose, and the Junior Woodchucks allowed him to give free rein to his imagination and send the ducks on wild adventures to strange lands. While these stories can be read for the pure enjoyment they provide, they do send messages to his readers.

Bibliography

Barrier, Michael. *Carl Barks and the Art of the Comic Book*. New York: Lilien, 1981.

Block, Patrick. "A Tribute to Carl Barks." *Lost River Star –Butte Valley Star* July 1995.

Cheryl Desforges

Barney and Friends (1992-), premier television for toddlers, once insulated by economic insignificance from the winds of political discord, has now attracted controversy worthy of its more profitable older sibling, teen programming. Children's live action video programming has come of age. How else could a character geared toward the mental capabilities of a two-year-old become a political issue on Capitol Hill?

Barney, a large purple dinosaur who sings with children, began innocently enough in 1988 as the brainchild of Sheryl Leach, a former elementary school teacher who noticed that most children's videos were geared toward older children who could follow the story line of an hour-and-a-half animated feature such as *The Little Mermaid*. Leach's two-year-old, whose attention might wander during an animated feature, would watch a shorter, live-action video with costumed characters and lots of music (*Wee Sing Together*), over and over again. Given that Nielsen ratings neglected viewers under the age of two, Leach recognized a market niche that was not being served—music videos for toddlers.

Leach developed a business plan to produce three half-hour live-action videos appropriate for toddlers and convinced her father-in-law to invest $1 million. Thus, the Lyons Group was born as a division of the closely held DLM Inc., a religious and educational publishing house based in Allen, TX. Although the children's video market was expanding as much as 30 percent a year, the Disney Company dominated the market, combining its merchandising muscle with an impressive film library.

Instead of pushing videos down the distribution pipeline like the Disney Company, Leach relied on sales at the retail level to "pull" distributors into carrying the videos. Employing a bottom-up strategy, Leach enlisted 17 friends and mounted a direct marketing telephone campaign aimed at stores that sold Disney and Sesame Street videos. To gain shelf space in toy stores for her new video character, Leach offered retailers a 50 percent discount instead of the 35 percent discount typical with competitor's products.

Once the videos were on the shelves, however, sales lagged, and retailers were clamoring to return unsold copies. "What we didn't realize," Leach explained in 1992, "is that exposure is so important." Advertising costs of $15,000 on Nickelodeon did little to remedy the problem.

Then, lightning struck—*People* magazine reporter called the Barney lyrics "stupid." Barney bashing had begun, and the ironic result was that within a few years sales of the videos climbed past the 300,000 mark. By 1992, Barney had his own television show on the Public Broadcasting Service (PBS) as well as enough merchandising contracts to make Ariel jealous.

Such was Barney's success that Richard Carlson, president of the Public Broadcasting Corporation, found himself defending public funding of the *Barney and Friends* program, explaining that Barney's owners would net only $7 million or $8 million in 1994 after taxes. Exposure, even of the most negative sort, created a merchandising bonanza estimated to gross $1 billion in revenue in 1994. Economically, Barney is the ultimate irony of the 1990s; his critics helped create his economic success by generating attention that his producers would never have been able to afford. Merchandising revenue of $1 billion is something even a low-budget, low-brow, purple dinosaur can appreciate.

As a cultural icon, Barney functions like an inkblot in a psychological Rorschach test. Adults project their own feelings about childhood onto this giggly, purple blob. "He is so pure and has such an easy laugh that our (adult) sarcastic sides come out," one defender explained; "Children just feel his innocence." A Barney detractor sees a darker "lesson for our times: Smart is bad. Dumb is good." For adults, Barney's blandness prompts our ambivalent feelings about powerlessness, simplicity, and fantasy.

Bibliography
Blumenthal, Karen. "How Barney the Dinosaur Beat Extinction, Is Now Rich." *Wall Street Journal* 28 Feb. 1992: B2.
Carlson, Richard. Interview on *Face the Nation*, CBS, 22 Jan. 1995.
Gorman, James. "Of All Dinosaurs, Why Must This One Thrive?" *New York Times* 11 Apr. 1993: B3.
Kastor, Elizabeth. "Play It Again, Pinocchio." *Washington Post* 23 March 1994: B1.
Twomey, Steve. "Of Love, Civility, and Other Dinosaurs." *Washington Post* 18 Nov. 1994: C1.

Janice Walker Anderson

Bars, taverns, and cocktail lounges are places where a person may consume alcoholic drinks away from home. In most cities and many smaller communities there are bars whose clientele may vary by age, occupation, ethnicity, gender, and sexual preference, as well as taste in recreation, music, decor, cuisine, and of course, beverages.

The terms for what can generically be called "bars" reflect both history and type. "Tavern" is the oldest, originally a colonial inn or dram-shop, and the term continues to be associated with places that serve a local blue-collar group, or that affect an Old English decor. The "bar," a long counter that made it possible to serve a larger number of people in a small space, developed in England in the 1830s and was soon exported to the frontier along with "saloon," an urban term that from the beginning bore connotations of immorality. In many cases the reputation was well deserved, as saloons were harbors for prostitution, criminals, graft, and drunkenness. From the 1820s, active temperance groups led to many city, county, and state laws prohibiting or restricting the sale of liquor, Maine being the first to have statewide prohibition in 1846. By 1919, over 30 states had restrictive laws, yet such groups as the Anti-Saloon League (national by 1895) also contributed to the emergence of "blind pigs," unlicensed covert bar operations. With the passage of the national Prohibition amendment in 1919, the term "speakeasy" replaced "blind pig."

Drinking tastes changed during the Prohibition era as cocktails gained in popularity, and for the first time, it became fashionable for American women to flout tradition and drink in bars. After the repeal of national Prohibition in 1933, many states and counties maintained local laws. Among these were laws against the word "saloon"; New York City's ban was not repealed until 1973. The local laws led to the advent of "roadhouses," bars located beyond the city limits or across a nearby "wet" border. Like saloon and speakeasy, the implication of immorality was strong for roadhouses, and since they were only accessible by automobile, they were associated with easy sex and drunken driving. According to Jim Hathaway, until the 1960s, all drinking places had an aura of furtiveness and guilt, so even as "cocktail lounges" came onto the scene in 1930s and 1940s, they still were dark, and, like most saloons and roadhouses, were heavily shuttered or curtained against prying proper eyes. Nevertheless their *moderne* decor and air of sophistication were attractive to women as well as men. Even more glamorous were "nightclubs" providing floor shows, big bands, dancing, food, and a black-tie dress code, along with cocktails.

In 1967, *Time* magazine reported a new development: "dating bars" (soon to be called "singles bars"), the first being Sullivan's in Manhattan: "Not only could a 'post-college' girl in her 20s enter without fear," says Hathaway, "but the dating bar also served as a meeting ground for women." Since then, bars have shed much of their furtiveness, with large windows, casual seating rather than private booths, and, in hotels and shopping malls, are more like European sidewalk cafes, the imbibers being separated from the passing throngs only by low planters, picket fencing, or velvet ropes.

Bar entertainments range from tavern arm-wrestling, pinball, and tavern-sponsored bowling and softball teams, to live acts performing oldies or arpeggios at piano bars, or jazz, folk, country, or rock groups. For much of the century, patrons of taverns and saloons provided their own music with tipsy renditions of songs celebrating or sentimentalizing alcoholic conviviality and guilt: "There Is a Tavern in the Town," "Frankie and Johnny," "Behind Those Swinging Doors," "Roll Out the Barrel," "Sparrow in the Treetop," "Pistol-Packin' Mama" and such maudlin favorites as "Sweet Adeline," "Melancholy Baby," and "As Time Goes By." Machine music entered bars in the later 19th century with player pianos and nickelodeons, later jukeboxes, and in the 1990s, karaoke.

Many bars have achieved popular notoriety beyond their locale: Judge Roy Bean's notorious Jersey Lily in Langtry, TX; Hinky Dink's saloon in Gay Nineties Chicago; McSorley's Bar in Lower Manhattan, immortalized by "Ashcan School" artist John Sloan (and the last *real* saloon, finally admitting women in 1970); the Round Table of the Algonquin Hotel in New York, where the Barrymores, H. L. Mencken, Alexander Woollcott, Dorothy Parker, Robert Benchley, and other notables of stage and journalism regaled each other with witty badinage, assured of publicity by hotel manager Frank Case (1870-1946); the Long Branch in Dodge City, KS, familiar to *Gunsmoke* fans as the territory of Miss Kitty and Sam, the bartender; the Coconut Grove in Boston, where 491 perished in a 1942 fire; and Gilley's

Saloon near Houston, with its capacity of 4,500. Among notable fictional bars are (from 1940s radio) Duffy's Tavern ("where the elite meet to eat, Duffy ain't here"); (from black and white television) cool-jazz Blue Note of *Peter Gunn*; and in the 1990s, Cheers, from the long-running show of that name, which even spawned look-alike real bars complete with replicas of the regulars, as well as *Cheers* trivia games and logo barware for the home.

In film, bars contributed at least two great conventions, the barroom brawl and the gangster nightclub. One of the earliest barroom melees was that of William S. Hart in the immoral town of *Hell's Hinges* (1917), and they continued as standard fare in Westerns from B to adult (*Shane*) to extravagant parodies in *The Great Race* and *Airplane* and pure raucous fun in *Smokey and the Bandit*. The nightclubs in films of the 1930s and 1940s probably did much to glamorize drinking, and to give unwonted social prestige to the club owner, whose personal welcome assured one of a choice table and an obsequious waiter to serve "the usual."

Curiously, there is a popular culture of temperance, too. Temperance songs livened the meetings of the Women's Christian Temperance Union (founded 1874), the Anti-Saloon League, and the Salvation Army. These have been treated humorously in the stage and film *Guys and Dolls* (1955), and the film *Hallelujah Trail* (1965). In 1854, Timothy Arthur (1809-85) wrote *Ten Nights in a Barroom, and What I Saw There*, a tale of the ruination of an entire village at the hands of the demon rum. Richard Erdoes describes it as "the drys' *Uncle Tom's Cabin*." Read aloud at countless rallies and church meetings, it was soon transformed into a play and a musical that was highly popular for over 50 years. Possibly the only rival in popularity to *Ten Nights* was Carry Nation (1846-1911), who at age 54 started a campaign of attacking saloons with a hatchet, destroying bottles, glasses, the invariable bar-mirror, and paintings of nude women. In a single day in Wichita, KS, she trashed 114 places, achieving nationwide fame. She became stagestruck and gave lectures between acts at burlesque theaters and on Coney Island. She played the part of the heartbroken mother in an adaptation of *Ten Nights*; it was, a reporter said, "a smashing success."

Bibliography

Brown, John Hull. *Early American Beverages*. Rutland: Tuttle, 1966.

Cavan, Sherri. *Liquor License: An Ethnography of Bar Behavior*. Chicago: Aldine, 1966.

Erdoes, Richard. *Saloons of the Old West*. New York: Knopf, 1979.

Hathaway, Jim. "A History of the American Drinking Place." *Landscape* 29.1 (1986): 1-9.

Fred E. H. Schroeder

See also

Sports Bars

Baseball Films. While many people might consider the notion of a baseball film genre as oxymoronic, its history is both lengthy and rich. In fact, what was probably the first motion picture ever produced in the U.S. was Thomas Edison's *Ball Game*, which was made on May 20, 1896—a peep show photographed from a single position behind home plate that showed some action from an actual baseball game. The first full-fledged baseball movie was a filmed dramatization of *Casey at the Bat*, produced by the Edison Company in 1899; while it was fiction, most of the earliest baseball films were newsreels of real action, such as the Essanay-produced 1909 Detroit-Pittsburgh Baseball Series.

The year 1909 marks the legitimate beginning of the baseball film era, with *His Last Game*, a cowboys-and-Indians diamond drama, soon followed, in that first decade, by the likes of *Take Me Out to the Ball Game* (1910), *Hal Chase's Home Run* (1911), *Love and Baseball* (1914), *Right Off the Bat* (1915), and *Baseball, An Analysis of Motion* (1919).

While there were more than two dozen baseball films during the 1920s and early 1930s, the popularity of Babe Ruth served best to capture both our national imagination and that of Hollywood. As Linda K. Fuller has noted, "The real story of the success of baseball films is not in the batting box, but at the box office. From the beginning, filmmakers were quick to realize the added box-office potential of the day's baseball stars, so it wasn't long before some of them began appearing, usually as themselves, in dramatized films as well as in newsreels." Ever since Hal Chase played himself in a 1911 film, followed the next year by Chief Bender, Jack Coombs, and Rube Olding in *The Baseball Bug*, others joined the film fun: Christy Mathewson in *Love and Baseball* (1914), Mike Donlin and John McGraw in *Right Off the Bat* (1915), Ty Cobb in *Somewhere in Georgia* (1916), Frank Baker in *Home Run Baker's Double* (1914), Jack Johnson in *As the World Rolls On* (1921), and Babe Ruth in *Babe Comes Home* (1927), as well as a number of shorts produced by Universal Pictures, like *Fancy Curves, Just Pals,* and *Slide, Babe, Slide*. Also, Roger Maris, Mickey Mantle, Ralph Houk, Whitey Ford, and other actual players have made film appearances.

Most baseball films fall into the following categories:

CARTOONS: *Boulevardier from the Bronx* (1936), a Warner Brothers' Merrie Melodies production featuring an all-bird cast of "good guys" beating a baseball team of city slickers; *Baseball Bugs* (1946)—Bugs Bunny trying to play all nine positions; the 1946 Disney-RKO musical fantasy *Make Mine Music*, which features a Jerry Colonna rendition of "Casey at the Bat"; and *Abner the Baseball* (1961), a cartoon tracing the life of a baseball named Abner. The *Peanuts* character Charlie Brown has spawned his own set of baseball-related cartoons, including *Charlie Brown's All-Stars* (1966) and *It's Arbor Day, Charlie Brown* (1983).

COMEDIES: *Giants vs. Yanks* (1923), a baseball game waged by the Our Gang kids; Buster Keaton in *College* (1927); *Elmer the Great* (1933), with Joe E. Brown as the usual egomaniacal bumbler; Abbott and Costello's famous Who's on First routine in *Naughty Nineties* (1945); *Rhubarb* (1951), about the cat who inherits ownership of the Brooklyn Dodgers; and *The Bad News Bears* (1976) and its many sequels. *Major League* (1989) was a highly successful baseball spoof, which also spawned a sequel.

PROMOTIONS: *Ninth Inning* (1942), a noteworthy official American League production dedicated to the memory of Yankee great Lou Gehrig, the "Iron Man"; *Little League Baseball* (1949), chronicling the sport's development, the highlight being a play-by-play of the 1948 World Series as announced by Ted Husing; and the 1987 28-minute documentary *A League of Their Own*, directed by Mary Wallace, in honor of the All-American Girls Professional Baseball League (see entry) players' reunion, which inspired Penny Marshall's 1992 film of the same name.

INTERNATIONAL FILMS: While American baseball films have traditionally been box-office poison when it comes to exportation, only two countries have also been involved in the genre: Japan produced *I'll Buy You* (1956), *Youth* (1968), and *The Ceremony* (1971), and Korea produced *Just the Beginning* (1977). Tom Selleck stars in an embarrassment called *Mr. Baseball* (1992), as an American player demoted to playing on a Japanese team.

BIOGRAPHICAL FILMS: Baseball greats have been featured in a number of motion pictures, including Gary Cooper as Yankee Lou Gehrig in *Pride of the Yankees* (1942), which won him an Oscar nomination and another for Teresa Wright as wife Eleanor, and featured Irving Berlin's famous song "Always"; *The Babe Ruth Story* (1948), based on the book by Bob Considine and starring William Bendix as the Sultan of Swat; Jimmy Stewart as the one-legged White Sox pitcher Monty Stratton trying to make a comeback, encouraged by wife June Allyson in *The Stratton Story* (1949); *The Jackie Robinson Story* (1950), with the athlete playing himself in the story about breaking major league's color barrier; Dan Dailey as pitcher Dizzy Dean in *The Pride of St. Louis* (1952); Ronald Reagan as pitcher Grover Cleveland Alexander in *The Winning Team* (1952); and *Fear Strikes Out* (1957), with Anthony Perkins as Jimmy Piersall, suffering a nervous breakdown. Interestingly, there has been recent interest in baseball biographies, such as the story of Shoeless Joe Jackson in *Eight Men Out* (1988) and *Field of Dreams* (1989), as well as John Goodman's portrayal of *The Babe* (1991).

BASEBALL FILMS ABOUT BASEBALL: *Kid from Cleveland* (1949), with George Brent playing a sportswriter while Cleveland Indian owner Bill Veeck, manager Lou Boudreau and other team members play themselves; William Bendix at first a critic, then an umpire himself in *Kill the Umpire* (1950); *Max Dugan Returns* (1983), a Neil Simon comedy with Charlie Lau, then-coach of the Chicago White Sox, having a major supporting role; and *Jose Canseco's Baseball Camps* (1989).

MUSICALS: *Take Me Out to the Ball Game* (1949) cast Esther Williams as owner of an 1890 ballclub whose double-play combination was featured in the song "O'Brien [Gene Kelly] to Ryan [Frank Sinatra] to Goldberg [Jules Munship]"; Tab Hunter as a married, middle-aged Washington Senators fan who sells his soul to the devil for a chance to become the world's greatest baseball player in *Damn Yankees* (1958)—featuring the songs "Whatever Lola Wants," "Heart," and "Shoeless Joe from Hannibal, Missouri."

According to H. M. Zucker and L. J. Babich, there are three basic cinematic sports themes: triumph of the underdog, the fall (and sometimes resurrection) of the mighty, and the sporting event as pretext. Among baseball films, an early prototype of the underdog notion was *Pinch Hitter* (1917), focusing on a shy boy at a small college who becomes the butt of pranks and jokes before becoming the game-winning hero; *Roogie's Bump* (1954) concerns the ghost of a baseball star who helps the neighborhood wimp become an instant sports sensation (*Angels in the Outfield* [1951; remade 1994] has a similar premise). How one can make a living post-baseball is the theme of *The New Klondike* (1926), as well as *Adventures of Frank Merriwell* (1936); *Bang the Drum Slowly* (1973), with Robert DeNiro as an average ballplayer dying of Hodgkin's disease; *Long Gone* (1987), about a minor league baseball manager given a second chance; *Stealing Home* (1988), with Mark Harmon as a washed-up player; and *Pastime* (1991), about a pitcher who can't face his pending retirement. Under the "event as pretext" category one might include *Death on the Diamond* (1934), a mystery about someone murdering members of the St. Louis Cardinals; *The Natural* (1984), based on Bernard Malamud's magical-mythical novel on heroism, with baseball as a backdrop; or *Amazing Chuck & Grace* (1987), an interesting cross between an anti–nuclear war and a sports movie. The history of the game and its centrality to American culture is captured in Ken Burns's 9-part documentary *Baseball* (1994).

The baseball film genre, which spans nearly a century, shows that we have long been fascinated by both the heroes and the foibles inherent in our national sport; its future at this point on the Big Screen seems quite secure. In the words of A. Bartlett Giamatti, late commissioner of Major League Baseball, "If baseball is a narrative, it is like others—a work of imagination whose deeper structures and patterns of repetition force a tale, oft-told, to fresh and hither-to unforeseen meaning."

Bibliography

Boswell, Thomas. *How Life Imitates the World Series.* Garden City: Doubleday, 1982.

Cohen, Marvin. *Baseball the Beautiful.* New York: Link, 1974.

Durso, Joseph. *Baseball and the American Dream.* St. Louis: Sporting News, 1986.

Fuller, Linda K. "The Baseball Movie Genre: At Bat or Struck Out?" *Play & Culture* 1990.

Giamatti, A. Bartlett. "The Story of Baseball." *New York Times* (1989).

Guttmann, Allen. *From Ritual to Record: The Nature of Modern Sports.* New York: Columbia UP, 1978.

Zucker, H. M., and L. J. Babich. *Sports Films.* Jefferson: McFarland, 1987.

Robert Baird

See also
Sports and Popular Literature
Women in Baseball

Baseball Re-creations, the result of the marriage between radio and baseball, were dependent on the medium's ability to broadcast the "home and away" schedule of a given team. But innovative sportscasters of the 1920s patented a cost-effective method for covering road games that became a part of radio production procedures for nearly four decades: "re-creation." Instead of traveling with the team, announcers produced dramatizations of road games in the studio, based on information furnished by telegraph or telephone from the stadiums of opposing teams.

Major league sportscasters such as Red Barber, Harry Caray, Mel Allen, and Ted Husing (and even Ronald Reagan, who re-created Chicago Cubs' games for WHO in Des Moines) relied on this method of broadcasting games played away from home until the mid-1950s. However, re-creation continued even longer at stations covering the minor leagues, because limited fan and advertiser support still made the prospect of full-schedule coverage financially unattractive. Therefore, sports announcers who entered the profession as late as the 1950s found re-creation to be an expected qualification. Re-creation was finally abandoned by most minor league sportscasters in the early 1970s.

Since a broadcast without the accompanying sounds of the game—crowd noise, vendors, the crack of the bat, and organ music—sounded cold, impersonal, and somewhat naked, announcers who attempted these dramatizations were also required to have a vivid imagination and superior production ability. Without the benefits of modern recording methods, early re-creators became quite adept at manufacturing their own ballpark sound effects: striking a wooden object with a pencil to simulate the crack of the bat against the ball, speaking into a reverberant trash can to simulate the public address system, or hitting a wallet with a clenched fist to imitate the ball coming into contact with the catcher's mitt. Primitive transcriptions of baseball crowd noise completed the re-creator's simulation of the stadium ambiance. Beyond such embellishments, announcers relied on basic theatrical talent to successfully feign the excitement of describing a home run or the pacing of a typical pitching sequence.

Bibliography

Barber, Red. *The Broadcasters.* New York: Dial, 1970.

Catsis, John. *Sports Broadcasting.* Chicago: Hall, 1995.

Smethers, J. Steven. *Re-Creation in Sports Broadcasting: An Oral History.* Columbia: U of Missouri P, 1991.

Smith, Curt. *Voices of the Game.* South Bend: Diamond, 1987.

J. Steven Smethers

Baseball Stadiums both create and reflect popular culture. No other sports locale has this distinction. One hockey arena is largely interchangeable with another; distinctive features of basketball arenas are few and far apart; and the variety in football stadiums ends at the field of play. Baseball stadiums are, however, more than mere stages. Baseball, it has been suggested, like a liquid, takes the shape of the container. Ballparks offer a panorama of popular culture, and in doing so, they create memories and traditions that perpetuate the culture.

A visit to any ballpark involves certain constant rituals. Even before the game begins, there is the choreographed ritual of batting practice, the performance of the national anthem, and the ceremonial first pitch. Then comes the traditional baseball fare of peanuts (and the peanut vendor with his banter and distance tossing of the bags), hot dogs, and beer, the music between innings and during lulls in the action (often from a stadium organist so integral to the culture of the game that the organist's name is known even to casual fans: Nancy B. Hepply at Dodger Stadium, Nancy Faust at Comiskey Park, Eddie Layton at Yankee Stadium), the seventh inning stretch and the singing of "Take Me Out to the Ball Game," and promotional dates, including bat day, ball day, old timers day, and photo day.

The fans are often a microcosm of their cities—or at least the popular stereotypes of their cities. In Toronto the fans are unfailingly polite and frequently all but silent; at Shea and Yankee Stadiums in New York, there is never a moment's doubt about the fans' feelings towards any given play or player; in Los Angeles the fans are enthusiastic but laid-back, and the stadium is rarely full before the third inning or after the seventh. The vendors, too, with their regional accents, are reflections of the culture of the city. And if there are more than three kinds of beer and more than three kinds of sausages available, you can only be at County Stadium in Milwaukee.

Between the pacing of the game and the panorama of the play, with its simultaneous action spread across the field, the game seems to have been designed to frustrate television coverage and to embrace radio. The voice and unique style of Harry Caray heard on a radio meant a Cubs game was in progress somewhere in the night; the banter of Phil Rizzuto and Bill White was for years part of the identity of the Yankees; what would the Dodgers be without the reassuring narration of Vince Scully—and, years ago in Brooklyn, of Red Barber.

In the 1960s and 1970s cities outdid themselves to see who could build the largest most multipurpose stadium. Recently the pendulum has, with a vengeance, swung the other way. While fans bemoan the loss of the unique and intimate stadiums (old Comiskey in Chicago with its close-in seating, Crosley Field in Cincinnati with its uphill climb in the outfield; Ebbets Field in the heart of Brooklyn), cities now compete to build truly unique parks as distant from each other and deserving of the name "park" as the multipurpose ovals of the '60s and '70s were alike and deserving of the name "stadium": Camden Yards in Baltimore, Jacobs Field in Cleveland, the Ballpark at Arlington in Texas, Coors Field in Denver. Even Kaufman Stadium in Kansas City, a modern but intimate park, is ripping out its artificial surface and for the first time installing a grass playing field.

Bibliography

Angell, Roger. *Late Innings*. New York: Simon & Schuster, 1982.

Boswell, Tom. *Why Time Begins on Opening Day*. Garden City: Doubleday, 1984.

Reidenbaugh, Lowell. *Take Me Out to the Ball Park*. 2d ed. St. Louis: Sporting News, 1984.

Justin J. Burke
Scott M. Martin

Basie, Count (William "Bill") (1904-1984), one of the true legends of the swing era, was—and continues to be—one of

Count Basie. Photo courtesy of Sound Recording Archives, Bowling Green State University, Bowling Green, OH.

the most influential forces in the history of jazz and one of its best-ever bandleaders and pianists. Born at Red Bank, NJ, Basie grew up across the Hudson River from New York City; his mother gave him his first lessons at the piano, but it was in New York that he heard Harlem stride pianists such as James P. Johnson, Willie "The Lion" Smith, and particularly Fats Waller, who not only gave the teenager some informal instruction but also recommended Basie to be his replacement in the Katie Crippen and Her Kids act that made its way around the "chitlin' circuit," playing to black audiences. When the act collapsed in 1927 in Kansas City, Basie found himself stuck there and made his living for several months by playing in silent theater houses. The next year, Basie hooked up with Walter Page's Blue Devils; Page would stay with Basie in one band or another for the next 20 years, and Jimmy Rushing, another Blue Devil, also would be a major figure in Basie's own band later on.

In 1929, after leaving the Blue Devils and knocking around with two minor area bands, Basie joined Bennie Moten's Kansas City Orchestra, and other members of the Blue Devils followed shortly thereafter. Basie stayed with the band for six years until Bennie Moten died in 1935; the band stayed together under Bennie's brother Buster, but Basie pulled out with several other members to form the Barons of Rhythm, which one source claimed to be, at the time, "quite simply the most classy and propulsive unit in the history of music." The Barons enjoyed a long run at the Reno Club in Kansas City; their radio appearances in 1936 prompted contracts with Decca and with a national booking agency, and the Count Basie Orchestra, as it now was known, put out several hits in the late 1930s, including "One o'Clock Jump" (1937) and "Jumpin' at the Woodside" (1938). The storied rhythm section of Jo Jones (drums),

Freddie Green (guitar), and Walter Page (bass) drove the group to national prominence, as did the work of Lester Young (see entry) on tenor sax and Buck Clayton on trumpet, all "comped" by Basie's freshly minimalist piano style (he had called himself a "non-pianist"), later reflected in solo styles such as that of Thelonious Monk.

Although by 1940 the group's reliance on more standardized written arrangements had tended to curtail much of the creativity that originally had constituted the group's attractiveness, Basie's orchestra enjoyed tremendous popularity through the 1940s with a number of outstanding instrumental soloists and also vocalists such as Jimmy Rushing and Helen Humes. Financial difficulties caused a reconfiguration of the band in 1950, a downsizing that left the group at six to nine members for a couple of years until he could rehire an entire big band in 1952. In 1954, the band toured Europe, and in 1957 Basie's orchestra became the first black band ever to play at the Waldorf-Astoria in New York; they stayed for a four-month run. That year, *The Atomic Mr. Basie* featured arranger Neal Hefti's work in stereo and was hailed as an instant classic. During the next several years, Basie's band appeared in films (*Sex and the Single Girl* and *Made in Paris* among them). They also worked with many other heavy-hitters in the business, including Frank Sinatra, Fred Astaire, Sammy Davis, Jr., and Tony Bennett. Basie's landmark 1963 tour of Japan was a hit as well. Arranging for Basie proved to be a career-maker for Quincy Jones (see entry), now one of the most powerful producers in the business.

By the late 1960s most of the original band members except for Freddie Green had gone; still, the band was in demand for appearances and recordings, including the 1979 *Afrique*, arranged by Oliver Nelson and featuring Albert Ayler and Pharoah Sanders (among others) on saxophone in a new-jazz style that shook up some of the old Basie fans. Also during the 1960s and 1970s, Basie was persuaded to record many popular tunes, some of them in a big-band swing flavor, presumably in an attempt to "stay current" and to capture some of the market then being lost to pop and rock acts. These recordings met with limited acclaim at best, and in 1975 a new association with Pablo Records gave Basie the freedom to go back to the swing style that had made him popular in the first place. Increasingly poor health during the late 1970s and early 1980s forced him to perform from a wheelchair at times, and Basie died in Hollywood, a year after Catherine, his wife of many decades, had died.

Basie's contributions to jazz over his very long and popular career generally are acknowledged to be manifold. Among other contributions, Basie's rhythm section helped to establish the four-beat stress as a new norm in jazz; drummer Jones kept the four-beat pulse more in the closed hi-hat than in the bass drum, thereby changing the feel of the rhythmic pulse by taking the "thump" out of it; and Page's "walking" bass left the pianist's left hand free to go solo, if needed, rather than bang out bass notes on the keyboard, thus making possible Basie's minimalist solo style, which passed up ostentatious displays of technical virtuosity for a melodic line that played off, rather than overpowered, the rhythmic character of the music. As George Benson has said, Basie's music doesn't depend on the soloist; rather, "it swings with you or without you. It doesn't need *you*. It's got legs."

Bibliography
Bourne, Michael. "George Benson: Back to Basics, Back to Basie." *Down Beat* Jan. 1991: 16-19.
Freeman, Don. "My Biggest Thrill? When Duke Roared Back: Basie." *Down Beat* Feb. 1994: 31.
Kernfeld, Barry, ed. *The New Grove Dictionary of Jazz.* London: Macmillan, 1988.
Larkin, Colin, ed. *The Guinness Encyclopedia of Popular Music.* Vol. 1. Middlesex, U.K.: Guinness, 1992.

Stephen Finley

Baskets. The U.S. has always had a rich tradition of basketmaking. Most people think of baskets as containers that are coiled, twined, or plaited, created to hold items such as flowers, eggs, grains, or other foods. The broader category of basketry also includes hats, fish traps, pocketbooks, cradles and cradleboards, ornaments, mats, furniture, and even shelters created with basketry techniques. Basketry techniques have also been combined with clay to create containers that hold liquids. While most baskets are meant to be functional, today many artists with formal training incorporate basketry techniques into sculptural forms. Although these objects are nonutilitarian, they are often still referred to as baskets.

Basketry in the U.S. began as an art of necessity. Native Americans, African Americans, and the Pilgrims needed baskets to carry on their daily activities. In Appalachia, baskets were used for measurement as well as hauling and storage. Among farmers, the need for baskets decreased with the introduction of new tools and machinery. Many baskets became almost obsolete, such as the winnowing fan and the rye coil bread basket. These, and other such baskets, were replaced by boxes, paper bags, and large tin cans.

Some basketmaking groups have continued their cultural traditions of making baskets for hundreds of years. Many African Americans in Mt. Pleasant, SC, continue to make seagrass baskets the way they were taught by older family members. This art form has been practiced, uninterrupted, in this area for over 300 years. It has been traced back to Africa, and today over 1,500 African Americans in the Low Country still coil these traditional baskets. The seagrass has been disappearing because of increased urbanization, and the weavers now purchase their grasses in order to continue making baskets.

Generally speaking, while Native American baskets have stylistic traits identifiable with a particular group or tribe, individual artists, even when working within their tradition, make variations. Sometimes artists may take great liberties, as with the Papago artists who make containers using colored telephone wire. Today, basketry classes are held all over the United States. Basketry groups have formed, and basketry conferences are not uncommon, although they were more frequent in the 1970s and '80s than they are today.

Bibliography
James, George Wharton. *Indian Basketry.* New York: Dover, 1972.

Pullen, Rob. *The Basketmaker's Art: Contemporary Baskets and Their Makers.* Asheville: Lark, 1986.

Rossbach, Ed. *Baskets as Textile Art.* New York: Van Nostrand, 1973.

Kristin G. Congdon

Batman, one of the lasting icons of American youth, debuted in May 1939 in *Detective Comics* 27, created by artist Bob Kane and writer Bill Finger, and the Caped Crusader has been striking fear into the hearts of criminals ever since. After seeing his parents slain during a robbery, Batman dedicated his life to fighting crime, putting in years of mental and physical training to bring himself to the peak of human perfection. He maintains the secret identity of bored millionaire playboy Bruce Wayne as a cover for his activities.

Much of Batman's appeal stems from the approachability of his origin; while none of us are really aliens from another planet or superpowered mutants, we all could make ourselves more skilled through dedicated application and study. Almost a year after Batman first appeared, he was given a partner, Dick Grayson, an orphaned circus acrobat who adopted the identity of Robin, the Boy Wonder. (The current comic book Robin is the third; the first grew up, and the second was killed by reader vote in a phone-in poll.)

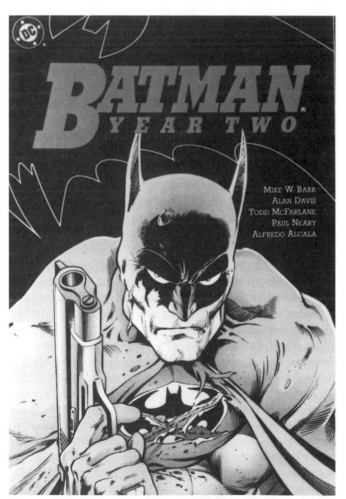

Batman. Photo courtesy of Popular Culture Library, Bowling Green State University, Bowling Green, OH.

In January 1966, the *Batman* TV show (see entry below) premiered and ushered in an age of camp on both the screen and the printed page. The next significant revamp of the character took place in 1986, with Frank Miller's *The Dark Knight Returns*. This four-issue series, set in a dystopian near future, revitalized the comics industry, ushering in an era of "grim and gritty" books and making comics more acceptable for older readers. Batman's large "rogue's gallery" includes such famous villains as the Joker and Catwoman. In addition to his continuing run in *Detective Comics* and *Batman,* the character has historically appeared in *The Justice League of America, World's Finest* (team-ups with Superman), and *The Brave and the Bold* (team-ups with a variety of other heroes). In addition to many special projects, his titles currently include *Shadow of the Bat, Legends of the Dark Knight*, and *The Adventures of Batman and Robin,* which is based on the animated TV cartoon.

Bibliography

Barr, Mike W. "The Batman." *Encyclopedia Mysteriosa.* Ed. William L. DeAndrea. New York: Prentice-Hall, 1994. 20-21.

Daniels, Les. *DC Comics: Sixty Years of the World's Favorite Comic Book Heroes.* Boston: Little, Brown, 1995.

Vaz, Mark Cotta. *Tales of the Dark Knight: Batman's First Fifty Years: 1939-1989.* New York: Ballantine, 1989.

Johanna L. Draper

Batman, the movie (1989), directed by Tim Burton (see entry), was the year's top money-maker, generating about $250 million in ticket sales; film-related merchandise generated twice that much income during the same period. The film was followed by the 1992 Burton-directed sequel, *Batman Returns*, which was also that year's top money-maker, generating $163.7 million in ticket sales, and by *Batman Forever* (1995), directed by Joel Schumacher.

Featuring Michael Keaton as Batman, Burton's *Batman* portrayed the character of millionaire Bruce Wayne as a psychologically torn man who was driven to become a vigilante crime fighter in response to the childhood trauma of witnessing the murder of his parents by a criminal who would, years later, become the Joker. The film focused on Batman's struggle against the Joker (who blamed Batman for his disfigurement in a chemical accident) and Batman's romance with Vicki Vale, but the psychological development of the criminal and crime fighter received most of the attention.

Tim Burton's interpretation of *Batman* appears to have been influenced by two DC Comics reinterpretations of Batman: *Batman: The Dark Knight Returns*, Frank Miller's highly praised 1986 four-issue series that reintroduced psychological realism in an "alternate universe" story of Batman in his 50s coming out of retirement only to be labeled a criminal for his attempts to battle a de-institutionalized Joker and mutant youth gangs and, eventually, even Superman, as Batman attempts to restore order to a Gotham City in decay, and *Arkham Asylum*, Frank Morrison's graphic novel (published, after several delays, in 1989), which explored Batman and the Joker's link through obsession and madness as Batman confronts the Joker-led criminally insane inmates who have taken over Arkham Asylum. These darker narrative elements were extended into the film's Oscar-winning production design by Anton Furst, combining German Expressionist and Gothic design elements to create a threatening and alienating Gotham City, underscored by a Wagnerian soundtrack by Danny Elfman interspersed with popular songs by Prince for the Joker.

The combination of psychologically traumatized characters in a city (and a story) that reflects their internal realities was extended in *Batman Returns*. For *Batman Forever*, Val Kilmer took over the role of Batman; this film introduced Batman's sidekick, Robin (Chris O'Donnell).

Batman and its sequels continued the casting tradition begun in the television series (see next entry) of guest star villains. In addition to Jack Nicholson's Joker, *Batman* also represented Billy Dee Williams in a cameo role as the villain "Two-Face." *Batman Returns* cast Danny DeVito as the Penguin and Michelle Pfeiffer in the role of Catwoman. In *Batman Forever*, Tommy Lee Jones became Two-Face, while Jim Carrey was the Riddler.

In addition to the feature-length film versions, two 15-part serials were released in the 1940s: *Batman* (1943), starred Lewis Wilson as Batman and Douglas Croft as Robin battling Japanese spies, and *Batman and Robin* (1949) starring Robert Lowery and John Duncan battling a criminal mastermind named the Wizard (William Fawcett). The success of *Batman* also inspired a successful daily Fox television animated series (see the following entry).

Bibliography

Barol, Bill. "Batmania." *Newsweek* 26 June 1989: 70-74.

Corliss, Richard. "Battier and Better." *Time* 22 June 1992: 69-71.

Gerani, Gary. *Batman Returns: Official Movie Souvenir Magazine.* Brooklyn: Topps, 1992.

Marriott, John. *Batman: The Official Book of the Movie.* New York: Mallard, 1989.

Rodman, Harold A. "They Shoot Comic Books, Don't They?" *American Film* 14.7 (May 1989): 34-39.

Greg Metcalf

Batman, the TV show (1965-1968) burst onto an America already infatuated with popular art and culture. It gently mocked the establishment by making its heroes bigger squares than Mitch Miller and Lawrence Welk combined, and let the villains have all the fun. Besides, the kids loved it. After the 1960s TV show ended, however, it tended to hobble those trying to take comics seriously. Every article written about comics was nailed to a headline with "Pow! Zap!" or "Holy Somethingorother!" in it. Not until the 1980s could Batman be taken seriously again.

The show was designed to resemble comic book action as closely as possible, using bright hues (also good for selling color TVs) and tilted camera angles. Some scripts were adapted from the comic books, and a few were written by Bill Finger, Batman's co-creator. Adam West was cast over Lyle Waggoner for the lead. Burton Gervis, a youthful 21-year-old with no acting experience but an athletic build, walked into the studio office and was hired as Robin, changing his name to Burt Ward. The cast included former matinee

Adam West, the original "Batman" of television, here as a celebrity attraction at the "World of Wheels" auto show, Sioux City, IA, 1980. Photo courtesy of Mark McDermott.

idol Neil Hamilton as Commissioner Gordon and Madge Blake as Aunt Harriet, added to quiet the hint that Bruce Wayne and Dick Grayson were closet homosexuals (Aunt Harriet had been in the Batman comics since 1964, after Alfred the butler was temporarily killed off). George Barris, "King of the Kustomizers," built a Batmobile out of a 1957 Ford Futura concept car.

The pilot was shot with Frank Gorshin as the Riddler and Jill St. John as his moll, and West was constantly admonished not to sneak in sight gags to prove he wasn't really that stiff. The show was designed to be broadcast on two nights each week, with a serial-style cliffhanger ending the first half. The visual "Biffs" and "Pows!" were created to save money on the fight scenes. William Dozier, the show's executive producer, was tagged at the last minute to read the "Meanwhile, at stately Wayne Manor..." narrations.

Actors who normally avoided TV lined up to play special guest villains and villainesses. Frank Sinatra allegedly sought, but lost, the role of the Joker to Cesar Romero. Other villains included Burgess Meredith as a perfectly perfidious Penguin and slinky dancer Julie Newmar as Catwoman.

A quickie feature film was shot after the first season. The movie broke with the style of the TV show and was a bomb. The show's novelty began to wear off in the second season. For the third season, 1967-68, *Batman* was trimmed to one episode a week and brought in Yvonne Craig as Batgirl, a character who had just debuted in the comic series, driving a purple motorbike with a big yellow bow in back. But the stories went from camp to self-parody. Audiences got tired, and *Batman* got canceled in March 1968.

Batman was immediately picked up by Filmation and added to its *Superman* cartoon series, now *The Batman/Superman Hour*, with Olan Soule voicing Batman and Casey Kasem as Robin. They repeated their roles in several seasons of Hanna-Barbera's *Super Friends*, starting in 1973. West and Ward reprised their roles in Filmation's *New Adventures of Batman* in 1977, aided by the prankish imp Bat-Mite, a transplant from the gimmicky comics of the early 1960s.

By the 1990s, Batman's credibility had been restored, first by Frank Miller's gritty *The Dark Knight Returns* comic, then by Tim Burton's movies (see entries above). Warner Communications, which now owned DC Comics, aired *Batman: The Animated Series* from 1992 through 1995. While it was tied to the feature *Batman Returns*, the design on this series was more in homage to the Fleischer Brothers' Superman shorts of the 1940s. Gotham City gained a dark deco look, achieved by painting backgrounds on black board.

Batman: The Animated Series, shown on the Fox network, was a marked departure from any other American TV cartoon. The characters had motivations, however melodramatic: Batman was tortured by the memory of his murdered parents, Catwoman tried to reform and work for the environment, the Clock King was an anal-retentive seeking revenge on the mayor for making him late, Two-Face was physically and emotionally scarred, and the Mad Hatter was driven by unrequited love. This cartoon won high ratings among kids in its afternoon slot, topping the Disney afternoon bloc in most markets. It also won two Emmy Awards. *Mask of the Phantasm: Batman the Animated Movie* appeared in 1993. 1999 brought *Batman Beyond* (WB), with a retired Bruce Wayne in his seventies coaching a new Batman, Terry McGinniss.

Bibliography

Alvarez, Gabriel, and Kevin Burke, eds. "The Dark Knight Returns." *Film Threat* Feb. 1994: 8.

Desris, Joe. "Episode Guide: Batman." *Cinefantastique* Feb. 1994: 11-62.

Fleischer, Michael L. *The Encyclopedia of Comic Book Heroes, Vol. 1: Batman.* New York: Collier, 1976.

Garcia, Bob. "Batman, the Animated Series: The 90s New Dark Knight." *Cinefantastique* Feb. 1994: 68-111.

———. "Batman: Camping Up the Comics." *Cinefantastique* Feb. 1994: 8-63.

Garcia, Bob, and Nancy Garcia. "Episode Guide: Batman, The Animated Series." *Cinefantastique* Feb. 1994: 70-111.

Mark McDermott

Battlestar Galactica (1978-1979), at $40 million for 12 episodes including a three-hour pilot, was the most expensive television series ever filmed. The plot was biblical, the art direction Egyptian, and the concept straight out of Erich von Daniken's *The Chariots of the Gods* (1968). During a Munich-like peace conference which the human leader says will offer the tribes "the first peace we have known for a thousand years," the Cylons, robots manipulated by the reptilian Imperious Leader, attack the humans and nearly wipe them out. The survivors of the 12 human colonies in a ragged collection of space ships clustered around the one surviving battlestar set out to escape the Cylons and to discover the settlement of a lost tribe of humans—located on a distant planet called Earth. The fleet is led by the paternal Commander Adama (Lorne Greene). His crew includes his two surviving children Apollo (Richard Hatch) and Athena (Maren Jensen) and their friend Starbuck (Dirk Benedict), Apollo's stepson Boxey (Noah Hathaway), and Boxey's robotic dog, Muffit II.

The proportions of the framework should have allowed for a long run. Indeed, though located in outer space and "another time," the series did address issues of current concern. For example, when Apollo's wife, Serena (Jane Seymour), is killed by the Cylons, Boxey must face the grief of losing a mother, and Captain Apollo encounters many of the dilemmas of single parenthood. Unfortunately, much of the writing did not live up to the spectacular effects, and the show was canceled after one season. Despite the size of the budget and the short duration of the series, *Battlestar Galactica* was a financial success.

Bibliography

Asimov, Isaac. "Sci-fi Gets Zapped by Special Effects in Space Wars Films." *Dallas Times Herald* 17 Sept. 1978: K-7.

Buck, Jerry. "*Battlestar Galactica* Has Interesting Concept." *Dallas Morning News* 17 Sept. 1978: 4C.

Janet P. Sholty

Beach Boys, The, are a musical group whose status as American pop icons was confirmed in 1983 by President Ronald Reagan. Public outrage over the group's being banned by Secretary of the Interior James Watt from performing at a Washington, DC, Fourth of July celebration on the Washington Monument grounds led to the president's upbraiding Watt and inviting the band to perform at the White House.

The three Wilson brothers, Brian (1942-), Carl (1946-) and Dennis (1944-83), were the sons of Audree and Murry Wilson, a machinery salesman and failed songwriter. Singing was part of life in the otherwise inharmonious Wilson home, so it was no surprise when the Wilson brothers, along with cousin Mike Love (1941-) and their friend Al Jardine (1942-), formed a singing group, first dubbed the Pendletones, and later the Beach Boys.

Brian Wilson, who never thought of the Beach Boys as a conventional 1960s pop group, was the first pop artist to write, produce, perform, and arrange his own material with *Surfer Girl* (1963). Under his creative leadership, 1963-1964, the Beach Boys recorded four albums of catchy California pop songs that made them stars.

In 1965, a mental breakdown as well as his desire to concentrate on writing and producing led Brian to stop touring with the group. Recording the instrumental tracks with a group of top-flight studio musicians (including future pop star Glen Campbell), the group would add the vocals when they returned to Los Angeles from the road. *Smile* (out of which came "Good Vibrations") became the most famous unreleased album of all time.

With Brian's breakdown, Carl Wilson took over the creative leadership of the Beach Boys. Working with studio leftovers from the *Smile* sessions, *Smiley Smile* (Capitol Records, 1967) was released to mediocre reviews. Termed "a bunt, not a grand slam" by Carl, *Smiley Smile* was the first album with the production credit going to the Beach Boys and not Brian.

The Beach Boys continued to release albums that received mixed critical and commercial acceptance. The most notable of these, on the Warner Bros. label, were *Sunflower* (1970), *Surf's Up* (1971) with tracks from the 1967 *Smile* session, *Holland* (1972), and *Fifteen Big Ones* (1976), prematurely hailed as Brian's "comeback."

In 1988, the Beach Boys were elected to the Rock and Roll Hall of Fame. The continuing popularity of the Beach Boys was confirmed in 1989 when another of their celebrations of sun and surf, "Kokomo" (co-written by Mike Love), hit the top of the charts to become their biggest chart success since 1966.

Bibliography

Gaines, Steven S. *Heroes and Villains: The True Story of the Beach Boys*. New York: New American Library, 1986.
White, Timothy. "Back from the Bottom." *New York Times Magazine* 26 June 1988: 24+.
Wilson, Brian, with Todd Gold. *Wouldn't It Be Nice: My Own Story*. New York: HarperCollins, 1991.

Martin R. Kalfatovic

Beale Street, east of the Mississippi in Memphis, is one of the most famous streets in the world of jazz. Walking east from the Mississippi riverfront up Memphis's storied Beale Street, one comes upon a small urban park, with a statue dedicated to the park's namesake, W. C. Handy. Except for Schwab's Department Store across the street, this park is all that remains of the legendary mile and a half of urban landscape once known as "the Main Street of Negro America." Despite being created and remembered mostly by people who could not leave a written record of their memories, Beale Street's legacy has survived its origin to become a significant part of American and even world culture. The history of Beale Street is the history of how African-Americans shed the crippling legacy of slavery while maintaining a distinctive and valuable culture. Ostensibly a tribute to "the Father of the Blues," the monument on Beale memorializes, even more than Harlem, the area that best represented the locus of African-American culture in the first half of this century. For W. C. Handy was less the father of the blues than transcriber of the music that could be heard night and day, indoors and out, on Beale.

Like the great river that runs beside it, Beale Street began and thrived as a confluence of various cultures, black, white, and Native American. The land that would become Memphis originally belonged to the Chickasaws, who sold it to the U.S. government in 1818 for five cents an acre. Beale Street itself first came into existence in the 1830s, when most blacks who lived there were likely to be found in the slave quarters, though there were a few free blacks who owned property there as well. After the Civil War, however, the white mansions of Beale Street receded before the flood of newly freed blacks who came to Beale Street to begin what would ultimately become the transformation of the South from a strictly agrarian culture to an industrial and urban one. By the 1920s Beale Street was the mecca of southern black culture, the center of its social life, and a promise of opportunity, exerting its influence and appeal through the 1960s. Although it was said that on Beale, Greeks owned the restaurants, Jews owned the pawnshops, and Italians owned the entertainment, African Americans understood Beale Street to be the place where they could throw off the social and psychological burden of being stigmatized for one's color and celebrate it instead. Beale Street was a magnet for the rural blacks of Arkansas, Mississippi, and western Tennessee, drawing them in with its promise of good times and a better way of life. Long before it became a catchphrase of the civil rights movement, black was beautiful on Beale.

Since the 1980s, Memphis has been rediscovering Beale's heritage, and an effort has been made to recapture its historical significance. Lansky's Men's Wear, where Elvis Presley developed his fashion sense when he was not honing his musical chops during the amateur contests at the Palace Theater, has been turned into the Center for Southern Folklore, where one can learn about Beale Street's most famous graduates: Handy, Jimmy Lunceford, who directed a band that rivaled Duke Ellington's, B. B. King, Bobby "Blue" Bland, and Johnny Ace (together known as "The Beale Streeters"), Furry Lewis, Gus Cannon, Big Bill Broonzy, Robert Wilkins, and even Robert Johnson. B. B. King himself has opened up a blues club, one of many on refurbished Beale Street, meant to keep the spirit of the street, the blues, alive.

Though Beale Street is mostly a museum now, it is a breathing one. Memphis still stages public festivals on and near Beale Street. On the corner of Hernando and Beale, where W. C. Handy stands, one can hear echoes of the past as street bands still gather to play the blues, even if the audience is comprised mostly of tourists. This park, once the center of Beale Street's social life, home to preachers and blues singers alike, no longer is as vibrant as it was, but lives on as a monument to the fertile African-American culture that at one time moved and had its being there. Moreover, because people from all over the world come to marvel at what once took place here as a matter of course, Beale Street retains its distinctive, heterogeneous cultural flavor.

Bibliography

Booth, Stanley. *Rythm* [sic] *Oil*. New York: Pantheon, 1991.
McKee, Margaret, and Fred Chisenhall. *Beale Black and Blue*. Baton Rouge: Louisiana State UP, 1981.

Timothy L. Parrish

Beany and Cecil, a little boy with a propeller-topped yarmulke and his friend the "Sea Sick Sea Serpent," were television staples throughout the 1950s and '60s. Their humor tickled both kids and adults, and their influence is seen in today's cartoons.

For Bob Clampett, the Beany and Cecil pair was another phase in a long creative career. As an animator and director at Warner Brothers, he created Tweety Bird, defined Bugs Bunny, and directed most of their wackiest adventures. In 1946, a talent raid brought Clampett to Columbia's Screen Gems studio, but only as a story man, not director. He left shortly and gravitated toward television.

Time for Beany started in February 1949 on Paramount's KTLA as a 15-minute puppet serial, five days a week throughout the year. Its many fans included Jimmy Stewart,

Albert Einstein, George Bernard Shaw, and Groucho Marx, who wrote that "it's the only kid's show adult enough for my daughter Melinda to watch." *Time for Beany* won Emmys for best children's show of 1949, 1950, and 1952, and lost to *Lassie* for 1954. Cecil's voice, Stan Freberg, provoked controversy by being nominated for best actor of 1950 against José Ferrer and Sid Caesar (the winner was comedian Alan Young, the voice of Uncle Scrooge on *Duck Tales*).

Captain Horatio K. Huffenpuff of the Leakin' Lena was based on Baron Munchausen and Professor Challenger from *The Lost World*, one of Clampett's favorite movies. "Uncle Cap'n's" get-rich-quick plans led Beany and crew on their fabulous adventures. When trouble reared its head, Captain Huffenpuff was first to retreat ("There goes a brave coward," Cecil would remark), leaving Beany and Cecil to save the day.

Cecil, too, was inspired by *The Lost World*. With no arms, Cecil's mouth conveyed expression, like the later Kermit the Frog. The animated Cecil was based on the puppet Cecil's moves and expressions. The heavy, Dishonest John, was part melodrama villain, complete with black cape and "Nyah-Hah-Hah!" and part used-car salesman. He was a "happy villain" who often hollered "Help, Cecil, Help!" when his own plots backfired.

Clampett decided to produce Beany and Cecil as a theatrical cartoon series in 1959, making *Beany and Cecil Meet Billy the Squid* as a demonstration. United Artists liked it, but made Clampett come up with 104 story ideas over the weekend before signing anything. The first few cartoons were shown in theaters overseas, but during production, UA sold the series to Mattel. The toymaker wanted a replacement for the Casper cartoons running on their prime-time *Matty's Funday Funnies* show on ABC. Beany and Cecil had their animated TV debut in January 1962. Clampett got 78 cartoons made.

Since the cartoons were self-contained gag episodes instead of serial adventures, Clampett brought over many of the "punniest" characters and locales from the puppet show, such as Marilyn Mongrel, Careless the Mexican Hairless, Peking Tom Cat, Tear-a-Long the Dotted Lion, No Bikini Atoll.

After the prime-time run ended in December 1962, ABC showed *Beany and Cecil* on daytimes and weekends through 1967. The entire cartoon series was released on home video by RCA-Columbia in the mid-1980s, and syndication films of the puppet show turn up on collector's videos and in broadcast museums.

With continuing interest in *Beany and Cecil*, ABC revived the series for fall of 1988, with Bob Clampett's widow and son, Sody and Robert, supervising. John Kricfalusi, fresh from Ralph Bakshi's *Mighty Mouse: The New Adventures*, produced and directed. However, the principals had a falling out over whether the show should be wild and contemporary like *Mighty Mouse* had been, or just recycle the old cartoons. ABC stranded the cartoon at 7:00 a.m. Saturday morning, then canceled it after six weeks.

Bibliography

Brasch, Walter M. *Cartoon Monickers: An Insight into the Animation Industry.* Bowling Green, OH: Bowling Green State U Popular P, 1983.

Brooks, Tim, and Earle Marsh. "Matty's Funday Funnies." *The Complete Directory to Prime Time Network TV Shows, 1946-Present.* 4th ed. New York: Ballantine, 1988. 498.

Grossman, Gary H. *Saturday Morning TV.* New York: Dell, 1981.

Korkis, Jim. "The Beany and Cecil Story by Bob Clampett as told to Jim Korkis." *Cartoon Quarterly* Winter 1988: 25+.

Lenburg, Jeff. "Beany and Cecil." *The Encyclopedia of Animated Cartoons.* New York: Facts on File, 1991. 284-86.

Mark McDermott

Beatles, The, a British rock and roll group, appeared on the Ed Sullivan *Toast of the Town* TV show on February 9, 1964. When the Beatles performed twice on the hour-long show before an audience of screaming teenagers and smiling adults, they had conquered America. Ed Sullivan exorted the girls to control themselves. The Beatles performed five songs, including "I Saw Her Standing There" and "I Want to Hold Your Hand." This performance drew an audience of 70 million, or 60 percent of all American television, and this began Beatlemania.

The term Beatlemania was coined October 13, 1963, during the Beatles' appearance on *Sunday Night at the London Palladium.* This live TV show was viewed by more than 15 million, and, suddenly, the English sported Beatle haircuts, affected Beatle-style clothing, and talked with a Liverpool scouse slang. It had only been a few years since the band began in the small northern English port city, Liverpool.

In 1957, John Lennon (1940-1980), a Liverpool student at the Quarry Bank School, formed a skiffle band, the Quarry Men. Skiffle music, emphasizing homemade or crude instruments, was influenced by Lonnie Donegan's 1956 hit "Rock Island Line." Then on July 6, 1957, Lennon played at the Woolton Parish Church and met a young guitar player, Paul McCartney (1942-). Then a young guitarist, George Harrison (1943-), was brought in to join the group. After playing in and around Liverpool, the Quarry Men slowly disintegrated.

Only three members of the band persisted—John Lennon, Paul McCartney, and George Harrison continued to play, with their roots in American rock and roll. They changed their name in October 1959 to Johnny and the Moondogs. After auditioning unsuccessfully for British promoter Carroll Levis, they considered giving up their musical dreams.

While working some local Liverpool gigs for Alan Williams, they met young drummer Pete Best (1941-) and he joined the group. After listening to Buddy Holly and the Crickets, the band changed its name to the Beatles. A booking in Hamburg, Germany, for club owner Bruno Koschmider, brought the Beatles into the seedy Indra Club, where they performed eight hours a night and developed a solid following. Soon they graduated to the plush Kaiserkeller Club and became overnight celebrities. It was here that the Beatles covered American rock and roll tunes by Buddy Holly, Carl Perkins, the Coasters, Jerry Lee Lewis, Gene Vincent, and Elvis Presley, and they began writing the songs which made them famous.

While the Beatles were in Hamburg they added Tony Sheridan on a cover version of Ray Charles's "My Bonnie." The Beatles gave this record to Liverpool disc jockey Bob Wooler, who played it regularly at teen dances. Soon people were asking where they could purchase "My Bonnie."

Brian Epstein, who managed the record department at the NEMS store in Whitechapel, was asked to order "My Bonnie" by the Beatles. Epstein, who prided himself on his knowledge of music, had never heard of the group. He found out that the Beatles were performing at a former jazz cellar, the Cavern, and, with his assistant Alistair Taylor taking notes, he wrote out a management agreement.

After signing the Fab Four, Epstein had their hair cut in the distinctive Beatle cut and outfitted the boys in fashionable suits. He also replaced drummer Pete Best with Richard Starkey (1940-). His stage name was Ringo Starr and he was the last piece in the puzzle.

On New Year's Day 1962, the Beatles auditioned for London Records but they were not offered a recording contract. Epstein used his contacts within the music business to secure a recording contract. The Beatles signed with Parlophone Records, a novelty label, and producer George Martin began crafting their hit sound.

The Beatles' first British hit, "Love Me Do," was released on October 5, 1962, and was only a moderate hit. With each subsequent release their popularity soared. By late 1963 the term Beatlemania was used to describe their impact upon England. Their breakthrough single "I Want to Hold Your Hand" brought the Beatles a brief American tour and a chance to perform on Sullivan's popular TV show. Capitol Records signed them to an American recording contract and spent an inordinate amount of money publicizing their first American album, *Meet the Beatles,* which sold 5 million copies.

As the 1960s evolved the Beatles were ahead of their time not only in music but in dress, manners, and morals. After a series of smash American albums, in 1967 the Beatles released the *Sgt. Pepper's Lonely Hearts Club Band* album and it was hailed by *Rolling Stone* magazine as the most influential rock album ever released. The psychedelic music contained in *Sgt. Pepper's Lonely Hearts Club Band* revolutionized rock and roll and helped to popularize an intricate, complex, and innovative approach to rock music.

In 1967, the Beatles were suddenly in a precarious financial position when they were informed that they had a two-million-pound tax bill. So they formed their own corporation and established Apple Records to release their own material. From August 1968 the Beatles produced one hit after another, including "Hey Jude," "Revolution," "Get Back," and "The Ballad of John and Yoko."

But personal, financial, and musical difficulties doomed the Beatles. The Lennon-McCartney songwriting combination began to unravel. Their partnership was dissolved on December 31, 1970, when a lawsuit in the London High Court decreed that their business affairs be put into the hands of an official receiver who would handle the Beatles' affairs.

Bibliography

Coleman, Ray. *Lennon: The Definitive Biography*. New York: HarperCollins, 1985.

The Beatles when they first began performing. Photo courtesy of Sound Recording Archives, Bowling Green State University, Bowling Green, OH.

DeWitt, Howard A. *The Beatles: Untold Tales*. Fremont: Horizon, 1983.

——. *Paul McCartney: From Liverpool to* Let It Be. Fremont: Horizon, 1992.

Norman, Philip. *Shout: The True Story of the Beatles*. London: Hamish Hamilton, 1981.

Howard A. DeWitt

See also
Hard Day's Night, A

Beauty and the Beast (1987-1990), a CBS television series, was touted as a contemporary retelling of the 18th-century folk tale. The female lead of Catherine Chandler was played by Linda Hamilton, whose role as Sarah Connor in *The Terminator* (1984) was reprised to critical acclaim in *The Terminator 2: Judgment Day* (1991). A beautiful and rich lawyer who was brutally attacked and disfigured, Chandler was rescued from Central Park by Vincent, a mysterious figure of beastly appearance and almost superhuman strength. He was played by Ron Perlman, who had previously donned beastly makeup for his roles in *Quest for Fire* (1982) and *The Name of the Rose* (1986). The series focused on the empathic and increasingly romantic relationship between Catherine, who became an assistant district attorney after her beauty was restored with plastic surgery, and Vincent, who inhabited and protected a secret world of outcasts hidden in subterranean New York City.

The series was canceled in the middle of its third year, but edited episodes appeared on the conservative Family Channel during the 1990-91 season. *Beauty and the Beast* persists in worldwide syndication and retains a strong cult following in fandom.

Bibliography
Bacon-Smith, Camille. *Enterprising Women: Television Fandom and the Creation of Popular Myth*. Philadelphia: UP of Pennsylvania, 1992.
Gross, Edward, ed. *Above & Below: A Guide to* Beauty and the Beast. New York: Image, 1990.
Hearne, Betsy. *Beauty and the Beast: Visions and Revisions of an Old Tale*. Chicago: U of Chicago P, 1989.

Rhonda Harris Taylor

Beauty Contests and Pageants, popular throughout America, are a generic type of competition in which a ranking, judging, or measurement of contestants takes place based on some explicit or implicit standard of beauty. Beauty contests or their precursors seem to have existed throughout recorded history and throughout the world's cultures, varying in form, degree of structural complexity, and even in their social or symbolic significance.

Among the oldest references to a beauty contest is the myth of the Judgment of Paris. In this Greek myth, a golden apple was given to the most beautiful goddess on Olympus. Cinderella offers another example. In this story, a ball was held so that the prince could choose a wife from among the kingdom's beauties. Other such ancient tales include the legend of Scheherazade, and from the Bible story of Esther.

Although beauty contests were not established as structured, generic forms until the 20th century, contests where a queen or a king was selected existed with abundance and regularity in 19th-century America. One example is the 19th-century May Day celebration, in which girls selected one from among themselves to be Queen of the May. Another example is the selection of Twelfth Night King and Queen. In this 19th-century tradition, a ring and a bean were baked into two separate cakes. The man who found the ring and the woman who found the bean were chosen king and queen of the evening.

Contests where beauty was a primary and explicit criterion did not emerge until the onset of the Industrial Revolution. Industries associated with leisure sprang up, including carnivals, fairs, and seaside resorts. Women were among the many gimmicks used to attract a paying audience to the new world of relaxation, amusement, and entertainment. Just as freaks, animals, and Indians were flaunted by P. T. Barnum, Buffalo Bill Cody, and others, so too were women.

By the end of the century, the photographic beauty contest would be used by a large number of newspapers as a publicity gimmick. The bathing beauty contest did not emerge until the changing of social attitudes towards bathing. By the late 1800s, bathing for recreational and therapeutic purposes became socially acceptable forms of leisure activities in the U.S. Men, women, and children entered the waters laden with the heavy layers of the period's bathing outfits. The first documented bathing beauty contest was held at Rehoboth Beach, DE, in 1880. The contest also set specific standards. A contestant had to be no more than 25 years old, a minimum of five feet, four inches tall, and a maximum of 130 pounds.

Although by 1920 the bathing beauty contest concept was already in existence, and although many other elements associated with pageantry existed in isolation, it was not until Atlantic City's Fall Frolic of 1921 that all these elements were combined into a new form—the bathing beauty pageant. In 1920, Atlantic City's Business Men's League sponsored a week-long event one week after Labor Day to extend the business associated with the Labor Day weekend. The Fall Frolic of 1920 did not include a beauty contest, but the next year Harry Finley, an Atlantic City newspaperman, suggested that a beauty contest should be part of the Fall Frolic of 1921. Finley proposed that a popularity contest run by newspapers in various cities would increase their circulation. The most popular girl selected in each of the cities would win a trip to Atlantic City. The Hotelmen's Association agreed to entertain each lady, who would, in turn, compete against the other intercity champions. The event, which combined pageantry, recreation events, and theatricality with a beauty contest, was dubbed by the press with such names as "The Atlantic City Pageant," "the Super Carnival," and "the Second Annual Pageant." With each subsequent year, the line of demarcation between the pageantry aspect and the contest portion of the event became more and more blurred. Eventually, the contest became the event, with all the pageantry and entertainment becoming peripheral components. It would not be until 1940 that this event would be officially called the Miss America Pageant, considered by many to be the archetype of all future beauty pageants.

In 1927, the Atlantic City pageant was discontinued. It was revived in 1933 and again discontinued. In 1935, the pageant was once again revived and called the Showman's Variety Jubilee. In 1938, a talent competition was added to the swimsuit and evening-gown portions of the contest. Scholarships were added to the award roster in 1945. Eventually, scholarships would become the Miss America Pageant system's raison d'être. In 1947, an interview was added to the competition elements, and in 1954 the pageant finals were first broadcast on ABC.

The Miss America Pageant would be the source of other pageant systems. In 1951, Miss America, Yolande Betbeze, refused to pose before cameras in a swimsuit. Her unbending attitude instigated a rift between the Miss America Pageant and its sponsor, Catalina Swim Wear. Catalina subsequently discontinued its sponsorship of the Miss America Pageant and allied itself with Universal International. The result was the Miss Universe Pageant in 1952. Pageants were now an accepted and popular concept worldwide. Miss Universe's popularity would rival Miss America's. The Miss Universe system would have national preliminaries including the Miss USA Pageant, founded in 1952. Other international pageants would surface, including Miss World, also established in 1952.

Through the years beauty contests of all kinds have proliferated. There has been a contest for all seasons and occasions. There have been teen pageants, children's pageants and senior's pageants; pageants for married women, fat women, petite women, and nude women; male pageants, gay pageants, drag pageants, bodybuilding pageants, and on the local scale, "wet T-shirt" and "wet-panty" contests in bars. Beauty contests have helped promote everything from beer, to subways, to tanning oil. By the early 1990s, Pay-Per-View's *Bikini Opens* on cable television had become lucrative enterprises. According to *Pageantry* magazine, there are now approximately 3,500 registered American pageant systems with over 3.5 million competitors each year.

Bibliography
Banner, Lois. *American Beauty*. New York: Knopf, 1983.
Deford, Frank. *There She Is: The Lives and Times of Miss America*. New York: Viking, 1978.
Panati, Charles. *Extraordinary Origins of Everyday Things*. New York: Harper, 1987.
Riverol, A. R. *Live from Atlantic City: The History of the Miss America Pageant Before, After, and in Spite of Television*. Bowling Green, OH: Bowling Green State U Popular P, 1992.

A. R. Riverol

Beavis and Butt-head, animated characters created by Mike Judge, first appeared in September 1992 on MTV's *Liquid Television* series as the stars of "Frog Baseball." Going on to become stars of their own MTV series, beginning in March 1993 and ending in November 1997, these addled adolescents garnered high ratings, gained immense popularity, and sparked constant controversy. In the show, these two sniggering, cretinous, libidinous teenagers attended Highland High but spent most of their time watching and commenting on music videos.

Within months of its premiere, an Ohio mother claimed that the series led her five-year-old son to set fire to his family's mobile home, causing the death of his two-year-old sister. Shortly thereafter, Senator Ernest Hollings denounced the show during Senate hearings linking television to violence. MTV's response consisted of moving the show to a late-night berth, editing references to fire from existing episodes and prohibiting such references in new ones, and running a disclaimer before each episode.

Such controversies in no way impeded the show's success. In November 1993, the duo's first book, *This Book Sucks*, was published and became a best-seller. The following month, they starred with Cher in a video of "I Got You Babe" to promote their CD, *The Beavis and Butt-head Experience*. On Super Bowl Sunday in 1994, MTV lured football fans away from that halftime show by presenting Beavis and Butt-head in the Butt Bowl.

Beavis and Butt-head held the distinction of being the most popular show on MTV for two years. Further, the series was successful in persuading such celebrities as comedian Bob Goldthwait, late-night talk-show host David Letterman, MTV news anchor Tabitha Soren, and comedic actor David Spade to provide voices on episodes. Another measure of the show's success was the animated series *Daria*, a spinoff debuting in 1997 and starring Daria Morgendorffer, a fellow student at Highland High. In 1996, Beavis and Butt-head starred in the feature film *Beavis and Butt-head Do America*, with the stars' creator, Mike Judge, serving as director and co-writer.

In 1997, Judge, who had done much of the animation for the first two seasons, supervised production on the series, and provided most of the voices, left *Beavis and Butt-head*

An interactive Beavis and Butt-head at a Consumer Electronics Show. Photo courtesy of Mark McDermott.

for *King of the Hill*, another animated series he created. The series continued without Mike Judge until November 28, 1997, when "Beavis and Butt-head Are Dead," the last original episode, aired.

Bibliography
"Beavis and Butt-Head." *alt.culture*. Online. Internet. 9 March 1998.
"Beavis and Butt-Head Are Dead—For Now." *USA Today* 4 Feb. 1998. Online. Internet. 9 March 1998.
"Beavis & Butt-Head Bite Big One (Heh, Heh) After 4 Years." *Wichita Online* 26 Nov. 1997. Online. Internet. 9 March 1998.
Lawson, Terry. "Big-Screen Debut of Beavis and Butt-Head." *Detroit Free Press* 20 Dec. 1996. Online. Internet. 9 March 1998.
"Leave It to Beavis and Butt-Head." *The Sacramento Bee* 25 Nov. 1997. Online. Internet. 9 March 1998.
Slavin, Glenn. "Beavis and Butt-Head Do America." Online. Internet. 9 March 1998.
Wallner, Chris, and Chris Forman. "The Beavis and Butt-Head FAQ." Online. 9 March 1998.

Linda R. Hill

Bebop (also known as bop, or rebop) is a jazz style that incorporates harmonic dissonance, shifted accents, and long, subtly inflected melodic lines. The music is typically played at very fast tempos. Although bebop certainly had its musical precedents, it was nevertheless characterized as a revolution in jazz by both its supporters and detractors when it emerged in post–World War II America. It continues to be popular with jazz audiences, and many elements of the bebop style have been adopted by contemporary jazz musicians.

Jazz historians trace the development of bebop as a distinct jazz style to the early 1940s. Jazz innovators like guitarist Charlie Christian and drummer Kenny Clarke laid the groundwork for this musical revolution. Christian's style was characterized by a heavy use of dissonance, solos consisting of long series of uninflected eighth notes, and irregular phrasing—all of which became standard practice for bebop musicians. Kenny Clarke's innovations included a shifting of the ground beat from the bass drum—with its large, thudding sound—to the lighter top cymbal. This drumming style provided for an easier musical flow, and consequently created more musical space for the pyrotechnic improvisations of later bebop soloists.

During this early period, New York nightclubs like Minton's and Monroe's became the venues for all-night jam sessions in which the various elements of the style were synthesized. Much has been written about the musical one-upmanship prevalent at these now-famous jam sessions. The breakneck tempos, frequent chord changes, and odd phrasings had the effect—often intended—of keeping inferior musicians off the stand. "The modulations we manufactured were the weirdest," Dizzy Gillespie once told jazz historian Marshall Stearns, "especially if some new cat walked in with his horn and tried to sit in with us." What emerged from these sessions was nothing less than a new musical force. Alto saxophonist Charlie Parker and trumpeter Gillespie are given the lion's share of the credit for "inventing" bebop, with important contributions attributed to pianist Thelonious Monk, bassist Nick Fenton, drummer Kenny Clarke, and others.

Early beboppers—most notably Charlie Parker and Dizzy Gillespie (see entries)—were among the first to incorporate into jazz the advanced harmonies already common in European concert music. More significant perhaps were the beboppers' rhythmic inventions. These included a shift in phrasing from the first and third to the second and fourth beats of a measure, and the playing of long melodic lines without the pronounced syncopation typical of the earlier swing period in jazz. The standard bebop composition consisted of a unison chorus, followed by a series of solos based on the chorus's chord changes, and a concluding repetition of the initial unison chorus. Except for the slower ballads, tempos were typically in excess of 300 beats per minute, highlighting the bebop musician's concern for technical proficiency. Not everybody welcomed this new way of playing jazz. The beboppers' characteristic use of the diminished seventh chord with its flatted fifth and their other harmonic innovations offended the tastes of some older jazz musicians. Eddie Condon, one of the founders of the Dixieland revival movement, spoke for many of these musicians when he commented, "We don't flat our fifths, we drink 'em." Louis Armstrong once referred to bebop as "that modern malice."

In 1945, the Musicraft and Guild labels released what are generally considered to be the first bebop recordings, which have since become jazz classics. The Prestige label later reissued these recordings under the title *In the Beginning*, including such bop standards as "Salt Peanuts," "Shaw 'Nuff," and "Hot House." The disc featured Parker on alto saxophone, Gillespie on trumpet, Cozy Cole and Sid Catlett on drums, Slam Stewart and Curly Russell on bass, pianist Al Haig, and guitarists Remo Palmieri and Clyde Hart. These and other bebop classics emerged at the end of a two-year ban on recordings that had been imposed by the American Federation of Musicians. This ban contributed to the public's sense that the "new" music had no precedent, and the postwar American public was predictably shocked by its "sudden" appearance. Early bebop tunes had mixed effects on jazz audiences. To some, the music sounded harsh and chaotic. Bebop's supporters, however, were won over by its surprising shifts and turns, by its open rebellion against standard musical practice, and by the cool virtuosity of its best musicians. Jazz audiences accustomed to dancing to the easy swing of the big bands were now required to sit down and listen to this challenging new "music for music's sake."

There is some dispute over the origin of the word "bebop." The typical account has it that "bebop" and its variant "rebop" were onomatopoeic inventions designed to mimic the sounds of the new music, in much the same way that the nonsense syllables of scat singers mimic the instruments of the jazz ensemble. Musician Budd Johnson gives this account of the word's origin: "[Dizzy Gillespie] would sing, and actually, that's how I think it got its name, bebop. Because he would be humming this music, and he'd say, 'Ooop bop ta oop a la doo bop doo ba'.... And the cats would say, 'Sing some more of that bebop,' and actually, I think that's how it got its name, because that's the way he would have to sing it to make you get the feeling that he wanted you to play with." Another account attributes the word's origin to a shortened form of the Spanish exclamation "*arriba!*" ("up!" or "go!")—not a surprising theory, given Latin music's pervasive influence on jazz.

Bibliography

Collier, James Lincoln. *The Making of Jazz*. New York: Dell, 1978.

Gitler, Ira. *Swing to Bop*. New York: Oxford UP, 1985.

Rosenthal, David H. *Hard Bop*. New York: Oxford UP, 1992.

Stearns, Marshall W. *The Story of Jazz*. New York: Oxford UP, 1956.

Tirro, Frank. *Jazz: A History*. New York: Norton, 1977.

G. Albert Ruesga

Bee Gees, The, with over 25 Top 40 singles, is one of the most successful all-brother groups. The band's amazing harmonies made them an instant hit during the 1960s when pop songs emphasizing harmonic vocal styles dominated the charts. The core of the band, which began performing in 1958, is Barry Gibb, vocals (1946-), and twins Maurice (bass, vocals) and Robin (vocals) (1947-).

The trio's first chart-topping single, "New York Mining Disaster 1941" (#14), was released in 1967, and their first album, *Bee Gees 1st*, hit #1. They performed on *The Ed Sullivan Show* in March 1968 to rave reviews and released their second album, *Horizontal* (#12), which featured the single "I've Got to Get a Message to You" (#8). Robin left the group for a solo career in 1969, after which Barry and Maurice continued as the Bee Gees and released the adventurous double album, *Odessa* (#20). *The Best of the Bee Gees* also was released and went gold. Barry and Maurice produced the ill-fated British TV program *Cucumber Castle* (1970), starring Maurice's new bride, the Scottish pop singer Lulu, and Vincent Price.

The brothers settled their differences and re-formed their trio in 1971, releasing *2 Years On*, which spawned the #1 single "How Can You Mend a Broken Heart." The Bee Gees did not have another #1 single until their 1975 "Jive Talkin'," taken from the *Main Course* album (#14). The band began its foray into disco in 1976 by releasing the single "You Should Be Dancing" (#1). Subsequently, it released *Children of the World* (#8) and its single "Love So Right" (#3); however, it was not until the release of the soundtrack from the 1977 movie *Saturday Night Fever* (see entry; starring John Travolta), that the Bee Gees became a household name.

With this soundtrack, the Bee Gees helped to define the disco era with the #1 songs "How Deep Is Your Love," "Stayin' Alive," and "Night Fever." The Bee Gees received a Grammy for Best Pop Vocal Performance in 1978 and continued to release #1 singles throughout 1978 and 1979, including "Too Much Heaven," "Tragedy," and "Love You Inside Out." As a result of its performance on the *Saturday Night Fever* soundtrack, the band received recognition for Album of the Year, Best Arrangement for Voices, and Best Producer of the Year at the 1979 Grammy Awards.

Although a 20-track compilation, *Bee Gees Greatest*, released in 1980, went platinum and topped the album charts, the 1980s saw the band's popularity wane. In 1983, the band contributed to another movie starring John Travolta, *Staying Alive*, and the single, "The Woman in You," peaked on the charts at #24. The brothers Gibb pursued various solo projects and did not release another Bee Gees album until their 1987 *E.S.P.* (#96).

Tragedy struck the Bee Gees when their brother Andy Gibb, well known for his songs "Love Is Thicker Than Water" and "Shadow Dancing," died in early 1988. The band released *One* in 1989, and its #7 title track put the Bee Gees back into the charts. The band continued to tour and occasionally released albums including *High Civilization* (1991) and *Size Isn't Everything* (1993). In 1995, the band contributed their cover of "Will You Still Love Me Tomorrow" to the Carole King tribute, *Tapestry Revisited*, and in 1996 released another greatest hits package. The Bee Gees helped define the disco sound and the image of the 1970s and still performs to sold-out audiences.

Bibliography

Bee Gees. *Bee Gees Anthology: Tales from the Brothers Gibb a History in Song 1967-1990*. Milwaukee: Hal Leonard Publishing, 1991.

English, David. *Bee Gees: The Legend of Barry, Robin, and Maurice Gibb*. London: Quartet Books, 1984.

Leaf, David. *Bee Gees: The Authorized Biography*. New York: Pinnacle, 1980.

Rees, Dafydd, and Luke Crampton. *Encyclopedia of Rock Stars*. New York: D. K. Publishing, 1996.

Robert G. Weiner

Belafonte, Harry (1927-), was one of the most influential folksingers of the 1950s and 1960s, a major popularizer of calypso and other Caribbean musics. Born Harold George Belafonte, Jr., in New York, to parents from Jamaica and Martinique, he grew up with West Indian culture. From 1935 to 1940 he lived with his parents in Jamaica before returning to New York. After navy service in World War II, he worked in maintenance and garment industry jobs, then studied acting, eventually joining the American Negro Theater. But acting proved unsatisfying, with few black roles, and he began singing in clubs in the late 1940s. Belafonte signed with Capitol as a pop singer and did some touring. But he had limited success and soured on pop music, opting instead to open a restaurant in Greenwich Village in 1950 that featured folk music. There he began to perform Caribbean music, occasionally examining the folk music archives at the Library of Congress. In 1951 he joined with guitarist Millard Thomas to work up an act. His successful bookings at the Village Vanguard and the Blue Angel got him an RCA record contract, after which he toured the country and joined the cast of *John Murray Anderson's Almanac,* which featured folk songs. The show was adapted for CBS-TV broadcast in June 1955, and Belafonte's performance captivated a national audience. He then played the lead in Oscar Hammerstein's musical play *Carmen Jones* and toured with the folk-music-laced *Three for Tonite*.

He began recording and had a string of hits with a West Indian flavor, including "Jamaica Farewell" (1956), "Mary's Boy Child" (1956), "Day-O (The Banana Boat Song)" (1957), "Island in Sun" (1957), and "Coconut Woman" (1957). Other Caribbean tunes he popularized included "Brown-Skin Girl," "Come Back Liza," and "Matilda." The success of these songs greatly expanded the scope for American popular music. Before the mid-1960s only the Weavers could rival him as folksingers with a mass audience. These recordings and his well-attended concerts also spurred U.S. interest in calypso music in the mid-1950s. Indeed, his LP *Calypso* became the first album in history to sell over a million copies and one of RCA's top sellers ever, spending 31 weeks at the top of the national charts. Belafonte issued many albums that sold well from the mid-1950s through mid-1960s. "Day-O," based on a Trinidad work song, was his all-time biggest selling single.

Ironically, although closely identified with Trinidad calypso in the popular mind, some of his Caribbean-flavored songs actually derived from either the folk and calypso-like *mento* music he heard as a child in Jamaica or the popularized versions adapted or written by other New Yorkers of West Indian heritage, such as Lord Burgess (author of, among others, "Jamaica Farewell" and "Come Back Liza") and Lord Melody. But Belafonte was a versatile talent with wide musical interests. He also recorded and helped popularize American folk songs ("John Henry," "Midnight Special"), folk-tinged songs ("Scarlet Ribbons"), blues ("Jump Down, Spin Around"), black spirituals ("My Lord, What a Mornin'"), romantic songs ("Try to Remember"), international songs (the Israeli "Hava Nageela"), and even the occasional topical song ("These Three Are on My Mind," about the assassinations of the Kennedys and Martin Luther King). In a 1957 poll of high school students, Belafonte tied with Perry Como as the fourth most popular singer, trailing behind only Pat Boone, Elvis Presley, and Tommy Sands.

Along with Pete Seeger and the Weavers, Belafonte helped spur the folk music revival of the later 1950s and early 1960s. Some rock historians believe he was an important source for the gradual merging of folk and rock music that later produced 1960s folk rock. He was also noted as a singer of songs and superb stylist. His choral group, the

Belafonte Folk Singers, were a major influence on popularized folk-based groups such as the Kingston Trio; indeed, the Kingstons acknowledged this debt by including some Caribbean material popularized by Belafonte (such as "Zombie Jamboree" and "All My Sorrows") in their repertoire. Belafonte's several albums of material recorded in concert at Carnegie Hall in 1959-60 (which well convey his electrifying style), as well as his 1962 Christmas album, are considered among his greatest achievements. He appeared in various Broadway shows in the 1950s, in movies like *Carmen Jones* (1954) and *Island in the Sun* (1957), and soon began frequent television work, including performances on popular variety shows. When his recording career waned in the later 1960s he became more active as both an actor and producer, making TV specials for NBC on black themes; he had roles in films like *Buck and the Preacher* and *Uptown Saturday Night*. Later he developed his own film and publishing companies.

His political activism for human rights also increased. He began promoting the civil rights movement in the early 1960s, even incorporating appeals for support of "freedom riders" and voting rights into his popular concerts. Later he became known for his work with UNICEF and his key role in the *USA for Africa* famine relief appeal. Belafonte focused consistent attention on the racist apartheid system in South Africa; in 1988 he issued an album about the South Africa system, *Paradise in Gazankulu.*

Bibliography

Baggelaar, Kristin, and Donald Milton. *Folk Music: More Than a Song.* New York: Crowell, 1976.

Brand, Oscar. *The Ballad Mongers: Rise of the Modern Folk Song.* New York: Minerva, 1962.

Hardy, Phil, and Dave Laing. *The Faber Companion to 20th-Century Popular Music.* London: Faber, 1990.

Hill, Donald. *Calypso Calaloo: Early Carnival Music in Trinidad.* Gainesville: UP of Florida, 1993.

Shaw, Arnold. *Belafonte: An Unauthorized Biography.* Philadelphia: Chilton, 1960.

Craig A. Lockard

Belushi, John (1949-1982), lived his short life synonymous with drug abuse and wild excess. His acting and comedy is overshadowed by his death, which has become a tabloid cliché revisited every time another Hollywood star overdoses on drugs or alcohol.

Belushi first came to the public's attention as a member of the cast of Chicago's influential Second City comedy team. His intense energy and raucous attitude were already evident, and he was constantly pushing the envelope of his comedy. Local reviews made it increasingly clear that he was the "star" of Second City.

Thus, in 1972, when Tony Hendra, the producer-director of *National Lampoon* magazine's satirical musical review *Lemmings*, was assembling his cast, he stopped by Second City to see Belushi. The actor's energy and unpredictability so fascinated Hendra that he offered him a role.

Lemmings received rave reviews and drew sellout audiences, in no small part due to Belushi. Supposed to run for

only six weeks, it ran for ten months. At the end of the run, Belushi decided *National Lampoon* best suited his brand of comedy, so he went to work as a writer, director and actor in the *National Lampoon Radio Hour*. In his biography, *Wired* (later made into a movie), Bob Woodward suggests that it was during this time that Belushi began to use cocaine heavily.

In the spring of 1975 Belushi was invited to join the regular cast of a new television show, *Saturday Night Live* (*SNL*; see entry). The cast, which also included Chevy Chase, Dan Aykroyd, and others, billed themselves as the "Not Ready for Prime Time Players," and set about redefining American television comedy in the irreverent image of Britain's *Monty Python's Flying Circus.* When Chase departed for Hollywood at the end of the first season, Belushi became the new favorite. His most memorable performances included a lunatic weatherman, a Samurai warrior with a short fuse and a long sword, a resentful leader of a band of killer bees, and Joe Cocker.

Like Chase, Belushi was also looking toward Hollywood, beginning his movie career with a bit part in Jack Nicholson's poorly received comedy-Western *Goin' South* (1978). Months before it was released, however, his second movie project was in the theaters and thrilling audiences. Returning to *National Lampoon*, he was cast as the gross undergraduate Bluto Blutarsky in John Landis's *National Lampoon's Animal House* (1978; see entry). The low-budget movie became the biggest earner of the year, critics attributing much of its success to Belushi. He wasn't so fortunate with his next movie, a more serious comedy, *Old Boyfriends* (1979), or in Steven Spielberg's *1941* (1979). To the public, Belushi was Bluto and the Samurai.

Meanwhile, Belushi and Aykroyd were collaborating on sketches for *SNL*, most notably ones involving the Blues Brothers, a pair of bad boy warm-up performers in dark suits and sunglasses. They followed up their television success with a best-selling album and a promotional tour, and then decided to quit television and concentrate on their movie and music careers.

The Blues Brothers, directed by Landis, opened in 1980 to a mixed reception. The *Animal House* audience loved it, seeing the return of the Belushi they had missed in his other movies. Belushi then moved on to his first dramatic role as reporter Ernie Souchak in *Continental Divide* (1981).

Belushi's return to comedy, on *Neighbors* (1981) with Aykroyd, was a critical and box office disaster, in no small part due to the director's idea of having the partners switch roles, with Belushi playing the straight man to Aykroyd's quirky neighbor. The experience convinced Belushi that he needed more control of his movie projects, so he began working on a revision of the script for his next role in a movie to be called *Noble Rot*. He envisioned the role as a return to the Bluto character that his audience was demanding. However, by this time he was taking heroin. He died of a drug overdose before completing the film.

Bibliography.

"Belushi, John." *Current Biography Yearbook*, 1980.

Jacklin Belushi, Judy. *Samurai Widow.* New York: Carroll & Graf, 1990.

"John Belushi." *People Weekly*. Special Issue. Summer 1989: 70.

John Belushi: Funny You Should Ask. Prod. Sue Nadell-Bailey. Videocassette. Weller/Grossman Productions, 1994.

Langdon, Dolly. "The Search for John Belushi." *People Weekly* 11 June 1984: 102-4+.

Woodward, Bob. *Wired: The Short Life and Fast Times of John Belushi.* New York: Simon & Schuster, 1984.

John J. Doherty

Ben-Hur (1880) was a blockbuster of blockbusters, both as novel and movie. The pursuit and exploitation of such best-sellers has been one of Hollywood's prime preoccupations for almost as long as there have been movies. In the case of *Ben-Hur*, the collective history of the interaction between the original novel and the movies (and the theater) is the stuff of which legends—and epic films—are made.

Written by Lew[is] Wallace, a Union general in the Civil War, *Ben-Hur* went on to become the best-selling American novel of the 19th century and has been in print ever since. While it is essentially an inspirational work (albeit an action-packed one) of historical fiction, its subtitle, *A Tale of the Christ,* indicates that its narrative is set against the backdrop of the life of Jesus; the story is framed by the birth of Christ and the Crucifixion. The action is centered in the Holy Land and, in essence, follows the sufferings of Judah Ben-Hur and his family at the hands of the Roman army of occupation. While much of the story focuses on his desire for revenge against his former friend, the ambitious Roman soldier Messala, Judah eventually comes to believe in the message of peace and brotherhood preached by Jesus.

The novel's initial impact was overwhelming. It is credited with removing much puritanical opposition to fiction and reached a huge audience whose religious views had previously discouraged reading a novel. Its popularity led to Marc Klaw's and Abraham Erlanger's immense and expensive stage production. Replete with large crowd scenes, sea battle, and chariot race, it opened in late 1899 and is still regarded as one of the most spectacular theatrical productions ever.

In 1921, the rights were sold to a consortium (for $600,000), which in turn offered them for sale at the then-astronomical price of $1 million. Unfortunately, this hefty price tag put the property out of everyone's reach. However, the following year the Goldwyn company, on the lookout for a prestigious subject, struck an unprecedented deal by which they would produce a high quality adaptation in return for half the profits.

The production was put in the hands of June Mathis, Goldwyn's powerful head scenarist, who decided, among other things, that *Ben-Hur* would be filmed in Italy and Egypt. What followed was one of the most turbulent productions in all of film history. The planned film, which included staging a full-scale sea battle as well as building the enormous Circus Maximus and Joppa Gate sets, would have been daunting enough under the best possible circumstances. However, director Charles Brabin and his crew were beset by labor disputes and countless delays in Mussolini's Italy as

Photo courtesy of Popular Culture Library, Bowling Green State University, Bowling Green, OH.

well as a general aura of chaos that seems to have engulfed the entire company.

Back in Hollywood, however, the Goldwyn company merged with the Metro and Louis B. Mayer companies to form Metro-Goldwyn-Mayer (MGM); Mathis was dismissed, Brabin was replaced by Fred Niblo, and the title role went to Ramon Novarro instead of George Walsh. Eventually the entire production, still suffering from problems, returned to Hollywood.

The film itself (1925) is a magnificent achievement. Its enormous sets, which were in part realized via some ingenious special effects work, are among the most impressive ever created for the screen and its action sequences among the most memorable. The legendary chariot race is often cited as one of the greatest action sequences ever filmed. For the most part the film is skillfully acted—Carmel Myers's Iras, and to a lesser extent Francis X. Bushman's Messala, being the only exceptions worth noting—and Ramon Novarro stands out as a very appealing hero. It surpasses its celebrated 1959 remake in overall impact and excellence. Kevin Brownlow does not exaggerate in describing it as "a sort of Dunkirk of the cinema: a humiliating defeat transformed, after heavy losses, into a brilliant victory."

Like its 1925 predecessor, the 1959 remake came at a critical point in MGM's history. However, this time around it did not represent a bold beginning, but rather an attempt to recapture the grandeur that was MGM—and in so doing, save the studio. The finished film more than lived up to the hoopla that surrounded its planning and production. Particularly noteworthy are its massive sets and meticulous attention to historical accuracy and detail; filmed in the MGM Camera 65 widescreen process, and featuring an impressive stereophonic soundtrack scored by Miklos Rosza, it can accurately be described as an awesome experience. Charlton Heston's Judah Ben-Hur is strong and aggressive as well as warm and intelligent. Outstanding in supporting roles are Stephen Boyd and Jack Hawkins (British actors handled the Roman roles in order to emphasize differences of class and culture) and Hugh Griffith. While the film is essentially faithful to the Wallace novel, it does present a somewhat more secularized interpretation. At the end, however, there is no question of Judah's conversion to Christianity.

The film was a tremendous popular and box-office success and won a record 11 Academy Awards for 1959, including those for best picture, director, actor (Heston) and supporting actor (Griffith). Significantly, while an Academy Award nomination for best screenplay was among its 12 nominations, this is the only category in which *Ben-Hur* failed to win on Oscar night. One can also argue that the film represents the final crowning achievement of both MGM, greatest of all film studios, and the studio system itself.

Bibliography
Brownlow, Kevin. *The Parade's Gone By...* New York: Knopf, 1968.
Hay, Peter. *MGM—When the Lion Roars.* Atlanta: Turner, 1991.
Magill's Survey of Cinema. English Language Films; First Series. Vol. 1. Englewood Cliffs: Salem, 1980.
Magill's Survey of Cinema. Silent Films. Vol. 1. Englewood Cliffs: Salem, 1982.
Morsberger, Robert E., and Katherine M. Morsberger. *Lew Wallace: Militant Romantic.* New York: McGraw-Hill. 1980.
Fred Guida

Bennett, Tony (1926-), one of America's more prominent and long-lasting popular singers, finally had his career fading until, in early 1994, he became the subject of a nationally telecast program focused on his later career. The program told how Bennett's son, through skillful management and public relations and a lot of determination, helped Bennett resurrect his failing career (for the second time). It also showed that Bennett was still performing ballads and other older-style songs, most notably "I Left My Heart in San Francisco," the song that he made famous and that made him famous. These facets of the program suggested that nothing basically had changed since Bennett had begun his vocal career in the early 1950s. Yet when the program turned to the audiences Bennett was delighting in the 1990s, there was clear evidence that there had been a substantial shift in his fan base. Not only was Bennett still pleasing middle-aged and older audiences, but starting with his second revival in the 1980s, teenagers and young adults also began to flock to his concerts. These younger fans, in addition, were not confined to clean-cut youth apparently from middle-class fami-

lies. Male earrings, tattoos, and biker garb could be spotted in the audiences profiled on the television program.

Born Anthony Dominick Benedetto in Queens, NY, Bennett pursued, for a while, commercial art studies at the Manhattan School of Industrial Art. After serving in the army in World War II, he received some vocal training from Miriam Spirer. Inspired in part by the talents of Mabel Mercer, "a singer's singer" who also influenced Frank Sinatra, Peggy Lee, Nat King Cole, Johnny Mathis, and Barbra Streisand, Bennett decided on a vocal career. In his youth, he had been a singing waiter in a Queens Italian restaurant, and after the war made occasional appearances as a singer. Until he became a successful full-time entertainer, however, he took interim jobs, such as a hotel elevator operator.

His first break came in 1950. He was a contestant on *Arthur Godfrey's Talent Scouts* (his first television appearance) and also on *Songs for Sale,* hosted by Jan Murray. As a result of his television work, he appeared in a Greenwich Village nightclub at a time when Pearl Bailey was at the top of the bill. During this important nightclub gig, Bob Hope heard Bennett and had him join Hope's national touring company. After the tour with Hope, Bennett was "discovered" by yet another major show business figure, Mitch Miller. As a creative director at Columbia Records, Miller furthered the careers of a number of famous artists, including Rosemary Clooney, Johnnie Ray, Johnny Mathis, Doris Day, Guy Mitchell, and Jo Stafford. In 1950 Miller asked Bennett to record an old song by lyricist Al Dubin and composer Harry Warren, "The Boulevard of Broken Dreams" (1933). After this disc became Bennett's first successful recording, he followed up with several other records in 1951, Hank Williams's "Cold Cold Heart," Arthur Hammerstein and Dudley Wilkinson's "Because of You," Fred Wise and Al Frisch's "I Won't Cry Anymore," and Renée Borek, Carl Nutter, and King Guion's "Solitaire." All of these were hits, and *Cash Box* called him the year's No. 1 male vocalist. Other nightclub and television appearances were also very successful, and in 1953 he had his first smash hit, "Rags to Riches." The creators of "Rags to Riches" were Richard Adler and Jerry Ross (see entry), who were to take Broadway by storm with the brilliant musicals *Pajama Game* (1954) and *Damn Yankees* (1955).

Another huge success came with Bennett's recording of "Stranger in Paradise" in 1955. The song, from the 1953 Broadway hit *Kismet,* was a blend of lyrics by George "Chet" Forrest and Robert Wright and music borrowed from the Russian composer Alexander Borodin. Bennett's recording was on the charts for 16 weeks, and reached No. 1 in sales. Other late 1950s recordings were Bernice Petkere's 1933 "Close Your Eyes" in 1955, Ted Varnick and Nick Acquaviva's "In the Middle of an Island" in 1957, and lyricist Carolyn Leigh and composer Cy Coleman's pair of 1958 songs "Firefly" and "It Amazes Me." Despite these successes, rock and roll, which was not compatible with Bennett's talents and disposition, more or less pushed him into the background by the end of the 1950s.

His career was revived in 1962 by a single song. Douglass A. Cross and George Cory had written the tender ballad

"I Left My Heart in San Francisco" in 1954. Bennett received two Grammys for that monumental recording. "I Left My Heart in San Francisco" became his theme song and became so closely associated with him that one tends to overlook all his other fine recordings. Among the other records by Bennett after 1962 were "The Good Life" (1963), written by Sacha Distel and Jack Reardon; "I Want to Be Around" (1959, recorded in 1963), written by Johnny Mercer and Sadie Vimmerstedt; "Who Can I Turn To (When Nobody Needs Me)" (1964), written by Leslie Bricusse and Anthony Newley; "For Once in My Life" (1965), written by Ronald Miller and Orlando Murden; "Love Story" or "Where Do I Begin" (1970), written by Carl Sigman and Francis Lai; and "The Summer Knows" or "The Theme from *The Summer of '42*" (1971), written by Alan and Marilyn Bergman.

All of these were older-style songs, not rock pieces, which, along with revivals of earlier compositions, were the kind of song Bennett had in his repertory over the decades. Among the older songs Bennett recorded were "Chicago" (1922) by Fred Fisher, "Get Happy" (1930) by lyricist Ted Koehler and composer Harold Arlen, "Strike Up the Band" (1930) by lyricist Ira Gershwin and composer George Gershwin, "Just One of Those Things" (1935) by Cole Porter, "Tenderly" (1947) by Jack Lawrence and Walter Gross, "Far Away Places" (1949) by Joan Whitney and Alex Kramer, and "Moments to Remember" (1955) by lyricist Al Stillman and Robert Allen. He also made albums focusing on Count Basie, Irving Berlin, Duke Ellington, and Rodgers and Hart, as well as on Christmas songs.

Bennett never deviated from this sort of repertory even when his career was eclipsed in the years before 1962 and again in the 1970s. His steadfastness paid off, as demonstrated by his first revival in 1962 and his second revival in the 1980s. His career spans two generations and his style and winning ways bridge the gap between the generations.

Bibliography

Ewen, David. *All the Years of American Popular Music.* Englewood Cliffs: Prentice-Hall, 1977.

Jasper, Tony. *Tony Bennett: A Biography.* London: Allen, 1984.

William E. Studwell

Benson, George (1943-), has carved out a place in music history for himself with a career far more wide-ranging in repertoire, artistic skill, and longevity than most casual fans imagine.

Benson was born in Pittsburgh. A nightclub singer by the time he was eight years old, he recorded "It Should Have Been Me" in 1954 at the age of 11 and formed his own rock and roll band in 1960 at 17. Benson moved to New York City in the early 1960s, but not before he had begun to establish himself as a first-rate guitarist. From 1962 to 1965, Benson played for Brother Jack McDuff, with whose quartet he performed at the Antibes-Juan-les-Pins Jazz Festival in 1964 and in a television broadcast from Stockholm with Jean-Luc Ponty. He also worked with Herbie Hancock and Wes Montgomery, who was perhaps the most significant influence on Benson's guitar playing, a style characterized by smoothness, agility, and nontraditional lines borrowed from other types of music.

Benson won a Columbia contract in 1966 and was a sideman on Miles Davis's 1968 album *Miles in the Sky*; he also served as a sideman for other big names, such as Freddie Hubbard, Ron Carter, Billy Cobham, and Lee Morgan. On Benson's own albums, Davis, Earl Klugh, and Joe Farrell appeared, a sign that the music world was taking his talent quite seriously. In 1969, Montgomery died, and Benson was widely believed by critics to be the logical successor to Montgomery in the vein of inoffensive but smoothly skilled music that he had played.

In 1970, Benson covered the entire Beatles album *Abbey Road* with his own *The Other Side of Abbey Road*, a reinterpretation of every cut on the album. This sort of cover (along with his own original work in the popular vein) became one of his career tracks, an enormously lucrative one that included work on music for films and several original jazz-pop hits (like "Give Me the Night" and "On Broadway") that netted him enough money to keep him working in his second track, traditional jazz and blues. The money-making covers usually were totally redone, often to the point of unrecognizability but almost always to at least some critical acclaim and the support of audiences.

In the more traditional mode, Benson worked with Earl Klugh, Aretha Franklin, and more recently Count Basie and his orchestra. Occasionally, Benson would touch both tracks, as when he recorded Nat King Cole's "Tenderly" and "Nature Boy." For his part, Benson has contended that it was his work in jazz that established him as an artist rather than a mere celebrity.

Benson's collaboration with Count Basie, and after Basie's death the Count Basie Orchestra, was typically serendipitous and fruitful. Benson performed with Basie at Carnegie Hall in 1983 and got interested in playing big band music. After getting some hints from Basie that he wanted to record with him, Benson went home after the concert and wrote "Basie's Bag." Basie loved the song and Benson began to gather other material for an album, but before they could get it rolling, Basie died. Benson later revived the project, and the result was 1990's *Big Boss Band*, a mix of old and new that won rave reviews from both critics and fans.

Throughout his career, audiences have hooked into Benson's musical trademark, the playing of a guitar line, often an impossibly complex one, while singing in exact unison with the line. Benson considers himself a singer first, but he believes his most lasting contribution to be as a guitarist, somewhat as Nat King Cole's work as a pianist is in some ways even more historically significant than his popular vocal legacy.

Bibliography

Bourne, Michael. "George Benson: Back to Basics, Back to Basie." *Down Beat* 58.1 (1991): 16-19.

Kernfeld, Barry, ed. *The New Grove Dictionary of Jazz.* London: Macmillan, 1988.

Larkin, Colin, ed. *The Guinness Encyclopedia of Popular Music.* 4 vols. Middlesex, U.K.: Guinness, 1992.

Stephen Finley

Bergen, Candice (1946-), is best known as an actress for the comedic talents she displayed as the title character in the award-winning television sitcom *Murphy Brown* (CBS, 1988-97; see entry). Her other credits include her rich and varied career for more than 20 years as a cover-girl model, photojournalist, author, and film star.

Bergen's success as a comedic actress might have been genetic, as she suggested to interviewers, but it was long in arriving. As a child she had grown up in the rarefied atmosphere of Hollywood's golden age. She had all the benefits and liabilities of being the only daughter of the famous ventriloquist Edgar Bergen (see next entry) and of the former model Frances Westerman. But she also had grown up in the shadow of an unusual sibling rival, the wise-cracking puppet Charlie McCarthy, with memories of her father balancing her on one knee and the puppet on the other and seeming to make two dummies speak. In her early acting career unkind critics had said, "If you think Charlie was the wooden one, wait till you see his sister in ————."

After the best schools in Hollywood and a year at a Swiss boarding school, she attended the University of Pennsylvania for two years. However, she spent so much time in New York working as a successful cover-girl model (*Vogue, McCall's*) that she flunked out of school. Modeling meant she became fully self-supporting at the age of 19 and led to her first film role in *The Group* (1966). In her next 12 films she was often locked into Ice Queen roles, admired for her flawless beauty but criticized for her lack of acting ability. Her best known roles were in *The Sand Pebbles* with Steve McQueen (1966), *Carnal Knowledge* with Jack Nicholson (1971), and *The Wind and the Lion* with Sean Connery (1975).

Her real interest during that period was in travel and photojournalism. In her outstanding autobiography, *Knock Wood* (1984), she apologized for her lackluster performances, explaining that she selected film roles most often for their interesting locations. In the movie *Gandhi* (1982), she played the role of the photojournalist Margaret Bourke-White, a role she might have played in real life. She also worked as a TV journalist on *AM America* and *Today*, and wrote magazine articles about diverse topics from Charlie Chaplin to a Masai witch doctor.

Her comic potential was glimpsed initially in several guest appearances on NBC's *Saturday Night Live*. Her real turning point came in *Starting Over* (1979) as Burt Reynolds's ex-wife, a surprisingly funny, piano-pounding composer, in which she showed the world how badly a girl could sing, and was nominated for an Academy Award as best supporting actress. In *Rich and Famous* (1981), a *roman a clef* film covering 20 years in the lives of two successful women writers, she played the role of a smug gushing housewife who wrote lucrative potboilers.

In September 1980 Bergen married the Paris-based film director Louis Malle (*Pretty Baby, Atlantic City, My Dinner with André*, and *Au Revoir les Enfants*), and in 1985 their daughter, Chloe, was born. In a surprising interview for *Playboy* magazine, she explained that those two events were the most special in her life, and without her family she could not imagine being able to bear the pain of playing Murphy Brown, the successful journalist whose only close relationship is with her house-painter.

Bibliography
Bergen, Candice. *Knock Wood.* New York: Linden, 1984.

Ann Schoonmaker

Bergen, Edgar (1903-1978), is famous for his ventriloquist radio act which surprisingly became one of radio's most popular programs. A home audience cannot see whether a ventriloquist moves his lips. But from their debut on Rudy Vallee's (1903-1978) *Royal Gelatin Hour* in 1936, through their own shows sponsored by Chase and Sanborn (1937-48), Coca-Cola (1949-52), Richard Hudnut (1952), Kraft (1954), and CBS, Bergen and his dummy Charlie McCarthy clicked until 1956. Perhaps their appeal had less to do with Bergen's agile larynx than with the way he exploited proven themes. Restrained, parental, didactic, Bergen contrasted to Charlie's cocky self-indulgence.

Other entertainments had conditioned fans to enjoy battles between responsible and chaotic characters. *The Katzenjammer Kids* discomfited their elders; infantile Stan Laurel sabotaged the relatively mature Oliver Hardy; Baby Snooks began to pester "Daddy" Higgins in 1936; Red Skelton's "mean widdle kid" tormented Gramma in 1937. Bergen's duels with Charlie were sparked by the latter's incivility. Although dressed in upper-crust top hat, tuxedo, and monocle, he spoke like the feisty newsboy whose features Bergen copied. Sometimes his bluntness ("So help me, I'll mow yuh down!") seemed appropriate. W. C. Fields, a regular for the first five months, loathed him. They traded insults about Fields's red nose or Charlie's flawed family "tree." Even when Charlie spoke politely, his motives remained selfish.

Beautiful women like Dorothy Lamour, Rosalind Russell, and Jane Powell stimulated him. Two other dummies emphasized additional divisions. Mortimer Snerd arrived in 1938, a good-willed, simple-minded bumpkin. A foil to Charlie's street smarts, Mortimer profited from radio's benign view of country folk. Mortimer spoke like Walt Disney's Goofy and eliminated the tragedy hovering around Dust Bowl-era farmers. Spinster Effie Klinker, introduced in 1944, pursued men as eagerly as Charlie hunted women. Cast members also highlighted Charlie's traits. MC Don Ameche, suave star of *Betty and Bob*, pointed up Charlie's lack of sophistication; as John Bickerson, Ameche duplicated the dummy's bumptiousness. Ray Noble, the poised orchestra leader, reminded audiences that Charlie's school experience was negative and his escapades with pal Skinny Dugan nearly criminal. Pat Patrick arrived in the late 1940s as flutey-voiced Ercil Twing. His distraught plea ("Fray-unds, I say, fray-unds") emphasized the show's continual balancing of harmony and disruption.

On film, Charlie and Edgar retained their split roles: *Look Who's Laughing* (1941) has Edgar help the Fibber McGees in a land purchase. *Here We Go Again* (1942) casts him as a shy scientist. In both, Charlie flirts, brags, and (impersonated by a small actor) runs unsupervised.

Bibliography
Dunning, John. *Tune In Yesterday: The Ultimate Encyclopedia of Old-Time Radio, 1925-1976.* Englewood Cliffs: Prentice-Hall, 1976.
Harmon, Jim. *The Great Radio Comedians.* Garden City: Doubleday, 1970.
Packer, Eleanor. *A Day with Charlie McCarthy and Edgar Bergen.* n.p.: McCarthy, 1938.

James A. Freeman

Berkeley, Busby (1895-1976), famous for having created the Hollywood film musical (see Musical Films) as a genre distinct from the stage musical, combined imaginative photography with spectacular scenery, military formations, geometric designs, beautiful women, and in some production numbers, dramatic action to realize a scope and vision unobtainable on the live stage. His innovations inspired major Hollywood studios until, in the late 1950s, the musical declined, victim of rising costs, failing studio systems, and competition from television.

Born Busby Berkeley William Enos in Los Angeles, Berkeley, son of players with the Frawley Repertory Company, first appeared on stage at the age of five. He regularly accompanied his mother to the theater and toured with her. Sent to Mohegan Lake Military Academy in New York, from which he graduated in 1914, Berkeley joined the army when the United States entered World War I. In France, he was charged with parade drill. He devised intricate formations, giving section leaders instructions that allowed the detailed maneuvers to be performed without spoken orders. In Germany, after the Armistice, he was assistant entertainment officer. From these experiences, he learned the stagecraft, the demands of popular audiences, and a fascination with the choreographed movements of masses of people that contributed to his unique Hollywood style.

After the war, he acted, produced, and directed road and stock companies. Although he never studied dance, he became dance director (the word "choreographer" was rarely used) for 21 Broadway shows, including *A Connecticut Yankee* (1927), *Present Arms* (1928), and the *Earl Carroll Vanities of 1928.* His Broadway work familiarized him with the visual patterning of female bodies and lavish costumes that brought audiences to Florenz Ziegfeld's *Follies* from 1907 to 1931 and to its competitors, including the *Vanities*, and the extravagant scenery that had been a feature of popular revues since the 1860s (see Revue).

Unimpressed by what he had seen of film musicals, Berkeley reluctantly accepted Samuel Goldwyn's invitation in 1930 to direct dances for the film version of Eddie Cantor's stage hit *Whoopee.* He stayed in Hollywood as dance director for a number of MGM, Universal, and Goldwyn films, including Cantor's *The Kid from Spain* (1932).

Darryl F. Zanuck, Warner Brothers production head, sensed that a different kind of musical could succeed and gave Berkeley freedom and an unlimited budget. In films from *42nd Street* (1933), *Footlight Parade* (1933), *Roman Scandals* (1933, for Goldwyn), to *Dames* (1934), and *Gold Diggers of 1935*, Berkeley created a distinctly cinematic musical form. He hired only beautiful and intelligent chorus women and allowed the camera eye to caress the face of each individually. Increasingly complex diagonal angles, traveling shots, and rhythmic cutting were designed in advance and worked out with his dancers, and production numbers were shown in their entirety.

Berkeley's influence was apparent in such films as *Flying Down to Rio* (1933) and *The Great Ziegfeld* (1936). His work continued, although his reputation waned. His later credits include, among many others, *Babes in Arms* (1939), *Strike Up the Band* (1940), *Babes on Broadway* and *Ziegfeld Girl* (1941), *For Me and My Gal* (1942), *The Gang's All Here* (1943), *Take Me Out to the Ball Game* (1949), and *Million Dollar Mermaid* (1952). In 1962, interest in his work was revived by the San Francisco Film Festival, followed by tributes in New York, London, Munich, and Vienna. In 1971, at age 75, he was supervising producer for a successful Broadway revival of *No, No, Nanette* with Ruby Keeler. He died in Palm Desert, CA.

Bibliography
Delamater, Jerome. *Dance in the Hollywood Musical.* Ann Arbor: UMI Research, 1981.
Mordden, Ethan. *The Hollywood Musical.* New York: St. Martin's, 1981.
Pike, Bob, and David Martin. *The Genius of Busby Berkeley.* Reseda: CFS, 1973.
Sennett, Ted. *Hollywood Musicals.* New York: Abrams, 1981.
Thomas, Tony, and Jim Terry with Busby Berkeley. *The Busby Berkeley Book.* Greenwich: New York Graphic Society, 1973.

Betty Richardson

Berlin, Irving (1888-1989), was one of America's early and great composers of folk-like popular songs. He became a fixture in the musical world, successfully creative for about half a century. With more than 1,000 compositions, including at least 10 real classics and a number of standards, he was the king of popular music during the first half or so of the 20th century. He wrote scores for 20 Broadway musicals, yet although he did very well on Broadway, he did much of his best work away from this genre. So, when one thinks of Berlin, one cannot focus chiefly on his shows. For in contrast to Cole Porter, Rodgers and Hart, Rodgers and Hammerstein, Jerome Kern, and the Gershwin brothers as a team, all contemporaries, he was not primarily linked to his own Broadway musicals. Like George Gershwin, who switched to other modes when he composed his three classical masterpieces, Berlin was more successful with the music he wrote for his 17 movie musicals, his army revues, the songs interpolated in the musicals of others, and the many separately published songs.

Israel Baline was born in Temun, Siberia, the youngest of eight children in a poor family headed by the cantor of a small synagogue. When Israel was four, his village was ravaged by one of the periodic pogroms encouraged by the tsars. The Baline family fortunately escaped death, and soon after the incident left Russia for America. At the age of 14

Berlin left home and earned a marginal existence by singing popular songs indoors and outdoors. Sometimes he would get steady singing engagements, but always for low pay. By the time he was 18 he became a singing waiter at Pelham's Café in New York's Chinatown. While there he learned to play piano by ear (self-taught, and preferring the black keys), and he also started to write songs. In 1907 he composed his first song, the lyrics for "Marie from Sunny Italy." On the sheet music was printed "I. Berlin," and Israel Baline had become Irving Berlin. The next year he wrote both words and music for "The Best of Friends Must Part" and for "She Was a Dear Little Girl." The latter song ended up in a Broadway musical, *The Boys and Betty* (1908).

Berlin left the Chinatown restaurant for another position as a singing waiter at a more prestigious location in 1909, and continued his songwriting. Although he did not create any really memorable songs until 1911, some of his compositions before then aided the careers of Eddie Cantor and Fanny Brice. In 1911, Berlin became a famous artist with three enduring songs. "Woodman, Woodman, Spare that Tree" appeared in the 1911 *Ziegfeld Follies.* "Everybody's Doin' It" (1911) was probably the main song in the turkey-trot dance craze of that era. Most of all, he wrote "Alexander's Ragtime Band," the first of his classics, in 1911. Berlin began to create complete scores for Broadway. *Watch Your Step* came in 1914 and *Stop! Look! Listen!* in 1915. While most of Berlin's works at the time were syncopated ragtime pieces, he wrote a good non-ragtime piece, "Play a Simple Melody," for *Watch Your Step.* Bing Crosby and his son Gary were to revive it in a 1950 recording. At about the same time, Judy Garland and Fred Astaire revived "I Love a Piano," from *Stop! Look! Listen!* in the 1948 classic film *Easter Parade.*

Despite two prestigious collaborations during the World War I era, with Victor Herbert on "The Century Girl" (1916) and with George M. Cohan on "Cohan Revue of 1918," Berlin did not produce any more notable songs until after his 1918 induction into the Army. While stationed at a camp in New York State, Berlin created an all-soldier show, *Yip, Yip, Yaphank* (1918). The production included a good standard, "Mandy," plus the rousing classic "Oh, How I Hate to Get Up in the Morning" introduced by Berlin. When World War II rolled around, Berlin wrote another all-soldier revue, *This Is the Army* (1942). That show introduced another memorable song, "This Is the Army, Mr. Jones" and featured Berlin, then in his mid-fifties, personally reviving "Oh, How I Hate to Get Up in the Morning."

Another Berlin classic appeared in 1927. "Blue Skies" was inserted in Rodgers and Hart's 1926 musical *Betsy,* which was already running. Al Jolson sang "Blue Skies" in the pioneering film *The Jazz Singer* (1927) and also in his movie biography *The Jolson Story* (1947). Bing Crosby sang it in the 1946 film *Blue Skies* and in the 1954 film *White Christmas* (with Danny Kaye). In 1929 Berlin created the lively standard "Putting on the Ritz," which appeared in the 1930 film of that name. Between 1930 and 1932, Berlin lost his confidence and wrote nothing. But after an earlier unpublished song, "Say It Isn't So," was successfully introduced

by Rudy Vallee in 1932, he regained his zeal for composition. The year 1932 also saw another fine standard, "How Deep Is the Ocean," and the big hit "Let's Have Another Cup o' Coffee." The latter song appeared in Berlin's musical *Face the Music* and was later used to promote a major brand of coffee on the radio.

In 1933, one of Berlin's better musicals, *As Thousands Cheer,* produced one of his best songs, the classic "Easter Parade" (originally, the song had been written with another lyric: "smile and show your dimple"). In 1942, Bing Crosby sang "Easter Parade" in the film *Holiday Inn,* and in 1948 Judy Garland sang it as she strutted down the avenue in the film *Easter Parade.* Also in the 1933 show was the brash standard "Heat Wave." Berlin wrote another standard, "Cheek to Cheek," for the 1935 film *Top Hat* (see entry), starring Fred Astaire and Ginger Rogers. Another film, *On the Avenue* (1937), introduced the enduring "I've Got My Love to Keep Me Warm."

After a trip to Europe in 1938, Berlin in a highly patriotic mood wrote "God Bless America." Introduced on radio by Kate Smith in November 1938, "God Bless America" was published in 1939 and since then has been a tremendous favorite and one of the U.S.'s unofficial national anthems. Mostly for this outstanding song, President Dwight Eisenhower presented Berlin with a gold medal. In 1942, another of Berlin's greatest songs, "White Christmas," was introduced by Bing Crosby in the film *Holiday Inn.* That dreamy Christmas classic has become a holiday phenomenon, with many recordings and a 1954 movie, *White Christmas,* honoring it. Another notable song, "Happy Holidays," was also in *Holiday Inn.*

Berlin continued his streak of genius with his greatest musical, *Annie Get Your Gun,* in 1946. With Ethel Merman as Annie Oakley, the show presented several fine Berlin songs, "Anything You Can Do," "You Can't Get a Man with a Gun," "Doin' What Comes Natur'lly," "Sun in the Mornin'," "They Say It's Wonderful," "The Girl That I Marry," and most of all the blockbuster "Show Business" (or "There's No Business Like Show Business"). With enough memorable songs to create two or three successful productions, *Annie Get Your Gun* is among the elite of Broadway musicals. Subsequent musicals produced the hits "Let's Take an Old-Fashioned Walk" (in *Miss Liberty,* 1949) and "It's a Lovely Day Today" plus "The Best Thing for You" (in *Call Me Madam,* 1950). Berlin's final Broadway show, *Mr. President* (1962), left nothing of consequence.

Probably Berlin's last top song was "Count Your Blessings" (1952), introduced by Bing Crosby and sung again by him in a duet with Rosemary Clooney in the 1954 film *White Christmas.* With his career effectively approaching closure in the 1950s, Berlin could count his many blessings. An unparalleled talent in American popular song, Berlin wrote the best Christmas song of the 20th century, the best secular Easter song, the unofficial theme song of the entertainment industry, one of the U.S.'s unofficial national anthems, and many other good compositions. As one of his early songs proclaimed, Berlin did "Say It with Music."

Bibliography

Bergreen, Laurence. *As Thousands Cheer: The Life of Irving Berlin.* New York: Viking, 1990.

Ewen, David. *The Story of Irving Berlin.* New York: Holt, 1950.

Freedland, Michael. *Irving Berlin.* New York: Stein & Day, 1974.

Studwell, William E. *The Popular Song Reader.* New York: Haworth, 1994.

William E. Studwell

Berry, Chuck (1926-   ), is generally regarded not only as the seminal influence in the emergence and early development of rock and roll but also as a pivotal figure in bridging the gap between black and white musical cultures. Influenced by such blues, jazz, and pop performers as Louis Jordan, Muddy Waters, T-Bone Walker, Charlie Christian, Big Joe Turner, Frank Sinatra, and Nat King Cole, Berry, in turn, has inspired, influenced, and, through covers of various of his songs, ensured the early commercial success of an equally wide range of popular performers not only of his own, but succeeding generations.

Berry's own recording career began in 1955 when, hopeful of placing a number of demo tapes with an independent record label, he went to Chicago, where Muddy Waters, impressed by Berry's talent, referred him to Leonard Chess of Chess Records. Berry played Chess a demo tape of a blues number, "Wee, Wee Hours," but Chess was more interested in the country-influenced "Ida Red," the title of which, upon Chess's recommendation, Berry changed to "Maybellene." Chess took a dub of "Maybellene" to New York and encouraged legendary disc jockey/promoter Alan Freed to play it on his radio show. The song created a sensation (due in part, as Berry has explained, to the clarity of his enunciation, which distinguished him from other black performers), and following its release in May 1955, it quickly sold a million copies and reached No. 5 on the national singles charts. The song marked Berry's arrival as a major songwriter and led, over the next several years, to a series of now classic singles, such as "Roll over Beethoven," "Too Much Monkey Business," "No Money Down," "School Day" (1956); "Rock and Roll Music" (1957); "Sweet Little Sixteen," "Little Queenie," "Carol," "Johnny B. Goode," "Reelin' and Rockin'," "Memphis" (1958); and "Almost Grown" and "Back in the USA" (1959). Berry's reputation was further augmented by his appearance in a number of early rock and roll films, including *Rock, Rock, Rock* and *Mr. Rock and Roll* (1957) and *Go Johnny Go* (1959).

With the appearance, during the 1960s, of such diverse musical styles as folk rock, beach music, and disco, the popularity of hard-driving '50s-style rock experienced a decline in popularity. Still, Berry's influence was discernible in such unlikely contexts as the Beach Boys' "Surfin' USA" (a direct transposition of "Sweet Little Sixteen" to the California beach scene), Bob Dylan's "Subterranean Homesick Blues" (a derivative tribute to "Too Much Monkey Business"), and most dramatically, and ironically, across the Atlantic, as numerous groups such as the Kinks, the Animals, Gerry and

Chuck Berry. Photo courtesy of Sound Recording Archives, Bowling Green State University, Bowling Green, OH.

the Pacemakers, and, most notably, the Beatles and the Rolling Stones lionized Berry as a cult hero and, by way of homage, reprised many of his hit singles from the previous decade. Berry himself recorded a body of new material, including "Nadine," "You Never Can Tell," "Promised Land," and "No Particular Place to Go."

Curiously, it wasn't until 1972 that Berry scored his first No. 1 single, with the release of "My Ding-a-Ling," a novelty song with transparent sexual overtones recorded live at a Coventry, England, concert the same year. More memorable songs such as "Sweet Little Sixteen," "School Day," and "Johnny B. Goode" never rose higher than No. 2, 3, and 8, respectively, on the national charts. As previously, Berry continued to tour extensively, often appearing in various nostalgia concerts organized and promoted by Richard Nader; and in 1974 he was one of the featured performers in *American Hot Wax*, an affectionate tribute to the early days of rock and roll. An unexpected acknowledgment of Berry's enduring influence and reputation occurred in 1977 when a compilation album including "Johnny B. Goode" (the sole "rock" entry) and additional selections by Bach, Mozart, Beethoven, and Louis Armstrong, among others, was placed in the capsule of *Voyager 2* to provide anyone "out there" with a crash course in the planet's musical evolution.

Signal events in Berry's "later career" (though his most memorable live performances still reveal a seemingly ageless vitality) include a homecoming concert at the Fox Theater in St. Louis in 1986 to commemorate his 60th birthday; the release of *Hail! Hail! Rock 'n' Roll* (1987), a documentary tribute to Berry's life and career, which, in addition to concert footage, features interview segments with Berry himself as well as interpolated testimonials by such admirers as B. B. King, Little Richard, Jerry Lee Lewis, Eric Clapton, Bruce Springsteen, Willie Dixon, and Keith Richards; and the publication in 1988 of *Chuck Berry: The Autobiography*, in which Berry provides his own version of such controversial episodes as his alleged violation of the Mann Act (1959) and his later conviction for tax evasion (1979), both of which resulted in prison sentences. Whatever the regrettable legal complications that disrupted his personal and professional life, the release in 1988 of *Chuck Berry: The Chess Box*, a three-volume retrospective of Berry's career, ranging from "Maybellene" (1955) to the then-current "Bio" (1975), reconfirmed the proper focus of Berry's lifetime achievement and the incontestable basis for his continuing popularity: the music itself.

More than any other popular songwriter of his generation, Berry chronicles, in such songs as "School Day," "Sweet Little Sixteen," "Little Queenie," and "Almost Grown," what it was like to be young and growing up in the 1950s; and such subjects as sex, fast cars, dancing, hanging out, and the evangelical appeal of rock and roll itself have proved equally relevant to succeeding generations.

Though a comprehensive review of Berry's discography reveals a variety of musical styles, ranging from blues, rockabilly, and country-western to jazz and calypso, his most familiar musical trademarks will no doubt remain the urgent, high-pitched guitar introductions, the ringing guitar licks, the driving backbeat and the frenetic, break-neck speed typical of such classic numbers as "Carol," "Roll Over Beethoven," and "Johnny B. Goode" that have become synonymous with rock 'n' roll. No less distinctive are the inimitable features of Berry's performance style: his spontaneous and often impish interaction with the audience; his seductive insinuation of gesture and intonation; and, of course, his legendary "duck walk."

Bibliography
Berry, Chuck. *Chuck Berry: The Autobiography.* New York: Harmony, 1988.
DeWitt, Howard A. *Chuck Berry: Rock 'n' Roll Music.* 2d ed. Rock & Roll Series: No. 12. Ann Arbor: Popular Culture, 1985.
Lydon, Michael. "Chuck Berry." *Ramparts* 8 (Dec. 1969): 47-56.
McGee, David. "Chuck Berry." *The Rolling Stone Album Guide.* Ed. Anthony DeCurtis, James Henke, and Holly George-Warren. New York: Random House, 1992.
Reese, Krista. *Chuck Berry: Mr. Rock 'n' Roll.* New York: Proteus, 1982.

Michael Wentworth

Best Years of Our Lives, The (1946). According to press releases, a 1944 *Time* magazine article inspired Sam Goldwyn to make a movie that would address the problems of returning World War II veterans. He commissioned MacKinlay Kantor, author of *Andersonville*, to write the novel that was to become the basis for *The Best Years of Our Lives*. Kantor's *Glory for Me*, a blank-verse epic poem full of social commentary, however, was utterly unacceptable to Goldwyn, and the book sat on the shelf for the remainder of the war. But director William Wyler and author Robert Sherwood then did a screenplay that toned down the more radical elements of the book.

Best Years follows the efforts of three ex-servicemen (played by Harold Russell, Fredric March, and Dana Andrews) in their efforts to remaster the tempo of civilian life. The winner of seven Academy Awards including best picture, the film met with universal praise, particularly for its realism. Wyler cast a double-amputee to play Homer, chose store-bought clothes over costumes, and kept close-ups to a minimum. Motion picture critic Philip Hartung found Wyler's direction so realistic that "in spite of the fact that his cast has several top-ranking stars, [he] has succeeded in making these people as real as your own neighbors." *Best Years* is the most endearing of the films that depict the postwar social problems of returning World War II veterans—a list that includes *Pride of the Marines* (1945), *Home of the Brave* (1949), and *The Men* (1950)—and remains a staple of holiday television programming.

Bibliography
Anderegg, Michael. *William Wyler.* Boston: Twayne, 1979.
Friedland, Michael. *The Goldwyn Touch: A Biography of Sam Goldwyn.* London: Harrap, 1986.
Hartung, Philip T. "Pursuit of Happiness." *Commonwealth* 45 (13 Dec. 1946): 230-31.
Marx, Arthur. *Goldwyn: A Biography of the Man behind the Myth.* New York: Norton, 1976.
Roffman, Peter, and Jim Purdy. *The Hollywood Social Problem Film: Madness, Despair, and Politics from the Depression to the Fifties.* Bloomington: Indiana UP, 1981.

Steven L. Davis

Bester, Alfred (1913-1987), is generally recognized as one of the major early innovators in the field of science fiction. His novels and short stories laid the groundwork for many of the thematic and stylistic innovations of the authors of the 1960s and 1970s. Both Samuel Delany and Harlan Ellison cite him as a major influence in their own work.

Bester began writing science fiction in 1939 and wrote primarily for fun. He edited the magazine *Holiday* for ten years, worked as a writer of television and radio screenplays, and wrote for DC Comics. Bester's entire science fiction opus is relatively small, consisting of five novels and several collections of short stories.

Science fiction in the 1930s-50s, dominated by figures such as John Campbell and Isaac Asimov, was an action-adventure genre defined by speculative treatment of technologies based in the hard sciences. Alfred Bester's work was revolutionary in two major respects. First, he introduced psychology into the genre. Second, Bester created experimental narrative styles, principally using radical typographies, which laid the foundation for the literary experimentation of the 1960s and 1970s. He incorporated this creative treatment of language into classic structures of the murder mystery or the space opera. His work is known for larger-than-life characters, continuous melodramatic action, and his acute, satiric sense of humor.

His classic novel *The Demolished Man*, rejected by virtually every publisher in the field during the 1950s because it failed to conform to their ideas of the science fiction formula, won the first Hugo Award (bestowed by the Science Fiction Writers of America for the best works of the year) in the novel category in 1953.

Bester also explored the relationship between language, consciousness, and the senses in the typography of *The Stars My Destination* (1956), a revenge story based on *The Count of Monte Cristo*. Many of the characters are melodramatic and larger-than-life in this innovative space opera. The novel expresses Bester's optimism about human potential in that the hero, Gully Foyle, is a common man who transcends his criminal past to become a savior of humanity.

Alfred Bester was also known for acute satires of the upper class, of which he, himself, was a part, in stories such as "Ms Found in a Champagne Bottle" and "Travel Diary." His innovative treatment of the "last man" cliché in "Adam and No Eve" illustrates his talent in exploding the conventions of the genre.

Bibliography
Ellison, Harlan. "Introduction." *Angry Candy*. New York: Plume, 1988.
Platt, Charles. "Alfred Bester." *Dream Makers*. New York: Berkley, 1980.

Kristi S. Long

Beverly Hillbillies, The (1962-1971). To the strains of Jerry Scoggins on the banjo and guitar instrumentals of bluegrass legends Lester Flatt and Earl Scruggs, *The Beverly Hillbillies* premiered on September 26, 1962, and television viewers learned the story of the mountaineer family who struck it rich in oil and promptly moved to Beverly Hills, the better to live the life of millionaires. The idea for taking a backwoods family and transplanting them to jet-age California came to series creator Paul Henning on a driving tour in 1959.

For nine seasons, until September 7, 1971, Americans watched the Clampett family from the Ozarks drive their 1921 Oldsmobile flatbed truck into the heart of Beverly Hills each week. Panned by the critics for its corn-pone humor, *The Beverly Hillbillies* nonetheless became a cultural institution almost overnight. Three weeks after first airing, the CBS show became the most popular on television, a position it held for two years, remaining in the Top 20 until 1970. The cast included Jed Clampett (Buddy Ebsen), his daughter Elly May (Donna Douglas), Granny (Irene Ryan), and cousin Jethro (Max Baer, Jr.), along with their banker neighbor (Raymond Bailey) and his secretary (Nancy Kulp). In addition to two spinoffs—*Petticoat Junction* and *Green Acres*—the show also generated a wealth of *Beverly Hillbillies*

paraphernalia. A parodic documentary, *The Legend of the Beverly Hillbillies*, aired on CBS May 24, 1993, and was highly watched. Also in 1993, Twentieth Century-Fox's *The Beverly Hillbillies Movie* premiered with an entirely new cast, but the production was critically trounced.

Bibliography
Cox, Stephen. *The Beverly Hillbillies*. New York: Harper, 1993.
Shayon, Robert Lewis. "Innocent Jeremiah." *Saturday Review* 5 Jan. 1963: 38.
Story, David. *America on the Rerun*. New York: Citadel, 1993.

Roger N. Casey

Beverly Hills, 90210 (1990-2000), was an hour-long teen-oriented relationship drama on the Fox network. In spite of poor early reviews, *Beverly Hills, 90210* became a "monster hit among teens, at times reaching a phenomenal 50% of teenagers watching television" in 1991.

When the program premiered, the ensemble cast included mostly unknown young actors: Jason Priestley as handsome good-guy Brandon Walsh, a wholesome teenager who lives in Beverly Hills with his parents and twin sister, Brenda; Ian Ziering as rich, blond, handsome, arrogant and spoiled Steve Sanders; Brian Austin Green as David Silver, an overly sincere underclassman who tries too hard to fit in with the upper-class students; Luke Perry as Dylan McKay, a rich ultra-cool rebel and recovering alcoholic.

Primary female cast members included Shannen Doherty as Brandon's twin sister, Brenda, the wholesome Minnesota teenager who develops an increasingly "bitchy" persona; Jennie Garth as blonde, sexy, loose, and sometimes snobby Kelly Taylor, Brenda's best friend, and Steve's ex-girlfriend. Gabrielle Carteris as Andrea Zuckerman, the bright, achieving editor of the school newspaper who comes from the "poor" side of town; and Tori Spelling, the real-life daughter of producer Aaron Spelling (see entry), as Donna Martin, a beautiful southern California blonde eternal virgin who is always exquisitely attired in designer clothing. This primary cast remained intact until the fall of 1994 when Shannen Doherty left the program amid rumors of being fired. Other continuing characters were added for the 1994 season, most notably Tiffani-Amber Thiessen as Valerie Malone, a pot-smoking and trouble-making daughter of Walsh family friends, who moved into Brenda's room.

Unlike many of Spelling's productions, which have often been criticized for being sensationalistic, *Beverly Hills, 90210* distinguished itself in its effective portrayal of teen issues. The show was very popular with young people, who believed that *90210* provided an honest and realistic view of the concerns confronting their generation.

In 1993, the cast of characters graduated from high school and began their first year of college at California University. The show continued to focus on issues, with a particular emphasis on collegiate issues such as adjustment to college, pregnancy, fraternity and sorority pressures, sexual harassment, and student-faculty relationships—and to be one of the most successful Fox programs. It stimulated the development of many copy-cat programs.

Bibliography
James, Caryn. "90210 Goes to the Head of the Class." *New York Times* 4 Aug. 1991: 29.
Lowery, Brian. "Is Fox Endangering Mass Appeal?" *Variety* 3 June 1991: 27-31.

Ginny Schwartz

Bewitched (1964-1972), the humorous fantasy-sitcom, examined the marriage of sorceress Samantha (Elizabeth Montgomery) to advertising executive Darrin Stephens (Dick York; Dick Sargent). Although she aimed to be a normal homemaker, Samantha frequently employed her magical powers. Besides having to adapt to Samantha's witchcraft, Darrin constantly contended with his supernatural mother-in-law, Endora (Agnes Moorehead), who despised her daughter's mortal spouse. While *Bewitched* provided its viewers an escape from the tumult of the 1960s, some episodes dealt with vital issues of the period. *Bewitched* featured a cast of memorable characters including Darrin's imperious boss, Larry Tate (David White); Samantha's blundering Aunt Clara (Marion Lorne) and flirtatious cousin Serena (Montgomery); Gladys Kravitz (Alice Pearce; Sandra Gould), the Stephens's prying neighbor; Uncle Arthur (Paul Lynde), Endora's obnoxious brother; gregarious physician Dr. Bombay (Bernard Fox); bashful maid Esmerelda (Alice Ghostley); and Samantha and Darrin's supernatural offspring, Tabitha (Erin Murphy; Diane Murphy) and Adam (David Lawrence; Greg Lawrence).

Bewitched was created by Harry Ackerman and Bill Dozier of Screen Gems and television writer Sol Saks. During its eight-year run, the program earned 22 Emmy nominations. *Bewitched* enjoyed immense popularity. In its initial season, the supernatural comedy finished second in the ratings (behind *Bonanza*) with a 31.0 Nielsen rating. *Bewitched* remained in the Top 20 through the 1968-69 season, and was the top program on ABC for four years. Several television shows, including *I Dream of Jeannie* and *Tabitha,* were inspired by *Bewitched.*

Bibliography
Pilato, Herbie J. *The Bewitched Book: The Cosmic Companion to TV's Most Magical Supernatural Situation Comedy.* New York: n.p., 1992.

S. K. Bane

Bierce, Ambrose (1842-1914), was an important American author of horror fiction writing at the turn of the 20th century. His macabre short stories, only a relatively small portion of his total writings, provided a significant literary bridge between the work of Edgar Allan Poe in the 19th century and H. P. Lovecraft in the 20th century (see entries).

Born in Ohio, and later serving in the Union Army during the Civil War, Bierce eventually found himself in San Francisco, pursuing a career in journalism that would eventually make him both famous and infamous. Between 1867 and 1871, he published a variety of short writings—poems, essays, and sketches—in a number of San Francisco–based periodicals, including William Randolph Hearst's *San Francisco Examiner,* where, in 1887, he resurrected his cynical editorial column, "Prattle." Later, he disappeared in Mexico while observing Juarez's revolution; several of his biographers conjecture that he died in 1914 at the battle of Ojinaga.

Bierce's important short story collections include *Tales of Soldiers and Civilians* (1891), revised and retitled as *In the Midst of Life* (1898), and *Can Such Things Be?* (1893). In his macabre short fiction, he explores such diverse subjects as the Civil War and the American frontier. Several of his tales, such as "The Damned Thing" (1893) and "Moxon's Master" (1903), are also frequently credited as representing the early development of American science fiction. In works like "Incident at Owl Creek Bridge" (1891) and "Chickamauga" (1891), Bierce fundamentally transformed the horror story by making its language more contemporary and by emphasizing psychological realism over traditional gothic clichés.

Bibliography
Davidson, Cathy N. *The Experimental Fictions of Ambrose Bierce.* Boston: Hall, 1984.
Grenander, M. E. *Ambrose Bierce.* New York: Twayne, 1971.
Woodruff, Stuart C. *The Short Stories of Ambrose Bierce: A Study in Polarity.* Pittsburgh: U of Pittsburgh P, 1964.

Gary Hoppenstand

Big Little Books were publications proving that little could be big. Whitman Publishing Company of Racine, WI, published the first Big Little Book (BLB) in 1932. This book, about 4 inches wide, 4 and 1/2 inches tall, and 1 and 1/2 inches thick, was entitled *The Adventures of Dick Tracy,* and featured a reprinted segment (though not the first) from Chester Gould's famous newspaper strip. In the course of the next 16 years, hundreds of titles appeared (published by Whitman and about a dozen competitors and imitators), each of which sold thousands and hundreds of thousands of copies. Most BLBs adapted and reprinted famous newspaper comic strips of the day. These books usually featured a page of text on the left page and a frame from the strip reprinted on the facing right page. The comic strip frame reprinted on the right was often devoid of its original word balloons—this text was altered, adapted, and reprinted on the left. Many of these books numbered 424 and more pages in length. In some cases, BLBs were "All Pictures Comics" and simply reprinted one comic strip frame, in its entirety, on each page.

The most popular comic strips BLB showcased were Dick Tracy, Little Orphan Annie, Mickey Mouse, Donald Duck, Flash Gordon, Buck Rogers, and Popeye. Less frequently, but still quite importantly, BLBs found their source material in motion pictures, movie serials, radio dramas, and even early motion picture animation. Motion picture BLBs differed slightly from comic strip BLBs, often a bit taller and wider on the surface, and a little less deep or long in page count (5 inches x 5 1/2 inches x 7/8 inches, and about 256 pages). Also, motion picture BLBs were generally not as lavishly illustrated—their illustrations were black and white photographic stills from the movies which appeared on every fourth or sixth page. *Lions and Tigers Starring Clyde Beatty* (1934) is an example of the usual motion picture BLB. BLBs based on radio dramas were relatively few in number, and

Big Little Books. Photo courtesy of Popular Culture Library, Bowling Green State University, Bowling Green, OH.

presented a unique problem. These books were dependent on illustrations provided especially for them. These black and white line drawings were generally not the level of quality of the drawings found in newspaper strip BLBs.

The golden age for the BLB ran from 1932 to 1938. In 1938, with its highly commercially successful product imitated and exploited by other publishers—in fact, the term Big Little Book, now quite generic—Whitman Publishing decided to retitle its product line Better Little Books. Hence, the silver age of BLBs was ushered in. It lasted until about 1949. BLB history from 1950 until the 1980s (when, due to rising production costs, the last Whitman products could not maintain their competitively low cover prices) is divided into several shorter periods. During these years, there were a series of New Better Little Books, a series of BLBs based on several popular television programs of the 1950s, a 36-title Big Little Book series (1967-69), and several occasions in the 1970s and 1980s that brought paperback reprints of classic BLB titles and new stories altogether.

In the 1930s and 1940s, BLBs were sold for pennies, often averaging 10 cents, sometimes less, sometimes 15 cents, and sometimes they were given away free as premiums or incentives to buy grocery store items. Cocomalt was a milk drink mix that offered such premiums. Retailers bought BLBs by the lot, for a percentage—often 60 percent—of the retail price.

Bibliography

Lowery, Lawrence F. *The Collector's Guide to Big Little Books and Similar Books*. Danville: Educational Research and Applications, 1981.

Roberts, Garyn G. *Dick Tracy and American Culture: Morality and Mythology, Text and Context*. Jefferson: McFarland, 1993.

Thomas, James Stuart. *The Big Little Book Price Guide*. Des Moines: Wallace-Homestead, 1983.

Garyn G. Roberts

See also
Feature Books

Bill Cosby Show, The (1969-1971), cinched the career of an actor already well established. By 1969, Bill Cosby (see

entry) had assembled an impressive television track record. In 1965, Cosby became the first African-American actor to land a starring role in a dramatic series, *I Spy*. In 1967 and 1968, Cosby won Emmy Awards as best lead actor for his *I Spy* efforts. The following year, Cosby's variety special won an Emmy for outstanding variety series. Thus, it came as no surprise when NBC latched onto Cosby's rising star and gave him his own sitcom—*The Bill Cosby Show*—in 1969.

Cosby's entry, a warmhearted series about the personal and professional life of a Los Angeles high school gym teacher, was only one of several sitcoms in its time to feature African Americans; Diahann Carroll's *Julia* and Lloyd Haynes's *Room 222*, two other sitcoms with serious overtones, debuted in 1968 and 1969, respectively. Part of the networks' efforts to reverse many of the negative African-American television images of the past—as well as to appease the NAACP's complaints regarding African Americans in TV—each of these shows seemed to represent a shift toward a growing trend of equitable media treatment.

Acting in his first sitcom, Cosby was able to hone a unique comedy style that in 1984 would make his second sitcom, *Cosby*, a No. 1 Nielsen hit (see entry). Unfortunately, *The Bill Cosby Show* did not fare as well; while first season ratings placed the program in 11th place, it failed to register in the Top 20 during the next season; the show was dropped in 1971. *Julia* met with a similar fate, placing 7th in 1968, but falling off the charts—and the network's schedule—by 1971. *Room 222*, which was never a major success, was kept on the air for five years by ABC, which, as the No. 3 network, had nothing to lose by broadcasting a marginal show.

Unfortunately, *The Bill Cosby Show* and similar sitcom efforts failed to translate into long-term equity for African-American TV images. While sophisticated shows such as *The Mary Tyler Moore Show* and *All in the Family* presented racial issues, neither of the shows featured blacks in anything other than occasional supporting roles. While later series such as *Good Times* or *The Jeffersons* had black casts, many African Americans felt the programs contained stereotypical behavior.

Bibliography

Brooks, Tim, and Earle Marsh. *The Complete Directory to Prime Time Network TV Shows, 1946-Present*. 4th ed. New York: Ballantine, 1992.

Brown, Les. *Les Brown's Encyclopedia of Television*. Detroit: Visible Ink, 1992.

Fuller, Linda K. *The Cosby Show: Audiences, Impact, and Implications*. Westport: Greenwood, 1992.

Sackett, Susan. *Prime Time Hits*. New York: Billboard, 1993.

Michael B. Kassel

Billboard/Poster Art and Advertising. Outdoor advertising, consisting of many forms, including posters, three-dimensional objects, and billboards (greatly enlarged "posters"), is considered the oldest ad medium. The three-dimensional objects include oversized product-package models, painted walls, telephone-kiosk displays, transit/rail platforms, and bus shelter displays. The Institute of Outdoor Advertising claims that this medium is the final reminder of

Michael Jordan's and Bugs Bunny's first appearance together on a Chicago billboard for Nike. Photo courtesy of Mark McDermott.

a firm's product or service. It bridges the gap between in-home ad messages and out-of-home purchases.

The first posters in America were mere announcements of sales, auctions, and related events. The pictorial sign came into prominence in Philadelphia, before the Revolution. Many were simply non-illustrative, even around the mid-1880s. For a long time signs were the chief means of advertising for most businesses. In the early 1800s the first illustrated posters, like newspapers, used stock printer's cuts. In time, however, woodcuts would be commissioned. In the 1830s and 1840s America's growing cities found merchants touting their wares: elegant clothes, musical instruments, and tobacco.

Until the 1890s, posters had been made from either woodcuts or lithographic plates, but the development of halftone printing made possible the reproduction of photography or original art. Various sizes of billboards existed, mostly used for show business purposes, but in time, the size and popularity of this oversized poster medium increased.

Circus advertising represented the state of the art in billboard advertising during the latter 1800s and continued strongly during the first half of the 1900s. While in the early days, few laws concerning poster and billboard placement existed, even then, to assure reasonable permanence, permission had to be sought. Soon, laws would evolve to regulate these ad forms, and today, they are, in some cases, severely limited by them. The increase in auto traffic on the open road introduced billboards to these areas, and traveling

habits of Americans and others served as perfect vehicles for billboards. In addition, busy city intersections and squares became perfect places for billboards.

The billboard era between 1900 and 1945 encompassed product advertising to its fullest, along with patriotic messages during two world wars, among other things. Advertising agencies started to pay more attention to the use of illustrations early in this period, using them for more than mere attention-getters. In addition, advertising research came into prominence, and included poster and billboard usage.

However, it was after World War I that not only the billboard but the testimonial came into prominence; these could also complement one another in advertising. Billboard artists depicted Americans during the 1930s as they wished they could be, and therefore "fantasy" played a huge part in ads of these years. The great increase of large electric signs during the 1920s is also an advertising phenomenon of the era. The 1920s saw the economy as well as advertising take severe downturns, severely affecting virtually every facet of America's people. The rise of the billboard of the 1920s as used by advertisers, even in whole campaigns, made a great impact upon product promotion. The use of color in signs and billboards helped advertisers manipulate buyers' emotions.

During the mid-1930s, there arose the trend to use photography in advertising. Pure realism, via photos, seemed the order of the times. As the Depression ended, however, another misery hit: World War II. While billboards still contained product messages, they tended to be far more patriotic, and the war effort was a major feature.

After the end of the war, advertising was ready to promote new peacetime products and services now available to it. The 1950s ushered in the painted billboard throughout the world. These were bigger, sleeker, glossier than printed poster counterparts. More stylized, subjective ad treatments became common.

Commercial and fine art began exchanging many ideas, and it was often the commercial use of an art trend that made it far more acceptable to the public. While family values were stressed, there was a more monied youthful market that attracted advertisers, who offered attractive and even sexy ads to capture attention and wallets. With the advent of boom trucks, sign rotation became a natural result. Changes in the 1950s also saw an increased use of photography and the move to present larger ad images. Billboards adapted to the needs, including less text and more illustration. Advertising and new art styles were indicators of cultural trends and helped to create them.

In the 1960s op, pop, and psychedelic art became powerful tools in advertisers' hands and very successfully helped simulate sales. Color became an important tool to manipulate viewers' perceptions. Elaborate designs, reminiscent of the art nouveau period, abounded. The link between pop and commercial art was so close during the 1960s that it actually brought about a marriage of the two. The spectacular use of billboard color deepened the freshness and appeal of this outdoor medium.

The 1970s ushered in an era of superrealism, whereby products, especially foods, needed to be depicted on billboards in vivid detail. The painters of this school call themselves photorealists or super realists. This was the final, inevitable link between fine art and commercial art, bringing them within the same boundaries.

Photorealism's painters usually worked from photographs. Although photorealism throughout the 1970s was at the vanguard of the traditional arts, the 1980s did not usher in a single school or movement. While studies have repeatedly shown the effectiveness of billboard advertising, all was not well during the decades of the 1960s and 1970s, with more and more laws emerging to control the outdoor devices. Highway beautification and increased concern for the environment (the latter more intense in the 1980s and 1990s) also have taken their toll on billboards and other signs.

The large, 30-sheet billboards are being studied by many companies in relation to high placement, and size-reduction may have some answers to the problems of the future. City planners and urban developers seem ready to accept smaller-sized outdoor signage. Three-dimensional displays, usually via inflatable product-related objects, may provide one answer; even holography, though difficult, is being explored.

Bibliography

Danna, Sammy R. *Advertising and Popular Culture.* Bowling Green, OH: Bowling Green State U Popular P, 1992.
Fox, Charles Philip, and Tom Parkinson. *Billers, Banners and Bombast.* Boulder: Pruet, 1985.
Fraser, James. *The American Billboard 100 Years.* New York: Abrams, 1991.
Gallo, Max. *The Poster in History.* New York: New American Library, 1972.
Henderson, Sally, and Robert Landau. *Billboard Art.* San Francisco: Chronicle, 1981.
Margolin, Victor, Ira Brichta, and Vivian Brichta. *The Promise and the Product: 200 Years of American Advertising Posters.* New York: Macmillan, 1979.

Sammy R. Danna

Billiards, more popularly called pool, has a history of 500 years. Mary Queen of Scots, during her imprisonment in the 16th century, lamented when she was denied her billiards table. Billiards is mentioned in Shakespeare's *Antony and Cleopatra*, and appears as an aside in *The Mikado*. Gilbert and Sullivan discuss the dangers of billiards and the need to avoid the "sharper" who pretends to be a poor player, entraps his opponent in a wagered contest, and then walks off with the winnings.

During the 19th century players began to use chalk on the tips of their cues. In Britain this was known as "side," while in America it came to be known as "English." This allowed players to upgrade their precision and to slice or swerve the ball.

In the 1930s snooker took over from billiards as the major professional form of the sport. In the U.S. the game is supervised by the Billiard Congress of America, and there is now a professional tour circuit for male and female players. Among the inductees into the Billiard Congress of America Hall of Fame are the celebrated Willie Mosconi (pocket billiards world champion 15 times between 1940 and 1957) and Charles C. Peterson. According to Ralph Hickok, Peterson was the "missionary of billiards" because of the manner in which he captivated the attention of college students and servicemen.

The game can be an intriguing filter through which to examine major social themes. In the movie *The Deer Hunter* (1978) collegiality and male companionship are heightened as the steel workers sip Rolling Rock beer and "shoot pool." Unquestionably, the best pool-room movie of all time is *The Hustler* (1961). The black and white format captures the dark and smoke-filled caverns that were the pool-rooms of the period. Paul Newman looks like a snooker player down on his luck as he falls afoul of an underworld gambling syndicate. The starring role nevertheless is Jackie Gleason as the extraordinary "Minnesota Fats," in real life known as Rudolf Walter Wanderone, Jr. Fats may be big and burly but his shot making is magnificent. A follow-up sequel with Paul Newman and Tom Cruise, *The Color of Money* (1986), never matched the atmosphere and competitive chicanery exhibited in *The Hustler*.

In any account of billiards the name Joe Davis (1901-1978) deserves pride of place. While the Australian Walter Lindrum (1898-1960) became the first stellar touring professional and established fame and fortune from his skills as a cue-man, it was England's Davis who legitimized the game and made himself, and the sport, as acceptable in the living room as it was in the workingman's pub and in the exclusive gentlemen's club.

Bibliography

Adelman, Melvin L. "Neglected Sports in American History: The Rise of Billiards in New York City. 1850-1871." *Canadian Journal of History of Sport* 12.2 (1981): 1-28.

Bury M. "The Social Significance of Snooker: Sports-Games in the Age of Television." *Theory, Culture, and Society* 3.2 (1986): 49-62.

Craven, R. R. *Billiards, Bowling, Table Tennis, Pinball, and Video Games: A Bibliographic Guide*. Westport: Greenwood, 1983. 163.

Cuddon, J. *The International Dictionary of Sports and Games*. New York: Schocken, 1979.

Hickok, R. *New Encyclopedia of Sports*. New York: McGraw-Hill, 1977.

Scott A. G. M. Crawford

Bingo is a popular, relatively low-cost game of chance played for cash and prizes. Players purchase bingo squares, along the top of which appear the letters B-I-N-G-O. Each letter heads a column of five randomly generated, preselected numbers within a set of 15: the B column, for example, includes 1-15, and on a given bingo square, the numbers 12, 4, 7, 9, and 10 may appear. The I column includes five numbers between 16 and 30, and so on through O, which includes five numbers between 61 and 75. The middle square is usually "free"—players are credited with filling that space before the game even begins. A "caller" chooses numbers at random, and players mark the called numbers that appear on their cards, winning when their marked squares correspond to a preannounced pattern. Common winning patterns include the simple bingo (five squares in a straight line), double or triple bingos, the "picture frame" (all the outside squares), the "kite with a string" (four squares in a corner, with a diagonal line attached), and the "blackout" (all squares), as well as more complex patterns. Bingo is closely related to keno and lotto, games in which players first select numbers and then win if their numbers match those randomly chosen.

Bingo's origins are obscure, but it is clear that bowl games related to lotto and bingo existed among Native American tribes before European exploration here. To play these games, players would place two-sided objects such as fruit pits, stones, or nut shells into a bowl. They would then bet on how the pieces would fall, smack the bowl against the ground or rocks to make the pieces fly into the air, and then settle their bets according to the results. These bowl games may have inspired lotto, the earliest recorded description of which appeared in 1778. American keno dates from the early 1800s. Bingo itself has existed in essentially the form it takes today all this century. In the 1930s, during the Great Depression, a variety of bingo called screeno was played in movie theaters: as an incentive to buy tickets, theater managers would distribute free bingo squares to patrons, and games were played between features.

Until the early 1980s, bingo was most often played in Elks' lodges, Catholic churches, school fairs, or other similar *ad hoc* locations, with beans or poker chips for markers, on single squares for small stakes (about $5 to $50 per game). The proceeds went largely to benefit the game's sponsor. Since 1980, though, the game has become high-tech and big-stakes, played in vast halls dedicated specifically to bingo, with special equipment, by serious players eager to win big pots. Whereas formerly callers selected numbers at their own pace, now sophisticated bingo machines equipped with timers beep when it is time for the next number—about every 15 seconds. Video monitors lining the bingo hall's walls show the forthcoming number before it is read. Other display boards show all numbers called so far and the pattern required for a win. Using specially designed markers called daubers, which look and work like oversized highlighter pens, players mark called numbers on sheets printed with one, three, six, or most often nine bingo squares. Many players buy multiple sheets, playing as many as 18 to 36 squares per game. Each square has its own serial number, and all squares' numbers are fed beforehand into a computer. When a player achieves the required pattern and calls "Bingo!" a technician enters the winning square's serial number into a computer, verifying the win on-screen.

As domestic dependent sovereignties, Native American reservations are not subject to state civil law; Native Americans themselves may regulate all games not prohibited by state law. (Most states allow bingo.) This means that Native American bingo halls' earnings are not subject to local, state, or federal taxes, and that pots can be as large as tribes choose to make them. Larger pots attract larger crowds, and tax-free status maximizes profits; Native American bingo has therefore enjoyed great success. (By mid-1993 there were 152 Native American–run bingo halls in the U.S.) Their phenomenal growth has contributed substantially to the popularity of bingo generally, so that bingo is now a $13-billion-a-year industry and an important part of American popular culture.

Bibliography

"Bingo." *The New Encyclopedia Britannica Micropaedia*. Vol. 2. London: Encyclopedia Britannica, 1993. 218.

Eadington, William R. "Gambling." *The Americana Annual*. New York: Encyclopedia Americana, 1982. 224.

Moore, W. John. "A Winning Hand?" *National Journal* 17 July 1993: 1796-1800.

Pasquaretta, Paul. "On the 'Indianness' of Bingo: Gambling and the Native American Community." *Critical Inquiry* 20 (1994): 694-714.

Brian Cowlishaw

Biography (1962-1964), the Peabody Award–winning syndicated series, was developed by independent television producer David L. Wolper (credited for the 1958 *The Race for Space*). This weekly half-hour program hosted by Mike Wallace was a retrospective of the lives of 20th-century personalities and celebrities. These historic biographical documentaries were presented in narrative form and structure. Each production presented the subject's triumphs and failures. Often treated in a personal manner, the study of each subject was noncontroversial. *Biography* was wholesome entertainment. The show made drama from life. It displayed to the audience an objective educational lesson in history.

Compiled from actual newsreel footage of major political and cultural events, the 39 *Biography* episodes chronicled a gamut of famous lives, from Winston Churchill and Babe Ruth to Mohandas K. Gandhi and Adolph Hitler. Sponsored by Chemical Bank N.Y. Trust, the first show examined the public life of former New York Mayor Fiorello LaGuardia. This show covered the better-known events of the mayor's career, focusing in on the man rather than the Depression era. His story was told by use of still photographs, depicting his younger years, and archive film of his election and tenure in office.

Cable television helped to revitalize *Biography* in the 1990s, on *David L. Wolper Presents* and *A&E's Biography*. Seen on the Arts & Entertainment Network, these presentations feature the wide collection of documentary telecasts from the Wolper Production archives.

Bibliography

Bluem, William A. *Documentary in American Television.* New York: Hastings, 1965.

Hamond, Charles Mongomery. *The Image Decade: Television Documentary, 1965-1975.* New York: Hastings, 1981.

Marc, David, and Robert J. Thompson. *Prime Time, Prime Movers.* Boston: Little, Brown, 1992.

Michael Espinosa

Biondi, Dick (1932-), was the first of the Top 40 DJ screamers, the "Wild Eye-talian," leader of a generation and consternation of parents from coast to coast. Radio programmers, stung by the payola scandals of 1959, took the power to pick records away from announcers. They adopted the Top 40 format, with playlists determined by consultants or from national trade charts. Because every rock 'n' roll station now played the same records, they needed more personality to attract listeners. It was into this void that Dick Biondi arrived.

A native of Endicott, NY, Biondi landed his first radio job in nearby Corning at the age of 19. Three months later he was fired by a new station manager. Bitten by the radio bug, Biondi ended up at KSYL in Alexandria, LA. He was expected to play Glenn Miller, but discovered rhythm & blues in the clubs across the tracks. By 1953, he was playing R&B on the weekend *Jammin' Jive* show, until he left the next year to return north. Dick turned up in Youngstown, PA, where he brought Jerry Lee Lewis and Elvis Presley in for concerts, and was probably the first DJ to play Gene Vincent's "Be-Bop-a-Lula." At an Elvis show he was emceeing, Dick asked the "Pelvis" to autograph his shirt, then jumped into the crowd. Biondi required several stitches and very little of the shirt survived.

In 1958, WKBW in Buffalo, NY, offered Biondi a chance to fill the shoes of George "Hound Dog" Lorenz, who had brought R&B to the Niagara Falls area. Hound Dog initiated many tricks subsequently picked up by Biondi and other Top 40 jocks: reading weather and commercials over instrumentals to keep the music flowing, and "rocking the

pots"—twisting the volume knobs to punch the beat. Biondi commanded the airwaves with his screaming "Wild Eye-talian" delivery, which he had picked up from sports broadcasters, and commanded 50 percent of the Buffalo market.

On May 2, 1960, Chicago's WLS-AM went from a farm-oriented country station to a 50,000 watt rock 'n' roll beacon. The station hired Biondi along with the cadre of DJs that brought full-time Top 40 to Chicago and eventually to the rest of the ABC-owned and -operated stations. Within a year he was at the top of the heap and an idol to Chicago kids. At a benefit show in 1961, Biondi ended up trapped in a stadium ticket office, surrounded by police, because fans were literally tearing off his clothes. He had a regional hit record with "On Top of a Pizza" but was later fired.

Dick's firing was a step upward—to KRLA in Los Angeles. The Beach Boys brought him a tape of "Surfer Girl" the night they recorded it. He announced concerts at the Hollywood Bowl, introducing the Beatles and the Rolling Stones to the West Coast.

Biondi was fired and rehired by KRLA, then returned to Chicago in 1967. WCFL was knocking at the gates of WLS' Top-40 heaven, and the Screamer was there through urban riots and the Democratic Convention. Biondi brought "Super 'CFL" to the top of the ratings before the program director got fed up with him in 1973.

By 1983, old WLS teammate Bob Sirott looked up Biondi for a "where are they now" TV feature. Because of the story, Biondi was invited to Chicago for an oldies record hop, and then the morning drive on Top 40 WBBM-FM. In 1984, he switched to WJMK-FM's new '50s-'70s oldies format. He is now heard there every night, part of a stable of original Chicago Top 40 DJs, playing the hits they made famous. In 1994, Biondi was named among over 60 DJs to be part of an exhibit on disc jockeys at the Rock and Roll Hall of Fame and Museum in Cleveland.

Bibliography

Biondi, Dick. *Cruisin' 1960.* Increase Records, INCD, 1960.

Feder, Robert. "Chicago Rock Jocks Joining Hall of Fame." *Chicago Sun-Times* 10 Nov. 1994: 49.

Hopkins, Jerry. Liner notes. *Cruisin' 1960.* Increase Records, INCD, 1960.

Reich, Howard. "Biondi Redemption: For Deejay Dick, Rock 'n' Radio Still Hold the Ultimate Meaning of Life." *Chicago Tribune* 31 July 1988: Arts 4.

Smith, Wes. *The Pied Pipers of Rock 'n' Roll: Radio Deejays of the 50's and 60's.* Marietta: Longstreet, 1989.

Mark R. McDermott

Bird, Larry (1956-), the quintessential white ballplayer, large, a good shot but not much of a leaper, Larry the Legend, a.k.a. Larry Bird, the hick from French Lick, IN, hardly seemed destined to play a revolutionary role in propelling the National Basketball Association from a league "based on size, strength, and pounding the ball inside in order to shoot from near the basket into one based on quickness, agility, and spreading the court to increase the pace of the game." That is exactly what Larry Bird, along with Earvin Magic Johnson, did in the 1980s as the prototypes of the new "versatile big men." No longer was offensive strategy dictated by picks and set plays and pounding the ball into the big men but instead was now predicated on the individual and his athletic ability.

This "basketball revolutionary from America's heartlands" was born in West Baden, IN. He attended Springs Valley High School, where he became one of the Hoosier state's legendary prep superstars. At his last high school game, 4,000 people attended the contest, although officially the town had a total population of only 2,100.

Bird was drafted by the Boston Celtics in 1979 and would remain with them through the 1991-92 season. His NBA career was spectacular. He scored 40 points or more in 52 games and had four games in which he scored 50 or more points. He scored 2,000 points in four consecutive seasons. He was also the first NBA player to shoot 50 percent from the floor and more than 90 percent from the free throw line. He is only one of five players in the NBA to have over 5,000 assists and score more than 20,000 points. His total statistics in the NBA are truly amazing: 21,791 points, 1,556 steals, 0.886 FT percentage, 8,974 rebounds, 5,965 assists and 897 games played. He carried a 24.3 scoring average to lead all Boston Celtic players.

After his retirement, Larry worked in the Celtics' front office. He then took the job as the head coach of the NBA Indiana Pacers. Returning to his home state, Bird has been able to instill a work ethic in his players and a commitment to team play. In 2000, his team was able to take the Los Angeles Lakers to a dramatic seven-game NBA championship series before losing.

Bibliography
Italia, Bob. *Larry Bird*. Minneapolis: ABDO, 1992.
Kavanagh, Jack. *Sports Great Larry Bird*. Springfield, NJ: Enslow, 1992.
Rosenthal, Bert. *Larry Bird: Cool Man on the Court*. Chicago: Childrens, 1997.

Lawrence E. Ziewacz

Bixby, Bill (1934-1993), in a career devoted almost exclusively to television, was one of the first actors to portray the gentle hero. In several series, Bixby played characters who were sensitive as well as strong, and who rarely resorted to force.

Bixby was born in San Francisco. He attended public schools there; in high school he was active both in theater and debate. In 1956 he received a degree in speech and philosophy from the University of California at Berkeley. After a short stint in the army, he moved to Hollywood, where a modeling job led to a test for a part in *The Many Loves of Dobie Gillis* and later to a featured role in *My Favorite Martian* (1963-66).

Bixby's role as Tom Corbett in *The Courtship of Eddie's Father* (1969-72) was one of the first in television to feature a single father raising a young child alone, and Corbett was unusual among television fathers in that he was openly affectionate. His role as Anthony Blake in *The Magician* (1973-74) added ingenuity to sensitivity. As a magician, illusionist, and escape artist with a shady past, Blake was more likely to solve the weekly dilemma with a clever ruse than with strength. In *The Incredible Hulk* (1978-82), developed from the Marvel comic book, Bixby played a gentle man with a fearful secret, always looking for ways to support the research that would help him rid himself of his alter ego, the green hulk (played by bodybuilder Lou Ferrigno).

In addition to these three series, Bixby directed the ABC miniseries *Rich Man, Poor Man* (1976) and produced and directed the BBC/PBS series for children *Once upon a Classic*. His concern for children and children's programming also led him to co-host *The Puzzle Children* (1976) with Julie Andrews. At the time of his death from cancer, Bixby was directing the second season of *Blossom*.

Bibliography
Kennedy, Maggie. "Bixby Crusades for Kids' TV." *Dallas Times Herald* 23 Sept. 1976: C-2.
Richmond, Ray. "Bixby Remembered as a Class Act." *Los Angeles Daily News* 23 Nov. 1993: F-1.
Thomas, Bob. "Bixby Incredibly Happy Hulk-ing." *Dallas Times Herald* 14 Sept. 1978: C-1.

Janet P. Sholty

Black Church Women are an ever-growing force in American politics, religion, and society in general. The black church is a term applied to seven denominations whose leadership and membership are overwhelmingly composed of African-descended people living in the U.S. These denominations are the African Methodist Episcopal Church; African Methodist Episcopal Zion Church; Christian Methodist Episcopal Church (originally Colored Methodist Episcopal Church); National Baptist Convention, USA, Inc.; National Baptist Convention of America, Unincorporated; Progressive National Baptist Convention; and Church of God in Christ. The approximately 2,600 predominantly black congregations in the United Methodist Church and the host of independent churches and spiritual churches whose membership is composed of African Americans must also be considered when considering women and the black church. Black Baptist churches may maintain dual affiliation with a black church denomination and the American Baptist Convention.

Approximately 70 percent of the members of historically black churches are women. Women are most often relegated to roles of exhorter, missionary, lay reader, musician, choir member, caterer, hostess, secretary, clerk, vacation Bible school director, teacher, and office holder in the women's department in the church. Women are rewarded for participation in these activities and often sanctioned for attempts to assume other roles in the church. The most prestigious position available for laywomen is that of Church Mother. The honorific title is an embodiment of the respect the African American communities hold for the older members of the society and an implicit accolade acknowledging comportment, longevity, and degree of service to the church. Women's departments often hold power, as seen when women in the Church of God in Christ vetoed the preacher's choice to head the church after the death of its founder.

In response to such constraints from the time of the northern migration of African Americans during the beginning of the 20th century, which climaxed during the First World War, many African-American women established and pastored independent churches. Over 50 percent of the female membership of the black church who become ordained serve as pastor in white denominations. White denominations are generally perceived as being less oppressive and presenting fewer obstacles to use of one's skills and talents. Most of these clergywomen pastor African-American congregations in the white denominations.

Women have served the black church as unofficial preachers and pastors even when they were denied ordination. Jarena Lee of the African Methodist Episcopal Church preached in the black church in the 18th century even though she was never ordained by the bishops of the church. Among 19th-century African-American women preachers were Elizabeth, whose surname and denomination are unknown; Julia Foote, of the African Methodist Episcopal Zion Church; and Amanda Berry Smith, of the African Methodist Episcopal Church. These women also preached without being ordained.

The African Methodist Episcopal Zion Church became the first black church to officially ordain women when Julia Foote was ordained deacon in the New York Annual Conference in 1884. Mary J. Small was ordained deacon in 1894 and elder in 1898. In the African Methodist Episcopal Church, Sarah Hughes was ordained deacon in 1886 by Bishop Henry McNeal Turner. However, this ordination was nullified by the other bishops of the church on the grounds that church law forbade the ordination of women. It was not until 1948 that African Methodist Episcopal Church law was amended to allow for the ordination of women. The Christian Methodist Episcopal Church began ordaining women in 1954, although it was not until 1966 that they were granted all the rights and privileges accorded to their male colleagues. Today many Baptist churches still do not ordain women. The first record of ordination of women in the National Baptist Convention, USA, Inc., or the National Baptist Convention, Unincorporated, occurred somewhere in the period 1960-70 after the sudden death of pastor-husbands. Ordination of women in all three instances was allowed to enable the wives to officially carry on the husband's work and serve the respective local churches as pastors. As of 1990, the Church of God in Christ still did not ordain women to serve as pastors.

Since the late 1980s some black female theologians have begun using the paradigm of womanism in their theologizing. Womanism has its roots in the African-American folk notion of a girl assuming behavior that is acceptable only at an older age ("girl you actin' womanish"), and blossomed into an archetype of the black woman's experience after publication of Alice Walker's book *In Search of Our Mothers' Gardens* (1983). A Womanist Theology Unit has been established in the American Academy of Religion.

Bibliography

Higginbotham, Evelyn Brooks. *Righteous Discontent.* Cambridge: Harvard UP, 1993.
Hull, Gloria T., Patricia Bell Scott, and Barbara Smith, eds. *All the Women Are White, All the Blacks Are Men, But Some of Us Are Brave.* Old Westbury, NY: Feminist, 1982.
Lincoln, Eric C., and Lawrence H. Mamiya. *The Black Church in the African American Experience.* Durham: Duke UP, 1990.

A. Washington

Black College Radio began at Hampton University in Hampton, VA, which became the nation's first historically black college to receive a noncommercial radio station license. WHOV-FM was awarded a license by the Federal Communications Commission in 1964.

Other historically black colleges and universities to follow suit in applying for and receiving noncommercial radio station licenses include Shaw University (NC) in 1968; Clark College (GA) in 1974; Grambling Station University (LA), Jackson State University (MS), Langston University (OK), Lincoln University (PA), and Savannah State College (GA), all in 1975; Florida A&M University in 1976; Fayetteville State University (NC) and Morgan State University (MD) both in 1977; Wiley College (AL) in 1978; Texas Southern University in 1979; and Norfolk State University (VA) in 1980.

Radio at the historically black colleges and universities can be traced back to World War II. Many of these colleges offered technical training to the "Negro" student as part of the nation's war preparation effort. In addition, several broadcast stations around the country supplemented their regular on-air programs with African-American participants to call attention to the increasing role of the American "Negro" in radio broadcasting.

In 1943, the NBC Blue Network broadcast a special program from Howard University in Washington, D.C., to discuss the black college and university in America. The school's president, Dr. Mordecai Johnson, and other noted black educators participated. Bennett College in North Carolina also initiated programs about blacks on both WBIG radio in Greensboro and WBT radio in Charlotte. Atlanta University broadcast a popular radio series in the 1940s over WGST in Atlanta entitled *People's College Radio Hour* that featured noted black educators and scholars, including Dr. W. E. B. DuBois.

The growth and popularity of radio at historically black colleges and universities has been accompanied by several of these stations joining National Public Radio (NPR) and American Public Radio (APR) as affiliates, thus placing them in the ranks of full-service noncommercial public radio stations. Howard University eventually became the first black college to be awarded a noncommercial public television station license.

Bibliography

Lash, John. "The Negro and Radio." *Opportunity* Oct. 1943.
Tinney, James S., and Justine J. Rector. *Issues and Trends in African-American Journalism.* Washington, DC: UP of America, 1980.

Frank W. Johnson, Jr.

Black Mask (1920-1951), published monthly between April 1920 and July 1951 (twice a month in 1923 and 1924) for 340 issues, was the most significant and influential detective pulp magazine. Of its half-dozen editors, the most important were George W. Sutton, Jr., Philip C. Cody, and Joseph T. Shaw, who introduced and nurtured the development of hard-boiled detective fiction between 1923 and 1936. Carroll John Daly contributed stories about private detective Race Williams beginning in 1923; shortly thereafter, Dashiell Hammett's first Continental Op story, "Arson Plus," followed. Hammett's fiction subsequently became the model for the writers who followed him, including Erle Stanley Gardner, Raymond Chandler, and George Harmon Coxe. One reason for the continued success of *Black Mask* was the use of series characters. Critics acclaimed the magazine for its creation of a new type of detective story, and aspiring writers fought to appear in its pages.

The detective story was among the most popular in the pulp format. It has been estimated that between the 1920s and the early 1950s, as many as 178 different pulp magazine titles appeared on the newsstands. Many survived only a few issues, but among those that lasted for many years and are still remembered are Street & Smith's *Detective Story Magazine* (1915-49), the first detective pulp; *Dime Detective* (1931-53); *Clues* (1926-43); *Thrilling Detective* (1931-53); and *Spicy Detective* (1934-42). Related to detective pulp magazines were the hero pulps with continuing characters like *The Shadow* (1931-49), *The Phantom Detective* (1933-53), and *The Spider* (1933-43). The advent of the paperback market, lessening popular interest in mystery short stories, and evolving cultural trends resulted in the demise of pulp magazines by the 1960s, but they remain significant artifacts in popular culture history.

Bibliography

Cook, Michael L. *Mystery, Detective, and Espionage Magazines*. Westport: Greenwood, 1983.

Hagemann, E. R. *A Comprehensive Index to* Black Mask, *1920-1951*. Bowling Green, OH: Bowling Green State U Popular P, 1982.

Nolan, William F. *The Black Mask Boys*. New York: Morrow, 1985.

Shaw, Joseph T., ed. *The Hard-Boiled Omnibus*. New York: Simon & Schuster, 1946.

J. Randolph Cox

Black Oak, Arkansas, has been made famous by the white Spandex–clad, bulging-crotched, long-haired, rebel leader of the South's foremost sexually explicit rock band emerging from the quagmires of northeastern Arkansas. Jim Mangrum and his motley crew of Arkansas axe-men gave the small Arkansas town of Black Oak notoriety with their unique form of "hot 'n' nasty—raunch 'n' roll." The band's original members, lead singer Jim Mangrum, guitarist Rickey Reynolds, guitarist Stanley Knight, guitarist Harvey Jett (replaced by Jimmy Henderson in 1974), bass guitarist Pat Daugherty, and drummer Wayne Evans (replaced by Tommy Aldridge in 1972), were musically influenced by the blues, and musicians like Elvis Presley. Via their music they pursued their dream to get out of the poverty and drudgery of rural southern life.

In 1963, Mangrum, Reynolds, J. R. Brewer, and Keith McCain formed the Knowbody Else. After breaking into several local schools to steal better sound equipment and burglarizing the town of Black Oak's cotton gin to obtain money, the four were charged with several counts of burglary and grand larceny. They were convicted, and sentenced to eight, eight-year terms at the Arkansas State Penitentiary, but the state suspended the sentences. Brewer and McCain then quit the group, and Daugherty, Jett, and Knight joined the band.

During the mid-1960s this new lineup fought and played their way through the rough Arkansas bar scene, until the sheriff of Craighead County ordered them to leave the area. After kicking around the South, and cutting a record for Stax in 1969, they decided to travel to Los Angeles, where they dropped the name the Knowbody Else, and adopted Black Oak, Arkansas. After seeing them perform at the Corral Club in Topanga Canyon, CA, Ahmet Ertegun, the president of Atlantic Records, offered the band a contract. They readily accepted, and in 1971 the band released its first gold record, *Black Oak, Arkansas*.

Black Oak, Arkansas had a strong influence upon southern culture and rock music. The band gave millions of dollars to southern charities and organizations. In 1974, for example, they built a school for the community of Oakland, AR. Since this new school had replaced the last one-room school in the state, several dignitaries, including future president Bill Clinton, attended the ribbon-cutting ceremony. In fact, the governor of Arkansas was overjoyed with the generous offer and proclaimed October 6, 1974, Black Oak Arkansas Day. Moreover, in the mid-1970s several members of the band were officially honored as Arkansas citizens of the year.

Also, Black Oak, Arkansas had a major influence upon southern rock music. Their monetary success compelled the record industry to notice other southern rock bands in the 1970s. They helped open the way for hard southern rock when the band appeared on Wolfman Jack's *Midnight Special* four times, performed on *Don Kirshner's Rock Concert*, and played at the California Jam. Other rock musicians such as Lynyrd Skynyrd, Marshall Tucker, .38 Special, and Molly Hatchet followed in Black Oak's footsteps. In addition, rock notables, such as David Lee Roth, claimed to have patterned their stage personalities after Mangrum. In retrospect, Black Oak was the first heavy metal rock group from the South, and it created a new "hillbilly metal" rock sound.

Bibliography

Hutson, Cecil Kirk. "Black Oak Arkansas: An Analysis of How Black Oak, Arkansas Reflected and Rejected Rural Southern Culture." Master's thesis, Arkansas State University, 1990.

——. "Cotton Pickin', Hillbillies and Red Necks: An Analysis of Black Oak, Arkansas and the Perpetual Stereotyping of the Rural South." *Popular Music and Society* 17.4 (1993): 47-62.

——. "Rebel Yell: An Examination of the Violent Legacies of Two Southern Musical Groups." *1994 Proceedings of the Southwest/Texas Popular Culture and American Culture Associations*.

Shiras, Ginger. "Black Oak Arkansas: Catching Up on Family Doings of Multimillion Dollar Rock Band." *Arkansas Gazette* 23 Jan. 1977.

Zabawski, Brian. "Black Oak Arkansas." *Crawdaddy* May 1972: 46.

Cecil Kirk Hutson

Black Radio Deejays date back to the 1920s. Sherman H. "Jocko" Maxwell was one of the nation's early African-American trailblazers in American radio and worked at WRNV in New York in 1929. He later worked at WNJ in Newark, and in 1934, when he was only 23, he was heard twice a week on WHOM in New Jersey. Maxwell would eventually do sportscasts over station WLHT in New York and WWRL in Long Island.

Among other African Americans also heard on radio during the 1930s, Nat D. Williams is said to have been the first black radio announcer in America. His *Amateur Night on Beale* went on the air in 1937 on WHBQ radio in Memphis, TN. There are a number of African Americans who were reportedly the "firsts" to be on the radio in America, although there have been no documented historical accounts that prove who really was the first black deejay or announcer.

Mississippi native Jack L. Cooper, for instance, could be heard on stations in Chicago as early as 1938. In 1941, he launched *The All Negro-Hour* on station WSBC in that city. Another Chicago black radio personality would soon replace Cooper on radio as the nation's premier black deejay. The Rev. Arthur B. Leaner, also known as Al Bensen and "Ole Mushmouth," launched his radio career from his church in Chicago on station WGES. Before his death in 1980, he had amassed a fortune after having started a record company and becoming a concert promoter.

Lightfoot Solomon ("Elder") Michaux is probably more unfamiliar to casual readers of radio history than others. Michaux became known in 1929 as the "Happy I Am Preacher," when he began broadcasting a weekly one-hour religious program on WJSV in Washington, DC. His radio program gained wide popularity and was the only one to be retained by the Columbia Broadcasting System in 1932 when the network became the new owners of WJSV.

Hal Jackson, a vice president of New York's Inner City Broadcasting, is also touted as the first black sportscaster on radio. He began his career on WOOK-AM in Washington, DC, in 1939. Jackson later became host of a radio program on ABC Network Radio in 1951 and eventually joined NBC television as host of *Frontiers of Faith* in 1968.

Well-known black radio announcers and television deejays like Black Entertainment Television's (BET) Donnie Simpson, Frankie Crocker of New York's WBLS-FM radio, and Dallas/Chicago announcer Tom Joyner were preceded in the field of on-air radio announcing by these and other trailblazing black radio announcers who earned their way into the lives and hearts of the American radio audience during the formative years of the industry (see also the next entry).
Bibliography
Ashcraft-Webb, Lillian. *About My Father's Business: The Life of Elder Michaux.* Westport: Greenwood, 1981.
Brooks, Tim, and Earle Marsh. *The Complete Directory to Prime Time Network TV Shows, 1946-Present.* 4th ed. New York: Ballantine, 1981.

Newman, Mark. *Entrepreneurs of Profit and Pride: From Black Appeal to Radio Soul.* New York: Praeger, 1988.
Tinney, James S., and Justine J. Rector. *Issues and Trends in Afro-American Journalism.* Washington, DC: UP of America, 1980.

Frank W. Johnson, Jr.

Black Radio Networks developed along with the civil rights movement and demands for more black-oriented programming. Media and advertising executives were also beginning to recognize the purchasing power of the black community.

The father of the first black radio network was Leonard Evans, a black Chicago advertising executive. On January 19, 1954, the National Negro Network (NNN) was the first radio network to provide programming, coast to coast, exclusively to "colored people," and enlisted some 40 radio stations in its inaugural broadcast. The network's programming format included gospel music, rhythm and blues, wire-copy, news summaries, and a popular, dramatic transcription serial, based on black life. At one point, the short-lived network boasted a list of advertisers including the Pet Milk Company, Philip Morris, William Wrigley, A&P Supermarkets, Coca-Cola, Firestone Tire Company, Buick, General Electric, and Westinghouse.

Jay Levy, another black businessman, launched Black Audio Network (BAN) during the height of the civil rights movement in 1968. Blacks had begun to demand more equal opportunities as on-air personalities, writers, reporters, and news anchors. In fact, BAN was created because of a demand by radio stations to hire blacks to gather and report news of the assassination of Dr. Martin Luther King, Jr. BAN fed news items and reports by telephone from New York to affiliate stations on a daily basis. Another black radio network to use black news reporters and news makers to provide news coverage to black programmed stations was Third World Media News (TWMN), which went on the air in 1971.

In 1972, the first permanent black radio network, Mutual Reports, was launched by the Mutual Broadcasting System (MBS) from Washington, DC; Mutual Reports eventually became Mutual Black Network (MBN). C. Edward Little, a white man who had served as president of MBS, is given credit for launching both MBN and a Spanish-speaking service known as Mutual Spanish Network. MBN's format included a five-minute newscast on the hour, sportscasts, special programs, and in-depth public affairs items.

In 1973, Eugene Jackson launched the nation's second permanent black radio network, National Black Network (NBN), in New York. The popularity of MBN and NBN increased as the number of radio stations owned by blacks grew. One of the largest black-owned radio station groups, the Sheridan Broadcasting Company, eventually purchased MBN and changed the network's name to the Sheridan Broadcasting Network (SBN) in 1979. Sheridan is headed by black businessman Ronald Davenport, and is based in Pittsburgh, PA.

Black radio network ownership grew even more in 1982 when New York–based Inner City Broadcasting purchased NBN. Inner City is owned by black businessman Percy

Sutton, a former Manhattan borough president and owner of several radio stations, as well as the famous Apollo Theater. In 1991, black radio network ownership took another turn when the nation's two black-owned radio networks, SBN and NBN, merged to create the American Urban Radio Networks (AURN), which in 2000 continues to be the only black-owned radio network.

Bibliography

Abarbanal, Albert, and Alex Haley. "A New Audience for Radio." *Harper's* Feb. 1956.

Feretti, Fred. "The White Captivity of Black Radio." *Columbia Journalism Review* Summer 1970.

Johnson, Frank W., Jr. "History of the Development of Black Radio Networks in the U.S.: 1954-1993." *Journal of Radio Studies* 2.2 (1993-94).

Frank W. Johnson, Jr.

Bloch, Robert (1917-1994), best remembered for his novel *Psycho* (1959), which Alfred Hitchcock made into the famous film of the same title in 1960, wrote hundreds of short stories, novels, radio plays, movie screenplays, television dramas, and other popular fictions. Raised in the Midwest, he eventually settled in Los Angeles, where as an author he made significant contributions to the genres of fantasy, horror, mystery fiction, science fiction, and more. A dominant subject in his work is the probing of psychopathology; many of his stories explore sexual or emotional disturbance culminating in grisly behavior and violence. Others incorporate elements of comedy and parody, while still others showcase his vast knowledge of world and literary history. A trademark of Bloch tales is the twist ending, and he has been tabbed "the 20th century's O. Henry."

His first major story, "The Feast in the Abbey," appeared in the January 1935 issue of *Weird Tales*. Between 1935 and 1952, Bloch published 67 works of short fiction in *Weird Tales* alone; his work also appeared in other magazines such as *Amazing Stories*, *Fantastic Adventures*, *Imaginative Tales*, *Unknown Worlds*, and *Unusual Stories*, and showed the strong influence of H. P. Lovecraft (see entry). Bloch's first hardcover book was a collection of short tales published by August Derleth's Arkham House of Sauk City, WI, *The Opener of the Way* (1945), and several other collections followed. Among the author's many novels are *The Kidnapper* (1953), *Spiderweb* (1953), *Firebug* (1962), *The Star Stalker* (1968), *Psycho II* (1982), and *Psycho House* (1990). Bloch's stories were also the basis for several motion pictures, and he wrote for television, including three episodes for the original *Star Trek* series. Numerous writers (including Stephen King and Ray Bradbury) have acknowledged Bloch's influence.

Bibliography

Bloch, Robert. *The Early Fears.* New York: Tor, 1994.

——. *Once around the Bloch: An Unauthorized Autobiography.* New York: Tor, 1993.

Larson, Randall D., ed. *The Complete Robert Bloch: An Illustrated Comprehensive Bibliography.* Sunnyvale: Fandom, 1986.

Garyn G. Roberts

Block, Martin (1903?-1967). The show most often given credit for initiating the modern disc jockey movement was Martin Block's *Make Believe Ballroom* on WNEW in New York City. Block's *Ballroom* began in February 1935 during the trial of Bruno Hauptmann for the kidnapping of the Lindbergh baby. Martin Block, who had started working at WNEW in December 1934 after moving to New York from California, was a $20-a-week staff announcer who was engineering the broadcasts of the trial from the station.

Block convinced Bernice Judis, the station manager, to let him use phonograph records to fill some of the gaps between trial segments. When the next recess arrived, Block introduced and played several records. His manner of presentation, however, was unique. Block pretended that the show was a live broadcast from a giant dance hall with a glittering chandelier. He, then, was the master of ceremonies introducing the songs as if the bands were actually there.

In time, Block's *Make Believe Ballroom* became the nation's preeminent disc jockey show, and, during various periods, it was broadcast over the Mutual and ABC networks. It was even syndicated over the Voice of America briefly. Block, then, was the first popular icon of the jockey genre and also its first millionaire.

Bibliography

Fornatale, Peter, and Joshua Mills. *Radio in the Television Age.* Woodstock: Overlook, 1980.

"Martin Block Parlays a $20 a Week Idea into a New Radio Pattern." *Variety* 8 Feb. 1950: 33.

Passman, Arnold. *The Deejays.* New York: Macmillan, 1971.

Charles F. Ganzert

Blondie, rising out of the lower Manhattan musical scene cranked up by the Velvet Underground and the New York Dolls in the late 1960s and early 1970s respectively, was one of the most successful groups to come out of the new wave movement. The group formed by pairing former Playboy bunny Deborah Harry (1945-) with the backup group of her earlier girl vocal group the Stilettos. With Harry on vocals, Chris Stein (guitar), Jimmi Destri (keyboards), Gary Valentine (bass), and Clem Burke (drums), Blondie began playing CBGB's, the New York City nightclub operated by Hilly Kristal and generally acknowledged as the birthplace of New York City's punk and new wave movements.

In 1976 Blondie recorded their first single, "X-Offender," and their subsequent self-titled album on the small Private Stock label as the corporate music industry had yet to embrace the burgeoning new wave movement. By 1977, that was no longer the case, as the band's contract was bought out by Chrysalis records to include previously recorded material. When the second album, *Plastic Letters*, was released, it included a remake of Randy and the Rainbows' 1976 hit "Denise," beginning Blondie's U.K. hit run while the LP broke into the U.S. album charts.

In 1981 Blondie outdid themselves once and for all with their *Autoamerican* album, which bore the fruit of two No. 1 singles, the reggae-tinged "The Tide Is High" and the rap-influenced "Rapture." The album itself reached the No. 7

position on the U.S. album chart and was the group's most successful to date.

On the heels of Blondie's success, Harry released a solo LP, *KooKoo* (1981), which was a Top 40 album but failed to provide a substantial single. As happens with many groups after several successful releases, in 1981 *The Best of Blondie* compilation was released and reached No. 30 in the charts. In 1982, Blondie recorded their last album, *The Hunter*, which provided the minor hit "Island of Lost Souls," their last U.S. chart single. That same year the group announced its split and Harry took roles in films, most notably *Videodrome* (1983) and *Hairspray* (1988). She would also go on to record two more solo albums, *Rockbird* (1986) and *Def, Dumb and Blonde* (1989). In 1988, an album of critically reviled remixes of Blondie's hits, *Once More into the Bleach*, belied the group's originality and punky pop qualities.

Bibliography
Bangs, Lester. *Blondie*. New York: Simon & Schuster, 1980.
Rees, Dafydd, and Luke Crampton. *Rock Movers and Shakers*. New York: Billboard, 1991.
Robbins, Ira. *The Trouser Press Record Guide*. New York: Collier, 1991.

Hugh Foley

Blood Sports have generally been ignored in recent writing in both the sociology of sport and the history of sport. Richard Hummel's *Hunting and Fishing for Sport* (1994) is a seminal and pioneering study. He defines blood sports as "those events constructed by humans for sporting purposes which result in harm or death to specified animals." Hummel clusters his chapters around major themes and issues, and these microstudies are set against a wider focus, the dynamics of conflicting values and contrasting moral crusades in a constant state of agitation because of the controversial and divisive nature of these activities.

Hummel identifies four critical issues. The first is blood sports as an area of investigation, and the ongoing battles over the legitimacy of blood sports. His second theme is the interrelationship of technology and fair play. Hummel addresses the question of whether animals stand a sporting chance of surviving and escaping. His third area of concern is man-animal interactions as sport, and he illustrates this with the role of trophy seeking. Finally, Hummel looks at blood sports in the context of popular culture. Sport hunting in narrative films is examined, as are hunting and fishing topics as covered in boys' books.

Blood sports have a history as long as mankind itself. By the 19th century in America, according to Elliott Gorn and Warren Goldstein, cockfighting and bull- and bear-baiting went on in New York, Philadelphia, and Baltimore. Rat-baiting took place in bars, at hotel stables, and in specially designed pits. The Sportsman's Hall in New York had room for 250 avid fans who might pay as much as $5 to watch a champion dog fight. Then, as now, the debate raged about the ethical dimensions of these activities. By the mid-19th century, cruelty to animals grew to be as important an issue as the debasement of humankind, to those who would outlaw blood sports.

A century ago the number of journalists, essayists, and academics writing about blood sports was considerable. That is not true today. Neither the 1988 nor the 1992 *Directory of Scholars* (North America Society for Sport History) lists blood sports in the topical index.

For a cleverly constructed and revealing study of a contemporary sports subculture, Fred Hawley's examination of cock fighting in Northwest Louisiana is exemplary. Two central issues explored by Hawley are the roles of women associated with cockfighters, and the fact that personal honor and masculinity are interwoven into the game or contest ethos.

Philosophically and ethically, blood sports are a paradox. George Bernard Shaw observed, "When a man wants to murder a tiger he calls it sport, when a tiger wants to murder him he calls it ferocity."

Bibliography
Cone, Carl B., ed. *Hounds in the Morning: Sundry Sports of Merry England*. Lexington: UP of Kentucky, 1981.
Gorn, Elliott J., and Warren Goldstein. *A Brief History of American Sports*. New York: Hill & Wang, 1993.
Hawley, Fred. "Cockfighting in the Piney Woods: Gameness in the New South." *Sport Place* 1.2 (1987): 19-26.
Hummel, Richard. *Hunting and Fishing for Sport: Commerce, Controversy, Popular Culture*. Bowling Green, OH: Bowling Green State U Popular P, 1994.
Palmatier, Robert A., and Harold L. Ray. *Sports Talk: A Dictionary of Sports Metaphors*. Westport: Greenwood, 1989.

Scott A. G. M. Crawford

Blood, Sweat, and Tears, also known as BS&T, was an innovative New York City–based musical group that fused rock, jazz, and blues. The group was formed by keyboard player, songwriter, and vocalist Al Kooper (1944-). Kooper's career started in the 1950s as a member of the group the Royal Teens. He also had several successes as a songwriter, including the 1965 Gary Lewis and the Playboys' "This Diamond Ring." Kooper's credits as a session musician included the well-known organ accompaniment to Bob Dylan's "Like a Rolling Stone."

Kooper joined a blues/rock group, the Blues Project, in 1967. The Blues Project was formed in 1965 by guitarist Danny Kalb and drummer Roy Blumenfeld. It included a loose collection of jazz, folk, and blues musicians who played in Greenwich Village clubs. The group's signature song was "Flute Thing," which featured flutist Andy Kulberg and other group members in extended solos that were sometimes bluesy, other times psychedelic.

But the Blues Project was wracked by personality conflicts. When Kalb became ill in October 1967, the group broke up. Katz and Kooper began playing regularly at New York's Cafe Au Go Go with drummer Bobby Colomby and bass player Jim Fielder. The four added a brass section consisting of Fred Lipsius, Dick Halligan, Randy Brecker, and Jerry Weiss, and Blood, Sweat, and Tears was formed.

The group got its name from an all-night jam session featuring Kooper, B. B. King, and Jimi Hendrix. Kooper did not notice that he had cut his hand until the morning light.

When he saw that his organ keyboard was covered with blood, the name came to mind.

BS&T's first album was the highly acclaimed, if less than commercially successful, *Child Is Father to the Man* (1968). The LP featured songs by Harry Nilsson, Randy Newman, and Gerry Goffin and Carole King. Lipsius contributed the group's brass arrangements. But the group soon began to suffer from the same kinds of personality conflicts that beset the Blues Project, culminating in an onstage battle between Kooper and Weiss.

Colomby and Katz, who had more of a flair for mainstream pop music, took charge of BS&T's musical direction. They hired Chuck Winfield, Lew Soloff, and Jerry Hyman to replace the departing Brecker and Weiss, expanding the brass section from four to five musicians. But the most significant change in the band was the addition of a powerful front man, British singer David Clayton-Thomas.

The new Blood, Sweat and Tears self-titled debut album was a smash hit in the spring of 1969. It topped the U.S. album charts for seven weeks and earned a Grammy Award for album of the year. It produced three million-seller singles, the first being a cover of the Motown ballad "You've Made Me So Very Happy." The second hit single was a Clayton-Thomas composition, "Spinning Wheel." In the single version, the trumpet solo was edited out, and listeners to Top 40 stations were not aware of the group's jazz influences. In November, the group released an upbeat, honky-tonk version of Laura Nyro's "And When I Die."

The group gained notoriety in 1970 for embarking on a tour of Eastern bloc countries including Rumania, Yugoslavia, and Poland. BS&T's third album (the second since Kooper's departure) was appropriately titled *Blood, Sweat and Tears 3*. It also reached the No. 1 spot on the charts in August 1970. The LP produced two Top 30 singles, "Hi-De-Ho" and "Lucretia MacEvil."

In the summer of 1971, the group released the album *Blood, Sweat and Tears 4*. The band, like its album titles, began to sound repetitious, although the album reached No. 10 on the charts. Two singles from *Blood, Sweat and Tears 4* were minor successes, "Go Down Gamblin'" and "Lisa, Listen to Me." BS&T also had a minor personnel change, with horn-player Dave Bargeron replacing Jerry Hyman.

The group rapidly deteriorated after the fourth album with Jerry Fisher replacing Clayton-Thomas and the departure of arranger Fred Lipsius. Guitarist Steve Katz left the group in late 1972 after the release of the album *New Blood*. In 1973, the group released *No Sweat*. The band's brass section was in such a state of flux that it often changed from concert to concert. The lead vocalist changed again, with Jerry LaCroix replacing Fisher.

David Clayton-Thomas returned in the summer of 1974 and the group recorded three disappointing albums between then and 1976, *Tell Me That I'm Wrong*, *New City*, and *More Than Ever*. Columbia Records dropped BS&T in 1976, and the last original member, Bobby Colomby, left shortly thereafter. Clayton-Thomas reassembled the group for two albums on the ABC label, but neither was successful. Colomby produced the first of those, *Brand New Day*, in 1977.

Colomby and Clayton-Thomas retained the rights to the group's name, which was changed in 1975 to Blood, Sweat and Tears Featuring David Clayton-Thomas. The group occasionally got together again for concerts.

Bibliography

Romanowski, Patricia, and Holly George-Warren. *The New Rolling Stone Encyclopedia of Rock & Roll.* New York: Fireside, 1995.
Stambler, Irwin. *Encyclopedia of Pop, Rock, and Soul.* New York: St. Martin's, 1989.

Ken Nagelberg

Bloodworth-Thomason, Linda (1947-), has been called by *Time* magazine "the closest thing TV has to an advocacy producer" and listed by *Newsweek* as one of the nation's "cultural elite." Creator, co-producer, and principal writer of three successful prime-time series broadcast in the 1990s, she has been one of the few women in the television industry to obtain such power.

Linda Bloodworth, from Poplar Bluff, MO, graduated with a Bachelor of Arts from the University of Missouri. She moved to Los Angeles in the early 1970s to work for the *Wall Street Journal* in advertising and later the *Los Angeles Daily Journal* as a reporter. She then taught for two years as an instructor of English literature at a high school in Watts before beginning her career as a freelance writer.

When Bloodworth met actress Mary Kay Place (*Mary Hartman, Mary Hartman* on TV; *The Big Chill* in film), Place suggested they write a script together. Based on their efforts, producer Larry Gelbart asked them to be the first women writers for *M*A*S*H* in the mid-1970s. Together they wrote three scripts and Bloodworth wrote an additional two for the series. She continued over the next few years to write for others. In 1982 Bloodworth created *Filthy Rich* for CBS, a spoof of the popular prime-time serial *Dallas*. Concerned with the members of a Memphis family trying to live by the dictates of the recently deceased head of the clan who had taped his will, the series had a strong beginning in summer, but soon lost its large audience and was canceled in less than a year. She also created *1st & Ten*, a half-hour comedy set in the world of professional football, for pay cable network Home Box Office (HBO) in 1984.

Bloodworth-Thomason made her most important collaboration in 1983 when she married Harry Thomason, a native of Arkansas whom she met at Columbia Pictures Television. The two formed Mozark Productions and in 1985 they produced their first project, *Lime Street*. An hour adventure series starring Robert Wagner (previously seen in *Hart to Hart* on TV), the show was canceled after only a few episodes when the young actress (Samantha Smith) who portrayed one of Wagner's daughters was killed in a plane crash. Smith had become famous when she wrote to Soviet leader Yuri Andropov urging peace and was invited to visit.

Much better luck came with the Thomasons' next series, *Designing Women* (see entry), a half-hour comedy that debuted on CBS in 1986. Created by Bloodworth-Thomason, it was co-produced by both Thomasons. Set in Atlanta, it was centered on four women who worked in an interior design business located in the home of one of them. Although the series lost much of its audience when CBS moved it from their popular line-up on Monday nights (which included *Murphy Brown* and other shows targeted to women), viewer outcry convinced the network to renew the series and put it back to its original time slot. Despite some problems with actress Delta Burke and a few cast changes, it enjoyed a seven-year run of original episodes.

With *Designing Women* Bloodworth-Thomason became the first American writer in television history to write 35 consecutive episodes of a series, and out of the first 100 shows, she wrote 65. Through her characters, most notably Julia and Mary Jo, Bloodworth-Thomason addressed important topics such as wife abuse, child abuse, world hunger, and sexism. In "The Strange Case of Clarence and Anita" she even showed clips from the Thomas/Hill hearings where, as the Senate considered Clarence Thomas for a position on the Supreme Court, he defended himself against charges of sexually harassing Anita Hill years earlier.

The next successful series Bloodworth-Thomason created for CBS was *Evening Shade*, which debuted in 1990 and lasted four years. Featuring film star Burt Reynolds, the show centered around a high school football coach, his attorney wife, played by Marilu Henner (formerly in the critically acclaimed TV comedy *Taxi*), and their family. Once again, Bloodworth-Thomason was focusing on southern culture, only this time in Arkansas, home state of her husband and their good friend, future president Bill Clinton. In July 1992 the Thomasons produced *The Man from Hope*, the acclaimed documentary on Bill Clinton presented at the Democratic National Convention where he was nominated for president. After Clinton was elected, the Thomasons were often referred to as "First Friends" and President Clinton was criticized for all his Hollywood connections.

The debut of *Hearts Afire* in 1992 gave Bloodworth-Thomason three comedy series in prime time that year. The show started out in Washington, DC, but also ended up in the South. John Ritter (from the 1970s hit TV comedy *Three's Company*, and the 1980s critically acclaimed dramedy *Hooperman*) portrayed John Hartman, an aide for a conservative senator and Markie Post (from the popular TV comedy, *Night Court*, begun in the late 1980s) played Georgie Ann Lahti, a liberal journalist who became the senator's speech writer.

In 1990 CBS gave the Thomasons a multimillion-dollar contract for five shows over eight years (*Hearts Afire* was the first). With it, Bloodworth-Thomason had become one of an elite group of writer-producers who, according to the *New York Times*, were guaranteed not only financial security but also the freedom to produce their own ideas in prime time. She has received many awards for her writing, including numerous Emmy and Writer's Guild nominations. Her shows have also received a number of civic and cultural awards, including the Humanitarian Award from Funders Concerned about AIDS and the Genii Award from American Women in Radio and Television. In 1992 Bloodworth-Thomason received the first Freedom of Speech Award from Americans for Democratic Action, an organization founded by former First Lady Eleanor Roosevelt.

Bibliography
Alter, Jonathon. "The Cultural Elite." *Newsweek* 5 Oct. 1992: 30-41.
Marc, David, and Robert J. Thompson. *Prime Time, Prime Movers*. Boston: Little, Brown, 1992.
McNeil, Alex. *Total Television*. 3rd ed. New York: Penguin, 1991.
Spangler, Lynn. "Designing the Thomas/Hill Hearings on *Designing Women*: Creative and Business Influences on Content." *He Said, She Said, We Listened: A Communication Perspective on the Hill/Thomas Hearings*. Ed. Paul Siegel. Cresskill: Hampton, 1995.
Zoglin, Richard. "Sitcom Politics." *Time* 21 Sept. 1992: 44-47.

Lynn C. Spangler

Bloom County (1980-1989) was created, written, and drawn by Berkeley Breathed. The world-famous comic strip was based on characters and ideas Breathed formulated and developed during his years at the University of Texas drawing *Academia Waltz* for the *Daily Texan* (1978-79). The strip appealed to both adults and children, containing political and philosophical themes.

A fanciful, if anxiety-ridden examination of life in the 1980s, *Bloom County* (*BC*) was presented through the eyes of sensitive, intelligent children and animals, and the somewhat mentally bruised, jaded, and very imaginative adults with whom they associated. The characters were somewhat familiar, but hardly stock: a strung-out cat named Bill; the wheelchair-bound Vietnam vet, Cutter John; the smarmy Steve Dallas; the psychoanalyst's dream, Opus; the precocious, intellectual, 10-year-old child Milo Bloom; the sensitive 10-year-old child Binkley, living with monsters in his anxiety closet and pipe dreams under his bed; and Oliver, an intelligent child who spends a great deal of time building nuclear devices and questioning the universe. *BC* featured "dandelion breaks"—a sort of timeout from reality, and from anxiety about life and females—elections supporting Bill for President (and Opus for "Veep"), *Star Trek* adventures, utterances of "ack," and bits of poetry. Breathed's comic strip examined the culture and politics of the 1980s, leaving few stones unturned. Subjects of discussion and parody included the "Left," the "Right," machismo, the Moral Majority, James Watt, Creationists, David Stockman, football, the Royal Couple, the Reagans, consumerism, and drugs—each subject depicted in its own shame and glory.

Breathed denies that *Bloom County* was a blend of Walt Kelly's *Pogo*, with its political views and philosophical musings, and Charles Schulz's *Peanuts*, with its anxious, adult-children-type characters, claiming that he never remembers reading such strips. When *Bloom County* ended in 1989, Breathed replaced the famous comic strip with the short-lived, somewhat darker in tone Sunday feature, *Outland*, which was a sort of sequel to *Bloom County*. At the end of its run, *Bloom County* was being published in more than 1,000 newspapers.

Bibliography
Breathed, Berkeley. *Bloom County Babylon: Five Years of Basic Naughtiness*. Boston: Little, Brown, 1986.

——. *Bloom County: Loose Tails*. Boston: Little, Brown, 1983.

——. *Classics of Western Literature: "Bloom County" 1986-1989*. Boston: Little, Brown, 1990.

——. *Politically, Fashionably, and Aerodynamically Incorrect: The First Outland Collection*. Boston: Little, Brown, 1992.

Goulart, Ron. *The Encyclopedia of American Comics: From 1897 to the Present*. New York: Facts on File, 1990.

Virginia Woods Roberts

Blue Highways (1982), by William Least Heat Moon, arguably the greatest American travel narrative of the 20th century, describes the journey of a man of mixed descent, Sioux and Caucasian, after being laid off as a college instructor. The narrative prefigures many 1990s preoccupations, with diversity and economic heartlessness and even the breakup of the American family. The title of the book comes from the map representation of secondary roads by blue lines. The story is of the events that the author experiences on these roads as he circles the United States beginning from Missouri, traveling eastward, then northward, westward and then eastward again.

Bibliography

Perrin, Noel. *New York Times Book Review* 6 Feb. 1983: 1.

Tammaro, Thom. "Lost in America: Steinbeck's *Travels with Charley* and William Least Heat Moon's *Blue Highways*." *Rediscovering Steinbeck: Revisionist Views of His Art, Politics, and Intellect*. Ed. Cliff Lewis and Carroll Britch. Lewiston: Mellen, 1989.

William R. Klink

Blume, Judy (1938-), is perhaps the most commercially successful American writer of books for children and problem novels for young adults in the 20th century. Her works are passionately sought by her readers if often abhorred by their parents. She began to write at age 27, with two young children, "determined to write the kinds of books that weren't there for me when I was growing up. Books about real life and real feelings."

Blume probes subjects that have always inspired anxiety in young people, as well as concerns peculiar to today's adolescents. Her topics range from obesity, the onset of menstruation, and sibling rivalry to the integration of a neighborhood and coping with the violent death of a parent. With the publication of *Are You There, God? It's Me, Margaret*, Blume's fame was ensured. Girls from childhood through the teenage years identify with Margaret as the new student in school, her search for religious identity, and her desire for the onset of puberty.

Blume is adept at realistic dialogue and humor, and is fine-tuned to the minutiae of her readers' daily lives. Other notable titles include *Tiger Eyes* (1981), about a Hispanic family, *Deenie* (1973), and *Then Again, Maybe I Won't* (1971). Some of her works have been cited as notable books by the American Library Association, and she is generally highly regarded by teachers and critics. Margaret remains the character for which she is best known, but five-year-old

Fudge of *Superfudge* (1980) and *Fudge-a-Mania* (1990) may eclipse her as he is serialized on television.

Bibliography

Weidt, Maryann. *Presenting Judy Blume*. Boston: Twayne, 1989.

Linda Burns

Board Games, from their earliest religious forms to their contemporary commercial forms, have provided players with countless hours of enjoyment. Whether the games have as their themes divinations of the gods, the piety of individuals, or the interminable quest for wealth and power, they also provide observers with an interesting glimpse into the values of the cultures from which they emerge. Bound most formally by the principles of competition, skill, and luck, board games have formed an important component of leisure-time activity in almost every civilization.

The earliest known example comes from a royal cemetery in Mesopotamia and is housed in a museum in Brussels, Belgium. Found along with ivory game pieces, this board game dates from 4000 to 3500 B.C. The Egyptian game senet, a forerunner of all backgammon games, dominated the ancient world. Archaeologists even found a senet set in the tomb of King Tutankhamen. Backgammon traveled from Egypt to Europe, appearing first in England as early as 1645. Most early games, like the 18th-century A Journey through Europe and Game of Virtue Rewarded and Vice Punished, had religious or educational significance.

Board games first appeared in the U.S. in the mid-19th century, when Mansions of Happiness and Piety met with great popularity. European immigrants brought board games with them to the U.S., and craftspersons and other individuals made a large variety of boards by hand. When not in use, board games often served as wall decorations in 19th-century dwellings. In the 1850s, early game manufacturers Milton Bradley and Parker Brothers began to manufacture lithographed boards, but homemade boards remained popular into the early 20th century, when cheap paper boards rendered the homemade variety obsolete.

As the nation's values changed, so did its board games. As early as the 1890s, games like Up to Klondyke offered players a taste of the excitement of the California gold rush or other money-making possibilities, and by the 1930s the emphasis of most board games had shifted from the spiritual to the secular. In the midst of the Great Depression board games reached a new height in popularity and since then have followed economic cycles, finding the greatest popularity in times of economic hardship. It was also in the 1930s that board games emphasizing business principles and the art of making money took precedence in the industry.

The early-20th-century recognition of childhood and then of adolescence as specific cultural experiences also affected the development of the board games industry. Parents began to expect that children's leisure activities would in some way shape their values by teaching them to think, to play in a group, and not incidentally, to learn the art of competition. Manufacturers took this lead and introduced educational children's games, but money-making often formed the basis of the education. Two contemporary games, Meet Me at the Mall, and Mall Madness, for instance, encourage girls to practice their shopping skills. Television has also had a major impact on the industry; television shows and board games often share themes and characters.

Gender is an important factor in the design and content of board games for children. Game boards and boxes feature pinks and pastels for girls, camouflage greens and browns for boys. Indoor worlds provide the settings for girls' games while boys' games feature the great outdoors. Girls' games often promote dependency on boys or men. In Heartthrob: The Dream Date Game and Sweet Valley High: Can You Find a Boyfriend in Time for the Big Date? girls learn that they need boyfriends to complete their self-definition. For boys, war games remain extremely popular; in 1990, 200 war-related board games filled the nation's toy store shelves. The Gulf War inspired several new ones: A Line in the Sand and Arabian Nightmare: Desert Storm. Boys, in their leisure play, learn nothing of girls but a great deal about fighting for power.

Adults, who purchase approximately 20 percent of all board games sold in the U.S., form a small but significant target audience. Adults generally prefer trivia and word games, and longtime favorite Scrabble and newer favorite Trivial Pursuit continually rank high in adult sales. Money-making values inform many adult games, and Monopoly, played by children and adults, has reached over $100 million in worldwide sales. Most adult games centering on money provide a more sophisticated challenge than do the children's mall games, but one, It's Only Money, has players traveling around a shopping mall visiting stores that feature popular brand-name products.

Two American board games, Monopoly and Scrabble, merit special attention here, as they are an important part of the nation's game-playing identity. Monopoly, probably the most famous board game in the U.S. if not the world, has disputed origins. The most common story of its invention, while false, fits American notions of Horatio Alger–like success, attributing it to Charles Darrow, an unemployed salesman suffering the effects of the Great Depression and dreaming about the money-making possibilities available in Atlantic City. The real story differs a bit and starts with a woman, Elizabeth Magie Phillips, who invented and patented the Landlord's Game in 1904. A Quaker, single-tax enthusiast, and follower of Henry George, Phillips designed a game to promote her own irreverent attitude toward business. She introduced the Landlord's Game to George Parker of Parker Brothers, who had already purchased one of her games, Mock Trial, but Parker decided this game was too political to sell well. Phillips sold the Landlord's Game on her own, and it became especially popular on college campuses. Harvard and Princeton students made some of their own changes, including a name change to Monopoly, and the enterprising Phillips incorporated the most successful of those changes into her game. Charles Darrow, the unemployed salesmen, then stepped in, combining Monopoly with Finance, a popular game from the Midwest. Darrow's friend Ruth Hoskins suggested they change the place names to

Board Games. Photo courtesy of Popular Culture Library, Bowling Green State University, Bowling Green, OH.

match real places in Atlantic City; true Monopoly enthusiasts know that they misspelled the name of Marven Gardens. Parker Brothers purchased the new version of the game in 1935, and Monopoly saved the ailing company, which sold 2 million sets in two years.

Scrabble, the popular word game, has also achieved worldwide fame with dozens of annual tournaments, 200 licensed clubs, 9,000 players attending club meetings, and 7,000 subscribers to Scrabble Players News. Invented in 1933 by Alfred Butts, Scrabble hit the mass market in 1949 and became tremendously popular in 1952. Game manufacturers Selchow & Righter acquired rights to the game in 1953, and by the end of their first year they had sold 1.1 million sets and secured more than 10 million players. The first Scrabble dictionary was published in 1978, and current records estimate the number of Scrabble players at 33 million.

Milton Bradley, the first board game manufacturer in the U.S., entered the market in 1861 with The Checkered Game of Life. This board game offered its players two possible outcomes: happy old age or financial ruin. During the Civil War Milton Bradley introduced several pocket games, Games for Soldiers, initiating a long tradition of war games in the United States. He introduced other Civil War–related games as well: Patriot Heroes and Who's the Traitor? The second company to publish board games, Selchow & Righter, entered the market in 1867. Scrabble provided them with sales and fame, but Selchow & Righter, even with Scrabble, went out of business, and Milton Bradley acquired the rights to Scrabble. The third company to enter the U.S. board game market, Parker Brothers, did so in 1883. George Parker launched his board game career with Banking and invented over 100 additional games by the time he died in 1953.

Today's four game and toy manufacturing giants, Parker Brothers, Milton Bradley, Mattel, and Fisher-Price, account for over half of the $6 billion worth of sales in the toy industry. Of that total, 20 percent comes from board games; sales of board games reached $1.2 billion in 1991. Although fantasy games and computer games have challenged the stronghold that toy manufacturers have had on the leisure time of both children and adults, board games continue to sell. Trivial Pursuit, for example, invented when Canadians Chris Haney and Scott Abbott grumbled about having to buy a whole new Scrabble set to replace a few pieces, has had enormous success, selling more than 60 million sets in 33 countries and in 19 languages. The successes of Trivial Pursuit and Pictionary, another recent game, have caused manufacturers to pay attention once again to small-time inventors and not to rely strictly on the inventors they hire. Game manufacturers have also made computer versions of the most popular board games: Parker Brothers introduced an electronic version of Monopoly for use on Nintendo's Game Boy system. And board games continue to follow current social trends. "Green" or environmental games have found a market among children and adults, with Pollution Solution and Save the Whales ranking high in sales for educational board games.

Bibliography

Barol, Bill. "Game Boards." *American Heritage* 41 (Feb. 1990): 30-31.

Costello, Matthew J. *The Greatest Games of All Times*. New York: Wiley, 1991.

Ollman, Bertell. *Class Struggle Is the Name of the Game: True Confessions of a Marxist Businessman*. New York: Morrow, 1983.

Scanlon, Jennifer. "Boys-R-Us: Board Games and the Socialization of Young Adolescent Girls." *Images of the Child*. Ed. Harry Eiss. Bowling Green, OH: Bowling Green State U Popular P, 1994.

Seiter, Ellen. *Sold Separately: Children and Parents in Consumer Culture*. New Brunswick: Rutgers UP, 1993.

Jennifer Scanlon

Bob Newhart Show, The (1972-1978), **Newhart** (1982-1990), and **Bob!** (1992-1993) are all dependent upon one entity—the "Button Down Mind" of Bob Newhart (1929-). Indeed, Newhart's ability to create sanity while surrounded by surrealism and insanity has become the hallmark of each of his shows. After all, it was Newhart, the midwestern accountant-turned-comic, who had become famous for his outlandish comedy routines based on telephone conversations with people like Abraham Lincoln and Sir Walter Raleigh; his albums featuring such skits, produced in the early 1960s, sold millions. Newhart found similar success in television, with *The Bob Newhart Show* and *Newhart* each garnering respectable TV audiences.

The Bob Newhart Show, produced by MTM, and created by *Mary Tyler Moore Show* veterans David Davis and Lorenzo Music, was based on relevant topics divided between the home life and the work of a Chicago psychologist, Robert Hartley. As a psychologist, Newhart could remain stuffy and conservative as his job opened him up to America's changing values and mores. His group therapy sessions provided a great deal of comic interaction among widely diverse, highly defined neurotic characters. Bob also interacted well with his often petty and selfish co-workers, who included dentist Jerry Robinson (Peter Bonerz) and secretary Carol Kester (Marcia Wallace).

Bob's wife, Emily (Suzanne Pleshette), an elementary school teacher who later became a principal, was one of the first TV wives with an aura of sensuality, and the Hartleys became one of the first TV couples to be featured sleeping in a queen-size bed.

Newhart decided to end the series in 1978. Four years later, Newhart returned to sitcoms in *Newhart*, in which he played Dick Loudon, a Vermont inn owner and TV talk show host. Like *The Bob Newhart Show*, *Newhart*'s setting provided a constant influx of strange small-town characters and hotel guests who played well against Newhart's established centering character.

Newhart's second and third seasons represented some of the finest, most inventive comedy on television, but in later years the show's surrealism got out of hand, giving it a *Green Acres* feel and making the show less believable. Much of this was due to the introduction of Larry, Darryl, and Darryl, three inbred backwoods characters whose greeting "Hi, I'm Larry, this is my brother Darryl, and this is my other brother Darryl" became a much-repeated sentence in the mid-1980s.

Newhart remained a popular series through 1990, when the cast again decided to end the series. In a nod to the first sitcom's success, the last *Newhart* episode featured Dick Loudon waking up as Robert Hartley in his old Chicago apartment, lying next to Suzanne Pleshette as Emily Hartley; this rendered the entire *Newhart* series nothing more than a dream.

Newhart, a popular TV favorite who can literally have a show any time he wants, encountered his second blow in 1993, with cancellation of *Bob!*, featuring Bob as a Chicago comic book artist. (Newhart's first cancellation occurred in 1962 when NBC canceled his comedy/variety series, also called *The Bob Newhart Show*.)

Newhart's style, though quite subtle, had a profound impact on television sitcoms, proving that a put-upon, centering character could help launch a more surrealistic brand of humor. While viewers may have outgrown him, they have not outgrown the precedents he set for sophisticated surrealistic comedy.

Bibliography

Brooks, Tim, and Earle Marsh. *The Complete Directory to Prime Time Network TV Shows, 1946-Present*. 4th ed. New York: Ballantine, 1992.

Feuer, Jane, Paul Kerry, and Tise Vahimagi. *MTM: "Quality Television."* London: BFI, 1984.

Meisler, Andy. "Bob." *New York Times* 11 Oct. 1992.

Michael B. Kassel

Bobbsey Twins, The, are the protagonists of a popular, long-running juvenile series published under the Stratemeyer Syndicate pseudonym "Laura Lee Hope." There are two sets of twins: blond-haired, blue-eyed, plump Flossie and Freddie (age four in early titles; six in later ones) and their older siblings, dark-haired, dark-eyed, slender Nan and Bert (aged eight and subsequently twelve). All live with their parents in fictional Lakeport, a town at the head of Lake Metoka, where Mr. Bobbsey owns a lumber business.

The twins' character and circumstances have altered radically since their inception in 1904. Most changes occurred after 1960, when the series was extensively revised to reflect contemporary sensibilities. Originally, the books combined cozy family activities with material comforts and wish-fulfillment. The Bobbseys traveled widely, visiting friends and relatives who welcomed the twins into their homes, planning special excursions and proffering gifts. Though the twins frequently helped others by solving minor mysteries, early titles highlighted their domestic adventures and triumphs. Books from the 1940s and 1950s incorporated a growing emphasis on consumerism and tourist attractions, while the 1960s turned the children into amateur detectives—junior versions of fellow Syndicate products Nancy Drew and the Hardy Boys—less interested in playing than pursuing clues.

The greatest modifications appeared in the New Bobbsey Twins series, which began in 1987: the family no longer kept resident domestic help; Mrs. Bobbsey acquired a part-time job as a reporter; and Nan and Bert joined a rock band.

Bibliography

Billman, Carol. *The Secret of the Stratemeyer Syndicate: Nancy Drew, the Hardy Boys, and the Million Dollar Fiction.* New York: Ungar, 1986.

Johnson, Deidre. *Edward Stratemeyer and the Stratemeyer Syndicate.* New York: Twayne, 1993.

Mason, Bobbie Ann. *The Girl Sleuth: A Feminist Guide.* Athens: U of Georgia P, 1995.

Deidre Johnson

See also
Children's Literature
Stratemeyer Syndicate, The

Bochco, Steven (1943-), has been one of Hollywood's strongest television writer-producers, a creative, irreverent experimenter. His landmark success in the 1980s with *Hill Street Blues* (1981-87) and *L.A. Law* (1986-93) marked him as one of Hollywood's major talents and creators of dramatic series. These two shows were not only ratings winners with young, upwardly mobile viewers but were also critically acclaimed. Between the two series, Emmys were awarded seven times for best dramatic series. *Hill Street Blues* set the record for awards for a dramatic series, winning 26 Emmys overall. Bochco himself won nine Emmys for the two shows.

Bochco's formula for success was based on these patterns: (1) multiple storylines, sometimes extending for weeks; (2) large ensemble casts with clearly defined, sometimes bizarre, characters; (3) scripts built around relevant social issues such as gay bashing, breast implant liability, or social responsibility of corporate America; (4) merging intense drama with black comedy (such as a woman witness revealing her breast implants on the witness stand to justify fighting a divorce by her husband); (5) frequent sexual references; and (6) use of a shaky, hand-held camera, shooting straight with no cutaways.

Despite his scripts laden with social issues, Bochco has distanced himself from the so-called Hollywood cultural elite. He emphatically insists that television is "first and foremost a selling medium, not an art medium, not an entertainment medium."

Bochco's success with *Hill Street Blues* and *L.A. Law* led to his signing a precedent-setting $50 million contract with ABC, calling for ten pilot series over six years. Included among these series were the minor successes *Hooperman* and *Doogie Howser, M.D.*; the colossal failure *Cop Rock*, an extremely expensive MTV-like police series that flopped almost immediately; another failure, the adult cartoon *Capitol Critters;* and the controversial successes *Civil Wars* and *NYPD Blue*.

Civil Wars first aired as a mid-season replacement show in 1991 and was controversial from the beginning. Created for ABC about one of Bochco's most successful specialties, lawyers, the series centered around lawyers handling bitter divorce cases. After screening the first episode, ABC demanded major revisions, saying the show was too grim and too uncommercial. The series broke new ground by featuring its star, Mariel Hemingway, completely nude—a first for prime-time television family viewing hours.

Bochco's next series also brought about massive controversy. With *NYPD Blue* (see entry), first airing in 1993, advertisers withdrew from the beginning. Affiliates refused to run the premiere because of the steamy, partially nude sex scenes and many affiliates still refused to run the show even

The Bobbsey Twins. Photo courtesy of Popular Culture Library, Bowling Green State University, Bowling Green, OH.

after its first successful year. However, it appears that the publicity only accelerated the ratings. *NYPD Blue* is another hard-edged police drama with all of Bochco's signatures, such as well-publicized nudity and raw language. Consequently, each episode is preceded by a "viewer discretion" disclaimer warning viewers against nudity and language.

Bibliography
Brown, Les. *Les Brown's Encyclopedia of Television*. New York: Visible Ink, 1991.
Current Biography Yearbook. New York: Wilson, 1991.
Mandese, Joe. "Courtroom TV." *Advertising Age* 21 Nov. 1994: 13.
Marc, David, and Robert J. Thompson. *Prime Time, Prime Movers*. Boston: Little, Brown, 1992.
Zoglin, Richard. "Bochco under Fire." *Time* 27 Sept. 1993: 81.

Sheri Carder

Bodybuilding, which has reached almost manic proportions in recent American society, is a complex term. In a sociological sense it is closely tied to body image and in a psychological sense it has links with the concepts of self-esteem, self-worth, and the traditional troika of mind, body, and soul. Fifty years ago bodybuilding was a virtual global craze and was known as physical culture. Today, physical culture is used to describe systems of sport, physical education, and recreation in what were formerly the Iron Curtain countries.

In the late nineteenth and twentieth century there emerged numbers of "strong men" who toured the world and touted their sculpted bodies as testaments to the virtue of scientifically lifting weights. There was the Scotsman Donald Dinnie, who was a champion wrestler and a Highland Games athlete of renown. He would throw the hammer in the afternoon and lift weights on a music hall stage in the evening.

Health gurus such as Bernarr MacFadden and Eugene Sandow became international celebrities by showing off their weight-trained physiques and espousing a bizarre mixture of sensible training and exercising routines (the use of dumbbells, Indian clubs, barbells, etc.) and adding ideas on healthy living and nutrition. Charles Atlas (see entry) became a male model and touted his exercise course.

Historian John Fair, in a 1987 essay on Bob Hoffman, outlined the golden years of American weight lifting (the 1940s to the 1960s) and then traced its decline up to the 1980s. Bob Hoffman, despite being the founder of the York Barbell Company, was unable to win over an American public increasingly captivated by the jogging and tennis booms of the 1970s and 1980s. Hoffman's attempt to market weight-lifting (bodybuilding) as a method for inculcating American values and high ideals seemed out of sync with the times, especially in view of the exhibitionist nature of bodybuilding competitions and the dangerous use of steroids to achieve bulk and muscle mass. Nevertheless, there has been a bodybuilding renaissance.

There have always been strong men in Hollywood movies. Several epics of the 1950s and 1960s used a transnational base (American actors in an Italian setting) to star former champion bodybuilders such as Steve Reeves and

Photo courtesy of Popular Culture Library, Bowling Green State University, Bowling Green, OH.

Mickey Hargitay in B movies. By 1990, however, the situation was such that an ex–Mr. Universe, Arnold Schwarzenegger (13 World Champion bodybuilding titles from 1964 to 1990), became a leading box-office draw (see entry). Other actors such as Jean-Claude Van Damme ("The Muscles from Brussels"), Sylvester Stallone, and the late Jason Lee have continued to popularize the "built body" as an integral aspect of movies.

Two American documentaries, *Pumping Iron* (1977) and *Pumping Iron II: The Women* (1985) are informative insights on the bodybuilding subculture. The growing popularity of women's bodybuilding is seen by some to be tied to issues of gender equity and empowerment. Sadly, in *Pumping Iron II*, the female bodybuilders Rachel McLish and Bev Francis seem portrayed in a stereotypical fashion. Bodybuilding competitions have received exposure and coverage on ABC-TV's *Wide World of Sports* and on ESPN.

Bodybuilding's popularity has also contributed to the marketing of a line of health foods and dietary supplements ("power" food and drinks) and to the expanding number of powerlifting gyms.

Bibliography
Bednarek, J. "Pumping Iron or Pulling Strings: Different Ways of Working Out and Getting Involved in Body-Build-

ing." *International Review of Sociology of Sport* 20.4 (1985): 239-61.

Fair, John D. "Bob Hoffman, the York Barbell Company, and the Golden Age of American Weight Lifting, 1945-1960." *Journal of Sport History* 14.2 (1987): 164-88.

Hatfield, Frederick C. *Power: A Scientific Approach.* Chicago: Contemporary, 1989.

Klein, Alan. *Little Big Men: Bodybuilding Subculture and Gender Construction.* Albany: SUNY P, 1993.

Lingis, Alphonso. "Orchids and Muscles." *Journal of the Philosophy of Sport* 13 (1986): 15-28.

Lipsyte, Robert. *Arnold Schwarzenegger: Hercules in America.* New York: HarperCollins, 1993.

Scott A. G. M. Crawford

See also
Atlas, Charles

Bogart, Humphrey (1899-1957), actor, was born in New York City. He was expelled from Phillips Academy in Andover, Massachusetts, served in the navy in World War I, and was a road company manager and stage manager at Brady's New York film studio before his screen debut in a 10-minute short, *Broadway's Like That* (1930).

Although lacking the cult status of his posthumous stardom of the 1960s—an image summed up by Jean-Paul Belmondo's admiring gaze at the studio photo from *The Harder They Fall* (1956) in *Breathless* (1959)—Humphrey Bogart still occupies an important role in film history. Ironically, he became a bigger star following his death, when the Bogart icon seemed to define the alienated, self-reliant, and skeptical persona admired by youthful audiences reacting to the contemporary Cold War and Vietnam eras. But in his lifetime, Bogart never achieved the degree of success seen in his posthumous stardom. During his career, he always appeared a highly unusual leading man whose chief characteristic was often one of brooding exhaustion as opposed to dynamic action, a feature noted by Louise Brooks in *Lulu in Hollywood*. Both the man and star image reveal significant personal and cultural relationships to changing occupational and historical patterns within American society.

Despite Bogart's image as a Warner Brothers proletarian hero (or "city boy" in Robert Sklar's terms), the real man came from a privileged New York family. He performed many lackluster upper-class juvenile roles on Broadway before beginning his film career. Bogart began as a stage actor without having the benefit of the dynamic theatrical attributes that brought contemporaries James Cagney and Paul Muni to the notice of Hollywood. Between 1930 and 1935, he played a number of bland, second-leads in movie roles little different from his stage performances in Hollywood while commuting back and forth from Broadway. However, Leslie Howard's insistence that Bogart repeat his stage performance as Duke Mantee in the film version of *The Petrified Forest* (1936) provided the first step towards eventual stardom. Although Bogart's performance appears mechanical and overtly low-key today, it is the first sign of the qualities of brooding personal isolation and existential angst that would characterize his later screen roles.

Despite his success in *The Petrified Forest*, Warner Brothers never developed Bogart's potential, choosing instead to cast him in 28 films as second lead. More often than not, they were gangster films in which he played the villain to more dynamic stars such as James Cagney in *The Roaring Twenties* (1939) and Edward G. Robinson in *Brother Orchard* (1940). When the studio attempted to cast him against type, as in *The Return of Dr. X* (1939), the results were as embarrassing as his mad artist Dracula figure in *The Two Mrs. Carrolls* (1947). But although film historians usually date the Bogart image as beginning with *The Maltese Falcon* (1941), it is perhaps the John Huston–scripted *High Sierra* (1941) which is the most significant. As Louise Brooks shrewdly observes, the first film revealed that "too much dialogue betrayed the fact that his miserable theatrical training had left him permanently afraid of words." However, in *High Sierra*, Bogart's Roy Earle revealed both the isolated nobility that would later characterize the alienated heroes of *Casablanca* (1943) and *Key Largo* (1948) as well as that "threatening exhaustion" seen in *The Treasure of the Sierra Madre* (1948).

The Bogart persona blossomed out into full expression in *Casablanca*, a film uniting both past and future aspects of the actor's star persona. As a former anti-Fascist activist, Rick is now the "forgotten man" of *Gold Diggers of 1933* lamenting the lost potentials of romance and political activism in his North African retreat. However, both the return of Ingrid Bergman's Elsa and his lost 1930s ideals result in a significant uniting of the political and personal in a more potent dialectical manner than before. At the end of *Casablanca*, Bogart's Rick accepts his loss like Roy Earle in *High Sierra*. But unlike his doomed gangster predecessor, Rick joins with his formerly jaded Vichy counterpart (Claude Rains) to participate in the "good war." *Casablanca* was an important film not just for the Bogart persona but in reaffirming the audience's sense of a selfless, idealistic American identity ideologically crucial for another "noble crusade" in World War II. Rick's newfound virtues of integrity and dogged persistence would also characterize Bogart's Philip Marlowe in *The Big Sleep* (1946), Hawks's Hemingway hero in *To Have and Have Not* (1944), and Rick's postwar counterpart in *Key Largo* (1948). Such wartime ideals would be also relevant for post-war society if circumstances permitted their full realization.

However, the changing mood of postwar society and the McCarthy era would put these attributes into abeyance. Instead, the personal would take precedence over the political and Bogart's late-1940s persona would develop the rugged determinism and individualism seen in earlier portrayals. If the goal-orientation did not develop into insanity and corruption as in *The Treasure of the Sierra Madre* and *The Caine Mutiny* (1954), it would also lead to an extension of the world-weariness and cynicism seen in Bogart's more alienated performances in *In a Lonely Place* (1950), *Deadline–U.S.A.* (1952), *Beat the Devil* (1954), *The Left Hand of God,* and *The Desperate Hours* (both 1955).

However, despite the world-weariness and tendencies towards inertia seen in many performances, the strongest appeal of the Bogart legacy remains the figure of an actor deciding to fight on against overwhelming odds even when no victory is possible, as in *Dark Passage* (1947) and *Knock on Any Door* (1949). Although containing a different ending from the more pessimistic Budd Schulberg novel, *The Harder They Fall* (1956) concludes with Bogart's formerly tarnished but now redeemed sportswriter engaged on a seemingly hopeless crusade to eliminate both boxing and a corrupt system from American life. The endeavor appears futile as embodied by an actor tired, aged, and dying. But the nobility of the pursuit evokes images of earlier ideals followed by Roy Earle, Rick, and Philip Marlowe, who are all outcasts of society. Although the actor played many roles in different films, the quintessential Bogart persona remains relevant today even in the changed circumstances of an American society different from the actor's generation and a later one awarding him cult status.

Bibliography

Brooks, Louise. *Lulu in Hollywood*. New York: Knopf, 1982.

Cahill, Marie. *Humphrey Bogart: A Hollywood Portrait*. New York: Smithmark, 1992.

Eyles, Allen. *Humphrey Bogart*. London: Sphere, 1990.

Pettigrew, Terrence. *Bogart: A Definitive Study of His Film Career*. London: Proteus, 1981.

Sklar, Robert. *City Boys: Cagney, Bogart, Garfield*. Princeton: Princeton UP, 1992.

Tony Williams

Bold and the Beautiful, The (1987-), a soap opera created by William J. Bell and Lee Phillip Bell, first aired on CBS. The show's first storylines centered about the lives of two families, the rich and powerful Forresters, and the middle-class Logans. In much the same tradition as *The Young and the Restless, The Bold and the Beautiful* was steeped heavily in beautiful people and strong production values; it was set in the Los Angeles fashion industry. Bell had originally intended to cast attractive actors who were new to daytime television audiences. For many of the key roles, this was done. At the same time, however, he cast several *Young and Restless* graduates: John McCook as Eric Forrester, Jim Storm as Bill Spencer, Lauren Koslow as Margo Lynley, as well as Susan Flannery, formerly of *Days of Our Lives*, as Stephanie Forrester.

Within three years, this half-hour soap rose to No. 3 in the ratings, beating out many of the more experienced, older, hour-long soaps. One device the Bells used, both boldly and beautifully, to accomplish this was the cross-over storyline involving the interactions of characters from *The Young and the Restless* and *The Bold and the Beautiful*.

Bibliography

Copeland, Mary Ann. *Soap Opera History*. Lincolnwood: BBD Promotional Book (Mallard), 1991.

Schemering, Christopher. *The Soap Opera Encyclopedia*. New York: Ballantine, 1987.

Barbara J. Irwin

Bonanza (1959-1973), one of television's most successful Western series, the story of a prosperous family of ranchers, was set in the vicinity of Virginia City, NV, during the Civil War period soon after the discovery of the fabulous Comstock Silver Lode. Widower Ben Cartwright, patriarch of the all-male clan and owner of the 100,000-acre Ponderosa Ranch, had three sons by three different wives. Adam, the oldest of the half-brothers, was the most serious, thoughtful, and balanced, and the likely successor to his father as manager of the sprawling Cartwright holdings. "Hoss," the middle son, was a mountain of a man who was as gentle as he was huge, sensitive, and at times naive. Little Joe was the youngest, most impulsive, and most romantic of the Cartwrights.

Bonanza differed from the majority of television Westerns in that it emphasized the bonds of affection between four strong men. Although constantly engaging in family scrapes, father and sons clung together to protect the family name and the family property from corrupt and thieving outsiders.

Producer David Dortort was concerned about the damage television had been doing to the image of the American father. He was being portrayed as a "buffoon" and "an incompetent" and Dortort wanted to reinstate him as the head of the American household in his depiction of the patriarch of the Cartwright family. Ben Cartwright was not only a father his sons could respect, but a stern, though gentle, role model for fathers across the land.

In keeping with his philosophy that television creates its own stars, Dortort chose relatively unknown actors to portray the four major characters. In the pivotal role of Ben, Dortort cast Canadian actor Lorne Greene. Pernell Roberts, however, had some previous stage experience when he was cast as the eldest son, Adam.

Perhaps Dortort's most fortuitous casting selection was his choice of six-foot four-inch, 300-pound Dan Blocker to play the role of Hoss. When Dortort cast Michael Landon in the role of the impetuous and romantic 17-year-old Little Joe, Landon had not yet reached his 22d birthday. Landon was, however, both intelligent and talented and fit comfortably into the role that he was to play for some 14 years.

After a somewhat slow beginning, *Bonanza* became the most watched television program of any genre during the 1960s. It reached No. 17 in the Nielsen ratings during its second season, zoomed to No. 2 during the third year, and held the No. 1 position from 1964 to 1967. The show never left the Top 20 until its final season, when it was canceled after the death of one of its most popular leads, Dan Blocker, and a shift from its familiar Sunday evening time slot. Only *Gunsmoke* with 20 successful seasons could boast a longer TV run.

Two unsuccessful attempts to revive the series were later made by Dortort. In 1987 he produced a syndicated two-hour TV film entitled *Bonanza: The Next Generation* and in 1993, after Michael Landon's death, another potential pilot, *Bonanza: The Return,* was aired by NBC. Although both films featured several siblings of the original cast members, neither generated high enough ratings to justify the launching of a weekly series.

Bibliography

Shapiro, Melany. *Bonanza: The Unofficial Story of the Ponderosa*. Las Vegas: Pioneer, 1993.

Yoggy, Gary A. *Riding the Video Range: The Rise and Fall of the Western on Television.* Jefferson: McFarland, 1995.

Gary A. Yoggy

Bond, James, is the hero in a series of spy fiction novels beginning with *Casino Royale* (1952), created by Scottish-born author Ian Fleming (1908-1964). Bond is an agent of the British Secret Service, headed by "M," and is licensed to kill in the line of duty, as is signified by the "00" code number in his identification "007."

In *From Russia with Love*, Bond is said to have a "dark, clean-cut face, with a three-inch scar" down the side, and a "finely drawn but cruel mouth." He is an athlete, a connoisseur, a sophisticate, and a man of carnal appetites who pursues willing women as sexual conquests.

In 1961, President John F. Kennedy revealed that Fleming's fifth Bond novel, *From Russia with Love* (1957), was one of his 10 favorite books. Following this announcement came the period of the Bond phenomenon in the U.S. and throughout the world—characterized by the great popularity of the novels, and the prodigious success of the series of films, beginning with *Dr. No* in 1962, featuring Sean Connery (see entry) as Bond. Later actors playing Bond include Roger Moore, Timothy Dalton, George Lazenby, and now Pierce Brosnan, though none achieved the critical or popular acclaim of Connery in the role.

While James Bond's attitudes derive from Fleming's own, he has outlived his creator not simply because of his film fame but because Bond was a phenomenon who touched, and allayed, a deep anxiety within the collective Western consciousness. Fleming presented in the character of Bond a reassuring if anachronistic heroic fantasy wherein all threats to Western civilization were thwarted through superior intelligence, technology, and moral worth.

Bibliography

Amis, Kingsley. *The James Bond Dossier.* New York: New American Library, 1965.

Benson, Raymond. *The James Bond Bedside Companion.* New York: Dodd, 1988.

Del Buono, Oreste, and Umberto Eco. *The Bond Affair.* London: Macdonald, 1966.

Photo courtesy of Popular Culture Library, Bowling Green State University, Bowling Green, OH.

Hibbin, Sally. *The Official James Bond Movie Book.* New York: Crown, 1987.

Pearson, John. *James Bond: The Authorized Biography of 007.* New York: Morrow, 1973.

Rosenberg, Bruce A., and Ann Harleman Stewart. *Ian Fleming.* Boston: Twayne, 1989.

Nicholas Ranson

Book Cover Design. To accurately speak of a book cover is to refer to its binding. The binding—comprised of the sewing, boards, and outer "skin" of manuscript codices—until recently was an artifact made to last for generations. To ensure their status as highly coveted, precious objects, book covers and spines were lavishly ornamented, not only with gold tooling on select leather or other animal hides, but with chased or sculptured gold and silver, carved ivory, jewels and embroidery. The protective boards, typically made of solid wood, also were wrapped in luxurious fabrics like velvet, silk or cloth interwoven with gold.

The craft of bookbinding and cover decoration developed simultaneously in several disparate countries. Islamic bookbinding had its origins in the highly skilled leathercraft of Christian Syria and Egypt. The Near Eastern approach to book design differed radically from the heavily incised and ornamented covers of medieval Europe. Mohammedan craftsmen favored motifs such as circular or almond-shaped medallions, usually centered on the cover and complemented by austere typography framed with interlacing bands or other geometrical arabesques. In the 15th century, Islamic bookcraft was to heavily influence Italian binding, particularly in Venice, the center of Italy's book trade during the Late Renaissance. In the 17th century, the most significant binding innovations originated in France. The lavish, gold-tooled "fanfare" bindings, based on decorative fans, lace and embroidery patterns of the time, set the standard throughout Europe.

In England in the 1840s, the introduction of cloth binding and the invention of machinery to join book pages to their covers threatened to eliminate traditional hand-sewn and decorated books. It was not until the end of the 19th century that fine binding was rejuvenated by visionary poet and socialist William Morris, who founded Kelmscott Press in 1891 in West London. His crowning glory, completed in 1896 shortly before his death, is *The Works of Geoffrey Chaucer,* which took his consortium of illustrators, calligraphers, and binders 23 months to print and features over 110 original woodcuts and a magnificent cover of interlaced vines and floral motifs, blind-tooled in imported leather and joined by silver clasps.

In the Morris tradition, Franz Weisse of Hamburg, and Pierre Legrain of Paris began a remarkable revival in binding design in the years between the two world wars. Between 1917 and 1919, Legrain introduced the idioms of cubist and abstract art into book cover design, an innovation that continues in Paris today, where binders work in tandem with world-renowned contemporary artists. Even before Legrain's seminal work, serious book collectors and publishers commissioned fine artists to create limited edition books as early as the 1880s. So-called artist books were often one of a kind, usually hand-painted directly onto the blank cover by artists who often decorated the spine and back cover as well. A short list of well-known commissioned artists includes Salvador Dali, Henri de Toulouse-Lautrec, and Joan Miro. More recently, American artists Benjamin and Deborah Alterman, with their 1987 precious metals design for Herman Melville's *Billy Budd, Sailor,* and Philip Smith's 1967-68 colorful inlaid leather cover for Shakespeare's *King Lear,* show that the bookbinding tradition is very much alive.

Although a relatively new development in book cover design, the illustrated book jacket is an important artifact that has reflected changes in popular culture since the 1920s. The book jacket (or dust jacket) was a plain paper covering created in England in the 1830s to protect clothbound books from the soot and fog blanketing London. But it was the Americans, with their penchant for salesmanship, who transformed the unassuming book jacket into a powerful mini-poster, designed to compete with a growing magazine trade and the burgeoning movie industry of the 1920s-40s.

Books and their decorated covers have been admired and collected for nearly 15 centuries. The art and craft of bookbinding, having survived the machine age, television, and the Internet, appears destined to continue to document, reflect, and influence the chapters of human culture for many years to come.

Bibliography

Bearman, Frederick A. *Fine and Historic Bookbindings from the Folger Shakespeare Library.* Washington, DC: Folger Library, 1992.

Febvre, Lucien, and Henri-Jean Martin. *The Coming of the Book.* London: Thetford, 1984.

Heller, Steven, and Seymour Chwast. *Jackets Required.* Vancouver: Raincoat Books, 1995.

Lewis, Roy Harley. *Fine Bookbinding in the Twentieth Century.* New York: Arco, 1985.

Olmert, Michael. *The Smithsonian Book of Books.* Washington, DC: Smithsonian Books, 1992.

Mark Zust

Boombox, The, also known as a "jam box" or "boogie box," is a portable, stereophonic radio receiver, usually with a cassette-tape-recorder/player. While the trend in portable radios in the 1950s and 1960s was toward miniaturization, the boombox was an attempt to provide sound quality approaching that of indoor stereophonic components. Boomboxes were first developed in Japan in the early 1970s and provided good-quality sound in a small package. They became popular household items because many Japanese did not have room for larger component systems in their relatively small houses and apartments.

Boomboxes first appeared in the U.S. in the mid-1970s, and they became especially popular among African-American and Hispanic youths in inner-city neighborhoods. As a result, the derogatory term "ghetto-blasters" is often used to describe boomboxes. The higher powered amplifiers in boomboxes require more and larger batteries than previous battery-powered radios and cassette players. The combination of bulky batteries and large speakers often brings the size of the boombox to that of a suitcase. These boomboxes are often hoisted onto the shoulders as their owners walk down city streets.

The basic boombox contains an AM/FM receiver, a cassette playback deck, and two speakers. The speakers are sometimes detachable, giving better stereo separation when the boombox is stationary. More advanced boomboxes include separate high and low frequency speakers for each channel and/or a second tape deck to allow copying of cassette tapes. They may also contain "graphic" frequency equalizers that allow for more control over the volume of various frequency bands than the single tone control or bass and treble controls of simpler radios and cassette players. In the 1990s, boomboxes often offer a compact disc (CD) player in addition to the cassette deck.

The significance of the boombox as a cultural symbol was illustrated in the 1989 motion picture *Do the Right Thing,* directed by acclaimed African-American director Spike Lee (see entry). In one scene, a young African-American man, Radio Raheem, refuses to turn down his boombox in a pizza parlor. The Italian-American restaurant owner smashes the boombox with a baseball bat, inciting a riot that ends in the destruction of the restaurant and the death of Raheem. The scene is accompanied by the Public Enemy song, "Fight the Power," first heard on the boombox when Raheem enters the restaurant.

Kenneth M. Nagelberg

Boop, Betty (1930-1939), an animated cartoon character, was a product of the Fleischer Studios. The earlier cartoons enjoyed a resurgence of popularity from the 1980s on, including a fan club. Betty first appeared as a chimera with floppy dog ears and a girl's legs, singing a song popularized by Helen Kane, the "Boop-oop-a-doop Girl" (1904-1966). The ears transformed into long earrings, the character was given a name, and until the Production Code domesticated Betty Boop, she was a wide-eyed bosomy ingenue scantily clad in a frilly strapless miniskirt, one trim leg sporting a fancy garter. There were many spinoff products such as dolls, candy, and a comic strip (1934-37). In 1934, Helen Kane brought suit against the Fleischers and distributor Paramount for misappropriation of "boop" and "boop-oop-a-doop" but lost the case because a black entertainer, Baby Esther, was proven to have sung the words before either Helen or Betty.

Bibliography

Solomon, Charles. *Enchanted Drawings: The History of Animation.* New York: Knopf, 1989.

Fred E. H. Schroeder

Boston, the classic-rock band distinctive for its glittery power-rock sound, has produced only four albums since its phenomenal 1976 debut due to artistic perfectionism and to acrimonious but ultimately landmark litigation with the record industry.

Boston essentially is guitarist Tom Scholz (1947-) an MIT graduate who in 1971 in his apartment building's cellar began making demo tapes of songs he had written, involving only a drummer, and, for vocals, Brad Delp (1951-).

(Scholz later used his engineering experience to invent various devices for the electric guitar.)

"More Than a Feeling," destined to be Boston's first smash hit in 1976, was actually recorded in 1971. Scholz remained unsuccessful at soliciting record companies until late in 1975, when the tapes' refreshing rock sound (during the heyday of discomania) caught the interest of Epic Records, a subsidiary of CBS. The company required live auditions; so the rest of the band's original lineup was assembled: Barry Goudreau (1951-) on guitar, Fran Sheehan (1949-) on bass, and Sib Hashian (1949-) on drums.

Boston's self-titled first album was released in August 1976 and went gold in 7 weeks, platinum in 11, and double platinum in 16—at the time the most successful debut album in history. "More Than a Feeling" hit the charts in September 1976 and became a rock classic. *Don't Look Back* was released in 1978, then the band essentially split, while Scholz began painstakingly slow work on a third album, so slow that he ended up in a $20 million breach-of-contract suit with CBS that was settled, in his favor, in 1990. MCA then released *The Third Stage* in 1986 and *Walk On* in 1993.

In spite of criticism labeling their music "dork-rock" and bemoaning the "formulaic virtuosity," which gave rise to false rumors in the past that the songs were written by a computer, Boston struck upon and has proven its successful formula for a rich and popular rock music sound.

Bibliography

Crowe, Cameron. "The Band from the Platinum Basement: Boston." *Rolling Stone* 10 Aug. 1978: 37-42.

Dannen, Fredric. *Hit Men.* New York: Time Books, 1990.

Goodman, Fred. "Tom Scholz: Boston's Next Stage." *Rolling Stone* 6 Oct. 1988: 22.

Romanowski, Patricia, and Holly George-Warren. *The New Rolling Stone Encyclopedia of Rock & Roll.* New York: Fireside, 1995.

Young, Charles. "Boston's Sounds of Science." *Rolling Stone* 2 Dec. 1976: 14, 19.

Michael Delahoyde
Maureen Smith

Bowling, a game in which the participant rolls a ball of 8 to 16 pounds down a lane to score points by knocking down ten pins in one attempt (for a strike) or two (for a spare), is achieving great popularity on the casual, amateur, and professional levels. Bowling is a cultural pastime and popular ritual that levels social boundaries of class, race, age, gender, and disability, by celebrating solidarity through team interaction; it invites, as a ritual of unity, a spirit of community for players of varying backgrounds and skill levels, while it subverts the primacy of individualism.

Currently, bowling takes place under the auspices of the American Bowling Congress (ABC), founded in 1895 as the ruling body for men's bowling, and the Women's International Bowling Congress (WIBC), established in 1916. The popularity of bowling is due, in part, to network and cable television coverage of the sport.

Power and excitement have been integral parts of the game since its inception in ancient Egypt. Bowling supposedly dates from around 3200 B.C., based on the discovery of objects similar to present-day bowling equipment in the tomb of an Egyptian child of that period. Players in ancient Rome used a game similar to bowling for practice in war maneuvers. By the medieval period, the idea of bowling as a leveling of social authority became evident with the game called skittles, which was popular among the peasantry in England. Medieval Germany, by contrast, brought a sense of community to the development of bowling with the game called kegling, in which participants attempted to knock down pins representing the "heathen" to prove to their church that they led a virtuous life. If they failed, they were deemed "sinful." Kegling was so enjoyable that players indulged in it outside of church confines, and the game spread to other parts of Europe, eventually being brought to the New World. In 1622, Dutch immigrants established the game of ninepins in America, and it was subsequently amended in the later 1800s, after the game of ninepins had been outlawed, by a clever sportsman who added the tenth pin as a way of subverting the law. From that point, indoor bowling became the norm.

Evident from its history, bowling is a game of subversion. Originally a game for ancient Egyptian aristocrats, bowling is now the game of the common man. Even though bowling allows for the breakdown of social barriers, it also upholds values of the dominant culture: hard work, achievement, competitiveness, and fair-mindedness. Bowling etiquette and good sportsmanship reflect as well as extol the cultural values of democratic capitalism, teaching skills needed to survive in a competitive world.

Bibliography

Grinfelds, Velma. *Right Down Your Alley: The Complete Book of Bowling.* 3d ed. Englewood: Morton Activity Series, 1992.

Mackey, Richard T. *Bowling.* 3d ed. Palo Alto: Mayfield, 1980.

Martin, Joan L., Ruth E. Tandy and Charlene Agne-Traub. *Bowling.* 7th ed. Madison: Brown & Benchmark, 1994.

Granetta L. Richardson

Brackett, Leigh (Douglass) (1915-1978), author of numerous short stories, novels, motion picture screenplays, and more, was one of the top woman writers of 20th-century science fiction specifically and popular literature generally. Her science fiction stories were often but not always space operas reminiscent of Edgar Rice Burroughs's *John Carter of Mars* tales. She also wrote Western and detective fiction. Influenced by past literary tradition, Brackett was an important teacher of aspiring authors. Ray Bradbury (see next entry) may have been her most famous student, and Bradbury himself acknowledges an extensive debt to Brackett. (The pair collaborated on a now-legendary short pulp novel, *Lorelei of the Red Mist* [1946].)

Leigh Brackett is remembered for contributions to pulp magazines like *Planet Stories, Startling Stories*, and *Thrilling Wonder Stories*; her Eric John Stark Mars adventures (which appeared in two series—one in the 1940s, one in the 1970s); her screenplays—including a 1946 adaptation (with William Faulkner) of Raymond Chandler's *The Big Sleep*, a landmark John Wayne vehicle entitled *Rio Bravo* (1958), and her last major work, the script for the second *Star Wars* movie, *The Empire Strikes Back* (1979); and more. Her novel *The Long Tomorrow* (1955), a classic tale of post-apocalypse America, is reflective of the Cold War era in which it was written and has been critically celebrated. Brackett married popular author Edmond Hamilton and both influenced and was influenced by his work. Like Robert Bloch, she was one of those rare, "special" authors who was highly emulated, revered, and truly loved by her fellow writers.

Bibliography
Brackett, Leigh. *The Book of Skaith*. Garden City: Doubleday, 1977.
——. *The Long Tomorrow*. New York: Ballantine, 1974.
——. *People of the Talisman/The Secret of Sinharat*. New York: Ace, 1964.
Hamilton, Edmond. *The Best of Leigh Brackett*. Garden City: Doubleday, 1977.

Garyn G. Roberts

Bradbury, Ray(mond) (Douglas) (1920-), an author of near legendary proportions, has proven himself a magician of words and teller of universal tales that incorporate myths, beliefs, and related symbols such as iconography, character types, rituals, themes, motifs, and settings that define both American and world popular cultures. He draws heavily upon personal experience and cultural inheritance, and relies on the history of ideas, free word association, and the potential of imagery and color through language.

Bradbury's short stories, novels, stage plays, screenplays, poems, and radio plays appeal to all ages, and his dexterity with issues of youth and age, and coming of age, make his writing significant and meaningful to a wide-ranging public. He has always drawn heavily from his personal experiences, making autobiography the largest overriding thematic element of his work. Bradbury is a visionary who is sensitive to the emotions, idiosyncrasies, and wonders that comprise the human experience. If at times the logic of his stories is suspect, his ability to evoke profound emotion and keen insight into the human experience makes matters of plotting and logic relatively unimportant.

Bradbury's first professional sale, "Pendulum," was co-authored with Henry Hasse and appeared in the November 1941 issue of *Super Science Stories*, a popular fiction or pulp magazine. Bradbury, however, had a variety of short stories published in science fiction and fantasy fanzines as early as January 1938. By the mid-1940s, Bradbury was regularly appearing in several nationally circulated pulp magazines.

Some of his early contributions to *Weird Tales* and other such periodicals were the beginnings of his first major story: stories of the "Dark Carnival." In these tales, Bradbury used the traveling carnival as a metaphor for life. His first published book, a collection of Dark Carnival stories, weird tales, and macabre fantasies entitled *Dark Carnival*, was published in 1947. This was subsequently revised and reappeared in 1955 as *The October Country*. By 1962, several of

themes and ideas from the Dark Carnival stories were adapted, synthesized, and expanded into the novel *Something Wicked This Way Comes*. Ultimately, four Bradbury short story collections have been framed by the Dark Carnival mythos. Between and beyond *Dark Carnival* and *The October Country* there were *The Illustrated Man* (1951) and *The Small Assassin* (1962). Bradbury published a second Dark Carnival novel, a tribute to the private-eye mysteries of writers like Dashiell Hammett, Raymond Chandler, and others entitled *Death Is a Lonely Business,* in 1985.

The genres and related story types that Ray Bradbury has created and contributed to since those early pulp days are numerous. A representative list includes the Dark Carnival stories, gothic tales, weird tales, dark fantasy, weird menace, detective fiction, and science fiction. Bradbury writes not only genre fiction, he crosses between genres, and even ignores such categorization all together. For example, *Dandelion Wine* (1957) and *Fahrenheit 451* (1953) fall neatly into no specific genre. *Fahrenheit 451* is a futuristic novel dependent neither on science fiction, fact, nor horror fiction for its ultimate message. It is influenced by George Orwell's *1984*, but is uniquely Bradbury. Its author claims that, like Orwell's novel, *Fahrenheit 451* was designed to prevent a potential future, not predict one.

The subjects and social issues addressed in the fiction of Ray Bradbury are some of the most poignant and profound of the human experience. Here are found detailed discussions of religions of various sorts, youth, age, death and dying, nature and the environment, life and living, family and friends, race, gender, love, sex, eros, the rural community, a variety of geographical locales, and much more. The episodic novel *The Martian Chronicles* (1950), among other things, is best appreciated as an environmental allegory. In the 1940s and early 1950s, Bradbury was writing intelligent, insightful stories about ethnicity and race relations and about gender long before such stories became fashionable. Stories like "The Big Black and White Game" and "The Other Foot" told more about racial harmony than many before or since; stories like "I'll Not Look for Wine" and "Cora and the Great Wide World" featured women with great stamina and independence and individual identity.

Bradbury's best novels are often episodic, i.e., they are a carefully woven series of short stories. He has published four major volumes of poetry and has written a number of successful and critically acclaimed stage plays and motion picture screenplays. Since the 1950s, Bradbury stories have been adapted for several comic book series. From the late 1980s through 1990, Bradbury himself adapted his stories for *The Ray Bradbury Theater* television series.

Ray Bradbury's recent short story collection, *The Toynbee Convector* (1988), is as fine a collection as he has ever done and his recent novel (again episodic in organization), the fictionalized autobiography *Green Shadows, White Whale* (1992) is considered one of his finest. It recounts Bradbury's experiences with famed movie director and mogul John Huston, and the making of the movie *Moby Dick* (which Bradbury scripted), in the mid-1950s. Bradbury's appeal is universal—it transcends all generations and is appeal is universal—it transcends all generations and is timeless. He is one of the 20th century's most important storytellers and allegorists.

Bibliography
Nolan, William F. *The Ray Bradbury Companion: A Life and Career History, Photolog, and Comprehensive Checklist of Writings.* Detroit: Gale, 1975.
Olander, Joseph D., and Martin H. Greenberg, eds. *Ray Bradbury.* New York: Taplinger, 1980.

Garyn G. Roberts

Bradley, Marion Zimmer (1930-1999), popular author of fantasy novels, published her first work in 1953, the short stories "For Women Only" and "Keyhole," which appeared in *Vortex Science Fiction 2.* Bradley's first novel, *The Door through Space,* was published in 1961. This was quickly followed by *Seven from the Stars* (1962). Most of her early works can be easily classified as space opera, and often appear as fantasy genre novels including some sword-and-sorcery evidencing thinly veiled scientific premises. At the time Bradley was first writing, there was no good market for fantasy fiction, so she incorporated scientific elements into her work to make them salable.

Bradley is recognized as one of the top three women writers of science fiction/fantasy. (André Norton and Anne McCaffrey are the other two.) She is best known for her Darkover series, a group of books written over the last thirty years. These provide a strong sense of the author's evolution in social-political thought (many of her works celebrate feminist and humanist ideals) as well as her maturation as a writer. Bradley's later works are less science fiction and are more fantasy and historical fantasy. Her best-selling Arthurian novel, *The Mists of Avalon* (1983), is written entirely from the female characters' points of view, and depicts the conflict between paganism (seen as feminist) and Christianity (seen as patriarchal). She followed *The Mists of Avalon* with *Firebrand* (1987), a novel of ancient Greece with similar themes.

Bradley's writing is highly reminiscent of work done by Leigh Brackett (see entry), C. L. Moore, Abraham Merritt, Henry Kuttner, André Norton, and others. She likewise has influenced a number of up-and-coming authors in the 1980s and '90s, such as Mercedes Lackey, Jennifer Robeson, Diane Paxton, and others. Bradley produced a continuing series of anthologies featuring works she feels have particular merit and fit the genre. These include *Swords and Sorceresses* (begun in 1984) and *Spells of Wonder* (1989). The magazine she founded in 1988, *Marion Zimmer Bradley's Fantasy,* continues to do the same thing.

Bibliography
Bradley, Marion Zimmer, ed. Introduction. *Spells of Wonder.* New York: DAW Books, 1989.
Clute, John, and Peter Nicholls, eds. *The Encyclopedia of Science Fiction.* New York: St. Martin's, 1993.
Frank, Janrae, Jean Stine, and Forrest J. Ackerman. *New Eves: Science Fiction about the Extraordinary Women of Today and Tomorrow.* Stamford: Longmeadow, 1994.

Virginia Woods Roberts

Brand, Max, was the legendary pen name of Frederick Faust (1892-1944), one of America's greatest authors of Western fiction. Faust's childhood in Seattle had left him bitter and literature provided a means for escape. Faust had been virtually on his own since he was orphaned at the age of 13, but he attended the University of California at Berkeley, paying his own way by working full-time.

In common with many pulp writers, he yearned to be accepted as a serious writer and to excel in higher forms of writing. Ironically, Faust was the ultimate pulp writer, producing over 600 published books and articles under at least 20 pseudonyms. He wrote over 400 novels in a number of genres. Brand was his most famous pen name; under it he wrote detective stories, the Dr. Kildare series, and stories of other genres in addition to his Westerns. It was his Westerns for which he was best known.

His first Max Brand story was published on June 23, 1917, in *All-Story Magazine.* His first Western, *The Untamed,* was published in 1919. Interestingly, his own experiences of the "real West" were unsatisfying and he wrote that as a Westerner he found the West "disgusting." That disgust, however, did not keep him from providing stories for *Western Story Magazine.* In turn, the money Faust made from his incredible productivity—he could write 50 pages a day—supported him and his family in a villa in Florence that he filled with original masterpieces.

When the Depression caused a decline in the pulps, Faust moved to the slicks, often using his own name. His works appeared in *Harper's, Collier's, Esquire,* and other "respectable" magazines. He also worked in Hollywood at MGM, where he had success with the adaptation of his Destry novels and his Dr. Kildare stories. Unfortunately, Hollywood led to an increase in his drinking and depression about his career and personal life. In 1944 he became a war correspondent, but he was killed when hit in the chest by a shell fragment.

In spite of his desire to be taken seriously as a poet or writer of more serious works, it is Faust's enormous output as a pulp writer able to master the deepest roots of American culture that ensures him serious consideration. Faust tapped deep themes in American culture and understood the American psyche. His emphasis on the individual over society was never so well achieved in other Westerns. Instinctively, his weaving of European myths underscored the mythic dimensions of the Western itself and his own writing did much to place the American Western into the category of myth and legend, moving it into new areas.

Bibliography
Bloodworth, William. "Max Brand (Frederick Faust)—1892-1944." *Fifty Western Writers: A Bio-Bibliographical Sourcebook.* Ed. Fred Erisman and Richard W. Etulain. Westport: Greenwood, 1983.
Cawelti, John G. *Adventure, Mystery, and Romance: Formula Stories as Art and Popular Fiction.* Chicago: U of Chicago P, 1976.
——. *The Six Gun Mystique.* Bowling Green, OH: Bowling Green State U Popular P, 1971.
Easton, Robert. *Max Brand: The Big "Westerner."* Norman: U of Oklahoma P, 1970.

Faust, Frederick S. *Cheyenne Gold*. New York: Warner,

Frank A. Salamone

Brando, Marlon (1924-), before, during, and even after his prime, won acclaim as one of America's greatest actors; in recent years, however, erratic behavior and personal tragedy have come close to overshadowing that greatness.

Born in Omaha, NE, and raised there and in Illinois, Brando set off for New York in 1943, enrolling in Erwin Picador's Dramatic Workshop at the New School for Social Research. At the Dramatic Workshop he met and became the protégé of Stella Adler, a proponent of the Stanislavsky Method. After performing in summer stock theater the following summer, he won the role of Nels in the Broadway play *I Remember Mama*, a role he played for 16 months.

The young actor's first stage triumph came in 1947 in Tennessee Williams's *A Streetcar Named Desire*. Chosen by Williams to play the part of Stanley Kowalski, Brando ignited audiences and critics alike with the brilliance of his interpretation. During this period, he was also a member of the advanced class at the newly formed Actors Studio.

Brando's first film role was that of a disabled veteran in *The Men* in 1950. He prepared for this role by living as a paraplegic at a VA hospital for the three weeks of rehearsal. He reprised the role of Stanley Kowalski in Elia Kazan's film version of *A Streetcar Named Desire* the following year, earning an Academy Award nomination for best actor, the first of four consecutive nominations. Brando's success as Kowalski legitimized Method acting, paving the way for such actors as James Dean, Paul Newman, and Robert DeNiro (see entries).

Brando's next two Academy Award nominations for best actor were for his performances as Zapata, the Mexican revolutionary, in *Viva Zapata!* in 1952 and as Marc Antony in *Julius Caesar* in 1953. He won his first Oscar for his performance as Terry Malloy, the boxer who could have been a contender, in *On the Waterfront* in 1954. That same year he played a rebellious biker in *The Wild One*.

Subsequent film roles included that of Napoleon in *Desirée* in 1954; Sky Masterson in the musical *Guys and Dolls* in 1955; Sakini in *The Teahouse of the August Moon* in 1956; Major Gruver in *Sayonara* in 1957; and Christian Diestl in *The Young Lions* in 1958.

In 1961, Brando made his directorial debut in the Western *One-Eyed Jacks*, starring in the film as well. In his next film role, as Fletcher Christian in *Mutiny on the Bounty* (1962), Brando continued to exhibit his penchant for difficult, unruly behavior. His next films, *The Ugly American* in 1962, *Bedtime Story* in 1963, *Morituri* in 1964, *The Chase* in 1965, and *The Appaloosa* and *A Countess from Hong Kong* in 1966 were critical failures as well. Brando's performance in the film adaptation of Carson McCullers's *Reflections in a Golden Eye* (1967) was his best in years, but critics panned the film and did not single him out for praise. Brando's reputation as an actor continued to plummet in *Candy* and *The Night of the Following Day* in 1968.

Although the critical response to his performance in the 1969 film *Burn!* was mixed rather than uniformly negative,

Brando despaired of being considered for the role of Don Corleone in the film version of Mario Puzo's *The Godfather*, to be directed by Francis Ford Coppola. Nevertheless, Puzo wanted him for the role and launched a campaign that ultimately succeeded when Paramount insisted that he undergo a screen-test and Brando agreed to the condition. His powerhouse performance in the role of the aging don in the 1972 film won critical acclaim and resulted in another Academy Award nomination for best actor. He decided to refuse the award in the event that he won it, sending Sacheen Littlefeather in his place to explain that Hollywood's treatment of American Indians made it impossible for him to accept the award.

Brando was again nominated for an Academy Award for best actor for his performance in *Last Tango in Paris*, the 1973 film directed by Bernardo Bertolucci, a film controversial for its sexual explicitness. In it he played the part of a lonely middle-aged widower obsessed by a beautiful young woman. Although he did not win the award, his financial earnings from the movie were stratospheric by the standards of the day.

Brando continued to profit handsomely from films in which he agreed to appear, earning $16.5 million for *The Missouri Breaks* in 1976, $3.5 million for Francis Ford Coppola's *Apocalypse Now*, based on Joseph Conrad's *Heart of Darkness*, also in 1976, a reported $15 million for *Superman* in 1978, and $3 million plus a percentage of the gross for *The Formula* in 1979.

Brando continues to command huge sums for his film roles (*Christopher Columbus*, 1992; *Juan de Marco*, 1995; and *The Island of Dr. Moreau*, 1996) and will remain a giant in film regardless of the roles he chooses to play.

Bibliography

"Brando Verite." *GQ* Nov. 1994: 258.

Brodkey, Harold. "Translating Brando." *New Yorker* 24 Oct. 1994: 78-85.

Manso, Peter. *Brando: The Biography*. New York: Hyperion, 1994.

Linda R. Hill

Break Dancing, or breaking, was an element of the adolescent hip-hop culture that originated in the Bronx, New York, in the mid 1970s. DJs extended the music breaks (part of a tune in which the drums take over) into long instrumentals. Breaks were isolated by using two copies of the record on twin turntables and playing the one section over and over. This style of music was known as beats or break beats.

A new form of dancing was established in the Bronx to complement this new style of mixing records. When DJs extended the breaks into instrumentals, break boys, or B-Boys, would dance. This new type of dance was termed "breaking" because the dance would take place during these breaks in music. Although breaking competitions have often been viewed as a nonviolent means to beat an adversary, sometimes competitions would end in fights.

Although breaking was very much a freestyle dance, two distinctive styles were developed in breaking, the Electric Boogie and acrobatic breaking. The Electric Boogie was contributed by black and Hispanic California youths. This style of breaking consists of a pop-like motion in a joint that the B-Boy moves from joint to joint. The effect is that the dancer has been electrified and the movement of the electricity courses through his body. The Electric Boogie also incorporates sinuous movements through limb and torso defining a wave throughout the body. The dancer will also "glide" (a slithering sideways motion) and "moon walk" (a backwards gliding motion). Other moves included joint popping, freezes, mime, and robotic imitations.

Rock Steady Crew introduced an acrobatic element with gymnastic moves to breaking. The crew was formed in 1977, with membership including the top dancers from other crews (urban celebrities like Jimmy D., Jimmy Lee, Mongo Rock, and Spy). Crazy Legs had to battle the leader, Jimmy D., to obtain membership in the crew. All of the members lacked formal dance training. Their dance moves were created from watching other B-Boys and karate movies. This type of breaking used the head, neck, shoulders, back, hands, and other unlikely body parts to become the tip of a human spinning top. Combined with acrobatic stunts, gymnastics, and martial-arts-derived movements, breakers created highly energetic dance moves such as the "windmill," "hand glide," "handstand pirouettes," and "helicopters."

Breaking was an urban street movement until the 1983 movie *Flashdance*. In this movie, a brief appearance was made by Rock Steady Crew. Jennifer Beals watches a few of the B-Boys' moves and then incorporates those moves into her final, climactic dance routine. This movie attracted millions of adolescents to breaking. Other movies such as *Breakin'* and *Beat Street* (both 1984) helped to move the hip-hop culture into the mainstream. Michael Jackson offered another boost to the commercialization of breaking. His jerky, robotic movements, and moonwalking steps were viewed by millions of people through his music videos. Praised by the conventional and talented Fred Astaire, Michael Jackson received national attention as perhaps the greatest contemporary dancer.

By 1985, hip-hop music shifted toward a harsher, rebellious music. Rap artists such as Run-D.M.C. and L. L. Cool J created music that sounded sparse, brutal, and slow. This new sound made the fast-paced style of breaking difficult. As hip-hop music evolved into rap that focused on violence, racial disharmony, and drugs, breaking receded into the background.

Bibliography
Fernando, S. H., Jr. *The New Beats: Exploring the Music, Culture, and Attitudes of Hip Hop.* New York: Anchor, 1994.
Toop, David. *Rap Attack 2: African Rap to Global Hip Hop.* London: Pluto, 1984.

Lynn A. Powers

See also
Hip Hop

Breakfast Cereals, heralded as scientific food that would restore vitality and health, took the country by storm near the end of the 19th century. Had it not been for the mid-19th-century health movement that attacked the consump-

Photo courtesy of Popular Culture Library, Bowling Green State University, Bowling Green, OH.

tion of meat and other rich foods for corrupting the body and the morals, the world might never have heard the phrase "snap, crackle, and pop," an advertising slogan of the Kellogg Company. Under the onslaught of the heavily advertised new cereals of the 1890s and 1900s, the standard heavy breakfast of steaks or chops, potatoes, eggs, bread, and pancakes gave way to flaked, granulated, shredded, and puffed cold cereals with names like Force, Zest, and Brittle Bits.

The early inventors and producers of cereal made a variety of health claims for their products. The Kellogg Company called their Apetizo "The Great Hemoglobin Producer" while the National Food Company urged customers to eat shredded wheat instead of meat since it was "more easily digested and much more nutritious." Advertising for Post's Grape-Nuts (grape here referring to grape sugar or glucose produced by starch conversion in the manufacturing process) claimed it steadied the nerves and made blood red. C. W. Post, a former real estate developer, also referred to his cereal as "brain food" on his promotional lecture tours. Enriched cereals appeared on the market after World War II under an order of the War Food Administration, which also required that white flour and bread be supplemented nutritionally.

The booming breakfast industry of the early 1900s put Battle Creek, MI, on the map, as more than 40 manufacturers set up in business to cash in on the health associations created by Dr. John Kellogg's (brother of the breakfast food baron, William K. Kellogg) Sanitarium. Another breakfast cereal location of note was Niagara Falls, where the Quaker Company operated a showplace factory called the Palace of Light, which drew vacationing honeymooners by the hundreds each day.

Appealing to children was also an early marketing discovery of cereal makers, who hit upon the idea of stuffing boxes with premiums right from the start. Around 1905 Quaker, which had introduced its puffed rice by shooting it from eight bronze cannons at the St. Louis World's Fair the year before, packed children's rings in boxes, along with spoons and kitchen gadgets. A 1934 Quaker radio campaign featured Babe Ruth, with baseballs as prizes for boxtop collectors. The Depression also inspired a Ralston Purina campaign, the first to tap the cowboy craze. Because sales of

115

their animal feeds fell dramatically in the 1930s, Ralston boosted cereal profits by getting the leading cowboy of the day, Tom Mix, to lend his name to their radio show. During the 17 years *Straight Shooters* was on the air, hundreds of premiums were offered, including framed photos of Mix with Tony the Wonder Horse. Other cereal makers followed suit, with General Mills sponsoring the *Lone Ranger* show and Quaker Oats sponsoring Roy Rogers. Premiums advertised on the shows included magic bullets, sirens, and comic books. But of all the premiums ever offered, probably the most popular was that of Quaker Oats/Mother's Oats in which 21 million deeds to one-inch-square plots of land in Alaska were given away in 1955, a tie-in to the *Sgt. Preston of the Yukon* TV show.

Sugared cereals and their Saturday morning TV commercials were the target of a new set of food reformers in the 1970s who claimed that cereals were non-nutritious junk food that hooked young children on sugar and mindless consumerism. Manufacturers responded by increasing nutrients in cereals and bringing out a number of "natural" products. With the aging of the baby boom cohort and thus of the population as a whole, cereals have honed marketing strategies around adult health concerns once again.

Bibliography

Belasco, Warren J. *Appetite for Change: How the Counterculture Took on the Food Industry, 1966-1988.* New York: Pantheon, 1989.

Carson, Gerald. *Cornflake Crusade.* New York: Rinehart, 1957.

Heide, Robert, and John Gilman. *Box-Office Buckaroos: The Cowboy Hero from the Wild West Show to the Silver Screen.* New York: Abbeville, 1989.

Marquette, Arthur F. *Brands, Trademarks and Good Will: The Story of the Quaker Oats Company.* New York: McGraw-Hill, 1967.

Mirabelle, Lisa, ed. *International Directory of Company Histories. II. Electrical and Electronics—Food Services and Retailers.* Chicago: St. James, 1990.

Jan Whitaker

Brinkley, John Romulus (1885-1942), the notorious "goat-gland man," was one of the renegade borderblasters of the 1930s who appreciated that radio waves pay no attention to lines on a map and contributed bizarre episodes to the chronicle of American broadcasting by beaming his advertising across the Rio Grande to North America during radio's golden age.

Brinkley was born in the Smoky Mountains of North Carolina. A newspaper account in 1912 placed him in nearby Knoxville, TN, where he operated a men's clinic. By 1923 Brinkley had moved to tiny Milford, KS. There he became licensee of the state's first radio station, KFKB. Through his *Medical Question Box* program, Brinkley established a mail-order drug business. He advised listeners who wrote to him with medical problems to purchase prescriptions sold by number at participating pharmacies throughout KFKB's coverage area. When Brinkley began "transplanting" tissue from the gonads of Toggenburg goats into human beings, Milford hospital became the 20th-century site of the Fountain of Youth for middle-aged men seeking sexual rejuvenation.

In 1930, the American Medical Association pressured the Kansas State Medical Board to revoke Brinkley's license because of the goat-gland operations. That same year, the Federal Radio Commission revoked his broadcast license for KFKB on the grounds that the *Medical Question Box* did not serve the public interest. The resourceful Brinkley quickly sold KFKB. In 1931, he established a powerful Mexican station, XER, at Villa Acuna, Coahuila, across the river from Del Rio, TX. The "Sunshine Station Between the Nations" was heard in most of the U.S. at night. In addition to Brinkley's medical advice, XER featured fortune tellers and country-and-western musicians.

Soon after establishing XER, Brinkley returned to Kansas, where he unsuccessfully campaigned for the office of governor in 1932. The following year, Brinkley demolished his hospital in Milford and moved his employees and equipment to Texas, where he built two hospitals along the Rio Grande to serve his radio listeners. One specialized in prostate treatments, the other in rectal problems. During Brinkley's years on the border, his annual income was estimated at more than $1 million.

Brinkley sought a more central location for his activities and moved much of his operation to Little Rock, AR, in 1938. The Brinkley empire began unraveling the following year, after he lost a libel suit against Dr. Morris Fishbein of the American Medical Association. Numerous former patients then filed lawsuits against Brinkley. Troubles with the Internal Revenue Service and U.S. postal authorities followed. Brinkley developed serious health problems in 1941, about the time the Mexican government expropriated XER. He died the following year.

Bibliography

Fowler, G., and B. Crawford. *Border Radio.* Austin: Texas Monthly, 1987.

Price, J. D. "Superpowers and Borderblasters, Part III." *Broadcast Programming and Production* 5.3: 15+.

Robert M. Ogles

Broadside magazine (1962-79; 1982-85) was started by Sis Cunningham (formerly of the Almanac Singers; see entry), Gil Turner, and Pete Seeger in New York City. The first issue of *Broadside* included songs by Sis Cunningham, Malvina Reynolds, and Bob Dylan. The main thrust of *Broadside* was to publish the actual lyrics and sheet music for current topical songs: the sheet music included both melody and chordal accompaniment. In the first issue they wrote, "Many people throughout the country today are writing topical songs, and the only way to find out if a song is good is to give it wide circulation and let the singers and listeners decide for themselves. *Broadside*'s aim is not so much to select and decide as to circulate as many songs as possible and get them out as quickly as possible."

Songs such as "Blowin' in the Wind," "There But for Fortune," "The Ballad of Ira Hayes," "Plastic Jesus," "Talkin' John Birch Blues," "Ramblin' Boy," "Bottle of

Wine," and "Last Thing on My Mind" were found in the early pages of *Broadside*.

Broadside was widely circulated by the folk-singing public, college students, and others. There were also other *Broadside* magazines, the *Boston Broadside* and *Los Angeles Broadside*. The New York *Broadside* was best known for printing the lyrics and music for the early songs of Bob Dylan, Phil Ochs, Eric Andersen, Malvina Reynolds, Arlo Guthrie, Julius Lester, Earl Robinson, F. D. Kirkpatrick, Waldemar Hille, Pete Seeger, Nina Simone, Patrick Sky, Tom Paxton, Ernie Marrs, Len Chandler, Joan Baez, Janis Ian, Buffy Sainte-Marie, Peter LaFarge, and many others. By the end of the 1970s *Broadside* published a few yearly issues and then stopped publication.

In 1982 Norman Ross and Jeff Ritter gained permission to revive the magazine in New York City and succeeded in publishing monthly issues for three years. Acoustic music with a political side had become popular again and the songs of many grassroots singers and organizers were published. In this period *Broadside* also published special issues with songs on issues such as the environment, Native Americans, and children.

Bibliography

Dunson, J. "*Broadside:* Ten Years—One Thousand Songs." *Sing Out* 21.5 (1972): 1-2.

Gleason, Ralph J. "Perspectives: 'Cover' Versions and Their Origins." *Rolling Stone* 7 June 1973: 7.

Oliver, P. "O, Freedom." *Jazz Monthly* Dec. 1965: 16-17.

Jeff Ritter

Brown, Fredric (William) (1906-1972), was a prolific writer of enthralling, high quality popular fiction (mostly science fiction and detective fiction) which was marked by a sardonic, even macabre sense of humor. Like several successful authors of the pulp magazines during the first half of the 20th century (including Walter B. Gibson, author of *The Shadow*), Brown was a journalist. His first novel was a work of detective fiction titled *The Fabulous Clipjoint* (1947); his first science fiction novel, *What Mad Universe* (1949), is an "alternate universe" tale, and is highly autobiographic—the story's protagonist is an aspiring author of pulp fiction. Several other science fiction and detective novels followed, including *Madball* (1953) and *Martians, Go Home* (1955), a science fiction tale rich in humor. Brown had many novels and shorter works—some very short, only a few lines in length—published in science fiction, fantasy, detective fiction, horror, and "weird" pulps; many of these were collected in the 1950s and '60s in book form. In the mid- and late 1980s, Dennis McMillan published 20 volumes of Fredric Brown's writing; these were primarily reprints of pulp magazine stories from the 1940s and '50s. The works of Fredric Brown are staples for enthusiasts and scholars of both science fiction and detective fiction.

Bibliography

Bloch, Robert, ed. *The Best of Fredric Brown*. Garden City: Doubleday, 1976.

——. *Carnival of Crime: The Best Mystery Stories of Fredric Brown*. Ed Francis M. Nevins, Jr., and Martin H. Greenberg.

Carbondale: Southern UP, 1985.

——. *Homicide Sanitarium: Fredric Brown in the Detective Pulps*, Vol. 1. Belen: Dennis McMillan, 1984.

Seabrook, Jack. *Martians and Misplaced Clues: The Life and Work of Fredric Brown*. Bowling Green, OH: Bowling Green State U Popular P, 1993.

Garyn G. Roberts

Brown, James (1933-), the "godfather of soul," may be the most important figure in the history of rhythm and blues. He was born near Augusta, GA, into difficult circumstances. By the age of four his parents separated, and he lived with a succession of relatives in Macon, GA, one of whose home doubled as a house of prostitution. Literally dirt poor, he often went to school without shoes and was once sent home for wearing, in Brown's words, "insufficient clothes." As a child he was inspired by the musical short films of Louis Jordan, and he soon learned that he could earn money by singing and dancing in the streets and in local amateur shows. By the time he was 15 he had performed with numerous gospel groups, formed his own rhythm and blues group, quit school, and become involved in various criminal schemes. Soon he found himself doing 8-16 years hard labor for automobile theft. Largely due to his outstanding baseball skills, Brown was released to the family of Bobby Byrd, with whom Brown founded his epochal singing group, the Famous Flames, and one of the most extraordinary careers in the annals of American music was underway.

Brown's early career was spent working talent shows, fraternity parties, and dives trying to build a name for himself; he sometimes doubled for Little Richard, who often had to leave his tour. Brown got his big break in 1956 when Ralph Bass, King Records' talent scout, heard a radio station pressing of the Famous Flames' "Please, Please, Please." When that song reached No. 6 on the rhythm and blues charts, the Famous Flames became James Brown and the Famous Flames. At this time Brown was a part of the rhythm and blues mainstream, and his music resembled other popular groups of the time, such as the Dominoes, Hank Ballard and the Midnighters, and the "5" Royales.

Brown did not have another hit for two years, the gospel-tinged "Try Me," and by then Sid Nathan, the owner of King, was close to dropping Brown from the label. From this time to 1962 Brown played hundreds of live shows, cultivating the live persona that would earn him the name "the hardest working man in show business." Playing with the best band in rhythm and blues (Brown fined them for every missed note), Brown turned every show into the highest drama. He sported flashy suits, changing as many as seven times in one performance, wore an outrageous pompadour that took hours to create and only 15 minutes to destroy, wrapped himself in a cape, and danced with a grace and verve that would inspire Michael Jackson. Each night he staged his own mock death, miraculously returning from the grave for one more chorus of "Please, Please, Please." The 1962 landmark *Live at the Apollo* captured Brown driving his fans to the brink of ecstasy and exhaustion. Interestingly, since Nathan refused to give

Brown the money to make the record, Brown, with the help of his booking agent, Ben Bart, put up the money himself. The result was the biggest selling rhythm and blues album of all time; it reached No. 2 on the pop charts. Many consider it to be the greatest live album ever recorded.

James Brown's years of hard work and unwavering self-confidence exploded in 1964-65 with the release of a series of singles which revolutionized American popular music. "I Got You," "Out of Sight," and the suggestively titled "Papa's Got a Brand New Bag" forever changed the direction of rhythm and blues, pointing to Brown's even more radical music of the late 1960s and 1970s and, ultimately, funk, hip-hop, and rap. Beginning with these singles Brown followed through on the rhythmic possibilities only hinted at in "Please, Please, Please," "I'll Go Crazy," and "Think." Brown's music surrendered melody and chord changes to emphasize percussive and rhythmic variety. Musicologist Robert Palmer notes that Brown made rhythm the basis of his sound. While Ray Charles recorded country and western music with strings, Brown created polyrhythmic masterpieces like "Cold Sweat," "I Can't Stand Myself," and "I Don't Want Nobody to Give Me Nothing (Open Up the Door, I'll Get it Myself)," which brought out into the open the African heritage of African-American music.

Even without a song as openly militant as "Say It Loud—I'm Black and I'm Proud," Brown would have become an emblem of African-American pride. Not only his music but his way of carrying himself as a self-made, unapologetically black man made him a hero of epic proportions to the black community. Brown's popularity and inventiveness continued through the mid-1970s until the popularity of disco replaced his harder edged funk, and he seemed to suffer a creative dry spell.

Still, Brown's peak lasted for 20 years, an astonishing achievement given that Brown was no mere interpreter but the creator of a new sound. Moreover, as a sideline to his own career, Brown produced records for many of his band members and associates (collected in *Soul Pride* and *James Brown's Funky People,* vols. 1 and 2) which display a genius for arranging and producing that was always at the heart of his own music. Maceo Parker, Fred Wesley, Pee Wee Ellis, Bootsy and Catfish Collins all apprenticed under Brown before joining George Clinton's Parliament and Funkadelic outfits. Like Miles Davis in jazz, whose jazz-fusion movement Brown partially inspired, Brown's bands have served as a testing ground for the best soul and funk players of his era. While legal problems slowed down his career in the 1980s, his music remains ever-present. In 1986, he had a Top 10 single with "Living in America" and continues to record. More important, his rhythmic experiments paved the way for hip-hop and rap.

Bibliography

Brown, James, with Bruce Tucker. *James Brown: The Godfather of Soul.* New York: Macmillan, 1986.
Guralnick, Peter. *Sweet Soul Music.* New York: Harper, 1986.
Hirshey, Gerri. *Nowhere to Run: The Story of Soul Music.* New York: Times, 1984.
Palmer, Robert. "James Brown." *The Rolling Stone Illustrated History of Rock & Roll.* New York: Rolling Stone, 1993.
Rose, Cynthia. *Living in America: The Soul Saga of James Brown.* London: Serpent's Tail, 1990.

Timothy L. Parrish

Brown, Margaret Wise (1910-1952), one of our more important authors of children's literature, was born in New York City. She published over 100 original children's books, as well as adaptations, translations, stories, and poems. Her books feature the work of 40 different illustrators, reflecting her exacting demand that the visual design be perfectly suited to the text. In 1935, Brown joined an experimental writing group led by Lucy Sprague Mitchell, a pioneer of the "here and now" approach to children's literature that sought to enter the child's world, to see through a child's eye. Brown's *The Noisy Book* (1937) and its numerous sequels reflect this practice.

Her best works include *The Runaway Bunny* (1942) based on an old French love song with the reassuring message that, wherever the bunny goes, his mother will find him and care for him; *The Little Island* (1946), which features the setting of her summer house in Maine and won a Caldecott Medal for the illustrator, Leonard Weisgard; *The Little Fur Family* (1946), originally bound in rabbit skin; *Mr. Dog* (1952) about a small boy and a dog, each of whom "belonged to himself"; and *Don't Frighten the Lion!* (1942), where a dog is dressed up like a little girl in order to gain admittance to the zoo.

Brown's biggest success, *Goodnight Moon* (1947), which has sold over 4 million copies, consists of an enumeration of the familiar things surrounding a child going to bed. The illustrations by Clement Hurd are in strong primary colors, yet the effect is soothing. Much of Brown's work has endured because she enters the child's world without sentiment, but with emotional truthfulness, wonderment, and respect.

Bibliography

Marcus, Leonard. *Margaret Wise Brown: Awakened by the Moon.* Boston: Beacon, 1992.

Mary Welek Atwell

Browne, Jackson (1948-), singer-songwriter, was born in Heidelberg, Germany. At the age of three, Browne and his family moved to Los Angeles, where Browne grew up. He studied music at an early age, and by his late teens excelled on the piano and guitar. Success came first in the form of songwriting; when Browne was 17, his song "These Days" was recorded by Tom Rush. In 1967, Browne moved to New York City, where he spent a year working in clubs, writing songs, and playing in the fledgling Nitty Gritty Dirt Band. Upon his return to Los Angeles in 1968, Browne found that his reputation as a songwriter had preceded him to the West Coast. His songs have been recorded by such artists as Joe Cocker, Joni Mitchell, Gregg Allman, the Eagles, the Nitty Gritty Dirt Band, the Byrds, Linda Ronstadt, Nico, and the Jackson 5.

In 1969, Browne opened for Linda Ronstadt at Hollywood's Troubador Club. Three years later he released his first album, *Jackson Browne,* with Asylum Records, a chart hit with such singles as "Doctor My Eyes" and "Rock Me on the Water." This same year, the Eagles covered Browne's "Take It Easy," which he co-authored with Eagles member Glenn Frey. His debut album was followed by *For Everyman* (1973), *Late for the Sky* (1974), and *The Pretender* (1976). This four-year stretch was marked by an introspective, confessional style, particularly in *The Pretender,* which followed the suicide of his first wife, Phyllis. During this period, Browne was accompanied by musician David Lindley. The themes of his songs at this point include the ambiguity of love as salvation and as a prison.

Following the confessional albums, Browne's music began to take on a hard rock style and a political tone. Browne also financially supported the documentary film *No Nukes* in 1980 and was involved in Amnesty International. He claimed that his previous style of the "intimate, confessional and introspective song really had its time" while he was "wistful, searching bleary-eyed for God in the crowds." *Lawyers in Love* (1983) satirizes the Cold War warriors. Browne's visit to Nicaragua inspired a series of protest songs on the album *Lives in the Balance* (1986), which addresses American foreign policy, specifically U.S. involvement in Central America. *World in Motion* (1989) tackles such issues as apartheid and the arms race. During Browne's "political" period, his songs concentrated on social concerns, including the struggle in the cities and the peace in the countryside, and the hopes of a better world and fears of apocalypse.

In 1993, Browne released his first album in four years, *I'm Alive* (Elektra). The songs for this album were written over four years, during which the singer-songwriter was ending his relationship with actress Daryl Hannah. The album included the songs "Miles Away" and "All Good Things," which, among others, suggest the mentality of a survivor of a tumultuous relationship.

Bibliography

DeCurtis, Anthony. "Jackson Browne." *Rolling Stone* 15 Oct. 1992: 138-39.

Hardy, Phil, and Dave Lang. *Encyclopedia of Rock.* New York: Schirmer, 1988.

Kot, Greg. "Jackson Browne Refocuses on Jackson Browne." *Chicago Tribune* 11 Nov. 1993: 5:1, 5.

Moritz, Charles, ed. *Current Biography Yearbook.* New York: Wilson, 1989.

Stambler, Irwin, ed. *Encyclopedia of Pop, Rock, and Soul.* New York: St. Martin's, 1974.

Lynnea Chapman King

Brubeck, David Warren (1920-), one of popular music's noted innovators, was born in Concord, CA, grew up on a 45,000-acre cattle ranch managed by his part-Indian father, studied piano with his mother, graduated from the College of the Pacific in 1942, served in the army during World War II, took lessons briefly with Arnold Schoenberg, and pursued further musical studies at length with Darius Milhaud at Mills College in Oakland, CA. Brubeck's early training in classical music equipped him with a variety of compositional techniques and harmonic concepts borrowed from the "serious" side of the familiar contrast between high art and popular culture. Some percipient colleagues—including clarinetist Bill Smith, tenor saxophonist Dave Van Kriedt, bassist Jack Weeks, trumpeter Dick Collins, drummer-vibist Cal Tjader, and alto saxophonist Paul Desmond—joined with Brubeck as pianist in various small groups whose work culminated in recordings made in the late 1940s. In this music, presaging the so-called Third Stream movement that emerged on the East Coast a decade later, classical forms abound—for example, in Van Kriedt's "Fugue on Bop Themes" or in Brubeck's arrangement of "The Way You Look Tonight," both of which draw upon formal devices borrowed from Bach and the other Baroque masters of counterpoint.

After Brubeck had partially recovered from a nearly fatal swimming accident, his musical experiments continued with the formation of the Dave Brubeck Quartet, which began in 1951 and lasted until 1967—always featuring Paul Desmond (see entry) on alto with a succession of bassists and drummers. The sound developed by this quartet in general and by Desmond in particular came to epitomize the so-called West Coast School of jazz, distinguished from the East Coast School of hard bop by its cooler, more formally structured, smoother style of delivery. Playing often at the Blackhawk in San Francisco and recording for Fantasy and Columbia Records, Brubeck and Desmond produced highly abstract, often contrapuntal, and sometimes comically disjointed versions of such familiar standards as "Let's Fall in Love," "Look for the Silver Lining," "Little Girl Blue," or "Jeepers Creepers." Sometimes distracted by a tendency to grow heavy-handed or bombastic, Brubeck acquired an underground reputation among musicians for destroying pianos with his bare hands. Indeed, Brubeck's greatest strength as a pianist was then and has remained his ability to "comp" (short in jazz lingo for "ac*comp*any") by laying down a harmonically rich layer of chords that respond sensitively to the soloist's improvisations. Such comping provided the perfect foil for the soaring saxophonic lyricism of Desmond.

With these assets, the quartet impressed a whole generation of jazz fans, winning Brubeck a spot on the November 8, 1954, cover of *Time* magazine. In the mid-1950s, the group toured extensively, playing a steady stream of concerts on college campuses, and cranking out a new LP every three or four months. As the quartet's repertoire expanded, it featured many of Brubeck's own compositions—"Two-Part Contention" or "One Moment Worth Years"—a few of which have gone on to become jazz standards: "The Duke," "Summer Song," or "In Your Own Sweet Way." The group made some beautiful and critically acclaimed concept albums—*Dave Digs Disney*; *West Side Story*; *Gone with the Wind*; *Southern Scene.* Brubeck and Desmond also experimented with the then-unconventional time signature of 3/4 (i.e., triple as opposed to duple meter or, in other words, jazz waltzes) and with the superimposition of 6/4 (with two triplets per measure) against 4/4 or 2/2 (with two strong downbeats to the bar). These new rhythmic inventions appear, for example, in the quartet's mid-1950s recordings of "Lover" and "Someday My Prince Will Come." Perhaps fittingly, these experiments in time led to the quartet's greatest commercial success—a popular hit called "Take Five," composed by Desmond around a recurrent pattern of five beats to the bar and included on the album *Time Out*, which became the first million-selling LP by a jazz instrumental group.

By the mid-1960s, this assault on the boundaries of rhythm and meter had pretty much run its course. The quartet returned to playing the classic jazz standards in albums of tunes by Matt Dennis (*Angel Eyes*), Richard Rodgers (*My Favorite Things*), and Cole Porter (*Anything Goes!*). The quartet disbanded in 1967, and Brubeck turned his attention to three new types of artistic activity.

First, in the late 1960s and early 1970s, Brubeck undertook a series of concerts and recordings in collaboration with the baritone saxophonist Gerry Mulligan (*Compadres*; *Live at the Berlin*; *The Last Set at Newport*). Second, Brubeck turned his formal training in the direction of more ambitious large-scale compositions for orchestra (*The Light in the Wilderness*; *The Gates of Justice*; *Truth Is Fallen*; *Upon This Rock*; *To Hope! A Celebration*; *Joy in the Morning*). Third, Brubeck began a stream of musical projects involving his rapidly maturing children—Chris on trombone and electric bass, Danny on drums, and Darius on keyboards (*Two Generations of Brubeck*; *Brother, The Great Spirit Made Us All*).

Brubeck's more recent recordings find him playing the piano pretty much the way he has played it for 50 years (*Back Home*; *Reflections*; *Quiet As the Moon*). Sometimes heavy handed, occasionally pounding the ivories, often mixing elements of stride with harmonically bombastic block chords, repeatedly tinkling with ideas that seem to go nowhere, Brubeck has proven in his solos that his greatest accomplishments as a jazz pianist have always resided in his sensitive accompaniment of others.

Bibliography
Hall, Fred. *It's about Time: The Dave Brubeck Story*. Fayetteville: U of Arkansas P, 1996.

Morris B. Holbrook

Buck Rogers, one of early science fiction's heroes, was born in 1928-29, when *Amazing Stories* serialized Philip Francis Nowlan's (1888-1940) *Armageddon 2419 A.D.* Nowlan's storyline centered around the adventures of the hero (a member of the USAF) after that hero had been transported 500 years into the future. In many ways, the storyline evidenced thematic elements found in Washington Irving's "Rip Van Winkle" (1819-20) and in Edgar Rice Burroughs's *A Princess of Mars* (1912, the first John Carter of Mars novel).

Nowlan's creation was soon adapted for a variety of popular media. On January 7, 1929, *Buck Rogers* debuted as a daily comic strip drawn by Dick Calkins (1895-1962); in March 1930, *Buck Rogers* premiered in Sunday newspaper comic sections. The Sunday feature ended in June 1965, and the daily comic was terminated in June 1967. Stories of Buck Rogers have appeared in Depression-era Big Little Books (see entry), motion picture serials, two television series, and a motion picture. *Buck Rogers* Big Little Books

were very popular, and, like those featuring Chester Gould's *Dick Tracy*, Harold Gray's *Little Orphan Annie*, Alex Raymond's *Flash Gordon*, and *Mickey Mouse* and *Donald Duck*, had some of the largest numbers assigned to them. In 1939, Universal produced a 12-chapter movie serial entitled *Buck Rogers*, starring Buster Crabbe (1907-1983), the Olympic swimming champion who also played Flash Gordon in the serials. There were two *Buck Rogers* television series—one done in 1950-51 by ABC, one by NBC in 1979-81. In 1979, a *Buck Rogers* movie featuring actors from the NBC TV series was produced (Gil Gerard as Buck, Erin Gray as Wilma Deering). Other important characters in the *Buck Rogers* saga include Dr. Huer (a "good guy"), Killer Kane (Buck's archenemy), and Princess Ardala.

Bibliography
Clute, John, and Peter Nicholls, eds. *The Encyclopedia of Science Fiction*. New York: St. Martin's, 1993.
Dille, Robert C., ed. *The Collected Works of Buck Rogers in the 25th Century*. New York: Chelsea, 1969.
Lowery, Lawrence F. *The Collector's Guide to Big Little Books and Similar Books*. Danville: Education Research and Applications, 1981.

Garyn G. Roberts

Buffalo Springfield is best remembered for its 1967 protest-rock anthem, "For What It's Worth," but any attempt to pigeonhole this stylistically wide-ranging and enormously influential rock group as either protest music, folk-rock, country rock, Latin rock, or introspective musical poetry would be inaccurate. For at various times in their brief history (1966-68), this quintet composed of folk-trained but adventurous musicians contributed to the development of all of these genres while creating their own distinctive sound.

Lured by the sound of California folk-rock (the Byrds, most notably), and determined to form a band of his own, Stephen Stills drifted from New York to Los Angeles. Meanwhile, Richard Furay—an old friend of Stills from New York—encountered Neil Young (see entry) in Greenwich Village and was captivated by Young's new songs. By late 1965, Furay had joined Stills in L.A. on the latter's promise of a band in the works.

That dream remained elusive until March 1966, when, sitting in traffic on Sunset Boulevard, Stills and Furay spotted a long black hearse with Neil Young at the wheel and passenger Bruce Palmer, a bassist who had played with Young briefly in a Motown group. That night, the four made plans to form a band. They were soon joined by Dewey Martin, a Canadian drummer just off a stint with the Dillards, a bluegrass-folk-rock band. The new group took the name Buffalo Springfield from a sign on a steamroller paving the street outside the house where they were rehearsing.

The quintet began playing an eight-song repertoire ranging from harder-edged folk-rock songs like Stills's "Sit Down, I Think I Love You," to Furay's "Go and Say Goodbye"—a country-rock prototype—to an orchestral arrangement of Young's earnestly questioning and introspective "Nowadays Clancy Can't Even Sing." (All three would appear on their first album, *Buffalo Springfield*, in early 1967.) With much creative promise, the group nevertheless had difficulty finding steady work until Chris Hillman of the Byrds landed them a six-week stay at the Whisky-a-Go-Go, a well-known Hollywood club. Shortly thereafter, they were opening for well-established bands and signing a recording contract.

With the release of their second (and definitive) album late in 1967, *Buffalo Springfield Again*, the band dropped any semblance of folk-rock in favor of more straight-ahead rockers like "Mr. Soul" (Young's dark portrait of the rock star syndrome) and Stills's "Bluebird." There were also country-tinged Furay compositions and Young's experimental and orchestral-sounding epic, "Broken Arrow." Like many Young compositions, the song was oblique and poetic —an evocation of mood—in contrast to the more literal songwriting styles of Stills and Furay.

Buffalo Springfield began to self-destruct with the departure late in 1967 of Palmer, whose bass and personality had balanced the creative, sometimes explosive, tension between Young and Stills. Young also began a series of unexplained absences, eventually leaving the band for good in 1968, shortly after the completion of *Last Time Around,* the final Buffalo Springfield album (excluding compilations). Engineer Jim Messina replaced Palmer as bassist, joining Richie Furay on several songs before both left to form the country-rock band Poco. Stills, whose Latin influence was strongly felt on that final album ("Uno Mundo," among others), soon teamed up with David Crosby and Graham Nash (departed from the Byrds and the Hollies, respectively) in 1968 through a mutual friend, Joni Mitchell.

As country rock developed into a dominant genre in the 1970s, nearly all of its practitioners imitated, with varying degrees of success, the archetypal Buffalo Springfield sound of acoustic guitars overlaid with electric, many infusing their Latin- and jazz-rock sounds as well.

Bibliography

Costa, Jean-Charles. Liner notes. *Buffalo Springfield.* ATCO SD2-806, 1973.

Marsh, Dave, and John Swenson. *The Rolling Stone Record Guide.* New York: Random House-Rolling Stone, 1979.

Stuessy, Joe. *Rock and Roll: Its History and Stylistic Development.* Englewood Cliffs: Prentice-Hall, 1990.

Whitcomb, Ian. *Rock Odyssey: A Musician's Chronicle of the Sixties.* New York: Doubleday-Dolphin, 1983.

Zimmer, Dave. *Crosby, Stills, and Nash: The Authorized Biography.* New York: St. Martin's, 1984.

Chris J. Magoc

Bugs Bunny, probably the most seen and best loved cartoon character in the history of animation, continues to grow in popularity. The character has permeated American culture and is as omnipresent as any media creation can be. Bugs's brash energy and "in-your-face" attitude may be seen as quintessentially "American" and has endeared him to generations of fans.

In 1938, Ben Hardaway and Cal Dalton directed *Porky's Hare Hunt*, a cartoon featuring Porky chasing after a screwy rabbit. The rabbit was much like the early Daffy Duck and also the early Woody Woodpecker, who would appear a few years later at the Walter Lantz studios. Not surprising, since Hardaway (known as "Bugs") had a hand in bringing all three characters to the screen, the legend goes that the screwball rabbit was referred to by the Warner Brothers cartoon staff as "Bugs' Bunny," hence his eventual name.

At heart, Bugs is a version of the trickster animal, a popular folklore motif. Br'er Rabbit comes to mind, as does the Hare who races the Tortoise in the noted Aesop fable. (Bugs battled the Tortoise no less that three times himself.) Other animated rabbits had starred in cartoons, notably Oswald the Lucky Rabbit, and Disney's Max Hare. But they failed to have the staying power of Bugs.

Several cartoons with prototypes of Bugs appeared at Warner Brothers, beginning in 1937 with Frank Tashlin's *Porky's Building*. Hardaway tried again after the aforementioned *Porky's Hare Hunt* and Chuck Jones also utilized a similar rabbit character. Jones soon tried again with *Elmer's Candid Camera* (1940), in which Elmer is trying to take wildlife photographs of a Bugs-like rabbit. However, the "true" Bugs did not appear until Fred "Tex" Avery's 1940 *A Wild Hare*. Finally, the Bugs that millions would come to know was evident in full form, including being voiced by Mel Blanc (1908-1989), with an accent created by crossing Bronx vocalizations with Brooklynese.

In the 1950s Jones had modified Daffy into a jealous, short-tempered character, a perfect foil for the unflappable and always-in-control Bugs. Jones's best use of Daffy is in *Duck Amuck* (1953), where Daffy is at the mercy of an unmerciful animator, who torments him by changing Daffy's shape and location at will—and is finally revealed to be Bugs himself. It shows Jones's character-based approach in full flower, and is a perfect gag—if you know Bugs's character. Jones scored with the deadpan operatic parody *What's Opera Doc?* (1957), which puts Elmer and Bugs's eternal rivalry in a lavish, mock-Wagnerian setting, with Elmer as Siegfried and Bugs as Brunhilde singing lyrics set to some of Wagner's themes.

Other animation directors at Warners turned out some excellent Bugs cartoons, and some efforts were nominated for Academy Awards. But it was not until 1958 with Friz

Photo courtesy of Popular Culture Library, Bowling Green State University, Bowling Green, OH.

Freleng's *Knighty Knight Bugs* that the coveted Oscar was awarded to a Bugs Bunny cartoon.

In 1959, Warners released much of its past cartoon product to television, and by 1964 production of new Bugs Bunny theatrical films was halted. But Bugs didn't retire. New appearances on prime-time television specials and commercials, theatrical compilations, and Saturday morning television shows kept the rabbit active. Every television market ran the old cartoons, which proved to be as popular with new generations as they had been originally.

Holiday specials made up of both old cartoon segments and new sequences (often directed by Friz Freleng) became television staples. In 1975 *Bugs Bunny Superstar,* a documentary including several complete vintage cartoons, was released theatrically. Five compilation films followed; then Bugs appeared in new films like *Who Framed Roger Rabbit?* (1988) and *Box Office Bunny* (1990).

In 1996 Bugs again returned to the big screen in *Space Jam*, a combination live-action/animated film that had Bugs solicit the help of sports star Michael Jordan when cartoonland is invaded by outer space baddies. Fans may have been surprised at Bugs needing help—but it was still good to see him and his pals back in action. A year later Bugs did the seemingly impossible and was commemorated on a U.S. postal stamp. Getting on a stamp was previously a posthumous act, but since when did Bugs need to follow the rules?

Bibliography

Adamson, Joe. *Bugs Bunny: Fifty Years and Only One Grey Hare.* New York: Holt, 1990.
——. *Tex Avery: King of Cartoons.* New York: Popular Library, 1975.
Friedwald, Will, and Jerry Beck. *The Warner Brothers Cartoons.* Metuchen, NJ: Scarecrow, 1981.
Gebert, Michael. *From Goopy Geer to Gütterammerdung: The Development of the Warners' Weltanschauung.* Zurich: Felix Meierhof, 1990.
Maltin, Leonard. *Of Mice and Magic: A History of American Animated Cartoons.* New York: New American Library, 1980.

Benjamin K. Urish

See also
Warner Brothers Cartoons

Bullwinkle Show, The (NBC 1961-1962; ABC 1964-1973; NBC 1981-1983; syndicated 1964). As successor to Jay Ward's *Rocky and His Friends*, *The Bullwinkle Show* continued to showcase the wit and animation talents of animator Jay Ward and chief writer Bill Scott as they promoted the lovable simpleton Bullwinkle J. Moose to the position of star and host of his own show (see Rocky and Bullwinkle). Keeping the series format used in *Rocky and His Friends,* this half-hour episode consisted of a main storyline broken into two segments. New episodes written for this series, however, placed the blunt and egocentric, if gentle-minded, Bullwinkle in the lead role as Rocket J. Squirrel retreated to the position of sidekick. With Rocky putting a check on Bullwinkle's impulsiveness and trying to keep him out of harm's way, the two friends otherwise continued in their efforts to put a stop

to the exploits of Pottsylvanian spies Boris Badenov and Natasha Fatale as they carried out the instructions of the "Krumlin's" midget mastermind, Mr. Big, and his Nazi-like officer, "Fearless Leader." With Bullwinkle in the lead position the two friends foiled Boris and Natasha's plans to bring about the demise of American society in ever-wackier fashion. In the episode "Banana Formula," for example, Bullwinkle kept the secret of the silent explosive "Hush-a-Boom" unintentionally to himself when he slipped on a banana peel and swallowed the sought-after formula.

As in *Rocky and His Friends*, the main storyline of each episode of *The Bullwinkle Show* was intersected by brief (usually 3 1/2 minutes) mini-episodes of six component series: "Aesop and Son," "Fractured Fairy Tales," "Peabody's Improbable History," and "Mr. Know It All" carried forward from *Rocky and His Friends* with the addition of two new component series, "Bullwinkle's Corner" and "Dudley Do-right of the Mounties." "Bullwinkle's Corner" found Bullwinkle alone on center stage as he issued verbose if nonsensical pronouncements, tapped out limericks, "clocked" a nursery rhyme on time, and read wandering sonnets and equally aimless poems such as "I Shot an Arrow in the Air."

Neither *Rocky and His Friends* nor *The Bullwinkle Show* received top ratings until after 1964 when *Bullwinkle* was in its original run and both series were in syndication. However, as the children raised on Rocky and Bullwinkle in the 1960s became parents themselves by the late 1980s, they created a nostalgic resurgence of demand for the series that was reflected in as much as spurred by Disney's February 1991 release of the set of six videocassettes of original episodes (reaching sales of over 2 million copies in the first six months).

Responding to the groundswell of adult interest and affection for Rocky and Bullwinkle, PBS aired an hour-long special, *Of Moose and Men: The Rocky and Bullwinkle Story,* in March of 1991. Before the year ended, individual *Rocky* and *Bullwinkle* celluloid stills representing 1/24 second of time in animated film (known as "cels") had sold for over $1,000 each and Nintendo had come out with a Rocky and Bullwinkle video game. Furthermore, a feature film, *The Adventures of Rocky and Bullwinkle*, was released in June 2000.

Bibliography

Brooks, Tim, and Earle Marsh. *The Complete Directory to Prime Time Network TV Shows, 1946-Present.* New York: Ballantine, 1995.
Erickson, Hal. *Television Cartoon Shows: An Illustrated Encyclopedia, 1949 through 1993.* Jefferson City: McFarland, 1995.

Pam Steinle

Bumper Stickers offer one of the few means available to the average citizen in modern urban society to interject messages into the environment of mass-mediated communication. Through bumper stickers, individuals can publicly express their perspectives on political and social issues, proclaim their individuality, or use their vehicles as mobile bill-

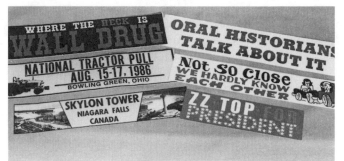

Some of the messages on bumper stickers are whimsical. Others are serious attempts to communicate messages of importance to those employing the medium. However, aside from religious statements and symbols, there are few expressions of philosophy on bumper stickers or car window decals. Photo courtesy of Popular Culture Library, Bowling Green State University, Bowling Green, OH.

boards to advertise various products. These messages reflect and shape the opinions, fears, interests, and the very essence of our society and the experience of its individuals.

In addition to the classic bumper sticker, several other forms of car signs have evolved. These include window decals or stickers, license plate frames with messages, customized license plates, and "silly yellow signs" attached to windows by suction cups.

The most frequent messages displayed on bumper stickers and car signs are expressions of self-identity. Of the 1,518 messages recorded in a study of 2,160 vehicles in California, the majority (56 percent) provided information about the status, occupation, recreational activities, school, or other sources for self-identifying information about the vehicle owner or users. The second most frequent category of messages was commercial products (17 percent of all messages), followed by "other" displays, mostly stuffed animals (10 percent), philosophical expressions (9 percent), ideological/ political statements (5 percent), and public service/safety messages (3 percent). The large proportion of self-identity messages is indicative of a need to communicate individuality and group identity in social settings where interactions are largely anonymous and impersonal.

Bibliography
Case, Charles E. "Bumper Stickers and Car Signs: Ideology and Identity." *Journal of Popular Culture* 26.3 (1992).
de Lauwe, Paul-Henry Chombart. "Oppression, Subversion and Self-Expression in Daily Life." *International Social Science Journal* 35.2 (1983).
Godbout, Oscar. "Sticker Styles." *New York Times Magazine* 14 April 1957.

Charles E. Case

Bungee Jumping, diving from heights with restraints that stop the fall just before the jumper hits solid earth or water, is one of the newest of the fad sports (see Thrill Sports). Bungee jumpers usually dive from a 130-foot-high tower, though sometimes from a bridge or a high building. A towel is placed around the ankles, a thick nylon band is wrapped around the towel, and a bungee cord, the length based on the participant's weight, is clipped onto the band. The factors that determine how far a bungee cord will stretch include

elasticity and the weight of the jumper. Jump experts use a physics equation to determine how far jumpers will fall in order to ensure a safe jump.

New Zealanders visiting Vanuata in the 1970s were amazed to watch islanders jump from towers tethered to strong vines, a practice that had gone on for hundreds of years. The New Zealanders found that technological advances meant there were resilient and incredibly elastic materials that could be used to duplicate the experience. They, young recreational enterprisers, in a country not bound by a series of safety laws, started marketing the activity, which, by the 1980s, arrived in California and became a sensation.

Sue Lebrecht writing in *Mademoiselle* (1994) sums up the philosophical conundrum posed by bungee jumping. While it is at the apex of vertigo-seeking "thrill" activities— experts say the rush of adrenaline is greater than that of sky-jumping, sky-diving, and aerobatics—is it sheer insanity or a meaningful experience? Perhaps both if one reads William Safire's witty narrative in the *New York Times Magazine* (1993).

Bibliography
Lebrecht, Sue. "High Risk, High Thrill-Fitness." *Mademoiselle* 40.19 (1994): 182-85.
McNulty, Karen. "Booiinngg!!!" *Science World* 48.11 (1992): 14.
Safire, William. "Bungee Jumping." *New York Times Magazine* 4 Apr. 1993: 16.
Sterba, James P. "Anthropological Roots." *Wall Street Journal* 1 June 1993: A1.
Thigpen, David. "Bungee Jumping Comes of Age." *Time* 15 April 1991: 50.

Scott A. G. M. Crawford

Bunyan, Paul, representing the American ethic of hard work, is a folklore hero, a larger-than-life lumberjack who chopped down the forests of the upper Midwest, the Northwest, and even traveled to Florida and California swinging an ax and using farm implements; he was also a champion rotary driller in the Pennsylvania mines. Accompanying this giant who combed his beard with a pine tree was Babe the Blue Ox, whose breadth between horns was 42 ax handles and a plug of chewing tobacco.

Drawn from "gang-lore" around logging campfires in the 19th century, legends of Paul Bunyon, later Anglicized as "Bunyan," chronicle his creating the St. Lawrence River, the Puget Sound, and the Rocky and Appalachian Mountains, as well as the Black Hills and the Grand Canyon, while conquering the frontier of the North Country. Because he cut all the trees in North Dakota, Bunyan was said to have caused the cold weather that sweeps from the Canadian borders across the midwestern U.S. Other folktales describe how he invented the grindstone and devised a sawmill that ran backwards. By 1860, stories of Paul Bunyan permeated the logging communities and his reputation was complete.

Bunyan's fame has been recorded in the oral tradition and kept alive in numerous literary accounts, ranging from a host of juvenile books and stories to his adaptation by classic authors like John Dos Passos in *1919* (1932) and Carl Sandburg in *The People, Yes* (1936). Bunyan's popularity in the Depression was pervasive, not merely because of his working-class origins and pioneer grit, but also because he was made to stand for populist ideals: his giant flapjacks and huge dinner table fed a company; his warfare against the mosquito saved the masses from suffering; his brawny skill on the rotary driller validated mineworkers. He is also remembered on roadways and byways across America, imaged forth in giant statuary and preserved in local monuments.

Bibliography
Bowman, James. *The Adventures of Paul Bunyan*. New York: Century, 1927.
Felton, Harold, ed. *Legends of Paul Bunyan*. New York: Knopf, 1950.
Marling, Karal Ann. *The Colossus of Roads: Myth and Symbol along the American Highway*. Minneapolis: U of Minnesota P, 1984.

Carolyn Lott

Burlesque, far more than merely an avenue for striptease dancing and ribald humor, developed as a vibrant theatrical arena related to vaudeville, Broadway revues, and other venues of performance (see Revue; Vaudeville). Burlesque's influence went beyond the theatrical world into politics, courtrooms, the health movement, and even marriage counseling.

What is recognized as American burlesque theater came into being in the first third of the 19th century. However, it was not until 1866 that a popular stage parody, *The Black Crook,* and an all-female revue show, *Lydia Thompson and Her British Blondes*, both began touring the U.S. in the growing burlesque arena. Their popularity paved the way for the formation of the theatrical form that came to be known as "classical American burlesque."

Burlesque touring companies soon formed, fusing the elements of the earlier hit shows: broad comedy and attractive women. Star comic performers in often ribald parodies of classical works and female chorus lines became a staple. Audiences could count on conventions being mocked and authority being ridiculed. Over time, a basic revue format developed and certain skits became standard. There was cross-pollination between vaudeville and burlesque, each serving as a training ground for the other. Many comics, singers, and dancers rose through the ranks of both entertainment forms. Vaudeville booking agents began to solidify their power and attempted to "clean up" vaudeville at the turn of the century, while burlesque retained and even enhanced its raucous reputation. The White Rats, a vaudeville performers union, called a series of strikes in 1916-17, and eventually lost. Many strikers were blacklisted by vaudeville bookers and theater owners, and found a haven in burlesque.

This helped to precipitate the next age of burlesque, which began in the 1920s and extended until the end of World War II. It is this latter age that most think of when the term "burlesque" is mentioned, because this period marked the first generation of striptease performers.

Burlesque folklore relates several stories pertaining to the birth of modern striptease, most tracing it to an occurrence involving a vigorous shimmy dance by Hinda Wasseau, who incorporated her accidental disrobing into future performances. Regardless of how the modern striptease started, it became a burlesque fixture by the early 1930s.

Scantily clad dancers had also been featured since the start of burlesque's first golden age, but usually in a formalized chorus setting. Olios (specialty numbers, often performed in front of the curtain while scenery is changed) also featured star female singers and dancers. All of these elements coalesced into the striptease. Striptease offered individualism (a strong cultural trait of America) and added a more explicit level of provocation (tease caused by process of strip). In time, the specialty (olio) dancers, who had been subordinate to the comics and variety performers, became their equals. As World War II ended and classical burlesque began its disintegration, the striptease performers gained preeminence.

The most famous was Gypsy Rose Lee (1913-1970) who parlayed her fame to the Broadway stage, motion pictures, and her own touring revues. She also wrote two best-selling novels (*The G-String Murders*, later filmed as *Lady of Burlesque*; and *Mother Finds a Body*) and an autobiography (*Gypsy*), which was adapted into a hit musical and has been filmed twice so far.

The final banning of burlesque in New York City in 1942 is traced to performers who flashed too often and too long, particularly Margie Hart. With New York burlesque a thing of the past, burlesque as a theatrical form began a slow death.

At the same time, live theater itself as a popular entertainment form was on the decline due to the double punch of radio and motion pictures. With the pinnacle of the theatrical world, New York City, removed from burlesque's grasp, the top comics began to abandon burlesque for revue shows and nightclubs. This only increased burlesque's reliance on striptease to secure an audience. As television took hold during the 1950s, burlesque all but vanished, with only a handful of nightclubs carrying burlesque-style reviews. The ensuing decades would see burlesque return as nostalgia, either cleaned up for television or presented as regional theater and Broadway shows. Striptease and nude dancing continued in various arenas, ranging from the hard-core sex industry to aerobics and even as a form of marital therapy.

Bibliography
Allen, Robert C. *Horrible Prettiness: Burlesque and American Culture*. Chapel Hill: U of North Carolina P, 1991.
Corio, Ann, with Joseph DiMona. *This Was Burlesque*. New York: Grosset & Dunlap, 1968.
Lee, Gypsy Rose. *Gypsy: A Memoir*. New York: Simon & Schuster, 1986.
Minsky, Morton, and Milt Machlin. *Minsky's Burlesque*. New York: Arbor House, 1986.
Sobel, Bernard. *Burleycue: An Underground History of Burlesque Days*. New York: Farrar, 1931.

Benjamin K. Urish

Burma-Shave, the main product of the Burma-Vita Co. of Minnesota, is famous for having placed advertising sign-series by the sides of roads and highways of America. This unusual campaign remained a well-known, unique, popular culture icon for almost 40 years. The first ads appeared in 1927 with the last ones removed in 1963, soon after Burma-Shave had been sold.

The first sign-series ad, on wooden signs approximately 100 feet apart, was placed in Minnesota in 1927: "SHAVE THE MODERN WAY/NO BRUSH/NO LATHER/NO RUB-IN/BIG TUBE 35c DRUG STORES/BURMA-SHAVE." It would be 1929 before the first rhyming jingles would appear along roadsides. The first was "EVERY SHAVER/NOW CAN SNORE/SIX MORE MINUTES/THAN BEFORE/BY USING/BURMA-SHAVE." Finally, the last sign-series to appear was one of 17 in 1963: "OUR FORTUNE/IS YOUR/SHAVING FACE/IT'S OUR BEST/ADVERTISING SPACE/BURMA-SHAVE."

Some 600 different sets of the mini-billboards appeared between 1927 and 1963. At the peak of the campaign in the early 1950s, about 7,000 sets of these whimsical ad signs appeared along numerous roads in 45 states. Soon after the Burma-Vita company was sold to the Philip Morris Company in that year, the nostalgic popular culture roadside rhymes had entered the realm of history. Fittingly, a set of Burma-Shave signs was presented, in the mid-1960s, to the Smithsonian Institution.

Bibliography

Crain, Rance. "Superhighway Needs Burma-Shave Signs." *Advertising Age* 31 Jan. 1994: 18.

Goodrum, Charles, and Helen Dalrumple. *Advertising in American: The First 200 Years.* New York: Abrams, 1990.

Lyons, Richard D. "Allen G. Odell, 90; Burma Shave Executive Linked Beards to Bards" (Obituary). *New York Times* 22 Jan. 1994: A-10.

Margolin, Victor, Ira Brichta, and Vivian Brichta. *The Promise and the Product.* New York: Macmillan, 1979.

Rowsome, Frank. *Verse by the Side of the Road.* New York: Penguin, 1990.

Sammy R. Danna

Burns, George, and Gracie Allen, one of entertainment's most successful teams, are perhaps most remembered for their groundbreaking television show (1950-58), but their accomplishments are just as notable in other areas of entertainment.

George Burns (1896-1996) and Gracie Allen (1902-1964, also given as 1906-1964) became a team in 1922, but both had been in show business for years prior to their partnership. George Burns began performing while a child of seven as a member of the Pee-Wee Quartette. School got in the way of bookings and Burns eventually devoted himself to his career as a vaudevillian, doing a variety of acts with partners and alone. Burns danced, skated, sang, worked with animals, and did comedy. He often changed his professional name so as not to lose jobs from managers who might have seen him and been less than thrilled. In the early 1920s Burns finally found success, first with singer Sid Gary, and then with Billy Lorraine, doing impersonations.

Gracie Allen was part of an act in which she and her sisters danced, featuring the Irish Clog. The act was incorporated into another act, Larry Reilly and Company, the Allen sisters being the "Company." In 1922 Lorraine and Burns were breaking up and some of the Allen sisters were ready to give up show business. A friend suggested that Allen catch Lorraine and Burns, thinking she might be able to work with Lorraine. Things worked out differently.

Burns and Allen developed a standard boy-girl flirtation act, a vaudeville staple. At their debut, Gracie played straight and George was the comic. Burns realized the audience was responding well to Gracie and they switched roles. The team developed a routine called "dizzy," which featured Gracie in a "dizzy dame" role with Burns trying to make her acquaintance. This was a common type of act in vaudeville (Matthews and Ayers or Block and Sully for example), but Burns and Allen played it differently. Gracie made perfect sense in a twisted sort of way, and Burns's response was not just mounting frustration but bemused affection. The act would finish with a dance number showcasing Allen's talent more than Burns's.

By the spring of 1923 the team was getting good bookings and a new act titled Lamb Chops brought them further success. By 1926 they had reached the pinnacle of vaudeville, the Palace theater in New York. They were also married that year. While Gracie was certainly the star of the act, Burns was responsible for selecting and preparing material, a function he continued throughout their career. They continued touring vaudeville to great success.

In 1929 they went to England, where they were also a hit and started appearing on British radio. Upon their return to the U.S. they began making a series of highly popular short subjects for Paramount, with George doing much of the writing. The success of the shorts got them work on radio, and in 1933 they had their own series on CBS. Burns helped devise a running gag in which Allen was looking for her lost brother. Soon Gracie was all over the CBS airwaves, interrupting other shows unannounced with her search. The gag even spilled over to NBC when Burns and Allen appeared on the Rudy Vallee program. Burns and Allen's show was formatted as a grab bag of music, cross-talk, and skits until the early 1940s, when it became a sitcom.

Paramount thought Burns and Allen should stop their series of shorts and put them into feature films, usually in co-starring roles. They made 12 co-starring features for the company from 1932 to 1939. They co-starred with Bing Crosby four times, W. C. Fields twice, Jack Benny twice and once with Bob Hope, among other Paramount stars. However, their best film may be RKO's *A Damsel in Distress* (1937), starring Fred Astaire. Burns and Allen get to do a few choice routines, and even dance in two wonderful numbers. In their next Paramount film, *College Swing* (1938), Gracie got to sing, doing a fine job. Gracie followed these successes by starring in two mystery comedies without George, *The Gracie Allen Murder Case* (1939) and *Mr. and Mrs. North* (1941). In both films her convoluted way of looking at events helps solve the mystery.

The change to a sitcom format in 1942 set the stage for the radio show's successful transfer to television in 1950. The television show was an immediate hit and remained so until it went off the air in 1958, due to Gracie's retirement. *The George Burns and Gracie Allen Show* featured much of what had made the radio show such a success, with the addition of George (and only George) now being aware that he and the others were in a show. Burns bantered with the audience and watched the plots unfold with the same bemusement he expressed at all of Gracie's antics. When outsiders would wonder how George could tolerate Gracie's antics, he would respond, usually before they had formulated their question, "I love her, that's why." It became the title of his first autobiography, published in 1955. The shows would usually end with a re-creation of a vaudeville bit, with Gracie telling George about her crazy relatives until time was up and George would request, "Say 'goodnight,' Gracie."

After Gracie retired, George tried to carry on with the show, now on NBC and titled *The George Burns Show,* with much of the same cast. It lasted only one season, but Burns enjoyed success as a frequent guest star and producer, his McCadden production company having several hit series, including *Mr. Ed.* In 1964 he tried again with the series *Wendy and Me,* but it too lasted only one season. That same year, Gracie died.

Burns continued his career by making numerous personal and television appearances, a record album, and producing. Then, after not appearing in films for 36 years, he returned to the screen in *The Sunshine Boys* (1975), a movie version of the hit play about two bickering old vaudevillians. Burns won an Oscar for his portrayal. He wrote another autobiography, *Living It Up,* and stared in another hit film, *Oh God!* in the title role. Burns starred in two sequels to the film.

Burns was a hot property, continuing to make television and personal appearances in addition to more films. His acting in 1979's *Going in Style* is particularly fine, and is equaled by his touching performance in the made-for-TV film *Two of a Kind* (1982). In 1980 he had a hit record with the song and album *I Wish I Was 18 Again,* a song he had been singing in his act for some time. He followed this up with three more albums and starred in a 1988 film that used the song's title and premise.

Burns continued as a one-man industry, turning out humor books, exercise and performance videotapes, and biographies. Two of the biographies stand out, 1989's *All My Best Friends,* about his show business cronies; and *Gracie: A Love Story,* an affectionate tribute to his partner.

Bibliography
Blythe, Cheryl, and Susan Sackett. *Say Goodnight, Gracie!: The Story of Burns and Allen.* New York: Dutton, 1986.
Burns, George. *Gracie: A Love Story.* New York: Putnam, 1988.
——, with Cynthia Hobart Lindsay. *I Love Her, That's Why!* New York: Simon & Schuster, 1955.
Maltin, Leonard. *Movie Comedy Teams.* New York: New American Library, 1985.

Benjamin K. Urish

Burns, Ken (1953-), is one of public television's most celebrated and prolific producers. He has fashioned a long list of major Public Broadcasting Service (PBS) specials, addressing a wide range of topics from American history, such as *The Brooklyn Bridge* (1982), *The Shakers: Hands to Work, Hearts to God* (1985), *The Statue of Liberty* (1985), *Huey Long* (1986), *Thomas Hart Benton* (1989), *The Congress* (1989), *The Civil War* (1990), *Empire of the Air* (1992), *Baseball* (1994), and *The West* (1996), which have all won awards and recognition from both professional and scholarly organizations and at international film festivals.

Ken Lauren Burns was born in Brooklyn, NY, and grew up in Ann Arbor, MI. He is a 1975 graduate of Hampshire College in Amherst, MA, where he studied under still photographers Jerome Liebling and Elaine Mayes, and received a degree in film studies and design. Upon graduation, he and two of his college friends started Florentine Films and struggled for a number of years doing freelance assignments, finishing a few short documentaries before beginning work in 1977 on a film based on David McCullough's book *The Great Bridge* (1972). Four years later, they completed *The Brooklyn Bridge*, which won several honors including an Academy Award nomination, thus ushering Burns into the ambit of public television.

While editing *The Brooklyn Bridge* in 1979, Burns and one of his collaborators, Amy Stechler, moved Florentine Films to Walpole, NH; they later married in 1982 and now have two daughters, Sarah and Lilly. Much about Ken Burns's career defies the conventional wisdom: He operates his own independent company in a small New England village more than four hours north of New York City, hardly a crossroads in the highly competitive and often insular world of corporately funded, PBS-sponsored productions. His television career is a popular and critical success story in an era when the historical documentary generally holds little interest for most Americans.

Ken Burns's chronicles are populated with seemingly ordinary men and women who rise up from the ranks of the citizenry to become paragons of national (and occasionally transcendent) achievement, always persisting against great odds. *The Brooklyn Bridge*, for example, described by the film's "chorus of voices" as "a work of art" and "the greatest feat of civil engineering in the world," is the "inspiration" of a kind of "Renaissance man," John A. Roebling, who died as the building of the bridge was beginning; and his son, Washington Roebling, who finished the monument 14 years later through his own dogged perseverance and courage, despite being bedridden in the process. In *The Shakers: Hands to Work, Hearts to God*, Mother Ann Lee emerges as another "American original," a former factory worker and English immigrant, who comes to upstate New York on the eve of the Revolutionary War and pioneers a peculiarly American religious movement.

Ken Burns is best known, of course, for his 11-hour documentary series *The Civil War* (see entry), whose overwhelming popularity in September 1990 made him a household name. Much of the success of the series must be credited to the extent with which Burns makes this 130-year-old conflict immediate and comprehensible to a contemporary audience. The great questions of race and continuing discrimination, of the changing roles of women and men in society, of big government versus local control, and of the individual struggle for meaning and conviction in modern life, all form essential parts of Burns's version of the war.

He adopted a similar strategy with *Baseball*. This 20-hour history of the sport debuted over nine evenings in September 1994. Nearly double the length and costing twice the budget ($7 million) of *The Civil War*, "*Baseball*," he says, "is as much about American social history as it is about the game," as it examines such issues as immigration, assimilation, labor and management conflicts, and, most important, race relations. Similarly, the story of the American West (told in an 8-part series), he believes, is "at once the story of a unique part of the country and a metaphor for the country as a whole." Recent Burns television miniseries (all on PBS) include: *Lewis & Clark: The Journey of the Corps of Discovery* (1997), *Thomas Jefferson* (1997), *Frank Lloyd Wright* (1998), *Not for Ourselves Alone: The Story of Elizabeth Cady Stanton and Susan B. Anthony* (1999), and *Jazz* (2000).

Bibliography
Edgerton, Gary. "Ken Burns—A Conversation with Public Television's Resident Historian." *Journal of American Culture* 18.1 (1995).
Marc, David, and Robert J. Thompson. *Prime Time, Prime Movers*. Boston: Little, Brown, 1992.
Toplin, Robert Trent. *Ken Burns'* The Civil War. New York: Oxford UP, 1996.

Gary Edgerton

Burton, Tim (1958-), has combined an offbeat sense of humor and an obsession with the grotesque to create some of the most unlikely Hollywood movies in recent history. Most of his movies have been extremely popular, and several have been critically acclaimed.

Born in Burbank, CA, Burton became an apprentice animator at the Disney Studios, where he directed several short films, culminating in *Frankenweenie* (1984). His first feature was *Pee-wee's Big Adventure* (1985), followed by the bizarre *Beetlejuice* (1988) and two dark, menacing Batman films (1989, 1992; see entry). He also created the story and characters for the animated *Tim Burton's The Nightmare Before Christmas* (1992).

Whether reanimated dog, superhero, monster (*Edward Scissorhands*, 1990), or talentless hack (*Ed Wood*, 1994), Burton's heroes are outsiders, whom society cannot accept or who are dissatisfied with society. The difference between these figures and ordinary people is clearly what Burton loves about them, and invariably these characters are depicted as braver, better-natured, and more creative than society's "normal" members. Although society usually cannot accept a Burton hero, and although the hero suffers from this rejection, the real loss, these movies tell us, is society's. There is never any real suggestion that the frustrated hero, who is often an artist, should try to change in order to gain acceptance. Burton's films stress the importance of being oneself, no matter how weird that self may be, and the need to work to make one's dreams happen, no matter how impossible those dreams are.

Bibliography
Ansen, David, with Donna Foote. "The Disembodied Director." *Newsweek* 21 Jan. 1991: 58-60.
Burton, Tim. *Burton on Burton*. London: Faber, 1995.
Gliatto, T. "And to All a Good Fright." *People* 22 Nov. 1993: 73-74.
Handelman, D. "Heart and Darkness." *Vogue* July 1992: 142+.

Linda Anderson

Bury My Heart at Wounded Knee (1970), by Dee Brown, was what he called "a narrative of the conquest of the American West as the victims experienced it." Mainstream society thought little about an event that has since gained mythic proportions, the battle between 350 Hunkpapa Sioux and 300 men from the late Lt. Col. Custer's Seventh Cavalry on December 29, 1890, at Wounded Knee, SD. To white historians, the battle marked the end of Indian resistance to westward expansionism; to Indians, it became a rallying cry for unity and the civil rights long denied them.

Brown's account traces the history and symbolism of the event, arguing that the battle was the consequence of a government policy rooted in mythical misconceptions about Native peoples, the frontier, and the motives of white settlement. *Bury My Heart* changed the popular image of the American Indian. The stereotype of the "blood-red savage" was replaced to a great extent by the myth of the native as environmentalist, naive and apolitical, victim of Euro-American technology as well as its greed and fear. Recently, such studies as Gary Nash's *Red, White, and Black* (1974) present a more balanced view of Indian peoples as separate and successful cultures that prospered long before the arrival of Europeans, though Brown's more pitiful image has prevailed in the popular mind.

Brown's account also galvanized the American Indian Movement. In 1973, 200 members of that group occupied Wounded Knee for 69 days, demanding government action to rectify the sorry plight of many contemporary Native peoples.

Bibliography
Axtell, James. *The European and the Indian: Essays in the Ethnohistory of Colonial North America*. New York: Oxford UP, 1981.
Josephy, Alvin. *The Indian Heritage of North America*. New York: Knopf, 1991.
Miller, David Humphreys. *Custer's Fall: The Native American Side of the Story*. New York: Meridian, 1985.

Patricia W. Julius

Bushnell, Nolan K. (1943-), incited the video game revolution of the 1970s. As the founder of Atari, he perfected the coin-operated video game played at the neighborhood video arcade (see entry), then brought it into the home. Though maligned, the video game (see entry) created new expectations that viewers could control their televisions, and it anticipated acceptance of home computers and video.

Bushnell began playing with microcomputers while working for Ampex in California's Silicon Valley, and by 1970, had adapted the hacker classic Spacewar into a coin-op game called Computer Space. The game proved too complicated for bar patrons, and failed to sell.

Undaunted, Bushnell and fellow Ampex engineer Ted Dabney pooled $500 to start their own business, named "Atari" from an expression in the Japanese game go. Their engineer, Al Alcorn, designed a Ping-Pong game that any barfly could learn. It was tested in a Sunnyvale, CA, bar and became so popular it broke down, jammed with quarters. Pong came out in November 1972 and eventually sold 8,000 games in an industry where 3,000 was considered a hit.

Atari produced other coin-op games while working on a Home Pong set. Magnavox already introduced a home video game called Odyssey in 1972, but Atari's Home Pong, aided by an exclusive distribution deal with Sears, outsold Odyssey by 50 percent when it came out in 1975.

The next step was an interchangeable cartridge game, introduced with Fairchild's Channel F in 1976. Bushnell was so involved with Atari's video cartridge system (VCS) that he turned down a chance to finance one of his consultants, Steve Jobs (see entry), in developing the Apple home computer. Instead, Nolan sold Atari to Warner Communications for $26 million.

Atari's VCS appeared for the 1977 Christmas season. Sales were modest until a boom in video games started in 1979 with Space Invaders, which Atari licensed for its VCS. Atari was also riding high with its coin-ops Asteroids and Missile Command, which also became hits as home cartridges. By 1982, Atari controlled 80 percent of the video game market.

With Atari producing 70 percent of Warner Communications' profits, the parent firm clamped corporate policy on a company that had been started by free-spirited hackers. The names of Atari programmers were company secrets. Many programmers left to start third-party game companies like Activision and Imagic, whose product was much better than Atari games. Atari's decline in quality was exemplified by its anemic E.T. spinoff and Pac-Man conversion.

Sales skidded in December 1982. Home computers had arrived at popular prices, and they played better games. Atari's 400 and 800 computers could not play the VCS cartridges. By 1984, Atari became a huge liability for Warner, which sold it to Jack Tramiel (see entry), founder of Commodore Electronics.

Bushnell, meanwhile, started Pizza Time Theatre in 1977. The family restaurant chain, later named Chuck E. Cheese for its robot mascot mouse, makes most of its profit from arcade and video games and now has over 250 outlets in North America. In 1991, Bushnell became chairman of Octus Inc., which sells software products for Novell network systems.

Bibliography

Cohen, Scott. *Zap: The Rise and Fall of Atari*. New York: McGraw-Hill, 1984.

Fisher, Lawrence M. "New Chief and Name for Office Automation." *New York Times* 19 Oct. 1991: Sec. 1: 37.

Landrum, Gene N. *Profiles of Genius: Thirteen Creative Men Who Changed the World*. Buffalo: Prometheus, 1993.

Mark McDermott

Byrds, The (1964-1973), one of the most influential bands in the history of rock 'n' roll music, was originally formed as the Jet Set in Los Angeles in mid-1964, changing their name to the Byrds by the fall of that year—both appellations reflected leader Jim (later Roger) McGuinn's fascination with flight. The group originally was comprised of McGuinn, David Crosby, Chris Hillman, Gene Clark, and Mike Clarke. All of the members, prior to forming the Byrds, had played with popular folk groups: McGuinn with the Limeliters and the Chad Mitchell Trio (as well as a folk set in Bobby Darin's nightclub act); Gene Clark backed the New Christy Minstrels, while Crosby played for Les Baxter's Balladeers; Hillman had learned a mixture of bluegrass and folk while playing for the Scottsville Squirrel Barkers. But by 1963, these folk-trained musicians had grown weary of the increasing banality and commercialization which then characterized much of both folk and rock 'n' roll music in America.

For McGuinn, as for other musicians of the time, Bob Dylan maintained the honest integrity of pure folk music, while the Beatles and the British invasion were revitalizing the creative edge of American rock 'n' roll by infusing it with African-American rhythm and blues. It was this perceived musical space between Dylan and the Beatles within which the Byrds would create a unique sound.

The first attempt to do so—a Beatlesque tune entitled "Please Let Me Love You"—failed miserably in the fall of 1964. After seeing the popular success that year of groups like the Animals ("House of the Rising Sun"), the Byrds turned to stylizing Dylan. Their rendition of his "Mr. Tambourine Man" marked the emergence of the Byrds' trademark sound: rhythmically upbeat, formally perfect, and pleasantly harmonic. The title song (by Pete Seeger) to their second album, *Turn, Turn, Turn* (1965), became the group's second No. 1 hit in nine months.

In 1966 Gene Clark left the group to pursue a solo career, signaling the onset of a protracted period of internal division and splintering of the band that plagued the Byrds until their ultimate demise in 1973. The shakeup, though, like others which followed, also brought a burst of artistic creativity; the Byrds began to suffuse fresh musical influences into a folk-rock genre grown stale amid the briskly changing cultural climate of the mid-1960s. "Eight Miles High," the group's third hit single, epitomized the countercultural zeitgeist of creative experimentation in 1966 and was the highlight of their album that summer, *Fifth Dimension*. Beyond its suggestion of LSD "flight," musically the song featured strange chord progressions and an electrified evocation of Eastern music—what came to be called raga rock. It was David Crosby, in fact, who introduced George Harrison to the sitar sounds of Ravi Shankar, influencing much of the Beatles' music from this era. Crosby's song from the same album, *What's Happening?!?!*, was an equally adventurous foray into jazz-rock.

After serious musical disputes with McGuinn, Crosby was fired from the Byrds and in 1968 teamed up with Stephen Stills and Graham Nash. Electing to not fill Crosby's vacancy, the Byrds nevertheless continued to explore new musical boundaries. Their 1968 album, *The Notorious Byrd Brothers*, was an eclectic mix of folk-rock, political protest, psychedelic sound effects (à la the Beatles' 1967 *Sgt. Pepper*), electronic manipulation, and most significantly, a clear country sound. The latter influence, typified by such songs as "Change Is Now," was even more clearly felt in the Byrds' next album, *Sweetheart of the Rodeo*, marking the band's pivotal role in the development of the country rock genre which dominated much of 1970s rock music.

The Byrds continued to suffer from personnel losses when Hillman and Gram Parsons (the latter had joined for *Sweetheart*) both left in 1968 to form the Flying Burrito Brothers. Although the soundtrack of the 1969 film *Easy Rider* employed a few Byrds' songs, what followed was a slow descent in musical creativity and musical success. After a brief reunion of the original five Byrds in 1973, McGuinn formally disbanded the group to pursue a solo career as a singer-songwriter, joining a growing list of folk-country rock artists (James Taylor and Jackson Browne, to name two) for whom, again, the Byrds had helped pave a musical trail with similarly introspective and acoustic work. Other members of the band continued to perform solo and in various combinations until 1990, when McGuinn, Crosby, and Hillman reunited for several appearances and a boxed set collection of Byrds music. The Byrds were formally recognized for these contributions in 1993 when they were inducted into the Rock and Roll Hall of Fame.

Bibliography

Burt, Rob, and Patsy North, producers. *West Coast Story*. Secaucus: Chartwell, 1977.

Crosby, David. *Long Time Gone: A Biography*. New York: Doubleday, 1990.

DeCurtis, Anthony, and James Henke. *The Rolling Stone Illustrated History of Rock & Roll*. New York: Random House, 1992.

Gillett, Charlie. *The Sound of the City*. New York: Pantheon, 1983.

Stuessy, Joe. *Rock and Roll: Its History and Stylistic Development*. Englewood Cliffs: Prentice-Hall, 1990.

Zimmer, Dave. *Crosby, Stills, and Nash: The Authorized Biography*. New York: St. Martin's, 1984.

Chris J. Magoc

Cagney, James (1899-1986), began his climb to stardom because he fit a stereotype. In 1933, during the filming of *Lady Killer* (1933), Darryl F. Zanuck sent to his crew of writers a memo detailing the studio's requirements for the Cagney persona: "He has got to be tough, fresh, hard-boiled, bragging—he knows everything, everybody is wrong but him—everything is easy to him—he can do everything and yet it is a likable trait in his personality." During the 1930s, Cagney both affirmed and challenged Zanuck and later Hal B. Wallis's dictates. Cagney's uptempo acting style—the rat-a-tat-tat of his reedy voice—and his distinctly Irish-puck appearance, created a decidedly Lower East Side aura. However, behind the anarchic energy, the leaning forward, the clenched fists, was not only dynamic explosiveness but, according to Lincoln Kirstein, a man hiding fear "from himself and the world."

James Cagney was born in New York City. Although studio publicity promoted stories about a tough East-Side upbringing and life above a saloon, Cagney was, in fact, raised in the modest middle-class neighborhood of Yorkville. Two of his brothers became doctors. Cagney's father died during the influenza epidemic of 1919-20 and afterward Cagney with wife Frances (Bill) toured vaudeville before he began playing leads on Broadway in 1925. Al Jolson discovered Cagney and Joan Blondell in Broadway's *Penny Arcade* (1929) and sold its rights to Warner Brothers under the stipulation Cagney and Blondell re-create their roles. They did, in Warners' renamed *Sinners' Holiday* (1930). A series of small roles followed before Cagney electrified audiences as the indomitable Tom Powers in *Public Enemy* (1931).

The film is famous for an enduring still in which Cagney, with lips pursed, hair awry, and eyes enraged, smashes a grapefruit in Mae Clarke's face. But it was Tom's contempt for assimilation—"Aw that sucker. He's too busy going to school. He's learning how to be poor"—that alarmed educators and reformers. In 1932-33, a group of Chicago sociologists warned that immigrant youths would over-identify with certain screen stars and surrender their parents' values for the falsely "Americanized" ones on screen.

Warner Brothers shifted their narrative emphasis from lost world losers to common men trying to make it in America. *Taxi* (1932) was Cagney's first film to take on this new role. His Matt Nolan is a working-class hot-head who is reformed through an Irish woman's tenderness. *Taxi* also suggests a link between Cagney and New York's immigrants. It opens with a setpiece: Cagney and a Jewish American speaking Yiddish, while an Irish-American cop haplessly stands by, not understanding a word. The police officer represents authority (controlling the large immigrant mass from Eastern Europe); Cagney mediates that authority.

Regardless of how Cagney's image was read by immigrants and sociologists, he was not happy with how he perceived Zanuck and the Warner Brothers scriptwriters to have structured his persona. A devout Catholic and a shy, soft-spoken man off screen, he was tired of roughing up women and playing street punks, on screen. Three times (1932, 1934, 1936) he walked off the studio lot to protest his typecasting. In March 1936, Cagney won a breach of contract suit against Warners when studio publicity inadvertently billed Pat O'Brien's name above Cagney's in a *Ceiling Zero* (1936) six-sheet. The victory, however, appeared hollow. No previous star had won such a momentous decision and with Warner Brothers appealing, the other majors were afraid to hire Cagney. But on July 11, 1936, six days before his 37th birthday, fledgling Grand National took a chance on Cagney.

For Grand National, a small company with only 28 exchanges who tried to sell their product as "down to earth entertainment," Cagney made two films, *Great Guy* (1936) and *Something to Sing About* (1937). The first film borrowed from the plot of *G-Men* (1935), except Cagney no longer fought public enemies but white-collar crooks "who cheat the housewife." His second film, a musical, represented a decisive break from his Warner Brothers past. *Something to Sing About* mixes Cagney's biographical legend with fiction to create an imagistic wish-fulfillment: Cagney as hoofer, singer, and a gentleman with women. It was a box-office failure. Cagney returned to Warners just prior to Grand National's fold.

To enhance Cagney's return, Warner Brothers immediately teamed him with old pal and co-star Pat O'Brien in *Boy Meets Girl* and the classic *Angels with Dirty Faces* (both 1938). For the latter film, his performance as Rocky Sullivan received an Academy Award nomination and the New York Critics Award for best actor.

By the 1940s, Cagney's image had radically changed under the pressures of the Martin Dies "communist" innuendoes. With war raging in Europe the competing images in Cagney's persona (the anarchic individual at odds with the collective; the Irish American trying to make it in WASP society) were transformed into a homogenized pro-U.S. figure. The plight of the immigrant was replaced by Warners' all-American front to the Axis. *Yankee Doodle Dandy* (1942) culminated the change as Cagney's simultaneity was galvanized into a singing, dancing superpatriot. Cagney won an Academy Award for his dynamic performance.

Following a second try at independence (United Artists, 1943-48), the post–World War II Cagney struggled to maintain a contemporary persona. Much of his New York City audience had grown up and moved to the suburbs. Too old and lace-curtain Irish to remain an ethnic in-between, the postwar Cagney bifurcated into two types: a strong-willed patriarch (*13 Rue Madeleine* [1946], *Come Fill the Cup* [1951], *Run for Cover* [1955], *These Wilder Years* [1956], *One, Two, Three* [1961]), or a completely insane figure who needed to be destroyed (*White Heat* [1949], *Kiss Tomorrow Goodbye* [1950], *A Lion Is in the Streets* [1953], *Shake Hands with the Devil* [1959]).

On March 18, 1974, more than 50 million Americans watched Cagney accept the American Film Institute's second annual lifetime achievement award. Although he had fought Zanuck, Wallis, and the studio's construction of his "tough, fresh, hard-boiled" image, he embraced it in his acceptance speech, thanking the tough city boys of his past. James Cagney died on Easter Sunday, 1986.

Bibliography

Forman, Henry James. *Our Movie Made Children*. New York: Macmillan, 1933.

Kirstein, Lincoln (as Forrest Clark). "James Cagney." *New Theatre* 2 (Dec. 1935): 15+.

McGilligan, Patrick. *Cagney: The Actor as Auteur*. San Diego: Barnes, 1982.

Naremore, James. *Acting for the Cinema*. Berkeley: U of California P, 1988.

Sklar, Robert. *City Boys: Cagney, Bogart, Garfield*. Princeton: Princeton UP, 1992.

Tynan, Ken. "Cagney and the Mob." *Sight and Sound* May 1951: 12-16.

Grant Tracey

Cagney & Lacey (1982-1988) began as a CBS made-for-television movie in 1981. The television movie featured Tyne Daly as Mary Beth Lacey and Loretta Swit as Christine Cagney. A decision by CBS and creators Barbara Corday, Barbara Avedon, and Barney Rosenzweig to generate a series in 1982 resulted in a new Cagney since Swit had prior commitments to *M*A*S*H*. Meg Foster replaced Swit. Low rating caused the series to be canceled, but popular demand and public pressure brought the program back in 1983 with Foster replaced by Sharon Gless.

Cagney & Lacey was a new kind of program. Barbara Corday had shown her husband, Barney Rosenzweig, Molly Haskell's *From Reverence to Rape: The Treatment of Women in the Movies*. Corday proposed a television program featuring women, but capitalizing on the buddy films made popular by Paul Newman and Robert Redford—*Butch Cassidy and the Sundance Kid* (1969) and *The Sting* (1973). Television had already created buddy series with men; *Starsky and Hutch* (1975-79) and *Simon & Simon* (1982-83) were very popular. Corday and Avedon suggested the female buddy concept and were given the go-ahead with the suggestion that they use Ann-Margret and Raquel Welch. The pilot showed two police officers assigned to the hooker squad and used as decoys.

By the opening of the television show, the women did not work decoy but were members of the precinct assigned to robberies, assaults, and murders. The show was a far cry from "cute" women shows like *Charlie's Angels* (1976-81) and paved the way for other buddy shows like *Kate & Allie* (1984-89) and programs starring independent and strong-willed women like *Designing Women* (1986-93) and *Murphy Brown* (1988-97) (see Women's Roles in Series Television).

Besides being a ground-breaking program for the charac-terization of women, *Cagney & Lacey* also portrayed a realistic side of police life and private lives of officers similar to that of *Hill Street Blues* (1980-87) and *L A. Law* (1986-94), and by extension *Lou Grant* (1977-82) and *St. Elsewhere* (1982-88).

Bibliography

D'Acci, Julie. *Defining Women: Television and the Case of Cagney and Lacey*. Chapel Hill: U of North Carolina P, 1994.

Thompson, Robert J. *Television's Second Golden Age: From Hill Street Blues to ER*. New York: Continuum, 1996.

Donna Waller Harper

Cahn, Sammy (1913-1992), one of America's most important composers of popular songs, was born Samuel Cohen in the Lower East Side of Manhattan, the only son of Polish immigrants. The family did not have a lot of money, but still managed to provide violin lessons for Cahn and piano lessons for his four sisters. While in his teens, Cahn played the violin at Catskill Mountain resorts and became a member of a small Dixieland band called the Pals of Harmony. After being allowed to drop out of high school, Cahn worked at various low-paying jobs for a few years. At 16 he devised his first lyric, "Like Niagara Falls, I'm Falling for You." Soon he discovered he had some real ability to write song lyrics, though even he probably never imagined that he would become one of America's most facile and talented lyricists.

In the early 1930s Cahn teamed up with his friend Saul Kaplan (to be known as Saul Chaplin), and started the first of his three significant collaborations. During the 1930s, Cahn and Chaplin wrote music for Milton Berle, Phil Silvers, Danny Kaye, Bob Hope, and Frank Sinatra as well as creating a large number of other songs. Their first notable composition was "Rhythm Is Our Business" (1935), which became the theme for the Jimmie Lunceford band.

Cahn and Chaplin collaborated on their first smash hit, "Bei Mir Bist Du Schoen" in 1938. Adapting a Yiddish song they had heard in 1936, Cahn wrote English lyrics and Chaplin wrote an arrangement to match. A then-unknown vocal trio, the Andrews Sisters, recorded the song for Decca and the disc sold more than a million copies. As a result, the Andrews Sisters were launched on their career as the best female vocal group of the era. In 1940, after Vitaphone Studios closed its doors, Warner Brothers, who owned Vitaphone, sent Cahn and Chaplin to Hollywood to write movie songs. However, for two years Warners just ignored them although paying them salaries. This caused Chaplin to end his artistic relationship with Cahn and turn toward a new career, movie producing, at which he did quite well. Meanwhile, Cahn continued as a lyricist and in 1942 had a big break. He and Chaplin had done some songwriting work for Republic Pictures while waiting for Warners to give them some kind of assignment. After Chaplin left, Republic asked Cahn to collaborate with composer Jule Styne on the music for the 1942 film *Youth on Parade*. Frank Sinatra introduced their song, "I've Heard that Song Before," which became a top hit and began Cahn's second important collaboration.

With Styne, Cahn wrote a number of memorable songs, including one Academy Award winner. For the movies, they wrote "I'll Walk Alone" for *Follow the Boys* (1944), "Five Minutes More" for *The Sweetheart of Sigma Chi* (1946), "It's Magic" for *Romance on the High Seas* (1948), and "Three Coins in a Fountain" for the 1954 movie of that title. The last song gave Cahn the first of his four Oscars. Ironically, the Oscar-winning Cahn-Styne song came about only because of a temporary reunion for the occasion. The team had split up in 1948 for purely artistic reasons. Cahn liked Hollywood; and Styne, who was to become a top composer for musicals, including *Gentlemen Prefer Blondes* (1949), *Bells Are Ringing* (1956), *Gypsy* (1959), and *Funny Girl* (1964), preferred Broadway. Before the 1948 parting, Cahn and Styne also wrote several top songs away from the silver screen. "Saturday Night Is the Loneliest Night of the Week," (1944), "Let It Snow, Let It Snow, Let It Snow" (1945), and "It's Been a Long, Long Time" (1945) are all standards.

Subsequent to the termination of the productive Cahn-Styne partnership, Cahn wrote a number of songs with various collaborators, including "Be My Love" (1949) with Nicholas Brodsky, sung by Mario Lanza in the film *Toast of New Orleans*, "Because You're Mine" in the 1952 film of that name, again with Brodsky as the composer and Lanza as the vocalist, and "Teach Me Tonight" (1954) with Gene DePaul, popularized by Jo Stafford. Also, while still working with Styne, Cahn was the co-lyricist with Phil Silvers and Johnny Burke on the 1944 ballad "Nancy with the Laughing Face." The composer for this last song was Jimmy Van Heusen (whose given name was Edward Chester Babcock); he was to be Cahn's most important songwriting partner.

Starting in 1955, Cahn and Van Heusen produced a batch of fine standards, many for Frank Sinatra (see entry). In 1955 came "The Tender Trap" for the film of that name, introduced by Sinatra. That same year "Love and Marriage" was introduced in a television adaptation of Thornton Wilder's *Our Town*. Cahn and Van Heusen won Emmys for that song and for their music for the 1966 Gene Kelly television special, *Jack and the Beanstalk*. In 1957 came "All the Way," introduced by Sinatra in the film *The Joker Is Wild*. "Come Fly with Me" (1958) was a top recording by Sinatra. "High Hopes," one of Cahn and Van Heusen's most charming songs, was introduced by Sinatra in the 1959 nonmusical film *A Hole in the Head*. "The Second Time Around" was yet another song introduced by Sinatra in a movie, the 1960 production *High Time*. In 1964, the two collaborated on the excellent and enduring ballad "My Kind of Town (Chicago Is)," sung by Sinatra in the musical film *Robin and the Seven Hoods*. It became not only a theme song for the city but also a repertory favorite for Sinatra and a building block for Cahn's reputation.

Three of the Cahn-Van Heusen songs won Oscars, "All the Way," "High Hopes," and "Call Me Irresponsible" (from the 1963 film *Papa's Delicate Condition*), making a total of four Oscars and two Emmys for Cahn.

Bibliography

Cahn, Sammy. *I Should Care*. New York: Arbor House, 1974.
Ewen, David. *All the Years of American Popular Music*. Englewood Cliffs: Prentice-Hall, 1977.
——. *American Songwriters*. New York: Wilson, 1987. 78-82.
Studwell, William A. *The Popular Song Reader*. New York: Haworth, 1994.

William E. Studwell

Cain, James M. (1892-1977), an early hard-boiled novelist, began his career as a reporter for the *Baltimore American* and the *Sun*. There he met H. L. Mencken, who exerted considerable influence on his thinking. Their mutual contempt for materialist, middle-class values helped sustain a lifelong friendship. These ideas found their way into Cain's novels, raw stories of people on the make whose naive faith in the promise and integrity of the American dream inevitably leads them to victimization and ruin. Fascinated by the criminal underside of American life, and susceptible to the misogyny of the hard-boiled literary culture he emulated, Cain's stories often featured beguiling but villainous women who fostered the destruction of these hungry dreamers.

Such patterns surface in his best-known fiction, beginning with *The Postman Always Rings Twice* (1934), *Double Indemnity* (1936), *Serenade* (1937), *Mildred Pierce* (1941), *Past All Dishonor* (1946), and *The Butterfly* (1947). Critical reception of Cain's novels generally mingles praise with nagging suspicion of their content and value. Though all of Cain's fiction is not of equal merit, at his best he is more than merely a technician operating upon vulgar, sleazy material as some critics like James T. Farrell have suggested. Cain's swift, taut narratives and spare prose capture a world of stark and sometimes brutal passions. In those scenes in *Postman* and *Double Indemnity* where his lovers conjure their dark schemes, his dialogue rises to the level of incantation. In his preface to *The Butterfly*, Cain writes of his interest in the terrifying wish that comes true, and of his intention as a writer to open "a forbidden box." His quintessentially American fiction addresses the nation's fascination with outlaws, crime, and violence.

Bibliography

Farrell, James T. *Literature and Morality*. New York: Vanguard, 1947.
Frohock, W. M. *The Novel of Violence in America*. Dallas: Southern Methodist UP, 1957.
Hoopes, Roy. *Cain: The Biography of James M. Cain*. New York: Holt, 1982.
Madden, David. *Cain's Craft*. Metuchen: Scarecrow, 1985.
——, ed. *Tough Guy Writers of the Thirties*. Carbondale: Southern Illinois UP, 1950.

Bill Mistichelli

See also
Chandler, Raymond
Crime Fiction

Calloway, Cabell "Cab" (1907-1994), one of America's most stagey band leaders, was born in Rochester and raised in Baltimore, where he began working very early as a drummer and an emcee. After moving to Chicago in the late 1920s, he worked as both a singer and a dancer with his sister Blanche; in 1929, he became the lead vocalist first for the Missourians and then for the Alabamians, a group with whom he performed in New York. Soon, Calloway began working again for the Missourians, also in New York, and it was that group's long-running appearance at the Savoy Ballroom that marked the first widespread public attention for Calloway's eccentric, exaggerated style. His oversized zoot suit, complete with a wide-brimmed hat that nearly dwarfed him and a watch chain that dusted the floor behind him as he walked, became visual trademarks, but even more than that, his distinct vocal style, along with his call-and-response games with the audience, marked him as a unique performer.

Soon after he became the big draw for the band, Calloway's bunch renamed itself Cab Calloway and His Orchestra and got perhaps its biggest break of all in 1931 when it replaced Duke Ellington's group at the Cotton Club, a move loosely alleged to have had something to do with the Mafia and its influence on the owners of the club. Radio broadcasts from the club helped make the band known to a national audience, and in 1934 the band toured Europe. Calloway recorded several hits in the next few years and also appeared in films, including 1943's *Stormy Weather*, in which he performed "Sunday in Savannah" and "Geechy Joe." (Other films included *The Big Broadcast* [1932] and *The Singing Kid* [1936].) In 1934, the group toured Europe.

Calloway and his collection of musicians continued to enjoy success and made several more recordings until 1948, when they finally broke up; afterward, Calloway himself began to work on stage (*Porgy and Bess, Bubbling Brown Sugar, Hello, Dolly!*). He continued to make appearances in various venues over the next few decades, mostly for audiences that came to see his unique style. Calloway had a significant role in 1980's *The Blues Brothers*, in which he was able to perform "Minnie the Moocher" much as he had 50 years before at the Cotton Club, this time in a resplendent white tuxedo. A year later, Joe Jackson recorded Calloway's "Jumpin' Jive," and in 1987 Calloway appeared with daughter Chris in "His Royal Highness of Hi-de-ho: The Legendary Cab Calloway."

On October 7, 1993, on the South Lawn of the White House, President Bill Clinton honored Calloway with the National Medal of Arts and the Charles Frankel Prize in the Humanities. Less than a year later, on June 12, 1994, Calloway suffered a severe stroke and died at home in White Plains, NY.

Calloway's outrageous style often put jazz purists ill at ease, especially early in his career, but his popularity was long-lasting and marked by several periods of resurgence in audience affection. Collections of his work include *Club Zanzibar Broadcasts* (1981), *Kicking the Gong Around* (1982), *Cab & Co.* (1985), *Cab Calloway Collection—20 Greatest Hits* (1986), *Missourians* (1986), *The Cab Calloway Story* (1989), and *Hi-De-Hi* (1991).

Bibliography
"Head Hep Cat Calloway Dies at 86." *Lubbock Avalanche-Journal* 20 Nov. 1994: 15A.
Holland, Bill. "Three U.S. Music Legends Honored By White House." *Billboard* 23 Oct. 1993: 23.
Kernfeld, Barry, ed. *The New Grove Dictionary of Jazz.* London: Macmillan, 1988.
Larkin, Colin, ed. *The Guinness Encyclopedia of Popular Music.* 4 vols. Middlesex, U.K.: Guinness, 1992.

Stephen Finley

Calvin and Hobbes (1985-1995). Bill Watterson was the sole creative force behind this story of a fairly typical six-year-old child named Calvin and his stuffed (to all but Calvin) toy tiger Hobbes, Calvin's playmate, co-conspirator, and conscience. This newspaper strip, like many influential humor comics such as Winsor McCay's *Little Nemo in Slumberland*, George Herriman's *Krazy Kat*, Walt Kelly's *Pogo*, and Crockett Johnson's *Barnaby*, worked primarily on two levels. The slapstick level was the stuff of Hank Ketcham's *Dennis the Menace,* where competition with the opposite sex (i.e., little girls), parents, teachers, and other authority figures led to outrageous and humorous complications. (While Margaret was Dennis's foil, Suzy was Calvin's nemesis.)

What made *Calvin and Hobbes* stand out from other comic strips of the 1980s and 1990s was its level of fanciful philosophy (indeed, the two were named for the 16th-century theologian and the philosopher). Calvin's imagination forced him to investigate major modern fictions like mystery fiction (as is the case with the "Tracer Bullet" storylines), science fiction (as evidenced in sagas of "Spaceman Spiff"), dino-saur fantasies, and tales of superheroes. His macabre imagination created worlds of headless snowmen and a "trans- mogrifier"—which Calvin created before considering the consequences of his act. Throughout, Hobbes was the sidekick in the spirit of Inspector Clouseau's Kato, keeping Calvin alert for the next attack, or simply asking, "Do you think we should do this?"

Bibliography
"Cartoonist Retiring *Calvin and Hobbes*." *A. P. Wire Service* 10 Nov. 1995.
Jones, Tim. "As Calvin Would Say, 'Me, Worry?'" *Chicago Tribune* 12 Nov. 1995, Sec 5: 4.
Watterson, Bill. *The Calvin and Hobbes Tenth Anniversary Book*. Kansas City: Andrews & McMeel, 1995.

Virginia Woods Roberts

Calypso is a musical form that originated in the English-speaking islands of the eastern Caribbean, especially Trinidad, and enjoyed sporadic periods of modest popularity in the United States between the 1920s and 1960s. Rooted in traditions brought by West African slaves, for whom the music became a major form of expression, and mixed with various European influences, calypso (or *kaiso*) developed as an assertion of Afro-Caribbean identity, providing a forum for protest, satire, and celebration in defiance of colonial strictures. In Trinidad it became closely identified with the pre-Lenten carnival, utilizing elaborate instrumental backgrounds heavy with brass and percussion. Carnival and calypso became closely identified with the black working class, as an opportunity for both collective and self-expression, a platform for sociopolitical or personal commentary, and escape from the drudgeries of daily life. Conservative observers considered the music déclassé and colonial governments sought to repress it as subversive; only later did elite West Indians perceive it as a unique local cultural form.

From its original base in folk culture, calypso was harnessed to anticolonial agitation from the 1930s to 1950s, culminating in independence. Politics and topical commentary remained an important component of calypso, but many calypso songs dealt with the eternal verities of sex, romance, gender relations, and having a good time. The leading calypsonians adopted flamboyant costumes and names like Atilla the Hun, Growling Tiger, Lord Executor, King Radio, and Mighty Sparrow. Ironically the only Trinidadian music recorded between 1914 and 1937 was done in New York, mostly by West Indians resident there such as Sam Manning, Lionel Belasco, Gerald Clark, and Wilmoth Houdini (Wilmoth Hendricks). Houdini was the most important and prolific recording artist between 1927 and 1940, even offering some protest songs such as "Poor But Ambitious."

During the 1920s there was a vogue for West Indian culture in Harlem, spurred by Caribbean immigrants and the political activities of Jamaican exile Marcus Garvey. Beginning in 1934, several calypsonians traveled to the U.S. to record; later a Trinidad-based recording industry would emerge. Calypso developed a modest following in the U.S. and Britain, keeping expatriate West Indian performers employed for several decades and also providing a market for Caribbean-based musicians. Furthermore, Trinidad calypsonians, whose work faced government censorship, were able to record politicized songs in New York in the 1930s; hence American aficionados helped sustain political calypso in late colonial times.

During and after World War II American military forces were stationed in Trinidad, spurring the evolution of calypso. Records were now made for a growing number of fans in the U.S., so the genre achieved considerable international popularity. American-based artists like Houdini, Duke of Iron, and Sir Lancelot maintained a following in the 1940s; several Trinidad musicians also had successful engagements in New York. A Trinidad calypso song, Lord Invader's "Rum and Coca Cola," became a massive American hit for the Andrews Sisters. The lyrics about "mother and daughter working for the Yankee dollar" were viewed in Trinidad but not in the U.S. as a satirical commentary on the degradation the presence had brought to island women. Several mainstream artists recorded the occasional calypso-flavored tune, such as Ella Fitzgerald's jazzy version of Houdini's "Stone Cold Dead in the Market."

Despite its exotic flavor and catchy rhythm, calypso never achieved lasting popularity in the U.S. The biggest boost came in the mid and late 1950s from Harry Belafonte (see entry), who had lived in Jamaica as a child, but the brief fascination he engendered did not endure. Perhaps calypso's greatest legacy in the U.S. has been rap music (see entry), which has clear affinities with both early Trinidad calypsos and Jamaican *dub*.

Bibliography

Bergman, Billy. *Hot Sauces: Latin and Caribbean Pop.* New York: Quill, 1985.

Hill, Donald R. *Calypso Calaloo: Early Carnival Music in Trinidad.* Gainesville: UP of Florida, 1993.

Rohlehr, Gordon. *Calypso and Society in Pre-Independence Trinidad.* Tunapuna: Rohlehr, 1991.

Shaw, Arnold. *Belafonte.* Philadelphia: Chilton, 1960.

Warner, Keith Q. *Kaiso! The Trinidad Calypso. A Study of the Calypso as Oral Literature.* Washington, DC: Three Continents, 1982.

Craig A. Lockard

Camcorder Journalism. The camcorder is an electronic image- and sound-recording device that combines optics, imagery, and audio processing, and recording into one integrated system. The combination of camera/recorder and the broadcast television process have changed the way we perceive daily events.

The camcorder evolved from a primitive, bulky, separate camera and recorder into a single unit that easily fits into the palm of the hand. The ability to hand-hold a television imaging device and record sensational, sometimes disturbing images, has profoundly affected the process of newsgathering and reporting.

Camcorder journalism may represent journalism's ultimate goal, the ensuring of an enlightened populace necessary for preserving democracy. It literally puts the power to inform millions in the hands of anyone having access to a camcorder. In America, the camcorder has quickly become a necessary artifact in our family and social, ritual life. The broad-based ownership of a potential news recording device has created an unprecedented opportunity for the public to "eyewitness" everything from a walk-by shooting at the White House, to murders and disasters, to home video footage of O. J. Simpson and his children.

News directors and the public refer to amateur camcorder footage as being "more real" than staged re-enactments or standup commentary. Because of this perception, local and network news departments will pay from $50 to $500 for important camcorder news footage. The camcorder's true ability to portray reality is, in fact, as limited if not more limited than human observation. Restrictive fields of view, time limits, lens distortion, limited contrast range, low resolution, and limited audio input and reproduction severely compress and distort the "reality" of any camcorder records.

Electronic camcorder journalism, whether professional or amateur, has had a long technological development as well as extensive historical precedent of "on the scene" news reporting. Although the immediacy of TV news increased in the 1960s with low-light film stocks and transoceanic jet travel, on-the-scene news reports shot during the Vietnam War were still a film record of events played on live nightly newscasts. The late 1960s introduced the first truly portable camera/ recorder, the Sony 1/2-inch black-and-white "Porta-Pak," which provided the basis for the next revolution of camcorder journalism.

The advent of the 3/4-inch U-matic video format provided the networks with the first video recorders capable of broadcast quality color that could be used in the field. Although in the early 1970s this equipment was still heavy and cumbersome, it was widely accepted. Most network news departments used this equipment along with a camera operator, a VCR/sound person, and usually a standup reporter throughout the 1970s and 1980s.

Has the camcorder and its instant journalism already seen its apex? Camcorder TV shows such as *Cops* (see entry) have high ratings and are prime examples of camcorder *vérité* documentary. Other shows such as *Eyewitness Video*, a half-hour prime time video news show, have faded from public interest. News departments, whether local, national, or international (CNN), have a continued interest in soliciting amateur and professional camcorder footage to incorporate into their news programming. It seems likely, as networks scale down their international news offices in efforts to save money, independent news providers will flourish.

Bibliography

Aufderheide, Pat. "Vernacular Video." *Columbia Journalism Review* Jan. 1995.

Luft, Greg. "Camcorders: When Amateurs Go after the News." *Columbia Journalism Review* Sept. 1991.

William Prior

See also
Electronic News Gathering
Television Dramatic-Reality Programming

Campbell, Ramsey (1946-), British author, has made his name writing horror fiction. His novels, set in Campbell's native Liverpool, generally concern the lives of ordinary people thrust into extraordinary circumstances. Everyday events take on disturbing colorations; mundane details become terrifying. Campbell's early work was strongly influenced by H. P. Lovecraft (see entry); by the early 1970s, however, Campbell adopted the more densely atmospheric style for which he is best known.

Among his better-known books are *Demons by Daylight* (1973), a collection of stories probing the hideous that underlies the quotidian world of work and home; *The Face That Must Die* (1984); *Obsession* (1986); and *Strange Things and Even Stranger Places* (1993). Campbell has also published short fiction in magazines and anthologies. He has won numerous awards for his work, including the British Fantasy Award and the World Fantasy Award, which he has received several times.

Bibliography

Crawford, Gary William. *Ramsey Campbell.* Mercer Island: Starmont, 1988.

Jonathon S. Epstein

Captain Kangaroo (1955-1984) was a network children's staple. Captain Kangaroo, the star of the show, was termed the Gentlest Pied Piper on Television. For many of those years it was the only network children's program on television and aired, until CBS's disastrous decision to move it to an earlier time, at 8:00 A.M. It contained a mixture of cartoons, stories, songs, and sketches, over which Bob (Robert James) Keeshan, its creator and star, presided.

Keeshan (1927-), born in Lynbrook, NY, was the third of four children. He had two brothers and a sister. His father was a supervisor of a grocery store chain. Keeshan grew up in Forest Hills, Queens, in a childhood he says was "delightfully free from worries or...insecurities."

Keeshan began his career at 16 as an after-school NBC page. Upon graduating from high school, he entered the Marines. After being discharged he returned to NBC and became its fourth-floor receptionist at Radio City. Keeshan attended pre-law classes at Fordham University.

All plans of becoming a lawyer were dropped, however, when he became an assistant to Buffalo Bob Smith, architect of the *Howdy Doody* show (see entry). Smith had a successful program entitled *Triple B. Ranch*. Most of Keeshan's work had been done for Smith and he accepted his offer to become his assistant. His primary duties were to handle props and talk to the children who were to appear on the program. Keeshan was quite good at dealing with the youngsters.

One day, he decided to dress as a clown and bring some props on the set. The audience howled with appreciation. For five years after that incident, Keeshan played Clarabell the Clown (1947-52), a character he created for *Howdy Doody*. This early exposure nurtured Keeshan's flair for entertaining youngsters. However, he was not totally happy with working for Smith, who, he said, had not only the last word but all the words. Additionally, Keeshan was not happy with the violence on kids' shows.

While still on the program, he had met Jack Miller, who became his co-producer of *Captain Kangaroo*, and discussed his ideas of what a children's show might be. He and Miller agreed on the basics: that a program should not talk down to kids, should emphasize values and feelings, and should be non-violent. So strongly did these feelings become that Keeshan quit his work with *Howdy Doody* and was unemployed for eight months.

On *Time for Fun* (1953-55), a WABC noontime program in New York City on which he played Corky the Clown, Keeshan secured his career. He won the right to screen the cartoons he showed and rejected the racist and violent ones. He also began to stress manners, health, and safety—three staples of the later *Captain Kangaroo* format. During his last year as Corky he also developed a new character, that of an old Alpine toymaker on *Tinker's Workshop* (1954-55).

In July 1955, Keeshan and Miller had entered a competition sponsored by CBS executives. The executives wanted a children's program and had asked six programs to compete. They chose *Captain Kangaroo*. On October 3, 1955, Keeshan began *Captain Kangaroo* and that became the focus of his creative attention for the next 29 years, making Keeshan portrayer of the longest-running series character in television history. The program featured regular characters such as Mr. Green Jeans (Hugh Brannum, the only other live actor), Mr. Moose, Bunny Rabbit, Dancing Bear, Debra, and other puppets (worked by Cosmo "Gus" Allegretti).

The Captain of the Treasure House, a location strewn with objects that Keeshan carefully chose to intrigue youngsters, wore a pouch-like jacket from which he took his name. From those pouches he would pull out various surprises. Keeshan precisely chose his white wig and mustache and small Captain's cap to present an approachable but also venerable figure. He wrote a good portion of his scripts with the aid of staffers who were also parents. Keeshan emphasized what today is called "values education."

His principled stand on commercials—he retained the right to accept sponsors or not and to monitor their method of presentation—left the show under-subscribed for much of the early period of its run. By the early 1960s, however, the program brought in millions of dollars in revenue. Basically, parents trusted what the Captain sold.

The Captain's legacy lives on in the videos of his programs, which are readily available, and in the programs that have followed his lead, most notably *Sesame Street* (see entry). Keeshan's longtime producer, David Connell, left *Captain Kangaroo* in 1968 to produce *Sesame Street* for PBS.

Keeshan has won many awards, the Peabody Award for children's programs (1958), the Sylvania Award, the approval of the Parent Teachers Association, and virtually every award and seal of approval possible for a children's program. Keeshan is the founder and director of a national child-care corporation and remains quite concerned with children's issues.

Bibliography

Brown, Les. *Encyclopedia of Television*. Detroit: Gale Research, 1992.

Keeshan, Bob. *Growing Up Happy*. New York: Doubleday, 1989.

Moody, Kate. *Growing Up on Television*. New York: McGraw-Hill, 1980.

Terrace, Vincent. *Encyclopedia of Television Series, Pilots, and Specials: 1974-1984*. Vol. 2. New York: Zoetrope, 1985.

——. *Fifty Years of Television*. New York: Cornwall, 1991.

Frank A. Salamone

Carlin, George (1937-), is the thinking man's comic. His irreverent style of humor has shocked and entertained audiences for four decades. In 1963, this future counterculture guru and icon for iconoclasts began performing solo in folk clubs and early comedy houses, where audiences were receptive to his offbeat humor, blunt language, and strange takes on popular culture. Such characters as his stoned "Hippy Dippy Weatherman" and sloshed "Wonderful Wino" were now born; ironically, it was their popularity that landed him on television, the ultimate conservative medium. Exploding onto the tube in the mid-1960s, Carlin appeared 58 times in 1965 and 1966 alone, on programs like the Mike Douglas and Merv Griffin shows. With over 130 appearances on *The Tonight Show*, his fame as a comedian soared.

Joining the radical and disaffected counterculture, Carlin now found a ready-made audience for his outrageous cynicism, biting sarcasm, and iconoclastic, off-the-wall humor. With his hippie attire and manner, he became the very image of the visible counterculture. And as its comedic voice, he filled his act with anti-establishment themes, including his famous—or infamous—verbal attack on censorship, the now classic and wildly hilarious "Seven Words You Can Never Say on Television." When television finally opened itself to

irreverent satire and daring parody by broadcasting the first *Saturday Night Live* (see entry) in 1975, it is quite natural that Carlin, that champion of free speech and the "seven deadly words," was the guest host.

Over the years, Carlin has won numerous Grammys and Cable Ace Awards, and he has garnered many more Emmy and Grammy nominations. In 1996, he won a Cable Ace Award for his HBO concert, *Back in Town*. Carlin has starred in over nine HBO Comedy Specials, and has appeared in many Hollywood films and starred as a New York cabbie in his own Fox TV sitcom (1994-95).

Although his conservative critics never get beyond what they deem his profanity and obscenity, Carlin's comic genius certainly transcends simple scatalogy and explosive and arbitrary expletives for their pure shock value. For four decades now, the weird world of George Carlin has helped his many fans perceive their world with a greater, if ironic, clarity of vision.

Bibliography

Carlin, George. *Brain Droppings*. New York: Hyperion, 1997.

——. *Sometimes a Little Brain Damage Can Help*. New York: Hyperion, 1984.

Esquire 82 (Dec. 1974): 122+.

"George Carlin." *Current Biography Yearbook: 1976*. Ed. Charles Moritz. New York: Wilson, 1976. 76-79.

Newsweek 69 (9 Jan. 1967): 41.

Village Voice 10 Aug. 1976: 10+.

Wayne Scott

Carousel Horses are prized for their blend of realism and fantasy. The colorful wooden animals were the principal carved figure on carousels, also known as a Merry-Go-Round or Carry-Us-All, at the turn of the 20th century. The use of carousels was recorded as early as 1831 in Dayton, OH, and in some rural sections of the U.S. around 1828. On the East Coast, modern machine-powered carousels were introduced in the 1880s. The beginning of carousel horse carving, in the U.S., parallels the arrival of immigrants from various parts of Eastern Europe between 1870 and 1910. Carl Landow, a German immigrant, is credited with building one of the first hand-turned carousel rides. William F. Mangeles invented the mechanical jumping horse mechanism and C. W. Parker obtained its first patent.

Carousel horses have distinctive qualities associated with three manufacturing styles: the Philadelphia, the Coney Island, and the Country Fair style. These predominant styles recognize the diversity of carvers and their aesthetic aspirations.

The Philadelphia style is characterized by its striking realism: well-formed legs, perfectly shaped heads, and spectacularly detailed accessories. Horses were divided into outer-row standers and inner-row figures. Outside row standers were the largest and most elaborately carved steeds. Inner-row petite horses were carved to attract young children. Early carved horses were fully detailed on only the right side, because of the counterclockwise motion of the carousel. By the early 1900s, several manufacturers produced carousels. The Philadelphia Toboggan Company was one of the first, organized by Henry B. Auchy and Chester E. Albright in 1900. Others were the Dentzel Factory; Norman and Evans Company; Armitage Herchell Company; J. P. Marqua Company; C. W. Parker Manufacturing Company; American Carouselle and Toy Company; and the United States Merry-Go-Round Company. In the 1920s, the Dentzel Factory reported that it received approximately $18,000 for a three-abreast horse carousel and $24,000 for a four-abreast machine. Dentzel and the Philadelphia Toboggan Company both carved the Philadelphia-style carousel horse.

Gustav Dentzel, a German immigrant and cabinetmaker, began his carousel manufacturing business in 1867. His beautifully carved horses were posed lightly prancing, jumping, and in a powerful gallop. Dentzel mimicked European traditions and experimented with carving techniques and two-story carousels. In 1903, Salvatore Cernigliaro, a Sicilian woodcarver, joined Dentzel's staff and contributed a flair for soft curves, garlands, drapery, and fanciful ornamentation. The playful quality that characterized his carvings added a touch of fantasy to the realism of the earlier Philadelphia-style carved horses.

A master carver, Daniel Muller, worked for Dentzel's company as well as for the Philadelphia Toboggan Company. Muller's horses had flamboyant features: tightly trimmed roached-hair manes, bridle roses, tassels, and secondary carved sidesaddle figures: eagles, monkeys, clowns, nudes, and the American flag. Rear saddle adornment showed a full range of animal heads, oak leaves, or possibly a jester's face. Muller was also interested in suits of fish-scale armor and clad his carved horses in full-face "chamfron" or chain mail blankets, holsters, guns, swords, canteens and other military gear.

The Coney Island style horse, revered for its simple realism, was developed in 1876 by Charles Looff, a furniture carver from Schleswig-Holstein. Gold and silver manes added an exaggerated touch of flash and fantasy. Looff's horses graced carousels in magnificent poses, with their front left leg raised. He carved eagles, lions, cherubs, birds, foxes, rabbits, and lambs to embellish the saddle and trappings. In the early 1900s, master carver Charles Carmel continued to carve carousel horses in his small studio on Coney Island, despite a drop in carousel-horse manufacturing. He joined and introduced the Coney Island style to the Philadelphia Toboggan Company in 1920. The Coney Island style is named in connection with the first carousel opened at the Charles Feltman restaurant on Coney Island. Master carvers in this style also included Marcus C. Illions, William F. Mangeles, Solomon Stein, and Harry Goldstein.

The County Fair carousel horses were designed for traveling carnivals, which introduced carousels into the U.S. in the early 1800s. Early Midwest carousel horses were suspended by rope and chains and called "flying horse swings." The County Fair steed had a "sleeked-down" lean posture. Carousel promoters traveled to one-night-stand carnivals from North Dakota to Texas. The carved horses were small and compact with interchangeable legs and heads. Their box-like bodies were easy to transport. The "star-gazer" or "nose-in-the-air" pony was a favorite figure. The dramatic outstretched jumper was regularly adorned in the Midwest with a cowboy,

Carousel horses.

flag, corn, or sunflower carved as a decorative sidesaddle motif. Most County Fair horses were carved in North Tonawanda, NY, the carousel capital of the U.S. until C. W. Parker Manufacturing Company opened for business in 1894 at Abilene, KS.

Historically, carousels derived from a game of Arabic origin adopted by Spanish crusaders around 800 A.D. In Italian, *carosello* means "little war." In early carousel games, players rode spinning wooden horses on a manually turned device. Riders attempted to catch clay balls filled with scented oil. A brass ring was suspended in the center of the ride and challenged players to demonstrate their jousting expertise. In the 17th century, similar contests in France attracted the aristocracy. They were entertained by knights wheeled wildly around on a hand-cranked carousel at high speeds.

In the U.S., Gustav Dentzel adapted the steam engine and Charles Looff, Jr., harnessed electricity to turn the mighty merry-go-round. The industrial age freed workers to pursue leisure activities, and the advent of electric power begat such innovations as the trolley and railroad system. Entrepreneurs built amusement parks at the end of lines to encourage transportation and increase profits. The golden age of carousel horses was from 1905 to 1925 and mirrored changes in society's industrial progress.

Bibliography

Dinger, Charlotte. *Art of the Carousel*. Green Village: Carousel Art, 1988.

Mann, William, Peggy Shank, and Marianne Stevens. *Painted Ponies: American Carousel Art*. Millwood: Zon, 1986.

Weedon, Geoff, and Richard Ward. *Fairground Art.* New York: Abbeville, 1983.

Don H. Krug

Carpenter, Mary Chapin (1958-), is one of the more prominent members of a group of female vocalists whose music finds its roots in different genres, making it difficult to say exactly into what category her music falls—a fact explained at least partly by Carpenter's eclectic, well-traveled background.

Perhaps the distinguishing characteristic of Carpenter's personal story is the leisurely pace at which she emerged as a national-level star. The daughter of a *Life* magazine executive, Carpenter lived a privileged existence as a child that included the advantages of exposure to all sorts of music. Although Carpenter was more interested in skating than in music during her early years, she gravitated toward writing music after the family moved back to the U.S. from Tokyo. Still, it was not until May 1989 that an agreement between her own company and EMI/SBK to publish her songs prompted her to concentrate full-time on music.

In 1990, Carpenter's appearance at the Country Music Awards show gained her valuable national exposure. The performance was arranged at the last minute by the show's producer to showcase Carpenter's unrecorded "The Opening Act," a humorous song about the trials of opening for better-known artists. Despite her fears that the song might be perceived as vicious or whiny, the crowd gave her a standing ovation, and from that time on she became a national name, appearing in such diverse venues as David Letterman's show, *CBS This Morning*, *Cosmopolitan,* and the *Wall Street Journal.* Two 1992 Grammy nominations for "Down at the Twist and Shout" also boosted her career; her 1992 *Come On Come On*, which went gold within 30 days of its release and platinum in six months, has produced several megahits and a Grammy, a CMA best female vocalist award and an Academy of Country Music award for female vocalist of the year (although the album was given a relatively lukewarm reception by some critics). *Stones in the Road* (1994) has included two hit singles thus far: "Shut Up and Kiss Me" and "Tender When I Want to Be."

Carpenter's style has been widely described as "realism tempered by dry humor" with "no self-pity." Although her songs are often about women who act decisively and responsibly, Carpenter claims that her songs are not meant as political diatribes.

Bibliography
Bufwack, Mary A., and Robert K. Oermann. *Finding Her Voice: The Illustrated History of Women in Country Music.* New York: Holt, 1995.
Larkin, Colin, ed. *The Guinness Encyclopedia of Popular Music.* 4 vols. Middlesex, U.K.: Guinness, 1992.
"Mary Chapin Carpenter." *Current Biography* 55.2 (1994): 20-23.
Rev. of *Come On Come On.* Mary Chapin Carpenter. *Rolling Stone* 3 Sept. 1992: 68.
Rev. of *Come On Come On.* Mary Chapin Carpenter. *Stereo Review* 57.9 (1992): 79.

Stephen Finley

Carrier Current and Cable Radio grew out of a little radio engineering experiment in 1936 by two Brown University freshmen that would become an industry. The technology existed as early as the 1910s in limited military applications, known then as "wired wireless" radio. But George Abraham and David Borst discovered it independently, based on their curiosity about radio.

Using a hand-built, very low-power AM transmitter (under one watt), the collegians took advantage of the campus buildings' metal framework to help carry the radio signal to each dormitory room and be heard on students' home receivers. They purposely broadcast at AM 600, below the FCC-assigned frequencies used in their area, to avoid interference with licensed stations and to avoid incurring their (or the government agency's) wrath.

The term "gas pipe networks" was coined as a result of the students' stringing wire through the steam tunnels typically found beneath the dormitories of the time, that helped bring the station's signal to buildings other than that where the broadcasts originated. However, if it over-radiated, nearby city telephone pole wires would also carry a station—allegedly in one case, for hundreds of miles.

In 1941, the Brown alumni had founded the Intercollegiate Broadcast System (IBS), an association to support the creation and ongoing development of these carrier current stations. By the late 1940s, over a dozen such stations were on the air. Besides holding conferences and publishing a newsletter, IBS began a small rep service to help bring national advertising to these stations, eventually superseded by the more successful (and also student-run) Ivy Network rep firm. The latter survived until 1971, when campus interest had largely switched to FM broadcasting. Ironically, cigarettes and beer were among campus radio's biggest advertisers, two product categories that these stations were later prohibited by law and campus policy, respectively, to promote.

The careers of thousands of today's top executives and talent in professional radio, ranging from syndicated shock-jock Howard Stern to former FCC chairman William Henry to *Prairie Home Companion* creator Garrison Keillor, began on campus carrier-current stations.

As it does not need a cable hookup, carrier current continues to exist only slightly below its peak in the 1970s of over 400 campus stations. However, the trend is toward upgrade from carrier current to cable radio, especially in the mid-1990s with the emergence of institutions fully wired for high-capacity video, voice, and data. The same wire should carry cable radio to a new level in the years to come.

Bibliography
Bloch, Louis M. *The Gas Pipe Networks: A History of College Radio, 1936-46.* Cleveland: Bloch, 1980.
Brant, Billy G. *The College Radio Handbook.* Blue Ridge Summit: TAB Books, 1981.

Glenn Gutmacher

See also
College Radio

Cars, The, were a pioneer group in new wave music. By 1977-1978, the punk rock movement was giving way to new wave, largely a music industry term agreed upon to avoid using the harsher punk tag. Empowered by the new stripped-down and left-of-center approach to rock 'n' roll, bands began surfacing across the country with a quirky pop sound. Progenitors of this style included Devo, the B-52's, Pere Ubu, and the Cars.

Formed by longtime songwriting and performing partners Ric Ocasek and Benjamin Orr, the Cars were successful from the airing of their first demo tape of "Just What I Needed" on Boston radio stations. The group's first album was recorded in just two weeks, and once on the U.S. album charts, stayed there for 139 weeks, selling well over a million copies.

Known for such other songs as "My Best Friend's Girl," "Good Times Roll," and "Let's Go," all hits in 1978 and 1979, the Cars' style is described in the *Trouser Press Record Guide*: "Singer/songwriter Ric Ocasek pursued the trail of ironic, sometimes wistful romanticism" blazed by David Bowie and especially Bryan Ferry...virtually interchangeable lead singers Ocasek and bassist Ben Orr ride a slick, pulsing current generated by Elliot Easton's skittish guitar, Greg Hawkes' poised synths and ex-Modern Lover David Robinson's booming drums."

The second Cars album, *Candy-O*, released in 1979, was a Top 10 album in the U.S. as was the 1980 *Panorama*, which provided the Top 40 single "Touch and Go." Soon after, the group bought a studio in Boston and band members produced a variety of groups individually before recording yet another Top 10 album, *Shake It Up*, the title track of which hit the Top 10 in 1982.

After Ocasek released a solo album to fair commercial success in 1983, the group recorded *Heartbreak City*, which gave them three major hits in 1984: "Drive," "Magic," and "You Might Think." The computer-generated video for "You Might Think" won first prize in the First International Music Festival in St. Tropez, France. The album itself reached No. 3 on the U.S. charts.

After two more singles, "Hello Again" and "Why Can't I Have You," landed in the Top 40, Ocasek, Easton, and Orr all released solo albums. Ocasek charted "Emotion in Motion" and Orr had a minor hit with "Stay the Night" from those albums. Easton's LP climbed to No. 99 on the U.S. album charts and stalled.

The final Cars album, *Door to Door*, appeared in 1987. Although the album had a Top 20 single, "You Are the Girl," it was the first Cars album to fall short of a million sales and by early 1988 the band publicly called it quits. In 1991, Ocasek released *Fireball Zone*, a solo album, produced by Nile Rodgers, who also produced David Bowie's "Let's Dance."

Bibliography

Goldstein, Toby. *Frozen Fire: The Story of the Cars*. Chicago: Contemporary, 1985.

Rees, Dafydd, and Luke Crampton. *Rock Movers and Shakers*. New York: Billboard, 1991.

Robbins, Ira, ed. *The Trouser Press Record Guide*. New York: Collier, 1991.

Hugh Foley

Carson, Johnny (1925-), one of TV's most successful talk show hosts, began his TV career in Omaha, NE, in 1948 after having had a successful radio career. By the mid-1950s CBS was hailing Johnny Carson as "a bright young comic." In 1951 after Carson moved to Los Angeles, he began hosting a well-received but unsuccessful local show called *Carson's Cellar*.

Carson's big break came when he began writing monologues for Red Skelton. This led to a stint as host of the 1954 summer quiz show *Earn Your Vacation*. Also in 1954 Carson was asked to substitute host for Red Skelton on his CBS comedy show (see entry). Both critics and CBS were convinced Carson could carry his own variety show; *The Johnny Carson Show* was the result. It started out early in 1955 as a daytime series, but by the spring of 1955 was ready for prime time. The format relied heavily on comedy sketches, many created by Carson himself, as well as some singing.

In 1957, Carson was asked to host an ABC daytime quiz show in New York. The memorable *Who Do You Trust?* (originally called *Do You Trust Your Wife?*) was in danger of cancellation and was being renewed on a month-to-month basis. Art Stark was named the producer when Carson joined the show. Both he and Johnny felt it was a trap to restrict the show to just husbands and wives, though it was the general rule.

On this show, Carson developed some of the gimmicks and techniques he would use on *Tonight*. In the fall of 1958, Carson needed a new announcer, someone who could be a foil for his jokes as well. That was the beginning of the Johnny Carson–Ed McMahon duo that would last for several decades. In September of 1962 Carson and McMahon left the show to become the new host and announcer on NBC's *The Tonight Show*, which Jack Paar had left in March of that year.

Carson also brought along Stark as new staff producer, who settled on a structure for *The Tonight Show* that is still being followed, notably the opening monologue. Unlike Paar, Carson stressed events in the news; the show was taped live and without canned laughter. Watching Carson's well-loved idiosyncrasies became a nightly ritual for millions of viewers.

Some of the greatest moments in telecast history of *The Tonight Show Starring Johnny Carson* were perhaps when guest Ed Ames (who had a role as Mingo on the TV series *Daniel Boone*) demonstrated how to throw a tomahawk; and when Tiny Tim wed Miss Vicki on December 17, 1969. Mostly the show succeeded because of its cozy familiarity and the fact that Carson listened well and put the focus on the guest. Carson also often enlisted the audience as collaborators, with everything from the chorus of straight lines that arose from the studio audience whenever he complained about the weather ("How hot was it?") to his ubiquitous savers—the ad libs meant to salvage jokes that bombed. For standup comics, a *Tonight* gig was always TV's most important door-opening break.

In 1971 Carson cut back to doing four shows a week, and in 1972 the show moved permanently from New York to Burbank. Carson's irregular appearances opened the door for a flood of substitute hosts. Joan Rivers was the one and only guest host from September 1983 until 1986, when she quit to go head-to-head unsuccessfully with *The Tonight Show*. Jay

Leno was named exclusive guest host in the fall of 1987 and became heir to the throne in 1992 after Carson retired.

In 1991, Carson announced his final broadcast date to be May 22, 1992. On that Friday night, Carson appeared without guests and simply reminisced with a selection of clips from past shows, presenting a collage of the past 30 years on *The Tonight Show*.

Bibliography

DeCordova, Frederick. *Johnny Came Lately: An Autobiography*. New York: Simon & Schuster, 1988.

Metz, Robert. *The Tonight Show*. New York: Playboy, 1980.

Connie Wineland

Carson, Rachel (1907-1964), influential nature writer, acquired her twin loves of writing (she began publishing at age 11) and nature as a child growing up in rural Pennsylvania. After earning a master's degree in marine biology in 1932, she worked for the U.S. Bureau of Fisheries, then wrote pamphlets on wildlife refuges for the Fish and Wildlife Service. But it was her essays, such as "Undersea" in the *Atlantic Monthly* in 1937, that caught the public's attention—not only for their lyrical, evocative prose but for their interest in the beauty and complexity of strange life forms.

Carson's sea books—*Under the Sea Wind* (1941), the best-selling and award-winning *The Sea around Us* (1951), which Irwin Allen turned into a popular documentary film in 1953, and *The Edge of the Sea* (1955)—all generate a sense of wonder about the oceans and the fabulous creatures that inhabit them. For Carson, respect for the earth must begin with a "sense of wonder," and it must begin early. Indeed, she wrote a book for children with that title, published posthumously in 1965.

The sea books made Carson famous, but it was *Silent Spring*, published in 1962, two years before her death, that made her legendary. A truly monumental work, it profoundly influenced public policy and changed history. *Silent Spring* describes, in lucid and engaging prose despite its technical subject matter, the devastating effects of DDT and other toxic pesticides. The book prompted President Kennedy to establish a commission to investigate the hazards of pesticides, and more broadly, galvanized the modern environmental movement.

Bibliography

Brooks, Paul. *The House of Life: Rachel Carson at Work*. Boston: Houghton Mifflin, 1972.

Gartner, Carol B. *Rachel Carson*. New York: Ungar, 1983.

McCay, Mary A. *Rachel Carson*. New York: Twayne, 1993.

White, Fred D. "Rachel Carson: Encounters with the Primal Mother." *North Dakota Quarterly* 59 (1991).

Fred D. White

Carter, Lin(wood) (1930-1988), is the prolific author of a variety of fantasy and science fiction tales, mainly in what has been called the "sword and sorcery" genre, as well as a leading critic of fantasy fiction. In addition to publishing a great many individual novels and short stories, he is the author of several series of interrelated novels, including the Callisto,

Great Imperium, Green Star Saga, World's End, Godwane Epic, Lemurian, and Zarkon, Lord of the Unknown books. All his works explore the recurring theme that humankind has a need for myths and heroes to provide consolation. This theme is demonstrated forcefully in *As the Green Star Rises* (1975). The novels in the Godwane series, such as *The Warrior of the World's End* (1974), show Carter's fascination with the gallery of superheroes who people his magical, faraway worlds.

Carter has also worked as an editor for a variety of science fiction and fantasy collections, notably his efforts as editorial consultant for the Ballantine Adult Fantasy series. In 1973 he published *Imaginary Worlds: The Art of Fantasy*, considered a classic survey of fantasy literature. He is also highly regarded for his scholarly work on J. R. R. Tolkien and H. P. Lovecraft.

In 1951, Carter began work with L. Sprague de Camp on the *Conan the Barbarian* revisions, based on Robert E. Howard's unfinished manuscripts, completing twelve volumes by 1965, and did the same for Howard's *King Kull* series. In 1972, Carter received the Nova Award for his works.

Bibliography

Bleiler, E. F., ed. *Supernatural Fiction Writers: Fantasy and Horror*. New York: Scribner, 1985.

Solomon Davidoff

Cartland, Barbara (1902-2000), was one of the most prolific and recognized writers in the contemporary world. Known as "Queen of the Romance," Cartland authored over 300 books, primarily romantic and gothic novels. (She wrote as both Barbara Cartland and Barbara McCorquodale, the latter her married name.)

Beginning with her first novel, *Jig-Saw* (1925), through the three quarters of a century since, Cartland established her creative formula, which she varied little over the years, though the earlier works demonstrate a freshness and density missing in the later, more prescriptive novels. Characteristically, Cartland stories feature innocent, passionate, and beautiful heroines caught up in whirlwind lives and beguiled by aristocratic, gallant, and savvy suitors who initiate in the heroine a romantic awakening. Typically, the novels end with the union of the lovers as they face a future of ecstatic togetherness in which the mysteries of love promise to abide.

Despite the relative sameness of the plots of these romantic stories, buyers have continued to undergird Cartland's position on the pedestal of best-sellerdom. As critics of her work note, her fiction affirms a conservative, even retrograde social philosophy, celebrating feminine capitulation, class hierarchy, and ennobled individualism, values that need romantic underpinnings to seem plausible in the modern ethos. In the earlier novels, such as *Jig-Saw, Sweet Punishment* (1931), *Dangerous Experiment* (1937), and others, Cartland allowed the reader to glimpse the darker side of the romantic sensibility that seems more unalloyed in later novels like *A Frame of Dreams* (1975), *Kiss the Moonlight* (1977), *The Treasure Is Love* (1979), *Pure and Untouched* (1981), and a host of others.

Bibliography
Cloud, Henry. *Barbara Cartland, Crusader in Pink.* New York: Everest, 1979.
Robyns, Gwen. *Barbara Cartland: An Authorized Biography.* Garden City: Doubleday, 1985.

Liahna Babener

Cartoons: Theatrical and Television. From the first theatrical shorts of the silent era to the enormously popular television show *The Simpsons* of today, animation has captured the hearts and imaginations of children and adults alike. There are few symbols around the world that are more recognizable than Mickey Mouse. Merchants have capitalized on the popularity of and nostalgia for animation with Warner Brothers and Disney stores in nearly every shopping mall across the United States.

Animated films first debuted in America in 1906 with *Humorous Phases of Funny Faces* (see Animation [Early], above). *Gertie the Dinosaur*, the first film to feature fluid movement, and the *Colonel Hezza Liar* series, considered the first commercial-cartoon release, aroused great interest in animation. Stars of the silent era included the *Out of the Inkwell* series' Koko the Klown and Felix the Cat.

The celluloid or "cel" is considered the single greatest change in cartoon production. Characters could be inked and painted on clear cels and laid over stationary backgrounds. Other time-saving inventions and devices such as the "rotograph" and multiplane camera increased the quantity and quality of animation; however, it was sound that rescued animation from a slow death.

Song Car-tunes, a series of "bouncing ball sing-a-long" films produced in 1924, were the first synchronized sound cartoons. The first talking picture in 1927, Al Jolson's *Jazz Singer*, helped popularize sound pictures. The first widely distributed synchronized sound cartoon was Disney's *Steamboat Willie* in 1928, featuring Mickey Mouse. Color films shortly followed. Disney had exclusive rights to three-color Technicolor (see entry) from 1932-35, leaving other studios to use an inferior two-color process.

The studio system had a tremendous impact on animation. Bray, Hearst, and Barre, the main studios in the 1910s, as well as Paramount, MGM, and Warner Brothers, were instrumental in creating animation, but Disney arguably "defined" it. Walt Disney established the idea of individual personalities of characters and good storytelling. He produced *The Three Little Pigs*, the most popular animated short subject of all time. Other studios struggled, imitating Disney's *Silly Symphonies* series with *Merrie Melodies* (Warner) and *Happy Harmonies* (MGM).

Because of enormous production costs, full-length feature animation was a gamble, a gamble Disney has monopolized. *Snow White and the Seven Dwarfs* (see entry), released in 1937, was the first full-length animated feature. Disney followed with a series of fairytales over the years, from *Pinocchio* (1940) to *Beauty and the Beast* (1991). Though a commercial failure at the time of its release, *Fantasia* (1940), animation choreographed to classical music, was a critical success.

A few adult-oriented animated films have been successful: 1968, the Beatles' *Yellow Submarine*; 1971, *Fritz the Cat*, the first X-rated cartoon feature; and 1988, *Who Framed Roger Rabbit?*, which grossed over $100 million.

The mid 1930s saw the first cartoon "stars," and Warner Brothers, with the help of Mel Blanc's voice, launched more important characters than any other studio (see Warner Brothers Cartoons). Porky Pig debuted in 1935, Daffy Duck and Egghead (who later developed into Elmer Fudd) in 1937. Bugs Bunny (see entry) first spoke the immortal line "Eh, what's up Doc?" in 1940. Cartoons became funny instead of just cute. In the mid to late '40s, Warner Brothers added Tweety and Sylvester, Pepe LePew, Foghorn Leghorn, the Tasmanian Devil, Yosemite Sam, Roadrunner, and Wile E. Coyote.

The first made-for-TV special was *Mr. Magoo's Christmas Carol* in 1962. Christmas offered popular holiday animation: *How the Grinch Stole Christmas* (1966); *Frosty the Snowman* (1969); and *A Charlie Brown Christmas* (1965; credited as the only one that actually mentions Jesus). The Charlie Brown holiday series covering Halloween to Arbor Day is second only to Dr. Seuss as the longest running series of cartoon specials in television history.

In the 1960s, networks created an all-cartoon Saturday morning schedule (see Children's Network Programming). DePatie-Freleng Enterprises joined Hanna-Barbera as leading suppliers of Saturday morning kiddie shows. Japanese cartoon producers began to import fully animated fantasy/adventure series such as *Speed Racer*, re-edited and re-dubbed into English.

Animated shows airing during prime time have achieved an adult audience. The first made-for-television cartoon series to air on prime time was *The Flintstones* (1960-66; see entry), based on the sitcom *The Honeymooners* (1955-56). Other contemporary prime-time shows were derived from successful characters from popular live-action programs: *Top Cat* (1961-63, 1965-68) from *The Phil Silvers Show* (1955); *Calvin and the Colonel* (1961-62) from *Amos 'n' Andy* (1951-53), and later *Wait Till Your Father Gets Home* (1972-74) from *All in the Family* (1971-79).

The Simpsons (see entry), which first aired on the Fox Network in 1989, overtook *The Flintstones* as the longest running prime-time animated series in history. *The Simpsons'* popularity spawned a series of animated programs, many featuring bathroom humor. The 1990s saw the premiere of *Ren & Stimpy* (1991; see entry), which quickly became the most popular cable television series ever, *Beavis and Butt-head* (1993; see entry), and *South Park* (1997). One character on *South Park*, Kenny, dies a violent death every episode; his head falls off and his body is eaten by rats. Other adult-oriented animated series include *Duckman* (1994-97), *King of the Hill* (1997), and *Dr. Katz* (1995).

To cut costs, an estimated 90 percent of American television cartoons are produced in Asia. Cultural differences, however, make successful animation more difficult. Many of the major studios have offices in the Philippines where there is more Western influence.

The popularity of animation continues to increase with advances in technology. Disney's *Toy Story* (1995), the industry's first computer-animated movie (along with *Toy Story II*, 1999), and *TuneLand*, the world's first interactive cartoon in CD-ROM, appear to be the wave of the future. Poorly redrawn color Porky Pig cartoons are being replaced with new, computer-colorized versions. The new computer technology known as "motion capture" attaches sensors to human actors and transfers motion information to a powerful computer, further blurring the line between real and fantasy.

Bibliography

Maltin, Leonard. *Of Mice and Magic: A History of American Animated Cartoons*. New York: McGraw-Hill, 1980.

McConville, Jim. "HBO Creates Animation Division: HBO Animation Will Focus on Adult-Oriented Fare." *Broadcasting & Cable* 126.42 (7 Oct. 1996): 76.

Rothenberg, Randall. "Tooning Out TV." *Esquire* 127.2 (Feb. 1997): 46-47.

Thornton, Emily. "That's Not All Folks: Asia Gets Serious about Drawing Cartoons." *Far Eastern Economic Review* 158.25 (22 June 1995): 86-87.

Patrice A. Oppliger

Cash, Johnny (1932-), known as the "Man in Black," remains a mainstay of contemporary music and culture. He was the fourth of seven children born in Kingsland, AR, to a lower-class farming family. Cash grew up knowing what hard work was, as he lived much of his youth on the family farm. While he was exposed to southern gospel music by the Baptist missionaries in his family, Cash grew up listening to a wide range of musical styles, including traditional folk music, blues, and country. Cash always enjoyed artists like the Carter family, Jimmie Rodgers, and Ernest Tubb; he was firmly rooted in the music of the South.

Cash's musical career began after he did a four-year stint in the Air Force (1950-54), during which he bought a guitar and practiced regularly. The music bug took hold when he was discharged, and Cash went to Memphis to seek his fortune. With his band, Johnny Cash and the Tennessee Two, which included his friends Marshall Grant on bass and Luther Perkins on guitar, he auditioned for Sam Phillips' Sun Records. A drummer was added in 1955, and the name changed to the Tennessee Three. While Cash impressed Phillips, his sound was still a little too gospel to produce dollar signs in Phillips's eyes. Phillips told Cash to tune up a bit and return for another audition. In early 1955, he finally signed with Sun and recorded "Cry, Cry, Cry," a local hit, and "Hey Porter," but it was not until Cash recorded "Folsom Prison Blues" (1956) that he sold a million records. This song was inspired by a movie Cash saw while in the Air Force. Cash also recorded some songs that were not released until the mid-1980s, with Sun artists Elvis Presley, Jerry Lee Lewis, and Carl Perkins, in "The Million Dollar Quartet." The hit songs "So Doggone Lonesome" and "I Walk the Line" were recorded in 1956. Cash also popularized his version of the old fiddle tune "Orange Blossom Special." In the short history of Sun Records, Cash became its biggest selling artist.

Cash signed with Columbia Records in 1958, and continued to record hits for both the country and pop charts. These included "You're the Nearest Thing to Heaven" (1958), and "Don't Take Your Guns to Town" (1959). The 1960s were a time of terrible personal turmoil for Cash. The death of country star Johnny Horton and increasing drug and alcohol abuse amplified his feelings of depression. In spite of personal problems, Cash continued to record and produce million-selling singles like "Ring of Fire" (1963) and "Understand Your Man" (1964). Other singles included "Ballad of Ira Hayes" (1963) and "Guitar Pickin' Man" (1967).

It was not until Cash married June Carter, daughter of Maybelle of the famous Carter family, in 1968, that he began to reclaim his personal life. Carter, a member of Cash's touring group, was like "Manna Sent from Heaven." In the late 1960s, Cash released two successful live albums, *Johnny Cash at Folsom Prison* (1968) and *Live at San Quentin* (1969). He also made a big hit with the Carl Perkins tune "Daddy Sang Bass" (1968). Cash hosted his own variety television program from 1969 to 1971.

In the 1970s, Cash continued to record and tour, and was a top country seller with "Man in Black" (1970), "Any Old Wind That Blows" (1972), and "Ghost Riders in the Sky" (1978). Cash also produced and narrated a religious documentary, *The Gospel Road*, in 1973, and recorded several gospel records.

The 1980s seemed like one of Cash's busiest periods. He was inducted into the Country Music Hall of Fame in 1980, and, in 1982, rejoined Carl Perkins and Jerry Lee Lewis for *The Survivors*. Cash released a critically acclaimed album of acoustic songs, *Johnny 99* (1983), and was a founding

Photo courtesy of Sound Recording Archives, Bowling Green State University, Bowling Green, OH.

member of one of the first country superstar groups, the Highwaymen, with Waylon Jennings, Willie Nelson, and Kris Kristofferson (1985). An album with the same title was released, to the delight of country fans everywhere; then *Highwaymen Two* was released in 1990. He again rejoined the Highwaymen in the spring of 1995 for the album *The Road Goes on Forever*. In 1986, Cash again joined with Jerry Lee Lewis, Carl Perkins, and the late Roy Orbison to record *The Class of 55*. He also wrote his fictional account of the life of Saint Paul, *Man in White*. In the late 1980s, reissues, compilations, and box sets were released. Cash continued his high profile presence in the 1990s. He was asked to contribute vocals on the million-selling album, *Zooropa*, by the rock band U2, and in 1994 he released his highly hyped and critically acclaimed album, *American Recordings*, which transcended all boundaries and ages.

Cash has released more than 50 albums since 1955, and he has received seven Grammy Awards and countless Country Music Association Awards. He has acted in numerous television shows and movies, including *Columbo*, the television railroad documentary *Ridin' on the Rail, Gunfight* (1970), *Thaddeus Rose and Eddie* (1978), *North and South* (1985), and *Stagecoach* (1986).

Bibliography

Cash, Johnny. *Johnny Cash: Lyrics 1955-1995*. New York: St. Martin's, 1995.

——. *Man in Black*. Grand Rapids: Zondervan, 1975.

——. *Man in White*. San Francisco: Harper, 1986.

Dolan, Sean. *Johnny Cash*. New York: Chelsea, 1994.

Dunn, Jancee. "Johnny Cash." *Rolling Stone* June 1994: 35.

Rob Weiner

Castle, William (1914-1977), was the creator of some of the most idiosyncratic technical innovations to appear in American motion-picture theaters as gimmicks that accompanied the horror films he produced and directed. Castle was occasionally associated with important, high-budgeted pictures—as associate producer of *The Lady from Shanghai* (Orson Welles, 1948) and producer of *Rosemary's Baby* (Roman Polanski, 1968)—but the majority of his film work was spent on directing B movies for Columbia Pictures during the 1940s and 1950s. He is best known in film history, however, for the various gimmicks he used to promote a series of horror films he produced and directed for Allied Artists and Columbia between 1958 and 1965.

The "King of the Gimmicks" was born William Schloss, Jr., in New York City and became interested in show business when, at age 13, he saw a stage performance of *Dracula* starring Bela Lugosi. Castle's first job in theater came in 1929, when Lugosi recommended Castle for the post of assistant stage manager of a *Dracula* touring company. This job was quickly followed by work as an actor and stage manager for Jules Leventhal's Broadway version of *An American Tragedy* (1930), a job, according to Castle, that he got by pretending to be Samuel Goldwyn's nephew. Castle also performed opposite Marjorie Main in *Ebb Tide*, at the New Yorker Theater in 1931, and held other theater jobs during the early 1930s.

From 1934 to 1939, however, Castle found it increasingly difficult to find Broadway work, and in 1939 leased the Stony Brook Theater in Connecticut after its previous summer stock company, Orson Welles's Mercury Players, traveled to Hollywood to begin *Citizen Kane* (1941). The popularity of the Stony Brook productions—including *Not for Children*, starring Ellen Schwannecke (the star of the controversial German film *Maedchen in Uniform* [1931]), and *This Little Piggy Had None*, a horror play—earned Castle a job interview with Harry Cohn, co-founder and production supervisor for Columbia Pictures.

Castle was hired at Columbia, spent three years working on different Columbia productions in minor capacities, and then directed his first film, *The Chance of a Lifetime*, in 1942. *Chance* was the sixth film in Columbia's profitable Boston Blackie series of B movies, and between 1942 and 1948 Castle would mostly direct films designed to be entries in other long-running series, such as the Whistler series (including *The Whistler* [1944] and *Mysterious Intruder* [1946]), and the Crime Doctor series (*Crime Doctor's Warning* [1945], *Just Before Dawn* [1946], and others). Perhaps his most notable film of this period was *When Strangers Marry* (1944), a highly respected noir made when Harry Cohn loaned Castle out to Monogram pictures; Castle landed the job as associate producer of *The Lady from Shanghai* after Orson Welles praised his work on *When Strangers Marry*.

In 1948, Castle left Columbia for Universal-International Pictures, a relatively new company formed from the merger of Universal Studios with the independent International Pictures in 1946. Castle directed *Johnny Stool Pigeon* (1949), *Undertow* (1949), *The Fat Man* (1951), *Hollywood Story* (1951), and *Cave of Outlaws* (1951) at Universal-International, and *It's a Small World* (1950), an exploitation vehicle about a midget who is abused in the "tall" world before finding happiness in a circus, for Eagle-Lion films. He then returned to Columbia and directed a long string of B movies for producer Sam Katzman, including *Fort Ti* (1953, exhibited in 3-D), *Slaves of Babylon* (1953), *Jesse James vs. the Daltons* (1954, also in 3-D), *The Americano* (1954, made when Castle was loaned out to RKO), *New Orleans Uncensored* (1955), and *The Houston Story* (1956).

In 1957, Castle left Columbia and ventured into independent production, inventing the gimmicks and directing the horror films that established his reputation. The first film in the Castle "gimmick cycle" was *Macabre* (1958), inspired by the French film *Diabolique* (Henri-Georges Clouzot, 1955) and based on *The Marble Forest*, a novel by "Theo Durant," a pseudonym for 13 mystery writers who were members of the San Francisco chapter of the Mystery Writers of America. The film was co-produced by Robb White, the screenwriter responsible for all of the Castle gimmick films from *Macabre* to *Homicidal* (1961) and father of National Public Radio commentator Bailey White. Castle and White invested $90,000 of their personal money to finance production, and shot *Macabre* in nine days. The film concerns a plot to murder a doctor by convincing him that his daughter has been buried alive; Castle used the gimmick of a $1,000 insurance policy in order to promote the film.

After negotiating the policy with Lloyd's of London, Castle had theater managers pass out a "Beneficiary Agreement" that all *Macabre* patrons were invited to sign that stated, "The Producers of the film MACABRE undertake to pay the sum of One Thousand Dollars in the event of the death by fright of any member of the audience during the performance." (The policy also included a disclaimer: "I understand that if I have a known heart or nervous condition the One Thousand Dollars [$1000] is not payable.") Castle toured to promote *Macabre*, often arriving at premieres of the film in a closed coffin taken out of the back of a hearse by pallbearers hired for the occasion.

Castle's next independent production was *The House on Haunted Hill* (1958), starring Vincent Price in the role of Frederick Loren, an eccentric millionaire who offers five strangers $10,000 each to spend the night in a haunted mansion. The Castle gimmick for this film was "Emergo," a black box located on the side of the movie screen that held a skeleton designed to fly over spectators' heads at the point in *Haunted Hill* when Loren's skeleton emerges from a vat of acid to attack his unfaithful wife Annabelle (Carol Ohmart). Projectionists were instructed to press a button that would release the skeleton and have it travel through the theater attached to a wire.

Castle's next film also included his most infamous gimmick. *The Tingler* (1959), also starring Vincent Price, hypothesized that every human being has a small creature—a tingler—that lives in the spinal column and feeds on its host's fear; the only way for humans to keep the tingler at a manageable size is to scream and release fear out of their bodies. Price plays a doctor who discovers the existence of tinglers, and removes one from the back of a mute woman who died of fright. For this film, Castle came up with the gimmick of "Percepto": seats in the movie theater designed to deliver low-level electric shocks to their occupants. Castle personally introduces the film with a warning that "some of the sensations—some of the physical reactions—that the actors on the screen will feel will also be experienced for the first time in motion picture history by certain members of this audience." When the tingler escapes from Price and attacks the patrons and projectionist of a movie theater inside the story world, the screen of the actual film of *The Tingler* goes black, as Price's voice on the soundtrack says, "Ladies and gentlemen, please *do not* panic. But scream! Scream for your lives! The Tingler is loose in this theater!" This warning was immediately accompanied by the electric "tingles" provided by the wired seats.

Castle's next three films for Columbia, *13 Ghosts* (1960), *Homicidal* (1961), and *Mr. Sardonicus* (1961), all relied on gimmicks in order to attract audiences. *13 Ghosts* concerns a family that moves into a mansion full of ghosts that can only be seen with a special pair of goggles; audience members were given "Illusion-O" cardboard glasses that had the same effect. *Homicidal*, a *Psycho* pastiche about a sexually-ambiguous murderer, offered the "Fright Break": near the climax of the film a bright clock appears on the screen and Castle's voice invites audience members too scared to endure the climax to leave and get their money refunded before the clock ticks away 45 seconds. *Mr. Sardonicus*, a film about an evil 19th-century baron whose face becomes disfigured while robbing his father's grave, featured the "Punishment Poll," where the audience voted whether or not Sardonicus should die for his crimes at the end of the film.

After *Mr. Sardonicus*, Castle moved away from outrageous promotion. *Zotz!* (1962), a Disney-like fantasy about a nebbish (Tom Poston) who acquires a powerful magic coin, featured the innocuous gimmick of giving out replicas of the zotz coin to theater patrons. Castle continued to produce and direct horror films—a remake of *The Old Dark House* (1963), and two films starring Joan Crawford, *Strait-Jacket* (1964, script by Robert Bloch) and *I Saw What You Did* (1965)—but none of the movies were promoted with the over-the-top gimmicks typical of *The Tingler* or *The House on Haunted Hill*. In what John Waters calls Castle's "last, and most touchingly pathetic" gimmick, some of the seats in theaters exhibiting *I Saw What You Did* were equipped with seat belts to keep spectators from jumping fearfully out of their seats. Castle's last films with his production unit include *Let's Kill Uncle* (1966), *The Busy Body* (1967), *The Spirit Is Willing* (1967), a horror film spoof, and *Project X* (1968).

Castle received unprecedented critical acclaim for his production of *Rosemary's Baby* (1968). Afterwards, Castle suffered a number of health problems, including kidney stones and uremic poisoning, that limited his participation in motion picture production until his death in 1977. His last projects included directing and producing *Shanks* (1974), a horror-fantasy show casting Marcel Marceau in two roles, producing and co-writing *Bug!* (1975), and acting roles in *Shampoo* (1975), *Day of the Locust* (1975), and *The Sex Symbol* (1974), a TV movie starring Connie Stevens. Castle died at age 63 after suffering a heart attack at his Beverly Hills home.

Bibliography

Castle, William. *Step Right Up! I'm Gonna Scare the Pants off America*. New York: Putnam, 1976.

Waters, John. "Whatever Happened to Showmanship?" *Crackpot: The Obsessions of John Waters*. New York: Macmillan, 1986.

Craig Fischer

Catcher in the Rye, The (1951), J. D. Salinger's first novel, is the prototypical coming-of-age tale for the post–World War II generation. Salinger's disaffected hero-narrator is Holden Caulfield, a 17-year-old expelled from several prep schools, who rails against society's phoniness and his own betrayals: by seemingly benevolent adults, by the values of his schoolteachers, by young women with lovely looks but little imagination. A figure of innocence poised between adolescence and adulthood, Holden—like his predecessor Huckleberry Finn—is the archetypal American boy in search of self, experience, and the American Dream.

Not simply a postwar phenomenon, *Catcher* has achieved true cult status. One of the most popular works of modern fiction, it is also one of the most frequently censored books by conservative critics, who condemn its allegedly obscene language and countercultural attitudes. *Catcher in the Rye* retains a remarkable hold on the cultural imagination, most notoriously in Mark Chapman's 1980 killing of John Lennon, an act supposedly influenced by Chapman's misreading of the novel.

Bibliography

Bloom, Harold, ed. *Holden Caulfield*. New York: Chelsea, 1990.

French, Warren, ed. *J. D. Salinger, Revisited*. Boston: Twayne, 1988.

Lundquist, James. *J. D. Salinger*. New York: Ungar, 1979.

Salzman, Jack, ed. *New Essays on* The Catcher in the Rye. Cambridge: Cambridge UP, 1991.

Barbara Lupack

CATV, Cable TV, Coaxial Cable, Fiberoptics. Community antenna television systems (CATV) originated in the late 1940s. They consisted of a large antenna erected at an elevated location, such as a hill to serve a community in a valley or a tall building to serve city dwellers. Since radio waves induce a current in any conductor they contact, such as an antenna, the antenna would intercept TV transmission signals that were then retransmitted via air or wire to homes within the community.

CATV systems have been replaced by pure cable systems, in which the signals travel solely as electric currents through wires. Cable systems, like telephone systems, use coaxial cable, which means that the two conductors have a common center, unlike an electrical wire, in which the two conductors are parallel. Cable systems normally transmit at alternating currents of 40 to 300 MHz, whereas telephone systems normally transmit at lower frequency alternating currents of 300 to 5000 Hz. Cable systems also include amplifiers to boost the current as it travels and filters to selectively block out certain signals, so as to control access to premium cable TV.

Early cable systems supplied a limited number of stations, due to limitations of the carrying capacity of coaxial cable and the need to feed the signals at existing VHF channel frequencies. Improvements in coaxial cable capacity and the use of UHF channel frequencies have substantially increased the number of stations available on most cable systems. Cable-ready television receivers now permit the use of VHF and UHF channels with a direct cable feed; however, the cable stations generally appear on channels other than their broadcast channels to avoid interference.

Some local television stations, primarily independent stations carrying local sports broadcasting and/or classic movies, are now seen nationally as a result of cable. WTBS (channel 17 from Atlanta) is probably the best known, with WOR (channel 9 from New York) and WGN (channel 9 from Chicago) not far behind. The advent of cable has also resulted in the nationalization of local religious shows, which had been relegated to UHF stations, as well as the development of religious networks, such as CBN, the Christian Broadcasting Network.

While the development of local cable stations has followed along the lines of UHF, the development of national cable TV networks more closely parallels the development of national magazines. One of the first was CNN, a cable network dedicated to news (see entry).

Like CNN and CBN, most national cable TV networks are dedicated to a specific niche market. ESPN is sports; CNBC is business news (with the ticker running from the opening to the closing of the NYSE, AMEX, and NASDAQ). The Weather Channel is past, present, and predicted weather around the world, while the Travel Channel is travel around the world. Court TV shows live trials and commentary thereon, and C-SPAN (see entry) shows live congressional hearings and votes, as well as coverage of Parliament for matters of international interest. Comedy Central spotlights standup comedians, as well as reruns of vintage sitcoms; E! Entertainment TV is the *Variety* of the cable; MTV (see entry) and VH-1 are music videos.

Cable today is a trunk-and-branch system, with the signals traveling one way from the source to the subscriber. The advent of fiberoptic cable, in which signals are transmitted as light waves, should make cable systems two-way, permitting interactive communications. An optical fiber is comprised of a transparent material clad in a protective material, whereby the light is internally reflected within the fiber with a loss of less than 1 percent per mile. While refreshing the light requires complex equipment, such equipment is only needed every 30 to 60 miles, depending on the quality of signal required. Current fibers can carry up to 300 million bits per second; the introduction of single mode fibers should push this to as high as 10 billion bits per second. More significantly, some 100,000 such fibers can be bundled in a cable less than one-half inch in diameter. Some cable systems have already started using fiberoptic cable; others are now installing it.

In the cable television industry the top four companies, in terms of customer reach in the 1990s, are far less known but would include Tele-Communications, Inc., Time Warner (see entry), Cox Cable, and Cablevision Systems Inc. These are companies that own cable television franchises with millions and millions of customers under legal monopolies and hence define power and profit in the new world of cable TV.

Bibliography

Baer, W. S. *Cable Television: A Handbook for Decisionmaking*. New York: Crane, Russakt, 1974.

Broadcasting & Cable Yearbook 1994. New Providence: Bowker, 1994.

Brown, L. *Encyclopedia of Television*. 3d ed. Detroit: Visible Ink, 1992.

Sloan Commission on Cable Communications. *On the Cable: The Television of Abundance*. New York: McGraw-Hill, 1971.

Claire Koegler

See also

Closed-Circuit and Cable-Access TV

Television Broadcasting—VHF and UHF

Television Technology

Cavanaugh, Peter C. (1941-   ), known as Peter C. on the AM airwaves, was born in Syracuse, NY. He was a major

Midwest innovator of radio programming strategies from the 1960s to the 1980s. He began broadcasting in high school in 1957, and as an undergraduate student at Le Moyne College, he worked as a disk jockey. Then he moved around the country for several years taking positions with WTAC-AM in Flint, MI; as program director at KSO-AM in Des Moines, IA; then to WTLB-AM in Utica, NY; and returning as disk jockey with WTAC-AM in 1966, where he remained until 1978. He advanced to general manager and vice president first at WTAC-AM and later at WWCK-FM/WLQB in Flint. From 1983 to the early 1990s, he helped run Reams Broadcasting.

As an innovator, Cavanaugh experimented with a number of radio programming strategies (see Radio Formats). In 1967 he began a nightly two-hour *WTAC Underground* show, moving a Top 40 AM station to the fore as a disseminator of the alternative music of the era. Cavanaugh continued the alternative music show, later titled *The Cave,* until 1970. In the late 1970s, he opened a time slot for *Radio Free Flint,* socially aware public affairs programming, run by Michael Moore, who later made the documentary film *Roger and Me* (1989). In his last year (1979) at WTAC-AM, Cavanaugh introduced *The Beat Never Stops,* a fusion format of rock, soul, and disco music. While at WWCK-FM/WLQB-FM Cavanaugh inaugurated a station targeted to women, WWMN-FM, Flint's New Woman.

In early 1987, he was responsible for a pioneering experiment with the now-popular Oldies format (1950s to mid-1960s rock and roll) at WCWA, Reams's AM outlet in Toledo, OH. Both WWCK-FM of Flint and WIOT-FM of Toledo won *Billboard*'s Album-Oriented Rock Station of the Year Award during Cavanaugh's association with these FM outlets.

Bibliography

Guilford, D. "Goodbye, Peter C." *Flint Journal* 24 April 1983: D-1.

Kenneth G. Bielen

CBS Television Network, The, ranks as one of the three most important programming services in the 50-year history of television broadcasting in the United States. In the late 1940s and early 1950s, with the superior comedy of Jack Benny and Burns and Allen, to the superior news coverage by Edward R. Murrow and company, CBS was the network most Americans turned to. From the 1950s, as Americans acquired their first sets, through to the days before cable television became a force in the mid-1980s, CBS led the way in network power, profits, and prestige. Long-running No. 1 hits from *All in the Family* to *60 Minutes* could be found on the network with the eye symbol.

Long No. 1 in the overall ratings—through the 1960s and 1970s—CBS took to calling itself the "Tiffany Network." Founder and chief operating officer William S. Paley insisted on a fastidious image, in graphics, decor, and news quality. Paley set the tone by insisting his news be the best, and he willingly cross-subsidized news from profits made by the entertainment side. Company president Frank Stanton carried CBS to greater and greater earnings, at least until ABC took over prime-time first place in 1976.

CBS began as a radio network in 1927, as the United Independent Broadcasters, to challenge mighty NBC, then owned by the leading manufacturer of radios, the Radio Corporation of America (RCA). William S. Paley purchased controlling interest in CBS in 1929, and was associated with the company until his death in 1990. As radio grew during the Great Depression, CBS prospered, and after World War II the company was poised to enter television broadcasting.

Through the 1950s, 1960s, and into the 1970s CBS was TV's ratings leader—at night and during the daytime hours. Its hit programs defined the history of television broadcasting success in the United States, from *I Love Lucy* to *The Dick Van Dyke Show,* from Burns and Allen to Phil Silvers, from *Gunsmoke* to *Kate & Allie.*

Paley, more than any other individual, brought the Hollywood star system to network television. Indeed in the late 1940s, by restructuring lucrative deals with vast tax advantages, Paley brought to CBS the biggest stars from radio: Edgar Bergen, Arthur Godfrey, Ed Sullivan, Jack Benny, and Red Skelton, to name but a few. With its advantageous position on the dial in many cities, number "2" when there was no number "1," CBS could be and was seen by more and more Americans as families paid the required $500 to purchase a black and white television set.

Paley constantly heralded CBS's news division as the network's shining star. Through the glory days of the 1960s and 1970s Walter Cronkite represented the news anchor as father figure. Indeed few doubt that when "Uncle Walter" began to sour on the Vietnam War, President Lyndon B. Johnson lost his last chance at turning the American people to supporting his overseas adventure.

But as early as the 1960s, Paley anticipated a world where CBS would have competition, and began to diversify his corporate creation. He had lost his battle, a decade earlier, to dominate color television, and so in the 1960s went outside broadcasting to invest. Paley purchased book publishers and set up toy subsidiaries. CBS Records became the top music company in the world. For a time CBS even owned the New York Yankees baseball team.

During the network era of television in the United States (the 1960s and 1970s) CBS-TV offered up television programs unrivaled in popularity. In February 1983 the final episode of the long-running hit *M*A*S*H* drew the largest audience in television history for a single program. Thereafter, however, there was more bad news than good. New CBS shows all too often proved to be rating duds. In April 1986, after six straight years as the top-rated television network, CBS finished in second place. Lower finishes would soon arrive. In September 1987, infuriated when a tennis broadcast ran into his time slot, CBS news anchor Dan Rather walked off the set and, for seven long minutes, the fabled CBS eye was simply a blank screen. By April 1988 CBS finished third in the ratings for the first time since the earliest days of television.

It seemed that Paley was unable (or unwilling) to groom a successor. During the 1980s CBS's weak leadership could not protect the company from takeover attempts. Paley eventually turned to a friend, Lawrence A. Tisch of Wall Street investment giant Loews Corporation, for help and advice. As the 1980s turned into the 1990s Tisch, not Paley, was running CBS. Tisch systematically sold the toy making, records, and publishing interests. In the 1980s, with cable TV and home video drawing away more and more viewers, CBS's power and profits shrank.

By the beginning of the 1990s CBS was the simple sum of only its television network, owned and operated TV stations (five, all VHF), and radio stations. Unlike the well-diversified ABC and NBC, CBS under Tisch took no interest in cable or other new TV technologies. Nevertheless, CBS stabilized in the 1990s. While CBS in 1994 lost key long-term affiliates and the rights to NFL broadcasts to Rupert Murdoch's upstart Fox network, David Letterman did take over late night from Johnny Carson's successor Jay Leno.

By late 1995, however, the network was ripe for takeover: Westinghouse bought CBS for $5.4 billion and began to diversify the company. In May 2000, Viacom, owner of cable channels MTV and VH-1, as well as a film studio, bought CBS for $44 billion, creating a conglomerate expected to rival the newly merged Time Warner–America Online and Walt Disney Co., owner of ABC (see entries).

Bibliography

Castleman, Harry, and Walter J. Podrazik. *Watching TV: Four Decades of American Television.* New York: McGraw-Hill, 1982.

MacDonald, J. Fred. *One Nation under Television.* New York: Pantheon, 1990.

Paley, William S. *As It Happened: A Memoir.* New York: Doubleday, 1979.

Reel, Frank. *The Networks: How They Stole the Show.* New York: Scribner's, 1979.

Smith, Sally Bedell. *In All His Glory: The Life of William S. Paley.* New York: Simon & Schuster, 1990.

Douglas Gomery

CD-ROM Publications. Compact Disc—Read Only Memory began its publishing explosion in 1993. Although audio-only CDs revolutionized the music industry in the 1980s and CD-ROM technology existed in 1985, the high price of the optical laser drives needed to read the digitized data on CD-ROM discs limited their use to corporate library storage (340,000 pages of text per disc). When the cost of drives began to drop drastically in 1992, their appeal to home computer buyers grew. By the end of 1993, 7 million CD-ROM drives were installed and by mid-1994, half the consumer PCs were shipped with built-in drives. Apple increased sales of laser drives from 50,000 in 1992 to a million in 1993. In response, software development boomed. The capacity of CD-ROMs made video, music, speech, and animation possible.

Reference works were 40 percent of 1993 sales. In mid-1994, *Compton's Encyclopedia* was the best-selling CD-ROM of all time. Digital encyclopedias outsold printed versions 3-to-1, threatening paper-based publishers. Games were 30 percent and home education, including "edutainment," 17 percent. Other software included catalogs, X-rated titles, books, magazines, coffee-table books, travelogues, phone directories, and photograph storage. The number of CD-ROMs for sale has continued to increase.

Bibliography

Boroughs, Don L. "Profits on a Platter." *U.S. News & World Report* 25 Apr. 1994: 69-72.

Samuels, Gary. "CD-ROM's First Big Victim." *Forbes* 28 Feb. 1994: 42-44.

Shaffer, Richard A. "Birth of a Genre." *Forbes* 28 Mar. 1994: 114.

Janet Valade

Censorship in Popular Music, 1950s-present, has always been desired by many parents and religious groups. The most widely publicized censorship case in popular music involved rap group 2 Live Crew, and other attempts to censor popular music artists in the 1980s and 1990s have largely revolved around rap music (see entry). However, popular music was an outspoken and controversial form, a dissenting voice, threatening to authority, from its earliest manifestations, long before the advent of rap.

By the 1960s popular music grappled often with censorship based on its lyric content. The Rolling Stones changed the lyric of "Let's Spend the Night Together" to "Let's Spend Some Time Together" at Ed Sullivan's insistence. Jefferson Airplane was fined several times for not honoring clauses in its performance contracts that prohibited verbal abuse. Country Joe McDonald was fined for saying "fuck" during a performance in Massachusetts. During the 1960s, too, many songs were banned by the BBC for explicit drug references (including the Beatles' "With a Little Help from My Friends").

Not until the late 1980s did the government intervene in the distribution of popular music. Fueled in part by the organization of the Parent's Music Resource Center (PMRC) by the wives of various Washington luminaries (Tipper Gore and Susan Baker are the most prominent founders) and renewed fundamentalist lobbying, Congress, in particular the Senate Commerce Committee, held hearings over lyric content in popular music. In 1985, the Recording Industry Association of America (RIAA) agreed to the PMRC's request for labels on sound recordings to warn of explicit lyric content.

The case involving 2 Live Crew came to a head in 1990. In June 1990, a record store owner in Fort Lauderdale, FL, was arrested and convicted on obscenity charges for selling 2 Live Crew's "As Nasty As They Wanna Be" (though the recordings were labeled). The store owner and the group were found not guilty. 2 Live Crew's record sales during this time skyrocketed.

Anxiety over legal confrontations has prompted a major record label, MCA Records, to create a committee to screen lyrics before they are released on record. Clauses concerning the record company's sole approval of commercially satisfactory recordings are standard in recording contracts. It is doubtful that censorship issues in popular music will ever be resolved to the satisfaction of all participants.

Bibliography

Hill, Trent. "The Enemy Within: Censorship in Rock Music in the 1950s." *Present Tense: Rock and Roll and Culture.* Ed. Anthony DeCurtis. Durham: Duke UP, 1992.

Pally, Marcia. *Sex and Sensibility: Reflections on Forbidden Mirrors and the Will to Censor.* Hanover: UP of New England, 1994.

Walser, Robert. *Running with the Devil: Power, Gender, and Madness in Heavy Metal Music.* Hopewell: Ecco, 1993.

Steve Jones

Centennial (1978-1980), the longest television Western miniseries ever made, was an adaptation of James Michener's mammoth 909-page novel about the American West. Michener's 1974 bestseller could be described as part history, part soap-opera, part editorial (on environmental issues), but always moving and exciting.

From the beginning, the filming of Michener's epic novel was the most ambitious project ever attempted by television. It was initially budgeted by Universal Studios at $1 million per hour (or $26 million total for the entire series—more than four times the cost of *Roots*). The final cost, however, was in excess of $30 million. The cast literally included thousands, all shooting was done "on location," and an entire town was constructed near the South Platte River in Colorado.

John Wilder as executive producer assembled a cast of epic proportions to breathe life into seven generations of Michener characters. Dominating the story during the early episodes were Robert Conrad (of *The Wild Wild West*) as the French-Canadian trapper Pasquinel, and Richard Chamberlain (see next entry; star of *Dr. Kildare*) as the red-bearded Alexander McKeag—a tall, shy, rather elegant mountain man who Pasquinel rescues from the Cheyenne and who becomes his partner.

Unfortunately, the series peaked in the opening episode with a rating of 23.4 and never again reached that level in the Nielsens. The final average for the entire 12 episodes was 19.5, placing it 33rd out of the 112 ranked series for the 1978-79 season. This would have been considered a reasonable rating for most programs, but *Centennial* was decidedly not "most" programs. At a cost of $1,150,000 per hour, it was the most expensive series produced to that date.

Bibliography

Marill, Alvin H. *Movies Made for Television: The Telefeature and the Mini-Series 1964-1986.* New York: Zoetrope, 1987.

Yoggy, Gary A. *Riding the Video Range: The Rise and Fall of the Western on Television.* Jefferson: McFarland, 1995.

Gary A. Yoggy

Chamberlain, Richard (1935-), a rare actor in American entertainment, may have peaked in success too early for his own good. The great Shakespearean actor Sir Cedric Hardwicke was the man who warned Richard Chamberlain in 1961, "You're doing it backward. You're a star before you've learned how to act!" Richard Chamberlain was a star then, and he has remained a stellar performer, equally at home in the theater, in feature films, or in television.

Born George Richard Chamberlain in Beverly Hills, CA, he became interested in acting at Pomona College in Claremont; then, after a brief stint in the army, he attempted to find work in Hollywood. His early feature films included

Secret of the Purple Reef (1959), *A Thunder of Drums* (1959), and *Twilight of Honor* (1962). He landed six roles in television shows before 1961, including parts on *Gunsmoke* and *Bourbon Street Beat*, but he is best known as the title character in NBC's successful pioneer medical drama *Dr. Kildare* (1961-66; see entry).

In spite of critical praise and a growing mastery of his talent, none of the feature films in which he appeared propelled him to top stardom. When he was excellent, as in *The Lost City of Gold* (1987), the film was panned; when the film succeeded, as did *The Three Musketeers* (1973), his role was a minor one. His ability was to play the "pure" hero, but with the elimination of such characters from feature film leads, particularly after 1972-73, his greatest opportunities came in television productions.

Among the miniseries and made-for-television movies in which he played with distinction, the following are perhaps the best remembered: *The Count of Monte Cristo* (1975), *Centennial* (1978; see entry), *Shogun* (1980), *The Thorn Birds* (1983), and *Wallenberg: A Hero's Story* (1985). Despite his many successes, Chamberlain has never been awarded a Tony, Emmy, or Oscar.

Richard Chamberlain achieved in the role of Jim Kildare a rare synthesis of rightness for the part, readiness to portray the character's age and psycho-emotional state, and audience popularity; the character certainly belongs among the legendary personal triumphs of television's first half century.

Bibliography

Ryder, Jeffery. *Richard Chamberlain: An Unauthorized Biography.* New York: Dell, 1988.

Siegel, Barbara, and Scott Siegel. *Richard Chamberlain: An Actor's Life.* New York: St. Martin's, 1989.

R. D. Michael

Chandler, Raymond (1888-1959), was the premier stylist of hard-boiled detective fiction in America, and remains one of the most important, most influential, and finest writers in that genre. He was born in Chicago but moved with his mother to England as a young boy, where he was raised and educated. After a series of civil servant and journalistic jobs in Europe and wartime experience, he settled permanently in the United States, married in 1924, and began a career as an executive in the southern California oil industry.

Chandler came late to writing, publishing his first story, "Blackmailers Don't Shoot," in *Black Mask* in 1933. A reader of pulp detective magazines for entertainment, Chandler was influenced by the hard-boiled writing of Dashiell Hammett (see entry) and the objective style of Ernest Hemingway. He wrote and published 21 short stories—12 of them later reprinted in *The Simple Art of Murder* (1950)—in pulp magazines from 1933 to 1941, and reworked three of the stories into his first novel, *The Big Sleep* (1939), which firmly established his reputation. This and other novels such as *Farewell, My Lovely* (1940) and *The Lady in the Lake* (1943) brought him popular fame and were made into memorable films.

The formula Chandler perfected in *The Big Sleep* led to seven book-length variations featuring the detective persona of Philip Marlowe (see entry). The novels are distinguished by first- person narration, uncommon characters, and a pattern of action so convoluted that even Chandler could not always figure it out. In his essay "The Simple Art of Murder" (1944), Chandler described his conception of the detective: "Down these mean streets a man must go who is not himself mean, who is neither tarnished nor afraid...he is the hero." Marlowe's sense of honor is his hallmark: he can be hired but never bought.

Later in his career, Chandler worked as a screenwriter. He received Academy Award nominations for his adaptation of the James M. Cain novel *Double Indemnity* (1944), directed by Billy Wilder, and *The Blue Dahlia* (1946), an original screenplay. He also wrote the script for Alfred Hitchcock's *Strangers on a Train* (1951). Along with Hammett, Chandler changed the face of American detective fiction, helping to create the hard-boiled tradition; his fictional renditions of southern California are unsurpassed. He was the president of Mystery Writers of America in 1959, and received the Mystery Writers of America's Edgar for screenplay in 1946 and for novel in 1954. Chandler's wife died in 1954 after a long illness; thereafter, Chandler drank heavily, wrote little, and became ill himself. Since his death in 1959, his reputation and popular appeal have grown consistently.

Bibliography

Fine, David, ed. *Los Angeles in Fiction: A Collection of Original Essays.* Albuquerque: U of New Mexico P, 1984.

Gross, Miriam, ed. *The World of Raymond Chandler.* New York: A & W, 1977.

MacShane, Frank. *The Life of Raymond Chandler.* New York: Dutton, 1976.

Speir, Jerry. *Raymond Chandler.* New York: Ungar, 1981.

Wolfe, Peter. *Something More Than Night: The Case of Raymond Chandler.* Bowling Green, OH: Bowling Green State U Popular P, 1985.

Stephen Soitos

See also

Crime Fiction	Mystery and Detective Fiction
Mystery Awards	Regional Mysteries

Chaney, Lon (1893-1930), and **Lon Chaney, Jr.** (1906-1973), are both remembered chiefly for their roles in horror films. Over time, their legacy as famous movie monsters has overwhelmed the diversity of their work. Even today, Lon Chaney, Sr., is considered above all to be the first true master of movie makeup. His nickname, "the man of a thousand faces," has become the standard way of identifying him. During his heyday, the favorite joke around Hollywood (and apparently one of Chaney's as well) was "don't step on that—it might be Lon Chaney!"

Alonzo Chaney was born on April Fools' Day in Colorado Springs, CO. His parents were both deaf mutes, and many people hypothesize that this contributed to his abilities. To communicate with deaf-mute parents would certainly require development of terrific facial and body control. Despite his father's wishes (he initially apprenticed Lon to be an interior decorator), Lon wanted to be in show business.

During his teen years, Lon worked in vaudeville, specializing in comedy and dance, traveling all over the country. He worked with his brother, John, who ran a touring acting company at the turn of the century. In Oklahoma City Lon met and married Cleva Creighton in 1905. The following year, Creighton Chaney (later "Lon, Jr.") was born. The Chaneys eventually ended up in Hollywood, where Lon tried to break into motion pictures.

Part of the mystique and enduring fascination with Chaney is undoubtedly due to his love/hate relationship with fame. He obviously enjoyed creating extraordinary characters (with or without special makeup) and seems to have worked and practiced very hard to become a great actor. Some of his makeup techniques are understood as laying the groundwork for screen makeup in general. One of Chaney's common habits was to film himself in makeup, improvising with characters to see how they looked on film. This is the forerunner to modern screen and makeup tests.

The senior Chaney made over 150 films in all, eventually commanding huge salaries. He was voted most popular male star by theater owners in both 1928 and in 1929. His biggest hits have been remade often (*Hunchback of Notre Dame* in 1937, 1957, 1982; *Phantom of the Opera* in 1943, 1962, 1983, 1989, 1990), but never really surpassed. In 1957, James Cagney portrayed Chaney in the moving though highly romantic biography *Man of a Thousand Faces*. Part of Chaney's legacy, though, is his son, whose underrated work has been recovered in recent years.

Lon, Jr., was originally given his mother's maiden name. Young Creighton Chaney was close to his mother and was crushed when his father divorced her (at the time, Creighton was told that his mother had died). Lon, Jr., was reluctant to change his name, constantly wary of his father's ever-looming shadow.

In 1937, he married Patsy Beck and legally changed his name to Lon, Jr. When things looked absolutely hopeless, Chaney got the part of Lennie in *Of Mice and Men* (1940). His work was very well received by critics and audiences.

Of Mice and Men's success led to a long-term contract with Universal Studios. The studio, eager to exploit his father's name, cast him primarily in thrillers and monster pictures. A role in *One Million B.C.* (1940—not to be confused with the similarly titled Raquel Welch remake in 1966) as a crippled and disfigured tribe leader suggested he was ready to fill his father's shoes.

Lon Jr.'s most famous role came in 1941, playing long-suffering Lawrence Talbot, the title character of *The Wolf Man*. This movie remains the definitive version of the tale of lycanthropy. With makeup by Universal's master, Jack Pierce, Chaney provided the character with just the proper amount of pathos.

He portrayed Count Dracula (in the generally well-liked *Son of Dracula*, 1943), Frankenstein's monster (*The Ghost of Frankenstein*, 1942), and the Mummy (*The Mummy's Tomb*, 1942; *The Mummy's Ghost*, 1944; and *The Mummy's Curse*, 1944). He was also the star of a weak collection of fantasy/horror films called the Inner Sanctum series.

Bibliography
Beck, Calvin Thomas. *Heroes of the Horrors*. New York: Macmillan, 1975.
Blake, Michael. *Lon Chaney: The Man behind the Thousand Faces*. Vestal: Vestal, 1993.
Brosnan, John. *The Horror People*. New York: St. Martin's, 1976.

Michael Goldberg

Chapbooks were early popular publications which circulated throughout England and America from the mid-17th century through the early 19th century. Chapbooks were small, inexpensive books or pamphlets that generally contained retellings of earlier popular sources such as oral folk tales, medieval romances, fairy tales, legends, religious stories, and adventures. They were constructed of folded papers equaling 12 to 32 unbound pages and measuring about 4 by 6 inches. The printed text was decorated with woodcut illustrations that usually coincided with the subject matter. Traveling peddlers sold them to people living in the outlying areas for about a penny each. These inexpensive prices allowed the poorer classes, women, and young people access to materials once available primarily to the privileged classes.

By the 1800s, the interest in chapbooks had waned, but new writers briefly revived the market by offering original material with hand-colored illustrations—*The Comic Adventures of Old Mother Hubbard and Her Dog*, *Jack Spratt*, and *The History of the House That Jack Built*. These later chapbooks more closely resemble today's nursery rhyme books and children's readers, but for the adult and adolescent reader, the chapbook lingers in such popular genres as crime stories, science fiction, fantasy, Westerns, and romance novels.

Bibliography
Neuberg, Victor E. *Chapbooks: A Bibliography of References to English and American Chapbook Literature of the Eighteenth and Nineteenth Centuries*. London: Vine, 1964.
——. *The Penny Histories: A Study of Chapbooks for Young Readers over the Centuries*. New York: Harcourt, 1968.

Elena J. P. Marts

Chaplin, Charles (1889-1977). Over the history of comedy, no comedian has ever achieved the universal popularity or comic mastery of Charlie Chaplin. Even today, more than 70 years after the glory days of silent films, there is immediate recognition of Chaplin's "Little Tramp" character—the oddly dressed fellow with the mustache, twirling cane and shuffling, "east-and-west feet" who made his debut in the 1913 silent one-reeler entitled *Kid Auto Races in Venice*. The consensus is that at the pinnacle of Chaplin's golden career, he was the most popular film personality in the world. Not only was he a master at comic invention, but he proved himself an able writer/director/ producer/musician, functioning in one or more of those roles in more than 80 films.

Born in London, Chaplin must have fashioned his Tramp character after much of his own life. His mother was often hospitalized and his father died of alcoholism, which forced Chaplin and his older half-brother to live in poverty and frequently in the streets. He and his brother spent two years in an orphanage. While filling in for his mother, who tried to support the family as a musician, Chaplin made his first professional appearance at the age of five. By the time he was eight, Chaplin was a member of the Eight Lancashire Lads, a touring music hall troupe. From there Chaplin gained performance experience with other touring groups, joining the Fred Karno Pantomime Troupe at the age of 17 and eventually becoming a key player in that group. Chaplin was signed to a contract with Keystone Studio in 1913 while on a tour to America, and made his first appearance in a one-reeler film entitled *Making a Living*.

He left the studio in 1915 to sign with Essanay Studio, which released that year one of his funniest films, *The Tramp*. He made several moves to other studios, but at Mutual he began making some of his most famous films, such as *The Pawnshop* (1916), *The Immigrant* (1918), and *East Street* (1916). On the strength of these films with their clever, fresh, and hilarious comic approaches, Chaplin became a world-famous silent star.

After his move to First National Studios, he produced some of his finest classic films such as *A Dog's Life* (1918) and *A Day's Pleasure* (1919). In 1919 Chaplin joined with artists Mary Pickford, Douglas Fairbanks, and D. W. Griffith to create a company called United Artists. Their goal was to achieve more freedom as artists and exercise more artistic control over the production of films. Chaplin's most famous feature, *The Gold Rush* (1925), took two years to make, and marked the beginning of a period of a slower artistic output for the comic.

Despite the fact that new technology had every studio in Hollywood making "talkies," Chaplin seemingly ignored the trend and made *City Lights* (1931), featuring his original musical score and sound effects but no dialogue. The opinion was that the film would fail miserably in competition with "talkies," but it was the fourth biggest grosser of the year.

Fifteen years after the end of the silent film era, Chaplin played two speaking roles in his first all-talking movie, with *The Great Dictator* (1940), his second talking film, becoming the biggest hit of the year. The film was a comic attack on fascism, with Chaplin playing the role of a Jewish barber (a character similiar to his trademark "tramp") and Hynkel (a character based on Adolf Hitler).

The late 1940s and 1950s brought a decline in Chaplin's popularity due in some part to his abandonment of his trademark comic characters and his venturing into dark humor. Also, Chaplin's left-wing political views drew criticism during the "red" witchhunts of that period. Many were suspicious because Chaplin had never sought U.S. citizenship.

Chaplin's last two films fell short of audience's and critics' expectations, yet in 1971, Hollywood awarded the memorable comedian an honorary Academy Award and celebrated him with a long-standing ovation. His own birth country honored Chaplin with knighthood.

Bibliography
MacIntyre, Diane. *Tramp*. New York: HarperCollins, 1996.
Robinson, David. *Chaplin: His Life and Art*. New York: McGraw-Hill, 1985.

Siegel, Scott, and Barbara Siegel. *American Film Comedy*. New York: Prentice-Hall, 1994.

Barbara Anderson

See also
Slapstick

Charles, Ray (Robinson) (1930-), one of America's leading popular musicians, was born into a poor backwoods family in Albany, GA, but moved to Greenville, FL, while still a baby and grew up in this country setting. For reasons that do not appear to have been definitively diagnosed (probably glaucoma), he began to lose his eyesight and was completely blind by the age of seven. Ray's family sent him to the State School for Deaf and Blind Children in St. Augustine, FL. Charles emerged from this institution at age 15, orphaned but with proficiency in Braille and with enough competence on the keyboard (plus clarinet and alto saxophone) to begin working as a professional musician in Jacksonville, Orlando, and Tampa.

Charles's musical roots lie primarily in gospel music, blues, jazz, rhythm and blues, and even country. As a performer, he drew upon Charles Brown, Louis Jordan, and Nat "King" Cole as early stylistic influences. Indeed, Ray's earliest recordings feature a trio with the piano-bass-guitar instrumentation popularized by Nat Cole and with some vocal performances that sound so much like Cole as to encourage a listener to confuse the two. Also, Charles shares with Cole and Brown an uncanny ability to accompany himself on the piano, swinging powerfully on the keyboard while singing to full effect with unique rhythmic and melodic complexities. Further, fusing disparate borrowings into an idiosyncratic voice, Charles drew on a diversity of musical genres that not only emphasized jazz, blues, gospel, and rhythm and blues but subsequently encompassed Latin music, British rock, and country.

Charles's recordings for Atlantic during the early to late 1950s–collected in *The Birth of Soul*—represent the manner in which his youthful innovations drew upon diverse influences to prepare the way for the soul movement to follow. Often, Charles borrowed tunes straight from the church, set secular lyrics to them, and performed them in a gutsy style uniquely his own ("I've Got a Woman"; "Hallelujah I Love Her So"; "Talkin' about You"; "What'd I Say"). In 1959 "What'd I Say" became Charles's first million-seller.

His gospel-drenched singing produced a hit recording in 1960 when Charles changed record companies and moved to ABC-Paramount to record "Georgia on My Mind." Subsequent imitators have included Sam Cooke, Lou Rawls, Al Green, and Aretha Franklin (whose work has, in turn, given birth to a whole secondary line of subsidiary followers like Patti LaBelle, Deniece Williams, Natalie Cole, and Whitney Houston) as well as practitioners of "blue-eyed soul" ranging from the Righteous Brothers to Michael Bolton. Ironically, these less creative disciples have sometimes enjoyed far greater commercial success than the original progenitor himself. But—at his best—as in performances like "Hallelujah I Love Her So," "What Would I Do Without You," "Alexander's Ragtime Band," "California, Here I Come," "Margie," "It Makes No Difference Now," "You Are My Sunshine,"

"Let's Go Get Stoned," "Yesterday," "America," "Is There Anyone Out There?," or "Still Crazy After All These Years" —Charles demonstrates how he earned his famous nickname: "The Genius."

Bibliography
Balliett, Whitney. *American Singers*. New York: Oxford UP, 1988.
Charles, Ray, and David Ritz. *Brother Ray: Ray Charles' Own Story*. New York: Dial, 1978.
Heilbut, Anthony. *The Gospel Sound: Good News and Bad Times*. New York: Limelight, 1985.
Palmer, Robert. Notes to *The Birth of Soul*. Atlantic 7-82310-2, 1991.
Pleasants, Henry. *The Great American Popular Singers*. New York: Simon & Schuster, 1974.

Morris B. Holbrook

Charlie Daniels Band, The, is one of the more popular groups that helped define southern country-rock, a musical genre (at one time tentatively called "raunch & roll") that combines several existing styles: rock 'n' roll, rhythm and blues, and country and western. Thus, the Charlie Daniels Band ranks among such groups as the Allman Brothers Band, Lynyrd Skynyrd, the Marshall Tucker Band, and ZZ Top. Daniels himself, who progressed from respected session musician to major country artist, is known for both his delight in and incorporation of an eclectic assortment of other musical styles in addition to his hard-core southern country-rock.

Charlie Daniels (1936-) was born in rural Wilmington, NC. He took up the guitar at age 15 and soon also mastered the mandolin and fiddle, playing regularly at square dances and school proms with friends in a bluegrass band called the Misty Mountain Boys. In the late 1950s with a group called the Rockets he traveled throughout the U.S. In Fort Worth, TX, local producer Bob Johnston had the group record a song called "Jaguar," at which point the group changed its name to the Jaguars and continued touring the South with Charlie honing his skills as guitarist, fiddler, and songwriter. An early credential came in 1963 when Elvis Presley recorded "It Hurts Me," a Daniels composition.

By 1967, Johnston had ascended Columbia Records' corporate ladder and invited Daniels to work in Nashville. There, Daniels learned bass and banjo while serving as a studio musician on albums by artists such as Pete Seeger, Al Kooper, and Flatt and Scruggs. He contributed to three albums by Leonard Cohen (and traveled with his band in the late 1960s), and played on Bob Dylan's *Nashville Skyline* (1969), *Self Portrait* (1970), and *New Morning* (1970), and on Ringo Starr's 1970 album *Beaucoup of Blues*.

In 1971, a first album for Charlie Daniels himself was released on Capitol Records; and in 1972 he put together his own band and started touring. The Charlie Daniels Band made their chart debut in 1973 with the album *Honey in the Rock,* which included their first U.S. Top 10 hit single, "Uneasy Rider," something of an anti-redneck novelty piece that Daniels has called his "most unlikely hit song." The band's late 1974 release of *Fire on the Mountain* was a

151

greater success, containing the songs "No Place to Go," Charlie's virtuoso performance of "Orange Blossom Special," and the band's signature song, "The South's Gonna Do It Again," which secured for them their first gold record. The Charlie Daniels Band was honored with invitations to play at the Grand Ole Opry (August 1976 and again in April 1978) and also performed at the inaugural ball for President Jimmy Carter.

The band's most notable success came with the 1979 release of *Million Mile Reflections* and its international hit single "The Devil Went Down to Georgia," which won the Charlie Daniels Band a Grammy for the best country vocal performance by a duo or group.

Bibliography

Stambler, Irwin, and Grelun Landon. *The Encyclopedia of Folk, Country, and Western Music.* 2d ed. New York: St. Martin's, 1989. 161-63.

Towne, Phil. "Charlie Daniels' Volunteer Jam." *Down Beat* May 1985: 52-53.

James Sirotzki
Michael Delahoyde

Charlotte's Web (1952), written by E. B. White, is a fantasy novel for children about the inhabitants of a New England barnyard: Wilbur, a runt piglet who is saved from the ax by young Fern Avery; Templeton, a self-centered rat who comes to the rescue in spite of himself; and Charlotte, a worldly spider who serves as Wilbur's protector, mother, and friend. Charlotte prevents Wilbur from becoming Christmas ham by weaving words about him into her web. The humans who view Charlotte's messages conclude that Wilbur is a remarkable pig, and as a result, Wilbur is assured a long and happy life.

Charlotte's Web has achieved lasting stature among readers of all ages (including a film version in 1973) because its enduring themes are the primal lessons of life itself—lessons of birth and growth, selfless love, loss, and the acceptance of inevitable death.

Bibliography

Neumeyer, Peter F. "The Creation of *Charlotte's Web*: From Drafts to Book." *The Horn Book* (Oct. 1982 and Dec. 1982).

Nodelman, Perry. "Text as Teacher: The Beginning of *Charlotte's Web*." *Children's Literature* 13 (1985).

Laura Obbink

Chautauqua is a term applied to several kinds of popular adult education programs of the later 19th and 20th centuries. The name derives from Chautauqua Lake in western New York state, where, in 1874, Methodist minister John H. Vincent (1832-1920) established a summer school for Sunday school teachers on a woodsy shore near a steamboat landing. Originally it was a 15-day session with the participants living in tents, but it soon evolved into a summer-long series of lectures, discussions, concerts, and dramatics with regular attendees building permanent cabins in styles from rustic to Queen Anne. One of the innovative features for the Sunday school teachers was a model of the Holy Land with the lakeshore serving as the Mediterranean coast (this was

one of the exciting aspects of a juvenile book, *Four Girls at Chautauqua* [1876] by "Pansy" [Isabella MacDonald Alden, 1841-1930], which was followed by two more volumes in the series).

Four years after the founding, Vincent developed a way of sustaining the Chautauqua experience throughout the year with the Chautauqua Literary and Scientific Circle home reading program. In 1891 there were 180,000 enrollees, 12 percent of whom had completed four years and graduated. In the first 20 years there were 10,000 reading circles nationwide. Meanwhile the summer program—active to this day—had a virtual who's who of lecturers and performers, among them Teddy, Franklin, and Eleanor Roosevelt, Jane Addams, Thomas Edison, Henry Ford, George Gershwin, and philosopher William James.

The first Chautauqua spawned imitation "permanent" Chautauquas nationwide, as many as 200 in 31 states by 1900. Most of these had pavilions or tenting areas on a lake or river where many regulars would spend a summer vacation, much as at Chautauqua Lake. These were called permanent to distinguish them from the circuit or tent Chautauquas developed in 1903 by Keith Vawter (1872-1937), who had worked for the successful Boston booking agent James Redpath (1831-91). Redpath had taken the pre–Civil War lyceum, which was started in 1826 by Josiah Holbrook (1788-1854) as a network of towns engaged in self-improvement with some sharing of guest lecturers, and turned it into a glittering array of well-paid star speakers on one-night stands: among lyceum favorites were Ralph Waldo Emerson, the Reverend Henry Ward Beecher, humorists Bill Nye and Mark Twain, Hoosier poet James Whitcomb Riley, and feminists Elizabeth Cady Stanton and Susan B. Anthony. Lyceum circuits spread wide as railroads covered the nation. Keith Vawter combined the lyceum circuit idea with Chautauqua's summer outdoor format, and, as with other outdoor entertainments of the time, used tents instead of depending upon public halls.

This method of bringing culture to the people began in 1903; by the peak year of 1924 there were dozens of tent circuits reaching an estimated 12,000 towns and close to one-third of the nation's population. Although many of the performances were far from educational—Swiss bellringers, chalk-talk artists, magicians, corny melodramas and community sing-alongs—the rural audiences clamored for Shakespeare and opera stars as well. The staple fare, though, was still lecturers: the romantic traveler Richard Halliburton, U-Boat commander Count Felix von Luckner, muckraking historian Ida Tarbell (whose writing career began as an editor for the reading circles' *Chautauquan Magazine*), Milwaukee socialist Emil Seidel, and Russell Conwell (whose "Acres of Diamonds" lecture was delivered over 6,000 times in 40 years that spanned both lyceum and Chautauqua, and earned enough so that he could found Temple University in Philadelphia). Far and away the most popular tent Chautauqua attraction was the Great Commoner, William Jennings Bryan.

The original summer Chautauqua is thriving, and its reading circles continue in a modified format. In the 1980s circuit Chautauquas were revived in a number of states as a means of disseminating culture programs sponsored by state humanities committees of the National Endowment for the Humanities. North Dakota's programs were performed in tents, while in its dozen years of existence, the Minnesota Chautauqua reached over 100,000 people in parks, schools, churches, fairs, and festivals. As with the circuit Chautauquas and later lyceums, sustaining a balance between popular appeal and thought-provoking continuing education was an unending challenge, but like its predecessors, the humanities Chautauquas have succeeded in bringing live lecturer-performers to rural communities.

Bibliography

Bode, Carl. *The American Lyceum; Town Meeting of the Mind.* New York: Oxford UP, 1954.

Case, Victoria, and Robert Ormond Case. *We Called It Culture: The Story of Chautauqua.* Garden City: Doubleday, 1948.

Horner, Charles F. *Strike the Tents: The Story of the Chautauqua.* Philadelphia: Dorrance, 1954.

Morrison, Theodore. *Chautauqua: A Center for Education, Religion, and the Arts in America.* Chicago: U of Chicago P, 1974.

Fred E. H. Schroeder

Cheap Trick is a pop musical group that is both praised and criticized. In 1969 Rockford, IL, natives Rick Nielsen, Brad Carlson, and Tom Peterson released an album under the moniker Fuse, then toured as Sick Man of Europe before forming Cheap Trick with Rockford folk vocalist Robin Zander in 1973. Ira Robbins writes of their style in the *Trouser Press Record Guide*, "Drawing primary inspiration from the Move and Beatles, Cheap Trick synthesized a loud and brilliant rock powerdrive and backed it up with shows that while formulaic and gimmicky in the extreme, had all the punch and spirited good humor that older, tired arena bands lacked."

Although the band got off to a slow start in the U.S., Cheap Trick's first and second album went gold in Japan, prompting the band to go to Tokyo, where they ran into unexpected "Trickmania." Their show at the Budokan Arena sold out in two hours, and the group wisely decided to record the concert and release it as *Cheap Trick at Budokan*, which stayed on the U.S. album charts for a year. The album also provided Cheap Trick's first trip into the U.S. Top 10 with the single "I Want You to Want Me" in 1979. The album itself sold over 3 million copies in Japan and was the group's first million seller in the U.S.

The followup to *Budokan* was Cheap Trick's fourth studio effort, *Dream Police*, a Top 10 album and the title track of which made the Top 40 in 1979. As the 1980s dawned, Nielsen, Zander, and Carlson contributed to John Lennon's *Double Fantasy* LP and released a mini-album of 1970s leftovers that was a Top 40 album in the U.S. Cheap Trick hooked up with Beatles producer George Martin in 1980; the result was the Top 40 hit "All Shook Up."

Cheap Trick only had moderate success keeping on the charts until 1988, when their ballad "The Flame" was No. 1

in the U.S. The single's success helped sales of the album from which it was taken, *Lap of Luxury*, with the group using outside writers to return them to form. The band's version of "Don't Be Cruel" hit No. 4 in the same year and became the first Elvis Presley cover to reach the Top 10 since his death. In 1990, Zander's duet with Heart's Ann Wilson, "Surrender to Me," from the movie *Tequila Sunrise,* made the Top 10 and the group scored again with "Can't Stop Falling Into Love" later in the year.

Bibliography

Rees, Dafydd, and Luke Crampton. *Rock Movers and Shakers.* New York: Billboard, 1991.

Robbins, Ira. *The Trouser Press Record Guide.* New York: Collier, 1991.

Hugh Foley

Checker, Chubby (1941-), is best known as the popularizer of the early 1960s dance called the twist. The Philadelphia native was born Ernest Evans. While he was working as a chicken plucker, his boss was so impressed with Evans's singing talents that he brought Evans to the attention of Kal Mann of the Philadelphia-based Cameo-Parkway Records in December 1958.

American Bandstand impresario Dick Clark (see entry) and his wife, Bobbie, discovered Evans when they visited Mann at Cameo-Parkway. The Clarks were particularly impressed by Evans's imitations of late 1950s performers, including Fats Domino. Bobbie Clark suggested that since he was not as hefty as Fats, he could be called a "chubby checker," and the nickname stuck. Chubby Checker recorded a novelty song for the Clarks, "The Class," in which he imitated Fats Domino, the Coasters, Elvis Presley, and the Chipmunks.

Hank Ballard and the Midnighters recorded the original versions of "The Twist," and it was a modest success on the rhythm and blues charts. Clark was bombarded with requests for the song during the summer of 1959. He suggested that Checker record the song, and the cover version of "The Twist" was produced in 35 minutes. The Cameo-Parkway release was accompanied by heavy promotion on *American Bandstand*. Checker performed the accompanying dance and so did the enthusiastic teenaged audience.

Checker proved able to adapt to the short life of the early 1960s dance crazes. "Pony Time" was a No. 1 hit in February 1961 and helped push the pony as the next dance fad. In August, Cameo-Parkway released "Let's Twist Again" to celebrate the first anniversary of the twist. The single reached No. 8 on the charts and sparked a new wave of interest in the dance. It also earned a gold record and a Grammy for best rock 'n' roll record of the year.

The twist spread to fashionable night spots like the Peppermint Lounge and to other countries. Checker was invited to sing "The Twist" on the *Ed Sullivan Show* in October 1961, generating new interest in the original song. When "The Twist" was re-released, it hit No. 1 again in January 1962—the only time in U.S. recording history that a single reached No. 1 on two separate releases. Checker also had a hit with a variation of the twist, "The Fly," in the fall of 1961.

"Slow Twistin'," a duet with Dee Dee Sharp, hit No. 3 on the charts in April 1962. The success of the twist was prolonged by that song, another single, "Twistin' Round the World," and Checker's appearance in the summer 1962 film *Don't Knock the Twist.*

But in November 1962, Checker promoted two other dance fads with the two sides of a single—"Limbo Rock" and "Popeye (The Hitchhiker)." The limbo was the more successful dance and song, and "Limbo Rock" reached No. 2 in December. As he had done with the twist, Checker kept the dance going by recording a followup, "Let's Limbo Some More" in the spring of 1963.

Checker promoted another dance, the bird, with the No. 12 hit, "Birdland," in June 1962. He tried unsuccessfully to cash in on the surfing craze with "Surfin' Party," then promoted the twist one more time with "Twist It Up" in August 1963.

Checker had a series of non-dance minor hits: "Loddy Lo" (December 1963) and its B-side, "Hooka Tooka" (February 1964); "Hey Bobba Needle" (April 1964); and "Lazy Elsie Molly" (July 1964). He also tried to ride the short-lived swim fad with "She Wants T'Swim" (September 1964) and even a British dance craze, the Freddie, with "Let's Do the Freddie" (May 1965).

In 1966, Checker recorded his last hit for Cameo-Parkway, "Hey You! Little Boo-Ga-Loo." He signed with Buddah Records in 1969 but achieved little commercial success on that label. Checker made a minor comeback in 1982 with the dance LP *The Change Has Come* on MCA Records. In 1988, he recorded a rap version of his first hit, "The Twist (Yo' Twist)," with the Fat Boys. The single peaked at No. 16 in August 1988.

Bibliography
Romanowski, Patricia, and Holly George-Warren. *The New Rolling Stone Encyclopedia of Rock & Roll.* New York: Fireside, 1995.
Stambler, Irwin. *The Encyclopedia of Pop, Rock, and Soul.* New York: St. Martin's, 1989.

Ken Nagelberg

Cheerleading is synonymous with sports. Once only associated with football and basketball, cheerleaders are now seen at other sporting events such as swim meets, track and wrestling competitions, and volleyball games. In recent years physical skills have become the dominant attribute of many squads, so much so that college scholarships are offered and competitions are held by two groups, the National and the Universal cheerleading associations. Meanwhile, professional cheerleaders have successfully combined entertainment, sex, and athletics to create a popular and lucrative industry.

Today most major professional sports teams have a cheerleading squad or pep team. Professional cheerleaders have been the subject of made-for-TV movies, featured guests on talk shows and telethons, and celebrity spokespersons for major advertising campaigns. The most notable and celebrated squad among professional cheerleading teams is undoubtedly the Dallas Cowboy Cheerleaders. An amateur squad composed of male and female high school cheerleaders represented the Dallas Cowboys in the 1960s, but as the football team rose in popularity so did their cheerleading squad. In 1972, the Dallas Cowboy Cheerleaders, immortalized as "America's Sweethearts," were formed, thus introducing professional cheerleading to America.

Cheerleading, as it is known today, originated in 1898 at the University of Minnesota. Johnny Campbell, an undergraduate at the university, was the first person to stand before a group of spectators at a sporting event and lead a group cheer. Prompted by the crowd's less than enthusiastic support of the losing Gophers, Campbell was compelled to encourage the Minnesota fans to support their team vocally. Campbell's leadership led to the selection of a group of male students who would lead cheers at football games. In addition to claiming the origins of cheerleading, the University of Minnesota was the first school to incorporate gymnastics into the activity.

Uniforms have changed as fashion trends have evolved. The female collegiate uniform of an above-ankle skirt, sweater boasting a felt megaphone and the first letter in a school's name, oxfords, and bobby socks has been replaced with short skirts, sleeveless shirts that often expose the midriff, and expensive athletic shoes. Like many collegiate basketball and football teams, some schools have athletic shoe contracts to outfit their cheerleading squads.

Famous former cheerleaders include pop star Paula Abdul, former Miss America and cable-television personality Phyllis George, actor Jimmy Stewart, and former president Dwight D. Eisenhower. However one may view cheerleading and its participants, it is an anticipated, celebrated, and entertaining aspect of sporting events on all levels.

Bibliography
Froiland, Paul. "Where Cheerleading Was Born." *Cheer Magazine* 1.1 (1993): 13+.
Hanson, Mary Ellen. *Go! Fight! Win! Cheerleading in American Culture.* Bowling Green, OH: Bowling Green State U Popular P, 1995.
Hart, Elaine, and Randy L. Neil. *The All-New Official Cheerleader's Handbook.* New York: Simon & Schuster, 1979.
May, Phyllis. "Cheerleading and Twirling." *Encyclopedia of Southern Culture.* Ed. William Ferris and Charles Reagan Wilson. Chapel Hill: U of North Carolina P, 1989. 1215-16.

Teresa Hollingsworth

Cheers (1982-1993), a TV sitcom set in a bar of that name in Boston, was created by James Burrows, Glen Charles, and Les Charles. During its 11-year run, the show received 111 Emmy nominations, but it barely survived its first season. Despite critical praise, ratings were quite low. A mid-season cameo appearance from Cheers' local Congressman, none other than then-Speaker of the House Tip O'Neill, drew viewer interest. In the show's second season, it reached the Top 10, where it stayed for seven years of its 11-year prime-time tenure.

The show's primary focus for the first five seasons was on the relationship between Cheers' bartender-owner Sam

Malone (Ted Danson), a former Red Sox pitcher recovering from alcoholism, and the intellectual barmaid Diane Chambers (Shelley Long). Adding to the fun were barmaid Carla (Rhea Perlman), bartender Woody (Woody Harrelson), who replaced "Coach" (played by Nicholas Colasanto, who died in 1985), and patrons such as regular beer-drinkers Norm (George Wendt), Cliff (John Ratzenberger), and Frasier Crane (Kelsey Grammer). (The success of the Frasier character led to Grammer's Emmy-winning spinoff of that name.) After the fifth season, coworker Rebecca Howe (Kirstie Alley) became Sam's love interest.

Bibliography

Long, Rob. "Three Cheers." *National Review* 7 (June 1993): 62-63.

Van Hise, James. *Where Everybody Knows Your Name: Cheers.* Las Vegas: Pioneer, 1992.

Waters, Harry F., and Charles Fleming. "Raise a Glass for 'Cheers.'" *Newsweek* 17 May 1993: 60.

Roger N. Casey

Chenier, Clifton (1925-1987), was a leading and influential zydeco musician. The self-styled Black King of the South, Clifton Chenier (rhymes with "veneer") was born in rural Louisiana near Opelousas. Like other zydeco musicians, Chenier began his musical career playing harmonica and tapping or rubbing spoons on a *frottoir*, a washboard that hangs over the shoulders like a metal smock or vest, serving as a soundboard. Tuning his instrument with paper clips, Chenier perfected and legitimized this percussive sound, called spoons, now a staple in New Orleans's French Quarter as well as in rural dance halls and honky tonks all over Cajun country.

In the late fifties and sixties, with his Red Hot Louisiana Band, Chenier performed on the piano accordion primarily at black dance halls between New Orleans and Houston. The success in 1954 of "Cliston Blues" promoted Chenier to the top of the ranks of zydeco (a Creole musical form sung in both French and English; see entry).

After a decline in popularity in the early 1960s, Chenier was resurrected later in the decade by Houston's black churches, from whom he soon learned to demand a share of the gate. His father, Cleveland Chenier, joined him on *frottoir*, and the two made a hit in 1965 with "Louisiana Blues," which illustrates his rich patois. His 1967 hit "Monifique" was followed in 1970 by "Tu le ton son ton" and in 1975 by "Jambalaya."

In the 1970s Chenier toured England, Germany, Scandinavia, and France, where they fell in love with his Louisiana French; the country that credits itself with discovering American jazz discovered zydeco and opened a door to some of Chenier's best years. After winning a European contest over 500 other accordionists, he was touted as the King of Zydeco and began wearing a gaudy rhinestone-studded crown wherever he played. In the early 1980s the King took his sound to Montreux, where he turned the Swiss jazz festival into a romping, stomping zydeco party.

Americans responded to his popularity in Europe. He played the San Francisco Jazz Festival in 1977 and the Blues Festival in 1982. During his heyday, Chenier performed throughout the United States and recorded under a variety of labels, including Specialty Records and Arhoolie. At his peak, he played with Elvin Bishop, Gatemouth Brown, Ray Charles, Lightnin' Hopkins, B. B. King, Big Mama Thornton, Big Joe Turner, and Johnny Winter. Les Blank's *Hot Pepper* (1973) is one of several documentary films about the King of Zydeco.

In spite of successes that led to a Grammy in 1984 for best ethnic album, *I'm Here!*, Chenier always played a Louisiana circuit. Heirs apparent to his throne included Rockin' Dopsie and the Twisters, Buckwheat Zydeco, Terrance Simien's Mallet Playboys, Nathan Williams, and C. J. Chenier, Clifton's son. But when the King died in 1987, he left a vacuum that nature, in spite of her reputation, was slow to fill.

Bibliography

Ancelet, Barry Jean. *Cajun Music and Zydeco.* Baton Rouge: Louisiana State UP, 1992.

——. *The Makers of Cajun Music.* Austin: U of Texas P, 1984.

Lichtenstein, Grace, and Laura Dankner. *Musical Gumbo.* New York: Norton, 1993.

Bonnie Elgin Todd

Cheyenne (1955-1963), the first and most successful loner-Western on television, premiered on ABC. *Cheyenne* depicted the exploits of Cheyenne Bodie, a wandering frontier scout as learned in the ways of the Indian as those of the white man.

To play this charismatic hero Warner Brothers chose a handsome, muscular unknown actor named Clint Walker. *Cheyenne* was the first Western to be one hour in length. It was also Warner Brothers' longest-running series, lasting for eight seasons. The show gradually rose in the Nielsen ratings and from 1957 through 1960 it finished in the Top 20.

In 1958, Walker walked off the set and demanded a new contract. While Walker was "on strike," the studio brought in a new actor, Ty Hardin, to play a character very similar to Cheyenne Bodie named Bronco Layne. The program alternated with *Sugarfoot*, but the name of the series remained *Cheyenne*.

If imitation is the sincerest form of flattery, then *Cheyenne* must have been the most flattered Western on television. Nearly 20 *Cheyenne* clones rode the video range during the late 1950s and 1960s (see Television Westerns). *Cheyenne* was finally canceled by ABC in 1963.

Bibliography

Brooks, Tim, and Earle Marsh. *The Complete Guide to Prime Time Network and Cable TV Shows, 1946-Present.* New York: Ballantine, 1995.

Yoggy, Gary A. *Riding the Video Range: The Rise and Fall of the Western on Television.* Jefferson: McFarland, 1995.

Gary A. Yoggy

Chicago, as the group which introduced the use of horns into rock 'n' roll at the end of the 1960s, is considered a jazz-rock pioneer. Classified with the band Blood, Sweat and

Tears in this regard, Chicago's initial jazzy sound, jazz-style improvisation, and blending of these with blues and classical influences gave way in the 1970s to ballads which, though rather formulaic, dominated pop charts throughout the decade. The group also succeeded in the 1980s, so that over the years they have produced several dozen hit singles, most of these in the Top 40.

The group coalesced in the late 1960s, with Terry Kath on guitar and vocals; Robert Lamm on keyboards and vocals; Peter Cetera on bass and vocals; James Pankow on trombone; Lee Loughnane on trumpet; Walt Parazaider on woodwinds; and Danny Seraphine on drums. With the exception of Lamm, who grew up in Brooklyn, NY, all original members were from Chicago; thus the name (they had earlier called themselves the Big Thing).

In 1969, they recorded their debut album for Columbia. The two-record set, *Chicago Transit Authority*, contained the hit single "Does Anybody Really Know What Time It Is?" and went gold, staying on the charts into 1971 and even reappearing for several years afterwards.

The band shortened its name to Chicago. Their second album was also a double-record set, *Chicago* (1970), including the hit singles "Make Me Smile," "25 or 6 to 4," and "Color My World." The third album, *Chicago III* (1971), was yet another two-record set, emphasizing musical suites. Still in 1971, a four-record set, *Chicago Live at Carnegie Hall*, was released, albeit against the band's wishes due to the quality of their performance (a result of the producer's interference on stage). *Rolling Stone* called it "probably the worst live album in history"; but it too went gold, as did all of Chicago's 1970s albums, often due to hit singles such as "Saturday in the Park" from *Chicago V* (1972), "Just You 'n' Me" and "Feelin' Stronger Every Day" from *Chicago VI* (1973), and "(I've Been) Searchin' So Long" and "Wishing You Were Here" from *Chicago VII* (1974).

In 1974, Brazilian percussionist Laudir De Oliveira joined as an eighth member. After the *Chicago's Greatest Hits* album in 1975, *Chicago X* in 1976 became No. 1 in the U.S. and the U.K. and earned the group Grammy Awards for the hit single "If You Leave Me Now" as best pop vocal performance by a group and best arrangement.

Despite the death of Terry Kath in 1978, various replacements, and the departure of Cetera for a solo career in 1985, the group continued to flourish. The biggest seller in the group's history, *Chicago XVII* (1984), went multi-platinum due to two more hit singles: "Hard Habit to Break" and "You're the Inspiration." In 1998 the group's roman-numeraled series reached *XXV (The Christmas Album)*.

Bibliography

Hohman, M. "The Chicago Papers." *Down Beat* 16 Jan. 1975: 13-15, 42.

Larkin, Colin, ed. *The Guinness Encyclopedia of Popular Music*. Vol. 1. Middlesex, U.K.: Guinness, 1995.

Siders, H. "Chicago: Jazz-Rock Pioneers." *Down Beat* 29 Oct. 1970: 12-13.

Catherine Olson
Michael Delahoyde

Children's Book Illustrators, while an important feature of earlier children's books, did not become a significant native tradition in America until the later 19th century. With the work of Howard Pyle (1853-1911), American illustration finally came into its own. A one-man movement, Pyle exerted incalculable influence by stressing character, action, and understanding of his subjects, and his books led readers of all ages into the magical lands of King Arthur and Robin Hood. Pyle's students (sometimes called the Brandywine School) included Maxfield Parrish (see entry), Elizabeth Shippen Green, Jessie Wilcox Smith, Harvey Dunn, N. C. Wyeth, and Frank Schoonover. About the same time came other memorable illustrators: Frederic Remington, whose roistering cowboys and vigorous Indians are now legendary; A[rthur] B[urdett] Frost, one of the best artists of rural life, renowned for illustrating Joel Chandler Harris's *Uncle Remus* stories; Reginald B. Birch, known for illustrating *Little Lord Fauntleroy*; E[dward] W[indsor] Kemble, illustrator of *Uncle Tom's Cabin* and selected by Mark Twain to do the artwork for *Huckleberry Finn*; and Daniel Carter Beard, whose satirical pen and ink drawings gave Twain's *A Connecticut Yankee in King Arthur's Court* a special edge.

American illustration in the late 19th and early 20th centuries was also greatly influenced by the rise of children's magazines (see entry). In addition to Pyle, Frost, and Birch, contributors to the magazines included some of the finest artists of the day, such as Harrison Cady, Winslow Homer, Edwin Abbey, and John La Farge, as well as cartoonist Thomas Nast (see entry). In the next several decades, advances in printing technology helped to lower production costs and liberate illustrators to explore diverse media: line, pencil, or wash drawings, lithographs, watercolor, tempera, gouache, even collage.

The Caldecott Medal, established by the American Library Association in 1938 to recognize the outstanding American picture book of the year, has honored many exceptional illustrators, notably Robert McCloskey, who mastered the comic anecdote in works like *Make Way for Ducklings;* Leo Lionni, who used his graphic design skills to develop innovative techniques; Ludwig Bemelmans, creator of the *Madeline* books; Marcia Brown, three-time medal winner and author of *Stone Soup* and other folk tales; Ezra Jack Keats, remembered for bold, beautiful interpretations of inner-city minority children; Roger Duvoisin, prolific writer-illustrator; Theodore Seuss Geisel, the beloved "Dr. Seuss" (see entry), whose Horton, Cat in the Hat, and other characters are staples of children's literature; Maurice Sendak (see entry), critically acclaimed writer and illustrator of imaginative works like *Where the Wild Things Are*; John Steptoe, whose vibrant interpretations of folk stories draw heavily on black culture; William Steig, a successful cartoonist who turned to children's illustration late in his career; and Chris Van Allsburg, creator of works like *Jumanji* and *The Polar Express* that explore the relationship between reality and dreams.

Bibliography

Bader, Barbara. *American Picturebooks from Noah's Ark to the Beast Within*. New York: Macmillan, 1976.

Bland, David. *A History of Book Illustration: The Illuminated Manuscript and the Printed Book.* London: Faber, 1969.

Estes, Glenn. *American Writers for Children since 1960: Poets, Illustrators, and Nonfiction Authors.* Detroit: Gale Research, 1987.

Klemin, Diana. *The Art of Art for Children's Books: A Contemporary Survey.* Greenwich: Murton, 1982.

Marantz, Sylvia, and Kenneth A. Marantz. *The Art of Children's Picture Books: A Selective Reference Guide.* New York: Garland, 1988.

Barbara Lupack

Photo courtesy of Popular Culture Library, Bowling Green State University, Bowling Green, OH.

Children's Literature was not considered a separate readership until at least the 1600s. Until the modern era, reading matter for children was designed primarily to convey practical advice and foster moral and spiritual betterment.

Through the Middle Ages, children were viewed as little adults, and childhood served as a training ground for adulthood. When William Caxton established England's first printing press in 1476, the material he printed for children was based on the idea that they should only read what would instruct them, such as *Caxton's Book of Curtesye* (1477), which contained rules of personal hygiene. The three books he printed that still rank among children's classics, *The History of Reynard the Fox* (1481), *The Fables of Aesop* (1484), and *The Death of Arthur* (1485), were meant originally for an adult audience. What popular literature children were exposed to came in the form of an oral tradition, including fables, folk tales, Bible stories, romances, epics, ballads, and performances by wandering minstrels and players.

The influence of Christianity, especially Puritanism, resulted in popularized versions of conversion, sainthood, didactic lessons, and stories from the Bible. John Foxe's *Book of Martyrs* (1563) dramatized the horrors of religious martyrdom and was given to children; James Janeway's *A Token for Children* (1671) impressed juvenile piety. The conviction that even young children harbored Satanic influences prompted John Bunyan's *Pilgrim's Progress* (1678), the story of a Christian soul on a pilgrimage through the world of sin to the heavenly paradise. Bunyan's saga was filled with theological moralizing but was still a moving story with compelling characters and high adventure. It remained a widely read children's book through the 19th century.

In the U.S., the first early juvenile book of importance was *The New England Primer*, published by 1691, which began its rhyming alphabet, "In Adam's fall/We sinned all." The pious thrust continued throughout the 18th century with such works as *Mary Lathrop, Who Died in Boston* (Perkins & Marvin, 1831), a story meant to guide children to righteous behavior through the lesson of Mary's virtuous death. In the 19th century, Samuel G. Goodrich, writing under the pseudonym of Peter Parley, put out numerous biographies of famous men and various pedantic non-fiction works. Jacob Abbott wrote of a boy named Rollo who bore up well under endless moralizing as he was shifted from one location to another. The second half of the century saw the didactic stories of Martha Farquharson, pseudonym of Martha Finley, whose Elsie Dinsmore books run to 26 volumes.

Notwithstanding the edifying mission of much children's literature well into the 19th century, by the 1700s, different views of children had begun to take hold, reflected in the literature of chapbooks, cheaply published pulp books that featured mostly folk tales and familiar fables (see entry). Though not expressly for them, chapbooks were popular with children, creating a new market for non-didactic juvenile reading matter. As early as 1632, John Amos Comenius, a Czech educational reformer, advanced the notion that children could be enticed to learn through interesting and appealing reading matter. John Locke's *Some Thoughts Concerning Education* (1693) stressed that children should be taught through play rather than force-fed knowledge through fear of God.

The first true imaginative literature written specifically for children was thus about to appear. The popularity of a number of works written for adults but read and loved by children helped to hurry this development: Charles Perrault's *Tales of Mother Goose* in 1696, a collection of fairy tales including "Sleeping Beauty" and "Cinderella"; and later, adventure stories like Daniel Defoe's *Robinson Crusoe* (1719), and Jonathan Swift's *Gulliver's Travels* (1726).

In 1744, a time when middle-class life began to center around home and family, John Newbery published the first in a line of books for children, *A Little Pretty Pocket-Book*. These books were intended chiefly for children's pleasure, though they retained a didactic tone. Newbery's success paved the way for others and led to a fusion of educational and entertainment objectives in children's literature. Jean-Jacques Rousseau advanced the idea that an educational program should allow the unimpeded unfolding of a personality that was by nature good, thus dispensing with the need to entice children to virtue through moral tutelage.

This idea drove the 19th-century Romantic movement in England and the U.S., which emphasized the intuitive wisdom and natural optimism that children possess. The Romantics also stressed the value of an age-old tradition as a source of cultural knowledge, residual in the stories and folklore of the common people rather than the educated literati, the upper classes, or the clergy. The importance of this shift cannot be overstated. It enabled the rise of a true popular literature in the West.

The brothers Grimm's collections of German folk tales, first published in 1812 and 1816, unleashed a flood of folk literature to readers across Europe, a trend followed by an appetite for fairy tales and folk fables in America as well. The emergence of folk literature brought with it other forms of writing for children that enhanced entertainment and reduced moralizing. An American professor, Clement Moore, wrote *A Visit from St. Nicholas* (later known as *The Night Before Christmas*) in 1822, still the classic Christmas poem for children (see entry). Lucretia Hale authored a series of stories about the Peterkin family in magazines, which were eventually collected into a widely read book in 1880. Nathaniel Hawthorne's retelling of Greek mythology, *A Wonder-book for Girls and Boys* (1853), was a refreshing antidote to the didacticism still in place in the era, though it is not as highly respected today because of a tendency to talk down to children, and because the gods and heros are pictured as overly childish. William Taylor Adams, writing as Oliver Optic, produced adventure stories for boys, and Horatio Alger (see entry) wrote *Ragged Dick* (1867) and other stories that popularized the "rags-to-riches" genre while celebrating the spunk and resourcefulness of American children. Joel Chandler Harris's Uncle Remus tales began a serious use of American racial folklore.

Beginning in the 19th century, adventure stories for children beguiled young readers (see also Adventure Fiction). In response to the abiding popularity of books like *Robinson Crusoe, Gulliver's Travels*, and *Ivanhoe* (1820), many adventure tales were published as short fiction in the various children's magazines like *St. Nicholas* or *The Youth's Companion* that flourished from mid-century onward, but adventure evolved into a book-length genre for young readers as well. Johann Wyss's *Swiss Family Robinson* (1812) was written to mimic *Robinson Crusoe* and featured a family ensconced on a tropical island. James Fenimore Cooper's pioneer novels, especially *The Last of the Mohicans* (1826), found a ready audience in children, as did Richard Henry Dana's *Two Years Before the Mast* (1840), recounting the author's own travels on the high seas.

All the ingredients of adventure—danger, derring-do, search for treasure, faraway places, colorful characters—were encompassed in Robert Louis Stevenson's splendid *Treasure Island*, first serialized in 1881 and 1882 in *Young Folks*, issued as a book in 1883. Young Jim Hawkins's escapades with the buccaneers and the memorable pirate captain Long John Silver—a villain with heroic qualities—remain as vivid today and as appealing to young readers as they were a century ago. Other Stevenson novels (*Kidnapped*, 1886, and *The Black Arrow*, 1888), also won over juvenile readers with their outlaw bands, secret identities, and dramatic rescues.

Translations of Jules Verne's science-fiction adventures (*Journey to the Center of the Earth*, 1864; *Twenty Thousand Leagues under the Sea*, 1869; and *Around the World in Eighty Days*, 1872) enlarged the parameters of the adventure genre, and capitalized on the technological revolution happening in the latter part of the century. Animal stories for children often feature adventure plots; Rudyard Kipling's *The Jungle Books* (1894-95) combined exotic locations and animal worlds, as in the story of Mowgli, a boy raised in the jungle by a wolf pack and befriended by bears and panthers. *The Yearling* (1939), *Lassie Come-Home* (1940), *Big Red* (1945), *Little Vic* (1951), *Old Yeller* (1956), and *Where the Red Fern Grows* (1961) show how the friendships and adventures shared by animals and children serve as vehicles for growth toward adulthood.

A separate category of juvenile literature, the syndicated series, evolved in America in the early 20th century, with the Stratemeyer Syndicate (see entry) leading the way. The Horatio Alger and Elsie Dinsmore series demonstrated that inexpensive, fast-paced mass produced books commanded a large audience among children. Edward Stratemeyer capitalized on this market, at first writing his own sequence of boys' books with American wars as the setting, then limiting his participation to outlining stories and hiring writers to flesh them out. The syndicate produced the Rover Boys, the Bobbsey Twins, the Motor Boys, the Hardy Boys, Nancy Drew, Tom Swift, and more than 60 other series (see entries).

Many of the teen series Stratemeyer started continue today (albeit modified to reflect changing tastes, attitudes, and heroic ideals among young people), along with other adolescent romances such as the Babysitters Club, Sweet Valley Twins, and Sweet Valley High (see Adolescent Romance Fiction). Similar sequences for younger readers are Lois Lowry's Anastasia books and Betsy Byars's Bingo Brown series. Another less respected but successful genre of books for all ages is the Choose Your Own Adventure series first developed by Edward Packard and Ray Montgomery, which allow readers to reread the books several times, choosing a different route to the end of the story each time.

Other notable trends in children's literature include fantasy, poetry, biography, and realism. Important works of fantasy span the modern age, starting with L. Frank Baum's *The Wizard of Oz* in 1900; at midcentury, E. B. White's beloved *Charlotte's Web* (1952; see entry); and later, Madeleine L'Engle's creative meshing of science fiction, theology, myth, and history in her *Time Trilogy* (beginning with *A Wrinkle in Time* in 1962)—all of which have remained popular classics since their publication. *The Hobbit* (1938) and the trilogy *Lord of the Rings* (1965), by J. R. Tolkien (see entry), were originally written for adults but have garnered a sizable juvenile audience. The imaginary "Middle-earth" setting of *The Hobbit* and its fantastical dwarfs, wizards, trolls, and dragons are particularly inventive. Lloyd Alexander's five-book high fantasy, which began in 1963 with *The Book of Three*, is another popular staple. Beginning with *Harry Potter and the Sorcerer's Stone* (1997), J. K. Rowling's series featuring an orphan who discovers he's a wizard topped the best-seller lists by fascinating both adults and children. In July 2000 the fourth book was published.

Stories of toys that come alive, a subcategory of fantasy, have long been popular with children. Living toy stories gain much of their appeal by transfiguring the domestic details of everyday life into magical fantasy—dolls, stuffed animals, and other familiar objects in a child's world become invested with extraordinary and beguiling properties. Some stories, like Hans Christian Andersen's "The Steadfast Tin Soldier" (1838, translated into English in 1846), Margery Bianco's *The Velveteen Rabbit* (1922), and the original Raggedy Ann and Raggedy Andy series (beginning with *Raggedy Ann Stories*, 1914, written and illustrated by Johnny Gruelle), work their magic by bringing toys to life at night, while children sleep. Others, like Carl Collodi's *Adventures of Pinocchio* (1881), present toy figures interacting directly with both talking animals and people. In A. A. Milne's *Winnie the Pooh* (1926; see entry), the toys are stuffed animals given imaginative life periodically by the child and his father, but return happily to their inanimate existence after storytelling time.

Poetry has always attracted children but enjoyed its heyday in America in the 19th century. Readers balanced beloved English authors (Shakespeare, Burns, Wordsworth, Coleridge, and others), available in handsome, elaborately illustrated editions, with newly popular American counterparts (Emerson, Longfellow, Holmes, Whittier, Poe, and later Eugene Field, James Whitcomb Riley, and others), whose works were published in separate editions as well as in anthologies, magazines, newspapers, almanacs, school texts, and other media. In the 20th century, notables such as Robert Frost, Carl Sandburg, Ogden Nash, John Ciardi, David McCord, Nancy Willard, and Shel Silverstein (see entry) continued to produce verse for juvenile readers, though poetry as a genre has declined in popularity and influence since at least World War II. Modern poetry for children has moved continuously away from the didacticism, sentimentality, and instructive thrust of an earlier age; newer writers emphasize humor, the oddities and eccentricities of contemporary life, and introduce darker, more ironic themes.

Children's biography has been a staple for juvenile audiences since the 19th century, told both in factual chronological narratives and fictionalized versions, and usually focusing on the lives and careers of noteworthy people—presidents, political leaders, and first ladies; war heroes; pioneers; inventors and scientists; authors; business leaders; medical heroes and heroines; and other citizens whose contributions to society have been deemed admirable. Biography is a popular genre for young readers because it conveys history and information through storytelling. Jean Fritz demonstrated that life histories could interfuse meticulous research and palatable narration. *And Then What Happened, Paul Revere?* (1973) and *Bully for You, Teddy Roosevelt!* (1991) demonstrate her lively approach. *Abraham Lincoln, Friend of the People* (1950), by Clara Ingram Judson, is a classic of the genre. Younger readers still enjoy *Ride on the Wind* (1956) by Alice Dalgliesh, about Charles Lindbergh, and now have Maryanne N. Weidt's *Stateswoman to the World: A Story about Eleanor Roosevelt* (1991). Well-known biographers for children include, among others, David Adler, Ingri and Edgar d'Aulaire, James Daugherty, Doris Faber, F. N. Monjo, Eloise Greenfield, Diane Stanley, and Elizabeth Yates.

In realistic fiction, American writers came to the fore-front by the latter half of the 18th century and remain the leaders of this mode. *Little Women* (1868-69), by Louisa May Alcott (see entry), with its excellent characterizations and vivid re-creation of domestic life, led the way. Mark Twain carried realistic fiction into a more blunt world beyond the security of the traditional family structure. In works like *The Adventures of Tom Sawyer* (1876) and *The Adventures of Huckleberry Finn* (1884), he offered youthful protagonists who went against the rules of society and yet remained attractive and morally admirable, enabling Twain to employ popular fiction for children as a tool for social and political condemnation. Frances Hodgson Burnett combined the domestic ethos of earlier writers like Alcott with a more modern understanding of dysfunctional families in stories like *Little Lord Fauntleroy* (1886) and *The Secret Garden* (1911). Laura Ingalls Wilder's *Little House* series was at the forefront of a group of excellent realistic fiction books in the 1930s and 1940s. These include Carol Ryrie Brink's chronicle of a pioneer family, *Caddie Woodlawn* (1935); Eleanor Estes's stories about the Moffet family (1941-43); Nancy Barnes's *The Wonderful Year* (1946), set on an apple ranch in Colorado; Marguerite de Angeli's *Thee, Hannah!* (1940), about a Quaker girl's rebellion; and Doris Gates's *Blue Willow* (1940), depicting a poor migrant family's struggles and triumphs. Esther Forbes's *Johnny Tremain* (1943) offered a strongly patriotic portrayal of the American Revolution in the cultural context of international conflict and the approaching cold war.

In the 1960s, realistic fiction for children shed the last vestiges of sentimentalism and veered away from narratives that promoted an old-fashioned sensibility and traditional family structures. Now, led by Louise Fitzhugh's *Harriet the Spy* (1964), children's books plunged into a candid exploration of all of the social ills, including alcoholism, divorce, murder, rape, and drug abuse. Judy Blume (see entry), taking a particular sociological problem as the center for each of her books, was instrumental in this shift. White teenage girls were her market, and they made her the best-selling writer of a literature that spoke to a new readership interested in finding expression for their real concerns, such as the arrival of menstruation and emerging sexuality. Yet many books of contemporary realism have reflected a moralizing tendency that, though not so heavy-handed or pious as in prior ages, nonetheless proffered a socially correct worldview that some have criticized.

Fortunately, the field of children's realism is such a large and diverse subgenre that excellent writers have moved it beyond narrow didacticism. Many skilled authors are currently producing among the best realistic fiction ever written for children and adolescents. A list inevitably leaves out many, but notable among them are Katherine Paterson, Robert Cormier, Virginia Hamilton, Zibby Oneal, Beverly Cleary, Patricia MacLachlan, Laurence Yep, Bruce Brooks, S. E. Hinton, Paul Zindel, and Mildred Taylor. While adolescent literature has only recently come to be defined as a separate field, many writers address both markets, demonstrating the vibrant imaginative output for young readers.

Bibliography

Aries, Philippe. *Centuries of Childhood.* New York: Knopf, 1962.

Lystad, Mary H. *From Dr. Mather to Dr. Seuss: Two Hundred Years of American Books for Children.* Boston: Hall, 1980.

MacDonald, Ruth K. *Literature for Children in England and America from 1646 to 1774.* Troy, NY: Whitson, 1982.

Meigs, Cornelie, et al. *A Critical History of Children's Literature: A Survey of Children's Books in English.* New York: Macmillan, 1969.

Townsend, John Rowe. *Written for Children: An Outline of English-Language Children's Literature.* New York: Lippincott, 1983.

Harry Eiss
Ronald Reichertz
Liahna Babener

See also
Children's Book Illustrators

Children's Magazines have been with us for over 200 years but their role in society has always been unclear. Boasting more than three million subscribers, *Highlights for Children* (1946-) is an enduring contemporary example of the juvenile miscellanies that flourished after the American Civil War. Its masthead—"Fun with a Purpose"—poses the editorial challenge that has faced children's periodicals since 1789, when *The Children's Magazine* lasted only four seminal issues: Is it possible to edify and entertain at the same time?

Cultural historian R. Gordon Kelly argues that *The Children's Magazine* was too much "wrapped in the sober mantle of pedagogy," boring youngsters with a milk-and-water version of adult prescriptions. More successful was the philosophy that undergirded a later children's periodical: "Most children do not want to be bothered nor amused nor petted," observed Mary Mapes Dodge in 1873 as she embarked upon her fabled 42-year editorship of *St. Nicholas,* an attitude that suggests why *St. Nicholas* became the preeminent children's magazine of its day.

By the 1840s, reform-minded organizations from the American Sunday School Union to the American Temperance Union produced the bulk of children's weeklies. On the commercial side were the wider-read secular publications like *Merry's Museum* (1841-72) and *The Youth's Companion* (1826-1929). When Erastus S. Beadle brought out *The Youth's Casket* (1852), a prototype for the successful series of dime fictions that would define *Frank Leslie's Boys and Girls Weekly* (1867-83), the rough-and-tumble world of adventure joined the genteel and the repentant as a third niche for 19th-century concepts of childhood, though all such periodicals retained a didactic bent and reflected the broader cultural project of infusing ideals of democratic citizenship into youthful readers.

The late 19th and early 20th centuries represented the commercial and artistic golden age of children's periodicals, when a pantheon of literary miscellanies flourished. *St. Nicholas* alone featured the initial serializations of *Little Lord Fauntleroy, Tom Sawyer Abroad,* and *The Jungle Book.* With the growth of other media—radio, and eventually television and film—the miscellanies began a gradual decline.

With the introduction of magazines like *Girls Companion* (1902-49), *Boys' Life* (1911-), and *The American Girl* (1917-79), the dominant modern trend of segmenting the youth market into gendered categories had begun. As children's magazines have become more specialized, they have been designed to appeal to more circumscribed age categories. For example, *Humpty Dumpty* is for children aged 4 to 6; *Children's Playmate* is for those aged 6 to 8, and *Child Life* is written for those aged 9 to 11. Ethnic divisions—*Ebony Jr!*—are a further development of this century.

Many children's magazines are used for instructional purposes by schools. In the 1940s, 1950s, and 1960s, the *Weekly Reader* served as a prominent pedagogical aid. *Junior Scholastic,* which focuses on social studies, is still issued. Other contemporary magazines that serve educational functions include *Scholastic Sprint* for language arts; *Scholastic Dynamath* and *Zillions* for math; *National Geographic World* and *Ranger Rick* for nature; *Science World* and *Odyssey* for science; *Calliope* for history; and numerous others built around subject matters of academic and general interest. Literary periodicals no longer valorize the classics, focusing instead on more contemporary writers and themes; *Lady Bug* is for very young children, and *Stone Soup* features stories, poems, reviews, and art by children.

In the 1990s, when magazines like *Nintendo Power* compete with perennial stalwarts like *Sesame Street Magazine,* it is evident that the abiding debate about whether children's magazines should entertain or instruct remains central to the genre, affirming that the study of American children's periodicals probably tells us more about the imperatives of adults than it will ever reveal about children.

Bibliography

Kelly, R. Gordon. *Children's Periodicals of the United States.* Westport: Greenwood, 1984.

——. *Mother Was a Lady: Self and Society in Selected American Periodicals, 1865-1890.* Westport: Greenwood, 1974.

Mott, Frank Luther. *A History of American Magazines.* 5 vols. Cambridge: Harvard UP, 1938-68.

Richardson, Selma K. *Magazines for Children: A Guide for Parents, Teachers, and Librarians.* Chicago: American Library Association, 1991.

Dale Rigby

See also
Children's Book Illustrators

Children's Network Programming. "Tomorrow's children, through the great new medium of Television, will be enrolled in a world university before they leave their cradles.... Think what this means." So proclaimed a 1945 advertisement for the Allen B. DuMont Laboratories, and within a very few years what has come to be known as the "television generation" was born. Television sets became available for purchase by the general public in 1946 and by 1947 children were already being encouraged to "tune in" as audience members by televised puppets Howdy Doody and Jerry

Mahoney, and their respective human co-hosts, "Buffalo Bob" Smith, and Paul Winchell. When WABD New York broadcast America's first full day of programming on September 21, 1948, it was a schedule created "for the whole family," yet one which clearly distinguished between programs intended for adults and those intended for children. The full-day schedule was "designed to coincide with the average housewife's routine," explained Mortimer Loewi of DuMont Labs; "when the housewife has to wash the dishes or fix luncheon, for instance, there will be programs designed to keep preschool children occupied and out of her way."

Children's television is distinguished by the following factors: (1) they are programs created with an audience of children aged 2-12 in mind; (2) attempting to capture the attention of children rather than adults, these programs are predominantly scheduled in non-prime time hours; and (3) it is the only television genre to develop primarily through independent stations and syndicated programming rather than at the network level. Historically, the earliest children's programs were the variety or mixed entertainment shows which combined the humor and melodrama of puppetry with musical entertainment, animated theater shorts (early cartoons), and games played by adult hosts with a "live studio audience" composed of children. *Howdy Doody* (1947-60) and *The Paul Winchell Show* (with Jerry Mahoney), which ran in syndication from 1947 through the late 1950s, are the earliest examples of this programming, followed by two-time Emmy winner *Judy Splinters* (late 1940s-early 1950s), *Rootie Kazootie* (1952-54), *Children's Corner* with future public television "neighbors" Fred Rogers and Josie Carey (1955), the *Mickey Mouse Club* (1955-59), the various Shari Lewis shows (from "Hi, Mom" of 1957 to *Lamb Chop's Play-Along* in 1991), and the enduring *Kukla, Fran, and Ollie* (NBC, 1949-54, ABC, 1954-57, NET, 1969-70, and PBS, 1970-71) with puppets "little man" Kukla, Oliver J. Dragon, and host Fran Allison.

Early programming intended for children also included a number of "educational" shows that originally aired on network and independent commercial television stations. Beginning with schoolteacher Pat Meikle's genteel instruction in art and literature from the cozy setting of *The Magic Cottage* (DuMont, 1949-53), the 1950s saw the introduction of NBC's equally magical exploration into science with experiments conducted by the engaging Don Herbert (*Mr. Wizard,* 1951-65) as well as the first electronic preschool, *Ding Dong School* ("taught" for NBC by Dr. Frances Horwich, 1952-56 and syndicated in 1959), and its independent station alternative and competitor, *Romper Room*, syndicated in 1953. In 1955, Sonny Fox began his three-year stint as a children's tour-guide, leading excursions around the world on the junior travelogue, *Let's Take a Trip* and CBS opened its own network preschool named after its tutor, *Captain Kangaroo* (see entry). *Winky Dink and You* (CBS, 1953-57 and continuing in syndication) made the most innovative use of the television medium. Host Jack Barry encouraged children at home to "help out Winky Dink" by drawing on their own television screens with a wax crayon to provide a missing link or prop (i.e., a crosswalk needed to get Winky

Dink—"and you"—across the street safely) so that each day's adventure could continue.

Both children's variety and educational formats faltered commercially in the early 1960s and would primarily survive through the establishment of non-commercial "public television" networks such as National Educational Television (NET, 1962), which would become the Public Broadcasting Service (PBS) in 1969 (see Children's Public Television). The commercial networks made only tentative attempts at similar programming, such as ABC's *Schoolhouse Rock* (originating in 1972 as a series of "educational inserts"), *Take a Giant Step* (NBC, 1971-72), and *Rainbow Sundae* (ABC/O&O, 1974-75). Hence, the two earliest television formats intended explicitly for children, educational and variety programming, have been sustained primarily on public television and presently constitute a minor portion of commercial network programming.

Animal series constituted a third category of early programming intended for children but which were in actuality the first "family shows," as the writers reached out to include adult viewers through weekly melodramas. 1954 saw the introduction of two series built around "man's best friend": as German shepherd Rin Tin Tin came to the rescue of his human companions each week, Lassie the collie (see entry) began an 18-year series of original adventures, undergoing six changes in program format before Lassie was called home for the final episode in 1972. Following the lead of these canine American heroes, horses were the next group of stars from the animal kingdom. In 1955, *Fury* (also known as *The Brave Stallion*) began his 11-year run on NBC protecting his human caretakers from the dangers of marauding strangers, natural disasters, and wild animals, while *My Friend Flicka* appeared in a similar series focused around the relationship of mutual nurturing between the gentle Flicka and members of her human family (CBS, 1956-59, ABC, 1959-61, CBS, 1961-64), and in 1960, *National Velvet* was translated from novel and film into a series highlighting Velvet's steed and companion, King. By the mid-1960s, a porpoise named *Flipper* (1964-67) as well as Judy the chimpanzee and Clarence the lion of *Daktari* (1966-69) joined television's canine and equine stars in dramatic series targeted for "family" audiences.

There is, however, a fourth category of network programming that meets the distinguishing criteria for children's television and which has been commercially successful in sustaining corporate sponsors as well as keeping the attention of the audience of children. It is the televised cartoon: animated programming that is intended for and watched by children aged 2 to 11 (see Cartoons: Theatrical and Television).

Many of the early televised cartoons (i.e., *Popeye, Roadrunner*) were the short animated strips produced for use in movie theaters, simply transferred to television broadcasting. With sound film moving at the speed of 24 frames per second, theatrical animation was a creative art in which each individual frame was completely redrawn to achieve a fluid portrayal of an infinite variety of complex character movements. "Fully animated," more than half of the frames in the televised theatrical cartoons (as well as the early "made for television" cartoons which soon joined them) were wholly unique drawings. Earning the nickname "radio with pictures," cartoon dialogue duplicated or at best elaborated upon the narrative unfolding through the visual action on screen. Indeed, the voices of cartoon characters became at least as memorable as their on-screen animation: if there is a common voice echoing in the post-World War II American imagination, surely it is that of Mel Blanc in one of his various incarnations as *Porky Pig* or *Bugs Bunny* (ABC and CBS, 1960-75); their pals Daffy Duck, Sylvester the Cat and Tweety; Barney Rubble of *The Flintstones* (ABC, 1960-66; rebroadcast on NBC, 1967-70) and Mr. Spacely of *The Jetsons* (ABC/CBS/NBC, 1962-75).

When cartoonist Walter Lantz created *Woody Woodpecker* (ABC, 1957-58, syndicated 1958; NBC, 1970-72), it was his wife, Grace, who gave voice to Woody's familiar if annoying woodpecker's call. Working together, the Lantzes were only one of several creative teams in the emerging film animation industry. The joint efforts of Jay Ward and Alexander Anderson produced television's first cartoon series, *Crusader Rabbit,* in 1949, but it was the hybrid productions of Bill Hanna and Joe Barbera that demonstrated how truly fertile collaborative efforts could be. Appropriately, a cat-and-dog team were the stars of Hanna-Barbera's first cartoon for television (as well as the first cartoon to air on Saturday mornings), *Ruff and Ready* (NBC, 1957-60 and 1962-64, then syndicated), which was followed by a stream of successful cooperative ventures in syndication and network television. Huckleberry Hound's slow-paced search for his role in life (1958) was countered by the manic antics of the more members of the Hanna-Barbera cast: mice Pixie and Dixie, Yogi Bear and Boo Boo (see entry). Mr. Jinks the cat, and Hokey Wolf. In 1959, Hanna-Barbera produced *Quick Draw McGraw*, spoofing adult Westerns of the 1950s with their equine sheriff attempting to maintain law and order with the help of Baba Looey the burro, Doggie Daddy (Deputy Dawg) and son Auggie Doggie, and introducing the mouse detective team, Snooper and Blabber. The next year, Hanna-Barbera gave Deputy Dawg his own show, syndicated *Wally Gator* in his adventures with Snagglepuss, and created *The Flintstones* (see entry). As the 1960s came to a close, Hanna-Barbera dominated children's television, as nearly all of the preceding programs continued in syndication in addition to *Touché Turtle* (syndicated 1962), *The Jetsons*, *Peter Potamus* (syndicated 1964), *Space Ghost* (CBS, 1966-68), *Herculoids*, *Moby Dick and the Mighty Mightor*, and *Shazzan!* (all CBS, 1967-69), and kidvid's animated best friend, *Scooby-Doo* (CBS, 1969-74), among others.

Such cartoons quickly began to dominate children's television (especially on Saturday mornings) and brought with them some less admirable elements, most of which were due to an emphasis on profitability. "Limited" animation, for instance, sacrificed visually fluid movement for a less costly bottom line. Furthermore, the programming was repetitious: by the end of the 1960s, networks were playing episodes of even moderately successful series an average of six times over two years.

But by far most noticeable was the proliferation of advertising during children's programming, ever since the first toy commercial (for Mattel's "Burp Gun") aired in 1955 during the *Mickey Mouse Club*. In the late 1950s and into the 1960s, up to 16 minutes per hour of network programming on Saturday and Sunday mornings was commercial "non-program material" (even as the industry code ceiling for prime time was 9.5 minutes).

In the late 1960s, this trend eventually resulted in toy-based programming or program-length commercials (PLCs), first seen in the animated *Hot Wheels* series (ABC, 1969-71) based on the tiny toy race cars of the same name brought out by Mattel in 1968. The existence of the animated characters usually preceded the production of related toys and food items; however, combined efforts in the late 1970s among executives of the American Greeting Card Corporation, General Mills, and General Mills' Kenner Toys led to the simultaneous creation of a doll and a greeting card character, "Strawberry Shortcake" (1980), who was soon to appear in a series of animated television "specials" as well as on a line of lunch boxes, school accessories, and toiletry items.

Long before the multi-industry birth of "Strawberry Shortcake," the favorable ratings and related sales figures of PLCs were accompanied by public consternation which led to the formation of industry watchdog organizations such as Action for Children's Television (ACT, founded by critic Peggy Charen in 1968). ABC eventually withdrew the *Hot Wheels* series in response to a critical opinion statement issued by the Federal Communications Commission (FCC) in 1969 regarding network commercial policies. As PLCs continued to appear on local stations and on network "specials," ACT strengthened and supported the FCC's 1974 policy statement barring PLCs and calling for the use of audio-visual devices such as "pop-up" educational minutes and pro-social "mortar messages" to demarcate program and commercial boundaries.

Federal deregulation in 1984 meant that commercial policies ceased to be an FCC consideration for license renewal and the network PLC race was on. The mid-1980s saw the beginning of an apparently endless line of PLCs ranging from the candy-based *Gummi Bears* to the robotic toy-based *Transformers*. Pop-ups and pro-social messages continue in use at present but function as segues rather than separators, allowing an intertextual flow between programs and advertisements that fosters the perception of children's television as a seamless and comprehensive universe. While some critics see this unification of entertainment, information, and suasion as a particularly insidious form of propaganda when produced for an audience of assumedly naive and impressionable children, others like critic Tom Engelhardt have pointed out that it is exactly in this sense that children's commercial programming is "our truest educational television" and that it is "propaganda" only as it is "meant to sell our own lives to our children."

The validity of Engelhardt's claim is evident in the actual content of children's television. If all television genres demonstrate the pervasively ideological nature of commercial programming, nowhere are the "ruling ideas" and values of post-war America as predominant and explicit as they are in the world of children's television. This is especially true for animated programming where the nearly uniform representation of American society has historically been, and for the most part remains, ethnocentrically middle-class in its value orientation and homogeneously WASP in the wielding of economic and political power.

The earliest cartoons made specifically for television, *The Telecomics* (NBC, 1950-51, also known as *The NBC Comics*; CBS, 1951; syndicated and withdrawn), rotated four animated series which directly responded to these concerns. Simultaneously addressing fears of personal invasion and alienation, two of the four *Telecomics* series had central characters who were lifted out of their dissatisfactory lives and gained heroic stature by becoming "crime-fighters": *Danny March* as the orphaned "tough kid" who turned his street-smarts to fighting crime and became the Mayor's "personal detective," and Eddie Hale, who trained to be a prizefighter to please his father, instead pursuing his own dream of becoming a musician, only to emerge as *Kid Champion*, fighting for justice and championing the dreams of others.

As children's programming expanded throughout the 1950s and into the early 1960s, animated heroes engaged in similar one-on-one struggles for identity and justice as their wit and cunning provided slapstick entertainment but with one major difference: they were no longer human heroes but were instead animals or other anthropomorphized beings. In addition to the earlier *Crusader Rabbit, Casper the Friendly Ghost* (1953), crows *Heckle and Jeckle* (1955), *Ruff and Ready, Woody Woodpecker, Porky Pig, Bugs Bunny* and *Roadrunner* (1949), *Huckleberry Hound, Quick Draw McGraw, Hokey Wolf, Wally Gator,* and *Touché Turtle*, we have, to name just a few, the adventures of *Mighty Mouse* and *Yogi Bear* (syndicated 1958), *Lippy the Lion* (and his laconic hyena sidekick, Hardy Har Har; syndicated 1962), penguin *Tennessee Tuxedo* (syndicated 1963), *Magilla Gorilla* (syndicated 1964), and *Felix the Cat* (syndicated 1960), whose magic black bag was sought after by the animated human secondary characters, the Professor and Poindexter. A comparison of this abbreviated list against the relative absence of human characters other than *Gerald McBoing-Boing* (CBS 1956-58), the *Telecomics* heroes, the ever-resourceful *Popeye* (syndicated 1958), hapless hunter Elmer Fudd of the *Bugs Bunny Show*, and boy-child Beany of *Beany and Cecil* (syndicated 1961; see entry), more than suggests that while Americans found humor in the foibles and frustrations of these non-human characters as they struggled against evildoers, fought with their neighbors, and generally tried to outwit each other in situations and contexts that otherwise replicated contemporary society, the use of human characters in such all-too-familiar circumstances was avoided as a more likely source of ire in the copacetic context of the immediate postwar period.

Secret passages and underground activities were also the subject of *Tom of T.H.U.M.B.* (ABC, 1966-69), which was the first cartoon to reflect the specific sociopolitical context of America's increasingly controversial involvement in Vietnam: it chronicled the investigations of two miniature human heroes, young American Tom and his Asian assistant "Swinging Jack," agents of a "secret United States government office" known as the "Tiny Humans Underground Military Bureau." Tom and Jack soon had equally tiny counterparts on *Fantastic Voyage* (ABC, 1968-70), which traced the adventures of the "C.M.D.F.," the secret U.S. government "Combined Miniature Defense Force" whose agents were capable of reducing evil problems as well as evil persons to microscopic size. While the presentation of heroic characters as team members of covert agencies seeking power and control through information management may imply the resourcefulness and implied goodness of bureaucratic institutions, the miniaturization of the human characters as well as the extensive use of acronyms to convey human agency indicates an imaginative perspective that is overwhelmed by the world-at-large (and perhaps by the world-at-war) and dehumanized through bureaucratic abstractions. As an imaginative construct, the necessary existence of the "C.M.D.F." reveals a view of the United States as a nation faced with conflicts too large in scale to be "handled" and in need of some (scientific) magic that might bring the conflicts down to a more "manageable size."

As protest against America's involvement in the war in Vietnam reached its peak, a new series was introduced that returned to the earlier model of the individual American hero. In *Here Comes the Grump* (NBC, 1969-71), a magic land was put under the "curse of gloom" by the evil Grump. American hero Terry and his dog Bob are magically transported to help Princess Dawn, unaffected by the curse and searching for "the secret cave of the whispering orchids" where the "crystal key" that will break the curse is hidden. Structured to highlight the essential nature of the struggle between forces of good and forces of evil in the context of an unknowable and mystical foreign land, *Here Comes the Grump* also offered a parable of justification and explanation for American expansionist involvement in foreign lands. Ironically, no matter how successful Terry's episodic efforts were, his frustrating failure to actually oust the Grump was necessary to sustain the series narrative from week to week. Hence, as the United States commitment in Vietnam continued in similar fashion toward defeat, *Here Comes the Grump* continued with only momentary victories for Terry, and it was the mysterious and impenetrable nature of the native culture which explained Terry's inability, despite his good intentions and his ingenuity, to end the reign of the evil Grump.

If Terry's failure to achieve his objectives was defensible, in the animated programming of the late 1960s to the mid-1970s, human characters overall did not fare very well in managing much less mastering the world around them. Various sorts of "bumblers" were the hapless lead characters of several short-lived series, with a very few, such as *George of the Jungle* (ABC, 1967-70), enjoying somewhat longer lives. In this klutzy version of *Tarzan* ("Watch out for that tree!"), a cry for help or an observation of some injustice led the inept George to swing—or crash—his way to the rescue. A secondary series of episodes within the *George of the Jungle* time slot followed the adventures of "Super Chicken," a mild-mannered scientist who concocted a secret formula ("super sauce") transforming him into a daring crimefighter. While recalling the earlier *Telecomics* plotlines of heroes Danny March and Kid Champion, Super Chicken's reliance on his "super sauce" rather than on his own force of character paralleled the late 1960s need for magical assistance evident in *Tom of T.H.U.M.B.* and *Fantastic Voyage*.

Yet another compatriot on *George of the Jungle* was Tom Slick the dull-minded race driver, a secondary series which served to introduce automobile racing as a regular subject for animated children's programming. By 1968, *Wacky Racers* (CBS, 1968-70) brought the driver-as-villain to the cross-country racing world through melodramatic characterization of Dick Dastardly, and the Japanese production of *Speed Racer* (syndicated 1967) highlighted both car and driver as it tracked the daring routes of a young driver and his "Special Formula Mark Five." It was not until 1969, however, with the creation of *Hot Wheels* (ABC, 1969-71) that the automobiles themselves became the central cast of characters.

While many of the early (pre-1966) cartoon series with their anthropomorphized characters would continue in syndication throughout the 1970s, with the notable exception of the "displaced" *Flintstones* and *Jetsons*, few of the series developed in the mid to late 1960s would survive into the 1970s. The decade opened with the children's literary classic *The Wind in the Willows* loosely translated into a cartoon version for *The Reluctant Dragon and Mr. Toad* (ABC, 1970-72); however, such literature-based series would once again be given wider berth on public broadcasting qua educational networks rather than in the commercial market. Instead, the writers and producers of commercial children's television turned to popular culture for its models: a rock group became the prototype for the animated cast of *The Osmonds* (ABC, 1972-74), animation revived beloved animal star Lassie for *Lassie's Rescue Rangers* (ABC, 1973-75), and two new series, *My Favorite Martians* (CBS, 1973-75) and the *New Adventures of Gilligan* (ABC, 1974) were animated versions of popular situation comedies.

Similarly, Hanna-Barbera's *Super Friends* (ABC, 1973-77) followed adventures of superhuman comic book heroes Aquaman, Batman and Robin, Superman, and Wonder Woman, who (along with teenage "Wonder Twins" Wendy and Marvin and their sidekick, Wonder Dog) formed the animated "Justice League of America." Presuming the insufficiency of mere mortal human beings in the face of contemporary problems, the Superfriends met at the "Hall of Justice" in Washington, DC, made individual and cooperative use of their superhuman powers to "fight injustice, right that which is wrong and serve all mankind," and regrouped at the end of each episode with their pro-social and pro-environmental missions accomplished. Syndicated in 1983 and rebroadcast on ABC from 1981-85, the success of *Super Friends* led to the production of four spinoffs (*The All-New Super Friends Hour*, ABC, 1977-78; *Challenge of the Super Friends*, ABC, 1978-79; *The World's Greatest Super Friends*, ABC, 1979-80; *The Super Friends Hour*, ABC, 1980-81) which combined re-runs with new episodes that extended and revised the original format and characterizations.

Extraordinary capabilities were also granted on *Wheelie and the Chopper Bunch* (NBC, 1974-75)—in this case to anthropomorphized vehicles rather than human characters—as protagonist Wheelie the Volkswagen engaged in weekly struggles to limit and fend off the mischievous deeds and evil forays of the motorcycle "Chopper Bunch." Short-lived as a series in itself, *Wheelie and the Chopper Bunch* is of particular note as the precursor to the numerous series featuring vehicles as super-heroes that would come to distinguish commercial children's programming in the 1980s and into the 1990s. Although network programming explicitly for children experienced a temporary decline of over 50% between 1979 and 1983 (from an average of 11.3 hours per week to a mere 4.4 hours), independent stations filled the gap with expanded afternoon blocks of syndicated series, and, with de-regulation in 1984, syndicated series took the lead in the renewed market of "program-length commercials" (PLCs).

Emerging in the pro-defense "Star Wars" context of the Reagan administration, several of the new PLCs featured superheroes who defended "the universe" against both native and "alien" evil forces and resolved conflicts through high-tech intergalactic combat. Expanding upon the successful format of the *Superfriends* series, *He-Man and the Masters of the Universe* (syndicated 1983; see entry) were animated heroes with high-tech weaponry who were engaged in an endless battle against evil forces seeking to wreak havoc upon the civilized universe. In a spinoff series introduced two years later, *She-Ra: Princess of Power* (syndicated 1985; see entry), He-Man's sister used her "sword of protection" to achieve gender equality as well as repeated victories over a group of evildoers known as "the horde"—all of which (sword, villains, and She-Ra herself) were also available from Mattel for at-home parallel play.

If the *Superfriends* were the plot prototype for *He-Man* and *She-Ra*, President Reagan's metaphorical construct of a technologically advanced "evil empire" which the "forces of good" must prepare equally high-tech defenses against was played out in an even more lucrative pair of PLCs: *Challenge of the Gobots* (syndicated in March of 1986; character products c. Tonka) and *Transformers* (syndicated in September of 1986; character products by Hasbro). Both *Gobots* and *Transformers* featured the use of transformable robotics and presumed an adversarial universe in which benevolent leaders sought to protect citizens at large against attack and invasion from power-hungry dictators and tyrants.

Children's programming in 1990 included the extension of He-Man in the *New Adventures of He-Man* (syndicated 1990) along with arrival of the earthbound PLC *Teenage Mutant Ninja Turtles* (CBS, 1990) promoting pro-social values of brotherhood and altruism along with the strike and shield defense techniques of the martial arts. The *Mighty Morphin Power Rangers* (Fox, 1993-present; produced by Saban Entertainment and character products by Bandai America) appeared and became an instantaneous cultural phenomenon. Like the animated human team of the *Gobots* series, the Power Rangers are a real-life group of culturally diverse teenagers who transform or "morph" into fighting dinosaur robots called "Dino-Zords." They have become Power Rangers through the instruction of their leader

Zordon, "the force of good," who regularly reminds the Rangers that "the power of the universe is in your hands." As a live-action rather than an animated series, Power Rangers has led the toy market through the sale of costumes and life-size props as well as toy "action figures." As might have been expected, the fall of 1994 saw "copycat" series such as the syndicated *V.R. Troopers* and *SuperHuman Samurai Syber-Squad* (both produced by Saban Entertainment) as well as USA Network's *Tattooed Teenage Alien Fighters from Beverly Hills*.

The highly successful *Bobby's World* (Fox, 1988-96) was a sustained anomaly in this hyperreal world of animated superheroes. Created by comedian Howie Mandel, *Bobby's World* followed the literally down-to-earth adventures of toddling four-year-old Bobby Generic. Another anomaly is Nickelodeon's Emmy-winning *Rugrats* (1991-), which views the world through the eyes of toddlers. Nevertheless, the PLC is still alive and well, in such shows as *Pokémon* (WB, 1998-), based on the extremely popular card and video games produced by Nintendo.

If Peggy Charen's description of children's commercial television as "an animated world of meanness and mayhem" is understandable, it is one that misses the fundamental significance of children's television as a cultural institution, reflecting adult beliefs and values as it offers a realm of hopefulness and empowerment to the next generation. Writing in response to attempted censorship of children's literature in Britain, G. K. Chesterton argued that "fairy tales do not give the child the idea of the evil or the ugly; that is in the world already.... What fairy tales give the child is his first clear idea of the possible defeat of bogey." Whatever else we might bemoan about the world of children's commercial television, its animated evildoers and superheroes are in fact part of an imaginative universe that is in the final analysis *pro-child*.

Bibliography

Comstock, George, and Haejung Paik. *Television and the American Child.* San Diego: Academic, 1991.
Engelhardt, Tom. "Children's Television: The Shortcake Strategy." *Watching Television.* Ed. Todd Gitlin. New York: Pantheon, 1987.
MacDonald, J. Fred. *One Nation under Television.* New York: Pantheon, 1990.
Palmer, Edward L. *Children in the Cradle of Television.* Lexington, MA: Heath, 1987.
Woolery, George. *Children's Television: The First 35 Years, 1946-1981.* Metuchen, NJ: Scarecrow, 1985.

Pamela Steinle

Children's Public Television has always been situated on the edge of culture and entertainment, not sure of its place and role. The corporate culture surrounding the pre-World War II development of radio and television contrasted sharply with a simultaneously emerging culture concerned with the scientific rearing of children. Trying to fit an educational agenda, such as co-opting newly opened channels for the public good, into an inherently commercial enterprise resulted in an awkward mixing of the two cultures.

In 1950, the Joint Committee (later renamed Council) on Educational Television was formed. While it attracted only moderate public interest, it paved the way to a series of research studies, underwritten by the Ford Foundation, to tabulate the number of violent scenes depicted on commercial television. Educators hoped that they could use these tabulations as evidence that counterprogramming, in the form of reserved educational channels, was needed.

In 1952, the Federal Communications Commission (FCC), under Frieda B. Hennock, agreed by establishing Channels 2 through 13 in the VHF (very high frequency) band and 70 new channels in the UHF (ultra high frequency) band as educational channels. Hennock had effected a creative compromise. Tapping the higher frequency channels had long been advocated by the commercial broadcasters, who felt themselves increasingly crowded on the existing frequencies. And Hennock's "price" for opening up the new frequencies was to immediately set aside channel access for educational and public interest television programming. Unfortunately, her solution to balancing the two competing interests proved shallow, since she had not provided for the financing of these new educational stations. America's first educational station, KUHT in Houston, went on the air in May 1953. Los Angeles's KTHE debuted shortly thereafter, but quickly failed and folded by Christmas. The main stumbling block continued to be money.

In 1953, Fred McFeely Rogers (1928-), struck by the insane comedic antics of early television performers, believed that the medium had far greater potential and apprenticed himself at NBC. Rogers excelled in the medium, advancing to floor director on *The Kate Smith Hour* within a short two years. In 1953, Rogers abruptly left commercial television, his interest piqued by plans to open WQED-TV, Pittsburgh's proposed public television station made available by Hennock's channel access arrangement a year earlier. One of the dozens of stations loosely affiliated under the banner of National Educational Television (NET), WQED-TV was not even on the air when Rogers joined. Within a year, however, Rogers and co-producer Josie Carey debuted with *Children's Corner*, a half-hour puppet show that aired on WQED from 1954 until 1961. Rogers and Carey's *Children's Corner* won the 1955 Sylvania Award as the best locally produced children's television show in America. It was a good beginning.

At the same time that Rogers was helping to put WQED (Channel 12) on the air, similar initiatives were underway in Boston and New York. New York's educational television began on WNET (Channel 13) and Boston's on WGBH (Channel 2). In some parts of the country, universities or community organizations tried to start their own stations, responding to the continuing support of the Ford Foundation and to the Kennedy administration's Educational Television Facilities Act of 1962, which provided $32 million in grants for new station construction. These grants enabled in-classroom instructional television to operate in thousands of elementary schools across America, offering primarily arts, music, and religious instruction. Overall, however, growth for NET was belabored by high setup costs, low-quality programming, and a still undefined audience.

National Educational Television remained in stasis until 1967, when the Carnegie Commission, created as a privately financed presidential commission by Lyndon B. Johnson in 1965, authorized a broad sweeping review of educational television's management, programming, and audience. The assessment was long overdue. By the end of 1967, there were 132 local educational stations nominally affiliated with NET, reaching nearly three-quarters of all American households. Children's programming, which had been Commissioner Hennock's primary interest in 1952, was frequently bypassed in favor of public affairs and cultural programming. Ironically, children were becoming increasingly isolated from educational television.

In January 1967, the Carnegie Commission on Educational Television issued its report, *Public Television: A Program for Action*. The commission urged dissolving the bureaucratic and loosely organized NET system and replacing it with a more centralized organization that could create as well as distribute original programming and serve as a focal point for what the commission titled "public," rather than the more exclusive "educational" television. Equally important, the Carnegie Commission stressed a return to NET's original emphasis on children's programming, especially preschool programming, in order to give lower income or minority children an early introduction to literacy.

President Johnson, fulfilling his Great Society agenda, acted swiftly on the Carnegie Commission's recommendations. On November 7, 1967, he signed the Public Broadcasting Act, which created the nonprofit Corporation for Public Broadcasting (CPB), a centralized agency that distributes federal grant allocations to local stations. The commission had advocated CPB's creation to guarantee a smoother and more predictable cash flow to public television. Shortly thereafter, the reorganization of American public television was completed with the Carnegie and Ford Foundation-sponsored formation of the Public Broadcasting Service (PBS), a membership organization that distributes programming to the increasingly large number of local public television stations. With a strong central core in place, plans were made to launch an experimental children's educational program that would test both the workability of the new system and the very future of children's public television itself. That experiment was called *Sesame Street*.

Without a doubt, *Sesame Street* has become one of the most influential and popular programs in the history of television, public or commercial. From its debut on November 10, 1969, to its 25th anniversary in 1994, *Sesame Street* had earned 51 Emmy Awards, two George Foster Peabody Awards, four Parents' Choice Awards, and an Action for Children's Television (ACT) Special Achievement Award.

The maiden project of the Children's Television Workshop (CTW, founded in 1968 by Lloyd Morrisett and Joan Ganz Cooney) was an experimental preschool educational show that would teach basic instruction in mathematical and language literacy using the clipped pace, rapid imaging, and catchy jingoes proven successful on children's network television, especially in cartoons and commercials. To create and monitor the curriculum content of the show, CTW amassed an impressive educational advisory board made up of the most prominent names in preschool educational theory, psychology, and practice. Each script was carefully constructed, debated, and then reconstructed to meet well-defined cognitive, social, and affective goals. To translate those goals to the screen, Cooney hired one of America's leading young puppeteers, Jim Henson, to create the cast of characters that have become the physical embodiment of preschool education on television (see Jim Henson Productions).

The simplicity and sincerity of Henson's Muppets (a unique blend of marionette and puppet) combined with the real literacy skills that children were quickly learning made *Sesame Street* into a renowned hit. The show proved that public television, even children's educational television, could work. It was not a foregone conclusion before 1970 and the success of the show secured the economic viability and educational legitimacy of children's educational programming on public television. A second show with equally important ramifications for children's television was *Mr. Rogers' Neighborhood*, a children's show hosted by *Children's Corner* veteran Fred Rogers.

CTW launched its second educational show, *The Electric Company,* in 1971 as a reading series for children 7 to 10 years old. In 1980, *3-2-1 Contact* followed, then in 1987, *Square One TV*, two math shows for those 8 to 12 years old. In 1972, Boston's WGBH created *The Spider's Web*, a 30-minute show of stories, poetry, and folk songs. In the last decade, *Reading Rainbow*, *Zoobilee Zoo*, *Big Blue Marble*, *Zoom*, *Shining Time Station*, *Lamb Chop's Play-Along, Barney,* and *Arthur* have captivated child audiences and proven the viability of children's educational programming. Still, funding issues continue to be the paramount obstacle confronting the Corporation for Public Broadcasting and the Public Broadcasting Service as they seek to fund and distribute high-caliber programming.

To wrest some control over its own funding, CTW has aggressively licensed its *Sesame Street* characters, to provide revenues to offset the vagaries of federal and corporate funding. In 1993, CTW generated over $30 million in licensing revenues and launched a series of *Sesame Street* boutique stores, drawing upon the successful outlets owned and operated by Walt Disney Productions.

Bibliography

Barnouw, Erik. *Tube of Plenty: The Evolution of American Television*. 2d ed. New York: Oxford UP, 1990.

Cater, Douglass, and Michael J. Nyhan, eds. *The Future of Public Broadcasting*. New York: Praeger, 1976.

Fischer, Stuart. *Kids' TV: The First 25 Years*. New York: Facts on File, 1983.

Palmer, Edward L. *Television and America's Children: A Crisis of Neglect*. New York: Oxford UP, 1988.

Polsky, Richard M. *Getting to Sesame Street: Origins of the Children's Television Workshop*. New York: Praeger, 1974.

Kathleen D. Toerpe

Children's Radio has played a significant part in the history of broadcasting. During radio's golden age (roughly 1930 to 1955) children's programs were an important segment of the free entertainment aired to millions of listeners on a daily basis. Children's radio took over the airwaves every afternoon after school, and the 5:00 to 6:00 P.M. time slot became known as the children's hour. Shows were also scheduled in the surrounding time periods. Saturday morning, which became the home of children's television programming, also had some children's radio programs. Most featured storytellers and radio "uncles" and targeted the younger child. But the late afternoon shows were taken over by the genre known as thriller dramas, roughly equivalent to television's action adventure shows. These programs made up the vast majority of children's radio, and set the tone for children's television.

Most of the thrillers were serials, with the cliffhanger endings guaranteed to keep the youngsters tuning in day after day. The earliest radio serial was *Little Orphan Annie*, which came to the air in 1931 from the comic strip. Many of the serial thrillers were adapted from comic strips, including *The Adventures of Superman*, *Dick Tracy*, and *Flash Gordon*. The children's programs generally fell into six categories, five of them thrillers. Shows featuring adventuresome schoolboys and schoolgirls included *Little Orphan Annie* and *Jack Armstrong, the All-American Boy*. Children of the 1930s and 1940s were fascinated by airplanes; popular shows featuring aviators and adventurers were *Captain Midnight and the Secret Squadron*, *Sky King*, and *Terry and the Pirates*. Superheroes and other crimefighters included *The Adventures of Superman, Dick Tracy,* and the *Green Hornet*. The largest category was the Western, with the most popular of all children's shows, *The Lone Ranger*, plus movie Western heroes *Hopalong Cassidy* and *Tom Mix Straightshooters*. Space adventures included *Buck Rogers in the 25th Century* and *Flash Gordon*. The sixth category, educational and storytelling included some of the earliest children's programs. *American School of the Air,* for instance, came on CBS in 1930 and was heard in many of the nation's schools. *Let's Pretend* came on the air in the same year as *The Adventures of Helen and Mary*, telling stories and fairy tales. *Big Jon and Sparkie* was among the latest additions to children's radio programming, coming on the air in 1950.

Radio seems to be experiencing a resurgence of interest in children's programs. A "new" concept was introduced in 1993—radio stations programming exclusively for younger children. The Children's Satellite Network, a Minneapolis-based syndicate, hoped to fill this gap with affiliates in several major markets programming for children of school age and preschoolers. Some of the programs offered are *Storytime, Alphabet Soup, All-American Alarm Clock, Kid Stuff,* and the only call-in talk show for children, *What Would You Do If...?* Children's music favorites are also included in the daily programming. Also, several local stations across the country have produced programs designed for children. This trend would seem to indicate that children's programming will once again be part of radio though it may never be as popular as it once was.

Bibliography
Boemer, Marilyn. *The Children's Hour: Radio Programs for Children, 1929-1956*. Metuchen, NJ: Scarecrow, 1989.
"Drive-time Radio Tuned in to Kids." *Dallas Morning News* 6 May 1993: 10C.
Dunning, John. *Tune In Yesterday*. Englewood Cliffs: Prentice-Hall, 1976.
Turow, Joseph. *Entertainment, Education, and the Hard Sell: Three Decades of Network Children's Television*. New York: Praeger, 1981.

Marilyn Lawrence Boemer

Christian Radio Music Formats. Contemporary Christian music (CCM) is unique in that it is defined primarily by its lyrical content rather than by a musical style. CCM runs the gamut from easy listening–flavored pop music to the radical extremes of grunge and speed rock. There are two separate realms of Christian music radio; the approximately 60 Christian stations nationwide broadcasting primarily music, and the more than 250 weekly CCM radio shows aired on stations around the country.

The full-time Christian radio stations use several musical formats. On the more traditional end of the scale are "inspirational" music stations that broadcast easy-listening instrumental music (e.g., Maranatha! Strings) and the lightest of the light in CCM (e.g., Steve Green). These stations target older listeners and often dedicate a portion of the broadcast day to popular preaching or talk shows such as Dr. James Dobson's *Focus on the Family*. The inspirational format is most representative of what early Christian radio music formats were like, traditional religious music interspersed, often as little more than filler, between talk programs.

Christian adult contemporary (AC) stations follow a light pop format. Artists like Sandi Patti and Steven Curtis Chapman are representative of the musical style that targets women but tries to appeal to a wide age range of both men and women. Guitar solos are buried in the mix or are edited for AC stations during remixing. Lyrically and musically, AC hit songs tend to be upbeat and positive. Christian hits radio (CHR) stations play a format similar to their Top 40 counterparts, with Michael W. Smith, John Gibson, Crystal Lewis, and even the rap of DC Talk representative of the musical style.

Whatever the format, there is a tendency to play those songs that have overtly religious lyrics that are simple, direct, and, most often, positive or uplifting. Artists who use "religious" language (e.g., "Praise the Lord") are more likely to gain radio exposure than artists who write more obscure lyrics.

Christian rock finds its radio home among the weekly radio shows aired over secular rock stations, college stations, and sometimes on full-time Christian stations that use a lighter music format. Shows range from two to four hours in length. Chris MacIntosh's *Rock and Soul Gospel* on WCWP in New York City is one of the longest running Christian rock shows in the nation. These shows play the most hip and progressive Christian music including Christian alternative (e.g., Daniel Amos), metal (e.g., Mortal), and arena rock (e.g., Magdalen). Occasionally, some rock artists will release a pop-oriented song that will receive airplay on CHR or AC stations, but their prime exposure to potential fans is through the weekly shows.

CCM probably accounts for 5 to 6 percent of all music sales in the U.S. Among CCM artists there are two clear orientations. Most CCM artists define themselves as ministers who are involved in evangelism and edification. Lyrically, their music tends to either be a gospel message addressed to the nonbeliever or a message of encouragement for the believer. An increasingly vocal minority of CCM performers are defining themselves as artists whose art simply reflects their Christianity. Lyrically, their music often presents political and social commentary from a Christian perspective or, as does most popular music, simply celebrates human relationships.

Bibliography

Howard, Jay. "Contemporary Christian Music: Where Rock Meets Religion." *Journal of Popular Culture* 26.1 (1992): 123-30.

Romanowski, William. "Roll Over Beethoven, Tell Martin Luther the News." *Journal of American Culture* 15.3 (1992): 79-89.

Jay R. Howard

See also
Alternative Contemporary Christian Music
Radio Formats

Christian Songs have had a lasting impact on American culture. Probably the most dominant religious figure in the U.S. since World War II has been William Franklin "Billy" Graham (1918-). Preaching to millions throughout North America and the world via live or televised services, Graham has become very well known in most sectors of American life. He and the hymn long associated with the Billy Graham Crusade have in a way become icons of mass culture. The song, "How Great Thou Art," became part of the Graham repertory in the 1950s soon after American Stuart K. Hine published English lyrics for the 19th-century Swedish hymn in 1949. The original song consisted of an old Swedish folk tune and Swedish lyrics written by Carl Boberg in 1886. Singer George Beverly Shea, with a splendid low-range voice, did much to popularize the song while with the Graham Crusade.

Perhaps the best hymn at least partly created in the U.S. is "Amazing Grace." The lyrics were written in 1779 by John Newton, an English hymn writer and clergyman. The melody is anonymous, first appearing in the 1831 publication *Virginia Harmony*. Despite the significant geographical and time differences, the words and music of "Amazing Grace" fit together extremely well. The song is well imbedded in the American national conscience, being a standard at police funerals and playing a crucial role in one episode at the Cheers bar, in the long-running television series of the 1980s and 1990s.

Another general hymn important in American life is "Ave Maria." Among the number of hymns so titled, the most famous was written in 1825 by Austrian composer Franz Schubert and inspired by the 1810 poem "Lady in the Lake" by Sir Walter Scott. This composition has often been sung by popular singers like Perry Como. The second famous "Ave Maria" was written by French composer Charles Gounod in 1859, basing the piece on music by the German master Johann Sebastian Bach.

"Blest Be the Tie that Binds" and "Lord, Dismiss Us with Thy Blessing," which have inched over into almost folk status, are both favorites to end religious services. They both were written by English hymn writer and author John Fawcett. "Blest," created in 1782, is paired with a melody by Swiss composer Johann Georg Nageli. "Lord," published in 1773, is linked with an anonymous 1794 melody that has been used with a number of lyrics. Another very familiar hymn, "Faith of Our Fathers," is almost a cliché in the religious history of the U.S. The 1849 words were by Frederick W. Faber, the tune by Englishman Henri F. Hemy.

"Glory Be to the Father," also known as "Gloria Patria" or the "Lesser Doxology," is an almost universal element in Protestant services. The words date back to the third or fourth century and the various melodies used include a medieval chant and two modern chant-like tunes, by German-American Christoph Meineke (1844) and American Henry W. Greatorex (1851). The other "doxology" omnipresent in the U.S. is "Praise God from Whom All Blessings Flow," usually associated with the passing of the collection plate. The 16th-century words are by English bishop Thomas Ken, and the 16th-century melody probably by Louis Bourgeois, a choirmaster in Geneva, Switzerland.

Five well-known compositions are "God of Our Fathers," "Hallelujah Chorus," "Holy, Holy, Holy," "Hymn to Joy," and "A Mighty Fortress Is Our God." The booming "God of Our Fathers," which like "Faith of Our Fathers" has sometimes had its lyrics altered because of the presence of the allegedly sexist term "fathers," was written in the late 19th century by musician George W. Warren and lyricist Daniel C. Roberts, both Americans. It is a staple of Protestant churches. The "Hallelujah Chorus," from "The Messiah," is familiar to a wide segment of American society, being used in animated cartoon, movies, and television advertisements. The entire "Messiah," created in England in 1742 by George Frederick Handel and lyricist Charles Jennens, is performed by the general public in various "do-it-yourself Messiah" events throughout the U.S. "Holy, Holy, Holy," perhaps the greatest of Christian songs, is another English hymn strongly entrenched in American culture. The early 19th-century words were by Reginald Heber and the 1861 melody by John Bacchus Dykes. The magnificent "Hymn to Joy," from the fourth movement of Beethoven's Ninth Symphony (1824), has been used for several hymns and a number of mass culture situations such as movies and television. Only a bit into the popular domain is Martin Luther's famous 1529 hymn "A Mighty Fortress Is Our God."

Two quieter songs are "The Little Brown Church in the Vale" and "The Lord's Prayer." "Little Brown Church," a folk-like composition, was written in 1865 by William Savage to honor his rural church in northeast Iowa. "The Lord's Prayer" uses the biblical text and a 1935 melody by

American Albert Hay Malotte. This low-key song is probably sung more outside of church than in it. Another significant hymn in the U.S. is "Nearer, My God to Thee," with 1841 words by English lyricist Sarah F. Adams and 1856 music by the famous American hymn composer Lowell Mason. "Nearer, My God" has been used in films and in a classic joke. A man is driving down a country road progressively fast. With each increase in speed, a hymn comes to mind. When he reaches 100 mph, the appropriate song is "Nearer, My God to Thee."

Four other hymns that are a part of general American culture are "The Old Rugged Cross," "Onward, Christian Soldiers," "Rock of Ages," and "Swing Low, Sweet Chariot." "The Old Rugged Cross," a fixture of fundamental Protestantism and hence the common American, was written in 1913 by American George Bennard. "Onward, Christian Soldiers," 1864 words by English writer Sabine Baring-Gould and 1871 music by Sir Arthur Sullivan of Gilbert and Sullivan fame, is such a well-known march that a number of sectors of American society are familiar with it. The term "Rock of Ages" is used throughout the popular culture of the U.S., for example, as the title for a history of rock and roll. The 1776 words were by Englishman Augustus Toplady, and the 1830 melody by American Thomas Hastings. "Swing Low, Sweet Chariot," an African-American spiritual, is not only one of the best American hymns, but has been parodied and used in various mass media.

Four Easter songs are classics of U.S. popular culture. One would expect Irving Berlin's secular 1933 "Easter Parade," the theme of the 1948 film of that title starring Fred Astaire and Judy Garland, to be so. But the totally religious "Christ the Lord Is Risen Today," which uses an anonymous 1708 English melody with 1739 poetry by the great English hymn writer Charles Wesley, is so well known that it overflows into general life. The lesser known "Low in the Grave He Lay," an 1874 song by American Robert Lowry, was very popular among Protestant fundamentalists in the late 1800s and the first half of the 1900s. The African-American spiritual "Were You There When They Crucified My Lord?" is a poignant part of American culture.

Three songs are especially associated with Thanksgiving. "Come Ye Thankful People, Come," with 1844 lyrics by Englishman Henry Alford and 1858 tune by Englishman George J. Alford is popular enough to have been used in, among others, the "Peanuts" animated Thanksgiving special. "Over the River and through the Woods," an anonymous secular American piece of uncertain date and with no particular relation to Thanksgiving, is most usually associated with the November holiday. The most famous Thanksgiving piece, "Prayer of Thanksgiving" or "We Gather Together to Ask the Lord's Blessing" was written in 1597 by Adrianus Valerius of the Netherlands, using a Dutch folk tune. The American musicologist Theodore Baker wrote the English words in 1894.

A popular song for American funerals is "Abide with Me," with 1847 lyrics by English poet Henry Francis Lyte and 1861 melody by English musician William Henry Monk. Weddings frequently use Richard Wagner's famous wedding march from the 1850 opera *Lohengrin* on the way to the altar, and Felix Mendelssohn's lively recessional after the ceremony. Mendelssohn's music is from his classical masterpiece *A Midsummer Night's Dream* (1842). Another piece long associated with weddings is "Oh Promise Me," from American Reginald DeKoven's 1890 operetta *Robin Hood*. English lyricist Clement Scott wrote the lyrics. None of these three famous wedding songs are from religious sources. Hymns commonly pass over into secular popular culture, and nonreligious songs often become associated with religious holidays and events.

Bibliography

Companion to the Hymnal: A Handbook to the 1964 Methodist Hymnal. Nashville: Abingdon, 1970.

Haeussler, Armin. *The Story of Our Hymns.* St. Louis: Eden, 1952.

Julian, John. *A Dictionary of Hymnology.* New York: Dover, 1957.

Reynolds, William Jensen. *A Joyful Sound: Christian Hymnody.* 2d ed. New York: Holt, 1978.

Routley, Erik. *Hymns and Human Life.* 2d ed. Grand Rapids: Eerdmans, 1959.

William E. Studwell

See also
Christmas Songs
Gospel Song/Gospel Hymn

Christie, Dame Agatha (1890-1976), who also published novels as Mary Westmacott, was named a Dame of the British Empire in 1971 to recognize her position as the world's best-known writer of mystery and detective fiction. The honor was well deserved, as Christie's 97 books have sold over a billion copies in English and have been translated into countless other languages; paperback reprints of her novels abound. Her play *The Mousetrap* (1952) is the longest-running production ever. Her name is automatically twinned with mystery fiction; she is virtually inseparable from her genre.

Christie's first novel, *The Mysterious Affair at Styles* (1921), was an early example of the golden age of detective fiction, with the emphasis on the now-classic whodunit. Writers in the Detection Club—Christie, G. K. Chesterton, and Dorothy L. Sayers, among others—promised to eschew jiggery-pokery and play fair with their readers. Christie's forte was the puzzle novel focused on plotting and ingenious planting of clues and insinuating details that adumbrate the solution to the mystery. Her murder investigations revolve around a small cast of suspects—whether in a country house in England or on an archeological expedition in Egypt—with more than enough motive and opportunity.

Among Christie's half dozen detectives are the enduring prototypes Jane Marple (see entry), Ariadne Oliver, and Hercule Poirot (see entry). Unlike her golden age contemporaries who favored handsome, upper-class male detectives (notably, Lord Peter Wimsey and Albert Campion), Christie created eccentric, improbable sleuths: an elderly village spinster; an absent-minded writer; and a retired foreign dandy with an accent.

Christie's talent for overturning the conventions of detective fiction and her readers' expectations can be seen in her decision to make the first-person narrator the culprit in *The Murder of Roger Ackroyd* (1926), and all the suspects the killers in *Murder on the Orient Express* (1934). She not only situates crime and evil in the middle of the most comfortable and secure settings but also challenges every assumption a reader might make about why, how, and who-dunit.

Bibliography

Bargainnier, Earl. *The Gentle Art of Murder: The Detective Fiction of Agatha Christie.* Bowling Green, OH: Bowling Green State U Popular P, 1980.

Gill, Gillian. *Agatha Christie: The Woman and Her Mysteries.* New York: Free, 1990.

Maida, Patricia, and Nicholas B. Spornick. *Murder She Wrote: A Study of Agatha Christie's Fiction.* Bowling Green, OH: Bowling Green State U Popular P, 1982.

Sanders, Dennis, and Len Lovallo. *The Agatha Christie Companion: The Complete Guide to Agatha Christie's Life and Work.* New York: Berkley, 1989.

Kathleen Gregory Klein

See also
Cozy Mysteries
Feminist Detective Fiction
Mystery and Detective Fiction

Christmas Decorations, beginning in traditional German folk culture in America, by the end of the 19th century had entered mainstream American culture as commercially mass-produced, material objects. Germans who settled in Pennsylvania brought the tradition of the Christmas tree to America with them. In 1832, Professor Charles Follen of Cambridge, MA, decorated a tree with candles, baskets of sugar plums, dolls, and gilded egg shells. In 1851, Mark Carr sold Christmas trees in New York City. In 1856, President Franklin Pierce displayed the first decorated tree in the White House. In 1882, the first electrically lighted Christmas tree in New York City was decorated at the home of Edward Johnson, a colleague of Thomas Edison at Edison Electric. John C. Heap (d. 1884) at Westinghouse suggested sales of such lights to the public, but not until the 1890s did General Electric become the first company to commercially distribute electric Christmas lights. In 1903, the Ever-Ready Company commercially offered string lights called festoons, and the Kremenetzky Electric Company distributed figurative miniature lights. Between 1920 and 1950, Popeye, Little Orphan Annie, Dick Tracy, and Disney cartoon-figure electric lights illuminated American Christmas trees. Between 1945 and 1950, Carl Otis invented BubbleLites (containing methylene chloride, which boils at low temperatures) for Montgomery Ward. The 1970s brought flashing midget lights or twinkle lights, usually produced in Japan or Taiwan.

Americans of the 19th century decorated their Christmas trees with apples, cookies, cranberry strings, fruits, marzipan, nuts, raisins, Springerle, and unshelled peanuts. These trees provided a functional display of edibles, and trees decorated with small gifts provided a functional display of gifts. Other early Christmas decorations included angels, candy canes, chains, dolls, gilded nut shells, stars, stockings, and paper ornaments.

Stores in the U.S. started selling Christmas ornaments in the 1870s, including butterflies, crosses, diamonds, and lead stars created by Nuremberg toy makers, blown glass ornaments (*Kugel*) from Lauscha, Germany, and wax angels, animals, and Christ childs. By 1875, American merchants sold celluloid toys, soldiers, dolls, and birdhouse ornaments. A Nuremberg factory in 1875 manufactured silver foil icicles. In 1880, Frank W. Woolworth began selling blown-glass ornaments, and angel hair became available. Between 1880 and 1910, Dresden manufacturers created glass ornaments, and gold cardboard camels, storks, peacocks, pianos, and sailboats and used by Americans for Christmas decorations. In the 1890s, German ornament manufacturers added cotton to Santas and angels, Czechoslovakian manufacturers created glass-beaded wire designs for ornaments, and the Japanese manufactured lanterns and parasols for decorations on American Christmas trees. Christmas tree ornament hooks were on sale by 1892. That same year, blown-glass storybook characters, vegetables, fruit, fish, and tinsel garland from France became available. Honey-combed paper bells were first made in 1908. In 1910, Sears and Roebuck began selling glass ornaments by mail; by 1918 American ornaments replaced German ornaments because of World War I. By 1938, Brooklyn glassblowers created glass Christmas balls, and by the next year, Corning was mass producing glass balls. Between 1940 and 1950, because of war with Germany, Max Eckardt (importer of German ornaments) expanded manufacturing of glass balls in his own ShinyBrite Company in America. Today, several companies, like Hallmark Cards, produce limited edition signed and numbered Christmas ornaments.

German-speaking Moravians in early 19th-century North Carolina and Pennsylvania practiced *putzing*—making tiny figures to decorate outdoor Christmas trees in Christmas tree yards. From this practice, outdoor Christmas decorations evolved. Pennsylvania Germans constructed the outdoor creche or nativity scenes *(Putz)*, a specific form of *putzing*. *Putz* or "ornament" is from the German verb *Putzen*, "to decorate" or "to dress or adorn." Once Christmas decorations moved out of doors, entire communities often gathered for the decorating of an outdoor tree. Franklin County, IA, residents in 1868 trimmed their first community tree with candles, popcorn garlands, and red apples. Early electrically lighted community trees appeared in San Diego in 1904, in Pasadena in 1909, in New York, Boston, and Cleveland in 1912, and in Philadelphia in 1914. Cities today frequently decorate entire streets, court houses, and other public buildings. Nativity scenes adorn many American homes today whether Protestant or Catholic, and late-20th-century adaptations of nativity scenes are often peopled with Star Wars, Batman, or other secular figures. Some Americans light and otherwise decorate the entire exteriors of their homes, and they may fill their yards with various outdoor Christmas decorations, both secular and religious. In some cities, individual homes and neighborhoods compete for annual prizes for the best decorations.

Bibliography
Barnett, James H. *The American Christmas: A Study in National Culture.* New York: Macmillan, 1954.
Bauer, John E. *Christmas on the American Frontier, 1800-1900.* Caldwell: Caxton, 1961.
Chalmers, Irena. *The Great American Christmas Almanac: A Complete Compendium of Facts, Fancies, and Traditions.* New York: Penguin, 1988.
Feingold, Helen, and Mary L. Grisanti. *The Joy of Christmas.* New York: Barron's, 1980.
Waugh, Dorothy. *A Handbook of Christmas Decorations.* New York: Macmillan, 1958.

Larry D. Griffin

Christmas Songs are more popular in the U.S. than anywhere else. The U.S. has produced more famous Christmas songs than any other country but England, and in the 20th century has been clearly dominant. Though perhaps best known for nonreligious holiday songs, the U.S. has also created its share of religious carols, all of which have found their way into the popular domain. Because Christmas songs are performed and heard by the American masses, even by non-Christians, year after year, even the most sacred of Christmas carols have become a continuing part of popular culture.

The first important American Christmas song appeared in 1839. In that year the famous American hymn composer Lowell Mason probably wrote the melody for the internationally celebrated carol "Joy to the World!" The uncertainty about the authorship of the music is due to the strange notation "from Handel" which accompanied the tune when it was published with English poet Isaac Watts's 1719 words in an 1839 collection.

The first significant all-American carol was "It Came Upon the Midnight Clear." The words were written in 1849 by clergyman Edward Hamilton Sears and the music in 1850 by journalist Richard Storrs Willis. With its skillful lyrics and gentle, rolling melody, it is perhaps the second-best-known religious Christmas piece from the U.S. In 1857 there was a double Christmas bonus. "We Three Kings of Orient Are" was written by John Henry Hopkins for his Vermont nieces and nephews at Christmastime. Though some persons disparage the song because the phrase "three kings" is not actually in the Bible story of Jesus' birth, the flowing processional has been a favorite with children and adults for many years. Also in 1857 came "Jingle Bells," possibly the best-known American Christmas song. It was created by James S. Pierpont for use by Boston Sunday school children.

In 1863, the American poet Henry Wadsworth Longfellow wrote "Christmas Bells," a partly Christmas, partly pacifist lyric, as a reaction to the horrors of the Civil War. When paired with an 1872 tune by English composer John Baptiste Calkin, "I Heard the Bells on Christmas Day" was born. Today, a mid-20th-century tune by Johnny Marks is often used to replace Calkin's melody. Perhaps the best-known religious carol from the U.S. is "O Little Town of Bethlehem" (1868), by Philadelphians Phillips Brooks and Lewis H. Redner. Clergyman Brooks's lyrics were inspired by a trip to the Holy Land, and organist Redner's melody by a deadline. Sometime in the 1860s or late 1850s, Ohioan Benjamin R. Hanby wrote the delightful "Up on the House-top." Around the same time, he may have written the similar "Jolly Old Saint Nicholas," an anonymous piece created sometime between the 1850s and the early 20th century.

It would not be until 1932, however, that the next burst of Christmas creativity would take place. In between the 1860s and the 1930s, only two significant Christmas songs would appear. The lyrics for "Away in a Manger" were first published anonymously in 1885, with its most famous melody created by James Ramsey Murray in 1887. When Murray first printed his tune, he put the notation "Luther's Cradle Hymn" with it, making some believe the whole carol was by Martin Luther, the 16th-century Protestant reformer. Another carol created around the turn of the century was the African-American spiritual "Go Tell It on the Mountain." This rousing song has been attributed to Frederick J. Work.

In 1932, the second outstanding period of Christmas song creation began. Lyricist Haven Gillespie and composer J. Frederick Coots collaborated on "Santa Claus Is Comin' to Town." One of the most popular and most profitable of holiday songs, it was introduced by the entertainer Eddie Cantor on his radio program in 1934. The well-known folklorist John Jacob Niles wrote one of the 20th century's best religious carols, the haunting "I Wonder As I Wander," in 1933. It was based on a folk song heard in North Carolina. "Winter Wonderland" was created in 1934 by lyricist Richard B. Smith and composer Felix Bernard. In 1936, Peter J. Wilhousky devised some lyrics to go with a 1916 melody by Ukrainian Mykola D. Leontovich, thus creating "Carol of the Bells," the light, lively song that has been used in champagne commercials on television.

In 1940, Irving Berlin wrote "White Christmas" for the 1942 film *Holiday Inn.* Popularized by Bing Crosby and many others, "White Christmas" was the most successful holiday song of the century, and quite possibly the most famous secular American Christmas song ever. It is rivaled only by "Jingle Bells." Another classic appeared in 1942, this time the perennial 1822 poem "'Twas the Night before Christmas" by Clement C. Moore set to some music by Ken Darby. "I'll Be Home for Christmas," a sentimental mid-World War II ballad, was written in 1943 by lyricist Kim Gannon and composer Walter Kent. A bit later Judy Garland made an exquisite recording of "Have Yourself a Merry Little Christmas," written in 1944 by lyricist Ralph Blane and composer Hugh Martin.

The post-war period saw several top songs. Mel Torme and Robert Wells's classic holiday composition "The Christmas Song" or "Chestnuts Roasting on an Open Fire" appeared in 1946. Two good novelties that same year were Donald Gardner's "All I Want for Christmas Is My Two Front Teeth," re-recorded in 1948 by Spike Jones and his ensemble of lunatics, and "Here Comes Santa Claus," written by Gene Autry and Oakley Haldeman and recorded by Autry. Another of Autry's recordings, Johnny Marks's blockbusting "Rudolph the Red-Nosed Reindeer" (1949), was the second-most-successful holiday phenomenon after "White

Christmas." It spawned several television specials, including one using the voice of Burl Ives. Also generating holiday specials was the 1950 "Frosty the Snow Man," by lyricist Walter E. Rollins and composer Steve Edward Nelson. Jimmy Durante was the narrator for one of the "Frosty" specials. In 1951, "Silver Bells" was introduced by Bob Hope in the movie *The Lemon Drop Kid*. The accomplished songwriting team of Ray Evans and Jay Livingston wrote this delicate classic.

After 1951, good holiday songs became rarer. Tommie Connor wrote the novelty "I Saw Mommy Kissing Santa Claus" in 1952. "Home for the Holidays," a perennial favorite, was created by lyricist Al Stillman and composer Robert Allen in 1954. The best rock Christmas song, "Jingle Bell Rock," was devised in 1957 (exactly one century after "Jingle Bells") by Joseph C. Beal and James R. Boothe. In 1958, "The Little Drummer Boy," which had its own television special, appeared. Originally written under the title "Carol of the Drum" by Katherine K. Davis in 1941, the song became "The Little Drummer Boy" later, with added credits to Henry V. Onorati and Harry Simeone. The most recent American Christmas song of note was the religious piece "Do You Hear What I Hear?" created in 1962 by Noel Regney and Gloria Shane. Following that 1962 song, no Christmas composition written in the U.S. was particularly successful except for "Grandma Got Run Over by a Reindeer," the 1983 novelty that faded away after a few years.

Bibliography

The Christmas Carol Songbook. Milwaukee: Leonard, 1991.
Del Re, Gerald, and Patricia Del Re. *The Christmas Almanack.* Garden City: Doubleday, 1979.
Studwell, William E. *The Christmas Carol Reader.* New York: Haworth, 1995.
——. *Christmas Carols: A Reference Guide.* New York: Garland, 1985.

William E. Studwell

Circus in America's tradition of fantasy, incredibly broad appeal, and remarkable longevity mark it as arguably one of the most important popular entertainment forms in American history, if not, as P. T. Barnum (1810-1891) declared in 1865, the "Greatest Show on Earth." While its basic elements have remained intact, it has endured because its shape and meaning have evolved in response to alterations in American society. The circus's antecedents can be traced back to ancient Rome and Egypt. However, it was only with the rise of industrialized society and commercialized leisure that the circus became structured as we know it today.

The first American circus was established in 1793 by John Bill Ricketts in Philadelphia. However, Ricketts's circus, which many historians credit as a favorite entertainment of President George Washington, still was not in the form we would recognize today. The early shows did not travel, and there were no menageries, parades, or elephants, and no tents. The label "circus" was attached to any combination of equestrian acts, jugglers, clowns, and acrobats who performed in a ring. Yet born literally with the new republic, the circus grew as rapidly as the nation. By 1815 dozens of companies existed and began to tour. In 1825, J. Purdy Brown's show became the first to use a tent. From 1830 to 1850 the circus became more mobile, using wagons and even riverboats to reach communities outside the eastern cities (the first circus arrived in St. Louis in 1826, and Chicago in 1836). The menagerie with its exotic wild animals (America's first zoo) was added during these years as was the sideshow with its human abnormalities ("freaks") and objects and strange beings from exotic foreign locations.

Until the Civil War, however, the circus's cultural importance remained rather circumscribed due to moral injunctions in New England and the South against traveling entertainments. Though the view of public entertainments as immoral began to fade by the War of 1812, many communities still retained laws prohibiting circuses. The early anti-circus laws usually seemed to be based on a perception that the circus was an alien presence that disturbed communal harmony. After all, the circus brought strangers into town who practiced a craft that often seemed magical. The performers exhibited their bodies in ways that refined or religious societies often found lewd. Their traveling lifestyle, moving together from town to town in a mixed group, appeared disorderly and even immoral. The circus people clearly disrupted good social order.

Despite their nefarious reputations, circuses continued to exist during the antebellum years, for they offered the public a fantasy world vastly different from everyday life. It was the magic that the laws attempted to ban that allowed the circus to survive despite its lack of ethics. While they kept a close eye on their wallets, and viewed everyone on the lot with suspicion, the public still marveled at the performances of aerialists, wirewalkers, and clowns. One of the earliest circus legends, Dan Rice (1823-1900), made a reported $1,000 a week during the 1850s as a clown. He was a national figure acquainted with the societal elite, and a friend of presidents Andrew Jackson, Zachary Taylor, and Abraham Lincoln. As his career demonstrated, the circus, though tainted, was viable because it was so wondrously unique.

After 1865 rail travel allowed the circus to play more lucrative venues and to increase in size. It also facilitated improved performance quality since the wearisome and filthy necessity of all-night wagon travel was eliminated. The first transcontinental railroad circus was Dan Castello's show in 1869. In 1872 Barnum's circus went out entirely on rails. As circuses grew in size and popularity so did the tent. In order to keep performances close to the audience as the tents were expanded, Barnum and his partner W. C. Coup's single-ring circus became two rings in 1872. When James Bailey joined his circus to Barnum's in 1881 the three-ring circus was born (European circuses never did adopt this style). In 1840 a large tent was 85 feet in length; Barnum & Bailey's 1890 tent was over 460 feet. In the major shows personnel numbered from about two dozen to nearly 2,000. The shows became so big that by 1905 the Ringlings needed 83 rail cars to carry their show.

By far, the largest and most spectacular circus production was created when Bailey joined up with Barnum in 1881. While Barnum usually gets much of the credit for making the circus popular during its golden age, his partners Coup and Bailey were the ones who ran the shows and made them financially solvent. Coup created the loading and logistic systems that made train shows profitable, and he also added the second ring. Bailey expanded into three rings, and his inclination toward grandiose spectacle made Barnum & Bailey a larger-than-life national institution.

Barnum's contribution should not be dismissed, however. It was his method of operation created during his museum years (1841-68) that the circus, vaudeville, the cinema, and even theater would follow thereafter. Barnum bowdlerized his museum, making it acceptable to the growing middle-class's sensibilities. He forbade alcohol and purged his business of prostitutes and any grift. As he often exclaimed, his shows were honest, wholesome, and educational, and they appealed to all classes. His success caused many to imitate his methods; consequently Barnum in large measure is responsible for setting the standard for what became labeled the "Sunday School" circus, such as Barnum & Bailey or the Ringling Brothers (1882-1917).

The circus was popular because it presented a series of features never before seen in America. It became valued for disseminating everything that was new in the world. It was the circus that first brought electricity to the public (Bailey's show was illuminated with electricity in 1879 three years prior to Edison's initial lighting of one New York street). The forerunner of the movie, the kinetoscope, was first seen by a large segment of the American people at the Ringling show in 1894. Many people caught their first glimpse of such wonders as the automobile and the telephone while under the big top.

After Bailey's death in 1906, the Ringling Brothers purchased Barnum & Bailey. In 1917, the two shows combined into the supershow that continues to exist today: Ringling Brothers and Barnum & Bailey. The Ringlings were never the innovators that Barnum, Bailey, and Coup were, and their desire to remain true to tradition perfectly suited the temper of the times. Due to increasing expenses, technologic changes, and the Depression, many of the old circuses disappeared, and by the mid-1930s the Ringlings controlled almost all the major circuses. Even though the Ringling circus also came close to extinction, it and a few smaller shows staggered through into the 1940s and 1950s.

The circus was so ingrained as an American tradition that when in 1956 the Ringling show ceased to perform under canvas it was described as a national disaster. Some said that losing the tent was not only the death knell of the circus, it foreshadowed dire social consequences. Of course the move was not the end of the world, and taking the circus indoors essentially saved it. The costs of the big top, and the fact that few communities had enough open area near the rail yards to erect a tent, made the move quite practical. Though this action rescued the circus, it was considered so threatening to tradition that up until 1970 Ringling was still having to defend the move.

As a result of its steadfastness to a formula of tradition and "family values," Ringling has once again become a financial success. Its resurgence has been duplicated by many smaller shows. As the nation seemed to be in the throes of a spiritual if not social collapse during the late 1960s and 1970s, the circus was able to satisfy a wide spectrum of the American populace with its old-fashioned shows. The focus on a family show emphasizing the past continued into the 1980s and 1990s. One man characterized the circus in 1985 as "an ancient tradition of human entertainment." A reporter in 1993 stated that Ringling endured because it managed to "maintain the old-fashioned charm and timeless appeal of the traditional circus."

The circus, though, might be going through yet another transmogrification in the 1990s. Since 1977, when Paul Binder created the Big Apple show, there has been a resurgence of the single-ring tented circus in America. The Big Apple's success with a format offering less spectacle and more high-quality single acts, and the fact that one-ring shows are generally cheaper to stage, has led other circuses to return to a single ring (Circus Vargas switched in 1993).

The stunning success of the Canadian import Cirque du Soleil also is reshaping the circus's appeal (it can be considered "American" since it plays almost all of its dates in the United States). This show might be called the postmodern circus, with its single ring, harlequin-dressed and -masked performers, a theatrical thematic format, and fusion-jazz/rock music accompaniment. From performers who slither onto the stage, to the lack of vendors, announcers, or animals, there is practically nothing in this show that resembles the traditional circus (save for remarkably skilled performers). Its immediate success after its arrival in 1988 (there is a permanent unit in Las Vegas) has influenced the staging and style of some established U.S. circuses, including Ringling.

Bibliography

Culhane, John. *The American Circus*. New York: Holt, 1990.
Durant, John, and Alice Durant. *Pictorial History of the American Circus*. New York: Barnes, 1957.
Hammerstrom, David Lewis. *Big Top Boss: John Ringling North and the Circus*. Champaign: U of Illinois P, 1993.
May, Earl Chapin. *The Circus from Rome to Ringling*. New York: Dover, 1963.

Doug A. Mishler

Citizen Kane (1940) is generally acclaimed as one of the finest movies produced in America, a Mercury Production for RKO Radio Pictures, produced, directed, co-written by, and starring Orson Welles (see entry). It opened at the RKO Palace on Broadway in New York on May 1, 1941.

Amid the cultural, economic, technological, geopolitical, and philosophical upheavals since World War II, one thing that has remained constant is the almost universal critical consensus that *Citizen Kane* is the Great American Film. Though there is no single element in *Citizen Kane* that cannot be found in earlier films by others or in previous theater or radio work by Welles himself, perhaps it is this quality of the original excitement of discovery that pervades the film, the imaginative make-believe that it is the very first film ever made, that best explains its capacity to arrest, dazzle, and overwhelm even the most resisting viewer, and to continue to do so after no matter how many repeat viewings. A related factor is the iconoclasm of its subject. Charles Foster Kane is modeled on the notorious yellow journalist William Randolph Hearst, one of the most influential figures in American public life in the early decades of the 20th century. Most recently, Hearst had been one of the most bitter opponents of Franklin D. Roosevelt's liberal New Deal politics, of which Welles was an ardent supporter, and contemporary audiences would have recognized in the film a politically motivated attack. The film also stirs deeper resonances. Kane is an authentically American creation, the entrepreneur-tycoon, who appears perhaps not first but certainly most definitively in Benjamin Franklin's autobiography and figures prominently in the fiction of Henry James, William Dean Howells, Theodore Dreiser, and F. Scott Fitzgerald. Many believe that if there is a central trait that characterizes Americans, it is a preoccupation with worldly success and its concomitant product, fame. Popular culture analyst Robert Warshow speculated that the preoccupation also extends to the obverse, the inevitable loss of self or soul that accompanies the spectacular rise. *Citizen Kane* tells both sides of the story—of a man (as the reporter investigating Kane's life puts it) "who got everything he ever wanted, and then lost it." And adds: "Maybe Rosebud was something he couldn't get or something he lost."

Rosebud is also deeply resonant. Unquestionably the sled is the most famous prop in movie history; it is also the most enigmatic. In the most general sense, Rosebud is a transcultural symbol that has stood variously for life, virginal innocence, sexuality, and death. Within the film it also has contradictory meanings, of a mystery that will either reveal everything about Kane's life (as the newsreel producer speculates) or won't reveal anything (as the reporter concludes). Some of those who worked on the film projected their own special associations onto it—for screenwriter Herman Mankiewicz, it was reminiscent of another toy (a bicycle) he himself had owned as a child; for Welles, it was the knowledge that "Rosebud" was Hearst's pet name for the private sexual parts of his mistress, Marion Davies, the model for Kane's second wife, Susan Alexander. Rosebud has been subjected to endless explanation, from the ridiculous to the sublime, and has become as widely known and alluded to as other great symbols in American narrative such as a white whale, a scarlet letter, a raft on the Mississippi, and the green light on a dock.

While the film is unquestionably the product of Welles's genius, it is also the result of one of the most successful collaborations in the history of Hollywood. They later denied it, but Welles and his co-writer, Mankiewicz, knew from the beginning that they were taking on one of the most powerful figures in contemporary American life, and they proceeded audaciously and almost scandalously. During planning and production, at the creative center was a triumvirate of Welles, art director Perry Ferguson, and cinematographer Gregg Toland. Ferguson executed the construction of the unusually large number of sets called for by the script at an astonishingly low cost, most notably the Great Hall at Xanadu, where optical trickery (hanging sheets of black velvet in the empty spaces, which registers photographically as an illusion of depth) causes the eye to see a great deal more than is actually there. Toland, the most daringly innovative cinematographer in the history of Hollywood, always had his camera rigged with the newest technical gadgetry, and it is said that there was a running game between Welles and him during the shooting, with Welles daring Toland to achieve an effect and Toland baiting Welles to think up an effect he thought couldn't be achieved. At the heart of the cinematographic plan is a clash of visual styles that suggests the polarity of Kane himself—needle-sharp daylight scenes, with images approaching the crispness of documentary still-photography, for the youthful figure of dynamic energy; the harsh and foreboding darks and lights of German expressionism for the aged tyrant withdrawn to Xanadu in defeat and despair. Perhaps most famous is Toland's extreme deep-focus cinematography, with the foreground and background and all planes between in equally sharp focus (in contrast to the standard shallow-focus studio style). Also on the creative team was Bernard Herrmann, the greatest composer in Hollywood history. He and Welles together worked out the musical ideas—the two central themes, "power" (first heard in the opening two bars of the score in muted brass) and "Rosebud" (first heard as a vibraphone solo when the glass ball appears); motifs for the characters (the *Dies Irae* for Bernstein, elegant waltzes for Kane's first wife, Emily, jazz for Susan); *Salaambo*, the opera for Susan's debut, French Oriental in genre, richly orchestrated in the manner of Richard Strauss, with a libretto from Racine's classic play *Phédre*. *Citizen Kane*, wrote one remarkably astute contemporary reviewer, "is the work of many artists and yet, with and above that, the work of one, as great works of art in any medium have always been."

Bibliography

Carringer, Robert L. *The Making of* Citizen Kane. Berkeley: U of California P, 1985.
Citizen Kane. Criterion Collection CAV Laserdisc, 1992.
Kael, Pauline. *The* Citizen Kane *Book*. Boston: Little, Brown, 1972.

Robert L. Carringer

Civil Religion in America. In addition to those well-established and historically shaped denominations of the American religious scene, Christianity, Judaism and now, increasingly, Islam, there exists another well-defined and elaborate system of beliefs and rituals that has come to be known as "civil religion." This religion requires the same serious study as do the other religions of America. Throughout the course of American history, there have been several formative events that have focused the American religious sensibility, such as the Revolutionary War, the writing of the Declaration of Independence, and the Civil War. These events have been given a religious cast not only by American preachers and theologians, but by the very men and women who took part. And the same religious themes of redemption, rites of passage, entrance to the promised land, and sacrificial death that course through these pages of American history have been present in 20th-century history as well.

During the Revolutionary War, the theme of redemption was commonly heard from the pulpits of Protestant clergymen. Some referred to George Washington as a kind of Moses, leading the revolutionary forces away from bondage into the promised land. Indeed, Thomas Jefferson, in his own inaugural address, stated: "I shall need, too, the favor of that Being in whose hands we are, who led our fathers, as Israel of old, from their native land and planted them in a country flowing with all the necessaries and comforts of life."

When the founding fathers discussed the nature of the seal of the United States and what should be depicted, one suggestion was to have the seal display a pillar of fire and a cloud leading the American people to safety. These images appear in the Old Testament's account of Moses leading his people out of the desert into the promised land where they were led by a pillar of fire at night and clouds by day.

With the advent of the Civil War, the theme of sacrificial death enters the imagery of civil religion. It was a catastrophe so deeply dividing America and the American psyche that it ultimately found expression in religious terms. In Abraham Lincoln's Gettysburg Address there are themes of death, sacrifice, and rebirth. Symbolized in the very life and death of Lincoln himself, these themes of sacrificial death and vicarious suffering were eloquently put forth in that brief address, when President Lincoln used words such as "conceived in liberty," "created," "dedicated" and "a new birth of freedom," and "We have come to dedicate a portion of that field as a final resting place for those who here gave their lives that the nation might live." These utterly profound words of Lincoln gave the battlefield an infinite significance. It was the place of sacrificial death.

Since the Civil War, Memorial Day celebrations have taken the role of ritual expressions of sacrificial death. They are major events for the whole community, where the population rededicates itself to the "martyred" dead and to the idea of sacrifice and to the theme of loyalty to American values. In this view, Thanksgiving Day also fits into the rituals of civil religion because it involves the family in the annual recitation of the litany of appreciation for all the good things that America has to offer its citizens. One could also mention the annual celebrations of Presidents' Day and the Fourth of July as events that evoke gratitude and patriotism, which are the virtues of this national religion.

In the 20th century the religious themes of redemption and sacrificial death are played out often enough, but the theme of messianism is most clearly seen in the New Frontier and Great Society programs of Kennedy and Johnson, respectively. These two presidents, especially, were able to mobilize civil religion to attain certain national goals. Indeed, every president has continued to mention God, some have even urged prayer, and all have expressed the hope that God will continually bless America, this promised land, this home for refugees, this land of opportunity, this place where, in John Kennedy's words, "God's work must truly be our own."

Bibliography

Bellah, Robert. *Beyond Belief: Essays on Religion in a Post-Traditional World.* New York: Harper, 1970.

James Prest

Civil War, The (1990), premiered over five consecutive evenings, September 23-27, 1990, amassing the largest audience for any series in public television history. Ken Burns's 11-hour documentary version of the war between the states acted as a kind of lightning rod for a new generation, attracting a great deal of praise and attention, as subsequent research indicated that nearly half the audience would not even have been watching television at all if it had not been for *The Civil War*.

The series, a production of Ken Burns's Florentine Films in association with WETA-TV in Washington, boasted many of the filmmaker's usual collaborators, including his brother and co-producer, Ric Burns, writer Geoffrey C. Ward, and narrator David McCullough. *The Civil War* took an estimated five years to complete and cost nearly $3.5 million, garnered largely from support by General Motors, the National Endowment for the Humanities, and the Corporation for Public Broadcasting.

Burns (see entry) employed 24 prominent historians as consultants on the project, melding together approximately 300 expert commentaries and another 900 first-person quotations from Civil War-era letters, diaries, and memoirs, read by a wide assortment of distinguished performers, such as Sam Waterston, Jason Robards, Julie Harris, and Morgan Freeman, among many others. Writer, historian, and master raconteur Shelby Foote emerged as the onscreen star of *The Civil War*, peppering the series with entertaining anecdotes during 89 separate appearances.

Bibliography

Edgerton, Gary. "Ken Burns—A Conversation with Public Television's Resident Historian." *Journal of American Culture* 18.1 (Spring 1995): 1-12.

Marc, David, and Robert J. Thompson. *Prime Time, Prime Movers.* Boston: Little, Brown, 1992.

Toplin, Robert Brent, ed. *Ken Burns's* The Civil War: *Historians Respond.* New York: Oxford UP, 1996.

Gary Edgerton

Clancy, Tom (Thomas L., Jr.) (1947-), an immensely popular writer of military and espionage thrillers, began his career as an insurance agent. Poor eyesight prevented him from entering the armed forces, so he made his personal perceptions of the conflict between institutionalized and individual right and wrong the foundation for his fiction. His writing career began with the publication of *The Hunt for Red October* in 1984. The novel, later made into a successful film, concerns a U.S.-Soviet race to capture a defecting Russian submarine captain and his high-tech ship. It features CIA intelligence specialist Jack Ryan. Having found his stride as a popular writer, Clancy has continued steadily to produce tales of high-stakes international intrigue and danger.

Red Storm Rising (1986) tells of the dangers of a non-nuclear World War III. In *Patriot Games* (1987), Clancy reintroduces as his protagonist Jack Ryan, who unwittingly endangers his own and his family's lives by foiling an IRA assassination attempt upon members of the British royal family. In *The Cardinal of the Kremlin* (1988), Ryan forestalls the potential use of a controversial laser weapon, and in *Clear and Present Danger* (1989) he combats powerful South American drug merchants.

Clancy's recent fiction—*The Sum of All Fears* (1991), *Without Remorse* (1993), *Debt of Honor* (1994), *Executive Orders* (1996), and *Rainbow Six* (1998)—continues in this vein. Clancy's work is most often recognized for its familiarity with state-of-the art military hardware and crime-fighting and intelligence-gathering techniques, earning his works the label of techno-thrillers. He is also admired for complex but fast-paced plots and an authentic-seeming knowledge of the inner circles of power in government, business, and the military high command, a knowledge he also puts to use in works of nonfiction.

Bibliography

Henderson, Leslie, ed. *Twentieth-Century Crime and Mystery Writers*. Chicago: St. James, 1991.

McCormick, Donald, and Katy Fletcher. *Spy Fiction: A Connoisseur's Guide*. New York: Facts on File, 1990.

Ryan, William F. "The Genesis of the Techno-Thriller." *Virginia Quarterly Review* 69.1 (1993): 24-40.

Thomas, Evan, and Richard Sandza. "The Art of the Techno Thriller." *Newsweek* 8 Aug. 1988: 60-65.

Thomas B. Frazier

See also
Spy Fiction
Thriller, The

Clark, Dick (1929-), "America's oldest teenager," was significant in transforming the record business into an international industry, reigning as host of the popular music show *American Bandstand* for nearly four decades. Before the clean-cut Clark began as host in July of 1956, rock 'n' roll was viewed by most adults as vulgar, low-class music which had been almost exclusively the domain of black artists. Due in large part to exposure on Clark's hugely popular, five-afternoons-a-week program broadcasting rock 'n' roll into the homes of the American public, the popularity of this newly emerging musical genre among white teenagers caused an industry-wide effort to "whiten" the music in order to bolster record sales. White artists began an attempt to seize the rock 'n' roll domain from black artists, who then had to resist efforts by the industry to reclassify them as rhythm and blues singers.

Clark, a canny entrepreneur who got his start at an upstate New York radio station at the age of 17, has built a video and entertainment empire worth over $200 million today. *American Bandstand*, a teen-oriented show that originated in Philadelphia's blue-collar south side, became a national institution as the longest-running network television show in history, enabling Philadelphia for a time to become the pop music capital of the world. Clark, the host with the "All-American Boy" image, decided who would appear on the show, which in 1959 was besieged by 750,000 unfilled ticket orders from the bobby-sox crowd clamoring for a chance to do The Slop, The Hand Jive, The Bop, Stroll, Circle, or Chalypso, the most popular dance steps of the day (see Rock 'n' Roll Dancing). *American Bandstand* became the springboard for launching the careers of most of rock's early stars such as Bill Haley and the Comets, Buddy Holly, Connie Francis, Bobby Darin, Fabian, Ritchie Valens, and Chubby Checker (see entry).

Despite being the target of Congressional payola investigations that ruined the careers of many of his contemporaries in the industry, Clark, the man who once remarked, "I don't make culture, I sell it," witnessed and very often directly influenced the changing styles and countless revolutions of popular music and culture during the past 40 years, forging the country's first teenage constituency, and becoming the first television personality to simultaneously host regular series on all three major television networks.

Bibliography

Clark, Dick, and Richard Robinson. *Rock, Roll and Remember*. New York: Crowell, 1976.

Jackson, John A. *American Bandstand: Dick Clark and the Making of a Rock 'n' Roll Empire*. New York: Oxford UP, 1997.

Sanjek, Russell, and David Sanjek. *American Popular Music Business in the 20th Century*. New York: Oxford UP, 1991.

Barbara Anderson

Clark, Mary Higgins (1929-), is a leading writer of romantic suspense fiction. Her background in advertising and later in writing radio scripts provided the creative fodder for her eventual career as a mystery author. Clark's first major publication, *Aspire to the Heavens: A Biography of George Washington* (1969), received little positive critical or commercial recognition, but her 1975 mystery novel, *Where Are the Children?*, placed her on best-seller lists, as have all of her subsequent novels: *A Stranger Is Watching* (1977); *The Cradle Will Fall* (1980); *A Cry in the Night* (1982); *Stillwatch* (1984); *Weep No More, My Lady* (1987); *While My Pretty One Sleeps* (1989); *Loves Music, Loves to Dance* (1991); *All Around the Town* (1992); *I'll Be Seeing You* (1993); *Remember Me* (1994); *Let Me Call You Sweetheart* (1995); *Silent Night* (1995), *Moonlight Becomes You* (1996), *Pretend You Don't See Her* (1997); *You Belong to Me* (1998); *All through the Night* (1998); and *We'll Meet Again* (1999).

Clark's characteristic style features worlds of suspense confined within rather limited geographical settings, and adroit psychological probing of her characters. Her novels depict episodes of danger and terror that enter the lives of ordinary people, particularly—in most of her later works—professional women who encounter unexpected menace and romance that are interlinked. Many of her plots center around victimization of children or threats to or from within families, resolved through quiet but determined acts of bravery by her protagonists.

Bibliography

Bestsellers: Books and Authors in the News. Detroit: Gale Research, 1990.

Contemporary Authors. Vols. 81-84. Detroit: Gale Research, 1979.

Contemporary Authors, New Revised Series. Vol. 36. Detroit: Gale Research, 1992.

Reilly, John M., ed. *Twentieth-Century Crime and Mystery Writers*. New York: St. Martin's, 1985.

Whissen, Thomas. "Mary Higgins Clark." *Great Women Mystery Writers: Classic to Contemporary.* Ed. Kathleen Gregory Klein. Westport: Greenwood, 1994. 66-68.

Thomas B. Frazier

See also

Crime Fiction Romantic Horror
Gothic Mysteries Thriller, The
Regional Mysteries

Clarke, Arthur C(harles) (1917-), as was Isaac Asimov (1920-1992), is a scientist who writes science fiction. Born in the United Kingdom, Clarke earned college degrees in physics and mathematics. His first professional publication was the science fiction story "Loophole," which appeared in the April 1946 issue of *Astounding (Science Fiction)*, but his first professional sale was the science fiction tale "Rescue Party," published by *Astounding* in May 1946. His first two novels appeared in 1951. These were *Prelude to Space* and *Sands of Mars.* Also during 1951 Clarke's short story "Sentinel of Eternity" was published in *10 Story Fantasy.* This story became the basis for the Stanley Kubrick motion picture classic *2001: A Space Odyssey.* (Clarke and Kubrick co-authored the screenplay; Clarke later wrote the novel based on that writing.) In the 1960s, '70s, and '80s, Arthur C. Clarke spent much of his writing effort on works of nonfiction, though he continued to publish an occasional science fiction short story or novel. In 1973, he received extensive critical acclaim and several major literary awards for his science fiction epic, *Rendezvous in Rama.* In December 1995 Arthur C. Clarke was nominated for the Nobel Peace Prize.

Bibliography

Clute, John, and Peter Nicholls, eds. *The Encyclopedia of Science Fiction.* New York: St. Martin's, 1993.
McAleer, Neil. *Arthur C. Clarke: The Authorized Biography.* Introduction by Ray Bradbury. Chicago: Contemporary, 1992.

Garyn G. Roberts

Clarke, Kenny (1914-1985), drummer, composer, and multi-instrumentalist, pioneered an approach to drumming that helped define the style of jazz known as bebop (see entry). Clarke was part of a small group of young black jazz players, including Thelonious Monk, Dizzy Gillespie, and Charlie Parker, who invented what came to be called bebop in a series of jam sessions at such Harlem clubs as Minton's in the early 1940s.

Clarke also played a part in two of the most important post-bebop movements in modern jazz. He helped to shape cool jazz of the 1950s, first as a participant in the seminal Miles Davis/Gil Evans "Birth of the Cool" recording sessions (1949-50); and, although he left the group after three years, Clarke also helped found the Modern Jazz Quartet, a pioneering chamber jazz ensemble whose relaxed sophistication exemplified "cool." Clarke was also present for the birth of hard bop (also known as soul jazz)—a style that added blues and gospel to bebop—on the famous Miles Davis *Walkin'* recording session in 1954 that shaped the public perception as well as musical direction of jazz in the late 1950s

and early 1960s. He was further influential during that decade in his role as the house drummer for Prestige Records, playing with many emerging modernists.

In 1956, Clarke moved to Paris, where his most notable work came with the Clarke-Boland Big Band. He never returned to reside in the U.S., where he felt artists were not respected.

Bibliography

Feather, Leonard. *Inside Jazz.* New York: Da Capo, 1977.
——. *The New Encyclopedia of Jazz.* New York: Horizon, 1960.
Gitler, Ira. *Jazz Masters of the Forties.* New York: Macmillan, 1966.
Russell, Ross. *Bird Lives! The High Life and Hard Times of Charlie "Yardbird" Parker.* New York: Charterhouse, 1973.

Lynn Darroch

Classical Mysteries, perhaps the most popular type of mystery and detective fiction in America, began with the first mystery stories in the 1840s—the Dupin tales of Edgar Allan Poe (see entry)—and ended just before the start of the golden age. Poe had read the quasi-fictional *Memoirs* of the French detective Eugène Vidocq (1828-1829) when he created the first fictional detective, C. Auguste Dupin, in "The Murders in the Rue Morgue" (1841). In this and two other stories, "The Mystery of Marie Rogêt" (1842), and "The Purloined Letter" (1844), Poe invented most of the basic situations, character types, and narrative conventions that the classical detective story employs and that later varieties must either use or react against. These include the observant and astute detective described by a less perceptive narrator-friend, the bumbling policeman who seeks the sleuth's expertise, and the brilliant criminal adversary who is almost a mirror image of the detective but on the wrong side of the law. Like many later fictional investigators, Dupin acts as both an armchair detective who solves cases merely by reading newspaper accounts and an agent who actively investigates the crime scene in a baffling locked-room murder; he also enjoys staging a dramatic revelation of the truth at the end of his adventures.

In 1866, Metta Victoria Fuller Victor, writing as "Seeley Regester," became the first American woman to write a detective novel, *The Dead Letter: An American Romance.* In 1878 Anna Katharine Green published *The Leavenworth Case: A Lawyer's Story*, in which a police detective, Ebenezer Gryce, solves the case, though the story is narrated by Everett Raymond, the lawyer of the subtitle—possibly because policemen were still very much *infra dig* at this time in the popular imagination. The story revolves around circumstantial evidence that points first at one of the murdered man's nieces, then at the other. Romance and melodrama play large parts in both *The Dead Letter* and *The Leavenworth Case*, as they do in the books of Mary Roberts Rinehart (1876-1958), the best known of which is *The Circular Staircase* (1908). A name has been given to this school of fiction by the regretful "Had I but known..." spoken by Rinehart's heroines, whose insights come just too late to prevent further mayhem.

American mysteries of the period between 1890 and 1920 parallel the British in several respects, two being the interest in science and the popularity of Robin Hood figures who flout the law. The interest in science grows naturally from a story form based on positivism and realism. Jacques Futrelle created his technological whiz kid detective, Augustus S. F. X. Van Dusen, in *The Thinking Machine* (1907). William MacHarg and Edwin Balmer, in *The Achievements of Luther Trant* (1910), have Trant using the infant science of psychology as a detection method. Craig Kennedy, in *The Silent Bullet* (1912) by Arthur B. Reeve, wields flashy pseudoscience to expose rigged roulette wheels and solve locked-room murders.

Lawbreakers are also a natural development in mystery fiction, since from the beginnings (for example, in "The Purloined Letter"), detectives used extralegal means to bring about their ends. On the other side of the law in classical American crime fiction is O. Henry's Jeff Peters, the Gentle Grafter, in a series of stories collected under that title in 1908. Not so gentle is the amoral lawyer Randolph Mason, created by Melville Davisson Post; in *The Strange Schemes of Randolph Mason* (1896), the lawyer counsels his clients how to murder and commit other crimes without fear of prosecution.

Post was responsible for another, distinctively American development in his creation of Uncle Abner, a Scripture-quoting backwoods detective who frequently discovers that what looks like a criminal act is merely God's stern justice worked out in a freak accident. Story titles like *The Angel of the Lord* and *An Act of God* reflect such divine retribution. The stories are collected in *Uncle Abner: Master of Mysteries* (1918), which ushers out the classical period. Afterward came the milder puzzle stories of the golden age of detective fiction (see entry) and the pervasive violence of the hard-boiled mysteries.

Bibliography

Haycraft, Howard. *Murder for Pleasure: The Life and Times of the Detective Story*. New York: Carroll, 1984.
Panek, LeRoy. *An Introduction to the Detective Story*. Bowling Green, OH: Bowling Green State U Popular P, 1987.
Steinbrunner, Chris, and Otto Penzler. *Encyclopedia of Mystery and Detection*. New York: McGraw-Hill, 1976.
Symons, Julian. *Bloody Murder: From the Detective Story to the Crime Novel*. New York: Mysterious, 1992.

Michael Cohen

See also

Clavell, James (1925-1994), an Australian by birth, immigrated to the United States in 1953, where he remained to forge a career in the arts as a novelist, screenwriter, and film director. The definitive experience of his prior lifetime was his three-and-one-half-year incarceration in the Japanese prisoner of war camp at Changi, near Singapore, an event that shaped his outlook and provided material for much of his fiction. Best known for his epic popular novels of Asia, Clavell began his writing career with original screenplays,

including the 1958 version of *The Fly*, along with *The Great Escape* (1963); *To Sir, with Love* (1967); and *The Last Valley* (1971), among others, which he also directed and produced.

King Rat (1962), Clavell's first novel, a story based directly on his experiences at Changi, probes the psychic devastation that prison camp survivors must endure and offers a keen look at the evils of militarism. A popular book, *King Rat* was adapted to film in 1965. But it was *Tai-Pan, A Novel of Hong Kong* (1966), that established Clavell as an international best-selling author. The story of the British founder of Noble House, a Hong Kong trading company founded in the 19th century, was the first in his series of interrelated Asian sagas, later followed by *Noble House: A Novel of Contemporary Hong Kong* (1981), a massive 1,207-page volume, and *James Clavell's Gai-Jin: A Novel of Japan* (1993).

Clavell also wrote *Whirlwind* (1986), set in Iran in the early days of the Iranian revolution, but his most celebrated book was *Shogun: A Novel of Japan* (1975), the tale of a British sailor who makes a life among the warlords of feudal Japan in the 17th century. *Shogun* gained fame among a second wave of readers when it was adapted as a television miniseries in 1980, produced by Clavell and starring Richard Chamberlain (see entry) in his most memorable screen role.

Bibliography

Doug, Stella. "James Clavell." *Publishers Weekly* 24 Oct. 1986: 54-55.
"Obituaries: James Clavell." *Current Biography* Nov. 1994: 58.

Liahna Babener

Cleopatra (1963) ranks as one of the most overpublicized, scandal-plagued, and expensive films ever made. Director Joseph L. Mankiewicz asserted that the ill-fortuned movie "was first conceived in emergency, shot in hysteria, and wound up in blind panic." Walter Wanger produced the feature for Twentieth Century-Fox, which was almost financially destroyed by the film's staggering cost, an estimated $44 million. Mankiewicz, Ranald MacDougall, and Sidney Buchman penned the screenplay, which was based on the ancient writings of Plutarch, Suetonius, and Appianus, and *The Life and Times of Cleopatra* by Charles Marie Franzero (1957). The principal cast included Elizabeth Taylor (Cleopatra), Richard Burton (Mark Antony), Rex Harrison (Julius Caesar), Pamela Brown (High Priestess), George Cole (Flavius), Hume Cronyn (Sosigenes), Cesare Danova (Apollodorus), Kenneth Haigh (Brutus), Martin Landau (Rufio), and Roddy McDowall (Octavian).

Films concerning the famous Egyptian ruler dated back to 1899, and such actresses as Theda Bara (1917), Claudette Colbert (1934), Vivien Leigh (1946), and Rhonda Fleming (1953) had played Cleopatra. Initially, Wanger, whose resume included *Stagecoach* and *Invasion of the Body Snatchers*, and Twentieth Century-Fox president Spyros Skouras envisioned a modest movie starring Joan Collins in the title role. They also considered Susan Hayward and Audrey Hepburn for the part. However, Taylor was hired to portray Cleopatra after Twentieth Century-Fox agreed to pay her the phenomenal sum of $1 million against 10 percent of the gross. Early on, Peter Finch was hired to play Caesar and the role of Antony went to Stephen Boyd. Rouben Mamoulian was set to direct the screenplay by novelist Nigel Balchin. Shooting began in September 1960 but trouble was not long in coming. Production shifted from Hollywood to Rome, then to Pinewood Studios outside London. Taylor's poor health slowed filming, which was halted in November. In January 1961 Mamoulian, who had shot only a little over ten minutes of usable film, resigned.

Skouras hired Mankiewicz, director of such movies as *All About Eve, Julius Caesar, Guys and Dolls,* and *Suddenly, Last Summer,* to replace Mamoulian. Like Taylor, Mankiewicz commanded a high price for his services. Besides paying his salary and expenses, Twentieth Century-Fox purchased the new director's production company. Mankiewicz deemed Mamoulian's footage unusable, and then set out to rewrite the script. He also substituted Harrison and Burton for Finch and Boyd. To acquire Burton, then starring on Broadway in the successful *Camelot,* Twentieth Century-Fox paid $50,000 to buy out his contract. Production ceased in March due to Taylor's health problems. Following a tracheotomy, the stricken actress required a lengthy period of rest.

Mankiewicz finished shooting in July 1962. Because his movie ran over seven hours, he planned to release *Cleopatra* as two feature films, the first examining the Egyptian monarch's relationship with Caesar and the second concentrating on her affair with Antony. In the meantime, though, Skouras had been forced to step down, and Darryl F. Zanuck, his replacement at Twentieth Century-Fox, ordered Mankiewicz to cut *Cleopatra* into a single film.

Finally, on June 12, 1963, the controversial feature made its world premiere at New York's Rivoli Theatre. Although the 243-minute epic received an Academy Award nomination for best picture of 1963, it lost to *Tom Jones.* Harrison was nominated for best actor, but the Oscar went to Sidney Poitier. However, *Cleopatra* won Academy Awards for cinematography, costume design, art direction/set direction, and special effects.

Bibliography

Film Facts 6.22 (4 July 1963).

Geist, Kenneth L. *Pictures Will Talk: The Life and Films of Joseph L. Mankiewicz.* New York: Scribner, 1978.

Solomon, Jon. *The Ancient World in the Cinema.* New York: Barnes, 1978.

Vermilye, Jerry, and Mark Ricci. *The Films of Elizabeth Taylor.* Secaucus: Citadel, 1989.

S. K. Bane

Cliff, Jimmy (1948-), one of the so-called godfathers of reggae and the best-known reggae artist after Bob Marley (see entry), was among the earliest popularizers of Jamaican music. Cliff sought early in his career to achieve international fame by blending the styles of reggae and American popular music.

Jimmy Cliff was born James Chambers in Somerton near Montego Bay, Jamaica. His musical interests, especially his love for American rhythm and blues, brought him at age 13

to Kingston. There he worked with several producers, most importantly with Leslie Kong, the Chinese-Jamaican owner of a record-store cum ice-cream shop named Beverley's. Cliff convinced Kong (soon to be a key figure in the Jamaican record industry until his death in 1969) that his song "Dearest Beverley" would naturally boost business. The teenage Cliff was signed as Lesley Kong's first artist on the Beverley's label in 1962. During the early 1960s, Cliff imitated American rhythm and blues music and had two local hits, "Hurricane Hattie" and "Daisy Got Me Crazy." When ska emerged as a native genre (soon to evolve into rock steady and then reggae), Cliff joined a delegation of Jamaican ska singers for a government-sponsored tour of the U.S. and to the 1964 World's Fair in New York. Island Records producer Chris Blackwell was impressed, signed Cliff, and brought him to England in 1965 where, based on Island's distribution potential, he hoped to gain fame. Cliff's first British album, *Hard Road to Travel* (1967), sold poorly, but his songs and his unusual, quavery, tenor voice gained him a devoted club following. In 1968 during a tour of Brazil, where his composition "Waterfall" won the Brazilian Song Festival, Cliff wrote a consciously international song, "Wonderful World (Beautiful People)." Released in the U.S. by A & M Records, the song became a U.K. Top 10 hit and the first international reggae hit in 1969.

The late 1960s saw much of his best work: the poignant "Sitting in Limbo" and "Many Rivers to Cross," and "Viet Nam," written as a mother's letter concerning her son's death. The 1969 album, *Jimmy Cliff,* enjoyed considerable success, as did later work for other artists such as the songs "Let Your Yeah Be Yeah" for the Pioneers and "You Can Get It If You Really Want" for Desmond Dekker. Cliff's rendition of the Cat Stevens song "Wild World" in 1970 signaled his pop leanings, soon confirmed on the 1971 non-reggae album, *Another Cycle,* recorded at trendy Muscle Shoals. This tendency, designed to propel him into quicker international success, lost Cliff fans from among the reggae purists.

Stardom actually came when a friend of Blackwell's, Perry Henzell, gave Cliff the starring role in *The Harder They Come* (1973)—the first film produced in Jamaica by Jamaicans—based on the story of a cop-killer who in 1948 was slain by police in a gun battle near Kingston harbor.

His subsequent albums—*Unlimited* (1973), *Struggling Man* (1974), *House of Exile* (1974), and *Music Maker* (1974)—were too unfocused for Cliff to cement his status as reggae's leading star, and Bob Marley claimed that position.

While releasing albums continually, with occasional hits such as "Beyond the Boundaries" and "Bongo Man," Cliff also toured extensively, appearing at international festivals and in concert films, and enjoying tremendous popularity in Nigeria, where he maintains a second home. After his 1978 album *Give Thanx,* Cliff traded in WEA for his own label, the Jamaica-based Sunflower Records, whose subsidiary Oneness was designed to promote young Jamaican musicians. After *Bongo Man,* a 1980 concert film which celebrates African culture, and his albums *I Am the Living* (1980) and *Give the People What They Want* (1981), Cliff signed with CBS, who produced *Special* (1982), *Power and the Glory* (1983), *Cliff Hanger* (1985, with members of Kool and the Gang on production and backup instrumentals), and *Hanging Fire* (1987). In 1986 Cliff co-starred with Robin Williams, Peter O'Toole, and Twiggy in the film *Club Paradise*, a comedy set in a ramshackle Caribbean resort. In recent years Cliff remains active, releasing or contributing to albums yearly, such as *Images* (1990), *Reggae Greats* (1991), and *Breakout* (1992).

Bibliography
Davis, Stephen, and Peter Simon, *Reggae Bloodlines*. New York: Da Capo, 1992.
Garland, Phyl. "Cliff Hanger." *Stereo Review* 51 (Jan. 1986): 79.
Santoro, Gene. "Fela Anikulapo Kuti and Jimmy Cliff." *The Nation* 13 Aug. 1990: 176+.
"Scandal Ska." *The Nation* 13 Nov. 1989: 597.
Simels, Steve. "The Real Jamaican Ska." *Stereo Review* 58 (Sept. 1993): 102.

Michael Delahoyde
Erik Williams

Cline, Patsy (1932-1963), one of the most popular and influential talents of any musical genre, not only continues to sell millions of records but also to influence singers from Dolly Parton to Linda Ronstadt to Wynonna Judd. Patsy Cline's unique and compelling style defines a crossover appeal that seems to continually lure new fans and admirers.

Born Virginia Patterson Hensley in the Shenandoah Valley of Virginia, she grew up in rural America as a fan of "hillbilly music" on the radio. She quit high school at the beginning of her sophomore year to help support her family, who had by then moved to Winchester, VA. To earn additional money, she sang at fraternal organizations and in assorted honky-tonks in northern Virginia, eastern West Virginia, and western Maryland. In 1952 she professionally became "Patsy" Hensley as the star vocalist at the Brunswick, MD, Moose Hall. In 1953 she married Gerald Cline in Frederick, MD; she continued to use her new name even after she divorced Cline and married Charles Dick in 1957.

Patsy Cline's break came on the radio in Washington, DC. This led to a local television show, with Jimmy Dean and Roy Clark, and innumerable concerts, all set up by impresario Connie B. Gay. A three-month crest of popularity came during the spring of 1957 after she was a winner on *Arthur Godfrey's Talent Scouts,* singing what became her first hit, "Walkin' after Midnight."

After innumerable struggles through 1960 and into 1961, Patsy Cline finally made it in a big way with "I Fall to Pieces" and "Crazy." During the subsequent 18 months before her death early in March of 1963, Patsy Cline pioneered career possibilities for female country singers. She played in Las Vegas and at Carnegie Hall. Song after song reached the top of the charts, in particular "She's Got You."

Since 1963 her 100 recordings have been forever in print. Millions love her *Greatest Hits*. Indeed it seems as if Patsy Cline's influence unceasingly grows. Admirers redo her vocal arrangements; avant-garde singer k. d. lang named her band the Reclines in Patsy's honor. Her genius lives on through her remarkable recordings.

Bibliography
Bufwack, Mary A., and Robert K. Oermann. *Finding Her Voice: The Saga of Women in Country Music*. New York: Crown, 1993.
Jones, Margaret. *Patsy*. New York: HarperCollins, 1994.
Malone, Bill C. *Country Music, U.S.A*. Austin: U of Texas P, 1985.
Millard, Bob. *Country Music*. New York: Harper, 1993.
Nassour, Ellis. *Honky Tonk Angel*. New York: St. Martin's, 1993.

Douglas Gomery

Clio Awards are presented in an annual competition by the advertising and commercial production industries for the best advertisements. Originally presented by the American TV and Radio Commercials Festival in 1960, the Clios became the envy of the industry and eventually eclipsed all other coveted advertising awards. To the advertising industry a Clio is tantamount as the Oscar in film, the Tony in theater, the Emmy in television, and the Grammy in music. Awards are presented for product campaigns and for craft categories such as cinematography, editing, and writing. Awards are for both American-made and international commercials.

Founded by Wallace Ross in 1959, the first Clio Awards were presented for excellence in U.S. television advertising. Winners received a gold statuette designed by George Olden, called a Clio after the mythological Greek muse of history, the proclaimer, glorifier, and celebrator of history, great deeds. and accomplishments. Ross expanded the awards in 1966 to include international TV and cinema and U.S. radio in 1967.

Under the direction of Bill Evans for the next two decades as a for-profit organization, the Clios carried considerable prestige. Evans added U.S. print in 1971, international print in 1972, international radio in 1974, U.S packaging design in 1976, U.S. specialty advertising and international packaging design in 1977, U.S. cable in 1983, and Hispanic competition in 1987.

The Clio Awards are determined by a peer system of judging. More than 1,000 advertising professionals, living in the U.S. and foreign cities, judge the entries in their specific areas of expertise. The judges are instructed to vote solely on the creative merits, considering whether the ad was an effective piece of sales communication, whether it would affect and motivate an audience, whether it was both believable and tasteful, and whether it employed imaginative techniques to support the sales message.

Past Clio Award winners (selected to the Clio Hall of Fame) include the James Garner/Mariette Hartley commercial for Polaroid One Step Cameras, when Garner jokingly suggests that it's so simple even a woman can use it. Hartley threatens to have a thousand women boycott him as spokesman. Another winner for a nonprofit organization was the Department of Transportation "Drinking and Driving can kill a friendship" ad, featuring liquor-filled glasses attempting a toast to good times and good friends, when the glasses clash and break.

Bibliography
Brown, Les. *Les Brown's Encyclopedia of Television.* New York: Zoetrope, 1991.
Lafayette, John. "Clio Chaos." *Advertising Age* 24 June 1993: 3, 60.
Riordan, Steve, ed. *Clio Awards: A Tribute to 30 Years of Advertising Excellence, 1960-1989.* New York: Clio Enterprises, 1989.
U.S. News and World Report 1 July 1991: 1.

Sheri Carder

Clogging is a dance of rhythmic footwork, which usually minimizes other movements of the body. Cloggers may use percussive or light footwork; they may emphasize toes, heels, or the whole foot; they may keep the feet close to the floor, or include kicks, hops, jumps, or chugs; and their steps may make sounds or be silent. In clogging, the knees bend and stretch with each beat, and the emphasis is downward on the beat. Related terms are flatfooting, old style buck dancing, and jig dancing. Clogging and its related forms are known in two ways: as social dances within some European American, Native American, and African-American communities, especially in the Central Appalachian and Ozark regions, and as individual and team performance or competition forms supported by national or local organizations. These footwork dances are believed to be a blending of dance styles of African, Native American, and British Isles origins.

Around 1970, the Green Grass Cloggers in North Carolina invented a new style by combining Western Club Square Dance figures in four-couple sets with steps learned from social cloggers and precision and freestyle teams, and steps they created. Steps are sometimes synchronized, and the high energy style uses loosely dangling arms, legs, and torso, and head-level kicks.

Social and theatrical forms of clogging have existed in the U.S., mutually influencing each other, since at least the early 1800s. Clogging was a customary feature of minstrel and medicine shows. The early 20th-century folk dance education movement introduced such clogging and character dance into schools with books like Helen Frost's *The Clog Dance Book*, which detailed steps and actions.

The first documented formal clogging competition was Bascom Lamar Lunsford's 1928 Asheville Mountain Dance and Folk Festival. Dancers in eight-couple groups, not yet teams, competed for monetary prizes to "strictly mountain tunes." Teams evolved by the mid-1930s, practiced more complicated steps and developed costumes, in part to satisfy the tourism demand. In the 1940s and 1950s, clogging teams appeared regularly on Nashville's *Grand Ole Opry* (see entry).

Bibliography
Hall, Frank. "Improvisation and Fixed Composition in Clogging." *Journal for the Anthropological Study of Human Movement at New York University* 3 (1984-85): 200-17.
Matthews, Gail. "Cutting a Dido: A Dancer's Eye View of Mountain Dance in Haywood County, N.C." Master's thesis, Indiana University, 1983.

Spalding, Susan Eike, and Jane Harris Woodside, eds. *Communities in Motion: Dance, Community, and Tradition in America's Southeast and Beyond.* Westport: Greenwood, 1995.
Stearns, Marshall, and Jean. *Jazz Dance: The Story of American Vernacular Dance.* London: Macmillan. 1968.

Susan Eike Spalding

Closed-Circuit and Cable-Access TV should be credited for bringing the power of the medium to the people. Beginning in the 1970s, local cable systems began establishing channels for public use, partly under pressure from the governments of the communities that gave them their franchises to build and operate there. This led to the creation of PEG access, or public, educational and governmental access channels. In the 1980s, many towns had included additional demands for the cable systems in the franchise initiation or renewal agreements. Systems had to provide free use of equipment and training for members of the community who wished to produce programming, and provide air time to show it.

Colleges, noticing the inherent public relations and educational benefits, and the availability at no cost, were among the first to jump on this bandwagon. Colleges and high schools often received their own educational access channel on the system to program as they wished. To eliminate the inconvenience of people having to go physically to the cable system to produce shows and for other educational purposes, many campuses built their own TV production studios in order to send their channel's program feed directly to the cable system head-end. Schools that merely had TV production classes whose resulting videos ended up sitting on a shelf now found increased interest among students and faculty to produce thanks to the incentive of having their works seen by a town-wide potential audience. However, time and budgets prevented schools from producing nearly enough programming to fill the broadcast day, and they were not in a position to purchase much programming, so a scrolling calendar of campus and community events typically ran in a continuous loop during the hours between actual programs.

Besides colleges, towns themselves organized to produce occasional programs, usually coverage of municipal board meetings and other official functions on a government access channel. Public access channels carried shows by the general public—from local gossip talk shows to sports interviews to creative dramas or comedy sketches. Though some people preferred to produce their shows at home and provide videotape or feed it to the cable system (as in the popular "Wayne's World" comedy films and TV sketches of the early 1990s), many took advantage of the cable system's facilities and did it all there. In the 1980s, the development of public access centers in many localities, often funded through a portion of the franchise fee paid by the cable operator, allowed for the public to produce shows in a separate place.

These channels were purposely run in a mostly noncommercial fashion and were not subject to the pressures on commercial media to develop mass-appeal, formulaic programming to maximize audience ratings and thus advertising income. Therefore, access programming has tended to reflect a more eclectic range of programming, including some avant-garde material that would rarely be accepted by a commercial network, and a more raw, less rehearsed style.

College TV was among the first to produce computer-generated animation shows and telecast nonmainstream sports such as lacrosse, volleyball, and soccer, on a regular basis. Campus versions of existing TV genres such as the soap opera, news, public affairs, comedy, drama, and documentary also offered an interesting spin on these established formats.

However, even the increased interest in producing programs locally could not fill the broadcast day without excessive repeat telecasts. Fortunately, with the rapid development of satellite technology in the 1990s, the number of networks offering programming geared to colleges had increased dramatically, and schools did not want to be left behind in benefiting from TV's educational potentials. Therefore, many colleges acquired relatively low-cost satellite dishes to receive some of these many new networks, such as SCOLA (foreign language news), U Network (best student-produced works), and distance-learning services.

Often simultaneously, colleges built closed-circuit TV systems to carry that programming throughout the campus for the benefit of residents and in-classroom instruction. Many large corporations have similar in-house TV systems. Today's setups often include multichannel services similar to local cable, including the entertainment networks available at home, as well as on-line/interactive offerings and more education-oriented program/network choices than typically offered by commercial cable.

Bibliography

Engelman, Ralph. *The Origins of Public Access Cable Television, 1966-1972.* Columbia: Association for Education in Journalism and Mass Communication, 1990.

Fuller, Linda K. *Community Television in the United States: A Sourcebook on Public, Educational and Government Access.* Westport: Greenwood, 1994.

Nicholson, Margie. *Cable Access: Community Channels and Productions for Nonprofits.* Washington, DC: Benton Foundation, 1990.

Glenn Gutmacher

Clowns and clowning in the U.S. constitute a rich blending of types and styles. The clowns of the U.S. have their roots in European culture, with antecedents recorded as far back as ancient Grecian burlesque. Clowns are magical figures, licensed to cross the boundaries of culturally sanctioned behavior and by crossing them, demonstrate the boundaries' existence. Clowns are freakishly marked by their costume and makeup; and, while clowns are primarily viewed as mirth makers, their status as magical outsiders also makes them figures of cultural unease.

The term "clown" can have a variety of inferences, from the court jester "fool" of the Middle Ages to the merry prankster of Elizabethan theater to the modern comedian, but the most common association is the white-face makeup, red-nosed circus clown. The contemporary circus clown is a fusion of several European clowning traditions. The painted clown face, the most obvious marker of clown status, is of Germanic origin. From France came the Pierrot and the Harlequin, the dancing acrobatic clowns. Italy supplied the sad or serious clowns named Pantaloon, a name given to their characteristic baggy trousers, eventually giving the name for all trousers: "pants." Each of these traditions relied on pantomime and slapstick for their humor, from delicate mime to the more raucous slapstick.

Clowns had become a fixture of theatrical productions by the 1500s, either as the focal character or as comic commentary or relief. The modern circus clown has its roots in a commedia dell'arte character who acted as a foil for the Harlequin character. This character gradually became the contemporary clown, largely due to the innovations by performer Joseph Grimaldi (1779-1837), who essayed the character in the early 1800s. Clowns still refer to each other as "Joeys" in his honor. By the middle of the 19th century, such clowns were a fixture of American circuses.

Clown types fall into several categories, with 20th-century America giving birth to the latest addition to the clown pantheon, the character clown. Emmett Kelly, Sr. (1898-1979) became the most famous clown of his time with his "Weary Willie" hobo characterization, an example of the character clown. Such character clowns can be any type of recognizable persona: police and firefighters are common character clowns.

The red-nosed, white-faced portly clown is called a grotesque and is the clown who will perform cartoon-like sight gags and engage in set-pieces. Two of the most noted of these clowns in the United States were Felix Adler and Lou Jacobs. Jacobs bears the singular distinction of appearing on a U.S. postage stamp while still alive, albeit his appearance was in the guise of his clown persona. The character clowns, especially the hobos, can do this as well, with the touch of pathos usually missing from the grotesques. The Auguste clown is also white-faced, and is usually the aggressor, with other clowns on the receiving end of their actions. Auguste clowns often retain their characteristic markings while essaying character roles.

American vaudeville and burlesque created another clown variation since those comedians were usually overtly marked by costume and makeup. Many tramp and hobo comedians were on the stage and certainly influenced Emmett Kelly and his hobo clown compatriots. Quite a few of the baggy-pants (Pantaloon again?) comedians of the stage transferred to the silent and early sound cinema with their characterizations virtually intact. The character clown markings are evident in many comedians and their personae throughout the silent era and into the sound, as evidenced by the Three Stooges' hairstyles, Groucho Marx's painted-on mustache, and Charlie Chaplin's shoes and cane, to cite but a few noted examples. In time, the marking has become less overt, though the status of screen and television comedians as a type of clown is clearly evident, since they each serve much of the same sociocultural functions in many of the same ways.

In a step that almost brought clowning back to its Middle Ages forms, the U.S. in the late 1900s saw clowning fuse with magic, acrobatics, dance, mime, and other activities. People could hire clowns for all sorts of social functions, as kings and queens with their own jesters at hand. Labeled party clowns and looking much like their circus counterparts, these clowns were able to juggle, do simple magic, and make animal shapes out of twisted balloons.

Related to the party clown is the street mime, so designated because of the penchant for open-air public performances. Street mimes use only white-face makeup and liner, no red hair or bulbous noses. They do not speak but enact standard mime routines and exercises.

Clowns are also a staple of rodeo performances (see Rodeo). Rodeo clowns entertain audiences between competitions and events, usually by poking fun at macho cowboy stereotypes. But their main function is to distract the animals and draw their attention away from the riders when the riders are thrown or dismount. Ultimately all clowning probably serves a serious social purpose, but the purpose of a rodeo clown's antics are quite explicit and immediate.

One of America's most famous clowns is Bozo the Clown. Bozo became a fixture in American homes due to his children's television program which began in 1959. Larry Harmon, the man behind the clown, smartly adapted Bozo to changing times, and also licensed others to perform and make appearances as Bozo under his strict supervision. Bozo became a mass-market figure as Bozo dolls, puppets, games, books, and other toys were sold. "What a Bozo!" became a phrase of amused disparagement at someone's unseemly antics. Another television clown, Clarabell from *The Howdy Doody Show*, failed to have Bozo's staying power. Bob Keeshan, the first Clarabell, also appeared on television as Corny the Clown, before gaining greater fame as Captain Kangaroo (see entry).

The jack-in-the-box clown from the popular toy lent its name and image to a restaurant chain, but it is clown Ronald McDonald, the national mascot for McDonald's restaurant chain, who may be the most recognizable clown of all time. Ronald comes from a land of anthropomorphic food and brings joy not so much from his clowning as through his dispensing of McDonald's products.

Clown figures also became symbols of charitable events and even religious functions as people "clowned for Christ." In the Broadway show *Godspell*, the role of Jesus was performed in clown-face. Corporate clown Ronald McDonald sponsors a series of Ronald McDonald Houses as lodging for families of hospitalized children.

Bibliography

Disher, M. Wilson. *Clowns & Pantomimes*. New York: Blom, 1968.

Kelly, Emmett, with F. Beverly Kelley. *Clown*. New York: Prentice-Hall, 1954.

McVicar, Wes. *Clown Act Omnibus: Everything You Need to Know about Clowning Plus over 200 Clown Stunts*. Colorado Springs: Meriwether, 1987.

Sanders, Toby. *How to Be a Compleat Clown*. New York: Stein & Day, 1978.

Willeford, William. *The Fool and His Scepter: A Study in Clowns and Jesters and Their Audience*. Evanston: Northwestern UP, 1969.

Benjamin K. Urish

CNN (Cable News Network) has been self-dubbed "the world's most important network." When the channel first signed on to cable systems around the U.S. on June 1, 1980, the description may have seemed rather presumptuous. After all, media mogul Ted Turner's vision of a 24-hour news channel appeared at best to have a remote chance to succeed. Despite its critics, Atlanta (GA)-based CNN has expanded exponentially to cover the globe. Beamed via satellite to more than 200 countries, CNN has indeed become "the world's most important network."

Originally a cable television curiosity, CNN's status in the world of electronic journalism has grown to epic proportions. News operations of the major broadcast networks are typically limited in scope. They must coexist with entertainment programming that is frequently given priority over the news. CNN is nothing but news, allowing the network to cover events for longer periods of time and in greater detail than broadcast networks. CBS, NBC, and ABC have been forced to follow CNN's lead in many instances. However, while CNN has been able to raise advertising rates and increase revenues, the broadcast networks have lost millions of dollars on their news operations. Often, the networks' normal advertisers are not willing to spend their money for anything other than entertainment. When programs are preempted for news, the networks lose the ad money that would have been generated.

Often CNN's news product is rough in comparison to traditional, packaged television news, but the approach has been effective. Sometimes the style is even riveting for the viewer, as exemplified by CNN's detailed and lengthy coverage of the Persian Gulf War, the Challenger tragedy, the William Kennedy Smith rape trial, the Clarence Thomas Supreme Court confirmation hearing, the O. J. Simpson case, and numerous other important news events. CNN's timeliness in getting stories to the public more than makes up for the rough edges.

CNN has had its criticism, but none more biting than for parts of its Persian Gulf War coverage. CNN's initial coverage of the war was praised, as the network was the only one with people shrewd enough to get a live telephone feed from a Baghdad hotel to television screens worldwide. Three CNN reporters, John Holliman, Peter Arnett, and Bernard Shaw, described the U.S. bombing raid on Baghdad. Even Iraq's Saddam Hussein watched CNN's coverage. However, when CNN's Arnett was allowed to stay in the country, his censored reports were attacked as being mere dissemination of Hussein's propaganda to the world. CNN was unapologetic, and defended the importance of its coverage. Basically, the network's philosophy is to let international figures have their say, and to allow viewers to make their own judgments.

CNN has spawned U.S. competitors over the years, none of them as successful. The network's chief competition in world news has come from BBC World Service Television. To meet the challenge, CNN created CNN International (CNNI). World Service Television is considered extremely credible and traditional. BBC executives prefer scheduled newscasts over breaking news, which is CNN's trademark style.

CNN Headline News, originally called CNN2, was begun on January 1, 1982. Also a success story, the channel uses CNN's resources in a half-hour, around-the-world type of format done in a more traditionally packaged news presentation.

Bibliography

Bibb, Porter. *It Ain't as Easy As It Looks: Ted Turner's Amazing Story*. New York: Crown, 1993.

Smith, Perry M. *How CNN Fought the War: A View from the Inside*. New York: Carol, 1991.

Westin, Av. *Newswatch: How TV Decides the News*. New York: Simon & Schuster, 1982.

Wiener, Robert. *Live from Baghdad: Gathering News at Ground Zero*. New York: Doubleday, 1992.

W. A. Kelly Huff

Coe, David Allan (1939-), a tattooed eccentric, is a superb country singer/songwriter and self-promoter. His decade of greatest success was the 1970s, with such hits as "Long-haired Redneck," "If That Ain't Country," and a tune penned by Steve Goodman, "You Never Even Called Me by My Name." His *Greatest Hits* (1978) went platinum. Near sublime are his brilliantly conceived and executed concepts albums (e.g., *David Allan Coe Rides Again* and *Human Emotions* of 1977), but Coe also gained fame for two songs recorded by others: "Would You Lay with Me in a Field of Stone" a hit for Tanya Tucker in 1974, and "Take This Job and Shove It" for Johnny Paycheck (1977), the latter serving as the basis for a successful Hollywood film. The competitive showmanship emerges in his insistence that he, and not the pretender, Glen Campbell, is the "original Rhinestone cowboy" and in his more recent magic acts in Las Vegas.

Born in Akron, OH, Coe spent nearly 20 years in and out of various correctional institutions. A self-trained musician, he fled to Nashville in 1969 and attempted to break into the music industry. Despite his greatest period of productivity in the 1970s, Coe's first No. 1 hit came with "The Ride" in 1983—a song, ironically, not written by himself. Other hits from the early 1980s include "Mona Lisa Lost Her Smile," but his split with Columbia in 1986 (ostensibly broken by Coe when Columbia dropped his friend Johnny Cash) left him without a recording contract, after having released 21 albums for them (excluding "hits" packages). In 1988 Coe moved to Branson, MO, where he opened The Rhinestone Cowboy Store and Museum, and continued to tour the U.S. regularly, appearing occasionally in Europe. In the early 1990s he released three albums on his own independent label: *1990 Songs for Sale, Standing Too Close to the Flame*, and *Granny's Off Her Rocker,* the latter superior to the other two and representative of Coe's talent as both composer and performer.

Bibliography

Clarke, Donald. *The Penguin Encyclopedia of Popular Music*. London: Penguin, 1990.

Nash, Alana. *Behind Closed Doors: Talking with the Legends of Country Music*. New York: Knopf, 1988.

Wiseman, Rich. "David Allan Coe's Death Row Blues: Rhinestone Ripoff?" *Rolling Stone* 1 Jan. 1976.

Rebecca A. Umland
Samuel J. Umland

Coffeehouses are public places of refreshment where the main beverage served is coffee. Coffeehouses sometimes provide informal entertainment or serve as meeting places for intellectual discussions. Coffee, introduced into Europe and North America in the 17th century, grew increasingly popular following the opening of the first coffeehouse in London in 1652. Most European cities had such establishments by the late 17th century, and the first North American colonial coffeehouse was founded in St. Mary's City, MD, in 1689. Centers of gossip and gambling in that era, coffeehouses were places where business was transacted, newspapers were read, and literary, philosophical, and political opinions were exchanged. They also provided patrons with pens, paper, and ink, serving as mailing addresses as well as accepting letters for mailing.

During the 1800s, coffeehouses were gradually displaced by the home delivery of mail, the growth of daily newspapers, and the appearance of private clubs. They reemerged as part of New York City's Greenwich Village milieu of clubs, galleries, salons, and theaters in the early 20th century.

Espresso, brewed by forcing steam through finely ground darkly roasted coffee beans, became popular in the 1940s and was the main beverage served in coffeehouses that sprang up in urban areas and around college campuses. Coffeehouses became favorite hangouts of the Beat Generation in the 1950s. There were Beat coffeehouses in every American city with a population of over 100,000 by the early 1960s. New York's Greenwich Village, San Francisco's North Beach, and Venice West in southern California, with their low rents, friendly bistros, and reputations for tolerance, were seen as retreats from "square" society.

By the end of the decade, hippie coffeehouses throughout the country were offering folk music, serving as community centers for the youth counterculture, and providing political contacts and counseling for Vietnam War draft resisters.

Christian coffeehouses emerged in the early 1970s as part of the Jesus Movement (see entry), itself a spinoff from the hippie counterculture. Operated both independently of and by established churches and denominations, the idea was to provide fellowship for religious believers while appealing to the "unsaved" who might never go to a traditional church. Christian coffeehouse founders envisioned their establishments as alternatives to worldly bars and clubs. Offering much the same atmosphere as hippie hangouts, Christian coffeehouses were marked by low-key and subtle religious witnessing.

Coffeehouse culture emerged again in the 1990s amidst a public craze for coffee. As retail sales of specialty beans and beverages doubled during the decade, people sought pleasant surroundings for camaraderie and cappucino. Coffeehouses came above ground in the mid-1990s. Upscale establishments attracted affluent professionals, parents with children, and retirees. Offering numerous varieties of coffee, large magazine and newspaper racks, well-stocked book shelves, and clean bright facilities, these places were stark contrasts to bohemian and student coffeehouses with their discarded couches, unmatched tables and chairs, and dingy, often basement-like surroundings. The appearance of nationwide corporate chains was testimony to the appeal of such places even as they were criticized for driving local proprietors out of business.

Bibliography

Bizjak, Mary. *Coffee Crazy: A Guide to the 100 Best Coffeehouses in America.* Sacramento: Tzedakah, 1995.

Heise, Ulla. *Coffee and Coffeehouses.* West Chester: Schiffer, 1987.

Morse, Minna. "Across the Country, It's All Happening at the Coffeehouse." *Smithsonian* Sept. 1996: 104-13.

Michael Hoover

Coleman, Ornette (1930-), along with Louis Armstrong, Charlie Parker, and Miles Davis, is one of the greatest innovators and musicians in jazz. His revolutionary saxophone playing, with his exceptionally human-like sound and intonation, his rhythmically free phrasing, and his unique approach to harmony and melody, was a profound influence on the styles of such jazz greats as Sonny Rollins, John Coltrane, Lester Bowie, George Russell, and Jimmy Giuffre. He has trained several generations of musicians in "harmolodics"—his unique and profound system of improvisation. Coleman's music paved the way for the avant-garde jazz movement. Many of his compositions have become jazz standards, and he has written screenplays for several movies.

Coleman's early career is replete with stories of the difficulties he faced as an individualist in a world that expected conformity. Born in Fort Worth, TX, at 15 Coleman took up the saxophone; within a year he was backing up traveling blues musicians such as Joe Turner. Coleman gained a reputation as a specialist in entertaining the audience by jumping on tables and "walking the bar," in the style of Big Jay McNeely.

Coleman soon developed his own sound and style, and this earned him the dislike of many musicians and audiences. He was fired from the Silas Green Minstrel Show for teaching his music to one of the horn players. Later, while on tour with blues singer Pee Wee Clayton, he played some of his new concepts during a sax solo at a dance concert. This so infuriated some of the members of the audience that after the concert they ambushed him, smashed his horn to pieces, and then severely beat him up.

At 20, Coleman had already written hundreds of compositions, so when he was fired from Clayton's band while in Los Angeles he stayed there. He sought out musicians to play his compositions but most jazz musicians were unable to play them. Coleman taught his new concept, harmolodics, to trumpeter Don Cherry, drummers Billy Higgins and Ed Blackwell, and bassist Charlie Haden.

In 1958, record producer Lester Koening agreed to release two of Coleman's records on his label, Contemporary Records. These recordings led to a stint at New York City's famous club the Five Spot in November 1959 that caused an uproar in the jazz community. Many famous jazz musicians came, out of curiosity, to see Coleman play. The great drummer Max Roach was so infuriated by Coleman's music that he punched him in the mouth. Miles Davis claimed that Coleman sounded like he was "all screwed up inside," and

legendary trumpeter Roy Eldridge said, "I think he's jiving." Critics' reactions were equally varied. Other musicians, such as John Lewis, Jimmy Giuffre, Sonny Rollins, and Art Pepper, felt that Coleman's music was a major breakthrough. The great John Coltrane (see entry), then at the height of his powers, began to study with Coleman.

In the late 1960s and early 1970s Coleman frequently performed and recorded with his new drummer, his ten-year-old son Denardo, whom Coleman lauded for his free and expressive style. Coleman also frequently played with tenorman Dewey Redman, drummer Ed Blackwell, and bassist Charlie Haden, with whom he released numerous recordings on Blue Note records.

During this period Coleman also bought himself a home in the SoHo neighborhood of New York City: a loft large enough for concerts and performances. Numerous musicians lived with him there, including composer and reedman Anthony Braxton and violinist Leroy Jenkins. Rock-influenced guitarist James "Blood" Ulmer moved in, and began playing with Coleman, learning harmolodics. By the mid-1970s electric bassist Jamal Adeen Tacuma and drummer Ronald Shannon Jackson had joined the band, playing free jazz over funky rock grooves. Coleman called the group "Prime Time," and they began recording on the Antilles label in 1979. Soon Tacuma and Jackson had moved on to creating their own successful bands using harmolodics, and Coleman had replaced them with yet another younger set of musicians. Since then Prime Time has been Coleman's main project, although he frequently appeared with other artists from Pat Metheny to Jerry Garcia, and was often commissioned to compose and perform. One of his latest projects was collaborating with the composer Howard Shore on the soundtrack for the film *Naked Lunch* (1991).

Bibliography

Litweiler, John. *Ornette Coleman: A Harmolodic Life.* New York: Morrow, 1992.

Spellman, A. B. *Four Lives in the Bebop Business.* New York: Random House, 1966.

Eric Pakula

College Fight Songs are the energy and muscle of college sports. For basketball fans, "March Madness" means the National Collegiate Athletic Association (NCAA) is sponsoring its annual tournament to determine that year's champion of men's college basketball. (There also is a women's version at about the same time.) For music fans, the colorful and exciting tournament (sometimes called "the big dance") is also a time to experience the songs played by the bands of the 64 colleges and universities whose teams have merited inclusion in the sports contest. However, if one listened carefully and continually to the music performed by these pep bands during the 1980s and 1990s, it seemed at times that all the ensembles involved became overwhelmed by a musical "March madness" and knew only one piece—a five-note tidbit from the "Hootchy Kootchy Dance." This famous dance, often played to accompany belly dancing, was probably written by Sol Bloom during the 1893 Chicago World's Columbian Exposition. The melody has been adapted into parodies such as "Oh, they don't wear pants/On the southern side of France" and has been the inspiration for "borrowing" by other songs. The curious version used by so many college bands over and over again, the first five notes repeated once (which is the opening of a rock song), became the rage of so many college bands by the 1980s that the numerous good fight songs of the various colleges almost seemed to be secondary.

The first composition specifically written for college use, "Fair Harvard," appeared in 1836, set to a traditional tune. In 1872 the 19th century's best known college song, Cornell University's "Far Above Cayuga's Waters" was published. The lyrics were by two Cornell students, Archibald C. Weeks and Wilmot M. Smith, who used H. S. Thompson's 1858 ballad "Annie Lisle" as the source for the melody. Around the turn of the 20th century, some of the most famous fight songs began to be created. Louis Elbel wrote the stunning and proud "The Victors" for the University of Michigan in 1898. "On Wisconsin," the superb and much borrowed 1909 song, was written for the University of Wisconsin by composer William Thomas Purdy and lyricist Carl Beck. Other early fight songs are "Yale Boola," written in 1901 by A. M. Hirsh (the bouncy tune was later used by the University of Oklahoma for their rouser "Boomer Sooner"); "The Bull Dog," another Yale University song, created in 1911 by the great Cole Porter, then a student at Yale; "Down the Field" (1911), written by musician Stanleigh R. Freedman and lyricist C. W. O'Connor (the melody of this smooth Yale classic has been borrowed by the University of Tennessee and the University of Oregon); "The Eyes of Texas" (1903), with lyrics by John Lang Sinclair set to the tune for the anonymous 1894 American composition "I've Been Working on the Railroad" (later, "The Eyes of Texas" was incorporated into the official fight song of the University of Texas, "Texas Fight"); "Anchors Aweigh" (1907), by Alfred H. Miles and Charles A. Zimmerman, a splendid march used as the official song of both the U.S. Navy and the U.S. Naval Academy; "Semper Paratus," a highly stimulating composition by Francis S. Van Boskerch (used both by the U.S. Coast Guard and the Coast Guard Academy); "Notre Dame Victory March" or "Cheer, Cheer for Old Notre Dame" (1908), by the brothers Michael J. Shea and John F. Shea, probably the best known and possibly the best composed college fight song; and "The Maine Stein Song" (1910), with lyrics by Lincoln Colcord and music by E. A. Fenstad, adapted from one of Johannes Brahms's Hungarian dances (Rudy Vallee later made this lively song internationally famous).

Later fight songs include "Rambling Wreck from Georgia Tech" (1919), "Our Director March" (1926) by F. E. Bigelow, "Rice's Honor," "The Air Force Song" (1939) by Canadian-born Robert M. Crawford, and "Fight On for USC," also known by the generic title "Fight On," written for the University of Southern California in 1948 by Milo Sweet and Glen Grant.

Other notable and/or interesting fight songs, all of uncertain date, are Ohio State University's smooth and moving "Across the Field," written by W. A. Dougherty, Jr.; Clem-

son University's "Fight Song," which uses the very playful, lively, and anonymous tune for "Tiger Rag" (1917); the sweeping and dramatic "Hawaii Five-O," written by Mort Stevens for the television police series (an unofficial song of the University of Hawaii); the University of Georgia's "Glory, Glory to Old Georgia," which somewhat ironically uses the famous 19th-century tune for "The Battle Hymn of the Republic;" and the University of Colorado's "Glory, Glory, Colorado," which uses the same powerful melody.

Bibliography

Bailey, Dee. "College Songs." *New Grove Dictionary of American Music.* Vol. 1. Ed. H. Wiley Hitchcock and Stanley Sadie. London: Macmillan, 1986.

O'Brien, Robert F. *School Songs of America's Colleges and Universities: A Directory.* New York: Greenwood, 1991.

Studwell, William E. "College Fight Songs: An Essay and Bibliography." *Music Reference Services Quarterly* 3.4 (1994).

——. "The Top College Fight Songs." *The College Finder.* Ed. Steven R. Antonoff. New York: Ballantine, 1993. 443-44.

William E. Studwell

College Radio, as a culture, reflects the contemporary climate on the campus. As an outlet for the student population, it acts as a venue into the campus itself. The college radio station offers a true alternative to programming not commercially available or viable. The best indicator of this trend is the programming of alternative music that reflects the diverse lifestyles of a college culture. "College radio" encompasses stations operating on college and university campuses, including two-year colleges.

Initially, college radio stations were developed as experimental stations. Today, college radio broadcasting exists in many forms in addition to the standard FM and AM radio station. Carrier current/wired-wireless, and closed-circuit offer campuses additional outlets. An even more recent offering is the FM cable access station provided to schools through local cable TV systems or on-campus networks (see Carrier Current and Cable Radio).

The purposes and structures of college radio are many. Often an alternative to commercial radio, its programming can span many music genres, from rock to folk, jazz to metal, reggae to rap, gospel to tejano, and classical to country (see Radio Formats). Spoken word poetry, alternative-perspective news, religious, and political programming also often find a home on college radio. College radio is the training ground for tomorrow's broadcasters, providing the student an opportunity to practice techniques in broadcasting. Because most campus radio stations are under the auspices of an academic department within the college or university, the presence of the station can complement actual coursework. The stations are generally supervised by a faculty advisor or staff manager who oversees the administration and operation of the station on a day-to-day basis, providing needed continuity as student staffs change year to year.

Funding for stations varies greatly, with the bulk traditionally coming from student fee support or general academic funds. Some stations also solicit program underwriting support, listener contributions, and outright donations, which are important because advertiser/commercial content is severely restricted by law on noncommercial stations. The ongoing broadcasts provided by college radio function as public relations arms for the schools themselves. Often college radio stations are the only outlets for such broadcasts as campus sports and news. In regard to the colleges' and universities' perceptions of college radio, one advantage is that the institutional image is enhanced every time a well-programmed station identifies itself as affiliated with the school. Overall, as with commercial stations, the underlying premise of the college radio station is to serve the community, whether it be the campus community or the community at large, but in unique ways it is often geared to underserved segments of the population.

Some of the major umbrella organizations that support college radio are the Broadcast Education Association and the National Association of College Broadcasters. Numerous college radio stations are network affiliates of National Public Radio (see entry), offering well-known programming such as *Morning Edition* and *All Things Considered*.

Bibliography

Brant, Billy G. *The College Radio Handbook*. Blue Ridge Summit: TAB, 1981.

Samuel J. Sauls

Coltrane, John (1926-1967), a cult hero in popular music, was born in Hamlet, NC. In his short life, he sowed the seeds that influenced an entire generation of musicians. Perhaps no musician while still alive has received the extreme adulation given to "Trane." There were those who viewed him as a kind of messiah, a font of holiness.

Coltrane developed trends already present in jazz and creatively fostered others. While developing bop trends in harmonization to their ultimate logical conclusion with his stream of sound style of the 1950s, he also explored simpler modal style and free jazz, which emphasized melodic development free from confining chordal progressions. Like other innovators, he never entirely abandoned use of one style while moving toward another.

Both his parents were musical and he grew up in a musical environment. His father died when Coltrane was 12 years old, but his mother kept the family together and provided him with economic and emotional stability. She moved to Philadelphia where jobs were more plentiful in the World War II economy but sent money home to support him and aid her parents.

Upon graduation in 1943, Coltrane moved to Philadelphia to be with his mother. There he studied alto saxophone at the Orenstein School. As was said of him many times in his life, he impressed people with his seriousness, discipline, and eagerness. These studies were interrupted when he was drafted into the navy. Coltrane spent his naval career playing in the navy band in Hawaii.

Upon his discharge, he resumed his saxophone studies. Soon after, he played in a number of rhythm and blues bands, most notably that of Eddie "Cleanhead" Vinson. The spectacle of the serious Coltrane tossing horns to Vinson in a vaudeville setting is hard to imagine, but that is what he did and did well according to contemporary accounts. By this time, he had switched to tenor sax, originally so as not to compete with Vinson.

Unfortunately, Coltrane's various addictions in addition to music began to catch up with him at this time. He was an alcoholic, heroin user, heavy smoker, and addicted to sweets. He managed to kick all his habits, except his sugar addiction. Coltrane's sweet tooth cost him all his teeth, since he refused to have his cavities filled, and all his teeth ultimately decayed and were removed.

However much that may have cost him tonal clarity in his later career, his dental problems did not affect his articulation earlier in his profession. From 1949 to 1951, he played with Dizzy Gillespie's band and made his first recorded solo with that group.

In 1952, he resumed work with Earl Bostic's rhythm and blues band. Bostic, like Cleanhead Vinson, was primarily noted for his work on alto saxophone. His rhythm and blues style in the early 1950s exposed Coltrane to large dance audiences and emotional reactions to music once again.

Coltrane left Bostic to work with his early idol, Johnny Hodges. Hodges had left Ellington for a brief time to head his own band, one that has been underrated or forgotten over the years. In 1954, Hodges fired Trane because his heroin addiction had made him erratic and undependable.

Once more he returned to Philadelphia, where he suffered from physical and emotional problems. In this period, he met Juanita Grubbs, known as Naima. What is perhaps his most beautiful composition was named after her. In 1955 he and Naima married, and he seems to have sorted out his problems to the extent that he was able once again to resume playing.

He became part of Miles Davis's classic 1955 quintet. By this time, his style had incorporated elements of Charlie Parker and Coleman Hawkins. While Coltrane could play gorgeous melodic lines like Parker, in the 1950s he generally preferred to construct arpeggio-like vertical runs at breakneck speed. The style reflected the searching that characterized his life and personality.

Alcohol and drug abuse cost him his job with Miles Davis in 1957. However, Coltrane picked up his career with a stunning engagement with Thelonious Monk at the Five Spot in Manhattan. Working with Monk was worth more than all the theory courses one could take. Coltrane perfected his sheets-of-sound style with Monk, while absorbing Monk's unique approach to harmonic conception.

In 1960, Coltrane struck out on his own and began to develop other styles of playing. In his 1959 *Giant Steps* album he showed his ability to develop an older style while moving into a newer one. His *My Favourite Things* album (1961) marked a return to jazz of the soprano saxophone. Although it had been used over the years since Sidney Bechet had mastered it, notably by Johnny Hodges, no one had really turned it into a popular jazz instrument used on a regular basis by a major jazz figure. Coltrane was open in his acknowledgment of Bechet's influence on his soprano work.

Even in the midst of his freest experiments, *Ascension* (1965-66) and *Expression* (1967), when he recorded with Freddie Hubbard, Archie Shepp, Eric Dolphy, Pharoah Sanders, and Rashid Ali, Coltrane never totally abandoned his love of harmony and melody. *Expression*, his last recording, includes elements from all his periods. Certainly, Coltrane died at the top of his form, intonation problems or not. His creative flow had not dried up, and it is reasonable to assume that had he lived he would have continued to develop new areas without neglecting those through which he had passed.

Bibliography

Cole, Bill. *John Coltrane*. New York: Da Capo, 1993.

Fraim, John. *Spirit Catcher: The Life and Art of John Coltrane*. West Liberty: Greathouse, 1996.

Nisenson, Eric. *Ascension: John Coltrane and His Quest*. New York: St. Martin's, 1993.

Priestly, Brian. *John Coltrane*. London: Apollo, 1987.

Frank A. Salamone

Columbia has long been one of Hollywood's most important moviemaking and television-producing factories and continues that function at the close of the 20th century. Columbia was the first Hollywood studio taken over by a Japanese company, Sony, giving the studio impressive capital backing. Yet in its early years, Columbia struggled simply to exist in what was known as "Poverty Row." During the years just prior to the coming of sound, dozens of fly-by-night Hollywood producers attempted to become the next Metro-Goldwyn-Mayer. Columbia Pictures was one of only two that made it (Warner Bros. being the other).

Columbia's success came because of two brothers: Harry Cohn, the archetypal cigar-chomping movie mogul, and Jack Cohn, a quieter New York City-based insider. Both were tough negotiators and skilled businessmen. Beginning in 1924, the brothers Cohn marshaled their forces to create movies on the cheap and then distribute them first across the U.S. and by 1931 around the world. Unlike the major Hollywood studios of the 1930s and 1940s, Columbia could never afford to buy a circuit of theaters.

Columbia came of age in 1934 with the release of Frank Capra's *It Happened One Night*, which swept the Academy Awards. Harry Cohn had signed Clark Gable and Claudette Colbert for that film because MGM and Paramount bosses wanted to "punish" their ungrateful stars. But such a coup was not business as usual for Columbia. Typically, during the 1930s, Columbia relied on "B" Westerns, serials, and shorts to stay in business. Today the studio is too often only remembered for its rare high-cost productions: Frank Capra's *Mr. Deeds Goes to Town* (1936), *Lost Horizon* (1937), George Stevens's *Penny Serenade* (1941), *Talk of the Town* (1942), *The Jolson Story* (1946), and its sequel (1949).

But the efforts of Western heroes Buck Jones and Gene Autry enabled the studio to remain consistently in the black. Popular series focused on Boston Blackie and the Lone Wolf. Serials included *Batman* and *Terry and the Pirates*. The antics of the Three Stooges were a favorite with children.

The Cohn brothers responded well to the coming of television and prospered further. In 1951 Columbia established Screen Gems to produce television series and distribute films and series to television. Using these profits Columbia then began to distribute the significant works of such filmmakers as David Lean, Elia Kazan, Otto Preminger, and Fred Zinnemann. Columbia was responsible for *From Here to Eternity* (1953), *On the Waterfront* (1955), *The Caine Mutiny* (1954), and *The Bridge on the River Kwai* (1957).

The Cohn brothers ruled Columbia until their deaths—Jack in 1956 and Harry in 1958. Abe Schneider and Leo Jaffe succeeded the Cohns, and under their leadership Columbia continued to prosper with *Lawrence of Arabia* (1962), *A Man for All Seasons* (1966), *Guess Who's Coming to Dinner* (1967), *To Sir, with Love* (1967), *In Cold Blood* (1967), and *Oliver!* (1968). In 1969 Columbia distributed *Easy Rider*. Ray Stark, producer of *Funny Girl* (1968), emerged as Columbia's principal hit-maker, and television series rolled out regularly from the studio lot.

The 1970s were not kind to Columbia. The studio lost $50 million in 1973 and cost-cutting became the order of the day. Columbia sold its Gower lot and moved in to share operations at Warners' Burbank studio. It suffered a publicity nightmare when executive David Begelman was accused of embezzling millions of dollars.

Columbia needed help, particularly financial support, and got it when mighty Coca-Cola bought Columbia and took charge. Coca-Cola brought a research-oriented, marketing philosophy to the movie business, where instinct and intuition had long proven the business methodology of choice. Coca-Cola tried to harness the creative energies in Hollywood by having traditional business-school-trained executives formulate strategies to optimize sales and rentals from "movie software." Despite a series of skillful attempts at cross-promotional advertisements for soft drinks and movies (for example, Diet Coke and Steve Martin's *Roxanne*), Coca-Cola never was able to create a true blockbuster film and in 1988 looked to spin off Columbia Pictures.

Ownership changed in October of 1989. That month the Sony Corporation, the giant electronics manufacturer from Japan, agreed to pay more than $3 billion for Columbia Pictures as well as assume more than $1 billion of Columbia's debt. Sony acquired not only an ongoing movie and television studio, but an extensive library of nearly 3,000 movies and 23,000 television episodes.

The biggest surprise of the Sony takeover was the price it agreed to pay to sign two top Hollywood executives—Peter Guber and Jon Peters. The duo, the powers behind such hit movies as *Rain Man*, broke their multiyear contract with Warner Bros. to run the "new" Columbia for a fee that amounted to more than $500 million. Even the most cynical of Hollywood observers were surprised that Sony was willing to give Warners half ownership in its Columbia Record Club and its share in the Burbank Studio in order to sign Guber and Peters.

The results into the 1990s have been mixed. Columbia remains one of six major studios that continue to dominate Hollywood filmmaking and television production.

Bibliography

Dick, Bernard F. *Columbia Pictures*. Lexington: U of Kentucky P, 1992.

Gomery, Douglas. *The Hollywood Studio System*. New York: St. Martin's, 1986.

Hirschhorn, Clive. *The Columbia Story*. New York: Crown, 1989.

McClintick, David. *Indecent Exposure*. New York: Morrow, 1982.

Douglas Gomery

Columbo (1971-1977), an unconventional television cop show, should not have worked, but it did. The show was not a whodunit, but a how-will-he-unravel-it. The murderer appeared first, the credits signaling which guest star the audience should track. The murder was plotted, planned, and executed before the viewer's eyes. Well into the drama, Columbo arrived. The sparring began.

Peter Falk (1927-) fashioned the disheveled Lt. Columbo into one of the most enduring and endearing figures in television history. Character and actor were so closely associated, it is difficult to imagine that the role was originally offered to Bing Crosby. Antecedents for this character could be Jimmy Stewart's folksy lawyer in *Anatomy of a Murder* (1959), Edward G. Robinson's canny insurance claimsman in *Double Indemnity* (1944), and Falk's own disorganized barrister in the short-lived but memorable *Trials of O'Brien* (1965), but Falk made shambling Columbo into an institution. Winning three best actor Emmys during the show's original seven-year span, Falk has been periodically coaxed back for two-hour *Columbo* specials ever since.

Audiences were introduced to Columbo in a pair of TV movie pilots, *Prescription: Murder* (1968) and *Ransom for a Dead Man* (1971). *Columbo* then became part of *NBC's Mystery Movie* series, which first aired on Wednesdays and then shifted to Sundays. *McCloud* (Dennis Weaver) and *McMillan and Wife* (Rock Hudson and Susan Saint James) were the other original components of the series, alternating with the *Columbo* episodes.

Other shows launched from this format included *Hec Ramsey* (Richard Boone), *Amy Prentiss* (Jessica Walter), *McCoy* (Tony Curtis), *Quincy, M.E.* (Jack Klugman), and *Lanigan's Rabbi* (Art Carney and Bruce Solomon). NBC introduced additional programs in the rotating *Wednesday Mystery Movie* slot: *Madigan, Cool Million, Banacek, Tenafly, Faraday & Company*, and *The Snoop Sisters*. None proved as durable as *Columbo*.

Bibliography

Brooks, Tim, and Earle Marsh. *The Complete Directory to Prime Time Network and Cable TV Shows, 1946-Present*. New York: Ballantine, 1995.

McNeil, Alex. *Total Television: A Comprehensive Guide to Programming from 1948 to the Present*. New York: Penguin, 1991.

Karen Koegler

Comedians, Standup, in the second half of the 20th century, became one of the most popular and ubiquitous entertainers.

The exact origins of standup comedy are lost in history. In Western culture, standup comedy might be traced back to the figure of the fool which inhabited the cot of the Egyptian pharaohs of the Fifth Dynasty. In English-speaking countries, the familiar tradition of the medieval royal fool or jester was a practice which was carried up into the 18th century. The role of the fool was to provide entertainment for royal or noble households.

Over time, many elements from the fools' repertoire were incorporated into the theater. The most famous fools were improvisers as well as performers of set-pieces, the majority of which they created themselves.

The music hall grew out of tavern entertainments (established to get around theatrical licensing laws). By the middle of the 19th century, the format was well developed; it flourished until after World War I. These two strains, the fool and the music hall, came together in the United States around 1865 when Michael Bennet Leavitt invented burlesque (see entry—a type of entertainment not to be confused with classical theatrical burlesque). Leavitt's burlesque was intended for men only.

Paralleling burlesque was another form of entertainment that featured comedians, vaudeville (see entry). Vaudeville, too, started out in much the same vein as the English music hall. By the 1870s, instead of following the same path as burlesque, vaudeville was on its way to becoming family entertainment. The format was similar to that of burlesque, but the comedy was not as coarse and the "leg shows" were omitted. The life of vaudeville was relatively short. By the 1920s, its demise was imminent, promulgated to a large extent by the emerging cinema, especially when the talkies arrived on the scene. Vaudeville had been home to a large number of America's best and favorite comedians. Jack Benny, Fred Allen, George Burns, Gracie Allen, Milton Berle, Henny Youngman, Red Skelton, Joey Bishop, Jack E. Leonard, Buddy Hackett, and a host of others honed their skills on the vaudeville circuit (much of which consisted of stops at Jewish resorts in New York state's Catskill Mountains).

When radio became available to a majority of American households in the 1930s and 1940s, a great many of these comedians transferred to this new medium of entertainment (Benny, Fred Allen, and Burns and Allen had their own radio programs). Most of those who had moved into radio also were featured prominently in the motion pictures of the time, some creating careers in film that lasted well into the 1980s. The same phenomenon occurred with the rising popularity of another new form of technology, television. Berle, starring in his own *Texaco Star Theater* (see entry), became one of the most popular entertainers ever on the new medium.

Indeed, in the past 50 years, television has been the prime exhibition ground for standup comedians. Beginning in the 1950s and 1960s, Jack Paar and Steve Allen, along with Joey Bishop, were instrumental in establishing late-night television as a home for standup comedians. Dick Cavett, Johnny Carson, David Letterman, and Jay Leno, who started out in standup, graduated to being hosts of these shows and continuing the tradition of spotlighting standup comedy on their programs. Today, a whole new generation of standup comedians (almost all of whom became famous on the comedy club circuit) has made the transition to television with sitcom shows of their own—Gabe Kaplan, Jerry Seinfeld, Roseanne Barr, Garry Shandling, Paul Reiser, Tim Allen, Ray Romano, Paul Rodriguez, Ellen DeGeneres, Brett Butler, Jeff Foxworthy, Paula Poundstone, and Drew Carey, to name a few.

Television has not been the prime training ground for standup comedians. This distinction belongs to the clubs, night and comedy. Will Rogers, Bob Hope, Jerry Lewis, Bob Newhart, Woody Allen—these names are associated with work in the nightclubs (and in some cases the speakeasies) of the 1920s through the 1950s. In the 1950s, though, nightclubs went into a decline, to a large extent due to the variety of competition presented by television. Comedy clubs replaced them. In 1963, the only showcase club in the United States was the New York Improv (where Freddie Prinze, Jimmie Walker, Robert Klein, David Brenner, Rodney Dangerfield, Kaplan, Bill Cosby, Cavett, and Steve Landesberg got their starts). Since then, clubs have proliferated. Clubs such as the Comedy Store in Los Angeles (an early venue for Richard Pryor and Robin Williams) and Pips in Brooklyn (where Klein started) highlighted newcomers and old-timers alike, and people went to hear them in droves. Acts either washed out quickly or became professionally polished. A circuit was established, in part supported by other media—Home Box Office specials, followed by programs on Showtime and Cinemax and finally a comedy channel, Comedy Central, along with the focus on *Saturday Night Live* (see entry), for instance—and standup comedians found that they could make a living on the road. The clubs boomed in the 1980s, and at the end of that decade it was estimated that over 300 of them existed. People such as Eddie Murphy (who was strongly influenced by Pryor) and Robin Williams became household names (and went on to establish careers in the movies).

Among today's performers, harking back to standup comedy's beginnings, there are those who specialize: political humorists (Mort Sahl—who influenced Lenny Bruce—Pat Paulsen, and Mark Russell); insulters (like Don Rickles), whose performances are reminiscent of the medieval flyting (verbal abuse) contests; and crazies (people such as Steve Martin, Andy Kaufman, Sam Kinison—a protégé of Dangerfield's—and "Bobcat" Goldthwait). These categories seem to have been established since early in the history of genre. However, the second half of the 20th century has also been a time of change in the composition of the performers—color and gender moved from white male to encompass black and Latino men and women of all races. This is at least in part due to the ubiquitousness of that commonizer, television, which enters more homes in America than indoor plumbing. Exposed to nationally televised programs featuring standup comics, minorities felt at home exploring their own perspectives on American life through this medium. Flip Wilson starred in his own comedy show; Bill Cosby was a regular on *The Tonight Show*; Red Foxx moved from off-color jokes in predominantly black night spots to a popular situation comedy; and Andy Griffith showed that even white males who were not northern in accent could succeed. The ethnic humor of black comedians George Wallace and Sinbad has replaced that of other minority jokesters, particularly the Jewish (Myron Cohen and Jack Carter), of two or three decades ago (though a strong Jewish influence has been present throughout, with today's practitioners including Alan King, Jackie Mason, Shelley Berman, and Shecky Greene). Louis Anderson made being fat funny. Phyllis Diller, Joan Rivers, and Rita Rudner proved that they could be as popular as the men.

Four standup comedians who can be singled out for both their uniqueness and their representiveness are Dangerfield, Lenny Bruce, George Carlin, and Richard Pryor (see entries).

Bibliography

Bruce, Lenny. *How to Talk Dirty and Influence People.* Englewood Cliffs: Simon & Schuster, 1965.

Carlin, George. *Sometimes a Little Brain Damage Can Help.* Philadelphia: Running, 1984.

Dangerfield, Rodney. *I Couldn't Stand My Wife's Cooking, So I Opened a Restaurant!* Middle Village, NY: Jonathan David, 1972.

Goldman, Albert. *Ladies and Gentlemen—Lenny Bruce!!* New York: Random House, 1974.

Haskins, Jim. *Richard Pryor: A Man and His Madness.* New York: Beaufort, 1984.

Kofsky, Frank. *Lenny Bruce: The Comedian as Social Critic and Secular Moralist.* New York: Monad, 1974.

Pryor, Richard. *Pryor Convictions and Other Life Sentences.* New York: Pantheon, 1995.

Russell, Dave. "Varieties of Life: The Making of the Edwardian Music Hall." *The Edwardian Theatre: Essays on Performance and the Stage.* Ed. Michael R. Booth and Joel H. Kaplan. Cambridge: Cambridge UP, 1996. 61-85.

Smith, Ronald L. *Who's Who in Comedy: Comedians, Comics and Clowns from Vaudeville to Today's Standups.* New York: Facts on File, 1992.

Williams, John A., and Dennis A. Williams. *If I Stop I'll Die: The Comedy and Tragedy of Richard Pryor.* New York: Thunder Mouth, 1991.

Steven H. Gale

Comic Book Autobiography is a new entry in self-revelatory prose. Many comics creators have produced autobiographies (e.g., Harvey Kurtzman), but few of them have done so in the art form for which they are famous. While cartoonists have long included autobiographical elements in their works (e.g., Sheldon Mayer's "Scribbly" stories, Charles Schulz's *Peanuts*, Alex Toth, and Will Eisner's recent works), strictly autobiographical comics originated in the often self-published works of the "underground comix" movement.

Noted figures who have produced autobiographical comics include Robert Crumb, Trina Robbins, Matt Groening, Linda Barry, Chester Brown, and Art Spiegelman, whose Pulitzer Prize-winning *Maus*, though ostensibly his father's biography, is actually Spiegelman's autobiographical account of trying to "get to know" his father. Arguably, the most important figure in autobiographical comics is Harvey Pekar, who, since the mid-1970s (and in collaboration with a number of artists), has been chronicling his life in annual issues of *American Splendor* (1976-). From the late 1980s to the early 1990s, national recognition of Pekar's work (trade paperback collections, television appearances, news articles, critical reviews) probably did more than anything else to generate the spate of autobiographical comics that appeared during that time. Certainly many of those who followed Pekar have tried to emulate his brutally honest (and almost self-denigrating) approach—though unfortunately without emulating his focus and pacing. Most recently, a near-fatal bout with cancer provided the impetus for Pekar's *Our Cancer Year*, a moving work done in collaboration with his wife, Joyce Brabner, and artist Frank Stack.

Bibliography

Brabner, Joyce, and Harvey Pekar. *Our Cancer Year*. New York: Four Walls Eight Windows, 1994.

Eisner, Will. *A Contract with God and Other Tenement Stories*. Princeton: Kitchen Sink, 1986.

Reynolds, Richard. *Super Heroes: A Modern Mythology*. Jackson: UP of Mississippi, 1994.

Spiegelman, Art. *Maus: A Survivor's Tale*. 2 vols. New York: Pantheon, 1986; 1991.

Toth, Alex. *Alex Toth*. Northampton: Kitchen Sink, 1995.

Witek, Joseph. *Comic Books As History: The Narrative Art of Jack Jackson, Art Spiegelman, and Harvey Pekar*. Jackson: UP of Mississippi, 1989.

Daryl R. Coats

Comic Book Superheroes have some roots in folklore, mythology, religion, pulp magazine adventure heroes, and science fiction, but the superhero first came into its full form in American comic books (see next entry). The first comic book superhero (and the one from whose name the term derives) was Jerry Siegel and Joe Shuster's Superman, who first appeared in 1938 in the first issue of *Action Comics*. It has been reasonably argued that Superman's appearance is the most important event in the history of American comics. Certainly it led to an explosion of publishers and provided some form of direction for a directionless medium—and it seemed to fix the perception that many readers, nonreaders, and publishers have of comics. Even comics fandom, in dividing the history of comics into "ages" (e.g., golden age, silver age), does so on the basis of the appearance of superhero comics (*Action Comics* No. 1; *Showcase* No. 4; *Giant-Size X-Men* No. 1).

For the most part, the first superheroes were very crude and simplistic, often the work of writers and artists not much older than the children targeted as their audience. Hundreds of superheroes saturated newsstands in the early 1940s, but despite the popularity of such characters as Batman, Captain Marvel, Plastic Man, Wonder Woman, the Human Torch, Sub-mariner, Captain America, and the Justice Society of America, most superheroes were very short-lived. By the end of World War II almost all of them were gone, and very few superheroes were published during the 1950s. The 1960s, however, witnessed a resurgence in the popularity of superheroes, during which the "Marvel Age of Comics" revolutionized the superhero genre with its depiction of flawed

Marvel's Spider-man, a flawed hero. Photo courtesy of Popular Culture Library, Bowling Green State University, Bowling Green, OH.

heroes (e.g., Spider-man; the Hulk) who had more trouble solving their personal problems than they did foiling villains—and by restoring a "relevancy" that had been missing from the genre since the late 1940s (see Marvel Comics).

In the 1970s, superheroes came more and more to dominate the steadily declining comics market. Whereas other genres at this time apparently had mostly casual readers, superheroes had devoted fans. (The superhero "renaissance" of the 1960s was accompanied by the growth of comics fandom, much of which regarded the superhero genre more fondly than it did the others.) By the 1980s, publishers DC and Marvel were deriving most of their sales from comics shops supported by superhero fans. Consequently, they began to focus almost exclusively on producing superhero comics. Although the superhero genre in the 1980s still was often childishly repetitive, several superhero comics of the period received much media and critical attention, among them Frank Miller's *The Dark Knight Returns* (see Batman) and Alan Moore's and Dave Gibbons's *Watchmen*. The "sophistication" of such works contributed to the two dominant approaches to superhero comics of the 1990s: an imitative, "grim and gritty" approach that made heroes out of Wolverine and Spawn and "bad girls," which often destroyed and darkened earlier superheroes (e.g., Green Lantern and Iron

Man both became villainous murderers); and a reactionary, more lighthearted, revisionist approach that sought to re-create the more innocent superheroes of earlier decades, but with a more sophisticated and almost ironic edge (e.g., *1963* and *Big Bang Comics*).

Bibliography
Reynolds, Richard. *Super Heroes: A Modern Mythology.* Jackson: UP of Mississippi, 1994.

Daryl R. Coats

Comic Books, as a medium of communication, were made technically possible by earlier arts and media: European illustration and woodcuts, journalism, color printing, greeting cards, romances, pulp magazines, photography and early film with storyboards.

Serialized adventure comic strips (see next entry) were key to the coming of age of the book-length comic in the 1930s, especially after the 1929 syndication of *Tarzan*, which set the standard both for art and story. *Buck Rogers, Dick Tracy,* and *Terry and the Pirates* soon followed. In May 1939, Batman emerged in issue 27 of *Detective Comics,* preceded by the first publication of Superman in the June 1938 issue of *Action Comics*. While adventuring rose in the 1930s, other domestic and regional subtexts got on board, such as *Blondie, L'il Abner,* and *Mickey Mouse* in comic strip format.

The onset of World War II found many cartoonists sympathetic to the Allied cause, even before the U.S. joined the war. Comic strips and books bloomed with new heroes despite the decreasing supply of chemicals to color the frames. After the war as comics settled down to crime, romance, and humor, new strips emerged, like *Pogo* (1949) and *Peanuts* (1950), both of which added social commentary and morality over the humor.

Other trends include Dell, Disney, and Archie Comics as well as *Classics Illustrated*. By the 1960s Marvel Comics (see entry) began its pantheon of existential superheroes while underground comics like *The Fabulously Furry Freak Brothers* and *Zap! Comix* also mirrored the controversies of the times. As Marvel rose to become a titan of the industry, new syndicated strips like *B.C., Doonesbury,* and *Hagar the Horrible* gained high-profile readership. Japanese and other international influences generated the look and feel of upscaled graphic novels in the 1980s. *Batman* and *Superman* were reinvented to rival the new style with its abundant color palette. *Watchmen* further celebrated the new style with post-modern narrative strategies, both as a story in its own right and as a self-reflexive commentary on the history of comics.

Comics did not thrive without controversy. EC Comics (Educational Comics) ironically began as Bible-oriented but with slowing sales branched into *Tales from the Crypt, Weird Stories,* and others. A Dr. Wertheim spearheaded a morality campaign at the gory excesses. Senator Joseph McCarthy championed the investigation into comics, resulting in a comic book code. With the onslaught EC eventually turned to *MAD,* a magazine which regularly lambasted the sorts of hypocrisy levied against recalcitrant comics.

Sex comics emerged during the underground years of the 1960s, though various lewd strips had predated them by many years. Currently there are gay and lesbian entries, like *Dykes to Watch Out For* and *Meat Men*. Naturally, Tom of Finland's earlier illustrations of beefy men on the make gave over to overt eroticism in ways that more mainstream publications only hinted at, with skintight costumes and cut and buffed bodies. In the meantime, sports trading cards have opened to cheesecake and single-frame erotic robots.

Finally, numerous role-playing games have their corresponding comic books, and there are fanzines of *Star Trek* which feature comics and stories of Spock and Kirk, most often called slash fiction. After Superman "died" in the early 1990s, comics branched more into high quality production standards, including multicolor, lack of ads, and a self-contained look for each issue.

Photo courtesy of Popular Culture Library, Bowling Green State University, Bowling Green, OH.

Bibliography
Couperie, Pierre, et al. *A History of the Comic Strip*. Trans. Eileen B. Hennessy. New York: Crown, 1968.

Lupoff, Dick, and Don Thompson. *All in Color for a Dime*. New Rochelle: Arlington, 1970.

McCloud, Scott. *Understanding Comics*. Northampton: Kitchen Sink, 1993.

Reynolds, Richard. *Super Heroes: A Modern Mythology*. Jackson: UP of Mississippi, 1992.

Spaulding, Amy. *The Page As a Stage Set: Storyboard Picture Books*. Metuchen: Scarecrow, 1995.

Carl Holmberg

Comic Strips are generally believed to have begun in 1896 with the debut of Richard F. Outcault's *The Yellow Kid*. Commissioned by the *New York World* as a means of attracting readers by use of humorous color inserts every Sunday, *The Yellow Kid* epitomizes the type of drawing and storyline that dominated the early years of the form. Crudely drawn, colored yellow because that was the easiest color to reproduce (thus coining the term "yellow journalism"; see entry), it was crammed with illustrations and text in the style of the editorial and political cartoons of the previous 200 years. The Kid, who lived in Hogan's Alley, was street-wise and a representation of the ethnic diversity of Hogan's Alley and America. Outcault's strip was written phonetically, as comic strips like Rudolph Dirks's *The Katzenjammer Kids*, George Herriman's *Krazy Kat*, and Harry Hershfield's *Abie the Agent* would continue to do well into the 1930s.

Early comic strips borrowed material from recognizable sources such as fables, folklore, and vaudeville. They would soon incorporate elements of contemporary culture like newspaper headlines. A single Sunday comic strip often filled an entire newspaper page, and was printed in four or five colors, plus black and white. As the popularity of comic supplements to newspapers grew, so did various rivalries between publishers. This led to the business phenomena and techniques of syndicates and syndication. Comic strips of the 1910s and 1920s introduced "girl strips" such as Cliff Sterrett's *Polly and Her Pals* (begun 1912), Martin Branner's *Winnie Winkle* (begun 1920) and Russ Westover's *Tillie the Toiler* (begun 1921). In the 1920s, newspapers also featured adventure strips such as Roy Crane's *Wash Tubbs* (begun 1924) and Harold Gray's *Little Orphan Annie* (begun 1924).

The Great Depression was a watershed era for newspaper comics as it was for American mass entertainment media in general. The 1930s were marked by the continued success of humor and adventure strips and introduced newcomers like Chic Young's *Blondie* (begun 1930), Chester Gould's *Dick Tracy* (begun in 1931; see entry), and Milton Caniff's *Terry and the Pirates* (begun 1934). There were many more. In the 1940s, many of the newspaper strips which originated in the 1920s and 1930s continued and thrived. Such was the case of Gould's *Dick Tracy* and Gray's *Little Orphan Annie*. Humor strips centered around an extended family or neighborhood, popular since the earliest days of the modern comic strip, also continued to flourish. Young's *Blondie*, from this group of comic strips, would eventually become one of the most-read newspaper strips of all time. The most popular newspaper comics of the 1940s had circulations in the tens of millions and were showcased in many hundreds of tabloids nationwide.

Of the many important newspaper comic strips emerging in the 1940s, Dale Messick's *Brenda Starr* (begun 1940) is one of the most significant. Created, written, and drawn by Messick, *Brenda Starr* was a topnotch adventure/detective/ thriller story featuring sharp, detailed, and inventive illustrations and a beautiful, progressive, intelligent, and self-assured heroine. By the 1950s, that decade when Charles Schulz first brought us Charlie Brown's gang in *Peanuts* (begun 1950), it became increasingly apparent that comic strips were undergoing a change in format—newspaper editors were making them smaller, fitting several Sunday strips on one page and downsizing daily strips. It is only recently that comic strip creators, writers, and artists have had any significant creative or licensing control over their art forms. For the most part—and Milton Caniff's *Steve Canyon* (begun 1947) was a landmark exception here—newspapers have always owned the comic strips, hiring and firing creators, writers, and artists over a range of minor and major disputes.

One hundred years after the advent of comic strips as a marketing tool, the medium appears to be taken for granted. Old standards in often compromised forms carry on; only a handful of truly innovative works have appeared in recent decades. Of these, Berkeley Breathed's *Bloom County* and Bill Watterson's *Calvin and Hobbes* are most noteworthy (see entries).

Bibliography

Blackbeard, Bill, and Dale Crain, eds. *The Comic Strip Century: Celebrating 100 Years of an American Art Form*. Northampton: Kitchen Sink, 1995.

Blackbeard, Bill, and Martin Williams, eds. *The Smithsonian Collection of Newspaper Comics*. Washington, DC: Smithsonian Institution, 1977.

Emery, Edwin, and Edwin H. Ford, eds. *Highlights of the History of the American Press*. St. Paul: U of Minnesota P, 1954.

Goulart, Ron. *The Encyclopedia of American Comics from 1897 to the Present*. New York: Facts on File, 1990.

Horn, Maurice, ed. *The World Encyclopedia of Comics*. New York: Chelsea, 1976.

Virginia Woods Roberts

See also
Radio and Cartoons

Community Radio in the U.S. is one of the few loci of people-based politics and culture. It is predicated on the continually active interchange of responsibility between broadcaster and listener. The listeners come to the station as active participants in the creation of programming to share with others having similar concerns, as well as with the larger society within the range of the station's signal. The station is a center for community communications and cultural creation, acting as diverse voices of, by, and for the participating public rather than a centralized, monolithic source to them.

Community radio has become the primary voice for politically and culturally marginalized populations, presenting compelling programming produced by and for AHANA (African, Hispanic, Asian and Native American) peoples, gays and lesbians, the elderly, children, the physically challenged. Funding comes primarily from listener subscription, community fundraising, and occasional gifts from progressive foundations.

The first such station, KPFA in Berkeley, CA (begun by Lewis Hill in 1949), remains on the air to this day. It is affiliated with four sibling stations of the Pacifica Foundation, which are located in Los Angeles, New York, Houston, and Washington, DC. Programming on these stations has been culturally diverse, including live poetry readings by such people as Allen Ginsberg and Lawrence Ferlinghetti, programs by pacifists discussing their opposition to the Korean, Vietnam, and Gulf wars, eclectic mixtures of classical, rock, folk, blues, jazz, hip-hop, electronic, and international folk music that can be heard nowhere else on the dial, or collages of spoken word and music.

These and roughly 40 other urban community stations try to be focal points for the variety of dispossessed communities in their area. The KRAB Nebula, named after station KRAB in Seattle, WA, is organized collectively. Their public affairs programs lean heavily toward community access by participation in panel discussions, listener call-in programs, and debates.

Two urban stations that have successfully incorporated participation by AHANA peoples for the bulk of their programming have been KPOO-FM San Francisco and WPFW Washington, DC. KPOO-FM calls itself "Poor People's Radio," and has had active participation by the city's Latino, Asian, Filipino and Native American communities. WPFW provides jazz, blues, and public affairs programming for the minority communities in and around the nation's capital.

There are roughly 100 stations in smaller, more homogeneous communities. These range from KILI-FM, the "Voice of the Lakota Nation" in Porcupine, SD, to various stations in college and university communities, to a virtual one-person station in a housing project in Springfield, IL. KILI includes programming in native languages, as does KCAW, "Raven Radio," in Sitka, AK.

Two organizations represent the interests of community radio. The NFCB (National Federation of Community Broadcasters) is headquartered in Washington, DC, and is the lobbying agency for its approximately 120 members around the country. AMARC (the French acronym for the World Association for Community Radio Broadcasters) is housed in Montreal, Quebec, Canada. It is a resource for the worldwide community radio movement, providing workshops on station management and structure, programming content, and community outreach efforts.

The Baha'i religion also has an extensive international community radio effort. One of their stations, WLGI-FM, is in Hemingway, SC. It acts as a community outreach project for the local area.

Despite their tenuous existence, community radio stations have, for more than 50 years, pointed the ways for the possibilities of radio, providing a continuing forum for unconventional ideas in politics, the arts, and community affairs. As such, they have been unique cultural resources in their communities.

Bibliography
Girard, Bruce. *A Passion for Radio: Radio Waves and Community.* Montreal: Black Rose, 1992.
McKinney, Eleanor. *The Exacting Ear.* New York: Pantheon, 1966.
Strauss, Neil, ed. *Radiotext(e).* New York: Semiotext(e), 1993.

John L. Hochheimer

See also
Black Radio Networks
Native American Radio
Radio Formats

Computer Art refers to any aesthetic formation based on logical or numerical transposition of given data produced with the aid of electronic mechanisms. This definition encompasses many possibilities and allows inclusion of not only computer images and objects that emulate conventional drawing, painting, photography, and sculpture but also works that extend beyond conventional art-world constraints, including computer-controlled environments, electronically mediated interactive displays such as video games, and multimedia events such as films or performances.

The evolution of computer art has been shaped and influenced by the contexts of computer development and application. Much early imagery evolved out of U.S. military research. The earliest examples of computer art were produced in the 1940s on analog machines, resulting, for example, in Herbert W. Franke's images of cathode ray oscilloscope patterns and Ben F. Laposky's images of electrical oscillations of varying time functions. In the 1960s the first digital images presented as art were produced. These images took the form of alphanumeric hard copy from teletypes, line printers, and flat-bed plotters. Initial efforts in computer art came from scientists and mathematicians. An excellent collection of early images, made by such famous names in the history of computer art as A. Michael Noll, Kenneth Knowlton, and Charles Csuri, is found in *Computer Graphics—Computer Art* by Herbert W. Franke (1971). Noll was a mathematician, Knowlton worked in the Bell Telephone Laboratories, and Charles Csuri was a professor of art at the Ohio State University. A collaborative work by Csuri and computer scientist James Shaffer titled *Sine Curve Man* was awarded first prize in the 1967 computer art contest of the magazine *Computer and Animation.*

Cynthia Goodman's book *Digital Visions: Computers and Art* (1987) provides a comprehensive discussion of computer art from the early 1960s through the mid-1980s. A key figure in digital photography is Nancy Burson, whose melded digitized images of portraits of famous personalities (including Reagan and Chernenko) and combinations of images of different kinds of animals produced surreal statements and meanings. She is well known for her Age Machine, an interactive computer station that automatically ages the subjects of her photographs.

Today, computer art is ubiquitous—it is found in television, video games, commercial graphics software packages, museums and galleries, and movies (especially for special effects; see the next entry). Access to the computer as an art tool is now available to millions of people through a myriad of relatively inexpensive software packages, including the award-winning Kid Pix (released in 1991 from Broderbund Software). The program, developed by Craig Hickman, who teaches computer art and information design at the University of Oregon, received the Software Publishers Association Award for best user interface program in 1991. The original graphics program available for commercial use, called MacPaint, created the standard for the Apple Macintosh user interface. Kid Pix continues but also expands this interface, incorporating multimedia options, or a combining of sound, text and graphics.

Another approach in computer art involves interactive imaging and image processing. Computer scientist Myron Krueger, who has been refining cybernetic concepts for almost 20 years, has developed a new art form he calls Responsive Environments. Krueger describes the Responsive Environment as a unique melding of aesthetics and technology, dependent upon a collaboration between the artist (creator) and the audience (viewer). The characteristic that differentiates computer art, as defined by Krueger, from most other forms of art is that it incorporates the real life of the viewer/participant in a dynamic and integral way.

The notion of interactivity reached new dimensions in the 1990s with the combination of telecommunications and participation, creating one of the first telecommunications art events on a global scale. The Electronic Mural Project, featured at the 1992 SIGGRAPH art show, allowed the real-time transmission of text, graphics, paintings, video, and other multimedia elements as they were created through the use of off-the-shelf Apple Macintosh hardware and software applications. The network connected artists working in different locations (in this case Chicago, San Francisco, San Jose, Toronto, and Tokyo) to create artworks together.

It is still difficult to find much information about computer art in traditional art magazines or museums and galleries. However, as soon as one steps out of the conventional art world, the prominence of computer art as a component of popular culture, and the attendant computer art community, becomes all too evident. One very important journal, bridging the artistic and scientific communities, is *Leonardo: Journal of the International Society for the Arts, Sciences and Technology*. Two key international organizations, publishing journals and holding annual meetings, are SIGGRAPH (Special Interest Group for Graphics of the Association for Computing Machinery) and NCGA (National Computer Graphics Association). Electronic data bases, available through a number of public and private computer networks, also provide extensive, often interactive information about computer art, as well as local to international special interest groups.

Bibliography
Franke, Herbert W. *Computer Graphics—Computer Art.* 2d ed. Berlin: Springer-Verlag, 1985.
Goodman, Cynthia. *Digital Visions: Computers and Art.* New York: Abrams, 1987.
Leonardo: Journal of the International Society for the Arts, Sciences and Technology 26 May 1993.
SIGGRAPH. *Association for Computing Machinery.* 11 West 42nd Street, NY 10036.

Linda F. Ettinger

Computers and Movies are close relatives, and computers contribute to both plot and technology of movies. Ever since "computer" became a common word, "thinking" machines have had movie prominence. An early major film with a major role for a computer was *2001: A Space Odyssey* (1968), in which Hal, a quiet-voiced, chess-playing computer, goes berserk. Computers in control, causing problems for humans, are common in movies. In *Demolition Man* (1993), this plot is played for laughs, e.g., the computer issuing citations for swearing. *Wargames* (1983) is serious in depicting the computer mistakenly beginning a countdown to nuclear attack. Extreme versions of computer-in-control can be seen in *Terminator* (1984) and *Terminator 2* (1991), when a future computer engages in a war to exterminate humankind, and in *The Matrix* (1999). Computers often are useful machines, as in the *Star Trek* series I-VI (1979-91; see entry). Less frequently, computers are charismatic, such as the robots C-Threepio and R2D2 in the *Star Wars* saga (1977-83, 1999; see entry).

Computer animation has contributed to faster and cheaper production of cartoons, with over a dozen being made in early 1994. Computers have also been used to integrate digitally animated characters into traditional film, as in *Jurassic Park* (1993; see entry), which featured incredibly realistic dinosaurs. (Steven Spielberg's Amblinmation Studio [see entry] has since focused on computer animation.) Since then, computers have fueled the explosion of special-effects based films.

Bibliography
Darlin, Damon, and Joshua Levine. "Stars Who Don't Throw Hissy Fits." *Forbes* 28 Feb. 1994: 94-98.
Maltin, Leonard. *Movie and Video Guide.* New York: Plume, 1994.

Janet Valade

Computers and Popular Culture now develop concurrently. To illustrate the computer-mediated character of contemporary experience, imagine yourself during a typical day of work, shopping, or recreation. Remember the green "power is on" glow of omnipresent video display terminals at airports, libraries, and checkout counters in retail stores. Recall the frequent whine of hard disks, the hum of cooling fans for processing units and laser printers in offices or homes where people are word processing, desktop publishing for the church, playing games, using CD-ROMs for reference or entertainment, or "surfing" the Internet (see entry).

A detailed view of the computer scene can be developed by examining some of the main genres of popular culture study: heroes and celebrities, games, communities, fiction, and popular commentary. To address these subjects is to touch upon popular speech, icons, and several other manifestations of popular culture embedded in the culture of computing.

HEROES AND CELEBRITIES. "The two Steves"—Wozniak and Jobs (see entries)—founded Apple Computer in the mid-1970s and temporarily made us believe that corporate culture might change significantly. They appeared as near teenagers from the Silicon Valley of California with countercultural sensibilities. They had been nurtured by the "hacker" culture. Not surprisingly, they created a more casual, hipper style of business. IBM suffered much when attacked by the two Steves and other microcomputer entrepreneurs.

For almost a decade the markets for personal microcomputers were defined by a series of improbable and unpredictable characters who had no rational business expectation to succeed in territories for which no prior career had really trained them. Jack Tramiel (see entry), for example, was a cigar-smoking Polish immigrant who created the now defunct Commodore Computers. His background was retailing office equipment and hand calculators. The engineer Nolan Bushnell (see entry) invented Pong, the first commercial computer game, testing it successfully in a bar. He founded Atari Computers, also now defunct.

The 1970s and 1980s were a time when these improbable people suddenly flashed to celebrity and then, like meteors, disappeared from celebrity space as their companies crashed or jettisoned their entrepreneurial talents in favor of more traditional managers. The one perpetual star in the sky during the age of micros was Bill Gates (see entry) of Microsoft, who had the vision to acquire the planet's largest self-made fortune—and then to become in 2000, at a mere age of 45, "the world's richest man." Less spectacular than these commercial giants are quiet figures like Grace Hopper, the naval mathematician and programmer. Or Ted Nelson (see entry), an early advocate of uncloaking the computer priesthood so that ordinary people could enjoy the powers of computing. His views were influential in the hacker community.

GAMES. One of the most seductive commercial applications of microprocessor technology has been entertainment for young people. The video arcade (see entry) entered American life in the 1970s, substantially displacing the pinball machine. The seductive machines have violent video imagery and an addictive pull for the coins of the players, most of whom are young boys or men with tastes for blowing things up or rescuing captive maidens. Many communities were alarmed by the character decay they saw in these dark arcades and passed ordinances to regulate them. A parallel entertainment industry developed around the home video games (see entry), manufactured as independent machines by companies like Atari, Nintendo, and Sega-Genesis, and also as microcomputer software.

Sherry Turkle, a Harvard psychiatrist who studied children in schools that were becoming highly computerized, reported in 1984 that many children were seeing themselves as "feeling computers, emotional machines." Hers was one of the first eloquent suspicions that children's prolonged encounters would create a new kind of human self that has trouble drawing boundaries between human personality and machine embodied activities. A significant extension of these early blurrings of self/computer is the personal home page on the World Wide Web. In these page frames individuals define themselves in part as the sum of their preferred connections to host computers in the universe of telecommunications. These phenomena suggest that computers are not mere instruments of purpose but presences that profoundly shape purpose and expression. Ted Nelson's concept of hypertext is instructive here; he described the effortless, nonlinear passage among linked documents as an ideal of information retrieval. The concept is modeled on how the mind moves fluidly among its associations. Yet, when embodied in the texts available through networked computers, it creates new forms of reading experience. An even more radical departure from ordinary linear reading is hypermedia, which provides simultaneous nonlinear access to sound, images, and text. This is the ideal pursued in successful CD-ROM products that provide multiple experiences through a single computer screen equipped with sound system.

ELECTRONIC COMMUNITIES. Computerized discussion forums have become important nodes where people gather for sharing perspectives, animosities, hobbyist interests, and information. Commercial online services, vast computer bulletin boards for the nation, became popular with millions of computerists in the late 1980s and 1990s. Intimate "electronic families" develop in the community online services, where there is emphasis on electronic friendship and caring. Ironically, many of the linkages and technologies for these human encounters grew out of the Internet, whose early origins were military and academic. Both the commercial and the community services are centers of popular culture. One of the first ethnographic descriptions of these new communities is by Howard Rheingold (1993). While optimistic about the quality of personal relations that are possible in faceless electronic encounters, he fears that the Internet will be trivialized if it is swamped with the "infotainment" products that commercial forces may be eager to provide.

FICTIONS. Hollywood and the television networks have been eager to offer interpretations of computer presence through movies and television programs. It is routine in the 1990s to include a flickering computer as normal equipment in an office, a police station, a news room, a military command center, or a spaceship. Computers are as prominent in contemporary production sets as telephones in the soap opera.

Novels about the computer exhibit a wide range of reactions. The darker visions emphasize the computer's tendency to lead us toward destruction or, at the least, perverted cultures. William Gibson's *Neuromancer* (1984) was the first novel to receive the triple crown of science fiction awards: the Hugo, Nebula and Philip K. Dick. It was Gibson who coined the word "cyberspace" and innocently led to the linguistic craze for attaching the "cyber-" prefix to anything associated with networked computers. As he defined it in *Neuromancer*, cyberspace is a disturbed "information matrix": "A consensual hallucination experienced daily by billions of legitimate operators, in every nation.... A graphic representation of data abstracted from the banks of every computer in the human system. Unthinkable complexity. Lines of light ranged in the nonspace of the mind, clusters and constellations of data." Gibson's perspective, developed further in *Burning Chrome* (1986) and *Count Zero* (1986), is thematically coherent with a strand of culture called "cyberpunk," a technologically sophisticated evolution beyond the counterculture of the 1960s and 1970s.

LITERATURE OF COMMENTARY. A celebrative vision of a computer-saturated future is found more easily in nonfiction commentaries. Christopher Evans's very widely read book *The Micro Millennium* (1979) is the most extravagant and hopeful of the prophecies. After describing his depression over civilization's condition, he rhapsodically declares, "Man, for so long the sole and undisputed master of the planet, will no longer have to face the universe alone. Other intelligences, initially comparable, and later vastly superior, will stand by his side." Evans goes so far as to suggest a new form of religion in which human beings might formally worship computers as "deities" in the form of "ultra intelligent machines." Other best-selling authors like Alvin Toffler in *The Third Wave* (1980) and John Naisbitt in *Megatrends* (1982) have proclaimed the trend, the inevitability, and the desirability of a more intensely computerized "information society." Less sweeping in scope, but equally celebratory have been writers like Seymour Papert, who in *Mindstorms* (1980) advocated an intensive computerization of childhood education.

Effusive praise for computers and their creation has been matched word for word by pessimistic best-selling authors like Theodore Roszak, whose *The Cult of Information: The Folklore of Computers and the True Art of Thinking* (1986) sees extensive reliance on computers as a failure to understand thinking and the requirements of democracy. A more alarmist popular book was Joseph Weizenbaum's *Computer Power and Human Reason* (1976). It was Weizenbaum who developed the program "Eliza," the computerized psychological counseling program that many persons could not distinguish from a real psychiatrist—despite its absurdly incoherent responses to remarks by patients. Weizenbaum was an active alarmist in discouraging military reliance on computer systems that remove human judgment from response to perceived military threats. Another popular literary voice decrying the perils of the computer age is Clifford Stoll, whose *The Cuckoo's Egg* (1989) created a picture of extensive security breaches occasioned by untended computers at American defense installations. His later *Silicon Snake Oil: Second Thoughts on the Information Highway* (1995) is an informed, sardonic assessment of the craze for electronic information communication.

The innovative dynamic of computerization is built upon increasing the speed of every function and every component part of the computer that serves it. This has meant that "the latest" microcomputer products have shelf lives measured in mere months. Some slightly new device or program is always better than its predecessor. The new is thus condemned to technological obsolescence at the moment of its birth. What has been said here about computers will be at least partially out of date at the moment it is read. That is both the triumph of the computer and an intimation of daily cultural tragedy. The computers in our midst have increasingly forced us to discard or to revise what we knew as the familiar truth. We do not finally know whether we are moving toward a higher consciousness or merely suffering from the symptoms of infomania. We hope that we can restrain our merely technological excitement (recently labeled "technophilia") and subordinate our inventions to rational and caring social purposes. A difficult and interesting social struggle lies ahead.

Bibliography

Evans, Christopher. *The Micro Millennium*. New York: Viking, 1979.

Gibson, William. *Neuromancer*. New York: Ace Books, 1984.

Hanson, Dirk. *The New Alchemists: Silicon Valley and the Microelectronics Revolution*. Boston: Little, Brown, 1982.

Levy, Steven. *Hackers: Heroes of the Computer Revolution*. Garden City: Anchor, 1984.

Rheingold, Howard. *The Virtual Community: Homesteading on the Electronic Frontier*. New York: HarperPerennial, 1994.

Turkle, Sherry. *The Second Self: Computers and the Human Spirit*. New York: Simon & Schuster, 1984.

John S. Lawrence

Coney Island entrepreneurs, in the late 19th century, pioneered the American amusement park as an enclosed space in which customers experienced the technological sublime of roller coasters and cycloramas. Patrons wandered through cultural bazaars of shows and foods; they witnessed spectators suddenly transformed into spectacles by hidden devices and agents. Coney thus evolved from a seaside resort for rich New Yorkers, gamblers, and beach-goers into a nickel empire of competing amusement parks, eateries, and attractions that entertained urban masses and tourists along Surf Avenue between Coney Island Beach and Brighton Beach in Brooklyn, NY. The pastoral vistas and dignified promenades of Central Park and Prospect Park were not found between Surf Avenue and the tawny sand beach to the south. Instead, Coney Island looked ahead to a 20th-century popular culture in which the public became thrilled participants, titillated voyeurs, and seduced consumers. Six Flags, Busch Gardens, Disneyland, "gong shows," and disaster spectacles all have roots there (see Theme Parks).

Essential to Coney's transformation of the public's recreational pleasures were its sandy beaches, facing south away from New York City and toward the Atlantic breakers that curled around Rockaway Point. After the Civil War, Coney's massive hotels and bathing pavilions helped to popularize sea-bathing. By the early 1900s, bathers shed pantaloons and blouses for suits that accentuated body lines and revealed more flesh. Postcards and stereoscopic views showed men and women flirting and striking provocative poses. Visitors mailed these tokens of modern freedom all over the world; 250,000 postcards left Coney Island in one day in 1907.

Coney Island has endured not just in postcards and photos but films, music, toys, resorts, even food (a "Coney" is a hot dog with condiments galore on the bun). It has symbolized life's ups and downs, slapstick, romance, and both the gritty and glamorous sides of New York. Almost from the beginning, the roller coaster and Ferris Wheel were symbols of tumult and thrill. This usage can be seen vividly in the backdrop shots of the Cyclone and Thunderbolt in modern cinema like *The Little Fugitive* (1953), *The Pick-Up Artist* (1987), and *Shakedown* (1988). Coney always has figured in comedy, especially burlesque and slapstick. Indeed, the come-hither sales icon of Steeplechase Park was a demoni-

cally grinning mask. In early silent film shorts, King the Horse plunged off the pier at Steeple Chase. Keystone Cops flopped and slid through rides in Fatty Arbuckle and Buster Keaton's *Fatty at Coney Island* (1917). In *Annie Hall* (1977), Woody Allen's character traced his neurotic behavior to growing up in a house beneath Coney's rampaging Thunderbolt roller coaster. However, the movie *It* (1927) defined Coney in film. A flapper, played by Clara Bow (later called the It girl), romances a handsome playboy; she is seen at landmarks like the Ritz Hotel and rides at Coney. Henceforth, Coney was the scene for cute meets and romance, as in *The Crowd* (1928), *The Symphony of Six Million* (1932), and *Coney Island* (1943). Grittier images of decayed Coney and its environs appeared in the gang fantasy *The Warriors* (1979). *The Boardwalk* (1979) inverted the Coney film formula of young lovers by focusing on an aged couple in a decayed neighborhood. Paul Mazursky's *Enemies: A Love Story* (1989) played against the formula by concentrating on the torturous romances of a Jewish refugee from Nazi Germany.

Coney also has produced pop music and been its subject. Sophie Tucker, Al Jolson, Eddie Cantor, and Phil Silvers played at Henderson's Music Hall on Surf Avenue, while Jimmy Durante sang in local saloons and George Burns harmonized in the Pee-Wee Quartette on the beach. Like film, pop music has used Coney as a background for young romance. In "Coney Island Steeplechase," Lou Reed sang of "you and me...cling[ing] to each other" on a roller coaster. In "Under the Boardwalk," the Drifters captured the innocent sensuality of the seaside amusement parks along the East Coast before the 1970s: "Under the Boardwalk/Out of the sun./Under the Boardwalk/Man, we'll be having some fun." "On a blanket with my baby, is where I'll be," the group sang, recalling as well the sounds of the carousel and smells of hot dogs and french fries. Aerosmith's recent homage to Coney youth in "Bone to Bone (Coney Island White Fish Boy)," on the other hand, expressed the hard realism of a grittier time, with its reference to a Coney Island White Fish Boy (a condom washed up on the beach or from a storm drain).

Bibliography

Kasson, John F. *Amusing the Million: Coney Island at the Turn of the Century*. New York: Hill & Wang, 1978.

McCullough, Edo. *Good Old Coney Island: A Sentimental Journey into the Past*. New York: Scribner's, 1957.

Pilat, Oliver, and Joe Ranson. *Sodom by the Sea: An Affectionate History of Coney Island*. Garden City, NY: Garden City, 1941.

Stanton, Jeff. "Coney Island History Site." http://naid.sppsr.ucla.edu/

Harry Hellenbrand

Connery, Sean (1930-), well known for his resistance to Hollywood glamour, repeatedly has stated that he finds little remarkable about what he does for a living: "There's nothing special about being an actor. It's a job, like being a carpenter or a bricklayer, and I've never stopped being amazed at the mystique people attach to my business."

Sean Connery was born Thomas Connery, a truck driver's and charlady's son, in Edinburgh, Scotland. He attended the Edinburgh School of Art, but left school at age 15 to join the Royal Navy. After being discharged due to ulcers, Connery worked as a bricklayer, lifeguard, truck driver, and coffin polisher, although he reportedly dreamed of becoming a soccer player. While working this odd assortment of jobs, Connery had time to begin bodybuilding, the results of which led to modeling assignments and to a part in the chorus of the touring company of *South Pacific* (1951-53). Connery was competing in the Mr. Universe contest when he learned of the casting call for that show. After his touring stint, Connery honed his acting skills by performing wherever possible, and by the late 1950s he had earned small roles in films and significant roles on British television, including the BBC production of *Requiem for a Heavyweight* (1956).

While his television future looked bright, his film career had rather stalled out when he was chosen to play James Bond, the central character of Ian Fleming's spy adventure novels. The year was 1962, and the film was *Dr. No*. Immediately Connery became synonymous with James Bond (see entry) to audiences everywhere. While playing James Bond (a character Connery describes as "a cardboard booby") made Connery an overnight star and thereby ensured his future, it would be accurate to describe his relationship to those films as a complex one. Officially, however, Connery ceased his formal relationship with these Agent 007 films because he felt the gadgetry that had once enhanced the films' playfulness had taken over the films entirely.

Among Connery's best-known films are two sci-fi cult favorites: *Outland* (a futurist *High Noon* set on Io, one of Jupiter's moons) (1981) and *Highlander* (1986). When director Steven Spielberg decided to make *Indiana Jones and the Last Crusade* (1989), he set out to cast Connery for at least two reasons. First, since Harrison Ford, who plays Indiana Jones, takes up so much of the available energy on the screen it would take someone of Sean Connery's stature and presence to stand up to him. Second, since the series of action-adventure *Indiana Jones* films grows from the Bond tradition, it just made good sense to cast the actor with the most personal knowledge of, and audience recognition with, the genre. Connery read the script and accepted the role on the condition that he be allowed input into the character of Dr. Henry Jones, Indiana's father.

Connery also had input on his character in *The Hunt for Red October* (1990), in which he plays a Soviet submarine captain who defects. The resulting film was a blockbuster hit worldwide that stayed on the U.S. list of Top 10 films for four months, earning $120 million. Another—less successful—Russian tie-in came with Connery's role as Barley Blair in the film version of John le Carré's *The Russia House* (1990).

More recently Connery has played characters who have placed themselves outside the system in order to operate to maximum efficiency. For instance, in *Medicine Man* (1992), he plays biochemist Robert Campbell, a scientist gone native, who has spent the last six years in a rain forest in Brazil, searching for a cure for cancer. In *Rising Sun* (1993), Connery plays philosopher-patriarch John Connor—a role that novelist Michael Crichton wrote with Connery in mind. In the same vein, in *The Rock* (1996) he played an ex-con, a former resident of Alcatraz, and in *Entrapment* (1999), an art thief.

He has appeared in more than 50 films, yet only once has he received an Academy Award—for his portrayal of veteran Irish cop Jimmy Malone in Brian De Palma's *The Untouchables* (1987).

Bibliography
Fong-Torres, Ben. "Connery. Sean Connery." *American Film* May 1989: 28.

Parker, John. *Sean Connery*. Chicago: Contemporary, 1993.

Roberta F. Green

Connick, Harry, Jr. (1967-), was born in New Orleans. He studied piano with Ellis Marsalis and began his career on Bourbon Street as a jazz pianist who could play in many styles. Soon it became obvious that he had great singing ability and the jazz vocalist Marion Cowings gave him voice lessons. Connick still occasionally plays strictly instrumental gigs with his trio in a totally jazz setting.

However, he is in great demand as a singer-bandleader who possesses a clean-cut image but reminds audiences of a young Frank Sinatra. His brash stage presence is a throwback to the 1940s and 1950s performers whom he obviously appreciates. That it is not simply "camp" was made obvious by his *When Harry Met Sally* soundtrack (1989), for which he both performed and composed. The soundtrack won numerous awards and Connick's career has continued its ascent.

Bibliography
Gammond, Peter. *Oxford Companion to Popular Music*. New York: Oxford UP, 1991.

Frank A. Salamone

Contra Dancing, or country dancing, as it is practiced in today's traditional New England style, is a vigorous immersion in living history (except for the comfortable, everyday clothes, and a few electronic aids). The prompter gives a short walk-through, the band swings into a strongly phrased jig or reel, and couples progress up and down the hall using a short series of "zesty" figures: balances, buzz-step swings, allemandes, stars, chains, circles, and heys. Ten minutes later, having done the figures with 15 or so other couples, everyone swings their partner one more time, thanks them for the dance, and finds another partner for the next dance.

The dance form, many of the figures, and some dances in current use, were included in the first dance book in English, *The English Dancing Master*, published by John Playford in 1651. By the time Playford published his last volume in 1728, contras, "longways for as many as will," had become by far the most popular of the English country dances.

According to James Morrison in *American Country Dances of the Revolutionary Era 1775-1795*, "Country dances [contras] were the most popular of the social dances done by all ages and all classes of society in America during the latter part of the 18th century. By the 1780s Americans began calling these dances 'contra dances,' probably derived from the French term contradanse." Ballroom manuals of the 19th century contained extensive lists of contras. In *The Country Dance Book* (1950), Ralph Page, New England caller, author, and leader of the contra dance revival, stated that over 2,000 American contras had been published since 1790.

During the time of maximum popularity for the contra, French dancing masters introduced the square dance to the U.S., first cotillions and then quadrilles, and longways dances gradually became less popular. The dominant social dancing trend of the second half of the 19th century was toward couple dances—waltzes, polkas, schottisches, mazurkas, and two-steps, and away from group dances. The quadrilles proved more adaptable than the contras, both geographically and as a dance form. In many areas of the country dance programs included only a token contra like the ubiquitous Virginia Reel. The tradition was kept alive, just barely, by Henry Ford in the 1920s, then by Ralph Page, until there was a nationwide increase in the 1980s, especially among urban professionals who enjoy historical reenactment. In the 1990s, there were over 500 English and American country dance groups.

Bibliography

Holden, Ricky. *The Contra Dance Book*. Newark: American Squares, 1965.

Jennings, Larry. *Zesty Contras*. Wellesley Hills: New England Folk Festival Association, 1983.

Page, Ralph, and Beth Tolman. *The Country Dance Book*. Brattleboro: Stephen Greene, 1976.

Sanella, Ted. *Balance and Swing*. New York: Country Dance Society, 1982.

David R. Peterson

Cooke, Sam (1931-1964), the central figure in the transformation of gospel music into soul, was born in Clarksdale, MS. Part of the great black migration from the plantation to the industrial northern cities, Cooke was actually raised in Chicago. He began his career when he was a boy, singing with his brothers and sisters in a gospel group called the Singing Children. By the time Cooke was 15, he was the lead singer for the Highway Q.C.'s, a teenage gospel quartet. Then, at 19, Cooke became the lead singer for the Soul Stirrers, the most popular and influential gospel group of the time. Cooke soon became the biggest star the gospel circuit ever had, exuding sexual charisma with a preternatural cool. At this point, one would have thought Cooke's career was set. To the shock and dismay of most, Cooke left the gospel circuit in 1956 to pursue pop music's wider audience on the Keen label and, by 1960, for RCA.

Gospel music's loss became soul music's gain as he brought its style, if not its message, to a broader audience. Cooke, who began as imitator of the man he replaced in the Soul Stirrers, R. H. Harris, built on his predecessor's discoveries in helping to shape soul. Besides bringing the lead singer of a quartet out front, and then setting him off against a second lead, Harris revived the West African tradition of singing falsetto. By the time Cooke went solo, he was a master of the type of singing that Harris practiced and, crucially, he had developed his own style.

When Sam Cooke's first crossover hit, "You Send Me" (1957), sold over a million copies and landed on the pop charts, Cooke proved that there was a market for the "down home"—that is, the southern, rural, and black—singing that characterized gospel music. The career of Otis Redding or Al Green would have been inconceivable without Cooke's example. Aretha Franklin said of Cooke, "When I saw he went pop, you know, outside church, that's what made me say, 'I want to sing that stuff, too.'" Most of Cooke's pop records, especially his early ones like "Only Sixteen" (1959), "Wonderful World" (1960), and "Cupid" (1961),

lacked the intensity, even the greatness, of his gospel records like "Wonderful" or "Jesus, Wash My Troubles Away" (1956). Nevertheless, despite frequent charges to the contrary, these records retained vestiges of Cooke's gospel sensibility and as his career progressed his gospel heritage became increasingly prominent. A song like "Bring It On Home to Me" (1962), with Cooke's soaring melisma and his call-and-response duets with Lou Rawls, as well the singer's promise of salvation, could have been torn out of the Soul Stirrers' songbook. Finally, triumphantly, there was his posthumous release, "A Change Is Gonna Come" (1965).

One of the most important records in the history of soul music, this song united the conflicting strains of Cooke's career. Written in response to Bob Dylan's civil rights anthem, "Blowin' in the Wind," Cooke, as Martin Luther King, Jr., would four years later, sang of having seen the promised land. Against lyrics such as "I go to the movie/I go to downtown/Somebody keep telling me don't come around" (which RCA excised from the original release), Cooke, in his most moving gospel voice, sings, "I know a change is gonna come." In so doing, Cooke made explicit the African-American quest for spiritual and social freedom that had always been implicit in the spirituals of gospel music. Ultimately, the civil rights movement and soul music were reflections of each other, both coming out of the black southern church, both insisting on African-American pride and self-determination.

Bibliography

Guralnick, Peter. *Sweet Soul Music*. New York: Harper, 1986.

Heilbut, Tony. *The Gospel Sound: Good News and Bad Times*. New York: Simon & Schuster, 1971.

Hirshey, Gerri. *Nowhere to Run: The Story of Soul Music*. New York: Times Books, 1984.

Timothy L. Parrish

Cooper, Gary (1901-1961), one of Hollywood's most accomplished and popular actors, was born Frank James Cooper in Helena, MT, to English immigrants. His parents were among the leading citizens of the town. His father was a lawyer and an elected justice of the Montana Supreme Court.

In 1922, he enrolled in Grinnell College in Iowa. After two years, he left to join his parents in Los Angeles. The young Cooper had hoped to pursue a career as a newspaper cartoonist. Unable to find work, he was encouraged by friends from Montana already playing in Westerns to join them as a stunt man and extra. Cooper rapidly rose from bit player to star.

After two years as an extra, he played the supporting male lead in the 1926 production of *The Winning of Barbara Worth,* starring Vilma Banky and Ronald Coleman. The gentlemanly Coleman was the actor Cooper claimed to admire most, and both survived the transition from silent films to sound. By 1928, Cooper was a leading man at Paramount. Within 10 years he would become one of the most popular and loved screen actors in the history of the industry.

During his career, Cooper was fortunate to work with Hollywood's most talented players and directors in some of the best films produced by the studio system. His first talkie, *The Virginian* (1929), was directed by Victor Fleming and also starred Walter Huston. The role established Cooper's image as a Western hero. In the film, Cooper actually said to Huston, "If you want to call me that—smile," not as film legend has it, "Smile when you say that."

In 1930, he starred in *Morocco* with Marlene Dietrich in her American debut. Director Josef von Sternberg got Cooper to play his part with a menace inconsistent with his emerging persona. Cooper refused to work with Sternberg again. *City Streets* (1931) was directed by Rouben Mamoulian and was Sylvia Sydney's first Hollywood film. It is one of Cooper's few performances as a gangster. In 1932 he starred with Helen Hayes in Frank Borzage's adaptation of Hemingway's *A Farewell to Arms*. The film made the author and the actor lifelong friends. In his adventure films, Cooper exemplified the Hemingway ethic of grace and courage under pressure. The commercially successful *Lives of a Bengal Lancer* (1935) was directed by Henry Hathaway and reinforced Cooper's image as the stoical hero. It was followed by Frank Capra's *Mr. Deeds Goes to Town* (1936). Cooper received his first Academy Award nomination for his role as Longfellow Deeds. The film established him as a popular hero and began a seven-year period in which Cooper achieved his greatest popularity.

In *The Plainsman* (1936), directed by Cecil B. DeMille, Cooper plays the legendary Wild Bill Hickok. In 1937, he was the highest paid actor in the industry. *The Real Glory* (1939), directed by Henry Hathaway, is set in the Philippines during the insurrection against the American occupation following the Spanish-American War. In 1939, Cooper also starred in William Wellman's version of *Beau Geste*. The film fulfilled every boy's idealistic dream at the time of honor, sacrifice, and comradeship. Along with Walter Brennan, who won an Academy Award as Judge Roy Bean, Cooper starred in William Wyler's *The Westerner* (1940); Brennan and Cooper worked together in Cooper's most successful films. Frank Capra's *Meet John Doe* (1941) gave Cooper the chance to perfect his portrayal of the average American with whom he was to become permanently identified. Also in 1941, he won his first Academy Award for his role as Sgt. Alvin York, the American hero of World War I. *Sergeant York* was directed by Howard Hawks. The following year he received the academy's nomination for *The Pride of the Yankees*. Directed by Sam Wood, Cooper's portrayal of baseball great Lou Gehrig is assumed by many to be his best role. His recitation of Gehrig's farewell speech is one of the classic moments in film. *Balls of Fire* (1942) is a light comedy directed by Howard Hawks. Cooper plays one of seven shy college professors giving shelter to a stripper helping them compile the slang section of a dictionary. For his part as an American partisan in the 1943 screen adaptation of Hemingway's *For Whom the Bell Tolls*, Cooper was again nominated for an Academy Award. Directed by Sam Wood, the film was Ingrid Bergman's first in the U.S. Hemingway asked that Cooper be cast as the lead and critics believe the character in the novel was modeled on Cooper.

The Depression years and World War II were the time of Cooper's greatest popularity. He was the highest paid actor in the industry and regarded by audiences as the representative American. At the height of his greatest triumphs, Cooper's career began to slip. In *Along Came Jones* (1945) he plays a shy and awkward drifter who is mistaken for a killer. The film did poorly at the box office. The public was unwilling to pay to see Cooper in roles that compromised his image as a Western hero.

As Marshall Will Kane in *High Noon* (1952), Cooper came back to win his second Academy Award. Directed by Fred Zinnemann, the film brings together all the elements of the Cooper image familiar to audiences since *The Virginian*. Critically acclaimed as a "classic" Western, *High Noon* is his most memorable film.

In William Wyler's *Friendly Persuasion* (1956) Cooper plays the patriarch of a family of Southern Indiana Quakers during the Civil War. The film received Oscar nominations for best picture and director. In Billy Wilder's *Love in the Afternoon* (1957), Cooper is an aging millionaire playboy in love with a young Audrey Hepburn. The film showed his talent for biting, sophisticated comedy.

After *High Noon*, Cooper was able to choose his roles. Critics argue he was seeking material appropriate for his age and development as an actor. The audience wanted him to stay in character and was unwilling to accept him in roles inconsistent with the Cooper image.

He plays a coward in *They Came to Cordura* (1959), an older man having an affair with his daughter's roommate in *Ten North Frederick* (1958), and is suspected of murder in his last film, *The Naked Edge* (1961). They are among his least satisfying performances.

Shortly before his death, Cooper narrated a television special, *The Real West*. Through photographs and personal accounts, the documentary debunks the mythic West invented by Hollywood and pays tribute to the settlers who, as Cooper's parents, brought civilization to the frontier.

In his personal life, Gary Cooper was not the democratic hero he played in his best films. Married to the daughter of the president of the New York Stock Exchange, he was at home in the high society of Europe and the United States. A wealthy and sophisticated gentleman and sportsman, Cooper opposed the populism of the New Deal while playing a hero of the masses. A conservative champion of wealth and privilege, he nevertheless personified for a generation of Americans their ideal of the common man.

Bibliography

Dickens, Homer. *The Films of Gary Cooper.* New York: Citadel, 1970.

Jordan, Rene. *Gary Cooper.* New York: Pyramid, 1974.

Kaminsky, Stuart. *The Life and Legend of Gary Cooper.* New York: Pyramid, 1980.

Schickel, Richard. "Gary Cooper." *The National Society of Film Critics on the Movie Star.* Ed. Elisabeth Weis. New York: Viking, 1981.

Swindell, Larry. *The Last Hero: A Biography of Gary Cooper.* New York: Doubleday, 1980.

Jim Ferreira

Cooper, James Fenimore (1789-1851), in the series of novels known as the Leatherstocking Tales, virtually invented both the American novel and the American Western. In these works, five epic novels published between 1823 and 1841 spanning the life of frontiersman Natty Bumppo, also known as Deerslayer, Leatherstocking, and Hawkeye, Cooper captured the new nation's soul as it encountered its physical and psychological boundaries. In Cooper's hands, the frontier became a symbol of, and a battleground over, the meaning of America.

In the first of the series, *The Pioneers* (1823), Cooper began an American version of Sir Walter Scott's Waverley novels, a national saga of heroic struggles in the wilderness. Though it was the first written, *The Pioneers* was actually fourth in the Leatherstocking plot sequence. Set in the decade after the Revolutionary War in frontier Ohio, the novel introduces a middle-aged Natty Bumppo, a man alone, with no family and no strong ties to keep him from following his destiny, along with his enduring companion, the Indian Chingachgook.

In *The Last of the Mohicans* (1826), Cooper places his hero back in time to the French and Indian War when he is at the peak of his powers, and among Mohican tribesmen, whom he romanticizes. The story focuses on the hostilities between various Indian groups, and on the fate of two white women who are captured and imprisoned by enemy tribes. Cooper planned *The Prairie* (1827) to be his final book in the series. Leatherstocking, wifeless and alone and now transplanted farther West to the plains, is old and dies reconciled to changing times but still firm in his belief that the old way was best.

Cooper was not the first author to discover that he could not so easily dispose of a popular hero. Therefore, in *The Pathfinder* (1840), he presents Natty and his Eden in their early maturity when all seemed possible. Finally, in *The Deerslayer* (1841), he writes of Natty's youth and of his romantic encounter with a young white woman amid the Indian wars of the 1740s, a romance that Natty ultimately forswears in favor of the primitive life that will be his enduring fate.

The Leatherstocking series established Cooper as the foremost author of the West until a later generation of authors addressed the conflict between the pastoral and progressive views of America. Cooper wrote a substantial body of fiction, including *The Spy* (1821), his first successful work; *The Pirate* (1822), a seafaring novel; and a late fictional trilogy known as the Littlepage Manuscripts, depicting the class divide in upper New York state where Cooper's family had been landowning gentry. *The American Democrat* (1838) is a treatise articulating Cooper's skepticism about democracy as a political system.

Bibliography
Barker, Martin. *The Lasting of the Mohicans: History of an American Myth.* Jackson: UP of Mississippi, 1995.
Walker, Warren. *Plots and Characters in the Fiction of James Fenimore Cooper.* Hamden: Archon, 1978.
Wallace, James D. *Early Cooper and His Audience.* New York: Columbia UP, 1986.

Frank A. Salamone

Cops (1989-) each week has a cameraperson carrying a mobile shoulder-held video camera riding along in a squad car as it makes its rounds. *Cops* contains elements of *cinema vérité:* no actors, scripts, narrator, or reenactments. Each episode begins with the theme song "Bad Boys" by the reggae group Inner Circle, which seems to mock the alleged criminal's plight: "Whatcha gonna do when they come for you?" The viewer is then afforded a voyeuristic examination of "unfiltered reality" as the camera rides with the police.

Cops premiered on the Fox-owned and operated stations and later that year was carried nationwide by its affiliated stations. Although the series continues to generate good ratings for Fox, and in syndication, there have been several concerns voiced about *Cops*. Some have argued that what is most disturbing about the series is not the image of its protagonists but what writer D. Friedman called the "odor of exploitation." Others have argued that even though a disclaimer prefaces every episode ("all of the suspects are considered innocent, until proven guilty in a court of law"), the camera and lens tend to act as what writer D. Waters called an "electronic jury. No matter that none of them [perpetrators] may ever be convicted of anything. In the eyes of viewers, conditioned by the arresting denouements of *Miami Vice*, the mere click of the handcuffs may be enough to establish guilt."

Bibliography
Friedman, D. "True Grit [*Cops*]." *Rolling Stone* 6 April 1989: 26.
Katz, Jon. "Covering the Cops: A TV Show Moves in Where Journalists Fear to Tread." *Columbia Journalism Review* Jan./Feb. 1993: 25-30.
Waters, D. "TV's Crime Watch Gets Real: Fox's *Cops* Is the Last Word in Video Vérité." *Newsweek* 15 May 1989: 72.

Daniel A. Panici

See also
Television Dramatic-Reality Programming

Corea, Chick (1941-), generally considered by jazz fans and critics to be one of the most prolific composers in the field, was born to Spanish-American parents in Boston and named Armando Corea, Jr. Like his contemporary and sometime collaborator Herbie Hancock, Corea was a child prodigy as a classical pianist. He did not become interested in jazz until his high school years. After high school he attended the Berklee School of Music in Boston, where he met other musicians with whom he would collaborate later, such as vibraphonist Gary Burton. In the early 1960s Corea was mastering the bop style of jazz and was influenced by pianists Bud Powell, Bill Evans, Horace Silver, and especially McCoy Tyner. From Tyner he copied, then used his own creativity to develop, uses for the interval of the fourth in both melodic and harmonic devices. Corea began to be admired by musicians when he played and recorded with members of Horace Silver's quintet. Blue Mitchell's album *The Things I Do* displays the young Corea's mastery of the bop style (see Bebop). His first major engagement was with saxophonist Stan Getz. It was with Getz that his playing and composing began to be noticed by musicians and critics alike. During this period Corea composed "Windows" (influenced by Bill Evans), "Litha," which used the fourth interval, and "LaFiesta," which was based on a familiar flamenco chord progression and the Phrygian mode.

In the late 1960s, Corea, along with bassist David Holland and drummer Barry Altschul, formed a trio called Circle. This group began to explore avant-garde styles of jazz. In addition to the other influences already identified—a recorded example is *The Song of Singing* (1970)—Corea was also influenced by contemporary classical composers, most notably Béla Bartók. During this period Corea also contributed to the Miles Davis albums *In a Silent Way, Bitches Brew,* and *Black Beauty.* In addition to Davis, Corea recorded with other jazz stalwarts, such as drummer Roy Haynes and bassist Miroslav Vitous on *Now He Sings Now He Sobs.* This album reveals the contemporary classical and free-form jazz-style influences on Corea.

In 1972, Corea formed a group called Return to Forever. The first edition of this group featured saxophone/flutist Joe Farrell, bassist Stanley Clark, Brazilian percussionist Airto Moriero, and vocalist Flora Purim. The ensemble's sound was light but rhythmic. "Spain" and "LaFiesta," two of Corea's most popular compositions, were recorded with this group on *Light As a Feather* (1973). Also on this album are "500 Miles High," and "You're Everything," very popular in the early 1970s.

The second edition of Return to Forever became one of the prime examples of jazz/rock fusion. The saxophone/flute was eliminated, Al Dimeola was added on guitar, Lennie White replaced Moriero on drums, and Corea began to use synthesizers. The most popular album by this Return to Forever group was *The Romantic Warrior* (1976), which contained "No Mystery" and "Vulcan Worlds."

From 1977 to the middle 1980s, Corea recorded and toured with various groups which included musicians he worked with earlier as well as younger but very technically able musicians. He also performed some duet concerts and recordings with Gary Burton and Herbie Hancock. During this period he returned to using more Latin American sources as well as becoming more influenced by the music of Bartók. Some of the albums produced were: *The Leprechaun* (1976), *Music Magic* (1977), *Mad Hatter* (1978), *Secret Agent* (1978), and *Tap Step* (1980). Among the musicians on these albums were Alan Vizutti on trumpet, Bill Watrous and Jim Pugh on trombones, and Al Jarreau and Gayle Moran on vocals. He was also commissioned by Woody Herman to write a three-movement composition for Herman's big band called "Suite for Hot Band" (on *Chick, Donald, Walter and Woodrow*).

In the mid 1980s, Corea formed a five-member ensemble with a group of young virtuoso musicians, notably bassist John Patitucci. The rest of the group included Dave Weckl on drums, Eric Marienthal on saxophones, and Frank Gambale on guitar. The group was called the Elektric Band, and Corea composed many new compositions for them. Their first recording was *Elektric Band* (1986). The compositions were somewhat reminiscent of the (rock-influenced) second Return to Forever unit. In 1988 the band recorded the more critically acclaimed *Eye of the Beholder,* with compositions much more diverse in style than the first recording. By this session, Corea had mastered the use of the continually developing digital keyboards. The compositions display a contrast between the acoustic and electronic instruments. The album also highlights Corea's prodigious talent as an improviser who can work in a variety of styles and contexts. For contrast from the electronic sounds, the Elektric Band would present a portion of their concerts on acoustic instruments, the highlights of which were duets between Corea and Patitucci. This led to a recording called *Akoustic Band,* which was made by just three members of the group (Corea, Patitucci, and Weckl). In this recording they play old standards, such as "My One and Only Love," "Autumn Leaves," "Someday My Prince Will Come," plus new versions of older Corea compositions, such as "Spain" and "Circles." The improvisations by Corea and Patitucci are very inventive and varied.

In the 1990s, Corea continued to work with versions of the Elektric and Akoustic bands plus appearing as a guest on many GRP recordings.

Bibliography

Megill, Donald D. *Introduction to Jazz History.* Englewood Cliffs: Prentice-Hall, 1993.
Toner, John. "Chick Corea: Return to Forever." *Down Beat* July 1994: 66.
Woodard, Josef. "Chick Corea: Piano Dreams Come True." *Down Beat* Sept. 1988: 16-19.

Frank Ferriano

Corman, Roger (1926-), is one of the most successful independents in Hollywood history. He produced his first feature, *The Monster from the Ocean Floor* (Wyott Ordung, 1954), for $12,000, and sold it to the Lippert Releasing Company for $60,000. With the profits from *Monster*, Corman produced *The Fast and the Furious* (1954), a race car drama starring Dorothy Malone and John Ireland, and directed by Ireland.

The Fast and the Furious was purchased by American International Pictures, a newly formed distribution exchange that used Corman's film to negotiate an advance from exhibitors that would pay for three more features. As critic Mark Thomas McGee notes, "This was the beginning of American International Pictures." During the next five years (1955-59), Corman produced and directed 18 films for AIP in several different genres, including Westerns (*Five Guns West* [1955], *Oklahoma Woman* [1956]), science fiction (*Not of This Earth* [1957], *It Conquered the World* [1956], *Attack of the Crab Monsters* [1957]), teenage exploitation (*Rock All Night* [1957], *Sorority Girl* [1957]), and crime films (*Swamp Women* [1955], *Machine Gun Kelly* [1958]). Corman also provided AIP with such low-budget oddities as the sword and sandal "epic" *The Saga of the Viking Women and Their Voyage to the Waters of the Great Sea Serpent* (1957), the horror comedy *A Bucket of Blood* (1959), and the crime-film-meets-exotic-travelogue movies *Naked Paradise* (1956) and *She Gods of Shark Reef* (1958). He also served as the producer—but not director—for AIP's *Night of the Blood Beast* (Bernard Kowalski, 1958) and *Attack of the Giant Leeches* (Bernard Kowalski, 1959).

In 1959, prompted by his belief that AIP was both controlling his work and "getting a disproportionate share" of the profits from his movies, Corman founded the Filmgroup, his own production and distribution company. Corman's first movie for the Filmgroup, *The Wasp Woman* (1959), was successful, and over the next four years Corman directed and produced *Atlas* (1960), *The Last Woman on Earth* (1960), *Ski Troop Attack* (1960), and *Creature from the Haunted Sea* (1961) for distribution by his own company. Other movies handled by the Filmgroup include *The Beast from Haunted Cave* (Monte Hellman, 1960) and *Dementia 13* (Francis Ford Coppola, 1963). The Filmgroup remained active until late 1963, when Corman realized that he did not have enough time and energy to be a distributor while continuing to produce and direct. The Filmgroup gradually faded into inactivity and obscurity.

Corman then developed his own production facility and distribution company, New World Pictures, and adhered to the same low-budget, high-profit practices pioneered by AIP. Specializing in quickies that tapped into profitable, established genres, New World released biker films (*Angels Die Hard* [Richard Compton, 1970], *Angels Hard as They Come* [Joe Viola, 1971]), soft-core pornography (*The Student Nurses* [Stephanie Rothman, 1970], *Night Call Nurses* [Jonathan Kaplan, 1972]), science fiction movies (*Battle Beyond the Stars* [Jimmy Murakami, 1980], *Galaxy of Terror* [B. D. Clark, 1981], *Forbidden World* [Allan Holzman, 1982]), women-in-prison films (*The Big Doll House* [Jack Hill, 1971], *The Hot Box* [Joe Viola, 1972]), disaster spectacles (*Tidal Wave* [Shiro Moriana and Andrew Meyer, 1975], *Avalanche* [Corey Allen, 1978]), and car chase movies (*Eat My Dust* [Charles Griffith, 1976], *Grand Theft Auto* [Ron Howard, 1977]). New World also released quirky cult items like *Death Race 2000* (Paul Bartel, 1975) and *Rock 'n' Roll High School* (Allan Arkush, 1979). Personnel who worked on these and other New World films included Lorne Greene, John Sayles, Gary Busey, David Carradine, Martin Scorsese, Jonathan Demme, Mia Farrow, Sylvester Stallone, Rock Hudson, and the Ramones.

In 1983, after 13 years of activity, Corman sold New World's name and distribution arm to lawyers Harry Evans Sloan, Lawrence Kuppin, and Larry Thompson for nearly $17 million. Corman, however, was never paid the money his pictures earned, and so he sued New World in 1985. The settlement allowed Corman to reenter film distribution as a new company, Concorde/New Horizons. Concorde has emerged as a production leader in the direct-to-video market, pre-selling such genre titles as *The Dirt Bike Kid* (Hoite Caston, 1986), *Deathstalker II* (Jim Wynorski, 1987), and *Body Chemistry* (Kristine Peterson, 1990) to video stores. Corman's most recent projects have included a return to direction with *Frankenstein Unbound* (1990) and the formation of a comic book company, Roger Corman's Cosmic Comics, with titles like *The Little Shop of Horrors* and *Rock 'n' Roll High School,* designed to franchise recognizable Corman fare.

Corman's overemphasis on profit and the business end of filmmaking is best illustrated by the title of his autobiography, *How I Made a Hundred Movies in Hollywood and Never Lost a Dime.* Although several of his films—including *A Bucket of Blood* and *The Raven*—are charming and fun, the grim, factory-like product that constitutes the bulk of his career indicates that Corman never truly realized his creative potential as either a director or producer.

Bibliography

Chute, David. "The New World of Roger Corman." *Film Comment* March-April 1982: 27-32.

Corman, Roger, with Jim Jerome. *How I Made a Hundred Movies in Hollywood and Never Lost a Dime.* New York: Random House, 1990.

McGee, Mark Thomas. *Roger Corman: The Best of the Cheap Acts.* Jefferson: McFarland, 1988.

Craig Fischer

Corwin, Norman (1910-), came to CBS in 1937 after working in journalism and public relations. Shortly afterward, Corwin began production on *Norman Corwin's Words without Music*, a series modeled on his earlier *Poetic License*, a radio program of dramatized poetry which retained most of the original lines.

Already recognized as a creative force in radio, Norman Corwin became radio's unofficial laureate as the U.S. became involved in World War II. Besides working on the wartime programs *This Is War!* (1942), *An American in England* (1942), *Transatlantic Call* (1943), and *Columbia Presents Corwin* (1944), Corwin wrote the radio plays that consecrated the war, dedicated the United Nations, celebrated victory in Europe, and considered the meaning of victory over Japan: *We Hold These Truths* (12/15/41), *Word from the People* (4/25/45), *On a Note of Triumph* (5/8/45), *14 August* (8/14/45), and *God and Uranium* (8/19/45). "The Lonesome Train," a program he had directed, laid President Roosevelt to rest. After the war, as Chief of Special Projects for the United Nations, Norman Corwin was called on to commemorate the passage of the Universal Declaration of Human Rights: *Document A/777* (March 26, 1950).

Recipient of the Wendell Wilkie One World Award and author of the series *One World Flight* (1947), Corwin left network broadcasting in 1948 when CBS president William Paley offered unacceptable terms in a new contract. Since then he has written successfully for film, stage, television, and print.

Bibliography

Bannerman, R. LeRoy. *Norman Corwin and Radio.* University: U of Alabama P, 1986.

Barnouw, Erik. *A History of Broadcasting in the United States.* Vol. 2. New York: Oxford UP, 1968.

Kostelanetz. "The Radio Dramatist Norman Corwin." *American Drama* Spring 92.

MacDonald, J. Fred. *Don't Touch That Dial!* Chicago: Nelson-Hall, 1979.

Stanley D. Harrison

Cosby, Bill (1937-), one of America's most influential entertainers, began his comedy career in the 1960s, with small gigs in New York and elsewhere. After establishing himself in the standup circuit, Cosby was quickly recruited to push the envelope in another direction. He was asked to star alongside Robert Culp's Kelly Robinson as a tough, Rhodes scholar/CIA agent, Alexander Scott, in the TV series *I Spy* (1964-69; see entry). Although inexperienced as an actor, Cosby soon relaxed into the role, which brought him more recognition. With the success of *I Spy*, Cosby was a household name, a television star. His groundbreaking role brought him the title the "Jackie Robinson of TV," the first black actor to have a primary heroic role on television (see African Americans and Entertainment TV).

Eventually the spy craze waned and so did *I Spy*. Next for Cosby was the role of teacher Chet Kincaid on *The Bill Cosby Show* (1969-71; see entry above). At this time, the *New York Times* ran two articles with opposing views of Cosby's stance in the public eye. But the show did not achieve the success of *I Spy*.

Still, Cosby concerned himself with bettering the standards of TV programming, not just for blacks but for all people. At the University of Massachusetts, he eventually finished his doctorate in education in the 1970s while producing quality children's programming like *Fat Albert and the Cosby Kids* (1972-84; see entry). Realizing the power of supportive guidance and education as depicted on the show, Cosby took some of his earnings from his successes and reinvested them into the educational system. A handful of universities have received donations from Cosby, the largest of which was a $20 million donation to Spelman College. He also made donations to aid earthquake victims in California and to children's hospitals, which he has frequently visited.

The Cosby Show (1984-92; see next entry) marked a new beginning for Cosby, NBC, and sitcoms in general (see Sitcom) As of the early 1980s, the sitcom was slogging off and, from Cosby's perspective, was not holding up the model he promoted of a supportive family, but rather, demeaning the family through contrived humor. So, he stepped in with a new show. Logically, *The Cosby Show* is centered on Bill Cosby: his character, Heathcliff Huxtable, is virtually Bill Cosby, an upper-class professional who supports his family with love and humor. In this way, the show focused on Cosby's world view: that everyone can live in peace with respect for others and that black people can, honestly and realistically, achieve upper-class status (Heathcliff is a gynecologist and his wife, Claire, a lawyer). Like *I Spy*, *The Cosby Show* provided an exceptional model, a testament to the potential of the traditionally underprivileged. The show won three Emmys in 1985.

After staying in the Top 10 for most of its eight-year run, *The Cosby Show* lost viewers to more cynical 1990s shows like *Roseanne* and *The Simpsons* and, in 1992, the Huxtables said good-bye. With the help of some key investors, Cosby, who was worth $30 million at the time, wanted to buy NBC so that he could, in effect, order the network to fulfill his hopes of a higher standard of TV viewing. This plan never materialized.

A spokesman for many big corporations (Jell-O, Texas Instruments, IBM, and many others), and the author of various books, including *Fatherhood* (1986) and *Time Flies* (1987), and numerous recordings of his comedy sketches, Cosby has continued to be a formidable figure in popular culture, despite his checkered past of successes and failures. His attempts at making a big screen career have never achieved the same amount of success as his TV career. The movies he did with director Sidney Poitier, *Uptown Saturday Night* (1974), *Let's Do It Again* (1976), and *Piece of the Action* (1977), are the only ones that stand out of a long line of forgettable films, the latest of which is *Jack* (1996). On the small screen, Cosby is most powerful. By reteaming with Phylicia Rashad (his wife on *The Cosby Show*), Cosby succeeded again in the aptly titled *Cosby* (1996).

Bibliography

Adler, Bill. *The Cosby Wit: His Life and Humor.* Oklahoma City: Quill, 1989.

Fuller, Linda K. *The Cosby Show: Audience, Impact, and Implications.* New York: Greenwood, 1992.

Smith, Ronald L. *Cosby: The Life of a Comedy Legend.* New York: Prometheus, 1997.

Robert Baird

Cosby Show, The (1984-1992), was the most popular television series of the 1980s, and the program held almost single-handedly responsible for the rejuvenation of the situation comedy (see Sitcom) and the return of NBC to the top of the Nielsen ratings. *The Cosby Show* finished up its first season at No. 3 in the ratings and made it to No. 1 the following year, where it stayed for the next three seasons before finishing as No. 2 to *Roseanne* in the 1989-90 season. Only *All in the Family*, at five seasons, stayed at the top longer since the Nielsen ratings began in 1960.

The year before *The Cosby Show* premiered, only three of the top 22 Nielsen shows were sitcoms, but by its third year that number had risen to 12. The show's success was a burst of inspiration for comedy creators, especially giving new life to family shows and African-American-oriented comedies.

The concept of *The Cosby Show,* originally the brainchild of Bill Cosby and NBC president Brandon Tartikoff, was finalized by Cosby and producers Ed. Weinberger and Michael Leeson. Cosby originally wanted the show's married couple to be much more working class. When the show finally premiered, however, Cosby played Heathcliff (Cliff) Huxtable, a successful New York obstetrician with an equally successful lawyer wife, Clair (Phylicia Allen, later Phylicia Rashad). They had five children, ranging from college-age to preschool.

The focus of *The Cosby Show* was definitely the family. Cliff and Clair were rarely shown at work, and because Cliff had an office at home, there was hardly ever a time when a parent was not home. Such family values were welcome at the height of the Reagan 1980s and contributed greatly to the show's popularity. Part of its appeal also lay in the simplicity of the family's problems and the ease with which they were solved each week, much in the tradition of such family sitcom precursors as *Father Knows Best, Leave It to Beaver*, and *The Brady Bunch*.

By 1986, one out every four homes was watching *The Cosby Show*, making it one of the highest-rated series ever.

The episode of January 22, 1987, was viewed by 36.1 million people, the third highest rated episode of a weekly series ever to that time. The show also generated a short-lived spin-off, *A Different World* (1986). After eight years, however, facing competition from programs like *Roseanne* and *The Simpsons*, Cosby decided to call it quits while still relatively at the top.

Bibliography

Hamamoto, Darrell Y. *Nervous Laughter: Television Situation Comedy and Liberal Democratic Ideology*. New York: Praeger, 1989.

Jones, Gerard. *Honey, I'm Home! Sitcoms: Selling the American Dream*. New York: Grove-Weidenfeld, 1992.

McNeil, Alex. *Total Television: A Comprehensive Guide to Programming from 1948 to the Present*. 3d ed. New York: Penguin, 1991.

Morrow, Lance. "Video Warriors in Los Angeles." *Time* 11 May 1992.

Teachout, Terry. "Black, Brown, and Beige." *National Review* 18 July 1986.

Paul R. Kohl

Cosell, Howard (1918-1995), was born Howard William Cohen in Winston-Salem, NC, the son of Isadore and Nellie Cohen. His father was a Polish immigrant who took his family to Brooklyn soon after Howard's birth.

Howard attended public schools and was a stellar student at Alexander Hamilton High, where he worked on the school's newspaper. Cosell majored in English literature at New York University and graduated Phi Beta Kappa. He also received a law degree from NYU and edited the law review, passing the New York bar exam in 1941 at the age of 23. During World War II, Cosell was a major in the U.S. Army Transportation Corps. He married Mary Edith "Emmy" Abrahams, who preceded him in death in 1990.

After World War II, he began a law practice and also became involved in representing the Little League of New York. In 1953, he was asked to host a show on which Little Leaguers asked Major Leaguers questions. Cosell accepted and did the show for free for three years. After that he abandoned his law practice to become a media broadcaster full time.

During the 1960s, Cosell was part of ABC's innovative Olympics coverage. He was a particularly adamant spokesman against racism. At the 1968 Olympics when track and field athletes such as Tommie Smith gave the "black power gesture," Cosell was very sympathetic in his interview and was roundly criticized. Similarly, when Muhammad Ali declared himself a conscientious objector, Cosell rushed to his defense. Cosell's give-and-take interviews with a brash and boastful Muhammad Ali made them both media celebrities and set the dramatic stage for the championship bouts.

Undoubtedly, Cosell's major achievement was his role on the *Monday Night Football* telecasts of ABC beginning in 1970. Roone Arledge's theory was that putting Cosell in the booth with Don Meredith and Frank Gifford would inject an "entertainment element into it other than the foot-ball game itself." That is exactly what happened. *Monday Night Football* became an entity unto itself and Cosell became the star and brought a freshness and honesty to sports journalism. He connected social and critical issues to the world of sports and questioned the underlying business structure of sports as well as its uneven record of fairness and equality. Because of his outspokenness, Howard was either loved or hated.

Bibliography

Cosell, Howard. *Cosell*. Chicago: *Playboy*, 1973.

——, with Peter Bonventre. *I Never Played the Game*. New York: Morrow, 1985.

Lawrence E. Ziewacz

Cosmopolitan (1886-) is a women's magazine published in its current incarnation by Hearst Magazines Corporation. For the past 30 years, until recently under the auspices of Helen Gurley Brown, famous for her *Sex and the Single Girl* (1962), *Cosmopolitan* has been a publication that caters to the lifestyle and interests of the hedonistic woman (career-oriented or domesticated). The "Cosmo" girl who appears on each cover represents the aesthetic philosophy of Ms. Brown—she is a woman who is beautiful and alluring in an obvious way. Articles focus on all aspects of the sensuous woman, and may also, peripherally, consider job-related issues. Most of the magazine is made up of advice columns, ranging from personal finances and travel items to concerns over sexual performance. Sex is the mainstay of the "Cosmo" girl and all interviews, beauty columns, or horoscopes relate to the female body, or to romance in one way or another. Sentimental short stories and selections from newly published novels and biographies add literary interest to the magazine. Its advertisements include items such as naughty lingerie, body-sculpting devices, cosmetics, perfume, and specialty erotic articles that underscore the magazine's editorial policies and emphasize "having it all." This magazine addresses a readership somewhere between *Ladies' Home Journal* and the *Victoria's Secret* catalog.

Bibliography

Katz, Bill, and Linda Sternberg Katz. *Magazines for Libraries*. 7th ed. Providence: Bowker, 1992.

Schneirov, Matthew. *The Dream of a New Social Order: Popular Magazines in America, 1893-1914*. New York: Columbia UP, 1994.

Mona Phillips

Costain, Thomas B(ertram) (1885-1965), a Canadian by birth who made his literary career in the U.S., is best known as a historical novelist. Several of his works, such as *The Black Rose* (1945), *The Silver Chalice* (1952), and *The Darkness and the Dawn* (1959), were international best-sellers; he also wrote a four-volume history of the Plantagenet kings, *The Conquerors* (1949), *The Magnificent Country* (1951), *The Three Edwards* (1958), and *The Last Plantagenets* (1962), that enjoyed the kind of popularity usually reserved for fiction.

Costain's work, fiction and nonfiction, is driven primarily by an affirmation of democracy against forms of political tyranny. This theme is visible in his Plantagenet saga as he highlights the struggles of peons and serfs to gain a modicum of political autonomy and critiques the autocratic mentality of royalty. In *The Darkness and the Dawn*, a chronicle of Attila the Hun and his times, Costain exposes both the violent destructiveness of the Huns and the corrupt degeneracy of their enemies, the Romans, valorizing the plainsmen in their democratic strife against both rulers. The hero of *The Black Rose* is a baseborn Saxon who gains knighthood and vindicates his clan against the powerful Normans. In *The Silver Chalice*, the early Christians are venerated for their bravery, resourcefulness, and communalism. Alongside political themes, Costain's novels foreground romance, usually between men of inferior class standing and noble women who must overcome the cultural and familial divide. Costain's legacy is his ability to vitalize history with the human passions that transcend the boundaries of time, enabling contemporary readers to empathize with figures across the ages and continents.

Bibliography

Authors Speak for Themselves: Autobiographical Sketches of 48 Leading Authors, Fall 1950. New York: Herald Tribune, 1950.

Liahna Babener

Costello, Elvis (1955-), with his skinny tie and Buddy Holly horn-rimmed glasses, burst on the music scene in the seminal punk/new wave year of 1977. Though the singer/songwriter would later be called the Cole Porter of his generation for the intricate word-play in his lyrics, it was as the poet of revenge and guilt that, in 1977, he was distinguished from the radical politics of the Clash and the anarchism of the Sex Pistols.

Born Declan Patrick MacManus in London, MacManus's father was Ross MacManus, a big-band singer with Joe Loss, "the British Glenn Miller." Signed by the small British label Stiff Records and given the name Elvis Costello by label co-founder Jake Riviera (who remains as Costello's manager), MacManus took sick leave from his job to record his first album, *My Aim Is True* (Columbia, 1977). Produced by Nick Lowe (who had also signed with Stiff), the album included "Watching the Detectives" (No. 15 U.K.) as well as "Alison" (covered to Costello's disdain by Linda Ronstadt in 1978) and "(The Angels Wanna Wear My) Red Shoes." The success of the album in Britain led to Columbia Records signing Costello to an American contract.

Costello quit his day job, recruited a band, the Attractions (Steve Nieve, keyboards; Bruce Thomas, bass; Pete Thomas, drums), and recorded *This Year's Model* (1978). He released what is perhaps his most satisfying album in 1979, *Armed Forces* (Columbia), also one of his most popular (reaching No. 10 on the U.S. charts) and including the alternative radio favorites "Two Little Hitlers," "Accidents Will Happen," "Oliver's Army," and the Lowe-penned "(What's So Funny 'Bout) Peace, Love and Understanding." While on tour in Columbus, OH, to promote the album, Costello got into an infamous bar brawl with Stephen Stills that cemented his American image as the new "angry young man."

Costello's two albums of 1981, *Trust* and *Almost Blue* (both Columbia), confused fans and critics alike. *Trust*, a dark album that included the hit "Clubland," was quickly followed by *Almost Blue*, recorded in Nashville by noted country and western producer Billy Sherrill. It included covers of songs by Don Gibson, Gram Parsons, and Hank Williams.

Co-produced by Beatles associate Geoff Emerick, *Imperial Bedroom* (Columbia, 1982) was an over-produced concept album about love and deceit; the album included the single "Man Out of Time." Changing directions in 1983, Costello and the Attractions recorded *Punch the Clock* (Columbia), which included Costello's first U.S. Top 40 hit ("Everyday I Write the Book"), the up-tempo, peppy "Let Them All Talk," the haunting commentary on Britain's involvement in the Falkland's war, "Shipbuilding," and a bitter indictment of Britain's Prime Minister Margaret Thatcher titled "Pills and Soap."

Goodbye Cruel World (Columbia, 1984) included the hit "The Only Flame in Town," a duet with Daryl Hall of Hall and Oates. *King of America* (Columbia, 1986) featured an all-star cast of sidemen instead of the Attractions, and the song credits, for the first time in his career, were under the name MacManus. The album included "American without Tears," "Brilliant Mistake," and a cover of the Animals' "Don't Let Me Be Misunderstood." Costello rejoined the Attractions and producer Lowe for *Blood and Chocolate* (Columbia, 1986), an album poorly promoted by Columbia and ignored by record buyers.

In 1988, Costello was contacted by Paul McCartney with the idea of working on some songs together. This collaboration led to four songs on McCartney's *Flowers in the Dirt* (Capitol, 1989), including the hit "My Brave Face."

McCartney, along with Roger McGuinn, members of Tom Petty's Heartbreakers, and bassist Cait O'Riordan (whom he had married in 1986), appeared on *Spike* (Warner Bros., 1989), which included the MacManus-McCartney song "Veronica," his biggest American hit (U.S. No 19). *Spike* became Costello's eighth album to hit the U.S. Top 40, putting him in a five-way tie for second place in the album category. *Mighty Like a Rose* (Warner Bros., 1991), featuring a pensive Costello with a full beard on the cover, was a decidedly mixed followup to successful *Spike* and again included joint compositions with McCartney and O'Riordan.

Reunited with the Attractions (including Bruce Thomas, who wrote *The Big Wheel* in 1990, an attack on Costello thinly disguised as a novel) and Nick Lowe for *Brutal Youth* (Warner Bros., 1994), Costello found himself being accused of pandering to the past and received mixed reviews. *All This Useless Beauty* (1996) was also recorded with the Attractions, but *Painted from Memory* (1998) was an unusual collaboration between Costello and his songwriting idol, Burt Bacharach.

Bibliography

Gouldstone, David, Jeffrey Stock, and David Wild. *Elvis Costello—God's Comic*. New York: St. Martin's, 1989.

———. "Elvis Costello: The *Rolling Stone* Interview." *Rolling Stone* 1 June 1989: 63-68, 94.

Martin R. Kalfatovic

Cowboy Music is as old as sea songs, mountain songs, and general folk music. It is this older music riding the range. In 1910 a major New York publisher published John Lomax's *Cowboy Songs and Other Frontier Ballads*. This was the first time the general public was exposed to cowboy music. (N. Howard ["Jack"] Thorp, a working cowboy, had privately published a book two years previously, but it did not find a wide audience.) Lomax's book, revised and enlarged in 1938, contained songs from the oral tradition in the West, including "Git Along, Little Dogies," "Good-bye, Old Paint," "The Old Chisholm Trail," "The Dying Cowboy," "When the Work's All Done This Fall," "Little Joe, the Wrangler," "Billy the Kid," "Sam Bass," "Jesse James," "Rye Whiskey," "Red River Valley," "Texas Rangers," "Sweet Betsy from Pike," and "Home on the Range." A large number of these songs can be traced back to a writer or writers, although a few, such as "The Old Chisholm Trail," can only be traced to the oral tradition, with no known writers and each new singer making up new verses.

In 1927, sound was introduced to movies and by the 1930s the singing cowboy (see entry) emerged, beginning with Ken Maynard, who made the first singing cowboy movies, then Gene Autry, who took the genre to new heights beginning with his appearance in Maynard's 1935 film *In Old Santa Fe*. By World War II, the singing cowboy was firmly established with Autry, Roy Rogers, Tex Ritter, and numerous others starring in Western movies and making recordings. This era of singing cowboys lasted until the early 1950s, when television arrived.

Musically, cowboy songs can be traced back to British melodies, the same Scots-Irish influences that provided Appalachian folk songs. Other melodies came from Germany, with number of German immigrants settling in Texas in the late 19th century. As the people moved west, so did the songs. Most cowboys songs are essentially the same as American folk songs with the major difference being the lyrics, dealing with western themes. These themes include the working life of the cowboy, the western landscape and scenery, well-known events and story songs (like the Broadside ballads), famous outlaws, the gold rush, and songs of love, hearth, and home. The chief importance of cowboy songs lies in the subject matter. Because the cowboy is so quintessentially American and has become a hero in American popular culture, cowboy songs are significant because they helped create the image of the cowboy.

Bibliography

Allen, Bob. *The Blackwell Guide to Recorded Country Music*. Oxford: Blackwell, 1994.

Buckaroo: Visions and Voices of the American Cowboy. New York: Callaway, 1993.

Lewis, George H. *All That Glitters: Country Music in America*. Bowling Green, OH: Bowling Green State U Popular P, 1993.

Don Cusic

Gene Autry. Photo courtesy Sound Recording Archives, Bowling Green State University, Bowling Green, OH.

Cozy Mysteries invoke a fictional atmosphere of ease and contentment—a roaring fire, a comfortable armchair, a snoozing cat on one's lap, and a world howling outside. In William DeAndrea's words, "a cozy supposes belief in a benign universe." Violence is underplayed in the cozy world, a far cry from the mean and cynical streets of Raymond Chandler. The sleuth is usually an amateur, and the characters know each other, and, indeed, the murderer as well, making the crime's impact personal, immediate, and invasive.

No one exemplifies the cozy mystery better than Agatha Christie (see entry). In her 17 Jane Marple novels and short-story collections from 1930 to 1976, Christie set the standard of the serene English village concealing an ever-snaking thread of evil, and of the amateur sleuth whose seeming vagueness conceals a rapier insight into human nature. In Dame Agatha's time, American Phoebe Atwood Taylor provided in Asey Mayo an offbeat Cape Cod handyman who fixes mysteries in addition to performing his other duties.

Recent years have seen a virtual explosion in the cozy's popularity, including the establishment of "malice domestic," a new convention to celebrate them. Today's cozy sleuths appear in a wide spectrum of occupations and an expanding universe of locales. Katherine Hall Page's ex-caterer Faith Fairchild, a minister's wife in New England, produces luscious meals and solutions to the odd murder. Charlotte MacLeod's rollicking Sarah Kelling and Max Bittersohn solve mysteries among Kelling's pack of eccentric Bostonian relatives. Margaret Maron's Deborah Knott is a judge in a small North Carolina town. Joan Hess's widowed Claire Malloy runs her own bookstore in a small Arkansas town and investigates while dealing with an obnoxious teenage daughter. K. K. Beck's lighthearted "The Body in..." series features murder in unlikely locations. Susan Kenney's English professor Roz Howard ferrets out campus mysteries.

Although this genre of mystery fiction is dominated by female writers, characters created by male authors have made significant contributions, including Jon L. Breen's bookseller Rachel Hennings, Aaron Elkins's archaeologist Gideon Oliver, and M. D. Lake's campus cop Peggy O'Neill. Sleuths of color, such as Barbara Neely's maid Blanche White, are also represented. In whatever locale, the cozy provides a reassuring island of safe haven in the sea of hard-boiled detective fiction. In the end, good triumphs, and the universe disrupted by the crime is set right once more.

Bibliography

DeAndrea, William L. *Encyclopedia Mysteriosa: A Comprehensive Guide to the Art of Detection in Print, Films, Radio, and Television.* New York: Prentice, 1994.

Klein, Kathleen Gregory, ed. *Great Women Mystery Writers: Classic to Contemporary.* Westport: Greenwood, 1994.

Swanson, Jean, and Dean James. *By a Woman's Hand: A Guide to Mystery Fiction by Women.* New York: Berkley, 1994.

Elizabeth Foxwell

See also

Academic Mysteries

Classical Mysteries

Cross, Amanda

Golden Age of Detective Fiction

Had-I-But-Known Mysteries

Mystery Awards

Mystery and Detective Fiction

Credit Cards, popularly known as "plastic," are an economic phenomenon that transformed American consumer behavior from around 1960 on. They have contributed to the development of catalog marketing by way of toll-free telephone numbers, to telemarketing, and to fraud and widespread personal bankruptcy. Buying staple goods on monthly credit was common in the days of general stores and corner groceries, and oil companies such as Texaco introduced gasoline credit cards in the early 1920s. Following World War II, credit cards proliferated, especially for department stores and for travelers, who found themselves carrying an accordion-folded ribbon of cards for oil companies, hotels, car rentals, air travel and restaurants. In 1950, Diners' Club launched a comprehensive travel-and-entertainment card that eight years later was accepted at 17,000 outlets in 76 countries. The annual fee was $5, but Diners' Club raked in 7 percent on every charge. In 1958, American Express initiated a "war" in which the two rivals acquired or allied with various other credit cards such as Esquire Club, Gourmet Guest Club, Sheraton and Hilton Hotels, Avis, Hertz, Mobil and Amoco. The main thrust was "swank" outlets and business travel, and accounts were due in 30 days.

Paralleling these developments, bank credit cards were first introduced in 1951 by Franklin National Bank. It was in California, however, that the bank card began to challenge Diners' Club and American Express. California law allowed branch banks, and so the large Bank of America chain could provide credit statewide. In 1966, it went national with the Bank Americard (later VISA), with its characteristic blue, white, and yellow-striped card that could be issued for affiliated banks. Eastern banks objected to the central control, and in 1967 initiated the rival Master Charge (later MasterCard). The important distinction about the bank cards was "revolving credit," allowing customers to pay about 5 percent per month on their total charges. Essentially, the banks held the balance as a high-interest loan, by 1997 averaging 18.8 percent.

Department stores had pioneered in revolving credit, primarily as an alternative to "lay-by" monthly payments on furniture and appliances. But the effect on the popular consumer was a buy-now, pay-later psychology. By juggling VISA, Sears, Montgomery Ward, and Gimbels, consumers could acquire clothing, household goods, lawn furniture, power tools, tires and so on now, and a horrendous debt for later. Research showed that charging goods became habitual among new cardholders.

Bibliography

Friedman, John, and John Meehan. *House of Cards: The Troubled Empire of American Express.* New York: Putnam, 1992.

"Goodbye, Freebies—Hello, Fees." *Time* 12 Jan. 1998.

"On-the-Cuff Travel Speeds Up." *Business Week* 16 Aug. 1958.

Russell, Thomas. *The Economics of Bank Credit Cards.* New York: Praeger, 1976.

Fred E. H. Schroeder

Creedence Clearwater Revival was a successful rock band of the late 1960s, combining rhythm and blues, country, and "good times" rock 'n' roll into what group leader John Fogerty (1945-) called "swamp music." But the group's roots were anywhere but the swamps. Fogerty grew up in a poor neighborhood in the San Francisco Bay area. He is a self-taught musician who learned to play electric guitar, piano, saxophone, drums, and harmonica. Fogerty also had a unique gravelly voice.

Fogerty formed a trio with two childhood friends, bass player Stu Cook (1945-) and drummer Doug "Cosmo" Clifford (1945-). John Fogerty's brother, Tom (1941-), joined the band as rhythm guitarist, and they began to play clubs in the Bay area as the Blue Velvets.

Lead guitarist John Fogerty emulated African-American blues artists, including Muddy Waters and Howlin' Wolf. The Blue Velvets' first single, "Don't Tell Me No Lies," was released by Fantasy in November 1964, but Hy Weiss at Fantasy changed the group's name to the Golliwogs. Weiss chose the name because it "sounded British" so that they could capitalize on the success of British rock bands.

The Golliwogs were moved to Fantasy's new, teen-oriented subsidiary, and scored a moderate regional success with "Brown-Eyed Girl" in early 1966. Two followup releases sold poorly, and the band drifted for the next year after John Fogerty and Clifford were drafted.

The four original members reunited in early 1967, settling for a harder rock sound and renaming themselves Creedence Clearwater Revival. The name came from a friend's last name (Creedence), a local beer (Clearwater), and their intention to revive the blues sounds of the 1940s and 1950s. Meanwhile, John Fogerty had become good friends with Saul Zaentz, who bought Fantasy Records and signed the renamed band.

The band rehearsed and recorded two blues-flavored rock classics, Dale Hawkins's "Suzie Q" and Screamin' Jay Hawkins's "I Put a Spell on You." "Suzie Q" was released in early 1968 in two versions, a long album cut and a two-part single, with one part on each side. The single became a national Top 40 pick, and reached No. 11 on the national charts in late 1968.

In 1969, the band, now often abbreviated as CCR, recorded *Bayou Country*. The album was based on a Louisiana swamp theme, although none of the band's members had ever visited the bayou state. The album's first single, "Proud Mary," hit No. 2 on the charts, and was revived in cover versions by Elvis Presley and Ike and Tina Turner.

In the summer of 1969, CCR played the pop festival circuit and released a second million-seller LP, *Green River*, featuring "Green River," "Down on the Corner," and "Fortunate Son." In early 1970, CCR released *Willie and the Poor Boys*, which got its title from a line in "Down on the Corner." The biggest hits from this album were "Travelin' Band" and "Who'll Stop the Rain?" Later that year, Creedence Clearwater Revival released *Cosmo's Factory* with the group's seventh and eighth million-selling singles, the folk-rock ballad "Have You Ever Seen the Rain?" and the country-flavored "Lookin' Out My Back Door."

CCR slid rapidly after the departure of Tom Fogerty in January 1971. The remaining three members co-produced *Mardi Gras* in early 1972 (since Cook and Clifford had been upset with the dominance of John Fogerty in previous recording sessions). The LP was panned by reviewers, its only redeeming quality being the inclusion of an old single, "Sweet Hitchhiker."

Although the group disbanded in October 1972, CCR got lots of airplay in the 1970s through greatest hits compilations. In 1976, the 1969 recording "I Heard It through the Grapevine" was re-released as a single. John Fogerty released solo albums under his name and under the name the Blue Ridge Rangers before dropping out of the music scene in 1976. But he returned to recording in 1985, and his album *Centerfield* reached the top of the charts in the U.S.

Bibliography

Hallowell, John. *Inside Creedence*. New York: Bantam, 1971.

Romanowski, Patricia, and Holly George-Warren. *The New Rolling Stone Encyclopedia of Rock & Roll*. New York: Fireside, 1995.

Stambler, Irwin. *The Encyclopedia of Pop, Rock, and Soul*. New York: St. Martin's, 1989.

Ken Nagelberg

Crichton, Michael (1942-), is best known for his science fiction novels *The Andromeda Strain* (1969) and *Jurassic Park* (1990), both of which were made into movies, but he has also written several mysteries that blend classic formulas with provocative contemporary issues. Crichton grew up in New York, and graduated from Harvard Medical School in 1969. He financed his schooling by writing eight paperback thrillers under the pseudonym John Lange. As Jeffrey Hudson, he also wrote a whodunit, *A Case of Need*, depicting the false arrest of an abortion doctor in pre-Roe vs. Wade Boston, which won the Mystery Writers of America Edgar Award for best novel in 1968.

Later Crichton mysteries were issued under his own name. He won another Edgar for *The Great Train Robbery* (1979), a fact-based novel that details the exploits of a Victorian master criminal and explores the hypocrisy and class-based discrimination that riddled this supposedly moral society. *Rising Sun*, a police procedural that created controversy over its depiction of clashing Japanese and American cultures, appeared in 1992. Crichton continued to explore contemporary topics in *Disclosure* (1994), in which a man falsely accused of sexual harassment must identify the motives of the true criminal in order to save himself. Each of these novels has benefited from a successful film version. (*A Case of Need* appeared as *The Carey Treatment*.) Crichton himself directed *The Great Train Robbery*, and contributed to the adaptation of the other films. *Timeline* was published in 1999.

Bibliography

Contemporary Authors, New Revision Series. Vol. 40. Detroit: Gale Research. 99-102.

Contemporary Literary Criticism. Vol. 54. Detroit: Gale Research. 62-77.

Crichton, Michael. *Travels*. New York: Ballantine, 1989.

Trembley, Elizabeth A. *Michael Crichton: A Critical Companion*. Westport: Greenwood, 1996.

Elizabeth A. Trembley

See also

Medical Mystery

Mystery Awards

Thriller, The

Crime Fiction, or detective fiction as it was called until recently, began perhaps in the biblical account of Cain's murder of his brother Abel and God's questioning to establish the truth, and with the story of Susanna and her run-in with the Elders as recounted in the Book of Daniel. Later, Herodotus, the Greek historian called the Father of History (after 440 B.C.), recounted the theft of wealth in his story "The Thief Versus King Rhampsinitus."

Generally, however, modern detective fiction is dated from Edgar Allan Poe's short story "Murders in the Rue Morgue" (1841), featuring C. Auguste Dupin as an intellectual investigator, and was pushed rapidly ahead by the popularity of A. Conan Doyle's never-ending series about Sherlock Holmes beginning with "A Study in Scarlet" (1887).

Interest in crime fiction continues to grow with both authors and the reading public. Writers seem to find crime fiction easy to write, though not necessarily well. Readers find it intriguing both for its demands on the people who like to solve puzzles and because it seems to provide a sense of

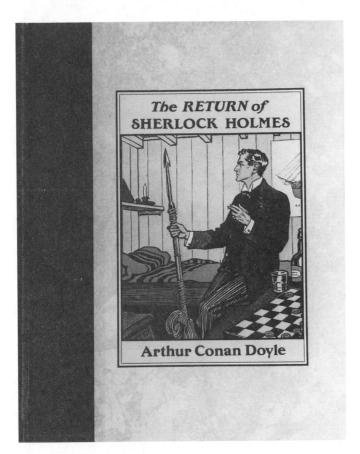

Photo courtesy of Popular Culture Library, Bowling Green State University, Bowling Green, OH.

safety and closure in a world that outside the pages of the fiction grows increasingly violent. It also provides an excellent setting for readers to learn about cultures and elements of societies about which they know little or nothing.

The range of areas and subject matter continues to expand, but generally crime fiction can be classified under the following types or genres: female; gay and lesbian, a growing type; "Golden Age" or "Cozies" or "Closed Room," the oldest modern type; hard-boiled, the prototypical American type; historical; "Little Old Ladies"; mixtures and modifications of various types; Native American and ethnic; plants and animals; police procedurals. They are discussed in this volume under several categories.

Bibliography

Albert, Walter. *Detective and Mystery Fiction.* San Bernardino, CA: Borgo, 1998.

Dove, George. *The Reader and the Detective Story.* Bowling Green, OH: Bowling Green State U Popular P, 1985.

Heising, Willetta L. *Detecting Men: A Reader's Guide and Checklist for Mystery Series by Men.* Dearborn, MI: Purple Moon, 1998.

——. *Detecting Women 2: A Reader's Guide and Checklist for Mystery Series Written by Women.* Dearborn, MI: Purple Moon, 1996.

Swanson, Jean, and Dean James. *Killer Books: A Reader's Guide to Exploring the Popular World of Mystery and Suspense.* New York: Berkley Crime, 1998.

Ray B. Browne

Crisis: Behind a Presidential Commitment (1963), the documentary chronicling the June 1963 integration of the University of Alabama, is a rich historical artifact, not only of the American civil rights movement, but also of the evolution of *cinema vérité* and the presidency of John F. Kennedy.

In the spring of 1963, the determination of two black students, James Hood and Vivian Malone, to exercise their educational rights by enrolling in the University of Alabama pitted the Kennedy administration against Governor George Wallace. Upon reading of the imminent confrontation, Greg Shuker, one of the filmmakers of Drew Associates, arranged through Attorney General Robert Kennedy to document the story of decision-making in the Justice Department as the events unfolded. Another member of Drew Associates, Jim Lipscomb, secured the consent of Governor Wallace to follow his activities in the showdown. Wallace had promised to defy the federal government by "standing in the schoolhouse door" rather than allow the campus to be integrated. The two students also agreed to participate in the filming.

Before it was aired, *Crisis: Behind a Presidential Commitment* was shown at Lincoln Center in the first New York Film Festival. When the program aired on NBC on October 21, 1963, it generated controversy and strong reactions. In the *New York Times*, TV critic Jack Gould questioned the sincerity of the key players. And New York's educational TV station, Channel 13, ran a half-hour panel discussion titled "Crisis: Presidency by Television," which explored the validity of the documentary. Editorialists took swipes at the program, noting "the President has no business in show business" and that it was an improper way to enlist sympathy for the civil rights movement.

Bibliography

O'Connell, P. J. *Robert Drew and the Development of Cinema Vérité in America.* Carbondale: Southern Illinois UP, 1992.

Watson, Mary Ann. *The Expanding Vista: American Television in the Kennedy Years.* New York: Oxford UP, 1990.

Mary Ann Watson

See also
Documentary Film
Drew, Robert

Crosby, Bing (1904-1977), one of the truly exceptional American singers of popular songs, was born Harry Lillis Crosby in Tacoma, WA. Raised in an large Irish-Catholic family, Bing, the fourth of seven children, grew up in comfortable circumstances in Spokane. While studying at Gonzaga University (1921-24), a Catholic institution operated by the Jesuit order in Spokane, Bing performed with a local band as a drummer and vocalist. By 1925 he played the vaudeville circuit with Al Rinker, as Two Boys and a Piano. His big break came in 1927, when Crosby and Rinker sang with Paul Whiteman's orchestra. When Harry Barris joined them they had national success as the Rhythm Boys, touring with big bands (1927-30).

By 1932, Crosby was America's most popular radio singer, and appeared in his first feature movie, *The Big Broadcast of 1932.* His rendition of "Pennies from Heaven" and "Where the Blue of the Night" (his signature tune) made him a movie star overnight and the most distinctive crooner of the 1930s.

In the 1930s, Crosby made a variety of movies—backstage epics (*Too Much Harmony* in 1933), campus capers (*College Humor* in 1933), Westerns (*Rhythm on the Range* in 1936), and South Sea musicals (*Waikiki Wedding* in 1937)—but he was best in lighthearted musical comedies. *We're Not Dressing* (1934) was a superb Paramount musical with fine songs for Bing and a strong supporting cast with Ethel Merman, Carole Lombard, George Burns, and Gracie Allen. *Anything Goes* (1936) was a Broadway adaptation with marvelous Cole Porter music and once again strong support by Ethel Merman. Crosby starred in 16 Paramount movies in the 1930s as Hollywood gradually learned to produce outstanding original musical comedies, and he always had hit songs in each film. Perhaps his best movie in this genre was *Sing, You Sinners* (1938) with Fred MacMurray and the young Donald O'Connor.

In 1940, Crosby made movie history when he was teamed with Bob Hope and Dorothy Lamour (see entries) in the first of six very popular "Road" pictures. With Crosby playing the witty smart guy to Hope's brash, leering fool and comic coward, and Lamour's exotic love goddess, the trio showed isolationist Americans the studio lot view of an exotic and goofy world.

Although Crosby introduced his most memorable song, "White Christmas," in the 1942 movie *Holiday Inn*, he is best remembered for singing it in the 1954 film *White Christmas*. In 1944 he became the first pop singer to win an Academy Award for best actor, for his sensitive performance as Father O'Malley in *Going My Way*. In a sense, this film typecast Crosby as the amusing and lovable Irish-American priest. Although he was cast as a priest in only three movies (*Going My Way*, *The Bells of St. Mary's* [1945], and *Say One for Me* [1959]), the war-weary public loved him in a clerical collar.

Bing Crosby's talent as a casual charmer on the screen was well established in more than 60 movies, but his skill as a dramatic actor is best revealed in *Country Girl* (1954), with Grace Kelly and William Holden. Kelly won an Oscar for her role as the wife of the alcoholic singer, Frank Elgin (Crosby). *A Yankee in King Arthur's Court* (1949), *Here Comes the Groom* (1951), and *High Society* (1956) are his other outstanding screen performances.

Bing made many forgettable films; nonetheless, 30 of his movies from 1934 to 1964 were listed among the top grossing films each year. Bing retired in 1957, but continued to appear in films and, occasionally, on television in the 1950s and 1960s.

Crosby married Wilma Winifred Wyatt (Dixie Lee) in 1930, and had four sons. After Dixie died in 1952, Bing married an actress, Olive Kathryn Grandstaff (Kathryn Grant), in 1957. They had three more children, and the whole family appeared in several television Christmas specials and a television series, *The Bing Crosby Show*, in 1964. His sudden death at a golf course in Spain ended 50 years of success in the entertainment business.

Photo courtesy of Sound Recording Archives, Bowling Green State University, Bowling Green, OH.

Bibliography

Barnes, Ken. *The Crosby Years.* New York: St. Martin's, 1980.

Bookbinder, Robert. *The Films of Bing Crosby.* Secaucus: Citadel, 1977.

Crosby, Bing. *Call Me Lucky.* New York: Simon & Schuster, 1953.

Crosby, Gary, and Ross Firestone. *Going My Own Way.* Garden City: Doubleday, 1983.

Morgereth, Timothy A. *Bing Crosby: A Discography, Radio Program List, and Filmography.* Jefferson: McFarland, 1987.

Peter C. Holloran

Cross, Amanda, is the pseudonym of Carolyn G. Heilbrun (1929-), a professor of literature retired from Columbia University, who has gained recognition as a feminist literary critic—the author of *Reinventing Womanhood* (1979) and *Writing a Woman's Life* (1988)—and as mystery writer Amanda Cross. Cross's series detective Kate Fansler, the protagonist of 12 novels beginning with *In the Last Analysis* (1964), like Heilbrun herself teaches in a New York City university and publishes feminist scholarship. The novels have academic settings, including Harvard in *Death in a Tenured Position* (1981), Oxford in *The Question of Max* (1976) and *No Word from Winifred* (1986), Wellesley-like Clare College in *Sweet Death, Kind Death* (1984), and Kate's own Columbia-like university in *Poetic Justice* (1970) and *A Trap for Fools* (1989). Kate's solutions draw heavily on celebrated authors and texts: Freud in *In the Last Analysis*, Joyce in *The James Joyce Murder* (1967), Antigone in *The Theban Mysteries* (1971), and John le Carré in *An Imperfect Spy* (1995), and its sequel, *The Puzzled Heart* (1998).

Though increasingly concerned with current feminist issues (*An Imperfect Spy* sets up an implied parallel between the gender war and the Cold War), the novels do not belong to the female hard-boiled detective fiction subgenre. Cross most closely resembles British detective novelist Dorothy L. Sayers (1893-1957), while Kate Fansler is reminiscent of Sayers's feminist protagonist Harriet Vane.

Bibliography

Bargainnier, Earl. *Ten Women of Mystery*. Bowling Green, OH: Bowling Green State U Popular P, 1981.
Fraser, Antonia. *New York Times Book Review* 14 Oct. 1990.
Matthews, Anne. *New York Times Magazine* 8 Nov. 1992.
Purcell, J. M. *Armchair Detective* Winter 1980.
Reddy, Maureen T. *Sisters in Crime*. New York: Continuum, 1988.

June M. Frazer

See also
Academic Mysteries
Cozy Mysteries
Feminist Detective Fiction

Cruise, Tom (1962-   ), one of Hollywood's clean-faced idols, was born Thomas Cruise Mapother IV in Syracuse, New York. Cruise, one of the 1980s "brat pack" kids, has been married twice. His first wife was actress Mimi Rogers. After their divorce, he married Nicole Kidman in 1981.

Cruise's debut film was 1981's *Endless Love*. It established him in a character he used in many subsequent roles, the childlike kid on the edge of adulthood. His character appears to want to be amoral but has an innate sense of decency that prevents him from going too far. In later films, Cruise was teamed with older, established actors who played father figures. These older actors—Dustin Hoffman, Paul Newman, Bryan Brown—were generally lavish in their praise of his acting ability and helped him toward achieving his goal of becoming a reputable actor.

Cruise has starred in a number of films, including *Losin' It* and *The Outsiders* in 1983 as well as the film that brought him his earliest widespread fame, *Risky Business* (1983). In *Risky Business*, he portrayed the epitome of Reagan's entrepreneurial capitalist, opening a whorehouse in his home while his parents are off on vacation. Again, he made it seem like a childish prank and all turned out well.

In 1986's *Top Gun*, he played a macho pilot, not giving much thought again to the morality of his actions. The emphasis was on the adventure and pure heroism. In 1988's *Rain Man* and 1989's *Born on the Fourth of July*, however, his acting showed a deepening maturity. In the latter film, he portrayed the real-life Ron Kovic, a disabled Vietnam vet who became a leader in the peace movement. He demonstrated in that film that he was able to go beyond playing just another pretty face. However, in his next film (*Days of Thunder*, 1990) he returned to an action character.

In the 1990s Cruise appeared in eight movies, in roles varying from a turn-of-the-century Irish immigrant (*Far and Away*, 1992), to a lawyer (*A Few Good Men*, 1992; *The Firm*, 1993), to a vampire (*Interview with the Vampire*, 1994), to a spy (*Mission Impossible*, 1996) to a sports agent (*Jerry Maguire*, 1996). In 1999 he starred in *Magnolia* and, along with Kidman, in *Eyes Wide Shut*, a dark film about sexual fantasy directed by Stanley Kubrick.

Bibliography

Gross, Edward. *Top Gun: The Films of Tom Cruise*. Las Vegas: Pioneer, 1990.
Themas, Nicholas, ed. *International Directory of Films and Filmmakers. Actors and Actresses*. Detroit: St. James, 1992.

Frank A. Salamone

C-SPAN, a cable television network, was launched on March 19, 1979, with live, gavel-to-gavel coverage of the U.S. House of Representatives from within the chambers of the House itself. It was the first time in U.S. history that citizens from all over the country were able to view their government in action. The initials were an acronym for Cable Satellite Public Affairs Network. A second companion network, C-SPAN2, was initiated in 1986, dedicated to televising the gavel-to-gavel proceedings of the U.S. Senate.

The C-SPAN networks were created as a unique private, nonprofit venture managed and funded entirely by the cable television industry itself. Contrary to public opinion C-SPAN and C-SPAN2 are not supported by the federal government or by any corporate sponsors. The programming is entirely free from commercials.

During the first 20 years of operation the programming on both channels became accessible 24 hours a day to more than half of the American viewing public, some 59 million cable households, and globally via satellite. Two audio networks were created in 1989 to provide a world perspective on public affairs, news, and cultural events. C-SPAN Audio 1 blends international English-language news programs, while C-SPAN Audio 2 airs the BBC World Service live from London. Educational support services continue to expand for teachers and students at schools and colleges, and a permanent archives department for all programming was established at Purdue University.

The inauguration of programming on C-SPAN was due to the confluence of four factors: (1) the vision of Brian Lamb, its primary founder, chairman of its board and CEO, as well as its most frequently recognized host; (2) the desire to televise proceedings of the House of Representatives by its members, especially Tip O'Neill, who had become Speaker of the House in 1977; (3) the reluctance of the networks and PBS to give away control of the cameras and programming in the House; and (4) the development of technology that had led to the formation of the cable industry by its leaders. Each of these factors was necessary, with timing providing the rare happenstance that creates history.

The first priority of programming on C-SPAN and C-SPAN2 continued to be the live, gavel-to-gavel sessions of the Houses of Congress whenever in session, any time of day or night. The second area of programming grew out of the second mandate in the mission statement: "To provide elected and appointed officials and others who would influence public policy a direct conduit to the audience without filtering or otherwise distorting their points of view." Regularly scheduled programs that fulfilled this clause included the *American Profile* series on national holidays that featured in-depth interviews with public officials as well as opinion and business leaders. *Road to the White House* programs provided special coverage of possible Democratic, Republican, and third-party candidates as they prepared for presidential campaigns.

The third unique programming feature of the C-SPAN networks was the regularly scheduled opportunities for television viewers to interact directly with guests. These programs had been mandated in the third clause of the mission statement: "To provide the audience, through the call-in program, with direct access to elected officials, other decision-makers and journalists on a frequent and open basis."

An additional service of C-SPAN has been to supply educators with tools for integrating C-SPAN programming into the classroom. Special programs were scheduled, such as *C-SPAN in the Classroom*. In 1990 an interactive computer service began carrying C-SPAN schedules as well as *C-SPAN Classroom*, which included lessons plans incorporating network programs. Teachers reported using C-SPAN programs to teach government procedures, comparative government, current events, critical thinking, and speech communications. Copyright clearance for educational use was given automatically without charge. C-SPAN also sponsored several grant programs for classroom equipment and fellowships for high school teachers and professors to attend special workshops in Washington. There were also special programs for students to interact with politicians, such as the *National Student Town Meetings*, begun in 1993 in cooperation with the Close Up Foundation and Scholastic, Inc.

One of the most innovative educational projects was the bright yellow C-SPAN school bus, which began traveling nationwide during 1993-94 school year visiting public schools and historical sites. This 45-foot customized motor coach had been designed as both a television production facility on wheels and an interactive media information station for teachers, students, and cable operators.

Bibliography

"Bringing Government to the People." *Broadcasting* 3 April 1989.

Geltner, Sharon. "Brian Lamb: The Man Behind C-SPAN." *Saturday Evening Post* Jan. 1986.

Krolik, Richard. "Everything You Wanted to Know about C-SPAN But Were Afraid to Ask." *Television Quarterly* 25.4 (1992).

Lamb, Brian. "Getting the Whole Truth." *Media Studies Journal* Winter 1996.

Ann Schoonmaker

Culp, Robert (1930-), in 1994, during an interview while he was making a reunion *I Spy* movie with Bill Cosby, labeled himself "a director first, a writer second, and an actor third." Yet Culp has been among the busiest actors of this century. Born in Berkeley, CA, he attended several colleges and enjoyed an athletic career. He went to New York and eventually won an Obie for his theater work.

Culp had appeared in more than a dozen shows on television when he won the lead in *Trackdown* (1957-59). The show had two formats; in each, Culp portrayed Hoby Gilman, Texas Ranger. The laconic, quick-thinking, quick-shooting role made the actor a household name. After the series was canceled, Culp became one of television's busiest guest stars. His roles on *Dr. Kildare, Bonanza,* and especially his three bravura achievements on *The Outer Limits,* are still remembered more than 30 years later.

After 40-some roles, he found another series, his greatest personal triumph, the phenomenally popular and quoted *I Spy* (see entry). The program was the brainchild of movie heavy Sheldon Leonard. He sought long and hard for the right man to team with inexperienced, bright ex-athlete Bill Cosby. Despite opposition from some southern elements, the pair worked brilliantly together as wisecracking, sincere espionage agents, on many levels including that of improvised dialogue. Shot entirely on foreign locations with television film and a portable generator, it remains the only series ever to have been shot in this manner. Culp won three Emmy nominations for his work in the series. It is still winning him fans in reruns.

After this legendary NBC role, Culp starred in miniseries, *Name of the Game, Greatest Heroes of the Bible,* and several *Columbo* episodes. His feature film career includes roles in *Bob & Carol & Ted & Alice* (1969), *Hickey and Boggs* (1972), *The Castaway Cowboy* (1974), and numerous others. In his third series, ABC's *Greatest American Hero* (1981-83), he portrayed Bill Maxwell, a pompous FBI agent recruited by aliens to help a schoolteacher to use a supersuit to fight criminals. His endearing performance was easily the show's finest asset.

The busy Culp has played scores of roles since that series was canceled. He was featured in such films as *Hannie Caulder* (1971) and, more recently, *Time Bomb* (1991) and *The Pelican Brief* (1993). He is most adept at playing outwardly calm but inwardly suffering characters, whether in comedic or serious style. He was part of a fourth series, which had a brief run in 1979, *Women in White*. A man with charm and imagination, Culp brings unusual grace to every role he undertakes.

Bibliography

Brooks, Tim. *The Complete Directory to Prime Time TV Stars, 1946-Present.* New York: Ballantine, 1987.

R. D. Michael

Cults form a portion of any portrait of American religious behavior. "Cult" is a loosely defined term, generally used to refer to those religious communities with smaller, fluctuating memberships, which often do not demand the exclusive allegiance of their followers, and whose followers share unique views that in general deny the importance of most worldly values.

Despite their differing theological orientations, cults share several organizational and social characteristics, although not all groups will exhibit all characteristics. Cults are usually rooted in the Protestantism of the 19th century and have undergone a conflict with the larger society over some aspect of either their theologies, interpretations of those theologies, or practices. Founders of these new groups are generally viewed as having charismatic qualities stemming from their ability to communicate with other-world entities and are frequently dubbed radical by conventional society because their beliefs are often innovative.

General use of the ascriptive term "cult" is one indicator that the subgroup is considered marginalized by the larger society. Marginality is not based on theological issues but instead is a reflection of a tension between the groups' practices and the society's normative, secular interests, a response with historical precedence. Cotton Mather considered the marginal religious groups of colonial America as possessing a capacity for challenging social norms and therefore considered them a potentially disruptive social element. Cults and other marginalized religious groups are legitimized by the larger society when they either delete the offending practice (The Church of Jesus Christ of Latter-Day Saints and polygamy, for example) or the larger society experiences a change in the particular, normative secular value in the direction of the marginalized religion (Jehovah's Witnesses and concerns of national security and loyalty, for example). Generally, but not always, the withholding of legitimization is based on the practice of stated beliefs, not the beliefs themselves, which increasingly the courts have held to be a matter of individual belief rather than institutionalized theology. The tolerance exhibited by American law is reflected in the tolerance granted by the dominant society to the religious cult.

Most earlier American religious participation, as competitive and varied as the denominations were, was well within the traditions of mutually inherited religious traditions. As the 18th century merged into the 19th, however, innovative religious groups began to appear. A common feature of the founders of these groups is that each considered that society had become too complex and disarrayed: natural human simplicity had been corrupted. A return to simpler, even primitive, ways would return human innocence and correct society's imperfections. Cults proliferated across the American landscape, most to disappear (the Oneida Community, for example), a few to form the basis for the development of new denominations (the Church of Christ, Scientist, for example, and the transformation of the dwindling Millerite cult into another authentic American denomination, the Seventh Day Adventists, both of which are extant and worldwide).

Alternate religious organizations became a concern for Americans in the last half of the 20th century. The term "cult," as used by the general public, began to take on connotations of fear and anti-Americanism. Eight movements in particular drew national attention: The Children of God, the Unification Church of America, the Divine Light Mission, the International Society of Krishna Consciousness, the Church of Scientology, the People's Temple, Rajneeshpuram, and the Branch Davidians. Most of these and other cult movements did not meet the definitional guidelines based on 19th-century cults. Most maintained large membership numbers and did insist on the exclusive allegiance of their followers. Many have followed the sects' example of withdrawal from society, and for some groups, there is intragroup pressure to conform. Additionally, most were derived from older religious traditions; therefore, the founders were not establishing radical, new religious traditions.

Bibliography

Bromley, David G., and Anson D. Shupe, Jr. *Strange Gods: The Great American Cult Scare.* Boston: Beacon, 1981.

Lehmann, Arthur C., and James E. Myers, eds. *Magic, Witchcraft, and Religion: An Anthropological Study of the Supernatural.* Palo Alto: Mayfield, 1985.

Marty, Martin E. *Pilgrims in Their Own Land: 500 Years of Religion in America.* Boston: Little, Brown, 1984.

Zaretsky, Irving I., and Mark P. Leone, eds. *Religious Movements in Contemporary America.* Princeton: Princeton UP, 1974.

Sydney Langdon

Cussler, Clive (1931-), born in Illinois and raised in southern California, is a best-selling popular novelist, the author of an adventure series featuring the heroic Dirk Pitt, an Air Force major assigned to work with the National Underwater and Marine Agency (NUMA). NUMA is a fictionalized version of an agency that Cussler himself heads, a nonprofit organization founded in 1978 to locate the relics of historically significant ships, planes, and other lost vehicles.

NUMA's missions provide the occasion for Pitt's many exploits, ranging from refloating the *Titanic* to recover "byzantium," a radioactive element, in *Raise the Titanic* (1977), to uncovering the secret behind the assassination of President Lincoln after locating his body in a Confederate submarine buried in the Sahara desert in *Sahara* (1992). Pitt, a hard-drinking, womanizing adventurer, is a somewhat autobiographical creation. His novels have been published in 28 languages. Other major works include *The Mediterranean Caper* (1973), *Iceberg* (1975), *Vixen 03* (1978), *Night Probe* (1981), *Pacific Vortex* (1982), *Deep Six* (1984), *Cyclops* (1986), *Treasure* (1988), *Dragon* (1990), *Inca Gold* (1994), and *Atlantis Found* (1999).

Bibliography

Jayroe, Walt. "PW Interviews: Clive Cussler." *Publishers Weekly* 11 July 1994.

Lambert, Pam. "Hard-Driving Clive." *People* 21 Sept. 1992.

Pat Tyrer

Cybill (1995-1997), a popular CBS situation comedy, starred Cybill Shepherd, who made her film debut as a high school beauty in *The Last Picture Show* (1971), about life in a small Texas town in the early 1950s. She gained television stardom in the detective comedy/drama *Moonlighting* (see entry), in the 1980s, but had to share the limelight and behind-the-scenes fighting with co-star Bruce Willis. A producer as well as star in *Cybill*, Shepherd's real life is the basis for her character, Cybill Sheridan, a middle-aged, struggling actress, divorced twice with children from each ex-husband (played by Tom Wopat from the popular 1980s comedy/adventure,

The Dukes of Hazzard, and Alan Rosenberg from the short-lived courtroom drama in the early 1990s, *Civil Wars*). Cybill had a 22-year-old married daughter, Rachel, and a 16-year-old daughter, Zoey, a sarcastic brat. Another important person in Cybill's life was her rich, alcoholic friend, Maryann, played by stage actress Christine Baranski.

Bibliography
Murphy, Mary. "Cybill Plays Cybill." *TV Guide* 7 Jan. 1995: 24-27.
Tucker, Ken. "Redesigning Women." *Entertainment Weekly* 13 Jan. 1995: 42-44.

Lynn C. Spangler

Dahl, Steve (1954-), is cited, possibly unfairly, as an early example of radio's "shock jocks." Throughout the 1980s, Dahl and his partner Garry Meier ran afoul of everyone from the Federal Communications Commission to the Archdiocese of Chicago, and fans loved it.

A Los Angeles area native, Dahl started his radio career at age 15 at tiny underground KAFY in Bakersfield, getting his break when a DJ passed out on the air. He had over two dozen radio jobs, 20 of which he was fired from. Dahl evolved his free-form style at WWWW in Detroit, where station management was negotiating a sale, and didn't keep an eye on him until he pulled in a 7.2 rating. When Dahl left for Chicago, he was replaced by young Howard Stern (whom Dahl later often accused of stealing his ideas).

After less than a year at progressive rocker WDAI, Dahl objected to a format change (to disco). WLUP-FM ("Chicago's Loop") hired him in 1979, where he shortly teamed with overnight announcer and Chicago native Garry Meier (1949-), forming *Steve & Garry's Breakfast Club.*

The pair played off their contrasting styles—funster Dahl rambled about anything that interested or annoyed him, until Meier's dry quip got them back to earth for a commercial. Steve Dahl recorded parody songs, created a raft of character voices, and held "Disco Demolitions." WLUP mysteriously fired the pair in 1981, but they were quickly hired back by the "new" WLS-FM, and continued their antics until 1986, when they returned to WLUP. In 1993, however, Meier quit the show, and Dahl ended up with an all-sports format morning show. That show suffered from competition with other sports stations, but Dahl found his feet again when he was teamed with lawyer turned irreverent sportscaster Bruce Wolf and was no longer required to talk exclusively about sports.

Bibliography

Dahl, Steve, and Garry Meier. *A Decade of Service* (2 audio cassettes). Shock Radio Inc. No. 101-102, 1989.

Feder, Robert. "Why Meier Got Fed Up." *Chicago Sun-Times* 1 Nov. 1993: 35.

Johnson, Steve. "Shocked Jock: Will Steve Dahl Survive?" *Chicago Tribune* (Sunday Magazine) 6 Nov. 1994: 15-20, 32.

Kening, Dan. "Thrown for a Loop." *Chicago Tribune* 9 Dec. 1993: 1.

Terry, Clifford. "Dahl-Meier, WLS Just Don't Match." *Chicago Tribune* 20 Feb. 1986: 13.

Widder, Pat. "Steve and Garry Part Ways—for Now—after 15 Years." *Chicago Tribune* 14 Sept. 1993: 22.

Mark McDermott

Dailey, Janet (1944-), one of the mainstays of the stable of Harlequin and Silhouette novelists, is the author of close to a hundred formula romances. Adept at the Harlequin fictional prescription, Dailey writes stories of fated lovers who undergo series of trials and overcome a series of obstacles, including, often, animosity against each other, to claim their destined union. Her first novel, *No Quarter Asked* (1974), established this pattern, from which she has seldom strayed during her 25-year career. Despite changing gender mores, she has stuck to a traditional profile for her hero (conventionally masculine, stoic but passionate, strong but vulnerable, often roguish or rebellious) and heroine (conventionally feminine, chaste but sexually awakened, resolute but craving surrender).

Bibliography

Dailey, Janet. *The Janet Dailey Companion: A Comprehensive Guide to Her Life and Her Novels.* New York: Harper-Collins, 1996.

Thompson, Jim. "It's Not What You Know, It's What You Learn." *Writer's Digest* Jan. 1986: 6.

Liahna Babener

Dallas (1978-1991), one of the most popular prime-time TV drama series of all time, was the story of a family of Texas oil and cattle barons that epitomized the greed and consumerism of the 1980s Reagan era. Not since *Peyton Place* in the 1960s had a prime-time drama soap appeared on television. *Dallas*, however, became the great escape for viewers, defining the American dream as "anything is fair in the pursuit of riches and power." With its emphasis on high living, the show was a distorted reflection of the decadent 1980s.

The basic plot of the show was the old Romeo and Juliet motif: the rivalry of the two former partners in the oil field, Jock Ewing, played by Jim Davis, and Digger Barnes (David Wayne; Keenan Wynn), later written out of the show with the character's death in 1980. Eventually, the mom-and-pop oil business, Ewing Oil, became the largest independent oil company in Texas, and the Ewing family lived in style at Southfork Ranch. The feud was escalated with the marriage of Bobby Ewing (Patrick Duffy) and Pamela Barnes (Victoria Principal). After Digger's death, his son Cliff (Ken Kercheval) continued the never-ending, and never successful, fight to destroy Ewing Oil with J. R. Ewing, the elder brother (Larry Hagman) as his chief nemesis.

Dallas first appeared on CBS in the spring of 1978 for a five-week trial run. The show was renewed for the 1979-80 season in the 10 p.m. Saturday time slot. As popularity increased later in the season, it was moved to Friday at 10 p.m. where it ruled that time slot for most of the 1980s. *Dallas* reached its height of popularity in 1980 with the "Who Shot J. R.?" episode. Over 300 million viewers sat glued to their television sets in 57 countries around the world to find out who shot J. R. The consummate model of marketing hype, the episode revealing the killer (his sister-in-law Kristen) garnered a 53.3 rating and a 76 audience share, meaning that every 3 out of 4 television viewers watched that episode. This record number of viewers would stand until outranked by the final episode of *M*A*S*H* in 1983.

When *Dallas* finished first in the ratings in the 1980-81 season, it was only the second time a dramatic series had ever done so (*Marcus Welby, M.D.* was the other). Ratings began to decline after 1986, when a bizarre plot twist cast an entire season as a dream, and favorite cast members left the show. By its final season in 1990-91, ratings had fallen to No. 61. The show ended with a two-hour episode depicting J. R. with his life and precious Ewing family in ruins: he'd lost his family, Ewing Oil, and Southfork.

Bibliography

Brooks, Tim, and Earle Marsh. *The Complete Directory to Prime Time Network TV Shows, 1946-Present.* New York: Ballantine, 1992.

Corliss, R. "Good-bye to Gaud Almighty." *Time* 29 April 1991: 72.

Gianakos, L. J. *Television Drama Series Programming.* Metuchen: Scarecrow, 1987.

Goodman, M., and T. Gold. "Sunset at Southfork." *People* 6 May 1991: 15-19.

Stern, Michael, and Jane Stern. *Encyclopedia of Pop Culture.* New York: HarperCollins, 1992.

Sheri Carder

Dances with Wolves (1990) is an Academy Award-winning, successful movie that evoked both approval and disapproval. The success of the film obviously had something to do with the romanticism of the noble savage and the fantasy of seeing Kevin Costner, an icon of middle America, "go Indian" as Civil War Lt. John Dunbar, who is assigned to what turns out to be an abandoned fort and slowly becomes part of a nearby Sioux village, and is named Dances with Wolves. And *Dances* follows a long tradition of earnest white men who have "gone Indian," witnessed in the historical and literary roots of Daniel Boone and Thoreau and in more direct cinematic forerunners like Jimmy Stewart in *Broken Arrow* (1950), Dustin Hoffman in *Little Big Man* (1970), and Richard Harris in *A Man Called Horse* (1970). Many critics complained that the film's sensibility celebrated contemporary Hollywood liberalism rather than an accurate history of the meeting of white and Sioux cultures during the 1860s. But romanticism of the noble savage and the going-Indian myth each have long historical and mythic roots in American culture, and Costner (himself part Cherokee), writer Michael Blake, and producer Jim Wilson explored and revised these ongoing threads in American thought.

Dances, too, is quite simply a finely made film. All the basic elements of filmmaking are gracefully deployed. The acting is outstanding in a genre not known for patient explorations of character; the cinematography of a reimagined Great Plains, of Cavalry blues, and Sioux buckskin and face paint, of horses, wolves, and buffalo, blends a wide-screen lushness with the austerity of a nature documentary; the editing is expert and the gliding camera moves into and away from characters at dramatic moments, complementing the restrained performances of all the actors.

Costner and Blake's *Dances with Wolves* alluded to and revised some major strains in American Romantic thought. The most traditional American literary move, however, is the form of Dunbar's spiritual quest toward self through nature, and the careful recording of his journey in a diary (prominently photographed and often read from by Dunbar in voiceover narration).

Bibliography

Ansen, David. "How the West Was Lost: This Time the Good Guys Wear War Paint." *Newsweek* 19 Nov. 1990: 67-68.

Baird, Robert. "Going Indian through *Dances with Wolves.*" *Film & History* 23 (1993): 91-102.

Robert Baird

Dangerfield, Rodney (1921-), grew up during the Great Depression, an era providing the impetus for the comedy success of older more cynical comedy clowns such as W. C. Fields, the Marx Brothers, and Mae West.

Dangerfield, like a number of performers of his day, got his big break when he was booked on television's *Ed Sullivan Show* and did the unimaginable: He made Sullivan laugh. From there he became a television talk show regular, appearing more than sixty times on *The Tonight Show*. On film, Dangerfield became the fast-talking, loud, obnoxious yet somehow lovable bumbler who dares to utter all the rude thoughts we all think but don't say.

Dangerfield's film credits include the role of comic villain in *The Projectionist* (1971); a hilarious supporting role in *Caddyshack* (1980); *Easy Money* (1983), a film which he also wrote and was his first starring role in a comedy; *Back to School* (1986), judged by most as his best film, which pokes fun at the hallowed halls of academia and was one of the first comedies to gross over $100 million. *Moving* (1988) and *Ladybugs* (1992) were both less well received and not nearly the commercial success of the others. In contrast to his comedic roles, Dangerfield accepted a dramatic role in Oliver Stone's *Natural Born Killers* (1994), in which he earned critical praise as a realistic "Father from Hell." A 1997 comedy was *Wally Sparks*.

Bibliography

Gehring, Wes D. "Personality Comedians As Genre: Selected Players." *Contributions to the Study of Popular Culture* 61. Westport: Greenwood, 1997.

Mast, Gerald. *The Comic Mind: Comedy and the Movies.* 2d ed. Chicago: U of Chicago P, 1979.

Siegel, Scott, and Barbara Siegel. *American Film Comedy.* New York: Prentice-Hall, 1994.

Barbara Anderson

See also

Comedians, Standup

Daniel Amos, which began as an acoustic quartet in Costa Mesa, CA, in 1974, has always been credited with being one of the leading forces in popular Christian music. While Larry Norman (see entry) is clearly the originator of modern Christian rock music, Daniel Amos (also known at various points as "D.A." and "da") must be recognized as the band that refined and extended the genre. The band's 1981 release *Alarma!* came at a time when Contemporary Christian Music (CCM) was primarily evangelistic tracks set to music or "praise" music written for the already converted (see Christian Radio Music Formats). The raw, aggressive, and angry *Alarma!* introduced a social consciousness into CCM. Lead singer and songwriter Terry Taylor, drummer Ed McTaggart, bassist Tim Chandler, and guitarist Jerry Chamberlain dared to talk about the church's indifference to hunger ("Faces to the Window"), belief that "bigger is better" ("Big Time/Big Deal"), and the tendency to withdraw from a hurting and broken world ("In My Room"). CCM would never be entirely safe again. The genre had learned to critique itself, the church, and the world.

Doppelganger (1982), the second volume of the Alarma! Chronicles, broke the ground for a thinking person's CCM. The album began with a paraphrase of T. S. Eliot's "Hollow Men." "Mall All over the World" simultaneously slammed the canned mass-produced CCM and the consumer culture it imitates. "New Car!" challenged the "Name it/Claim it" theology that thrived in televangelism. It was an outrageous mixture of sarcasm and exhortation wrapped in progressive new wave music that was uniquely Daniel Amos. The final two chapters of the Alarma! Chronicles, *Vox Humana* (1984) and *Fearful Symmetry* (1986), pondered the impact of technology on humanness and the struggle to find balance and peace in life. Throughout these and their five subsequent studio albums to date, Taylor's critical and insightful lyrics have been balanced with satire and self-depreciation.

Daniel Amos has expanded its activity in several directions. Most of the band members, along with several other CCM notables, have produced three discs full with humor under the moniker "The Swirling Eddies," a name borrowed from Dante's Inferno. Terry Taylor is a member of the Lost Dogs, a CCM supergroup composed of Taylor, Gene Eugene of Adam Again, Derri Daughtery of the Choir, and Mike Roe of the Seventy Sevens. Taylor is also one of the most in-demand CCM producers.

Bibliography

Baker, Paul. *Topical Index of Contemporary Christian Music*. Pinson: Music Helps, 1987.

Peters, Dan, Steve Peters, and Cher Merril. *What about Christian Rock?* Minneapolis: Bethany, 1986.

Jay Howard

Darin, Bobby (1936-1973), has been called the "angry young man" of rock 'n' roll. Always driven, Darin was a confident performer who deliberately distanced himself from rock 'n' roll. With a childhood ambition to be an actor and with what critics called an ordinary but pleasant voice, Bobby Darin used snapping fingers and fancy footwork to earn both a reputation as a master showman and a movie career.

Bobby Darin was born Walden Robert Cassotto. While some sources attribute the name Darin to a malfunctioning Chinese restaurant sign that read Mandarin, others claim that Darin chose the name from a telephone directory for luck. With heart troubles that began at eight when he had rheumatic fever, Darin often told reporters that he knew he would die young, and he died after heart surgery at the age of 37.

Fulfilling his childhood dream, Darin starred in his first film, *Come September*, in 1961. He also wrote the title song and theme for the film that was shot in Rome, where he met Sandra Douvan (Dee). The two were married on December 1, 1960, and had a son, Dodd Mitchell Cassotto. Other movies of Darin's included *Pressure Point* (1962), *If a Man Answers* (1962), *Too Late Blues* (1961), *State Fair* (1962), and *Hell Is for Heroes* (1962). He earned a best-supporting-actor nomination for his role in *Captain Newman, MD* (1962).

During the 1960s, Darin returned to the Top 10 in 1966 with his version of Tim Hardin's "If I Were a Carpenter." He also worked on Robert Kennedy's presidential campaign. Devastated by Kennedy's assassination, Darin recorded two protest albums, singing the songs of Laura Nyro, Tim Hardin, and Bob Dylan.

During the 1972-73 season, he had a weekly variety show on NBC. Darin also performed at prominent nightclubs, making his highlight appearance at the Copacabana in New York City on June 2, 1960. With 22 Top 40 hits, including "Dream Lover," "Clementine," and "Beyond the Sea," he was inducted into the Rock and Roll Hall of Fame in 1990.

Bibliography

Bleiel, Jeff. *That's All: Bobby Darin on Record, Stage and Screen*. Ann Arbor: Popular Culture Ink, 1993.

"Bobby Darin." *Current Biography Yearbook*. New York: Wilson, 1963.

Hochman, Steve. "Bobby Darin: A Reluctant Rocker in Hall of Fame." *Los Angeles Times* 17 Jan. 1990: F1: 2, 8.

"Rock & Roll Hall of Fame." *Rolling Stone* 8 Feb. 1990: 71-80.

Wolff, Carlo. "Seasons, Tops, Kinks, Who, Darin among 13 Giants Set for Jan. Rock Hall Induction." *Billboard* 4 Nov. 1989: 92.

Jill Talbot

Davis, Miles (Dewey) (1926-1992), became famous among both jazz buffs and people who know very little about the art form through a combination of intelligence, charisma, and self-awareness of his abilities. His success has rarely been equaled in jazz. Some critics note that he succeeded with less natural technical ability than most jazz stars. But he made his mark on American culture.

In 1945, Davis went to New York to study at the Juilliard School of Music. In a typical move, he tracked Charlie "Bird" Parker (see entry) down and moved in with him. Bird sponsored his career and used him on recordings and with his working band from time to time. Certainly, this work aided him in getting jobs with Benny Carter's band and then taking Fats Navarro's chair in the Eckstine band.

In 1949, Davis emerged as the leader of a group of Claude Thornhill's musicians, including Lee Konitz, Gerry Mulligan, and Gil Evans, and from that collaboration sprang *The Birth of the Cool* and the style of jazz named after it. But for the next few years Davis struggled with heroin addiction and did little artistically.

By 1954, however, Davis was heading toward the most artistically successful years of his life. The Davis style was fully matured. Davis attributes his sound to Freddie Webster, a St. Louis trumpet master. He also attributes his use of space to Ahmad Jamal, a pianist of great genius. That style of the 1950s and early 1960s was marked by use of the Harmon mute, 1/2 valves, soft and fully rounded tones, reliance on the middle register, snatches of exquisite melodic composition, and general absence of rapid-fire runs.

In the mid-1950s Davis again switched styles, pioneering the funk movement with songs like "Walkin'." The Advise Quintet, consisting of John Coltrane on tenor sax, Paul Chambers on bass, Philly Joe Jones on drums, and Red Garland on piano, was a band of all-stars and the stuff of which jazz legends are made. With the addition of Cannonball Adderley on alto sax, the sextet was able to use combinations and colorations that shaped the course of modern jazz.

Kind of Blue (1959), which featured pianist Bill Evans on a number of cuts, fueled the modal explosion in jazz. He also did a series of records with Gil Evans featuring a big band, including *Sketches of Spain* (1960).

Beginning in 1967 with *Nefertiti* and followed in 1968 with *Filles de Kilimanjaro*, Davis began incorporating rock elements into his work. He used Chick Corea (see entry) on electric piano and replaced his veterans with other younger men, including Tony Williams on drums, Ron Carter on bass, and Wayne Shorter on tenor sax. The success of these records, although somewhat short of his expectations, forced Davis to explore the genre further. That led to his use of John McLaughlin of the Mahavishnu Orchestra on *In a Silent Way* in 1969 and the all-out fusion album *Bitches Brew* the next year.

For a period of years, Davis stopped performing and rumors once again surfaced regarding his condition. In the early 1980s, he made a successful comeback with a funk-oriented group. Finally, at the Montreux Festival of 1992, Quincy Jones convinced Miles Davis to relive the work he had done with Gil Evans.

Davis died of pneumonia, leaving a rich legacy of music and enough fuel for controversy to satisfy jazz fans for many years.

Bibliography

Collier, Lincoln. *The Making of Jazz*. Boston: Houghton, 1978.

Feather, Leonard. *Encyclopedia of Jazz*. New York: Da Capo, 1984.

——. *The New Yearbook of Jazz*. New York: Horizon, 1958.

Gridley, Mark. *Jazz Styles*. Englewood Cliffs: Prentice-Hall, 1994.

Frank A. Salamone

Davy Crockett (1954-1955), Walt Disney's highly popular contribution to the TV Western, was taken from the Frontier segment ("tall tales and true from our legendary past") of the series *Disneyland*. Disney decided to tell the story of Davy Crockett in three hour-long episodes and asked studio writer Tom Blackburn to develop the storyline that took Crockett from the frontier to Congress and finally to his heroic death at the Alamo.

When the film was finally assembled, it fell short of the desired length. George Bruns, a new composer at the studio, wrote a song that fit the lines in Blackburn's script. The demand for "The Ballad of Davy Crockett" began when a small part of it was heard in the preview portion of the first *Disneyland* show. After the first episode aired, as the eighth installment of *Disneyland*, the avalanche began. Seventeen different versions of the song were recorded, selling over 10 million records and making it No. 1 on the *Hit Parade* for 13 weeks.

As Davy, Fess Parker, whom Disney had spotted in the 1954 science fiction film, *Them!*, became a star virtually overnight, and Buddy Ebsen, who played Davy's sidekick, George Russell, found his career suddenly rejuvenated.

The second and third episodes of the series, "Davy Crockett Goes to Congress" and "Davy Crockett at the Alamo," were even more successful. Nielsen ratings placed the number of viewers of the second program at more than half of all the people who were watching TV.

Two more hour-long Crockett stories were shown on *Disneyland*. The first of these, "Davy Crockett's Keelboat Race" (Nov. 16, 1955), pitted Davy and Georgie against the boastful riverboat captain Mike Fink. The second sequel, "Davy Crockett and the River Pirates" (Dec. 14, 1955), had Davy and Mike the best of friends, working together to thwart a gang of thieves preying on riverboats plying their trade on the Ohio River.

Bibliography

MacDonald, J. Fred. *Who Shot the Sheriff?* New York: Praeger, 1987.

Thomas, Bob. *Walt Disney: An American Original*. New York: Simon & Schuster, 1976.

Yoggy, Gary A. *Riding the Video Range: The Rise and Fall of the Western on Television*. Jefferson: McFarland, 1995.

Gary A. Yoggy

Day, Doris (1924-), America's most popular girl-next-door vocalist, was born Doris Kappelhoff in Cincinnati to a middle-class German-American family. After her parents' divorce, she and her older brother were brought up by their mother and eventually lost contact with their father. Doris was an indifferent student at local Catholic schools and ended her formal education after the tenth grade to pursue a show business career. Originally trained as a dancer, Doris switched to singing after severely breaking her leg in a car accident. Cincinnati bandleader Barney Rapp changed her last name to Day when he saw how well audiences responded to her rendition of the song "Day after Day." Singing jobs in the Cincinnati area quickly led to bigger things. While still a teenager, Doris Day toured the country with Bob Crosby and his Bobcats and with Les Brown and his Band of Renown, with whom she recorded "Sentimental Journey," one of the top hits of 1944.

After leaving the Les Brown band, Doris Day sang in nightclubs, on radio, and participated in a Bob Hope show tour of domestic military bases. Despite a lack of acting experience, Day was given a principal role in the Warner Brothers musical *Romance on the High Seas* in 1948. Day signed a seven-year contract with Warner and went on to make 16 more films for the studio, most of which were inexpensive musicals quickly shot on the backlot. She co-starred four times with fellow Warner contract singer/actor Gordon MacRae—*Tea for Two* and *The West Point Story* (both 1950), *On Moonlight Bay* (1951), and *By the Light of the Silvery Moon* (1953).

When her contract with Warner expired in 1955, Day placed her career in the hands of her manager and third husband, Martin Melcher, whom she had wed in 1951. (Day was previously married to trombonist Al Jorden, with whom she had a son, Terry, and to saxophonist George Weidler.) Melcher was given executive producer credit on most of Day's post-Warner films, though he rarely did anything except arrange for his wife to star in the picture. In MGM's *Love Me or Leave Me* (1955) she played troubled 1930s torch singer Ruth Etting. James Cagney played Etting's gangster boyfriend. Though much too vivacious a screen presence to be effective as a "Hitchcock blonde," Day nevertheless gave it a try in the director's inferior 1956 remake of his own 1935 film *The Man Who Knew Too Much*. This suspense film became the unlikely source of Day's biggest recording success, the bouncy novelty tune "Que Sera, Sera (Whatever Will Be Will Be)."

The following year Day starred in the screen version of the hit Broadway musical *The Pajama Game*. In 1959, Day co-starred with Rock Hudson in the glossy sex comedy *Pillow Talk,* for which she received her only Academy Award nomination.

She turned to television in 1968. *The Doris Day Show* was a weak offering and its premise was altered four times during its five-year run (CBS-TV, 1968-73). The personal popularity of its star, who still had a large following with the general public, if not with increasingly youthful and cynical movie audiences, was largely responsible for its success. Day also starred in musical/variety specials on CBS in 1971, 1972, and 1975. After leaving television Day effectively retired from show business. She makes her home in northern California and has been a high profile advocate of animal rights.

Bibliography
Current Biography 1954. New York: Wilson, 1955.
Hotchner, A. E. *Doris Day: Her Own Story*. New York: Morrow, 1975.
——. "Doris Day Today." *Ladies' Home Journal* June 1982: 75-77, 123-27.
Katz, Ephraim. *The Film Encyclopedia*. New York: Perennial Library, 1990.
Thomson, David, ed. *Biographical Dictionary of Film*. 2d ed. New York: Morrow, 1981.

Mary Kalfatovic

Days and Nights of Molly Dodd, The (1987-1988; 1989-1991), created by Jay Tarses with actress Blair Brown in mind, was a half-hour TV series about a divorced woman in her 30s who lives in New York City. The show was a pioneer in "dramedy," containing elements of both comedy and drama with no closure at the end of episodes and no laugh track. Highly critically acclaimed, the series initially achieved good ratings following *Cheers*. When NBC Entertainment President Brandon Tartikoff publicly lost faith in the genre, however, scheduling problems and decreasing ratings led to its cancellation. The fate of *The Days and Nights of Molly Dodd* became indicative of the changing television industry in the 1980s. Lifetime, promoted as the cable network for women, not only agreed to pick up the original 26 episodes from NBC; they also produced and cablecast 39 new ones between 1989 and 1991.

Although critics were quick to compare Molly Dodd with the single women on other series, particularly Mary Richards on the *Mary Tyler Moore Show* from the 1970s, Molly was quite different from her predecessors. She was friendly and open and intelligent, but she was also a very flawed character. Molly was not goal-oriented and had trouble making a commitment. She frequently changed jobs and boyfriends.

Bibliography
Brooks, Tim, and Earle Marsh. *The Complete Directory to Prime Time Network TV Shows, 1946-Present*. 5th ed. New York: Ballantine, 1992.
Milward, John. "A Baby, a 40th Birthday and a New Job." *TV Guide* 19 Jan. 1991: 28-29.
O'Connor, John J. "NBC Offers 'The Days and Nights of Molly Dodd.'" *New York Times* 13 Aug. 1987: C30.

Lynn C. Spangler

Days of Our Lives (1965-   ), one of TV's longest-running soap operas, was created by Ted Corday, Irna Phillips, and Allan Chase. Corday, the creative force behind this venture, relied heavily on the motifs of *The Guiding Light* and *As the World Turns* (see entries), which he directed and controlled in partnership with Irna Phillips. Thus, family drama was at the core of the new soap. Its opening epigraph, "Like sands through the hourglass, so are the days of our lives," incorporated the essence of the show.

The credit for *Days of Our Lives'* success was attributed to the hiring of William J. Bell as head writer in 1967. Like Ted Corday, Bell had worked under Irna Phillips on *Guiding Light* and *As the World Turns*. But it was Bell's vision to take *Days* out of the mold of the show's original realism into the realm of adult fantasy that sent the ratings soaring. The soap evolved from prolonged storylines featuring an out-of-wedlock pregnancy, a murder, and a complicated trial to bold, new mosaics of traumatic family suffering and medical and psychiatric melodrama, centering on rape, near-incest, interracial romance, and such never-presented-before subjects as artificial insemination. Bell remained as head writer until 1973 when he left to write his own soap, *The Young and the Restless*. New head writer Pat Falken Smith took over. Over the next several years, she worked her magic of high drama, warmth, compassion, and witticism into the soap's fabric.

In 1975, the soap expanded to one hour, continuing its roller coaster ride to the top. For eight years, *Days* remained firmly entrenched at the top of the highest rated soaps. It was nominated for the Emmy as outstanding dramatic series every year from 1973 to 1979, winning top honors in 1978, and it was nominated for outstanding writing every year from 1975 to 1978, winning the Emmy in 1976. In its January 12, 1976, issue, *Time* magazine broke tradition by featuring Susan Seaforth and Bill Hayes on its cover, and in its cover story, "Sex and Suffering in the Afternoon," named *Days of Our Lives* as the best soap opera.

Pat Falken Smith's departure over a contract dispute in 1977 marked the end of an era, as a new hurdle not only for *Days*, but for all the soaps, presented itself: social change. The demographics of the soap opera audience were changing and the challenge was meeting this change without discarding the very qualities that made the soaps popular with their loyal, older audience. The mantle of leadership changed hands, and *Days*—although immensely popular with the fans—has never been able to regain its position at the top.

Bibliography

Copeland, Mary Ann. *Soap Opera History*. Lincolnwood: BDD Promotional (Mallard), 1991.

LaGuardia, Robert. *Soap World*. New York: Arbor, 1983.

Russell, Maureen. *Days of Our Lives: A Complete History of the Long-Running Soap Opera*. Jefferson: McFarland, 1995.

Schemering, Christopher. *The Soap Opera Encyclopedia*. New York: Ballantine, 1987.

Mary Cassata

See also
Soap Opera
Soap Opera Writers and Producers

DC Talk, the hip-hop trio from Washington, DC, brought Christian music into the 1990s with stylistic borrowings from pop, soul, funk, and traditional gospel, but an emphasis on rap. More so than Christian rock, theirs seems an unlikely musical genre for conveying explicitly conservative religious messages, yet DC Talk has quite successfully pioneered this new form of Christian entertainment.

The group formed in 1987 at Liberty University in Lynchburg, VA (formerly Liberty Baptist College and founded by Jerry Falwell), after Toby McKeehan (1964-) of Annandale and Michael Tait (1965-) of the northeast DC area circulated cassettes of "Heavenbound," a hip-hop song McKeehan had written. After initial wariness (the school forbids rock music and dancing), the piece became a hit on campus. They added Kevin Max Smith (1967-) of Grand Rapids, MI, previously in another Christian band on campus, and chose the name DC Talk to signify both the group's rap style and their geographical origin (typically vital among hip-hop artists).

DC Talk attracted an enthusiastic Christian following at small parties and churches, and soon signed with ForeFront Records of Brentwood, TN, which became their home. Their self-titled first album, released in 1989, sold over 100,000 copies in its first year, which for Christian music constitutes a smash. *DC Talk* contained the song "Heavenbound," later to become a video, and announced the group's emergence on the Christian music scene. They next contributed two songs, "Yo Ho Ho" and "Reason for the Season," for 1990's *Yo Ho Ho Christmas*: a compilation album from contemporary

Christian artists. In 1991, they released their second album, *Nu Thang*. Music videos of "Nu Thang," "I Luv Rap Music," and "Heavenbound" began appearing even on secular networks such as BET.

In 1991 they appeared with headliner Michael W. Smith (the so-called "king of Christian crossover") on his "Go West Young Man" Tour and again in 1993 for his "Change Your World" Tour. Their third album, *Free at Last*, released in 1993, achieved platinum status. More a balanced group effort than the previous albums featuring McKeehan, *Free at Last* contained hit singles "Socially Acceptable," "The Hard Way," and their versions of the Bill Withers's standard "Lean on Me" and the classic rock song by the Doobie Brothers, "Jesus Is Just Alright." The platinum status of the 1993 album (which sat atop *Billboard*'s Christian charts for 34 weeks) led to DC Talk's winning a Grammy for contemporary Christian rock album of the year, *Billboard's* Contemporary Christian Artist of the Year as well as contemporary Christian album of the year, and two Dove Awards for song of the year from the Gospel Music Association—the first such awards ever given to a rap act.

Bibliography

Brown, Joe. "The Word Made 'Free.' " *Washington Post* 30 April 1993: W13.

Carpenter, Bill. "DC Talk, a Group on a Mission to Spread Gospel." *Washington Post* 1 May 1993: G1.

Darden, Bob. "Rappers Are the D.C. Talk of the Town." *Billboard* 11 Jan. 1992: 27.

Harrington, Richard. "Rolling On: The Word from DC Talk." *Washington Post* 13 April 1994: D7.

McAdams, Janine. "R&B Music's Winner's Circle Widens." *Billboard* 16 Jan. 1993: 19, 24.

Russell, Deborah. "Is DC Talk Losing Becuz of Its Religion?" *Billboard* 18 Jan. 1992: 51.

Cameron Lenahan
Michael Delahoyde

See also
Christian Radio Music Formats
Hip Hop

De Camp, L(yon) Sprague (1907-), a New York native, is the author of an ample body of fiction, scholarly texts, verse, scientific books for children, and other writings. He is best known for his science fiction and fantasy works, particularly stories featuring time and space travels. His first novel, *Lest Darkness Fall* (1941), an inventive and witty story considered a classic of science fiction, began the Viagens Interplanetarias series that now numbers over a dozen novels. Other notable titles in the series include *Rogue Queen* (1954), about a matriarchal society modeled on bee societies, *The Hand of Zei* (1963), a space adventure story, and *The Bones of Zora* (1983), about an interplanetary archaeological dig, written with his wife, Catherine Cook de Camp, a frequent collaborator.

De Camp has also collaborated with a number of other writers on important projects. His work with Fletcher Pratt produced the humorous Harold Shea series, of which *The Incomplete Enchanter* (1941) is especially familiar. De

Camp began work in 1951 with Lin Carter (see entry) on a series of Conan the Barbarian revisions, based on Robert E. Howard's unfinished manuscripts; he also paired with others, including Bjorn Nyberg, on the Conan project, and wrote his own novels featuring the Conan character, such as *Conan and the Spider God* (1980).

De Camp has been amply honored for his fiction, receiving a number of awards for his science fiction and fantasy, culminating in the prestigious World Fantasy Award for life achievement in 1984.

Bibliography

Bleiler, E. F. *Supernatural Fiction Writers: Fantasy and Horror.* New York: Scribner, 1985.

Solomon Davidoff

Dean, James Byron (1931-1955), was born in Marion, IN, achieved fame as a stage, television, and movie actor, then died in an automobile accident near Cholame, CA, at the age of 24, on September 30, 1955, while on his way to an auto race in Salinas, CA.

Despite his brief career, Dean has become a legend who represents the rebelliousness and uncertainties of youth. Dean created this anti-establishment image in just three major film roles over a period of 18 months: exhibiting the innocence and alienation of Cal in *East of Eden* (1954), embodying adolescent intolerance and urgency as Jim Stark in *Rebel without a Cause* (1955), and portraying the somewhat sinister, poor outsider underdog Jett Rink in *Giant* (1956). He is now seen as setting the stage for the restless youth movement of the 1960s.

Bibliography

Alexander, Paul. *Boulevard of Broken Dreams: The Life, Times, and Legend of James Dean.* New York: Penguin, 1994.

"As in '55, Restless Youth in the Heartland." *U.S. News & World Report* 25 Sept. 1995: 25.

Dalton, David, and Ron Cayen. *James Dean: American Icon.* New York: St. Martin's, 1984.

Holey, Val. *James Dean: The Biography.* New York: St. Martin's, 1997.

Spoto, Donald. *Rebel: The Life and Legend of James Dean.* New York: HarperCollins, 1996.

Phyllis Schmidt

Dean Martin Show, The (1965-1974), was a controversial TV series which spun off numerous summer replacements and its own replacement spinoff, *Dean Martin's Celebrity Roast,* as well as a syndicated series starring Dom DeLuise (1933-), who was a supporting comic in *The Dean Martin Show*. The last few seasons of *The Dean Martin Show* met with protests over the show's sexual humor and treatment of women.

Dean Martin (1917-95; see entry) first came to television with his partner Jerry Lewis as part of the NBC series *The Colgate Comedy Hour*. The series lasted from 1950 to 1955, and Martin and Lewis alternated hosting duties on the show with other performers during those years, making roughly 40 appearances. After the team split up in 1956, Martin made a

series of eight successful specials. The specials were all titled *The Dean Martin Show* and were all done for NBC. *The Dean Martin Show* debuted in 1965, to mixed reviews and only fair ratings. People tuned in to see Dean, but he was serving as little more than a singing emcee. The problem was addressed in the second season, with Martin performing in sketches and engaging in light banter with guests. The show ended the season in the Top 10 where it continued for most of its run.

Bibliography

Marx, Arthur. *Everybody Loves Somebody Sometime (Especially Himself): The Story of Dean Martin and Jerry Lewis.* New York: Hawthorn, 1974.

Terrace, Vincent. *Encyclopedia of Television Series, Pilots, and Specials, 1937-1973,* Vol. 1. New York: Zoetrope, 1986.

——. *Encyclopedia of Television Series, Pilots, and Specials, 1974-1984,* Vol. 2. New York: Zoetrope, 1985.

Tosches, Nick. *Dino: Living High in the Dirty Business of Dreams.* New York: Doubleday, 1992.

Benjamin K. Urish

Deep Throat (1972), directed, written, and edited by Gerard Damiano, opened quietly at the New Mature World Theatre in Manhattan's Times Square Area. The film explored new subject matter and portrayed sex in a manner never before seen in a pornographic film, and led the editor of *Screw* magazine, Al Goldstein, to proclaim that *Deep Throat* was "the best porno ever made." Word of the film and the exploits of its star, Linda Lovelace, began to spread eventually into the mainstream cinema audience. The film played to almost a quarter of a million people, grossing over a million dollars and exceeding any previous adult film before it was ordered to stop running in March of 1973.

Deep Throat served as the logical end to a long stream of what were called "nudies." These films ranged from portraying nudist colonies and stripteases and became more explicit as the 1960s came to a close. Russ Meyer's films, *The Immoral Mr. Teas* and *I Am Curious, Yellow,* highlight the shifting nature of adult cinema in the 1960s, but what separated *Deep Throat* from Meyer's "nudies" was that it did not leave the act of sex to the imaginations of its audiences. The sex was explicit and no longer a tease. What had previously been available in grainy black-and-white under-the-counter stag films was now appearing in color in the theaters in Times Square.

Although *Deep Throat* was taken from the theaters, it helped forge a place for sexually explicit media in the United States, and its eventual court case explored and tested the limits of the First Amendment.

Bibliography

Smith, Richard. *Getting into* Deep Throat. Chicago: Playboy, 1973.

Jason Landrum

DeForest, Lee (1873-1961), vital inventor in American electronic development, received his Ph.D. in physics from Yale University in 1899. In 1906, he created the three-element vacuum tube or audion, patenting it in 1907. To Sir Ambrose

Fleming's 1904 invention, the two-element "valve" detector, DeForest affixed a third element, the "trigger," a "grid" (piece of zigzag platinum wire) between the filament and the plate. (It was Thomas A. Edison who devised the one-element vacuum tube in 1883.)

The audion transformed the wireless detector into, among other things, the chief means of amplification for sending and receiving radio waves. Hundreds of millions of vacuum tubes were produced over the years, especially from 1920 through the 1950s. It was the invention of the transistor and later related radio devices which replaced the audion.

DeForest experimentally broadcast voice and music around the New York City area in 1907. In the spring, he organized the first of several unsuccessful business ventures, the DeForest Radio Telephone Company. While DeForest's ambition was "to beat Marconi" in the field of wireless communication, he never accomplished this goal.

Nevertheless, his contributions to radio are quite significant. He traveled to various parts of the U.S. to set up wireless equipment for broadcasting, or "narrowcasting," point-to-point communication. He is one of the true early radio broadcasting pioneers, along with Reginald Fessenden, Charles "Doc" Herrold, Alfred Goldsmith, E. M. Terry, and Frank Conrad. To be sure, the DeForest audion actually revolutionized wireless.

Although most of his domestic radio activities took place in the New York City area, DeForest did experiment elsewhere. One of the most famous early broadcasts was that of the immortal tenor Enrico Caruso from the New York Metropolitan Opera House on January 13, 1910.

In the summer of 1908, he set up technical equipment and broadcast from the Eiffel Tower in Paris. The feat amazed throngs of persons who heard the voice and lengthy phonograph music program reportedly from as far away as 500 miles. However the signal was more reliable at 25 miles from Paris.

In 1915, DeForest installed a 125-watt transmitter at the Columbia Gramophone Building on 38th Street and began daily broadcasts of phonograph music with Columbia as his "sponsor." He later moved the transmitting site back to his original High Bridge tower in the Bronx.

Bibliography

Barnouw, Erik. *A Tower in Babel: A History of Broadcasting in the United States.* Vol. 1. New York: Oxford UP, 1966.

Carneal, Georgette. *A Conqueror of Space.* New York: Liveright, 1930 (authorized biography).

Dunlap, Orrin E., Jr. *Radio's 100 Men of Science.* New York: Harper, 1944.

Levine, Israel E. *Electronics Pioneer: Lee DeForest.* New York: Messner, 1964.

Lewis, Tom. *Empire of the Air.* New York: HarperCollins, 1991.

Sammy R. Danna

DeMille, Cecil B(lount) (1881-1959), actor, playwright, and movie producer, is best remembered as one of the most successful directors in film history, with a career spanning 40 years. When his last movie, *The Ten Commandments,* pre-miered in 1956, DeMille had directed 70 films. While critics of the time generally regarded him as artistically shallow, audiences enthusiastically embraced most of his films, and some more recent critics have argued that his work deserves much higher regard.

DeMille's first film, *The Squaw Man* (1914), was based on a successful play and was one of the first full-length feature films produced in Hollywood, though the precedent for feature-length films had been set first by those brought to America from Europe. More important for DeMille's career, this initial effort was very successful at the box office.

DeMille's penchant for movie extravaganzas began in 1915 when he hired New York opera star Geraldine Farrar to play the lead in *Carmen.* This film increased DeMille's fame at a time when directors were usually little known. In 1916 he used Farrar again in *Joan the Woman.* This was one of his inspirational patriotic movies that he made in response to America's involvement in World War I. Others include *The Little American* (1917) and *The Whispering Chorus* (1918).

After the war, DeMille was able to anticipate the Roaring Twenties and made a series of films that catered to the nation's relaxed moral attitudes and desire for higher living following the sacrifices of the war effort. Like *The Cheat* earlier (1915), DeMille's films of this period featured rich families dealing with marital problems, often a struggle with extramarital temptation. These stories allowed DeMille to combine sexual content and a look at the lifestyles of the very wealthy.

After the postwar years DeMille found it necessary to respond to a moral backlash against Hollywood's looser treatment of sex. He now began making his biblical spectaculars, the first of which was DeMille's first version of *The Ten Commandments* (1923; see entry). DeMille promoted conventional values while still providing the sexual content of his earlier movies, which though it is implicitly condemned is nevertheless present.

This combination of sex and morality really wasn't new for DeMille. His films during the Roaring Twenties had actually endorsed conventional values, demonstrating that the institution of marriage should be honored and love within it nurtured. These ideals can be seen even in the titles of movies like *Don't Change Your Husband* and *Why Change Your Wife? The Ten Commandments* nevertheless struck audiences as more in tune with the restrained morality of the day, and it became one of the top grossing films for a number of years. Another of DeMille's biblical films, and yet another of the movie spectaculars, was *The King of Kings* (1927), which told the story of Jesus. This movie was immensely successful and is believed to have been viewed by some 800,000,000 people worldwide. Although DeMille was at first slow to accept sound with movies, *The King of Kings* signaled the end of his silent film period.

In 1934, DeMille's *Cleopatra* premiered, another box-office success. Although DeMille took liberties with his biblical and historical facts in the films of this era, they nevertheless provided welcome escapist entertainment on a grand scale for a nation weary from the Depression. In 1937 the first of his Western epics, *The Plainsman,* starring Gary

Cooper, came to the screen. It was followed by *Union Pacific* (1939), starring Barbara Stanwyck, and *Northwest Mounted Police* (1940), starring Gary Cooper. The Westerns, like the biblical movies, provide spectacular sets and landscapes, and again the good guys contend with godless enemies, this time the Indians.

DeMille made just six films during the 15 years between 1941 and 1956, but they included a couple of his biggest blockbusters, *The Greatest Show on Earth* (1952) and *The Ten Commandments* (1956). *The Greatest Show on Earth* is one of the rare later movies set in contemporary times. It starred Charlton Heston as the circus manager whose struggle to put on his grand show has been seen as symbolic of DeMille's own effort to provide his public with spectacular movies that entertain and offer a respite from the tedium of daily routines.

The Ten Commandments was a remake of his 1923 version of the movie. This time DeMille dropped all references to contemporary history and focused entirely on the story of Moses and the Israelites departing from Egypt. Unlike the original, the remake was filmed in Egypt using as many as 25,000 extras in a scene. The price tag was $13 million, a phenomenal sum at that time, some of which went to pay for the stunning Academy Award-winning special effects. Charlton Heston was again the star, this time playing Moses, while Yul Brynner played the pharaoh. It was the most spectacular of his movie spectacles, and it was his most successful at the box office. *The Ten Commandments* was also his 70th movie and the one with which he ended his career.

While critics at the time of his death were not overly generous in their praise of his work, he had nonetheless earned a number of honors. In 1949, DeMille was awarded a special Academy Award for 37 years of "brilliant showmanship." In 1952, *The Greatest Show on Earth* was given the Academy Award for best picture. In the same year DeMille was presented at the Academy Awards ceremony with the highly respected Irving Thalberg Award honoring him as a movie producer. He received the Milestone Award from the Screen Producers' Guild in 1956.

Bibliography

DeMille, Cecil B. *The Autobiography of Cecil B. DeMille.* New York: Garland, 1985.

Essoe, Gabe, and Raymond Lee. *DeMille: The Man and His Pictures.* New York: Castle, 1970.

Higashi, Sumiko. *Cecil B. DeMille: A Guide to References and Resources.* Boston: Hall, 1985.

Higham, Charles. *Cecil B. DeMille.* New York: Scribner, 1973.

Ringgold, Gene. *The Complete Films of Cecil B. DeMille.* New York: Citadel, 1985.

Alan Kelly

Demolition Derbies, in which stripped-down cars ram into each other until only one is left running, succeed with the general public despite their seeming lack of merit and are aimed at a relatively broad-based audience.

A common event at local fairs and special promotional events at race tracks, demolition derbies have developed their own unique entertainment features that resonate with the recreation needs, cultural identities, and lifestyles of a substantial number of people. In so doing, derbies have amassed large and loyal followings, including especially persons who have skills at getting the most mileage ("bang for the buck") out of older, used cars. Yet, derbies also may be appreciated on other levels. For a modest price, demolition derby patrons vicariously experience a dangerous, thrilling, and normally forbidden activity. For all involved, whether behind the wheel or in the stands, this experience provides an opportunity to engage in a conflict, cheer a hero, rail against a villain, and to honor the victor(s).

Bibliography

Hill, Graham. *Life at the Limit.* New York: Coward-McCann, 1970.

Setright, L. J. K. *With Flying Colors.* New York: Summit, 1987.

Seymour, Lois. *The Smash-up, Crash-up Derby.* New York: Orchard, 1995.

Linda S. Welker

DeNiro, Robert (1943-), actor, director, producer, is considered one of the preeminent actors of the American cinema. DeNiro was born in New York City, the son of two artists, Robert DeNiro, Sr., and Virginia Admiral. The young DeNiro began his acting career working with the famous Method acting coach, Stella Adler. He later continued his instruction in Method acting at the famous Actors Studio under the tutelage of Lee Strasberg. Two of the first three films in which he appeared were directed by his friend Brian De Palma (*Greetings,* 1968; *The Wedding Party,* 1969). After a number of other minor films, the year 1973 became a monumental period in DeNiro's early career. He achieved critical acclaim for his performances in the films *Bang the Drum Slowly* and *Mean Streets,* for which he received two New York Film Critics' Awards for best supporting actor. These prestigious accolades not only gained him the recognition needed to become a major figure in the film industry, but they are representative of the types of roles that DeNiro has pursued throughout his career.

In the 1970s DeNiro appeared in 13 films, several of which are ranked among the greatest films of all time. In 1974, DeNiro received his first Academy Award for best supporting actor for his portrayal of the young Vito Corleone in *The Godfather, Part II* (dir. Francis Ford Coppola). In addition to winning an Oscar in 1974, he was also nominated for his roles in *Taxi Driver* and the 1978 film *The Deer Hunter* (dir. Michael Cimino), which chronicled the effect of the Vietnam War on the lives of people from a small steel town in rural Pennsylvania. But it was in the 1976 film *Taxi Driver* (dir. Martin Scorsese) that DeNiro turned in one of his most well known and oft-quoted performances as the psychotic cabby Travis Bickle. DeNiro's famous line from the movie, *"You talkin' to me?"* has become part of the American lexicon, just as a line spoken by Method predecessor Marlon Brando in *On the Waterfront* (1954)—*"I coulda been a contender"*—also depicts the conflict facing the urban anti-hero in American culture. *Taxi Driver* also represents the quintessential example of life imitating art, when, five years after its release, John Hinckley, Jr., attempted to assassinate President Ronald Reagan, presumably in an ode to film character Travis Bickle and to impress actor Jodie Foster (who played a young prostitute in the film).

DeNiro won his second Oscar for best actor for his gritty, realistic portrayal of boxer Jake LaMotta in the 1980 film, *Raging Bull.* The film, directed by Scorsese, is often considered to be the greatest film achievement of the decade and one of the best films of all time. With an eye toward diverse and personal stories, DeNiro starred in two romance films, *Falling in Love* with Meryl Streep (1984, dir. Ulu Grosbard) and *Stanley and Iris* with Jane Fonda (1989, dir. Martin Ritt). He also portrayed a Jesuit priest in search of redemption in the poignant and political film *The Mission* (1986, dir. Roland Joffe), a bounty hunter in the box-office hit comedy *Midnight Run* (1988, dir. Martin Brest), and a psychologically wounded Vietnam vet in *Jacknife* (1989, dir. David Jones).

In addition, the size of the role has not been a predominant factor in DeNiro appearing in a variety of films. He played a barely recognizable urban plumber-cum-terrorist in Terry Gilliam's brilliant apocalyptic vision of the future, *Brazil* (1985), and he appeared on-screen for only ten minutes as Al Capone in *The Untouchables* (1987, dir. Brian De Palma). During the 1990s, DeNiro was twice nominated for Academy Awards—for his role as a catatonic patient in Penny Marshall's *Awakenings* (1990), and for his portrayal of vengeful ex-con Max Cady in the remake of the 1962 classic *Cape Fear* (1991, dir. Scorsese).

In 1988, DeNiro founded his own production company, Tribeca Productions, and with Jane Rosenthal, the Tribeca Film Center. *A Bronx Tale* in 1993 marked DeNiro's directorial debut. Since its inception, Tribeca Film Center has produced several other films, including *Cape Fear* (1991), *Thunderheart* (1992), *Marvin's Room* (1996), and *Wag the Dog* (1997). With the release of over 20 movies in the 1990s in which DeNiro has acted, he continues to be one of the most important and influential figures in American cinema today.

Bibliography

Agan, Patrick. *Robert DeNiro: The Man, the Myth, and the Movies.* London: Robert Hale, 1989.

Brode, Douglas. *The Films of Robert DeNiro.* New York: Citadel, 1993.

Dougan, Andy. *Untouchable: A Biography of Robert DeNiro.* New York: Thunder's Mouth, 1996.

McKay, Keith. *Robert DeNiro: The Hero Behind the Masks.* New York: St. Martin's, 1986.

Parker, John. *DeNiro.* London: Victor Gollancz, 1995.

Lori Liggett

Denver, Bob (1935-), simpleton Gilligan on the successful TV show *Gilligan's Island,* began his acting career at Loyola University of Los Angeles, and was plagued with stage fright but continued to perform in further shows until graduation. Then while working as an elementary school teacher, his big break came when at age 24 he landed the role of a teenager named Maynard G. Krebs in the TV series *The Many Loves of Dobie Gillis,* a situation comedy. Denver, one of the key members in a cast that originally included Warren Beatty and Tuesday Weld, was an audience favorite as Dobie's unacceptable beatnik friend who hates work and cultivates unconventional views. The show, airing from 1959 to 1963, attempted to provide a teenager's perspective on life and was television's first response to baby boomers reaching their adolescent years.

After *Dobie Gillis*, Denver was assigned the role that is his most significant contribution to popular culture. *Gilligan's Island* aired between 1964 and 1967 (see entry). As "The Ballad of Gilligan's Island" explains at the beginning of each episode, the cast was stranded on an island by a storm that swept them away during a three-hour boat tour out of Hawaii. The seven castaways each represent a different type of American, so viewers can easily identify with someone.

Television movies have reunited most of the cast on three occasions: in 1978, *Rescue from Gilligan's Island* was one of the highest-rated TV movies of the year; *The Castaways on Gilligan's Island* aired in 1979 with Gilligan and his buddies deciding to transform their island into a resort; and in 1981, *The Harlem Globetrotters on Gilligan's Island* brought the basketball team and a mad scientist to the island.

Denver has also reprised his role as Maynard G. Krebs in a couple of television movies. *Whatever Happened to Dobie Gillis* was broadcast in 1977 as a pilot movie for a new series which never materialized. Another reunion movie, *Bring Me the Head of Dobie Gillis*, aired in 1988, also with little success.

Immediately after *Gilligan's Island* Denver tried another TV series, *The Good Guys* (1968-70), a sitcom in which Denver played Rufus Butterworth, a cabbie and later part-owner of a diner. *Dusty's Trail* (1973) was a slapstick comedy and a Western version of *Gilligan's Island* created by the earlier hit's creator Sherwood Schwartz and in which all the characters of *Gilligan's Island* have their equivalents. Denver plays a guide to a wagon train that never can quite find its way west. One other syndicated series, *Far Out Space Nuts*, survived for a mere 16 episodes.

In the mid-'70s, Denver provided his voice for a couple of TV cartoon series, *The New Adventures of Gilligan's Island* and *Gilligan's Planet.* There have been a number of other projects throughout the years. He has made guest appearances on a variety of TV shows, including *The Perry Como Show*, *I Dream of Jeannie*, several *Love Boat* shows, *The Andy Griffith Show*, *ALF,* and *Baywatch.* Big screen appearances mostly date back to the 1960s and include B films such as *Take Her, She's Mine* (1963), *For Those Who Think Young* (1964), *Who's Minding the Mint?* (1967), and *The Sweet Ride* (1968).

Bibliography

Denver, Bob. *Gilligan, Maynard, and Me.* New York: Carol, 1993.

Green, Joey. *The Unofficial Gilligan's Island Handbook.* New York: Warner, 1988.

Javna, John. *Cult TV: A Viewer's Guide to the Shows America Can't Live Without.* New York: St. Martin's, 1985.

Johnson, Russell. *Here on Gilligan's Isle*. New York: Harper-Perennial, 1993.

Schwartz, Sherwood. *Inside Gilligan's Island: From Creation to Syndication*. Jefferson: McFarland, 1988.

Alan Kelly

Denver, John (1943-1997), one of the most prolific and best-known American songwriters of the latter 20th century, wrote and performed soft-spoken, environmentally oriented folk/country music which touched the hearts of millions. Born Henry John Deutschendorf, Jr., Denver became interested in performing music while an architecture student at Texas Tech University in Lubbock. Beginning in 1961, he played folk music in local coffeehouses and moved to Los Angeles two years later. In 1965, Denver successfully auditioned for one of the top folk groups of the mid-sixties, the Chad Mitchell Trio, and replaced Mitchell as the lead singer; the group played the coffeehouse and campus circuits.

Rhymes and Reasons (1969), Denver's first album, was not a success, but when the folk group Peter, Paul, and Mary recorded Denver's "Leaving on a Jet Plane," it reached No. 1. In 1971, Denver released *Poems, Prayers, and Promises* (No. 15), featuring the No. 1 single "Take Me Home, Country Roads," and by the time he released *Rocky Mountain High* (No. 4) in 1972, Denver was established as a pop music phenomenon. The title track (No. 9) sparked controversy because some people thought the song advocated marijuana use. However, Denver argued that the song was about the Colorado mountains. In 1974, *John Denver's Greatest Hits* spent three weeks at No. 1, becoming Denver's biggest-selling album; it contained the No. 1 "Sunshine on My Shoulders." Throughout the late 1970s, Denver continued to make hit albums, including *Back Home Again* (No. 1), *Windsong* (No. 1), *An Evening with John Denver* (No. 2), and *John Denver's Greatest Hits Volume 2* (No. 6), as well as hit singles including "Thank God I'm a Country Boy" (No. 1), "I'm Sorry" (No. 1), "I Want to Live" (No. 55), and "Like a Sad Song" (No. 36). Denver also guest-starred in various programs and variety shows on television and became known for saying "far out," "wow," and "Have a nice day."

Denver's special "Thank God I'm a Country Boy" in 1977 on ABC featured special guests Johnny Cash and Glen Campbell. That same year, Denver made his film debut in *Oh God*, with George Burns. In late 1979, Denver guest-starred on a Muppets Christmas special; his album, *A Christmas Together*, with the Muppets, was released in January 1980 and reached No. 26.

The late 1970s and the 1980s saw Denver's musical popularity wane, and his political and environmental activism rise. 1987 was a year in which Denver participated in numerous political and artistic ventures. He again starred with the Muppets in the Christmas special, "Julie Andrews and the Muppets." He also filmed and released several documentaries: *Rocky Mountain Reunion*, about endangered species (which won six awards), and *John Denver's Alaska: The American Child*. In 1988, he released *Higher Ground*, which entered the U.S. country charts, and asked the Soviet Union to consider sending him to the Mir Space Station. Denver

performed at the White House in 1989, and hosted an NBC television special, "In Performance at the White House." His 1995 *Wildlife Concert* was released in support of the Wildlife Conservancy, and peaked at No. 104.

Denver's musical career was beginning to take shape again, as interest in his music was rekindled with the 1996 release of Rhino Records' *The Rocky Mountain Collection*. However, tragedy struck on October 12, 1997, when an experimental airplane Denver was flying crashed into California's Monterey Bay, killing the 53-year-old singer. Released posthumously, *The Best of John Denver Live* peaked at No. 56 and *Celebration of Life: The Last Recordings* at No. 130. At the time of his death, Denver had more than twelve gold and seven platinum albums to his credit.

Bibliography

Clinton, William J. "Statement on the Death of John Denver." *Weekly Compilation of Presidential Documents* 33.42 (20 Oct. 1997): 1566.

Denver, John. *Take Me Home: An Autobiography*. New York: Harmony, 1994.

Kemp, Mark. "Country-Pop Star Dies in Plane Crash: John Denver, 1943-1997." *Rolling Stone* 774 (27 Nov. 1997): 24.

Rees, Dafydd, and Luke Crampton. *Encyclopedia of Rock Stars*. New York: DK Publishing, 1996.

Robert G. Weiner

Designing Women (1986-1993). "Get four women together and listen to them talk" is how creator, co-executive producer, and head writer Linda Bloodworth-Thomason (see entry) described the idea behind *Designing Women*, on CBS. Often referred to as a younger version of *The Golden Girls* (another CBS comedy starring four women, which debuted a year earlier; see entry), this series quickly established itself as a forum for the discussion of social issues and southern culture. The four original characters represented conflicting ideologies and sensibilities, so disagreements were inevitable. Julia Sugarbaker, played by Dixie Carter, co-owned an interior design firm in Atlanta with her sister, Suzanne, played by Delta Burke. While Julia, widowed mother of a grown son, was liberal and socially conscious, one might say Suzanne was socially unconscious; a former beauty queen who lived well off alimony from several husbands, Suzanne was self-absorbed and quick to judge people harshly. Mary Jo Shively (Annie Potts) was a divorced mother of two school-aged children, insecure about her body, but quite capable at her job and concerned about others. Charlene Winston (Jean Smart) was the small-town innocent, always ready to give people the benefit of the doubt; during the series, Charlene married the man of her dreams and eventually moved away with him and their baby. Often caught in the middle of the women's arguments, Anthony Bouvier (Meshach Taylor) was an African-American ex-convict who started out doing deliveries for them and later became a partner.

Designing Women was met with mixed criticism its first season. While some critics enjoyed its biting wit and sexual innuendos, others thought there was too much "male-bashing." Throughout much of its run, however, it enjoyed Top

10 status, continuing the audience flow from the popular *Murphy Brown* on Monday nights. When *Designing Women* was put on hiatus its first season, thousands of women rallied in a letter-writing campaign (as they have for other female-dominated series, such as *Cagney & Lacey*) to ensure its return.

Bibliography

Brooks, Tim, and Earle Marsh. *The Complete Directory to Prime Time Network TV Shows, 1946-Present*. 5th ed. New York: Ballantine, 1992.

Gunther, Marc. "CBS and the Steel Magnolia." *New York Times* 3 Mar. 1991: H29+.

Terrace, Vincent. *Television Character and Story Facts*. Jefferson: McFarland, 1993.

Zoglin, Richard. "Sitcom Politics." *Time* 21 Sept. 1992: 44-47.

Lynn Spangler

Desmond, Paul (1924-1977), one of America's more famous jazz musicians, was born in San Francisco as Paul Emil Breitenfeld. After a mysterious but apparently unhappy childhood mostly spent living with relatives in a suburb of New York, he spent three years in an army band, attended San Francisco State College, and changed his name to Paul Desmond (which he picked out of a telephone book) before embarking on his career as a charter member of the Dave Brubeck Quartet in 1951 (see Brubeck entry). Desmond's early style on alto was most remarkable for the fact that he copied no one but evolved a sound uniquely his own—light, airy, quintessentially cool, intricately crafted for structure, balance, and fascinating surprises contained within a coherent design and characterized by a consistent demonstration of wit. Desmond's intellectual flare—both musical and verbal—was legendary, showing up in his brilliantly clever interpolations of familiar songs into his own improvised solos.

During the early days of the Brubeck Quartet, the group performed extensively in the San Francisco area and recorded for Fantasy—with Desmond achieving such notable improvisational masterpieces as his solos on "This Can't Be Love," "Trolley Song," and "All the Things You Are." As the quartet's national fame developed, the group joined a larger record label (Columbia), hit the nightclub and college circuit, and recorded such commercial successes as *Jazz Goes to College*, *Dave Brubeck at Storyville: 1954*, *Jazz: Red Hot and Cool*, and *Jazz Goes to Junior College*.

The Brubeck Quartet with Desmond in tow traveled the globe, leaving a trail of recorded evidence on such albums as *In Europe*, *Jazz Impressions of Eurasia*, *Brubeck in Amsterdam*, *Jazz Impressions of Japan*, and *The Last Time We Saw Paris*. These recordings confirm that Desmond consistently rose to levels of improvisational genius, on demand, night after night. At home, the quartet recorded tributes to Walt Disney (*Dave Digs Disney*) and to the Old South (*Gone with the Wind* and *Southern Scene*). Desmond's famous jazz hit in 5/4 time called "Take Five," recorded on *Time Out* (1959), became a bestseller.

The day-to-day grind of operating the Brubeck Quartet finally took its toll in 1967 when Brubeck and Desmond dissolved the group and went their separate ways. Desmond retired in relative obscurity, emerging from time to time to participate in Brubeck reunions or to play in local jazz clubs. With the Canadian guitarist Ed Bickert, Desmond made some of his last and most beautiful recordings—*Pure Desmond*, *Live*, *Paul Desmond*, and *Like Someone in Love*. Also, for the first time, he played with the Modern Jazz Quartet (*The Only Recorded Performance*) and with trumpeter Chet Baker (*She Was Too Good to Me*).

It was with Chet Baker that Paul Desmond made his final appearance in the recording studio to play on the title tune for Baker's album *You Can't Go Home Again*. Desmond had grown so weak with the ravages of his terminal illness that he barely had the strength to complete this one track; he died, only a few weeks later, on Memorial Day. In his last recorded solo on this arrangement by Don Sebesky of the "Adagio" from Rachmaninoff's Symphony No. 2, Paul Desmond did not sound tentative or feeble. As so often throughout his career, he sounded resolutely pensive and ineffably sad.

Bibliography

Goldberg, Joe. *Jazz Masters of the 50s*. New York: Da Capo, 1965.

Hentoff, Nat. Tribute to Paul Desmond written for the *Village Voice* 22 Aug. 1977.

Lees, Gene. *Meet Me at Jim & Andy's*. New York: Oxford UP, 1988.

McPartland, Marian. "Perils of Paul: A Portrait of Desperate Desmond." *Down Beat* 15 Sept. 1960.

Ramsey, Doug. "Remembering Desmond." *Radio Free Jazz* Sept. 1977.

Morris B. Holbrook

Detective Comics is the longest-running, continuously published American comic book, the flagship title of the publisher now known as DC Comics. (The publisher's name derives from this publication's initials, and since 1940 all of its comics have carried a circular DC logo on their covers.) Originally published by a partnership involving Malcolm Wheeler-Nicholson, Harry Donnefeld, and Jack Liebowitz, *Detective Comics* first appeared in late 1936 or early 1937 and was one of the earliest American comics devoted to a single theme or genre. During its first two years, *Detective Comics* featured a number of recurring characters such as Slam Bradley, Cosmo, Speed Saunders, the Crimson Avenger, and even Fu Manchu, none of which quite caught on with readers. Initially, the comic did not sell as well as its publisher had hoped, and by 1938 a bankrupt Wheeler-Nicholson had sold his interest in the comic to his partners, who continued to publish it as part of a line of three titles. Similarly disappointing sales have often plagued the comic, reducing its publishing frequency in the 1970s and almost leading to its cancellation in the 1960s.

Detective Comics' sales improved dramatically in 1939 when it began featuring the adventures of one of the medium's earliest superheroes, "the Bat-Man" (now Batman; see entry). Batman became the comic's lead/cover feature—and its only continuously recurring character. Reduced

Photo courtesy of Popular Culture Library, Bowling Green State University, Bowling Green, OH.

to backup status, the comic's earlier recurring characters could not compete with Batman's popularity, and eventually all of them were replaced by other series characters who likewise could not compete and were in turn replaced. Despite its changing roster of backup features, however, *Detective Comics* remained an anthology title well into the 1980s; not until late in its existence did it become merely one of many Batman titles.

As Batman became more of a superhero and less of a detective, so *Detective Comics* began to lose the thematic focus suggested by its name. The appearance of the Boy Commandos (1942) and the Martian Manhunter (1955) as backup features are only the most obvious early indications of this shift in focus. By the 1960s, *Detective Comics* was featuring only one backup to each issue's Batman story, and until the mid-1970s that backup almost always featured a superhero and/or supporting character from Batman's own series. Twice in the 1970s and 1980s, *Detective Comics* briefly expanded its backup features as it became first a "100-page Spectacular" and later a "dollar comic" (incorporated with the discontinued title *Batman Family*), but with few exceptions these backups continued to feature only superheroes and Batman supporting characters. After both expansions, *Detective Comics* reverted to a single backup feature and finally became simply a solo title for Batman—a title whose stories now continue from and in stories published in Batman's other titles.

Bibliography

Daniels, Les. *DC Comics: Sixty Years of the World's Favorite Comic Book Heroes*. Boston: Little, Brown, 1995.
Fifty Who Made DC Great. New York: DC Comics, 1985.

Daryl R. Coats

Detective Film, understood as a crime film that places the process of detection at the center of action, originated in the early years of the silent era; a Sherlock Holmes film appeared in 1903. But it has flourished in the sound era. From the aphoristic wisdom of Charlie Chan, through the sophisticated banter of Nick and Nora Charles and the knowing wisecracks of Philip Marlowe, to the gritty street vernacular of Popeye Doyle and Harry Callahan, and beyond, dialogue has served both to characterize the detective protagonist and to provide an overall verbal texture as a primary source of the audience's pleasure and fascination.

Like its counterpart in print, the detective film has frequently been extended into the detective series (see Serials). Commonly in the early sound era, the success of an A picture, like *Bulldog Drummond* (1929) or *The Hound of the Baskervilles* and *The Adventures of Sherlock Holmes* (both 1939) generated a series of sequels, most of which were made at lower budgets, to fill the bottom half of the double feature that was standard at the time (see B Movie). This pattern was not universal. The series inaugurated by *The Thin Man* (1934) was given the A treatment throughout the six films that comprised it, although attention to quality obviously declined in the later entries. Some series, including those focusing on Charlie Chan, Ellery Queen, and Michael Shayne, consisted essentially of B pictures from the start. Later in the century, the detective series would become a staple of television.

The 1940s saw the emergence of a distinct subgenre of detective film, as the hard-boiled detective, usually a private investigator, became a dominant screen figure (see also Hard-boiled Detective Fiction). Two films played an especially significant role in inaugurating this subgenre. John Huston's *The Maltese Falcon* (1941) was based on the 1929 novel by Dashiell Hammett, which had already spawned two undistinguished film adaptations. But Humphrey Bogart's incarnation of Sam Spade as a cynical detective of questionable morals who may not be as crooked as his reputation would suggest, defined, as much as any single performance could, the essence of the hard-boiled hero. *Murder, My Sweet* (1944) was based on *Farewell, My Lovely*, one of the Philip Marlowe novels of Raymond Chandler. In its use of such features as flashback structure, voiceover narration, and a quasi-expressionistic visual style, characterized by distortion to suggest internal character states and by an emphasis on shadow, on darkness, on the night world as normative, Edward Dmytryk's film did much to shape the characteristic look and feel of American hard-boiled cinema.

The characteristics of *Murder, My Sweet* are often associated with an important subcategory of American film, called film noir, and during the 1930s and 1940s, the heyday of noir, many of the most effective hard-boiled detective films were also classics of this subcategory. In contrast to the breezy entertainments that were the detective films of the 1930s, these films defined a world of uncertainties and ambiguities, intellectual and ethical. The protagonist was often at least tainted by some compromise with corruption or marginalized by a refusal to compromise in an environment in which corruption has become the norm. The complex narrative structures and brooding visual styles of the films thus articulated a vision of darkness the films seem to share as a group, almost regardless of the filmmaker's identity. Howard Hawks's *The Big Sleep* (1946), from another of Chandler's Marlowe novels, sometimes attacked for narrative incoherence, in its portrayal of a hero (Bogart as Marlowe, this time) who must meet crises and make commitments with no assurance that his understanding will comprehend the dark complexities of the world in which he makes his way, captures an important aspect of the spirit of the hard-boiled detective film during the noir era.

Detective films represent a significant portion of the most successful and important films of the 1940s and 1950s, and the genre has remained an important component of the American cinema. The continuing viability of the private eye has been manifested in the Harper films (*Harper*, 1966; *The Drowning Pool*, 1975), in which Paul Newman played a detective based on Ross Macdonald's creation, Lew Archer. Alternative directions for the detective film were suggested by Robert Altman's *The Long Goodbye* (1973), which returned to Philip Marlowe, this time in a revisionist spirit that questioned the validity of Marlowe as a heroic ideal; and by Roman Polanski's *Chinatown* (1974), in which the private eye retained the position of morally compromised seeker but proved radically and tragically ineffective in action. And if *V. I. Warshawski* (1991), which introduced a female protagonist within the hard-boiled tradition, was a critical and commercial failure, it nevertheless opened up possibilities that will no doubt be further explored.

The protagonist of a detective film need not be in the usual sense a detective at all, and "Who done it?" need not be the organizing question. Alfred Hitchcock notoriously despised the whodunit formula and, with the exception of the British film *Murder!* (1930), managed to avoid it throughout his career. Yet *Rear Window* (1954), in which the protagonist is a wheelchair-bound photographer, and in which the identity of the killer is never in doubt, is centrally concerned with the process of detection, as are a number of other Hitchcock films.

The official police often played a secondary role in earlier detective films, but as the genre matured, characters like Harry Callahan and Popeye Doyle established the police detective as protagonist, even if one hesitates to use the word "hero." The hesitation arises from the invitation offered by films like Don Siegel's *Dirty Harry* (1971) and William Friedkin's *The French Connection* (1971) that we interrogate, rather than identify with, the values of the protagonist.

In inviting such an interrogation, these films suggest at least possibilities of the detective structure as a vehicle for probing some of the questions that trouble modern society. Films like Clarence Brown's *Intruder in the Dust* (1949) and Norman Jewison's *In the Heat of the Night* (1967) have effectively linked the detective interest to an exploration of racial tensions. And there is no reason to suppose that detective films, while retaining their identity, are incapable of probing still more deeply into the human condition. We may in fact apply to the detective film what Raymond Chandler said of the detective novel: a form capable of generating the best of the films mentioned here, as well as films of the caliber of Orson Welles's *Touch of Evil* (1958) and Hitchcock's *Vertigo* (1958), is not incapable of anything.

Bibliography

Cochiarelli, Joseph J. *Screen Sleuths: A Filmography*. New York: Garland, 1992.

Conquest, John. *Trouble Is Their Business: Private Eyes in Fiction, Film, and Television*. New York: Garland, 1990.

Everson, William K. *The Detective in Film*. Secaucus: Citadel, 1972.

Pitts, Michael R. *Famous Movie Detectives*. Metuchen: Scarecrow, 1979.

Tuska, Jon. *In Manors and Alleys: A Casebook on the American Detective Film*. New York: Scarecrow, 1988.

W. P. Kenney

Detective Sidekicks have been present in detective fiction since its beginnings, originating with Dupin's unnamed assistant in Edgar Allan Poe's "The Murders in the Rue Morgue" (1841). As in Poe, most sidekicks have served as foils to their brilliant counterparts or as narrators of the detectives' ratiocination. In the traditional mystery story, the sidekick functions as a surrogate for the reader, providing the immediacy of a first-person voice without giving away the case's solution, which the detective often intuits early on.

Though inferior to the detective, the sidekick often participates in the sleuthing process. While sometimes played for comic effect in film dramatizations, figures such as Doyle's Dr. Watson and Agatha Christie's Captain Hastings are written as serious men, well versed in the ways of the world and useful in emergencies. That the detective solves puzzles ahead of them suggests not their incompetence but the depth of the detective's insights. Lord Peter Wimsey's Bunter (in Dorothy L. Sayers) and Albert Campion's Lugg (in Margery Allingham) have lesser functions as servant/companions, and British procedurals often feature policemen of lower rank and social status than the chief inspector who aid in the detection process.

Although sidekick is an American term, American mystery writers have downplayed the sidekick's role. The quintessential sidekick is Archie Goodwin—the foil to Nero Wolfe—who first appeared in Rex Stout's *Fer-de-Lance* (1934). Wolfe's employee, he has complementary skills and can operate independently, venturing into the mean streets where Wolfe will not tread. Archie punctures Wolfe's hubris and moves the plot along. Most detective writers follow lone investigators (who narrate their own adventures), or convert sidekicks into full partners, as is appropriate in the streets where detecting is a police function and detectives must watch each other's backs. Some sidekicks, like Nora Charles in Dashiell Hammett's *The Thin Man*, are important for comic effects. Others appear only when needed in the plot, as does John D. MacDonald's Meyer, friend and financial consultant to Travis McGee.

The formulaic sidekick has evolved with detective fiction into a more fully developed variety of characters, such as Lottie Herschel and Mr. Contreras (in Sara Paretsky's V. I. Warshawski novels), friends of the detective who serve in various ways to aid her both personally and professionally. Given the richness of such characters and many others that might be cited, the formulaic sidekick probably will not be missed.

Frederic Joseph Svoboda

See also
Animal Detectives
Holmes, Sherlock
Poirot, Hercule

Devo, an American counterpart to British punk rock, assimilated punk, new wave, and performance art to create a musical product for popular consumption. Two Kent State University art students, Jerry Casale and Mark Mothersbaugh—joined by their brothers (Bob Casale and Bob Mothersbaugh) and Alan Myers—formed a band informed by avant-garde performance, punk-rock outrageousness, and the synthesized sound of German electronic pop groups such as Kraftwerk. The band's name derived from the members' radical philosophical manifesto of "de-evolution." When shortened to "Devo," their name also recalled the social deviance that they sought to embody.

The band toured widely during the mid-to-late 1970s, moving from Ohio to New York City and eventually to Los Angeles. Along the way they acquired several important champions: Iggy Pop, David Bowie, and Brian Eno. These established performers helped bring Devo to the attention of the pop music establishment, and Eno produced their debut album, *Are We Not Men? We Are Devo!* in 1978. However, they had already achieved significant success with two earlier singles that year, "Jocko Homo" and their cover of the Rolling Stones' "(I Can't Get No) Satisfaction."

Devo's obscurantist lyrics—promoting de-evolution—did nothing to prevent their rise to popularity. More albums followed: *Duty Now for the Future* in 1979; *Freedom of Choice* in 1980; *New Traditionalists* in 1981; *Oh, No, It's Devo!* in 1982. A single from *Freedom of Choice*, "Whip It," was their best-seller and marked the moment of their greatest popularity. Subtle suggestions of sadomasochism accompanied the danceable sound of "Whip It," which reached No. 14 on the record sales charts.

Taking their cue from performance artists such as Laurie Anderson, Devo used films and rear-screen projections of images to enliven their concerts. By 1977, they began showing their homemade films before each show. They later experimented with purely cinematic work, suggesting the title of and appearing in Neil Young's *Rust Never Sleeps* in 1979, and again in his *Human Highway* (1982). In 1984, they made a home video of their promotional clips, entitled *Are We Not Men?*

During the 1980s, as the influence of the new wave music that Devo helped to popularize began to dissipate into a less radical pop sound, Devo's fame declined. They recorded music for two Hollywood films in the 1980s, *Heavy Metal* and *Dr. Detroit*, but public interest was waning. In 1987 they released a CD of "Muzak" versions of their greatest hits, and followed in 1988 with another LP, *Total Devo*.

Bibliography

Devo: The Men Who Make the Music. Video. Produced by Chuck Stattler. Burbank: Warner Home Video, 1984.

Romanowski, Patricia, and Holly George-Warren. *The New Rolling Stone Encyclopedia of Rock & Roll.* New York: Fireside, 1995.

Joe Thomas
Don Bacigalupi

Diamond, Neil (1941-), a leading American composer and singer of popular music, was born in Brooklyn, NY. His interest in music started when he was a child. He sang with his friends on the streets of Brooklyn and was writing songs by the time he was 15 years old. As a teenager he spent all his spare time writing songs and singing. In the early 1960s, he marketed other people's songs and eventually became a staff writer for Sunbeam Music. By the mid-1960s, he was writing songs for a number of famous singers and bands, but he also wanted to gain recognition for performing his own work. After joining Bang Records, he had a series of his own hits, including "Cherry, Cherry" and "Kentucky Woman."

In the late 1960s he signed with MCA and had a series of hits again, including "Holy Holy" and "Sweet Caroline." His album *Brother Love's Travelin' Salvation Show* (1969) was widely successful. In September of 1970 Robert Hilburn of the *Los Angeles Times* attributed some of Diamond's success to his "high sense of drama," "powerful rock voice," and "effective" stage presence, as Irwin Stambler notes.

His single "Cracklin' Rosie" and his album *Gold* (1970) were on the Top 10 list and went gold. "Solitary Man" and "He Ain't Heavy, He's My Brother" swept the nation and were enormously successful. *Tap Root Manuscript* also went gold in 1970. In 1971, Diamond provided MCA with a deeply felt song called "I Am...I Said" and "Done Too Soon." In 1972, Diamond's one-man Broadway show ran for over 20 performances, and his two-album set, *Hot August Night*, recorded live, went gold.

After signing with a new record company, Columbia, he won a Grammy and a Golden Globe Award for the soundtrack from *Jonathan Livingston Seagull* (1973). Shortly thereafter, *Serenade* (1974), which contained "Longfellow Serenade," was released. Extremely well received, the single "Longfellow Serenade" climbed the charts quickly. Diamond's next album, *Beautiful Noise* (1976), was no exception and went platinum.

Diamond's second live album, *Live at the Greek*, went platinum in 1977. His duet with Barbra Streisand, "You Don't Bring Me Flowers," stayed at No. 1 for two weeks in December 1978. A spinal cord tumor interrupted his career in the late 1970s. Diamond then released another album, *September Morn* (1979), and starred with Laurence Olivier in *The Jazz Singer* (1980). Although *The Jazz Singer* was not considered a commercial success, the soundtrack produced several outstanding singles, such as "Love on the Rocks," "America," and "Hello Again."

In the 1980s, he did a TV special, performed in concert and made more albums, such as *Heartlight* in 1982, *Primitive* in 1984, *Headed for the Future* in 1986, and another double album recorded live, *Hot August Night II,* in 1987. Neil Diamond was inducted into the Songwriting Hall of Fame in 1984.

Bibliography

Grossman, Alan. *Diamond: A Biography.* Chicago: Contemporary, 1987.

Stambler, Irwin. "Neil Diamond." *The Encyclopedia of Pop, Rock, and Soul.* New York: St. Martin's, 1989.

Wiseman, Rich. *Neil Diamond, Solitary Star.* New York: Dodd, 1987.

Lee Ann Paradise-Schober

Dick, Philip K. (1928-1982), compared by some to Franz Kafka and Jorge Luis Borges, stands as the master of science fiction that questions the existence of objective reality. Born in Chicago, Dick moved with his mother in 1939 to California, where he remained for most of his life. Briefly in 1948, he attended the University of California, Berkeley, but dropped out to avoid an ROTC requirement. He worked in record and appliance stores from 1944 until 1952, when he made writing his career. Recognized as one of the most imaginative authors in the genre, Dick is noted for his ability to create complex plots and use multiple narrators effectively in his bleak tales. His themes include the individual's creation of a private version of reality and the struggle of the individual against authoritarianism.

Dick's first sale was the short story "Roog," which Anthony Boucher published in the *Magazine of Fantasy and Science Fiction* (February 1953), but because of the vagaries of publication schedules, the first of Dick's stories to appear in print was "Beyond Lies the Wub," published in *Planet Stories* (July 1952). Dick's first published novel, *Solar Lottery* (1955), was purchased by Donald A. Wollheim at Ace. Dick followed *Solar Lottery* with two story collections, five science fiction novels, and a dozen mainstream novels, but he could not find publishers for his mainstream works. One of them, the autobiographical *Confessions of a Crap Artist*, finally appeared in print in 1975, followed by several others.

The only Dick novel that won a Hugo Award—*The Man in the High Castle*—appeared in 1962. In 1963, Dick claims to have had a vision of an evil face staring at him from the sky. The experience led Dick to write his masterpiece, *The Three Stigmata of Palmer Eldritch* (1965), in which a false messiah offers followers a drug that will allow them to do anything they can imagine. *The Three Stigmata* introduced the motif of characters using drugs to alter their perceptions of reality, which appears regularly afterwards in Dick's fiction. Dick's best-known novel, *Do Androids Dream of Electric Sheep?* (1968), formed the basis of Ridley Scott's film *Blade Runner* (1982). The book was reissued in 1982 with the title *Blade Runner* and became Dick's best-selling book. In the book, the similarities between humans and androids is explored more fully than in the film. In 1974, Dick claims that VALIS (Vast Active Living Intelligence System), a transcendent and brilliant alien mind, entered him and provided him with insights. Dick's novel *VALIS* (1981) relates this experience. In *Radio Free Albemuth* (1985) Dick divides the adventures of his mystical experiences and life between two characters who live in a totalitarian version of the U.S.

Bibliography

Clute, John, and Peter Nicholls. *The Encyclopedia of Science Fiction.* New York: St. Martin's, 1993.

James, Edward. *Science Fiction in the 20th Century.* Oxford: Oxford UP, 1994.

Mackey, Douglas A. *Philip K. Dick.* Boston: Hall, 1988.

Platt, Charles. *Dream Makers.* New York: Berkley, 1980.

Brent Chesley

Dick Tracy (1931-), one of the icons of America's comicsland, by Chester Gould, first appeared in the *Detroit Mirror* on October 4, 1931. The first continuities began eight days later on October 12, establishing the origin and justification for the detective hero and his cause. These continuities debuted in the *New York Daily News,* where they continued, on the front page, for 45 consecutive years. The famous comic strip has appeared in many hundreds of national and international newspapers. Chester Gould (1900-1985) arrived in Chicago, from Oklahoma, in 1921 and spent the next 10 years working to get a big-time syndicated cartoon strip like those done by Sidney Smith (*The Gumps*) and Harold Gray (*Little Orphan Annie*) accepted for publication. He had some 60 lesser known comic strip series published in these years in a variety of nationally renowned newspapers.

In popular fiction, Chester Gould's *Dick Tracy* provided the archetypal police detective hero and police-procedural mystery formula. It inspired a radio show, two TV shows (live action and animated), a film (dir. Warren Beatty, 1990), and toys and video games. Assistants took over producing the strip in 1977, but Gould's message, celebrating a high personal and social morality, has endured and left an indelible legacy and mythology for generations past, present, and to come.

Bibliography

Galewitz, Herb, ed. *The Celebrated Cases of Dick Tracy 1931-1951.* 1970. Secaucus: Wellfleet, 1990. Press.

——. *Dick Tracy—The Thirties: Tommy Guns and Hard Times.* 1978. Secaucus: Wellfleet, 1990.

Maeder, Jay. *Dick Tracy: The Official Biography.* New York: Penguin, 1990.

Roberts, Garyn G. *Dick Tracy and American Culture: Morality and Mythology, Text and Context.* Jefferson: McFarland, 1993.

Garyn G. Roberts

See also
Comic Books
Comic Strips

Dick Van Dyke Show, The (1961-1966), is considered by critics and fans alike as one of the best written and most timeless sitcoms, placing second only to *I Love Lucy.* While *I Love Lucy* validated the sitcom as a successful TV genre, the *Dick Van Dyke Show* took the genre to a more sophisticated and realistic level (see Sitcom).

Significantly, it was the first sitcom to address both the work and home life of its main character, Robert Petrie. Rob's job as head writer for "The Alan Brady Show" became a focal point of the series. *The Dick Van Dyke Show* was also progressive in showing a woman who worked as an equal to the men (Rose Marie as writer Sally Rogers), and by refusing to avoid blacks. Furthermore, the series always featured blacks as responsible characters.

Comic Morey Amsterdam as comedy writer Buddy Sorrell, "The Human Joke Machine," served as the bridge between old-style humor and Rob's more progressive approach. Sorrell's main target was Mel Cooley, the sycophantic producer of "The Alan Brady Show." Cooley, played by veteran character actor Richard Deacon, was also a whipping boy for Alan Brady, a recurring character played by *Dick Van Dyke Show* creator Carl Reiner (1922-). Drawing from his experience as a young writer for Sid Caesar's *Your Show of Shows,* Reiner wrote the first 13 episodes of the series—originally titled *Head of the Family.*

Getting the series on the air proved quite a challenge for Reiner, who starred as Robert Petrie in the 1959 *Head of the Family* pilot. CBS was unimpressed with the pilot, but Reiner's agent sold the idea to Sheldon Leonard, the star producer at Danny Thomas Productions. Leonard felt the series could be a hit if Reiner was replaced by another actor; ironically, Reiner was deemed inappropriate for the autobiographical role he created.

Leonard fought hard to get CBS to accept the series. After an unsuccessful first season, in which *The Dick Van Dyke Show* was beaten in the ratings by *Perry Como* and canceled by CBS, Leonard got the network to renew the show. Dick Van Dyke (1925-), who was starring in the Broadway musical *Bye Bye Birdie*, was an unknown in television when chosen to star in the series. By the end of its run, however, Van Dyke and co-star Mary Tyler Moore (1936-) became perennial TV favorites. *The Dick Van Dyke Show* laid the foundation for Moore's 1970s sitcom *The Mary Tyler Moore Show* (see entry), one of the first sitcoms to exceed *The Dick Van Dyke Show*'s sophistication.

Bibliography

Brooks, Tim, and Earle Marsh. *The Complete Directory to Prime Time Network TV Shows, 1946-Present.* New York: Ballantine, 1992.

Weissman, Ginny, and Steven Sanders Coyne. *The Dick Van Dyke Show: Anatomy of a Classic.* New York: St. Martin's, 1983.

Michael B. Kassel

Digital Audio Broadcasting (DAB), also known as digital audio radio service (DARS), is an innovation that is expected to change or even replace radio broadcasting as we know it. DAB is an audio signal that offers compact disc sound quality and can be transmitted to consumers via satellite or terrestrial methods. On August 1, 1990, the Federal Communications Commission (FCC) initiated a Notice of Inquiry into DAB, and emotions in the broadcast industry have since run the gamut from fear to excitement. Some traditional broadcasters see DAB as a threat to their existence while others see DAB as a way not only to save radio, but to help it prosper.

The National Association of Broadcasters and much of the radio industry, however, believe that DAB's future is probably in-band. In-band means implementing DAB through existing AM and/or FM frequencies. For example, about 10 DAB channels can be employed using the same space now taken up by one FM frequency. But which system will emerge as the standard? Other than technological impact, the real opportunity offered by DAB is that it puts the U.S. squarely in a position to regain its world leadership role in setting technological communications standards—a position the U.S. lost in the 1980s era of deregulation, and exemplified by AM stereo.

Bibliography

Baert, Luc, Luc Theunissen, and Guido Vergult. *Digital Audio and Compact Disc Technology.* Newton: Butterworth-Heinemann, 1992.

Mirabito, Michael M. A. *The New Communications Technologies.* 2d ed. Newton: Focal, 1994.

Rumsey, Francis. *Digital Audio Operations.* Newton: Focal, 1991.

Talbot-Smith, Michael. *Broadcast Sound Technology.* Newton: Focal, 1990.

W. A. Kelly Huff

Digital Audio Tape (DAT) is a method for recording and playing back audio signals with sound quality equal to a compact disc (CD). The advantage of DAT over CDs is that DAT can also be used for recording.

Digital audio tape machines were first developed in Japan in the early 1980s. A coalition of Japanese electronics manufacturers adopted a single recording standard at the DAT Conference in 1985. But the recording industry's fears of losing money from illegal CD copying onto DATs delayed the availability of DAT machines for home users in the U.S.

Digital audio tape uses a combination of three technological advances in the 1960s and 1970s. The first was a system for converting analog audio signals into digital (on or off) pulses for recording and back to analog signals for playback. The second advance was the helical scanning technique previously used to record video signals onto magnetic tape. This method uses a spinning tape head that records in long diagonal tracks along the tape path as opposed to the much shorter paths in linear audio tape recording. The third development was the cassette packaging used in analog audio and video cassettes. The cassette frees users from having to thread and unthread the tape each time a tape is changed. DAT machines use a cassette similar to analog audio cassettes, except that the tape is a little wider than the analog cassette, and it has a high quality coating to record the frequency range of the digital signal.

In 1989, the U.S. Congress adopted a copy protection system based on placing a computer chip inside the DAT machine. The chip allows users to make a first generation copy from the original CD, but it marks that recording so no successive copies can be made. The first DAT machines were marketed in 1990. U.S. consumer response was weak because the recorders were five times as expensive as audio cassette recorders, blank tapes cost almost as much as prerecorded CDs, and analog audio cassettes cannot be played back on a DAT machine.

DAT recorders are, however, standard equipment in most radio stations. They provide superior recording quality to analog cassette and open reel recorders and they can be more accurately cued in a shorter time. DAT tape machines are also growing in popularity as data backup systems for personal computers. They can store over one gigabyte of computer data and access files within 20 seconds, far exceeding previous backup tape systems.

Bibliography

Horn, Delton T. *DAT: The Complete Guide to Digital Audio Tape.* Boston: Focal, 1991.

Watkinson, John. *An Introduction to Digital Audio.* Blue Ridge Summit: Tab, 1994.

Kenneth M. Nagelberg

Dilbert, the comic strip featuring the "Hero of the New Worker" of the same name along with co-workers of various species, was created by Scott Adams, a former applications engineer at Pacific Bell, who began sketching fellow employees during boring meetings. The growth curve for *Dilbert* has been phenomenal; it appears in more than 1,400 papers worldwide. It may be the most photocopied, pinned-up, downloaded, faxed, re-faxed, e-mailed, and snail-mailed comic strip in America. There is a Dilbert Zone web site and several books as well. *The Dilbert Principle: A Cubicle's-Eye View of Bosses, Meetings, Management Fads and Other Workplace Afflictions* was #1 on the *New York Times* bestseller list after just two weeks in print.

Dilbert highlights the tension between the bright, technology-empowered employee and the more traditional people who manage them. Even Bill Gates, the highly successful founder and CEO of Microsoft said, "Managing programmers is like herding cats." Dilbert and his supporting cast give us all a humorous look at the new breed of "cats" and the conflicts they face in today's workplace. As business managers look for solutions to these problems, *Dilbert* will be pointing out their faults with cynical humor and pointed remarks. Maybe they will even listen.

Bibliography

Adams, Scott. *The Dilbert Principle.* New York: Harper-Business, 1997.

The Dilbert Zone. http://unitedmedia.com/comics/Dilbert.

Herman, Roger E. *Turbulence! Challenges & Opportunities in the World of Work.* Akron, OH: Oakhill, 1995.

Douglas R. Laird

Dime Novels, one of America's notable contributions to mass distribution of literature, grew from a perceived need and opportunity. In 1860, Irwin P. Beadle conceived the idea of issuing inexpensive paper-covered novels in a continuous sequence and at a fixed price of ten cents. He called the series Beadle's Dime Novels and "dime novel" soon became a generic term for any book issued in this paperbound format, principally one with a plot of sensational adventure. The original Beadle books were stories of life on the American frontier, patterned after James Fenimore Cooper. By the 1880s stories of the frontier had been joined by detective stories, adventure tales, and science fiction.

Beadle & Adams (Irwin's partners were his older brother, Erastus, and Robert Adams) was the principal firm in this endeavor but soon had lively competition. The other major publishers of dime novels were George P. Munro, his brother Norman L. Munro, Frank Tousey, and Street & Smith. Dime novels came in several basic formats ranging from small four-by-six-inch booklets to larger quarto-sized leaves, and ran from 100 to 300 pages. Each format usually featured pictorial covers and black and white or colored illustrations.

The major publishers had their own regular authors and, in many instances, continuing characters who appeared in a series of novels. Beadle & Adams' principal authors included Mrs. Ann S. Stephens, Mrs. Metta Victor, Edward S. Ellis, Edward L. Wheeler, and Ned Buntline, some of whom also wrote for other publishers. George P. Munro became famous for books by "Old Sleuth" (a pseudonym for Harlan Page Halsey), while Munro's brother Norman published stories of detective Old Cap. Collier written by W. I. James. Norman Munro also published John DeMorgan, Weldon J. Cobb, and Harrie Irving Hancock. Frank Tousey was the publisher for a handful of writers who used so many pseudonyms and house names that the staff seemed larger than it was. Luis P. Senarens, Francis W. Doughty, John R. Musick, and Harry K. Shackleford were among the most popular and prolific. Street & Smith (a relative latecomer to the field) published Horatio Alger, Jr., Ned Buntline, Fredric Van Rensselaer Dey, Gilbert Patten, Col. Prentiss Ingraham, Luranna Sheldon, and Edward Stratemeyer (who later founded the Stratemeyer Syndicate; see entry).

While many of the authors went unrecognized behind pseudonyms, characters like Deadwood Dick, Old Sleuth, Nick Carter, Buffalo Bill, Young Wild West, Frank Reade, Jr., and Frank Merriwell were household names. Some of these have passed into legend where their names still stand for attributes of courage and patriotism. While the earliest dime novels were written with the adult reader in mind, gradually more titles were created for younger readers. The themes they presented shaped and preserved some of the prevailing notions of early American history. However, as early as 1916, motion pictures had replaced the dime novel as inexpensive entertainment.

Bibliography

Denning, Michael. *Mechanic Accents: Dime Novels and Working-Class Culture in America.* London: Verso, 1987.

Johannsen, Albert. *The House of Beadle and Adams and Its Dime and Nickel Novels.* Norman: U of Oklahoma P, 1950-1962.

Jones, Daryl. *The Dime Novel Western.* Bowling Green, OH: Bowling Green State U Popular P, 1978.

Noel, Mary. *Villains Galore: The Heyday of the Popular Story Weekly.* New York: Macmillan, 1954.

Randolph Cox

See also

Western Fiction

Dirty Harry (1971), Don Siegel's police drama, mirrors the "spread of urban violence and the resulting change in public opinion in favor of law and order" which took place in the early and mid 1970s, while simultaneously foregrounding the limitations of conventional law in the face of unfettered savagery (Baxter 246). The film focuses on the quest of "Dirty" Harry Callahan (Clint Eastwood), a San Francisco police inspector, to apprehend a maniacal killer called Scorpio. Using his own unconventional and only partially legal methods of justice, Callahan pursues and captures the murderer, later to discover that his actions, while initially successful, are legally inappropriate and have allowed the killer to go free. Undaunted, the killer hijacks a busload of schoolchildren, at which point Callahan takes justice into his own hands, kills the killer, and drops his police badge on Scorpio's body in a final comment on the inextricable nature of justice and violence in America's legal system. Though the film was criticized for its violence, it was highly popular, and Eastwood reprised the role of Dirty Harry in four more films: *Magnum Force* (1973), *The Enforcer* (1976), *Sudden Impact* (1983), which made famous the line "Go ahead, make my day!," and *The Dead Pool* (1988).

Bibliography

Baxter, John. *Dirty Harry. International Dictionary of Films and Filmmakers: Films.* 2d ed. Chicago: St. James, 1990. 245-46.

Milne, Tom. *"Dirty Harry." Sight and Sound* 41 (1972): 112.

Schickel, Richard. *Clint Eastwood: A Biography.* New York: Knopf, 1996.

Lynnea Chapman-King

Disco was, from the mid 1970s to the early 1980s, one of the most influential musical and social trends. From popular fashion to soft rock, from movies to hairstyle, disco became the rage. A descendant of rhythm and blues, and more contemporarily, Motown, disco swept the music world.

What began as essentially an African-American counter-cultural music quickly became mainstream. This mainstream popularity is the reason that disco is now disparaged in sarcastic, dismissive representations of 1970s culture. Artists such as the Temptations, the Spinners, and individuals like Carl Douglas ("Kung Fu Fighting") influenced the disco beat that was a reaction to the harder rock and the mellow 1970s pop. Most disco features a driving, 4/4 dance beat, though much lighter than the music of 1970s hard rock. The lyrics of disco contain themes from discontented love to new romance. However, one of the essential elements of disco is the centering of lyrics on dancing itself. Vicki Sue Robinson's "Turn the Beat Around" (which combines disco with jazz-style scatting), KC and the Sunshine Band's "Shake Your Groove Thing," Michael Zager Band's "Let's All Chant," and Donna Summer's "Last Dance" all focus on the act of dancing as paramount in life. Disco also was the first mainstream dance movement to capitalize on innovations in studio sounds and synthesizers, as evidenced in instrumentals like "Popcorn" by Hot Butter and strange extraterrestrial themes such as those from *Star Wars* and *Close Encounters of the Third Kind*, both by the group Meco.

Possibly the greatest media memory of disco is the movie *Saturday Night Fever* (1976; see entry). While its sequel *Staying Alive* did not do as well, *Saturday Night Fever* brought disco music and fashions to mainstream America. The soundtrack became one of the biggest sellers of the disco era, including songs by the Bee Gees, Yvonne Elliman, and the Tavares among others. The Bee Gees, con-

sisting of the Gibb brothers Robin, Barry and Maurice (see entry), soared to the top with hits like "Stayin' Alive," "Night Fever," and "Jive Talkin'." Their brother Andy shared in the disco heyday with hits like "(I Just Want to Be Your) Everything," "Shadow Dancing," and the mellower "(Love Is) Thicker Than Water." Some of the other big names in disco include Gloria Gaynor ("I Will Survive"), Van McCoy and the Soul City Symphony ("The Hustle"), the Village People ("YMCA"), and ABBA ("Dancing Queen").

Television quickly jumped onto the disco bandwagon with shows like *Solid Gold*, hosted by Marilyn McCoo (of the Fifth Dimension) and, later, Dionne Warwick. *Solid Gold* weekly counted down the top hits while ornately clad professional dancers danced. Disco influenced Broadway with hit musicals like Neil Simon's *They're Playing Our Song,* about a lyricist and a composer who fall hopelessly in love amid music reflective of disco dance hits.

Barry Gibb of the Bee Gees carried disco into his arranging and recording with Barbra Streisand. Streisand's albums *Wet* and *Guilty* reflect the influence of disco on her music. On *Wet*, Streisand teamed up with Donna Summer to record one of the last great disco dance numbers, "Enough Is Enough (No More Tears)." Country girls Olivia Newton-John and Dolly Parton added their voices to disco, also.

Disco ended when a new generation of music listeners turned their attention to singers like Madonna and groups like Wham.

Bibliography

DeCurtis, Anthony, and James Henke. *The Rolling Stone Illustrated History of Rock and Roll.* 3d ed. New York: Random House, 1992.

Goldman, Albert. *Disco.* New York: Hawthorne, 1978.

Radcliffe, A. Joe. *This Business of Disco.* New York: Billboard, 1980.

Mark K. Fulk

Discovery Channel, The, was lauched on June 17, 1985, by John Hendricks with a group of financial backers on Galaxy 1 satellite, transponder 22, with approximately 156,000 subscribers. The Discovery Channel (TDC) was the first cable television network to concentrate on nonfiction entertainment, focusing its diversified programming in the areas of nature ("In the Company of Whales," "America Coast to Coast"), science and technology ("Movie Magic," "The Secret Life of Machines"), history ("Discovery Journal," "Discovery Sunday"), human adventure ("Wings," "Safari"), world exploration ("Magical Worlds," "Arthur Clarke's Mysterious World"), informational/instructional entertainment ("Homeworks," "Great Chefs"), as well as international documentary programming ("Russia: Live from the Inside," "The Second Russian Revolution") and educational programming designed for the classroom. TDC also carries an exceptional number of public service announcements designed to raise environmental awareness, and in the 1990s it sponsored a tree planting program (160 million) in U.S. communities.

In 1990, TDC launched the Discovery Interactive Library, cable television's first entry into the interactive video market. The 1992 development of Your Choice TV, a Discovery subsidiary, helped organize the hundreds of new viewing options made possible by digital compression and video on demand.

Bibliography

Pagano, Penny. "John Hendricks' Big Adventure." *Channels* Oct. 1989.

Stump, Matt. "The Discovery Channel Looks for the Next Frontier." *Broadcasting* 11 June 1990.

Jennifer A. Machiorlatti

Disney Theme Parks, tourist attractions built under the aegis of the Walt Disney Company since 1955, are located in the U.S., Europe, and Japan. Disney theme parks have become the most popular tourist destinations in the world, attracting over 60 million people a year. Beginning with Disneyland, which opened in Orange County, CA, in 1955, to Euro Disneyland Paris, unveiled in France in 1992, Walt Disney's vision has reached global proportions. Other enterprises include the Walt Disney World complex (opened 1971 outside Orlando, FL) and Tokyo Disneyland in Japan (1983). Walt's conception of the theme park grew out of his dissatisfaction with dirty and disorderly amusement parks. He envisioned a utopian environment of cleanliness, safety, and order that would be entertaining and educational both for adults and children.

Drawing from European folk tales, children's literature, U.S. history, and his movies, Walt created several themes for the original Disneyland, including Adventureland, Tomorrowland, Fantasyland, and Frontierland. These themed lands are anchored by Main Street, USA, an idealized version of Walt's boyhood hometown, Marceline, MO, with a railroad at its entry point and Sleeping Beauty's Castle at its point of departure into the various lands. The design featured Hollywood-like stage sets through which visitors passed as if in a movie. Located along the park's perimeter, the attractions are spaced to control traffic patterns. Lands and attractions are thematically linked: Fantasyland (dreams, myth and magic); Frontierland (United States' past); Adventureland (exotic travel); and Tomorrowland (technology and the future). Fantasyland's "It's a Small World" emphasizes similarities over differences in the human family. Frontierland's "Tom Sawyer's Island" exalts rugged individualism. Adventureland's "Jungle Safari" stresses exploration and discovery. Tomorrowland's "Carousel of Progress" accentuates scientific and technological progress. The various attractions offer a diversity of experience while projecting security and harmony. Disneyland is a social space that celebrates middle-class virtues.

The Disney phenomenon was made possible by the multi-faceted changes in the United States following World War II. Technological innovations, growing affluence, and expansion of the entertainment industry converged to create mass consumption culture. In Disney's case, success can be attributed to television, which provided access into North American homes, allowing Disney both to advertise his theme park and to indulge children's fantasies (see Walt Disney Television). Viewers of the original *Wonderful World of Disney* Sunday night TV series (aired under various titles from the mid-fifties through the sixties) discovered their experience was incomplete without a visit to Disneyland. The commercial success of Disneyland, visited by one-fourth of the U.S. population in its first ten years, allowed Walt Disney to buy land in Florida and expand.

Walt Disney World began in November 1965 when Walt announced the purchase of 27,433 acres in Central Florida, a parcel larger than the island of Manhattan. A year later he unveiled plans revealing that from its inception, Walt Disney World was to be more than an amusement theme park. Unlike the cramped space of Disneyland, this expanse of land would protect the project from non-Disney development, as Walt created a new world of theme parks, hotels, and recreational facilities, but most important, a model city. Cooperating with Disney, the state of Florida created the Reedy Creek Improvement District (RCID), a self-governing jurisdiction that prohibited local political interference. Control over growth and development allowed the Disney company, after Walt Disney's death in 1966, to construct the following: the Magic Kingdom (1971); Fort Wilderness Resort and Campground (1971); Discovery Island (1974); Lake Buena Vista Shopping Village (now Disney Village Marketplace) (1975); River Country (1976); EPCOT, the Experimental Prototype Community of Tomorrow (1982); Typhoon Lagoon (1989); Disney-MGM, which lets guests "ride" the movies (1989); Pleasure Island (1989); Blizzard Beach (1995); the Disney Institute, Disney's Boardwalk, and Celebration, a planned residential community (all 1996); Disney's Wide World of Sports, Downtown Disney (both 1997); and Disney's Animal Kingdom (1998).

Interested in keeping people on its grounds, Disney began several hotel projects in the late 1980s which rival the parks themselves. Through arrangement with multinational hotel operators and the employ of world-renowned contemporary architects, the company has created hotel culture. Guests vacation in the Northwest woods (Wilderness Lodge), the Caribbean (Caribbean Beach Resort), or New Orleans (Port Orleans) without leaving their hotels. In 1994, Disney opened the All Star Sports Resort, its first moderately priced hotel, and in 1997, the Southwest-themed Coronado Springs Resort. The Dolphin and Swan Hotels are childlike fantasies with large concrete rooftop sculptures of classical dolphins and swans. As Disney theme parks re-create landscapes from other places and times, the Dolphin copies Florida's environment—sunlight, palm trees, hotel rooms, and shopping.

The first Disney theme park built outside the U.S., Tokyo Disneyland, replicates California Disneyland. The 115-acre park opened on August 13, 1983 at a cost of $1.4 billion. Opening day attendance broke the original park's record for a single day and Tokyo Disneyland now draws more visitors per year than the Magic Kingdom. Owned by the Oriental Land Corporation, a Japanese railroad and real estate firm, the park sits on a 600-acre landfill in Tokyo Bay. Disney designed the park, has a 45-year management contract, and collects royalties on its profits through a licensing agreement. While Disney receives about $40 million annually from Tokyo Disneyland, the park makes several hundred million dollars each year, having drawn 125 million visitors—the total population of Japan—in its first ten years. Disney and Oriental are building an adjacent $3 million ocean adventure park, Tokyo DisneySea, featuring seven seas and islands, that is scheduled to open in 2001.

Euro Disney Resort, located on 4,481 acres 30 miles outside Paris, opened on April 12, 1992 at a cost of $4 billion and is comprised of Disneyland Paris, six U.S.-themed hotels (Newport Bay, New York, Sequoia, Santa Fe, Cheyenne, and the Disneyland Hotel), a nighttime entertainment complex called Festival Disney, a convention center, a 27-hole golf course, and the Davy Crockett Campground. Euro Disneyland's Enchanted Kingdom adds three new attractions (the Visionarium, Alice's Curious Labyrinth, and a dungeon in Sleeping Beauty's Castle featuring a live-in dragon) and more sophisticated technology. Its version of Tomorrowland, Discoveryland, serves as a mini-EPCOT. To keep out inclement weather, protected corridors and covered arcades make 80 percent of visitors' time spent indoors. Built around a ten-acre artificial lake, the hotels, in movie-set fashion, allow guests to travel from New England to California.

While Tokyo Disneyland has been a smashing success, Euro Disney has suffered financial losses. In the midst of Euro Disney difficulties, the company announced plans to build a 100-acre historical theme park outside Williamsburg, VA, called Disney's America. The park's original projection included Native America (1600-1800, describing American Indian civilizations), Civil War Fort (1850-70, dealing with slavery and the Civil War), and the Industrial Revolution, depicted as a roller-coaster ride through a turn-of-the-century steel mill. Immediately, Disney received criticism of its plans—historians claimed history was being treated as a series of isolated events and would be trivialized and over-simplified. Further controversy erupted as environmentalists, preservation groups, and local farmers and homeowners united in opposition to Disney's plans. However, business leaders in the area predicted an economic boom from the jobs Disney would create, tourist dollars the park would bring in, and secondary economic development that would be generated. On March 13, 1994, following heated debate, the Virginia legislature approved a $163.2 million incentive package for Disney's America. But, surprised by the national debate that was hurting its image, the company cancelled the project in 1995.

Bibliography

Fjellman, Stephen. *Vinyl Leaves: Walt Disney World and America*. Boulder: Westview, 1992.

Francaviglia, Richard V. "Mainstreet USA: A Comparison/ Contrast of Streetscapes in Disneyland and Walt Disney World." *Journal of Popular Culture* 15.1 (1981): 141-56.

Schickel, Richard. *The Disney Version: The Life, Times, Art and Commerce of Walt Disney*. 1968. Rev. ed. New York: Touchstone, 1985.

Sorkin, Michael. "See You in Disneyland." *Variations on a Theme Park: The New American City and the End of Public Space*. Ed. Michael Sorkin. New York: Noonday, 1992. 205-32.

Wallace, Mike. "Mickey Mouse History: Portraying the Past at Disney World." *Radical History Review* 32 (1985): 33-57.

Michael Hoover
Lisa Odham Stokes

See also
Theme Park, The

Dr. Demento (Barry Hansen) (1941-), with his *Dr. Demento* radio show, has since 1971 brought fans ("Dementians" and "Dementites") the best and worst novelty records from the past and present. "The good Doctor" has beat the drum for classic acts like Spike Jones, Tom Lehrer, and Allan Sherman, and exposed new artists like "Weird Al" Yankovic (see entry). He has, by extension, amassed one of the world's largest private record collections.

Hansen's radio career began at Reed College in Portland, OR, a liberal arts school with a reputation as a hippie college. He spent part of the 1960s as a roadie for rock bands before settling in southern California. There, he studied for his Master of Arts in folk music at UCLA and got a job at free-form station KPPC in Pasadena. In 1971 he assumed the Dr. Demento persona to play "mad music and crazy comedy" full-time. The Doctor relied mostly on old records from his collection until the show was syndicated by Westwood One starting in 1976 (it is now syndicated by On the Radio Productions). The Doctor's home base has moved a few times, from KPPC to LA's KMET, where he did a live show with records that might not be allowed on some of his affiliates. When KMET changed to new age WTWV, he moved the show to KLSX.

Hansen's massive record collection has provided rare discs for TV productions and oldies anthologies. As a pop music expert, he has consulted on and contributed liner notes to several oldies collections, especially those put out by reissue label Rhino Records. He has also compiled several demented collections, including *Dr. Demento's Delights* (1975, Warner Bros.), *Dr. Demento's Dementia Royale* (1980, Rhino, including segues by the Doctor), a six-record set, compiled by decade, of *The Greatest Novelty Records of All Time* (1985, Rhino), and the *Dr. Demento 20th Anniversary Collection* (1991, Rhino).

Bibliography

Hansen, Barry. *Dr. Demento 20th Anniversary Collection* (liner notes). Rhino Records #R2 70743 (2 compact discs), 1991.

——. *The Rhino Brothers Present the World's Worst Records* (liner notes). Rhino Records RNLP 809, 1983.

——. *The Spike Jones Anthology* (liner notes). Rhino Records #R2 71574 (2 compact discs), 1994.

Popson, Tom. "Dr. Demento Hits the Tour Trail to Mark 20th Anniversary." *Chicago Tribune* 20 Sept. 1991, Sec. 7 ("Take Two" section).

"WPIX adds Dr. Demento." *Billboard* 28 April 1979.

Mark R. McDermott

Dr. Kildare (1961-1966) was a successful pioneer in TV medical drama, based on a series of novels by Max Brand that MGM had made into B movies in the late 1930s. Before the late 1950s, no hour-long medical series had ever been presented on network television. In 1961, both *Dr. Kildare* and *Ben Casey* premiered, and both became instant successes. Comparisons between the two series were inevitably offered. The surly, hairy-chested, visceral Casey, played by Vince Edwards, contrasted in every way with the clean-cut, Galahad-like James Kildare portrayed by Richard Chamberlain (see entry). *Kildare* was a bright, modern look at the world of medical practitioners; by comparison, *Ben Casey* looked dingy and decidedly old-fashioned. But the biggest difference between the two was that Casey was a neurosurgeon while Kildare was an intern (later a youthful resident). Each had a crusty old chief, played by Raymond Massey as Leonard Gillespie on *Kildare* and Sam Jaffe as Dr. Zorba on *Casey*. It was Kildare's youth, vulnerability, and curiosity that gave his show a decided edge in the generating of plot lines.

A consistent Top 10 Nielsen show despite strong competition, the show was revamped in the 1965-66 season. It became a twice-weekly half-hour show but was canceled at year's end. It was the one medical program in network television history that often transcended the "neurotic patient" or "doctor of the week" level of characterization. Some plots showed how rational physicians perform their daily work. The series led to several less-successful imitations, including *Medical Center, The Doctors,* and *Marcus Welby, M.D.* It has never been forgotten, and never equaled.

Bibliography

Brooks, Tim, and Earle Marsh. *The Complete Directory to Prime Time Network and Cable TV Shows, 1946-Present.* New York: Ballantine, 1995.

R. D. Michael

Dr. Seuss (Theodor Seuss Geisel) (1904-1991) is one of America's most-loved authors of children's literature. With the opening lines—"The sun did not shine/it was too wet to play/so we sat in the house/all that cold, cold wet day"—from *The Cat in the Hat* (1957), Dr. Seuss captivated a generation of children with an enthusiasm that has endured through the years. He was born Theodor Seuss Geisel in Springfield, MA. Children's literature came later in his life after success as an advertising cartoonist and documentary filmmaker. While attending Dartmouth College, Geisel began using his middle name as editor of the college humor magazine, a custom he retained throughout his professional career.

Dr. Seuss published his first children's book, *And to Think That I Saw It on Mulberry Street*, in 1937. That successful work was followed by *The Five Hundred Hats of Bartholomew Cubbins* (1938), *The King's Stilts* (1939), and *Horton Hatches an Egg* (1940)—certainly one of his most beloved stories. In these, he established a pattern of peopling his books with eccentric characters—usually animals and birds, but sometimes invented beings of no recognizable species, whose antics and foibles enable the introduction of simple, basic actions, concepts, and words. Some works, like *Horton*, also dramatize moral values.

Seuss's work took a detour during World War II, when he served under Frank Capra in the Army Signal Corps as head of the animation section. He made a series of patriotic films, winning Academy Awards for two documentaries. After the war he refocused his attention on children's literature, receiving Caldecott Honors for *McElligot's Pool* (1947), *Bartholomew and the Oobleck* (1949), and *If I Ran the Zoo* (1950). An Academy Award for best animated cartoon followed for *Gerald McBoing-Boing* (1951).

Dissatisfied with the boring Dick and Jane reading primers used in the 1950s, Seuss wrote *The Cat in the Hat* employing a controlled vocabulary list issued by the textbook division of Houghton-Mifflin. That book was the catalyst for Beginner Books, a special division of Random House with the cat as the logo and Dr. Seuss as the division head. Specific tactics were used to aid the child reader to master the text. For example, the familiar anapestic tetrameter rhythm was used to assist in word recognition. *Green Eggs and Ham* (1960) was written in response to a challenge to limit the text to only 50 basic vocabulary words. Seuss used 49. In 1968, he launched Bright and Early Books at Random House, using the names Theo LeSieg and Rosetta Stone for books he wrote but did not illustrate.

Seuss's later message books weave political commentaries throughout the story: *Yertle the Turtle* (1958) addresses totalitarianism; *The Lorax* (1971) promotes environmentalism; *The Butter Battle Book* (1984) critiques weapons proliferation. In 1984, Dr. Seuss received a Pulitzer Prize for his contributions to children's literature. The outpouring of sentiment upon his death is a testament to his impact on children and adults.

Bibliography

MacDonald, Ruth. *Dr. Seuss.* Boston: Twayne, 1988.
San Diego Museum of Art. *Dr. Seuss from Then to Now.* New York: Random House, 1986.

Sylvia Tag

Dr. Strangelove, or How I Learned to Stop Worrying and Love the Bomb (1964), directed by Stanley Kubrick (see entry), made its appearance on the screen after the first wave of fear about "the bomb" had already come and gone. The immediate post-1945 shock over what happened at Hiroshima and Nagasaki had waned somewhat, only to be replaced by a greater if more generalized fear driven by the development and testing of the hydrogen bomb. Except for the conclusion, in which Armageddon is barely averted, the plot of *Dr. Strangelove* owes much to Peter George's 1958 novel *Red Alert* (originally published in the U.K. as *Two Hours to Doom*). But the darkly comic treatment of the subject matter is Kubrick's (along with screenwriters Peter George and Terry Southern), with the help of memorable performances by Peter Sellers (who plays three different characters, including Dr. Strangelove), Slim Pickens (as Major "King" Kong, who eventually "drops" the bomb), George C. Scott (as General "Buck" Turgidson), and Sterling Hayden (as the fanatical general who sends a fleet of bombers to nuke the Russians).

The film's three main locations of action are in the "war room" somewhere near Washington, at the Burpleson air base headquarters of the Strategic Air Command, and on the flight deck of a B-52 bomber on watch at its "fail safe" position two hours from potential targets inside the Soviet Union. The most memorable of the three is the war room with 25 or 30 officials seated around a brightly lit giant circular table. It is here, for example, that we meet Dr. Strange-love, a skillfully blended composite of three leaders of American policy at the time: Edward Teller, a physicist involved in the development of both the atomic and hydrogen weapons; Henry Kissinger, who fled from Germany to America in the 1930s and became a major theoretician of the policy of "nuclear deterrence"; and Herman Kahn, whose study *On Thermonuclear War* had seriously considered the idea of a "doomsday device," though ultimately rejecting it as unreliable.

Unlike many other Kubrick films, *Dr. Strangelove* was immediately recognized by critics as a masterpiece. It also serves as an important look at the period of Cold War paranoia.

Bibliography

Boyer, Paul. "Dr. Strangelove." *Past Imperfect: History According to the Movie.* Ed. Mark C. Carnes. New York: Henry Holt, 1996. 266-69.

George, Peter. *Red Alert.* New York: Ace, 1958.

Kagan, Norman. *The Cinema of Stanley Kubrick: New Expanded Edition.* New York: Continuum, 1989.

Linden, George W. "*Dr. Strangelove or: How I Learned to Stop Worrying and Love the Bomb.*" *Nuclear War Films.* Ed. Jack Shaheen. Carbondale: Southern Illinois UP, 1978. 58-67.

Maland, Charles. "*Dr. Strangelove* (1964): Nightmare Comedy and the Ideology of Liberal Consensus." *Hollywood as Historian: American Film in a Cultural Context.* Ed. Peter Rollins. Lexington: UP of Kentucky, 1983.

John E. O'Connor

Documentary Film, or nonfiction film, has been an important part of American popular culture from the beginning of film history. Even before the invention of motion pictures, photographers such as Eadweard Muybridge, with his animal locomotion series, demonstrated the extent to which the camera might reveal to us what realist film theorist Siegfried Kracauer has called "life in the raw."

Thus it is no accident that "documentary" has its root in the Latin *docere*, to teach. John Grierson, prime mover of the British documentary movement in the 1920s, coined the term in a review of Robert Flaherty's *Moana* (1926). The film, he wrote, "being a visual account of events in the daily life of a Polynesian youth and his family, has documentary value."

Documentary was crucial to the early development of the cinema. Indeed, film history is said to have begun in 1895, when two brothers, Louis and Auguste Lumière, publicly exhibited their first program of short films in the basement of the Grand Café in Paris. With titles such as "Workers Leaving the Lumière Factory," "Arrival of a Train" and "Feeding the Baby," the Lumières' films—"actualities," as they called them—were brief slices of life captured by the camera. According to media historian Erik Barnouw, the Lumière programs were so popular that within two years they had approximately 100 operators at work around the world, both showing their films and photographing new ones to add to a steadily increasing catalogue. Many of the new enterprising film companies that sprang up at the turn of the century produced nonfiction titles, particularly travelogues.

But when filmmakers such as Edwin S. Porter and D. W. Griffith perfected editing techniques for the purposes of advancing the story ("the classical Hollywood style"), nonfiction films were quickly eclipsed in popularity by narrative film. Documentary assumed a subsidiary position, ultimately institutionalized in movie theaters as the "newsreel," one of a series of shorts shown before the feature attraction.

Nevertheless, newsreels retained a distinct appeal. Pathé News, for example, which was begun in the U.S. by the Frenchman Charles Pathé in 1910, proved so popular that by 1912 several other companies and studios—Hearst, Universal, Paramount, and Fox—entered the newsreel field.

Yet documentary has remained on the margins of Hollywood cinema, only periodically producing a feature-length work that has managed to find distribution in commercial theaters. The first of these was the landmark *Nanook of the North* (1922), about Inuit life in the Canadian north. Directed by Robert Flaherty, a former explorer and prospector with little prior training in cinematography, *Nanook* demonstrated that fictional techniques could be successfully employed in the documentary as well. Its distributor, Paramount Studios, even commissioned Flaherty to go to the South Pacific to "make another *Nanook.*"

In the 1930s, perhaps because of the momentous social changes wrought by economic failure, documentary emerged as a dominant form of cultural expression in America. A network of local film and photo leagues developed in major American cities as a response to the avoidance of controversial material by mainstream theatrical newsreels. Together the leagues produced a worker's newsreel that concentrated on documenting the intense labor activities of the early Depression period. Many important documentary filmmakers of the time were associated with the particularly active New York Film and Photo League, and later with Frontier Films, a socially committed production company that produced a series of important films about international politics beginning in 1936.

Under Franklin Roosevelt's presidency, the Resettlement Administration sponsored a photographic unit that included Walker Evans, Dorothea Lange, and others. It moved into documentary film with Pare Lorentz's *The Plow That Broke the Plains* (1936) and *The River* (1937), about the dust bowl and the Tennessee Valley Authority, respectively. Although various government agencies had previously sponsored documentaries, Lorentz's films were the first to garner serious attention and considerable theatrical distribution. Roosevelt established the U.S. Film Service in 1938, although it died by 1940 because Congress refused to appropriate the necessary funds, largely as a result of pressure from Hollywood studios, which viewed the initiative as unfair competition against the spirit of free enterprise.

During World War II, many governments relied on the propaganda value of documentary film. By the late 1930s, filmmaking in Japan and Germany had come under firm government control. In Great Britain, documentaries helped boost morale on the home front. In the U.S., the government entered film production again when Frank Capra, a major Hollywood director who in the 1930s had made a string of successful populist comedies, oversaw for the military the production of *Why We Fight* (1942-44), a series of seven documentaries designed to provide background information about the global conflict, so as to help shake Americans from their strong isolationist position. Later, a number of other important Hollywood directors accepted military commissions, and lent their filmmaking talents to documenting the war effort. Most notably, John Ford contributed *The Battle of Midway* (1944), William Wyler made *Memphis Belle* (1944), and John Huston made *The Battle of San Pietro* (1944) and *Let There Be Light* (1945).

With the domestic prosperity of the postwar years, government sponsorship of documentary in the U.S. disappeared. In this period, documentary production was sponsored largely by industry, often with pronounced ties to government interests, and so the films tended to be conservative in both style and content. Cold War paranoia also served as a strong disincentive to originality. In addition, through the 1950s the various newsreel series ceased production as their function was increasingly taken over by television.

At the same time, Hollywood feature films began absorbing the influence of documentary. *The Naked City* (Jules Dassin, 1948) and *On the Waterfront* (Elia Kazan, 1954), for example, featured actual locations in New York City to enhance their dramatic realism. Independent filmmakers such as Morris Engel (*The Little Fugitive*, 1953) and John Cassavetes (*Shadows*, begun in 1959 but not released until 1961) began making feature films with portable equipment, allowing for greater improvisation on the part of the actors.

The most notable exception to the new conservatism in documentary was the CBS-TV series *See It Now*, started in 1951 by Edward R. Murrow and Fred Friendly. Murrow's stature as a war correspondent and his high administrative position at CBS enabled him to produce the show with relative freedom. In 1953-54 he successfully exposed the demagoguery of Sen. Joseph McCarthy, a prime mover behind the Cold War blacklists and witch hunts.

In the 1960s with the development of new portable 16 mm equipment, the documentary film underwent a significant revolution. The new reflex (through the lens) capability meant that the previously bulky camera (which Richard Leacock had earlier referred to as a "sort of monster") no longer had to be the center of pro-filmic events but could follow them as they happened. For the first time filmmakers could enter into the very situation they were documenting as it happened—what Stephen Mamber has called an "uncontrolled cinema." The tripod was abandoned, and the camera gained a new mobility carried on the shoulder of the operator.

Thus was born a new observational style in documentary, one which allowed filmmakers to rebel against both the style and ideology previously identified with the Griersonian tradition. As a result, documentary experienced a simultaneous revitalization in North America and Europe. Although there are differences between the various national movements (British Free Cinema, the National Film Board of Canada's "Candid Eye" series, the French *cinema vérité* films of Jean Rouch and Chris Marker), they shared the premise that truth could now be discovered, not imposed, as a result of the new relatively unobtrusive technology.

In New York, a group of young filmmakers organized by Robert Drew (see entry below) in 1958 began making films for Time, Inc., in an attempt to achieve a more truthful "pictorial journalism," as Louis de Rochemont had described his *March of Time* newsreels. Known as the Drew Associates, the group included many of the pioneering figures of American observational cinema, including D. A. Penne-baker, Albert Maysles, and Richard Leacock. The Drew Associates sought to be invisible observers of events transpiring before the camera—ideally, like a "fly on the wall," in Leacock's famous phrase.

The Drew filmmakers were able to produce a remarkable series of 19 pioneering films for television, beginning with *Primary* and ending with *Crisis: Behind a Presidential Commitment* in 1963 (see entry). Together they constitute a singular moment in the history of television documentary, along with Frederick Wiseman's series of institutional documentaries broadcast irregularly on PBS and the vastly popular historical chronicles by Ken Burns (see entry).

This impetus of observational film reached its height in documentaries such as *An American Family*, Craig Gilbert's 12-part series broadcast on public television in 1973, which sought to capture the unadorned life of one particular family.

The heightened political polarization of the Vietnam era influenced the pronounced partisanship of many documentaries, as in the work of Peter Davis (*The Selling of the Pentagon*, 1971; *Hearts and Minds*, 1974). The former film, shown as a CBS news documentary, was broadcast in prime time and its examination of the military's public relations efforts in southeast Asia had considerable impact, resulting in part in the Pentagon's withdrawal of some of its war-promotion films. (Indeed, the widespread protest against the war itself was said to be fueled by the reality footage beamed into American homes on daily newscasts.) The introduction in the 1960s of video portapaks and public access of local cable TV allowed for grassroots concerns to be heard. Some filmmakers, such as Emile de Antonio, established themselves as counterculture heroes by making documentaries that exposed government corruption (*Point of Order*, 1964, about the 1954 Army-McCarthy Senate hearings) or challenged official policies (*Rush to Judgment*, 1967, about the report of the Warren Commission). Today much documentary practice continues to be politically engaged, and some films (*Harlan County, USA*, 1976; *The Panama Deception*, 1992) are able to find limited commercial distribution. The appeal of the engaged documentary has filtered down to mainstream popular culture in the exposé form of such shows as *60 Minutes*, the most successful nonfiction series in television history, on the air since 1968 (see entry).

Subcultures and various interest groups have used the documentary successfully to help develop a sense of identity and solidarity. In the 1970s feminist documentary filmmakers developed a distinctively intimate, "talking-head" style that promoted the shared discovery of mutual experience with the viewer, as in *With Babies and Banners* (1977) and *The Life and Times of Rosie the Riveter* (1980). Similarly, documentaries about gay issues, such as *Word Is Out* (1977) and *The Life and Times of Harvey Milk* (1984), appeared with the emergence of the gay pride movement in the 1980s. And much of the seemingly antithetical tradition of experimental or avant-garde film, especially since the emergence of the New American Cinema movement in the late 1950s, also has been informed by the documentary aesthetic, as in the "diary" style of Stan Brakhage or Jonas Mekas.

Many recent documentaries seek to uncover ambiguities of truth rather than a unified, singular truth. One of the most significant of these, *The Thin Blue Line* (1987), for example, foregrounds its constructedness with highly theatricalized reenactments of the murder it investigates, yet was so effective in exposing an apparent miscarriage of justice that it was largely responsible for getting the convicted man released after years of imprisonment. Stylistically, nonfiction films now often employ a more pronounced mixing of modes, combining elements of fiction and documentary, or creating an ambiguity concerning their documentary status, as in *Madonna: Truth or Dare* (1992). Others, such as the commercially successful *Roger and Me* (1989), establish an unabashedly personal tone reminiscent of the New Journalism of the 1960s, freely intermixing the personal voice of the reporter with the reportage.

Bibliography

Barnouw, Erik. *Documentary: A History of the Non-Fiction Film.* New York: Oxford UP, 1974.

Barsam, Richard. *Nonfiction Film: A Critical History.* New York: Dutton, 1973.

Ellis, Jack C. *The Documentary Idea: A Critical History of English-Language Documentary Film and Video.* Englewood Cliffs: Prentice-Hall, 1989.

Jacobs, Lewis, ed. *The Documentary Tradition.* 2d ed. New York: Norton, 1979.

Nichols, Bill. *Representing Reality: Issues and Concepts in Documentary.* Bloomington: Indiana State UP, 1991.

Scott, William. *Documentary Expression and Thirties America.* New York: Oxford UP, 1973.

Barry Keith Grant

See also
Television Docudrama

Dogs occupy an important place (as do all kinds of animals) in almost all aspects of popular culture. The prize for longevity goes to Nipper, an English mixed-breed terrier who was painted listening to his master's voice speaking from a cylinder phonograph. The painting was bought by the Gramophone Company, provided that the artist, Francis Barraud would paint out the cylinder and replace it with a gramophone disc. The American inventor of the disc recording, Emile Berliner, saw the painting in London, and on his return in 1900 registered the dog-and-trumpet and His Master's Voice as trademarks for what was to become the Victor Talking Machine Company and, in 1929, RCA Victor records. On record labels and in very collectible company premium ceramics and other objects, Nipper lives on. In the 1980s, Nipper acquired a pup named Chipper, and these live dogs appeared at trade shows and in television commercials. So popular was Chipper that the puppies were much sought after as they outgrew cuteness. Second in longevity is Tige, the rather nondescript bulldog companion of the early comic-strip character Buster Brown. The strip first appeared in 1902, but at the 1904 St. Louis World Fair, the artist, R. F. Outcault, met an executive of the local Brown Shoe Company who bought rights to Buster and Tige for their line of children's shoes. Long after the strip had ceased, they lived on in give-away comic books, radio ads (where "That's my dog Tige!" gained currency), and, of course, in the brand name shoes.

Other long-lived comic strip dogs were Little Orphan Annie's Sandy and Blondie and Dagwood's Daisy. Largely cast as supporting players with canine limitations, Sandy and Daisy could not match the popularity of Snoopy in Charles Schulz's *Peanuts* strip (see entry). Snoopy was originally just a sort-of-beagle pet of Charlie Brown's, but by the 1970s he began to upstage his owner, climbing trees to loom like a hungry buzzard, or fantasizing a life as a World War I air ace, challenging the Red Baron to dog-fights.

Animated cartoons brought Mickey Mouse's pet dog into being in 1930 as an anonymous bloodhound, but he soon was a star with the planetary name of Pluto. Goofy, originally Dippy Dawg in 1932, was more of a hayseed human with a houndlike head. Disney produced a full-length dog story in 1955; *Lady and the Tramp* had talking, singing dogs (cocker spaniel and mongrel terrier, respectively), but the animation derived from close observation of living animals. Disney's *101 Dalmatians* (1961) appealed to many with its doggy point-of-view and proved popular enough to deserve a whole new live-action remake in 1996.

For television, Terrytoons introduced in 1957 Tom Terrific, with Mighty Manfred, his mastiff-like Wonder Dog. The appeal was primarily for the Romper Room set, but when Hanna-Barbera Studios brought blue-pelted Huckleberry Hound into being in 1958, TV animated series began to touch older audiences. Their prime-time animated sitcom, the *Jetsons,* featured a futuristic Great Dane, Astro, the name being a play on Nick and Nora Charles' Asta. Asta, a wired-haired fox terrier in *The Thin Man* film series (1934-47), was mainly known for the trick of covering his eyes with his paws when trouble loomed.

In 1922, the German shepherd Rin Tin Tin appeared in *The Man from Hell's River.* His popularity became so great that he got top billing over humans, and with Darryl Zanuck writing some of his silent scripts, Rin Tin Tin kept the Warner Studio alive for several years. Other film dogs with some notoriety include Dorothy's Toto in the *Wizard of Oz* and Roy Rogers's Bullet. Disney Studios produced many dog films: *Old Yeller* (1957) and *The Incredible Journey* (1963) were serious dramas, while *The Shaggy Dog* (1957) and *Shaggy D.A.* (1976) are farces, featuring talking Old English sheepdogs. *The Incredible Journey* (1963) was faithful to Sheila Burnford's book with a yellow labrador retriever, a bull terrier, and a Siamese cat crossing the Canadian wilderness; the 1993 remake, *Homeward Bound,* moved it to California, softened animals to an American Staffordshire, a golden retriever, and a Himalayan cat, and provided them with voices and feminist wisecracks. *Homeward Bound II* (1996) had them lost in the San Francisco wilderness. St. Bernards, with all the popular traditions as rescue dogs (always with a cask of brandy) would seem naturals, but the adaptation of Stephen King's *Cujo* (1983) features a rabies-crazed Saint, while *Beethoven* (1992) and *Beethoven's 2nd* (1993) are genial comedy adventures. On television, of course, the best-known dog has been Lassie, the collie (see entry). Eddie, a pesky Jack Russell terrier, on *Frasier* (1993-), is a relative newcomer to the animal TV star ranks.

In popular literature, Jack London's *Call of the Wild* (1903) with a half St. Bernard sled dog and *White Fang* (1906) with a one-quarter dog, three-quarter wolf are harshly naturalistic and have the status of classics. Both were filmed more than once. For several generations, the best-known dog in literature may have been Dick and Jane's "Spot" in the basic primer series, but aside from Eric Knight's 1940 *Lassie Come-Home,* the most durable have been the collie stories of Albert Payson Terhune (1822-1942), beginning with *Lad: A Dog* in 1919. Eighty years later, ten Terhune titles are still in print.

Aside from fiction and the media, dogs are a vital part of American popular culture. The Westminster Kennel Club's annual show in Madison Square Garden boasts that it is the second oldest continuously held sporting event in the United States. The first Westminster Show was in 1877, while the Kentucky Derby was first run in 1875. "Conformation" shows (the "beauty contests" that validate the choicest breeding stock) are but one of the aspects of popular dog sports. Field trials for hunters and retrievers, Shutzehund for guard dogs, tracking and herding trials, obedience and agility trials (even some for non-pedigreed mixed breeds) are held all over the nation. Over 10,000 dog shows and trials are held annually under American Kennel Club rules. The World Wide Web has "virtual dog shows" for which proud dog owners submit photos of their pets. There are innumerable unofficial local dog events, such as frisbee-fielding contests, Halloween dress-up contests, and kids' dog parades. The commercial sport of racing greyhounds after a mechanical lure developed in the 1920s and there is a Greyhound Hall of Fame in Abilene, KS.

"Fad breeds" are those whose popularity shows rapid climbs and falls in AKC registrations, often influenced by movies: Saint Bernards and Dalmatians are two breeds whose popularity was influenced by the *Beethoven* movies and *101 Dalmatians.* The remake of the latter film prompted Dalmatian breeder clubs to alert the public to the importance of responsible breeders. "Back-yard breeders" of fad dogs have been shown to "ruin" blood-lines, as happened to cocker spaniels in the later 1940s.

Bibliography

The AKC's World of the Pure-Bred Dog. New York: Howell, 1983.

"Brown Shoe Company." *International Directory of Company Histories V.* Detroit: St. James, 1992.

Maken, Neil. "Nipper: Alive in Our Hearts and Very Collectible." *Antiques & Collecting* Aug. 1994.

Mandevill, John. "1996 Registration Statistics." *AKC Gazette* 114: 4.

Solomon, Charles. *Enchanted Drawings: The History of Animation.* New York: Knopf, 1989.

Fred E. H. Schroeder

Dolls, in all their variety, are among the earliest and most loved of American children's toys. Defined as replicas of the human form used as playthings, dolls function as children's companions—objects of affection to be clutched and treasured—but they also serve as important cultural reflectors. Changing trends in dolls shed light on the playing styles of children over the years, particularly the connection between toys and children's aspirations for the future. In addition, they reveal adult attitudes toward children, parenting, beauty, fashion, lifestyle, and media personalities, for it is primarily adults who design, manufacture, and purchase dolls. One whose image is transformed into a doll—such as Charlie Chaplin, Shirley Temple, or E.T.—is one highly recognized by society at the time, as well as reflective of some quality it values. Finally, dolls are the product of a manufacturing business, showcasing advances in technology and marketing strategies. Dolls in America express all of these functions.

Even before the first colonists arrived, American Indians sewed rag dolls for their youngsters, and in 1585, the first English colonists landing at North Carolina's Roanoke Island included dolls among their gifts for the Indians. As more settlers arrived in America, they brought with them dolls from Europe, such as a wooden doll that William Penn brought to Pennsylvania in 1699 (today regarded as one of the oldest surviving American toys).

The first patent for a doll was issued in the United States in 1858, and by the late 1800s, an American doll industry, accompanied by the production of doll houses and other paraphernalia, had begun to emerge. In many cases, however, dolls' heads continued to be imported from Europe and attached to American-made dolls' bodies. Philip Goldsmith (1844-1994), one of the first American doll makers, operated a Cincinnati factory that made and distributed dolls and dolls' bodies. He is representative of a group of early doll manufacturers who established factories in the Cincinnati, OH, to Covington, KY, region. Other doll makers set up businesses in the New York, Philadelphia, and New England areas.

Two of the best-known classic American doll makers were Rose O'Neill and Madame Beatrice Alexander. In 1909, O'Neill, of Wilkes-Barre, PA, drew a design for the cherubic Kewpie doll, which attained wide appeal over the years as various doll makers produced different versions of it. Madame Alexander, the daughter of a Russian native who opened the first doll hospital in the U.S., was born in 1895 and founded her own doll manufacturing company in New York in 1923. She began by making cloth dolls—many based on figures from literature—with painted faces showing detail and personality, a style prompting one journalist to write, "Not only does Madame Alexander put soles on her dolls but she also puts souls into them." Madame Alexander then embarked on the type of doll that would become her trademark: beautiful, idealized collectible dolls made, first, of rubber and, later, of plastics and vinyl. Regarding her dolls as objects of beauty, Madame Alexander noted in an interview in 1977 with Patricia Smith, "I believe that children should look like dolls and dolls [should] look like children. At a very early age, I became aware that the love of a doll by a child has the same depth as the love of a mother for her child." One of the oldest surviving American doll manufacturers, the Madame Alexander Doll Company continues to design elaborate dolls reflecting its founder's philosophy, and many of the dolls have become valuable collectibles.

The growth of the doll industry in America has been closely tied to historical events as well as to advancements in doll-making materials. Prior to World War I, the French and the Germans dominated the world's doll-making market. However, the war so disrupted doll manufacturing that they were unable to regain their command after the war, paving the way for American companies. After the war, as European doll makers tried to reclaim their popularity, American manufacturers priced their dolls far below their competitors and waged an advertising campaign urging Americans to buy domestically made dolls. "American dolls for Americans" and "Made in America for American boys and girls" became popular slogans. By the end of World War II, Germany had fallen as a world leader in doll manufacturing, and America gained a stronghold. Although Germany had been known for its high-quality bisque dolls, American doll makers showed incredible diversity in their types of dolls, producing—at various times, due to both aesthetics and availability—dolls of wood, wax, china, bisque, papier-mâché, cloth, celluloid, rubber, composition (sawdust and glue), plastics, and vinyl. As doll-making materials improved, becoming more durable, attractive, and innovative, American manufacturers adopted them.

A very popular doll from the early 20th century was created when Johnny Gruelle took an old, faceless rag doll, drew a face with button eyes and a red triangular nose, and gave it to his daughter Marcella. Dubbed Raggedy Ann, the doll became Marcella's favorite possession. Marcella contracted tuberculosis, and to entertain her, Gruelle made up stories featuring Raggedy Ann. Marcella died at the age of 14, and, in 1918, Gruelle published the stories as a tribute. In order to generate interest in the books, booksellers placed them in their store windows alongside Raggedy Ann dolls, and both sold. Raggedy Andy dolls followed, along with other characters from the stories, notably Beloved Belindy, an early black doll who was widely marketed in the Sears, Roebuck catalog.

Other popular dolls bore the image of media figures: film stars, such as Charlie Chaplin, Shirley Temple, Judy Garland, Jane Withers, Deanna Durbin, and Disney's animated creations; comic-strip characters, such as Popeye, Buck Rogers, and Superman; and radio personalities, such as Charlie McCarthy and Amos 'n' Andy. The Depression years were particularly dark for the doll industry, but coveted, media tie-in dolls—especially Ideal Toys' Shirley Temple, one and a half million of which were sold during 1934—

helped some companies stay afloat. The Shirley Temple doll's popularity during that period is telling: it suggests a reverence for the image of the happy, well-adjusted child at a time when the birthrate in America was down and many parents were unable to indulge their children because of economic hardships.

Although the pretelevision media had an unmistakable influence on the doll industry, the impact of television was much more dramatic and long-lasting. By the mid-1950s, doll manufacturers had the ability to reach the large audience of baby-boom children directly, through television advertising. Further, the production characteristics of television inspired doll makers to design new types of dolls that, in television commercials, would appear irresistible to viewers. Perhaps no company understood this better than Mattel Toys. In 1959, Mattel introduced an 11.5-inch plastic fashion doll named Barbie (see entry). Possessing large breasts, a tiny waist, well-formed legs, and a casual ponytail, Barbie appeared to be the perfect 1950s teenager—and little girls loved her. Because Barbie had no specific personality, girls could project on her any characteristics they wished; thus, she became a vehicle through which little girls could act out their dreams. Crucial to Barbie's popularity was her diverse wardrobe, which was heavily promoted on television. In the years that followed, Mattel provided Barbie with a boyfriend named Ken, various friends and relatives, regularly updated clothes and accessories, and a slew of possessions, including a house, Ferrari, and sauna. Although Barbie went on to become the most popular doll in history, she generated many critics who object to what she represents: blatant consumerism, an over-emphasis on sexual attractiveness, fashion, and leisure rather than more serious pursuits, and an exaggerated physical profile unattainable by real women. Nevertheless, Barbie inspired a host of other teenage fashion dolls, among them Tammy, Tressy, and Dawn.

Barbie was not the only doll to achieve popularity in the early television decades. Given the era's relative placidity, with its emphasis on the traditional family, it is not surprising that many infant and child dolls appeared, many sporting new features highlighted on television commercials. Mattel created a line of talking dolls, such as Chatty Cathy, Chatty Baby, and Charmin' Chatty, whose appeal was the novelty of their talking mechanisms. Also, unlike Barbie, these dolls had physical imperfections, such as buck teeth, a pot belly, or a need to wear glasses, making them more like real children. Other realistic dolls, most of them made of plastic and having rooted hair and eyes that opened and closed, appeared, each with a different gimmick: Betsy Wetsy drank and wet; Little Miss Echo contained a recording device that repeated what a child said; Kissy hugged and kissed; Bye Bye Baby waved goodbye; Baby First Step walked; and Baby Alive, advertised as "the closest thing to a real baby that any doll could be," did everything. By the 1970s, as many began to question traditional gender roles, baby dolls continued to flood the market, priming little girls, as dolls always have, for future roles as mothers.

In addition to charges of sexism, American doll makers and their advertisers have also met with accusations of racism. In *Sold Separately: Parents and Children in Consumer Culture*, Ellen Seiter notes that "U.S. designers of dolls have always glorified light skin, blond hair, blue eyes, tiny noses, and thin lips. When commercials are set in the upstairs bedroom and advertise the pinkest, most traditionally feminine toys—baby dolls, clay flowers, kitchens—toy commercials use only white models." Although ethnic dolls are under-represented among American doll manufacturers, some have gone on to achieve popularity, in some cases further promoting racist attitudes. For example, among rag dolls, the black mammy character, with her apron and head bandanna, has been a staple. More positively, Mattel was one of the first major American doll makers to take steps to promote ethnic dolls, introducing African-American Barbies in the 1960s and a series of multiracial dolls in the 1980s. A Julia doll, based on the Diahann Carroll character from the television show of the same name, joined the Barbie line in 1969, and, not surprisingly, Ideal countered the same year with its own black personality doll, Diana Ross of the Supremes.

Although toy manufacturers generally targeted dolls to girls, by the 1960s they developed new doll lines to tap the boys' market. Known as "action figures," boys' dolls entered the toy arena with a vengeance in 1964 when Hasbro introduced G.I. Joe. Although metal and paper soldiers had been sold in America since the 1800s, G.I. Joe marked a new direction in boys' dolls. Twelve inches tall, made of plastic with 21 moving joints and variations in hair and eye color, G.I. Joe bore the unmistakable image of a doll and thus became one of the first socially acceptable and commercially profitable dolls for boys. The first G.I. Joe series consisted of four World War II figures with uniforms and equipment reflective of the four branches of the U.S. military. But this was only the beginning. The G.I. Joe line underwent numerous expansions, adding, for example, a Jeep and the first black G.I. Joe in 1965 and a talking G.I. Joe in 1967. G.I. Joe racked up impressive sales until 1978, when Hasbro suspended the line. The official reason was the rising price of oil used in making the plastic for the dolls, but public sentiment opposing violence and war during the Vietnam era was also a factor.

Not surprisingly, G.I. Joe exerted a formidable influence on the doll industry. Despite public criticism against toys depicting violence, in 1975, Kenner unveiled its popular Six Million Dollar Man, and, in 1977, Star Wars action figures, produced by Kenner and MPC, sold three hundred million units, making them the year's blockbuster toys. The He-Man and the Masters of the Universe collection earned Mattel $35 million in 1984, and more recently, Teenage Mutant Ninja Turtles and Power Rangers, packaged with their weapons, have carried on the action toys trend. The popularity of these smaller action figures led to the return of G.I. Joe in 1982.

The 1980s saw the birth of toy-based television shows, also called program-length commercials (see Children's Network Programming). Animated programs such as *Strawberry Shortcake* and *My Little Pony* were designed expressly to promote doll lines. Kenner's Strawberry Shortcake became America's top-selling doll after she appeared on video, triggering sales of over $1 billion in Strawberry Shortcake dolls and related products. In the 1980s, Hasbro sold 150 million units of My Little Pony, which encompassed two classic elements of dolls' appeal, hair care and fashion.

Even without promotional television shows, however, other dolls broke sales records. Steven Spielberg's hit movie *E.T.* debuted in July 1982, and by September consumers had snatched up 15 million E.T. dolls. The extraterrestrial also went on to become the best-selling toy of the year's Christmas season. The following year, Coleco struck a chord with its Cabbage Patch Kids, distinctive infant, sculpted and stuffed fabric dolls, each given a different first and middle name. Customers hoping to "adopt" a Cabbage Patch Kid went to great lengths to get them since production was unable to keep up with the great demand. In 1984, there were sales of $5 million in Cabbage Patch Kids, and the following year $600,000. The dolls remained on the best-seller list until 1978, after which Coleco, which had pumped too much of its assets into a single product, filed for bankruptcy. The E.T., Cabbage Patch Kids, and troll doll crazes suggest that children crave, along with their perfect Barbies, imperfect, almost ugly, dolls that seem to be longing for care and affection.

By the 1990s, doll sales, including action figures, had dropped considerably, except for Barbie. At the same time, doll collecting emerged as one of America's fastest growing hobbies, suggesting a growing nostalgia for the past as well as a yearning for the objects of childhood. Dolls have remained one of children's most valued and familiar playthings, and if their history in America is any indication, their longevity, in some form or another, is ensured.

Bibliography

Anderton, Johana Gast. *Twentieth Century Dolls: From Bisque to Vinyl*. Rev. ed. Lombard: Wallace-Homestead, 1974.

Bach, Jean. *The Warner Collector's Guide to Dolls*. New York: Main Street, 1982.

Gerwat-Clark, Brenda. *The Collector's Book of Dolls*. Secaucus: Chartwell, 1987.

Seiter, Ellen. *Sold Separately: Parents and Children in Consumer Culture*. New Brunswick: Rutgers UP, 1993.

Stern, Sydney Ladensohn, and Ted Schoenhaus. *Toyland: The High-Stakes Game of the Toy Industry*. Chicago: Contemporary, 1990.

Kathy Merlock Jackson

See also

Toys

Domestic Appliances. Changes in the American home during the 19th and 20th centuries have centered in large part on the introduction of new appliances. Using the factory system as a model, 19th-century home planners and domestic theorists looked to mechanized gadgets and appliances to improve efficiency and decrease women's labor in caring for the home. Inventors registered patents for the early version of most modern appliances by the mid-19th century, often adapting their design principles from industrial equipment. While smaller hand-operated domestic tools were essentially perfected by the 1860s, larger appliances were not widely available until the early years of the 20th century, when technology, the invention of the small motor, and widespread electrification made them compact enough and sufficiently automated to be practical in the middle-class home. Advanced technology coupled with increased factory productivity, improved transportation, and a burgeoning advertising industry made most major appliances standard features of upper- and middle-class American homes by the 1930s. Nowhere were changes greater than in the kitchen. In little more than a century, cooking progressed from an open hearth to a gas or electric range. The only change in the technology of cooking since the early 20th century was the affordable production of microwave ovens in the 1970s and 1980s, but microwaves have not replaced traditional technology and are mainly used as auxiliary appliances.

As with the introduction of the range, the development of mechanical refrigeration dramatically changed the routine of early-20th-century households. No longer was grocery shopping a necessary part of each day. Basic designs for both electric and gas refrigerators existed in the 19th century, but technical obstacles, such as the unavailability of small electric motors, delayed their adoption for domestic use. Cumbersome refrigerators appeared in homes in 1919, featuring dark wood walls that made them look similar to the iceboxes they replaced. In the 1920s, General Electric and Kelvinator found ways to solve the size problem as well as the need for total automation, and mass production of refrigerators began.

Dishwashers and washing machines were designed and patented in the mid-19th century, but they were not manufactured for domestic use until after the turn of the century. Requiring hand cranking and constant attention from the women who operated them, these early models were questionable as labor-saving devices. These appliances point to the fallacy of assuming that automation in the home necessarily freed the woman from time spent on household duties. Several studies conducted in the 1970s concluded that the average amount of time spent on housework by full-time housewives remained relatively constant between 1920 and 1970 despite the introduction of numerous "labor-saving" appliances.

Small appliances proliferated during the first quarter of the 20th century, as lower production costs brought them within reach of the middle-class home. By the 1930s, consumers could purchase a wide variety of appliances: electric hot plates, grills, coffee makers, toasters, egg cookers, mixers, blenders, can openers, waffle irons, corn poppers, and bottle warmers, as well as room heaters and fans. Electric irons and vacuum cleaners ranked among the best selling of small appliances. Door-to-door sales were in large part responsible for the ubiquity of the vacuum cleaner in American homes.

From the early days of *I Love Lucy* through more contemporary television comedies, the stock kitchen scene of electrical appliances running out of control, wreaking havoc in the kitchen, suggests the mixed blessings and perceived fears of new technology for the home.

Bibliography

Cowan, Ruth Schwartz. *More Work for Mother: The Ironies of Household Technology from the Open Hearth to the Microwave*. New York: Basic, 1983.

Giedion, Siegfried. *Mechanization Takes Command: A Contribution to Anonymous History*. New York: Oxford UP, 1948.

Strasser, Susan. *Never Done: A History of American Housework*. New York: Pantheon, 1982.

Cristine Levenduski

See also

Kitchens

Domestic Decorations. Decorating the spaces in which we live is an important cultural practice, one in which we use materials and objects to show ourselves and others who we are, and that this space is "home." Most of us must face, at one time or another in life, taking up residence in a space that seems strange, impersonal, and uncomfortable. Domestic objects can have several functions that suit them for use in household display and decoration. They can be functional, they can communicate cultural meanings, and they can be pleasurable.

Besides utilitarian objects with decorative value, common types of decorative artifacts include photographs, heirlooms, souvenirs, pictures (original artwork or reproductions), holiday decorations, and trophies. The display of family photographs, a widespread practice among all social classes, according to sociologist David Halle, serves as an important sign of our relationships to others and our history of life experiences.

Souvenirs represent their extraordinary or unusual origins, recalling experiences of travel or important events which extended beyond the everyday routine. Souvenirs can be important means for remembering experiences which are associated with their acquisition. Displaying souvenirs may also communicate the general value a person places on travel, or afford the person a level of social status associated with worldly experience.

Pictures are another common type of domestic decoration, and may be one of a kind or mass-produced. Halle's research indicates that some subject matter preferences vary across different social classes: pictures of religious figures are more likely to appear in working-class homes, while abstract art is more likely to appear in the homes of the urban, upper-middle class. Depictions of calm, tranquil landscapes devoid of people are the most likely pictures to be prominently displayed in homes of all social classes. These landscape pictures reflect an orientation to nature as a place of retreat and leisure. For many urban and suburban residents, landscape pictures offer a substitute experience for nature; for others, landscape pictures evoke memories of pleasant experiences in nature.

Whether modest and casual or elaborate and formal, temporary decorating transforms domestic space into a sacred space for acknowledging the ritual time of passing seasons, religious observances, holidays, and secular celebrations.

Like other decorative artifacts, the trophy may function as a symbol, that is, a metaphoric representation of meanings that are not explicitly (or consciously) recognized or expressed. These meanings can be personal, but are also widely shared—albeit implicitly—by others in the culture. Thus, the trophy may symbolically express feelings of belonging, strengthen social bonds between the trophy's owner and other sport team members, generate fantasies of grander sporting triumphs, and so on.

The meanings imbedded in domestic decorations make the home a key site for learning and acculturation. The home is the primary site for children's initiation into cultural life. It is where they first encounter meaningful objects, learn cultural behavior from other family members, and actively engage in the process of developing their own cultural identities. The aesthetic and symbolic content of toys, room decorations, and family artifacts often make powerful and lasting impressions on a child's aesthetic preferences and cultural understandings. The cultural behaviors of older family members are often the primary models from which children develop their own behaviors for producing and using images and artifacts. African-American writer bell hooks vividly recalls how her grandmother, and her grandmother's house, were powerful influences on her developing knowledge of beauty and self: "From her I learn about aesthetics, the yearning for beauty that she tells me is the predicament of heart that makes our passion real.... Her house is a place where I am learning to look at things, where I am learning how to belong in space. In rooms full of objects, crowded with things, I am learning to recognize myself."

A key social factor affecting object relations, decorating practices, and the very notion of domesticity is gender. The gender designations associated with particular objects reflect fundamental cultural assumptions about the nature of masculine and feminine identities. Decorative objects that express fertility, nurturance, or seductiveness tend to be seen as feminine; while objects associated with strength, endurance, and bravery tend to be seen as masculine. Moreover, the rooms in a home may be designated and then decorated according to masculine or feminine qualities, depending on the symbolic and actual activities associated with the particular space. But by far, it is the feminine qualities associated with the concept of "domesticity" that have profoundly influenced the practices of home decoration. Thus, the domestic world connotes a place with qualities of life that distinguish it from the world of business and public life, a world that is designated as having masculine qualities.

The upper classes in the U.S. of the early 18th century followed the lead of their English counterparts. Thomas Jefferson's intense interest in architecture and interior design can be seen as simply an outstanding example of a common preoccupation of American and English gentlemen of his era. But as the century unfolded, vast social, economic, and political changes brought changes to the nature and function of American homes. American women's points of view on house design and decorating gained increasing dominance, in part due to the writings of women authorities like Catherine Beecher and Harriet Beecher Stowe. These influential women challenged the prevailing notions of a gentleman's house based solely on masculine ideas of visual order, retreat from the world, and a place of ease. They argued for the woman's perspective of the home as a place of domestic

work, and forcefully promoted Victorian ideals of domesticity and the role of women as the rightful directors of the family and household.

The eclecticism and density of Victorian decorations was challenged by the "industrial aesthetic," which characterized modernist styles of home decoration in the early to middle 20th century. In marked contrast to preceding tastes, modernist styles of home decoration favored the image of efficiency over coziness, and stripped-down austerity over complex patterns and furnishing arrangements. The domestic environment was, as much as possible, to imitate industrial and commercial environments. In this vision of the home, little value or space was given to the symbolic and signifying functions that decorative objects and memorabilia fulfilled for the inhabitants.

Today's home decorating practices reflect many of these historical precedents, but also influences from advertising, industry, and technology, as well as current social and cultural trends. We are constantly presented with visions of how American homes ought to be: in magazines, movies and television, advertising, museums, literature and art, and merchandise displays. From them we learn the exemplars of "home" that are currently dominant in the culture, and against which we are to evaluate our individual homes.

Bibliography

Csikszentmihalyi, Mihaly, and Eugene Rochberg-Halton. *The Meaning of Things: Domestic Symbols and the Self.* Cambridge: Cambridge UP, 1981.

Foy, Jessica H., and Thomas J. Schlereth, eds. *American Home Life, 1880-1930: A Social History of Spaces and Services.* Knoxville: U of Tennessee P, 1992.

Halle, David. *Inside Culture: Art and Class in the American Home.* Chicago: U of Chicago P, 1993.

hooks, bell. "An Aesthetic of Blackness." *Yearning.* Toronto: Between the Lines, 1990. 103-13.

Rybczynski, Witold. *Home: A Short History of an Idea.* New York: Viking Penguin, 1987.

Cathy Mullen

Donahue, "Big Daddy" Tom (1928-1975), widely recognized as the father of underground FM radio because of his radically different radio programming practices at KMPX-FM and later KSAN-FM, San Francisco, was born Thomas Coman in South Bend, IN. By age 19, Donahue had served with the U.S. Army doing criminal intelligence work. After his discharge, Donahue married his first wife, Grace, in 1948, and began his first radio job at WTIP-AM, Charleston, WV, as host of *Uncle Tom's Gabbin'*. After a brief stint at WINX, Washington, DC, in 1950, Donahue moved to then-jazz-formatted WIBG-AM, Philadelphia, in late 1950. While at WIBG, Donahue participated in local politics under his given name. During this same period, Donahue also began eating his way to "Big Daddy" proportions, expanding from a trim 175 pounds to an eventual weight of over 400 pounds.

In 1958, WIBG went to a Top 40 approach, mainly at the urging of Donahue. WIBG soon became a dominant AM rock 'n' roll station. Although Donahue and fellow WIBG announcer Bobby Mitchell were investigated for payola allegations during 1959-60, no formal charges were filed. However, Donahue and Mitchell left Philadelphia as a result. Mitchell went to San Francisco's KYA-AM, Donahue to Wilmington, DE, where he did a call-in show until joining Mitchell at KYA in 1961. Until 1965, Donahue and Mitchell operated a number of related businesses while at KYA, including a record label (Autumn Records), a nightclub, a music tipsheet, and a radio consultant service. Mitchell died of Hodgkin's disease in 1968.

In 1965, the FCC again investigated Donahue for allegations of payola and plugola. He was officially cleared of any wrongdoing. Between the time Donahue left KYA in 1965 and the time he began broadcasting on KMPX-FM, Donahue apparently experimented with hallucinogens while mulling over his ideas about radio programming. By the spring of 1967, Donahue had formulated a radio programming style that would be antithetical to the style of Top 40, a style reliant on personable announcers, a lack of hype, no jingles, and extended passages of music either as individual cuts or as theme montages. This style debuted on KMPX-FM on April 7, 1967, as "underground" or "progressive" rock. Its success coincided with the youth movement which converged on San Francisco during 1967's "summer of peace and love."

A disagreement with KMPX-FM owner, Leon Crosby, in March 1968, caused Donahue and most of the KMPX airstaff to migrate to Metromedia's KSAN-FM, where Donahue remained until his death, from a heart attack attributed to his excessive weight.

Bibliography
Krieger, Susan. *Hip Capitalism.* Beverly Hills: Sage, 1979.
Ladd, Jim. *Radio Waves: Life and Revolution on the FM Dial.* New York: St. Martin's, 1991.

Steven O. Shields

Donna Reed Show, The (1958-1966), was the very essence of wholesome TV sitcoms. At the start of every episode, Dad and kids each received a lunchbox and a kiss from a pretty woman wearing a crisp shirtwaist dress, a string of pearls, and an every-hair-in-place do. When they're gone, she leaned against the door and smiled to herself with satisfaction.

When the series began, Donna Reed (1921-86) was known mostly for wholesome parts in movies, her role in Frank Capra's *It's a Wonderful Life* (1946), and her Academy Award-winning role as Alma, a prostitute, in *From Here to Eternity* (1955).

On the show, she played Donna Stone, perfect mother, and perfect wife to husband Alex, a pediatrician. Alex was played by Carl Betz (1920-78), who later starred in *Judd for the Defense.* The Stones had two perfect children: Mary, played by Shelley Fabares, and Jeff, played by Paul Petersen. In the 1963-64 season, the Stones adopted another perfect child, Trisha, played by Petersen's real-life sister, Patty Petersen.

The series was nicknamed "The Madonna Reed Show." Reed herself despised her role, considering it a two-dimensional caricature created by a sexist Hollywood establishment. She received four Emmy nominations but never won, losing usually to Jane Wyman of *Father Knows Best.*

At its finale on September 3, 1966, the show was ABC's third-oldest prime-time series. It was produced by Reed's husband, Tony Owen, in association with Screen Gems. Reruns began on daytime TV in 1964.

Bibliography
Brooks, Tim, and Earle Marsh. *The Complete Directory to Prime Time Network and Cable TV Shows, 1946-Present.* New York: Ballantine, 1995.
Royce, Brenda Scott. *Donna Reed: A Bio-Bibliography.* New York: Greenwood, 1990.

Katie Hutchinson

Doonesbury (1970-   ), by Garry Trudeau (1948-   ), began as *Bull Tales* in the *Yale Daily News* in 1968. By October 26, 1970, the strip was titled after principal character Michael Doonesbury, and premiered in 28 newspapers. The strip focused on three core characters, Doonesbury, B. D., and Marvelous Mark Slackmeyer, but gradually began to build a core ensemble that would eventually include both fictional and factual celebrities and politicians, and over 40 regularly appearing characters. Always satirical, the strip gradually took on a more political focus as the core group, which originally interacted in a college atmosphere, eventually graduated and explored the "real world."

The strip currently is syndicated in over 1,400 national and international newspapers, often appearing on the editorial page and denounced on the floor of Congress. Trudeau believes that satire is an effective form of social control, because it is so unfair, forcing its target to react and thus lose the advantage. Trudeau has been awarded over 20 honorary degrees, became the first comic strip artist to win the Pulitzer Prize for editorial cartooning in 1975, and has been made a fellow of the American Academy of Arts and Sciences.

Bibliography
Trudeau, G. B. *The Doonesbury Chronicles.* New York: Holt, 1975.
——. *Flashbacks: Twenty-Five Years of Doonesbury.* Kansas City: Andrews & McMeel, 1995.
Satin, Allan D. *A Doonesbury Index: An Index to the Syndicated Daily Newspaper Strip "Doonesbury" by G. B. Trudeau, 1970-1983.* Metuchen: Scarecrow, 1985.

Solomon Davidoff

Doors, The, stands out among rock groups from the 1960s as both defining a part of the sound of that era and also in many ways going against the trends. Songs such as "Love Street" and "Universal Soldier" covered typical love and peace themes of the time, but just as often their music dealt with the darker side of human behavior in numbers such as "People Are Strange" and "The End."

Jim Morrison (1943-71), after graduating from Florida State University, met Ray Manzarek (1935-   ) while attending UCLA film school. Manzarek was impressed with Morrison's poetry and song lyrics. They recruited drummer John Densmore (1944-   ) and guitarist Robbie Krieger (1946-   ) from a band called the Psychedelic Rangers. Manzarek played a second keyboard to cover bass lines, freeing Morrison to concentrate on vocals. The Doors had signed with Columbia/CBS on the strength of an early demo. But during most of 1966, while they played clubs around Los Angeles, nothing much came of it, so they sought and obtained an early release.

Landing a regular spot at the Whisky-a-Go-Go, they were spotted by Elektra Records founder Jac Holzman and signed. Their first album, *The Doors,* released in January of 1967, became a million-seller, partly due to the airplay given to a shortened version of one of the tracks, "Light My Fire." *Strange Days* was released in October. By then Morrison had been charged with "indecent and immoral exhibition" at a Connecticut concert.

After two Top 40 singles, "Unknown Soldier" and "Hello, I Love You," the Doors released their third million-selling album, *Waiting for the Sun,* in July of 1968, which hit No. 1 on the U.S. charts. In connection with "Unknown Soldier" the Doors made a promotional film depicting Morrison being shot, well before what today are called videos.

In July of 1969, the group released their fourth album, *The Soft Parade,* including their third million-selling single, "Touch Me." In February of 1970, they released *Morrison Hotel,* which reached No. 4 on U.S. album charts and featured the single "Roadhouse Blues." In July they released the double album *Absolutely Live,* recorded at concerts earlier in the year, which became their sixth U.S. Top 10 album in three years.

On October 30, 1970, Morrison was sentenced in Miami for indecent exposure and using profanity in public, but remained free pending an appeal. The Doors had been performing sporadically in Mexico and the U.S., and gave what was to be their last show as a quartet on December 12 in New Orleans. They recorded the *L.A. Woman* album, which would be released in April of 1971 and included the hit singles "Love Her Madly" and "Riders on the Storm." It would also reach the U.S. Top 10. Morrison made spoken-word recordings of much of his poetry in December.

With *L.A. Woman* the Doors completed their obligations to Elektra and were negotiating with major labels for a new contract. In a telephone conversation with John Densmore, Morrison indicated that he was planning music for their next album. But on July 3, 1971, his long-time companion Pamela Courson reported finding Morrison dead of an apparent heart attack in the bathtub of their Paris apartment.

Several compilation albums followed, one featuring Morrison's recorded poetry along with music by the three surviving Doors. The group was the subject of a popular feature film by Oliver Stone in 1991. The Doors' popularity and sales of their music have, if anything, increased since Morrison's death. They made a profound impact on the music of their own time and have continued to influence musicians ever since.

Bibliography

Densmore, John. *Riders on the Storm: My Life with Jim Morrison and the Doors.* New York: Dell, 1991.

Hopkins, Jerry, and Danny Sugerman. *No One Here Gets Out Alive.* New York: Warner, 1981.

Sugerman, Danny. *The Doors: The Illustrated History.* New York: Morrow, 1983.

Tobler, John, ed. *Who's Who in Rock & Roll.* New York: Crescent, 1991.

Bruce Henderson

Douglas, Kirk (1916-), and sons **Michael** (1944-), **Joel** (1947-), **Peter** (1955-), and **Eric** (1958-), are all involved in the film industry, either as actors, directors, producers, or all of these. They often work together. Kirk has had leading roles in his sons' respective productions and, when they were very young, Michael and Joel were extras in some of their father's films and plays. Although Kirk Douglas admits that he never encouraged his sons to go into show business, they have all made a career out of it, especially Michael, who since the 1970s has become a successful Hollywood actor and producer.

Kirk Douglas, born Issur Danielovitch, was raised in Amsterdam, NY. His parents, Herschel and Bryna, both of Jewish origin, fled Russia around 1908 to escape the draft into the Russo-Japanese war. Issur was the only boy in a family of seven, and as a child he experienced great poverty. His father was a peddler who left home when Issur was a teenager. Issur had to start working when he was thirteen years old to help support the family. He became interested in acting in first grade, and in high school some of his teachers noticed his talent, and encouraged him to pursue his passion for acting. At an early age he knew that he wanted to become famous. He struggled his way through high school, graduating when he was 17, sometimes working three jobs in order to bring money home and save for college. Unable to support himself through college, he covered his first years of schooling by being part janitor, part gardener at St. Lawrence University at Canton, NY. In the following years he became very active in school activities, and was elected president of the student body.

Graduating with a B.A. in 1939, Douglas decided to pursue his acting career and aimed for one of the best schools in the field, the American Academy of Dramatic Arts in New York City. This is when Issur Danielovitch decided to become Kirk Douglas. Since Douglas could not pay for the school tuition, he persuaded the academy to create a scholarship for him after displaying his talent in a special audition. To support himself, he worked as a waiter and at other odd jobs, and in summer stock plays. He finally got a small role in a Broadway musical called *Spring Again.* After graduating from the Academy of Dramatic Arts, Douglas married a fellow actress, Diana Dill, with whom he had two sons, Michael and Joel. (After their divorce in 1951, Douglas married Belgian-born Anne Buydens in 1954.)

In 1942, he was sent to war. Wounded by friendly fire, he was discharged in 1944, worked as an actor for radio soap operas, and had a few modest roles in various plays. His break in theater came that year when he was chosen to replace Richard Widmark in a successful Broadway play, *Kiss and Tell.* Then, when his old classmate Lauren Bacall sent Hollywood executive Hal Wallis to interview Douglas for a movie role, the actor first rejected the offer since his true ambition was to become a star on Broadway. He finally conceded to work with Wallis, however, for lack of significant roles on stage.

Kirk Douglas had the rare privilege of starting his movie career in a relatively important part. He was offered the role of Barbara Stanwyck's weak husband in Lewis Milestone's *The Strange Love of Martha Ivers* (1946). In Hollywood, Douglas was immediately typecast as an antihero, usually a bully, and often a villain. Just after *The Strange Love of Martha Ivers*, Douglas was offered a more important part in a film noir by Jacques Tourneur called *Out of the Past* (1947), starring Robert Mitchum and Jane Greer. Then came *I Walk Alone* (1947), another film noir starring Burt Lancaster, who was to become a good friend of Douglas's. Kirk Douglas's true breakthrough in Hollywood came in 1949 with his role as a boxer in his eighth film, *The Champion*. This film marked both the beginning of the actor's total autonomy, and his new screen image as a tough guy.

Kirk Douglas is renowned for his sense of independence. He broke his contract with Hal Wallis a year after he went to Hollywood, and got out of his contract with Warner Brothers. Douglas eventually formed his own production company in 1955—named Bryna Productions, after his mother—and became a millionaire producing films as varied as *Spartacus*, *The Last Sunset*, and *Lonely Are the Brave*. As an actor working for different production companies including his own, Douglas has had a full career on screen, making more than 70 films—mostly in leading roles—as well as several plays. He also played several remarkable roles for television, including roles in *Amos* (1985), *Remembrance of Love* (1982), and the miniseries *Queenie* (1987), based on Michael Korda's best-seller. Kirk Douglas has collaborated with some of the most respected directors in Hollywood such as Joseph Mankiewicz (*A Letter to Three Wives*, 1949; *There Was a Crooked Man*, 1970), Elia Kazan (*The Arrangement*, 1969), Billy Wilder (*Ace in the Hole* and *The Big Carnival*, 1951), Stanley Kubrick (*Paths of Glory*, 1957; *Spartacus*, 1960), and Vincente Minnelli (*The Bad and the Beautiful*, 1952; *Lust for Life*, 1956). His favorite film—one he produced and starred in—is *Lonely Are the Brave* (1962), the story of a modern-day outlawed cowboy yearning for a better world. The two films Kirk Douglas directed, *Scalawag* (1973), inspired by *Treasure Island*, and *Posse* (1975), did poorly at the box office and did not impress the critics.

Michael Douglas has followed in his father's footsteps. Beyond having a successful career as an actor, he has produced numerous hits since the mid-1970s. His most remarkable achievement as a producer was his very first. After many years of trying, his father was still unable to finance the screen adaptation of Ken Kesey's novel *One Flew over the Cuckoo's Nest*. He chose the director Kirk Douglas had in mind all along—Czechoslovakian Milos Forman—and picked a striking cast of professional and amateur actors. *One Flew over the Cuckoo's Nest* was a major critical and financial success. It won all top Academy Awards in 1975, and was United Artists' top profit-maker to date. Michael Douglas produced another hit in 1984, *Romancing the Stone*, a romantic comedy in a cliff-hanger style starring himself, Kathleen Turner, and Danny DeVito. It was followed in 1985 by a sequel, *The Jewel of the Nile*. In 1993, Douglas produced *Made in America*, starring Whoopi Goldberg and Ted Danson.

As an actor, Michael Douglas has made over 20 films, among which are several hits. His first significant role was in the television series *The Streets of San Francisco*, as a young police officer. This role revealed him to the public and made of him a top television star. In 1979, he played a leading role in Jane Fonda's production of *The China Syndrome*. After *Romancing the Stone*, Douglas played in another hit directed by Oliver Stone. *Wall Street* (1987), a slick business thriller, gave Michael a chance to play a tough and cunning character in the tradition of his father's early roles. The same year, he was in Adrian Lyne's blockbuster *Fatal Attraction*. In 1989, Douglas teamed up again with DeVito and Kathleen Turner in the black comedy *War of the Roses* directed by DeVito. In 1992, Michael had the male lead in the controversial film *Basic Instinct* starring Sharon Stone as a best-selling novelist whose fiction reflected too well a dangerous reality. In 1993, *Falling Down* gave Michael Douglas an opportunity to play the challenging role of a bitter L.A. dweller, tired of it all after a nasty divorce, and ready to get even with the world.

Michael's brother Joel Douglas, and half-brother Peter, are also involved in producing movies. Joel's *King Cobra* (1998), is, to date, his only significant production. In 1980, 23-year-old Peter produced *The Final Countdown*, a World War II epic about the *Nimitz*, a nuclear-powered aircraft carrier. Kirk Douglas played the captain of the ship. In 1982, Peter produced a reasonably successful film called *Something Wicked This Way Comes*, adapted from a Ray Bradbury novel. Then there was *Fletch* in 1985, and in 1987, *A Tiger's Tale* starring Ann-Margret, which Peter wrote and directed as well.

Eric Douglas, Kirk's youngest son, shares his father's passion for acting and has often played in his movies. In *Remembrance of Love* (1982), Eric played Kirk's character as a young man. In *A Gunfight* (1971), a film produced by his father and financed by the Jicarilla Apache Indian tribe, Eric played the son of Kirk's character. Some of his most recent films are *The Flamingo Kid* (1984), *The Golden Child* (1986), *Honor Bound* (1989), and *Delta Force III: The Killing Game* (1991).

Bibliography

Douglas, Kirk. *The Ragman's Son: An Autobiography*. New York: Simon & Schuster, 1988.
Munn, Michael. *Kirk Douglas*. New York: St. Martin's, 1985.
Thomas, Tony. *The Films of Kirk Douglas*. New York: Citadel, 1991.

Marion Bermondy

Doyle, Sir Arthur Conan (1859-1930), the creator of Sherlock Holmes and the grandfather of all contemporary crime fiction, was born in Edinburgh to expatriate Irish parents. After studying medicine, Doyle established a practice in England, but eventually turned to fiction writing. In 1886, he composed the novel that would be published in *Beeton's Christmas Annual* (December 1887) as *A Study in Scarlet*, introducing the world to Mr. Sherlock Holmes (see entry). In 1891, after publishing a second Sherlock Holmes novel and

Photo courtesy of Popular Culture Library, Bowling Green State University, Bowling Green, OH.

beginning a series of Holmes short stories, Doyle gave up medicine altogether. By this time he had also completed *The White Company* (1891), the first of his historical romances, which he always valued more highly than his detective tales though it was the detective fiction that made his fortune and his fame.

Eventually the adventures of Sherlock Holmes and Dr. Watson would fill four novels (*A Study in Scarlet*; *The Sign of Four*, 1890; *The Hound of the Baskervilles*, 1902; and *The Valley of Fear*, 1915), along with 56 short stories (collected in five volumes: *The Adventures of Sherlock Holmes*, 1892; *The Memoirs of Sherlock Holmes*, 1894; *The Return of Sherlock Holmes*, 1905; *His Last Bow*, 1917; and *The Casebook of Sherlock Holmes*, 1927). Translations into numerous languages have made Holmes a universally recognized figure. To this day, he remains the preeminent fictional detective.

The immense popularity of the Holmes stories provided Doyle the liberty to pursue other interests as a writer. Historical fiction and science fiction were the two genres in which he enjoyed the greatest success. *The White Company* and *Sir Nigel* (1906) recount the adventures of 14th-century chivalric heroes; *The Great Shadow* (1892), *The Refugees* (1893), *Rodney Stone* (1896), and *Uncle Bernac* (1897) all transpire during the Napoleonic era. The Professor Challenger stories comprise Doyle's most important contributions to science fiction. The first, *The Lost World* (1912), is probably the best and certainly the most influential.

Doyle's patriotism led him to volunteer for service in the Boer War (1899-1902). In 1902, he published a popular defense of British aims and actions, *The War in South Africa, Its Cause and Conduct*, for which he was knighted. Doyle also composed histories of that war and of key British campaigns in World War I. By the 1920s, Doyle's energies shifted from patriotism to spiritualism. The supernatural had fascinated him since his early days as a doctor, and now he wrote and spoke widely on spiritualism, apparently never regretting this diversion of his talents into a crusade that appeared ridiculous to most of his contemporaries and to posterity. Though his cause was discredited, Doyle's personal integrity remained unblemished. He was, as he proclaimed in his epitaph at the time of his death in 1930, "Steel True and Blade Straight."

Bibliography

Carr, John Dickson. *The Life of Sir Arthur Conan Doyle*. New York: Harper, 1949.

Edwards, Owen Dudley. *The Quest for Sherlock Holmes*: *A Biographical Study of Arthur Conan Doyle*. Totowa: Barnes, 1983.

Green, Richard Lancelyn, and John Michael Gibson. *A Bibliography of A. Conan Doyle*. New York: Oxford UP, 1983.

Lellenberg, Jon L., ed. *The Quest for Sir Arthur Conan Doyle*. Carbondale: Southern Illinois UP, 1987.

J. K. Van Dover

Dracula (1897), a novel first published in England by Bram Stoker, has become one of the most visible, important, and enduring icons of Western popular culture, relived in countless stage dramatizations, cinematic adaptations, parodies and sequels by other authors, and in a succession of vampire tales published continuously over the last century.

Stoker's novel tells the story of the loathsome Count Dracula, an ancient vampire from a noble family who dwells in his Gothic castle in Transylvania where he lives the life of the undead: sequestered by day in an inanimate state in his coffin; prowling the world by night in search of victims to seduce, bite, and drain of their lifeblood. They in turn either die or are themselves transformed into vampires. When a London solicitor visits the castle on business, he discovers the horror that takes place there. Dracula follows him to London, where he unleashes his vampiristic mayhem on the unsuspecting Victorian populace, including a young woman who is both entranced and repulsed by him. Ultimately, he is destroyed by a determined doctor who pits science against the supernatural.

While Stoker's story emphasized Dracula's predatory nature and villainy, the character has gradually been reconstituted in various film and theatrical interpretations to evoke sympathy as one who is capable of taking life but who can bestow immortality on his beloved. And thus Dracula's victims have also come to be portrayed as his lovers. Early film versions emphasized Dracula's odium, as in F. W. Murnau's classic German film, *Nosferatu* (1922). Bela Lugosi's famous portrayals of Dracula in the stage adaptation by Hamilton Deane and John L. Balderson and in the 1931 movie retained the nefarious qualities of the Count, but humanized him, a trend continued in Christopher Lee's 1958 performance. The transformation was complete by the time of Francis Ford Coppola's 1992 film, *Bram Stoker's Dracula*, a story of star-crossed lovers struggling to reunite.

Bibliography

Carter, Margaret L. *Dracula: The Vampire and the Critics.* Ann Arbor: UMI Research, 1988.

Leatherdale, Clive. *Dracula: The Novel and the Legend: A Study of Bram Stoker's Gothic Masterpiece.* Brighton: Desert Island, 1993.

Skal, David J. *Hollywood Gothic: The Tangled Web of Dracula from Novel to Stage to Screen.* New York: Norton, 1990.

Wayne E. Hensley
Liahna Babener

See also
Horror Fiction
Horror Film

Dramatic Family Genre, The. As television became part of the family living room, it is not surprising that the living room became a major focus of television. While film and theater require a physical escape from the home, television—and network radio programming that preceded it—has remained a home-based medium whose entertainment generally reflects such themes. Consequently, the numerous families that dot the TV landscape make defining the dramatic family genre almost as difficult as defining the American family itself.

Many genres and subgenres contribute to the family drama. Westerns such as *Bonanza* (see entry) and *The Big Valley,* as well as adventure programs such as *Lassie* (see entry), each have elements of the dramatic family situation. Family-based sitcoms, from *Leave It to Beaver* to *Good Times,* also have varying degrees of dramatic involvement. In an America where the definition of family is constantly changing, even the office environments of sitcoms such as *The Mary Tyler Moore Show, WKRP in Cincinnati, Taxi,* and *Murphy Brown* revolve around a cast of workers who comprise a family, each with its own dramatic moments (see Sitcom).

However, as diverse as they are, most TV families are usually better off than their real-life counterparts. This is not only true of such obvious examples as *The Brady Bunch* or *Leave It to Beaver,* but of series featuring dysfunctional or nontraditional families, as well. *Bonanza*'s Cartwright boys, sons of three-time widower and family patriarch Ben Cartwright (Lorne Greene), always emerged healthy and victorious despite their respective mothers' absence. Engineer Bill Davis, portrayed by Brian Keith in the seriocomic *Family Affair,* raised a normal family despite his frequent business trips. New York magazine publisher Tom Corbett (Bill Bixby) was quite successful in raising his well-adjusted son Eddie (Brandon Cruz) in the dramedy *The Courtship of Eddie's Father.*

Extended and nuclear TV families, such as the Waltons of Depression-era Virginia or the Fitzpatricks of recession-era Flint, MI, also successfully fought the odds. Both families used love and togetherness to fight obstacles that would test the mettle of their hardiest real-life counterparts. Many

media scholars agree that this disparity between real and televised families has created a growing anxiety within American families themselves—it is as though viewers ask, Why aren't we as happy as they are?

There appear to be three major formats through which families are dramatically portrayed on television. The first posits the family in the everyday world, exploring the internal and external forces they face. The second places the family in a situation of adversity, showing how love and togetherness help them face tough times. The third—more popular in sitcoms than dramas—explores the one-parent/no-parent family in which uncles, step-parents and other nonbiologically related adults serve as guardians for a given set of children.

The oldest and most common format of both dramatic and comedic family programs features the family coping with everyday life. *Mama*, while considered one of the first TV sitcoms, has enough pathos to qualify as the first successful TV family drama, as well. Based on the Kathryn Forbes novel *Mama's Bank Account*, which became a successful play, musical, and film in the 1940s, the television series chronicled the Norwegian-immigrant Hansen family as they coped with life in turn-of-the-century San Francisco. Told through the eyes of eldest daughter Katrin, the live series opened each week with a sentimental montage of family album photos.

First telecast by CBS in 1949, the series enjoyed a successful eight-year run. According to *Prime Time Hits* author Susan Sackett, *Mama*'s appeal was found in the same family nostalgia evident today: "Just as today's audience seems to have romanticized the 'golden,' family-oriented decade of the '50s, the audience of the mid-20th century waxed nostalgic over this dramedy that hearkened back to a simpler era still—the turn of the century."

Through the 1950s and 1960s, the exclusive domain of the family appeared to be sitcoms and Westerns. *Life with Father, Father Knows Best*, and *The Donna Reed Show* were certainly played more for laughs than drama, although each show usually resolved to a tender or touching dramatic moment. Dramatic Westerns such as *Bonanza* and *The Big Valley* also involved family relationships, but their chief draw was found in their western settings.

It was not until the early 1970s that the general family in everyday life became the focus of a dramatic series; *The Smith Family* (ABC, 1971-72) starred Henry Fonda as Chad Smith, an L.A. police detective who struggled to balance his responsibilities of work and family. Like many shows of the early 1970s, the growing generation gap between Smith and his children—including a teenage son and daughter—provided the meat of the series' conflict. Although it ran only one season, the series reintroduced America to Ron Howard, last seen as Opie Taylor in *The Andy Griffith Show*. Three years later, Howard would join the Cunningham family in ABC's successful sitcom *Happy Days*.

In the late 1970s, the family drama genre began including more modern, relevant themes, with the most notable examples being two ABC series—*Family* (1976-80) and *Eight Is Enough* (1977-81). While both featured the family coping with everyday life, *Family* was the more dramatic—

or melodramatic—of the two. While it never reached the Nielsen Top 25, *Family* gave "everyday" life a new meaning, becoming the first family drama to broach such previously taboo topics as women's rights, promiscuity, drugs, homosexuality, and divorce (TV's first divorced mom premiered one year earlier when Bonnie Franklin portrayed Ann Romano in the 1975 CBS sitcom *One Day at a Time*). Programs such as *All in the Family* and *The Mary Tyler Moore Show*, as well as the more relevant dramas of the period, paved the way for *Family*'s dramatic explorations.

Family drew from a broad base of characters to create its plots. James Broderick and Sada Thompson, as sophisticated, liberal parents Doug and Kate Lawrence, saw their adult daughter Nancy (Meredith Baxter Birney) divorce, their son Willie (Gary Frank) drop out of college, and their teenage daughter Buddy (Kristy McNichol) face the pains of puberty. McNichol's sensitive, Emmy-Award winning portrayal brought her popularity beyond that of the series; Mego toys immortalized the young actress with a doll in her likeness.

Although not as hard-hitting as *Family*, *Eight Is Enough* consistently ranked high in the ratings during its five-year run. Presented in the hour-long dramatic format, it was sprinkled with light moments of comedy accompanied by a laugh track. Dick Van Patten, who played young Nels in *Mama*, was now the head of a family of eight children, most of whom were still living in the same house. Unlike *Family*, which consistently hit upon relevant themes, *Eight Is Enough* alternated between comic and relevant episodes. While Van Patten's character Tom Bradford was not initially a widower (which would place him in the one-parent/no-parent format), the sudden death of co-star Diana Hyland changed the focus of the series. Bradford soon remarried, however, and the series continued to focus on the large family's domestic problems. Reruns of the series serve as a time capsule of 1970s popular culture with disco, skateboarding, and bell-bottom outfits severely dating the series.

In 1977, NBC's *James at 15*, starring Lance Kerwin, made a critically acclaimed attempt at providing a more honest view of 1970s family life, particularly those matters affecting teenagers. However, it was not until 1988, when the ABC half-hour dramedy *The Wonder Years* debuted, that television provided its most honest—and popular—family portrait (see entry). Narrated through the recollections of teenager Kevin Arnold, played by Fred Savage, the late-1960s period piece concentrated on the pains of puberty in an honest and humorous manner. The family was equally believable; Kevin's father was far from perfect, his older brother Wayne was, at best, a jerk, and his sister Karen was too busy trying to find herself to find time for the rest of the Arnold clan. The show did particularly well in the ratings during its second season and, after its cancellation, found a lucrative life in syndication.

Dramatic family entries of the 1990s such as NBC's *Sisters* (1991-96) and ABC's *My So-Called Life* (1994-95) continued to bring relevance to the small screen, yet both failed to capture anything but a small-yet-devoted audience. Bring-

ing a more inclusive aspect to the dramatic family was ABC's *Life Goes On* (1989-92), which featured Christopher Burke as a teenager with Down's syndrome.

The family-facing-adversity format was certainly not an invention of the 1970s—stories of families facing tough times have frequently surfaced in American popular culture—but it certainly blossomed during that period in television. Two notable examples are *The Waltons* and *Little House on the Prairie*.

The Waltons (see entry), which debuted on CBS in 1972, was the brainchild of veteran film and television writer Earl Hamner, Jr., who narrated the series, a semi-autobiographical look at his childhood in Depression-era Virginia. While the Waltons certainly faced daily struggles, the majority of these were filtered through either the Depression or, as the series progressed, World War II.

Although it retired in 1981, *The Waltons* has become institutionalized in American popular culture. The episodic closing line—"Good night, John-Boy"—remains the verbal icon of the series, and has been parodied in various sketch comedies since its debut. The actors have returned to star in highly rated Walton family TV movies, the latest appearing in 1995. In 1992, the Walton's Mountain Museum was founded at Hamner's childhood home in Schuyler, VA; 6,000 fans turned out for the opening. Reruns of the series have become the flagship program of the Family Channel.

NBC tried to duplicate the success of *The Waltons* in 1975 with *The Family Holvack*, which also featured a southern, Depression-era family. While *The Family Holvack* lasted only one season, NBC had struck gold with *Little House on the Prairie* (1974-83), produced by series star Michael Landon. Based on the popular *Little House* books by Laura Ingalls Wilder, the series' adversity involved a homesteader family's survival in territorial Minnesota. Like the Waltons, the Ingalls family of *Little House* fame became institutionalized, with several TV movies appearing after the series' retirement.

While adverse situations of the past seemed acceptable family drama material, such was not the case for more contemporary examples. CBS's short-lived *The Fitzpatricks* featured the challenges faced by a contemporary family living in recession-era Flint, MI. Mike Fitzpatrick, played by Bert Kramer, was the loving father who worked overtime, and Maggie Fitzpatrick (Mariclare Costello) was the loving mother who took a job as a waitress to make ends meet for their four children, aged 10 to 16. Juxtaposed against Michael Moore's 1989 film *Roger and Me*, a documentary about Flint's economic devastation, *The Fitzpatricks* made the recession seem downright bearable. Oddly enough, while Moore had no trouble going after General Motors, *The Fitzpatricks* ignored the corporation's existence, making Mike a steel worker as opposed to an auto worker.

While the one-parent/no-parent format was incredibly successful in situation comedy—*Bachelor Father*, *The Lucy Show*, *Family Affair*, and *Diff'rent Strokes*, to name just a few—it has all but failed in the one-hour dramatic format. *The Monroes* (ABC, 1966-67) centered around five orphans, aged 6 to 18, left to fend for themselves as they fought for a homestead in the Wyoming territory. A decade later, NBC's *Mulligan's Stew* brought four orphaned children into the Mulligan family, already busy with three kids of their own. An obvious attempt to capitalize on the popularity of ABC's *Eight Is Enough*, the series aired only two months. The 1979 ABC drama *MacKenzies of Paradise Cove*, which centered on five orphans being raised by a crusty old fishing-boat operator in Hawaii, did not fare much better.

Bibliography

Brooks, Tim, and Earle Marsh. *The Complete Directory to Prime Time Network TV Shows, 1946-Present*. New York: Ballantine, 1992.

Denis, Christopher Paul, and Michael Denis. *Favorite Families of TV*. New York: Citadel, 1992.

Sackett, Susan. *Prime Time Hits*. New York: Billboard, 1993.

Taylor, Ella. *Prime Time Families*. Berkeley: U of California P, 1989.

Michael B. Kassel

Drew, Robert (1924-), a documentary filmmaker, after a stint as a fighter pilot with the Army Air Corps during World War II, wrote a story for *Life* magazine about the first U.S. jet fighter planes. He stayed on for the next ten years with the magazine as a correspondent and editor. During that time he worked with great photographers, such as Alfred Eisenstaedt, whose work captured excitement, spontaneity, and human emotion.

In early 1960, Time-Life offered to support Drew's efforts to develop more mobile, lightweight film equipment if he would work with the Time-owned stations in cultivating their documentary offerings. With a pared-down TV news film camera patched to a one-quarter-inch audiotape recorder, Drew and his team were ready to try their hands at a new style of documentary filmmaking with a film about the decision-making process in the Wisconsin presidential primary of 1960, which pitted John Kennedy against Hubert Humphrey.

With *Primary*, Drew introduced a new style of unscripted, sync-sound documentary known as *cinema vérité* to American television. It was a landmark piece of work for its innovation in technique and was awarded several honors, including the Flaherty Award for best documentary and the blue ribbon at the American Film Festival.

After the making of *Primary*, Robert Drew was recruited to make a television documentary for the ABC network on the subject of Latin America. The result was *Yanki, No!*, broadcast in the fall of 1960. The program, sponsored by the Bell and Howell camera company, was rife with haunting images.

The sponsor asked Drew for more programs to air as part of the *Bell and Howell Close-Up* series. With the help of Time, Inc., Drew formed Drew Associates and set up a research staff to find and develop story concepts. In their first season with the ABC series, Drew Associates produced six programs, including *The Children Were Watching*, which chronicled the integration of a New Orleans elementary school. The program captured the reprehensible behavior of mothers and fathers and grandparents opposed to integration as they congregated around the school to taunt black children.

Drew's production company included an impressive list of distinguished documentarians, including Richard Leacock, D. A. Pennebaker, Albert Maysles, Jim Lipscomb, Greg Shuker, Joyce Chopra, and Hope Ryden. Drew Associates was one of the first independent documentary companies to challenge and penetrate the dominance of internal network news departments in the production of documentaries.

In 1963 Drew Associates independently began shooting a film about the integration of the University of Alabama, which aired on NBC as *Crisis: Behind a Presidential Commitment* (see entry above).

The syndicated series *The Living Camera* appeared in late 1964 and was comprised of ten documentaries produced by Drew Associates during 1961 and 1962. Each film entered the life of its subject at a crucial period, often providing poignant portrayals. Among the stories were *Jane*, featuring the young and little-known actress Jane Fonda preparing for her first starring role in a Broadway play; *Eddie*, a portrait of race car driver Eddie Sachs prepping for the Indianapolis 500; and *The Chair*, which followed death-row inmate Paul Crump through the commutation of his sentence.

Drew's recent work includes projects such as *Life and Death of a Dynasty* (1991), the story of three generations of India's Nehru-Gandhi family. In 1993, Robert Drew received the career achievement award of the International Documentary Association.

Bibliography

Allen, Robert C., and Douglas Gomery. *Film History: Theory and Practice*. New York: Knopf, 1985.

Einstein, Daniel. *Special Edition: A Guide to Network Television Documentary Series and Special News Reports, 1955-1979*. Metuchen: Scarecrow, 1987.

O'Connell, P. J. *Robert Drew and the Development of Cinema Vérité in America*. Carbondale: Southern Illinois UP, 1992.

Rosenthal, Alan, ed. *New Challenges for Documentary*. Berkeley: U of California P, 1988.

Watson, Mary Ann. *The Expanding Vista: American Television in the Kennedy Years*. New York: Oxford UP, 1990.

Mary Ann Watson

See also

Documentary Film

Drive-in Theaters were an important development as one of the major organs for screening movies, when important social and economic forces led to transformation of the Hollywood motion picture industry after World War II. When middle-class Americans moved to the suburbs in record numbers after World War II, they also abandoned propinquity to the matrix of downtown and urban neighborhood movie theaters. Indeed, nearly all the increase in population in the U.S. after the World War II took place in the suburban rings around cities. Suburbs grew at a rate 15 times faster than any other segment of the country. More than one million acres of farmland were plowed under each year. Supported by Veterans Administration and Farmers Home

Administration mortgages, home ownership in the U.S. increased by nearly 50 percent from 1945 to 1950, and went up another 50 percent in the decade after that. By 1960, for the first time in the history of the U.S., more Americans owned houses than rented.

Drive-ins had been around since the mid-1930s. The origins of the drive-in go back to the Great Depression. The first drive-in came in June 1933 in Camden, NJ, just across the river from Philadelphia. This initial effort set the standard with semicircular rows of parking spaces accommodating 400 cars. Entrepreneur Richard Hollingshead correctly anticipated that patrons "would enjoy movies where they could dress as they please, smoke, talk, and eat supper at the same time."

With little suburban growth during the 1930s and none during World War II, the number of drive-ins at the end of the war stood at less than 25 theaters. Then the population growth and suburbanization thrust began. Now that necessary building materials had become available, thousands of drive-in theaters opened on former farmer's fields. By 1948, there were 800; in 1950 the data revealed 2,000; in 1956, drive-in numbers peaked at 4,000. By 1960, drive-ins accounted for one out of every five movie-viewing sites.

The 1950s deluxe drive-in typically included space for more than 2,000 cars, a snack bar, and a playground for the tots, the baby boomer children. Drive-ins could be counted on to sell about four times as much popcorn, candy, and soft drinks as the average indoor theater. Many drive-ins offered pizza, barbecued chicken, french fries, and onion rings—a cafeteria-like menu.

Drive-ins took direct aim at the suburban family, with its ever-growing number of young children, by tendering free passes to parents of newborns up to three months of age. A New Orleans drive-in installed a special indoor theater—equipped with 16mm—for children in high chairs. Children age 12 and below nearly always were admitted free; exhibitors knew children could not drive themselves to movies under the stars.

Additional services often went far beyond drawing families with small children. One Tennessee drive-in installed a while-you-wait laundry service. Others offered shuffleboard, horseshoes, miniature golf, wading pools, baby bottle warmers, fireworks exhibitions, petting zoos, facilities for the family cat or dog, and even free pony rides. Drive-ins borrowed from strategies of the movie palace. Screen tower backs were enlivened with flamboyant neon displays: the Rodeo drive-in in Tucson, AZ, featured a cowgirl twirling a neon lasso, while a giant cheerleader adorned the Campus drive-in outside San Diego, CA.

The strongest attraction of the drive-in seemed to be cheapness; baby boom families had little money since they were mortgaged to the hilt. For $2 a car any and all could have a fun night out. One slogan was "Come as you are in the family car." Still, price, convenience and informality could not clear the foggy windshield or improve the sounds from the tinny loudspeaker hooked to the car window.

Drive-in problems turned acute in the 1960s. Those located north of the Mason-Dixon line, for instance, regularly closed in the winter. Noise and fuss from "wild teens" led to special zoning ordinances. As the drive-in craze hit its peak, some owners even built motels nearby so mom and dad could escape the kids.

Most important, the land at the edge of town had become too valuable to remain a drive-in. Suburbanization continued unabated and the acres required for a drive-in could be more profitably employed as space for a score of new homes. As the receipts of drive-ins peaked and then began to ebb, exhibitors sought some sort of longer term and more permanent response to the suburbanization of America, to the television-in-every-household life. Drive-ins closed and the movies moved to the mall. Today less than 1,000 remain open, solely in an arc from Southern California to Florida, with all too rare exceptions in the North.

Bibliography

Austin, Bruce A. *Immediate Seating: A Look at Movie Audiences.* Belmont: Wadsworth, 1989.

Gomery, Douglas. *Shared Pleasures.* Madison: U of Wisconsin P, 1992.

Jackson, Kenneth T. *Crabgrass Frontier: The Suburbanization of the United States.* New York: Oxford UP, 1985.

Jones, Landon Y. *Great Expectations: America and the Baby Boom Generation.* New York: Random House, 1981.

Segrave, Kerry. *Drive-In Theaters.* Jefferson: McFarland, 1992.

Douglas Gomery

Drugs in American culture refer especially to various mind-altering and addictive "controlled substances." Their highest profile in popular culture is in tabloid stories of celebrity overdoses and party scandals in the worlds of movies, pop music, and professional sports. Among these notables were comics John Belushi and Chris Farley, actress/model Margaux Hemingway, and rock stars Jimi Hendrix, Janis Joplin, and Jim Morrison. The sheer number and variety of drugs that relate to non-celebrity popular culture is daunting. Medicinal drugs range from Rolaids to AIDs "cocktails," recreational drugs from the caffeine in colas to crack cocaine. In between are the semi-legitimate use of uppers and downers to augment performers' professional energies, and painkillers and muscle-enhancers for athletes' professional efficiency.

The implications for popular culture in medicinal drugs particularly refer to advertising. Prior to the passage of the Pure Food and Drugs Act in 1906, advertising for patent medicines was uncontrolled, claims were untested, and ingredients were undisclosed. Ingredients might be generally innocuous, as Lydia Pinkham's Vegetable Compound, which purported to ease all sorts of female complaints, or they might be potentially dangerous, as Mrs. Winslow's Soothing Syrup, which calmed colicky babes with a generous dose of narcotics. Hostetter's Bitters was a million-dollar tonic in the 19th century whose alcoholic content was 32 percent. All these were heavily advertised in newspapers and magazines and available by mail order as well as over the counter. Sears, Roebuck offered the patent remedies in the 1897 catalog, as well as cheaper generics including laudanum (tincture of opium) at $3 for a dozen 4 oz. bottles.

The most common ailments now as then are headaches, cramps, sleep disorders, upset stomachs and bowels, with all combined in flus and the common cold. Therefore, the most popular drugs numerically are not tabloid headliners, but remedies for everyday afflictions. The brand names are so embedded in American culture by way of media advertising that many are used as common nouns, such as Tums, Alka-Seltzer, Pepto-Bismol, Ex-lax, Ben-gay, Midol. Competition for these billion-dollar markets is fierce, and rival ads are familiar to all through television and mass magazines.

The same can be said about advertising for the three most popular "recreational" drugs, caffeine, nicotine, and alcohol, but unlike medicinal drugs, the advertising is often memorable in itself. A few examples of slogans are Maxwell House coffee's "Good to the Last Drop," Lucky Strike's "L.S./M.F.T.," and Miller Lite's "Less Filling! Tastes Great." Ad characters include Folger coffee's Mrs. Olson (whose Scandinavian accent was not deterred by the "G" in the product name), the glamorous feminists of Virginia Slims, and Joe Camel, and, for alcoholic beverages, Johnny Walker, Lord Calvert's "Men of Distinction," Budweiser's Clydesdales and Absolut vodka's protean bottle. Each of these drugs evokes popular ritual behaviors, from the ubiquitous coffee break and social patterns of lighting cigarettes to a whole spectrum of drinking manners (see Bars).

A survey of drugs as a topic in the entertainment media deserves to begin with *Reefer Madness* (1936), which Leonard Maltin calls "the grand-daddy of all worst movies." Its depiction of teenagers driven to insanity and death by a few puffs of pot made it a cult favorite in the 1960s. The Hays Office code forbade drugs in movies, although in the silents (as well as contemporary popular thrillers), scenes in Chinese opium dens were standard. The Prohibition era (1920-33) spawned a new popularity of illegal alcohol and of the gangsters who made booze available. Alcohol, therefore, was the driving force in *Public Enemy* (1931), *Scarface* (1932), *Roaring Twenties* (1939), the TV series *The Untouchables* (1959-62), and the film of the same name in 1987, as well as many other rum-running pictures. Hard drugs and organized crime were the subjects of the Oscar-winning *French Connection* (1971), *King of New York* (1990), and *Clear and Present Danger* (1994). *New Jack City* (1991), in addition to the usual violence, carried a clear anti-drug (crack cocaine) message.

For serious depictions of the effects of drugs on persons, Ray Milland as an alcoholic in *The Lost Weekend* (1945), Frank Sinatra as a heroin addict in *The Man with the Golden Arm* (1955), addict Don Murray in *A Hatful of Rain* (1957), and alcoholics Jack Lemmon and Lee Remick in *Days of Wine and Roses* (1962) are classics. Drunk scenes abound in films, usually with tipsy humor (*The Thin Man* [1934-47], although Nick and Nora Charles sober up as the series continues, *Harvey* [1950], *Arthur* [1981], etc.), but occasionally mixed with a degree of pathos, as with Robert Mitchum in *El Dorado* (1964).

Undoubtedly, the "golden age" for drugs and film art was the late 1960s, as directors employed various psychedelic effects of LSD trips and marijuana highs. In Britain, the Bea-

tles' *Yellow Submarine* (1968) is the classic, but in the U.S., Jack Nicholson's *The Trip* (1967) was quickly followed by *Psych Out* (1968), *Easy Rider* (1969), and *Woodstock* (1970). Twenty years later, Oliver Stone's biopic *The Doors* (1991) explored the drug-induced creativity of musician Jim Morrison, as well as his drug-induced death.

Until anti-smoking activism extinguished cigarettes as television sponsors and the industry banned them from films (probably the only censorship remaining), cigarette lighting, puffing, waving, and otherwise posing was the actor's stock-in-trade. In war films, lighting up for your wounded comrade was as much a cliché as the companionable post-intercourse smoking in bed.

In detective fiction, drug-pushing and smuggling is now one of the most frequent motives for murder and revenge, but the hard-drinking ever-smoking tough guys of Dashiell Hammett and Mickey Spillane are replaced by Robert Parker's and Sue Grafton's smoke-free tough guys and gals. In popular music, songs of bibulous celebration are as old as civilization, but in country-western lyrics, drink is often one of the evils. For hard drugs, the first lyric may be Cole Porter's frequently censored verse from *Anything Goes* (1934): "Some get a kick from cocaine/I'm sure that if/I took even one sniff/That would bore me terrific'ly too." In the rock era, marijuana and LSD were frequently the topic and/or creative impulse for songs (see Acid Rock); rap refers to the entire spectrum of street drugs, cautionary as often as not.

Drugs have also contributed to popular language. The slang terms for alcoholic beverages and stages of drunkenness (moonshine, sauce, tipsy, blotto, plowed, etc.) are boundless, as are slang terms for various street drugs; Jack Margolis in 1978 listed over a hundred synonyms for the then three most popular drugs, among the more colorful being black birds, chicken powder, sparkle plenties for amphetamine; brown sugar, joy powder, Mexican mud for heroin; blue heaven, cherry tops, orange mushrooms for LSD.

Bibliography

Cagin, Seth, and Philip Dray. *Born to Be Wild: Hollywood and the Sixties Generation*. Boca Raton: Coyote, 1994.

Margolis, Jack. *Jack S. Margolis' Complete Book of Recreational Drugs*. Los Angeles: Cliff House, 1978.

Walker, John, ed. *Halliwell's Filmgoer's Companion*. 12th ed. New York: Harper, 1997.

Young, James Harvey. *The Toadstool Millionaires: A Social History of Patent Medicines in America Before Federal Regulation*. Princeton: Princeton UP, 1961.

Fred E. H. Schroeder

du Maurier, Daphne (1907-1989), as the author of stories with rich atmospheric features and complex characters, won early affection from readers. These qualities made her work particularly translatable to the screen. A number of stories and novels, including *Jamaica Inn* (1936), *Rebecca* (1938), "The Birds" (1939), *Frenchman's Creek* (1941), *Hungry Hill* (1943), *My Cousin Rachel* (1951), *The Scapegoat* (1957), and "Don't Look Now" (1971), were made into memorable films.

Du Maurier's most famous work is her gothic romance novel *Rebecca*, an archetypal example of what is known today as the woman-in-jeopardy genre. The novel's first sentence, "Last night I dreamt I went to Manderley again..." is among the best-known opening lines in English literature. *Rebecca* won the 1938 British National Book Award and Alfred Hitchcock's charismatic 1940 film adaptation won the Oscar for best picture.

Du Maurier was named Dame of the British Empire in 1969, and was chosen for the Grand Master Award by Mystery Writers of America in 1978.

Bibliography

Bakerman, Jane. "Daphne du Maurier." *And Then There Were Nine...More Women of Mystery*. Ed. Jane S. Bakerman. Bowling Green, OH: Bowling Green State U Popular P, 1985.

Forster, Margaret. *Daphne du Maurier*. London: Chatto, 1993.

Winn, Dilys. *Murderess Ink: The Better Half of the Mystery*. New York: Bell, 1981.

Kate Grilley

DuBois, W(illiam) E(dward) B(urghardt) (1868-1963), American civil rights leader, sociologist, and writer, the descendent of French Huguenots and African slaves, was born in a small, mostly white New England town. DuBois was among the first important leaders to advocate complete economic, political, and social equality for African Americans.

DuBois attended Fisk University, the University of Berlin, and Harvard University, from which he received his Ph.D. He was invited to read his Harvard dissertation, later published as *The Suppression of the African Slave Trade to the United States* (1896), to the annual meeting of the American Historical Association. After two years of study in Europe, DuBois returned to the U.S. to begin his career as an educator, social worker, and writer. From 1897 to 1910 and again from 1932 to 1944, he taught history and economics at Atlanta University.

DuBois's seminal work in sociology, *The Philadelphia Negro: A Social Study* (1899), remained influential for 40 years. His best-known historical work, *Black Reconstruction* (1935), countered the misconceptions about the role of African Americans during the Reconstruction period. In *The World and Africa* (1947), DuBois sought to present an accurate account of African history. In addition to his scholarly work, DuBois was also a skillful novelist and essayist. *The Souls of Black Folk* (1903) gives a complex analysis of African-American psychology.

In 1909, DuBois co-founded the Niagara Association, which later became the National Association for the Advancement of Colored People (NAACP). During this time, DuBois came to national prominence because of his opposition to Booker T. Washington and his policy of accommodation to Jim Crow practices. DuBois and the other founders of the NAACP believed that African Americans should have complete economic, political, and social equality. DuBois became the editor of *The Crisis*, the NAACP's journal and leading publication of African-American opin-ion, and was instrumental in the Harlem Renaissance, a rebirth of blacks in the arts, in the 1920s.

Just after World War I, DuBois was instrumental in organizing the first Pan-African Congress. DuBois felt that the nonwhite people of the world should organize to oppose white colonialism. Four Pan-African Congresses were held, with the final one meeting in New York in 1927. This movement caused conflict within the NAACP leadership, for some felt that Pan-Africanism was essentially a form of self-segregation. DuBois also came under attack from Marcus Garvey's United Improvement and Conservation Association, which worked for the ultimate rule of Africa by Africans and African Americans.

In 1945, DuBois met Kwame Nkrumah and Jomo Kenyatta at the newly re-formed Pan-African Congress. Soon after, he was asked to leave the NAACP because of his political leftism. He then began working with Paul Robeson in the Council on African Affairs (CAA). The CAA raised funds for conferences and liberation movements while maintaining close contact with Nelson Mandela, Kwame Nkrumah, Jomo Kenyatta, and Walter Susulu. The group was charged with being a communist front, and for most of the 1950s, DuBois and Robeson were denied U.S. passports. However, in the latter years of that decade, DuBois was allowed to visit China and Eastern Europe. In 1961, he joined the Communist Party of the United States and emigrated to Ghana, where he died.

Bibliography:

DuBois, W. E. B. *Dusk of Dawn: An Essay Toward an Autobiography of a Race Concept*. New York: Schocken, 1968.

Lewis, David L. *W. E. B. DuBois: Biography of a Race, 1868-1919*. New York: Henry Holt, 1993.

Moore, Jack B. *W. E. B. DuBois*. Boston: Twayne, 1981.

Janice Snapp

Duffy's Tavern (1941-1951), a widely acclaimed radio comedy as conceived by Ed Gardner (who in real life claimed he drank only milk), was set in an old-fashioned, mirrored and sawdusty place that attracted "mostly ordinary people, but a few of the hoi polloi." Duffy, of course, was never around; Archie just talked to him on the telephone. That pretty much constituted the radio program.

There was never a dull moment at Duffy's, and each of its patrons helped give the dump a true Third Avenue touch. Most of the time there was a guest star—not just any star but the best and brightest that Hollywood and radio had to offer. *Duffy's Tavern* remained one of the most popular comedy shows on radio from 1941 to 1951.

Bibliography

Buxton, Frank, and Bill Owen. *The Big Broadcast: 1920-1950*. New York: Easton Valley, 1972.

——. *Radio's Golden Age: The Programs and Personalities*. New York: Viking, 1966.

Danning, John. *Tune in Yesterday: The Ultimate Encyclopedia of Old-Time Radio 1925-1976*. Englewood Cliffs: Prentice-Hall, 1976.

Gary A. Yoggy

Dumas, Alexandre (1802-1870), designated *père* to distinguish him from his son, Alexandre Dumas *fils,* also an author, was a French playwright and novelist. Although the product of a poor and somewhat disreputable background, Dumas determined to educate himself. Service at the household of the future King Louis-Philippe provided him with the opportunity he needed.

In 1829, Dumas wrote *Henri III et sa cour,* his first play, launching 20 years of successful dramas. Ten years later he added novels to his repertoire. Dumas was a master of the historical novel, featuring romance and derring-do. He obtained many ideas for his plots from collaborators, using his own skills to augment the plot and enliven characters. His best-known novels, popular with both European and American readers, include *The Count of Monte Cristo* (1845), *The Three Musketeers* (1844), and its two sequels, *Twenty Years After* (1845) and *La vicomte de Bragelonne* (1850). In addition to his famous historical romances, Dumas also wrote excellent travel books, children's stories, and essays. His fiction has claimed an enduring readership and a number of his stories, particularly *The Count of Monte Cristo*, have been memorably filmed.

Bibliography

Hemmings, F. W. J. *Alexandre Dumas, The King of Romance.* New York: Scribner, 1979.

Ross, Michael. *Alexandre Dumas.* Devonshire: David & Charles, 1981.

Frank A. Salamone

Duran Duran helped create another minor British invasion 20 years after the Beatles and the Rolling Stones took the U.S. by storm. Their musical talent in combination with their glamorous appearance and fashionable videos earned them a singularly devoted following in Britain and almost equal popularity in the U.S., primarily among teenage girls. Initially a new romantic group like Spandau Ballet, Adam and the Ants, and Depeche Mode, they usually dressed in frilly clothes and wore makeup when performing their synth-pop music (coined for the predominant role of the synthesizer).

An early incarnation of Duran Duran was formed in 1978 by Nick Rhodes on synthesizer and rhythm box and John Taylor, then lead guitar, with Steve Duffy covering vocals and Simon Colley on bass. The band's chic style emerged in reaction against the punk saturation of Britain's music scene at the time. Although briefly considering calling themselves R.A.F., they selected Duran Duran, the name of the villain in the campy sci-fi movie starring Jane Fonda and based on the French comic strip, *Barbarella* (1968), as the group played primarily at a Birmingham club named Barbarella's.

Duran Duran underwent tumultuous personnel changes in the early years. When Duffy and Colley left, Andy Wickett from the group TV Eye and Roger Taylor, drummer for the Scent Organs, took their places, both also from the Birmingham area. John Taylor moved to bass when Andy Wickett left; and a period followed during which they tried out roughly 10 singers and 20 guitarists. Finally Andy Taylor from Newcastle joined on guitar and Simon LeBon joined as lead singer.

EMI signed them in 1981 and they began achieving a consistent output of hit records, with their first single, "Planet Earth," receiving attention nationwide. In the same year, Duran Duran's eponymously titled first album was released. The single "Girls on Film" hit the Top 10 in the U.K. and also launched their ultimately successful video career. The group floundered in the U.S. until later videos on MTV generated interest and, in turn, radio play.

The photogenic quality of the band and the glamorous locales for the videos "Hungry Like the Wolf" and "Rio" helped the group achieve their superstar status in the U.S. The song "Hungry Like the Wolf" reached No. 3 on the American charts. The albums *Rio* (1982) and *Seven and the Ragged Tiger* (1983) hit platinum in the U.S. and the international market, and the 1984 single "Reflex" provided them with their first American No. 1 hit. In July 1985, Duran Duran charted their second U.S. No. 1 single with "A View to a Kill," the theme song for the James Bond film of the same name, the first Bond theme to hit that height.

By the mid-1980s, musical differences among the members made studio work tense. LeBon and Rhodes felt drawn toward more experimental music, and Andy and John Taylor were more interested in a heavier rock sound. The Taylors briefly collaborated with singer Robert Palmer, and Tony Thompson and Bernard Edwards formerly of Chic, and formed Power Station, whose single "Some Like It Hot" (1985) reached No. 6 on the U.S. charts. The rest of the band formed Arcadia, recorded the album *So Red the Rose* (1985), and also enjoyed mild success with the hit single "Election Day."

In 1993, their new album *Duran Duran* announced a confident return. The album reached No. 7 on the *Billboard* 200 in the U.S. on Capitol Records, and No. 4 in the U.K. on EMI, thanks to the single "Ordinary World," which charted not only in the U.S. and U.K. Top 10 but also worldwide after first going platinum in Argentina. The album's second single, "Come Undone," also hit the U.S. Top 10, and worldwide sales of the album quickly reached over 2 million. The group, now with a more mature image to match their true talent, has gained support from its original fans as well as from a new and much wider audience.

Bibliography

Bronson, Fred. *The Billboard Book of Number One Hits.* 3d ed. New York: Billboard Books, 1992.

Duffy, Thomas. "Duran Duran on Track for '93 World Comeback." *Billboard* 21 June 1993: 18, 53.

Romanowski, Patricia, and Holly George-Warren. *The New Rolling Stone Encyclopedia of Rock & Roll.* New York: Fireside, 1995.

Vitus Tsang
Michael Delahoyde

Dylan, Bob (1941-), iconoclast, rebel, mystic, fundamentalist, blasphemer, folkie, and poet. Known for his out-of-tune, raspy, almost non-musical singing voice, Bob Dylan has become a true cultural icon. He was born Robert Allen Zimmerman in Duluth, MN, into a middle-class Jewish family. Dylan spent his early youth in the town of Hibbing,

MN, where his father ran a furniture store. Not much is known about Dylan's early life except that he took to music at an early age and that he played the piano proficiently by the age of nine.

Dylan's musical style was influenced by the whole spectrum of popular music, including artists like Little Richard, John Lee Hooker, and Hank Snow. However, the most influential artists were folksinger Woody Guthrie and bluesman Big Joe Williams. Deeply influenced by Woody Guthrie's autobiography, *Bound for Glory*, Dylan, who took his name from his favorite poet Dylan Thomas, decided that he would follow Guthrie, his pied piper of music. He moved to New York in 1961 to perform in the burgeoning folk scene and to meet Woody Guthrie. Dylan visited Guthrie, who suffered from Huntington's disease, in a New Jersey hospital, where legend has it Guthrie passed the folk torch to Dylan.

Later that year Dylan's coffeeshop performances received an excellent review in the *Times*. Next, he came to the attention of Columbia Records producer John Hammond. He recorded his first album of old folk tunes, *Bob Dylan*, for Hammond in 1962. While this album failed to make a deep impression in the folk scene, his second album, *The Freewheelin' Bob Dylan* (1963), hit like a stick of dynamite. Songs like "Masters of War," "I Shall Be Free," the antinuclear "A Hard Rain's a-Gonna Fall," and the civil rights anthem "Blowin' in the Wind" spoke directly to a segment of American society that was disenchanted. Dylan enhanced his popularity with his emotional performances at the Newport Folk Festival (1963 and 1964) alongside such artists as Joan Baez, Peter, Paul, and Mary, and Pete Seeger (see entries). His next albums, *The Times They Are a-Changin'* (1964), *Another Side of Bob Dylan* (1964), *Bringing It All Back Home* (1965), and *Highway 61 Revisited* (1965), supported his role as the emerging voice of the counterculture, but Dylan himself never claimed this role.

In 1965, at the Newport Folk Festival, Dylan changed his whole image and musical style by going electric, much to the horror of many fans in the audience. He then toured with a band known as the Hawks, which later became the Band. He released one of the first of the double albums, *Blonde on Blonde* (1966). It was during this period that Dylan's songs began to be performed and electrified by artists like the Byrds, the Turtles, the Grateful Dead, and Jimi Hendrix, all of whom had hits with Dylan songs. A near fatal motorcycle accident in 1966 put Dylan out of commission for two years. When he reemerged, with the albums *John Wesley Harding* (1968) and *Nashville Skyline* (1969), he again changed musical styles. Both of these albums were traditional country, neither rock nor folk.

In the 1970s, Dylan again switched gears, recording introspective albums: *Self Portrait* (1970), *Planet Waves* (1974), *Blood on the Tracks* (1975), *Desire* (1976), and *Street Legal* (1978). The widely bootlegged *Basement Tapes*, recorded with the Band in the mid-1960s, was released in 1975. This album went straight to the top of the critics' best-for-the-year list. In 1975, Dylan also put together his touring troupe, the Rolling Thunder Revue, with T-Bone Burnett's Alpha Band, guitarist Mick Ronson, and folkie Ramblin'

Jack Elliott. Dylan's most massive undertaking yet, the tour received critical acclaim.

In 1979, Dylan surprised the world with another drastic change: he converted to Christianity and made a series of poor, Christian-oriented albums, including *Slow Train Coming* (1979), *Saved* (1980), and his best from this period, *Shot of Love* (1981). Many of his shows during this period were done in half empty halls for audiences who sometimes booed. In 1983, Dylan renounced his Christianity and converted back to Judaism; the release of *Infidels* in 1983 saw Dylan again addressing political topics.

Dylan released one of the first box-sets, *Biograph*, in 1985. Since then, many artists have followed this trend. Dylan had a very successful tour in 1986, backed by Tom Petty and the Heartbreakers, much to the delight of fans everywhere. These shows went so well that an HBO tour documentary was aired in 1987, and Dylan then did several sold-out stadium shows with the Grateful Dead as his backing band in the summer of 1987. A recorded tour documentary was released on the excellent *Dylan and the Dead* album in 1989. The Rock and Roll Hall of Fame inducted Dylan early in 1988. In the same year, Dylan participated in a very successful "superband" project when he joined with George Harrison, Jeff Lynne, Tom Petty, and Roy Orbison as the Traveling Wilburys. The first album, *Volume One*, shot straight up the pop charts, and is an excellent example of musical collaboration, but the second album in 1991 was less successful.

In the 1990s, Dylan went back to his folk roots and made two fine vocal solo records with acoustic guitar and a harmonica: *Good As I Have Been to You* (1992) and the Grammy-winning *World Gone Wrong* (1993). *Time out of Mind* (1997) earned critical acclaim as Dylan's best work in 20 years; it won three Grammy awards, including, for the first time in his career, best album.

Bob Dylan has released over 35 albums throughout his long career. He published several books: his novel, *Tarantula* (1970), *The Writings and Drawings of Bob Dylan* (1973), *Lyrics 1961-1985* (1985), and a collection of his drawings, *Drawn Blank* (1992). Several excellent documentaries have been made about Dylan, including *Eat the Document* (1969), *Don't Look Back* (1967), *Hard Rain* (1975), and *At Budokan* (1978). Dylan acted in several movies: *Pat Garrett and Billy the Kid*, with Kris Kristofferson (1973), *Renaldo and Clara* (1978), *Hearts of Fire* (1986), and Dennis Hopper's *Backtrack* (1990).

Bibliography

Hampton, Wayne. *Guerrilla Minstrels: John Lennon, Joe Hill, Woody Guthrie, and Bob Dylan*. Knoxville: U of Tennessee P, 1986.

McGregor, Craig, ed. *Bob Dylan: A Retrospective*. New York: Morrow, 1972.

McKeen, William. *Bob Dylan: A Bio-Bibliography*. Westport: Greenwood, 1993.

Michel, Steve. *The Bob Dylan Concordance*. Grand Junction: Rolling Tomes, 1992.

Richardson, Susan. *Bob Dylan*. New York: Chelsea, 1995.

Robert G. Weiner

Eagles, The (1971-1980), made an enormous impact on the country-rock music scene in the decade they were together, with more than 80 million record sales worldwide, four No. 1 albums, four Grammy awards, and five No. 1 U.S. singles: "Best of My Love," "One of These Nights," "New Kid in Town," "Hotel California," and "Heartache Tonight."

The original four members of the group were back-up musicians for Linda Ronstadt when her producer recognized their potential and introduced them to David Geffen of Asylum Records. Bernie Leadon, born July 19, 1947, in Minneapolis, MN, had been a banjoist with the Scottsville Squirrel Barkers (a bluegrass band), Hearts and Flowers, Dillard and Clark, the Corvettes (a Ronstadt back-up group), and the Flying Burrito Brothers. Glenn Frey, born November 6, 1946, in Detroit, MI, first played guitar for the Mushrooms. With J. D. Souther, he formed the duo Longbranch Pennywhistle. Discouraged because of an unsuccessful LP for Amos Records, they split; and Frey performed solo until he became lead guitarist in Ronstadt's band. Don Henley, born July 22, 1946, in northeastern Texas, initially played in Felicity, a jazz group that later became a country music band called Shiloh, led by Henley. This group disbanded, and Henley was soon induced by Frey to join Ronstadt's band. Randy Meisner, born March 8, 1947, in Scottsbluff, NE, was a bass player in 1962 with the Dynamics, a Nebraska group. He moved to Colorado and joined The Poor, but mediocre recordings resulted in the band's break-up. Meisner then joined Poco, recording with the band their first album, *Pickin' Up the Pieces* (1969). He then joined Rick Nelson and the Stone Canyon Band to make *Rick Nelson in Concert* (1970) and *Rudy the Fifth* (1971). His big break came when he filled in for Ronstadt's bass player and was asked to stay.

The group's first recording at Olympic Studios in London was released in June 1972; *The Eagles* included two U.S. hit singles: "Take It Easy," written by Jackson Browne and Glenn Frey, and "Witchy Woman," written by Don Henley and Bernie Leadon. *Desperado*, a widely acclaimed album in 1973 with a western theme, was the last recording made by the original four. In March 1974, the Eagles acquired a fifth member: lead guitarist Don Felder, born September 21, 1947, in Topanga, CA, added a harder rock feel to the country rock sound. The five's initial LP, *On the Border* (1974), an immediate success, included "Best of My Love," their first U.S. hit single. The title song from *One of These Nights* (1975) soon became a U.S. No. 1 hit.

Bernie Leadon, discontented, decided to leave the Eagles in December 1975 in favor of less stressful work with the Leadon-Georgiades group. Joe Walsh, born November 20, 1947, in Wichita, KS, formerly lead guitarist with the heavy rock James Gang, replaced Leadon. *Hotel California* (1976) set sales records as No. 1 in the U.S. for eight weeks

and also reached No. 1 in Europe. Don Henley and Glenn Frey were the lead vocalists, but Meisner and Walsh each had one song. The group's platinum album, *Their Greatest Hits 1971-1975* (1976), still ranks in sales as the U.S. all-time No. 2 record. Stories of squabbles and high living began to circulate. Randy Meisner left the band and was replaced by Timothy B. Schmit, born October 30, 1947, in Sacramento, CA. Schmit, like Meisner, had been a member of Poco, but Schmit was too late to save the Eagles, whose popularity had begun to decline.

The last two albums, *The Long Run* (late 1979) and the *Eagles Live* (1980), were disappointing. The critics gave them poor reviews; sales slipped, despite a fifth U.S. No. 1 single, "Heartache Tonight" (from *The Long Run*), that won their fourth Grammy as the best rock vocal performance by duo or group in 1979. In 1980, the group split up, primarily because of internal stress and pressures. Irving Azoff continued to manage Don Henley. Don Felder said years later that the band had seemed on the brink of breaking up when he first joined in 1974.

The last album before they regrouped in 1994, *Eagles Greatest Hits Volume 2*, was issued in 1982. Only Henley and Frey were markedly successful as solo performers in the 1980s, both having hit singles. While these musicians were separated, however, sales of Eagles music continued strong.

Band members were encouraged to resolve their differences when a tribute album in 1993, *Common Thread: The Songs of the Eagles* by Travis Tritt, Clint Black, and other country music stars, sold more than 3 million copies. A portion of the royalties aids Don Henley's Walden Woods Project, initiated by Henley in 1990 for the environmental protection of the area surrounding Walden Pond in Massachusetts.

In 1994 the reunited Eagles—Henley, Frey, Felder, Walsh, and Schmit—taped a two-hour show for MTV and began their *Hell Freezes Over* tour.

Bibliography

Larkin, Colin, ed. *The Guinness Encyclopedia of Popular Music*. Vol. 1. Middlesex, U.K.: Guinness, 1995.

Walters, Dave. "Desperados." *The Marshall Cavendish Illustrated History of Popular Music*. Vol. 15 (1978-79). New York: Marshall Cavendish, 1990.

Marion Barber Stowell

Earth, Wind and Fire, fusing soul, jazz, rock, and the polyrhythms of African music, produced a number of hit singles in the 1970s. The group also generated the No. 1 single by backing girl-group trio the Emotions, "Best of My Love," in 1977, and set the stage for lead vocalist Philip Bailey's Top 10 duet with Phil Collins, "Easy Lover," in 1984.

Maurice White, a session drummer for Chess Records who played with Chuck Berry, Etta James, and Jackie

Wilson, then a member of the Ramsey Lewis Trio, launched Earth, Wind and Fire at the height of the early 1970s funk movement, which included Kool and the Gang and Parliament-Funkadelic. The group catapulted to No. 1 status with their 1975 album *That's the Way of the World*, a soundtrack from an obscure movie that provided the No. 1 single "Shining Star." With this album, Earth, Wind and Fire's style cemented; as Joe McEwen describes it, "Cowbells, slight tango rhythms and snatches of James Brown bass lines stand[ing] side by side with delicate Latin beats and hard, insistent funk vamps."

Throughout the 1970s, Earth, Wind and Fire maintained a constant presence on the charts. Singles such as "Sing a Song," "Saturday Night," "Serpentine Fire," "Fantasy," a cover of Lennon and McCartney's "Got to Get You into My Life," "September," "Boogie Wonderland," and "After the Love Is Gone" easily made the group one of the decade's most successful. By 1980, Maurice White's production skills were requested to oversee albums by artists including Ramsey Lewis, Barbra Streisand, and Jennifer Holliday.

The early 1980s proved to be solid for Earth, Wind and Fire. However, the group was not able to reach its earlier successes after 1981's gold record "Let's Groove" spent a record-breaking 11 weeks at the top of the U.S. R&B charts. In 1984, claiming the need to rest, White disbanded the group and focused on his Kalimba production company, named after the African finger piano. Freed of his responsibilities as the group's vocalist, Philip Bailey recorded his duet with Phil Collins and experienced Top 10 success on both sides of the Atlantic, then recorded a series of pop and gospel albums. Bailey won best male gospel performance for his album *Triumph* at the 29th Grammy Awards.

Having achieved six double platinum and two platinum albums with numerous gold awards, Earth, Wind and Fire reunited in 1987 to continue their touring and recording. *Millennium*, in 1993, with Bailey, carried on their stylistic traditions and peaked at No. 39 on the pop album charts.

Bibliography

McEwen, Joe. "Funk." *The Rolling Stone Illustrated History of Rock & Roll*. New York: Random House, 1980.
Rees, Dafydd, and Luke Crampton. *Rock Movers and Shakers*. New York: Billboard, 1991.

Hugh Foley

Easter Eggs. Originating in Europe, the custom of decorating Easter eggs was brought by immigrants to the New World. The egg was a timeless and universal symbol of spring and rebirth which later became part of the Christian celebration of Jesus' resurrection. Associated with the soul, resurrection, and spiritual rebirth, eggs were an important part of death ceremonies, often being placed in tombs. Symbolizing transformation, they were also included in courtship and marriage rituals. The expression "don't put all your eggs in one basket" originated with German courtship rituals; by giving eggs to several men, a girl kept potential suitors guessing and lessened her chance of rejection. The English folk-practice of "pace-eggs" (or "paste-eggs") is a variation of the word *pasche*, or *paschal* (the Jewish tradition of Passover

which is also celebrated in spring), and dates back to a 4,000-year-old ritual struggle to overcome death. For centuries exchanging brightly decorated eggs expressed the good wishes, friendship, and esteem shared by giver and recipient. Over time, many of the old traditions involving eggs became incorporated into the Christian Easter celebration. The Roman practice of sending eggs as tokens of congratulations was adopted by third-century Christians; decorated eggs were blessed in church at Easter and given to friends for good luck charms.

Decorated eggs continue to be made as gifts, and preserved as precious heirlooms. Two of the traditional methods of egg decorating currently in use in America are etching and wax-resist. Intricate and difficult, these processes combine coloring with designs and patterns made by scraping the surface away from a colored egg, or by applying melted wax with the point of a pin, until an intricate design is gradually built up with layers of dyes and wax. Referred to as *pisanica* by Croatians, *kraslice* by Moravians, Czechs, and Slovaks, and *pysanky* by Ukrainians, the result is a spectacular combination of bright colors, geometric patterns, and animal and flower motifs. According to Ukrainian legend, the faith, patience, and creativity required to make *pysanky* hold the key to the world's fate; when *pysanky* is no longer practiced, demons will release an evil monster to destroy the world.

The colors used in egg decorating remain important. Purple dye is associated with royalty, wealth, and affluence because it was rare, expensive, and available only to the rich and powerful. Green is connected with the earth and conveys the hope for healthy abundant crops. Blue represents good health, brown represents contentment, black stands for remembrance, and white for purity and grace. Yellow is associated with spirituality, pink conveys a wish for success, and orange indicates attraction or desire. Red has come to represent Christ's blood and victory over death.

As the contemporary version of an ancient custom, egg decorating continues to be popular in the U.S. It provides a creative outlet, and a means of preserving traditions as well as creating new ones.

Bibliography

Hart, Rhonda Massingham. *Easter Eggs*. Pownal: Storey, 1993.
Newall, Venetia. *An Egg at Easter: A Folklore Study*. London: Routledge, 1971.

D. Ann Maukonen

Eastwood, Clint (1931-), usually comes in two varieties, either as a cheroot-smoking, poncho-wearing Western outlaw with near-superhuman powers or as an eternally calm police detective who wears dark shades and enacts a swift brand of justice, courtesy of Smith and Wesson. Movie audiences around the world have been attracted to the taciturn, always-in-control men that Eastwood usually plays. Even U.S. presidents have invoked the Eastwood image, as when Ronald Reagan used the famous "Go ahead. Make my day" line from *Sudden Impact* (1983) as he threatened Congress with vetoing a bill.

Born to a poor family in San Francisco, Eastwood worked a variety of manual labor jobs, including lumberjack, blast furnace worker, lifeguard, dock worker, gas station attendant, janitor, and foundation digger. After a stint in the army during the Korean War, he enrolled at Los Angeles City College and studied business administration. At the urging of friends he got a screen test with Universal Studios, and to his surprise, they signed him to a contract at $75 a week. At Universal (and later RKO) he secured several bit parts, but nothing more substantial developed. The bit parts included a lab technician in *Revenge of the Creature* (1955) and the Air Force pilot who drops napalm on the marauding spider in *Tarantula* (1955). He even appeared as a sailor in a Francis-the-talking-mule series entry, *Francis in the Navy* (1955). With bit part after bit part leading nowhere, Eastwood accepted an offer from CBS to co-star in a television series, *Rawhide* (see entry). Premiering in 1959 (and lasting for seven years and over 200 episodes), *Rawhide* featured Eastwood as cowpoke Rowdy Yates. He and co-star Eric Fleming played a cattle-driving team on a drive that never seemed to end.

After the series became a success, Eastwood received an offer to star in an Italian-Spanish-German production, *The Magnificent Stranger*, a Western with shades of Akira Kurosawa's *Yojimbo*. CBS initially refused to let Eastwood accept the role, but after he threatened to go AWOL, CBS relented. As filming commenced in Spain, Eastwood struggled with his character. Working with director Sergio Leone, he cut huge chunks of dialogue until the "Magnificent Stranger" became a nearly silent angel of death. Eastwood returned to America not particularly hopeful that the movie would bring him fame, and he settled down to more episodes of *Rawhide*. Several months later he read about a movie named *A Fistful of Dollars* that was setting box-office records in Italy. Eventually, he realized that *The Magnificent Stranger* and *A Fistful of Dollars* were one and the same. A letter from the movie's producer finally arrived, asking if Eastwood was interested in a sequel.

With the two movies that followed, *For a Few Dollars More* and *The Good, the Bad, and the Ugly* (released in the United States between January 1967 and March 1968), Eastwood found himself at the center of one of the most famous movie trilogies in history. Filmed by Sergio Leone with a flagrant disregard for the conventions of the American Western, these movies thrust Eastwood into the spotlight during the Vietnam War—a time in America's history when many people were losing faith in American institutions. In this climate, Eastwood's cynical, destructive Man with No Name injected the Western with a caustic dose of existentialism (see Western Films).

After the spaghetti Westerns, Eastwood starred in several American-made Westerns with strong Italian influences, such as *Hang 'em High* (1968) and *High Plains Drifter* (1973). However, in these post-Italian Westerns, American sensibilities surfaced (revenge being a much more acceptable human desire than greed in the language of the American Western). The movies use violence as a way of atoning for being Westerns, as if violence would legitimize the Western for audiences that didn't believe in the Old West anymore. *High Plains Drifter* in particular features one of the

most amoral central characters in motion picture history. Once again playing a character without a name, Eastwood rides into town as an avenging angel enacting vengeance against the town that cowered while outlaws killed their sheriff. Filled with stunning images, *High Plains Drifter* becomes a journey into hell itself.

Directed by Don Siegel, *Coogan's Bluff* (1968) was the first of Eastwood's crime dramas and it represented a transitional move, placing him in Western garb and positioning him between the West and the big city. When Eastwood next appeared in a crime drama, he played Harry Callahan in *Dirty Harry* (1971; see entry)—the role that solidified his persona.

Eastwood continued to play detective Harry Callahan in four sequels—*Magnum Force* (1973), *The Enforcer* (1976), *Sudden Impact* (1983), and *The Dead Pool* (1988)—until he considered the character "worked to death." Along the way he starred in a variety of action adventures (*Thunderbolt and Lightfoot* [1974] and *The Eiger Sanction* [1975]), Westerns (*The Outlaw Josey Wales* [1976] and *Pale Rider* [1985]), crime thrillers (*The Gauntlet* [1977] and *Tightrope* [1984]) and country-and-western comedies (*Every Which Way But Loose* [1978] and *Bronco Billy* [1980]). And he teamed with Siegel again, in the elegantly underplayed *Escape from Alcatraz* (1979).

From early in his career, Eastwood opted for greater control over his movies and established his own production company, Malpaso. In addition, he produced and directed many of his own movies, starting with *Play Misty for Me* in 1971 and including *High Plains Drifter*, *Breezy* (1973), *The Outlaw Josey Wales*, *Bird* (1988), *Unforgiven* (1992), and *A Perfect World* (1994). Appreciation for his directorial talents has grown over the years. In 1980, the New York Museum of Modern Art held a retrospective of Eastwood's work, and in 1985 the French government awarded him the Chevalier Des Arts et Lettres, while the Cinematheque Française held a retrospective in his honor. In 1993, he took home the best director and best picture Academy Awards for *Unforgiven*.

Striving to give his career greater breadth, Eastwood has directed (or starred in) several movies that don't fit into the Western or crime drama categories, such as *Bird* (1988), a biography of jazz legend Charlie Parker, and *The Bridges of Madison County* (1995), a romance based on the best-selling novel by Robert James Waller, but the old images have proven tough to shake. Even *Unforgiven* (1992) derives much of its power from the contrast it provides to Eastwood's typical Western persona.

Bibliography

Bingham, David. *Acting Male: Masculinities in the Films of James Stewart, Jack Nicholson, and Clint Eastwood.* New Brunswick: Rutgers UP, 1994.

Smith, Paul. *Clint Eastwood: A Cultural Production.* Minneapolis: U of Minnesota P, 1993.

Zmijewsky, Boris, and Lee Pfeiffer. *The Films of Clint Eastwood.* New York: Citadel, 1993.

Gary Johnson

Easy Rider (1969) is one of the most important movies to document the yearnings of the 1960s counterculture. At the same time, it explores a perennial American theme—the search for America by taking to the road. Cinematically, the film takes advantage of mobile cameras and rock music to celebrate the beauties of the American landscape. The combination of theme and technique worked evocatively in a low-budget film which reaped both critical kudos and rewards at the box office. (Jack Nicholson's acting career took off as a result of his performance in a supporting role.)

In the main title sequence of the film, Captain America (Peter Fonda) and Billy (Dennis Hopper, who also directs) make a symbolic drug deal which will finance their motorcycle trip across the continent from Los Angeles to Florida. Their commercial act symbolizes the misuses of America's resources by an exploitative society.

Midway through the road trip, the explorers meet George Hanson (Jack Nicholson), who articulates the basic query of the film: "This used to be a hell of a country.... I wonder what's gone wrong with it." The message seems to be mixed about what went wrong; both those who praise and those who condemn the counterculture of the 1960s will find evidence to support their positions.

The film celebrates the spirit of the new generation in the music of Steppenwolf; Crosby, Stills, and Nash; Jimi Hendrix; and Bob Dylan. Especially in the New Mexico and desert sequences, the coordination of music with colorful scenery is effectively united with moving camera to evoke a sense of both physical and spiritual liberation. Yet *Easy Rider* makes a judgment; America has gone astray and there are painful consequences of the choices we have made.

Bibliography

Easy Rider. Dir. Dennis Hopper. Columbia Tristar Home Video, 1969.

James, David. *Allegories in Cinema: American Film in the Sixties*. Princeton: Princeton UP, 1989.

Medved, Michael. *Hollywood vs. America*. New York: HarperCollins, 1992.

Reich, Charles A. *The Greening of America*. New York: Bantam, 1970.

Peter C. Rollins

Ed Sullivan Show, The (1948-1971), dominated the Sunday variety slot for CBS for almost a quarter of a century. The original broadcast on June 20, 1948, was as *Toast of the Town*, a title retained until June 25, 1955, when the program's title became *The Ed Sullivan Show*, a title kept until the program left the air on June 6, 1971. The 1948 broadcast included guests Eugene List, the comedy team of Dean Martin and Jerry Lewis, and the songwriting team of Richard Rodgers and Oscar Hammerstein; for this broadcast, all talent was paid $200.

The program always included Sullivan, a former columnist for the *New York Daily News* as emcee, the Ray Block orchestra, and the June Taylor Dancers (originally the Toastettes). Its format was similar to many other television programs with its comedy-variety format; however, in many other programs, the host was the center talent. Such was the case of *The Arthur Godfrey Show* (1948-59), *The Ken Murray Show* (1950-53), and *The Perry Como Show* (1948-63). The success of the Sullivan show was unique, for Sullivan himself displayed virtually no noticeable talent other than the ability to recognize talent and to know what the public wanted. Unlike the hosts of other programs, Sullivan never incorporated himself into skits or used the program to showcase his own talent, although he did eventually take minor roles in skits. Sullivan quietly and blandly introduced each act, but contributed nothing else on screen.

The program's place in history is due to its longevity (23 years) and its showcase of talent. Sullivan's program provided the television debut for such names as Martin and Lewis, Bob Hope, Lena Horne, the Beatles, Eddie Fisher, Dinah Shore, and Walt Disney. Although Elvis Presley had previously appeared on television, most of the public still views his appearance on Sullivan as his first because it was assuredly his most significant appearance.

Sullivan's success came at a time when other variety shows were equally popular. Only *The Red Skelton Show* (1951-71), *The Jackie Gleason Show* (1952-70), *The Lawrence Welk Show* (1955-71), and *The Andy Williams Show* (1958-71) enjoyed anywhere near the longevity of Sullivan. None of the programs showcased the wide variety of talent that Sullivan did.

Sullivan's leaving the air in 1971 was a move to modernize its lineup, according to CBS. Sullivan's absence left only *The Carol Burnett Show* (1967-79). Burnett's show, like other variety programs, still differed from Sullivan—Burnett had personal success as a comic and actress. The end of Sullivan's show for the most part was an end to the variety show in its truest sense. Virtually nothing akin to it has been regenerated on television. The idea of a non-talent hosting a show might be similar to video jockeys on MTV; they, however, do not pick the talent, but merely introduce it.

Bibliography

Bowles, Jerry. *A Thousand Sundays: The Story of* The Ed Sullivan Show. New York: Putnam, 1980.

Brooks, Tim, and Earle Marsh. *The Complete Directory to Prime Time Network Television Shows, 1946-Present*. New York: Ballantine, 1992.

Harris, Michael David. *Always on Sunday*. New York: Meredity, 1968.

Donna Waller Harper

Edison Cylinder, The, was one of the influential inventions that heralded the birth of the 20th century. Its development was tied to other inventions and projects Thomas A. Edison worked on, and was most closely allied to the telephone, telegraph, and radio. It originally came about as Edison was seeking a way to record telegraphic clicks that would enable operators to play back messages more slowly and at their leisure. Evolving in conjunction with these devices, the Edison cylinder should be viewed as one of the foundations of modern communication technology.

Edison invented the cylinder phonograph in 1877, though several other inventors, most notably Emile Berliner and Alexander Graham Bell, were working on similar

Edison Cylinder. Photo courtesy of Sound Recording Archives, Bowling Green State University, Bowling Green, OH.

devices. Using tin foil as the medium into which grooves were cut with a stylus, Edison filed for a patent on his device that year. The cylinder phonograph was originally meant to record the telephonic voice rather than music. It is primarily for that reason that the early phonograph was commonly referred to as a "talking machine." Indeed, its aural qualities left much to be desired, even when used for voice recording.

Edison established the Edison Speaking Phonograph Company to market the phonograph, and after initially paying less attention to it than to the telephone, resumed work on it in the late 1880s. Those efforts resulted in creation of wax cylinders instead of tin ones, and a motor to drive the cylinder. Edison also outfitted the phonograph with coin slots and leased it to arcades.

Bibliography

Frow, George L. *A Guide to the Edison Cylinder Phonograph.* St. Austell: Anthony, 1970.

Koenigsberg, Allen. *Edison Cylinder Records, 1889-1912, With an Illustrated History of the Phonograph.* New York: Stellar, 1969.

Welch, Walter L. *From Tinfoil to Stereo: The Acoustic Years of the Recording Industry, 1877-1929.* Gainesville: UP of Florida, 1994.

Steve Jones

See also
History of Sound Recording
Phonograph

Electrical Transcriptions (ETs) were recordings made exclusively for radio broadcasting from the late 1920s through the 1950s. ETs evolved from long-playing records designed for talking movies. Most broadcasters considered recorded programming inferior to live programming, but transcriptions were less expensive than live talent. The term "electrical transcription" originated as an attempt to evade government regulations requiring broadcasters to announce phonograph records. Technically, stations that played electrical transcriptions were not playing records and did not have to announce ETs as such.

Transcribed programs were usually recorded in one of three ways: in the studio of a company that specialized in transcriptions, through a direct line from a radio station control room, or directly from the air. The transcription used either live talent or dubs (re-recordings) from other recordings. In the case of dubbing, program producers usually chose material, such as music, from other transcriptions or records. The producers then re-recorded the selections onto one disc. Transcribing a dubbed program cost about one third as much as transcribing a program with live talent. For fast-breaking news events, the discs could be recorded right at the news scene with portable equipment. Many stations owned instantaneous recording equipment primarily for recording network programs directly from the phone line. These recordings then allowed broadcasters to air network programs at times more convenient than the networks' original broadcasts.

After World War II, magnetic tape (see entry) took the place of the disc. The tape recorder retained all the conveniences of the discs and eliminated most of the difficulties, including cost. Network quality tape recorders cost around $700 in 1949 while the same quality transcription systems cost upward of $2,000. The superior fidelity of tape, the longer recording time, the ability to reuse the tape, and the ease of editing expedited the switch from disc to tape.

Bibliography

Abbot, Waldo. *Handbook of Broadcasting.* New York: McGraw-Hill, 1937.

Healy, J. Dale. "Processing Radio Transcriptions." *Radio and Television News* Feb. 1950.

Lewis, Leonard. "Transcriptions—Why and How." *Printer's Ink Monthly* Dec. 1936.

"What Is a Transcription?" *Western Advertising* March 1937.

Jana L. Hyde

Electronic Banking and Automatic Teller Machines. Financial institutions in the United States and around the world are re-engineering their relationships with customers. Because of explosive advances in technology, traditional banking with cash and checks is converting to electronic banking with computers and software.

The most noticeable technology impacting electronic banking is the Automatic Teller Machine (ATM). The standard ATM allows a bank customer, with a plastic ATM card, which has a magnetic stripe encoded with account information, and a personal identification number (PIN), access to bank accounts and cash at ATMs all over the world. The use of ATM technology is surging as banks replace human tellers with a technology that works seven days a week and 24 hours a day.

A further innovation, the use of the ATM card as a debit card, has now begun to displace cash and credit cards as a means of payment. The dual ATM/debit card allows consumers to access their bank account at the point of sale. Instead of presenting cash, check, or a credit card to a merchant for a purchase, the customer uses an ATM/debit card to complete the transaction at the cash register. The plastic ATM/debit card is swiped through an on-line terminal, connected to a financial network that includes the customer's bank. The customer punches in a PIN, then the money is electronically transferred from the customer's bank account to the merchant's bank account. The transaction is completed immediately without cash or check.

The ATM/debit cards are quickly gaining acceptance nationwide. Retailers ranging from doctors' offices to fast food restaurants to supermarkets to dry cleaners are adopting this technology for their customers' payments. Several state and local governments are also accepting the ATM/debit card for tax and fine payments.

Not all consumers are willing to embrace the instant on-line debit of the ATM/debit card. The main concern is the loss of "float" inherent with payment by checks or credit card. This concern seems to be less apparent for those consumers who would have used cash as a form of payment. In some communities, a more technologically oriented generation of Americans have grown to expect point-of-sale technology in the marketplace.

The next evolution in bank card technology may soon surpass both the conventional ATM card and the ATM/debit card. This next generation of "smart cards" will look like the traditional plastic bank card with a major exception: the magnetic stripe will be replaced with computer microchips, which will allow the card to contain a portrait of the cardholder, along with all sorts of pertinent information, such as eligibility for senior citizen discounts, frequent flyer information, and so on.

Bibliography

Cohen, David R. "Diebold Inc." *The Value Line Investment Survey* 7 (1994): 1118.

Harrington, Joseph. "Dual ATM/Debit Cards Hope for Fee Income." *SI: Savings Institution* May 1991: 48.

Mannix, Margaret. "Checks Made of Plastic." *U.S. News and World Report* 14 March 1994: 72-74.

Philip K. Flyn

Electronic Field Production (EFP) refers to the application of cinematography techniques to video recording with portable television cameras. A video camera much the same size as a small motion picture camera is employed to record imagery in a scene one shot at a time. In the professional arena, the techniques and equipment are also called electronic cinematography, single-camera video production, or film-style videography. Professional equipment tends to be expensive and requires technical expertise for successful operation. At the amateur level, EFP can be referred to as electronic movie-making and home video. Consumer equipment is available in a number of relatively inexpensive and easy-to-use formats.

The future of electronic field production seems to indicate two complementary directions, one toward increasing sophistication of high-definition TV and advanced television systems for the professional to rival the quality inherent in the best motion pictures, and the other toward accessibility of similar technology by consumers. Distinctions between "professional" and "amateur" videography will tend to blur even further in the 21st century.

John Freeman

Electronic News Gathering (ENG) refers to the use of portable video cameras and recorders to videotape news events at the scene where they are happening. The term applies not only to the equipment but also to the procedures, techniques, and processes used by television reporters (broadcast journalists who write the news stories and appear on camera) and videographers (photojournalists who operate the camera/recorder) to gather news outside of their newsrooms and studios. ENG has liberated television news from the confines of the TV station and from the bulky, slow technology of 16mm newsfilm cameras that ENG replaced in the 1970s and 1980s.

The impact of ENG has been significant. It has changed the way TV news departments plan, produce, and present the news. News teams can report visually what is happening now, rather than what happened three or four hours earlier. ENG has changed audience perceptions of what television news means: more visual drama, more "live" reports and immediacy, more stories covered, and longer newscasts.

ENG equipment is characterized by relatively small, hand-held video cameras and videotape recorders (VTRs) easily operated by one person. These devices record the images and sounds of news events. The camcorder is the typical ENG device in current use. It combines camera and recorder in one compact, easy-to-use unit resting on the photojournalist's shoulder. ENG is used throughout the television industry, in local stations, at the broadcast networks, and on such cable networks such as CNN Headline News.

The world, because of ENG technologies and techniques, has changed visibly over the past 25 years. Not everyone agrees that the changes are entirely positive. Although television news contains more visual drama, immediacy and excitement, stories have become shorter. Some argue that the news has become more superficial, providing viewers with less of what they need to understand its significance and importance.

Bibliography

Musburger, Robert B. *Electronic News Gathering: A Guide to ENG*. Boston: Focal, 1991.

Yoakam, Richard D. *ENG, Television News and the New Technology*. Carbondale: Southern Illinois UP, 1989.

John Freeman

See also

Camcorder Journalism

Ellington, "Duke" (Edward Kennedy) (1899-1974), is regarded by most jazz musicians as the greatest composer of the 20th century. His work spans the history of African Americans in the U.S. Certainly, Ellington was aware of his position as a cultural interpreter to non-African Americans and bore that role with regal or, he might say ducal, dignity.

From Ellington's earliest professional days, Caribbean music played a direct part in his music. The drum kit of his band member Sonny Greer alone was persuasive. It was filled with all types of African and Caribbean percussion. However, the influence went deeper than that and indicated what was later termed "roots." Ellington was a proud man from a proud family. He was never ashamed of himself and consequently could not be ashamed of his ancestors.

Ellington began music lessons as a child but really picked up most of his music on the streets, listening to music from area clubs and on piano rolls. He was artistically talented and won both an NAACP art award and a scholarship to Brooklyn's Pratt Institute. After some thought, he declined the scholarship and turned to music. In 1918, he married Edna Thompson, who was pregnant with Ellington's only child, Mercer.

On December 4, 1927, Ellington began his run as pianist/composer/leader of a jazz orchestra playing at the Cotton Club, one of the more important engagements in jazz history. The run lasted into 1932, with breaks for movies and tours allowed. In addition to playing his music regularly, writing for the shows, and providing a basic income to keep his men together, the gig provided Ellington with a large radio audience who came to know his music. At this time, Ellington developed what he termed his "jungle sound," a use of various tonal colors through plunger mutes and such that he associated with Africa, a constant theme in his ever-evolving music.

In October 1930, Ellington had his first hit, which was titled *Dreamy Blues* but is better known today as *Mood Indigo*. Shortly after leaving the Cotton Club, Ellington went on his first European trip. That trip did not keep Ellington from writing. He developed the habit of writing on the road and a string of hits followed. In the midst of his hits, however, Ellington wrote more complex compositions, including *Daybreak Express, Blue Harlem*, and others.

Throughout the 1930s Ellington had a constancy of personnel that enabled him to compose with particular performers in mind. From 1939 to 1942, significant changes took place in the band: Billy Strayhorn, his alter ego, joined the band as a composer-arranger and sometimes pianist; Jimmy Blanton, the revolutionary bassist, and Ben Webster on tenor added a drive that the band needed.

Strayhorn composed the band's theme song, "Take the A Train," "Chelsea Bridge," and other tunes. Ellington composed "Warm Valley," "Harlem Airshaft," "Jack the Bear," and the musical *Jump for Joy* in Hollywood. He also wrote the pop tune, "I Got It Bad and That Ain't Good!" From 1943 to 1950 he began an annual series of concerts at Carnegie Hall. In 1943, he performed *Black, Brown and Beige*. Its lukewarm critical reception led Ellington to perform only selections from it for the rest of his life. Thanks to a recording ban in 1943, the performance was not recorded and released at the time.

In 1956, at the Newport Jazz Festival, a saxophone solo by Paul Gonsalves marked the return to widespread popularity of the Ellington Band. Ellington introduced his old chestnut, *Diminuendo in Blue and Crescendo in Blue*, as having an interlude by Paul Gonsalves. For whatever reason the saxophonist took an extended solo that brought the house to its feet.

The band never lost its popularity again. It went on world tours, represented the U.S. in State Department–sponsored tours, performed extended concert works, appeared on numerous TV shows, and in many ways became an embodiment of jazz itself. In 1957, Ellington was commissioned to write the Shakespearian suite *Such Sweet Thunder,* for the Stratford Ontario Shakespeare Festival. He also revised

Black, Brown, and Beige and recorded it with Mahalia Jackson. His recording of the *Duke Ellington Songbook* with Ella Fitzgerald and their joint appearance at Carnegie Hall were artistically and commercially successful.

Ellington introduced a number of innovations into jazz. Wordless vocals were first inaugurated with Adelaide Hall's singing on *Creole Love Call*. The three-minute record imposed a limit on creativity but Ellington surmounted it by placing performances over more than one recording. *Creole Rhapsody* and *Reminiscing in Tempo* both were released on this type of extended format in the early 1930s. Ellington even recorded an early stereo record for Victor, a record since released in LP format. He worked on the concerto for Barney Bigard, a clarinetist, and Cootie Williams, a trumpeter. He wrote extended pieces, sacred music, and otherwise up until his death.

Bibliography

Feather, Leonard. *Encyclopedia of Jazz*. New York: Da Capo, 1984.

——. *Encyclopedia of Jazz Yearbook*. New York: Horizon, 1958.

Gammond, Peter. *Oxford Companion to Popular Music*. New York: Oxford UP, 1991

Gridley, Mark. *Jazz Styles*. Englewood Cliffs: Prentice-Hall, 1994.

Peretti, Burton. *The Creation of Jazz*. Urbana: U of Illinois P, 1992.

Weinstein, Norman. *A Night in Tunisia*. Metuchen: Scarecrow, 1993.

Frank A. Salamone

Embroidery is practiced today by women (and some men) all over the U.S. Many women embroider as a solitary activity, learning from books or from an informal interchange with a friend or relative; some belong to organized groups, like a chapter of the Embroiderers' Guild of America; others learn it in school settings. Embroidery is adornment sewn onto a piece of fabric, clothing, or linen. The thread used may be thin like silk, or thick yarn like that used in crewel embroidery. Perhaps the most often used thread is embroidery floss, which may be purchased at most needlework and craft shops. Often hoops are used when stitching to keep the fabric taut. Embroiderers may create their own designs, embellish already designed patterns, or purchase and follow the directions in an embroidery kit.

Young girls in colonial America usually learned embroidery skills by creating samplers. More than 2,500 examples of samplers made before the end of the 18th century have been catalogued. Often verses became part of these samplers, reflecting a young woman's preoccupation with subjects such as religion, piety, duty, and death. A young girl stitching religious pieces not only strengthened her role as a domestic artist but also developed her role as a religious caretaker. Many early embroidered pieces were memorials that functioned like stitched paintings. Some samplers have provided historians with architectural documentation since stitchers in early America occasionally turned to community buildings for subject matter. So varied and ubiquitous were embroidered pieces in the U.S. that it has been said that one can "see American history through the eye of a needle."

Today women gather regularly to stitch and enjoy each other's company. Much of the credit for embroidery's continued popularity can be attributed to the Embroiderers' Guild of America, founded in 1958. It currently has more than 220 chapters in the U.S., Canada, and Mexico. Whether an embroiderer embellishes a baby bib or a tablecloth, it is clear that this art form is flourishing.

Bibliography
Callen, Anthea. *Angel in the Studio: Women in the Arts and Crafts Movement, 1870-1914.* New York: Pantheon, 1979.

Faxon, Alice, and Sylvia Moore, eds. *Pilgrims and Pioneers: New England Women in the Arts.* New York: Midmarch Arts, 1987.

Parker, Rozsika. *The Subversive Stitch: Embroidery and the Making of the Feminine.* London: Women's, 1984.

Kristin G. Congdon

English, Diane (1948-). With a contract worth about $40 million with CBS and a major hit television show to her credit, Diane English is one of the most influential television writer/producers in the U.S. Born in Buffalo, NY, she graduated from Buffalo State College with a major in education and minor in theater arts. After teaching high school for one year, she moved to New York City in the early 1970s, determined to become a playwright. She obtained a job as a secretary at WNET, the local PBS affiliate, which soon turned into an administrative position for the Television Laboratory, an outlet for experimental work. English also began a three-year stint writing a TV column for *Vogue* magazine in 1977. At WNET she eventually got the opportunity to edit and rewrite a film adaptation of Ursula LeGuin's novel *The Lathe of Heaven,* broadcast on PBS in 1980. Her subsequent nomination for a Writers' Guild Award helped to convince her that television was where her future lay. In 1977, English had married Joel Shukovsky, owner of an ad agency, whom she met at WNET. The couple moved to Los Angeles in 1981 to try their luck in the commercial television industry.

English has written scripts for several network TV movies, including *My Life As a Man* on NBC in 1984 and *Classified Love* on CBS in 1986. She also wrote for series television, including the short-lived *Call to Glory,* which debuted in 1984 on ABC and looked at the turbulent 1960s through the eyes of an Air Force family. The 1985-86 season, however, marked the debut of the first comedy series she created, produced, and wrote. *Foley Square* was also the first of three of her series on CBS that revolved around a single career woman with a sexually ambiguous name in a field dominated by men. Alex Harrigan was an assistant district attorney in New York City whose best friend was a man, also establishing precedent for her successors. Featuring both her professional and personal life in classic workcom fashion, the series lasted only one year. English's next project was *My Sister Sam* in 1986. Sam was a photographer whose teenage sister moved in with her after their parents died. Her best friend was her male next-door neighbor. Sam was portrayed by Pam Dawber, from the popular *Mork and Mindy* of the 1970s. Her sister was portrayed by Rebecca Schaeffer, tragically killed by a stalking fan not long after the series' two-year run.

In 1988, English introduced her first hit, *Murphy Brown* (see entry). Played by Candice Bergen, Murphy is a co-anchor of a network television newsmagazine. Compared by critics to *The Mary Tyler Moore Show* because of its single, female character in a newsroom, Murphy, unlike Mary Richards, did not mince words when it came to both her professional and personal life. Known for her tough investigative reporting and interviewing, Murphy is also a recovering alcoholic who spent time at the Betty Ford Clinic.

Co-executive producer with her husband, English created the series and was its head writer. Although it took a couple of seasons for *Murphy Brown* to become a Top 10 hit, it began garnering Emmy Awards from the beginning. Over its first four seasons, it took 15 Emmys, including one for the pilot episode, written by English.

In 1992, English and Shukovsky severed ties with *Murphy Brown* to form their own production company, Shukovsky English Entertainment. They no longer would have to share their profits with Warner Brothers, which owned that series, or any other studio. The first show to come out of the new company was *Love and War* (1992-95), which starred Jay Thomas and Susan Dey (formerly of the 1970s *Partridge Family* and the 1980s *L.A. Law*).

Bibliography
Alley, Robert S., and Irby B. Brown. *Murphy Brown: Anatomy of a Sitcom.* New York: Dell, 1990.

Brooks, Tim, and Earle Marsh. *The Complete Directory to Prime Time Network TV Shows, 1946-Present.* 5th ed. New York: Ballantine, 1992.

De Vries, Hilary. "Laughing Off the Recession All the Way to the Bank." *New York Times Magazine* 3 Jan. 1993: 19+.

Marc, David, and Robert J. Thompson. *Prime Time, Prime Movers.* Boston: Little, Brown, 1992.

Lynn C. Spangler

Entertainment Tonight (1981-), as the premier U.S. program of entertainment news and gossip, has had lasting influence on both the dominant media and the public's perception of entertainment. Since its debut, the show, popularly known as *ET,* has sparked a minor revolution in broadcast journalism, pioneering entertainment news coverage, while at the same time almost single-handedly changing how the entertainment industry sells its products.

From its first broadcast, which covered the previous evening's Emmy Award ceremonies in September 1981, the show's basic concept has remained steady, despite occasional changes in personnel and formats. The program is set up as a straightforward newscast, complete with anchors and correspondents, but with an approach that is more similar to *People* magazine. The focus is on entertainment news and gossip, with a steady supply of celebrity interviews and profiles, on-location visits to films, television programs, and music recording sessions, and other assorted tidbits. *ET's* strength is its immediacy. It broadcasts a daily, 30-minute episode on weeknights, followed by an hour-long weekend edition. Each episode is fed by satellite to local stations, many of which broadcast the program live. The show's most identifiable on-screen personalities have been Mary Hart, who joined the show as senior anchor in June 1982, John Tesh, who became co-host in 1986, weekend host Leeza Gibbons, and film critic Leonard Maltin.

Entertainment Tonight can perhaps be seen as the senior ambassador for show business. Though its structure is that of a news broadcast, it more closely resembles a promotional program for the entertainment industry. The program works to contribute to the public perception of show business as glamorous and glitzy, providing viewers with a steady stream of backstage access to awards shows and other exclusive celebrity events. Television series and specials, movies, music, books, and other entertainment media are regularly showcased in stories that undoubtedly prove invaluable to audience awareness of these works. As one of the top-rated syndicated programs in the country, *ET* can provide high-profile exposure that few if any other publicity outlets can equal.

Broadcast in more than 15 countries, and with correspondents reporting from all over the world, *Entertainment Tonight* at times takes on a global look. But it is dominated by the U.S. entertainment industry, and specifically Hollywood, where it is based. Because of *ET* and imitations like CNN's *Showbiz Today*, entertainment reporting and celebrity journalism now command more time in news broadcasts.

Bibliography
Brodie, John. "*ET*'s New Competitor Sets Flacks a-Flutter." *Variety* 24-31 July 1994: 1, 73.
Brooks, Tim, and Earle Marsh. *The Complete Directory to Prime Time Network and Cable TV Shows, 1946-Present.* New York: Ballantine, 1995.
Dugard, Martin. "Close-Up: John Tesh." *Runner's World* Nov. 1993: 42-44.
Freeman, Mike. "Entertainment Tonight Turns 3,000." *Broadcasting & Cable* 8 Mar. 1993: 30.
O'Brien, Maureen. "Entertainment Tonight: The Hot Button." *Publisher's Weekly* 30 Nov. 1992: 28.

Bob Mastrangelo

Escher, M. C. (1898-1972). In the 1960s, any self-respecting hippie haven was decorated with at least one perspective-bending, psychedelic poster by graphic artist M. C. Escher. However, few of those admirers were aware of the circumstances of his life or the sources of his fantastic creations, even though at that time the artist was alive and tolerably well. Interest in Escher's prints has continued to grow, and his distinctive, otherworldly designs adorn clothing and other products.

This tall, gaunt Dutchman grew up at the turn of the century expecting to become an architect. That would certainly seem an obvious career choice for a budding artist who was transfixed by the simple beauty of horizontal and vertical planes, symmetry and order. However, Escher was persuaded by an insightful college professor to consider a profession in graphic arts. Fortunately for those who are intrigued by the ingenuity of his artistic experiments, he chose a less-traveled path. That path began in Europe, often on foot.

It was on one of these junkets that Escher's imagination was seized by the intricate, interlocking tile designs in a Moorish palace, the Alhambra, in Spain. His letters and sketchbooks show that he was clearly enthralled. There, on those cool walls, the young printmaker saw solutions to puzzles that had vexed his creativity since childhood. Those glossy tiles profoundly influenced the somber Dutchman by giving substance to the whirling images that persisted in joining provocatively behind his eyes. The Alhambra confirmed his personal obsession, and Escher inwardly adopted a compelling mission, to express infinity.

In 1935, a move from the warm, lush landscapes of Italy to a somewhat more sterile Switzerland turned his artist's eye inward for solutions to an enigma that had always obsessed him, the regular and systematic division of a level surface, or plane, with intersecting figures. His precise and creative woodcuts began depicting crystalline structures instead of bridge spans and mushrooming hamlets. Escher started improvising on the way matter is naturally packaged and joined. He concocted impossible structures and ants crawling eternally on a latticed Mobius strip. Mathematics became an important tool, as his divisions of a plane became more intricate, elaborate, and colorful. His explorations were immediately embraced by crystallographers and mathematicians as beguiling representations of models used extensively in their fields. From those circles, he received appreciation and respect, an affinity that continues today.

A 1948 lithograph, "Drawing Hands," is often seen in public, decorating a teenager's ensemble or even a doctor's wall. This provocative print depicts duplicate hands rising from a paper and drawing each other's cuffs. Each of these hands is a simple, yet faithful image of Escher's left hand, captured in the act of translating visionary speculations to a single plane.

Bibliography
Bool, F. H., J. R. Kist, J. L. Locher, and F. Wierda. *M.C. Escher, His Life and Complete Work.* New York: Abrams, 1982.
Ernst, Bruno. *The Magic Mirror of M. C. Escher.* Norfolk: Tarquin, 1985.
Escher, M. C., and J. L. Locher. *The World of M. C. Escher.* New York: Abrams, 1989.
MacGillary, Catherine. *Fantasy & Symmetry: The Periodic Drawings of M. C. Escher.* New York: Abrams, 1976.

Susan Boot

ESPN and ESPN2 are 24-hour cable-television networks that broadcast live and taped sporting events, sports news, sports talk shows, music videos, game shows, and exercise programs. Sports channels that deal wholly or in part with sports programming, such as ESPN (Entertainment and Sports Programming Network) and ESPN2, Prime Ticket, SportsChannel, TNT (Turner Network Television), TBS (Turner Broadcasting System), and the Golf Channel are outgrowths of the 1980s concern with consumerist culture, and reflect several popular culture elements, including popular rituals (rites of unity and of season), popular formulas, sports icons, and sports heroes of American mass culture. These sports channels celebrate the achievement of those who have attained the American dream of wealth and success, the champion athletes and winning teams. Sports channels cover not only traditional sports such as basketball, baseball, football, tennis, golf, hockey, and auto racing, but also less traditional ones such as game fishing, go-cart races, yachting, surfing, women's beach volleyball, snooker, rodeo, and monster-truck events (see Sports on Television).

These sports, both the familiar and the unfamiliar, form the staple programming of ESPN. Today's ESPN and other sports networks continue to make innovative programming deals with other continents, such as Africa and Asia, and for other lesser-known sports, such as soccer, in order to expand a growing international sports audience. These networks keep up with technological trends such as ESPN's connection with Prodigy Computer Network (ESPNET), satellite transmission, interactive games, and pay-per-view programming.

The Rasmussen family founded ESPN on September 7, 1979, with Getty Oil as a partner. ABC agreed to purchase ESPN in 1984, and, in an attempt to attract a younger audience and to maintain the integrity of ESPN's programming for older viewers, ESPN2 came to the airwaves on October 1, 1993. Its style involves casual dress, "hip" music and graphics, bright and unusual colors, and perky deliveries of the sports news in an attempt to woo and to develop a future sports audience, especially since media observers feel that the youth of the 1990s do not seem to be particularly interested in sports.

For those individuals devoted to sports events, sports channels like ESPN help to create a sense of community for a sports audience that continues to expand. They represent an electronic rite of unity whereby, at all hours of the day, participants gather at the television shrine in order to celebrate the pleasures and pains of sports participation in one international congregation. Rites of season (concerned with the pattern of death and rebirth as reflected in the four seasons) occur with each new seasonal sport; for instance, spring and summer are observed with the re-appearance of *Baseball Tonight*. ESPN2 observes fall and winter rituals by having sportscasters dress in collegiate scarves and take on their version of Ivy League accents. Popular formulas occur on sports channels with the traditional "good-guy/bad-guy" binary for winners and losers, with land acquisition in the playing of sports like football, hockey, and basketball, and with imperial conquest, in sports like golf and tennis. These formulas represent American values of Puritan goodness, manifest destiny, and world prominence. Viewers of sports channels around the globe have the opportunity to celebrate world-renowned sports figures like Michael Jordan (1963-) and André Agassi (1970-); this celebration represents the global culture's desire to have all people be their best, to achieve the pinnacle of human success.

The programming itself on ESPN evinces respect for traditional American values. A program such as *Sports Center* gathers viewing participants together for ritual celebration of the day's achievements, functioning as a rubber stamp for values of success, ingenuity, physical prowess and physical beauty, and secular worship of human energy and resourcefulness. Other programs, such as the exercise and bodyshaping shows, emphasize secular values of attractiveness, personal magnetism, hard work, and self-worth, all values of the dominant culture.

Sports channels tend to uphold the values of the dominant culture. These values include personal integrity, fairness, *esprit de corps,* honesty, might, strength, physical and mental power; in other words, values that have helped the culture to achieve dominance. Sports play is reminiscent of the social and political games needed for the continuance of democratic capitalist systems, and sports channels serve as official spokespersons to disseminate those values.

Bibliography

Rasmussen, Bill. *Sports Junkies Rejoice! The Birth of ESPN.* Hartsdale: QV, 1983.

Whannel, Garry. *Fields in Vision: Television Sport and Cultural Transformation.* New York: Routledge, 1992.

Williams, Huntington. *Beyond Control: ABC and the Fate of the Networks.* New York: Atheneum, 1989.

Stephanie A. Richardson

Estleman, Loren (1952-), prolific popular author, was born in Ann Arbor, MI. Even while attending college at Eastern Michigan University, where he received his bachelor's degree in 1974, Estleman was working at professional journalism. He was a cartoonist and writer for the *Michigan Fed* from 1967 to 1970. He wrote for a variety of papers, including the *Ypsilanti Press*, the *Community Foto News* (where he was also editor-in-chief), and various other papers.

Estleman has excelled in three genres: mystery, Western, and a historical mystery with horror. His novel about Buffalo Bill, *This Old Bill* (1984), was nominated for the Pulitzer Prize. Estleman perceives mysteries and Westerns to be merely variations on the same theme. He believes that private eye mysteries are modern-day equivalents of the old Western. In both, it is the lone hero who must depend on his own resources and integrity to overcome great odds.

Bibliography

Crider, Bill. *Twentieth Century Crime and Mystery Writers,* 2d ed. New York: St. Martin's, 1985.

Dary, David. *Los Angeles Times Book Review* 21 Aug. 1983.

"Estleman, Loren D." *Contemporary Authors: New Revised Edition* 27 (1988): 151-58.

Frank A. Salamone

E.T., The Extra-Terrestrial (1982), one of America's most successful movie versions of a visit of an alien being, reportedly began as a small-scale film called *After School,* depicting children's late-afternoon activities, and eventually grew into an outright cultural phenomenon when the idea of an extraterrestrial was introduced. *E.T., The Extra-Terrestrial* is considered by some to be the greatest film ever made, or at least "the best Disney film Disney never made." Although other critics saw it as a sappy and manipulative "*Lassie* in science fiction drag" and an over-hyped, merchandising tie-in gimmick, the $359 million this Universal film made in its first year remains a record; and since its June 1982 release the picture has grossed well over $400 million, making it the single most popular movie in history to date.

Written by Melissa Mathison, scriptwriter for *The Black Stallion* (1979), the film was produced by Steven Spielberg (see entry) and Kathleen Kennedy with Spielberg directing. He and Mathison supposedly aimed straight for the anxieties and fantasies of children: including fear of losing a parent, homesickness, and empathy for vulnerable creatures. Indeed, Spielberg called *E.T.* his most personal and autobiographical movie.

The film tells the tale of an alien left stranded in the woods near a California suburb when its spaceship takes off to elude a team of faceless scientists, and 10-year-old Elliott, who discovers the creature, overcomes his fear, hides E.T. from the scientists, and helps the alien find its way home.

Beyond the impressive special effects by Dennis Muren of Industrial Light & Magic (George Lucas's studio), the film's most interesting achievement was the $1.5 million creature itself, referred to indiscriminately as "he" or "she" during filming, according to Spielberg. The large-eyed, long-necked, pear-shaped, leathery-skinned E.T. was created and operated by Italian sculptor Carlo Rambaldi. In addition to the electronic puppet, rubber suits were worn for some scenes by 2-foot 10-inch Pat Bilon, by legless youngster Matthew de Meritt, and by 2-foot 7-inch Tamara de Treaux.

E.T. pioneered tie-in merchandising. The film promotes Coke, Pez, and particularly Reese's Pieces (sales of which soared 85%). Universal contracted for more than 40 products: candy, chewing gum, socks, games, even *E.T.* ice cream (a dyed-green vanilla with Reese's Pieces). Film jokes similarly looked self-serving: Elliott's toy shark evoking Spielberg's *Jaws* (1975), the child's action figure of Lando Calrissian and the Halloween costume of Yoda both from Spielberg's *The Empire Strikes Back* (1980). But the strengths of the film could not be ignored and *E.T.* was nominated for seven Academy Awards (including best screenplay), winning for best sound, best visual effects, best sound effects editing, and best musical score (by John Williams), but losing best picture and best direction to *Gandhi*.

E.T.'s gimmick of an abandoned special effects creature was used in a spate of lesser films including *Baby: Secret of the Lost Legend* (1985) about a young dinosaur, *Hyper Sapien* (1986), and the most despicable rip-off, *Mac and Me* (1988), which pitches the intergalactic healing properties of McDonald's fast food. *E.T.* also inspired Neil Diamond's hit song "Turn on Your Heartlight," and spawned a ride at Universal Studios theme park. Melissa Mathison's sequel to *E.T.*, written in 1983, has not been filmed, yet.

Bibliography

Hardy, Phil, ed. *Science Fiction: The Aurum Film Encyclopedia*. London: Aurum, 1991. 374.

McCarthy, Todd. "Sand Castles: Steven Spielberg Interviewed." *Film Comment* May/June 1982. 53-59.

Palmer, William J. *The Films of the Eighties: A Social History*. Carbondale: Southern Illinois UP, 1993.

Michael Delahoyde

Ethnic Food. Until about 1970 the all-American dinner of choice was steak and baked potato, accompanied by a simple lettuce and tomato salad, and a dessert of ice cream or pie. Eating such a meal proclaimed that the diner had attained a degree of economic success and enough appreciation for the good things in life to be considered a "real" American. It appeared that the 1920s "Americanization" campaigns directed at changing immigrants' eating habits had been successful. Exotic ethnic foods had disappeared from diets, while a few foreign dishes had been adopted into the conventional cookbooks, proving that America was indeed a culinary melting pot.

But a culinary revolution that would redefine the all-American steak dinner as unhealthy and boring was already starting to boil. Ethnic food was about to make a comeback.

Since 1970, consumption of ethnic foods has been on the increase. Mexican salsa, a spicy blend of tomatoes and peppers, has recently surpassed ketchup as the nation's favorite condiment. The food industry attributes this shift to the health concerns of aging baby boomers who are looking for ways to enliven meals containing less fat, salt, and sugar. But it is also noteworthy that sauces are a type of food easily assimilated, since their strangeness can so easily be tempered by pairing them with familiar foods such as chips, bread, pasta, and such. Thus, salsa replacing ketchup is a much more likely occurrence than is cornmeal replacing wheat flour, for instance.

Rebellious members of the baby boomer generation led the critique of mainstream American diets in the 1970s. Charging that all-American food was bland, unhealthy, and ecologically unsound, young members of the antiwar, anti-bourgeois counterculture turned instead to Third World peasant foods. Dishes like Middle Eastern tabouleh, Indian curries, South American empanadas, and Mexican tortillas came to symbolize solidarity with the oppressed, opposition to American cultural imperialism (i.e., McDonald's around the world), and a rejection of the meat-and-potatoes ideal of normalcy.

Demand for more exotic spices and authentic ingredients took culinary rebels into small ethnic grocery stores and restaurants, helping to revive areas such as Boston's North End and Detroit's Greektown. Just as the bohemians of the first decade of this century had "discovered" Italian restaurants—then considered very exotic by mainstream Americans—the counterculture led the broader American public to Mexican, Indian, and Thai eating places. Restaurants are where most people, whether "natives" or "immigrants," first encounter food of other ethnic groups. Second-generation Mexican-American youth, for instance, eat hamburgers and french fries at McDonald's, while fourth-generation Iowa farmers try out tacos at Taco Bell.

In the last several decades, neighborhoods, towns, and even whole regions have embraced ethnic foods in festivals that draw throngs of visitors. Clambakes, crawfish boils, and kielbasa cookouts, for example, celebrate the respective culinary heritage of Anglo-Americans, Cajuns, and Polish-Americans.

Bibliography

Belasco, Warren. *Appetite for Change: How the Counterculture Took on the Food Industry, 1966-1988*. New York: Pantheon, 1989.

Brown, Linda K., and Kay Mussell, eds. *Ethnic and Regional Foodways in the United States*. Knoxville: U of Tennessee P, 1984.

Levenstein, Harvey. *Paradox of Plenty: A Social History of Eating in Modern America*. New York: Oxford UP, 1993.

———. *Revolution at the Table: The Transformation of the American Diet*. New York: Oxford UP, 1988.

Mariani, John. *America Eats Out*. New York: William Morrow, 1991.

Jan Whitaker

Ethnic Mysteries. The mystery genre has undergone an important evolution in recent years, opening its canon to writers and detectives of various ethnic backgrounds and thus creating a new subcategory. Rudolph Fisher's *The Conjure Man Dies* (1932) is usually considered the first black detective novel but was actually preceded by two earlier works. J. E. Bruce's *Black Sleuth*, published as a serial in *McGirt's Weekly* from 1908 to 1909, features an African-born detective who brings a black nationalist perspective on American society to the genre. Even earlier, the pioneer African-American writer Pauline Hopkins wrote *Hagar's Daughter* (1901-2), serialized in *The Colored American Magazine*. This novel previews the direction of much 20th-century African-American writing. It created a black female detective persona, celebrated the black vernacular in music and language, and depicted hoodoo as an affirmative element of black culture. Moreover, Hopkins showed that mystery novels, commonly the property of a white mainstream worldview, could be transformed for political and social ends.

Historically, most ethnic mysteries have been written by black males. Chester Himes proved the most prolific, producing ten detective novels between 1957 and 1969 set in Harlem, nine featuring his hard-boiled detective team of Coffin Ed Johnson and Grave Digger Jones. African-American writers have also contributed to the traditional subgenres of detective fiction. Dolores Komo created a memorable black private eye in *Clio Browne: Private Investigator* (1988). Eleanor Taylor Bland has written several police procedurals—beginning with *Dead Time* (1992)—about black homicide detective Marti MacAlister, who works with a white male partner in and around Chicago. Yolanda Joe's *Falling Leaves of Ivy* (1994) is a contemporary crime novel with an eastern university setting.

The recent popularity of African-American mystery writers such as Walter Mosley and Barbara Neely signals the genre's new trends. Mosley's books featuring detective Easy Rawlins, beginning with *Devil in a Blue Dress* (1990), take place predominantly in the Watts area of Los Angeles and explore the historical development of African-American issues from the period just after World War II until the early 1960s. In Barbara Neely's mysteries, such as *Blanche on the Lam* (1992), *Blanche among the Talented Tenth* (1994), and *Blanche Cleans Up* (1998), the detective is Blanche White, a black domestic worker. Neely's novels provide sophisticated examinations of contemporary class and race issues.

Representatives of other ethnic groups have also made a significant impact on detective fiction. Earlier in the century, writers such as Earl Derr Biggers and John P. Marquand created the Asian detectives Charlie Chan and Mr. Moto, but these ethnic personalities were presented stereotypically from a mainstream viewpoint. In the last two decades, a variety of ethnic mysteries have addressed questions of race, class, and gender from a nonmajority point of view. Tony Hillerman's novels feature Navajo tribal police detectives Joe Leaphorn and Jim Chee. Books such as *The Blessing Way* (1970), *Dance Hall of the Dead* (1973), and *A Thief of Time* (1988) use the mystery genre to explore Native American themes and concerns. Japanese-American Detective Sergeant Masao Masuto is the protagonist of E. V. Cunningham's mysteries, such as *The Case of the Murdered Mackenzie* (1984). Peter Bowen's series featuring French-Indian cattle-brand inspector Gabriel Du Pre, set in Montana, and Dana Stabenow's Alaskan mysteries profiling Aleut private investigator Kate Shugat demonstrate the diverse possibilities of the ethnic subgenre.

The achievements of ethnic writers, along with the works of women and gay authors, have dramatically widened the scope of the mystery field. For example, the black writer Nikki Baker has written mystery novels with a lesbian detective named Virginia Kelly solving crimes dealing with lesbian issues. Chicano author Michael Nava's books featuring Henry Rios, a gay California lawyer-sleuth, also demonstrate the richness of the ethnic sensibility, beginning with *Little Death* in 1986. A number of African-American writers have written inventive juvenile mystery novels with black characters. John Shearer's Encyclopedia Brown series depicts a police chief whose smart young son tackles unsolvable cases, and Virginia Hamilton's books, notably *The House of Dies Drear* (1968) and *The Mystery of Drear House* (1987), interweave episodes in African-American history like the Underground Railroad into contemporary mysteries. Walter Dean Myers's juvenile novels about life in the urban ghetto, including *Scorpions* (1988) and *Somewhere in the Darkness* (1992), do what the best mysteries have always done: stretch the genre into a vehicle to probe the most compelling issues of contemporary life.

Bibliography

Peck, David. *American Ethnic Literatures*. Pasadena: Salem, 1992.

Ruoff, A. La Vonne Brown, and Jerry W. Ward, Jr., eds. *Redefining American Literary History*. New York: MLA, 1990.

Simonson, Rick, and Scott Walker, eds. *Multi-Cultural Literacy*. St. Paul: Graywolf, 1988.

Stephen Soitos

See also

Feminist Detective Fiction

Gay and Lesbian Mysteries

Mystery Periodicals

Native American Crime Fiction

Evening Shade (1990-1994), a powerhouse TV comedy, was created by the husband/wife team of Linda Bloodworth-Thomason (see entry) and Harry Thomason. Evening Shade was the name of a sleepy little Ozark town populated by eccentrics; the show starred Burt Reynolds as Wood Newton, a former professional football player now returned to his hometown and condemned to being coach of the eternally losing high school football team. The talented ensemble comedic cast included Marilu Henner as Ava, Wood's wife and the local prosecuting attorney and mother of their four children, Hal Holbrook as her father and publisher of the local newspaper, Elizabeth Ashley as her aunt, Charles Durning as the town doctor, Ossie Davis as Ponder Blue, owner of the local rib joint and narrator/muse/moral-teller of each episode, Michael Jeter as the wimpy and inexperienced assistant football coach and high school math teacher, and Charlie Dell as the addled adult paperboy.

Following the incredible success of Bloodworth-Thomason's *Designing Women*, *Evening Shade* became one of the powerful comedies on the Monday night CBS line-up, designed especially to compete with *Monday Night Football*. Bloodworth-Thomason, a native of the Missouri Ozarks, and husband Harry, Arkansas bred, set out to design the show specifically from that region. She held a contest inviting nominations for the name of the town and, hence, the series. Even soon-to-be First Lady Hillary Clinton contributed some suggestions, including the winning entry, "Evening Shade." Bloodworth-Thomason wanted to "show you can have a really steamy, high-voltage, male-female Southern relationship within a marriage."

Bibliography
Brooks, Tim, and Earle Marsh. *The Complete Directory to Prime Time Network TV, 1946 Present*. New York: Ballantine, 1992.
Brown, Les. *Les Brown's Encyclopedia of Television*. New York: Visible Ink, 1991.
McNeil, Alex. *Total Television*. New York: Penguin, 1991.
Weisburg, Jacob. "Southern Exposure." *New Republic* 2 Nov. 1992: 13-16.

Sheri Carder

Exorcist, The (1971), is a gripping horror thriller, written by William Peter Blatty, that recounts a young girl's possession by the devil. One of the most popular novels of the era, and the basis for a riveting film (directed by William Friedkin) that had a phenomenal impact on its release in 1973, *The Exorcist* was partly responsible for a revival of interest in horror, the supernatural, and particularly deviltry and the occult.

The story traces the disturbing events that follow when 12-year-old Regan MacNeil, the daughter of an actress, entertains herself with a Ouija board (see entry) and an imaginary "friend" while her mother is filming a movie. The child's pastimes grow sinister, evolving into a series of strange noises, levitating furniture, and frightening transformations in her character. MacNeil's frustrated search to assuage her daughter's ailment leads her, as a last resort, to Damien Karras, a priest well versed in cases of spiritual possession. Preoccupied with his own despair over the frailty of

human agency in an evil world, Karras commits to helping her. When the Church-appointed exorcist perishes, Karras absorbs the demon into his own body before plunging to his death, thus affirming the power of human love over evil.

A controversial best-seller and chilling inquiry into the nature of evil, *The Exorcist* tackles philosophical polarities with sustained ambiguity and addresses the contemporary interest in what has been called the death of God while proffering an ultimately hopeful theme.

Bibliography
Blatty, William Peter. *William Peter Blatty on "The Exorcist": From Novel to Film*. New York: Bantam, 1974.
Creed, Barbara. *The Monstrous-Feminine: Film, Feminism, Psychoanalysis*. London: Routledge, 1993.

Kathleen Brosnahan Fish

Eyewitness to History (1960-1963) was television's first regularly scheduled half-hour coverage of the major news story of the week, national or international. This in-depth study of current events grew out of an irregular series of "instant specials" that began airing on CBS and evolved into a weekly, year-round program.

During its irregular time period, Walter Cronkite anchored reports on President Eisenhower's trips to Europe, Asia, and South America, Premier Khrushchev's visit to the U.S., and the Paris Summit in May 1960. When it became a regularly scheduled program in the fall of 1960, Charles Kuralt anchored, with reporting by, among others, Howard K. Smith, Ernest Leiser, Harry Reasoner, David Schoenbrun, Daniel K. Schorr, George Herman, Marvin Kalb, Winston Burdett, and Eric Sevareid. Cronkite returned on January 27, 1961, as anchor for the series' second regular season, when the title was shortened to *Eyewitness*. Charles Collingwood became its third and last anchor in April 1962, remaining through the last program on September 2, 1963. Leslie Midgley was the executive producer throughout the program's existence.

Presented on Friday nights from 10:30 to 11:00, *Eyewitness* was often put together at the last minute, scrapping nearly completed stories for a late-breaking crisis or disaster. Whether unrest in the Congo, racial strife in Georgia, Soviet cosmonauts orbiting the earth, or an airline collision over New York, the show aimed at the biggest story of the week, combining greatly polished scripts with compelling videotaped and filmed segments into crisply edited, highly informative programs.

Its hard news orientation and production values proved so successful that the program eventually caused its own demise. CBS had the expertise, personnel, and technology to provide in-depth coverage of the world's events on a daily basis—thus *Eyewitness* paved the way for the expanded half-hour *CBS Evening News* and the reporting, integrity, and prestige of the CBS News Division.

Bibliography
Brooks, Tim, and Earle Marsh. *The Complete Directory to Prime Time Television and Cable TV Shows, 1946-Present*. New York: Ballantine, 1995.

Cryder Bankes

Fad Diets. Around the turn of the century, a slim figure began to look attractive to people. This was new. Before that, a well-padded figure was prized as a sign of wealth and health. In 1878 a book entitled *How to Be Plump* advised readers to eat starchy foods and sweets. Eight courses were normal at dinner parties and the almost 200-pound actress Lillian Russell (1861-1922) looked just fine to her many fans.

A new model of the ideal woman, the Gibson Girl, based on the magazine illustrations of Charles Dana Gibson (1867-1944), suggested an emerging standard for women's looks for the new century. She was tall, lithe, and athletic looking. Millions of women would try to emulate her appearance for the rest of the century, in the process making dieting part of the rhythms of everyday life and building businesses selling low-calorie prepared foods, appetite suppressants, and exercise equipment into a multi-billion dollar industry. Men, too, would eventually join women on the weight-reducing bandwagon.

Dieting for the purpose of losing weight became a never-ending quest. Apart from World War II food shortages, and a brief postwar period when women retired from the workforce and had babies *en masse*, the slim ideal has reigned and dieting has shown no sign of slacking off. In 1992, 70 percent of all teenaged girls were said to diet and at least 20 percent of all retail food sales went for "light" and "diet" foods.

Significant moments in dieting history can be noted. In 1913 bathroom scales were first marketed. 1918 saw the publication of the first diet book to become a best-seller, Lulu Hunt Peters's *Diet and Health, with Key to the Calories*, which familiarized the public with the new concept of calories. Calories were counted on menus of the Childs' Restaurants chain as well as in some tearooms and hotel dining rooms in the 1920s. In the 1930s, the Hollywood 18-day 585-calorie diet of citrus fruit, Melba toast, green vegetables, and hard-boiled eggs became the rage—as did the public's fascination with celebrity dieters. In the 1940s diet zwieback and Ry-Krisp crackers came onto the market, supporting the erroneous notion that toast was less fattening than bread. In that same decade Esther Manz formed the first dieting organization, TOPS (Take Off Pounds Sensibly), modeling it on the newly formed Alcoholics Anonymous. Dietetic foods moved in the 1950s from drugstores onto supermarket shelves, capturing a larger market.

The 1960s marked a major increase in dieting activity. The liquid diet Metrecal was introduced into supermarkets, along with the tremendously popular diet colas. Jean Nidetch inaugurated Weight Watchers, which would eventually become a major business venture and produce its own successful line of food products. By the 1980s the production of diet books became intense, with 300 books in print, Stouffer's Lean Cuisine rehabilitated the low-status frozen dinner,

and New York socialite Babe Paley announced "You can't be too thin, or too rich," launching a decade which may well be memorialized as one in which lean young stockbrokers worked out in health clubs and drank no-calorie mineral waters.

Bibliography

Levenstein, Harvey. *Paradox of Plenty: A Social History of Eating in Modern America.* New York: Oxford UP, 1993.
——. *Revolution at the Table: The Transformation of the American Diet.* New York: Oxford UP, 1988.
Schwartz, Hillel. *Never Satisfied: A Cultural History of Diets, Fantasies, and Fat.* New York: Free, 1986.
Wyden, Peter. *The Overweight Society.* New York: Morrow, 1965.

Jan Whitaker

Family Rooms, first described in the 1850s as informal living rooms or second parlors, still are generally recognized as casual living spaces designed to accommodate the diverse recreational and social activities of the modern American family. The modern family room is often viewed as a natural extension of the rumpus, or recreation, room of the 1930s and 1940s, a special room designated for hobbies, parties, and games or as a children's playroom and, with the conversion from coal to less cumbersome heating sources, most often situated in the basement. During the late 1940s and early 1950s the family room assumed special prominence as a renovative option in older homes and as an integral component in newer homes; a development that can be directly related to various economic, sociological, and technological conditions that had a dramatic impact upon the size, composition, and leisure activities (both individually and collectively) of the postwar American family.

The increase in birth rate and family size, and a resulting diversification of age within the postwar American family, created the need for an informal living space to support various family activities that were no longer efficiently, or sufficiently, served by the formal setting and constraints of the traditional living room: children needed a space for play; adolescents needed a space where they could entertain friends; parents needed a space for their hobbies and their own casual social entertainment (e.g., bridge parties, cocktail parties, informal "get-togethers"); and the family as a unit required a space for shared group activities. The most common response to such diverse and multiple needs was the family room, the location, interior decoration, and function of which were generally dictated by such factors as climate, taste, income, and, perhaps most importantly, the number and ages of family members.

During the 1950s and 1960s, such popular magazines as *American Home, Better Homes and Gardens, House Beautiful,* and *House and Garden* frequently featured family room plans which, in spite of a seemingly open-ended range of recreational features, locations, and decor, typically underscored such characteristics as informality, versatility, and flexibility that have since become intimately associated with the family room. Such plans might recommend the conversion of a basement, garage, or attic or the development of multiple-use areas such as a combination family room-kitchen or family room-dining area. Other plans might focus on specific activities; hence, the family room-music center, the family room-game room, the family room-minikitchen, the family room-hobby room, the family room-guest room, and even such unusual combinations as the family room-laundry room and the family room-exercise room. Remodeling schemes would frequently highlight such functional and decorative features as built-in storage walls, modular storage systems, sliding glass partitions, accordion-style room dividers, polyurethane beams, streamlined furniture, low-maintenance flooring and paneling, and a built-in or portable fireplace.

Whatever the apparently inexhaustible options, the general correlation between the family room and informal recreational and social activity was consistent with a postwar sensibility that emphasized convenience, relaxation, comfort, and casual living. Fun and happiness evolved as the central goals of family life and the transaction of such goals, in terms not only of individual family members but of the family as a group unit, was most readily accommodated by the multi-purpose family room. Thus considered, the family room provides an instructive corollary to historian Elaine Tyler May's estimate of "the legendary family of the 1950s" as "the first whole-hearted effort to create a home that would fulfill virtually all its members' personal needs through an energized and expressive personal life."

Once vaguely designated in the 1940s as "the room without a name," the family room has since quietly, or noisily as the case may be, subsumed the original functions of the formal living room or parlor; has both stimulated and accommodated key sociological and technological developments; and, far from its original auxiliary status, has established itself as a permanent and indispensable living space in the modern American home.

Bibliography

Coontz, Stephanie. "*Leave It to Beaver* and *Ozzie and Harriet*: American Families in the 1950s." *The Way We Never Were: American Families and the Nostalgia Trap*. New York: Basic, 1992. 23-41.

Hague, William E. "The Family Room." *The Complete Basic Book of Home Decorating*. Garden City: Doubleday, 1968.

Mintz, Steven, and Susan Kellogg. "The Golden Age: Families of the 1950s." *Domestic Revolutions: A Social History of American Family Life*. New York: Free, 1988. 176-201.

Wright, Nelson. "The Room without a Name." *Tomorrow's House*. New York: Simon & Schuster, 1946. 76-80.

Michael Wentworth

Fanny Hill (1748), originally published in two parts as *Memoirs of the Life of Fanny Hill*, or the *Memoirs of a Woman of Pleasure*, was written anonymously by John Cle-

land, an English foreign official. In his groundbreaking survey of libertine literature, David Foxon characterizes the novel as "the first original English prose pornography, and the first to break away from the dialogue form into the style of the novel" (45). It is one of the most banned and prosecuted literary works in history, having been successfully prosecuted in England and the United States until 1963, when the United States Supreme Court held that its literary merit prevented it from being obscene (*Massachusetts v. Memoirs*, 1963).

Fanny Hill is the story of an innocent orphan girl forced into prostitution before meeting her true love and "living happily ever after." The work, written as two long letters and in the first person, is largely episodic and contains many sex scenes, albeit without four-letter words. Justice Clark, dissenting in *Massachusetts v. Memoirs*, summarized the plot: "The book starts with Fanny Hill, a young 15-year-old girl, arriving in London to seek household work. She goes to an employment office where through happenstance she meets the mistress of a bawdy house.... The remaining 200 pages of the book detail her initiation into various sexual experiences, from a lesbian encounter with a sister prostitute to all sorts and types of sexual debauchery in bawdy houses as a mistress to a variety of men. This is presented to the reader through an uninterrupted succession of descriptions by Fanny, either as an observer or participant."

The majority of the Supreme Court and many scholars have viewed the work as more than a series of sexual episodes, however, and have elevated it to the status of literature. Some scholars have concluded that the primary difference between *Fanny Hill* and other 18th-century works such as Richardson's *Pamela* and Defoe's *Moll Flanders* is the amoral ending and Fanny's enjoyment of sex. In addition to its role in establishing the episodic pattern that is the hallmark of literary and cinematic pornography even today, and serving as a major foundation for obscenity law in the United States, the work is studied today as part of the gender revolution in Europe in the 1690s.

Bibliography

Epstein, William H. *John Cleland: Images of a Life*. New York: Columbia UP, 1974.

Foxon, David. *Libertine Literature in England, 1660-1745*. New Hyde Park, NY: University Books, 1965.

Trumbach, Randolph. "Modern Prostitution and Gender in *Fanny Hill*: Libertine and Domesticated Fantasy." *Sexual Underworlds of the Enlightenment*. Ed. G. S. Rousseau and Roy Porter. Chapel Hill: U of North Carolina P, 1988.

Wagner, Peter. *Eros Revived: Erotica of the Enlightenment in England and America*. London: Seckler & Warburg, 1988.

William E. Brigman

See also
Pornography

Farmer, Philip José (1918-), credited with introducing sex into science fiction, has won three Hugo awards. The first was for his 1952 novella *The Lovers*, which, according to Donald Wolheim, made sex "a legitimate subject of science fiction extrapolation." *Riders of the Purple Wage* earned him a second Hugo in 1968; employing sustained Joycean punning, it investigates the balance between chaos and order, authority and individual vision, while celebrating human sexuality, energy, and guile. Farmer's inclusive vision and "wild invention" are perhaps best exemplified in the book which won him a third Hugo, *To Your Scattered Bodies Go* (1971), the first novel in his "Riverworld" series. Set on a planet on which the entire human race has been resurrected along the banks of a river 10 to 20 million miles long, "Riverworld" mixes fictional characters with such historical personages as Sir Richard Burton, Samuel Clemens, Tom Mix, and Hermann Goering.

Farmer's blending of individuals from ancient and modern cultures continually generates fresh, and often startling, insights. Throughout his career, he has exhibited a predilection for such vast canvases. Indeed, Leslie Fiedler suggested that "Farmer's larger attempt" has been "to subsume in his own works *all* of the books in the world that have touched or moved him." These books range from pulp fiction to classic literature, from scientific texts to sacred books. Farmer has, for example, explored and transformed the Tarzan story repeatedly. Among the rewrites, *Lord Tyger* (1970) brilliantly explores the character a "real" Tarzan might have developed, the underground classic *A Feast Unknown* (1969) analyzes the erotic and sadistic undertones of superhero fiction, and *The Jungle Rot Kid on the Nod* whimsically joins Edgar Rice and William Burroughs.

While *Tarzan Alive: A Definitive Biography of Lord Greystoke* (1972) demonstrates Farmer's extensive knowledge of popular literature, he has been equally adept at assimilating such serious writers as Melville, Jung, Freud, Robert Graves, and Joseph Campbell into his work. Born in North Terre Haute, IN, Farmer has spent most of his life in Peoria, IL. Farmer is a prolific and too frequently undervalued writer whose passions, from airships to Sufism and linguistics to Mycenae, recur in his more than 50 books and dozens of stories.

Bibliography

Brizzi, Mary. *The Reader's Guide to Philip José Farmer.* Mercer Island: Starmont, 1980.

Farmer, Philip José. *The Book of Philip José Farmer.* New York: Berkley, 1982.

Fiedler, Leslie. "Thanks for the Feast." *In Dreams Awake: A Historical-Critical Anthology of Science Fiction.* New York: Dell, 1975.

Steve Connelly

Fashion. An object that is currently in style is said to be fashionable or "in fashion." The term fashion is commonly used to refer to a transitory mode of dress, the latest style, and includes such things as hairstyles (see entry) and accessories. The desire to conform to current trends in dress is a form of collective behavior in which large segments of a population adopt and wear a certain style of clothing at a particular point in time. However, fashion is not limited to clothing and accessories or other items that adorn the human body. Consumer goods such as home furnishings as well as houses and automobiles also have a fashion component. The

speed with which fashion changes, particularly in dress, is related to the relative wealth of a society as well as to such issues as religion, the class system that is in place, and the educational level of the population. Since fashion is a many-faceted concept, the discussion that follows covers forces that affect fashion; the fashion business; and fashion change. Because of the complexity of discussing fashion cross-culturally, references used here relate to Western culture.

FORCES THAT AFFECT FASHION. To illustrate the forces which affect fashion, consider the social changes that have accompanied the women's movement in the 20th century and the effect on women's dress. For example, the change in the length of women's skirts from floor-length to miniskirt represents a transformation in the allowable limits of a woman's body that can be exposed to public view without fear of censure or even arrest. In less than a century, social norms shifted from requiring a woman to cover her entire body with floor-length skirts, long sleeves, and high collars, to sanctioning micro miniskirts, halter tops, and bikinis. Political forces, such as women securing the right to vote and becoming a part of the electoral process, were part of this transformation, as were economic forces. The latter relates to the relative wealth of a society and the amount of discretionary income that is available for the purchase of more than just the most basic consumer items. In the past several decades women have entered the job market in large numbers. Consequently, women dress for the job market. A trend toward women marrying later in life and having fewer children also affects the amount of discretionary income that is available. Demographics too are important, as younger consumers tend to be more involved with fashion. Ethnic populations also influence the fashion of the time.

There is a tendency to assume fashion relates only to women. However, the same social, political, economic, and demographic forces that influence women impact what men wear. Historically, men have frequently been the peacocks; males wearing earrings is not a new phenomenon. Although the business suit remains the accepted style of dress in the corporate world, an examination of 20th-century men's fashion indicates that a revolution took place for men as well as for women. Men's active sports clothing, a relatively new category of apparel that dates from the early 1950s, is a good illustration. Early in the century men dressed formally to play golf and tennis. Knickers or long flannel pants, a necktie, and often a coat, were worn. Shorts were not part of a man's wardrobe and swimsuits included a modest top. Today's athletic shoes, which have become a standard wardrobe item, are a result of late-20th-century technology. Some of the materials the shoes are made of didn't exist earlier in the century, and even the design involves the use of sophisticated computer technology.

THE FASHION BUSINESS. Today, the fashion business is global and few countries remain untouched by this giant multibillion dollar industry. Paris continues to maintain its reputation as the fashion capital of the world and has retained its image of elegance and glamour. This is at least partially due to government involvement, for fashion is one of France's three top exports. Worldwide, relatively few women purchase expensive designer ready-to-wear fashions, much less couture, which is made-to-measure clothing. The category of clothing that is mass fashion is much more economically important. However, high fashion continues to play an important role, and for economic reasons the French government continues to support its profitable fashion industry. Beginning in the 17th century with the regulation of France's luxury textile industry, the government has been involved. In 1868 the Chambre Syndicale de la Couture Parisian, which governs and regulates France's glamorous couture business, was established. It oversees the training of workers for the couture houses and the scheduling and coordination of events showing couturier's collections. Designers who wish to have the status and prestige that accompanies that title of Grand Couturier must be invited to open a Parisian design house and establish workrooms there. Today, it takes vast amounts of capital to open a couture house (there are only 22), and the biannual collections that feature dresses sometimes costing hundreds of thousands of dollars serve primarily as vehicles to publicize designers' very profitable licensed ready-to-wear and accessory businesses, as well as their fragrance lines.

The aura of glamour which surrounds the high fashion business is due in large part to promotion and involvement of the media, as well as the exclusivity which is related to the wealth and social standing of the individuals who buy and wear the latest styles. Well-known designers have accumulated worldwide prestige as well as great wealth. A more recent phenomenon is the international prestige, the superstar status, and the wealth which has accrued to the women who model clothing designed by internationally famous designers.

Other countries' involvement in the fashion business is relatively recent. Outside of France, the preeminent European country with a large fashion industry is Italy. Although smaller in size, Italian couture is organized much like that of France, with a governing body called the Camera Nazionale dell'Alta Moda Italiana. Italy is best known for its expensive ready-to-wear fashion, women's as well as men's. Both Spain (especially in Madrid) and Germany have small but established fashion businesses, and England is well known for its traditional tailored men's apparel. Since 1950 Japan has produced a number of world-famous fashion designers, such as Hanae Mori, one of the first Japanese designers to study in Paris after World War II.

The U.S. has also produced a number of internationally known designers, but does not have a structured couture business as in France. Nevertheless, New York City competes with Paris for the title of world fashion capital. Prior to World War II, most fashion influence in America came from Paris; this was also the case for other Western nations. Since the 1950s American designers have become internationally recognized for their ready-to-wear lines, particularly sportswear.

FASHION CHANGE. The importance of change in the fashion process is a concept that scholars have sought to understand since the late 19th century, with the ultimate goal of prediction. One of the first and most persistent theories explains the fashion process as one that is cyclical, one in which after a prescribed period of time, a style will repeat itself. Other theories suggest a vertical process in which a class system operates, with a trickling down of new styles. For example, as the upper class initiates new trends which are then imitated by individuals further down the social scale, fashion begins to trickle down. As this process continues the upper class adopts a new style which will continue to differentiate them from the lower classes. Another vertical theory, originating in the 1960s, suggests that fashion influences originate in the streets with the youth and trickle up to the upper classes. Although both theories are useful in explaining fashion change, the process is more complicated than this. Demographics, particularly the age of the population, as well as the status of the economy and the role of government are important to understanding fashion change.

Bibliography

Behling, D. U. "Fashion Change and Demographics—A Model." *Clothing and Textile Research Journal* 4 (Fall 1985): 18-23.

Breward, Christopher. *The Culture of Fashion: A New History of Fashionable Dress.* Manchester: Manchester UP, 1995.

Cunningham, Patricia A., and Susan Vosso Lab. *Dress in American Culture.* Bowling Green, OH: Bowling Green State U Popular P, 1993.

Field, G. A. "The Status Float Phenomenon." *Business Horizons* Aug. 1970: 45-51.

Laver, James. *Costume and Fashion: A Concise History.* Rev. ed. New York: Thames, 1995.

Dorothy Behling

Fast Food Chains. Although fast food is now virtually equated with chain restaurants, it actually pre-dates these businesses by many centuries. People on the move have always needed a hasty snack. Almost all cultures have long had a form of quickly prepared, hand-held food suitable for eating on the run. Often this food is sold by small operators along the roadside, as hot dog vendors continue to do in large cities in the U.S. Chain restaurants, on the other hand, are the product not only of complex industrial society, but also of a developed restaurant industry.

The first fast food chains, dairy lunches, date back to the late 19th century. Often started by milk deliverymen, these self-service eateries featured limited menus. They were nicknamed "one-arm joints" because of their wooden chairs with eating surfaces built onto one arm. The first, the Everett Dairy Lunch in New York City, opened in 1875 and sold milk, toast, and oatmeal along with the standard steaks and chops. Other successful chains included Dennett's, Childs', Stouffer's, Clark's, Kohlsaat, and the J. R. Thompson Dairy Bars. Most of these chains attained their maximum growth in the 1920s, with few exceeding 100 outlets.

The Horn and Hardart Automat chain, running what were perhaps the most famous self-serve restaurants of the early century, was a variant of the dairy lunch. Food was prepared out of sight, and placed in a wall of glass-fronted cubicles from which customers on the other side inspected and removed their selection after depositing the price in coins.

The first Automat opened in 1902 in Philadelphia; in 1912 a Times Square location was opened in New York City in an ornate Beaux-Arts style building sharply in contrast to the usual dairy lunch. The last remaining Automat closed in 1991.

Fascination with chain restaurants has long centered on their efficient operation, particularly on how quickly customers can be served. 1920s operators, the first to make use of efficiency experts, would have been impressed with Ray Kroc (1902-84), who streamlined service at McDonald's until a customer could be served burger, fries, and shake in 50 seconds. The Burger King chain tried to reduce service time to 15 seconds. Another goal of engineering the fast dining experience was to get the customer to move along after eating. Kroc, for instance, prohibited all amenities that would encourage patrons to linger, such as comfortable seating, jukeboxes, newspaper vending machines, and telephone booths.

McDonald's was a relative latecomer in hamburger chains, getting its start as a franchise operation in the 1950s. The first McDonald's, operated by Richard and Maurice McDonald, started in California as a drive-in with carhops. The McDonald brothers sold the business to Ray Kroc in 1961 for $2.7 million. The first hamburger chains arose in the midwest and southern midwest in the 1920s. White Castle began in 1921 in Wichita, KS, spreading eastward all the way to New York City by 1930. This chain was entirely standardized from its architecture down to its coffee preparation. The White Tower originated in Milwaukee, WI, in 1926. 1929 marked the start of White Tavern Shoppes in Shelbyville, KY, and Toddle House in Houston, TX. The Krystal began in 1932 in Chattanooga, TN. White Hut appeared in Toledo, OH, in 1935. Many of these chains constructed their buildings in factories and designed them to be portable, so that advantage could always be taken of better locations. Proximity to blue-collar workers and their travel routes was important because these were the primary customers. To serve all shifts, most of these restaurants were open 24 hours a day.

Hamburgers have been only one of the menu stars of the fast food business. Chicken, pizza, Mexican food, and pancakes have also formed the culinary basis of fast food restaurants. Church's Fried Chicken began in San Antonio, TX, in 1952. That same year Harland Sanders, a Kentucky motel and gas station operator, started selling his fried chicken recipe to restaurants. After he sold out in the 1960s he agreed to become a virtual living trademark of the Kentucky Fried Chicken chain, traveling around the country in his familiar white suit with string bow tie. Dave Thomas, founder of Wendy's, began his fast food restaurant career as a KFC employee. Pizza Hut started in 1958 in Wichita, KS.

The limitations of fast food restaurants—plastic food in a plastic environment—are well known and accepted by the broad American public as part of a trade-off that includes sanitary conditions, low prices, and familiarity. Periodically, criticism of fast food chains results in toned down exterior signage or the provision of nutrition information. Nevertheless, it would seem that one version or another of fast food eating places will survive and continue to spread throughout the world. For many chains, growth potential today lies outside this country; for instance, 143 of the 193 McDonald's opened in 1993 were outside the U.S. It is almost unnecessary to say that fast food restaurants, like American movies and music, represent the essence of American culture to much of the world. That Taco Bell has opened in Mexico City and has attracted Mexican customers is not surprising since everyone knows that Taco Bell is selling genuine American culture, not genuine Mexican food. But then all American fast food restaurants sell American culture.

But they do more than that. They also sell local culture by modifying the American atmosphere to local conditions. In Amsterdam, for example, because the citizens want a snack in their food day, McDonald's advertises as McSnack. The American fast food industry obviously satisfies a worldwide need. On December 7, 1998, *Time* named Ray Kroc as one of the Builders and Titans of the 20th Century because he "understood that we don't dine—we eat and run."

Bibliography
Langdon, Philip. *Orange Roofs, Golden Arches*. New York: Knopf, 1986.
Liebs, Chester H. *Main Street to Miracle Mile: American Roadside Architecture*. Boston: Little, Brown, 1985.
Mariani, John. *America Eats Out*. New York: Morrow, 1991.
Monninger, Joseph. "Fast Food." *American Heritage*. April 1988: 68-75.

Jan Whitaker

Fat Albert and the Cosby Kids (1972-1984). In the 1970s, producers of children's TV shows found themselves chafed by directives to de-emphasize violence and promote educational themes. Most shows that followed these edicts are now largely forgotten. The bright spot was *Fat Albert and the Cosby Kids*. It received plaudits from educators and was the first Saturday morning cartoon show to earn a commendation from Action for Children's Television.

In 1972, the comic and actor Bill Cosby (see entry) was preparing a variety series (*The New Bill Cosby Show*) and appearing in the PBS show *Zoom* as he worked on his education degree. As part of his course work, he and Filmation produced *Fat Albert and the Cosby Kids* for CBS. Cosby assembled his own team of educators and advisors to work out the lessons of the scripts. Considering that network advisors were excising the entertainment from other cartoons in order not to offend, *Fat Albert* turned out remarkably well.

Based on Cosby's earlier comedy routines reminiscing about growing up in Philadelphia, *Fat Albert* had begun three years earlier as a prime-time NBC special, "Hey, Hey, Hey, It's Fat Albert," with Cosby supplying most of the voices. The series played out urban hijinks in the *Dead End Kids* style, but dealt with serious topics like drugs, child abuse, literacy, tolerance, even fear of hospitals.

Fat Albert proved immediately successful, staying on CBS through 1984, then going into syndication. A second prime-time special, "Weird Harold," ran in 1973, and holiday specials aired in 1977 (Christmas and Halloween) and 1982 (Easter). Despite concerns over the cast's racial makeup, surveys showed most kids watching didn't even notice the characters were black.

Bibliography
Grossman, Gary H. *Saturday Morning TV.* New York: Dell, 1981.
Lenburg, Jeff. *The Encyclopedia of Animated Cartoons.* Rev. ed. New York: Facts on File, 1991.
Smith, Ronald L. *Cosby.* New York: St. Martin's, 1986.

Mark McDermott

Father Knows Best (1954-1963), which aired in prime time, set the standard for classic family situation comedy. The Andersons were average Americans, living in the typical midwestern town of Springfield. Each week viewers watched as Jim Anderson (played by Robert Young), an agent for the General Insurance Company, returned to his perfect home, complete with white picket fence. There he was greeted by his faithful and charming wife, Margaret (Jane Wyatt), and their three irresistible offspring, Betty (Elinor Donahue), Bud (Billy Gray), and Kathy (Lauren Chapin).

The Andersons were the ideal family of the 1950s. Americans related to the household dilemmas they muddled through each week and often tried to emulate the close-knit bunch. The Anderson children encountered all the usual entanglements associated with growing up. They attempted to assert their independence at times, often with mixed results. Dad and mom always came to their rescue, resolving the problem by the end of each episode.

The Anderson clan was so much the ultimate prototype of the American family that the U.S. Treasury Department asked the producers to film a special episode to help promote the 1959 Savings Bond Drive. In the episode, the Anderson children attempt to live under a dictatorship for just one day. Although never aired, this special program was distributed to civic organizations to stress the importance of preserving a strong democracy. *Father Knows Best* can still be seen today on many cable channels.

Bibliography
Brooks, Tim, and Earle Marsh. *The Complete Directory to Prime Time Network TV Shows, 1946-Present.* 3d ed. New York: Ballantine, 1985.
Lichter, S. Robert, Linda S. Lichter, and Stanley Rothman. *Watching America.* New York: Prentice-Hall, 1991.

Lynn Bartholome

Feature Books. David McKay Publishers began its "Feature Book" series early in 1937. Forerunners to what would eventually become recognized as a standard for comic books, the books measured about 8 1/4 inches wide, 11 1/4 inches tall, and 1/4 inch thick. It seems apparent that Feature Books took a good deal of their lead from Whitman Publishing's Big Little Books (see entry). The difference between the two was primarily in size and format, and the fact that Feature Books reprinted comic strips sequentially and largely unedited and unchanged. Like Big Little Books, McKay's product served as an important transitional medium between newspaper comic strips and comic books. In 1939, Dell Publishing introduced its oversized "Black and White Comics" series, which, except for publisher, were essentially identical to the McKay product. Between 1941 and 1943, Dell contin-ued the Black and White series as "Large Feature Comics." Prior to the advent of Feature Books and Dell's Black and White Comics series, even the most avid of newspaper comic strip readers had to wait months for their favorite newspaper strip storylines to reach fruition, and it was very likely that in that period of several months the reader would miss some of the daily installments.

In a sense, McKay's Feature Books and Dell's Black and White Comics were the equivalent of today's trade paperbacks that reprint contemporary comic strips like Charles Schulz's *Peanuts*, Jim Davis's *Garfield*, Jeff Mac Nelly's *Shoe*, and Bill Watterson's *Calvin and Hobbes*. Feature Books usually sold for ten cents apiece and featured famous comic strip characters like Chester Gould's Dick Tracy, Lee Falk and Phil Davis's The Phantom, Falk and Davis's Mandrake the Magician, E. C. Segar's Popeye, Milton Caniff's Terry and the Pirates, and Zane Grey's King of the Royal Mounted. These early forerunners of the comic book lasted until about 1948.

Bibliography
Overstreet, Robert M. *The Comic Book Price Guide.* 25th ed. Cleveland: Overstreet, 1995.
Roberts, Garyn G. *Dick Tracy and American Culture: Morality and Mythology, Text and Context.* Jefferson: McFarland, 1993.

Garyn G. Roberts

Female Sports Hero, The. Classical theories about the hero as portrayed in myth and literature, and consequently our understanding of the hero, are based upon the assumption that the hero is male. Similarly, the basic view of the sports hero, and consequently our understanding of the sports hero, is male. With women's entry into sport in the late 19th century, the first female sports heroes appeared. The challenges that they faced were significantly different, however. For a female, success and accomplishment in sport challenged the very notion of what it was to be female. Sport required independence, courage, physical action, and risk—qualities associated with masculinity. Sport was thought to be detrimental to child-bearing, and the female athlete therefore endangered her potential as a wife and mother. The female sports hero publicly challenged cultural views of the physical and emotional limitations of the female, her role as wife and mother, and the view of sport as the exclusive province of the male. In short, she challenged the status quo and the established order.

Although countless women have successfully faced these challenges in the 20th century, several have figured most significantly in altering society's views about females and the nature of modern sport. Among the more notable of these are: Eleanora Randolph Sears, Gertrude Ederle, Suzanne Lenglen, Mildred "Babe" Didrikson, Althea Gibson, and Billie Jean King.

It was Eleanor Randolph Sears who provided the first public expression of the challenge to society's views concerning women and sport. In the 1920s, Sears often drove a car and, while wearing men's clothing, was arrested for speeding. She played polo with men while riding astride. She is credited with popularizing squash for women; won more than 240 trophies in squash, tennis, and riding; and, in 1930 at the age of 46, became the winner of the first national squash tournament. She received much public attention when she walked from Providence, RI, to Boston while setting a pace which tired her male companions.

A more publicized challenge to the cultural view of female capabilities and the notion that sport was a male activity was provided by Gertrude Ederle. In 1926, only five men had successfully swum the English Channel. After failing in her first attempt, Ederle not only swam the channel, she did so in 14 hours and 31 minutes, breaking the record of the fastest man by two hours.

In many ways, Suzanne Lenglen, the tennis idol of the 1920s and sports' first international female hero and media star, embodied the female sports hero's quest more than either Sears or Ederle. Although Lenglen portrayed a feminine image which society found acceptable, she dominated tennis as no athlete—male or female—dominated a sport. Perhaps more importantly, Lenglen shocked the tennis world with her non-conforming behavior (both on and off the court), her revealing and stylish tennis attire, and her aggressive style of play.

The challenges of Sears, Ederle, and Lenglen found full expression in the life and accomplishments of Mildred "Babe" Didrikson. Didrikson was an all-around athlete who successfully competed at national and international levels in basketball, track and field, and golf—for which she was chosen the Greatest Female Athlete of the first half of the 20th century. According to Donald J. Mrozek, Didrikson was a self-possessed, independent outsider whose athletic achievements, manner, and tone "continued to moot her gender identification." Although Didrikson married, her participation in basketball and track and field, vigorous activities which were considered detrimental to child-bearing, revealed an obvious disregard for the perceived role of the female as wife and mother. Apparently Didrikson had the same disregard for the idealized view of the woman athlete. After the AAU restored her amateur status, which it had taken away, she refused reinstatement.

Althea Gibson did what these other heroes could not— oppose the racial bias in sport. In 1950, the U.S. Lawn Tennis Association ruled against her participation in the Forest Hills playoffs because she was black. Later the decision was reversed. Gibson went on to win the finals and broke the color barrier in tennis, emerging as the first black athlete, male or female, to receive national and international recognition in tennis. In 1957, she became the first black person to win the Associated Press's annual Woman Athlete of the Year.

The accomplishments of these sports heroes contributed to the growing demand in the last half of the 20th century for women's opportunity to participate in amateur sports (and support for that participation) and for equality of financial rewards in professional sports. The passage of Title IX of the Education Amendments Act in 1972 assisted in the development of women's collegiate sports. Billie Jean King led the challenge in professional sport, protesting in 1970 the disparity in money for tennis. Her victory over Bobby Riggs in

a 1973 "Battle of the Sexes" made her a hero in the larger context of both the women's sports movement and the women's movement. These female sports heroes challenged society's long held views regarding women, their roles in society, their physical and emotional capabilities, and the nature of modern sport.

Bibliography

Campbell, Joseph. *The Hero with a Thousand Faces.* Princeton: Princeton UP, 1973.

Gerber, Ellen W., Jan Felshin, Pearl Berlin, and Waneen Wyrick. *The American Woman in Sport.* Reading: Addison-Wesley, 1974.

Howell, Reet, ed. *Her Story in Sport: A Historical Anthology in Sports.* West Point: Leisure, 1982.

Mrozek, Donald J. "The Amazon and the American 'Lady': Sexual Fears of Women as Athletes." *From "Fair Sex" to Feminism: Sport and the Socialization of Women in the Industrial and Post-Industrial Eras.* Ed. J. A. Mangan and Roberta J. Park. London: Cass, 1987. 282-98.

Pearson, Carol, and Katherine Pope. *The Female Hero in American and British Literature.* New York: Bowker, 1981.

Susan J. Bandy

Feminist Detective Fiction. Although detective fiction featuring strong and independent women characters is increasingly popular, the category "feminist detective fiction" can be somewhat difficult to define. While some include novels by women about women detectives, others define it as works reflecting the feminist movement of the 1970s and 1980s. Yet others contend that there is an implicit, even irreconcilable, contradiction between the goals of feminism and the ideological assumptions and generic structure of the detective novel, which, they maintain, in its essential conservatism, functions always to shore up the institutions of patriarchy that have been threatened by crime.

If feminist detective fiction is characterized by the presence of spirited and intelligent women investigators whose resourcefulness triumphs over criminal doings, and who defy, subvert, or manipulate legal and social constraints to engage in detection, classical authors like Anna Katharine Green, Agatha Christie, and Dorothy Sayers in varying degrees may be said to fit the category. All provide an expansion of female possibilities as they involve their characters in murder, a violation of the conventional separation of the public (masculine) and private (feminine) realms. Green's spinster detective Amelia Butterworth overturns societal assumptions as well as the definition of acceptable feminine behavior. Through Miss Jane Marple, whose fluffiness masks a hard clarity of vision and knowledge of the world, Christie redefines the marginalized spinster as a powerful force of ethical intelligence. And in Sayers's *Gaudy Night* (1935), not only is Harriet Vane urged by Lord Peter Wimsey to take on the disagreeable and dangerous work of detection, but the novel looks toward, as Patricia Craig and Mary Cadogan suggest, "a more complex ethical structure in which values and virtues are not absolutely fixed."

The feminist movement of the 1970s and the 1980s, however, and the social changes which accompanied it, have stimulated a greater production of fiction showing women in roles other than victim or seductress. Series featuring amateur detectives (including those by Jane Dentinger, Margaret Maron, and Nancy Pickard) increasingly focus on independent women whose careers or personal lives bring them into contact with murder. These novels have shifted from the complexity of plot to an emphasis on the domestic lives of the characters and the societies in which they move. Amanda Cross's academic detective Kate Fansler has become less clearly associated with her classical roots as she has grown into a character who, as Maureen Reddy argues, "identifies *as* a woman and *with* other women." Barbara Neely's Blanche White, an African-American domestic worker, both suffers from and exploits the essential invisibility of her race, gender, and profession in order to solve mysteries, resolve problems, and invert (however temporarily) established structures of power—without reference to the police or the legal system.

The police procedural also has been changed by the feminist writers who have adopted it. Patricia D. Cornwell's Dr. Kay Scarpetta, the chief medical examiner of Virginia, works for the government but is continually reminded of her status as woman as well as of the political perversions of the system. Only personal relationships allow her to circumvent these. Katherine V. Forrest's lesbian detective Kate Delafield, a Los Angeles homicide cop, confronts violence from within the system but remains in uneasy relation to it.

But it is the genre traditionally most hostile to women, the hard-boiled detective novel, which has been most enthusiastically transformed, perhaps because of its method of exposing the layers of corruption endemic to society. The heroic, isolated male private eye (for whom woman is enemy and alien) has given way to the female private investigator—created by, among others, Marcia Muller, Sara Paretsky, and Sue Grafton—who struggles against fear and an impulse toward isolation. No longer is detection, as the title of P. D. James's 1972 novel makes clear, an unsuitable job for a woman. This new female hero unveils corruption in patriarchal institutions, but most often she must expose and remedy the corruption in that most central of social constructs, the family. Her task is often to counter the corruptive force of standard family structures by reconceptualizing families and communities as more open, non-traditional, and non-hierarchical arrangements—thus serving the feminist function of undermining the oppressive patriarchal order.

Lesbian detective fiction is even more radically transformative, pairing the process of detection with the process of coming to terms with one's sexuality and with one's identity in relation to an often hostile heterosexual world that attempts to enforce its patriarchal order through male violence. Lesbian detective fiction—as seen, for example, in the work of Barbara Wilson, Sandra Scoppettone, or Katherine V. Forrest—is about creating an image of community that includes a range of lesbian, gay, and heterosexual couplings. As lesbian detective fiction simultaneously reinvents womanhood and redefines community, it reaffirms the broader objectives of all varieties of feminist detective fiction.

Bibliography

Craig, Patricia, and Mary Cadogan. *The Lady Investigates: Women Detectives and Spies in Fiction*. New York: St. Martin's, 1981.

Klein, Kathleen Gregory. *The Woman Detective: Gender and Genre*. Urbana: U of Illinois P, 1988.

Littler, Alison. "Marele Day's 'Cold Hard Bitch': The Masculinist Imperatives of the Private-Eye Genre." *The Journal of Narrative Technique* 21.1 (Winter 1991): 121-35.

Reddy, Maureen T. *Sisters in Crime: Feminism and the Crime Novel*. New York: Continuum, 1988.

Sandels, Robert. "It Was a Man's World." *The Armchair Detective* 22.4 (Fall 1989): 388-404.

Susan Allen Ford

See also

Gay and Lesbian Mysteries

Ferber, **Edna** (1887-1968), was one of the leading popular novelists of the first half of the 20th century in America. She began her career as a newspaper reporter in Wisconsin, where she had spent her youth, but by 1911 had published her first novel, *Dawn O'Hara, The Girl Who Laughed*. Her breakthrough came in 1924 with *So Big*, a novel about the conflict between a mother, who values hard work and personal honor, and her son, who strives for material gain and celebrity. In the end, he achieves his goals but lives a bleak emotional life.

In this novel, which won the Pulitzer Prize, Ferber set forth a critique of the American Dream that is sustained through most of her subsequent works. The novel also turned a skeptical eye on the agrarian mythos of the nation; like other midwestern writers who undermined the cultural romance of rural life (Sinclair Lewis, Ruth Suckow, Hamlin Garland, and Edgar Lee Masters, especially), Ferber showed the hardscrabble underside of the family farm.

Most of her novels feature strong female protagonists who demonstrate admirable character as they struggle through romantic hardships and ethical dilemmas about money and status. *Show Boat* (1926), her best-known book, centers on a southern woman who marries a charismatic but reckless gambler who leaves her with a daughter she must support through a series of struggles. It also features an interracial romance, expanded because of its social importance when *Show Boat* was made into a celebrated stage musical in 1927.

Other notable Ferber novels include *Cimarron* (1930) and *Giant* (1952), epic novels of western lands and the conflicts over their settlement and growth, both featuring women of spirit and culture who marry lesser men; and *Saratoga Trunk* (1941), featuring a brash heroine of mixed blood who determines to avenge herself on her father's family until she comes to value love above retribution. *Giant* became a favorite Hollywood epic, starring Elizabeth Taylor and Rock Hudson, in 1956.

Ferber also collaborated with playwright George S. Kaufman to write a number of classic American dramas, including *Minick* (1925), based on a Ferber short story; *The Royal Family* (1927); *Dinner at Eight* (1932); and *Stage Door* (1936).

Bibliography
Goldsmith, Julie. *Ferber: A Biography*. Garden City: Doubleday, 1978.
Shaughnessy, Mary Rose. *Women and Success in American Society in the Works of Edna Ferber*. New York: Gordon, 1977.

Liahna Babener

Fibber McGee and Molly (1935-1957), a highly rated and consistently patriotic radio program, deftly portrayed a neighborhood of busybodies at the same time it championed a midwestern, middle-class, small-town community. Starring Jim and Marian Jordan, a husband-and-wife vaudeville team from Peoria, IL, and written by a former cartoonist, Don Quinn, the program slowly built a following that, during the war years, rivaled Jack Benny's and Bob Hope's and enabled it to become the top-rated show in 1941.

The show was centered around the mundane exploits of "knuckle-headed, know-it-all" Fibber McGee and the conversations he had with and advice he received from his wife and neighbors and acquaintances. A typical show would involve Fibber in the middle of an everyday task; the plot was really subordinate to the quirks and eccentricities of each character. In one program, Fibber decides to walk down to the corner to mail a letter. His feet become stuck in wet cement and, for the rest of the show, his neighbors' reactions and suggestions frustrate and irritate him as he attempts to free himself.

Marian Jordan's Molly was the long-suffering wife, who was ready, willing, and able to knock Fibber, her "dearie," down a few pegs. She also played one of the recurring, secondary characters, Teeny (Fibber called her "Sis"), a sweet-voiced, mischievous little girl who often interrupted Fibber's "big" plans. Other secondary characters included "Mr. Old Timer" (played by Bill Thompson); Mrs. Abigail Uppington (Isabel Randolph), a pretentious snob; and, most famous of all, Throckmorton P. Gildersleeve (Hal Peary), a smug, superior town official and next-door neighbor to Fibber and Molly. The character became so popular that he was spun off into a separate series, *The Great Gildersleeve* (1941-58; see entry). An African-American character, the Gildersleeve's maid Beulah, was also spun off into her own series.

The Jordans began their radio career in Chicago, starring in a 1920s daytime serial, *The Smith Family*. From 1931 to 1935, the couple teamed with writer Quinn on a series called *Smackout*, in which Jim Jordan played a neighborhood grocer in a small town who was "smack out" of everything but tall tales. It was this production that earned the notice of NBC, which gave the Jordans the half-hour Tuesday night time slot they held until 1953. In its remaining years on the air, *Fibber McGee and Molly* switched to a five-day-a-week, quarter-hour format.

Bibliography
American Magazine March 1942.
Dunning, John. *Tune in Yesterday*. Englewood: Prentice-Hall, 1976.
Firestone, Ross. *The Big Radio Comedy Program*. Chicago: Contemporary, 1978.

Richard L. Testa, Jr.

Fields, W. C. (1879-1946), comedian, born in Philadelphia, was the son of an impoverished Cockney immigrant who lived a life of extreme destitution and instability. Running away from home at the age of 11, he experienced near-starvation and violence, which undoubtedly appeared in the misanthropy and skepticism characterizing his screen performances. In this sense, the child became father to the later cinematic adult. But the adult's success in later Hollywood owed much to prevailing ideological circumstances surrounding the 1930s, the decade in which he achieved his major success.

Although Fields had great experience in vaudeville, often performing earlier versions of those roles he perfected upon the screen, both the grim conditions of the 1930s as well as sound technology were important factors consolidating his position. While audiences went to the movies for escapism, they also did not entirely wish to bask in illusionary worlds of exotic fantasy entirely removed from their actual circumstances. In an era when many brothers sought a dime and several "forgotten men" stood outside during *Gold Diggers of 1933*, W. C. Fields's screen persona as a con-man and misogynistic figure railing at authority figures such as bankers and constraining family circumstances must have struck a chord in many audiences. Similarly, the actor's rasping voice and caustic comments needed the sound technology of the 1930s to deliver his urban streetwise epithets. Like Mae West, Fields has associations with cynical attitudes toward late 19th-century moral codes still operating in society long after their redundant nature is apparent.

Fields's frustrated misogynistic patriarchs of *It's a Gift, You're Telling Me* (both 1934), *The Man on the Flying Trapeze* (1935), and *The Bank Dick* (1940) react in different ways against dominating wives, uncaring children, and obnoxious relatives only to escape temporarily and find the same familial constraints operating in the outside world, as the figure of the obnoxious controlling waitress in *Never Give a Sucker an Even Break* (1941) reveals. But even in these underdog aspects of the Fields persona dwells a recurring deep contempt for any institution and its representatives that save his comedic depictions from falling into the trap of sentimentality.

Fields first embodied this figure of the antiheroic conman in his screen debut, *Pool Sharks* (1915), and continued portraying this figure with subtle variations in *Sally of the Sawdust* (1925), *It's the Old Army Game* (1926), *If I Had a Million* (1932), *Tillie and Gus* (1933), *The Old Fashioned Way, It's a Gift* (both 1934), *Mississippi* (1935), *Poppy* (1936), *You Can't Cheat an Honest Man* (1939), and *My Little Chickadee* (1940). *Mississippi* is the most explicit representation of this 19th-century tradition since it is set on the riverboat location endemic to T. B. Thorpe's "Big Bear of Arkansas" and Herman Melville's *The Confidence-Man*.

If we are to believe Carlotta Monti's biography, the caustic comedian died on Christmas Day cursing everyone except his devoted mistress. Relegated to cameo roles since finishing his last starring feature, *Never Give a Sucker an Even Break* (1941), the old performer declined in health but maintained his iconoclastic cynicism to the end. But it was one having key roots within an American popular cultural tradition which still lives whenever his films are screened for future generations.

Bibliography

Gehring, Wes D. *Groucho and W. C. Fields: Huckster Comedians.* Jackson: UP of Mississippi, 1994.

——. *W. C. Fields: A Bio-Bibliography.* Westport: Greenwood, 1984.

Monti, Carlotta, with Cy Rice. *W. C. Fields and Me.* Englewood Cliffs: Prentice-Hall, 1971.

Rocks, David T. *W. C. Fields—An Annotated Guide.* Jefferson: McFarland, 1993.

Tony Williams

Film Presentation Venues. Once the original inventors of the cinema abandoned the idea of the peepshow in the late 1890s as the venue for watching film, the cinema became an industry based on projecting films to mass audiences. The exhibition of films became the final link in developing the film industry as a profitable set of businesses. Today we can see more films in more places (principally in multiplexes and on television) than at any time in history.

At first, about a century ago, audiences saw movies as part of other entertainments, in particular in vaudeville theaters and, during the summer, amusement parks. What gave impetus to the extraordinary rise in the movie business was the innovation of a theater which only presented movies— the nickelodeon (see entry). These small, makeshift theaters presented a series of short films from the news, documentary, comedy, fantasy, and dramatic genres.

Once the nickelodeon movement began in earnest in 1905, its rise was extraordinary. By 1910 estimates placed the number over ten thousand and attendance at some 26 million per week. But this success only inspired bigger theaters aimed at broad-based middle-class tastes. In the 1920s, with the rise of the movie palace, Balaban & Katz of Chicago taught the film world how to make millions in glorious surroundings.

The modern movie palace had begun with Roxy's opening of the 3,000-seat Strand Theatre in 1914 in New York. Samuel F. "Roxy" Rothapfel had gone back to the roots of the mass entertainment industry and tendered a live vaudeville show plus a movie show in a theater even grander than the legitimate theaters of the day. Balaban & Katz honed this basic set of ideas with such success that in 1925 founder Sam Katz was able to merge his company into the largest Hollywood studio, Famous Players–Lasky, which set the standard for Hollywood's presence on Main Street.

Balaban & Katz's success had commenced a mere eight years earlier with the opening of the Central Park Theatre in Chicago. Much of their success was due to carefully selecting the location of their theaters, not in the entertainment districts downtown but in what were then the suburbs of America's biggest cities. What gave Balaban & Katz its opening was the construction of urban mass transit systems at the turn of the century.

The company also sought to make their buildings attractions unto themselves. With the pride associated with the opening of a world's fair or new skyscraper, Balaban & Katz proclaimed and heralded their movie palaces as the finest in the world. Designs included elements from past architectural glories of France, Spain, Italy, as well as Moorish and later Art Deco renderings. Balaban & Katz had a policy of treating the movie patron as a king or queen, with services to customers including ushers who accepted no tips, free child care, smoking rooms, and painting galleries in the foyers and lobbies.

Balaban & Katz also emphasized stage shows. They became small-time vaudeville entrepreneurs, developing local talent into stars who could then make the circuit in their theaters. With popular but tasteful shows, they could attract the middle-class audience who had grown up on vaudeville. The late 1920s was the acme of the stage show, but with the coming of sound only popular singers and bands would ever be used, and only in flagship houses.

The company's air-conditioned theaters were a major draw. Movie trade papers noted the consistently high grosses during the summer months and could find no better explanation than the climatic comfort inside. Indeed, the take at the box office in the summer regularly exceeded the take during the normal peak months during the winter.

Location, architecture, service, stage shows, and air conditioning made the movie palace into an American institution. Balaban & Katz made money faster than anyone dreamed. Theaters were filled from morning to night. Prices at the box-office soared past five and ten cents, sometimes reaching $1 for the best seats on Saturday and Sunday nights.

With the merger with Famous Players in 1925, Sam Katz was able to successfully transfer the Balaban & Katz system to Paramount's national chain of theaters. Hollywood took notice and all the studios adopted the same techniques for their theater chains: Loew's, Fox, Warner Bros., and RKO. These vertically controlled chains ruled the nation's moviegoing habits until the U.S. Supreme Court forced divestiture in 1949.

The Great Depression changed the movie palace formula. Movie palaces were left to deteriorate and ushers fired. The one plus was the introduction of the concession stand to tender popcorn, soft drinks, and candy. The peak of attendance came during World War II, but only because patrons had few other entertainments from which to choose.

After World War II, Americans moved away from the movie palace theaters. The film industry's reaction was first to create theaters at the new crossroads, the intersection of highways. The drive-in, the auto theater, flourished during the 1950s and into the 1960s (see entry).

The second reaction came with the very image projected. CinemaScope, 3-D, and then Panavision wide-screen —in color—became the order of the day. These certainly differentiated film exhibition from the presentation of 4x3 black-and-white programming on that era's television.

But in the end television replaced the cinema as the place we watched most movies (see Television Movies). First came the re-running of older films late at night on TV stations throughout the nation, then the running of fairly contemporary films in prime time. During the 1970s came pay television with the presentation of uncut, uninterrupted films. HBO made this formula work for great profits. Finally in the 1980s came the advent of home video. With a VCR one could become one's own exhibitor, running films—through rental or purchase—wherever one wanted. High-definition TV (see entry) promises to transform watching films at home during the initial years of the 21st century.

Movie theaters still premiere films, but increasingly the home television set has become the principal venue for film exhibition, a far cry from the era of the movie palace. In the 1980s and 1990s the first-run theaters moved to the mall, and became another part of the general shopping experience. And so we have *multi*plexes, with a dozen screens offering a smorgasbord of choices of first-run Hollywood feature films in competition with subsequent-run fare at home.

Bibliography

Gomery, Douglas. *The Hollywood Studio System*. New York: St. Martin's, 1986.
——. *Shared Pleasures*. Madison: U of Wisconsin P, 1992.
Hall, Ben M. *The Best Remaining Seats*. New York: Bramhall, 1961.

Douglas Gomery

Fisher, Eddie (1928-), one of America's more popular singing stars, was one of seven children who grew up in a working-class Jewish neighborhood of South Philadelphia. Fisher began his professional career at 17, first in New York City, then, with the help of agent Milton Blackstone, who became a solid fixture in Fisher's often chaotic life, at Grossinger's Resort in the Catskills.

At Grossinger's in 1949, Blackstone arranged for Eddie Cantor to hear Fisher sing. Cantor took an immediate liking to the young singer and invited him along on Cantor's cross-country tour. The success of the tour and Cantor's endorsement led to RCA Victor signing Fisher to a recording contract. His early recordings on the RCA Victor Bluebird label (including "My Bolero"/"Foolish Tears" and "Sorry"/"Yesterday's Roses" 1949) failed to make the charts, but still sold in respectable numbers. In June 1950, Fisher was called on short notice to fill in at the important New Jersey nightclub, Bill Miller's Riviera. Receiving rave reviews for his performance in the *New York Times* and *Time*, Fisher started a whirlwind series of performances and RCA Victor moved him to its more prestigious Blackbird label. By the end of the year, he had been named the "Most Promising Male Vocalist of 1950" by *Billboard*. The first months of 1951 saw him performing at New York's famed Paramount Theater for $5,000 a week.

Called up for military service in 1951, Fisher spent the next two years touring the world with the Armed Forces Review. In 1953 he began hosting NBC-TV's *Coke Time* variety show, sponsored by Coca-Cola. Lasting nearly four years, the show led to Fisher's nickname as the Coca-Cola Kid. During this time, Fisher scored his biggest hits, "Count Your Blessings" and "Oh, My Pa-Pa."

On September 26, 1955, "America's Sweethearts," Fisher and Debbie Reynolds, were married. In the same year, Fisher had hits with "You Gotta Have Heart" and "A Man Chases a Girl" (with Reynolds singing the refrain, "until she catches him"). Fisher—in his first screen appearance—and Reynolds co-starred in the disastrous remake of *Bachelor Mother* (1939), entitled *Bundle of Joy* (1956), that bombed at the box office.

Between 1950 and 1957, Fisher had 35 Top 40 hits, with 19 in the Top 10. His four-year marriage to Reynolds had produced two children, Carrie and Todd (Carrie would go on to star in the *Star Wars* films before becoming a best-selling novelist). Elizabeth Taylor, motion picture superstar and her producer-husband Mike Todd, were close friends of the Fishers; in 1958, after Todd's death in a plane crash, Fisher and Taylor moved from a close friendship to a romance that would forever destroy his clean-cut image. Fisher and Taylor were married on May 12, 1959.

Fisher continued to headline in Las Vegas showrooms and other nightclubs across the country through the early 1960s. His last hit, "Games That Lovers Play," was released in 1966 and reached #45 on the charts. Early in his career, Fisher had become addicted to Methedrine, an amphetamine, administered by the infamous Dr. Max Jacobson. By the early 1970s, his self-destructive addiction to this and other drugs brought his career to an end.

Though vowing never to marry again, Fisher was briefly married to singer/actress Connie Stevens (1968-69), with whom he had two children (Joely and Trisha Leigh). Fisher had another brief marriage to Terry Richards (1975-76).

Bibliography

"Eddie Fisher." *Current Biography* (1954): 275-76.
Fisher, Eddie. *Eddie: My Life, My Loves*. New York: Harper & Row, 1981.
Greene, Myrna. *The Eddie Fisher Story*. Middlebury: Eriksson, 1978.

Martin R. Kalfatovic

Fitzgerald, Ella (1917-1996), overcame many obstacles on the way to becoming the "First Lady of Jazz." Though most sources list 1918 as her year of birth, Ella Fitzgerald was actually born on April 25, 1917, in the city of Newport News, VA. Her home life was difficult; her father left home while she was a toddler, and her mother was forced to support her alone.

Fitzgerald, like many other talented entertainers, learned her trade by copying the styles of artists whose music she admired. Her early influences included Bing Crosby, the Boswell Sisters (especially Connee Boswell), and Louis Armstrong. Her initial break came in 1934, when she won an amateur talent night competition at Harlem's Apollo Theater.

Fitzgerald's professional career began in 1935 when Chick Webb hired her as the female vocalist for his band. With Webb's band, she recorded such swing hits as "You'll Have to Swing It" and "A-Tisket, A-Tasket." During the mid-1940s, Fitzgerald became the only successful swing singer to make the shift into "bebop" music (see Bebop). Her recording of Lionel Hampton's "Flying Home" brought her firmly into the current era with its daring and precise use of "scat."

While Louis Armstrong is usually credited with inventing scat (a form of singing where nonsense syllables are sub-

Ella Fitzgerald. Photo courtesy of Popular Culture Library, Bowling Green State University, Bowling Green, OH.

stituted for an instrumental lead line), it is Ella Fitzgerald who brought the form to the musical forefront and popularized it with audiences outside the jazz realm. During those years, she toured with jazz great Dizzy Gillespie and recorded many hits, including "Lady Be Good," "Stairway to the Stars," and "Lover Man."

In the late 1940s and early 1950s, Ella began touring internationally. Having mastered the up-tempo popular songs, she began to work more ballads into her repertoire, proving her versatility. Her best-selling albums were recorded during the 1950s—the *Songbook* series and *Mack the Knife: Ella in Berlin*. The songs recorded during this era became popular with diverse audiences. Fitzgerald's fans included President John F. Kennedy, for whose Inaugural Gala she temporarily interrupted an overseas concert tour in 1961. She performed for only five minutes, then returned to Australia.

During her long career, Ella Fitzgerald worked with many of America's greatest popular musicians and singers: Duke Ellington, Frank Sinatra, Benny Goodman, Ray Charles, Oscar Peterson, and others. She earned the admiration and respect of critics and the approbation of audiences all over the world. In a business where appearances are so often stressed as necessary for success, her amazing range, her gifts for rhythm and pitch, and her supple, youthful voice allowed the once-portly, self-conscious artist to become a star. She continued performing into the 1990s, and her music continued to sell to a wide assortment of audiences.

Bibliography:
Nicholson, Stuart. *Ella Fitzgerald: A Biography of the First Lady of Jazz.* New York: Scribner's, 1993.

Katherine Doman

Flash Gordon (1934-), the influential comic strip by Alex Raymond, first appeared as a King Features Syndicate Sunday comic strip. Considered the archetypal "space opera," the series featured the conflict between Flash and his nemesis Ming the Merciless, despot from the planet Mongo. Accompanied by scientist Hans Zarkov and perpetual girlfriend Dale Arden, Flash engaged both enemies and friends of Earth within a baroque artistic style that stressed action, mystery, and romance. In 1936, Flash branched into comic books with the publication of *Flash Gordon in the Caverns of Mongo*. In 1937 it appeared in book form with the same title.

In 1944, Austin Briggs took over the development of the strip. Mac Raboy continued the series in 1948, and since then Dan Barry, Al Williamsen, and most recently Bruce Jones. Illustrators have included Harvey Kurtzman, Wally Wood, and Gray Morrow. Other story contributors have included Harry Harrison and Dan Jurgens, who completed a nine-part series for DC Comics in 1988.

In addition to its prominence as a daily comic strip, a single issue of the pulp magazine *Flash Gordon Strange Adventure Magazine* was published in December 1937, featuring "The Master of Mars" by James E. Northfield. In 1974-75, a six-part paperback series appeared, adapted by Ron Goulart and B. Cassiday.

Flash Gordon also made its way into radio; the popularity of its 1936 serial starring Buster Crabbe continues even today. The original 12-episode series was followed by the 15-part *Flash Gordon's Trip to Mars* in 1938, and *Flash Gordon Conquers the Universe* in 1940. Edited portions of the 1936 serial received theatrical release as *Spaceship to the Unknown* (1936) and *Perils from the Planet Mongo* (1936). *The Deadly Ray from Mars* was released in 1938 from the second serial, and *Purple Death from Outer Space* was the theatrical release from the edited 1940 serial.

In 1951, a short-lived series appeared on U.S. television. In 1974, a soft-porn parody, *Flesh Gordon*, was released. In 1980, Dino de Laurentiis released a feature-length film based on the original comic strip.

Bibliography
Benton, Mike. *Science Fiction Comics: The Illustrated History*. Dallas: Taylor, 1992.
Clute, John, and Peter Nicholls, eds. *The Encyclopedia of Science Fiction*. New York: St. Martin's, 1993.
Moskowitz, Sam. *Strange Horizons: The Spectrum of Science Fiction*. New York: Scribner's, 1976.
Sawyer, A. *Science Fiction Foundation Collection*. http://WWW.liv.ac.uk/÷asawyer/sftcl.html, 1996.
Scholes, Robert, and Eric C. Rabkin. *Science Fiction: History, Science, Vision*. New York: Oxford UP, 1977.

Marguerite Cotto

Flatt and Scruggs, with their band, the Foggy Mountain Boys, were the leading exponents in the 1950s and 1960s of a style of folk and country-western music known as bluegrass. Lester Raymond Flatt was born in Overton County, TN, in 1914; Earl Eugene Scruggs in Cleveland County, NC, in 1924. As boys, both were interested in performing music. When his time was not taken with school and chores, Flatt taught himself to play the guitar, and during the 1930s, he played for local groups. Scruggs began playing the banjo at the age of five and had invented his own style of picking, known as the three-finger approach, and a device used for making rapid tuning changes by the age of ten. Both men gained notoriety for their musicianship and in 1944 began playing with the "father of bluegrass," Bill Monroe, on the *Grand Ole Opry* stage. Flatt and Scruggs played with Monroe until 1948, when the two decided to form their own bluegrass band, the Foggy Mountain Boys.

Within only a few years, the new band had signed a recording contract and was featured on many radio stations in the American Southeast and some television shows, such as *Farm and Fun Time*. By 1953, the bluegrass players earned their own spot at the *Grand Ole Opry*. In the mid-1960s, Flatt and Scruggs continued to broaden their audience by landing their own syndicated television show as well as continuing to play folk, country-western, and bluegrass music festivals. Their rendition of the theme song for the hit comedy *The Beverly Hillbillies*, as well as occasional appearances on the show, allowed an even broader audience to appreciate the bluegrass performers' work. A version of the duo's "Foggy Mountain Breakdown" was featured in the 1967 film *Bonnie and Clyde*.

Awards the duo received include best instrumental group at the Country and Western Jamboree from 1955 to 1958, Music Reporter's 1961 most popular male stars, and *Billboard*'s 1963 favorite country group. With both individual and team-written songs such as "Foggy Mountain Special," "Earl's Breakdown," and "Songs of Our Land," Flatt and Scruggs laid the foundation of bluegrass music and, until the duo split in 1969, enjoyed much success.

Bibliography

Carlin, Richard. *The Big Book of Country Music: A Biographical Encyclopedia.* New York: Penguin, 1995.

McCloud, Barry. *Definitive Country: The Ultimate Encyclopedia of Country Music and Its Performers.* New York: Perigee, 1995.

Shestack, Melvin. *The Country Music Encyclopedia.* Toronto: KBO, 1974.

Stambler, Irwin, and Grelun Landon. *The Encyclopedia of Folk, Country & Western Music.* 2d ed. New York: St. Martin's, 1983.

Scott Baugh

The Flintstones (1960-1966), about a "modern Stone-Age family," was the first successful prime-time animated series on American television. Its continuing popularity can be seen not only in years of reruns and revivals, and the 1994 live-action feature, but in over 4,000 merchandise tie-ins from clothing to vitamins.

After their success with children's shows like *Huckleberry Hound* and *Yogi Bear*, William Hanna and Joseph Barbera were urged by Screen Gems (the television arm of Columbia Pictures) to develop a prime-time animated series. They worked out the concept of parodying current situation comedies, especially *The Honeymooners* and *Father Knows Best*, with the twist of setting them in a different historical era. Cartoonists Dan Gordon and Bill Benedict had the idea to use a Stone Age setting (although the Fleischer Studios produced a similar series of *Stone Age Cartoons* back in 1940). The concept was bought by ABC, and premiered Sept. 30, 1960. Voiced by Alan Reed, Jr. (Fred Flintstone), Mel Blanc (Barney Rubble), Jean VanderPyl (Wilma Flintstone), and veteran actress Bea Benaderet (Betty Rubble), *The Flintstones* finished the season in the Nielsen ratings' Top 20, and won a number of industry awards, including the Golden Globe, and an Emmy nomination for best comedy series of 1960-61.

A clear appeal of the series was its parody of sitcom formula plots, and there are elements of satire in the way modern consumer conveniences are turned into sight gags. One of the show's favorite gags was to have cameos by Stone Age versions of modern celebrities (Ann Margrock, Stony Curtis, etc.). The most popular gimmick was Wilma's pregnancy, ending with the February 1963 "birth" of their little girl, Pebbles. The next season the Rubbles adopted Bamm-Bamm, a little boy of incredible strength and a one-word vocabulary.

By the fifth and sixth seasons, the show began to use more storylines aimed at kids, with new neighbors the Gruesomes (a spin on *The Munsters* and *The Addams Family*), and magical space alien The Great Gazoo (Harvey Korman). The show was canceled after 166 episodes in 1966, but went immediately into syndication to find continued success. That same year, Columbia released *The Man Called Flintstone*, a theatrical feature spoofing James Bond.

The Flintstones were revived several times as Saturday morning series, starting in 1971 with *Pebbles and Bamm-Bamm*, pitting the adolescent pair in Archie-type hijinks, then in 1980 with *The Flintstones Comedy Show*. *The Flintstone Kids* (1986) followed the trend of presenting well-known cartoon stars as children.

The idea of a live-action movie languished for several years until Steven Spielberg brought the project through dozens of writers and lassoed John Goodman as the natural choice to play Fred. *The Flintstones* opened in May 1994, to good box office from audiences who wanted to see the original cartoon gags and catchphrases, though most critics were not impressed.

Bibliography

Brooks, Tim, and Earl Marsh. "The Flintstones." *The Complete Directory to Prime Time TV Shows, 1946-Present.* 4th ed. New York: Ballantine, 1988.

Halpin, Joan. "Animation Legend Visits in Cambria." *Central Coast Times* (Paso Robles, CA) 27 Aug. 1992: 1.

Lenburg, Jeff. *The Encyclopedia of Animated Cartoons.* Rev. ed. New York: Facts on File, 1991.

O'Neil, Thomas. *The Emmys.* New York: Penguin, 1992. 73-77.

Shaw, Scott. "The Bedrock Chronicles: The Evolution of the Flintstones." *Cartoon Quarterly* Winter 1988: 27-31.

Mark McDermott

Flynn, Errol (1909-1959), the most memorable of the pre-war swashbuckling Hollywood movie heroes, was born Errol Leslie Flynn in Hobart, Australia. A rebellious son of socially prominent Australians, he left school at age 17 to work on an Australian sheep ranch, as a customs officer, plantation manager and gold miner, a sailor, and an actor. Flynn traveled restlessly from 1927 to 1934 in Asia, France, and England before Jack L. Warner brought him to Hollywood. In 1934 Warner Brothers cast him in a series of B movies before his first major role in 1935, starring in *Captain Blood.*

He was always at his best in the swashbuckler or romantic melodrama, films such as *Captain Blood* (1935), *The Prince and the Pauper* (1937), *The Adventures of Robin Hood* (1938), or *The Adventures of Don Juan* (1948). In these unforgettable costume melodramas, Flynn defined the role of the aristocratic hero overcoming injustice and triumphing for his own personal glory and for the good of society. His "English" accent, good manners, sense of fair play, and wit charmed the women and wowed the boys. His dueling scenes were choreographed like musical comedy dance numbers. After some attempts at modern roles, Flynn returned to the swashbuckler role in *The Master of Ballantrae* (1953). With an aging Flynn as a Scottish rebel turned pirate, this movie foreshadowed the decline of his meteoric movie career.

In eight films, Flynn's leading lady was Olivia de Havilland (1916-), playing an aristocratic heroine, initially repelled by the disguised hero turned commoner, but eventually won over to his egalitarian morality. Her love enables him to triumph and to return to his social position in a better, fairer world. Flynn and de Havilland's final movie together was *They Died with Their Boots On* (1941), a sweeping historical view of Custer's Last Stand.

Classified 4-F due to malaria and cardiac problems, Flynn cinematically contributed to World War II in *Dive Bomber* (1941), *Desperate Journey* (1942), *The Edge of Darkness* (1943), and *Objective Burma* (1945). Like many stars, he resisted typecasting but found the studio adamant that he continue in big box office movies.

Underestimating the movies he made for the tyrannical Jack Warner, Flynn longed to play weighty roles. His more serious films, *The Sun Also Rises* (1957), *Too Much, Too Soon* (1958), playing his tragic friend, John Barrymore, and *The Roots of Heaven* (1958), demonstrated his dramatic skills as did earlier rare comedies like *The Perfect Specimen* (1937) and *Four's a Crowd* (1938). Best when working with strong directors, like Michael Curtiz in twelve films or Raoul Walsh in seven films, he also benefited from strong supporting actors like David Niven, Alan Hale, Anne Sheridan, Claude Rains, Basil Rathbone, and Henry Stephenson.

Bibliography
Flynn, Errol. *Beam Ends.* New York: Longmans, Green, 1937.

——. *My Wicked, Wicked Ways.* New York: Buccaneer, 1959.

Godfrey, Lionel. *The Life and Crimes of Errol Flynn.* New York: St. Martin's, 1977.

Thomas, Tony, Rudy Behlmer, and Clifford McCarty. *The Films of Errol Flynn.* New York: Citadel, 1969.

Valenti, Peter. *Errol Flynn: A Bio-Bibliography.* Westport: Greenwood, 1984.

Peter C. Holloran

Folk Rock is a term applied to music that combines elements of folk music, such as traditional stories and melodies, with the stronger beat and electrified instruments of rock music. The broader contemporary definition of folk music is generally applied to folk rock, meaning it includes much of what is written and performed by singer-songwriters even though it is not passed down by friends or families. Two strong influences led to folk rock: the folk revival that started in Greenwich Village in the late 1950s and early 1960s and the success of the Beatles in adapting folk harmonies to rock music and in combining electric and acoustic instrumentation, particularly in the film *A Hard Day's Night* (see entry).

The term folk rock was first used on a regular basis in 1965. In that year, the Byrds made two folk classics into No. 1 hit singles, Bob Dylan's "Mr. Tambourine Man" and Pete Seeger's "Turn, Turn, Turn." Also in 1965, Bob Dylan began to team up with rhythm and blues-oriented rock musicians, first at the Newport Folk Festival. His use of rock accompaniment generated a great deal of controversy, but songs like "Maggie's Farm," "She Belongs to Me," and "Like a Rolling Stone" became classics.

The use of electric instruments by folk musicians became common in the mid-1960s. Producer Tom Wilson added electric instruments to Simon and Garfunkel's "The Sounds of Silence," making it their first No. 1 hit. Their subsequent recordings alternated traditional folk songs like "Scarborough Fair" with rock songs like "Mrs. Robinson." Two of the mid-1960s most popular folk rock bands, the Mamas and the Papas and the Lovin' Spoonful, used acoustic instruments like the flute and autoharp along with rock instrumentation to produce the softer, "flower power" sounds of the psychedelic period.

Folk rock took a turn toward country music in 1967 with the formation of Buffalo Springfield in Los Angeles (see entry). They combined acoustic instruments, four-part bluegrass harmonies, and folk-influenced rock lyrics to produce two classic albums before breaking up. But each of the musicians went on to greater fame. Neil Young and Steve Stills became half of Crosby, Stills, Nash and Young, the most popular folk rock group at the end of the 1960s. Richie Furay and Jim Messina moved more in the country direction with the band Poco.

Other folk singer/songwriters joined the country-folk-rock bandwagon. Native New Yorker Jesse Colin Young moved to California and formed the Youngbloods, who scored a hit with the protest hit "Get Together" in 1969. Other country rock groups from California included the Nitty Gritty Dirt Band, which had a Top 10 single ("Mr. Bojangles"), and the Stone Poneys ("Different Drum").

The Nitty Gritty Dirt Band was the launching pad for singer/songwriter Jackson Browne, who co-wrote another L.A. band's first hit, the Eagles' "Take It Easy." Linda Ronstadt left the Stone Poneys for a solo career, while the Nitty Gritty Dirt Band returned to traditional music with the 1973 folk and country music triple album, *Will the Circle Be Unbroken.*

In the 1970s, folk rock split in two directions. The Eagles, Neil Young, and Jackson Browne (see entries) moved into progressively harder and louder rock as they began to play large auditoriums and stadiums. Others directed their songs to the growing "soft rock" audience of older and more conservative rock listeners. Carole King's 1971 *Tapestry* album is a good example of the latter trend. It stayed on the charts for six years and included mellow remakes of her successes as a soul-music songwriter, "Will You Still Love Me Tomorrow" and "(You Make Me Feel Like a) Natural Woman." James Taylor recorded numerous covers of old soul hits, including "How Sweet It Is" (1975) and "Handy Man" (1977), and he sang with Paul Simon on Art Garfunkel's 1978 hit, "Wonderful World."

The 1980s and 1990s saw a revival of folk rock music, much of it written and performed by women. The Indigo Girls and 10,000 Maniacs both show strong folk music influences, as do soloists Sarah McLachlan, Nanci Griffith, Shawn Colvin, and Tori Amos. The Counting Crows, although they look and use instruments similar to "grunge" bands, incorporate themes reminiscent of Bob Dylan in their hit singles "Mr. Jones" and "'Round Here." And the alternative band R.E.M.'s mysterious lyrics and Dylanesque vocals in songs like "Losing My Religion" and "What Is the Frequency, Kenneth?" are also suggestive of mid-1960s folk rock.

Bibliography
Laing, Dave, Karl Dallas, Robin Denselow, and Robert Shelton. *The Electric Muse: The Story of Folk into Rock.* London: Methuen, 1975.
Vassal, Jacques. *Electric Children: Roots and Branches of Modern Folkrock.* New York: Taplinger, 1976.

Kenneth M. Nagelberg

Follett, Ken (1947-), is a modern master of spy fiction, often compared to John le Carré in expertise and popularity. Born in Glamorgan, Wales, Follett moved from a career in journalism to full-time writing in 1978. His reputation was founded on *Eye of the Needle* (also called *Storm Island*), published in 1978, and on other popular novels such as *Triple* (1979), *The Key to Rebecca* (1980), *The Man from St. Petersburg* (1982), *On Wings of Eagles* (1983), *A Dangerous Fortune* (1993), and *The Third Twin* (1996).

Follett's novels often focus on a climactic historical moment of international crisis, when fictional plots are thwarted to preserve the facts of history as they are actually recorded. The plots usually revolve around the deadly personal conflict between an antagonist whose villainy threatens to undermine a historical outcome as readers know it to be, and a protagonist who must pull out the stops to defeat him. Follett does not rewrite history, but maintains suspense throughout his novels by including exciting chases, inventing cameo appearances by real figures like Churchill and Rommel, and introducing the moral and emotional tensions inspired by patriotism, sex, and violence. Follett's endings are abrupt, concluding in a dramatic culmination where the culprit is overcome and history as we know it is preserved.

Bibliography
Turner, Richard Charles. *Ken Follett: A Critical Companion.* Westport: Greenwood, 1996.

Deborah Weber Long

Follies, The, was a series of lavish musical revues produced by Florenz Ziegfeld (1867-1932) that dominated the American theater in the 1910s and 1920s (see Revue); the skimpily adorned Las Vegas showgirl and the spectacular production in which she appears are its last vestiges. Traditionally, Ziegfeld has been credited with inventing the form, but this credit is undeserved. America's first revue was *The Passing Show* of 1894, which featured spectacle, attractive girls, stage effects, topical humor, and skits parodying then-popular stage presentations. It resembled vaudeville in that it was a plotless show featuring a variety of acts. However, unlike vaudeville, all the show's material was created for this one production and its performers appeared throughout the night and not at just one place on the bill. From burlesque, the show drew its predilection for displaying attractive, unadorned females and for parodying other shows, while the 19th-century extravaganza provided the model for breathtaking sets and costumes. An immediate hit, *The Passing Show* influenced subsequent revues, including *The Merry Whirl* (1895) and *In Gay New York* (1896). By 1900, this form was well established on the New York stage.

What it needed to flourish was a genius, and that gentleman appeared in 1907. His name was Florenz Ziegfeld, a somewhat successful Broadway producer, known primarily for his marriage to French musical star Anna Held (1873-1918). It was his wife's idea that he mount a summer musical entertainment modeled on Paris's popular Folies-Bergère. Harry B. Smith (1850-1936), the show's librettist-lyricist, provided the production's title from the name of a popular newspaper column, "Follies of the Day." And so the *Follies of 1907* appeared, at a cost of $13,000, ran for 70 performances, and made a profit of over $100,000.

Ziegfeld, though possessing little in the way of a sense of humor, was able to hire funny people. When the *Follies* was at its height, Ziegfeld had as his regular comics Fanny Brice (1891-1951) for seven shows; Bert Williams (1874-1922), the country's greatest African-American comic, for eight shows; W. C. Fields (1879-1946) for seven shows; Will Rogers (1879-1935) for five shows; and Eddie Cantor (1892-1964) for five shows. The *Follies* became the tired businessman's ideal entertainment, providing more than enough jokes and bare flesh for a worthwhile night out. By 1911, his creation had become so closely associated with his name that Ziegfeld changed its title to *The Ziegfeld Follies* and so it remained even after he had died.

Such success was sure to spawn imitators, and the competition was not long in coming. In 1912, the Shubert brothers, Lee (1873-1953) and J. J. (1878-1963), America's foremost producers and theater owners, launched their own revue series, *The Passing Show* (1912-24). It featured parodies of popular shows, as had its namesake, as well as a female chorus of 80, and lasted through 12 editions. It introduced the newer, slimmer version of the chorus girl (beginning with the 1914 show), who replaced the heftier, hourglass-figured chorine in popularity. In 1919, former Ziegfeld dancer George White (1890-1939), utilizing some talent he had lured away from the *Follies,* introduced his *Scandals* (1919-39), which would run for 13 editions, mostly in the 1920s. The series emphasized dance (it popularized the Black Bottom in 1926) and employed outstanding songwriters, including George Gershwin (1898-1937), who worked on five editions, and the team of Buddy DeSylva (1895-1950), Lew Brown (1893-1958) and Ray Henderson (1896-1970), who worked on three shows. In 1921, Irving Berlin (1888-1989), who had provided the *Follies* with its theme song, "A Pretty Girl Is Like a Melody," opened a theater, the Music Box, to house his own lavish smart series, *The Music Box Revue* (1921-24). Finally, in 1923, lyricist-director Earl Carroll introduced *The Vanities* (1923-40), a series which would present nine editions, mostly in the 1920s. Usually featuring second-rate talent and production values, these shows emphasized a maximum display of female flesh in as tasteless a manner as possible, and proved to be extremely successful. By the late 1920s, both Carroll and White were dominating the revue field, Ziegfeld having abandoned it to them.

By the end of the decade, talking pictures had lured away many of the major revue stars and were presenting more spectacular scenic effects than could possibly be found on the stage, striptease burlesque was displaying more female anatomy than the major revues had ever attempted to exhibit, and the Great Depression had arrived to bankrupt the revues' financial support. As a result, by the early 1930s, the big, lavish, female revue was about as dead as the Roaring Twenties in which it had thrived.

Bibliography

Baral, Robert. *Revue: A Nostalgic Reprise of the Great Broadway Period.* New York: Oxford UP, 1962.

Bordman, Gerald. *American Musical Revue: From the Passing Show to Sugar Babies.* New York: Oxford UP, 1985.

——. *American Musical Theatre: A Chronicle.* 2d ed. New York: Fleet, 1992.

Ewen, David. *New Complete Book of the American Musical Theater.* New York: Holt, 1970.

Ziegfeld, Richard, and Patricia Ziegfeld. *The Ziegfeld Touch: The Life and Times of Florenz Ziegfeld, Jr.* New York: Abrams, 1993.

Richard M. Goldstein

Fonda, Henry (1905-1982), born in Grand Island, NE, started acting as a 20-year-old in the Omaha Community Playhouse. His first Hollywood role was as the star in *The Farmer Takes a Wife* (1935), which he had played on Broadway a year earlier. Fonda made his first major breakthrough with the title role of *Young Mr. Lincoln* (1939), fitting the standards of honesty and good-natured integrity suggested by Lincoln. The integrity of Fonda was once again realized in his Oscar-nominated portrayal of Tom Joad, who migrates with his family to California in the film adaptation of John Steinbeck's *The Grapes of Wrath* (1940). This distillation of the Depression-era experience has been secured in the hearts of the American audience because of Fonda's legendary "I'll be there" farewell speech. To the audience, Fonda's Joad *is* everywhere as a symbol of the American struggle to succeed.

Fonda's next great success demonstrates his reserved performance style; *The Lady Eve* (1943), one of his personal favorites, depicts Fonda as a shy millionaire buffoon, guarding himself from Barbara Stanwyck, a grifter on board a cruise ship. Fonda's penchant for comedy, as well as drama, won him accolades of appreciation and established him as one of the foremost stars during this time.

In 1943, *The Ox-Bow Incident* depicted the proceedings of a lynch mob, a harrowing Western in which Fonda plays a wandering cowboy who witnesses the event. From his perspective, the audience witnesses the horror of mob mentality and violence. In this film, Fonda's character stands for justice and humanity, ideals that are closely tied to Fonda's overall screen persona. Another conscientious triumph for Fonda's persona lies in his portrayal of Juror No. 8 in *12 Angry Men* (1957). At the beginning of the film, 11 of the 12 jurors are ready to convict a youth that stabbed his father, but No. 8 (Fonda) has a reasonable doubt. One by one, he patiently convinces the jurors and the audience of the defendant's innocence. His clarity and optimism are the virtues of his open mind, leaving the audience in simple admiration of his belief in humanity combined with intelligence. As No. 8, Fonda defines the American ideals of justice and democracy.

Unlike most film stars, Fonda remained involved in theater, perhaps because of the success he achieved as the titular *Mister Roberts*. In 1948, the play began its long run on Broadway, which ended in 1950; Fonda also starred in the 1955 film version. Aside from Tom Joad, this is the character most often identified with Fonda.

Henry Fonda's swan song performance in *On Golden Pond* (1981) marked the end of a magnificent career, but, also, reconciliation between the actor and his estranged daughter, Jane Fonda. The total immersion in his career combined with his generally withdrawn nature left Henry Fonda ill-equipped to deal with his precocious children, who eventually became actors themselves. The rift of alienation was bridged with *On Golden Pond*, which also united Fonda with a screen star who eluded his career, Katharine Hepburn. As the crochety Norman Thayer, Jr., Fonda is unapproachable, which well describes his offscreen personality, but, with her mother's (Hepburn) insistence, Chelsea (Jane) finds the warm affectionate parent that is just below the gruff, stern surface of her father. Although Fonda had received lifetime achievement awards from the Academy, the Golden Globes, and the American Film Institute, he still had not obtained the Academy Award for best actor. It was graciously bestowed on him a few months before his death for *On Golden Pond*, a thank you for being the conscientious voice of the nation for many years.

Bibliography
Collier, Peter. *The Fondas: A Hollywood Dynasty.* New York: Putnam, 1992.
Sweeney, Kevin. *Henry Fonda: a Bio-bibliography.* Westport: Greenwood, 1992.
Teichman, Howard. *Fonda, My Life.* New York: New American Library, 1991.

Robert Baird

Fonda, Jane Seymour (1937-), was born in New York City to Henry Fonda (see above) and his second wife, Frances Seymour Brokaw Fonda. Her acting career, apart from parts in a few school plays, began in 1954 when she appeared along with her father in the Omaha (NE) Community Theater production of *The Country Girl.* But she had still not decided on acting as a career and while at Vassar, she went to Paris to study art. After she returned from Paris, she became a model and, as an "establishment ingenue," she twice graced the cover of *Vogue.*

Her career interests became more focused in 1958 when she met Lee Strasberg and became his student at the Actors Studio. In 1960, she made her Broadway and Hollywood debuts. Both the play, *There Was a Little Girl,* and the film, *Tall Story,* were "frothy," but Fonda received rave reviews for her roles and ended up winning the New York Drama Critics Award as the "most promising new actress of the year."

Her 1965 marriage to French director Roger Vadim, considered the "Svengali of sex goddesses," was certainly a defining moment in her career. He attempted to mold her into another Brigitte Bardot through films such as *Barbarella* (1968) and in effect transformed her into the "sixties sexpot."

In the late 1960s, she took on the role of a social activist, speaking on an array of anti-establishment causes for the Black Panthers, Native Americans, and American GIs. In particular, she directed her energies to ending the war in Southeast Asia and in this context, formed the Anti-War Troupe with Donald Sutherland. The group attempted to mobilize American troops against the war, and toured military camps defying the expressed wishes of the Pentagon. In 1972, she co-produced *Free the Army*, a documentary detailing the tour. Her involvement in part led to her marriage to antiwar activist Tom Hayden in 1973, and the following year she made a controversial visit to North Vietnam. Her militant stance earned her the nickname "Hanoi Jane" and the wrath of the establishment and numerous right-wing groups.

Parallel to her activist role, her film career continued to evolve. In 1969, she was nominated for an Oscar for her portrayal of a 1930s marathon dancer in *They Shoot Horses, Don't They?*, which earned the New York Film Critics best actress award as well. Two years later she gave one of the best performances of her career in *Klute,* playing a New York call girl. The role won her another New York Critics award.

In the late 1970s, Jane Fonda rejoined the Hollywood mainstream, and established her dominance in commercial cinema through highly acclaimed films such as *Julia* (1977),

Coming Home (1978), *The China Syndrome* (1979), and *On Golden Pond* (1981). She was awarded an Oscar for best actress for *Coming Home* and received nominations for the other three. She particularly cherished her role in *On Golden Pond* because it was her first film with her father.

Her energies during the 1980s went toward producing and promoting a videotape, *Jane Fonda's Workout,* and several sequels, all of which were highly successful. Her political stance also became more moderate as she helped her then-husband Hayden get elected to the California State Assembly, and in a 1988 interview, she formally apologized to Vietnam veterans and their families for her actions during her 1972 visit to Hanoi.

The Jane Fonda of the 1990s has mellowed considerably and, since her marriage to media mogul Ted Turner in 1984, she has done little acting. But she still uses her status and considerable clout to make occasional forays into the world of activism. The central focus of her life for now, however, appears to be on her own family.

Bibliography
"Jane Fonda." *Current Biography Yearbook* 1988.
"Jane Fonda." *Movie Guide Database.* Internet. http://www.tvguide.com/movies/katz/2349.sml (23 Jan. 1998).
Spada, James. *Fonda: Her Life in Pictures.* New York: Doubleday, 1985.

Zia Hasan

Fonda, Peter (1939), son of the late Henry Fonda and younger brother of Jane (see entries above), has been an actor, producer, screenwriter, and director. He went from playing simple roles such as that of the boy-next-door to the nonconformist or rebel roles of *The Wild Angels* (1966) and *Easy Rider* (1969), which brought financial success and made him a celebrity. With its eclectic hippie-infused/motorcycle nonconformist, drug and sex themes coupled with its subliminal anti-violence and anti-war message (contrasting with its tragic and violent ending), *Easy Rider* has become a "cult classic." He both co-wrote and produced the film, which also included Jack Nicholson in his first starring role.

During the sixties, seventies, and eighties, Peter Fonda associated himself with various causes and became a symbol of the American counterculture that was nonpolitical. In 1971 Fonda directed *The Hired Hand*, a Western with praiseworthy acting. He continued to work in about two movies annually, but none was as successful as *Easy Rider.* Yet even in mediocre vampire films such as *Nadja* (1994), in which he portrayed Dr. Van Helsing, Fonda displays acting skills reminiscent of his father. The resemblance to his father is even clearer in *Ulee's Gold* (1997), in which Peter plays Ulysses "Ulee" Jackson, a Vietnam veteran who learns to cope with personal suffering by coming to understand that "there's all kinds of weakness in this world, and not all of it is evil." This role earned him an Oscar nomination as best actor.

Peter Fonda's daughter, Bridget Fonda (1964-), has also followed the family's calling, acting in such films as *Single White Female* (1992), *Point of No Return* (1993), and *A Simple Plan* (1998).

Bibliography

Lally, Kevin. "Fact Sheet—Peter Fonda." *E!Online*. n.p. Online. Internet 1 Jan. 1998. Available: http://e3.eonline.com/Fa...e/Bio/0,128,5461,00.html.

——. "Peter Fonda." *Cinemania Online*. n.p. Online. Internet 1 Jan. 1998. Available: http://207.68.14296/cin...ographies/PeterFonda.HTM.

——. "Q & A with Peter Fonda." *Rough Cut Q & As*. n. p. Online. Internet 1 Jan. 1998. Available: http://www.roughcut.com/main/drive1 97jul3.html.

——. "Ulee's Gold." *smartdev.com/reviews*. n.p. Online. Internet 1 Jan. 1998. Available: http://www.smartdev.com/reviews/ulegold.htm.

Mitali R. Pati
Eugene F. Wong

Food Art. Preparation and presentation of food, emphasizing beauty and symbolism beyond the utilitarian function, is common in all human cultures. Folk customs echoing prior religious rituals are manifested in varied forms from Easter eggs (see entry) to harvest arrangements of the bounty of the fields presented for judging at state fairs. Rites of passage are marked by decorated birthday and wedding cakes. Each cultural group and historical time period embeds traces of past and present beliefs and practices in such celebratory activities.

The contemporary United States is one of the most varied cultures ever to exist in this regard. Influences of ancient, medieval and contemporary Europe, ancient and modern Asia and Africa, as well as original North and South America impact postmodern California. In the Southwest, ethnic blends of contemporary Asian with Native American and Hispanic culture are evident in the ingredients and visual presentation of food. In Louisiana, French, West Indian, African, Spanish, and Vietnamese influences coexist. Food historians who trace the diffusions of culture by the extent of change in food practices such as the use of spices or the style of food combinations and presentations will be faced with interesting challenges when analyzing the recent varieties in the United States resulting from waves of immigration and changing cultural values. These result in both rapid and interesting changes as well as selective maintenance of prior cultural practices.

Publishers of periodicals, books, and videos employing artists, food stylists, and photographers to portray food preparation and presentation have increased in the last 15 years. Along with broadcast television, these publications allow us to see the lifestyles and practices of the rich and famous, of various ethnic groups, or of cutting-edge artists working in food art. In some of these publications high art and popular art join. Indeed, Andy Warhol participated as a table setting designer in the *New Tiffany Table Settings*, about table art in the households of prominent and famous people.

Coexisting with rapid change are the continuing practices of those populations within the United States who value certain aspects of their heritage and who maintain and express them in displays and activities involving food. Some of these are consciously designed to inform and educate others. Others are unexamined practices simply reenacted traditionally. The latter is the way in which food practices were most commonly learned and perpetuated prior to dynamic changes in travel, immigration, education, and mass media.

Traditional forms may be consciously re-created in the narrow sense of an immediate family's experience yet remain unconscious in the larger socio-historical sense. An example is one family's holiday cookies: The carved wooden cookie mold that belonged to a great-grandmother is removed from the shelf every Christmas and the recipe card that was recopied by grandmother and mother is consulted. The cookies are baked and presented to children in those special ways that reflect a remembered childhood. Certain preparation tools and serving plates are used and legends of St. Nicholas are recounted. A particular kind of cultural maintenance, an unselfconscious form of ancestral worship, is performed. The symbols carved into the cookie mold and their historical European origins and folk culture or religious meanings may not be consciously examined but their impact remains felt from generation to generation.

A cultural historian might point out that an examination of these molds across the centuries in certain areas of Europe would reflect larger artistic style and customs. Similarities of images extend from the pre-Christian era to the present. Contemporary artists making ceramic cookie molds and stamps for commercial sale continue to utilize this imagery. Similarly, the history of the importation of the ingredients across Europe or the origins of the practices involved in the presentation of the cookies may remain unexamined. However, they subtly influence the participants as they behave in taken-for-granted ways, making and eating the symbols of their heritage. These taken-for-granted activities of the dominant culture have often been portrayed on broadcast television and have permeated other immigrant populations.

The traditional practices of baking uniquely shaped and decorated breads, cakes, and cookies are related to a deep mythological, artistic, religious, and social history. These practices remain alive both unconsciously and as foci of deliberate perpetuation. The tie of these cooking activities to weddings, births, and deaths within the life cycle and to the cycle of holidays within the year assist in their continued survival. Piero Camporesi, in *The Magic Harvest: Food, Folklore and Society,* provides many examples of contemporary baked goods that reflect ancient rites and symbols of fertility and life. Recent variations on these themes include the light wedding cake encrusted in spun sugar sculptures (a 19th-century addition) and the very recent erotic bakeries that have sprung up in large cities in the United States. These bakeries create explicitly sculptured and decorated cakes and chocolate configurations that in many ways evoke the same themes that are more subtly communicated in the ancient forms described by Camporesi.

Traditional baking practices of Euro-American culture are paralleled by the practices of carving and arranging vegetables and fruits in Asian cultures. The beautifully prepared and presented foods of China, Japan, Thailand, and other Asian countries are influencing the dominant culture. The dominant culture utilizes common garnishes, such as the scallions, radishes, and tomatoes made into flowers, as well as adaptive traditional forms such as carved Halloween pumpkins. These have been joined by Asian sculptures such as melons carved with ancient symbols of good fortune, vegetables sculpted and rejoined into intricate butterflies, or elaborate artificial flower arrangements carved from various, often exotic, vegetables. Food art forms based on ceremonies and rituals of the past have been adopted in contemporary daily life. For example, the popularity of Japanese sushi within the mainstream culture has as much to do with its beauty of form and presentation as with its nutritional value. However, few who enjoy it realize that it was originally served as part of a ceremony involving food offerings for ancestors.

Cultural groups who have struggled to maintain their traditions may more consciously and deliberately present them. For example, Native American Hopis, having struggled to maintain unique agricultural and religious practices involving the planting, harvesting, and seed selection of corn, now enjoy the homage paid to them by those who appreciate the uniqueness of the beautifully colored corn that they produce. The legends and stories connected with the corn goddess, the seeds, the decorative corn grown from them, the prepared corn-based dishes and the art works created using the corn, and the ceremonies surrounding corn are now enjoyed by other segments of the population as well the originating group.

Fall state fairs are often the sites for a secular version of the celebration of the harvest bounty in contemporary culture. The presentation and judging of preserved fruits and vegetables at state fairs has been practiced within many areas of the United States. These carefully created food jars are judged not only on taste but on beauty. A 1990 text that celebrates the historical contribution of early homemaker food artists and places food preserving activities of contemporary food artists in the context of its increasing revival is *Perfect Preserves: Provisions from the Kitchen Garden.*

Many contemporary chefs have built the reputations of their small exclusive restaurants on the beauty, freshness, and purity (organically grown quality) of the ingredients of their cuisine. Their menus are illustrated with symbols of ecological harmony and their interviews speak to the need for human well-being to spring from ingesting produce that has been consciously and carefully grown, lovingly prepared, and beautifully presented.

Interest in edible flowers, herbs, and unusual vegetables such as the small purple potatoes of Peru as both beautiful and useful illustrate these changing attitudes. More people are taking part in small-scale home growing of exotic and beautiful salad greens and other forms of unusual produce. An aesthetic of harmony between the earth and human seeks expression in the preservation of biological diversity and beauty. This aesthetic perspective is expressed in texts and interviews that accompany the visual presentation of these food products.

Presentation of these designer vegetables upon appropriately hand-crafted or unique vessels also expresses a rebellion against the uniformity and mass production of food that has increasingly characterized daily life. The modern perspective on food began in the late 1890s but did not become widely accepted until after World War II. This perspective valued efficiency, mass-produced uniform quality, and quantity of food products.

By the late 1970s, the illustrations and instructions in popular magazines and books reflected a growing interest in the aesthetic and cultural aspects of food. The 1980s accelerated the growing interest in regional fresh ingredients, careful handiwork in preparation, and a renewed appreciation of time-consuming activities related to the aesthetic and cultural aspects of food. These included gardening, home food preparation and preservation, and the practices of the new "postmodern" chefs. These chefs integrate ingredients and presentation practices of many cultures in one dish. They adopt forms from visual arts as plate decorations and food decorations. For example, paper cutouts of Native American pottery designs are used as a template for sifting chocolate powder over desserts. Plates are painted with sauces before salads, main dishes, or desserts are carefully assembled upon them. Vegetables are arranged in both formal and symbolic arrangements to create a narrative history of the dish.

These practices are also portrayed in popular periodicals and cookbooks which are enjoying a rapidly increasing readership. Even readers who find the speed of life makes it increasingly difficult to engage in these practices appear to enjoy reading about them, hence participating vicariously. Some participate in the product and practices by eating at small restaurants. In addition, many have begun to enroll in cooking and gardening courses (replacing both the traditional way of learning and the modern surface-visual representation of the end product with disregard for process). Contemporary food art is richly varied and holds promise of continued exciting aesthetic and cultural development.

Bibliography

Camporesi, Piero. *The Magic Harvest: Food, Folklore and Society.* Cambridge: Polity, 1993.

Cary, Nora. *Perfect Preserves: Provisions from the Kitchen Garden.* New York: Stewart, Tabouri & Chang, 1990.

Loring, John, and Henry B. Platt. *New Tiffany Table Settings.* Garden City: Doubleday, 1981.

Beverly J. Jones

Ford, Harrison (1942-), first rose to prominence in 1977, portraying space pirate Han Solo in George Lucas's now-classic film *Star Wars* (see entry). However, despite being labeled an "overnight star" following his role in that film, Ford had been appearing in small roles in films and television for more than a decade.

Born and raised in the suburbs of Chicago by a Russian-Jewish housewife and an Irish-Catholic advertising executive, Ford appears to have had an unexciting childhood. He attended Ripon College in Wisconsin, majoring in philosophy and English, but flunked out shortly before graduation in 1964. After gaining some experience in summer stock, Ford headed out to Los Angeles, in the hope of finding work in films. Not long after his arrival, he signed with Columbia

Pictures, and made his film debut in 1966, with a bit part as a bellboy in *Dead Heat on a Merry-Go-Round.*

Unquestionably, Ford's breakthrough role was as Han Solo. It was an enormous success, but more importantly, it was his first role of any real dimension. Though some have criticized the lead characters of the film (and its sequels) as being secondary to the special effects and shallow, this is not wholly accurate. As Solo, Ford brought a degree of charisma to his role, raising it above the stereotype of a self-serving loner with the Hollywood "heart-of-gold." He continued to expand the character in the sequels, *The Empire Strikes Back* (1980) and *Return of the Jedi* (1983), obviously getting increasingly comfortable in the role, and bringing a higher degree of maturity to Solo. The role of Solo provided Ford with an unique opportunity to show off his skills, creating the combination of adventurer and wise-cracker that he would later more fully develop when portraying Indiana Jones.

Between *Star Wars* and its first sequel, Ford was the busiest of the film's three leads. However, Ford's films during this period were, for the most part, forgettable and offered little hope this newcomer would be able to transfer his success in a blockbuster to more lucrative roles.

In 1981, Ford was finally able to create for himself an acting identity that expanded beyond Han Solo. That was the year of Steven Spielberg's *Raiders of the Lost Ark*, which, like *Star Wars*, was a box-office record-breaker. In his role as Indiana Jones, Ford was able to display his considerable talents. Much of the film's success is credited to the imagination of co-writer Lucas and director Spielberg, but Ford also must be given his credit. Ford continued his role as Jones in two sequels, *Indiana Jones and the Temple of Doom* (1984) and *Indiana Jones and the Last Crusade* (1989), as a result becoming possibly even more identified with his Jones character than with Han Solo.

Ford followed his debut as Indiana Jones with one of the most unique roles of his career, playing bounty hunter Rick Deckard in Ridley Scott's *Blade Runner* (1982). In the decade since its release the film has developed a solid cult following, both on the basis of Scott's imaginative and bleak view of the future, and for Ford's commanding presence in the film.

Despite his success as Han Solo and Indiana Jones, Ford had not yet had the chance to shine in a complex, dramatic part. The opportunity finally came in 1985 with Peter Weir's *Witness*. Ford silenced his critics, and earned an Oscar nomination, with his portrayal of John Book, a Philadelphia detective who uncovers a drug ring in his department, and is forced to take refuge with the family of an Amish boy who witnessed a murder committed by a police detective.

Ford returned to the adventure film with Roman Polanski's *Frantic* (1988), but later that same year appeared in Mike Nichols's *Working Girl*, his first comedy since *The Frisco Kid,* nine years earlier. In the same way that *Star Wars* and the Indiana Jones films were reminiscent of Saturday matinees, *Working Girl* stirred up memories of the romantic comedies of the 1940s and 1950s. Ford clearly showed that he was just as capable of handling comedy, as he was at handling adventure and drama.

In *Presumed Innocent* (1990), Alan J. Pakula's adaptation of the Scott Turow novel, Ford played an adulterous lawyer accused of brutally murdering a fellow lawyer with whom he was having an affair. For Ford it was yet another strong performance that challenged his mainstream, heroic image.

Ford made yet another dramatic change in his image in *Regarding Henry* (1991). He played an unscrupulous lawyer, Henry Turner, who is brain-damaged after being shot in a hold-up, and begins a new life with the family from whom he had become alienated. The film has been justly criticized for trivializing the process of recovery that such a trauma would require, but Ford's performance is largely able to rise above the criticism.

As CIA analyst Jack Ryan in *Patriot Games* (1992), Ford returned to the familiar genre of action. Action is also the focus of *The Fugitive* (1993), based, like the earlier television series, on the story of Dr. Sam Sheppard.

Ford kept up the pace and variety of his career through the 1990s in such films as *Clear and Present Danger* (1994), *Sabrina* (1995), *Air Force One* (1997), *Six Days, Seven Nights* (1998), and *Random Hearts* (1999).

Bibliography

Bandler, Michael. "Acting the Hero." *American Way* 1 Feb. 1987: 36-45.

Kaplan, James. "Harrison Ford's Natural Drive." *Vanity Fair* 53.8 (Aug. 1990): 96-100, 147-50.

Robert Mastrangelo

Ford, **John** (1895-1973), who always abruptly introduced himself with, "My name's John Ford. I make Westerns," was born Sean Aloysius O'Feeney in Cape Elizabeth, ME. He did make some fine Westerns, but he also made a lot more—some of the most popular films of his generation. With the help of his older brother Francis, who had changed his name to Ford, John entered the motion picture industry at an early age. In 1896, the family moved to Portland, ME, and after graduating from Portland High School in 1913, John went to Hollywood to work with Francis, who was under contract at Universal Studios as a director-writer-actor. Beginning with a serial film called *Lucille Love—The Girl of Mystery* (1914), directed by his brother, "Jack" Ford (his new screen name) played bits in various segments, did stunts (often doubling for his brother), and served as a handyman/assistant. He even played a klansman in D. W. Griffith's *The Birth of a Nation.*

Ford got his first chance to direct in 1917 with *The Tornado*, which he remembers as "just a bunch of stunts." In the same year, however, he directed Harry Carey in *The Soul Herder*, the first of 26 films he would make with Carey and the one he considered his first as a director. A surprising success, this film developed the good-badman persona that would become Carey's popular trademark; it also marked the first appearance of Hoot Gibson in a Ford film. Ford's first feature film, *Straight Shooting,* also appearing in 1917 and starring Carey and Gibson, received critical acclaim for its combination of "raw action, infectious characters, compelling situations, and artful...photography" (Gallagher).

At a St. Patrick's Day dance in 1920, Ford met Mary McBride Smith, and they were married on July 3. Patrick was born in April 1921, and Barbara in December 1922. After making 39 pictures (28 of them features) for Universal, Ford signed with Fox in 1921, and on a trip to Europe, he visited the "Old Sod," his dear Ireland, and returned to the U.S. with a stronger sense of identity (changing his name back to John) and a commitment to Ireland that remained for the rest of his life. In 1924, he made one of the decade's top-grossing films; *The Iron Horse* made him internationally famous and put a Fox film for the first time on Broadway. But two years later, trying to repeat its success, Ford made a box-office flop with *Three Bad Men*, and he would not make another Western for 13 years. But by the late 1920s, concluding his apprenticeship as a film director, he had had some solid commercial successes for Fox.

The Informer (1935) was a high point in Ford's early career; it won four Oscars and was nominated for two others, in addition to winning a host of other awards from around the world. But Ford's position as Hollywood's top director was not secure until 1939-41, when he directed seven films that won 10 Oscars and 34 nominations.

The cast of *Stagecoach* (the first of three films in 1939) included John Wayne, Thomas Mitchell, Andy Devine, Claire Trevor, and John Carradine. Based on the short story "Stage to Lordsburg" by Ernest Haycox and scripted by Dudley Nichols, the film won two Oscars and has become a genre classic.

According to Andrew Sarris, *The Grapes of Wrath* (1940) transformed Ford "from a storyteller of the screen to America's cinematic poet laureate." It won two Oscars (best director and supporting actress) and five nominations; it was also selected by the New York Film Critics as best picture and Ford as best director for it and his next film, *The Long Voyage Home* (also 1940). Following closely upon Steinbeck's critically acclaimed novel (1939), *Grapes* mixes literary and documentary techniques with a strong dose of social consciousness.

The last of the seven films in this remarkably productive three-year period would be called, in today's parlance, a blockbuster. The star-studded *How Green Was My Valley* (1941) was designed to gain popularity (the second highest-grossing film during its year of release) and was intended to win awards (six Oscars, including direction, and five other nominations; in addition, Ford was chosen best director by the New York Film Critics).

The Fugitive (1946) was based on Graham Greene's novel *The Power and the Glory*. As Ford admitted, his company lost money on this film, and his next five Westerns were an attempt to put the company back in the black. Although they were meant to have box-office appeal, these films also reveal a marked change in Ford's directing style. With the cinematography focusing on the land (the dynamism of Monument Valley) and the sound track rendering celebrated folk tunes (like "She Wore a Yellow Ribbon"), these films usher in what Gallagher calls Ford's "Age of Myth."

The first, *Fort Apache* (1948), also the first of Ford's cavalry trilogy, loosely resembles Custer's "last stand." Based on the short story "Massacre," by James Warner Bellah, the film features the arrogant, vain, glory-seeking Col. Thursday (Henry Fonda) and his able captain, Kirby York (John Wayne). Thursday, against the advice of York and others, leads his men in a suicidal charge against Cochise.

Ford claims he tried to capture the color and movement of Remington's paintings in *She Wore a Yellow Ribbon* (1949), the second of the cavalry films, and the Technicolor did win an Oscar for photography. In this film and in *Rio Grande* (1950), the last of the trilogy, Ford continues his celebration of the cavalry ritual, highlighting the loneliness, self-sacrifice, and devotion to duty of the common soldiers.

The cavalry films and *Three Godfathers* (1948) were popular films, giving Ford money and status and allowing him to make some personal favorites; one of these was *Wagonmaster* (1950), a film some critics consider a masterpiece, but which received little attention at the time.

After three war films in the early 1950s, Ford made another personal favorite that turned out to be very successful—his top-grossing movie to that point. *The Quiet Man* (1952) won two Oscars, best director and best photography, was nominated for six others, and received a number of other awards as well. Shot on location in Ireland, filled with stars, and emphasizing the theme of family relationships, the film captured the hearts of most of America's movie audience; it may be Ford's most popular movie.

Mogambo (1953), starring Clark Gable, Ava Gardner, and a 24-year-old Grace Kelly (who was made a star by the film), outdid *The Quiet Man*'s popularity, at least in the early stages; it was the highest grossing of all Ford's films in the first year. Controversial at the time, *The Searchers* has grown notably in popularity and in critical esteem since its 1956 appearance. John Wayne gives a searing performance as the angry, alienated protagonist in this unforgettable film and has helped it become a standard offering not only in college courses on Westerns but in courses on American film throughout the country.

Ford's final period of significant filmmaking included *The Man Who Shot Liberty Valance* (1962), *Donovan's Reef* (1963), *Cheyenne Autumn* (1964), and *Seven Women* (1965). The films of this period tend to be more reflective, to look backward, even to challenge some of the myths his earlier films had celebrated or to dramatize issues previously overlooked.

Bibliography

Bogdanovich, Peter. *John Ford*. Berkeley: U of California P, 1978.
Gallagher, Tag. *John Ford: The Man and His Films*. Berkeley: U of California P, 1986.
Sarris, Andrew. *The John Ford Movie Mystery*. Bloomington: Indiana UP, 1975.

Leonard Engel

Ford, "Tennessee" Ernie (1919-1991), born in Fordtown and raised in Bristol, TN, was an icon of the 1950s and 1960s variety show circuit as well as a respected and successful country music artist and performer. During his career as a celebrity, which stretched from the 1940s to the 1980s, Ford earned his outstanding reputation as a singer and TV star by rendering pop tunes such as "Anticipation Blues," and "Mule Train" with his own jazzy style of country blues and cowboy songs, and by appearing in his own network radio show, hosting *The Ernie Ford Show* (a TV variety show), and holding regular spots on many other top-ranked TV shows.

Ford's upbringing, while not especially rural, did start him on the path to a musical career. He sang in the high school choir, played in the high school band, and at 18, worked his first job as a radio announcer at a local station. He then pursued classical music training at the Cincinnati Conservatory of Music after a tour in World War II and ended up on the West Coast working as a vocalist for cowboy style bands. It was during this time that he adopted the name "Tennessee Ernie." He met and married Betty Jean Heminger, with whom he had two sons, Jeffrey (Buck) and Brian, and decided to settle in California. At this time he struck up what became a lifelong friendship with Cliffie Stone (a prominent promoter/band leader/musician), an executive at the newly formed Capitol Records, who was to become Ford's mentor and manager for the remainder of his career.

Ford's professional music career began in 1948 with a Capitol recording contract. His own composition, "Shotgun Boogie," which remained on the Top 10 list for many weeks, led to so much acclaim that he was awarded his own radio show. His 1955 remake of Merle Travis's "Sixteen Tons," however, crystallized his career. The pencil-mustached pop and country singer had arrived. Ford's NBC TV variety show, which ran until 1961, followed on the heels of his release of "Sixteen Tons," and made him quite popular in American households. *The Ernie Ford Show* made Ford's expression "Bless your little pea-pickin' hearts" a national catchphrase.

After the six-year run of his variety show, Ford relocated to North California to spend more time with his wife and sons. In April of 1962, he returned to television, starring in a new weekday show for ABC, and eventually appeared as a guest on the *I Love Lucy* show. He then turned to more mellow musical pursuits and recorded country's first million-selling album, *Hymns* (1963), the first in a string of religious recordings. The addition of patriotic renderings to his religious songs propelled Ford's fame through the 1960s. His smooth voice and conservative manner, along with his renderings of mostly time-worn releases, secured his fame on into the early 1970s. He continued to turn out recordings until the mid-1970s with his release of his *25th Anniversary* album.

During his extended career, Ford recorded more than 100 albums of country, gospel, and other forms of music. His honors include the Medal of Freedom, America's Civilian Honor (1984), and induction into the Country Music Hall of Fame (1990). He died of advanced liver disease at the age of 72, ending a long and illustrious career, having achieved a lasting impact on the world of country music.

Bibliography

Carlin, Richard. "Tennessee Ernie Ford." *The Big Book of Country Music: A Biographical Encyclopedia*. New York: Penguin, 1995.

McCloud, Barry. "Tennessee Ernie Ford." *Definitive Country: The Ultimate Encyclopedia of Country Music and Its Performers*. New York: Perigee, 1995.

Shestack, Melvin. "Tennessee Ernie Ford." *The Country Music Encyclopedia*. Toronto: KBO, 1974.

Stambler, Irwin, and Grelum Landon. "Tennessee Ernie Ford." *The Encyclopedia of Folk, Country and Western Music*. 2d ed. New York: St. Martin's, 1983.

Carole L. Carroll

48 Hours. On September 2, 1986, CBS News presented a major two-hour prime-time special called *48 Hours on Crack Street*. The magazine-formatted documentary focused in on the central theme of the American drug crisis, and revealed a drug scene that was more extensive than most Americans ever realized. Unlike other news programs of its type, this special covered a story over a two-day period (hence the name). Eventually, after the success of *48 Hours on Crack Street*, it became the weekly series *48 Hours*. This news series managed to obtain a 20-share of the television viewing audience and covered such stories as "Moscow Vice," "Trauma," and "Spring Break." *48 Hours II* began airing in the fall of 1999.

Bibliography

Corry, John. "CBS on Crack." *The New York Times* 4 Sept. 1986.

Nichols, Bill. *Representing Reality*. Bloomington: Indiana UP, 1991.

Rosenthal, Alan, ed. *New Challenges for Documentary*. Los Angeles: U of California P, 1988.

Michael Espinosa

42nd Street (1933), directed by Lloyd Bacon and choreographed by Busby Berkeley (see entry), stands as the prototype of the backstage, chorus-girl-becomes-star film musical. The film endures as an important document of the early 1930s Warner Bros. studio style, exemplifying even in this customarily most escapist of genres the studio's characteristic, nitty-gritty "realism" and solid narrative efficiency.

42nd Street faithfully mirrors its contemporary world, drawing on the Great Depression not only for setting but also for narrative substance. The opening scene underlines the struggle for survival in New York's theater world that dogs each major character right up until the film's close. Julian Marsh (Warner Baxter), an established Broadway director, faces financial ruin from recent stock market losses and needs desperately another successful show. The near-starving, less prestigious hopefuls auditioning for the chorus face comparable compromises in order to have work on the stage, such as fresh-from-the-sticks Peggy Sawyer (Ruby Keeler), who faints during long rehearsals, apparently from not having had much to eat of late. The immediate alternative remains the explicit prostitution faced by actresses at the top as well as in the chorus, either to attain work on stage or to compensate for the lack of it. Wholly appropriate to the plot, this was Ruby Keeler's first film, launching her, like the character she played, into stardom. The sparse back stage and contemporary Manhattan settings provide much of *42nd Street*'s hard-edged visual texture. In addition to the authenticity of atmosphere and the strength of individual performances, critics at the time of the film's release praised Berkeley's elaborate and original staging of the major musical numbers, which skillfully integrated music and story.

Bibliography

Hoberman, J. *42nd Street*. London: BFI, 1993.

Roddick, Nick. *A New Deal in Entertainment: Warner Brothers in the Late 1930s*. London: BFI, 1983.

Rubin, Martin. *Busby Berkeley and the Tradition of Spectacle*. New York: Columbia UP, 1993.

Sennett, Robert S. *Setting the Scene: The Great Hollywood Art Directors*. New York: Abrams, 1994.

Steve Lipkin

Foster, Jodie (1962-), born Alicia Christian Foster in Los Angeles, has enjoyed a career remarkable on many counts, not the least of which is her transformation from an impressive child actor to a mature and self-possessed movie actress, one of the finest of her generation. Foster has not only overcome the difficult hurdle from childhood performer to adult actress, a transition that many of her predecessors and contemporaries have failed to achieve, but she has also managed to avoid the numerous pitfalls that accompany early success in the show business world. And she has accomplished these feats without being stereotyped into limited and limiting roles, with her intelligence, humanity, and humor intact.

Her precociousness and her unconventional upbringing in a cosmopolitan single-parent family define Foster's early film and television roles in the 1970s, as she appeared on such series as *Mayberry, R.F.D., The Courtship of Eddie's Father, Gunsmoke, The Partridge Family, Medical Center, Bonanza*, and the short-lived TV spinoff of the popular film *Paper Moon* (which starred her rival, Tatum O'Neal). Seemingly wise beyond her years, tomboyish, and street smart, the young Foster meshed her roles effectively with her personality. Director Martin Scorsese was the first filmmaker to use Foster's persona to full advantage and to take the girl into the difficult emotional terrain of true acting. Her small role in *Alice Doesn't Live Here Anymore* (1974), as a delinquent who tempts Alice's son into drinking Ripple wine, impressed not only the critics but Scorsese, who sought her out for the role of a 12-year-old prostitute in the highly acclaimed *Taxi Driver* (1976). Having to pass a psychological test in order to play the part, Foster would be changed forever, as an actress and as a person, by the role.

She appeared in several more films before she graduated from high school in 1981 and entered Yale University; that same year an obsessed fan of *Taxi Driver*, John Hinckley, Jr., attempted to assassinate President Reagan in order to attract Foster's attention.

After the trauma of the Hinckley episode and death threats by another crazed fan, Foster gradually moved back into the acting profession as she was finishing her college career (she received her B.A. in 1985). Her full return to acting came when she pursued the challenging role of Sarah Tobias in Jonathan Kaplan's 1988 film *The Accused*. Foster plays a tough but sexy lower-class young woman who is bru-

tally gang raped in a bar while the bar patrons cheer on the atrocities. When her yuppie lawyer (Kelly McGillis) cops a plea that allows the rapists to go free, Foster's character determines to regain her pride and achieve partial justice by prosecuting the onlookers who refused to stop the rape. For her efforts Foster was awarded the Oscar for best actress.

For *The Silence of the Lambs* (1991), the highly acclaimed adaptation of Thomas Harris's novel, Foster again had to actively pursue her role, as FBI trainee Clarice Starling, for director Jonathan Demme initially wanted Michelle Pfeiffer for the part. He soon realized the rightness of Foster for the darkness and fierceness of the role. In pursuit of a serial killer who murders and mutilates women, Starling must seek as an ally the diabolical psychologist Hannibal Lecter (Anthony Hopkins), who helps her to solve the crime by insinuating himself into her personal past. Not only did Foster win the Oscar for best actress, but the film was named best picture of 1991.

With these two Oscars for very powerful, emotionally wrenching roles, Foster established herself as an actress of the first rank, one capable of pleasing the critics and the audience with her honest and complex characterizations. This has allowed her new freedom to choose roles, from a cameo as a prostitute in Woody Allen's *Shadows and Fog* (1992), to a romantic role as a Civil War survivor who falls in love with the man who impersonates her dead husband in *Sommersby*, the 1992 remake of the French hit *The Return of Martin Guerre*, to a saloon hall girl in the movie version of the classic television Western *Maverick* (1994).

For the title role in *Nell* (1994), a strange backwoods woman who speaks her own language, Foster won a Screen Actors Guild Award for best actress. In *The Contact* (1996), she played a radio astronomer seeking an extraterrestrial encounter. She became a mother in 1998, and then starred in *Anna and the King* (1999), a nonmusical remake of the story told in *The King and I*.

The greatest gift of Foster's success, however, is her transition to director. It is easy to see why the script for *Little Man Tate* (1991) appealed to her and why the finished film has such sensitivity and appeal. The story centers on the life of a gifted child, played by Adam Hann-Byrd, who is torn between his loyalty to his hard-working single mom (Foster) and his fascination with his new intellectual mentor (Dianne Wiest). Much of Foster's own relationship with her mother as well as her youthful feelings of being different are invested in the film.

Bibliography

Cook, Pam, and Philip Dodd, eds. *Women and Film: A Sight and Sound Reader*. Philadelphia: Temple UP, 1993.

Corliss, Richard. "A Screen Gem Turns Director." *Time* 14 Oct. 1991: 68-72.

"Foster, Jodie." *Current Biography Yearbook 1992*: 200-04.

Hirshey, Gerri, "Jodie Foster." *Rolling Stone* 21 March 1991: 34-41, 88-89.

Horton, Robert. "Life Upside Down." *American Film* Jan.-Feb. 1991: 38-39.

Kennedy, Philippa. *Jodie Foster: A Life on Screen*. New York: Carol, 1996.

Miller, Linda R. "Victor of Circumstances." *American Film* Oct. 1988: 26-31.

Carol M. Ward

Foster, Stephen Collins (1826-1864), America's first professional songwriter and still among its best-known throughout the world, was the first musician whose work reached all segments and levels of American society. The youngest son in a middle-class Scots-Irish family in and around Pittsburgh, PA, he was influenced by the stories and songs of the ethnic groups swelling into that growing industrial center, and the music, books, and magazines his parents and older sisters brought into the home.

Foster wrote songs that were recognized as being distinctly American, yet were understandable to members of any nationality, race, or ethnic group. He studied the distinct and different styles that circulated primarily within their own immigrant groups, including the British parlor ballad, Scottish folk ballad, Irish melodies of Thomas Moore, German Lied, Italian aria, and—perhaps—the African-American spiritual, and incorporated their elements into his own melodic style, harmony, song form, and textual themes. That he succeeded in overcoming ethnic barriers is indicated by his publishers' boasts of the number of presses they had to keep operating to supply the demand for his songs; by the performance of his music on plantations, in northern parlors, by street musicians, and by concert recitalists; and by the adaptation of his words and melodies as folk songs. His earliest hit, "Susanna" ("Oh! Susanna"), became the theme song of the California Gold Rush in 1849, and can still be heard in many films, television shows, and cartoons representing the Old West. Foster's songs even overcame the barriers of the continent itself, and within weeks of their publication in New York were heard on the streets of England, Europe, and Asia, wherever trade routes carried sailors and passengers to and from the United States.

Contrary to myth, Foster was well educated. Also contrary to widespread assumption, Foster was no apologist or eulogizer for the Old South. He chose Southern themes for many of his songs because they were the stock-in-trade of the blackface minstrel shows, the most widely popular entertainment of the day, and hence the most effective medium through which to introduce new songs to a mass audience. (No mechanical media had yet been invented; Foster relied on royalties from the sale of sheet music for his income.) Stephen Foster was arguably the first white American songwriter to portray black characters with the same depth and range of human emotions and needs as the characters of his own race.

From his first tune performed in 1841 to the end of his career, Stephen Foster wrote or arranged 284 compositions, including 152 solo songs and four vocal duets with piano accompaniment, two unaccompanied vocal quartets, 28 hymns, six dances or character pieces for piano alone, one piece for piano four-hands, and two works for other instruments; he arranged 16 of his songs for guitar accompaniment, and his book *The Social Orchestra* (1854) contains 73 original works and arrangements of his own or other composers' works for chamber ensemble. He wrote his own words for most of his songs.

More than two dozen of Stephen Foster's songs have retained emotional significance and symbolic meaning. "The Old Folks at Home" ("Swanee River," 1851) adopted as Florida's state song, is the theme of a state park at White Springs; "My Old Kentucky Home" (1853) is the name of a state park at Bardstown, KY, and is that state's official song. Those, along with "Massa's in the Cold Ground" (1852) and "Old Black Joe" (1860), are among Foster's enduring tragic minstrel songs; "Susanna" (1847) and "Camptown Races" (1850) are his best-remembered comic minstrel tunes; and "Old Dog Tray" (1853), "Jeanie with the Light Brown Hair" (1854), "Hard Times Come Again No More" (1854), "Gentle Annie" (1856), and "Beautiful Dreamer" (1862) are among the sentimental ballads whose familiarity have not diminished.

Bibliography
Austin, William. *"Susanna," "Jeanie," and "The Old Folks at Home": The Songs of Stephen Foster from His Time to Ours*. 2d ed. Urbana: U of Illinois P, 1987.

Hamm, Charles. *Yesterdays: Popular Song in America*. New York: Norton, 1979.

Howard, John Tasker. *Stephen Foster: America's Troubadour*. 2d ed. New York: Crowell, 1953.

Root, Deane L. "The 'Mythtory' of Stephen C. Foster; or, Why His True Story Remains Untold." *The American Music Research Center Journal* 1 (1991): 20-36.

Saunders, Steven, and Deane L. Root, eds. *The Music of Stephen C. Foster: A Critical Edition*. Washington, DC: Smithsonian Institution, 1990.

Deane L. Root

Four Seasons, The, were a vocal group from New Jersey that recorded the largest number of records to hit the charts of any U.S. popular group and sold over 85 million records. The group's music was characterized by tight harmonies and the piercing falsetto of lead singer Frankie Valli (Frank Castelluccio, 1937-).

Valli's career started with a series of Newark-based recording groups in the early 1950s. After failing with recordings under the name Frank Valley and the Travelers, Valli joined a group called the Variety Trio, featuring Hank Majewski and Nick and Tommy DeVito. The group changed its name, first to the Variatones, and later to the Four Lovers. The Four Lovers appeared on television's *The Ed Sullivan Show* and scored a minor hit with "You're the Apple of My Eye" in 1956, but then broke apart as Valli tried unsuccessfully to start a solo career. In 1959 Valli reassembled the group as Frank Valli and the Romans, with Bob Gaudio replacing Nick DeVito.

In 1960, Hank Majewski left and was replaced by Nick Massi (Macioci). Record producer Bob Crewe used the group for backup vocals on various recordings. In February 1962, Gone Records released the quartet's recording of "Bermuda" under the name the Four Seasons. The group's new name has been attributed to the fact that Gone Records' office was across the street from New York City's famous Four Seasons restaurant or to the fact that the band used to play at a bowling alley bar named the Four Seasons Cocktail Lounge.

"Sherry," written by Bob Gaudio, was recorded by the Four Seasons in August 1962. It sold 180,000 copies for Vee Jay records the day after the Four Seasons performed it on the *Ed Sullivan Show*. In just four weeks, "Sherry" reached No. 1 and eventually sold 2 million copies. The group followed with another No. 1 hit, "Big Girls Don't Cry," penned by Gaudio and Crewe. In December 1962, the two hits were released on an album, *Sherry and 11 Others*, and a Christmas album was released simultaneously.

The Four Seasons' third million-seller single was "Walk Like a Man." It topped the charts for three weeks in March 1963, meaning the group had a No. 1 hit for 13 of 27 weeks. Other hits in 1963 included a remake of Fats Domino's "Ain't That a Shame" and "Candy Girl."

In the summer of 1964, the Four Seasons returned to the top of the charts with "Rag Doll," followed by three more successful singles that year, "Save It for Me," "Big Man in Town," and "Bye Bye Baby (Baby Goodbye)."

After Nick Massi left the group and was replaced briefly by Charlie Callelo and then Joe Long, the next hit was a Motown-styled dance song, "Let's Hang On." At the same time as the Wonder Who, they recorded a falsetto version of Bob Dylan's "Don't Think Twice, It's Alright," and Valli recorded his first solo single, "You're Gonna Hurt Yourself." Three more hits followed in 1966: the Motown-sounding "Workin' My Way Back to You," the classical-influenced "Opus 17 (Don't You Worry 'Bout Me)," and a revival of Cole Porter's "I've Got You under My Skin."

In 1967 and 1968, the Four Seasons scored with some minor hits, "Tell It to the Rain," "Beggin'," and "C'mon Marianne." The group showed its diversity again, recording a former Motown hit, "Will You Still Love Me Tomorrow" and the psychedelic-influenced "Watch the Flowers Grow." But the biggest hit of the period was Valli's solo effort, "Can't Take My Eyes Off of You."

In 1969, the group tried to cash in on the popularity of "concept albums" with *The Genuine Imitation Life Gazette*. The album and resulting singles were a failure and the group began a rapid downhill slide. The group was renamed Frankie Valli and the Four Seasons in May 1970. Original group member Tommy DeVito left, and Frankie Valli and the Four Seasons recorded one unsuccessful album for Mowest Records.

But Valli rebounded with a solo hit on Private Stock Records in 1975, the chart-topping million-seller, "My Eyes Adore You." Valli followed with his first disco-sound release, "Swearin' to God," in May 1975. Valli's solo comeback encouraged him to re-form the Four Seasons, although none of the original group members were included. The new Frankie Valli and the Four Seasons signed with Warner-Curb Records, and their first single, "Who Loves You," peaked at No. 3.

In March 1976, "December '63 (Oh, What a Night)" captured both the disco and nostalgia audiences and topped the charts for three weeks. The song was the Four Seasons' first No. 1 hit in 12 years. After some minor chart successes, mainly in Great Britain, Valli broke with the Four Seasons to pursue a solo career as a club act. The title song from the

1950s nostalgia film *Grease* earned him a platinum disk and topped the charts in August 1978.

The Four Seasons were reunited in 1984 to record a single with the Beach Boys, "East Meets West," and in 1985 for an album, *Streetfighter*.

Bibliography

Romanowski, Patricia, and Holly George-Warren. *The New Rolling Stone Encyclopedia of Rock & Roll*. New York: Fireside, 1995.
Stambler, Irwin. *The Encyclopedia of Pop, Rock, and Soul*. New York: St. Martin's, 1989.

Ken Nagelberg

Fox Television Network, The. In 1985 billionaire Australian-born press lord Rupert Murdoch began to fashion a U.S.-based corporate mass-media colossus. At the heart of his empire building was the establishment of a fourth over-the-air television network—Fox. By the mid-1990s Murdoch had established Fox as a contending TV network and had remade his media empire from one centered in newspapers and magazines to an electronic-oriented corporation positioned at the very heart of the information and entertainment superhighway.

Murdoch's first step was to buy half of Twentieth Century-Fox, the movie and television production studio, from Denver oilman Marvin Davis in 1985. Murdoch's next step was to acquire a core of television stations in the largest U.S. cities. For more than $1 billion, News, Inc., Murdoch's parent corporation, purchased the six Metromedia independent television stations, then not affiliated with any network. The six (one per market) were located in New York City (the largest television market in the United States), Los Angeles (the second largest), Chicago (third largest), Dallas, Washington, DC (eighth), Dallas (ninth), and Houston (tenth). Nearly one in five homes with television sets in the United States could tune in to one of these stations, providing the largest reach for any set of stations outside of those owned by ABC, CBS, and NBC. (Later Fox would buy shares in more TV stations.)

By the late 1980s, having acquired the remaining other half of Twentieth Century-Fox studio, Rupert Murdoch stood ready to launch his new TV network. The Fox Network simply represented the logical linkage of all Murdoch investments by uniting his well-positioned television stations with more than 100 other independent stations. The Fox Network reached but seven-eighths of rivals and in the beginning had only middling luck making hit series. The first attempts, in particular *9 to 5*, failed badly, as did a game show/beauty contest entry, *Dream Girl U.S.A*, and the much-heralded late-night entry *The Joan Rivers Show*. But from a base of only Sunday night programming, the Fox Network added more nights and developed hits like *Married...with Children*, *America's Most Wanted*, *Beverly Hills 90210*, and *Melrose Place* (see entries). In 1993, the Fox Network began, on a limited basis, telecasting seven nights a week.

But the key breakthrough show was the animated *Simpsons*, which premiered in January 1990 (see entry). Soon *The Simpsons* had become not only the new Fox television network's first top-rated series, but also the initial popular culture fad of the 1990s. By June of 1990, Bart and his dysfunctional family were on the covers of *Newsweek* and *Rolling Stone*, and a new era in network television, Fox-style, had commenced. It took more years of struggle, but by 1992 Fox's television network was making money.

This new network did not represent Murdoch's sole thrust into television. Fox's production of television programs (including *L.A. Law*) for the other three television networks was thriving, and its television "evergreens" such as *M*A*S*H* were making millions of dollars in TV syndication. Fox's *A Current Affair* was hated by critics, but drew such good ratings and cost so little that it drew millions more into Fox's bottom line.

Murdoch kept adding to his television empire in the United States by spending $3 billion for Walter Annenberg's *TV Guide*. This move added the nation's second-largest circulating magazine to Murdoch's already formidable media empire. But the early 1990s did not prove all glowing for Murdoch. The Fox Network stagnated as Murdoch refinanced his News, Inc.'s billion-dollar debt. In 1991, Murdoch sold nine magazines (including *The Racing Forum, Soap Opera Digest,* and *Seventeen*) to raise capital and protect his television network.

By the mid-1990s the centerpiece of the Murdoch empire had clearly become Fox, Inc. In 1994, Murdoch and his Fox Network seemed to have turned the corner. Murdoch personally outbid CBS for the rights to National Football League games, a contract that CBS had had for nearly four decades. *The X Files*, introduced in 1993, had also become a hit (see entry). In a remarkably short period of time the Fox television network and its allied media investments have made Rupert Murdoch one of the most powerful and most important persons in the creation of mass popular culture. This achievement ranks with the creation of NBC, CBS, and ABC, all of which required far more time to reach the status Fox did in but a half dozen years.

Bibliography
Block, Alex Ben. *Outfoxed.* New York: St. Martin's, 1990.
Shawcross, William. *Murdoch.* New York: Simon & Schuster, 1992.

Douglas Gomery

Foxfire (1967-) was a teaching experiment that grew into an educational philosophy, a quarterly magazine of "cultural journalism," and a series of books on the history, personalities, and folkways of the southern Appalachians. The Foxfire project originated in 1966 when Eliot Wigginton began teaching at the Rabun Gap-Nacoochee School, a private, church-related institution in northeastern Georgia. Failing to hold student interest with traditional literature and language instruction, Wigginton experimented with involving students in directing their own learning. An early venture was the preparation of a periodical, which students named *Foxfire*, first published in 1967.

The most successful articles were based on student interviews of "old timers" native to the southern Appalachians,

which attracted national attention. In 1972, Doubleday published the first *Foxfire Book*, drawn from these materials. It was subtitled: "Hog dressing, log cabin building, mountain crafts and foods, planting by the signs, snake lore, hunting tales, faith healing, moonshining, and other affairs of plain living." Ten more Foxfire books have been published, *Foxfire 11* in 1999.

The magazine and books attracted support from foundations, which, together with the book royalties, formed an endowment, currently administered by the Foxfire Fund, in Rabun Gap, Georgia. After experiments in cultural preservation and community development, the fund focused on Wigginton's original idea, an approach to teaching that invites students to participate in educational decisions and engages them in learning activities that lead to tangible products. Dissemination of these ideas and techniques is the responsibility of Foxfire Teacher Outreach, one activity supported by the fund.

Bibliography
Knapp, Clifford E. "Reflecting on the Foxfire Approach." *Phi Delta Kappan* 74.10 (1993): 779-82.
Puckett, John L. *Foxfire Reconsidered: A Twenty-Year Experiment in Progressive Education.* Urbana: U of Illinois P, 1989.
Wigginton, Eliot. "Foxfire Grows Up." *Harvard Educational Review* 59.1 (1989): 24-29.

Paul T. Bryant

Frampton, Peter (1950-), recorded the most popular live album in history, *Frampton Comes Alive,* which has sold over 15 million copies worldwide. This double album, recorded at San Francisco's Winterland Ballroom and released in April 1976, topped the pop charts at #1 for five weeks. It features three singles, "Show Me the Way" (#6), "Baby I Love Your Way" (#12), and "Do You Feel Like We Do" (#10).

Frampton began his rock career in 1966, at the age of 16, in a U.K. outfit called the Herd. In 1969, he formed the blues/hard rock band Humble Pie, and released *As Safe As Yesterday* and *Town and Country*, but he left that band in 1971 to pursue a solo career. After Frampton left, the band went on to release the albums *Smokin'* and *Eat It*, which are now considered rock classics. Frampton contributed some guitar tracks to George Harrison's massive solo project, *All Things Must Pass,* and went on to record his *Winds of Change* with guests Ringo Starr and Billy Preston.

Frampton formed Frampton's Camel in 1973 and released an album of the same name, which failed to chart. His two subsequent releases, *Something's Happening* (#25) and *Frampton* (#32), finally put him in the Top 40, but it was not until he released *Frampton Comes Alive* in 1976 that he garnered a chart-topping album and superstar status. His 1977 release, *I'm in You,* peaked at #2, as did the single from the title track. In 1978, Frampton starred in and recorded for the soundtrack of the film *Sgt. Pepper's Lonely Hearts Club Band.*

Frampton continued to release albums during the 1980s and 1990s, but never again had the chart success his work had achieved from 1976 through 1978. In 1987, he joined

David Bowie's Glass Spider tour as a side guitarist. *Shine On: A Collection*, a 30-song two-CD retrospective, was released in 1992, and the reggae band Big Mountain scored a hit covering Frampton's "Baby I Love Your Way" (#6). Frampton also toured with guitar legend Robin Trower throughout 1994 for his "Frampton Comes Alive Again" tour. Then in 1995, in an attempt to follow the success of his first live album, he released *Frampton Comes Alive II*, but this album failed to make a dent on the charts.

Bibliography

Daly, Marsha. *Peter Frampton*. New York: Ace, 1979.

Rees, Dafydd, and Luke Crampton. *Encyclopedia of Rock Stars*. New York: D. K. Publishing, 1996.

Robert G. Weiner

Frankenstein (1818) is the original and ultimate in horror fiction, the basis of numerous films (see next entry). When asked to write the definitive ghost story, 19-year-old Mary Shelley generated the classic novel *Frankenstein or The Modern Prometheus*, which was published in 1818. The title is significant because Victor Frankenstein can be equated to the ancient Titan, Prometheus, who formed human beings out of the clay of the earth. By exploring the deepest mysteries of creation, Frankenstein is also able to infuse life into an inanimate shell. Interestingly, as Isaac Asimov notes, this is the first tale in which life was created by a scientific means and not by divine intervention. Unlike Prometheus, however, Victor abandons his "child" upon its birth. So obsessed was the scientist in the creative endeavor that he did not bother to worry about the physical features of the creature. This oversight comes back to haunt Victor each time he gazes upon the horrific countenance of "the monster." After experiencing several months of a debilitating illness (brought on, no doubt, by the creature's proximity), Frankenstein retires to his father's home in Geneva, Switzerland, hoping that he can free himself forever of his parental (and moral) obligations.

But only in death can the creature be reunited with its creator, and the "split personality" be mended. While several stories have continued the Frankenstein saga by having the monster survive the ordeal and make its re-entrance into today's society (Aldiss, Estleman), the Shelley ending remains the most powerful one in the genesis genre to date.

Bibliography

Aldiss, Brian. "Summertime Was Nearly Over." *The Ultimate Frankenstein*. Ed. Byron Preiss. New York: Dell, 1991. 19-28.

Asimov, Isaac. "The Lord's Apprentice." *The Ultimate Frankenstein*. Ed. Byron Preiss. New York: Dell, 1991. 1-6.

Estleman, Loren D. "I, Monster." *The Ultimate Frankenstein*. Ed. Byron Preiss. New York: Dell, 1991. 136-45.

Iaccino, James F. "Frankenstein: The Alchemic 'New Age' Creator." *Psychological Reflections on Cinematic Terror: Jungian Archetypes in Horror Films*. Westport: Praeger, 1994. 93-107.

Pearson, Carol S. *The Hero Within: Six Archetypes We Live By*. San Francisco: HarperCollins, 1989.

James F. Iaccino

Frankenstein in Film. In the past 80 years, films on Frankenstein have proliferated. Randy Quaid has been the latest actor thus far to portray the monster in *Frankenstein* (1993, Poland), a forgettable film made for cable TV. Roger Corman, who had not directed a film in 20 years, in 1990 made an unexciting adaptation of Brian Aldiss's 1973 sci-fi time travel novel, *Frankenstein Unbound*. *Frankenhooker* (1990), with its sophomoric comedy slated toward the exploitation-cult splatter market, combined prostitutes, crack addiction, and the seedy 42nd Street milieu with a tongue-in-cheek anti-drug message. A more sophisticated but failed black comedy was Brian Yuzama's *Bride of Re-Animator* (1990), a bloody sequel to the 1985 original.

The 1980s contained several sumptuously mounted productions based on the history of the monster's creation, including Ken Russell's *Gothic* (1986) and Ivan Passar's *Haunted Summer* (1988). Franc Roddam's 1985 *The Bride* has splendid sets and an eye-catching laboratory sequence but misses the mark in casting Jennifer Beals and Sting in the lead roles. In the updating of the Frankenstein legend the quality of most 1980s films is appalling with the exception of Stuart Gordon's dark comedy thriller *Re-Animator* (1985), based on H. P. Lovecraft's character Herbert West. Dealing with the Frankenstein-like situation of socialized medicine, Lindsay Anderson's splendid British satire *Britannia Hospital* (1982) has a blood-soaked finale in which a doctor's creature created from spare parts literally goes to pieces. In the so-bad-it's-funny category there are *Frankenstein's General Hospital* (1988), *The Vindicator* (1986)—albeit with Stan Winston's impressive cyborg monster—and *Frankenstein's Island* (1981).

The 1970s witnessed the first interactive film of its kind to involve the audience viscerally, *The Rocky Horror Picture Show* (1975), a parody of 1950s science fiction and horror with a Frankenstein motif, which contained enough rock music and kinky sex to make it a midnight cult hit with American youth, and brazenly exposed the underlying psychosexual themes inherent in the subgenre to the surface. The definitive parody of the classic Frankenstein films, however, is Mel Brooks's *Young Frankenstein* (1974), lovingly imitating the black and white photography and camera movement of the 1930s classics and employing a rich expressive score while sending each convention up with hilarious sight gags and one liners. From the more serious tradition of Masterpiece Theatre are Jack Smight's *Frankenstein: The True Story* (1973), produced as a three-hour TV movie for American audiences, with James Mason's bizarre portrayal of Dr. Polidori, and the pictorially stunning *Victor Frankenstein* (1977, Ireland), whose adolescent creature, estranged from society, is turned into a juvenile delinquent.

The second golden age for the Frankenstein monster arrived in Britain in the late 1950s and lasted into the early 1970s, a period during which Hammer Films remade in color the Universal horror cycle of the 1930s with more liberal doses of sex, violence, and gore than had previously been seen. The first in the series, looking much more costly than its $250,000 price tag, *The Curse of Frankenstein* (1957), grossed millions and made its stars forever linked with the horror genre: Peter Cushing as the cerebral doctor, Christopher Lee as the monster (in this and five sequels), with Terence Fisher directing and Jimmy Sangester scripting. *Horror of Frankenstein* (1970) was the only one without Cushing. While British horror played to an adult audience (children were restricted from seeing domestic and imported horror by an "X" rating), the Americans catered to the juvenile crowd with *I Was a Teenage Frankenstein* (1957), parable-like in its use of a teenage monster with raging hormones and a narcissistic complex. Equally shoddy in its production values and acting is *Frankenstein's Daughter* (1958), in which another mad scientist attempting to make a girl into a super-human turns her instead into a robot-like monster. *The Mad Doctor of Blood Island* (1968) offered an appalling concoction of the Frankenstein, zombie, and Dr. Moreau stories, while William Baudine's last poverty row picture, *Jesse James Meets Frankenstein's Daughter* (1966), had the granddaughter transplant an artificial brain into Jesse's muscular moronic friend, proving that the marriage of horror and the Western needed more than a cross-genre novelty to make it work. In the same year a minor comedy made for TV but released theatrically, *Munster Go Home*, had the family inheriting Munster Hall only to find it the heart of a counterfeiting ring.

During World War II, Universal Pictures took their old menacing creations and revived them, believing that if one monster was frightening, three in the same film would have greater impact. Made as programmers (the most expensive being *House of Frankenstein*, at $354,000), they contained a fine supporting cast, including Cedric Hardwicke, Lionel Atwill, Evelyn Ankers, and George Zucco. All were well-mounted productions using existing sets which created a 19th-century ambiance with modern characters to populate them. The creature was played by Lon Chaney, Jr. in *The Ghost of Frankenstein* (1942), the first of the 1940s series and the last to star only one monster; Bela Lugosi, happy to get the part of the monster he had refused in 1931, appeared in *Frankenstein Meets the Wolf Man* (1943); the burly cowboy star, Glenn Strange, appeared as the monster in both *House of Frankenstein* (1944), where the monster, Dracula, and the Wolf Man are united for the first time, and *House of Dracula* (1945), the seventh and poorest in the series. The end came with the tamely humorous *Abbott and Costello Meet Frankenstein* (1948).

The decade of the 1930s, however, singlehandedly contributed to the establishment of the genre, especially through the advent of sound and the Great Depression. Universal, facing bankruptcy, embarked on a cycle of horror films under Carl Laemmle, Jr. that, at least until 1936, brought some money into the company's depleted coffers. The horror was not explained away as in many 1920s films, nor were its monsters as human as the ones that the senior Chaney had played. These creatures were presented as real beings. *Frankenstein* came immediately on the heels of *Dracula* (both 1931). James Whale, on the basis of two war films, replaced Robert Florey on the set, accepting the challenge of a fantasy film even though he had been offered a number of other projects to choose from. Lugosi, who tested for the creature but never wanted the part because the makeup hid his features, was replaced by Boris Karloff, whose work on *The Criminal Code* (1931) brought him to Whale's attention. As in many 1930s horror films, there are two "heroes" in *Frankenstein*: the conventional romantic one played by Colin Clive, the tormented scientist and lover, and his monster, the Romantic villain-hero, who is the mirror image of his creator and the more sympathetic of the two. The sets, camera set-ups, and acting (especially from the over-wrought doctor and the inarticulate pantomime of his creature) point back to the German expressionistic influence of the 1920s.

The film is based on two plays, Peggy Webbling's *Frankenstein: An Adventure in the Macabre* (1927) and John L. Balderston's *Frankenstein* (1930). Universal purchased the screen rights of both plays for $20,000 plus one percent of the world gross. It is from the Webbling play that the change in names from the novel arbitrarily occurs: Victor Frankenstein becomes "Henry," and his friend Henry Clerval becomes "Victor." Waldman, the "benign wizard" figure of 1930s horror films, is both a priest and a doctor in the Balderston play. Although Edward Van Sloan's character has been secularized in the film, he still voices moral opposition to Henry's experiments and, therefore, retains a hint of the priestly character he had in the play. Whale consummately cast his characters very close to Balderston's description: John Boles, a rather colorless actor groomed by the studio for leading roles, plays Victor Moritz in the film and is described in the play as a "normal young man...but not particularly intelligent," a perfect foil to Henry, played by Colin Clive, who is introduced in the play as "young, thin, nervous...but now at the point of hysteria." Whale ended the film with the death of Henry and the destruction of the monster.

Universal changed this to an upbeat ending to prepare the way for a sequel as it waited for the right director. Whale was hesitant after directing *The Old Dark House* (1932) and *The Invisible Man* (1933) to be typecast as a horror specialist, yet finally signed on for the sequel, *Bride of Frankenstein* (1935). With Franz Waxman's operatic leitmotivs to introduce the characters, the film opens with a framing device that takes place in 1816 at the time Byron was with the Shelleys in Geneva, but Whale deliberately avoids specificity here as well as in the main narrative. The somber 1931 film gives way in this flamboyant production to black humor from characters like Dr. Pretorius, played by Ernest Thesiger, whose prissiness and whimsicality in Whale's *Old Dark House* are fully orchestrated here. Against Karloff's objections, Whale demanded that the monster be given a voice which adds even more pathos to his Christ-like figure: he eats bread and wine at supper with Pretorius, is tied to a cross and, pointing to a "resurrection," bursts his prison bonds. At the decade's end Rowland V. Lee directed a stylish sequel, *Son of Frankenstein* (1939), with splendid stark expressionistic sets and impressive performances from Lugosi as Ygor, Basil Rathbone as the baron, Lionel Atwill as the prosthetic-armed police inspector, Krogh, and Karloff as the mutely sinister creature.

Finally, the silents offered two variations on the Shelley novel. In the Edison Company's *Frankenstein* (1910, 16 minutes) the monster, played by Charles Ogle, is defeated by the power of love and vanishes into thin air, leaving Frankenstein and his bride to live in peace. In 1915, the first American feature-length version, *Life without a Soul* (70 min.), boasted of extensive location shooting. Percy Darrell Stading played the awe-inspiring creature sympathetically with little makeup.

The success of this legend on film is as endurable as Shelley's novel and because the genre formula is constantly modified for new generations and to garner money at the box office, there is no reason to believe that Frankenstein will ever truly die at the hands of popular culture.

Bibliography

Brunas, Michael, John Brunas, and Tom Weaver. *Universal Horrors: The Studio's Classic Films, 1931-1946*. Jefferson: McFarland, 1990.

Hardy, Phil, Tom Milne, and Paul Willemen, eds. *The Encyclopedia of Horror Movies*. New York: Harper, 1986.

Riley, Philip J., ed. *Bride of Frankenstein* [Original 1935 Shooting Script]. Absecon: MagicImage Filmbooks, 1989.

Sevastakis, Michael. *Songs of Love and Death: The Classical American Horror Film of the 1930s*. Westport: Greenwood, 1993.

Michael Sevastakis

Franklin, Aretha (1942-   ), the most influential American female popular singer since Billie Holiday, was born in Memphis, TN. She eventually moved to Detroit, where her father, the Reverend C. L. Franklin, himself an impressive performer, directed the congregation at the New Bethel Baptist Church. Her mother left the family when Aretha was six, dying four years later, leaving Franklin to be raised by her father and the galaxy of gospel and rhythm and blues greats, Clara Ward, Mahalia Jackson, Marion Williams, Sam Cooke, and Dinah Washington, who were all frequent visitors to the Franklins' church and home.

By the time she was a teenager, she was a legend in gospel music circles, traveling its segregated circuit. When she was 14 her father arranged for her to record a live album of gospel music for Chess. More than an impressive document of a precocious teenager, *Songs of Faith* (now titled *Aretha Gospel*) revealed an unmistakable genius, and probably would have made her a legend if she had never done anything else. While Franklin might have followed in the footsteps of her gospel idols, she and her father always had their eyes on the pop market. Following the example of Sam Cooke, Franklin joined the world of secular music in 1960 when she signed with Columbia Records.

Acutely conscious that Franklin was the next link in the chain of great African-American female singers, producer John Hammond initially recorded Franklin in a jazz context. However, the type of jazz that Hammond favored had lost much of its cultural currency, if none of its greatness, and did not incite the depth of inspiration that Jerry Wexler would uncover in Aretha for Atlantic Records in the late 1960s. Still, Franklin did make great records with Hammond, best represented by "Today I Sing the Blues." After Hammond, Franklin was shuffled from producer to producer, recording cocktail jazz, pop standards, show tunes, blues, and even some incipient soul. It would be an injustice to a singer of Franklin's genius to imply, as often happens, that Franklin's six years with Columbia were a waste of her talent. No less an authority than Jerry Wexler considers her version of *Camelot*'s "If Ever I Would Leave You," a song often pointed to as an example of Columbia's waste of her talent, to be one of her greatest records.

As a producer, Wexler's brilliance consisted of letting Franklin be Franklin. Her prime coincided with the soul era, and it was her fate and achievement to become the purest expression of that moment. "Respect," "Dr. Feelgood," "(You Make Me Feel Like) A Natural Woman," "Chain of Fools," "Think," "The House That Jack Built," "See Saw," the hits exploded one after another, bringing her eight straight Grammy awards. From 1967 to 1972, Franklin released a series of albums unmatched by any other soul artist, with the possible exception of James Brown, and which deserve to be ranked alongside the great achievements of her predecessors, Bessie Smith, Billie Holiday, and Mahalia Jackson, as one of the treasures of American music.

Her transformation of Otis Redding's already magnificent "Respect" provides a good example of her accomplishment. What was a typical male appeal for domestic courtesy became in Franklin's hands a glorious declaration of female identity. Given the political climate of the time, the song became an anthem of African-American feminist pride. Franklin became the first African-American woman to capture the imagination of "mainstream" American society who could look her broad audience squarely in the eye, and not have to apologize for what she was.

By the mid-1970s, Franklin's career had lost its momentum, and her music since then has been erratic. As was the case for the other great singers of her era, the music changed, giving way in the late 1970s to disco, in the 1980s to techno-soul, which depends largely on synthesizers and other machine-made music, and then rap. She suffered personal difficulties as well. Her father lay in a coma from 1979 to his death in 1984, shot in the head by a thief.

Even during her heyday Franklin was an idiosyncratic, deeply personal singer. As a result, she has often been accused of suffering from lapses in taste in her choice of material, such as singing show tunes instead of soul. Actually, this willfulness is an essential part of her genius, and proves that her conception of herself has been larger than her fans have been able to comprehend. There is no form of American popular music that she has not graced. All of her post-Atlantic records have something memorable to recommend them. In 1987, as if to call her wayward fans home, she brought her career full circle, returning to her father's church to record the magisterial *One Lord, One Faith, One Baptism*, a glorious return to form and proof that this great singer has lost nothing. In 1994 she received the Lifetime Achievement Grammy, the highest award given by that organization.

Bibliography

Bego, Mark. *Aretha Franklin, the Queen of Soul*. New York: St. Martin's, 1989.

Gersten, Russel. "Aretha Franklin." *The Rolling Stone Illustrated History of Rock and Roll.* New York: Rolling Stone, 1976, 1993.

Guralnick, Peter. *Sweet Soul Music.* New York: Harper, 1986.

Hirshey, Gerri. *Nowhere to Run: The Story of Soul Music.* New York: Times, 1984.

Wexler, Jerry. *Rhythm and the Blues: A Life in American Music.* New York: Knopf, 1993.

Timothy L. Parrish

Freed, Alan (1922-1965), in the 1950s, became the first nationally recognized disk jockey to feature the emerging rhythm and blues and rock musical forms. During a time when many white platter-pilots were reluctant to play songs by African-American performers, Freed was not; and, as a result, he helped to advance the careers of a number of artists. He has also been credited with helping to popularize the term "rock 'n' roll."

Freed, who grew up in Salem, OH, began his career in radio as an announcer in New Castle, PA, after World War II, and by 1949 he had a popular music request show over WAKR in Akron, OH. In 1950, he moved to Cleveland and landed a job at WXEL-TV; however, by June 1951, Freed had returned to radio, hosting a record show over Cleveland's WJMO from six to seven o'clock in the evenings. Less than a month later, he moved over to WJW to host what became a very popular late evening request show, *The Moondog Show*, which focused on rhythm and blues.

Freed moved from Cleveland to New York City in July 1954 after signing with WINS radio for the largest salary paid to an independent rhythm and blues jockey up to that point—$75,000. However, blind street musician Louis "Moondog" Hardin objected to Freed's use of the Moondog moniker, and in December of 1954, he won a court injunction against Freed's use of the term. Freed changed the name of his WINS program to *The Rock and Roll Show*, and the age of rock began.

Freed moved to WABC in 1958, but he lost his prestigious radio program and a television program he hosted over WNEW-TV in 1959 as a result of the Congressional payola investigations. He pleaded guilty to a charge of taking bribes in 1962 and, subsequently, moved to the West Coast. Freed died at age 43 in Palm Springs, CA.

Bibliography
Fornatale, Peter, and Joshua Mills. *Radio in the Television Age.* Woodstock: Overlook, 1980.

Passman, Arnold. *The Deejays.* New York: Macmillan, 1971.

Sterling, Christopher, and John Kittross. *Stay Tuned: A Concise History of American Broadcasting.* 2d ed. Belmont: Wadsworth, 1990.

Charles F. Ganzert

Freedom Songs is a term for a broad category of music that revolves around the civil rights movement in the United States from roughly 1955 to 1966. The civil rights movement, which was aimed towards gaining equal civil rights for African Americans and the desegregation of American society, used many methods of protest such as sit-ins, marches, and demonstrations to move towards its goals. Music and singing was central to the group participation in these methods of protest. Freedom songs were popularized through word of mouth and through organizations such as the S.N.C.C. (Student Non-Violent Coordinating Committee) and the S.C.L.C. (Southern Christian Leadership Conference). The songs were also frequently published in music magazines such as *Broadside* and *Sing Out!*

Many of the freedom songs were actually adapted from earlier songs, usually hymns. Zilphia Horton is credited by Pete Seeger with changing the hymn "I Shall Overcome" to "We Shall Overcome" in 1946. Guy Carawan, of Tennessee's Highlander Folk School, is also credited with turning "I'll Be Alight" into "We Shall Overcome" and introducing it in Nashville sit-ins in 1960.

Other freedom songs include: "Ain't Gonna Let Nobody Turn Me Around," "Which Side Are You On?" "Hold On," "Woke Up This Morning," "Keep Your Eyes on the Prize, Hold On," "Oh, Freedom," "Ain't Gonna Let Segregation Turn Me Around," "Roll, Freedom, Roll," "If You Miss Me at the Back of the Bus," "Freedom Is a Constant Struggle," and "We'll Never Turn Back."

The Freedom Singers were probably the most famous group singing freedom songs, though many of the songs of the civil rights movement were recorded by performers such as Peter, Paul and Mary; Bob Dylan; Phil Ochs; Tom Paxton; Odetta; Joan Baez; Harry Belafonte; Pete Seeger; and others (see entries). The Freedom Singers included Charles Neblett, Bernice Reagon, Cordell Reagon, and Rutha Harris.

Many of the freedom songs from the civil rights movement were also adapted to other protest movements, such as the struggle for equality in South Africa in the 1960s and through the 1990s (see Protest Music). Many of these songs were also used by American protesters in the 1970s through the 1990s in the protests that called for divestment of South African holdings by universities and other institutions.

Bibliography
Carawan, Guy. *Sing for Freedom: The Story of the Civil Rights Movement through Its Songs.* Bethlehem: Sing Out, 1990.

Sanger, Kerran L. *"When the Spirit Says Sing!": The Role of Freedom Songs in the Civil Rights Movement.* New York: Garland, 1995.

Jeff Ritter

Friends (1994-), the weekly 30-minute NBC sitcom, narrates the ongoing tale of over 20 young people in New York City with whom members of the average American television viewing audience can easily identify. The appeal of this television show, created by Marta Kauffman and David Crane, is evident from excellent ratings, good reviews, and numerous Emmy nominations. The members of the cast of *Friends* include several very talented young American performers: Matthew Perry (Chandler Bing), Jennifer Aniston (Rachel Green), Courteney Cox Arquette (Monica Geller), Lisa Kudrow (Phoebe Buffay), Matt LeBlanc (Joey Tribbiani), and David Schwimmer (Ross Geller).

Lisa Kudrow won the Emmy award in 1997-98 for outstanding supporting actress in a comedy series for her performance as the spacy but lovable folk singer/massage therapist Phoebe Buffay. Kudrow has also been nominated for Golden Globe, Screen Actors Guild and American Comedy awards. Jennifer Aniston trained at New York's School of the Performing Arts. From off-Broadway stage productions, she went on to roles in several television series and in several feature films such as *Picture Perfect*, *She's the One*, *'Til There Was You*, and *Object of My Affection*. Courteney Cox Arquette made her television debut in 1984 in *As the World Turns*. David Schwimmer, who plays Monica's twice-divorced older brother Ross, has extensive stage experience, and has appeared in the films *The Pallbearer*, *Twenty Bucks*, *Crossing the Bridge*, *Since You've Been Gone*, and *Six Days, Seven Nights*. Matthew Perry is the son of actor John Bennett Perry, under whose guardianship his interest in acting blossomed. Other television performances by Perry include *Home Free* and *Sydney* as well as a recurring part on *Growing Pains*. Joey Tribbiani is played by Matt Leblanc, who started his career doing commercials in New York City.

Bibliography

"NBC: Friends." *NBC.com.* n.p. Online. Internet 6 Jan. 1998, 17 March 2000. Available: http://www. nbc.com/tvcen...ws/ friends.html.

Silverstein, Dan. "Dan's Shrine to *Friends*." 25 Sept. 1997. n.p. Online. Lycos 6 Jan. 1998. Available: http://www-scf. usc.edu/~dsilvers/friends1.html.

Mitali R. Pati
Eugene F. Wong

Frishberg, David L. (1933-), grew up in St. Paul, MN, studied music with various teachers, listened ceaselessly to jazz recordings, and graduated from the School of Journalism and Mass Communication at the nearby University of Minnesota in 1955. After moving to New York and working in advertising, Frishberg was soon devoting as much attention to late-night jazz sessions as to his "day job." His musical creations as a songwriter are replete with uncomplimentary and hilarious references to marketing ("Blizzard of Lies"), consumer behavior ("Let's Eat Home"), the business world ("Quality Time"), the information revolution ("The Sports Page"), the business cycle ("Long Daddy Green"), and the pernicious effects of greed ("Wheelers and Dealers").

As the 1960s progressed, Frishberg found himself increasingly busy as a jazz pianist—accompanying such singers as Carmen McRae, Odetta, Dick Haymes, and Fran Jeffries and playing in the house band at the old Half-Note club in a group that backed up visiting jazz luminaries like Bob Brookmeyer, Clark Terry, Al Cohn, and Zoot Sims. Blossom Dearie (a neighbor) helped to get Frishberg involved in writing songs. Together, they penned "Long Daddy Green." With Bob Dorough (creator of such gems as *Multiplication Rock*), Frishberg wrote "I'm Hip." With Alan Broadbent (the West Coast pianist/arranger), he wrote "Heart's Desire" and "Marilyn Monroe." With Johnny Mandel (who composed "The Shadow of Your Smile"), Frishberg wrote "You Are

There," "El Cajon," and "Brenda Starr." With Sam Frishberg (his then-wife), he created "Blizzard of Lies" and "Slappin' the Cakes on Me," both dedicated to the sort of sardonic commentary on the indelicacies of commerce and the foibles of lovers that have become Frishberg trademarks.

In 1971, Frishberg moved to Los Angeles, where he spent two years with Herb Alpert's Tijuana Brass and sought work as a songwriter or occasional composer of jingles in the L.A. television and movie studios. Frishberg registered his nostalgia for the Big Apple in his triumph of ambivalence entitled "Do You Miss New York?" Before long, however, he had settled into Hollywood and was turning out marvelously intricate rhymes for sports events ("Dodger Blue"), film soundtracks ("Brenda Starr"), and television productions (Mary Tyler Moore singing "Listen Here").

The contribution made to Frishberg's work by his own pianistic background cannot be overestimated. Other singers have increasingly performed his songs but few if any of these renditions have managed to attain the comic effect and musical wit that Frishberg generates on his up-tempo tunes when he sings and plays them himself ("You Would Rather Have the Blues," "Can't Take You Nowhere," "Blizzard of Lies," "My Attorney Bernie") or the pathos that he can achieve on his more pensive ballads if left to his own devices ("The Dear Departed Past," "Matty," "Sweet Kentucky Ham," "Green Hills of Earth").

Bibliography

Balliett, Whitney. *American Singers: Twenty-Seven Portraits in Song.* New York: Oxford UP, 1988.

Baseball's Greatest Hits. Videocassette. Rhino Home Video, 1990.

In New Orleans. Videocassette. Jack Sheldon. Featuring David Frishberg's solo performance of "I Was Ready." Leisure Video, 1989.

Morris B. Holbrook

Frontline (1983-), on the Public Broadcasting Service, was at first projected as a 26-hour-long investigative documentary series. The show was produced by a consortium (WGBH, Boston; WTVS, Detroit; WPBT, Miami; WNET, New York; and KCTS, Seattle), but WGBH and executive producer David Janning oversee every documentary. Almost two decades later the program is still on the air waves, more popular and controversial than ever.

The original format of the program utilized a host, Jessica Savitch. Tragically she was killed in an automobile accident later that fall and was replaced by Judy Woodruff. Later the show changed to a voice-over style featuring various narrators, the most prominent being Will Lyman. *Frontline* has offered a outlet for such filmmakers as David Harrison, Jim Gilmore, Michael Kirk, Noel Buckner, Stephen Talbot, and Orville Schell.

From the initial program, on the death of the Los Angeles Rams football team owner, the show has tackled a wide variety of topics: child abuse, civil rights, drugs, the National Park Service, baseball, and General Motors. Other programs covered international issues in Iran, the Soviet Union, and Central America.

Frontline was to overcome the initial roller coaster reviews and in 1984 went on to win a coveted Peabody Award for "overall excellence." *Frontline* repeated this accomplishment again in 1985 for "Crisis in Central America," in 1988 for a series on the 1987 election campaign, and five more times in the 1990s. It has also won numerous Emmys. The excellence of the program stems in no small measure from the writers and reporters, among them, Shelby Steele, Bill Moyers, Hodding Cotter, Judy Woodruff, James Reston, Jr., and Robert Krulwich.

The program persistently receives a mixed bag of kudos and criticisms by attempting to blend good journalism and provocative filmmaking. The "In Our Children's Food" episode was accused of perpetuating a pesticide myth. Such beliefs reflected a pervasive feeling that *Frontline,* as a PBS product, was thought to tread a liberal fine line even though the Public Broadcasting Company has been accused of succumbing to organized right-wing political pressure.

The credibility of the program was enhanced in 1993 when its documentary "Tabloid Truth" (directed by Richard Ben Cramer) served as the cornerstone for a scathing essay in the *New Yorker* on tabloid television.

Bibliography
Avery, Dennis T. *Wall Street Journal* 18 ed. (April 1993): 14.
Daily News Sunday. 13 Feb. 1994: 16-17.
Wolcott, James. *New Yorker* 69 (Feb. 1994): 92-94.

Richard Veteikes

Fuller, Samuel (1912-1977), writer, producer, and director, represented in his films a different story-world, a hyper-realism grounded in the traditions of the tabloid press and his combat experiences with the First Infantry Division. In the 1960s, Fuller said that he plotted his potboilers on a blackboard with different color chalk to make sure the composition of red (action), white (exposition) and blue (romance) was balanced. Fuller's collision of these modes was, in part, informed by his work as a crime reporter, 1929-31, on Bernarr MacFadden's *Evening Graphic*, a poor imitation of the *New York Daily News,* which specialized in sensational stories of sordid love, gangland crimes, and murder. Fuller found parallels between filmmaking and reporting: the cinematic close-up was like a headline. Several Fuller stories, *House of Bamboo* (1955), *Underworld U.S.A.* (1961), *Shock Corridor* (1963), and *The Naked Kiss* (1965), involve amoral reporter types, investigators who infiltrate a mob, an insane asylum, a small town to uncover truth. For Fuller's characters, danger lies in losing distance and getting too close to the aesthetics of the world they inhabit. Fuller's world of exaggeration, of shifts in moods, has its antecedent in the pages of the *Graphic*.

Fuller was born in Worcester, MA. By the age of 17 he was a crime reporter for the *Graphic*. He began writing short stories and pulp fictions around the same time, and in 1935 published *Burn Baby Burn*. In 1936 he wrote scenarios for films and collaborated on James Cruze's *Gangs of New York* (1938), and during the war years he fought in North Africa and Europe. A corporal, Fuller was awarded the Bronze Star,

the Silver Star, and a Purple Heart. After the war, Fuller returned to Hollywood and directed his first feature, the somewhat slow and plodding *I Shot Jesse James* (1949). But it was the following year that Fuller emerged as a star with *Steel Helmet* (1950). Made for $104,000 and shot in ten days at Griffith Park, the film, taken from the day's headlines, was the first to address the Korean War. *Steel Helmet* presents a battleground in which there are no rules. The film has a brutal intensity that mixes banality and nihilism to eschew patriotic pieties.

Not only do Fuller's characters comment on social issues, but the overall presentation of a Fuller film often shifts from narrative to expository discourse. A C.O. tells James Best in *Verboten!* (1958) that you can't tell a German from a Nazi. "Seems they found Hitler dead with a piece of paper in his fist on which he had written, 'I was never a Nazi.'" A shock edit follows with found footage of hollowed-out German planes, aerial images of a rubbled Berlin, a woman screaming, refugees walking streets, the Red Cross handing out food. These collisions, in essay format, comment on what Hitler's Nazism has wrought on the German people. In *Underworld U.S.A.* (1960), Fuller expands on the descriptive pause with three frozen images: Mencken's daughter lies dead on the street, discarded shoes and a mangled bicycle next to her; corrupt police chief Fowler kills himself and the exit bullet lodges in a portrait of the police force; Tolly lies dead in a back alley and as the camera tracks in on his clenched fist it transforms into a grainy newspaper still. All three images circumscribe the action and invite a viewer to ascribe meaning, to "write a caption." These images halt story time and ask that we consider them separate from story, as part of the text's larger discursive statements on crime. Exposition is the newspaper reporter's textual mode of social relevance.

Another dominant aspect of Fuller's style is narrative collisions across and within scenes. Fuller's aesthetic presents sentiment as something to be buried, repressed within the contrapuntal shock edits of violence. Within scenes Fuller's narrative voices (exposition, love, action) are also charged with competition. Following Mo's death in *Pick-up on South Street* (1952), an angry Richard Widmark pushes away Jean Peters. Peters cries because she loved Mo, and Widmark, remorseful, embraces her and apologizes. In response, Peters smashes a beer bottle over Widmark's head. Fuller's view of love and apparent domestic security is shattered by sudden acts of violence that indicate a post-traumatic poetics at the heart of his narratives.

Bibliography
Chatman, Seymour. *Coming to Terms: The Rhetoric of Narrative in Fiction and Film.* New York: Cornell UP, 1990.
Garnham, Nicholas. *Samuel Fuller.* New York: Viking, 1971.
Hoberman, J. "Three American Abstract Sensationalists." *Vulgar Modernism.* Philadelphia: Temple UP, 1991.
Server, Lee. *Sam Fuller: Film Is a Battleground.* Jefferson: McFarland, 1994.

Grant Tracey

G

Gable, (William) Clark (1901-1960), the straight-talking he-man who was for 30 years the King of Hollywood stars, was born in Cadiz, OH. He grew up in a Pennsylvania German family on a small farm there and in nearby Hopedale. By 1921, he had worked in Ohio and Oregon stock theaters. He moved to Hollywood in 1924, where he married Josephine Dillon, his acting coach. "Billy" Gable won some minor stage roles and was an extra in several movies. His stage appearance in a Texas stock company led to a successful 1928 Broadway debut as a leading man in *Machinal*, which resulted in an MGM contract in 1930.

After Gable married his second wife, Ria Langham, in 1930, he seemed destined for a successful movie career. The astute dean of Hollywood actors, John Barrymore, described him as "Valentino in Jack Dempsey's body." Clark Gable appeared in his first talkie playing a Western villain in *The Painted Desert* (1931) with silent-screen star Pola Negri. Leading roles followed rapidly, first in *Susan Lennox: Her Rise and Fall* (1931) with Greta Garbo; then in *Possessed* (1931) with Joan Crawford; in *Hell Divers* (1932) with Wallace Beery; in *Night Nurse* (1931) with Barbara Stanwyck; in *Red Dust* (1932) with Mary Astor and Jean Harlow; and in *Men in White* (1934) with Myrna Loy. Known more for his forceful personality rather than his acting skills, Gable's rugged good looks and straightforward masculine charm earned wide box-office appeal. Like John Wayne, Gable often played himself rather than submerging himself in the role as Spencer Tracy did. However, his versatility was not apparent until he won an Academy Award for Frank Capra's legendary romantic comedy, *It Happened One Night* (1934). Gable was the "King" thereafter, Hollywood's major romantic leading man in the movies' golden age.

Gable's major roles included parts in *China Seas* (1935), *Mutiny on the Bounty* (1935), *San Francisco* (1936), *Saratoga* (1937), and *Boom Town* (1940). His forte was playing the roguish hero, and casting Gable as Rhett Butler in *Gone with the Wind* (1939) was inevitable. Without a doubt, Rhett Butler was Gable's most memorable role, and critics were sympathetic but unforgiving when Timothy Dalton attempted to re-create the role in a 1994 television miniseries sequel, *Scarlett*. Gable dominates every scene and exudes the toughness of a dispossessed aristocrat devoid of scruples but determined to survive the Civil War and to succeed in the turmoil of the Reconstruction era. Rhett's last words to Scarlett, "Frankly, my dear, I don't give a damn," have become part of the American vernacular.

The death of Gable's third wife, screen actress Carole Lombard (1906-42), in an airplane crash cast a shadow over his career. She was a leading lady and popular comedienne in some 50 movies, daring to be wacky while glamorous, and her marriage to Clark Gable brought them both much happiness. After her death, the Hollywood community rejoiced when the shaken Gable resumed his public role as King on the MGM lot. During World War II, Gable served in combat as an Army Air Corps intelligence officer, winning an Air Medal and a Distinguished Flying Cross. The King's return to the silver screen was hailed by Hollywood in an unforgettable movie trailer declaring, "Gable's back and Garson's got him." But *Adventure* (1945) was one of the more unsuccessful MGM romantic pairings. Gable and Greer Garson simply did not have the screen chemistry to save this cumbersome comedy.

But Gable's performances in more than 70 films often benefited from his talented leading ladies, Joan Crawford in *Possessed*; Loretta Young in *Call of the Wild* (1935); Jean Harlow in *Red Dust* and *China Seas*; Vivien Leigh in *Gone with the Wind*; Lana Turner and Claire Trevor in *Honky Tonk* (1941); and, finally, Marilyn Monroe in *The Misfits* (1961). Outstanding co-stars, like Spencer Tracy in *Boom Town*, Wallace Beery in *China Seas*, and Charles Laughton in *Mutiny on the Bounty*, or strong supporting actors like Brian Donlevy and Charles Bickford in *Command Decision* (1948), and Gig Young in *Teacher's Pet* (1958), certainly gave added depth to Gable's efforts.

Gable's best postwar movies included *Command Decision*; a lusty remake of *Red Dust* called *Mogambo* (1953); then a large-scale Western, *The Tall Men* (1955); and a submarine yarn, *Run Silent, Run Deep* (1958). Gable returned to light comedy in *Teacher's Pet* (1958), but time and television had diminished Hollywood, and Gable's best work had been done. His final role was as a brooding cowboy in John Huston's uneven modern Western, *The Misfits*, with Marilyn Monroe in her last movie. Gable died from a heart attack shortly before completing the film. In it he was uncomfortable playing an aging 20th-century rodeo cowboy hunting wild mustangs on the vanishing frontier. His farewell performance in this anguished screenplay marked the end of the last real Hollywood he-man.

Bibliography

Garceau, Jean. *"Dear Mr. G—": The Biography of Clark Gable*. Boston: Little, Brown, 1961.

Kobal, John, ed. *Clark Gable*. Boston: Little, Brown, 1986.

Lewis, Judy. *Uncommon Knowledge*. New York: Pocket, 1994.

Samuels, Charles. *The King: A Biography of Clark Gable*. New York: Coward-McCann, 1962.

Tornabene, Lyn. *Long Live the King*. New York: Putnam, 1976.

Peter C. Holloran

Gambling. Legalized gambling has become one of America's premier growth industries; it has also become one of the nation's premier political and social issues. Gambling activity in the United States has fallen under the jurisdiction of the individual states. Each state has laws in place that restrict and control gambling activities. Some of these laws are by state constitution while others are statutory. In some states, communities are granted the power to enact local ordinances regarding gambling activities.

The majority of the states receive revenues from legalized gambling. Nevada state government derives a fourth of its annual revenue directly from gambling taxes. States hungry for new sources of tax revenue and economic development have liberalized their restrictions on gambling during the 1980s and 1990s. As a result, legalized gambling has become much more accessible for potential players. Forty-eight states allow gambling in some form. The variety of games allowed in these states is constantly growing.

Typically, gambling creates a picture of casinos in Las Vegas or Atlantic City. However, casino gambling composes only 34 percent of the total winnings nationwide. State lotteries constitute the largest share of the industry's winnings at 38 percent (see entry). Traditional gaming such as horse racing and bingo generates 7.5 percent and 4 percent of the prizes. Greyhound tracks, jai alai, sports betting (see entry), and other forms of gambling create lesser payouts.

The operators of gaming facilities naturally create odds in their favor. Losses as a percentage of wagering average approximately 4 percent for casinos, 20 percent for horse tracks, 20 percent for greyhounds, 25 percent for bingo, and a confidence-altering 49 percent for state lotteries.

As the gaming industry evolves, a new mixture of gambling is occurring. The majority of the states bordering the Mississippi River have legalized riverboat or dockside gambling. Several other states along other waterways such as the Ohio River have legalized the riverboat form of gambling or they are considering legalization.

Las Vegas-style theme park gambling was created, in part, to contend with a new source of gambling, American Indian Reservation gambling. Federal legislation under the Indian Gaming Regulation Act of 1988 allows American Indian tribes to offer gambling on their reservations if that type of gambling is already legally offered in their state. Nine states have agreements that allow various types of casino gambling on Indian property. The federal law is interpreted differently in each state, with Minnesota and Connecticut becoming the most active Indian-gaming states. The Mashantucket Pequot tribe in Connecticut has emerged as the highest volume Indian casino operator. Indian gaming is normally tax exempt and feebly regulated. These advantages have become a concern for traditional forms of gambling as they compete for the wagered dollars. Indian activists have also raised ethical and economic questions concerning reservation casinos and the welfare of their people.

Bibliography

"Casinos Move into New Areas." *Leisure Time.* Vol. 1 of *Standard & Poor's Industry Surveys.* New York: Standard & Poor's, 1993.

Dye, Thomas R. *Politics in States and Communities.* 8th ed. Englewood Cliffs: Prentice-Hall, 1994.

Findlay, John M. *People of Chance: Gambling in American Society from Jamestown to Las Vegas.* New York: Oxford UP, 1986.

Sasuly, Richard. *Bookies and Bettors: Two Hundred Years of Gambling.* New York: Holt, 1982.

Philip K. Flynn

Game Shows can be traced back as far as one wishes, to spelling bees, or Socrates interrogating the Sophists, or the Sphinx asking enigmatic riddles, but in their recognizably contemporary form, they began on the radio in the mid-1920s with such question-and-answer programs as *The Pop Question Game* and *The Brunswick Hour Musical Memory Contest* (DeLong). The 1930s brought such radio Q&A shows as *Uncle Jim's Question Bee* and *Professor Quiz* (Graham). By the 1940s, quiz and game shows represented about 25 percent of the programs on network radio (DeLong 89), and the Q&A radio format had reached a peak in popularity, commanding huge audiences with such favorites as *Pot o' Gold* (in which spinning a wheel of fortune produced big telephone giveaways for the lucky winners).

Many of the successful radio quiz shows from this era survived to reappear on television: *Dr. I.Q.* with silver dollars for prizes; *Information Please*, in which an expert panel tried to answer questions from listeners; *Quiz Kids*, featuring precocious question-answering children; *Truth or Consequences* (Ralph Edwards) and *People Are Funny* (Art Linkletter), with guests performing various light-hearted stunts; *Kollege of Musical Knowledge* (Kay Kyser) and *Stop the Music!* (Bert Parks), with questions based on a knowledge of music and the names of obscure pieces; *Ladies Be Seated* (Johnny Olson) and *Missus Goes a-Shopping* (John Reed King), which centered on the activities of consumers and featured the role of housewives; *Break the Bank* (Bud Collyer, John Reed King, Bert Parks) and *Take It or Leave It* (Garry Moore), which first introduced large cash prizes of over $1,000 (*Break*) and the double-or-nothing concept that made famous the phrase "The $64 Question" (*Take*).

The latter logic of huge rewards for the display of knowledge in high-stakes gambles characterized the smash hits that dominated the TV-quiz mania of the mid-to-late-1950s in such blockbuster prime-time financial extravaganzas as *The $64,000 Question* (Hal March, CBS, Tuesdays; see entry), *The $64,000 Challenge* (Sonny Fox, then Ralph Story, CBS, Sundays), *Twenty-One* (Jack Barry, NBC, Mondays; see entry), and *Tic Tac Dough* (Jack Barry, NBC, Thursdays; see entry), on which attractive, down-home, folksy contestants (policeman, housewife, cobbler, Marine, grandmother, minister, psychologist, salesman) displayed remarkable knowledge of esoteric topics (Shakespeare, the Bible, opera, cooking, baseball, jazz, boxing, theater). Cloistered in isolation booths (soundproofed and heated to produce sweating, shaking, and other symptoms of anguished intellectual effort), these contestants played for hitherto unimaginable sums of money that escalated, with the help of the beneficent sponsors (Revlon, Lorillard Tobacco, Geritol, Sominex), into the hundreds of thousands of dollars (for example, the top cash prize of $252,000 won by Teddy Nadler on *Challenge*). Perhaps inevitably, with these large cash prizes involved, corruption soon followed (see Stone and Yohn, *Prime Time and Misdemeanors*).

Even as the popular excitement over such charismatic quiz-show heroes as Charles Van Doren reached epic proportions (putting him on the cover of *Time*), rumors began to leak out concerning certain "controls" that had been employed to ensure the "entertainment" value of the big-money quiz programs—that some of the contestants had been pre-screened for what they did and did not know as a basis for preparing questions, had received hint-filled warm-ups to help them win, had been given instructions on how and when to lose, or had even been coached on what dramatic gestures and grimaces to use while "thinking" about their answers. After a disappointed contestant (Edward Hilgemeier) produced hard evidence of corruption on a show called *Dotto* (where another contestant had been given answers and had been foolish enough to write them down in a notebook purloined by Hilgemeier), a truly sore loser (Herbert Stempel) blew the whistle on the secret not only to his own success on *Twenty-One* but also to that of his massively popular opponent (Charles Van Doren). These revelations precipitated grand-jury inquiries, congressional hearings, FCC proceedings, scandal to the masterminds behind the rigged or fixed quiz shows (Dan Enright, Albert Freedman, Jack Barry), and humiliation to a few misguided "quizlings" caught with their hands in the cookie jar (Patty Duke, Xavier Cugat, Charles Van Doren). The scandal was the basis for the film *Quiz Show* (1994), directed by Robert Redford.

By 1959, the genre of high-stakes quiz-oriented giveaway bonanzas had reached its nadir. It had lost the kind of credibility on which it had depended as the basis for its national craze of popularity. An attempt to reintroduce an updated *$128,000 Question* in 1976—with larger prizes, improved question-guarding security, and first Mike Darrow but later Alex Trebek as host—lasted only a couple of seasons, and it remains to be seen whether the turn-of-the-20th-century revivals of the genre—*Who Wants to Be a Millionaire?*, *Twenty-One,* and *Greed* (see below) will endure. Fortunately for game-show fans, other formats stood waiting in the wings.

Specifically, various alternative types of game shows had emerged to provide formats as diverse as the minds of TV producers were capable of creating. For example, as developed with conspicuous success by Mark Goodson and Bill Todman, one format featured celebrity panelists trying to guess the answers to obscure secrets based on ambiguous clues. On *What's My Line* (1950-67), sponsored by Stopette spray deodorant, host John Daly led such panelists as Arlene Francis, Dorothy Kilgallen, Steve Allen, and Bennett Cerf toward the identification of a guest's occupation or mystery identity; the top prize for fooling the panelists was only $50; but Jefferson Graham in *Come on Down!* hints darkly that Kilgallen, who took her job very seriously, committed suicide after performing poorly on the show. On *I've Got a Secret* (1952-67), host Garry Moore's panel—consisting of people like Bess Myerson, Henry Morgan, Betsy Palmer, Faye Emerson, Jayne Meadows, Steve Allen, and Bill Cullen—tried to solve some intriguing mystery about the activities or background of otherwise nondescript visitors (Louis Armstrong's trumpet teacher, etc.). On *To Tell the Truth* (1956-67)—emceed by Bud Collyer—panelists Kitty

Carlisle, Peggy Cass, Tom Poston, Orson Bean, and others tried to figure out which of three guests was telling the truth about his real identity (with the two impostors purposely lying and only the real person pledged to give honest answers). In all three cases, the amounts of money involved were modest or nonexistent, with principal interest centering on the witty remarks made by the clever members of the celebrity panels.

A second type of format involving minimum money but lots of slapstick, hijinks, and showmanship appeared on the first TV game—namely, *Truth or Consequences* (invented and hosted first by Ralph Edwards, then by Jack Bailey, Bob Barker, and others)—which made the transition to television in 1941 and which asked contestants who missed questions to perform inane penalty stunts such as pushing walnuts across the floor with their noses. Comparable horseplay also appeared on *People Are Funny* (with Art Linkletter as host) when guests got hit in the face by cream pies or sprayed with seltzer bottles. Further mayhem reached its pinnacle of entertaining absurdity on Goodson-Todman's *Beat the Clock* with Bud Collyer putting cooperative victims through stunts in which they were given a few seconds to perform such visually amusing feats as stuffing balloons under their clothing without breaking them or balancing a baton dangling from a fishing rod on the bottom of a salad bowl attached to a helmet worn on their heads.

Another popular format from the 1950s, immune to accusations of corruption by virtue of its charitable purpose, focused on giving away small fortunes to people shown to be impoverished and desperately in need of help. On *Queen for a Day* (hosted by Jack Bailey), needy women received rewards in proportion to the magnitude of the personal suffering demonstrated in their tales of woe and gauged by applause-metered audience responses to their "maudlin sob stories" awash in "bathos and bad taste." Building on this premise, *Strike It Rich* (hosted by Todd Russell, then Warren Hull) gave destitute guests a chance to tell their tear-jerking stories, to play games for prizes, and—if lucky—to receive remunerative calls on the *Heart Line* (as when Fritz Kreisler phoned a deprived but musically gifted boy violinist to give him a Stradivarius). Exploitative in the extreme, this format has ultimately bestowed its most merciful gift by disappearing from the airwaves.

Another genre of TV game show from the 1950s focused on the comedic potential of the quiz format and drew its hosts from the ranks of full-fledged humorists. *Two for the Money* capitalized on the jocular talents of Herb Shriner and, later, Sam Levenson. *Do You Trust Your Wife?* featured Edgar Bergen with Charlie McCarthy and later became *Who Do You Trust?* with Johnny Carson and Ed McMahon. But nonpareil among emceeing comedians, Groucho Marx presided over *You Bet Your Life* from 1950 until 1961, running comic circles around his less keen-witted and oft-bewildered contestants, though opinions differ on whether his quips were ad-libbed (Graham) or carefully scripted (DeLong). Whatever the degree of Groucho's improvisational genius, beyond doubt, the point of his show was merriment rather than questions or prizes.

Still another popular format presented contestants with tricky questions about their everyday lives or their experiences as consumers and rewarded them with generous but not gargantuan prizes if they guessed the right answers. Precursors to this format included *The Missus Goes a-Shopping*, *Ladies Be Seated*, and *Consumer's Quiz*. But foremost among these consumer-oriented game shows, beginning on TV in 1956, *The Price Is Right* (see entry; hosted originally by Bill Cullen with announcer Don Pardo) posed questions about the cost of merchandise and therefore appeared, on the surface, to reward contestants for being knowledgeable about ordinary shopping activities. In a sense, this Goodson-Todman invention became the prototype for many or even most game shows of the future.

Many of the game shows described thus far continued into the 1960s and 1970s, often with the substitutions of new hosts or slightly revised formats. These included: *What's My Line* (revived in 1968 with Wally Bruner and then Larry Blyden hosting), *I've Got a Secret* (returning in 1972 with Steve Allen or Bill Cullen as host), *To Tell the Truth* (lasting into the 1980s with first Joe Garagiola and later Robin Ward in charge), *Truth or Consequences* (with Jack Bailey, Bob Barker, Bob Hilton, and Larry Anderson successively at the helm), *Beat the Clock* (with Jack Narz in 1969, Gene Wood in 1972, and Monty Hall in 1979), *Queen for a Day* (with Dick Curtis in the 1969 version), and especially *The Price Is Right* (re-emerging in 1972 with Bob Barker hosting and first Johnny Olson or later Rod Roddy announcing).

As the TV game shows moved into the 1960s and beyond, varieties multiplied to satisfy audiences' apparently insatiable desire for Trivia Writ Large. Though a review of game-show history (DeLong; Graham; Schwartz et al.) makes it clear that most have failed after a season or two—indeed, in the cases of *Fun and Fortune*, *Let's Celebrate*, and *You're in the Picture* (Jackie Gleason), after only one broadcast—others have shown greater staying power. On *Let's Make a Deal*, Monty Hall won appreciative kisses from eager contestants by encouraging them to dress in absurd costumes (clown, bride, sheriff, chef, cowboy, farmer, nurse, chicken), forcing them to choose between equally uncertain alternatives such as having what is in a box (could be a $1,000 bill or something worthless) versus taking home what's behind a curtain (could be a $6,700 car or a "zonk"), and then torturing them by revealing with gleeful delight what they could have won but lost because they made the wrong choice and ended up with nothing instead of something valuable (a car or a room full of furniture). As described in his autobiographical *Game Show King*, Chuck Barris invented increasingly bizarre ways for otherwise unremarkable people to humiliate themselves in public by reporting their sexual preferences (*The Dating Game*, hosted by Jim Lange), by revealing marital secrets (*The Newlywed Game*, with emcee Bob Eubanks), or by performing ineptly with embarrassing results (*The Gong Show*, presided over by Barris himself). *Hollywood Squares* allowed free reign for the humor of nine celebrity panelists (Morey Amsterdam, Jonathan Winters, Wally Cox, George Gobel, Charo, Paul Lynde, and others) while Peter Marshall (later John David-

son) steered contestants through their attempts to complete a tic-tac-toe sequence by guessing whether the panelists' funny answers were right or wrong. Borrowing the focus of *Match Game* (Gene Rayburn), *Family Feud* (Richard Dawson, later Ray Combs, then Louie Anderson) pitted five-person teams related by birth or occupation against one another in guessing what *other people* have said in response to simple questions. Merv Griffin's *Jeopardy!* tested real knowledge in a variety of categories by having three contestants race to provide questions for the answers given by the emcee (Art Fleming, later Alex Trebek).

By the late 1980s, these and other game shows were watched by over 100 million viewers per week, but were designed to appeal primarily to people who happened to be at home, within reach of the television, and badly in need of entertainment during the daytime or early evening hours—in other words, mostly young mothers, unemployed housewives, and retired people. Studies have shown that such viewers tend to watch the game shows *while* doing their housework and, indeed, that the format of the shows nicely complements the repetitive but frequently interrupted nature of such household chores.

In contrast to this hegemonic reading of the game-show subtext, other critics have emphasized the possibility of resistant interpretations. For example, just as a viewer of *I Love Lucy* could read Lucy as a dizzy redhead *or* as a crafty manipulator who always gets her way with the incompetent Ricky, one could view TV game shows as paeans to the power of purchasing *or* as opportunities for the empowerment of women by demonstrating their competence as consumers and their expertise on prices or other aspects of shopping. The empirical evidence casts doubt on the demonstration of such expertise (Holbrook), but the resistant readings remain a potential if perverse possibility.

By the early 1990s, technological advances made it possible for home viewers to play along interactively by dialing a "900" number and using their telephone keypads to record answers to questions flashed on the TV screen. On *Shuffle* and *Boggle*, Wink Martindale pauses three times per half-hour to give audience members a chance to dial and then to compete with other members of the viewing audience by responding as fast as possible to questions (via numbers on the telephone dial).

By the year 2000, TV game shows had begun to experience a resurgence. The hugely popular *Who Wants to Be a Millionaire?* (with daytime talk-show host Regis Philbin as emcee) brought both the big-money genre back to TV, and the game show back to prime time; *Greed* (with Chuck Woolery) and a revival of *Twenty-One* (with Maury Povich) are in the same mold. A new version of *Hollywood Squares* features Whoopi Goldberg as the center square. There is even a Game Show Network available on cable for especially dedicated fans.

Without making value judgments on the intellectual or aesthetic merits of TV game shows, it seems fair to point out that no genre has received more contemptuous treatment from media critics. First, serious scholars have punished the game shows with a widespread and not-so-benign neglect.

Second, scholars and media-industry observers who have noted the role of game shows have generally branded them with such insulting descriptions as "the jackpot in bad taste," "a vast wasteland," "popcorn for the mind," and "a neon-lit orgy of product plugola, group hysteria and psychological mayhem" or "the thorniest, stoniest area in the wasteland of television...infested with the scorpion of greed," "one TV form for which no one but a network vp has a kind word," and "a shoddy gambling device." Indeed, with such rare exceptions as *Jeopardy!* or *Tic Tac Dough*, contestants generally demonstrate little real knowledge or ability beyond a talent for making lucky guesses or throwing round objects at targets.

TV game shows appeal strongly to the rags-to-riches ethos of the American Dream. In the World of Game Shows, ordinary people are plucked from the masses, given what Andy Warhol called their 15 minutes of fame, and potentially rewarded with emblems of what every self-respecting member of the Consumer Culture wants to have—symbols of the Good Life, symptoms of Success, signs of Prosperity. As a social institution, game shows help to teach us the Glories of Consumption. As an example of Marketing Writ Large, they reinforce in us the desire to possess things like hot tubs, home gyms, motor bikes, and popcorn poppers—things we surely don't need, but things we certainly do want.

Bibliography

Barris, Chuck. *The Game Show King: A Confession.* New York: Carroll & Graf, 1993.

DeLong, Thomas A. *Quiz Craze: America's Infatuation with Game Shows.* New York: Praeger, 1991.

Graham, Jefferson. *Come on Down!!! The TV Game Show Book.* New York: Abbeville, 1988.

Holbrook, Morris B. *Daytime Television Game Shows and The Celebration of Merchandise: The Price Is Right.* Bowling Green, OH: Bowling Green State U Popular P, 1993.

Schwartz, David, Steve Ryan, and Fred Wostbrock. *The Encyclopedia of TV Game Shows.* 3d ed. New York: Checkmark, 1999.

Stone, Joseph, and Tim Yohn. *Prime Time and Misdemeanors: Investigating the 1950s TV Quiz Scandal—a D.A.'s Account.* New Brunswick: Rutgers UP, 1992.

Morris B. Holbrook

Game-Show Hosts, Hostesses, and Producers. Through the years, many hosts of television game shows have appeared over 200 days per year for season after season and, by dint of stamina if not charm, have built a loyal following of devoted viewers—sometimes despite or even because of abrasive or bland television personalities. Such emcees are often assisted with an added element of sex appeal provided by glamorous hostesses who wear provocative clothing, fondle the merchandise on display as prizes, and maneuver the contestants into the proper positions by grabbing their elbows and steering them around the stage. Meanwhile, a remarkably small number of producers or production companies have accounted for most of the big game-show hits. Sometimes illustrating this paradoxical triumph of quantity over quality, the more illustrious of these game-show emcees, hostesses, and producers include the following (in alphabetical order).

Bob Barker of *Truth or Consequences* and *The Price Is Right* (see entry) is a distinguished-looking, grandfatherly, perennially Emmy-winning, quintessential emcee. A walking avatar of self-contradiction, Barker insults both his staff and his guests even while inspiring the latter to hug and kiss him. He dresses like an investment banker and shows the male-chauvinistic mentality of a dirty old man. On the other hand, he stood up for "grey rights" by renouncing hair dye in 1987 and, subsequently silver-haired, has also supported animal interests by incessantly encouraging viewers to have their pets spayed or neutered. On the lawsuit for alleged sexual harassment, which was dismissed in 1995, see Dian Parkinson (later).

Chuck Barris of *The Gong Show* is clever enough to have invented and/or produced *The Dating Game*, *The Newlywed Game*, and *The $1.98 Beauty Show*—those media masterpieces of voluntary self-embarrassment. For some reason, Barris chose to play the fool in his dopey role as emcee of *The Gong Show*, but his autobiographical book called *The Game Show King* reveals him to be intelligent, insightful, amusing, and perhaps a little shy. Apparently, he intended *Gong* and *$1.98* as parody or satire, making him perhaps the first postmodern game-show designer and host.

Jack Barry of *Twenty-One* and *The Joker's Wild* was disgraced with partner Dan Enright in the game-show scandals (see previous entry), but he came back to host and/or produce with Enright such sequels as *The Generation Gap*, *The Reel Game*, *The Joker's Wild*, and *The New Tic Tac Dough*. Barry died in 1984; Enright in 1992.

Johnny Carson, the late-night talk-show host, got his television start in the mid-1950s as emcee for *Earn Your Vacation* and later hosted *Who Do You Trust?*

After hosting *American Bandstand*, Dick Clark survived the payola scandals of the 1950s to reemerge as a pleasant, almost venerable emcee of *Pyramid* (*$10,000, $20,000, $25,000,... $100,000*) plus other game and talent shows. Clark liked to second-guess losing *Pyramid* teams by illustrating how they could have provided better clues. His latest game-show gig is on *Winning Lines*.

Once the radio voice of Superman, Bud Collyer of *Break the Bank*, *Beat the Clock*, and *To Tell the Truth* became a fun-loving and enthusiastic, but dignified game-show host. Collyer sometimes operated on automatic pilot and fell back on clichés, as when a female contestant said that her husband had recently died and he replied, "Isn't that nice?" He always wore a bow tie and ate six eggs for breakfast every morning. Collyer died in 1969.

Bill Cullen of the early *The Price Is Right*, *I've Got a Secret*, *To Tell the Truth*, *Name That Tune*, and many others was the warm, friendly, and merry "dean" of game-show hosts. Cullen put contestants at ease and later fit naturally into his role as a celebrity endorser before the days of Michael Jackson and Madonna. During his long career, he participated in over 20 game shows as host or regular celebrity panelist. More than most, Cullen vividly illustrates the postmodern paradox by which game-show celebrities achieve star status primarily by appearing on the game or talk shows that generate their celebrity. He died in 1990.

John Charles Daly, Jr. served as a newsman for CBS radio before becoming the long-running moderator of *What's My Line?* Daly displayed a suave, debonair, dry sense of humor and a patrician attitude, especially when bantering with the likes of Bennett Cerf, Dorothy Kilgallen, or Arlene Francis. He bantered thus for 17 years, while continuing his career in news broadcasting, until his death in 1991.

Originally a British comedian and actor on *Hogan's Heroes*, Richard Dawson of *Family Feud* established a tradition of kissing female contestants, apparently with the approval of a viewer write-in poll. He partially redeemed himself in the eyes of liberals by making anti-establishment comments about the Republican administration and Vietnam.

Ralph Edwards of *Truth or Consequences* and *This Is Your Life* masterminded *T or C*, which ran a record 37 years on radio and TV. *T or C* had a town in New Mexico named after it. There one also finds Ralph Edwards Park and Ralph Edwards Street.

Dan Enright: See Jack Barry (earlier).

Bob Eubanks of *The Newlywed Game* played the role of a mischievous but good-natured co-conspirator, who helped guests embarrass themselves and kept the proceedings a hair's breadth above the level that would get his show canned by the FCC. Eubanks once described game-show emcees as "happy guys with big teeth."

Along with co-producer Bill Todman, Mark Goodson was the creative force behind such game-show classics as *What's My Line?*, *I've Got a Secret*, *To Tell the Truth*, *Beat the Clock*, *The Price Is Right*, *Password*, *The Match Game*, *Concentration*, and *Family Feud*. Self-described as *not* a big fan of TV but a patron of the arts, Goodson continued his career as sole producer after Todman retired and passed away in 1974. At least one Goodson show has appeared on the air every weekday since 1946. He died in 1992.

Merv Griffin of *Play Your Hunch* and *Keep Talking* also served as the host of a long-lived talk show. Griffin produced *Jeopardy!* (inspired by a joking remark from his wife) and *Wheel of Fortune* (based on the old word game "Hangman"). Ultimately, he sold his production company to Coca-Cola in 1986 for $250 million.

On *Let's Make a Deal*, Monty Hall played the role of an imaginative wizard who propounded almost scam-like "deals" to confound confused contestants and to throw them into existentially anguishing dilemmas in which they must choose between two chancy opportunities for big payoffs. He created the so-called "Monty Hall Problem," involving a choice between two doors, one with a goat and the other with a car behind it. This problem poses questions for probability theory that continue to perplex world-class mathematicians.

Warren Hull of *Strike It Rich* always seemed well intentioned but sentimental or even sappy in presiding over the revelation of tear-jerking sob stories.

Dennis James of *Cash and Carry*, *The Price Is Right*, and *Name That Tune* hosted the first network TV game show (*C&C*) on the DuMont Network in 1946. He continued as an emcee and announcer until his death in 1997.

After his lascivious beginnings on *The Dating Game* and *The Newlywed Game*, Jim Lange mellowed into a truly courteous, bespectacled emcee on *Name That Tune*. Lange has encouraged contestants even when they are hopelessly behind: "You didn't get it, but you were so close; anyway, the dental career is going great, hunh?"

Though viewed as "egghead" or "highbrow," Allen Ludden of *College Bowl* appeared on *Password*. He married Betty White a year after she appeared as a panelist on *Password*; see Betty White (later). Ludden died in 1981.

Wink Martindale of *Gambit*, *Tic Tac Dough*, *Shuffle*, *Trivial Pursuit*, and *Boggle* is a busy emcee and producer who compares himself to Santa Claus, wears loud ties plus a bad toupee, rushes at a furious pace, and cheerfully warns contestants that they are about to lose if they do not start getting more correct answers.

As the inspired comedic host of *You Bet Your Life*, Groucho Marx added new dimensions to the concept of inimitability, though opinions differ on the extent to which his lines were improvised as opposed to scripted. Marx died in 1977.

Polite, congenial, and relaxed, Garry Moore of *I've Got a Secret* seldom made waves—in short, a perfect gentleman from the 1950s. He died in 1993.

Dian Parkinson of *The Price Is Right* is a former Miss USA and was arguably the most overtly sexy of the female models who display the merchandise and fondle the prizes on *PIR* and comparable giveaway shows. Accompanied by other such "Barker's Beauties" as Holly Hallstrom and Janice Pennington on *PIR*, Parkinson fulfilled a destiny charted by Roxanne Rosedale on *Beat the Clock*, Bess Myerson on *The Big Payoff*, and Carol Merrill on *Let's Make a Deal*; see also Vanna White (later). Especially talented at displaying beds and mattresses while wearing low-cut negligees, Parkinson pushed sexiness to the point of self-satire before appearing in cover-story pictorials for *Playboy*, making a much-publicized pornographic videotape, and leaving *PIR* for greener pastures (which have included a lawsuit, dismissed in 1995, against *PIR*'s Bob Barker for alleged sexual harassment).

Once a singer, Bert Parks of *Break the Bank* got his start in the days of radio quiz shows where he was ubiquitous. Parks took *Break the Bank* to television in 1948 with Bud Collyer. His singing talent came in handy on *Stop the Music*, *Hold That Note*, and *Yours for a Song*. Parks also served as a smiling, upbeat, high-energy host for such short-lived shows as *Party Line*, *Balance Your Budget*, *Double or Nothing*, *Two in Love*, *Giant Step*, *Bid 'N' Buy*, *Masquerade Party*, and *County Fair*. His conspicuous role as singing emcee of the Miss America Pageant ended in 1976; he died in 1992.

Regis Philbin, of *Who Wants to Be a Millionaire?*, longtime co-host of the daytime talk show *Live with Regis and Kathie Lee*, asks repeatedly "Is that your final answer?" to contestants sitting in the "hot seat."

The yang to Bob Barker's yin, David Ruprecht of *Supermarket Sweep* is pleasant, polite, energetic, enthusiastic, young, informal, endearing. Ruprecht treats guests with respect and shares with apparent sincerity in their elation when they win the modest prizes available on this low-budget show.

Pat Sajak of *Wheel of Fortune* is a cheerful and cute foil for Vanna White (see later). Sajak has joked that "blandness just comes naturally to me," but he failed when he tried to trade on his loyal following by hosting a late-night talk show on CBS.

After inventing *The Price Is Right, To Tell the Truth,* and *Password*—produced by Goodson-Todman (see earlier)—Bob Stewart developed and produced *Pyramid*, based on the *Password* premise of one contestant's guessing words from clues given by another under time pressure.

Ray Combs of *Family Feud* resembled a somewhat shorter, rounder Pat Sajak. Good-humored but sporting a mountainous pompadour, he continued Richard Dawson's disconcerting habits by touching attractive female contestants and making comments about their physical charms. Dawson returned as host in 1994; Combs died in 1996.

Bill Todman, who died in 1974, was half of the inspired Goodson-Todman team (see earlier).

As the first game-show host to sport the dark, mustachioed look, Alex Trebek of *Classic Concentration* and *Jeopardy!* is serious, studious, and strict in asking the tough questions or rigidly following such *Jeopardy!* rules as beginning one's response with "What is...?"

In a profession dominated by men, the perennial celebrity panelist Betty White finally got to hostess her own short-lived game show *Just Men* in 1983 and promptly won an Emmy.

Possibly the best-known mannikin in America, Vanna White is famous for looking beautiful while uncovering letters on *Wheel of Fortune*. Her advice for those wishing to enter her profession? "Know your alphabet." See Pat Sajak (earlier).

A former country singer, Chuck Woolery of *Wheel of Fortune, Love Connection, Scrabble,* and *Greed* applies smooth, square-jawed charm to coaxing revealing details of first dates from the in-love and love-lorn guests on *Love Connection*. Woolery was man enough to admit on *Scrabble* that (like at least one bewildered viewer) he did not understand why "BACKS" was an answer to the clue "Sometimes they go out bowling."

Bibliography

Holms, John Pynchon. *The TV Game Show Almanac.* Radnor: Chilton, 1995.

Ryan, Steve, David Schwartz, and Fred Wostbrock. *The Encyclopedia of TV Game Shows.* New York: Facts on File, 1995.

Morris B. Holbrook

Gangster Film. Since the first feature-length gangster film, *Redemption*, was directed in 1915 by Raoul Walsh, a major figure in the development of the genre, the gangster film clearly existed at least in embryonic form in the silent era. But the genre came into its own at the beginning of the sound era. In part, this reflects the realities of the social environment. By the beginning of the 1930s, the gangster was a fact of American life. Al Capone was certainly one of the best-known Americans of the period and was nothing less than a folk hero to some.

According to the view of most film historians, three films established the definitive lineaments of the genre: Mervyn LeRoy's *Little Caesar* (1930), William Wellman's *The Public Enemy* (1931), and Howard Hawks's *Scarface* (1932). The gangsters portrayed respectively in these films by Edward G. Robinson, James Cagney, and Paul Muni embody alternatives to the moral givens of society at large, permitting the audience a vicarious suspension of moral codes. They are also doomed, and the inevitability of their downfall reaffirms the social order.

They seemed too heroic, in fact, in the eyes of those moralists for whom the gangster film was nothing more than a glorification of the criminal. And this reaction was at least a factor in the compromise of the mid-1930s. Films like William Keighley's *"G" Men* (1935, starring Cagney) and *Bullets or Ballots* (1936, starring Robinson) offered audiences many of the ingredients of the gangster films, including the stars, but offered in place of the gangster hero a protagonist who is on the side of the law, although placed by circumstances in an ambiguous relationship with the underworld.

A new, softer version of the gangster film emerged as the decade drew to a close. Michael Curtiz's *Angels with Dirty Faces* (1938) owes much of its considerable impact to a direct appeal, as powerful as it is hokey, to the emotions of the audience. Rocky Sullivan, the gangster hero played by James Cagney, feigns cowardice to discourage a group of tough city kids from following his criminal example. Cagney is also a good bad guy in Raoul Walsh's *The Roaring Twenties* (1939), a self-declared memory film that pays elegiac tribute to the age of prohibition, while assuring its audience that the sort of gangsterism the film depicts lies safely in the past. Humphrey Bogart, the bad bad guy of the two films just mentioned, and of a number of others as well, achieved stardom in Walsh's *High Sierra* (1941), playing a desperado who comes to a measure of self-understanding as he reaches the end of the trail.

As the gangster film evolved in the postwar years, a fruitful merger with film noir occurred. The moral ambiguity that characterized noir—the sense of a world, not merely a few individuals, gone wrong—lent an incisive new accent to films like Robert Siodmak's *The Killers* (1946), *Cry of the City* (1948), and *Criss Cross* (1949). The interest in location shooting that had arisen during the war, when materials and personnel required for the construction of sets were in short supply, generated the semi-documentary gangster film, exemplified by Henry Hathaway's *Kiss of Death* (1947). The ingredients of the classic gangster film and the enduring star power of James Cagney, now combined with the popular Freudianism of the 1940s, produced the mother-ridden gangster hero of Raoul Walsh's *White Heat* (1949). Cagney's Cody Jarrett is so powerfully realized in this film that many viewers perceive Edmond O'Brien's undercover cop as the villain of the piece; the gangster film was still not the genre for simple moral tales.

As the restrictive codes of earlier periods dissolved, gangster films turned to the exploration, and perhaps the exploitation, of an open amorality. Tales of dishonor among thieves, like John Boorman's *Point Blank* (1967) and Don Siegel's *Charley Varrick* (1973), abandon all pretense to absolutes, while acknowledging gradations between the organization men and the individualists who assume the role of protagonist. The formal and thematic boldness of Arthur Penn's *Bonnie and Clyde* (1967), focusing on the rural variant of the gangster, generated so many ambiguities that it reduced critics to a state of intellectual disarray.

Attention to organized crime as organized, rather than as the extended shadow of a few ruthless men, began to emerge as a dominant theme. *The Enforcer* (1951, credited to Bretaigne Windust but completed by Raoul Walsh) projects a chilling image of a force whose destructive presence is felt everywhere, while *Murder, Inc.* (1960, directed by Burt Balaban and Stuart Rosenberg) purports to tell the story of the syndicate, a word popularized by the Kefauver hearings of the early 1950s. The Mafia film achieves its apotheosis in Francis Ford Coppola's *Godfather* series (1972, 1974, 1990; see entry below), which compellingly merges a vivid family saga, a telling image of the immigrant experience, a trenchant study of left-handed upward mobility, and a provocative probe of the role of crime in American society.

If the films of Coppola and Leone encouraged viewers to recognize the epic dimensions of the gangster story, Martin Scorsese's *GoodFellas* (1990) provided an ironic counterstatement. While directly acknowledging the lure of gangsterism, that concern of the moralists of the 1930s, Scorsese presents Mafia chieftains and their underlings as ethical buffoons, men whose brutality reflects their lack of imagination and vision.

A drift toward nihilism can be detected in the gangster film of the 1990s. There is only one cop who has not himself descended to the criminal level by the end of Abel Ferrara's *King of New York* (1990); and his climactic insight that the issue is between himself and the gangster—that their conflict has no vital connection to the needs of society—isolates cop and criminal in a struggle as meaningless as it is bloody. Quentin Tarantino's *Reservoir Dogs* (1992) isolates its characters even further. Even though one of them is an undercover cop, they hardly exist beyond the immediate caper. The names by which we know them are the absurd noms de guerre (Mr. Blue, Mr. Pink) assigned by the leader of the operation. The violence of the film is chilling in itself and all the more so because in aid of no discernible moral vision. Tarantino used a similar approach for *Pulp Fiction* (1994).

For some, this nihilism may suggest that the genre is approaching exhaustion. Others may see in it a continued power to reflect the darker, frequently denied, realities of the surrounding society. Still others will regard it as nothing more than a fascinating new range of thematic possibilities.

Bibliography

Clarens, Carlos. *Crime Movies: From Griffith to the Godfather and Beyond.* New York: Norton, 1980.

McArthur, Colin. *Underworld, U.S.A.* New York: Viking, 1972.

McCarty, John. *Hollywood Gangland: The Movies' Love Affair with the Mob.* New York: St. Martin's, 1993.

Rosow, Eugene. *Born to Lose: The Gangster Film in America.* New York: Oxford UP, 1978.

Shadoian, Jack. *Dreamers and Dead Ends: The American Gangster/Crime Film.* Cambridge: MIT, 1977.

W. P. Kenney

Garbo, Greta (1905-1990), one of filmland's enigmas, having made 24 films in the United States for MGM, retired from movie-making and public life at the height of her stardom in 1941 at age 36. In terms of stories and supporting casts, many of her films are second or even third rate, but they are redeemed by her luminous screen presence and her fine acting ability. She is considered by many to have been the most beautiful actress in the history of film, and this, no doubt, was what drew people (women as much as men) to the theaters.

Garbo was born Greta Gustafsson in Stockholm. The Gustafssons lived almost in poverty in two shabby rooms for decades. When she was 14, her father, to whom she had been close, died, and the family members all had to get jobs. Greta worked as a barber's assistant and then as a model in a department store, but she also dreamt of becoming a great film star.

She was discovered by Erik A. Petschler in 1922 and appeared in his film, *Peter the Tramp*. Greta then received a scholarship to the Academy of the Royal Dramatic Theatre in Stockholm. While there, the prominent Swedish director Mauritz Stiller took an interest in her progress and she became his protégée. She changed her name to Garbo, which she and Stiller thought had greater international appeal, and starred in his picture *The Saga of Gosta Berling* (1924), when she was just 18. Then she starred in *Joyless Street* for Georg W. Pabst (1925). That same year, Louis B. Mayer was trolling Europe for talented directors; he saw Stiller's film and was anxious to sign him for MGM, but Stiller would not go without Garbo. In two years' time, however, it was Garbo and not Stiller who became hot property at MGM. Stiller's defeated return to Sweden devastated Garbo, as she had relied upon his strong artistic vision and personal advocacy. She was never to see her mentor again.

In the latter 1920s (still the silent era) her most famous films were *Flesh and the Devil* (1927), *Wild Orchids* (1928), and *The Kiss* (1929), all of which presented Garbo as the tragic fallen woman. William Daniels, the photographer for these and most of her films, liked to use the extreme close-up—normally too revealing a shot—to fill the screen with her face, and it transfixed audiences. Garbo became a huge star.

The films that provided Garbo's greatest roles were made near the end of her career: *Anna Karenina* (1935), *Camille* (1937), and *Ninotchka* (1939). Though the direction was stilted and she was surrounded by a wooden supporting cast, the title role in *Anna Karenina* fitted her talent and dignity. *Camille* was based on the life of Marie Duplessis (1824-1846), a legendary French beauty who, though born in poverty, had become the greatest of all French courtesans. It is considered by many commentators to have been Garbo's greatest dramatic role. For *Ninotchka*, which cheerfully satirized communism *and* democracy, Billy Wilder wrote most of the witty screenplay and Ernst Lubitsch, who specialized in sparkling, elegant comedies, directed. In it Garbo got a comedic turn as a coldly abstract Soviet emissary sent to Paris to censure three other emissaries suspected of having been seduced by capitalism. All of the supporting cast were superb, including Melvyn Douglas, who was hilarious as Garbo's determined suitor. Everything about the movie—the players, the brilliant dialogue, the photography—was top notch, and it is now widely accepted as a masterpiece.

In her retirement, Garbo led a quiet life of simplicity and leisure. But as time passed, the Garbo mystique increased rather than declined. Garbo became nearly obsessed with hiding from the media: she used false names, wore disguising clothes, and avoided public places. She also had friendships of some importance with the composer Leopold Stokowski, Gayelord Hauser (a health expert), and George Schlee (a financier), all of whom were commanding, visionary men as Stiller had been. Mostly, however, she was unattached, and over the years she appears to have wanted more and more time alone.

Bibliography

Paris, Barry. *Garbo: A Biography.* New York: Knopf, 1994.
Payne, Robert. *The Great Garbo.* New York: Praeger, 1976.
Sands, Frederick, and Sven Browman, *The Divine Garbo.* New York: Grosset & Dunlap, 1979.
Walker, Alexander. *Garbo: A Portrait.* New York: Macmillan, 1980.

April D. Wilson

Gardner, Erle Stanley (1889-1970), one of the most prolific and entertaining American mystery writers, delighted countless readers with Perry Mason novels and a wide range of other works. Born in Massachusetts in 1889, Gardner moved with his family to California when he was ten. After a failed attempt at college, Gardner became a professional boxer and eventually "read for the law" in various lawyers' offices. Admitted to the bar at the age of 21, he proudly claimed to be the only California attorney to have been sworn in with two black eyes from a boxing match. In the early 1920s, Gardner began writing for the pulps. When one of his stories appeared in *Black Mask*, his writing career took off. Some of his early work appeared under his own name, but Gardner also used various pen names, including Kyle Corning, A. A. Fair, Robert Parr, Dane Regley, and Les Tillray.

Gardner introduced fictional defense attorney Perry Mason (see entry) in *The Case of the Velvet Claws* (1933). A remarkably successful series ensued, and Gardner eventually authored 82 Mason novels. The Mason books are both formulaic and inventive. In each, Mason takes on difficult defense cases, and his combination of skilled sleuthing and keen lawyering brings about the vindication of his client. He is aided by a core of repeat support characters including private secretary Della Street, investigator Paul Drake, and seemingly formidable District Attorney Hamilton Burger, who is always bested by Mason. Mason's cases involve serpentine plots and subtle clues, and deftly meld the standard whodunit and the courtroom mystery.

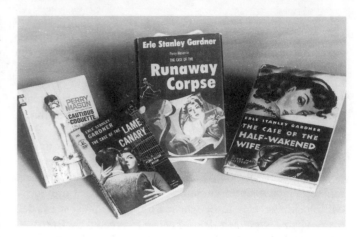

Photo courtesy of Popular Culture Library, Bowling Green State University, Bowling Green, OH.

Gardner's work, however, was not limited to Perry Mason. In an average year he would write two Mason novels; another novel as A. A. Fair, featuring tough, penny-pinching detective Bertha Cool and her cantankerous assistant Donald Lam; and various nonfiction works such as travel books about his beloved Mexico; as well as articles for magazines like *Life* and *Popular Science*.

Toward the end of his life Gardner kept a tight rein on the CBS series featuring Raymond Burr as Perry Mason, one of the most enduring television dramas ever. He also made "The Court of Last Resort" his pet undertaking. The "Court" consisted of Gardner and other criminal justice experts who reviewed the evidence that had been used to convict defendants claiming to have been falsely accused. Their deliberations appeared as a popular feature in *Argosy* and later were dramatized on television.

In the final year of his life, though he was suffering from cancer, Gardner remained productive. He dictated *The Case of the Fabulous Fake*, his final Perry Mason novel, along with a last A. A. Fair book and a nonfiction piece. He died having left behind a substantial literary legacy.

Bibliography

Hughes, Dorothy B. *Erle Stanley Gardner: The Case of the Real Perry Mason.* New York: Morrow, 1978.
Johnston, Alva. *The Case of Erle Stanley Gardner.* New York: Morrow, 1947.

David Ray Papke

See also

Golden Age of Detective Fiction
Legal Mysteries

Garfunkel, Art (1941-), a popular singer and actor, is best known as half of the folk-rock duo Simon and Garfunkel. Garfunkel has also had a secondary career as an independent singer and film actor.

Born in Queens, New York, Art Garfunkel met Paul Simon (see entry) during their sixth grade at Public School 163. The pair began to sing rock 'n' roll, making their first recording in a Coney Island booth for 25 cents. Subsequently, they enjoyed one chart success as Tom and Jerry with "Hey Schoolgirl," which reached #54 in 1956, and made an appearance on Dick Clark's *American Bandstand.* After going on to college, they briefly gave up performing rock as a duo, although each continued to sing and record individually. When they resumed their partnership, it was to sing Simon's own, folk-oriented compositions, doing so with some success in New York clubs and colleges. Late in their sophomore year, they were auditioned by Tom Wilson of CBS, which led to their debut album, *Wednesday Morning, 3 A.M.* (1964).

"Sounds of Silence" (1965) became their first major hit and elevated them instantly into the elite of a newly emerging genre, folk rock (see entry). Quickly established as peers to Bob Dylan and the Byrds, Simon and Garfunkel went on to produce some of the most popular and influential music of the late sixties. Their major hits included "Homeward Bound," "I Am a Rock," "Mrs. Robinson," and "Bridge over Troubled Water." Following the 1970 success of this last song and its eponymous album, the pair split up and, while continuing to be friends and occasionally working together—most notably for a 1981 benefit concert in Central Park—have essentially pursued separate careers.

Simon and Garfunkel's success had a three-part foundation: Simon's haunting, richly imagistic songs with their themes of lyricized alienation; Garfunkel's effortlessly lyrical, pitch-perfect tenor voice; and a shared passion for perfect craftsmanship. Although the latter concern made the recording of their albums a long and elaborate process, it resulted in records unmatched in their blend of lyrical power, vocal harmony, and opulent production.

Despite their successful pairing, each partner had strong and distinct individual goals, which led to their 1970 breakup. Garfunkel had an interest in acting and, having previously worked with director Mike Nichols while recording the soundtrack for *The Graduate* (1968), was cast for two Nichols films: *Catch-22* (1969) and *Carnal Knowledge* (1971). Critically acclaimed for this work, he would go on to give his best performance a decade later in Nicholas Roeg's *Bad Timing* (1981). His subsequent films, including *Good to Go* (1986) and *Boxing Helena* (1993), have been less successful.

Garfunkel has also continued to record regularly, covering standards and working with a variety of songwriters. His greatest success came during the seventies when, working primarily with Jimmy Webb, he produced albums such as *Angel Clare* (1973), *Watermark* (1975), and *Breakaway* (1977). He enjoyed a #1 U.S. hit with "All I Know" in 1973, but was more popular in Britain, where his "Bright Eyes," the theme song to the film *Watership Down,* and "I Only Have Eyes for You" both topped the charts. While he has continued to work regularly, he has neither had nor perhaps even sought the success of his earlier career, focusing instead upon his wide-ranging intellectual interests, a walk across America, and life with his second wife and their son born in 1990.

Bibliography

Romanowski, Patricia, and Holly-George Warren. *The New Rolling Stone Encyclopedia of Rock & Roll.* New York: Fireside, 1995.

Stambler, Irwin. *The Encyclopedia of Pop, Rock, and Soul.* New York: St. Martin's, 1989.

Iain Crawford

Garland, Judy (1922-1969), born Frances Gumm, the child of vaudeville performers, is widely considered one of the greatest entertainers of the 20th century. She is known for her work both in film (mostly MGM musicals) and in live concerts, which drew largely from her earlier film career. What is perhaps most notable about Garland is the wide range of her talent; she was known not only for her voice but also for her dramatic acting and her gift for comedy.

The extent of Garland's popularity and talent was and is apparent in the reception of her films and concerts. Her concerts sold out, and a recording of one of her best performances, *Judy at Carnegie Hall* (1961), received an unprecedented five Grammy Awards in 1962 and was the first double album to sell over a million copies. Garland films such as *Love Finds Andy Hardy* (1938), *Babes in Arms* (1939), *Babes on Broadway* (1942), *Meet Me in St. Louis* (1944), *The Harvey Girls* (1946), *Easter Parade* (1948), and *The Pirate* (1948) were and continue to be well loved by many, and Garland was nominated for best actress and best supporting actress for *A Star Is Born* (1953) and *Judgment at Nuremberg* (1961), respectively.

One of Garland's best and most popular films is *The Wizard of Oz* (1939), which was re-released in the theaters in the decades subsequent to its original release and which still airs regularly on television. In *Where the Girls Are*, media critic Susan Douglas writes that *Oz* addresses an important gap in film history—a gap that even her four-year-old daughter noticed: "Mommy, there should be more movies with girls." Douglas writes that *Oz*, which has "gripped [her] daughter's imagination" more than any other movie, is the only film—classic or contemporary—that she is happy to have her daughter embrace: "Finally, here's a *girl* who has an adventure and doesn't get married at the end.... Throughout the movie, [Garland's Dorothy] is caring, thoughtful, nurturing, and empathetic, but she's also adventuresome, determined, and courageous." Indeed, Garland received a special Academy Award for the best juvenile performance for her portrayal of Dorothy. Also notable is that even though *Oz* is generally regarded as a children's film, and even though Garland was only 17 when it was filmed, the film enjoys a devoted following among adults as well as children.

Talent, however, is not the only quality associated with Garland; she also has an image of having been one of Hollywood's most troubled stars, known in the later part of her career for her erratic behavior, drug and alcohol abuse, failed marriages, and suicide attempts. Although some saw this behavior as "spoiled," Garland was and is seen by many others as a tragic illustration of the perils of stardom. Her death in 1969 of a drug overdose certainly contributed to this image. It is striking that this image of her unhappiness—probably even more so than her talent—has characterized the memory of Garland. Despite her daughter Liza Minnelli's insistence that Garland was not nearly as unhappy as people believed, her image as the quintessential troubled star persists.

She was also an important figure for a more specific group: the gay community. Although several stars, such as Mae West, Bette Davis, Marilyn Monroe, Carmen Miranda, and Marlene Dietrich, are also popular in this community, it is Garland who is widely considered to be the "diva-of-gay-males'-divas." Film scholar Richard Dyer gives an excellent account of the Garland-gay male connection; he points out that many gay men see Garland's emotions as being intense and authentic and as somehow representing the experience of being gay in a homophobic society. Garland's image, Dyer explains, reflects several important aspects of gay culture: androgyny as in *Everybody Sing* (1938), *Summer Stock* (1950), and *A Star Is Born*; camp, especially in *Ziegfeld Follies* (1946) and *The Pirate*; and "a special relationship to ordinariness" in *The Wizard of Oz*, *Babes in Arms*, *Babes on Broadway*, *Little Nelly Kelly* (1940), *The Clock* (1945), and *Meet Me in St. Louis*.

Bibliography

Douglas, Susan. *Where the Girls Are*. New York: Times, 1994.

Dyer, Richard. *Heavenly Bodies: Film Stars and Society*. New York: St. Martin's, 1986.

Finch, Christopher. *Rainbow: The Stormy Life of Judy Garland*. New York: Grosset & Dunlap, 1975.

Fricke, John. *Judy Garland: World's Greatest Entertainer*. New York: Holt, 1992.

Judy Garland: The Secret Life of an American Legend. New York: Hyperion, 1993.

Kathy Evans

Gates, William "Bill" (1955-), born in Seattle, where he continues to live and rule Microsoft, Inc., is the living revenge of the nerds. He is reputed to be the first self-made billionaire and by 1995 had been declared by *Forbes* magazine "The World's Richest Man." So important to the world of the personal computer is Microsoft that most major publications feel compelled to profile him periodically. There is a growing journalistic industry devoted to Microsoft seismology, attempting to interpret the tremors induced by the heavy steps of the software behemoth.

A boyish, bespectacled lad, Gates stopped out of high school to be a software consultant at TRW. He later dropped out of Harvard to become a freelance software writer. Microsoft was formed in 1975 when he was a mere 20. The BASIC language interpreter he had written for the Altair microcomputer—in his dorm at Harvard—became the conceptual platform for several other BASIC programming languages needed for the growing population of Apples, Commodores, and Radio Shacks.

Gates's next grand opportunity was an invitation in 1980 to write the operating system for IBM's PC. Retaining the right to market the resulting MS-DOS independently of the contract with IBM, Microsoft sold millions of copies to the industry that adopted the IBM standard. His company also developed extremely popular software such as Works (integrated), Word (word processing), Excel (spreadsheet)

and Flight Simulator (game). Gates's next dream was Windows, a graphic interface that employed the icon and mouse—just as did the Apple Macintosh. Windows established itself as the dominant interface in the 1990s, compelling independent software developers to accommodate it and compete with Microsoft itself. Windows has had notorious bugs and balkiness. Millions of computer users have quested frenetically for hardware that has the capacity to make it run smoothly. Deficiencies of memory, storage capacity, screen resolution, and processor speed have driven the hardware industry in a way that produces obsolescence for products in very short periods of market history.

Microsoft, because of its size and dominance, is perpetually charged with intellectual theft and monopolistic practices. It is routinely sued by competitors and investigated by the U.S. Federal Trade Commission. In 2000, Gates and the Justice Department are trying to negotiate a settlement after a judge ruled Microsoft a monopoly. The judge ruled that Microsoft must be broken into two companies. Microsoft is appealing that decision.

Gates's personal career stands as one of the most remarkable within a remarkable industry. In an industry that has produced notable dropouts, bankruptcies, and even suicides, Gates has steadily maintained his discipline and vision, conquering a worldwide industry in a way unmatched by any other entrepreneur in history.

Bibliography

Moody, F. "Mr. Software." *New York Times Magazine* 25 Aug. 1991: 26ff.

Seabrook, John. "E-mail from Bill." *New Yorker* 10 Jan. 1994: 48-52.

Wallace, James. *Hard Drive: Bill Gates and the Making of the Microsoft Empire*. New York: Wiley, 1992.

John S. Lawrence

Gay and Lesbian Mysteries developed as a sub-category of mystery and detective fiction along with the emergence of more liberal sexual attitudes in the 1960s. The first gay detective was George Baxt's Pharaoh Love, an African-American New York City homicide detective and the protagonist of a series of comic novels from the late 1960s. Pharaoh Love, however, offers readers few insights into the problems faced by either blacks or gays and has not enjoyed widespread popularity.

A significantly more influential and important gay detective is Joseph Hansen's Dave Brandstetter. In a 12-novel series, from *Fadeout* (1970) to *A Country of Old Men* (1991), Hansen invents the gay hero. In contrast to the common pejorative stereotype of the male homosexual, Brandstetter, an insurance investigator, is conventionally masculine, brave, monogamous, caring, intelligent, and extremely skilled at his work.

Following the acceptance of Brandstetter, a sizable number of other gay detectives began appearing in the 1980s and 1990s. Hansen's heir-apparent seems to be Michael Nava, author of a series of novels featuring Henry Rios, a Mexican-American lawyer, starting with *The Little Death* (1986). Like Hansen, Nava is more concerned with probing the character of his protagonist and using his fiction as a vehicle to treat social issues than merely providing an entertaining mystery. Henry Rios must deal with discrimination because he is openly gay, prejudice because he is Mexican American, and complications caused by his lover's being HIV positive.

Other writers take different approaches. Some treat their characters in the traditional hard-boiled manner. For example, Richard Stevenson writes about Albany private investigator Donald Strachey and his lover, an assistant to a New York State legislator. Like other private eyes in the tough-guy tradition, Strachey speaks comic one-liners, but the novels stress issues such as euthanasia, police indifference to crimes against gays, and the outing of closeted homosexuals. Steve Johnson's Doug Orlando, an openly gay New York City police detective, confronts departmental bigotry and religious intolerance. Some writers employ a more comic tone. Tony Fennelly writes about New Orleans antique dealer Matthew Sinclair, who becomes involved in crimes, and Grant Michaels about Boston hairdresser Stan Kraychik, who constantly encounters dead bodies.

Lesbian detective fiction has grown in production and stature in recent years. Among lesbian detectives, two of the earliest and most influential are Barbara Wilson's Pam Nilsen and Katherine V. Forrest's Kate Delafield. Nilsen, part of a printing collective in Seattle, investigates crimes involving friends or coworkers. Three novels in the series, especially *Sisters of the Road* (1986), deal with feminist as well as lesbian issues. Delafield, a Los Angeles homicide detective, must cope with the death of her former lover, sexist attitudes on the police force, and becoming more open about her sexual preference.

Among more recent lesbian detectives are Sandra Scoppettone's Lauren Laurano, a NYC private eye; Ellen Hart's Jane Lawless, a Minneapolis restaurant owner; and Nikki Baker's Virginia Kelly, an African-American financial analyst in Chicago. M. F. Beal, Lauren Wright Douglas, Sara Dreher, Vicki P. McConnell, Rebecca O'Rourke, and Mary Wings have also created memorable fictions featuring lesbian investigators.

Gay identity and the mystery genre constitute a natural pairing, since both involve probing closeted lives and hidden truths. Not surprisingly, such mysteries have garnered a passionate following among homosexual audiences, but they have also won over a broad general readership, suggesting their permanent significance to the canon of detective fiction.

Bibliography

Baker, Robert A., and Michael T. Nietzel. *Private Eyes: One Hundred and One Knights*. Bowling Green, OH: Bowling Green State U Popular P, 1985.

Gorman, Ed, et al., eds. *The Fine Art of Murder*. New York: Galahad, 1993.

Klein, Kathleen Gregory, ed. *Great Women Mystery Writers*. Westport: Greenwood, 1994.

Slide, Anthony. *Gay and Lesbian Characters and Themes in Mystery Novels*. Jefferson: McFarland, 1993.

David C. Wallace

See also
Ethnic Mysteries
Feminist Detective Fiction

Gay and Lesbian Radio began in the 1960s, when several Pacifica stations began airing poetry and discussion shows related to the problems of gay men. College stations and public radio stations followed in the 1970s. One notable example was *Gay Dreams* on WXPN-FM, Philadelphia, a National Public Radio affiliate.

Gay and lesbian radio programming made several strides in 1992. In Boston, where one of the nation's first gay rights laws was passed, Modern Rock WFNX-FM debuted a 3 1/2 hour radio magazine show *One in Ten*. This show features a mix of news, entertainment, music, and call-in discussions on Monday nights. *HIV Talk Radio*, a 30-minute show that appeals to both the mainstream and gay/lesbian listeners, began airing at Adult-Alternative WNUA-FM, Chicago. Other commercial radio stations were not as fortunate in 1992. WFTL-AM aired *Queer Talk*, a 3-hour call-in talk show and WVCG-AM aired a news magazine show called *AlterNet*. Both shows aired for only 9 months in Miami.

The first attempt to market a 24-hour all-gay and lesbian format in America came in November 1992, when the K-GAY Radio Network began broadcasting from Denver, CO. Its programming was uplinked 24 hours a day to satellite dishes in North America, Canada, and the Caribbean. The network was promoted as the first daily media vehicle for the gay and lesbian community in North America. KXRE-AM, Colorado Springs, was its first network affiliate, but the station went bankrupt (due to financial problems unrelated to K-GAY). By June 1993, K-GAY's programming was test marketed in Austin, TX, on a local cable radio station. City officials, the local media, and a number of listeners supported the station, but the cable experiment failed after a few months. Almost one year after it started, K-GAY Radio Network, with only a few sponsors and a mostly volunteer staff, failed as well. K-GAY aired *A Way Out, Ground Zero, Speak Out America*, and other talk-oriented shows. In addition, K-GAY played adult alternative music, including college chart, adult contemporary, dance, acoustical, and gay and lesbian artists.

Only a handful of commercial radio stations broadcast local gay and lesbian programs. Nationally syndicated shows, such as *A Way Out*, have filled the void. In May 1994, another local talk show, *Lesbigay Radio*, debuted on WCBR-FM, North Chicago.

Bibliography

Boehlert, Eric. "Gay Radio Comes Out Commercially; New Shows Give Voice to Ignored Demo." *Billboard* 104 (50): 64, 66.

Herndon, John. "KGAY Offers an Alternative." *Austin American-Statesman* 1 July 1993: 17.

Nidetz, Steve. "'Lesbigay Radio' Is Breaking New Talk-Show Ground." *Chicago Tribune* 22 May 1994: 7 (Arts Plus).

Summer, Bob. "A Niche Market Comes of Age." *Publishers Weekly* 239, no. 29 (1992): 36-40.

Phylis Johnson

Gaye, Marvin (1939-1984), R&B musician, was one of Motown's greatest successes. His versatile tenor voice and his songwriting have inspired soul singers for decades. Crediting Ray Charles and James Brown for his own inspiration, Gaye in turn influenced such artists as Stevie Wonder and Michael Jackson.

Marvin Gaye was born in Washington, DC, and began his singing career at the age of five. While accompanying his father, a preacher, to a Kentucky religious conference, he sang "Journey to the Sky," and his father decided to have Marvin, Jr., continue to travel with him. Later, Gaye learned piano and drums, played organ in his father's church, and began singing in curbside doo-wop groups. While in high school, he won a talent show and attracted the notice of Harvey Fuqua, who later became a record producer with his own label and then Motown. After graduation, his father convinced him to enlist in the U.S. Air Force, which postponed his musical pursuits until he was discharged on psychological grounds. In 1957, after singing with popular Washington vocalists the Rainbows, Gaye formed his own group, the Marquees, who recorded "Wyatt Earp" on the OKeh label with the help of Bo Diddley, whom they backed until 1958.

In 1960 Fuqua brought Gaye to Detroit, and Gaye signed with Motown as a session drummer in 1961. He played for Smokey Robinson and the Miracles for two years while also making his own solo singles. His first album, *The Soulful Moods of Marvin Gaye*, was unsuccessful, but a single, "Stubborn Kind of Fellow" with back-up vocals by Martha Reeves and the Vandellas, became a national Top 50 R&B hit late in 1962. Over the next few years, Gaye enjoyed success with hits such as 1963's "Can I Get a Witness," 1964's "How Sweet It Is," and in 1965 his first two R&B No. 1 hits, "I'll Be Doggone" and "Ain't That Peculiar," both of which were also Top 10 hits on the pop chart.

Gaye was teamed in several duos, first in 1964 with Mary Wells for an album, *Together*, until she left Motown later in the year. He recorded with Kim Weston the moderately successful "What Good Am I without You" in 1964, "It Takes Two" in 1966, and the 1967 album *Take Two*, before she left for MGM. Then began his three-year pairing and friendship with Tammi Terrell, with whom he sang hits "Ain't No Mountain High Enough," "Your Precious Love," "Ain't Nothing Like the Real Thing," and "You're All I Need to Get By."

Gaye's most successful recording was the 1968 solo smash, "I Heard It through the Grapevine." Although already successful for Gladys Knight in 1967, the song now became a British hit too and proved one of Motown's best-selling singles, with Gaye's version considered classic R&B. The song was re-popularized in the 1983 film *The Big Chill* and in late 1980s advertisements for California raisins.

Upon Terrell's death in March of 1970, Marvin quit touring and was scarcely seen in the studio. He reemerged in 1971 with the release of "What's Going On," an introspective and socially conscious song, inspired partly by his brother Frankie's Vietnam experience. Followup hits "Mercy Mercy Me (The Ecology)" and "Inner City Blues" also showed a new philosophical side to Gaye. The resulting album *What's Going On* was a breakthrough for Motown.

In 1972, he wrote the soundtrack for the movie *Trouble Man* and in 1973 he released the sexually celebratory *Let's Get It On* album with its hit title track. Soon thereafter, *Diana and Marvin* was released—an album of duets with Diana Ross. Gaye's first stage appearance in almost five years at California's Oakdale Coliseum produced a critically acclaimed live album.

After a difficult divorce, the commercial failure of his double-album *Here, My Dear* (1978), and financial struggles with the IRS, Gaye lived in exile in Belgium. He recorded *In Our Lifetime* (1981) and *Midnight Love* (1982) with its hit "Sexual Healing." Gaye returned to performing in 1983, and returned to the U.S. when his mother needed surgery. He moved into his parents' house, where tension built between him and his alcoholic father. On April 1, 1984, the day before his 45th birthday, a dispute resulted in Gaye being shot twice and killed by Marvin, Sr., who later proved the slaying was an act of self-defense.

Gaye not only contributed significantly to Motown's success, but also helped shape the business in the 1970s when his independent attitude in producing and arranging his own albums led to Motown's allowing its stars more artistic freedom. Still, it is for his music that he has been dubbed the "number one purveyor of soul."

Bibliography

Davis, Sharon. *I Heard It through the Grapevine: Marvin Gaye, The Biography.* Edinburgh: Mainstream, 1991.

Ritz, David. *Divided Soul: The Life of Marvin Gaye.* New York: Da Capo, 1991.

Aimee Bernd
Michael Delahoyde

GE College Bowl (1953-1970), "the varsity sport of the mind," was a fixture on Sunday afternoons for more than a decade. Compared to other quiz shows, there was something refreshing about clean-cut college students competing for scholarships—for their alma maters, not themselves (totaling over a million dollars). Only *College Bowl* escaped untainted from the game show scandals of the 1950s and '60s (see Game Shows); it was for a time the only quiz program on network television.

The show, sponsored by *Good Housekeeping*, premiered on NBC radio as *College Quiz Bowl*, first using a three-way hookup to New York, later originating from the campus of one of the competitors. The moderator was Allen Ludden, a small-town disc jockey with an M.A. in English. In that first game, Northwestern University defeated Columbia. Six years later, Northwestern again was the victor, over Brown University, when the show debuted on CBS television, January 4, 1959, beginning an 11-year run as *GE College Bowl* and winning an Emmy and a Peabody Award along the way.

College Bowl continued through the turbulent 1960s with the only significant change coming when Allen Ludden, now a household name and face, left *College Bowl* for *Password* and was replaced by media professor Robert Earle, who provided an even more scholarly image. In the mid-

1960s, however, NBC induced GE to move *College Bowl* to that network and about the same time the pressures began that eventually led to its demise. Three factors combined to make 1969-70 *College Bowl*'s final season. Given prominence in the media was General Electric's petulant response to student anti-war protests against the giant corporation. Some executives felt that GE had given a great deal to higher education, and if these attacks were the thanks it got, there was no reason to continue. A second, more difficult problem—for new sponsors could have been found—was the growing popularity of professional football. *College Bowl* had enjoyed a long stay on what once was the quiet, nearly cerebral, programming of Sunday afternoon. When pro football boomed, *College Bowl* was often preempted, rescheduled at the convenience of the sports gods, and even moved to late Saturday afternoon. The third—and unpublished—reason was a falling-out between Don Reid and his partners in the ownership of the show. The differences among them proved irreconcilable and Reid let the show die rather than end up in court.

College Bowl, the game, lay dormant for about six years, but the company, College Bowl, Inc., endured under the leadership of Don Reid's son, Richard. It provided questions and resources for its High School Bowl game, nationally syndicated under many different names. The hiatus ended when College Bowl turned the organizing of the competition over to ACUI (The Association of College Unions International). Since 1977, College Bowl has become the flagship of ACUI's regional and national tournaments, contested in everything from billiards to backgammon.

Bibliography

Holms, John Pynchon. *The TV Game Show Almanac.* Radnor: Chilton, 1995.

Schwartz, David, Steve Ryan, and Fred Wostbrock. *The Encyclopedia of TV Game Shows.* 2d ed. New York: Facts on File, 1995.

Daniel J. Fuller

General Hospital (1963-), known as the "action" soap, is also, surprisingly, the strongest in friendships. It has fooled fans many times by coming back from the dead. The creation of Frank and Doris Hursley, the "first" *General Hospital (GH)* revolved around Dr. Steve Hardy (the late John Beradino) and Nurse Jessie Brewer (the late Emily McLaughlin). Friendship is unusual as a central dramatic relationship, and Steve and Jessie's lasted almost thirty years, until McLaughlin's death. It lasted through Steve's troubles with Audrey, eventually his wife (Rachel Ames, 1964-), and through Jessie's greater problems from philandering Dr. Phil Brewer (Roy Thinnes, 1963-66). Central in these early years, and still part of "Port Charles, NY," were lawyer Lee Baldwin (Peter Hansen, 1965-) and his son Scotty. In 1972, *GH* was No. 1 in the ratings; then, tired, it fell, until in 1977, cancellation was broached. The show was saved mainly by the introduction of Leslie Charleson as Monica Webber (now Quartermaine) and Kim Shriner as Scott Baldwin, and his pairing with Genie Francis as Laura Vining, lost daughter of the popular Dr. Leslie Williams (Denise Alexander). Even better, Douglas Marland was brought on as headwriter, and Gloria Monty as executive producer.

With the help of technologically adept directors, Monty tightened and speeded up the show. Marland created steamy stories in which Laura, at 15, murdered her middle-aged lover and her mother took the blame; Monica romanced Dr. Rick Webber (Chris Robinson) during a suspenseful hospital quarantine; and, to come between Laura and Scotty, he introduced a dynamic villainess, Bobbie Spencer (Jacklyn Zeman)—and her brother Luke (Anthony Geary). In a year, *GH* came from almost the cellar to No. 3 in the ratings.

Marland wanted to go slower than Monty in getting Luke and Laura together, and left. With Pat Fulken Smith as headwriter, the romance grew into a controversial rape (1979). Eventually, however, because of the popularity of the anti-hero Luke, and Geary and Francis's chemistry, the romance took over the show, and the country. When Luke and Laura married in 1981, Elizabeth Taylor was a guest and *Newsweek* put them on the cover.

Monty also took *GH* into fantastic action; e.g., Luke saving the world from freezing. In the early '80s, Francis and Geary went, and new adventurers came, but the focus, amid all the action, and the romantic melodrama as well, shows off the friendships. After a breakup, or a break in the action, comes a cup-of-tea or a buddy scene. Friendship, not romance, is what turns a *GH* character from outsider or villain into one who belongs.

But the action seems as necessary as the friendships. There was an attempt to bring Tony Geary back as Luke's gentle cousin Bill, but ratings plummeted and soon Bill was adventuring, and then he died in the returned Luke's arms (Geary playing both roles, of course).

In 1993, Claire Labine, co-creator of *Ryan's Hope* and six-time Emmy winner, became *GH*'s headwriter under producer Wendy Riche, and *GH* became a soap opera rich in what a veteran New York soap columnist called "womansense."

Bibliography

Groves, Seli. *The Ultimate Soap Opera Guide.* Detroit: Visible Ink, 1995.

Nochimson, Martha. *No End to Her: Soap Opera and the Female Subject.* Berkeley: U of California P, 1992.

Williams, Carol Trayn. *"It's Time for My Story": Soap Operas, Sources, Structure, and Response.* Westport: Praeger, 1992.

Carol Traynor Williams

Generations (1989-1991), a short-lived half-hour NBC soap opera, replaced *Search for Tomorrow* (see Soap Opera). Although other soap operas had incorporated African-American characters into racial storylines, *Generations* was daytime television's first fully integrated soap opera, the first to include from its inception a black family as part of its core. Created by Sally Sussman (who had previously written for William Bell's *The Young and the Restless*), *Generations* followed the lives of two Chicago families—the Whitmores and the Marshalls—who had been linked together for several generations. It was NBC's first network-owned soap opera, produced by NBC Productions. NBC heavily promoted *Generations* with their "Black and White in Color" campaign, which was designed, in part, to attract a significant proportion of the black audience, but more importantly because the network wanted *Generations* to hit the broadest possible market. Strong resistance from local affiliates led NBC to give stations the option of airing *Generations* at 12:00 or 12:30 Eastern time. Because of this flexibility, *Generations* managed to gather nearly complete clearance of U.S. television markets, thereby equaling the reach of other NBC soap operas.

The majority of the cast of *Generations* had no major soap opera credentials; however, when ratings lagged, the cast became peppered with familiar faces from daytime drama, including Debbie Morgan and Robert Gentry (both from *All My Children*), as well as film actors, including Richard Roundtree (*Shaft*) and Martin Hewitt (*Endless Love*).

Generations moved swiftly in the telling of its often provocative, well-thought-out stories. But one of the apparent problems that *Generations* had in winning a large and loyal audience was in its failure to truly integrate the black and the white experience. It was as though the stories of the blacks and whites ran on parallel tracks. From the beginning, the soap's mission was developed, for example, to exclude interracial romance and interracial marriage, perhaps a mistake in hindsight. Despite its efforts to remedy this with the introduction of Peter Whitmore, hinting at interracial complications, the soap was never truly given the chance to find itself. *Generations* was consistently rated at the bottom of the daytime serial contenders, and after less than two years of airtime, NBC announced its cancellation.

Bibliography

Copeland, Mary Ann. *Soap Opera History*. Lincolnwood: BDD Promotional (Mallard), 1991.

Barbara J. Irwin
Mary Cassata

Gershwin, George (Jacob) (1898-1937), born in Brooklyn, NY, of Russian descent, was a composer, songwriter, and pianist who transcended the bounds of popular music to become one of America's most beloved and influential musicians. Gershwin's interest in music began when, at the age of nine, he heard Anton Rubinstein's Melody in F. His family later purchased a piano for his older brother, Ira (see next entry), which George appropriated for his own use.

In 1914, he began work as a song plugger in Tin Pan Alley and a piano demonstrator for the Jerome H. Remick publishing firm. The song "When You Want 'Em, You Can't Have 'Em, When You Have 'Em, You Don't Want 'Em," published in 1916, was Gershwin's first composing success and was a minor hit for Sophie Tucker. Also in 1916, "Making of a Girl" was included in the Broadway musical *The Passing Show of 1916*. Gershwin then was commissioned to write music for a Broadway revue, *Half-Past Eight*, and also for a Broadway music comedy, *La La Lucille*. Gershwin's first major success was "Swanee," a song popularized by Al Jolson in 1919, in *Sinbad*. Gershwin then moved on to write songs for the *George White Scandals*, an annual revue, a position which he held until 1924. During this period, such songs as "I'll Build a Stairway to Paradise," "Do It Again," and "Somebody Loves Me" became popular songs of the time.

In addition to composing popular songs for revues and musical comedies, Gershwin worked on incorporating the styles and techniques of Tin Pan Alley into serious musical forms. His first attempt was a one-act tragic jazz opera entitled *Blue Monday*, which was cut from the *George White Scandals of 1922* after its opening night because of its melancholy nature. Because of this one performance, however, Paul Whiteman, the conductor of the *Scandals* orchestra, later commissioned Gershwin to write an extended piece for an all-American musical concert in Aeolian Hall. The result was *Rhapsody in Blue*, which premiered on Lincoln's birthday, February 12, 1924. The concert was conducted by Paul Whiteman, with Gershwin at the piano. Also in 1924, with his brother Ira Gershwin, who wrote the lyrics for many of George's songs, George Gershwin wrote his first musical, *Lady Be Good*, which starred Fred and Adele Astaire. Following *Lady*, the Gershwins wrote a series of musical comedies which included *Oh Kay* (1926), *Funny Face* (1927), *Rosalie* (1928), *Strike Up the Band* (1930), *Girl Crazy* (1930), and *Of Thee I Sing* (1931), which became the first musical comedy ever to win the Pulitzer Prize. These years of musical comedy were interspersed with additional serious music ventures, which included Concerto in F (1925), *An American in Paris* (1928), and *Second Rhapsody* (1930), in which Gershwin returned to the classical form of *Rhapsody in Blue*.

Gershwin's 1935 folk opera, *Porgy and Bess* (see entry), based on DuBose Heyward's novel, was his last major work and became one of his most performed works. The opera contained such hit songs as "Summertime," "I Got Plenty o' Nuttin," "Bess, You Is My Woman Now," "It Ain't Necessarily So," and "I Loves You Porgy." Following the completion of *Porgy and Bess*, the Gershwin brothers went to Hollywood in 1936, where they wrote songs for films which included "They All Laughed," "Let's Call the Whole Thing Off," and "They Can't Take That Away from Me," for *Shall We Dance* (1937), and "Nice Work If You Can Get It" and "A Foggy Day" for *A Damsel in Distress* (1937). In 1937, while working on *The Goldwyn Follies*, George Gershwin became ill, suffering from cystic degeneration of a tumor which could not be removed. He died on the operating table in California, at the age of 39.

Bibliography

Cross, Milton, and David Ewen. "George Gershwin." *The Milton Cross New Encyclopedia of the Great Composers and Their Music*. Garden City, NY: Doubleday, 1962.

Ganzl, Kurt. "George Gershwin." *The Encyclopedia of the Musical Theatre*. New York: Macmillan, 1994.

Gilbert, Steve. *The Music of Gershwin*. New Haven: Yale UP, 1995.

Hardy, Phil, and Dave Laing. "George Gershwin." *The Faber Companion to 20th-Century Popular Music*. Boston: Faber & Faber, 1990.

Rimler, Walter. *A Gershwin Companion: A Critical Inventory and Discography, 1916-1984*. Ann Arbor: Popular Culture, 1991.

Lynnea Chapman King

Gershwin, Ira (Israel) (1896-1983), one-half of one of America's leading musical teams, was born into a Jewish family of very modest means in New York City. Two years later, his brother Jacob/George was born. There were two younger children, Arthur and Frances. Though indifferent to formal schooling, Israel/Ira early on developed an enduring interest in a wide range of world literature, along with a talent for shaping limericks and other poetics. He and George were inseparably close despite marked differences in their personalities and life styles. Together they were responsible for some of America's finest popular music.

Ira Gershwin started his career by writing poetry for magazines, but all the while he was scanning the patterns and styles of successful song lyricists. In 1918, he collaborated with his brother on ragtime tunes, using the pseudonym "Arthur Francis." By 1924, however, Ira Gershwin had come into his own as a recognized lyric writer, associating with George for many songs, as well as in other musical projects. For the preparation of Gershwin's *Porgy and Bess*, Ira assisted librettist DuBose Hayward with some of the song lyrics for that show. After George's tragic illness and death in 1937, Ira Gershwin continued on with a highly successful career, contributing the poetic words for the melodies of such leading song composers as Harold Arlen, Vernon Duke, Johnny Green, Jerome Kern, Burton Lane, Arthur Schwartz, Harry Warren, Kurt Weill, and Vincent Youmans.

It was with Kurt Weill that Ira Gershwin truly launched his post-George career, writing the lyrics for the 1941 Broadway show *Lady in the Dark*. His lyrics fit the then-advanced ideas of that production, both as to content and style of stage presentation. Gershwin and Weill collaborated on other projects until Weill's death in 1950. Then there were numerous song lyrics for Hollywood films, memorably for the melodies of Jerome Kern for *Cover Girl* (including "Long Ago, and Far Away"), and for those by Harold Arlen for *A Star Is Born* (including "The Man That Got Away").

Over the years, Ira assumed custody of George Gershwin's artistic legacy, and concentrated on arrangements and revivals, performances and recordings, of such major works as *Rhapsody in Blue*, *An American in Paris*, and, of course, *Porgy and Bess* (see entry), which eventually reached the stage of the Metropolitan Opera House in New York City. He established the Gershwin Archive, combining his own lifelong collections of manuscripts, art works, and literature with all the holdings of his brother George. Clearly, they remained inseparable to the end, when Ira Gershwin died in Beverly Hills at the age of 85.

Bibliography

Kimball, Robert, ed. *The Complete Lyrics of Ira Gershwin*. New York: Knopf, 1993.

Rosenberg, Deena. *Fascinating Rhythm: The Collaboration of George and Ira Gershwin*. New York: Dutton, 1991.

Irene Heskes

Gettysburg (1993), a critically acclaimed docudrama depicting the three-day Civil War battle of July 1863, was originally intended as a miniseries to air on the Turner Network TNT. Translating well to the big screen, however, this powerful four-hour epic was first released to select theaters in late autumn of 1993. Shortly after its subsequent release on video, TNT began airing *Gettysburg* in late June and early July of 1994. According to residents of Gettysburg, PA, tourism noticeably increased in their already popular town once *Gettysburg* was released.

Based on Michael Shaara's Pulitzer Prize-winning *Killer Angels*, *Gettysburg* was a project that screenwriter and director Ronald Maxwell struggled for ten years to realize. Combining historical facts and fictive elements, *Gettysburg* is a realistic re-creation, filmed on and around the actual battle sites, of the unlikely events leading up to, and including, the bloodiest battle in American history. The film, structured chronologically, commences on June 30, 1863, the day prior to battle, and proceeds through some key engagements over the next three days, from both the Union and Confederate vantage points.

Gettysburg's adherence to historical detail, via the assistance of historical advisors Brian Pohonk and Pat Falci, gives the viewer a viable sense of how the Civil War was fought: its tactics, weaponry, flags, marching bands, uniforms, miscalculations, questionable victories and devastating defeats. Yet the story would be incomplete without the moments of human intimacy, the conflicting ideologies, the courage, honor, glory, compassion, and tragedy captured by the filmmaker.

Bibliography

Alleva, Richard. "Maxwell's Gettysburg." *Commonweal* 19 Nov. 1993.

Gettysburg. Acorn Publications.

Holden, Stephen. "When War Was All Glory, Bands and Death." *New York Times* 8 Oct. 1993.

The Making of Gettysburg. TNT Productions.

Therese Schramm

Ghost Stories have beguiled the popular psyche since the beginnings of culture. They have appeared anecdotally in literature since ancient Greece, and surfaced more vividly in the gothic novels of the late 18th century. But it was in the 19th century that the ghost story emerged as a fictional genre. Most ghost stories feature a spirit, benign or sinister, that haunts or appears to haunt a person or location.

Washington Irving popularized the conceit of the ghost as avenger in "The Legend of Sleepy Hollow" (1820); later, the influence of Edgar Allan Poe's tales in the 1830s and '40s established the short story as the chief mode through which ghosts would appear in fiction. Although few of Poe's tales may be classified as ghost stories per se, works such as "Ligeia" (1838) introduce fundamental features of the ghost story as it developed in the 19th century. Poe's creation of the unreliable first-person narrator as a means of conveying mysterious events influenced writers of classic ghost stories, such as Henry James. Later in the century, Ambrose Bierce (see entry) wrote macabre stories blending supernatural horror, sardonic humor, and surprise turns of plot.

A key practitioner of the genre in the 19th century was the English author Sheridan Le Fanu (1814-73). His tales, collected in *A Glass Darkly* (1872), exemplify some of the classic elements of the ghost story, particularly "Green Tea." This tale of a clergyman, Jennings, haunted by a red-eyed monkey visible only to himself, reflects the rich psychological dimensions of spectral fiction and epitomizes a central motif of the genre, the attention to an individual chosen to become the victim of a haunting. The same motif dominates in the works of other ghost story writers, including Henry James, M. R. James, and Edith Wharton. Le Fanu also introduces in "Green Tea" the figure of the psychic detective, a recurrent character in later works by Algernon Blackwood and William Hope Hodgson.

Many consider M[ontague] R[hodes] James (1862-1936) the master of ghost fiction in English. His stories first appeared in 1904 and have never been out of print. A distinguished British scholar, James wrote ghost stories in his spare time, mainly to entertain friends. He regarded Le Fanu as his master and helped bring about a resurgence in Le Fanu's popularity; however, James's own work is now widely seen as the classic prototype of the genre.

The ghost story is a powerful vehicle for commentary on the human world, as we know from Shakespeare's enduring versions of the genre, *Hamlet* and *Macbeth*, and from more contemporary practitioners, such as Daphne du Maurier, Stephen King, R. L. Stine, and others (see individual entries).

Bibliography

Briggs, Julia. *Night Visitors: The Rise and Fall of the English Ghost Story*. London: Faber, 1977.
Cox, Michael. *M. R. James: An Informal Portrait*. Oxford: Oxford UP, 1983.

Cyndy Hendershot
Anthony Oldknow

Ghostbusters (1984) became the highest grossing film of the year ($220 million) and the highest grossing comedy to that time. Dan Aykroyd hatched the original idea as a vehicle for himself and John Belushi. With the latter's death in 1982 (see entry), the film underwent major changes, including the collaboration of Harold Ramis and Aykroyd on the final script for Columbia.

The movie's plot is fairly simple. Three psychologists of the paranormal, Peter Venkman (Bill Murray), Raymond Stantz (Dan Aykroyd), and Egon Spengler (Harold Ramis), open their own business, called "Ghostbusters." Soon, they find the entire New York metropolitan area has an infestation of ghosts, a precursor to Judgment Day, and the safety of the world relies on their abilities and high-tech equipment. The film's wonderfully creative conclusion not only includes the one-liners of Bill Murray—who, upon seeing his possessed girlfriend (Sigourney Weaver) mutate into a canine guardian of Zool, turns to his colleagues and dryly comments: "OK, so she's a dog"—but also some magical and fantastic special effects, created by Richard Edlund, including an earthquake

outside of a Central Park high-rise and a 112-and-a-half-foot marshmallow man.

Although the original film did not offer many tie-in deals, the sequel, *Ghostbusters II*, filmed five years later with the original cast, offered a wide variety of opportunities for companies and consumers to ride on the *Ghostbusters* product bandwagon.

Bibliography

Magiera, Mercy, and Kate Fitzgerald. "*Ghostbusters* Spooktacular." *Advertising Age* 15 May 1989.
Schickel, Richard. "Exercise for Exorcists." 11 June 1984.
Shay, Don, ed. *Making Ghostbusters: The Screenplay*. New York: Zoetrope, 1985.

William C. Boles

Gibson, Bob (1931-1996), a folk musician, strongly influenced by the folk artistry of Pete Seeger, became one of the more influential folk-song collectors and performers of America. He centered his search in the Ohio Valley, tracing the development of songs, the way they became unconsciously modified from generation to generation. He also became interested in the music of the Caribbean, and before settling into full-time performing, he traveled through the Bahamas, collecting calypso music and work songs. He came back armed with priceless gems, such as "The Banana Song."

In addition to his banjo, which he mastered, Bob took up the 12-string guitar, which at that time was relatively uncommon. His performance on that instrument was near virtuoso quality. Many performers, such as Roger McGuinn, Gordon Lightfoot, John Denver, and Josh White, Jr., credit his playing with their decision to play the 12-string guitar.

In the late fifties and early sixties, Bob was everywhere there was folk music. He was a winner on Arthur Godfrey's Talent Scouts and subsequently appeared frequently on Godfrey's radio and TV shows. He appeared on television's *Hootenanny* often and performed in a one-man show at Carnegie Hall. He had a hit record, *Marching to Pretoria*. He wrote the hit songs "Abilene" and "Well, Well, Well," and his album made with Hamilton (then Bob) Camp, *Gibson & Camp at the Gate of Horn*, became a benchmark for folk music. (Even the Beatles are said to have been influenced by that album.)

Unfortunately, as the folk revival hit its peak, Gibson dropped out of sight for a while, due to his problems with drugs. When he did return in 1969, the trend had shifted enough that such huge fame never reached him again. He continued to be extremely productive, doing most of his work in Chicago. He wrote, produced, and co-starred in the play *The Courtship of Carl Sandburg* and co-wrote musical shows such as *Chicago: Living along the Green River*, with several Chicago writers, and *The Women in My Life*, with singer-songwriter Michael Smith. He wrote songs for children and performed as "Uncle Bob," touring the country sponsored by Osh-Kosh B'Gosh. This even developed into an Emmy-nominated television show called *Flying Whales and Peacock Tales*. He performed for a while with Tom Paxton and Anne Hills in a trio called Best of Friends.

His greatest love, though, always remained relating to his audiences. In his career, which spanned 40 years, he recorded 20 albums, wrote 150 songs, and influenced countless major entertainers. His life and career were cut short by the rare disease Progressive Supranuclear Palsy. He died in Portland, OR, at the age of 64, but through the ripple effects caused by his work, he is still influencing those who may not even be aware of the source for their music.

Bibliography

Baez, Joan. *And a Voice to Sing With*. New York: Simon & Schuster, 1987.

Erlewine, Michael, ed. *All Music Guide*. San Francisco: Miller Freeman, 1994.

Okun, Milton. *Something to Sing About*. London: Macmillan, 1968.

Sandburg, Carl. *The American Songbag*. New York: Harocurt Brace Jovanovich, 1927.

Carole Bender

Gilbert and Sullivan. Certainly a day does not pass without one of Gilbert and Sullivan's operettas being performed live somewhere in the United States. In addition, several of their better known collaborations have been made into motion pictures and television specials. While most adaptations are more or less faithful to the original source, Gilbert's lyrical prose and Sullivan's buoyant tunes are also the raw material for everything from commercial jingles to parodies and academic treatises.

Though they both had lengthy, productive and successful careers separately, William Schwenck Gilbert (1836-1911) and Arthur Seymour Sullivan (1842-1900) are forever linked because of their 14 comic operetta collaborations from 1871 to 1896. Gilbert was an erstwhile lawyer who turned to light verse and dramatic pieces to increase his income, producing over 50 dramatic works in addition to short stories and a continuing series of comic verse which he also illustrated, collectively titled *The Bab Ballads*. Most of Gilbert's work is nonsensical, a close relation to the works of Lewis Carroll and Edward Lear. Gilbert's guiding principle was the land of "Topsy-turvydom," a location where the "natural" social orders were reversed or generally scrambled. To this precept Gilbert added streaks of light satire and often blistering parody of the institutions and figures of his day. Gilbert published widely during the 1860s, and by the time of his first association with Sullivan he had earned a reputation as dramatist, critic, and humorist of high rank. Gilbert continued this prodigious output throughout the years of his partnership with Sullivan, and beyond.

Arthur Sullivan's special musical talent was recognized at an early age; he wrote incidental music for a production of *The Tempest* at the age of 19. In 1866, when Gilbert had his first big stage success with *Dulcamara*, Sullivan's *In Memoriam* overture solidified his standing as a composer. In fact, Sullivan came to see his work in light opera as a distraction from his more "serious" works. Sullivan did manage to define himself as the serious composer of his nation and generation with a variety of musical pieces as diverse as the songs "Onward Christian Soldiers" and "The Lost Chord,"

several dance music compositions, various oratorios, and even the grand opera *Ivanhoe*.

Gilbert and Sullivan first collaborated under the auspices of theatrical promoter John Holingshead, creating *Thespis,* a work spoofing the gods of Olympus. The piece was not entirely a hit, running for only 64 performances. All but fragments of the music has been lost, though Sullivan reused parts for later musical pieces.

It was not until their next joint effort, *Trial by Jury* (1875), that the duo hit their stride, mixing keen parody and dramatic nonsense with engaging melody, and strong orchestral structure. They soon became the darlings of Victorian society, and their popularity soared with such works as *H.M.S. Pinafore* (1878), *The Pirates of Penzance* (1879), and *The Mikado* (1885).

Musical comedy theater in the United States had consisted largely of costumed burlesques and tab show parody with occasional home-grown operetta, such as the works of Victor Herbert. The works of Gilbert and Sullivan crossed the ocean with ease, and many productions of their works were touring nationally and regionally, with the duo receiving no royalties due to copyright difficulties between Britain and the United States. The incredible success of *H.M.S. Pinafore* prompted numerous unsanctioned versions in an attempt to thwart such doings; for their next effort they premiered *The Pirates of Penzance* in the U.S.—to no avail; it, too, was "pirated."

The duo were so successful that a theater and theatrical company were founded solely for producing their works, the company being in continuous operation until its disbanding in 1982. By that time, Gilbert and Sullivan and their works had long since become cultural institutions.

Sullivan's aspirations for serious music and Gilbert's desire to reinvent theater eventually caused several rifts between them, not just artistically but personally and on a business level as well. They pursued outside projects and a break eventually occurred in 1889. It took four years to blow over, and the pair reunited in 1893 for *Utopia, Limited*. It is one of Gilbert's most vitriolic works, attacking British society foibles and presuppositions with a harshness he usually avoided. He even attacks earlier Gilbert and Sullivan works, possibly upset with having to compete with his younger self. Sullivan cleverly quotes from his earlier works, as usual fusing the music with the libretto in a fashion that enhances it beyond mere support. But not surprisingly, biting the hands that fed them did not result in a success, and with one more joint effort, *The Grand Duke* (1896), the partnership finally ended.

Bibliography

Asimov, Isaac. *Asimov's Annotated Gilbert & Sullivan*. New York: Doubleday, 1988.

Hayter, Charles. *Gilbert and Sullivan*. New York: St. Martin's, 1987.

Benjamin K. Urish

Gillespie, John Birks "Dizzy" (1917-1993), whose name is synonymous with jazz, was born in Cheraw, SC, and died in New York City. His accomplishments in jazz are enormous.

He was a pioneer in the founding of bebop along with Charlie Parker, whom he called "the other half of my soul." He worked with Afro-Cuban musicians to establish Latin jazz. He was a composer of note, an outstanding soloist, a leader of big bands and small combos, an entertainer to equal Louis Armstrong, and a serious teacher. Above all, he was a genuine human being, a true original.

Gillespie came from a large family. At the age of 12, he began playing trombone, then at age 15 the trumpet. Gillespie was largely a self-taught trumpet player, although he won a scholarship for his music. However, in 1935, he left college and at the age of 18 he went to Philadelphia and played in various bands, including those of Teddy Hill and Cab Calloway. Then he went to Harlem to play in various clubs; at this time he recorded a solo on Lionel Hampton's recording of "Hot Mallets" which many claim to be the first recorded bop solo.

In 1940, Gillespie met Charlie Parker and discovered that they both were working along the same lines. The partnership was a fruitful one and revolutionized modern music. Gillespie joined the Earl Fatha Hines Band, a kind of cradle of bop. Parker was also in that unit. In 1944, he went into the Billy Eckstine Band, a fully operational bebop unit, which Parker was also part of for a time. Unfortunately, because of the recording ban, the band was not widely documented although a few air checks do exist.

Gillespie went on to form his own big band, an Afro-Cuban unit. He often spoke quite movingly about the importance of Chano Pozo to his rhythmic experiments. The fact that Chano Pozo, a Cuban Santeria, could get three rhythms in playing songs such as "Cubano Be" and "Cubano Bop" intrigued him. Over the years, he continued to return to the big band format, one he preferred to his small groups. He often toured Europe, Asia, and Africa. Many of those tours were sponsored by the State Department as part of the Cultural Exchange program. Gillespie proved a fine ambassador and even half-seriously "ran" for president.

His United Nations Band continued the tradition and performed up until his death, and it has even occasionally returned in his honor since his passing. In continuing his tradition, it is a mixture of people from all over the world and features at least one outstanding young trumpet player. Gillespie loved to discover young trumpet players and to encourage their careers. The list of those young musicians includes Miles Davis, Lee Morgan, Clifford Brown, Chuck Mangione, and Jon Faddis.

In 1977, his somewhat flagging career was given a boost through the contribution of his protégé, Jon Faddis. Faddis had left Philadelphia as a teen to find Gillespie. He became Gillespie's alter ego and continued to perform with him, off and on, even after he had become a major jazz figure in his own right. In 1977, Faddis and Gillespie recorded at the Montreux Jazz Festival. The recording inspired Gillespie to one last great effort and his final period in jazz history as its elder statesman.

In spite of dental and other health problems, including the cancer that killed him, Gillespie had a number of other spectacular recordings up until his death. His fans realized that his playing had lost something in technique but had gained in emotional depth. Just prior to his passing, the Blue Note had a month-long celebration of his music. Gillespie performed with a different group every week, each marking a major phase of his career.

Bibliography

Dearman, Karen M. *Encyclopedia of Southern Culture.* Chapel Hill: UP of North Carolina, 1989.

Gammond, Peter. *Oxford Companion to Popular Music.* New York: Oxford UP, 1991.

Gitler, Ira. *Swing to Bop.* New York: Oxford UP, 1985.

Gridley, Mark. *Jazz Styles.* Englewood: Prentice-Hall, 1994.

Frank A. Salamone

Gilligan's Island (1964-1967) was part of the mid-'60s flurry of fantasy shows that included *Mr. Ed, Bewitched, My Favorite Martian,* and *I Dream of Jeannie.* Critics almost universally panned this CBS series about seven disparate characters stranded together on an uncharted island after a shipwreck. But *Gilligan's Island* took itself much less seriously than the critics did.

Created and produced by Sherwood Schwartz for Gladasya Productions in association with United Artists TV, *Gilligan's Island* starred Alan Hale, Jr. (1918-) as Skipper Jonas Grumby, Bob Denver (1935-) as first mate Gilligan, and Jim Backus (1913-89) as millionaire Thurston Howell III. Denver's character often seemed a reprise of the loony but lovable beatnik, Maynard G. Krebs, he'd played on *The Many Loves of Dobie Gillis* from 1959 to 1963. His trademark innocence was an essential part of the show; bossed, bullied, and badgered by nearly everyone, Gilligan is inept but well meaning. Hale had made a career of bluff, hearty roles. His Skipper calls Gilligan "little buddy" and has to be reminded anew in each episode of Gilligan's worth.

The last show ran on CBS on September 4, 1967, but the 98 episodes have had a long afterlife in syndication. Most of the cast was reassembled for three made-for-TV movies on NBC: *Rescue from Gilligan's Island* (1978); *The Castaways on Gilligan's Island* (1979); and *The Harlem Globetrotters on Gilligan's Island* (1981). The series also spawned two cartoon versions: *The New Adventures of Gilligan* (1974), and *Gilligan's Planet* (1983).

Bibliography

Johnson, Russell. *Here on Gilligan's Isle.* New York: Harper-Perennial, 1993.

Schwartz, Sherwood. *Inside Gilligan's Island: From Creation to Syndication.* Jefferson: McFarland, 1980.

Katie Hutchinson

Girlhood Stories. Stories about girlhood fit under the broader category of realism in children's literature, and frequently center on themes of family, making friends, developing moral attitudes and standards, growing toward personal and sexual maturity, facing romance, and coping with problems of the human condition (such as illness, aging, and death). While their readership is primarily female, many are adored across gender lines.

Photo courtesy of Popular Culture Library, Bowling Green State University, Bowling Green, OH.

Classic girlhood stories begin with Louisa May Alcott's *Little Women* (1868), the family chronicles of four sisters and their mother while their father is away at war, and Johanna Spyri's *Heidi* (1884), about a young girl's growing up in her grandfather's cottage in the bucolic Swiss Alps. Other time-tested classics include Kate Douglass Wiggin's depiction of a high-spirited girl in *Rebecca of Sunnybrook Farm* (1903), and L. M. Montgomery's *Anne of Green Gables* (1908) and its sequels, the very successful series of stories about a young orphan girl living on Prince Edward Island in Canada. Frances Hodgson Burnett's *The Secret Garden* (1910), and *Pollyanna* (1913) by Eleanor Porter, are two enduringly popular stories about orphans who must adjust to life.

The *Little House* books (1932) by Laura Ingalls Wilder, and Carol Ryrie Brink's story of a vivacious tomboy, *Caddie Woodlawn* (1935), deal with pioneer girlhood. Memorable girl characters who behave quite differently from the more traditional heroine are Astrid Lindgren's irrepressible *Pippi Longstocking* (1945); Karana in Scott O'Dell's *Island of the Blue Dolphins* (1960); Harriet in Louise Fitzhugh's *Harriet the Spy* (1964); and Robert Burch's *Queenie Peavy* (1966), who insists she will become a doctor, not a nurse. Lois Lenski's *Strawberry Girl* (1946) is set in rural Florida and tells of the life of a backwoods farm child.

Light fiction in the form of popularized series books enjoyed by pre-teen and early adolescent readers include the Babysitters Club books, *Sweet Valley Twins,* and *Sweet Valley High.* Some older series were built around the paradigm of the girl detective, including the phenomenal Nancy Drew mysteries, and the lesser known Dana Girls stories (both produced by the Stratemeyer Syndicate) and Trixie Belden mysteries—all using the mystery device to depict girlhood mores. The American Girl series focuses on girls in various historical periods.

More contemporary stories about girls include Judy Blume's *Are You There, God? It's Me, Margaret* (1970), about the onset of puberty, and Katherine Paterson's *Jacob Have I Loved* (1980), a sensitive portrayal of conflict between twin sisters when one believes the other is the adored family favorite. *Lyddie* (1991), also written by Pater-

son, treats a self-sufficient 19th-century New England girl who becomes a mill worker to save the family farm. Julie in Jean Craighead George's *Julie of the Wolves* (1972) struggles to survive in the harsh arctic tundra while she seeks to find her identity between her native society and the competing white society.

Bibliography

Norton, Donna E. "Genres in Children's Literature: Identifying, Analyzing, and Enjoying." *Children's Literature: Resources for the Classroom.* Ed. Masha Rudman. Needham Heights: Christopher-Gordon, 1989.

——. *Through the Eyes of a Child.* New York: Maxwell, 1991.

Ann de Onis

See also
Adolescent Mystery
Adolescent Romance Fiction

Gladys Knight and the Pips (1954-1989), performing together for three and a half decades, produced consistent hits that topped both the R&B charts and eventually crossed over to top the pop charts. The five-member singing group, who turned out hits for Motown Records during the 1960s and 1970s, has been hailed for their return to the roots of the soul of black rhythm and culture in America. When not recording, they headlined in Las Vegas, Atlantic City, and other cities, traveling the club and concert circuit.

Before the group's first No. 1 hit in 1961, the Pips shared duties, but Knight often sang lead. When "Every Beat of My Heart" hit the No. 1 spot with the 16-year-old Knight as the front woman, record producers urged the group to keep Knight as lead. Knight (1944-) first appeared on stage at the age of four with the Mount Moriah Baptist Choir, after her mother encouraged her to sing. During 1950-53, she toured Georgia and Alabama with the Morris Brown gospel choir, standing on a soapbox. At seven, she won the grand prize of $2,000 at the Ted Mack Amateur Hour performing a rendition of Nat King Cole's "Too Young."

Described as a gritty contralto, Gladys Knight joined with the Pips at an all-day birthday party for her brother Merlad, Jr. (Bubba) in September of 1952. Gladys, Merald, their sister Brenda, and cousins William and Elenor Guest improvised a singing group, and were named for James "Pip" Wood, a cousin, who became their manager and arranged gigs for them at local clubs. Performing pop, they were the Pips, but as a gospel group, they were known as the Fountaineers.

Gladys Knight and the Pips were opening for such major stars as Sam Cooke and Jackie Wilson by the time Knight was 13. Their first hit, "Whistle My Love" received little attention upon its release in 1957 through Brunswick recording company. Brenda and Elenor left the group and were replaced by cousin Edward Patten and Langston George. When the group was asked by a friend in New York to do a "sound check" for "Every Beat of My Heart," they were surprised when it was marketed by three different record companies. Although they made no money from it at the time, the song reached the R&B Top 20 in 1961, and eventually went gold. After two more recordings, including the Top 5 R&B hit, "Letter Full of Tears," Langston George left the group, making it a family quartet. They temporarily split when Gladys married at age 16.

In 1965, the group signed with Motown Records (see entry) and generated such hits as "Just Walk in My Shoes," "Take Me in Your Arms and Love Me," "I Don't Want to Do Wrong," and "If I Were Your Woman." It was their 1967 hit, "I Heard It through the Grapevine," that Gladys credited as their best song. Hitting No. 2 on the pop charts, it allowed the group to cross over, as she explained, into a new market: the whites. Although the group was successful, they were dissatisfied with their subservience in the hierarchy of Motown to such acts as the Supremes, Marvin Gaye, Smokey Robinson and the Miracles, claiming that Berry Gordy saved the best songs for these performers.

They joined Buddah Records in 1973 and released the LP *Imagination*, producing three gold singles, "Midnight Train to Georgia" that hit No. 1 in 1973, "I've Got to Use My Imagination," reaching No. 3 in 1974, and "Best Thing That Ever Happened to Me," hitting the No. 3 spot in 1974. The group received two Grammys for *Imagination*, for "Neither One of Us," and "Midnight Train." The group also had a hit single, "On and On," from the soundtrack they had written for the film *Claudine* in 1975.

Gladys Knight and the Pips broke up in 1989 when Knight went solo, making her debut at the Bally's Grand Hotel in Las Vegas. During the course of their 36 years together, the group's in-church, family-oriented origins highlighted with masterful timing and choreographed dance steps contributed to the acceptance of R&B and earned them the Second Annual Soul Train Heritage Award in 1988. The group also received four American music awards, an NAACP Image Award, and Billboard and Record World awards.

Bibliography

"Gladys Knight." *Current Biography Yearbook*. Ed. Charles Moritz. New York: Wilson, 1976.

"Gladys Knight & the Pips Still Sizzle after 35 Years Together." *Jet* 25 Jan. 1988: 57-61.

Johnson, Robert E. "Gladys Knight Goes Solo and Tells Why." *Jet* 8 May 1989: 56-57.

Little, Benilde. "Just Gladys." *Essence* Oct. 1991: 52-56.

Romanowski, Patricia, and Holly George-Warren. *The New Rolling Stone Encyclopedia of Rock & Roll*. New York: Fireside, 1995.

"'Soul Train' to Honor Gladys Knight." *Billboard* 12 March 1988: 25.

Jill Talbot

Gleason, **Jackie** (1916-1987), a loud-mouthed comic artist, began his professional life in 1933 in Brooklyn, NY. Though he started with a partner, he was soon working solo as a monologist and emcee. Gleason caught on and by 1940 was playing the better New York clubs and acted in the legitimate stage production of *Keep Off the Grass*. Gleason was spotted by Jack Warner, one of the Warner Brothers, and given a movie contract but failed to make his mark in the six films he appeared in from 1941 to 1943. Gleason continued his nightclub work and then went on tour with the stage comedy extravaganza *Hellzapoppin'* in 1943. He followed that up with the Broadway show *Along Fifth Avenue* the next year. In 1948, he made his television debut in *Toast of the Town*, later known as *The Ed Sullivan Show*.

His success in that venue led to his first series for the DuMont network in 1949-50, *The Life of Riley*. *Riley* had been a popular radio show starring William Bendix (1906-1964), but contracts kept Bendix from taking the TV series. Gleason got good notices, but the character of Chester A. Riley was so associated with Bendix that audiences never accepted Gleason in the role and the series was shelved after one season, until Bendix was able to take the role, where it had a successful run on NBC from 1953 to 1958.

Gleason was shifted to DuMont's *Cavalcade of Stars*, a hodge-podge variety show. The show set the format of sketches and music that Gleason was to follow on television for much of the next two decades. Gleason proved to be a master of the short comic sketch, utilizing a number of characters he had developed on stage and in nightclubs, as well as new characters. One new character which appeared in germinal form began as something of a Chester A. Riley, but soon blossomed into Gleason's most notable character, Ralph Kramden.

Gleason was lured from DuMont to CBS by an unprecedented two-year, $11-million contract which gave Gleason complete control over every aspect of his show, a control Gleason utilized. From the *Cavalcade of Stars* Gleason took the June Taylor Dancers and actor Art Carney (1918-) and a lot of ideas. *The Jackie Gleason Show* was a hit, especially the recurring sketches, now known as *The Honeymooners*, featuring the Ralph Kramden character.

Gleason's energies didn't stop at writing, producing, and acting. In 1953, he began composing soft, sentimental, heavily orchestrated music. The first album, *Music for Lovers Only*, was a surprise hit, selling over 500,000 copies. Nearly three dozen similar albums would follow in the next two decades, with equal success. Later in the year he televised his own production of a four-movement symphony-ballet he had written called *Tawny*. The soundtrack of the broadcast sold over a million copies.

Gleason then signed a $14 million two-year contract with CBS under the stipulation that *The Honeymooners* (1955-56; see entry) become a half-hour filmed show. Gleason broke the contract after the first year by not filming the 1956-57 season, and the 39 filmed *Honeymooners* shows from the 1955-56 season have been in constant syndication and are known among fans as the "Classic 39." Contrary to popular belief, they were not a runaway hit when first broadcast.

Gleason then took a break from television, returning to the stage in *The Time of Your Life* and winning a Tony for *Take Me Along* in 1959. He also returned to films, and was nominated for an Oscar for his work in 1961's *The Hustler*. He also got good reviews in 1962 for his work in *Requiem for a Heavyweight*, and the little-seen *Gigot*, in which he not only starred, demonstrating his pantomimic skills, but also wrote the story and music. Gleason played starring and guest roles in films throughout the sixties, usually coming off better than the films he appeared in, such as his hilarious and sensitive portrayal in the disappointing *How to Commit Marriage* (1969). The exception to this rule is *Papa's Delicate Condition* (1963), an excellent film with one of Gleason's strongest performances in which he introduced the Oscar-winning hit song "Call Me Irresponsible."

He tried hosting a game show in 1961 called *You're in the Picture*, but it bombed so badly that Gleason apologized for it on air the second week, and the show was turned into an interview program. 1962 saw *Jackie Gleason and His American Scene Magazine*, another variety series which was revamped in 1966 and retitled *The Jackie Gleason Show*. Both shows followed the pattern he had developed on his shows in the 1950s. Though consistently highly rated, the show was canceled as one of the victims of the demographic analysis that led to the large-scale revamping of the CBS schedule in 1970 and 1971.

Gleason made frequent guest appearances and a couple of specials for television in the early and mid 1970s. He returned to films and the stage in 1977, suffering a heart attack during a performance of *The Sly Fox* in 1977. That same year saw his definitive portrayal as a harried southern sheriff in the box-office hit *Smokey and the Bandit*. The film revitalized Gleason's career, and he returned to television, this time ABC, with a series of four new hour-long *Honeymooners* specials in 1977 and 1978. His film career unfortunately took the same turn as it had in the late 1960s, with Gleason never getting a role worthy of his talents until his last film, *Nothing in Common* in 1986. Television served him better with the HBO project *Mr. Halpern and Mr. Johnson* (1984), a superior work with Gleason acquitting himself well in a two-person film, along with Laurence Olivier (1907-1989). Gleason also repackaged the non-filmed *Honeymooners* skits and episodes for syndication and videotape release in 1986. Though a cut below the classic 39, they have pleased fans of Gleason and the series by showing a great comic artist in peak form.

Bibliography

Bacon, James. *How Sweet It Is: The Jackie Gleason Story.* New York: St. Martin's, 1985.

Terrace, Vincent. *Encyclopedia of Television Series, Pilots, and Specials, 1937-1973, Volume I.* New York: Zoetrope, 1986.

———. *Encyclopedia of Television Series, Pilots, and Specials, 1974-1984, Volume II.* New York: Zoetrope, 1985.

Weatherby, W. J. *Jackie Gleason: An Intimate Portrait.* New York: Berkley, 1992.

Benjamin K. Urish

Godfather, The, a trilogy of films directed and co-written by Francis Ford Coppola, focus on the Mafia family of Vito Corleone and examine the psychology and the culture of crime, as the Mafia develops from a crude secret society to a sophisticated brand of corporate government.

The Godfather, released in 1972, is an adaptation of Mario Puzo's novel of the same title. The film traces the fall of Vito Corleone (Marlon Brando) as a Mafia boss and the rise of his son Michael (Al Pacino) to his father's position in the crime family. Puzo's novel, published in 1969, was an enormous best-seller, and Paramount Studios bought the rights to the story in order to create an adaptation. Paramount executives were undecided on their choice of director, but eventually chose the little-known Coppola because his Italian-American ethnicity would help fend off anticipated clashes with Italian-American lobbying groups and the Mafia.

Despite production problems, *The Godfather* achieved enormous financial and critical success. Before the end of 1972, the film had become the all-time box-office champion, with estimated earnings of $150 million, and it won Academy Awards for best picture, best actor (Brando), and best screenplay. *The Godfather* would set the standard for films in future years in terms of financial success.

Coppola convinced Paramount to capitalize on *The Godfather*'s success with a sequel. He had two main objectives in making *The Godfather Part II* (1974). First, he wanted to dispel the notion that sequels are normally cheap imitations of their parent and he felt that the second film could be more ambitious than the first. Second, he was concerned with the ending of *The Godfather* because it appeared that he endorsed Michael's behavior. Coppola did not want to glamorize the actions of Michael Corleone in *The Godfather Part II*. The film focuses specifically on the decline of the Corleone empire and obscures any idealism that the audience may have felt from the first installment of the saga. *The Godfather Part II* earned about half of the money that *The Godfather* did, but it went on to dominate the Academy Awards in a manner that separated it from its parent. The film earned 12 nominations and won for best picture, best director, and best screenplay. *The Godfather Part II* became the only sequel to win an Academy Award for best picture.

The third installment of the saga, *The Godfather Part III*, began to take shape in late 1980s and was eventually released in 1990. Coppola gathered together many of the crew and cast that had worked on the previous two *Godfather* films. This film centers on Michael's attempt to return to innocence by making all of his businesses legitimate and focuses on the ultimately self-destructive psychological effects of abuse of power.

The films of *The Godfather* saga are almost universally regarded as compelling, richly textured, remarkably patient, and profoundly insightful in their exploration of a family, the abuse of power, and the culture of crime. *The Godfather* franchise is also recognized as an achievement to be emulated. Combining mass appeal with the profundity of an artistic endeavor is the legacy that the trilogy leaves for future filmmakers.

Bibliography

Cowie, Peter. *Coppola.* New York: Scribner's, 1990.

Jason Landrum

Godzilla, King of the Monsters! (1954), directed by Inoshiro Honda, was a tremendous international success, and for most Americans it was their first exposure to Japanese cinema.

Known as *Gojira* to the Japanese, *Godzilla* and its 17 sequels have spawned an enormous international franchise of video games, dolls, and T-shirts, and the character has become a cultural icon in Japan as well as the United States. The idea for the film was first developed by the film's executive producer, Tomoyuki Tanaka, after he saw the American film *Beast from 20,000 Fathoms* in 1953. He coupled his viewing of the American science fiction film with a true event that happened in Japan, the exposure to radioactive fallout of a Japanese fishing boat that sailed too close to an American hydrogen-bomb testing area. Originally, Tanaka had planned for the monster to be a giant octopus but changed his mind in order to make a film more like the 1933 American film *King Kong*. The atomic testing giving birth to a monster that destroys a civilization then becomes the driving force of the film's narrative.

Eighteen months after the premiere of *Godzilla* in Japan, Joseph E. Levine bought the film for American distribution and hired director Terry Morse to re-edit the film. The film was dubbed into English, and Morse shot additional scenes with Raymond Burr for the American release. One complaint about the American reissue was that it deemphasized the dangers of nuclear weapons. Although there are differing versions of the film, it went on to shatter box office records in Japan and for Japanese films in the United States, and the character of Godzilla has been compared to Mickey Mouse for its cultural importance to the Japanese. In addition, the film and character tremendously inspired the genre of science fiction in film and television not only in Japan but in the United States as well.

Bibliography

Broderick, Mike, ed. *Hibakusha Cinema*. London: Kegan Paul, 1996.

Buehrer, Beverly Bare. *Japanese Films*. Jefferson: McFarland, 1990.

Galbraith, Stuart. *Japanese Science Fiction, Fantasy, and Horror Films*. Jefferson: McFarland, 1994.

Maxford, Howard. *The A-Z of Horror Films*. Bloomington: Indiana UP, 1997.

Jason Landrum

Go-Go's, The (1978-1985), were an all-female band (as opposed to vocal group) from the post-punk era of the late 1970s, whose commercial success in the early 1980s marked a turning point in rock history for female musicians.

The group began as a comically inept novelty act in Hollywood, CA. Belinda Carlisle, a former high school cheerleader who nearly joined the seminal L.A. punk band the Germs, and Jane Wiedlin founded the band in 1978, admittedly on a whim and the lingering inspiration of having traveled to San Francisco to see the Sex Pistols' final performance. They recruited an inexperienced rhythm section of bassist Margot Olaverra, and drummer Elissa Bello, and asked another friend, Charlotte Caffey, a guitar veteran of numerous bands, including the Eyes with X's D.J. Bonebrake, to join.

They debuted as the Go-Go's, a name suggested by Wiedlin, with a 1 1/2-song set at the Hollywood club, the Masque. The following year, Gina Shock, who had toured briefly with cult film star Edie Massey and her Eggs, replaced Bello as the drummer. As they toured the punk circuit and rehearsed in earnest, the Go-Go's evolved from being regarded as a hilariously daring bunch of amateurs to a band with a bouncy pop-rock sound that echoed the melodic style of the new wave group Blondie from the New York punk underground.

On April 1, 1981, Miles Copeland, who, according to Caffey, "was the only one willing to take a chance on us," signed the Go-Go's to his I.R.S. Records roster. "Girl group" producer Richard Gottehrer, whose credits included two Blondie records, was hired to supervise the project. By the spring of 1982, the group's debut album, *Beauty and the Beat* (1981), reached the top of the charts, making the Go-Go's the first all-female band in rock history to have a No. 1 album. The album's success was propelled by two Top 20 singles that lingered on the charts, the gold "We Got the Beat" and "Our Lips Are Sealed" (co-written with Terry Hall of Britain's Specials and Fun Boy Three).

Female musicians during the 1980s were able to channel their inspiration into the realm of punk and forge successful careers out of the opportunity. By 1984 the group's cohesiveness began to unravel. Pressures from their sudden success, legal disputes over royalties, lack of enthusiasm, and drug and alcohol abuse were among the factors which contributed to the band's bitter breakup one year later.

After the split, each of the members pursued a solo career with only marginal critical and commercial success. Wiedlin's credits included a self-titled album (I.R.S. 1985), *Fur* (EMI 1988), and *Tangled* (EMI 1990). (She also appeared as Joan of Arc in the 1989 film *Bill and Ted's Excellent Adventure*.) Shock's only record was *House of Shock* (Capitol 1988). Valentine reunited with her former Girlschool bandmate Kelly Johnson and formed World's Cutest Killers. After assisting Carlisle with her first solo effort, Caffey founded the Graces, with Gia Ciambotti and Meredith Brooks, and released *Perfect View* (A&M 1989). Of all the post Go-Go projects, Carlisle's glamorized records—*Belinda* (I.R.S. 1986), *Heaven on Earth* (MCA 1987), and *Runaway Horses* (MCA 1989)—achieved the most success, including the hit singles "Mad about You" and "Heaven on Earth."

In 1990, the Go-Go's reunited briefly to perform for a charity event and a short tour, and I.R.S. released a compilation of their hits, *Go-Go's Greatest*. The box-set collection, *Return to the Valley of the Go-Go's*, followed in 1994.

Bibliography

O'Brien, Lucy. *She Bop: The Definitive History of Women in Rock, Pop, and Soul*. New York: Penguin, 1996

Thomson, Liz. *New Women in Rock*. London: Omnibus, 1982.

George Plasketes

Golden Age of Detective Fiction, The, frequently denotes a particular style of writing and set of conventions, but it also describes a time period. The seed for the golden age was planted in 1913 with the publication of E. C. Bentley's *Trent's*

Last Case. Bentley's novel featured a new naturalness, along with a literate writing style, engaging humor, more subtle drawing of character, and more emphasis on the central "puzzle" than had been seen before in mystery writing.

The golden age of detective fiction was the period between 1920 and roughly 1940 in England. Among others, Agatha Christie, Dorothy L. Sayers, Philip MacDonald, Freeman Wills Croft, Margery Allingham, Nicholas Blake, Anthony Berkeley (who also wrote as Francis Iles), and Ngaio Marsh published popular and influential novels that came to define the genre. Their work has several identifying characteristics. Compared to most earlier detective fiction, the stories, if not always the solutions, seem more plausible and more closely related to real life. The detective evolved from a person of dazzling brilliance but little real personality into a more human face, such as the spinster Jane Marple; the eccentric but endearing Hercule Poirot; the not-so-endearing Roger Sheringham; and the well-educated, kindly Inspector John Appleby, to name a few. Minor characters tended to be flat and stereotypical—dull-witted bobbies, patronizing butlers, sullen and "swarthy" foreigners, and others.

The puzzle dominated detective fiction during the early 1920s. Murder took place in locked-room settings, alibis were elaborately forged and impossibly complex falsehoods, and murder methods were wildly inventive. Also important was the idea of fair play—authors were expected to reveal enough clues for the reader to analyze and solve the case. When the narrator of Agatha Christie's *The Murder of Roger Ackroyd* (1926) proved to be the murderer, many readers felt they had not simply been tricked, but betrayed.

As the golden age moved into the 1930s, setting, character, and psychology became prominent, displacing the puzzle element as the mystery's heart. Novelists like Sayers, Allingham, Marsh, and Francis Iles demonstrated the stability of this trend.

In the United States, as in England, a few pre-1920 writers experimented with fictional features that would later be associated with the golden age tradition. In 1908, Mary Roberts Rinehart published *The Circular Staircase*, and continued to produce books until shortly before her death in 1958. Carolyn Wells followed Rinehart by one year, creating detective Fleming Stone who debuted in *The Clue* (1909) and appeared subsequently in most of Wells's 74 novels.

It was Willard Huntington Wright, however, writing under the name S. S. Van Dine (see entry), who is considered most influential and visible among the American mystery authors of the period. *The Benson Murder Case* was published in 1926, and Detective Philo Vance captured the reading public. Van Dine's second work, *The Canary Murder Case* (1927), broke all previous sales records for a detective novel. Van Dine's success seemed to unleash a flood of American talent, and the American golden age of detective fiction exploded.

While Van Dine's mysteries were still in the British tradition, though set in the U.S., Ellery Queen Americanized the golden age genre itself. The author "Ellery Queen" (see entry) was a pseudonym for two cousins, Frederic Dannay and Manfred B. Lee, who wrote as a team beginning with

The Roman Hat Mystery (1929). "Ellery Queen" was also the name of the novel's protagonist, a writer and amateur sleuth who assisted his father, police inspector Richard Queen. In the course of the next half century, Ellery Queen novels evolved in many ways. The earliest, however, represent the best of the golden age with intricate puzzles offered in the spirit of fair play and psychologically rich characterization.

Rex Stout (see entry), who began his Nero Wolfe series with *Fer-de-Lance* (1934), combined the best of the golden age with the best of the hard-boiled. A fat man who rarely leaves his home, Wolfe lives in an elegant New York brownstone where he raises orchids, drinks beer, eats well, and solves his cases using the footwork (and brainwork) of his tough, breezy, wise-cracking assistant, Archie Goodwin.

Other writers followed, expanding the limits of their detective characters and the limits of the golden age tradition: Mabel Seeley; Erle Stanley Gardner; Phoebe Atwood Taylor (writing also as Alice Tilton); Stuart Palmer; Craig Rice; Leslie Ford (writing also as David Frome); and Elizabeth Daly are important examples. Golden age mysteries thrived during the period between the two World Wars, but they live on in the cozy mystery, a format that places old-fashioned detection of traditional puzzles in contemporary settings.

Bibliography

Haycraft, Howard. *Murder for Pleasure: The Life and Times of the Detective Story*. 1941. New York: Biblo & Tannen, 1968.

Murch, A. E. *The Development of the Detective Novel*. New York: Philosophical Library, 1958.

Panek, LeRoy Lad. *Probable Cause: Crime Fiction in America*. Bowling Green, OH: Bowling Green State U Popular P, 1990.

Scott, Sutherland. *Blood in Their Ink*. London: n.p., 1953.

Skinner, Robert E. *The Hard Boiled Explicator: A Guide to the Study of Dashiell Hammett, Raymond Chandler, and Ross Macdonald*. Metuchen: Scarecrow, 1985.

Symons, Julian. *Bloody Murder*. New York: Mysterious, 1992.

Susan Peters

See also

Academic Mysteries	Detective Sidekicks
Adolescent Mysteries	Gothic Mysteries
Classical Mysteries	Mystery and Detective Fiction
Cozy Mysteries	Native American Crime Fiction
Crime Fiction	Regional Mysteries

Golden Girls, The (1985-1992), a breakthrough TV comedy series which aired on NBC and still runs in syndication, provided audiences with the first glimpse of how issues affected the elderly, especially women. Rather than providing a sinister view of four elderly women seeking refuge from the modern world after losing their husbands to death and divorce, the series gave audiences a sense of how older women, often displaced by society, muster their individual and collective resources to create a new, rich, friendship-based family.

Like many seniors, these women had moved to Miami in search of a new life. Dorothy Zbornack (Bea Arthur), a former English teacher, New Yorker, and divorcée, provided the dominant spirit with her logical, dependable, and straightforward approach to life. She was the rudder that held this female ship on course. Sophia Petrillo (Estelle Getty), Dorothy's widowed mother, became a family member when her nursing home, Shady Pines, burned down. Although some characters attributed Sophia's quixotic behavior to her stroke, they were at a loss to explain her sexy and outrageous quips. In contrast, Rose Nylund (Betty White), a Minnesota widow, brought her naive, farm perspectives to the household. Her frequent literal interpretations of events and situations that defy reason provided humorous double takes. Ironically, Rose's part-time job was that of a grief counselor. The owner of the women's home was Blanche Devereaux (Rue McClanahan), a Southern belle who never outgrew her adolescent lusty taste for men. The touching and hilarious interactions of these five women offered a refreshing view of women in their "golden" years.

Bibliography

Brooks, Tim, and Earle Marsh. *The Complete Directory to Prime Time Network TV Shows, 1946-Present.* New York: Ballantine, 1992.

Gold, Todd. "Golden Girls in Their Prime." *Saturday Evening Post* July 1986: 58-61.

Mourges, Denise. "Inspiration and Other Talents Behind Comedy." *New York Times* 22 Sept. 1985: L. I, 2.

Adelaide P. Amore

Golf in America was born on February 22, 1888, when John Reid, a transplanted Scot who is regarded as the father of American golf, invited four friends to play three improvised holes in a cow pasture in Yonkers, NY. Although golf had been played in several states prior to 1888, Reid and his friends became so enthusiastic that they founded St. Andrews Golf Club of Yonkers, America's first permanent club, on November 14, 1888. These excited golfing Americans encouraged Bob Lockhart, Reid's friend, to bring back more clubs and gutta-percha balls from Tom Morris's shop at St. Andrews, Scotland.

By 1895, golf flourished in America. There were 75 golf clubs in operation, and they wanted to organize so that there could be a national championship, particularly after there had been two national championships in 1894. Henry O. Tallmadge, secretary of St. Andrews, and others created the United States Golf Association (USGA) on December 12, 1894. The USGA has provided American golf with a central authority which establishes and enforces uniformity in the rules of play, a handicap system, an executive committee as a court of reference and final authority, and, most importantly, decides on what courses the championships would be played. The U.S. Men's Open was created for professionals, who were generally foreigners and who were regarded as being in a lower social stratum. The U.S. Men's and the U.S. Women's Amateur Championships were designed for Americans who golfed primarily for fun (see also next entry).

All three championships were held in 1895. The men's championships were held at Newport Golf Club, Newport, RI. Thirty-two men participated in the Amateur, which was won by Charles B. McDonald. Richard Peters, who perhaps suffered from yips, was disqualified for putting with a billiard cue. Horace Rawlings, a 21-year-old assistant pro, won the U.S. Open. In November, Mrs. Charles Brown captured the Women's Amateur at Meadow Brook Club, Hempstead, NY, with an 18-hole victory over Nellie Sargent. Beatrix Hoyt dominated the women's amateur with victories in 1896, 1897, and 1898. She remains the youngest champion at age 16; she retired from competitive golf at 21.

By 1900, 1,000 golf clubs existed in the United States. In order to learn golfing skills and to build golf courses, Americans imported United Kingdom golfers. Harry Vardon, the greatest player of the era, gave exhibitions which promoted golf and introduced A. G. Spalding & Bros.'s new guttie golf ball. Foreigners dominated the U.S. Open as Willie Anderson, a Scotsman, won four, three consecutively.

Johnny McDermott was the first native-born American to win the Open, in 1911 and 1912. However, in 1913, Francis Ouimet, a 22-year-old caddie, defeated the "invincible" Harry Vardon and Ted Ray in a playoff to become the first amateur to win an Open. Later, Charles "Chick" Evans won the Open and the Amateur in 1916, the first amateur to accomplish this feat. Ouimet and Evans stimulated amateur interest in golf, which reached its peak in the 1920s. Alexa Stirling captured three U.S. Women's Amateurs in 1916, 1919, and 1920.

Since professional golfers were lowly regarded, received low pay, and remained relatively obscure, Rodman Wanamaker in January 1916 suggested that the professionals develop a national organization. By July, they established the championship of the Professional Golfers' Association and held their championship at Siwanoy Country Club, Bronxville, NY; "Long" Jim Barnes won and received $500.

No American championships were held in 1917 and 1918. However, American golf dramatically improved, and by 1923, Americans were the best golfers in the world. Walter "The Haig" Hagen, golf's greatest match player, gained worldwide attention with his flamboyance and drive. With Hagen, the professional came out of the caddie shack and into the clubhouse. "The Haig," the first professional golfer to win and to spend $1 million, won 5 PGAs, 11 majors, and 60+ tournaments. Tommy Armour, Gene Sarazen, Macdonald Smith, Bobby Cruickshank, and Leo Diegel ignited Americans' golfing dominance. Ted Ray (1920), Gary Player (1965), and Ernie Els (1994, 1997) are the only foreigners to win the Open since Ray's victory.

From 1923-30, Robert Tyre Jones, Jr., America's greatest amateur, ruled both the amateur and the professional ranks. He won 13 national championships: 4 U.S. Opens, 3 British Opens, 5 U.S. Amateurs, 1 British Amateur. At 28, he retired from competitive golf. Glenna Collett Vare, the greatest women's amateur, won her first of 6 amateur titles in 1922.

During the 1920s, the golden age of golf course architecture began in America, dentist William Lowell invented the golf tee, and the USGA approved the use of steel shafts. American squads won the inaugural Walker Cup (1922) and Ryder Cup Matches (1927).

In 1920, 477 clubs had joined the USGA. By 1930, 1,154 courses of the 5,700-plus courses in the United States were members in the USGA. Nonetheless, golf course development nearly stopped because of the Depression and World War II. However, one of the greatest accomplishments in golf course design emerged when Augusta National Golf Club, the quintessential example of strategic design, opened in 1932.

Golfing equipment was improved and standardized during the 1930s. Gene Sarazen perfected the sand wedge, the USGA approved a new ball measuring 1.68 inches in diameter and weighing 1.62 ounces; Phil Young, owner of Acushnet, used X-rays to check every ball produced; and the USGA limited the number of clubs that a golfer could carry to 14.

The Curtis Cup was inaugurated in 1932. Lawson Little won 32 consecutive matches, including the U.S. and British Amateurs in 1934-35. Johnny Fisher won the Amateur with hickory shafts, while Johnny Goodman's victory at the 1933 Open is the most recent for an amateur.

Jimmy Demaret's victory at the Masters (see next entry), which he won for the next two years, and Ben Hogan's money title introduced the 1940s to golf. The Open was not held from 1942 to 1945, and the Masters was canceled from 1943 to 1945. Although many golfers served in the military, Byron Nelson's streak of 11 straight victories during the war years remains as one of sport's most spectacular accomplishments. In 1946, Patty Berg won the first Women's Open in Spokane, WA. In 1949, 11 women met in Wichita, KS, and formed the Ladies Professional Golf Association (LPGA).

Golf's modern era began after World War II; the pros played a new game because steel shafts, matched clubs, and improved golf course maintenance introduced lower scores. In 1953, the World Championship was broadcast on television, and purses topped $500,000. The hard-swinging Ben Hogan epitomized the new golfer with his Open wins in 1948, 1950, 1951, and 1953. Babe Zaharias won her third and last U.S. Women's Open in 1954, which was added to the USGA's roster of national championships in 1953. Arnold Palmer's emergence as "The King" began with his Amateur victory in 1954 and his win at his first professional tournament in 1955; however, "Arnie's Army" fell in love with his hitch of the pants, his lunging swing, and attacking approach to courses, particularly during the final rounds. Palmer's exuberant personality and charismatic appeal revolutionized golf.

In American golf 1960 was a significant year because Arnold Palmer shot a 65 at Cherry Hills in Denver to defeat the aging Hogan and the young Jack Nicklaus, golf's next superstar. Later, Palmer flew to Scotland to win the British Open, which indicated that major championships and golf were only hours away. Nicklaus's 1962 professional debut was a playoff victory over Palmer for the Open. The "Golden Bear" is known for his unmatched 22 majors, which reflects quality of victories rather than quantity. In 1965, Sam Snead won his 84th tour victory, which would be his last. In women's golf, Betsy Rawls won her 4th Open in 1960, and Mickey Wright won 13 of 32 events on the LPGA

Tour. Amazingly, in 1967, France's Catherine Lacoste became the only amateur ever to win the U.S. Women's Open.

The 1960s also introduced technological developments to the game as Ram Golf made a golf ball with a Surlyn cover; Spalding's Top-Flite, a solid ball with a Surlyn cover, was the first two-piece ball. Resorts started offering "golf packages"—rooms, meals, and green fees—at attractive prices at beautiful places like Myrtle Beach.

Title IX legislation enacted by Congress in 1972 provided equal opportunities for women athletes. In that same year, the Colgate-Dinah Shore, the first big money event for women professionals, debuted. Kathy Whitworth, who won the LPGA Player of the Year seven times in eight years, and Mickey Wright, who had 82 tour victories, dominated the early part of the decade. The latter part of the decade belonged to 1978 Rookie of the Year Nancy Lopez, whose remarkable domination included nine tournaments, five consecutively, and $189,813.

Jack Nicklaus, Lee Trevino, and Johnny Miller battled for the major tournaments (see next entry) during the early 1970s on the men's tour. Nicklaus became the first golfer to win the four majors twice in 1971, and in 1978 had won the four majors three times. In late 1977, Tom Watson, however, outdueled Nicklaus at the Masters and the British Open, and Watson became the dominant golfer in the early 1980s. Lee Elder was the first African American to qualify for the Masters in 1975 and to play in the 1979 Ryder Cup.

Nicklaus's fourth Open win in 1980 was a 72-hole record of 272; he later won his sixth Masters in 1986 at age 46, while Raymond Floyd won the Open at age 43. Tom Watson won the Open in 1982, and in 1983 he won his fifth British Open. Calvin Peete, with 13 victories, won more tour events than any golfer from 1978 to 1987. American golfers, however, were being challenged by a "foreign invasion" led by Seve Ballesteros's victory at the Masters in 1980. Ballesteros was joined by Germany's Bernhard Langer, Scotland's Sandy Lyle, Wales's Ian Woosnam, Australia's Greg Norman, and Britain's Nick Faldo. The European Ryder Cup team defeated the American team for the first time on American soil in 1987, and they won again three times since then.

Women golfers were also enjoying financial success as Kathy Whitworth became the first professional female to earn $1 million in career prize money in 1981; by 1985, she won her 88th career title, which is unequaled on any tour. Pat Bradley broke the $2 million in career prize-money barrier in 1986.

Golf and interest in golf boomed during the 1980s as courses were being constructed in the California deserts and even China in 1988, the USGA added the U.S. Senior Open in 1980, and Americans were bombarded with a video explosion as professionals and their teachers marketed golf instruction tapes.

In the 1990s, there are approximately 14,500 golf courses in the United States. Professional and amateur golf has improved, which can be seen by the quality of play and the amount of play. Although American golfers controlled the Open and the PGA, foreign golfers were beginning to assert their dominance, particularly in 1994 when they won the four majors. In the late 1990s, however, the American Tiger Woods was the player to watch; he won four major tournaments in just four years on the tour.

Women's golf, generally dominated by Americans, has also seen improvement in foreign golfers like Laura Davies and Liselotte Neumann; nonetheless, Patty Sheehan, Betsy King, Beth Daniel, Juli Inkster, and Dottie Mocherie have emerged as the most accomplished women golfers.

Although American golfers have traded in their hickory sticks for over-sized graphite clubs, the golfers' interest remains as it was in 1888 when John Reid and four friends enjoyed a short walk participating in a most mesmerizing outdoor activity.

Bibliography

Glenn, Rhonda, and Robert R. McCord. *The Whole Golf Catalog.* New York: Perigee, 1990.

Peper, George. *Golf in America: The First One Hundred Years.* New York: Abrams, 1988.

Michael Schoenecke

Golf's Major American Tournaments consist of, for men, the U.S. Men's Open Championship, the Professional Golfers' Association (PGA) Championship, the Masters Tournament, and the U.S. Men's Amateur Championship, and, for women, the U.S. Women's Open Championship, the Ladies Professional Golf Association (LPGA) Championship, the Nabisco-Dinah Shore Winner's Circle, and the U.S. Women's Amateur Championship. Most golfers, writers, and golf aficionados agree that the "majors" are the most difficult tournaments to win, that the winners earn fame for a lifetime, and that they are as close as the game comes to deciding the best golfers in the world; the names engraved on the trophies attest to the winners' golfing excellence.

Historically, the majors have the strongest fields because the U.S. has more first-class golfers than any other country, because the best foreign golfers are invited, and because other means of qualifying allow only the best to compete. As a result, a list of major winners reads like a litany of golf's elite players, which enhances the championships' unique atmosphere and tradition. The 1954 U.S. Open was the first televised broadcast of a major.

The U.S. Opens are the ultimate goal in American golf: they are this country's championships and the largest golf tournaments worldwide. The United States Golf Association (USGA), American golf's governing body, has overseen the Men's Open championships since 1895. The Men's Open was initially conducted at the Newport Golf Club, a nine-hole golf course, and four professionals, invited by the founding fathers, played 36 holes of match play. (Since 1898, the championship has been determined by stroke play.) The Men's Open was established primarily for professionals, who, because they were foreigners and better golfers, were not considered to be the social equals of amateurs. Since Ted Ray's 1920 victory, Gary Player (1965) and Ernie Els (1994, 1997) are the only foreigners who have won the Open.

Willie Anderson (1901, 1903, 1904, 1905), Robert T. Jones, Jr. (1923, 1926, 1929, 1930), Ben Hogan (1948, 1950, 1951, 1953), and Jack Nicklaus (1962, 1967, 1972, 1980) have each won four Opens. Only Sam Snead, who has won more golf tournaments than any other professional male golfer, never won an Open.

The first Women's Open, which was match play, was held in 1946 at the Spokane Country Club. All succeeding tournaments have been stroke play, and women's golf has grown in prestige because the USGA has conducted the Open since 1953. Seven of the first 12 Opens were won by former U.S. Amateur winners who had turned professional. Obviously the best golf in America was being played by professionals, but purse sizes and travel often prevented many exceptional amateurs from turning professional. Betsy Rawls (1951, 1953, 1957, 1960) and Mickey Wright (1958, 1959, 1961, 1964) have won four Opens; Nancy Lopez has never won an Open.

The Professional Golfers' Association's Championship was initially held in 1916; from 1916 to 1957, it was match play; since 1958, it has been stroke play. The PGA of America is the largest sports-related organization in the world, and their championship invites tour players, the best foreign golfers, and 40 club professionals to participate; as a result, Jack Nicklaus has argued that recent PGAs have the strongest fields in golf. Walter Hagen (1921, 1924, 1925, 1926, 1927) and Jack Nicklaus (1963, 1971, 1973, 1975, 1980) have won five titles.

The Ladies Professional Golf Association Championship was established in 1955 and it has been decided by stroke play since 1956. The LPGA Championship was dominated by Mickey Wright (1958, 1960, 1961, 1963) during its middle years, but Kathy Whitworth owns three titles. Joanne Carner has never won the LPGA championship.

The Masters Tournament, originally called the Augusta National Invitational Tournament for its first four years, was established in 1934. Augusta National Golf Club hosts this annual event, which was created by Robert T. Jones, Jr. As a result, the Masters exemplifies gentlemanly manners and graciousness as well as outstanding golf. Jack Nicklaus (1963, 1965, 1966, 1972, 1975, 1986) has won six of the green jackets given to the Masters champion.

In 1983, the LPGA decided that the Nabisco-Dinah Shore Winner's Circle, formerly known as the Colgate-Dinah Shore Winner's Circle (1972-81), would be its fourth major. The championship is held at Mission Hills Country Club, Rancho Mirage, CA. Amy Alcott (1983, 1988, 1991) has three titles, and, when she won in 1988, she and Dinah Shore dove into the pond guarding the 18th green.

The U.S. Men's and Women's Amateur Championships were conducted in 1895; the men's amateur, which covered three days of match play, was held at Newport Golf Club; the women's, an 18-hole event with lunch between nines, was hosted by Meadow Brook Club in Hempstead, NY. The Amateur championships were created for the golfer who played the game solely for enjoyment, and, in the early years, these golfers were Americans. During the second women's amateur the spectators' enthusiasm became so ardent that they had to be restrained behind a rope. Robert T. Jones, Jr., won 4 titles, and Glenna Collett won 6 events.

Jack Nicklaus, who focused on "the ones that count," won a remarkable 20 majors in 27 years against golf's toughest competition. As a result, Nicklaus is regarded as the greatest player in golf's first 100 years.

Bibliography

Graffis, Herbert Butler. *The PGA: The Official History of the Professional Golfers' Association of America.* New York: Crowell, 1975.

Peper, George, ed. *Golf in America: The First One Hundred Years.* New York: Abrams, 1988.

Steel, Donald. *The Guinness Book of Golf Facts and Feats.* Middlesex, U.K.: Guinness, 1982.

Michael Schoenecke

Gomer Pyle, U.S.M.C. (1964-1970), one of TV's surprise hits, was one of the most popular programs on television in its day, and still plays well in syndication. Indeed, Gomer Pyle, played by Jim Nabors, is one of the most recognizable and parodied characters from TV's past; Gomer Pyle's trademark phrases "Surprise, Surprise, Surprise" and "Shazam" still evoke a clear image of the character.

Although set at Camp Henderson, a Marine base in Los Angeles, *Gomer Pyle* was still a rural comedy; like the *Beverly Hillbillies,* Gomer just took the hayseed to the city. And, much like the rural comedies, its lesson was that city folk needed to relax before they all died of peptic ulcers.

Gomer Pyle's city vs. rural theme revolved around the relationship between kind-hearted, always faithful Marine private Gomer Pyle and his anxious, worldly-wise sergeant, Vincent Carter. Not since Laurel and Hardy was there a more perfect match between honest clown and scheming foil. No matter what Pyle did to please his sergeant, played convincingly by Frank Sutton, Carter was never satisfied.

Gomer Pyle was a spinoff from *The Andy Griffith Show* (see entry), in which Gomer worked as a gas station attendant at Wally's Filling Station. While the Gomer Pyle of *The Andy Griffith Show* was a bit sardonic, his own series found him more lovable and gullible. It was yet another successful show for producers Sheldon Leonard and Danny Thomas, who, along with Paul Henning, were the dominant forces in 1960s sitcoms.

Bibliography

Brooks, Tim, and Earle Marsh. *The Complete Directory to Prime Time Network TV Shows, 1946-Present.* 5th ed. New York: Ballantine, 1992.

Sackett, Susan. *Prime Time Hits: Television's Most Popular Programs.* New York: Billboard, 1993.

Michael B. Kassel

Gone with the Wind (1936), the most popular movie ever to be made in America, had its umpteenth second wind in the 1990s in the form of a sequel. Alexandra Ripley's *Scarlett* (1990), a long-awaited continuation of Margaret Mitchell's 1936 monumental *Gone with the Wind*, made it into cinematic form (as a TV miniseries in 1994) in roughly the same amount of time it took David O. Selznick working with "a cast of thousands" to make the movie against which all others would be measured.

The original *Gone with the Wind* (*GWTW*) has proved to be a tough act to follow. Although the sequel tried to replicate the scale of impact which was created in the late 1930s by Mitchell and Selznick, the world of the 1990s shows signs of having been seriously overexposed to such media mega-events as those attending the first release of *GWTW* upon the American public. One of the movie's central themes—that things today are gone tomorrow—has indeed become the expected pattern. *Gone with the Wind* is unique in that it has stayed so long.

Gone with the Wind is one of a very few great movies to come of a good book. Along the way, in majestic scale and scope, by demonstrating the virtue of stalwartness, *GWTW* became America's story of preference. Mitchell's narrative did brisk business for Macmillan when it was published. The millionth copy—hardcover, of course—was printed six months after official publication in June of 1936. It was the fastest-selling book in history, and as such, the fire that once burned Atlanta was re-ignited and set to rage again. In a flash, on July 7, 1936—with the book only on the market a week—Selznick put $50,000 (more money than ever before for an unknown writer's work) on the line for the film rights to *GWTW*.

The effort to develop a workable movie script from a novel of 1,037 pages proved daunting, but eventually revolving writers (Sidney Howard, Ben Hecht, Sidney Howard, Jo Swerling, Oliver H. P. Garrett, John Van Druten, Charles MacArthur, Winston Miller, John Balderstron, Michael Foster, Edwin Justus Mayer—even F. Scott Fitzgerald, in the dark twilight of his life) and evolving directors (Victor Fleming, with help from Sam Wood and W. C. Menzies and others after George Cukor was fired) worked the stars into the movie form that would define "big" in Hollywood for more than half a century. The fall of the genteel old South (with slavery represented—but not too meanly) was a romance just waiting to be rendered in film (the film medium had earlier gotten a big boost from *Birth of a Nation*, with D. W. Griffith's own southern angle). From the beginning, *GWTW* was mythic in scale.

Production cost ate up $3,700,000—a whopping lot of Depression-era dollars. 449,512 feet of film were shot—eventually worked down to the final print of 20,300 feet (220 minutes, a long sit in itself). In addition to the notables (Clark Gable, Vivian Leigh, Olivia de Havilland, Leslie Howard), there were many plum small parts (Hattie McDaniel's Mammy won her an Oscar, the first for an African-American performer) and room for 2,400 extras, 1,100 horses, and 450 wagons and ambulances. Then there were all the painted sets, to create Tara and Twelve Oaks and Atlanta, some 90 background images which successfully convinced audiences that they were seeing the South and the devastating effects of the Civil War upon that part of America. *GWTW* contributed significantly to the fact that the Civil War looms large in memory still.

Once production was finally complete in mid-1939, the mythos of the film's production grew as large as its onscreen story. It was said that a special dispensation was granted by Will H. Hays, head of the Motion Pictures Producers, who overruled Joseph Breen's refusal to allow Rhett his famous "Frankly, my dear, I don't give a damn" line. Selznick orchestrated the December 15 premiere at Loew's Grand Theater in Atlanta to have maximum impact. The author was there, the stars were there, the public was there, and the film was finally there. Soon, there were Oscars in abundance, eight awards, the most ever for a film at that time and the record until *Ben-Hur*'s 11 in 1959.

Selznick brought out the film again in 1941 and 1942, with record profits, but then sold the rights for $2.4 million to MGM, which kept the movie under wraps from 1943 to 1947, when audiences were again given a chance to see it and to love it. By the end of 1948, profits had cleared $9 million. The stage was set for the 15th year anniversary, and the 1954 CinemaScope wide-screen *GWTW* format proved as popular as ever. The Civil War centennial brought *GWTW* back for another smashing success, launching it back into first place for total rentals. A subsequent re-release, in 1967, helped *GWTW* keep pace with *The Sound of Music*.

America's bicentennial wouldn't have been complete without a reprise of *GWTW*, which was offered in a new venue. In June of 1976, America's greatest movie was broadcast to cable subscribers by HBO, and then, in a $5 million deal with MGM, NBC broadcast *GWTW* on two successive nights in early November that year. Despite having to put up with seemingly endless commercials, *GWTW*'s living room audience was faithful enough to put the showing in the Top 10 most-watched TV programs.

By 1978, CBS wanted a turn, paying the biggest fee ever ($35 million) for TV rights to 20 showings of *GWTW*. Next came media mogul Ted Turner, who went after the MGM film library in 1986, mainly to get *Gone with the Wind*. He got the movie itself, the film rights from CBS in 1987, and then dressed the old glory up to match its 1939 form in time for the 50th anniversary release. By that time, Margaret Mitchell's estate had given permission for the sequel that had long been anticipated. Ripley won the writing honor in a contest, and Warner Books secured publication rights in an auction. *Scarlett* did very well in both hardcover and paperback, setting up Warner's made-for-TV film project.

Bibliography

Bartel, Pauline. *The Complete* Gone with the Wind *Trivia Book*. Dallas: Taylor, 1989.

Edwards, Anne. *Road to Tara*. New Haven: Ticknor & Fields, 1983.

Harwell, Richard. Gone with the Wind *as Book and Film*. Columbia: U of South Carolina P, 1992.

Lambert, Gavin. *GWTW: The Making of* Gone with the Wind. Boston: Little, Brown, 1973.

Owen W. Gilman, Jr.

Good Morning America (1975-) is the two-hour morning news program on TV which premiered as part of the Entertainment Division of the ABC network. It was a revamped version of *AM America*, which had failed earlier that same year. The affable and genial host of the new show was David Hartman, the actor who had been a regular on the television series *The Virginian*, *The Bold Ones*, and *Lucas Tanner*.

The choice of an actor as host was a controversial move at the time because morning show hosts generally came from news backgrounds. NBC and CBS were more interested in hard news, and their morning shows were generally produced by their news divisions. Hartman represented a tactical decision by ABC's management to compete against NBC's *Today* show by offering a new form of programming, combining information and entertainment, which later became known as "infotainment."

Hartman was described as a friendly, avuncular presence with boundless energy and searching curiosity. In a way his informal relaxed style was akin to that of Dave Garroway, the first host of the *Today* show (1952-61). Just as Garroway was succeeded by hosts with solid news backgrounds, Hartman was eventually succeeded by Charles Gibson in 1987. The show was put together as a family concept on a living-room set with Hartman at the center joined by several regular cast members. Joan Lunden joined the show in 1980.

There were three major reasons for *Good Morning America*'s ability to start from scratch and outreach its rival morning shows in the ratings war. The first and primary reason was that it had been deliberately targeted at a specific audience—a typical 32-year-old working woman, to be precise—whereas the *Today* show was still designed to supply news and features for a general audience.

Another reason for the extraordinary success of *Good Morning America* was the ability of producers to attract and book celebrity guests. David Hartman was an enormous drawing card for other actors and actresses, since he knew many of them personally. Once the show was a ratings success, celebrities wanted to appear on it to be seen by more people.

The third reason was Joan Lunden's increasing popularity with the target group—other young women—who could identify with her as a working wife and mother of three children. While Hartman was still on the show, Lunden's role invariably had been that of a subordinate who did the lighter, fluffier features. Hartman would handle the interviews with Washington newsmakers, while she seldom even introduced a segment that had been produced in Washington. After Gibson became co-host, Lunden's role on the show was allowed to expand until she was fully co-equal with him, doing interviews with politicians as well as handling longer travel assignments. Over the years Lunden also became highly visible as a supermom with books and commercials, lectures and other television shows which made her an authority on wifehood and motherhood. As happened with other hosts on news programs and talk shows, she became a celebrity in her own right and left the show in 1997. When Gibson left the show in 1998, it floundered in the ratings until ABC brought back Gibson, along with newswoman Diane Sawyer, in January 1999, to help resuscitate the show.

Bibliography

Hammer, Mike. "Make Overs for Morning Shows." *TV Guide* 13 Apr. 1996: 41.

Marion, Jane. "Being No. 1 Is Icing on the Cake." *TV Guide* 25 Aug. 1990: 24.

Sherman, Eric. "*Good Morning America* Turns Fifteen." *Ladies' Home Journal* Nov. 1990: 132.

Ann Schoonmaker

See also
Television Talk Shows

Goodman, Benny (1909-1986), clarinetist and swing band leader, is probably the world's best-known jazz musician. Dubbed "The King of Swing" by the press in 1936, his band's headline-grabbing success at the Palomar Ballroom in Los Angeles on August 21, 1935, has gone down in history as the night the Swing Era was born.

A rags-to-riches story, Goodman was raised in Chicago's Jewish ghetto, then rocketed to fame and fortune before the age of 30. From that eminence in the entertainment industry he shaped the musical taste of millions. Goodman played a key role in one of the most powerful shifts in American culture in the 20th century—that period from 1935 to 1945 called the Swing Era, when jazz was synonymous with popular music and dance and the optimistic drive of that music defied the realities of economic depression and world war.

Goodman was the first bandleader to defy segregation practices when he hired black musicians for a public concert in a major venue in 1937, thus opening the field for integrated bands and the success of black entertainers in other fields. He traveled the world as a revered elder statesman of jazz after World War II, when he was also considered a master of both jazz and classical music. His classical concerts and recordings helped give jazz added respectability, as did his historic jazz concert at Carnegie Hall in 1938. Dozens of famous musicians, including Harry James, Gene Krupa, and Lionel Hampton, established their careers or gained fame while playing in Goodman's bands. Yet he remains a problematic figure in jazz history, both revered and reviled, one whose achievements have been alternately exaggerated or overly disparaged.

Born Benjamin David Goodman, one of 12 children of parents who were part of the second wave of Jewish immigrants to arrive in Chicago, he learned to play on a borrowed instrument in a synagogue band, but his study with one of the finest teachers of the day laid the foundation for his prodigious technical command on the clarinet. He was a working professional before the age of 14.

Goodman grew up with jazz in America, and he was in his teens during the "Jazz Age" in the early 1920s. He was influenced by both white and black practitioners of the early "hot" jazz style, and he absorbed the innovations of Louis Armstrong, which laid the foundation for the swing instrumental approach. Later, he began working with nationally known bands during the move from small Dixieland combos to larger jazz dance orchestras; he followed their format when he developed the prototype swing band of the 1930s.

His rise to fame paralleled the growth of radio in the United States, and the big break that prepared the ground for his emergence as "The King of Swing" was his band's appearances on the nationally broadcast radio show, *Let's Dance*, in 1934. By 1938, he was broadcasting to an estimated two million listeners three times a week, and the audience he helped create was responsible for the rejuvenation of the record industry, which reached new heights in 1939, when swing music accounted for 85 percent of all sales.

While Goodman continued to lead and record big bands as well as small groups after the Swing Era ended, his largest audience remained the generation that came of age during the 1930s and 1940s, jitterbugging in the aisles and bringing out the riot police when thousands were turned away from his overflowing performances. The excitement his performances occasioned in the 1930s rival the youthful frenzy stirred by Frank Sinatra, Elvis Presley, or the Beatles. Though he attempted to adapt to the changes brought by bebop in the late 1940s, he soon reverted to playing his older material. Despite a Hollywood movie of his life (1955) and continued recognition, after the mid-1950s Goodman was no longer an important influence. But music was his life, and he continued to perform until his death.

Bibliography
Collier, James Lincoln. *Benny Goodman and the Swing Era.* New York: Oxford UP, 1989.

Feather, Leonard. *The New Encyclopedia of Jazz.* New York: Bonanza, 1960.

Firestone, Ross. *Swing, Swing, Swing: The Life and Times of Benny Goodman.* New York: Norton, 1993.

Goodman, Benny, with Irving Kolodin. *The Kingdom of Swing.* New York: Stackpole Sons, 1939.

Schuller, Gunther. *The Swing Era: The Development of Jazz, 1930-1945.* New York: Oxford UP, 1989.

Lynn Darroch

Gospel Song/Gospel Hymn is a genre that, well over a hundred years after its development, remains a musical mainstay of American evangelical Christians. The word gospel means "good news," with the message of most gospel songs focusing upon (1) a loving God who freely offers salvation to helpless sinners through the death of His son Jesus, (2) a Savior who sustains believers amid the daily toils and temptations of life, and (3) the blessed hope of eternal life in a literal heaven. It is good news because it is available to all, and it is free.

Gospel hymnody's relative simplicity stems from its origin in the American Sunday School movement. By the 19th century it was felt children needed hymns in a language appropriate to their vocabularies and concrete ways of thinking. Thus, from the 1840s onward there developed a body of song particularly adapted to the Sunday School. By the 1870s there was a flourishing market of Sunday School (often called Sabbath School) songbooks, publishers, and successful writers.

Musically, Sunday School songs differed little from the popular song style of Stephen Foster. Tuneful diatonic melodies in major keys supported by simple harmonies and slow harmonic rhythms characterized these strophic songs of three to five stanzas. A repeated chorus or refrain concluded each stanza, driving home in summary fashion the simple message of the song. A predominance of eighth-notes and frequent use of compound rhythms provided a conspicuously lively feeling.

The most important Sunday School songwriters were Philip Bliss ("Wonderful Words of Life" words/music), William Bradbury ("Jesus Loves Me, This I Know" music), Fanny Crosby ("Blessed Assurance, Jesus Is Mine" words), William Doane ("Rescue the Perishing" music), and Robert Lowry ("Shall We Gather at the River" words/music).

In late 1871, Ira D. Sankey, a prominent Sunday School and YMCA worker, joined evangelist Dwight L. Moody of Chicago as his musical assistant. They soon began a successful evangelistic tour of England in which the widespread use of American Sunday School songs as both vocal solos and congregational hymns was one of the most novel features of their meetings.

The demand for these songs caused Sankey to publish the most popular for which he could secure copyrights as a modest 15-page, words-only pamphlet called *Sacred Songs and Solos* (London: Morgan & Scott, 1873). From such humble beginnings it continued to expand, eventually becoming a collection of 1200 selections, words and music.

After Sankey returned to the U.S., he combined his efforts with Philip Bliss, whose collection *Gospel Songs* (Cincinnati: John Church, 1874) was intended for adult use in prayer meetings and revival services as well as Sunday School. The result was *Gospel Hymns and Sacred Songs* (New York: Biglow & Main; Cincinnati: John Church, 1875), which eventually ran to six volumes and became the "bible" of gospel hymnody. Thus in the mid-1870s the Sunday School song was transformed into the gospel song.

Gospel hymnody quickly became identified as the music of urban revivalism as represented by songs like Bliss's "Hold the Fort" and Sankey's "The Ninety and Nine." It was also literally carried around the world by gospel musicians (such as Charlie Alexander, who popularized Charles Gabriel's "The Glory Song") and by missionaries whose use of gospel hymns was enthusiastically adopted by countless nationalities who still sing them today.

In the early 20th century, Homer Rodeheaver, music director for evangelist Billy Sunday, continued to popularize gospel songs (George Bennard's "The Old Rugged Cross") via his songleading and publishing business. The genre was also spread by means of phonograph records and radio stations like WMBI in Chicago. It was operated by Moody Bible Institute, an important training center for evangelists and gospel musicians. One of their graduates was John Peterson, the most successful of post–World War II gospel songwriters ("Heaven Came Down"), who promoted many of his songs as choral arrangements. The latest, and perhaps last, of the major contributors to the genre are Bill and Gloria Gaither, who have also popularized their songs ("Because He Lives") through recordings, public appearances, and Gaither Music Company.

Although few new gospel songs have gained wide acceptance, the genre remains the core hymnody of many denominational and non-denominational hymnals. In addition, gospel songs furnish the basis for countless choral and instrumental arrangements. While churchly hymns have usually represented the more authorized music of the church, the immense popularity of gospel hymns has clearly made them the folksong ("people's song") of American religious life.

Bibliography

Eskew, Harry, and James C. Downey. "Gospel Music." *The New Grove Encyclopedia of American Music.* Vol. II. London: Macmillan, 1986.

Hall, J. H. *Biography of Gospel Song and Hymn Writers.* New York: Fleming Revell, 1914.

Sizer, Sandra. *Gospel Hymns and Social Religion.* Philadelphia: Temple UP, 1978.

Mel R. Wilhoit

See also
Christian Songs

Gospel Spirituals have become difficult to define, since there is much diversification and splintering with other genres such as rhythm and blues, jazz, dance, rap, and Motown. Only two percent of the nation's total radio audience listens to gospel music, but spirituals have provided inspiration and guidance in education, family unification, voter registration, and minority-owned businesses.

Gospel spirituals, never forgotten, were popularized by demonstrators during the civil rights movement. New words were put to the melodies of the traditional spirituals, and, according to Martin Luther King, Jr., these freedom songs (see entry) when sung by the marchers inspired courage and hope for a better world in the future.

After World War II, WDIA, the first all-black-formatted radio station in the nation, began airing black gospel and rhythm and blues in Memphis and drew huge crowds to its concert benefits.

Two decades earlier, Chicago had established itself as the birthplace of gospel music. Thomas Dorsey began to publish spirituals, and church choirs and choral groups aired on Chicago radio. Dorsey, influenced by songwriter C. Albert Tindley and blues and jazz when growing up, became well known as a leading choir director, and earned national recognition for his experimentation in black gospel music styles that readily gained acceptance among whites. Dorsey wrote his first gospel song, "If You See My Savior, Tell Him That You Saw Me," in 1928.

Black gospel songs, like the early spirituals, were never sung the same way twice, and singers were encouraged to ad-lib the lyrics and to add their own interpretations to the music. This spirit of individuality was captured by Mahalia Jackson in her gospel renditions. After the Civil War, a number of new styles of black music—ragtime, jazz and blues—began to gain popularity in New Orleans, Memphis, and Chicago, and these new forms found their way into gospel spirituals.

Choirs like the Fisk Jubilee Singers began to harmonize, changing the way spirituals were sung. Black holiness churches, or holy roller churches, that sprang up in the South during the late 1800s began to shape the sound of the gospel hymns in white churches.

The first major collection of gospel spirituals and hymns, *Slave Songs of the United States*, was published after the Civil War in 1867. Characteristic of gospel spirituals were ritualistic shouts and dances, and lyrics with double meanings.

The slaves' desire to be free from oppression was often perceived by their masters as a desire for spiritual freedom. These spirituals, called Sorrow Songs, were a combination of biblical verses and personal slave stories.

The origin of gospel spirituals has been a long-standing debate among historians. Gospel spirituals, according to many researchers, are the true folk songs of the African American. Some plantation owners brought their slaves to church. Many slaves created their own versions of the songs that they heard, often changing the words and melodies to reflect their biblical interpretations, at their own gatherings. In many instances, slaves were forced to sing uplifting work songs and spirituals to reassure their owners of their happiness.

Another theory suggests that spirituals were the result of a fusion between the African and Caribbean story-songs and the British and European folk songs of the 17th and 18th centuries. In some parts of rural America, camp meetings brought together whites and blacks, as they listened together to traveling preachers. During these revivals, they shared in song.

Bibliography

Blackwell, Lois S. *The Wings of the Dove*. Norfolk: Donning, 1978.

Cusic, Don. *The Sound of Light*. Bowling Green, OH: Bowling Green State U Popular P, 1990.

Epstein, Dena J. *Sinful Tunes and Spirituals*. Urbana: U of Illinois P, 1977.

Lornell, Kip. *Happy in the Service of the Lord*. Urbana: U of Illinois P, 1988.

Phylis Johnson

Gothic Mysteries are rooted in the earlier tradition of the gothic novel, begun in 18th-century Europe as a literary vehicle for the popular interest in the Middle Ages characteristic of the time. Horace Walpole wrote the first of these, *The Castle of Otranto*, in 1764. Other well-known writers in the genre included Mrs. Ann Radcliffe, author of *The Mysteries of Udolpho* (1794), and Matthew Gregory Lewis, author of *The Monk* (1796). Gothic stories generally featured heroines beset by various forces of good and evil in medieval settings and melodramatic plots, and were extremely popular.

Later in the 19th century, the Brönte sisters developed the genre further in such works as *Jane Eyre* and *Wuthering Heights* (both 1847). In the early years of the 20th century, Mary Roberts Rinehart (see entry) employed the gothic style in works like *The Circular Staircase* (1908), adding a more contemporary twist to the gothic. In 1938, English novelist Daphne du Maurier (see entry) published *Rebecca*, a literary classic that fully established the hallmarks of the vintage gothic novel: a young and inexperienced heroine, an enigmatic hero who just might be a villain in disguise, and a setting in which the heroine feels out of her depth and therefore prey to the terrors which occur. The success of du Maurier's book, and of Alfred Hitchcock's subsequent Academy Award-winning film, helped prepare for the heyday of the contemporary gothic novel.

After *Rebecca*, the English writers Mary Stewart and Victoria Holt and the American Phyllis A. Whitney produced best-selling suspense fiction in the vein of du Maurier. Their success soon spawned imitators, and the neo-gothic boom had begun, though not all of the work published lived up to the standards set by the three leading authors, and subsequently "gothic" came to have a derisive connotation. Nevertheless, a number of other writers—including Joan Aiken and Jane Aiken Hodge, daughters of the American poet and critic Conrad Aiken; Velda Johnston; and Barbara Mertz (writing as Barbara Michaels and Elizabeth Peters)—have added quality works to the canon. As Barbara Michaels, Mertz often uses elements of the supernatural in her fiction, while as Elizabeth Peters she offers overtly feminist elements to the gothic canon. By the late 1970s, interest in the gothic began to fade, though well-established writers like Whitney, Holt, and Michaels/Peters have continued to publish. Recently, Mary Higgins Clark (see entry) has steered the gothic in the direction of romantic suspense, writing about spirited women characters who are caught up in mysterious and perilous situations, the resolution of which often involves a romantic partnership with a man.

Bibliography

MacLeod, Charlotte. *Had She But Known: A Biography of Mary Roberts Rinehart*. New York: Mysterious, 1994.

Swanson, Jean, and James Dean. *By a Woman's Hand: A Guide to Mystery Fiction by Women*. New York: Berkley, 1994.

Dean James

See also

Adolescent Mysteries	Horror Fiction
Classical Mysteries	Poe, Edgar Allan
Golden Age of Detective Fiction	Mystery and Detective Fiction
	Religious Mysteries
Had-I-But-Known Mysteries	Thriller, The

Grable, Betty (1916-1973), the famous pin-up model and star of numerous musical comedies, was not only the highest salaried woman in the United States at the end of and following World War II, but she was also voted by motion picture exhibitors as the No. 1 draw in their 1943 box office popularity list—a list which held her name in the Top 10 for eight consecutive years. Grable was especially popular with soldiers, five million of whom had pin-ups of her by the end of the war.

Grable's movie studio, Twentieth Century-Fox, drew attention and created hype about a particular part of her body featured in the pin-up: her legs. Although her legs came to be thought of as Grable's "natural assets," there was nothing "natural" about the way Fox used Grable's legs to make money; top executive Darryl Zanuck even referred to them as "a sure-fire commodity." Fox took advantage of this "commodity" in numerous ways. The film *Springtime in the Rockies* (1943), for instance, features a lengthy shot of a newspaper clipping about Vicki Lane, Grable's character; the lead-in to this "news" refers to Vicki Lane's legs as "famous." There was also a rumor that Grable's legs were insured at Lloyd's of London for a million dollars. This rumor was widely accepted as fact—so much so that at one point Grable made a joke to the effect of "If my legs really were insured for a million dollars, I would have cut them off long ago."

Grable's more tangible contributions to film history include a few dramas—*A Yank in the RAF* (1941), *I Wake Up Screaming* (1941), and *That Lady in Ermine* (1948)—as well as many musical comedies, including *Down Argentine Way* (1940); *Tin Pan Alley* (1940); *Moon over Miami* (1941), which has inspired the Denny's restaurant chain's trademarked ham and egg sandwich "Moons over My Hammy"; *Footlight Serenade* (1942); *Song of the Islands* (1942); *Springtime in the Rockies* (1943); *Coney Island* (1943); *Sweet Rosie O'Grady* (1943); *Pin-Up Girl* (1944); *Billy Rose's Diamond Horseshoe* (1945); *The Dolly Sisters* (1945); *Mother Wore Tights* (1947); *The Shocking Miss Pilgrim* (1947); *The Beautiful Blonde from Bashful Bend* (1949); and *How to Marry a Millionaire* (1953), a film which, co-starring Lauren Bacall and Marilyn Monroe, confirmed that Monroe had indeed taken Grable's place as the next "Fox blonde."

Before she starred in these films, Grable spent over ten years in Hollywood getting hired (and dropped) by several studios for bit parts. After her film career wound down, she did shows such as *Guys and Dolls* and *Hello, Dolly*, traveling to cities around the U.S. and Britain. She was married and divorced twice, once to actor Jackie Coogan and once to renowned bandleader Harry James, with whom she had two daughters. She died in 1973 of lung cancer.

Bibliography

Billman, Larry. *Betty Grable: A Bio-Bibliography*. Westport: Greenwood, 1993.

Gaines, Jane. "In the Service of Ideology: How Betty Grable's Legs Won the War." *Film Reader* 5 (1982): 47-59.

——. "The Popular Icon as Commodity and Sign: The Circulation of Betty Grable, 1941-1945." Ph.D. Diss. Northwestern University, 1982.

Renov, Michael. *Hollywood's Wartime Woman: Representation and Ideology*. Ann Arbor: UMI, 1988.

Kathy Evans

Grace under Fire (1993-1998), making its debut on ABC-TV, was an instant Top 10 hit, following its popular lead-in show, *Home Improvement*. After its surprising cancellation, it is now shown in syndication.

One of the many sitcoms starring a standup comic, *Grace* starred Brett Butler as Grace Kelly, a divorced mother of three in her mid-30s. The double meaning of the series title and the cultural irony of the main character having the same name as a beautiful actress-turned-princess set the tone of this sometimes serious comedy. Grace had divorced her alcoholic husband because he beat her, a scenario never before attributed to a major character in a sitcom. The series showed her struggling in an Alabama oil refinery to support her family, and helping her children with the emotional trauma of a neglectful father. To help, she had her best friend from high school, Nadine, who lived next door and was married to another good friend, Wade, a Vietnam veteran. During the first season, her sister, Fay, moved into town and was also there for emotional support and babysitting. The local pharmacist, Russell, was a good buddy and became her sister's lover. In the beginning of the second season, Grace's ex-husband, Jimmy, was introduced.

The relationship of Grace and Nadine (Julie White) was central to this series. Although Grace was a strong, often sarcastic woman, and the three-times divorced Nadine was somewhat insecure, the two were mutually supportive, as seen in their frequent heart-to-heart talks. Although Grace's financial independence and strong female friendships would indicate she might be a feminist, her survival was based on individual coping skills, not politics.

Bibliography

Kaplan, Michael. "Julie White's Life 'Under Fire.'" *TV Guide* 13 Aug. 1994: 26-27.

Murphy, Mary. "The Cynical Cinderella of Sitcoms." *TV Guide* 11 June 1994: 18-21.

Lynn C. Spangler

Graffiti, derived from the Italian word *graffiare*, means to scribble on a wall. As a singular noun the term graffiti is popularly accepted and commonly used to refer to both the plural and singular forms of this artistic expression.

Paleolithic caves, scattered throughout Europe, yield a cornucopia of both pictographs and writing. Some messages, distanced in time from the context in which they were formulated, remain mute, while others speak eloquently across time of everyday popular interests such as the hunt, the worship of nature, or dead ancestors and deities. A preoccupation with the human condition and the sensed finality of life is evident on walls in human settlements around the world. Drawn, etched and painted pictographs, the forerunner of writing, were universally used as late as the Bronze Age. The eruption of Mount Vesuvius and the resultant ruins of Pompeii in 79 A.D. provides us with good examples of how the invention of writing empowered people to communicate more extensively and publicly about everyday matters. When Mount Vesuvius erupted, its ashes preserved a number of writings, such as "Romula tarried here with Staphylus." From the Middle Ages through the early 17th century, English graffiti found on church walls was thought to be the work of the educated and upper class. It dealt with the lofty ideals of knighthood and the appeal of an afterlife. Later, in 18th-century England what had previously been regarded as private matters such as bodily functions, unresolved human relationships, and hopeful sexual fantasies became public dialogue as a result of the opportunities made possible by graffiti.

It was not until the 20th century, and more specifically the mid-1960s, that the practice of graffiti in the United States became so prolific that civic action had to be taken to quell its advancing tide. Its current output in the United States has outdone all other times and places in the bountiful production in kind and quality of work. Urban centers in the United States are home to a variety of graffiti subcultures linked by significant crosscurrents around the world. In the mid-sixties large urban centers such as Los Angeles, New York, Chicago, Philadelphia, and Seattle became fertile ground for the proliferation of three distinct forms of graffiti: tag, wildstyle and social/political graffiti. These categories of graffiti continue to be recognized as distinctly evolved styles emulated by enthusiasts around the world.

Tag graffiti originally appeared in New York City in the early sixties and swept across the United States. As far as it can be discerned, it began in the late sixties when a Washington Heights teenager started writing his nickname, Taki 183, on walls, subway stations, and public monuments. The sole motivation of the tag graffitist focused on a "hit and run" tactic of using large marking pens and aerosol spray paint to demark territory with a signature and not get caught. The idea was to take an alias—Taki 183, Risk-e, Cazal, Frank 207, Bozo, Jimbo, Misty, Rip—and by means of it achieve a style which, when repeated over and over again, communicated one's presence and ubiquity without fear of retaliation. The label "tag" has come to stand for a group of highly stylized letters in a format that makes the end result appear much like a commercial logo publicizing the alias of a graffitist or the code name of a "crew."

Wildstyle graffiti, in its early transitional phase, looked much like the menacing banality of tag graffiti. So much so, that when stylistic rendering of the letters failed to distinguish it sufficiently from tag graffiti, wildstyle graffitists began to focus their attention on size, color, and technique of execution as a way of elaborating its distinctive character.

Creating a word with "bubble" letters as many as five feet in height, filling in the outline in each letter with dots, diagonals, and zigzag lines, and creating a three-dimensional effect by outlining and fading out, produced highly spirited orchestrations of color and form in rhythmic patterns. As a result, wildstyle graffiti took on a look of complexity and originality of design that outdid tag grafitti. As well, the total disregard of the conventional figure/ground relationship evident in conventional artistic composition baffled the onlooker, who was inclined to see the work as chaotic. What is unique and remarkable about wildstyle is that it achieved its meaning and vitality on the street by capturing the attention of pedestrians.

To the bystander who is witness to tags and wildstyle graffiti and has no understanding of the game or its players, the marks may mean only the defacement of property or an act of empty conformity. Police officers suggest that while graffiti has traditionally been regarded as spontaneous isolated acts, tag graffiti may be considered a deliberate act of vandalism in that it is repetitive in intent.

Concurrent with the founding of tag and wildstyle graffiti, a series of provocative little remarks began to appear on downtown walls in urban centers. This work is popularly categorized as political/social graffiti and has been around since the beginning of time. With the advent of tag and wildstyle graffiti, it gained in notoriety. The work taunts pedestrians in a playful yet provocative manner with sayings such as, "Free love: Can you afford it?" "Despise authority," and "Post-atomic Cow: Precooked." The work was visually as well as socially provocative with the interfacing of graphic images and text. It exuded social and political satire, thus affirming through its medium a cosmic relationship with the plight of human beings over time and in other places. The alleyways, monuments, and streets of major urban centers such as New York, Los Angeles, Philadelphia, and Seattle became drawing boards for these graffitists, many of whom were traditionally trained artists. Consequently, several academically trained artists, taking their cue from the graffitists, turned to situating their ideas in the non-art context of graffiti in order to gain recognition. In New York, Jean-Michel Basquiat, Keith Haring, Jenny Holzer, Kathleen Seltzer, Kenny Scharf, and Richard Hambleton achieved success as up-and-coming stars when their work was declared as art by the New York art circuit.

Astute gallery owners observed the animated interaction between the public and these brash young upstarts and recognized a chance to inspirit an economically sluggish mainstream art scene. These artists-turned-graffitists infiltrated mainstream art accelerated by the idea of being seen with a difference by introducing their art on the street and making it answerable in the context of everyday life. Blurring the traditional lines of distinction between themselves and graffitists, they made it possible to become stars of the art world by changing the system in which art becomes significant.

Gaining insight into the origins of conventions that have historically driven human expression, as a way of understanding how standards are set and met, might appear frivolous. By understanding the liberties taken by graffitists within the conventions and the chronology of historical events over time we stand a chance of making sense of how we come to reify certain forms of human expression over others. The work of wildstyle and social/political graffitists described here has become recognized as an attempt to re-appropriate human expression away from the dominant culture of institutions purported to advance a view of human expression based on controls guaranteed in advance of innovation.

Wildstyle and social/political graffitists seem to be setting conditions for an active reworking of the ground of acceptance and rejection of human expression. First, the possible condemnation of graffiti as an offense with a threat of recrimination has come to be seen as a way for graffitists to promote their work while questioning ownership of the freedom and limits of expression. Second, subversive messages in street-smart graphics, utilizing popular corporate advertising gimmicks, provides free publicity while bringing into question strategies of mass cultural technique such as distribution, accumulation, and consumption. It is not the art product that is the exclusive focus of the reworking of the terrain; rather, it is the drama that is played out as bystanders, gallery owners, and anthropologists begin to invite the graffitist in. Herein lies the realization that the real artistry is in the drama of acceptance and rejection as much as it is in the residue left on the walls. The residue left as a mark on walls merely signals that the play is in progress. The rationale of conditions of acceptance and rejection of human expression, whereas in the past only certain phenomena got sanctioned, has, in the hands of the graffitist, drawn us into a dance that, however inadvertently, stands to rework the terrain on which the meaning of art as human expression rests.

Bibliography

Ferrell, Jeff. *Crimes of Style: Urban Graffiti and Politics of Criminality*. New York: Garland, 1993.

Larsen, Agnessa. *Graffiti on My Heart*. Seattle: Peanut Butter, 1994.

Rafferty, Patricia. "Discourse on Differences: Street Art/ Graffiti of Youth." *Visual Anthropology Review* 7.2 (1991): 77-83.

Reisner, Robert. *Graffiti: Two Thousand Years of Wall Writing*. Chicago: Henry Regency, 1971.

Pat Rafferty

See also
Hip Hop

Grafton, Sue (1940-), born in Louisville, KY, is the author of numerous film and TV screenplays but is best known for her widely read series of alphabetically titled detective novels beginning with *A Is for Alibi* (1984), and followed by, thus far, *B Is for Burglar* (1985), *C Is for Corpse* (1986), *D Is for Deadbeat* (1987), *E Is for Evidence* (1988), *F Is for Fugitive* (1989), *G Is for Gumshoe* (1990), *H Is for Homicide* (1991), *I Is for Innocent* (1992), *J Is for Judgment* (1993), *K Is for Killer* (1994), *L Is for Lawless* (1995), *M Is for Malice* (1996), *N Is for Noose* (1998), and *O Is for Outlaw* (1999).

Following the conventions of American hard-boiled detective fiction as adapted for the female detective by Marcia Muller, whom Grafton has called the "founding 'mother' of the contemporary female hard-boiled private eye," Grafton's novels feature Kinsey Millhone, a tough California female private investigator whose cases take her through the whole gamut of investigative activity, from routine stakeouts to violent encounters on the mean streets. In the tradition of her male precursors Dashiell Hammett, Raymond Chandler, and Ross Macdonald, Grafton makes particular use of the California milieu to symbolize both the idealism and the corruptibility of modern American society.

Like all hard-boiled private eyes, Kinsey competes with the police, but she also works closely with them, so the novels contain elements of the police procedural as well. In addition, Grafton often includes a secondary plot involving Kinsey's personal life, thus using the traditional hard-boiled detective's loner role to explore the complex psyche of a modern, self-sufficient woman who simultaneously resembles and contrasts with her creator. Kinsey's "biography is different," Grafton said in an interview in *The Armchair Detective*, "but our sensibilities are identical."

Bibliography

Grafton, Sue. *The Armchair Detective*. Winter 1989.

Klein, Kathleen. *The Woman Detective*. Urbana: U of Illinois P, 1988.

Reddy, Maureen. *Sisters in Crime*. New York: Continuum, 1989.

June M. Frazer

See also
Feminist Detective Fiction
Police Procedural
Regional Mysteries

Grand Ole Opry. In 1925, Nashville's National Life and Accident Insurance Company established its radio station with the call letters WSM, which stood for "We Shield Millions." Within the year, the *Grand Ole Opry* program had taken root in WSM programming, and a country music institution was born. On November 28, 1925, George D. Hay, the self-appointed "Solemn Ol' Judge," served as the announcer for the first WSM *Barn Dance*, featuring the white-bearded fiddler Uncle Jimmy Thompson. The one-hour program which aired Saturday nights at eight o'clock was an instant hit with listeners, and became a regular weekly feature on WSM. Hay continued as announcer for the *Barn Dance*, and recruited additional Tennessee musicians to perform regularly on the show, including Doctor Humphrey Bate, Uncle Dave Macon, Deford Bailey, the Fruit Jar Drinkers, and the Gully Jumpers.

For two years, the WSM *Barn Dance* aired weekly on Saturday nights following the NBC "Music Appreciation Hour," and officially became the *Grand Ole Opry* in May 1927. At the conclusion of the classical program preceding the *Barn Dance*, Hay introduced his country music show by saying, "Friends, for the past hour you've been listening to Grand Opera, but for the next we'll be listening to *Grand Ole Opry*!" The name stuck, and the popularity of the show continued to grow, with listeners packing the WSM studio to watch the live show as it aired on Saturday nights, prompting studio officials to build a larger studio to accommodate the crowds. As the *Opry* outgrew even the new 500-seat auditorium studio, the whole show was moved to the Hillsboro Theatre, and in 1939 to the War Memorial Auditorium studio, where a 25-cent admission fee was imposed in an effort to curb the size of the crowds. However, despite the charge, crowds of 3,000 or more viewed the show each week.

The quality of the performers on the *Grand Ole Opry* contributed to the popularity of the show, as from the early 1930s on, more modern, professional musicians like the Vagabonds were added to the line-up. In the mid-1930s, *Opry* acts began touring the nation, spreading the popularity of the country western sound. Harry Stone formed a booking agency to promote these road shows, and was largely responsible for the movement towards more modern music. During these years of growth, Hay was away from the station due to health problems, and when he returned to the studio full time in 1938, served only as scriptwriter and announcer, as Stone was now managing and booking the shows himself.

From 1925 to 1938, the emphasis of the *Grand Ole Opry* remained on instrumental performances. In 1939, however, with the introduction of fiddler/vocalist Roy Acuff, its focus shifted towards vocal performances, including such acts as Pee Wee King and the Golden West Cowboys, Minnie Pearl, Bill Monroe, Red Foley, and Hank Williams. In 1939, the show made its national radio debut on the NBC network under the sponsorship of Prince Albert Smoking Tobacco. The following year, its national exposure expanded with the release of the Republic Pictures feature film *Grand Ole Opry*, starring Roy Acuff and Uncle Dave Macon. These elements combined to draw larger crowds to the studio broadcasts, and consequently, in 1943, the program moved to Ryman Auditorium, where it remained for the next 30 years.

The growth and popularity of the *Opry* brought change to its programming, as honky tonk music was introduced to the show by Ernest Tubb, who played an electric guitar during a 1943 performance on the program. The following year, Bob Will's Texas Playboys became the first band to use drums in its *Opry* act, and in 1949, Hank Williams used a steel guitar in his act. Further changes included the rise of television and first *Grand Ole Opry* telecast in September 1950, and the retirement of George Hay in 1953. The number of regular performers on the program continued to grow throughout the 1950s and 1960s and included many of the top country musicians in the nation, such as Lester Flatt and Earl Scruggs, Marty Robbins, Hank Snow, Little Jimmy Dickens, Johnny Cash, the Everly Brothers, Porter Wagoner, Loretta Lynn, Dolly Parton, Mel Tillis, and others.

It was during these decades, however, that the *Opry* lost some of its best musicians. Hank Williams died in 1953, followed by Patsy Cline, Hawkshaw Hawkins, Cowboy Copas, Jack Anglin, Berry Jack Davis, Texas Ruby Owens, Jim Reeves, Ira Louvin, and Sam McGee, who were all killed in accidents in the 1960s. Despite these losses, the *Opry* continued to be successful and employed Nashville residents in recording studios, record pressing plants, talent agencies, and recording companies.

The 1960s and 1970s saw the *Grand Ole Opry* boast a roster of over 50 acts, and by 1974 the show had outgrown the Ryman Auditorium. National Life constructed a new 4,400-seat Grand Ole Opry House in a rural Nashville area, which was followed by the Opryland USA theme park and hotel. In the 1980s, the *Opry* and its parent company WSM were purchased by Gaylord Entertainment Corporation, and became a part of a conglomerate which included its own cable network, the Nashville Network. The resurgence of country music popularity in the 1980s and 1990s helped sustain the popularity of the *Grand Ole Opry*, and by 1994, *Opry* cast members numbered over 70, and continued to bring in capacity crowds. In the words of Judge George Hay, "The principal appeal of the *Opry* is a homey one. It sends forth the aroma of bacon and eggs frying on the kitchen stove on a bright spring morning. That aroma is welcomed all the way from Maine to California."

Bibliography

Carlin Richard. "Grand Ole Opry." *The Big Book of Country Music: A Biographical Encyclopedia*. New York: Penguin, 1995.

McCloud, Barry. "Grand Ole Opry." *Definitive Country: The Ultimate Encyclopedia of County Music and Its Performers*. New York: Perigee, 1995.

Sakol, Jeannie. "Grand Ole Opry." *The Wonderful World of Country Music*. New York: Grosset, 1979.

Stambler, Irwin, and Grelun Landon. "Grand Ole Opry." *The Encyclopedia of Folk, Country & Western Music*. 2d ed. New York: St. Martin's, 1983.

Lynnea Chapman King

Grant, Amy (1960-), is Contemporary Christian Music's (CCM) sweetheart, its biggest success story, and its most frequent target for criticism. Grant became the first CCM artist to reach the secular charts when her song "Find a Way" made *Billboard*'s Top 40. She followed that with another pop hit, "Next Time I Fall in Love (It Will Be with You)," a duet sung with Peter Cetera. Grant also was the first CCM artist to reach No. 1 on *Billboard*'s Hot 100 with "Baby, Baby." "Every Heartbeat" followed, also reaching the Top 20. The album that spawned her biggest hits, *Heart in Motion*, went triple platinum. Grant is also the only CCM artist to be involved in a national advertising campaign (for Target stores). In 1998, Grant released *Behind the Eyes*.

But Grant's success has come at a price. Her duet with Cetera led to rumors that she had left her husband, CCM songwriter Gary Chapman. The lack of a religious message in "Baby, Baby" and the rest of the album *Heart in Motion* fueled speculation Grant had forsaken her faith for crossover success. Controversy is not new to Grant. The cover of her 1979 release, "My Father's Eyes," featured a picture of the then-18-year-old college student with the top three buttons of her blouse unbuttoned. It spawned a furor in the ever-suspicious Christian community. Some have chosen to interpret Grant's success as a sign of "backsliding." They fear losing the Amy Grant of the *Age to Age* album, which was filled with memorable worship songs like "El Shaddai" and "Sing Your Praise to the Lord."

Indeed, in 1999 Grant did get a divorce from Chapman; in March 2000 she married country star Vince Gill, with whom she had made the 1994 *House of Love* album.

Bibliography

Harper, Sharon. "Amy Grant: She'll Be Home for Christmas." *Contemporary Christian Music* Dec. 1992: 24-27.

Millard, Bob. *Amy Grant: A Biography*. Garden City: Doubleday, 1986.

Newcomb, Brian Q. "Amy Grant: The Secret of Life." *Harvest Rock Syndicate* 1991.

Styll, John W. "Amy Grant: The CCM Interview." *Contemporary Christian Magazine* July/Aug. 1986: 30-35.

Jay R. Howard

Grant, Cary (1904-1986), born Archibald Alexander Leach in Bristol, England, began life as the only child of poverty-stricken parents. At age nine, following the institutionalization of his mother, he developed a love for the English music hall and procured part-time jobs at the Hippodrome and Empire theaters to accommodate this new passion. Leaving school at age 14, Leach joined the Bob Pender Troupe of comedians and acrobats, where he learned to dance, stilt-walk, and perform acrobatics and pantomime. In 1920, the troupe completed a tour of small English towns and departed for the United States, where they toured successfully for two years. At the conclusion of this tour, Leach opted to stay in New York City, and for five years worked as a placard walker and society escort.

While making the transition from comedian to screen actor, in 1927, Leach appeared in the stage production of *Golden Dawn*, following which he appeared in the musical

Boom, Boom (1929) and a summer season at the St. Louis Municipal Opera (1931). Moving to Los Angeles, he made a screen test for Paramount executive B. P. Schulberg, following which he signed a five-year contract with the studio. It was at this point that he made his film debut in the short *Singapore Sue* (1932) and changed his name to Cary Grant at the suggestion of the studio.

Grant's feature debut was in *This Is the Night* (1932), and he appeared in films with Marlene Dietrich (*Blonde Venus*, 1932) and Mae West (*She Done Him Wrong*, 1933) prior to achieving leading man status. His experience with the comedic troupe and the stage contributed to his success in the fast-paced screwball comedies of the late 1930s, *The Awful Truth* (1937), *Bringing Up Baby* (1938), and *His Girl Friday* (1940). In 1937, upon the completion of his contract with Paramount, Grant chose not to re-sign with the studio, instead forming his own production company, Grantart. In addition to his comedic film roles, he appeared in dramatic pictures as well, including *Penny Serenade* (1941) and *None But the Lonely Heart* (1944), for both of which he received Academy Award nominations. Additionally, Grant expanded his persona to include leading man characters in several Alfred Hitchcock films, *Suspicion* (1941), *Notorious* (1946), *To Catch a Thief* (1954), and *North by Northwest* (1959). He retired from the screen in 1966.

Cary Grant's screen personas were often characterized by a combination of elegance, wit, and sophistication, and possessed a mystique which attracted female characters played by Irene Dunne, Jean Arthur, Ingrid Bergman, Katharine Hepburn, Eva Marie Saint, and Grace Kelly, among others. Grant commented that his screen personas were "a combination of Jack Buchanan, Noel Coward and Rex Harrison. I pretended to be somebody I wanted to be, and, finally, I became that person. Or he became me." Although Cary Grant never received an Oscar for his performances, in 1969, he was honored with a Special Oscar for his contribution to motion pictures, as well as a Lifetime Achievement Award from the American Film Institute. He died from a stroke at age 82 in Davenport, IA.

Bibliography

"Cary Grant." *Brewer's Cinema: A Phrase and Fable Dictionary.* London: Cassell, 1995.

"Cary Grant." *International Dictionary of Films and Filmmakers 3: Actors and Actresses.* 3d ed. New York: St. James, 1997.

Monaco, James, ed. "Cary Grant." *The Encyclopedia of Film.* New York: Perigee, 1991.

Lynnea Chapman King

Grateful Dead, The, was the most enduring of the San Francisco-based acid rock bands. They continued to perform and record, followed everywhere by a fiercely loyal group of fans known as "Deadheads." The Dead's music was centered around the electric guitar wizardry of Jerry Garcia, and they were known for playing extended improvisational sets during long concerts.

Jerry Garcia, the leader, moved to Palo Alto after being thrown out of the U.S. Army in 1959. He began a long friendship with Robert Hunter, the lyricist for many of the Dead's songs. Garcia took up banjo in 1962 and played in a number of folk and bluegrass groups including the Thunder Mountain Tub Thumpers, the Zodiacs, and Mother McCree's Uptown Jug Stompers. The latter included guitarist Bob Weir (Robert Hall), Hunter, and drummer Bill Kreutzman, as well as others who would become non-playing members of the Dead "family."

The group added electronic composer Phil Lesh on bass and Ron "Pigpen" McKernan on keyboards and harmonica. They became more electric and their repertoire drifted toward rhythm and blues standards as they named themselves the Warlocks in 1965. That summer, the Warlocks became the house band for the LSD experiments conducted by Ken Kesey and His Merry Pranksters, the "acid tests" (see Acid Rock). Their music grew louder and more improvisational, and they got financial support from LSD chemist Owsley Stanley. Stanley also designed their state-of-the-art sound system. Garcia renamed the group the Grateful Dead, legend having it that the name popped out of the dictionary at him during one of the acid tests. In November 1965 they played the opening of Bill Graham's Fillmore Auditorium in San Francisco with the Jefferson Airplane.

The Grateful Dead moved to the Haight-Ashbury district of San Francisco and played numerous free concerts during 1966 and early 1967, including the first "Human Be-In" at Golden Gate Park. They also played a heavy concert schedule at the Fillmore and the Avalon Ballroom. The Dead recorded their first album for Warner Brothers in three days in May 1967. The eponymous album did not capture the intensity of their live performances, and it sold only moderately well.

The band began work on a second more experimental album in February 1968, adding a second percussionist, Mickey Hart, and electronic musician Tom Constanten. Hart's father Lenny also became their business manager. It took them six months to complete *Anthem of the Sun*, and the album left them deeply in debt to Warner Brothers. They performed at the major pop festivals in 1968 and 1969, including Woodstock. But their practice of giving free concerts and a second expensive studio album, *Aoxomoxoa*, extended their money problems.

In 1970, Garcia renewed his interest in folk and bluegrass music, working with a spinoff group, the New Riders of the Purple Sage. The Grateful Dead also released their first concert recording, *Live/Dead*, which included a 25-minute version of their crowd-pleaser, "Dark Star."

Constanten left the group before they recorded two highly acclaimed studio albums that took a different direction. *Workingman's Dead* and *American Beauty* included acoustic blues, folk, and country-flavored songs like "Casey Jones," "Friend of the Devil," "Box of Rain," and "Truckin'" (which included the Deadhead motto, "what a long, strange trip it's been"). Lenny Hart was arrested for embezzling money from the Grateful Dead, and his son Mickey quit the band. A second live album reached No. 25 on the charts, the group's best showing to date.

Both Garcia and Weir recorded solo albums in 1972, and the group toured in Europe with the husband and wife team of Keith and Donna Godchaux on keyboards and vocals. The triple-album chronicle of the tour, *Europe '72*, fulfilled their contract with Warner Brothers, and they started their own labels, Grateful Dead Records and Round Records (for side projects). Keyboardist Pigpen sustained liver damage from excessive drinking and left the group in 1972: he died the next year.

The Dead played the largest rock festival in Watkins Glen, NY, in July 1973. The group also recorded its first studio album in three years, *Wake of the Flood*, with a return to improvisational music, this time with jazz influences. The album reached No. 18 on the U.S. charts, and the 1974 *Grateful Dead from the Mars Hotel* peaked at No. 17. But the band effectively stopped performing for two years, recording *Blues for Allah* (with Hart back as the second percussionist) in the studio for United Artists in 1975.

They resumed touring in 1976 and signed with Arista Records, using producers from outside the Dead family for the first time on *Terrapin Station* (1979) and *Shakedown Street* (1979). The Grateful Dead also played three concerts at the foot of the Great Pyramid in Egypt, the last one coinciding with a lunar eclipse. Keith and Donna Godchaux were fired from the band in 1979 and replaced by keyboardist Brent Mydland. Keith Godchaux died in an automobile accident the next year. In 1980, the group released the album *Go to Heaven* and a moderately successful single, "Alabama Getaway."

Garcia's playing deteriorated in the early 1980s as he became more addicted to heroin, but the group continued to play benefit concerts and two major outdoor concerts, the U.S. Festival in California and the Jamaica World Music Festival, in 1982. Garcia finally began drug treatment in 1985 and the Grateful Dead regrouped in the summer of 1986. But Garcia's health failed again, and he lapsed into a five-day diabetic coma.

The Dead began work in the studio with Garcia again in early 1987 with Hunter again writing lyrics. *In the Dark* was the group's most successful album, reaching No. 6 and providing them with their first hit single, "A Touch of Grey." The Grateful Dead also toured with Bob Dylan that summer, and a concert album, *Dylan and Dead,* was released in 1989. Mydland died of a drug overdose in 1990, making him the third Grateful Dead keyboard player to die. Pianist Bruce Hornsby replaced Mydland to finish the tour and Vince Welnick was chosen as the permanent replacement. The group broke up after Garcia's death in 1996.

Bibliography

Brandelius, Jerilyn Lee. *The Grateful Dead Family Album.* New York: Warner, 1989.

Coupland, Douglas. *Polaroids from the Dead.* New York: Regan, 1996.

Grateful Dead: The Official Book of the Dead Heads. New York: Morrow, 1983.

Hunter, Robert. *A Box of Rain.* New York: Penguin, 1993.

Troy, Sandy. *One More Saturday Night: Reflections with the Grateful Dead, Dead Family, and Dead Heads.* New York: St. Martin's, 1992.

Kenneth M. Nagelberg

Graveyards. The designation of specified areas for the burial of the dead and, concomitantly, the erection of monuments at gravesites to mark the spot of individual burial and commemorate the person departed are among humanity's most ancient and widespread practices. In America, these elements of the constructed landscape, while incorporating features derived from European and other predecessors, have over time and space developed their own distinctive forms and purposes. For the student of American cultural history, they are important in at least three primary ways—as physical sites in themselves, as concentrated repositories of unique material artifacts, and as focal points for a wide variety of traditional practices.

The geographic siting, as well as the underlying philosophical concept of cemeteries in America, follows a distinctive evolutionary pattern closely linked to changing standards in taste and cultural values. With certain exceptions, the earliest organized burial sites in the colonies, unlike their European (primarily British) counterparts, did not as a general rule surround church structures, and thus were uncommonly known as "churchyards," preferring instead the more generically descriptive terms "burying ground," "burial ground," or "graveyard." The frequently used term "cemetery," deriving from the Greek word for sleeping chamber, would not gain general currency until the early 19th century, eventually to be challenged in our own time by the even more euphemistic "memorial park."

American art, it may truly be said, had its origins in the graveyard, and its medium was stone. Following several decades in which gravemarkers were fashioned of wood or roughly shaped fieldstone, the discovery of deposits of high-grade slate in the greater Boston area led in the mid-17th century to the adoption of this highly workable material as the memorial stone of preference among folk artisans and their patrons in the communities of eastern Massachusetts. Here, Puritan theological concepts became transformed into grim yet exceptionally beautiful folk artifacts which featured winged skulls, skull and crossbone combinations, and sometimes even whole skeletons, as well as various secondary death symbols (coffins, hour glasses, picks and shovels, imp-like figures with darts, scythes, etc.) carved in the tympanum (top central) area of the erect, tablet-style markers. Occasionally, the skill of individual carvers would produce remarkably dramatic visual allegories, such as the figures of Death and Father Time, each with their appropriate identifying features, snuffing out the candle of life. Intricate vegetative or geometric designs frequently decorated the side and bottom borders of these markers, while Latin inscriptions such as *Memento Mori* ("Remember Death") or *Hora Fugit* ("The Hours Fly") served as effective counterparts to the visually dominant mortality symbolism.

Burial grounds situated within the burgeoning urban areas of America were, by the early decades of the 19th century, rapidly becoming filled to capacity and viewed as both eyesores and community health hazards. New "rural cemeteries" were located outside existing urban boundaries, on sites specifically chosen for their topographical and horticultural qualities. Characterized by their tasteful blending of splendid monuments with other natural and ornamental features, they became sentimentalized landscapes of memory.

Gravestones in 19th-century American cemeteries were mainly of marble, and feature a rich and varied panoply of decorative symbolism, the most commonly recurring motifs being the hand with upraised index finger (signifying resurrection), the weeping willow tree (a generic mourning symbol, descendant of the urn and willow image popular in the previous century), and clasped hands (a contextually specific figure with several explanations).

The last phase in the evolution of America's graveyards—and that which has come to dominate the design of these sites in the 20th century—is the "memorial park," a generally nondescript landscape featuring markers, usually granite, set in precise rows flush to the ground surface and accompanied by a minimum of plantings or other decorative features. In hand with these developments have come a number of innovative and sometimes aggressive marketing techniques to ensure the commercial success of these largely privatized ventures, including the emphasis on "pre-need" sales (i.e., the financed purchase of cemetery plots and other services well in advance of their actual need) and the trend of memorial parks serving as "one-stop shopping" centers for funerary purposes. To many observers, such places and practices would seem to epitomize not only late-20th-century Americans' obsession with convenience, but also the enormous distance they have contrived to place between themselves and the fact of death itself.

In keeping with late-20th-century American lifestyles and philosophies, both the visual and verbal elements emerging with ever-increasing frequency on gravemarkers since the 1960s have tended to place strong emphasis upon the individual and upon things of this world, particularly occupational and recreational interests.

Traditional practices associated with American graveyards are widespread and vary considerably along historical, regional, and ethnic lines. The evolution of the typical American funeral—particularly its gravesite elements—from the elaborate processions of the Puritans and highly codified mourning behaviors of the Victorians to the essentially sanitized ceremonies of the present era serves as one telling indication of historic changes in the manner in which Americans have chosen to ritualize this significant rite of passage. Among the more interesting of regional patterns in cemetery-related ritual is the practice, widespread throughout much of the country's Upland South areas, of Decoration Day, an annual time of cleaning, repair, decoration, and socializing closely allied to concepts of familial and community solidarity.

In addition to all their other features and functions, graveyards have managed to provide the stimulus and focal point for an astounding variety of elements in American folklore and popular culture. From proverbial utterances such as "whistling past the graveyard" to superstitions and popular beliefs (e.g., "when a grave sinks early, another will follow soon") to blues and other musical forms (e.g., John Lee Hooker's "Graveyard Blues"), cemeteries provide a metaphorical context for a number of manifestations of folk wisdom and sentiment. Legends of all sorts, ranging from traditional ghostlore to accounts of weeping sculpted angels and telephones in mausoleums, feature cemeteries as their primary setting.

Graveyards in America, as indeed wherever they occur, are outdoor museums and laboratories—of history certainly, but also of art, architecture, ethnicity, regionalism, social patterns, and a host of other concerns vital to the understanding of cultural evolution.

Bibliography

McDowell, Peggy, and Richard E. Meyer. *The Revival Styles in American Memorial Art.* Bowling Green, OH: Bowling Green State U Popular P, 1994.

Meyer, Richard E., ed. *Cemeteries and Gravemarkers: Voices of American Culture.* Logan: Utah State UP, 1992.

——. *Ethnicity and the American Cemetery.* Bowling Green, OH: Bowling Green State U Popular P, 1993.

Sloane, David Charles. *The Last Great Necessity: Cemeteries in American History.* Baltimore: Johns Hopkins UP, 1991.

Richard E. Meyer

Grease (1978), directed by Randal Kleiser, and starring John Travolta and Olivia Newton-John, remains one of the most successful movie musicals of all time, earning about $100 million.

With music and story by Warren Casey and Jim Jacobs, *Grease* the play takes a nostalgic look at teenagers in the 1950s. A fairly simple boy-meets-girl romance, catchy '50s-style music, and plenty of humor kept the Broadway show running for delighted audiences for 3,388 performances, though it was not particularly well received by the critics.

The movie was designed to showcase two of the hottest stars of the late 1970s, John Travolta and Olivia Newton-John. Producers Allan Carr and Robert Stigwood signed Travolta before his mammoth success in *Saturday Night Fever* (1977, also produced by Stigwood). Newton-John, on the other hand, was cast shortly before shooting. She was one of the most successful female pop singers of the decade and she lobbied hard for the lead in *Grease.*

The film had high production values and the set-pieces, even the most generic, appeared fresh, energetic, and convincing. *Grease* contained such big hits as the title song (written for the film by Barry Gibb of the Bee Gees and performed by 1960s idol Frankie Valli), "Greased Lightning," "Hopelessly Devoted to You," and "You're the One That I Want" (also written especially for the movie, this song, performed by Travolta and Newton-John, spent 24 weeks on top of the charts). Eventually, the lovers are reunited and everything ends happily. In the tradition of big Hollywood musicals of earlier eras, the film finishes with a rousing production number ("We Go Together") during which all of the major characters are coupled together.

A sequel, unimaginatively entitled *Grease 2*, was released in 1982, with Michelle Pfeiffer and Maxwell Caulfield. Unfortunately, it was a pale shadow of the original.

Bibliography

Altman, Rick. *The American Film Musical.* Bloomington: Indiana UP, 1987.

Denisoff, R. Serge, and William D. Romanski. *Risky Business: Rock in Film.* New Brunswick: Transaction, 1991.
Richards, Stanley. *Great Rock Musicals.* New York: Stein, 1979.
Wallechinsky, David, and Amy Wallace. *The Book of Lists: The 90's Edition.* Boston: Little, Brown, 1993.
Whitburn, Joel. *Top Pop 1955-1982.* Menomonee Falls: Record Research, 1983.

Michael Goldberg

Great Gildersleeve, The (1941-1957). "Great" was the perfect epithet for Throckmorton P. Gildersleeve, main character of the radio show *The Great Gildersleeve*. A large man in the tradition of Shakespeare's pleasure-loving Falstaff, he was never mean. His very name combined dignity (Basil Gildersleeve was a famous Victorian classicist), social polish (one Throckmorton was an Elizabethan diplomat), and naughtiness (another rebelled against Elizabeth).

Gildy drove from NBC's Wistful Vista, where he had battled Fibber McGee (see entry), to Springfield and became radio's first successful spinoff. His new world embraced home, work and social life. Gildy's appetites kept housekeeper Birdie Lee Coggins (Lillian Randolph) busy. More feisty than most black radio domestics, Birdie moderated his pomposity by repeating herself ("You know what I said? That's right! That's what I said"). She also provided a mother surrogate for his live-in niece Marjorie Forrester (Lurene Tuttle, Louise Erickson, Marylee Robb) and nephew Leroy (Walter Tetley). Like other unmarried guardians (Donald Duck, Sky King), Gildy coped with the younger generation. Marjorie usually abided by his rules, but began dating and, after marrying Bronco Thompson (Richard Crenna) and bearing twins, set up her own house. Leroy gave little promise of accepting maturity: He reacted to his "Unk's" apparently foolish directions with an exasperated "Oh, for corn sakes."

The show also followed Gildy loitering through his job as Water Commissioner, sometimes aided by his simple secretary Bessie (Pauline Drake, Gloria Holiday). His campaign for mayor in 1944 floundered when he lost his temper on a political broadcast. Anyway, romance interested him more, but his amorous quests never led to the altar. His closest approach with Leila Ransom (Shirley Mitchell), a flirtatious southern widow, ended when her supposedly dead spouse turned out to be alive. Gildy's friends provided enough excitement to compensate for these losses. Judge Horace Hooker (Earle Ross), the "old goat" who monitored his care of Marjorie and Leroy, deflated his ego. So did Rumson Bullard (Gale Gordon), his wealthy and insulting neighbor.

Real life might have caused disaster because the original Gildy, Hal Peary, launched his own short-lived CBS show *Honest Harold* in 1950. Luckily, Willard Waterman, a friend of Peary's who often teamed with him on other shows, sounded like him and took over the lead until the show ended in 1957. Both men had fine singing voices and incorporated easy-listening songs into the plot. Peary starred in four amusing Gildersleeve films in the 1940s while Waterman took over the 1950s TV series.

Bibliography
Buxton, Frank, and Bill Owen. *The Big Broadcast 1920-1950.* New York: Viking, 1972.
Dunning, John. *Tune in Yesterday: The Ultimate Encyclopedia of Old-Time Radio, 1925-1976.* Englewood Cliffs: Prentice-Hall, 1976.
"Helpful Hints to Husbands." *Tune In* 4 (July 1946): 20-21.
"Throckmorton P." *Newsweek* 22 (13 Dec. 1943): 84.

James A. Freeman

Great Train Robbery, The (1903), is generally considered to be the first movie to tell a story with the use of imaginative editing. Directed by Edwin Stratton Porter (1870-1941) for the Edison Manufacturing Company in November 1903, the 11-minute movie also contributed to the new moving-picture technology's popularity and helped establish the economic viability of early theaters built solely for movies, nickelodeons. In fact, according to various studies of the early exhibition practices of theater owners, Porter's movie was so popular and created such a sensation that audiences would demand that it be re-shown immediately after they saw it for the first time.

The Great Train Robbery has a simple storyline: Two masked men enter a railroad telegraph office in the West and force the operator to signal an approaching train to stop and give the engineer a false order. The operator is bound and gagged. The men sneak on the train, kill a rail man, open a "valuables box" with explosives, kill a male passenger in full view of a crowd of passengers, escape with the engine car, throw a railroad man off the train, and join accomplices who await with horses. Meanwhile, the telegraph operator's daughter arrives at his office and unties him. He seeks the help of a group of cowboys, who are relaxing and dancing with women in a saloon. This organized posse leaves immediately, chases the robbers on horseback, and kills them. The most exciting moment for audiences was a close-up shot of one of the bandits, played by G. M. "Bronco Billy" Anderson, who points a revolver at the camera and pulls the trigger.

Two years after its production and release, on the day before Thanksgiving in Pittsburgh, PA, Harry Davis and John P. Harris opened their "nickelodeon" theater, which sat approximately 100 patrons. The first movie they exhibited was *The Great Train Robbery*. On the first day, they collected $22.50 in receipts; they made $76.00 on the next day.

The Edison Company sold their movie product as soon as they were completed. Post-production of *The Great Train Robbery* was finished in early December 1903. By Christmas, all the major film exchange companies in New York City were exhibiting it in theaters throughout Manhattan and Brooklyn. The American setting (many call the movie the first Western) and subject matter was said to have contributed to its popularity at that time. Besides Anderson, who played many roles in the movie, the performers were Walter Cameron, A. C. Abadie, Marie Murray, George Barnes, and Frank Hanaway. Anderson, whose real name was Max Aronson, a veteran of 100 Western shorts from 1907 through 1914, was given an honorary Academy Award in 1957.

Bibliography
Everson, William. *American Silent Film*. New York: Oxford UP, 1978.
Jacobs, Lewis. *The Rise of the American Film*. New York: Harcourt, Brace, 1967.
Jowett, Garth. *Film*. Boston: Little, Brown, 1976.
Sklar, Robert. *Movie-Made America*. New York: Vintage, 1975.

Richard L. Testa, Jr.

Green Acres (1965-1971), went far beyond the standard rural sitcom. Populated with characters more suitable for Alice's "Wonderland" than the farm belt, *Green Acres* was the epitome of surrealist situation comedy. Hot-tempered city lawyer–turned–country farmer Oliver Wendell Douglas (Eddie Albert) found his simple dream of owning a farm constantly complicated by his "malapropping" wife Lisa (Eva Gabor), lazy hired hand Eb (Tom Lester), hustling huckster Mr. Haney (Pat Buttram), absent-minded county agent Hank Kimball (Alvy Moore), and neighbors Doris and Fred Ziffel (Hank Patterson, Barbara Pepper, then Fran Ryan) whose "son" was a pig named Arnold. *Green Acres* was one of the most popular series of its time, perhaps because the show's insanity provided viewers a much needed escape from a changing, war-torn society.

Presenting a twist in rural comedies, *Green Acres* had Oliver Douglas escape from the city to live on a farm—this premise was clearly established in the 60-second opening theme, which has been committed to memory by even the most passive couch potato. The series divided its time between recurring gags, such as Lisa's hotcakes or the dilapidated farmhouse and tractor—both sold to sucker Douglas by Mr. Haney—and unusual storylines, such as Arnold's "Romeo and Juliet" affair with a dog named Cynthia. For all its escapism, this and other episodes often addressed deeper problems in our society, including prejudice and the emerging battle of the sexes.

Like many of the rural sitcoms, *Green Acres* was canceled when CBS president Bob Wood moved toward a more relevant schedule of programming in 1970. *Green Acres*, like many of the rural sitcoms, does very well in syndication. In 1990, CBS did a reunion episode, *Return to Green Acres*. In 1991, Nick at Nite, the MTV-owned classic sitcom cable network, did its own *Green Acres* retrospective during a marathon broadcast of the show's most popular episodes.

Bibliography
Brooks, Tim, and Earle Marsh. *The Complete Directory to Prime Time Network TV Shows, 1946-Present*. New York: Ballantine, 1992.
Cox, Stephen. *The Hooterville Handbook: A Viewer's Guide to* Green Acres. New York: St. Martin's, 1993.
Winship, Michael. *Television: Companion to the PBS Television Series*. New York: Random House, 1988.

Michael B. Kassel

Green, Anna Katharine (1846-1935), is important to the history of mystery and detective fiction because she could write a good "criminal romance" (her own preferred term), and consequently established the detective novel as a realistic form, with plausible plotting and credible characters. Her stories are inventive, and she is noted for devising ingenious murder methods, such as bullets pressed from ice crystals that melt on impact, leaving no trace. In addition, Green is the first American detective novelist to present real American backgrounds. Throughout her 40 volumes is the pervasive presence of New York City and—more occasionally—upstate New York in the last quarter of the 19th century.

Green was a generation behind Edgar Allan Poe, and as his successor as a mystery writer, she both drew from and departed from his work. Noting that the detectives she knew outside the fictional realm were "tame and uninteresting," Green made her literary detectives much the same, avoiding the eccentricities of Poe's Dupin. In her fiction one finds not the supreme detective and his bumbling auxiliary, but the conscientious professional policeman and his aristocratic sidekick who gains the policeman entrée into the upper-class circles where most crimes are committed in Green's world. All these elements form the pattern of the author's first and most famous novel, *The Leavenworth Case* (1878), which introduces Inspector Gryce, who figures in 11 novels and 2 short stories over the next 40 years.

Bibliography
Hayne, Barrie. "Anna Katharine Green." *Ten Women of Mystery*. Ed. Earl F. Bargainnier. Bowling Green, OH: Bowling Green State U Popular P, 1981.
Maida, Patricia. *Mother of Detective Fiction*. Bowling Green, OH: Bowling Green State U Popular P, 1989.
Welter, Barbara. *In Dimity Convictions: The American Woman in the Nineteenth Century*. Athens: Ohio UP, 1976.

Barrie Hayne

See also
Classical Mysteries
Feminist Detective Fiction
Regional Mysteries

Greene, **Lorne** (1915-1987), was barely 40 years of age when he was cast as the father, Benjamin Cartwright, on NBC's *Bonanza* television series in 1959 (see entry). As an actor, Greene projected the manly, intelligent nature of a perfect father figure. But he was more paterfamilias than patriarch because his ability was to project inward strength rather than overt sensuality. Despite his relative youth, the silver-haired Canadian with the classical training and rich voice rapidly became noted as one of the most successful leads to appear in this century. For 14 full seasons, "Pa" Cartwright guided his sons and hired hands, helping to keep the TV Western genre alive. *Bonanza* bridged the gap between action adventure and family-oriented programs; his sons "grew up" on screen; "Ben" remained the series' vital center.

Greene was born in Ottawa, Canada. After extensive education, acting training, and theatrical experience, he began his radio career during World War II. He became Canada's premier radio voice, then gained additional fame by writing and hosting his own news program for four years.

He migrated to the U.S. in the early 1950s as did other talented Canadian actors and directors. He gained work in feature films and more than a dozen series and anthology TV programs before *Bonanza* debuted. His credits include *Bronco, Alfred Hitchcock Presents,* and the *U.S. Steel Hour.* Equally gifted at serious or comedic acting, at home in any style, era, or school of performance, Greene also parlayed his *Bonanza* success through spoken records such as "Ringo," rodeo appearances with series co-stars Dan Blocker and Michael Landon, and guest appearances and narrational duties on TV specials and documentaries.

Greene was able to find other series that could benefit from his unusual strengths of energy, concentration, and professional preparedness. *Bonanza,* his greatest personal success, may have been behind him by 1973, but Greene was able to play other aspects of that role in many guises thereafter without his presentation losing any of its freshness. He appeared in the made-for-TV movie *Nevada Smith* (1975), *Roots* (1977), and the miniseries *The Moneychangers* (1976). But the busy actor soon made another series. He played Wade "Griff" Griffin in 1973, a retired police captain turned private investigator. When the show was canceled after a short run, Greene accepted a lead in *Code Red* (1981). It was a poorly conceived adventure program whose storyline revolved about Joe Rorchek, patriarch of a family whose business was firefighting and arson investigation. Prior to this project, Greene was granted his last great TV series lead. He played Commander Adama on *Battlestar Galactica* from 1978 to 1980. Much was expected of this high-budget, highly touted science fiction epic (see entry). Greene's towering portrayal of a man who was president, field marshal, father, and father-confessor to dozens was not enough to save the series from cancellation.

Greene's other TV credits were numerous. They included *The Alamo: Thirteen Days to Glory* (1987), *Highway to Heaven* (1985), and *A Time for Miracles* (1980). Greene also narrated a well-received ecological show called *Last of the Wild.* Later, he produced the series as *Lorne Greene's New Wilderness* (1982), contributing to the cause of global ecological preservation for which he cared so deeply. At the time of his death, Greene was preparing to star in the *Bonanza* revival project NBC was planning.

Bibliography

Brooks, Tim, and Earle Marsh. *The Complete Directory to Prime Time TV Stars, 1946-Present.* New York: Ballantine, 1987.

Brown, Mary Wale. *Reel Life on Hollywood Movie Sets.* Riverside: Ariadne, 1995.

R. D. Michael

Greeting Cards in ever-increasing variety attempt to satisfy the need for any occasion or sentiment in our society. There are cards of congratulations for births and condolences for death, and cards to celebrate birthdays for each year of a person's life in between. Birthday cards can be selected based on the relationship of the person, whether parent, spouse, sibling, other immediate family member, or friend. There are cards for engagements, wedding showers, anniver-

saries, separations, divorces, and second marriages. Cards can announce new addresses, invite guests to any type of party or occasion, or express thanks for gifts, hospitality, or acts of kindness. Congratulations for each accomplishment, for graduation from kindergarten through college, for a new job, or for promotions are common. There are cards expressing concern about illnesses, surgery, and recovery from a variety of addictions. For every holiday or special day there is a card beginning with New Year's and going through the calendar to Christmas and Hanukkah.

The emotional messages written or implied in each of these categories may be serious, comic, sentimental, insulting, or sexually suggestive. Cards in a wide range of prices may be purchased from card shops, supermarkets, convenience stores, or by mail order. Cards have also been sold door-to-door.

Some card designs are artistically created, some sport a photograph, abstract design, or they may feature animals, caricatures, flowers, landscapes, still life, men, women, children, modes of travel, sunrises, and sunsets.

Over the years many novelty cards have appeared. Phonograph-record cards play a pre-recorded musical tune or a message recorded by the sender. Perfumed sachets imbedded in the card add to romantic messages. Pop-up characters, pull-down tabs, and wheels add motion to cards. Reflective paper suggests a mirror. Microchips have made it possible to push a button and have a song or message played. Lace, fringe, deckled edges, and cut-outs have added to the design of cards.

Of the billions of cards sold annually, an increasing percentage of them fall into the category of non-occasion cards. These cards express a variety of sentiments unrelated to a specific occasion. One of the earliest producers of the non-occasion card was Susan Polis Schutz, who wrote poetry about relationships and nature. Along with her husband, she started Blue Mountain Arts. The trend toward the non-occasion card was eventually capitalized on by the larger card producers, such as Hallmark, American Greetings, and Gibson Greetings, which helped them to offset decreased sales with the demographic decline in births and the related smaller demand for birthday cards.

The growth in the greeting card industry may be attributed to commercialization of the variety of special days and holidays throughout the year. Special days, such as Mother's Day, Valentine's Day, St. Patrick's Day, Father's Day, Halloween, and Thanksgiving, along with holidays, like Easter, Hanukkah, Christmas, New Year's Day, and Rosh Hashanah, are promoted by merchants as opportunities for remembering others near or far. One failure at commercialization was the promotion of a Friendship Day on the first Sunday in August. There has been more success with adding Secretary's Day and Grandparents' Day to the special occasion calendar.

Licensing agreements for comic strip characters, and television and sports personalities, have added to the lucrative enterprise of greeting cards. A card can be an inexpensive gift in itself, or cards can be sent with a gift, money, or gift certificate. Cards are even sent with prepaid, long distance telephone calling credit, which encourages the recipient to use the credit in another American pastime, talking on the telephone.

The popularity of greeting cards predates the commercialization of holidays by enterprising merchants. Valentines were common in England as early as the Middle Ages. In medieval Germany, greetings were produced on parchment from a woodcut. In the mid-19th century, Christmas cards were used in England as a substitute for a handwritten note or a personal visit during the holidays. Sending Christmas cards was customary by the end of the century.

The ritual of exchanging Christmas cards spread to America in 1875. That year Louis Prang, a prominent Boston lithographer, decided to sell some of his cards in the United States as well as exporting them to Europe. His success signified the beginning of the first wave of the American greeting card industry. An important factor in this success was the establishment in 1863 of free postal service in the United States. Also Puritanism was declining, which allowed a more spirited and romantic celebration of Christmas. Popular writers like Charles Dickens and Washington Irving helped to promote Christmas celebrations and times of good cheer. The decline of the Puritan influence also helped establish Easter cards in the United States. Protestants associated the celebration of Easter with Catholicism, but in the 1890s it was accepted as a holiday and Easter cards became customary.

Several American companies were part of the second wave of greeting card popularity, which began early in the 20th century. Stationers, printers, and booksellers were diversifying by selling cards, with some producing their own lines. Three companies that began in that period are the leaders of the industry today.

Gibson Greetings was established in 1850 by the Gibson brothers in Cincinnati, OH. To their commercial paper sales, they added printed stationery and eventually greeting cards. At first they bought cards from Prang but then began to design and produce their own.

American Greetings was established in 1906 in Cleveland, OH, by Jacob Sapirstein, who enlisted the help of his nine-year-old son to help fill the orders of his home-based business.

Joyce C. Hall founded what was to become Hallmark in 1910 in Kansas City, MO. Storing his inventory under his bed, Hall ran a postcard distribution business while attending business college. Later bringing in his brother, he added greeting cards to his stock when he saw the quality and profit from post cards declining. Today with its diversified product lines, it has become the largest company in the industry.

Other contributors to the second wave of American greeting cards were Fred Rust of Kansas City, who founded the company that would become Rust Craft; Albert M. Davis of Boston; and Paul F. Volland of Chicago.

Until recently, ethnic and cultural differences were not often expressed in cards. Small producers and sellers have supplied some race-specific cards. Larger companies have relied on non-specific cards with flowers, animals, or landscapes to fill the void. With the growth of the non-Caucasian population in the United States, larger companies are beginning to introduce more diversity. However, newer ethnic holidays, such as Kwanzaa, are supplied by small, ethnic publishers.

Collecting cards, especially 19th-century ones, is now a popular hobby. There are several special collections in libraries, museums, and private collections. A selection of Prang sample books, used by salesmen, is held in the collection of the American Antiquarian Society at Worcester, MA.

Bibliography

Buday, George. *The History of the Christmas Card.* Detroit: Tower, 1971.

Chase, Ernest Dudley. *The Romance of Greeting Cards.* Cambridge: Cambridge UP, 1926.

Cheney, Lynne. "You Can Thank Louis Prang for All Those Cards." *Smithsonian* 8.6 (1977): 120-25.

Schmidt, Leigh Eric. "The Commercialization of the Calendar: American Holidays and the Culture of Consumption, 1870-1930." *Journal of American History* 78 (1991): 887-916.

Margo B. Mead

Grey, Zane (1874-1939), perhaps America's most famous author of Western fiction, was born Pearl Grey in Zanesville, OH. For a short time he was a dentist in New York City, but the success of two early novels convinced him to change professions. *The Spirit of the Border* (1903), the second of these, launched his career as a Western writer. Although

James Fenimore Cooper is widely held to be the originator of the American Western, the modern popular Western owes more to Owen Wister's *The Virginian* (1902), and to Grey (see Western Fiction).

Of Grey's 54 novels, *Riders of the Purple Sage* (1912) is the most famous. Its hero is a Texas Ranger who confronts and kills a gunslinger, posing as a judge, in retaliation for a past crime, and must now flee for his life from a posse. The ingredients that made *Riders* so popular became stock elements of Grey's subsequent novels. Set in ranch and cattle country, they center around the dramatic conflicts between strong, self-sufficient heroes—men of honor, loyalty, and chivalry—and the brutal villains who challenge their proprietorship of the West. Best known among them are *Desert Gold* (1913); *The Border Legion* (1916); *The U.P. Trail* (1918); *Call of the Canyon* (1924); *The Thundering Herd* (1925); and *Code of the West* (1934). A number of Western novels were published posthumously, including *Rogue River Feud* (1948), *Lost Pueblo* (1954), and others.

Writing in an era when the "old West" had passed into history and people were nostalgic for a world whose loss they mourned, Grey's writings both satisfied and fed the hunger for Western myths. He elaborated on Cooper's celebration of the American hero who faces life alone and welcomes his destiny, and further developed Cooper's basic symbolism of the West as American Eden. Grey's West was a pastoral terrain where melodramatic strife between heroic and nefarious characters reaffirmed standard American credos about opportunity, individualism, and courage.

Bibliography

Karr, Jean. *Zane Grey: Man of the West*. New York: Grosset & Dunlap, 1950.

Tranquilla, Ronald. "Ranger and Mountie. Myths of National Identity in Zane Grey's *The Lone Star Ranger* and Ralph Conor's *Corporal Cameron*." *Journal of Popular Culture* 24 (1990).

Frank A. Salamone

Griffith, Andy (1926-), one of television's most popular stars, born in Mt. Airy, NC, had a happy childhood in spite of his family's modest means. The adolescent Griffith developed an interest in music early, especially after watching the movie *Birth of the Blues* (1941), starring Bing Crosby and Mary Martin.

Griffith attended the University of North Carolina, where pursuing a divinity degree proved a bit too dry for his taste. He began to perform in university musicals, in which he was well received, and he thought for a time he might become an opera singer. He switched majors to music, graduating in 1949, and soon after married Barbara Edwards, a fellow music major. Feeling obliged to find a steady source of income, Griffith abandoned his ambitions for an opera career to become a high school music teacher in western North Carolina, but soon realized he was not an effective teacher.

Three years later, Griffith left the classroom to become an entertainer. Confronted with decidedly discouraging results from an audition for a New York musical, he concluded his forte was comedy rather than singing. He and his wife then put together an act, mailed out brochures themselves, and found steady work traveling around North Carolina performing for any civic gathering that would hire them. Andy had a bit of good luck when a representative from Capitol Records discovered and had recorded his monologue entitled *What It Was—Was Football*. The ensuing record sold well all over America, resulting in an invitation to appear in 1954 on the *Ed Sullivan Show*. Griffith flubbed this opportunity due to excessive nervousness. Refusing to become discouraged, he honed his skills in nightclubs, finally winning the lead part in the Broadway version of *No Time for Sergeants*.

It was in 1960 that Griffith initiated his most significant contribution to modern popular culture. Movie opportunities began to dry up, so he decided to try television. The idea for a new sitcom was tested in early 1960 with Griffith appearing as a small-town sheriff on *The Danny Thomas Show* (see entry).

The Andy Griffith Show began on October 3, 1960, and went on to become one of the most popular and enduring series in the history of television, lasting until its 249th episode was broadcast on September 16, 1968 (see entry). Winner of six Emmies, and consistently ranked among the Top 10 shows, it was No. 1 its final season. More than 25 years later, some 5 million viewers in America alone still watch the series daily in the form of syndicated reruns shown in some localities more than once daily, seven days a week.

There have been a couple of spinoff series. Jim Nabors, who played the simple-minded gas station attendant with a generous heart, went on to star as a simple-minded soldier with a generous heart in *Gomer Pyle, U.S.M.C.* Another spin-off, *Mayberry, R.F.D.* (see entry), aired after Griffith discontinued his own show. *Mayberry, R.F.D.* nearly duplicated the original series, with Ken Berry, like Griffith, playing a widower rearing a son.

Continued interest in *The Andy Griffith Show* generated a television movie reunion of most of the cast, entitled *Return to Mayberry*. This was the most-watched TV movie of the 1985-86 season. Many of the show's stars joined together again in February of 1993 for a presentation of clips from their favorite episodes.

Despite the show's No. 1 ranking during the 1967-68 season, Griffith decided to move on to other projects. He was to regret his decision, because the public liked him so much as Sheriff Andy Taylor he had difficulty finding a different niche. In 1970, Griffith tried another television series, *The Headmaster*, a comedy in which he plays Andy Thompson, headmaster of the Concord School, who contends with a variety of problems with the students and faculty. After this show lasted less than six months, Griffith tried to lure back his old audience with *The New Andy Griffith Show* (1971), a comedy series in which he plays a character called back to his hometown, a small southern town much like Mayberry, to serve as mayor. This series was also cancelled in its first season.

Griffith appeared in several made-for-television movies after *The Andy Griffith Show*. He starred, for example, in *Pray for the Wilderness* (1978), a version of *Deliverance*. In

1979, he starred in *Salvage*, in which he rockets to the moon to recover trash discarded by NASA. This show led to another attempted TV series, *Salvage 1*, which failed to last into a second season. In 1983, Griffith appeared in the TV movie *The Demon Murder Case*, in which he is a scholar of demonology who helps perform an exorcism. In the same year he played the villain in *Murder in Coweta County*, a TV film based on a real 1948 murder in Georgia. Other television projects included the miniseries *Fatal Attraction* (1984). Meanwhile big screen efforts included *Angel in My Pocket* (1969), with Griffith cast as a young minister coping with a new small-town congregation; *Hearts of the West* (1975), an off-beat comedy set in Hollywood; and *Rustler Rhapsody* (1985), a comedy satirizing old movie Westerns in which Griffith stars with Tom Berenger.

In 1986, Griffith appeared in the TV movie *Diary of a Perfect Murder*, and audience acceptance led later the same year to Griffith's second long-lasting television series, *Matlock* (1986-95), on which Griffith played a defense attorney. It never gained the degree of popularity of *The Andy Griffith Show*.

Bibliography

Beck, Ken, and Jim Clark. *The Andy Griffith Show Book*. New York: St. Martin's, 1985.

Harrison, Dan, and Bill Habeeb. *Inside Mayberry*. New York: HarperPerennial, 1994.

Kelly, Richard. *The Andy Griffith Show*. Winston-Salem: Blair, 1981.

Pfeiffer, Lee. *The Official Andy Griffith Show Scrapbook*. Secaucus: Carol, 1994.

Alan Kelly

Griffith, D(avid) W(ark) (1875-1948), actor, director and producer, was born in La Grange, KY, and joined the Meffert Stock Company of Louisville in 1897 as a supporting player. An actor for 10 years, he played the leading role in Edison's *Rescued from an Eagle's Nest* (1907), and worked with Biograph Studio (1907-13), Reliance Majestic (1913-15), Triangle Film Corporation (1915-17), Paramount-Artcraft (1917-19), First National/United Artists (1919-24), Paramount (1924-27), and United Artists (1927-31).

D. W. Griffith was (and still remains) a controversial figure both in terms of cinema history and contemporary culture. Usually categorized as the director of the racist *Birth of a Nation* (1915) or praised as the father of modern cinema, closer investigation of the director's life, work, and cultural relationship reveals an inherent complexity refusing easy and convenient definition. His 485 surviving films demonstrate the existence of a complex talent which can neither be defined as either totally conservative or progressive. If Griffith no longer retains his status as the inventor of cinematic techniques such as the close-up, parallel editing, changing camera angles, dramatic lighting, and intercutting, he is recognizably the key talent responsible for wielding these techniques together in a manner influencing cinema to the present day.

Although Griffith began in theater and moved to cinema, he still integrated many recognizable melodramatic techniques from his former interest into his new discipline.

Influenced by late-19th-century narrative tropes such as myths of the defeated South, realism, journalistic muckraking exposures, melodrama, and naturalism, he used these elements within his films. But their successful cinematic realization often characterizes his Biograph films rather than majestic narrative epics such as *Birth of a Nation*, *Intolerance* (1916), *Hearts of the World* (1918), and *America* (1924). It is easy to categorize the director as victim of a cultural crisis during the latter years of the Progressive era, when America rapidly changed its character due to factors of increasing industrialism, World War, modernity, and changing gender roles. However, despite previous views of Griffith's postwar films supposedly representing the director's retreat from social issues due to creative curtailment by the classical Hollywood studio system, several works such as *Broken Blossoms* (1919), *Way Down East* (1920), and *The Struggle* (1931) critically represent issues of race, gender, and family relationships current within American culture today. Questions of immigration, ideological treatments of corrupt cities and supposedly pure country, and alcoholism's effect on human relationships remain as important as they were in Griffith's lifetime. The films themselves often reveal significant motifs ignored by his detractors. The doomed love between the physically abused child-woman and a "yellow man" also corrupted by Western civilization; the heartless nature of agrarian country life; and the noble experiment's failure in the declining years of Prohibition were all issues whose complexities contemporary audiences sought to deny in favor of comforting cinematic pleasures.

Although *Birth of a Nation*, *Intolerance*, and *Hearts of the World* previously overshadowed the earlier Biograph work, present criticism concentrates upon the Biograph material both in terms of its relationship to contemporary narrative influences such as the naturalist school of fiction and its relationship to popular cultural and ideological issues.

Griffith's Populist Biograph shorts such as *A Corner in Wheat*, *A Child of the Ghetto* (1910) ironically reveal more sympathetic images of the plight of ethnic groups than works by eminent literary figures like Henry James, whose *American Scene* contains more racist images than *Birth of a Nation*. If the latter epic unconsciously gave rise to exploitative action and exploitation techniques dominating contemporary Hollywood cinema, Griffith's earlier work has significant parallels with so-called "muckraking" journalistic works which brought appalling conditions to public notice. Furthermore, despite Griffith's fascination with stereotypical virginal images within the star persona of Lillian Gish, more varied explorations of female roles appear in films such as *A Flash of Light* (1910), *The Painted Lady* (1912), and *The Mothering Heart* (1913). If *The Musketeers of Pig Alley* (1913) reveals Griffith as the accidental father of the social gangster film, the above-cited works also support Scott Simmon's claims for Griffith as "father of the woman's film." Finally, although many damn Griffith for *Birth of Nation*, examination of his other Southern works reveals a divergent picture depicting the director as a participant in a far more complex discourse of the South than has been hitherto supposed.

Bibliography
Griffith, D. W. *The Man Who Invented Hollywood: The Auto-biography of D. W. Griffith.* Louisville: Touchstone, 1972.
Gunning, Tom. *D. W. Griffith and the Origins of American Narrative Film: The Early Years at Biograph.* Urbana: U of Illinois P, 1994.
Schickel, Richard. *D. W. Griffith: An American Life.* New York: Simon & Schuster, 1984.
Simmon, Scott. *The Films of D. W. Griffith.* Cambridge: Cambridge UP, 1993.

Tony Willliams

Grimes, **Martha** (1931-), one of the more widely read authors of the golden age detective mystery, was born the daughter of a Pittsburgh attorney and a hotel owner, but the mystery fiction that has brought her critical acclaim is set in England, each story revolving around a particular pub which gives the work its title.

Because of her style and her works' settings, Grimes has been compared to such British mystery writers as Agatha Christie and Dorothy L. Sayers. Grimes gained her understanding of things English through frequent trips to England and extensive research. Her intricate mysteries bring together a continuing cast of characters: Scotland Yard detective Richard Jury, an appealing man with a melancholy sensibility and a romantic streak; Chief Superintendent Racer, an incompetent shirker; Jury's aristocratic friend and amateur assistant Melrose Plant; and Plant's American aunt Agatha, all introduced in Grimes's first novel, *The Man with a Load of Mischief* (1981). Grimes manages this cast of characters deftly, rendering them with an appealing mix of sincerity and satire.

Bibliography
Chambers, Andrea. "The Terribly English Mysteries of Martha Grimes Are a Welcome Addition to the Public Domain." *People Weekly* 2 Feb. 1987.
Contemporary Authors Vol. 113, 1985.
Henderson, Lesley, ed. *Twentieth-Century Crime and Mystery Writers.* Chicago: St. James, 1991.
Magill, Frank N., ed. *Critical Survey of Mystery and Detective Fiction.* Pasadena: Salem, 1988.
Major Twentieth-Century Writers. A Selection of Sketches from Contemporary Authors. Detroit: Gale, 1991.

Thomas B. Frazier

See also
Cozy Mysteries
Detective Sidekicks
Golden Age of Detective Fiction
Humorous Mysteries

Grisham, **John** (1955-), former attorney and self-confessed cynic about the legal profession, turned his knowledge of the law into five best-selling novels in four years. Born in Arkansas, Grisham attended the University of Mississippi law school, and passed the bar in 1981. After opening a private law practice in Southaven, MS, he quickly became disillusioned with the profession and eventually turned to writing fiction.

Between 1984 and 1987, Grisham wrote his first novel, *A Time to Kill*, which was rejected more than 20 times before 5,000 copies were published in 1989. It was his second novel, *The Firm* (1991), that catapulted him to his stature atop the popular charts, a position he has held almost continuously since then. *The Firm* is a fast-paced legal thriller about a novice attorney who accepts unwittingly a position with a Mafia-controlled law firm and finds his life in jeopardy once he discover's the firm's illegal doings. The success of *The Firm* was repeated when *The Pelican Brief*, about a young lawyer who uncovers a political plot to assassinate Supreme Court justices, was published in 1993 and became another runaway best-seller. Like the last book, *The Pelican Brief* culminated in a protracted flight by the heroine from her would-be killers.

After the success of *The Pelican Brief*, *A Time to Kill* was reissued in paperback, this time selling over three million copies. Grisham's career continued to flourish with two additional blockbusters, *The Client* (1992), and *The Chamber* (1994), both of which repeat Grisham's standard formula of a legal setting and an honorable protagonist caught up in a devious conspiracy no one else can unveil.

The dramatic conflicts, extended chase and escape plots, and the clipped dialogue of the books has made them especially suitable for screen adaptation. *The Firm* was filmed in 1993 along with *The Pelican Brief*, and *The Client* debuted in 1994. All three were box-office hits, further confirming Grisham's popularity. *A Time to Kill* was filmed in 1996. He continues to write best-selling fiction, including *The Rainmaker* (1995, film 1997), *The Runaway Jury* (1996), *The Partner* (1997), *The Street Lawyer* (1998), *The Testament* (1999), and *The Brethren* (2000).

Bibliography
"Grisham, John." *Current Biography* Sept. 1993: 21-24.
Matthews, Tom. "Book 'Em." *Newsweek* 15 March 1993: 78-81.

Richelle Kortering Hofman

See also
Legal Mysteries
Thriller, The

Grunge Music. The term grunge became a well-known part of popular culture during the late 1980s and early 1990s, referring to both a style of music and a style of dress. Grunge music is a hybrid of punk, heavy metal, and high energy rock 'n' roll; it is officially considered to have originated in Seattle, WA, and the Northwest U.S. Grunge is also defined as a style of dress which includes wearing flannel shirts, jeans with holes, and unkempt hair styles. During the early 1990s, many bands and musicians moved to Seattle seeking musical success. The music scene in Seattle in the 1990s is sometimes compared to the San Francisco music scene of the 1960s.

The roots of grunge can be traced to the Sub Pop record label, founded by Joe Poneman and Bruce Pavitt in 1987. Some of the bands included on the label included the influential Mudhoney, Screaming Trees, Dinosaur Jr., Soundgarden, and Nirvana. Pearl Jam and Nirvana are perhaps the two biggest grunge bands ever to come out of Seattle and enter the mainstream rock scene (see entries).

Nirvana released the ground-breaking grunge album *Nevermind* in 1991. Although the album was not an instant seller, by the middle of 1992 the band had become very successful because of its ability to tap into the often gloomy zeitgeist of its youthful fans. *Nevermind* went on to sell over 7 million copies, and the single "Smells Like Teen Spirit" hit the top of the pop charts at No. 6. The band gained national acceptance through media appearances and radio airplay, but Cobain's drug problems and tempestuous marriage to actress/singer Courtney Love (who was the leader of her own underground band, Hole) became a constant source of media attention. At the height of the band's popularity, in April 1994, the 27-year-old Cobain committed suicide. Cobain's death was considered a great loss to music lovers, especially his Generation X fans, who felt that he spoke for them.

Pearl Jam's history is a little brighter than Nirvana's. Pearl Jam toured around the Seattle area building a reputation, then secured a contract with Epic Records in 1991. Pearl Jam's music, high energy rock 'n' roll with a sound like that of heavy metal, as showcased in such songs as "Evenflow," "Alive," and the controversial "Rearviewmirror," was much more polished than other grunge bands, garnering the band a nationwide following. Pearl Jam even opened selected dates for the Rolling Stones' tour of 1997, a sure sign of mainstream success.

Other popular grunge bands are Alice in Chains, Temple of the Dog (which features members of Soundgarden and Pearl Jam), the Melvins (who are credited with actually being one of the first grunge rock bands), Love Battery, Supersuckers, and the Posies. The grunge label has also been applied to some classic rock 'n' rollers, notably Neil Young (see entry).

Bibliography

Azerrad, Michael. "Grunge City." *Rolling Stone* 628 (16 April 1992): 43-46.

Black, Suzi. *Nirvana: The Story of...*. New York: Omnibus, 1995.

Butt, Malcolm. *None Too Fragile: Pearl Jam and Eddie Vedder*. London: Plexus, 1997.

Harrison, Hank. *Kurt Cobain, Beyond Nirvana: The Legacy of Kurt Cobain*. Wilton, CA: Archives, 1995.

Humphrey, Clark. *Loser: The Real Seattle Music Story*. Los Angeles: Feral House, 1995.

Power, Martin. *Pearl Jam: Dark Corners*. New York: Omnibus, 1997.

Rees, Dafydd, and Luke Crampton. *Encyclopedia of Rock Stars*. New York: DK, 1996.

Sansevere, John, and Erica Farber. *Grunge: Inside Seattle's Music*. Racine WI: Golden, 1993.

Robert G. Weiner

Guest Stars on Television have been the backbone of both series and anthology shows from network television's beginnings. The job of a featured guest star, particularly a dramatic one, is immensely difficult. He/she has only one episode in which to establish rapport with the regular cast, project a personality, and enact the style, accent, manner, and period required by the storyline and the creator's intention. And if the guest succeeds in this, he/she runs the risk of being typecast in the same sort of role thereafter.

Television producers have tried to hedge against the failure of their projects in many ways. They eliminated anthologies to avoid the challenge of satisfying viewers with a wholly new milieu on a weekly basis. They gave series regulars massive salaries to ensure repetition of prior success. And they have consistently ignored or denigrated the guest artist, although viewers have just as assiduously cared about and appreciated these mostly unsung professionals.

Moreover, series leads are frequently played as "types," adhering to recent fads or predilections. But guest roles require the actor to be able to play almost any combination of elements among the spectrum of human possibility. And, exactly as the apron symbolizes the female's place in society or neckwear the male's place, the guest star symbolizes the filmmaker's view of "human-in-general." For in such roles, as in the choice of what individuals should enact them, the creator has no need to bow to any fad, any whim, any expectation.

The early years of television broadcasting offered guest artists a wide variety and large number of roles. Series commonly aired 39 episodes a year; other series running 13 weeks replaced them in the summer. This happy situation for guest stars and for viewers continued even after production was shifted from live to filmed recording. Many early series were anthologies (1946-57); nearly all were a half hour in length, and few had large continuing casts. Such shows did not offer guest artists much publicity. Yet work was relatively plentiful.

Between the years 1957-72, hour-long programs became usual. Guest-starring roles became longer but the size of continuing casts gradually increased. The number of series was curtailed and anthology programs were all but eliminated. In this era, guest artists received more publicity than at any other period of network history. However, jobs were fewer and many were being given only to those who were "attractive."

After 1972-73, the status of guest stars deteriorated. Sitcoms with large casts, special-effects activities, and other factors eliminated longer speaking roles. "Romantic" or "self-responsibility" philosophy was also eliminated in favor of "naturalism" or "characterization by categorical character flaws." Before the 1972-73 season, the majority of guest actors hired were Shakespearean-trained, over 30, and dramatic. After this date, guest stars were under 30, chosen for looks, and predominantly comedic, adding to the original and central false equation.

After 1972, producers began making more made-for-television films and introduced miniseries. But these developments merely reinforced the network czars' tendency to cant their product to a youthful market and further eroded the number of television acting jobs available. The content of these new films was normally mean-streets realism or fantasized parodies of normal behavior; for these projects, folk-speech-trained youths and sitcom performers were the usual choices. A few miniseries such as *Roots* (1977) and *Centennial* (1978) did hire trained actors.

The guest star and his/her role in some sense represent, subliminally or consciously, the producer's idea of "the human." But additionally, the guest star helps to shape the image of humanity within an entire culture. In any artistic medium, guest stars form the "universal background" against which leading stars shine.

Bibliography
Eames, J. D. *The MGM Story*. Avenal, NJ: Outlet, 1990.
Eisner, Joel, and David Krinksy. *Television Comedy Series*. Jefferson: McFarland, 1984.
Medved, Michael. *Hollywood v. America*. New York: Harper Perennial, 1992.

R. D. Michael

Guiding Light (1937- ; *The* was dropped in 1978) is the senior American soap opera. The work of Irna Phillips (see entry), the creator of soap opera, when *GL* started in 1937, it was mainly the sermons of "Dr. John Rutledge" (collections of which sold hugely). Procter and Gamble owns *GL*, now as then.

In the late 1940s, the "guiding light" became the family, specifically the German-American Bauer family of "Papa" Bauer (Theo Goetz, 1947-73). Unlike today, Papa spoke "ethnic" ("I'm tellin' ya somethin' ya don't know?"); and lived with his son Bill, and Bill's wife Bert (the beloved Charita Bauer, 1950-84; died February 28, 1985), bringing up their sons Mike and Ed. Bill's sister Meta was lively and always in trouble, and was hence the early focus of the show.

From June 30, 1952, to 1956, *GL* was on TV in the morning and radio in the afternoon. The Bauers moved from "Selby Flats, CA" (a Los Angeles suburb) to "Springfield," near Chicago. Bert, who at first drove Bill (perhaps into his alcoholism), became the family's strength, and the show's guiding light. In 1956, *GL* left radio. (In June 1952, 3-4 million listened; in 1953, 2.6 million, with 3.5 million watching.) And in 1956, Agnes Nixon became headwriter. Protégé of Irna Phillips, Nixon, in her first headwriting job, typically wrote an "issue" story (rare on soaps then): Bert's uterine cancer, discovered by an early PAP test.

Mike Bauer grew up fast, becoming *GL*'s leading male in the early 1960s. His daughter, Hope, hooked the Bauers to the next central family (introduced in the late 1970s), the Spauldings. Hope married the tycoon, Alan Spaulding, and gave birth to Alan-Michael who, in the late 1980s, became a new young *GL* hero.

In 1967, *GL* went to color, and in 1968, to a half-hour. Nixon left in the mid-60s, and after a time, in 1975, Jerome and Bridget Dobson took over as headwriters. *GL* won the 1980 Emmy for outstanding daytime drama; and in 1981 and 1982, the new headwriter, Douglas Marland, and his team won the writing Emmy, thanks mostly to his creation, Nola Reardon. Actress Lisa Brown's comic skills, and Marland's fantasies for movie-mad Nola helped *GL* win another Emmy for best show in 1982. But *GL* was slumping when, in 1983, it was taken over by producer Gail Kobe and writer Richard Culliton. Fresh from *Texas*, an ambitious soap failure, Kobe, Culliton, and, later, Pamela Long (Hammer) wrote the Bauer family back into focus and concentrated on young people.

Guiding Light's strengths have been acting (and casting), directing, for which it won the 1994 Emmy, but perhaps most of all, exceptional writing. The characterization of its men—often lesser in daytime drama—may be the richest in soap opera. From Roger Thorpe and Grant Aleksander's 1980s Phillip Spaulding, who thought he could do good with power and masked his greed from himself with that thought, to today's struggling young men, Alan-Michael Spaulding, the scion (Rick Hearst), and Frank Cooper, who owns a diner and a small, old house, and finally, to Buzz Cooper (Justin Deas), Vietnam veteran, lost for 20 years, and now home, still unable not to hurt the family he cherishes, *Guiding Light* was where to go to learn about men in the '90s.

The story of Ed and Maureen Bauer was 1993's strongest and one of soaps' most memorable. They were the core of *GL*, and their marriage was riven by his infidelity and ended with her car crash. Fans protested the firing of Ellen Parker (Maureen), but the writing and acting of this marriage made in heaven and killed by man was harrowing, beyond realism, universal, and almost worth the price of losing "Mo" and Ed in their "ordinary," everyday role as the heart of this story started so long ago, of the immigrant Bauer family. But the next generation grows, and the guiding light moves on.

Bibliography
Intintoli, Michael James. *Taking Soaps Seriously: The World of* Guiding Light. New York: Praeger, 1984.
Schemering, Christopher. *Guiding Light: A 50th Anniversary Celebration*. New York: Ballantine, 1986.

Carol Traynor Williams

Guns of Autumn, The (1975), a 90-minute "long form" CBS-TV documentary, examined the American recreational sport of hunting, as told by the hunter himself. Its echo still reverberates throughout society.

In many respects, *The Guns of Autumn*, which was written, directed, and produced by Irv Drasnin, was in part representative of the observational, reflexive, and expository modes of documentaries. Camera operators Greg Cooke and William Wagner followed on the heels of their subjects (the hunters) as they tracked and eventually killed their targets. Many scenes were filmed in a *vérité* style; in this method, the presence of the camera is comparable to what an actual participant or observer would experience, if placed in similar circumstances.

The narration was supplied by CBS news correspondent Dan Rather, who offered facts and statistics, revealing how technology had changed the odds of hunting in favor of the hunter; he mentions how man no longer needs to hunt for survival, but it remains a "savage" part of his past that cannot be wiped away.

Drasnin intentionally draws the viewer's attention through repetition of the use of still images. In a 15-second montage of slaughtered bears on the hoods of cars, the viewer is left with certain feelings and emotional impressions. The filmmaker's uses of these effects and devices are intended to expose and to stir reaction. The documentary did just that—even before its airing the network received much criticism and pressure from hunting enthusiasts.

At the start of the broadcast, CBS ran a discretion advisory stating that, "This program contains scenes of the death of animals that may be disturbing to some viewers." This warning helps to set the initial tone and mood of the documentary. The viewer actually witnessed dead and/or dying animals brutally displayed on the television screen. What made these images graphically startling was the repetitive use of tight close-up shots. Many of the animals killed on film were seen being gutted and skinned for easy transportation or for trophy preparation. The constant array of these graphic images provides for immense shock value.

Bibliography
New York Times 3 Sept. 1975, 5 Sept. 1975, 14 Sept. 1975, 17 Sept. 1975.
Nichols, Bill. *Representing Reality*. Bloomington: Indiana UP, 1991.
Rosenthal, Alan, ed. *New Challenges for Documentary*. Los Angeles: U of California P, 1988.

Michael Espinosa

Gunsmoke (1955-1975) holds the distinction of being the first "adult" television Western (see Television Westerns). The term "adult Western" was used by Norman Macdonnell and John Meston as early as 1952. They were trying to create a radio series that was different from other Westerns. Since the American public was accustomed, with only a few exceptions in literature and film, to the Western as a form of entertainment geared for children, why not design a Western which adults would enjoy? It was a question the answer to which revamped TV entertainment.

To accomplish this, Macdonnell, a director/producer, and Meston, a writer, sought to build a radio series that would rely on historical accuracy more than most other Westerns and that would be free from as many of the traditional Western clichés as possible. Their series would eliminate many of the things cowboys always did in Westerns, like the hero shooting better than anyone else, the cowboy calling his horse by name, and heroes in white hats and villains in black hats. The key element was to be the fallibility of the hero. This was perhaps their most important innovation—a hero who made mistakes. This fallibility would extend to all characters in the stories.

Gunsmoke was hailed as the forerunner of a new breed of Western in which mature plot, fuller human characterization, and intelligent theme, all enacted according to high dramatic standards, were combined to produce the most sophisticated Western drama in radio history. When the program moved to television in 1955, Charles Marquis Warren was added to the team to produce the show.

Fate was to determine that a relatively unknown actor, James Arness (see entry), would become television's quintessential Western hero. For more than three decades Arness personified the Western hero, towering head and shoulders—both physically and charismatically—over a multitude of television cowboy stars. First as Matt Dillon, the stoic and courageous marshal of Dodge City in *Gunsmoke* (1955-75), and later as Zeb Macahan, the tough, free-spirited mountain man in *How the West Was Won* (1977-79),

Arness became the most filmed actor in the history of cinema and television.

When it came time to cast Dillon's deputy, Chester, Warren already had Dennis Weaver in mind, having worked with him in *Seven Angry Men* (1955). The most experienced cast member selected for *Gunsmoke* was Milburn Stone as Doc Adams. Stone, a veteran of over 250 films, had worked for Warren in *Arrowhead* (1953).

The role of Kitty, saloon keeper and Dillon's love interest, was eventually given to Amanda Blake; it was her persistence as much as her acting ability that won her the part. Originally intended to be a saloon girl, like the character on radio, Kitty had to be changed on television to avoid offending viewers in the more broadly based medium.

Over the years, *Gunsmoke* was the recipient of many awards: *Look* Magazine's Annual Television Award in 1958 for Best Action Series; the Radio Television Daily All-American Favorite Western Show of the Year in 1958; Television Champions Award for Best Western in 1959 and again in 1969 and 1972. Many individuals—actors, writers, directors and technicians—were also recognized for their outstanding contributions.

As a Saturday night series *Gunsmoke* ranked in the Nielsen Top 20 from its second season until 1965, being first from 1957 through 1961. After being moved to Monday evenings in 1967, the series returned to the Top 20 and remained there until its final season.

There have been five made-for-TV *Gunsmoke* movies. Only the first one included any of the original characters other than Matt Dillon. (Kitty was seen in the first in 1987 as well as Doc, Chester, and others via flashbacks.) Each film achieved ratings which placed it among the Top 10 programs of the week, so it is not unlikely that additional *Gunsmoke* movies will be made as long as Arness is willing and able.

Bibliography
Barabas, SuzAnne, and Gabor. *Gunsmoke: A Complete History and Analysis of the Legendary Broadcast Series with a Comprehensive Episode-by-Episode Guide to Both the Radio and Television Programs*. Jefferson: McFarland, 1990.
Peel, John. *Gunsmoke Years: The Behind the Scenes Story*. Las Vegas: Pioneer, 1989.

Gary A. Yoggy

Guthrie, Arlo Davy (1947-   ), son of the late Woody Guthrie (see next entry), was born in Coney Island, NY. The Guthrie household was full of music and musicians who never hesitated to drop by. Guthrie, who began playing on an eight-dollar guitar when he was six, grew up under the musical tutelage of his father, Pete Seeger, Leadbelly, Sonny Terry, Bob Dylan, and other folk music giants. Together they reshaped the performance of folk songs.

Although Guthrie never saw his father perform, he began adapting Woody's songs at an early age. In junior high school Arlo wrote a parody of Woody's song "So Long, It's Been Good to Know You," about a math test, rather than the dust-bowl. Approximately seven years later, he took another one of Woody's forms, the talking blues, and made it his own in composing "Alice's Restaurant."

On Thanksgiving of 1965, Guthrie made the trip to Stockbridge that would form the setting for his most recognized song, "Alice's Restaurant." The song, which can run from 18 to 35 minutes, humorously details how Guthrie avoided serving in Vietnam because he was convicted of littering. The satirical song became quite popular with the antiwar movement and was the basis for a film version in 1969.

The success of "Alice's Restaurant" has overshadowed many of Guthrie's other talents. Guthrie has released 16 albums. In 1993, 25 years after his acting debut in *Alice's Restaurant*, Guthrie appeared in a brief ABC spring series called *The Byrds of Paradise*. Guthrie, however, is staying with music. He owns his own record company, Rising Son, his own charitable organization, the Guthrie Center, and a 250-acre farm outside of Stockbridge, MA.

Bibliography

"Arlo Guthrie." *New Yorker* 6 Jan. 1968: 18-21.

Guthrie, Arlo. *This Is the Arlo Guthrie Book.* New York: Collier, 1969.

Leventhal, Harold. Jacket notes. *Alice's Restaurant.* Arlo Guthrie. Reprise Records, Warner Brothers, 6267-2, 1967.

Stambler, Irwin, and Landon Grelun. *Encyclopedia of Folk, Country, and Western Music.* New York: St. Martin's, 1969.

Rusty Reed

Guthrie, **Woody** (1912-1967), was a prolific songwriter, many of whose songs have had lasting appeal. His creative lifespan lasted barely 20 years but holds a unique place in U.S. popular culture and musical history. And apart from his songs, poetry, and other works, he created a kind of cultural persona—the rambling musician who took on the role of spokesperson for the poor and dispossessed. Guthrie introduced the notion that popular music could have a political point and could have a role in social action.

Guthrie's biography illustrates a gradual transformation from a rural folksinger to a political activist who saw his music and other writing as an important social force. He was born in Okemah, OK, and grew up there and in Texas, where he attended school, probably until about 10th grade. After leaving school, he made a living doing odd jobs and singing, developing his skills on guitar and harmonica. Eventually, he left his wife and two daughters behind to travel to California with other migrant Dust Bowl refugees in the mid-1930s. There he sang in bars, worked in orchards, and eventually was signed to perform in a radio show on the progressive station KFVD, teamed first with his cousin Jack Guthrie, and then with Maxine Crissman, known as Lefty Lou.

In 1940, encouraged by the radical actor Will Geer, Guthrie moved to New York City. He began performing on radio, where he attracted the attention of folklorist Alan Lomax. In May 1940, Lomax persuaded RCA Victor to record Guthrie's "Dust Bowl Ballads." Lomax himself recorded Guthrie's songs and reminiscences for the Library of Congress, although these were not released until years later. Guthrie, along with Alan Lomax, Pete Seeger, Cisco Houston, Bess Lomax, and others, formed the Almanac Singers, who expressed their political activism through song (see entry). Guthrie abandoned his radio show, believing it was becoming too commercialized, and left New York for a short time. A believer in the New Deal, he signed on with the Bonneville Power Administration to write propaganda songs, and in one month in 1941, wrote many of his best-known songs, such as "Roll on Columbia," "Hard Traveling," and "Pastures of Plenty."

Guthrie returned to New York in 1941 and became an active member of the Almanac Singers, performing in union halls, political rallies, and "Hootenannies," the term they developed to refer to evenings of music and political commentary. During this period, Guthrie and others who were associated with the New York wing of the U.S. Communist Party believed fervently that socialist goals were real and attainable. Like Joe Hill and the Wobblies years before, they believed that music was an important part of the class struggle. Unlike Hill, who usually adapted hymns and popular songs, Guthrie introduced the folk styles of rural America to a mass audience.

This phase of his life ended with World War II, during which Guthrie served in the Merchant Marine. He supported the war effort, as a stand against fascism, and wrote propaganda songs like "Round and Round Hitler's Grave." After the war, he settled again in New York, forming People's Songs, a cooperative of singers and songwriters that included Seeger, Josh White, Sonny Terry, and others, who performed at concerts, political meetings and hootenannies. Guthrie's autobiography, *Bound for Glory,* had been published to critical acclaim in 1943. In 1945 he married dancer Marjorie Greenblatt; the youngest of their four children, Arlo, also became famous as a musician (see entry).

Nevertheless, the golden age of radical politics was over and many radicals left New York, although the folk revival scene remained as fertile grounds for the protest movement of the 1960s. Guthrie's personal life also deteriorated. His second marriage ended as his behavior became increasingly unpredictable due to the first signs of Huntington's disease. By late 1952, he was clearly ill, and in 1956 he was hospitalized. He lived on until October 1967, suffering a horrifying physical and mental decline, while his ex-wife Marjorie cared for him.

In his 20 years of productivity, Guthrie's output was prodigious, numbering thousands of songs, poems, journalistic pieces, and other writings. Although perhaps best known for his political songs, his subjects were many.

His "dustbowl ballads" were simple, folksy songs about hard times in the country—songs like "Tom Joad" and the famous "So Long, It's Been Good to Know You." Later, these songs took on a radical edge, as he sang of the "Union Maid," and the outlaw as hero in "Pretty Boy Floyd." In "Jesus Christ," he presents Jesus as a radical organizer and revolutionary. His most famous song, "This Land Is Your Land," was written in 1940 as a response to Irving Berlin's "God Bless America," asserting the common people's right to own America. And throughout his life, he wrote delightful children's songs that hold up well today, such as "Riding in My Car" and other "Songs to Grow On."

His songs foreshadow the fights against pollution, war, and the plight of migrant workers. His look was important; the unkempt hair, jeans, and salty language all became stylistic markers of the counterculture that began in the 1960s. Urban middle-class youths from comfortable backgrounds, such as Bob Dylan, Ramblin' Jack Elliott, and others consciously adopted Guthrie's mannerisms and singing style. Dylan visited Guthrie frequently during the last years of his life, and embraced him as a hero. The 1960s protest movement of Dylan, Joan Baez, Phil Ochs, Judy Collins, Tom Paxton, and so on would not have happened without the example of Woody Guthrie and Pete Seeger.

Bibliography

Guthrie, Woody. *Bound for Glory*. New York: Dutton, 1943.

Klein, Joe. *Woody Guthrie: A Life*. New York: Knopf, 1980.

Marsh, Dave, and Harold Leventhal, eds. *Pastures of Plenty: A Self Portrait, Woody Guthrie*. New York: HarperCollins, 1990.

Reuss, Richard A., ed. *A Woody Guthrie Bibliography: 1912-1967*. New York: Guthrie Children's Trust Fund, 1968.

S. Elizabeth Bird

Had-I-But-Known Mysteries are a type of mystery story that is read with pleasure but not taken seriously. They make up a sizable portion of present-day crime fiction.

Ogden Nash gave the derisive nickname Had-I-But-Known (HIBK) to the type of mystery story that features a female heroine who gets into danger, takes a risk—usually without being able to give any reasonable explanation for her behavior—and is saved at the last moment by a male detective. Such novels are usually narrated retrospectively, with many foreshadowing sentences, including variations on "had I but known then, what I know now...," rueing the lack of foresight or acuity that got her into the novel's dangerous predicament. HIBK novels typically include multiple murders and red herrings; they are prolonged by accidents, happenstance, unmotivated interferences, and lapses. Most such stories have confusing currents of strong emotion, and characters who forget to tell the detective important clues. In contrast to mysteries written solely as puzzles, HIBK fiction shows how crime or violence impacts everyday life. The best HIBK fiction offers realistic portrayals of the hardships and psychological damage resulting from violence and murder.

Mary Roberts Rinehart, one of the founders of the HIBK school, was the best-known and best-paid American author of her day. Writers who followed her lead include Mignon Eberhart, Dorothy Cameron Disney, Daphne du Maurier, Phyllis A. Whitney, Mary Stewart, Isabelle Holland, Judith Kelman, and Diane Mott Davidson.

Bibliography

Fleenor, Juliann E. *The Female Gothic*. Montreal: Eden, 1983.

Haycraft, Howard. *The Art of the Mystery Story*. New York: Simon, 1946.

——. *Murder for Pleasure: The Life and Times of the Detective Story*. New York: Carroll, 1941.

Klein, Kathleen Gregory. *The Woman Detective: Gender and Genre*. Urbana: U of Illinois P, 1988.

Mann, Jessica. *Deadlier Than the Male: Why Are Respectable English Women So Good at Murder?* New York: Macmillan, 1984.

Steinbrenner, Chris, and Otto Penzler. *Encyclopedia of Mystery and Detection*. New York: McGraw-Hill, 1976.

Kimberly J. Laird

See also
Classical Mysteries
Golden Age of Detective Fiction

Haggard, Merle (1937-), was born in Bakersfield, CA (known as "Nashville West," in part because country singer Buck Owens was also from there). Haggard spent most of his youth as a juvenile delinquent. He was sent to San Quentin on a burglary charge in 1958. Though he was paroled in 1960, Haggard received a full pardon in March 1972 from the then-governor of California, Ronald Reagan. Haggard is circumspect about his experiences in prison, but he clearly cashed in with such songs as "Sing Me Back Home," "Branded Man," "Mama Tried," and "I'm a Lonesome Fugitive," which was his first No. 1 hit in 1966. He had previously made the country charts, however, with a duet single, "Just between the Two of Us" (1964), sung with Bonnie Owens (Buck Owens's ex-wife), who, in 1965, became the second of Haggard's four wives.

Haggard had several crossover hits during this period, including "Okie from Muskogee" (1969) and "If We Make It through December" (1975). In 1970, he was named the Country Music Association's Entertainer and Male Vocalist of the Year; *Okie from Muskogee* was Album of the Year. The Academy of Country Music named him Male Vocalist five times from 1966 to 1974. An innovative and independent artist, Haggard experimented with concept albums and tributes to his precursors, with *Same Train, a Different Time* (1969), a Depression-era motif in praise of Jimmie Rodgers, and *Tribute to the Best Damn Fiddle Player in the World: My Salute to Bob Wills* (1970), credited with assisting the revival of western swing.

The 1980s also brought success for Haggard, especially in the duet genre, including an LP with country great George Jones, *A Taste of Yesterday's Wine* (1982), and the sublime *Poncho and Lefty* with Willie Nelson, which won the CMA Album of the Year in 1983. Haggard and Nelson recorded a fine second duet LP in 1987 with *Seashores of Old Mexico*. His hit singles included such songs as "Big City," "That's the Way Love Goes," and "Kern River" (1982-85); but his 1989 *5:01 Blues* on Epic is perhaps his best LP of the late 1980s.

Overestimating Haggard's talent and his influence on other artists would be difficult. He has recorded over 50 albums, and has managed to remain successful for over 25 years. Such luminaries as George Strait openly acknowledge Haggard's influence and express admiration for his abilities. Phil Ochs has criticized Haggard for misusing his great talent by writing unworthy songs like "Okie from Muskogee" (see entry) and "Fightin' Side of Me"; he referred to Haggard as possibly being "today's Hank Williams, who is still the foremost songwriter." Writer John Lomax III called Haggard "the finest American singer-songwriter of the post-Hank Williams era." An exceptional talent, Haggard's contribution to country music will remain considerable.

Bibliography

Clarke, Donald, ed. *The Penguin Encyclopedia of Popular Music*. London: Penguin, 1992.

DeCurtis, Anthony, and James Henke, eds. *The Rolling Stone Album Guide*. New York: Random, 1992.

Haggard, Merle, with Peggy Russell. *Sing Me Back Home: My Story*. New York: Pocket, 1981.

Nash, Alana. *Behind Closed Doors: Talking with the Legends of Country Music.* New York: Knopf, 1988.

Thompson, Stephen I. "Forbidden Fruit: Interracial Love Affairs in Country Music." *All That Glitters: Country Music in America.* Ed. George H. Lewis. Bowling Green, OH: Bowling Green State U Popular P, 1993.

Rebecca A. Umland
Samuel J. Umland

Haggard, Sir H(enry) Rider (1856-1925), important author of novels of fantasy and adventure, was born in Norfolk, England, trained as a barrister and spent extended time in South Africa, where he studied African customs and institutions before returning to England to begin a writing career. He is best known for two lengthy fictional series, the "Quatermain Adventures," and the novels featuring the immortal "She," also known as Ayesha and "She-Who-Must-Be-Obeyed." The Quatermain series represents a lasting contribution to the genre of adventure fiction, while *She* goes beyond that legacy to offer a definitive fantasy world and a sophisticated and compelling exploration of the eroticism of death. Haggard has influenced a number of U.S. writers.

The Quatermain series centers around the exploits of English hunter, explorer, and adventurer Allan Quatermain, introduced in *King Solomon's Mines* (1885). In that novel, Quatermain and fellow soldier of fortune Henry Curtis set out to find Curtis's brother, lost in Africa while seeking King Solomon's legendary mines. During their quest, the two become involved in a series of bloody African political quarrels. Though a contemporary reader is likely to be annoyed at the paternalistic characterizations of the Africans, the story is vivid and exciting. Over the next 40 years, Haggard wrote a series of sequels to the first Quatermain adventure, including such titles as *Allan Quatermain* (1887), *Allan's Wife and Other Tales* (1889), *The Holy Flower* (1915), *The Ancient Allan* (1920), and *Allan and the Ice Gods* (1927).

She (1886) is a fantastic tale involving the encounter in Africa between a contemporary Englishman and a woman from a century in the distant past who has the power to stay immortal. In her attempt to marry the Englishman, whom she recognizes as the reincarnation of a prior lover, she loses her supernatural powers and shrivels to a shrunken, monkey-like corpse. The character of She—powerful, beautiful, and deadly—was immediately received as an influential literary archetype. It was parodied by other writers and recast in a sequence of sequels by Haggard, including *Ayesha: The Return of She* (1905), *She and Allan* (1925), and *Wisdom's Daughter* (1923).

Bibliography
Higgins, D. S. *Rider Haggard: A Biography.* New York: Stein, 1981.

Katz, Wendy R. *Rider Haggard and the Fiction of Empire: A Critical Study of British Imperial Fiction.* Cambridge: Cambridge UP, 1987.

Pocock, Tom. *Rider Haggard and the Lost Empire.* London: Weidenfeld, 1993.

Richard Bleiler

Hairstyles and Hair Ornaments. Hairstyles are the deliberate manipulation of hair to achieve a certain look through cutting, curling, braiding, waving, crimping, dying, or the application of additions. Hairstyles are usually used to denote some sort of social status, or are seen as a flattering copy of someone in the public eye. In the past it was royalty who were imitated as the leaders in hairstyles, but today it is celebrities who set the looks which are copied. Hairstyles can be grouped into a few basic categories; long, short, elaborately upswept, augmented through additions, and artificially treated for color or texture.

The most basic of all hairstyles for European Americans is long straight hair, which has had a revival in the late 20th century for both men and women as hairstyles become softer and simpler. Young white women's hair is often left long and braided into a braid on either side of the head, a look popularized by the designer Byron Lars in his fashion shows. For men the trend toward long hair has also been popularized by musicians such as pop singer Michael Bolton and country western singer Billy Ray Cyrus. The late 1970s and early 1980s long hair phenomena for women was established by the television actress Farrah Fawcett in the TV show *Charlie's Angels*. She wore long hair with feathered, flipped back sides, a look which was one of the most widely copied in the decade. In the earlier 1970s long straight hair, parted in the middle, was the fashionable look as it was youthful and a breakaway from the fussy structured styles of the 1960s.

Part of the popularity for long straight hair in the 1970s was the interest in cultural identity, long hair having been worn by the Native Americans and promoted each week on television by pop singer Cher. Other television shows which helped to promote the long hair interest were situation comedies such as the *Brady Bunch* and the character portrayed by Peggy Lipton in the *Mod Squad*. Long hair for both men and women in the mid to late 1960s, however, was seen as a rejection of accepted, conventional hairstyles, and hippies (see entry) used their long hair as a badge of protest. The Beatles popularized longer hair for men in the mid 1960s.

The opposite extreme to long hair is short hair, which, although almost always acceptable for men, has had noticeable periods of interest for women. For women today, short hair is worn as an alternative look to the long youthful look. Actresses such as Winona Ryder and Madonna have popularized the look in recent years. The majority of men in the late 20th century also wear their hair short, in the same simple styles which evolved in the 1920s. In the 1980s many women followed the style of Lady Diana as she became a Princess, copying her short feathered hair. The 1970s saw the most popular of all short hairstyles on the Olympic Gold Medal ice skater Dorothy Hamill. Her "short and sassy" wedge cut is still referred to by her name. In the 1950s and 1960s it was Audrey Hepburn and Mia Farrow who promoted the gamine short-hair look, also approved by President Eisenhower's wife, Mamie, who wore her hair in a short rolled style with very short straight bangs. The housewives of 1950s and 1960s television also wore a short, easy-to-take-care-of style similar to that of Mrs. Eisenhower, including Donna Reed in *The Donna Reed Show* and Barbara Billingsley in *Leave It to Beaver*, setting the style for homemakers across the country. For men the period of the 1950s included two different looks, the crew cut or flat top, the haircut given to soldiers, and the greased-back high-topped pompadour popularized by singer Elvis Presley. 1940s women adopted a shorter hairstyle, as many women were working in factories and were concerned with safety and the danger of hair getting caught in equipment, this short-haired image being portrayed by the fictitious "Rosie the Riveter."

Elaborate upswept hair has had a revival in the late 20th century through the influence of Ivana Trump. Her signature blond upswept chignon which is left in slight disarray has become the classic evening style of the 1990s. The 1960s was the last period of truly structured styles being worn for every day, the short round bouffant with flipped ends being popularized by Jacqueline Kennedy. Mrs. Kennedy also wore her hair in very elaborate styles for evening, establishing the look for dressy affairs. The classic back-combed style of Mrs. Kennedy had an exaggerated counterpart also in the 1960s which was worn by celebrities such as Priscilla Presley, wife of singer Elvis Presley. This style required a great deal of back-combing, additional false hairpieces, and much hairspray to achieve monumental height, very reminiscent of the elaborate styles worn by the French court in the 18th century. The 1940s were also a period of elaborate upswept hair, popularized by the Hollywood film industry. Actresses such as Ginger Rogers, Dorothy Lamour, and Lana Turner all wore elaborate styles in their film roles.

The most elaborate little girl's hairstyle was developed in the 1930s by the image of child movie star Shirley Temple. Her ringlet style was made up of 56 individual curls and became the established norm for little girl's dress-up style in the 1930s and 1940s. The 1890s through the early 1920s were another period of elaborate upswept hairstyles, known as pompadour styles and popularized by the Gibson Girl drawings by Charles Dana Gibson. Prior to 1890, hairstyles were elaborate and either upswept or a mass of curls, usually dictated by the European royalty and made known in America through such publications as *Godey's Lady's Book* and *Peterson's*. In the 1880s, English beauty Lilly Langtry was followed for her fashion and hair trends, creating a slick upswept hairstyle with short frizzed bangs. In the 1850s, Queen Victoria established a unique and widely copied upswept style which was parted in the middle and pulled around her ears leaving them exposed. Swedish singer Jenny Lind also helped to set very simple styles of the 19th century with her softly pulled back, low bun style. Empress Eugenie of France and Empress Elizabeth of Austria both popularized center-parted hair dressed in long ringlets for everyday wear in the mid 19th century.

In recent years the largest use of hair additions and extensions is in the African-American community. Elaborate braided styles have emerged which require additional braids of both matching and contrasting hair colors. Singer Patti LaBelle has adopted and popularized this style, as has pop singer Queen Latifah. For the European American community wigs and hair additions were at their most popular in the late 1960s and early 1970s with the creation of the man-made hair fibers which were easy to take care of and permanently kept their styles.

Hair dye, which has been used since the time of the Egyptians, has been popularized in the 20th century as it is now possible to dye hair at home. Supermodel Linda Evangelesta and pop singer Madonna have both been instrumental in promoting the idea of repeatedly changing hair color. In the 1990s, red hair has become the color of choice, and has been seen on many top models as well as movie actresses such as Susan Sarandon and Geena Davis. The 1950s and 1960s were the decades of platinum blond, made popular by Marilyn Monroe and Jayne Mansfield. An even lighter shade of this color was popularized in the 1930s by glamour queen Jean Harlow. In the 1970s and 1980s the popular form of chemical treating of hair was the permanent wave or perming. The resulting style, whether long or short, was of soft full curls. In the early 1970s perming was used by European Americans to emulate the popular African-American "afro" in this period of cultural awareness. The permanent wave was used extensively in the 1930s to create the marcelled wave styles popularized by the movie stars of the early film industry.

Hair ornaments encompass any object which is used to decorate a hairstyle. In the late 20th century girls with their long hair are keeping it back with a ponytail holder called a scrunchie, a fabric tube sewn over a rubber band which creates a puff of fabric when used. Hairclips, both plain and with bows attached, and "Banana Clips" (plastic combs which interlock and form the shape of a banana) are also used to keep long hair back. The 1980s, known for its clean-cut preppie movement, popularized headbands and plaid hairbows. The 1970s and early 1980s saw hair combs which were decorated with ribbons and feathers to be worn to discotheques. Princess Diana in the 1980s wore one of the crown jewel necklaces as a band around her forehead, starting a craze for these jeweled bands. In the 1930s and 1940s jeweled clips were created to put into elaborate evening coiffures.

The personal expression of manipulating and decorating hair has been an ongoing process in the history of fashion. This form of adornment is used for decoration, or to define social status, and is usually copied from a public figure of high regard.

Bibliography

Batterberry, M., and A. Batterberry. *Mirror, Mirror.* New York: Holt, 1977.

Cooper, Wendy. *Hair.* New York: Stein & Day, 1971.

Trasko, Mary. *Daring Dos.* New York: Ingram, 1994.

Jeffrey Mayer

Haley, Bill (1925-1981), was a singer, guitarist, and bandleader credited by some as the father of rock 'n' roll music. Born William John Clifton Haley, Jr., in a Detroit suburb, he learned guitar as a teenager and formed several successive groups to play country and cowboy music. By the late 1940s he was working as a disc jockey and performing music on a small radio station in Chester, PA. Influenced by black musicians, especially the beat pattern of jump blues, he began introducing black stage antics and rhythm and blues songs into his act, modifying the sexually explicit lyrics for his white audience. Soon Haley began more purposefully developing a music style that combined aspects of western swing with a steady up-tempo beat and the electricity of black pop.

Haley changed his group's name to the Comets, and in 1951 they made their first successful record for Essex. By 1952 they were recording full-fledged rockers like "Rock the Joint" (which sold 75,000 copies). The Comets utilized many instruments, with Rudy Pompilli's saxophone, Al Pompilli's stand-up bass, and Haley's guitar crucial. Early songs such as "Rock the Joint" and "Rocket 88" (a cover of a black hit) represented an aggressive, high energy updating of rhythm and blues. Haley became convinced there was a substantial white audience for up-tempo danceable music, then proceeded to mine the rich vein of restless but bottled-up teenage energy. Their first major national hit, "Crazy Man Crazy" in 1953, is considered by some observers the first rock 'n' roll record to register on the *Billboard* pop charts. In 1954, after signing with major label Decca, Haley and the Comets recorded "Shake, Rattle and Roll" (a cover of Joe Turner's rhythm and blues song) and "Dim Dim the Lights." Haley's version of "Shake" sanitized some of Turner's raunchier lyrics; it quickly shot into the Top 10 in both the United States and Britain. Another early Haley song, "Rock a Beatin' Boogie," was also crucial to rock history; Cleveland disc jockey Alan Freed was reportedly so taken by the lyrics "Rock rock, rock everybody, roll, roll, roll everybody" that he coined the designation "rock 'n' roll" for the new sounds.

In 1955, "Rock around the Clock" (originally released with modest success in 1954) was featured in the youth alienation film *Blackboard Jungle*. Partly owing to its identification with a "rebel" film, the song quickly became a rock anthem and first true song of the emerging youth subculture, shooting to the top of the charts. This gave Haley an international reputation and established him as the first rock 'n' roll star. *Blackboard Jungle* also fostered the identification of rock with teenage rebellion. Eventually the record sold 22 million copies, making it one of the top-selling singles of all time. Between 1955 and early 1957 all Haley's records became hits, including "Razzle Dazzle" (1955), "Burn That Candle" (1955), "See You Later, Alligator" (1955), and "Rip It Up" (1956). "See You Later, Alligator" soon provided an essential of contemporary teen slang. His last major hit was "Skinnie Minnie" in 1958. Altogether he sold over 60 million records. Haley lacked the physicality and charisma of more sexual and youthful rockers such as Elvis Presley. He was married (with five children), paunchy, with an odd curl on his forehead, and looked middle aged. This fact became better known after his appearances in the films *Rock around the Clock* and *Don't Knock the Rock*. His popularity began to fade in 1957. Resisting any change in his style or image, he maintained his career into the 1970s largely through rock 'n' roll revival shows. Confusion about his rapid success, disillusionment with his career decline, and two failed marriages led to heavy drinking and mental illness. He died alone of a heart attack in Harlingen, TX, on February 9, 1981.

The Comets included some excellent musicians and have been described as the first true rock *band*. The guitar licks and drumming of "Rock around the Clock" were revolutionary in commercial recording. Haley made the first serious attempt (only partly successful) to blend three once-divergent streams of white pop, country, and black pop into one fusion. He can be recognized as the catalyst for popularizing black music with whites and successfully communicating to a wide audience. Haley's sound and image were essentially "white," somewhat corny and wholesome. His exuberant music proved irresistible to teenagers rebelling against the sedate mainstream pop but it ultimately lacked the alienation and provocation of rivals like Presley and Chuck Berry. Still it is hard to deny his seminal role in the creation of rock. Haley was unquestionably a rock pioneer who put together the crucial ingredients into a vibrant musical style which would endure in various forms beyond the 1990s. Haley wanted badly to be remembered as "the Father of Rock 'n' Roll" and many would agree. His major contribution was perhaps forging a particular embodiment to the musical expression of teenage assertiveness.

Bibliography

Brown, Charles T. *The Rock and Roll Story*. Englewood Cliffs: Prentice-Hall, 1983.

Ennis, Philip H. *The Seventh Stream: The Emergence of Rock 'n' Roll in American Popular Music*. Hanover: UP, 1992.

Swenson, John. *Bill Haley*. New York: Stein & Day, 1982.

Ward, Ed, et al. *Rock of Ages: The Rolling Stone History of Rock & Roll*. New York: Rolling Stone, 1986.

White, Timothy. *Rock Lives: Profiles and Interviews*. New York: Holt, 1990.

Craig A. Lockard

Hall, Tom T. (1936-), known as the "Nashville Storyteller," is most famous for his ballads. In the 1980s, he also began to gain acclaim for his fiction. During the 1970s, he published two nonfiction works—*The Songwriter's Handbook* (1976) and *The Storyteller's Nashville* (1979)—but he has since written *The Laughing Man of Woodmont Cove* (1982, 1991), *The Acts of Life* (1986), *Christmas and the Old House* (1989), *Spring Hill, Tennessee* (1990), and *What a Book!* (1996). Despite his success as a novelist and short-story writer, Hall is likely to remain best known for his early hit songs, such as "The Year that Clayton Delaney Died," "Old Dogs, Children and Watermelon Wine," "I Love," "Faster Horses," "Ballad of Forty Dollars" and also for penning "Harper Valley P.T.A."—a No. 1 pop and country hit for Jeannie C. Riley in 1968.

Born in the economically depressed town of Olive Hill, KY, Tom Hall (the T. was added later, "so no one would confuse me with Tompall Glaser") began his musical career with the Kentucky Travellers (1952-54) and worked as a DJ in Morehead, KY. He joined the army and served in Europe, where he began to write songs. When he returned to the United States in 1961, Hall continued to work as a DJ in both Roanoke and Salem, VA (among other places) and to compose songs which he regularly placed with Nashville luminaries such as Jimmy C. Newman, Bobby Bare, and Dave Dudley.

Hall's initial success as recording artist occurred in the late 1960s and early 1970s with top LPs such as *In Search of a Song, The Rhymer and Other Five and Dimers, For the People in the Last Hard Town,* and *Songs of Fox Hollow,* which included pop crossover hits such as "I Love" and "Watergate Blues" (1971-75). After something of a decline, Hall enjoyed a renewed success in the early 1980s with his LP *The Storyteller and the Banjoman,* a joint effort with Earl Scruggs, and with the hit single "Everything from Jesus to Jack Daniels."

For three years during the 1980s, Hall served as the host of *Pop Goes the Country,* a syndicated TV show, and he also rejoined the *Grand Ole Opry,* which he had quit in 1974, when it changed location. "I didn't move with it like furniture," Hall remarks, a statement indicative of his fierce independence, his integrity in a lemming business, and his no-nonsense humor.

Bibliography

Clarke, Donald. *The Penguin Encyclopedia of Popular Music.* London: Penguin, 1990.

Hall, Tom T. *The Storyteller's Nashville.* Garden City: Doubleday, 1979.

Nash, Alana. *Behind Closed Doors: Talking with the Legends of Country Music.* New York: Knopf, 1988.

Rebecca A. Umland
Samuel J. Umland

Hallmark Hall of Fame (1951-) has outlived all other live dramatic anthology shows of its kind. The concept was initiated and developed by Albert McCleery. It began as a half-hour show on NBC in 1951. Then in the summer of 1952, Hallmark premiered as *Hallmark Summer Theater* on NBC, sponsored by Hallmark Greeting Cards. With McCleery its producer-director and Sarah Churchill as its hostess, it expanded to the longer format and resurrected the "theater-in-the-round" style of staging and a minimum of props that had been used on NBC for Shakespearean productions (and in a series called *Cameo Theater*).

In its early days, *Hallmark*'s plays revolved around short stories highlighting some crisis or act of courage. Unlike many of the "big budget" live anthologies, *Hallmark* initially selected its talent from Shakespearean and classically trained artists, scouting Broadway and the Canadian repertories. Slowly, *Hallmark* began to focus on classical drama, especially Shakespeare, presenting shows that were expensively produced. Since the program originated from Hollywood, the casts of the dramas began to draw less from New York and Canada and more from the best artisans of the American entertainment industry employed on the West Coast.

What we regard as the excellence of Hallmark's productions began in 1954 with a two-hour version of *Hamlet* with Maurice Evans, followed by *Richard II* and *Macbeth* with Maurice Evans in 1954 with Mildred Freed Alberg as producer and George Schaefer as director. In 1955-56, Evans produced the series *Maurice Evans Presents* on the *Hallmark Hall of Fame,* and it included productions of Shaw's *The Devil's Disciple* and *Man and Superman* as well as Shakespeare's *Taming of the Shrew,* and *Twelfth Night. Hallmark* was the last show to run live dramas but it, too, changed over to videotape in the early 1960s. With the advent of videotape in 1960, *Hallmark* gave television its first taped Shakespeare, *The Tempest.*

In response to audience demand, *Hallmark* departed from its "high classical" format in the 1960s and started airing quarterly shows of off-Broadway productions, particularly popular musicals such as *The Fantasticks.* Memorable and Emmy-nominated dramatic performances include *Little Moon of Alban* (1958); *A Doll's House* (1959); *Kiss Me Kate; The Green Pastures* (1957); *Victoria Regina* (1961); *Johnny Belinda* (1958); *The Invincible Mr. Disraeli* (1962); *Macbeth* (1954); *The Patriots* (1963); *The Magnificent Yankee* (1964); *Inherit the Wind* (1965); *Eagle in a Cage* (1965); *Anastasia* (1966); *Elizabeth the Queen* (1967); *Saint Joan* (1967); *Teacher, Teacher* (1968); *A Storm in Summer* (1969); *Hamlet* (1970); *The Price* (1970); *The Snow Goose* (1971); *Gideon* (1971); *Beauty and the Beast* (1976); *Peter Pan* (1976); *Taxi* (1977); *The Last Hurrah* (1977); *All Quiet on the Western Front* (1979); *The Hunchback of Notre Dame* (1981); *The Marva Collins Story* (1981); *Camille* (1984); *Love Is Never Silent* (1985); *Promise* (1986); *Pack of Lies* (1986); *Foxfire* (1987); *My Name Is Bill W.* (1988); *The Tenth Man* (1988); *The Shell Seekers* (1989); *Caroline?* (1989); *Decoration Day* (1990); and *Sarah, Plain and Tall* (1990).

Bibliography

O'Neil, Thomas. *The Emmys.* New York: Penguin, 1992.

S. P. Madigan

Hamlisch, Marvin (1944-), composer, pianist, and conductor, hails from New York City. His father, Max, was a Viennese accordion player who arrived in America in November 1937 with his wife, Lilly. A daughter, Terry, was born shortly thereafter. Young Marvin was quickly recognized for his ability to reconstruct on the piano songs that he heard on the radio and, thus, was enrolled at age six in the Preparatory Division of the Juilliard School of Music (New York).

Hamlisch's first professional work in the Broadway/popular music world came through Buster Davis in 1963. Davis hired Hamlisch to be a rehearsal pianist and chorus director/arranger for the show *Funny Girl.* This job introduced him to the rising star of the show, Barbra Streisand, with whom a long professional association developed. Additional recognition came in 1965 when his song "Sunshine, Lollipops, and Rainbows" was recorded by Leslie Gore and made a respectable showing on the *Billboard* chart. He also worked as a rehearsal pianist for the *Bell Telephone Hour* television show. Hamlisch's great ear and fast-paced working style brought him to the attention of producer Sam Spiegel, who, in 1967, hired Hamlisch to score the film *The Swimmer.* Shortly thereafter he worked on films with Woody Allen and Jack Lemmon.

The 1970s were particularly successful for Hamlisch beginning with stints as musical advisor to both Ann-Margret and Groucho Marx. However, it was through composing and arranging that he achieved widespread name recognition. In 1973, he composed the music for the film *The Way We Were* and adapted ragtime music of Scott Joplin for the film *The Sting*. At the 1974 Academy Awards ceremony, Hamlisch was recipient of three: for the score of *The Way We Were*, for the song of the same name (recorded by Streisand; words by Alan and Marilyn Bergman), and for the arrangement of Joplin's music. In that same year he began work on the Broadway show *A Chorus Line*, which earned him both a Tony Award and a Pulitzer Prize in 1975. Many Americans have the opportunity to hear Hamlisch's music daily; he composed the theme song for the ABC television show *Good Morning America* and for other shows.

His personal relationship with lyricist Carole Bayer Sager led them to write the music for a show titled *They're Playing Our Song* by Neil Simon, which opened on Broadway in February 1979. Hamlisch and Bayer Sager also penned such pop hits as "Nobody Does It Better"; Carly Simon's version reached #2 on the charts. Hamlisch has said that he thinks first of what a song should say—what meaning it has in a scene. He considers the function before he thinks about the music.

Bibliography

"Hamlisch, Marvin (Frederick)." *Current Biography* 1976.

Hamlisch, Marvin, and Gerald Gardner. *The Way I Was.* New York: Scribner's, 1992.

Linda Pohly

Hammett, Dashiell (1894-1961), did not originate the hard-boiled detective, but he created a number of the major characters of that subgenre of mystery fiction. With the Continental Op, the wise-cracking Sam Spade, and the high-living Nick and Nora Charles, Hammett brought the detective story to new heights in the 1920s and 1930s. The author's life, however, was as interesting as those of his characters, and he remains an intriguing figure decades after his death.

Samuel Dashiell Hammett was born in Maryland and educated in Baltimore, but left school at age 14 when his father became too ill to work. After holding a variety of ill-paying jobs, he joined the Pinkerton Detective Agency in 1915. During the next two years, and again after World War I, he traveled the country as a member of the nation's most famous firm of investigators. While many of the stories Hammett later told about his life as a "Pinkerton" may have been embellished if not entirely fictitious, nevertheless the realism he brought to his writing convinced readers that the author knew the techniques of "working a case." After World War I, Hammett settled in San Francisco. Over the next ten years, while fighting a recurrent case of tuberculosis, he continued to work part time as a detective for Pinkerton and later turned to writing advertising copy. During these years, Hammett wrote most of the fiction that gave him fame and fortune.

Hammett quickly found an audience in *Black Mask* (see entry), one of the new pulp magazines created to serve the growing American appetite for short fiction. By the mid-1920s, Hammett's clipped, edgy prose style along with his major character, the Continental Op—a nameless investigator for the Continental Detective Agency—had become well known. With the help of Joseph Shaw, *Black Mask*'s editor, Hammett's wrote tales of mob violence, blackmail, double-dealing, and murder that set the standard for the hard-boiled detective story, outstripping Carroll John Daly, Erle Stanley Gardner, and other famous pulp writers.

In the late 1920s, Hammett turned to the full-length novel, publishing five highly significant works between 1929 and 1934: *The Dain Curse* (1929), *Red Harvest* (1929), *The Maltese Falcon* (1930), *The Glass Key* (1931), and *The Thin Man* (1934). Several of these featured memorable detective heroes. The Continental Op reappeared in *The Dain Curse*, a mystery about family corruption and religious scams, and *Red Harvest*, a novel probing the tainted politics in a Western mining town. Nick and Nora Charles made their appearance in *The Thin Man* (see entry) as a society couple whose sophisticated urban lifestyle is as much the subject of the story as the mystery that is interwoven into it. Most enduring is Sam Spade of *The Maltese Falcon*, the hard-boiled detective par excellence, whose cool cynicism and embattled sense of honor have come to define the form. Hammett's detective protagonists have been frequently imitated, but seldom if ever equaled. Despite his successes, after completing *The Thin Man* in 1934, Hammett stopped writing fiction. Hammett worked as a scriptwriter in Hollywood and became politically active in anti-fascist causes. After World War II he resumed his leftist activities, and became a victim of the McCarthy witch hunts. He died shortly thereafter, his health broken, his income impounded by the IRS, and his writing career a thing of the past.

Bibliography

DeAndrea, William L. *Encyclopedia Mysteriosa*: *A Comprehensive Guide to the Art of Detection in Print, Films, Radio, and Television.* New York: Prentice-Hall, 1994.

Herron, Don. *The Dashiell Hammett Tour.* San Francisco: City Lights, 1991.

Reilly, John, ed. *Twentieth Century Crime and Mystery Writers.* New York: St. Martin's, 1985.

Steinbrunner, Chris, and Otto Penzler, ed. *The Encyclopedia of Mystery & Detection.* New York: McGraw-Hill, 1976.

Fred Isaac

See also

Crime Fiction

Hard-boiled Detective Fiction

Regional Mysteries

Hammond Electric Organ, The, was the first mass-produced musical instrument which generated sounds by electrical means. The organ, invented by Laurens Hammond of Chicago, was patented in 1935 and first displayed in public at the Industrial Arts Exhibit at Rockefeller Center in New York City. The Hammond company began full-scale production in 1936 and continued manufacturing organs according to the original design until 1974.

The original design used an electro-mechanical tone generation system based on moving parts. The heart of the system is a synchronous motor originally developed by Laurens Hammond for use in electric clocks. The motor turns a shaft at a steady speed, and gears on the shaft turn a series of tone wheels which generate the organ's sounds. A total of 91 tone wheels serve the two 61-note keyboards and 25-pedal clavier.

The sound produced by the Hammond tone wheel system is quite pure—almost like that generated by an electric oscillator or a flute. The sounds of other instrumental colors, such as violins or clarinets, are approximated by mixing various pitches of the tone wheels at different strengths. This is accomplished by a series of drawbars which control the amplitude of selected tone wheels. Most Hammond organs have two sets of drawbars per keyboard, plus a number of preset combinations. Each set has nine drawbars each. There are only two drawbars for the pedal clavier.

Had the Hammond drawbar system gone far enough, it could have come much closer to generating the sounds of brasses, strings, and diapasons than it actually does. In fact, all Hammond drawbar settings are similar to one another and are really just variations on a flute sound. A Hammond can produce approximately 30 distinctly different tones, and these are sufficient for it to serve as a reasonable substitute for a pipe organ in many situations. In addition to tone wheels and drawbars, Hammonds use a sustain and vibrato to add variety to the sound. A favorite combination for many years has been a Hammond organ connected to a Leslie speaker, which uses rotating horns and baffles to disperse the sound in all directions.

Bibliography

"All Hail the King: The Hammond B-3." *Keyboard Magazine* Nov. 1991.

Dorf, Richard H. *Electronic Musical Instruments.* New York: Radiofile, 1968.

Henry B. Aldridge

Hanks, Tom (1956-), versatile movie actor, film director, and screenwriter, captured the attention of movie and television audiences early in his career. His comedic and dramatic talent is comparable to that of Cary Grant, Jimmy Stewart, Henry Fonda, Gary Cooper, and Steve Martin.

Hanks's film roles take him from the wild-eyed husband-to-be in *Bachelor Party* (1984) to the voice of the cool and even-handed toy sheriff, Woody, in Walt Disney's *Toy Story* (1995) and *Toy Story 2* (1999). He honed his acting skills playing a variety of film characters: a wise yet innocent simpleton named Forrest Gump, a forlorn and lonely widower, a small child trapped in an adult's body, a brave astronaut facing potential death, a manager for an all women's baseball league, and a homosexual attorney seeking dignity and respect in his battle with AIDS. Two of these won him Academy Awards for best actor: *Philadelphia* (1993) and *Forrest Gump* (1994).

Born in Concord, CA, Hanks began his acting career in television, starring in *Bosom Buddies*, a sex farce about two young ad executives who seek shelter in an all-women's hotel. Hanks also appeared in television guest roles in *Happy Days* and *Family Ties*. He also starred in made-for-television movies, directing and performing in *Fallen Angels* (1993).

Hanks made his first appearance as director and screenwriter with *That Thing You Do!* (1996), which chronicles the story of a small-town Pennsylvania rock band seeking fame and fortune during the early years of rock 'n' roll. His role as a soldier in Steven Spielberg's *Saving Private Ryan* (1998), a World War II story about a soldier facing the ordeals of the Normandy invasion, earned him yet another Oscar nomination. He also starred in the film adaptation of Stephen King's *The Green Mile* (1999).

Bibliography

Hanks, Tom. "Peaking Tom." Interview by Brian D. Johnson. *MacLean's* 107.28 (11 July 1994): 52-55.

Troy, Carol. "It's a Cool Gig." *American Film* 15.7 (April 1990): 20.

Kenneth Dvorak

Hansen, Joseph (1923-), has emerged as the most famous, respected, and influential writer of gay mysteries. For many years a would-be author who tried unsuccessfully to publish novels, Hansen worked as a bookstore clerk, radio announcer, and magazine editor. His recognition as a writer began in 1970 with *Fadeout*, the first of 12 mysteries featuring Dave Brandstetter, a death-claims investigator for an insurance company. At the start of the series, the 44-year-old Brandstetter, who is homosexual, is mourning the death from cancer of his lover of 20 years. *Fadeout* establishes Brandstetter as an admirable gay character: monogamous, intelligent, caring, and professionally skilled.

Unlike many mystery writers, Hansen has used "real time" in the series, allowing Brandstetter to reflect on the changing world around him, to develop new ties (such as a long-term relationship with Cecil Harris, a young African-American television reporter), and to face the problems of aging. Throughout the series, Hansen uses the mystery format to comment on social issues such as racism, environmental pollution, abused children, AIDS, and the prevalence of violence in American society. Hansen brought the series to a conclusion with Brandstetter's death in *A Country of Old Men* (1991).

Hansen has also written short stories featuring heterosexual detective Hack Bohannon, and several novels about gay life such as *Living Upstairs* (1993).

Bibliography

Baker, Robert A., and Michael T. Nietzel. *Private Eyes: One Hundred and One Knights.* Bowling Green, OH: Bowling Green State U Popular P, 1985.

Slide, Anthony. *Gay and Lesbian Characters and Themes in Mystery Novels.* Jefferson: McFarland, 1993.

Winks, Rubin W. *Colloquium on Crime: Eleven Renowned Mystery Writers Discuss Their Work.* New York: Scribner's, 1986.

David C. Wallace

See also
Crime Fiction
Gay and Lesbian Mysteries

Happy Days (1974-1984), a nostalgic sitcom about the 1950s, created by Garry Marshall (see entry) and produced by Paramount, was originally to be about an innocent high school kid, Richie Cunningham, his slightly more worldly friend, Potsie Weber, and another friend, Ralph Malph. The three attended Jefferson High in Milwaukee, WI, and hung out at Arnold's Drive-In. Richie's dad, Howard, ran a hardware store, and his slightly dippy mom, Marion, stayed home to take care of husband, children, and house. In addition to Richie, the Cunninghams had a college-age son, Chuck, and a 12-year-old daughter, Joanie.

To give the show a bit of spice, the producers added a mother's nightmare, a greasy-haired, leather-jacketed, motorcycle-riding drop-out named Arthur "Fonzie" Fonzarelli, adeptly played by Henry Winkler. Street-smart Fonzie had a way with women, and soon the relationship between Richie and Fonzie became the focus of the show with "The Fonz" advising Richie on matters of the heart and life in general. The Fonz, with his leather jacket and his signature thumbs-up gesture, grew into a cultural phenomenon, and the popularity of the show increased until in 1976-77, it was the No. 1 program on television.

Because of its popularity, *Happy Days* was able to attract a host of guest stars. Such diverse personalities as Hank Aaron, the Amazing Randi, Frankie Avalon, Dr. Joyce Brothers, Morgan Fairchild, Lorne Greene, Happy Hairston, Tom Hanks, Cheryl Ladd, June Lockhart, Penny Marshall, Sean McDonough, Phil Silvers, Buffalo Bob Smith, Cindy Williams, and Robin Williams were a few visitors to grace the show. Penny Marshall and Cindy Williams, who played Richie and Fonzie's tough-girl dates, became the lead characters of the spinoff series *Laverne and Shirley* (1976-83; see entry).

Changes were made in the show over the years. Richie's older brother disappeared altogether, the high school friends went to the University of Wisconsin in Milwaukee, and Fonzie moved into the apartment over the Cunninghams' garage. By the 1980s, Richie and Ralph had graduated from college, joined the army, and were shipped out to Greenland. Richie stayed in touch, even marrying his sweetheart, Lori Beth, over the phone with the Fonz as stand-in. Fonzie became increasingly mainstream until, as the show ended, he was Dean of Boys at George S. Patton Vocational High School. The focus of the show moved to the younger generation, Joanie and her boyfriend, Chachi (Fonzie's cousin), and their rocky relationship. A spinoff show, *Joanie Loves Chachi,* only lasted about a year. There was also an animated version of the series, *The Fonz and the Happy Days Gang,* which aired from 1980 to 1982.

In 1992, ABC aired a *Happy Days* reunion. Fonzie hosted the event and was joined by the regular cast: Tom Bosley (Howard Cunningham), Marion Ross (Marion Cunningham), Ron Howard (Richie), Anson Williams (Potsie), Don Most (Ralph Malph), Scott Baio (Chachi), Al Molinaro (Alfred), Pat Morita (Arnold), and series creator Garry Marshall. Erin Moran (Joanie) was unable to attend. The 90-minute show consisted of clips from the series, including bloopers and out-takes, and reminiscences from the cast.

Bibliography
"Happy Days Fans Club—Reunion 1992." Online. Internet. 7 March 1998. Available: http://www.infosquare.it/fonzie/ereunio.htm.
"Happy Days: Notable Guest Appearances." Online. Internet. 7 March 1998. Available: http://www.geocities.com/TelevisionCity/9835/notable.html.
"Happy Days: Show Information." Online. Internet. 7 March 1998. Available: http://geocities.com/TelevisionCity/9835/show.html.
"International Happy Days Fan Club." Online. Internet. 7 March 1998. Available: http://www.infosquare.it/fonzie/.
"Upcoming Happy Days episodes on Nick-at-Nite." Online. Internet. 7 March 1998. Available: http://www.geocities.com/TelevisionCity/9835/upcoming.html.

Barbara Basore McIver

Hard Day's Night, A, Richard Lester's 1964 presentation, is characterized as "the single most important event in the Beatles's own history" (Monaco 26). Joined by family, friends, and business associates, George Harrison, John Lennon, Paul McCartney, and Ringo Starr star as themselves in this film which captures 36 hours in their travels. Musical performances in the film include "I Should Have Known Better" and "Can't Buy Me Love," among others, and are alternately incorporated into the "plot" of the film as performances on television or before a live crowd, as well as without the illusion of an actual performance, as in the rendering of "Can't Buy Me Love."

Lester draws on various film techniques to achieve the effects of this film, including a "blend of cine-verite (hand-held camera, location shooting, improvised performances, and a generally casual approach towards filming) and modernism (a self-conscious use of film technique, anti-realist editing, and cinematic pastiche)" (Hill 374). The film served to transform movies about pop stars from the earlier "let's put on a show" format to the "a day in the life of..." formula, as in later "rockumentaries" such as Lester's *Help* (1965) and Madonna's *Truth or Dare* (1991) (Hill 373).

Bibliography
Hagen, Ray. "A Hard Day's Night." *Films in Review* 15.8 (1964): 503-5.
Hill, John. "A Hard Day's Night." *International Dictionary of Films and Filmmakers: Films.* 2d ed. 372-74.
Monaco, James. "Some Late Clues to the Lester Direction." *Film Comment* 10.3 (1974): 25-31.
Sarris, Andrew. "A Hard Day's Night." *Confessions of a Cultist: On the Cinema, 1955-1969.* New York: Simon & Schuster, 1970.

Lynnea Chapman-King

Hard-boiled Detective Fiction, sometimes called the "tough guy school," originated as an American subgenre of mystery fiction. Carroll John Daly and Dashiell Hammett (see entry) wrote the first hard-boiled short stories for *Black Mask* in the 1920s. Soon after, both authored novels that established the style and formulaic elements of hard-boiled detection: Daly's *The Snarl of the Beast* (1927), and Hammett's *Red Harvest* (1929). While Edgar Allan Poe, in "The Murders in the Rue Morgue" (1841), provided the first literary model for a detective, the hard-boiled sleuth is as much a descendant of James Fenimore Cooper's Natty Bumppo, hero of the Leatherstocking tales, the prototype for the capable, solitary figure who epitomizes the early fictional private eye. Sources as diverse as late-19th-century dime novels, Owen Wister's classic Western, *The Virginian* (1902), and Ernest Hemingway's spare narrative style also influenced hard-boiled writing. From its inception, hard-boiled fiction has been almost entirely an urban genre, examining the criminal underside of modern American life.

Almost from the start, the genre began to evolve in varying directions. Daly's Race Williams, the first hard-boiled detective, is an affluent New Yorker, while Hammett's Continental Op (Op being short for "operative"; the character is never named) works out of the Continental Detective Agency's San Francisco office. Both narrate their own stories, a dominant device in hard-boiled fiction, but Williams, whose boasting and violent predilections foreshadow Mickey Spillane's Mike Hammer, contrasts sharply with the more dispassionate Op, who employs violence only selectively.

Attitudes toward women range from the sentimentality of Daly's Williams to the sexual detachment of the Continental Op. The misogyny latent in Hammett's portrait of Brigid O'Shaughnessy, who seduces and deceives detective Sam Spade in *The Maltese Falcon* (1930)—and turns out to be the murderer—initiates a pattern emulated by numerous hard-boiled writers, whose detectives, jaded by female treachery, steer clear of romantic involvement. Raymond Chandler's Philip Marlowe (see entry), introduced in *The Big Sleep* (1939), eschews women as contaminating and lethal, and Thomas B. Dewey's series character Mac, from his first appearance in *Draw the Curtain Close* (1947), isolates himself from female contact. Not all early detectives are as sexually austere: Brett Halliday's Michael Shayne, a Miami private eye first featured in *Dividend on Death* (1939), exhibits a marked interest in women.

Other, more contemporary attitudes appear in the postwar generation of hard-boiled detectives. John D. MacDonald's Travis McGee, who debuts in *The Deep Blue Good-by* (1964), ruminates extensively on the meaning of his relationships with and feelings about women, and other series detectives such as William Campbell Gault's Brock Callahan, Bill Pronzini's Nameless, and Robert B. Parker's Spenser achieve intimate involvements with women. While most early hard-boiled detectives reject marriage or, as happens to Ross Macdonald's Lew Archer, become separated from wives and children because of the compromising and alienating nature of their work, more recent characters sustain permanent love relationships and family contacts.

With time, hard-boiled fiction came more closely to resemble traditional novels of manners and morals. Joseph T. Shaw, editor of the pulp magazine *Black Mask* (see entry), from 1926 to 1936, required an action-focused narrative with frequent violent interludes. Chandler, however, was resolved to combine a hard-boiled plot with a greater consciousness of language, a more pointed critique of American cultural values, and a sharply realized sense of atmosphere. In this regard he set the standard for later writers such as Ross Macdonald, who openly acknowledged Chandler's influence, and John D. MacDonald.

In addition, Chandler—concerned with developing the sort of hero he describes in his celebrated essay, "The Simple Art of Murder" (1944)—produces in Marlowe a more psychologically complex and morally insightful character who serves as an exemplar for many subsequent writers. Ross Macdonald's Archer represents a variation on Chandler's model, less himself the subject of the fiction than a conduit into the lives of the people in his cases. Loren D. Estleman's Amos Walker and Jonathan Valin's Harry Stoner maintain the tradition of the isolated, lonely private eye.

Writers like Erle Stanley Gardner, Hammett, Chandler, and other pulp practitioners made New York, San Francisco, and Los Angeles the most popular settings for early hard-boiled fiction, but by the later decades, the fictional worlds expanded to the rest of America. Chandler and Hammett in particular used California as a symbol of the despoiled American Dream and the national fixation on money, glamour, and artifice. Later writers have broadened the base, showing the criminality of American life to be pervasive. McGee operates in Ft. Lauderdale, Spenser in Boston, Michael Z. Lewin's Albert Samson in Indianapolis, John Lutz's Alo Nudger in St. Louis, Walker in Detroit, James Crumley's Milo Milodragovitch in Montana, and Sara Paretsky's V. I. Warshawski in Chicago.

One feature of the hard-boiled novel which has remained relatively constant is the background from which the detectives emerge. Almost all male private investigators have either a police background or investigative experience, either for a district attorney's office or a private security company. In addition, most self-employed male detectives have left such employment, usually because they were unable to conform to or could no longer sanction the politics or ethical practices of the organization. Female hard-boiled detectives continue this pattern, underscoring the iconoclastic bearing of most fictional private eyes: Sue Grafton's Kinsey Millhone and Linda Barnes's Carlotta Carlyle are ex-policewomen, and while Paretsky's Warshawski, introduced in *Indemnity Only* (1982), is a lawyer, she is also the daughter of a Chicago policeman whose old friend and fellow officer Lt. Bobby Mallory attempts to control and protect her. V. I.'s rejection of his interference is the series' version of the private eye's traditional inability to function as a member of the police force.

The uneasy affiliation between the police and the private investigator constitutes a long-running fictional conceit in hard-boiled literature. The Continental Op, with his agency's resources, sometimes functions as an extension of the police, arresting people and helping to interrogate suspects. Hammett and Chandler often portray the police as expedient, corruptible, and pugnacious. Despite their independent calling and their personal antagonism to the system, however, most detectives rely on a working relationship with the police and retain a personal contact on the force.

More recent fictional detectives take the genre in new directions, while still maintaining its defining features. Vietnam, for example, has replaced World Wars I, II and Korea, as the conflict which brought many of them to maturity; Les Roberts's Milan Jacovich and Jeremiah Healy's John Francis Cuddy both served as military policemen in that war. Allusions to earlier hard-boiled detectives continue to stress the genre's development. Love relationships and family involvements also remain staples. Jacovich, though divorced, frequently houses his two sons, establishing a familial subtheme to the stories. Steven Dobyns's Charlie Bradshaw, a Saratoga Springs private detective, futilely tries to avoid his ex-wife and his successful cousins, and even, on occasion, works for his mother. Millhone and Warshawski reluctantly allow older grandfather figures to protect them on occasion, despite their feminist discomfort with such chivalry. Women detectives including these and Barnes's Carlyle, though independent and unmarried, tend to cluster themselves inside affectionate and supportive networks and extended families of mostly women.

Despite the diversity of settings, protagonists, and storylines seen in contemporary hard-boiled detective fiction, the classic features of the genre, particularly its depiction of the venality of the American mean streets, continue to define this enduringly popular form.

Bibliography

Cawelti, John G. *Adventure, Mystery, and Romance: Formula Stories as Art and Popular Culture*. Chicago: U of Chicago P, 1976.

Durham, Philip. *Tough Guy Writers of the Thirties*. Ed. David Madden. Carbondale: Southern Illinois UP, 1968.

Geherin, David. *The American Private Eye: The Image in Fiction*. New York: Ungar, 1985.

Grella, George. *Detective Fiction: A Collection of Critical Essays*. Ed. Robin W. Winks. Woodstock: Countryman, 1988.

Nolan, William F. *The Black Mask Boys: Masters in the Hard-Boiled School of Detective Fiction*. New York: Morrow, 1985.

Lewis D. Moore

Hardin, Tim (1941-1980), though usually labeled a "folk singer," initially thought of himself as a blues musician and, later, as a jazz artist. However, none of these categories does justice to Hardin's unique, powerful, and deeply personal contribution to contemporary popular music.

Slight of build and small of stature, interested in music and acting, Hardin was already an anomalous figure in working-class Eugene, OR, by the time he graduated from high school in 1959. Though desperate to break from his parents and flee the stultifying confines of his home town, Hardin never considered college.

Hardin moved to Greenwich Village in 1964 and acquired a manager, Erik Jacobsen, who arranged for an audition with Columbia Records. The 15 songs he recorded were an often awkwardly arranged mix of traditional blues and his own compositions. Worse yet, Hardin was so stoned on marijuana that he passed out in the studio.

In 1965, Hardin signed with the newly formed Verve/Forecast label. His first album, *Tim Hardin 1*, was released in July 1966. Vastly superior, in every way, to the Columbia demo tapes, it contained such classics as "Don't Make Promises," "It'll Never Happen Again," "Misty Roses" (later covered by Colin Bluestone), "Reason to Believe" (covered by Rod Stewart and many others), and the superb "How Can We Hang on to a Dream," which was released as Hardin's first single six months before the album appeared. Clearly, Hardin was rapidly reaching the height of his powers as a singer and songwriter.

Hardin's second LP, *Tim Hardin 2* (released in April 1967), was even more incisive and focused than his first. Dubbed "one of the ten best from the '60s" by critic Colin Escott, it featured such classics as "Red Balloon," "Black Sheep Boy," "Lady Came from Baltimore" (later covered by Scott Walker), "Tribute to Hank Williams," and probably Hardin's best-known tune, "If I Were a Carpenter," which soon became a huge hit—for Bobby Darin, much to Hardin's chagrin. (Later, successful cover versions were recorded by the Four Tops, Johnny Cash and June Carter, Bert Jansch, and others.)

After four years of inspired composing, Hardin's creative wellsprings suddenly ran dry. His next few albums featured virtually no new material. A jazz-tinged live recording, at Town Hall, NYC (*Tim Hardin 3*, 1968), was followed by a company-mandated knockoff of the old Columbia demo tapes (*Tim Hardin 4*, 1969), a sub-par album that galled Hardin. The subsequent release of two compilations in 1969 (*The Best of Tim Hardin* and *This Is Tim Hardin*) seemed to confirm the end of Hardin's most vital period. When he finally did release new material, *Suite for Susan Moore and Damion*, on the Columbia label in April 1969, the result was an overproduced and maudlin confessional album that chronicled the dissolution of his marriage.

In ill health and frustrated by the fact that everyone except himself seemed to make hits of his songs, Hardin relocated to England in 1971. He lived there for the next seven years.

Hardin returned to the United States in 1979. In April 1980, he teamed with Don Rubin, his executive producer and music publisher from his days with Verve/Forecast, and undertook an American comeback album. Ten new songs were written and the recording was underway when Hardin was found dead of a heroin overdose in Los Angeles on December 29, 1980. He had just turned 39.

After Hardin's death, Columbia brought out *The Shock of Grace*, a 1981 compilation of his later work. In 1982, a small independent label released *The Homecoming Concert*, recorded live in Eugene in 1979. Polygram Records followed suit with a *Memorial Album* in 1982 and a massive 47-song compilation album on two CDs in 1994.

Bibliography
Larkin, Colin, ed. *Guinness Encyclopedia of Popular Music 3*. London: Guinness, 1995.
Pareles, Jon, and Patricia Romanowski. *The Rolling Stone History of Rock & Roll*. New York: Fireside, 1983.
Stambler, Irwin. *The Encyclopedia of Pop, Rock and Soul*. New York: St. Martin's, 1977.

Robert Niemi

Hardy Boys, The, a juvenile mystery series, was launched in 1927 with the publication of *The Tower Treasure* by "Franklin W. Dixon," issued by the Stratemeyer Syndicate (see entry). So the boy detectives would be more credible, they were made the sons of world-famous private investigator Fenton Hardy, who served as mentor to the teenage sleuths. Their role was to discover the clues while he interpreted them. Edward Stratemeyer's idea was to adapt popular adult detective fiction to a juvenile market, and his strategy was immensely successful. The Hardy Boys mysteries are still avidly read by young audiences, boys and girls alike.

Stratemeyer did not himself write the stories; he outlined the plots but hired contract writers to compose them for a set sum. Canadian author Leslie McFarlane, as "Franklin W. Dixon," wrote 22 of the early Hardy Boys books, the last in 1947, when other anonymous writers took over the series. Between 1959 and 1973, the sequence of 38 mysteries was revised at the same time that new mysteries continued to be produced. This project made older stories more contemporary, removed the overt racism, and changed the style to appeal to a younger grade-school audience. Hardy Boys books continue to be produced; the 100th mystery, *The Secret of Island Treasure,* was published in 1990. A racier murder mystery series intended for a young adult audience was introduced in 1987 by Simon & Schuster, who now own the syndicate. Despite the television-style depiction of action and violence in these, conservative moral codes forbidding swearing, sex, and drugs continue to prevail.

Bibliography
Billman, Carol. *The Secret of the Stratemeyer Syndicate: Nancy Drew, The Hardy Boys, and the Million Dollar Fiction*. New York: Ungar, 1986.
Deane, Paul. *Mirrors of American Culture: Children's Fiction Series in the Twentieth Century*. Metuchen: Scarecrow, 1991.
Dizer, John. *Tom Swift and Company*. Jefferson: McFarland, 1982.
Johnson, Deidre. *Edward Stratemeyer and the Stratemeyer Syndicate*. New York: Twayne, 1993.
McFarlane, Leslie. *Ghost of the Hardy Boys: An Autobiography*. Toronto: Methuen, 1976.

Jacqueline Reid-Walsh

Harris, Susan (1942-), a prolific writer and producer of television situation comedy, grew up in Westchester County in the shadow of New York City. Although she never received a degree, she studied English literature at both Cornell and New York universities. She broke into the television business in 1969 when a friend with connections on the set of *Then Came Bronson* (1969-70) gave her script to the producer. This short-lived dramatic series about a newspaper reporter who searches for the meaning of life on a motorcycle after the death of a friend was the start of her career as a television writer, although comedy quickly became her specialty.

Harris was then given the opportunity by NBC to create her own show. The result was the critically acclaimed *Fay* in 1975. A situation comedy starring Lee Grant, the show dealt with the new independence and sexuality of a middle-aged, divorced woman. Unfortunately, it became a victim of network politics and the short-lived concept of "family viewing time" adopted by the television industry to keep the first hour of prime time suitable for viewing by all family members; the series was canceled after only three broadcasts.

Although Harris announced soon after that she was hoping to write her way out of the television business by working on plays, ABC gave her the opportunity to create another series. *Soap* (see entry) made its debut in 1977, but even before it aired, thousands of letters of protest poured into the network. A satire of the soap opera genre, the prime-time comedy serial had storylines dealing with subjects such as homosexuality, premarital sex, adultery, alien possession, and satanism. The negative press probably helped the show stay in the Top 20 for three out of its four years on the air.

A spinoff of *Soap, Benson* debuted on ABC in 1979 and remained on the air until 1986. Benson had been the wise-cracking African-American servant on *Soap*; in his own show he ran the household of the governor of an unknown state and eventually became lieutenant governor. The success of *Benson* was followed by three disappointments: *I'm a Big Girl Now* in 1980 about a divorced woman with a child who moves in with her dad, *It Takes Two* in 1982 about a doctor/lawyer couple, and *Hail to the Chief* in 1985 about the first female president of the United States, the latter two starring Patty Duke.

With her next try, however, Harris had a hit on her hands. *The Golden Girls* (see entry) debuted in 1985 and showcased three actresses who had been in popular comedies in the 1970s: Beatrice Arthur, former star of *Maude*; Rue McClanahan, best friend from *Maude*; and Betty White, the "Happy Homemaker" from *The Mary Tyler Moore Show*. Estelle Getty played Dorothy's mother, Sophia, a feisty, sarcastic octogenarian, who also shared a house with the three women in Miami after her retirement home burned down. Over the series' seven years on CBS, it won several Emmy awards, including best comedy in its first two years. Harris was also nominated for her writing on the series.

In 1988, *Empty Nest* was spun off from *The Golden Girls,* with the widowed Dr. Harry Weston, played by Richard Mulligan of *Soap* fame, whose two grown daughters lived with him. *Nurses*, which debuted in 1991, was yet a third Harris comedy set in Miami. With all three NBC shows on Saturday night during one season, Harris was able to run a common storyline through them—the theme one night was coping with an impending hurricane. *Good and Evil*, the second Harris comedy debuting in 1991, did not fare as well as the Saturday night line-up. An off-the-wall comedy about two sisters with opposite personalities, it lasted only one month.

Since 1976, Harris has been a partner with her husband, Paul Junger Witt, and Tony Thomas, the son of legendary comedian Danny Thomas. She has been a major innovative force in Witt-Thomas-Harris Productions, creating the series and writing many of the scripts. She has received many awards, including the Emmy, the Humanitas Award, and the Hollywood Foreign Press's Golden Globe Award.

Bibliography

Brooks, Tim, and Earle Marsh. *The Complete Directory to Prime Time Network TV Shows, 1946-Present*. 5th ed. New York: Ballantine, 1992.

David, Marc, and Robert J. Thompson. *Prime Time, Prime Movers*. Boston: Little, Brown, 1992.

Montgomery, Kathryn C. *Target: Prime Time—Advocacy Groups and the Struggle over Entertainment Television*. New York: Oxford UP, 1989.

Lynn C. Spangler

Hart, Lorenz (1895-1943). Before there were Rodgers and Hammerstein, the most successful creators of Broadway musicals in American theatrical history, there were Rodgers and Hart. Ironically, Hart's premature death came only several months after the March 31, 1943, premiere of Rodgers and Hammerstein's greatest show, *Oklahoma!*

One of the finest musical collaborations of the 1920s, 1930s, and early 1940s, Rodgers and Hart in their time almost rivaled George and Ira Gershwin. Lorenz Milton Hart, born in New York City of well-to-do parents on May 2, 1895, first met Rodgers in 1918. Richard Rodgers (1902-79), then only 16, had been writing songs for about two years. In 1917, he had produced both words and music for an amateur production in New York. A friend of the Rodgers family brought Rodgers to the Hart home hoping that Hart, who by then had gained a reputation for writing witty and clever poetry, would work with young Rodgers. Rodgers demonstrated his musical talent to Hart, and Hart elaborated to Rodgers his unconventional ideas about lyric writing. The meeting led to a very productive 23-year-long collaboration, which resulted in 27 significant shows.

Soon the pair were turning out songs, and in 1919, one of their pieces, "Any Old Place with You," was inserted in the musical *A Lonely Romeo*. Later that year Rodgers and Hart wrote all the songs for *Fly with Me*, a Columbia University Varsity Show. Rodgers was then enrolled at Columbia, and Hart earlier had attended the university but without graduating. Hart, who had always excelled in language, had studied journalism and dabbled in college shows. *Fly with Me* caught the eye of Lew Fields, a Broadway entrepreneur who was planning a new show, *Poor Little Ritz Girl*. Fields already had gotten eight songs from the great Sigmund Romberg, who after his successful 1917 operetta *Maytime* was on the threshold on being a top composer on Broadway. Fields had Rodgers and Hart write seven additional songs. The 1920 production was a modest success, and Rodgers was praised for his musical skill and Hart for his imaginative

and well-crafted lyrics. Yet it would be several years before they had another Broadway opportunity.

In 1925, the Theatre Guild contacted the duo about contributing songs for a fundraiser which was scheduled for just two performances. Rodgers and Hart in a short time created a dozen songs. The show *The Garrick Gaieties* was such a hit that it was transferred to Broadway, where it ran for about half a year. "Manhattan," a brilliant and still popular ballad from this show, was their first hit. In 1926 the pair did four shows, which produced only two hit songs: "The Blue Room" and "Mountain Greenery."

The next Rodgers and Hart musical, however, *A Connecticut Yankee* (1927), was to be one of their better ones. Among the songs was "Thou Swell," a clever blend of the language of the Arthurian era and 20th-century America. Another very good song in the show was "My Heart Stood Still," which originally had been introduced in *One Damn Thing After Another*, another Rodgers and Hart musical which opened in London earlier in 1927. Their next six productions were not particularly successful, only resulting in three notable songs. "You Took Advantage of Me" appeared in *Present Arms* (1928), the fine standard "With a Song in My Heart" in *Spring Is Here* (1929), and "Ten Cents a Dance" in *Simple Simon* (1930).

In 1931, Rodgers and Hart wrote their first songs for Hollywood. *Love Me Tonight* (1932) produced three of their top creations for the movies, "Mimi," sung by Maurice Chevalier, "Isn't It Romantic," sung by Chevalier and Jeanette MacDonald, and the classic "Lover," sung by MacDonald. Perhaps their best song connected with a film was the perennial "Blue Moon." Originally written with different lyrics as "The Bad in Every Man" for the 1934 film *Manhattan Melodrama*, "Blue Moon" was issued independently of the movie. After returning to Broadway, the pair wrote the score for *Jumbo* (1935), a fairly successful show starring Jimmy Durante. That musical included one of Rodgers and Hart's finest compositions, "The Most Beautiful Girl in the World." *On Your Toes* (1936) produced another standard, "There's a Small Hotel," plus the extraordinary ballet scene "Slaughter on Tenth Avenue" by Rodgers.

Their best score was probably the one for *Babes in Arms* (1937). Three standards, "The Lady Is a Tramp," "I Wish I Were in Love Again," and "Where or When?" came from that show, plus the good novelty "Johnny One Note" and the perennial classic "My Funny Valentine." The next year, *I Married an Angel* (1938) gave the world the title song plus "Spring Is Here," and *The Boys from Syracuse* (1938) introduced two standards, "Falling in Love with Love" and "This Can't Be Love."

The most successful Rodgers and Hart musical was *Pal Joey* (1940), which in its first run was moderately well received, but which was acclaimed in its 1952 revival. The revival won two awards and had the longest run for a revived musical up to that time. The score was not nearly as good as the one for *Babes in Arms*, but *Pal Joey* had a compelling plot and one blockbuster song, "Bewitched, Bothered and Bewildered."

Rodgers and Hart's last musical was *By Jupiter* (1942), which had no outstanding songs. When the pair was offered

Oklahoma!, Hart rejected the opportunity and suggested that Rodgers replace him with another lyricist. But the long collaboration of the songwriting team produced a number of enduring and fine songs. Ironically, Hart, the very talented wordsmith who wrote so many love songs, was a failure in love and had a troubled life in his final years (by the late 1930s). His masterpiece "Bewitched, Bothered and Bewildered" is a perfect description of Lorenz Hart as an individual.

Bibliography

Green, Stanley. *Rodgers and Hammerstein Fact Book.* New York: Rodgers & Hammerstein, 1955.

Hart, Dorothy. *Thou Swell, Thou Witty.* New York: Harper & Row, 1976.

Marx, Samuel, and Jan Clayton. *Rodgers & Hart: Bewitched, Bothered and Bedeviled.* New York: Putnam, 1976.

Richard Rodgers Fact Book with Supplement. New York: Lynn Farnol Group, 1968.

Rodgers, Richard. *Musical Stages: An Autobiography.* New York: Random House, 1975.

William E. Studwell

See also
American Musical Theater

Harvest of Shame: C.B.S. Reports (1960) chronicles the plight of the American migrant farmworker. For nine months prior to the completion of the TV documentary, producer David Lowe followed the route of farmworkers from Florida to New York state, as they migrated north in search of the harvest and employment. Using photographic record and direct interview, he and renowned radio and TV reporter Edward R. Murrow documented their circumstances and gave voice to farmworkers' stories, conducting interviews and seeking answers. Murrow speaks directly to the viewer as he narrates the film. From the onset, the filmmakers prod at the hearts and consciences of the more fortunate in America by repeatedly exposing the extreme poverty, deplorable working and living conditions, and obvious exploitation of the migrant farmworker. To ensure that the viewer is aware of the worthiness of these forgotten Americans to pursue the "American Dream," Lowe and Murrow bring to our attention, via dialogue, narration, and images, the farmworkers' adherence to the long-held American ideals and values of religion, family, hard work, and patriotism. *Harvest of Shame* remains an unsurpassed passionate cry for social justice.

Bibliography

Bluem, A. William. *Documentary in American Television: Form, Function, Method.* New York: Hastings, 1965.

"The Excluded Americans." *Time* 5 Dec. 1960.

Kendrick, Alexander. *Prime Time—The Life of Edward R. Murrow.* Boston: Little, Brown, 1969.

Persico, Joseph E. *Edward R. Murrow—An American Original.* New York: McGraw-Hill, 1988.

M. Therese Schramm

Harvey Comics (1939-) was America's most successful publisher of comic books for children, especially *Casper, the Friendly Ghost* and *Richie Rich*. At their peak in the 1970s, they published the same characters in dozens of titles, balancing new material with a large inventory of reprints.

Brothers Alfred and Leon Harvey's first series, *Speed Comics*, was dated October 1939, just a year after Superman's first appearance. Their costumed heroes included Shock Gibson, the Blazing Scarab, Jungleman, and the Human Meteor.

Pocket Comics (1941) proved unpopular with retailers because its small size made it easy to steal. It did introduce one of the first female comic crimefighters: glamorous movie star Linda Turner, who donned a mask and a skimpy black outfit to fight Nazis and criminals as the Black Cat. Today, collectors seek out her stories as "good girl" art.

The brothers had better luck with their adaptation of the *Green Hornet* radio show from 1942 to 1949. They also reprinted several comic strips, like *Joe Palooka, Li'l Abner, Mary Worth,* and *Dick Tracy*.

The longest-lived comic strip adaptation was *The Sad Sack,* George Baker's trod-upon "average soldier" from the army's *Yank* magazine. Harvey's reprints began in 1949, when the Sack's misadventures in civilian life were syndicated to the newspapers. Sack never caught on in civvies, so when the strip died in the early 1950s, Baker put his creation back in the army for new comics stories. The series lasted 33 years.

Following World War II, Harvey, like other publishers, joined whatever genre seemed popular at the time. The Black Cat's title, for example, changed to *Black Cat Western,* then *Black Cat Mystery*. Harvey's crime and horror comics of the early '50s were likely no worse than others, but they seemed to have been cited most often by Frederick Wertham's 1953 anti-comics polemic *Seduction of the Innocent*. The most damning illustration used was the lurid cover of a Harvey one-shot entitled *Teen-Age Dope Slaves,* subtitled, in smaller lettering, *As Exposed by Rex Morgan, M.D.*

In 1959, Paramount sold Harvey all rights to Casper and the gang. They immediately repackaged the movie shorts as *Harveytoons,* replacing the Paramount title card with their jack-in-the-box mascot. ABC ran the shorts on its Sunday afternoon *Matty's Funday Funnies,* sponsored by Mattel Toys. The next year, the show moved to Friday evenings, one hour before ABC's new hit, *The Flintstones*. *Harveytoons* appeared on prime time until 1962, when Mattel replaced them with *Beany & Cecil*.

Harvey returned to ABC in 1963 with the Saturday morning *New Casper Cartoon Show*. The series was directed by Seymour Kneitel, who had directed the Casper series for Paramount, and introduced a supporting cast from the comics: Wendy the Good Little Witch, Nightmare the Galloping Ghost, and the Ghostly Trio (another Harvey creation, Hot Stuff the Little Devil, must not have been wholesome enough for TV). Both the Paramount shorts and the new Casper cartoons were also syndicated around the world.

While other humor and children's comics were dying off in the 1960s and 1970s, Harvey continued to add titles for its popular characters. They maintained a tight "house" art style to ensure that new stories were indistinguishable from old ones, which enabled the heavy use of reprints. By 1977,

Harvey had over 30 Richie Rich titles on the stands, including *Richie Rich Millions*, *Richie Rich Billions*, and *Richie Rich Zillionz*.

In 1989, the Harvey family sold its characters to Jeffrey A. Montgomery, who resumed publication as Harvey Comics Entertainment, Inc. Montgomery continued the family tradition by issuing not only several "Casper" and "Richie Rich" titles, but eight titles with the New Kids on the Block.

While comics publishing proved unprofitable, Montgomery had more success promoting the Harvey characters in other media. Macaulay Culkin starred in a *Richie Rich* movie in 1994, followed by a *Casper* feature from Steven Spielberg. Harvey Entertainment also syndicated a *Baby Huey* cartoon, produced in the style of *Ren and Stimpy*.

Bibliography

Benton, Mike. *Superhero Comics of the Golden Age: The Illustrated History*. Dallas: Taylor, 1992.

Brooks, Tim, and Earle Marsh. *The Complete Encyclopedia to Prime Time Network TV Shows, 1946-present*. 4th ed. New York: Ballantine, 1988. 498.

Lenburg, Jeff. *The Encyclopedia of Animated Cartoons*. New York: Facts on File, 1991. 58-59, 368-69.

Maltin, Leonard. *Of Mice and Magic: A History of American Animated Cartoons*. New York: New American Library, 1980. 305-16.

Mark McDermott

Harvey, Paul (1918-), was at one time one of the most influential radio commentators in the United States. Approximately 23 million people listen each day to his programs, which are broadcast on over 1,500 stations. Inducted into the National Radio Hall of Fame in 1990, Harvey has been a leading radio personality since the 1960s. In 1994 Harvey received a Peabody Award for career achievement in radio.

Born in Tulsa, OK, Paul Harvey Aurandt began volunteer work at the age of 14 in a local radio station. He worked at a number of radio stations in the 1930s and joined the Office of War Information during World War II. He was drafted into the army in 1943 and received a medical discharge in 1944. After leaving the army, he changed his name to Paul Harvey and moved to Chicago to pursue a radio career. He joined ABC radio in the late 1940s and built his early reputation as a staunch conservative.

Harvey's morning and noon program of "news and comments" is an amalgamation of the day's headlines, celebrity reports, "agribusiness" news, humorous anecdotes, references to amusing bumper stickers ("bumpersnickers"), and long-term marriages of his listeners ("tournament of roses"). The common person and small-town values are highlighted in each broadcast: a heroic deed; a family tradition; a unique event. Another measure of his popularity is his impact on contemporary language. He is credited with inventing such words as "Reaganomics," "skyjacker," and "guesstimate."

Bibliography

Nimmo, Dan, and James E. Combs. *The Political Pundits*. New York: Praeger, 1992.

Short, Brant. "'Hello Americans': Paul Harvey and the Rhetorical Construction of Modern Agrarianism." *Journal of Radio Studies* 1 (1992): 43-54.

Brant Short

Have Gun Will Travel (1958-1963). The "hero" of this TV success was a professional gunman named Paladin (Richard Boone). Paladin sold his services to almost anyone who could afford them, but he was far from your average illiterate, unrefined gunslinger. This Western soldier of fortune was decidedly different. He clearly functioned within the Western genre, but managed to break the genre's stereotypes, and he quickly became TV's most interesting nonconformist.

Have Gun Will Travel was endowed with action and interesting plots by such distinguished writers as Sam Peckinpah. Paladin was called upon to do an astonishing variety of things in pursuit of justice—from dashing across the desert on a camel to bargaining with an Armenian vintner for his daughter's dowry on behalf of a bashful Texan.

Have Gun Will Travel was an overnight hit, ranking in the Top 5 programs during its first season on the air. From 1958 to 1961, it was the No. 3 program on television, behind two other Westerns—*Gunsmoke* and *Wagon Train*. Even the show's theme song, "The Ballad of Paladin," was a hit record during the early 1960s. The show's popularity soon declined, however, and it was canceled at the end of the 1962-63 season.

Bibliography

Brooks, Tim, and Earle Marsh. *The Complete Directory to Prime Time Network and Cable TV Shows, 1946-Present*. New York: Ballantine, 1995.

Yoggy, Gary A. *Riding the Video Range: The Rise and Fall of the Western on Television*. Jefferson: McFarland, 1995.

Gary A. Yoggy

Hawaii Five-0 (1968-1980) was a long-running television series that presented both adventure and dramatic episodes. Fundamentally, it was a police show that bridged the gap of time and taste between hero-centered police dramas of the late 1950s and graphically depicted "action" entertainments of the 1970s and 1980s. The central character was pirated from the Jim Kildare, Eliot Ness quintessential "pure" hero type; however, the series achieved a strong ingredient of local Hawaiian color that set it apart from other crime dramas. Location shots, folk-speaking minor and major characters, and its detailing of police techniques stamped it as a genuine attempt to exhibit some aspects of policemen's work in an exotic setting.

From its debut on CBS in 1968 and for twelve seasons thereafter, the show broke new ground in television. It kept one incorruptible man its moral center; its producers pioneered the use of twin mainland and island production facilities; and they also foreshadowed both of television's next two philosophical changes—toward "mean streets" details and toward "mysticism"—by introducing both extensive local color and a superhuman element into hero Steve McGarrett's persona. From the first, Jack Lord was the program's star. A veteran of many guest performances on quality series such as *Combat, The Untouchables,* and dozens more, the actor had had a near-miss series in *Stoney Burke* before being tapped for the role that was to make him famous. He was known as a demanding yet technically proficient actor. Lincolnesque features, a firm, quiet voice, and an unemotional style contributed to his ability to make his part believable. His assets contrasted sometimes almost too strongly with the boyish enthusiasm of his co-star, James MacArthur playing Danny "Danno" Williams.

The show's producers made a necessary and commendable effort to exhibit on McGarrett's staff the Islands' mix of races. Nightclub performer Zulu was hired to play Kono Kalakaua and dignified Kam Fong to play Chin Ho Kelly. Later, other officers were played by Al Harrington (Ben Kokua 1972-74); Herman Wedemeyer (Duke 1972-80); Harry Endo (Che Fong 1972-80); Moe Keala (Truck Kealoha 1979-80); William Smith (James "Kima" Carew 1979-80); and Sharon Farrell (Lori Wilson 1979-80).

The long-running series inspired many imitations; we probably owe *Magnum P.I., Big Hawaii, Island Son, Hawaiian Heat, Shogun, Blood and Orchids, The Hawaiians,* and other shows at least partly to *Hawaii Five-0*'s pioneering efforts. Strong stories and picturesque locales make it popular in reruns.

Bibliography

Brooks, Tim, and Earle Marsh. *The Complete Directory to Prime Time Network and Cable TV Shows, 1946-Present.* New York: Ballantine, 1995.

R. D. Michael

Hawking, Stephen (1942-), British theoretical physicist and popular best-selling author, is considered by his fans as the next Einstein. Hawking is famous for his theories on the big bang origin of the universe, black holes, and the worm holes featured so often in *Star Trek* episodes. In fact, in 1993, he made a cameo appearance on the show. Hawking is popular not only for his theories, but for communicating his knowledge to people who aren't scientists. Hawking's book, *A Brief History of Time* (1988), has done a great deal to popularize physics, especially astronomy. It chronicles scientists' attempts to understand the universe, from Galileo and Newton, to Einstein and physicists of today.

While a graduate student at Cambridge, Hawking was diagnosed as having Lou Gehrig's disease, a crippling ailment which causes a disintegration of muscle control but leaves the mind intact. As disease has taken his physical powers from him, Hawking has come to live a life of the mind. He is now confined to a wheelchair, unable to speak. He communicates with a speech synthesizer and a computer which he operates by clicking a mouse-like device.

Fortunately, Hawking chose a career in which his ailment doesn't hinder him much. As a theoretical physicist, Hawking spends his days thinking. Hawking's goal is to find the one grand unified theory that will explain the origins of the universe and everything in it. He believes that this will be accomplished by combining the two greatest intellectual achievements of this century: Einstein's theory of general relativity and quantum mechanics. Hawking is optimistic that this theory will be found within the next two decades.

Bibliography

Asler, Jerry, Gerald Lubenow, and Maggie Malone. "Reading God's Mind." *Newsweek* 13 June 1988: 56-59.

Boslough, John. *Stephen Hawking's Universe.* New York: Morrow, 1985.

Jenkins, Helen R. "On Being Clear about Time: An Analysis of a Chapter of Stephen Hawking's *A Brief History of Time.*" *Language Sciences* 14 (Oct. 1992): 529-44.

Linda Foss

Hawks, Howard (1896-1977). Few filmmakers in the history of Hollywood have worked in as many genres as Howard Hawks—from gangster and detective dramas to screwball comedies and musicals, from Westerns and war dramas to science fiction and epics. He has taken us from the muddy front-line trenches of World War I to the fog-shrouded mountain passes of the Andes, from the dusty savannahs of Africa to the dimly lit backstreets of the City of Angels. And along the way, his movies, spanning a career of nearly 50 years, have become hallmarks of the Hollywood system at its best. In many cases it is difficult to discuss a genre without referring to Hawks. (Try discussing Westerns without *Red River* [1948] or *Rio Bravo* [1958], for example, or try discussing the gangster/detective genre without *Scarface* [1932] or *The Big Sleep* [1946].)

Furthermore, Hawks's movies contain some of the most memorable moments in cinema history, such as Katharine Hepburn destroying Cary Grant's reconstructed dinosaur skeleton in *Bringing Up Baby* (1938), or Cary Grant barking orders over the telephone while Rosalind Russell pounds out a newspaper story in *His Girl Friday* (1940), or Gary Cooper in *Sergeant York* (1941) picking off Germans one-by-one as he gets their attention by gobbling like a turkey, or Lauren Bacall instructing Humphrey Bogart on how to whistle— "You just put your lips together and blow"—in *To Have and Have Not* (1944), or John Wayne, insane with rage, nicking Montgomery Clift with gunshots to force him to draw in *Red River*, or Marilyn Monroe slinking through a seductive "Diamonds Are a Girl's Best Friend" number in *Gentlemen Prefer Blondes* (1953). These scenes, and many others, have become part of the heritage of American cinema.

Hawks's silent movies are generally regarded as unremarkable; however, *The Air Circus* landed on the *New York Times* list of the ten best films of 1928. His first all-talking movie, *The Dawn Patrol* (1930), attracted attention with its naturalistic use of dialogue. Hawks said, "The dialogue before that reminded you of a villain talking on a riverboat." Dialogue would continue to be a hallmark of Hawks's movies throughout his career—whether it be the rapid-fire, overlapping exchanges of *Twentieth Century* (1934) and *His Girl Friday* or the sparseness of *Rio Bravo*.

His movies reveal his presence through the consistent development of plots and characters built around a similar set of concerns. In general, the dramas are about a group of men isolated from the rest of society—whether it be by sheer distance, as in the case of Harry Morgan, the fishing captain in *To Have and Have Not*, or by the danger of their professions, as in the race car drivers of *The Crowd Roars* (1932). These characters fight to survive and to maintain their self-respect against forces that are often stacked against them.

The comedies, on the other hand, subvert the heroes by placing them in situations that they clearly don't control. *Bringing Up Baby*, for example, throws Katharine Hepburn (who rambles nonstop throughout the movie) into the world of a paleontologist played by Cary Grant. She dismantles his world piece by piece, bone by bone, leaving him running through the countryside dressed in a woman's bathrobe. *Ball of Fire* (1941) tosses the streetwise Barbara Stanwyck into an enclave of professors, who quickly become the Seven Dwarfs to her Not-So-Snow White.

In these scenarios, women are usually outsiders that challenge the order of the self-enclosed male societies and make the heroes question their roles. Lauren Bacall makes Humphrey Bogart question his isolation in *To Have and Have Not* and Zita Johann breaks up the stability of the all-male group of fishermen in *Tiger Shark* (1932). Additional conflict results from within the group itself, usually because of a team member who has failed to obey the rules and must now pay a terrible penance. Richard Barthelmess in *Only Angels Have Wings* (1939) is responsible for the death of another pilot. In order to earn readmission to the group, he must now take all of the toughest assignments. Dean Martin in *Rio Bravo* plays a drunken deputy who in order to earn readmission must confront a bar-full of paid gunslingers and somehow survive.

His penchant for revealing traits through the actions of characters allowed Hawks to become a shrewd judge of acting talent. As such he is credited with discovering a wide range of actors, including Montgomery Clift, Ann Dvorak, Paul Muni, Angie Dickinson, Lauren Bacall, Jane Russell, and Carole Lombard. And even actors he didn't discover frequently found themselves delivering the performances of their careers in his films. John Ford, for example, was shocked when he saw John Wayne's performance in *Red River*: "I never knew the big son of a bitch could act" (*Hawks on Hawks* 116).

Hawks's only film noir, *The Big Sleep* (based on the Raymond Chandler novel), takes place in a world where murders are committed and never explained. Its streets are dark and forbidding, filled with hired killers and decaying office buildings forever cloaked in ink-black shadows. At one point during the filming, Hawks cabled Chandler asking for the identity of a murderer. Chandler wired back "I don't know either."

Rio Bravo takes place in a town where the respectable common citizens are largely absent, replaced by hired gunmen and barkeepers. Hawks made *Rio Bravo* as a reaction to *High Noon*. He thought that any self-respecting sheriff wouldn't "go running around town like a chicken with his head off asking for help." Sheriff John T. Chance (John Wayne) actually warns people about being on his side: "Anybody that sides in with me right now is liable to find themselves up to their ears in trouble." *Rio Bravo* takes place in austere settings while a deadly, ominous pallor hangs in the air. The haunting refrains of "The Cutthroat Song"

played by a Mexican band provide Wayne and his cohorts, a drunk (Dean Martin) and an old man (Walter Brennan, the quintessential Hawks' supporting actor), with no relief.

Hawks's comedies replace violence and danger with chaos and humiliation. In *Gentlemen Prefer Blondes*, a wonderfully gaudy extravaganza of mercenary beauties in action, the gold-digging Lorelei (Marilyn Monroe) gets stuck in a porthole during an ocean cruise, and in *Monkey Business* (1952), a wild, frantic funhouse of a movie, Cary Grant and Ginger Rogers revert to children after they drink a youth potion.

Throughout his career, Hawks only received one Oscar nomination as director (for *Sergeant York*). Only in 1975 did the Academy finally recognize his lifetime contribution by presenting him with an honorary award. Hawks's movies play to a rather limited set of concerns (usually revolving around honor, courage, and redemption), but any narrowness of his world is offset by the consistency and clearness of his vision. In his tales of men and women working together in groups, Hawks conveyed both the despair of isolation and the optimism of love and rebirth, and in the process he imprinted upon his movies the signature of an artist.

Bibliography

Mast, Gerald. *Howard Hawks, Storyteller*. New York: Oxford UP, 1982.

McBride, Joseph, ed. *Focus on Howard Hawks*. Englewood Cliffs: Prentice-Hall, 1972.

——. *Hawks on Hawks*. Berkeley: U of California P, 1982.

Wood, Robin. *Howard Hawks*. Garden City: Doubleday, 1968.

Gary Johnson

Hayes, **Isaac** (1942-), more than anyone other than James Brown, revolutionized the possibilities for black popular music in the 1970s. As a Stax Records house songwriter he had earlier helped to define soul music in the second half of the 1960s.

Hayes started out dirt poor, born into a sharccropping family in Covington, TN. When he was a year and a half, his mother passed away. By the age of seven he had relocated to Memphis, where he was brought up by his grandmother. Intoxicated with music, Hayes began playing saxophone in junior high while also singing doo wop with friends. In need of money, Hayes accepted an early 1960s New Year's Eve job as a piano player with Memphis rhythm and blues journeyman Jeb Stuart.

Anxious to record, Hayes had auditioned unsuccessfully twice for Stax, once as a member of the doo wop Ambassadors and later as a pianist with Calvin Valentine and the Swing Kings. In late 1963, he finally got his foot in the door as a member of baritone saxophonist Floyd Newman's ensemble. Newman was a regular part of the Stax house band and had been given the chance to cut his own single. Hayes co-wrote the A-side, "Frog Stomp," and, in the process, made an impression on Stax owner Jim Stewart. Regular Stax keyboardist Booker T. Jones was in college, and Stewart began calling Hayes for sessions whenever Jones was unavailable. By the time he was 23, Hayes had played on such classic recordings as Otis Redding's "Respect" and Wilson Pickett's "In the Midnight Hour."

As Hayes played on an ever-increasing number of Stax sessions, he began contributing as a writer and arranger. He eventually formed an incredibly successful songwriting partnership with former doo wop rival David Porter. The Hayes-Porter team went on to write and produce every Sam and Dave hit including "Soul Man," "When Something Is Wrong with My Baby," "Hold On, I'm Comin'," "I Thank You," and "Wrap It Up." They also wrote and produced hits for Mable John, Carla Thomas, Johnny Taylor, the Soul Children, and the Emotions.

In 1968, he recorded his first solo album, *Presenting Isaac Hayes*. A piano-bass-drums trio effort, Hayes tentatively experimented with extended, improvisatory structures that synthesized elements of jazz, rhythm and blues, and easy listening. The album was released with little fanfare and received little notice.

In 1969, Hayes was granted a second solo shot as Stax mounted a massive 27-album release with the intention of developing an "instant" black catalogue to replace the one they had lost when they separated from Atlantic. Hayes was given total freedom and elected to record away from Stax and without Booker T. and the MG's, opting to use the Bar-Kays rhythm section and Marvell Thomas and recording at Memphis's Ardent studio instead. He also elected to forgo his own compositions, covering songs by the likes of Burt Bacharach and Jim Webb. The resulting album, *Hot Buttered Soul*, was released nearly as an afterthought among new products by virtually every Stax star. To everyone's surprise, it became the biggest-selling album Stax had released up to that point, and Hayes quickly became one of the biggest stars in popular music.

Hot Buttered Soul combined jazz, classical, rhythm and blues, rock, pop, and easy listening elements. The net result was an album that could fit most radio formats of the time. Hayes enjoyed nearly unprecedented crossover success, hitting the top rungs of *Billboard*'s rhythm and blues, pop, classical, and easy listening charts. *Hot Buttered Soul* proved that black artists could record album length projects and that the black populace was eager to buy them. As odd as this may seem, in 1969 this was a revelation to the music industry. Hayes's breakthrough paved the way for similarly ambitious album-length projects by Marvin Gaye, Stevie Wonder, Curtis Mayfield, and Parliament/Funkadelic.

Several equally impressive albums followed on the Stax subsidiary Enterprise, and later on ABC and Polydor Records. The most important was the 1971 soundtrack for the film *Shaft,* which garnered Hayes an Oscar for the title track. Hayes's immense popularity with the black audience led to his being dubbed the "Black Moses." He became and remains an important symbol of black achievement and possibility.

In the 1980s, Hayes spent most of his time developing an acting career, appearing infrequently on stage. In 1989, the Smithsonian Institution spent two days honoring the compositions of Isaac Hayes and David Porter. Hayes's most recent albums are *Branded* (1995) and *Raw and Refined*

(1996); he also is the voice of Chef in the animated television comedy show *South Park* (1997-).

Bibliography
Bowman, Rob. Monograph included in *The Complete Stax/Volt Singles 1959-1968*. Berkeley: Atlantic Records, 1991.
——. Monograph included in *The Complete Stax/Volt Soul Singles Vol. 2: 1968-1971*. Berkeley: Atlantic Records, 1993.
Guralnick, Peter. *Sweet Soul Music*. New York: Harper & Row, 1986.
Hirshey, Gerri. *Nowhere to Run*. New York: Times, 1984.

Rob Bowman

Healing and the Mind, with Bill Moyers (1993), a five-part Public Broadcasting Service series (with a companion book that has been on the best-seller list), asks the question: "Do our emotional lives affect our physical state of health?" Moyers's quest for the answer takes him from China to the United States; from large university hospitals to small clinics; from Taoism and Buddhism to basic Christian principles. His expositions range from T'ai Chi to biofeedback, meditation to drug therapies, revealing the benefits and usefulness of each, through direct address, interviews and observations. Moyers's nonthreatening demeanor and obvious skepticism make him an appropriate host for explaining the mind-body connection to a Western "prove-it-to-me" society. His prior accomplishments as a widely acclaimed and respected television journalist and editor with CBS News and PBS lend enormous credibility to this work.

Bibliography
"Bill Moyers: Dialogue on Film." *American Film* June 1990.
"Mind over Malady." *Time* 1 March 1994.
"Mind over Medicine." *People Weekly* 15 March 1993: 63-64.
Moyers, Bill. *Healing and the Mind*. New York: Doubleday, 1993.
Zurawik, David. "American Originals—Bill Moyers." *Esquire* Oct. 1989: 138-48.

Therese Schramm

Health Food tends to turn conventional food prestige scales upside down, with the most humble grains and vegetables taking top place and meat tumbling to bottom. The versatile peanut is a prime example. It has been the basis for a number of health foods, among them vegetarian steaks and chops and a milk substitute. And, for over 100 years, the health food movement has had a love affair with the most popular peanut product, peanut butter.

It was first cranked out by a St. Louis doctor in 1880, for a patient who could eat no meat. Its high protein content recommended it to other vegetarians and it achieved higher production by the end of the century. Dr. John Kellogg (brother of William K. Kellogg of cereal fame), director of the Battle Creek Sanitarium, and a member of the vegetarian Seventh Day Adventists, began making it in his institution around 1903. In 1912, a Virginia company was founded exclusively to make peanut butter. Its two brands, Golden Tint and Old Reliable, were shipped throughout the country.

In 1914, Macy's sold peanut butter along with yogurt, whole wheat, and other health food items. Until about 1940, peanut butter, like clam broth, beef tea, and grape juice, was sold primarily in drug stores.

In the late 1960s, the peanut butter sold in supermarkets came under attack by a resurgent, counterculture health food movement which reviled it (along with a host of food products made by major manufacturers) for its added salt, sugar, and preservatives. Pure peanut butter made of nothing but ground peanuts soon became an icon of the new organic food movement and a staple of the nonprofit food cooperatives which sprang up in metropolitan areas and college towns. Many of these grew into major health food chains which survive today, increasingly offering a wide range of gourmet foods alongside the traditional brown rice, granola, and tofu.

Interest in health foods in America can be traced back to the 1830s as a spinoff of temperance campaigns. Former preacher Sylvester Graham (1794-1851) kicked things off with lecture tours in which he stressed the value of whole grain breads. The graham cracker was named for him, though he would hardly approve of the addition of white flour in most brands today. Seventh Day Adventists took up his message and opened health resorts, restaurants, and food stores around the world early in the 20th century.

California proved a fertile ground for sowing the health food message. In the 1920s and 1930s a number of stores and restaurants specializing in natural foods flourished there. Ella Brodersen's Health Way Cafeteria operated in the 1930s in San Francisco. A Seventh Day Adventist who had lived in the South Pacific, Brodersen served roasts made of vegetables and melba toast, juices of dandelion or turnip, and tropical breadfruit accompanied by honey and melted butter. The 1930s saw a growth in the public's attention to health foods, led perhaps by Hollywood stars' attraction to Gayelord Hauser, who advocated eating five "wonder foods" (blackstrap molasses, brewers' yeast, powdered skim milk, yogurt, and wheat germ) to stay youthful. Not too surprisingly, California once again became the launching ground for the revived health food movement of the late 1960s, which was closely tied to critiques of American capitalism and imperialism.

Bibliography

Belasco, Warren J. *Appetite for Change: How the Counterculture Took on the Food Industry, 1966–1988.* New York: Pantheon, 1989.

Carson, Gerald. *Cornflake Crusade.* New York: Rinehart, 1957.

Ensminger, A. H., M. E. Ensminger, J. E. Konlande, and J. R. K. Robson. *Foods and Nutrition Encyclopedia. Vols. 1 and 2.* Clovis: Pegus, 1983.

Jan Whitaker

Hearst, William Randolph (1863-1951), American editor, publisher, and politician, created a media empire with its roots in sensationalism but gained reforms by exposing social injustice and corruption. The most excessive of his brand of news became known as "yellow journalism" (see entry), which reached its apex in the circulation battle with Joseph Pulitzer's *New York World* in covering the Spanish-American War. Hearst's *New York Journal* alone averaged 1.5 million in circulation a day.

Hearst's sex and scandal themes remain as powerful news values today. Supermarket tabloids and many magazines, TV programs, and mainstream press mirror Hearst's "gee whiz" slogan. Millions of people daily read the Hearst Corporation's newspapers, magazines and books. Millions more watch its TV stations and cable networks—A&E and Lifetime—or listen to its radio stations. Its magazines include *Good Housekeeping, Cosmopolitan, Esquire, Redbook, Harper's Bazaar,* and *Popular Mechanics.* Begun in 1901, the Good Housekeeping Institute enjoys an international reputation serving consumers, still using its famous seal of approval.

Hearst's King Features comics—some dating to the 1930s—are household words. Early strips included *Blondie, Ripley's Believe It or Not!, Krazy Kat, Betty Boop, Popeye,* and *Flash Gordon.* Added were *Hagar, Hi and Lois, Beetle Bailey, Family Circus, Spiderman, Dennis the Menace,* and others.

TV newscasts are descendants of the movie newsreels Hearst pioneered. Metrotone News shown in movie theaters thrilled viewers worldwide. His first newsreel was of Woodrow Wilson's inauguration in 1913. Hearst began movie production in 1914 with the 21-week serial *The Perils of Pauline.* Others included *Broadway Melody, Captain Blood,* with Errol Flynn, and *Peg o' My Heart,* starring showgirl Marion Davies, who was to become Hearst's life-long companion.

The man and his papers themselves made interesting topics. The 1902 play *The Front Page* was a hit comedy by Charles MacArthur and Ben Hecht about their days on Hearst's Chicago newspapers. Four movie versions followed; critics recommend the first, vintage 1931. Orson Welles's 1941 movie *Citizen Kane* (see entry), loosely patterned after Hearst's life, is considered among the best films ever.

Born in San Francisco, the only child of wealthy miner and senator George Hearst, William was expelled from Harvard for a prank. He then worked for the *New York World* as a reporter. The *World* blended crusading with sensationalism, fighting injustice while printing crime and scandal. At 23, he revived his father's *San Francisco Examiner,* improving upon the *World*'s style of enterprise, sensationalism, and idealism. High salaries helped recruit the best journalists and authors, such as Richard Harding Davis, Frederic Remington, Ambrose Bierce, Mark Twain, Jack London, and Stephen Crane.

Hearst served as U.S. Congressman for New York and was defeated in a bid for the presidency. He swung the presidential nomination for Franklin Roosevelt in 1932. He was one of the world's richest men, worth $220 million in 1935. He built castles and filled them with art treasures. His $30 million San Simeon complex was given to the state of California in 1958. A technological innovator and expert writer, Hearst edited almost until his death. He died at age 88 in Beverly Hills, CA.

Bibliography
O'Donnell, James F. *100 Years of Making Communications History*. New York: Hearst Professional Magazine, 1987.
O'Loughlin, Edward T. *Hearst and His Enemies*. 1919. New York: Arno, 1970.
Swanberg, W. A. *Citizen Hearst*. New York: Collier, 1961, 1984.

John L. Griffith

Heavy Metal is a term used to describe rock music that is characteristically loud, has instrumentation centered around the electric guitar, and incorporates lyrics that deal with death, violence, and the occult. It is a music genre that is distinctly male: almost all of the performers and over 90 percent of its audience are men.

The use of the words *heavy metal* is attributed to a line in the 1968 Steppenwolf song, "Born to Be Wild," a hit single that was also featured as background for a cross-country motorcycle sequence in the film *Easy Rider*. Steppenwolf was one of many late 1960s "power trios" that used lead guitar, bass, and drums, all greatly amplified. Other early heavy metal groups in the United States included Vanilla Fudge, which added an organ in its plodding remakes of soul hits; Mountain, best known for its powerful hit single, "Mississippi Queen"; and Grand Funk Railroad, with a toned-down version of metal in its 1973 hit single, "We're an American Band."

In Great Britain, the musical characteristics of early heavy metal were combined with an interest in the occult by Led Zeppelin and Black Sabbath in the early 1970s. The only U.S. equivalent during that period was Alice Cooper. But Cooper was more sarcastic, and his stage antics included chopping up baby dolls to the music of songs like "Love It to Death." Cooper had major Top 40 successes with "I'm 18" and "School's Out" in 1972 among post-psychedelic-era adolescents.

Other groups became more serious about death and Satanism in the late 1970s, and parents and civic leaders voiced concern about the effects of heavy metal music. They often pointed to Blue Oyster Cult's 1976 hit, "Don't Fear the Reaper," which appeared to advocate suicide for unrequited teenage lovers. The Australian group AC/DC was cited as the favorite rock group by serial killer Richard Ramirez, and the music of Black Sabbath's former lead singer, Ozzy Osbourne, was implicated in teen suicides.

Groups like Van Halen, Kiss, and Great Britain's Def Leppard converted the music of heavy metal into commercial success with elaborate costumes and stage shows featuring smoke bombs and spectacular lighting.

The success of the these groups was further buoyed by the advent of the MTV music television network in 1981. Groups like Twisted Sister, Motley Crue, Ratt, and Quiet Riot became a mainstay of the network's early menu of music videos. But the videos drew criticism for being violent, sexist, or satanic, and MTV and copycat video networks and programs responded to pressure by cutting back on the number of heavy metal videos.

Deprived of airplay from MTV and the commercial radio stations who looked to MTV as an example, heavy metal went underground. Audiences began listening to heavy metal in small clubs, at first on Los Angeles's Sunset Boulevard and later in cities across the U.S. Some groups continued to play large stages and garnered radio airplay. These included Poison, Guns 'n' Roses, and some of the early MTV bands. They even recorded ballads like Poison's "Every Rose Had Its Thorn" and Extreme's "More Than Words." Meanwhile, underground heavy metal split into a number of subgenres.

"Speed metal" features extremely fast and aggressive guitar playing, best exemplified by the group Metallica, one of the few underground metal bands to gain a national following. In the early 1990s the group gained Grammy Award recognition.

"Thrash metal" is influenced by the 1980s punk music bands. Its lyrics are often related to social issues such as racism. The band Anthrax is a good example of thrash metal, and they made music history by touring and recorded with rapper Ice-T.

"Industrial metal" is a small subgenre that combines the machine-like sounds of industrial music with the gruesome lyrical themes of heavy metal. Ministry is a good example of a group in the industrial metal category.

"Death metal" has generated a great deal of criticism from conservative political, religious, and civic leaders. This subgenre features songs that deal in graphic terms with death, often using imagery of corpses and mutilation. The premier death metal band of the 1980s and 1990s is Slayer, and their repertoire includes songs about Nazi doctor Josef Mengele and serial killer Ed Gein. The most extreme of these groups, "black metal" bands like Morbid Angel, use extremely deep and distorted vocals and instrumentals. Death metal stage performances and album covers are often filled with gruesome or sacrilegious symbols and photographs.

The most extreme form of heavy metal music is known as "grindcore" for its grinding sound and for the influence from the "hard core" offshoot of punk music. Grindcore bands attempt to be the most extreme of metal bands—the loudest, the fastest, the most gruesome. Like the hardcore groups, they often record a large number of very short songs on their albums, some as short as 20 seconds.

The "progressive metal" movement began in the 1990s with the group Dream Theater. Proponents of this type of metal music consider themselves more "serious" musicians, combining elements of the progressive rock or "art rock" movement of the early 1970s with the power of 1980s heavy metal.

Heavy metal gained respect at the end of the 1980s as it began to appeal to college audiences. In 1989, the first Grammy Award for heavy metal was awarded, although it went to a group many metal purists did not consider to be heavy metal—Jethro Tull. Groups such as Alice in Chains, Tool, and Helmet became accepted as part of the 1990s alternative music scene.

Bibliography
Hale, Mark. *Head Bangers: The Worldwide Megabook of Heavy Metal Bands*. Ann Arbor: Popular Culture, 1993.

Walser, Robert. *Running with the Devil: Power, Gender, and Madness in Heavy Metal Music.* Hanover: UP of New England, 1993.

Weinstein, Deena. *Heavy Metal: A Cultural Sociology.* New York: Lexington, 1991.

Kenneth M. Nagelberg

Heinlein, Robert A. (1907-1988), called the dean of American science fiction authors and compared by some to Mark Twain, has probably affected more readers than any other American author in the genre. Heinlein's concerns include characters coming of age and the need for intelligent, quirky, and often cantankerous people to propel the human race forward.

Heinlein's first story, "Life-Line," appeared in the August 1939 issue of John W. Campbell's *Astounding Science Fiction.* By 1941, Heinlein supplied Campbell's magazine with more stories than any other author. After World War II, Heinlein worked to expand the reach of science fiction. He published stories in the *Saturday Evening Post* and other magazines previously closed to the genre. He created a series of juvenile novels noteworthy for not talking down to their readers. *Have Spacesuit—Will Travel* (1958) is considered the best of these. Heinlein's influence extended to film and television. Using his juvenile novel *Rocket Ship Galileo* (1947) as a basis, Heinlein wrote the screenplay for George Pal's film *Destination Moon* (1950). Another of Heinlein's juvenile novels, *Space Cadet* (1948), provided the inspiration for the early television series *Tom Corbett, Space Cadet* (1951-54). Heinlein's *Starship Trooper* (1959) won a Hugo Award, but critics wrongly claimed that the novel—which celebrates coming of age in the military—revealed the author to be a fascist.

In fact, Heinlein's political philosophy is libertarian, as evidenced by *The Moon Is a Harsh Mistress* (1966), a novel championed by libertarians. Heinlein's *Stranger in a Strange Land* (1961), the first science fiction novel to appear on the *New York Times* best-seller list, explored a lifestyle of free love and emotional sharing, which led characters to truly understand one another. *Stranger* became a favorite of members of the 1960s and 1970s counterculture. Unfortunately, the San Francisco *Chronicle* reported that the murderer Charles Manson had been inspired by *Stranger*. In fact, at the time of the murders Manson had neither read the novel nor heard of Heinlein, but this false accusation continues to appear in publications about the author.

In later novels such as *The Number of the Beast* (1980), Heinlein explored various time-travel paradoxes which allowed one large family to interbreed again and again without adverse effects upon the progeny. The later novels also draw together a number of characters from the author's earlier books. Born in Butler, MO, Heinlein graduated from the U.S. Naval Academy at Annapolis in 1929. His naval career was cut short in 1934 when he developed tuberculosis. After attempting several other pursuits, Heinlein turned to writing in 1939. During World War II he served as a civilian research engineer for the navy, but in 1947 he returned to writing science fiction.

Bibliography

Clute, John, and Peter Nicholls. *The Encyclopedia of Science Fiction.* New York: St. Martin's, 1993.

Heinlein, Robert. *Expanded Universe.* New York: Ace, 1980.

James, Edward. *Science Fiction in the 20th Century.* Oxford: Oxford UP, 1994.

Stover, Leon. *Robert A. Heinlein.* Boston: Hall, 1987.

Brent Chesley

He-Man and the Masters of the Universe (1983-1985), a half-hour animated series, first appeared on television in the fall of 1983, airing on 166 television stations across the country in the weekday "after school" time slot. He-Man himself was of course already familiar to preschool and elementary school children as an "action figure" toy introduced by Mattel in 1982. The show quickly became the exemplar of toy-based programming; by 1984, the He-Man doll was the second best-selling toy in America and by the mid-1980s, its producer, Filmation Associates, had reached over $1 billion in annual licensed product sales—split almost equally between the various toys produced by and copyrighted to Mattel and other novelty products.

Mattel and Filmation Associates had certainly "plugged in" to some aspect of the American imagination, since within the first year of the series premiere, *He-Man* gained an audience of 9 million viewers predominantly boys aged four to seven. By the mid-1980s, *He-Man* was maintaining sixth place in the ratings of the Top 10 children's commercial programs and reaching a documented 81 percent of American homes. Interestingly, an estimated one-third of the *He-Man* audience was girls aged four to ten, and when He-Man's "twin sister" *She-Ra, Princess of Power* (see entry) emerged in her own series in late 1985, she quickly surpassed *He-Man* in the ratings, ranking in fourth place and reaching 84 percent of American households.

She-Ra aside, it is He-Man who has become the quintessential "Superman in other worlds." Starting out each episode as a meek and mannered young boy named Adam, when he raises his sword and utters the magic incantation "By the power of Greyskull, I have the power!" Adam turns into the heroic He-Man, described best as an animated "Prince Valiant with Arnold Schwarzenegger's physique." Often mounted on his battle-armored horse Stridor, He-Man then proceeds to vanquish the nefarious schemes of his archenemy Skeletor, resident of Snake Mountain ("the Realm of Evil"), or the destructive plans of the equally detestable opponents Clawful, Tri-Klops, and Evil-Lyn.

Even so, the valorous *He-Man* has been identified as one of the most offensive toy-based "program-length commercials" by Peggy Charen's industry watchdog organization Action for Children's Television (see Children's Network Programming). Critics of *He-Man* (as well as well as *She-Ra*) have argued that the violent actions and themes of the show in combination with the production and use of toys that replicate characters children have seen portrayed in violent ways and settings compound the sanctioning of violence and consequently increase aggression in play. Filmation Associates and Mattel have attempted to maintain a clear social conscience in this regard through the employment of educational and psychological consultants in program development.

Bibliography

Erickson, Hal. *Television Cartoon Shows: An Illustrated Encyclopedia, 1949 through 1993.* Jefferson: McFarland, 1995.

Pam Steinle

Henderson, Fletcher (1898-1952), is generally considered one of the most important transitional figures in the development of big band jazz. The bands he directed from 1923 through the middle 1930s displayed a marked transition from early jazz to the swing style.

Henderson was born in Cuthbert, GA, into a middle-class black American family. He graduated from Atlanta University in 1920 and then began graduate study at Columbia University in New York. Harry Pace, owner of Black Swan records, hired Henderson to be musical director and accompany most of the performers as a solo pianist or leader of a small ensemble.

By 1923, Henderson had collected a nucleus of musicians including saxophone-clarinetists Coleman Hawkins and Don Redman. Henderson also hired Redman as the chief arranger for the new band. The group played at the Club Alabam for one year and then moved to the Roseland Ballroom where it was an almost permanent fixture for five years. Henderson was able to recruit some of the top black musicians for his band. In addition to Redman and Hawkins, there were trumpeters Rex Stewart and Joe Smith, clarinetist Buster Bailey and alto saxophonist Benny Carter. In October 1924, Louis Armstrong joined the band for a one-year stay and caused quite a sensation as the most exciting jazz soloist of that period. Musicians both black and white flocked to the Roseland to hear him. Because there was continuous music, the Henderson band would alternate with white bands, but to the chagrin of some of the white bandleaders the dancers seemed to favor Henderson's ensemble.

In 1934, it looked as if the Henderson band was going to be hired by the Cotton Club, but at the last moment Jimmy Lunceford's band was hired. There were other disappointments in this period, but one fortunate thing was that John Hammond, the jazz critic and recording supervisor, took an interest in Henderson, as he had done with other black performers such as Bessie Smith and Count Basie. He secured Henderson some engagements, record dates, and, most importantly, persuaded Benny Goodman to commission arrangements from Henderson for a new band he was forming. Many of Goodman's early hits were scored by Henderson, including "King Porter Stomp," "Down South Camp Meeting," "Sometimes I'm Happy," and "Blue Skies." "Christopher Columbus," which was incorporated into "Sing Sing Sing," was a huge success for Goodman even though Henderson recorded it before any other band.

In addition to his arranging contributions, Henderson must be remembered for hiring many outstanding jazz musicians, including trumpet players Louis Armstrong, Rex Stewart, Roy Eldridge, Cootie Williams, Joe Smith, Henry "Red" Allen, and Emmett Berry; saxophone/clarinetists Coleman Hawkins, Chu Berry, Benny Carter, Ben Webster, Russell Procope, Buster Bailey, and Don Redman; trombonists Jimmy Harrison, Dicky Wells, J. C. Higginbotham, and Benny Morton; bassists John Kirby and Israel Crosby; and drummers Sid Catlett and Kaiser Marshall.

Bibliography

Allen, Walter C. *Hendersonia: The Music of Fletcher Henderson and His Musicians.* Highland Park, NJ: n.p., 1973.
Dews, Margery P. *Remembering: The Remarkable Henderson Family.* Chicago: Adams, 1973.
Megill, Donald D., and Richard S. Demory. *Introduction to Jazz History.* Englewood Cliffs: Prentice-Hall, 1993.

Frank Ferriano

Hendrix, Jimi (1942-1970), has been considered by many as the most electric of American rock music's many electric guitarists. His legendary status comes, however, as a result of recording only four studio albums before his death from an overdose of barbiturates.

Hendrix was born Johnny Allen Hendrix in Seattle, WA, the son of an African-American father and a part-Cherokee mother. At the age of four, his father renamed him James Marshall Hendrix, which put a curse on him, according to Native American beliefs that naming a person twice divides their spirit in two.

His father tried to develop young Jimmy into a performer, hoping the boy would become a professional dancer. But Jimmy was more interested in playing the guitar, and he got his first one at age 12. Hendrix played the instrument left-handed, turning the guitar upside down.

Hendrix enlisted as a paratrooper in the U.S. Army in 1959. He was shunned by most of his comrades because of his strange habits, like sleeping with and talking to his guitar. Jimmy was also known for experimenting with the guitar's amplifier and vibrato bar as he tried to imitate the high-pitched drone of airplane engines.

He was discharged with back injuries in 1961, and began playing guitar for a number of performers under the pseudonym Jimmy James. He teamed up with his army buddy, bass player Billy Cox, and went to Nashville to play local clubs. He also toured for a while in 1963 with Little Richard's band.

In 1965, Hendrix formed his own band, Jimmy James and the Blue Flames. He spent some time in the recording studio, releasing a minor local hit in Los Angeles, "My Diary." While his recordings were similar to other 1960s soul groups, his onstage performances were more dramatic. The same year, Hendrix moved to New York City, where he was influenced by the bohemian lifestyle of Greenwich Village.

Hendrix's talents were becoming well known in New York City, especially among visiting British rock musicians. Chas Chandler of the Animals encouraged Hendrix to go to London, where, in September 1966, they recruited drummer Mitch (John) Mitchell and bass player Noel (David) Redding to form the Jimi Hendrix Experience.

The band released its first single, "Hey Joe," an updated version of a folk song, in December on the British Polydor label. The song was a Top 10 hit, and reports of Hendrix's onstage histrionics added to his appeal. In March 1967, the single "Purple Haze" (a reference to a type of LSD) was released in England and climbed to No. 3 on the charts there. The Jimi Hendrix Experience went on tour in April, with Hendrix playing the guitar with his teeth and setting it on fire at the end of his set.

The group's first album, *Are You Experienced?* was released in England in May 1967. It eventually climbed to No. 2 on the British charts. The group was invited to play at the Monterey Pop Festival in June at the urging of Paul McCartney.

Meanwhile, Warner Brothers signed the group to its Reprise label, and *Are You Experienced?* climbed to No. 5 on the U.S. charts in the fall of 1967. The group's second album, *Axis: Bold as Love,* was released in December, and "Foxy Lady" was a minor success as a single in January 1968.

The Jimi Hendrix Experience began experiencing internal problems, and Hendrix ended up in a Swedish jail after a fight with Redding. As *Axis* climbed to No. 3 on the U.S. charts, audiences were unhappy with Hendrix's restraint on stage. He was focusing more on his music and less on theatrics.

Smash Hits, a re-release of the Jimi Hendrix Experience's first four singles and four songs from *Are You Experienced,* reached No. 6 on the charts in April 1968. Hendrix spent most of the second half of 1968 in a recording studio. In September, Hendrix had his first successful single in the U.S. with his remake of Bob Dylan's "All along the Watchtower." The double-LP *Electric Ladyland* was released amid controversy in October 1968 because Hendrix appeared with nude women on the album sleeve.

In May of 1969, Hendrix was arrested in Toronto and charged with possession of heroin. He was eventually acquitted, but the arrest raised suspicions about whether Jimi was addicted to hard drugs. The Jimi Hendrix Experience played its final concert in San Diego in May, and Hendrix was never able to keep a band together for any significant period of time after that.

Hendrix joined up with former army friend Billy Cox and drummer/vocalist Buddy Miles for recording sessions in the summer of 1969. Experience drummer Mitch Mitchell rejoined Hendrix and a loose collection of musicians called the Electric Sky Church at the Woodstock Festival in August. Hendrix's wailing, howling performance of "The Star Spangled Banner" was a highlight of the festival and the film *Woodstock.*

Hendrix, Miles, and Cox reunited as the Band of Gypsys in January 1970, playing the Fillmore East in New York. The concert was recorded and released as the album *Band of Gypsys* on Capitol Records to compensate a former manager. The group split after Hendrix walked off stage during their second concert. Hendrix flew to Hawaii for filming of the motion picture, *Rainbow Bridge.* He recalled Mitchell to replace Buddy Miles, and Hendrix, Mitchell, and Cox performed as the new Jimi Hendrix Experience.

In 1969 and 1970, Hendrix devoted much of his time to construction of a state-of-the-art recording studio, Electric Lady, in New York City. Hendrix began recording in the Electric Lady studio in July 1970. He also performed sporadically in August and September, but many of his performances were poorly received. On September 18, he was found dead of an overdose of barbiturates. Most accounts considered the overdose accidental.

Hendrix's last planned album, *The Cry of Love,* was released in March 1971. It was to be part of a concept album, *The First Rays of the Rising Sun,* and it peaked on the U.S. charts at No. 3. A flood of recordings of unreleased Hendrix sessions included the LP *Rainbow Bridge* and the single "Dolly Dagger." Producer Alan Douglas was given control of over 500 hours of studio tapes, from which he edited three albums, *Crash Landing* and *Midnight Lightning* (both in 1975) and *Nine to the Universe* (1980).

Bibliography

Dannemann, Monika. *The Inner World of Jimi Hendrix.* New York: St. Martin's, 1995.

Hendrix, Jimi. *Cherokee Mist: The Lost Writings.* New York: HarperCollins, 1993.

Mitchell, Mitch. *Jimi Hendrix: Inside the Experience.* New York: St. Martin's, 1994.

Ken Nagelberg

See also
Acid Rock

Henning, Paul (1911-), was a television producer whose rural sitcoms, along with those of Danny Thomas Productions, dominated Nielsen ratings in the 1960s. Henning's biggest hit, *The Beverly Hillbillies*, was a Top 5 show from its 1962 debut until its 1970 cancellation. Although popular viewership continued to support Henning's shows, in 1970 CBS replaced all of its rural sitcoms with more contemporary and relevant programs.

Henning was born in Independence, MO. Although he was trained as a lawyer, his ambition since childhood was to become a singer. Working his way through law school, Henning took a job at a local radio station, doing everything from on-air singing to sweeping the studio. By the time Henning received his law degree, he had sold a script to *The Fibber McGee and Molly Show* (see entry). When Henning was invited to become a staff writer for the show, he moved to Chicago where its production was based.

In 1940, Henning moved to Los Angeles, where he eventually worked as a writer for the *George Burns and Gracie Allen Show.* When *Burns and Allen* transferred to television in 1950, Henning followed. It was during this period that Henning met Al Simon, the pioneering producer who had devised the multiple film camera system for Ralph Edwards's quiz show *Truth or Consequences* (1950). Simon would later produce many of Henning's sitcoms.

Henning's first production was *The Bob Cummings Show* (1961), which was later syndicated as *Love That Bob.* Although Henning enjoyed the experience of writing for urban-based characters, he desired to create a show based on the Southern characters he had developed a fondness for during his youth. This led Henning to *The Beverly Hillbillies* (see entry), which, upon its 1962 debut, became one of television's few runaway hits, staying in the Nielsen Top 20 throughout its nine-season run. The show's success earned Henning approval from CBS to produce and debut any program he chose, sight-unseen by the network.

Confirming the network's faith in his ability, Henning produced two more hits for the network—*Petticoat Junction* (1963-70) and *Green Acres* (1965-71). While *Petticoat Junction* was quite reserved in its characters and content, *Green Acres* was a surrealistic romp which featured funny, believable characters placed in unbelievable circumstances (see entry). There was a close connection among all Henning's shows, and recurring characters from *The Beverly Hillbillies*, *Petticoat Junction* and *Green Acres* would occasionally appear on each other's programs.

Henning's characters remain popular today. Both *Green Acres* and *The Beverly Hillbillies* were the subjects of 1980 TV movie reunions, and *Green Acres* became one of the sitcoms included in the Nick-at-Nite classic sitcom cable network's lineup. All three of Henning's rural sitcoms continue to do well in syndication.

Bibliography
Brooks, Tim, and Earle Marsh. *The Complete Directory to Prime Time Network TV Shows, 1946-Present*. New York: Ballantine, 1992.
Brown, Les. *Les Brown's Encyclopedia of Television*. Detroit: Visible Ink, 1992.
Marc, David, and Robert J. Thompson. *Prime Time; Prime Movers*. Boston: Little, Brown, 1992.

Michael B. Kassel

Hennock, Frieda Barkin (1904-1960), was sworn in as a Federal Communications Commissioner on July 6, 1948, becoming not only the first woman to serve on the FCC, but also the catalyst precipitating a series of policy decisions that created a foundation for the system of public broadcasting that exists in the United States today.

Frieda B. Hennock was born in Kovel, Poland, the youngest of eight children. In 1910, the family moved to the United States, settling in New York. Hennock received her L.L.B. degree from Brooklyn Law School in 1924, and at age 21 was admitted to the New York bar. At first she handled criminal and corporate law cases. Later she and a colleague established the law firm of Silver and Hennock. When that partnership dissolved, she worked independently for several years before joining Choate, Mitchell and Ely.

Politically, Hennock was active in the Democratic party in New York, working in election campaigns and raising funds for several candidates. When a vacancy occurred at the FCC in 1948, Hennock's name was suggested to President Harry S. Truman. Truman nominated her and the Senate confirmed the appointment.

During her tenure as an FCC commissioner, Frieda Barkin Hennock was an outspoken critic of violence in television programming and growing monopolies in the broadcast industry. She was equally outspoken about the potential for television to serve the educational needs of the public and dedicated her efforts to shaping the policies that made public television possible.

Bibliography
"Frieda Hennock." *Current Biography: Who's News and Why, 1948*. New York: Wilson, 1949.
Frieda Hennock personal papers. The Schlesinger Library, Radcliffe College, Cambridge, MA.
Morgenthau, Henry. "Dona Quixote: The Adventures of Frieda Hennock." *Television Quarterly* 26.2 (1992): 61-73.
Powell, John Walker. *Channels of Learning: The Story of Educational Television*. Washington, DC: Public Affairs Press, 1962.
Robertson, Jim. *TeleVisionaries*. Charlotte Harbor: Tabby House, 1993.

Lucy A. Liggett

See also
Children's Public Television

Hepburn, Audrey (1929-1993), born Edda van Heemstra Hepburn-Ruston, in Brussels, Belgium, reflected that magical mixture of captivating charm, waif-like innocence, and regal beauty more completely than did any other female film star of the 1950s and 1960s. Raised amid the ashes of World War II, having spent her childhood in Nazi-occupied Holland, Hepburn was a real-life Cinderella who would like to fulfill many of her childhood dreams through the illusions manufactured by the Hollywood Dream Factory. While stars such as Rita Hayworth and Grace Kelly would actually marry into royalty, throughout her 40-year career, Hepburn would project the aura of a beloved real-life princess.

In many of the 20 films she starred in, from *Roman Holiday* (1953) through *My Fair Lady* (1964), Hepburn played various versions of this Cinderella-Princess figure, a young woman magically transformed by love or some other equally powerful force. In *Roman Holiday*, the princess attempts to find romance free of her royal status. In *My Fair Lady*, Hepburn's Cockney flower-girl is transformed into a pseudo-princess by Rex Harrison's Pygmalion-like Professor Higgins. In Billy Wilder's *Sabrina* (1954), Hepburn is a chauffeur's daughter who is pursued by Humphrey Bogart and William Holden as two socialite brothers and modern Prince Charmings. In the 1956 film version of Tolstoy's *War and Peace*, the aristocratic Hepburn seeks love during the chaos of the Napoleonic Wars. And in Billy Wilder's *Love in the Afternoon* (1957), she is a vulnerable yet confident non-princess romantically involved with Gary Cooper as an aging Prince Charming. In *Funny Face* (also in 1957), seven years prior to *My Fair Lady*, it is Fred Astaire playing Pygmalion as photographer who orchestrates Hepburn's metamorphosis from timid salesgirl into one of the fashion world's most famous models. According to Stanley Donen, the film's director, Hepburn's character changes from a "caterpillar to a butterfly."

In her two 1959 films, *Green Mansions* and *The Nun's Story*, there is nothing of the princess or the waif, but much emphasis on one of Hepburn's other cinematic traits—ethereality. In the former film, she is an enchanting, bird-like jungle sprite in the Amazon basin; in the latter, she is a young woman undergoing a series of serious spiritual transformations. In the early 1960s, Hepburn appeared in two very different kinds of film unlike any she had yet done: *The Unforgiven* (a 1960 Western focusing on Comanche raids on the Texas frontier) and *The Children's Hour* (a 1962 censored version of Lillian Hellman's disturbing drama of lesbianism and the relationship between innocence and evil). During this same decade, Hepburn starred in four of her finest films: *Breakfast at Tiffany's* (1961), *Charade* (1963), *My Fair Lady* (1964), and *Wait Until Dark* (1967). While her Holly Golightly character in Blake Edwards's *Breakfast at Tiffany's* presents another variation on the Cinderella and transformation motifs, in *Charade*, Hepburn is a trusting and innocent widow enmeshed in a series of events in which the other characters go through a number of identity shifts and transformations as they try to locate a hidden treasure she may possess.

Hepburn's Eliza Doolittle in *My Fair Lady* once more highlights the Cinderella-Princess motif, beautifully realized in the scene in which the former flower-vendor descends an ornate staircase as a stunningly beautiful, refined, and elegant lady. Following an uninspired typical caper film *How to Steal a Million* (1966), Hepburn's 1967 *Wait Until Dark* is an edge-of-your-seat thriller.

In addition to this moody thriller, Hepburn also starred in the equally dark *Two for the Road,* which focused on the collapse of a marriage, on the Cinderella dream gone bad. In 1979, she returned to Hollywood and her film career. It was appropriate that she begin this second phase of her career with *Robin and Marian*, set some 20 years after the events of most Hollywood Robin and Marian romances. This film with Sean Connery as Robin appealed to her because she said it gave her the chance to find out what happens after the typical "They lived happily ever after" endings of most fairy tales and romances. Always aware of the conflict between dream and reality, she shared with the cinematic Marian a sense of life's tarnished romance. Turning away from the Hollywood lifestyle, she retired once more in 1979.

She acted on her lifelong affection for children and joined UNICEF in 1988 as a Goodwill Ambassador on behalf of the world's children. As a voice for UNICEF's Children's Fund, she gave children hope and worked to end the suffering caused by AIDS, war, famine, and all forms of disease. Hepburn constantly challenged people everywhere to take responsibility for the children of the world.

Since her death and the April 27, 1993, memorial tribute to her at the United Nations, Audrey Hepburn has been honored throughout the world by scores of political figures, artists, and entertainers. An Audrey Hepburn Memorial Fund to promote basic education for children traumatized by war and famine in Ethiopia, Somalia, and Sudan, has been established. In the year prior to her death, she had received the Presidential Medal of Freedom from President George Bush. She also received the Humanitarian Award from the Congress on Racial Equality, the Screen Actors Guild Award, and a posthumous Academy Award for Humanitarian Service at the 1993 Oscar ceremony.

Bibliography

Morley, Sheridan. *Audrey Hepburn: A Celebration*. London: Pavilion, 1995.

Paris, Barry. *Audrey Hepburn*. New York: Putnam, 1996.

Walker, Alexander. *Audrey: Her Real Story*. New York: St. Martin's, 1994.

Wayne H. Scott

Hepburn, Katharine (1909-), the most honored American motion picture actress of all time, was born in Hartford, CT. She began her movie career in 1932, and is primarily known for her work in the 1930s for RKO Radio Pictures, especially *Morning Glory* (1933), *Little Women* (1933), and *Alice Adams* (1935); her co-starring vehicles with Cary Grant, *Sylvia Scarlett* (1936), *Bringing Up Baby* (1938), *Holiday* (1938), and *The Philadelphia Story* (1940); and her nine movies made with co-star Spencer Tracy, from *Woman of the Year* (1941) to *Guess Who's Coming to Dinner?* (1967). She has been admired and criticized for portraying strong-willed characters that, it is said, resemble herself.

Hepburn won four Academy Awards for movies in which she appeared as the lead actress: *Morning Glory, Guess Who's Coming to Dinner?, The Lion in Winter* (1968), and *On Golden Pond* (1981). She was nominated for the award on eight other occasions. In 1990, she was honored by the John F. Kennedy Center for the Performing Arts.

Hepburn graduated from Bryn Mawr College in 1928. There, she became interested in drama, though she was not deemed to be overly talented. After graduation, she immediately signed with producer Edwin H. Knopf, whom she reportedly pressured into giving her a chance as a bit player in stage plays. After an initial reluctance, her father helped her financially while she pursued a stage career.

In 1928, she was fired from a leading role in *The Big Pond* and from a part in *Death Takes a Holiday*. She was also fired from *The Animal Kingdom* (1932). At the time, she was labeled "snobbish" by her acting contemporaries, "difficult" by her directors, and "impossible" by reporters who found that she did not grant interviews. Her first stage success was in *Art and Mrs. Bottle* (1931), though her first real hit was *The Warrior's Husband* (1932), which she later claimed was popular because it was "a leg show." Having earned $79.50 a week for *The Warrior's Husband*, she demanded and received $1,500 a week from RKO for her first movie, *A Bill of Divorcement* (1932), in which she was presented to movie audiences, opposite co-star John Barrymore, by director George Cukor.

At RKO, she followed her debut by playing an aviator in *Christopher Strong* (1933) and then received plaudits for *Morning Glory* and *Little Women* that same year. With the Academy Award in hand, she returned to Broadway in *The Lake*, but her performance was not greeted enthusiastically. When she returned to RKO, she was assigned box office flops *Spitfire, Break of Hearts*, and *The Little Minister* (all 1934).

In 1935, she received some praise for *Alice Adams*, but more derisive comments for *Sylvia Scarlett*. After three more failures, *Mary of Scotland* (1936), *A Woman Rebels* (1936), and *Quality Street* (1937), producer Pandro S. Berman gave her a role in *Stage Door* (1937) with box office winner Ginger Rogers, assigned her to *Bringing Up Baby,* and asked her to be in the B movie *Mother Carey's Chickens*. Hepburn decided to buy up the remainder of her contract for $220,000 at this point and RKO happily accepted. She filmed *Holiday* for Columbia and then went home to Connecticut.

At this crossroads in her career, Philip Barry, who had written *Holiday* for the stage, visited Hepburn at her home and convinced her to play the lead in his new stage play, *The Philadelphia Story*. The 1939 play was a success (it had 417 performances) and, surprisingly to movie industry insiders, so was the MGM filmed version in 1940, with Hepburn, Grant, and James Stewart.

After this success and industry recognition that she was a box office attraction once again, she began a long collaboration with Spencer Tracy. They also had a romantic relationship, which many movie reviewers claimed was evident on screen. Their first movie together, *Woman of the Year*, was a box office success, but their next three movies were received indifferently: *Keeper of the Flame* (1943), *Without Love* (1945), and *Sea of Grass* (1947). Two movies in the late 1940s, *State of the Union* (1948), and *Adam's Rib* (1949), and two movies in the 1950s, *Pat and Mike* (1952) and *Desk Set* (1957), were popular. *Guess Who's Coming to Dinner* was Tracy's final movie (he died shortly after filming was completed) and accorded the pair even more critical acclaim.

Movies made after 1940 without Tracy and for which Hepburn received plaudits include *The African Queen* (1951), *Summer Madness* (1955), *Suddenly, Last Summer* (1959), and *Long Day's Journey into Night* (1962). During the 1950s, she was cited by the House UnAmerican Activities Committee as a Communist sympathizer; this contributed to a second, modest career decline.

Bibliography

Edwards, Anne. *A Remarkable Woman*. New York: Morrow, 1985.

Hepburn, Katharine. *The Making of "The African Queen"; Or, How I Went to Africa with Bogart, Bacall and Huston and Almost Lost My Mind*. New York: Knopf, 1987.

———. *Me: Stories of My Life*. New York: Knopf, 1991.

Richard L. Testa, Jr.

Herbert, Victor (1859-1924), one of America's most beloved composers of popular music, was born in Dublin, Ireland. After his father died when Herbert was an infant, his mother remarried a German physician and the family moved to Stuttgart, Germany. Demonstrating an early talent for music, he studied cello. He toured Europe for a while, played in various ensembles, and in 1883 performed one of his own early classical works, a suite for cello and orchestra. Later he was to write several other classical works, including two serious operas. Shortly after marrying in Vienna in 1886, he and his wife sailed to the United States, which he would make his home for the rest of his life.

In America, he was a cellist in orchestras and chamber ensembles, a music teacher, and a conductor. His wife, Theresa Förster, was a soprano at the Metropolitan Opera Company while Herbert was in the cello section of that company's orchestra. Starting in 1893, he was the leader of a renowned New York military band, and from 1898 to 1904,

conductor of the Pittsburgh Symphony Orchestra. Up to 1894, all of his activities were related to serious music. Then he began to move away from classical music somewhat by writing his first work for the American musical theater. *Prince Ananias* (1894) was a light opera of no consequence except that it introduced the American public to the melodic and graceful music of Victor Herbert. In the next few years, he wrote several other light operas, including *The Wizard of the Nile* (1895), a significant success which was revived a few times, the even more successful *The Serenade* (1897), and *The Fortune Teller* (1898), perhaps the best of his early works. By the time he composed *The Fortune Teller*, an operetta, he had definitely passed over into the popular domain. "Gypsy Love Song" or "Slumber On, My Little Gypsy Sweetheart" (lyrics by Harry B. Smith), which appeared in *The Fortune Teller*, was one of Herbert's best songs, and supposedly his own favorite.

Herbert's finest period, however, was in the first decade of the 20th century. *Babes in Toyland* (1903) was a smash success. That show included Herbert's two most enduring songs, the brilliant instrumental "March of the Toys" and the nostalgic favorite "Toyland." Lyricist Glen MacDonough wrote the words for "Toyland." *Mlle. Modiste* (1905) was another success. *The Red Mill* (1906), one of Herbert's best, included the memorable songs "The Isle of Our Dreams" and "Every Day Is Ladies Day" (a delightful comedic piece). Henry Blossom was the lyricist for the 1906 classic. Yet another Herbert classic, *Naughty Marietta* (1910), featured several fine songs, including the outstanding and enduring love song "Ah, Sweet Mystery of Life." Also in *Naughty Marietta* were "Italian Street Song," "Tramp, Tramp, Tramp along the Highway," and "I'm Falling in Love with Someone." The lyrics for all the songs in *Naughty Marietta* were by Rida Johnson Young. *Naughty Marietta* was more or less the end of Herbert's ride at the top. Two subsequent operettas, *Sweethearts* (1913) and *Eileen* (1917), were musically consequential, but were not particularly appealing to the public in spite of a top-selling song, "Thine Alone" (lyrics by Henry Blossom), from *Eileen*.

In total, Herbert wrote over 40 operettas. He wrote many fine melodies in the old-fashioned romantic style in these stage works, presenting touches and tastes of classical music to popular audiences. A 1902 lawsuit claimed that he used more than a little from the classical arena, claiming that all of Herbert's works were copied and unoriginal. Herbert easily beat the lawsuit. By the next year, when Herbert began his most brilliant period with *Babes in Toyland*, nobody would dare challenge the artistry of this dominant figure in American culture.

Bibliography

Kaye, Joseph. *Victor Herbert: The Biography of America's Greatest Composer of Romantic Music*. Freeport: Books for Libraries Press, 1970.

Purdy, Claire Lee. *Victor Herbert, American Music Master*. New York: Messner, 1945.

Waters, Edward N. *Victor Herbert: A Life in Music*. New York: Da Capo, 1978.

William E. Studwell

Here's Lucy (1968-1974), starring Lucille Ball (see entry), became one of TV's most popular shows. Though the title of her shows changed through the years, Ball continued as a great favorite of television audiences, and her characters varied only slightly. She was famous for her low comedy and her physical stunts. Extending the immense popularity of the *I Love Lucy* series that ran almost continually on CBS from 1951 until her retirement from serial television in 1974, *Here's Lucy* was the last of the successful Lucy incarnations.

Tackling a series on her own, without husband Desi Arnaz, Lucille Ball established herself alone as the first lady of American television with the first of her long-running series, *The Lucy Show* (1962-68). *Here's Lucy* and *The Lucy Show* differed from the *I Love Lucy* shows. In *I Love Lucy*, Lucy was the scatter-brained, inept housewife, no-hope want-to-be performer, and comedic centerpiece to Desi's straight man. After the Arnaz/Ball divorce in 1960, which also ended the currently playing *Lucille Ball-Desi Arnaz Show* comedy hour with guest stars, Lucy left weekly television.

When Lucy returned in 1962 in *The Lucy Show*, Vivian Vance (Ethel from the original series) accompanied her. Also starring was Gale Gordon. Lucy was a widow with two children, living in suburban Danfield, CT, and sharing her home with her divorced friend Vivian Bagley, and son Sherman. Both women were desperately looking to snag new husbands and Lucy eventually went to work part-time for Mr. Mooney.

In 1968, *Here's Lucy* was the direct successor with only a slight change in format and major cast changes. This time, Lucy lived in Los Angeles and she had a full-time job. Lucy starred as Lucille Carter, an overzealous secretary at her brother-in-law's employment agency. She was still a widow with two children but they were now named Kim and Craig (played by her real-life children, Lucie and Desi). Gale Gordon continued as the blustery, ever-suffering foil and starred as her brother-in-law and her boss, head of the Unique Employment Agency ("Unusual Jobs for Unusual People"). Mary Jane Croft replaced Vivian Vance as Lucy's best friend and sidekick.

Taking advantage of Ball's popularity in television sitcoms, all three Lucy shows played Mondays at 9 p.m., giving CBS first place in ratings virtually every season Ball was with the network. The series continued on CBS until 1974, when Lucille Ball retired from situation comedy. Each of the sequential Lucy shows demonstrated decreasing popularity: though Lucille Ball was awarded back-to-back Emmys as best actress in a continuing comedy series in 1967 and 1968 for *The Lucy Show*, the *Here's Lucy* program won no Emmys. A reprise in 1986, entitled *Life with Lucy*, lasted only six weeks.

The Lucy Show had placed in Nielsen's Top 10 most popularly rated shows each year it ran; *Here's Lucy* also began in the Top 10 for the first three seasons, but fell to the Top 20 for the next two seasons, and finally out of the Top 20 for its last season.

Bibliography

Brown, Les. *Les Brown's Encyclopedia of Television*. New York: Visible Ink, 1991.

Grey, Frances. *Women and Laughter*. Charlottesville: UP of Virginia, 1994.

Marsh, Earle, and Tim Brooks. *The Complete Directory to Prime Time Network TV, 1946-Present*. 5th ed. New York: Ballantine, 1992.

Sheri Carder

Herman, Gerald "Jerry" (1933-), Broadway composer and lyricist, was born in New York City to Harry Herman, a summer camp owner, and Ruth Sachs Herman, a schoolteacher. Herman was brought up in Jersey City, NJ, where he graduated from Henry Snyder High School. Initially interested in a career in interior decoration, Herman attended New York's Parsons School of Design. He later studied drama at the University of Miami.

A self-taught musician, Jerry Herman's first shows had brief off-Broadway runs (*I Feel Wonderful*, Theatre de Lys, 1954; *Nightcap*, a late night revue, Showplace, 1958; *Parade*, Players Theatre, 1960). The music of Jerry Herman was first heard on Broadway when he contributed the opening number, "Best Gold," to the revue *From A to Z* (1960, 21 performances). The following year saw Herman's first Broadway musical, *Milk and Honey* (1961, 543 performances), a story of American travelers in Israel. The show's title song was a rousing number, Herman's strongest suit as a composer, and the ballad "Shalom" also stood out. *Milk and Honey* received mixed reviews and its relatively long run was chalked up to its being about Israel and thus attracting the interest of New York's large number of Jewish theatergoers. Another reason for Jewish interest was the presence of Yiddish theater legend Molly Picon (making her Broadway debut) in a featured role. *Milk and Honey* was the first Broadway show to run more than 500 performances without making a profit. The failure of this solid, if minor, hit to return its investment signaled the start of troubled times for the Great White Way.

Herman's next show, *Hello, Dolly!* (1964, 2,884 performances), a musical version of Thornton Wilder's play *The Matchmaker*, is among the most profitable Broadway productions of all time. As was the case with *Milk and Honey*, however, Herman's music was not considered the primary reason for the show's popularity. Gower Champion's direction, Carol Channing's star turn performance, and most importantly, producer David Merrick's publicity gimmicks were given more credit than composer Herman for making *Hello, Dolly!* a smash. After Channing left the show, Merrick installed a series of famous Dollies, including Ginger Rogers, Betty Grable, Martha Raye, and Phyllis Diller. In 1967, a new production of *Hello, Dolly!* was mounted with an entirely African-American cast headed by Pearl Bailey. Finally, Broadway legend Ethel Merman, for whom *Hello, Dolly!* had been written (she turned it down), assumed the role with great fanfare in 1970.

Jerry Herman followed *Hello, Dolly!* with *Mame* (1966, 1,508 performances), the story of a wealthy, iconoclastic Manhattanite who takes in her orphaned nephew from the midwest. *Mame* was based on the play *Auntie Mame* by Jerome Lawrence and Robert E. Lee which was in turn based on the novel of the same name by Patrick Dennis (who took his story from the exploits of his real life aunt). There was also a popular *Auntie Mame* film in 1958. After many Broadway divas such as Mary Martin, Ethel Merman, and Rosalind Russell (who had played Mame in the straight play and film versions) turned down the role, it was given, with some reluctance, to Angela Lansbury, a film actress with little experience in the musical theater. Despite this inauspicious beginning, *Mame* was a great success not only with audiences but also with critics (most of whom had been left cold by *Hello, Dolly!*) and established Angela Lansbury as an important stage star. *Mame* is a better integrated show than *Hello, Dolly!* Most of the score's numerous upbeat production numbers ("It's Today," "Open a New Window," "We Need a Little Christmas," and the familiar title song) advance the plot and establish the likeable Mame's cheerful outlook.

A string of failures after *Mame* caused many to regard Jerry Herman as a "tunesmith" whose old-fashioned style could not compete with rock operas and the sophisticated works of Stephen Sondheim. Four well-publicized, big-budget Herman shows—*Dear World* (1969, 132 performances), a musical version of Jean Giradoux's play *The Madwoman of Chaillot*; *Mack and Mabel* (1974, 65 performances), the story of silent movie director Mack Sennett and actress Mabel Normand; and *The Grand Tour* (1979, 61 performances), based on Franz Werfel's play *Jacobowsky and the Colonel*—all failed to please audiences or critics sufficiently. *Mack and Mabel*, however, has achieved a cult status and many people consider it Herman's best score if not his best show. Herman bounced back with *La Cage aux Folles* (1983, 1,761 performances), a flashy musical version of the French film of the same name. In the 1980s, a revue of Jerry Herman songs, entitled *Jerry's Girls*, enjoyed a lengthy national tour and opened on Broadway in December 1985 with Dorothy Loudon, Chita Rivera, and Leslie Uggams. In recent years, Herman has devoted much of his time to raising funds in the fight against AIDS.

Bibliography

Bloom, Ken. *Broadway: An Encyclopedic Guide to the History, People, and Places of Times Square*. New York: Facts on File, 1990.

Mordden, Ethan. *Better Foot Forward: The History of American Musical Theatre*. New York: Grossman, 1976.

Newman, Jeffrey L. "Inside Herman's Head." *The Advocate* 29 June 1993: 83-85.

Suskin, Steven. *Show Tunes 1905-1985: The Songs, Shows, and Careers of Broadway's Top Composers*. New York: Dodd, Mead, 1986.

Mary C. Kalfatovic

Herman, Woodrow Charles ("Woody") (1913-1987), one of America's more popular, influential and long-lasting swing orchestra leaders, born in Milwaukee, began his long and distinguished musical career while still in grade school, singing and tap-dancing in local clubs before touring in vaudeville as a singer. He soon took up the saxophone and later the clarinet, and by his mid-teens was playing in dance bands. He became the featured soloist and vocalist with the Isham Jones Orchestra, which disbanded in 1936. However, the band's core musicians elected him leader of what became "The Band That Plays the Blues," and the 1939 hit, "Woodchoppers' Ball," firmly established the Herman band.

The early 1940s brought changes in personnel and a gradual shift in style to swing, and by 1944, Herman was leading the band that was to become known as the First Herd. Among this illustrious group were powerhouse players such as trumpeters Neal Hefti and Pete Candoli, trombonist Bill Harris, tenor saxophonist Joe "Flip" Phillips, and the hot rhythm section of Ralph Burns, Billy Bauer, Chubby Jackson, and Dave Tough. Igor Stravinsky was so impressed with its sound that he composed "Ebony Concerto" for the band in 1945, which Herman's Herd premiered in a critically acclaimed concert at Carnegie Hall the following year. Despite the First Herd's popularity, Herman temporarily disbanded because of financial difficulties and personal problems in late 1946. The following year, though, he was back with his Second Herd, which reflected a modern approach to big-band music, playing bop-influenced music by Jimmy Giuffre, among others. The remarkable saxophone section, including Herbie Steward on alto, Stan Getz and Zoot Sims, tenors, and Serge Chaloff, baritone, led to the moniker the "Four Brothers" band. During this period Herman's band was the first prominent big band to move from swing to a more advanced, bebop style that eventually became known as progressive jazz.

Herman folded the band in the early 1950s, but formed the Third Herd almost immediately. Because the Herds were recognized for their precision, intensity, and innovation, the new band attracted first-rate musicians, including Red Rodney, Urbie Green, Kai Winding, Richie Kamuca, Bill Perkins, Monty Budwig, and Jake Hanna. Nat Pierce wrote many fine arrangements, as well as played piano. Herman's first European tour was in 1954. The times seemed hostile to big bands, and the Herman band struggled to keep its music alive. During the 1960s and 1970s, personnel and stylistic changes led to uncounted new Herds and to various informal names, such as the Swinging Herd and the Thundering Herd, which suggested both the style and force of the music. The Herds toured extensively, including several international tours, throughout the 1960s, 1970s, and early 1980s. In 1976, Herman played at Carnegie Hall, celebrating the 40th anniversary of his first appearance there. In 1986, he celebrated 50 years as a bandleader with a major U.S. tour featuring longtime sideman Frank Tiberi and several alumni players, and culminating in a gala concert at the Hollywood Bowl.

Herman made over 100 recordings, with million-selling records such as "Woodchoppers' Ball," and had over 50 Top 40 songs between 1937 and 1952. His swinging First Herd topped the polls (*Down Beat* 1945; *Esquire* 1946-47), performed on Herman's own *Wildroot Show* on network radio, and garnered his first record that went gold, "Laura." The Herds appeared in six movies in the 1940s. Among the Herman standards were "Caldonia," "Woodchoppers' Ball," "Four Brothers," "Early Autumn," and his signature theme, "Blue Flame." Numerous honors and awards were bestowed on Herman over the decades. He won several Grammys, and in 1987, was honored with a gold star bearing his name in Hollywood Boulevard's Walk of Fame.

One of the most durable figures in jazz and big bands, Herman persevered through the waning popularity of the big-band sound, mounting financial problems, and failing health. In the early 1980s, he was in residence at The Woody Herman Club in New Orleans and later in the St. Regis Hotel in New York. One of the true legends of jazz and big band music, Woody Herman died after a long illness.

However, he continues to influence musicians and excite audiences through numerous excellent recordings that showcase the spirited intensity of the First Herd, the sheer virtuosity of the Second Herd, the many world-class musicians who got their big break with one of the Herds, and his uncompromising standards.

Bibliography

Deffaa, Chip. *Swing Legacy*. Metuchen: Scarecrow, and the Institute of Jazz Studies, Rutgers U, 1989.

Larkin, Colin, ed. *The Guinness Encyclopedia of Popular Music*. Middlesex, England: Guinness, 1992.

Schuller, Gunther. *The Swing Era*. New York: Oxford UP, 1989.

Walker, Leo. *The Big Band Almanac*. New York: Da Capo, 1989.

Ellen Day

Heroes (both male and female) have been with us since the first families had to raise children. Heroes acted as models for behavior and for growing up. Adults, likewise, have always had other persons whom they admired for their accomplishments, looks, thoughts or general being.

Two aspects of heroics, however, have changed through the years and centuries. In the past, heroes took some time in developing, especially among adults. Some kind of heroic action, above and beyond the everyday, was required, like leading a successful war effort, saving a life under hazardous and threatening conditions, providing spiritual uplift. In other words, the term *hero* was applied only after more than a mere superior action had been performed. Heroes, like good wine, took some time in maturing.

Heroes took some time in developing because, second, the means of communicating their heroic actions were slower than they are now, their heroic actions consequently took longer to be known, and also once achieved lasted longer than they do now. Of course, from the beginning people could be heroes to a single individual, to a family or small group, but ordinarily when we think of hero we think of the designation applied to larger groups.

In the electronic age, though heroes serve the same basic purpose they have always served, they are strikingly different. Now heroic status is granted an individual for only slight cause. Thus, we have dozens of rock heroes, movie heroes, sports heroes, and heroes of a hundred other kinds, whose only accomplishment is that they entertain us, sometimes very well, in what they do. Elvis Presley's main accomplishment was singing in an entertaining way. Sports heroes who because of natural abilities are able to outperform most of us are awarded heroic status, though they might be doing only "what comes naturally."

The ways we create heroes have also changed. In the past, notoriety which could be accomplished only after an extended time through print and oral means now is achieved instantly. The electronic media broadcast within minutes anything that is done above normal. Often, too, because the media must have people and events to talk of, the slightest action is blown up into something extraordinary. If somebody dives into a river and saves a drowning person, he or she is generally named a hero though in fact all that person has done is perform perhaps a "heroic" deed. In the past, "heroic deeds" did not make heroes. So present-day heroes are easily created.

They also often are soon forgotten. *People* magazine and CNN may create heroes on Monday, but often by Friday, other, newer heroes have replaced them. So what the media create, the media can take away. Perhaps it is proper for the modern hero to be on the platform receiving medals for only a moment. Creating and having heroes, at least for adults, is, after all, kids' stuff. Children need models. Adults should be their own models. It can easily be believed that among a properly educated adult population there is no need for heroes. In a democracy everybody should be his or her own hero. Political equality should eventually lead to social, financial, cultural equality of opportunity—and perhaps accomplishment.

If so, then the term *heroic* might well be reduced to *admired*, and then the public might stop rewarding certain "heroes" that we have created benefits that the true *hero* would not want.

Bibliography

Browne, Ray B. *Heroes and Humanities: Detective Fiction and Culture*. Bowling Green, OH: Bowling Green State U Popular P, 1986.

Browne, Ray B., and Marshall Fishwick. *The Hero in Transition*. Bowling Green, OH: Bowling Green State U Popular P, 1983.

Browne, Ray B., Marshall Fishwick, and Michael T. Marsden. *Heroes of Popular Culture*. Bowling Green, OH: Bowling Green State U Popular P, 1972.

Ray B. Browne

See also
Female Sports Heroes
Sports Heroes and Heroines

Heyer, Georgette (1902-1974), popular English writer, published 40 historical romances and 12 thrillers during a long and successful career. She is best remembered as one of the originators of the Regency romance, a genre that remains hugely popular with American readers. Her most unusual and well-known mystery is *Penhallow* (1942), about a woman who commits a murder for which she is never caught, despite her desire to be apprehended.

Although Heyer's historical fiction covers a range of periods, she focused chiefly on the Regency, the last nine years of the reign of George III, assembling a wealth of materials on the language and mores of the age. Her writing owes much to two forebears, the Baroness Orczy, creator of the Scarlet Pimpernel, and Jane Austen. The Regency romances show a progressive movement from novels of adventure, such as *These Old Shades* (1926), to comedies of manners, like *The Nonesuch* (1962). They generally present a conservative view of society, where class and wealth are of prime importance, alongside the personal virtues of her protagonists.

Bibliography

Hodge, Jane Aiken. *The Private World of Georgette Heyer.* London: Bodley Head, 1984.

Helaine Razovsky

High-Definition Television (HDTV), has also been called, among other things, advanced television (ATV), ultra-definition television (UDTV), improved-definition television (IDTV), and enhanced-definition television (EDTV). The Federal Communications Commission (FCC) prefers ATV, because HDTV is seemingly limited to the video picture. ATV can include other technological enhancements. The broadcast industry and general public tend to favor HDTV as a descriptor, and the term has become more or less synonymous with advanced television. Definition is the key word in HDTV, however, and it refers to the quantity of visible detail one can see in a picture shown on the television screen. In other words, definition is the clarity or sharpness of the television picture as the viewer sees it. HDTV also features a wider screen than is found on normal television sets.

The standard for television picture definition in the United States was established in 1941 by the National Television System Committee (NTSC), and it has not been changed since. NTSC standard pictures contain 525 lines of information. As the number of lines is increased, the picture becomes sharper. In Europe the standard is 625 lines, which means the picture is much more detailed than in the U.S.

HDTV is said to offer the consumer movie caliber video and compact disc quality audio. When HDTV is approved for broadcast by the FCC, it will be the third major technological enhancement for over-the-air television since the NTSC standards were set more than 50 years ago. The first was color in 1954, and the second was multichannel television sound (MTS), better known to consumers as stereo TV.

Broadcast HDTV also requires much more spectrum space than NTSC. While the normal NTSC television signal requires a tremendous amount of frequency space, HDTV needs even more. The HDTV signal, which carries as much as ten times more information than color television, needs considerably more bandwidth. Digital processors can eliminate much of the unneeded information. But even digital HDTV can demand as much space as that which is currently occupied by two NTSC stations.

Although interest in HDTV goes back many years, the FCC officially began its work in 1987. When the FCC became involved, HDTV was analog and similar to technology developed in Japan. Japan was first to develop broadcast HDTV, albeit using analog technology. By 1990, General Instruments (GI) had developed an all-digital system. Soon, all proposed U.S. HDTV systems were converted to digital technology, giving the U.S. a clear technical lead in HDTV development. Japanese analog HDTV is incompatible and cannot be upgraded to digital.

For successful HDTV to be achieved, however, there will still be a rather long period of transition. To accomplish the change effectively, it will be necessary to assign additional channels to broadcast stations in order to transmit simultaneously both NTSC and HDTV signals until receivers saturate the marketplace. HDTV receivers cost considerably more than NTSC receivers, and consumers probably will not purchase them in great volume until prices become more reasonable.

Bibliography

Gilder, George. *Life after Television.* New York: Whittle Direct, 1990.

Grant, August E. *Communications Technology Update.* 3d ed. Boston: Focal, 1994.

Mirabito, Michael M. A. *The New Communications Technologies.* 2d ed. Boston: Focal, 1994.

Watkinson, John. *The Art of Digital Video.* 2d ed. Boston: Focal, 1994.

W. A. Kelly Huff

See also

Television Technology

Highways. In the beginning of the 19th century, Thomas Jefferson (1743-1826) and his Secretary of the Treasury Albert Gallatin (1761-1849) proposed an ambitious plan for the building of a national road system that they felt was necessary to bind the vast new country. They saw communication, through the post and the press, as crucial to the development of the young democracy in an era where data traveled over real highways, not informational ones. Only a few of Jefferson's plans were realized, however, and most roads during this period were nothing more than paths that followed natural geographical lines and old Indian trails. The National (Cumberland) Road, from Cumberland, MD, to Wheeling, WV, was begun in 1807, but most of the highway development in this period was instituted by private corporations, often with state support.

It was the railroad that settled and connected the sprawling country. Most of the great national road projects would not be started until after the introduction of the Model T in 1908. In his attempt to make his product accessible to every family, Henry Ford (1863-1947) managed to place the automobile at the center of the American dream. Less concerned with securing 40 acres and a mule, many people now saw as inalienable their right to own a car and to be provided with a place to drive it. Recreation was the primary catalyst for the building of the most ambitious early automobile roads. The dream of a coast-to-coast, paved highway especially for cars was not inspired by a need to deliver the mail or to transport troops. The plan was hatched by two fellows who sold cars and their accessories. Henry Joy (1864-1936) was president of the Packard Motor Company, and Carl Graham Fisher (1874-1939) owned a company that manufactured headlights when, in 1912, they teamed up to campaign for and promote what would become the Lincoln Highway. The plan was to pay for the road with money supplied by auto-related companies. It didn't take a genius to figure out how much rubber could be burned from Washington to San Francisco, and

Goodyear signed right up. Under the guidance of the Lincoln Highway Association, little sections of pavement popped up all along the route, courtesy of companies, social organizations, and towns that did not want to be passed by. Several other highways were conceived, and many were built on promotional campaigns based on the Lincoln Highway Association model. The Lincoln Highway itself, however, was not completed until the federal government stepped in to supply funding and an official name, U.S. Route 30. This was made possible by the Federal Aid Road Act of 1916 and the Federal Aid Highway Act of 1921, both of which established a policy for federal support for highway building, supposedly for the purpose of speeding the mails.

Before long, the road was elevated to a form of art. The "parkway," which had been originated in the 1850s and 1860s by Frederick Law Olmsted (1822-1903), the designer of New York City's Central Park, was, in fact, a long, thin park with a road in the middle. With the support of people like Robert Moses (1888-1981), divided highways augmented by artistic bridges and natural surroundings were appearing in New York and elsewhere.

But for all the parkways' beauty, congestion and ugliness soon became the rule on many roads, which still passed through heavy commercial areas. There were also many excellent roads, like the Pennsylvania Turnpike, which opened in 1940 with four divided lanes and no speed limit from Pittsburgh to Harrisburg. But they would not efficiently be linked until the introduction of the Interstate Highway System. Inspired by Germany's autobahns, high-speed, limited-access superhighways that began opening in the mid-1930s, President Eisenhower championed the idea of a comprehensive system of national, linked roadways, and by 1956 a Highway Trust Fund was established to federally finance, through taxes on gas and auto products, 90 percent of the interstate project (the other 10 percent was paid for by the individual states). By 1978, nearly every large city was linked by nonstop, limited-access, divided highways.

Cultural analysts have recently begun to look at roads as "texts," and books have appeared in the last several years on such "masterpieces" as the Lincoln Highway, the New Jersey Turnpike, and Route 1, the 2,500-mile concrete slab that extends from Fort Kent, ME, to the Florida Keys. At the top of the canon of highway-texts, however, is Route 66, a strip of pavement that from 1926 to 1985 served the manifest destinies of millions of tourists, transients, and truckers between Chicago and the Pacific. If, as roadside scholar Chester Liebs observes, the highway is like a movie (all motorists see basically the same scenes through a cinemascope-shaped windshield), then Route 66 is the classic, the *Citizen Kane* of the American road.

In its heyday, this road was the subject of a network TV series, a hit parade single, a Steinbeck novel, a Woody Guthrie song, and an assortment of other tributes. It officially ceased to exist in the mid-1980s, having been absorbed or bypassed by more modern interstates, but since then it has resurfaced as the reigning road of the retro revolution. A new generation of nostalgic travelers—many of them baby boomers who remember first experiencing it from the jammed way-back of the family station wagon—are once again searching for kicks on what John Steinbeck called "the Mother road." Three books on Route 66 were published between 1988 and 1990, the TV series was rerun and remade in the early nineties, and the shield-shaped route signs came down only to spring up a few years later in trendy, painfully authentic-looking diners across the U.S.

In some areas, the history of the American road has now come full circle. The slow, dangerous unpredictability of the early frontier roads has given way to the slow, dangerous unpredictability of the urban freeway. This is nowhere more apparent than on the notorious L.A. freeway system. Officially inaugurated with the opening of the Arroyo Seco Parkway in 1940, the freeways of Los Angeles now stand in the popular imagination as an enduring symbol of modern technology run amok.

Bibliography

Gillespie, Angus Kress, and Michael Aaron Rockland. *Looking for America on the New Jersey Turnpike*. New Brunswick: Rutgers UP, 1989.

Liebs, Chester. *Main Street to Miracle Mile*. Boston: Little, Brown, 1985.

Malcolm, Andrew H., and Roger Straus III. *U.S. 1: America's Original Main Street*. New York: St. Martin's 1991.

Patton, Phil. *Open Road: A Celebration of the American Highway*. New York: Simon & Schuster, 1986.

Wallis, Michael. *Route 66: The Mother Road*. New York: St. Martin's, 1990.

Robert J. Thompson

See also
Roadside Attractions

Hillerman, **Anthony (Tony) Grove** (1925-), dean of Native American crime fiction authors, was born and raised in the dust-bowl poverty of rural Oklahoma among the Indians indigenous to that area. After World War II, Hillerman worked as a journalist, a professor of journalism and eventually a full-time writer of both nonfiction and fiction. His nonfiction highlights the natural beauty and cultural richness of the Southwest.

But it is his innovative move into the Navajo-based ethnic detective novel that has proved to be his major contribution. Hillerman wrote three mysteries featuring the mature, assimilated Navajo Tribal Police officer Joe Leaphorn (*The Blessing Way,* 1970; *The Dance Hall of the Dead,* 1973; and *Listening Woman,* 1978), then three featuring the younger, more self-consciously ethnic Jim Chee (*People of Darkness,* 1980; *The Dark Wind,* 1982; and *The Ghostway,* 1984). His next five works paired Leaphorn and Chee together (*Skinwalkers,* 1986; *A Thief of Time,* 1988; *Talking God,* 1989; *Coyote Waits,* 1990; and *Sacred Clowns,* 1993). While all make the Navajo detectives protagonists, three are set in specific tribal pueblos. Thus, not only Indian-white, but intertribal Indian relations are factors in the stories.

Hillerman's Navajo mysteries are notable for their knowledgeable and respectful use of indigenous history and customs, both as crucial plot devices and as ways to evoke a powerful sense of place. Most important, however, are the Indian values which provide the novels' moral and thematic center. Foremost among these is the Navajo concept of *hozho*, which expresses the interrelatedness of everything in the natural and human social worlds. Hillerman received the "Special Friend to the Dineh" award from the Navajo Nation in 1987, "as an expression of appreciation and friendship for authentically portraying the strength and dignity of traditional Navajo culture."

Bibliography

Erisman, Fred. *Tony Hillerman*. Boise: Boise State UP, 1989

Freese, Peter. *The Ethnic Detective*. Essen: Verlag Drei Blaue Eule, 1992.

Greenberg, Martin, ed. *The Tony Hillerman Companion*. New York: HarperCollins, 1994.

Hieb, Louis A. *Tony Hillerman: From* The Blessing Way *to* Talking God */A Bibliography*. Tucson: Gigantic Hound, 1990.

George L. Scheper

See also

Ethnic Mysteries	Regional Mysteries
Native American Crime Fiction	Religious Mysteries

Hindenburg Broadcast, The (1937). The *Hindenburg* and Herb Morrison are inseparably linked, each remembered because of the other. The explosion of the German dirigible at Lakehurst, NJ, on May 6, 1937, remains in our memory because of Morrison's poignant radio narration, while Morrison's name is synonymous with the *Hindenburg* broadcast. Yet it was not a live broadcast at all, but rather a recording that was not heard on radio until the following day.

Morrison was a radio announcer at WLS in Chicago when he flew to New Jersey, courtesy of an American Airlines promotion, to witness the one-year anniversary of transatlantic flights by the *Hindenburg*. Morrison wanted to test recording equipment for possible use in news coverage of special events. So it was that he and recording engineer Charles Nielsen were in Lakehurst that fateful evening, recording a description of a routine landing, when the giant airship suddenly burst into flames and crashed.

The *Hindenburg* left Frankfurt, Germany, on May 3 and arrived at Lakehurst the afternoon of May 6. Delayed by weather, the landing began just after 7:00 p.m. Herb Morrison had begun his narration with a description of the dirigible as it approached the runway, with the engineer recording his words onto a 16-inch disc, when suddenly the *Hindenburg* burst into flames. Herb Morrison's emotional account has been replayed countless times since. With an anguished voice, he called it "one of the worst disasters in the world" and cried, "Oh the humanity."

With only 36 fatalities among the 98 on board, the *Hindenburg* does not rank among the worst disasters of the 20th century. But the dramatic account by Herb Morrison has made it endure in our memory.

Bibliography

Barnouw, Eric. *A Tower in Babel*. New York: Oxford UP, 1966.

Bliss, Edward, Jr. *Now the News; The Story of Broadcast Journalism*. New York: Columbia UP, 1991.

Poindexter, Ray. *Golden Throats and Silver Tongues: The Radio Announcers*. Conway: River Road, 1978.

Lynn Hinds

Hinton, S(usan) E(laine) (1950-), the "mother" of young adult literature, wrote the ground-breaking book *The Outsiders* when she was 16. Growing up a tomboy, a loner, and a voracious reader in Tulsa, OK, she found that "there was no 'young adult' literature. If you were through with the horse books and not ready for adult books there wasn't much to read except 'Mary Jane Goes to the Prom' books, and I couldn't stand to read that stuff. So I wrote *The Outsiders* partly because I wanted something realistic to read that dealt with teenagers."

The Outsiders is a straightforward novel about growing up and addresses a universal theme, the social warfare between the "in" group and the "out" group, a focus that continues to define Hinton's work. The novel—fast paced and lively—is told from a teenage boy's viewpoint. In fact, Hinton writes so convincingly from this perspective that many of her readers are surprised to discover that "S. E." is really "Susan Elaine."

Hinton's novels deal with the realities of contemporary teenagers. Many of her fictional topics were earlier considered taboo for teen readers, such as changing sexual mores, premarital pregnancy, illegitimacy, one-parent or no-parent homes, drugs, violence, and death. Hinton's heroes are teenage boys from the "out" group who face the problems of maturation amid cultural forces hostile to their survival: gangs, absent or abusive parents, lack of role models. Her direct style, ear for teen lingo, action-oriented plots, and empathy with young people's concerns appeal to even the most reluctant of teen readers.

Four Hinton novels have been made into films: *The Outsiders* (1967), *That Was Then, This Is Now* (1971), *Rumble Fish* (1975), and *Tex* (1979), and several have won literary honors. *The Outsiders* has been particularly recognized as an outstanding adolescent book.

Bibliography

Daly, Jay. *Presenting S. E. Hinton*. Boston: Twayne, 1989.

Whissen, Thomas R. *Classic Cult Fiction: A Companion to Popular Cult Literature*. New York: Greenwood, 1992.

Linda Lattin Burns

Hip Hop is often equated with rap music in the popular media. Actually the term denotes an aesthetic that was developed in the black and Puerto Rican ghettos of New York and Philadelphia in the early to mid 1970s. The three main media of the hip hop aesthetic are rap, graffiti, and breakdancing. In addition, hip hop extends into painting (Jean Michel Basquiat), film (Charlie Ahearn), fashion design (Cross Colors, Dapper Dan), poetry (Marisela Norte), and a variety of other creative media.

In the early days of rap music, DJs would initiate impromptu street parties by performing publicly. They would often power their systems by tapping into street lamps (referred to as "lamping"). Fab 5 Freddy, host of MTV's "Yo MTV Raps," writer and denizen of the downtown art scene, remembers early DJs like Master D and Grandmaster Flowers setting up their sound systems in the parks of Brooklyn.

Hip hop "writers" (graffiti artists), like DJs, adopt self-styled street names (i.e., Futura 2000, Legend). It is the writing of these names that constitutes two of the three main forms of hip hop graffiti. The first of these forms is "tagging." A tag is a stylized signature written in ink marker, spray paint, shoe polish, grease pencil, or paint stick. The next level of writing, "throw-ups," consists of larger names written in bubble, block or similar styles. In throw-ups, the outlines of the letters are done in one color and filled in with another. Examples of the most sophisticated form of writing are called "pieces." Pieces are large, elaborate, polychromatic murals. Some of the common elements of pieces are text, cartoon characters, background, abstract geometrical forms, and the writer's tag.

Breakdancers, like "writers," rappers, and their fans, often band together to form crews or posses. The crew functions as a support system and source of local identity for its members. Tricia Rose, author of *Black Noise: Rap Music and Black Culture in Contemporary America,* posits (via Arthur Jafa) that the defining stylistic themes of hip hop are flow, layering, and ruptures in line. These themes are well illustrated by the choreography of breakdancing. Ruptures in line are created by moves like popping and locking, which consist of snapping joints into angular positions and freezing them there. But by popping and locking a consecutive series of joints, one after the other, the rupture in line achieves a flowing semi-liquid effect. Last, by mirroring each other's moves, and intertwining their bodies to create new forms, two dancers can create a complex sense of layering.

Until the early '80s, when it began to achieve some commercial success, hip hop functioned entirely at the street level. Artists created, performed, and distributed their work independently. Even after ten years of commercialization, hip hop still reflects its origins. As its performers gain more national exposure, it is becoming a political as well as cultural force to be reckoned with.

Bibliography

Brewer, Devon D. "Hop Hop Graffiti Writers' Evaluations of Strategies to Control Illegal Graffiti." *Human Organization* 51 (Summer 1992): 188-95.

Nelson, Havelock, and Michael A. Gonzales, eds. Foreword. *Bring the Noise, A Guide to Rap Music and Hip-Hop Culture.* Fab 5 Freddy. New York: Harmony, 1991.

Perkins, William Eric. *Droppin' Science: Critical Essays on Rap Music and Hip Hop Culture.* Philadelphia: Temple UP, 1996.

Rose, Tricia. *Black Noise: Rap Music and Black Culture in Contemporary America.* Hanover: Wesleyan UP/UP of New England, 1994.

Ross, Andrew, and Tricia Rose, eds. *Microphone Friends: Youth Music and Youth Culture.* New York: Routledge, 1994.

Shaw, Arnold. *Black Popular Music in America: From the Spirituals, Minstrels, and Ragtime to Steel, Disco, and Hip-Hop.* New York: Schirmer, 1986.

Shomari, Hashim A. *From the Underground: Hip Hop Culture as an Agent of Social Change.* Fanwood: X-Factor, 1995.

Mark Harrison

See also
Break Dancing
Graffiti
Rap

Hippies emerged within the United States as part of the 1960s counterculture. Adherents of the hippie movement were often characterized by unconventional hairstyles and clothing; experimentation with drugs, meditation, and other methods of enhancement of personal awareness; investigation of alternative religious beliefs and practices; and experimentation with nonconventional forms of sexuality and family life. While its cultural influence peaked during 1965-67 and then declined somewhat, the movement had a substantial impact upon American society; even after 40 years the movement continues to possess enclaves of vitality and to attract new followers.

Its core began as a bohemian aesthetic movement in the early 1960s, centered in the East Village of Manhattan and especially the Haight-Ashbury region of San Francisco. Early participants drew much of their inspiration from the Beat poets and writers of the 1950s exemplified by Jack Kerouac and Allen Ginsberg, as well as from folk/protest musicians such as Joan Baez. This original hippie "scene" underwent extremely rapid development following Bob Dylan's synthesis of the folk and rock music genres, the arrival of the Beatles and "British Invasion" rock music, and the popularization of psychedelic drugs by Timothy Leary, Ken Kesey, and underground chemist A. Owsley Stanley.

The assassination of JFK, the subsequent assassinations of Martin Luther King, Jr., and Robert Kennedy, America's continued involvement in Vietnam, the eventual suppression of campus anti-war protests, and the ejection of white persons from an increasingly militant civil rights movement, tended to undermine confidence in the American political process and radicalize the youth. Many formerly politically active young persons now felt alienated from utilitarian industrial capitalist values; such persons often chose to "drop out" of mainstream society in order to experiment with alternative hippie lifestyles in an attempt to discover a more meaningful and authentic existence.

In general, hippies were eclectic thinkers who were more concerned with underlying attitudes than ideology. It is probably safe to say that most sought a new society founded upon individual self-expression, cultivation of intense experiences, and noncompetitive, nature-friendly communitarianism. The hippie ethic of self-expression was manifested in many ways, most obviously in terms of appearance. The women, but especially the men, tended to wear their hair much longer than the larger society. Clothing was distinctive, often mixing and matching bright colors (especially tie-dyes), ornate embroidery, and leather work with rural, Victorian, and/or American Indian fashions. Vehicles and homes could also be decorated in a similar informal manner.

Even more important than the visual arts was music. Early hippies tended to listen to and elaborate upon folk music and labor protest songs. These artistic forms, and their underlying political concerns, were soon combined with the rock and roll popularized by the Beatles into myriad new musical styles.

Given their predilection for self-expression and spontaneity, it is not surprising that the hippies tended to see much of American culture as suffering from various forms of needless repression. Some of this the hippies felt was self-induced, but even more was perpetrated by a "system" which demanded mindless conformity in exchange for providing a false sense of collective security. At times the hippies tried to wake up the larger society to its plight through the use of confrontational tactics. More often, however, they would attempt to free themselves from the corrupting influence of society through the pursuit of unmediated experience. This was part of the rationale for the movement's heavy use of drugs, particularly marijuana and hallucinogenic drugs such as LSD and, less frequently, STP and mescaline; such drugs were thought of as both enhancing creativity and allowing the perception of levels of reality, perhaps even divine reality, inaccessible to the Western waking mind.

A desire for a more intimate, less class-stratified existence, combined with both a longing for participatory democracy and a distrust of bureaucracy, led many to experiment with communitarian living. Such experiments could include experimentation with alternative forms of sexuality and family arrangements, including polygamy, "polyfidelity" (group marriage), and open relationships, as well as tolerance of homosexual unions.

Though remaining influential, the hippie movement entered a period of decline after 1967. Part of this was due to excessive media attention given to events such as the "First Human Be-in" and the "Summer of Love." Publicity from these events caused the two major centers of hippie activity, Haight-Ashbury and the East Side of Manhattan, to be deluged with so many runaways, social malcontents, and criminals that the local economies collapsed. As a result, much of the movement was dispersed into smaller rural settlements across the U.S.

A second reason was linked to demographics: the youth culture of the 1960s was in part propelled by a disproportionate number of young persons coming of age at the same time, and an unusually large number of these persons going on to enter colleges that were unprepared for influxes of this size. By the early 1970s the numbers of college-age youth were decreasing, while colleges had become more adept at handling large student bodies.

A third reason for the decline was a combination of internal conflict, aging, and disillusionment. By 1970, some hippies had come to advocate violent, revolutionary social change, while others preferred a path of inner transformation and political quietism. Furthermore, as the initial novelty of the movement wore off, and as the hippies themselves grew older, a large number of men and women simply married and reentered mainstream American culture. Commercialization also exacted a price; hippie rock music and fashions became valuable commercial commodities, and the original message of the movement was diluted by mass merchandizing and concert promotion. Finally, there was a smaller but disproportionately influential group of persons who became disenchanted with the drugs and sex within the movement while not finding the meaning that they desperately desired, and went on to seek meaning in Eastern-inspired faiths (e.g., Krishna Consciousness, Transcendental Meditation, Divine Light Mission), Christian sectarian groups (the Jesus Movement), and more psychologically oriented human potential groups (est).

The extent to which the hippie movement influenced American culture is contested. The movement's aesthetic impact was enormous. Hippie-derived eclectic dress and hairstyles remained influential for a decade, with denim remaining a fashion staple to the present day. Similarly, many of the musical forms originating among the hippies remain current, while Woodstock continues to be paradigmatic within the rock music and concert industries.

The hippies' social agenda, however, met with much more modest results. Drug use is still regarded as a criminal activity. Furthermore, despite its radical egalitarian rhetoric, the movement had difficulty transcending its bourgeois origins: participants tended to come from, and were often supported by, middle- and upper-middle-class families. Only modest numbers came from working-class backgrounds or ethnic minorities. Furthermore, sexual roles within the movement frequently reflected those found in the larger society.

In spite of setbacks and commercialization, the hippies remain influential in America. Religious historian Timothy Miller suggests that the New Age movement is one of the substantial legacies of the hippies; further investigation reveals that the movement has also had a significant influence upon Protestant evangelicalism. The hippies were also instrumental in popularizing and staffing the early environmental movement.

Bibliography

Melville, Keith. *Communes in the Counter Culture: Origins, Theories, Styles of Life.* New York: Morrow, 1972.

O'Neill, William L. *Coming Apart: An Informal History of America in the 1960s.* Chicago: Quadrangle, 1971.

Smith, Timothy. *The Hippies and American Values.* Knoxville: U of Tennessee P, 1991.

Wagner, Jon, ed. *Sex Roles in Contemporary American Communes.* Bloomington: Indiana UP, 1982.

John M. Bozeman

See also

Acid Rock   Protest Music

Jesus Movement   Woodstock

Hirt, Al (1922-1999), an exceptionally skilled and influential jazz trumpet musician, was born in New Orleans, LA. Trained in symphony music, not traditional jazz, he was a trumpet virtuoso from an early age. His basic jazz training came from work in the big bands, and his associations there are remarkable. He worked with Tommy Dorsey, Ray McKinley, and others.

Hirt's big decade was the 1960s, during which he had 17 albums on the charts. Pete Fountain was an early and frequent associate in that period. For a time Al Hirt had his own club in New Orleans.

Although he received criticism for his success from jazz hardliners, he kept his good humor. He was an influence on Wynton Marsalis and a close friend of Ellis Marsalis, Wynton's father.

Bibliography

Larkin, Colin, ed. *The Guinness Encyclopedia of Popular Music.* Middlesex, England: Guinness, 1992.

Rose, Al, and Edward Souchon. *New Orleans Jazz Family Album.* Baton Rouge: Louisiana State UP, 1967.

Frank A. Salamone

Hispanic Music in the United States is one of the oldest musical traditions. The four-string Spanish guitar accompanied explorers, soldiers, and colonists to the Southeast (Florida, 1521), the Southwest (Texas, 1598), and up the Mississippi River from New Orleans to St. Louis (Louisiana Territory, 1762-1800). Spanish songs from Majorca were still alive in St. Augustine (est. 1565) when Spanish colonial exiles from Cuba founded Key West and then Ibor City (Tampa) in the 19th century. Old ballads are still being collected in the Southwest, especially in New Mexico.

The music of the Southwest includes the traditional *mariachi* trio of stringed instruments, romantic songs with guitar, and sprightly topical ballads. The latter significantly influenced American country music, the Spanish *guitarra* even threatening the fiddle of Anglo tradition. Songs from the Southwest like "Cielito lindo" and "Carmen Carmela" or the Cuban "La paloma" via Florida would jump cultural barriers to become standards in the U.S. by the time phonographs became common household appliances in the earlier 20th century. By the 1940s the *mariachi* was becoming urbanized, now including trumpets. At times in more recent years *mariachi* music has made significant appearances in mainstream American music: Herb Alpert and the Tijuana Brass (see entry) or Ritchie Valens's rendition of an old traditional song, "La Bamba."

In 1911, the Argentine tango via Paris became the American dance craze, followed briefly by the Brazilian *maxixe*—both forms bombed out by the xenophobic guns of World War I. Otherwise, many Hispanic musical traditions would remain within the confines of the Spanish-speaking areas of the U.S. until after the popularization of radio in the 1920s. Prohibition sparked tourism to Cuba, where Americans became addicted to rumba with rum at elegant Havana supper clubs. In the meantime, continuing immigration from the Caribbean to Florida and to New York created a growing demand for Cuban and Puerto Rican music. A young concert violinist from Spain, Enric Madriguera, formed a popular orchestra in New York, and by 1924, was supplying the Cuban *danz* to Americans in supper clubs and on radio and record. A brief American tour by Spain's Raquel Meller brought castanets and melodies like *Valencia* and *El relicario* into vogue. At this time Rudolph Valentino (see entry) brought back the Argentine tango, in a more authentic ver-

sion, only to be eclipsed by a Cuban rumba, the "Peanut Vendor," featured in the movie *Cuban Love Song* (1930) and performed on stage in New York in 1931. The two major numbers in Vincent Youmans's score for the movie *Flying Down to Rio* (1933) are "Orchids in the Moonlight" (tango) and "Carioca" (rumba). In his 1934 Broadway musical, *Jubilee*, Cole Porter introduced his Caribbean-styled "Begin the Beguine." Henceforth the "Latin number" would remain a staple of American stage and screen, eventually to produce parodies like "South America, Take It Away," Peggy Lee's "Mañana," or Pearl Bailey's "Takes Two to Tango."

But the greatest stylistic impact on American music in modern times is from the Caribbean. The Prohibition era addicted American nightclubbers in Havana to Cuban music, which in the 1920s became increasingly influenced by American instrumentation, the Charleston, and the foxtrot. Cuban orchestras, heavy on percussion (maracas, bongó, güiro, cencerro, and timbal), blended their flutes, and trumpets, and pianos with American saxophones while speeding up the tempo of their 2/4 *danz* to create the hybrid *rumba*. Americans were enchanted, only to find themselves touristically disenfranchised by the collapse of Wall Street. Cuban musicians deserted the empty dance floors of Havana, flocking to Miami, New York, and Chicago, where happy clients went back into their dance. Cuban-styled music, whether American- or Cuban-composed, became an integral part of American music continually evolving from *rumba*, to *conga*, slower *bolero*, to *mambo*, and *cha-cha*. Pan-Caribbean music shares many characteristics with Cuban music including, especially, the *bolero* format. Urban composers from coastal Mexico and from Puerto Rico shared popularity with the Cubans in the period of intense Caribbeanization of American music. Cautiously in the later 1920s, American orchestras began to imitate Cuban percussive style with ingenious substitutes: woodblock, triangle, rim shots on snare drum, even washboard and brush for the *güiro*. A notable example is Ted Weems's 1934 recording of "Heartaches." Indeed the Cuban percussive array appears to be the inspiration for the American drum battery as developed, for example, by Gene Krupa. By 1940, some of the Cuban instruments would become standard in American orchestras.

The Cuban revolution, victorious in 1959, had musical consequences in the United States. Cuban *mambo* and *chachá* were immediately replaced with the Dominican *merengue*, the Brazilian *bossa nova*, and the *calypso* (see entry) from Trinidad. Brazilian music, also similar to Pan-Caribbean style including percussion and heavy on guitar, had been in competition with Cuban music in the United States from the arrival of Carmen Miranda to Broadway in 1939, thence to Hollywood. Indeed her main production number in *Weekend in Havana* (1941) is curiously enough a Brazilian *samba*. One is tempted to see revenge for the earlier *Flying Down to Rio* (1934) which inappropriately features a tango and a rumba! Hollywood, more often than not, stripped gears with Hispanic music.

All the while Artie Shaw and Stan Kenton, Dizzy Gillespie with Chano Pozo, and Machito and Tito Puente continued to synthesize and re-synthesize Caribbean and American music: *pachanga, boogalú* Latin disco, and *salsa*. The strands no longer disentangle.

Bibliography

Robb, John Donald. *Hispanic Folk Music of New Mexico and the Southwest*. Norman: U of Oklahoma P, 1980.

Roberts, John Storm. *The Latin Tinge: The Impact of Latin American Music on the United States*. New York: Oxford UP, 1979.

Spottswood, Richard K. *Ethnic Music on Records: A Discography of Ethnic Recordings Produced in the United States, 1893-1942*. 7 vols. Champaign: U of Illinois P, 1990.

Theodore S. Beardsley, Jr.

Historical Crime Fiction is one of the fastest growing types in the genre. All areas of history are being covered, especially ancient history. The number of authors and periods covered are increasing for several reasons. The first is practicality. Crime fiction, like fiction in general, seeks new and exotic settings as subject matter. Historical crime fiction provides ideal settings. So far the oldest setting for such a story is among the Australian Aborigines of 35,000 B.C. This story, "Death in the Dawntime," by F. Gwenplaine MacIntyre, develops under the assumption that the Aborigines were as skilled in physical tracking then as they were when the British settled Australia in the 18th century.

Historical crime fiction provides ever-expanding new cultures as settings and feeds a growing interest in history. Such fiction is somewhat different in development from its conventional modern counterpart. Since it has to create or re-create the culture in which the participants live, the historical crime novel must present reality in setting so that the reader's interest is maintained. In doing so, often the author pays less concern with the guilt and punishment of perpetrators than with setting. The episode is thus frozen in a historical moment, and to that extent resembles the modern golden age mystery. But it does not at all qualify as a "cozy" novel because its action grows out of and spills over into all of society. It bears only the outside limits of its historical period.

Historical crime fiction has another spill-out effect which may or may not be a primary goal but which becomes a primary or unintended result. In order to be credible, the historical setting must be detailed and authentic. Thus, the book becomes a history lesson, both as entertainment and as instruction. Throughout history, entertainment and education (or entertaining education) have served as enlightenment and the development of democracy. Historical crime fiction, then, serves at least three beneficial purposes beyond the mere unraveling of a mystery: (1) it teaches history; (2) it shows the development of political and cultural systems through the ages; and (3) it provides excellent reading and problem-solving in an unusual setting. The following authors and their works demonstrate the range and power of historical crime fiction.

Elizabeth Peters, under her real name of Barbara Mertz, is a noted Egyptologist. Writing as Elizabeth Peters and Barbara Michaels, she has authored numerous crime fiction novels, including *The Curse of the Pharaohs* (1981), *The Mummy Case* (1985), *Lion in the Valley* (1986) and *The Snake, the Crocodile and the Dog* (1992). In all, Victorian Egyptologist Amelia Peabody Emerson and her irascible husband, renowned archaeologist Emerson, and their son Ramses, for one reason or another wind up at the site of some Egyptian ruins to investigate a murder.

Lynda S. Robinson is a recent comer to crime fiction, this time to Egypt—Memphis and Thebes—during the short reign of Pharoah Tutankhamen, King Tut. In *Murder in the Place of Anubis* (1994), the sacred place of embalming has been desecrated with a murdered corpse. Though the corpse is of the hated scribe Hormin, Tut's "eyes and ears," Lord Meren must discover the murderer before the priests use the murder to undermine his authority. *Eater of Souls* (1997) sets out to unravel the horrifying mystery of why the streets of Memphis are littered with bodies of innocent people. If this mass murder is not the work of the Devourer, the eater of souls, then what mortal is? The streets are littered with fascinating life as well as with multiple deaths.

Classical Greece is the site for several novelists and short story writers. One of the interesting novelists is Anna Apostolou, almost certainly one of the many pseudonyms of P. C. Doherty. Apostolou's *A Murder in Macedon* (1997) takes place in Macedon, in 336 B.C. when Philip is about to celebrate his glorious reign. At the beginning of the celebration, before the eyes of all the monarchs and dignitaries, he is stabbed to death. Suspicion immediately falls on his former wife, witch Queen Olympias, and her son Alexander, who rumor says was not the son of Philip after all. To clear his name so that he can rule his vast kingdom, Alexander must clear the mystery of whether the assassin acted alone or in concert with other conspirators.

Margaret Doody, Canadian-born one-time professor at the University of California, has written one murder mystery featuring Aristotle, Socrates' competitor for the best teacher's award of ancient Athens. In *Aristotle Detective* (1978), when a prominent citizen is killed by a bow and arrow, Aristotle and a young lad who does the legwork reason out the guilty party. Athens is authentically detailed and Aristotle wears a different personality from the one we usually associate with him.

Rome, especially during the last century B.C., is a popular site for historical crime fiction. Wallace Nichols (1888-1967) is generally called the grandfather of the Roman detective story. His investigator is Sollius, the slave detective. Because slaves in Rome could be at the same time very visible or virtually invisible, they served as good investigators.

John Maddox Roberts has at least four novels about Rome from 70 B.C. onward. Roberts uses as his investigator the long-lived member of a noble family who actually lived for many years before 93-91 B.C. As a young and as yet unimportant Roman civil servant, Decius Caecilius Metellus investigates many serious threats to Rome. In *The Sacrilege* (1992), he delves into the sacrilege committed by a corrupt politician who dressed as a woman and infiltrated a sacred female rite presided over by Caesar's wife, Pompeia.

Steven Saylor is a prolific author of novels about Rome from the time of 80 B.C., the period of Cicero, Marc Antony, and Pompey the Great. Saylor's agent is Gordianus the Finder. Though not of noble blood, through service to the political leaders Gordianus the Finder has achieved wealth, independence, and influence in Rome. As investigator and speaking in the name of the rulers, he wanders through the homes and offices of Roman officials and through the streets of a chaotic and dangerous Rome. In so doing, he chronicles with revealing detail what it meant to live in an overcrowded Rome and listen to the Senators Cicero and Marc Antony and witness their constant effort to sway the mob and grab power. Saylor's novels are particularly rich in details concerning the Rome of the last years before the birth of Christ and revealing descriptions of the Romans whose identities have come down as household names.

Classical China is represented by two authors, one from the period, and one who writes about it. Lord Bau, from the Sung Dynasty (about 1000), who appears in many short stories from the period, solves crimes, rights wrongs, and protects the poor and weak. Judge Dee, in a series of novels by Robert Van Gulik, is a traveling magistrate who goes from destination to destination, discovers crimes and injustices, and brings the offenders to justice.

Historical Britain is, perhaps logically, the favorite country for historical crime fiction. Bruce Alexander writes a series about 18th-century London, with all the filth and corruption of that capital at that time. His novels develop around Sir John Fielding, who had founded the Bow Street Runners, a police force, and Jeremy Procter, a 14-year-old orphan just arrived in London. Alexander's stories superbly re-create London and involve intriguing mysteries.

P. C. Doherty, who holds a doctorate from Oxford, is by far the most prolific historical crime novelist working today and is unexcelled in his coverage and details of history. As Doherty, he has written a series based on Chaucer's *Canterbury Tales*, including *A Tournament of Murders* and *An Ancient Evil*. More importantly, he has written ten novels using Sir Hugh Corbett, Edward I's clerk and spy, to investigate murder, generally multiple slayings in 14th-century Oxford. As Paul Harding, Doherty has created the 14th-century Southwark Dominican parish priest Brother Athelstan, who is assistant to the Coroner of the City of London, fat, hard-drinking Sir John Cranston. Cranston and Athelstan, among other adventures, investigate the throat-cut murder of the Constable of the Tower of London, behind locked doors (*Red Slayer*, 1994) and, after the death of King Edward III, the murder of merchant prince Sir Thomas Springall, while the empty throne waits for the crowning of ten-year-old Richard. As Michael Clynes, Doherty has written some half dozen adventures of Sir Roger Shallot, a Falstaffian character during the reign of Henry VII. As C. L. Grace, Doherty has expanded his coverage to include a series featuring Kathryn Swinburne, a physician and chemist in 15th-century Canterbury.

Robert Lee Hall does in crime fiction what Benjamin Franklin did in real life. Hall takes the American humanitarian physicist and philosopher to London, where he is called upon to exercise his wisdom in solving murders. In *Benjamin Franklin Takes the Case* (1988), Franklin investigates a brutal murder to exonerate a servant who is covered with blood and naturally accused of the murder. The servant boy turns out to be Franklin's friend and helper in solving other mysteries as they arise.

Another side of 18th-century London life is told by Lillian De La Torre, pseudonym of Lillian de la Torre Bueno McCue (1902-1993), who wrote numerous short stories and four novels about Dr. Samuel Johnson, the real lexicographer and editor of the first dictionary of the English language, and his rakish, first-class biographer James Boswell. Her settings, characters and stories are real, but the solutions are fiction.

American historical crime fiction is much more limited than that of other countries for obvious reasons. Peter J. Heck, however, has written four such novels about one of America's gaudiest periods, the so-called Gilded Age, as Mark Twain labeled it. Heck's stories involve Mark Twain on a journey or at the end of one, and all four play on the titles of Twain's own books. James Brewer's series of books are set along the Mississippi just after the Civil War.

Bibliography

Browne, Ray B., and Lawrence Kreiser. *The Detective as Historian*. Bowling Green, OH: Bowling Green State U Popular P, 2000.

Winks, Robin. *The Historian as Detective*. Chapel Hill: U of North Carolina P, 1967.

Ray B. Browne

History of Sound Recording, The: 33, 45, and 78 RPM Records. Sound recording revolutionized entertainment so completely that 20th-century civilization might have taken quite a different path had it not been for audio technology. From its beginning in the 19th century, changes in and exploitation of audio technology have defined both popular music and specific periods in American culture.

Although there is some debate as to who first actually thought of recording and playing back sound on a mechanical device, Thomas Edison is given credit for inventing such a device—the phonograph (see entry)—in 1877. For Edison, using a hand-cranked rotating cylinder, sound waves focused by an acoustic horn, were indented vertically on tin foil (see Edison Cylinder). In 1888, this process was rethought by Emile Berliner. He incised sound laterally onto a flat revolving wax disk. From an audio point of view the Edison-cylinder approach was a better device. The sound was louder, the recording surface produced less hiss than the disk, but because of ease of operation and better promotion by entrepreneurs supporting the disk—the Victor Company, the Columbia Phonograph Company, and the American Graphophone Company—by 1929 Edison's cylindrical machine eventually disappeared.

Both early cylinder and disk players operated by hand cranks at speeds ranging from 60 to 160 revolutions per minute (RPM). The precise speed depended on the specific machine being used to record the cylinder or disk, the company who produced the recording, the year the recording was made, and the available play-back equipment. In any event, slowly the standard for the disk reached 78 RPMs.

The sound quality of early 78 RPM disks in no way approached the standard of the later LP or of today's compact disk. The hard recording surfaces left noisy bits of shellac or wax in the grooves, which produced annoying hiss upon playback. The pressure of the six ounce stylus leveled the fine groove undulations of any frequency above 2000 Hertz. The inherent physical differences of the groove speed between the outside and inside of the disk caused a loss of both upper and lower frequencies. These technological limitations meant that only certain types of music and musicians could benefit from audio technology.

With the electric recording system, developed in 1924 by Joseph P. Maxfield and Henry C. Harrison of Bell Laboratories, instead of musicians performing at a very loud intense level into a conical horn which moved a relatively inflexible diaphragm against a course cutting stylus which cut a ragged groove into a relatively rigid recording medium, performers now merely sang or played at a natural level into a microphone. The sound would then be electronically amplified and used to drive a magnetic groove-cutting head. With this new method the limited frequency response of the acoustic recording method (3,200 Hertz top) was increased to 4,200 hertz. The result was a performance with warmth and a sense of naturalness unheard on record before.

This new sound recording technique opened the door for many new artists. One was not required to have an exceptionally strong voice like so many of the performers of the pre-electric period. This new electric recording equipment, which was portable enough to be transported from venue to venue, meant people like Ralph Peer and Alan Lomax were able to record performers like country artist Jimmie Rodgers and rural blues artist Leadbelly, artists who generally did not perform in major metropolitan areas, thus opening entire genres of music to new audiences.

During the war, Decca Recording Company in England developed a recording system sensitive enough to distinguish the subtle differences between British and Germany submarines. Using a lightweight stylus and a new electrical feedback loop in the cutting head, the hissing noise usually heard on recordings was dramatically reduced and the frequency range was extended to 14,000 Hertz. This "Full Frequency Range Recording"—ffrr—was commercially marketed in the U.S. in 1946 on the London label.

The advent of the lightweight sapphire stylus, with operating pressures of around 1 1/2 ounces, meant that Vinylite, a synthetic plastic more resistant to scratches, could now be used effectively as a recording medium. In 1948, the Columbia Recording Company did just that. By reducing the coarse 3 mil groove of the 78 RPM record to a 1 mil microgroove; by increasing the number of lines per inch from about 90 in the 78 RPM recording to 224-300; and by reducing the recording speed to 33 1/3 RPMs, the long playing (20-25 minutes) "Hi Fidelity" record (the LP) emerged.

The technological advantages of the LP had important implications for the entire recording industry. Almost immediately its existence put pressure on other recording companies to embrace the LP as a new standard for sound reproduction. But as much pressure as the LP put on the entire industry, RCA resisted the move. Instead, in January 1949, they introduced an alternative recording device—the microgroove 45 RPM Vinylite record. Although technically very similar in design to the LP, its playing time was generally only five to seven minutes. Its introduction ushered in the technological "battle of the speeds."

Attempts at stereophonic recording—the illusion of spaciousness from two distinct sound paths to the ears—had been undertaken during the thirties. In 1931, Alan D. Blumlein patented two methods of stereophonic recording, the vertical/lateral method and the 45/45 method. In 1952 Emory Cook brought out a record with two separate but continuous grooves—one for the right channel, the other for the left—that was played by two pickups attached to one tone arm. In 1957, the Whistler Company developed a stereophonic cutting head using Blumlein's 45/45 method, and in 1958, a commercially viable stereophonic LP was born.

Coincidental to the development of the LP was the evolution of magnetic tape recorders (see entry). When recording technicians discovered that the magnetic recorder was an excellent device for capturing sound faithfully (frequency response up to 20,000 Hertz) around 1948, audio producers began manipulating the devices and the sound on the tape. Ultimately, producers found that an ensemble could be recorded discretely on individual recording tracks and mixed together in new and creative ways. And the stereophonic disk, with its two channels, was the primary medium in which the audience heard the new music.

This new use of technology ultimately established distinct aesthetic concerns in recorded music. Today, the classical ensemble is recorded differently, and sounds differently, from the pop ensemble partly because of the different aesthetic concerns associated with the way technology is used. And to a large extent the specific defining factor of a particular genre of recorded music—its "sound"—lies in the way technology is specifically used to capture or produce the sound. Rock music in the 1960s was rock music because of rock production techniques. Disco music of the 1970s depended on specific disco production techniques using specific recording technology.

With the end of the 33, 45 and 78 RPM recordings comes an end to specific production techniques and old sounds. With the development of digital technology new sounds have appeared (sampling) and the evolutionary process continues.

Bibliography

Dearling, Robert, and Celia Dearling. *The Guinness Book of Recorded Sound*. Middlesex, U.K.: Guinness, 1984.

Read, Oliver, and Walter L. Welch. *From Tin Foil to Stereo: Evolution of the Phonograph*. Indianapolis: Sams, 1976.

Welch, Walter L., and Leah Brodbeck Stenzel Burt. *From Tinfoil to Stereo: The Acoustic Years of the Recording Industry 1877-1929*. Gainesville: UP of Florida, 1994.

William F. Shea

Hitchcock, Alfred (1899-1980), one of America's most successful movie directors, like the Beatles, masterfully cultivated the image of the lovable Englishman for millions of infatuated Americans. In a career begun in London and influenced by German Expressionism, Hitchcock's films were profoundly rooted, again, like the music of the Beatles, in American popular forms.

Hitchcock's first film job was writing titles for silent films produced for Paramount's Famous Players–Lasky (London branch). Moving quickly up the ranks to director, Hitchcock began making thrillers in Britain that drew worldwide attention (*The Lodger,* 1926; *The Man Who Knew Too Much,* 1934; *The 39 Steps,* 1935), but little respect from an English press enamored of high art. Partially because of this lack of hometown respect, and certainly because of the greater resources of Hollywood, Hitchcock came to America in 1939, a contract with David O. Selznick in hand. His first film made in America, *Rebecca* (1940), won the Oscar for best picture and was the beginning of a long and successful career in Hollywood. Forty years later, when Hitchcock personally accepted his knighthood in January of 1980, his failing health kept him from receiving the honor in Britain. Instead, Hitchcock's knighthood was conferred on a set at Universal Studios, Hollywood, CA. When he died three months later, Hitchcock was, by nearly everyone's accounting, one of America's greatest film directors.

Hitchcock created an unmistakable style which he lavished on the suspense thriller, a genre not always treated with great care and artistry. While difficult to describe, this Hitchcockian style has been often imitated, elaborated, and parodied, and now exists far beyond Hitchcock's own canon. At its most simple, the style seems a blend of the haunting, odd melodies of composer Bernard Herrmann (a frequent Hitchcock collaborator); a gliding camera that never rose above a sleepwalker's pace; a penchant for uncluttered, sometimes overly composed images; and, when shooting in black-and-white, an understated German Expressionism, and, when shooting in Technicolor, a reserve with color that found expression through an elaborate reliance on earth-tones and pastels.

Although Hitchcock always preferred to discuss style and formal manipulation, critics have attributed thematic and philosophical depth to his films. Hitchcock's stock as an artist had its greatest surge in the mid 1950s, when various French critics and directors associated with the *Cahiers du Cinema* film journal found Hitchcock's work a profound exploration of guilt and redemption, thought to derive from the director's early Catholic/Jesuitical upbringing. One obvious thematic tension in Hitchcock's films is a careful balance between a dark pathos which often turns into a barely constrained terror and a gallows humor that carries over from slapstick to whimsy to the bleakest of satire. This means, for viewers, that Hitchcock's films are scary and funny, sometimes at the same time, as when Bruno Antony (Robert Walker) shows a society matron how to strangle someone in *Strangers on a Train* (1951), his lesson quickly becoming dangerous. This tension between death/aggression and life/civility can be seen in dozens of scenes where Hitchcock stages murderous activity right under everybody's noses: in the lobby of the United Nations; on an Isle of Love at an amusement park; on the face of Mount Rushmore; during a child's birthday party at a beach-front home.

One thing which kept Hitchcock's films from suffocating under his highly noticeable style and formulas was the director's lifelong commitment to experimentation with film form. These experimental impulses were not always complete successes, as in *Lifeboat* (1944), where the director tried to make a Hollywood film restricted to the single location of a drifting lifeboat, and in *Rope* (1948), where Hitchcock composed a murder mystery in real time and with the appearance of one long take (i.e., no apparent edits). Hitchcock's insistence on pushing film form and convention eventually paid off nicely, contributing to what many consider one of cinema's greatest treasures: *Rear Window* (1954). In *Window,* Hitchcock restricted himself to a small apartment complex and its courtyard, and offered up a tight thriller that was as eloquent a philosophical statement on the nature of film viewing (and gossip, and voyeurism, and male fear of commitment) as we have.

By the mid 1950s, Hitchcock's name was so widely known and respected that television executives offered the director an unprecedented deal for a television series. *Alfred Hitchcock Presents* capitalized more on Hitchcock's persona than his directorial talents. Lasting a decade (from 1955 to 1965), Hitchcock's various incarnations on network television were, especially in their first five years, massively successful. Hitchcock's primary contributions to the series were his name, his unforgettable profile (sketched by the director himself), and his wry introductions for each episode (written by Jim Allardice). Gounod's "Funeral March of the Marionette," used to open and close each show, seemed to musically capture Hitchcock's jovial attitude toward the macabre. With his name now something of a seal of approval for stories of suspense, horror, and murder, it was not long before one could find pulp fiction collections endorsed by the master of suspense.

An examination of the cast and crew for a masterpiece like *Vertigo* (1957) reveals the extent to which Hitchcock's great films were works of collective genius. Saul Bass, the most innovative and original of title designers ever to work in Hollywood, began his collaboration with Hitchcock on *Vertigo,* offering a mesmerizing geometric opening that evoked the film's theme of obsession. Later, Bass would design the opening titles for *North by Northwest* and *Psycho,* and contribute so much input into *Psycho*'s famous shower scene that some have claimed Bass as the scene's author. Bernard Herrmann (Hitchcock films and a handful of Hitchcockian films like *Sisters* and *Cape Fear*) composed a profoundly poetic and haunting score for *Vertigo.* Robert Burks (11 Hitchcock films) served as cinematographer and George Tomasini (9 Hitchcock films) edited the film. Edith Head, a veritable institution of Hollywood costuming (11 Hitchcock films), provided her usual elegant fashion sense of color and line. One of Hitchcock's favorite actors, Jimmy Stewart, rendered in *Vertigo* one of his career-best performances, while Kim Novak played the cool blonde in what was certainly *her* career best.

In *North by Northwest* (1959) Hitchcock perfected a type of big-budget Hollywood thriller that would influence films well into the '90s. Using big stars and impressive locations that spanned familiar urban cityscapes and the American countryside, Hitchcock sent Cary Grant and Eva Marie Saint through a convoluted mistaken-identity plot that expertly titillated 1950s viewers with their Cold War fears and Monroe-era sexual infatuations.

With *Psycho* (1960), Hitchcock single-handedly revitalized the American horror genre and ushered in a form of horror that was both more viscerally aggressive (Herrmann's screeching violins and Tomasini's staccato editing) and more profoundly troubling (a boy-next-door type ultimately shown to harbor a boundless psychopathology). A significant influence on the later slasher genre, *Psycho*'s intensity seemed to signal a shift in American film treatment of violence, sexuality, and psychological aberration that would extend far beyond the horror film. *The Birds* (1963), Hitchcock's other full-blown horror film, has only lately been appreciated for its role in formalizing the environmental-monster-disaster subtype that had been associated before with 1950s science fiction films like *Them*. In other words, Hitchcock shifted the apocalyptic from science fiction to horror. After *The Birds*, monstrosity and social anarchy could derive as easily from human psychology as from scientific meddling.

In the late 1960s, Hitchcock's films betrayed a clear slowing. Such films as *Torn Curtain* (1966), *Topaz* (1969), and *Family Plot* (1976) fell far short of the great films of the 1950s and early '60s. Long plagued with health problems brought on by indulgences in food and spirits, Hitchcock died on April 29, 1980, but not before his knighthood, a lifetime achievement award from the American Film Institute, and widespread recognition that this son of an English greengrocer had quite possibly created the finest body of films in the history of cinema.

Bibliography

Spoto, Donald. *The Dark Side of Genius: The Life of Alfred Hitchcock*. New York: Ballantine, 1984.

Truffaut, François. *Hitchcock*. New York: Simon, 1984.

Wood, Robin. *Hitchcock's Films Revisited*. New York: Columbia UP, 1989.

Robert Baird

H-Net is an Internet-based group of discussion lists from humanistic and historical disciplines which announced itself to the world in December 1992. By late June 1993, it had three lists in operation with 500 pioneer subscribers. By July 1994 it had 28 public lists that reached over 12,500 subscribers in 50 countries, with about one million messages a month. H-Net met the growth challenge by adding new lists in specialty areas, new editors and a few non-moderating staff. Most were college professors at smaller schools from every part of the USA, plus Canada, Australia, Britain, Italy, and Japan. The editors were all volunteers who contribute their time out of sense that they were shaping the new communications system in academe. By the year 2000 there were over 80 lists, on topics such as history and computing, African history and culture, oral history, and regional history.

To look behind the scene, consider H-Net's second-largest list, H-AmStdy. In March 1995 it had 1,250 subscribers representing all 50 states and DC, plus 140 others from 35 foreign countries. Among the subscribers were the directors of American Studies programs at 60 colleges, 80 full professors, 130 associate professors, and 408 assistant professors. (Computer users tend to be younger scholars.) Subscribers came from 620 different institutions, with strong representation from the large graduate programs. Two out of three were faculty or graduate students in an American Studies program, with the rest drawn from English, history, and numerous other departments, libraries, and museums. They received an average of 44 messages a week, every week of the year. In 1994 this one list posted about 500 research related queries and 280 calls for papers. Its threads ranged from "Advice on Developing New American Studies Programs" and "Antiheroes in Oppositional Cultures" to "Wrestling in the 1950s" and "Zines." Many "threads" involved dozens of contributions, such as those on "Disney history," historical consciousness, multiculturalism and postmodernism, the relationship of American Studies to the social sciences, and home front culture during World War II. All subscribers discussed their own background, teaching and research in entries in an alphabetical "white pages" assembled by the editors.

The H-Net lists have become one of the major communications media for humanities scholars, with notable impact on teaching, research, and community involvement. They have by far their greatest impact on people at the periphery of academe—graduate students, independent scholars, professors at smaller colleges, professors in other disciplines for whom history is a secondary interest. The lists have these people talking to one another, and discovering that they too are part of the "Republic of Letters," that their ideas count, that their teaching innovations and problems are of national interest, that scholarship no longer is a monopoly of famous graduate schools.

Richard Jensen

Hoffman, Dustin (1937-), one of Hollywood's more versatile and successful actors, was born in Los Angeles, and educated at Los Angeles High School and Santa Monica City College. He was involved with the Pasadena Playhouse, 1956-58, then made his Broadway debut in *A Cook for Mr. General* (1961) and his film debut in *The Tiger Makes Out* (1967).

The Hoffman character is often an unfortunate victim of circumstances, ceaselessly combating negative forces surrounding him, constantly engaged in a tensely neurotic tournament with whatever blocks his progress. Even his low-key, autistic Raymond Babbitt in *Rain Man* (1988), which won an Oscar, exhibits an air of quiet desperation, suggesting the presence of turbulent forces attempting to break out of the character's imprisoning shell of disability. Hoffman's manifold acting persona reflects the destabilizing world of post-1950s America, in which nobody ever feels secure in anything whether in personal assurance of identity or relationship to historical change.

Dustin Hoffman's predominant traits of vulnerability and insecurity appeared earlier in his career with his acclaimed performance in *The Graduate* (1968). Yet, even then, the character was never a spontaneous creation. It was more a calculated naturalistic creation by an actor far older than his graduate character. His following films continued the actor's quest for versatility and confinement within the respective roles. In *Midnight Cowboy* (1969), he portrayed the doomed and vulnerable urban counterpart to the illusionary westerner persona adopted by Jon Voight in a film showing the death of a buddy tradition begun by American writers such as J. Fenimore Cooper. The odds were against his survival as they were for believing the claims of Hoffman's Jack Crabb of *Little Big Man* (1970) in being not just the oldest man in America but the sole survivor of Little Big Horn. In Arthur Penn's celebrated Western, Hoffman's Jack Crabb exhibited not just Shakespeare's axiom of each man playing many roles in his lifetime but anticipations of later postmodernist axioms concerning the impossibility of any person achieving a fixed historical position in American society.

In *Straw Dogs* (1971), Hoffman's pacifist professor flees from American campus life disrupted by the Vietnam war to seek refuge in rural Cornwall. But he discovers not just the violence he sought to escape from but also those peculiarly American atavistic traits which characterize his own culture. After brutally killing the invaders of his hearth, he expresses uncertainty over his next direction in the climax of the film. Bob Fosse's *Lenny* (1974) saw Hoffman play a character destroyed both by the forces of American puritanical conservatism as well as those cultural demons attacking him from within. His 1976 Jewish roles as Carl Bernstein in *All the President's Men* and Babe Levy in *Marathon Man* presented the Hoffman character as a potential victim of dark forces equally at home both within the American Dream and the nightmare side of the European enlightenment. During 1979, he gained his first Academy Award for a role in *Kramer vs. Kramer* of threatened husband combating another new "enemy" on the American scene—feminism— by showing that sensitive male Ted Kramer was a far better mother than his former wife. It anticipated his later role in *Tootsie* (1983) where his Michael Dorsey character proved he could play a woman much better than the real thing. In the 1990s Hoffman continued to take on a wide variety of roles, from a deliciously nasty Captain Hook in *Hook* (1991), to a doctor dealing with a deadly virus in *Outbreak* (1995), to a movie producer asked to create a war as part of election politics in *Wag the Dog* (1997), to a scientist dealing with a strange craft in *Sphere* (1998).

While Hoffman's several attempts at comedy have been less than successful (*Who Is Harry Kellerman and Why Is He Saying Those Terrible Things about Me?* [1971], *Straight Time* [1978], and *Ishtar* [1987]) and his one attempt at a screen lover forgettable (*John and Mary,* 1969), his most effective performances have often been in classical theater not always transferable to film. His London stage performance in Peter Hall's *The Merchant of Venice* and acclaimed 1984 Broadway performance as Willy Loman in *Death of a Salesman* reveal an actor aiming at a virtuosity not always effective on the most plastic medium of cinema. As if recog-

nizing this, Hoffman's highly made-up and parodic performance as Mumbles in *Dick Tracy* (1990) testify to this. He is an actor whose roles are really diverse in an attempt to achieve the most naturalistic dimensions possible.

Bibliography

Brode, Douglas. *The Films of Dustin Hoffman*. Secaucus: Citadel, 1983.

Freedland, Michael. *Dustin: A Biography of Dustin Hoffman*. London: Virgin, 1989.

Lenburg, Jeff. *Dustin Hoffman, Hollywood's Anti-Hero*. New York: St. Martin's, 1983.

Tony Williams

Holiday, Billie (Eleanora Halliday) (1915-1959), has been, not so arguably, the most influential female jazz vocalist in history. Perhaps only Louis Armstrong has exerted more overall influence on vocals. Holiday, herself, attests to his influence along with Bessie Smith's on her style. In fact, she ran errands for a local madam in Baltimore just so she could listen to their recordings in the brothel. Basically, Holiday approached her music in the same manner as a jazz instrumentalist, more specifically, like Louis Armstrong on trumpet.

She employed great tonal variation, used vibrato to significant effect, reshaped melodic lines, and molded lyrics to fit her emotions. She had superb diction, honed in numerous dives on her way up. Her ear was excellent and her taste and innate honesty came through even after her voice had faded from self-abuse.

Holiday was born in Philadelphia, PA, and raised in Baltimore, MD. She moved to New York in 1928 or 1929. In 1933, John Hammond "discovered" her singing in Monette's club. Hammond had gone to hear Monette sing the blues. Instead he found Holiday filling in for her. He gave Holiday her first press notice, a positive one, in *Melody Maker*. In the same year she changed her name to Billie Holiday, taken from her favorite actress, Billie Dove. She also made her first recording, which was with Benny Goodman.

In 1935, she opened at the Apollo Theater and recorded her first sides with Teddy Wilson, "I Wished on the Moon," and "Miss Jones to You." These sold well, and a classic formula for recording Holiday was born—simply surround her with fine musicians and sit back. From 1935 to 1942, she released a series of recordings with Lester Young, whom she had nicknamed Prez. These are considered among the best jazz records ever made.

In 1939, she opened at Cafe Society, a big career move. "Strange Fruit," about a southern lynching, became a hit in spite of the fears of Decca. In fact, Milt Gabler received permission to issue it on his own Commodore label because it was considered too controversial.

It was this ability to convey the essential emotions of a tune that led Milt Gabler, longtime A & R man at Decca, to present Holiday as a "pop" singer. By that, he meant to have her sing songs from what is now often termed "The Great American Songbook" instead of blues or "fast" numbers. More specifically, however, he meant "torch" songs, such as "Lover Man," "Don't Explain," "Crazy, He Calls Me," and

"Good Morning, Heartache." Not to consider her performance of these songs "jazz" would be to question the meaning of jazz itself. On these slower numbers, one can truly appreciate her alteration of rhythm to convey her reading of the meaning of the lyrics, a trick she certainly learned from Armstrong but had reinforced by her long association with Lester Young and Teddy Wilson.

Holiday was so popular at one point in her career, the 1940s, that she helped bring down Jim Crow practices in jazz. As she remarked, she and Teddy Wilson, her pianist, were often the only black faces on 52nd Street, known as "Swing Street." Even earlier, in 1937, she worked with Artie Shaw's popular big band. Shaw insisted that club owners in Kentucky, where the band was touring, allow her to use the same entrance as other band members. Moreover, Shaw refused to allow her to stay anywhere else but in Kentucky's best hotels.

But Holiday suffered from many personal problems, including bad luck with men and a heroin addiction that eventually killed her. In 1947, she began serving a long prison sentence for drug use. Upon her release she had a triumphant Carnegie Hall engagement, but it was clear that her problems were not over and her voice was failing her.

A 1956 Carnegie Hall concert timed to coincide with her autobiography, *Lady Sings the Blues*, provides a retrospective of her career. That and a triumphant Newport Jazz Festival appearance in 1957 demonstrated that, although her voice no longer had the sweetness it once did, she had lost none of her ability to infuse a song with *her* meaning and emotion. Indeed, one of the more memorable moments in jazz came in December 1957, not long before her death. CBS decided to televise a live jazz program on its *Omnibus* series. Holiday could not believe she was to appear in jeans instead of a gown. The crowning moment of that superb telecast was the reunion of Lester Young and Billie Holiday. It was their first meeting in a number of years and also their last. Holiday's look as she gazes at the President of the Tenor Saxophone says it all. Her own solo on Milt Gabler's "Fine and Mellow" redefined the meaning of the blues. All the pain of her star-crossed life emerged in that twelve-bar form.

Bibliography

Gabler, Milt. *Billie Holiday: The Complete Decca Recordings.* 1991.

Gammond, Peter. *Oxford Companion to Popular Music.* New York: Oxford UP, 1991.

Holiday, Billie, and William Dufty. *Lady Sings the Blues.* Garden City: Doubleday, 1956.

Peretti, Burton. *The Creation of Jazz.* Urbana: U of Illinois P, 1992.

Placksin, Sally. *American Women in Jazz.* New York: Wideview, 1982.

Taylor, Billy. *Jazz Piano.* Dubuque: Brown, 1982.

Frank A. Salamone

Holiday Decorations. During culturally specified occasions of festivity, religious observation, or commemoration known as holidays, and at related events such as celebrations of the life-cycle, homes and other buildings are sometimes customarily adorned with evergreens, flowers, fruits, vegetables, ribbons, drawings, candles, signs, and many other items. Domiciles and places of business are in this way marked, much as participants in rituals are marked by special clothing, face and body paint, masks, tattoos, and so forth. Ritual theorists such as Victor Turner see this as a means of suggesting that the individual occupies a special status, often a transitional stage between two social roles in life, e.g., single-married. In a parallel way, people frequently signal participation in the "time out of time" of social and calendrical festivals by decorating homes and other buildings. This custom has existed since at least the time of Julius Caesar and the Roman era, when evergreens were displayed during the year-end festivals of Saturnalia and Kalends.

In the contemporary period, Christmas remains the day for which people decorate most extensively, both indoors and outside, but people are decorating increasingly for other annual holidays and seasons. In fact, seasonal decoration of one sort or another can frequently be found adorning a single house through the entire year. The display of "harvest" fruits and vegetables is appropriate from September through November. At Halloween, the pumpkins are carved into jack-o'-lanterns and images of witches, ghosts, bats, and otherworldly or nocturnal creatures are added, but these are removed shortly after October 31, while the Indian corn, squash, and uncarved or painted pumpkins generally remain through to Thanksgiving before giving way to the evergreens and electric lights of Christmas. Some people display wreaths for all the holidays, or add and subtract various holiday symbols on a single wreath as appropriate: a red ribbon and a heart in February, a green ribbon and a shamrock in March. After the Easter symbols of rabbits, eggs, and perhaps a specifically Christian item, flowers and flags are most common through May and the summer holidays from Memorial Day through Flag Day, the Fourth of July, and Labor Day.

In addition, people display the flag of their alma mater on days of important sporting contests, and may publicly adorn their houses for other special events or unusual times. People decorate for the Super Bowl and the International Olympics, and a great many people displayed yellow ribbons or facsimiles during the Gulf War, and before that, during the period when American citizens were held hostage in Iran. Indeed, the range of potential decorations is extensive, and the items chosen may have very different meanings according to the contexts for which they are used. In some parts of Ireland, for instance, it was once customary to put a lit candle in a window in each of the four walls of a house at Halloween, in the belief that the souls of departed family members would be returning to their home; or alternatively, as a protection against malevolent spirits on this night of wandering souls. The custom is similar to that of placing electric candles in windows at Christmas, which are sometimes said to light the way for the Christ child, or for Santa Claus. However, even these examples, as closely related as they are, show significant differences in purpose and underlying beliefs, and reflect varying national and regional traditions. Other decorative acts, such as placing a jack-o'-lantern on one's porch, is not an intrinsically magical, religious, or spiritual act; it is instead generally emblematic of family activities.

The range and use of decorations varies widely. Holiday decorations are derived from the symbolism appropriate to the seasonal event. Their presence inside and outside signals the occurrence of a special period of time and help creates the feelings thought to be appropriate to that time. They also signal the participation by both domestic and commercial establishments in the culturally defined flow of time and special events. A sign of the growth in popularity of such decorations is the extent to which they have become commercialized. Following the model of Christmas lights, electric lights are commercially available in the shape of jack-o'-lanterns for Halloween, carrots and eggs for Easter, and even flags for the Fourth of July. Another example is the availability of seasonal flags appropriate for various holidays and times of year, which are increasingly common.

An interesting development is the rise of public decorations for rites of passage of the life-cycle. Houses are decorated for births, birthdays, homecomings, and retirements. Ironically, the practice of displaying a black wreath on the front door to indicate the death and wake of a family member has all but disappeared, along with the home wake itself. The use of signs and balloons to announce births, birthdays, and retirements, however, is often done in an anonymous way. The passers-by on the street (or the highway) do not know the individuals referred to. This may reflect a shifting sense of neighborhood community. Rites of passage traditionally require witnesses to note the social changes. With the rise of house decorations, the witnesses become the general (anonymous) public.

Decorating for holidays, rituals, and other festivals and celebrations, then, while a very old custom, is enjoying a widespread growth in contemporary American society, in terms of both when decorations are displayed, and what the decorations are. The contexts they reflect and the range of meanings they express is as varied as the population itself. We can say, however, that holiday decorations have become a year-round phenomenon and a major form of popular culture.

Bibliography

Santino, Jack. *All around the Year: Holidays and Celebrations in American Life.* Urbana: U of Illinois P, 1994.

——. "The Folk Assemblage Autumn: Tradition and Creativity in Halloween Folk Art." *Folk Art and Art Worlds.* Ed. John Michael Vlach and Simon Bronner. Logan: Utah State UP, 1992.

——. "Yellow Ribbons and Seasonal Flags: The Folk Assemblage of War." *Journal of American Folklore* 105.415 (1992): 19-33.

——, ed. *Halloween and Other Festivals of Death and Life.* Knoxville: U of Tennessee P, 1994.

Jack Santino

See also

Christmas Decorations

Easter Eggs

Holly, Buddy (1936-1959), was a singer, guitarist, and composer who became one of the most important and innovative figures of early rock 'n' roll. Charles Hardin Holley was born in Lubbock, TX, to a family that loved country music (Jimmie Rodgers and the Carter Family). A precocious musical talent who learned piano and guitar, at 13 he formed a group that performed what they called "Western bop" at high-school dances and on local radio. After opening for a Bill Haley concert, Holly made some country-flavored demonstration records for Decca between 1954 and 1956 but they were not commercially successful. A shared bill with Elvis Presley inspired Holly's transition to rock 'n' roll. He formed a new group, the Crickets, whose members included drummer Jerry Allison, bass guitarist Joe Mauldin, and guitarist Niki Sullivan. Holly is credited with first popularizing the two-guitar, bass and drum lineup that became the rock standard.

In early 1957, Holly and the Crickets traveled to Clovis, NM, to record for Norman Petty, an innovator of multitrack recording well suited to Holly's unique guitar style. Once he obtained a contract with Brunswick, some of Holly's songs soon rocketed to the top of the national charts. "That'll Be the Day" (cowritten with Jerry Allison) became their first hit in 1957, even reaching No. 2 in the rhythm and blues charts; it was followed by "Oh Boy" (1957), "Not Fade Away" (1957), "Everyday" (1957), "Peggy Sue" (1957), "Think It Over" (1958), "Maybe Baby" (1958), and "Rave On" (1958). Several of these songs, most notably "Peggy Sue" (which reached No. 3), were released without the Crickets. Later Holly would issue other important songs, including "It's So Easy to Fall in Love" (1958), "Heartbeat" (1959), and Paul Anka's "It Doesn't Matter Anymore" (1959).

By 1958, Holly's career was in flux. He toured Britain with the Crickets, achieving massive popularity there. But soon he tired of touring and sought more independence; he left the group to pursue a solo career, angrily splitting with his mentor and manager Petty. Holly moved to New York, the hometown of his new wife, Puerto Rico-born Maria Elena Santiago. A restless spirit, he began taking acting lessons. His new backing group included future "country outlaw" superstar Waylon Jennings, whose first record Holly produced, on bass guitar and backing vocals. In need of cash to further his career, Holly and his band embarked on a concert tour with pop stars like Ritchie Valens and the Big Bopper (J. P. Richardson) that soon developed problems in the frozen Midwest. On February 3, 1959, after a concert in Clear Lake, IA, Holly was tired and wanted to get to their next stop, Morehead, MN. Having chartered a plane whose pilot proved inexperienced, Holly was killed in a plane crash that also took the lives of Valens and Richardson. He was 22 years old. Ironically the Crickets were preparing to rejoin Holly in the Midwest. This tragic event was immortalized as "the day the music died" by Don McLean in his 1970 hit "American Pie," symbolizing both the end of pioneering rock music and perhaps also the loss of innocence that characterized the turbulent 1960s to follow. After receiving news of the tragedy the Morehead organizers hired a replacement band headed by a then-unknown local musician named Bobby Velline (later Bobby Vee), who specialized in Holly songs, to continue the tour; besides establishing his own successful career Vee would also provide the first job for young Holly-inspired Minnesotan Bobby Zimmerman (later Bob Dylan). The Crickets continued as a group for some years with fluctuating personnel, remaining popular in Britain.

Holly cultivated something of a rebel image in his songs and style, as well as in his electrifying live performances, yet he also reflected a certain innocence in contrast to the hard-edged Elvis. Unlike Bill Haley or Elvis Presley, Holly's music betrays little black influence; the western swing and country base seems more obvious, although he sometimes performed songs by Chuck Berry (with whom he toured). Yet in 1957 the Crickets became the first white group to play New York's Apollo Theatre, whose managers apparently thought the act was black.

Holly's synthesis of diverse country, pop, and gospel influences, along with Chuck Berry's stylings, have been described as the two major influences on 1960s rock. John Lennon chose the name "Beatles" as a take-off on Crickets, whose name also had two meanings (Holly once considered naming his own group the Beetles). The British group the Hollies were named after their musical hero in 1963. Holly was the initial influence on Rolling Stone Mick Jagger. It is not difficult to spot clear Hollyesque strands in the music of Creedence Clearwater Revival, Tommy Roe, the Beatles ("I'll Follow the Sun"), Gerry and the Pacemakers ("It's Going to Be All Right"), the Kinks, and the Mersey School generally. Both George Harrison and Johnny Cash emulated Holly's guitar playing. Rockers like Linda Ronstadt, Blind Faith, the Rolling Stones, and the Grateful Dead recorded his songs. In the 1970s, Elvis Costello cultivated a Holly-inspired appearance; later Marshall Crenshaw would be widely compared to Holly. In 1979, the film *The Buddy Holly Story* (starring Gary Busey in the title role) chronicled his brief but fabulous career. His biographer, John Goldrosen, believes Holly's music so closely mirrors the optimistic American spirit it can never die. Ultimately he stands with Haley, Presley, Berry, Jerry Lee Lewis, Little Richard, and Fats Domino as one of the seminal figures in early rock.

Bibliography

Goldrosen, John. *Buddy Holly: His Life and Music*. New York: Quick Fox, 1979.

Laing, Dave. *Buddy Holly*. London: Studio Vista, 1971.

Tobler, John. *The Buddy Holly Story*. London: Plexus, 1979.

Ward, Ed, et al. *Rock of Ages: The Rolling Stone History of Rock & Roll*. New York: Rolling Stone, 1986.

White, Timothy, ed. *Rock Lives: Profiles and Interviews*. New York: Holt, 1990.

Craig A. Lockard

Hollywood Boulevard may, to the casual viewer, appear rundown, perhaps even tawdry, but along either side of it remain perhaps the clearest reminders of the golden age of Hollywood, the 1920s and 1930s, and its eclectic architecture: Spanish, English Tudor, American Colonial, Art Deco, Mayan, Chinese.

Among the famous edifices that actually line Hollywood Boulevard perhaps the best known is Mann's Chinese Theatre, originally Grauman's Chinese Theatre (see entry). Built in 1927 for $2 million, the Chinese Theatre is famous in part for its forecourt, in which nearly 200 stars have left their footprints and signatures in cement as part of the Hollywood Walk of Fame (see below).

Another theater further down Hollywood Boulevard is the Pantages Theater, built as a movie palace in 1930 and operating today as a legitimate theater, while retaining all of the original detail work, both inside and out. Also on Hollywood Boulevard is the El Capitan Building, an erstwhile theater built in 1926 by Hollywood pioneer Charles E. Toberman. Originally home to Loew's Hollywood theater (Hollywood's first legitimate stage theater), the six-story, 97,000-sq. ft. building was converted for use as a movie theater in 1941. While over the years the building has housed a variety of corporate offices, in 1984 it was sold for $2.8 million to investors interested in renovating the Hollywood landmark.

Close by the Chinese Theatre is the Roosevelt Hotel, built in 1927 and decorated inside and out in the Spanish Revival style. Home to stars and site of various film productions, the Roosevelt was renovated in 1984-85 for a reported $25 million. Among the areas restored are the Blossom Room, the hotel's ballroom and site of the 1929 Academy Awards dinner, and the hotel's pool.

Also of note along Hollywood Boulevard is Capitol Records (once home to such monumental recording stars as Peggy Lee and Nat Cole), the first round office building ever built. At the time of its erection (1955), the building was touted as remarkably efficient, with 85 percent of its floor space open to active use. Built for $2 million, the 13-story, concrete and glass office building gives the illusion that it is floating above its lot, due in large part to its small first floor (90 ft. in diameter).

The legendary center of Hollywood, the corner of Hollywood and Vine, looks rather undistinguished today. A plaque posted there in 1953 by the Board of Supervisors, the Broadway-Hale Department Store chain, and the Historical Society of Southern California reads: "Hollywood was given its name by pioneers Mr. and Mrs. Harvey H. Wilcox. They subdivided their ranch in 1887 and called two dirt crossroads Prospect Avenue and Weyse Avenue. Prospect Avenue, the main artery, was renamed Hollywood Boulevard and Weyse Avenue became Vine Street. This was the origin of Hollywood and Vine."

Also worthy of note is the Hollywood Walk of Fame. Proposed in 1955 by Hollywood Chamber of Commerce member Harry Sugarman, the walk was meant to "immortalize Hollywood's icons with sidewalk stars." In fact, the first eight placed in 1958 still remain at the corner of Hollywood Boulevard and Highland Avenue: Olive Borden, Ronald Colman, Louise Fazenda, Preston Foster, Burt Lancaster, Edward Sedgwick, Ernest Torrence, and Joanne Woodward. Today nearly 2,000 stars grace Hollywood Boulevard.

In 1935, Frederick's of Hollywood moved into the former Kress & Co. building, launching a lingerie department store on Hollywood Boulevard, and over the years the building and the company have maintained their flamboyant image and business. Once recognizable by its purple facade

Norma Talmadge, Mary Pickford, and Adolph Zukor were among the first stars to leave their marks at Mann's Chinese Theatre (formerly Grauman's). Photo courtesy of Mark McDermott.

and hot pink awnings, the building underwent a $300,000 facelift in 1989.

Another site of interest located at the corner of Hollywood Boulevard and Highland is the Max Factor Beauty Museum, opened in 1984 in honor of its founder and in commemoration of the company's 75 years in business. Included in the Art-Deco building are a huge variety of memorabilia dating back as far as 1904, with everything from cosmetic pulverizing machines to vintage Max Factor ads. Beyond revolutionizing the makeups used in Hollywood productions, Factor also invented many of the cosmetics more generally worn today, including false eyelashes, lip gloss, and pancake makeup.

Other landmarks along Hollywood Boulevard have had less success surviving over the years. For instance, the Garden Court Apartments, home to such Hollywood notables as studio executive Louis B. Mayer, director Mack Sennett, and comic actor Fatty Arbuckle, was declared a historic monument in 1981 but demolished in 1984 due to disrepair and vandalism. Additionally, the fabled Brown Derby Restaurant—where Clark Gable proposed to Carole Lombard and where Marlene Dietrich made Hollywood headlines by wearing slacks in public—was demolished in 1994.

Bibliography

Coppa and Avery Associates. *Architecture and Preservation in California: A Guide to Historic Sites, Historic Homes and Churches.* Monticello: Vance, 1981.

Futagawa, Yukio. *California Architecture.* Tokyo: A.D.A. Edita, 1985.

Harris, Frank. *A Guide to Contemporary Architecture in Southern California.* Los Angeles: Watling, 1951.

Roberta F. Green

Hollywood Ten, The, is a group of eight screenwriters and two directors who were imprisoned for contempt of Congress and blacklisted by the motion picture industry. In October 1947, a Congressional committee subpoenaed these ten plus nine other Hollywood figures to testify about alleged "un-American activities." Of the 19, 16 were screenwriters. The majority of the 19 belonged or had belonged to the Communist Party.

The House Un-American Activities Committee (HUAC) called 11 of the 19 as witnesses. Playwright Bertolt Brecht testified politely and left immediately for East Germany. The remaining ten, apparently the individuals against whom the committee had the most evidence, had supported reelection of Franklin Roosevelt, opposed fascism in Europe, and favored progressive unions in Hollywood. HUAC suspended the hearings before calling any other subpoenaed witnesses.

Many of the Hollywood Ten had active, successful careers in 1947. Dalton Trumbo counted among the highest-paid screenwriters, while Lester Cole stood ready for promotion to writer-producer at MGM. Although young, Ring Lardner, Jr., had already won an Academy Award. Writer

398

Adrian Scott and director Edward Dmytryk (see entry) had contracts at RKO. Albert Maltz, a writer popular at the studios, chose to freelance. The remaining four—writers John Howard Lawson, Samuel Ornitz, and Alvah Bessie, and director Herbert Biberman—had lapsed or modest careers.

Causes for the imprisonment and blacklisting of the Hollywood Ten lie in the politics of the time, and the character of the film industry. Anticommunist efforts grew during the 1940s. In 1944, the Motion Picture Alliance for the Preservation of American Ideals formed, including union leader Roy Brewer, actors Gary Cooper, Robert Montgomery, and Ronald Reagan, and studio executives Jack Warner and Walt Disney. This association invited Congress to investigate alleged subversion at the studios.

Congressional representatives opposed to the New Deal readily agreed, for hearings investigating Communist activity in Hollywood served them well. The hearings helped anti-New Deal politicians win elections, allowed them to attack Roosevelt appointees, and generated welcome publicity.

Under the direction of J. Parnell Thomas (R-NJ), HUAC held hearings to establish that the few pro-Russian films (*Mission to Moscow*, Curtiz, 1943, for example) made during World War II constituted evidence of Communist subversion. Thomas suggested that writers had injected films with Communist propaganda, and that the Roosevelt administration had improperly pressured Hollywood to produce pro-Soviet films. Given that Russia was an ally and that the federal Office of War Information supported production of those films along with many other patriotic war films, testimony by "friendly" witnesses proved neither of Thomas's points convincingly.

Motion picture producers initially minimized HUAC's concern over Communist influence in Hollywood, testifying that they guarded against subversion from their personnel. Several directors, writers, and actors formed a Committee for the First Amendment to defend Hollywood against governmental intrusion. This group flew Humphrey Bogart, Lauren Bacall, Groucho Marx, and others to Washington to protest HUAC's hearings.

Support from within the industry evaporated as the Ten testified and were cited for contempt. Matching the rudeness of HUAC Chair Thomas, some of the Ten belligerently argued with and shouted at him. The Committee for the First Amendment returned to Hollywood, while producers met in New York to formulate containment policy. Fearing boycotts from anticommunist groups, producers reacted as they had to previous external threats—they vowed internal regulation.

Publicly, producers proclaimed they would not knowingly employ Communists. In practice, this meant a blacklist only of the Hollywood Ten. The Ten found no work at the studios while they unsuccessfully appealed their convictions, nor were they hired after they served their sentences of 6-12 months. (Convicted of taking kickbacks, J. Parnell Thomas joined two of the Ten in a Connecticut prison.) Some of the Hollywood Ten took menial jobs. Cole worked in a warehouse and Bessie at a nightclub. Some left the country for England (Scott) or Mexico (Maltz). Some sold scripts using the names of other writers ("fronts") or pseudonyms. Trumbo won an Academy Award in 1956 for *The Brave One*, penned under the name Robert Rich.

The industry's containment strategy failed when HUAC reopened hearings in 1951. Witnesses either gave names of fellow "subversives," or faced blacklisting. Producers fired 324 people by the end of 1951. The blacklist did not end until the 1960s, by which time it had ruined many careers and lives.

Bibliography
Carr, Robert K. *The House Committee on Un-American Activities, 1944-1950*. Ithaca: Cornell UP, 1952.
Ceplair, Larry, and Steven Englund. *The Inquisition in Hollywood: Politics in the Film Community, 1930-1960*. Berkeley: U of California P, 1979.
Cogley, John. *Report on Blacklisting: I. Movies*. New York: Fund for the Republic, 1956; rpt. ed. New York: Arno and the *New York Times*, 1972.
Cole, Lester. *Hollywood Red*. Palo Alto: Ramparts, 1981.
Navasky, Victor S. *Naming Names*. New York: Viking, 1980.

Denise Hartsough

Holmes, Sherlock, is without doubt the most famous fictional detective of all time, one of the most widely recognized characters in literature, and the subject of more films than any other fictional character (see next entry). The creation of British writer Arthur Conan Doyle (see entry), Holmes first appeared in December 1887 in the pages of *Beeton's Christmas Annual*, where his investigation of a murder, *A Study in Scarlet*, was narrated by his fictional friend and associate, Dr. John H. Watson. The story's popularity led to a second long narrative, *The Sign of the Four*, in 1890. Finally, in July 1891, the first of 56 short stories chronicling Holmes's adventures was published in *The Strand*. These were eventually collected into five volumes: *The Adventures of Sherlock Holmes* (1892), *The Memoirs of Sherlock Holmes* (1894), *The Return of Sherlock Holmes* (1905), *His Last Bow* (1917), and *The Casebook of Sherlock Holmes* (1927). Two additional novels, *The Hound of the Baskervilles* (1902) and *The Valley of Fear* (1915), complete the canon authored by Doyle. Many unauthorized accounts of Holmes's exploits—parodies and pastiches—appeared during Doyle's era and have continued to see print ever since.

The full measure of Sherlock Holmes's appeal lies in Doyle's first-rate story-telling, inventive plots, and memorable characterizations. *The Hound of the Baskervilles* is usually regarded as Doyle's supreme achievement in this regard. The stories also capture the rich atmosphere of Edwardian England, complete with gaslights and hansom cabs, that continues to attract readers. The address of Holmes's London flat, 221B Baker Street, has become familiar around the world.

In 1893, midway through Holmes's fictional career, Doyle sought to dispatch his creation in a fatal encounter with the Napoleon of Crime, Dr. Moriarty, at the Reichenbach Falls. Popular demand and financial considerations led to Holmes's return in 1901 and full resurrection in 1903.

Upon learning of his companion's supposed death, Dr. Watson eulogized him as "the best and wisest man whom I have ever known." Millions of readers have shared Watson's sentiments.

Bibliography

Harrison, Michael. *The London of Sherlock Holmes*. New York: Drake, 1972.

Starrett, Vincent. *The Private Life of Sherlock Holmes*. Chicago: U of Chicago P, 1960.

Tracy, Jack. *The Encyclopedia Sherlockiana*. Garden City: Doubleday, 1977.

J. K. Van Dover

See also
Classical Mysteries

Holmes, Sherlock (in Film), has appeared more than any other fictional character, having been portrayed in well over 100 European and American films. Included are more than 40 feature-length sound films. Many of the films were early silent shorts, so an exact number is unavailable; however, in 1991, Granada Television estimated that 117 men had performed the role of Holmes. While all of these films feature the detective created by Arthur Conan Doyle, the majority are not directly based on the plots of Conan Doyle's stories. The drawings of Sidney Paget, the stories' original illustrator, who gave Holmes his deerstalker cap, have prevailed as the visual standard for Holmes performers.

Holmes first appeared on the screen in a 1903 silent film titled *Sherlock Holmes Baffled*, a short American film produced by American Mutoscope and Bioscope Company. While Holmes films were steadily produced in America and Europe, it was not until a 1912 series of two-reel films that the original stories were used as the basis of the films. This series, featuring Georges Treville, a French actor, as Holmes, was apparently made with Conan Doyle's collaboration.

Those actors who have most strongly been identified with the detective are those who portrayed him in series. Eille Norwood was the first film actor to become firmly identified with the role of Holmes. Beginning in 1921, Norwood starred as Holmes in three annual series of British Sherlock Holmes two-reelers, and the six-reel productions of *The Hound of the Baskervilles* (1921) and *The Sign of the Four* (1923). A contemporary contender to Norwood's Holmes was William Gillette, an American actor who had written the play, *Sherlock Holmes*, for himself in 1899, with pieces of *A Scandal in Bohemia* and *The Final Problem* and, establishing something of a precedent for screen Holmeses, a romance added to the literary Holmes's apparently celibate life. Gillette's linkage with the role resulted from his regular revivals of the play on the stage and in a 1935 radio adaptation, although Gillette also starred in a silent film version of the play in 1916. (In 1922, Gillette's play was filmed again in a version starring John Barrymore.) Clive Brook laid a temporary claim to the role as the first of the talking film Holmeses in three American films, beginning with *The Return of Sherlock Holmes* in 1929. It was in these films that the detective was first relocated into contemporary times; the second film, *Paramount on Parade*, presented Holmes dying in a comedy sketch with Paramount characters Philo Vance and Fu Manchu. Brook's British contemporary Arthur Wontner has been widely acclaimed as the greatest and most accurate of the screen Holmeses for his five performances beginning with *The Sleeping Cardinal* (*Sherlock Holmes' Fatal Hour*) in 1931, but Wontner is largely unknown because his films have been unavailable to wide audiences in the years since their release.

By contrast, Basil Rathbone's Holmes has been steadily available to the American public, insuring that the actor has become the most pervasive image of Sherlock Holmes. Rathbone and Nigel Bruce, who continued in the film tradition of portraying a buffoonish avuncular Dr. Watson, were first paired by Twentieth Century-Fox in the very successful *The Hound of the Baskervilles* (1939). An immediate sequel, *The Adventures of Sherlock Holmes* (officially based on the Gillette play) was rushed out the same year.

Since the Rathbone films, Holmes films tend to present "realistic" interpretations of the detective based in the values and popular theories of identity of their day. Often grounding their claims to authenticity in the discovery of new Watson manuscripts, these films present Holmes as increasingly involved in real historical events with real historical personages.

All three of these adjustments can be seen in the most noted of the post-Rathbone films, Billy Wilder's *The Private Life of Sherlock Holmes* (1969). Wilder presents a Holmes (Robert Stephens) who is deceived into assisting a ring of pre-World War I German spies in exposing a British submarine experiment which, incidentally, explains Loch Ness monster sightings. Reflecting its time of release, brother Moriarty's secret work for the government is presented more critically than in Conan Doyle's stories. The film is probably best remembered for its implication, made less obvious in the final edit, that Holmes is homosexual.

The Seven Per Cent Solution (1976) revealed Moriarty to be an innocent mathematician onto whom Holmes (Nicol Williamson) has projected his cocaine-induced paranoid delusions. Watson (Robert Duvall) tricks Holmes into consulting Sigmund Freud (Alan Arkin) before the two solve a case. Both *A Study in Terror* (1965, British) and *Murder by Decree* (1979, Canadian-British) found Holmes (John Neville and Christopher Plummer) solving the Jack the Ripper murders.

Child-oriented Holmes stories include the Steven Spielberg-produced *Young Sherlock Holmes* (1985), which recounts the schoolboy meeting of Holmes, Watson, and Moriarty. The young Holmes (Nicholas Rowe) is moved to play detective in equal parts by attempts to impress a girl and by the suppressed psychological trauma of having interrupted his mother's infidelity; the film ends with Holmes doing an Indiana Jones turn in an Egyptomaniacal finale. *The Great Mouse Detective* (1986), Walt Disney's animated adaptation of Eve Titus's *Basil of Baker Street* presents a mouse and rat version of the Holmes stories, with Holmes's feet making a brief cameo at the beginning of the film.

There have been numerous film parodies of the Holmes character, notably Gene Wilder's *The Adventures of Sherlock*

Holmes's Smarter Brother (1975), *Without a Clue* (1988), which revealed that Dr. Watson was the true brains of the operation, and the darkly comic *They Might Be Giants* (1971).

Among television films, the most iconically significant may be *Sherlock Holmes in New York* (1976), which finds Roger Moore as Holmes and Patrick MacNee as Watson pursuing Moriarty (John Huston) to America, where the possibility is raised that Holmes has sired a son by actress Irene Adler (Charlotte Rampling). Charlton Heston also essayed the role in *Crucifer of Blood* (1991), adapted from a stage adaptation of *The Sign of the Four*. Finally, Jeremy Brett, who played Watson to Heston's Holmes in the stage production of *Crucifer of Blood*, portrays Holmes in the Granada television series which has been seen in America as part of the PBS *Mystery* series as well as on the A&E channel. The Granada series intends to produce faithful adaptations of all of the Conan Doyle Holmes stories and novels, leading to the replacement of the buffoonish Watson with more soldierly portrayals (first by David Burke and then Edward Hardwicke) and the disappearance of Holmes's deerstalker cap from urban cases.

Bibliography

Davies, David Stuart. *Holmes of the Movies: The Screen Career of Sherlock Holmes.* New York: Bramhall, 1978.

Eyles, Allen. *Sherlock Holmes: A Centenary Celebration.* New York: Harper, 1986.

Haydock, Ron. *Deerstalker!: Holmes and Watson on Screen.* Metuchen: Scarecrow, 1978.

Steinbrunner, Chris. *The Films of Sherlock Holmes.* Secaucus: Citadel, 1978.

Greg Metcalf

Holt, Victoria, is a pseudonym for one of the world's best-selling writers, the late Eleanor Hibbert (1906-1993). Born in London and educated privately, Hibbert also wrote variously as Jean Plaidy, Eleanor Burford, Kathleen Kellow, Ellalice Tate, and Philippa Carr. As Jean Plaidy she wrote over 80 novels on various periods of English and French history, but as Victoria Holt she became a hugely popular and successful author in the United States. With the publication of the first Holt novel, *Mistress of Mellyn* (1960), many wondered whether Daphne du Maurier or Mary Stewart could be writing these popular tales of suspense under a pseudonym. Throughout the 1960s and 1970s, the heyday of the romantic suspense or gothic novel, Holt became a regular on the best-seller lists along with others who excelled in this genre, particularly Mary Stewart and Phyllis A. Whitney.

Holt's stories follow a loose formula. Their protagonists are young women of gentle birth but impoverished circumstances, forced to rely upon others for their security, most often in Victorian England, though Holt made one foray into the present with *Bride of Pendorric* (1963), one of her best works. Sometimes the author takes her heroines away from England itself, to Australia or the Far East, as in *The Pride of the Peacock* (1976) and *The House of a Thousand Lanterns* (1974). Whatever the setting, Holt's heroines find themselves in danger from an unnamed menace as they attempt to

unravel a mystery or discover a past secret that affects their own future. They endure terror amid villainy and madness and find self-knowledge before a brooding hero provides a rescue. Holt's stories offer rich atmosphere and compelling psychological portraits.

Bibliography

Hinckley, Karen. "Victoria Holt." *Twentieth-Century Crime and Mystery Writers.* Ed. Lesley Henderson. Chicago: St. James, 1991.

Lambert, Bruce. *The New York Times* 21 Jan. 1993.

Mussell, Kay. "Victoria Holt." *Twentieth-Century Romance and Historical Writers.* Ed. Lesley Henderson. Chicago: St. James, 1990. 327-31.

Who's Who 1993.

Dean James
Charlene E. Bunnell

See also

Gothic Mysteries
Thriller, The

Home Alone (1990), a family comedy written and produced by John Hughes (*Uncle Buck*) and directed by Chris Columbus, scored a direct box-office hit for Twentieth Century-Fox. The sequel—*Home Alone 2: Lost in New York* (1992)—and the usual commercial fallout inevitably followed. Starring Catherine O'Hara, John Heard, Joe Pesci, Daniel Stern, and John Candy, *Home Alone* also gave Americans child-star Macaulay Culkin; his line "I don't think so" soon became famous.

Eight-year-old Kevin McCallister (Macaulay Culkin) is accidentally left behind in Chicago while family and relations visit Paris over Christmas. Kevin's mother (Catherine O'Hara) realizes the mistake, flies back to Scranton, and from there travels to Chicago (the McCallister residence) in a rented van with John Candy, the "Polka King of the Midwest." Thus the film actually alternates between Kevin's adventures in the home and those of his mother on the road. Recalcitrant son and anguished, guilt-ridden mother are finally reunited at home just in time for Christmas.

Kevin enjoys having the house to himself, but his cute domestic adventures soon turn serious. Two clownish thieves, Joe Pesci (Harry) and Daniel Stern (Marv), plan on robbing the houses in Kevin's white, upper-class neighborhood.

Kevin's successful defense of his house provides *Home Alone* with its most hilarious scenes. He booby-traps the house with such ingenious weapons as toy cars scattered over the floor, paint cans which drop on the thieves, a red-hot doorknob, and his brother's pet tarantula. The sequence matches explosive slapstick comedy with seemingly indestructible cartoonish characters.

Home Alone 2: Lost in New York is repetitive, less funny, and far more violent than *Home Alone*. Kevin again is separated from his parents at Christmas (they fly to Miami while he flies to New York). Culkin again outwits Pesci and Stern (now The Sticky Bandits) in a violently booby-trapped house. Of the two, *Home Alone* is the film that audiences will remember.

Bibliography

Ansen, David. "Walt and the Waif: *Home Alone 2: Lost in New York*. Directed by Chris Columbus." *Newsweek* 23 Nov. 1992: 76-77.

Moore, Suzanne. "Film: Out of Time." *New Statesman and Society* 14 Dec. 1990: 28-30.

"Reviews: *Home Alone*." *Variety* 19 Nov. 1990: 79.

Ian Wojcik-Andrews

Homicide: Life on the Streets (1993-), a police drama that debuted on NBC following the Super Bowl, has been almost universally praised for its writing, direction and "gritty realism." Academy Award-winner Barry Levinson co-executive produced *Homicide* with Tom Fontana (*St. Elsewhere*). Levinson joined a number of big-name filmmakers—including Oliver Stone, David Lynch, Steven Spielberg, George Lucas, John Sayles—who launched critically acclaimed TV series in the early 1990s. Levinson started his entertainment career in 1963 as a TV production assistant. In 1974 and 1975, he won Emmys for his writing on *The Carol Burnett Show*, before moving to film. Although Levinson did not write any early *Homicide* episodes, and he directed only the series' Emmy-winning debut program, *Homicide* successfully translated Levinson's cinematic skills and themes to the TV cop-show genre.

Based on Baltimore writer David Simon's *Homicide: A Year on the Killing Streets* (1991), the show is filmed in the port city, adding to the show's authenticity. Many critics found Baltimore's row houses, downtown hotels, and neighborhood bars a welcome visual contrast to typical prime-time locales.

Homicide may be television's first prime-time drama to use only the hand-held camera. The free-wheeling camera movement, jump cuts, and double edits create a tense, improvisational *mise-en-scène*. While rare in dramatic TV, critics note that *Homicide*'s stylistic techniques are fairly common in documentary film and "reality-based" television like the Fox Network's *Cops* (see entry).

Bibliography

Beale, Lewis. "Barry Levinson's 'Homicide' Kicks Off in a Big Way." *Los Angeles Times* 31 Jan. 1993.

Carter, Bill. "Pure Baltimore, Right Down to the Steamed Crabs." *New York Times* 24 Jan. 1994.

David Weinstein

Homosexuality as represented in popular media parallels American political, legal, and social attitudes. Thus, for much of the 20th century homosexuality was "in the closet" and did not appear in the mainstream. Graffiti in toilet stalls sought and directed gays to covert assignations, and conversely prompted "gay-bashing" threats and dirty jokes. Gay bars existed, but always at the peril of raids, both official and unofficial. Imported homosexual literature and illustrations were available among other erotica from rare book dealers, ranging in quality from Aubrey Beardsley to French postcards. All this was illegal, and to keep the repression of homosexuality in perspective, it might be noted that the New York Court of Appeals "Desmond Decision" ruling (that nudity as such was not indecent) was in the mid-1950s, while it was not until 1967 that the Supreme Court sanctioned frontal nudity. Sex of any explicit nature has until recently been *sub rosa* in America.

The topic of homosexuality entered American popular culture in an unlikely runaway best-seller, Dr. Alfred Kinsey's ponderous statistical study of *Sexual Behavior in the Human Male* (1948). The "Kinsey Report" estimated that at least 50 percent of the male population experiences some sort of overt homosexual behavior between adolescence and old age. In the subsequent study of the *Human Female* (1953) Kinsey and his co-authors reported that 28 percent of American females had had lesbian experiences. Regardless of the fact that the Kinsey Report has been largely discredited, its impact on popular perceptions of sexuality was real. However, the standard cross-reference in libraries continued to be "Homosexuality—See Sex Perversion" until 1955, and the titles of articles in popular newsmagazines in the fifties were "Curable Disease?" "Delicate Problem," "Hidden Problem," "Guilt or Sickness," etc. Such negative and pathological labeling colored the images of homosexuality in the entertainment industry.

Lillian Hellman's 1934 stage tragedy *The Children's Hour*, about a malicious girl accusing her boarding school teachers of lesbianism, was adapted for film in 1936 as *These Three*, but was so bowdlerized that the lesbianism was lost. Robert W. Anderson's 1953 stage drama about a prep-school-boy who is accused of homosexuality, *Tea and Sympathy*, met a similar fate when filmed in 1956, despite scripting by the playwright and the original Broadway cast. The year 1962 is something of a watershed in Hollywood film, with William Wyler's remaking *These Three* under the original title of *The Children's Hour*, and now more faithful to the play. In the same year, Allen Drury's 1959 political novel *Advise and Consent* was filmed, graphically depicting the seamier side of gay bars and male prostitution, as well as the vulnerability to blackmail of participants in same-sex acts. Also released in 1962 was *Walk on the Wild Side* with Barbara Stanwyck in the role of the lesbian madam of a New Orleans bordello. In all these, homosexuality is depicted as a tragic condition.

The Boys in the Band (1970) and *Cabaret* (1972), both adaptations from Broadway productions, tempered the stereotype with bittersweet gaiety. Blake Edwards's comedy musical *Victor/Victoria* (1982), a remake of a 1933 German film, was regarded by critics as "sexually harping," "grotesque low comedy," "depressingly crude," but it showed gays thoroughly enjoying themselves in Parisian night life of the 1930s, as well as exploring ambivalent attitudes among the sexes. In an unusual exchange, the movie was successfully adapted for the stage a decade later, perhaps reflecting changed public attitudes. Before the "Hays Office" Production Code of 1930 established a quarter-century of film censorship (see Production Code), there was at least one classic episode in *Morocco* (1930) where, in her first Hollywood role, Marlene Dietrich, dressed in male formal attire, plants a solid kiss on another woman's mouth.

A 1996 documentary, *The Celluloid Closet*, provides an excellent history of homosexuality in film with clips from over 100 films, interviews, and perceptive commentary. It postulates changing stereotypes of film homosexuality. As a butt of comedy, gays were depicted as mincing, coy, smirking clowns in the 1920s, later as sexually unthreatening "sissies." Outside of comedy, homosexuals were depicted as pitiable "nature's mistakes" or as sinister seducers of the innocent. As the subject became more open in the 1960s the stereotypes moved more toward depicting homosexuals as victims of society. Teen flicks had a standard device of hazing "faggots." In 1982, 20th Century-Fox came out of the celluloid closet with great fanfare, previews of *Making Love* announcing its "bold" and "gentle" examination of a genuine love relationship between two men. Rock Hudson's press release from a hospital in Paris announcing his having AIDS (of which he died in 1985) shocked the general movie-going public into recognizing the reality of homosexuality in Hollywood. The AIDS crisis also spurred writers and producers to make films that attempted to avoid stereotypes and show gays, lesbians, and their relationships with balance and understanding. Among these were *The Living End* (1992), *Philadelphia* (1993), *Go Fish* (1994), and *Boys on the Side* (1995). In pop music, the Village People (see entry) addressed these issues. It may be worth mentioning that pornography, too, came out of the closet. Sexually explicit "how-to" and homosexual "late night" fantasies became readily available in videos for sale or rental.

During the decades of film censorship, filmmakers often "wrote between the lines" to include homosexuality, and it became something of a parlor game for gays and lesbians to find such gems as unmistakably gay scenes in Laurel and Hardy skits, *Calamity Jane* (where Doris Day sings a gay/lesbian favorite, "My Secret Love"), Sal Mineo's infatuation with James Dean in *Rebel without a Cause*, *Ben-Hur* (where Gore Vidal wrote in a gay relationship, but didn't let Charlton Heston in on it), or *Pillow Talk* (where gay Rock Hudson plays a straight pretending he is gay). Judy Garland (see entry) has also been embraced by the gay community. In comic books, Wonder Woman and Batman were similarly scrutinized for homosexual subtexts.

Transvestism in real life is usually homosexual in purpose; in media it may be, but often is simply a comic device, especially with men dressing as women. *Some Like It Hot* is a good example, despite the ambiguity of the last shot, where it appears that Joe E. Brown is going to marry "Geraldine" (Jack Lemmon). *Halliwell's Filmgoer's Companion* lists over 75 examples under "transvestism," and this doesn't include television dragsters such as Milton Berle, Lucille Ball, and RuPaul.

At the century's end, homosexuality in popular culture has made great strides toward openness and respect. The furtive, sordid, and dangerous gay districts of mid-century receded, and gays and lesbians have been instrumental in urban renewal in historic districts nationwide such as in San Francisco, New Orleans, and Key West, while Fodor's added gay travel guides to their highly regarded publications in the 1990s. However, the mere fact that guides to non-discriminatory accommodations are needed is indicative of continuing prejudice. Talk radio brings this to the fore on a daily basis, and when Lynn Johnston's daily comic strip *For Better or For Worse* introduced a gay character in the late 1990s, several newspapers suspended the strip.

Bibliography
"A Delicate Problem." *Newsweek* 14 June 1954.
Epstein, Rob, and Jeffrey Friedman. *The Celluloid Closet.* Documentary film produced for HBO. 1995.
Moore, F. Michael. *Drag! Male and Female Impersonators on Stage, Screen and Television.* Jefferson, NC: McFarland, 1994.
Walker, John, ed. *Halliwell's Filmgoer's Companion 12th ed.* New York: HarperPerennial, 1997. (Entries "AIDS," "Homosexuality," "Transvestism.")

Fred E. H. Schroeder

See also
Gay and Lesbian Mysteries
Gay and Lesbian Radio

Honeymooners, The (1955-1956), was originally conceived and presented as a short skit on Jackie Gleason's 1951 DuMont variety show, *The Cavalcade of Stars.* After several seasons of the variety show, Gleason wanted a change: the result was the innovative situation comedy *The Honeymooners.* The repackaged incarnation was filmed live, in front of a studio audience, without interruptions or revisions. This filming process, just as in *I Love Lucy*, allowed for the show's permanence and preservation through reruns.

Gleason (see entry) portrayed the blue-collared bus driver Ralph Kramden. He (Ralph) and his wife Alice (played by Audrey Meadows) survived on the near edge of poverty. The Kramdens meagerly resided in a grey, shabbily furnished one-bedroom tenement flat on 358 Chauncey Street, Brooklyn. They were without the simplest of amenities, such as a telephone or an electric refrigerator. His friend and lodge brother, the simple-minded sewer worker Ed Norton (played by Art Carney), lived with his wife Trixie (Joyce Randolph) upstairs from Ralph and Alice. The Nortons dwelled in dissimilar comfort, compared to the Kramdens—having purchased their furnishings on credit.

At the time they made the show, CBS had little faith in Gleason's vision. They believed that the variety show, not the situation comedy, should be the network's mainstay. The viewing audience also demonstrated less than favorable enthusiasm. *The Honeymooners* dropped from 2nd to 20th place in the Nielsen ratings. Presently in rerun syndication, *The Honeymooners* is considered a timeless and celebrated staple of American entertainment. Besides the original 39 episodes, Gleason and CBS attempted a revival of *The Honeymooners* in the late '60s, but this venture was canceled in 1970. Since then, the 1980s discovery of *The Honeymooners: The Lost Episodes* (kinescopes) has given present audiences a glimpse into the genesis of the original 39 masterpieces. Asked why *The Honeymooners* has endured the test of time, Jackie Gleason responded, "Because they were funny."

Bibliography
Bluem, A. William. *Documentary in American Television.* New York: Hastings, 1965.

Hamond, Charles Montgomery. *The Image Decade: Television Documentary: 1965-1975.* New York: Hastings, 1981.
Marc, David, and Robert J. Thompson. *Prime Time, Prime Movers.* Boston: Little, Brown, 1992.

Michael Espinosa

Hood Ornaments. Americans' love affair with the automobile and desire to express individuality has led to competitive and flamboyant customizing, recently displayed in vanity license tags, fancy wheel covers, bright color schemes, bumper stickers, and objects stuck with suction cups to windows. One of the earliest methods to personalize an automobile was the use of a hood ornament or mascot, as it is called by automobile enthusiasts and collectors. Current styles of sleekness and more stringent safety standards discourage the use of ornaments on late-20th-century cars. In 1896 when automobiles were in their infancy, an Englishman, Lord Montagu of Beaulieu, placed a bronze statuette of St. Christopher, patron of travelers, on the dash of his Daimler. From this humble beginning the hood ornament fad spread east and west of England.

One of the earliest American hood ornaments was a 1909 copyrighted gnome called Gobbo, God of Good Luck. Its designer, Louis V. Aronson, was also responsible for many other ornaments. Lalique, a French jeweler and designer, worked with glass to fashion works of art which were widely and often poorly copied by other European and American glass and crystal makers. In the 1920s hood ornaments were combined with motometers or calorimeters to indicate the water temperature in the radiator, until the indicator moved inside to the dash.

Some car manufacturers adopted specific ornaments for their models as standard equipment or after-market accessories, such as Chrysler's winged hat of Hermes, Cadillac's herald, the Pontiac Indian, and the DeSoto warrior. There also were many commercial manufacturers offering accessory or after-market ornaments in a wide variety of styles and prices. Finer pieces, usually sold through jewelry or specialty stores, were made in bronze and silver. Pot metal or pewter, as less-expensive pieces and often direct copies of better quality designs, were sold through automobile magazines and catalogs as well as in-store displays.

The ultimate individuality was displayed by the famous who had their own custom ornament, as with Jackie Coogan's self-portrait of "The Kid," Rudolph Valentino's coiled cobra, and cowboy Tom Mix's silver saddle. Trademarks and logos were also widely used, with the Michelin tire man and the goose from Red Goose Shoes as examples. During wartime, patriotic themes of flags, eagles, and miniature Statues of Liberty appeared. Membership in fraternal organizations could be proclaimed with organizational emblems. Cartoon characters, including Disney and Warner characters, were popular. Abraham Lincoln, Charlie Chaplin, and Richard Nixon represent the famous personalities who were immortalized as mascots. Mostly held in private collections, representatives of the thousands of hood ornaments are catalogued in several books.

Bibliography
Boynton, Larry. "1,000 Mascots: 25 Years of Collecting Established the Extraordinary Auto Mascot Collection of Tom Nebel." *Mobilia: The Marketplace for Automobilia* May 1994: 34-36.
Smith, Dan. *Accessory Mascots: The Automotive Accents of Yesteryear, 1910-1940.* San Diego: Dan Smith, 1989.
Williams, William C. *Motoring Mascots of the World.* Rev. and expanded ed. Portland: Graphic Arts Center, 1990.

Margo B. Mead

Hooker, John Lee (1917-), the King of the Boogie, was born in Clarksdale, TN, near the Mississippi border. As with so many other performers, there is a dispute about the date of his birth. Some writers list 1917 and some 1920. He came from a large family of sharecroppers, being one of eleven children. Since his family could not afford music lessons, Hooker was self-taught on the guitar.

He used his talents to escape the poor life of a sharecropper. He headed out from Memphis to the North and in 1943 arrived in Detroit. There he recorded "Boogie Chillen'" and began his rise to prominence. He has since recorded over 500 records. At a time when other country blues singers were considered too rough and uncultivated for changing African-American tastes, Hooker became and remained popular. Throughout his career he has managed to remain the center of attention in spite of changing styles.

In the 1950s he was quick to see the potential of the Blues Revival movement and quickly joined it, some would say led it. He returned for a time to an acoustic guitar and gathered a large white following, influencing a number of rock musicians along the way. These included the Animals, Yardbirds, Spencer Davis Group, Groundhogs, and others.

In 1960, he was a hit of the Newport Festival and in 1962 went on a European tour with the American Folk and Blues Festival. He continued to move into the rock scene in the 1960s and 1970s, where he was revered as a founding father. In 1970, he recorded an influential and successful double album with Canned Heat. The King of the Boogie has continued to record successfully into the 1990s.

Bibliography
Herzhaft, Gerard. *Encyclopedia of the Blues.* Fayetteville: U of Arkansas P, 1992.
Wilson, Charles Reagan, and William Ferris, eds. *Encyclopedia of Southern Culture.* Chapel Hill: U of North Carolina P, 1989.

Frank A. Salamone

Hope, Bob (1903-), has been a major figure in the American entertainment industry for over 50 years. He was born in Eltham, Kent, in England, as Leslie Townes and emigrated with his family to Cleveland at age four. In spite of his family's humble circumstances (his father was a stone mason and Leslie was the fifth of seven children), he had dancing and singing lessons as a boy. He briefly attempted a boxing career after high school. His show business career began in 1920 in vaudeville theaters. He made his Broadway debut as one half of a musical comedy team in 1927 in *The Sidewalks* *of New York*. Taking the stage name Bob Hope, he developed his vaudeville abilities and his superb comedic skills at monologue in Ohio supper clubs and in Chicago. Eventually he moved on to headliner billing on the RKO circuit, leading to a 1932 hit in *Ballyhoo*.

Hope's Broadway career included feature roles in *Roberta* (1933), *Say When* (1934), *The Ziegfeld Follies of 1935*, and *Red Hot and Blue* (1936). Hope's radio appearances in 1935 were so successful that he had his own radio program by 1938. His Hollywood career began in 1937 with *The Big Broadcast of 1938*, which made "Thanks for the Memories" both a hit record and Hope's lifelong signature tune as well as the title of his next movie. Subsequent movies included classic performances in *College Swing* (1938), *My Favorite Blond* (1942), *Let's Face It* (1943), *Monsieur Beaucaire* (1946), *Paleface* (1948), and *Fancy Pants* (1950). Although he appeared in over 50 major films, Hope's film career may be best remembered for his teaming with Bing Crosby, a showbiz pal with whom he shared a mutual interest in golf, and Dorothy Lamour, a fellow Paramount studio star, in a series of seven "road" pictures, beginning with *Road to Singapore* (1940) through the embarrassingly out-of-date *Road to Hong Kong* (1962). This series perfectly met the longing of wartime America for light-hearted, escapist, uncomplicated, and good-natured humor. The films allowed Hope an outlet for leering, perfectly timed gags. Crosby could display both his humor and his vocal talents, while Lamour's showgirl figure, together with her vocalizing, gave Paramount studios the perfect recipe for box office success.

Hope's underrated talent as a dramatic actor and dancer was revealed in *The Seven Little Foys* (1955) and *Beau James* (1957). But comedy remained his forte in movies such as *The Lemon Drop Kid* (1951), *Casanova* (1953), and *A Global Affair* (1964). Critics consider his sequel *Son of Paleface* (1952), with Roy Rogers and Trigger, a comedy classic.

In *Let's Face It* (1943), Hope re-created Danny Kaye's role in the Cole Porter hit Broadway comedy. His performance benefited from the brassy character of Betty Hutton as well as from strong supporting roles played by ZaSu Pitts, Eve Arden, Phyllis Povah, and Dave Willock. American wartime audiences were ready for escape entertainment and this timely, topical movie about the funny and risqué side of army life fit the bill. World War II would mark a turning point in Hope's career.

In 1942, Bob Hope took a troupe of USO entertainers on tours in every theater of operations to entertain American and Allied troops. He would tour in Africa, England, Wales, Ireland, Scotland, Sicily, Alaska, the Aleutians, and the Pacific theater. This military showbiz career continued during the Korean, Vietnam, and Gulf Wars, cementing Hope's ties to the Pentagon as well as to establishment Washington leaders. In *White Christmas* (1954), Bing Crosby and Danny Kaye reworked this theme, but not as successfully as Hope's own television specials. His Christmas tours to entertain homesick American soldiers and sailors overseas became an annual tradition. Beginning in 1948 with a band, a comic, and a few leggy starlets to supplement Hope as the wisecracking, leering, golf-club-swinging master of ceremonies, Hope earned widespread respect and admiration for bringing holiday cheer to remote (and sometimes dangerous) military outposts around the globe. Hollywood recognized Hope's troop shows and extensive charitable work with Special Academy Awards in 1940, 1944, and 1952. In 1969, he received the Presidential Medal of Freedom for these patriotic efforts as a comedic Cold War warrior.

By the Vietnam era, however, Hope's brand of comedy found far less favor with the young, restless, and hipper Vietnam troops. The same humor that had so delighted their fathers was beginning to leave a generation of sons unappreciative. The sexual revolution of the 1960s had made Hope's wise-guy leers and risqué jokes seem dated and out of touch with a new generation. At some Vietnam shows, Hope was even booed by American troops. Many infantry grunts demonstrated resentment at the large-scale defensive effort that they had to mount in order to provide protection and security for the Hope show, which was performed before a relatively small number of garrison troops. The Pentagon, grateful for Hope's past as well as his present efforts, committed generous logistic and financial support to the Hope troupe. In *For the Boys* (1991), James Caan portrayed the generation gap that an aging Hope-ish World War II song and dance man encountered with the new generation of fighting men in Vietnam.

As a businessman, Hope proved shrewd. Once his popularity was assured, he drove hard—one of his agents said wicked—bargains for his talents. He created Hope Enterprises, Inc., to manage his show business ventures and maximize the profitability of his efforts in films, broadcasting, music, and publishing. Beyond show business, Hope invested in major sports teams (both the Cleveland Indians and the Los Angeles Rams), resorts, real estate, oil and food, and other business enterprises. His success as an entrepreneur was solidly demonstrated by the wealth which he managed to accumulate.

In 1950, Hope made a successful transition to television, with his own TV programs and frequent guest appearances, especially on Johnny Carson's *Tonight Show*. A long and successful career in every aspect of show business gave him star status that approached the level of a contemporary cultural icon. In 1968, he received a special Peabody Award for his many years on television. In 1986, Hope was honored by the Museum of Broadcasting in a six-week-long tribute to his more than 50 years in radio and television. In a one-day seminar, Hope, at age 82, still displayed his vintage form as a master of ceremonies par excellence and king of the one-liners. By 1990, though, reviews of his *Don't Shoot, It's Only Me: Bob Hope's Comedy History of the United States* indicated that the book, like Hope himself, "comes off rather like an attenuated, pretentious, heavy-on-the-patriotism Bob Hope special!" Hope's age, as well as his dated approach to comedy, had become painfully evident. In 2000 Hope is no longer performing.

Bibliography
Faith, William Robert. *Bob Hope: A Life in Comedy.* New York: Putnam, 1982.
Hope, Bob. *Don't Shoot, It's Only Me: Bob Hope's Comedy History of the United States.* New York: Putnam, 1990.
Thompson, Charles. *Bob Hope: Portrait of a Superstar.* New York: St. Martin's, 1981.

James P. Hanlan

Horror Fiction is as old as the earliest narrative traditions in Western culture. Odysseus, for example, visits the land of the dead in Homer's *The Odyssey.* Witches appear in Shakespeare's *Macbeth,* a ghost in Shakespeare's *Hamlet.* The first true horror novel was Horace Walpole's *The Castle of Otranto* (1764), which should also be considered the first popular fiction novel. The gothic formula, as established by Walpole, remained the dominant type of horror fiction for a number of years, reaching its apex in Matthew Gregory Lewis's *The Monk: A Romance* (1796) and in Charles Robert Maturin's *Melmoth the Wanderer* (1820). In the typical gothic horror story, human will is subverted by Fate; the castle is the story's dominant symbol, its hidden passages and dark chambers often embodying repressed, irrational emotions or perverted sexual urges that overtake the individual's rational will. The supernatural controls and subverts the world of nature. Personified evil (both psychological and supernatural) exists side-by-side with mere mortals and influences the mortal sphere. Nightmares invade the real world, possessing substance and vitality, and they portend disaster when social or sexual taboos are violated.

The publication of three early gothic novels not only split the horror genre into other formula categories, but also established new genres in the process. The first of these gothic novels, *Vathek* (published in an English version in 1786) by William Beckford, read like a Arabian fairy tale, mimicking and emphasizing exotic and grotesque elements found in Middle Eastern folk legends. Beckford's novel became one of the first examples of modern fantasy.

The second important work to split from Walpole's gothic model was Ann Radcliffe's *The Mysteries of Udolpho* (1794). Radcliffe retained the Gothic castle as a fictional fixture, and, like Walpole, built her story around a victimized heroine, but she replaces overtly supernatural elements with suspense. Radcliffe seduces her reader into thinking that the supernatural may intrude at any moment into her plot, but it never actually does; what appears to be supernatural has a rational explanation. Radcliffe thus redirected the gothic mode toward romantic suspense. She also expanded the length of the gothic narrative, helping to make the "triple-decker" novel—a lengthy novel published in several volumes—fashionable.

The third significant novel to split from the original gothic source was Mary Shelley's *Frankenstein* (see entry), first published in 1818, which introduced a philosophic dialogue about the morality of humanity's quest for knowledge, basically arguing the point that there are some things—like the creation of life—best left to God. Shelley also incorporated scientific elements into her story; it is Victor Franken-stein's misuse of science that creates the monster. Thus, *Frankenstein* charts that point when the gothic tale branched into the modern science fiction story.

One of the most popular mass print mediums in 19th-century England was the "penny dreadful." These inexpensive "story papers" often featured lurid and graphic depictions of fictional and semi-fictional crime, as well as outright horror, such as the sensational monster formula story *Varney the Vampire; or, The Feast of Blood* (1845), anonymously published but frequently attributed to James Malcolm Rymer. The serial magazine, like the *Strand Magazine,* best known today as the magazine that published Arthur Conan Doyle's Sherlock Holmes stories, eventually replaced the penny dreadful.

The type of horror story that came to dominate the Victorian period in England was the ghost story (see entry). Often, such stories dealt with family curses, the resolution of some past crime, or the moral transformation of those individuals who come into contact with ghosts. Charles Dickens's *A Christmas Carol* (1843) was the most famous example of the ghost story as moral allegory. Joseph Sheridan Le Fanu's stories in *In a Glass Darkly* (1872) also proved extremely influential. In the early 20th century, a number of British authors published excellent supernatural fiction, including Arthur Machen, Algernon Blackwood, Oliver Onions, and E. F. Benson. The ghost story achieved its greatest recognition, however, in the work of two writers: M. R. James, whose first published collection, *Ghost Stories of an Antiquary* (1904), is a landmark in the history of the horror genre, and Henry James, whose complex short novel, *The Turn of the Screw* (1898), has delighted readers for years as they argue whether the ghosts are real or a figment of the main character's disturbed imagination.

In America, the gothic narrative provided the foundation upon which was built a new, national literature. Washington Irving and Charles Brockden Brown transplanted the Old World gothic formula to New World literary soil and in the process created new horror formula variants. Like Walpole, Irving used folk tales and legends as the basis for his horror stories, like "The Legend of Sleepy Hollow" and "Rip Van Winkle," that were anthologized in *The Sketch Book* (1820). Brown employed various gothic horror motifs in his novels *Arthur Mervyn* (1799) and *Ormond; or, The Secret Witness* (1799), but in two particular novels, *Wieland* (1798) and *Edgar Huntly; or, Memoirs of a Sleep-Walker* (1799), psychological horror was central. Brown's influence led to the dominance of the psychological horror story in 19th-century American literature.

Robert Montgomery Bird, for example, published several novels, such as *Sheppard Lee* (1836) and his Indian-hating frontier adventure *Nick of the Woods* (1837), that emphasized aberrant psychology as horror. Edgar Allan Poe (see entry) was an expert at writing both traditional European gothic horror tales, like "The Fall of the House of Usher" (1839), and American psychological horror stories, such as "The Black Cat" (1843) and "The Tell-Tale Heart" (1843). Several significant authors of the period, including Nathaniel Hawthorne and Herman Melville, fused the psychological horror story with allegorical romance, a formula that prevailed in American horror fiction until Fitz-James O'Brien (see entry).

Though relatively unknown to contemporary readers, O'Brien, in a handful of short horror stories such as "The Diamond Lens" (1858) and "What Was It?" (1859), helped to reconceptualize the horror genre in America by utilizing both science fiction elements, contemporary settings, and more realistic characters. O'Brien was one of the first to finally break Walpole's far-reaching grip on the horror story by dispatching with long-standing gothic narrative motifs, such as the castle setting, the vulnerable heroine, and the stock supernatural devices. In essence, O'Brien transformed the horror narrative from romance to realism, from tale to short story. His work influenced the next generation of horror writers in America, Ambrose Bierce and Robert W. Chambers (see entries).

Bierce and Chambers were the two authors instrumental in moving the horror genre into the 20th century. Bierce's two anthologies, *In the Midst of Life* (also titled *Tales of Soldiers and Civilians*, 1891) and *Can Such Things Be?* (1893), demonstrated how the horror story could be used as dark satire; his Civil War stories, in particular, were effective satiric accounts of the grisly and pointless tragedy of the American Civil War, and of war in general.

Though Chambers's contributions to the horror genre comprised only a relatively small portion of his total literary output—he mainly wrote light romance novels—his overall influence was undeniable. His collection of horror fiction entitled *The King in Yellow* (1895) and his novel *The Maker of Moons* (1896) provided a number of the narrative motifs—such as obtuse references to unknown horrors, books and other texts as horror icons, ambivalent resolution of plots, and pessimistic visions of the human condition—that led to the creation of the dark fantasy horror story that became H. P. Lovecraft's hallmark (see entry). His dark fantasy stories of the 1920s and 1930s, published exclusively in pulp magazines, gained momentum from society's horror concerning the mass destruction caused by World War I.

In the period between the two World Wars, the horror fiction market was dominated by pulp magazines like *Weird Tales* and others. Following World War II and the decline of the pulps, the popular horror story made its way into both comic books and paperbacks, the print mass media that replaced the pulp magazine.

During the 1960s and 1970s, two British literary disciples of H. P. Lovecraft, Ramsey Campbell (see entry), and Brian Lumley, achieved both critical and popular recognition for their horror fiction. Following the publication of his first anthology, *The Inhabitant of the Lake and Other Less Welcome Tenants* (1964), the prolific Campbell quickly dispensed with the Lovecraftian influence and explored innovative areas of dark fantasy. Lumley's early writing, as in *The Caller of the Black* (1971), also exhibited Lovecraft's influence, but in recent years he has ventured into a new type of horror fiction, the epic horror story, with his "Necroscope" series of novels.

In the U.S., despite the efforts of several horror writers like Shirley Jackson, the author of *The Haunting of Hill House* (1959) and *We Have Always Lived in the Castle* (1962), and Robert Bloch (see entry), the author of *Psycho* (1959), both of whom helped to successfully resurrect both the traditional gothic and psychological horror formulae of earlier years, the horror story languished until the publication of three novels that created a new formula, the domestic horror story, featuring victimized women and children and the dysfunctional family as central protagonists.

Ira Levin's *Rosemary's Baby* (1967), Thomas Tryon's *The Other* (1971), and William Peter Blatty's *The Exorcist* (1971) were all instrumental in reconfiguring the contemporary horror genre by enlarging its audience to include women readers who had traditionally preferred gothic romance. Levin, Tryon, and Blatty brought these readers back to the fold, and in the process demonstrated the potent commercial appeal of popular horror melodrama, thus paving the way for a newer generation of horror writers like Dean R. Koontz (see entry), John Saul, V. C. Andrews, and Robert R. McCammon.

Stephen King (see entry), in particular, demonstrated in his first novel, *Carrie* (1974), as well as in numerous subsequent best-sellers, the tremendous mass appeal of the horror story. King and Peter Straub have also helped to popularize the epic horror formula. King's *The Stand* (1978) and *It* (1986), their collaborative book, *The Talisman* (1984), and Straub's ongoing "Blue Rose" series of novels that includes *Koko* (1988), *Mystery* (1990), and *The Throat* (1993), have helped to make the epic horror novel a favorite among contemporary readers. In the mid-1980s the six-volume *Books of Blood* series by Britisher Clive Barker (see entry) revolutionized the genre with a new horror formula called "splatterpunk," a story that blended a postmodern cultural rebellion against authority—as also seen in punk rock music of the early 1980s in England—with a visceral and graphic depiction of violence. Splatterpunk fiction is also the province of American writers John Skipp, David J. Schow, and Craig Spector, among others. Barker, though, has recently turned to the epic novel format. His massive works like *Weaveworld* (1987) and *Imajica* (1991) have successfully blurred the formulaic distinctions between horror and high fantasy. Another writer of epic horror novels, Anne Rice (see entry), has returned the horror genre full circle back to its gothic origins in her several best-selling horror series including the "Vampire Chronicles" and the "Lives of the Mayfair Witches." Rice recaptures the gothic motifs of her distant predecessors, Monk Lewis, Ann Radcliffe, and Mary Shelley, combining these traditional components with a contemporary portrait of sexual and gender diversity and a sophisticated eroticism, proving once again the flexibility and eternal appeal of the horror genre.

Bibliography

Barron, Neil, ed. *Horror Literature: A Reader's Guide*. New York: Garland, 1990.

Birkhead, Edith. *The Tale of Terror: A Study of the Gothic Romance*. New York: Russell, 1963.

Carroll, Noel. *The Philosophy of Horror: or, Paradoxes of the Heart*. New York: Routledge, 1990.

Grixti, Joseph. *Terrors of Uncertainty: The Cultural Contexts of Horror Fiction.* London: Routledge, 1989.

Gross, Louis S. *Redefining the American Gothic: From* Wieland *to* Day of the Dead. Ann Arbor: UMI Research, 1989.

Gary Hoppenstand

See also
Vampire Fiction

Horror Film in America has always enjoyed a hospitable atmosphere. If its history were plotted on an Electrocardiograph, it would show a long life punctuated by periods of intense activity, and near arrest (no horror films released in 1937 and 1938)—but never, not yet, the terminal flatline. The periods of activity, both economic and aesthetic, have been in the early 1930s (*Dracula, Frankenstein, The Mummy*); in the early 1940s (*Cat People*); in the beginning of the 1960s (*Psycho, The Haunting*); at the end of the 1960s (*Night of the Living Dead, Rosemary's Baby*); and in the mid 1970s (*The Exorcist, Jaws, Texas Chainsaw Massacre, Halloween*). The 1980s and 1990s brought a stabilization of horror's significant place within popular culture, bringing gluts of remakes, sequels, slasher variations, television-to-film outings, omnibus horror films, and countless Stephen King work-ups. Amidst such predictable output one still found the occasional aesthetic breakthrough (*Silence of the Lambs,* 1991) or economic blockbuster (*Jurassic Park,* 1994). But at this point American horror seems dependent on the "old masters" of the 1970s who continue to search, in a rather scatter-brained, shotgun approach, for the next defining moment of film terror: *Wes Craven's New Nightmare* (1994), George Romero's *The Dark Half* (1993), John Carpenter's *In the Mouth of Madness* (1995). Even the rare horror newcomers of note, director/screenwriter Sam Raimi (*Evil Dead,* 1983; *Evil Dead II,* 1987; *Darkman,* 1990; *Army of Darkness,* 1993) and writer/director Clive Barker (*Hellraiser,* 1987; *Nightbreed,* 1990; *Candyman,* 1992), have not stimulated the horror genre with the type of breakthrough film—*Dracula, Psycho, Halloween*—capable of launching the next progression in the American horror film.

The horror genre contains a sprawling hodge-podge of settings, story patterns, and subgeneric mutations. This is because no setting, theme, or formula necessarily dominates or lastingly achieves horror's prime goal: the stimulation of negative affects in a viewer or reader. Fear, disgust, startles, and doubt are the stuff of the horror genre, and such subjective affects are stimulated by widely different narrative, thematic, and stylistic treatments. Some general concerns, though, have consistently helped in the generation of horrific affects: the supernatural, the monstrous, psychological aberration, madness, physical decay, and, of course, the threat, prolongation, desire for, and certainty of death. And a little sex. The fuzziness of the horror genre may also result from the ease with which Hollywood film genres cross-breed.

Horror and science fiction have intermingled to produce some of the best examples of either genre: *The Thing, Invasion of the Body Snatchers, Alien.* Likewise, the recent success of the thriller genre, a close cousin of horror, has

Friday the 13th. Photo courtesy of Popular Culture Library, Bowling Green State University, Bowling Green, OH.

insured no small number of horror/thriller half-breeds: *Dead Calm* (1989), *The First Power* (1990), *Pacific Heights* (1990), *Jennifer 8* (1992), *Single White Female* (1992), *Knight Moves* (1993), *Blink* (1994). Other dramatic modes and genres have frequently been coupled with horror: fantasy and fairy tale (*The Company of Wolves,* 1984; *Army of Darkness,* 1993; *Nightbreed,* 1990) and comedy (*Bride of Frankenstein,* 1935; *An American Werewolf in London,* 1981; *Re-Animator,* 1985; *The Lost Boys,* 1987; *Buffy the Vampire Slayer,* 1992; *Innocent Blood,* 1992). But if contemporary horror films benefit from a decades-long lineage of generic development and enrichment, this was not always the case.

As early as 1910 the Edison studio produced a 16-minute *Frankenstein.* In 1919, Robert Wiene's *The Cabinet of Dr. Caligari* became a tremendous international success, its German Expressionist style influencing art trends far beyond film. But *Caligari* proved too unique and odd to provide a repeatable horror formula or aesthetic. Three years later, the German experiment in film horror continued with F. W. Murnau's *Nosferatu,* a brilliant and powerfully intimidating film that was little seen in America in the 1920s due to its illegal status (Stoker's wife used legal means to suppress the film in Britain and America since it was an illegal production of her husband's novel). Influenced by the occasional German import and still developing, the horror film in 1920s America was largely associated with two men.

Lon Chaney (1883-1930; see entry), the "man of a thousand faces," used his legendary skills in makeup and physical transformation to develop a parade of grotesques and villains who helped establish our first notions of the cinematic monster. His most successful films were gothic historical pieces: *The Hunchback of Notre Dame* (1923) and *The Phantom of the Opera* (1925). *The Unholy Three* (1925) served as Chaney's first outing with horror director Tod Browning, who would direct nine more Chaney films, many of which, like *The Unholy Three*, were set in the odd and cruel world of the carnival sideshow, a setting Browning had personal experience with. This early association of horror with the freakish, side-show setting of carnival and second-rate circus would continue with *The Unknown* (1927), *Freaks* (1932), and *West of Zanzibar* (1928). In *London after Midnight* (1927), Chaney presented the first feature-length depiction of a vampire in American cinema.

While Chaney would have no influence on America's first widely successful horror film, both German Expressionism and Tod Browning would make overt contributions to Universal's *Dracula* (1931), starring Bela Lugosi (see entry). After successful theatrical stagings in Britain and America, *Dracula* finally made it to film, casting the generic mold of the vampire film subgenre (one of the most frequently filmed topics in all of cinema), and providing a formula that Universal would follow in creating the first horror boom in American cinema.

Nearly all the early Universal horror films offered moments of visual greatness and narrative invention that have reached far and wide in popular culture. Although the obvious influences were on American film, Universal's monsters became such icons that they simply became part of the popular landscape. The influence of James Whale's *Frankenstein* (1931), immortalized through Boris Karloff's performance, Jack Pierce's makeup, and Whale's gothic aesthetic, extends through decades of Halloween costumes, advertising imagery, and children's toys, recycled so often that young viewers might perfectly appreciate parodies like John Hughes's *Weird Science* (1985) and Tim Burton's *Frankenweenie* (1982/1992) without seeing the originals.

Other Universal films would mark the "classic" versions of their distinctive horror subgenres: *The Old Dark House* (1932, James Whale); *The Mummy* (1932, Karl Freund); *The Invisible Man* (1933, James Whale). According to many critics, the pinnacle of Universal horror came in 1935 with *Bride of Frankenstein*, James Whale's already campy exaggeration of the conventions the director himself had helped fix in his first treatment of Mary Shelley's monster. Universal would continue eating its own horror tail well into the 1940s, beginning with comedians Bud Abbott and Lou Costello, who first entered the studio's horror product in *Hold That Ghost* (1941), and ending with a "monster revival," where Universal sought to cram as many of their famous monsters in a single film as they could (five being the record): *Frankenstein Meets the Wolf Man* (1943), *House*

of Frankenstein (1944), and *House of Dracula* (1945). The 1930s did not belong solely to Universal. Paramount funded Rouben Mamoulian's 1932 version of the often-filmed Stevenson novel *Dr. Jekyll and Mr. Hyde*. Given a plum role—playing two distinct personalities—and rising to the occasion, Fredric March captured a best actor Oscar in the nearly always snubbed horror genre (only a handful of major Oscars have gone to horror films: Kathy Bates for *Misery* [1990], Ruth Gordon for *Rosemary's Baby* [1968], and the near-sweep of *Silence of the Lambs*—which some purists do not even count as horror).

While Universal was recycling its horror catalogue during the 1940s, an intelligent novelist got involved in B-movie horror production at RKO studio. Not a director but a hands-on producer in the model of David Selznick, Val Lewton would oversee a series of B-movie horror features that pushed the subtle, offscreen evocation of fear and horror further than any previous works. In *Cat People* (1942, Jacques Tourneur) the film's threat is seen mostly in shadow and glimpsed once in the flesh, the literal presence of the leopard forced on Lewton by studio authorites. In *I Walked with a Zombie* (1943, Jacques Tourneur) Lewton developed a key element of his suggestive horror: a context where supernatural threats are undercut by naturalistic and psychological explanations. In *The Leopard Man* (1943, Jacques Tourneur) Lewton traded in a supernatural monster for a psychological one, offering an early model of the horror of human psychopathology that has come to dominate much of the thriller and horror genres after *Psycho*. Both *The Body Snatcher* (1945, Robert Wise) and *Bedlam* (1946, Mark Robson) tap horrific historical events: the grave diggers of Great Britain and the brutal treatment of the insane in London's infamous "Bedlam," the 18th-century St. Mary of Bethlehem hospital.

"Purebred" horror films of note were few and far between during the 1950s. Universal offered one last monster in *Creature from the Black Lagoon* in 1954, banking as much on the film's 3-D presentation as on its new "gill-man" monster. Science fiction, like *The Blob*, engulfed many of horror's conventions and much of its imagery during America's Cold War years. Both the space race and the development of atomic energy contributed to a horror of technology greater than anything the good Dr. Frankenstein had ever animated. Some of the best of these science fiction and horror hybrids were *The Thing* (1951, Christian Nyby & Howard Hawks), *Invaders from Mars* (1953, William Cameron Menzies), *Them!* (1954, Gordon Douglas), and *Invasion of the Body Snatchers* (1956, Don Siegel).

As a number of 1950s science fiction films became deathly serious and socially progressive, the horror film turned to good, schlocky fun under the showman's hand of campy horror director William Castle (see entry). Castle's horror films used promotional and theatrical gimmicks that slyly played with and commented upon the conventions and effects of the horror genre. In *House on Haunted Hill* (1958), spectators thrilled to flying plastic skeletons that soared above their heads in theaters. With *Macabre* (1958), viewers could purchase insurance policies against the possibility of "death by fright." Far less whimsical was Castle's later stint as producer of *Rosemary's Baby*.

Although a British enterprise, Hammer Studios revitalized the classic Universal horror subgenres in the late 1950s with *The Curse of Frankenstein* (1957), which used director Terence Fischer and actors Peter Cushing and Christopher Lee in the first of many Hammer horror products, nearly all of which brought Universal's monsters up to date with bold color and explicit presentations of sex and violence. Before Hammer's horror boom was over, Fischer and company had modernized Universal's mummy, Dracula, werewolf, Stevenson's Jekyll and Hyde, Arthur Conan Doyle's Sherlock Holmes, and other lesser icons of the horror pantheon.

Psycho, Alfred Hitchcock's low-budget elaboration of Robert Bloch's short story about the infamous serial killer/cannibal Ed Gein, marks the most radical transformation in film horror: the monster now requires little makeup, the setting no gothic castle, the narrative a new set of rules that allow for the stylish slaughter of a film's protagonist. Ironically, British director Michael Powell's *Peeping Tom* was released in the same year as *Psycho* and unflinchingly covered the same issues of voyeurism, sexual psychopathology, and mother fixation. Yet Powell's film and the critical response to it nearly ended his career while Hitchcock's film and the critical response to it brought an embarrassment of riches.

Many others would follow *Psycho*'s success in the 1960s. Hard-boiled action director Robert Aldrich would begin a new horror formula by casting Hollywood's aging leading ladies in roles as psychopathic gothic grotesques: Bette Davis and Joan Crawford in *What Ever Happened to Baby Jane?* (1962) and Davis and Olivia de Havilland in *Hush...Hush, Sweet Charlotte* (1965). At the other end of the horror spectrum, *Psycho* would inspire the first "splatter film," Herschell Gordon Lewis's *Blood Feast* (1963). Filmed in nine days for something like $70,000, it showed how a careful presentation of gore effects could offset bad acting and incompetent production values and still turn a profit. Hitchcock's stint in pure horror would include only one other film, *The Birds* (1963). Less impressive or influential than *Psycho*, *The Birds* nonetheless invigorated the horror genre's "old dark house" formula and its exploration of the primal spatial fears of entrapment and violation.

The relentless elaboration of group psychology under siege in an enclosed space depicted in *The Birds* was explored by younger horror directors, including George Romero, who traded in Hitchcock's birds for zombies in his *Night of the Living Dead* (1968). Romero would contribute two more zombie films, forming a trilogy—*Dawn of the Dead* (1978) and *Day of the Dead* (1985). Besides zombie pictures, Romero has offered slightly off-kilter versions of familiar horror subgenres. Especially interesting is his *Martin* (1978), a vampire story centered on a disturbed young man whose belief in his own vampirism proves just as deadly as any supernatural agency.

Like Romero, many of the post-studio system generation of horror filmmakers would begin their careers on independent and ultra low-budget features. Wes Craven's infamously violent and terrifying *Last House on the Left*

(1972) launched a new horror subgenre of the rape-revenge formula. Craven offered up another low-budget success with *The Hills Have Eyes* (1977), where a feral human "family" attempts to cannibalize an extended family lost in the wilds of Arizona. Craven's biggest success, though, was his *Nightmare on Elm Street* (1984), which intelligently expanded on the slasher formula and began a new horror franchise in Freddie Krueger, whose fedora hat, knife-studded glove, and burned visage would grace six sequels and millions of rubber masks, toys, and T-shirts. Before returning to Freddie with a self-reflexive neo-parody in which the director plays himself screenwriting an out-of-control Freddie as the film unfolds—*Wes Craven's New Nightmare* (1994)—Craven presented *The People under the Stairs* (1991), an ambitious but didactic elaboration of the old-dark-house formula where Reaganomics is lampooned through an incestuous pair of slum lords who prey on the local working classes until they are foiled by the film's atypical protagonist, a brave young African-American boy.

No survey of American horror would be complete without mention of producer and director Roger Corman (see entry). Corman's low-budget production technique and keen sense of exploitation fare helped him acquire one of the largest filmographies in Hollywood: over 200 films, a good number of which turned a profit. Corman's early days were spent making films for the low-budget AIP (American International Pictures—1956-79). There, Corman made a series of horror films based on variations and combinations of Edgar Allan Poe stories. This "Poe cycle" began with *House of Usher* in 1960 and continued with seven more pictures, including *The Pit and the Pendulum* (1961), *Tales of Terror* (1962), *The Raven* (1963), *The Masque of the Red Death* (1964), and *The Tomb of Ligeia* (1964). Like the Hammer horror films, Corman used bold colors and explicit displays of sexuality and violence to refresh the horror genre. The Poe cycle is also distinguished with the presence of Vincent Price, horror's most famous postwar actor, who appears in seven of Corman's eight Poe films. Corman continues, in the 1990s, producing and directing low-budget horror films. Corman's most recent directorial effort was yet another attempt to update one of Universal's classic monsters: *Frankenstein Unbound* (1990). Most active now as a producer, Corman remains committed to the horror genre, with film such as *The Terror Within II* (1992), the *Jurassic Park* imitation *Carnosaur* (1993), *Dracula Rising* (1993), and *To Sleep with a Vampire* (1993).

Since the 1970s, a number of directors have consistently worked in horror, providing many near-misses and quite a number of powerful and original horror works. David Cronenberg's investigations of biological and technological horrors have been consistently original, if not always completely successful (*Rabid*, 1977; *Scanners*, 1981; *Videodrome*, 1983; *The Fly*, 1986; *Dead Ringers*, 1988). In 1990, Cronenberg played his largest acting role to date, a stint as the main villain in Clive Barker's *Nightbreed*. Like Cronenberg, John Carpenter has been consistently interesting as a director of horror features. Beginning in 1974 with *Dark Star*, originally a graduate school project mounted with schoolmate Dan O'Bannon (himself a respected horror screenwriter), Carpenter has, besides directing and producing horror films, written screenplays and musical scores for a number of the most original and offbeat horror films of the last 15 years: *Eyes of Laura Mars* (1978); *The Fog* (1980); *Escape from New York* (1981); *The Thing* (1982); *Christine* (1983); *Prince of Darkness* (1987); *They Live* (1988). Carpenter's greatest success was with *Halloween* (1978), one of the most financially successful films in history ($325,000 cost vs. $80 million in global sales).

Carpenter's numerous tracking shots from the killer's point of view, the electronic score for the film, and his precise manipulation of film space to hide, occlude, and reveal the "boogie man" for maximum effect resulted in a horrific symphony as powerful and influential as any American horror film, ever. The entire slasher subgenre (including *Friday the 13th*, 1980, and its many sequels) can be seen as an attempt to repeat Carpenter's formula and style in order to repeat his financial success.

Mining the Hitchcock vein, Brian De Palma differs from Hitchcock in one crucial manner: De Palma blends the thriller and horror elements that Hitchcock typically kept more distinct. *Sisters* (1973) displays an elaborate manipulation of split-screens and carries the Hitchcockian style and sensibility into a post-1960s setting in a way Hitchcock himself never really achieved; *Frenzy* (1972), utilizing on-location but soon-to-be-demolished produce markets in Covent Garden, undercut its contemporary London setting with a nostalgia uncharacteristic of Hitchcock. In 1976 De Palma yoked his neo-Hitchcockian style with a Stephen King property, providing with *Carrie* one of the few exceptions to the rule that Stephen King's fiction loses in the translation to film. De Palma's horror films have frequently been criticized for their foregrounding of violence against women, the director's obvious stylistic signature probably drawing attention where other horror violence remains more transparent: *Obsession* (1976), *The Fury* (1978), *Dressed to Kill* (1980), *Body Double* (1984), *Raising Cain* (1992).

Roman Polanski's four horror films make up a small but worthy part of his total filmography. *Repulsion* (1965) remains many people's most intense psychological horror; *Rosemary's Baby* (1968) brought the same emphasis on feminine psychological fears to a mainstream audience, helping, in the process, to resurrect the horror genre after the first wave of *Psycho* imitators dried up. Polanski's *Fearless Vampire Killers* (1967) is one of a handful of horror comedies that is as funny as it is frightening.

Francis Ford Coppola began his career with a Roger Corman horror film, *Dementia 13* (1963), and recently returned to the genre with a much fatter wallet for *Bram Stoker's Dracula* (1992). Coppola's *Dracula* was one leg of the most recent attempt to revitalize the Universal classic monsters, a campaign which included two other mainstream directors, Mike Nichols, who helped Jack Nicholson translate the werewolf format into a contemporary analysis of aggressive business practices in *Wolf* (1994) and Kenneth Branagh, who turned to Robert DeNiro in an attempt to top Boris Karloff's performance as Frankenstein's monster in *Frankenstein* (1994). Then, of course, there is Stanley Kubrick, whose translation of Stephen King's *The Shining* is considered by many as one of the best film treatments of any of that author's works. The best one-shot effort of all, though, must go to William Friedkin, whose work on William Peter Blatty's novel *The Exorcist* proved to be one of the most successful and socially significant horror films of all time.

Because of its emphasis on affect and its viability at extremely low budgets, the horror genre has entertained as much narrative, thematic, and stylistic experimentation as any other American film genre. Tobe Hooper gave America one of its goriest and cheapest nightmares with *The Texas Chainsaw Massacre* (1973). Joe Dante, one of the many who began his career with Roger Corman, directed two popular, socially parodic horrors in the early 1980s: *The Howling* (1981) and *Gremlins* (1984). While the films of David Lynch are nearly unclassifiable, they remain powerfully horrific and unsettling. Closest to the horror genre are Lynch's *Eraserhead* (1978), *Blue Velvet* (1986), and *Wild at Heart* (1990). Stuart Gordon's gory send-ups of H. P. Lovecraft material have been praised and enjoyed: *Re-Animator* (1985) and *From Beyond* (1986).

Ken Russell brought his flamboyant style to two horror features, *Gothic* (1986), a hallucinatory chronicle of the night in 1816 when Mary Shelley and Dr. Poliadori first dreamt Frankenstein's monster and the vampire at the challenge of Lord Byron and Percy Shelley, as well as a version of *The Lair of the White Worm* (1988), one of Bram Stoker's *other* horror novels. While women make up a tiny fraction of horror filmmakers, a few notable works have been produced: Kathryn Bigelow's *Near Dark* (1987) blends multiple American film genres (Western, road-picture, romantic comedy, coming-of-age teen picture, etc.) around the core vampire myth with great skill and charm; Stephanie Rothman, another Corman protegé, has provided some horror films of interest: *Blood Bath* (1966) and *The Velvet Vampire* (1971).

Usually associated with low-budget exploitation fare, the horror genre has been driven by the blockbuster as much as any genre. Indeed, some of the biggest blockbusters of all time are fully or partially situated in the horror genre: the *Exorcist* (1973, William Friedkin), *Jaws* (1975, Steven Spielberg), the *Alien* trilogy (1979, 1986, 1992), *Poltergeist* (1982), and *Silence of the Lambs* (1991, Jonathan Demme). The most successful film of all time, *Jurassic Park* (1993, Steven Spielberg), blended science fiction and horror to inspire global fear, startles, and disgust. While the dinosaur subgenre appears unlikely to spawn a new subgenre as *Halloween* did with the slasher film, the success of *Jurassic Park* in using computers to generate frightening monsters may herald horror's next phase, whose hulking forms we can only dimly make out on the horizon of American cinema.

Bibliography

Brunas, Michael, John Brunas, and Tom Weaver. *Universal Horrors: The Studio's Classic Films, 1931-1946*. Jefferson: McFarland, 1990.

Fischer, Dennis. *Horror Film Directors, 1931-1990*. Jefferson: McFarland, 1991.

Hardy, Phil. *The Encyclopedia of Horror Movies*. New York: Harper, 1986.

Siegel, Joel E., and Val Lewton. *The Reality of Terror*. New York: Viking, 1973.

Skal, David J. *The Monster Show: A Cultural History of Horror*. New York: Norton, 1993.

Robert Baird

See also
Frankenstein in Film
Slasher Films

Houses in America, aside from those designed individually by professional architects, should be regarded as expressions of popular culture. At one end of the scale of styles are the dwellings built according to folk traditions from local natural materials. Native American lodges, hogans, and pueblos are the clearest instances, but pioneer first homes are also representative. However, as in the case of log buildings and sod houses, these were not necessarily part of the cultural baggage of the immigrants so much as patterns that spread from first settlers to the subsequent waves.

The other extreme of popular domestic architecture is mass produced, using manufactured materials such as plywood, steel studs, laminated beams, synthetic resin ("Formica") walls, ultraviolet-resistant window glass, fiberglass ceilings, modular bathrooms. Mobile homes, fully furnished and needing only a concrete pad and connections for utilities, exemplify this end of the scale.

The variants between the extremes seem infinite. Electrified pueblos with furnishings from Sears Roebuck, prairie pioneers in shanties built of discarded packing cases and tarpaper, suburban ramblers "stick-built" by contractors according to plans purchased from Sunday newspaper features, pre-cut and prefabricated mail-order homes, "cookie-cutter" identical apartments in high-rise urban renewal projects begin to hint at how many aspects of mass production, mass marketing, and popular taste influence the houses we live in.

There is also a vast industry that feeds the popular culture of home-building, injecting high style into the mass media. Mail-order catalogs and magazines such as *Ladies' Home Journal* and *House Beautiful* are among the earliest of these periodical tastemakers. The editor of the *Journal*, Edward Bok (1863-1930), initiated house plans as a regular feature. It was in these pages that Frank Lloyd Wright's "Prairie Houses" were introduced to the American public in 1901. Such mass dissemination of house plans had been anticipated in pattern books as early as the 18th century for carpenters, and then in the 19th century in elaborately ornamented volumes for consumers. These were usually arranged from modest little "starters" to full-blown gothic and Queen Anne mansions. Two of the earliest and most influential books were Andrew Jackson Downing's *Architecture of Country Houses* (1850) and Calvert Vaux's *Villas and Cottages* (1857), but many followed, often titled with the author/architect's name, such as *Holly's Country Seats* (1866), *Bicknell's Village Builder* (1872), and *Hobb's Architecture* (1876). A particularly interesting work on popular architecture was Charles Dwyer's *The Immigrant Builder; or Practical Hints to Handymen, Showing Clearly How to Plan and Construct Dwellings in the Bush, on the Prairie, or Elsewhere Cheaply and Well, with Wood, Earth, or Gravel* (1872, 1884), which may mark the first time that traditional construction methods were converted from oral transmission to national distribution.

There was little academic interest in popular architecture in America until the 1970s; art historians were interested in the big name architects and major public structures rather than anonymous builders and modest pattern-book dwellings. One exception was Harold Shurtleff's *The Log Cabin Myth*, edited posthumously by Samuel Eliot Morison for publication in 1939. Shurtleff, research director for Rockefeller's Colonial Williamsburg reconstruction, demonstrated that the idea of colonial pioneer log cabins was actually a backward view from the famous 1840 "Tippecanoe and Tyler Too" presidential campaign. In Europe and England interest in what came to be called *vernacular architecture* accelerated after World War II and, by 1954, a Vernacular Architecture Group had been formed in Britain. Not surprisingly, their interest was in regional styles of rural structures built from local materials. In Scandinavia, similar research was spurred by the development of outdoor folk museums. In the U.S., we can probably credit cultural geographers such as Fred Kniffen as starting to look seriously at folk styles, and Henry Glassie's *Folk Housing in Middle Virginia* (1975) as a landmark, providing, as it did, a typological program for examining folk-vernacular houses, barns, and outbuildings. Research at several outdoor museums (notably Colonial Williamsburg and Lincoln's New Salem) in the 1930s antedates these, and has undergone much correction and refinement, both in these places and many other museums and historic sites. Interest in non-folk vernacular is much more recent, probably spurred as much by the historic preservation movement and the *Old-House Journal* as by scholars in popular culture and social history.

It is generally agreed that the real watershed in American popular domestic architecture was in the 1830s because of several technological advances: rail transport, improved steel blades for power sawmills, the replacement of costly hand-forged nails with cut-iron, and, in the 1880s, steel wire nails. These made possible the invention of a new, peculiarly American method of construction, the *balloon frame*, whereby lightweight slender boards could be quickly nailed to form a house frame that only required sheathing for floors, walls, and roof. With some modifications, this is essentially how wood houses continue to be constructed. The significance of the railroad is that as the frontier moved from the eastern forests into the prairies, it became possible to ship standardized dimension lumber and cheap nails to stations where a settler might be able alone to load housing material into a wagon, and with little or no help build a house. The first such buildings appeared in the village of Chicago, contributing to rapid growth (and destruction by fire in 1872).

Most authorities now divide American vernacular architecture into pre- and post-railroad. Before the railroad, there were local and regional styles using available materials and handcrafting; after, standardized lumber and dimensions (2 by 4, 2 by 10; studs and joists 16 inches on center, etc.) produced a national structural skeleton. There are, however, many variations in *form*, some deriving from older traditions such as the *shotgun*, a gable-front, usually single-story arrangement of three or four rooms in line (a West African import by way of the Caribbean), or the *I-house*, side-gabled, one or two stories of two rooms, one deep. Other forms developed along with mass suburban developments, such as the *four square* and *bungalow*. House forms, therefore, reflect the arrangement of rooms, stories, doors, chimneys, and roofs and gables. The number of forms that are common in American houses defies final definition, as typologies range from a dozen to as many as 67 formal patterns. (McAlesters' *Field Guide* below is particularly comprehensive.)

Visually, though, there is even greater variety, for Americans discovered historic styles of architecture by mid-19th century, and often the slightest architectural details applied to a traditional-formed balloon frame will mark it as Classical Revival (e.g., a triangular pediment above the door) or Gothic Revival (e.g., scroll-sawed pendants at the porch corners). Alan Gowans's *The Comfortable House* identifies the period from 1890 to 1930 as the time when suburban building was most given to variants on historic styles. The popular culture aspect then went well beyond pattern books and magazine plans, for this was the time when mail-order homes were in their heyday. Pre-cut and/or prefabricated homes with all millwork finished were shipped to order to be assembled by numbered parts on site. Best known were the Sears Roebuck mail-order homes, but there were many competing companies offering designs with such names as The Windermere, The Milford, The Oxford, The Alhambra, The Plaza. Following the Great Depression and World War II, mail-order houses declined and the postwar building boom was in large tracts where developers arranged several simple designs along curved streets, all ready for GI Bill of Rights mortgagees. The Levittowns of William Levitt were the epitome, their rapidly constructed one-and-a-half-story "minimalist colonial" houses with unfinished upstairs thereby contributing to the do-it-yourself boom. It is in the postwar period also that vacation house-trailers transmogrified into "mobile homes," their wheels used only for transportation from factory to more or less permanent sites. In the 1980s, historic styles were applied to single and double mobile homes, somewhat disguising their production-line origins with mansard and gable roofs, federal doorways, cupolas, and so forth.

The place of the house—the single-family detached residence—in American culture is central. Jan Cohn in *The Palace or the Poorhouse* asserts that "the house has been, and continues to be the dominant symbol for American culture," while Spiro Kostof in *America by Design* equates the house with the American Dream. In literature as well houses are symbols for success, as in William Dean Howells's *The Rise of Silas Lapham* (1885) and F. Scott Fitzgerald's *The Great Gatsby* (1925). Three masterpieces of Hollywood underscore the centrality of the dream and the symbol.

"Tara" is as well known as Scarlett O'Hara; no one can forget Charles Foster Kane's obsession for his fictional San Simeon; and it would be downright unAmerican not to know what Dorothy's words are as she regains consciousness. "Be it ever so humble, there's no place like home" wrote John Howard Payne in 1823, and his Home, Sweet Home on Long Island is but one of the many humble houses that are shrines to Americans. Stately homes attract visitors worldwide, but Americans, as Jan Cohn notes, are drawn to "biographical" sites of little or no architectural interest, such as the John Wayne birthplace in Winterset, IA, the Eisenhower home in Abilene, KS, or the Jesse James home in St. Joseph, MO (complete with the fatal bullet hole in the wall).

Halliwell's *Filmgoer's and Video Viewer's Companion* lists more than four dozen titles with houses as "the dramatic center," including various haunted houses. In comedy, there is a recurrent theme of the problems that urbanites encounter as they become house owners/restorers/builders, as in *George Washington Slept Here* (1942), *The Egg and I* (1947), *Mr. Blandings Builds His Dream House* (1948), and *Please Don't Eat the Daisies* (1960). The television series *Green Acres* (1965-70) was in this genre. In most situation comedies, though, the house as such does not appear, as the action centers in the living room.

Bibliography

Cohn, Jan. *The Palace or the Poorhouse: The American House as Cultural Symbol.* East Lansing: Michigan State UP, 1979.

Gowans, Alan. *The Comfortable House: North American Suburban Architecture, 1890-1930.* Cambridge: MIT, 1986.

Kostof, Spiro. *America by Design.* New York: Oxford UP, 1987.

McAlester, Virginia, and Lee McAlester. *A Field Guide to American Houses.* New York: Knopf, 1989.

Stevenson, Catherine Cole, and H. Ward Jandl. *Houses by Mail: A Guide to Houses from Sears, Roebuck and Company.* Washington: Preservation, 1986.

Fred E. H. Schroeder

How the West Was Won (1978-1979) premiered to high ratings as a six-hour TV miniseries in February 1978. The series returned to the ABC schedule in September 1978, billed as "the longest motion picture ever made." More accurately, it was the longest single-story television program produced to that time, surpassing *Roots* from the previous year.

During the 1978-79 season, MGM presented 20 hours of connected plot beginning with two three-hour segments produced on a budget of $12 million. Filmed in Colorado, Utah, Arizona, and California, *How the West Was Won* utilized three Indian villages (one Sioux, one Arapaho, and one renegade), a Mexican town, a complete frontier town, an Army encampment, a robber's hideout, a cave, a mine, and Bent's Fort, a historical monument located in La Junta, CO. Over 1,700 animals were needed, including over 400 buffalo, a herd of cattle, oxen, mules, burros, pigs, goats, dogs, and cats, and the standard quota of horses. It was truly an ambitious undertaking even by Hollywood standards.

All the expense and attention to detail paid off. During its first season, *How the West Was Won* earned higher ratings than any recent television Western, finishing the year in 17th place on the Nielsen list. It was renewed for another season in a slightly altered format, with each story completed in a two-hour weekly episode. In the spring of 1979, *How the West Was Won* dropped to 46th place in the Nielsen ratings and was canceled.

Although the plots switched back and forth between the major characters, with one usually focusing on Zeb Macahan (James Arness), one on his nephew Luke (Bruce Boxleitner) and one on Aunt Molly (Fionnula Flanagan) and the other Macahan siblings, occasionally two or all three of the storylines would come together. The focal character, however, was always Zeb. Whether negotiating with the Indians for the release of a visiting Russian count, helping a mountain man rescue his son from the Indians, or trying to prevent a bloody war between the Army and the Indians, Arness dominated every scene in which he appeared.

An appreciation of the dignity and worth of the Indians the white man slaughtered when settling the West was a recurring theme in *How the West Was Won*. Zeb felt a genuine respect for Indian life and culture. He once had taken an Indian maiden for his bride and she had given him a son. With both now dead, Zeb simply tried to keep the peace.

Bibliography

McNeil, Alex. *Total Television: A Comprehensive Guide to Programming from 1948 to the Present.* New York: Penguin, 1991.

Yoggy, Gary A. *Riding the Video Range: The Rise and Fall of the Western on Television.* Jefferson: McFarland, 1995.

Gary A. Yoggy

Howard, Robert E. (1906-1936), a native Texan, wrote prolifically for the weird, Western, and action pulp magazines, creating in the process a number of memorable series characters, of which Conan the Barbarian is the best known. He effectively created the subgenre of "sword and sorcery" fiction. Early in his career, he came under the influence of H. P. Lovecraft (see entry), a lasting inspiration for his work. Most of Howard's stories were published in *Weird Tales*, including his first, "Spear and Fang" (1925), about a handsome Cro-Magnon woman evading would-be rapists. The story's combination of fast-paced action, prehistoric characters, and sexual violence prefigured much of the author's later work.

There followed a succession of stories featuring series characters: Solomon Kane, a dour 16th-century Puritan swordsman; King Kull, a massive barbarian living around 100,000 B.C.; Bran Mak Morn, a chief of the Picts engaged in constant battles against the invading Romans; and Conan the Barbarian, a dweller in the pre-glacial world, who defeats sorcery through a combination of brute strength, courage, and luck. In this last series, Howard traces Conan's career from his early days as a scavenging burglar to his period as a freebooter and pirate, and eventually to his rise to power as a future king. (Later writers, including Lin Carter and L. Sprague de Camp in collaboration, wrote a series of novels based on the Conan character.)

Howard created bizarre and imaginative mythical worlds, suffused with magic and wizardry, driven by violence and vengeance. Despite his early death by suicide, his fiction lives on and continues to influence countless readers and writers.

Bibliography

Cerasini, Marc A., and Charles E. Hoffman. *Robert E. Howard.* Mercer Island: Starmont, 1987.

Herron, Don. *The Dark Barbarian: The Writings of Robert E. Howard: A Critical Anthology.* Westport: Greenwood, 1984.

Schweitzer, Darrell. *Conan's World and Robert E. Howard.* San Bernardino: Borgo, 1978.

Richard Bleiler

Howdy Doody (1947-1960) for more than ten years supplied entertainment for America's kids. "Hey, kids! What time is it?" Buffalo Bob asked the very young. "It's Howdy Doody time," they screamed back from the in-studio Peanut Gallery and from homes across the nation.

The red-haired marionette Howdy Doody, perhaps the embodiment of early American television's innocence, began his career as the "alter-voice" of Bob Smith (1917-1998). The show first aired on NBC in December of 1947 as *Puppet Television Theatre* and was a vaudeville-like combination of puppet theater—featuring precision Rockette-like dancers—and live acts, including French poodles brought by the Gaudsmith Brothers from Radio City Music Hall.

In this first show, Howdy himself did not appear but was concealed in Bob Smith's lower desk drawer. Children were invited to write to Howdy to tell him what kind of entertainment they would like. This ploy was popular, for subsequent shows saw Howdy emerge from the desk drawer wearing his signature plaid shirt, neckerchief, cowboy boots, and ear-to-ear, freckle-faced grin. Buffalo Bob (Bob Smith), arrayed in a cowboy shirt and jeans, was the MC for the show. Doodyville puppet regulars included Phineas T. Bluster (the mayor), Dilly Dally, and Flub-a-Dub. Human regulars were Cornelius Cobb (Nick Nicholson), Chief Thunderthud (Bill LeCornec), and Princess Summerfall Winterspring (Judy Tyler). Lowell Thomas joined the show for travelogs. Clarabell the Clown (Bob Keeshan, then Lew Anderson) was also a regular. The mute Clarabell communicated with sprays of seltzer, never speaking, except on the last show, when he said, "Good-bye, kids."

The first show of its kind, *Howdy Doody* was also a landmark in other ways. It spun off the major kiddie show *Captain Kangaroo* with Bob Keeshan, the original Clarabell, as Captain Kangaroo. Too, broadcasting live with children in the Peanut Gallery gave spontaneity and unpredictability to the show because, as Buffalo Bob acknowledges, "We never knew what the kids were going to say in the Peanut Gallery" (Fritz 2).

In the mid-'50s in an effort to compete with ABC's highly successful *Mickey Mouse Club*, Howdy moved from the pre-dinner hour to Saturday mornings at 10:00. The same characters continued, with the addition of Gumby, an animated clay character.

Despite its increasingly limited appeal, the show lasted 13 years, an unusual feat for the early medium. One of the reasons for its continuation may be that although the show changed little, every year brought new children to watch. Also, the show displayed some technical virtuosity which may have attracted older viewers, experimenting with split-screen in the late '40s—Buffalo Bob in New York and the puppets in Chicago—and adding color in the mid-'50s—a fairly controversial move since, as one writer put it, "the brats won't know the difference" (*Variety* 14 Sept. 1955).

By the '60s, the show was gone, but in 1987, "It's Howdy Doody Time: A 40-Year Celebration" was staged during the holiday season to commemorate Howdy's 40th birthday. It seemed apparent that Howdy and his show had not aged gracefully, and the patronizing ethnic attitudes of the '50s (particularly toward Native Americans) were still uncomfortably visible. His creator died in 1998 at the age of 80.

Bibliography

Fritz, Steve. "Howdy Doody Goes on the Block." *Mania: Hey, Kids! What Time Is It?* Online. Internet. 6 Jan. 1998. Available: smash.mgz.com/tv/features/buffalobob.html.
"Kids' TV in the Fifties." Online. Internet. 6 Jan. 1998. Available: www.fiftiesweb.com/kids.htm.
"Say Kids What Time Is It!" Online. Internet. 6 Jan. 1998. Available: www.contees.com/HowdyDoody/welcome.html.
"Steve's Collectibles—Howdy Doody." Online. Internet. 6 Jan. 1998. Available: www.tiac.net/users/sblenus/hdspec.htm.
Variety Television Reviews. Ed. Howard H. Prouty. 15 vols. New York: Garland, 1989.

Barbara Basore McIver

How-to Literature makes up a large body of nonfiction which offers descriptions of processes used to carry out tasks. The genre includes works ranging from instructions, to advice, to informative presentations of information needed to complete tasks. Books and articles are generally heavily illustrated with photos and drawings.

How-to literature has a nearly inexhaustible market in the U.S. with regular publication in newspapers, magazines and books on a variety of subjects. How-to books often top the best-seller lists and the entire genre has experienced phenomenal growth in the last few years. Accounting for only 12 percent of the book market in 1969, by 1989 how-to books accounted for 18 percent of all new books published in the United States. The 1990 issue of *Writer's Market* identifies more than 150 publishers of how-to books. This genre holds an even bigger share of the market in magazines. One result of this tremendous surge in popularity is the advent of how-to bookstores—shops dedicated solely to merchandising this genre.

Common topics of how-to books and magazines include cooking, self-help, animals, sports, childcare, mechanics, electronics, decorating and hobbies. One particularly active category is sports, with golf leading the way. Sports books tend to come from smaller publishers and book publishing spinoffs of major sports magazines (e.g., *Golf Digest*, *Sports Illustrated*). Few sports books sell well in the short term, but are looked at as long-term investments for the publishing house, and the introduction of sports videos and their infomercials to the marketplace has caused a drop in the popularity of sports books.

How-to books have been with us since the earliest attempts at publishing. We have examples of cookbooks from Rome and Turkey that date back to before the time of Christ. But by far the most popular of the ancient how-to books were the libri secretorum, or Books of Secrets.

Libri secretorum books were books of recipes and formulas of various kinds. They often included medical procedures, magic, parlor tricks, and cooking recipes. Many of them dealt with traditional lore about the natural properties of plants, animals, and minerals. The foremost of these arts in terms of the amount of literature produced was medicine.

Early "recipe books" were written in a variety of mediums. In the late third or early fourth century, the Egyptian papyri volumes of *LeydenX* and the *Stockholm Papyrus* were written. Between them, they contained 250 recipes, 100 for imitating precious metals and the rest for dying fabrics or counterfeiting precious stones. While we have examples of this type of literature that date back to the second century (*Kyranides*, a book of Hellenistic magic), according to William Eamon, the "age of the how-to book" was the 16th century, particularly in Italy. The 1555 version of *Secreti* by Alessio Piemontese went through more than 70 editions and Giambattista Della Porta's *Magia Naturalis*, written in Latin, had almost 20 editions. The most popular book of the Middle Ages, though, was the pseudo-Aristotelian *Secretum Secretorum*, but today, the most widely recognized 16th-century how-to book that survives is Niccolò Machiavelli's *Prince*.

Bibliography

Eamon, William. *Science and the Secrets of Nature: Books of Secrets in Medieval and Early Modern Culture*. Princeton: Princeton UP, 1994.
Sargent, Sy. *How to Collect How-To Books—Managing the How-To Collection and Learner's Advisory Services: A How-To-Do-It Manual for Librarians*. New York: Neal Schuman, 1993.
Weyr, Thomas. "Sports by the Book." *Publishers Weekly* 235.7 (17 Feb. 1989): 21-32.
Writer's Market. Cincinnati: Writers Digest, 1990.

Michael W. Gos

H-PCAACA is an Internet-based academic discussion list of the Popular Culture and American Culture Associations. These associations developed under the leadership of Ray Browne at Bowling Green State University. The list is affiliated with H-Net, a large group of discussion lists from humanistic and historical disciplines (see entry). Using the listserv software administered by University of Illinois-Chicago and Michigan State University, H-PCAACA can communicate with hundreds of people around the world daily.

In these electronic lists, where the subscribers are also contributors, there is a steady flow of information and lively discussion about methods, issues, current films, conferences, calls for papers or book chapters. Using the evolving technology of gophers and the World Wide Web, the list can also make permanently available program announcements, member lists, and other data vital to a functioning international organization. Finally, H-PCAACA is also an important book review medium. In dealing with popular print materials, a book has often been remaindered before its review can appear in a paper scholarly periodical. Waiting times of two years are common. Electronic publication, on the other hand, can take place as quickly as it has been reviewed editorially. H-PCAACA was formed at the initiative of Peter Rollins, who with John Lawrence, served as its first moderator.

John Lawrence

Hubcaps are the removable covers that attach to the center area of the exposed side of an automobile wheel. They serve both an instrumental and an aesthetic purpose. The instrumental purpose is to protect the hub or center wheel area and axle from harmful debris. This practical function has changed with closer fitting components that reduced harmful materials from penetrating the wheel/axle area. Form and function are connected and aesthetic features are affected by innovations such as durable lightweight materials and metal alloys. Until the 1970s, hubcaps were made from cast iron and steel. Advances in technology introduced aluminum, plastics, and composite materials into hubcap design. In the 1990s, standard chrome-plated and aluminum hues have been replaced with a host of colors: red, white, black, gold, and more. Hubcaps continue to change, since they were first used on the Newton Reaction Carriage in 1680. For example, in the 1920s, steel replaced cast iron and wooden wheels. Over the years, hubcaps have been differentiated into partial components: centercaps, trim-rings or beauty-rings, and full covers or wheel covers.

Centercaps are small decorative disks used to cover the center axle of the auto and are made from metal, aluminum, or durable plastic materials. Varying in design, centercaps are colorful accents which provide a sense of stylish elegance or simple ruggedness. Meanings and values associated with these features are a matter of advertising fads, fashions, and conventions. For example, two- and three-bar spinner or "knock off" center caps were a flashy accent to the rally automobile. Spinners are the accent feature of stainless steel spoke wheels. Introduced into the commercial market in the 1930s, they continue to maintain a high profile in current collector markets. In the late 1960s, federal safety standards banned two- and three-bar spinners from manufacture in the United States.

Trim-rings are partial hubcaps, open in the center, and attached to the outside edge of the steel wheel rim. They are used alone, in combination with centercaps, or with colored wheel rims to heighten the aesthetic overall wheel design. Trim-rings or beauty-rings are typically featured on small economical compact vehicles.

Full wheel covers are a product of the late 1920s. Aerodynamic considerations in the 1980s and 1990s introduced solid disks with optical spin grooves as common auto attire. In the 1960s and 1970s, stainless steel spoke wheel covers were manufactured to resemble the more costly spoke wheel rims of the 1930s. Metal covers in the 1960s were emblematic of society's changing conditions. Clear plastic and enameled logos occupied the center portion of the full wheel cover. In the late 1940s, small, eight- to nine-inch "baby moon" hubcaps were the fad. But by the early 1950s, they were replaced by the full-size moon disk. This wheel cover was dome shaped with no air valve and originally made of aluminum. It was designed to screw into pre-cut grooves in the wheel rim. Its aerodynamic design, reminiscent of earlier racing vehicles at the turn of the century, attracted street rod owners.

Hubcaps are not just side-dressing anymore. The 1994 Orange Show Art Car Ball, in Houston, TX, advertised a Hubcap Hullabaloo Dinner. No hubcaps were served. Some people collect and display hubcaps on their buildings, fences, and/or make hubcap sculpture. It's hard to miss the sign promoting 12,000 hubcaps located near Interstate 70, on the outskirts of Claysville, PA. In Columbus, OH, Hubcap Annie is the queen of the full wheel cover, and her hubcap business is well established. It is rare not to see at least one hubcap, full wheel cover, centercap, or trim ring displayed at a local flea market, antique mall, or swap shop.

Bibliography

Berg-Flexner, S., ed. *The Random House Dictionary of the English Language.* 2d ed. New York: Random, 1987.

Ludvigsen, K., and D. Burgesswise. *The Encyclopedia of the American Automobile.* Great Britain: Edinburgh, Morrison & Gibb, 1977.

Ruiz, M., et al. *One Hundred Years of the Automobile, 1886-1986.* New York: Gallery, 1985.

Don H. Krug

Hudson, Rock (1925-1985), one of Hollywood's more durable and popular stars, was born Roy Harold Scherer, Jr., in the Chicago suburb of Winnetka, IL, to a working-class family. He was later adopted by his stepfather and during his adolescence and early adulthood was known as Roy Fitzgerald.

Fitzgerald was homosexual, and it was through friends he made in the southern California gay community that he met agent Henry Willson. Willson was impressed by the handsome, affable, and very tall (6 ft., 4 in.) young man and took him on as a client. Willson had Fitzgerald's teeth fixed and changed his name to Rock Hudson. Fitzgerald detested this new name and even after decades of fame as Rock Hudson he continued to think of himself as Roy Fitzgerald. Willson secured a one-year contract for Hudson with director Raoul Walsh. Rock Hudson made his movie debut in Walsh's *Fighter Squadron* in 1948. Ambitious and cooperative, Hudson worked hard at the studio's "acting school" and dutifully escorted young Universal actresses on dates arranged for publicity purposes. When told that his high-pitched voice did not suit the leading man image the studio was developing for him, Hudson made regular trips to the desert to scream at the tops of his lungs. His permanently damaged vocal chords produced lower tones.

During his apprenticeship at Universal, Hudson appeared in small roles in more than a dozen films. Most notable among these early films are two Anthony Mann-directed Westerns, *Winchester '73* in 1950, and *Bend of the River* in 1952, both starring James Stewart. Two years later, the tear-jerker *Magnificent Obsession*, directed by Douglas Sirk and co-starring Jane Wyman, made Rock Hudson a star. Its box-office success led to an immediate reteaming of Hudson and Wyman in another Sirk-directed soap opera-like film, *All That Heaven Allows* (1955). Hudson gave some of his best dramatic performances under the direction of Sirk, who was able to see past the actor's rugged exterior and bring out his vulnerable side. It was for the George Stevens-directed *Giant* in 1956, however, that Hudson received his only Academy Award nomination.

The risqué comedy *Pillow Talk* (1959), co-starring Doris Day, showed Hudson could handle comedy and was at his most likable when sending up his macho image. He made two more comedies with Doris Day—*Lover Come Back* (1961) and *Send Me No Flowers* (1964)—as well as a number of similar films with other actresses, most notably the Howard Hawks-directed *Man's Favorite Sport?* with Paula Prentiss in 1964.

In the mid-1960s, Hudson's career floundered. Although other actors of his generation such as Paul Newman and Steve McQueen were more popular than ever, studio-creation Rock Hudson was viewed as an anachronism by independent-minded "new Hollywood." His very name bespoke of old-fashioned, studio-system phoniness. Hudson struggled along for a few years, making indifferently received action pictures and one notorious failure, the World War I romantic drama *Darling Lili* (1969) with Julie Andrews. With interesting movie roles no longer coming his way, Hudson reluctantly turned to television. In *McMillan and Wife* (NBC, 1971-77), a weak variation on the *Thin Man* series, Hudson played San Francisco police commissioner Stewart McMillan and Susan Saint James was his younger, hipper wife, Sally. Hudson disliked television and drew little satisfaction from starring in a hit series, the scripts of which he considered of poor quality. He took more pride in his theatrical ventures during this period, including an extensive tour of the musical *I Do! I Do!* with his friend Carol Burnett. Hudson was lured back to television with a new series, a detective show called *The Devlin Connection*. Production was delayed in 1981 when Hudson, a heavy smoker and enthusiastic meat eater, underwent coronary bypass surgery. When *The Devlin Connection* finally aired on NBC in the fall of 1982, it was canceled after three months.

When Hudson accepted the role of romantic millionaire Daniel Reece on the popular nighttime soap opera *Dynasty* in 1984, he already knew he was suffering from AIDS. He left the series after one season when he became too ill to continue working. After unsuccessful medical treatment in Paris, he died at his home in Los Angeles.

Bibliography

Annual Obituary. Detroit: Gale, 1986.

Hudson, Rock, and Sara Davidson. *Rock Hudson: His Story.* New York: Morrow, 1986.

Katz, Ephraim. *The Film Encyclopedia.* New York: Perennial Library, 1990.

Thomson, David. *Biographical Dictionary of Film.* 2d ed. New York: Morrow, 1981.

Mary Kalfatovic

Hugo Award. Renowned as the "father of the science fiction magazine," Hugo Gernsback (1884-1967) helped define and further create a popular literary genre (i.e., science fiction) which has thrived ever since. The most prestigious fan award in science fiction, and one of the most sought after trophies of writers of this genre and in general, the "Hugo" Award is named for this influential editor and publisher. Gernsback had been guest of honor at the 1952 World Science Fiction Convention in Chicago; beginning with the 1953 convention in Philadelphia, achievement awards presented at these "fan" gatherings were declared "Hugos." (Science fiction's "Nebula" and "Philip K. Dick" awards, for example, are conferred by different groups of "professional" writers.) Since 1952, Hugo Awards have been made in several classes, and these classes have varied over the years. Usually, Hugos are presented for achievements in fiction writing, but have also been given for outstanding illustrating/artwork, editing, diverse media presentations, and more. The award itself is a model of a rocket ship sitting upright on its tail fins. Alfred Bester earned the first Hugo in 1953 for his novel, *The Demolished Man.* Gernsback, himself, was presented with his namesake award at the 18th World Science Fiction Convention in 1960.

Bibliography

Clute, John, and Peter Nicholls. *The Encyclopedia of Science Fiction.* New York: St. Martin's, 1993.

Roberts, Garyn G. "Hugo Gernsback." *Dictionary of Literary Biography 137: American Magazine Journalists, 1900-1960, Second Series.* Ed. Sam G. Riley. Columbia: Bruccoli Layman Clark, 1994. 96-103.

Garyn G. Roberts

Humor: A Paradoxical Overview. Surprise, incongruity, irony, and paradox are among the features that make people smile or laugh at pictures, stories, jokes, and commercial messages, as well as at the slipping-on-a-banana-peel events that happen in real life. These features characterize not only individual jokes, but also the whole field of humor, where we see such paradoxes as health care workers championing the healing and preventative powers of laughter for both mental and physical ailments, while a whole raft of special interest groups protest humor as damaging.

In the 1990s, especially, humor collided with ideas of political correctness. Paramount Films, for example, apologized and removed a billboard advertising *Crazy People* from a location near the South Florida State Hospital in Pembroke Pines. The billboard had been especially offensive in showing a cartoon-style drawing of a cracked egg with waving arms and the large-print caption, "Warning: Crazy People Are Coming." ABC apologized to the mayor and citizens of Cleveland who were offended at Jerry Van Dyke's promotion piece for his new show *Coach* in which he said that even if the Cleveland Browns beat the Denver Broncos, they would still lose "because they have to go back to Cleveland." And according to newspaper articles and talk shows, men all over the country were offended by the hundreds of joking variations-on-a-theme told in relation to John Wayne Bobbitt having his penis severed by his angry wife.

While on one level women were quick to protest their traditional role as the butt of sexist humor, at another level they also began to protest the old saw about females not having a sense of humor. In the '90s, the percentage of stand-up comedians who are female increased from something like 3 percent to over 20 percent. In a review of Regina Barreca's *They Used to Call Me Snow White, But I Drifted: Women's Strategic Use of Humor*, the *New York Times* (September 1, 1991) observed that "Good Girl Donna Reed has been replaced by Roseanne...; Mrs. Brady has been eclipsed by Mrs. Bundy," and American society has come to accept a woman who can "snap back an answer as well as snap her gum."

Such "serious" women's magazines as *Mirabella's*, *Elle*, and *Harper's Bazaar* added humorous features, and even such respected career women as Supreme Court Justices Sandra Day O'Connor and Ruth Bader Ginsburg went along with a joke by wearing the "Hers-and-Hers" T-shirts presented to them by the National Association of Women Judges. On the front the T-shirts read "The Supremes" and on the back, "I'm Sandra, Not Ruth," or "I'm Ruth, Not Sandra."

At the same time that protesters were bringing about an era of what some critics called "creeping nice-ism" and "new blandness," comedians as well as ordinary citizens were developing a penchant for sick or gallows humor—those grim jokes that could be recycled from the Jonestown suicide story, to the Challenger explosion, to the Jeffrey Dahmer case, to the fire at the Branch Davidian complex in Waco. A contributing factor is that as mass media writers, performers, and producers were forced to compete for the attention of readers, listeners, and viewers, they worked to find information that would strike viewers as new and intriguing. Also, because of fax machines, electronic mail, television, radio, and easy access to long distance phone calls, a truly funny joke could make its way around the country within a few hours. As a result, American comedians, desperate for "new" material, began startling their audiences with insults, sexual references, scatology, and what most surprised the rest of the world, disaster humor. One effect was to normalize shocking jokes so that they lost their sting, while another was to lend a stamp of approval, almost a granting of moral permission, to ordinary people to ask such riddles as the following. They were printed in the *New York Observer* (May 3, 1993) in a story about how Wall Street traders create, adapt, and spread the jokes as part of the "rat-a-tat" telephone manner which they use with potential clients.

Q: *Who's doing the cleanup at the Waco cookout?*
A: Jeffrey Dahmer, with a bottle of barbecue sauce!
Q: *How do you pick up a girl in the Branch Davidian compound?*
A: With a Dustbuster!
Q: *Why did the Branch Davidians commit suicide?*
A: They wanted to keep up with the Joneses!

A less distressing effect of mass media competition has been to make advertisers more amenable to using humor, first to attract and hold the attention of potential customers (especially with television commercials), and second to leave listeners or viewers with a pleasant feeling toward the advertised product.

As people have noticed the many paradoxes involved with humor, both its creation and its appreciation have come under a new level of scrutiny as an academic topic. Various organizations and universities regularly sponsor conferences and other humor-related events. The International Society for Humor Studies, founded in 1987, has a quarterly journal and an annual conference. Several other groups sponsor more specialized conferences on such topics as health and humor, humor in literature, or the humor of a particular country or ethnic group. During the 1992 winter term, the University of Michigan College of Liberal Sciences and Arts offered "The Comedy Semester," in which 13 courses were offered across several departments so that students could "explore the phenomenon we call comedy from a variety of perspectives." For the past few years, Skidmore College in Saratoga Springs, NY, has hosted an Annual National College Comedy Festival combining education and entertainment.

Bibliography

Barreca, Regina. *They Used to Call Me Snow White...But I Drifted: Women's Strategic Use of Humor*. New York: Viking, 1991.

Blair, Walter, and Hamlin Hill, eds. *American Humor: From Poor Richard to Doonesbury*. New York: Oxford UP, 1987.

Dressner, Zita, and Nancy Walker, eds. *Redressing the Balance: America Women's Literary Humor from Colonial Times to the 1980s*. University: UP of Mississippi, 1988.

Nilsen, Don L. F. *Humor Scholarship: A Research Bibliography*. Westport: Greenwood, 1993.

Don L. F. Nilsen
Alleen Pace Nilsen

Humor and Art, until recently, were considered low brow in combination, if not downright vulgar, despite more than a few authorized works, including those of George Bellows (1882-1925) and the Ashcan School. All eight of the gifted Ashcan painters held jobs as cartoonists or magazine illustrators at one time. Pop Art painters of the 1960s, such as Roy Lichtenstein, Andy Warhol, and Jasper Jones, regularly drew humor into their works, pulling from comic-strip images for subjects and in the case of Lichtenstein, parodying other art or concealing jokes for the art-initiated.

Four categories of humorous art stand out. Humorous illustration includes subgenres dealing with book, magazine, newspaper, advertising, and decorative art. Norman Rockwell's paintings of Americana, Maurice Sendak's children's illustrations and mood-setting drawings accompanying newspaper and magazine articles all belong here (see entries), as does humorous decorative art, whether it is on book jackets, record album covers, or greeting cards. Since the 1930s, advertisers have recognized the vast potential of humorous art, applying it to products, everything from the Charles Atlas bodybuilding program (remember "Hey Skinny!") to breakfast cereals and insurance.

Among the cartoons are gag, social satire, and political or editorial. Gag cartoons depend upon simplicity and directness to relay a joke or humorous incident, and are usually drawn on a freelance basis for magazines. With the demise of many general interest magazines that were the seedbeds of gag cartoons, the genre is in a precarious state. Social satire and political/editorial cartoons fare much better. Most newspapers have political cartoons today, either syndicated or local (see entry).

Comic strips and their derivatives, comic books and animated cartoons, are the most widely read and viewed form of humorous art. They reach deep into American history (although "The Yellow Kid" of 1895 is celebrated as the first), have inspired other artists, and have profoundly affected popular fads, fashion, and even the language.

The long tradition of caricature, which attempts to capture the nuances of a person through humor, often by comparing human and animal traits, has not found a hospitable marketplace in recent years as the outlets dwindle and editors and publishers shy away from using it.

Although caricatures and gag cartoons are not as popular and prevalent as in their heydays before and slightly after World War II, the other forms of comic art have prospered. Generally, humor in art has become acceptable, and even respectable, because of more tolerance and understanding of the fine art community and zealous promotional activities and professionalization among the cartooning and graphic arts groups.

Bibliography

Lent, John A. *Comic Books and Comic Strips in the United States: An International Bibliography*. Westport: Greenwood, 1994.

Staake, Bob. *The Complete Book of Humorous Art*. Cincinnati: North Light, 1996

John A. Lent

See also

Cartoons: Theatrical and Television
Comic Books
Comic Strips

Humor and Ethnicity. Humor that deals with various ethnic groups and nationalities, members of religious, racial, linguistic, cultural, or national groups such as Jews, Poles, Italians, and Irish, has been common in America. Generally speaking, ethnic humor is made by members of in-groups about members of out-groups—those different from the person generating the humor. But in some cases ethnic groups tell ethnic jokes about themselves.

In dealing with ethnic humor, in addition to considering the subject of the humor, ethnic groups, we can also deal with the form of the humor, the techniques of humor generally used in ethnic humor, and the themes found in this humor. The most common forms of ethnic humor are jokes and riddles, jokes being understood as short narratives with a punch line. Riddles take the form of questions and answers. Ethnic humor generally involves techniques such as stereotyping, insult, imitation, ridicule, and the use of dialect. This humor focuses on alleged personality traits, physical characteristics, beliefs and common behaviors.

A brief sampling of ethnic riddles about Poles (their stereotype is that they are stupid), Italians (their stereotype is that they are dirty and often members of the Mafia), and young Jewish American women (their stereotype is that they don't cook and avoid sex) follows:

Q. *What has an IQ of 375?*
A. Poland.
Q. *Why do Italian men wear such pointy shoes?*
A. So they can kill bugs when they crawl into the corners.
Q. *How does a JAP (Jewish American Princess) get exercise?*
A. "Waitress!" (waving her arms frantically).

Other common stereotypes about ethnic groups in America are that the Irish are drunkards, that Mexicans are lazy, that the English are snobs, the Scots are cheap, Jews are materialists and cheap, and that African Americans are sexual supermen and criminals.

Ethnic humor can be understood as ascribed deflation of ethnic groups by other groups. In contemporary America, ethnic humor is not looked upon with favor, due, in part, to the multicultural nature of our society and to the refusal of ethnic groups to accept being ridiculed. Although the aggressive content of ethnic humor makes it unpleasant for the group being ridiculed, ethnic jokes may often be seen as a functional alternative to physical aggression and violence. Ethnic humor is, then, a means by which some people express their hostility and anger verbally rather than physically.

Ethnic humor, like all humor, reveals a good deal about the political arrangements and the preoccupations of various groups and subcultures in societies. The decline in the popularity of ethnic humor in America shows that various groups who were typically the subjects of this humor have enough status and power to make attacking them—in public, at least—unacceptable now. Though ethnic humor is not considered permissible in public forums and the mass media, it still flourishes in our folklore.

Bibliography

Berger, Arthur Asa. *An Anatomy of Humor*. New Brunswick: Transaction, 1993.

Davies, Christie. *Ethnic Humor around the World*. Bloomington: Indiana UP, 1990.

Dundes, Alan. *Cracking Jokes: Studies of Sick Humor Cycles and Stereotypes*. Berkeley: Ten Speed, 1987.

Arthur Asa Berger

Humor and Medicine. The possibilities of humor playing beneficial roles in health care are arousing curiosity and enthusiasm around the globe—especially Australia, Japan, India, and some Moslem countries. Health care professionals throughout the world are exploring possible roles for humor in their work. And health care professionals are becoming interested in the value of humor in their own lives.

Many organizations have formed during the past several decades, structured to provide support and interactive networking for the increasing number of believers in the value of humor. *Nurses for Laughter* was activated during the early 1980s and experienced enthusiastic reception during its relatively brief life. *The Humor Project*, centered in Saratoga Springs, NY, has persisted successfully since its inception in

1980 as a semi-private, semi-public venture. The American Association for Therapeutic Humor, headquartered in St. Louis, MO, has developed as a dynamic organization for communication, interaction, and coordination. It has recently initiated a program of regional and national meetings and conferences.

Exploration of the beneficial roles played by humor in health care is not limited to hands-on, intuitive experience of enthusiastic caretakers and providers. Formal studies have provided substantial data giving firm justification for belief that humor is good for health care. A pioneer study was carried out at the Andrus Gerontology Center of the University of Southern California (Los Angeles) and was reported favorably (Andrus Volunteers). Exploration of humor benefits in treatment of patients in Lyckorna Primary Health-Care Centre (Motala, Sweden) provided a positive report (Ljungdahl). Norman Cousins's individual experience with health care use of humor received worldwide attention and gave impetus to much similar personal and/or institutional experimentation with how humor may contribute to treatment, to quality of life during disease, even to health maintenance or disease prevention. Many laboratory, scientifically controlled studies have also been carried out, providing factual data which is consistent with the clinical and experiential information (Fry). Laboratory data has been obtained that demonstrates generally favorable effects during mirthful laughter on most of the major physiologic systems of the body. Evidence strongly suggests that response to humor is a total body experience. The medical psychological values of humor are similarly widely documented (Nahemow et al.).

Bibliography

Andrus Volunteers. *Humor: The Tonic You Can Afford.* Los Angeles: Goldenera, 1983.

Cousins, Norman. *Anatomy of an Illness as Perceived by the Patient.* New York: Norton, 1979.

Fry, William F. "The Biology of Humor." *Humor: International Journal of Humor Research* 7 (1994): 111-26.

Goldstein, Jeffrey H. "Therapeutic Effects of Laughter." *Handbook of Humor and Psychotherapy.* Ed. William F. Fry and Waleed A. Salameh. Sarasota: Professional Resource Exchange, 1987. 1-19.

Ljungdahl, Lars. "Laugh If This Is a Joke." *Journal of the American Medical Association* 261 (1989): 558.

Nahemow, Lucille, Kathleen A. McCluskey-Fawcett, and Paul E. McGhee. *Humor and Aging.* Orlando: Academic, 1986.

William F. Fry

Humor in Literature. Humor is the most nationalistically defined of the literary genres, and the development of American literary humor mirrors the nation's history. Benjamin Franklin wrote satiric, witty essays modeled after English high comedy. Most humor produced during colonial days did not approach the intellectual subtlety of Franklin's works, however, and the paradigm for critics has depended upon the frontier tradition—the roughness of the frontier and how American humor reflects that roughness in a physical, brutal stereotype (especially in the writings from the Old Southwest—A. B. Longstreet, W. T. Thompson, G. W. Harris, T. B. Thorpe) which includes boasting and exaggeration. While Franklin was producing erudite essays, the precursors of Old Southwest humorists were creating a different heritage.

Thus, American humor is a combination of the colonial tradition, epitomized by T. C. Haliburton, and that of the Old Southwest, which is an outgrowth of the backwoods genus. The figures of the Yankee and the backwoodsman emerged early and full-bodied as the prototype of the American character. Ironically, these are contradictory types: Yankee humor was "gradual," "pervasive," "subtle," spare, and the Yankee stood alone; backwoods humor was "broad," "grotesque" "macabre," and profuse, and backwoodsmen appeared in pairs (Rourke 76).

In 18th-century Hartford, CT, the Hartford Wits (J. Trumbull, T. Dwight, J. Barlow) became famous for their light verse. After the turn of the century, Washington Irving continued the high humor tradition in *A History of New York* (1809). High humor incorporated American themes, characters, and locales, but was English in accent.

Among the first to introduce frontier language and manners into humor was J. K. Paulding. J. R. Lowell's *Bigelow Papers* (first series, 1848) exemplifies dialect humor linking Yankee lore and the comic fiction of the late 19th century. Lowell was also editor of the *Atlantic Monthly* (founded 1857), which gave impetus to the dominant local color movement in the 1870s and 1880s. The inclusion of humorous sketches in newspapers was an important element in the development of American humor as practiced by Artemus Ward, David Ross Locke, Josh Billings, Finley Peter Dunne, and Ambrose Bierce, who wrote in the vernacular, with popular idioms and spelling.

This background helped produce Mark Twain, America's premier humorist. Twain included these elements in his writing, yet he is superior to his predecessors because his style and significant themes, particularly in *The Adventures of Huckleberry Finn* (1884), are derivative but transcend that background and make his work universal and unique.

Meanwhile, the Romantic movement flourishing in Europe moved across the Atlantic. By century's end, the shift from Romanticism began, and the mainstream confronted new perceptions as a result of World War I. Nevertheless, humor was thriving in a number of venues. The Roaring Twenties/Jazz Age opened new possibilities of expression. In Harlem, Langston Hughes created the character Jesse B. Simple. In contrast, college humor magazines were fertile grounds for humorists.

Beginning with *American Magazine and Monthly Chronicle* in 1757, American humor magazine history is filled with successful entries, the *New Yorker* being preeminent. The concept of high humor in the United States was reestablished in the journal, and many important humorists contributed to and defined the *New Yorker* style, as pursued by Robert Benchley, Dorothy Parker, S. J. Perelman, and James Thurber.

Centering on the "Little Man" character, this humor is human, cultivated, sensitive. The polished style is lyrical, gentle, relaxed, urbane. Though the writers may appear dilettantish, they are not foppish, silly, or stupid. They are quiet, amused, wistful, romantic, wise but innocently foolish. If their personae are pretentious at the beginning of a story, they are not at the end.

Related to magazine humor is comic newspaper writing from *American Magazine* to *The Spirit of the Times* to the present. George Ade, Damon Runyon, and Will Rogers in the early 20th century were more tempered than were the writers of the Old Southwest, but there is a distinct connection between these authors. There is a similar connection with contemporary writers such as Andy Rooney, Art Buchwald, Erma Bombeck, and Dave Barry. Newspaper humorists write about quotidian events, in the vernacular, and fill their writing with references to popular culture.

American humor remains a mixture in the 20th century. William Faulkner's novels contain humor related to that of the Old Southwest; the literary black, ironic humor of Vladimir Nabokov, J. D. Salinger, Joseph Heller, and Kurt Vonnegut, Jr., and the Jewish novelists Saul Bellow, Bernard Malamud, and Philip Roth is akin to the Yankee tradition.

On the stage, native humor has been present since Royall Tyler's *The Contrast* (1781). Stage comedy since has seldom risen above the popular level of musical comedies or a Neil Simon.

Regionally, Eastern humor is associated with the urban centers, is knowing, sophisticated, understated, self-deprecatory, ironic; cruelty and physical violence are mainstays in the South and the Southwest; Midwestern humor is down to earth, filled with rural horse sense expressed in proverbs glorifying the simple and distrustful of sophistication (a humor predominating from the 1930s through the 1950s, propelled by radio); raw, untamed, exaggerated Western humor is less prevalent.

Diversity is inherent in American humor to a greater extent than in most national literary humors—America is the great melting pot literarily as well as racially. While there are momentary differences throughout the country's history and various locales, a pattern extends across time and geography. Whether the Yankee, the backwoodsman, or the *New Yorker* paradigm is used, American humor is characterized by a blend more diversified and complicated than the traditional stereotype suggests.

Bibliography

Cohen, Sarah Blacher. *Comic Relief: Humor in Contemporary American Literature*. Detroit: Wayne State UP, 1992.

Holiday, Carl. *The Wit and Humor of Colonial Days*. Williamstown: Corner House, 1975.

Rourke, Constance. *American Humor: A Study of the National Character.* 1931. Tallahassee: Florida State UP, 1986.

Steven H. Gale

Humorous Mysteries. In the real world, combining comedy with corpses is considered tasteless, but in the fictional world, murder and humor have had a long partnership. American readers have long delighted in the dry wit and keen-edged satire of such British writers as Agatha Christie, Ngaio Marsh, Margery Allingham, Dorothy L. Sayers, Michael Innes, and Edmund Crispin, as well as in more recent British authors, like Patricia Moyes, Robert Barnard, Paula Gosling, Reginald Hill, and Sarah Caudwell, who display similar comic virtuosity. The humorous genre has a clearly established history in the United States as well. S. S. Van Dine, creator of the witty and urbane Philo Vance, and Ellery Queen quickly gained popularity in the 1920s. Later, Phoebe Atwood Taylor's mysteries gain humor from ironic titles (*Dead Ernest* features a victim named Ernest), comic characters, and farcical situations. Rex Stout introduced the wisecracking Archie Goodwin and his orchid-growing employer Nero Wolfe; and writing as A. A. Fair, Erle Stanley Gardner originated the witty Bertha Cool. The last few decades have seen a marked increase in humorous mysteries, highlighted by authors such as Charlotte MacLeod, Elizabeth Peters, Donald Westlake, Joan Hess, Kathy Trocheck, Charlaine Harris, Susan Dunlap, and Carole Nelson Douglas. Perhaps as contemporary life becomes more violent and complicated, the need for order is irrevocably joined with the need for laughter.

Bibliography

Keating, H. R. F. "Comedy and the British Crime Novel." *Comic Crime*. Ed. Earl F. Bargainnier. Bowling Green, OH: Bowling Green State U Popular P, 1987.

Susan L. Peters

See also

Mystery Parodies

Huston, John (1906-1987), was among the generation of American film directors that came of artistic age in the 1940s and were esteemed in the mass public imagination as among the most accomplished in Hollywood, a member of a rich company: Elia Kazan, Joseph Mankiewicz, Preston Sturges, Billy Wilder, and Fred Zinnemann, to name a few, in addition to John Huston. These individuals also each underwent a disorienting rollercoaster so far as the critical community is concerned, alternately extolled and abused.

Born to an itinerant journalist, Rhea Gore, and his celebrated actor father, Walter (who memorably embodied his son's ability to laugh in the face of failure in *The Treasure of the Sierra Madre* [1948]), John Huston acquired his love of language, admiration for actors, and propensity for literary adaptation virtually through genetic infusion. Prior to becoming a director, he trained in the visual arts, published fiction in H. L. Mencken's *American Mercury*, wrote for various newspapers, acted with the renowned Provincetown Players, and entered the motion picture industry as a scriptwriter, first at Universal and later for the more prestigious Warner Brothers before making his justly celebrated debut with *The Maltese Falcon* (1941).

Huston's career, like that of many of his professional peers, temporarily took a sideline when the United States entered World War II. He served in the U.S. War Department as a member of the Army Pictorial Service, completing three films in the process: *Report from the Aleutians* (1943), *The Battle of San Pietro* (1945), and *Let There Be Light* (1946).

Huston directed best when he endeavored to do the least; when he had a thematic or technological cross to bear, the results frequently proved overwrought if not unbearable. That appears to be the case with *The African Queen* (1951) and *Moulin Rouge* (1952), the former an inspired act of casting that collapses under the weight of an inadequate sense of place while the latter amounts to an exercise in art direction rather than compelling narrative. There are the other altogether dispensable efforts from this period—*The Barbarian and the Geisha* (1958) and *The Roots of Heaven* (1958)—that may well have helped Huston pay off his ever recurring debts but gave the spectator little return for his admission. On the other hand, *Moby Dick* (1956), while not a complete success, aspires to and achieves a sense of grandeur that one finds in few of the director's films. *Beat the Devil* (1954), a jeu d'esprit that dispenses with conventional narrative prescriptions, deserves its cult reputation as one of Huston's most likable and light-hearted efforts. *Heaven Knows, Mr. Allison* (1957), an underrated film, remains one of those rare occasions when Huston just let two well-drawn characters— a war-weary marine (Robert Mitchum) and a stranded nun (Deborah Kerr)—interact with understated results.

The 1960s found Huston often the subject of publicity (his locations frequently were the setting for inspired journalism) rather than critical accolades. More than once, his budgets exceeded any substance discernible on screen, as was the case with *The Bible...In the Beginning* (1965) and his portions of the multi-directed *Casino Royale* (1968). *The Unforgiven* (1960), *The Misfits* (1961), and *Freud* (1962) each exhibit considerable intelligence and Huston's penchant for inspired casting, but once again thematic aims exceed adequate results. Other productions of the time remain pleasant, unstrenuous exercises that stretched neither Huston nor his audience: the narratively concatenated thriller *The List of Adrian Messenger* (1963) and the period pieces *Sinful Davy* (1969) and *A Walk with Love and Death* (1969). Two highlights from the period, however, remain: *The Night of the Iguana* (1964) and *Reflections in a Golden Eye* (1967). He brought to the potentially overheated and bombastic writing of Tennessee Williams and Carson McCullers his customary even-handed and unaggressive approach to narrative and characterization, turning what might have been turgid into transcendent evocations of wayward souls at odds with circumstances.

The final two decades of Huston's career include some of his most accomplished films. Unlike a number of his peers, he not only managed to continue to work in an industry that appeared to identify age with ossification but also tackled demanding material with a deftness that one observed in few of his earlier films. He also proved to be a photogenic and facile actor, though one often employed more for the gravity of his presence and the sonorousness of his voice than whatever skills he might bring to a part. Two roles do stand out: his comic depiction of the self-assured Secretary of State under President Theodore Roosevelt, John Hay, in the period piece *The Wind and the Lion* (1975) and most particularly his venal patriarch Noah Cross in Roman Polanski's *Chinatown* (1954), a character David Thomson describes as "a terrible charismatic paradox, a bastard and an aristocrat." So too was his directorial acumen often squandered, during the early 1980s most of all; who recalls *Phobia* (1980) or *Victory* (1981) and how many wish to forget *Annie* (1982)? Commentators at the time dismissed two spy thrillers, *The Kremlin Letter* (1970) and *The Mackintosh Man* (1973), which in retrospect contain acidic expressions of Huston's nihilistic fascination with entropy and futility. That predilection for gazing into the void colors as well Huston's 1984 adaptation of Malcolm Lowry's *Under the Volcano* (in which Albert Finney's tour de force as an alcoholic is obscured by the director's uncertain grasp of a more than likely unfilmable novel), *Prizzi's Honor* (1985) (which promoted the career of his talented daughter, Anjelica), and his valedictory effort, *The Dead*.

For all that has been written about Huston, he remains an underappreciated and not wholly comprehended director. His oversized legend (both self-created and the product of memoirs as well as roman à clef) obscures his all too human aptitudes and liabilities. A number of perspectives would prove ripe for reconsidering his career. First, his relationship to literary texts and predetermined canons, the majority of his works being adaptations; second, the gender dynamics of his narratives. While driven almost without exception by males, the stress on their behavior permits an examination of the complexity of masculinity. Third, as committed as Huston is to unfilled quests, one could through the films reexamine our national predilection for the gospel of success and aversion to any form of failure. Clearly, much as the most accomplished work of Huston's oeuvre came in the final decades of his life, more fully considered analyses of his career lie ahead of us, as elusive and potentially as rewarding as a Maltese Falcon, a buried treasure, or a white whale.

Bibliography

Cooper, Stephen. *Perspectives on John Huston*. New York: Hall, 1994.

Huston, John. *An Open Book*. New York: Knopf, 1980.

Studlar, Gaylyn, and David Pesser. *Reflections in a Male Eye: John Huston and the American Experience*. Washington: Smithsonian Institution, 1993.

David Sanjek

Hutto, J(oseph) B(enjamin) (1926-1983), is notable among modern blues musicians for his gritty vocals and raucous slide guitar work. As a prominent figure on the Chicago music scene in the early 1950s, Hutto played an important part in urbanizing the blues.

Like many Chicago blues musicians, Hutto came to the city from the rural South. One of seven children, he was born in Blackville, SC, and raised in Augusta, GA, in a farming family with strong religious beliefs. After his father's death in 1949, J. B.'s mother relocated the family to Chicago in hopes of better employment opportunities.

Hutto started his performing career as a drummer for a local band, Johnny Ferguson and His Twisters. He later tried piano before settling on the guitar, which he played with a bottleneck or metal bar called a "slide" on his left hand. As a leader, he named his first band the Hawks (as would be the case with all of his later bands), and they quickly developed a reputation as one of the loudest, most dynamic groups on the Chicago club circuit. The Hawks' first recording, a 45 rpm single featuring "Pet Cream Man" and "Lovin' You," was released on Chance Records, a small, Chicago-based label, in 1954.

In the 1960s and 1970s, Hutto's declamatory vocals, stinging guitar solos, colorful stage-wear (most notably, exotic hats), and energetic performing style appealed to fans raised on the visual theatrics of rock and roll. Similarly, his music appealed to rock fans interested in the roots of the genre.

Hutto's repertoire included blues standards such as "Dust My Broom," made famous by his musical idol Elmore James, popular songs such as "Summertime," and original compositions. As a lyricist, Hutto was noted for his double entendres and emotionally direct lines about lost love. Of songwriting in general, Hutto once said, "You write a song like a man, not a boy, but a man that's saying something about his life." The popularity of Hutto's music is in part attributable to the cathartic quality of the blues.

Hutto recorded and performed in venues across the country through the early 1980s. His last album, *Slippin' and Slidin'*, was recorded three months prior to his death on June 12, 1983. Hutto won *Down Beat* magazine's International Critics Award for Rock-Pop-Blues group deserving of wider recognition in 1969 and was inducted into the Blues Foundation's Hall of Fame in 1985. His legacy has been carried on by his nephew, slide guitarist Ed Williams, who performs some of Hutto's music with his band Lil' Ed and the Blues Imperials.

Bibliography

Harris, Sheldon. *Blues Who's Who: A Biographical Dictionary of Blues Singers*. New Rochelle: Arlington House, 1979.

Herzhaft, Gerard. *Encyclopedia of the Blues*. Fayetteville: UP of Arkansas, 1992.

Rowe, Mike. *Chicago Blues: The City and the Music*. New York: Da Capo, 1975.

Santelli, Robert. *The Big Book of Blues: A Biographical Encyclopedia*. New York: Penguin, 1993.

Weld, Dave. "Living Blues Interview: J. B. Hutto." *Living Blues: A Journal of the African-American Blues Tradition* 30 (Nov. 1976): 14-24.

Mark Madigan

Hypertext. Hypertextuality embodies the way users read and write with a computer. Hypertext refers to nonlinear reading and writing, and linking documents together. An example would be clicking on a word or button in a program and a new concept or feature appears on the screen. These experiences have become common on the World Wide Web and in CD-Rom instructional materials. The term "hypertext" was coined by Ted Nelson (see entry) in 1965, but the concept of linking documents is old. The poet Samuel Coleridge envisioned links between literary works. And, in the 1930s, a proposal to build a machine that could retrieve associated documents in libraries was printed in the *Atlantic Monthly*. Databases, networks, gophers, and "hot links" on the Internet reflect this desire to connect documents. Because hypertext is supposed to work like the human mind, by association, many computer programmers see it as the ultimate information retrieval system. Since the advent of personal computing, futurists have been discussing the freedom of hypertext environments. Some see hypertext as a completely new form of literacy, where readers can add their thoughts to larger documents and writers can connect their works to the works they cite. In 1987, several organizations were formed to discuss and promote hypertextuality. Since then software tools for creating "hyperfictions," Internet hypertexts, and training hypertexts have been developed. Many software Help systems use hypertext features so that users don't have to scroll through long lists of text.

Bibliography

Evans, Tim. *10 Minute Guide to HTML*. Indianapolis: Que, 1995.

Nielsen, Jakob. *Multimedia and Hypertext: The Internet and Beyond*. Boston: AP Professional, 1995.

Tittel, Ed, and Steve James. *HTML for Dummies*. Foster City: IDG, 1996.

William E. Studwell

See also

Computers and Popular Culture

I Spy (1965-1968) was a revolutionary spy show in many ways. It was the first television program to star a black actor—Bill Cosby—in an ongoing mainstream role. As such it established Cosby as a star (see entry). Cosby played Alexander Scott, trainer and manager to international tennis champion Kelly Robinson (Robert Culp). But the two were actually undercover agents for an American spy organization who traveled to exotic locales each week.

Throughout its three-year run on NBC, the program remained high in the ratings. It did not focus on Cosby's race nor did it ignore it. By showing a close relationship between a black and white man as "natural," it did more for racial harmony than more preachy television approaches.

Robert Culp (see entry) had made his mark in the film *PT 109* in 1963. He also demonstrated talent as a writer and director for *I Spy*. Much of the repartee between Culp and Cosby was ad-libbed and resulted from the genuine friendship between them. Cosby stated that Culp taught him everything he knew about acting and was a bit embarrassed to win three Emmys in a row while Culp received none. In 1994, a two-hour special reunited Cosby and Culp in their original roles.

Bibliography

Brown, Les. *Encyclopedia of Television*. Detroit: Gale Research, 1992.

Meyers, Richard. *TV Detectives*. San Diego: Barnes, 1981.

Terrace, Vincent. *Encyclopedia of Television Series, Pilots and Specials: 1937-1973*. Vol 1. New York: Zoetrope, 1985.

——. *Encyclopedia of Television Series, Pilots and Specials: 1974-1984*. Vol 2. New York: Zoetrope, 1985.

—. *Fifty Years of Television*. New York: Cornwall, 1991.

Frank A. Salamone

Ian, Janis (1951-), is an American-born singer/songwriter whose first record, "Society's Child," was also a controversial popular song in the late 1960s. Ian was born Janis Eddy Fink in 1951 in New York City. She adopted her performing name after her brother's middle name, Ian.

Music figured early in her life, since her mother was a music teacher. Ian began writing folk songs while she was in junior high school. One of her songs, "Hair of Spun Gold," was published in the folk magazine *Broadside* when she was just 12 years old.

Ian's first release was a song she wrote in 1966 while waiting to see her high school guidance counselor. "Society's Child" spoke in intimate terms about an interracial romantic relationship between teenagers. The lyrics were written from the point of view of a white girl whose friends, parents, and teachers disapprove of her dating an African-American boy.

The lyrics of "Society's Child" proved too controversial for many radio stations. In April 1967, however, Leonard Bernstein included the song on one of his CBS television specials, *Inside Pop: The Rock Revolution*. The special was designed to show that many of the current popular songs were complex enough to be taken as seriously as classical music. Janis Ian played the song on the program with the accompaniment of the New York Philharmonic Orchestra.

The song reached No. 14 on the U.S. singles chart, and her debut album also sold well. But in 1968, Ian's second album, *All the Seasons of Your Mind*, barely made the Top 200. And a third album released that same year, *The Secret Life of J. Eddy Fink*, did not chart at all. Ian abandoned her career, married, and moved to Philadelphia.

Ian returned to public life in 1971, playing concert dates and recording an album for Capitol Records, *Present Company*. The album did not sell well. In 1973, Roberta Flack scored a hit with Ian's song "Jesse." Buoyed by the song's success, Columbia Records signed Ian and in July 1974 released the album *Stars*, which included Ian's version of "Jesse." The autobiographical title song earned heavy airplay on FM stations.

The next year, Ian recorded "At Seventeen," another intensely personal song about an ugly duckling who compares herself to the "perfect faces" she sees around her. Ian wrote the song in 1973 while she was divorced, destitute, and living with her mother. It reached No. 3 on the singles charts and earned Ian a Grammy. The single was included on her second Columbia album *Between the Lines*, which reached No. 1 and went gold. Her next seven albums sold progressively worse, although they were produced by top producers and featured well-known backup musicians.

In 1982 Ian left Columbia Records, married again, and moved to Los Angeles. She took up acting lessons and recorded a duet with Mel Torme of her song "Silly Habits." The song was nominated for a Grammy Award.

Janis Ian's third recording career started ten years later with the album *Breaking Silence* (1993), the title of which, according to Ian, was a double entendre to announce that she was gay. Ian has continued to tour and to record: *Revenge* (1995), *Hunger* (1997), and *god & the fbi* (2000).

Bibliography

LaBlanc, Michael L. *Contemporary Musicians: Profiles of the People in Music*. Detroit: Gale, 1991.

Pareles, John. *The Rolling Stone Encyclopedia of Rock and Roll*. New York: Rolling Stone/Summit, 1983.

Stambler, Irwin. *Encyclopedia of Pop, Rock, and Soul*. New York: St. Martin's, 1977.

Ken Nagelberg

IBM, or "Big Blue" in popular culture, is one of the wealthiest, best-known corporations in the world. Brushing off clone makers, and facing down a federal antitrust suit, the giant sold reputation and security as well as hardware, and became the most admired American corporation of the

1970s and 1980s. While the early 1990s were difficult for IBM—losses in 1993 exceeded $8 billion as the mainframe giant failed to adjust quickly to the personal computer revolution—the company has since rebounded.

IBM originated from the company that Herman Hollerith started in the 1890s to sell punch cards and card readers to government bureaus and insurance agencies. New owner Thomas Watson renamed the company "International Business Machines," expanding into electric typewriters and other office machines. Watson built a highly motivated and disciplined sales force. The inside motto was "THINK," but users were warned not to "fold, spindle or mutilate" the cards. This phrase became the basis for countless cartoons and jokes that linked the mainframe computer with repressive central authority.

Bibliography

Fishman, Katherine Davis. *The Computer Establishment.* New York: Harper & Row, 1981.

Richard Jensen

See also
Mainframe Computers

Identity Christians first came to the attention of the general public in 1985, when the Federal Bureau of Investigation revealed that several armed robberies and the murders of Denver radio talk show host Alan Berg and several young men had been committed by a band of "white racist terrorists" called variously "The Order," "Bruders Schweigen," and the "White American Bastion." The subsequent trials and convictions of some 30 persons—male and female—for crimes related to the activities of this group signaled a "chilling trend in racist activity," according to the Anti-Defamation League of B'nai B'rith in a report mailed to potential contributors.

Ten Identity Christian group leaders were also charged in a plot to overthrow the U.S. government in 1987, but were ultimately acquitted. Other organizations, such as the Citizens Freedom Foundation and Center for Democratic Renewal, have not only challenged the legitimacy of the religious beliefs held by those involved in the Order and like-minded groups, but have called such doctrines "cult-like and deserving criminal prosecution."

The primary goal of the Identity Christian (or Christian Identity movement) is to do battle against a "satanic cabal" that has infiltrated the dominant institutions of society, such as the media, schools, and churches. This cabal is trying to subvert "God's will" by promoting equal rights for "unqualified ethnic and racial minorities, non-Christian religions, and moral perversion." Most Identity believers see the Order, a faction of the larger group, as being too extremist and, ultimately, as a hindrance to the general acceptance of Identity beliefs, although most do believe that a revolution to save the white race may well be necessary at some point.

Identity Christians veer sharply away from fundamentalists in asserting their belief that through studying the Bible true seekers will find "convincing proof that the Anglo-Saxon, Celtic, Scandinavian, Germanic and related peoples, often called 'the Christian nations,' are the racial descendants of the tribes of Israel...[and that] the United States and Canada uniquely fulfill the prophesied place of the regathering of all the tribes of the Israel of God."

Identity Christians also seek to establish a paradise within the United States and hope to do so once non-whites (or "mud peoples") disappear, which they believe will happen eventually, either through deportation or race wars. Some believers have sought to establish such a paradise in the northwestern United States and southern Canada, where land is relatively inexpensive and plentiful—and where few minorities can be found.

Identity believers, like most conservative Christians, want to return God to public life, in the belief that once that happens, life will improve dramatically. Identity, of course, goes much further in advocating that certain minorities be eliminated from all society, an act they feel will also return God to society. And many seek to return laws based on biblical principles to our legal sysem, as do Christian Reconstructionists.

Bibliography

Barkun, Michael. *Religion and the Racist Right: The Origins of the Christian Identity Movement.* Chapel Hill: UP of North Carolina, 1994.

Bulter, Richard G. *Who Are the Aryan Nations?* 1987.

Coates, James. *Armed and Dangerous: The Rise of the Survivalist Right.* New York: Hill and Wang, 1987.

Flynn, Kevin, and Gary Gerhardt. *The Silent Brotherhood.* New York: Free, 1990.

"The Hate Movement Today: A Special Report." Anti-Defamation League of B'nai B'rith, 1988.

Larson, Viola. *Identity: A Resurrection of the Third Reich?* 1989.

Linda Collette

I'll Fly Away (1991-1993), in just two seasons, was one of the most honored television programs. Producers and writers Joshua Brand and John Falsey made television history in 1992 when their two series, *I'll Fly Away* and *Northern Exposure*, were nominated for an unprecedented 31 Emmy Award nominations.

I'll Fly Away's charged drama is set in the South of the late 1950s and into the 1960s, as racial upheaval ushers in the civil rights movement. Sam Waterston played a district attorney, Regina Taylor his housekeeper, Lilly Harper. The series has been compared to the novel *To Kill a Mockingbird*; Lilly Harper's name suggests Harper Lee, author of the novel. *I'll Fly Away* captured audiences with its gripping historical drama about a time when hope, perseverance, and personal commitment held a dream for a new, more tolerant America even if the realization of this dream has not fully been achieved.

Among its many accomplishments *I'll Fly Away* and its cast garnered a Peabody Award, two Humanities Awards, two Emmys, 22 Emmy Award nominations, a Producer Guild Award, American Television Awards, Golden Globe Awards, Directors Guild Awards, 1992 Quality Awards for Viewers for Quality Television, the TV Critics Association Award, and three 25th Annual NAACP Image Awards. But the best award that this program had was its intensely loyal viewers, who are given credit for not only keeping it on

NBC for a second season, but also for the decision by the Public Broadcasting Service to continue the series and produce the film *I'll Fly Away: Then and Now* (1993).

Bibliography

Berman, Marc. "Reviews: *I'll Fly Away*." *Variety* 14 Oct. 1991: 247.

Collum, Danny Duncan. "*I'll Fly Away* Is a Worthy Step Toward Civil-Rights Genre." *National Catholic Reporter* 18 Oct. 1991: 17.

Zoglin, Richard. "They Were All Heroes." *Time* 11 Oct. 1993: 82-84.

Jennifer A. Machiorlatti

Indians in Film and Television is a fundamentally important subject in contemporary society because, for the past century, Hollywood studios have dictated popular images of American Indians. Critics have bemoaned the film industry's depiction of Indians as hostile warriors who merely obstruct western settlement, or as noble savages doomed to extinction. Rarely, they seem to say, have Hollywood Indians gone beyond these formulaic stereotypes.

The release of Kevin Costner's *Dances with Wolves* (1990) appeared to have ushered in a new wave of pro-Indian films. Costner's multimillion-dollar epic, which captured seven Academy Awards (including best picture), proved to be a box-office bonanza, and Hollywood eagerly followed with other sympathetic Indian sagas: *Thunderheart* (1992), *The Last of the Mohicans* (1993), *Geronimo: An American Legend* (1993), and Disney's animated musical, *Pocahontas* (1995). Critics hailed *Dances with Wolves* as being the first film to cast Indian actors in lead roles, the first to incorporate Native American dialogue, and the first to portray Indians sympathetically. The fact is, filmmakers had been experimenting with these same themes since the early 1900s.

The movies' initial depictions of American Indians were, in part, influenced by the dime novels, Wild West shows, and stage plays of the "noble savage" that were firmly embedded in American culture. These earliest films were silent and only several minutes in length: *The Sioux Ghost Dance*, made in 1894 by the Thomas Edison studios, was actually a "kinetoscope" film viewed through a peephole. The brief sequence was nothing more than several Indians beating on drums and stomping around the stage in full regalia of breechcloth and headfeathers.

The early silent years brought a variety of Native American images to the screen. The films were short—usually 10 to 15 minutes in length—and their stories were often simplistic, but the absence of studio monopolies and censorship organizations allowed movie producers more diversity and creativity. Indian-themed pictures were especially popular from 1910 to 1912, when studios released approximately 12 to 15 per month.

Popular literary tales of American Indians frequently became a source for movie stories. Edison studios reenacted the classic tale of John Rolfe and his marriage to the Indian princess in *Pocahontas* (1908), and in 1907, the Independent Motion Picture Company brought Henry Longfellow's immortal poem *Hiawatha* to the screen, followed in 1910 by its sequel, *The Death of Minnehaha*. The American Mutoscope and Biograph Company produced the screen's first version of Helen Hunt Jackson's poignant tale, *Ramona* (1910). There was even *An Indian Romeo and Juliet* (1912), in which a young Huron man falls in love with an (enemy) Mohawk maiden.

American movie pioneer D. W. Griffith (see entry) brought a variety of Indian images to the screen. *The Redman and the Child* (1908) was Griffith's first Western and arguably his best: an Indian warrior rescues a kidnapped white boy and avenges the death of the boy's grandfather by killing the outlaws. In the final scene, the Indian paddles the canoe back to the campsite, with the child safely asleep by his side. In other Griffith films, Indians might besiege a family's cabin (*Fighting Blood*, 1911) or attack a covered wagon (*The Last Drop of Water*, 1911) but their behavior was often provoked by villainous whites. In *The Battle at Elderbush Gulch* (1914), the Sioux Indians terrorize a community of innocent settlers when their chief is cruelly assassinated by a white man.

Griffith's contemporary, Thomas H. Ince, occasionally explored the cultural aspects of Indian life. In 1911, Ince transported a tribe of Oglala Sioux Indians from Pine Ridge, South Dakota, to his scenic ranch in California's Santa Monica Mountains. For the next several years, Ince produced more than 80 Westerns that included Native Americans as subjects. One of them, *The Invaders* (1912), is the story of Sioux retaliation against the invasion of railroad surveyors upon their lands.

The transition to feature-length films (1912-13) brought longer and more complex Indian stories to the screen. The all-Indian idyllic love tales of D. W. Griffith and other artists became less popular as films began to grapple with Indian/white intermarriages, racial discrimination, and cultural marginality. *The Squaw Man* (1914), based upon Edwin Milton Royle's popular stage play, shows the tragic demise of an Indian woman's marriage to a white man. Not all Indian/white marriages were doomed, however; in *The Heart of Wetona* (1919), a Blackfeet woman ultimately chooses a life with her white husband rather than remain with her tribe.

The "marginal man" theme of an educated Indian who is scorned by both white civilization and his own people was also popular. Alan Hale's *Braveheart* (1925), based upon William C. de Mille's 1905 play, *Strongheart*, told the story of an educated Yakima Indian who must face society's prejudice as well as his tribe's ostracism. In *The Half-Breed* (1916), directed by Allan Dwan and produced by D. W. Griffith, the mixed-blood hero flees to the secluded wilderness in order to escape the town's bigotry. Matinee idol Douglas Fairbanks plays the title role.

Other, bolder films condemned federal Indian policies. George Seitz's *The Vanishing American* (1925), based upon a Zane Grey magazine serial, delivers a sharp indictment against the country's corrupt and mismanaged Indian reservations.

The silent film era introduced many talented Indian actors. Although non-Indians (including black Americans and Japanese) frequently portrayed Indian characters, a few notable Native Americans occasionally performed in key roles. Lillian St. Cyr, a Winnebago Indian known in Hollywood as "Red Wing," portrayed the lead in the 1914 version of *The Squaw Man*. Chief John Big Tree, a Seneca Indian, began in silent films and became a regular in the Westerns of director John Ford, including *The Iron Horse* (1924), *Drums along the Mohawk* (1939), and *She Wore a Yellow Ribbon* (1948). Chief Yowlache (Yakima), an established singer and actor, appeared in many silent films, including the title role in *With Sitting Bull at the "Spirit Lake Massacre"* (1927). Conversely, celebrated Cherokee statesman, writer, and comedian Will Rogers rose to stardom in films as a non-Indian before his untimely death in 1935.

A few talented Native Americans became movie directors. James Young Deer, a Winnebago Indian, was head of production for the French-owned Pathé Frères studios in Los Angeles. From 1911 to 1913, Young Deer directed more than 100 Indian- and Spanish-themed films. His short films were thematically versatile in content, often portraying American Indians as heroes (or heroines) alongside two-dimensional white characters. Edwin Carewe, a quarter Chickasaw, began as an actor for the Lubin Manufacturing Company and years later rose to the rank of director in major Hollywood studios. Carewe's career spanned more than 30 years in the movies, and he was best noted for directing the third screen version of *Ramona* in 1928, starring Dolores Del Rio.

The advent of "talking" pictures in the late 1920s did not immediately alter the Indian's screen image. While Raoul Walsh's mega-budget *The Big Trail* (1930) plummeted at the box office and consequently buried the cowboy epic for several years, Indians began to appear outside the Western genre. *The Silent Enemy* (1930), for example, dramatizes the Ojibwa Indians' struggle against hunger before the arrival of the Europeans and employed an all-Indian cast. Other key films highlight native tradition and take a close look at Indian survival against white civilization. Metro-Goldwyn-Mayer's *Eskimo* (1933), spoken in the Inuit language with English titles, shows how European contact corrupts an isolated Native Alaskan community. Warner Brothers' *Massacre* (1933) exposes the neglect of America's Indians living on reservations, and the only screen version of Oliver La Farge's widely acclaimed tale, *Laughing Boy* (1934), reveals white exploitation of Navajo culture.

Indian/white intermarriages surface again in the early 1930s, often with ambiguous results. Paramount's *Behold My Wife!* (1934) shows a wealthy eastern man who marries an educated Apache woman in order to spite his parents. The Academy Award-winning *Cimarron* (1930), a much overlooked liberal Western for its time, is the story of the Oklahoma Land Rush, which includes the successful marriage of the hero's white son to the family's Indian servant. On the other hand, *Call Her Savage* (1932) casts the coquettish Clara Bow in the title role as a half Indian and half white woman whose romances with Caucasian men repeatedly end in disaster. Only when the heroine settles down with her half-breed suitor does she find happiness.

The rise of the "B Westerns" in the mid-1930s endlessly recycled the most simplistic plots of good vs. bad Indian characters. Costly scenes of Indian attacks or buffalo stampedes were reused in subsequent pictures, and whites in Indian makeup would serve as inexpensive substitutes for Indian extras. Movie serials popularized the Indian-as-villain and ally in titles such as *The Last of the Mohicans* (1932), *The Miracle Rider* (1935), and *The Lone Ranger* (1938), the latter featuring "Chief Thundercloud" (Cherokee) as the screen's first Tonto. (Jay Silverheels, of Canadian Mohawk descent, later portrayed Tonto in the popular 1950s television series of the same name.)

By the mid-1930s, Hollywood had reestablished the 19th-century belief in a Manifest Destiny—the concept of American expansion across the continent—with cowboys as heroes and Indians obstructing the path to western settlement. From Cecil B. DeMille's *The Plainsman* in late 1936, which immortalizes Wild Bill Hickok and Buffalo Bill Cody, to John Ford's *Stagecoach* in 1939, in which the Apaches are mowed down like blades of grass, these Western pictures cast Indians as unwelcome aliens in their own land, and left an indelible mark on the American mind.

With the outbreak of World War II, the Japanese and the Nazis became the screen's new villains, while Indians emerged as America's allies. Indians serve North American interests in DeMille's *Northwest Mounted Police* (1940), a story of the uprising of the Métis (the French and Indian mixed bloods) against the Canadian government in Saskatchewan. In Warner Brothers' *They Died with Their Boots On* (1941), another biography of George Armstrong Custer, the Army officer becomes the personal guardian of the Sioux people and even refers to Crazy Horse as his brother.

Indian policy changed in the 1950s as Congress approved a sweeping measure known as "Federal Termination." The program eliminated the Indian's special wardship status with the U.S. government by encouraging Native American assimilation into white society (namely, reservation lands dissolved and Indians relocated to urban areas). Hollywood lost no time in advocating this policy of "racial inclusion" in Westerns dealing with Indian/white relations. Delmer Daves's *Broken Arrow* (1950), a true story about the friendship between a U.S. mail rider and the Apache Indian chief Cochise, displays conspicuous tolerance and sympathy toward its Indian characters while proposing assimilation as a solution to the "Indian problem." The film's success spurred the popular television series *Broken Arrow* (ABC, 1956-58), which reiterates the postwar ideal of a peaceful Indian/white coexistence. Other television Westerns preached the same theme: *Brave Eagle* (CBS, 1955-56), *Cheyenne* (ABC, 1957-63), *Wagon Train* (ABC, 1957-65), and *Yancy Derringer* (CBS, 1958-59).

Later Westerns shed some of their idealism while becoming more skeptical of white attitudes. In Otto Preminger's *River of No Return* (1954), a priest observes: "I came here to administer to the Indians. I think the white man will need me more." John Ford's *The Searchers* (1956) suggests that savagery is innate to both races when the white protagonist mutilates dead Indians and kills buffalo in order to deplete the Indians' food supply. In *Trooper Hook* (1957), a captive white woman and her half-breed son become outcasts among the frontier community because she had relations with an Indian man.

Don Siegel's *Flaming Star* (1960) examines the plight of the half-breed (played by popular rock singer Elvis Presley) as he fought against an embittered society and found peace only outside its boundaries. A similar story occurs in Delbert Mann's *The Outsider* (1961), the tragic account of Indian and World War II hero Ira Hayes (Tony Curtis), who is unable to accept the hypocrisy of his celebrity status within American society. In *Hombre* (1967), Paul Newman plays a white man raised by Apaches who returns to an intolerant civilization. Resentment against the country's involvement in Vietnam along with a distrust of society's institutions dominates Arthur Penn's *Little Big Man* (1971), based upon Thomas Berger's popular novel and featuring the Canadian Indian actor Dan George (Squamish) as Old Lodge Skins. (George's memorable performance earned him an Academy Award nomination for best supporting actor.) Similarly, Ralph Nelson's *Soldier Blue* (1970) depicts the U.S. Army as relentless murderers in its graphic re-creation of the Cheyenne and Arapaho massacre at Sand Creek, CO. Robert Altman's *Buffalo Bill and the Indians, or Sitting Bull's History Lesson* (1976) debunks America's legend of William Frederick Cody and portrays him as a pompous, egotistical showman.

As the decade saw a sharp decline in the Westerns' popularity, Indians began to appear "outside" society's boundaries. *One Flew over the Cuckoo's Nest* (1975) confines its characters to a state mental hospital, with its mute patient (played by the Creek Indian actor Will Sampson) as the story's hero. *Harry and Tonto* (1974) places an adventurous old man in the same jail cell with Dan George. Occasionally, Hollywood mixed Indian mysticism with contemporary horror: both *The Manitou* (1978) and *Nightwing* (1979) resort to Indian spiritualism to explain the unexplainable.

Television struggled to fill the gap with pro-Indian sagas that attempted to rewrite American history in order to "balance" the record. *I Will Fight No More Forever* (ABC, 1975), the story of Chief Joseph of the Nez Perce, boasted that "real" Indians played Indians; *Mystic Warrior* (ABC, 1984), based upon Ruth Beebe Hill's controversial novel *Hanta Yo!*, favored Indian lifestyle over white civilization; and the miniseries *Roanoak* (PBS, 1986) claimed authentic Ojibwa dialogue.

Elliot Silverstein's *A Man Called Horse* (1970), the tale of an aristocratic Englishman who is captured and tortured by the Sioux, brought angry demonstrators to its premiere in Minneapolis. Members of the activist American Indian Movement, in particular, labeled the film's graphic portrayal of the sacred Sun Dance Ceremony as "humiliating and degrading." (The movie's popularity brought two sequels: *The Return of a Man Called Horse* in 1976 and *Triumphs of a Man Called Horse* in 1984.) Another troublesome issue was the casting of British actor Trevor Howard as the Indian

lead in *Windwalker* (1980), a story of the Cheyenne and their struggle against their traditional Crow enemies.

The release of Kevin Costner's *Dances with Wolves* (1990), however, revived an interest in the Indian-as-subject, both in film and in television. Two years later, Michael Apted's *Thunderheart* (1992) set its volatile story within the politically divided Oglala Sioux nation during the turbulent 1970s.

Television responded with its own version of Custer's Last Stand in ABC's *Son of Morning Star* (1991). This two-part story juxtaposes the Indians' point of view with personal recollections of Custer's friends and family. A year later, Home Box Office television presented *The Last of His Tribe* (1992), in which Graham Greene (Oneida) delivers a memorable performance as Ishi, California's last Yahi Indian. Recent television series include regular Native American characters: CBS's *Northern Exposure* and *Dr. Quinn, Medicine Woman,* as well as episodes from *X Files* and *Kung-Fu: The Legend Continues.*

Michael Mann's *The Last of the Mohicans* (1992) simply reworked James Fenimore Cooper's century-old Leatherstocking tales. The fabled story of how Hawkeye and his faithful companions defeat their Huron enemy, Magua, has been a favorite among filmmakers since D. W. Griffith's *Leather Stocking* in 1909. Indian activist Russell Means played the elderly Chingachgook; Cherokee actor Wes Studi portrayed Magua with an intensity that earned him high critical praise.

A year later Studi played the title role in *Geronimo: An American Legend* (1993), Hollywood's third version of the Chiricahua Apache's campaign against the U.S. Army. *Powwow Highway* (1988) casts Gary Farmer (Mohawk) in the lead role as Philbert, a good-natured fellow who teaches his cynical companion to rediscover his Indian identity. *The Dark Wind* (1991), based upon the Tony Hillerman novel and again featuring Gary Farmer, investigates a mysterious reservation murder that reveals the tensions between Navajo and Hopi cultures. *Silent Tongue* (1992), written and directed by the Pulitzer Prize-winning playwright Sam Shepard, is the haunting story of an Indian woman's ghost (played by Indian actress Sheila Tousey) caught between the world of the living and the dead. *Where the Rivers Flow North* (1992) reveals how an old Yankee logdriver and his irrepressible housekeeper (played by Cree/Métis actress Tantoo Cardinal) must combat the region's first hydroelectric dam, which threatens their self-sufficient livelihood.

Recently, American Indian filmmakers have themselves created a viable alternative to mainstream Hollywood movies. Cable television has provided a visible format: in 1992, the Public Broadcasting Service aired *Surviving Columbus*, a Pueblo perspective on 500 years of European contact, produced by an all-Indian crew.

The Turner Broadcasting System has also opened its doors to talented Native American artists, both in front of and behind the camera. *The Native Americans: Behind the Legends, Beyond the Myths* is a combined television series of documentaries and dramas portraying Indian history, life, and culture.

Despite their noticeable appearance in contemporary film and television, however, Hollywood's Indian artists continue to face many obstacles. Studios still insist upon casting non-Indians in Indian roles, often pointing to the actor's celebrity status as necessary for box-office appeal. Examples abound: A. Martinez in *Powwow Highway* (1988), Lou Diamond Phillips in *Renegades* (1989) and *The Dark Wind* (1991), Kevin Dillon in *War Party* (1989), and Val Kilmer in *Thunderheart* (1992). The problem is magnified when these non-Indian celebrities establish Native American identities *ex post facto* to ward off criticism for playing Indian characters.

Another problem is Hollywood's visible lack of American Indian directors. Although Indian artists have made headway in cable television, more and more non-Indians continue to make feature films about Native Americans. Yet, talented Indian filmmakers steadily emerge from the Native American Film and Video Festival (New York) and the American Indian Film Festival (San Francisco), and their enthusiastic receptions point to a growing demand for a Native American perspective. A few have even created their own production companies: noted Choctaw filmmaker Phil Lucas is the owner of Phil Lucas Productions, Inc., and Hanay Geiogamah (Kiowa/Delaware) is president of the Los Angeles-based Native American Media Enterprises, Inc. The current resurgence of Indian pictures in Hollywood, however, should prompt the film industry to take a closer look at these Native American artists.

Bibliography

Bataille, Gretchen M., and Charles L. P. Silet. *The Pretend Indians: Images of Native Americans in the Movies*. Ames: Iowa State UP, 1980.

Hilger, Michael. *From Savage to Nobleman: Images of Native Americans in Film*. Lanham: Scarecrow, 1995.

O'Connor, John E. *The Hollywood Indian: Stereotypes of Native Americans in Films*. Trenton: New Jersey State Museum, 1980.

Angela Aleiss

See also
Native American Crime Fiction
Western Films

Indy 500, The, is an annual, internationally famous, 500-mile, 200-lap automobile race held at the Indianapolis Motor Speedway Racetrack in Indianapolis, IN, on the Sunday immediately preceding Memorial Day. The "Old Brickyard" is a 2-1/2 mile oval track, and the race draws over 300,000 spectators annually to watch sleek, high-tech racing machines that can top 200 miles an hour.

Though not the fastest or the longest race, this springtime rite of season is considered to be auto racing's premier event. The race is the culmination of a month of spectacle—"The Thirty Days of May"—that includes a festival, the crowning of a queen, and the excitement of time trials which determine a 33-car field. Spectacle continues with race-day festivities, which include a salute to the United States of America with the playing of "The Star Spangled Banner," a salute to God with an invocation by a clergyman, and a salute to the state of Indiana with the singing of the song "Back

Home Again in Indiana." The actual race is opened by the famous command, "Gentlemen, start your engines!" which has been altered to "Lady and Gentlemen, start your engines!" each time that a woman has participated in the race.

The race is surrounded by signs of the media. After years of being covered only by live worldwide radio broadcast on the syndicated WIBC Mutual Network, ABC Sports began a tape-delay worldwide television broadcast of the race in 1971. In 1986, ABC Sports switched its coverage of the race to a live worldwide television broadcast. Recently, the time trials in the weeks preceding the race have begun to be covered on ESPN. Additionally, each car in the race is covered by advertising for the companies and businesses that have sponsored its entry.

The race incorporates a car culture's fascination with speed, technical innovations, driver skills, and danger of high-speed crashes.

Bibliography

Bloemaker, Al. *500 Miles to Go: The Story of the Indianapolis Speedway*. New York: Coward-McCann, 1961.

Carnegie, Tom. *Indy 500: More Than a Race*. New York: McGraw-Hill, 1987.

Kleinfield, Sonny. *A Month at the Brickyard: The Incredible Indy 500*. New York: Holt, Rinehart & Winston, 1977.

Reed, Terry. *Indy, Race and Ritual*. San Rafael: Presidio, 1980.

Raymond Schuck

Inner Sanctum (1941-1952), the famous suspense radio program with its creaking door and macabre sense of humor, was broadcast on various networks. Produced and directed during its entire run by Himan Brown, it was much imitated; Brown used his successful format in directing a revival of radio drama, *The CBS Radio Mystery Theater* (1974-80).

Though famous stars appeared as guests on *Inner Sanctum*—Boris Karloff, Mercedes McCambridge, Peter Lorre, and Claude Rains, to name a few—the real stars of *Inner Sanctum* were the sound effects. Brown believed that sound on radio was as important as words. In an interview in the mid-1940s, Brown claimed that "many shows are written around sound effects....I use sound unashamedly. In a program like *Inner Sanctum*, where mood is of the essence, I believe in a minimum of writing."

The program (hosted by Raymond E. Johnson, 1941-45, then Paul McGrath) premiered on the NBC Blue Network; it was broadcast on Tuesday nights for the first 11 shows, then moved to Sundays through 1942. The following year, CBS bought *Inner Sanctum* and it remained on the network, on various nights, until 1950. ABC ran the stories in 1950-51. CBS broadcast a sustaining summer series in 1952; the final show was heard on October 5, 1952.

Bibliography

Dunning, John. *Tune in Yesterday: The Ultimate Encyclopedia of Old-Time Radio, 1925-1976*. Englewood Cliffs: Prentice-Hall, 1976.

Life 16 (7 Feb. 1944): 45-46+.

New York Times 18 Aug. 1946: II:7:2.

Richard L. Testa, Jr.

Internet, The, is a technological system that has become comparable in impact and importance to the railway and the automobile of the 19th and 20th centuries. The computer revolution that swept America after the introduction of the IBM Model 360 in 1965 resembled the changes wrought by railroads. Computers organized people's lives, and made the economy, the government, and education more productive, but they were not easily accessible to ordinary mortals. Mainframes were multimillion-dollar installations operated by a priesthood of white-coated technicians. Their liturgical language was not Latin but FORTRAN and COBOL. They set the schedules and the routes that everyone had to use.

When personal computers began arriving in quantity in the 1980s, the old Mainframe Establishment tried to stop, impede, or control the shift toward decentralized computing. It was no use, for by the early 1990s personal computers packed more power than giant mainframes of a decade earlier, cost 1/1000 as much, and featured software that was as easy to learn as driving a Model T. Word processing meant that people could enter and control their own words, without the intervention of a secretarial staff. Spreadsheets meant that junior staffers could analyze complex data sets and build models of the sort that previously cost tens or hundreds of thousands of dollars to handle. A valuable breakthrough came in the program *Notes* by Lotus (which became part of IBM in 1995). *Notes* allowed work teams to share textual information in an intuitive fashion, and the team could be geographically dispersed. Text no longer had to be filtered through faxes (or "snail mail"), and the delay factor implicit in collaborative work was strikingly lessened. The limitation of the personal computer (PC) lay in connectivity. In bureaucracies, the PCs were connected to local servers, which contained only the information and programs selected by management.

PCs in the academic world were generally not controlled by managers, thus allowing for much greater "freedom." Most students used the freedom to play complex games, of course, while a few created programs that made them millionaires before graduation. The Internet was created in 1969 by the U.S. Defense Department, but quickly taken over by the National Science Foundation (NSF), which supervised it until 1995. The Internet was originally designed for easy communication among research scientists and engineers. By the early 1990s, its "e-mail" functions gave it broad popularity among academics with modems. E-mail proved a fast, free, highly convenient communications mechanism. (Smaller schools set up a rival system called "Bitnet" that performed much the same e-mail role. Bitnet faded away after 1994.)

The Internet is free—or at least it appears that way to users. The economics depends on the availability of cheap telecommunications. In the 1980s, the telephone industry recabled America and most other industrialized countries with fiber optics. The materials are thin strands of glass that carry not electricity but flashes of light. The flashes can be encoded as digital signals, and the less expensive fiber optic can thus replace copper wires. The carrying capacity ("bandwidth") of fiber optic cable is so large that telephone companies sold their excess capacity very cheaply. College computer centers formed regional cooperatives. These co-ops used dues from colleges to purchase large blocks of bandwidth. The dues were low—perhaps $50,000 a year for a major university—and provided virtually unlimited message capacity. The cost of e-mail messages fell to less than one penny per hundred messages—virtually free, and certainly less than the cost of hiring the technical people at the computer centers who handled Internet chores and wrote software. True to its co-op origins, the computer centers donated the software they wrote for free distribution. For example, the University of Minnesota developed and gave away "gopher" programs that allowed easy, menu-driven access to files stored on a mainframe. CERN (the European Laboratory for Particle Physics in Switzerland) wrote and gave away the "World Wide Web" software in 1991; the Supercomputer Center at the University of Illinois donated "Mosaic" in 1994.

By the mid-1990s, NSF pulled out of the Internet business and numerous commercial providers moved in. Tens of thousands of commercial accounts were established, as business began exploring a new marketing frontier. Commercial providers like CompuServe, Prodigy, America Online, and Microsoft Network connected millions of people directly to the Internet (and to moderately expensive additional services). Slogans like "the information highway" told people that a revolutionary change was at hand of a magnitude comparable to railroads or automobiles, but no one could fathom just what free information was good for. With most information and software "free," it was not immediately obvious how people were making money on the Internet. The answer was that communications giants (telephone and cable utilities, computer companies, and publishers) were pouring millions into the system in order to establish a presence, hoping that eventually the market share would translate into a huge revenue stream.

The first major service on the Internet was person-to-person e-mail. It was like having free telegrams. But if messages could be sent to one address free, then why not to many addresses at once? Evan Thomas created "Listserv" software for Bitnet that provided a simple, reliable e-mail publications system. A "list" could be created on a mainframe, and people could subscribe via e-mail. The subscribers could post and answer messages to each other. Thousands of e-mail lists formed, each narrowly focused.

The greatest breakthrough in Internet connectivity was the creation of the "World Wide Web" (invented in Switzerland) and easy-to-use web browsers, especially Mosaic (invented at the University of Illinois-Urbana in 1994) and Netscape. The "net is free" and so the WWW software, and indeed the Mosaic and Netscape browsers, are all free as well. These programs (all given away free) greatly simplified the problem of connecting to one point or another. They allowed text to move, and also graphics, sound, and visuals. The WWW was interactive. Unlike television, where producers in Hollywood determined what appeared on the screen and when, the WWW gave individuals a freedom of action akin to the advance of automobiles over railroads. The WWW technology meant that people now could control not only their own postal system, but their own video networks as well, communicating with all parts of the world effortlessly and at (nearly) zero cost. Newspapers and magazines, alarmed at the trend, began establishing on-line editions so that subscribers could create their own newspaper. Most people were just browsers ("lurkers"), but they drew exhilaration from the immediacy of the new medium, and the sense of listening to and interacting with the best minds in the world. The radical transformation of the economics and access of communications was bound to have startling impacts on the popular culture.

Negative commentators have worried about the loss of human contact—suggesting that typing on a keyboard is somehow less human than writing in ink or speaking into a telephone. With many millions of American workers accustomed on their jobs to the advantages and disadvantages of computers, the scattershot attacks by the neo-Luddites had little or no impact. The openness of the Internet system made it much too easy for advertisers to "spam" hundreds of thousands of people simultaneously with unwanted messages. There was little or no "law and order" on the Internet. Like the Wild West, the Internetters responded to spammers with vigilante attacks and virulent "flames." When the easy availability of hard-core pornography on the Internet became an issue in 1995, Internetters drew up in a circle, demanding utter freedom for whatever messages they wanted to send in their domain.

According to a poll by National Public Radio, the Kaiser Family Foundation, and Harvard's Kennedy School of Government released in February 2000, "enthusiasm for computers and the Internet runs wide and deep," though there is a "digital divide" which separates those with lower incomes, less education, and especially those over the age of 60. Nevertheless, there are some concerns about the Internet, particularly over children's access to strangers and pornography, as well as over privacy. By the holiday season of 1999-2000, shopping via the Internet was becoming much more popular, and advertising for "e-businesses" was becoming widespread.

Bibliography

Baczewski, Philip, et al. *The Internet Unleashed*. Indianapolis: Sams, 1994.

Kurland, Daniel J. *The Net, the Web, and You: All You Really Need to Know about the Internet—And a Little Bit More*. Belmont: Wadsworth, 1996.

Manger, Jason J. *The Essential Internet Information Guide*. New York: McGraw-Hill, 1995.

"Survey Shows Widespread Enthusiasm for High Technology." NPR Online. Available: http://www.npr.org/programs/specials/poll/technology/index.html; 3 April 2000.

Richard Jensen

See also
Computers and Popular Culture

Iron Butterfly was a popular rock group in the late 1960s that achieved notoriety for their "In-A-Gadda-Da-Vida," a classic of acid rock (see entry). The group formed in San Diego in 1966, but moved to Los Angeles to play in the growing club scene there.

Iron Butterfly was led by Omaha native Doug Ingle, the son of a church organist, and drummer Ronald Bushy, from Washington, D.C. Ingle was responsible for much of the group's characteristic sound, including the throaty lead vocals and warbling organ sounds. Other members of the original band were three San Diego natives, Jerry Penrod (bass), Danny Weis (guitar), and Darryl DeLoach (vocals), all of whom left before the group's hit single and album were recorded.

In March 1968, Iron Butterfly reassembled with St. Louis-native Lee Dorman on bass guitar and Boston's Erik Braunn on guitar and backup vocals. The group toured in the spring as the opening act for the Doors and the Jefferson Airplane. They also gained some recognition when two of their songs were included in the motion picture *Savage Seven*.

The album *In-A-Gadda-Da-Vida* reached No. 4 on the LP charts in the U.S. and sold 3 million copies. It remained on the Top 200 chart for 140 weeks, 81 of them in the Top 10. *In-A-Gadda-Da-Vida* also was Atlantic Records' biggest seller to date.

The album cut of the title song ran 17 minutes and was widely played by progressive rock stations in its entirety. The song was also noted for its long drum solo, which was edited out of the single version. The single version was also mildly successful, peaking at No. 30 in October 1968. Iron Butterfly's success with *In-A-Gadda-Da-Vida* led to bookings at a number of the major rock music festivals in 1968 and 1969, including the Newport Pop Festival, the Miami Pop Festival, and the Atlantic City Pop Festival.

Their second album, *Ball*, was released in early 1969 and eventually reached No. 3 on the charts. Later that year Mike Pinera and Larry Reinhardt replaced Erik Braunn; this lineup recorded *Iron Butterfly Live* and *Metamorphosis* (both 1970). It peaked at No. 20 on the charts, but no singles were released from the album. The group, however, did record the title song from the motion picture *Easy Rider*.

The group split up and gave a farewell concert on May 23, 1971, after selling seven million albums in their three years together. Guitarist Braunn and drummer Bushy tried to revive the group in 1975 and recorded two unsuccessful albums for MCA Records before splitting again.

Bibliography

Pareles, Jon, and Patty Romanowski. *Rolling Stone Encyclopedia of Rock & Roll*. New York: Summit, 1983.

Stambler, Irwin. *The Encyclopedia of Rock, Pop and Soul*. New York: St. Martin's, 1977.

Ken Nagelberg

Ironside (1967-1975) was a 60-minute crime drama on NBC that aired 120 episodes plus the original pilot. Chief Robert Ironside of the San Francisco Police Department is on vacation when an assassin shoots him with a high-powered rifle. The shot cripples him and confines him to a wheelchair. Unwilling to retire passively, Ironside manages to get himself appointed to a consultancy with the San Francisco Police Department, complete with his own unit and a specially equipped van. The police commissioner, played by Gene Lyons, permitted Ironside to live in the police headquarters' attic. The original unit consisted of Sergeant Eve Whitfield (Barbara Anderson), Sergeant Ed Brown (Ed Galloway), and Marc Sanger (Dan Mitchell), a reformed convict and Black Power advocate, who was Ironside's personal assistant.

The show became less preachy and more concentrated on good, action-oriented entertainment as it went on. The performers grew into their roles. The program's success was due to its better-than-average plotting, good acting, and the presence and skill of its lead actor, Raymond Burr (see entry).

Bibliography
Brown, Les. *Encyclopedia of Television.* Detroit: Gale Research, 1992.
Meyers, Richard. *TV Detectives.* San Diego: Barnes, 1981.
Terrace, Vincent. *Encyclopedia of Television Series, Pilots and Specials: 1937-1973.* Vol. 1. New York: Zoetrope, 1985.
——. *Encyclopedia of Television Series, Pilots and Specials: 1974-1984.* Vol. 2. New York: Zoetrope, 1985.
——. *Fifty Years of Television.* New York: Cornwall, 1991.

Frank A. Salamone

It Happened One Night (1934), the first movie to win all five major Academy Awards, became a critical and popular success despite the indifference, during various stages of its production, of the eventual winners: the stars, Clark Gable and Claudette Colbert; the studio, Columbia; and even the screenwriter, Robert Riskin, and the director, Frank Capra. The movie helped usher in the "screwball comedy" period of Hollywood filmmaking (see entry), and was much imitated. The story centered on the unlikely and inevitable union of two young people, a society heiress and a working-class newspaper reporter, who meet at the same time they are both attempting to find themselves and understand their place in American society. A 1956 Columbia remake, *You Can't Run Away from It*, was a critical and commercial failure.

The screenplay for *It Happened One Night* was adapted from a *Cosmopolitan* magazine story by Samuel Hopkins Adams, "Night Bus." Columbia bought the property for $5,000. The female lead was offered to and turned down by Myrna Loy, Margaret Sullavan, Miriam Hopkins, and Constance Bennett. Capra and Riskin were ready to give the project up—until Capra's friend, Myles Connolly, convinced him to alter the main characters slightly so audiences would feel more sympathetic toward them. Peter Warne's character was changed from a "party-waist painter" to a "tough, crusading reporter." Ellie Andrews's character became sympathetic, for her "bratty" nature was now said to be due to her being "bored" with being an heiress.

With the changes, Capra approached other actresses—and was still turned down. Finally, he offered Colbert $50,000 for four weeks' work. MGM's studio head, Louis B. Mayer, offered Clark Gable to Columbia; Mayer wished to "punish" Gable by sending him to "Siberia." The movie made Gable a star. Another star was the American landscape: location shooting of real buses, coffeeshops, highways, and "auto camps" (motels) helped keep costs down. Cinematography was by Joseph Walker. The 105-minute movie was edited by Gene Havlick. Supporting actors included Roscoe Karns, Ward Bond, Eddie Chandler, Alan Hale, and Wallis Clark.

Bibliography
Bergman, Andrew. *We're in the Money.* New York: New York UP, 1971.
Capra, Frank. *The Name above the Title.* New York: Vintage, 1971.
Schatz, Thomas. *Hollywood Genres.* Philadelphia: Temple UP, 1981.
Sikov, Ed. *Screwball.* New York: Crown, 1989.
Sklar, Robert. *Movie-Made America.* New York: Vintage, 1975.

Richard L. Testa, Jr.

It's a Wonderful Life (1946), the first Hollywood project undertaken by Frank Capra after his separation from the military, gave him the opportunity to continue promoting the ideals of Americanism he had recognized in such pre-war films as *Mr. Deeds Goes to Town* (1936) and *Mr. Smith Goes to Washington* (1939), and focused the nation's attention upon so adroitly in his *Why We Fight* series of films for the War Department between 1942 and 1945. What this film does even more pointedly than his other works is to concentrate on an ordinary American citizen, not a war hero or a man of great accomplishments, to demonstrate the value that one life can have for the fabric of family and community.

The idea for the film came from a "Christmas card," a 24-page story entitled "The Greatest Gift" which writer Van Doren Stern had printed as a pamphlet and mailed to his friends at Christmas 1938. The film focuses on George Bailey (Jimmy Stewart), who is prevented from committing suicide by a well-intentioned but somewhat dim-witted guardian angel who allows George to see what life in his home town would have been like if he hadn't been born.

Although it was successful in its original theatrical release, annual Christmas-time television reruns are primarily responsible for transforming *It's a Wonderful Life* into an icon of American culture. It remains, as well, convincing evidence of Capra's religious faith and civic heroism.

Bibliography
Basinger, Jeanine. *The* It's a Wonderful Life *Book.* New York: Knopf, 1986.
Capra, Frank. *The Name above the Title: An Autobiogrpahy.* New York: Macmillan, 1971.
Carney, Raymond. *American Vision: The Films of Frank Capra.* Cambridge: Cambridge UP, 1986.
Fishgall, Gary. *Pieces of Time: The Life of James Stewart.* New York: Scribner's, 1997.
Hawkins, Jimmy. It's A Wonderful Life: *The Fiftieth Anniversary Scrapbook.* Philadelphia: Courage, 1996.

John E. O'Connor

ℐ

Jack Benny Program, The (1932-1955), the most successful and critically acclaimed comedy series of radio's golden age, was broadcast weekly. First written as a comedy-variety show, it evolved into a situational comedy. Jack Benny (born Benjamin Kubelsky, February 14, 1894, in Waukegan, IL; died December 26, 1974) and his ensemble cast made a smooth transition to television during the 1950s and, after the radio show left the air, appeared on weekly telecasts until 1965. Benny's contemporaries and self-proclaimed disciples have made clear through the years that his program was the most influential and closest to perfection in form; a diverse group of comedians, from George Burns, Goodman Ace, and Fred Allen during the radio days, to Steve Allen, Jack Paar, and Johnny Carson in the television era, have all acknowledged their debt to Benny and his mastery of the humor of self-ridicule.

Benny's character was vain, pompous, and exasperatingly stingy, yet audiences loved him anyway. Fred Allen claimed that Benny was "the best-liked actor in show business"—a considerable achievement considering the character that was created for him. His foils on the program were his real-life wife, Mary Livingstone, who played his girlfriend of the same name; his announcer Don Wilson; his Irish tenors, primarily Kenny Baker and, after 1939, Dennis Day; his band leaders, most notably Phil Harris and, later, Bob Crosby; and his butler/valet Rochester Van Jones, played by Eddie Anderson.

Benny was a 20-year veteran of the vaudeville circuits when his broadcast career began. Appearing on Broadway in Earl Carroll's *Vanities*, Benny was asked to appear on *New York Daily News* columnist Ed Sullivan's CBS radio program, *Broadway's Greatest Thrills*. An advertising representative for Canada Dry heard the March 1932 broadcast and persuaded Benny to host their weekly series on NBC (1932) and CBS (1933). Benny's shows were later sponsored by Chevrolet (NBC, 1933-34), General Tire (NBC, 1934), General Foods (NBC, 1934-42, *The Jell-o Program*; NBC, 1942-44, *The Grape Nuts and Grape Nuts Flakes Program*), and the American Tobacco Company (NBC, 1944-48 and CBS, 1949-55, *The Lucky Strike Program*).

Some of *The Jack Benny Program*'s best-known gags were Benny's age (which eventually was stuck at 39); his violin playing; his exasperated expressions "Well!" "Oh, for heaven's sake!", and "Now cut that out!"; his vault where he kept all of his money; the train station announcer's cry "Anaheim, Azusa, and Cucamonga!"; his feud with Fred Allen (see entry); the innovations of comic commercials and satirical versions of current movies; and, probably most famous of all, his pause and irritated response to a robber who threatens "Your money or your life!": "———I'm thinking it over!"

Bibliography
Benny, Joan, and Jack Benny. *Sunday Nights at Seven*. New York: Warner, 1990.
Benny, Mary Livingstone, and Hilliard Marks. *Jack Benny: A Biography*. Garden City: Doubleday, 1978.
Fein, Irving A. *Jack Benny: An Intimate Biography*. New York: Putnam, 1976.
Newsweek 9 Feb. 1943.
Time 28 Oct. 1935.

Richard L. Testa, Jr.

See also
Sitcom

Jackson 5, The, was one of the most sensational singing groups to be discovered by the end of the 1960s. The Jackson 5, led by 11-year-old Michael, and his four brothers Jermaine, Tito, Marlon, and Jackie, created a unique sound and energetic dancing style that was to change American music and music in the world forever. The five brothers were fresh, young, full of energy, and made music-business history when their first singles topped the record charts and became No. 1 in 1970. The chart toppers included "I Want You Back," "ABC," "The Love You Save," and "I'll Be There."

Hailing from humble beginnings in Gary, IN, the five were the eldest sons in a family of nine born to steelworker Joseph Jackson and his wife, Katherine. When their father discovered his sons had talent, he devoted himself into shaping them into a well-rehearsed group that covered Motown and other soul/R&B hits of the day. The group performed at places like talent shows and Harlem's Apollo Theater and were opening acts for many artists. All during this time, Michael was studying the on-stage movements, choreography, and the ways successful artists worked a crowd. These singers included such masters as James Brown, Sam and Dave, Jackie Wilson, Diana Ross, Etta James, and even his older brother Jermaine, who was a mentee of Marvin Gaye.

The Jacksons were discovered when a performer and producer, Bobby Taylor, saw their act at Chicago's Regal nightclub. He introduced them to Motown's Berry Gordy, and Gordy took a hands-on interest in the group. Gordy, who had now moved to California from Detroit, matched them with "the Corporation," a Motown production team that groomed them to become the No. 1 singing group.

In January 1970, their first production, "I Want You Back," reached No. 1 on the pop R&B charts. Their next hit, "Let It Be," replaced the Beatles' top position that April. By the summer of 1970, the Jackson 5 was headlining 20,000-seat auditoriums, and the Jackson cult was in full swing.

The Jackson 5 tenure at Motown lasted until 1975, and by that time the nation's mania was disco. They also turned their attention to the disco movement with hits like "Dancing Machine," which reached No. 2 in 1974. When the group moved to the Epic label in the middle 1970s, they shortened their name to the Jacksons and began writing and producing their own material. The Jacksons wrote a trio of dance/R&B albums titled *Destiny, Triumph and Victory* that were released in the late seventies and early eighties. In 1984, their highly publicized *Victory* tour turned out to be the last Jacksons' project to include brother Michael, who was by now a superstar in his own right, and a prominent entertainment figure in the world (see next entry).

Bibiography

"The Jackson Five 1997, Performers." *Rock and Roll Hall of Fame and Museum*. Internet. 7 Jan. 1998. hhtp://www.rockhall.com/induct/jackson5.html.

Michael Jackson
Peggy Stevenson Ratliff

Jackson, Michael (1958-), began performing with his four older brothers in 1964 in their home town, Gary, IN. Motown Records signed the Jackson 5 in 1969 and moved the entire Jackson family to California for incorporation into the music industry's star-making machinery.

Starting in 1971 with the Top 10 hit "Got to Be There," Michael also made solo recordings, establishing himself as an individual child star. It was already obvious that Michael was a major talent and the linchpin of the family act. Probably the first sign of Michael's apparent weirdness was his 1972 smash hit "Ben"—a love song to a rodent (and a touching number at that).

The next several years were a time of fewer and smaller hits for the brothers, who moved to Epic Records and changed their name to the Jacksons in 1975. Michael, playing the Scarecrow in the 1978 film musical *The Wiz* (an adaptation of *The Wizard of Oz*), became friendly with the multitalented Quincy Jones, the film's musical coordinator. This led to Jones producing Michael's breakthrough solo album, *Off the Wall*, released in 1979.

Michael had already been a star continuously since 1969, but during the 1980s his stardom reached mammoth proportions. A pivotal event was his electrifying performance on the NBC-TV special *Motown 25* in May 1983. After the Jacksons had sung a medley of their hits, Michael, as if emerging from a cocoon, brought the house down with his new hit, "Billie Jean." His choreography included the Moonwalk, a dance step that seems to defy the laws of physics.

Michael's album *Thriller*, produced by Quincy Jones and released late in 1982, became the best-selling album of all time and spawned an unprecedented seven singles, all of which became Top 10 hits. Jackson took full advantage of MTV as a new medium of record promotion, overcoming an alleged MTV bias against black artists and expanding the aesthetic boundaries of music video with his clips "Billie Jean" (1982), "Beat It" (1983), and "Thriller" (1983).

Jackson's career during the 1980s was a succession of commercial, financial, and artistic superlatives. He was the ultimate crossover artist and in fact the ultimate entertainer. The child star had apparently grown up, but there were signs of trouble. At the same time that the video productions *We Are the World* (1985), *Man in the Mirror* (1988), and *Michael Jackson: The Legend Continues* (1988) emphasized Jackson's social conscience and larger-than-life qualities, press reports suggested that he was quite eccentric.

In September 1993, Jackson was accused in a civil suit of molesting a 13-year-old boy. Jackson denied the charges but cut short his world tour. News media widely reported details of the suit's allegations and an investigation into the matter by the Los Angeles police. No criminal charges were filed against Jackson, and the civil suit was settled out of court in early 1994. Nevertheless, entertainment pundits speculated that Jackson's career was effectively finished. Although his record sales continued unabated, PepsiCo canceled its $10-million sponsorship deal with Jackson. A sensational press eagerly reinterpreted his entire career in light of the unproven 1993 accusations. Jackson's alleged character flaw turned the King of Pop into a modern-day tragic hero.

The shy and reclusive Jackson became the subject of more speculation in 1994 when he married Lisa Marie Presley, Elvis's daughter. Their marriage didn't last long; Jackson then unexpectedly married Debbie Rowe and fathered two children. Meanwhile, he released his first two-CD set, *HIStory: Past, Present and Future, Book 1* (1995), a mixture of old and new material, which received good reviews.

Bibliography

Jackson, Michael. *Moonwalk*. New York: Doubleday, 1988.

Marsh, Dave. *Trapped: Michael Jackson and the Crossover Dream*. Toronto: Bantam, 1985.

Rees, Dafydd, and Luke Crampton with Barry Lazell, eds. *Book of Rock Stars*. Middlesex, U.K.: Guinness, 1989.

Swenson, John. "Michael Jackson." *The Rolling Stone Illustrated History of Rock & Roll*. 3d ed. Ed. Anthony DeCurtis and James Henke with Holly George-Warren; original ed. Jim Miller. New York: Random House, 1992. 648-55.

Terry, Carol D., comp. *Sequins & Shades: The Michael Jackson Reference Guide*. Ann Arbor: Pierian, 1987.

Gary Burns

James, P. D. (1920-), is a widely acclaimed novelist whose works incorporate a mystery rather than a creator of puzzles. Her characters are complex, her style highly literate, and her sense of place extraordinary in detail and atmosphere. While acknowledging the presence of evil, her novels celebrate the restoration of order, affirming, in her words, "an understandable universe." Strongly influenced by the writings of Dorothy L. Sayers and Margery Allingham, James's first mystery, *Cover Her Face* (1966), introduced Inspector Adam Dalgliesh, an intense, committed policeman who is also a published poet, and the protagonist of nine subsequent mysteries. James also created Cordelia Gray, a private investigator featured in two books, including *An Unsuitable Job for a Woman* (1973), recognized as an early example of feminist mystery fiction.

James is noted for creating powerfully atmospheric settings that also function symbolically, such as the nuclear power station that suggests a morally contaminated world in *Devices and Desires* (1989), and the church rectory in *A*

Taste for Death (1986) where murder occurs as a reminder of the profane directions of modern life. Indeed, her primary fictional theme is the decline of moral certitude in a troubled contemporary society. Not surprisingly, Dalgliesh, though a meticulous and accomplished detective, exhibits increasing disillusionment and pessimism as the series progresses, as in *Original Sin* (1995) and *A Certain Justice* (1997).

In addition to detective fiction, James has written a science fiction novel, *The Children of Men* (1992), and a psychological thriller, *Innocent Blood* (1980). Her works have influenced many recent mystery writers, including Frances Fyfield and Elizabeth George.

Bibliography

Gidez, Richard B. *P. D. James*. Boston: Twayne, 1986.
Siebenheller, Norma. *P. D. James*. New York: Ungar, 1981.

Susan L. Peters

See also
Crime Fiction
Feminist Detective Fiction
Golden Age of Detective Fiction

Janssen, David (1930-1980), was the actor best known for his most notable role: Dr. Richard Kimble in the television adventure series, *The Fugitive* (1963-67). In this role Janssen played the part of a man running for his life, a doctor who had been unjustly convicted for killing his wife but freed in a train accident en route to the penitentiary.

Janssen played the lead character in three other television series: a debonair detective in *Richard Diamond, Private Detective* (1957, 1959-60); a treasury agent working for the government in *O'Hara* (1971-72); and a retired, disabled cop working as a private detective named Harry Orwell in *Harry O* (1974-76).

Although Janssen was never quite successful in establishing a film career, he carried major roles in over 21 telefilms between 1970 and 1980 and played in more than 28 single episodes of other series, including *Zane Grey, Route 66, Police Story,* and *Centennial*. He was considered a thoroughly professional actor who had come up through the system, respected by both cast and crews. A charismatic man, with a reputation for drinking and ladies, he died prematurely in 1980 of a heart attack.

Bibliography

Brooks, Tim. *The Complete Directory to Prime Time TV Stars, 1946-Present*. New York: Ballantine, 1987.
Janssen, Ellie. *David Janssen, My Fugitive*. Hollywood: Lifetime, 1994.
Proctor, Mel. *The Official Fan's Guide to* The Fugitive. Stamford: Longmeadow, 1995.

Ann Schoonmaker

Jaws (1975), produced by Richard D. Zanuck and David Brown, and directed by a young Steven Spielberg (see entry), came at the end of a cycle of disaster movies that includes such films as *Earthquake* (1974) and *The Towering Inferno* (1974) and inaugurated the cycle of the scary summer film blockbuster that takes advantage of schools' summer vacations to draw in young audiences. The story, based on the 1974 novel by Peter Benchley, concerns a shark attack off the shores of the fictional New England resort community of Amity. Sheriff Brody (Roy Scheider), who has moved to Amity from New York with his wife Ellen (Lorraine Gary) and family, is convinced by the town's Mayor Vaughan (Murray Hamilton) not to publicize the attack or to close the town's beaches during the profitable Fourth of July weekend. After the shark attacks several other swimmers, Brody feels such remorse that he joins ichthyologist Hooper (Richard Dreyfuss) and shark-hunter Quint (Robert Shaw) to seek out and destroy the marauding shark.

Although predictably attacked by those critics most out of touch with such a popular cultural event, the movie often received critical praise for its special effects and for its use of those effects to develop suspense and to manipulate its audience, even when the audience knows it's being manipulated. Critics also often praised the acting of the film's stars: Richard Dreyfuss, Roy Scheider, and Robert Shaw.

In its first week, *Jaws* grossed $14 million, and it went on to become the first film to gross $100 million during its initial release. Moreover, *Jaws* became a cultural phenomenon, endlessly alluded to in comedy monologues, television sketches, political cartoons, and practical jokes. The movie's familiar musical title theme, by John Williams, became as instantly recognizable a signal of foreboding as had the *Psycho* and *Twilight Zone* themes before it. So successful a film naturally spawned three sequels—in 1978, 1983, and 1987—and an amusement park ride, a key attraction at the Universal Studios tour. In the first of the sequels, *Jaws 2*, Scheider returns as Sheriff Brody, who thinks that a shark is once again stalking swimmers near Amity, but who finds that no one believes him. The second sequel, *Jaws 3-D*, was, as the title implies, filmed in 3-D and starred Dennis Quaid as Brody's adult son now working in a Marineland-like ocean park owned by Louis Gossett, Jr. In the third sequel, *Jaws the Revenge*, Lorraine Gary returns to her role as Ellen Brody, who fears her family is being destroyed intentionally by sharks. None of these films enjoyed anything like the critical or commercial success of the original, which remains a powerful cultural icon of the destructive unknown.

Bibliography

Benchley, Peter. *Jaws: The Final Draft Screenplay*. Hollywood: Script City, 1986.
Erickson, Glenn. "*Jaws*." *Magill's Survey of Cinema: English Language Films, First Series*. Ed. Frank N. Magill. Englewood Cliffs: Salem, 1980. 863-65.
Goldman, Peter, with Martin Kasindorf, "*Jaws*mania: The Great Escape." *Newsweek* 86.4 (28 July 1975): 16-17.
Harris, Eleanor. "*Jaws*: The Movie That Almost Got Away." *Readers Digest* 107.641 (Sept. 1975): 142-45.
Jaws. Tolmca: Film Analysis Series, 1983.
Lindsey, Robert. "'*Jaws*,' Setting Records, Helps Revitalize Movies." *New York Times* 8 July 1975: 37.
"Summer of the Shark." *Time* 105.26 (23 June 1975): 42-51.

Robert Chamberlain

Jazz Singer, The (1927), was the movie that effectively ended the silent film era. Warner Brothers, attempting to become a major studio and to reverse declining film attendance in the 1920s due to competing with radio, had invested $3 million in Vitaphone experimentation and pilot films before producing this feature-length movie, but other studio heads were skeptical. Audience response and revenues from *The Jazz Singer*, however, proved that sound was unquestionably the direction of the future. Both *The Jazz Singer* and Warner's next sound film, *The Singing Fool* (1928), were made for approximately $500,000. *The Jazz Singer* brought in $3.5 million in U.S. rentals alone; *The Singing Fool* brought in more than $5 million and became the highest grossing film of the next decade. *The Jazz Singer* combined silent passages, subtitles, brief dialogue passages, and six songs. The technique showed the flatness of silent acting and subtitles when contrasted with "natural" dialogue and vigorous singing. Even the script emphasized the contrast between past and present.

Part of *The Jazz Singer*'s success was due to the enormous popularity of its star, Al Jolson (see entry), who played Jakie Rabinowitz. The script, from a Samuel Raphaelson story, "The Day of Atonement," roughly paralleled Jolson's early life. (Adapted for the stage as *The Jazz Singer*, the play, starring George Jessel, had been a hit of the 1925-26 Broadway season.) The silent film comes to life when, after a tearful singing of "Dirty Hands! Dirty Face!" Jolson tells his audience aloud, "You ain't heard nothin' yet," and launches into a powerful singing of "Toot, Toot, Tootsie! Goo'bye." (Other Jolson songs include "Mother of Mine," "I Still Have You," and "My Mammy.") Later, with his screen mother (played by Eugenie Bresserer), Jolson speaks and sings "Blue Skies."

Audience demand for the film was such that Jolson almost immediately began *The Singing Fool*. This film, directed by Lloyd Bacon, is about a singing waiter, an unfaithful wife, and a dying child. It is also partly silent, partly in sound. *The Singing Fool* co-starred Josephine Dunn and Betty Bronson; its songs include "It All Depends on You," "Golden Gate," "There's a Rainbow Round My Shoulder," "The Spaniard That Blighted My Life," "I'm Sitting on Top of the World," and "Sonny Boy." "Sonny Boy" is said to be the first recorded song to sell a million copies.

Bibliography

Finler, Joel W. *The Hollywood Story*. New York: Crown, 1988.

Freedland, Michael. *Jolie: The Al Jolson Story*. London: Allen, 1985.

Goldman, Herbert G. *Jolson: The Legend Comes to Life*. New York: Oxford UP, 1988.

Kiner, Larry F., and Philip R. Evans. *Al Jolson: A Bio-Discography*. Metuchen: Scarecrow, 1992.

Sennett, Ted. *Warner Brothers Presents*. New Rochelle: Arlington, 1971.

Betty Richardson

Jefferson Airplane, The, was one of the seminal musical groups of the psychedelic era and has had continued success through numerous personnel and name changes in the 1970s and 1980s. The group was one of the few acid-rock groups that were able to balance commercial success with musical innovation and a strident political stance.

The Jefferson Airplane was formed by aspiring actor Marty Balin (Martyn Buchwald), who had belonged to a folk group, the Town Criers. Balin met guitarist Paul Kantner at a club in San Francisco, and they recruited guitarist Jorma Kaukonen and vocalist Signe Toly (later Signe Anderson) to form a folk-rock band. The group was named for a match that is split at one end to serve as a "roach clip" for a marijuana cigarette.

Drummer Jerry Peloquin and bassist Bob Harvey were replaced by Skip Spence and Kaukonen's friend Jack Casady respectively before the first album, *Jefferson Airplane Takes Off*, was recorded in December 1965. In the fall of 1966, Signe Anderson became too pregnant to perform, and drummer Spence left to help form Moby Grape. Anderson was replaced by Grace Slick, a former fashion model who had been the lead singer of the Great Society along with her then-husband Jerry and her brother-in-law Darby. She also brought along two Great Society songs that would launch the Airplane to success, "Somebody to Love" and "White Rabbit."

The group's first album with Grace Slick and new drummer Spencer Dryden, *Surrealistic Pillow*, was recorded in June 1967. The album earned a gold record and reached No. 3 on the charts, and the single "Somebody to Love" peaked at No. 5. Later that summer the psychedelic anthem "White Rabbit" reached No. 8 on the charts, despite the fact that many radio stations banned the song because it advocated drug use.

The next year the Jefferson Airplane recorded *After Bathing at Baxter's*, a critically acclaimed album that was not as successful as the previous one. The album lacked a hit single, featured a nine-minute psychedelic jam, "Spayre Change," and sparked a battle with RCA over the use of the word "shit." The group played numerous concerts and rock festivals in 1967 and 1968, and released another album, *Crown of Creation*, in November 1968.

Crown of Creation reached the Top 10 on the album charts. Progressive radio stations played several songs from the album, including the title cut, "Lather," and "Triad," a David Crosby ballad about a ménage à trois. But the group began suffering from internal struggles as Balin fought with Slick for the vocal spotlight.

Slick was hospitalized in January 1969 with a growth in her throat, and the group released an album of earlier live performances, *Bless Its Pointed Little Head*. That spring the group recorded its most political album, *Volunteers*. The group's contract with RCA gave them complete control over the record, and the company was unable to edit out the phrase "up against the wall, motherfuckers" from "We Can Be Together." But the album also included some of the group's most mellow harmonies on "Good Shepherd" and "Wooden Ships."

The Jefferson Airplane did not fare well in the following months. Kaukonen and Casady began devoting more time to a side project, a traditional music duo called "Hot Tuna." In 1970, Dryden left to join the New Riders of the Purple Sage and Balin was arrested for drug possession. When Slick became pregnant by Kantner that summer, the remainder of the group had to stop touring, and Kaukonen and Casady took Hot Tuna on the road.

Kantner became increasingly interested in science fiction, and he and Slick recorded *Blows against the Empire* under the name Paul Kantner and the Jefferson Starship. Balin officially left the Jefferson Airplane in April 1971, and that summer the group released its first album, *Bark*, on their own label, Grunt Records.

Kantner and Slick released a second album (this time under their own names) in December 1971. *Sunfighter* featured a photograph of the couple's child China on the cover. In the spring of 1972, the Jefferson Airplane re-grouped for one last album, *Long John Silver*. That summer, Quicksilver Messenger Service bass player David Freiberg joined the group for a tour, the last under the name Jefferson Airplane.

Kantner, Slick, and Freiberg recorded a disappointing album, *Baron von Tollbooth and the Chrome Nun*, and Slick failed in a solo bid with *Manhole*. In 1974, Kantner and Slick reformed the Jefferson Starship with Freiberg, former Turtles' drummer Johnny Barbata, and 19-year-old lead guitarist Craig Chaquico. But the group's work had nothing in common with its earlier recordings.

The new Starship was highly melodic and made no references to drugs, social protest, or outer space. They had a string of hit singles, including "Miracles" (No. 3, 1975), "With Your Love" (No. 12, 1976), "Count on Me" (No. 8, 1978), and "Runaway" (No. 12, 1978). Kantner quit the band in 1984 and forced the group to drop the word Jefferson from its name.

Under the name Starship, they recorded several pop hits, including three No. 1 singles, "We Built This City" (1985), "Sara" (1986), and "Nothing's Gonna Stop Us Now" (1987). The original Jefferson Airplane (minus Spencer Dryden on drums) regrouped in 1989, but they met with little critical or commercial success.

Bibliography

Larkin, Colin. *Guinness Encyclopedia of Popular Music.* Vol. 3. Middlesex, U.K.: Guinness, 1995.

McDonough, Jack. *San Francisco Rock: The Illustrated History of San Francisco Rock Music.* San Francisco: Chronicle, 1985.

Stambler, Irwin. *The Encyclopedia of Pop, Rock and Soul.* New York: St. Martin's, 1989.

Kenneth M. Nagelberg

Jefferson, Clarence ("Blind Lemon") (1897-1929), the founder of Texas blues, was born on a farm 50 miles east of Dallas, TX. Because of his disability, music became his only way to make a living, although he did wrestle for a time in Dallas in 1917. He gained a strong local reputation for his competence and then began to make trips outside Texas in the 1920s. His high, clear voice aided his career. Jefferson worked with Leadbelly in Dallas. He played Hawaiian guitar to Leadbelly's mandolin. It was also in Dallas that he worked with Josh White. Both White and Leadbelly are said to have served as guides for Jefferson.

Jefferson's style was characterized by very marked bass notes and arpeggios. He incorporated large elements of the flamenco guitar style which Mexican cowboys had introduced into Texas. This intriguing style captured the attention of a bazaar show impresario in Dallas who recorded Jefferson and sent the demo record to Paramount Records. The A & R man at Paramount, Mojo Williams, signed Jefferson, who became a major success in the 1920s.

During the 1920s, he recorded 90 songs, including "Matchless Blues," "Cannon Ball Moanin'," "D. B. Blues," "'Lectric Chair Blues," "Prison Cell Blues," and the song that became the origin of Jefferson's legend in the 1960s, "See That My Grave Is Kept Clean." It was, in fact, after a party given during a trip to Chicago to make a recording that he died. He left the party and lost his way in a storm. He was found dead the following morning in a snowdrift.

In the 1950s, Jefferson became the idol of the Blues Revival. Groups and performers such as the Rolling Stones and Bob Dylan were strongly influenced by Jefferson's style. Fans searched for and in 1967 found his grave so that it could be kept clean as he begs in his famous song. The best collection of his work is the double album on Yazoo records, *King of the Country Blues*.

Bibliography

Barlow, Bill. *Encyclopedia of Southern Culture.* Chapel Hill: U of North Carolina P, 1989.

Herzhaft, Gerart. *Encyclopedia of the Blues.* Fayetteville: U of Arkansas P, 1992.

Welding, Pete, and Toby Byron. *Bluesland: Portraits of Twelve Major American Blues Masters.* New York: Dutton, 1991.

Frank A. Salamone

Jenkins, Charles Francis (1867-1934), American inventor, was responsible for the development of the first practical electronic-mechanical television system. While little of Jenkins's technology remains in use today, he was one of the first inventors to realize the scientific possibility and public desire for the transmission of moving images.

Born in Dayton, OH, Jenkins achieved his first major success in 1894 through his invention of an improved motion picture projector. During that same year, Jenkins wrote several articles proposing systems that could transmit television images. While his earlier proposals were later proven impractical, Jenkins developed a successful method for the radio transmission of photos, which he successfully demonstrated on October 3, 1922. One year later, Jenkins gave a more popular demonstration of the successful radio photo transmission of a picture of President Harding.

After developing a prismatic ring system that replaced the motion picture projector shutter, Jenkins became convinced that if the scanning rate of the rings could be increased, the transmission of moving images would be possible. On June 13, 1925, two years after successful experiments in his lab, Jenkins publicly demonstrated the first successful transmission of a motion picture—a film featuring a windmill that sped up and slowed down. Jenkins promised that "the process would be perfected until baseball games and prize fights could be sent long distances and reproduced on a screen by radio."

In 1928, using his crude, low definition system, Jenkins began a series of regular broadcasts for television experimenters and hobbyists. Jenkins's broadcasts, along with those of several other experimenters, lasted until 1933, an era that television historian Joseph Udelson calls the low-definition television boom period.

Bibliography

Brown, Les. *Les Brown's Encyclopedia of Television.* Detroit: Visible Ink, 1992.

Udelson, Joseph H. *The Great Television Race.* University: U of Alabama P, 1982.

Michael B. Kassel

Jeopardy! (1964-1975; 1984-) is a long-running television quiz show famous for its challenging trivia and its added twist, that contestants must phrase their responses in question form. In its first incarnation, *Jeopardy!* was a very popular daytime quiz show featuring emcee Art Fleming and announcer Don Pardo. The original *Jeopardy!* was a serious game show, akin to the Sunday afternoon quiz program *College Bowl* (1959-70). The original program's set was spartan and its questions were valued at only one-tenth of the later show's amounts. The program's current host and executive producer is Alex Trebek (1940-), whose suave personality has been integral to the show's continuing success.

With its sister production, the perennially perky game show *Wheel of Fortune*, *Jeopardy!* has dominated the ratings for syndicated early evening TV shows for over a decade and has been fantastically profitable for their creator-producer Merv Griffin and for distributor King World.

Bibliography

DeLong, Thomas A. *Quiz Craze: America's Infatuation with Game Shows.* New York: Praeger, 1991.

Fiske, John. "Quizzical Pleasures." *Television Culture.* New York: Routledge, 1987. 265-80.

Lidz, Franz. "Television for $1000: The World's Toughest Game Show. What Is 'Jeopardy!'?" *Sports Illustrated* 70.1 (May 1989): 94-98+.

Trebek, Alex, and Peter Barsocchini. *The "Jeopardy!" Book: The Answers, the Questions, the Facts and the Stories of the Greatest Game Show in History.* New York: HarperPerennial, 1990.

Kathryn H. Fuller

See also
Game Shows

Jesus Movement, The, was a Christian revival that began within the hippie counterculture of the late 1960s and early 1970s (see Hippies). New converts professed a charismatic, evangelical Christian faith while retaining those portions of the countercultural lifestyle (such as music, dress and communitarian living arrangements) that could be reconciled with their new convictions. In spite of occasional misunderstandings with more mainstream elements of American religiosity, the movement had a considerable impact upon the shape of youth outreach within American mainline denominations. The Jesus Movement also led to the formation of a number of new Christian sects and denominations both within the U.S. and abroad.

The roots of the Jesus Movement can be found in David Wilkerson's Teen Challenge, a Pentecostal ministry founded in the early 1960s and broadly aimed at young persons with drug addictions. By 1967, a number of youth evangelists were, independently and unknown to each other, starting outreaches specifically targeting members of the counterculture. Among the earliest of these were Christian coffeehouses and store-front ministries such as Arthur Blessit's His Place (Hollywood) and Ted Wise's Living Room (Haight-Ashbury). These initial efforts were soon followed by those of other evangelists who began to set up their own missions to alienated youth; included in this number were Linda Meissner's Jesus People's Army (Seattle and Vancouver), David Berg's Children of God (Huntington Beach), Chuck Smith's Calvary Chapel (Anaheim), and Jack Sparks's Christian World Liberation Front, or CWLF (Berkeley).

Theological views were usually based in the Pentecostal-Holiness tradition, emphasizing personal moral purity and devotion, biblical literalism, and belief in contemporary miracles such as faith healing, prophecy, and visions; many groups also held millennialist views. Most participants within the Jesus Movement believed that Christian faith and love were best expressed within groups, rather than in isolation. Ministries in the movement thus tended to foster intimate friendships based upon a shared experience of faith. Such attitudes were in part responsible for the rapid multiplication and spread of Christian communes. Hundreds, perhaps thousands, of these houses came into existence during the 1970s; the largest of these, the Shiloh communities, peaked at some 187 homes.

While the Jesus Movement's influence was widespread, the informal nature of the phenomenon and the mobility of participants makes it difficult to chart the growth of the movement accurately. The movement probably was at its zenith from about 1968 to 1973. Persons joining at the beginning of this time period were generally hippies who had become disillusioned with the drugs, sex, and eclectic religiosity of the counterculture. Later, as the number of hippies began to diminish in the wake of the decline of the counterculture, their numbers were supplemented by an influx of youth from mainline religious backgrounds who were seeking a more religiously committed way of life.

By 1974, the movement seems to have entered a period of decline. Part of this decrease was due to "media fatigue"; the movement had become so well known that it was no longer considered newsworthy. However, it is also true that many of the ministries were rather unstable. Groups frequently had a high membership turnover rate, while authority often centered upon a small senior leadership or minister-and-spouse pair operating independently of institutional ties. Such a structure meant that a scandal, divorce, or even a disagreement between elders could result in a group's demise; it also meant that the Jesus Movement as a whole was weakened on occasions in which a minister began teaching doctrines regarded as heretical within the broader Christian community. The Shiloh communities, for example, collapsed after a split in the upper-level leadership; the large Children of God ministry, on the other hand, caused a tumult after the group's leader, the colorful but highly eccentric "Moses," David Berg, attempted to modify traditional Christian understandings of marriage and sexuality.

In spite of its ephemeral nature, the movement also gave rise to several successful denominations as well as a number of sectarian bodies. For example, the CWLF, after growing into a sizable body and undergoing several internal reorganizations, eventually joined the Antiochian Orthodox Christian Church. Another group, Calvary Chapel, is now an active charismatic body with about 600 member churches in the U.S. and about 150 affiliates abroad; roughly a third of the American congregations have memberships of 1,000 or more. Similarly, the Vineyard Christian Fellowship now claims some 420 congregations (plus another 300 overseas) and is also extremely active.

Several large communal bodies exist as well. Jesus People USA, now affiliated with the Evangelical Covenant Church, is now one of the largest single communal settlements in the U.S. Claiming some 500 members, the group publishes *Cornerstone*, a well-known Christian magazine, runs a large music ministry (including the Resurrection Band, a popular Christian heavy metal group), as well as doing inner-city mission work in Chicago. The Messianic Communities (formerly the Northeast Kingdom Community Church), with a membership of between 1,000 and 1,500 members, has developed into a strongly sectarian body that has adopted a lifestyle that appears to parallel that of the communal Anabaptists. The Family (formerly known as the Children of God) also continues to grow, now numbering some 9,000 members; however, given the group's unusual past, it is uncertain at present whether or not it will be able to gain acceptance as a legitimate denomination in the near future.

In addition to the groups just mentioned, a sizable number of other small Jesus Movement-inspired ministries continue to exist both in America and abroad. These include the Jesus People Information Center (Sacramento), the Jesus Inn (Tulsa), the Jesus Army (Northampton, UK), and Jesus People, Inc. (Perth, Australia).

Bibliography

Adams, R. L., and R. J. Fox. "Mainlining Jesus: The New Trip." *Society* 9 (Feb. 1972): 50-56.

Baker, Paul. *Contemporary Christian Music*. Westchester, IL: Crossway, 1985.

Bozeman, John. "Jesus People, USA: An Examination of an Urban Communitarian Religious Group." M.A. Thesis, Florida State U, 1990.

Di Sabatino, David. "The History of the Jesus People Movement." M.A. Thesis, McMaster U, 1994.

Enroth, R., E. E. Ericson, Jr., and C. B. Peters. *The Jesus People*. Grand Rapids: Eerdmans, 1972.

Jacobson, C. K., and T. Pilarzyk. "Faith, Freaks, and Fanaticism: Notes on the Growth and Development of the Milwaukee Jesus People." Paper read at the annual meeting of the Society for the Scientific Study of Religion, Boston, Oct. 1972.

Melton, J. G. *Encyclopedic Handbook of Cults in America*. New York: Garland, 1986.

John M. Bozeman

See also
Coffeehouses

Jetsons, The (1962-1963). As every successful television show begets a spinoff, so it was with the animated show *The Flintstones* (see entry). Hanna-Barbera followed their first prime-time venture with *The Jetsons*, another takeoff on TV situation comedies. This time, it presented a typical sitcom family in the 21st century. Though *The Jetsons* didn't have the same memorable sight gags or catchphrases as *The Flintstones*, the show's ultra-retro-modern look and its jazzy theme song are well remembered. In 1962, though, the fad for prime-time cartoons was fading. *Bugs Bunny* and *Bullwinkle* had departed the previous season, *Beany and Cecil* was canceled that December, and *The Jetsons* lacked the grown-up humor of the other shows. The futuristic family lasted out the season, leaving *The Flintstones* to carry on in 1963.

However, ABC immediately put the 24 shows on Saturday morning, and they remained on the air, bouncing among all three networks until 1983. In 1984, Hanna-Barbera produced 41 new episodes and offered the show for local syndication. Another ten episodes were produced in 1987. Hanna-Barbera also made ten feature-length cartoons that year for first-run syndication, including the team-up we were waiting for, *The Jetsons Meet the Flintstones*. The show remained popular enough to be spun off into *Jetsons: The Movie* in 1990.

Bibliography

Brooks, Tim, and Earle Marsh. *The Complete Directory to Prime Time TV Shows, 1946-Present*. 4th ed. New York: Ballantine, 1988.

Erickson, Hal. *Television Cartoon Shows: An Illustrated Encyclopedia, 1949 through 1993*. Jefferson: McFarland, 1995.

Lenburg, Jeff. *The Encyclopedia of Animated Cartoons*. Rev. ed. New York: Facts on File, 1991.

Mark McDermott

Jewell, Frederick Alton (1875-1936), early 20th-century composer, bandmaster, and publisher, was born in Worthington, IN, one of seven children that made up the Jewell Family band between 1885 and 1894. He left home to join the circus band at about age 16. From 1891 to 1901 he worked with the Gentry Brothers Dog and Pony Show, first as baritone horn player and then as conductor.

In 1902 Jewell was hired as a baritone player with the Ringling Brothers Circus, a much larger organization with a big-top band of 27. Jewell played with and directed the band of the Sells-Floto show during the 1905 and 1906 seasons, during which time he also began to see his compositions enter the repertoire of other bands and to gain experience conducting for theatrical stock companies. He returned as assistant conductor and soloist to the Ringling organization in 1907. From 1908 until 1910 he served as director of the prestigious Barnum and Bailey Circus band, after which time he abruptly left the rigors of circus travel.

In 1912 Jewell returned to his hometown of Worthington to work with a town band and a touring theatrical troupe. He was lured back to the circus by the Hagenbeck-Wallace organization as "Musical Director" of a 31-piece band in 1916, but settled in Fairfield, IA, in 1918 as town band leader. From 1919 until 1923 he directed the Iowa Brigade Band headquartered in Oskaloosa and taught music in the public schools. In 1920 he formed his own publishing company which released his own works and those of others. Jewell's work with school and municipal ensembles continued upon his return to Indiana in 1923.

As a composer he is remembered for more than one hundred marches and other works including trombone smears and waltz sets. His marches were intended for practical use as circus accompaniment, as street parade pieces, as entertainment and competition repertoire for town and lodge bands, and for educational literature. He was especially adept at writing for various skill levels and instrument combinations. Marches from his pen that have retained a place in band repertoire include "E Pluribus Unum," "The Screamer," "Gentry's Triumphal," and "Quality-Plus."

Jewell's significance in American culture lies in his broad-based musical activity at a time when many Americans depended on bands as resources for musical entertainment and education. Even circus bands presented concerts of both popular and "classical" music (much in transcription) for audiences before and between the circus shows. Likewise, the 1920s was a time of substantial growth of instrumental music in American public schools. Jewell was at the forefront not only as a teacher but as a composer of music suitable for such situations and performance levels.

Bibliography
Braathen, Sverre O. *Circus Bands, Their Rise and Fall.* Evanston: Instrumentalist, 1958.
Conrad, Charles P. "Fred Jewell (1875-1936): His Life as Composer of Circus and Band Music, Bandmaster, and Publisher." D.A. diss., Ball State U, 1994.
Prince, Richard E. "Fred Jewell—One of the Best!" *Circus Fanfare* 22.4 (20 Aug. 1992): 18-21.

Linda Pohly
Charles Conrad

Jewelry. Unique design, a three-dimensional sculptural quality, and its function as decoration qualify jewelry as both a fine art and an applied art. Appreciated for its aesthetic appearance, the beauty of jewelry serves to flatter the wearer, which affords jewelry an intimacy not associated with other art forms. As with other arts, jewelry is subject to, and reflective of, changes in aesthetic values. Over the past few hundred years, the gradual elevation of jewelry to its present status as a "fine art" has resulted in its production being increasingly dominated by specialists. However, during the late 1970s, jewelry began to be recognized as a popular art form by growing numbers of people.

Jewelry is influenced by many aspects of the cultural environment, such as economics, clothing fashions, architecture, history, myth, religion, aesthetic values, and politics, which may determine its design and function, as well as how much is worn, when, and by whom. Western art (inspired by ancient Greece) reflects a preference for the harmony and balance of formal, symmetrical design, whereas Eastern art demonstrates an inclination to the dynamics of informal and asymmetrical design, which is considered visually exciting. In Europe it was considered "fashionable" to emulate those in power by mimicking their style of dress and jeweled adornment, but ancient Aztecs of lower classes were forbidden to wear precious stones and metals, which were reserved only for the ruling class. Economic and technological changes also influence the design and production of jewelry; refining precious metals allowed their use for both cast (or molded) and hand-crafted jewelry, and industrialization and the greater availability of precious stones allowed people of lower economic status access to jewelry at affordable prices.

American aesthetics have been greatly influenced by those of Europe; American jewelry has adopted and modified traditional European designs, and American trends in jewelry often parallel European trends. The display of jewelry has long denoted success in American and European culture (especially the latter, where it was worn in increasing quantities until after the French Revolution, when simpler and less showy fashions were considered to be more aesthetically pleasing). The 19th-century preference of decorative over precious pieces anticipated modern costume jewelry, as did the popularity of original designs which incorporated ancient coins, mosaics, and motifs inspired by other time periods and cultures (as a result of archaeological discoveries). The increased availability of gems, the social importance of the rising business class, and the development of mass production techniques changed the character and aesthetics of jewelry in the late 1800s, when jewelry once again indicated success. Even those of modest means could emulate the elite by purchasing less expensive imitations of fashionable jewelry, which led to a showy extreme similar to that exhibited in Europe prior to the French Revolution. However, also evolving at this time was the American folk art of button "memory strings," which were easily created from inexpensive and readily available materials. Less pretentious than status jewelry, these neckpieces consisted of attractive and unusual buttons that were given to girls by friends and family members. They also functioned in a way similar to that of friendship quilts, in that the owner could relate the history of each button and the story of its acquisition.

Jewelry design in the 20th century illustrates a change in aesthetics which occurred due to a number of factors. As had occurred after the French Revolution, the post–World War I economy made the excessive show of wealth unfashionable. Dressmakers were less interested in jewelry due to the more casual dress styles, which included short skirts (as well as shorter hair lengths), and less distinction between day and evening attire. New trends in the arts and new archaeological discoveries demanded a corresponding innovation in jewelry. Art Nouveau (1890-1920) popularized retrospective motifs of fluid, endlessly intertwined patterns inspired by East Indian, Egyptian, Islamic, Renaissance, and Oriental art, and the introduction of the Russian ballet in the 1920s also influenced jewelry design. In 1925, African bone and ivory art, the discovery of Tutankhamen's tomb, functionalism, and the development of Cubism combined to create Art Deco, which made Egyptian colors and patterns fashionable in jewelry, as well as other forms of art.

The United States experienced a renaissance in all mediums after World War II. Reaction to the machine aesthetic (which had defined product design of the 1920s and 1930s), and an emphasis on simplicity, resulted in new expressions which reflected both modern art and the "primitivism" of African and Oceanic sculpture. The 1946 Museum of Modern Art exhibit of modern jewelry design focused on the vitality and spirit of innovative concepts, unusual materials, and an eclecticism which recognized many aesthetic trends. Contemporary design continued in popularity through the 1950s with an emphasis on freedom of expression and imagination.

The continued redefinition of jewelry (as well as other art forms) in the 1960s resulted from cultural and political turmoil, the influence of counterculture, and a rise in popular culture. Assertive individualism brought a change in aesthetic values which favored socially relevant rather than precious art. These elements were reflected in pop jewelry, which elevated comic strip characters (and other popular images and objects) to icon status, and funk jewelry, which used organic, sensual forms and sexual imagery to shock. "Primitivistic," folk, and ethnic elements continued to be important to contemporary jewelry design, which included large hoop earrings, bracelets with attached rings (inspired by India and the European "Bohemian" culture), "hippie" beads (also inspired by non-Western cultures), and "peace signs" (which were political statements symbolic of the anti-war movement). During this era, jewelry (for the first time since the French Revolution) became more fashionable for men.

Rediscovery and redefinition during the 1970s again led to innovation, variety, and the expanded design of jewelry, in addition to unusual placement on the body (head, torso, upper arms, legs, breasts, hips, and shoulders). A pluralistic period, the 1970s and 1980s borrowed imagery from abstract to mannerist, while inexpensive nontraditional materials and combinations of materials continued to be investigated (cork, iron, stainless steel, aluminum, paper, tin, pewter, brass, copper, enamel, common stone, plastic, fossils, fabric and fibers, glass, found objects, clay, wood, bone, shells, seeds, feathers, and mechanical parts). Gold chains (worn to accent the style of clothing popular at discos) and crucifixes (made popular by rock star Madonna) replaced "hippie beads" and peace signs. "Punk" rock generated its own fashion and jewelry, the most visible example being the safety pin. First used for body piercing and shock value, the safety pin has found its way into popular jewelry making and has proven highly adaptable for imaginative and complex designs (such as Egyptian-style collar necklaces). Trends at this time also included "junk jewelry," and rhinestones, which became enormously popular. Found at flea markets, thrift stores, and rummage sales, old costume jewelry was inexpensive and easily reassembled or combined with other pieces to create inventive new pieces.

Jewelry of the 1990s is considered to be America's most exciting and stimulating current form of personal expression. While modern jewelry continues to borrow from antiquity, it also takes new directions which address contemporary cultural and conceptual issues. It may be nostalgic (peace signs have made a comeback), express humor and emotion, provide a personal narrative, or refer to anything from Christianity to popular culture. Representing a positive reaction against conservative, expensive, and ostentatious designs which have become clichéd, popular jewelry is less bound to past traditions of form, function, materials, and value. Crossing cultures as well as time periods, it is designed and executed using new, inexpensive, and easy-to-use materials such as plastics which may be melted and formed, and synthetic polymer clays (such as Das and Fimo) which may be formed and allowed to harden. These materials can be made to imitate the appearance of other materials including semi-precious stones, crystal, metal, or wood. New processing techniques, such as low-temperature silver solder (for home silversmithing), kilns (for melting and molding crushed glass for beads), and small stationary torches (for "lamp-working," or forming glass beads by hand), allow an endless variety of home-made jewelry.

No longer restricted to professionals and specialists, or precious stones and metals, today's jewelry is a delightful combination of fun and fashion that makes inspired and innovative use of a variety of accessible materials. Jewelry's ability to transform the wearer physically and psychologically, and its tradition of being both utilitarian and symbolic, are maintained in popular jewelry which represents a tactile, intimate, and visually intriguing decorative art that expresses personal exploration, and the appreciation of the human body as an arena for artworks.

Bibliography

Dormer, Pete, and Ralph Turner. *The New Jewelry Trends & Traditions*. London: Thames & Hudson, 1985.

Huges, Graham. *Modern Jewelry*. New York: Crown, 1963.

Moody, Jo. *The Book of Jewelry*. New York: Simon & Schuster, 1994.

Scarisbrick, Diana. *Jewellery*. London: Batsford, 1984.

Trustees of the British Museum. *Jewellery through 7000 Years*. Woodbury, NY: Barrons, in association with British Museum Publications, 1976.

D. Ann Maukonen

Jim Henson Productions and the Muppets. In 1954, James Maury Henson (1936-1990), fresh from high school, lobbied hard for a puppeteer's job at a local Washington, DC, television station, WTOP. Henson was not so much interested in puppets as he was in getting involved in the newest cultural medium, television. Any job would have suited him as long as it involved television. Like millions of other American children in the 1940s and 1950s, television for young Henson was a magical doorway into images and experiences that both nurtured and stretched the limits of his own considerable creativity. What Jim Henson and television created together revolutionized Americans' daily entertainment and education. It was nothing less than the creation of a new civilization of earthly creatures, half marionette and half puppet, amusingly christened by Henson as "Muppets."

In 1955, Jim Henson created a five-minute show called *Sam and Friends*, which aired two times each day, first before the early evening *Huntley and Brinkley Report* and then before the late night *Tonight Show*, then hosted by Steve Allen. One of Sam's friends was an indistinguishable lizard-like creature made from an old green coat. The creature's name was simply "Kermit"; he would not become "Kermit the Frog" for several more years. Sam and Kermit satirized the current topics of the day, told corny jokes, and lip-synched to popular tunes.

A simple act of technical creativity, however, gave Henson's Muppets a realism that set them apart. Instead of working behind a curtain or screen, or breaking the realism completely by placing the puppet on one's lap, Henson and his partner and wife, Jane Nebel, held the Muppets high over their heads while simultaneously watching a viewing monitor of the Muppets' faces. That way, Henson saw exactly what the audience saw; facial expressions and bodily motions could be adjusted as necessary, and the entire realism of the craft was preserved.

Henson and Nebel worked on *Sam and Friends* until 1961, then entered a three-year stint working Rowlf the Dog for *The Jimmy Dean Show*. The show paired Rowlf and Dean (1928-) in skits together, relying on the interaction between the two stars, with Rowlf garnering more fan mail than the popular singer. Audiences were not sure what to make of Rowlf; he was obviously a puppet but he seemed so human. Appearances for Henson and his increasingly large trunk of Muppets followed on the *Ed Sullivan Show*, the *Today Show*, and in dozens of commercials hawking everything from coffee to dog food to IBM products. The event that enshrined Jim Henson and his Muppets as icons of American culture, however, was the 1969 debut of the experimental children's show, *Sesame Street* (see entry). Henson was ambivalent at first about the new project. His form of puppetry had been aimed at adults; he simply was not accustomed to dealing with a preschool audience. But Henson also had young children of his own and his interest was piqued by producing puppetry segments that were technically sophisticated yet accessible to a juvenile market. The earliest *Sesame Street* Muppets continue to be the most popular: Kermit, Bert and Ernie, Big Bird, Oscar the Grouch, Grover, and the ever-hungry Cookie Monster.

Proud though he was of his continuing success on *Sesame Street*, Henson yearned to go back to adult television, to be able to explore through comedy and parody adults' needs for knowledge, security, and power. In March 1975, Henson produced a pilot show called *The Muppet Show: Sex and Violence*. The show had little to do with either but satirized the extent to which television's critics had debased the medium Henson loved. The American networks passed on the show, but Henson found an ally in Briton Lord Lew Grade, who produced and distributed the program for Henson in first-run syndication. It aired in the U.S. on local stations to fill up the dead time after the evening news but before prime time. The show was quickly a hit, ran a respectable five seasons, and introduced to American audiences, among others, Kermit's love-interest and antagonist, Miss Piggy, and the never quite defined character, the Great Gonzo.

By its fourth season, *The Muppet Show* aired in over one hundred countries, but Henson and his staff felt increasingly constrained by the show's format: backstage at a theater with characters constantly coming and going with little opportunity for in-depth character development. Henson's Muppets became truly anthropomorphized not in *Sesame Street*, not in *The Muppet Show*, but in the series of Muppet movies: *The Muppet Movie* (1979), *The Great Muppet Caper* (1981), *The Muppets Take Manhattan* (1984), *The Muppet Christmas Carol* (1992), *Muppet Treasure Island* (1996), and *Muppets from Space* (1999). As popular as the furry Muppets were, Henson's creative energy needed more outlets. In 1982 and 1986 respectively, Henson released *Dark Crystal* and *Labyrinth*, two adult dramas in which newly created Muppet characters such as Jen, Kira, and Hoggle examined the timeless topic of good and evil. Henson's latest films virtually recreated the art of puppetry by combining it with radio control, the art of "animatronics" also popularized in the *Teenage Mutant Ninja Turtle* films, for which Henson's freelance Creature Shop created the four anthropomorphized turtles, and the *Dinosaurs* series (1991-94). But Henson, though still enthralled by the seemingly limitless possibilities of television, was ultimately less concerned with the gadgetry of his films than with their message.

American audiences have been extraordinarily receptive to Henson's and his associates' messages. In 1999, *Sesame Street* celebrated its 30th anniversary and has won over 50 Emmys, among numerous other broadcasting and parents' awards. The *Muppet Show*, *Jim Henson's Muppet Babies* (an animated cartoon, 1984-), *Fraggle Rock* (1983-86), *Dinosaurs*, and the various Muppet movies are all enjoying healthy receipts since their video release. And Henson Productions has continued to produce new programming after Henson died of a violent streptococcus infection in May 1990. Three years earlier, Henson had been inducted into the Television Academy's Hall of Fame and, in 1993, was posthumously inducted into the Broadcasting and Cable Hall of Fame.

Bibliography

Finch, Christopher. *Jim Henson: The Works, the Art, the Magic, the Imagination*. New York: Random House, 1993.

——. *Of Muppets and Men: The Making of* The Muppet Show. New York: Knopf, 1981.

Henson Associates. *The Art of the Muppets: A Retrospective Look at Twenty-Five Years of Muppet Magic*. New York: Bantam, 1980.

Owen, David. "Looking Out for Kermit." *New Yorker* 16 Aug. 1993: 30-43.

Kathleen D. Toerpe

See also

Jobs, Steven Paul (1955-), made a significant impact on the world of computing by his early 20s when, with Steve Wozniak (see entry), he built the first Apple microcomputer and founded Apple Computer, Inc. in 1976. The original Apple was followed by a series of improved versions that gave Apple dominance in the market it did so much to create. As much as any individual, Jobs contributed to the folklore of Silicon Valley, which suggested that anyone could do anything, that the old-style hardware corporation (IBM, for example) could not survive the attack of the quick, wily counterculture kids emerging from hackerdom. He was a college dropout who took Eastern religions seriously and considered the priesthood as an alternative to business.

Jobs lacked the engineering background of Wozniak and moved toward a role as visionary Chairman of the Board. Pressing forward as a futurist, he was fascinated by the graphic user interface (GUI) developed and mysteriously ignored at Xerox's Palo Alto Research Center (PARC). The GUI's icons and its mouse pointer offered a far friendlier aspect than the tyrannical flashing cursor that demanded a perfectly keyboarded command. Jobs's first GUI machine was the Lisa (1983)—a quick failure—and then the Macintosh in 1984, a barely functional machine whose birth limitations almost permanently destroyed Apple's credibility with business users.

Jobs eventually resigned in anger and set up his own company, NeXT. He tried to take many of Apple's employees with him, provoking lawsuits from Apple. He built his new dream machine, an elegant high-performance workstation. Evaluators praised it, but the unique operating system failed to stimulate the independent software developers needed to insure its viability. The NeXT hardware fizzled in the early '90s while the software continued to attract interest. But Jobs, who had become one of the world's wealthiest men, had not lost his fortune. He had merely been surpassed by the company he had first founded and by another outsized wunderkind of his own generation, Bill Gates, whose Windows graphic interface threatened by mid-90s to swallow every competing operating system.

Bibliography

Butcher, Lee. *Accidental Millionaire: The Rise and Fall of Steve Jobs at Apple Computer.* New York: Pantheon, 1988.

Levy, Steven. *Insanely Great: The Life and Times of Macintosh, the Computer that Changed Everything.* New York: Viking, 1994.

Rose, Frank. *West of Eden: The End of Innocence at Apple Computer.* New York: Viking, 1989.

John S. Lawrence

Joel, Billy (1949-), is a singer-songwriter-pianist who has been one of the most successful U.S. recording artists from the 1970s to the present. His songs are an almost contradictory mix of romantic ballads like "I Love You Just the Way You Are" and New York City street-thug rants like "Big Shot."

In 1971, Joel signed as a solo artist for Family Productions, recorded his first album, *Cold Spring Harbor*, and went on his first tour. But the album was accidentally recorded at the wrong speed. Joel, disgusted with the rock music business, moved to Los Angeles and began playing a piano bar as Billy Martin (Martin is his middle name).

Meanwhile, Philadelphia radio station WMMR had been airing a recording of the song "Captain Jack," the story of a depressed teenager in suburbia. The enthusiastic audience response to the song encouraged Columbia Records to sign Joel. His first Columbia album, *Piano Man*, with its self-referential title cut, was released in 1974.

In 1975, Joel returned to New York City, where he found his songwriting energy renewed. His second album, *Streetlife Serenade*, featured another song filled with self-references, "The Entertainer." His next album, *Turnstiles*, was recorded under less than ideal circumstances in July 1976. The best-known song from the album was a celebration of Joel's return to New York City, "Say Goodbye to Hollywood."

In September 1977, Joel introduced the romantic ballad "Just the Way You Are," on television's *Saturday Night Live*. The song became a million seller, reaching No. 3 on the U.S. charts in February 1978 as well as winning two Grammy Awards. The album *The Stranger* produced three other Top 40 singles—"Movin' Out (Anthony's Song)," "Only the Good Die Young," and "She's Always a Woman." It eventually became the second-biggest-selling LP in the history of Columbia Records.

Joel followed with another million-seller album, *52nd Street* in January 1979. The LP, which topped the U.S. charts for eight weeks, included his second million-seller single, "My Life," and won two Grammy Awards.

Joel repeated his success in 1980 with the album *Glass Houses*, which earned him a Grammy for best male rock vocal performance. *Glass Houses* included his second chart-topping single, the 1950s-retro song "It's Still Rock 'n Roll to Me." In February 1981, Joel's first live album, *Songs from the Attic*, reached No. 8 on the U.S. record charts. Joel's next album, *The Nylon Curtain*, took a decidedly more political stance than earlier recordings, especially with "Allentown," about unemployed factory workers in Allentown, PA.

Joel's next album, *An Innocent Man*, was nonpolitical, focusing instead on musical styles of the 1950s and 1960s. The album was released in September 1983 and sold over 2 million copies. The LP produced 2 million-selling singles, the No. 1 hit "Tell Her about It," and No. 3 hit "Uptown Girl," in which Joel mimicked Frankie Valli's falsetto vocals. The music video for "Uptown Girl" featured Christie Brinkley, Joel's fiancée at the time.

The album *The Bridge*, a return to more serious topical songs, was released in the summer of 1986. It included a piano duet with soul/blues legend Ray Charles, "Baby Grand." While *The Bridge* reached No. 7 on the U.S. charts, it did not produce any notable singles. In 1987 Joel toured the U.S.S.R. and recorded the concert in Leningrad on *Kohuept*.

Joel released the album *Storm Front* in 1989. The album included a number of topical songs, including the chart-topping single, "We Didn't Start the Fire," a chronicle of major events in politics and entertainment during the four decades of rock and roll. The album reached No. 1 in January 1990.

In 1993, Joel released *River of Dreams*, which included the No. 1 single, "River of Dreams." He did a stadium tour with Elton John (see next entry) in 1994. He was inducted into the Rock and Roll Hall of Fame in 1999.

Bibliography
Geller, Debbie. *Billy Joel: An Illustrated Biography.* New York: McGraw-Hill, 1985.
McKenzie, Michael. *Billy Joel.* New York: Ballantine, 1984.
Rolling Stone. *The Interviews: A Twenty-fifth Anniversary Special.* New York: Straight Arrow, 1992.

Ken Nagelberg

John, Elton (1947-), the British artist, has the distinction of being the only pop music artist to have a Top 40 hit every year for over 25 years. John's tribute to the late Princess Diana, "Candle in the Wind 1997" was the biggest-selling single of all time.

Born Reginald Kenneth Dwight, John had an interest in music from a very early age. He was four when he started taking piano lessons, and eleven when he first attended the Royal Academy of Music. Throughout the 1960s, John performed with a rock/blues band, Bluesology (which included frontman Long John Baldry). After the demise of Bluesology, John auditioned for Liberty Records; while he failed to impress the executives, they put him in contact with songwriter Bernie Taupin (1950-), with whom he started a legendary songwriting partnership. However, John and Taupin did not actually meet until after they had written some 20 songs through correspondence.

John's first album from his collaboration with Taupin, *Empty Sky*, was released in 1969 on a small label; by 1970, however, John had signed with MCA Records and released *Elton John*, which entered the charts at No. 4. Its single, "Your Song," peaked at No. 8. John's next album, *Friends*, the soundtrack for a British film, reached No. 36. John had his first No. 1 album with *Honky Chateau* in 1972, followed by another No. 1 album, *Goodbye Yellow Brick Road*, in 1973.

In late 1974, John recorded his version of the Beatles classic "Lucy in the Sky with Diamonds" (No. 1) with John Lennon guesting; Elton John later became godfather to Lennon's son, Sean. In 1975, John appeared in Ken Russell's fantasy film *Tommy*, which was based on the Who's rock opera of the same name. By 1977, when Taupin moved to Los Angeles, the John/Taupin partnership temporarily dissolved. Tired from life on the road, John announced he was done touring, but he returned to the stage 15 months later. John's first album without Taupin lyrics, *A Single Man*, was released in 1978 and hit the charts at No. 15.

John had a continuous string of hits in the 1980s, including "I Guess That's Why They Call It the Blues," "Sad Songs Say So Much," and "I'm Still Standing." In 1983, John released *Too Low for Zero*, his first album with Taupin since 1976. *Too Low for Zero* peaked at No. 25. Throughout the 1980s, John continued to tour and record, contributing to a project led by singer Dionne Warwick to raise money for AIDS research. The single, "That's What Friends Are For" (1985), also featured Gladys Knight and songwriter Stevie Wonder and became one of the biggest singles of the year.

In 1988, John's live version of "Candle in the Wind," from the double *Live in Australia* album and recorded with an Australian orchestra, became a hit, peaking at No. 6. The song, dedicated to Marilyn Monroe, was originally recorded on *Goodbye Yellow Brick Road* in 1973.

John has released albums throughout the 1990s and has remained a top-selling live act. John and Taupin were inducted into the Songwriters Hall of Fame in May 1992. Hit singles released during the 1990s include "The One," "Can You Feel the Love Tonight," and the No. 1 duet with George Michael, "Don't Let the Sun Go Down on Me."

In 1994, John was inducted into the Rock and Roll Hall of Fame and embarked on an ambitious stadium tour with vocalist/songwriter Billy Joel (see entry). John's 1995 album, *Made in England*, debuted at No. 13 and in 1997 *Big Picture* reached No. 9 on the album charts. In June 2000 John and Tim Rice won a Tony for the score to *Aida*. He also provided music for the films *The Lion King* (1994) and *The Road to El Dorado* (2000).

Bibliography
Bernardin, Claude, and Tom Stanton. *Rocket Man: Elton John A-Z.* Westport: Praeger, 1996.
Gambaccini, Paul. *A Conversation with Elton John and Bernie Taupin.* New York: Flash, 1976.
Goodall, Nigel. *Elton John: A Visual Documentary.* New York: Omnibus, 1993.
John, Elton. *In His Own Words.* New York: Omnibus, 1994.
Norman, Philip. *Elton John.* New York: Fireside, 1993.
Rees, Dafydd, and Luke Crampton. *Encyclopedia of Rock Stars.* New York: DK, 1996.
Taupin, Bernie. *The One Who Writes the Words for Elton John.* New York: Knopf, 1976.

Robert G. Weiner

Jolson, Al (1886-1950), was the first modern mass entertainment star. Trained in minstrel shows and vaudeville, where he learned his sentimental and comic themes and openly emotional song style, he projected his voice through theaters before the use of microphones. He synthesized vocal elements from his Jewish cantor father's tradition with cadences from ragtime and, later, jazz. With these, he mingled whistling, gestures, improvisations, dance steps and the ability to communicate with each member of his audience. Advancing technology allowed him to attract new audiences through records, films, and wartime military and hospital appearances. During much of the period between 1917 and 1950, he was known as "The World's Greatest Entertainer."

Jolson was born Asa Joelson in Seredzius, Lithuania; the date generally given is May 16, 1886. His father came to the U.S. in 1890, settling in Washington, DC, and sending for his family four years later. While his father urged him to remain within the family's orthodox Jewish tradition, Jolson was quickly secularized and Americanized. He and his brother Hirsh (they renamed themselves Al and Harry Jolson) performed for coins in the streets and, by age 11,

Jolson had begun to run away from home to find work in show business.

Jolson appeared with a carnival, with a traveling circus, and on various vaudeville circuits, among others. His first success came in San Francisco, shortly after the 1906 earthquake. There, too, he met the first of his four wives: Henrietta Keller (1907-19), Ethel Delmar (1922-16), Ruby Keeler (1928-40), and Erle Galbraith (1945-), who survived him.

His New York success came with *La Belle Paree* (1911). Already working primarily in blackface, then a generally unquestioned convention derived from minstrel shows and as accepted as the stock stage Irishmen and Jews of the period, Jolson created his stock blackface character, Gus, for *Vera Violetta* (1911). While not starring in these shows, he quickly dominated critical and audience attention. Other shows included *Dancing Around* (1914), *Robinson Crusoe, Jr.* (1916), and *Sinbad* (1918), in which he introduced George Gershwin's song "Swanee." *Bombo* (1921) introduced the hit song "April Showers."

His first authenticated records were cut in 1911 for Victor Records; his first film performance was the short *Honeymoon Express* in 1913. His radio debut came in 1922 when his voice was heard along the eastern seaboard and apparently was piped into hospital wards for World War I wounded. He appeared in a number of other short films and began a film, *Black Magic*, for D. W. Griffith in 1923. Dissatisfied with early footage, he abruptly quit. Griffith sued. Nevertheless, in 1923, Jolson signed to do the history-making talking film, *The Jazz Singer* (see entry).

With Jolson's songs and improvised comments, *The Jazz Singer* (1927) brought the silent film era to an end. Warner Brothers followed this success with *The Singing Fool* (1928), *Say It with Songs* (1929), *Mammy* (1930), and *Big Boy* (1930). In 1933, United Artists released *Hallelulah, I'm a Bum*, a failure. By 1935, when Jolson starred with his then-wife, dancer Ruby Keeler, in *Go into Your Dance*, his career seemed over. Swing music had supplanted jazz for the time, and Jolson's sentimentalism was out of tune with Depression-era audiences. He was relegated to a series of supporting roles and cameo appearances.

But in 1948, he was given his own radio show, the *Kraft Music Hall*. This revival of popularity motivated Columbia Pictures to film *The Jolson Story* (1946), which became that studio's greatest money-making film to that time. The film starred Larry Parks as Jolson, but Jolson dubbed all the songs, as he did again for the sequel *Jolson Sings Again* (1949). Jolson himself was briefly seen in the first film, dancing to "Swanee."

His career revived, Jolson nonetheless volunteered as an overseas entertainer at the outbreak of the Korean War. His ill health and the conditions under which he performed some 160 wartime shows led to his death from a heart attack on October 23, 1950.

Bibliography

Anderton, Barrie. *Sonny Boy! The World of Al Jolson*. London: Jupiter, 1975.

Fisher, James. *Al Jolson: A Bio-Bibliography*. Westport: Greenwood, 1994.

Freedland, Michael. *Jolie: The Al Jolson Story*. London: Allen, 1985.

Goldman, Herbert G. *Jolson: The Legend Comes to Life*. New York: Oxford UP, 1988.

Kiner, Larry F., and Philip R. Evans. *Al Jolson, A Bio-Discography*. Metuchen: Scarecrow, 1992.

McClelland, Doug. *Blackface to Blacklist: Al Jolson, Larry Parks, and "The Jolson Story."* Metuchen: Scarecrow, 1987.

Betty Richardson

See also

Vaudeville

Jones, Curtis (1906-1971), was a musician whose own life story remarkably parallels the development and dissemination of "country blues." The popularity of this genre of African-American folk music spread from the Mississippi delta and eastern Texas throughout the South at the beginning of the 20th century and internationally some 60 years later.

Born one of seven children near Naples in the northeast part of Texas, Curtis was exposed to blues early in life through family and neighbors. By age 10 he had begun learning the guitar, but as a teenager he developed his true talent, playing piano. During these early years, when not working on the farm or the railroad, Curtis joined with friends to perform in local vaudeville shows. At about the age of 16, he headed to Dallas, where he worked as a singer/pianist in local bars. Alex Moore (aka Papa Chittlins) heard Curtis and had him play in a recording session in 1925. The record unfortunately was never issued, but Jones's personal playing style and blues interpretation were being formed, a lightly layered style later described as economical and unassuming.

In 1937, Curtis recorded what has been called his signature piece, "Lonesome Bedroom Blues," soon a national hit. Riding the tide of popularity, he also recorded on the Bluebird and OKeh labels; however, he had no significant successes from among approximately 100 songs he recorded in the late 1930s and early 1940s. He worked in local Chicago clubs, but his heyday already seemed over. Jones virtually dropped out of sight during the 1940s.

In 1959, while living in a Chicago slum, Jones was sought out by Jacques Demêtre, a French blues critic. This meeting led to a revival of Curtis's career in the 1960s, when he recorded again, this time with the Prestige-Bluesville and Delmark labels, and in 1962 he moved to France to begin touring Europe. He benefited from the so-called blues revival at this time, accepting engagements in France, England, Germany, Poland, Switzerland, Belgium, Morocco, and Tunisia. In 1964, sparked by his London appearances (and what is now his most acclaimed album, *Curtis Jones in London*), *Rhythm & Blues Monthly* began publishing "The Curtis Jones Blues Story," an uneven but colorful and engaging series of autobiographical articles written by Jones from his home in France.

Jones reached the pinnacle of his modest success with "Lonesome Bedroom Blues" and was more or less rejected by American audiences afterwards, but his life replicates the vicissitudes in the development of the blues from its south-

445

ern origins through its Chicago urbanization and ultimately to its revival and legitimization in the 1960s among formal musicians and scholars.

Bibliography

Harris, Sheldon. *Blues Who's Who: A Biographical Dictionary of Blues Singers*. New Rochelle: Arlington House, 1979: 291-92.

Jones, Curtis. "The Curtis Jones Blues Story." *Rhythm & Blues Monthly* (from early 1964 through late 1965, most issues available through the Blues Archives, Oxford, MS).

Catherine Olson
Michael Delahoyde

Jones, George (1931-), has been considered the quintessential country singer with his voice able to convey the essence of a country song—the humor, pathos, struggle, sincerity and homespun philosophies that embody country lyrics.

Born in Saratoga, TX, he moved to Beaumont, TX, in 1942 where his father worked in the shipyards. At 12, Jones was busking on street corners and in stores; at 14 he ran away to Jasper, TX, where he performed on station KTXJ before he returned to Beaumont in 1947 and performed with Eddie and Pearl on KRIC. In 1949, Jones was in the band that played behind Hank Williams but, because he was so awed by his idol, Jones "never hit a lick," although afterwards he received some advice from Williams. Jones performed at KRIC and KTRM in Beaumont, was jailed for failure to pay child support, and then joined the Marine Corps in November 1951. He spent most of his time at Camp Pendleton in California and performed in clubs in the San Francisco area.

Upon his return home to Beaumont in November 1953, Jones signed with a local record label, Starday, which had been started by Pappy Daily and Jack Starnes; by the end of 1954, he had released four singles; he also worked as a disc jockey for KTRM in Beaumont during this time. Jones's first national hit came for Starday in 1955 with "Why, Baby, Why," followed by several more before Pappy Daily joined Mercury Records in Nashville as a producer and brought Jones along. At Mercury (a subsidiary), Jones had a string of hits from 1957 to 1962 that included "White Lightning" and the sad ballads he became known for. Beginning with "Window Up Above" in 1960, Jones established his image as a country ballad singer; this song was followed by others such as "Tender Years" and "She Thinks I Still Care." In the 1960s he recorded hits such as "The Race Is On," "Take Me," "Walk through This World with Me," "When the Grass Grows over Me," and "A Good Year for the Roses" for several other labels.

During this period he married Tammy Wynette (February 16, 1969; see entry) and their show became the most popular on the road, billed as "Mr. and Mrs. Country Music." He recorded a number of duets with her after he signed with Epic, the label she was on, in 1972. A string of hits followed, including "The Grand Tour" and "We Can Make It," before their marriage ended in divorce in 1975.

A turbulent personal period followed, although Jones continued to release hit songs, mostly autobiographical, such as "These Days (I Barely Get By)," "Her Name Is," "If Drinkin' Don't Kill Me (Her Memory Will)," and "He Stopped Loving Her Today," which many consider to be the quintessential country song. During the 1980s and '90s, Jones became the godfather of the new traditionalists in country music, who looked to George Jones as their hero and idol as they brought country music back to its traditional roots.

Bibliography

Allen, Bob. *George Jones: The Life and Times of a Honky Tonk Legend*. Secaucus: Carol, 1994.

Carlisle, Dolly. *Ragged but Right: The Life and Times of George Jones*. Chicago: Contemporary, 1984.

Jones, George. *I Lived to Tell It All*. New York: Villard, 1996.

Don Cusic

Jones, Quincy Delight (1933-), is known as one of the most eclectic and durable producers in the music industry. He began his career as a jazz trumpeter and has since distinguished himself as a pop/R&B/producer/composer/arranger.

Born on the South Side of Chicago, he is the son of a carpenter and a mother who was confined for mental illness much of his early life. At 14, he met Ray Charles, then 16; in addition to working and "jamming together," Charles schooled Jones in the fundamentals of blues, bebop, and musical arrangements.

The young Jones and Charles were employed at a pristine Seattle tennis club, where from 7 to 10 in the evening they would perform to accompany the dinner. Then the two would play R&B for strippers and comedians in such black clubs as the Black and Tan, the Rocking Chair, and the Washington Educational Social Club. When the paid "gigs" were over, Jones would gather with such musicians as Cecil Young, Gerald Brashear, and Ray Charles at the Elks Club, where they would play hardcore bebop until four or five in the morning. It was these early experiences that laid the foundation for Jones's eclectic musical background as a producer/arranger.

At 15, Jones joined Lionel Hampton. During this time Charlie Parker became friends with him, and Clark Terry, a member of the Count Basie band, tutored him. He also began playing the trumpet in Billie Holiday's band. Later, he took a break and began studies at Boston's Berklee College of Music. Eventually he went to Paris to study under Nadia Boulanger.

He rejoined Lionel Hampton's big band in 1951 and quickly became renowned in jazz circles as an arranger and composer. He added his artistic touch to sessions with Ray Charles, Dinah Washington, Duke Ellington, Cannonball Adderley, Billy Eckstine, and others.

In the 1960s he began to branch out, producing records, scoring Hollywood soundtracks and becoming the first African-American executive at a major American label, Mercury Records, where he joined as a R&B man. There, he began to make a name for himself as an artist in his own right when he recorded his own music such as *The Birth of a*

Band as well as producing pop hits like Leslie Gore's 1963 smash, "It's My Party." In 1969 he signed with A&M Records, an association that lasted 12 years.

The year 1963 found Jones composing his first film score, for Sidney Lumet's *The Pawnbroker* (1965). By the early 1990s he had written music scores for some 50 movies, including: *In Cold Blood, Cactus Flower, The New Centurions, The Slender Thread, In the Heat of the Night, For Love of Ivy, The Anderson Tapes,* and *Bob & Carol & Ted & Alice.* He also created themes for TV shows like *Ironside* and *Sanford and Son.* In 1971, he produced the *Duke Ellington Special* for CBS. Almost two decades later he would become the co-owner with Time Warner of Quincy Jones Entertainment, Inc., and produce TV programs like *Fresh Prince of Bel Air* and *The Jesse Jackson Show.* In 1985, he not only wrote the music score but was the executive producer of *The Color Purple.*

In 1978, he scored Lumet's film, *The Wiz,* and made the acquaintance of Michael Jackson (see entry). Their friendship led to three blockbuster albums produced by Jones: *Off the Wall* (1979), *Thriller* (1982), which won eight Grammy Awards and would go on to become the best-selling pop album in history, and *Bad* (1987).

Jones's success with these three projects was but a single expression of his creative and eclectic genius. In 1981, he launched his own record label, Qwest Records. The next year he became the most honored member at the 24th annual Grammy Awards ceremony when he garnered a total of five Grammys including best producer of 1981. His production of "We Are the World," a recording session for the USA for Africa relief effort, raised $50 million for Ethiopian famine victims and became the biggest-selling hit single of the 1980s. His 1991 solo album, *Back on the Block,* sold more than 3 million copies and resulted in Jones collecting six Grammy awards. In July of 1991, Jones produced the 25th annual Montreux Jazz Festival in Europe. In the fall of 1992, he founded *Vibe* magazine, which he considers the voice of hip-hop.

His six decades of achievement were not without difficulties. In 1974, he suffered two brain aneurysms. His three interracial marriages all ended in divorce. On the positive side, with 25 Grammy Awards, he has more nominations than anyone else in the history of pop music. It is because of his loyalty to African-American music that he successfully institutionalized "crossover" and has become one of (if not the) greatest pop-music producers in the world.

Bibliography

George, Nelson. "The Many Worlds of Quincy Jones: 40th Anniversary." *Billboard* 9 Dec. 1989.

Horricks, Raymond. *Quincy Jones.* Tunbridge: Hippocrene, 1985.

Michael Washington

Jones, Spike (1911-1965), remembered primarily as a comic bandleader with a flair for manic melodies, was a skilled, serious musician who provided popular music audiences a form of structured revolt against both mainstream and classical music tastes during and following World War II.

Lindley Armstrong Jones was born in Long Beach, CA. An only child, he developed a sense of independence and an interest in music at an early age. Later, Spike—a nickname that resulted from his father's job as a railway depot agent—said in interviews that he first had become interested in percussion when a chef at the depot rattled forks, knives, and other kitchen utensils in unusual rhythms.

When Jones was 12, he joined with some teenaged musicians to form a dance band. By the time he graduated from high school in 1929, Jones had developed a reputation in the Los Angeles music scene as a respectable and reliable drummer. Working constantly, he got his first real break in 1936 when he was hired to fill in with the Victor Young Orchestra, one of Hollywood's most popular and prolific bands. By continually adding special sound effects to his repertoire, Jones soon had all the movie studio and radio show work he could handle. Considering himself a pretty good comic, he persistently sought out gadgets that could be used or abused into making unusual sounds.

Jones also began collecting musicians. For a few months in 1940, he managed the Feathermerchants, a dance combo that featured spontaneous, vaudeville-style comedy sketches in its act. The Feathermerchants' failure fueled Jones's eagerness to start his own band. Working with an expanding troupe of musicians, singers, and songwriters, Jones created a distinctive slapstick style from burlesque, with detailed choreography.

Jones and his band, now billed as Spike Jones and His City Slickers, made their first recordings in August 1941, but it was the troupe's third trip to RCA's studios that made Jones and his sound a national phenomenon. Written for a Donald Duck cartoon short, "Der Fuehrer's Face" was issued in late 1942; its brassy, belittling style was the loud, collective laugh of a nervous nation. Rollicking lyrics—sung in a garbled German to the accompaniment of a fractured oompah band—were punctuated by a toy rubber "razzer."

Despite the runaway success of "Der Fuehrer's Face," Jones and the City Slickers found themselves cultivating their celebrity on radio, since the wartime musicians' union strike barred them from recording. By the time the band returned to the recording studio in late 1944, Jones had added more sound effects and more seasoned musicians—and had developed a more pointed assault on popular music. "Cocktails for Two," the City Slickers' best-selling record ever, was a representative example. A post-Prohibition ballad, the City Slickers' version starts in a "sweet" big-band style that lulled the audience into familiar complacency—that is, until a band member screams and police whistles, car horns, and gunfire ring out. While popular songs were frequent fodder for Jones's musical slapstick, he also carved up classical works, turning Rossini's "William Tell Overture" into a horse race and riddling Liszt's "Liebestraum" with crashes and razzing brass instruments.

After the war, Jones accelerated his experimenting (briefly, he even staged a "straight" 30-piece band, the Other Orchestra) and began nearly a decade of nonstop touring. Jones had a late-1940s success on radio with *Spotlight Revue,* which was broadcast from wherever the band was performing at the time. Although he maintained his popularity into the mid-1950s, Jones's exaggerated slapstick faced fierce competition from television and changing tastes in popular music. As late as 1953, Jones had a minor success with "I Went to Your Wedding," a takeoff on a Patti Page hit, but Jones never seemed to figure out how to mock rock and roll. Instead, he shifted his musical attention in his later years to Dixieland jazz, the classics, and topical subjects.

A chronic smoker, Jones never was in good health. Although he was diagnosed with emphysema in 1960, Jones continued live performing but died after a severe attack. His music was kept alive by like-minded music manglers such as Peter Schickele (also known as P. D. Q. Bach) and an unlikely range of American creative artists who have claimed Spike Jones as an important influence, from comedian George Carlin to cult novelist Thomas Pynchon.

Bibliography

Dunning, John. *Tune in Yesterday: The Ultimate Encyclopedia of Old-Time Radio 1925-1976*. Englewood Cliffs: Prentice-Hall, 1976.

Hansen, Barry (Dr. Demento). *Notes for Musical Depreciation Revue: The Spike Jones Anthology*. Rhino R2 71574 (1994 compact disc).

Mirtle, Jack, with Ted Hering. *Thank You Music Lovers: A Bio-discography of Spike Jones and His City Slickers, 1941-to 1965*. New York: Greenwood, 1986.

Young, Jordan R. *Spike Jones and His City Slickers: An Illustrated Biography*. Beverly Hills: Disharmony, 1984.

Chris Foran

Jones, Tom (1940-), with a voice ranging from baritone to tenor, an interest in a wide scope of musical expression, and an energetic sensuality, successfully synthesizes disparate aspects of American and British culture. Born Thomas Jones Woodward, the son of a coal miner in Pontypridd, South Wales, he was heir to the rich tradition of poetry and song of the Welsh laborers. He began singing at an early age, in church, in school, and in his home, where he would ask his mother to "pull the drapes and announce me" ("Tom Jones—The Man" 2).

As a young man, he was less interested in school than he was in music and the pleasures of youth. At 16, he left school; at 17, he had a wife and son. To support his family, he worked a variety of jobs including builder's laborer and vacuum cleaner salesman. By 1963, he was also performing at night in the working-class clubs with his own group, "Tommy Scott and the Senators." Gordon Mills, an established performer eager to branch out into songwriting and management, came to see Tom work. Immediately impressed, Mills took him to London, but promoting him was not easy because "He sounded black and moved like Elvis" ("Tom Jones—The Man" 2). But the two persisted, finally securing a contract with Decca Records. The first single was not successsful, but the next, "It's Not Unusual" written by Mills, was an international hit. Considered too hot by the sedate BBC Radio, it was aired by an off-shore station. The next year found Tom Jones opening for the Rolling Stones at London's Beat City and performing with the Spencer Davis Group.

His early inspiration came from such diverse singers as Tennessee Ernie Ford, Little Richard, Big Bill Broonzy, and Jerry Lee Lewis, among others. These influences helped create the gold singles and albums that followed in the 1960s: "Green Green Grass of Home," "Delilah," "Help Yourself," "Love Me Tonight," "I'll Never Fall in Love Again," *Tom Jones Live*, and *Tom Jones in Las Vegas*. In 1969, six of his albums were certified gold, and Jones branched out into another entertainment genre as ABC signed him to a contract for a music-variety show titled *This Is Tom Jones*, which was recorded in London and Los Angeles. The show ran until 1971. The gold hits continued into the '70s with "I (Who Have Nothing)," "She's a Lady," and *Tom Jones Live at Caesar's Palace*. Between 1973 and 1986, Jones continued to record and to perform for sell-out audiences internationally.

In 1987, he again moved to another genre, this time to a British musical play titled *Matador,* for which he recorded the score. A cut from that album, "A Boy from Nowhere," reached No. 2 in the British charts and prompted a resurgence of requests for "It's Not Unusual" in London clubs. Re-released, the song attracted a new generation of Tom Jones fans.

Jones was back in the Top 10 in 1988, when he collaborated with the British avant-garde group the Art of Noise on Prince's *Kiss*. Jones appeared in the video, which won the MTV award for Breakthrough Video of the Year. Again Jones was crossing demographic barriers.

In the early '90s, he performed at benefits, including the 30th Anniversary of Amnesty International, and had his own television series on the British network ITV, *Tom Jones: The Right Time*, with guest artists such as the Chieftains, Joe Cocker, David Gilmore, Daryl Hall, Cyndi Lauper, and Stevie Wonder.

Jones provided an animated serenade on the hit comedy show *The Simpsons* and participated in a stage performance of fellow Welshman Dylan Thomas's *Under Milkwood*. In 1994, he released *The Lead and How to Swing It,* an original album.

Bibliography

"An Evening with Tom Jones." Online. Internet. 17 Dec. 1997. Available: www.musiccircus.com/tj.html.

"Jones/Bio." Online. Internet. 17 Dec. 1997. Available: kspace.com/KM/spot.sys/Jones/pages/bio.html#chrono.

"Tom Jones at the Metro: Chicago January 11, 1995." *Entertainment Avenue!* Online. Internet. 17 Dec. 1997. Available: www.e-ave.com/c_hall/unk_rev/tjones2.html.

"Tom Jones, Special Guest Voice in 'Marge Gets a Job.'" Online. Internet. 17 Dec. 1997. Available: www.foxworld.com/simpsons/epi9f05.htm.

"Tom Jones—The Man!" Online. Internet. 17 Dec. 1997. Available: www.kensai.com/tomjones/.

Barbara Basore McIver

Joplin, Janis (1943-1970), is considered the premier white blues-rock singer. Her reputation for hard drinking, drug use, and promiscuous sex, however, often eclipsed her achievements as a performer and recording artist. Her public success did not carry over into private happiness, as epitomized by her statement, "Onstage I make love to 25,000 people, then I go home alone." She died of a drug overdose after a brief but influential recording and performing career.

Joplin was born in Port Arthur, TX. She was often regarded as an "ugly duckling" in high school, which made her status as one of the sex symbols of the 1960s even more remarkable. Joplin withdrew into a world of music and art as a teenager. She began singing in clubs in Austin and Houston and joined the Waller Creek Boys at the age of 17.

Joplin ran away and hitchhiked to San Francisco in 1963. There she became a part of the growing folk-blues movement. She performed solo and with singer-guitarists like Jorma Kaukonen, who later became the lead guitarist for the Jefferson Airplane. She also became involved with drugs in San Francisco, but she decided to leave the hippie scene in early 1966. Joplin returned to Texas and attended the University of Texas. She also began making plans for marriage. She continued her singing, this time with a country band at the "outlaw" bar, Threadgill's.

But she returned to California in June 1967 after being summoned to join the blues-rock band Big Brother and the Holding Company. In June 1967, Janis Joplin received tremendous accolades for her performance at the Monterey Pop Festival. Her show was captured on film by noted documentarian D. A. Pennebaker in the 1969 film *Monterey Pop*. Bob Dylan's manager, Albert Grossman, was impressed and signed Joplin and her group. In August, "Big Brother and the Holding Company" was released by Mainstream and reached No. 60 on the U.S. charts.

In August 1968, Columbia released Big Brother's first album, shortening the title from the more suggestive *Dope, Sex, and Cheap Thrills* to *Cheap Thrills*. The live recordings were of poor quality, but they captured the raw energy of Joplin's concert performances. The album also featured cover art by acclaimed psychedelic comic-book artist R. Crumb. *Cheap Thrills* reached No. 1 on the U.S. charts in October and stayed there for eight weeks. The LP also produced two successful singles, "Down on Me" and "Piece of My Heart," and the latter peaked at No. 12 on the charts.

But the band broke up in December, and former Big Brother guitarist Sam Andrews and Joplin formed a new group, Janis and the Joplinaires, in February 1969. The group was renamed the Kozmic Blues Band and toured the United States and England with fluctuating lineups in the spring and summer. Andrews left the band, and the group subsequently became more soul-oriented. The Kozmic Blues Band's only album, *I Got Dem Ol' Kozmic Blues Again*, peaked at No. 5.

In May 1970, Joplin formed a touring group, the Full Tilt Boogie Band, with bassist Brad Campbell of the Kozmic Blues Band and some new musicians. The group followed a busy concert schedule in the summer and began recording sessions in September. Midway through the sessions, however, Janis Joplin died in her room at the Landmark Hotel in Hollywood on October 4, 1970. Her death was ruled an accidental heroin overdose by the coroner, although many suspected it was a suicide.

The unfinished recording sessions were released as the album *Pearl*, which reached No. 1 for nine weeks in early 1971. Her recording of fellow-Texan Kris Kristofferson's "Me and Bobby McGee" on that album became a rock classic. The song had a very different style than those in Joplin's earlier recordings. "Me and Bobby McGee" had a country-folk quality, and both the lyrics of the song and the way it was sung conveyed an attitude of despair that many think represented Joplin's depression at the time. *Pearl* also included the minor hit "Cry Baby." But the B-side of that single, the a capella tongue-in-cheek ballad "Mercedes Benz," is far better known.

Joplin is memorialized in numerous recordings and biographies and a television documentary. In 1972, Columbia released *Janis Joplin in Concert*, featuring her with Big Brother and the Holding Company on one side and with the Full Tilt Boogie Band on the other. The album peaked at No. 4 on the charts. The next year, *Janis Joplin's Greatest Hits* reached No. 37.

The television documentary *Janis* included performances from her Texas days (1963-65) as well as recordings from television performances with the Full Tilt Boogie and Kozmic Blues bands. Some critics consider the documentary too sympathetic to Joplin, however, since it was produced in cooperation with her family. A two-disc recording from the soundtrack was released in 1974. In 1980, *Anthology* was released, followed by the LP *Farewell Song* in 1982.

In 1979, singer-actress Bette Midler played a role based loosely on Joplin's life in the motion picture *The Rose*. The best-known written account of Joplin's life is *Buried Alive* by Myra Friedman (1973). In 1992, her sister Laura wrote a biography, *Love, Janis*, based on letters Janis Joplin had written home to her family. Laura Joplin also wrote a musical play by the same title that debuted in 1994.

Bibliography

Dalton, David. *Piece of My Heart: A Portrait of Janis Joplin*. New York: Da Capo, 1991.

Friedman, Myra. *Buried Alive: The Biography of Janis Joplin*. New York: Harmony, 1992.

Joplin, Laura. *Love, Janis*. New York: Villard, 1992.

Kenneth M. Nagelberg

Joplin, Scott (1868-1917), earned the title "The King of Ragtime Writers" by introducing classical elegance into the new popular genre during the heyday of classic ragtime, from the late 1890s until World War I when flashy Tin Pan Alley imitations predominated. Even though he thought the term "ragtime" to be "scurrilous" and devoted energies to grander projects such as ragtime ballet and opera, his piano rags have been declared America's equivalent to Mozart minuets, Chopin mazurkas, and Brahms waltzes.

Joplin was born into a fairly musical Texarkana family. When his father purchased second-hand a square grand piano, Scott taught himself how to play until news of the 11-year-old prodigy spread, whereupon an old German immigrant musician offered young Scott free tutoring. Joplin hit the road as an itinerant pianist, playing in honky-tonks, brothels, and gambling houses, and eventually using St. Louis as his home base. He organized a small orchestra in which he played piano and cornet at the 1893 Chicago World's Fair, and in 1895, toured with his brothers Will and Robert in a male octet he apparently had formed in Texarkana years earlier. This group, the Texas Medley Quartette, traveled to Syracuse, NY, where Joplin sold his first two songs, both sentimental parlor fare.

In the mid-1890s, he settled in Sedalia, MO (which became known as the "Cradle of Classic Ragtime" because of Joplin), attended George R. Smith College for Negroes to supplement his musical education, played locally, taught music, and published a waltz and two marches. The Maple Leaf Club at which Joplin played provided the name for his first and most famous rag. Late in 1899, after being rejected by two publishing houses (one of which did accept his "Original Rags"), "Maple Leaf Rag" was published by John Stark, a 59-year-old Sedalia music dealer who ultimately published about one-third of Joplin's compositions. When piano works typically sold outright for under $25, Joplin received a lucrative $50 and royalties of a penny per copy sold. "Maple Leaf Rag" sold well, kept selling, and eventually became the most famous and most recorded of all piano rags.

With the success of "Maple Leaf Rag," Joplin quit performing and devoted himself to teaching and composing. In addition to composing piano rags, he undertook his first more ambitious project: *The Ragtime Dance*, a folk ballet which he staged in 1899 and which Stark reluctantly published with its choreographic directions (now lost) in 1902.

Joplin met ragtime composer Joseph Lamb and by lending his own name as arranger helped to promote sales of "Sensation Rag" (1907). Meanwhile his own rags grew more sophisticated: though lyrical and structurally sound, earlier pieces such as "Cleopha" (a favorite of the Sousa Band from 1902), "Elite Syncopations" (1902), and "The Chrysanthemum" (1904) seem to pale next to the masterful "Gladiolus Rag" (1907), the introspective "Wall Street Rag" (1909), or the experimental "Euphonic Sounds" (1909). Joplin also published his instructional "School of Ragtime" in 1908 and began work on another ragtime opera, *Treemonisha*.

A financial dispute with Stark dissolved their relationship in 1909; Joplin subsequently published the *Treemonisha* score himself. He became so involved with orchestrating this opera that little else was published during the last years of his life. He was able to finance one performance at Harlem's Lincoln Theatre in 1915; but with no scenery, costumes, lighting, or orchestra, the work gleaned no support (nor was it performed successfully until 1972). Depressed over the opera and afflicted with syphilis, Joplin began to deteriorate, and he lost pupils. He composed only fragments, and took up and abandoned projects such as the orchestration of his earlier rags. He died April 1, 1917, the day America entered World War I.

Although the 1940s saw some renewed interest in ragtime, a tremendous revival emerged in the 1970s with the New York Public Library's publication of Joplin's works, pianist Joshua Rifkin's rag performances in concert halls, and productions of *Treemonisha*. Primarily, though, the 1973 film *The Sting* and its Academy Award-winning score—including "The Entertainer" (1902), "Pine Apple Rag" (1908), and "Solace" (1909)—repopularized Joplin (although Marvin Hamlisch was often given credit for more than arranging and adapting Joplin's music for the film). "The Entertainer" even climbed into the Top 10 on the pop charts in May 1974. A posthumous Pulitzer Prize in 1976 and commemorative postage stamp in 1983 provided further honors for the man who remains the most famous composer of ragtime music.

Bibliography

Blesh, Rudi. "Scott Joplin: Black-American Classicist." *Scott Joplin: Collected Piano Works*. New York: New York Library, 1971. xiii-xl.

Blesh, Rudi, and Harriet Janis. *They All Played Ragtime*. New York: Oak, 1971.

Gammond, Peter. *Scott Joplin and the Ragtime Era*. New York: St. Martin's, 1975.

Haskins, James, and Kathleen Benson. *Scott Joplin: The Man Who Made Ragtime*. Garden City: Doubleday, 1978.

Michael Delahoyde
Yong Peng Chen

Jordan, Michael (1963-), the man who transformed the National Basketball Association into a global entity and enticed millions of new fans to professional basketball arenas, began his career as a skinny 6′ 6″ kid from Wilmington, NC. Born in Brooklyn, NY, Michael attended Wilmington Laney High School and as a sophomore averaged 23 points a game for the junior varsity but was not selected to the varsity team. He worked hard on his game over the summer and made the varsity in his senior year, averaging 23 points a game.

He received a scholarship to play at the University of North Carolina under the tutelage of legendary coach Dean Smith. His freshman year at North Carolina, Jordan made the last-second jump shot that allowed the Tar Heels to capture the 1982 NCAA championship. He was chosen the consensus national college player of the year in 1984 and played a crucial role in the 1984 USA Olympic Basketball team's winning the Olympic Gold Medal in Los Angeles.

In 1984, Jordan was drafted by the Chicago Bulls of the National Basketball Association. Jordan was NBA Rookie of the Year in 1984-85 and made the NBA All-Rookie Team in that year, also. He would go on to play on five NBA World Champion teams in 1990-91, 1994-95, 1995-96, 1996-97, and 1997-98. In the 1987-88 season, he was the first NBA player to capture the scoring title (37.1 points a game) and also to be named the Defensive Player of the Year. He led the league in scoring for seven consecutive seasons from 1986-87 through 1992-93, until David Robinson broke the string. He was a nine-time NBA First Team All Star, made the All NBA Defensive First Team seven times, and was the NBA Defensive Player of the Year in 1998. He was the NBA's most valuable player five times—1988, 1989, 1990, 1991, 1992, 1993, and NBA Finals Most Valuable Player six times in 1991, 1992, 1993, 1996, 1997, and 1998.

Michael Jordan's appeal was in his ability to take the game to a higher level via his high-flying leaping ability whereby he seemed to simply soar through the air. In fact, he came to be known as "Air Jordan" with the Nike Shoe Company marketing the "Air Jordan" shoes that became the standard premier product of an industry ready to skyrocket itself to record profits.

Although he took a brief retirement to play minor league baseball from October of 1993 to March of 1995, Jordan came back to help the Bulls win the NBA championships in 1996, 1997, and 1998. He retired again after that season but has since come back to the Bulls in a front office job.

Bibliography

Donnelly, Sally B. "Great Leapin' Lizards!" *Time* 9 Jan. 1989: 90-91.

Kertes, Tom. "80's Basketball." *Sport* Oct. 1989: 50-52.

Naughton, Jim. *Taking to the Air.* 1992.

Ribomsteom, Jereme F. "Air Jordan: How Much Jordan, How Much Air?" *Sport* Mar. 1986: 86.

Lawrence E. Ziewacz

Journal of Popular Culture (JPC), The (1967-), and ***The Journal of American Culture (JAC)*** (1978-), are the publishing arms of the Popular Culture Association and the American Culture Association (see entries). Both journals were founded by Ray B. Browne, who still serves as editor. Published quarterly, *JPC* has dedicated itself to bringing humanistic study to all parts of everyday culture in the United States and around the world. As the premier journal in the study of popular culture, *JPC* has had a profound influence on other academic publications in the humanities and social sciences. Published quarterly, *JAC* has dedicated itself to bringing humanistic study to all parts of American culture and its relationship to other cultures around the world. It has had a significant influence on other academic publications in the U.S. and abroad that study American culture. The journals have always been housed at Bowling Green State University, Bowling Green, OH 43403.

Bibliography

Browne, Ray B. *Against Academia.* Bowling Green, OH: Bowling Green State U Popular P, 1989.

Peter Rollins

Judds, The, was one of America's more successful musical family groups. Naomi Judd was born Diana Ellen Judd in Ashland, KY, in 1946; in 1964 Naomi gave birth to her first child, Christina Claire Ciminella, now known as Wynonna. Theirs is a classic rags-to-riches story. Naomi harmonized while Wynonna learned to play guitar in their Kentucky home that did not have a television or a telephone.

They moved to Nashville, TN, in 1979. Eventually they were given the opportunity to audition in the RCA boardroom, got their first recording contract, and released their first album in 1984. Influenced by Bonnie Raitt and Joni Mitchell, Wynonna supplied the "strong soulful voice and Naomi added the harmonies" and stage presence (Kingsbury, Axelrod, and Costello 380).

Their list of awards seems endless. In 1985, their album, *Why Not Me?* went gold, and they won a Grammy for best country performance by a duo or group. They also won a Country Music Award for "Why Not Me?"

In 1986, they received another Grammy for "Grandpa (Tell 'Bout the Good Old Days)" and another Country Music Award in the vocal group of the year category. During the same year, *Rockin' with the Rhythm* went gold and platinum. The years to follow proved to be equally successful for the Judds. In 1987 the Judds' album *Heartland* went gold, and they won vocal group of the year from the Country Music Association. More award-winning songs included "Give a Little Love" and "Love Can Build a Bridge."

As a result of complications due to hepatitis, Naomi Judd was forced to retire from the music business. The Judds' final concert at Murphy Center in Murfreesboro, TN, was broadcast as a pay-per-view event on cable television in 1991. Naomi Judd went on to write a book in 1993 entitled *Love Can Build a Bridge,* which became a best-seller. Wynonna continued her career as a solo artist. Her first solo album, *Wynonna* (1992), was a huge success and went gold and platinum. She has since released five more albums, the latest *New Day Dawning* (2000).

Bibliography

Judd, Naomi. *Love Can Build a Bridge.* New York: Ballantine, 1993.

Kingsbury, Paul, Alan Axelrod, and Susan Costello, eds. *Country: The Music and the Musicians.* New York: Abbeville, 1994.

Lee Ann Paradise-Schober

Jump Rope Rhymes. Scholars have found evidence of jumping rope as a boy's sport of physical endurance and skill prior to the 17th century. Sometime during the American migration from farms to towns, jumping rope became a young girl's activity, and accompanying rhymes became an integral part of its protocol, evolving in active folk tradition over the last 150 years. In the more than 600 rhymes collected, subject matter ranges from domestic life to fantasy to amorous adventure and teasing, with some rhymes directing the activity itself. Rhymes reflect the child's world; they may also parody the violent and political adult world.

Photo courtesy of Popular Culture Library, Bowling Green State University, Bowling Green, OH.

Photo courtesy of Popular Culture Library, Bowling Green State University, Bowling Green, OH.

Many jump rope rhymes replicate domestic life, often in a fantastic or exaggerated way: setting the table ("Mabel, Mabel, set the table/Don't forget the red hot pepper"); a new baby ("Momma had a baby, his name was Tiny Tim./I put him in the bathtub to teach him how to swim./He drank up all the water./He ate up all the soap./He couldn't eat the bathtub/'Cause it wouldn't go down his throat"); sibling disputes ("Johnny broke a milk bottle/Blamed it on me./I told Ma/Ma told Pa./Johnny got a lickin'/So Ha, Ha, Ha."); toys ("Teddy Bear, Teddy Bear, turn around./Teddy Bear, Teddy Bear, touch the ground"). Some verses have jumping rules imbedded, such as "red hot pepper," which prompts the rapid turning of the rope to test the agility and endurance of the jumper, or contain commands the jumper must obey, like "turn around" and "touch the ground."

Rhymes often express familiar girl-boy jostling: "Along came _____ and kissed her on the cheek./How many kisses did she get that week?" (Pepper until she misses). And some have suggestive variations: "Cinderella dressed in yellow/Went up stairs to kiss her fellow./Made a mistake and kissed a snake./Came down stairs with a bellyache./How many doctors..." While these rhymes may reflect underlying social and sexual tensions, their formulas and commonplaces also direct the jumping game itself.

Bibliography

Abrahams, Roger. *Jump Rope Rhymes: A Dictionary*. Austin: U of Texas P, 1969.

Cole, Joanna, and Stephanie Calmson. *Miss Mary Mack: and Other Children's Street Rhymes*. New York: Morrow, 1990.

Orbach, Barbara C. *Rhymes of Children: A Select Bibliography of English Language Materials*. Washington, DC: Library of Congress, 1980.

Maryellen Hains

Jurassic Park (1993), directed by Steven Spielberg (see entry) and based on the 1990 best-seller by Michael Crichton, turned that year into the biggest in box-office history (with Americans spending $5 billion at the movies). Costing $63 million to produce, the movie grossed a record-breaking $870 million worldwide; and the approximate $346 million it earned domestically is second so far only to the $359 million brought in by Spielberg's own *E.T.* in 1982.

The June 11 premiere of the film launched the 1993 summer blockbuster-movie season. Even before the opening, though, consumers devoured *Jurassic Park* paraphernalia due to the intensive, worldwide merchandise licensing of MCA Inc., parent company of Universal Pictures. The anticipation gave a boost to companies that had offered dinosaur merchandise for years.

Techno-fiction writer Michael Crichton (see entry), best known previously for *Westworld* (1973)—in which robots run amok in an amusement resort—was reluctant to cash in on dinosaur mania with his 1981 screenplay, which also suffered from being written from a child's perspective. He shelved the piece until 1989, by which time, since the mania had not waned and as Crichton had become increasingly concerned about the commercialization of genetic engineering, he revised the work as a novel.

The title of the film refers to a kind of amusement park, situated (according to the story) on an island off Costa Rica, featuring live dinosaurs cloned from the DNA extracted from dinosaur blood preserved inside fossilized mosquitoes. Responsible for the park is entrepreneur John Hammond (Richard Attenborough). For an inspection of the project, Hammond lures paleontologists Alan Grant (Sam Neill) and Ellie Sattler (Laura Dern), his own grandchildren Tim (Joseph Mazzello) and Alexis "Lex" Murphy (Ariana Richards), chaos-theory mathematician Ian Malcolm (Jeff Goldblum), and an ultimately disposable investment lawyer (Martin Ferrero). When the computer systems architect of the park (played by Wayne Knight) shuts down power in order to steal dinosaur embryos, the electrified fences no longer protect the tour group from the animals, and soon the T-rex and velociraptors are terrorizing the guests.

From the start of the film project, Spielberg prioritized the realism of the dinosaurs, demanding as much full-scale footage as possible over stop-motion post-production, even if manipulating a convincing-looking dinosaur strained robotic capabilities. Unlike the stately, lumbering reptiles seen in previous dinosaur movies, *Jurassic Park* would depict the animals according to up-to-date paleontological thinking—that dinosaurs were probably agile, warm-blooded, and birdlike. Spielberg also intended that the film not be another "slasher" dinosaur movie; but despite a few surviving tranquil moments with dinosaurs, the film remains a tense creature feature.

The real stars of the film are said to be Stan Winston, Phil Tippett, Dennis Muren, and Michael Lantieri, leaders of the special effects teams. They created the vicious velociraptors (alternately animatronic puppets used for stationary shots, and humans in raptor suits for agile movements), the partially fictionalized dilophosaur with its expanding cowl, the brachiosaur (hydraulically operated by crane for broad movements of the body, controlled by cable and radio for facial movements), and the terrifying tyrannosaur (choreographed manually by using a scale model linked to the full-size rig through computerized interface).

Industrial Light and Magic (founded by George Lucas for new visual effects in *Star Wars*) was responsible for the vistas of grazing animals, the 50-foot-tall grazing brachiosaur, the stampeding herd of gallimimus, and even some shots of the T-rex.

Although critical consensus held that the story and characterization were disappointing—merely flat characters running from monsters—and that the film was gimmicky in terms of programmed surface thrills, the dinosaurs themselves were universally considered impressive. Concern was raised over young children seeing the PG-13 movie, due more to its intensity than gore (which had actually been toned down from the book). The film also gave rise to questions, indeed some panic, about DNA cloning and the current state of molecular genetics. Responsible scientific voices repeatedly tried to calm the scare fueled by a sensational press. But, finally, it was the dinosaurs themselves that galvanized enthusiasm.

Such enthusiasm, of course, required a sequel, *The Lost World: Jurassic Park* (1997), which finds some of the dinosaurs having survived on another island. In this film the focus is on protecting both the world from the animals and the animals from the world, in the form of greedy entrepreneurs who want to establish them in a zoo in the U.S. *The Lost World* actually has a T-rex terrorizing San Diego, à la Japanese monster movies.

Mark Dippé, co-visual effects supervisor for ILM on *Jurassic Park*, asserts that "dinosaur films have always been the classic effects films." Indeed, key special effects have been developed over the years specifically for dinosaur movies, beginning with Willis O'Brien's stop-motion techniques in *The Lost World* (1925) and *King Kong* (1933). Stop-motion continued animating the dinosaurs in such films as *Lost Continent* (1951), *The Beast from 20,000 Fathoms* (1953), *One Million Years B.C.* (1966), *The Valley of Gwangi* (1969), and *When Dinosaurs Ruled the Earth* (1971). Photographically enlarged lizards, iguanas, and crocodiles have been used, with various fins attached and often to the outrage of the ASPCA, in *One Million B.C.* (1940), *Journey to the Center of the Earth* (1959), and *The Lost World* (the 1960 remake). Even films relying on men wearing rubber suits, such as *Unknown Island* (1948), *Godzilla* (1956), *Gorgo* (1961), and *The Last Dinosaur* (1977), and those relying on puppets, like *The Land That Time Forgot* (1974), are more impressive than those which simply make use of stock footage from earlier dinosaur films: *Two Lost Worlds* (1950), *Untamed Women* (1952), *King Dinosaur* (1955), *Teenage Caveman* (1958), and *Valley of the Dragons* (1961). These effects, and the newer radio-control technology and cable-driven puppets, used in *Baby: Secret of the Lost Legend* (1985), all may gradually become extinct due to the success and popularity of the full-motion computer animation first seen in *Jurassic Park*.

Bibliography

Carnes, Mark C. *Past Imperfect: History According to the Movies*. New York: Holt, 1995.

Gifford, Denis. *A Pictorial History of Horror Movies*. London: Hamlyn, 1973.

Kilday, Gregg. "Hollywood Scores Big." *Entertainment Weekly* 21 Jan. 1994: 32-33.

Shay, Don, and Jody Duncan. *The Making of* Jurassic Park. New York: Ballantine, 1993.

Michael Delahoyde

See also
Computers and Movies

Kansas City Jazz, also known as Southwest jazz or Kansas City blues, was a unique style of jazz characterized by specific musical structures that began to appear on recordings from Missouri, Texas, and Oklahoma about the mid-1920s. The style typically was characterized by these features: 8- to 12-bar blues phrasing; a flexible repertoire; simple changes memorized by the band and played with an emphasis on rhythmic backup for solos; emphasis on saxophones, both for solos and accompaniment; and later (1930s), development of the walking bass and increased use of the hi-hat (closed cymbals).

The musical lineage of K.C. jazz included influences from orchestral ragtime, which was particularly strong in Missouri, and the vocal blues of the rural South and the Southwest; moreover, the music was distinctly different from the jazz that had developed in urban areas such as New Orleans, New York, and Chicago.

Early on, Bennie Moten's band, some of whom later split to form Count Basie's group, were K.C. practitioners; the fact that the group tended to get the best musicians in the area undoubtedly helped the new style to catch on. Besides Moten's group, Alphonso Trent in Dallas, Troy Floyd in San Antonio, and walking bassist Walter Page in Oklahoma City all led bands that specialized in and helped to evolve Kansas City jazz. Later bands such as those of Basie, Jay McShann, Andy Kirk, and Harlan Leonard, along with the Jeter-Pillars Orchestra, performed in the K.C. style. Sometime between 1935 and 1940, the elements of Kansas City jazz became subsumed in (and contributed to) the new swing era.

Bibliography

Kernfeld, Barry, ed. *The New Grove Dictionary of Jazz*. London: Macmillan, 1988.

Pearson, Nathan W., Jr. *Goin' to Kansas City*. Urbana: U of Illinois P, 1987.

Stephen Finley

Karloff, Boris (1887-1969), is best known for his horror roles, but he was an underrated actor of scope, depth, and variety. Remembered mainly for his film work, Karloff worked extensively on stage, and in radio and television. So beloved and in demand was he that, by the time of his death, a half dozen features awaited posthumous release.

He was born William Henry Pratt to a large family of upwardly mobile British civil servants (one brother was eventually knighted); his choice of career made him the "black sheep" of the family and may have prompted his name change to Boris Karloff sometime in 1910.

During the silent era Karloff worked in a variety of bit and supporting roles in films, earning a featured part in *The Bells* (1926) as a mesmerist who helps bring a murderer to justice. He worked in features, shorts, and serials; for major studios and on poverty row. By the time Holly- wood was shifting to sound, Karloff had over 50 films to his credit.

Karloff broke through into stardom when he was given the role turned down by Bela Lugosi, that of Frankenstein's monster. The 1931 film was a huge financial success, and is a genuine classic. Karloff's superior pantomime abilities gave the monster a depth of character—a sense of true humanity—that the film might have failed without. Remakes and sequels without Karloff would demonstrate time and again how truly impressive Karloff is in this film, as well as his subsequent two appearances as the monster in *The Bride of Frankenstein* (1935) and *The Son of Frankenstein* (1939).

Between the time Karloff finished *Frankenstein* and its resulting success after being released, he had acted in six more films. Then he made three films which not only solidified his stardom, but demonstrated his versatility: *The Old Dark House, The Mask of Fu Manchu,* and *The Mummy,* each released in 1932. Karloff had earned popular fame and the respect of his peers.

Having worked under horrendous conditions (especially for *Frankenstein* and *The Mummy*) which caused later health problems (Karloff had persistent back and leg problems, necessitating braces for the last two decades of his life), Karloff became one of the founders of the Screen Actors Guild in 1933 and was active in its development. Throughout his career Karloff also continued to accept supporting roles if he found them intriguing, often creating memorable screen moments, as in 1934's *The Lost Patrol* and *The Comedy of Terrors* three decades later.

One of Karloff's best acting efforts is his take on the "good twin/bad twin" plot in *The Black Room* (1935). Karloff's performances are superb at every level, and set a high mark for such roles. Beyond that, however, Karloff crafted a brilliant third performance when one twin is forced to impersonate the other.

In 1941 Karloff had one of his greatest stage successes parodying himself in *Arsenic and Old Lace.* It became a staple, and Karloff returned to it throughout his career. After starring as Chinese sleuth Mr. Wong in five films from 1938 to 1940, he spent the first half of the 1940s starring in several B-movie mad-scientist melodramas.

Karloff hosted radio shows, and continued his film career. Most notable of his 1940s films are his work in three films for producer Val Lewton, *The Body Snatcher* (1945), *Isle of the Dead* (1945), and *Bedlam* (1946). The films are moody, atmospheric period-piece costume pictures—with the horror element as superbly understated as Karloff's delicate performances.

Karloff's soft-spoken and lilting British accent was an asset on radio, and he hosted several radio series and made numerous appearances in the medium. Nor did he abandon the stage, appearing in several productions until his health no longer was up to it. In addition to the revivals of *Arsenic and Old Lace,* he starred in *On Borrowed Time* first in 1946, and revived the play continuously until his last performance of it in 1960. He scored a big success on Broadway as Captain Hook in *Peter Pan* for over 300 performances in 1950-51, but his last and greatest success was in *The Lark,* which ran for over 200 performances in 1955-56.

Television also kept the busy actor working throughout the 1950s, though he still managed to make 11 features. Karloff's first series, *Col. March of Scotland Yard,* was syndicated in 1953-54 and he appeared on numerous game shows during the decade, giving fans a welcome glimpse of his humor, gentleness, wit, and erudition. Karloff was a welcome guest star on television from his first appearance in 1949 until his last made shortly before his death. Other series were attempted, the most successful being *Thriller,* which he hosted and sometimes acted in from 1960 through 1962. His most lasting television work was to narrate and give voice to the title character in *How the Grinch Stole Christmas,* first broadcast in 1966. Karloff had made many recordings of children's stories over the years, and the soundtrack album of Grinch earned him his only Grammy.

The best film of Karloff's latter career, however, is *Targets* (1968), a well-made, wonderfully acted film in which Karloff plays an old Hollywood horror film star who feels his films can't compete with the horrors of modern life, such as mass killings. By now, Karloff was a living cultural icon. As with his star-making role as the Frankenstein monster, without Karloff's insightful and moving performance, the film would be in danger of collapsing in upon itself.

Bibliography

Bojarski, Richard, and Kenneth Beales. *The Films of Boris Karloff.* Secaucus, NJ: Citadel, 1976.

Buehrer, Beverly Bare. *Boris Karloff: A Bio-Bibliography.* Westport: Garland, 1993.

Mank, Gregory William. *Karloff and Lugosi: The Story of a Haunting Collaboration.* Jefferson, NC: McFarland, 1995.

Nollen, Scott Allen. *Boris Karloff: A Critical Account of His Screen, Stage, Radio, Television, and Recording Work.* Jefferson, NC: McFarland, 1991.

Ben Urish

Kate & Allie (1984-1989), making its debut on CBS, like *Cagney & Lacey* (see entry) before it, excited many women viewers because of the emphasis on the friendship of the two female leads. The series was created by Sherry Koben, who was inspired to do the show after finding many divorced women with children at her tenth high school reunion. Kate McArdle and Allie Lowell, best friends since childhood, decided to share Kate's Greenwich Village apartment in New York City for mutual financial and emotional support. The series focused on their trials and tribulations as they attempted to raise their children, deal with ex-husbands, establish and maintain careers, and engage in the world of dating in their thirties. Kate was played by Susan Saint James, formerly the wife on the police drama *McMillan and Wife.* Jane Curtin, originally on NBC's late night comedy-variety show, *Saturday Night Live,* portrayed Allie.

Before the end of the series, Allie remarried, but the strong friendship with Kate remained. With Allie's husband away most of the time (he was a sports announcer), Kate moved in and the two continued their catering business. While neither woman ever had to struggle financially as do most real-life single parents, their creation of their own kind of family demonstrated the potential strength of nontraditional households as two-parent families became less the norm in American culture.

Bibliography

Brooks, Tim, and Earle Marsh. *The Complete Directory to Prime Time Network TV Shows, 1946-Present.* 5th ed. New York: Ballantine, 1992.

Ehrenreich, Barbara, and Jane O'Reilly. "No Jiggles. No Scheming. Just Real Women as Friends." *TV Guide* 24 Nov. 1984: 6-10.

McNeil, Alex. *Total Television.* New York: Penguin, 1991.

Lynn C. Spangler

Kaufman, Murray "the K" (1926-1981), was a radio personality in the New York market from 1958 to 1967. He was the consummate example of the disk jockey as creative artist, performer, and entrepreneur. Born in Richmond, VA, he entered show business at the age of nine. In 1958, he replaced Alan Freed (see entry) at WINS-AM. Kaufman's "Swingin' Soiree" held down the 6 to 10 p.m. time slot until March 1965. He played music for "Submarine Race Watchers" and punctuated sentences with the word "baby." Although he catered to the rock music audience, he opened every radio show with a Sinatra recording.

Kaufman came into national prominence after Ringo Starr acknowledged him at a Beatles press conference at Idlewild Airport on February 7, 1964. He broadcast from the Beatles' Plaza Hotel rooms, traveled with the group to their first concert (Washington, DC) and to Florida, and billed himself as "the Fifth Beatle." Kaufman introduced the idea of the disk jockey as the audience's "inside" contact to the artist. With transatlantic calls to the Fab Four, he quenched rumors that McCartney was to marry actress Jane Asher and that the Beatles had decided to stop touring in January 1965.

Although Murray the K drew disrespect from new-breed musicians, the Beatles maintained ties with him. In 1967, manager Brian Epstein and Beatle George Harrison paid visits to Kaufman's broadcast. In May 1969, Kaufman participated in the Plastic Ono Band's "Give Peace a Chance" recording.

Kaufman hosted (or co-hosted with his wife, Jackie "the K") compilations of Top 40 "oldies" including *Golden Gassers for Hand Holders* (1963) and *The Fifth Beatle Gives You Their Favorite Golden Gassers* (1964). Kaufman authored one book about music, *Murray the K Tells It Like It Is, Baby* (1966). He played himself in the 1978 film about Beatlemania, *I Wanna Hold Your Hand.*

Bibliography

London, Herbert I. *Closing the Circle: A Cultural History of the Rock Revolution.* Chicago: Nelson-Hall, 1984.

Marsh, Dave. *Before I Get Old: The Story of the Who.* New York: St. Martin's, 1983.

Pollock, Bruce. *When Rock Was Young: A Nostalgic Review of the Top 40 Era*. New York: Holt, 1981.
Sklar, Rick. *Rocking America: An Insider's Story*. New York: St. Martin's, 1984.

Kenneth G. Bielen

Keaton, Buster (1895-1965), along with Charlie Chaplin and Harold Lloyd, was one of the three great clowns of silent film. From 1920 to 1923, he produced and starred in no fewer than 20 two- and three-reelers, including such classics as *One Week, Cops, The Boat*, and *The Electric House*. From 1923 to 1927, Keaton turned to feature-length films, producing and starring in ten comedies that are among the treasures of world cinema. His masterpiece was *The General* (1926), about a locomotive chase during the Civil War. Keaton appeared in several MGM talkies during the early 1930s, but these were minor efforts compared to his great work in the silents.

Keaton was born in Piqua, KS, where his parents, Joe and Myra, were performing with a traveling show called the Mohawk Indian Medicine Company. Christened Joseph Frank Keaton, he was given his nickname by the magician and escape-artist Harry Houdini, who was also a member of the troupe.

Until 1923, Keaton made mostly shorts. There was one undistinguished feature, *The Saphead* (1920), which was a commercial success and established him as a star. But *The Saphead* was made before Keaton had perfected the manner and style characteristic of his best work. For his best work Keaton developed an on-screen personality as distinctive, though not as artificial, as that of Chaplin's Little Tramp. He played a serious, dignified young man struggling to cope with bewildering circumstances. If he did not smile, it was not because he lacked a sense of humor—it was because he was too puzzled or too polite. His seriousness was an essential part of his humor. Keaton knew better than anyone that the funniest scenes are the ones not played for laughs.

Keaton's first film after switching from shorts to features was *The Three Ages* (1923), a parody of D. W. Griffith's *Intolerance*. But it was *Our Hospitality*, released in the same year, that established him as a filmmaker of the first rank. *Our Hospitality*'s combination of comedy, adventure, and plot easily surpassed anything being done by the other film comics. It introduced one of Keaton's grand themes, the naive innocent making his way through a rough-and-tumble world, as Keaton's hero, a citified Easterner, is exposed to the wilds of New Jersey.

Keaton continued to make two features each year. In 1924, there was *Sherlock Jr.*, in which he played a movie projectionist who becomes part of the movies he is showing. This was followed by Keaton's greatest commercial success, *The Navigator*, in which we find him at sea on a deserted schooner.

Keaton's next three efforts—*Seven Chances* (1925), *Go West* (1925), and *Battling Butler* (1926)—were not as good; but then came *The General* (1926), one of the great films of all time. Unquestionably Keaton's masterpiece, this Civil War epic featured a spectacular locomotive chase, much acrobatic derring-do, and an irresistibly sweet romance.

Two more films, the very good *College* (1927) and the splendid *Steamboat Bill Jr.* (1927), brought Keaton's great creative period to a close. The cyclone near the end of *Steamboat Bill Jr.* is one of the most admired sequences in all of Keaton's films.

In 1928, Keaton signed with MGM, a move he would later call the biggest mistake of his life. The films he made for MGM during the next five years, including some in which he was teamed with Jimmy Durante, were quite popular. But he was not good at verbal humor, and Keaton seems oddly out of place.

Keaton's reputation was revived somewhat in 1947 when he made a series of successful personal appearances in Paris. In 1952, Charlie Chaplin—who, unlike Buster, had remained a big star—used him for a sequence in *Limelight*, and the public was again reminded of who Keaton once was. It was the only time the two great comedians ever appeared together. In 1957 there was a not-very-good screen biography, *The Buster Keaton Story*, starring Donald O'Connor. Keaton published an autobiography, *My Wonderful World of Slapstick*, in 1960. Five years later he was dead of cancer.
Bibliography
Blesh, Rudi. *Keaton*. New York: Macmillan, 1966.
Robinson, David. *Buster Keaton*. Bloomington: Indiana UP, 1969.

James Rachels
See also
Slapstick

Keillor, Garrison (1942-), one of today's stars on National Public Radio (NPR), is best known for humorous monologues about life in the imaginary town of Lake Wobegon, MN. Born Gary Edward Keillor in Anoka, MN, he grew up in Brooklyn Park, MN, graduated from Anoka High School in 1960, and continued his education at the University of Minnesota (1960-62 and 1963-67), where he earned a B.A. in English in 1966 and completed one year's work toward an M.A. degree. While in college he wrote for the campus newspaper, edited the literary magazine, won the Academy of American Poets contest, and worked for radio stations. Keillor began his association with public radio in November 1969, when he began supporting his work as a poet by hosting *The Morning Program* on KSJR in Collegeville, MN, the original station of the Minnesota Educational Radio (MER) network. He has remained affiliated with the network, now Minnesota Public Radio, except for brief breaks in 1971, 1973-74, and 1987-88.

When MER established KSJN-St. Paul as its flagship station in October 1971, Keillor's *Morning Program* moved to St. Paul and was rechristened *A Prairie Home Companion*, the first of two Keillor shows to carry that title. This first show, which ran until April of 1982, had an eclectic format of recorded music and announcer talk during the weekday morning drive-time slot. Here Keillor invented Lake Wobegon as the backdrop for a series of mock commercials (because public radio eschews advertising) for dubious products, beginning with vacation home sites behind Jack's Auto Repair alongside an overgrown puddle aptly dubbed Lake Wobegon. As the reference to Minnesota's lakes suggests, this version of *PHC* (1974-1982) was strictly local; Keillor's international recognition as a radio humorist came from the second *PHC*, which featured live music and comedy performances in the Saturday evening dinner slot.

The variety show was inspired partly by Keillor's 1974 report on the *Grand Ole Opry* for the *New Yorker* magazine and partly by limitations of the morning show format and the KSJN studio, which was too small to accommodate the folk musicians whom Keillor had begun inviting to perform live for the weekday *PHC*. The new program combined country and folk music with humor of varying sophistication, from mock commercials for Bob's Bank ("in the green mobile home.... Save at the sign of the sock") and parodies of radio dramas (complete with exaggerated old-time sound effects) to lengthy narratives about eccentric and lonely members of Lake Wobegon society. Broadcast nationally over the American Public Radio network beginning in May 1982 (after NPR declined its option), *PHC* became famous for these droll stories that began, "It's been a quiet week in Lake Wobegon, my home town," and meandered through tall fictions, autobiographical reminiscence, psychological representation, and moral commentary before concluding with wonder at a town "where all the women are strong, all the men are good-looking, and all the children are above average."

As the radio stories grew from pseudo-commercial "spots" into 30-minute personal narratives *cum* religious parables, which cast Keillor's fictitious experiences as lessons for listeners, evidence of Lake Wobegon's entrance into the popular culture mounted. Listeners sent in photographs of the Chatterbox Cafe, Hotel Minnesota, Bob's Bank, and other local landmarks; the *St. Paul Pioneer Press and Dispatch* listed the town in their annual index; the American Automobile Association debated including Lake Wobegon on maps of Minnesota. Eventually the town acquired a full-scale comic history and geography, which Keillor detailed in his novel *Lake Wobegon Days* (1985), whose success (44 weeks on the *New York Times* hardcover best-seller list) increased attention to Keillor and his radio show.

The show closed on June 13, 1987, when Keillor moved from St. Paul to Copenhagen, claiming discomfort with celebrity and a desire for privacy following his 1986 marriage to a Danish national, Ulla Skaerved. Fatigue may also have figured in his decision. By mid-1987 he had not only written all the comic and narrative materials for two radio shows (about 2500 hours' worth between 1974 and 1987), but also published a novel, nearly 50 stories in the *New Yorker*, and a dozen op-ed pieces for Minneapolis newspapers. Twenty-nine of these writings appeared in the first edition of *Happy to Be Here* (1981), and five more were added for the second (1983). In addition, Keillor and NPR published recordings of selected monologues—*The Family Radio* (1982), *Tourists* (1983), *News from Lake Wobegon* (1983), *Ten Years on the Prairie* (1984), and *Gospel Birds* (1985)—as well as a spoken books version of *Lake Wobegon Days* (1986).

A collection of Lake Wobegon stories, *Leaving Home* (1987), appeared, with unintended irony, shortly after his return to the U.S. in September 1987, when he settled in New York City and joined the staff of the *New Yorker*, writing pieces for "The Talk of the Town" and short fiction. Another collection, *We Are Still Married* (1989), combined radio and *New Yorker* material. On November 25, 1989, he inaugurated *American Radio Company of the Air*, a live variety show broadcast by NPR from three locations in New York before finally roosting, in the fall of 1992, at St. Paul's World Theatre, the former home of *A Prairie Home Companion*. Like his old show, *American Radio Company* featured a live Saturday evening broadcast of music, humor, and a Lake Wobegon monologue, but the new show contained less country music and more urban humor. As was the case in 1974, however, Keillor's return to radio stimulated rather than conflicted with his writing. A second novel, *WLT: A Radio Romance*, appeared in 1991, and *The Book of Guys*, another collection of literary and radio humor, in 1993. In July 1993, he decided to abandon the format of *American Radio Company*, which he now saw as "so broad no one could remember it," and revive *A Prairie Home Companion*'s focus on contemporary folk performers. The program resumed on October 2, 1993.

Although Keillor's place in America's comic pantheon may ultimately rest on his books, his importance to American popular culture undoubtedly centers on his contributions to radio. Chief among these is his reinvention of oral story-telling for a radio audience. Lake Wobegon has a history, landscape, popularity, and complexity reminiscent of Faulkner's Yoknapatawpha County, but the Minnesota town evolves week by week, year by year, as Keillor's listeners join in the conspiracy to build fictitious commercials, tongue-in-cheek news reports, and announcer talk into a parallel Minnesota universe. As a result, what began as an upper-midwestern folk version of the *Grand Ole Opry* revived live radio as an electronic hearth.

Bibliography

Larson, Charles U., and Christine Oravec. "*A Prairie Home Companion* and the Fabrication of Community." *Critical Studies in Mass Communication* 4 (Sept. 1987): 221-44.

Lee, Judith Yaross. *Garrison Keillor: A Voice of America.* Jackson: UP of Mississippi, 1991.

Scholl, Peter A. *Garrison Keillor.* New York: Twayne/Macmillan, 1993.

Judith Yaross Lee

Kelley, David E. (1956-), first achieved personal recognition as the award-winning executive producer, creator, and writer for two of Hollywood's most successful dramatic series: *Picket Fences* (CBS, 1992-96) and *Chicago Hope* (CBS, 1994-), as well as numerous awards for his earlier work as executive producer and head writer of *L.A. Law* (1986-94).

The formats for all three series were comparable: ensemble casts, richly drawn characters wrestling with topical social issues, personal and professional problems, and occasional quirky scenes and peculiar characters. *L.A. Law* featured a group of legal partners, their clients, and court cases in downtown L.A.; *Chicago Hope*, the staff and members of a medical/surgical team in a metropolitan teaching hospital. In *Picket Fences* the locale shifted to a small Wisconsin town where the sheriff, his physician wife, their children and other local citizens dealt with personal issues and the spread of urban problems often requiring legal intervention.

Kelley had taken an improbable path to success in the television industry, and his shows reflect his previous legal background. A native of Maine, he was a graduate of Princeton (1979) and Boston University Law School (1983). He never had any ambition to earn a living as a writer nor had he taken a college writing course. While working as a member of a Boston law firm, he wrote his first screenplay, *From the Hip*, simply as a form of escapism. Upon seeing the film, *L.A. Law*'s co-creator Steven Bochco hired Kelley as legal consultant and writer. When Bochco left to create other series (*NYPD Blue*), Kelley then replaced him. Kelley continues to be active in television with several series on the air, notably *Ally McBeal* (Fox, 1997-) and *The Practice* (ABC, 1997-), both Emmy winners.

Bibliography

Coe, Steve. "The Dramatic License of David Kelley." *Broadcasting and Cable* 12 June 1995: 16-19.

Streisand, Betsy. "The Write Stuff." *US News and World Report* 20 Nov. 1995: 81.

Thompson, Robert J. *Television's Second Golden Age: From Hill Street Blues to ER.* New York: Continuum, 1996.

Ann Schoonmaker

Kelly, Grace (1929-1982), famous as movie star and wife of royalty, was born Grace Patricia Kelly in Philadelphia. Like many young New York actors in the early 1950s, she found the newly emerging medium of television a place to gain valuable experience. She played a number of roles on such programs as *Hallmark Hall of Fame*, *Philco Television Playhouse*, and *Studio One*.

Kelly's screen debut in Twentieth Century-Fox's suspense drama *Fourteen Hours* in 1951 did little to advance her career. Kelly spent the summer of 1951 performing in a variety of plays at Denver's Elitch Gardens Theatre. While in Denver she received word that she had landed the role of Gary Cooper's Quaker fiancée in the now-classic Western *High Noon*. The part was largely plot business that required her to do little but look blond and virginal. Though it is now, arguably, the most famous movie in which she appeared, *High Noon* did not make Grace Kelly a star. When Metro-Goldwyn-Mayer chief Dore Schary offered her a seven-year contract, Kelly accepted the offer. She was soon off to Africa to shoot *Mogambo*, a big-budget Technicolor remake of the 1932 Clark Gable adventure romance *Red Dust,* with Gable repeating his role and Kelly taking Mary Astor's "good girl" supporting role. Released in late 1953, *Mogambo* marked the beginning of the Grace Kelly phenomenon. She was nominated for the best supporting actress Oscar and made the cover of *Life* magazine in April 1954, with "This Year of Grace" as the caption.

She appeared in three Hitchcock films—*Dial M for Murder* (1954), *Rear Window* (1954), and *To Catch a Thief* (1955). They are generally considered her best work, though it was for the George Seaton–directed drama *The Country Girl* that she won the best actress Oscar of 1954. Kelly was never a great actress (she herself later admitted that she left acting before fully developing her talent).

While filming *To Catch a Thief* in the south of France in 1955, Grace Kelly met Prince Rainier of the then-little-known principality of Monaco. The two were married in the cathedral at Monte Carlo in April 1956. The wedding was accompanied by a torrent of publicity and is one of the earliest examples of the unprecedented power of television to create a worldwide media event out of something that is not inherently of great importance. The couple eventually had three children—Caroline, Albert, and Stephanie. Kelly never officially retired from acting and in 1962 accepted, with her husband's reluctant approval, the title role in Hitchcock's *Marnie*. She withdrew from the project when it seemed that a return to the screen would jeopardize her hard-won acceptance by the people of Monaco, who had initially viewed her as something of an American interloper. On September 13, 1982, Princess Grace suffered a cerebral hemorrhage while driving on the curving roads above Monte Carlo. She died the following day, two months short of her 53rd birthday.

Bibliography

Current Biography 1955. New York: Wilson, 1955.

Englund, Steven. *Grace of Monaco: An Interpretive Biography.* Garden City: Doubleday, 1984.

Katz, Ephraim. *The Film Encyclopedia.* New York: Perennial Library, 1990.

Thomson, David. *Biographical Dictionary of Film.* 2d ed. New York: Morrow, 1981.

Mary Kalfatovic

Kenton, Stan (1912-1979), born in Wichita, KS, was one of America's innovators in popular music. His boyhood ambition was to become a baseball player, but his mother preferred he be a pianist. The family moved to California, where Kenton found a job with Everett Hoagland's band at the Rendezvous Ballroom in Balboa Beach. After working with several other bands he formed his own ensemble in 1941. The band was heard on the radio via the *Balboa Bandwagon*. Musicians were intrigued with Kenton's arrangements, which featured strong syncopations and unusual harmonies, influenced by the Jimmie Lunceford Band (a very popular black dance band of that period). The band moved to the Palladium Ballroom in Los Angeles, where it attracted more attention. This engagement led to an offer to play at the Roseland Ballroom in New York City.

When this engagement did not go well, Kenton decided to reorganize and try a different arranging style. Kenton's new band received a break when jazz critic Dave Dexter, Jr., signed it to the new Capitol Record Company. The band's first record date featured Kenton compositions "Artistry in Rhythm," which was its theme song, and "Eager Beaver," plus Duke Ellington's "Do Nothing Till You Hear from Me." "Eager Beaver," a typical swing-era riff piece (with some original Kenton touches), was an instant success. Kenton began to have other arrangers, like veteran Gene Roland, contribute scores to the band. Two young players who went on to greater fame were tenor saxophonist Stan Getz, and trombonist Kai Winding. Kenton's trombone sections had a unique sound that can be traced back to Winding's tenure with the band.

In 1946, Kenton hired a young arranger, Pete Rugulo, who would be the first of a series of experimental arranger/ composers who would be hired by Kenton. He also increased the size of the brass section to ten players, five trumpets and five trombones including a bass trombone. After successful dates at New York's Pennsylvania Hotel and Paramount Theater, more hits on Capitol Records, and critical acclaim from jazz periodicals *Down Beat* and *Metronome,* Kenton disbanded his band in 1948 because of physical exhaustion.

In late 1949, Kenton reorganized a band (an orchestra actually) called the Innovations in Modern Music Orchestra, which totaled 43 members including a large string section. The music was a mixture of jazz and contemporary classical music. Although interesting for the musicians involved, the music was not commercial enough for financial success. After one tour and several recording dates Kenton gave up this band for a more conventional big band. His early 1950s band and again in the early 1960s were two of his best from a pure jazz perspective.

For several years in the early 1960s Kenton added to his brass section four mellophoniums, a hybrid instrument which is a combination French horn mellophone and cornet. This was one of Kenton's favorite bands. One of Kenton's greatest achievements was his role in promoting jazz education. In the early 1960s he lent his name and when possible participated in summer jazz camps and clinics. From 1964 to 1967 Kenton formed another large ensemble using French horns, tuba, and extra percussion. This group served as a resident jazz orchestra which he called the Los Angeles Neophonic Orchestra. Once again new compositions were commissioned by Kenton for this ensemble. In 1968, Kenton was invited to participate in the Tanglewood Symposium, an attempt to influence the course of music education. After his participation, at which Kenton strongly suggested the teaching of jazz in American music education, he became more active in presenting jazz clinics.

Kenton launched another ambitious project in the early 1970s to form his own publishing and recording company called Creative World. By this time rock and roll had become the popular music of young people and Capitol Records, under newer management, was more interested in promoting rock groups and singers. He reissued his older Capitol recordings, as well as the recordings of other Capitol jazz artists. By 1973, Creative World had a 100,000 name mailing list to primarily high schools and colleges. In the late 1970s, the constant travel and other abuses on his body took its toll. Kenton continued leading his band on the road until his death, but was only a shell of his earlier enthusiastic personality. His will emphatically stated he did not want a "ghost band," that is, a band using his name and library and directed by an ex-Kenton band member, or another musician.

Bibliography
Arganian, Lillian. *Stan Kenton: The Man and His Music.* East Lansing: Artistry, 1989.
Lee, William F. *Stan Kenton: Artistry in Rhythm.* Los Angeles: Creative, 1980.

Frank Ferriano

Kern, Jerome David (1885-1945), one of America's most famous and best-loved composers of popular music, was born in New York City into a Jewish family of comfortable circumstances. Kern was the youngest of nine children, only three of whom survived beyond birth. His grandfather served as the beadle/sexton at Temple Emanu-El on Fifth Avenue, New York City. Early on, he received music lessons and in his teens already was recognized as a musically talented and gifted pianist. Young Kern soon found employment as a song-plugger for various music firms on Tin Pan Alley, and in 1902 published his first song. In 1903, after taking courses in piano and composition at the New York Musical College, he went to Europe for a year of advanced musical studies in Germany, and then found music work in London. Kern soon returned to America, where he embarked upon an active musical career of popular songwriting.

Extremely prolific from the start, Kern began to craft the songs for a series of revues and shows on Broadway, and then for London theaters. He also found his musical way into the Hollywood film industry. Likely the most significant of his theatrical contributions was the full score for *Show Boat,* which premiered in 1927, an elaborately devised musical based upon a novel by Edna Ferber. In the 1990s, it was revitalized in its unabridged original version for new presentation on recordings, and then was prepared for staging in Canada and the U.S. As a result, the work has been cited as a "classic" in the historic annals of American entertainment for both its musical numbers and its sociocultural scenario. While *Show Boat* remains the product of the late 1920s, it seems in many respects to be artistically advanced for its era.

Kern's melodic creations followed the style of European operettas, with tune patterns that remain lastingly comfortable for the repertoires of professional entertainers. His musical output was amazingly substantial, and his collaborative lyricists, whose notable roster included Dorothy Fields, Ira Gershwin, Oscar Hammerstein, Otto Harbach, E. Y. (Yip) Harburg, and Johnny Mercer, meshed very well with Kern's musical ideas. In his book *Jerome Kern: His Life and Music,* Gerald Bordman lists 887 songs written by Kern.

Kern became highly successful not only as a songwriter but also as a publisher, and at one time was vice-president of the T. B. Harms Publishing Company. While he always acknowledged his Jewish background, he was not associated in any way with Jewish music. Nevertheless, there have been attempts to ferret out Judaic motifs in his melodies, as for example in "Old Man River," as well as elements of old Yiddish folksong in some of his ballads. Kern led a pleasantly affluent life with his family, and died in New York City.

Bibliography
Bordman, Gerald. *Jerome Kern: His Life and Music.* New York: Oxford UP, 1980.

Ewen, David. *The World of Jerome Kern: A Biography*. New York: Holt, 1960.

Freedland, Michael. *Jerome Kern*. London: Robson, 1978.

Kreuger, Miles. *Show Boat: The Story of a Classic American Musical*. New York: Oxford UP, 1977.

Irene Heskes

Kershaw, Doug (1936-   ), born in Teil Ridge, LA, is a fiddler and singer who became known as the "Ragin' Cajun" or the "Louisiana Man." Inspired by his mother, a fiddler and singer, but without formal musical education, Kershaw had no rules to go by, so he set no limits on himself. Over the years, he developed his own style of playing rhythm, melody, and lead, all at the same time, in an attempt to get as much from his instrument as it had to give.

Popular on the regional circuit for years, Kershaw took his hard-driving, shrill, and strident southern Louisiana folk music national in the early 1960s. With his brother Rusty, Kershaw recorded "Louisiana Man" and "Make Me Realize" in 1960, and "Diggy Liggy Lo" in 1961. A series of releases followed on a variety of labels, Hickory, Mercury, RCA Victor, and Princess, but the duo disbanded in 1964, after which Doug became known as much for his gymnastic approach to the fiddle as for his music. His early solo recordings include "Diggy Liggy Lo" (1969), "Mama Said Yeah," and "Natural Man" (1971), and, *de rigueur* for any fiddler, "Orange Blossom Special" (1970). Kershaw became the first Cajun singer to make it big nationally.

Bibliography

Broven, John. *South to Louisiana: The Music of the Cajun Bayous*. Gretna: Pelican, 1983.

Hardy, Phil, and Dave Laing. *The Faber Companion to 20th-Century Popular Music*. London: Faber, 1990.

Larkin, Colin. *Guinness Encyclopedia of Popular Music*. Vol. 3. Middlesex, U.K.: Guinness, 1995.

Bonnie Elgin Todd

Keyes, Frances Parkinson (née Wheeler) (1885-1970), a Southerner by birth, began publishing novels when her husband was governor of New Hampshire. One of the century's most popular writers, Keyes enjoyed her heyday with readers from the 1940s to the 1960s, when she produced a series of grand, sweeping novels with old-fashioned, romantic storylines, appealing aristocratic characters, and atmospheric settings. After the death of her husband in 1938, Keyes spent much of her time in New Orleans, where she discovered a rich vein of fictional material that would dominate her subsequent writings and beguile the public for the next several decades.

Keyes's earlier novels, such as *The Old Gray Homestead* (1919) and *Queen Anne's Lace* (1930), were set in New England and Europe. But her fiction about Creole culture in Louisiana, including such works as *Crescent Carnival* (1942), *Steamboat Gothic* (1952), *Victorine* (1958), and *The Chess Players* (1960), remains her most celebrated. In these novels, she created multigenerational sagas of Southern life, richly detailed accounts of the customs and daily worlds of New Orleans' faded aristocracy and its colorful old world ambiance, accounts that were bolstered by meticulous

research into regional history and anthropology. *Dinner at Antoine's* (1948), her best-known novel, incorporated the New Orleans lore for which she was famous, but added a mystery to the mix.

Keyes also wrote nonfiction. During her husband's tenure as a U.S. senator, she gained notoriety for a column she contributed to *Good Housekeeping*, "Letters from a Senator's Wife." Later, her conversion to Catholicism occasioned a spiritual autobiography, *Along a Little Way* (1940), and several hagiographic biographies of Catholic figures.

Bibliography

Keyes, Frances Parkinson. *All Flags Flying: Reminiscences of Frances Parkinson Keyes*. New York: McGraw-Hill, 1972.

Warnick, Robert. "The Queens of Fiction." *Life* 6 April 1959.

Liahna Babener

King, B. B. (1925-   ), born Riley King, is the preeminent exponent of the urban blues style. King was born on a plantation near Indianola, MS, a site that became the title of one of his successful albums. He was one of five children. When his parents broke up, he was four years old. He moved with his mother to Kilmichael, where he sang in a quartet at school. When she died in 1934, he returned to Indianola where he remained until 1946. In that year, he moved on to Memphis, TN.

In Memphis he divided his time between singing at the W. C. Handy Theater with the Palace Theater Beale Streeters and being a disc jockey at WDIA. It was at WDIA that he received his nickname "Beale Street Blues Boy," later shortened to B.B. The Beale Streeters included Bobby "Blue" Bland, Johnny Ace, and Earl Fast, young men who became giants in the blues idiom. Because of King's influence, most of the blues performers who followed him were more jazz-oriented than their predecessors.

In 1950, King had his first hit, which he has kept part of his repertoire, "Three o'Clock Blues." The tune went to the top of the rhythm and blues list. For the next 20 years, King worked the "Chitterling Circuit" and performed 300 one-night stands, which he interrupted once a year for long gigs at the Regal, Apollo, or other similar theaters. Finally, recognition of his influence on white rock players led to a triumphant 1968 tour that ended his need to perform one-nighters.

King's "The Thrill Is Gone" (1970) gave him the major breakthrough crossover hit he had been seeking. It gave him a wider audience without sacrificing his core followers. Some of his other hits include "Sweet Sixteen," "Everybody Wants to Know Why I Sing the Blues," "Nightlife," "The Thrill Is Gone," "Lucille," "Paying the Cost to Be the Boss," and "Nobody Loves Me But My Mother and She Might Be Jiving Too!"

Bibliography

Barlow, Bill. *Encyclopedia of Southern Culture*. Chapel Hill: U of North Carolina P, 1989.

Feather, Leonard. *Encyclopedia of Jazz*. New York: Da Capo, 1984.

Herzhaft, Gérard. *Encyclopedia of the Blues*. Trans. Brigitte Debord. Fayetteville: U of Arkansas P, 1992.

Sawyer, Charles. *The Arrival of B. B. King: The Authorized Biography*. New York: Da Capo, 1982.

Frank A. Salamone

King, Carole (1942-), star performer of popular music, was born in Brooklyn as Carole Klein to an insurance salesman father and schoolteacher mother. Interested in music from an early age, she took the stage name Carole King at age 16 when she released the single "Goin' Wild" (1958) for ABC/Paramount.

Attending Queens College with future music stars Neil Diamond and Paul Simon, King was briefly in an all-girl band, the Co-Sines. She dropped out after her freshman year to marry chemistry major and fellow music lover Gerry Goffin. Together, the two began to write songs. Neil Sedaka introduced the couple to music publisher/impresario Don Kirshner, who signed them to a contract with his publishing firm, Aldon Music. Working out of the famed Brill Building, the unofficial headquarters of the music business, alongside such writers as Sedaka, Barry Mann, and Cynthia Weil, Goffin and King began churning out songs.

"Will You Still Love Me Tomorrow?" sung by the Shirelles, was their first hit, entering the charts in November 1960 and reaching No. 1 on January 30, 1961. The songs Goffin and King would write in the next few years would become the soundtrack for the early years of the 1960s. Just a few of these include "Some Kind of Wonderful" (The Drifters, 1961); "Every Breath I Take" (Gene Pitney, 1961); "Take Good Care of My Baby" (Bobby Vee, 1961); "Go Away, Little Girl" (Steve Lawrence, 1962); "Up on the Roof" (The Drifters, 1962); "The Loco-Motion" (Little Eva, 1962); "He's a Rebel" (Crystals, 1962); "Chains" (The Cookies, 1962); "Don't Say Nothin' Bad (About My Baby)" (The Cookies, 1962); "One Fine Day" (The Chiffons, 1963); and "I Can't Stay Mad at You" (Skeeter Davis, 1963).

Goffin was the primary lyricist of the team with King providing the music. King had another important role, the recording of the demos of songs that would be used to shop the songs around to performers. In 1962, King had her first hit as a recording artist with the release of "It Might as Well Rain Until September." The mid-1960s saw a change in the music industry with more performers beginning to write their own songs. Goffin and King continued to write hit songs for others, including "Just Once in My Life" (Righteous Brothers, 1965) and "(You Make Me Feel Like) A Natural Woman" (Aretha Franklin, 1967), but the heyday of their career had passed. In 1968, King and Goffin divorced and their creative partnership ended. King moved to Southern California and joined a band, the City, that recorded one album, *Now That Everything's Been Said* (1969). But the album was not a hit and King's stage fright kept the band from touring.

James Taylor, just then beginning his solo career in 1969, was impressed with a number of King's recent songs, including "You've Got a Friend," and encouraged her to go solo. Touring with Taylor and the positive, though not over-whelming success of her first solo album, *Writer: Carole King* (Ode, 1970), gave her the encouragement to continue as a solo artist. Her next release would become a phenomenon.

Tapestry (Ode, 1971), with its simple structure and expression of basic values, stood out from the postpsychedelic rock of the early 1970s. It, along with the works of Taylor, would inaugurate the softer, singer-songwriter era. Selling over ten million copies by 1973, the album won King four Grammy Awards and stayed on the charts for nearly seven years. Including the hit songs "You've Got a Friend," "I Feel the Earth Move," "So Far Away," "It's Too Late," and "Where You Lead," the album also contained remakes of King and Goffin's "(You Make Me Feel Like) A Natural Woman" and "Will You Still Love Me Tomorrow?"

King's third solo album, *Music*, released the same year as *Tapestry*, received mixed reviews. She recorded four more albums on the Ode label: *Rhymes & Reasons* (1972), *Fantasy* (1973), *Wrap around Joy* (1974; which included the No. 2 hit, "Jazzman"), and *Thoroughbred* (1976), then through the mid-1990s almost a dozen more albums for various labels, including two as a result of collaboration with children's writer Maurice Sendak, but none duplicated the incredible success of *Tapestry*.

Following on the heels of her 1973 free Central Park concert that was seen by over 70,000 people, King shed much of her stage fright and has become a popular touring attraction. In 1988, King and Goffin received National Association of Songwriters' lifetime achievement award.

Bibliography
"Carole King." *Contemporary Musicians*. Vol. 6. Ed. Michael L. LaBlanc. Detroit: Gale, 1989. 128-30.

"Carole King." *Current Biography* (1974): 201-3.

Garr, Gillian G. *She's a Rebel: The History of Women in Rock and Roll*. Seattle: Seal, 1992.

Ressner, Jeffrey. "Nonperformers." *Rolling Stone* 8 Feb. 1990: 82.

Martin R. Kalfatovic

King Kong (originally released by RKO in 1933 and re-released in 1938, 1942, 1946, 1952, and 1956) is not only one of the greatest horror/fantasy films ever made but one of the greatest movies of all time. Its title character has also become a universally recognizable icon in American popular culture. The film offers an intriguing twist on the fable of beauty and the beast, for in Kong's willingness to leave his jungle kingdom in pursuit of Ann Darrow (played by a blonde-wigged Fay Wray) lies the seeds of his own destruction. Carl Denham (played by Robert Armstrong) shackles Kong and puts him on display in New York as "The Eighth Wonder of the World" before the giant ape breaks free and takes his doll-like beloved to the top of the Empire State Building, where machine guns from biplanes destroy him.

A collaborative effort in the extreme, the film was produced and directed by Merian C. Cooper and Ernest B. Schoedsack, who also played the pilots in the biplane that eventually shoots down Kong. (David O. Selznick served as executive producer, who raised enough cash at financially strapped RKO to keep the film in production.) Based on a story by Cooper and Edgar Wallace, the screenplay was written by James A. Creelman and Ruth Rose. (Cooper allegedly conceived the basic premise of the scenario while walking through New York and imagining an immense ape looming over the Empire State Building.) The film's title evolved from *The Beast* to *Kong*, to *King Ape*, to *The Eighth Wonder of the World*, and finally to its eventual title.

King Kong is most famous for the special effects wizardry of Willis O'Brien, who was assisted by models created by Marcel Delgado. (O'Brien and Delgado had worked together eight years previously on the dinosaurs in *The Lost World*.) The great ape himself was really six 18-inch puppets, though a giant foot, paw, and head (20 feet high and operated by technicians using levers and compressed air) were also used in the film footage. Most shots showing Kong carrying Fay Wray either in the jungle or in New York involve the puppet gorilla, with an animated doll in its hand. Via stop-motion photography on miniature sets, against the backdrop of glass paintings, Kong was able to interact with live actors. Ingenious editing also assisted in making the trick photography seem remarkably convincing. In addition to Kong himself, the film features realistic animations of a tyrannosaurus rex, a stegosaurus, a brontosaurus, a pterodactyl, and a giant snake. Although the special effects techniques were primitive by today's standards, they were pioneering efforts that influenced movie-making for many decades.

All subsequent attempts to exploit the Kong mystique have been disappointing. *Konga* (1960), a British film that attempted to capitalize on Kong's popularity, dramatizes a mad scientist's experiment with growth serum, which eventually results in the transformation of a chimpanzee into a gigantic gorilla. In Japan, Toho Company's *King Kong vs. Godzilla* (1962) offered a 150-foot-tall Kong (three times his height in the 1933 original), played by an actor in a silly gorilla costume. The battles between the two giant monsters are ludicrous to say the least. At the end of the film, Kong defeats Godzilla and swims back to his jungle isle. In *King Kong Escapes* (1967), Toho Company's sequel to *King Kong vs. Godzilla*, a pathetic confrontation of Kong and a mechanical monster known as Mecha-Kong leads to rather predictable results.

The 1976 remake, also entitled *King Kong*, a Dino de Laurentiis production, starred Jeff Bridges, Jessica Lange, and Charles Grodin in an updated version of the tale exploiting the oil crisis prevalent at the time. The film was based on a screenplay by Lorenzo Semple, Jr. (perhaps best known for his scripts for the *Batman* TV show) and featured music by John Barry. Despite its multimillion-dollar budget (which dwarfed the original's $650,000) it did not feature any dinosaurs as foils for Kong, which is one of the many reasons for its failure at the box office. Moreover, a giant mechanical ape proved ineffective in most scenes, so that makeup artist Rick Baker had to play the role in his own gorilla suit. This ill-conceived remake was followed by a formulaic sequel, *King Kong Lives* (1986), starring Linda Hamilton, in which scientists revive Kong after his fall from the World Trade Center by means of an artificial heart. Kong

and a female counterpart have a baby Kong in the jungles of South America prior to being killed.

It is a testament to the enduring quality of the original *King Kong* that the fairly recent remake has been nearly forgotten while the 1933 classic still has the power to evoke both terror and empathy. Kong's fatal infatuation with Fay Wray may have been the perfect escapist tonic for Americans in the grip of the Depression, but the story of the beauty who killed the great beast has attained archetypal status in our celluloid mythology.

Bibliography

Geduld, Harry, and Ronald Gottesman, eds. *The Girl in the Hairy Paw: King Kong as Myth, Movie, and Monster.* New York: Avon, 1976.

Goldner, Orville, and George E. Turner. *The Making of* King Kong*: The Story behind a Classic Film.* New York: Ballantine, 1975.

Ted Billy

King, Larry (1933-), television interview-show host, was born Lawrence Harvey Zeiger in Brooklyn, the son of Russian immigrants. The stage name "King" was invented for him by a Miami radio station manager. By the mid-1960s, King had developed a casual interview style that would be the basis for his later national fame. He broadcast nightly from a Miami restaurant, interviewing patrons, whether regular customers or visiting celebrities. In addition to the nightly interview program (featuring a parade of visiting stars), King also conducted a weekly TV show, wrote columns for several Miami newspapers, and was color commentator for Miami Dolphins' football broadcasts.

After a period of personal problems, in 1978 King took the microphone at Mutual's all-night national radio talk show. The network had tried twice previously to launch such a program and twice had failed. Only 28 stations carried King's show when it debuted, but the number of stations grew into the hundreds through the 1980s.

The 1985 addition of *Larry King Live* weeknights on television's Cable News Network (CNN) raised King's profile, especially in Washington, where both the radio show and the CNN program originated. Each became "a national town meeting," as King described them.

King's talk show was CNN's highest-rated regular program. By the standards of the traditional networks, however, the ratings were not very high. But ratings were less important than forging the new frontier of cable. Because CNN was viewed in more than 150 countries around the world, King saw possibilities to "promote understanding, involvement, inter-connection." By 1992 King had become an important part of the talk-show phenomenon, especially after H. Ross Perot announced his candidacy for president on King's show (see Television Talk Shows).

The workload of the nightly program on CNN prompted moving the radio show to daytime in early 1993; then it was abandoned in 1994, replaced by a radio simulcast of the CNN talk-show. King was also active in print with a weekly column in *USA Today* and six autobiographical books. King or his programs have won the Peabody Award, the National

Association of Broadcasters' Radio Award, and ACE Awards for excellence in cable television. In 1992, he was inducted into the Broadcasting Hall of Fame.

Bibliography

Burns, Robert. "Bush on 'King' as Perot Works on His Strategy." *Houston Post* 6 Oct. 1992.

King, Larry, with Emily Yoffe. *Larry King by Larry King.* New York: Simon & Schuster, 1982.

King, Larry, with Mark Stencel. *On the Line.* New York: Harcourt, 1993.

Rosenstiel, Thomas B. "The Talk-show Phenomenon." *Houston Chronicle* 31 May 1992.

Ed Shane

King, Martin Luther, Jr. (1929-1968), Baptist minister, civil rights activist and writer, led the civil rights movement in its quest for peace, freedom, and democracy. In 1964, he became the youngest Nobel Prize laureate in history. During his life, King received hundreds of awards and honors. Perhaps the ultimate honor for King and his work for justice and equality was the passage of a bill by the Congress of the United States to create a national holiday on the third Monday of January in observance of his birthday.

Born in Atlanta, GA, King was the son and grandson of middle-class Baptist ministers who served as pastors of Ebenezer Baptist Church in Atlanta. He was educated in the public schools of Atlanta, and at the age of 15 was admitted to Morehouse College. Upon graduating from Morehouse in 1948, King was called to enter the ministry, and was admitted to Crozer Theological Seminary, where he became the first African-American student body president. He was graduated with the highest grade point average in his class.

After hearing a lecture by Mordecai Johnson, president of Howard University, on the use of nonviolence in the struggle for racial equality, King became interested in the teachings of Mahatma Gandhi, whom Johnson had met in India. When he acquired his bachelor of divinity degree in 1951, King was admitted to Boston University, where he earned a doctorate in systematic theology. While he was in Boston, King met Coretta Scott, whom he married in 1953.

The following year King was installed as pastor of the Dexter Baptist Church in Montgomery, AL. A little more than a year later, King led the Montgomery bus boycott, which subsequently engendered the Supreme Court ruling that Alabama state laws requiring segregation of buses were unconstitutional. King's account of the boycott, *Stride toward Freedom,* was published in 1958.

In 1957, King helped organize the Southern Christian Leadership Conference (SCLC). He served as the organization's president for the rest of his life. King and the SCLC received international attention for the promotion of nonviolent direct action in the struggle for African-American freedom. The SCLC was involved in many programs including voter registration, political education, and economic development. The SCLC's goal was to destroy segregation and, simultaneously, to empower the African-American community.

Because of the demands of the civil rights movement, King decided to move back to Atlanta, where he became co-pastor of the Ebenezer Baptist Church. He continued to organize nonviolent resistance including marches, sit-ins, freedom rides, and other forms of protest. These tactics appealed to both African Americans and liberal whites and gained King national attention as he helped lead numerous protests throughout the South. He was arrested and jailed many times. In 1963, he wrote "Letter from Birmingham Jail" a reply to eight clergymen who had criticized his mass demonstration tactics. The letter became the centerpiece for the book *Why We Can't Wait* (1964).

The Birmingham campaign led to the historic March on Washington on August 28, 1963. An interracial audience of over 250,000 listened to a number of speakers plead for equality and justice in every aspect of American life. The most memorable speech was King's "I Have a Dream," which electrified the crowd in attendance as well as those who watched at home on their televisions. Partly because of the March on Washington, Congress passed the Civil Rights Act of 1964, giving the federal government the power to enforce desegregation of public places and outlawing discrimination in employment. In December 1964, King was awarded the Nobel Peace Prize.

King continued to lead campaigns in both the North and South, addressing broader issues to improve the quality of life for all Americans. In 1967, King linked the civil rights struggle with opposition to the war in Vietnam. Although he was often criticized for his views, his moral convictions compelled him to speak.

On April 3, 1968, while addressing a group in support of a garbage workers' strike in Memphis, TN, King delivered his last speech, "I've Been to the Mountaintop." The following day he was shot to death while standing on the balcony of his room at the Lorraine Motel.

Bibliography:

Branch, Taylor. *Parting the Waters: America in the King Years, 1954-63.* New York: Simon & Schuster, 1988.

Garrow, David. *Bearing the Cross: Martin Luther King, Jr. and the Southern Christian Leadership Conference.* New York: Morrow, 1986.

King, Coretta Scott. *My Life with Martin Luther King, Jr.* London: Hodder & Stoughton, 1970.

Janice Snapp

King, Stephen (1947-), is the most popular and best-selling horror novelist ever, with well over 80,000,000 books in print. He also remains one of the most prolific authors working today, with several dozen novels (counting those written under his "Richard Bachman" pseudonym), five short-story collections, eight screenplays, and a nonfiction critical study to his credit.

King's novelistic debut, *Carrie* (1974), coincided with the early 1970s revival of public interest in horror following the successes of *Rosemary's Baby* (1967) and *The Exorcist* (1971). *Carrie*, the story of a young girl with telekinetic powers who enacts vengeance on those who have been cruel to her, began King's remarkable ascendancy to the top of the best-seller lists, a position he has almost never relinquished.

King creates contemporary fairy tales within the context of a modern existence that devalues imagination and denies the human need for magic. His engagingly colloquial style complements this approach, as does the strong presence of the supernatural in most of his work. Some novels (The Dark Tower series; *The Talisman*, co-authored with Peter Straub; *The Eyes of the Dragon*) take place at least partly in a magical realm paralleling and occasionally intersecting our own reality. Even those narratives set in a recognizably modern America are populated, especially in King's early fiction, with familiar monster archetypes from cinema and popular folklore (the vampire, the demon, the werewolf, the zombie, the extraterrestrial invader, and others). Significantly, in the nonfiction study *Danse Macabre* (1981), King points to 1950s B movies as primary influences on his developing imagination.

King's work tends to focus repeatedly on the wonders and dangers of cognitive growth from childhood to maturity. In many ways, he speaks eloquently for our present-day concern over childhood neglect or abuse as an origin of social evil. This child-in-jeopardy plot is central to *The Shining* (1977) and *Firestarter* (1980). Adolescents are particularly vulnerable to corruption after years of mistreatment, ostracism, or indifference as we see in Carrie, *The Stand*'s Harold Lauder (1978), and *Christine*'s Arnie Cunningham (1983). Often, dark forces are residual in nature, as in *Cujo* (1981) and *Pet Sematary* (1983).

In earlier works, King emphasized traditional horror conventions, as in *'Salem's Lot* (1975), the first of his novels to be adapted for TV (1979), and *The Dead Zone* (1979); many of the later novels, while retaining grisly elements, probe psychological themes, such as *Misery* (1987) and *The Dark Half* (1989). In March 2000 King published the novella "Riding the Bullet" on the Internet. Online book stores were overcome by an estimated 500,000 orders.

Bibliography

Beahm, George, ed. *The Stephen King Companion*. Kansas City: Andrews, 1989.

Collings, Michael R. *The Many Facets of Stephen King*. Mercer Island: Starmont, 1985.

Winter, Douglas E. *Stephen King: The Art of Darkness*. New York: New American Library, 1986.

Philip Simpson

King World is the syndicator of the most popular daily television shows in North America. Starting from a library of Hal Roach movies and old TV series, King World now distributes *Wheel of Fortune*, *Jeopardy!* and *The Oprah Winfrey Show*. The company was founded in 1964 by the late Charles King (he has been succeeded by his sons, Roger M. King as chairman of the board, and Michael King as chief executive officer). King World's original stake was made with television rights to Hal Roach's *The Little Rascals/Our Gang* shorts, the 14 Basil Rathbone *Sherlock Holmes* films, and the *East Side Kids*, *Mr. Moto*, and *Charlie Chan* features. Its library of TV series includes *Topper* and the Westerns *Branded* and *The Guns of Will Sonnet*. By holding TV, theatrical, and home video rights to its library, King World has

been instrumental in exploiting them by keeping the characters in the public eye, with everything from calendars and T-shirts to home video re-releases and revival films, like a Saturday morning *Little Rascals* cartoon (1982), the 1994 feature, and various revivals of *Topper*. This has also led to the unpopular colorization of the *Topper* and *Sherlock Holmes* films.

New FCC regulations implemented in the early '80s were intended to encourage local television stations to fill their prime time access slots (7:30-8:00 p.m. EST) with original programming instead of off-network reruns. One result of this new environment was the production of first-run syndicated shows. King World entered the new market in 1983 by producing a syndicated version of *Wheel of Fortune*, a staple of NBC's daytime game show lineup since 1975. *Wheel*'s popularity encouraged its creator, Merv Griffin, to attempt a revival of his *Jeopardy!* (see entry). The new *Jeopardy!* also became a smash hit, usually scoring as the second most popular syndicated show behind *Wheel of Fortune*. Oprah Winfrey was hosting a local talk show, *A.M. Chicago*, on WLS-TV when she attracted national attention and an Oscar nomination for her role in *The Color Purple*. She and King syndicated *The Oprah Winfrey Show*, through her Harpo Productions, for the 1986-87 season (see entry).

King World's first self-produced show was the tabloid newszine *Inside Edition*, which premiered in January of 1989 on 147 stations. Another magazine show, *American Journal*, debuted in 1993. The company also distributes *Mr. Food* inserts for local news and magazine shows. Other shows distributed by King World included *Rolonda* (a talk show hosted by Rolonda Watts), the *Les Brown Show*, and a failed revival of *Candid Camera*. The company co-produced a cartoon show, *Wild West C.O.W.-Boys of Moo Mesa,* with the Ruby-Spears studio, that aired over ABC in the 1992 season.

Bibliography

King, Michael. Biography. King World public relations packet, 1994.

King, Roger M. Biography. King World public relations packet, 1994.

"Michael and Roger King: 'It Always Gets Back to Software.'" *Broadcasting and Cable* 13 Sept. 1993: 17-24.

Noglows, Paul. "King World's Caper: Clone Its Winners." *Variety* 25 Jan. 1993: 46, 131.

Mark McDermott

Kingston Trio, The (1957-1967), formed in 1957 in San Francisco, originally consisted of Bob Shane (1934-), Nick Reynolds (1933-), and Dave Guard (1934-   ). After Guard left the singing group in 1961 and was replaced by John Stewart (1939-), the Trio carried on until it disbanded in 1967. In the late 1960s Bob Shane purchased the rights to the group's name, and has continued the group since. He and Reynolds reunited in the late 1980s. During their peak popularity, from 1958 through 1964, the Trio had few rivals but many imitators (e.g., the Brothers Four, the Lettermen).

The group's first album, *The Kingston Trio*, was released by Capitol in June 1958. It was the single "Tom

Dooley," however, about a man hanged for murder, that cemented the group's success, reaching the No. 1 position on *Billboard*'s Top 40 chart in December 1958. Although the song had been discovered and performed by Frank Proffitt and had also been recorded by Frank Warner on Elektra in 1952, the Kingston Trio's version became a hit. The group's success was so colossal that Capitol released four Trio albums within the next year alone, attempting to cash in on the exposure provided by "Tom Dooley." *At Large* (1959), the group's fourth LP, stayed at the No. 1 spot for 15 weeks, and is one of the best-selling folk albums of all time. It yielded another hit single, "M.T.A.," about a man doomed forever to ride the Boston Mass Transit Authority train because he hasn't the money to get off. During the years 1958-63 the Trio had 17 Hot 100 entries (or debuting singles) and seven gold records.

Close-Up, released in the fall of 1961, was the debut album by the "new" Trio. This Trio's second single, "Where Have All the Flowers Gone?" (written by Pete Seeger), released in January 1962, became the first of many popular singles; it was followed by "One More Town," "Greenback Dollar," and "Reverend Mr. Black," the latter release of 1963 being one of the group's most successful singles behind "Tom Dooley." *Time to Think*, released early in 1964, yielded the Trio's last charting single, "Ally Ally Oxen Free," a Rod McKuen penned tune, but the album also contained the Trio's moving version of the Clancy Brothers' "The Patriot Game." The song failed to chart as a single, as did the Trio's final single for Capitol, "Seasons in the Sun" (though it became a smash hit for Terry Jacks in early 1974). The group released one more album for Capitol, *Back in Town*, in May 1964, the 20th album in six years.

The Trio moved to Decca in late 1964 and released four albums. According to critics, the best of these was *Stay Awhile*, released in May 1965. The final album, *Children of the Morning*, was released early in 1966; by June of 1967, the group decided to call it quits. The live album *Once upon a Time*, released in 1969, consisted of material recorded in 1966.

Bibliography

Blake, Benjamin. *The Kingston Trio on Record*. Naperville: Kingston Korner, 1986.

Callot, Robin, and Paul Surratt. Liner Notes. *The Kingston Trio: The Capitol Collector's Series*. By the Kingston Trio. Capitol CDP 7-92710-2, 1990.

Clarke, Donald, ed. *The Penguin Encyclopedia of Popular Music*. London: Penguin, 1990.

Samuel J. Umland
Rebecca A. Umland

Kirby, Jack (1917-1994), was among the most prolific and influential creators of American comic books. Alone, and in collaboration with Joe Simon and Stan Lee, he created memorable characters like Captain America, the Fantastic Four, the X-Men, and the New Gods, and originated the romance and "kid gang" genres. Although he had acrimoniously parted company with Stan Lee and Marvel Comics in 1970, Stan still refers to Jack as "the king."

Born Jacob Kurtzberg, Kirby grew up in the slums of New York's Lower East Side. He managed to acquire a taste for science fiction and literature, even though getting caught with a book usually ensured a beating from local gangs. Without formal art training, Kirby studied first book illustrators, then the movies and comic strips. In 1936, he got his first illustration job at Lincoln Newspaper Syndicate, supplying comics to weekly newspapers. From there he went to Max Fleischer's animation studio as an in-betweener on *Popeye*. While drawing cels that filled in movement between the animator's main drawings, Jack learned about action and how to draw exciting fight scenes.

Kirby broke into comic books at Will Eisner's studio. He drew several stories for *Jumbo Comics* (No. 1, dated September, 1938), using a variety of pen names before settling on "Jack Kirby." By 1940, he was drawing his first costumed hero, the newspaper strip version of Fox Publications' Blue Beetle. He met Joe Simon, an editor at Fox, and the two began a partnership by collaborating on *Blue Bolt*.

In 1941, Simon and Kirby were hired as editors for Martin Goodman's Timely Comics, the forerunner of Marvel Comics (see entry). By then, America was still trying to stay out of the war, but many comics creators, mostly young lower-class Jewish men with relatives in Europe, felt America had to wake up to Hitler's threat. Simon and Kirby responded with the patriotic hero Captain America. Simon and Kirby's ten-issue tenure on *Captain America* solidified their storytelling style.

Kirby split with Simon in 1956, during a collapse in the comics industry. He tried to break into syndication, created the adventurous quartet *Challengers of the Unknown* for DC (debuting in *Showcase* No. 6, Jan.-Feb. 1957), and even rejoined Simon, by then an editor at Archie Comics, to revive the company's 1940s heroes the Fly and the Shield.

Kirby came back to Marvel, then called Atlas Comics, in 1956, looking for freelance work. He found the company about to shut down and had to grab a drawing board from the movers, promising editor Stan Lee he'd draw some salable stories. In two years, Marvel became marginally profitable, propelled by Kirby's stories of Godzilla-sized monsters, given outrageous names by Lee: Fin Fang Foom, Grottu, Moomba, Zzutak, or The Thing That Shouldn't Exist. Finally, Martin Goodman told Lee to give costumed superheroes another shot. The result was the milestone *Fantastic Four* No. 1 (Nov. 1961) which featured, for good measure, another giant Kirby monster on its cover.

The new superheroes sold well, so Lee created more, with Kirby designing them and illustrating at least their first few adventures. Among them were the Incredible Hulk, the Mighty Thor, Ant-Man, the X-Men, Sgt. Fury, and the Avengers. He had worked on the first Spider-Man story before Lee gave the job to Steve Ditko, and designed Iron Man's armor for series artist Don Heck.

Kirby introduced readers to his Fourth World in the pages of *Superman's Pal, Jimmy Olsen*, wherein the red-headed reporter encountered the clones of the original Newsboy Legion. Together, they uncovered a cosmic conspiracy involving Clark Kent's new boss, Morgan Edge, and leading to Darkseid, Kirby's most implacable villain. In three new titles, *New Gods, The Forever People,* and *Mister Miracle,* Kirby detailed Darkseid's complex machinations in search of the "anti-life equation," which would bring the entire universe under his heel. Darkseid's name, plus the fact that his foes, the New Gods, were in communion with a cosmic guide called "The Source," seemed to have made an impression on filmmaker George Lucas.

Though *New Gods* was avidly followed by comics fans, his dialogue proved unequal to Lee's purple prose. DC abruptly canceled the titles, and Kirby worked at a few more projects before returning to Marvel. He wrote a Watergate-era White House conspiracy plot for *Captain America,* who also saved the country for the Bicentennial. Kirby applied his "cosmic" formula to a comics adaptation of *2001: A Space Odyssey.*

Kirby created *Captain Victory and the Galactic Rangers* in 1981 for Pacific Comics, one of the first "independent" publishers which allowed creators to retain rights to their characters. The next year, he drew *Destroyer Duck,* a fundraising comic for Steve Gerber, who was suing Marvel to establish ownership of his creation, *Howard the Duck.* The fan press reported that Kirby might sue Marvel for his characters himself, and Marvel refused to return Kirby's old artwork unless he relinquished any claim of ownership. The parties finally came to an agreement including a gag order on public discussion, but fans excoriated Stan Lee for appearing to take the Marvel corporate line against his former collaborator.

Kirby finally slowed down in the late 1980s, after a career in which he is estimated to have averaged a page of comics every day for 50 years. Before his death, he was working on a "Kirbyverse" project for the comics division of the Topps trading card company, in which other artists and writers would create stories from characters he created and owned.

Bibliography

Benton, Mike. *The Comic Book in America: An Illustrated History.* Dallas: Taylor, 1989.
——. *Superhero Comics of the Golden Age: The Illustrated History.* Dallas: Taylor, 1992.
——. *Superhero Comics of the Silver Age: The Illustrated History.* Dallas: Taylor, 1991.
Goulart, Ron. *The Comic Book Reader's Companion.* New York: HarperCollins, 1993.
Horn, Maurice, ed. *The World Encyclopedia of Comics.* New York: Chelsea House, 1976.

Mark McDermott

Kitchens, which first appeared as separate rooms in American homes during the late 18th and early 19th centuries, have changed dramatically during the past two centuries, yet the issues and themes central to their design and marketing have remained remarkably consistent. Domestic theorists of the 19th century argued for making kitchens more efficient by applying scientific principles from the industrial world to the home. In the latter half of the 20th century, the connection between the kitchen and the public world continued, with the office gradually replacing the factory as the model of efficiency; kitchen plans in 1980s women's magazines include a "work center" with a prominently placed computer to bring the kitchen into the same technological sphere as the corporate world. The changes in kitchen design reflect not only technological advances, but also changes in cultural attitudes toward women.

From the 19th century onward, kitchen designs reflect a tension between the desire for efficient organization of smaller spaces and the symbolic need to make the kitchen a gathering place for the family. In colonial American homes, the hearth was the literal and symbolic center of family life. Although domestic theorists continued to perpetuate this ideal by referring to later kitchens as the "heart" or "soul" of the home, 19th-century kitchens, occupied in upper-class homes primarily by servants, were walled off from the living area of the house. Well into the 20th century, when servants were less common and the housewife worked alone in the kitchen, no moves were made to end her isolation by opening the kitchen; instead designers praised the efficiency of the I, U, or L-shaped kitchens and of the smaller, enclosed kitchens patterned after ships' galleys and kitchens in Pullman railroad cars, with everything in easy reach. In the 1950s, this concern for efficiency manifested itself in step-saving designs, based on time and motion studies, that emphasized careful placement of major appliances and work surfaces. One of the most visible efforts to conserve human energy was the introduction of islands, a feature appearing in an array of shapes and sizes in plans of the 1960s.

Plans of the 1970s began to entice the family into the kitchen with built-in stereos and televisions placed strategically over the table or snack bar. Several design guides from this period also feature fireplaces or brick archways around electric ovens, reminiscent of the colonial hearth. Kitchens in contemporary households also serve as family communication centers where messages are exchanged between family members seldom occupying the room at the same time. Collectible kitchen magnets—marketed widely in mail-order catalogs, novelty stores and souvenir stands—to hold the messages are displayed on refrigerator doors in most homes.

Not until the middle of the 20th century, when women became more prominent in the public sphere, did kitchens begin to open into the rest of the house. Initially openings into the kitchen were little more than pass-through windows that allowed the cook, who was also the hostess, to more conveniently transport food from the kitchen to the dining room. By the 1950s, the walls between kitchens and dining areas began to disappear. They were replaced by room dividers or by peninsulas with cabinets over them, which provided more counter and storage space. Picture windows above sinks, standard in designs of the 1940s and 1950s, opened kitchens to the outdoors, as did skylights and sliding glass doors in the environmentally conscious 1960s and 1970s.

Even as kitchens became more open, advertisements for kitchen appliances and furniture continued to reinforce the gendered image of kitchens, showing only women working in them and labeling kitchen decor as the site for women's creativity. Changes in appliance colors became the most visible mark of kitchen decor, from the pastel colors of the 1950s to the earth tones of the 1960s and back to the white and off-white tones in the 1980s and 1990s. Wood and wood-like surfaces became popular as a way to blend kitchen decor with the rest of the house. Only in the late 1970s do men begin to appear in advertisements, and remodeling guides begin to offer plans for "his and hers" kitchens, which include two side-by-side stoves, sinks, and counters.

Bibliography

Cowan, Ruth Schwartz. *More Work for Mother: The Ironies of Household Technology from the Open Hearth to the Microwave.* New York: Basic Books, 1983.

Strasser, Susan. *Never Done: A History of American Housework.* New York: Pantheon, 1982.

Wright, Gwendolyn. *Moralism and the Modern Home: Domestic Architecture and Cultural Conflict in Chicago: 1873-1913.* Chicago: U of Chicago P, 1980.

Cristine Levenduski

See also
Domestic Appliances

Knitting is a way of making a mesh fabric by looping a continuous yarn through itself. (Although knitting is usually lumped with crochet, its structure is completely different.) Most knitters think of knitting as having two basic stitches, knit and purl, but these are actually two methods for obtaining the same effect. The basic knitted fabric, called stockinette, is smooth on the front and bumpy on the back and is created by alternating rows of knit and purl stitch. The other basic fabric, garter stitch, has raised horizontal lines formed on both sides and is constructed of all knit or all purl stitches. Knitted fabrics can range from luxuriously drapable silks to plastic dish scrubbers, from dense woolens to light and airy lace. Knitting's versatility, the simplicity of its tools, and its portability all help to account for its continuing popularity.

The basic tools of knitting are yarn and needles. The relation between the size of the yarn and the diameter of the needle determine the size of the loop formed and the properties of the finished fabric. Heavy yarn knit with small diameter needles results in thick and inelastic fabric; the same yarn knit on large needles results in a stretchy mesh. Any kind of yarn or pliable wire that can be looped around a knitting needle can be used to create a knitted fabric. While woolen yarns are now thought of as the most traditional fiber for knitted garments, knitting in cotton, linen, and silk threads is equally old.

Although the public perception is that knitting is an age-old technique, textile scholars generally believe that knitting was developed around the Mediterranean sometime between the 7th and the 12th century. It spread only with the development of metalworking technology that made possible the production of wires of uniform diameter which could be used as knitting needles. Limited at first to the production of hats and stockings, knitting was later adopted as a way of making all kinds of garments, from fine cotton petticoats to heavy felted jackets. Given that knitted fabric is supremely adapted to comfortable garments worn close to the body—gloves, underwear, caps and especially socks—it has never had the prestige of other methods of textile manufacture. While there are isolated indigenous traditions of knitted fabrics in various parts of the world (not all produced by the Western two-needle method), modern knitting has been spread around the world by Westerners, especially missionaries.

Knitting remains a lively craft in the U.S. Unlike Europe, where knitting is taught in schools, knitting in the U.S. is generally passed on through families or social groups, and is often associated with a return to the ethnic heritage of the knitter. But knitters are also likely to learn from a friend, a knitting class held by a shop, or an adult education program. While fashion sometimes highlights hand knits and propels a boom in the hand knit industry—the most recent one was the huge growth of interest in hand knits in the eighties fostered by mainstream fashion designers like Perry Ellis—probably the most common reason for starting to knit or beginning to knit again is the birth of children. Those who knit without regard to fashion or babies are attracted by knitting's endless variety coupled to its economy of means: in one consumer survey knitters polled said that they produced on average six projects in a year. The popular image of the isolated knitter at home also obscures the long-standing tradition of knitting groups which make items for fund-raising fairs for churches and schools. The only part of the popular image that is true is that knitting is a craft practiced nearly exclusively by women: according to one industry survey (Hobby Industries of America), 88 percent of knitters are women. Knitting is a craft practiced across all classes, educational levels, and ethnicities by working women, professionals, and homemakers.

There are recurring efforts to expand the use of knitting beyond clothing, as in the wall hangings of Mary Walker Phillips, whose work is in the collection of the Museum of Modern Art. Although its mass popularity waxes and wanes, in an age when knitting a homemade garment may in fact be more expensive than buying its equivalent retail, knitting persists as a symbol of the power of hands to make beautiful objects with only the simplest tools.

Bibliography

Harvey, Michael. *Patons: A Story of Handknitting.* Ascot: Springwood, 1985.

MacDonald, Anne L. *No Idle Hands: The Social History of American Knitting.* New York: Ballantine, 1988.

Phillips, Mary Walker. *Creative Knitting.* St. Paul: Dos Tejadoras, 1986.

Royce, Beverly. *Notes on Double Knitting.* Pittsville: Schoolhouse, 1994.

Rutt, Richard. *A History of Hand Knitting.* Loveland: Interweave, 1989.

Margaret Bruzelius

Koch, Howard (1902-1995), is famous for having written the script for *The Invasion from Mars*, the radio show which nearly scared everybody to death. Having received his L.L.B. (Bachelor of Law) from Columbia University in 1925, Howard Koch moved away from New York City, the place of his birth, and began his adult life in Hartsdale, NY, as a small-town lawyer. His occupation, however, failed to satisfy him, so Koch undertook a writer's apprenticeship by taking time at the office to study *The Butter and Egg Man* (1925), a drama by George S. Kaufman, crafter of well-constructed Broadway plays. His own initial efforts were uneven, but with *The Lonely Man* (1935), a play in which Abraham Lincoln returns to confront the various slaveries daunting Depression-era America, Koch was successful in his desire to integrate a strong social awareness with dramatic form. It was on the strength of this play that Koch began to write for radio. John Houseman had read and liked Koch's play, so, in 1938, as co-producer with Orson Welles for a new radio series, *Mercury Theatre on the Air*, Houseman decided to hire Koch to script the program. Three weeks later, Koch was assigned to adapt H. G. Wells's *The War of the Worlds* for broadcast. Although Koch declared that under no circumstances could it be made interesting or credible to modern American ears, he managed to script *The Invasion from Mars*, and on October 30, 1938, this play, written in news-bulletin form, sounded so credible that at least 1,200,000 Americans flew into panic. Koch had written what turned out to be perhaps the most famous dramatic program in the history of radio.

His accomplished writing for radio's *Mercury Theatre* brought Koch to the attention of Hollywood, where Warner Brothers hired him in 1939. As a screenwriter, Howard Koch wrote or shared credit for notable films including *The Sea Hawk* (1940), *Sergeant York* (1941), and *Casablanca* (1943). His work on *Casablanca*, co-authored with Julius and Philip Epstein, earned Koch an Academy Award for best screenplay and strengthened his reputation for being able to handle projects with overtly political elements. His ease in writing about politics, developed during years in the theater, doubtlessly influenced Jack Warner to ask Koch to work on his next project, Joseph Davies's best-selling *Mission to Moscow*. The film, made at the insistence of President Roosevelt and considered patriotic in 1943, portrayed a sympathetic attitude toward the Soviet Union; the same film, however, was deemed subversive by the House Un-American Activities Committee in the fall of 1947. Subpoenaed to appear before HUAC, Koch became one of the original Hollywood 19, unfriendly witnesses who announced they would not cooperate with the committee (see Hollywood Ten). Though HUAC did not call him to appear on that occasion, the committee had had its effect; Koch became "graylisted" in Hollywood. A "possible subversive," able to find work in Hollywood with only diminished frequency, his status remained unchanged until his work on *The 13th Letter* (1951) succeeded in getting Koch "blacklisted."

In European exile, he adopted the name Peter Howard, wrote the screenplay for *The Intimate Stranger* (1956) (*Finger of Guilt* in the U.S.), and was unable to get his name off the list of "unemployables" until 1961. In his return to Hollywood, Koch scripted *Loss of Innocence* for Columbia Pictures and worked on four more pictures, the last in 1974. Still, Koch and Hollywood managed to revive fully their positive working relationship.

Bibliography

Corliss, Richard. *The Hollywood Screenwriters*. New York: Discus, 1972.

Koch, Howard. *The Panic Broadcast*. Boston: Little, Brown, 1970.

Morseberger, Robert E., et al., eds. *American Screenwriters*. Vol. 26 of *Dictionary of Literary Biography: American Screenwriters*. Detroit: Gale Research, 1984.

Navasky, Victor S. *Naming Names*. New York: Viking, 1980.

Stanley D. Harrison

Kool and the Gang (1964-) was started as a high school jazz combo in 1964 by Robert "Kool" Bell, whose father played bass with pianist Thelonious Monk. The group is one of the earliest exponents of the 1970s funky big band sound typified by the Ohio Players, B.T. Express, L.T.D., and Parliament-Funkadelic.

Their first single, the funky instrumental "Kool and the Gang," released just as the youngest members of the band graduated high school, riffed and grooved its way onto the U.S. single charts in 1969. Kool and the Gang broke into the Top 10 with 1974's "Jungle Boogie," the band's first million-selling single, and followed it up three months later with its second million-seller, "Hollywood Swinging." Both of these tunes set the non-stop groove standard Kool and the Gang would continue to mine through "Rhyme Time People," "Spirit of the Boogie," "Summer Madness" (also featured in the movie *Rocky*), "Caribbean Festival," and "Open Sesame." "Open Sesame" (1977) would be their last hit for three years as a result of the burgeoning disco movement; it somewhat ironically kept Kool and the Gang in the ears of listeners by being included on the *Saturday Night Fever* (see entry) movie soundtrack that eventually sold over 25 million copies.

Searching for a new direction in 1979, Bell recruited soul vocalist James Taylor, who became the primary vocalist of the 1980s and the voice on their biggest hits of that era. Produced by Eumir Deodato, a 1973 hitmaker with "Also Sprach Zarathustra," *Ladies Night* was the band's first million-selling album and provided two Top 10 singles, the title track and "Too Hot." Both songs feature a smooth groove enhanced by the sweet vocals of Taylor, but it is the good-time tune "Celebration" of 1981 that gave the band its first No. 1 single and sold over 2 million copies in the U.S. *Celebrate*, the album from which it's taken, hit the Top 10 on the U.S. charts.

Throughout the 1980s, Kool and the Gang proved to be one of pop's most durable acts with a string of Top 40 hits and gold and platinum albums. In 1989, Taylor left the group to work on a solo career and the band's *Sweat*, sans Taylor, struggled commercially, setting the stage for a spate of well-earned and fulfilling funky retrospectives.

Bibliography

McEwen, Joe. "Funk." *The Rolling Stone Illustrated History of Rock and Roll*. New York: Random House, 1980.

Nite, Norm N. "Rock On." *The Illustrated Encyclopedia of Rock 'N' Roll, The Modern Years: 1964–The Present*. New York: Crowell, 1978.

Rees, Dafydd, and Luke Crampton. *Rock Movers and Shakers*. New York: Billboard, 1991.

Hugh Foley

Koontz, Dean R(ay) (1945-), whose novels have sold over 70 million copies, is usually classified as a horror writer, though his work is more of a hybridization of various genres designed to deliver action-packed stories. Often his target audience is the young adult reader.

Koontz combines elements of romance, horror, fantasy, science fiction, and mystery in his plots, which usually feature supernatural or technological atrocities. Romantic narratives often feature lovers whose passion redeems them as they defeat the evil that has hurt or stalked them. Some novels emphasize a mystery plot with a puzzle introduced in the opening pages, such as *Dark Tears,* in which the source of the menace that is threatening people is eerily unknowable. In works like *Demon Seed* (1973), *Watchers* (1987), and *Midnight* (1989), Koontz blends psychic and mechanistic malice. *Strangers* (1986) features aliens who colonize human minds, and *Darkfall* (1984) describes voodoo forces marshaling their power to take over a city and then the world.

Koontz has also published fiction under a spate of pseudonyms, including David Axton, Brian Coffey, Deanna Dwyer, John Hill, Leigh Nichols, Anthony North, Richard Paige, and Owen West. His versatility of subject matter, theme, and genre promises continued interest in his work.

Bibliography

Kies, Cossette. *Presenting Young Adult Horror Fiction*. New York: Twayne, 1992.

Munster, Bill, ed. *Sudden Fear: The Horror and Dark Suspense Fiction of Dean R. Koontz*. Mercer Island: Starmont, 1988.

Carl Holmberg

Kovacs, Ernie (1919-1962), famous TV personality, began his show business career in Philadelphia in 1950. His first TV stint was a half-hour, twice-weekly daytime cooking show on an NBC network local affiliate called *Deadline for Dinner* (1950-52). At the same time Ernie began to emcee a 15-minute commercial for the Ideal Manufacturing Company of New Jersey called *Pick Your Ideal*. This local weekly afternoon show featured two models wearing nearly identical outfits, one from an expensive fashion source, the other a cut-price knockoff from Ideal. A viewer who sent her name to WPTZ might be telephoned by Ernie on the air and asked to pick the Ideal outfit, and if she guessed correctly she won it as a prize. This show debuted August 22, 1950, and ran until August 9, 1951.

Then WPTZ asked Ernie to host a new daily early-morning show called *3 to Get Ready,* which debuted on November 27, 1950, as the first television wake-up show in the country. The success of this show (which lasted through the spring of 1952) convinced the NBC network to give Ernie a national airing, and so from March to June 1951, the 15-minute *Time for Ernie* was broadcast nationally weekday afternoons. *3 to Get Ready* continued to air locally until March 28, 1952. In the spring of 1951 WPTZ put Ernie on another local show one afternoon a week. *Now You're Cooking*, a mixture of recipes for housewives, which Ernie would demonstrate, and plugs for Nat-Gas Company, lasted only until June 12. However, NBC, which had been quite pleased with Ernie's success, scheduled him into his first nighttime show. *Ernie in Kovacsland* was a nationally broadcast summer replacement show, bowing in at the 7:00-7:30 p.m. Monday to Friday time slot on July 2 to August 24, 1951, highlighting its star's repertoire of nutty characterizations and slapstick comedy. It was a forerunner of the later Kovacs shows. Appearing as a vocalist on this show was Edith Adams, whom the star would later marry.

While Ernie continued to do the daily *3 to Get Ready* (which was soon to be replaced by the *Today* show) and the twice-weekly *Deadline for Dinner*, NBC added another show to his schedule, *Kovacs on the Corner*, a late-morning, 30-minute nationally broadcast show modeled after the radio feature *Allen's Alley*. This show aired weekdays January–March of 1952.

After Kovacs's stint with NBC ended, WCBS-TV was eager to test Kovacs's strength with New York daytime audiences. They offered Ernie *Kovacs Unlimited*, a comedy variety show (April 1952–January 1954). CBS rewarded Kovacs's midday success with a network nighttime show, *The Ernie Kovacs Show*, which aired for the first three months of 1953, opposite Milton Berle's *Texaco Star Theater* on NBC. After he had been at CBS a year, the network scheduled him into another prime-time slot, but only as a panelist on a game show called *Take a Guess,* which lasted only from June to September 1953. Between 1954 and 1960, Kovacs appeared on four more prime-time quiz shows: *One Minute Please* (DuMont, July 1954 to February 1955); *Time Will Tell* (DuMont, August to October 1954); *What's My Line* (CBS, August to November 1957); and *Take a Good Look* (ABC, October 1959 to July 1960 and October 1960 to March 1961).

Almost exactly one year after CBS axed *The Ernie Kovacs Show*, DuMont was eager to enter the late-night arena. The new *Ernie Kovacs Show* premiered in April 1954, going up against the *Steve Allen Show*. The show was popular, but not enough to save a failing fourth-place network.

For a couple of weeks in the fall of 1955, Kovacs was substitute host for Steve Allen on *Tonight!* NBC also found a slot for the new *Ernie Kovacs Show* midmorning weekdays, hoping to steal some viewers away from Arthur Godfrey; it ran from December 1955 to July 1956. Television's fourth *Ernie Kovacs Show* premiered in July 1956, and ran through the summer, filling Sid Caesar's Monday night slot, and receiving an Emmy Award nomination for best new series for 1956. Still under contract to NBC, Ernie accepted an offer to do *Tonight* (Steve Allen was hosting it Wednesday through Friday), and so became the official Monday-Tuesday host from October 1956 to January 1957. After that, Ernie found himself much in demand as a guest star on television programs, and between 1957 and his death in 1962, Ernie made 37 guest appearances on different NBC and CBS network shows, and played various roles in 10 feature films.

Bibliography
Rico, Diana. *Kovacsland: A Biography of Ernie Kovacs.* New York: Harcourt, 1990.
Walley, David. *Nothing in Moderation: A Biography of Ernie Kovacs.* New York: Drake, 1975.

Connie Wineland

Kraft Television Theater (a.k.a. *Kraft Theater* then, in June 1958, *Kraft Mystery Theater.* NBC: May 7, 1947–Dec. 1947, Jan. 1948–Oct. 1958; ABC: Oct. 1953–Jan. 1955). Announcers: Ed Herlihy (1947-1955) and Charles Stark (1955). Producers and directors: Stanley Quinn, Maury Holland, Harry Hermann, Richard Dunlap, Fielder Cook, William Graham, Norman Morgan, David Susskind, Robert Herridge, Alex March, George Roy Hill, and Buzz Kulik. This famous series was sponsored by Kraft Foods, one of the major supporters of live television drama during the 1950s, and was one of television's most prestigious programs. Both NBC and ABC ran *Kraft Theater* series, at one time simultaneously, so that by the end of its run, it had presented more than 650 plays. *Kraft* enjoyed a generous budget which allowed it to hire large casts, elaborate sets, and the best playwrights, directors, and producers of the day. Audiences enjoyed classic drama (Shakespeare, Ibsen) and contemporary authors and dramatists (Tennessee Williams, Agatha Christie, Rod Serling), and were introduced to unknown writers who vied during the 1955-56 season for a $50,000 prize for the best original play (entries were judged by Helen Hayes, Walter Kerr, and Maxwell Anderson; the prize went to William Noble for "Snap Finger Creek," telecast on February 22, 1956). During the mid-1950s several youth-oriented episodes were presented to attract younger audiences. During April 1954, *Kraft* experimented with color broadcasts intermittently, a trial that became permanent in July 1956. Its awards include Emmys and/or Emmy nominations for best dramatic program (1952, 1953); various individual awards for "Patterns" (1955); various awards for "A Night to Remember" (1956); and in 1958, an Emmy nomination for best single performance by an actress, Maureen Stapleton in "All the King's Men."

Bibliography
Boddy, William. *Fifties Television.* Urbana: U of Illinois P, 1990.
O'Neil, Thomas. *The Emmys.* New York: Penguin, 1992.
Sturcken, Frank. *Live Television.* Jefferson: McFarland, 1990.

S. P. Madigan

Krantz, Judith (1927-   ), one of America's more popular authors, acknowledges that she is not a "literary writer." Instead, she sees herself as a storyteller who creates fairy tales in which her vulnerable heroines triumph over personal tragedies to find love. Her books move through the world of the "beautiful people," providing readers with richly detailed backgrounds and engaging plots. Krantz did not publish her first novel, *Scruples* (1978), until she was 51, but that book remained on the *New York Times* best-seller list for nearly a year and established her reputation as a leading popular author.

Judith Tarcher Krantz grew up in New York City. Her early career was in fashion publicity and editing, culminating in her position as contributing West Coast editor of *Cosmopolitan* from 1971 to 1979, but by the end of the decade she had turned to writing full time. *Scruples* was followed by a succession of popular novels, including *Princess Daisy* (1980); *Mistral's Daughter* (1982); *I'll Take Manhattan* (1986); *Till We Meet Again* (1988); *Dazzle* (1990); *Scruples Two* (1992); and *Lovers* (1994). Several of Krantz's novels, including *Scruples* and *Mistral's Daughter,* have been adapted as television miniseries. Krantz continues to have novels on the best-seller list.

Bibliography
See, Lisa. "PW Interviews: Judith Krantz." *Publishers Weekly* 16 May 1986: 58-59.
Sutton, Roger. "The Booklist Interview: Judith Krantz." *Booklist* 1 Oct. 1992: 240-41.
Yellin, Jessica. "Pomp and Judith Krantz." *Los Angeles Magazine* April 1996: 26.

Jody L. Flynn

Kubrick, Stanley (1928-1999), was an expatriate film director whose place as one of the most important American directors of the latter 20th century rests on just 10 films: *The Killing* (1956), *Paths of Glory* (1957), *Lolita* (1962), *Dr. Strangelove Or: How I Learned to Stop Worrying and Love the Bomb* (1964; see entry), *2001: A Space Odyssey* (1968), *A Clockwork Orange* (1971), *Barry Lyndon* (1975), *The Shining* (1980), *Full Metal Jacket* (1987), and *Eyes Wide Shut* (finished after his death in 1999). He also acted as director on *Spartacus* (1960) after the producer/star, Kirk Douglas, fired the original director, but he lacked significant control over the film and has since disowned it. Known for technical virtuosity, he was also known for his wickedly funny critiques of modern decadence and violence. Though he operated in England since 1960, Kubrick's films remained rooted in American culture and values.

Born in the Bronx, Kubrick began as a photographer for *Look* magazine. When he became interested in filmmaking, V. I. Pudovkin's book, *Film Technique*, was the only text he studied thoroughly. He also studied the films of Pudovkin, Sergei Eisenstein, Max Ophuls, and Orson Welles, whose works his films most resemble.

Significantly, like those whom he studied, Kubrick believed that the irreducible craft of filmmaking is editing. Kubrick edited very tightly, rejecting dissolves and other methods of gradual movement in favor of swift cuts. He often used Pudovkin's method of juxtaposition to create meaning in the mind of the viewer. Most famous is the jump cut from the soaring bone to the spaceship in *2001*. This tells the audience two things with masterful economy: that the discovery of the tool-weapon led mankind on a quest for technological mastery; and that the arms race began long before 1946. Extending Pudovkin's principle of juxtaposition, Kubrick also intentionally clashed music with visuals in order to create or intensify meaning. A famous example is the lushly romantic "Try a Little Tenderness" that accompanies an opening shot of B-52s in *Dr. Strangelove*. Without the music, the viewer might be awed by the spectacle of planes refueling in air, but with the music the viewer has to see this as airborne copulation, and the absurdity of it, the twisted intertwining of sex and technological destruction, resonates throughout the rest of the film.

Kubrick is important for more than his technical mastery, however. Along with Woody Allen, Martin Scorsese, Francis Ford Coppola, and others, Kubrick emerged in the late 1950s as part of the film industry's transition from the production of popular *movies* to "elite" *films*. Competition from television and the success of foreign "art films" such as *Shoot the Piano Player* and *La Dolce Vita* among urban, educated audiences provided a market for filmmakers who were interested in making highly distinctive films that were often critical of contemporary society and politics. These new films often celebrated individuality and presented non-traditional heroes struggling against mainstream society.

Kubrick's films both participate in and satirize this trend. With the exception of Dax in *Paths of Glory*, Kubrick presents truly abnormal protagonists. Humbert Humbert can only be sexually attracted to pubescent "nymphs" in *Lolita*; Alex's idea of individuality is violence in *A Clockwork Orange*; Jack Torrence subconsciously desires to murder his wife and child in *The Shining*. In general, Kubrick's characters suffer from an inability or unwillingness to be guided by a moral point of view, and they avoid responsibility for their actions by devising "foolproof" plans of protection. But such avoidance only leads to worse consequences, as in *Dr. Strangelove*, where both the Americans and the Soviets have devised "fail-safe" mechanisms of nuclear destruction (i.e., "deterrence") which are easily set in motion by unforeseen events.

American critical response to Kubrick's work is mixed, though all of his mature works have their enthusiasts. *Paths of Glory*, which is habitually compared to Renoir's anti-war classic *Grand Illusion*, and *Dr. Strangelove* were immediately recognized as masterpieces among critics. *2001*, though it baffled and/or bored many reviewers at the time, was extremely popular with audiences and later widely embraced by critics. It is still the best science fiction film ever made. The rest of his films, however, have not enjoyed the same embrace.

Discussions of Kubrick inevitably come around to one issue and one movie: violence and *A Clockwork Orange*. *Clockwork* is the best example of Kubrick's trademark combination of humor and horror, and when the film appeared in 1971, commentators from *Time,* the *New Yorker,* and *Catholic News* praised it to the skies. The film and Kubrick won the New York Critics awards for best film and best director that year. But many others objected to its extremely violent content.

Kubrick, however, considered *Clockwork* to be flawless and his best work. He has said in published statements and interviews that the main character, Alex, had to be thoroughly evil in order to make the point that removing free choice is unacceptable in every case. In this way he faulted the Western genre for depicting the evil of lynchings only when an innocent person's life was at risk—as if it was not *always* wrong to hang a person. Nothing justifies or could be more dangerous in his view than the obliteration of moral choice, and this is what *Clockwork* dramatizes.

Bibliography

Agel, Jerome, ed. *The Making of Kubrick's 2001.* New York: New American Library, 1970.

Coyle, Wallace. *Stanley Kubrick: A Guide to References and Resources.* Boston: Hall, 1980.

Nelson, Thomas Allen. *Kubrick: Inside a Film Artist's Maze.* Bloomington: Indiana UP, 1982.

Phillips, Gene D. *Stanley Kubrick: A Film Odyssey.* New York: Popular Library, 1975.

Walker, Alexander. *Stanley Kubrick Directs.* New York: Harcourt, 1972.

April D. Wilson

Ladies' Home Journal, The (*LHJ*), dates back to 1879, when Cyrus Curtis invited his wife, Louisa (née Knapp), to contribute a woman's column to his newly created *Tribune and Farmer*. Soon the column grew to a full page, then to a full-blown woman's supplement, then, in December 1883, to a magazine in its own right.

Curtis started an aggressive search after advertisers in 1889, when he also hired a new full-time editor, Edward Bok. The press lampooned Curtis's choice of a bachelor journalist to direct his ladies' magazine, but Bok saw the magazine's money-making potential. Under Bok's direction, Louisa Knapp's magazine became popularly known as "the monthly Bible of the American home."

Bok tried to raise the *Journal*'s status by seeking out popular writers to provide its fiction and articles. The *LHJ* was never a literary magazine, but Bok managed to attract some of the literary stars of his day, among them Rudyard Kipling, Arthur Conan Doyle, Sarah Orne Jewett, Hamlin Garland, William Dean Howells, and Elizabeth Stuart Phelps. Bok even convinced Theodore Roosevelt to contribute a column and had Benjamin Harrison write about life at the White House. In addition to these celebrity offerings, he regularly ran articles on the lives of famous women, such as those featured in his Clever Daughters of Clever Men series.

Bok used his editor's page to speak directly to his readers, involving them in some of the most controversial issues of the day. He carried out a persistent campaign against patent medicines and discussed such explosive topics as sex education, alcoholism, mental illness, and slums. In 1906, he undertook a daring campaign to educate the public about venereal disease. When he received complaints about his frankness, he declared: "The domestic nature of a magazine does not impose cowardice upon it."

Whether in spite of or thanks to the hard-hitting editorials, the *LHJ* continued to reign as the No. 1 selling women's magazine during Bok's time at the helm. After Bok retired in 1919, however, the publication passed through a string of editors and went into decline. Then, in 1935, the *Journal* was revivified by a husband and wife editorial team, Bruce and Beatrice Blackman Gould. The Goulds reinjected a social conscience into the *LHJ*. They took up some of Bok's causes and added a few of their own, addressing such subjects as VD, mental illness, education in the slums, alcoholism, birth control, divorce, and teenage sexuality.

When the Goulds retired in 1962, they left the *LHJ* facing some tough issues. Feminists were beginning to attack the magazine for containing too much advertising (ads had become virtually inseparable from the text) and for failing to address the concerns of the modern woman. These criticisms came to a crisis on March 18, 1970, when a group of women media workers staged a sit-in at the offices of publisher and editor-in-chief, John Mack Carter.

As a result of the sit-in, the *LHJ* agreed to run a special feature on the women's movement later that year. Many felt, however, that this was only a token gesture. A decade later, the *Journal*, having survived the rocky and competitive 1970s, found that it did not have to change to suit the times because the times were changing to suit it. Benefiting from the "new traditionalist" movement that saw many women refocus on motherhood as a career, the *LHJ* successfully reclaimed in the 1980s its historic position as one of the top-selling women's magazines in America.

Bibliography

Steinberg, Salme Haiju. *Reformer in the Marketplace: Edward W. Bok and* The Ladies' Home Journal. Baton Rouge: Louisiana State UP, 1979.

Tebbel, John, and Mary Ellen Zuckerman. *The Magazine in America, 1741-1990*. New York: Oxford UP, 1991.

Wood, James Playsted. *Magazines in the United States*. 3d ed. New York: Ronald, 1971.

Dawn Henwood

Lamour, Dorothy (1914-1996), famous as the sarong-lady in her work with Bing Crosby and Bob Hope in their "Road" pictures, was born Mary Leta Dorothy Slaton in New Orleans, and took a variant of her stepfather's name (Lambour) as her stage name. She began her show business career as a singer with band leader Herbie Kay (Kaumeyer), with whom she would eventually share a brief marriage. She achieved celebrity status following her 1931 Miss New Orleans title. Lamour would appear in 50 major motion pictures from 1936 through 1964. She benefited first from her contacts with the NBC radio network and then from the studio contract system.

Lamour's stunning beauty and her singing talent made *Jungle Princess* (1936), her film debut co-starring with Ray Milland, an instant hit at the box office. Her collaboration with Bing Crosby and Bob Hope (see entries) in the famous "road pictures"—*Road to Singapore* (1940), *Road to Zanzibar* (1941), *Road to Morocco* (1942), *Road to Utopia* (1946), *Road to Rio* (1948), *Road to Bali* (1953), and *Road to Hong Kong* (1962)—would ensure Lamour's status as one of Hollywood's premier celebrities. The road series fit the bill for wartime America.

By 1962, though, the road series had long since run its course. Lamour settled into semiretirement and raised three sons with Bill Howard (William Ross Howard III), with whom she enjoyed a long marriage from 1943 until his death in 1978. Her autobiography, *My Side of the Road* (1980), looked back on a long and successful Hollywood career. The latter stages of her career included a tour with *Hello, Dolly!* and a brief nostalgic comeback in 1982 at New York City's Ibis nightclub, where she had appeared many years before when it was the Versailles. Reviews indicated that while

Miss Lamour was no longer sarong-able, she was attractive and appropriately matronly with a singing voice still strong and assertive.

Bibliography

Lamour, Dorothy. *My Side of the Road.* Englewood Cliffs: Prentice-Hall, 1980.

James P. Hanlan

L'Amour, Louis (1908-1988), is primarily known for his famous and significant novels of the Western genre. However, his writings encompassed a much wider sphere. L'Amour, a voracious reader, wrote book reviews which he submitted to the *Sunday Oklahoman* as early as 1930. At that time, several small journals of his poetry were published, one at Emory University; these were later collected and published under the title *Smoke from This Altar* (1990).

The first of L'Amour's short stories was entitled "Anything for a Pal" and appeared in the pulp magazine *True Gang Life* in 1935. His early stories were of the Far East or the prize-fighting ring rather than the West. The first of L'Amour's full-length novels to be published was *Westward the Tide* (1949). It was released exclusively in England and did not appear in America for 27 years. In 1950, L'Amour signed with Doubleday to write, under the name Tex Burns, four novels based on the Clarence Mulford character Hopalong Cassidy. However, because of the growing popularity of the television series of the same name, the publishers asked L'Amour to rewrite Cassidy to match the new image. Although L'Amour yielded to the rewrite, he refused to acknowledge authorship of *The Rustlers of West Fork* (1951), *Trail to Seven Pines* (1951), *Riders of High Rock* (1951), and *Trouble Shooter* (1951). The first novel published under his own name and released in the United States was *Hondo* (1953), later made into a feature film starring John Wayne. L'Amour continued to write over 100 novels, all currently in print. His works have been translated into 20 languages, and 45 of his novels and short stories have been made into feature films or television movies. His books have sold over 230 million copies, making him one of the best-selling authors in modern literary history.

Some of L'Amour's novels have settings other than the West, such as *The Walking Drum* (1984), set in 12th-century Europe, and *The Last of the Breed* (1986), set in the USSR. L'Amour also wrote a series of novels about the Sackett Family, tracing it from Elizabethan England to their settling in America to the western expansion.

L'Amour did all of his own research, often walking the land on which a story was to occur. His personal library of over 17,000 volumes contained numerous diaries and journals from the pioneer era. He was also noted for strong character development. By stripping the characters of the outward constraints of law and order, L'Amour opens the inner door of human nature. Several of his novels, including *Ride the River* (1983) and *The Cherokee Trail* (1982), are based on strong women characters.

In 1983, L'Amour was the first novelist to be awarded the Congressional Gold Medal in recognition of his life's work. L'Amour was also awarded the Medal of Freedom by

Photo courtesy of Popular Culture Library, Bowling Green State University, Bowling Green, OH.

President Reagan in 1984. Daniel J. Boorstin, historian and Pulitzer Prize-winning author, in writing the introduction for L'Amour's memoir, praises the lesson "in open-mindedness and literary clarity" which L'Amour's life teaches.

Bibliography

Gale, Robert L. *Louis L'Amour.* 1985. Boston: Twayne, 1992.

L'Amour, Beau. Afterword. *The Rustlers of West Fork.* By Louis L'Amour. New York: Bantam, 1992.

L'Amour, Louis. *Education of a Wandering Man.* New York: Bantam, 1989.

Tompkins, Jane. *West of Everything: The Inner Life of Westerns.* New York: Oxford UP, 1992.

Sue Boonstra

Lancaster, Burt (1913-1994), appeared in nearly 70 films during his 40-year career. The variety of his roles is amazing: acrobat, convict, pirate, gunfighter, boxer, football hero, journalist, con man, evangelist, soldier, and Italian nobleman. Four times nominated for an Academy Award as best actor, he won an Oscar for his performance in *Elmer Gantry* (1960). In addition to his work in front of the camera, he also became a producer and director. In many ways Burt Lancaster represents the best of Hollywood's golden age.

Born Burton Stephen Lancaster in the East Harlem section of New York City, he graduated from DeWitt Clinton High School at the age of 16. Attending New York University on an athletic scholarship, he became a physical education major, playing basketball and baseball as well as taking part in boxing, track, and gymnastics.

After two years Lancaster left NYU and, with his boyhood friend Nick Cravat, formed the acrobatic team Lang & Cravat. From 1932 to 1939 the team presented their act in vaudeville, carnivals, and circuses, and were even featured in Ringling Brothers. But in 1939 an infected finger forced Burt to abandon acrobatics. For the next three years, he worked at various menial jobs. Drafted into the army in 1942, he served three years, then went to New York City. While riding in an elevator with a Broadway producer who assumed he was an actor, he was asked to audition for a part in a play. Lancaster got the part and, although the play had a short run, it led to several movie offers. He signed a contract with producer Hal Wallis and moved to Hollywood.

Making his film debut as a prizefighter in *The Killers* (1946), Lancaster was an instant success with both the public and the critics. During the next two years, he made two other "tough guy" films before portraying the sensitive son of a war profiteer in the 1948 film adaptation of Arthur Miller's play *All My Sons*. That role represented quite a change for Lancaster, and again the critics were pleased. At about this time, he formed his own movie company, Norma Productions, and arranged for Warner Brothers to distribute his company's movies while he would appear in theirs. The happy result was that Warners distributed such swashbucklers as *The Flame and the Arrow* (1950) and *The Crimson Pirate* (1952), both throwbacks to the glorious days of Douglas Fairbanks, Sr. In these films Lancaster displayed his great acrobatic ability. He also put his athletic talent to use in *Jim Thorpe—All American* (1951), a biography of the famous football hero. Again showing his versatility, he appeared as Doc, the husband of brooding Shirley Booth in the 1952 film adaptation of William Inge's play *Come Back, Little Sheba*. The following year Lancaster received his first Academy Award nomination for best actor in *From Here to Eternity* (1953), playing Sgt. Warden, a "man's man who's also a ladies' man," to quote film critic Pauline Kael.

During the next several years, Lancaster continued to display the range of his acting talent, giving some of his best performances. He starred opposite Anna Magnani in *The Rose Tattoo* (1955) and Katharine Hepburn in *The Rainmaker* (1956). In *Sweet Smell of Success* (1957), he played an egomaniacal Broadway gossip columnist who used his column to advance or destroy careers. During this period he continued to portray action heroes in films such as *Vera Cruz* (1954), *Gunfight at the O.K. Corral* (1957), *Run Silent, Run Deep* (1960), and *The Unforgiven* (1958).

In *Elmer Gantry* (1960), he portrayed a revivalist preacher equally adept at selling salvation or vacuum cleaners. Expelled from the ministry for seducing another preacher's daughter, Gantry put his charm and eloquence to work as a traveling salesman. But he got back into the "religion business" by joining the troupe of a lovely evangelist (Jean Simmons). Lancaster's Gantry defined for all time the fast-talking, womanizing Bible Belt evangelist. His riveting performance took the Oscar for best actor, beating out Laurence Olivier and Spencer Tracy.

Two years later Lancaster once again expanded his dramatic repertoire by playing the lead in *Birdman of Alcatraz*, a convicted killer whose only companions during 40 years of solitary confinement were birds. It was a difficult part, one which afforded Lancaster little opportunity to assert his imposing physical presence. But he succeeded so well that he received his third nomination for best actor.

Lancaster's popularity declined in the 1960s and 1970s despite strong, perceptive performances in Luchino Visconti's *The Leopard* (1963), *The Professionals* (1966), *The Swimmer* (1968), Bernardo Bertolucci's *1900* (1976), and *Go Tell the Spartans* (1978). But he bounced back in 1980 as Lou, an aging small-time gangster in Louis Malle's masterpiece, *Atlantic City*. Lancaster's touching, finely etched performance earned him his fourth best actor nomination.

More recently Lancaster played the eccentric CEO of a multi-national corporation in Bill Forsyth's *Local Hero* (1983), and even parodied his own macho image in *Tough Guys* (1986), co-starring with his long-time friend Kirk Douglas.

Bibliography

Fishgall, Gary. *Against Type: The Biography of Burt Lancaster.* New York: Scribner, 1995.
Fury, David. *Cinema History of Burt Lancaster.* Minneapolis: Artist's, 1989.
Windeler, Robert. *Burt Lancaster.* New York: St. Martin's, 1984.

John Hayward
Robert Sprich

Lassie is the fictional female collie dog whose story became the subject of films, a radio show (1946-49), two TV series, animated cartoons, and even comic books. When author Eric Knight completed his novel *Lassie Come-Home* (1940), he probably had no idea he had just created a cultural icon that would support a canine dynasty into the next century. He had not even set out to write a full-length novel—his dog, Toots, was the inspiration for a short story that he later expanded into the novel at the request of a publisher.

The book was an immediate success and only a few months after its release California dog trainer Rudd Weatherwax heard a rumor on the MGM lot that the studio had just paid $10,000 for the rights to the story. He hurriedly went home to retrieve from an actor friend the collie named Pal that he had given him after he was unable to break his habit of chasing motorcycles. Pal auditioned for the lead role, but the part went to a female of show dog quality and he was hired only as the stunt dog. When the chosen star refused to swim across a river, however, Pal jumped right in and came out on the other side the star of the movie. Human stars of the film included Roddy McDowall, Donald Crisp, Edmund Gwenn, Nigel Bruce, Elsa Lanchester, and Elizabeth Taylor. Although it was originally treated as a B children's movie, when *Lassie Come Home* was previewed by MGM executives and studio head Louis B. Mayer, Mayer was reportedly moved to tears and immediately ordered more scenes shot to enhance the picture and an all-out effort by the publicity department to promote it.

After the success of *Lassie Come Home* (1943), Mayer had the dog's image added to MGM's gallery of motion-picture artists and six more movies were released: *Son of Lassie* (in which Pal starred with June Lockhart, 1944), *Courage of Lassie* (1946), *Hills of Home* (1948), *The Sun Comes Up* (1949), *Challenge to Lassie* (1950), and *The Painted Hills* (1951). Only the last was less than very successful. By the end of 1951, MGM felt that the Lassie phenomenon had run its course and released Pal and Weatherwax from their contract with all the rights to the name and trademark of Lassie in exchange for $40,000 the studio owed them.

But the phenomenon was not over, and after a successful period of public performances, Weatherwax was approached by television producer Bob Maxwell with an offer to have Pal film a pilot episode for a new show about a dog and his family. CBS in 1954 quickly picked up the new show, Campbell's Soup became a permanent sponsor, and the show, at first starring George Cleveland, Jan Clayton, and Tommy Rettig, was assigned the Sunday evening time slot it was to remain in for 17 years. While it was never the No. 1 show on television, it was always in the Top 20 and first in its time slot. When Rettig began to outgrow his part a new interest was introduced in the form of the orphan child Timmy, played by Jon Provost. But with the death in real life of actor George Cleveland in 1957, a complete cast change was made and the farm was sold to a new couple, Ruth and Paul Martin, who adopt Timmy. After one disastrous season with Cloris Leachman playing Ruth and Jon Shepodd playing Paul, the parents' parts were re-cast with June Lockhart and Hugh Reilly, and the family most people remember Lassie living with was complete for the period from 1959 to 1964. Ratings and soup sales coincided with the critics' assessment that this was an excellent show, and it won two Emmys in the first three years.

No matter who the family was, Lassie was always the star of the show. By the time Jon Provost joined the show, Pal was no longer playing Lassie; he was being played by Pal's own son, Lassie, Jr. But no one seemed to notice. The original Pal, around whom the image of the heroic dog was created and who in real life was credited with saving the lives of three people in a boating accident, died in 1958 at the age of 18.

In the 1964 season, the cast changed again, and Lassie, after a three-part farewell episode that sent the Martins to live in Australia, went to live first with neighbor Cully Wilson and then with Ranger Corey Stuart (Robert Bray) and began his Ranger years.

In 1971, the FCC ordered prime time moved back an hour, which effectively killed Lassie's time slot. CBS canceled the show, which promptly continued in syndication for two more years at a new time, 7:30 p.m., and with a new family, a farm family called the Holdens. Despite the updated family and a number of big name guest stars, however, the show did not seem to work and in September 1974 Lassie left the screen after 20 years and 592 episodes.

After Lassie left the air CBS created a Saturday-morning cartoon version called *Lassie's Rescue Rangers* in 1973, depicting Lassie as a kind of superdog. It was a show Rudd Weatherwax hated. In 1978, producer Jack Wrather tried to reassemble a cast for a new Lassie show, set in an urban environment and addressing contemporary issues, but none of the networks was interested in the show and the episodes filmed were patched together for a television movie. Another film, *The Magic of Lassie*, starring Jimmy Stewart, Stephanie Zimbalist, and Mickey Rooney, premiered in September of 1979 at Radio City Music Hall, the same place *Lassie Come Home* premiered in 1943, but this film just broke even. Another television show came in 1989, *The New Lassie*, with Will Nipper and Wendy Cox as the two children, who now live in the suburbs, and Dee Wallace Stone and Christopher Stone as the parents. The show did well in the ratings and was No. 2 in syndicated weekly children's programming, but the adults the sponsors wanted were not attracted and the series lasted only two seasons.

In 1991, *TV Guide* declared Lassie one of television's "unsinkable stars." The rights to Lassie are now owned by Broadway Video, the production company of *Saturday Night Live*. Another Lassie film was released in the summer of 1994 to good reviews. One of Lassie's young charges was now exchanging earrings with his girlfriend, but, as critic Roger Ebert said, "It's somehow reassuring these days, to see a movie where there's no problem Lassie can't solve." In 1997 another TV series premiered on the Animal Planet cable channel.

Bibliography

Collins, Ace. *Lassie: A Dog's Life—The First Fifty Years*. New York: Penguin, 1993.

Mary Ann Simet

Latinos and TV. While Latinos have made many inroads in other areas, there is a striking lack of U.S. Latinos in prime-time TV programs. In 1995, the number of Latinos working in the networks as characters on TV programs was said to be around 1 percent, "a decrease from 3 percent that Latinos represented in 1955 and the images of Latinos were more negative than those of other cultures or minorities" (Braxton and Breslauer). The words of the noted Latino actor Ricardo Montalban best characterize this situation: "At first, for a long time we were ignored. Today we are under represented, and often misrepresented."

Throughout the history of TV, Latinos have worked as producers, directors, characters, and writers. Not all Latinos represented on TV were in fact of Latino heritage. Further, many Latino characters were represented in stereotypical fashion. A historical treatment of Latinos in TV must begin with the *I Love Lucy* show of the 1950s. This program was produced by Desi Arnaz (1917-1986) and he also starred in the comedy with his then-wife Lucille Ball. The comedy featured the life of a Cuban band leader, Ricky Ricardo, and his zany American wife. In addition to being a success and leader of classic series, this show presented the first important Latino star and also served as a model for several full-length motion pictures.

In real life, Arnaz was an authentic Cuban bandleader who worked with the noted Xavier Cugat. Arnaz also was the musical director of *The Bob Hope Show*, after World War II. Along with Cugat, Arnaz was also a popularizer of Latin, in particular, Cuban music in the U.S. In terms of technical innovations for TV, Arnaz is remembered for introducing the TV sitcom three-camera method of production, which subsequently became widely used. Some have classified the Ricky character as typical of the so-called Hispanic male buffoon. In the show he was often depicted as being very handsome, a highly volatile Latin who frequently reverted to using Spanish with long chains of expletives. As late as 1991, in a special broadcast "Desi and Lucy: Before the Laughter" (CBS), he was described as an "irresponsible Latin lover."

In the 1970s, Alejandro Rey was featured as a playboy character—Latin-lover type—opposite Sally Field in ABC's comedy *The Flying Nun*. Another popular and yet controversial series of the decade was NBC's *Chico and the Man* (1974-78). In this comedy, Freddie Prinze, of Puerto Rican background, plays a Mexican American and starred alongside Jack Anderson in a series about two characters who work in a garage in East Los Angeles. The late '70s and early '80s brought a dramatic series, *CHIPS*, about the California Highway Patrol, which starred Erik Estrada. During the same period, ABC produced *Fantasy Island* with the noted Mexican actor Ricardo Montalban (1920-), who played Mr. Roarke and provided his island visitors with their most desired wishes. Montalban, born in Mexico City, played many roles on Broadway before going into films both in Mexico and the U.S. He was often cast as a typical "Latin lover." Early on, he was successful in obtaining several roles in episodes of *The Loretta Young Show*. Montalban has also been an important spokesperson for the establishment of better opportunities for Latinos in film and television.

In the '80s the short-lived comedy *a.k.a. Pablo* starred Latino comic Paul Rodriguez. The program also featured Hector Elizondo, who would later appear on TV during the late '80s and early '90s.

The '80s provided TV viewers with a few Latinos in dramatic as well as comedic roles. The first of these was *Hill Street Blues* on NBC, which starred Rene Enriquez, who played Lt. Ray Calletano in a police force series. From 1984 to 1989, noted Latino actor Edward James Olmos (1947-) played a police officer who headed the Miami police force on the popular series *Miami Vice*. Olmos, originally from Los Angeles, has worked as an actor, composer, producer and director. He began his entertainment career as a rock musician and has also had a successful career in the movies. Olmos is often seen as one of the most positive Latino characters on prime-time TV and film.

Latino Jimmy Smits starred in NBC's popular *L.A. Law*. After leaving *L.A. Law* in 1991, he went on to work in ABC's *NYPD Blue*. The '90s also provided viewers with such comedies as Fox's *House of Buggin*, which features John Leguizamo, who is also the producer of this comedy. Latino comedy in the '90s can be best exemplified by *Culture Clash*, which includes Herbert Siguenza, Richard Montoya, and Ric Salinas. Latinos have also had some important

roles in science fiction and science-oriented programs such as *Star Trek*, *Voyager*, and *Sea Quest*. Robert Beltran has worked in *Star Trek* and Marco Sanchez has been featured in *Sea Quest*.

Other Latinos who have worked on prime-time TV are Liz Torres in *The John Larroquette Show*, Rita Moreno in *The Cosby Mysteries*, and Daphne Zuñiga of *Melrose Place*. From 1990 to 1991, Elizabeth Peña starred along with Danny Sheridan in NBC's *Shannon's Deal*. Some cite the lack of Latinos on TV to be associated with the failures of such features as ABC's *Viva Valdez* (1976), ABC's *a.k.a. Pablo* (1984), and CBS's *Frannie's Twin* (1992). While there are some exceptions and breaks in the traditional representation of Latinos with stereotypes and negative images, there is still much work to be done in promoting Latinos in all areas of the television industry.

Bibliography

Braxton, Greg, and Jim Breslauer. "Casting the Spotlight on TV's Brownout." *Los Angles Times* 5 March 1995.

Hadley-Garcia, George. *Hispanic Hollywood. The Latins in Motion Pictures.* New York: Carol, 1990.

Reyes, Luis, and Peter Rubie. *Hispanics in Hollywood: An Encyclopedia of Film and Television.* New York: Garland, 1994.

Subervi, Federico. "Media." *The Hispanic American Almanac.* Ed. N. Kanellos. Detroit: Gale, 1993.

Subervi, Federico, et al. "Television." *Handbook of Hispanic Cultures in the U.S.: Sociology.* General ed. N. Kanellos. Houston: Arté Publico, 1994. 312-17.

Rafael Chabrán

Laugh-In (1968-1973) first appeared as an hour-long special on NBC. The special was a hit and NBC premiered the series as a mid-season replacement in January of 1968. The hour-long show was an immediate and unqualified success and won an Emmy for its 1968-69 season.

The hosts, straightman Dan Rowan (1922-1986) and comic Dick Martin (1922-), served as go-betweens for the audience and the rest of the show. Their more traditional comedy routines centered the show in familiar territory. *Laugh-In* was a burlesque-styled revue show, a sort of *Hellzapoppin'* built on contemporary events and social commentary.

Aside from sociopolitical humor, the show pushed the boundaries of television censorship by dealing in topics such as sexuality, drugs, and the Vietnam War and using sexual innuendo and double entendre. The show was notorious enough to warrant a full-time censor, the first such incidence in television history.

A large cast of supporting performers changed as the years went by. Among the more notable were Goldie Hawn, who portrayed a "dumb blonde" in the first seasons and went on to win an Oscar for *Butterflies Are Free* (1970) and has had a long and successful film career since then. Lily Tomlin appeared sporadically in films, though her greatest success has been with her one-woman shows. Henry Gibson came to the show as an established supporting actor and continued working as such after the show's end. In addition to the regulars, the show stitched in numerous guests for one-liners and cutaways labeled "Quickies." Guests were unannounced, but instantly recognizable, and ranged from Richard Nixon to Ringo Starr.

The success of the show created a few imitators, *Hee-Haw* being the longest lasting and *Turn-On* being the briefest. Other variety shows tried to adapt part of the *Laugh-In* style with varying degrees of success. It also brought numerous catchphrases to the American consciousness, including "You bet your sweet bippy," "Look that up in your Funk and Wagnall's," "Sock it to me" (from the song "Respect"), and several others. *Laugh-In* was one of the first shows to have explicit social commentary at its core, and as such marks entertainment television's coming of age.

Bibliography

Brodhead, James E. *Inside Laugh-In #3*. New York: New American Library, 1969.

Maltin, Leonard. *Movie Comedy Teams*. New York: New American Library, 1985 (1974, 1970).

Original Cast. *Direct from Beautiful Downtown Burbank: Laugh-In '69*. California: Reprise Records, 1969.

Terrace, Vincent. *Encyclopedia of Television Series, Pilots, and Specials, 1937-1973*. Vol. 1. New York: Zoetrope, 1985.

——. *Encyclopedia of Television Series, Pilots, and Specials, 1974-1984*. Vol. 2. New York: Zoetrope, 1985.

Benjamin K. Urish

Laverne and Shirley (1976-1983) was a tremendously popular situation comedy set in Milwaukee in the late 1950s, about two twenty-something working-class women who lived and worked together. Primarily a physical comedy, *Laverne and Shirley* debuted in the No. 1 spot with the highest Nielsen ratings in a decade of television. It remained among the top two positions in annual ratings for four years, holding the top position after the 1978-79 television season. A number of factors served to make this program a hit from the very beginning. The blue-collar status of the two central characters, who fought fiercely for and proved their independence as women in the 1950s, appealed to viewers across social boundaries. The program made viewers laugh at being human because the central characters, as well as their co-stars, played everyday characters who had problems and feelings like anyone else.

The characters of Laverne and Shirley made their debut in an episode of the very popular television sitcom *Happy Days* (see entry), as tough-girl characters who were the dates of lead characters Richie Cunningham and Fonzie (Arthur Fonzarelli). *Happy Days* producer Garry Marshall, brother of Penny Marshall (Laverne), decided to develop these female characters and created the idea of *Laverne and Shirley* as a 1970s version of *I Love Lucy*, because he realized that no one was doing low physical comedy on television in the mid 1970s. *Laverne and Shirley* is a rare example of a spinoff that proved to be as popular as the parent series. Fonzie occasionally appeared on *Laverne and Shirley*, showing up to visit his female friends and adding to the popularity of the spinoff program. *Laverne and Shirley*'s weekly time-slot between *Happy Days* and *Three's Company*, another popular sitcom, also helped to boost its viewing numbers.

Laverne and Shirley's characters are among television's first feminists because of their constant battle to make it on their own and to be recognized as individuals. The theme song, "Making Our Dreams Come True" (by Charles Fox and Norman Gimbel, and sung by Cyndi Grecco), reiterates the idea of independence that characterizes *Laverne and Shirley*.

In 1978-79, the show suffered a drop in the ratings, causing the producers to seek new material, and ultimately a new location, for the program. In the fall of 1980, the entire *Laverne and Shirley* crew moved to Burbank, CA. Frank and Edna DeFazio were the first characters to move, opening a restaurant named Cowboy Bill's. The others soon followed, all attempting to better their situations in a new environment. In Burbank, the title characters both took jobs at Bradburn's Department Store. Many of these California episodes centered on Laverne and Shirley attempting to make it as movie actresses.

In 1982, Cindy Williams (Shirley) became pregnant and was written off the show. Her character married an army medic named Walter Meany, who was assigned duty overseas. Penny Marshall's character went it alone for several episodes, with Williams appearing in occasional episodes, but the loss of the consistently funny chemistry between Laverne and Shirley, coupled with rising competition from other programs such as *The A-Team*, made the program wane in popularity. The show went off the air in the spring.

Although it was a huge success, *Laverne and Shirley* wasn't without its critics: some critics referred to the show as TV junk food. In 1976, a *Time* article claimed that *Laverne and Shirley* should be voted the worst new sitcom for "sheer witlessness." Regardless of what critics said about the program, the public loved it. A Saturday morning cartoon version of Laverne and Shirley even aired from October 1981 to September 1983.

Bibliography

Ball, Aimee L. "Laverne and Shirley." *Redbook* Oct. 1976: 4+.

Berman, Ronald. "Sitcoms." *Journal of Aesthetic Education* 21.1 (Spring 1987): 5-19.

Hoey, Robert. *Laverne and Shirley: The Only Fan Site on The Web*. http://www.geocities.com/Hollywood/Lot/6143/indexnav.htm, accessed 7 March 1998.

Jones, Gerard. *Honey, I'm Home*. New York: Grove Weidenfeld, 1992.

Marc, David. *Comic Visions: Television Comedy and American Culture*. Boston: Unwin Hyman, 1989.

McNeil, Alex. *Total Television: A Comprehensive Guide to Programming from 1948 to the Present*. New York: Penguin, 1991.

Newcomb, Horace, and Robert S. Alley. *The Producer's Medium*. New York: Oxford UP, 1983.

Ross, Ronald E. *Character Visualization in 1970's Television Situation Comedy*. Ph.D. diss. U of Missouri-Columbia, 1993.

Mary Anne Hansen

Lawn Ornaments. Lawn and garden ornaments have a long history in elite cultures, including the courtyard traditions of ancient Rome, Islamic Spain, and Renaissance Italy, the "eye-catcher" statuary and architectural follies of 18th-century England, as well as Zen-inspired Japanese tea-gardens. Aspects of each of these have influenced popular ornaments. A medieval vernacular tradition that continues is the household and wayside religious shrines which can be found in Europe and in Roman Catholic neighborhoods in large cities and rural areas of such regions as Quebec, Iowa, Wisconsin, and the Hispanic Southwest.

The display of popular nonreligious objects such as flamingos, birdbaths, and planters coincides with the development of the vernacular American open front yard in the 1870s. Suburban grounds began to imitate elite traditions with iron deer, concrete birdbaths, gazing globes, and summerhouse gazebos. On smaller lots, decorative hitching posts (the well-known jockey or stable boy still persists) and birdbaths surrounded by geometric floral plantings were very likely the earliest, along with iron and wicker lawn furniture available from Sears Roebuck in the 1890s. In the early 20th century, designs for jigsawed "garden sticks" were featured in popular magazines and industrial arts classes. Popular subjects were nursery rhyme characters, lines of ducklings or skunks as well as more complex whirligigs, miniature windmills, and carts. These have continued, often responding to popular themes, such as Walt Disney characters. Recycled objects were utilized from the 19th century on, often with an air of nostalgia as wagon wheels, milk cans, and other farm implements became obsolete. Following World War II there was an efflorescence of junk ornaments, especially fences and planter-rings made from tires, planters fashioned from hot-water-heater tanks, wringer washing-machine tubs, toilets, and old-fashioned bathtubs up-ended to form grottos for displaying religious images in front yards. A significant characteristic of all popular American yard ornaments is the orientation to the passersby rather than for private vistas, as in the elite traditions.

In the 1960s, plastics and fiberglass technologies immensely enlarged the lawn ornament industry, although not diminishing the homemade cottage products. Flamingos, which had become popular in the 1920s as jigsawed figures with springsteel necks, flourished in three dimensions, and by the 1980s gained ambivalent meanings as both the butt of ethnic joke cycles, e.g., "What do flamingos have on their front lawns? Pink (ethnic minority of your choice)"; and at the same time becoming a vogue among landscape architects and designers. Old bathtubs being no longer available, fiberglass reproductions were manufactured to provide cowls for the Blessed Virgin Mary. Plastics also made possible the more limited but nonetheless popular reproduction of authentic Renaissance and oriental statuary and fountains in museum shops and garden supply catalogs.

The variety and originality of vernacular and popular lawn ornaments defies classification, but some of the more common types are: statuary, wooden silhouettes, planters, rural mailboxes, birdhouses, whirligigs, wind socks, and "found objects" such as driftwood and old machinery. There are definite regional, ethnic, religious and occupational subcategories. For example, south Florida shows a preponderance of nautical themes, while midwestern farms will often have images of the livestock they produce. Concrete geese, elaborately dressed in a variety of costumes, became a popular regional type in the 1980s along the upper Ohio River. Italian, Hispanic, and Eastern European Roman Catholic neighborhoods have shrines and grottos.

Bibliography

Curtis, J., and D. Helgren. "Yard Ornaments in the American Landscape: A Survey along the Florida Keys." *Journal of Regional Culture* 4.1.

Grampp, C. "Social Meanings of Residential Gardens." *The Meaning of Gardens*. Ed. M. Francis and R. Hester. Boston: MIT, 1990.

Moore, K. "Gazing Globes." *Fine Gardening* 23.

Schroeder, F. "The Democratic Yard and Garden." *Outlaw Aesthetics*. Bowling Green, OH: Bowling Green State U Popular P, 1977.

Fred E. H. Schroeder

Lawrence Welk Show, The (1955-1982), was a cultural mainstay on American television for its 27-year run. Combining cover versions of classic Broadway and movie soundtracks, and even the "mod" sound of groups like the Byrds and the Association, the show became a cipher for translating and performing the cultural norms.

The show debuted opposite Phil Silvers's *Your Show of Shows*. As it happened, Welk's popularity actually pushed its competition off the air. Welk (see entry), already in his fifties when the show debuted, had been a bandleader and accordion maestro since the early days of radio in the 1930s. By the time the show premiered, Welk's "champagne music" style had already developed. This style, like the bubbles of champagne, was light, fun, and entertaining. In 1955 Welk and his band had their first and only No. 1 hit—the song "Calcutta," which went to gold later that decade.

Lawrence Welk ended his show in 1982, and died in March 1992, at 89 years of age. The show continues as a favorite in syndication on many PBS stations, and former members of the show such as Jo Ann Castle, Myron Floren, Ken Delo, and others continue to tour in the summers in tribute to Welk.

The show is also remembered for its wealth of talent, both orchestrally and vocally. Though none of the groups or individuals had highly noted careers, many did modestly well in and out of the Welk circle. The Lennon Sisters—Janet, Kathy, Dianne, and Peggy—who were discovered by Welk's son Larry, had a modestly successful recording career because of Welk's influence and their talent. Pete Fountain continued from Welk's show to become a famous clarinetist. Jo Ann Castle still remains a fabulous ragtime pianist, touring the country as both a solo act and part of the Welk ensemble.

Bibliography

Katz, Susan. *The Lawrence Welk Scrapbook*. New York: Grosset, 1978.

Sanders, Coyne Steven. *Champagne Music: The Lawrence Welk Show*. New York: St. Martin's, 1985.

Welk, Lawrence. *You're Never Too Young.* Englewood Cliffs: Prentice-Hall 1981.

Mark K. Fulk

See also
Mystery Awards
Spy Fiction

le Carré, John (David John Moore Cornwell) (1931-), British author, has turned spy fiction into an established subgenre of the novel and placed himself securely in the hierarchy of John Buchan, Eric Ambler, and Graham Greene. Le Carré's best work includes *The Spy Who Came in from the Cold* (1963), which Graham Greene considered the best espionage novel he had ever read, the novel that established le Carré's reputation in both the U.S. and Britain and earned him the Edgar Award. Other significant works include *A Small Town in Germany* (1968); the three novels that form the Smiley trilogy (*Tinker, Tailor, Soldier, Spy*, 1974; *The Honorable Schoolboy*, 1977; and *Smiley's People*, 1979); *The Looking-Glass War* (1965); *A Perfect Spy* (1990); and *The Night Manager* (1993).

The major themes of le Carré's fiction are the search for identity, the prevalence of secrets (family and institutional), and the inevitability of betrayal, along with a larger sense of disillusionment about the moral underpinnings of nationalism and the alliance of Western powers since the onset of the Cold War. The central character of his most successful novels is George Smiley, the scholar turned spy who has worked himself up to a position of high leadership in British intelligence, M.I. 6. Smiley's sustained rivalry with his opposite number, Karla the Soviet spymaster, his uneasy alliance with his fellow agents, and his troubled marriage constitute ongoing storylines that undergird le Carré's broader fictional vision. The pairing of the two adversaries is meant to underscore fundamental likenesses between them, thus calling into question the legitimacy of East-West enmity and the high ground that the West has always used to validate its spying activities. In recent years, le Carré has had no trouble adapting his spy fiction to the end of the Cold War in such novels as *Our Game* (1995), *The Tailor of Panama* (1996), and *Single & Single* (1999).

A commercially successful movie of *The Spy Who Came in from the Cold* with Richard Burton as the protagonist, Alec Leamas, was made in 1965; later movies have included *The Little Drummer Girl* (1984), a drama of the Israeli-Palestinian conflict, and *The Russia House* (1990), with Michelle Pfeiffer as the Russian spy who entraps a British publisher, played by Sean Connery.

Bibliography

Barley, Tony. *Taking Sides: The Fiction of John le Carré.* Philadelphia: Open UP, 1986.

Beene, Lynn Dianne. *John le Carré.* New York: Twayne, 1992.

Bloom, Harold, ed. *John le Carré: Modern Critical Views.* New York: Chelsea, 1987.

Monaghan, David. *Smiley's Circus: A Guide to the Secret World of John le Carré.* New York: St. Martin's, 1986.

Wolfe, Peter. *Corridors of Deceit: The World of John le Carré.* Bowling Green, OH: Bowling Green State U Popular P, 1987.

Nicholas Ranson

Leave It to Beaver (1957-1963) was a family sitcom focused on the Cleavers: father Ward (Hugh Beaumont), mother June (Barbara Billingsley), and sons Wally (Tony Dow), and Theodore, also known as "Beaver" (Jerry Mathers). Considered today as little more than high camp fun, and often grouped with programs that David Marc refers to as "Aryan melodramas," the Cleaver family remains one of the most popular in TV history for various reasons.

Although Beaver was the cute kid that brought viewers in, Ward Cleaver, played convincingly by minister-turned-actor Hugh Beaumont, was the show's heart. Unlike other TV fathers, Ward had a pretty solid back story which helped explain his vacillation between "old-fashioned horse whipping" and modern psychological parenting, a struggle being experienced by 1950s viewers as well. Money didn't come easily to Ward, who was often seen hard at work—albeit at an undefined job—in his office or den. Ward tried to balance love and respect while teaching his boys the value of hard work.

Contrary to popular myth, Ward was not a perfect father. Often against June's wishes and warnings, Ward would dispense bad advice, inadvertently set a bad example, or lose his temper with his children. Unlike Jim Anderson, Ward did not always know best; however, Ward was willing to learn. The episodes ended with love and kisses because Ward and June were able to empathize with their children, who also made an effort to see their parents' point of view. Thus, kids appreciated Beaver and Wally's struggle to understand their parents, and parents appreciated Ward and June's struggle to understand their kids.

Also, this show had touches of realism. While the Cleavers, like other fifties TV families, were too perfect, the rest of their home town, Mayfield, was quite dysfunctional. Town terror Eddie Haskell (Ken Osmond), for instance, was an incorrigible delinquent.

Series creators Bob Mosher and Joe Connelly, who both came from single-parent homes, paid special attention to the experiences of their—and their children's—childhoods in creating episode plots. While the problems on *Leave It to Beaver* are often considered mundane, many consider them funny morality plays that speak to universal issues. Today's family sitcoms may have more relevant problems, but the themes of peer pressure, dating, and getting along in school are just as real today as they were in the 1950s. Furthermore, several *Leave It to Beaver* episodes featured more relevant topics, such as homelessness, divorce, and alcoholism.

Today, the Mayfield characters—particularly Eddie Haskell and Beaver Cleaver—show up frequently as popular culture icons displayed on T-shirts or trendy greeting cards. A mid-1980s CBS TV movie, *Still the Beaver,* launched a short-lived syndicated revival titled *The New Leave It to Beaver.*

Bibliography

Brooks, Tim, and Earle Marsh. *The Complete Directory to Prime Time Network TV Shows, 1946-Present.* New York: Ballantine, 1992.

Jones, Gerard. *Honey, I'm Home: Sitcoms Selling the American Dream*. New York: St. Martin's, 1992.

Marc, David. *Comic Visions: Television Comedy and American Culture*. Boston: Unwin Hyman, 1989.

Michael B. Kassel

Led Zeppelin (1968-1980), the British quartet considered the godfathers of heavy metal/hard rock, is the second-biggest-selling act of all time (outsold only by the Beatles), with overall sales of over 63 million recordings. The group included Jimmy Page (1944-), guitars; Robert Plant (1948-), lead vocals; John Paul Jones (1946-), bass and keyboards; and John Bonham (1948-1980), drums. Their impact on American rock 'n' roll cannot be overestimated.

They were signed to Atlantic Records in 1969 and released their debut album *Led Zeppelin*. With its unique sound, a hybrid of blues, and hard and acid rock, the album was an immediate success and reached the Top 10 of the U.S. pop charts. The band also toured, receiving rave audience reviews as well as critical acclaim.

The band's second album, *Led Zeppelin II* (also 1969), garnered the band its only gold Top 10 and gold single, "Whole Lotta Love." By the time they released *Led Zeppelin IV* (also known as the *Four Symbols*, the *Runes Album*, or *ZOSO*) in 1971, the band was well on its way to becoming superstars. *Led Zeppelin IV* is the band's best-known album (charting at No. 2), containing such classics as "Black Dog," "Rock 'n' Roll," and the epic eight-minute "Stairway to Heaven."

Their first No. 1 album, *Houses of the Holy* (1973), showed Led Zeppelin expanding on their musical repertoire by including hints of reggae and soul. The band formed their own label, Swan Song, in 1974, which released subsequent Led Zeppelin albums as well as records by the highly successful hard rock group Bad Company.

Led Zeppelin recorded and released the double album *Physical Graffiti* in 1975. Again, the group showed its flair for the experimental with this album, its sound (especially Page's unique sitar work) making it the most diverse album in their career. This album also spawned one of Led Zeppelin's signature songs, "Kashmir." Another No. 1 album, *Presence*, followed in 1976; it contained the 10-minute opus "Achilles Last Stand." The band released the concert film and soundtrack album *The Song Remains the Same* (taken from a show in New York City in 1973). *In through the Out Door* was released in 1979; Led Zeppelin used an unusual marketing ploy for this album, releasing it with six different sleeves.

In 1980, the group embarked on its first full-scale European tour in seven years. However, the band was struck by tragedy in September when drummer John Bonham was found dead, having choked in his sleep after a drinking bout. The band decided not to continue as Led Zeppelin but released *Coda,* an album comprised of various unreleased material, in 1982, which again put the group in the Top 10.

The 1980s and 1990s saw the band members embark on various successful solo activities, including tours, albums, and session work. In 1985, the surviving members of Led Zeppelin regrouped for a short performance at the Live Aid festival with Genesis drummer Phil Collins. The band performed in 1988 (with John Bonham's son Jason) for a short set at Madison Square Garden in New York for Atlantic Records' 40th anniversary; they again performed for a five-song set at Jason Bonham's wedding reception.

Page and Plant performed without Jones for a highly successful tour and album. Their MTV special, "Unledded," was one of MTV's highest-rated programs, and their album *No Quarter* (1994) debuted at No. 4, going platinum within a month of its release. A Led Zeppelin-related album, *Kashmir, The Symphonic Led Zeppelin* (an album of Led Zeppelin songs done in a symphonic style), and a collection of old radio recordings were released in 1997. The radio recordings, released as Led Zeppelin's *The BBC Sessions*, charted at No. 12 and went platinum. Despite having only one Top 10 single in their entire history, Led Zeppelin remains the most successful album-oriented rock 'n' roll band in history.

Bibliography

Cole, Richard, and Richard Trubo. *Stairway to Heaven: Led Zeppelin Uncensored*. Scranton: HarperCollins, 1992.

Davis, Stephen. *Hammer of the Gods: The Led Zeppelin Saga*. New York: Boulevard, 1997.

Halfin, Ross, ed. *The Photographer's Led Zeppelin*. Los Angeles: Two Thirteen Sixty-One, 1995.

Kendall, Paul, and Dave Lewis, ed. *Led Zeppelin in Their Own Words*. New York: Omnibus, 1995.

Rees, Dafydd, and Luke Crampton. *Encyclopedia of Rock Stars*. New York: DK, 1996.

Robert G. Weiner

Ledbetter, Huddie ("Leadbelly") (1889-1949), also known as Walter Boyd, but better known as Leadbelly for his strength and deep voice, was perhaps America's most notorious and influential folk singer. He was born in 1885, or 1889 (there is some dispute) near Mooringsport, LA. His parents owned 65 acres of land and Leadbelly was a prodigious worker.

His mother and two uncles were musicians and taught him to play. Eventually, he played piano, mandolin, and accordion, as well as the guitar. Soon he was drifting to Shreveport's Red Light District to play piano, always with a Colt snuggled in his belt. He drifted on to Dallas, where he met Blind Lemon Jefferson (see entry) and performed with him. Like Blind Lemon, he also employed flamenco flourishes in his playing. In spite of his growing musical success, he returned to farming each summer near New Boston, TX.

Here began a series of imprisonments (for assault and murder) and escapes that led to his incarceration in a Texas labor camp in 1920. Even in prison, however, Leadbelly was encouraged to sing and was brought out as a showpiece for guests. One of those guests was the governor of Texas, Pat M. Neff. On January 15, 1925, Governor Neff pardoned Leadbelly, although it is fair to note that there is a dispute over whether Leadbelly was pardoned or had served his full term.

Unfortunately, in 1930, five men jumped Leadbelly. He wounded them in self-defense but was sentenced to ten years at hard labor. Once again a plea for mercy managed to get him pardoned. This time his plea was recorded by John and Alan Lomax, two ethnomusicologists, and presented to Governor O. K. Allen of Louisiana, who pardoned Leadbelly in August of 1934.

Leadbelly and John Lomax then began a 6,000-mile tour of the South, including its prisons. Leadbelly acted as Lomax's informant and managed to elicit valuable musical performances for him. He knew which questions to ask and often began singing himself to prime the pump.

After the tour, Leadbelly went to New York, where he became the darling of the sophisticated set. He did, however, have one more prison term to serve, again for assault, in 1939-40. He had a radio show from time to time and performed in many settings. Recordings of these programs demonstrate his ease in conversation and ability to communicate with an audience. He played his 12-string guitar and sang in a primitive and powerful style. There is some dispute about his ability as a blues singer and his "watering down" of his style in Greenwich Village. His attempt in 1936 to play blues for a black audience failed, and few black artists appear to have followed in his stylistic footsteps. However, his recorded vocals leave no doubt about his musical ability and his well-deserved reputation.

Bibliography

Gammond, Peter. *Oxford Companion to Popular Music.* New York: Oxford UP, 1991.

Herzhaft, Gérard. *Encyclopedia of the Blues.* Fayetteville: U of Arkansas P, 1992

Larkin, Colin, ed. *The Guinness Encyclopedia of Popular Music.* Middlesex, U.K.: Guinness, 1992.

Wilson, Charles Reagan, and William Ferris, eds. *Encyclopedia of Southern Culture.* Chapel Hill: U of North Carolina P, 1989.

Wolfe, Charles K. *The Life and Legend of Leadbelly.* New York. HarperCollins, 1992.

Frank A. Salamone

Lee, Spike (1956-), is the most important African-American filmmaker of our generation and one of the finest directors working in America today. After fighting his way into the white-dominated movie business with the independent hit *She's Gotta Have It* (1986), Lee has managed to use major studio financing and distribution in order to write, direct, and act in original films that tackle such controversial issues as interracial relationships and ideological divisions in the African-American community. Lee has also proven to be an astute businessperson, aggressively marketing his films through merchandise (such as the "X" baseball hats that accompanied *Malcolm X*) and published production diaries. Lee's ability to create intelligent and formally innovative films, and to promote such films to a mass audience, defies "high concept" contemporary filmmaking and is an encouraging sign for the future of cinema as art rather than product.

Lee was born Shelton Jackson Lee in Atlanta, the oldest of five children. Culture played an integral part in the Lee household; Lee's father, Bill, is a distinguished jazz bass violinist who has scored several of his son's films, and his mother, Jacqueline Shelton Lee, taught African-American literature to high school students. (She also gave her son the nickname "Spike.")

In 1977, two significant events occurred in Lee's life; his mother passed away, and in the summer of 1977 he made his first film, *Last Hustle in Brooklyn*, a Super-8 work that incorporated documentary footage of the looting in Harlem and Brooklyn the day after the New York blackout.

After his graduation from Morehouse in 1979, Lee spent the summer interning for Columbia Pictures, and then attended film school at New York University's Tisch School of the Arts. At Tisch, Lee met cinematographer Ernest Dickerson, whose talents would later make indelible contributions to Lee's films. Lee's first graduate school film was *The Answer* (1980), a 20-minute parody of D. W. Griffith's *Birth of a Nation* (1915), and in his three years at NYU (1979-82) Lee made two other short films, including *Sarah* (1981) and his hour-long thesis project, *Joe's Bed-Stuy Barbershop: We Cut Heads* (1982). *Joe's Bed-Stuy Barbershop*, in particular, earned Lee serious attention, winning him a student director's Academy Award from the NYU faculty and a broadcast date for the film on New York Public Television.

Lee earned his master's degree from NYU in 1982 and for the next two years worked at a number of odd jobs in order to earn money for the production of one of his original screenplays. He began *Messenger* in 1984, a film, in his words, about "a bike messenger who has to become the head of his household when his mom dies of a heart attack." But after dealing with exorbitant union costs and an unethical producer who failed to find money to complete the film, Lee was forced to shut the *Messenger* shoot down and lost $50,000 in personal money and private donations in the process. Lee still describes the failure of the personal, semi-autobiographical *Messenger* as the most painful moment of his filmmaking career.

In 1985, Lee founded his own production company, 40 Acres and a Mule Filmworks, and began work on a new project, *She's Gotta Have It*. With only $12,000 in the bank, Lee raised money during production and post-production through a combination of grants (including $18,000 from the New York State Council of the Arts), loans, and personal donations (including a small stipend from Bill Cosby). *She's Gotta Have It* was economically shot in twelve days, and post-production lasted two months; its ultimate cost was $175,000. After earning praise for the film at the San Francisco Film Festival, and winning the *Prix de la jeunesse* for best new film at Cannes, Lee sold *She's Gotta's* distribution rights to Island for $475,000, and the movie proved to be a big hit with art-house and African-American spectators, earning over $8 million at the box office.

Based on the success of *She's Gotta Have It,* Lee moved 40 Acres and a Mule Filmworks into its own building in the Fort Greene section of Brooklyn. He also went into production on *School Daze* (1988), directing the shoot at Morehouse College and Atlanta University. When the film began to exceed the small $4 million budget provided by Island, Columbia bought the project and financed its completion cost of $6.5 million. *School Daze* is an ambitious examination of the light- and dark-skin tensions between African Americans at a fictional southern black college.

After leaving Columbia over *School Daze's* botched distribution, Lee went to Universal for *Do the Right Thing*

(1989), a powerful chronicle of the disintegration of social relations between whites and blacks in New York City's Bedford-Stuyvesant neighborhood.

Mo' Better Blues (1990), Lee's fourth film, was designed as his reaction to movies by whites about black musicians, such as *Round Midnight* (1986) and *Bird* (1988). *Mo' Better Blues* concentrates on Bleek Gilliam (Denzel Washington), an egotistical but supremely talented trumpeter, and his unstable relationships with the other members of his band.

Lee returned to the topic of black-white (and black-Italian) interaction with his next film, *Jungle Fever* (1991), an explicit examination of interracial sexual relationships. Some reviewers found *Jungle Fever* challenging and exciting; other reviewers were less complimentary (and less insightful), however, and *Jungle Fever* only brought moderate crowds into theaters.

Lee's next film was his most ambitious to date, a movie version of *The Autobiography of Malcolm X*. In its preproduction and production stages, the *Malcolm X* (1993) project involved Lee in a number of public controversies. After first persuading veteran director Norman Jewison to give up his position on a Malcolm X film already under studio development, Lee was then censured in the press by commentators who disagreed with his belief that only a black director could do justice to *The Autobiography*.

Crooklyn (1994) was an affectionate, semi-autobiographical portrait of a family growing up in middle-class Brooklyn in the 1970s. (Unfortunately, the film did poorly at the box office.) Lee's 12th feature film, *He Got Game* (1998), focuses on one of his great loves, basketball. In addition to his feature films, Lee has also directed music videos, commercials, and short films for MTV and *Saturday Night Live*. Lee has also branched out into other ventures, including his own New York City clothes boutique and his own comic book imprint, "Comics from Spike," through Dark Horse publishing.

Bibliography

Dyson, Michael Eric. "Film Noir." *Tikkun* 4.5 (1989): 75-78.

Guerrero, Ed. *Framing Blackness: The African American Image in Film.* Philadelphia: Temple UP, 1993.

Klein, Joe. "The City Politic: Spiked?" *New York* 26 June 1989: 14-15.

Lee, Spike. *Five for Five: The Films of Spike Lee.* New York: Stewart, Tabori, & Chang, 1991.

——. *Gotta Have It: Inside Guerrilla Filmmaking.* New York: Simon & Schuster, 1987.

Perkins, Eric. "Renewing the African American Cinema: The Films of Spike Lee." *Cineaste* 17.4 (1990): 4-8.

Craig Fischer

Lee, Stan (1922-), American comic book writer, editor, art director, promoter, and "father of Marvel Comics" (see entry), was one of America's more influential figures in the literature of comic books. Born Stanley Lieber, Lee began his comics career in 1940 at his uncle Martin Goodman's Timely Comics. By the mid-1940s, Lee was Timely's editor-in-chief and main writer, and even that early in his career, he

Photo courtesy of Popular Culture Library, Bowling Green State University, Bowling Green, OH.

demonstrated a propensity for promoting comics (as evident in his 1947 book *Secrets Behind the Comics*). For the most part, however, Lee's career during the 1940s and 1950s was not very distinguished, possibly because he was required to follow Goodman's publishing philosophy of saturating the market with comic books that took advantage of the latest trends. Lee's workload was so massive during this period that he began developing what later was known as the "Marvel method" of writing comics: giving an artist only a plot synopsis of a story, which Lee (or another scripter) would caption and dialogue after the story's pencilled art was completed. Usually a story's artist collaborated with Lee in developing its plot, but artists such as Jack Kirby (see entry) and Steve Ditko (1926-) often plotted stories by themselves.

In 1961, Lee and artist Jack Kirby produced the first issue of *Fantastic Four* and ushered in "the Marvel Age of Comics." Over the next three years Lee and his "bullpen" of artists and secondary scripters co-created such characters as the Hulk, Spider-man, the X-Men, Thor, Iron Man, Dr. Strange, and Daredevil, laying the foundation for a revolution in the superhero genre: "super heroes with super problems." Unlike those of other companies and earlier times, Marvel's superheroes bickered, faced handicaps, and struggled with self-doubts and inner conflicts. Although his role in actually creating characters and stories during this time has generated much controversy over the last decade, there can be no doubt that Lee (as editor-in-chief) was responsible for allowing all of Marvel's superheroes to co-exist in one universe, for shamelessly promoting those superheroes through columns in the comics and through the Merry Marvel Marching Society fan club, and for infusing his scripts with a very witty and endearing writing style.

In the late 1960s, Lee became publisher of Marvel Comics, and since then his output as a writer has dwindled to the point that now he rarely writes more than the syndicated Spider-man newspaper comic strip. Since the mid-1970s, however, Lee has very much been the visible representative of Marvel Comics on the lecture circuit, on television and radio (providing introductions and narration for Marvel programming), at promotional events and news conferences, and at comics conventions. Currently he works in Hollywood, overseeing attempts to make movies, cartoons, and television series based on those superheroes he helped to create in the 1960s.

Bibliography

Goulart, Ron, ed. *The Encyclopedia of American Comics.* New York: Facts on File, 1990.

Horn, Maurice, ed. *The World Encyclopedia of Comics.* Vol. 4. New York: Chelsea, 1983.

Daryl R. Coats

Legal Mysteries, complete with stirring courtroom scenes, have long been part of American popular literature. Legal mysteries combine an interest in the investigative aspect of criminal cases with the intellectual challenge of putting together a defense or prosecution, the marshalling of evidence, the interrogation of witnesses, and the vindication or condemnation of the defendant. Too, such stories address the larger question of justice in contemporary society.

Early fiction about lawyers featured both heroic do-gooders—men from small towns with good Protestant values—and sinister pettifoggers, citified characters who exploited opponents and clients alike. Frederick W. Thomas's *Clinton Bradshaw or, The Adventures of a Lawyer* (1835) and Thomas H. Shreve's *Drayton: A Story of American Life* (1851) are noteworthy examples. In the late 19th and early 20th centuries, the image of heroic attorneys remained largely unchanged, but villainous ones came to be portrayed as corporate tools or shysters. Lawyers affiliated with big business appeared in Albion W. Tourgee's *With Gauge and Swallow, Attorneys* (1889), Rex E. Beach's *The Spoilers* (1905), and several popular novels by Winston Churchill. Shysters were given an ethnic tinge, predominantly Jews and Irish Catholics, and were depicted disparagingly.

The most intriguing turn-of-the-century fictional lawyer was Randolph Mason, the creation of Melville Davisson Post. A social Darwinist, Mason specialized in criminal defense work and appeared in *Pearson's Magazine* as well as several

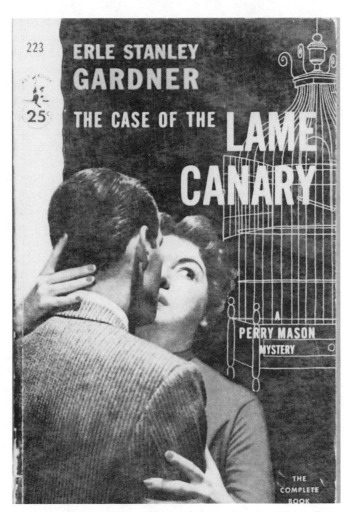

Photo courtesy of Popular Culture Library, Bowling Green State University, Bowling Green, OH.

bound collections. The Mason stories remained favorites— "The Corpus Delicti," a famous example, still has its readers—but Post himself tired of the enterprise and built a second popular series around the non-lawyerly Uncle Abner.

After World War I the most acclaimed fictional lawyer for American readers was Ephraim Tutt, created by attorney Arthur Train. Based in Manhattan, Tutt sallied forth in old-fashioned top hat and cutaway on behalf of the underdog. Rich in wry humor, Tutt's exploits appeared primarily as short stories in the *Saturday Evening Post*, but Train also wrote a Tutt novel, Tutt "autobiography," and Tutt "casebook." The Tutt stories continued to appear during the Depression years, but the newest member of the fictional bar was Erle Stanley Gardner's Perry Mason. Like Post and Train, Gardner was a lawyer, and he created for Mason the type of exciting legal practice rare in real life. Mason appeared in 82 novels and the resourceful attorney never failed to exonerate his client and find the true perpetrator as well, customarily in a dramatic courtroom revelation.

From the 1940s until the 1960s, a number of more serious legal novels also appeared. They include John Barth's *The Floating Opera* (1956); James Gould Cozzens's *By Love Possessed* (1957); Harper Lee's *To Kill a Mockingbird* (1962); and Robert Traver's *Anatomy of a Murder* (1958). In several of these works, the villainous lawyer is no longer a corporate tool or a shyster but an ambitious, biased district attorney. Driven to convict, these prosecutors resemble Hamilton Burger, whom Perry Mason routinely bested. Noxious prosecutors can still be found in contemporary legal fiction such as George V. Higgins's delightful Jerry Kennedy novels, and *The Client* (1993), by lawyer/novelist John Grisham. However, prosecutors can also be heroic or complexly presented. In *Presumed Innocent* (1987), the first of several lawyer novels by attorney and writer Scott Turow, prosecutor Rusty Sabich is himself brought to trial for the murder of Carolyn Polhemus, a fellow lawyer. In recent years, legal thrillers have frequently topped best-seller lists. Writers specializing in this genre include Grisham and Turow, Richard North Patterson, Steve Martini, Jay Brandon, Grif Stockley, and Philip Friedman.

Fictional lawyers who pursue a civil practice are less common, probably because the potential for a stirring storyline is diminished. Louis Auchincloss, a trusts and estates attorney in a large Wall Street firm, published a number of novels involving corporate law practice, including *Powers of Attorney* (1963) and *The Partners* (1974). John Jay Osborn, Jr., perhaps best known for his law school novel *The Paper Chase* (1971), also authored *The Associates* (1979), about corporate lawyers. Barry Reed's *The Verdict* (1980) reaches its climax in a dramatic civil trial pitting a solo practitioner against the assembled lawyers for a large hospital.

Bibliography

Baker, Donald G. "The Lawyer in Popular Fiction." *Journal of Popular Culture* 3.3 (1969): 493-516.

Bloomfield, Maxwell. "Law and Lawyers in American Popular Culture." *Law and American Literature*. Ed. Carl S. Smith, John P. McWilliams, and Maxwell Bloomfield. New York: Random House, 1980.

Breen, Jon L. *Novel Verdicts: A Guide to Courtroom Fiction*. Metuchen: Scarecrow, 1984.

Papke, David Ray. *Journal of Legal Education* 1988.

David Ray Papke

See also
Mystery and Detective Fiction

Legends or tall tales are part of the lifeblood of America, given our cultural penchant for hyperbolic bravado. The authorship of folk literature is usually unknown and unimportant relative to the content of the story. Such stories endure in part because they convey the customs, superstitions, and beliefs of ordinary people who emerge as brave and resourceful. Historically, legends—like that of King Arthur and the Round Table—were passed down through the centuries, often in the form of the epic tale, a long story about heroic exploits written in verse and featuring archetypal characters like tricksters, wise elders, and heroic figures. European settlers brought the legends of *The Odyssey, Beowulf,* and Robin Hood with them across the Atlantic. Traditionally, such legends included religious figures and royalty.

In America common folk were incorporated into the narratives. Tall tales featured heroes and heroines based on the real people who subdued the wilderness. The stories were often regional in setting and lingo, and prone to exaggeration. Paul Bunyan (see entry), Calamity Jane, and Pecos Bill were braggarts who chopped, shot, and lassoed with an energy that reflected the idealism of the frontier. Johnny Appleseed persevered in taming the wilderness for agriculture, and John Henry represented a country that was moving towards urbanization.

Native Americans use legends as a means of communicating tribal values and beliefs. Common themes are living with harmony in nature, respect for age and wisdom, and learning to place the needs of the larger group or families ahead of the individual. Legends reflect particular regions and tribes. The Oneida value the rights of animals, specifically the wolf. The Lakota often interact with the buffalo, and the heroes of the Inuit venture out onto the unpredictable ocean to overcome its perils. The trickster is a familiar figure in Native American legends; shape-shifters like the raven, coyote, and rabbit move between animal and human domains.

Africans brought legends that became adapted and filtered through the experience of slavery. Zomo, a rabbit trickster, became the basis for the popular character of Brer Rabbit written by Joel Chandler Harris in the 19th century. Cleverness, self-sufficiency, and wit were Brer Rabbit's weapons against oppression. Many recent stories celebrate the courage of ordinary African Americans who rose to overcome difficult circumstances; some recount episodes on the Underground Railroad from the perspective of the conductors and travelers.

Hispanic legends of the American Southwest show influences from a geographic area that includes Mexico, South and Central America, and Cuba. The stories of the Aztecs, Mayans, and Incas often dealt with the interactions between gods and humans. These tales blended with the Catholic narratives brought by Spanish explorers. Southwest Native American groups, such as the Apache and Pueblos, contributed trickster characters like Coyote. Despite the variety of cultures that constitute Hispanic legends, the narratives successfully blend and overlap because they reflect deeply shared human characteristics.

Bibliography

Battle, Kemp P. *Great American Folklore: Legends, Tales, Ballads, and Superstitions from All across America*. Garden City: Doubleday, 1986.

Norton, Donna. *Through the Eyes of a Child*. New York: Merrill, 1991.

Sherman, Richard. *Legends, Lies, and Cherished Myths of American History*. New York: Morrow, 1988

Wolkomir, Richard. "If Those Cobras Don't Get You, the Alligators Will." *Smithsonian* Nov. 1992: 166-77.

Sylvia Tag

Leiber, Fritz (1910-1992), one of America's most honored fantasy writers, is also recognized for his work in the horror and science fiction genres. After studying at the University of Chicago and attending theological seminary, he worked as an actor, a drama teacher, and a minister before turning his talents to fiction in 1939. He is best known for his supernatural fantasies and a form of the genre sometimes designated as "sword and sorcery" fiction.

Leiber's supernatural tales transplant familiar fantasy trappings into contemporary metropolitan settings, beginning with "Smoke Ghost" (1941) and continuing through *Conjure Wife* (1943) and *Our Lady of Darkness* (1977). That novel is set in contemporary California; under the urban veneer lies a subtly revealed and profoundly frightening horror. Leiber's science fiction works, such as *Gather Darkness!* (1943), *The Green Millennium* (1953), and *Destiny Times Three* (1957), mix supernatural elements with commentary on the dark implications of technology and the corruption of politics.

His most influential work is a classical fantasy cycle featuring the adventurous characters Fafhrd and the Grey Mouser, introduced in his first published story ("Two Sought Adventure," 1939), and continuing at the time of his death. The earlier stories in the series reflect the influence of traditional fantasy writers such as Robert E. Howard and feature voyages into strange and magical worlds populated by bizarre characters and swashbuckling enemies. The later stories establish new fantasy conventions, eschewing sword and sorcery clichés in favor of humor and satire. The Fafhrd and Grey Mouser stories have been collected in a number of volumes, including *The Three Swords* (1989) and *Swords' Masters* (1990), and two novels, *The Swords of Lankhmar* (1968) and *Swords and Deviltry* (1970).

Bibliography

Carter, Lin. *Imaginary Worlds: The Art of Fantasy.* New York: Ballantine, 1973.

Staircar, Tom. *Fritz Leiber.* New York: Ungar, 1983.

Daryl R. Coats

Leonard, Elmore (1925-), a celebrated author of crime fiction, published his first short story in *Argosy* in 1955. For the next 14 years he wrote only Westerns; four of these were adapted as films: *3:10 to Yuma, The Tall T, Hombre,* and *Valdez Is Coming.*

By 1969, his fictional directions began to change. That year, he published two crime novels, *The Big Bounce* and *The Moonshine War,* and subsequently, movies based on his screenplays were released, *Joe Kidd* (1972), and *Mr. Majestyk* (1974).

Following the release of the novel *Fifty-Two Pickup* in 1974, Leonard hit a productive stride that has not declined. He has published a novel nearly every year since 1976. Notable titles include *Swag* (1976); *The Switch* (1978); *Gunsights,* his final Western (1979); *City Primeval* (1980); *Cat Chaser* (1982); *Stick* (1983); *Glitz* (1985); *Touch* (1987); *Killshot* (1989); *Rum Punch* (1992); *Pronto* (1993); and *Be Cool* (1999).

Leonard gained national attention with the publication of *Glitz,* a best-selling work that brought national attention to his darkly comic depiction of the criminal underclass as it interweaves itself into the American mainstream. His success with *Glitz* earned Leonard the cover of *Newsweek* (22 April 1985), where he was called "the best American writer of crime fiction alive—and perhaps the best ever." The author's effectiveness derives from his sharp sense of character and setting, particularly his remarkable ear for dialect and dialogue. His protagonists range from con artists to law officers, and he captures them with equal authenticity. Leonard avoids plot formulas; in *Maximum Bob* (1991), one of his best works, he shatters his readers' expectations about which major protagonist will survive.

Bibliography

Geherin, David. *Elmore Leonard.* New York: Continuum 1989.

Most, Glenn. "Elmore Leonard: Splitting Images." *Western Humanities Review* 41.1 (Spring 1987): 78.

Prescott, Peter S. "Making a Killing." *Newsweek* 22 April 1985.

Sutter, Gregg. "Advanced Man: Researching Elmore Leonard's Novels, Part 2." *The Armchair Detective* 19.2 (Spring 1986): 160.

——. "Getting It Right: Researching Elmore Leonard's Novels." *The Armchair Detective* 19.1 (Winter 1986): 4.

David K. Jeffrey

See also

Crime Fiction

Thriller, The

Leonard, Sheldon (1907-1997), was an actor turned television producer whose association with Danny Thomas made him one of the most successful producers of the 1960s. Sheldon Leonard was executive producer for a number of popular programs, including *The Danny Thomas Show, The Dick Van Dyke Show, The Andy Griffith Show,* and *Gomer Pyle, U.S.M.C.* Leonard proved instrumental in the careers of such TV favorites as Dick Van Dyke and Mary Tyler Moore, and also helped develop the talent of Jerry Paris, a *Dick Van Dyke Show* character actor who became a successful director and producer for Garry Marshall's *Happy Days.*

Leonard began his career as an actor; by the time he entered television, he had appeared in more than 140 movies, mostly playing gangsters or gamblers. Leonard started working as a radio actor and writer in the 1950s; in 1953, he expressed an interest in television directing. Leonard's agent at William Morris went to another of the firm's clients, Danny Thomas, who was receptive to letting Leonard work as an assistant director for *Make Room for Daddy* (1953). Leonard proved quite adept at directing, and by the end of the sitcom's first season, Thomas made Leonard its director and producer.

As Danny Thomas parlayed his sitcom's success into a major production empire that he called the "Supermarket of Sitcoms," Thomas formed a partnership with Leonard. Under Thomas, Leonard went on to develop and executive produce *The Andy Griffith Show* (1960), as well as its spin-offs *Gomer Pyle, U.S.M.C.* (1964), and *Mayberry R.F.D.* (1968). Leonard is also credited with saving *The Dick Van Dyke Show* (1961), which, at the end of its first season, was canceled by CBS.

In addition to his work in sitcoms, Leonard also produced *I Spy* (1965), which starred Robert Culp and Bill Cosby. Leonard's hand in *I Spy,* the first dramatic series to feature a black character, is not surprising; indeed, during Leonard's experience on *The Dick Van Dyke Show,* black characters were often featured in responsible, non-stereotypical roles.

One of Leonard's few failures included the off-beat sitcom *My World and Welcome to It* (1969), which starred William Windom as a Thurberesque cartoonist whose overactive imagination often got the best of him. *Big Eddie* (1975), in which Leonard starred as a reformed gambler, also failed to capture an audience.

Bibliography

Brooks, Tim, and Earle Marsh. *The Complete Directory to Prime Time Network TV Shows, 1946-Present.* New York: Ballantine, 1992.

Brown, Les. *Les Brown's Encyclopedia of Television.* Detroit: Visible Ink, 1992.

Marc, David, and Robert J. Thompson. *Prime Time, Prime Movers.* Boston: Little, Brown, 1992.

Thomas, Danny, and Bill Davidson. *Make Room for Danny.* New York: Putnam, 1991.

Michael B. Kassel

Lerner and Loewe. Lyricist Alan Jay Lerner (1918-1986) and composer Frederick Loewe (1901-1988) were masters of the musical play during its heyday in the 1940s and 1950s. Though not innovators (their shows followed the pattern of integrated music, lyrics, dance, and plot established by Rodgers and Hammerstein), Lerner and Loewe gave the genre a sense of romance and magic that was distinctively their own. The musicals of Lerner and Loewe have proven extremely popular in revival.

Alan Jay Lerner, generally acknowledged as the dominant figure in the partnership, was born in New York City. His wealthy family (his father owned the Lerner Shops, a chain of women's clothing stores) sent him to Bedales, an English public school, the Choate School in Connecticut, and Harvard University, from which he graduated in 1940. Lerner began his career writing radio scripts, but his real interest was in the theater.

Frederick Loewe was born in Berlin to Austrian parents. His father was Edmund Loewe, a well-known singer in operetta. A child prodigy at the piano, Loewe gave his first public concert at age 13. After World War I, Loewe came to the United States with his family (his father had been engaged to star in American productions). For the next two decades Frederick Loewe had a checkered career, working as a boxer, cowboy, and a pianist at restaurants and theatrical rehearsals. By the late 1930s, several of his compositions (with words by various lyricists) had been sung in Broadway revues, but Loewe enjoyed no major success until teaming up with youthful Alan Jay Lerner.

Lerner and Loewe met in 1942 at the Lambs Club, a New York theatrical club to which they both belonged. Their first collaboration was a rewrite of a show called *Salute to Spring* that Loewe had written a few years earlier with another lyricist. The rewritten show, called *Life of the Party*, was produced in Detroit in October 1942.

Although the easy-going, middle-aged Loewe and the intense young Lerner did not become close friends (and never would), they continued to work together. Lerner and Loewe's next two shows—*What's Up?* in 1943 and *The Day Before Spring* in 1945—had brief runs on Broadway and were soon forgotten (though the latter show received mostly favorable reviews). It was the romantic fantasy *Brigadoon* (1947, 581 performances) that began their remarkable string of successes. The story of two American hunters who stumble upon a Scottish village that appears only once every hundred years, *Brigadoon* established the Lerner and Loewe style with its lushly romantic score and fanciful plot (by Alan Jay Lerner, who would write the book to all their shows) extolling the power of love.

Lerner and Loewe temporarily broke up after *Brigadoon*. With composer Kurt Weill, Lerner wrote *Love Life*, an idealized portrait of pre-industrial America. Directed by Elia Kazan and starring Nanette Fabray, *Love Life* (1948, 252 performances) was a minor hit though it has not been well remembered. Lerner then wrote the screenplay to the musical film *An American in Paris,* for which he won an Academy Award. Lerner and Loewe eventually reunited to create *Paint Your Wagon* (1951, 289 performances), a tale of the California gold rush. Avoiding the Western-setting hokiness such as that found in Irving Berlin's *Annie Get Your Gun* a few seasons earlier, *Paint Your Wagon* focused on romantic love (Lerner and Loewe's favorite theme) and the loneliness of life on the frontier. The show's best-known song is the rousing but plaintive "They Call the Wind Maria."

One of the most celebrated musicals of all time is Lerner and Loewe's *My Fair Lady* (1956, 2,717 performances), a musical reworking of G. B. Shaw's *Pygmalion.* *My Fair Lady* jettisoned most of Shaw's social commentary and turned *Pygmalion* into a romance between its principal characters, a linguistics expert, Professor Higgins, and Cockney flower-seller Eliza Doolittle (played by Rex Harrison and Julie Andrews). Nevertheless, much of Shaw's acerbic tone was retained and, ironically, this most successful Lerner and Loewe collaboration is their least characteristic work. The score contains just one heart-on-sleeve romantic ballad —"On the Street Where You Live." Numerous songs in *My Fair Lady* became familiar, especially "Wouldn't It Be Loverly?," "Get Me to the Church on Time," and "I've Grown Accustomed to Her Face."

Lerner and Loewe returned to the romantic fantasy style of *Brigadoon* with the sumptuous 1958 musical film *Gigi,* a delicate tale of a 19th-century Paris girl being trained as courtesan by her worldly grandmother. *Gigi* won the Academy Award for best picture and its title song earned Lerner and Loewe an Academy Award for best song. Other well-known songs from Gigi are "Thank Heaven for Little Girls," and "I Remember It Well."

Also in typical Lerner and Loewe style was *Camelot* (1960, 873 performances), a medieval fantasy centered around the legendary Arthur/Guenevere/Lancelot love triangle. Although weighed down with a long, lumbering book (the show ran four hours during out-of-town tryouts and desperate tinkering continued even after its Broadway opening), *Camelot*, which starred Richard Burton, Julie Andrews, and Robert Goulet, was enormously popular. An excellent score compensated for weaknesses in the overall production.

Camelot's score offered equal measure of Lerner and Loewe's greatest strengths—unabashed romance and clever, subtle wit.

Frederick Loewe retired after *Camelot*, citing health reasons. Though he had indeed suffered a massive heart attack in 1958, it was suspected that Loewe had simply lost interest in work now that he was a wealthy man. Just as Loewe had not enjoyed much success before teaming up with Alan Jay Lerner, Lerner did not enjoy much success after their partnership ended. An attempt at collaboration with Richard Rodgers in the early 1960s did not work out due to artistic and personal differences. Lerner's post-Loewe years saw only two minor hits—*On a Clear Day You Can See Forever* (1965, 280 performances), a look at reincarnation and extrasensory perception, with music by Burton Lane, and *Coco* (1969, 332 performances), a musicalized life of French couturiere Coco Chanel, with music by André Previn. Katharine Hepburn, making her first and only appearance in the musical theater, played Chanel, and her star presence was largely responsible for *Coco*'s relatively long run.

All of Lerner's later works were failures: *Lolita, My Love*, a musical version of the Nabokov novel with music by John Barry (1971, closed before reaching Broadway); *1600 Pennsylvania Avenue*, a look at the U.S. presidency with music by Leonard Bernstein (1976, 7 performances); *Carmelina*, based on the film *Buona Sera, Mrs. Campbell*, with music by Burton Lane (1979, 17 performances); and *Dance a Little Closer*, a musical version of Robert E. Sherwood's antiwar play *Idiot's Delight*, with music by Charles Strouse (1983, 1 performance).

Bibliography

Lees, Gene. *Inventing Champagne: The Worlds of Lerner and Loewe*. New York: St. Martin's, 1990.

Lerner, Alan Jay. *On the Street Where I Live*. New York: Norton, 1978.

New York Times. Obituaries: Alan Jay Lerner, 15 June 1986: 1, 31; Frederick Loewe, 15 Feb. 1988: 1, 19.

Suskin, Steven. *Show Tunes 1905-1985: The Songs, Shows, and Careers of Broadway's Top Composers*. New York: Dodd, Mead, 1986.

Mary C. Kalfatovic

See also
American Musical Theater

Letterman, David Michael (1947-), host of *The Late Show*, left Indianapolis for Los Angeles in 1975, and broke into show business doing standup at the Comedy Store and writing jokes for Jimmie Walker (*Good Times*) and Paul Lynde (*The Hollywood Squares*). During this time he got a spot on the *Gong Show* and had small parts in short-lived shows such as *Peeping Times*, *The Starland Vocal Band Show* (1977), and *Mary* (1978), a variety show starring Mary Tyler Moore. He went on to become one of TV's most famous talk show hosts.

His big break came when he caught the eye of the *Tonight Show* staff. After his standup routine on November 26, 1978, Johnny asked him to come over and sit on the couch, a sign of acceptance. In record time, after only three appearances on *The Tonight Show*, Dave was asked to guest host. He went on to guest host 51 times, while continuing to appear at the Comedy Store and making guest appearances on the *Gong Show*, *$20,000 Pyramid*, and one episode of *Mork and Mindy*.

In April of 1979, NBC offered Dave a two-year contract to do a morning variety show after the *Today Show*. *The David Letterman Show* premiered at 9 a.m., June 23, 1980, and aired for 19 weeks. NBC wanted Letterman to do cooking demonstrations and mix song and dance with guest interviews; however, Dave's style of comedy was out of place in the midmorning time slot and soon the show was cut from 90 to 60 minutes. After just a few weeks on air, and a number of complaints from housewives about the format, NBC notified Dave that the show would be canceled in four months. With nothing to lose, Letterman pulled out the stops and did the show the way he wanted, as a comedy show. Letterman and his girlfriend/head writer Merrill Markoe developed and introduced some pieces which were to become famous later on *Late Night with David Letterman,* including "Stupid Pet Tricks" with Dave's dog Bob, remotes to Chinatown, and other bits where Dave would go out of the studio with a camera crew. The final show aired October 31, 1980, but NBC did not give up on Dave's brand of humor.

When NBC decided to cancel *Tomorrow* with Tom Snyder, they offered Dave another chance, but this time following the *Tonight Show* in the 12:30 to 1:30 a.m. slot. The show premiered on February 1, 1982 as *Late Night with David Letterman*. *Late Night* had some of the familiar elements of the *Tonight Show,* but Dave developed his own sarcastic style. His monologue poked fun at events of the day, politicians, and even the woman who repeatedly broke into his home. Dave bantered with Paul Shaffer, the leader of "The World's Most Dangerous Band" (a four-member rock band). Some of the most popular bits on *Late Night* included "Stupid Pet Tricks," "Stupid Human Tricks," "Touch with Greatness," and the nightly "Top-Ten List." Other bits included "Viewer Mail," and "Small Town News," where he would highlight unintentional humor from small-town newspapers.

After Johnny Carson announced that he would retire from *The Tonight Show,* the top replacement candidates were David Letterman and Jay Leno. Conflicting rumors circulated that NBC was going to offer the position first to Letterman, but ultimately NBC chose Jay Leno. When it became apparent that Letterman might leave the network, NBC offered him the show, but not until Leno's contract ran out in 1994. Dave switched to CBS and moved into a time slot opposite NBC's *Tonight Show* hosted by his friend Jay Leno.

The Late Show with David Letterman premiered on August 30, 1993, on CBS in the 11:30 p.m.-12:30 a.m. time slot. CBS spent a reported $14 million renovating the Ed Sullivan Theater and signed a $14 million a year, three-year contract with Letterman, which doubled his $7 million a year salary at NBC.

The Late Show was not a carbon copy of *Late Night*; Dave changed his appearance and began wearing expensive suits instead of his traditional sport coats, khaki pants, and tennis shoes. Paul Shaffer remained music director with the same band members as *Late Night*, though adding new musicians as well as a brass section, becoming the "CBS Orchestra." It was a kinder and gentler David Letterman during interviews. NBC claimed rights to many of the old standards of *Late Night* as "intellectual property," including the top ten list, which became the "Late Show Top Ten." *The Late Show* has been able to keep the fans from *Late Night* while gaining a new audience.

Bibliography
Alder, Bill. *The Letterman Wit: His Life and Humor.* New York: Carroll & Graf, 1994.
Carter, Bill. *The Late Shift: Letterman, Leno and the Network Battle for the Night.* New York: Hyperion, 1994.
Latham, Caroline. *The David Letterman Story.* New York: Watts, 1987.
Lennon, Rosemarie. *David Letterman: On Stage and Off.* New York: Pinnacle, 1994.

John D. Wineland

LeVay, Anton Szandor (1930-1997), founder in 1966 of the Church of Satan, established himself as perhaps the most prominent and controversial figure of the modern occult culture. The roots of LeVay's movement lie as much in show business as magical studies. As a teenager, he joined a circus and worked as an animal trainer, handling eight lions by age 17. He also performed on the organ and a number of exotic musical instruments. After quitting the circus, he worked as a musician at amusement parks and carnivals and, occasionally, tent revivals. At these religious gatherings, LeVay says he observed traits of hypocrisy in Christianity.

LeVay also maintained an interest from an early age in magic and rituals. By age 12 he had already read popularized anthologies of magic such as *Albertus Magnus* and *Sixth and Seventh Books of Moses.* Finding these lacking, LeVay began a lifelong search for truly powerful magic rituals that cumulated in the publication of his *The Satanic Rituals* in 1972, a collection of what he considered to be the most authentic rituals throughout history.

The Satanic belief system developed by LeVay is somewhat different from the traditional Christian view of evil. It encourages the indulgence of human instincts, but attempts to channel them to positive ends. LeVay defines Satan not as a force of cosmic evil to be worshipped, but rather as a metaphorical representation of individuality, the refusal to live within hypocritical social constraints.

The eccentric glamour of the Church of Satan attracted a number of followers from the Hollywood film industry, most notably Jayne Mansfield, a well-known actress who pitched LeVay's philosophy to many of her influential celebrity contacts. In his efforts to reach a wider audience, LeVay even agreed to play the Devil in a scene in the 1969 film *Rosemary's Baby.*

Although the Church of Satan, as well as many other occult organizations, is often accused of widespread conspiracies, human sacrifice, and other illegal activities, extensive investigations have found little evidence of this. LeVay renounced human sacrifice as well as animal sacrifice and the mistreatment of animals.

Bibliography
Barton, Blanche. *The Secret Life of a Satanist.* Los Angeles: Feral House, 1990.
Freedland, Nat. *The Occult Explosion.* New York: Putnam, 1972.
Victor, Jeffrey S. *Satanic Panic.* Chicago: Open Court, 1993.

Curtis Shumaker

Lewis, C(live) S(taples) (1898-1963), famous science fiction author, born in Belfast, Northern Ireland, completed his education in England, where he made his career as a Cambridge University don and a writer of a diverse range of literary works, including science fiction and fantasy, poetry, children's literature, criticism, and reminiscence. The entire canon of his work was affected by his deeply held Christian beliefs, which are articulated and imaged forth in his fiction as well as in his theological essays.

Lewis wrote a number of stories and novels that meld fable and science fiction. *Out of the Silent Planet* (1938), *Perelandra* (1943), and *That Hideous Strength: A Modern Fairy Tale for Grown Ups* (1945) comprise what has been called Lewis's "space trilogy." The stories are set on Mars, Venus, and Earth, respectively, and feature characters called "eldils," a cross between space aliens and angels, who oversee the interplanetary domain. Lewis's outer space world, unlike the sterile futuristic worlds of other science fiction authors, resembles rather a Christian Utopia, into which the author also mixes Arthurian iconography. *The Screwtape Letters* (1942), another adult fantasy novel, is Lewis's best-known work.

Lewis also published a series of children's novels known as the Narnia tales, comprised of seven books beginning with *The Lion, the Witch, and the Wardrobe* (1950), chronicling the adventures of eight children from Earth who gain access to the mythical land of Narnia.

Bibliography
Ford, Paul F. *Companion to Narnia.* San Francisco: Harper, 1980.
Holbrook, David. *The Skeleton in the Wardrobe: C. S. Lewis's Fantasies, A Phenomenological Study.* Lewisburg: Bucknell UP, 1991.
Manlove, C. N. *The Chronicles of Narnia: The Patterning of a Fantastic World.* New York: Twayne.

Solomon Davidoff

Lewis, Jerry (1926-), famous for work in TV and movies, first came to television with his partner, Dean Martin (1917-1996), as part of the NBC series *The Colgate Comedy Hour.* The series lasted from 1950 to 1955, and Martin and Lewis alternated hosting duties on the show with other performers during those years, making roughly 40 appearances.

After the team split up in 1956, Lewis made a series of eight successful specials from 1957 through 1960. The specials, all done for NBC and all but one titled *The Jerry Lewis Show,* featured Lewis in comedy sketches and song numbers. Some of the sketches were blueprints or run-throughs of material he would later use in his films and personal appearances. In the early 1960s, Lewis gained positive notice when he substitute hosted *The Tonight Show*. There was talk of Lewis taking over the show when Jack Paar stepped aside, and when that didn't happen Lewis got an offer from ABC to develop his own talk show. Lewis came up with a weekly two-hour extravaganza that would combine elements of his successful NBC specials with the *Tonight Show* format. *The Jerry Lewis Show* was much ballyhooed and debuted in the fall of 1963 and ended its run by Christmas of that same year, considered one of the biggest flops in television history.

Lewis made no network specials or series until 1967, when he returned to NBC with an hour-long variety series also titled *The Jerry Lewis Show* and using the format of his NBC specials of 1957-60. The fact that his former partner had a hit series (*The Dean Martin Show*) on the same network may have spurred Lewis to try harder. He did, running the range of his talents and comic characters in the same manner of Jackie Gleason and Red Skelton. Lewis re-created some of his best bits from his film efforts and worked well with a variety of guest stars, but it was not enough. The show ended its run after two seasons.

Lewis then concentrated his television work on the annual Jerry Lewis Muscular Dystrophy Association Labor Day Telethon he organized and hosted, and infrequent talk show appearances. In the 1980s, he starred in a cycle of the *Wiseguy* series and later a made-for-TV movie, *Fight for Life*. In 1984, he shot five episodes of a celebrity talk show he hosted called *The Jerry Lewis Show,* intending the show to be syndicated. It was not picked up for production. In the 1990s he made more series guest and talk show appearances in addition to continuing the telethon.

Bibliography

Gehman, Richard. *That Kid: The Story of Jerry Lewis.* New York: Avon, 1964.

Marx, Arthur. *Everybody Loves Somebody Sometime (Especially Himself): The Story of Dean Martin and Jerry Lewis.* New York: Hawthorn, 1974.

Terrace, Vincent. *Encyclopedia of Television Series, Pilots, and Specials, 1937-1973.* Vol. 1. New York: Zoetrope, 1985.

——. *Encyclopedia of Television Series, Pilots, and Specials, 1974-1984.* Vol. 2. New York: Zoetrope, 1985.

Benjamin K. Urish

Lewis, Jerry Lee (1935-), considers himself to be the "King of Rock 'n' Roll" but most of the world refers to him as "The Killer." Lewis's wild and arrogant stage antics, such as setting his piano on fire, kicking the piano bench across the stage, playing standing up, or even playing with his toes, earned him this title.

Lewis was born in Ferriday, LA. The son of a farmer, Lewis was deeply immersed in gospel and "Southern hillbilly" lifestyles. He showed a keen propensity for piano playing at an early age, and was greatly influenced by traditional country artists like Hank Williams and Jimmie Rodgers. He also enjoyed the Mississippi Delta blues and the music of swing and jazz artists; singer Al Jolson and pianist Cecil Grant had a tremendous influence on his playing style. When he was a kid, he and his two cousins, Jimmy Swaggart and Mickey Gilly, often snuck out to clubs to listen, from outside, to the music being played.

At 14, Lewis made his first paid public performance, outside of a Ford dealership, for which he was paid $13 for playing hillbilly and gospel tunes. At 14, he also was married for the first of many times.

In 1955, after Sun Records president, Sam Phillips, sold Elvis Presley's contract for $35,000, Phillips began looking for another artist who would appeal to youths in both presence and music. While Carl Perkins and Johnny Cash were both under contract to Sun, they did not have the flamboyant look and presence that Phillips wanted. Lewis had worked at the studio as a session piano player before Phillips gave him his big break. His first recording was a cover of Ray Price's "Crazy Arms." While this song was good, it did not have the punch Phillips was looking for. However, in 1957-58, Lewis recorded what became Sun Records' two biggest hits, "Whole Lotta Shakin' Goin' On" and "Great Balls of Fire." Although these songs were not written by Lewis, they were his biggest hits; he also scored hits with "High School Confidential" and "Breathless." "Whole Lotta" was released in 1957, and after an appearance on *The Steve Allen Show,* Lewis was an overnight sensation. "Great Balls of Fire," released in 1958, furthered Lewis's popularity and mystique, and he advanced his career by appearing in (and singing the title tracks for) two films, *Jamboree* and *High School Confidential.*

Throughout his life, Lewis was plagued by controversy and scandal. In addition to his wild stage antics, his personal life was filled with wild parties, drugs, and weird happenings. Just as he was on the verge of becoming one of the biggest stars in the music world, his fame dropped, almost overnight, when he mishandled an interview with the press about his marriage to a 13-year-old.

In the late 1950s and early 1960s Lewis had top country hits with the songs "Carry Me Back to Old Virginny" and a cover of Ray Charles's "What'd I Say," and he appeared in the movie *Young and Deadly* in 1960. Throughout the mid-1960s, Jerry Lee recorded several moderately successful country records on Smash Records, including his 1966 success *Country Songs.*

During the 1970s, Lewis continued to record and tour with many of the rock 'n' roll revival shows. Lewis played Las Vegas and the casino circuit for a while. However, in Europe the controversy surrounding his marriage was soon forgotten; by the mid-1960s, Lewis again was drawing big crowds and selling many records.

In 1981, Lewis had a near-fatal stomach operation, which took him several years to recover from. In his typically arrogant fashion, Lewis declined to contribute to the Rolling Stones' 1983 release, *Undercover* (which turned out to be the Stones' worst project), but he did get together with his former Sun mates, Carl Perkins and Johnny Cash, to record *The Survivors* in 1982, and he joined them again (along with Roy Orbison) to record *Class of '55* in 1986. "The Killer" was inducted into the Rock and Roll Hall of Fame in 1986, the first year inductions took place. Throughout the 1980s several reissues, box sets, and unearthed live recordings were released to critical acclaim. The year 1989 saw the release of the Jerry Lee Lewis story in the film *Great Balls of Fire*, starring Dennis Quaid as "The Killer." One of the things that makes Jerry Lee unique in the culture of rock 'n' roll is that he was the first white piano (instead of guitar) player to make rock songs that became worldwide hits.

Bibliography

Busnar, Gene. *Superstars of Country Music*. New York: Messner, 1984.

Lewis, Jerry Lee. *Killer!* London: Century, 1993.

——. *Whole Lotta Shakin' Going On: The Life and Times of Jerry Lee Lewis*. New York: Hyperion, 1994.

Lewis, Myra. *Great Balls of Fire: The Uncensored Story of Jerry Lee Lewis*. New York: St. Martin's, 1989.

Tosches, Nick. *Hellfire: The Jerry Lee Lewis Story*. New York: Dell, 1989.

Rob Weiner

Lewis, Shari (1934-1998), the puppeteer/ventriloquist, and her most famous creation, the long-lashed, squeaky-voiced Lamb Chop, provided knock-knock jokes to several generations of five-, six-, and seven-year-olds. Shari Lewis and Lamb Chop emerged in 1991 from programming mothballs remarkably well suited to address a current desire for "quality" (read educational) children's programming.

Lewis's professional career began when she was 18 with an appearance on television in *Arthur Godfrey's Talent Scouts*. Small parts with her puppets on the *Captain Kangaroo Show* led to a regular spot on that program. In 1960, Lewis and Lamb Chop graduated to their own show on NBC, which lasted only three seasons. In 1963, NBC decided to replace live-action children's programming with cartoons.

Lewis then continued her show on stage, in special TV and movie appearances, and in videos; she also wrote more than 60 books. After a hiatus from television of more than 25 years, Shari Lewis and Lamb Chop returned to entertain a new generation of children with magic tricks, riddles, stories, and songs in *Lamb Chop's Play Along* on PBS in 1991, until her death from cancer in 1998.

Bibliography

Dickinson, A. "Dishing up Lamb Chop: On PBS, Shari Lewis's Second Generation." *Washington Post* 4 April 1994.

Elber, Lynn. "Children's Entertainer Shari Lewis Dies of Cancer at 65." Associated Press 4 Aug. 1998. Online. LEXIS-NEXIS Academic Universe. 16 May 2000.

Rensin, D. "Shari Lewis: One-on-one with Lamb Chop's Mom." *TV Guide* 29 Oct. 1994: 49-52.

Janice Walker Anderson

Lichtenstein, Roy (1923-1997), along with artists such as Andy Warhol and Claes Oldenburg, developed the art style that is known as Pop Art; *Newsweek* called Lichtenstein "pop art's Mr. Rogers." The son of a prosperous realtor, he grew up in Manhattan. Lichtenstein studied art in high school, at the Art Students League in New York, and at the Ohio State University.

Lichtenstein's purpose was not to glorify popular culture; rather, he wanted to make a comment on the deadening effect it could have on an unsuspecting public. Claiming not to be a moralist, Lichtenstein wanted his viewers to make up their own minds on the commercialization of our culture and its ubiquitous production of things. His appropriation of so-called low art to a "high art" level was intended to be humorous.

Lichtenstein's works look like blown-up comic strips. He used bright colors, bold outlines, and forms which are flat and stylized. His signature mark is the Ben Day dot, made by laying a metal screen on his canvas and spreading paint over it with a roller. He would later rub the paint smooth with a toothbrush so as to decrease any painterly characteristics. The result is a look that is immediately recognizable as both Lichtenstein and comic strip.

Some of his most popular works are comic-like images of girls created largely from the early to mid-1960s. They have cartoon balloons with comments such as "I don't care! I'd rather sink—than call Brad for help!" and "That's the way—it should have begun! But it's hopeless!" Another states, "Oh, Jeff...I love you, too...but...." They had titles like *Drowning Girl*, *In the Car*, *Hopeless*, and *We Rose Up Slowly*. These are clearly soap opera images which are not heroines, but appeal to the male ego. Lichtenstein did not invent them, and as he replicated them, he was fairly faithful to the original image.

Bibliography

Coplans, John, ed. *Roy Lichtenstein*. New York: Praeger, 1972.

Waldman, Diane. *Roy Lichtenstein*. New York: The Guggenheim Museum, 1993.

Kristen Congdon

Life. The tremendous success of *Life* magazine during its two periodical incarnations underscores the remarkable power of photojournalism to capture the imagination of the American public as it chronicles the evolving nature of international popular culture, art, and history during the 20th century. Founded in 1935 by Henry Robinson Luce, the magazine's first managing editor, *Life* appeared for the first time in a November 1936 issue aptly featuring the photo of a baby's birth and the caption, "Life Begins." Marked throughout its publication history by the enduring quality of its photography, *Life* sold out its initial issue in a mere four hours—a harbinger of the unqualified journalistic success that defines the magazine's remarkable print run. Regular features of the magazine during its initial incarnation as a weekly included the "Big News-Picture Story of the Week," "On the American Newsfront," and "The President's Album."

Life's remarkable ability to capture photographically the events that dramatically altered the culture of the U.S. and the world found its roots in the magazine's award-winning coverage of World War II. During this era, *Life*'s staff photographers—the envy of its competitors—included such luminaries as Margaret Bourke-White, Alfred Eisenstaedt, Thomas McAvoy, and Peter Stackpole, among others, and their heroic efforts resulted in a variety of death-defying, close-up shots taken in often perilous conditions. The work of Bourke-White as she photographed her own rescue from a torpedoed freighter in the Mediterranean in 1942 and Robert Capa's memorable photographs of the 1944 D-Day invasion on the Normandy beaches, among other photographic endeavors by *Life* photographers, remain hallmarks in the annals of wartime photography. Although military censorship and the difficulties of relaying film back to the U.S. often posed obstacles to the magazine's publication during this era, *Life*'s stunning coverage of the war resulted in its astounding growth in its weekly circulation from 2.8 million copies in 1940 to more than 5 million at the end of the decade.

During the 1950s and 1960s, *Life* entered its most influential period as America's leading national magazine. Under the guidance of the magazine's new managing editor, Edward K. Thompson, *Life* now featured a standard of writing that matched the high quality of its photojournalism. Under Thompson's leadership, the periodical published the work of such writers as Graham Greene, Robert Penn Warren, Evelyn Waugh, Ernest Hemingway, and James Michener, while also publishing the memoirs of such luminaries as former President Harry S. Truman and Sir Winston Churchill, among others. In addition to expanding its coverage of fashion, film, and entertainment during this era, *Life* also devoted its pages to investigative reporting, focusing particularly upon such stories as the McCarthy communist hearings in 1950, the Kefauver Committee hearings regarding organized crime in 1951, and school desegregation and the protest marches in Alabama during the mid-1950s. During the 1960s, *Life* afforded particular attention to the grandeur and, ultimately, tragedy of the John F. Kennedy presidency, as well as to the escalation of the Cold War with the Soviet Union and the rapidly evolving popular culture of the 1960s. Following Luce's death in 1967, the magazine's enduring financial problems—fostered largely by the sheer volume of the periodical's press run, as well as by the expenses required to maintain *Life*'s high publication standards—confronted future managing editors of *Life*, including Ralph Graves, who effected drastic budget cuts in 1969 and 1970 in an effort to save the struggling publishing juggernaut from certain bankruptcy despite the magazine's remarkable circulation in 1970 of more than 7 million copies.

The specter of financial collapse forced the managing editors of *Life* to scale back circulation to 5.5 million subscribers. Following additional budget cuts and further reductions in staff, *Life* ceased publication with its December 29, 1972, issue. From 1973 to 1977, the magazine continued to appear through the publication of two special issues a year, and in 1978 publisher Charles Whittingham revived *Life* as a monthly publication. Still devoted to the publication of high-quality photojournalism, the magazine maintained an annual readership of nearly 2 million subscribers for some time, although well short of the status of its predecessor as a cultural and historical icon. In 2000 it ceased publication once more, though special issues are planned.

Bibliography
Douglas, George H. *The Smart Magazines*. Hamden: Archon, 1991.
Hamblin, Dora Jane. *That Was the Life*. New York: Norton, 1977.
Nourie, Alan, and Barbara Nourie, ed. *American Mass-Market Magazines*. New York: Greenwood, 1990.
Wainwright, Loudon. *The Great American Magazine: An Inside History of Life*. New York: Knopf, 1986.

Kenneth Womack

Life and Legend of Wyatt Earp, The (1955-1961), was unusual among the previously make-believe world of television Westerns (see entry). Not only was it more or less based on fact, it developed its characters over a period of six years in a continuing story involving politics and family relationships as well as standard Western action. In many ways it resembled a serial drama.

Most of the early episodes allegedly were based on historical events in the life of the West's most famous lawman. Every effort was made to create sets and costumes that were accurate, even to the make of Earp's gun, the Buntline Special. The scripts followed Earp from his arrival in Ellsworth City, KS, through his career in Dodge City and Tombstone, AZ, concluding with a five-part dramatization of the famous gunfight at the OK corral.

The show brought actor Hugh O'Brian (1925-) from obscurity to fame. When O'Brian strode before the cameras as Wyatt Earp, he assumed the manner and confidence of the deadly lawman. He had studied old photos and donned the tight trousers with a narrow gray-on-black stripe, shiny gold vest with a daisy design, string tie, long-sleeved shirt, black sombrero, and black boots that Earp commonly wore.

The Life and Legend of Wyatt Earp established a pattern that was used by other television Westerns based on actual historical characters, such as *Bat Masterson*, *Jim Bowie*, and Pat Garrett in *The Tall Man*. In its quality of production and success in capturing the spirit of a man and his era, the series set a high standard for others to emulate.

From the start, *The Life and Legend of Wyatt Earp* was a ratings success. It was ranked in the Nielsen Top 20 for three out of its six years, and reached sixth during the 1957-58 season.

Bibliography
Brooks, Tim, and Earle Marsh. *The Complete Directory to Prime Time Network and Cable TV Shows, 1946-Present*. New York: Ballantine, 1995.
Yoggy, Gary. *Riding the Video Range: The Rise and Fall of the Western on Television*. Jefferson: McFarland, 1995.

Gary A. Yoggy

Lights Out (1934-1939, 1942-1943, 1945, 1946, 1947) was radio's definitive horror program. All others were judged by its standards, and many of its plots are still recalled by those who heard them originally or on reissued tapes. The stories of the man whose wife turned into a small cat, or the chicken heart that expanded to fill the world, or the man who turned inside-out in a diabolical fog rival those of Edgar Allan Poe in intensity and shock.

491

The program was created by Wyllis Cooper, an NBC staffer, in 1934 as a local Chicago program to be run on WENR. It played after midnight for 15 minutes. On April 17, 1935, it went on the NBC Red network as a late-night Wednesday network program. Since it went on after midnight, it was able to be as frightening as it desired without fear of scaring the kiddies.

Arch Oboler (see entry) took over the program in 1936 and expanded its already famous sound effects while honing his own prodigious writing skills. He opened the program with church bells and a gong and ended it with the wind coming up. Throughout there were always inventive sound effects: frying bacon to simulate a body frying in the electric chair; dripping molasses to suggest blood oozing from a body; cooked spaghetti being squished to suggest cannibalism; hammering spare ribs to imitate breaking bones; and various other ingenious devices.

Lights Out attracted numerous well-known movie stars. Boris Karloff was a natural for the program and appeared many times. Oboler's strong scripts provided an incentive beyond that of being associated with an unusual program.

The first version of *Lights Out* ended after the August 16, 1939, program. Oboler had tired of competing with his own previous programs and had moved to the West Coast to start his soon-to-be-famous *Playhouse* series. However, when he needed money in 1942, he revived the program, now on CBS for one-half hour from New York. It had two brief runs as a summer replacement in 1945 and 1946. In 1947, it ran for one month on the Mutual Network beginning on July 16. The efforts of Boris Karloff and its originator, Wyllis Cooper, failed to revive the program.

In common with many other radio programs, *Lights Out* was brought to television. Frank Gallup made a memorable host for its three-year television run. Some of the old scripts were revived and adapted for television. New ones were added to its repertoire. Since 1952, *Lights Out* lives in the memories of its fans and on "classic" tapes.

Bibliography
Dunning, John. *Tune in Yesterday.* Englewood Cliffs: Prentice-Hall, 1936.
Macdonald, J. Fred. *Don't Touch That Dial.* Chicago: Nelson-Hall, 1979.

Frank A. Salamone

Limbaugh, Rush Hudson, III (1951-), well-known conservative talk show host, grew up in Cape Girardeau, MO, a quintessential midwestern small town. Limbaugh began his radio career at the age of 16 at a hometown station, later working at stations in Pittsburgh and Kansas City. He got out of radio in 1979 to become director of group sales for the Kansas City Royals. But radio was still his first love, and he returned to it in 1984 at KFBK in Sacramento. There he developed much of the style that would carry him to New York City and national prominence.

Since he burst onto the national scene with his syndicated radio talk show (1988-), Limbaugh has become a "one-man media theme park of the '90s." His three-hour, daily radio show is heard by more than 20 million people each week—the most listened-to radio program in history. His syndicated television show (1992-96) did well in the late-night market. His monthly newsletter has more than 400,000 subscribers and his two books—*The Way Things Ought to Be* (1992) and *See, I Told You So* (1993)—made publishing history by becoming instant best-sellers. *People* magazine named Limbaugh one of its "25 most intriguing people" of 1993. He has also appeared on *CBS This Morning, Good Morning America, Sunday with David Brinkley, Meet the Press, Nightline, The Tonight Show, Donahue, Charlie Rose,* and a Barbara Walters special.

Limbaugh is the self-proclaimed "Doctor of Democracy," but others like to call him "the most dangerous man in America," a title Limbaugh also relishes. He calls himself "just a harmless, lovable little fuzzball...with talent on loan from God."

Bibliography
Colford, Paul D. *The Rush Limbaugh Story: Talent on Loan from God.* New York: St. Martin's, 1993.
Eastland, Terry. "Rush Limbaugh: Talking Back." *The American Spectator* Sept. 1992: 22-27.
Jacobs, Donald Trent. *The Bum's Rush: Phrases and Fallacies of Rush Limbaugh.* Boise: Legendary, 1994.
Limbaugh, Rush. *See, I Told You So.* New York: Pocket, 1993.
U.S. News & World Report 16 Aug. 1993: 27-35.

Jack Hodgson

See also
Talk Radio

Little Big Man (1964) is a Western novel by Thomas Berger (1924-), the author of *Neighbors* (1981) and *The Feud* (1983). The only Western Berger has written, *Little Big Man* is a comic parody of hallowed Western mythology, retelling many of the central historical events of the 19th-century West through the viewpoint of 111-year-old antihero Jack Crabb, by his account the only survivor of the Battle of Little Big Horn.

His tale constitutes a satirical revision of the Western and provides a significant revaluation of the romance of the West; it also predicts the increasingly affirmative image of Native Americans that followed. *Little Big Man* was adapted to film in 1970, starring Dustin Hoffman.

Bibliography
Landon, Brooks. *Thomas Berger.* Boston: Twayne, 1989.
Madden, David W., ed. *Critical Essays on Thomas Berger.* New York: Hall, 1995.

Reuben Ellis

Little Engine That Could, The, is one of the best known and most enduring stories for very young children. Its enchanting and optimistic refrain, "I think I can. I think I can," has become part of the American lexicon since its first official publication by Watty Piper in 1926. The history of *The Little Engine That Could* can be traced back to 1910, when Mabel Caroline Bragg published "The Pony Engine" in *Kindergarten Review*, but the story's oral roots actually go back to the 1880s, the glory days of the steam engine.

Beyond its unique appeal, the story is representative of a class of literature for youngsters featuring machines that come to life or exhibit human characteristics. Virginia Burton's *Mike Mulligan and His Steam Shovel* (1939) presents a normally inanimate object who is able to feel emotion. Mary Anne, the steam shovel, is "VERY SAD" at being made to feel obsolete by electric and diesel shovels. Though she doesn't speak, her long-lasting friendship with Mike, her operator, is shown throughout. In the end, Mary Anne's digging skills are vindicated and she and Mike find a useful place for themselves in the contemporary world. Burton also wrote *Katy and the Big Snow* (1943), a validation of American technological know-how that also celebrates perseverance and community spirit.

Other famous machine stories include Hardie Gramatky's *Hercules* (1940), about the adventures of a courageous horse-drawn fire engine, and *Little Toot* (1939), featuring a feisty tugboat; Graham Greene's *The Little Train* (1952) and *The Little Steamroller* (1950); and Gertrude Crampton's *Scuffy the Tugboat* (1946), about a self-important little toy vessel who overreaches and is rescued back to the safety of the bathtub.

Bibliography
Haviland, Virginia, ed. *Books before Five: Speeches and Essays by Louise Seaman Bechtel*. New York: Macmillan, 1969.

Dale Rigby
Mary E. Beardsley Land
Liahna Babener

Little Orphan Annie (1924-), the comic strip by Harold Lincoln Gray (1894-1968), was originally envisioned as about a boy. However, Captain Joseph Medill Patterson, comic strip mogul of the *New York News* and the *Chicago Tribune*, suggested that "Gray put skirts on the kid and call her Little Orphan Annie"—a name derived from the title of a once-famous James Whitcomb Riley poem. Gray did, and the comic strip succeeded beyond all expectations.

Harold Gray was born on his parents' farm in Kankakee, IL. He was a graduate of Purdue University, worked in the *Chicago Tribune* Art Department, and was a veteran of World War I. Gray's famous comic strip, with its legendary title character, her dog Sandy, her adopted father Daddy Warbucks, and a myriad of friends and foes, was launched in the *New York Daily News*. Storylines featured Horatio Alger-like "rags to riches" themes, celebrated moral goodness and hard work, and the inevitable (as Gray saw it) triumph of "good" over "evil." *Little Orphan Annie* was particularly popular in the 1920s and 1930s, perhaps due to themes of hope for good people down on their luck (as many people were during the Depression). Annie, herself, was the star of a radio show sponsored by Ovaltine drink mix, and was the focus of a Broadway musical which debuted in April 1977.

After Harold Gray died in 1968, there were several unsuccessful writers and artists who tried to carry the strip forward. Finally, as of the December 9, 1979, installment of *Little Orphan Annie*, Leonard Starr brought Harold Gray's strip back to respectability.

Bibliography
Blackbeard, Bill, and Martin Williams, eds. *The Smithsonian Collection of Newspaper Comics*. Washington, DC: Smithsonian, 1977.
Galewitz, Herb, ed. *Great Comics Syndicated by* Daily News-Chicago Tribune. New York: Crown, 1972.
Goulart, Ron. *The Encyclopedia of American Comics from 1897 to the Present*. New York: Facts on File, 1990.

Garyn G. Roberts

Lloyd, Charles (1938-). Lloyd's story is among the most idiosyncratic in jazz history. From 1966 to 1968, he enjoyed unprecedented commercial success while garnering international critical raves as the savior of jazz's artistic integrity. He was instrumental both in brokering the fusion between rock and jazz that would prove so influential throughout the 1970s, and in the marriage of jazz and orientalist spirituality that would captivate many musicians in the same period. His time in the sun was as brief as it was intense: by 1969, the musician that one critic had hailed as "the likeliest candidate to succeed" Sonny Rollins and John Coltrane had retired to obscurity, making comebacks in the 1970s and 1980s but never gaining anything close to his original prominence.

Lloyd was born in Memphis, and apprenticed himself on alto saxophone as a teenager to local luminaries Phineas Newborn, Booker Little, George Coleman, and Hank Crawford. He also paid dues in Bobby Bland's blues outfit. Lloyd began studies in dentistry only to move to Los Angeles and the jazz life in 1956, where he spent six years at USC as a composition student. He also began a casual association with avant gardists Eric Dolphy and Ornette Coleman. In 1961, he joined drummer Chico Hamilton's group, cutting his teeth in bandleading skills as its arranger and manager; switching to tenor in 1962, he entered Cannonball Adderley's sextet.

Hamilton's ensembles always had an experimental bent, and Adderley had long been at the forefront of the populist "soul" reaction to the academicism of bebop. Lloyd thus formed his own band in 1964 under a remarkable cross-pollination of influences. But Lloyd's first two albums, *Discovery* and *Of Course, Of Course*, received little attention. In 1966, however, Lloyd and George Avakian put together a remarkable group of young unknowns—Keith Jarrett on piano, Jack DeJohnette on drums, and Cecil McBee on bass (later Ron McClure)—and launched a Barnumesque promotional scheme. The Charles Lloyd Quartet released *Dream Weaver*, and the group was a hit.

Musically, Lloyd's tenor style was an unremarkable imitation of John Coltrane (whose music was becoming increasing inaccessible concurrent with Lloyd's rise). His popularity seemed to rest on his ability to embody all things to all audiences—traditional jazz aficionados and young psychedelics both claimed him as one of their own—in a time when all boundaries seemed in flux. The quartet broke up in 1969, and Lloyd was heard from sporadically until the mid-seventies, when he recorded some listless pop offerings in collaboration with former Beach Boy Mike Love and spiritual leader Maharishi Mahesh Yogi. His career took a remarkable twist in 1982, however, when the 18-year-old French pianist

Michel Petrucciani urged him out of seclusion and back into jazz. This led to a brief association with Blue Note records; Lloyd now records on ECM, where his modal style gels effectively with the German label's cool Euro-aesthetic.

Bibliography
"Charles Lloyd: Way Out, Way In." *Playboy* Dec. 1962: 220.
Crocker, R. "Charles Lloyd: New Journey." *Down Beat* Jan. 1973: 13.
"Dolphins on a Wave: Charles Lloyd, Prophet of New Wave Jazz." *Time* 3 Feb. 1996: 32.
Giddens, Gary. "Weatherbird: Something Borrowed, Something Blue (One Night with Blue Note Concert at Town Hall)." *Village Voice* 19 Mar. 1985: 68.

Rick Perlstein

London, Jack (1876-1916), during the first two decades of the 20th century, was the most famous writer in the U.S. Through determination and relentless self-promotion, he successfully overcame illegitimacy, an impoverished and vagrant childhood, and a grinding succession of manual laboring jobs (salmon canner, pin-boy in a bowling alley, gold miner, jute mill worker, coal shoveler, and laundry worker) to become a preeminent writer of tales of dangerous adventure. Many of London's stories are set in the Arctic and the South Seas, but no matter the setting, as a body they present the author's idiosyncratic combination of Socialist and individualist ideas. During his apprenticeship as a writer, London had read heavily in political philosophy and social science, including the works of Darwin, Marx, Malthus, Mill, Nietzsche, Spencer, and others, all of which helped to shape his worldview.

The Call of the Wild (1903) was London's fourth book and first success, and has remained in print since its publication. It describes the fate of Buck, a civilized dog stolen from a sunny California ranch and taken to Alaska to work as a sled dog. Buck's ancestral memories reawaken, and after his master is killed, he reverts to his primitive heritage and becomes the frightful Ghost Dog of the North. *White Fang* (1906) reverses the theme of *The Call of the Wild*, depicting a savage dog moving from the north to California; in its portrayal of the redeeming powers of civilization, it is less convincing than the earlier novel.

The Sea Wolf (1904) and *Martin Eden* (1909) are also among London's more notable novels. They contain autobiographical elements and reflect ideas gleaned from Nietzsche and Spencer. *The Sea Wolf* is dominated by the indomitable Captain Wolf Larsen, and *Martin Eden* describes the drive of a young sailor to overcome his naivete and low origins to achieve social status and romance, a quest culminating in bitter suicide. *The Iron Heel* (1908), told retrospectively by a narrator from the future, depicts a political revolution wherein capitalist interests band together to create a repressive society, policed by the Iron Heel, until it is overthrown in the distant future to be replaced by a collectivist utopia. He also wrote a number of short stories with science fiction themes, including "Goliah" (1908) and "When the World Was Young" (1910).

Richard Bleiler

Photo courtesy of Popular Culture Library, Bowling Green State University, Bowling Green, OH.

Lone Ranger, The (1933-1957). Some three months after Hopalong Cassidy's television debut in 1949, *The Lone Ranger* joined him on the video range and became one of the most famous and influential programs in the United States. Another hero from the B-Western mold, but one created especially for radio, *The Lone Ranger* had first premiered on Detroit radio station WXYZ in late January 1933.

Businessman George W. Trendle, owner of the station, discovered that the Western, which had been so successful on the movie screen, had not yet been adapted for radio. He also believed that there was a lack of wholesome, well-written, and appealing programs for children. Influenced by the assumption that children are less critical and can coax their parents into buying the sponsor's product, Trendle decided to develop a Western drama for children.

The creation of Trendle's proposed series was a "cooperative" effort headed by Buffalo, NY, scriptwriter Fran Striker using suggestions from WXYZ staff director Jim Jewell and Trendle himself. Gradually, the concept took on the familiar characteristics of the Ranger as he is known today: a Texas Ranger, sole survivor of an ambush; wearing a mask to conceal his true identity; riding a great white horse, eventually named Silver; silver bullets as his "calling card"; an Indian companion (Tonto) with whom to talk.

Within five years of its inception, the adventures of the Lone Ranger were being released in novels, comic strips, comic books and motion pictures. The Ranger was first adapted for the screen in 1938's 15-chapter serial, *The Lone Ranger*, in which Lee Powell played the title role. A year later, another serial, *The Lone Ranger Rides Again*, was released with Bob Livingston as "the masked rider of the plains."

Filming for the television version began on June 21, 1949, a full 16 years after the Ranger's radio debut. Clayton Moore was signed to play the Lone Ranger and Jay Silverheels, a full-blooded Mohawk by birth from Ontario, Canada, became TV's Tonto. General Mills, radio sponsor of the series, also underwrote the video version at an average production cost of $12,500 for each of the first 52 episodes. The outdoor scenes were filmed at locations in Utah and in California at Corriganville, Iverson's Ranch, Big Bear, and Sonora first for Hal Roach Studios and later for General Services Studios.

The series debuted on the home screen for ABC on September 15, 1949, and was carried by 90 stations coast-to-coast. The first three episodes presented the familiar story of how the Lone Ranger had received his name and his mission in life at Bryant's Gap. Within a year the Thursday night show was in the Nielsen Top 10 with a viewing audience of some 5 million people. It was ABC's highest rated program all season and the highest-rated television Western up to that time.

After the 1950-51 season, Moore reportedly threatened to quit unless he received a substantial raise. Trendle balked at his demands and hired John Hart to replace him, apparently believing the audience would not realize a switch had been made under the mask. John Hart could be described as little more than adequate as the Ranger, although he remained in the role for two seasons, filming 52 episodes. In 1954, Trendle wisely rehired Moore, who played the Ranger in the final 91 episodes.

Through much of the 1950s, the series had the distinction of being broadcast on two major networks. ABC aired the prime-time broadcasts and CBS owned the Saturday afternoon rerun rights. In 1960, NBC telecast *The Lone Ranger* on Saturday mornings. The network telecasts ended September 23, 1961, and thereafter episodes have been syndicated.

Bibliography

Harmon, Jim. *Radio Mystery and Adventure and Its Appearance in Film, Television, and Other Media.* Jefferson: McFarland, 1992.

Holland, Dave. *From out of the Past: A Pictorial History of the Lone Ranger.* Granada: Holland House, 1988.

Rothel, David. *Who Was That Masked Man? The Story of the Lone Ranger.* San Diego: Barnes, 1981.

Van Hise, James. *The Story of the Lone Ranger.* Las Vegas: Pioneer, 1990.

Gary A. Yoggy

Lonesome Dove (1989), the CBS television miniseries, was based on a novel by Larry McMurtry (see entry) that had won wide critical acclaim and had become an almost instant best-seller. It was clear that the film version of this tale about three Texas ranchers on a cattle drive would not be an ordinary movie. Logistics alone precluded that from happening: eight hours of air time (less commercials), a budget of nearly $20 million, a big-name cast, and a devastating 16-week shooting schedule involving massive location shifts, dozens of sets, 89 speaking parts, 1,000 extras, 90 production people, 1,400 head of cattle, 100 horses and 30 wranglers. Though it was being produced for the home screen, the film's scale was a vast throwback to the bygone days of such large-screen epics as *The Alamo* and *How the West Was Won*.

A superb cast of veteran actors was assembled to fill the lead roles. The incomparable Augustus McCrae was played by the Academy Award-winning actor Robert Duvall. Tommy Lee Jones, a Harvard-educated native Texan who raises cattle and horses on his ranch in San Saba, TX, seemed equally perfect for the role of Captain Woodrow F. Call. The central female character in *Lonesome Dove* is Lorena Wood (Diane Lane), the town prostitute at the Dry Bean Saloon. Lorena joins Call and McCrae's cattle drive to Montana and is subsequently kidnapped by a renegade half-breed and his gang of cutthroats. Sold to a band of traders, she is rescued by Gus. The role of Clara Allen, Gus's long-lost love, was given to Oscar-winner Anjelica Huston. Danny Glover was cast as Joshua Deets, the cowboy tracker and long-time friend of Gus and Call.

In addition to being the story of fascinating relationships among unforgettable characters, *Lonesome Dove* is the exciting story of a hazardous cattle drive from Texas to Montana dramatized in the second and third parts. Jack Spoon (Robert Urich), on the lam from the law in Arkansas where he accidentally killed the town dentist, spins a romantic yarn about his travels to Montana, a land so lush and beautiful it would be the ideal spot for a cattle ranch. For Call this is an opportunity for one last adventure, one last test of manhood. For Gus, the drive will provide a chance to see once more the only true love of his life—Clara Allen, a woman who rejected him to marry a more stable and reliable horse trader in Ogallala, NE. And so, against Gus's better judgment, he reluctantly agrees to Call and Spoon's plan for a cattle drive to Montana.

While earning almost universal critical acclaim, *Lonesome Dove* was also a huge commercial success by nearly every criterion. It scored the biggest miniseries ratings triumph in five television seasons and made money for the network from its first airing alone—rare for a miniseries.

A Western on television had not generated such critical acclaim and financial rewards since the golden age of TV Westerns during the late 1950s and early 1960s. This enthusiasm called for a sequel: *Return to Lonesome Dove* aired on CBS in 1993.

Bibliography

Busby, Mark. *Larry McMurtry and the West: An Ambivalent Relationship.* Denton: UP of North Texas, 1995.

Jones, Roger Walton. *Larry McMurtry and the Victorian Novel.* College Station: Texas A&M UP, 1994.

Yoggy, Gary. *Riding the Video Range: The Rise and Fall of the Western on Television.* Jefferson: McFarland, 1995.

Gary A. Yoggy

Lost in Space (1965-1968) was a successful television series aimed at a young audience, relating the adventures of the Robinson family as they attempted pioneering in another galaxy. Though taking advantage of a science fiction format, the series was structurally related to such 1950s situation comedies as *Leave It to Beaver, Ozzie and Harriet,* and *The Donna Reed Show.* Because of overpopulation, the earth launched the Jupiter II carrying the Robinson family to settle a planet in orbit around Alpha Centauri. A stowaway, Dr. Zachary Smith (Jonathan Harris), sabotages the ship, throwing it hopelessly off course. The episodes entail the Robinsons' attempts to get back on the way to their destination and Smith's attempts to return to earth. In addition to Smith, the Robinsons, and their three children, the cast included a pilot, and an amiable robot who combined scientific intelligence with the qualities of a pet, a playmate, and a nursemaid.

The concept for the series, developed by the producer Irwin Allen, derived immediately from the comic book series *The Space Family Robinson* and ultimately from the novel *The Swiss Family Robinson* by Johann Rudolph Wyss (1813). The influence of the feature film *Forbidden Planet* (1956) is also apparent in the series, both in theme and in visual design. The shipwreck on a hostile planet is a frequent plot device, and like the earth ship in *Forbidden Planet*, the Jupiter II is saucer-shaped. Robby the Robot is also clearly an ancestor to the robot belonging to the Robinson family.

The special effects were simple, even given the technology of the time. Though both parents are scientists, the plots never revolve about scientific theory. Neither do the Robinsons encounter problems of life support, though those issues loomed large both in the comic book narratives and in the original novel. The simplicity of the episodes was unattractive to many adult science fiction fans, but serious science fiction was never the object of the series. Rather, the plots revolve around issues of family loyalty and cooperation. A characteristic plot involved Will Robinson (Billy Mumy) faced with a moral choice, his alternatives acted out by the "good child" robot and the "bad child" Dr. Smith. Though set in space and attended by melodrama, adventure, and farce, the series was a fable designed to promulgate morality in the young.

Bibliography

CBS News Releases 15 Sept. 1965; 30 Sept. 1965; 7 July 1967.

Naha, Ed. *The Science Fictionary.* New York: Sea View, 1980.

Peel, John. *The Lost in Space Files.* Canoga Park: PSI FI Movie, 1986.

Van Hise, James. Lost in Space: *25th Anniversary Tribute Book.* Las Vegas: Pioneer, 1990.

Janet P. Sholty

Lotteries. Across America state lotteries have become one of this country's surprising growth industries. Tens of billions of dollars worth of lottery tickets are sold each year in the United States. Lottery players spend well over $100 per capita in states with legalized lotteries, and the numbers are growing.

Political expedience has allowed the lottery rage to develop. Several states have promoted the use of the lottery to the extent that it has become an obsession for many of the players, and the advertising often does not make clear the odds of winning (lower, actually, than other forms of gambling). Further, the economic burden falls mainly on lower-income persons, who tend to devote a larger percentage of their income to lotteries than those with higher incomes. However, concerns over compulsive gambling and the regressiveness of the lottery tax have been overwhelmed by the sensation of lottery prizes.

State governments have commonly felt fiscal stress since the early 1970s. Economic downturns and taxpayer revolts have become a contemporary challenge for the states while demands for services from state governments have steadily increased. As a result, state governments have been probing for new sources of tax revenues. A key new source of this tax revenue is now being derived from state lotteries. Over two-thirds of the states now offer lotteries.

In reality state lotteries are simply a voluntary tax with a financial game of chance attached at long odds. Almost one-half of the money wagered will be lost or, in essence, forfeited to the state as a tax. The money voluntarily lost by the taxpayer/gambler is utilized to cover the cost of operating the lottery, with the remainder reverting to the state treasury.

Each state generates lottery games with different methods of play. These methods are dictated by state law or by state constitution. Lotto, daily numbers games, and instant lotteries have become common games for most state lotteries. In lotto, the player will typically select six numbers. Each week, or every two weeks, the official lotto numbers are posted. If the players' numbers match the official numbers, a prize is awarded. A $2 lotto ticket has often exceeded $100 million in payout for the winner. If no one chooses the winning numbers, the jackpot rolls over and compounds. Large rollovers often make headline news. If multiple players pick the correct number, the jackpot will be divided among them. Daily numbers is a computerized version of the illegal numbers game long popular in many American cities. A three- or four-digit number is selected randomly each day and a fixed payoff is paid to players with matching numbers. Instant lottery allows a player to purchase a ticket and scratch a surface covering to reveal if a prize has been won.

Bibliography

Bingham, Richard D., and David Hedge. *State and Local Government in a Changing Society.* 2d ed. New York: McGraw-Hill, 1991.

Browning, Edgar K., and Jacquelene M. Browning. *Public Finance and the Price System.* 4th ed. New York: Macmillan, 1994.

"Casinos Move into New Areas." *Leisure Time.* Vol. 1 of *Standard & Poor's Industry Surveys.* New York: Standard & Poor's, 1993.

Clotfelter, Charles T. *Selling Hope: State Lotteries in America.* Cambridge: Harvard UP, 1989.

Watts, Tim J. *State-Run Lotteries: A Bibliography.* Monticello: Vance, 1991.

Philip K. Flynn

Lou Grant (1977-1982), a drama series on CBS, by exploring compelling issues with intelligence and compassion, stood out among comedy and action series of the period. It was a spinoff of a popular situation comedy, *The Mary Tyler Moore Show* (CBS, 1970-77; see entry), which co-starred actor Edward Asner as the gruff but endearing news director of a television station. In a unique move, the new series transplanted the character from a half-hour comedy to an hour-long drama that portrayed life at a metropolitan daily newspaper.

Nearly all of the two dozen newspaper dramas that had aired before *Lou Grant* were inauthentic, usually featuring reporters as crime-solving sleuths. The acclaimed Watergate film *All the President's Men* (1976) strongly influenced producers Gene Reynolds, Allan Burns, and James L. Brooks as they created the series. The series was a hit within the television industry and with critics, who hailed its realistic portrayal of journalism. It became a symbol of the medium's ability to offer quality programming. Among its numerous honors were a Peabody Award (1978) and 13 Emmy Awards, including those for outstanding drama in 1979 and 1980. Despite such acclaim, *Lou Grant* earned only average ratings during the regular television season.

Lou Grant ended amid controversy seldom seen in the medium. Asner, the president of the Screen Actors Guild and a vocal liberal, publicly supported humanitarian aid for El Salvador. His conservative critics claimed he had aided leftist rebels fighting the U.S.-backed government and had failed to distance the union from his personal views, charges Asner refuted. Three months of contentious debate, including calls for sponsor boycotts, climaxed with the cancellation of the series. Although CBS cited falling ratings for its action, others believed the network had succumbed to outside pressures.

The circumstances behind the demise of *Lou Grant* overshadowed its legacy as a groundbreaking series that preceded *Hill Street Blues* (NBC, 1981-87), *St. Elsewhere* (NBC, 1982-88), and other realistic dramas of the 1980s.
Bibliography
Daniel, Douglass K. Lou Grant: *The Making of TV's Top Newspaper Drama.* Syracuse: Syracuse UP, 1996.
Tener, Jane, Paul Kerr, and Tise Vahimagi, eds. MTM *"Quality" Television.* London: BFI, 1984.

Douglass K. Daniel

Louis, Joe (Joseph Louis Barrow) (1914-1981), has been considered one of the best heavyweight boxers of all times and is known for having done "as much for blacks in the sport of boxing as Jackie Robinson did for baseball." Born in Alabama to sharecroppers Munroe and Lillie Barrow, Joe was the seventh of eighth children. His mother divorced his father and moved to Detroit.

An indifferent student at Brewster Trade School, Joe became interested in boxing matches and decided to attempt a boxing career. He lost his first bout in 1932 but went on to win 50 bouts, 43 by knockouts, and losing only four. Powerful, quick, possessing the power to jab with either hand and to also deliver compact punishing punches with hammerstroke impact, Louis became the prototype of the new heavyweight contender.

Louis turned professional on July 4, 1934, when he knocked out Jack Kracken in the first round. This began a string of 27 straight victories for Louis, whose victims would include former champions Primo Carnera and Max Baer. However, in 1936, at Yankee Stadium, he faced the German boxer Max Schmeling, who administered a sound beating to Louis and dropped him in the 12th round with a knockout.

Coming back from this adversity, Louis strung together seven straight victories to earn a title shot at the heavyweight crown held by James J. Braddock. The two met on June 22, 1937, at Chicago's Comiskey Park. Although dropped to the canvas early in the bout, Louis bounced back to knock Braddock out in the eighth round. Louis became a hero for many urban black youths as he attained the championship belt last held by an African American, Jack Johnson, in 1908.

Joe Louis then compiled a series of victories which hardly tested him, so that he was frequently criticized for fighting a "Bum of the Month." However, his rematch with Max Schmeling in June of 1938 solidified Joe's reputation as a hero for all Americans, not just African Americans. With anti-Nazi feeling running rampant, Schmeling was portrayed as an example of the "master race" by the media.

Louis dispatched Schmeling with a knockout in 2.04 of the first round, after administering one of the most vicious beatings in the history of boxing and also having one of the quickest ends to a heavyweight bout on record. Total gate receipts for the bout were over a million dollars.

Louis was regarded as a hero by all Americans for having dispensed with a representative of the "master race." African Americans could be truly proud of Louis, and all Americans could approve of his exploits over a representative of Hitler's Nazism. White Americans also approved of the fact that Louis was cut from a different bolt of cloth than the infamous heavyweight champion Jack Johnson, who was often criticized for "gloating over white opponents and consorting with white women." Louis's private life was one of discretion and reflected his need for privacy.

During World War II, Louis gave exhibition matches as a member of the Armed Forces but in his quiet way fought discrimination. He supported Jackie Robinson when Jackie was facing a court-martial over insubordination regarding a refusal to go to the back of a bus, and he threatened to quit giving exhibition matches if the army insisted that separate theater entrances were utilized for American forces in Britain.

Louis continued fighting after the war but retired in 1949 after beating Jersey Joe Walcott in a rematch. However, bad financial investments and a poor choice of advisers left Joe in debt. In 1950, he returned to boxing and lost a fifteen-round decision to champion Ezzard Charles. He boxed nine more times but retired permanently after being knocked out by Rocky Marciano on October 26, 1951.

In order to satisfy his debt to the IRS for back taxes, he served as a greeter at Caesars Palace in Las Vegas, where he lived the last years of his life with distinction and recognition as the honored ex-champion.

Bibliography
Astor, Gerald. *And a Credit to His Race: The Hard Life and Times of Joe Louis Barrow, a.k.a. Joe Louis.* New York: Dutton, 1974.
Barrow, Joe Louis, Jr., and Barbara Munder. *Joe Louis: 50 Years an American Hero.* New York: McGraw-Hill, 1988.
Mead, Chris. *Champion: Joe Louis, Black Hero in White America.* New York: Scribner, 1985.

Lawrence E. Ziewacz

Louisville Slugger, The, Hillerich and Bradsby's famous baseball bat, has, over the past century, become an institution. It has been transformed from "A bat" to "The bat." "A bat" is something used to hit a baseball or a softball. For such purposes any bat will do. "The bat," however, is the chosen implement of heroes. "The bat" is used to win games, hit home runs, or win batting titles. For such purposes you cannot use just any bat; you have to have "The bat." "The bat" holds the promise of future exploits on the field of play and the acquisition of greater glory. The Louisville Slugger is "The bat" of choice for sandlotters and major leaguers.

The transformation of the Louisville Slugger from any bat to the bat of choice began with notions connecting product craftsmanship with batting success. The creation of the Louisville Slugger, a customized bat designed to meet the specific requirements of the user, developed from the interaction of technical wood-turning skill and baseball experience. Bud Hillerich, the 1884 creator of the Louisville Slugger, was a skilled wood turner who worked in his father's wood customizing business. Equally important, Bud played semi-pro baseball during the early 1880s in Louisville's city league.

Hillerich made his own customized baseball bats. He adjusted the size, weight, and taper of the bats based on their performance. This concept was further enhanced when members of the Louisville Eclipse team sought Hillerich's services as bat maker for the team.

Endorsements by popular major league stars influenced the process of transformation. Pete Browning (1861-1905) typifies how the relationship between Louisville Slugger baseball bats and batting excellence developed. Browning was "the Louisville Slugger." He was born in Louisville, grew up on the city's playing fields, and became synonymous with baseball slugging excellence. Early in 1884 Browning, faced with a batting slump, sought Bud Hillerich's help. Bud made a special bat for Browning. The next day Browning went 3 for 3, and the legend of the Louisville Slugger began.

The autograph model Louisville Slugger, introduced with the Honus Wagner model in 1905, further spread the notion that batting success required the right implement—the Louisville Slugger. The importance of the autograph model was two-fold. First, it functioned as the epitome of endorsement. When famous sluggers like Babe Ruth used a personalized bat with their name on it, the implication was that the Louisville Slugger had something to do with their phenomenal deeds at bat.

Second, the autograph model Louisville Slugger was more than mere endorsement. In the hands of youthful sandlotters, autograph models became instruments of imagination and dream. For example, an adult baseball buff admitted recently that as a youth, swinging an Ernie Banks autograph model Louisville Slugger, he became a great shortstop, performing prodigious deeds with his special bat. For him, the Louisville Slugger was not just any bat. It was a handcrafted weapon with magical powers, the implement of heroes. Such tales help inform about the how and why of the Louisville Slugger's transition from "A bat" to "The bat."

Bibliography
"A Baseball Player Called Pete." *Louisville Magazine* 20 Jan. 1959: 7-10.
Dudley, Bruce. "Every Knock Is a Boost for the Louisville Slugger." *Louisville Herald Magazine* 12 May 1913: 8-10.
Hardy, Stephen. "Adopted by All the Leading Clubs: Sporting Goods and the Shaping of Leisure, 1800-1900." *For Fun and Profit: The Transformation of Leisure into Consumption.* Ed. Richard Butsch. Philadelphia: Temple UP, 1990. 71-101.
"Still Top Slugger at 75." *Louisville Magazine* 20 Jan. 1959: 7-10.
Van Borries, Philip. "The Original Louisville Slugger." *Louisville Magazine* 10 May 1984: 42.

Lawrence W. Fielding
Lori K. Miller

Love Story (1970), Erich Segal's short novel, was a phenomenal success from its publication, heralded by *Time* magazine as ushering in "a new era of romanticism." A modern-day Cinderella story, the novel retroactively tells of the relationship between a wealthy Harvard student and an Italian-American scholarship student at Radcliffe. Appearing simultaneously in hardcover and in condensed form in *Ladies' Home Journal,* the novel was turned into a blockbuster film that same year. The film recouped its production costs within three days; the paperback release of *Love Story* sold over 5 million copies in its first edition.

Segal's experience as a Hollywood screenwriter makes the book's dialogue sharp and reflective of late 1960s colloquial speech. Its climactic statement, "Love means not ever having to say you're sorry," has become a cliché among its millions of readers, who nonetheless continue to add to the over 21 million copies sold.

Bibliography
Corliss, Richard. *Talking Pictures: Screenwriters in the American Cinema.* Woodstock: Overlook, 1974.
Larson, Charles R. "Why *Love Story?*" *Journal of Popular Culture* 4 (1971).
Meyer, Nicholas. *The Love Story.* New York: Avon, 1971.

Melody M. Zajdel

Lovecraft, H(oward) P(hillips) (1890-1937), now acknowledged as one of the foremost American writers of fantastic literature, was denied recognition during his lifetime. Publishing exclusively in pulp magazines, primarily *Weird Tales,* Lovecraft escaped the attention of the critical establishment and mainstream readers. Following his death, only the devoted efforts of literary friends, known as "the Lovecraft circle" and including such writers as August Derleth and Robert Bloch (see entry), kept his work from obscurity until he was discovered by genre aficionados and gradually a broader audience.

Lovecraft's influence on modern horror and fantasy fiction cannot be underestimated (see Horror Fiction). His short tales written during the early 1920s and subsequent novels in the later '20s and '30s evoke a peculiar cosmic horror: a sense of the smallness of humankind's glories and follies against the titanic energies of an infinite universe. Lovecraft's protagonists are usually intellectuals or scientists whose curiosity leads to a crippling recognition of the utter irrelevancy of humanity in the cosmos. In the series of stories dubbed "the Cthulhu Mythos," extraterrestrial, prehuman entities possessed of godlike powers threaten the earth's inhabitants with annihilation. The rare human victories are temporary; madness and death are the only certainties.

In his work, Lovecraft created a full pseudomythical cosmology around the struggle between the "Old Ones" and humanity that revitalized gothic horror traditions with a modernist sensibility. His stories are collected in *The Outsider and Others* (1939) and *Beyond the Wall of Sleep* (1943). Among his novels are *The Dream-Quest of Unknown Kadath* (1926); *The Case of Charles Dexter Ward* (1926); and *At the Mountains of Madness* (1931).

Bibliography

Burleson, Donald R. *H. P. Lovecraft: A Critical Study.* Westport: Greenwood, 1983.
Carter, Lin. *Lovecraft: A Look behind the Cthulhu Mythos.* New York: Ballantine, 1972.
Long, Frank Belknap. *Howard Phillips Lovecraft: Dreamer on the Nightside.* Sauk City: Arkham, 1975.
Schweitzer, Darrell. *The Dream Quest of H. P. Lovecraft.* San Bernardino: Borgo, 1978.

Philip Simpson

Ludlum, Robert (1927-   ), has authored more than 20 successful popular novels (three under the names of Jonathan Ryder and Michael Shepherd). A former Marine, actor, and producer, Ludlum turned to fiction in the early 1970s.

Ludlum's first book, *The Scarlatti Inheritance* (1971), establishes a recurrent theme in his fiction, the insidious and corruptive power of money. Other characteristics of a trademark Ludlum novel include a highly complex plot involving conspiracy, an international stage, and a rampantly violent atmosphere. The typical Ludlum hero is a character in over his head, such as John Tanner in *The Osterman Weekend* (1972). In three novels (*The Bourne Identity*, 1980; *The Bourne Supremacy*, 1986; and *The Bourne Ultimatum*, 1990), all built around the character of Jason Bourne, the many-layered world of the terrorist Carlos the Jackal is presented. Many of the novels reverberate with World War II echoes where the enduring Nazi influence is traced through flashbacks into contemporary times. Notable film versions of Ludlum books include *The Osterman Weekend* (filmed in 1983) and *The Holcroft Covenant* (1978, filmed in 1985 with Michael Caine).

Bibliography

Greenberg, Martin H., ed. *The Robert Ludlum Companion.* New York: Bantam, 1993.
Merry, Bruce. *Anatomy of the Spy Thriller.* Montreal: McGill-Queen's UP, 1977.

Nicholas Ranson

See also
Spy Fiction

Lugosi, Bela (1892-1956), was born Bela Blasko in Hungary (later a part of Rumania) in the town of Lugos—which he later adapted to become his surname. His father was a successful baker and the family prospered, until his death in 1894. Lugosi studied to become a locksmith, but soon gave it up for acting, making it his profession by 1901.

Lugosi appeared in all manner of venues and roles, touring with stock companies and picking up work wherever he could find it. Repertory theater provided expansive experience for the young actor, from bit parts to leading roles. By 1910, Lugosi was considered a rising star to take note of, and good work was plentiful.

World War I interrupted his career, with Lugosi serving for almost two years and being wounded twice. Returning from the front, he resumed his career in Hungary and was also married in 1917. That same year was also the first time he appeared in motion pictures. In order to appeal to non-Hungarian audiences, Lugosi used the name Arisztid Olt, a name he abandoned upon leaving Hungary just over two years later.

Legitimately fearing for his life due to the political turmoil in Hungary, Lugosi fled to Vienna, but could not find work. He went to Berlin, where he was able to obtain work (often starring) in films in Germany's exploding motion picture industry. Lugosi came to the USA in 1921. He tried to begin a Hungarian acting troupe, but was unable to make it successful. He struggled with English and began to rebuild his career on stage and in film. Though he was considered a romantic leading man in Europe, in the USA his accent and acting style typed him in villainous roles.

Lugosi had minor successes in both media as the twenties continued. In 1927, he was offered the role that would change his life: that of Dracula in a stage version of the famous novel (see entry). Reviews indicate that the play had some staging problems, but the force of Lugosi's mesmerizing performance held the play together and it played Broadway for over 250 performances before going on tour. Lugosi revived the play several times throughout his life, even touring in it as late as 1951.

Lugosi had made seven sound film appearances before *Dracula* was brought to the screen in 1931. As Lugosi entered his late 40s, he achieved stardom. Lugosi made four more films before the impact of Dracula set in. A full year passed between the release of *Dracula* and his next starring film, *Murders in the Rue Morgue* (1932), the film role he chose, having turned down the role of Frankenstein's monster. Loosely based on the Edgar Allan Poe mystery, the film was not the big hit Lugosi or Universal Studios had hoped for.

Lugosi's other starring follow-ups to *Dracula* were also near misses in their time. Though esteemed today, the brooding and atmospheric *White Zombie* (1932) failed to get wide release. The lackluster *Chandu the Magician* (1932) fared no better.

Lugosi bounced back in 1933 as the ape/human "teller of the law" in *Island of the Lost Souls* and seemed to settle in to a career of intriguing supporting roles in major productions, while starring in lower budget efforts from smaller studios.

His teaming with Boris Karloff in *The Raven* (1935) is a remarkable turn, going beyond the "mad-scientist" stereotypes to the point of creating them anew. However, his best appearance with Karloff was four years later in *The Son of Frankenstein*. Here Lugosi co-starred as Ygor, a man who survived hanging and found the revived monster, whom he befriends to enact revenge on the jury which condemned him to death. Lugosi steals the picture, and reprised his role three years later in *The Ghost of Frankenstein*. Lugosi's Ygor is a perfectly realized performance, and many consider it his finest screen moment.

Though most of Lugosi's low-budget starring vehicles have little to offer other than Lugosi himself, occasionally the pieces fell into place. One such minor gem is 1941's *The Invisible Ghost*, in which Lugosi's performance as a grieving widower (or is he?) is underplayed to great emotional impact.

Lugosi's career faltered a bit, but he was still working fairly steadily throughout the early and mid-1940s. One highlight is *The Return of the Vampire* (1944), an enjoyable horror outing with Lugosi in fine form. After 1946, Lugosi's career stalled, though he would certainly make more films, his turn as Dracula in *Abbott and Costello Meet Frankenstein* (1948) being perhaps the best.

He worked on stage, doing personal appearance tours with a "mad-scientist" act, or scenes from *Dracula*, even occasionally appearing in *Arsenic and Old Lace*. Television appearances were infrequent. Lugosi went in search of good film roles, but nothing much was offered. Roles parodying his past success in *Bela Lugosi Meets a Brooklyn Gorilla* and *Mother Riley Meets the Vampire,* both from 1952, were all he could gain, except for three films for the notorious director Ed Wood, Jr. He had just begun work on the third film when he died in August of 1956.

Bibliography

Bojarski, Richard. *The Films of Bela Lugosi.* Secaucus, NJ: Citadel, 1980.

Lennig, Arthur. *The Count: The Life and Times of Bela "Dracula" Lugosi.* New York: Putnam's, 1974.

Mank, Gregory William. *Karloff and Lugosi: The Story of a Haunting Collaboration.* Jefferson, NC: McFarland, 1990.

Svehla, Gary J., and Susan Svehla, eds. *Bela Lugosi.* Baltimore, MD: Midnight Marquee, 1995.

Ben Urish

Lupino, Ida (1918-1995), actress, director, producer, writer, composer—her list of motion picture and television credits attests to her versatility and her creative contributions in both entertainment industries. Ida Lupino was born into one of England's oldest theatrical families in London. Her father was noted music hall comedian Stanley Lupino, her mother actress Connie Emerald. Following the family tradition, Lupino made her first stage appearance as a child and by age 15 was studying at the Royal Academy of Dramatic Art. Film director Allan Dwan cast her in *Her First Affair* (1932). With her bleached hair and penciled eyebrows, she was promoted as Britain's Jean Harlow. Then Paramount brought her to the United States, intending for her to play Alice in *Alice in Wonderland*. Following a screen test, studio executives cast her instead in a series of ingenue roles.

Dissatisfied with the direction her career was taking, Lupino let her hair grow out and her eyebrows grow in. Cast in William Wellman's *The Light That Failed* (1939), Lupino gained recognition as a dramatic actress. A series of challenging roles followed in such films as Raoul Walsh's *They Drive by Night* (1940) and *High Sierra* (1941), Charles Vidor's *Ladies in Retirement* (1941), Michael Curtiz's *The Sea Wolf* (1941), Vincent Sherman's *The Hard Way* (1942), which won her the New York Critics best actress award, and Jean Negulesco's *Road House* (1948).

In 1949, Ida Lupino, Collier Young (her second husband), and Anson Bond formed Emerald Productions and produced *Not Wanted* (1949). When director Elmer Clifton suffered a heart attack, Lupino stepped in and finished directing the film. Later that year Bond left the partnership and the company was reorganized as The Filmmakers by Lupino, Young, and Malvin Wald. Of the nine feature films completed before The Filmmakers became inactive in 1954, Lupino directed six. Lupino also co-wrote the scripts for several of these films.

As employment opportunities in the motion picture industry narrowed in the early 1950s, more Hollywood stars turned to television. In 1952, Ida Lupino joined Dick Powell, Charles Boyer, and David Niven in the anthology drama series *Four Star Playhouse*. In 1956, she was hostess and star for a series of television dramas syndicated as *The Ida Lupino Theatre*. In 1957, Lupino and Howard Duff (her third husband) developed and starred in *Mr. Adams and Eve*. This situation comedy was built around the efforts of a film star couple to maintain a normal life. It lasted for 68 episodes and earned Lupino two Emmy nominations as best actress in a comedy series. From the early 1950s through the late 1970s, Lupino regularly appeared in a wide variety of roles in as wide a variety of series, from *Wild Wild West* and *Batman* to *Columbo* and *Charlie's Angels*. She continued to act in motion pictures and received a best supporting actress nomination from the New York Film Critics and the National Society of Film Critics for her work in *Junior Bonner* (1972).

More significant than Lupino's work as a television actress was her work as a television director. In 1956, Collier Young, producer of *On Trial*, convinced her to direct Joseph Cotten in "The Trial of Mary Seurat." The producer of *Have Gun, Will Travel* signed Lupino to direct an episode for that series. She quickly became known as a director who could handle action stories. Assignments followed to direct episodes for *Alfred Hitchcock Presents, The Untouchables,*

Kraft Suspense Theater, Twilight Zone, The Fugitive, The Big Valley, and others. Not content to be typecast as an action director, Lupino also directed comedy (*Gilligan's Island* and *Bewitched*) and drama (*Mr. Novak* and *Dr. Kildare*). In all, Lupino directed well over 100 television films and episodes.

Bibliography

Heck-Rabi, Louise. *Women Filmmakers: A Critical Reception*. Metuchen: Scarecrow, 1984.

Lupino, Ida. "Me, Mother Directress." *Action* May-June 1967: 14-15.

Stewart, Lucy Ann Liggett. *Ida Lupino As Film Director, 1949-1953: An Auteur Approach*. New York: Arno, 1980.

Weiner, Debra. "Interview with Ida Lupino." *Women and the Cinema: A Critical Anthology*. Ed. Karyn Kay and Gerald Peary. New York: Dutton, 1977.

Whitney, Dwight. "Follow Mother, Here We Go, Kiddies!" *TV Guide* 8 Oct. 1966: 15-18.

Lucy A. Liggett

Lux Radio Theater (1934-1955), successful for 20 years on radio, debuted on Sunday afternoons over NBC as a program that adapted Broadway plays for radio presentation. However, the show was in serious trouble following its premiere, even after a move to Monday evenings on CBS. Its ratings dropped four points within a year.

Danny Danker of the J. Walter Thompson advertising agency was sent in to save the program. After some investigation, he suggested the program move from New York City to Hollywood. Louella Parsons's *Hollywood Hotel* had broken the ice by demonstrating that radio appearances by major movie stars did not endanger their box office appeal but appeared to enhance it.

Within two years, the program began adapting Hollywood dramas. On June 1, 1936, Cecil B. DeMille (see entry) began his 10-year tenure as "host/producer." *Lux Radio Theater* became a hit and remained popular. Full adaptations of major movies were presented, often with the original stars. In addition to presenting Myrna Loy and William Powell in 1936's hit, *The Thin Man*, Clark Gable and Claudette Colbert reprised their roles in 1939's *It Happened One Night*, while Jimmy Cagney and his pal Pat O'Brien starred again in *Angels with Dirty Faces*. Bogie and Bacall returned to *Casablanca* and Jimmy Stewart, Cary Grant, and Katharine Hepburn retold *The Philadelphia Story*. Bogart and Walter Huston again searched for *The Treasure of the Sierra Madre*.

In the DeMille years, the program was lavish, as befitted his reputation. There were 25 musicians in the orchestra, a large cast, and major stars. Even though stars such as Joan Crawford were often terrified by the live mike in front of 30 million listeners, they generally performed well. They were aided by the supporting players and writers of the highest quality.

DeMille left the program only when a dispute with the union, AFTRA, forced him off the air in 1945. AFTRA had assessed each member $1.00 for its organizing work. DeMille, who hated unions and feared their growing strength, refused to pay. He took the case to the court and lost. The court ordered DeMille to pay the $1.00 or leave the show. He left, and visiting host/producers such as Walter Huston and Lionel Barrymore filled out the year.

In 1946, William Keighly, who had done some movie directing in the early 1930s and was a solid radio man, became the show's producer. Keighly had been the head of the Motion Picture Services in the Army Air Corps. He stayed with *Lux Radio Theater* for six years, 1945-51. Frank Woodruff, who had actually been the program's director, then got the title. John Milton Kennedy announced the program throughout the 1940s and Ken Carpenter in the 1950s.

On June 28, 1954, CBS dropped the program and it returned to NBC, its original home. It ran on Tuesday nights from September 14, 1954, to its final broadcast on June 7, 1955. Although *Lux Radio Theater* was not the only series to present movie adaptations, it was the first and best to do so, consistently in the Top 10 radio programs.

Bibliography

Billips, Connie J. *Lux Presents Hollywood: A Show-by-Show History of the Lux Radio Theatre and the Lux Video Theatre, 1934-1957*. Jefferson: McFarland, 1995.

Dunning, John. *Tune in Yesterday*. Englewood Cliffs: Prentice-Hall, 1936.

Macdonald, J. Fred. *Don't Touch That Dial*. Chicago: Nelson-Hall, 1979.

Frank A. Salamone

Lynch, David (1946-), is perhaps popular American cinema's principal exponent of surrealism. Beginning as the creator of one of the most successful and esteemed cult films of all time, he has brought his unusual vision to Hollywood and often, although not always, successfully met the demands of both art and commerce.

Born in Missoula, MT, Lynch spent his childhood in the Pacific Northwest, a setting he was to use for some of his work. Originally intending to be a painter, he studied art at various schools before graduating from Philadelphia's Pennsylvania Academy of Fine Arts in 1967. While in art school, he became interested in filmmaking and before and after graduating made several short films, mainly animated. After moving to Los Angeles, he supported himself and his family by working at various jobs while filming his first feature, *Eraserhead* (1978), which took several years to complete.

In addition to directing *Eraserhead*, Lynch served as the film's screenwriter, producer, designer, and editor, and worked on the film's impressive, if sometimes nausea-inducing, special effects. *Eraserhead*, a film that manages to be powerful and memorable, as well as grotesque and disgusting, has attained the status of a cult classic.

Hollywood apparently felt that *Eraserhead* qualified Lynch to deal with the story of the appallingly deformed John Merrick, and *The Elephant Man* (1980) became his second feature film. A commercial and critical success, *The Elephant Man* earned eight Academy Award nominations, including one for best director.

Lynch's first color feature, *Dune* (1984), reportedly cost more than $45 million, originally ran more than two-and-a-half hours, and was a disaster both critically and financially.

Perhaps betrayed by an attempt to remain true to the spirit of Frank Herbert's ponderous science-fiction novel, or perhaps defeated by its epic length, Lynch produced a film that, while echoing his characteristic interest in the innocent outsider hero in a grotesque world, is humorless and predictable.

Blue Velvet (1986) earned Lynch another Academy Award nomination for best director and showed up on various lists of best films not only of its year, but of its decade. In Lynch's typical but distinctive style, the movie combines elements of comedy and mystery in a manner designed to keep the audience continually off balance. Opening with impossibly idyllic scenes of the small town of Lumberton, the film quickly spirals into an examination of the dark underside of contemporary America.

Perhaps Lynch's most generally accessible film, *Wild at Heart* (1990) was also a critical success, winning the Palme d'Or at the Cannes Film Festival. As in many of Lynch's other films, the narrative is frequently interrupted by flashbacks, dreams, and visions, culminating in one of the characters experiencing a vision of Glinda, the Good Witch from *The Wizard of Oz*, who functions as a *dea ex machina*.

From 1989 to 1991, Lynch ventured into television with the series *Twin Peaks* (see entry), which recounts the investigation into the murder of a beautiful high-school student, Laura Palmer. In 1992, Lynch released a movie "prequel" to the series, *Twin Peaks: Fire Walk with Me*.

Lynch returned to movies with *Lost Highway* (1997), a suspenseful horror film. In 1999 Lynch directed, surprisingly, a Disney film. *The Straight Story* chronicles an older man's journey via riding lawnmower across America's heartland. Lynch has also continued working as an artist.

Bibliography

Alexander, John. *The Films of David Lynch*. London: Letts, 1993.

Kaleta, Kenneth C. *David Lynch*. New York: Twayne, 1993.

Linda Anderson

Lynyrd Skynyrd (1970-1977), a Jacksonville, FL, band, successfully utilized regional cultural traits to become one of the best hard rock groups in the United States. Lead singer Ronnie Van Zant, guitarist Allen Collins, guitarist Gary Rossington, keyboardist Billy Powell, bassist Leon Wilkeson, guitarist Ed King (quit in 1974), drummer Bob Burns (replaced by Artimus Pyle in 1975), and guitarist Steve Gaines (joined in 1976) understood the youths who listened to their music and were able to speak for a generation of young southerners.

In 1965 the nucleus of Lynyrd Skynyrd (Van Zant, Collins, and Rossington) met in junior high school and formed the band My Backyard, which tried to imitate Otis Redding, Jimmy Reed, Bo Diddley, Eric Clapton, Jimmy Page, and Jeff Beck. By 1970 they decided to name themselves after a high school gym teacher, Leonard Skinner, who had punished them for their long hair. By 1971, the band members had dropped out of high school, added Wilkeson and Powell to the lineup, shifted to their own material, and started performing on the rough bar circuit of the Deep South.

The band performed on this circuit for several years until Al Kooper discovered it while scouting groups for MCA's Sounds of the South label in 1972. Although numerous critics praised the group's first album, the rest of the nation did not initially recognize the band's remarkable talents until Pete Townshend got the group employed as an opening act for the Who's Quadrophenia tour in 1973. Under the new management of Peter Rudge, promoter of the Who and the Rolling Stones, Lynyrd Skynyrd was unchallenged as the leading southern rock and roll band for four years, recording six albums. Their best-known hit was "Sweet Home Alabama," which reached No. 8 in 1974. Unfortunately, on October 20, 1977, the airplane carrying the band crashed near Gillsburg, MS. Steve Gaines, backup singer Cassie Gaines, Van Zant, and three roadies were killed. This ended the band.

In the mid-1980s several former members tried to reestablish themselves in the rock world. Rossington and Collins formed the Rossington Collins Band, and Pyle toured with his own group. Although in the late 1980s Lynyrd Skynyrd reorganized under the leadership of Johnny Van Zant (Ronnie's younger brother), it never regained its former status.

The major significance of Lynyrd Skynyrd was that it emerged in a time when white southerners longed for the Old South's self-gratifying romantic myths. When the band made references to the Confederacy, waved Confederate flags, wore "Rebel" uniforms, and played "Dixie," their popularity did not decline among working-class southern whites. Instead, their reputations soared among the "good ol' boy" element. In the final analysis, Lynyrd Skynyrd became an outlet for young white southerners, particularly blue-collar males, after they and the rest of the nation began to question whether the southern image was dead. Through the use of Confederate memorabilia, the band reassured white southerners that they were still a unique group of people, that their philosophy of life was still viable in the contemporary world, and that their history would be preserved.

Bibliography

Christgau, R. "Lynyrd Skynyrd: Not Even a Boogie Band Is As Simple As It Seems." *Creem* 7 (Aug. 1975): 25-30.

Hutson, Cecil Kirk. "Rebel Yell: An Examination of the Violent Legacies of Two Southern Musical Groups." *1994 Proceedings of the Southwest/Texas Popular Culture and American Culture Associations*.

Malone, Bill C. *Southern Music, American Music*. Lexington: UP of Kentucky, 1979.

Yoder, Edwin M., Jr. "The Dixiefication of Dixie." *Dixie Dateline: A Journalistic Portrait of the Contemporary South*. Ed. John B. Boles. Houston: Rice University Studies, 1983.

Cecil Kirk Hutson

Macarena, The, is a dance which became one of the strongest public fads of 1996. The song which accompanied the body movements was supposedly written and originally performed by the Spanish flamenco duo Los del Rio. The Macarena consists essentially of music and words ("give your body joy, Macarena, that your body is to give joy and good things") and actions of hands and hips. The hands touch various parts of the body—arms, head, neck, etc., and the hips gyrate when the hands reach that part of the anatomy. Perhaps because the Macarena is so simple and involves physical action, it became famous immediately with nearly everybody throughout much of the civilized world: mothers singing and doing it and teaching it to their kindergartners; disc jockeys throughout the word airing and "doing" it; politicians of all leanings performing it. Perhaps its transitory race had begun to decline when public figures began to make jokes about it, and Vice President Al Gore "performed" it with no motion of his body and no change of expression on his very immobile face. Maybe the Macarena was destined to have a short, though joyful role, in the popular culture of the musical world.

Bibliography
Newsweek 30 Dec. 1996, 6 Jan. 1997: 109.
Schwartz, Jerry. The Associated Press. 29 Dec. 1996.

Ray B. Browne

Macdonald, Ross, pseudonym of Kenneth Millar (1915-1983), was one of the more admired and prolific authors of hard boiled mysteries, creating the memorable series character Lew Archer. Within the mystery genre, he also wrote novels with nonrecurrent protagonists, as in *Meet Me at the Morgue* (1953) and *The Ferguson Affair* (1960), as well as works of criticism. Macdonald received a doctoral degree in English literature, reviewed books for the *San Francisco Chronicle*, and taught in Ontario. His wife, Margaret Millar, herself was an accomplished mystery writer.

Macdonald is best known for the Lew Archer books. In that series, the author expands the detective genre with Archer doubling as amateur psychologist, moving through the moral landscape of a less-than-idyllic California of the 1960s and 1970s. Strongly influenced by Raymond Chandler, Macdonald's books are slices of contemporary California life, chronicling the way the failed quest for the American dream becomes a recipe for crime and corruption. Many novels probe private emotional pathology and disturbed sexual history, as in *The Galton Case* (1959) and *The Chill* (1964). Later works, such as *Sleeping Beauty* (1971) and *The Underground Man* (1973), enlarge on such themes but add an environmental consciousness, using industrial waste and urban pollution as symbols of the despoliation of the American landscape.

For his many accomplishments Macdonald received the Crime Writers Association Silver Dagger Award in 1965; the Mystery Writers of America Grand Master Award, 1973; and the Popular Culture Association Award of Excellence, 1973.

Bibliography
Bruccoli, Matthew. *Ross Macdonald*. San Diego: Harcourt, 1984.
Grogg, Sam L. "Interview with Ross Macdonald." *Dimensions of Detective Fiction*. Ed. Larry Landrum. Bowling Green, OH: Bowling Green State U Popular P, 1976.
Pry, Elmer. "Lew Archer's 'Moral Landscape.'" *Dimensions of Detective Fiction*. Ed. Larry Landrum. Bowling Green, OH: Bowling Green State U Popular P, 1976.
Schopen, Bernard. *Ross Macdonald*. Boston: Twayne, 1990.

Donna R. Casella

See also
Mystery Awards
Regional Mysteries

Madonna (1958-), having sold over 75 million records by 1990, was at that point arguably the most famous entertainer in the world. Only ten years earlier, the woman born Madonna Louise Veronica Ciccone had been completely unknown. Her rapid rise to fame began inauspiciously in 1982 with the recording of two 12-inch dance singles: "Everybody" and "Burning Up/Physical Attraction" and the low-budget video clips that accompanied them. On a promotional tour of dance clubs (mostly gay clubs) that year, singing to backup recordings and flanked by two male dancers, she demonstrated the major themes that would pervade her career: raw ambition and abundant self-confidence; streetwise and often controversial sexuality; and a penchant and talent for creating mystique through image.

After the release of her eponymous 1983 debut album, Madonna's songs reached the top of the pop charts with unprecedented regularity. Her first six albums produced 20 hit singles. Her songs were often steeped in pop clichés and borrowed stylistic riffs, but were catchy enough to appeal to mass audiences. While her early compositions contented themselves with predictable themes of love, romance, and dating, Madonna eventually broadened her scope to write songs about more substantial topics, including teenage pregnancy ("Papa Don't Preach") and child abuse ("Oh Father").

In 1985, on the eve of a major LiveAID benefit concert, *Playboy* and *Penthouse* magazines simultaneously published a series of nude photographs of Madonna made in 1979. She responded by confronting the issue directly and with some humor, appearing on stage in a demure, full-length coat and teasing the audience with chastisements for its prurience. Her 1989 music video "Like a Prayer" (directed by longtime collaborator Mary Lambert) caused Pepsi to drop her from a $5 million endorsement contract.

Throughout her career, Madonna has constructed image after image for herself, unabashedly borrowing elements from other cultures, from past media icons, and from earlier eras. Her early streetwise look relied heavily on New York's African-American and Puerto Rican street and dance floor cultures, with the addition of provocative lingerie and punky accessories. She unashamedly blended these with traditional Catholic motifs such as crucifixes and communion vestments. After a number of looks borrowed from glamorous Hollywood film legends, she settled on Marilyn Monroe, usurping from Monroe's image wholesale. Her 1984 video for "Material Girl" (the title of which would become a press epithet) even re-created one of Monroe's famous song and dance numbers: "Diamonds Are a Girl's Best Friend" from the film *Gentlemen Prefer Blondes*. In the 1990s she took on two more images, starring as Eva Perón in the film version of *Evita* (1996), and becoming a mother. A veritable chameleon of images, Madonna exploited the power and seduction inherent in each of her borrowed images.

Bibliography

Frank, Lisa, and Paul Smith, eds. *Madonnarama: Essays on Sex and Popular Culture*. Pittsburgh: Cleis, 1993.

James, David. *Madonna: Her Complete Story*. Lincolnwood: Publications, Ltd., 1991.

Lloyd, Fran. *Deconstructing Madonna*. London: Batsford, 1993.

Schwichtenberg, Cathy. *The Madonna Connection: Representational Politics, Subcultural Identities, and Cultural Theory*. Boulder: Westview, 1993.

Sexton, Adam, ed. *Desperately Seeking Madonna: In Search of the Meaning of the World's Most Famous Woman*. New York: Delta, 1993.

Joe Thomas
Don Bacigalupi

Magazine-Format Television Programs, one of the oldest and most durable program formats in television history, have in recent years ridden the crest of a wave of public demand for informational programming and proliferated on the dozens of cable networks which emerged in the 1980s and 1990s. Deriving its broad appeal from its multiple and varied segments, or features, and characteristic mix of lighter and weightier topics, the magazine-format program is uniquely positioned to serve an audience with widely varying interests and attention spans. Moreover, this format allows producers to adjust the segment length to fit the topic, thereby keeping coverage lean and efficient and audience interest high and focused.

Like *Time* or the *New Yorker*, magazine-format shows fold their contents between two consistently distinctive and easily identifiable covers such as the *60 Minutes* ticking clock face. Within these covers are features tied together by a persistent unifying theme which triggers audience expectations, such as *20/20*'s investigative reporting, recurring features, like Andy Rooney's commentary on *60 Minutes*, and by one or more regular hosts or reporters the viewers can expect to see each time, such as *Wall Street Week*'s Louis Rukeyser or the famous *60 Minutes* team, led since the series' inception in 1968 by Mike Wallace. An early magazine-format cultural and public affairs series, *Omnibus* (see

entry), derived much of its image from the striking and powerful presence of its urbane, unflappable Cambridge-educated host, Alistair Cooke, who greeted and bade farewell to viewers and led them carefully through the various segments of each 90-minute program.

Now the rule for virtually all commercial broadcasting, multiple sponsorship set magazine-format series apart in the early years of television. NBC president Sylvester (Pat) Weaver devised this strategy for *Today* and other programs to wrest control of programming away from advertisers accustomed to buying whole blocks of air time and placing in them whatever they wanted. Although Weaver was pursuing network programming control, the TV-Radio Workshop's Robert Saudek insured producer control over *Omnibus* through this strategy (aided by grants from the Ford Foundation) about the same time.

As was true of so many other program genres and formats, the magazine show originated in radio and made the jump to television in the post-World War II TV boom. The first prime-time magazine show was *Television Screen Magazine*, which aired on NBC from November 17, 1946, through July 23, 1949. A weekly half-hour program, it was a true potpourri of film and live features, with some regular "departments," and a host who was identified as the "editor." In 1949 and 1950, ABC aired *Action Autographs*, with a focus on interesting personalities, performers, and commentators on a broad variety of human interest stories—what came to be called lifestyle features.

Within a few years, prototypes of the various magazine-format programs now plentiful on network and cable began to appear. In 1951, NBC fielded *American Inventory*, a weekly news and feature show, and the weekly half-hour news summary and analysis program emerged in the mid-1950s with CBS's *American Week* (1954) and NBC's *Chet Huntley Reporting* (1957-63), followed by CBS's *F.Y.I.* (1960), NBC's *David Brinkley's Journal* (1961-63 and occasionally thereafter) and *Here and Now* (1961), and ABC's *Howard K. Smith—News and Commentary* (1962-63) and *ABC Scope* (1964-68). The longest running of these shows, *Washington Week in Review*, was introduced on the new Public Broadcasting Service in 1970 and is still going strong. Most of these shows were held together by the common theme of news recapping and the strong personality of the program host, usually a network nightly news anchor.

Sports magazines were quick to blossom as well. In 1949, CBS ran a 15-minute recap called *This Week in Sports*, and NBC offered *The Herman Hickman Show* (1952-53) and in summers from 1950 to 1955 *The Gillette Summer Sports Reel*. Each of these included features and interviews as well as sports news summaries.

Other types of TV magazines included early entertainment news and celebrity gossip shows, like the DuMont network's *Broadway to Hollywood—Headline Clues* (1949-54), a hybrid which included a quiz segment along with the celebrity interviews, news, reviews, and lifestyle features. Science and technology journals were anticipated by DuMont's *Johns Hopkins Science Review*, which aired from 1948 to 1954. America's fascination with the bizarre, which would spawn a host of reality-based truth-is-stranger-than-fiction shows in the 1980s and 1990s, was presaged by the original—*Ripley's Believe It or Not*, first on NBC in 1949-50 and then in revival on ABC from 1982 to 1986. Other precursors included NBC's *I'd Like to See* in 1948-49, and a close imitation, *You Asked for It*, which ran on the DuMont network in 1950-1951 and switched to ABC for a long run until 1959. The gimmick was that viewers would send in requests for oddities and the program would put the called-for item or event on the air. *You Asked for It* was also revived in syndication, once in 1972-77, a second time in 1981-83 with Rich Little as host, and a third time through cable in 1991 on the Family Channel.

In a class by itself and never duplicated was the aforementioned *Omnibus*, which ran for eight seasons in the 1950s. It encompassed an extraordinary range of cultural, historical, scientific, human interest, and public affairs features, producing both films and live studio demonstrations, illustrated lectures, and dramatic and musical performances. Specifically aimed at a middlebrow audience, *Omnibus* saw itself quite clearly as a kind of weekly *Life* magazine of the air and set out to show that excellent educational programming could be both entertaining and commercially viable. In some respects, the Sunday morning magazines, *Sunday Today* and CBS's *Sunday Morning with Charles Kuralt* resembled *Omnibus* in their relaxed, but dignified mood, deliberate pacing, and widely varied but generally middlebrow features. *CBS Sunday Morning* even shared the sunburst logo with *Omnibus*.

Of all the magazine-format programs, the one-hour newsmagazine has undeniably been the most significant over the long term exemplified by the overwhelming success of CBS's *60 Minutes* (see entry). Far too numerous to detail here, the abundance of these programs attests to the vitality and appeal of this format.

Bibliography
Brooks, Tim, and Earle Marsh. *The Complete Directory to Prime Time Network TV Shows, 1946-Present*. 5th ed. New York: Ballantine, 1992.
Brown, Les. "Magazine Concept" and "Magazine Format." *The New York Times Encyclopedia of Television*. New York: Times Books, 1977.
Carroll, Raymond. "Television Documentary." *TV Genres: A Handbook and Reference Guide*. Ed. Brian G. Rose. Westport: Greenwood. 242-43.
Eastman, Susan Tyler, Sidney W. Head, and Lewis Klein. *Broadcast/Cable Programming*. 2d ed. Belmont: Wadsworth, 1985.

William M. Jones

Magnetic Tape Recording. The tape recorder was theorized in 1888 by Oberlin Smith as a piece of string dipped in glue and coated with iron filings. In 1893, Valdemar Poulsen, a Danish engineer, used wire to store magnetic impulses that could reproduce sound. In 1921, magnetic tape was first proposed. But it required further electronic development such as the 1924 Western Electric Corporation patent permitting electrical sound recording. In the same year, the loudspeaker supplanted the use of headphones. In 1930, Germany's I. G. Farben industrial company created the first magnetic tape, and Germany's development of tape recording was in advance of any others.

Major recording innovations were introduced in the beginning of the 1940s. In 1943, both optical film and wire recorders were used to document the Allied invasion of Europe at the Normandy beaches. Home tape machines such as the Brush Soundmirror using Scotch 100 paper tape supplied by the 3M Company were beginning to appear in the consumer market, but fell far short of professional requirements.

In 1945, Armed Forces (U.S.) Col. John T. Mullin was part of a Signal Corps team investigating the military applications of German electronic technology. He was told by a British officer about a tape recorder at a Frankfurt, Germany, radio station being operated by the Armed Forces Radio Service that had exceptional musical quality. There Mullin found German technicians working for AFRS using Magnetophone audio tape recorder/players. The technological improvements of a constant speed transport, plastic tape impregnated or coated with iron oxide, and the employment of a very high frequency mixed with the audio signal to provide "bias" was what improved the fidelity.

The first two machines acquired were turned over to the Signal Corps, and Col. Mullin disassembled two other machines and shipped them to his home in San Francisco. In 1946, Mullin rewired and reassembled the Magnetophone machines and went into a partnership with Bill Palmer for movie sound-track work, using those machines and the 50 reels of tape he had acquired.

In October 1946, Mullin and his partner Palmer attended the annual convention of the Society of Motion Picture Engineers. He demonstrated the machine to the sound heads of MGM and 20th Century-Fox and the chief engineer of Altec Lansing. Mr. Mullin was then invited to an Institute of Radio Engineers meeting in May 1947 to demonstrate the German Magnetophone. It was there employees of Ampex saw and heard the tape recorder. Shortly thereafter Ampex began its own developmental project.

In 1947, the technical staff of the *Bing Crosby Show* on ABC arranged to have Mullin re-record original disk recordings of the show on ABC onto tape and then edit them. Crosby had been with NBC until 1944, doing the *Kraft Music Hall* live, but did not like the regimen imposed by live shows. Because NBC would not permit recorded programs, Crosby took a year off and returned on the newly formed ABC network when his new sponsor, Philco, and ABC agreed to let him record on electrical transcriptions. That process required cutting a record and re-recording (sometimes two or three generations) and quality of sound suffered. In July 1947, after the initial demonstration of editing, John Mullin was invited to give a demonstration of his equipment for Bing Crosby's producers by taping live side-by-side with transcription equipment the first show for the 1947-48 season in August at the ABC-NBC studios in Hollywood.

Bing Crosby Enterprises then negotiated financing for Ampex for exclusive distribution rights and Mullin was employed to record the Crosby show on his original German equipment until the Ampex machines would become available. With the original German tape-recorders and 50 rolls of BASF tape, Mullin's first recorded demonstration show of August 1947 was broadcast over ABC on October 1, 1947.

In April 1948, Alexander Poniatov and his team of engineers at Ampex in Redwood City, CA, introduced the first commercial audio tape recorder based on the Magnetophone as Ampex Model 200. The first two, serial numbers 1 and 2, were initially presented to John Mullin and numbers 3-12 went into service at ABC. To meet the contract requirements, Mullin gave his machines to ABC and later received Nos. 13-14 for his contribution. Mullin joined Bing Crosby Enterprises in 1948 and recorded his shows and others at ABC until 1951. Bing Crosby Enterprises, as the exclusive distributor for Ampex products, sold hundreds of recorders to radio stations and master recording studios.

In 1951, Mullin and other engineers were spun off as the Bing Crosby Electronic Division to handle development of audio instrumentation and video recording. In 1956, the Electronic Division became the Minicom Division of 3M, where Mullin served as head of engineering and Professional Recorder Development Manager until his retirement.

Bibliography

"Creating the Craft of Tape Recording." *Hi-Fidelity* April 1976.
Hickman, R. E. B. "The Development of Magnetic Recording." *American Broadcasting.* Ed. Lawrence Lichty and Malachi Topping. New York: Hastings House, 1975.
Mooney, Mark. "The History of Magnetic Recording." *Hi-Fi Tape Recording.* n.p: n.d.
Mullin, John T. "The Birth of the Recording Industry." *Billboard* 18 Nov. 1972.
——. "History of Recorded Sound: Edison through Tape-Recording." Speech Communication Association Presentation. 1976.

Marvin R. Bensman

Magnum, P.I. (1980-1988), was generated as a television series when CBS sought to continue the use of the Hawaiian sets and facilities previously used by Jack Lord's *Hawaii Five-0* (1968-80). CBS turned to Tom Selleck to star as Thomas Sullivan Magnum, a former naval intelligence officer and Vietnam veteran. In return for free residence at the Robin Masters estate, Magnum provided the security for the never-present Masters, whose voice was provided by Orson Welles, 1981-85.

By the time Tom Selleck landed the role of Thomas Magnum, he had been a professional actor for 16 years. He had not had great success in the movies prior to the series, having starred in the mega-flop *Myra Breckinridge* (1970), but he had seen great success in television, having done numerous commercials as well as a role in the popular daytime soap opera *The Young and the Restless* (1973-). This success came after having been the losing bachelor on *The Dating Game* (1973) and having had guest appearances on *The Rockford Files* (1974-80).

Selleck chose to pattern his Magnum more along the lines of James Garner's James Rockford than on other preceding detectives. He chose not to be the droll and virtually infallible Joe Friday of *Dragnet* (1952-70) or the ever-infallible Perry Mason of *Perry Mason* (1957-74). Instead, Thomas Magnum was easy-going, fallible, and flawed. He was frequently beaten, shot at, chased, and often did not "get the girl."

The success of the series is often attributed to Selleck's self-deprecating style as well as to the ensemble cast. Tension and conflict were always provided by Magnum's run-ins with Higgins (John Hillerman), a former sergeant major of the British army who tended to Masters's estate and business as well as his Dobermans, Zeus and Apollo. Magnum's fallibility was seen in his near fear and animosity with the dogs. Magnum was usually able to enlist the aid of his pals, T. C. (Roger Mosley), a helicopter pilot, and Orville "Rick" Wright (Larry Manetti), owner of the King Kamehameha nightclub.

Magnum, P.I. may well have been one of the final private eye shows, but the use of the ensemble cast has continued with such programs as *Hill Street Blues* (1980-87), *Designing Women* (1986-93), *Murphy Brown* (1988-97), and many others.

Bibliography

Brooks, Tim, and Earle Marsh. *The Complete Directory to Prime Time Network and Cable TV Shows, 1946-Present.* New York: Ballantine, 1995.
McNeil, Alex. *Total Television: A Comprehensive Guide to Programming from 1948 to the Present.* New York: Penguin, 1991.

Donna Waller Harper

Main Street is a commonplace name for the primary commercial corridor in small- and medium-sized towns across America. During its heyday between 1870 and 1920, Main Street was the center of everyday life, and the focus of public ceremony and display. As such, Main Street often enjoyed a distinct social and visual intensity, expressed in bustling activity and informal socialization along typically flat-faced rows of narrow brick buildings. But Main Street is more than a place, for it symbolizes values and beliefs fundamental to American identity. It represents the egalitarian small town marketplace, where one can find a familiar face and a fair deal. Despite this, Main Street was often a gritty and discordant business district, a place where American writers Sinclair Lewis and Sherwood Anderson also found narrow-mindedness, bigotry, and ugliness.

These often contradictory images of Main Street exist in American popular culture, from the familial and embracing streets of the *Andy Griffith Show*'s Mayberry, to the vulnerable and dangerous false-front towns of countless Westerns. During the 1930s mural programs of the Federal Arts Project, Main Street was a figurative representation of a strong community life, free from the fears and frustrations of economic depression. For politicians, the image of Main Street often serves as a means to promote their understanding of American values and middle-class common sense. It is not surprising then, that the Walt Disney Company welcomes visitors to its theme parks with the nostalgic Americana of

"Main Street, U.S.A.," with its sterilized, high Victorian facades.

Geographically, Main Street is an artifact of the American road, and reflects the economic and technological adaptation to a rectilinear landscape. While central marketplaces along primary roads were common in colonial cities, the expansion of the railroads and the creation of numerous towns during the 19th century diffused the Main Street landscape inland. Working within the gridiron land survey (1785), many towns were plotted with provisions for both residential and commercial development. As populations grew and economies prospered, increasing land prices concentrated commerce along primary transportation routes, usually close to the rail lines that provided ready access to merchandise from across the country. Often named Main Street, these areas took on the function as the local marketplace to satisfy consumer demands. Later, Main Street attracted a variety of civic and quasi-public institutions.

Architecturally, Main Street represents a manufactured vernacular design that tried to find balance between the spatial constraints of densely packed narrow lots, and the aesthetic tastes of local communities. Boosters often promoted Main Street as an emblem of civic pride, exalting local materials and craftsmanship that differentiated their town from all others. While wood was the most prevalent building material for commercial structures before 1850, brick surpassed wood due to its added substantiality, fire protection, and ability to provide a variety of colors and textures to structures. By the 1870s, however, builders had access to industrially produced millwork (windows, molding and door-frames, etc.) that increasingly economized building costs, while standardizing the look of Main Streets across the country. Pre-cut wood, cast iron, pressed copper, and molded terra cotta, stone, and later concrete products allowed builders to transform simple commercial facades into Italianate, Gothic, Romanesque, Second Empire, and classical structures. These styles changed with popular fashions, from the Victorian eclecticism favored by the 1870s, to the streamlined modern and Art Deco buildings of the 1920s and 1930s. Artistic and exotic styles were often reserved for movie theaters, arcades, and other entertainment establishments that promised romance and adventure behind their doors.

By the mid-19th century, advertising signs also became an integral part of the Main Street landscape. The names and merchandise of individual shops were promoted by a variety of hand-painted windows, painted walls, and hanging signs. Main Street offered America its first glance at standardized commercial signage, from the future national chain stores, such as Piggly Wiggly, A&P, Woolworth's, and McCrory's, to products like Uneeda Biscuit and Coca-Cola. Typically, these forms of advertisements were subtle and did not overshadow the facades of the buildings themselves. The larger billboards associated with contemporary commercial strips also emerged at the end of the 19th century, but were usually erected along railroads, streetcar lines, and upon hillsides to catch the attention of an ever-transient population. Because it was the center of community life and supported a variety of civic and economic functions, Main Street was often the first to receive lights, curbs, and pavement, frequently at the urging of increasingly powerful local business associations.

With the understanding that Main Street comes in a variety of forms, historian Richard Longstreth developed a typology for differentiating them based upon the spatial composition of streetscape facades along a shared block. While many variations exist, perhaps the most prevalent in small- and medium-sized towns is the "two-part commercial block." Derived from the "shop-house" of medieval European cities, two-part commercial blocks have a first floor "shop," with additional upper stories often subdivided into offices, apartments, or meeting halls. In contrast, the "one-part commercial block" is a simple decorative facade on a one-story building, much like the lower level of two-part structures. While many still exist, these buildings often acted as urban claim stakes to hold land with the intent of building something more substantial in the future. Ornamentation followed the same patterns of other commercial buildings, but it was less elaborate since it was widely believed they would be replaced. Unlike the "decorated sheds" identified by Denise Scott Brown and Robert Venturi, buildings within one-part blocks are usually conventional and unified in design, and not an exaggeration of a particular element designed to entice customers along the highly competitive commercial strips.

During the early 20th century, the increasing decentralization of public space had a tremendous impact on Main Streets across the U.S. As the automobile reshaped many American social and commercial experiences, new spaces were created to fulfill our needs to shop and be entertained. Commercial ventures spread outward with residential districts, oriented to the needs of the automobile. The ability to park and maneuver a car became primary concerns for most consumers who lived in new suburban developments away from the cluttered urban centers. Ironically, it was the old guards of the local business associations who lobbied for improved roadways, believing that with every car came a potential customer.

Seen by local planners as antiquated and serving no function in modern society, many Main Street districts were destroyed by urban renewal in the 1950s and 1960s. Many more of those that survived entered a period of marked decline as consumers increasingly patronized new strip malls along modern roadways that offered the convenience of ample parking space and access to large chain stores, such as Wal-Mart, which targets small- and medium-sized towns. In the past two decades, Main Street revitalization became a primary goal of state and local historic preservation agencies, to promote economic growth and cultural appreciation for older commercial districts. The National Trust's "Main Street Program," for instance, established a greater awareness of the viability of revitalizing American Main Streets based upon the nostalgia for quaint streetscapes and Victorian ways of life. Main Street has experienced a comeback through these efforts to find new ways to enshrine the narrow streets and diverse facades, and reinterpret them for a new generation of potential customers.

Bibliography
Gottfried, Herbert, and Jan Jennings. *American Vernacular Design, 1870-1940*. Ames: Iowa State UP, 1988. Rpt. New York: Van Nostrand Reinhold, 1985.

Jackle, John A. *The American Small Town: Twentieth-Century Place Images*. Hamden, CT: Archon, 1982.

Liebs, Chester H. *Main Street to Miracle Mile: American Roadside Architecture*. Boston: Little, Brown, 1985.

Longstreth, Richard. *The Buildings of Main Street: A Guide to American Commercial Architecture*. Washington, DC: Preservation, 1987.

Rifkind, Carole. *Main Street: The Face of Urban America*. New York: Harper, 1977.

Michael G. Bennett

Mainframe Computers conspicuously entered American life in 1965 when IBM introduced its Model 360. This multi-million-dollar machine was quickly adopted by large businesses, government agencies, and universities. Although it used transistors instead of vacuum tubes, the mainframe ran hot and required special air-conditioned facilities, and was always attended by white-coated technicians. IBM dominated the worldwide computer market. Rivals (the "seven dwarfs") could match IBM's technology, but not its reputation. Technological advances every year brought bigger and faster mainframes and hastened the restructuring of most bureaucratic enterprises around mainframes. The mainframe centralized computing power high in an organization, where legions of FORTRAN and COBOL programmers wrote codes that harnessed raw computing power to specialized tasks. Bureaucracies expanded, assigning lower echelons the task of preparing forms for keypunched data cards. Most jobs were simple and routine ("stupid"), such as the rapid processing of routinized data forms such as monthly electric bills. By the 1970s, distributed processing allowed clerks to use terminals connected directly to the mainframe. These were "dumb" terminals without their own computing power. The 1970s saw upstart companies introducing smaller, much cheaper "minicomputers" with the power of the older mainframes. By the early 1990s, the mass introduction of personal computers ("microcomputers") radically undercut the market for both mainframes and minis.

Bibliography
Dertouzos, Michael, and Joel Moses, eds. *The Computer Age: A Twenty Year View*. Cambridge: MIT, 1979.

Richard Jensen

Making of a President-1960, The (1963), was an award-winning documentary visually encapsulating the presidential election of 1960, first broadcast just three weeks after President Kennedy's death.

Adapted from Theodore H. White's Pulitzer Prize-winning book, this 90-minute documentary followed the presidential race between John F. Kennedy and Richard M. Nixon. *The Making of a President-1960* retraced the campaign trail from its grassroots beginnings in the fall of 1959, to the primary and election campaigns, ending with Kennedy's ultimate inauguration. More comprehensive than penetrating, it generated an understanding of the shape and scope of the electoral process. Focused and swiftly moving, this production gave the 1963 television viewer a "back stage" look into something rarely seen before. This was apparent in the famous 1960 television debate (which marked the outcome of the race). A camera operator filmed the candidates one-half hour before the telecast; Kennedy's demeanor was composed, while Nixon's appearance was more anxious. *The Making of a President-1960* showed scenes of scheming and tension within the parties. It also presented a glimpse into the decision-making process of political strategists.

Credited for their contributions, besides author White and executive producer David Wolper, were producer-director Mel Stuart and editor William T. Cartwright. The original music was composed and conducted by Elmer Bernstein and the film was narrated by Martin Gabel. *The Making of a President-1960* was the recipient of five Emmy Awards. It is not only a poignant political record but also a timeless slice of history—a slice of history that touched the grieving hearts of the American people one December day in 1963.

Bibliography
Marc, David, and Robert J. Thompson. *Prime Time, Prime Movers: From* I Love Lucy *to* L.A. Law. Boston: Little, Brown, 1992.

Michael Espinosa

Mamas and the Papas, The, were a singing group from the mid-to-late 1960s and early 1970s that combined soaring harmonies and wistful folk-rock lyrics. John Phillips, chief songwriter and arranger for the group, came from a series of doo-wop and folk groups. His biggest early success was with the group the Journeymen, which also included Scott McKenzie and Dick Weissman. Scott later had a hit with John's song "San Francisco (Be Sure to Wear Flowers in Your Hair)," which topped at No. 4 on the charts and became the anthem for the Summer of Love (1967). The Journeymen broke up in 1963, though Phillips continued the group without McKenzie or Weissman. The New Journeymen included John's wife, Michelle, Marshall Brickman and, after Brickman's departure, Denny Doherty. Doherty was the connection with the fourth member of the group, alto Cass Elliot, who had hailed from the Chicago group the Big Three. She had joined with Doherty in a group called the Mugwumps.

The Mamas and the Papas' first album, *If You Can Believe Your Eyes and Ears*, was a critical success on its release in 1966. Releases included the soaring "California Dreamin'," "Go Where You Wanna Go," and "Monday, Monday" (their only No. 1 hit). Later that year, their self-titled second album was released. The hits kept rolling with "Words of Love," "Dancing in the Street," "I Saw Her Again Last Night," and others. After the release of the second album, divisions in the group, already difficult since John had initially refused to let Cass join the group, got worse. Michelle was temporarily expelled after an affair with Doherty.

By 1967, the group's third album, *The Mamas and Papas Deliver*, was released. Included were hits "Dedicated to the One I Love," "Creeque Alley" (a song about the group's history and formation), and "Look through My

Window." That year the group was also involved in forming one of the earliest rock festivals, Monterey International Pop Festival. John and Michelle were key organizers of this event, and also the four were featured performers (although tensions among its members were so high that Doherty almost refused to show).

By the later sixties, the Mamas and Papas were becoming more immersed in drugs and the hippie lifestyle. The group had begun to fissure after Michelle's affair with Doherty, but the division now became more severe. Mama Cass, more confident in her solo abilities, wanted to begin a solo career. Their fourth group album came out in 1968, with mediocre critical reception. The album, *The Papas and the Mamas,* released "Twelve Thirty (Young Girls Are Coming to the Canyon)," "For the Love of Ivy," and "Safe in My Garden"—none of which were big hits. Also released was Mama Cass's biggest solo hit, "Dream a Little Dream."

At this point, Mama Cass and other group members went their separate ways. Cass, spurning the appellation "Mama," released her first solo album, *Dream a Little Dream.* Phillips produced his solo album, *John Wolf King of L.A.,* a folk album remembered for the song "Mississippi." However, the group was still under contract for one more album. The group, now practically at each others' throats, reunited for the *People Like Us* album, released in 1971.

Michelle would later release her own solo album, *Victim of Romance,* and become a regular on the TV series *Knots Landing.* Cass went on to release five more albums and became a success as a Las Vegas headliner, but she died of a heart attack in London in July 1974.

In 1982, John Phillips reformed the group, calling them the New Mamas and Papas. In the new group were John, Denny Doherty, Spanky McFarlane (formerly of Spanky and Our Gang), and John's daughter Mackenzie Phillips (previously on the sitcom *One Day at a Time*). Doherty would later leave and be replaced by former Journeyman Scott Mackenzie. The New Mamas and Papas toured the United States, playing small gigs in major cities and on the nostalgia circuit. John Phillips wrote a No. 1 hit for the Beach Boys, "Kokomo."

Bibliography
Phillips, John. *Papa John: An Autobiography.* New York: Dell, 1986.
Phillips, Michelle. *California Dreamin': The True Story of the Mamas and the Papas.* New York: Warner, 1986.

Mark K. Fulk

Man from U.N.C.L.E., The (1964-1968), a humorous spy adventure series on NBC, became a national fad despite a poor start. Inspired by Ian Fleming's James Bond, *The Man from U.N.C.L.E.* concerned the adventures of two agents, American Napoleon Solo (Robert Vaughn) and Russian Illya Kuryakin (David McCallum), who worked for Alexander Waverly (Leo G. Carroll), the head of United Network Command for Law and Enforcement (U.N.C.L.E.), an international organization combating crime. U.N.C.L.E.'s foe was a nefarious agency known as the Technological Hierarchy for the Removal of Undesirables and the Subjugation of Human-

ity (T.H.R.U.S.H.). In every episode, Solo and Kuryakin enlisted the aid of an ordinary individual in the battle against T.H.R.U.S.H. Guest stars, playing T.H.R.U.S.H. villains and the common people who assisted the U.N.C.L.E. agents, were an important element of the series. *The Man from U.N.C.L.E.*'s celebrity guests included Joan Crawford, Vincent Price, Telly Savalas, Jack Palance, Joan Collins, Leonard Nimoy, William Shatner, Lee Meriwether, Rip Torn, Slim Pickens, Carroll O'Connor, Ricardo Montalban, Leslie Nielsen, Jack Lord, Nancy Sinatra, Mary Ann Mobley, Martin Landau, Jill Ireland, and Sonny and Cher.

Despite a host of nominations, *The Man from U.N.C.L.E.* never captured an Emmy. Still, the program won numerous honors, including a Golden Globe Award for best TV series in 1966. Moreover, McCallum, who became a sex symbol during the show's run, received the Motion Picture Costumers' Adam and Eve Award for most popular actor of 1965. The American Legion also praised *The Man from U.N.C.L.E.* as the best family entertainment series for 1966. The program's immense popularity inspired the creation of other spy series such as *Honey West, Mission: Impossible, The Wild, Wild West, I Spy,* and *Get Smart,* which spoofed *The Man from U.N.C.L.E. The Girl from U.N.C.L.E.,* a spin-off, aired during the 1966-67 season and starred Stefanie Powers as April Dancer and Noel Harrison as Mark Slate. Eight MGM *Man from U.N.C.L.E.* films were released, including *To Trap a Spy, The Spy with My Face, One Spy Too Many,* and *How to Steal the World.* These movies, made by combining television episodes with extra footage of a more mature nature, grossed over twelve million dollars.

In 1983, the series reappeared in a new 90-minute CBS television movie, *The Return of the Man from U.N.C.L.E.: The Fifteen Years Later Affair.* Guest stars included George Lazenby, Keenan Wynn, and Patrick MacNee, and Vaughn and McCallum reprised their roles as heroic U.N.C.L.E. agents Solo and Kuryakin.

Bibliography
Anderson, Robert. *The U.N.C.L.E. Tribute Book.* Las Vegas: Pioneer, 1994.
Heitland, Jon. *The Man from U.N.C.L.E. Book: The Behind-the-Scenes Story of a Television Classic.* New York: St. Martin's, 1987.

S. K. Bane

Mancini, Henry (1924-1994), has a prominent place in the history of film and music because of the many film soundtracks and theme songs he composed and scored. Mancini began his musical training by studying with arranger Max Adkins at age 14; he entered the Juilliard School of Music in 1942. He sent some of his arrangements to bandleader Benny Goodman, who encouraged him to continue. While in the Armed Forces during the 1940s, Mancini joined the Army Air Force Band at the recommendation of another prominent bandleader, Glenn Miller.

Mancini worked on and off during the late 1940s and early 1950s, scoring films with moderate success, but received his first Oscar nomination for the score to the film *The Glenn Miller Story* in 1954; Mancini also scored *The*

Benny Goodman Story in 1956, his life intersecting once again with the famous figures who encouraged and inspired him. Mancini became even more well known for his scoring of the Orson Welles movie *Touch of Evil* in 1958. His biggest break, however, came when he did the theme song for the television series *Peter Gunn* in 1959. This song was later covered by artists like Emerson, Lake and Palmer and Art of Noise. The *Peter Gunn* theme firmly established Mancini as a sought-after composer and earned him Grammys for best arrangement and album of the year. During the 1960s, Mancini's career as a composer/arranger began to take off. Some of his most popular theme songs included: "Moon River" (1961), from the movie *Breakfast at Tiffany's*, which peaked on the national charts at No. 11 and featured the lyrics of Johnny Mercer; "Love Theme from Romeo & Juliet," which reached No. 1 in May of 1969 and went gold; and "(Theme from) Love Story," which reached No. 13 in February of 1971. Other famous Mancini works include his instantly recognizable scores for *The Pink Panther* (1964), *Wait Until Dark* (1967), *Mommie Dearest* (1980), and *That's Dancing* (1985).

After Mancini died of liver and pancreatic cancer, several Mancini tribute albums were released, including *Shots in the Dark*, *Days of Wine and Roses*, and James Moody's *Moody Plays Mancini*. In the mid-1990s, interest in Mancini's work was renewed due to new interest and popularity of lounge/"bachelor-pad" music, of which Mancini was one of the founders. Mancini made over 50 albums throughout his career, and won four Oscars, over 25 Grammys, and numerous other awards.

Bibliography

Jones, Dylan. *Ultra Lounge: The Lexicon of Easy Listening*. New York: St. Martin's, 1997.

Mancini, Henry, and Gene Lees. *Did They Mention the Music?* Lincoln, WI: Contemporary, 1989.

Scheurer, Timothy. "Henry Mancini: An Appreciation and Appraisal." *Journal of Popular Film & Television* 21.1 (Spring 1996): 34-43.

Robert G. Weiner

Mann, Michael (1943-). It is rare that one man can redefine the look of prime-time television and influence the fashion industry, but Michael Mann with *Miami Vice* in 1984 did both. The show, which cost an estimated $1.2 million per episode, transformed Miami into a pastel paradise with a dark underbelly where the vice-cops wore Armani, no socks, and earrings. The "Miami Vice look" was soon something to be found both on screen and in stores.

The creator of this phenomenon, Michael Mann, grew up in Chicago and later attended the University of Wisconsin at Madison, where he intended to become an English major but instead found film. Mann enrolled in the International Film School in London from 1965 to 1967. He began directing commercials and documentaries. When the Paris riots broke out in 1968, he used his contacts to obtain inside footage that he sold to NBC. He directed a self-proclaimed "abstract little art film," *Jaunpuri*, which won the Jury Prize at the 1971 Cannes Film Festival.

Mann returned to the U.S. that year and moved to Hollywood, where he expected "to score a gig in 30 days or something." He and his wife ended up selling chili at the Venice Canal, and 30 days turned to three years. Eventually Mann started writing episodes for 1970s cop shows *Starsky and Hutch* and *Police Story*. He also created the pilot episode for *Vega$* starring Robert Urich.

The success of *Vega$* gave Mann the edge in persuading ABC to allow him to direct a script he had co-written with Patrick J. Nolan called *The Jericho Mile*. Filmed in Folsom Prison, *The Jericho Mile* starred Peter Strauss as the story's central figure, Rain Murphy. Mann shared an Emmy for best writing in a limited series or special and won the Directors' Guild of America's Award for his work in 1980.

Mann's next project was to direct a feature film of his own screenplay called *Thief* (1981), which he also executive produced. While the film had a distinct look, driving soundtrack, and good performances, critics and audiences found it too bleak and masochistic. His next film, *The Keep* (1983), is a metaphysical World War II story about a squad of German soldiers guarding a mysterious medieval castle in the Carpathian Alps. Mann described it as "a fairy tale about the nature of fascism."

But it was with *Miami Vice* (see entry), for which Mann was the executive producer, that he found a near-perfect melding of sight, sound, and story. Literally conceived by Brandon Tartikoff as MTV cops, *Miami Vice* set the trend for a distinct style, pace, use of colors, and especially music not previously seen on the small screen. Perhaps this was because Mann approached each episode as if it were for the big screen. The series made instant stars of its leads, Don Johnson as Detective Sonny Crockett and Philip Michael Thomas as Detective Ricardo Tubbs, the two best-dressed undercover vice cops to hit the small screen. Edward James Olmos as their boss, Lieutenant Martin Castillo, also gained recognition and status in the public eye.

The show received 15 Emmy nominations in its first season and remained in the Top 10 for its first two seasons as it explored not just the idea of vice, but existential questions of the nature of evil. Once the show was moved opposite *Dallas* in its third season, the ratings fell and the newness wore off. However, its impact on the culture continued.

Mann created another stylish police series for NBC in 1986. *Crime Story*, which he executive produced during its two-year run, was set in Chicago and Las Vegas of the early 1960s and focused on an elite squad of detectives, led by Lieutenant Mike Torello (Dennis Farina), fighting the mob and, in particular, Torello's nemesis, Ray Luca (Anthony Denison).

The same year that *Crime Story* appeared, Mann also directed a cinema feature, *Manhunter*. The film is based on Thomas Harris's novel *Red Dragon* and introduced the character of Hannibal Lecter (Brian Cox) to film audiences. As in the later, more popular, *Silence of the Lambs*, Lecter is used to help emotionally vulnerable FBI agents track down a serial killer.

After *Miami Vice* finished production, Mann continued to focus on crime, but from a documentary approach. He executive produced two series adapted from Elaine Shannon's book, *Desperados,* about the Mexican and Columbian drug trade. The first, *Drug Wars: The Camarena Story* (1990), won an Emmy Award for its look at the events leading to the death of American federal narcotics agent "Kiki" Camarena. The second, *Drug Wars: The Cocaine Cartel* (1992), focused on the Medellin cartel.

The Last of the Mohicans (1992) saw Mann directing, co-producing, and co-writing (with Cameron Crowe) James Fenimore Cooper's story set against the French and Indian Wars for a 1990s audience. In 1995 Mann returned to the subject of crime as producer, co-director, and writer for *Heat,* an action film set in Los Angeles. His latest film, *The Insider* (1999), the true story of a tobacco company whistle-blower, earned him Oscar nominations for best picture, director, and co-writer (with Eric Roth).

Bibliography

Hirschberg, Lynn. "Michael Mann." *Rolling Stone* 17 Dec. 1987: 163-64.

Mann, Michael. *Current Biography* Jan. 1993: 41-45.

Marc, David, and Robert J. Thompson. *Prime Time, Prime Movers: From* I Love Lucy *to* L.A. Law. Boston: Little, Brown 1992.

Rochlin, Margy. "Vice Is Nice..." *American Film* Sept. 1986: 20-25.

Smith, Gavin. "Michael Mann: Wars and Peace." *Sight & Sound* Nov. 1992: 10-15.

Elizabeth W. B. Schmitt

Mann's Chinese Theatre (originally Grauman's Chinese Theatre). On May 18, 1927, Grauman's Chinese Theatre, located at 6925 Hollywood Boulevard, hosted its first premiere, Cecil B. DeMille's *King of Kings.* An estimated 50,000 persons crowded Hollywood Boulevard to see the parade of stars who had paid $11 apiece to attend the opening. In the reviews the next day, the theater received nearly as much press as did the film, with Hollywood columnist Louella O. Parsons declaring it "probably the most important motion picture premiere the world has ever seen." Since that date, many other landmark films have premiered there, including *The King and I* (1956), *Giant* (1956), *West Side Story* (1961), *Breakfast at Tiffany's* (1961), *Mary Poppins* (1964), and *Butch Cassidy and the Sundance Kid* (1969). Arguably "the most famous movie palace in the world," Grauman's has supplied the glamour integral to the presentation of the art of filmmaking.

Designed in 1927 by the architectural firm of Meyer & Holler (with actual design work done by architects Raymond Kennedy and D. R. Wilkinson and designer John Beckman), the theater was not intended to be authentically Chinese, but instead to echo the more delicate period of Chinese-influenced Chippendale. The ground-breaking ceremony was held on January 5, 1926, with silent-film star Norma Talmadge (aided by Chinese actress Anna May Wong) turning the first shovelful of earth with a gold-plated shovel and then operating a steam shovel. The theater took over a year to build and cost approximately $2 million.

Originally, the theater sat 2,258 audience members, was 90-feet high at its tallest point, and sported a 40-foot-high

The elaborate pagoda entrance in the courtyard of Mann's Chinese Theatre (formerly Grauman's), Hollywood, Sept. 9, 1988. Photo courtesy of Mark McDermott.

masonry facade, with four ornate obelisks creating a gateway. Although it was located in the center of Hollywood (on a lot that was actually once an orange grove and the home of actor Francis X. Bushman from 1913 to 1915), the theater was landscaped in such a manner as to transport audiences from Southern California to another place and time: vines cascaded from giant bronze planters and palm trees reached far beyond the bronze pagoda roof underlaid with immense red piers covered with huge iron masks. Gargoyles directed the spray from two 10-foot-tall fountains, lighted at night by jeweled lamps. Two Ming Dynasty Heaven Dogs, imported by Sid Grauman in 1927, guarded either side of the front entrance.

Also well known is the forecourt of the theater, where nearly 200 footprints, handprints, and signatures in the cement immortalize such "celebrities" as movie stars, public officials, and military servicemen. Some of the more amazing entries include the imprints of Roy Rogers's horse's hooves, Jimmy Durante's nose, Al Jolson's knees, Betty Grable's legs, and George Burns's cigar. Included in more traditional fashion are Fred Astaire, Humphrey Bogart, Gary Cooper, Joan Crawford (who wrote, "To Sid—May this cement our friendship"), Bing Crosby, Bette Davis, Olivia de Havilland, Cecil B. DeMille, Kirk Douglas, Henry Fonda, Clark Gable, Cary Grant, Jean Harlow, Rita Hayworth, Charlton Heston, Alan Ladd, Dorothy Lamour, Sophia Loren, Marilyn Monroe, Jean Simmons, Frank Sinatra, John Wayne, Elizabeth Taylor, Shirley Temple, and Jimmy Stewart, among many, many others. Two time capsules and nearly a dozen plaques commemorate and anticipate historical and technological achievements.

In 1973, Ted Mann purchased the Chinese Theatre, drawing a variety of criticisms for changing the name from Grauman's to Mann's Chinese Theatre. Since that time, Mann has added two adjacent theaters (the Chinese II and the Chinese III). Also, in 1984, Mann upgraded the sound system, adding the Lucasfilm THX Sound System. On December 3, 1998, the theater—renovated and refurbished—opened again with a showing of *The Ten Commandments,* tickets $1.50, in an effort to revitalize downtown Hollywood.

Bibliography

Endres, Stacey, and Robert Cushman. "Hollywood's Chinese Theatre." *Hollywood at Your Feet.* Los Angeles: Pomegranate, 1992.

Pierson, Robert. "The Urban Soul: Hollywood." *Los Angeles Magazine* Sept. 1985: 212.

Roberta F. Green

Marathons. The popularity of the jogging boom in the 1960s, greatly helped by Dr. Ken Cooper's various publications on what he called "aerobics," seemed to energize vast numbers of Americans. Marathons, which in the 1950s were seen to be somewhat odd and suffered from low participation and spectator turnout, became transformed into national festivals where literally thousands of people of all ages set off to complete a race course of 26 miles and 385 yards. Frank Shorter (gold medal in the 1972 Olympics and silver medal in 1976) and Bill Rodgers (winner of the Boston and New York City marathons four times each from 1975 to 1980) became the first American superstars of more than running, as well as the most important promoters of the sport.

Over the last two decades, the Boston (founded 1897) and New York (started in 1976) Marathons have established themselves as the world's premier long distance races. Entries are now selective, and the prize money now awarded makes them into sporting events of the first order. In 1999, 31,807 athletes completed the New York Marathon.

The marathon's fixed distance of 26 miles, 385 yards, was the distance of a race from Windsor to the finish line opposite the Royal Box, in the White City Stadium at the 1908 London Olympics. The name marathon comes from the legend of a Greek soldier called Philippides who ran from Marathon to Athens to convey news of a victory over the Persians in 400 B.C. That distance was 22 miles.

The marathon has provided many occasions of athletic triumph and tragedy. At the 1908 Olympics, an Italian, Dorando Pietri, entered the stadium first but he was in a state of collapse and had to be helped across the finishing line. In 1954, at the Empire Games marathon, the favorite, Jim Peters of England, entered the stadium and then, within sight of the finish line, collapsed and, tragically, could not continue to take what had seemed a certain gold medal.

In 1967, Katherine Switzer became the first official woman entrant in the Boston Marathon. Her various attempts to be accepted as a legitimate long distance runner stand as a testament to an era that denied women equal athletic opportunity. Only in 1984 did the International Olympic Committee allow women to compete over the marathon distance. The winner of that race at the Los Angeles Olympics was Joan Benoit in a time of 2 hours 24 minutes, 52 seconds.

Unofficial world record holders for the marathon are Moroccan Khalid Khannouchi, with a time of 2 hours, 5 minutes, and 42 seconds, in Chicago in 1999, and for women, Tegla Loroupe of Kenya, at 2:20:47 in the 1998 Rotterdam Marathon. At the 1996 Olympics in Atlanta the winners of the marathon were Josia Thugwane of South Africa (men) and Fatuma Roba of Ethiopia (women).

Significantly, champion handicapped competitors on board wheelchairs at the Boston and New York marathons finish more than 30 minutes in front of the rest of the field.

Bibliography

Arlott, J., ed. *The Oxford Companion to World Sports and Games.* London: Oxford UP, 1975. 644-45.

Gynn, R. W. H. *Guinness Book of the Marathon.* Enfield: Guinness Superlatives, 1984. 168.

Scott A. G. M. Crawford

Marley, Bob (1945-1981), the Third World's first international superstar, a champion of human rights, and "musical high priest" of Rastafarianism, remains Jamaica's best-known musical artist, especially to American audiences.

Robert Nesta Marley was born in Nine Miles, St. Ann's Parish, Jamaica. With childhood friend Neville Livingston (later Bunny Wailer), Marley listened to the American music played on Jamaican radio: Ray Charles, Curtis Mayfield, the Drifters. Marley and Livingston soon met Peter McIntosh (later Peter Tosh), another teen with musical ambitions.

In 1962, Jimmy Cliff introduced Marley to recording entrepreneur Leslie Kong, resulting in Marley's first singles: "Judge Not," and "One Cup of Coffee." But he sought success with Livingston and McIntosh—the trio named the Wailing Wailers because as ghetto kids they were "born wailing." That their voices did not mesh gave them a unique raw sound appropriate for their street-inspired songs. In 1963 they released their first single, "Simmer Down." This ska number topped Jamaican charts for two months in 1964, and was followed by singles such as "Rude Boy," "It Hurts to Be Alone," "Rule Them Rudie," and "Bend Down Low," most evoking the Kingston slums' street-rebel lifestyle.

By 1967 Marley's music began to reflect his social and religious consciousness. With McIntosh (now Tosh) and Livingston (now Wailer), he formed the Wail 'N' Soul label, which failed very quickly. In 1970, with producer Lee Perry and brothers Aston and Carlton Barrett (on bass and drums) from his studio band, the Wailers recorded what would become classic reggae tracks such as "Soul Rebel," "400 Years," "Small Axe," and "Duppy Conqueror." They formed another label of their own, Tuff Gong, and, sporting dreadlocks and by now all Rastafarians, recorded "Trench Town Rock" and the songs later to comprise the albums *African Herbsman* and *Rasta Revolution*.

American pop star Johnny Nash benefited from collaboration with Marley, whom he met while scouting out new material in Jamaica. Marley's "Stir It Up" became an American hit in 1973 on Nash's *I Can See Clearly Now* album, which contained other Marley tunes. By 1972 the entire band was struggling in England until Marley approached the white Jamaican promoter of reggae, Chris Blackwell of Island Records, who financed use of superior facilities for a whole album—this at a time when reggae usually sold only in singles. *Catch a Fire* (1973), followed by the first British and American tour of a reggae band, ignited the group's gradual international fame.

Their second album, *Burnin'* (1973), contains the tracks "I Shot the Sheriff" (an American hit for Eric Clapton in 1974) and "Get Up Stand Up." Peter Tosh and Bunny Wailer, unhappy with the Island contract, dropped out to go solo, whereupon Marley assembled the I-Threes (wife Rita Marley, Marcia Griffiths, and Judy Mowatt) to supply vocals, renamed the group Bob Marley and the Wailers, and, with other eventual members Al Anderson on guitar, Bernard "Touter" Harvey and Earl "Wire" Lindo on keyboards, and Tyrone Downie, continued touring.

Marley's album, *Natty Dread*, recorded late in 1974, contained sharp critiques of Jamaican living conditions, such as "Them Belly Full (But We Hungry)." A live version of "No Woman No Cry" recorded at London's Lyceum and featured on *Bob Marley and the Wailers Live!* (1975) gave the group their first U.K. hit, and both *Natty Dread* and the next album, *Rastaman Vibration* (1976), saw success on American charts due to outstanding performances during the ensuing U.S. tours.

In the late 1970s, due to political tension in Jamaica, Marley went back and forth from recording in London to touring in Jamaica. He also made his first visit to Africa, which inspired *Survival* (1979), a militant album providing the soon-to-be-liberated Rhodesia with an anthem: "Zimbabwe." During a 1980 U.S. tour, Marley became ill with cancer and died the following year.

Marley's Medal of Peace, awarded by the United Nations in 1978, his Order of Merit (Jamaica's highest honor, awarded a few weeks before his death), and his induction into the Rock and Roll Hall of Fame in 1994 testify to the importance of his legend and the love of his fans.

Bibliography
Barrett, Leonard E., Sr. *The Rastafarians.* Boston: Beacon, 1988.
Davis, Stephen. *Bob Marley.* Garden City: Doubleday, 1985.
Palmer, Robert. "One Love." *Rolling Stone* 24 Feb. 1994: 38-41, 67.

Alex Richardson
Michael Delahoyde

Marlowe, Philip, may be the most famous fictional private investigator in American literary history. Working out of a third-floor walkup in a downtown Los Angeles office building, Marlowe appears in several short stories and seven celebrated novels by Raymond Chandler (see entry). Earlier characters named Carmody, Dalmas, Malvern and Mallory, in the pulp fiction Chandler wrote for *Black Mask* magazine, eventually became the memorable Marlowe, whose ironic wit, moral alienation, and failed romanticism remain prototypical features of the hard-boiled detective hero.

First appearing in *The Big Sleep* (1939), Marlowe might be called an American middle-class existential hero. He sets out on a lonely quest to right the sins of the world. The multifaceted irony of his vision indicts the corruption of the human spirit. Marlowe is best represented in the early novels like *Farewell, My Lovely* (1940), *The High Window* (1942), and *The Lady in the Lake* (1943). Suspicious of both police and witnesses, Marlowe carves an independent course through the complicated snares of these stories. His vision is clearer and less sentimental in these than in the later books, *The Little Sister* (1949) and *The Long Goodbye* (1953). The Marlowe of *Playback* (1958), Chandler's last novel, appears world-weary and weak, beaten down by the relentless progression of human frailties he has investigated. When he died in 1959, Chandler left unfinished *Poodle Springs*, a novel in which he married Marlowe off to an heiress—a disappointing end for such a hero. The novel was later completed by Robert Parker.

Bibliography
Dictionary of American Biography. Documentary Series, Vol. 6. New York: Scribner, 1964.
Durham, Philip. *Down These Mean Streets a Man Must Go: Raymond Chandler's Knight.* Chapel Hill: U of North Caroline P, 1963.
Wolfe, Peter. *Something More Than Night: The Case of Raymond Chandler.* Bowling Green, OH: Bowling Green State U Popular P,1985.

Stephen Soitos

Marple, Miss Jane. Between 1928 and 1976, Jane Marple, elderly amateur detective from St. Mary Mead, appeared in 12 novels and 20 stories by immensely popular British mystery writer Agatha Christie (see entry). She has also been seen on stage, in films, and on television, played by such distinguished actresses as Margaret Rutherford, Helen Hayes, Angela Lansbury, and Joan Hickson. Christie's spinster sleuth fit the times—post-World War I England was full of unmarried women—and a tradition of female detectives that began with Miss Butterworth, the creation of American writer Anna Katharine Green, and continues today with such characters as Corinne Holt Sawyer's Angela Benbow and Eleanor Boylan's Clara Gamadge.

Miss Marple remains popular in the U.S. because of Christie's bamboozling skills and the many film and television adaptations of the novels and stories in which she appears. But she also appeals because, in a world of chaos and injustice, it is comforting to imagine that a kindly, determined Miss Marple can protect the innocent and punish the guilty.

Bibliography
Hart, Anne. *The Life and Times of Miss Jane Marple.* New York: Berkley, 1985.

Sanders, Dennis, and Len Lovallo. *The Agatha Christie Companion: The Complete Guide to Agatha Christie's Life and Work*. Rev. ed. New York: Berkley, 1989.

Shaw, Marion, and Sabine Vanacker. *Reflecting on Miss Marple*. New York: Routledge, 1991.

Marty S. Knepper

See also
Cozy Mysteries
Golden Age of Detective Fiction

Married...with Children (1987-1995), a situation comedy about the surreally dysfunctional Bundy family, premiered on the Fox Network. Set in Chicago, *MWC* stars Ed O'Neill as shoe salesman and former high school football great Al Bundy, the sole support of his ungrateful family: red-headed, Spandex-clad wife Peg (Katey Sagal), promiscuous and profoundly stupid daughter Kelly (Christina Applegate), and terminally uncool son Bud (David Faustino). *MWC* was a ground-breaking, often-attacked parody of wholesome family life, with the Bundy parents feeling that they'll never be happy, because they're married...with children.

Unlike most situation comedies about family life, *MWC*'s humor was caustic and raunchy, often pushing the limits of good taste, and after the first few episodes, the characters and action took on a cartoon-like quality. Nearly every episode featured scantily clad women, scatological humor, and sex jokes dealing with everything from Al's impotence and Kelly's promiscuity to masturbation.

Nevertheless, *MWC* was one of the Fox Network's most popular shows, and is widely syndicated.

Bibliography
Brooks, Tim, and Earl Marsh. *The Complete Directory to Prime Time Network and Cable TV Shows, 1946-Present*. New York: Ballantine, 1995.

Crawford, Allan Pell. "Not the Huxtables." *Reason* Dec. 1989: 56-57.

"Raunch on a Roll." *Broadcasting* 21 Nov. 1988: 27-30.

June Michele Pulliam

Marsalis, Wynton (1961-), born in Breaux Bridge, LA, to a family of musicians, appeared at New Orleans Jazz and Heritage Festival in Danny Barker's Marching Band as a pre-teen. At 14 he performed Hayden's Trumpet Concerto in public. He spent time at the Berkshire Music Center at Tanglewood as a teenager and then moved on to the Juilliard School of Music. In 1980, he received further training in Art Blakey's Jazz Messengers.

At one point, he and his brother Branford (1960-), a saxophonist, were both in the Messengers, long a training ground for fine young musicians. Soon, however, Wynton Marsalis left the Messengers temporarily and toured with Herbie Hancock, Ron Carter, and Tony Williams. That tour led to Marsalis's first album as a leader. In 1982, he left the Jazz Messengers permanently and formed his first quintet. His brother Branford was featured on tenor and soprano saxophones. The quintet was a commercial and artistic success, but in 1983 Marsalis left it to tour with Hancock once again.

In 1984, Marsalis won the jazz Grammy for "Think of One" and a classic Grammy for *Bach Trumpet Concertos*. In that same year he recorded in London with Raymond Leppard and the National Philharmonic Orchestra. Although Marsalis teaches a master class in Mozart at Juilliard, he has limited his classical recording because he feels it takes him too far away from jazz performance.

Bibliography
Gammond, Peter. *Oxford Companion to Popular Music*. New York: Oxford UP, 1991.

Gridley, Mark. *Jazz Styles*. Englewood Cliffs: Prentice-Hall, 1994.

Kernfeld, Barry, ed. *The New Grove Dictionary of Jazz*. Vol. 2. New York: Grove's Dictionaries of Music, 1988.

Frank A. Salamone

Marshall, Garry (1934-), television and film producer, is primarily known for his ABC hit sitcoms that dominated the mid-to-late-1970s Nielsen ratings. While Marshall's biggest hit, *Happy Days*, spawned two successful spinoffs, his quest for Nielsen rating success caused him to make compromises that harmed his earlier reputation for quality programming. Indeed, Marshall's popular ABC sitcoms pose a stark contrast to the quality programs he had been involved with earlier, including *The Dick Van Dyke Show* and *The Odd Couple*.

After a brief stint with his first career choice, journalism, Marshall became a gag writer for television performers such as Jack Paar, Rip Taylor, and Bill Dana. In the early 1960s, Marshall took a job as staff writer for *The Joey Bishop Show* (1961), where he was teamed with writer Jerry Belson. Marshall and Belson soon became a successful writing team, producing scripts for a number of long-running, critically acclaimed shows such as *The Danny Thomas Show* (1953) and *The Dick Van Dyke Show* (1961).

While Marshall and Belson's first venture as producers—*Hey Landlord* (1966)—was a flop, the pair received critical acclaim for their ABC sitcom based on Neil Simon's hit play and movie *The Odd Couple* (1970). Because ABC was then the third-place network, *The Odd Couple* failed to capture a large audience; however, the critically acclaimed sitcom continues to do well in syndication.

Marshall's first attempt at garnering younger viewers was *The Little People* (1972), an NBC sitcom starring Brian Keith and Shelley Fabres; the show failed. Marshall's next effort was the CBS series *Me and the Chimp* (1972), considered by many critics to be the worst sitcom in TV history.

Marshall's luck changed in 1974 when his series *Happy Days* debuted on ABC (see entry). Marshall's compromises regarding quality are clearly evident in *Happy Days*, which, in its first season, began as a well-written filmed sitcom that took a fun-yet-meaningful look at family life in the 1950s. One of the first season's more interesting recurring characters was a hood named Arthur "Fonzie" Fonzarelli, played by Henry Winkler. As Fonzie struck a chord with the American public, the series soon deteriorated to little more than a vehicle to showcase this developing icon of "cool." Series stars Ron Howard and Tom Bosley were shoved aside as the popular Fonzie dominated each episode.

As the 1970s progressed, Marshall churned out more *Happy Days*-based sitcoms. First came *Laverne and Shirley* (1976-83), which featured the antics of two single women employed at a Milwaukee brewery. The next series was *Mork and Mindy* (1978-82), little more than a vehicle for the singular comedy talents of Robin Williams. To show how far *Happy Days* had strayed from reality, *Mork and Mindy*, a contemporary series about an alien coming to earth, began as a spinoff episode from the 1950s-based *Happy Days*.

Laverne and Shirley and *Mork and Mindy* were wildly successful shows, joining *Happy Days* in the Nielsen Top 5. The final *Happy Days* spinoff, *Joanie Loves Chachi* (1982), based on the developing romance between *Happy Days* character Joanie Cunningham and Fonzie's cousin Chachi, was not as successful.

In 1979, perhaps in an effort to reclaim his reputation, Marshall created the series *Angie,* which starred Donna Pescow as a blue-collar waitress who married a millionaire. The series met with initial success that quickly faded, and Marshall's phenomenal prime-time prominence—much like ABC's brief flirt with first place—came to an end. One of Marshall's last TV efforts before moving on to film was a remake of *The Odd Couple* (1982), this time starring African-American actors Ron Glass and Demond Wilson. Using many of the same scripts from the original *Odd Couple*, the short-lived series failed to capture a sizable audience.

It was not until Marshall entered film that he was able to prove himself capable of producing works that combined popular appeal with a quality tone. His film credits include *Young Doctors in Love* (1982), *The Flamingo Kid* (1984), *Nothing in Common* (1986), *Beaches* (1989), and others.

Bibliography

Brooks, Tim, and Earle Marsh. *The Complete Directory to Prime Time Network TV Shows, 1946-Present.* New York: Ballantine, 1992.

Brown, Les. *Les Brown's Encyclopedia of Television.* Detroit: Visible Ink, 1992.

Marc, David, and Robert J. Thompson. *Prime Time, Prime Movers.* Boston: Little, Brown, 1992.

Michael B. Kassel

Marshall Tucker Band, The, recorded and released its first long-playing record album on the Capricorn Records label based in Macon, GA, in 1973 just as southern rock was exploding onto the national music scene. Along with Alabama's Wet Willie, the Spartanburg, SC, band added a new, fascinating dimension to the southern rock musical legacy solidly established by the Allman Brothers Band. Their unique, homegrown blend was a dash of Jethro Tull and the Grateful Dead here, a heavy dose of country music there, and a little western cowboy music thrown in for good measure. The Top 10 hit "Heard It in a Love Song" epitomized the sound of the Marshall Tucker Band, with its mix of Tex-Mex guitar, country lead vocals, and a flute.

The Marshall Tucker Band of the 1970s featured a six-person lineup led by the Robert Johnson, thumb-picking style of lead and steel guitarist and part-time lead vocalist Toy Caldwell. Caldwell's brother Tommy played bass guitar, percussion, and sang background vocals. The other four members of the original band were George McCorkle, rhythm and acoustic guitar and percussion; Paul Riddle, drums; Doug Gray, lead vocals and percussion; and Jerry Eubanks, alto sax, flute, percussion, and background vocals. The Marshall Tucker Band explored the free-form instrumental jam with guitarist Toy Caldwell making use of, and expanding upon, the major pentatonic scale in the tradition of Duane Allman and Jerry Garcia. A strong rhythm section provided a solid background for Toy Caldwell and woodwinds specialist Jerry Eubanks to improvise upon.

The Marshall Tucker Band's seventh album, 1978's *Together Forever*, was the first release to be solely recorded by the band members. Breaking from customary procedure, no guest artists were featured on the album. From 1973 to 1978, the Marshall Tucker Band's original lineup recorded two platinum albums, *Searchin' for a Rainbow* (1975) and *Carolina Dreams* (1977), and five gold albums, all on the Capricorn label: *The Marshall Tucker Band* (1973), *A New Life* (1974), *Where We All Belong* (1974), *Long Hard Ride* (1976), *Together Forever* (1978), and *Greatest Hits* (1978). The group's other albums were less successful. After Capricorn Records filed for bankruptcy in 1978, the band recorded and released five albums for Warner Brothers: *Running Like the Wind* (1979), *Tenth* (1980), *Dedicated* (1981), *Tuckerized* (1981), *Just Us* (1983), and *Greetings from South Carolina* (1983). *Still Holdin' On* (1988) was recorded for Mercury Records, and *Southern Spirit* (1990), *Still Smokin'* (1992), and *Walking Outside the Lines* (1993) were released by Cabin Fever Music.

The Marshall Tucker Band has always been a rock group, but its lasting legacy has been primarily through country music. The band's influence is heard in the work of country music performers such as Waylon Jennings, Hank Williams, Jr., Travis Tritt, and Charlie Daniels.

Bibliography

Larkin, Colin, ed. *The Guinness Encyclopedia of Popular Music.* Vol. 2. London: Guinness, 1992.

Romanowski, Patricia, and Holly George-Warren, eds. *The New Rolling Stone Encyclopedia of Rock & Roll.* New York: Fireside, 1995.

White Adam. *The Billboard Book of Gold & Platinum Records.* New York: Billboard, 1990.

W. A. Kelly Huff

Martin (1992-1997), a situation comedy that aired on the Fox network, was ranked as the fourth most popular television program watched by African Americans. The program was about the life of Martin Payne, a Detroit radio talk-show host. It starred comedian Martin Lawrence as Martin, Tisha Campbell as Gina, Martin's girlfriend/fiancée; Carl Anthony Payne II as Cole, a close friend of Martin; Thomas Mikal Ford as Tommy, another close friend of Martin; Tichina Arnold as Pam, Gina's best friend; Garrett Morris as Stan, the owner of the radio station where Martin works; and Jonathan Gries as Shawn, a white co-worker of Martin.

In an interesting innovation, Martin Lawrence also plays several minor characters: Mrs. Payne, Martin's mother; Sheneneh, Martin's neighbor; Otis, a gray-haired security guard; Jerome, a middle-aged playboy; Roscoe, a profane, street-smart little boy who lives in Martin's neighborhood, and others.

Some criticized *Martin*, saying that it was nothing more than a variation on the usual stereotypical, racist buffoonery that too often traps African-American comedy. Others felt that Martin and other characters on the show were funny, realistic depictions of people who live in the African-American community.

Bibliography

Collier, Aldore. "Martin Lawrence, Tic Campbell and Co-Stars of *Martin* Win Laughs and Fans." *Jet* 8 Mar. 1993: 56-58.

Smith, Daniel. "Martin Lawrence." *Rolling Stone* 11 Nov. 1993: 20.

Whitehead, Colson. "Single Black Male: *Martin/Hangin' with Mr. Cooper.*" *Village Voice* 22 Sept. 1992: 47-48.

Angela E. Chamblee

Martin, Dean (1917-1996), found career success in various media, including stage, screen, television, and recordings. While best known as a relaxed crooner or light comic actor, Martin also turned in several notable dramatic portrayals in his wide-ranging career.

Born in Steubenville, OH, Dean Martin began his show business career by singing with local bands as early as 1934, copying Bing Crosby as much as he could. By the late 1930s he was developing his own style, and playing clubs throughout Ohio. The early 1940s saw Martin slowly getting better and better bookings, mostly in clubs. Martin became the vocalist for the Sammy Watkins Orchestra, and was soon heard on live radio broadcasts in Cleveland. In 1944, he left the Watkins band and went to New York to become the house singer at the Riobamba, a nightclub. Even better bookings ensued and late in 1944 Martin caught the attention of comedian Lou Costello, who took an interest in Martin's career, paying for a nose-job and getting him better work.

While playing the club circuit in 1946, Martin met a rising comedian named Jerry Lewis (see entry) and the two formed a partnership that catapulted them into the big time, playing the best clubs and theaters. Martin also made his first professional recordings in 1946.

By 1948, the team had their own radio show and Martin was recording for Capitol Records, where he would remain for almost 14 years. With Capitol behind him, Martin's records started appearing on the charts. In 1949, the team began their series of successful films for Paramount, and the next year they became part of the rotating stars of the *Collegiate Comedy Hour* on NBC, a job they continued through 1955.

The team was very popular, turning out at least two films a year in addition to their live shows and television series. In 1953, a song from their film *The Caddy* was Martin's seventh hit, but first to break into the Top 10. The song, "That's Amore," only made it to No. 2, and it was not until "Memories Are Made of This" two years and several hits later that Martin finally had a No. 1 song.

In 1956, the team went their separate ways. Martin's career faltered through 1957 with no hit songs and one poorly received film, *Ten Thousand Bedrooms*. The club work continued, however, and 1958 saw a dramatic turnaround with a surprisingly strong serious performance in the film *The Young Lions* and four song hits. Martin also returned to television in number of specials. More hit films followed, including the classic *Rio Bravo* (1959), as did the hit songs. Martin left Capitol Records in 1961 and recorded for Reprise/Warner Brothers for the next dozen years.

Martin then added musicals and light comedies to his serious films, appearing in a two or three features a year including *Bells Are Ringing* (1960), *Ocean's Eleven* (1960), *Kiss Me, Stupid* (1964), and *The Sons of Katie Elder* (1965). At the same time, he was setting records with his nightclub shows and still having hit songs. His biggest hit from this time was "Everybody Loves Somebody Sometime," which pushed the Beatles out of the No. 1 position in 1964. Martin charted 27 more times in the next decade, including the smash "You're Nobody 'Til Somebody Loves You."

Martin began a television show which bore his name in 1965 (see entry). The show lasted nine seasons, and was followed by another decade of over 30 *Celebrity Roasts* and nearly a dozen variety specials.

In 1966, Martin starred in the first of four comic-adventure Matt Helm films, parodies of the James Bond series. A fifth was planned but never made. Instead, Martin played a key supporting role in the hit movie *Airport* (1970), which spawned three sequels and started the "disaster" cycle.

After nearly a decade off the charts, Martin had two hits in 1983, "My First Country Song" and "Since I Met You Baby," the latter helped by a music video which gained heavy rotation on MTV, first as a joke, and then for real. The rest of the 1980s saw Martin begin to slow down on all fronts, eventually announcing his retirement in 1990.

Bibliography

Marx, Arthur. *Everybody Loves Somebody Sometime (Especially Himself): The Story of Dean Martin and Jerry Lewis.* New York: Hawthorn, 1974.

Terrace, Vincent. *Encyclopedia of Television Series, Pilots, and Specials, 1937-1973.* Vol. 1. New York: Zoetrope, 1985.

——. *Encyclopedia of Television Series, Pilots, and Specials, 1974-1984.* Vol. 2. New York: Zoetrope, 1985.

Tosches, Nick. *Dino: Living High in the Dirty Business of Dreams.* New York: Doubleday, 1992.

Benjamin K. Urish

Marvel Comics revitalized the genre of costumed superheroes in the 1960s. Editor and chief writer Stan Lee (see entry) crafted characters with fantastic abilities, but human flaws: Spider-Man battled not only villains, but self-doubt, guilt, and ulcers, and he had to sneak out of his Aunt May's house to do it. The Incredible Hulk and the Thing would have preferred to go without their powers, while members of the Fantastic Four or the Avengers argued and quit on a regular basis. While DC Comics' stories were heavily plotted and

Photo courtesy of Popular Culture Library, Bowling Green State University, Bowling Green, Oh.

mystery oriented, Marvel's stories were driven by character. The "Marvel method" gave the artist more say in the story, and allowed for rousing fight scenes and cosmic settings.

The company that became Marvel was started as Western Fiction Publishing in 1932 by Martin Goodman, publisher of pulp magazines like *Complete Western Book*, *Star Detective,* and *Marvel Science Stories*. In 1939, Goodman went into comics by contracting with Funnies, Incorporated, a studio of artists and writers that packaged comics for other publishers. Their first project, *Marvel Comics* No. 1 (dated November 1939), included two of Marvel's seminal characters. Bill Everett's "Sub-Mariner," the water-breathing Prince Namor of Atlantis, was more of a modern-day Marvel villain: waging war on "the surface world" for despoiling his kingdom. Co-star Carl Burgos's "Human Torch" was his thematic opposite; when they began fighting each other, Namor destroyed New York City just for openers.

Goodman followed the industry practice of publishing through several paper companies for tax purposes. *Marvel Comics*, rechristened *Marvel Mystery Comics* with No. 2, was published under the Timely Comics imprint, the name applied by fans to all their comics of this period. Some of the Timelys also displayed a small "Marvel comic" logo.

Timely started an in-house "bullpen" of writers and artists, including the team of Joe Simon and Jack Kirby. Their first success was *Captain America* (March 1941), one of a string of patriotic heroes slugging it out with "Japanazi" fifth columnists well before Pearl Harbor.

Marvel's biggest character debuted in a throwaway story for the last issue of *Amazing Fantasy* (No. 15, August 1962). When bookish Peter Parker received superpowers from an irradiated spider's bite, he stitched his Spider-Man costume only to make money on television, then a thief he couldn't be bothered to capture later murdered his uncle. Spidey was a hero unlike any before him: neurotic, unsure of himself, and obliged to earn funds by selling pictures of his fights to a newspaper editor who hated him. Yet he baited the deadliest villains with jokes, and when faced with hopeless odds, found the strength within to turn the tide, a nobility shared by many Marvel heroes.

The Marvel reader of the 1960s was part of a fraternity called "Marveldom Assembled." Stan Lee gave full story credits to artists, inkers, and letterers, plus nicknames like Stan "The Man" Lee, Johnny "Ring-A-Ding" Romita, and of course, Jack "King" Kirby (see entry). The entire comic engaged the reader with Stan's wordplay, from Thor's mock Shakespearean dialogue to the carnival huckster house ads. The forsaken text page had become "Marvel Bullpen Bulletins," with chatty goings-on, news and "Stan's Soapbox." The real "True Believers" joined the "Merry Marvel Marching Society," or wrote clever letters to the editor in hopes of winning a "No-Prize" (when fans complained they hadn't received the No-Prizes, a fancy envelope was mailed—with No Prize inside).

Marvel's popularity was growing, but Marvel's circulation was stymied. DC allowed them to distribute only eight titles a month, so to give Spider-Man his own title, Lee had to cancel *The Incredible Hulk*. New heroes buddied up in anthology titles: The Sub-Mariner and the Hulk were in *Tales to Astonish*, the Human Torch and Dr. Strange in *Strange Tales*. Marvel soon had enough characters to form another team, *The Avengers*. They recovered Captain America from suspended animation in an iceberg, and later broke up, leaving Cap to lead a new team.

In 1968, Marvel got a new distribution deal, and was now able to launch dozens of new titles. The Hulk, Captain America, Thor, and others finally got their own books, and Sgt. Fury appeared in both the World War II milieu and the James Bond age as *Nick Fury, Agent of S.H.I.E.L.D.* There was even a *Captain Marvel*: no relation to Fawcett's classic character, but an alien spy who switched sides to defend the Earth. Stan was at his moralizing best with the *Silver Surfer* (August 1968), the former herald of the world-devouring villain Galactus, now wandering the world with Christ-like musings on the human race.

The Marvel age effectively ended in 1972, a year that started with Lee lecturing on comics in Carnegie Hall. Marvel had just taken on the Comics Code Authority by issuing, without Code approval, a Spider-Man story dealing with drug addiction. Its success forced the Code to revise many of its 1950s-era rules. Then Goodman retired, having sold the company to Cadence Industries, and Stan advanced from editor-in-chief to publisher, relinquishing his day-to-day duties.

Marvel has continued to issue flops, hits, and true trendsetters since then. Roy Thomas and Barry Smith adapted *Conan the Barbarian*, Robert E. Howard's character from *Weird Tales*, which revived the sword-and-sorcery genre. Chris Claremont revitalized the *X-Men* by blending cosmic soap opera with misunderstood teenage mutants, characters immediately familiar to the adolescent fans that now bought comics at specialty retail stores. In the 1980s, Marvel's reliance on spinoff "X-" books led many fans to deride their "Teenage Mutant Ninja" clichés, and inspired two independent publishers to create *Teenage Mutant Ninja Turtles* in 1984.

Marvel's fortunes in television and movies have been somewhat spotty. The syndicated *Marvel Super Heroes* of 1966 was a hit despite its limited animation. Spider-Man and the Fantastic Four each spawned three cartoon series, while the X-Men appear weekdays and Saturdays on the Fox network. "Spidey" was a feature of PBS's *The Electric*

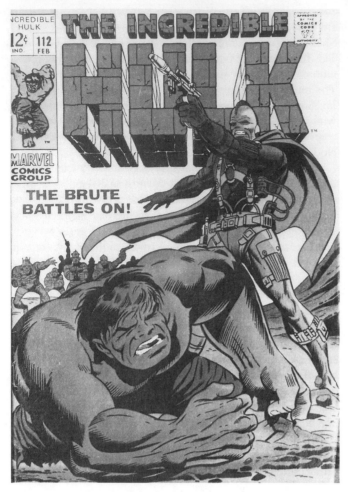

Photo courtesy of Popular Culture Library, Bowling Green State University, Bowling Green, OH.

Company. Bill Bixby and Lou Ferrigno starred as *The Incredible Hulk* (CBS, 1978-82), with a plot formula borrowed from *The Fugitive.* Its success led to a string of live-action *Spider-Man, Captain America,* and *Doctor Strange* TV movies. In 1996, a TV-movie of the mutant spinoff *Generation X* appeared on Fox.

In movies, Marvel's brightest spot remains Republic Studios' 1944 *Captain America* serial. The only other character to hit theaters was *Howard the Duck,* a brilliant satire in comics, but a George Lucas-produced goose egg on screen in 1986. *The Punisher,* starring Dolph Lundgren, went straight to cable and video in 1989, as did a *Captain America* feature in 1990. A low-budget *Fantastic Four* feature was shelved upon completion in 1993, when a bigger-budget film was announced. James Cameron signed to direct a *Spider-Man* feature but the project was bogged down in lawsuits. Stan relocated to California as president of Marvel Films to pitch the characters to Hollywood.

Comics have made Marvel a major entertainment conglomerate. It was sold to Roger Corman's New World Pictures in 1986, then purchased in 1989 by the Andrews Group. Now called the Marvel Entertainment Group, they acquired the trading card company Fleer, and independent publisher Malibu Comics. Of greatest concern to retailers was Marvel's 1994 acquisition of comics distributor Heroes

World, which was then named its exclusive distributor. Other publishers reacted by signing exclusive deals, forcing retailers to order comics from several distributors at once. This development arose as prices climbed, driving sales down. Marvel started 1996 with a splashy *DC versus Marvel* crossover series, but also with hundreds of layoffs and a halving of its comics output.

Bibliography

Benton, Mike. *The Comic Book in America: An Illustrated History.* Dallas: Taylor, 1989.

——. *Superhero Comics of the Golden Age: The Illustrated History.* Dallas: Taylor, 1992.

——. *Superhero Comics of the Silver Age: The Illustrated History.* Dallas: Taylor, 1991.

Daniels, Les. *Marvel: Five Fabulous Decades of the World's Greatest Comics.* New York: Abrams, 1991.

Horn, Maurice, ed. *The World Encyclopedia of Comics.* New York: Chelsea, 1976.

Mark McDermott

Marx Brothers, **Chico** (Leonard 1886-1961), **Harpo** (Adloph, 1888-1964), **Groucho** (Julius 1890-1977), **Zeppo** (Herbert 1901-1979), and, early on in their careers, **Gummo** (Milton, 1893-1977), vaudeville players of the 1910s and Broadway stars of the 1920s, achieved their lasting place in American popular culture through the movies they made in the 1930s. They belonged to the generation of vaudeville comics that made it big in film during the early sound era: W. C. Fields, Mae West, George Burns and Gracie Allen, Jack Benny, and Bob Hope.

I'll Say She Is, starring the Marx Brothers, opened on Broadway in May 1924. It was a combination of the best routines the brothers had been doing for years plus a smattering of singing and dancing numbers and piano and harp interludes. (A scene from this show featuring the brothers oafishly mimicking Maurice Chevalier was filmed as a Paramount publicity short in 1931 and can be seen in the 1982 documentary, *Marx Brothers in a Nutshell.*) They quickly became the toast of the New York literati, and frequently joined a group of prominent luminaries who met at the round table in the Algonquin Hotel. Chico joined the Thanatopsis Club, an exclusive literary poker club, and reeled in producer Sam Harris and writer George Kaufman for their next two Broadway shows, *Coconuts* (1925) and *Animal Crackers* (1928).

These shows were major hits on Broadway for years. Then, after the Wall Street crash of 1929, Groucho and Harpo were wiped out financially—Chico was always broke due to his gambling. They needed more money, and fortunately the film industry was mining Broadway talent for the new "talkies."

Coconuts (1929) and *Animal Crackers* (1930) were filmed by Paramount without changes. The next three films they did systematically reduced the staples of American high culture to comic rubble. *Monkey Business* (1931) portrayed rich society snobs as little more than gangsters putting on airs. *Horse Feathers* (1932) sent up the university as a locus for corruption and foolishness. *Duck Soup* (1933), their masterpiece, ruthlessly satirized democracy and the institutions of government.

When they signed with MGM (a contract that gave them an unprecedented 15 percent of the gross profits on the two pictures), they committed themselves to character changes and new plot standards. After *A Night at the Opera* (1935), MGM removed the social centers of the films to class-neutral locations which guaranteed a larger audience but removed some of the sting from the brothers' comedy. They also added serious love stories, longer, glitzier production numbers, plot-driven motives for the piano and harp solos, and climactic chase sequences (using stand-ins) at the ends. As Gerald Mast has observed, this meant that Marx Brothers films no longer satirized "serious" movie conventions. Altogether, the changes watered down the Marx Brothers' comedy and transformed them from the foes of propriety and elitism into the nutty champions of true love. Nevertheless, *A Night at the Opera* and *A Day at the Races* (1937) were very funny, and were bigger hits than any of their earlier pictures had been. Their next four films (one of which they did for RKO) were moderately well received, but it was clear that they were past their prime. After *The Big Store* (1941), the brothers went their separate ways professionally, but were mostly retired. Chico formed a successful nightclub band called "Chico Marx and His Ravellis." Harpo did some occasional television and performed with his harp. Groucho had small roles in several films and became a big star on television as the acerbic host of the quiz show *You Bet Your Life* (1947-61). They also made a few more films together, the best of which, *A Night in Casablanca* (1946), was an amalgamation of their funniest plots and routines.

Bibliography

Bergen, Ronald. *The Life and Times of the Marx Brothers.* New York: Smithmark, 1992.

Marx, Groucho, and Richard J. Anobile. *The Marx Bros. Scrapbook.* New York: Perennial, 1973.

Marx, Harpo. *Harpo Speaks!* New York: Geis, 1961.

Mast, Gerald. *The Comic Mind: Comedy and the Movies.* Chicago: U of Chicago P, 1979.

Tiersma, Peter Meijes. *Language-Based Humor in the Marx Brothers.* Bloomington: Indiana University Linguistics Club, 1985.

April D. Wilson

Mary Tyler Moore Show, The (1970-1977), was the prototypical classic TV situation comedy. At the entrance to CBS Studio City's Sound Stage Two is a plaque that reads, "On this stage a company of loving and talented friends produced a television classic." Hailed by critics and honored by numerous television awards, *The Mary Tyler Moore Show* not only meets the definition of a classic, but stands as one of the major groundbreaking sitcoms of the early 1970s, defining a new era of relevance in the sitcom genre and proving that TV could entertain, enlighten, and keep up with the changing times.

In essence, the series answered the question posed by its theme song: "How will you make it on your own?" This was not only appropriate for main character Mary Richards

(Mary Tyler Moore, 1936-), but for the many American women viewers who were finding themselves either divorced or single by choice. Mary Richards was TV's first truly liberated woman who saw the possibility of having both a career and a family.

While women's liberation and contemporary issues were a part of the show, the heart of its appeal was due to the strong character comedy derived by the talented ensemble cast. With Mary's life divided between the WJM newsroom—where she worked as associate producer—and her Minneapolis apartment, Mary's co-workers and friends became her family, something that has become the norm on sitcoms today.

Mary's best friend, Rhoda Morgenstern (Valerie Harper), a strange mix of liberated career woman and nymphomaniac, provided a perfect counterpart to Mary, whose Midwestern values often collided with Rhoda's East Coast cynicism. Between the two was Phyllis Lindstrom (Cloris Leachman), a parody of psychobabble know-it-alls. The characters eventually won their own spinoffs, *Rhoda* (1974-78) and *Phyllis* (1975-77).

The other half of the show was devoted to Mary's TV newsroom job. Her boss and mentor was the tough-yet-lovable Lou Grant (Ed Asner). After *The Mary Tyler Moore Show* ended, Asner continued with a more serious Lou Grant character in the CBS drama *Lou Grant* (1977-82; see entry). Rounding out the news staff were Ted Baxter (Ted Knight), the empty-headed newscaster, Gavin MacLeod as the wise-cracking Murray Slaughter, and, later, Betty White as the over-sexed, hypocritical Sue Ann Nivens, and Ted's girlfriend Georgette (Georgia Engles).

The Mary Tyler Moore Show was born out of CBS's desire to woo Moore back to series television. Disappointed by a failing movie career, Moore parlayed the CBS offer into what soon became one of television's most respected production companies, Mary Tyler Moore Enterprises, owned by her and then-husband Grant Tinker. The pair enlisted James L. Brooks and Allan Burns to create the series. While Mary was originally slated to play a divorcée, CBS executives feared TV was not quite ready for that. Another reason for Mary's change to single woman was the network's fear that viewers would think Moore had divorced Dick Van Dyke, whom she starred with as Laura Petrie in the successful *Dick Van Dyke Show*, a classic in its own right (see entry).

The series enjoyed a great deal of success, and, like *The Dick Van Dyke Show*, was ended by choice. The final episode focused on Mary saying good-bye to her newsroom friends, who, all except for Ted, had been fired by the new station owner.

Moore, a perennial TV favorite and movie actress, has yet to find a vehicle that can equal her sitcom's success. While Moore is no longer connected with MTM Productions, she and Grant Tinker had developed the company into a staple producer of quality sitcoms such as *Rhoda, Phyllis*, and *WKRP in Cincinnati* (1978-82), as well as hard-hitting dramas including *Lou Grant, The White Shadow* (1978-81), *Hill Street Blues* (1981-87), and *St. Elsewhere* (1982-88).

Bibliography

Brooks, Tim, and Earle Marsh. *The Complete Directory to Prime Time Network TV Shows, 1946-Present*. New York: Ballantine, 1992.

Feuer, Jane, Paul Kerr, and Tise Vahimagi, eds. *MTM: Quality Television*. London: BFI, 1984.

Michael B. Kassel

M*A*S*H (1972-1983). *M*A*S*H* first appeared as a best-selling novel (1968) written by Richard Hooker, pen name of Richard Hornberger, a doctor who had served in a Mobile Army Surgical Hospital (a MASH unit) during the Korean War. The novel was made into a hit movie (1970) directed by Robert Altman, featuring, among others, Gary Burghoff, the only member of the movie cast to appear in the TV series. After initial problems with low ratings, *M*A*S*H* on TV finally scored the mass media hat-trick by becoming one of the most successful sitcoms in television history.

The heart of the series was actor Alan Alda, who, as Hawkeye Pierce, fought the insanity of war with not only his surgical skills but also his humor, alcohol abuse, and women chasing. Unlike his tentmate and best friend Trapper John McIntyre (Wayne Rogers), later replaced by B. J. Hunnicut (Mike Farrell), Hawkeye had no respect for authority; after all, it was those in authority who started and perpetuated the war he so desperately hated. Alda eventually became the creative consultant for the show, and wrote many of the sitcom's most brilliant scripts.

The original cast was rounded out by Henry Blake (McLean Stevenson), the 4077th's bumbling-yet-lovable leader; Frank Burns (Larry Linville), the spineless wimp held captive by his secret desires; Margaret "Hot Lips" Houlihan (Loretta Swit), a career army nurse who was turned on by military order and authority; Radar O'Reilly (Burghoff), the Teddy-bear-toting corporal who kept the unit together; and Father Francis Mulcahy, the chaplain (William Christopher).

The first-season episodes failed to find an audience, causing some fear that the show was too graphic, but for the second season a move to Saturday evenings after the hit *All in the Family* made the difference. *M*A*S*H* began scoring Top 10 ratings that would last into the next decade.

In the second season a couple of characters were dropped, some modified, and transvestite Corporal Max Klinger (Jamie Farr), a character borrowed from Joseph Heller's *Catch-22*, was added. Klinger's cross-dressing scheme to get a discharge on the grounds of insanity became an integral part of the insanity of war that surrounded the group of young doctors and nurses. As actors left the series, and as public moods and consciousness changed, the series became more serious—and, as some argue—less humorous. The characters drifted toward 1970s enlightenment—including Hawkeye, who dropped his womanizing—and *M*A*S*H* lost some of its biting edge.

M*A*S*H remained an innovative show throughout its run. In 1975, when McLean Stevenson decided to leave the series, the producers took advantage of the moment to show

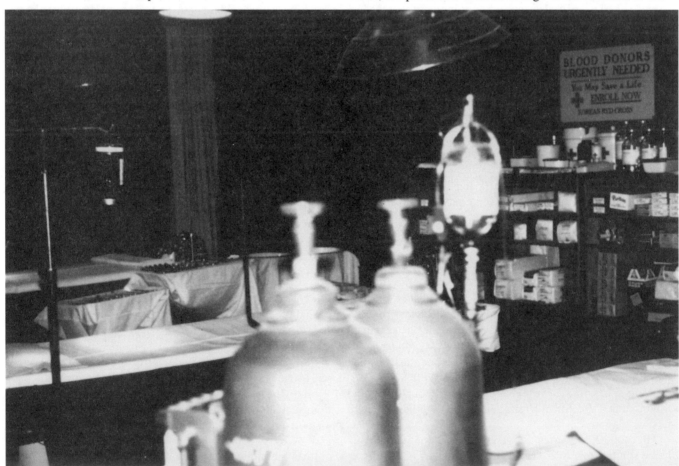

The Operating Room set from *M*A*S*H* rebuilt for display at the Smithsonian. Photo courtesy of Mark McDermott.

the horrors of war. After a first act of light farewells, the tone grew more serious with an emotional good-bye between Blake and Radar, who had developed a father-son relationship. The episode ended with Radar walking into the operating room to announce that Colonel Blake's helicopter had been shot down over the Sea of Japan. Much to the first-run viewer's surprise, *M*A*S*H* had killed off one of its major characters.

With such a creative series, it was only matter of time before the writers ran out of steam. The series had already lasted nine years longer than the Korean War, so amidst much hype and fanfare, the final episode—a 2 and 1/2-hour special—was broadcast in February 1983. One of the most watched events in television history, the episode revolved around Hawkeye, the rock of sanity, recovering from a chilling nervous breakdown. The following year, Jamie Farr, William Christopher, and Harry Morgan, who had replaced Stevenson as Colonel Sherman Potter, went on to star in an updated version of the series, *After M*A*S*H*. The public, however, failed to respond, and the new series was canceled after its first season.

Bibliography

Brooks, Tim, and Earle Marsh. *The Complete Directory to Prime Time Network TV Shows, 1946-Present.* New York: Ballantine, 1992.
Kalter, Suzy. *The Complete Book of* M*A*S*H. New York: Abrams, 1988.
Waldron, Vince. *Classic Sitcoms.* New York: Collier, 1987.

Michael B. Kassel

Mason, Perry. In the course of 60 years, fictional defense attorney Perry Mason has become the most recognized lawyer character in American popular culture. Mason first appeared in Erle Stanley Gardner's novel *The Case of the Velvet Claws* (1933). Himself a veteran lawyer in southern California, Gardner (see entry) projected his own devotion to unpopular defendants onto Mason, continuing the series through 82 novels.

Before World War II ended, eight Perry Mason novels were Pocket Books best-sellers and Perry Mason also appeared on radio and in the movies. Gardner originally thought of these dramatizations chiefly as ways to promote his novels. However, listeners and viewers loved Mason as much as readers did. The half-hour radio dramas were popular for a dozen years, and Warner Brothers produced seven feature films, the best of which starred Warren Williams.

In the late 1950s, Perry Mason attracted a considerable following on television. Determined to maintain tight control over the series, Gardner reviewed scripts, chose actors, and fought to preserve his pet character's integrity. Gardner wanted Mason to be clever and heroic, but refused to let him be a "smart aleck." In each episode, Mason functioned as a detective in the first part, and a trial lawyer in the concluding segment, where his client was usually vindicated in dramatic fashion and the guilty party exposed. The successful formula and Raymond Burr's winsome portrayal won loyal viewers.

The CBS series—co-starring Barbara Hale as secretary Della Street and William Hopper as detective Paul Drake—

ran from 1957 to 1966, and was one of the most acclaimed in television history. In 1973, NBC tried unsuccessfully to revive the series with Monte Markham as Mason, but fans identified Burr with the role. In 1985 he returned with Barbara Hale in a series of two-hour made-for-television movies, until his death in 1993.

Bibliography

Kane, Patricia. "Perry Mason: Modern Culture Hero." *Heroes of Popular Culture.* Ed. Ray B. Browne, Marshall Fishwick, and Michael T. Marsden. Bowling Green, OH: Bowling Green State U Popular P, 1972.
Kelleher, Brian, and Diana Merrill. *The* Perry Mason *TV Show Book: The Complete Story of America's Favorite Television Lawyer.* New York: St. Martin's, 1987.
Papke, David Ray. *Juris Doctor.* August 1973.
Sokolsky, Anita. *Yale Journal of Law & the Humanities.* 1990.
Stark, Steven D. *University of Miami Law Review.* 1987.

David Ray Papke

See also
Legal Mysteries

Mathis, Johnny (1935-), was born John Royce Mathis in San Francisco, CA, the fourth of seven children. The family lived in a basement flat in the Fillmore district, a poor and largely African-American section of San Francisco. Both parents worked for local millionaires—his mother as a domestic and cook, and his father as a handyman and chauffeur. Clem Mathis, who had been a vaudeville performer during the 1920s in his native Texas, recognizing his son's outstanding singing ability very early, managed to buy him a second-hand piano, began giving eight-year-old Johnny piano lessons, and taught him his first song, "My Blue Heaven."

During the following years Johnny Mathis continued singing in church affairs and amateur productions; at 13 he began taking singing lessons. In addition to his singing, Johnny Mathis served as a student leader—the first African-American student body president of his junior high and treasurer of his high school graduating class—and excelled as an athlete. However, a slight spinal defect prevented Mathis from becoming a professional athlete, so he prepared for a career teaching English.

Throughout his schooling Mathis never lost interest in singing, and while in college he sang in amateur jazz ensembles and in San Francisco nightclubs for extra money. It was during one of the jam sessions in 1955 at the famed Black Hawk that co-owner of the club Helen Noga decided to become his manager and initiated his professional singing career. Eventually, Noga introduced Mathis to Columbia Records executive George Avakian. Initially reluctant to abandon college for the chance at becoming a professional singer, Mathis went to New York at Avakian's request and recorded his first album while performing at many of the city's hotspots. Mathis's first effort, a jazz-based album called *Johnny Mathis: A New Sound in Popular Song* fell flat, and Avakian brought in the head of Columbia's singles department, Mitch Miller, to rework Mathis's sound. Miller suggested that Mathis steer away from jazz and toward romantic ballads, even though this move resisted the growing influence of rock 'n' roll. Mathis's romantic crooning earned him a place in the popular music scene.

With his first single release, "Wonderful! Wonderful!" Mathis became an instant hit, and together with three other singles, "It's Not for Me to Say," "Chances Are"/"The Twelfth of Never," and "No Love [But Your Love]"/"Wild Is the Wind," Mathis reached gold-record status in 1957. His *Johnny's Greatest Hits* album released in 1958 remained on *Billboard* album charts for a world record 490 weeks and sold over 2 million copies. Over the 40 years of his long career, Mathis has remained the only singer to have four albums on the charts at the same time and has registered a total of 50 gold and platinum records. Mathis has sold over 100 million records worldwide and has remained on the popular music charts for more time than any other singer besides Elvis Presley and Frank Sinatra. Mathis also appeared and performed in several movies, including *Lizzie* in 1957 and *A Certain Smile* in 1958.

At a time when the popular music scene was so heavily influenced by rock 'n' roll, Mathis disarmed audiences with his romantic crooning. He was influenced by Ella Fitzgerald, Billy Eckstine, Johnny Nash, Sarah Vaughan, Peggy Lee, and (Mathis's personal favorites) Nat King Cole and Lena Horne. Although his velvety plush voice, which has been described as choir-boy innocence hooked with a hint of romantic seduction, set Mathis apart from other singers of the time, Mathis's sheer talent and versatility as an artist have allowed his music to endure.

Bibliography

Current Biography, 1965, 1993.

Larkin, Colin, ed. *Guinness Encyclopedia of Popular Music.* Vol. 4. Middlesex, U.K.: Guinness, 1995.

Pareles, Jon, ed. *Rolling Stone Encyclopedia of Rock & Roll.* New York: Summit, 1983.

Scott Logan Baugh

Maude (1972-1978), a TV sitcom produced by Norman Lear, was spun off from *All in the Family* (see entry) in 1972 and featured Beatrice Arthur in the title role. A wealthy middle-aged suburbanite, Maude was a political liberal and an outspoken feminist. She was already familiar to viewers from her verbal battles with her cousin Edith Bunker's husband, Archie—battles Maude usually won. *Maude* was a radical innovation because, unlike *All in the Family*, which focused on a blue-collar household, the show invaded upper-middle-class suburban life and injected it with a rhetoric of race, class, and political dichotomy.

Although Maude was supportive of women's causes, she herself did not firmly cling to the belief that women must bond with one another in order to be unified. Throughout the course of the series, she did not have one truly supportive relationship with another woman. Her daughter Carol was her critic; Vivian (Rue McClanahan), her best friend of 30 years, her rival and judge; and her housekeepers, Florida Evans (Esther Rolle), and Mrs. Naugatuck (Hermione Baddeley), her subordinates.

While often humorous, *Maude* was at times disturbing as it dealt with both realistic and controversial issues. After suffering a decline in ratings during the 1977-78 season, producers announced some major cast changes. Maude was to move to Washington, DC, and begin a career in politics. But before this could happen, Bea Arthur announced that she was leaving the show. The producers conceded that no one else could fill her shoes, so *Maude* ended its prime-time run.

Bibliography

Bartholome, Lynn. "Loud-Mouthed and Liberated: The Women of Norman Lear." *Popular Culture Review* 5 (Feb. 1994).

Brooks, Tim, and Earle Marsh. *The Complete Directory to Prime Time Network TV Shows, 1946-Present.* 3d ed. New York: Ballantine, 1985.

Lichter, S. Robert, Linda S. Lichter, and Stanley Rothman. *Watching America.* New York: Prentice-Hall, 1991.

Marc, David. *Comic Visions: Television Comedy and American Culture.* Boston: Unwin Hyman, 1989.

Lynn Bartholome

Maverick (1957-1962) depicted the adventures of the Maverick brothers, Bret (James Garner) and Bart (Jack Kelly), who were everything traditional TV heroes were not. They were sneaky, lazy, interested more in money than in honor, and exceedingly slow with a six-gun. One of the most important distinctions of *Maverick* was its humor, a quality notably absent in most Westerns. *Maverick* refused to take itself too seriously and its efforts at tongue-in-cheek comedy proved to be, in the words of one critic, "a breath of fresh air in an increasingly self-righteous environment." Some of the funniest and best-remembered episodes were spoofs of other TV Westerns.

Another unique aspect of *Maverick* was its determined effort to avoid the usual Western plots, sometimes even adapting stories from literary classics. Creator Roy Huggins found ideas for stories in some pretty unlikely places: Shakespeare's *Othello*, *The Wrecker* by Robert Louis Stevenson, Euripides' *Alcestis*, Aristophanes' *Lysistrata*, *A Tale of Two Cities* by Charles Dickens. But most plots followed a formula involving an interesting swindle, scheme, or method of cheating.

When *Maverick* first appeared on ABC, September 22, 1957, it was only one of some 32 Westerns on television, and it was brashly pitted against the toughest competition on the air. In a few weeks it had beaten all three in the ratings and by the second season had won over most critics. A key ingredient of the series was its star, James Garner. Garner, although appearing like the standard hero (he was 6 feet, 3 inches tall, with a determined gaze, youthful vigor and good looks), was actually more like the character he played. When Garner left the series after the third season, Warner Bros. decided to replace him with the British-educated cousin Beauregard. To play Beau, Warners brought in one of their contract players, London-born Roger Moore, from *The Alaskans,* which had just been canceled.

There were two attempts to revive the popular series: *Young Maverick* (1979-80), which featured Charles Frank as cousin Beau's son Ben, and *Bret Maverick* (1981), starring James Garner in his old role. Neither caught on with the public, however, and both were canceled after one season. A theatrical film released in 1994, starring Australian actor Mel Gibson as Bret Maverick and Garner as his "Pappy," did quite well at the box office.

Bibliography

Barer, Burl. *Maverick: The Making of the Movie and the Official Guide to the Television Series.* Boston: Tuttle, 1994.
Yoggy, Gary A. *Riding the Video Range: The Rise and Fall of the Western on Television.* Jefferson: McFarland, 1995.

Gary A. Yoggy

Max Headroom (1987-1988), "twenty minutes into the future," featured a character who debuted in a TV movie on Britain's Channel Four in April 1985. Originally conceived as "host" of a music-video program, the character of Max (Matt Frewer) was fashioned as a computer-generated image by music video producers Rocky Morton and Annabel Jankel, authors of a book about computer graphics, and Peter Wagg. Morton and Jankel then made a movie intended to kick off the music-video series and as a sort of backstory or creation myth for the character of Max.

The TV movie was a success, and Cinemax followed with a biweekly Max Headroom "talk show" in the fall of 1985. Coca-Cola began using Max as a "spokesthing" in TV commercials the following spring. It is probably in this incarnation that Max reached his widest audience, achieving a "76 percent name recognition among teenagers" and bringing New Coke some success in the 1980s "cola wars."

The *Max Headroom* episodic TV series premiered on ABC in March 1987. The series was a critical success but a ratings failure. It returned in the fall of 1987 for a short run, with a couple of episodes held back until spring of 1988.

The premises of the American series were identical to those of the British TV movie: Edison Carter (Frewer) is a TV reporter working in the near future for Network 23, a broadcasting company epitomizing the excesses of real-world, present-day commercial broadcasting. Investigating apparent wrongdoing by his own network, he crashes his motorbike into a parking lot gate containing the phrase "Max Headroom [i.e., low clearance] 2.3 m[eters]." Carter's unconscious body is recovered by the network, where resident brat-prodigy Bryce Lynch feeds Carter's personality and memories into a computer, so as to keep the high-rated Carter alive as an artificial image. The scheme backfires, as the computer image takes form as a sarcastic talking head named Max Headroom (the last words Carter saw before crashing). Meanwhile, Carter himself is rescued and recovers completely, in time to root out the evil at 23 and ponder his slightly monstrous video doppelgänger Max.

In later episodes Carter roams a bombed-out urban cyberpunk hell, carrying a video camera with which he conducts ambush-style exposés and crusades, often for live broadcast. Back at network headquarters, "controller" Theora Jones (Amanda Pays) tracks Carter's movements on a computer screen and feeds him instructions, which he hears through an earpiece. Network brass and hacker-genius Lynch (movie, Paul Spurrier; series, Chris Young) variously encourage or impede Carter, depending on the situation.

Max Headroom, who exists only as a TV picture, randomly pops up to comment on the action.

Max's image was created by applying 4 1/2 hours' worth of makeup to Matt Frewer and inserting a computer-generated, abstract backdrop behind him. Special shooting techniques and the mixing of film and videotape gave Max his jerky, robotic, glitchy appearance. Voice-processing contributed further to the impression of Max as an artificial being.

Bibliography

Berko, Lili. "Simulation and High Concept Imagery: The Case of Max Headroom." *Wide Angle* 10.4 (Fall 1988): 50-61.
Chisholm, Brad. "On-Screen Screens." *Journal of Film and Video* 41.2 (1989): 15-24.
Landon, Brooks. "Max Headroom." *Cinefantastique* 18.1 (1987): 29, 58.
Roberts, Steve. *Max Headroom: 20 Minutes into the Future.* New York: Random House, 1986.

Gary Burns

Mayberry, R.F.D. (1968-1971). Television viewers of the 1980s and 1990s have become accustomed to extravagantly publicized final episodes of successful programs like *Cheers* and *M*A*S*H*. In the 1960s, however, *The Andy Griffith Show* ended its eight-year network run without fanfare by dissolving into *Mayberry, R.F.D.* The following decade, *All in the Family* ended similarly by becoming *Archie Bunker's Place.* Many of *Mayberry, R.F.D.*'s characters were introduced in the last few episodes of *The Andy Griffith Show.* *Mayberry, R.F.D.* lasted for 78 episodes.

Mayberry, R.F.D. was necessitated because General Foods, sponsor of *The Andy Griffith Show*, did not want to give up the ratings-rich show. Griffith and his producer Sheldon Leonard maintained ownership of *Mayberry, R.F.D.*, and some of *The Andy Griffith Show*'s original characters continued their roles. The premise of the show remained familiar. Ken Berry had joined *The Andy Griffith Show* in 1968 as Sam Jones, a farmer and city councilman. Like Sheriff Andy Taylor, Jones was a widower raising a young son named Mike, played by Buddy Foster. Frances Bavier remained as Aunt Bee and kept house for the Joneses until 1970. George Lindsey played Goober Pyle until the conclusion of the series. County clerk Howard Sprague (Jack Dodson) remained, as did fixit shop owner Emmett Clark (Paul Hartman) and his wife, Martha (Mary Lansing).

Mayberry, R.F.D. continued the success of *The Andy Griffith Show.* In its last year on the air, it was No. 7 in the ratings. But in 1971, CBS canceled all of its successful rural-based shows in an attempt to shake a presumed hick image, even though *Mayberry, R.F.D.*, like its predecessor, was more reality-based than shows like *Green Acres.*

Bibliography

Beck, Ken, and Jim Clark. The Andy Griffith Show *Book.* New York: St. Martin's, 1985.
Kelly, Richard. *The Andy Griffith Show.* Winston-Salem: John F. Blair, 1981.
McNeil, Alex. *Total Television: A Comprehensive Guide to Programming from 1948 to the Present.* New York: Penguin, 1991.

Pfeiffer, Lee. *The Official* Andy Griffith Show *Scrapbook.* New York: Citadel, 1994.

W. A. Kelly Huff

McBain, Ed, pseudonym of Evan Hunter (1926-), whose other aliases include Curt Cannon, Hunt Collins, Ezra Hannon, and Richard Martsen, writes fast-paced and convincingly realistic police procedurals and thrillers. He is best known for his more than 50 87th Precinct novels, in which a close-knit team of police detectives moves through daily frustrations to solve crimes and deal with the aftermath of violence. Some of the best of these include *He Who Hesitates* (1965), *Downtown* (1989), and *Vespers* (1991). McBain has also created attorney Matthew Hope in a series of novels that just as effectively captures Florida's sleaziness. Best known among the Hope books are *Rumpelstiltskin* (1961), *Snow White and Red Rose* (1985), and *Cinderella* (1986).

McBain's experimental plots (multiple story lines; murderous narrator; locked-room mystery; a recurring super villain, The Deaf Man) keep his procedurals fresh and exciting. A McBain novel is tough and realistic but tempered by humor, irony, and compassion.

Bibliography

Dove, George N. *The Boys from Grover Avenue: Ed McBain's 87th Precinct Novels.* Bowling Green, OH: Bowling Green State U Popular P, 1985.

Gina Macdonald

McCullough, Colleen (1938-), with her most famous novel, *The Thorn Birds* (1977), secured her place in popular literary history. McCullough is the Australian author of several other novels and continues to produce romantic sagas that captivate the reading public. Most of her stories feature intense but impeded passion between unlikely or illicit lovers and revolve around the competing claims of love and duty: *The Thorn Birds* traces the forbidden affair between a young woman and a Catholic priest (it was made into a television miniseries in 1983 starring Richard Chamberlain); *Tim* (1974) features a lonely but successful woman who falls in love with a man who is considerably younger and mentally retarded; *An Indecent Obsession* (1981) explores the romantic conflict lived by a war nurse over her fiancé and a patient under her care. With *The First Man in Rome* (1990), the first of a trilogy of novels set in the late days of the Roman republic, McCullough has shifted from romantic sagas to political life.

Bibliography

Mitgang, Herbert. *Words Still Count with Me: A Chronicle of Literary Conversations.* New York: Norton, 1995.

Morris, Gwen. "An Australian Ingredient in American Soap: *The Thorn Birds* by Colleen McCullough." *Journal of Popular Culture* 24.4 (1991): 59-69.

Steinberg, Sybil. "PW Interviews: Colleen McCullough." *Publishers Weekly* 14 Sept. 1990: 109-10.

Liahna Babener

McEntire, Reba (1955-), emerged as the premier female country music artist at the end of the 1980s and beginning of the 1990s. McEntire has a country background, having grown up in rural Oklahoma, but she has a jazz voice; she embodies the idea of a woman whose career and ambition has been liberated by feminism, but who still retains traditional values about home and family.

Born in Kiowa, OK, young Reba McEntire grew up in a rodeo family; her father and grandfather were both champion rodeo performers. Reba was a barrel racer in rodeos but preferred to sing, which she did as a group with her brother and younger sister. In 1974, her performance of the national anthem at the National Rodeo Finals in Oklahoma City was heard by Nashville recording artist Red Stegall; he then helped her obtain a recording contract from Mercury Records.

McEntire released her first single in 1976, but she would not achieve chart success until 1980 when "(You Lift Me) Up to Heaven" hit the Top 10; however, it was not until 1982 that she put together a string of hits, beginning with "I'm Not That Lonely Yet," "Can't Even Get the Blues," and "You're the First Time I've Thought about Leaving." In 1986, she released the song "Whoever's in New England" from the album by the same title; this album, and accompanying videos, brought McEntire the Country Music Association Entertainer of the Year award later that year. The following year she divorced her first husband, then married her road manager as her career advanced further with a series of hit singles and albums and an appearance in the movie *Tremors*. But in March 1991 tragedy struck when the plane carrying her band crashed in San Diego, killing all on board. However, ten days later she performed at the Academy Awards in Los Angeles and within a couple of months had formed a new group and continued touring.

Female artists who succeed in country music are those who can relate to females in the audience; Reba McEntire follows a select few (Kitty Wells, Patsy Cline, Loretta Lynn, and Tammy Wynette) who have achieved success in this field by articulating the woman's point of view, establishing an honesty and integrity in her recordings and performances and establishing herself as a spokesperson and role model for women.

Bibliography

Bufwack, Mary A., and Robert K. Dermann. *Finding Her Voice: The Illustrated History of Women in Country Music.* New York: Holt, 1995.

Legget, Carol. *Reba McEntire: The Queen of Country.* New York: Fireside, 1992.

McEntire, Reba. *Reba: My Story.* New York: Bantam, 1994.

Don Cusic

McGee, Travis, the hard-boiled detective, an ex-football player and Korean War veteran, was introduced by John D. MacDonald in *The Deep Blue Good-by* (1964). He appears in 21 novels published between 1964 and 1985, some of which feature a long-time friend and cohort, Meyer. The final novel in the series is *The Lonely Silver Rain*, in which McGee discovers an unknown daughter, Jean, the child of a woman he had met in *Pale Gray for Guilt* (1968). Readers can distinguish the McGee novels from others authored by MacDonald by the presence of a color in the title.

Bibliography
Benjamin, David A. "Key Witness: J. D. MacDonald." *New Republic* 26 July 1975.
Geherin, David. *John D. MacDonald.* New York: Ungar, 1982.
Hirshberg, Edgar W. *John D. MacDonald.* Boston: Twayne, 1985.
Moore, Lewis D. *Meditations on America: John D. MacDonald's Travis McGee Series and Other Fiction.* Bowling Green, OH: Bowling Green State U Popular P, 1994.

Lewis D. Moore

See also
Detective Sidekicks
Hard-boiled Detective Fiction

McGinley, Phyllis (1905-1978), was an award-winning and enduringly popular author. Best known for her poetry, primarily light verse, she also wrote juvenile books, essays, and musical lyrics. As a body, her work validates traditional social and family attitudes; she has been described as a defender of suburbia and housewifery. First publishing her poetry in *The New Yorker* and local newspapers in the 1930s, 1940s, and 1950s when there was a strong market for light verse, she earned a wide following for her comic depictions of middle-class life.

More consistently cheerful than her peers Ogden Nash, Dorothy Parker, and W. H. Auden, McGinley's criticism of a variety of modern social phenomena—psychiatry, progressive education, the battle of the sexes, war—is delivered ironically in the context of ordinary, typical events. Her most popular books of poetry include *One More Manhattan* (1937), *A Pocketful of Wry* (1940), *Husbands Are Difficult* (1941), and *Love Letters* (1951). *All Around the Town* (1948), an alphabet book set in Manhattan, *The Most Wonderful Doll in the World* (1950), and *The Year without a Santa Claus* (1957) are titles familiar to younger readers.

McGinley won the St. Vincent Millay Memorial Award in 1954, the Pulitzer Prize in 1960 for *Times Three: Selected Verse from Three Decades with Seventy New Poems* (1960), and numerous other writing awards, including several from Catholic organizations such as the Catholic Writers Guild and the Catholic Institute of the Press.

Bibliography
Wagner-Martin, Linda. *Phyllis McGinley.* New York: Twayne, 1971.

Mary Siobhan Sullivan

McGinniss, Joe (1942-), author of many kinds of books, began his career in journalism. After the publication of *The Selling of the President* (1969), he wrote primarily nonfiction novels, a form pioneered by Truman Capote's *In Cold Blood* (1966) that had evolved from the techniques of New Journalism. McGinniss's *Fatal Vision* (1983) retold the story of Jeffrey MacDonald, the Green Beret doctor convicted of murdering his wife. It was followed by *Blind Faith* (1989), and *Cruel Doubt* (1991), similarly dense and probing examinations of criminal cases, told with a novelist's sensitivity to language, character, and dramatic tension. Television movies based upon these best-selling books confirmed McGinniss as

preeminent in the emerging field of true crime writing, along with other writers, including Anne Rule and Jack Olsen.

Susan Weiner

McKuen, Rod (1933-), gained broad fame in the 1960s and 1970s as the most popular poet of the era. His three books, *Stanyan Street and Other Sorrows* (1966), *Listen to the Warm* (1967), and *Lonesome Cities* (1968), sold almost 2 million copies in three years, and all secured a position on the *Publishers Weekly* year-end Top 10 list, a rare feat for a poet. Since then, his 33 volumes of poetry have remained in demand and have been translated into 30 languages.

McKuen, a native Californian, began writing, reading, and performing his poems and lyrics in the 1950s, in places like San Francisco's Jazz Cellar, along with beat poets Jack Kerouac and Allen Ginsberg. His work is characteristically confessional in tone, focusing on his struggles with love relationships, his engagements with specific places and pets, and his nostalgic albeit existential reflections. McKuen's appeal to commonplace experiences and emotions is the strength of his work and has won him both the Carl Sandburg and Walt Whitman poetry awards. He has succeeded in being, as he has said, "a poet read" rather than "one who postures for posterity."

Although best known as a poet, McKuen's achievement as a composer is also significant. He has written over 1,500 songs, numerous symphonic and concert pieces, and eleven major film scores. Worldwide, he has 40 gold and platinum records and has been nominated for both the Pulitzer Prize in music (for *The City*) and the Oscar (for the scores of *The Prime of Miss Jean Brodie*, 1968, and *A Boy Named Charlie Brown*, 1970).

Bibliography
Disch, Thomas M. *The Castle of Indolence: On Poetry, Poets, and Poetasters.* New York: Picador, 1995.
McKuen, Rod. *Finding My Father: One Man's Search for Identity.* Los Angeles: Cheval, 1976.
Peters, Robert. *Where the Bee Sucks: Workers, Drones and Queens of Contemporary American Poetry.* Santa Maria: Asylum Arts, 1994.

Melody M. Zajdel

McLean, Don (1945-), is best known for writing and performing the 1972 song "American Pie," a chronicle of rock and roll's first two decades. McLean was born in the New York City suburb of New Rochelle. He decided on a musical career at an early age, and he began playing folk music concerts in high school.

In his college days at Villanova University, McLean played alongside Jim Croce before he began performing in clubs on the U.S. East Coast and in Canada. He met several folk music legends, including Lee Hays, Brownie McGhee, and Josh White. After a steady gig at New York City's Club Lena, he was appointed the "Hudson River Troubadour" in 1968 by the New York State Council of the Arts. In partial fulfillment of the appointment, McLean traveled the river valley north of New York City, giving three concerts a day in communities.

In 1970, a small record label, Mediarts, released McLean's first album, *Tapestry*. The album had previously been rejected by 34 labels. United Artists bought Mediarts and re-released the album in 1971. UA also released Don McLean's single "American Pie," an 8-minute, 36-second-long ode to rock and roll. Top 40 radio stations played the song despite its length, and it hit the top of the U.S. record charts at the end of the year.

A second single from McLean's 1971 *American Pie* album, "Vincent," was released in the spring of 1972. About painter Vincent Van Gogh, the song reached No. 12 on the U.S. charts. Another song from that album, "And I Love You So," was a hit for Perry Como in 1973.

McLean's self-titled third album was moderately successful, with a minor hit in the song "Dreidel." But McLean's career fizzled quickly in the mid-1970s, largely because he refused to play "American Pie" in concert. Most of his recordings in that period were cover versions of early rock hits like "Crying in the Chapel" and Buddy Holly's "Everyday." McLean signed with Nashville's Millennium Records in 1980 and had a hit single the same year with a remake of Roy Orbison's "Crying." He continued moving toward country music and recorded *Love Tracks* for Capitol Records in 1988.

Ken Nagelberg

McLendon, Gordon (1921-1986), a native of Paris, TX, was a radio station owner and an important program innovator who helped lead the radio industry through the troubled evolutionary period of the 1950s. After World War II, the emerging television industry swept away radio's traditional programming, personnel, and profits, and brought the golden age of radio to an end. McLendon was one of a small group of young, rogue managers who were willing to leave behind the established business practices of the golden age to establish a new order in radio.

From the beginning, McLendon tried to develop an approach to programming at his stations that was different from others in the same market. One significant effort during his early years was the Liberty Radio Network. During his time at KLIF, a station he and his father had established in 1947 in the Dallas area, McLendon introduced an on-air persona called "The Old Scotchman" who narrated sporting events. Unlike most sports broadcasters today who simply attend the games they announce, "The Old Scotchman," working from the KLIF studios, re-created the excitement of the games by reading telegraphed accounts with sound effects added for realism.

The Liberty Network, however, was forced to fold in spite of its financial success. Major league baseball denied McLendon the right to rebroadcast their games, and the courts upheld the decision. Without its hallmark sports programming, the Liberty Network was compelled to suspend operations and to declare bankruptcy in May 1952.

To fill the program void created by the demise of the Liberty Network, McLendon turned to a disk jockey-oriented music and news programming approach for inspiration. During 1953, KLIF filled its air time with popular music shows, and in 1954, it became the most popular station in its market.

Encouraged by his success with popular music, McLendon, along with Todd Storz, Gerald Bartell, and the stations owned and operated by the Plough pharmaceutical firm went on to develop a systematic approach to programming based on disk jockeys playing the most popular records mixed with station promotions, weather, and local news. This approach became known as Top-40 radio.

Bibliography

Glick, Edwin. "The Life and Death of the Liberty Broadcasting System." *Journal of Broadcasting* Spring 1979: 117-35.

MacFarland, David. *The Development of the Top 40 Radio Format.* New York: Arno, 1979.

——. "The Liberty Broadcasting System." *American Broadcasting: A Source Book on the History of Radio and Television.* Ed. Lichty Lawrence and Malachi Topping. New York: Hastings, 1975.

Charles F. Ganzert

McMurtry, Larry Jeff (1936-), leading author of books about the West, was born in Wichita Falls, TX, and raised on the family ranch near Archer City, TX, where he was exposed to the eccentricities of small-town life and the experiences of working cowboys, both of which he would later incorporate into his Western novels. McMurtry received his BA in English from North Texas State University in 1958 and his MA from Rice University in 1960, following which he was granted a Wallace Stegner Fellowship in fiction by Stanford University for 1960-61. Returning to Texas, he taught at Texas Christian University in Fort Worth in 1961-62 and Rice University in 1963-64. McMurtry left teaching temporarily with a Guggenheim Fellowship in 1964, and in 1965 returned to teach at Rice, where he stayed until 1969.

Throughout these years of study and teaching, McMurtry was writing as well. In addition to reviewing books for the *Houston Post* and writing articles about Texas for periodicals, he began publishing his first novels. Set in Thalia, a small town very similar to McMurtry's hometown of Archer City, the novels *Horseman Pass By* (Harper, 1961), *Leaving Cheyenne* (Harper, 1963), and *The Last Picture Show* (Dial, 1966) make up the Thalia trilogy. Like many of McMurtry's later novels, all three of the Thalia novels were adapted for film. *Horseman Pass By* was released in 1963 by Paramount under the title *Hud*, which starred Paul Newman and Patricia Neal, who won an Oscar for her role. *Leaving Cheyenne* was the basis for the film *Lovin' Molly* (Columbia, 1963), directed by Sidney Lumet and starring Blythe Danner in the title role. The final Thalia novel, *The Last Picture Show*, was adapted for a film of the same name (Columbia, 1971), which won a Motion Picture Academy of Arts and Sciences nomination for best screenplay, in addition to Cloris Leachman's Oscar for best supporting actress.

Following the release of *In a Narrow Grave* (1968), a compilation of his essays on Texas, McMurtry moved from Houston to the Washington, DC, area in 1969, where he taught creative-writing courses at George Mason and American Universities until 1971. Leaving academia, he opened a rare-book store, Booked Up, and continued to write novels. His next three books, *Moving On* (1970), *All My Friends Are Going to Be Strangers* (1972), and *Terms of Endearment*, (1975) form the Houston trilogy, which focus on urban living in Texas. *Terms of Endearment* was adapted to film and released in 1983 by Paramount, and received Oscars for best director, actress, scriptwriter, supporting actor, and best picture. Based on his experiences with Hollywood, McMurtry published *Film Flam: Essays on Hollywood* in 1987.

McMurtry's next three novels are unique in that they are not set in Texas. *Somebody's Darling* (1982) deals with a Hollywood film director, *Cadillac Jack* (1982) is set in Washington, although it is presented through the eyes of a visiting rodeo rider from Texas, and *Desert Rose* (1983) focuses on a topless dancer in Las Vegas. *Desert Rose* began as a screenplay which was composed during a break from working on what would later become *Lonesome Dove* (1985). The epic tale of three Texas ranchers on a cattle drive to Montana, *Lonesome Dove* won the Pulitzer Prize for fiction in 1986 and was adapted for an eight-hour miniseries in 1989 (see entry). CBS also broadcast *Return to Lonesome Dove* in 1993, a miniseries which was not based on a McMurtry novel.

While McMurtry's novels have conveniently divided themselves into groups of three up to this point, the books beginning with *Lonesome Dove* cannot be so easily classified, except to say that they alternate between novels which deal with the West of present day, and those which focus on the Old West. The first of these returns to the lives of the characters in the Thalia trilogy, *Texasville* (1987), and deals with the same small town of *The Last Picture Show*; however, the Old West has been completely obliterated in favor of present-day industry and materialism. The 1991 film by the same title incorporates several members of the film *The Last Picture Show*. However, in his next book, McMurtry leaves behind the West of the present, and draws upon the legend of Billy the Kid in *Anything for Billy* (1988). By contrast, *Some Can Whistle* (1989) picks up the story of Danny Deck, the main character in *All My Friends Are Going to Be Strangers*. Moving back to the Old West, *Buffalo Girls* (1990) uses the letters of Calamity Jane to tell the story of her life.

Evening Star (1992; film version, 1996) returns to the Texas of the present and to the character Aurora Greenway, from *Terms of Endearment*. McMurtry then moves back to the days following *Lonesome Dove* with its sequel, *Streets of Laredo* (1993). In 1995, CBS aired a miniseries of the same name, starring James Garner. Rounding out the *Lonesome Dove* tale is *Dead Man's Walk* (1995), a prequel to the original story. Working in collaboration with Diana Ossana, McMurtry published *Pretty Boy Floyd* (1994), which deals with the notorious gangster of the 1930s. Also in 1995, Simon & Schuster published *The Late Child. Walter Benjamin at the Dairy Queen: Reflections at Sixty and Beyond* appeared in 1999. Though still writing, McMurtry is now a resident of Archer City, TX, where he grew up, and has developed one of the largest used bookstores in the world. Through this bookstore, he hopes to rehabilitate Archer City and to encourage the use of and love for books.

Bibliography

Neinstein, Raymond L. *The Ghost Country: A Study of the Novels of Larry McMurtry.* Berkeley: Creative Arts, 1976.
Peavy, Charles D. *Larry McMurtry.* Boston: Twayne, 1977.
Schmidt, Dorey, ed. *Larry McMurtry—Unredeemed Dreams: A Collection of Bibliography, Essays, and Interview.* Edinburg: School of Humanities, Pan American University, 1978.

Lynnea Chapman King

Media Coverage of Soap Operas. Soap operas, a mainstay of radio and television programming since the 1930s, have themselves become the subject of much mass media coverage, including magazines, books, newspaper columns, newsletters, broadcast features and storyline updates, telephone services, and computer discussion groups.

In total, nearly three million readers keep up with their soap operas regularly via magazines. *Soap Opera Digest*, a biweekly publication, leads the soap opera magazines in terms of circulation, with subscription and single-copy sales totaling nearly one and a half million. The *Digest* first hit the newsstand in 1975, making it one of the most successful soap opera magazines in terms of its longevity. Editorial content includes synopses of soap opera storylines, interviews with and news items about the soap opera creative community, as well as lifestyle features on beauty, fashion, food, and parenting. A spinoff publication, *Soap Opera Digest Presents*, is published on an irregular schedule, but still reaches 500,000 readers, with each issue covering a particular soap opera theme (for example, soap opera weddings). Another large-circulation magazine, *Soap Opera Weekly*, was first published in 1989 and sells over one-half million copies each week, primarily through single-copy sales.

Several other soap opera magazines offer similar content to readers, including *Soap Opera Illustrated*, *Soap Opera Magazine*, and *Soap Opera Update*. Each of these publications has a readership of 250,000 to 300,000. Sterling McFadden magazines has what it refers to as the Women's Group, a collection of soap opera-oriented magazines totaling over 300,000 readers. This group of magazines includes *Daytime Digest, Daytime TV, Daytime TV Presents, Daytime TV's Greatest Stories*, and *Soap Opera Stars*, all of which are meant to provide entertainment for female readers by concentrating on daytime television personalities. The television networks have also published their own soap opera magazines which provide information related to the soaps airing on their respective networks (e.g., NBC's *Daydreams*, ABC's *Episodes*).

The soap opera has spawned publication of many books over the years. The majority are trade publications, which provide information on the history and development of the soap opera form, behind-the-scenes accounts of the soap opera industry, as well as comprehensive storyline summaries of individual soaps and biographies of soap opera actors. Among the most comprehensive books of this sort are Robert LaGuardia's *Soap World* (1983), and Christopher Schemering's *The Soap Opera Encyclopedia* (1985, 1987). Many other trade books written about soap operas offer plot summaries and behind-the-scenes gossip, and are heavily illustrated with photographs, past and present, of the soap operas and their actors. Among these would be Paul Denis's *Inside the Soaps* (1985), and Mary Ann Copeland's *Soap Opera History* (1991).

Some soap opera actors have turned writers themselves, authoring autobiographies which include a heavy dose of soap opera. Ruth Warrick of *All My Children* wrote *The Confessions of Phoebe Tyler* (1980), which chronicles not only the life of the actress herself, but also provides a behind-the-scenes look at *All My Children*. Mary Stuart's *Both of Me* (1980) provides readers with an account of her own life, as well as an insightful history of *Search for Tomorrow*.

Capitalizing on the popularity of the romance novel, the Pioneer Communications Network launched a series of books in the mid-1980s based on the soap operas themselves. The books offered readers backstory and insight into characters, without actually paralleling the stories as they unfolded on the screen. Books in the "Soaps and Serials" series were published monthly for *The Young and the Restless, Days of Our Lives, Guiding Light, Another World, As the World Turns, Dallas, Knots Landing,* and *Capitol* and were available to readers in bookstores, drug stores, department stores, convenience stores, and supermarkets.

In addition to trade books, the academic press has its own contributions to the books written about soap operas. Although soap operas had been studied since the 1940s by the academic community, the genre did not become fully recognized as an area of legitimate scholarly inquiry until the 1970s. Mary Cassata and Thomas Skill co-authored *Life on Daytime Television,* a pioneering academic publication which provided an analysis of the content of daytime drama and won praise by *Choice* as the best academic book of 1983. Other books followed, including Muriel Cantor and Suzanne Pingree's *The Soap Opera* (1983), examining the soap opera's social and historical context; Michael Intintoli's *Taking Soaps Seriously: The World of* Guiding Light (1984), an ethnographic study of the longest-running soap opera; Carol Williams's *It's Time for My Story* (1992), and Marilyn Matelski's *Soap Operas Worldwide* (1999), among others.

Rounding out the print media, hundreds of newspapers across the country provide weekly soap opera updates, storyline synopses, and answers to viewers' questions, primarily through syndicated columns. Newsletters dedicated specifically to soap operas include the weekly, comprehensive *Soap Opera Now!* as well as fan-club-produced publications highlighting individual soaps. Television and radio provide audiences with soap opera coverage in a variety of forms.

A recent development has been the entry of nontraditional media into the coverage of soap operas. Soap opera viewers are now able to access storyline synopses and behind-the-scenes information via 900 number telephone services. These services often feature messages prerecorded by soap opera actors. Computer online services also allow subscribers to interact with soap opera fans and actors, participate in opinion polls, view and print photographs, and order merchandise.

Bibliography

Cantor, Muriel G., and Suzanne Pingree. *The Soap Opera.* Beverly Hills: Sage, 1983.

Cassata, Mary, and Thomas Skill. *Life on Daytime Television: Tuning-in American Serial Drama.* Norwood: Ablex, 1983.

Copeland, Mary Ann. *Soap Opera History.* Lincolnwood: Mallard, 1991.

Denis, Paul. *Inside the Soaps.* Secaucus: Citadel, 1985.

Intintoli, Michael James. *Taking Soaps Seriously: The World of* Guiding Light. New York: Praeger, 1984.

LaGuardia, Robert. *Soap World.* New York: Arbor, 1983.

Schemerings, Christopher. *The Soap Opera Encyclopedia.* New York: Ballantine, 1985.

Matelski, Marilyn J. *Soap Operas Worldwide: Cultural and Serial Realities.* Jefferson: McFarland, 1999.

Williams, Carol. *It's Time for My Story.* Westport: Praeger, 1992.

Barbara J. Irwin
Mary Cassata

Medical Mystery is a popular subgenre that shows readers' fascination with the enigmas of illness and untimely death. Key issues in such stories are the vulnerability of human flesh, and the blind trust people place in medical science to maintain patients' best interests and to cure. Medical mysteries may depict the violation of that trust by doctors who become "mad scientists," lusting after fame or valuing their work above ethical concern about human experimentation. The sleuth who uncovers such abuse is frequently another medical professional who recognizes the evil pattern and upholds humane values by uncovering the reckless practice. Current masters of this form include Robin Cook, Michael Crichton, and Michael Palmer.

Another version of the medical mystery portrays health professionals in the role of forensic experts, reading clues from diseased persons, corpses, and the crime scene, and by developing theories about the lethal events, whether induced by human villains or microbes. Such sleuth figures are usually medical examiners or epidemiologists. Best known in this genre is Patricia Cornwell, whose detective, Kay Scarpetta, is a pathologist. Crichton's *The Andromeda Strain* (1969) is another popular example. Sometimes a nonfiction medical mystery, such as Richard Preston's *The Hot Zone* (1994), also succeeds as a best-seller.

Bibliography

Accardo, Pasquale J. *Diagnosis and Detection: The Medical Iconography of Sherlock Holmes.* Rutherford: Fairleigh Dickinson UP, 1987.

Herbert, Rosemary. *The Fatal Art of Entertainment: Interviews with Mystery Writers.* New York: Hall, 1996.

Stookey, Lorena Laura. *Robin Cook: A Critical Companion.* Westport: Greenwood, 1996.

Trembley, Elizabeth A. *Michael Crichton: A Critical Companion.* Westport: Greenwood, 1996.

Harriette C. Buchanan

See also
Crime Fiction

Mellencamp, John Cougar (1951-), a driving force in rock music, was born in Seymour, IN, the second of five children. Son of an electrical engineer and former beauty queen, John joined his first band when he was in the fifth grade.

In 1975, he graduated from Vincennes University, and in 1976 he recorded his first album, *Chestnut Street Incident.* Using the name John Cougar, Mellencamp made two other albums called *John Cougar* and *Nothing Matters and What If It Did?* Real commercial success, however, did not arrive until 1982 when his album *American Fool* topped the charts and went platinum. Two especially popular songs from the album were "Jack and Diane" and "Hurts So Good."

Wanting to make the transition away from the name John Cougar to the name John Mellencamp, Mellencamp used the name John Cougar Mellencamp for his next two albums, *Uh Huh*, released in 1983, and *Scarecrow* in 1985. With the transition underway, *Lonesome Jubilee* was released with the name John Mellencamp in 1987.

Socially and politically active, Mellencamp organized Farm Aid with Willie Nelson and Neil Young in 1985. The song "Small Town" from the *Scarecrow* album reached No. 6 on the charts in December of 1985 and reflected some popular sentiment about small town life.

Home movie clips strung together in a lighthearted way made the music video for "Cherry Bomb" entertaining for viewers. Along with "Cherry Bomb," other songs from the *Lonesome Jubilee* album such as "Paper in Fire" appealed to the blue-collar worker as well as the corporate executive. Other Mellencamp albums that crossed social boundaries were *Big Daddy* (1989), *Whenever We Wanted* (1991), and *Human Wheels* (1993) as well as *Dance Naked* (1994).

Bibliography

Holmes, Tim. *John Cougar Mellencamp.* New York: Ballantine, 1985.

Romanowski, Patricia, and Holly George-Warren. *The New Rolling Stone Encyclopedia of Rock & Roll.* New York: Fireside, 1995.

Torgoff, Martin. *American Fool: The Roots and Improbable Rise of John Cougar Mellencamp.* New York: St. Martin's, 1986.

Lee Ann Paradise-Schober

Melodrama in Film rocks the heart. Diverse as D. W. Griffith's *Way Down East* (1919) and George Stevens's *A Place in the Sun* (1951) may be in style, character, and setting, they share the basic, common core of melodrama: domestic conflict (often aggravated by class differences) foregrounding the repression and release of emotion, for audience as well as characters. The melodic rise and fall of emotion clarifies the moral system at work in the world of the film.

In its general movement film melodrama emphasizes the domestic, the familial, the maternal. The iconography of melodrama, its consistent, recurring imagery, lingers over kitchens, living rooms, stairways, and bedrooms. Within these household spaces melodrama unfolds complex permutations of intra- and extra-familial relationships. Melodrama offers clear and emphatic narrative instruction on the range of possible responses to family-based conflict. Outcomes constantly weigh relevant moral values. Our informal "one and two hankie" ratings suggest how effective melodramas are in teaching us how to respond to character and situation. At the same time melodrama sets the stage for emotional display, it shows pressures revolving around family life to be the sources of the repression of individual desire. Melodramas tend to tell stories of strong characters struggling to break the bonds that keep them from attaining their (our) greatest wishes.

Melodrama remains an enduring, flexible form. Today's "disease-of-the-week," "don't-touch-my-kid," made-for-TV docudramas, along with their afternoon, serial soap opera cousins, have family lines extending to the 19th-century novel and theater. Television's preference for "real-life" stories that feature the display of emotions and morals clearly indicates the depth of audience investment in melodrama. The production frequency and box office returns of feature film melodrama remain high. When other kinds of stories are fashioned melodramatically, it points to the flexibility of the form: the mainstream genre of film melodrama is eminently adaptable, allowing for a larger mode of narrative presentation in many other film genres. The family "unit" becomes "extended" in this sense to encompass figurative families in a wide variety of settings, including, for example, concentration camp victims (*Schindler's List*, 1993), army units in the war film (*Platoon*, 1986), the tribal teepee in the Western (*Dances with Wolves*, 1990), courts of law (*Regarding Henry*, 1991), and even forest fire fighters (*Always*, 1989). In all cases, as befits melodramatic form, characters must balance their desires against the counterweight of social propriety in their struggles to find the right courses of thought and action.

The agelessness of its themes, like the universal applicability of its conflict structures, guarantees the durability of melodrama. Forced family separation, almost a fixation of Movie of the Week melodramas in the early 1990s, has predecessors in films of the early 1920s (*Orphans of the Storm*, 1921) and the 1930s (*Make Way for Tomorrow*, 1937). The family remains the bulwark against the economic stresses that would tear it apart. Tough times, whether in the depressed 1930s or the recessed 1980s and 1990s, warrant the guidance and inspiration of the living by the dead. (How else could *A Guy Named Joe* return in *Always*? The spirits of the *Topper* series and those rejoined at the ends of *Three Comrades* and *Wuthering Heights* establish models for hope followed more recently by *Ghost* and even *The Return of the Jedi*.) Bette Davis's fatal blindness in *Dark Victory* (1939), like Debra Winger's cancer in *Terms of Endearment* (1983), serve to cast their victims' relationships with husbands, friends, and families as studies in courage. A brief list of other long-term thematic arenas in film melodramas includes "other" women, lost (true) love, mother love, social problems, and "coming of age" conflicts. Through all the stress and strain caused by poverty, divorce, illness and/or death, main characters in melodramas consistently offer case studies in coping with pressure and repression from within and outside of the family.

While notable melodramas of the 1960s and 1970s continue to set their protagonists against traditionally melodramatic obstacles such as literal and figurative distance (*A Man* and a Woman, 1966) and fatal illnesses (*Love Story*, 1970), they also continue a tradition of topicality that fueled the novels of Charles Dickens and the films of D. W. Griffith. *Coming Home* (1979) views the horrors of the war in Vietnam through the prism of the liberation from traditional, repressive roles of an army wife (Jane Fonda). Her affair with a paraplegic veteran (Jon Voight) puts her onto a new level of political and emotional awareness; unfortunately these same changes help precipitate violence from and ultimately the suicide of her husband (Bruce Dern). Personal liberation that rends apart a family receives a different value in *Kramer vs. Kramer* (1979) when Meryl Streep leaves her husband (Dustin Hoffman) to find herself, only to return later to try to sue for custody of their son.

Perhaps the greatest difference between melodramas of the 1950s and those made in subsequent decades is that the more recent films often show the family as an equally (potentially) repressive, yet more vulnerable mainstay against disruptive forces. *The Last Picture Show* (1971) views "coming of age" problems of the immediately earlier decades (exemplified by mid-1950s James Dean films such as *Rebel without a Cause, East of Eden*, and even *Giant*) from a later vantage point.

Most mainstream melodramas argue for the greater good that will result from the individual accepting a position subordinate to the family. Francie, in Elia Kazan's *A Tree Grows in Brooklyn* (1945), must consider sacrificing her desire for education in order to help support her fatherless family; George Bailey's commitment to Bedford Falls continually disrupts his plans for education and travel in Frank Capra's *It's a Wonderful Life* (1946); and in David Lean's 1946 film Laura mulls her "brief encounter" with another man while in her sitting room with her husband, who's "glad she's back" from her brief foray away from marriage. William Wyler's *Best Years of Our Lives* (1946) examines the tension between socioeconomic constraints and the needs and desires of individuals, as it contrasts the homecoming of three newly returned veterans.

Film melodramas of the 1930s laid the groundwork for the valorization in the post-war films of necessary individual self-sacrifice, clearly placing the sustenance of the family above individual desires. These films situate central preoccupations of the genre (family unity; pressures from illness, poverty, competing loves; children coming of age; social problems) in and around families necessarily united in the face of the Great Depression. Films such as Frank Borzage's *A Man's Castle* (1933), John Stahl's *Imitation of Life* (1934), Leo McCarey's *Make Way for Tomorrow* (1937), and King Vidor's *Stella Dallas* (1937) center on individuals' contributions to the family unit, and depict the home as a potential refuge from external exigencies.

Melodrama, in all its enduring forms and flexibility, offers us the melodic interplay of emotional display and concealment, making moral issues clear, accessible, immediate, and meaningful.

Bibliography
Affron, Charles. *Cinema and Sentiment*. Chicago: U of Chicago P, 1982.
Brooks, Peter. *The Melodramatic Imagination*. New Haven: Yale UP, 1974.
Elsaesser, Thomas. "Tales of Sound and Fury." *Monogram* 4 (1972): 2-15.
Heilman, Robert D. *Tragedy and Melodrama: Versions of Experience*. Seattle: U of Washington P, 1968.
Lang, Robert. *American Film Melodrama: Griffith, Vidor, Minelli*. Princeton: Princeton UP, 1989.

Steve Lipkin

Melrose Place (1992-1997) was an hour-long relationship drama on the Fox TV network. This evening soap premiered immediately following *Beverly Hills, 90210*. *Melrose Place* was a spinoff of *90210*, and attempted to capture the *90210* audience. Originally, *Melrose* was intended to address the issues of working twenty-somethings as opposed to the *90210* focus on the problems of privileged high-school students. However, after dismal early reviews, *Melrose* was retooled to focus less on realistic issues, and more on the melodramatic themes of other successful evening soaps.

The show was produced by Aaron Spelling, who also produced the monster hit *90210* for Fox. Darren Star is the creator, executive producer, and sometimes writer for both *90210* and *Melrose Place*.

Melrose Place became a popular culture sensation, with cover stories in dozens of popular magazines including *People, TV Guide, Entertainment Weekly,* and *Rolling Stone,* as well as dozens of cast appearances on television entertainment programs and TV talk shows.

Bibliography
Brooks, Tim, and Earle Marsh. *The Complete Directory to Prime Time Network and Cable TV Shows, 1946-Present.* New York: Ballantine, 1995.
Wild, David. "*Melrose Place* Is a Really Good Show." *Rolling Stone* 19 May 1994: 49-53.

Ginny Schwartz

Mercer, Johnny (1909-1976), who, like Oscar Hammerstein II and Sammy Cahn, was one of the leading song lyricists of the middle third of the 20th century, is most frequently connected with the songs he wrote with composer Henry Mancini (see entry) in the early 1960s. In 1961, Mercer and Mancini wrote the dreamy classic "Moon River" for the movie *Breakfast at Tiffany's*. That one song won an Oscar and two Grammys, was recorded well over a hundred times, and brought considerable fame to Mercer and Mancini as well as to Andy Williams, who crooned it in the film and adopted it as his theme song.

Mercer also provided the lyrics for "Days of Wine and Roses," from the 1962 film of that name, and for "Charade," from the 1963 film of that name. Both fine melodies were again by Henry Mancini. "Days of Wine and Roses," like "Moon River," won an Oscar each for Mercer and Mancini plus two Grammys. Mercer's excellent work with Mancini was the cap on a splendid songwriting career that went back to the 1930s.

Born in Savannah, GA, to an old southern family, John H. Mercer showed musical aptitude at an early age. At six months he supposedly could repeat any tune sung to him by his aunt. He studied piano and trumpet and at age 15 wrote his first song, "Sister Suzie Strut Your Stuff." About 1,500 songs later, a few years before his death due to complications from brain tumor surgery, Mercer became the first president and a founder of the Songwriters Hall of Fame. He did not live to see its doors open in January 1977, but he was most certainly one of its prime inductees. Involved with more than 70 movies and seven Broadway musicals, he successfully collaborated with several top composers, had 14 songs reach No. 1 on *Your Hit Parade,* and to top it all was a founder and president of Capitol Records.

Bibliography

Ewen, David. *American Songwriters.* New York: Wilson, 1987. 279-82.

Mercer, Johnny, Ginger Mercer, and Bob Bach. *Our Huckleberry Friend: The Life, Times, and Lyrics of Johnny Mercer.* Secaucus: Lyle Stuart, 1982.

Studwell, William E. *The Popular Song Reader.* New York: Haworth, 1994.

William E. Studwell

Merman, Ethel (1909-1984), one of the greatest stars of the American musical theater, was born Ethel Agnes Zimmermann in the New York City borough of Queens. As a child during World War I, Merman sang at army camps in the New York area. After graduating from William Cullen Bryant High School, she pursued a singing career while working as a secretary in the daytime. It was during this period she decided to shorten her last name from Zimmermann to Merman. Engagements at Manhattan nightspots and in vaudeville shows led to Merman being cast in George and Ira Gershwin's *Girl Crazy* (1930, 272 performances). In the secondary role of Kate Fothergill, the unknown Merman stole the show with her rendition of "I Got Rhythm," the first of countless hit songs that she would introduce throughout her illustrious career.

Merman's brassy style proved surprisingly adaptable to the more dramatically complex "book musicals" that began to dominate Broadway in the mid-1940s. She eased herself into the new genre with Irving Berlin's *Annie Get Your Gun* (1946, 1,147 performances), in which she portrayed legendary sharpshooter Annie Oakley. Produced by Rodgers and Hammerstein, *Annie Get Your Gun* offered typical Merman belting ("I Got the Sun in the Morning" and "There's No Business Like Show Business") and clowning ("I'm an Indian, Too" and "You Can't Get a Man with a Gun"), but also required her to tone down for heartfelt love songs ("They Say It's Wonderful" and "I Got Lost in His Arms"). Merman and Berlin teamed up again for *Call Me Madam* (1950, 644 performances), a lighthearted political satire. Merman's next show was an even weaker star vehicle called *Happy Hunting* (1956, 412 performances), with music and lyrics by Harold Karr and Matt Dubey. The greatest success in Merman's later career was undoubtedly *Gypsy* (1959, 702 performances), with a score by Jule Styne and Stephen Sondheim. The youthful Sondheim was originally set to write both music and lyrics, but Merman, having been dis-

pleased with the *Happy Hunting* score by young newcomers Karr and Dubey, insisted on a composer with more experience for *Gypsy,* and Sondheim was relegated to words only.

Merman herself became embittered when the part of Mama Rose in the film version of *Gypsy* went to Rosalind Russell. Vowing to never again set foot on Broadway, Merman turned down the lead in *Hello, Dolly!* which Jerry Herman had written especially for her. Merman's refusal led to *Hello, Dolly!* becoming a great success for Carol Channing. Merman reneged on her promise and did participate in two more Broadway productions, although *Gypsy* was the last new musical in which she was involved. In 1966, Merman starred in a well-received, limited-engagement revival of *Annie Get Your Gun* at Lincoln Center (1966, 78 performances). In March 1970 she assumed the role of Dolly Gallagher Levi in *Hello, Dolly!* Merman's presence renewed interest in the now six-year-old show, and her eight-month stint as Dolly helped it break the record for longest-running Broadway production, then held by *My Fair Lady.*

Ethel Merman appeared in a number of movies but the screen never captured the dynamism of her stage persona. Merman's films include *Kid Millions* (1934) and *Strike Me Pink* (1936), both with Eddie Cantor, *Alexander's Ragtime Band* (1939), and *There's No Business Like Show Business* (1954), both built around the music of Irving Berlin, and the film versions of *Anything Goes* (1936) and *Call Me Madam* (1953).

Bibliography

Bloom, Ken. *Broadway: An Encyclopedic Guide to the History, People, and Places of Times Square.* New York: Facts on File, 1990.

Bryan, George B. "Ethel Merman." *Notable Women in the American Theatre: A Biographical Dictionary.* Westport: Greenwood, 1989.

Schumach, Murray. "Ethel Merman, Queen of Musicals, Dies at 76." *New York Times* 16 Feb. 1984: A1, D26.

Thomas, Bob. *I Got Rhythm!—The Ethel Merman Story.* New York: Putnam, 1985.

Mary C. Kalfatovic

Metro-Goldwyn-Mayer (MGM) was surely the most famous of the Hollywood studios of the 1930s and 1940s. Its "Leo the Lion" trademark stood for the greatest stars and the top stories. Its stars, from Greta Garbo to Clark Gable, ranked atop the pantheon of Hollywood. But with the rise of television, since the mid-1950s, MGM has barely hung on. The second half of the 20th century has not been kind to the studio that once claimed more stars than in all the heavens.

From a purely business perspective, through the 1930s and 1940s, the MGM studio simply functioned as a highly publicized subsidiary of Loew's, Inc., a fully integrated movie company, based in New York City, which also owned a highly profitable movie theater chain. Indeed, from MGM's creation in 1924 as a studio to supply films for Loew's theaters through 1954, no more mighty operation existed in the American film industry. MGM films played Loew's theaters from New York to Los Angeles, but also were booked into movie houses owned by other studios as well.

MGM's method of film production reflected boss Nicholas M. Schenck's conservative business philosophy. MGM concentrated on top-drawer feature films, but also delivered far more. MGM publicly projected an image as the Tiffany of studios, but, in fact, during MGM's best years, the 1930s, the studio made far more money with films starring Marie Dressler and Mickey Rooney than with Greta Garbo and Spencer Tracy. Through its golden age, MGM produced all kinds of films including jungle adventures (the *Tarzan* series), slapstick comedies (Stan Laurel and Oliver Hardy in *Sons of the Desert*, 1933), and the satire and burlesque of the Marx Brothers (*A Night at the Opera*, 1935, and *A Day at the Races*, 1937). During the 1930s MGM also began producing cartoons (see Animation).

During the 1940s, MGM again led the way, becoming closely associated with Technicolor musicals, produced by Arthur Freed, such as *Meet Me in St. Louis* (1944) with Judy Garland and directed by her husband Vincente Minnelli, and *Singin' in the Rain* (1952), starring Gene Kelly and co-directed by Kelly and Stanley Donen. But again MGM needed to make movies for all possible customers, and so the lot in Culver City, CA, also turned out low-budget series such as the *Dr. Kildare* and *Hardy Boys* family films, and the animated *Tom and Jerry* cartoons.

Loew's, Inc. alone fought the decrees by the United States Supreme Court which ordered the company to split its theatrical holdings from its Hollywood studio. By 1959, when the company agreed to split off its theaters from its studio, MGM was in serious financial trouble, with no experience in an age which demanded both television and movie production. Famed studio boss Louis B. Mayer was long gone. His replacement, Dore Schary, introduced more serious subjects to MGM's production schedule such as *Intruder in the Dust* (1949), an adaptation of a William Faulkner novel, and *Quo Vadis* (1951), starring Robert Taylor and Deborah Kerr. But serious fare only lost more money. In 1955, Nicholas M. Schenck decided to retire; Dore Schary left a year later.

Thereafter violent corporate struggles became the order of the day. MGM never fully recovered as a succession of executives tried to revive its former glory. Hits emerged infrequently, usually from unexpected sources: Elvis Presley starred in *Jailhouse Rock* (1957); a re-make of *Ben-Hur* turned out to be the top-grossing film of 1960 and a multiple Oscar winner; a novel about the Russian revolution, *Dr. Zhivago* (1965), made Julie Christie a star.

In 1969, Kirk Kerkorian, an airline mogul, purchased controlling interest in MGM simply to gain a symbol for his new Las Vegas hotel. In the early 1970s, MGM turned to low-budget films, including the wildly successful black exploitation film *Shaft* (1971). But this strategy did not help, and in October 1973 in an announcement which shocked Hollywood, the once mighty MGM declared to the world it was abandoning the movie-making business.

The "death" of MGM film production was short lived. MGM came back to filmmaking in 1980 when Kirk Kerkorian formally split MGM into a hotel empire and a movie company and a year later acquired United Artists. But through the 1980s, few hits came from MGM/UA, principally the regular release of James Bond films. Kirk Kerkorian made money selling off parts of the company. At one point he sold MGM to Ted Turner, only to buy it back again, without the movie library. Lorimar-Telepictures took over what remained of MGM's fabled back lot.

No one was surprised in early 1990 when Kirk Kerkorian sold controlling interest in MGM to Italian Giancarlo Parretti, owner of Pathé. (United Artists, an MGM subsidiary through the 1980s, lost its unique corporate identity as part of the Pathé merger.) MGM-Pathé ran into immediate troubles covering the loans it acquired to take over MGM. MGM-Pathé hits came rarely, although *Rain Man* in 1989 achieved critical and financial success. By the 1990s, the company was spending more time in bankruptcy court than in movie houses, and few expected the once-mighty MGM to survive into the 21st century.

MGM survives principally on television. In 1986, Ted Turner acquired the classic MGM film library and a couple of years later created a complete cable television network, TNT, to showcase his collection. Thus, cable subscribers around the world now—in the comfort of their own home—view the greatest productions of one of the greatest studios of Hollywood's golden age of filmmaking.

Bibliography

Bart, Peter. *Fade Out: The Calamitous Final Days of MGM*. New York: Morrow, 1990.

Crowther, Bosley. *The Lion's Share*. New York: Dutton, 1957.

Gomery, Douglas. *The Hollywood Studio System*. New York: St. Martin's, 1986.

Higham, Charles. *Merchant of Dreams*. New York: Fine, 1993.

Torgerson, Dial. *Kerkorian*. New York: Dial, 1974.

Douglas Gomery

Miami Vice (1984-1989) was fast-action drama. The concept came from Brandon Tartikoff, then president of NBC entertainment, as he searched for programming for the 1984-85 season. Noting the popularity of music videos and especially the MTV cable channel, Tartikoff looked for ways to attract the younger viewer who increasingly was tuning out the established networks in favor of alternative programming. Tartikoff's idea was to use the music channel's style, texture, mood, and storytelling technique within a traditional network genre. Tartikoff's MTV cops would become *Miami Vice*.

Hired to write the pilot was Anthony Yerkovich, of *Hill Street Blues*, who made the decision to shoot on location in Miami. Relative unknowns Don Johnson and Philip Michael Thomas were cast as undercover vice detectives Sonny Crockett and Ricardo Tubbs. Michael Mann (see entry) was hired to direct and later became the show's producer.

The pilot aired on September 16, 1984, and finished second in the weekly ratings. The rest of the first season saw declining ratings, but strong word-of-mouth and 15 Emmy nominations, including an Emmy for co-star Edward J. Olmos, helped to build an audience for the show's second season. The series finished ninth overall in 1985-86. Additionally, Tartikoff's goal was realized; *Vice*'s audience included viewers who normally did not watch Friday night network television.

There were a number of reasons for *Miami Vice's* popularity. Most of them were related to the show's innovations. Foremost was the use of music videos; it was the first network series to fully utilize them. Structurally, the videos not only served as bridges between scenes, they often substituted for dialogue or helped to explain the motivation of the actors. Sometimes, as with Glenn Frey's "Smuggler's Blues," they even provided the basic plot. Thematically, the videos often added depth to the viewer's understanding of the character. And when the rock music was combined with a stunning visual, the overall effect was quite sensory—especially when compared to the rest of prime-time television. Jan Hammer, as music director, is usually given credit for at least some of the show's initial success. The sometimes very large royalty payments, however, added significant costs to what was already an expensive series to produce.

Ratings began to decline in the fourth season as the series became more like the rest of the cop show genre, and the show finished 53d in the ratings in its fifth and final season.

Bibliography
Brooks, Tim, and Earle Marsh. *The Complete Directory to Prime Time Network and Cable TV Shows, 1946-Present.* New York: Ballantine, 1995.
Janeshutz, Trish, and Rob MacGregor. *The Making of* Miami Vice. New York: Ballantine, 1986.

John Matviko

Michaels, Barbara, is a pen name of best-selling gothic and romance novelist Barbara Gross Mertz (1927-), who also writes mysteries as Elizabeth Peters. She draws on her own background as an Egyptologist in the various Peters novels, many of which feature archaeological settings or historical mysteries whose solutions must be uncovered from layers of time, such as *The Dead Sea Cipher* (1970), *The Murders of Richard III* (1974), and *The Curse of the Pharaohs* (1981).

Though critics favor her Peters novels, her major popular stature, however, has been achieved as Barbara Michaels, writer of romances with supernatural and/or historic elements. In novels like *The Master of Blacktower* (1967), *Sons of the Wolf* (1967), *The Dark on the Other Side* (1970), *Greygallows* (1972), *The Wizard's Daughter* (1980), and others, Michaels employs stock elements from the gothic repertoire of witchcraft and black magic, sorcery, bloodlust, ghosts, and werewolves. In more recent fiction, such as *Someone in the House* (1981), *Shattered Silk* (1986), and *Smoke and Mirrors* (1989), Michaels has emphasized psychological pathologies as the source of the chills.

Bibliography
Klein, Kathleen Gregory, ed. *Great Women Mystery Writers: Classic to Contemporary.* Westport: Greenwood, 1994.

Liahna Babener

Michener, James A. (1907-1997), is known for his massive popular novels capturing the unique cultures of exotic places and chronicling epochs in human history. His subject locales range from Hawaii to Japan to Israel to outer space; to each, he dedicated vast research, opulent details, and a full-bodied story that often begins in the outreaches of prehistoric time and extends to the future. Despite the sheer size and volume of his best-selling sagas, and the breadth of his milieu, Michener consistently drew a huge and loyal readership, and the publication of each new novel was an eagerly awaited event.

After an early academic career and service in the navy during World War II, where he was stationed in the South Pacific, Michener turned to fiction, publishing *Tales of the South Pacific* (1947), a powerful and atmospheric evocation of the American war effort that led to the Pulitzer Prize in 1948 and to the celebrated Rodgers and Hammerstein musical, *South Pacific*. His island experience also generated several subsequent novels, including *The Bridges at Toko-Ri* (1953), *Sayonara* (1954), *Hawaii* (1959), and *Caravans* (1963), all but *Caravans* being adapted to motion pictures. In *Hawaii*, Michener's successful storytelling formula—panoramic tales of places told through the evolution of their natural history and the unfolding of human events through fictional characters placed in real historical situations—was perfected.

Subsequent novels extended the formula to other storied locations: *The Source* (1963), traces Israel's history through the ages and views the Holy Land through diverse religious and ethnic perspectives; *Centennial* (1974) is a sweeping account of Colorado through the interconnected stories of over 70 characters; *Chesapeake* (1978) treats Eastern Maryland; and *The Covenant* (1980) is a stirring history of South Africa. Though these novels exhibit an established format, they are not replications of each other; each tells a dramatic and engaging story and reflects in abundant detail the distinctive cultural world of its subject. Other novels of this type include *Poland* (1983), *Texas* (1985), *Alaska* (1988), *Caribbean* (1989), and *Mexico* (1992). *Space* (1982) applies the epical frame to space exploration, paying tribute to the ingenuity and pioneering spirit that Michener saw symbolized in America's space program.

Though best known for his grand novels, Michener wrote other fiction, such as *The Drifters* (1971), about a group of hippies who travel through the Iberian peninsula, and a substantial body of nonfiction, including travel literature, history, essays on the arts, and autobiography. Taken as a whole, his work might be characterized as a mesmerizing window unto worlds beyond and before commonplace American life.

Bibliography
Becker, George. J. *James A. Michener.* New York: Ungar, 1983.
Day, A. Grove. *James A. Michener.* Boston: Twayne: 1964.
Hayes, John. P. *James A. Michener.* Indianapolis: Bobbs-Merrill, 1984.
Kings, John. *In Search of Centennial.* New York: Random, 1978.

Liahna Babener

Mickey Mouse Club, The (1955-1958), was a children's television show that aired on weekday afternoons on ABC and sparked a national phenomenon. Although it ran for only three years, it is important for its popularity among the baby-boom audience, as well as for its ability to showcase the new medium of television.

The year 1955, when *The Mickey Mouse Club* premiered, was a banner year for Walt Disney. It marked the release of a new animated film, *Lady and the Tramp*, a Davy Crockett craze spawned by programming aired on the *Disneyland* television show, and the opening of the theme park Disneyland. The last of these is certainly connected to the birth of Disney's *Mickey Mouse Club* show. Mickey Mouse, the friendly host and designated symbol of Disneyland, had not made a cartoon since *The Simple Things* in 1953, in part because animators had difficulty providing appealing storylines for what had evolved into a squeaky-clean character. *The Mickey Mouse Club* was an attempt to revitalize interest in Mickey at a time when his movie career had stalled.

Overwhelmingly, it worked. Beginning on October 3, 1955, *The Mickey Mouse Club*, which aired weekdays from 5 to 6 p.m. on ABC, celebrated the character of Mickey Mouse, whose name was chanted and spelled out in the show's theme song. At the peak of the show's popularity, 75 percent of America's households tuned in regularly.

In addition to giving attention to Mickey Mouse, the series was important for other reasons. First, it broke new ground in television by being one of the first shows specifically designed for the child audience. However, its creators did not underestimate children's tastes and did not talk down to the children. *The Mickey Mouse Club* evolved into a variety show for youngsters, featuring cartoons, singing and dancing segments, nature footage, newsreels about children, and daily serials, such as *Corky and White Shadow, The Hardy Boys, Adventures in Dairyland*, and, the most popular of all, *Spin and Marty*. It further entertained its audience by designating different days, such as "Anything Can Happen Day" or "Fun with Music Day," which added variety to the show's standard routine.

Also crucial to the success of *The Mickey Mouse Club* was a group of spirited youngsters dubbed "the Mouseketeers," who wore mouse-ear caps, sang the show's theme song, and acted in various segments. These children, led by Jimmy Dodd, possessed a spontaneous, unassuming quality; they were not actors. When assembling the Mouseketeers, Disney instructed his producer Bill Walsh to seek normal, happy children rather than trained actors for the roles, and the strategy worked. Children all over America seemed to embrace the Mouseketeers, in part because they appeared to be just like them. Of all the Mouseketeers, the best known was Annette Funicello, a dark-haired Italian American who was the daughter of an auto mechanic. Walt Disney himself discovered Annette at a dance class and was taken by her sincerity and girl-next-door appearance. So, too, was the television audience. At the height of her popularity, Annette received as many as 6,000 fan letters a week—ten times more than the other Mouseketeers. *The Mickey Mouse Club* show proved to be Annette's springboard to a movie career. She later appeared in Disney live-action comedies, such as *The Shaggy Dog* and *Babes in Toyland*, before co-starring in

a series of American International Pictures' beach films with Frankie Avalon. She also found fame as a recording artist.

Given the appeal of Annette, Darlene, Karen, Cubby, and the other Mouseketeers, *The Mickey Mouse Club* reached as many as 90 percent of the nation's children each day, thereby attracting advertisers of toys and other youth products. The most notable of these was Mattel, which advertised a new product, the Burp Gun, on the show and within approximately eight weeks filled orders for 1 million units of the product, doubling the company's sales volume.

Despite the groundbreaking popularity of *The Mickey Mouse Club*, audience and advertiser interest in the show eventually declined. By its third year, *The Mickey Mouse Club* was reduced from one hour to one-half hour, and the following year, after attaining a poor 20.0 rating, it was canceled and replaced by *Rin Tin Tin*. Although it lasted only three full seasons, *The Mickey Mouse Club* captured the interest of the baby boom audience, who, in turn, were more likely to buy Mickey Mouse byproducts, thereby generating more profits for Disney. Thus, the show proved to be important in popularizing the Disney empire as well as the new medium of television and, specifically, children's programming.

In 1977, *The New Mickey Mouse Club* reached the air with its producers' expectation that it would create the same sensation for a new generation that the original *Mickey Mouse Club* did 22 years earlier; but the show fizzled. (Future teen singers Britney Spears and Christina Aguilera were among this second generation of Mouseketeers.) Nevertheless, *Mickey Mouse Club* mouse-ear caps continue to sell well at the Disney theme parks, reminders of the reign of one of the most popular children's shows in television history.

Bibliography

Bowles, Jerry. *Forever Hold Your Banner High: The Story of the Mickey Mouse Club and What Happened to the Mouseketeers.* Garden City: Doubleday, 1976.

Jackson, Kathy Merlock. *Walt Disney: A Bio-Bibliography.* Westport: Greenwood, 1993.

Keller, Keith. *Mickey Mouse Club Scrapbook.* New York: Grosset & Dunlap, 1975.

Rovin, Jeff. *Of Mice and Mickey: The Complete Guide to the Mickey Mouse Club.* New York: Manor, 1975.

Schneider, Cy. *Children's Television.* Lincolnwood: NTC, 1989.

Kathy Merlock Jackson

Military Songs are patriotic compositions usually specifically written for a branch of the U.S. Armed Forces or for a particular war. America's most recent major conflict, the unpopular Vietnam War, 1961-73, for example, spawned a top popular song "The Ballad of the Green Berets," which was also a military song. Written in 1966 by Sergeant Barry Sadler, who had participated in the war, "The Ballad of the Green Berets" was the last significant U.S. military song.

The first important military composition was the famous "Yankee Doodle." Appearing in the American colonies about two centuries before Sadler's ballad, no later than the 1760s, it was adopted by the American revolutionaries as their primary musical piece in the Revolution of 1775-83. The tune may have been influenced by a British tune, and the lyrics may have been written around 1755 by an English physician, Richard Shuckberg, to mock the appearance of the colonial troops who were then allies of the British.

The next major U.S. conflict, the War of 1812 against the British, did not inspire any well-known or enduring songs. But the bloody Civil War of 1861-65 inspired several songs of consequence. On the Union side there were "Battle Hymn of the Republic," "When Johnny Comes Marching Home," "Tramp, Tramp, Tramp," and "The Battle Cry of Freedom." The magnificent "Battle Hymn of the Republic," which is still a favorite among many sectors of American culture, was the main war song of the North. Its lyrics were written in December 1861 by social worker and poet Julia Ward Howe after she heard some Union troops singing "John Brown's Body." The melody of that song, possibly a product of American camp meetings, first appeared in print in 1857. The new song with Howe's inspired lyrics and the "John Brown" melody was printed in 1862. "When Johnny Comes Marching Home" was probably written by renowned Irish-born bandmaster Patrick Gilmore (also known as Louis Lambert) in 1863. It remains a well-known favorite in the late 20th century. Less enduring but still significant were George Frederick Root's "Tramp, Tramp, Tramp" (1863) and "The Battle Cry of Freedom" or "Rally 'Round the Flag" (1861). Root could be called the poet laureate of the Union cause.

On the Confederate side was "Dixie," the main battle song of the Southern troops. Ironically, "Dixie" was probably created by a Northerner, Daniel Decatur Emmett. (The authorship of the lyrics is not certain.) It was first performed in a New York City minstrel show in 1859. Although not a big hit in the New York show, the song became a sensation in New Orleans after appearing in a theatrical production in 1860. From there it became the musical symbol of the Confederacy when the war started one year later.

The next major conflict, the Spanish American War of 1898, inspired no top song of its own. Instead, it borrowed Gilmore's "When Johnny Comes Marching Home," which was very popular in the Civil War, and made it even more prominent. Soon after the United States officially entered World War I (1914-18), in April 1917, the famous entertainer and composer George M. Cohan was struck by patriotic fervor and wrote a swaggering march entitled "Over There." The leading military song in the U.S. during the war period, the almost arrogant composition with the memorable line "the Yanks are coming" remains a favorite.

The most devastating war of the 20th century, World War II (1939-41), spawned a number of military songs. They included "Comin' in on a Wing and a Prayer" (1943) by lyricist Harold Adamson and composer Jimmy McHugh and "Praise the Lord and Pass the Ammunition" (1942) by Frank Loesser, who later was to become a leading Broadway composer with hits like *Guys and Dolls* (1950). "Praise the Lord and Pass the Ammunition" was controversial because of its mixture of militarism and religion. Less remembered are highly aggressive World War II pieces like "Remember Pearl Harbor" (1941) by lyricist Don Reid and composer Sammy Kaye and "We Did It Before" (1941) by lyricist Charles Tobias and composer Cliff Friend. The opening lines of the last song were "We did it before and we can do it again," meaning beat the Germans. The Korean Conflict of 1950-53 had no well-known songs associated with it.

The official song of the Army is "The Army Goes Rolling Along," an adaptation of the famous "The Caissons Go Rolling Along." Written in 1907 by Edmund L. Gruber, a career Army officer, while he was stationed in the Philippines, the brilliant "Caissons" march, originally intended for a reunion of the 5th Artillery Regiment, became a fixture after being published in 1918. Even more renowned is the Navy's official song, the sparkling "Anchors Aweigh" which was written in 1907 by two Navy men, Alfred H. Miles and Charles A. Zimmerman. At about the same time Francis S. Van Boskerck wrote "Semper Paratus" ("always prepared"), the rousing theme of the Coast Guard.

"Semper Fidelis" ("always faithful") is the official song of the Marine Corps. Written expressly for the Marines by John Philip Sousa in 1888 while Sousa was leader of the Marine Band, this lively march is one of the finest compositions by the "March King." Another famous song directly associated with the Marines is "The Marines' Hymn" or "From the Halls of Montezuma." Published with anonymous lyrics in 1918, "The Marines' Hymn" uses a stirring tune created in 1868 by French classical composer Jacques Offenbach for his light opera *Genevieve de Brabant*. In 1939, Canadian-born Robert M. Crawford composed the uplifting "The Air Force Song," also known as "The Army Air Corps Song" and "The U.S. Air Force Song." Its spirited melody and inspired lines, such as "Off we go into the wild blue yonder," came on the eve of World War II, the first conflict in which the U.S. extensively used aircraft.

Bibliography

Bowman, Kent A. *Voices of Combat: A Century of Liberty and War Songs, 1765-1865*. New York: Greenwood, 1987.

Browne, C. A. *The Story of Our National Ballads*. New York: Crowell, 1960.

Fuld, James J. *The Book of World Famous Music: Classical, Popular, and Folk*. 3d ed. New York: Dover, 1985.

Heaps, Willard Allison, and Porter W. Heaps. *The Singing Sixties: The Spirit of Civil War Days Drawn from the Music of the Times*. Norman: U of Oklahoma P, 1960.

Leipzig, Virginia, and Howard Harnne, eds. *Liberty Sings: An Anthology of America's National and People Songs*. Secaucus: Warner Bros., 1987.

William E. Studwell

Miller, Glenn (1904-1944), was the perfect myth in the making. The death of the celebrated bandleader at the early age of 40 when his plane disappeared en route from England to Paris cast him into the role of a cultural legend. Born in Clarinda, IA, a small rural town in the southwestern part of that state, Alton Glenn Miller studied trombone and at the age of 17 played in an ensemble led by Boyd Senter. After his stint with Senter in 1921, Miller played for Ben Pollack in 1926, Smith Ballew from 1932 to 1934, and also was in the orchestra for several Broadway musicals in the early 1930s. By the mid-1930s, he not only had gained a reputation as a fine trombonist but as a very good arranger. In the spring of 1934 he joined the Dorsey Brothers band as a trombonist and arranger.

In 1935, Miller left the Dorseys and switched to Ray Noble's ensemble. While with Noble, Miller studied composition under Joseph Schillinger. It was during these studies that he composed, as an exercise, the melody for the song we now know as "Moonlight Serenade." This student exercise was to become one of the very best songs of the big band or swing era, and Miller's only significant composition. The first lyrics used with the melody, written by Edward Heyman, were entitled "Now I Lay Me Down to Weep." When Miller later formed his own band and wanted to use his compellingly sweet and soft melody as his ensemble's theme song, he searched for more appropriate lyrics. In time Mitchell Parish's lyrics, "Moonlight Serenade," became the mate for Miller's melody.

After working with Noble and also Glen Gray, Miller formed his own band early in 1937. His group made some recordings for Decca Records, including Miller's arrangements of "Peg o' My Heart" (written in 1913 by Fred Fisher and Alfred Bryan) and "Moonlight Bay" (written in 1912 by Edward Madden and Percy Wenrich). His band also appeared at the Raymore Ballroom in Boston and the Blue Room of the Roosevelt Hotel in New Orleans.

During his seven years as a bandleader, Miller was associated with many songs. But the compositions he is most closely linked with, in addition to this own "Moonlight Serenade," were "In the Mood," "Chattanooga Choo-Choo," "Sunrise Serenade," "Little Brown Jug," "American Patrol," "Tuxedo Junction," "Elmer's Tune," and "A String of Pearls."

Glenn Miller has left behind many fine recordings, two very successful early 1940s films, *Sun Valley Serenade* and *Orchestra Wives*, and most of all, a style or sound. Nowhere is the legacy of Miller's sound any more evident than in a uniquely brilliant recording of "Jingle Bells" made after Miller's death by Tex Beneke, Ray Eberle, and the Modernaires. If Miller had done nothing else but provide the style and humor which was in this rendering of the old Christmas favorite, he still might be remembered.

Bibliography
Bedwell, Stephen F. *A Glenn Miller Discography and Biography*. London: Glenn Miller Appreciation Society, 1956.
Flower, John. *Moonlight Serenade: A Biodiscography of the Glenn Miller Civilian Band*. New Rochelle: Arlington, 1972.
Simon, George Thomas. *Glenn Miller and His Orchestra*. New York: Crowell, 1974.
Way, Chris. *"In the Miller Mood": A History and Discography of the Glenn Miller Service Band 1942-1945*. [S.I.]: S. Way, 1987.
Wright, Wilbur. *The Glenn Miller Burial File*. Southhampton: Wright, 1993.

William E. Studwell

Mills Brothers, The, one of the most popular singing groups of the 1930s and 1940s, actually were two groups: a foursome that turned their voices into a seven-piece jazz band, and a tightly harmonizing quartet that specialized in warm nostalgia. Both groups influenced generations of popular singers.

John, Jr. (born 1910), Herbert (1912), Harry (1913), and Donald Mills (1915) started singing together as kids, in a church choir in their home town of Piqua, OH. Later, when John, Jr., bought a guitar, they started trying more secular music. But instead of lining up additional instruments, the Mills brothers used their voices to mimic their accompaniment. By himself, John, Jr., provided the four-piece rhythm section, strumming a guitar and humming the bass part. The other three brothers combined cupped hands and voice control to "play" a trumpet and two saxophones—all in perfectly balanced harmony. The sound they created proved an ideal vehicle for the popular jazz music of the late 1920s and early 1930s. The foursome's syncopated style allowed enough flexibility that each of the brothers could toss in an "instrumental" solo—really more of a reined-in vocal scatting.

After polishing their act at small Ohio theaters, the Mills Brothers in 1925 auditioned to perform on Cincinnati radio station WLW, which at the time had one of the strongest signals in the country. Performing on different programs under different names, the quartet attracted the attention of CBS radio talent scouts, who signed them to a three-year contract—the first black artists to star in their own national radio show.

From 1931 to 1935, the quartet scored hits with everything from ragtime ("Tiger Rag") to swing ("It Don't Mean a Thing If It Ain't Got That Swing"). They even tried "instrumentals," delivering wordless renditions of songs such as Duke Ellington's multilayered "Caravan." The group also provided vocal/musical accompaniment for a number of the era's top recording artists, including Duke Ellington, the Boswell Sisters, and Bing Crosby.

In January 1936, John, Jr., died of pneumonia. The remaining brothers performed for some months as a trio, until their father, John, Sr., took over his namesake son's role as bassist. His joining the group coincided with a shift in the Mills Brothers' sound. By the late 1930s, the instrument-mimicking and scatting were gone. In their place, the revamped Mills Brothers provided slick, sentimental, four-part harmonies.

Unlike most of the singing groups trying to emulate their style, the Mills Brothers continued performing and recording long into the rock-and-roll era. When John, Sr., retired in 1957, at the age of 67, Herbert, Harry, and Donald continued performing, touring the world as a trio. Although firmly identified by their nostalgic sound, the three Mills Brothers occasionally crossed over into rock's domain; the group cracked the Top 20 as late as 1968. But their connection to and evocation of an earlier time kept their recording and performing in check. Age took its toll as well; Harry Mills died in June 1982.

Bibliography
Feather, Leonard. *The Encyclopedia of Jazz*. New York: Horizon, 1960.
Friedwald, Will. *Jazz Singing: America's Great Voices from Bessie Smith to Bebop and Beyond*. New York: Scribner, 1990.

Simon, George T. *The Best of the Music Makers*. Garden City: Doubleday, 1979.

Chris Foran

Mingus, Charles (1922-1979), developed into a Duke Ellington think-alike. Jimmy Blanton is usually credited with developing virtuoso bass playing while changing the course of Duke Ellington's band. Blanton died of tuberculosis in his early twenties and Charles Mingus is generally regarded as his musical successor, including his musical connection with Ellington.

Although Mingus played only briefly with Ellington's band (he had to be fired because of his temper), he remained fascinated with Ellington's music and often claimed to be writing music in the style that Ellington *should* be composing. Even a cursory listen to Mingus's music evokes strong memories of Ellington.

Mingus was, then, an influential bass player, a composer-arranger of note, and a bandleader whose groups exerted wide influence and featured sterling musicians who had to struggle to maintain their individuality against the challenge of Mingus's music. His music, like Ellington's, is hard to pin down in a few words, for like his idol, Mingus saw no boundaries in good music.

The period of his greatest popularity was the late 1950s. Columbia Records released two albums in the then-fashionable "funk" style, which combined blues and gospel. Instead of cashing in on that fame, Mingus, typically, refused to make any more such albums and continued to diversify. He released albums in a wide variety of styles: progressive, third stream, bop, free jazz, and others. He even turned his hand to film scoring.

In the midst of all this activity, he recorded an album, related to a film score, with Duke Ellington and Max Roach, entitled *Money Jungle*. The album remains a delight. It displays the performers at best, obviously enjoying themselves and their work.

Mingus's best recordings have the same characteristics as the best of Ellington's work. They mix composed and improvised formats in such a manner that it is often difficult to note which portions are improvised or written. Preset patterns spring up in the midst of improvised solos, interrupting the soloist and forcing him to respond to new challenges rather than to rely on cliché runs. Mingus also speeded and slowed the tempo, and changed styles in mid-composition,

In many ways, Mingus's groups resembled a workshop in which composition and performance were always in flux. He received great cooperation from his colleagues, to the point of their willingness to change styles to give him certain Ellington effects on certain compositions. Just how much of Mingus's work was in flux has been made clearer in the Mingus revivals that have flowered in the late 1980s and 1990s as various Mingus Dynasty groups have arisen to play his music. Great feats of cooperative reconstruction have led to the assembling of his "Epistrophy" composition, among others.

Bibliography

Collier, James Lincoln. *The Making of Jazz*. Boston: Houghton Mifflin, 1978.
Feather, Leonard. *Encyclopedia of Jazz*. New York: Da Capo, 1984.
——. *The New Yearbook of Jazz*. New York: Horizon, 1958.
Gridley, Mark. *Jazz Styles*. Englewood Cliffs: Prentice-Hall, 1994.
Weinstein, Norman. *Night in Tunisia*. Metuchen: Scarecrow, 1993.

Frank A. Salamone

Minnie Pearl, one of country music's most popular and most beloved stars, is the alter ego of Sarah Ophelia Colley (1912-1996), born in Centerville, TN. Her time-honored, down-home, "Minnie Pearl" hayseed act won her generations of fans and earned her the long-standing title "Queen of Country Comedy." Pearl's wide-brimmed straw hat with its dangling $1.98 price-tag, her cotton, thrift-store, "yeller" dress, and infamous "How-dee! I'm just so proud to be here!" greeting are recognizable even by people who rarely listen to or follow the trends of country music. Pearl was more like a friend to her audience rather than a show business act. Colley herself has described Pearl as "apple pie and clothes dried in the sun and the smell of fresh baking bread."

Colley, unlike her counterpart Pearl, was raised in a well-educated family, surrounded by classical music and literature, and educated at Ward-Belmont College, an elite finishing school in Nashville. She studied and showed promise in the field of dance, and, after teaching dance locally, was hired by a small Atlanta company, the Wayne P. Sewall Co., as a dramatic coach and worked with directors who staged amateur productions in small Southern towns. While working in Baileytown, AL, during her fifth year as a dramatic coach, she stayed with a local family, and met the prototype for her Minnie Pearl act. Her host family's Grande Dame was a great teller of tales, and Colley began to develop and perform monologues she used to promote the productions she was helping to direct.

Colley's father, Thomas, died in the late 1930s and she returned home to care for her ailing mother and began to work as a dramatic instructor for children. She soon revived her hayseed character, and gave a performance at a local bankers' meeting. She adopted Centerville's nearby railroad crossing, Grinder's Switch, as Minnie Pearl's hometown, and took her act to the *Grand Ole Opry* for an audition. She was awarded a broadcast to be aired at 11:05 p.m., well after prime listening time had expired, for fear her act might offend rural listeners. These concerns proved to be ungrounded, as Pearl soon became one of the *Opry*'s most popular acts. She became a permanent member in 1940, at the age of 28, and performed well into the 1980s. In 1966, she hit the Top 10 list with her Starday monologue single, "Giddyap—Go Answer" and appeared on many variety shows and major syndicated series including *The Today Show* and *Tonight* to *Dinah!* and an infamous gig on *Hee-Haw*. Her awards and honors include Nashville's "Woman of the Year" (1965) and induction into the Country Music Hall of Fame in 1975.

Bibliography
Carlin, Richard. "Minnie Pearl." *The Big Book of Country Music: A Biographical Encyclopedia.* New York: Penguin, 1995.
Sakol, Jeannie. "Minnie Pearl." *The Wonderful World of Country Music.* New York: Grosset & Dunlap, 1979.
Shestack, Melvin. "Minnie Pearl." *The Country Music Encyclopedia.* Toronto: KBO, 1974.
Stambler, Irwin, and Grelun Landon. "Minnie Pearl." *The Encyclopedia of Folk, Country and Western Music.* 2d ed. New York: St. Martin's, 1983.

Carole L. Carroll

Minow, Newton N. (1926-), will always be remembered as the man who called American television "a vast wasteland" when he addressed the National Association of Broadcasters on May 9, 1961, as the newly appointed chairman of the Federal Communications Commission (FCC) under President John F. Kennedy.

During the 1950s, the broadcast industry had grown comfortable in the expectation of nothing more than moderate regulation from the federal government. The FCC grappled with technical issues, but was little involved with the programming responsibilities of broadcasters. This passive stance was not entirely a matter of legal limitations, but rather philosophy. John Kennedy entered the Oval Office with a different belief. The liberal activism of his campaign rhetoric was translated into action in his plans for regulatory agencies. For broadcasters, Minow's Senate confirmation hearing in February 1961 was a portent of trouble ahead. He was clearly an idealist. To his interrogators he said, "I do think that the Commission has a role in encouraging better programs, and I am determined to do something about it."

When Newton Minow delivered the famous "vast wasteland" speech, he articulated to the American public a hopeful vision of what television could become. To the broadcast community, though, the speech ushered in a new era of strict regulation with a controversial emphasis on program content. The broadcast policies of the New Frontier described in the address included stiffer enforcement of license-renewal procedures and support of legislation that would give the FCC more direct control over the networks.

The irony of Minow's chairmanship is that his most significant contributions to American broadcasting produced little sensation. His push for the All-Channel Receiver Bill that required TV sets to be capable of receiving UHF stations, for legislation to aid educational television, and for the formation of the Communications Satellite Corporation (COMSAT), ultimately led to greater choice and program diversity.

Bibliography
Watson, Mary Ann. *The Expanding Vista: American Television in the Kennedy Years.* New York: Oxford UP, 1990.

Mary Ann Watson

Mission: Impossible (1966-1973) was a 60-minute program on CBS that combined foreign intrigue with intricately executed feats of espionage. During its life, the I.M.F. (Impossi-ble Mission Force) team solved 171 cases. The plots were incredibly detailed but carefully laid out. The original cast included Barbara Bain, Martin Landau, Greg Morris, and Peter Lupus, with Steven Hill as the Force's leader during the first year. He was replaced by Peter Graves. After four seasons Leonard Nimoy, as the magician, and Lesley Warren took over for Bain and her husband, Martin Landau, who had played the master of disguise. Bruce Geller was the executive producer for Paramount TV.

The program's opening has become a cult classic. Generally, Graves's character entered a phone booth where he listened to a tape that would self-destruct. The opening for the first season, however, was different from the one most viewers remember. For that season, Steven Hill was the leader of the I.M.F. and the opening began "Good Morning, Mr. Briggs." It ended with "Please dispose of this tape in the usual manner." Hill's character would then throw it into a vat of acid or a furnace or dispose of it in some such manner. The tape gave him his instructions, should he accept the assignment.

Neither Hill nor his successor, Peter Graves, ever refused an assignment. There were differences between the two leaders and the tone of the program, however, that each headed. Hill showed real moral concern for his assignments and drew the line at some operations. He refused to engage in assassination, stating that such an act was unequivocally against policy. That moral ambiguity left the show when Graves replaced him after the first season.

The I.M.F. engaged in covert activities that in the light of the Cold War may have been acceptable to some, but too much thought would lead to serious questions regarding the ethics of their operation, as it had in the program's first year. Both Graves and Hill were warned that, "If you or any member of the I.M. Force be caught or killed, the Secretary will disavow any knowledge of your actions."

Bibliography
Brown, Les. *Encyclopedia of Television.* Detroit: Gale, 1992.
Meyers, Richard. *TV Detectives.* San Diego: Barnes, 1981.
Terrace, Vincent. *Encyclopedia of Television Series, Pilots and Specials: 1937-1973.* Vol. 1. New York: Zoetrope, 1985.
——. *Encyclopedia of Television Series, Pilots and Specials: 1974-1984.* Vol. 2. New York: Zoetrope, 1985.
——. *Fifty Years of Television.* New York: Cornwall, 1991.

Frank A. Salamone

Mister Ed (1961-1966), a half-hour situation comedy of the early 1960s, embodied all that is fanciful in an era of Cold War and the threat of nuclear annihilation. America found escapism in an animal that was more intelligent than his human companions, a horse that could solve a crisis, dole out words of wisdom, maintain a sense of humor, and offer relief in a time of anxiety and upheaval.

The premise of the *Mister Ed* show explored the relationship between a talking horse named Mr. Ed and his friend Wilbur, an architect who worked out of his home office next to Mr. Ed's stall. The main characters, aside from Ed, were Wilbur Post, played by Allan Young, and Connie Hines as Wilbur's wife, Carol. Larry Keating (1961-64) played the next-door neighbor Roger Addison; with Edna Skinner (1961-64) his spendthrift wife, Kay. Later Leon Ames (1964-66) played the next-door neighbor Gordon Kirkwood, replacing Keating; Florence MacMichael (1964-66) was Gordon's wife, Winnie. Additionally there were such celebrity guests as Zsa Zsa Gabor, Clint Eastwood, and Mae West.

Mister Ed ran for a total of 143 episodes. A Filmways Production, first airing on January 5, 1961, it was acquired by CBS for syndication in October of the same year for their prime-time fall lineup. Classified as a fantasy situation comedy, it lasted until September 4, 1966. While the original pilot, *The Wonderful World of Wilbur Pope*, produced by George Burns, never aired, the subsequent *Mister Ed* series, produced by Arthur Lubin, went on to capture over 40 percent of the viewing audience at its peak, and won a 1962 Golden Globe Award for best television show.

Bibliography
Brook, Tim, and Earle Marsh. *Compete Directory to Prime Time Network and Cable TV Shows, 1946 to Present.* New York: Ballantine, 1995.
Brown, Les. *Les Brown's Encyclopedia of Television.* 3d ed. Detroit: Gale Research, 1992.
Maltin, Leonard, ed. *Leonard Maltin's TV Movies and Video Guide.* New York: Plume, 1991.
Scheuer, Steven, ed. *Movies on TV and Video Cassettes.* New York: Bantam, 1989.
Thompson, Robert. "A Dissertation on Mr. Ed?" *New York Times* 147 [national ed.] (15 Oct. 1997): B1+.
Young, Alan. *Mr. Ed and Me.* New York: St. Martin's, 1995.

Mary Timmons
Matthew Bashore

Mister Rogers' Neighborhood (1970-78; 1979-). Few series, of any type, have tackled the issues that the PBS children's series *Mister Rogers' Neighborhood* has. Fred McFeely Rogers (1928-), an ordained Presbyterian minister with a special ministry to the public through the media, has specialized in low-key presentation to children since his first programs in the 1960s, the forerunners of his current series. He has produced over 650 shows, many of which are out on videotape.

Rogers, who has degrees in music, psychology, and theology, deals with values and using those values to deal with feelings and fear. He has an uncanny way of understanding and talking to young children, emphasizing the value of each one. "People will like you just the way you are," he states at least once per program. He seems to understand the uncertainty that children have in being sure they are really accepted. Rogers takes great care to separate fact from fantasy. His technique is to discuss a fear or concern in a straightforward manner and then to treat that problem in his "Neighborhood of Fantasy," employing a form of play therapy.

This does not mean that the telecast is not entertaining. Rogers understands that in order to get his message across, he must capture and keep the attention of the children whose parents turn them on to the program. The set is a copy of his own home. For each show, he enters his front room singing "Won't You Be My Neighbor" and dons a comfortable sweater. (His original sweater is in the Smithsonian.)

On that set appear various continuing characters: Mr. McFeely, King Friday, Lady Elaine, and others. Real people are mixed with puppets. Famous guests pop up from time to time and some of the best jazz on TV has been part of the program. The music generally makes a point and tends to be soothing.

Bibliography
Brown, Les. *Encyclopedia of Television.* Detroit: Gale Research, 1992.
Collins, Mark, and Margaret Mary Kimmel, eds. Mister Rogers' Neighborhood: *Children, Television, and Fred Rogers.* Pittsburgh: U of Pittsburgh P, 1996.
Moody, Kate. *Growing Up on Television.* New York: McGraw-Hill, 1980.
Terrace, Vincent. *Encyclopedia of Television Series, Pilots and Specials: 1937-1973.* Vol. 1. New York: Zoetrope, 1985.
——. *Fifty Years of Television.* New York: Cornwall, 1991.

Frank A. Salamone

See also
Puppets on Television

Mitchell, Margaret (1900-1949), was the Georgia-born author of what is perhaps the most celebrated popular novel of the 20th century, *Gone with the Wind* (1936). Margaret Mitchell produced little else of enduring significance, though she need not have. *Gone with the Wind* is imbedded in the American psyche as the dominant national epic, its passionate characters and romantic Civil War saga having taken on mythic status in the sixty years since the novel was first published. As a literary work, and later as a landmark film (directed by Victor Fleming and starring Vivien Leigh and Clark Gable; see entry), *Gone with the Wind* stands at the pinnacle of American popular culture. It remains the best-selling book in history, aside from the Bible.

Gone with the Wind, set in Civil War Georgia, tells the story of Scarlett O'Hara, the self-centered and passionate daughter of an Irish plantation owner. Scarlett is in love with Ashley Wilkes, a member of the neighboring gentry, but he is betrothed to another woman. Much of the story concerns her abiding passion for Wilkes, though they both marry others and the war intervenes to ravish their homesteads and drive them to poverty and desperation. Scarlett's persistence enables her to survive the war, keep Tara, the family plantation, from economic ruin and Yankee occupation, and ultimately, to establish herself as a successful businesswoman in post-war Atlanta.

The author of this remarkable novel was herself rather unremarkable. Mitchell grew up in a middle-class household in Atlanta, where she was told heroic stories of the Civil War and the economic aftereffects of the conflict. Her family instilled in her strong ideas about character, determination, and the quest for upward mobility, all of which eventually found their way into her portrait of Scarlett O'Hara, the immortal heroine of *Gone with the Wind*. Indeed, much of her life's history was fodder for the novel: her cerebral fiancé, who died in World War I, may have been the model for Ashley Wilkes, the effete aristocrat for whom Scarlett pines for most of the story; her first husband, with his brash good looks and roguish masculinity, seems to have been the prototype for Rhett Butler; her own father was re-created in Gerald O'Hara; and the family's lost plantation likely was the inspiration for Tara.

For several years after her brief stint at Smith College, Mitchell was a columnist for the *Atlanta Journal*. There she developed her natural skills as a writer, experimenting with several short stories and unfinished novels before beginning what would become *Gone with the Wind* in 1926, a work that took her the better part of eight years to complete. The novel met with extraordinary success upon its publication in 1926: it was an immediate best-seller, was purchased by Hollywood for a considerable sum, and won the Pulitzer Prize the next year.

Her premature death in 1949, from injuries sustained when, as a pedestrian, she was struck by an automobile, had the mark of eerie culmination, since she had twice before been injured in serious car accidents. Though she would not write another novel, Mitchell's legacy is no less prolific, since *Gone with the Wind* remains the most popular novel ever written. In 1992, American author Alexandra Ripley wrote a sequel, *Scarlett*, a long and lively book that only demonstrates by contrast the achievement of the original.

Bibliography

Edwards, Anne. *Road to Tara: The Life of Margaret Mitchell*. New Haven: Ticknor, 1983.

Farr, Finis. *Margaret Mitchell of Atlanta: The Author of* Gone with the Wind. New York: Morrow, 1965.

Liahna Babener

Mitchum, Robert (1917-), was born in Bridgeport, CT, to a Norwegian immigrant mother and a half Scots-Irish and half Blackfoot Indian father. Fatherless at age two, Mitchum spent much of the Great Depression as a boxcar-hopping hobo. He worked as a dishwasher, ditch digger, coal miner, longshoreman, and "bum fighter." In 1942, he joined a Long Beach Theater Guild and starred in several productions, and in 1943, he appeared in 18 movies, playing heavies and small supporting parts in Westerns, war films, comedies, and other dramas. In 1944, he starred as the psychotic murderer in Monogram's *When Strangers Marry*. RKO was taken with Mitchum's performance and signed him to a seven-year contract. At RKO Mitchum, as the ill-fated existential protagonist Jeff Bailey, made perhaps his most famous film, *Out of the Past* (1947).

Over subsequent years Mitchum added to his "bad boy" legend through a series of collisions with the law. In 1949, Mitchum served a 60-day prison term on "the charge of conspiracy to possess marijuana." In 1951, "Bob (Trouble) Mitchum," as one of the fan magazines labeled him, knocked out Top 10 heavyweight Bernie Reynolds in a barroom brawl. Both of these scandals, rather than ruining his career, strangely enhanced it. RKO parlayed Mitchum's rebelliousness to full effect in several projects, including such warm Christmas fare as *Holiday Affair* (1949), in which widow Janet Leigh must decide between gentlemanly lawyer Wendell Corey and nonconformist drifter Mitchum.

Underneath Mitchum's "don't-give-a damn" attitude is a subtle current of sadomasochism. Mitchum is destroyed by alcohol, money, and wild women in *Lusty Men* (1951). Not heeding U.S. marshals, moonshiner Mitchum tries to make one final run and skids across an oil-slicked road block to an electrified end in *Thunder Road* (1958). After defiantly grinding a cigarette into the hand of one of Raymond Burr's goons, Mitchum is severely beaten in *His Kind of Woman* (1951). These undercurrents of sadomasochism become pure sadism in Mitchum's splendidly repellent roles as perverted preacher Harry Powell (*Night of the Hunter* [1955]) and reptilian ex-con Max Cady (*Cape Fear* [1962]).

In the 1940s and 1950s, the weary and sardonic Mitchum would have made the perfect Philip Marlowe. Unfortunately, he did not play the role until he was in his late fifties, but his performance in *Farewell, My Lovely* (1975) is among the best of his later characterizations.

Mitchum's image as a man's man (no wonder a deodorant bears his name) and loner hides his vulnerability. About his acting, Mitchum said, "my career is mostly a result of successfully showing up on time and not bumping into the camera."

Bibliography

Ebert, Roger. *A Kiss Is Still a Kiss: Roger Ebert at the Movies*. New York: Andrews, McMeel, & Parker, 1984.

McBride, Joseph. *Hawks on Hawks*. Berkeley: U of California P, 1982.

Peary, Danny. *Guide for the Film Fanatic*. New York: Simon & Schuster, 1986.

Roberts, Jerry. *Robert Mitchum: A Bio-Bibliography*. Westport: Greenwood, 1992.

Silver, Alain, and Elizabeth Ward, eds. *Film Noir: An Encyclopedic Reference to the American Style*. New York: Overlook, 1988.

Grant Tracey

Monk, Thelonious Sphere, Jr. (1917-1982), the man bebop haters loved to caricature, was an authentic musical genius. Although labeled as a bopper, he refused to regard himself as such and often told his sidemen not to "be playing no bop on my music!"

He was born in Rocky Mount, NC, but at four years old he moved with his family to Manhattan. Quite properly, Monk's identification with New York is now officially recognized, for at the height of the infamous cabaret card system, when Monk could not work in Manhattan's clubs, he refused to go on the road. The area is now known as Theolonius Monk Circle.

In 1944, at almost 27 years of age, Monk made his first studio recording. Coleman Hawkins, a swing player who loved the new music, chose Monk to play piano in his quartet. Hawkins encouraged many of the younger musicians and gave them opportunities to be heard by the jazz audience.

It was also in 1944 that the first recording of "'Round about Midnight," sometimes listed as "'Round Midnight," was made. Cootie Williams, another Ellingtonian trying his hand at his own band, is credited with co-authorship. In any case, Monk was the first person to record this now-standard jazz composition. For years most jazz fans knew Monk as the composer of "'Round Midnight" and a shadowy pianist whom many musicians praised but few fans outside New York City ever saw.

After working with Dizzy Gillespie and Charlie Parker, among others, in the middle 1940s, Monk finally recorded as a leader with his sextet for Blue Note. In 1950, he appeared as a sideman with Charlie Parker and in 1952, with Miles Davis on Prestige and again in 1954. He and Davis, however, did not get along. Davis found Monk's sense of harmony distracting and he asked him not to play while he was soloing. In 1954, Monk recorded his first solo album.

Finally, in 1955, he moved to Riverside Records and they knew how to promote him. From that time on, there were no more complaints about not being able to find Monk's records or seeing him perform. A number of these 1950s records are generally considered masterpieces and required for complete jazz collections. *Brilliant Corners* with Gigi Gryce on alto sax and Sonny Rollins on tenor sax proved particularly stunning to those not familiar with Monk's direction.

Monk's seminal collaboration with John Coltrane at the Five Spot in 1957 resulted in the release of only one recording. That recording, however, was enough to demonstrate the influence that Monk had on Coltrane's development. For Monk, it meant greater public attention and commercial success. He went on tour. In 1959, he led a larger group, a small band, at Town Hall. In 1962, he signed with Columbia Records and in 1964, he made the cover of *Time* magazine. During 1971-72, he was reunited with Dizzy Gillespie and other old colleagues in the Giants of Jazz group, which toured overseas to great success.

At this time, Monk made a series of solo and trio records in London that showed him at the peak of his powers. And in typical enigmatic fashion, he essentially retired. There were five more performances left to his career upon his return to the U.S., three at Carnegie Hall and two at Newport.

Bibliography
Megill, Donald D., and Richard S. Demory. *Introduction to Jazz History*. Englewood Cliffs: Prentice-Hall 1993.
Monceaux, Morgan. *Jazz: My Music, My People*. New York: Knopf, 1994.
Williams, Martin T. *The Jazz Tradition*. New York: Oxford UP, 1993.

Frank A. Salamone

Monkees, The, have the distinction of being the first "made for television" rock band. The television show and its namesake band were patterned after the Beatles' successful film, *A Hard Day's Night*. Both the Beatles' film and *The Monkees* featured the bands in a series of madcap situations, each culminating in a song. A minimal plot was used to tie the sequences together, but adoring audiences seemed not to care.

In creating the TV show, which debuted in August 1966, producers Bob Rafelson and Bert Schneider decided the best way to create an instant rock sensation was to select the four members of the band based on their acting skills, image, and interaction rather than on musical skills. After auditioning over 400 would-be Monkees, the producers settled on Mickey Dolenz, Davy Jones, Peter Tork, and Mike Nesmith (see entry). Only Tork and Nesmith had any musical experience.

The Monkees' musical image was carefully crafted by Don Kirshner, who hired songwriters Tommy Boyce and Bobby Hart as the music producers. Boyce and Hart wrote the group's first single, "Last Train to Clarksville," which was released six weeks before the show's debut. All of the instruments for this and the other early Monkees' hits were played by the group The Candy Store Prophets.

The group's records became showcases for Kirshner's troupe of songwriters. Hits included Neil Diamond's "I'm a Believer" and "A Little Bit Me, a Little Bit You," Neil Sedaka's "When Love Comes Knockin' at Your Door," and John Stewart's "Daydream Believer."

The success of *The Monkees* TV show and the Monkees' records was followed by a concert tour in early 1967. By now, the group was becoming more proficient at playing instruments, and they battled with Kirshner over the right to play their own music on records as well as in concert. The Monkees won the battle and played most of the instrument tracks on their third album, *Headquarters*.

But the Monkees' own music was not popular. They produced one more album as a group, *Pisces, Aquarius, Capricorn and Jones Ltd.*, and an album of cuts by the individual group members, *The Birds, the Bees, and the Monkees*. As their record sales dropped, so did their TV ratings, and *The Monkees* was axed after 58 episodes in August 1968.

Bibliography
Baker, Glenn A. *Monkeemania: The True Story of the Monkees*. New York: St. Martin's, 1986.
Dolenz, Micky, and Mark Dego. *I'm a Believer: My Life of Monkees, Music, and Madness*. New York: Hyperion, 1993.
Reilly, Edward. *The Monkees: A Manufactured Image—The Ultimate Reference Guide to Monkee Memories and Memorabilia*. Ann Arbor: Pierian, 1987.

Ken Nagelberg

Monroe, Bill (1911-1996), born in Rosine, KY, to a long line of musicians, was a singer, guitarist, mandolinist, fiddler, songwriter, and bandleader who blended together existing elements of blues, country, and folk music to become the "Father of Bluegrass." As a young man, Monroe learned music not only from his family, but also from the local black musicians of western Kentucky, and specifically, black blues guitarist Arnold Shultz. These two influences, according to Monroe, contributed largely to his development as a musician, and, in turn, the development of bluegrass.

In 1927, Bill and his brothers Charlie and Birch formed a band and performed locally and toured the South and Midwest as they gained popularity. Two years later, at the age of 18, Monroe joined his brothers in Indiana where they became regulars on a radio program. When Birch dropped out of the trio, Bill and Charlie continued performing as the Monroe Brothers, and from 1934 to 1938 the two recorded 60 songs for Victor's Bluebird label, including their first hit, "What Would You Give in Exchange for Your Soul?" In

1938, Charlie formed a band called the Kentucky Pardners and Bill began the first of many Blue Grass Boys bands with Cleo Davis, Art Wooten, and Amos Garin. Bill's band with its new bluegrass sounds gained instant popularity, and in 1939, was asked to join the *Grand Ole Opry*. Later members of the Blue Grass Boys included Lester Flatt, Earl Scruggs, Don Reno, Gordon Terry, Carter Stanley, Mac Wiseman, Jimmie Martin, Sonny Osborne, and Sam and Kirk McGee.

Throughout the 1940s, the Blue Grass Boys traveled with *Opry* tent shows in the South and signed first with Columbia Records, and then with Decca, which later became MCA. During this time, the group recorded such hit songs as "Blue Moon of Kentucky," "Will You Be Loving Another Man," "Molly and Ten Brooks (The Racehorse Song)," "Sweetheart You Done Me Wrong," and "I'm Going Back to Old Kentucky." Their best-selling songs were "Kentucky Waltz" and "Footprints in the Snow." In the 1950s, Monroe composed and recorded his more autobiographical songs as "Uncle Pen," "My Little Georgia Rose," "I'm on My Way to the Old Home," "Letter from My Darling," and "In Despair." His albums included *Knee Deep in Blue Grass* (1958, Decca), *Bluegrass Rumble* (1962, Decca), *The High Lonesome Sound of Bill Monroe* (1966, Decca), and *Bill Monroe & His Bluegrass Boys* (1970). His popularity reached such heights that when Elvis Presley auditioned for the *Grand Ole Opry* in 1954, he sang "Blue Moon of Kentucky."

Monroe formed an alliance with Ralph Rinzler in the 1960s, a young mandolin player who introduced him to the folk-revival movement and many younger musicians, persuaded Decca to re-release Monroe's recordings of the 1950s on LP, and became Bill's agent, booking him with many prestigious folk festivals. This involvement with folk festivals exposed Monroe to a whole new generation of listeners, and he continued to be popular with younger audiences throughout the 1970s and 1980s, touring college campuses throughout the U.S. He served as the host for the annual bluegrass festival in Bean Blossom, IN, which resulted in two live albums during the mid-1970s: *Bean Blossom* and *Bean Blossom '79*. In 1970, Monroe was elected to the Country Music Hall of Fame, and in 1971, he was inducted into the Nashville Songwriters Hall of Fame. His fame had spread to such lengths that he toured Europe, Canada, and Japan in the 1970s. Monroe received a Grammy Award in 1988 for best bluegrass recording (vocal or instrumental) for his album *Southern Flavor*, and in 1993 was the charter inductee into the Bluegrass Hall of Fame and received the Grammy's Lifetime Achievement Award. His later albums include *Bill Monroe and Friends* (1983, MCA), *Bluegrass '87* (1987, MCA), and *Mule Skinner Blues* (1991, RCA). Following a cancer scare in the early 1980s and a broken hip in 1994, Bill Monroe died.

Bibliography

Carlin Richard. "Bill Monroe." *The Big Book of Country Music: A Biographical Encyclopedia*. New York: Penguin, 1995.

McCloud, Barry. "Bill Monroe." *Definitive Country: The Ultimate Encyclopedia of Country Music and Its Performers*. New York: Perigee, 1995.

Shestack, Melvin. "Bill Monroe." *The Country Music Encyclopedia*. Toronto: KBO, 1974.

Stambler, Irwin, and Grelun Landon. "Bill Monroe." *The Encyclopedia of Folk, Country & Western Music*. 2d ed. New York: St. Martin's, 1983.

Lynnea Chapman King

Monroe, Marilyn (1926-1962), has been the subject of more books than any other Hollywood movie star. As an icon of American popular culture, her few rivals in popularity include Elvis Presley and Mickey Mouse. Accordingly, her image adorns everything from collector plates and coffee mugs to T-shirts and children's lunch buckets.

The interest in her is not hard to fathom: no other star has ever inspired an audience to such a wide range of emotions—from lust to pity, from envy to remorse. Her name immediately evokes images of her beauty and playfulness—Marilyn bedecked in diamonds and surrounded by tuxedoed male suitors or Marilyn squirming in pleasure as she stands on a subway grate and gusts of air billow her dress skyward.

Marilyn Monroe was born in Los Angeles as Norma Jean Baker or Mortenson. She never knew her father and his identity has never been determined. When Norma Jean was only 16 years old, a friend of her mother arranged for her to marry a factory worker, James Dougherty. Initially she enjoyed the security that married life offered her, but after Dougherty left home for military service during World War II, Norma Jean underwent a change. She began modeling and soon filed for divorce.

In 1946, Norma Jean signed with Twentieth Century-Fox as part of its stable of young starlets and changed her name to Marilyn Monroe. Her first part was in *Scudda Hoo! Scudda Hay!* (1948). Her performance, however, a single word ("Hi!"), ended up on the cutting room floor. After a year of little work, she was released from her contract. Next, Columbia Pictures signed her to a six-month contract and featured her as second lead in *Ladies of the Chorus* (1949), but when the contract expired, Norma Jean was left unemployed.

Without a studio contract, she nonetheless found small roles in two movies: *Love Happy* (1949) with the Marx Brothers and *A Ticket to Tomahawk* (1950). In *Love Happy*, Marilyn appears on screen for only seconds, wiggling across the screen while Groucho rolls his eyes in wonder.

John Huston's *Asphalt Jungle* (1950) proved to be an important turning point in her career. She was only featured in three scenes, but the scenes were crucial and her kittenish performance lingered in the minds of movie producers. She soon played a somewhat similar role in *All about Eve* (1950). Once again her time on screen was small, but her lines were choice material, presenting her character (Miss Caswell) as a counterpoint to the movie's central character. Miss Caswell will do whatever it takes to get ahead, including give herself to producers.

Thereafter, Marilyn was always in demand; she starred in 11 movies during the next two years. Many of these movies were nothing more than fluff, but she also starred in two demanding dramas, *Clash by Night* (1952) and *Don't Bother to Knock* (1952). In the latter, she played a psychotic babysitter, a woman so scarred by her past that she takes out her frustration and confusion on children. As would happen in some of her other movies (most notably *The Misfits* [1961]), Marilyn's own fragility and sadness are displayed so clearly that it is often difficult to watch her.

Monkey Business (1952) gave her one last chance to hone her comedic acting as a supporting player before the real push toward stardom began. At this time, Marilyn met Joe DiMaggio and their courtship soon became fodder for gossip columnists across the country. Two years later they married.

Niagara (1953) was the first movie sold with Marilyn's name above the titles. Advertisements prominently featured Marilyn, equating her sexual allure with the rush of water over Niagara Falls.

Marilyn quickly followed *Niagara* with one of her best-loved roles, as Lorelei in *Gentlemen Prefer Blondes* (1953). This is the movie most responsible for making her a star, showcasing her comedic and singing talents with incendiary results. Her performance of "Diamonds Are a Girl's Best Friend" is quite possibly the quintessential image of Marilyn. This role allowed her to solidify her persona as the gold digger who can be stupid to please men but witty when necessary. "I can be smart when it's important," says Lorelei, "but most men don't like it."

How to Marry a Millionaire (1953) allowed her to continue in a similar vein as she played a hopelessly myopic gold digger who is too vain to wear glasses and therefore constantly crashes into walls, and *There's No Business Like Show Business* (1954) allowed her to showcase her singing again (but, curiously, in a supporting role). *River of No Return* (1954) was forced upon her by Twentieth Century-Fox, and she struggled through the production.

Her next movie, Billy Wilder's *Seven Year Itch* (1955), treats her as a male fantasy, a sexually available young woman with the mind of a child. Monroe brings the role an ethereal quality that transcends the often juvenile tone of the humor. This was the movie that showed her standing over the subway grate.

Marilyn's work took a toll on her relationship with DiMaggio, and after only nine months, Marilyn announced a divorce. As the pressures of the spotlight began to wear her down, she left Hollywood for New York, where she studied method acting at the Actors Studio with the Strasbergs.

After a year in New York, Marilyn finally returned to Hollywood, but not before she and Arthur Miller had fallen in love. Several months later they married. Marilyn then starred in a role carefully chosen to showcase her progress as an actress—Cherie in *Bus Stop* (1956). With Josh Logan directing, Marilyn had one of her most pleasant experiences as an actress.

The Prince and the Showgirl (1957) found her mismatched with Laurence Olivier and struggling against what she perceived as his patronizing attitude. Soon thereafter she spent a two-year hiatus from moviemaking while playing the role of a New York wife and battling depression and insomnia with drugs.

Marilyn returned before the cameras in Billy Wilder's *Some Like It Hot* (1959). Her tardiness and absenteeism were long legendary, but now the troubles were compounded as she requested take after take until she was convinced her performance was perfect.

Her next movie was *Let's Make Love* (1960). Meanwhile, Arthur Miller was at work on the screenplay for her next movie, *The Misfits* (1961). The distance between her character, Roslyn, and the actress is small. Roslyn is a fragile, vulnerable woman, hurt by past relationships and unsure of her future. Shot in austere settings, the movie presents a bleak world of lonely people struggling to survive. The movie contains Marilyn's greatest dramatic performance.

Marilyn started *Something's Got to Give* in the spring of 1962, but problems soon developed as she appeared on the set just 12 times in the first month of shooting. Twentieth Century-Fox eventually decided to continue *Something's Got to Give* without Marilyn, so they fired her and filed a breach-of-contract lawsuit. Two months later, her housemaid found her dead in bed, a collection of prescription drugs on the nightstand.

Bibliography

Guiles, Fred. *The Life and Death of Marilyn Monroe*. New York: Stein & Day, 1984.

Monroe, Marilyn. *My Story*. (Written by Ben Hecht with additional material by Milton Greene.) New York: Stein & Day, 1974.

Rollyson, Carl. *Marilyn Monroe: A Life of the Actress*. New York: Da Capo, 1993.

Spoto, Donald. *Marilyn Monroe: The Biography*. New York: HarperCollins, 1993.

Gary Johnson

Moonlighting (1985-1989) was a hip 1980s comic/detective show inspired by the 1940 film *His Girl Friday*, which had starred Cary Grant and Rosalind Russell. The ABC show was reminiscent of the sexual warfare displayed by other famous screen couples: Tracy and Hepburn, Bogart and Bacall, Gable and Lombard. In *Moonlighting*, Cybill Shepherd (playing Maddie Hayes) and Bruce Willis (playing David Addison) costarred as mismatched private-eye partners. Maddie was strictly upscale, a former high fashion model, who was an iceberg to the core. Until cast in *Moonlighting*, Bruce Willis was a virtual unknown, but the chemistry was there between the two. Addison's cocky and crude New Jersey attitude both repelled and attracted Maddie Hayes and the sexual tension between the two resulted in the fastest verbal foreplay ever displayed on prime-time television.

The most interesting twist of the show was the fact that the verbal combat rather than physical sex caused the relationship tension. Unlike the Hollywood movies or even the made-for-TV movies of the 1980s, several television series used the mind-over-body route to keep the action sizzling between the male/female co-stars. Other series utilizing "The Big Tease" included *Remington Steele, Scarecrow and Mrs. King, Who's the Boss?* and *Cheers*.

The scripts for *Moonlighting* ran almost double (100 pages) the length for a standard 60-minute detective show. Much of the dialogue was overlapping, with Maddie and David simultaneously talking to themselves or breaking the "fourth wall" by talking directly to the camera, even commenting on the plot itself. Many episodes began with the stars doing out-of-character skits and commenting on the show, even before the story began. The witty, inventive dialogue and script were immensely popular with viewers; ratings improved from 20th place in 1985-86, to 9th place the following year.

Conflict between director and stars led to the producer's (Glenn Gordon Caron) departure from the show (along with three of the writers) in the 1988-89 season, leaving the show to finish 41st in the ratings in its last season. Clever to the end, the show's final episode spoke of its own demise. A silhouetted producer asked the characters, "Can you really blame the audience? A case of poison ivy's more fun than watching you two lately."

Bibliography

Brooks, Tim, and Earle Marsh. *The Complete Directory to Prime Time Network TV Shows, 1946-Present.* 5th ed. New York: Ballantine, 1992.

Brown, Les. *Les Brown's Encyclopedia of Television.* New York: Visible Ink, 1991.

McNeil, Alex. *Total Television.* New York: Penguin, 1991.

People Magazine 22 May 1989: 112-113.

People Magazine Sept. 1993: 98-101.

Thompson, Robert J. *Television's Second Golden Age.* New York: Continuum, 1996.

Larry Gunter

Moorcock, Michael (1939-   ), born in London but now a resident of Texas, is the World Fantasy Award-winning author of science fiction and fantasy literature. When only 17, he edited the little-known British magazine *Tarzan Adventures*, and in 1964, he became the chief editor of *New Worlds*, an important publication in British science fiction. He has played a major role in the early and continued growth of the genre, publishing over a hundred books himself.

Moorcock is perhaps best known for his Eternal Champion series of tales of the apocalyptic struggle between good and evil. These include *The Elric Saga*, *The Books of Corum*, the *Runestaff Histories*, and the *Eternal Champion Trilogy*. His speculative science fiction includes *The Dancers at the End of Time*, a series of novels that recount the final, hedonistic days of a dying and decadent human race. Many of his novels use fantastical plots and settings to probe obliquely contemporary global issues such as Cold War alliances and enmities or the domestic politics of Margaret Thatcher's England. Other works include *Behold the Man* (1969), for which Moorcock won the Hugo Award and *Gloriana* (1978), a book satirizing the court of Elizabeth I that earned him the World Fantasy Award for literature.

Bibliography

Bilyeu, Richard. *The Tanelorn Archives: A Primary and Secondary Bibliography of the Works of Michael Moorcock, 1949-1979.* Altona: Pandora, 1981.

Bleiler, E. F., ed. *Science Fiction Writers.* New York: Scribner, 1982.

Nicholls, Stan. "Memoirs of a Loony Dictator." *Starlog* 7 (1991): 79-85.

Platt, Charles. *Dream Makers: The Uncommon Men and Women Who Write Science Fiction.* Vol. 1. New York: Berkley, 1980.

Stephen Chenault

Moore, C(atherine) L(ucille) (1911-1987), published her first story in the November 1933 issue of *Weird Tales*. The tale, a wild space opera set on Mars and featuring a hero named Northwest Smith, was entitled "Shambleau." The story received great reader response and became a turning point for science fiction. Moore, born in Indianapolis, would soon become one of the most important and highly revered writers of science fiction. As was the case with her contemporary, Leigh Brackett (1915-1978), Moore championed women writers of science fiction. Like Brackett, she was influenced by the popular pulp magazines and sci-fi authors of her youth—particularly *Amazing Stories* and Edgar Rice Burroughs. In turn, she influenced a whole generation of new, women sci-fi authors. In the 1930s and 1940s particularly, Moore was a regular contributor to both *Weird Tales* and *Astounding (Science Fiction)*, and she published in other magazines as well, such as *Unknown (Worlds)* and *Famous Fantastic Mysteries*. She had two primary series characters; one was Northwest Smith (introduced in "Shambleau") and the other was a strong-willed female warrior named Jirel of Joiry (introduced in "Black God's Kiss" in the October 1934 issue of *Weird Tales*). During the years of her marriage (1940-58) to famous sci-fi author Henry Kuttner (1914-1958), Catherine L. Moore collaborated with Kuttner on a number of short stories and novels, often under the Lewis Padgett pseudonym. However, in 1957, Moore published her own novel entitled *Doomsday Morning*. After the death of Kuttner, Moore turned to writing for television; her grand science fiction writing was all but over.

Bibliography

Moore, C. L. *The Best of C. L. Moore.* New York: Ballantine, 1975 (edited with an introduction by Lester Del Rey).

Padgett, Lewis (psd. for C. L. Moore and Henry Kuttner). *Robots Have No Tails.* New York: Gnome, 1952.

Garyn G. Roberts

Morgan, Lorrie (1962-   ), is one of those singers whose life could serve as the subject for any number of country songs. Her father, George Morgan, was a popular country singer himself (although Hank Williams once called him a "cross-eyed crooner" and deemed "stupid" his 1949 No. 1 hit "Candy Kisses"). George Morgan had a heart attack while helping a friend install a CB antenna on his roof; he recovered well enough to watch his 13-year-old daughter sing "Paper Roses" as her debut on the *Grand Ole Opry* on his birthday, but in a few days he underwent open-heart surgery and died at 50 years of age on July 7, 1975. Lorrie appeared regularly at the *Opry* after that and recorded a duet with her father posthumously in 1979, "I'm Completely Satisfied with You," that made the charts.

Morgan signed her first record contract in 1979, but the relationship was unsuccessful, and she spent several more years at the threshold of stardom, but never quite achieving it. In 1986, Morgan married Keith Whitley, an up-and-coming country star who was just coming into the limelight about the time he and Morgan were wed. His success spurred her to greater achievement, including 1989's *Leave the Light On*, her debut album. But Whitley was a hard-core alcoholic. All efforts to keep his habit in check failed, however, and Whitley died in 1989 of alcohol poisoning at home. Morgan, on encouragement from Whitley, was on a promotional tour when the tragedy occurred.

Shortly after Whitley's death, Morgan's recording of "Dear Me" shot to the Top 10, and the singer had to handle the painful mix of burgeoning success and notoriety, which she had waited for all her life, with the grief that still dominated her and her children's lives. In rapid succession, "Out of Your Shoes" and "Five Minutes" made it to the No. 1 spot in 1989-90. As with her father, Morgan recorded a posthumous duet with Whitley, "'Till a Tear Becomes a Rose," a sentimental and popular success.

Morgan's 1991 album *Something in Red* hit it big with the title song and other hits such as "We Both Walk" and "Except for Monday," along with covers of "Tears on My Pillow" and George Jones's "A Picture of Me without You." *Watch Me* (1992) featured the title cut, "Half Enough," and "I Guess You Had to Be There"; 1994's *War Paint* included "My Night to Howl" and "If You Came Back from Heaven."

Bibliography

Bufwack, Mary A., and Robert K. Derman. *Finding Her Voice: The Illustrated History of Women in Country Music.* New York: Holt, 1995.

Dougherty, Steve, and Jane Sanderson. "The Heartbreak Is Real for Country Singer Lorrie Morgan, Whose Husband, Keith Whitley, Died as Her Career Took Off." *People* 7 May 1990: 177-79.

Larkin, Colin, ed. *The Guinness Encyclopedia of Popular Music.* 4 vols. Middlesex, U.K.: Guinness, 1992.

Stephen Finley

Morrow, "Cousin Brucie" (1932-), is a rock 'n' roll disc jockey who is located in the New York area but has achieved national prominence. He was born in Brooklyn, NY, and attended New York University where he majored in communication arts.

Cousin Brucie began his professional career at New York's WINS. He soon moved to WABC and remained there from 1961 to 1974. It was at WABC that he reached the height of his fame and popularity, creating such characters as Bermuda Shwartz. At the time, WABC was *the* rock 'n' roll station in the metropolitan New York area. He moved to WNBC but remained there a relatively brief time. He is now working at WCBS-FM, which has a Golden Oldies format. He has a local and national program, *Cruisin' America*.

Bibliography

Morrow, Cousin Brucie, and Laura Baudo. *My Life in Rock 'n' Roll Radio.* New York: Beach Tree, 1987.

Frank A. Salamone

Morse, Carlton E. (1901-1993), a prolific writer of dramatic radio programs, was born in Jennings, LA, but grew up on a farm in southern Oregon. After his family moved to Sacramento, Morse began to write for the school newspaper. He worked as a newspaper reporter until, in 1929, NBC in San Francisco hired him as a staff producer-writer.

During his tenure in radio (1929-59), Morse was the driving force behind 45 serials, or strip shows, for which he often acted as the producer, writer, director, and casting agent. Despite this show of creative energy, Morse's fame rests not on the vast body of his work but primarily on the lasting reputations of two of his programs, *One Man's Family* and *I Love a Mystery*. *One Man's Family*, the highlight of Morse's career, was based on John Galsworthy's *The Forsyte Saga* and, as such, chronicled the life and times of Henry Barbour's family and his family's family in a run which lasted from 1932 to 1959 and comprised 3,256 episodes.

A virtual fixture in radio, Morse failed in his attempts to write for television. Most significantly, the TV version of *One Man's Family* (1949-52; 1954-55) flopped before both prime and daytime audiences. It was only after Morse, in his mid-eighties, established his own publishing company, Seven Stones Press, that he again had a reliable outlet for his writing. He published six novels, including *Killer at the Wheel*, in his last decade.

Bibliography

"Carlton E. Morse; Created Radio's 'One Man's Family.'" *Los Angeles Times* 28 May 1993.

Dunning, John. *Tune in Yesterday.* Englewood Cliffs: Prentice-Hall, 1976.

Lamparski, Richard. *Whatever Became of...?* New York: Bantam, 1976.

Stanley D. Harrison

Morton, (Ferdinand) "Jelly Roll" (1885-1941), is one of the more fascinating and influential jazz figures who contributed immensely to the creation of the American art form. According to jazz historian Alan Lomax, he was actually born Ferdinand La Menthe, near New Orleans. His father was a carpenter and itinerant trombone player and deserted the family when his son, Ferdinand, was very young. Ferdinand took the name of his stepfather (Morton). The family was a fairly well-to-do African-American Creole family whose residence has been reported to be at the corner of Frenchman and Robertson in New Orleans.

As a youth Morton experimented with the trombone, harmonica, violin, and guitar, but ultimately the piano became his chosen instrument. Unlike many African-American jazz musicians who came from poor backgrounds, Morton was fortunate enough to have received classical piano instruction, which proved to be quite valuable in his later years.

His mother died when he was quite young and he went to live with his great-grandmother, who was a strict Creole Catholic. When she discovered that he had been playing piano in the sporting houses of Storyville, she threw him out of the house when he was only 15 years old. From that time on he was constantly on the move and, in addition to his music, worked as a pool player, bell hop, pimp, tailor, nightclub manager, and even as a boxing promoter.

One of Morton's trips carried him to California, where he stayed from 1917 to 1922. He played in San Diego, Los Angeles, and in one of the remaining Barbary Coast dives in San Francisco. During that time he performed from Tampico, Mexico, to Vancouver, B.C. Critic William Russell has argued that the California trip was one of Jelly's happiest times. He sported a big car and diamonds, and the trip was one of the more prosperous times of his life.

Perhaps his most famous band was the Red Hot Peppers, which was formed in 1926 for a series of recordings by Victor. The instrumentation included Omer Simeon, clarinet; Andrew Hilaire, drums; Johnny Lindsey, bass; Morton, piano; Johnny St. Cyr, banjo; Edward "Kid" Ory, trombone, and George Mitchell, trumpet. Recording in Chicago, this band cut 57 very successful sides. Morton was a perfectionist and insisted that the ensembles be performed precisely as he planned. On *Dead Man Blues* he added Barney Bigard and Darnell Howard on clarinets, featuring this clarinet trio. The Red Hot Peppers continued in New York and then went on the road in 1929 and 1930. Many of Morton's future replacements, such as Bubber Miley, Joe Nanton, Johnny Hodges, and Wellman Braud, later played for Duke Ellington.

In 1938, Alan Lomax found Jelly and had him make a jazz recording for the Library of Congress. He cut 12 long-play albums of his compositions and traditional jazz numbers. In addition to his singing and playing, he narrated a summary of his own life and provided information on other key jazz figures with whom he had been associated. He spent the last year of his life in California, where he died in a Los Angeles hospital.

Bibliography

Blesh, Rudi, and Harriet Janis. *They All Played Ragtime*. New York: Grove, 1959.

Feather, Leonard. *From Satchmo to Miles*. New York: Da Capo, 1980.

Hentoff, Nat. *The Jazz Life*. New York: Da Capo, 1975.

Lomax, Alan. *Mister Jelly Roll*. Berkeley: U of California P, 1973.

Bruce M. Mitchell

Motion Picture Advertising comes in a number of different forms. Advertising that promotes movies appears in newspapers, magazines, and on posters in store-fronts. Point-of-purchase ads at the theater site, including posters, marquis and lobby displays, are regularly used. In addition, there are trailers, previews of coming attractions, and on-screen product advertisements that are shown before or after feature films.

The common advertising term "cooperative ads" can aptly be applied to local movie marketing. While it is more prevalent in newspaper advertising, radio and TV play an important role in cooperative movie advertising. Local theaters are usually no longer able to provide sufficient promotion on their own. Movies have a short shelf life and ad companies are pressured to make their mark the first time. If an ad fails, new ads must be developed quickly and these must be immediately successful. Many of the former promotional gimmicks, such as grand premieres, major star appear-

ances, and slick magazine ads used in the golden years of motion pictures are no longer feasible.

Motion picture market research of the past has proved difficult for a number of reasons. While the film industry has analyzed the effectiveness of film titles, star names, and other easily probed subjects, the nature of the business makes such efforts especially difficult and costly. Since films are a curious blend of artistic and commercial ingredients, the industry is prevented from employing more traditional forms of product testing. Advertising, therefore, has proved to be the major movie promotional tool.

Film advertising is now more important than ever, since potential patrons have other choices for movie entertainment. If they desire to see a movie, they do not necessarily need the theater. They can view it on television, cable, or on-air, or they can wait a few months for new releases to appear at video stores.

In more recent years, classic movie posters have again gained attention. What began in 1900 in America is still a valuable contribution to popular culture. Although circuses, carnivals, Wild West shows, legitimate stage shows, and so forth used poster art for advertising long before motion pictures, the movie industry has made invaluable contributions to this ad vehicle. Contributing to any poster's worth are style, artistry, aesthetic and informational appeals. While film firms competed with one another, the industry leader in the "glory days" was MGM. It was almost always considered the industry pacesetter. Movie poster collections became most prevalent in the last two decades and contribute immensely to the study of the history of motion pictures and to the archives of American popular culture.

Publicity and exploitation in the film industry basically copied general advertising practices in other industries. Star publicity and tie-ins were in place by 1915. Always paramount in motion picture advertising is the local angle of time and place where a particular film can be seen. While national campaigns might have some benefit, the local angle was still priority. It was the early 1930s when national advertising became a consistent and normal practice among major firms. One of the significant innovations in film advertising practices has been redefining audience from "everyone" to those most likely to be attracted to the movie. When films gained First Amendment status in 1952, some of these constraints disappeared, but ads must still consider good taste and specific market requirements.

By the 1970s, film companies subscribed to a host of marketing procedures, most of which have been used in the past in one form or another. Within the 1980s, market segments not previously considered were commissioned specifically for them. For instance, Twentieth Century-Fox prepared two campaigns for *Making Love* (1982)—one aimed at homosexuals.

In recent years, the film industry has divided marketing into promotion/exploitation, publicity, and advertising much the same as had been practiced as early as the 1920s. In reality, this indicates that advertising techniques are still geared to voicing the industry's historical objective—

attracting the attention of potential customers and winning their patronage.

Bibliography

Noah, Emil T., Jr. *Movie Gallery*. Fort Lauderdale: Noah, 1980.

Rebello, Stephen, and Richard Allen. *Reel Art: Great Posters from the Golden Age of the Silver Screen*. New York: Abbeville, 1988.

Schapiro, Steve, and David Chierichetti. *The Movie Poster Book*. New York: Dutton, 1979.

Staiger, Janet. "Announcing Wares, Winning Patrons, Voicing Ideals: Thinking about the History and Theory of Film Advertising." *Cinema Journal* 29.3 (Spring 1990).

Sweeney, Russell C. *Coming Next Week: A Pictorial History of Film Advertising*. South Brunswick: Barnes, 1937.

Sammy R. Danna

Motown is really the story of Berry Gordy, Jr. Gordy, born in Detroit in 1929, was the product of a black middle-class family that stressed achievement. For the longest while Gordy was the nonachiever in the family, failing as a boxer and a record store owner before becoming an unhappy Lincoln-Mercury assembly-line worker. His 3-D Record Mart had specialized in jazz. Although it did not last very long, Gordy learned a number of valuable lessons from the experience. Perhaps the most important was that if one wanted to make a lot of money with music, one needed to understand the taste of one's prospective clientele. Gordy began studying what was being played on radio in the Detroit area. He was specifically interested in analyzing what ingredients were necessary to sell to both black and white Americans.

Once his analysis was completed, Gordy turned to songwriting, scoring hits in the late 1950s with Jackie Wilson ("Reet Petite," "To Be Loved," "Lonely Teardrops," "That's Why I Love You So," and "I'll Be Satisfied"), Marv Johnson ("You've Got What It Takes"), and Barrett Strong ("Money"). At the same time that he was writing songs, Gordy was also freelancing as an independent producer using rented equipment. In 1958, he met Smokey Robinson in Jackie Wilson's manager's office. Gordy began working with Robinson's group, the Miracles, and Robinson and Gordy became songwriting partners. The first Miracles singles crafted by Gordy and Robinson were leased to Chess and End. Dissatisfied with sales, promotion, and royalty payments (let alone the fact that one of the labels tried to "steal" the group), Gordy, at Robinson's urging, borrowed $800 from his family and started the Tamla label. Over time, a number of other label imprints were put into operation, including Motown, Gordy, and Soul. Effectively, it was all one company that became extraordinarily successful. Between 1960 and 1970, the Motown group of labels released 535 singles, of which 357 (67 percent) charted. In 1966, that ratio increased to 75 percent. Most major record companies do well if one out of 15 releases charts. In that same decade, Motown achieved 79 Top 10 hits, which averages out to one every six weeks. Such success was unprecedented in the record industry.

The Tamla/Motown operation was situated in a house that Gordy rented at 2648 West Grand Boulevard in Detroit. Gordy lived on the second floor, used the first floor for offices, and renovated the garage into a cramped studio. Virtually every Motown recording through 1968 was cut in that garage. Gordy would eventually buy the property as well as six other houses on the street. Each house would have a separate function (i.e., sales, choreography, grooming, etc.). In 1968, the company's main base of operations moved to a multi-story office building on Woodward and in 1970 Motown moved west to Los Angeles.

The label's first major success was the twelfth release on Tamla, the Miracles' October 1960 single "Shop Around." A No. 1 R&B and No. 2 pop record, "Shop Around," with its AABA structure, breaks, sax solo, and background vocal riffs, harked back to the sounds of rhythm and blues in the 1950s. More important, it put the label on the map and provided some much needed cash flow.

With Martha Reeves and the Vandellas' "Heat Wave" in 1963 the Motown sound had begun to emerge in embryonic form. The song was written by two brothers, Eddie and Brian Holland, and Lamont Dozier. Gordy personally trained all of his songwriters. His analysis of the charts several years earlier led him to believe that songs should be written in the first person and that they should tell a story that in one way or another was left unresolved. This formula was extremely successful.

Gordy believed in capitalism to the nth degree. At Motown the labor force was compartmentalized. Writers wrote, singers sang, bass players played bass, etc. In the 1960s, with rare exceptions, individuals did not cross functions. Talent was thought of as labor that was paid to execute, not to think. The writers were the engineers who designed the product. Everyone else just worked on the assembly line. A number of artists found this very frustrating, leading to large numbers of defections when contracts expired in the late 1960s. To keep artists such as Stevie Wonder and Marvin Gaye, Gordy had to loosen this control in the 1970s.

Gordy adopted the concept of vertical integration. Motown was not only a record company, it was also a booking agent and management firm. This obviously created a number of conflicts of interest that would later lead a number of artists to bitterly complain.

The Supremes (eventually renamed Diana Ross and the Supremes) were Motown's greatest success story. Between 1964 and 1969, 16 Supreme records appeared in the pop Top 10, 12 of those reaching No. 1. The only artists with greater commercial success in this period were the Beatles.

In the 1960s, there was a readily identifiable "Motown sound." Gordy used the same studio, the same few writing teams, and the same basic set of musicians for every record cut in Detroit. The latter were known as the Funk Brothers. The core of the group was James Jamerson, bass; Benny Benjamin, Richard Allen, or Uriel Jones, drums; Robert White, Eddie Willis, Joe Messina and/or Marv Tarplin, guitars; Early Van Dyke, keyboards; Jack Ashford, percussion and vibes; and Mike Terry and Beans Bowles, saxophones.

Although there was some variation between writing teams and individual artists, the following nine points, specific to Holland-Dozier-Holland's productions on the Supremes, summarize the essence of the mid-sixties Motown sound: (1) The essential groove was a flat 4/4 feel with little or no backbeat. (2) The lead vocal was to be young sounding with little or no playful voicedness (this is obviously quite specific to the Supremes. Groups such as the Temptations and the Four Tops featured much more complex singers). (3) Background vocals were generally in unison with little or no edge. (4) Songs were structured with multiple refrains and introductions often contained parts of one of the refrains. (5) Instrument solos were all but eliminated. (6) The lead instrument was commonly a non-rock or R&B instrument (e.g., vibes on the Supremes' "Stop! In the Name of Love," English horn on the Four Tops' "Bernadette"). (7) The mix was extremely dense and muddy. (8) Reinforcing the highly integrated mix, arrangements utilized a large number of timbral congruencies (e.g., footstamping, handclapping, snare, hi-hat, and tambourine parts were often combined to create one composite timbre). And (9) the high end of the sound spectrum was emphasized. In addition, Motown's lyricists routinely employed a high degree of craft via the use of alliteration, double and internal rhymes, word-sound images, and so on.

In 1970, Berry Gordy moved Motown to Los Angeles, expanding into films with *Lady Sings the Blues, Mahogany,* and *The Wiz.* Several of the session musicians remained in Detroit. Two years earlier, Holland-Dozier-Holland had left the company. Several artists had followed suit. In the next two decades Motown would continue to enjoy a high degree of success, charting with a diverse array of artists including the Commodores, Lionel Richie, the Jackson 5, Teena Marie, and Rick James. But any sense of a unique, readily identifiable sound was long gone. For all intents and purposes, Motown was now just another record company, specializing in rhythm and blues. In 1988, Berry Gordy surprised and shocked many by selling the company to MCA Records.

Bibliography

George, Nelson. *Where Did Our Love Go?* New York: St. Martin's, 1985.

Singleton, Raynoma Gordy. *Berry, Me, and Motown.* Chicago: Contemporary, 1990.

Waller, Don. *The Motown Story.* New York: Scribner, 1985.

Rob Bowman

Mountain Bikes generally do not traverse an alpine pass. Instead, mountain bikes are more likely to be found on American city streets, their riders ascending nothing steeper than a curb. Since its appearance in the early 1980s as a specialized off-roader, the bike's popularity has exponentially picked up speed: inflating a sagging bike industry, shoving aside the once-ubiquitous 10-speed, and spreading out from Yosemite Park to Central Park. By 1999, more than 30 million mountain bikes were being ridden on roads and trails in the U.S.

Whereas many recreational bikers found the drop-handle bar, thin-tire, stiff-frame 10-speed of the 1970s maladapted to stop-and-go city riding and dangerous on off-road riding, the mountain bike is at home in both. Its "fat" tires, durable frames, gel-filled seats, upright handlebars, 21 gears, and thumbshifters are extremely user-friendly. The public first saw commercial versions of the copyrighted "Mountain-Bike" in 1981. Two years later, sales of mountain or "all-terrain" bikes reached 200,000. In 1993, mountain bikes accounted for 8.4 million out of the 8.7 million adult bikes sold in the U.S. that year, and sales have continued to grow.

Bibliography

King, Dave. *The Mountain Bike Experience: A Complete Introduction to the Joys of Off-Road Riding.* New York: Holt, 1996.

Leslie, David. *The Mountain Bike Book.* London: Ward Lock, 1995.

Oliver, Peter. *Bicycling: Touring and Mountain Bike Basics.* New York: Norton, 1995.

Perry, David B. *Bike Cult: The Ultimate Guide to Human-Powered Vehicles.* New York: Four Walls, 1995.

John A. Kinch

Mountaineering is the act of climbing mountains. But rather than simply a hike up a peak with little or no danger of serious accident, it is usually associated with "high risk" activity because of steep and difficult climbing which requires specialized knowledge about technical climbing gear (ropes, crampons, etc.) and mountain terrain (negotiating glaciers, steep rock walls, etc.).

While first designated a sport by English mountaineers holidaying in the Alps in the late 19th century, mountaineering has links with adventure, discovery, and exploration. Mountaineering is an intensely cross-cultural sport, so in some respects it is difficult to separate American mountaineering from international mountaineering.

As with the international scene, American mountaineering intersects with a wide array of cultural currents. Issues of the natural environment, individualism, the aesthetics of adventure, folklore, romanticism, mysticism, philosophy, and psychology are but a sampling of mountaineering's cultural diversity. Although mountaineering might be considered an esoteric subculture, it is increasingly mainstreamed through Hollywood films, the advertising industry, television and magazine exposure, corporate sponsorship of expeditions, educational programs, and the adventure tourism industry. Significantly, today and in the past it has had ties with national and international political currents. For instance, expeditions have promoted national identity; they have symbolically represented international cooperation; they have produced anti-imperialist narratives; and they have addressed feminist issues.

American mountaineering has produced an immense body of literature, whether nonfiction narratives, fiction, magazines and journal articles, or films. While there are numerous histories of mountaineering, there is little work done exclusively on the cultural history of mountaineering. Significant magazines which capture the pulse of contemporary mountaineering are *Climbing, Rock and Ice* and *Summit.* Similarly, Roper and Steck's *The Best of Ascent* is a helpful barometer of mountaineering culture. Films like *The Eiger*

Sanction and *Cliff Hanger* have brought the dangers, excitement, and spectacular scenery of mountaineering to mass audiences and spurred popular interest in the sport.

Bibliography

Blum, Arlene. *Annapurna: A Women's Place.* 1980. San Francisco: Sierra Club, 1983.

Neate, Jill. *Mountaineering Literature: A Bibliography.* 2d ed. Seattle: Cloudcap, 1987.

Roper, Steve, and Alan Steck. *The Best of Ascent: Twenty-Five Years of the Mountaineering Experience.* San Francisco: Sierra Club, 1993.

Salkeld, Audrey, and Rosie Smith, eds. *One Step in the Clouds: The Sierra Club Omnibus of Mountaineering Fiction.* London: Diadem, 1990. 2d ed. San Francisco: Sierra Club, 1991.

Unsworth, Walt. *Hold the Heights: The Foundations of Mountaineering.* Seattle: Mountaineers, 1994.

Peter L. Bayers

Mrs. Miniver (1942), adapted from Jan Struthers's sentimental *London Times* serial of English family life, was one of the most successful films of the World War II era. With production beginning at MGM before Pearl Harbor, the film's pro-British tilt promised to bring it under congressional investigation along with other films that purportedly encouraged U.S. involvement in the war. Since it opened in 1942, however, *Mrs. Miniver* dodged such scrutiny and became the most popular film of the year, winning six Academy Awards, including those for best picture, director (William Wyler), and actress (Greer Garson).

U.S. critics praised *Mrs. Miniver.* Bosley Crowther proclaimed it "the finest film yet made about the present war." British critics, on the other hand, decried its sanitized portrayal of English family life and neglect of those who suffered most during the war, namely the working classes of the industrial cities.

Bibliography

Baker, M. Joyce. *Images of Women in Film: The War Years, 1941-1945.* Ann Arbor: UMI Research, 1978.

Crowther, Bosley. *New York Times* 5 June 1942: 23.

Slide, Anthony. "Mrs. Miniver." *Magill's Survey of Cinema: English Language Films.* 1st Series. Ed. Frank Magill. Englewood Cliffs: Salem, 1980. 1131-33.

Steven L. Davis

Ms Magazine (1971-) embodies in its title recognition for women who would not be defined by their marital status. From its inception it addressed feminist concerns on a wide array of topics, with editorial direction from such prominent feminists as Gloria Steinem, Betty Friedan, and Kate Millett. In its original version, which lasted 20 years, the magazine enjoyed significant popularity.

Unlike other women's magazines, *Ms* did not focus upon the home, or upon the woman as sex object. *Ms* features included a gossip column and expository articles of interest to its primarily well-educated white middle-class heterosexual female readership. Celebrities of all ages were featured on its covers, linked to articles of wide appeal to women, such as "What to Do Until the Sex Therapist Arrives." Its literary contribution to the magazine milieu was impressive, including authors such as Alice Walker, Margaret Atwood, and Alice Munro. Unlike other women's magazines of its time, *Ms* focused on a woman's mind rather than her body. Eventually *Ms* readers marginalized into special interest groups espousing causes such as lesbian rights, abortion, racial issues; and readership declined.

In 1991, a second version of the magazine, *Ms., the World of Women,* replaced the original *Ms.* Like the original magazine, it is advertising-free but it is more news-oriented, addressing news issues and the arts, as well as providing film and book reviews. The new *Ms* addresses the issues which factionalized the original publication, such as "Eco-feminism," the "Accidental Activist," and "Race: Can We Talk?" Because of its focus on topics of special interest to particular groups, its editorial policy appears to be the converse of the synthesizing and unifying policies of the original publication, and its claim that it is the "best of the original *Ms*" has yet to be proven. This magazine is published bi-monthly.

Bibliography

Katz, Bill, and Linda Sternberg Katz, eds. *Magazines for Libraries.* 7th ed. n.p.: Bowker, 1992.

Working Press of the Nation 1995: Magazine and Internal Publications Directory. Vol. 2. 45th ed. New Providence: Bowker, 1994.

Mona Phillips

MTV. On August 1, 1981, a new cable network program was launched into the homes of millions of viewers. The thought of music videos 24 hours a day was a teenager's dream; consequently, MTV has become, possibly, the most successful entity on cable network. Since its inception, MTV has attracted advertising from the biggest in corporate America and has influenced the youth-through-college culture of America to alter its dress, language, and general lifestyle.

When MTV began, at the beginning of the Reagan era, MTV was targeted almost exclusively at young whites. MTV's early leanings were conservative, but it seldom espoused those ideals. Perhaps one reason MTV targeted whites was that in the early days of cable, the system was usually tested in upper-middle-class neighborhoods, and when it did reach the inner cities, few could afford it initially. With cable becoming more affordable, MTV wisely showed its adaptability, e.g., its *Yo! MTV Raps* program becoming the main disseminator of a relatively new interracial rock youth culture centered on rap music and "hip hop street culture."

During its first decade, MTV successfully pursued innovation while expanding into Europe and South America. The days of a bubbly and wholesome Martha Quinn (MTV's first video DJ) are over. A typical scene now is of supermodel Cindy Crawford on location in Paris interviewing Paul Gautiler on how he became the wardrobe designer for Madonna's world tour.

According to critics, MTV's novelty may be that it tries to reach everyone under 35: "headbangers' ball" to reach the white audience, "liquid TV" for those who like animation and odd themes, and "the grind," with scantily clad women.

MTV's influence on the social fabric of America is unquestionable. During cable TV's infancy, it was the rally cry "I want my MTV," from a song by Dire Straits, that made kids demand that their parents get cable TV. Otherwise faceless aspirants such as Michael Jackson and Madonna were transformed overnight into virtual icons with worldwide stature and success. MTV introduced the world to MC Hammer, the Beastie Boys, Sinead O'Connor, and Wilson Phillips. Moreover, MTV revolutionized commercials and created new styles of TV shows. The success of Ray Charles's Diet Pepsi commercial, for example, is attributed to the MTV style by ad agency execs.

Beyond the undebatable truth that MTV can show more videos per hour than any other network, there is good reason to believe that the program has attempted to communicate to modern young people that, beyond music, Pepsi, and pizza, there is a world that needs their attention. Through MTV, viewers have been urged to become environmentally aware and politically conscious. In the 1992 presidential campaign, MTV urged viewers to register and vote through several rock star-studded advertisements, and "rock the vote" was a drive that prompted nearly one million Americans to become politically involved, if only to get out and vote.

In addition to its efforts in the political arena, MTV has displayed a sense of responsibility to keep its viewers informed about safe sex. MTV regularly airs updated versions of a program, *Sex in the 90's*, which takes viewers into college-age homes to talk about their views on sexual issues which range from female condoms to homosexuality. Records show that MTV often advocates safe sex not only for protection from pregnancy, but also from disease. In its best form, MTV has urged its viewers to think responsibly.

MTV also broke new ground with the phenomenally successful cartoon show *Beavis and Butt-head* (see entry), about a pair of delinquent teenagers who watch and comment on MTV videos. There is little question that successful commercial ideas in America not only generate a lot of money, but also shape the conscience and values of a significant part of society. Few would disagree that, for better or worse, MTV has impacted on the youth culture of America both now and for many years to come.

Bibliography

Denisoff, R. Serge. *Inside MTV*. New Brunswick: Transaction, 1988.

Goodwin, Andrew. *Dancing in the Distraction Factory: Music Television and Popular Culture*. Minneapolis: U of Minnesota P, 1992.

Kaplan, E. Ann. *Rocking around the Clock: Music Television, Postmodernism, and Consumer Culture*. New York: Routledge, 1989.

J. H. Esperian

Muddy Waters (McKinley Morganfield) (1913-1983), one of the most famous blues singers, was born in Rolling Fork, MS. After his mother's death in 1918, he moved to Clarksdale, where he lived with his grandmother. Like so many other blues singers and guitarists, he was self-taught.

He began playing around his home area and soon was in the Silas Green Tent Show along with Big Bill Broonzy.

In the 1940s, he was discovered by Alan Lomax, who aided his career. In 1943, he moved to Chicago, where his career gained steam under the influence of performers like Big Bill Broonzy, Sunny Boy Williamson, and others. In 1946 he made his first professional record with Leroy Foster and Sunnyland Slim (Andrew Luandrew). Soon after, he had his own band filled with top performers.

Muddy Waters quickly acquired his own nickname, so important to blues performers. Quite rightly, because of his influence, he was tagged the Godfather of the Blues. In the 1950s he had, perhaps, the finest blues band in the country. In addition, his work on electric guitar in the Delta blues idiom had a strong influence on rock musicians, whose acknowledgment of that influence gave his own career a boost. He toured Europe successfully after the "British Invasion" of America and became a folk hero in the 1960s.

Among his hits are "Mojo Hand," "Got My Mojo Working," "My Home's in the Delta," "Rollin' and Tumblin'," "Long Distance Call," and "I Can't Be Satisfied."

Bibliography

Gammond, Peter. *Oxford Companion to Popular Music*. New York: Oxford UP, 1991.

Larkin, Colin, ed. *The Guinness Encyclopedia of Popular Music*. Middlesex, U.K.: Guinness, 1992.

Welding, Pete, and Toby Byron. *Bluesland: Portraits of Twelve Major American Blues Masters*. New York: Dutton, 1991.

Wilson, Charles Reagan, and William Ferris, eds. *Encyclopedia of Southern Culture*. Chapel Hill: U of North Carolina P, 1989.

Frank A. Salamone

Muller, Marcia (1944-), is often credited with initiating the contemporary female hard-boiled private investigator in mystery fiction. A Michigan native transplanted to California, Muller worked as a secretary, social researcher, and merchandising manager before turning to writing. She published her first detective novel, *Edwin of the Iron Shoes*, in 1977, introducing series character Sharon McCone, an independent investigator and the protagonist of 18 additional novels in a sequence that continues today. Muller has also created two amateur sleuths, Elena Oliverez and Joanna Stark, who appear in limited detective series; edited several anthologies; and written uncollected short fiction in other genres. Her McCone novels, set in California, have brought her the most sustained readership and critical attention.

While her early novels rely on the classical puzzle form of the mystery, Muller's later books have become darker and more complex. Beginning with *There's Something in a Sunday* (1989), her works reflect the hard-boiled influence of writers like Ross Macdonald. More thematically coherent, they explore societal problems such as violence against women, the politics of the 1960s, government-sponsored witch hunts, and the corporate ethos of the 1980s and 1990s.

Bibliography

Isaac, Frederick. "Situation, Motivation, Resolution: An Afternoon with Marcia Muller." *Clues* 1984.

Klein, Kathleen Gregory, ed. *Great Women Mystery Writers: Classic to Contemporary.* Westport: Greenwood, 1994.

Susan Allen Ford

See also
Feminist Detective Fiction
Regional Mystery

Multimedia Science. Interactive educational CD-ROMs (Compact Disc Read-Only Memory), a combination of video, audio, and animation, are revolutionizing how children learn. Classrooms, called Multisensory Learning Environments, have become natural habitats for the interactive generation that has grown up playing Nintendo and fast-forwarding VCRs. This new method of teaching stimulates a number of cognitive skills: symbolizing, reasoning, pondering, reflecting, calculating, judging, visualizing, imagining, devising, inventing, and inferring. CD-ROM programs stimulate many cognitive skills simultaneously using audio, video, and animation. The brain's basic tools—imagery, association, and meaning—all come into play, increasing the speed of learning and the amount of information retained. CD-ROM formats make the child the most important component of the learning experience, discovering answers through active participation instead of being a passive recipient of information provided by a teacher or book. This interaction is the key to educational CD-ROMs and their greatest advantage as a teaching tool.

The approach used to build cognitive skills when using CD-ROM programs is, to a great degree, controlled by the child. Children who may be slow in developing one area of cognition can still be successful in the learning process by using stronger cognitive skills while improving less developed ones.

Interactive educational CD-ROMs put the fun back in learning and allow children the opportunity to be major players in their educations. Realistic visuals and sound, with the ability to access information as quickly as a child can absorb it, make CD-ROM programs remarkable and effective teaching tools.

Bibliography
Brown. Eric. "The Edutainment Boom." *New Media* Dec. 1994: 50-57.
Hanson, Andrew J., Tamara Munzner, and George Francis. "Interactive Methods for Visualizable Geometry." *Computer* July 1994: 65-70.
Patton, Phil. "Let Your Child Choose." *Computer Life* Oct. 1994: 145-46.
Wallis, Claudia. "The Learning Revolution." *Time: Special Issue* Spring 1995: 49-51.

Theresa L. Glavin

Multitrack Recording is the process of recording separate audio signals on parallel tracks so that they can be played back simultaneously. Open-reel multitrack recorders may have up to 48 separate tracks that will later be combined into the final stereo recording. These tape recorders use wider tape, one-half to two inches wide, as compared to conventional open-reel recorders, which use quarter-inch magnetic tape.

Prior to 1960, most music recordings were mixed before they were recorded onto tape. The audio signals from individual microphones were combined in the desired proportions as instruments were played and as vocalists sang. Recordings were made on a single-track recorder, or on two tracks if the recording was in stereo. No changes in sound quality of or balance among the individual instruments or vocals could be made after the recording session.

Musician and inventor Les Paul was the first artist to overdub, or combine music from one session with music from earlier sessions. In his 1948 record "Lover," he recorded his first track on a phonograph disc transcription machine, then played back the record and recorded on a second machine, adding additional instrumentation. Paul later experimented with two-track magnetic tape recorders to play back a recording from one track, mix in new sounds, and record the combination on the second track.

Multitrack recorders were available for music recording by the mid-1960s, and producer George Martin used four-track recording to produce the Beatles' *Rubber Soul* album in 1965. In early 1966, the Beach Boys made the most extensive use of multitrack recording and overdubbing to date to produce the single "Good Vibrations."

The Beatles' *Sgt. Pepper's Lonely Hearts Club Band* marked a turning point in multitrack recording in 1967. The group spent four months and $75,000 to record the album in its four-track Apple studio. Voices and instruments were distorted and manipulated to produce startling new sounds that could not be reproduced in concert. Bits of tape were edited together to produce the swirling circus sounds of "Being for the Benefit of Mr. Kite," and a 40-piece orchestra was mixed into the epic "A Day in the Life."

U.S. musicians soon began using similar techniques as recorders were upgraded to eight and twelve tracks. Jimi Hendrix's Electric Lady studio, built in 1969, was the first to use 24-track recording. By the end of the decade, it was commonplace for American rock groups to record in 16-track studios like the Record Plant.

The development of high quality four-track cassette recorders brought multitrack recording within the range of many smaller production studios in the 1970s. Many U.S. rock musicians began producing multitrack recordings in their homes and making cassette copies for local distribution.

In the late 1980s and 1990s, many musicians switched to digital recording techniques to take advantage of the higher audio quality of compact discs. Computer-based recording and mixing systems allow digital storage of an almost infinite number of tracks, limited only by storage space. The computer-stored tracks can be controlled and mixed before being permanently recorded on tape.

Kenneth M. Nagelberg

Munsters, The (1964-1966), was a 1960s sitcom that successfully transformed the horror genre from film to television for comedic purposes. Like its rival, *The Addams Family*, which ran concurrently, this show perpetuated the myth of the 1950s nuclear American family, albeit, on the surface, a perverse one.

Like previous sitcoms (notably *Leave It to Beaver,* which shared the same writing staff and production company as *The Munsters*), this horror spoof emphasized the traditional values of the American middle-class family: marriage, commitment to one's spouse and family, respect for authority and, subsequently, one's elders, and love and understanding of others, no matter how perplexing their actions or appearance. Accordingly, *The Munsters* was an idyllic vision set amid a macabre backdrop.

Bibliography

Fisk, John. *Television Culture.* London: Routledge, 1989.

MacCabe, Colin, ed. *High Theory/Low Culture: Analysing Popular Television and Film.* Manchester: Manchester UP, 1986.

Marc, David. *Demographic Vistas: Television in American Culture.* Philadelphia: U of Pennsylvania P, 1984.

Mitz, Rick. "*The Addams Family/The Munsters.*" *The Great TV Sitcom Book.* 1980. New York: Perigee-Putnam, 1988.

Anita M. Vickers

Mural Painting, the modern movement in the U.S., is a form of creation identified with cities, both in the larger group of murals with their emphasis on social issues and the smaller but more visible group of often huge *trompe l'oeil* murals found in downtown business districts. The first group are usually undertaken with community support or completely unofficially, while the latter works are commissioned by the owners of commercial buildings. Both types of murals address large and diverse audiences.

The recent interest in mural painting began in 1967, when a group of 20 black artists painted the *Wall of Respect* on the South Side of Chicago, and white artists produced some decorative paintings on apartment house walls in New York City. Within two years, Hispanic and multicultural groups had joined them in producing murals in half a dozen American cities. These artists varied in their level of training and background. They drew on the style and imagery of both the government-funded American mural movement of the Great Depression—itself inspired by the work of the Mexican muralists of the early 20th century—and the broader Western tradition of mural painting that flows from ancient times, through the Italian Renaissance, and into American narrative art history.

Mural painting in the U.S. can be traced to the extant wooden panels from the Clark House of Boston, decorated in a style derived from English landscape work and dating to 1712-14. Those panels, and similarly designed works painted in Virginia later in the century, were flat but colorful, and included a number of human figures in and among the scenery. Not until 1800 did fresco decoration appear. Subjects included landscapes, emblems and insignia, representations of specific ships and homes, and copies of English and European paintings of renown. All of these murals were confined to the interiors of buildings, setting a pattern that was to be maintained through the middle of the 20th century.

The first major public murals in this country were painted for the Rotunda of the U.S. Capitol by John Trumbull, between 1817 and 1824. He painted four 12-by-18-foot canvases documenting the events of the American Revolution. Because there was some opposition to the entire plan, the four other murals in the Rotunda were approved only after sectional politics decreed that other artists get the work in the 1840s. Thereafter, almost all mural painting in this country was either historical in subject and located in public buildings or similar to the fanciful landscapes painted by the African-American landscapist Robert Duncanson for Nicholas Longworth's Cincinnati mansion in 1840. These 9-by-7-foot works were painted directly on the wall, in oil, and are the largest of any domestic murals painted before the Civil War.

The first golden age of American public mural painting took place in the last quarter of the 19th century, inspired both by the patriotism that was generated by the Centennial celebrations, and by the growing interest in the work of the French muralist Pierre Puvis de Chavannes, who was largely responsible for the revival of interest in allegorical murals. Artists trained in the academies of Europe and the U.S. were responsible for most of the works that were to appear in state capitols, public libraries, and other public buildings, with scenes from American history and allegories of American progress dominating the subjects. Leading American examples of this work were William Morris Hunt's murals for the New York State Capitol Building, those by John La Farge for Trinity Church in Boston, John S. Sargent's works in the Boston Public Library, and those by Mary Cassatt for the Woman's Building at the Columbian Exposition. This kind of work was the norm through the 1920s, when the onset of the Great Depression created new opportunities and a new attitude toward mural painting in this country.

The modern era of mural painting that began in the mid 1960s differed from all prior mural painting in several significant ways: the site of the murals was outdoors and often in poor neighborhoods; the various sources of patronage and funding changed; the degree of training of the artist or groups of artists was more varied; the range and variety of the subjects being depicted was unlimited; the intended impact on the public and the reaction to the work in their communities expanded. For the first time in Western art's history, the murals were painted on the exterior of buildings rather than as part of an internal scheme of decoration; this incorporates a tacit assumption of the impermanence of the work, a substantial change in mindset for patron, artist, and audience. All of these aspects of the 1960s mural experience are still the factors that define the movement and the genre 40 years later.

Allan D'Arcangelo painted the first decoratively oriented murals in 1967, in New York, and both decorative and illusionistic murals soon appeared in the often depressed commercial areas inhabited by artists. This type of mural, often either geometric or abstract in design, was developed by the group City Walls, and immediately received the support of architects, city planners, and members of the corporate world. When increasing involvement of professional artists turned City Walls into the Public Arts Fund and the Los Angeles-based Fine Arts Squad, the aesthetics that informed the work was that of the fine arts world, not that of the masses. The *trompe l'oeil* work of painters like Richard Haas, which opened artificial windows through the buildings or presented photorealistic panoramas of the countryside, were painted with the sponsorship and support of the official business community, with a light-hearted touch, and yet were meant to please all segments of the public. Not exclusively the province of white artists, but usually produced by professionals with no commitment to either the mural form or social agendas, these works have been referred to as urban-environmentalist paintings. With the twin values of supporting artists while enhancing and improving the appearance of the urban environment, their objectives are close to those behind the creation of the New Deal programs of the 1930s. Painted in a variety of styles, and noticeably lacking in references to human activity, the work is often site-specific but otherwise totally interchangeable from area to area, from city to city.

The work of ethnic and minority artists, on the other hand, has continued in the direction established in the earliest works done in Chicago, Detroit, and Boston. Voicing the twin concerns of lack of official support for minority artists in public museums in their cities and the wish to express the values of the community, the artists and their supporters created an outdoor museum of and for their particular community. And while ornament and decoration have been incorporated into most of the murals, the thematic orientation has been the dominant concern of all involved in the process. Far from assuming a value-free aesthetic, the artists quite forcibly espoused the need to express and evoke the deepest struggles and aspirations of the community. These artists did not, and do not, just go home from a day's painting; they usually live in the area, and participate in the planning, local organizations, and activities of which the murals are one single component.

If the artists who work on illusionistic or abstract images reflect one major direction of the public art programs of the Depression, the mostly minority artists who work in the neighborhoods of the inner city most clearly reflect an interest in the Mexican muralists of the 1920s and the Latin American propensity for utilizing walls in order to convey specific messages or articulate issues of social concern. In addition to negotiating or appropriating the walls of buildings, railroad embankments, bus stops and park benches, vacant billboards, and other surfaces have been serviced by the muralists, even in competition with solo graffiti artists who use the spaces for their more personal statements. The work of modern muralists in this country is primarily figurative, with a fairly shallow stage setting as the spatial frame for the compositions. The figures are large and often sculptural in feeling, recalling the effects of the Mexican painter David Siquieros, who had begun to incorporate actual three-dimensional forms into his work in the 1940s and 1950s. Figures often overlap each other and individual body parts or even entire figures are often exaggerated, in the service of enhancing the dramatic effect of the representation.

In the black and Latino communities, the historical origins and/or mythic roots of the people are evoked through the adoption of African or pre-Columbian heros, facial types, and symbols. Color and design elements also refer to the heritage and continuity of the community's people. In the Chicano community murals in Los Angeles and Chicago, it is not unusual to encounter portraits of figures associated with the Mexican revolution on the same wall and as a statement about contemporary life in the barrio. Race wars, police brutality, long lines at government offices, and other issues of urban poverty are depicted, often including extremely unflattering images of the police, government bureaucrats, and corporate and official America. The difference between these works and those painted in Mexico in the 1920s is that the negative images in the Mexican works referred to a colonial past while those painted in American cities address the issues of the current social order. Thus, while the work of José Orozco and Diego Rivera portrayed a discredited past, the young and middle-aged muralists in American cities were crying out for change in the conditions of the people in the community in which they lived and worked. Among the many murals that depicted the pains of discrimination in the present, the Chicago mural painted by 40 Japanese-American high school and college students is almost unique in depicting the history of their experience as negative and the present in more positive terms. In general, the anger and frustration of the people living in sight of the murals was being depicted: the artists avoided the nostalgia so often found in the 1930s public art in favor of a clarion call to action and reform. In many of the poorest urban ghettos, it has been the teenagers—often teenagers in high schools that contained WPA-sponsored murals illustrating generally sanctioned subjects from the majority culture's concept of American history—that have demanded new murals. They ask that the contemporary works depict the American history that they know. In a number of cases, the new murals commissioned in response to public pressure have been placed side by side with the traditional murals painted in the 1930s. In George Washington High School in San Francisco, to cite one of the best-documented examples, a graduate of the school spent parts of six years painting a history of black, Latin, and Native Americans adjacent to those that depict Washington as a slave-owning plantation lord.

By the mid-1970s, many of the distinctions that were part of the creation of the first murals were being blurred by the well-meaning and enthusiastic support of both the broader art establishment and certain political forces that saw a positive side to what had originally been viewed with suspicion by the political and business communities. Whereas only a few elected officials supported the work of the pioneering muralists in the major cities, in the late 1960s, more and more began to see the values of self-pride, community support, and the involvement of youth and young adults in such activities. The fact that the community valued the paintings, kept them remarkably free of vandalism and graffiti, and often pressed for funding for additional murals, became sufficient reasons for official support. Sadly, political endorsement for mural projects was seldom based on artistic reasons.

State and local arts councils, usually supported by funds from the National Endowment for the Arts and often with additional matching funds from businesses and private foundations, encouraged mural projects in the communities. Since soon after the inception of the mural movement, there were workshops that supported minority artists who would teach techniques to local residents. There were also funded summer programs to involve inner-city youth in these projects, and new competitions for community designs were organized. All of these activities were a typically American pragmatic response to the problems of inner-city life while recognizing programs that would have the support of the affected communities.

The modern mural movement continues today, as new ethnic groups in changing neighborhoods discover the appeal of community murals and often adapt prior styles and formats to their own ends. Unfortunately, there is some abrasion in multi-faceted communities, where there is no identification with the area as the locus of community pride and spirit. In the lower East Side of New York, in the Uptown area of Chicago, and in other polyglot communities, the aspirations and perceptions of one group often clash with another. In almost all cases, the good will of the artists and the community leaders have led to sometimes lengthy and drawn-out negotiations and compromises. In certain cases, a greater understanding and respect for each other's culture has been the welcome result. In some of the most dramatic cases, working together on murals has caused rival gang members to collaborate on a mural rather than trying to kill each other over turf.

Forty years after the first contemporary murals were painted, new works are being commissioned, another generation of artists have taken up the practice of mural painting, and the sites selected for murals are more diverse.

Bibliography
Cass, Caroline. *Modern Murals*. New York: Whitney Library of Design, 1988.
Cockcroft, Eva, John Weber, and James Cockcroft. *Toward a People's Art: The Contemporary Mural Movement*. New York: Dutton, 1977.
McKinzie, Richard D. *The New Deal for Artists*. Princeton: Princeton UP, 1973.

David M. Sokol

Murder Ink, the first bookstore devoted exclusively to the sale of mystery fiction, opened in New York City in 1972. By 1985, there were 30 mystery bookstores nationwide, and by 1995, the number had grown to over 80, along with another 30 mail-order and by-appointment-only dealers. The rapid proliferation of such stores reflects the great popularity of the mystery, which currently commands the largest readership of any fictional genre.

Along with book sales, some mystery bookstores produce newsletters, hold classes, sponsor author signings and readings, and administer conferences. Such specialty stores may promote new or established writers, as well as cater to their customers' interests. Along with Murder Ink, among the better known mystery bookstores are the Mysterious Bookshop in New York City; the San Francisco Mystery Bookstore in San Francisco; Mysterious Galaxy in San Diego; the Raven in Lawrence, KS; the Mysterious Bookshop in Bethesda, MD; the Mystery Bookstore in Dallas, TX; the Poisoned Pen in Scottsdale, AZ; the Rue Morgue in Boulder, CO; Booked for Murder in Madison, WI; Murder by the Book in Houston, TX; Mysterybooks in Washington, DC; the Sleuth of Baker Street in Toronto, Canada; and Murder One in London, England.

Bibliography
Ames, Katrine. "Murder Most Profitable" *Savvy Woman* Jan. 1989: 33-34.

Janet A. Rudolph

Murder, She Wrote (1984-1996) was a highly successful one-hour CBS mystery series, one of the few series in television history that featured the sole lead character as a middle-aged woman. It stands as one of the most popular series of the decade even though it is a formula whodunit. The series was created by Richard Levinson, William Link, and Peter S. Fisher, the same creative team who did *Columbo* and *Ellery Queen*.

The show stars Angela Lansbury as Jessica Fletcher, a widowed mystery writer who is often called upon by the local sheriff or town doctor to solve real crimes. Because Jessica is a mystery writer, her everyday life often parallels her best-selling detective novels.

The show's formula is the same as all successful TV whodunits—there are a number of clues which must be pieced together in order to solve the crime. Like *Perry Mason*, the action suggests several different perpetrators and the audience must usually wait until the end of the show for Jessica to solve the crime. The plots are complicated and the pacing is brisk. Other regulars include Tom Bosley, who played the sheriff, William Windom as Dr. Seth Haslett, and Michael Horton as Jessica's nephew.

The never-ending appeal of the formula led *Murder, She Wrote* to be ranked among the Top 10 shows nearly every season.

Bibliography
Brooks, Tim, and Earle Marsh. *The Complete Directory to Prime Time Network and Cable TV Shows, 1946-Present*. New York: Ballantine, 1995.
Brown, Les. *Les Brown's Encyclopedia of Television*. New York: Visible Ink, 1991.
Goodman, Mark. "Angela Lansbury." *People* Sept. 1993: 98-101.
McNeil, Alex. *Total Television*. New York: Penguin, 1991.

Larry Gunter

Murphy Brown (1988-1997) was a hit, classy comedy about television itself, in the area of broadcast news. Inevitably, it will be compared to *The Mary Tyler Moore Show* because it centered around a woman in the newsroom, surrounded by an ensemble cast. Yet Murphy Brown is a far cry from sweet Mary Richards.

The popularity of *Murphy Brown* was attributable to three factors: its appeal to women, its constant mirroring of the real world of broadcast, and its political agenda. Both *Murphy Brown* and its producer, Diane English (see entry), represented the new power being acquired by women in Hollywood. Like others shows on television, *Roseanne,*

Designing Women, Hearts Afire, Love and War, and *Dr. Quinn, Medicine Women*, this show featured a strong, independent-minded heroine (played by Candice Bergen) adept at handling men who refused to take them seriously. By 1990, women had 46 percent of TV roles, compared with only 30 percent of movie roles, signifying the shift to more opportunities for women in television as writers, directors, producers, and some senior executives. The shift toward more strong female roles on television has less to do, however, with social responsibility by the networks, than it does with the fact that women television viewers outnumber men by 3 to 2. Additionally, TV advertisers set a premium on female viewers aged 18-49 because these women are considered to make the majority of the buying decisions in American households.

Finally, *Murphy Brown* seemed to blur the lines of media, politics, TV, and reality. Twenty years earlier, Norman Lear's *All in the Family* introduced the idea of situation comedies uttering social commentary while getting laughs. Other TV movies and drama shows (e.g., *L.A. Law*) also began to tackle headline-making issues. Diane English insists that her goal was to entertain, not to politic, but also admits that she deliberately created Murphy Brown as a liberal Democrat. In all, entertainment television is being thrust into the political arena more than ever before. Overall, the show demonstrated acerbic wit and intelligence along with its fascination with real world TV.

Bibliography

Brooks, Tim, and Earle Marsh. *The Complete Directory to Prime Time Network and Cable TV Shows, 1946-Present.* New York: Ballantine, 1995.

Brown, Les. *Les Brown's Encyclopedia of Television.* 3d ed. Detroit: Gale Research, 1992.

Gregor, A. "Designing Women." *Maclean's Magazine* 29 March 1993: 40-41.

Martel, J. "The Year in Television." *Rolling Stone* 10, 24 Dec. 1992: 195+.

Zoglin, R. "Sitcom Politics." *Time* 21 Sept. 1992: 44+.

Sheri Carder

Murphy, Eddie (1961-), a supreme mimic, was born Edward Regan Murphy in the Bushwick section of Brooklyn, NY, son of a police officer (Charles) and a telephone operator (Lillian), stepson of a Breyers ice cream foreman (Vernon Lynch). When he was three years old, his parents divorced, his mother had to be hospitalized for a lengthy period, and Eddie and his older brother, Charles, were placed with a woman jokingly credited with the reason he became a comedian: a "kind of black Nazi."

He briefly attended Nassau Community College to study theater but quit school when he was hired—after six auditions, as an "extra," later becoming a regular cast member, on *Saturday Night Live* from 1980 to 1984. Murphy especially became known for his characters, like an adult Buckwheat from the Little Rascals' *Our Gang* series; an irreverent Gumby-like persona; militant black film critic Raheem Abdul Muhammad; or Mister Robinson, a ghetto take on public television's Mister Rogers. Also, Eddie Murphy became famous for his biting imitations of Stevie Wonder, Muhammad Ali, Bill Cosby, and Jerry Lewis.

The comedian's film career, however, is what has advanced him as an icon. It began in 1982 with *48 Hours*, in which he played a fast-talking dude released from prison to help co-star Nick Nolte as a policeman track down two killers in two days. *Coming to America* (1988), the authorship of which became a cause célèbre, had him as an African prince searching for an independent lifelong companion, while *Harlem Nights* (1989), which Eddie Murphy wrote, produced, and directed as well as starred in, concerned nightclub owners in the 1930s. His charismatic charm was at the core of *Boomerang* (1992), a $42 million hit where the ego-maniacal womanizer meets his match in Robin Givens, and *Distinguished Gentleman* (1993), as a political creature who successfully runs for Congress.

In addition to the motion pictures, Eddie Murphy has also had great success with his albums. His first, labeled *Eddie Murphy*, released in 1982 from a live performance at the Comic Strip, was nominated for a Grammy as best comedy album. Soon to follow were *Eddie Murphy: Comedian* (1983), that nabbed the coveted Grammy, and an album of songs, *How Could It Be* (1984).

While Eddie Murphy has come under attack for not visibly supporting black causes, *Ebony* has documented that he has steadily worked behind the scenes by donating to organizations like the Martin Luther King, Jr., Center for Nonviolent Social Change, and at the 1988 Academy Awards he publicly chided the Academy for having awarded only three Oscars to blacks in its 60-year history.

Eddie Murphy's movies have grossed more than $1 billion worldwide, a triumph for which the National Association of Theater Owners named him "Star of the Decade" at ShoWest in 1992.

Bibliography

Gross, Edward. *The Films of Eddie Murphy.* Las Vegas: Pioneer, 1990.

Parish, James Robert. *Today's Black Hollywood.* New York: Pinnacle, 1995.

Willburn, Deborah A. *Eddie Murphy.* New York: Chelsea, 1993.

Robert Baird

Murray, Bill (1950-), unlike many of his *Saturday Night Live* colleagues, has made a successful changeover from TV to movies. Murray first achieved recognition in 1977 when he replaced Chevy Chase on the second season of *Saturday Night Live*. On this show he perfected his smartass character, embodied in the lounge singer Jerry, with his mock-sincere "And I mean that, really." Since his first major motion picture, *Meatballs* (1979), Murray has progressed from a smugness that bordered at times on the insufferable to a broadness of sensibility that allows the cynicism to coexist with romanticism. His psychic investigator in the *Ghostbusters* films (1984, 1989) and the camp counselor in *Meatballs* responded to all forms of authority or conventional social behavior with a raised eyebrow, a deft quip. At the same time, these figures, as well as that of Dustin Hoffman's roommate, whom he played without billing in *Tootsie* (1982), seemed detached, incapable of or unwilling to connect with a broader social world.

Murray then acted in and co-wrote the unsuccessful and dramatically vague remake of Somerset Maugham's *The Razor's Edge* (1984). In the wake of its commercial and critical failure, he embarked on a five-year hiatus from the screen save for a cameo in the overproduced musical version of *The Little Shop of Horrors* (1986), reprising Jack Nicholson's memorable appearance in the original 1960 Roger Corman film as the masochistic nebbish, Wilbur Force.

Murray's most recent work suggests a reexamination and refinement of the smartass persona, amplifying the figure's vulnerability and desire for romantic attachments. That kind of sensitivity, albeit the object of humor in *Quick Change* (1990), dominates Murray's most recent work: *Mad Dog and Glory* (1993), *Groundhog Day* (1993), *Ed Wood* (1994), and *Rushmore* (1998).

Murray's most successful film, *Groundhog Day*, fully displays his skillful range of behavior, from the smug to the sentimental. Murray portrays a meteorologist trapped in Punxsutawney, PA, during the annual groundhog festival who is mired in a timeloop that forces him to relive the day again and again. The delicate nuance of the transformation of yet another Murray smartass into a romantic hero reinforces how deft the actor has become.

Bibliography

Connelly, Christopher. "The Man You Are Looking for Is Not Here." *Premiere* Aug. 1990: 56-64.

Hill, Doug. *Saturday Night: A Back Stage History of* Saturday Night Live. New York: Beach Tree, 1986.

Solman, Gregory. "The Passion of Bill Murray." *Film Comment* Nov. 1993: 5-8.

Write, Timothy. "The Rumpled Anarchy of Bill Murray." *New York Times Magazine* 20 Nov. 1988: 38-39.

David Sanjek

Museum of Broadcast Communications, The, in Chicago, is a major resource and archive for students of radio and television. The museum was founded in 1987 by political correspondent Bruce DuMont, nephew of television and network pioneer Allen B. DuMont. Its chairman is Arthur C. Nielsen, Jr., retired chairman of the A. C. Nielsen Co. The museum is supported by archival donations and grants from the many media-related firms based in Chicago.

Originally located in the lobby of an apartment complex south of the downtown Loop, it moved in 1992 to Michigan Avenue and Washington Street, in the Chicago Cultural Center (the original public library building). Its archives hold over 6,000 television shows, 50,000 radio broadcasts, and 8,000 TV commercials, available for casual viewing or study. Some of its resources include the Lynn "Angel" Harvey Radio Center, named for Mrs. Paul Harvey, from which DuMont moderates the nationally syndicated *Inside Politics* talk show, and radio historian Chuck Schaden hosts *Those Were the Days,* an anthology of old radio shows, each Saturday afternoon. Schaden's fans have raised funds to honor Chicago native sons with an Edgar Bergen exhibit

(with Charlie McCarthy and Mortimer Snerd), a re-creation of *Fibber McGee*'s closet to supplement a collection of the show's scripts, and a Jack Benny exhibit, complete with vault. There are several vintage radio and television sets and related items like Ovaltine mugs and Little Orphan Annie decoder rings. A TV camera used in the first 1960 Nixon-Kennedy debate (at WBBM-TV in Chicago) is on view near a studio where visitors can make souvenir videotapes of themselves reading news and weather TelePrompTer copy. A series of special programs and exhibits has focused on subjects like country music on the air, women on television, and Walt Disney's TV work.

The museum is home to the Radio Hall of Fame, founded by the Emerson Radio Corporation in 1988 and administered by the museum since 1991. Nominations are chosen by a steering committee, then voted on by Hall of Fame members, radio executives, and historians for induction each November.

Bibliography

DeVore, Sheryl. "Airways Archive." *Americana* Nov. 1990: 13.

Mark McDermott

Museums. Curators of the representative, the remarkable, and the impressive, American museums are a ready index of contemporary cultural values and ideas. While universities offer certificates in generic Museum Studies, the American museum system today is as complex and diverse as the American society it strives to serve.

Charles Willson Peale (1741-1827) created the first American museum in 1785 in Philadelphia's Independence Hall as a combination of theater, community center, and exhibits of historic value as well as those appealing to popular taste. Unlike European museums, where the visitor wandered at will through halls festooned with objects meant to inspire feelings of beauty, majesty, or patriotism, Pcalc introduced an American innovation—the guided tour. Peale set the pattern for the typical 19th-century museum: a combination of mermaids, mummies, and mastodons, loosely organized, broad-based, and inventoried rather than catalogued, displaying bones from the latest archaeological dig alongside portrait paintings of the colonial gentry. Harvard's noted Peabody archaeological museum began life touting a "Cabinet of Curios," including shrunken heads that fascinated the commonalty well into the 1960s. Turn-of-the-century paleontologists from Philadelphia's Academy of Natural Sciences thought nothing of hijacking the fossil discoveries of their colleagues to better induce the novelty-hungry public to part with the price of admission. By 1842, when celebrated showman P. T. Barnum (1810-1891) assembled an eclectic mix of natural history displays, curiosities, freak shows, and performers and dubbed it his American Museum in New York, he was not so much creating a trend as following a well-established precedent.

As America grew, so did the dichotomy between the museum as elite "improving" gallery and treasure house such as the Pennsylvania Academy of the Fine Arts (1805), and the popular entertainment agenda of Barnum. Not until

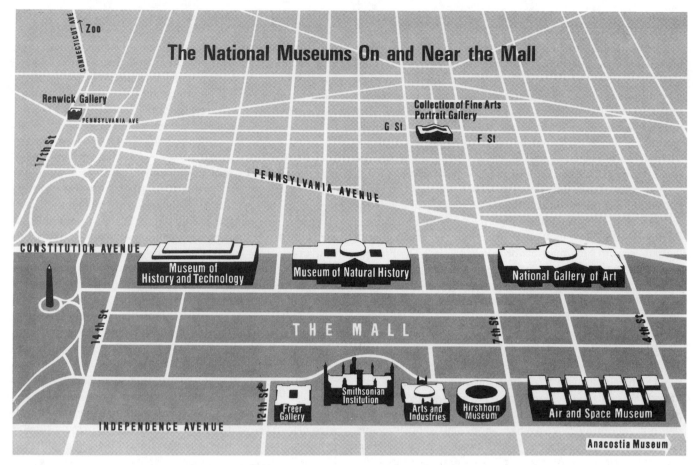

The National Museums On and Near the Mall

the third quarter of the nineteenth century did the scales tip firmly on the side of the museum as a repository of "high" culture. The newly minted captains of industry, Carnegie, Morgan, Freer, Mellon, Frick, and Whitney, endowed collections and museums with their family names and fortunes. Under the tutelage of Harvard's Charles Eliot Norton (1827-1908) and his student Bernard Berenson (1865-1959), they created the fine art museum as we know it today—unabashedly Eurocentric and conspicuously awe-inspiring in its porticoed majesty.

The collection of museums that make up the Smithsonian Institution (1846), the world's largest, found a middle ground with offerings ranging from the fine arts of the National Gallery and Hirshhorn to those of more general appeal, from dinosaur bones to the "Star-Spangled Banner" to the *Spirit of St. Louis,* prompting the nickname "the nation's attic."

Art and cultural museums, in particular, have asserted themselves as secular shrines of civilization. Showings have been expanded into popular culture subjects: animation at the Whitney, pop artists at the Corcoran; state icons at the Kansas State Historical Society, popular culture influences on art at the Museum of Modern Art, and television heritage at the Smithsonian.

History museums and historic homes convey awe and national pride, and the science museum is tied to American reverence for technology ("mechanic arts"), innovation, and the promise of the future. For most of this century, the museum establishment, ranging from cloister-like repositories of wealth to open-air living history re-creations such as

Colonial Williamsburg, have been key institutions for encouraging upward mobility based on the cultivation of taste and knowledge.

In the 1990s, American museums were again in a state of flux, the focus shifting away from specialization, preservation, and inspiration and toward general education. Contemporary exhibits are mandated as audience-centered, a scripted experience intelligible to a diverse general public and away from the more purely object-based conventions of the specialist scholars, collectors, and curators. The distanced and disinterested paradigm of the glass case, printed text, and isolated artifact is being replaced by the holistic experience, aided by the digital revolution: interactive computers, laser disks, and virtual reality.

The war of cultural taste waged between the high art museum and the commercial or popular museum continues. Barnum's contemporary equivalents, Ripley's Believe It or Not Museums and the Guinness Museum of World Records, have established successful outposts in major cities. These cater to the ongoing fascination with the grotesque, bizarre, exotic, and the sensational, where exhibits play at the extremes of the natural and manmade world: two-headed calves, the world's tallest human and largest domino game, and a cable car made of matchsticks. The circus, carnival, and midway tradition continues in evidence at the roadside museum of natural wonders (see Roadside Art), the commercial wax museum, multimedia shows and rides themed to a city's history, or the home/museums enshrining popular/historical figures like Elvis Presley's Graceland, the Gene Autry

Western Heritage Museum, the Babe Ruth House, Edgar Allan Poe House, Zane Grey Museum, and Liberace Museum. Even presidential museums and libraries, with their obvious historic worth, can be said to benefit from this mythic and celebrity allure, as well as the charm of history.

Advances in communications technology have been a mixed blessing for the museum community. On one hand, they have reshaped the way museums communicate to their public, expanding the universe of exhibits from the original and authentic to simulated materials, replicas, and images on video screens which may be manipulated in ways impossible with fragile, priceless, or unique artworks or cultural artifacts. On the other hand, the popularity of theme parks (see entry), the total-immersion communications medium of Disneyland, EPCOT Center, and Sea Worlds, has raised the expectations of the public as to how information is transmitted. The Franklin Institute, America's first science education museum, designed its Futures Center along theme-park lines, and IMAX and OMNIMAX large-format theaters are becoming an expensive but *de rigueur* centerpiece to attract video- and theme-park-raised generations conditioned to absorbing and interpreting multi-layered images and data. For them, the traditional static display and velvet rope are no longer even contenders.

Decreases in public funding since the late 1970s have forced museums to think and act in business terms about professional management, marketing, public relations, and income-generating aspects like shops and special events. Efforts to increase the numbers and diversity of the audience are giving rise to visitor studies; conventions geared to a Eurocentric middle class are giving way to those more in line with the "bottom-up" consciousness of the New Social History of the 1970s and 1980s. Resulting "new museum" configurations have been developed to meet the needs of a diverse audience, including traveling exhibits, discovery centers, and outreach programs. The introduction of multimedia and live performance not only serves to attract and keep video-raised audiences but also opens up new opportunities for communicating highly complex and emotion-laden subjects. The difficult, controversial, and complex "unthinkable" issue of genocide mounted by the United States Holocaust Memorial in Washington, DC, combines traditional museology with theme park and theater, using film, architecture, artifacts, music, and images to create a total visual and visceral narrative rather than an assemblage of historical artifacts.

Bibliography

Alderson, William, ed. *Mermaids, Mummies, and Mastodons: The Emergence of the American Museum.* Washington, DC: American Association of Museums, 1992.

Hein, Hilde, and Zahava Doerig. "The Museum Experience: Literature and Reality." Washington, DC: Association of Science and Technical Centers, 1989.

Leon, Warren, and Roy Rosenzweig, eds. *History Museums in the United States.* Urbana: U of Illinois P, 1989.

Naisbitt, John, and Patricia Aburdene. *Megatrends 2000.* New York: Morrow, 1990.

Sherman, Daniel, and Irit Rogoff, eds. *Museum Culture.* Minneapolis: U of Minnesota P, 1994.

Margaret J. King

Music in Motion Pictures. One of the great attractions of motion pictures is the music that accompanies the story. Sometimes it's a full orchestra highlighting action in an epic such as *Jurassic Park* (1993), at others it's a popular singer making a movie debut such as Whitney Houston in *Bodyguard* (1992), or it could be a collection of familiar tunes that add commentary to the unfolding story such as *Sleepless in Seattle* (1992). Movies are made for music.

Film was never a completely silent art. When film was first shown, music provided the appropriate psychological clue for audiences learning how to react to the new media. When the Lumières showed their first commercial film in December 1895, there was piano accompaniment. As film audiences grew in size, the live musical accompaniment also expanded from the piano to a small orchestra. By 1913, theater orchestras were able to purchase catalogues that included music for specific moods or dramatic moments. Smaller theaters used Wurlitzer organs for a wide range of both music and sound effects (see Theater Organs).

Possibly the first composer to write directly for a film was French composer Camille Saint-Saëns, who was commissioned by the Comédie Française to write music for *L'Assassinat du Duc de Guise* (1908). Saint-Saëns's contribution became his Opus 128 for strings, piano, and harmonium. D. W. Griffith demonstrated the power of wedding music with the edited screen image when he sent a score to each theater showing *The Birth of a Nation* (1915). Although little of the music was original, for example the galloping klansmen riding to Wagner's "Ride of the Valkyries," the selected melodies fit their assigned scenes and became leitmotifs when they were repeated throughout the film.

When talkies began with *The Jazz Singer* (1927), studio executives hesitated to use Griffith's pioneering musical concept. They feared that audiences watching a movie might question the source of music unless they could see a radio or the scene was taking place in a nightclub with the band in the background. The breakthrough that used music to drive the story took place with two movies in 1932, *Bird of Paradise* and *King Kong. King Kong* was a musical sensation because the entire film was accompanied by music that used themes for each character, especially Kong. Both films included completely original scores by Max Steiner, a Viennese-trained musician and composer. Steiner's demonstration that music can augment the drama started the movie music "golden age." The importance of film music was recognized with Academy Awards for best song and best score in 1934.

More than any other composer, Steiner broke new ground for using original composition for film background. Starting at RKO in 1930, Steiner moved to Warner Brothers in 1936 and eventually wrote scores for over 300 films, including *Gone with the Wind* (1939). It was Steiner who pioneered the division of musical responsibility into composition and orchestration. The composer determined where the music should accompany the scene and sketched out the melody; then the melody would be passed to an orchestrator who determined the instruments and arranged the film score. Steiner also created the "click track." Because a score is usually added after the film has been edited, the composer was provided with an early print that had perforations in the sound track, interrupting the dialogue and producing a noticeable click at regular intervals. This permitted the musical score to be written in time with the events appearing on the screen and created a perfect marriage of picture with music.

In film, music becomes a story-telling device; it can build up scenes and point to the exact emotion one should experience. A well-written score creates atmosphere for the story. It can be historical or comical, explain a character, establish the location, or even be part of the story. Because movies are the sum of a collection of parts, it is the music that ties those parts together. It can provide the transition from a scene of emotional intensity to one of lightheartedness. A good musical score can cover filmed mistakes, make transitions appear seamless, and even save a film the way Dimitri Tiomkin's hit song "Do Not Forsake Me" saved *High Noon* (1952), a film that preview audiences had despised.

Alfred Newman, music director at Twentieth Century-Fox, was the most decorated Hollywood musician, with nine Academy Awards, but only one, *The Song of Bernadette* (1942), was for composing an original score. Other awards were for musicals that he always claimed were group efforts. The score for *Bernadette* was the first to be released as a commercial recording on a 78 rpm Decca album in 1943. That also meant an appreciative audience could collect songs and scores they enjoyed and studios could increase their income by selling soundtracks.

Hit songs improved the public appeal of a film, and no composer in Hollywood was better at creating a memorable melody for a film than Russian-born Dimitri Tiomkin. By saving *High Noon* with a song that narrated the film, Tiomkin initiated the trend of songs accompanying the film credits. Although other composers imitated Tiomkin, including Henry Mancini with "Moon River" for *Breakfast at Tiffany's* (1964), none was as commercially successful over an extended period as Tiomkin. Tiomkin later composed "Thee I Love" for *Friendly Persuasion* (1956) and "Green Leaves" for *The Alamo* (1960) and guaranteed their success by using popular artists to introduce the songs before the films were released.

Movie composers have constantly pushed musical horizons to enhance their films. In 1945, Miklos Rozsa used an electronic instrument, the theremin, to create an eerie sound for Alfred Hitchcock's *Spellbound*. British director Carol Reed found Anton Karras playing the zither, an Austrian folk instrument, in a Viennese nightclub and commissioned him to write the score for *The Third Man* (1949). Alex North composed the first jazz-oriented score for the New Orleans locations of *A Streetcar Named Desire* (1951). Louise and Bebe Barron created an entirely electronic score for MGM's science fiction film *Forbidden Planet* (1956), and Vangelis took electric music into new areas with his synthesizer music for *Chariots of Fire* (1982), winning an Oscar for its score.

Film music has been written by amateurs and renowned composers. Charlie Chaplin hired composers, including David Raskin (*Laura,* 1944), to listen to him whistle and hum tunes that he wanted for *Modern Times* (1936). Classi-

cal composers have written scores for films they later adapted for the concert hall. Virgil Thompson was commissioned by the government's Resettlement Administration to score *The Plow That Broke the Plains* (1936), but was even more noted for his score for *Louisiana Story* (1948), which won a Pulitzer Prize. Aaron Copland's emphasis on Americana helped the scores for *Of Mice and Men* (1940) and *The Red Pony* (1949), and both became orchestral suites. John Williams, who conducted the Boston Pops Orchestra, frequently included his scores from movies, including *Star Wars* (1977), and *E.T., The Extra-Terrestrial* (1982), in pops concerts.

Although the lush, romantic orchestral sound initiated by Max Steiner is still the most prevalent form of music for motion pictures, the need for studios to reach the largest audience has seen them explore pop songs, electronic scores, native folk instruments, and even acid rock to increase the popularity of their films. People attend films to see the picture, but they also listen to the sound and by doing so encourage film composers to constantly seek out new ideas.

Bibliography

Kalinak, Kathryn. *Settling the Score: Music and the Classical Hollywood Film*. Madison: U of Wisconsin P, 1992.

Larson, Randall D. *Musique Fantastique: A Survey of Film Music in the Fantastic Cinema*. Metuchen: Scarecrow, 1985.

Prendergast, Roy M. *Film Music: A Neglected Art*. New York: Norton, 1992.

Thomas, Tony. *Music for the Movies*. South Brunswick: Barnes, 1973.

Arthur R. Jarvis, Jr.

Musical Films. Once inventors found a way to synchronize sound and motion, it was but a few short years to the Hollywood musical. The great days of the musical lasted about 25 years, until the mid-1950s. One of the finer, if not the finest musical, *Singin' in the Rain* (1952), is often used to mark the end of the great musical. It was a remake, also fitting, of one of the first screen musicals. Its story was rather typical of musical plots. In this case, Debbie Reynolds's character dubs in the voice and sings for a silent star who cannot make the transition to talkies. Gene Kelly's character is the charming leading man who falls in love with Debbie Reynolds's character. Donald O'Connor is the comic sidekick, and all, of course, works out well in the end.

But the story did not ever really matter. The music in musicals was written by America's great composers and lyricists: George Gershwin and his brother Ira, Cole Porter, Irving Berlin, Johnny Mercer, Harry Warren, Dorothy Fields, Richard Rodgers and Lorenz Hart, Oscar Hammerstein, Hoagy Carmichael, and others of fine ability. Their work was sung and danced by equally fine performers in their fields: Gene Kelly, Fred Astaire, Ginger Rogers, Bing Crosby, Rita Hayworth, Dick Powell, Frank Sinatra, Louis Armstrong, Lena Horne, Cab Calloway, Cyd Charisse, Tony Martin, Betty Grable, and just about every swing musician whom the producers could lure to bring his band in front of the cameras.

Although *The Jazz Singer*, the 1927 movie that introduced sound to the movies, featured Al Jolson and his music, the musical appeared dead by 1932 until Busby Berkeley revived it with *42nd Street* (1933) and Astaire and Rogers teamed up in *Flying Down to Rio* (1933). Berkeley's dazzling use of dancers to form a human kaleidoscope captured the audience's fancy. Crazy camera angles surprised and delighted the viewer and offered an escape from the dreary Depression world.

Jeanette MacDonald and Nelson Eddy became a Hollywood musical team about the same time as Fred Astaire and Ginger Rogers. They provided an alternative of sorts to the Astaire style. Their films tended toward operetta while Astaire and Rogers mastered the musical comedy form. MacDonald and Eddy appeared in a number of operettas, including *Naughty Marietta* (1935), *Rose Marie* (1936), *Maytime* (1937), *The Girl of the Golden West* (1938), *Sweethearts* (1938), *New Moon* (1940), and *Bitter Sweet* (1940). In 1942, they appeared in a musical comedy, Rodgers and Hart's *I Married an Angel*. The pairing of the two in a musical comedy underscored the fact that the operetta form was slow to change with the times while the musical comedy was keeping pace with the coming of the Second World War.

The film musical had virtually died in 1939 with the return of prosperity. The coming of World War II saw a resurgence in its popularity and in 1944, Hollywood produced 75 musicals, making the musical the most popular genre of its day. The musical provided an opiate for the public during a traumatic period. As one critic notes, the musical has always been a cheerleader during America's 20th-century bad times. The team of Astaire and Rogers personified the versatility of the form and its increasing popularity.

Fred Astaire and Ginger Rogers (see entry) were first teamed in *Flying Down to Rio* and were billed fourth and fifth respectively. Astaire had sharpened his prodigious abilities in partnership with his sister, Adele. When she broke up the act, he went into the movies. But no one seriously expected him to become a star. That evaluation changed, however, when he and Rogers danced together.

Although Ginger Rogers was never to be the dancer Astaire was, there was an indefinable magic in their pairing. They made ten films together, the last being *The Barkleys of Broadway* in 1949 for MGM, the only one they did not make for RKO. Astaire and Rogers achieved great intimacy in their roles, even though they did not share their first screen kiss until their eighth film, *Carefree*. They were able to convey a great deal through their playfulness, glances, and fluidity of movement that spoke far more than mere words.

Because of Fred Astaire and Gene Kelly and their need for partners for the romantic interest that all good musicals required, many women were given opportunities in musicals. Being a great dancer, however, was not always enough to be a great dance partner, as Eleanor Powell and Ann Miller discovered. Both were exceptional dancers but were better as solo performers.

Rita Hayworth, however, was a fine dancer who did make a fine partner. Her innate sexiness added great interest to her dance numbers and she starred with both Kelly, once, and Astaire, twice. Her sequences with these men are still classics and excite interest.

Judy Garland, of course, was an exceptional vocalist and her voice was, perhaps, the greatest wonder in *The Wizard of Oz* (1939). This now-classic fantasy based on Frank Baum's fairy tales set in Kansas featured not only the teen-aged Garland but the great singing and dancing talent of Ray Bolger. One of his dances is so good that it had to be cut from the film for diverting attention from the flow of the action. Fortunately, it has survived and is available on the anniversary video of the film. The film had the great comic acting of Bert Lahr, Jack Haley, Frank Morgan, and Margaret Hamilton. The 1939 production also helped establish the viability of Technicolor, already a process over 20 years old by that time. However, it would take about another 20 years for Technicolor or one of its variations to be used as a regular procedure rather than to underscore "romantic" films.

Perhaps the sexiest dancer of the late Hollywood musicals was Cyd Charisse, who was in constant trouble with the censors. Gene Kelly cast her as the vamp in *Singin' in the Rain*'s Broadway ballet. Although Charisse had been in films since the 1940s, it was this role that made her a star. She managed to survive her battle with the censors who were always checking her cleavage and the length of her leotard to star in *Brigadoon, It's Always Fair Weather, The Band Wagon*, and *Silk Stockings*. The first two films were with Kelly and the latter two with Astaire. Charisse appeared sexy whenever she moved. The censors never caught on to the fact that it did not matter how many clothes she wore or did not wear; her sexiness was in her grace and movement.

Very different in style and appeal from Charisse was Leslie Caron, who appeared with Kelly in *An American in Paris* (1951) and Astaire in *Daddy Long Legs* (1955). Her gamine-like quality appealed to the same fans who loved Audrey Hepburn. She was sweet, vulnerable, and very talented in an understated manner. Caron was a classically trained ballet dancer and ideal for the "experiments" Kelly was carrying out in incorporating ballet sequences into his films. The trend was begun on the stage with *Oklahoma!* and Kelly had worked a ballet sequence into *On the Town* (1949); there had also been one in *Lady in the Dark* (1964). Other ballet sequences made their way into films, but it was the success of *The Red Shoes* in 1949 that made *An American in Paris* possible and Caron an American success, which she capitalized on in *Lili* (1953), *Gigi* (1958), and other films.

There has been much debate on the reasons for the demise of the film musical after the 1950s. There were great musicals after that time. Most, however, tended to be remakes of Broadway successes: *Funny Girl, Grease, Gypsy, On a Clear Day, West Side Story, My Fair Lady, A Funny Thing Happened on the Way to the Forum, A Chorus Line, The Sound of Music, Hello, Dolly, Mame, Little Shop of Horrors*, and many others. They *looked* like filmed stage productions rather than the sleek productions of Hollywood's glory days.

The only production company "still making 'em the way they used to" is Disney. Beginning with 1989's *Little Mermaid*, and continuing with *Beauty and the Beast, Aladdin*, and *The Lion King*, Disney has consistently produced classic Hollywood musicals. It is not a new insight that Disney's classic animated films, like *Snow White and the Seven Dwarfs, Cinderella, The Jungle Book*, and others were really Hollywood musicals in cartoon form.

Certainly, *Who Framed Roger Rabbit?* was a logical extension of Gene Kelly's dancing with Hanna and Barbera's Tom and Jerry or Uncle Remus singing with that Mr. Bluebird on his shoulder. Disney had almost made a version of *Alice in Wonderland* with Mary Pickford long before he made *Snow White*. It would have featured animation and live action. The classic Hollywood films seemed to defy the laws of nature and leap over and through the screen. Perhaps only animation can preserve their memory.

In spite of its shortcomings, the Hollywood musical in its classic form was a masterpiece of entertainment. It was truly cinematic in its presentation, delighting in what was still a new medium. The appearance of sound was a natural factor in the genesis of the musical. The revolution in dance begun in ballet and spreading to Broadway provided further impetus for development of the form. The incorporation of color, especially after the success of *The Wizard of Oz,* further changed the musical. The continuing improvement in technology, conception, and understanding of the medium's full potential all contributed to a form of entertainment that delighted millions and has become a significant part of our cultural heritage.

Bibliography

Flatow, Sheryl. "Great Gals, Great Gams." *A&E Monthly* May 1994: 22-25.

Hirschhorn, Clive. *The Hollywood Musical.* New York: Portland House, 1991.

Kreuger, Miles, ed. *The Movie Musical: From Vitaphone to "42nd Street" as Reported in a Great Fan Magazine.* New York: Dover, 1975.

Woll, Allen L. *The Hollywood Musical Goes to War.* Chicago: Nelson-Hall, 1983.

Wollen, Peter. *Singin' in the Rain.* London: BFI, 1992.

Frank A. Salamone

See also
American Musical Theater

My Three Sons (1960-1972) was a vehicle for its star, film actor Fred MacMurray (1907-1991), who'd had a career in B movies, mostly comedies. The series was conceived as *The Fred MacMurray Show*, but MacMurray refused the title, believing he would have to work harder in a show with his name on it. In the 1950s and 1960s, he became Walt Disney's most popular dad, appearing in children's movies like *The Shaggy Dog* and *Son of Flubber*. His low-key charm was crucial to *My Three Sons*, in which he played Steven Douglas, a West Coast aerodynamics engineer and widower living in the town of Bryant Park with his, yes, three sons.

The show was a kind of hybrid of *Bachelor Father* and *Father Knows Best*. In the first episode, Steve is chased by a predatory woman at the same time he's telling Chip to be nice to the little girl who has a crush on him. Chip escapes; Steve has a harder time. The cardigan-sweatered, bemused Steve is helped out at home by the boys' gruff, lovable, house-keeping, apron-wearing grandfather, Bub O'Casey, played by William Frawley, who'd won fame as Fred Mertz on *I Love Lucy* (1951-57).

Frawley left the show midway through the 1964-65 season for health reasons, and was replaced by William Demarest (1892-1983), a veteran of vaudeville and film. Demarest played the gravel-voiced, lovable, apron-wearing ex-Navy man, Uncle Charley. Frawley and Demarest succeeded in these sexually ambiguous roles, possibly because they were not themselves sexually ambiguous men. In an early episode, Chip must write a composition about the best mom in the neighborhood, and chooses Bub.

Like many sitcoms, *My Three Sons* was a bland comedy of manners. One kid might call another "bean brain." What was different was the father, who, for once, was not a jerk, and the laugh track, which was unobtrusive. The show ranked in the Top 20 for seven of its 12 seasons.

Bibliography

Brown, Les. *Les Brown's Encyclopedia of Television.* Detroit: Visible Ink, 1992.

McNeil, Alex. *Total Television: A Comprehensive Guide to Programming from 1948-Present.* New York: Penguin, 1980.

Mitz, Rick. *The Great TV Sitcom Book.* New York: Perigee.

Katie Hutchinson

Mystery and Detective Fiction, one of the most enduring and versatile forms of popular literature throughout the world, has captured the American imagination for more than 150 years. In fact, American authors contributed many of the innovations which have shaped and defined this genre. Mystery and detective fiction has a history with distinct periods, and includes many specialized subgenres; it has played an influential role in the development of other literary modes as well.

Mysteries obey certain established generic conventions. They feature a central conundrum or secret in the plot—usually a crime—which is solved by someone through the act of detection. Readers often compete with their fictional heroes to solve the mystery at hand, and expect authors to fairly reveal all clues. Fictional sleuths can be professional or amateur; individuals, partners, or a group of people; and of either gender, any race, and virtually any age. Mystery fiction is closely related to but distinct from several related genres, including spy fiction, thrillers, and true crime. Spy fiction focuses on international politics and intrigue in a realistic and often unresolved situation, as in the novels of Ken Follett and John le Carré; it may also present a more romantic and swashbuckling portrait of the spy figure, as in Ian Fleming's James Bond stories. Thrillers, like those written by Robert Ludlum, Tom Clancy, Dick Francis, and Michael Crichton, withhold information from readers in order to keep them on the edge of their seats, presenting an unpredictable and exciting world. True crime writing, popularized by such writers as Joe McGinniss, Anne Rule, and Jack Olsen, generally focuses on murder in factual accounts of crimes, investigations, and their legal aftermaths.

The earliest period of detective fiction, classical mysteries (see entry), began in America in the 1840s when Edgar

Allan Poe wrote what many consider the first true detective stories, starring the amateur sleuth C. Auguste Dupin and his nameless sidekick. The three Dupin tales create the plot conventions, characters, and narrative style which define other classical mysteries. Following Poe, American women also influenced the development of the genre. Anna Katharine Green created characters whom later authors imitated: a professional police detective, a lawyer, a nosy spinster-sleuth, and a youthful single female amateur. Perhaps the most famous classical detective figure in America and throughout the world is Arthur Conan Doyle's Sherlock Holmes. In Holmes novels and short stories from 1887 through 1927, Doyle popularized patterns begun by Poe.

The 1920s initiated what is now considered the golden age of detective fiction (see entry), lasting until 1940. Novels of British origin achieved tremendous popularity at home and in America, and remain well loved today. Golden age authors such as Agatha Christie, Dorothy L. Sayers, Margery Allingham, and Ngaio Marsh greatly influenced the genre for all time. They have even gained new popularity through recent television adaptations of their works. The earliest successful American author of the golden age was S. S. Van Dine, whose Philo Vance books were best-sellers in the 1920s. Ellery Queen's novels added a distinctly American tone and remained popular for nearly 50 years. Rex Stout's Nero Wolfe stories appeared toward the end of the golden age, but continued many of the genre's distinct traditions, modified for the growing sophistication of American audiences.

The next important era in the mystery developed in reaction to, then simultaneously with, the golden age. Hard-boiled detective fiction (see entry) is a distinctly American mode, born of dissatisfaction with the British emphasis on upper-class settings, polished characters, and tidily solved puzzles. Hard-boiled authors depicted situations meant to be more realistic, more in touch with the experience of the common reader. Dashiell Hammett and others contributed hard-boiled short stories to pulp magazines such as *Black Mask* in the late 1920s, and soon novels in this mode began to appear. Hammett's Sam Spade, Raymond Chandler's Philip Marlowe, and Mickey Spillane's Mike Hammer are perhaps the best known of the hard-boiled detectives, and delineate the characteristics of the genre. Loners, they work for themselves as private investigators, struggle to make financial ends meet, and narrate their own stories to readers. They rigorously pursue their own codes of honor and justice, whether or not these coincide with the law. They talk tough and act tough, not afraid to meet violence or dish it out when they have to. They lack sentimentality, distrust authority, and pursue women who attract them. This atmosphere of unadorned, often cruel realism also developed in the novels of James M. Cain. Though his mysteries did not feature private detectives, Cain's spare prose and stark, brutal settings developed from and influenced hard-boiled fiction.

Since World War II, the contemporary period of mystery and detective fiction has seen an even broader expansion of the genre. Both golden age and hard-boiled styles continue today, in modified and updated forms. Cozy mysteries (see entry), such as those by Martha Grimes, have adapted the charming atmosphere, the relatively small cast of characters, and the happy ending standard in golden age detection. Postwar hard-boiled fiction has retained many of the traditional characteristics, but has sharply modernized its attitudes to reflect a broader social canvas. John D. MacDonald's Travis McGee, Robert B. Parker's Spenser, and Ross Macdonald's Lew Archer are not as isolated as Spade and Marlowe; they establish meaningful, long-term relationships with both women and men, and in some cases even depend upon partners. Marcia Muller, Sara Paretsky, and Sue Grafton have introduced professional women investigators such as Sharon McCone, V. I. Warshawski, and Kinsey Millhone, who bring feminist concerns to the mean streets.

The contemporary period has also added new forms to the genre, the most popular of which is the police procedural (see entry), in part a reaction against both golden age and hard-boiled styles of fiction, which share a pejorative view of the police. Police procedurals portray police as heroes, solving crimes as part of their professional duties. Ed McBain's series featuring members of the 87th Precinct are the best known of these novels; other popular authors include Joseph Wambaugh and Lillian O'Donnell.

Other types of mystery and detective fiction have begun to develop since the 1970s, reflecting more diverse social interests. Crime fiction, which addresses the psychological aspects of crime, criminals, and victims, has surged in popularity through the works of such authors as P. D. James, Elmore Leonard, and Ruth Rendell. Medical mysteries (see entry) also feature the psychology of fear. America's cultural diversity is reflected in novels featuring ethnic groups and situations that appeal to multiracial audiences or depict gay and lesbian life. Writers like Tony Hillerman and Joseph Hansen, for example, have introduced Native American and gay detectives whose personal lives serve as indexes to the subculture from which they originate. Recent authors have also diversified the settings of American detective fiction, introducing readers to varied regional locales through their works, such as Jonathan Valin's Cincinnati, J. J. Vance's Seattle, or Sandra Prowell's Montana. Others concentrate their efforts in a specific historical period, such as Walter Mosley's post-war Los Angeles. Some more adventurous authors even feature animals as investigators. This specializing trend has in no way narrowed the appeal of these current novels; rather it has enlarged the already manifold readership of the mystery.

Genres related to mystery and detective fiction have undergone parallel growth during the last century and a half. For instance, gothic fiction emerged as a popular mode in the late 18th century, but strongly influenced mystery fiction, especially in the works of Poe. Gothic mysteries (see entry) generally feature picturesque atmospheres, melodrama, and the warring forces of good and evil. Famous contemporary gothic writers include Daphne du Maurier, Victoria Holt, and Mary Higgins Clark, who place their relatively young and innocent heroines in situations with ever-escalating terrors, under the protection of mysterious males who may turn out to be either hero or villain.

Similarly, adolescent fiction has existed since Louisa May Alcott's girlhood stories of the middle 1800s. But adolescent mysteries (see entry) are a distinctly American contribution to popular culture, coming into their own between the world wars. While many of the early books and periodicals targeted young male audiences, probably the most enduring and influential figure of the adolescent mystery is Nancy Drew. Since her appearance in 1930, Nancy Drew has set the standard for youthful detective heroes, whatever their gender.

Other subgenres of mystery and detective fiction are defined by their focus on specific settings or character types. Locked-room mysteries, developed by Poe and popularized in puzzle novels, continue to mystify readers. Academic mysteries (see entry) involve higher education faculty and administration, and address the complexities of that environment. First popularized in the golden age, contemporary academic mysteries, such as those written by Amanda Cross, fall into the cozy category. Similarly, legal mysteries (see entry) feature attorney protagonists and explore issues of jurisprudence and justice. Erle Stanley Gardner's Perry Mason has captured the popular audience's admiration through novels and television from 1933 until the present. More recently, the best-selling fiction of Scott Turow and John Grisham has newly energized the legal mystery. In the same way, religious mysteries (see entry) feature clerical sleuths from many denominations whose dealings in their specialized worlds set the stage for investigation. Like academic mysteries, these stories also rose to popularity in the golden age; they have recently expanded to include non-Christian religious perspectives. Religious mysteries focus on morality, with wrongs set right through God's human agents.

The long-standing and continued popularity of mystery and detective fiction has led to several cultural developments beyond the literature itself. Bookstores specializing expressly in mystery and detective fiction such as Murder Ink (see entry) have sprung up across the country. They also market the many mystery periodicals (see entry) and fanzines which cover everything from new mystery books to author interviews. A number of organizations devoted to detective fiction sponsor mystery awards (see entry), such as the Edgar or Agatha, that bring prestige and fame to the lucky author-winners. And finally, for those enthusiasts who simply cannot satisfy their predilection for mysteries through reading, mystery weekends (see entry) are held all across the country which enable fans to participate in the solving of a staged crime.

William Reynolds
Elizabeth A. Trembley

See also

Mystery Awards extend formal recognition to writing achievement in the field. The Edgar Awards, named for the creator of the detective story, Edgar Allan Poe, are presented annually by the Mystery Writers of America, honoring works published that year in mystery and detective fiction. Awards go to the best novel, best first novel, best paperback original novel, best short story, best factual crime account, best critical or biographical study, best juvenile story, and best young adult story. The Edgar is a prestigious award and assures a writer of significant acknowledgment and stature in the literary world. Winners receive gilded statuettes of Poe.

In addition to the Edgar, several other awards are granted authors annually for achievement in the field of mystery writing. The Agatha Awards, named for Agatha Christie, are conferred by Malice Domestic, Ltd., the nonprofit literary corporation that hosts a yearly convention saluting "mysteries of manners" or cozy mysteries as they are often called. Recognition is granted in the categories of best novel, best first novel, best short story, and best nonfiction work. Agatha recipients are given teapots engraved with the Malice skull and crossbones.

The Anthony Awards, named for writer-critic Anthony Boucher, are conferred by those attending the Bouchercon, the largest mystery convention in the world. Anthony categories include best novel, best first novel, best true crime book, best short story, best collection of stories, and best critical work.

The Macavity Awards, named for the curious feline Macavity of T. S. Eliot's *Old Possum's Book of Practical Cats*, are selected by members of Mystery Readers International, the largest organization of mystery fans in existence. Certificates recognize best novel, first novel, short story, and nonfiction or critical work.

The Shamus Awards are chosen by the Private Eye Writers of America and awarded for work in the private eye genre: best novel, best paperback original, best first novel, and best short story. The Edgar is the best known of the writing awards, but to receive any of these is a notable achievement.

Bibliography

DeAndrea, William L. *Encyclopedia Mysteriosa: A Comprehensive Guide to the Art of Detection in Print, Films, Radio, and Television*. New York: Prentice, 1994.

Klein, Kathleen Gregory, ed. *Great Women Mystery Writers: Classic to Contemporary*. Westport: Greenwood, 1994.

Rudolph, Janet. *The Armchair Detective*. 1993, 1994.

Elizabeth Foxwell

Mystery Parodies. With its conventional characters and formulaic structure, mystery fiction has provided writers with ample material for parody (the exaggerated mimicry of an artistic or literary genre, or the humorous imitation of the style of an author). In the U.S., parodies of mystery and detective fiction appear primarily in two literary forms—the short story and the play.

Several important American authors have written parody mysteries, among them James Thurber (*The White Rabbit Caper*, 1953); S. J. Perelman (*Farewell, My Lovely*

Appetizer, 1943); Woody Allen (Match Wits with Inspector Ford, 1972); and Garrison Keillor (Jack Schmidt, Arts Administrator, 1979). Less famous contributors to the genre include John Sladek (The Purloined Butter, 1981) and John Harris (Monastic Mayhem: An Echo of Eco, 1986).

Mystery parodies for the stage—generally written for and produced by community theaters, little theater organizations, and student drama groups—generally provide comic mimicry of established detectives or make fun of well-known mystery stories or subgenres. A common type takes advantage of the public's unflagging interest in Sherlock Holmes, sometimes in the guise of a character with a name like Nick Sherlock. Other famous literary detectives are parodied as Nancy Sketch, the Hardly Brothers, Miss Maple, and a playwright who claims to have written Dial M for Morose, for example. Cynthia Mercati's Trixie, the Teen Detective and the Mystery of the Gravestead Manor (1985) mimics teenage detectives like Nancy Drew; William Gleason's The Prime Time Crime (1977) parodies television crime shows; and Tim Kelly's The Butler Did It (1977) pokes fun at the cozy mystery. Blair Graeme's Murder at the OK Corral (1991) takes aim at TV Westerns, while The Soapy Murder Case (1979) spoofs television soap operas.

Bibliography

Pronzini, Bill. Gun in Cheek: A Study of "Alternative" Crime Fiction. New York: Coward, 1982.

Swanson, Jean, and Dean James. By a Woman's Hand: A Guide to Fiction by Women. New York: Berkley, 1994.

E. D. Huntley

See also
Humorous Mysteries
Mystery and Detective Fiction

Mystery Periodicals. The success of the mystery story in the mass market has been paralleled by the proliferation of a diverse range of mystery review periodicals, "fanzines," and journals. The Mystery Readers Journal focuses on specific subjects such as religious mysteries, sports mysteries, and the ethnic detective. Mystery and Detective Monthly is a "letterzine" written almost completely by subscribers, recounting their recent readings, favorite authors, and other mystery-related news. The Drood Review of Mystery features reviews of fiction and reference books. Mystery News uses a tabloid format to discuss new fiction in categories such as suspense, espionage, and hard-boiled. Mystery Scene is the professional magazine of the industry, featuring publisher news and author interviews. Clues, an academic journal devoted to mystery literature, is published by the Popular Press. Murder Is Academic serves as a forum for professors teaching crime fiction.

There are also fanzines devoted to single authors, including The Bony Bulletin (Arthur W. Upfield), The Dorothy L. Sayers Society Newsletter, The Friends of Elizabeth Peters Newsletter, Most Loving Mere Folly (Ellis Peters), the Lilian Braun Newsletter, The John Buchanan Journal, The Perry Mason Newsletter, and The Columbo Files. Numerous publications are devoted to Sherlock Holmes.

Bibliography

Cook, Michael. Mystery, Detective, and Espionage Fiction: A Checklist of Fiction in U.S. Pulp Magazines, 1915-1974. New York: Garland, 1988.

——. Mystery, Detective, and Espionage Magazines. Westport: Greenwood, 1983.

Janet A. Rudolph

Mystery Plays. William Gillette's Secret Service (1896) may be the first stage presentation of the mystery genre; certainly, Gillette's Sherlock Holmes (1899) provided the great detective with his stage debut. Since then, the mystery play has enjoyed a vibrant history in the United States. The year 1912 marked the appearance of Bayard Veiller's Within the Law, a melodramatic stage mystery about the revenge of a working girl who turns the tables on the man responsible for her imprisonment on false charges. Melodrama dominated the early years of the American detective play. Most of these now-forgotten dramas featured mystery clichés such as sliding panels and bookshelves, creaky stairs, missing fortunes, wills read at midnight, hidden jewels, and mysterious strangers. Hurricanes or snowstorms cut off the inhabitants of houses from contact with any source of help; characters bemoaned their plight in contrived speeches. Most of these plays were plot-driven; characterization was amusing but stereotypical at best.

Despite the tremendous popularity of melodrama with theater-goers, other interesting plays that can be classified as mysteries were staged before the 1950s, such as George M. Cohan's Seven Keys to Baldpate (1913), Elmer Rice's On Trial (1914), Mary Roberts Rinehart and Avery Hopwood's The Bat (1920), Susan Glaspell's Trifles (1920), John Willard's The Cat and the Canary (1922), Philip Dunning and George Abbot's Broadway (1926), Mae West's Diamond Lil (1928), and Eugene O'Neill's Mourning Becomes Electra (1931).

During the 1950s, the crime play and the courtroom drama replaced the melodramatic mystery on the American stage. Two major examples of these newer genres are Frederick Knott's Dial M for Murder and Herman Wouk's The Caine Mutiny Court Martial, both produced in 1952. The 1960s introduced several additional mystery subgenres to the stage: the psychological thriller, the naturalistic crime drama, the mystery parody, and the backstage mystery. Frederick Knott followed the success of Dial M with two more plays: Write Me a Murder (1961) and Wait Until Dark (1966). Important mystery plays from the next decade include Eric Bentley's Are You Now, or Have You Ever Been (1972), Mario Fratti's Victim (1978), and Ira Levin's Deathtrap (1979).

While drama with roots in detective fiction still appears on stage, many detective plays of the last two decades are British imports, the work of such playwrights as Tom Stoppard and Anthony Shaffer. Recent American mystery dramas include Mark D. Kaufmann's Evil Little Thoughts (1992), Nathan Mayer's Beyond a Reasonable Doubt (1992), and Paula Volsky's The Bastard of Bologna (1992). Although mystery plays are no longer a staple of American commercial theater, they are alive and well in college and high school productions, community theaters, dinner theaters, and regional repertory and stock companies. The reasons for the genre's popularity are easy to understand. Mystery plays tend to have fairly large casts, ensuring that nearly everyone in an amateur company has a role, and many lead characters are women, the dominant group in many community and school theater circles; also, sets are simple to create, and mystery plays are guaranteed crowd pleasers. Interestingly, the mystery plays most likely to appear on community stages in America are those of British writer Agatha Christie.

Bibliography

Baker's Plays. 1994 Catalog.

Carlson, Marvin A. *Deathtraps: The Postmodern Comedy Thriller.* Bloomington: Indiana UP, 1993.

Dramatic Publishing Company. 1994 Catalog.

Kaye, Marvin, ed. *Sweet Revenge: Ten Plays of Bloody Murder.* New York: Fireside Theater, 1992.

Steinbrunner, Chris, and Otto Penzler, eds. *Encyclopedia of Mystery and Detection.* New York: McGraw-Hill, 1976.

Winn, Dilys. *Murder Ink: The Mystery Reader's Companion.* New York: Workman, 1977.

E. D. Huntley

See also

Holmes, Sherlock

Legal Mysteries

Mystery Parodies

Mystery/Suspense Drama. America's fascination with mystery and suspense literature made the genre a natural for broadcast audiences. Since television's debut, nearly every programming season has seen its share of mystery programs, with at least one series per decade emerging in the Nielsen Top 10. While first-run suspense programs seemingly vanished from the airwaves in the early 1970s, they had accounted for some of the most popular and critically acclaimed programming of TV's golden age.

Outside of literature and pulp fiction, television mystery and suspense programs find their roots in radio, which provided a perfect vehicle for such programs. Indeed, dialogue and sound effects helped create a unique program for each listener. Network radio series such as *The Shadow* delighted audiences for years, while programs such as *Lights Out, Suspense, Mr. and Mrs. North,* and *The Clock* made the successful transfer to television.

The first network television mystery series was *Barney Blake, Police Reporter,* which debuted on NBC in April 1948. The series featured Gene O'Donnell as a newspaper reporter who solved homicides. Another early crime mystery series was *Chicagoland Mystery Players*; two years before its 1949 DuMont network debut, the series was broadcast locally in Chicago. During its Chicago run, the solution to each week's mystery was revealed in the following day's *Chicago Tribune.* This sort of dual-media gimmick was also used in the ABC series *Stand By for Crime,* a live police drama also originating from Chicago. Viewers were invited to phone in their solution before the criminal was revealed. *Stand By for Crime* also earned a place in TV history on January 11, 1949, when it became the first Chicago show to be linked to eastern audiences. Series star Myron Wallace, who

played Lt. Anthony Kidd, eventually changed his first name to Mike and moved from acting to journalism; the series was Mike Wallace's first network appearance.

By the early 1950s, mystery and suspense programs accounted for nearly 50 percent of television programming, with a number of these series featuring continuing characters. Hard-boiled detective Mike Barnett was the principal player in *Man against Crime,* which debuted on CBS in 1949. The popular, violent series was later broadcast by DuMont and NBC through 1956. NBC's *Martin Kane, Private Investigator* was another successful TV sleuth airing on NBC between 1949 and 1954.

Boston Blackie, a popular character from pulp fiction and low budget films, became a syndicated TV series in 1951. Mark Saber, a suave British detective solving crimes in a large U.S. city, aired first on ABC, then on NBC from 1951 through 1960.

Some of the continuing sleuths were part-time detectives. Anna May Wong portrayed one of the first female detectives— an art gallery owner and part-time detective—in DuMont's short-lived 1951 series *The Gallery of Mme. Lui-Tsong.* John Cassavetes played jazz pianist *Johnny Staccato,* who solved crimes in between sets with such jazz musicians as Barney Kessel and Red Norvo. *Johnny Staccato,* which began on NBC in 1959, switched to ABC in its final 1960 season.

It was the dramatic anthology, however, that provided the bulk of the mystery and suspense drama in the 1950s. While anthologies specific to mystery and suspense abounded, examples of the genre were also popular in general dramatic anthologies such as *Kraft Theater, Philco TV Playhouse,* and *Playhouse 90.*

One of the best suspense anthologies of the early 1950s was *The Web* (CBS, 1950-54; NBC, 1957), which featured adaptations of stories written by the Mystery Writers of America. The series was the first TV show to be awarded the Edgar Allan Poe Award for excellence in presentation of suspense stories. Surprisingly, the producers of the series, Mark Goodson and Bill Todman, later became successful producing such game shows as *Truth or Consequences* and *The Price Is Right.* A unique golden age suspense series was *DuMont's Hands of Mystery* (1949-51). The weekly program used no props or sets, but derived its drama from its dialogue, camera angles, and lighting.

Many of these golden age series were quite graphic and violent, fostering great concern over the effects these shows had on viewers—particularly children. Riding on the heels of concerns regarding the media's role in juvenile delinquency, Congress in 1951 began investigating the problem. Before the government could intervene, however, the networks established their own television code to help to avoid censorship.

The two most significant series of the 1950s and early 1960s were *Alfred Hitchcock Presents* and Rod Serling's *The Twilight Zone,* two suspense anthology programs that reflected the unique styles of their producers.

Hitchcock was not interested in working for television until MCA executive Lew Wasserman, hot on the idea of using the famous director, offered Hitchcock a $129,000 per week contract which included script and casting supervision as well as opportunities to direct several of each season's half-hour dramas. Airing on CBS from 1955 to 1960, the series expanded to an hour when it moved for two years to NBC. In 1963, the series returned to CBS, only to return for its final season on NBC in 1954. Hosted by Hitchcock, whose morbid sense of humor introduced and concluded each episode, most of the stories had an O. Henry flavor. Numerous stars such as Joseph Cotton, Jessica Tandy, and Claude Rains appeared.

Sponsors and the network had several problems with the series. First of all, many of Hitchcock's dramatic villains virtually got away with their murders. The network soon made Hitchcock, in his epilogues, provide a clear message that justice was ultimately served. Sponsors also had a problem with Hitchcock's incessant brow-beating of their commercial interruptions; however, when sponsors found that Hitchcock's barbs improved sales, they eventually left the host alone.

Alfred Hitchcock Presents, while a Top 10 hit in first-run, lay dormant until 1985 when, five years after Hitchcock's death, the series was revived—hosted by a colorized Hitchcock created from footage from the original series. After the NBC attempt foundered in 1986, first-run episodes were aired during the 1987-88 season on the USA Network. Cable network *Nick at Nite* began running complete, uncut versions of the original series in the late 1980s.

Unlike Hitchcock, Rod Serling eagerly greeted the opportunity television afforded young writers. In 1951 Serling began freelancing scripts for such anthologies as *Hallmark Hall of Fame*, *Lux Video Theater*, *Suspense,* and *Studio One*. His big break came with a dramatic script called "Patterns," which centered on the drama of a corporate power struggle. "Patterns" became the first live drama to be re-performed by popular demand, winning Serling immediate fame and his first Emmy.

Serling went on to write feature films as well as scripts for *Playhouse 90*, for which he wrote his most famous teleplay, "Requiem for a Heavyweight." When he announced that he was devoting his attention to a new weekly science fiction series, many felt Serling was taking a step down. No one knew the tremendous potential *The Twilight Zone* would have.

While never a Top 10 hit during its first run, the CBS series (see entry), which aired from 1959 to 1965, has become a classic which has thrived in syndication. While labeled a science fiction anthology, there were just as many episodes dealing with such suspense themes as survival and alienation.

Serling's clipped, sardonic style of narration has become the object of parody in countless comedy sketches, and the series' four-note theme has become one of the most famous in TV history. The series was revived in both a 1985-87 CBS network version, as well as an 1987-88 syndicated version. A *Twilight Zone Magazine* appeared in the early 1980s and a feature film was released in 1983.

Another popular program of the late 1950s/early 1960s was *Peter Gunn*, more memorable for its music than its plots. The Henry Mancini theme, recorded by the Ray Anthony Orchestra, hit No. 8 on the *Billboard* Top 60 in 1959. The song was successfully covered by two other bands, with an Art of Noise version making the *Billboard* Top 60 in 1986. During the series' first run, Mancini released two popular RCA albums featuring music from *Peter Gunn*.

Viewers were also delighted by the wildly successful *77 Sunset Strip* (ABC, 1958-64). While the series starred Efrem Zimbalist, Jr., and Roger Smith as detectives Stuart Bailey and Jeff Spencer, the real star of the series was Edd Byrnes's character Gerald Lloyd Kookson III. Known affectionately as "Kookie," the hip character quickly made famous such phrases as "a dark seven" (a depressing week), the "ginchiest" (the greatest), and "piling up the z's" (getting some sleep). The series spawned a host of ABC imitations, including *Bourbon Street Beat*, *Surfside 6*, and *Hawaiian Eye*. None of the knock-offs were as popular as the original, whose appeal faded in the mid-1960s.

Into the 1960s, a series of short-lived programs featuring private detectives emerged, each with a unique twist. Anthony George and Doug McClure starred in the CBS series *Checkmate* (1960-62), in which the two detectives worked to prevent homicides. Howard Duff played the title role of *Dante*, a 1960-61 NBC series which focused on an underworld figure who had turned legit. Gene Barry played millionaire police captain Amos Burke in *Burke's Law*, a 1963-65 entry from ABC, and Patrick O'Neal starred as pathologist Daniel Coffee in the 1960 CBS series *Diagnosis Unknown*.

One of the most significant series from this era was ABC's daytime drama *Dark Shadows* (1966-71), which featured the supernatural antics of the Collins family, which had fallen prey to its 200-year-old family vampire, Barnabas. A nighttime version of the series in 1991 failed to recapture its 1960s faddish appeal; however, the original series is now offered on videocassette and the show continues to generate a cult following. The same is true of the British suspense series *The Prisoner*, created and produced by series star Patrick McGoohan. Although the series ran only one season on CBS (1968-69), its episodes have become top sellers in the home video market.

The 1960s also brought the debut of *Mannix* (CBS, 1967-75), which featured Mike Connors in the title role. The long-running drama was considered one of the most violent detective series of the era; during its heyday, the comedy team Bob and Ray, during their weekly radio show, often parodied *Mannix*'s senseless violence.

Mannix was one of the first TV series to feature the chase scene, now a staple of both cop and detective dramas. It was also one of the first detective series to feature an African-American actress, with Gail Fisher playing Mannix's girl Friday, Peggy Fair.

Several African-American detective programs also appeared during the 1970s, with the CBS series *Shaft* and the NBC series *Tenafly* both running one season in 1973-74. While *Shaft* featured the same sort of action and stereotypes of the feature film upon which it was based, Harry Tenafly, played by James McEachin, was a dedicated family man who divided his time between his home life and work as a detective.

Suspense appeared to be given a new life in the 1970s with Rod Serling's *Night Gallery* (NBC, 1970-73) and *Kolchak: The Night Stalker* (ABC, 1974-75). However, neither was successful in capturing a sizable audience, despite the fact that *The Night Stalker*, which featured a reporter who confronted supernatural criminals, was based on ABC's highest-rated TV movie of 1974.

Columbo (see entry), one of the most significant series of the decade, earned more than popular and critical acclaim —it introduced a new fictional detective whose fame rivals that of Hercule Poirot and Sherlock Holmes. *Columbo* was the brainchild of *Mannix* creators Richard Levinson and William Link. But Columbo was quite unlike Mannix—or any other detective TV had seen. Devoid of car chases, sexy women, or rough and tumble action, each *Columbo* turned on the shrewd tenacity of the LAPD's premier homicide detective. Although Columbo worked for the police department, he was seldom seen interacting with other cops, making *Columbo* a true mystery series.

Columbo, which aired as one of four series within *The NBC Mystery Movie* (1971-77), was TV's first reverse-whodunit. Each episode opened with the audience seeing the murderer commit what he or she believed to be the perfect crime. Columbo's task was to unravel the clues that would convict the murderer, who was invariably wealthy, respectable, and professional. Perhaps Columbo's popularity was due to the fact that he was an everyday person, always underestimated by his adversaries, but he emerged successful in the end.

Like other fictional detectives of his stature, Columbo has been parodied in sketch comedies. His worn trench coat, old Jaguar convertible, and ever-present cheap cigar have each become pop-culture icons. After quitting the show, series star Peter Falk revived the character in several ABC-TV movies.

Another nontraditional detective was found in *The Rockford Files* (NBC, 1974-80). Although the series had its share of love interests and action, the Travis McGee-like Rockford, played by James Garner, was a reluctant hero who would rather relax at his beachfront trailer than take a case that may lead to physical harm. Nevertheless, Rockford often became the target of mob-backed criminals who popped up in a series of complex plot twists. The series has done well in syndication and its Mike Post theme hit No. 10 on the *Billboard* Top 60 in 1975.

The 1980s was certainly the decade of the private investigator, with such wildly successful series as *Magnum P.I.* (CBS, 1980-88), *Mike Hammer* (CBS, 1984-87), and *Simon & Simon* (CBS, 1981-88). *Remington Steele* and *Moonlighting* brought back the popular *Thin Man*-inspired romantic detective couple. *Moonlighting* (see entry), starring Cybill Shepherd and Bruce Willis, was particularly effective for its "breaking-the-fourth-wall" humor which often poked fun at the series itself. *Moonlighting*'s Al Jarreau theme song made it to No. 23 on the *Billboard* charts in 1987, and the series brought superstardom for Willis, who has since gone on to feature films.

By far, the most popular series of the 1980s has been *Murder, She Wrote* (see entry). Done in classic whodunit fashion, *Murder, She Wrote* provides viewers with just enough clues to solve the case, which may account for its popularity. While mystery and suspense offerings no longer account for 50 percent of prime time programming, *Murder, She Wrote* stands as an example of the genre's longevity.

Bibliography

Boddy, William. *Fifties Television*. Urbana: U of Illinois P, 1993.

Brooks, Tim, and Earle Marsh. *The Complete Directory to Prime Time Network TV Shows, 1946-Present*. New York: Ballantine, 1992.

Dawidziak, Mark. *The Columbo Phile*. New York: Mysterious, 1989.

Sackett, Susan. *Prime Time Hits*. New York: Billboard, 1993.

Zicree, Marc Scott. *The Twilight Zone Companion*. Los Angeles: Silman-James, 1989.

Michael B. Kassel

Mystery Weekends. Murder mystery weekends, derived from the old parlor murder games of the 1920s, offer up a range of mystery-related activities such as games, dramatic productions, and especially large-scale staged entertainments during which participants compete to solve mysteries. Such theatrical events often take place on trains and ships, at ranches, restaurants, hotels, and resorts. They can occur over cocktails or dinner, or may extend over a weekend or even a week in which the mystery-solving venture is combined with leisure activity and the amenities.

The American mystery event craze began with the first Mohonk Mystery Weekend sponsored in 1977 by Dilys Winn, owner of New York's Murder Ink bookstore, and held annually since, an elaborate three-day pageant concluding with team solutions to a mystery created especially for the occasion. At present, over 200 companies in the United States alone actively write and perform mystery events. Some involve actors while others have guests play the roles; most are based on a script and feature clues such as simulated police memos, autopsy reports, and crime scenes, as well as opportunities for personal interrogation. Whatever the format, the event must always challenge amateur gumshoes, who pay to attend.

Bibliography

Dunn, Jerry Camarillo, Jr. "Murder They Wrote." *National Geographic Traveler* Jan. 1995: 24-28.

Edwards, Karen S. "Murder Most Merry." *Americana* Aug. 1990: 55-58.

Newman, Julia. "Getting Away with Murder." *Travel & Leisure* Nov. 1986: 26-36.

Janet A. Rudolph

Nancy Drew. In 1930, capitalizing on the popularity of the Hardy Boys mysteries with girl readers, Edward Stratemeyer created a girls' detective series featuring a 16-year-old heroine in *The Secret of the Old Clock*. She was Nancy Drew, "amateur sleuth," eventually to be the protagonist of more than 200 adventures and a familiar icon in American popular culture with her roadster convertible and Titian blond hair. In successive books, *The Hidden Staircase* (1930), *The Bungalow Mystery* (1930), and down through the long list of cases, Nancy and her chums Bess and George and boyfriend Ned solve crimes that baffle adults.

As with the Hardy Boys books, Stratemeyer used anonymous ghostwriters to construct the books, for which he provided titles and story outlines. For many years, his Stratemeyer Syndicate (see entry) kept a tight lid on the real identity of "Carolyn Keene." Recently it has been revealed that journalist Mildred Wirt Benson penned 23 of the early titles. Benson's legacy to the character is her adventurous and assertive nature. Stratemeyer's daughter, Harriet Adams, claimed to have written a number of the books, and was still closely involved with the series at the time of her death in 1982.

Between 1959 and 1977, the earlier 34 books in the sequence were updated, cleansed of their racist allusions, and shortened to make them more appealing to contemporary—and younger—readers, a move that prompted critics to charge that Nancy had been robbed of her maturity and autonomy in the revision process. Simon & Schuster bought the syndicate in 1984, and has continued to produce Nancy Drew books. At present, the publishers are issuing two concurrent series, one for grade-school readers (which has restored the more intrepid, risk-taking elements of the character), and one for young adult readers. This latter Nancy Drew Casefiles series combines murder mystery and adolescent romance fiction formats, wherein the plots have become more sensational, and Nancy's interests in boys and fashion have been augmented.

Bibliography

Billman, Carol. *The Secret of the Stratemeyer Syndicate: Nancy Drew, The Hardy Boys and the Million Dollar Fiction Factory*. New York: Ungar, 1986.

Caprio, Betsy. *The Mystery of Nancy Drew*. Trabuco Canyon: Source, 1992.

Craig, Patricia, and Mary Cadogan. *The Lady Investigates: Women Detectives and Spies in Fiction*. New York: St. Martin's, 1981.

Mason, Bobbie Ann. *The Girl Sleuth: A Feminist Guide*. Old Westbury: Feminist, 1975.

Plunkett-Powell, Karen. *The Nancy Drew Scrapbook*. New York: St. Martin's, 1993.

Dean James
Jacqueline Reid-Walsh

Nast, Thomas (1840-1902), a man who was to achieve both national acclaim and condemnation as a political cartoonist and satirist in America, was born in Landau, Germany, to a father who played the trombone in a Bavarian military band. They moved to New York when the boy was six, and lived in Greenwich Village. Nast's talent for drawing revealed itself early, and after sporadic attempts at formal education and some classes at the National Academy of Design, Nast secured his first job as an illustrator for *Leslie's Weekly*, at the age of 15. His early work—drawings on wooden engraving blocks—documented prize fights and local scandals; he also drew illustrations for *Gil Blas* which he exhibited at the National Academy. The precariousness of the economics at *Leslie's* sent the young man into freelance work for other New York papers, and resulted in a trip to England to document a major fight. Nast then joined the volunteer forces in Italy supporting Garibaldi, and saw the campaign through to its conclusion in 1860. He worked for the *News* and then briefly for Frank Leslie again, before starting his 24-year-long career with *Harper's Weekly* in 1862.

Nast was a great supporter of Lincoln, and his always positive illustrations of the Union cause earned the tribute from Lincoln that "Thomas Nast has been our best recruiting sergeant." A man who could produce both savage caricatures and sentimental patriotic evocations, Nast became a major force in American presidential campaigns for the next several decades, from his support of Lincoln and Grant to his attacks on James Blaine in 1884.

But it was not so much his ability to zero in on the physical characteristics of his subjects that earned Nast such renown, but rather his cutting commentary on the ways each had dishonored the public's trust. The artist is justifiably best remembered for taking on Tammany Hall, and particularly his relentless attacks on the "Ring" dominated by William M. "Boss" Tweed. Though several of the individual cartoons, "Let Us Prey," "Too Thin," and "The Tammany Tiger Loose," continue to appear in cartoon anthologies and illustrated histories of New York in the 1870s, it was the unrelenting consistency of the attack that helped bring down the corrupt government. Though publicly and privately threatened, and despite substantial financial offers to travel in Europe to study art, Nast maintained his dedication and zeal in pursuing the attack.

He continued to produce images for *Harper's* as well as going on the lecture circuit, and finally mortgaged his home to take over the *New York Gazette*, later to become *Nast's Weekly*. It failed in 1893, and facing debts and a public that was losing interest in his work, he continued to freelance while doing several large-scale historical paintings relating to Lee's surrender at the end of the Civil War. In deep financial straits, he accepted the position of consul in Guayaquil, in Ecuador, but died there of yellow fever a few months after his arrival in 1902.

Bibliography
Hoff, Syd. *Boss Tweed and the Man Who Drew Him.* New York: Coward, 1978.
Keller, Morton. *The Art and Publication of Thomas Nast.* New York: Oxford UP, 1968.
Paine, Albert Bigelow. *Thomas Nast.* New York: Chelsea, 1980.

David Sokol

National Enquirer, The, epitomizes America's weekly supermarket tabloid newspapers, those compendia of gossip, sensational stories, and self-help pieces which saturate and guide the gossips of America (see Tabloid Newspapers). It owes its success to the late Generoso (Gene) Pope, who established the current tabloid format. Pope bought the struggling 30-year-old paper in 1952, trying various formats before settling for gore, having noticed how auto accidents drew crowds. Until 1968, the paper built its circulation of over a million on stories and photos of horrific murders and accidents, with a sprinkling of unexplained mysteries, human interest tales, and vicious celebrity gossip.

Circulation then stalled, and Pope turned his attention to supermarkets as a new sales outlet, creating the "family-style" tabloid to fit the grocery store check-out line. This marketing move was crucial to his success, along with the decision to publish weekly, removing the need to compete with daily newspapers. Pope's marketing techniques successfully wooed a largely blue-collar readership, of both men and women.

Unlike British tabloids, which feature nude women and explicit stories about sex, the *Enquirer* made its name on celebrity innuendo, "feel-good" human-interest tales, and simplified medical and self-help stories. By the 1980s, the *Enquirer* was selling over 4 million copies a week, and circulation still hovers around 2 million. In 1989, after Pope's death, it was sold to MacFadden Holdings for a reported $412 million.

The style and content of the *Enquirer* and its imitators, though despised by critics, have had a far-reaching impact on many genres of popular culture, from gossip magazines to daily newspapers and television news.

Bibliography
Bernard, George. *Inside the* National Enquirer*: Confessions of an Undercover Reporter.* Port Washington: Ashley, 1977.
Bird, S. Elizabeth. *For Inquiring Minds: A Cultural Study of Supermarket Tabloids.* Knoxville: U of Tennessee P, 1992.

S. Elizabeth Bird

National Lampoon's Animal House (1978) was one of the successful and influential movies of its year. Directed by John Landis and written by Harold Ramis, Douglas Kenney, and Chris Miller, this inexpensive ($2.7 million) film featured a drunken, slovenly group of partying, beer-guzzling, know-nothing fraternity boys, circa 1962. The film's emphasis on parties, drinking, sex, and gross-out humor captivated the nation and played on the dark side of American youth culture and entertainment.

The star of *National Lampoon's Animal House* was John Belushi (see entry), a *Saturday Night Live* regular, in his first movie role. The film also featured actors who went on to larger roles in the 1980s, including Thomas Hulce, who played Mozart in the film version of Peter Shaffer's *Amadeus*; Stephen Furst, who was a regular on NBC's *St. Elsewhere*; Karen Allen, who played opposite Harrison Ford's Indiana Jones in *Raiders of the Lost Ark*, and Kevin Bacon, who starred in *Footloose*.

Television executives quickly recognized the success of *Animal House* and all three networks created shows focusing on Greek life as winter replacements. NBC introduced *Brothers and Sisters* and CBS offered *Co-ed Fever*. Neither one lasted long. ABC successfully acquired the rights to the film and the characters. They held over some of the original cast, including John Vernon, who played Dean Wormer, and Stephen Furst, and the pilot even was written by the movie's scriptwriters. However, the show, for obvious reasons, was unable to sustain the antic, perverse humor of the original R-rated film.

Animal House not only changed the party scene of college students, but also proved to be a major boost for the magazine *National Lampoon*. It was their first foray into the world of movies, and this film indicated they could successfully make the transition from print into film. They have since gone on to produce a number of feature films, including the widely successful vacation movie series, *National Lampoon's Vacation* (1983), *European Vacation* (1985), *Christmas Vacation* (1989), and *Vegas Vacation* (1997), starring Chevy Chase and Beverly D'Angelo.

Bibliography
Darlin, Lynn. "Toga! Toga! Toga!" *Washington Post* 26 Sept. 1978.
Rich, Frank. "Princely Palaces, Animal Houses." *Time* 22 Jan. 1979.
——. "School Days." *Time* 14 Aug. 1978.
Shah, Diane K. "To-ga! To-ga! To-ga!" *Newsweek* 2 Oct. 1978.

William C. Boles

National Public Radio (NPR), a successful alternative to commercial radio, was incorporated February 26, 1970, by the Corporation for Public Broadcasting (CPB) to interconnect a network of affiliated noncommercial radio stations. Unlike the Public Broadcasting Service (PBS), the television service created by CPB, NPR was to be responsible for producing programming to be delivered via the network. It has grown into one of the most influential voices of responsible news in the United States.

The first programming transmitted on the newly established NPR was live coverage of the Senate Vietnam hearings on April 19, 1971. Later that same year, a national newsmagazine, *All Things Considered*, debuted and remains one of NPR's most popular programs. Two years after its initial broadcast, *All Things Considered* won the Peabody Award for its live coverage of the Senate Watergate hearings.

Every week, an estimated 14.5 million people listen to the diverse programming provided by National Public Radio. There are more than 600 National Public Radio member stations currently operating in the U.S., and they take, on the average, 22 percent of their daily schedules from the programming menu provided by the network. These affiliates, while not required to carry any set amount of network programming, continue to deliver increasing numbers of radio listeners nationally.

Unlike commercial broadcast networks that often pay affiliated stations for carrying network programming, NPR member stations must subscribe to those NPR services they wish to broadcast. Currently, about 60 percent of the network's operating income comes from member stations, with less than 4 percent coming from the government. Contributions from the private sector are from two primary sources: the individual station's membership (in the form of individual listener contributions), and private businesses, which pay for program production or for carrying programs on individual stations. Recognition for these contributions comes from on-air acknowledgments called underwriting announcements. Federal law prohibits noncommercial radio stations from airing commercials, or any type of announcement considered promotional for the sponsoring business.

Much of the programming offered by NPR is news or informative in nature. Among those National Public Radio news programs that have been available to affiliates are: *Morning Edition*, a daily news program transmitted live via satellite from the NPR studios in Washington, DC, a program which debuted in 1979; *Weekend Edition*, a Saturday news magazine first broadcast in November 1985; and its most recent addition, *Talk of the Nation*, a live call-in program, which debuted in 1991. NPR's news gathering operation includes domestic news bureaus in Washington, New York, Chicago, and Los Angeles, as well as bureaus in London, Berlin, and Moscow.

Best known for its news and information programs, National Public Radio also provides programming to its member stations concerning the arts and culture. These offerings include *Performance Today*, a portrait of the classical music world; *Afropop Worldwide*, featuring African music and the related musical sounds of Brazil, Columbia, Haiti, Cuba, Paris, and London; and *NPR Playhouse*, one of the few remaining outlets of the classic art form of radio drama.

Increasingly, National Public Radio is an alternative source for radio listeners seeking in-depth news, information, and coverage of popular culture. As virtually the only source for such programming as dramatic radio presentations and world music, and the alternative journalistic view for such significant world events as the war in the Persian Gulf and the nomination of Supreme Court Clarence Thomas, National Public Radio has become the epitome of the ideals of noncommercial public broadcasting.

Bibliography

Collins, Mary. *National Public Radio: The Cast of Characters*. Washington, DC: Seven Locks, 1993.

NPR Online. Available: www.npr.org. 25 April 2000.

Witherspoon, John, and Roselle Kovitz. *The History of Public Broadcasting*. Washington, DC: Current Newspaper, 1987.

Thomas Birk

Native American Crime Fiction is developing rapidly as a subgenre. The reasons are three-fold. Crime fiction, in general, depends on new and preferably exotic fields in which to expand. Many authors, both Indian and non-Indian, feel that the American dominant society owes the Indians restitution for all the injustices inflicted upon those people through the years; several other authors merely want to use Indian—and reservation—society as a good setting for entertaining stories, and if they teach something positive about Indian society and negative about white mistreatment of those people, then all the better. Finally, there is a growing body of Indian scholars and authors of crime fiction who are using this medium to express their insights into Indian-white cultures and conflicts from the point of view of inside Indian society or partially outside.

One of the oldest and most respected authors of Indian crime fiction is Anthony Grove "Tony" Hillerman (see entry), ex-journalist and academic administrator. Hillerman has written a dozen and a half novels about two protagonists individually and together: Joe Leaphorn, introduced in *The Blessing Way* (1970) and Jimmy (Jim) Chee, introduced in *People of Darkness* (1980), and the two together originally in *Skinwalkers* (1986).

The Hopis of New Mexico and northeastern Arizona are treated realistically by Jake Page in five novels to date, all of which showcase a large, blind sculptor named Mo Bowdre. The latest, *A Certain Malice* (1998), is one of the more profound and searching books in crime fiction or any other literature.

James D. Doss writes of the Utes of Wyoming, Colorado, and Utah. His first novel, *A Shaman Sings* (1994), sets the pattern for his development in the kind of mysticism which seems unique to Indians.

Margaret Coel writes of the Arapahos of Wyoming. In *The Eagle Catcher* (1995), her first novel, she introduces her two main characters, Father John O'Malley, head pastor of St. Francis Mission, and Vicky Holden, Indian lawyer who is dedicated to protecting Indians from white injustices.

Peter Bowen writes of two of the genre's most amusing characters in a loose but distinct group. The characters are Gabriel Du Pre, an inspector of cattle brands, and his girlfriend Madelaine, a lusty sounding board for and governor of Du Pre's rage. In *Coyote Wind* (1994), his first novel, Bowen sets the stage for his development of a unique people, the Metis, who are distinctly Montanan.

Aimee and David Thurlo have written some 30 novels, but their strongest series, beginning with *Blackening Song* (1995), revolves around the Navajos and a protagonist named Ella Clah.

One of the stronger voices today is Dana Stabenow, who grew up in a half Aleut-half Filipino family in Alaska. She writes of the Aleuts, who are distinct from the dozen other kinds of people living in our 49th state and are not Native Americans. Stabenow's heroine is Kate Shugak, a young dynamo of action and amusement. From *A Cold Day for Murder* (1992), Stabenow's first novel about her, she has grown in adventure and importance through seven novels to date.

Three outstanding authors with Indian blood are Jean Hager, Mardi Oakley Medawar, and Louis Owens. Hager (one-sixteenth Cherokee) writes of two protagonists, one male and one female. In *The Grandfather Medicine* (1989), she creates Mitchell Bushyhead, Chief of Police of a small Oklahoma town, and in *Ravenmocker* (1992) she begins to develop Molly Bearpaw, Investigator of the American Advocacy League. Mardi Oakley Medawar is an Eastern Band Cherokee living in North Carolina. Her two novels to date, *Death at Rainy Mountain* (1996) and *Witch of the Palo Duro* (1997), are filled with Kiowa lore and mysticism.

One of the more promising Indian authors is Louis Owens, of Choctaw-Cherokee-Irish descent and a professor at the University of New Mexico, Albuquerque. He writes a somewhat more intellectualized and angry series, beginning with *The Sharpest Sight* (1991), in which Indians live uncomfortably in and at least rhetorically antagonistic to the dominant white society.

Other authors use Indian culture only incidentally or as background for conflicts which flare in the larger white society. Thomas Perry, author of several conventional adventure novels, writes of Jane Whitefield, a Seneca woman who is in the "research and consulting" business, in which she aids people who need to disappear and change identities. Her method is to use her friends and relatives in the Seneca and Iroquois nations to assist in the changing of identities.

Perhaps most amusing is J. F. Trainor, whose heroine, Angela Biwaban, is an Anishinabe princess. Trainor uses her and her adventures to successfully spoof Western and American adventures and heroes. She is the female Lone Ranger who scoffs at Nero Wolfe as an "old couch potato."

Bibliography

Deloria, Philip J. *Playing Indian.* New Haven: Yale UP, 1998.

Dilworth, Leah. *Imagining Indians in the Southwest.* Washington: Smithsonian Institution P, 1996.

Owens, Louis. *Mixedblood Messages: Literature, Film, Family, Place.* Norman: U of Oklahoma P, 1998.

Rollins, Peter C., and John E. O'Connor. *Hollywood's Indian: The Portrayal of the Native American in Film.* Lexington: UP of Kentucky, 1998.

Ray B. Browne

See also
Ethnic Mysteries
Regional Mysteries

Native American Radio. In 1972, the first Native–owned and operated radio station went on the air in Bethel, AK. During the next two decades a total of 24 Native–owned and operated stations would be licensed and become increasingly important.

Most Native–owned radio stations are located in the western U.S. The largest concentrations of stations are in Alaska and the southwest states of New Mexico and Arizona. Others are scattered about Oregon, California, Colorado, North and South Dakota, Wisconsin, Alabama, North Carolina, and New York. Only four Native radio stations are located east of the Mississippi River. Oklahoma, which has the second largest Native population of any state, has no Native–owned and operated radio stations.

One goal of many Native stations is to preserve what remains of local Native languages and cultures. Many broadcast traditional stories, news, and other information in local dialects. Native stations serve as forums for discussing social problems. Local news, public affairs, and call-in programs are common, as are reports by tribal governments and agencies. Entertainment directed at the interests of local Natives, including popular music, is another goal of Native stations. Programming in Native languages ranges from over 90 hours per week at KTDB-FM (Navajo) in New Mexico, to no native language programming at WASG-AM (Creek) in Alabama, and WYRU (Lumbee) in North Carolina, where the Native languages have been lost.

Native radio is no longer restricted to local service. Since 1987, National Native News has been broadcasting daily newscasts to more than 200 noncommercial radio stations across the United States over the National Public Radio (NPR) network. Since 1977, the Native American Public Broadcasting Consortium (NAPBC) in Lincoln, NE, has been helping to develop and distribute Native-produced programs to mainstream media. In 1993, the NAPBC received federal funding to create a new satellite interconnection system that will be used to distribute national Native radio programming even more extensively.

Other groups are helping develop Native American radio. The Indigenous Broadcast Center, created in 1990, trains Native radio personnel. The Southwest Native Radio Coalition, a regional group of noncommercial stations, sponsors joint training and other grant-related projects.

Bibliography

Brigham, J. C., and B. L. Smith. "Native Radio in the United States: A New Oral Tradition." *Many Faces: Media and Diversity.* Ed. S. Biagi. Belmont: Wadsworth, 1994.

Lightcloud, J. "Native American Radio: Broadcasting and Two-Way Communications Serving the American Indian. You Can Hear Them Too!" *Popular Communications* Oct. 1990: 9-10.

Smith, B. L., and J. C. Brigham. "Native Radio Broadcasting in North America: An Overview of Systems in the United States and Canada." *Journal of Broadcasting and Electronic Media* 36.2 (1992): 183-94.

Jerry C. Brigham
Bruce L. Smith

See also
Community Radio

Nature Magazines can be broadly categorized into two types: those focusing on environmentalism, and those emphasizing outdoor recreation. The most widely circulated nature periodicals are *Sierra*, *Audubon*, and *Outside*. While their editorial content sometimes overlaps, *Sierra* and *Audubon* stress ecological issues and natural history, while *Outside* is primarily devoted to recreation.

Sierra, the oldest of the three, shares its roots with modern environmentalism. It was first published in 1893 as *Sierra Club Bulletin* to speak for the preservation organization started by John Muir. Today, while *Sierra* maintains its environmental emphasis, its 500,000 readers can also peruse articles on diverse topics from outdoor fiction to eco-psychology. *Sierra* thus presents environmentalism as both politics and a lifestyle.

Audubon also originated with the conservation movement that expanded into American popular culture at the turn of the century. It was first published in 1899 as the official voice of the Audubon Society. With a contemporary circulation of half a million, *Audubon* focuses on conservation and natural history (especially of birds), and features important nature writers.

First published in 1976, *Outside* is a product of the 1970s boom in outdoor recreation. By concentrating on outdoor activities like climbing, hiking, camping, cycling, and others, *Outside* promotes recreational adventuring, and features travel, fitness, destinations, celebrities, and equipment reviews.

Beyond these three leading nature magazines, U.S. readers may choose from a range of smaller publications. Some, like *Climbing* or *Backpacker,* are devoted to specific activities, while others, such as *Western Outdoors*, focus on regions. Broadly speaking, *National Geographic*, the laureled magazine of international geography, appeals also to readers of nature periodicals since it often highlights the dramatic landscapes and natural phenomena of the world's many exotic locales.

Bibliography

Herr, Serena. "It's Not Easy Being Green." *Publish* July 1993: 18-23.

Hochwald, Lambeth. "A Women's Gym without the Walls." *Folio: The Magazine for Magazine Management* 1 Nov. 1995: 34.

Kauchak, Therese. "People to Watch: Bryant Inside and Outside." *Advertising Age* Oct. 1990: 516-17.

Fred Lifton

NBC, the National Broadcasting Company television network, is the oldest and one of the most influential television programming services in the history of television in the U.S. From its creation in the mid-1940s, for four decades NBC-TV functioned as the most famous unit of the Radio Corporation of America. In 1986, NBC was purchased by manufacturing giant General Electric and since then has functioned as a highly profitable, yet quite small, division of one of the world's largest corporations.

NBC links some 210 over-the-air television stations around the United States, offering programming 24 hours a day. It is famous for its morning *Today* show, afternoon soap operas (including the popular *Days of Our Lives*), early evening newscasts, prime-time series such as *Friends* and *Law & Order*, and the late night *The Tonight Show.*

NBC also owns and operates six over-the-air TV stations, based in New York City, Los Angeles, Chicago, Washington, Miami, and Denver. These six stations reach more than 20 percent of the households with television in the U.S. To show how much this core of owned and operated TV stations meant to General Electric, consider that in 1987 General Electric was willing to spend $270 million to acquire WTVJ-TV in Miami.

The 1986 merger that brought NBC under the General Electric corporate umbrella was significant. In retrospect it proved to be one of the biggest deals of the "Go-Go Mergers and Acquisitions Era" of the 1980s. The purchase price was in excess of $6 billion. But unlike rivals ABC, CBS, and Fox, NBC is buried in General Electric, which in terms of sales, gross profits, assets, and market value ranks in the Top 10 largest corporations headquartered in the United States. Critics often ask whether NBC can fairly report news that involves its massive corporate parent.

General Electric did expand NBC's reach. During the late 1980s, NBC paid $10 million for a significant share in Visnews, an international video news service. This agreement gave Visnews the right to sell NBC news programming to 400 clients in 84 countries around the world. At the same time NBC also designated the Australian Television Network as its first overseas affiliate.

In 1993, NBC and Credit Lyonnais, the vast and influential French bank, acquired a majority share in the largest programming service, the Super Channel, in Europe. NBC runs the Super Channel, an advertising-supported satellite service based in London, and seeks to reach more than 50 million TV homes across Europe. Gradually NBC adds programming to the Super Channel that it has already created for its network in the U.S. News, sports, and entertainment shows plus the content of cable's CNBC now flow into the Super Channel lineup.

NBC did not neglect investments in the U.S. It has heavily invested tens of millions of dollars in the News Channel. Based in Charlotte, NC, the NBC News Channel acts as a 24-hour-a-day clearinghouse to NBC's more than 210 affiliates. The News Channel brings to network shows (like NBC's *Today* and NBC's *News at Sunrise*) reports from around the United States, principally from affiliate stations.

NBC has a long and proud history. Founded by radio manufacturer RCA in the mid-1920s, by 1930, NBC had two radio networks and was the most powerful corporate force in radio broadcasting. Pioneering the manufacture of television sets, RCA founder and long-time chief executive officer David Sarnoff put the NBC television network on the air after World War II. Indeed, through the 1950s and 1960s, color broadcasting by NBC-TV helped RCA lead the world in selling color television sets. NBC also innovated with *Today, Tonight,* and the variety show format, in particular starring TV's first great personality—Milton Berle.

In the 1970s and 1980s, NBC participated in the glory days of network television. Top 10 shows included *Sanford and Son, Little House on the Prairie,* and *The A-Team.* But if there was an apex in NBC programming, it came in the mid-1980s. Thursdays led NBC's drive to ratings superiority under new leader Grant Tinker. *The Cosby Show,* along with *Family Ties, A Different World,* and *Cheers* (in various combinations), ranked as the top shows in all of television from 1985 through 1990.

Bibliography

Alexander, Alison, James Owers, and Rod Carveth. *Media Economics: Theory and Practice.* Hillsdale: Erlbaum, 1993.

Bilby, Kenneth. *The General: David Sarnoff and the Rise of the Communications Industry.* New York: Harper, 1986.

Castleman, Harry, and Walter J. Podrazik. *Watching TV: Four Decades of American Television.* New York: McGraw-Hill, 1982.

MacDonald, J. Fred. *One Nation under Television: The Rise and Decline of Network Television.* New York: Pantheon, 1990.

Tichy, Noel M., and Stratford Sherman. *Control Your Destiny or Someone Else Will: How Jack Welch Is Making General Electric the World's Most Competitive Company.* New York: Doubleday, 1993.

Douglas Gomery

Uniforms and mementos of the Negro League, at the Baseball Hall of Fame and Museum, Cooperstown, NY. Photo courtesy of Mark McDermott.

Negro Leagues in segregated baseball have a long and embarrassing history. Baseball has long been considered America's national pastime. By the 1990s, the growing interest in baseball history and its relationship to American society, reflected in such phenomena as Ken Burns's 1994 television documentary, *Baseball,* a series of symposia on baseball and society at Cooperstown, and a growing library of books on socioeconomic aspects of baseball, had elevated the sport in America's consciousness to the position of a social barometer. In truth, baseball had always occupied that position, especially regarding race relations in the United States.

Blacks were largely excluded from professional organized baseball throughout the 19th century, sometimes by explicit directive, at other times by informal "gentlemen's agreements." Some exceptions occurred. Bud Fowler (1858-1913) played for several white minor league teams; and Moses Fleetwood Walker (1857-1924) caught for Toledo in the American Association (then a major league) in 1884. By the end of the 1880s, however, the door of organized baseball had closed tightly against blacks. All that remained for black players was to form their own teams and leagues.

The first two decades of the 20th century saw the continued rise in popularity of baseball in the black community. Chicago became the baseball center for blacks, as it became the capital city of jazz during the 1920s. One of the baseball giants of this period, Andrew "Rube" Foster (1879-1930), became playing manager of the Chicago Leland Giants and, in 1909, led the team into the Park Owners Association, an organization in which all teams had to own their stadiums. The Chicago Giants stadium, which included 3,000 grandstand seats and 400 box seats, was at the time the most impressive black-owned stadium in all of baseball. Foster later formed his own team, the Chicago American Giants, and was the guiding force behind creation of the Negro National League. The league played its first games in 1920, with Foster as the league's president. For his accomplishments as a manager, organizer, and executive, Foster earned the title "the father of black baseball." Foster's accomplishments, however, transcended sport. What he helped establish was the largest black-run business in the country.

Black baseball, with the rest of the nation, was hit hard by the Great Depression. The Negro National League even folded in 1931. Recovery picked up speed in 1933 with the creation of a new Negro National League (extensively funded by underworld figures) and continued throughout the 1930s with the inauguration of annual East-West All-Star Games, barnstorming tours against major league teams, baseball tournaments in Denver and Wichita, and establishment of a Negro American League in 1937 (minus the criminal influence of the new NNL).

The popularity of the Negro leagues would continue throughout most of the 1940s. In 1944, for example, the East-West game drew 46,247 fans, while the major league All-Star Game attracted only 29,589. Much of black baseball's popularity was due to the style of play (with an emphasis on speed—bunts, hit-and-run plays, stolen bases) and, of course, to the exciting players who starred for the teams, many of whom were as famous within the black community as the greatest stars of the white major leagues—sometimes more famous. The Negro leagues in the 1920s, 1930s, and 1940s featured such legendary players as pitcher LeRoy "Satchel" Paige (1906-82), third baseman William "Judy" Johnson (1900-89), catcher (and one of the greatest sluggers of all time) Josh Gibson (1911-47), and center fielder James "Cool Papa" Bell (1903-91).

From the early days of black baseball, the black community delighted in seeing black baseball heroes outplay their white counterparts in hard-fought exhibition games. Rube Foster earned his nickname by outpitching the great major-leaguer Rube Waddell (1876-1914) in 1902. In later years, fans filled stadiums to watch Satchel Paige duel Dizzy Dean (1911-74), who called Paige the best pitcher that he had ever seen.

The integration of the big leagues in 1947 with the arrival of Jackie Robinson (1919-72) also had its down side. Integration, even on the playing field, was slow in coming. Not until 1959, when Pumpsie Green (1933-) joined the Boston Red Sox, did every major league team employ at least one black player; and still by the late 1990s few blacks were to be found in managerial or executive positions—and

573

none owned major league teams. Some members of organized baseball had argued in the early 1940s that integrating the majors would destroy the Negro leagues; this prophecy, which many saw as just an excuse for excluding blacks, proved true. The Negro National League disbanded after the 1948 season as the majors began to attract the best of its players. The Negro American League continued through 1960 but with declining support.

Bibliography

Ashe, Arthur R., Jr. "A Hard Road to Glory, 1988." *Baseball: The African-American Athlete in Baseball*. New York: Amistad, 1993.

Peterson, Robert. *Only the Ball Was White*. 2d ed. New York: McGraw-Hill, 1984.

Riley, James A. *The Biographical Encyclopedia of the Negro Baseball Leagues*. New York: Carroll & Graf, 1994.

Rogosin, Don. *Invisible Men: Life in Baseball's Negro Leagues*. New York: Atheneum, 1983.

Ward, Geoffrey C., and Ken Burns. *Baseball: An Illustrated History*. (Companion volume to Burns's PBS television series.) New York: Knopf, 1994.

Edward J. Rielly

Nelson, Theodor ("Ted") Holm, who coined the terms "hypertext" and "hypermedia," turned an information retrieval idea into a utopian ideal for expression and liberation through computers and became a culture hero among computer hackers. In 1960, Nelson was at Harvard, intending to become a writer and a filmmaker, when he took a class on computers. Over the course of several years, he wrote about computers, denouncing their use by a "priesthood" (*Computer Lib 4*) of computer specialists to control information for large organizations. He called for "a new era of personal computing" (*Computer Lib 7*). Nelson became influential in 1974 and 1975 with two very different versions of *Computer Lib*, an eclectic collection of thoughts and pasted pictures. The second version was occasioned by the arrival of the first personal computer, the Altair. Nelson saw it as a fulfillment of his predictions; however, the self-published futurist has often been accused of taking credit after the fact. Other books include *Literary Machines* (1982) on hypertext and literature. Nelson's liberationist visions have inspired software developers. Nelson's Xanadu, a hypermedia tool that could connect all of the world's electronic documents, has never materialized, but its influence on such multimedia software as Apple's Hypercard and the World Wide Web is obvious. In the 1990s, many of his predictions seem to be coming true, and he still works on Xanadu.

Bibliography

Nelson, Theodor H. *Computer Lib/Dream Machines*. Redmond: Microsoft, 1987.

——. *Literary Machines*. Sausalito: Mindful, 1982.

David Norton

Nelson, Willie (1933-), brought together the country and rock audiences beginning in the 1970s and reestablished Texas as a creative center for country music. In so doing, he became a leading influence in American country music.

Willie Nelson grew up in Abbott, TX, near Waco, and was influenced by the western swing of Bob Wills, other Texas acts such as Lefty Frizzell, Hank Thompson, Floyd Tillman, and Bill Boyd and the Cowboy Ramblers, as well as the pop acts he heard on the radio. He began writing poems and songs when he was five and joined his first band, a German polka group, the Johnny Paycheck Band, when he was 12. After high school he entered the Air Force briefly, then began a series of jobs as a disk jockey, Bible salesman, and whatever else he could find to support his wife and three children.

Willie Nelson recorded his first song, "No Place for Me," in 1957 while he was working as a disk jockey in Vancouver, WA. He moved back to Texas and settled in Pasadena, near Houston, where he worked as a disk jockey and guitar teacher for Paul Buskirk. Desperate for money, Nelson sold two of his songs, "Family Bible" and "Night Life," to Buskirk; "Family Bible" was recorded by Claude Gray for the Houston-based Big D Records and became a hit. Nelson moved to Nashville in 1960 and met Hank Cochran, who signed him to a songwriting contract with Pamper Music, and he became a professional songwriter with hits by Patsy Cline ("Crazy"), Billy Walker ("Funny How Time Slips Away"), Faron Young ("Hello Walls"), Ray Price ("Night Life"), and others.

Nelson began recording in 1962 but, although he had a string of chart records, never achieved success as an artist until 1972, when he moved back to Texas after his Nashville home burned. Beginning in 1973, Nelson released some critically acclaimed albums for Atlantic, *Shotgun Willie* and *Phases and Stages;* then, in 1975 recorded and released the album *Red Headed Stranger* for Columbia, which had the hit single "Blue Eyes Crying in the Rain." Also in 1973, Willie Nelson began his annual Fourth of July picnics in Texas where "hippies and rednecks" sat down together for Willie Nelson's music. With his crossover success as an artist and his "outlaw" image that challenged the Nashville business establishment, Nelson had gained wide recognition.

After *Red Headed Stranger,* Nelson recorded a number of albums that were both critical and commercial successes. He recorded duet albums with a number of old friends (Roger Miller, Webb Pierce, Waylon Jennings, Faron Young, Merle Haggard, Ray Price, Leon Russell), a tribute album to Lefty Frizzell, and an album of old standards, *Stardust*, that stayed on the country charts over ten years. He also appeared in a number of movies, including *Electric Horseman* (1979)*, Honeysuckle Rose* (1980)*, Barbarosa* (1982)*, Songwriter* (1984)*,* and *Red-Headed Stranger* (1986).

In 1973, Willie Nelson was inducted into the Nashville Songwriters Hall of Fame, and in 1993, he was inducted into the Country Music Hall of Fame.

Bibliography

Country Music Foundation. *Country: The Music and Musicians from the Beginnings to the 90's.* New York: Abbeville, 1994.

Nelson, Susie. *Heart Worn Memories: A Daughter's Personal Biography of Willie Nelson.* Austin: Eakin, 1987.

Nelson, Willie. *Willie: An Autobiography.* New York: Simon & Schuster, 1988.

Don Cusic

Nesmith, Robert Michael (1942-), was making a name for himself (and his sometime-pseudonym, Michael Blessing) in the burgeoning Los Angeles folk-rock musical scene in the mid-1960s when he answered the casting call which turned him into a Monkee (see entry). Often, and unfairly, described as "the talented one," the recalcitrant Nesmith was one of the manufactured group's harshest critics and was foremost in establishing their musical independence and their pioneering forays into country-rock music. He became instrumental in establishing the Monkees as an important American country-rock group.

Nesmith left the Monkees in 1969 to form the First National Band for RCA Records, with whom he cultivated the image of "Papa nez," sort of a cosmic cowboy, or, as RCA stated in a rare attempt to promote his work, "A Cowboy for Today's America." Though scoring some success with the singles "Joanne" and "Silver Moon," Nesmith's album sales were miserable. His peculiar blend of country and western (emphasis on the latter) and rock, best described as unclassifiable, was acclaimed by those critics not put off by his Monkees past, but at the time, being an ex-Monkee was definitely unhip, and radio programmers hadn't a clue of what to do with him.

After three more albums, Nesmith and RCA parted company, and he started his own record company, the Pacific Arts Corporation. The first Pacific Arts product was an ambitious mail-order book-with-a-soundtrack, *The Prison*, in 1975, which also toured as a stage show. Other albums followed, and despite a strong cult following, Nesmith continued to be overlooked. His style was never static, as he continually built upon his country/western/rock core with whatever happened to interest him, from blues and jazz to tropical and Latin influences. His writing ranged from love songs to metaphysical meanderings, progressively marked with wit, whimsy, and gentle humor. Though Nesmith the musician enjoyed limited commercial success, his songwriting skills have done well for such artists as Linda Ronstadt with "Different Drum" and "Some of Shelly's Blues" (also covered by the Nitty Gritty Dirt Band), Loretta Lynn with "I've Never Loved Anyone More," co-written with Linda Hargrove, and "Mary, Mary" for the Paul Butterfield Blues Band and Run-D.M.C.

In the 1980s, Nesmith increasingly turned his attention toward video, and he became one of the medium's most outspoken proponents. Producing and compiling rock videos and films into specialized programming for television resulted in *Popclips* on the Nickelodeon network. He ultimately sold this idea to Warner Brothers/American Express, who turned it into MTV. Continuing with rock videos, as well as comedy spots for NBC's *Saturday Night Live* and ABC's *Fridays*, and boosted by inheriting half of his mother Bette Nesmith Graham's Liquid Paper fortune, Pacific Arts abandoned audio completely for video and issued the first exclusively-for-home-video music and comedy revue, *Elephant Parts*, in 1981.

Elephant Parts won the first Grammy Award for video, in 1982, and its formula was used for a television series for NBC, *Television Parts*, hosted by Nesmith, in 1985. Compilations from these shows entered the video market as *Television Parts Home Companion* (1985) and *Dr. Duck's Super Secret All-Purpose Sauce* (1986).

For a while, motion pictures competed with video for Nesmith's attention as he became involved in the production of such films as *Timerider* (1983), *Repo Man* (1984), *Square Dance* (1987), and *Tapeheads* (1988). Meanwhile, his Pacific Arts made a name for itself as a source of quality materials of both popular and elite culture interest and the distributor of PBS Home Video.

Bibliography

Larkin, Colin, ed. *Guinness Encyclopedia of Popular Music.* Vol. 4. Middlesex, U.K.: Guinness, 1995.

Stambler, Irwin. *The Encyclopedia of Pop, Rock, and Soul.* New York: St. Martin's, 1989.

Allen Ellis

New York Philharmonic Young People's Concerts (1958-1978), from its inception, was an enormous critical and popular success, and these informative music lessons are recognized today as one of television's greatest contributions to music and arts education. Much of the appeal of this series (which aired on CBS four times a season) can be attributed to its charismatic host and adept writer, the music director of the New York Philharmonic, Leonard Bernstein (1918-90). Instead of sanctifying classical music, he broadened its appeal by analyzing its rudiments and illuminating its intricacies. Refusing to erect artificial distinctions between "art" music and vernacular forms, Bernstein drew for his televised concerts for children from the masters as well as from rock, folk, and jazz.

The Young People's Concerts had been a Philharmonic concert hall tradition since 1924 under conductor Ernest Schelling. In 1930, the orchestra began its affiliation with CBS, which continued to broadcast over radio about five annual Young People's Concerts until 1957. Although Schelling quickly became the country's acknowledged leader in the field of children's music appreciation, there were others, including the grandfatherly Walter Damrosch, who hosted a weekly daytime radio series, *Music Appreciation Hour*, over NBC between 1928 and 1942.

Some of these earlier presentations, however, were long, pedantic, and boring, and continued to consecrate the canon of symphonic music. In the hands of Leonard Bernstein, a champion of contemporary and American music, and through the commanding medium of television, the *Young People's Concerts* found the perfect forum to which greater audiences were drawn.

Bibliography

Burton, Humphrey. *Leonard Bernstein.* New York: Doubleday, 1994.

Chapin, Schuyler. *Leonard Bernstein: Notes from a Friend.* New York: Walker, 1992.

Shanet, Howard. *Philharmonic: A History of New York's Orchestra.* New York: Doubleday, 1975.

Geoffrey S. Cahn

New Yorker, The (1925-), remains one of the most influential weeklies in the modern publishing world, featuring—in addition to its award-winning selections of cartoons and photography—the works of many of the most gifted authors, poets, and essayists of the 20th century. Although the *New Yorker* now stands as one of the most successful American publishing ventures, a steady decline marked its early sales returns. After an initial sales run of 15,000 copies, the magazine averaged a circulation of a mere 8,000 copies during its first two years of publication. By the early 1950s, however, the *New Yorker* enjoyed a weekly circulation of more than 400,000 copies—a figure unheard of for a magazine devoted to literature and humor. The brainchild of journalist Harold Ross, the *New Yorker* found the roots of its success in a nation caught in a slow evolution from a rural to an urban society, and Ross brilliantly marketed the fledgling magazine in an effort to capture the interests of this new breed of Americans yearning for the sophisticated trappings of the metropolitan lifestyle.

In addition to its inclusion of high-quality prose, verse, and artwork, the *New Yorker* continues to offer its readers coverage of significant contemporary events and personalities, criticism regarding the latest cinematic, theatrical, and artistic openings, and a weekly entertainment guide devoted to New York City.

Following Ross's death in 1951, William Shawn became the magazine's editor-in-chief, and, while maintaining the *New Yorker*'s special reputation for the high quality of its literary and artistic offerings, guided the magazine to its record circulation in the mid-1980s of more than 500,000 copies. During his tenure as the *New Yorker*'s editor, the periodical featured the work of a number of significant American writers, including the wares of such luminaries as John Updike, Garrison Keillor, John McPhee, and Sylvia Plath, among others, while also supplementing its impressive staff of house writers with figures such as the esteemed film critic Pauline Kael. The *New Yorker* entered a decidedly different era in its publication history with the selection in 1992 of Tina Brown, the former editor of the slickly redesigned second incarnation of *Vanity Fair*, as its editor-in-chief in place of Shawn's beleaguered successor, Robert Gottlieb. The cover of Brown's October 1992 inaugural issue of the magazine depicts the image of a street punk riding by carriage through Central Park, and while such a parodic maneuver raised the ire of many of the *New Yorker*'s most dedicated readers, under Brown's editorship, the magazine continues to maintain its allegiance to its own tradition through the publication of many of its regular features, particularly the "Talk of the Town" department and the magazine's well-known biographical "Profiles." The *New Yorker* also includes an expansive selection of criticism, featuring essays by a number of well-respected literary and cultural critics, among them Henry Louis Gates, Jr., and Edward W. Said, while also showcasing the work of award-winning photographers such as Annie Leibovitz.

Bibliography

Douglas, George H. *The Smart Magazines*. Hamden: Archon, 1991.

Kunkel, Thomas. *Genius in Disguise: Harold Ross of* The New Yorker. New York: Random House, 1995.

Peterson, Theodore. *Magazines in the Twentieth Century*. Urbana: U of Illinois P, 1964.

Kenneth Womack

Newman, Paul (1925-), perennial and premier actor-director-producer, was educated at Kenyon College, OH (economics major), and at Williams Bay (WI) Repertory Company (1950). Temporarily working in his father's family sporting goods store and realizing his unsuitability for the small-business conformist ideal of early '50s American life, Newman moved to New York, gaining experience in theater and the Golden Age of American live television and attending the Yale Drama School and Actors Studio (1951-52). He made his Broadway debut in *Picnic*, winning a Warner Brothers contract (1953). His screen debut was in *The Silver Chalice* (1954).

As a major star, Paul Newman has lasted over 40 years. Initially categorized as a 1950s "rebel hero" (along with Marlon Brando, Montgomery Clift, and James Dean), he has been able to avoid being tied to a particular decade or acting type. While James Dean's premature death resulted in his fixed canonization as a 1950s icon and Marlon Brando's sporadic work demonstrates a more eccentric star signification, Paul Newman's career is more consistent. Whether as alienated, existential hero (*Somebody Up There Likes Me*, [1956], *The Hustler* [1961]) or redemptive middle-aged survivor (*The Color of Money* [1986]), Newman's development illustrates a 1950s liberal recognition of changing historical eras and a personal sensitivity to socially progressive artistic issues. At the same time, his work denotes a desire to escape stereotyping by ephemeral fashions and an endeavor to remain consistent by modifying his star persona according to the demands of age and historical change.

Although traces of the handsome "hunk" persona remain in his later portrayals in *The Verdict* (1982) and *The Color of Money*, they become embedded within a mature personification revealing indications of an earlier rebelliousness now modified by increasing years. Whatever the conclusion of later films, the Newman persona retains its integrity and growth solidified by growing wisdom. While aging results in more eccentric (*Blaze*, 1989) and stoical characterizations (*Mr. and Mrs. Bridge*, 1990), Newman's main image will always remain that of the sensitive loner, whether as young antihero (*The Left Handed Gun* [1958], *Hud* [1963], *Cool Hand Luke* [1967]) or regenerated middle-aged survivor (*Fort Apache: The Bronx* [1980], *Absence of Malice* [1982]).

Films such as *The Left Handed Gun, The Hustler, Sweet Bird of Youth* (1962), *Hud*, and *Cool Hand Luke* reveal Newman gradually developing a persona subtly articulating deep internal insecurities, desiring some form of consistent personal integrity. *Harper* (1966) and *Cool Hand Luke* reveal the gradual emergence of this latter quality, one inherent within a particular mode of star performance and not entirely dependent upon the actor's handsome persona. By the time of *Butch Cassidy and the Sundance Kid* (1969),

Newman had achieved his key persona, one also allowing him to counterpoint the challenge of a younger rival (Redford) with an assured stance of performance understatement. In *The Sting* (1973), both Newman and Redford equally match each other in open complimentary performance style.

Despite his achievements, Newman's work also reveals several inconsistencies and failures. His comedy films—*Rally Round the Flag, Boys!* (1958), *A New Kind of Love* (1963), *Lady L.* (1964), and *The Secret War of Harry Frigg* (1967)—illustrate his awkwardness and inabilities in succeeding at this format. Undoubtedly an accomplished actor, capable of non-star character roles (*Adventures of a Young Man* [1962]), Newman has developed his major star persona mostly in association with directors formed within the same liberal climate as Newman himself—Martin Ritt, Sydney Pollack, and Sidney Lumet. These talents are often associated with films internalizing social tensions and liberal issues within personalities and performances. A contrast thus exists between the more explicit *WUSA* (1970)—no matter how sincere Newman's intentions were—and more subtle works such as *Hombre* (1967), *Absence of Malice,* and *The Verdict.* It is more than coincidental that Newman's development coincides with the artistic evolution of these directors. All belong to the same historical era, one (Ritt) being a survivor of the blacklist. Furthermore, a star's development and persona is often dependent upon a collaborative process rather than isolated, individual, choices. Differences between the artistic achievements and audience reception of aberrant Newman works, such as his comedies, Huston collaborations (*The Life and Times of Judge Roy Bean* [1972], *The Mackintosh Man* [1973]), and Altman films (*Buffalo Bill and the Indians, or Sitting Bull's History Lesson* [1976], *Quintet* [1979]) appear to support this.

Following *Butch Cassidy and the Sundance Kid,* George Roy Hill's second Newman film, *The Sting,* extended the star's acting abilities into a more antiheroic, foul-mouthed persona, shocking many of Newman's audience and critics. This reveals less the failure of director and star but more how anchored Newman's understated, liberal star-image was.

Martin Ritt's Newman films reveal a development of a 1950s antiheroic loner persona in *The Long Hot Summer* (1958) toward the more amoral, vulnerable loner figure in *Hud,* and the aloof, alienated, reluctant savior character in *Hombre.* It was a process finally achieved after the less successful *Paris Blues* (1961) and the highly eccentric character cameos in *Adventures of a Young Man* and *The Outrage* (1964).

Describing Newman as "an Everyman, an ordinary character of integrity who must take a stand to make a difference," Sydney Pollack intuitively understood the Newman persona as an embodiment of the way in which an American audience wished to see a character fulfilling those very traits of an American democratic ideal transcending both politics and historical eras. Embodying a character trait sporadically appearing in American cinema from Frank Capra to Spencer Tracy, Newman probably owes his star status more to Pollack than to any other director. While Newman's association with directors such as Otto Preminger (*Exodus,* 1960) and Alfred Hitchcock (*Torn Curtain,* 1966) were unsatisfactory,

Pollack and Lumet tapped into Newman's intuitive qualities for their successful ventures in *Absence of Malice* and *The Verdict.*

Newman's acting ventures with his wife, Joanne Woodward (*The Long Hot Summer, Rally Round the Flag, Boys!, From the Terrace* [1960], *Paris Blues, A New Kind of Love, Winning, WUSA,* and *Mr. and Mrs. Bridge*), are often variable in quality. Their best collaborations often involve Newman behind the camera, as *Rachel, Rachel* (1968), *The Effect of Gamma Rays on Man-in-the-Moon Marigolds* (1972), *The Shadow Box* (1981), and *The Glass Menagerie* (1987) reveal. His *Glass Menagerie* production was obviously made in awareness of Hollywood's dilution of his previous Tennessee Williams roles in *Cat on a Hot Tin Roof* (1958) and *Sweet Bird of Youth.*

As he advances into his seventh decade, Newman's abilities develop further into mature understatement (*Fat Man and Little Boy* [1989], *Mr. and Mrs. Bridge, Nobody's Fool* and *The Hudsucker Proxy* [1994], *Twilight* [1998], *Message in a Bottle* [1999], and *Where the Money Is* [2000]) and the inevitable progression into character roles. But his consistent star persona ensures his continuance as a major influence in American cinema and culture.

Bibliography

Dumano, Elena. *Paul Newman.* New York: St. Martin's, 1989.

Godfrey, Lionel. *Paul Newman, Superstar: A Critical Biography.* New York: St. Martin's, 1978.

Quirk, Lawrence J. *The Films of Paul Newman.* Secaucus: Citadel, 1981.

Stern, Stewart. *No Tricks in My Pocket: Paul Newman Directs.* New York: Grove, 1989.

Tony Williams

Nicholson, Jack (1937-), has embodied through his acting career what Bogart and Brando did for audiences of the 1940s-60s: the sympathetic outsider who commands our respect—or at least attention—even if he fails miserably or chills our hearts. John Joseph Nicholson, Jr.'s own life has certainly given him adequate preparation for developing this unsettling but fascinating screen persona. Born and raised in Neptune City, NJ, in a family with two much older sisters, a beautician mother, and an absent father, Jack proved to be a bright student but a deportment problem in school. Whatever sense of inner turmoil he might have had in those early years was finally brought into stark focus in 1974 when *Time* magazine researchers uncovered the shock that his "sister" June, 17 years his senior, was actually his mother and his other "sister," Lorraine, was his aunt. Only Lorraine was alive at the time to confirm the truth, so he never knew his mother in that capacity, even though he followed her to Los Angeles in 1954 rather than going to college and was in frequent contact with her during his early career.

From an office boy job at MGM he advanced to acting classes (where he met Roger Corman and future roommate Robert Towne), then his first role (as the star of Corman's *Cry Baby Killer* [1958]), followed by a decade of acting—and some producing and writing—in low-budget, mostly forgotten films, except for his part as Wilbur Force, the masochist dental patient in the cult classic original version of *The Little Shop of Horrors* (1960). Some of his connections from these early assignments would pay off, though, such as Peter Fonda and Dennis Hopper as actors for Nicholson's script of the acid odyssey *The Trip* (1967)—although Nicholson had a major frustration in that a part which he wrote for himself was given to Bruce Dern. Nicholson also co-wrote and co-produced *Head* (1968) as an offbeat vehicle for TV's the Monkees (see entry), which began his long directorial collaboration with Bob Rafelson (who, with Bert Schneider, had created the Monkees in 1966).

In 1969, Rafelson, with Schneider and Steve Blauner, formed BBS Productions, the company that bankrolled Hopper and Fonda's rambling free-spirit saga, *Easy Rider* (1969). Nicholson was sent in to bring some control to the project, quickly took the part of young lawyer George Hanson from departing Rip Torn, and catapulted to public notice seemingly overnight. As Hanson, Nicholson displayed the trademarks that would make him famous in dozens of later roles: a clear insight into the problems of "the system," a melancholy attitude toward his inability to bring about change in an unforgiving world, and an alternately hostile/maniacal response to the insanity he sees around him.

Easy Rider won Nicholson a supporting actor Oscar nomination, as did one of his most recent roles as the homicidal patriot Colonel Nathan Jessup in Rob Reiner's *A Few Good Men* (1992); however, most of his non-winning nominations have come as best actor, for *Five Easy Pieces* (1970), *The Last Detail* (1973), *Chinatown* (1974), *Prizzi's Honor* (1985), and *Ironweed* (1987). Nominations led to victories for *One Flew over the Cuckoo's Nest* (1975) (actor), *Terms of Endearment* (1983) (supporting actor), and *As Good As It Gets* (1997) (actor), making him one of the few performers to win in both categories. His directing attempts have not proven to be so successful, but he has acted for many of the best directors in contemporary cinema, sometimes in small or offbeat parts just for the opportunity, including Michelangelo Antonioni (*The Passenger* [1975]), Hal Ashby (*The Last Detail*, written by Towne), Milos Forman (*Cuckoo's Nest*), John Huston (*Prizzi's Honor*), Elia Kazan (*The Last Tycoon* [1976]), Stanley Kubrick (*The Shining* [1980]), Vincente Minnelli (*On a Clear Day You Can See Forever* [1970]), Arthur Penn (*The Missouri Breaks* [1976]), and Roman Polanski (*Chinatown*, for which Towne won an Oscar for best original screenplay). Even more extensive are his connections with Rafelson (*Five Easy Pieces*, *The King of Marvin Gardens* [1972], *The Postman Always Rings Twice* [1981], *Man Trouble* [1982]) and Mike Nichols (*Carnal Knowledge* [1971], *The Fortune* [1975], *Heartburn* [1986], *Wolf* [1994]). And while his friend Warren Beatty is not usually considered one of the great directors, he did win the Oscar for *Reds* (1981), in which Nicholson plays a smoldering Eugene O'Neill to Diane Keaton's Louise Bryant, prior to her final journey to join John Reed (Beatty) in Russia.

While the body of Nicholson's notable work is too lengthy for full analysis, a brief tour of his most memorable roles reads like a catalog of significant modern American films. Following his wild incongruity of searing commentary, drunken blathering, and football helmet motorcycle attire in *Easy Rider*, he moved on to full stardom and character development in *Five Easy Pieces*. Bobby Dupea is another son of a respected family who cannot live up to his social expectations, so he abandons his career as a concert pianist for a roving life of odd jobs, casual affairs, and bowling alleys. He returns home for an explanation, if not a reconciliation, for his dying father but finally abandons his hick girlfriend (Karen Black) and heads for the last frontier in Alaska. This film also contains his classic moment of frustration with inhumane contemporary life as he asks a waitress for an order of toast not listed on the menu. She's resistant, even when he offers to order a chicken salad sandwich on toast but hold the chicken salad. His abrupt, climactic clearing of the table has achieved mythic proportions as the perfect reply of an angry citizenry overwhelmed with bureaucracy, social deterioration, and a lost sense of innocence.

After Nicholson's slightly sagging career was forcefully revived with *The Last Detail*, he soon found himself involved in some truly classic performances. The first of these was as J. J. ("Jake") Gittes, a cocky but overwhelmed private detective in *Chinatown*. The film is a fine metaphor for the imponderable actions of human nature, set against a devastating drought in 1930s Los Angeles. As Davie Locke in *The Passenger*, Nicholson was probably the only major American actor who could so comfortably fit the story of a man who exchanges identities with a dead hotel neighbor, then explores his new life to any conclusion, ending as government agents execute him assuming he is Robertson, an arms smuggler. His memorable role as Randle McMurphy in *One Flew over the Cuckoo's Nest* also involves identity shifting and eventual death. However, we welcome his demise this time as an escape from the tunnel-vision mentality of Nurse Ratched (Louise Fletcher) and as inspiration for the escape of Chief Broom (Will Sampson). Again, this seemed the perfect role for Nicholson, whose smartass demeanor balances his genuine concern for the treatment of his fellow patients with his independent spirit too free to exist in a repressive social structure.

In various ways, most of Nicholson's roles could be said to embody his perceived persona, which at times has been quite wild and cantankerous, but what the public does not always see is the artistic drive he has to find nuances and refinements for his characters. Thus, he may seem to just broadly parody himself as the demonically possessed writer-turned-hotel-operator in *The Shining* or to hardly act at all as the astronaut-turned-party animal in *Terms of Endearment*. Still, the sense of evil comedy that he brings to each role is necessary to balance the somber atmosphere of both films, certainly contributing to their success.

Building on his image and his reputation, Nicholson seemed inevitable as both the lusty, devilish Darryl Van Horne in *The Witches of Eastwick* (1987) and the crazed Joker in *Batman* (1989). Both of these proved to be commercial successes, but they pale as acting challenges compared to his poorly grossing yet effective *tours de force* with Meryl Streep, *Heartburn* and *Ironweed*. His potential as a director was dealt close to a fatal blow with *The Two Jakes* (1990), *Chinatown*'s sequel, despite a script by Towne and Nicholson's reprise of J. J. Gittes. *The Evening Star* (1996), the sequel to *Terms of Endearment*, with both Nicholson and Shirley MacLaine reprising their roles, was also unsuccessful.

There were no such problems in Nicholson's dual presence at Christmas 1992 in *A Few Good Men* and *Hoffa*, or in *As Good As It Gets* (1997), which won Nicholson an Oscar for his role as Melvin, a reclusive author with obsessive/compulsive disorder.

Other notable films in his career include *The Raven* (1963), *Hell's Angels on Wheels* (1967), *Drive, He Said* (1971, director, co-producer, and co-writer), *Goin' South* (1978, director), and *Broadcast News* (1987). Recent films include *Mars Attacks* (1996) and *Blood and Wine* (1997).

Bibliography

Brode, Douglas. *The Films of Jack Nicholson*. Secaucus: Citadel, 1987.

Canby, Vincent. "Big Labor's Master of Manipulation [*Hoffa*]." *New York Times* 25 Dec. 1992.

Downing, David. *Jack Nicholson: A Biography*. New York: Stein, 1984.

Shepherd, Donald. *Jack Nicholson: An Unauthorized Biography*. New York: St. Martin's, 1991.

Sragow, Michael. "Tell It to the Marines [*A Few Good Men*]." *New Yorker* 14 Dec. 1992.

Ken Burke

Nickelodeon, The, the first movie theater, functioned as a small, uncomfortable makeshift theater, usually a converted cigar store, restaurant, or skating rink, made to look like a vaudeville theater. In front, large hand-painted posters announced the movies for the day. Inside, the screenings of news and dramatic shorts lasted about one hour. Nickel theaters tempted the public inside with gaudy posters. The nickelodeon box office often was ringed by electric lights flashing a multitude of colors, reminding passersby that here was a modern marvel, in an age when few had electricity at home.

The interior of the nickel show was more sedate. The auditorium, typically the only room inside, was little more than a converted screening room, long and narrow, darkly lit. Between 50 and 300 simple wooden chairs or benches provided seating. A "stage" was a simple platform positioned up front. The 9-by-12-foot screen was simply attached to the back wall. A piano accompanied the silent films.

Costs of day-to-day operation of the typical nickel theater were low and profits high. *Variety* estimated that weekly expenses amounted to usually no more than $200, requiring only 60 patrons per show to break even. Others who came provided pure profit. Thus, in 1907, *Variety* told its readers: "Three years ago [December 1904] there was not a nickelodeon, or five-cent theatre devoted to moving-picture shows, in America." By 1910, *Variety* reported more than 100 in Chicago alone.

Myth often replaced fact about such dynamic growth. It is not true that the nickelodeon existed solely in the ghettoes of New York City. Thousands of small-town entrepreneurs followed suit; by 1910, nearly all of America's urban communities—of any size—had a permanent movie show.

But theater owners who desired to make even more money quickly abandoned the nickelodeon and sought a more well-off clientele who could and would pay higher prices. During the second decade of the 20th century, movie theater owners took direct aim at the emerging American urban middle class. The original nickel price soon gave way to admission prices of ten cents and more. To lure the "family trade," the former nickelodeon owner looked to the "New American woman" and her children, setting up "tea hour" screenings. If women and children came, the owner had a stamp of respectability that could lead (and did lead) to more money and a more favorable image in the community. In 1909, *Moving Picture World* had correctly predicted that the nickelodeon would soon be part of the past, and movie theaters would take their place, "seating five hundred to a thousand [patrons], most of them giving a mixed bill of vaudeville and motion pictures." The prediction was an understatement, but the large movie palaces likewise eventually were replaced by small but comfortable theaters.

Bibliography

Bowser, Eileen. *The Transformation of Cinema, 1907-1915*. New York: Scribner's, 1990.

Fell, John L. *Film Before Griffith*. Berkeley: U of California P, 1983.

Gomery, Douglas. *Shared Pleasures*. Madison: U of Wisconsin P, 1992.

Nasaw, David. *Children of the City: At Work and at Play*. Garden City: Anchor, 1985.

Peiss, Kathy. *Cheap Amusements*. Philadelphia: Temple UP, 1983.

Douglas Gomery

"Night Before Christmas, The" (1823). Undeniably the most influential Christmas poem ever written, Clement Clarke Moore's "A Visit from St. Nicholas" (author's title) has shaped the secular image of Christmas. Moore (1779-1863) was a professor of biblical learning at New York City's General Theological Seminary. He published works on history, government, natural science, and religion, but it is the simple 56-line poem, with its sprightly anapestic meter and its indelible first lines ("'Twas the night before Christmas, when all through the house/Not a creature was stirring, not even a mouse") and final lines ("Happy Christmas to all, and to all a good night"), that gives Moore his place in literary history.

In 1822, Moore drew on local legend and customs, as well as his own fertile imagination, to produce a Christmas present for his children. Tradition has it that a friend, delighted by the joy and originality of the poem, sent it to the editor of the *Troy Sentinel*, who published it anonymously on December 23, 1823. It would be over a decade before Moore acknowledged his authorship.

The influence of the poem cannot be overestimated. Every portly Santa in the mall, every plastic reindeer on the lawn; from Tim Allen in *The Santa Clause* to Tim Burton's

The Nightmare Before Christmas; from "Rudolph, the Red-Nosed Reindeer" to the dozens of cartoons and picture books that tell and retell the story—each owes its existence to "The Night Before Christmas."

Bibliography
Patterson, Samuel White. *The Poet of Christmas Eve: A Life of Clement Clarke Moore*. New York: Morehouse-Gorham, 1956.

Albert Solomon

Nightline (1979-), one of TV's longest-running and most famous night shows, began on November 4, 1979, when a group of Americans was taken hostage from the embassy in Iran. Believing, like everyone else, that the hostage situation would not last long, ABC News committed itself to a 15-minute broadcast about the situation, to run late each weeknight "for the duration." The special report coverage, titled *The Iran Crisis: America Held Hostage*, began on November 8, anchored by Frank Reynolds. Ted Koppel soon took over the anchor spot, and a few months later, *The Iran Crisis* evolved into *Nightline*, one of television's staple forums of information and entertainment.

Anchor Ted Koppel had been with ABC for 17 years and was working as its State Department correspondent when *The Iran Crisis* made him famous almost overnight. He soon won a reputation as one of the medium's finest interviewers—in a class with Mike Wallace, Bill Moyers, and Charles Kuralt—through his thorough preparation, no-nonsense questions, listening skills, and the calm but determined insistence that guests answer his questions without evasion. Under his leadership, *Nightline* has become a major forum for the world's most prominent and important people. Guests have included South African President Nelson Mandela and former President F. W. de Klerk, King Hussein of Jordan, Colonel Muammar Qaddafi of Libya, Nobel Peace Prize winner Desmond Tutu, Rajiv Gandhi, PLO leader Yasir Arafat, and Presidents Bush, Reagan, and Carter, and former Presidents Nixon and Ford. An interview with Austrian President Kurt Waldheim won an Emmy in 1989.

Nightline is also responsible for introducing to TV a new programming idea, that of the "town meeting." Using panelists, call-ins, radio simulcasting, and reports and audiences from its affiliates, *Nightline* created a brand-new, participatory news show. Topics on its Town Meeting broadcasts have included AIDS, Wall Street and the economy, the issue of legalizing drugs, and the changes in South Africa. A memorable show, on April 26, 1988, was the Town Meeting of Jews and Israelis, broadcast from Israel.

Koppel was born in Lancashire, England, and moved to the U.S. with his parents when he was 13. He has a B.A. in Liberal Studies from Syracuse University, and an M.A. in Political Science and Mass Communications Research from Stanford. He started his career as a desk assistant at WMCA Radio in New York, then, at the age of 23, joined ABC News as a full-time general assignment reporter in 1963. As a foreign correspondent, he covered Vietnam, then worked as the ABC bureau chief in Hong Kong and as ABC News anchor. He has two Peabody Awards and seven DuPont-Columbia Awards, including, for his week-long series from South Africa in 1985, the first Gold Baton ever bestowed.

Bibliography
Brown, Les. *Les Brown's Encyclopedia of Television*. Detroit: Visible Ink, 1992.
Castleman, Harry, and Walter Podrazik. *Watching TV: Four Decades of American Television*. New York: McGraw-Hill.
McNeil, Alex. *Total Television: A Comprehensive Guide to Programming from 1948 to the Present*. New York: Penguin, 1980.

Katie Hutchinson

Nightmare on Elm Street, A (1984), a successful horror movie written and directed by Wes Craven, was released by New Line Cinema. The movie cost $1.8 million to make but went on to gross $23 million. This film introduced one of the most unusual and gruesome heroes in American cinema—Freddy Krueger. Actor Robert Englund portrayed Krueger in the original motion picture and its five sequels that together have made $250 million. The success of the films translated into a merchandising phenomenon known as Freddymania.

Photo courtesy of Popular Culture Library, Bowling Green State University, Bowling Green, OH.

A Nightmare on Elm Street creator Wes Craven is best known for his work in the horror genre. Among his films are *Last House on the Left* (1972), *The Hills Have Eyes* (1977), *Deadly Blessing* (1981), *Swamp Thing* (1982), *The Serpent and the Rainbow* (1988), *Shocker* (1989), and *The People under the Stairs* (1991). His talents, however, are not limited to cinema and horror. He co-created the failed television fantasy comedy *The People Next Door* (1989) and also directed episodes of the new *Twilight Zone* television series (1985-88).

A Nightmare on Elm Street, despite its small budget, is a well-produced motion picture with an impressive visual impact. Director of photography Jacques Haitkin manages to capture the reality of everyday small-town suburban America and the surreal nightmare images in the dreams. The concept that became the *Nightmare* films originated in 1979 when Wes Craven read a newspaper article about nightmares. According to Craven, "the first story was about young men who were having severe nightmares and were not willing to sleep again. They would try to stay awake for a day or more and when they finally fell asleep they would die in their sleep—apparently from suffering another, even more severe nightmare."

The sequels show Freddy torturing and killing as many adolescents as possible. These films include *A Nightmare on Elm Street 2: Freddy's Revenge* (1985), *A Nightmare on Elm Street 3: Dream Warriors* (1987), *A Nightmare on Elm Street 4: The Dream Master* (1988), *A Nightmare on Elm Street 5: The Dream Child* (1989), and *Freddy's Dead: The Final Nightmare* (1992). Wes Craven was little involved with these sequels, although he and Bruce Wagner did write the original story to *Nightmare 3: Dream Warriors*. Robert Englund, on the other hand, has played Freddy Krueger in all of the *Nightmare* pictures. Both were involved in the final entry in the series, *Wes Craven's New Nightmare* (1994), a self-reflexive piece about the making of the original film.

Bibliography

Canby, Vincent. "Screen: 'Nightmare.'" *New York Times* 9 Nov. 1984: C10.

Cooper, Jeffrey. *The Nightmare on Elm Street Companion.* New York: St. Martin's, 1987.

Gilmore, Mikal. "Fab Freddy: How the Villain of *Nightmare on Elm Street* Became a Hero for Our Times." *Rolling Stone* 6 Oct. 1988: 91-94.

Novak, Ralph. "A Nightmare on Elm Street." *People Weekly* 27 May 1985: 12.

Russo, John. "Wes Craven." *Scare Tactics.* New York: Dell, 1992. 177-84.

Wiater, Stanley. "Wes Craven and Robert Englund" (interviews). *Dark Visions: Conversations with the Masters of the Horror Film.* New York: Avon, 1992. 47-56, 67-75.

William Chamberlain

See also
Horror Film in America
Slasher Films

Nirvana both symbolized and inaugurated a new era in mainstream popular music when the band's *Nevermind* LP joined releases by Garth Brooks and Michael Jackson at the top of the *Billboard* charts in early 1992. After band leader Kurt Cobain's 1994 suicide, *Rolling Stone*'s David Fricke wrote that Nirvana "made commercial-rock radio sound alive again, like a weapon again."

Hit singles "Smells Like Teen Spirit," "Come As You Are," "Lithium," and "In Bloom" were raw, angry, and, most of all, contradictory. The songs were alternately loud and soft, sincere and sarcastic, sloppy and slick. Dressed in their old, torn T-shirts and sweaters, the three band members seemed to contradict contemporary notions of pop stardom as they appeared on TV and in magazines next to fashionable artists like Michael Jackson and U2.

Cobain and bassist Krist Novoselic had started playing in bands together as teenagers in Aberdeen, WA, a small logging town about a hundred miles southwest of Seattle. In 1987, the high school friends adopted a temporary drummer and recorded a demo tape. The following year, Sub Pop, a small Seattle label that was becoming trendy in alternative circles, released a single with two of the demo's tracks: "Love Buzz" and "Big Cheese."

Nirvana recorded its debut album, *Bleach* (1989), for $606.17. The critically praised release sold 35,000 copies, at the time a high figure for an alternative rock record, and received college radio airplay. Sales were helped by the band's association with Sub Pop and Seattle's "grunge" sound, a combination of punk and the heavy-guitar rock of 1970s metal bands like Black Sabbath and Led Zeppelin (see Grunge Music).

The band added drummer Dave Grohl before recording their next release, *Nevermind*. They also left Sub Pop for Geffen. Cobain got more than he, Geffen, and most other observers of the music scene expected with the release of *Nevermind* in September 1991. Despite limited promotion and airplay at first, the record sold 200,000 copies in its first three weeks of release. Sales soared after MTV placed "Smells Like Teen Spirit" into heavy rotation in October.

Many commentators have noted that Nirvana's *Nevermind* proved to the music industry that "alternative" bands could be profitable. After *Nevermind*, record companies successfully marketed alternative bands like Pearl Jam, Stone Temple Pilots, the Smashing Pumpkins, Soul Asylum, and Green Day. Nirvana cleaned its musical attic after *Nevermind*, releasing a collection of rare tracks and B-sides: *Incesticide* (1992).

Despite sounding more raw than its predecessor, *In Utero* debuted at No. 1 when it was released in October 1993. Nirvana supported the album with a tour of relatively small arenas and ballrooms, then traveled to Europe for some more dates. After a March 1 show in Munich, Germany, the band had to cancel their remaining concerts due to Cobain's sore throat. While resting in a Rome hotel two nights after the Munich concert, Cobain overdosed on tranquilizers and alcohol. He emerged from a coma after 20 hours and was allowed to leave the hospital three days later. The drug use of Cobain and his wife, Courtney Love of the band Hole, had been a source of media interest and speculation from the time Nirvana became popular in 1990. Cobain committed suicide in his Seattle home on April 5, 1994.

Bibliography
Arnold, Gina. *Route 666: On the Road to Nirvana*. New York: St. Martin's, 1993.
Azerrad, Michael. "Live through This: A Year on the Road with Nirvana." *Rolling Stone* 2 June 1994: 55-56.
——. "Nirvana." *Rolling Stone* 16 Apr. 1992: 35-41.
Rolling Stone. *Cobain*. Boston: Little, Brown, 1994.

David Weinstein

Nixon, Agnes (1927-), one of television's most significant women, began her career in daytime drama as a writer for soap opera queen Irna Phillips (see entry), but surpassed her mentor when she was inducted into the Television Academy Hall of Fame in 1994, becoming the first in the "soap" industry to win such an honor. Thirteen years before that, she was the first woman and first writer to win the Trustees Award from the Academy of Television Arts and Sciences for her 30 years of achievement in television.

Agnes Eckhardt was raised in Nashville, TN, and later majored in speech and drama at Northwestern University. She sold a radio play while still in school and, determined to be a writer, showed it to Irna Phillips. Phillips was impressed and immediately hired her as a dialogue writer for *Woman in White*, one of Phillips's radio serials based in Chicago. Six months later Nixon moved to New York City to become part of the golden age of live television drama. She wrote additional dialogue in scripts for *Studio One* (CBS, 1948-58), *Robert Montgomery Presents* (NBC, 1950-57), *Armstrong Circle Theater* (various networks, 1950-63), and *Cameo Theater* (NBC, 1950-52, 1955). In 1951, she married Chrysler executive Robert Nixon, settled in Pennsylvania, and had four children in five years.

The same year, Nixon, with Roy Winsor, created *Search for Tomorrow*, daytime television drama's first successful show; she also wrote the first three months of it. In 1953, Nixon began writing for *The Guiding Light* at the request of Phillips and was its head writer from 1958 to 1966. During this time she was also writing for *As the World Turns* and *Another World*, both Phillips serials. In 1968, she was asked by Procter and Gamble, producer of several television soaps, to take over *Another World*. Under her tutelage, the serial went from near cancellation to No. 2 in the ratings. The year 1968 also saw the debut of the first serial Nixon created, produced, and wrote, *One Life to Live* (see entry). Two years later, she introduced another creation, the ever-popular *All My Children* (see entry). In 1983, *Loving* debuted, co-created with Douglas Marland, a long-time co-worker and collaborator. Set at a college campus, it was introduced as a prime-time movie the night before it made its debut. In other efforts to expand her audience, Nixon also took her soaps beyond the usual interiors to on-location shooting. She again briefly ventured into prime-time writing with the miniseries *The Manions of America* (ABC, 1980), co-written with Rosemary Anne Sisson.

Nixon began introducing social issues into serials when she was head writer at *The Guiding Light* (see entry). In the early 1960s she introduced a storyline about uterine cancer. Her own creations, *One Life to Live* and *All My Children*, however, took even more chances in the late 1960s and early 1970s on ABC. In the former, Nixon introduced groups of people previously excluded from daytime drama, including African Americans and Jews. Between the two shows, social issues, such as abortion, infertility, depression, child abuse, and problems associated with the Vietnam War were all part of her storylines, making Nixon's programs not only relevant but quite popular.

Bibliography
Allen, Robert C. *Speaking of Soap Operas*. Chapel Hill: U of North Carolina P, 1985.
David, Marc, and Robert J. Thompson. *Prime Time, Prime Movers*. Boston: Little, Brown, 1992.
Gilbert, Annie. *All My Afternoons*. New York: A & W, 1979.
Schemering, Christopher. *Guiding Light: A 50th Anniversary Celebration*. New York: Ballantine, 1986.
——. *The Soap Opera Encyclopedia*. New York: Ballantine, 1985.

Lynn C. Spangler

Noah, **Peter**, one of the many famous "hyphenates" in the television industry, has developed-produced-written and sometimes directed several prime-time television series. An English major in college, Noah was a songwriter and playwright. Writing plays led to his entry into television with *Mr. Sunshine*, a short-lived half-hour comedy on ABC in 1986 about a blind college professor. His next, and more important, association was with Ed Weinberger, former writer on *The Mary Tyler Moore Show* and creator of *Taxi*, two quality comedies of the 1970s.

Noah worked with Weinberger for three years. Through that association he was on three prime-time series. Noah was executive producer on NBC's successful *Amen,* which began in 1986. Starring Sherman Helmsley of *The Jeffersons*, this half-hour comedy was about a deacon, his family, and church members. The following year, Noah produced *Mr. President*, starring George C. Scott. On the fledgling Fox network, it lasted only one year. *Dear John* was more successful on NBC, beginning in 1988. Starring Judd Hirsch of *Taxi* fame, the show centered around a singles support group at a community center. Noah co-developed the series and served as an executive producer. Before that series left the air, Noah took over the romantic comedy *Anything But Love* (see entry) on ABC in 1986 after its first six episodes. Earning a "co-developed" credit, he also became executive producer and head writer of the series. In 1991, he made his directorial debut on the show.

In 1992, Noah obtained a three-year contract with Warner Bros. Television for comedy development. For them he was creator and executive producer of *Cafe Americain*, a comedy set in Paris and starring Valerie Bertinelli. The show lasted only one season (1993-94). He was also executive producer, director, and writer for the half-hour comedy *The Ties That Bind*, a mid-season replacement for the 1994-95 television season about the lives of a young couple with a child.

He also created a short-lived comedy about nerdy kids, *Dweebs* (1995), co-created *Mr. Rhodes* (1996-97), and is executive producer for *Ladies Man* (1999-).

Bibliography
Brooks, Tim, and Earle Marsh. *The Complete Directory to Prime Time Network TV Shows: 1946-Present.* 5th ed. New York: Ballantine, 1992.
McNeil, Alex. *Total Television.* 3d ed. New York: Penguin, 1991.

Lynn C. Spangler

Norman, Larry (1947-), is the most significant artist in the creation of contemporary Christian music (CCM). In 1987, *Harvest Rock Syndicate,* a magazine for the rock-oriented CCM fan, released its critics' poll of the best Christian rock albums released prior to 1980. Norman's album *Only Visiting This Planet* (1972), hailed as the "Sgt. Pepper of Jesus Rock," was No. 1. *Planet* included CCM's first anthem ("Why Should the Devil Have All the Good Music"), along with several other CCM classics ("I Wish We'd All Been Ready" and "The Outlaw") and songs with sociopolitical commentary ("Six O'Clock News"). Norman's *In Another Land* (1975) was ninth, *So Long Ago the Garden* (1973) was 11th, and *Upon This Rock* (1969) was 24th. In addition, Norman was the producer of the No. 2 and 4 albums in the critics' choice list, Randy Stonehill's *Welcome to Paradise* and Daniel Amos's *Horrendous Disc.* No other artist had more than two albums on the list.

The field of Christian rock was born when Norman left his band, People, following artistic differences with Capitol Records. In 1969, he released a solo album, *Upon This Rock,* which is generally recognized to be the first true Christian rock album. In the years to follow, Larry would simultaneously be hailed as the "father of Christian rock" and marginalized both in the secular rock music world (for being too religious) and in a burgeoning CCM industry (for being too rock oriented in his music). Sometimes the marginalization was self-created. After releasing a "rough" version of his *Something New under the Son* (1981) album, Norman dropped out of the CCM industry. Since then he has primarily released his work on his own Phydeaux label (named after Larry's dog) via mailing list.

Norman is critical of the CCM industry, suggesting it has evolved away from the evangelistic thrust and purity of message to a point where record companies are primarily concerned with record sales. He also charges that most CCM is poorly done both musically and lyrically. Those on the alternative end of the CCM spectrum still agree with Norman's diagnosis.

Bibliography
Platt, Karen. "The Original Christian Street Rocker: Larry Norman." *Contemporary Christian Music* Mar. 1981: 8-11, 25.
Scott, Martin. "The Kodon Interview with Larry Norman: Pioneer of Christian Rock." *Kodon* Feb. 1980: 3-6.
Jay R. Howard

North by Northwest (1959), a fast-paced thriller movie blending wit and danger, is one of Alfred Hitchcock's important movie creations (see entry). It broke attendance records at Radio City Music Hall and made $6.5 million in the U.S.—a good return on a film budgeted at $4 million. The film was over a year in writing, planning, and production. Producers tried to cut the film down from its long running time, but Hitchcock had an ironclad contract giving him final cut.

The film explores 1950s Cold War fears, "organization man" anxieties, disorientation, and most important, disturbing questions of identity in a world fraught with illusion. Cary Grant plays Roger O. Thornhill, a Madison Avenue advertising executive whose business is to make people believe what is not. The irony, and plot, begins when Thornhill is mistaken by enemy spies for George Kaplan, a secret agent who does not even exist but has been "invented" by a CIA-type organization to decoy the enemy spies' attention away from the real agent, Eve Kendall (Eva Marie Saint). In vain Thornhill tries to convince suave villain Phillip Vandamm (James Mason) that he is not Kaplan. Ernest Lehman's exciting script takes Thornhill from New York City to Chicago to the dramatic final chase atop Mt. Rushmore all in just a few days; the audience, like Thornhill, is bewildered; and the film's title reflects a baffling world where the only orientation is mere physical direction.

Bibliography
Bogdanovich, Peter. *The Cinema of Alfred Hitchcock.* Garden City: Doubleday, 1963.
LaValley, Albert, ed. *Focus on Hitchcock.* Englewood Cliffs: Prentice-Hall, 1972.
Spoto, Donald. *The Art of Alfred Hitchcock: Fifty Years of His Motion Pictures.* New York: Doubleday, 1992.
———. *The Dark Side of Genius: The Life of Alfred Hitchcock.* Boston: Little, Brown, 1983.
Truffaut, François. *Hitchcock.* New York: Simon & Schuster, 1967.

Don Florence

Northern Exposure (1989-1995), an atypical hour-long dramatic series that premiered quietly on CBS in April 1989, was set in the backwoods village of Cicely, AK, a small town that never was but many fans and critics wished could be. Hallmarks of the series were its richly drawn, eccentric characters and its evolving sense of community. The show compensated for its lack of violence, sex, and profanity with its depth of characterizations combined with decidedly quirky storylines. After two short runs of only eight episodes as summer replacements in 1989 and 1990, CBS gave an extraordinary order for an extended run of 50 episodes to the series' co-creators and executive producers, Joshua Brand and John Falsey.

In the pilot episode viewers were transported to Cicely along with the village's reluctant new resident physician, Dr. Joel Fleischman (Rob Morrow). A recent graduate of Columbia medical school, Fleischman had expected to repay Alaska for his medical school scholarship by practicing in Anchorage. When he was forced to work in Cicely, he was enraged. He termed it involuntary servitude and began conniving to find a way to escape—legally.

During the first season the primary focus was upon Fleischman's sense of culture shock and his resistance toward adjusting to his environment. In Cicely nothing turned out to be what he expected. Each of the primary characters displayed surprising inconsistencies. The Native American "driver" Ed (Darrin E. Burrows) who met him at the bus stop revealed odd bits of what later turned out to be an encyclopedic knowledge of American pop culture. The town's patriarch, Maurice Minnifield (Barry Corbin), was a retired astronaut with avaricious dreams of strip malls for Cicely. The owner of the local pub, Holling Vancour (John Cullum), was a 63-year-old man living with an 18-year-old former beauty queen, Shelly (Cynthia Geary). Fleischman mistook his landlady, Maggie O'Connell (Janine Turner), for a hooker. She turned out to be a bush pilot with her own plane who had grown up in a wealthy suburb of Detroit. The sparks that flew between them continued to engender much of the series' charm and suspense. As the series progressed, viewers watched through Fleischman's eyes while he continued to meet new people and his personal and cultural stereotypes fell apart.

Although ratings for the series were rarely high, the show continued to win multiple awards and critical acclaim. Besides numerous Emmys, the show also was given a unique award in 1995 by the Screen Actors Guild for distinction in promoting intercultural understanding.

Bibliography

Chunovic, Louis. *The Northern Exposure Book: The Official Publication of the Television Series.* Secaucus: Carol, 1995.

Nance, Scott. *Exposing Northern Exposure.* Las Vegas: Pioneer, 1992.

Thompson, Robert J. *Television's Second Golden Age.* New York: Continuum, 1996.

Ann Schoonmaker

Nursery Rhymes. In the U.S. the term "nursery rhyme" can refer to a number of verse forms for young children, including lullabies, Mother Goose rhymes, riddles, finger plays, street chants, parodies, counting-out rhymes, tongue twisters, and others. Some of these poems are part of our established literary heritage while others are a part of the oral tradition of the child's world, passed on from child to child in school yards and neighborhoods everywhere.

Scholars have posited that all cultures have simple, rhythmic, onomatopoeic songs and rhymes for children. In the U.S. the child is usually introduced to poetry by his or her parents in the form of Mother Goose rhymes (such as "Jack and Jill," "Peter Peter Pumpkin Eater," or "Hey, Diddle, Diddle") and lullabies (such as "Rock-a-Bye Baby"), readily available in anthologies and special editions for young people.

Some of the most popular rhymes are interactive and use repetition to teach the child to anticipate the next line and participate in the physical play. Examples are "Pat a cake, pat a cake, baker's man" and "This little pig went to market/This little piggy stayed home." Interactive rhymes for older children depend on suspense and wordplay. Here for example the first speaker (1) knows the joke, and the second speaker (2) is ignorant of it and gets caught in a trap: 1. "I am a gold lock." 2. "I am a gold key." / 1. "I am a silver lock." 2. "I am a silver key." / 1. "I am a monk lock." 2. "I am a monk key."

Scholars have identified a number of possible sources for nursery rhymes, which reflect a rich historical and cultural heritage: street cries ("Hot-Cross Buns"); fragments of ballads or broadsides ("Johnny over the Water"); historical personages ("Old King Cole" about a 3rd-century monarch, and "Mistress Mary, Quite Contrary" about Mary Queen of Scots); ancient charms ("Rain, Rain, Go Away"); and teaching devices ("A was an apple, B bit it").

Nursery rhymes introduce the child to the variety of forms English poetry takes: narrative ("Sing a Song of Sixpence"); lyric ("Ride a Cock-horse to Banbury Cross"); cumulative ("This Is the House That Jack Built"); quatrain ("Cock-a-doodle-do"), couplet ("Ding, Dong, Bell"). They contain almost all the poetic devices found in English literature from alliteration to symbol, although sometimes in a broad and exaggerated fashion. Even the extended metaphor of the Anglo-Saxon riddle can be found in the wordplay of the traditional nursery rhyme like "Humpty Dumpty," where the rhyme as whole constitutes a conundrum whose answer is "egg": "Humpty Dumpty sat on a wall/Humpty Dumpty had a great fall./All the King's horses and all the King's men/Couldn't put Humpty together again."

Bibliography

Knapp, Mary, and Herbert Knapp. *One Potato, Two Potato: The Secret Education of American Children.* New York: Norton, 1976.

Newell, William Wells. *Games and Songs of American Children.* New York: Harpers, 1903; rpt. New York: Dover, 1963.

Rollen, Lucy. *Cradle and All: A Cultural and Psychoanalytical Reading of Nursery Rhymes.* Jackson: UP of Mississippi, 1992.

Maryellen Hains

NYPD Blue (1993-) marked the 1990s return to the television cop genre for producer Steven Bochco (see entry), whose TV vita features award-winning productions (*Hill Street Blues*) and co-creations (*L.A. Law, Doogie Howser M.D.*). This gritty cop show, originally starring David Caruso as Detective John Kelly, Dennis Franz as Detective Andy Sipowicz as well as James McDaniel, Amy Brenneman, and Nicholas Turturro, comes close to the real world happenings of New York City cops by offering viewers partial nudity, violence, and explicit language. All elements helped expand horizons in American television. Complaints by television watchdog groups resulted in an introductory "viewer discretion advised" message before each broadcast. Profanity and nudity were also why nearly one-fourth (57) of ABC's 225 affiliates refused to carry the premiere, an unprecedented number of preemptions for a network series not on the air yet.

NYPD Blue does not focus so much on violence, but on characters whose lives are touched by the frantic feel of New York and its inexhaustible supply of criminal prototypes. Shot on film in a cinema vérité style, the program communicates a blunt realism. In its first season alone, *NYPD Blue* explored mob membership and violence, handgun ownership, rape, missing children, corruption in law enforcement, racism, domestic violence, and drug and alcohol abuse. But

NYPD Blue also takes the viewer out of the precinct and into the lives of its characters. Since the first season, for instance, viewers have seen Kelly replaced by Bobby Simone (Jimmy Smits), who became involved with fellow detective Diane Russell (Kim Delaney), but died at the close of the 1997-98 season (Rick Schroder as Detective Daniel Sorenson then joined the cast). Meanwhile, Sipowicz married, had a child with, and was left by assistant district attorney Sylvia Costas (Sharon Lawrence).

Bibliography

Douglas, Susan. "Signs of Intelligent Life on TV." *Ms.* May 1995: 78-81.

Lear, Frances. "Lunch." *Lears* Nov. 1993: 16-17.

Leland, John. "Blue in the Night." *Newsweek* 13 Dec. 1993: 56-59.

Rensin, David. "Steven Bochco." *TV Guide* 14 Aug. 1993: 14-19.

Thompson, Robert J. *Television's Second Golden Age.* New York: Continuum, 1996.

Zoglin, Richard. "Bochco under Fire." *Time* 27 Sept. 1993: 81.

Jennifer Machiorlatti

Oboler, Arch (1909-1987), one of radio's most prolific dramatists, was a student of electrical engineering at the University of Chicago in 1934 when he submitted a fantasy radio drama, *Futuristic*, to NBC. The network bought and performed the play during the opening ceremonies of Radio City in New York. By 1935, Oboler was writing full time for NBC, scripting playlets for *Grand Hotel*. A decade later, Arch Oboler had become one of radio's most prolific dramatists. He produced almost 800 radio plays while becoming one of the very few radio artists who worked in the triple capacity of writer, director, and producer.

His ascent to prominence began when, in 1936, he took over the after-midnight horror series *Lights Out* (see entry) from its creator, Wyllis Cooper. Oboler's use of sound effects to maximize drama began to distinguish his work from other radio fare. Motivated by the desire to expand his artistic skills beyond the horror genre, Oboler left *Lights Out* in 1938. His next radio play was *The Ugliest Man in the World*. The chief developer of stream-of-consciousness writing for radio explored the possibilities of interior monologue in this play, and his effort earned him an NBC contract to write the dramatic series *Arch Oboler's Plays* (1939-40, 1945).

Personal success coinciding as it did with German aggressions in Europe, Oboler concentrated on writing antifascist and beat-the-Axis dramas (e.g., *Ivory Tower, Hate)*. More significantly, a year before Pearl Harbor, he dropped his commercial contracts and, for 18 months, gave full time without pay to write war plays for government-endorsed broadcasts. After writing *Everyman's Theatre* (1940-41) and *Plays for Americans* (1942), Oboler revived *Lights Out* (1942-43) in order to regain some monetary stability. Again secure financially, he worked on *Free World Theatre* (1943), his series designed to illustrate the war and peace aims of the United Nations, and *Everything for the Boys* (1944), a collaboration between actor Ronald Colman and Oboler that provided fighting Allied servicemen with whatever dramatic entertainment they wanted. Oboler concluded his career in network radio with a second run of *Arch Oboler's Plays*. The Peabody Award-winning play *Night* came from this series.

In 1945, Oboler's article "Requiem for Radio" predicted the demise of dramatic radio at the same time that its author turned to writing for the movies. Most notable here, Oboler's screen version of *Escape* (1940), Ethel Vance's anti-Nazi novel, had already earned him repute as a screenwriter. After the successful release of *Five* (1951), his brilliant work of science fiction presented as a piece of reportage, Oboler wrote, directed, produced, and made a fortune from the first 3-D feature, the mediocre *Bwana Devil*, for which he received the first award of the Academy of Stereoscopic Arts and Sciences (1952).

Over succeeding decades, he continued to write for radio, movies, and the theater, and he headed Oboler Productions. Arch Oboler died of heart failure.

Bibliography

Barnouw, Erik. *A History of Broadcasting in the United States*. Vol. 2. New York: Oxford UP, 1968.

Dunning, John. *Tune in Yesterday*. Englewood Cliffs: Prentice-Hall, 1976.

MacDonald, J. Fred. *Don't Touch That Dial!* Chicago: Nelson-Hall, 1979.

New York Times 22 March 1987.

Newsweek 1 March 1943.

Stanley D. Harrison

O'Brien, Fitz-James (1828-1862), an Irish-American writer who also produced journalism, poetry, and drama, is today remembered in American culture for his fantasy stories, which deftly interweave psychological and supernatural events. *The Diamond Lens* (1858) and *The Lost Room* (1858) are among his finest works. In the former, the protagonist is obsessed with creating the perfect lens. He does so through a combination of creative science and magic, but his endeavor leads him to murder. His narrative could be madness, and this ambiguity exists also in *The Lost Room*. In that story, a narrator returns to find his dark, gloomy room brightly lit, taken over by mysterious revelers who cause him to be evicted. Now there is only a blank wall where the room once existed. His early death as a volunteer in the Civil War notwithstanding, O'Brien remains the most inventive American fantasist between Poe and Henry James.

Bibliography

Hoppenstand, Gary. "Robots of the Past: Fitz-James O'Brien's *The Wondersmith*." *Journal of Popular Culture* 27.4 (1994): 13-30.

Richard Bleiler

Ochs, Phil (1940-1976), influential musician, never had a "hit" album. Yet it is a testament to his genius that recordings unreleased during his lifetime continue to emerge, and a full account of his contribution to American music has yet to be made. That Ochs fell short of stardom and failed to receive the full recognition he deserved may be explained in part by the rigid generic categories that his music ultimately transcended; his compositions range from those of angry, righteous (and sometimes ironic) social protest in the folk vein to lyrical, highly romantic ballads in which one can detect a strong country music influence.

Ochs was born in El Paso, TX. His father was a doctor, and he moved his family to upstate New York when Ochs was only a few years old. When he was a teenager, the family moved again, this time to Far Rockaway, Queens. He attended the Staunton Military Academy in Virginia, and then entered Ohio State University in the late 1950s, majoring in journalism. His first singing group was called "The Singing Socialists," later changed to the less inflammatory "Sundowners." He moved to New York City in the early 1960s and became a part of the folk revival taking place there.

His first professional gig was at Gerde's Folk City in Greenwich Village in August 1962, a little over a year after Bob Dylan had debuted there. Eventually, Ochs moved to the forefront of the protest movement, and became its balladeer. Though he had been composing songs for a number of years, his first album, *All the News That's Fit to Sing*, was not released until 1964, and contained both the Woody Guthrie–influenced "Power and the Glory," as well as his tribute to Guthrie, "Bound for Glory." His second album, *I Ain't Marchin' Anymore*, released early in 1965, contained the infamous "Draft Dodger Rag" as well as the overtly pacifist title track, which led to his being banned from broadcast from American radio and TV. As a result, he never appeared on music shows designed for white middle-class teenagers such as *Hootenanny* or *American Bandstand*. The ban did not prevent him from remaining active in the antiwar and civil rights movements during the mid-1960s, however. His superb third album, *In Concert*, was his most "successful," making it to 149 on the *Billboard* charts in 1966.

He spent much of the early 1970s traveling outside of the U.S. Then, in October 1973, while in Dar-es-Salaam, Tanzania, Ochs was allegedly mugged and choked so severely that his vocal chords were permanently damaged. If the harm to his voice was bad, the damage to his temperament was worse. Only one more album was released in his lifetime—*Gunfight at Carnegie Hall* (1974), a live album—and it was released only in Canada. While staying at his sister's home in Far Rockaway, Ochs hanged himself. He was only 35 years old.

Bibliography

Clarke, Donald. *The Penguin Encyclopedia of Popular Music*. New York: Penguin, 1989.

Eliot, Marc. *Death of a Rebel: A Biography of Phil Ochs*. 1979. Rev. ed. New York: Franklin Watts, 1989.

Marsh, Dave, and John Swenson, eds. *The New Rolling Stone Record Guide*. New York: Random House, 1983.

Samuel J. Umland
Rebecca A. Umland

Odd Couple, The, has become a vernacular expression in America. In the more than 30 years since its first appearance, Neil Simon's play has gone through several incarnations: a multitude of stage productions, a movie, and two television series. As a result, the characters of Oscar Madison and Felix Unger have become staples in American culture, their very names becoming identifiable terms for excessive sloppiness and neatness.

Upon its premiere on Broadway in March 1965, *The Odd Couple* was an instant and enormous success, running for more than two years. It was, at its base, a remarkably simple idea. Two men, one divorced and the other recently thrown out by his wife, share an apartment on Riverside Drive in New York City. Their personalities, however, are vastly different. Oscar Madison is a blatant slob, and Felix Unger an obsessive cleaner. They clash inevitably and early, and in a matter of weeks there is all-out war. Simon's script turns what could have been a very predictable story into a sharp and fresh production. Though the arguments are frequent and real, they are never mean-spirited, and the friendship is never truly jeopardized. This is crucial to its success, as the play is surely as much about friendship as it is about differences. Walter Matthau (1920-2000), playing Oscar, and Art Carney (1918-), as Felix, each received public and critical praise for their comic turns, and the play picked up Tony awards for Matthau as best actor, as well as for Simon's script, Mike Nichols's direction, and Oliver Smith's set design.

The success of the play was such that a film version seemed inevitable. The film arrived in 1968, with Simon adapting his own screenplay, and Gene Saks directing. Matthau, because of his enormous success in the role on the stage, was the only logical choice to play Oscar. Jack Lemmon, however, was brought in to play Felix.

The premise of the story made it perfectly suited for adaptation into a television series, beginning in the fall of 1970. The characters were only slightly developed in the course of the play and movie, but the potential for further developing the characters (or, expanding the caricatures) seemed limitless in a sitcom format. The series did not radically change the story; it simply exaggerated it. The play's theme remained intact. It was still a story of two friends trying to live together and manage after divorce, and as always, the comedy relied heavily on the interplay between the two leads and their clashes in lifestyles. As played by Jack Klugman and Tony Randall, Oscar and Felix became, respectively, even more sloppy and more finicky. Though the series was very faithful to the theme and situation of the play, some minor changes were still made.

Since it left television in 1975, *The Odd Couple* has been the subject of a number of high-profile revivals, though rarely with the large public and critical success that it has been greeted in the past. The first major revival came in October of 1982, when the television series returned, under the title of *The New Odd Couple*. This time around, Demond Wilson played Oscar, and Ron Glass portrayed Felix. Unfortunately, by that time the original series had met with such success in syndication that the public seemed little interested in watching a new series when they could watch the old one almost any day of the week. As a result, the new show disappeared from the air after less than a season. A Broadway revival then was attempted in 1985, but with some major revisions to the original play. Simon rewrote his script, changing the gender of the characters. Sally Struthers appeared as finicky Florence, and Rita Moreno was sloppy Olive. However, switching the gender of the characters required much revision to the script, and the result was a public and critical reaction that was hardly enthusiastic. In 1993 Klugman and Randall reunited for the made-for-TV *The Odd Couple: Together Again*. In *Odd Couple II*, with an original screenplay by Neil Simon (1998), Matthau and

Lemmon again play the mismatched pair, now stuck in a car together on the way to the wedding of their children in Los Angeles.

Bibliography
Brooks, Tim, and Earle Marsh. *The Complete Directory to Prime Time Network TV Shows, 1946-Present.* New York: Ballantine, 1988.
Guernsey, Otis L., ed. *The Best Plays of 1964-1965.* New York: Dodd, 1965.
Rich, Frank. "'Odd Couple,' A Remix and Rematch." *New York Times* 12 June 1985, Sec. 3: 21.
Roddick, Nick. *Magill's Survey of Cinema, English-Language Films: First Series, Vol. 3.* Ed. Frank N. Magill. Englewood Cliffs: Salem, 1980. 1234-36.
Simon, Neil. *The Odd Couple: A Comedy in Three Acts.* London: Samuel French, 1966.

Bob Mastrangelo

"Okie from Muskogee" (1969), written by Merle Haggard (see entry) and his drummer, Edward Burris, became a No. 1 hit on country charts by capturing Middle America's reaction to the social turbulence of the late 1960s; it opens: "We don't smoke marijuana in Muskogee/And we don't take our trips on LSD." The album *Okie from Muskogee* became Haggard's first gold record; he immediately tripled his annual income to $1 million; and he won the 1970 Country Music Association Awards for best single, best album, top male vocalist, and entertainer of the year.

The song was reintroduced into American culture when Hank Williams, Jr., remade it for the soundtrack of the award-winning movie depicting Vietnam combat, *Platoon* (1986).

Bibliography
Hemphill, Paul. "Merle Haggard." *Atlantic* Sept. 1971: 98-103; rpt. in *The Good Old Boys.* New York: Simon & Schuster, 1974. 123-37.
Shestack, Melvin. "Merle Haggard." *The Country Music Encyclopedia.* New York: Crowell, 1974.

Douglas Brown
Michael Delahoyde

Oliver, Joe "King" (1885-1938), one of America's musical royalty, worked long and hard at his craft. In 1900, Joe Oliver joined his first parade band in his home town of New Orleans. By 1904, he was substitute cornetist for the Onward Brass Band. Until 1910, he played with a number of bands in New Orleans: the Allen Brass Band, Original Superior Orchestra, Eagle Band, Magnolia Band, and filled in for Manuel Perez, Bunk Johnson, and others. He also worked with Richard M. Jones and his Fair Hot Hounds. Soon, however, he became the predominant cornetist in the area and was named "King" of the horn players, replacing the legendary Buddy Bolden. After that time, he led his own bands and was no one's substitute.

Oliver was also a composer of note and had an eye for young talent for his much-in-demand bands. His contributions are too often overlooked because of the enormous talent of Louis Armstrong, his protégé (see entry).

Oliver, however, made many of his own contributions. In 1918 he joined a Chicago band, and in 1920 he led his own group there. In 1922 he formed the Creole Jazz Band, with Armstrong on second cornet and the Dodds brothers on drums and clarinet.

In 1924, Armstrong struck out on his own. Oliver, however, continued with the Dixie Syncopators, a larger version of the Creole Jazz Band geared toward playing dance music. This band featured saxophones, not yet considered a real jazz instrument.

Oliver did quite well for a time. Wild Bill Davison, a trumpet player much influenced by Armstrong, remembers that King Oliver could hold his own with Satch. He reports that one night he was present when Armstrong and Oliver exchanged 125 choruses of "Tiger Rag." Armstrong always acknowledged the debt to the man he called "Papa Joe" Oliver.

By 1930, Oliver's solo career was over. He had lost his teeth and was unable to play the cornet any longer. He did, nevertheless, lead a number of small orchestras from 1930 to 1936. He was unable to earn a living in music and came to a sad end. He ran a small fruit stand in Queens and was the janitor in a pool hall.

Bibliography
Peretti, Burton W. *The Creation of Jazz.* Urbana: U of Illinois P, 1992.
Rose, Al, and Edmond Souchon. *New Orleans Jazz: A Family Album.* Baton Rouge: Louisiana State UP, 1967.
Williams, Martin T. *King Oliver.* New York: Barnes, 1960.
Wilson, Charles Reagan, and William Ferris, eds. *Encyclopedia of Southern Culture.* Chapel Hill: U of North Carolina P, 1989.
Wright, Laurie. *Walter C. Allen & Brian A. L. Rust's "King" Oliver.* Chigwell: Storyville, 1987.

Frank A. Salamone

Omnibus (1952-1966). Imagine the Public Broadcasting Service and the Discovery and Arts & Entertainment cable networks all rolled into one weekly 90-minute program. That was *Omnibus,* a unique cultural and public affairs television program that established a new television format and set a high standard for entertainment and educational programming on commercial television. With urbane, witty Alistair Cooke as host, interviewer, and occasional writer, it became a television magazine of the liberal arts.

An early magazine-format program, *Omnibus* was conceived and developed by James Webb Young, a former advertising executive who became head of the Ford Foundation's Fund for Adult Education, and Robert W. Saudek, Peabody Award-winning producer and ABC vice president, as a bold answer to the claim that educational television could not survive on commercial networks. Financed by the Ford Foundation as well as commercial sponsors, and produced by the Television-Radio Workshop under Saudek's direction, *Omnibus* combined different types of feature segments of widely varying length, focusing on the visual and performing arts, science, history, and public affairs, with an emphasis on both contemporary and classic live drama and music.

In each of the first five seasons (1952-56 on CBS, 1956-57 on ABC), *Omnibus* broadcast 26 90-minute programs (24 in 1955-56). In 1957-58, *Omnibus* aired 14 90-minute shows; in 1958-59, 15 60-minute shows; and in 1960-61, 7 60-minute shows, for a total of 164, always on Sunday afternoons or evenings.

Certainly the longest-running series combining the performing arts and public affairs in commercial television history, *Omnibus* won widespread praise for providing the best that television could offer and attracted and held a loyal audience, ranging from about 4 million homes in the first season to 5.7 million in the 1958-59 season. By 1958, it had won over 65 awards, including several Emmys.

Omnibus pioneered combining the use of grants from the Ford Foundation and the strategy of multiple sponsorship to achieve a high degree of editorial independence. It was created by a wholly new type of production company, the Television-Radio Workshop, an entity which was able both to receive Ford grants and make commercial sponsorship agreements, thus paving the way for later nonprofit workshop companies, such as the Children's Television Workshop. In 1957, the Ford Foundation ended its relationship with the workshop and sold the rights to all its productions to Robert Saudek Associates, which produced *Omnibus* commercially for three more seasons.

Omnibus expanded and developed the magazine-format genre by pioneering the use of unequal program components as short as a 30-second slow-motion film of a jackrabbit's run, and as long as 90 minutes each for Puccini's *La Bohème*, Shakespeare's *King Lear*, and Homer's *The Iliad*, timing its segments to fit the subject and never interrupting a feature or dramatic element for a commercial. *Omnibus* stressed live broadcasting, using remotes, in-studio illustrated lectures by famous experts, live musical and dance performances, and live drama to draw the viewer into an intimate and personal entertainment environment. In addition to Alistair Cooke, later known for his *America* series and as the host of PBS's *Masterpiece Theatre* for 21 years, *Omnibus* made into television personalities composer-conductor Leonard Bernstein, drama critic Walter Kerr, scuba-diving pioneer Jacques Cousteau, and McCarthy-era lawyer Joseph N. Welch. It captured on film before their passing such key figures in American culture as Grandma Moses, Frank Lloyd Wright, James Thurber, William Faulkner, Fred Allen, Raymond Loewy, Leopold Stokowski, and William Saroyan.

Omnibus also created the miniseries and the docudrama to deal with larger subjects, such as Lincoln's early years (five segments), the Adams family (four parts), and the U.S. Constitution (three parts), always stressing the actual words of historic figures placed in a dramatic context.

As its sunburst logo suggested so strongly, *Omnibus* was like the sun, revealing, enlightening, and enlivening, a prototypical miniature of the kind of programming and funding later embraced by PBS. Astonishingly diverse and committed to excellence, it set a standard which commercial television has seldom reached since.

Bibliography
Krolik, Richard. "Television's Adventure in Culture: The Story of *Omnibus*." *Television Quarterly* 25.3 (1991): 5-10.
Saudek/"Omnibus" Collection, Cinema Archives, Wesleyan University, Middletown, CT.

William M. Jones

See also
Magazine–Format Television Programs

One Life to Live (1968-) is an American soap opera created by Agnes Nixon (see entry). It reflected 1968, with a Jewish lead (Dave Siegal), an Irish family and a Polish one (the Rileys; the Woleks), African-American characters, and issues: Carla Gray (Ellen Holly) passing for white (and, dramatically, for the first four months of *OLTL*, passing with the audience as well); drug addiction; and the single motherhood chosen by Cathy Craig, a *Banner* reporter.

The *Banner* of "Llanview, PA," was owned by the Lord family, and they brought the melodrama. Victor Lord died in 1976, and 18 years later, his daughter, Victoria, triumphed in convicting his wife Dorian of the murder (wrongly). Through the years, Viki's father-obsession regularly burst out via her "tough broad" alter-ego, Nikki Smith. Erika Slezak has played both roles since 1971 and won three Emmies. Nancy Pinkerton was the first Dorian Lord Callison (1973-77); Robin Strasser, the longest-running and current Dorian.

Nielsen ratings for the ABC show rose steadily, and it went to an hour in 1978. Storylines in the 1980s were more heavily melodramatic than when the series began. By the late 1980s, under headwriter S. Michael Schnessel (1987) and executive producer Paul Rauch, *One Life to Live* went all the way to gothic: storylines took place in heaven and in the Old West. In the early 1990s, producer Linda Gottlieb and headwriter Michael Malone pushed the soap envelope with a New Age heroine. Susan Bedson Horgan became the producer in 1994, bringing yet another vision to *One Life to Live*.

Bibliography
Marc, David, and Robert J. Thompson. *Prime Time, Prime Movers: From* I Love Lucy *to* L.A. Law. Boston: Little, Brown, 1992.

Carol Traynor Williams

One Man's Family (1932-1959), the longest-running serial in radio history, has been identified as the wellspring of radio and television soap opera. But Carlton E. Morse (1901-1993), author of the series, adamantly maintained that he had never written a soap opera, that soap operas foreground plot and drop characters in to tell the plot, whereas his programs featured characters and their relationships, from which came plot. His distinction respected, *One Man's Family* might better be called a family saga, a long-running show which depicts a whole family and gives approximately equal emphasis to each member. For almost three decades, Morse's family saga moved with the slowness of life itself as it patiently chronicled the lives of the Barbours, an upper-middle-class, strongly patriarchal family living in the Sea Cliff area of San Francisco.

The program went off the air rather suddenly on May 8, 1959. Facing increasing competition from television, NBC wrote to Morse and asked him to bring his show to a natural conclusion. Morse wrote back: "The show's been on 27 years. What kind of conclusion except that people are just not there anymore." And that is the way the show ended. However, before leaving the air, *One Man's Family* had left its mark. This vastly popular middle-class morality tale had successfully made radio's most sustained argument on behalf of the "traditional American family."

Bibliography
"Carlton E. Morse: Created Radio's 'One Man's Family.'" *Los Angeles Times* 28 May 1993.
Dunning, John. *Tune in Yesterday.* Englewood Cliffs: Prentice-Hall, 1976.
Lawrence, Jerome, ed. "*One Man's Family* Program." *Off Mike.* New York: Essential, 1944.
MacDonald, J. Fred. *Don't Touch That Dial!* Chicago: Nelson-Hall, 1979.

Stanley D. Harrison

Open End (1958-1987) was a quintessentially New York talk show that brought its host, David Susskind (1920-1987), to the attention of the American public (in 1966 it was retitled *The David Susskind Show*). The syndicated series, which originated on WNTA before moving to WNEW and WPIX, quickly became a forum for movers and shakers. Guests like Norman Mailer, Adlai Stevenson, Robert Kennedy, Dore Schary, Truman Capote, James Baldwin, and Marlon Brando were probed while seated around a coffee table in a sparse studio set with ladders and kleig lights visible in the background.

The weekly program was open-ended—of undetermined length, lasting as long as the discussion stayed lively. Susskind believed that freely unfolding talk could sustain viewer interest. He realized the potential of conversational gamesmanship to be both entertaining and edifying—and he was an indefatigable interviewer. In May 1960, for instance, he interrogated Richard Nixon for almost four continuous hours—Susskind puffing cigarettes and sipping coffee, while the Vice President hardly budged.

Despite its popularity, *Open End* was never a money-maker. In the early 1960s, Susskind was paid $39.00 per program. Nevertheless, it was his favorite pastime. Prepping for each Sunday night's program kept him sharp. The program explored issues from politics and civil rights to the sexual revolution.

In 1966, along with the change in title, the format changed to a standard two-hour program that was taped with a studio audience. By then, controversial talk shows that focused on a single issue were becoming a TV standard and David Susskind had become a fixture in American popular culture. His rococo language skills and frequently pugnacious demeanor were the stuff of parody.

Bibliography
Watson, Mary Ann. "*Open End*: A Mirror of the 1960s." *Film & History* Sept. 1991.

Mary Ann Watson

Oprah Winfrey Show, The (1986-   ), is the most popular syndicated talk show in television history. Presiding over what has been called a national group therapy session, Winfrey herself (see entry) has been described as "the host most responsible for ushering in the age of confession."

Watched by more than 15 million viewers daily, and seen in more than 111 foreign markets, the show has been at the top since its national debut. Winfrey was hired to take over a locally produced morning talk program called *A.M. Chicago* on January 2, 1984. Within months she had done the unthinkable—trouncing Phil Donahue's popular show, which had ruled in that city for more than a decade. Within a year the show had expanded to an hour, and it was later renamed *The Oprah Winfrey Show*.

Winfrey's show was modeled on Donahue's, the only game in town for serious talk. *Rolling Stone* described that genre as "wandering host, smug experts, glum victims, jump-right-in audiences, all that endless jabbering about problems, problems, problems." Like him, she weaved her way through the audience, microphone in hand, and she even copied his hand-shaking routine with the audience after the show. But Winfrey was less politically oriented, less intellectual, and much more emotional than Donahue. She was as earthy and brassy as he was detached and acerbic; she bubbled, joked, and even took off her shoes on occasion. Her most noted traits were her compassion and ability to empathize, what was called her "touchy-feely" style.

Despite the multiplying of daytime talk shows in the 1990s and their descent into dysfunction, Oprah has remained above the fray, even becoming an influential voice in the publishing world with her on-air "book club."

Bibliography
Gerosa, Melina. "What Makes Oprah Run?" *Ladies' Home Journal* Nov. 1994: 200+.
Noglows, Paul. "Oprah: The Year of Living Dangerously." *Working Woman* May 1994: 52+.
Reynolds, Gretchen. "The Oprah Myth." *TV Guide* 23 July 1994: 8+.
Woods, Geraldine. *The Oprah Winfrey Story: Speaking Her Mind—An Authorized Biography.* Minneapolis: Dillon, 1991.
"A Year to Remember: Oprah Grows Up." *TV Guide* 7 Jan. 1995: 14+.

Carole D. Parnes

Osmonds, The, a wholesome family pop group of the 1970s, appealed to Americans turned off by the preceding decade's rebellious and unkempt musical acts. As strict Mormons, the clean-cut Osmonds were noted for abstaining from tobacco, alcohol, and caffeinated beverages. Singing siblings Alan (b. 1949), Wayne (1951), Merrill (1953), Jay (1955), Donny (1957), Marie (1959), and Jimmy (1963) were among the leading practitioners of "bubblegum rock," a genre named for its popularity among adolescents and lack of musical or lyrical depth.

The four eldest Osmond brothers began singing as a barbershop quartet in the late 1950s. Among the group's early achievements was winning a Kansas City barbershop convention in 1960. Encouraged by their success, the brothers moved with their parents from Ogden, UT, to work for a summer as street singers at Disneyland. In 1962, Andy Williams, Sr., who had seen them perform in California, suggested that they audition for his son's popular television variety show. This began a seven-year association with the *Andy Williams Show*, which introduced the Osmonds to the American public. During their tenure with Williams, the Osmonds added brothers Donny and Jimmy and sister Marie to the act.

Television exposure led to a major label recording contract for the Osmonds. In 1971, their first single, "One Bad Apple," became a No. 1 hit. Several hits followed, including "Down by the Lazy River," "Crazy Horses," and "Hold Her Tight." At the height of the Osmonds' success, Donny and Marie also pursued solo careers. Donny's first hit, "Go Away Little Girl," rose to the top of the charts in 1971. Marie's first solo record, "Paper Roses," sold over a million copies in 1972. Donny and Marie hosted their own television variety show from 1976 through 1979.

In the early 1980s, the Osmond Brothers (Alan, Wayne, Merrill, and Jay) switched from rock and roll to country music. They were named Best New Country Group by *Billboard* magazine in 1982. Jimmy retired from performing and turned to managing the group and other family enterprises. In addition to performing, the family owns and operates a theater in Branson, MO.

As Donny and Marie grew into their 20s, their teen idol status was left behind. Donny had his last Top 10 hit in 1989 with "Soldier of Love." In 1992, he began acting in the lead role of Andrew Lloyd Webber's *Joseph and the Amazing Technicolor Dreamcoat*. Marie continued to tour as a singer and acted as well. In 1999 Donny and Marie returned to television with a morning talk show.

Bibliography

Daly, Marsha. *The Osmonds: A Family Biography*. New York: St. Martin's, 1983.
Dunn, Paul H. *The Osmonds: The Official Story of the Osmond Family*. New York: Avon, 1977.
McMillan, Constance Van Brunt. *Donny and Marie Osmond: Breaking All the Rules*. New York: EMC Paradigm, 1977.
Scott, Barry. *We Had Joy, We Had Fun: The Lost Recording Artists of the 70s*. New York: Faber & Faber, 1994.
www.osmond.com.

Mark Madrigan

Ouija is a board game and modern folk magic artifact commonly used as a medium for divination and communication with discarnate entities. Ouija—a compound of the French and German words for "yes"—was invented in 1892 by American Elijah J. Bond. He sold his patent to William Fuld, "the father of Ouija," who popularized the product. Fuld sold the patent to the Parker Brothers company in 1966. The game equipment consists of a miniature table with a small window built into the top, and a board with the letters of the alphabet, the numbers zero through nine, and the words "yes" and "no" written on it. Participants rest their fingers on the miniature table which moves around the board to spell out messages.

Bibliography

Covina, Gina. *The Ouija Book*. New York: Simon & Schuster, 1979.
Gruss, Edmond C. *The Ouija Board: A Doorway to the Occult*. Phillipsburg: P&R, 1994.
Morgan, Keith. *How to Use a Ouija Board*. London: Pentacle, 1992.

Eric Alden Eliason

Our Gang (1922-1944). The brainchild of pioneer comedy producer Hal Roach, the *Our Gang* comedies were a long-running series of short films dedicated to a celebration of the American childhood. They were not the first films to feature children, but they quickly emerged as the best. Much of their success and longevity can be credited to the fact that most of the films were produced at Hal Roach Studios, which specialized in great short comedies. The studio was known for its warm, familial atmosphere and the films benefited particularly from the presence of Roach himself and director Robert McGowan, who was responsible for many of the best films in the series.

The history of the production, distribution, and titling of these films is extremely complex; however, briefly stated, the films were originally produced and released theatrically from 1922 through 1944. Although they have come to be known by a variety of names used more or less interchangeably, the series was originally intended to be called *The Hal Roach Rascals* or *Hal Roach's Rascals*. However, drawing inspiration from the title of the initial production in the series, the films quickly acquired the appellation *The Our Gang Comedies* or simply *Our Gang*.

In 1938 Roach sold the entire *Our Gang* unit to MGM. In the late 1940s Roach re-obtained his rights to the films that were not actually produced by MGM (although MGM kept the *Our Gang* name) and the talkies were successfully released to television in the mid-1950s as *The Little Rascals*.

Although many actors stayed with the series for several years, cast turnovers were frequent as individual members approached adolescence. In its various incarnations the gang usually included an interesting mixture of physical types, such as chubby Joe Cobb, who would be replaced by Norman "Chubby" Chaney. At various times one member would emerge as a leader—Mickey Daniels in the silents, Jackie Cooper briefly in the early 1930s and then the popular Spanky McFarland. Various members from Pete the Pup to the one-and-only Carl "Alfalfa" Switzer also became particular favorites. The gang included female members: Mary Kornman, Jean Darling, Darla Hood; and black children were always equal and welcome members: Ernie Morrison, Allen "Farina" Hoskins, Matthew "Stymie" Beard, Billie "Buckwheat" Thomas. While one can cite examples of where the films occasionally reflect some of the accepted racial attitudes and assumptions of their day, the overall picture presented in these films is one in which race is a virtual non-issue, with everyone having an equal share in the ups and downs of childhood.

While there is no one definitive *Our Gang* film, it is useful to note that the series can basically be divided into three groups: the Roach silents, the Roach sound films of the 1930s, and the MGM productions of the late 1930s and 1940s. Of these three groups, only the Roach sound films are widely known today. It is largely through their widespread availability on television and home video, under the more or less generically used name of *The Little Rascals*, that the *Our Gang* legend continues to grow. Key films from this group include *Pups Is Pups* (1930), *Teacher's Pet* (1930), *Dogs Is Dogs* (1931), *Free Wheeling* (1932), and *Glove Taps* (1937). Interestingly, while it is by no means one of the best entries, *Bored of Education* won the 1936 Academy Award for best short subject.

Bibliography

Maltin, Leonard, and Richard W. Bann. *The Little Rascals: The Life and Times of Our Gang*. New York: Crown, 1992.

Fred Guida

Our Miss Brooks (1948-1957) was originally a radio show about everyone's favorite English teacher, Connie Brooks. Played by Eve Arden (1912-1990; see entry), she united two separate roles: attractive, wry, single working woman; and schoolteacher, like Miss Spalding on *Life with Luigi* and some of the Great Gildersleeve's flames. The show's popularity came from her stressful yet funny encounters with her landlady, students, principal, and fellow teachers, played by such noteworthies as Jane Morgan, Richard Crenna, Gale Gordon, and Jeff Chandler.

All revolved about Arden herself. Typed as a wise-cracking show business gal in films like *Stage Door* or *At the Circus*, she balanced dignity with wit on radio. Arden won an Emmy and an honorary membership in the National Education Association. A TV series (1952-56) and film (1956), both also with Arden, further chronicled Miss Brooks's successful career.

Bibliography

Arden, Eve. *Three Phases of Eve: An Autobiography.* New York: St. Martin's, 1985.

Brooks, Tim, and Earle Marsh. *The Complete Directory to Prime Time Network and Cable TV Shows, 1946-Present.* New York: Ballantine, 1995.

Shriner, Dejay J. "*Our Miss Brooks.* An Alphabetical List of All Programs Believed to Be in Circulation." Houma: typescript, 1989, 1990, 1992.

James A. Freeman

Outer Limits (1964-1965), the famous TV science fiction anthology, began each episode with the appropriate atmospherics. "There is nothing wrong with your television set; do not attempt to adjust the picture. We are controlling transmission... You are about to participate in a great adventure; you are about to experience the awe and mystery which reaches from the inner mind to the *Outer Limits*," the Control Voice (Vic Perrin) intoned over black and white interference patterns on the television screen, introducing the weekly episode of *Outer Limits*.

This science fiction series invaded television with film noir scripts and a philosophic twist. Episodes employing many of the conventional elements of science fiction—body snatchers, shape changers, time travel, space invaders—examined issues of language and communication, social responsibility and personal choice in scripts which were decidedly somber in tone.

Because of the unusual degree of creative control exercised by producer Joseph Stefano, successful science fiction writers, including David Duncan, Louis Charbonneau, and Arthur Leo Zagat, agreed to contribute scripts to the series. Harlan Ellison adapted his own short stories for the scripts of "Soldier" and "Demon with a Glass Hand," and the Clifford D. Simak story "Goodnight, Mr. James" was produced as "The Duplicate Man." The quality of the scripts, in turn, attracted well-known performers, such as Cliff Robertson, William Shatner, Robert Duvall, and Vera Miles.

In *Outer Limits,* the special effects were relatively simple, usually intended to be suggestive rather than realistic. The black and white format lent itself to high contrast and stylized design underlining the themes of sharp moral choice.

While Stefano's first 33 episodes pleased science fiction and drama fans, executives at ABC objected to the intellectual and philosophic cast of the series. The network replaced Stefano with Ben Brady in the fall of 1964, in an attempt to stress action and adventure, but the remaining episodes lacked depth and complexity, and the series was canceled in January of 1965. It remained in syndication through 1981, and in 1986 PBS produced a documentary, *The Outer Limits: The Official Companion.*

Bibliography

Naha, Ed. *Science Fictionary.* New York: Sea View, 1980.

Premiere: ABC Press Release. 9 Sept. 1963; 22 Apr. 1964; 11 Sept. 1964; 17 Sept. 1964; 14 Oct. 1964.

Janet P. Sholty

Page, Betty (Bettie Mae) (1923-), arguably the most popular pin-up girl of the 1950s, was called the Queen of Hearts, the Queen of Curves, and the Queen of Bondage. Decades after her disappearance from public view in 1957, Bettie is royal again as the Queen of Comics with superhero status. Bettie (misspelled as Betty, which stayed with her public image) was born in Nashville, TN, educated on a Daughters of the American Revolution scholarship as a teacher, and hoped to be a movie star, but became an underground model and fashion icon.

Bettie moved to New York in 1948 to pursue a theatrical career, one marriage behind her. As her acting break failed to materialize, she paid her way as a photographer's and artist's model. Working frequently with brother and sister team Irving and Paula Klaw for *Movie Star News* and other adult and art magazines, she used her Cleopatra-esque black pageboy hairdo, with trademark bangs, and her hourglass figure as the props for her natural style with photographers. It is estimated that between 20,000 and one-half million photos were taken of her, ranging from shots taken by amateurs in camera clubs to those by highly successful professionals such as model-turned-photographer Bunny Yeager. Her poses and attitudes ran the gamut from girl-next-door innocence to playful bondage, always with direct and honest sex appeal.

Whether due to the Kefauver Committee crackdown on pornography of the late '50s or her age (34), Betty disappeared in 1957. She reemerged on paper in 1982 in comic form when Dave Stevens created the comic book character "Betty," the hero's girlfriend, in the *Rocketeer* series. As interest in this now elusive and legendary siren increased, Betty could be seen as the inspiration for several publications including *The Adventures of Betty Page* and *The Betty Pages*.

When finally tracked down by *Lifestyles of the Rich and Famous* and others, Bettie granted interviews but refused to be photographed. Bettie Page preferred to be remembered as the legendary sexual, flirtatious, beautiful Betty Page of the '50s who continues to inspire art and fashion alike.

Bibliography

Cook, Kevin. "My Story: The Missing Years." *Playboy* Jan. 1998.

Essex, Karen. *Bettie Page: The Life of a Pin-Up Legend.* Los Angeles: General, 1996.

Foster, Richard. *The Real Bettie Page: The Truth about the Queen of the Pin-Ups.* Secaucus: Carol, 1997.

Henry, Buck. "The Betty Boom." *Playboy* Dec. 1992: P122+.

Silke, Jim. *Bettie Page: Queen of Hearts.* Milwaukie, OK: Dark Horse Comics, 1995.

Yeager, Bunny. *Betty Page.* Köln: Taschen, 1996.

——. *Bunny's Honeys.* Köln: Taschen, 1994.

Suzie Sims-Fletcher

Pageantry, a dynamically celebratory form of public history, was wildly popular during the first part of the 20th century. Historical pageantry grew out of post–Civil War civic celebrations commemorating significant local or national events (Fourth of July, Founders' Days, the American Revolution and the Civil War, civic and industrial processions, monument dedications, relic displays). A metamorphosis began as the "genteel cultural elite" increasingly took control of these celebrations. In the late 19th century, these members of patriotic and historical societies believed that patriotic and civic celebrations must be more than entertaining parades, firework displays, and general frivolity. Such occasions could be used more purposefully, in their estimation, "not only to disseminate patriotism and morality but also to spread art and culture" (Glassberg 32). By the first two decades of the 20th century, historical pageants, utilizing local amateur participants, were being performed outside. The events depicted community history and development by combining music, dance, and drama within a specific vision —one where an idealized past smoothly transformed into a progressive future.

The Progressive Era emphasis on professionalization found its way into historical pageantry as well. In 1913, those who wished to control the so-called purity of pageantry and see their collective vision become a national one founded the American Pageant Association. Its ideals were dispersed and shared with people through training programs, publications, and conferences. Composed of a small group of "artists, educators and social workers" who "attempted to assert technical and artistic standards" upon those who wished to follow their lead, the association allied itself with the Drama League. The league, founded in 1911, was composed of academic dramatists as well as "concerned" professionals who saw their work as a response to the "crass commercialism" of popular theater. The league attempted to revitalize American drama by encouraging its use as positive social force.

Professional playwrights, dancers, musicians, and educators joined in promoting pageantry as a "movement for art and democracy." Those who believed they could change society through pageantry included playwright Percy Mackaye and his sister Hazel, dancers Isadora Duncan, Ted Shaw, and Ruth St. Denis, musicians Arthur Farwell and Frederick S. Converse, and educators George Pierce Baker and Frederick H. Kock. They and others presented pageants both outside and inside—any place there was a space large enough to serve their needs.

Ironically, pageantry's themes seldom included troublesome issues such as labor, woman's suffrage, and the problems of Native and African Americans.

By the late 1910s the force of the American Pageant Association had lessened considerably, and it was finished by 1930. Pageants, however, continued to be performed for a variety of reasons, as they are to this present day.

Bibliography

Glassberg, David. *American Historical Pageantry: The Uses of Tradition in the Early Twentieth Century.* Chapel Hill: U of North Carolina P, 1990.

Prevots, Naima. *American Pageantry: A Movement for Art and Democracy.* Ann Arbor: U.M.I. Research, 1990.

Richard L. Poole

Paramount Pictures long functioned as one of Hollywood's dominant studios and continues that function as the 20th century draws to a close. Created during the mid and late 1910s by Adolph Zukor (1873-1976), the company since then has frequently reigned as Hollywood's top money maker, in particular through the 1920s, 1940s, and 1970s. Today the company leads the way in seeking methods by which to re-invent Hollywood to adapt to the 21st-century world of new video technologies.

During the mid-1910s, as the company was being put together, Paramount was simply the name of the distribution arm of the Famous Players-Lasky motion picture studio, named for a strategy of filmmaking ("Famous Players in Famous Plays") and a key founder, producer Jesse Lasky. But it was Hungarian immigrant Adolph Zukor who, as the first great movie mogul, created the first mighty Hollywood studio colossus. Adolph Zukor integrated a moviemaking operation on Melrose Avenue in Hollywood with a worldwide network of film distribution with a chain of several hundred movie palaces and created a corporate giant.

By 1925, when Famous Players-Lasky merged with Balaban & Katz (the leading movie theater operation of its day), thus adding the final piece to its Publix motion picture theater chain, the corporate production and distribution divisions were merged and renamed Paramount Pictures. By 1930, Publix owned and operated more than 1,200 theaters, playing to more patrons than any movie-house operation in film history. This development also meant that Paramount owed millions of dollars in mortgages on those theaters.

That became a corporate drag in the Great Depression, and during the early 1930s Paramount was financially reorganized. Such renowned films as Mae West's *I'm No Angel* (1933) and *Belle of the Nineties* (1934) and the Marx Brothers' *Coconuts* (1929) and *Horse Feathers* (1932)—all favorites today—only contributed to the company's money-losing efforts through the Great Depression. In 1935, when the dust settled, Paramount Pictures, Inc. became the appellation for the company as a whole—filmmaking, film distribution, and a national chain of nearly 1,000 theaters. Paramount had done well through the late 1920s—with such hits as *Wings* (1927)—but the studio's golden age of profitability came after re-organization and particularly with the boom in moviegoing associated with the Second World War. In 1936, Barney Balaban was placed in charge. He ruled with a conservative corporate strategy which earned Paramount ever-increasing profits, cresting in 1946 with a record $40 million.

Y. Frank Freeman, who ran the studio in California, relied on proven concepts and stars to turn out feature films and short subjects. For example, Paramount plucked Bing Crosby and Bob Hope from radio, and their "Road" pictures proved the most profitable series of feature films made during Hollywood's golden age. Cecil B. DeMille also created hit after hit: *Union Pacific* (1939), *Northwest Mounted Police* (1940), and *The UN Conquered* (1946). Preston Sturges added his sparkling comedies, including *The Great McGinty* (1940), *The Lady Eve* (1941), and *The Miracle of Morgan's Creek* (1944).

Paramount's money-machine began to unravel in 1949 when Balaban acceded to the U.S. Supreme Court's order to divest its theaters. Paramount Pictures became simply a production and distribution company. Through the 1950s Paramount had trouble dealing with television. VistaVision, the studio's widescreen process, could not make up for a lack of stars. Paramount produced only occasional hits such as Hal Wallis's *Gunfight at the O.K. Corral* (1957) and *Becket* (1964). Only a string of Elvis Presley musicals consistently made money. Corporate red ink began appearing in 1963. Barney Balaban retired a year later.

In the fall of 1966, a giant conglomerate, Gulf & Western Industries, stepped forward and purchased Paramount. Charles Bluhdorn became Paramount's president; he hired former actor, Robert Evans, to revitalize the studio in California. Evans tried and failed with such mega-musicals as *Darling Lili* (1970) and *Paint Your Wagon* (1969). It was not until 1972, with the release of Francis Ford Coppola's *The Godfather*, that Paramount began to make its comeback as a studio.

During the late 1970s and early 1980s, Paramount, under Barry Diller and Frank Mancuso, again became one of Hollywood's leading studios. Hits flowed regularly from the Melrose Avenue studio: the *Star Trek* films (and television shows), the Eddie Murphy films, and even television spin-offs such as the feature film *The Untouchables* (1987), and later another television series of the same name. In 1989, Gulf & Western was changed to Paramount Communications, Inc. After a prolonged bidding war, in 1994, diversified media giant Viacom Inc. bought the studio for $10 million; it is now called Paramount Pictures.

Bibliography

Eames, John Douglas. *The Paramount Story.* New York: Crown, 1985.

Edmonds, I. G., and Reiko Mimura. *Paramount Pictures and the People Who Made Them.* New York: Barnes, 1980.

Gomery, Douglas. *The Hollywood Studio System.* New York: St. Martin's, 1986.

Sobel, Robert. *The Rise and Fall of Conglomerate Kings.* New York: Stein & Day, 1984.

Zukor, Adolph. *The Public Is Never Wrong.* New York: Putnam, 1953.

Douglas Gomery

Paretsky, Sara (1947-), is the author of a series of hard-boiled mystery novels featuring feminist detective V. I. Warshawski, one of the best known and most admired heroines of the genre. Paretsky turned to fiction writing after earning an M.B.A. along with a doctorate in history from the Univer-

594

sity of Chicago in 1977, and a subsequent career in business. Influenced by the women's movement of the 1960s, Paretsky combined her feminist views with her attraction to the mystery form, creating the female private investigator Warshawski in *Indemnity Only* (1982). That novel introduced readers to what would become Paretsky's recurring themes: loyalty, parental love, independence, self-esteem, and an unrelenting tenacity in tackling established institutions. Later books pit Warshawski against such corrupt professional societies as medicine (*Bitter Medicine*, 1987); politics (*Bloodshot*, 1988, and *Burn Marks*, 1990); industry (*Deadlock*, 1984, and *Burn Marks*); and religion (*Killing Orders*, 1985). While investigating cases in the Chicago in which she was raised, Warshawski champions social causes such as the homeless, minorities, family, and the abused.

Paretsky also co-founded Sisters in Crime, a national organization of women detective fiction writers that has brought more exposure to women writers.

Bibliography

Henderson, Lesley, ed. *Twentieth-Century Crime and Mystery Writers*. Chicago: St. James, 1991.

Klein, Kathleen Gregory. *The Woman Detective: Gender and Genre*. Urbana: U of Illinois P, 1988.

Mary Clark-Upchurch

See also

Detective Sidekicks

Feminist Detective Fiction

Hard-boiled Detective Fiction

Regional Mysteries

Parker, Charlie "The Bird" (1920-1955), jazz alto saxophone player and composer, is considered one of jazz's most innovative and influential musicians. His ability to improvise long, complex, and organically unified solos awed his fellow musicians; his cool, effortless virtuosity dazzled his audiences. He and fellow musician Dizzy Gillespie are often credited with the development of bebop, a jazz style which, in the 1940s, quickly upstaged the swing and Dixieland styles of earlier musicians.

Parker was born in a suburb of Kansas City. His father, Charles Parker, Sr., a song-and-dance man, soon drifted away from the family, and his mother, Addie, was left with the responsibility of raising the young Parker. She helped launch her son's musical career by buying him a leaky alto saxophone when he was in high school. Largely self-taught, he joined a high school dance band called the Deans of Swing, but soon dropped out of school. After working in several bands, Parker made his way to New York in 1938.

It was around this time that Parker began to sit in on the now-famous after-hour jam sessions at New York clubs like Minton's and Monroe's. Led by Parker and other jazz innovators, the musicians at these jam sessions synthesized the various elements of bebop and created a new music that both shocked and delighted the American public. By 1944, Charlie Parker was at the center of the bebop revolution; his influence on jazz musicians was more or less universal. Despite a heroin addiction (which he acquired in the early 1940s), three unsuccessful marriages, and an insatiable appetite for food, drugs, and women, Parker was able to continue producing outstanding music until his untimely death on March 12, 1955. Bassist Charles Mingus was once quoted as saying, "Bird is not dead: he's hiding out somewhere, and he'll be back with some new shit that will scare everyone to death." Indeed, after Parker's death, "Bird lives!" became a favorite saying of his fans. Among many tributes to Parker's creative genius was Clint Eastwood's 1988 film, *Bird*.

Most of Parker's music falls into one or another of three categories: (1) blues tunes (Parker was once described as a "blues player caught in the age of anxiety"), (2) slow ballads, and (3) up-tempo original compositions, many of these based on the chord changes of popular songs. This last category includes such widely recorded standards as "Anthropology," "Au Privave," "Confirmation," and "Ko-Ko." In February and May of 1945, Parker and Gillespie produced what are generally considered to be the first bebop recordings. Reissued by the Prestige label under the title *In the Beginning*, the tunes included such bop standards as "Salt Peanuts," "Shaw 'Nuff," and "Hot House."

Bibliography

Collier, James Lincoln. *The Making of Jazz*. New York: Dell, 1978.

Crow, Bill. *Jazz Anecdotes*. New York: Oxford UP, 1990.

Gitler, Ira. *Swing to Bop*. New York: Oxford UP, 1985.

Reisner, Robert George. *Bird: The Legend of Charlie Parker*. New York: Citadel, 1962.

Russell, Ross. *Bird Lives!* New York: Charterhouse, 1973.

Stearns, Marshall W. *The Story of Jazz*. New York: Oxford UP, 1956.

G. Albert Ruesga

Parlor Entertainments were home-centered indoor amusements, mainly for family and friends, many of which exploited the physical arrangement of the Victorian parlor. By the mid-19th century the parlor had become the symbolic focus of widely accepted ideals of family and home in American Victorian life. The parlor contained the best furnishing and most impressive decoration the family could provide and helped to assert the family's identity in the community. It became a place for personal activities such as reading, Bible study, drawing, needlecraft, and other domestic arts; and it accommodated gatherings for social and religious pursuits and a variety of pastimes and entertainments.

A display of family pictures was a common feature of the parlor, made possible by the development of photography, and viewing the family album was a cherished activity. In the latter part of the century the stereopticon brought three-dimensionality to the pictures, and the "magic lantern" made showings to a roomful of guests possible.

Music, too, formed a staple of 19th-century home life, assisted by both the widespread distribution of affordable sheet music and by the inventions of affordable and versatile musical instruments. In Philadelphia, John Isaac Hawkins (1799-1845) produced an upright piano with excellent musical qualities and an attractive appearance. About 1840, the "parlor organ," or "reed organ," emerged and became ubiquitous in American parlors by the end of the century.

In more affluent homes the front parlor was apt to be separated from a back parlor by a sizeable archway equipped with portieres or pocket doors. This arrangement provided a ready-made theatrical environment by using the back parlor as a stage and the front parlor as an auditorium. Skits, poetry readings, renditions of famous speeches, and scenes from popular plays, novels, or short stories were frequently staged for an audience of family and visitors. Scripts of holiday pageants and other dramatic entertainments were written and sold especially for such presentations.

Tableaux vivants, also called "living pictures" or "living statues," enjoyed great popularity from about 1875 into the early 20th century. Imitating more elaborate presentations on the commercial variety stage, family performers costumed themselves to represent the characters in well-known paintings, sculpture, or even scenes described in literary sources. They posed in stage-like settings made to look as much like the original picture as possible. Portieres between the parlors were opened to reveal the "living picture," often with a musical selection or poetry reading as accompaniment. A series of related pictures might provide a full evening's entertainment.

The parlor was also the setting for a wide range of games for children and adults alike. Many variations of the well-known "Blind Man's Bluff" were popular; all involved teasing a blindfolded player until he caught and guessed the identity of one of his tormentors. "Pin the Tail on the Donkey," now almost exclusively a children's birthday party game, was once also a favorite adult pastime.

Other activity games such as "Drop the Handkerchief" and "Musical Chairs" provided opportunities for courting couples to engage in socially acceptable flirting and physical contact. Games such as "Spin the Bottle" and "Postman" directly fostered courting behavior. In addition, games often resulted in penalties or forfeits which allowed the winner to require a kiss or compliment from the loser. Frequently, of course, one might intentionally "lose" in order to pay the forfeit to a particular winner.

There were many varieties of storytelling games, frequently designed for comic results. In "The Family Coach," for example, each player took the name of a character in a familiar story ("Mrs. Wiggs of the Cabbage Patch" was a common choice) and whenever the character name was mentioned, that player had to jump up, turn around, and sit back down, or perform some other silly action. Naturally, hilarity made the tale difficult to follow, and mistakes resulted in appropriate forfeits.

Several memory and guessing games, popular at the turn of the century, are still played. For instance, one player begins, "I'm going to visit my aunt, and with me I'm taking my *toothbrush*." Then each player repeats the sentence, adding a new item to the list. Even adults still enjoy "Who Am I?"—now more commonly known as "Twenty Questions." One player assumes the identity of a famous person and answers "Yes" or "No" to questions from the other players, until the identity is guessed or the questions are exhausted.

Games sometimes took the form of practical jokes and were limited only by the ingenuity of those who created them. The "Obstacle Race" provides a suggestive example: Unsuspecting players were brought into a room one by one and shown an obstacle course of objects arranged on the floor. The player is then blindfolded and told to walk to the other side of the room without touching the obstacles. Surreptitiously, however, the objects have been quietly removed. The delight, of course, is to watch the player's exaggerated efforts to avoid the nonexistent obstacles and to shout warnings and encouragement for further confusion. The player then gets to watch the next person's effort.

Although some of these activities still survive, the development of automobiles and motion pictures took families away from their parlors, while phonographs, radios, and later, television replaced home-grown entertainment with manufactured popular culture. The parlor disappeared to reappear as the much less formal family room.

Bibliography

Beaver, Patrick. *Victorian Parlor Games*. New York: Thomas Nelson, 1974.

Clark, Clifford Edward, Jr. *The American Family Home, 1800-1960*. Chapel Hill: U of North Carolina P, 1986.

Grier, Katherine C. *Culture and Comfort: People, Parlors and Upholstery, 1850-1930*. Rochester: Strong Museum, 1988.

Stevenson, Louise L. *The Victorian Homefront: American Thought and Culture, 1860-1880*. New York: Twayne, 1991.

Jack W. McCullough

See also
Board Games
Family Rooms

Parrish, Maxfield (1870-1966), was the single most popular American artist of the early 20th century. When the American reading public increased during the early 1900s, illustrators attained celebrity status. At this time, mass-produced works of art (art prints in particular) were made especially for this new mass audience, for whom reproductions suitable for framing were available at affordable prices. This proved to be the perfect environment for the skilled, witty, and imaginative artistry of Maxfield Parrish.

Although his works were commercially successful, Parrish's induction into the Academy of American Artists in 1897 signified recognition of artistic talent beyond the purely commercial. He also received honors from organizations such as the National Academy of Design, and the Architectural League of New York. His work was commissioned nearly as often by private patrons and collectors, as advertisers.

Born Frederick Parrish in Philadelphia, PA, Parrish took his grandmother's maiden name (Maxwell) to create his professional name. He was raised in privilege, traveled extensively in Europe, and attended school in Paris. During this time, he frequented museums and became familiar with classical art and architecture, fine music, and literature. Parrish was particularly influenced by the Pre-Raphaelites' blend of naturalism, fantasy, and romanticism. The painting and sculpture he viewed at the Fine Arts building at the Chicago World's Fair in 1893 also left a strong impression; he dreamed of creating ideal cities with wondrous architectural groupings.

While studying architecture in 1888 at Haverford College, Parrish dropped out in order to paint full time (he was awarded an honorary degree from Haverford College in 1914). He took painting classes at the Pennsylvania Academy of Fine Art, audited classes at the Drexel Institute, and from 1892 through 1900 experimented with nearly every medium, from etching to photography. In 1904, one of his paintings was purchased by the St. Louis Museum of Art; in 1913, he was invited to become head of Yale University's Art Department (he declined, preferring to stay on his estate, "The Oaks," in New Hampshire, to paint), and an exhibition of his illustrations and paintings was held in 1925, in New York.

Maxfield Parrish's career began with a mural he painted for the University of Pennsylvania thespian society in 1894. Its success led to the exhibition and publication of his work, which gained him national attention. Parrish was commissioned for a magazine cover by *Harper's Bazaar* in 1895, and produced political cartoons for the *New England Homestead* in 1896. His fame increased with the popularity of his illustrations for *Mother Goose in Prose* (by L. Frank Baum, who also authored *The Wizard of Oz*), the success of which led to his providing illustrations for a number of other books, including Wagner's *Ring of the Nibelung* (by F. J. Stinson for *Scribner's Magazine* in 1898), Washington Irving's *Knickerbocker's History of New York* (a satirical history which parodied colonial New York, and for which Parrish's illustrations were equally amusing) in 1899, *The Golden Age* (by Kenneth Grahame) in 1899, and its sequel, *Dream Days,* in 1902. Parrish also delighted the intellectual establishment with his illustration of John Milton's *L'Allegro,* in 1901, and *Italian Villas and Their Gardens* (by Edith Wharton) in 1903. His critical and popular success continued with his illustrations for *The Arabian Nights* (Kate D. Wiggin and Nora A. Smith, eds.) in 1909, *A Wonderbook and Tanglewood Tales* (by Nathaniel Hawthorne) and *Poems of Childhood* (by Eugene Field) both in 1910, and his masterpiece, and last illustrated book, *The Knave of Hearts* (by Louise Saunders) in 1925. The magazines Parrish contributed to most consistently include *Collier's, Century Magazine, Harper's Weekly, Harper's Monthly, Harper's Round Table, Harper's Young People, Hearst's Magazine, Illustrated London News, Ladies' Home Journal, Life* (the humor magazine preceding the picture magazine of the same name), and *Scribner's Magazine.* Parrish became especially well known for his imaginative and humorous advertisements for a variety of products from candy and cosmetics, to cameras and Colgate products.

Parrish's illustrations were geared to the reproductive techniques suitable for both weekly magazines and the highest quality art prints. They were reproduced from original oil paintings created by a laborious technique to ensure aesthetic beauty and technical perfection. Parrish achieved the bold, luminescent colors characteristic of his works by alternating transparent glazes of pure pigment with layers of varnish to achieve the desired tint. A particular tint, still referred to as "Parrish blue," is so brilliant, it was mistakenly speculated to be composed of powdered lapis lazuli. Reproduction required a complex printing of up to 14 separate lithographs and press runs in order to successfully produce the colors of the original painting.

Maxfield Parrish's commercial career spanned four decades. His popularity waned during the Depression, when sentimental themes seemed trite, and cheap imitations had flooded the market. His audience also changed with the popularity of radio and moving pictures, and with the later advent of television and modern and abstract art. Brown and Bigelow Publishing Company continued to contract his less directly commercial work—landscapes inspired by New Hampshire, Arizona, and Italy, depicting rural buildings (churches, farmhouses, mills), ponds, trees, meadows, and mountains. Parrish believed these works provided an outlet for the city-dweller's imagination, and he focused only on landscapes through the 1950s. His work regained some of its former popularity with the changing aesthetics and criticism of 1960s Pop Art and 1970s New Realists and photo realists, which inspired a revival of interest and retrospective exhibitions.

Bibliography

Cutler, Laurence S., Judy Goffman, and the American Illustrators Gallery. *Maxfield Parrish*. New York: Crescent, 1993.
Ludwig, Coy. *Maxfield Parrish*. New York: Watson-Guptill, 1973.

D. Ann Maukonen

Parton, Dolly (1946-), is a larger-than-life figure in country music; in her songwriting, recording, movies, and personal appearances (as well as personal appearance), she has shown a knack for getting attention. She has also worked hard to achieve respectability with her fame and has generally succeeded; although she has confronted the image of the "dumb blonde" head on and been the object of numerous jokes from comedians about her wigs and breast size, she has come to be known as a talented writer and performer and an astute, shrewd businesswoman.

Dollie Rebecca Parton was born in Locust Ridge, TN, in Sevier County, located at the foot of the Smoky Mountains. The fourth of 12 children, she grew up in poverty with a burning ambition to be a star. She received her first guitar when she was 8 and at 13 began appearing on the "Cas Walker Show" in Knoxville. Her first recording was "Puppy Love" for a small independent label. The day after she graduated from high school in 1964 she moved to Nashville, where she made the rounds as a songwriter; the first hit she wrote was "Put It Off Until Tomorrow," recorded by Bill Phillips in 1966. In 1967, she signed with Monument Records and released two singles, "Dumb Blonde" and "Something Fishy," before she joined the *Porter Wagoner Show* after his previous female singer had left. She appeared regularly on his syndicated TV show, on tours with him, and recorded duets with him on his label, RCA; she also signed with that label and emerged as a solo artist. Her first solo hit was "Mule Skinner Blues (Blue Yodel No. 8)," an old Jimmie Rodgers song, in 1970; this was followed by

"Joshua," "Coat of Many Colors," "Touch Your Woman," and "Jolene." In 1973, Parton left the *Porter Wagoner Show* but he continued to produce her recordings and help guide her career; however, in 1976, she severed all ties with Wagoner and set out to broaden her appeal into the pop market. With the movies *9 to 5*, in which she co-starred with Jane Fonda and Lily Tomlin (and wrote and sang the title number) and *Best Little Whorehouse in Texas*, Dolly Parton proved she could make it in Hollywood as well as Nashville. Also during the 1980s she had a network variety show on ABC, *Dolly*, which did not survive; however, she continued to write and record hit songs.

Although her success as a movie star and recording artist are obvious, she has also achieved a great deal of unheralded success as a songwriter (she wrote "I Will Always Love You" as well as numerous other songs) and businessperson (she established "Dollywood" in the Smoky Mountains, which is a major tourist draw and provides employment in that economically disadvantaged region).

Bibliography

Bufwack, Mary A., and Robert K. Dermann. *Finding Her Voice: The Illustrated History of Women in Country Music.* New York: Holt, 1995.

Country Music Foundation. *Country: The Music and the Musicians from the Beginnings to the 90's.* New York: Abbeville, 1994.

Parton, Dolly. *My Life and Other Unfinished Business.* New York: HarperCollins, 1994.

Don Cusic

Partridge Family, The (1970-1974), the TV show, chronicled the fictional adventures of a musical family on the road in their multi-colored bus and at their California home. The Friday prime-time show created a pop music sensation worth 20 million albums and millions of dollars of merchandise. The show's star, David Cassidy, has called *The Partridge Family* "the last gasp of innocence in America."

In the first episode, the five Partridge children hold a recording session in their garage. When they ask mom to sing backup, they wind up with a hit, "I Think I Love You," a song which indeed climbed to No. 1 in the charts by the week of November 21, 1970, and sold 4 million copies.

The cast featured Shirley Jones (1934-), star of stage and movie musicals such as *Oklahoma!* (1955) and *Carousel* (1956) and Academy Award winner for her performance in *Elmer Gantry* (1960). Jones played Shirley Partridge, a widowed suburban mother who headed this musical group. David Cassidy (1950), Shirley Jones's real-life stepson (she married actor Jack Cassidy [1927-76] in 1956), was cast as 16-year-old teen heartthrob, Keith Partridge. Distinctive for his flyaway shag hair, Cassidy in real life, too, did have musical talent and enjoyed pop stardom. Former fashion model Susan Dey (1952-) played 15-year-old Laurie, habitually committing herself to good causes and bedeviling Keith. Danny Bonaduce (1959-) played the mercenary 10-year-old Danny, the band's bassist. Wily Danny enjoyed rankling the band's manager, Reuben Kincaid, portrayed with neurotic distraction by Dave Madden, formerly of *Laugh-In.* Jeremy Gelbwaks (1961-) was 7-year-old drummer Christopher during the show's first season only; he was replaced by Brian Forster (1961-), whose show-biz family included grandfather Alan Napier (Alfred the butler on TV's *Batman*). Semi-entity Tracy, the 5-year-old tambourinist, was played by Suzanne Crough (1963-), a child actress in commercials. Blending the traditional TV family's wholesomeness with mod 1970s culture and fashion, this "instant" group acquired an intensely loyal following. The series ranked among the Top 20 according to Nielsen ratings for both the 1971-72 and 1972-73 seasons.

The Partridge Family albums could claim vocals only from Cassidy and Jones, and she mostly background; studio musicians did the rest. The pre-fab strategy was successful though, as their first two albums, produced by Bell Records, hit the charts. Five subsequent albums through 1973 fared less spectacularly.

The Partridge Family, despite the sugary overlay, was more progressive than most domestic comedy. Jones helped pioneer the role of single mother/working woman without the show being obsessed with finding the family a husband/father.

Bibliography

Allis, Tim, et al. "The Boys Are Back" and "By the Way... Whatever Happened to the *Other* Partridge Kids?" *People Weekly* 1 Nov. 1993: 66-70, 73-74.

Brooks, Tim, and Earl Marsh. *The Complete Directory to Prime Time Network TV Shows.* New York: Ballantine, 1988.

Cassidy, David. *C'mon Get Happy: Fear and Loathing on the Partridge Family Bus.* New York: Warner, 1994.

Melissa Stout
Michael Delahoyde

Pass, Joe (1929-1994), born Joe Passalaqua, was a highly regarded guitar soloist and vocal accompanist. In his late teens, he played with a number of big bands, including Tony Pastor and Charlie Barnet. He accompanied both Sarah Vaughan and Ella Fitzgerald and was a sideman for Oscar Peterson. The range of his playing was remarkable.

In common with many other musicians of his generation, Pass was hooked on drugs. From the early 1950s into the early 1960s, he went into virtual obscurity, playing anywhere just to get money to feed his habit. He served prison time for that addiction. However, in 1961, he and other musicians who were members of Synanon recorded and released an album which marked his comeback.

Still, he remained in the relative shadows of studio recordings and vocal accompanist until the release of his 1973 album, *Virtuoso*. Since that time, he was highly regarded as a leading figure on his instrument and in great demand. He recorded duets with Zoot Sims, Count Basie, Oscar Peterson, and Jimmy Rowles, among others.

Bibliography

Enstice, Wayne, and Paul Rubin. *Jazz Spoken Here: Conversations with Twenty-Two Musicians.* Baton Rouge: Louisiana State UP, 1992.

Gammond, Peter. *Oxford Companion to Popular Music.* New York: Oxford UP, 1991.

Kernfeld, Barry, ed. *The New Grove Dictionary of Jazz.* New York: Grove's Dictionaries of Music, 1988.

Sallis, James, ed. *The Guitar in Jazz: An Anthology.* Lincoln: U of Nebraska P, 1986.

Frank A. Salamone

Patriotic Songs. The U.S. has, in effect, four national anthems. The official one is, of course, "The Star Spangled Banner." The story of Francis Scott Key writing the lyrics while watching the British bombarding Fort McHenry, near Baltimore, in 1814 is very familiar. Soon after, Key, a lawyer, published his poem along with an indication that it should be sung to the tune of "The Anacreontic Song." Ironically, the melody that was to be used with Key's anti-British lyrics was of British origins. "The Anacreontic Song" was an anonymous drinking song published in London around 1779-80. Though unofficially regarded as the national anthem by the military for years, "The Star Spangled Banner" was not recognized as the official anthem until 1916. In that year Woodrow Wilson declared the song to be official by executive order, and in 1931 Congress fully legalized the song's national anthem status. Perhaps part of the reason that Wilson made the 1916 declaration was to counteract a challenger to "The Star Spangled Banner." In 1910, "America the Beautiful" was published and soon there was a strong but unsuccessful movement to make it the national anthem. The tune had been written in 1882 by musician Samuel A. Ward and the lyrics in 1893 by English literature professor Katherine Lee Bates. (The words were first published in 1895.)

There are two other sometime pretenders to the title of national anthem: "America" and "God Bless America." The well-crafted words for "America" or "My Country 'Tis of Thee" were written in 1831 by Bostonian Samuel Francis Smith. When Smith published his poem in 1832, he unwittingly chose, from a German music collection, the melody for the national anthem of Great Britain, "God Save the King." (At the time the U.S. was still at odds with England.) That melody, possibly the world's best known, was published anonymously in London in 1744. The other unofficial national anthem is Irving Berlin's 1939 rouser, "God Bless America." All of these three unofficial anthems are very frequently performed on occasions when "The Star Spangled Banner" is not mandated by custom.

Besides these four, there are a number of other notable American patriotic songs, in addtion to military songs (see entry). In 1812, "Hail to the Chief" was published in New York. The brisk march tune was anonymous, and the words were derived from Sir Walter Scott's 1810 poem "Lady of the Lake." Although the song has been long associated with the U.S. presidency, being first performed in 1845 at the inaugural of James Polk, the "chief" in the song refers not to the leader of the U.S. but an imaginary leader in the Scottish Highlands. No matter, for the words are rarely used.

Another anonymous American song is "Columbia, the Gem of the Ocean," published in 1843. It was the first anthem-like song to be completely American. Its melody is outstanding and the song could be a challenger for the honor of official national anthem if it were not for the confusing lyrics, which refer to "Columbia," a long-ago obsolete term for the U.S.

The end of the 19th century and the early 20th century were graced by a number of excellent marches by the American march king, John Philip Sousa. He wrote about 100 marches, of which about ten are still quite popular. They include "Semper Fidelis" (1888), written for the Marine Corps, "The Washington Post March" (1889), "The Thunderer" (1889), "El Capitan" (1896), "Hands across the Sea" (1899), and his masterpiece, "The Stars and Stripes Forever!" (1897).

Early in the 20th century, several outstanding patriotic pieces appeared. In 1904 George M. Cohan strutted to his composition "Yankee Doodle Boy" or "I'm a Yankee Doodle Dandy" in his musical *Little Johnny Jones.* Two years later, he introduced his enduring rouser "You're a Grand Old Flag" in his 1906 musical *George Washington, Jr.* That same year "The National Emblem March" was written by otherwise obscure bandmaster Edwin E. Bagley. "National Emblem" is possibly the most performed American military-style march, after "The Stars and Stripes Forever." Furthermore, like "Stars and Stripes Forever," "National Emblem" has a widely circulated parody, "Oh the monkey wrapped his tail around the flagpole."

The World War II era saw the appearance of several patriotic songs. "Don't Sit under the Apple Tree" was a 1939 composition by lyricists Lew Brown and Charles Tobias set to a jazzed-up version of the melody for "Long, Long Ago!" (c. 1835) by English writer Thomas Haynes Bayly. "Apple Tree," with a bouncy recording by the Andrews Sisters, was one of the patriotic hits of the war. Also written around that time was "This Is My Country" (1940), created by lyricist Don Raye and composer Al Jacobs. A third notable song of the war period was "We Will Overcome," which first appeared in 1945. The lyrics of a 1900 poem by C. Albert Tindley, "I'll Overcome Some Day," were modified and set to a melody possibly written in 1945 by Roberta Evelyn Martin. Around 1960 the title was changed again, to "We Shall Overcome," and the song became the symbol of the 1960s civil rights movement.

Bibliography

Anderson, Gillian B., ed. *Freedom's Voice in Poetry and Song.* Wilmington: Scholarly Resources, 1977.

Browne, C. A. *The Story of Our National Ballads.* Rev. by Willard A. Heaps. New York: Crowell, 1960.

Elson, Louis Charles. *The National Music of America and Its Sources.* Boston: Page, 1915.

William E. Studwell

Paxton, Tom (1937-), one of the most productive and durable of American folk singer-songwriters, has recorded more than 30 albums since his first in 1962. Paxton was born in Chicago, but his family moved to Oklahoma when he was ten years old. His music is strongly influenced by dust-bowl folk singers like Oklahoma's Woody Guthrie. As a drama major at the University of Oklahoma, he was taken by the music of the Weavers and began scribbling lyrics. After graduation he joined the Army.

Paxton's army years included a stint in New York City, where he was exposed to the blossoming Greenwich Village folk scene. Paxton began serious songwriting and began performing at the Gaslight Club in 1962. The club issued his first album, but he did not come to national attention until Elektra Records released the LP *Ramblin' Boy* in 1965. The title song became Paxton's trademark, and it was covered by a number of other folk singers.

Paxton's music became increasingly politicized on his second Elektra album, *Ain't That News*, also released in 1965. The anti-war songs included "Lyndon Johnson Told the Nation" and "Buy a Gun for Your Son." His 1966 album *Outward Bound* was also a success, although it lacked the political acerbity of *Ain't That News*.

Paxton became a popular concert performer in the mid-1960s, mixing romantic folk ballads like his classic "The Last Thing on My Mind" with witty political commentary. He also wrote and performed a number of children's songs, including the ever-popular "The Marvelous Toy" and "Going to the Zoo" (covered by Peter, Paul, and Mary). The hootenanny tradition of good-time folk music emerged in songs like "Bottle of Wine."

Paxton recorded four more albums for Elektra, *Morning Again* (1969), *The Things I Notice Now* (1969), *Tom Paxton 6* (1970), and *The Compleat Paxton* (1971), the last a double-LP set recorded live. In 1970 Paxton shifted his critical pen toward the environment, writing "Whose Garden Was This?" which became a mainstay among environmental activists. The next year he moved to England and recorded *How Come the Sun* for Reprise. Paxton turned more toward political satire in the early 1970s, but continued to lash out at U.S. presidents in his "Talking Watergate." Paxton recorded two more albums for Reprise, *Peace Will Come* (1972) and *New Songs for Old Friends* (1973), with London folk singer Ralph McTell.

Paxton then formed his own label and recorded *Something in My Life* (1975), *New Songs from the Briar Patch* (1977), and *Heroes* (1978). *Heroes* signaled a return to political commentary with topical songs including "White Bones of Allende" and "Born on the Fourth of July."

After nearly a five-year leave of absence from the recording studio, he returned with a string of albums starting with *The Paxton Report* (1981). He then began recording for Flying Fish, a Chicago record label specializing in bluegrass and blues recordings. *Even a Grey Day* (1983) focused on folk ballads and included an updated version of "The Last Thing on My Mind." Paxton continued his interest in children's music in the 1980s with the album *The Marvelous Toy and Other Gallimaufry*. But he also recorded satirical albums, such as the live LP *Politics*, and *One Million Lawyers...and Other Disasters* (1986). The latter includes a song that became a concert favorite, an ode to the "Me Generation" entitled "Yuppies in the Sky," sung to the music of Vaughn Monroe's "Riders in the Sky."

Paxton then recorded several more albums of songs for children, did a series of musical commentaries for National Public Radio, and began translating into English popular songs by European artists. *It Ain't Easy,* released in 1992,

blends topical songs and folk ballads. *Wearing the Time* was released in 1994.

Bibliography

Larkin, Colin, ed. *Guinness Encyclopedia of Popular Music.* Vol. 4. Middlesex, U.K.: Guinness, 1995.

Ken Nagelberg

Pay-Per-View (PPV) bypasses the need for home video stores by instantly delivering a movie or event directly into a consumer's living room with the push of a button. PPV networks provide a variety of programming, ranging from movies to wrestling to tax assistance, sometimes 24 hours a day. The major players include five-channel Request Television and Viewer's Choice, Action Pay-Per-View, adult networks Spice and Playboy Television, smaller networks such as Cable Video Store, Adult PPV, and TheaterVision, as well as stand-alone services like KBLCOM, which operates not by satellite but by video or laser disc. The convenience of never having to leave your home to watch a movie or event, however, has yet to take off with subscribers. Studios continue to release movies to PPV 30-90 days after home video, while special events that draw a million viewers are few and far between. Due to numerous setbacks such as lack of cable channel space and poor customer awareness, the PPV industry thus far has been a financial disappointment.

In 1977, Warner Cable originated the concept of PPV when it launched the experimental cable system called QUBE in Columbus, OH. QUBE, with eight PPV channels, proved unsuccessful in Columbus and in six other cities from 1981 to 1983. Not until Request Television and Viewer's Choice launched their programming by satellite in 1985 did the PPV industry start to grow.

However, the PPV industry remained in a holding pattern until 1990 because of the explosion of the home video market in 1985. The main problem was addressability: the term for the number of subscribers connected to a particular cable service. Few homes were addressable, and the procedure for ordering movies was complicated and time-consuming. Now, most cable systems have 1-800 numbers for customers to order PPV, or "impulse" ordering systems which allow events to be purchased by the push of a button on a converter box.

PPV may have a bright outlook after all. Reregulation has created an impetus for operators to look at PPV as a future revenue source. Must-carry rules have limited what little channel space is already available, and PPV is unregulated. Time-Warner's 15 PPV channel Quantum system in Queens, NY, and various other multichannel systems are getting tremendous buy rates, serving as an early model for PPV's staying power until digital compression allows systems to double or triple their existing channel capacity. Regional sports have proven to be a moderate success, such as PASS's Detroit Red Wings hockey or ESPN's college football games. PPV has demonstrated its ability to succeed, but it will take more aggressive efforts on the PPV retailing side to be more competitive with home video in the future.

Bibliography

Katz, Richard. "Action Packed." *Cablevision* 19 Oct. 1992: 39-42.

——. "PPV Promotions: Special Report." *Cablevision* 10 May 1993: 39-51.

——. "Sexual Revolution." *Cablevision* 22 March 1993: 19-23.

——. "Wrestling Fights Back." *Cablevision* 18 Oct. 1993: 37-40.

West, Don, ed. "The Reluctant Steed of PPV." *Broadcasting and Cable* 24 Jan. 1994: 106-10.

Kevin S. Sandler

Peanuts (1950-2000), the comic strip by Charles Schulz (1922-2000), grew from an inauspicious beginning in only seven newspapers to one of the most popular comic strips of all time. The strip is a tale of childhood, with its hapless hero, Charlie Brown, bearing the brunt of bad luck and his dog Snoopy leading a fulfilling life of fantasy and adventure. While the strip premiered with only these two and the characters Shermy and Patty, more were introduced over the years. Other characters include Lucy the fussbudget, Linus the gentle scholar, Schroeder the Beethoven devotee, and Peppermint Patty the sports lover. The delay in introducing characters was planned, so that audiences would have time to see the characters grow and become used to them. Even so, *Peanuts'* ensemble cast grew to over 25 characters who appeared with varying degrees of frequency. While the plot generally dealt with how suburban six-year-olds see the world and deal with its various trials and tribulations, Christian theological themes were occasionally discussed in an explicit manner.

Unlike the creators of many other comic strips, Schulz did all the work on his creation, from writing each strip to drawing every aspect of the finished product. At the age of 77, Schulz had announced that he was retiring—and thus the strip was ending—and had stopped doing the daily strips when he died the night before his final Sunday strip was to be published, with its simple farewell message of gratitude to fans and the poignant statement: "how can I ever forget ...Charlie Brown, Snoopy, Linus, Lucy...."

Peanuts had appeared in over 2000 newspapers worldwide, and spun off into two musical plays, four feature films, over 40 animated television specials, books, toys, a successful line of greeting cards, and countless other products and advertising campaigns. The command ship and lunar module of the 1969 Apollo Ten mission were named after Charlie Brown and Snoopy, respectively. Schulz received countless awards, including two Reuben awards (1955 and 1964) and a best humor strip of the year award (1962) from the National Cartoonists Society and a Humorist of the Year Award from Yale (1958).

Bibliography

Goulart, Ron, ed. *The Encyclopedia of American Comics: From 1897 to the Present*. New York: Facts on File, 1990.

Horn, Maurice, ed. *The World Encyclopedia of Comics*. New York: Chelsea, 1976.

Johnson, Rheta Grimsley. *Good Grief: The Story of Charles M. Schulz*. West Sussex: Ravette, 1989.

The Oakland Museum Art Department, ed. *The Graphic Art of Charles Schulz: A Catalog of the Retrospective Exhibition*. Oakland: Oakland Museum, 1985.

Schulz, Charles M. *Peanuts Jubilee: My Life and Art with Charlie Brown and Others*. New York: Ballantine, 1976.

Solomon Davidoff

Pearl Jam (1990-). Coming out of the Seattle scene which had risen to prominence in the mid-1980s via what was popularly called the "grunge" movement, Pearl Jam became one of the most successful rock bands of the early 1990s with two multi-platinum albums, *Ten* and *Vs*. Both albums were billed as "alternative" releases, but are as influenced by the vocals of Steppenwolf's John Kay and U2's Bono, the funky wah-wah guitar of Jimi Hendrix, the bass work of Rush's Geddy Lee, the big-kick drum sound of Led Zeppelin, and the introspective lyrics of R.E.M.'s frontman Michael Stipe, as much as any aspect of the punk or underground rock movements.

Pearl Jam formed when the Seattle band Mother Love Bone dissolved after singer Andrew Wood overdosed and two of the remaining members, Stone Gossard (guitars) and Jeff Ament (bass), who had originally been in pioneer grunge outfit Green River together, decided to put together a new group. After recruiting Mike McReady on guitar and Soundgarden's Matt Cameron on drums, the band recorded a tape of loose instrumentals and sent the tape out to a variety of people, including former Red Hot Chili Peppers drummer Jack Irons. Irons passed the tape on to Eddie Vedder, who had been playing with San Diego band Bad Radio. He penned some lyrics to the songs, recorded vocals over the instrumental tracks at home and sent the tape off. Two weeks later, Vedder found himself in Seattle recording with Gossard, Ament, McCready, and drummer Dave Krusen. After a brief stint under the name Mookie Blaylock, an NBA player, the group decided on the name Pearl Jam, after a recipe made by Eddie's great-grandmother. Vedder told *Rolling Stone* in 1991, "Great-grandpa was an Indian and totally into hallucinogenics and peyote. Great-grandma used to make this hallucinogenic preserve...."

In 1991, *Ten* was released and by 1994 sold nearly 6 million copies with its radio-friendly sound which lended itself to repeated airplay and sensitive lyrics that appealed to legions of disaffected youth. In 1993, Pearl Jam released its sophomore effort, *Vs.*, which entered the charts at No. 1 by virtue of its predecessor (though many critics felt it was even better). 1994's *Vitalogy* also debuted at No. 1, selling more than 4 million copies. After adding their old friend Jack Irons on drums, the band also served as Neil Young's backup group for his 1995 album, *Mirror Ball*. Pearl Jam has released three more albums, all on the Epic label: *No Code* (1996), *Yield* (1998), and *Live on Two Legs* (1998).

Bibliography

Crowe, Cameron. "5 Against the World." *Rolling Stone* 28 Oct. 1993: 50-59, 88.

Neely, Kim. "Right Here, Right Now." *Rolling Stone* 31 Oct. 1991: 15-16.

Robbins, Ira. *The Trouser Press Record Guide*. New York: Collier, 1991.

Romanowski, Patricia, and Holly George-Warren, eds. *The New Rolling Stone Encyclopedia of Rock & Roll.* New York: Fireside, 1995.

Hugh Foley

Peck, Eldred Gregory (1916-), born in La Jolla, CA, attended first San Diego State University and then the University of California, Berkeley, where he was initially a premed major. On a trip to New York City, Peck saw Vera Zorina in *I Married an Angel*, following which he returned to Berkeley so inspired that he withdrew from the pre-med program, changed his major to English, and joined a campus theater group. Upon graduating from Berkeley in 1939, Peck moved to New York City, where he won a scholarship to the Neighborhood Playhouse School of Dramatics and studied under Sanford Meisner for two years. His first plays, *Morning Star*, *The Willow and I*, and *Sons and Soldiers*, attracted the attention of Hollywood and led to his film debut in Jacques Tourneur's *Days of Glory* (1943).

Peck's first starring role in *The Keys of the Kingdom* (1944) earned him an Oscar nomination, as did *The Yearling* (1946), *Gentleman's Agreement* (1947), and *To Kill a Mockingbird* (1962), for which he received the best actor award for his portrayal of Atticus Finch. His roles commonly found him as a morally uncompromising authority figure, a fairminded reformer, or the "fundamentally good man who rises to the moral demands of the occasion" (*International Dictionary* 940), although interspersed are others which demonstrate his ability convincingly to portray darker characters, including *Spellbound* (1945), *Duel in the Sun* (1947), *Twelve o'Clock High* (1949), and *Moby Dick* (1956). Peck's career spans five decades, and includes the TV miniseries *The Blue and the Gray* (1982) and a touring one-man show, *A Conversation with Gregory Peck*, in 1995.

Peck's film persona of moral and social leader is mirrored by his personal involvement in many artistic and social causes. He was instrumental in founding the La Jolla Playhouse in 1948, became a charter member of the National Council on the Arts in 1965, chairman of the American Cancer Society in 1966, a member of the Board of Trustees of the American Film Institute (1967-69), and served as president of the Academy of Motion Picture Arts & Sciences. For these efforts, he was rewarded with the Jean Hersholt Humanitarian Award in 1967 and the Life Achievement Award by the American Film Institute in 1989.

Bibliography

"Gregory Peck." *Brewer's Cinema: A Phrase and Fable Dictionary*. London: Cassell, 1995.

"Gregory Peck." *International Dictionary of Films and Filmmakers 3: Actors and Actresses*. 3d ed. Detroit: St. James, 1997.

Monaco, James. "Gregory Peck." *The Encyclopedia of Film*. New York: Perigee, 1991.

Lynnea Chapman King

Peckinpah, Sam (1925-1984), began his career as writer and director in television when the TV Western was at the height of its popularity in the late 1950s. Ironically, his switch to directing Western films in the early 1960s corresponded to the decline of that genre in the late 1960s and early 1970s. In fact, Peckinpah's popular but controversial film *The Wild Bunch* (1969) is often hailed as one of the films that put the deciding nail in the coffin of the traditional Western. Peckinpah, however, directed other films that reached a large audience, and he gained notoriety in the popular imagination for "graphic violence" in his films and for "legendary exploits" in his life and in his dealings with the Hollywood film industry.

David Samuel Peckinpah was born in Fresno, CA, and as a child spent long periods of time on a cattle ranch belonging to his grandfather, Denver Church, in Crane Valley (near Peckinpah Mountain). He later referred to this time as the happiest in his life, like a lost Eden. However, his relationship with the school system in Fresno was stormy (an early sign, perhaps, of the difficulty he would have with authority figures), and his parents finally sent him to San Rafael Military School, where he earned more demerits than anyone else in the school's history. After a brief stint with the Marines in 1945, he attended Fresno State College, graduating with a B.A. in drama in 1949. He took a Master's degree from the University of Southern California, writing his thesis on Tennessee Williams.

His first break in the film industry came with Allied Artists as third assistant casting director for Don Siegel, who urged him to write for television. Ten episodes of the CBS *Gunsmoke* series, produced in 1955-56, were written by Peckinpah, and in 1958 he directed his first television film, "The Knife Fighter," for the *Broken Arrow* series. He also directed "The Sharpshooter" in the same year, which became the pilot for a popular new series called *The Rifleman*. Peckinpah's concluding experience with the TV Western came in 1959-60 when he co-wrote and directed several episodes for NBC's *The Westerner*.

In 1961, Peckinpah directed his first feature film, *The Deadly Companions*. This was followed by *Ride the High Country* (1962), shot by Lucien Ballard, the cinematographer who would collaborate with Peckinpah on many of his features. MGM released it as the second half of a double feature, but to the studio's chagrin, it received good reviews and eventually became one of Peckinpah's most popular films.

Peckinpah's next major project was *Major Dundee* (1965), and this, too, became embroiled in controversy. Believing it too long, the studio cut several important scenes, damaging the narrative coherence and undermining Peckinpah's artistic vision, although it is still considered an important film in his canon. Then Peckinpah was fired after working only four days as director of *The Cincinnati Kid*. This incident coupled with the rumors about *Dundee* caused Peckinpah to be blacklisted by the Hollywood film industry for about two years. But during this time, he adapted and directed for television Katherine Anne Porter's short novel *Noon Wine*, which was hailed as a major artistic achievement.

Peckinpah began the second phase of his career as director of *The Wild Bunch* (1969), now considered his masterpiece, but then considered excessively violent and bloody.

Following closely after Arthur Penn's *Bonnie and Clyde*, *The Wild Bunch*, too, was about "good" bad people who set themselves on a path toward glorious self-destruction. But in technique and style, *The Wild Bunch* goes far beyond the famous slow-motion finale of *Bonnie and Clyde*. *The Wild Bunch* provokes, exhilarates, and disturbs, but the violence is not gratuitous. Reviled by many at the time for what one major critic called "moral idiocy," the film actually focuses on moral ambiguity and repeatedly dramatizes various levels in the conflict between appearance and reality (which Peckinpah had introduced in his first feature film, *The Deadly Companions*). *The Wild Bunch* was seen by many as an allegory on the Vietnam War and/or as a dark comment on the nature of violence in American life. *The Ballad of Cable Hogue* (1970) extends the mythic possibilities suggested in *The Wild Bunch*. Reviews appearing right after the film's release were mixed, and *Ballad* did not do well at the box office. However, like *The Wild Bunch,* it, too, has experienced a renewal of perceptive critical attention.

Straw Dogs (1971), which depicts how a mild-mannered mathematician (Dustin Hoffman) on sabbatical leave in England is provoked to extremely violent action, revived the violence controversy initiated by *The Wild Bunch*, with some critics finding it even more loathsome. However, in general the popular press saw the film not as an endorsement of violence but as a graphic dramatization of it as an essential ingredient in human nature.

Junior Bonner (1972), about a rodeo, had hardly any violence and was liked by critics, but was not a commercial success. In 1972, *The Getaway* also appeared, starring Steve McQueen and Ali MacGraw, along with members of Peckinpah's repertory company (Ben Johnson and Slim Pickens). Although not a Western, the film is set in the West and there are chases and shootouts. *The Getaway* was a major box-office success, grossing $25 million, and secured, at least for a while, Peckinpah's position as a bankable director.

The following year, 1973, saw what some people believe was the last *real* Western made by Peckinpah (or anyone else), *Pat Garrett and Billy the Kid.* Starring James Coburn as Pat Garrett and Kris Kristofferson as Billy, the film reprises Peckinpah's themes of the closing of the West and the decline of traditional, Western values, especially those developed through male bonding. In spite of cutting by MGM, the film received positive reviews and did reach a wide audience.

Most reviewers at the time disliked his next film, *Bring Me the Head of Alfredo Garcia* (1974), but later critics responded differently. Terence Butler found the film "the most Gothic of all Peckinpah's movies,...a somber examination of the death-wish mentality that has haunted the director." *The Killer Elite* (1975) caused strong critical reaction as well.

Peckinpah's next film, *Cross of Iron* (1977), is set during World War II on the Eastern Front in 1943. Starring James Coburn, Maximilian Schell, and James Mason, the film presents its pacifist message through horrific scenes of warfare. Cut by 15 minutes for release in this country and barely marketed, it received high critical praise but did not do well at the box office.

Peckinpah's final years were not happy ones: the battles with Hollywood studios and executives continued, his films (*Convoy* [1978] and *The Osterman Weekend* [1983]) diminished in quality, and his health failed. He died of a heart attack when he was 59.

Bibliography

Bliss, Michael. *Justified Lives: Morality and Narrative in the Films of Sam Peckinpah.* Carbondale: Southern Illinois UP, 1993.

Butler, Terence. *Crucified Heroes: The Films of Sam Peckinpah.* London: Fraser, 1979.

Seydor, Paul. *Peckinpah: The Western Films.* Urbana: U of Illinois P, 1980.

Simmons, Garner. *Peckinpah: A Portrait in Montage.* Austin: U of Texas P, 1976.

Wakeman, John, ed. *World Film Directors.* Vol. 2. New York: Wilson, 1988.

Leonard Engel

Pee-wee's Playhouse (1986-1991) opened to a Saturday morning TV audience accustomed to cartoons like *He-Man* and *She-Ra*. Children, along with their older siblings and parents, responded by making Pee-wee's combination of live-action sketches, Claymation, and animation one of the most highly rated Saturday morning programs throughout its six-season run on CBS. Critics also applauded actor Paul Reubens's multiple-Emmy Award-winning program for its humor, creativity, pedagogy, and general weirdness.

Paul Reubens (1952-) had honed his Pee-wee act on comedy club stages, HBO, and late night TV before starring in a hit film, *Pee-wee's Big Adventure*, in 1985. Claymation and special effects artists Peter Rosenthal and Stephen Oakes had won a number of awards for their work on MTV. Already popular in the underground comix world for *Jimbo*, Gary Panter collaborated with Wayne White and Ric Heitzman to design the colorful, kitschy set. In Pee-wee's surreal playhouse, plush chairs talked and grabbed people, while ice cubes danced in the freezer and dinosaurs played tennis.

Critics praised the children's program for its "progressive" messages. The androgynous Pee-wee and his friends gently encouraged viewers to be comfortable with their sexual identities and desires. In addition, *Pee-wee's Playhouse* was the most multicultural children's show of its time.

CBS saw *Pee-wee's Playhouse* as a "prestige program," designed to differentiate the network from tired, syndicated cartoons that other stations ran on Saturday mornings. CBS also hoped that the program would appeal to adults. It did. Like popular children's shows from TV's early days, such as *Kukla, Fran and Ollie* and *The Soupy Sales Show, Pee-wee's Playhouse* garnered a loyal adult following: over a third of the viewers were over 18.

Pee-wee's Playhouse was also less obviously geared towards selling children merchandise than were other popular kids' shows. However, Pee-wee had licensing agreements with 27 manufacturers to produce such items as pajamas, wristwatches, lunch boxes and talking dolls. Another film, *Big Top Pee-wee* (1988), added to his popularity.

But after Reubens was arrested for indecent exposure on July 26, 1991, most manufacturers hastily discontinued their Pee-wee products. While CBS and Reubens had mutually decided to end the show in April 1991, the network canceled five reruns that were to have aired through the end of that summer.

Bibliography

Barth, Jack. "Television: Pee Wee TV." *Film Comment* Nov. 1986: 78-79.

Brown, Les. *Les Brown's Encyclopedia of Television.* 3d ed. Detroit: Gale Research, 1992.

"Pee Wee's Big Bucks Adventure." *Adweek's Marketing Week* 6 March 1993: 20.

Penley, Constance, and Sharon Willis, eds. *Male Trouble.* Minneapolis: U of Minnesota P, 1993.

David Weinstein

Pentecostal/Charismatic Movement, The, is a religious movement emphasizing the outpouring of the Holy Spirit on believers, as on the day of Pentecost, characterized by speaking in tongues (glossolalia), healing, and prophecy. Pentecostal refers to churches such as the Assemblies of God which arose from the revivals of glossolalia at the turn of the century. Charismatic refers to members of mainline denominations who participate in Pentecostal experiences. The main theological difference between the two groups is that Pentecostals generally believe that the baptism of the Spirit should be accompanied by tongues, while most Charismatics do not hold this view.

Although speaking in tongues has emerged spasmodically since biblical times, the 20th-century Pentecostal movement in the United States begins with Charles Parham, a young minister at Bethel College in Topeka, KS. At a New Year's Eve service in 1900, Parham stopped preaching to pray and "lay hands" on one of his students, Agnes Ozman. As a halo appeared to surround Miss Ozman's head and face, she broke into several tongues. Several days later while praying in an upper room, other members of Parham's group burst into tongues.

In 1906, one of Parham's followers, William James Seymour, carried the message to Los Angeles. Seymour, the descendant of African slaves shipped to America, opened up a meeting place in a ghetto in Azusa Street. The meetings drew crowds and Azusa Street became a center of ecstatic outbursts and "miracles," with men and women crowding the building and speaking in tongues. By the participants' accounts, recorded in their newspaper *The Apostolic Faith,* visions, physical demonstrations, and falling prostrate were routine. Several Pentecostal historians such as Iain MacRobert hold that the Azusa Street phenomenon, from which the current movement has arisen, was a manifestation of West African religion, emerging from descendants of the slave trade.

When the Azusa Street revival finished, the Pentecostal movement suffered some setbacks: bitter divisions resulting in racial segregation, antagonism from fundamentalist quarters, evangelists' scandals, and public opposition. Nevertheless, revivals continued in bursts, and the movement became notably strong in the southern states. Once overseas it expanded rapidly, especially in Africa, Europe, and Latin America.

Up until 1960, Pentecostal beliefs were heterodox, and participants were thought to be on the lunatic fringe of Christianity. Then an event occurred which was a watershed in the history of Pentecostalism. On April 13, 1960, Dennis J. Bennett, rector of St. Mark's Episcopal church in Van Nuys, CA, announced to his congregation that he had experienced the baptism of the Spirit and speaking in tongues. Despite pressure from several members, he refused to leave the ministry. A new phase in church history began in which Pentecostal experiences spread through mainline denominations. This became known as the Charismatic renewal.

Seven years after Bennett's announcement, the renewal extended to the Catholic church. In 1967 four Catholics experienced the baptism of the Spirit and speaking in tongues, and this was followed by a much publicized outbreak of tongues at a Catholic prayer meeting at Notre Dame University. By the late 1970s, the Charismatic renewal had peaked, and in 1980, the World Council of Churches gave it official recognition.

Today Pentecostal churches are well established and many have adopted a more subdued style of worship. Notwithstanding several televangelists' scandals and a decline in overt displays of enthusiasm, the movement has continued to expand, predominantly through the rise of independent Pentecostal churches. It is one of the fastest growing religious movements worldwide.

Bibliography

Anderson, Robert Mapes. *Vision of the Disinherited: The Making of American Pentecostalism.* New York: Oxford UP, 1979.

Bennett, Dennis J. *Nine O'Clock in the Morning.* Plainfield: Logos, 1970.

Bloch-Hoell, Nils. *The Pentecostal Movement: Its Origin, Development, and Distinctive Character.* Oslo: Universitetforlaget, 1964.

MacRobert, Iain. *The Black Roots and White Racism of Early Pentecostalism in the USA.* New York: St. Martin's, 1988.

Synan, Vinson. *The Holiness-Pentecostal Movement in the United States.* Grand Rapids: Eerdmans, 1971.

Heather Kavan

People Weekly (1974-), commonly referred to as *People,* featured Mia Farrow on the cover of its first issue. It had a $500,000 advertising campaign and an initial run of 1.4 million copies. The brainchild of Marian Heiskill, wife of the former chairman of the board of *Time,* Andrew Heiskill, *People* deftly merges glossy photography with reports and commentary on the personalities and lifestyles of newsworthy individuals, particularly celebrities from television and the movies. The weekly's heavy use of photography underscores its stylistic debt to its periodical precursors, especially *Photoplay* and *Life. People*'s first managing editor, Richard Stolley, calls such a format "personality journalism": "This is a magazine devoted *entirely* to people—we don't deal with issues; we don't deal with events; we don't deal with debates. We deal *only* with human beings."

Because nearly two-thirds of the magazine's circulation derives from its newsstand sales, *People*'s cover remains the most significant factor regarding the success of a particular issue. *People* targets women as its primary audience, and their interest in the magazine and its cover account for more than two-thirds of the periodical's circulation. For this reason, a 1975 issue featuring Howard Cosell on the cover ranks as one of *People*'s poorest selling issues, while during the 1970s and the 1980s, perennial cover favorites included Cher, Princess Grace, Elizabeth Taylor, Farrah Fawcett, Michael Jackson, and Jacqueline Onassis, among others.

In addition to each issue's cover story, *People* also features a number of weekly items, including, until 1985, the "People Puzzle," the "People Picks" section devoted to brief book, film, and television reviews, and, during the late 1980s, the expanded "In This Issue" section offering photographs and anecdotes in an effort to draw further attention to each issue's contents. Marian Heiskill's brainchild continues to exceed all of the magazine's initial publishing expectations. *People* annually ranks among the top five periodicals in advertising revenue, weekly circulation, and profitability. While the magazine rarely strays from Stolley's dictum regarding "personality journalism," *People* nevertheless remains essential to any understanding of the American approach to entertainment, celebrity, and lifestyle since its inception in the mid-1970s.

Bibliography
Nourie, Alan, and Barbara Nourie, eds. *American Mass-Market Magazines*. New York: Greenwood, 1990.
Taft, William H. *American Magazines for the 1980s*. New York: Hastings, 1982.

Kenneth Womack

Perkins, Carl (1932-), known as a "southern man's" rocker, began his public career with his famous song "Blue Suede Shoes," which became a worldwide hit in early 1956. Perkins, born in Lake City, TN, was one of three sons of the only white sharecropper in western Tennessee. However, growing up in poverty did not deter Perkins in his passionate pursuit of a musical career. As a little boy, Perkins sat by the side of an old, black cotton picker who taught him licks on a guitar. During the late forties Perkins and his two brothers Jay and Clayton formed the Perkins Brothers, which played western music in various honky tonks in Tennessee. However, it was not until Perkins heard Elvis Presley sing a cover of Arthur Crudup's "That's All Right Mama" in 1954 that he was inspired to follow the rockabilly trend.

In 1955, Perkins went to Sam Phillips's Sun Records, in Memphis, to seek fame, fortune, and a recording contract. He was successful, and he recorded his biggest hit, "Blue Suede Shoes," in December 1955. This song was inspired by an incident he had witnessed at a live show, where there was a young country boy who was proudly displaying a new pair of shoes he was wearing. The song hit the Top 10 in both the U.S. and the U.K. However, it was not until Elvis Presley did his version in 1956 that the song gained worldwide recognition. Unfortunately, Perkins's success did not last very long. On the way to a television appearance on *The Perry Como Show* in March 1956 he was in a near-fatal car accident which put him out of commission for several months and eventually led to the death of his brother, Jay. Thus it was Elvis Presley who sang "Blue Suede Shoes" on television and made the song a huge success.

While Perkins had several minor country hits in the late fifties, with "Your True Love Ways" and "Dixie Fried," his career never regained the momentum it once had. Despite this, Perkins's influence on rock music continues, and he is cited by many musicians, among them guitarist Eric Clapton. Then, in the early sixties, the Beatles recorded several of Perkins's songs, including "Honey Don't," "Matchbox," and "Everybody's Trying to Be My Baby." In the mid-sixties, Perkins toured and recorded with Johnny Cash for ten years. He often appeared on Cash's late-sixties TV show, and even wrote the hit "Daddy Sang Bass," for Cash in 1968. Perkins also toured with sax great Ace Cannon, and in the late seventies and early eighties he toured, and occasionally recorded, with his two sons. In 1987, he was inducted into the Rock and Roll Hall of Fame.

Bibliography
MacPhail, Paul. *Rockabizzy Ambassador*. London: MacPhail, 1989.
McGee, Dave. "Interview with Carl Perkins." *Rolling Stone* 19 April 1990: 73-77.
Perkins, Carl. *Disciple in Blue Suede Shoes*. Grand Rapids: Zondervan, 1978.

Rob Weiner

Person to Person (1953-1961) was televised live, via coaxial cable, to the homes of over 600 stars of stage, screen, and television, prominent musicians, sports figures, and scientists, leaders in business, fashion, and dance, as well as major politicians and world leaders. It was independently produced as an entertainment program by Edward R. Murrow, John A. Aaron, and Jesse Zousmer and sold to CBS.

Murrow, sitting in a stuffed chair in a comfortable living room studio set in New York and looking into an oversized television monitor, became the "guest" of the people on his program. Usually going into the homes of two "hosts" during each half-hour program, Murrow first visited with Roy Campanella, the Brooklyn Dodgers catcher, and the conductor Leopold Stokowski and his wife, Gloria Vanderbilt.

Quickly becoming a popular Friday night prime-time fixture for most of its eight-season run, *Person to Person* was television's first version of *Lifestyles of the Rich and Famous*. After exchanging pleasantries, Murrow would usually ask if he might be given a tour of the home or apartment, often stopping to admire a favorite painting, valued object, or prized trophy.

Bibliography
Brooks, Tim, and Earle Marsh. *The Complete Directory to Prime Time Network and Cable TV Shows, 1946-Present*. New York: Ballantine, 1995.
McNeil, Alex. *Total Television: A Comprehensive Guide to Programming from 1948 to the Present*. New York: Penguin, 1991.

Cryder Bankes

Peter, Paul, and Mary (1961-), one of the most influential and enduring folk/rock groups from the 1960s, is comprised of Paul Stookey (1937-), Mary Travers (1937-), and Peter Yarrow (1938-). The group formed in 1961 in Greenwich Village in New York City. Combining social awareness and folk classics, the group has remained a force in folk music while exploring and expanding the range of what folk comprises. They released two of the defining songs of social protest, "If I Had a Hammer" and "Blowin' in the Wind," in 1962. Dedicated to the innovative folk music and poetic lyrics of Bob Dylan, the threesome has recorded not only his "Blowin' in the Wind," but also "Don't Think Twice, It's Alright" and, more recently, the wonderful "It Ain't Me, Babe." Furthermore, they have written their own music and explored the talents of writers Gordon Lightfoot ("Early Mornin' Rain") and John Denver ("Leaving on a Jet Plane"), making these and other songs big hits.

Their first album was *Peter, Paul and Mary* (1962), containing some excellently performed standard folk tunes and up-tempo Christian numbers. The repertoire includes the standard "500 Miles," "If I Had a Hammer," and "Where Have All the Flowers Gone," as well as the mournful "Lemon Tree," the rousing "If I Had My Way," and the gospel "This Train."

Their release of Dylan's "Blowin' in the Wind" came during this time, recorded as a single and not included in an album until their 1963 album *In the Wind*. The later sixties brought more experimentation in form, including a more psychedelic and free-floating sound in *The Peter, Paul and Mary Album* (1966) and *Late Again* (1968).

In between these two albums came their more rock-oriented *Album 1700* (1967). In this album, the group garnered several hits, including "Leaving on a Jet Plane," "I'm in Love with a Big Blue Frog," and "I Dig Rock and Roll Music," a song replicating and dedicated to the Mamas and the Papas.

The celebratory *Ten Years Together* (1970), a chronology of their hits, included their most remembered song, "Puff the Magic Dragon," originally released on *Peter, Paul and Mommy* (1969). This album chronicles the group's development without excluding or downplaying their commendable and continuing commitment to pacifism.

In the 1970s the group members went their separate ways for a while, though there were no major solo hits except for Paul Stookey's recording of "The Wedding Song." By the end of the decade, the group had reunited. *No Easy Walk to Freedom* (1987) caused quite a controversy because of their bold and energetic anger against U.S. involvement in El Salvador and Central America. In 1990, *Flowers and Stones* launched their Gulf War-era concerts, including a return to their roots with Dylan's "It Ain't Me, Babe," and the spiritual "I Shall Be Released" (originally included by the group on their 1968 *Late Again*).

The group has done many concerts broadcast on public television, including *Twenty-Five Years Together*, a Christmas concert, and *Peter, Paul and Mommy Too* (and a corresponding album). The group continues to appeal to the young and the old with its message of peace and solidarity.

Bibliography
Larkin, Colin, ed. *Guinness Encyclopedia of Popular Music.* Vol. 4. Middlesex, U.K.: Guinness, 1995.
Stambler, Irwin. *Encyclopedia of Pop, Rock and Soul.* New York: St. Martin's, 1989.

Mark K. Fulk

Petra (1972-) is Contemporary Christian Music's (CCM) original and biggest-selling rock band. Formed in 1972 when the Bill Gaither Trio was the hottest thing in Christian music, Petra launched a career that includes more than 20 albums. Bob Hartman, lead guitarist, principal songwriter, and only original member still with the band, has seen 12 different bandmates come and go.

Over time, the band members have come to recognize that their biggest audience is church youth who are also in need of ministry. To that end, Petra has included nationally known speaker Josh McDowell and his "Why Wait?" sex seminars in some of their tour dates. Petra has also won accolades from youth pastors for their *Petra Praise: The Rock Cries Out* (1989), a specialty album designed to get church youth involved in musical praise. Petra's first two albums, *Petra* (1974) and *Come and Join Us* (1977), due to poor marketing and censorship, were not successful.

However, Petra's third album, *Washes Whiter Than* (1979), including "Why Should the Father Bother?" became an immediate Christian radio success and Petra was on its way to becoming a major influence in CCM. The band followed with a series of albums (from *Never Say Die* [1981] to *God Fixation* [1998]), utilizing a spiritual warfare motif and featuring ballads for radio airplay, power pop praise songs, and flat-out rockers. *Petra Praise 2* was released in 1997.

Bibliography
Darbin, Bob. "Gospel Lectern." *Billboard* 7 Jan. 1989: 27.
Donaldson, Devlin. "Band on the Move." *Contemporary Christian Magazine* Nov. 1983: 32-35.
Larkin, Colin, ed. *Guinness Encyclopedia of Popular Music.* Middlesex, U.K.: Guinness, 1995.

Jay Howard

Peyton Place (1956), the novel by Grace Metalious, has come to serve as a metaphor for the steamy, seamy underside of a superficially respectable community, school, or workplace. Grace Metalious was the wife of a high school principal and mother of three, living in a rundown house in Gilmanton, NH, when she outraged community members with her tale of child abuse, sadomasochism, incest, sexual initiation, abortion, patricide, and teen pregnancy. After publication of the novel, one of the best-selling novels in U.S. history at the time of its publication, Metalious and her children were harassed by neighbors who thought the book was about Gilmanton.

Although it was positively reviewed in the *New York Times*, *Peyton Place* was likely to be hidden from disapproving parents who considered the book trashy. The book was banned in Rhode Island and in Allen County, Indiana. A Texas drugstore owner was fined for selling it to a teenager. Canadian customs banned it for its "indecent or immoral character," and it was banned in South Africa until 1978. Its legacy includes young adult novels that deal frankly with topics of sex, incest, violence, or abuse, such as S. E. Hinton's *The Outsiders,* Judy Blume's *Forever,* and Tabitha King's *One on One.* On a less positive note, Pocket Books published nine new books spinning off tales of various Peyton Place denizens, including *Carnival in Peyton Place, Thrills in Peyton Place,* and *Nice Girl from Peyton Place.*

Peyton Place was re-created as a popular, Oscar-nominated movie (1957) and as television's first prime-time soap opera, its 514 episodes running on ABC from 1964 to 1969. Both film and television show were sanitized versions of Metalious's original work. Within a month, *Peyton Place's* popularity had placed ABC at No. 1 in the Nielsen ratings for the first time. The careers of actors Ryan O'Neal and Mia Farrow were established in their roles of Rodney Harrington and Allison MacKenzie. The show then ran as a daytime serial for two years in the 1970s and as a two-hour NBC movie, *Peyton Place: The Next Generation,* in 1985.

Bibliography

Brower, Sue. "Peyton Place." *Encyclopedia of Television.* Ed. Horace Newcomb. Chicago: Fitzroy Dearborn, 1997.

Dodson, James. "Pandora in Blue Jeans." *Yankee* Sept. 1990: 92-97ff.

Metalious, Grace. *Peyton Place.* New York: Julian Messner, 1956.

Toth, Emily. "Fatherless and Dispossessed: Grace Metalious as a French-Canadian Writer.*" Journal of Popular Culture* 15.3 (Winter 1981): 28-38.

——. *Inside Peyton Place: The Life of Grace Metalious.* Garden City, NY: Doubleday, 1981.

Christine Whittington

Phil Silvers Show, The (1955-1959), during the formative years of television, helped define the genre. Several decades later *The Phil Silvers Show* hardly dates at all; its speed, invention, and skilled ensemble playing rank it among the finest of television's early comic masterworks. Mythical Fort Baxter, isolated in Kansas, provided the perfect setting for this satire on Cold War Army existence. Master Sergeant Ernest "Ernie" Bilko (Silvers), a military lifer, played a con man who never succeeded. With little to do, Bilko spent most of his time trying to make it big through one scam or another, which always and predictably backfired.

The Phil Silvers Show, originally titled *You'll Never Get Rich,* did so well that it knocked Milton Berle off Tuesday nights. The Bilko scripts were issued in book form, and Phil Silvers (1912-1985) and his platoon became fixtures in the ever-expanding number of America's TV households.

The creative force behind *The Phil Silvers Show* was one of television's earliest producer-writers, Nat Hiken. One of the funniest programs was "The Case of Harry Speakup," by Hiken with Coleman Jacoby and Arnie Rosen. Hysterically, and with a speed we associate with the modernism of MTV, Bilko helps induct a chimpanzee into the Army.

It is a testimony to the program's originality that it never could be cloned. In the 1963-64 television season came NBC's *The New Phil Silvers Show,* where Silvers played Harry Grafton, a plant foreman in a large corporation, again always trying (unsuccessfully) to get rich.

Bibliography

Berle, Milton. *Milton Berle: An Autobiography.* New York: Delacorte, 1974.

Hiken, Nat. *Sergeant Bilko.* New York: Ballantine, 1957.

Marc, David, and Robert J. Thompson. *Prime Time, Prime Movers.* Boston: Little, Brown, 1992.

Silvers, Phil. *The Laugh Is on Me.* Englewood Cliffs: Prentice-Hall, 1973.

Douglas Gomery

Phillips, **Irna** (1901-1973), "Queen of the Soaps," was the most important force in creating what became known as soap opera on radio and, later, less pejoratively, daytime drama on television. Born in Chicago, after receiving her M.A. degree in drama from the University of Illinois, she taught in Dayton, OH, for five years. In 1930, after acting in several radio productions at WGN in Chicago, Phillips decided to pursue a full-time job in the entertainment industry. She began on a daytime talk show called *Thought for the Day*, and was later asked to create a continuing family story to run for ten minutes a day. *Painted Dreams* (1930-33) was the result—radio's first soap opera, about an Irish widow struggling to raise a large family. Phillips both wrote and acted in this popular serial, and, when WGN refused to sell it to a national network, she sued them, claiming the soap was her property. While the lawsuit went on for years, Phillips created a similar program, *Today's Children* (1933-38; 1943-50), for NBC, making it the first radio network soap opera. She also created and wrote for *The Road of Life* (NBC, 1937-59), *Woman in White* (various, 1938-42), *The Right to Happiness* (various, 1939-60), *Lonely Women* (NBC, 1942-43), *Masquerade* (NBC, 1946-57), *The Brighter Day* (NBC, 1948-52), and the only soap still to survive from its radio days, *The Guiding Light* (1937-56). On a tenth soap, *Judy and Jane* (NBC, 1932-43), she was a writer only.

Phillips moved into television in 1949 by adapting *Today's Children* into *These Are My Children* for NBC. *The Guiding Light* made its television debut in 1952 on CBS, where it remains today (see entry). Phillips created and wrote for an additional seven other daytime dramas: *The Road of Life* (CBS, 1954-55), *The Brighter Day* (CBS, 1954-62), *The Edge of Night* (CBS/ABC, 1956-84), *As the World Turns* (CBS, 1956-present), *Another World* (NBC, 1964-99), *Days of Our Lives* (co-created, NBC, 1965-present), and *Love Is a Many Splendored Thing* (CBS, 1967-73). The two that debuted in 1956 expanded the usual 15-minute time slot to a half-hour format.

Phillips actively wrote scripts for several soaps until her death, remaining fairly conservative in story content.

Bibliography

Allen, Robert C. *Speaking of Soap Operas.* Chapel Hill: U of North Carolina P, 1985.

Gilbert, Annie. *All My Afternoons.* New York: A & W, 1979.

Marc, David, and Robert J. Thompson. *Prime Time, Prime Movers.* Boston: Little, Brown, 1992.

Schemering, Christopher. *Guiding Light: A 50th Anniversary Celebration*. New York: Ballantine, 1986.

———. *The Soap Opera Encyclopedia*. New York: Ballantine, 1985.

Lynn C. Spangler

See also
Nixon, Agnes
Soap Opera
Soap Opera Writers and Producers

Phonographs can be traced back to 1857, when the French scientist Leon Scott invented the phonautograph, a prototype of the cylinder phonograph. Twenty years later another French scientist, Charles Cros, devised the Phone-Graphos (though it was never built) and his plans inspired Emile Berliner ten years later to invent the gramophone, essentially the first sound recording machine. At about the same time Thomas Edison was experimenting with recording on paraffin cylinders (see Edison Cylinder).

The early phonograph reproduced sound within a very limited dynamic range, and its characteristics for the reproduction of music were described as tinny and unmusical. Essentially it relied on a horn or tube to transmit sound to (or from, in the case of playback) a needle cutting grooves in a malleable medium like wax. It was not until the 1920s, when electricity and the vacuum tube made possible the amplification of sound (for both recording and playback), that the phonograph's quality began to improve. Initially the phonograph was not intended to be a musical device but was developed for voice recording (for dictation, telephone recording, and the like).

Regardless of the purposes for which it was intended, the phonograph was immediately popular and commercially successful from the start. However, it took many years before recordings could be mass produced, as no means for "pressing" cylinders existed. Berliner's gramophone edged out Edison's invention for that reason, as the flat disc lent itself to the industrial process more readily. The gramophone was a superior device for audio reproduction. Regardless of audio quality, audiences clamored for recordings of virtually any sound, much as they were willing to watch Edison's film of Fred Ott sneezing solely for the novelty of the experience. By the 1930s the record industry was an important player in the entertainment field, rivaling the film industry.

During World War II the diversion of raw materials needed to press records meant that the phonograph's popularity reached a plateau. Immediately thereafter, though, the vinyl long-playing record (LP) became the *de facto* consumer audio standard. The stereo disc was introduced in 1958 and quickly gained acceptance, and the price of records was low enough that the medium gained ever-greater popularity with youth. The rise of rock 'n' roll and other popular music forms was due in part to the ready availability of records. Sales continued to increase until the late 1970s, when a combination of forces (including the popularity of the audio cassette) caused a sales slump. By the 1980s phonograph records were being displaced by the compact disc, and fewer and fewer phonographs were being manufactured. Perhaps the "last

Photo courtesy of Sound Recording Archives, Bowling Green State University, Bowling Green, OH.

hurrah" for the phonograph is its use for the creation of hip-hop and rap music (see entries) in the late 1970s and early 1980s. DJs, primarily in New York, used turntables to mix songs and "scratch" breaks and beats together. By the late 1980s even that use of the phonograph was supplanted by digital media, in the form of the digital sampler.

Bibliography
Marty, Daniel. *The Illustrated History of Phonographs*. New York: Dorset, 1989.

Welch, Walter L., Leah Brodbeck, and Stenzel Burt. *From Tinfoil to Stereo: The Acoustic Years of the Recording Industry, 1877-1929*. Gainesville: UP of Florida, 1994.

Steve Jones

See also
History of Sound Recording

Pickford, Mary (1892-1979), legendary actress, was born Gladys Louise Smith, in Toronto, Ontario. Mary Pickford made her stage debut at age five when her father's death forced her to become the primary source of support for her family. In 1907, after years of touring with her devoted mother, Charlotte, brother Jack, and sister Lottie, she appeared in the legendary theatrical impresario David Belasco's production of *The Warrens of Virginia*. It was he who christened her Mary Pickford. In 1909, with no further theatrical work on the horizon, she reluctantly turned to the much disdained motion picture business at American Biograph under the direction of D. W. Griffith.

She began making feature-length films in 1913 with the Famous Players Film Company, and throughout the teens her popularity, power, and earnings increased dramatically. Always an extremely hard worker and a very astute businesswoman, she studied all aspects of the filmmaking process and constantly sought and received more creative control over her films. As a result, most of her films were highly polished productions that were both popular and profitable. Key films from this period include *Hearts Adrift* (1914), *Tess of the Storm Country* (1914), *Rags* (1915), *The Poor Little Rich Girl* (1917), *Stella Maris* (1918), and *Daddy Long Legs* (1919). Early in 1919, she became one of the founding members of United Artists and was able to exercise complete creative and financial control over her career. (Her partners in the United Artists deal were Douglas Fairbanks, Charlie Chaplin, and D. W. Griffith.) In less than a decade, she had become the first female movie mogul—and "America's Sweetheart."

Her films were less frequent in the last decade of the silent era and, although she remained enormously popular throughout the world, her fans were not entirely pleased with several attempts to shift from her traditionally youthful screen persona into adult roles. Key films from this period include *Pollyanna* (1920), *Suds* (1920), *Little Lord Fauntleroy* (1921), a remake of *Tess of the Storm Country* (1922), and *Little Annie Rooney* (1925). In 1928, in a drastic attempt to change her image, Pickford cut her famous blond curls in favor of a more contemporary style. The following year she made her first talkie, *Coquette*, in which she played a modern sophisticate. She earned an Academy Award for her performance, but her new image was not popular with her fans. She would release only three more features—*The Taming of the Shrew* (1929), co-starring husband Douglas Fairbanks, *Kiki* (1931), and the very underrated *Secrets* (1933)—before retiring from the screen in 1933.

As to her personal life, Pickford was married three times. In 1920, she married Douglas Fairbanks, one of the most famous and popular male stars of all time. (The previous year she had divorced her first husband, actor Owen Moore.) The couple quickly became icons of Hollywood royalty for an international audience that was in love with the movies—and with them. Their home, the legendary Pickfair (a combination of their last names), was a focal point of the Hollywood social scene and further enhanced the fairy tale aura that surrounded their relationship. However, their marriage was not always a happy one and the couple divorced in 1936. The following year Miss Pickford married actor Charles "Buddy" Rogers, with whom she lived until her death.

Mary Pickford was essentially a comedienne, although her body of work reveals a very accomplished dramatic actress as well. In fact, most of her films employ a masterful blend of both qualities. While she did play many "little-girl" roles, in the bulk of her films she played a young girl and not a child. In some films her character would grow up within the story and on several occasions she departed from this image for an adult role. While most of her films were rich in sentiment and genuine pathos, they were also very funny and never became morbid or mawkish. Her characters were warm and charming, but also feisty, independent, and intelligent. It should also be noted that while there was incredible variety in the subject matter of Miss Pickford's films, they frequently reflected her impoverished childhood and, as such, contain an undercurrent—in many cases much more than an undercurrent—of what can only be called social commentary. In this regard, her work often has much in common with that of Chaplin, with whom she had a long and stormy personal and professional relationship.

Bibliography

Brownlow, Kevin. *The Parade's Gone By...* New York: Knopf, 1968.

Eyman, Scott. *Mary Pickford, America's Sweetheart.* New York: Fine, 1990.

Herndon, Booton. *Mary Pickford and Douglas Fairbanks.* New York: Norton, 1977.

Pickford, Mary. *Sunshine and Shadow.* New York: Doubleday, 1955.

Wagenknecht, Edward. *The Movies in the Age of Innocence.* Norman: U of Oklahoma P, 1962.

Fred Guida

Ping-Pong (Table Tennis) found itself making headlines all over the world in 1971. The Chinese extended an invitation to U.S. table tennis players to come to Peking. This effectively ended the impasse in China-USA relations, and was the first officially sanctioned China-America cultural exchange in two decades. The phrase "Ping-Pong diplomacy" came into being.

The game is played by individuals or two-person teams. The object is to hit a hollow plastic or celluloid ball over the net. Every five serves there is a service rotation. A winning game goes to 21 points unless it is tied at 20. The winner is then the first player or team to gain a two-point advantage. The wooden table is 9 feet long by 5 feet across, and 2 1/2 feet high. The net is 6 inches high, and the minimum playing space required is 20 feet by 40 feet.

For many years the bat (otherwise known as a paddle or racket) surface was pimpled rubber and the standard grip was the orthodox, "shake hand," grip. Then the Chinese introduced the penholder, now known as the oriental, grip. This technique, while it arguably reduces the volleying power of shot-making, means that defensive shots can be made with a flicking motion of thumb and index finger.

The game of table tennis emerged toward the end of the 19th century, and J. A. Cuddon notes that the matopoeic name "Ping-Pong" was coined in the 1890s (and later trademarked) when the sport enjoyed a short-lived stint, as a craze and fad.

The International Table Tennis Federation was founded in 1926 with its headquarters at Hastings, Sussex, England. While it has never reached the status of a minor sport in the United States, in certain countries it ranks as a major sport, and China, with several million registered players, continues to dominate the World Championships in men's and women's events, closely followed by Japan, Korea, and the various republics that formerly made up the Soviet Union. At the 1988 Seoul Olympics, table tennis was introduced for the first time.

Bibliography

Arlott, J. A., ed. *The Oxford Companion to World Sports and Games*. London: Oxford UP, 1975.

Craven, R. R. *Billiards, Bowling, Table Tennis, Pinball, and Video Games: A Bibliographic Guide*. Westport: Greenwood, 1993.

Cuddon, J. A. *The International Dictionary of Sports and Games*. New York: Schocken, 1979.

Hodges, Larry. *Table Tennis: Steps to Success*. Champaign: Human Kinetics, 1993. 151.

Parker, Donald, and David Hewitt. *Table Tennis*. New York: Sterling, 1989. 80.

Scott A. G. M. Crawford

Pink Floyd (1965-) is one of the most successful touring and album bands in the history of rock 'n' roll. They have been described as the "most anonymous supergroup on earth" because most people can scarcely identify a band member, either by picture or by name. The band's striking visual symbols are as easily identifiable as their music (examples include cows, prisms, bricks, and beds).

This British quartet, formed in 1965, originally included Syd Barrett (1946-) on guitars, Richard Wright (1945-) on keyboards, Nick Mason (1945-) on drums, and Roger Waters (1944-) on bass. Waters, Wright, and Mason were architecture students who joined up with Barrett to form what started out as an R&B band. After several name changes, Barrett named the band Pink Floyd after the American bluesmen Pink Anderson and Floyd Council. The band eventually abandoned the R&B format for a more improvisational, psychedelic format, playing as the house band for proto-rave "Spontaneous Underground" parties at the Marquee club in London.

Pink Floyd released their first album, *Piper at the Gates of Dawn*, in August 1967; this release is called a classic example of psychedelic rock and is the only full-length album with Barrett as the principal songwriter and leader of the band. Barrett, the only real drug user in the band, became a heavy LSD user and began to lose his grip on reality. Pink Floyd did, however, manage to do a short tour with Jimi Hendrix at the end of 1967. In 1968, it was becoming apparent that Barrett's increasingly unstable behavior was harming the band, and his friend David Gilmour (1944-) was brought in on guitar to augment Pink Floyd's live performances so that Barrett could do songwriting at home. For a brief period, then, the band had five members; however, it was soon evident that Barrett was not capable of serving as a band member in any capacity.

Pink Floyd released its second album, *Saucerful of Secrets*, in June of 1968. The album consisted of a mix of earlier tracks with Barrett and newer material with Gilmour on guitar, and it marks the beginning of Waters's new role as leader and main songwriter for the band. Critics lambasted the band for going on without Barrett, but *Saucerful* proved the Floyd was willing to take chances; the album's title track is an 11-minute opus of minimalist experimentation.

The group released a soundtrack to the Barbet Schroeder movie *More* (1969), about two heroin addicts' descent into despair. The album hit the U.K. charts at No. 9, but failed to enter the U.S. charts. Pink Floyd also released the double album *Ummagumma* in October of 1969, in which one disc is concert material and the second contains solo songs done by each of the band members. While these experimentations may seem minor today, at the time, the work was hailed as unique. *Ummagumma* finally made the U.S. charts in January 1970. It hit the Top 100 and launched Pink Floyd's popularity in the U.S.

Two Pink Floyd albums were released in late 1971: the singles and outtakes compilation, *Relics*, which has several covers, one drawn by Mason, and a critical favorite, *Meddle*. The latter marked Floyd's true rise to stardom in America, hitting the U.S. charts at No. 70; it contained a concert favorite, the 20-minute "Echoes."

In 1972, Pink Floyd debuted a live suite, "Eclipse," which in March became *Dark Side of the Moon*, their seminal concept album. It broke records by being on the U.S. Top 200 pop charts for over 740 weeks, and selling over 20 million copies worldwide. A single, "Money," hit No. 13 and *Dark Side* was the first album to feature Waters as the sole lyricist for the band, a trend which continued until 1987.

Pink Floyd continued to tour throughout 1974, and attempted to record an album without musical instruments; this project, *Household Objects*, was eventually dismissed. In 1975 Floyd's masterpiece, *Wish You Were Here*, consisting of minimal lyrics and lush instrumental passages, was released. It featured a piece dedicated to Barrett, "Shine on You Crazy Diamond."

Pink Floyd took a break from touring in 1976, but reemerged with *Animals* and a world tour in 1977. *Animals* was Waters's response to the punk rock movement and a commentary on society. It was the first album to have only Waters and Gilmour as contributors, and it hit the U.S. charts at No. 3.

Two Pink Floyd members released solo albums in 1978—Gilmour's *David Gilmour* and Wright's *Wet Dream*. In December 1979, the double album and magnum opus *The Wall*, the story of a rock star's journey into madness, was released. In 1982, Waters worked with director Alan Parker on a film version of *The Wall*, a film-length music video with the Boomtown Rats' vocalist, Bob Geldof, as the main character Pink. Waters also published his first book, *The Pink Floyd Lyric Book*.

1983's *Final Cut* featured Waters, Gilmour, and Mason with studio musicians; it charted at No. 6 in the U.S. and was one of Floyd's worst-selling albums. Nevertheless, it was a landmark in recording history because of its use of holographic sound techniques in the studio.

In 1984, Gilmour, Waters, and Wright released solo albums. Waters and Gilmour toured separately to half-filled arenas, and Wright recorded with Dave Harris as a synth-pop duo, Zee. In 1985, Mason released another, mostly instrumental, jazz album, *Profiles,* with guitarist Rick Fenn, and toured with jazz player Michael Mantler. Waters left Floyd in 1985, assuming that would mark the end of the band;

Gilmour and Mason, however, released *A Momentary Lapse of Reason* in September 1987. Enraged by this, Waters tried to keep the album and subsequent tour from happening, causing one of the most bitter battles in the history of rock 'n' roll. Gilmour and Mason were able to keep the name Pink Floyd, and enlisted the help of Wright (as a salaried player) and studio musicians for the album and tour. With Gilmour as leader and main songwriter, *Momentary* reached No. 3 on the charts and the tour sold out. Waters also released and toured behind a solo album, *Radio Kaos.*

Floyd released the live album, *Delicate Sound of Thunder* (No. 11) in 1988. In 1990, Waters resurrected *The Wall* by staging an all-star performance at the Berlin Wall, releasing the concert as a video and album (No. 52).

A Floyd tribute album by the Alex Bollard Assembly, *Pink Rock*, was released in 1991. In 1992, Waters released another solo album, *Amused to Death*; Floyd released the box set *Shine On*, and in 1993, a Barrett outtake album, *Opel*.

In 1994, Floyd again reconvened (without Gilmour) to release *The Division Bell*, which hit the charts at No. 1; Wright was once again a full-fledged member of Pink Floyd, contributing material to the new album. The band (along with session musicians) toured and revived the old Barrett tune "Astronomy Domine," to much praise from fans.

The band won a Grammy for Best Rock Instrumental Performance for the song "Marooned" on *Division Bell* in March of 1995 and released *Pulse* (No. 1), a tour document containing a live performance of the complete *Dark Side of the Moon*. In 1996, Pink Floyd was inducted into the Rock and Roll Hall of Fame.

Bibliography

Jones, Cliff. *Another Brick in the Wall: The Stories behind Every Pink Floyd Song*. New York: Broadway, 1996.

Mabbett, Andy. *The Complete Guide to the Music of Pink Floyd*. New York: Omnibus, 1995.

MacDonald, Bruno, ed. *Pink Floyd through the Eyes of Its Fans, Friends, and Foes*. New York: Da Capo, 1997.

Rees, Dafydd, and Luke Crampton. *Encyclopedia of Rock Stars*. New York: DK, 1996.

Schaffner, Nicholas. *Saucerful of Secrets: The Pink Floyd Odyssey*. London: Sidgwick & Jackson, 1992.

Robert G. Weiner

Pioneer Radio Stations saw their birth in the years around 1920. Two stations, KDKA of Pittsburgh, and WWJ of Detroit, have jousted for years in the battle for recognition as the first established station. Both stations went on the air in 1920, and they have continued as broadcast stations to date. Backed by the Scripps-owned *Detroit News*, WWJ, first known as amateur station 8MK, went on the air on August 20, 1920. The Radio News and Music Company, formed by associates of radio pioneer Lee DeForest, held the license to 8MK, which broadcast from a second-floor "radio phone room" in the *Detroit News* Building. A broadcast license was issued to the *Detroit News* on October 15, 1921, and the call letters of station WBL were first established. The letters were changed to WWJ on March 3, 1921, as the station continued with a format of "voice and phonograph music."

WWJ was the first to broadcast news when it reported results of the Michigan primary on August 31, 1920, to several hundred listeners. From that time on, the station carried news as a daily part of its format. The *Detroit News* viewed the station as a service to the public and as a way to sell papers. Other newspapers in Kansas City, Milwaukee, Chicago, Los Angeles, Louisville, Atlanta, and Dallas soon followed suit.

KDKA officially first broadcast on election night, November 2, 1920. Powered by a 100-watt transmitter located in a shack on top of a Westinghouse manufacturing facility in East Pittsburgh, KDKA broadcast returns of the victory of Warren G. Harding over James M. Cox in the presidential race to an audience of a few thousand listeners. It was started as experimental station 8XK by Westinghouse employee Frank Conrad. After receiving a license, Westinghouse moved the station into broadcasting, relocating the operation from a shack to a tent. When the tent blew over in a storm, the company built a studio with draped walls to improve acoustics and provide areas for a piano, phonograph player, and an announcer. The station was the first to create public interest in purchasing radio receiving sets. Later, KDKA became the first to transmit religious programming when it broadcast an Episcopalian service on January 21, 1921. Throughout 1921, the station broadcast a series of public speeches by national figures. In April 1921, the station gave a blow-by-blow account of a boxing match. The following summer, KDKA covered a tennis match and a baseball game, thus demonstrating the viability of sports coverage.

WJZ in Newark, NJ, was another Westinghouse-owned station that went on the air in September 1921. Like the crude beginnings of sister-station KDKA, WJZ started out in a partitioned portion of the ladies' lounge in the Westinghouse manufacturing plant in Newark. WJZ-pioneered practices and methods were implemented by stations nationwide. The station became the first non–college radio station to broadcast classes for credit in 1923. Stations WEAF in New York and WLS in Chicago quickly followed by broadcasting lectures in 1924. WJZ developed announcers to accompany the evening programming. Announcers wore tuxedos and were known by initials, to allow them to retain a bit of anonymity and have a private life. Thomas H. Cowan was known as ACN (Announcer Cowan, Newark) when he first broadcast over WJZ in October 1922. One of the first broadcasts of a musical band came in 1921 when WJZ broadcast the Vincent Lopez group in a weekly 90-minute format. Following the sports broadcasting example of sister-station KDKA, WJZ broadcast the World Series in 1922. The series was linked to other stations using Western Union lines. Drama on radio did not become popular until the 1930s, but WJZ captured the interest of listeners when it broadcast "The Perfect Fool" with Ed Wynn in 1922.

WEAF in New York (now WNBC) also pioneered many practices that were later adopted by other stations. Owned by AT&T, the station was praised by radio engineers for its sophisticated studio and excellent transmitter when it went on the air on August 16, 1922. The first commercial, as it was called by AT&T, was broadcast on August 28, 1922. Costing $100, the 15-minute pitch for a cooperative housing complex was repeated over five days and aired during the early evening. Tidewater Oil, American Express, and Gimbel's Department Store followed within the year. The first sustained vaudeville and variety show appeared in January 1923. The first weekly news commentary began on WEAF in October 1923, featuring *Brooklyn Eagle* assistant editor H. V. Kaltenborn. He later became known as one of the most distinguished news reporter-commentators. Perhaps the most famous announcer of the early 1920s came from WEAF. Graham McNamee created a large following with his sports broadcasts.

All of these stations contributed to some aspect of the newly created radio industry. However, the most visible station was WEAF in New York City. It became a model for stations nationwide.

Bibliography

Archer, Gleason L. *History of Radio to 1926*. New York: American Historical Society, 1938; New York: Arno, 1971.

Charnley, Mitchell V. *News by Radio*. New York: Macmillan, 1948.

MacDonald, Fred J. *Don't Touch That Dial! Radio Programming in American Life from 1920 to 1960*. Chicago: Nelson-Hall, 1979.

Sterling, Christopher H., and John M. Kittross. *Stay Tuned: A Concise History of American Broadcasting*. Belmont: Wadsworth, 1990.

Ed Adams

Pirate Radio. Unlicensed radio broadcasting is most often considered the domain of European pirate radio. But unlicensed broadcasts are not a rare phenomenon in the United States. And, as the film *Pump up the Volume* (1990) demonstrated, pirate radio broadcasting is a part (albeit a small part) of the rebellious myths of popular music. The Federal Communications Commission (FCC) has pursued a policy of fining and arresting unlicensed broadcasters, and those caught by the FCC often claim their First Amendment rights are violated by such FCC action.

According to Kirk Baxter, president of the Association of Clandestine Radio Enthusiasts, a radio listeners' group, from 50 to 100 pirate stations operate in the U.S. at any given time, varying from studio-quality broadcasts to low-fi sound. Two generalizations can be made about unlicensed broadcasting in the U.S. First, most pirate radio broadcasters rely on rock music for their programming, albeit they argue they provide an alternative to commercial radio. Second, most unlicensed broadcasts occur outside standard AM and FM radio bands.

Pirate broadcasting came into being early on in radio's history, in part because until 1927 the airwaves were not regulated. The best-documented examples of pirate radio come from England, where pirate radio thrives. Although most people associate British pirate radio with the well-known ship-based transmissions of Radio Caroline, one can trace the roots of pirate broadcasting there to programming from Radio Normandy and Radio Luxembourg. Though not themselves pirates, these stations broadcast English-language programs from the European continent toward Britain to escape the BBC's stranglehold on broadcasting—and advertising.

Unlike U.S. pirates, who tend to broadcast sporadically, the U.K. pirates broadcast virtually around the clock, and they solicit advertising from large, corporate sponsors. Also in contrast to U.S. pirates, who are usually individuals engaged in radio as a hobby, the U.K. pirates operate their stations for profit. Moreover, the U.K. station owners are usually in some way financially affiliated with music publishing firms or record companies. In contrast to the U.K. pirates, U.S. pirate radio stations operate on shoestring budgets, broadcast irregularly, do not solicit advertising, and keep a very low profile. Broadcasts often include comedy, or are seasonal (around Halloween, Christmas, etc.), in part because this is a time when FCC agents tend to have days off and because holidays provide the pirates with time away from school or work for their broadcasting.

It is not difficult, with a little effort, and a lot of time and patience, to tune in pirate broadcasts. Although the programming may not be particularly adventuresome, with its comedy spots and phony advertisements it is nonetheless a change from commercial radio.

Bibliography

Baron, Michael. *Independent Radio*: *The Story of Independent Radio in the United Kingdom*. Lavenham: Dalton, 1975.

Harris, Paul. *When Pirates Ruled the Waves*. Aberdeen: Impulse, 1968.

Hinds, John, and Stephen Mosco. *Rebel Radio*: *The Full Story of British Pirate Radio*. London: Pluto, 1985.

Yoder, Andrew. *Pirate Radio*: *The Incredible Saga of America's Underground, Illegal Broadcasts*. Solana Beach: High Text, 1996.

——. *Pirate Radio Stations: Tuning in to Underground Broadcasts*. Blue Ridge Summit: TAB, 1990.

Steve Jones

Planet of the Apes (1968) began what could only be described as a science fiction phenomenon. Over a period of six years, five films were produced by the late Arthur P. Jacobs, and in the subsequent years the films have proven durable, finding new and loyal fans with each generation through multiple showings on television.

The original film's obvious drawing card was its uniqueness, based on a novel by Pierre Boulle. Unlike other science fiction films, *Apes* did not focus on technological predictions and gadgets, but instead looked back at primitive society, emphasizing plot and imagination over special effects. Indeed, the only real special effect in the film was its Oscar-winning makeup.

The film depicts an astronaut's confrontation with, and attempt to escape from, a civilization where apes possess intelligence, while humans are reduced to the state of speechless animals. In the ape society, the three species are divided into strict social roles. The chimpanzees are the society's intellectuals, the orangutans occupy the power positions of government and administration, while the gorillas are the society's military. As for humans, they live in the surrounding jungle, and are routinely hunted by the gorillas for sport and used by the chimpanzees for scientific experiments. This reversal of roles at first causes repulsion, until it becomes apparent that the apes merely use humans the way that today humans use apes.

Four sequels—*Beneath the Planet of the Apes* (1970), *Escape from the Planet of the Apes* (1971), *Conquest of the Planet of the Apes* (1972), and *Battle for the Planet of the Apes* (1973)—continued the examination of violence and social structure, as well as the anti-nuclear, anti-war message.

Bibliography

Donaldson, Leslie. "Planet of the Apes." *Magill's Survey of the Cinema—English Language Films, First Series 3*. Ed. Frank N. Magill. Englewood Cliffs: Salem, 1980.

Greene, Eric. Planet of the Apes *as American Myth: Race and Politics in the Films and Television Series*. Jefferson: McFarland, 1996.

Maronie, Samuel James. "Apes of Wrath." *Fangoria* June 1980: 28-30.

Robert Mastrangelo

Platform Tennis was invented in 1928 in Scarsdale, NY, as an all-weather alternative to court or lawn tennis, and in its early years it was primarily played in the Northeast. Platform (or "paddle") tennis is exclusively a doubles game, played with a perforated wood or metal paddle and a sponge rubber ball, which can be played off the 12-foot screen that surrounds the playing surface. Its inventors were Fessenden Blanchard and James K. Cogswell, with the first platform built on Cogswell's property. The first official set of rules was published by the American Platform Tennis Association in 1974. Although the sport is primarily a recreational outlet, there is a professional circuit in which players compete for prize money.

Bibliography

Iseman, Jay. *Play Paddle*. New York: Dutton, 1976.

Platform Tennis: Playing Your Best Game with 7 Time National Champion Rich Maier. Videotape. Westport: Custom Video, 1989.

Russell, Doug. *Contemporary Platform Tennis*. Chicago: Contemporary, 1978.

Robert C. Johnson

Platoon (1986). More than a quarter-century after the first Americans were killed in Vietnam during a rocket attack near Bien Hoa in 1959, Hollywood released its most widely successful treatment of that war. Oliver Stone's *Platoon* became, for many, the definitive cinematic treatment of that long and hotly debated war. As the first film to present a simple narrative that was neither relentlessly gung-ho (*The Green Berets*, 1968); redemptively melodramatic (*Coming Home*, 1978); symbolically hallucinogenic (*Apocalypse Now*, 1979); or baldly cartoonish (*Rambo: First Blood Part II*, 1985), *Platoon* filled a void in American popular culture. By adopting resonant narrative patterns—the *Bildungsroman*; an allegory of good and evil; and classical tragic structure—*Platoon*, like the best Hollywood films, felt right to millions of viewers who had seen it all before somewhere: in evening news reports from the war, in World War II combat films, and, more distantly, in Melville's *Moby Dick*, one of Stone's self-professed influences.

Platoon follows the story of Chris (Charlie Sheen), a young man whose sense of duty compels him to drop out of college in order to enlist in the U.S. Army. Nicknamed "Crusader" for joining while others were drafted, Chris's tour of duty is followed from his first arrival in country to his last copter extraction out of combat. In between, Sheen's young innocent learns of rage, atrocity, and death, but his most important battles are internal, where he struggles with a divided allegiance to the two guiding forces of his platoon, Sgt. Barnes (Tom Berenger), obsessed, like Captain Ahab, with duty, and Sgt. Elias (Willem Dafoe), whose fury is tempered with paternal concern.

After years of struggling to have his film made, Stone soon saw *Platoon* garner $140 million at the box office. Nominated for eight Academy Awards, *Platoon* won for best picture, best director, film editing, and sound. The other four nominations were well deserved: Dafoe and Berenger for best supporting actor, Stone for best screenplay, and Robert Richardson for best cinematography. But the most inspired contribution to the film went without a nomination: composer George Delerue's use of Samuel Barber's "Adagio for Strings" gave *Platoon* an elegiac largeness sufficient to temper the blood and thunder of Stone's combat scenes. While most film critics and public commentators praised *Platoon* for its realism and power, a minority of significant critics, like Pauline Kael, spoke of "too much romanticized insanity" and reiterated the familiar complaint against Stone (see entry) that his films are frequently overwrought.

Bibliography

Baird, Robert. *Perceptions of* Platoon: *Vietnam Myth or Vietnam Reality?* Stillwater: Oklahoma State UP, 1989.

Kael, Pauline. *5001 Nights at the Movies*. New York: Holt, 1991.

McCombs, Phil. "Veterans, Reliving the Pain." *Washington Post* 16 Jan. 1987: B1.

Robert Baird

Playboy (1951-) is the literary embodiment of the lifestyle and philosophy of its founder, Hugh Hefner (1926-). The magazine was first published in 1951 and has remained the most popular men's magazine of its type. It is classified for libraries as "adult" because of its colorful nude photographs, its naughty cartoons (including the now-famous "Vargas Girl"), and its "Playboy Advisor" column, which deals with sexually explicit questions in a thorough and humorous way. It boasts an array of famous contributors such as Gore Vidal and Dan Greenberg, and its fiction is generally carefully selected and well written. *Playboy* originally pandered to the lusts and fantasies of the unmarried male, but in the age of AIDS and other sexually transmitted diseases, promiscuity is no longer as fashionable as it once was. Perhaps reflecting shifting public opinion, the magazine is now published by Hefner's daughter, Christie, although it continues its focus on male heterosexual virility.

Bibliography

Dines, Gail. "I Buy It for the Articles: *Playboy Magazine* and the Sexualization of Consumerism." *Gender, Race, and Class in Media: A Text-Reader*. Ed. Gail Dines and Jean M. Humez. Thousand Oaks: Sage, 1995.

Katz, W., and L. S. Katz, eds. *Magazines for Libraries.* 7th ed. New York: Bowker, 1992.

Miller, Russell. *Bunny: The Real Story of* Playboy. New York: Holt, 1984.

Weyr, Thomas. *Reaching for Paradise: The Playboy Vision of America.* New York: New York Times, 1978.

Working Press of the Nation: Magazines and Internal Publications Directory. Vol. 2. 45th ed. Burlington, VT: Reed, 1994.

Mona Phillips

Playhouse 90 (1956-1961), named for its 90-minute format, was one of the finest and most ambitious dramatic anthology series of television's "Golden Age." Armed with its large budget, *Playhouse 90* hired the best actors, producers, directors, and writers to present live the most provocative subject matter of the era. Initiated by CBS executive Hubbell Robinson, Jr., and producer Martin Manulis midway in the death of live television, *Playhouse 90* was committed to the notion of presenting a 90-minute drama every week so that people would know on a regular basis where they could find a quality program to watch. Before it, dramatic anthology was available to viewers on an occasional and largely irregular basis, often in alternating program format.

During the first season, all *90*'s presentations were aired live. The series opened with Rod Serling's adaptation of Pat Frank's novel *Forbidden Area*, followed by Serling's stunning *Requiem for a Heavyweight* (see entry), which won what were then all the major honors and awards in broadcasting. During the 1957-58 season roughly one drama each month was filmed in advance, by different production teams, or, as in the case of *A Town Has Turned to Dust*, was performed live with embedded video segments, a novelty in its day. During the third season, many of the plays were made using videotape, then a relatively new process.

Playhouse 90 died because of internal squabbles among its talented producers and the burden of maintaining its high production values. Its last telecast as a regular series was on January 21, 1960. A total of eight more shows aired on an irregular basis in different time slots through May 18, 1960, and a series of reruns was presented weekly during the summer of 1961 and was resurrected in its original format in the early 1970s.

Bibliography

Boddy, William. *Fifties Television.* Urbana: U of Illinois P, 1990.

Brooks, Tim, and Earle Marsh. *The Complete Directory to Prime Time Network Television Shows, 1946-Present.* New York: Ballantine, 1992.

O'Neil, Thomas. *The Emmys.* New York: Penguin, 1992.

Sturcken, Frank. *Live Television.* New York: McFarland, 1990.

S. P. Madigan

Poe, Edgar Allan (1809-1849), remains one of the most important, inventive, and influential writers in American literature, whose contributions to mystery and detective fiction and gothic literature are signal. His impact on a diverse range of subsequent authors (Nathaniel Hawthorne, Rudyard Kipling, Arthur Conan Doyle, Jules Verne, George Bernard Shaw, Robert Louis Stevenson, Henry James, Charles Baudelaire, William Faulkner, Jorge Luis Borges, and legions of others) is profound, and he has generated global inspiration.

Born in Boston, the second child of itinerant actors, Poe was orphaned at age two and became the ward of John Allan, a wealthy merchant. After several years in England with the Allan family, Poe was raised in Richmond. A series of misdirected career starts, a failed stint in the Army, and a lifetime dispute with his stepfather over Poe's gambling debts and irresponsible behavior caused an alienated Poe to move northeast, where he sought a life in letters. He published his first book, *Tamerlane and Other Poems* in 1827, then additional collections of poetry in 1829 and 1831. His literary credentials established, Poe embarked on a career as author, editor, journalist, and lecturer—producing tales, poems, and reviews for a succession of newspapers and popular journals and acquiring a reputation for brilliance, instability, and intellectual arrogance. In May 1836, he married his 13-year-old cousin Virginia Clemm. *The Narrative of Arthur Gordon Pym* appeared in 1838, *Tales of the Grotesque and Arabesque* in 1839, and *Tales* in 1845. The enormous popular success of "The Raven" led to the publication of *The Raven and Other Poems* (1845). Poe's physical and emotional health were often poor, and after his wife died in 1847, his behavior became increasingly erratic. In 1848, he published his last major work, the "prose poem" *Eureka*, but died under mysterious circumstances the following year.

Premier among Poe's fictions are his gothic and horror tales, atmospheric works that explore the dark recesses of the human mind. Poe manipulates gothic conventions to depict perverse and maniacal behavior and to conceptualize evil, terror, and the unknown. In tales like "Ligeia" (1838), "William Wilson" (1839), "The Black Cat" (1843), "The Tell-Tale Heart" (1843), and "The Cask of Amontillado" (1846)—stories of crime, obsession, and morbidity—an underlying irony operates to call into question the narrators' perceptions of events and protestations of innocence as grotesque distortions of reality. Poe's genius is to proffer a fictional world in which a range of possible explanations for the bizarre events is possible—supernatural, psychological, imaginary, or factual—leaving readers both illuminated and mystified.

Poe's tales of "ratiocination" have earned him the title of "Father of the Detective Story." His clever detective M. Dupin solves a series of lurid crimes in "The Murders in the Rue Morgue" (1841), "The Mystery of Marie Roget" (1842), and "The Purloined Letter" (1844) by employing deductive reasoning and a kind of poetic imagination. The ratiocinative tales thus establish the conventions of the detective genre in the 19th century: an eccentric and visionary sleuth whose powers of insight and analysis and methodical approach enable him to solve cases that baffle the hapless police; a nameless narrator, companion to the detective, who charts his adventures and acts as a kind of liaison with the reader; a mystery that defies common sense but ultimately affords a rational solution; a denouement that enables the triumph of the detective over a brilliant criminal adversary; a sense of order restored and justice vindicated.

Bibliography

Mabbott, Thomas Ollive, ed. *The Collected Works of Edgar Allan Poe.* Cambridge: Harvard UP, 1969.

Muller, John P., and William J. Richardson, eds. *The Purloined Poe. Lacan, Derrida, and Psychoanalytic Reading.* Baltimore: Johns Hopkins UP, 1988.

Quinn, Arthur Hobson. *Edgar Allan Poe: A Critical Biography.* New York: Cooper Square, 1969.

Thomas, Dwight, and David K. Jackson. *The Poe Log.* Boston: Hall, 1987.

Thompson, G. R. *Poe's Fiction: Romantic Irony in the Gothic Tales.* Madison: U of Wisconsin P, 1973.

David Cody
Diana Reep
Liahna Babener

See also

Classical Mysteries · Gothic Mysteries
Detective Sidekicks · Holmes, Sherlock
Doyle, Sir Arthur Conan

Poirot, Hercule, the dapper fictional detective with the egg-shaped head and the formidable "little grey cells," first appeared in Agatha Christie's *The Mysterious Affair at Styles* (1920), narrated by his long-time companion Captain Hastings. Best-selling mystery writer Christie (see entry) penned a series of 33 novels and 53 short stories featuring Poirot, ending the series back at the Styles estate in *Curtain* (1975).

Unlike the rugged male hero so popular in hard-boiled American literature and film, the eccentric Poirot reflects his Continental roots and classical literary forebears: he dresses formally, speaks fractured English, wears flamboyant mustaches, and uses his brains, not muscles, to entrap ruthless murderers. Yet the little Belgian detective is greatly popular in the United States with readers who have kept the series in print and enjoyed film and television embodiments of Poirot, performed most notably by Albert Finney, Peter Ustinov, and BBC Television's David Suchet.

Bibliography

Bargainnier, Earl. *The Gentle Art of Murder: The Detective Fiction of Agatha Christie.* Bowling Green, OH: Bowling Green State U Popular P, 1980.

Hart, Anne. *The Life and Times of Hercule Poirot.* New York: Putnam, 1990.

Palmer, Scott. *The Films of Agatha Christie.* London: Batsford, 1993.

Sanders, Dennis, and Len Lovallo. *The Agatha Christie Companion: The Complete Guide to Agatha Christie's Life and Work.* 2d ed. New York: Berkley, 1989.

Marty S. Knepper

See also

Detective Sidekicks
Golden Age of Detective Fiction

Police, The (1977-1983), drew from the multi-faceted talents and influences of its members to become one of the most successful popular groups of the 1980s. While many bands coming out of the punk and new wave movements placed panache above technique, the Police featured three accomplished musicians who stretched rock's traditional boundaries by incorporating elements of jazz, reggae, and progressive rock into their music.

The group started in 1977 as the brainchild of American drummer Stewart Copeland, who had gone to the U.K. in 1975 and played with progressive rock band Curved Air. Copeland recruited Gordon Sumner, a.k.a. Sting, from jazz-combo Last Exit and French punk guitarist Henri Podavani. Veteran guitarist Andy Sumners, ex-Soft Machine and the Animals, replaced Padovani after the group's first single, "Fall Out," was released. Soon after the trio solidified, they recorded and released their first album, *Outlandos D'Amour,* in 1978. The LP provided the group with its first hit, the reggae-tinged "Roxanne," inspired by the Parisian red light district. The single received little attention in the U.K. but became popular on college radio in the U.S.

Although the Police's second album, *Regatta de Blanc* (1979), did well on the U.S. album charts, it only furnished one minor hit single, the catchy "Message in a Bottle." Not until *Zenyatta Mondata* (1980), with its instrumental excellence and bubblegummish "De Do Do Do, De Da Da Da," did the band have a Top 10 hit in the U.S. both on the album and singles charts. In 1981, *Regatta de Blanc* won a Grammy for Best Rock Instrumental Performance and "Don't Stand So Close to Me" hit the Top 10. The Police were on a run, and the following LP, *Ghost in the Machine*, released in late 1981, produced two Top 40 hits, "Every Little Thing She Does Is Magic" and "Spirits in the Material World." The album itself peaked at No. 2 on the album charts. In 1982, the band again won Grammy awards, for Best Rock Vocal Performance by a Duo or Group for "Don't Stand So Close to Me" and Best Rock Instrumental Performance for "Behind My Camel."

All that remained for the Police to accomplish in the U.S. was to garner a No. 1 album, and they did so in 1983 with *Synchronicity,* which supplied the band with its only No. 1 single, "Every Breath You Take," and which won the band two more Grammys. *Synchronicity* was the group's final studio album, after which the members embarked on solo careers, with Sting having the most success in popular music.

Bibliography

Goddard, Peter, and Philip Kamin. *The Police Chronicles.* New York: Beaufort, 1984.

Goldsmith, Lynn. *The Police.* New York: St. Martin's 1983.

Rees, Dafydd, and Luke Crampton. *Rock Movers and Shakers.* New York: Billboard, 1991.

Tobler, John, ed. *Who's Who in Rock and Roll.* New York: Crescent, 1991.

Hugh Foley

Police-Detective TV Programs. From Jack Webb's sonorous "All we want are the facts, ma'am" to today's *NYPD Blue*, police-detective programs have long been a staple of television entertainment. The gap in the years between these two programs belies the similarities in each of these "cop" shows. The dead-pan seriousness and matter-of-fact account at the end of each *Dragnet* show seem far removed from the hectic intensity of *NYPD Blue*, yet each series is representative of sincere but not always successful attempts to re-create police "reality." Real police work is probably not as cut-and-dried as Jack Webb seemed to want us to believe; and perhaps modern police procedure is neither as emotional nor as intense as *NYPD Blue* portrays it. What remains consistent about television police drama is that each becomes a cultural morality tale about crime and punishment.

Attempts at reality in cop shows are not recent innovations. The first police drama on television was probably *Man against Crime,* which starred Ralph Bellamy and ran on CBS from 1949 to 1953 (and in reruns as *Follow That Man*). *Dragnet* made the successful move from radio to television in 1952 and enjoyed a seven-year run. Jack Webb starred in and directed the show, and it was his insistence on its *cinema vérité* style, with its clipped diction and no-nonsense plots, which made *Dragnet* a touchstone for all later police shows.

One of the first series to use an actual city as location was *The Lineup* (CBS, 1954-59). The on-location shots did much to lend verisimilitude to the police drama, and since the city was San Francisco, the location became the star. This was proven true when, in rerelease, CBS changed the series' name to *San Francisco Beat.*

A 1958 movie proved to be the impetus for the ABC 1958 season entry into realistic police drama: *Naked City* (1958-63) had recurring stars but was a type of anthology of the "eight million stories" in New York City. Its fast-paced, black-and-white camera work showed New York as it had not been seen before and set the standard for later on-location police dramas.

A half-hour ABC series from 1967 to 1968, entitled *N.Y.P.D.* gave an even more authentic documentary look to its short stories; the use of 16mm film to dramatize actual stories from New York City police files made this short-lived series a unique attempt by a major network to present police work in a realistic format.

Added to the NBC 1967 season was a new concept with a familiar face: *Ironside* (1967-75, with Raymond Burr of past seasons' *Perry Mason*) had as its plot gimmick crime and punishment viewed from the wheelchair of San Francisco's chief of detectives. What made this series work was the strong presence of Burr and his curmudgeon character's deductive questioning techniques.

Another crime series from ABC, this one from 1976-77, was *Most Wanted,* which featured Robert Stack. Its primary claim to fame is that it engendered later docudrama series such as *America's Most Wanted* (1988-), *Unsolved Mysteries* (1988-) and others of that genre.

The NBC anthology series *Police Story* (1973-77) had as its production consultant Joseph Wambaugh, former policeman and best-selling author (who was also responsible for the 1973 NBC miniseries of his novel *The Blue Knight,* which went on to CBS as a weekly series in the 1976-77

season). Wambaugh's authority and experience as a policeman was evident within the stories. With no recurring stars, *Police Story* became a showcase for television talent of the seventies.

Another NBC anthology, *The NBC Mystery Movie* (1971-77), gave viewers different (and lighter) approaches to police and detective work, with *McMillan and Wife,* *McCloud,* and *Columbo.* The first, a drama which featured a police commissioner and his wife, was a romantic crime show in the tradition of Nick and Nora Charles, although one might note that Mrs. McMillan was hardly as clever or as sophisticated as Nora Charles. Another offering was Dennis Weaver in *McCloud,* a police-detective show which could have been subtitled *Matt Dillon's Sidekick Rides into New York City.* While *McCloud* was billed as a police drama, the cowboy elements often took over.

Also part of the *Mystery Movie* anthology was one of the best entries in television police drama, one that still has occasional new episodes in production. In *Columbo* (1971-77; see entry), Peter Falk created his rumpled, loveable character who seemed the opposite of the detective-novel hero. Indeed, the title character was the oxymoron of detectives: the policeman who seemed dumber than even Inspector Lestrade (of Holmes's fame) but who actually was as cunning as Holmes himself. *Columbo* remains one of the few original contributions of television in its portrayal of the detective on the small screen.

The seventies seemed to be the decade of police drama, including some rather silly entries, such as *The Mod Squad* (ABC, 1968-73), a police series in which the writers expected audiences to believe that a police department would hire as undercover cops a former car thief, a black radical from Watts, and a part-time teen-aged prostitute. The youth culture and the city of Los Angeles were the stars.

The silly seventies also spawned *The Rookies* (1972-76), which found some good actors trapped in some bad scripts. Kate Jackson, Georg Stanford Brown, and Michael Ontkean all went on to find better scripts and better series. The other unlikely cop show which enjoyed success had Robert Blake as an undercover cop in *Baretta* (1975-78), a series in which a cockatoo took second billing but often stole the show.

Television attempted 1940s period shows, with both *Ellery Queen,* for one season in 1975, and the less-polished *City of Angels,* of the same season. The first remained true to the bookish character of the detective novels (and to the original television *Ellery Queen,* which ran sporadically from 1950 to 1959), while the latter was a smorgasbord of the Chandler type of California P.I. (already done to perfection by Humphrey Bogart in his portrayals of both Spade and Marlowe on the large screen). In the former, Ellery Queen, charmingly played by Jim Hutton, was not the policeman but only assisted his father, a New York City policeman, in solving the case each week. *City of Angels* was really a private eye series whose main charm was in offering glimpses of a Los Angeles which no longer exists.

Best known for its 1973 premiere as a TV movie entitled *The Marcus-Nelson Murders, Kojak* (1973-90) was shot on location and, like *Naked City* before it, became one of the best in-depth looks at New York City. *Kojak* won many fans, as much for the eccentric hero, played masterfully by Telly Savalas, as for its innovative ideas about law enforcement. The show did, however, raise some social issues which separated it from the action/hero program so popular in the sixties and seventies. Representatives from this last category were *Dan August* (1970-75), *Starsky and Hutch* (1975-79), and *CHIPS* (1977-83), where the chase and the final shoot-out became formulas for success.

Location became the star in two different shows set in Hawaii: *Hawaii Five-0* (1968-80) and *Magnum, P.I.* (1980-88) used the beautiful backdrop of the Islands to augment the plots, although *Hawaii Five-0* (see entry) did explore some ethnic problems of native Islanders as they related to crime. *Magnum* (see entry) was primarily a pretty face in a flashy car, another version of the California P.I. syndrome.

Decent scripts and even better acting elevated two police dramas above their contemporaries: *The Streets of San Francisco* (1972-77) from the seventies and *In the Heat of the Night* (1988-94), a seventies movie transferred to eighties' and nineties' television.

The public's fascination with forensic evidence and how science can assist police was perhaps best represented on television by NBC's 1976 entry entitled *Quincy* (1976-83), with Jack Klugman in the title role. The hero was not a cop but a Los Angeles County Medical Examiner, and like Perry Mason in the courtroom, Quincy was able to solve crimes in the pathology laboratory.

Two shows from the 1980s which have greatly influenced both video art and popular culture are *Hill Street Blues* (1981-87), in which the roaming camera gave the viewers a heightened sense of a real (chaotic) police station, and *Miami Vice* (1984-89; see entry), where the attitude (and the wardrobe) of the individual detective once more emphasized the anti-hero code of Chandler and Hammett. It can be said of *Hill Street* that it changed the audience's expectation of cop shows—so much so that today many of the most popular police dramas are the real-life, camera-on-the-run type of action.

Miami Vice affected viewers in a different way: The first action show which used current, popular rock music as background (and even some rock stars as guest actors), *Miami Vice* also had the effect of illustrating the gritty, yet opulent lifestyle associated with Florida.

One of the most unlikely cop shows ever to see eleven episodes was Steven Bocho's *Cop Rock* in the fall of 1990. The scripts and the camera work were typical of *Hill Street Blues* and lauded by critics. What the viewing audiences could not seem to accept was singing and dancing cops. Even clever numbers like the roll call "Let's Be Careful Out There" (a parody of the well-known *Hill Street* phrase) could not vindicate this musical cop show to the audience and to the ratings.

Fall of 1992 saw no fewer than seven reality-based cop shows aired on network prime time. *Top Cops* (1990-93), developed by TV producer Sonny Grosso, a former narcotics detective, had as its primary motive the fight against the bad cop stereotype which permeated the media after the Rodney King beating in Los Angeles.

One of the nineties' first major television censorship battles centered around ABC's 1993 entry into the police line-up—an hour-long drama entitled *NYPD Blue* (see entry). With a collage opening of New York City reminiscent of *Miami Vice*'s fast-paced pre-show gambit, and a theme song by Mike Post from *Hill Street Blues* fame, *NYPD Blue* relies upon suggested images, rather than true reality, to imply its themes. True to *Naked City* and to its nominal predecessor, *N.Y.P.D.*, *NYPD Blue* shows New York City at its grittiest and grimiest. *Law and Order* (1990-), which combines a cop show with a legal drama, is also set in New York.

Bibliography

Brown, Les. *Les Brown's Encyclopedia of Television*. New York: Zoetrope, 1982.

Gianakos, Larry James. *Television Drama Series Programming: A Comprehensive Chronicle, 1975-1980*. Metuchen: Scarecrow, 1981.

Grant, Judith. "Prime Time Crime: Television Portrayals of Law Enforcement." *Journal of American Culture* 16.1 (1992): 57-68.

Louise Conley Jones

Police Procedural refers to the subgenre of mystery and detective fiction in which the mystery is solved by the police as part of their professional duties. Critics agree that the first police procedural is Lawrence Treat's *V As in Victim* (1945), featuring Detective Third Grade Mitch Taylor of New York's 21st Precinct. Procedurals became popular in the 1960s, perhaps as a reaction to the classical and hard-boiled subgenres, with their consistently disparaging view of the police. Originally an American form, procedurals today are set in jurisdictions throughout the world, from Sweden to South Africa. Nonetheless, the best-known series, the one considered the benchmark, is that of American author Evan Hunter. Writing as Ed McBain (see entry), Hunter introduced the first of his 87th Precinct novels, *Cop Hater*, in 1957, and to date, the series contains more than 50 books. McBain's novels effectively define the genre.

One distinguishing characteristic of the police procedural is that there is often no single hero in a story. The characters, like real professionals, work together as a team. In some series, a repertory collective of characters is established, and a different protagonist surfaces in each novel. Thus, the various members of McBain's 87th Precinct squad take turns in the role of hero, and the canon honors the cooperative relationship of the team.

The method for solving crimes also helps define the police procedural. The investigative process involves a set of established professional procedures for collecting evidence, interviewing witnesses, examining crime scenes, and conducting forensic inquiries. Procedurals emphasize that it is such routine methods rather than individual acts of brilliant intuition that solve cases.

Procedural novels reflect a realism less visible in other forms of detective fiction. Authors deliberately show the working life of the police as it is enacted daily. Readers see the unpalatable aspects of the job, like low pay, long hours, and lack of esteem from the surrounding community. The group dynamics are often highlighted, re-creating in fiction the friendships and hostilities that exist among any group of people who work together. As they would in actual practice, characters investigate a number of cases simultaneously, often remarking on the luxury of fictional detectives to focus on just one puzzle at a time. At the end of a typical procedural, the main cases are solved but minor cases still await resolution. Realism is also achieved by depicting the characters' personal lives.

The overriding characteristic of this subgenre is its favorable portrayal of law enforcement. Neither bumpkins nor geniuses, cops are drawn as honest, hardworking professionals who do difficult, dangerous, and often thankless jobs. Police corruption is recognized but treated as an aberration and the mark of a failed professional, rather than an endemic threat.

Noted American police procedural authors and their series cops include John Ball's Virgil Tibbs stories; Rex Burns's Gabriel Wagner; Susan Dunlap's Jill Smith series; Katherine Forrest's Kate Delafield; Chester Himes's Grave Digger Jones and Coffin Ed Johnson books; Elizabeth Linington's Ivor Maddox; Margaret Maron's Sigrid Harald novels; Lillian O'Donnell's Norah Mulcahaney; Elizabeth Linington writing as Dell Shannon's Luis Mendoza; Lawrence Treat's Mitch Taylor and Jub Freeman; Dorothy Uhnak's Christie Opara novels; Hilary Waugh's Frank Ford, Frank Fellows, and Frank Sessions; and Colin Wilcox's Frank Hastings.

Bibliography

Dove, George N. *The Police Procedural.* Bowling Green, OH: Bowling Green State U Popular P, 1982.

Symons, Julian. *Bloody Murder: From the Detective Story to the Crime Novel.* New York: Mysterious, 1992.

Joan G. Kotker

See also
Crichton, Michael
Mystery and Detective Fiction
Wambaugh, Joseph

Political Advertising has become so much a component of modern American politics that candidates devote more attention to the selection of media consultants and "spin doctors" than they do to running mates. In its many manifestations, advertising reigns supreme at all levels of our political process. The candidate for municipal office must walk the district pounding on doors and fending off small dogs, but the difference between failure and success is often lawn signs, a printed brochure, postcards targeted to friends of supporters, and media ads. At the congressional, state, and national levels, most monies not needed for staff and travel are routinely allocated to advertising a candidate's virtues (and an opponent's grave character defects and apostasy on the issues) in print, on radio, and especially on television. Many scholars regard the dawn of the modern era in American politics as the summer of 1952, when Dwight D. Eisenhower's Republican campaign advisors hired a Madison Avenue advertising agency to produce and deploy a series of TV "spot" commercials promoting Eisenhower. One featured

Photo courtesy of Popular Culture Library, Bowling Green State University, Bowling Green, OH.

little animated elephants dancing in a circle while singing, "We like Ike, you like Ike, everybody likes Ike!" Democratic opponent Adlai Stevenson tried to respond by "talking sense to the American people" in televised addresses 15 to 60 minutes in duration. Fewer viewers were inspired than bored, the dancing elephants ruled the little screen, Eisenhower won in a landslide, and the nature of American elective politics was altered forever.

Yet political advertising is not a recent phenomenon in American politics or popular culture. The cartoons and broadsides created by Benjamin Franklin to promote his 1754 Albany Plan of Union were political advertising in its purest sense, as were the circular letters of the revolutionary committees of correspondence, Thomas Paine's pamphlet "Common Sense," and the lurid Paul Revere engraved prints portraying the 1770 Boston Massacre as a slaughter of the innocents. Thomas Jefferson's immortal Declaration of Independence was surely more, but was also carefully crafted political advertising for the aborning republic. During the early national period, proponents of the Federalists and opposition Jeffersonians advertised their positions at public rallies by wearing on their hats twigs, bucktails, or cockades. Ceramic pitchers imported from Liverpool advertised the greatness of Jefferson and James Madison and the perfidy of the Alien and Sedition acts imposed by the Federalists. Fine inlaid Sheffield razors were marketed in 1807 bearing such slogans as "a true Washingtonian," "a true Jeffersonian," and "a true Madisonian." Such wares ran the risk of violating what political culture scholar J. M. Heale has labeled the protocol of the "mute tribune," that an early party or candidate not commit the sin of overweening ambition by openly soliciting support, but they did enjoy brisk sales.

Such protocols of virginal innocence vanished from American politics abruptly after the 1824 presidential election. Tennessee senator Andrew Jackson led a field of four in both the popular and electoral votes, but was denied the presidency when Speaker Henry Clay supported runner-up John Quincy Adams in the House of Representatives. This did not bother the Jackson loyalists, but when Adams offered to Clay the position of Secretary of State (traditionally a stepping-stone to the White House), Jackson and his supporters were outraged. The 1828 campaign began at once, and in the process all genteel curbs on political advertising fell victim, once and for all, to partisan spleen. The Jacksonians put together a national network of weekly newspapers to promote the "Hero of New Orleans" and prototypical agrarian "Farmer of Tennessee" and to denigrate Adams as an overeducated effete snob who had supplied a teenage maid for the Russian czar, married a woman of loose morals, held membership in a Masonic lodge, and squandered public funds on a billiard table and other gaming devices for the White House. Adams's forces responded in kind.

The battle served to stimulate innovation in advertising. Clever entrepreneurs took advantage of the popular vogue for "Old Hickory" by marketing for profit such advertising devices as metal lucky tokens, shanked garment buttons, silk and cotton bandannas, silk ribbons, glass tumblers and flasks, ceramic pitchers and plates, papier-maché snuff boxes, velvet thread boxes, and tortoise-shell combs promoting Jackson. During an era when politics was local and political events participatory, Jackson's lieutenants made creative use of such rites as the planting of hickory saplings and raising of hickory poles, the wearing of hickory sprigs when "store-bought" badges were unavailable, and the staging of such mass events as parades and barbecues. Although political music was not new, Noah Ludlow's "The Hunters of Kentucky," an immensely popular air celebrating Jackson's victory at New Orleans, served in effect as our first real political commercial set to music. This innovative campaign elected Jackson in a landslide, revolutionized American political etiquette, and created an enduring niche for advertising in the electoral process.

Jackson's National Republican opposition then reorganized under the Whig banner, but it took them longer to exploit political advertising to exact revenge upon the Democrats. After Jackson's vendetta against the Bank of the United States prompted the Panic of 1837 and Jackson heir Martin Van Buren proposed an "independent subtreasury" in lieu of reviving the national bank, Whig critics flooded the land with satirical paper banknotes and copper medalets making mock of Old Hickory, Van Buren, and Senator Thomas Hart Benton, who so despised paper currency that coins were popularly known as "Benton mint-drops." The Missourian later described this funny money as "caricatures and grotesque pictures and devices intended to act on the thoughtless and ignorant through appeals to their eyes and passions"—in short, effective mass advertising!

Then in 1840, the Whigs exhibited a true mastery of the advertising arts in a campaign that still stands as a disreputable monument to civics as carnival, the "Tippecanoe and Tyler too" campaign on behalf of William Henry Harrison and John Tyler. That year the Whigs went "down to the people," portrayed their patrician nominee improbably as a simple backwoods frontiersman, abjured creation of a party platform (which, they said, only encouraged candidates to lie) in favor of such pithy slogans as "Tippecanoe and Tyler too" and "Van, Van is a used-up man," and carried the day in an exhibition of popular political mass marketing seldom rivaled since. Soon Whig loyalists crossed the thin line between fancy and downright fraud by transforming Harri-

son, a Virginia blueblood with a stately Ohio River mansion, into the simple rustic "Farmer of North Bend" who lived in a humble log cabin and replenished perspiration from the plough with copious swigs of hard cider.

However absurd, the metamorphosis of Harrison into a backwoods agrarian prompted a participatory fervor unrivaled in the history of American politics. For two or three-day rallies 100,000 gathered in Baltimore, Nashville, and Dayton, 60,000 at Bunker Hill, and "fifteen acres of men" at the Tippecanoe battlefield in Indiana. Parades were staged on the grand scale of a Cecil B. DeMille, and Whig women donned virginal white dresses to ride floats with banners thanking Old Tip for saving their mothers from fates worse than death at the hands of British and Indian adversaries. Such events begat thousands of mass-produced or handmade banners, transparencies, parade flags and standards, silk ribbon badges, and other visual devices to advertise Harrison and Tyler. Buckskin balls as large as ten feet in diameter were painted with partisan slogans and rolled from town to town. Throughout the land Whigs gathered to construct Harrison headquarter log cabins, inevitably equipped with barrels of hard cider. Cabins were put on wheels to serve as parade floats.

That creative promotional advertising can serve worthy political purposes was made manifest during the 1860 Republican campaign waged to elect Abraham Lincoln. A somewhat obscure Illinois attorney with little national exposure, Lincoln was advertised extensively and effectively as the "railsplitter of the West," a brainstorm of friend Richard Oglesby that dramatized at once Lincoln's rise from humble origins, the mystique of the frontier, and the dignity of free labor. This symbolism turned the homely, hulking lawyer from an advertising nightmare into a boon. Split rails adorned party headquarters and led Republican parades. They graced newspaper mastheads, transparencies, banners, and brass medalets. Marching units in Lincoln parades, often bearing such names as the Railsplitters or Rail Maulers, toted wooden axes and ax torches. Although his campaign featured a cogent balance of ideological imperatives as well, creative advertising did much to make possible the Lincoln presidency, the enunciation of a new nation on the killing fields of Gettysburg, emancipation for four million slaves, and the preservation of the American Union.

Two major innovations in political advertising accompanied the 1860 campaign. One was the genesis of the most spectacular of all American political art forms, the torchlight parade. The most lavish of these events in 1860 took place in New York on October 3, with a parade of more than 10,000 Lincoln loyalists for an audience of hundreds of thousands. The other key innovation was the introduction of photography to convey the visual images of candidates to partisans formerly afforded only artists' sketches. James Buchanan inaugural ribbons in 1857 bore engravings from photographs taken by a young and relatively unknown Mathew Brady, but 1860 marked the advent of the camera in American campaigning, with ribbons and prints featuring the handiwork of Brady and other photographers to promote Lincoln, John Bell, Stephen Douglas, and John C. Breckinridge. The "ferrotype," a small photograph encased in brass and produced from thin iron plates treated with a wet collodion solution, became a popular 1860 novelty. More than 160 varieties were produced and sold as miniature badges. It is difficult to overstate the importance of photography in a political culture predating motion pictures, photojournalism, and television, a culture of intense partisan passions starved for visual images of its champions.

During the postwar Victorian era, participatory politics remained an American passion, with voter turnouts of 80 to 90 percent the rule rather than the exception. In the heyday of local political clubs, the torchlight parade, mass rally, and holiday barbecue or ox-roast provided millions with both entertainment and renewal of party solidarity. Imitating the flamboyant decorative arts of the era, increasingly gaudy multicolored lapel badges supplanted ferrotypes and ribbon badges grew larger and more ornate. Perhaps the major initiative in political advertising during the period was the copious array of partisan decorative items produced and purchased to reach beyond the public arena and bring politics into the home. Among them were ornamental ceramic pitchers, plates, bowls, and "intaglio" tile trivets and glass paperweights, plates, and frosted figural decanters. Along with such mementos as political sewing boxes, pincushions, and thread, and other items featuring First Lady Frances Folsom Cleveland, they also provide persuasive evidence of the extraordinary importance placed on the good will of American women by major parties and producers who catered to them during the heyday of the "cult of domesticity" before suffrage.

The 1896 contest between William McKinley and William Jennings Bryan, regarded by political scientists as one of very few key realignment elections, was also a watershed race in terms of political advertising. Possibly the most emotion-charged of all American presidential races, 1896 was not only a struggle between candidates and parties but a clash of monetary ideologies and regional cultures. It was at once a glorious last hurrah for the politics of local participation and the dawn of a new age in the marketing of candidacies. Under the adept aegis of Marcus Alonzo Hanna, the McKinleyites waged the first truly modern, national campaign for the White House, with centralized control over fundraising and every aspect of promotional propaganda. Faced with an empty till and a hostile press, Bryan took to the rails to wage our first barnstorming appeal, traveling more than 18,000 miles to deliver 600 speeches to 5 million voters.

Perhaps the major 1896 innovation in political advertising owed less to evolving political culture than it did to simple Yankee ingenuity, for the celluloid campaign button made its debut in American politics that year. Developed in 1868 by two brothers seeking a substitute for ivory billiard balls, celluloid became our first commercially successful plastic, but for 25 years enjoyed limited use in the political process. Then in 1893, a patent was granted to Amanda Lougee of Boston for a clothing button with a textile surface covered with a thin layer of celluloid. By 1896, her patent was the property of the Whitehead & Hoag Company of Newark, NJ, and campaign lapel badges began to appear featuring a printed paper disk under celluloid set into a metal

collet with a fastening device. No other innovation in American political advertising gained acceptance so rapidly or on such a massive scale. Often wholesaling for a penny or less apiece, the celluloid button was much less expensive than any other type of lapel badge and much more durable. More than a thousand known varieties were produced to promote McKinley and Bryan in 1896, and within a few years all competing types of lapel badges were fading from the scene.

Next to the celluloid button, the most popular avenue of political advertising during the early years of the century was the penny postcard. Set free from a government monopoly in 1898, the postcard made its political debut in 1900, really caught on in 1904, attained the peak of its popularity in 1908, remained a very important avenue of partisan expression in 1912, and then declined dramatically (along with picture postcards for other purposes) as a result of the advent of the folded greeting card mailed in an envelope. During the 1908 contest between William Howard Taft and William Jennings Bryan, postcards were printed and used in several hundred varieties, including many intricate multicolored designs that rivaled and often replicated the most aesthetic of the celluloid buttons. Inexpensive and personally persuasive when mailed to a relative or friend, the postcard has remained a staple of American political advertising in local contests. Another promotional fad during this period was the political watchfob, very popular up to World War I but then doomed by the genesis of the wristwatch.

Perhaps the major innovation in political advertising during this period came in response to America's growing love affair with the automobile and the open road. In 1920, political decals were displayed in automobile windows and license plate attachments made their debut in 1924, the year that Calvin Coolidge's "Lincoln tour" motor caravan initiated motorized campaigning in the United States. Oilcloth coverings for spare tires enjoyed a vogue until after the 1932 campaign, when auto manufacturers began to store spare tires inside trunks. Bumper stickers, the advertising vehicle that rendered such pioneer accessories obsolete, did not make their debut until 1956, although nonadhesive prototypes were used as early as 1932. The political billboard made its debut alongside American highways in 1940, with one variety portraying a pretty little girl asking, "Daddy, what's a democracy?" and her father replying sagely, "It's America with Willkie!" Among the less noteworthy innovations in political advertising wrought by new technologies were 1920 electric glass window signs promoting James M. Cox and 1940 miniature "Hoosier Favorite/Willkie" airport wind socks.

Since the 1950s, the dominance of television and a continuing trend toward voter independence and apathy have contributed to a decline in traditional modes of political advertising. Buttons have become increasingly limited to the faithful who attend party rallies, caucuses, conventions, and inaugural celebrations, more collectibles than advertising artifacts. Throwaway stickers with no pins have become the vogue. In part, this trend is due to a growing introspection among Americans, a belief that their political persuasion is a private concern. This does much to explain a steadily increasing reliance upon bumper stickers for personal political advertising, for the bumper of an automobile driving on freeways or parked alongside curbs provides a cushion of anonymity a button on the lapel does not. The substitution of vinyl stickers that peel off easily for the old paper adhesive models requiring sandpaper or blowtorches has added to the public acceptance of bumper stickers.

Since the advent of Ike's dancing elephants in 1952, television has become the superhighway of American political advertising and, in the process, backroom operatives raised in the ethic of participatory party politics have given way to media experts with no roots in the political process. The 1960 contest between John Kennedy and Richard Nixon featured JFK's annihilation of Nixon in a series of four debates, but did not exhibit a mastery of the medium on either side for advertising purposes. The inherent meanness of television advertising, geared to slick visual exploitation and the limited attention span of the presumably prototypical voter, was first made manifest during a trio of Lyndon Johnson one-minute spots portraying Republican nominee Barry Goldwater as a real-life Dr. Strangelove in 1964. One featured hands tearing up a Social Security card. Another overlaid children with ice cream with a nuclear blast, a reminder of Goldwater's Senate vote against the nuclear nonproliferation accords. The third, probably the most devastating (and inherently unfair) commercial ever to air on American television, began with a pretty little girl plucking petals from a daisy and ended with the countdown for a nuclear detonation, with a stentorian voice-over suggesting that only Johnson could save the planet from evolving into a charred, radioactive cinder!

Savaged by public exposure and television in 1960, Richard Nixon utilized TV commercials to win the White House in 1968 through the genius of Republican media master Roger Ailes. While his opponent, Hubert Humphrey, endured the slings and arrows of unwashed activists, Nixon restricted his TV appearances to carefully staged forums with hand-picked participants reminiscent of a Pat Boone musicale. Ailes's commercials, meanwhile, featured visions of happy children riding tricycles, pert cheerleaders, idyllic sunsets, and productive minority workers juxtaposed against footage of riots in Chicago, street crime, and the lonely visage of a white woman in high heels shadowed down a deserted, rainy inner-city street by the sounds of menacing footsteps as the voice-over intoned solemnly, "Nixon *is* the America that you remember and long for again." Despite the protests raised by such media authorities as Joe McGinniss and political professionals raised to know the difference between right and wrong, the Ailes formula has become more the rule than the exception in recent campaigns. In 1972 Nixon was well served by a mix of television spots featuring him as a high-minded national statesman and opponent George McGovern as a reckless radical hell-bent on bankrupting the treasury with profligate social spending. The latter, done mainly by nominal Democrat John Connolly, attested to two salient trends in recent TV political advertising, a gathering nastiness and a tendency to shift the attack ads to sources not officially linked to the candidate, for purposes of deniability.

This trend was aided immensely by wholesale post-Watergate revisions in the 1971 Federal Election Campaign Act, a Supreme Court ruling, and subsequent congressional action which limited permissible campaign expenditures while increasing greatly the ability of independent political action committees (PACs) to spend money to influence elections. Unfettered by standards of civility and factual accuracy expected of a candidate and central campaign committee, PACs have given Americans some memorable 30- and 60-second television spots in recent years. This has dovetailed with, but also contributed to, an ongoing decline in voter confidence in both major parties, government at all levels from the court house to the White House, and the media. Jimmy Carter was served superbly in 1976 by Gerald Rafshoon's media message of the politics of hope and national renewal, but very poorly in 1980 by ads featuring on-the-street interviews with Californians who portrayed Ronald Reagan as a demented and dangerous fanatic from the far right fringe of our political spectrum. This attests to a truism in political advertising, that the best ads do little or nothing to change minds but much to reinforce existing beliefs and prejudices. Thus the most notorious "PAC attack" in recent times, the 1988 George Bush TV spot blaming Michael Dukakis for Willy Horton, a black felon on prison furlough who raped and murdered a woman, was less damaging in itself than was Dukakis's belated and unconvincing response, perceived as his "wimp factor" albatross. Only in 1992 did the pendulum begin to swing against such commercials, for at all levels utilizing television the purveyors of negativism did poorly.

Political advertising is by no means limited to campaigns for public office, as a plethora of TV and radio spots and print ads promoting or castigating NAFTA, universal health care reform, and the "Brady bill" for handgun control attests. In a political process that seems to run more from poll to poll than from term to term, advertising has become an almost daily part of American politics. From bucktails and twigs as hat ornaments through television, advertising has evolved hand in hand with, and often in advance of, the system of statecraft. Talk of possible voting by means of the Internet prompts speculation over the changes, both in political advertising and in government itself, to be wrought by the new interactive technologies.

Bibliography

Combs, James. *Polpop: Politics and Popular Culture in America.* Rev. ed. Bowling Green, OH: Bowling Green State U Popular P, 1991.

Diamond, Edwin, and Stephen Bates. *The Spot: The Rise of Political Advertising on Television.* 3d ed. Cambridge: MIT, 1992.

Fischer, Roger A. *Tippecanoe and Trinkets Too: The Material Culture of American Presidential Campaigns.* Urbana: U of Illinois P, 1988.

Jamieson, Kathleen Hall. *Packaging the Presidency: A History and Criticism of Presidential Campaign Advertising.* New York: Oxford UP, 1984.

McGinniss, Joe. *The Selling of the President, 1968.* New York: Penguin, 1969.

Roger Fischer

Political Cartoons are a form of visual-verbal commentary on topical, political, and social issues that appear in daily newspapers and some weekly magazines. By synergistically combining iconic, visual imagery and distilled, verbal commentary or dialogue, and employing various visual and literary tropes including satire, irony, symbolism, metaphor, allegory, exaggeration, parody, caricature, etc., these cartoons have the potential to entertain, provoke, or enlighten. In democratic societies with a free press, political cartoonists are often seen as watchdogs who can check the excesses of government and industry through trenchant satire and humiliating caricature. We may take for granted in the United States that these artists can practice their craft without fear of punishment, but there are many places in the world where satirists are regularly censored or punished for ridiculing public figures.

Although political cartoons are now a minor genre of visual entertainment, in the 18th and 19th centuries they had a much greater impact on political and social life, since they were one of the only sources of visual information for societies in which a large portion of the population was, to some degree, illiterate. In the United States in the 1870s, Thomas Nast (see entry)—considered by many to be the greatest American political cartoonist of the 19th century—toppled a corrupt political machine in New York City with his visual satire. So feared were these cartoonists by public officials, that several bills were introduced in state legislatures at the turn of the century which, if they had passed, would have banned political caricature.

With the rise in popularity of other visual media at the start of the 20th century such as film, comic strips, and television, political cartoons were no longer read as widely by everyday citizens, or feared as deeply by political figures. Although a few cartoonists such as Herblock and Garry Trudeau still succeed in enraging their targets and creating public debate with their work, political cartoons for the most part are now seen as a form of benign and entertaining commentary. Debate over the primary purpose of these cartoons—whether they should primarily be entertainment, or indignant, reformative satire (or some combination of these extremes)—continues in the field to this day.

Changes in printing technology have had a great impact on the evolution of political cartoons. In the 18th century the printing process for art—wood or metal engraving—was so laborious and time-consuming that large staffs of artists were employed to etch various sections of an original sketch onto small wood blocks that would later be joined to reconstruct the entire image. Visual satirists thus had difficulty addressing topical, day-to-day events, and creating a distinctive style. Editorial cartooning became much more topical and widespread when the technology of lithography was introduced into the United States in the 1830s. This allowed a single artist to draw directly onto a limestone slab with a crayon and have his image—after being treated chemically and applied with ink—transferred directly to the printed page. This streamlining of the craft helped to introduce a golden age of political cartooning in the latter half of the 19th century, in which newspapers and weekly, comic magazines peppered their pages with timely caricature and intricate, visual, political allegories. The introduction of photoengraving technology in 1915 further streamlined the reproduction process, allowing editors to shrink and manipulate images with greater ease. This simplification of the craft, combined with the introduction of national syndicates, put many small-town cartoonists and art technicians out of work. Since then, the genre has been dominated by well-paid, star cartoonists who work for large metropolitan papers and have their nationally oriented work syndicated to smaller-market papers. The ranks of professional political cartoonists have begun to dwindle in recent years as more and more papers, faced with growing financial pressures, opt to run inexpensive, syndicated cartoons rather than pay large salaries to staff cartoonists. The rise of new technologies such as the World Wide Web, which allows a cartoonist to bypass the mediations of editors and syndicates, promises to bring more changes to the medium.

Bibliography

Hess, Stephen, and Milton Kaplan. *The Ungentlemanly Art.* New York: Macmillan, 1975.

Murrel, William. *A History of American Graphic Humor, 1747-1865.* New York: Whitney Museum of American Art, 1933.

——. *A History of American Graphic Humors, 1865-1938.* New York: Whitney Museum of American Art, 1938.

Press, Charles. *The Political Cartoon.* Teaneck: Fairleigh Dickinson UP, 1981.

Kerry D. Soper

Polka Dances. The polka is a fast couple dance in 2/4 time or 4/4 cut time, with a heavy accent on the first beat of the measure. The basic characteristics are fast turns in closed dance position (1/2 turn per measure) using a two-step preceded by a hop (or lift) in each measure.

The music and songs are diverse, varying with ethnic background and instrumentation: accordion or concertina, tuba ("oompa" bands) or bass guitar (Mexican) or electric guitar, horns and/or woodwinds, keyboard, violin, harp, drums, and the African-American banjo. Some related dances are in 3/4 time: the Swedish hambo and polskas, the polka-mazurka, and Polish obereks.

The polka was originally a Czech peasant dance from Eastern Bohemia. Dance historians claim to have traced its invention to a specific hippity-hop half-step by a peasant girl on a Sunday in 1830 (*pulka* is Czech for "half-step"). In 1840, a dancing teacher from Prague exhibited the polka in Paris with tremendous success. It swept the Continent, challenging the waltz for dancing supremacy, and arrived in New York by 1844.

The polka became so pervasive in Europe—of course Germany and Poland, but also in Irish Ceili dances, Scandinavia, France, the Scottish skip-change step, and in various English and Spanish dances—that as it evolved as a folk dance in the United States there are now almost as many styles as there are dancers.

Many American adults objected to the sensuous, closed frontal dance hold, the fast solid polka beat, and heavy breathing of dancers (one reverend claimed to have witnessed several deaths by dancing), preferring genteel contras and quadrilles for their children—thus probably assuring the popularity of the polka and contributing to the decline of contras and quadrilles in the latter half of the 19th century.

The low point for polkas was reached with the introduction of 20th-century American dances: first the novelty ragtime dances, then the foxtrot, charleston, jitterbug (Lindy), tango and other Latin American dances, jazz, and rock 'n' roll. But the polka, popularized on television by Lawrence Welk and on radio by Frankie Yankovich, the Six Fat Dutchmen, and others, remained strong in German and Polish communities, especially at traditional wedding ceremonies and community festivals.

Finally, in the 1970s and 1980s country-western dancers rediscovered polkas and schottisches. They revised the steps to fit hoedowns and popular country and western tunes, often changing the closed dance position to nonpartnered line dances.

Bibliography

Casey, Betty. *Dance across Texas*. Austin: U of Texas P, 1985.

Harris, Jane A., Anne M. Pittman, and Marlys S. Waller. *Dance a While*. New York: Macmillan, 1988.

Stephenson, Richard M., and Joseph Iaccarino. The *Complete Book of Ballroom Dancing*. Garden City: Doubleday, 1980.

David R. Peterson

Popeye (1929-) first appeared as a comic strip character in cartoonist Elzie Crisler Segar's *Thimble Theatre*, a popular serial strip published in the *New York Evening Journal* since 1919. In 1933, Paramount Pictures produced the first animated Popeye cartoons for theater distribution, totaling 234 Popeye "theatrical shorts" by 1954. In September of 1956, these cartoons were televised for the first time on local television stations in New York and Chicago under syndication to Associated Artists Productions. When Los Angeles station KTLA introduced *Popeye the Sailor* in 1956, the series was hosted by cartoonist Tom Hatten. Following KTLA's successful format, in the late 1950s the syndicated series became associated across the nation with the personalities of its local television hosts, such as Buffalo's "Captain Bob." Consequently, by 1960, *Popeye the Sailor* was the No. 1 syndicated television cartoon, airing on some 150 stations nationwide. Between 1961 and 1963, King Features created an additional 220 cartoons produced specifically for television, appearing in combination with the original theatrical shorts in the retitled *Popeye* (syndicated 1961, King Features). Successful in syndication, Popeye did not appear on the national networks until the late 1970s when CBS aired the *All-New Popeye Hour* (1978-81), and the *Popeye and Olive Comedy Show* (1981-83). Both of these network series included new episodes produced by Hanna-Barbera for King Features after 1978. While the 1980 film musical *Popeye* (starring Robin Williams as Popeye and Shelley Duvall as Olive Oyl) was a box-office failure, Paramount still released it for the home video market in 1981 and 1989.

Photo courtesy of Popular Culture Library, Bowling Green State University, Bowling Green, OH.

From comic strip to network series to film, Popeye's adventures and exploits were most often rooted in an "eternal triangle." As landlocked but nonetheless love-starved sailors, Popeye and his disagreeable rival Brutus (Bluto) vied for the spurious attentions and affections of the rail-thin and pickle-nosed "beauty" Olive Oyl. As their episodic contests progressed from verbal sparring to physical fighting, Brutus had the advantages of greatly outsizing the scrawny Popeye and the willingness to use trickery and unfair tactics. However, just as Brutus seemed destined to win each match, Popeye would chug down his trademark can of spinach, giving the necessary strength to his multi-directional "twisker sock" wind-up punch to knock Brutus out of the running.

In the 1990s, Popeye was featured in two very different institutions in American life: the 1991 "Popeye Meets Warhol" Great American Comics Exhibit at Houston's Museum of Fine Arts, and the 1994 publication of the best-selling *Easy Piano Cartoon Tunes* by Hal Leonard. All across the country children of the 1990s are plinking out the melody and perhaps singing to themselves, "I yam what I yam, and that's all I yam, I'm Popeye the Sailor Man!"

Bibliography

Grandinetti, Fred. *Popeye: An Illustrated History of E. C. Segar Characters in Print, Radio, Television, and Film Appearances, 1929-1993*. Jefferson: McFarland, 1994.

Harvey, Robert C. *The Art of the Funnies: An Aesthetic History*. Jackson: UP of Mississippi, 1994.

London, Bobby. *Mondo Popeye*. New York: St. Martin's, 1988.

Sagendorf, Bud. *Popeye: The First Fifty Years*. New York: Workman, 1979.

Pam Steinle

Popular Culture Association, The (1970-), was founded by a group of academics unhappy over the direction being taken by other academic groups in the study of everyday life in America and around the world. The founders consisted of Carl Bode, Ray B. Browne (who became and remained Secretary/Treasurer), John G. Cawelti, Marshall W. Fishwick, and Russel B. Nye. All believed that in a democracy, academics should study democratic institutions as evidenced in everyday activities. To these academics, popular culture meant all aspects of culture, including, but not limited to, entertainment. At first felt as a threat to conventional academia, the Popular Culture Association grew rapidly and served as a catalyst to other areas in the humanities and social sciences to include everyday culture in their interests. The PCA was immensely successful in rounding out fields of interest and studies in all levels of education. The PCA has always been housed at Bowling Green State University, Bowling Green, OH 43403. The association publishes the quarterly *Journal of Popular Culture* (see entry).

Bibliography

Browne, Ray B. *Against Academia.* Bowling Green, OH: Bowling Green State U Popular P, 1989.

Peter Rollins

Popular Press, The (1970-   ), was established as the publishing arm of the Center for the Study of Popular Culture at Bowling Green State University, with Ray B. Browne as Director, and Pat Browne as Editor (now Director). In 1970, virtually no academic press would publish any material on popular culture, so the Popular Press, though *de facto* the Bowling Green State University Press, faced serious problems, not in getting manuscripts but in marketing the finished books. But working with the membership of the newly established Popular Culture Association, the Popular Press demonstrated to the world at large that materials of everyday culture, in the U.S. and abroad, were of interest to and value for academics throughout their institutions. By 1995, nearly every press in the U.S. had begun devoting large percentages of their production to popular culture subjects. What had originally been a single voice in a large industry became in fact only one of hundreds.

Bibliography

Browne, Ray B. *Against Academia.* Bowling Green, OH: Bowling Green State U Popular P, 1989.

Peter Rollins

Porches, Patios, and Decks. In most of the world's cultures and for as long as human beings have constructed dwellings, outdoor living space has been part of the basic domicile. Traditionally, the external living space has been a practical necessity, a place of community ritual, or a combination of the two. While the porches, patios, stoops, verandahs, and decks of United States vernacular architecture are, like their predecessors, practical adjuncts of the primary structure and ritual spaces, their significance and history are peculiarly American.

Although an actual history of attached outdoor living structures in North America has yet to be written, such spaces have always been included in its dwellings. Even before European exploration began, certain non-nomadic Indian civilizations such as the Mississippian tribes sheltered the area outside their front doors for work and built edifices with porch-like extensions for religious rituals. Most of those cultures, however, were vanishing before colonization and therefore would have had little influence on early European-American porches and porticos. The earliest European manifestation of an American porch area seems to have been the patios or courts of Spanish Colonial dwellings in Florida and Southwest North America. But the most significant influences on early outdoor living extensions in the rest of the country seem to have been English and French colonials and the African slaves who arrived on this continent by way of the Caribbean.

The most pervasive, the most American, and the most enduring outdoor living space seems to be the front porch. By front porch, most people mean a roofed structure attached to and extending across much of the front of a building, supported on the public side by two or more posts or columns. From the 1830s through the 1930s, such structures were attached to nearly every dwelling built in the U.S. and to many public establishments as well. In the Southeast, however, where high temperature and high humidity made exterior living space for work and leisure necessary through much of the year, such structures antedate the Victorian front porch by many years.

The American front porch is a truly multicultural development. Research has shown that the earliest North American colonial front porches were probably built onto the fronts of basic cabins by African slaves, who brought the idea from Haiti. Architectural evidence suggests that these structures were later imitated by whites who themselves needed the fresh air and work space. Roughly contemporary with the development of the traditional front porch in the central southern states were the galleries in Louisiana and South Carolina. In parts of those states, the French-inspired gallery—surrounding the Acadian style house; the second-story galleries of New Orleans row houses; and those that run alongside the first floor (above the ground floor) of early Charleston houses—provided the outdoor living space. The porticoes on Monticello and the buildings Thomas Jefferson designed for the University of Virginia are very much European, but George Washington's Mount Vernon could derive as much from the porch on the slave cabins as from the French galleries and Graeco-Roman tradition. In part because of its culturally diverse origins, the front porch is considered by many to be the most American of all vernacular structures.

Throughout their heyday, front porches served both practical and social functions. While the homes of 19th- and early 20th-century people of means had back porches, breezy outdoor work spaces in which chores could be done and hygiene seen to, working-class houses often had one door and one porch. Thus for many early Americans the front porch served as laundry, cannery, workshop, reception room, summer bedroom, and washroom. For the moderately affluent, the front porch was social and public, the back porch private and functional. For the rest, the front porch was all of the above, relying on knowledge of social codes to protect occupants from undue exposure during private rituals. Porches were considered to be so necessary in those decades that few dwellings were built without them and they were added to houses that had been clean and spare across the front; houses without porches became the rare exception.

In the Southeast, porches were also integral parts of public spaces. Every store had its porch where the men could both enjoy the breeze and shoot it while their wives shelled peas on the one at home. Downtown commercial buildings, in the South, had offices upstairs which could be reached by external steps to the ubiquitous second-floor galleries. And courthouses, churches, and banks were seldom constructed without some version of the be-columned front portico.

No discussion of outdoor living space would be complete without attention to the stoops on row houses in the cities of New England and the midatlantic states. Since these houses, almost flush with the sidewalk, had no room for outdoor living space, their residents commandeered the stoops to serve the ritual social function the front porch served in roomier rural areas: neighborhood gathering places, cooler spots less isolated than the indoors for light portable work, sites for conducting disagreeable business with people who would be unwelcome in the sanctity of the home.

The century of the American porch was also notable for the forms devised for ever more external living space. The front and back porches were joined by other outdoor accouterments. Second-floor galleries extending around most of the house and balconies, often tucked under the roof of a columned front porch on the Big Houses of the Deep South, provided "air conditioned" comfort for members of the household who wished to avoid the public space downstairs. The sleeping porch made its debut in the 19th century and stayed around to be screened and touted for its health-giving properties in the 1920s and '30s. Screen porches themselves on any or all sides of the houses became necessary outdoor rooms as soon as screen was available.

In the 1930s, perhaps in part because of tight money and a new respect for streamlined functionality in all design, porches began to disappear. At first, they retreated to the side and behind the houses. With the increased availability of the telephone and the gradual extension of car ownership to the less affluent classes, the front porch as a social institution ceased to be necessary. The advent of air conditioning made hot weather endurable without porches, and television began to obviate the need for frequent social contact. Porches added expense in a culture that began to look on home ownership as a right and sought ways to build houses for less; thus, they were less likely to be built on new houses. And because porches were the most expensive and difficult parts of any structure to maintain, they were often removed from older houses as well.

For a time in the mid-20th century, outdoor living space almost disappeared from North American homes (the exception being southwestern patios), but citizens of the United States would not be kept indoors for festive occasions. Thus, in the 1950s, patios and decks began to sprout up all over the country. By this time, privacy had become a primary concern, so that these new external structures were at the back—occasionally on the side—of the house and sheltered by extended walls, fences, or hedgerows. The space was no longer a place for casual entertaining but open only to invited guests who went through the house to arrive at the event. Patios can be distinguished from decks in that they are actual extensions of the house (and are often surrounded on two or three sides by it) and are constructed of the same materials; decks are invariably wood and are usually added

on. Even when decks are part of the original building plan, they are separate structures attached to the house—seldom if ever integral parts of it. Decks and patios rarely have roofs, although screening and covering those spaces has become increasingly widespread.

Decks and patios suggest more active leisure activities than do porches. Decks particularly seem to be the domain of the male who has often built them—as a leisure time activity—and who operates the barbecue and the portable bar with which they are furnished. Decks and patios are appropriate places for entertaining business associates.

For several decades, decks and patios have dominated suburban life, but the American South never completely gave up the porch. The Southern ranch houses of the last half of the 20th century usually featured small nonfunctional porches. Usually no wider than four feet, they were furnished for display rather than for use. Often such "porches" are furnished with antiques—a churn, a bench, even an old rocker. But the porches—even the front doors—are not used. People enter the air-conditioned house from the carport.

While porches, patios, decks, stoops, and verandahs are themselves significant American cultural entities, they are also signifiers in other media. A front porch on a house in a movie, book, or television program indicates gracious living, innocence, simpler times, and usually the South or the West. In *To Kill a Mockingbird* (1962), for example, Atticus tells his children the facts of Southern life and the obligation of the judicial system on a porch swing. In cities, outdoor living space and a sense of community are wrested from the unforgiving concrete; in *Do the Right Thing* (1989), stoops are commandeered for community communication. Private but often loud family business can be conducted on upstairs galleries, as in *Cat on a Hot Tin Roof* (1958) and *The Long Hot Summer* (1958).

Patios and decks in the media, however, usually suggest lost innocence and marketplace values. Poolside patios in California are homes equally to displays of scantily clad flesh and nefarious business dealings. Hollywood moguls court starlets and cut raw deals with equal zeal, and private eyes such as Columbo gain egress to unappealing people and information through patio doors. In the media, decks signify the aspiring middle class, immoderate alcohol consumption, and small regard for the natural environment.

There will always be decks, patios, courts and verandahs, but Americans seem unwilling to give up the front porch as a symbol of neighborliness, community, and gracious living. In the late 1980s, porches began to make a comeback. Communities in regions as varied as Florida, New England, and the upper Midwest are recommending— in some cases requiring—that new houses be built with front porches. The rationale seems to be that such public/ private space encourages a sense of community and, in a few cases, that even the possibility that someone may be occupying the porch could discourage crime. The most important reason, however, is that stressed-out Americans seem to be trying to recapture a lost innocence and sense of openness that only outdoor living space on the front of the house can provide.

Bibliography
Beckham, Sue Bridwell. "The American Front Porch: Women's Liminal Space." *Making the American Home*. Ed. Marilynn Motz and Pat Browne. Bowling Green, OH: Bowling Green State U Popular P, 1989.
——. "The Front Porch: A Legacy of American Cultural Plurality." *The World and I* 7 (1992).
Caspar, Dale E. *A Review of Decks, Patios, and Other Outside Construction Projects in the 1980s*. Monticello: Vance Bibliographies, 1987.
Kahn, Renee. *Porches*. Washington: Preservation P, 1986.
Vlach, John Michael. "Architecture." *The Afro-American Tradition in Decorative Arts*. Cleveland: Cleveland Museum of Art, 1970.

Sue Bridwell Beckham

Porgy and Bess (1935), the American opera by George and Ira Gershwin and DuBose Heyward, is acknowledged as a major cultural artifact. It is a mirror of African-American social history which, in spite of its many successes, has generated remarkable controversy.

Porgy and Bess focuses on an urban black community residing on Catfish Row in Charleston, SC, around the turn of the century. Written as a novel, *Porgy*, in 1925, by DuBose Heyward, the story is simple. Porgy, a crippled beggar who transports himself in a goat-drawn cart, falls in love with Bess, a "fallen woman" dominated by the powerful Stevedore Crown. Crown kills Robbins, one of the town residents, in the course of a crap game and flees. When he returns for his woman, Bess, he himself is killed in a fight with Porgy. While Porgy is in jail, Bess is enticed to New York by a flashy urban gambler, Sportin' Life. Porgy heads off to New York in search of Bess.

The first New York production of *Porgy and Bess* opened at the Alvin Theatre. Todd Duncan and Anne Brown sang the leading roles, with John Bubbles, Georgette Harvey, Abbie Mitchell, Ruby Elzy, J. Rosamond Johnson, and Helen Dowdy in smaller roles. Just days after the opening, it became apparent that there would not be a run at the box office. The show closed after 124 performances and was taken on the road.

George Gershwin never saw the first revival of his opera on the West Coast in early 1938, again with Todd Duncan and Anne Brown starring and Meryl Armitage producing. In January of 1942, Cheryl Crawford produced a second revival. With Duncan and Brown as Porgy and Bess, this production was cut down and streamlined, becoming a critical and financial success.

The third major revival was the Blevins Davis/Robert Breen production in 1952. William Warfield now played Porgy with Leontyne Price as Bess and Cab Calloway as Sportin' Life. To rave reviews it returned to play 305 performances in New York City. In 1954 this company, with Martha Flowers as Bess, Le Vern Hutcherson as Porgy, and Maya Angelou as Ruby, returned to Europe to play at La Scala in Milan and in 1955-56 in the Middle East, Latin America, and Russia.

The 1959 film, starring Sidney Poitier, Dorothy Dandridge, Sammy Davis, Jr., Pearl Bailey, Brock Peters, and produced by Otto Preminger, was a commercial failure. During the sixties, producer Ella Gerber put on 21 different productions worldwide. In 1976, under the direction of Jack O'Brien, the Houston Grand Opera put on an uncut version of the opera with Donnie Ray Albert as Porgy and Clamma Dale as Bess. Finally in 1986, the opera had its fullest and most faithful rendition since its 1935 premiere: in Boston at the Metropolitan Opera House. Starring Simon Estes and Grace Bumbry, the opera was heralded as the ultimate establishment embrace of the work.

Ironically, *Porgy and Bess* mirrors in many ways the history of blacks in America: its hybrid and dynamic nature, its tenacity in the face of countless successes and failures, its gradual acceptance into legitimate society, and its tentative embrace by the very society out of which it emerged and matured. The social and political implications of *Porgy and Bess* for the African-American community are very real: some see it as a positive example of integration and discovery, while others view it negatively as a white interpretation of black culture that was patronizing and degrading. *Porgy and Bess* provided its performers unprecedented opportunities to display their talents and, in the process, change some attitudes.

Bibliography
Alpert, Hollis. *The Life and Times of* Porgy and Bess: *The Story of an American Classic*. New York: Knopf, 1990.
Dizikes, John. *Opera in America: A Cultural History*. New Haven: Yale UP, 1993.

William Shea

Porno for Pyros. Formed from the ashes of Jane's Addiction, Porno for Pyros is the incarnation of vocalist Perry Farrell's rock and roll notions. Farrell was born Simon Bernstein in Queens, NY, and lived on Long Island and in Miami before moving to Southern California, where he took a job in a vitamin factory. After giving that up, Farrell began lip-synching at a Newport Beach bar.

Farrell's first group, Psi-Com, only released a tape and an LP in 1984 and 1985. As that group broke up, Farrell went about forming Jane's Addiction with Dave Navarro (guitar), Eric Avery (bass), and Stephen Perkins (drums). The group released a live album in 1987 and their first studio LP, *Nothing's Shocking*, in 1988. Although Jane's Addiction remained a cult and college radio success and *Nothing's Shocking* was nominated for a Grammy, the group's real success came with the follow-up album, *Ritual de lo Habitual*, which eventually sold more than a million copies with its punchy production and multi-mooded songs.

Jane's Addiction ended not long after the event that really launched "alternative" music's stranglehold on no less than half a million concert fans in the summer of 1991: Lollapalooza. Dreamed up by Jane's Addiction's booking agent Marc Geiger and drummer Stephen Perkins, the traveling festival was inspired by the U.K.'s Reading Festival, an annual three-day festival of music. Farrell lined up the Butthole Surfers, Ice-T, Living Colour, Sioxsie and the Banshees, the Rollins Band, and Jane's Addiction. After the 21-city tour, a few more shows, and a final performance in the buff in Hawaii, Farrell declared Jane's Addiction through.

Together with drummer Perkins, Farrell recruited guitarist Peter DiStefano, and bassist Martyn LeNoble, and put together the group named after an occasion when a fireworks flyer was found in a magazine advertising triple-X-rated S&M videos. The group's self-titled LP was released in 1993, with the first single, "Orgasm," released exclusively to strip clubs throughout the U.S. *Good God's Urge* was released in 1996.

Bibliography

Arnold, Gina. *Route 666: On the Road to Nirvana*. New York: St. Martin's, 1993.

Handelman, David. "Jane's Addiction." *Rolling Stone* 7 Feb. 1991: 68-71.

Robbins, Ira. *The Trouser Press Record Guide*. New York: Collier, 1991.

Hugh Foley

Pornography is a term ambiguous in both origin and meaning. The term is normally used to indicate sexual material that the speaker/writer finds objectionable. Most people would use the word "erotica" to refer to sexual materials of which they do not disapprove. The most non-pejorative usage is to define "pornography" as the explicit depiction of sexual organs and sexual practices for the purposes of entertainment or sexual arousal. In this sense, pornography is virtually universal, although often limited to the upper classes. Graphic depiction of sexual organs and acts can be found in prehistoric caves; ancient Greek and Roman writings such as those of Aristophanes, Catullus, Horace, Ovid, and Petronius were often erotic; sexual intercourse is featured on the walls of the brothel at Pompeii; and Roman sculptures of the god Priapus were common, apparently used as good luck charms. During the Middle Ages pornography was widespread. It is found in Chaucer, the French farces of the 14th and 15th centuries, the arts of Renaissance Florence, and Elizabethan ballads and poetry. Some non-Western cultures have an even stronger erotic content, as evidenced by *The Thousand and One Nights* and the *Kama Sutra*. Several non-Western religions, most notably Tantra, are highly sexual when viewed by the non-believer.

Although explicit sexual portrayals are ubiquitous, their treatment in art, literature, and law changed significantly between the Renaissance and the French Revolution. The primary force underlying the change was the increased availability of erotic material to the masses as a result of the invention of the printing press and the resultant growth of literacy. The rediscovery of the sexual materials of the Greeks and Romans also played a role. Prior to the 16th century, sexually explicit material was designed primarily for the social elite. Pornography emerged as a distinct societal concern as it became part of mass popular culture. As the audience for sexually explicit materials increased, its character changed. Earlier erotic works had intertwined sexual material with other elements such as religion and politics. The pattern continued in the early modern pornographic age. Although the ideological use of sexually explicit material continued into the 17th and 18th centuries, and is still used today, a new form had become dominant by 1660. The development was so dramatic, and took place in such a brief period, that some scholars refer to it as "the invention of pornography."

The new pornography was different in being sex-centered: its hallmark was the self-conscious aim of arousing sexual desire in the reader. Although it was not without political, social, or religious content, pornography now presented amoral sexual gratification as a clear alternative to traditional values. Sometimes it was necessary to disguise the message by pretending to catalog sexual perversions that should be avoided, but the impact of the presentation of the perversions was so great that the admonition was obliterated. (The process was repeated again in the 1960s and 1970s to try to give adult movies "redeeming social significance.")

The standard pornographic form, a dialogue between whores, was established by Pietro Aretino's *Ragionamenti* (1534-36). It was to be the dominant form of prose pornography for over two centuries. The form was overshadowed, but not completely replaced, by the new novel form which developed in mainstream literature in the 18th century. Although there were several major earlier French publications, the novel which defined the new pornographic genre was John Cleland's *Fanny Hill* (1748-49; see entry).

The next stage in the development of the early modern pornographic tradition was the work of the Marquis de Sade, which has been characterized as the ultimate reductio ad absurdum of pornography: the annihilation of the body in the name of desire. Sade intended his work as a philosophical critique of the Enlightenment, but is best remembered for his catalog of bizarre, violent sexual practices: his *120 Days of Sodom* listed more than 600.

The development of the new concept of pornography can be seen in the invention or re-creation of the term itself. Etymologically, the term is grounded in ancient Greek, and was used in French, in 1769, in the classical sense to refer to writing about prostitutes and prostitution. However, the word *pornography* appeared for the first time in its new usage in the *Oxford English Dictionary* in 1857. The 1864 edition of *Webster's Dictionary* also contained a definition of "pornography."

It is impossible to discuss pornography in the Western world without discussing censorship. Early censorship was aimed at the anti-clerical aspects of pornography and only incidentally at the sexual. Heresy, blasphemy, treason, and sedition were severely punished. Sexually explicit representations alone were not. Sir Charles Sedley's conviction (1663) is often cited as the first obscenity conviction. However, he was actually prosecuted for getting drunk, removing his clothes, uttering profane remarks, and pouring urine on a crowd of onlookers.

Apparently the common law courts in 17th- and 18th-century England viewed obscenity as only actionable in ecclesiastical courts. Probably the first true obscenity conviction was Edmund Curll's 1727 conviction for the publication of his *Venus in the Cloister, or the Nun in Her Smock*. While it could be argued that the conviction was designed to protect religion, that is unlikely since the work was anti-clerical in a regime which was also anti-clerical. The obscenity prosecution of John Wilkes in 1770 for his *Essay on Woman* was also politically motivated.

The history of the English experience with sexually explicit materials is largely paralleled by the American experience. The first real obscenity case in the United States was *Commonwealth v. Sharpless* in 1815. Six years later, the first true American obscenity law was passed and the first major obscenity trial (involving *Fanny Hill*) was held. There were no significant federal prosecutions until 1873, when Anthony Comstock persuaded Congress to pass a federal anti-obscenity statute. The first major Supreme Court decision on obscenity was *Roth v. United States* (1957). The case, and its progeny, are grounded in the belief that it is possible to formulate a legal mechanism capable of distinguishing between erotica and erotic realism on the one hand (which some perceive as beneficial to society) and obscenity on the other hand (which is perceived as harmful to society). Implicit in the Court's formulation is an assumption that the artistic quality, style, context, etc., of a sexually explicit presentation mitigate its presumed negative impact. Thus, the current formulation (*Miller v. California*, 1973) allows a jury to weigh the artistic and social value of a sexually explicit item against its offensiveness to local community norms.

Social conservatives have always challenged the assumption that sexually explicit materials could be saved by their artistic quality or social value. From their perspective, the capacity of explicit sexual materials to corrupt and deprave the members of society, especially the most susceptible members, is the overriding factor. Sexually explicit materials, they argue, are *per se* harmful and must be suppressed.

In the last two decades some feminists have organized against sexually explicit material based on the belief that pornography, which they distinguish from erotica, objectifies females and is harmful. While feminists are far from monolithic in their views on the issue, many are suspicious of the art-pornography distinction and would outlaw any representation that they perceive as objectifying and degrading women. Efforts to modify the law in the United States to reflect this view have been rebuffed by the Supreme Court. The Court has maintained a distinction between pornography—which some characterize as erotica and erotica realism—and obscenity—defined as hardcore pornography which has no redeeming artistic, medical, or social value. Canada, on the other hand, not bound by a history of First Amendment jurisprudence, has accepted the feminist formulation of pornography and the underlying assumption that it causes social harm. The result has been censorship of items that are widely available in the United States. Ironically, Canadian authorities have confiscated feminist literature in disproportionate numbers.

The controversy over the definition and regulation of pornography is likely to continue because it reflects values about the appropriate role of sexuality, sexual practices, and gender roles in society.

Bibliography

Hunt, Lynn, ed. *The Invention of Pornography*: *Obscenity and the Origins of Modernity, 1500–1800*. Cambridge: MIT P, 1993.

Kendrick, Walter M. *The Secret Museum*: *Pornography in Modern Culture*. New York: Viking, 1987.

Wagner, Peter. *Eros Revived: Erotica of the Enlightenment in England and America*. London: Secker & Warburg, 1988.

William E. Brigman

See also
Deep Throat
Production Code/Ratings System

Portable Radio. As wireless telegraph and telephone systems were commercialized in the United States during the first two decades of the 20th century, ship-to-shore messages and other private communications ("radio-grams") dominated the new medium. Often with homemade receivers and transmitters, youthful amateurs eavesdropped on these transmissions and communicated with each other. Sometimes they built compact sets that could be taken along on picnics and camping trips. Although called "portable wireless," these sets needed wires for operation—a ground connection and antenna—and could be heard only through headphones. A few manufacturers, notably Hunt and McCree of New York, sold portable wireless outfits to amateurs during this era (pre-1921), but the genre had a minuscule market.

With the advent of commercial entertainment broadcasting in late 1920, radio receivers began to enter American homes by the millions. Technical developments like the vacuum tube, which amplified feeble signals, allowed radios with horn speakers to become a focal point of evening social activities.

Powered by batteries, the pre-1927 home radio was somewhat portable. Thus a few adventurers took them along in place of portable phonographs on automobile excursions. Recognizing an interest in "outdoor" radios, some companies began to sell sets designed to be portable; their features included handles, rugged carrying cases, built-in speakers and battery compartments, and a "loop" antenna that at last freed the portable radio from ground and antenna connections. But because of the many vagaries of reception in the country, the portable radio's market shrank quickly and disappeared. As a result, few true portables were marketed between 1926 and 1939.

The first portable radios of essentially modern design were the Operadio 2 (1923), the Westburr Six (1923), and the Zenith Companion (1924). Anticipating a boom, more than a dozen other companies were soon selling portable radios. The best-performing sets, like the Operadio 2, weighed around 30 pounds with batteries; one bemused observer of the time remarked that such radios were about as portable as a steamer trunk. These state-of-the-art portables, usually with 6 tubes, cost a princely $200 or so.

Beginning in the late '20s a few companies such as Motorola offered add-on car radios. Soon these products enjoyed great success. In 1935 alone, more than 1 million add-on car radios were sold by 43 companies at $30 to $70 each. By the end of the decade, 20 percent of cars rolling off Detroit's assembly lines had built-in radios. In this specialized guise, the portable radio—more mobile than portable—thrived.

In early 1939, radio makers quickly brought to market a new generation of portables that made it possible for Americans, wherever they were, to monitor the progress of the new apocalypse.

By 1940, manufacturers began to offer $20 sets in camera-style plastic or metal cases weighing about 6 pounds—small enough to slip into a coat pocket. Portable radios did appeal to consumers in the pre-war years, and nearly four million were sold before civilian radio production was halted in April 1942.

During the post-war years, an astonishing variety of portables was sold by more than four dozen manufacturers, ranging from the Belmont Boulevard, the world's first radio small enough to slip into a shirt pocket, to the Zenith Transoceanic, a suitcase-size multiband receiver. The most popular models (at $20 to $50) were about the size of a lunch box, with cases of colorful plastic, which could be either plugged into house current or used with batteries. With their sporty, carefree image, these sets especially appealed to younger Americans, becoming a "must have" for college students. Portable radios, symbol of leisure, were also the perfect gift for Americans of all ages. More than 15 million post-war portables, all based on the technology of the vacuum tube, were sold before the appearance, in late 1954, of the first transistor radio.

The world's first transistor radio—the Regency TR-1, a 4-transistor shirt-pocket set—was the result of a collaboration between transistor-maker Texas Instruments and I.D.E.A., a small electronics company. Manufactured in Indianapolis, IN, the Regency TR-1 was put on sale in time for Christmas 1954 (at $49.95 plus earplug and carrying case). During the following two years, every American radio company added transistor portables to their lines.

In late 1957, the Japanese company SONY exported a shirt pocket transistor radio to the United States. The SONY TR-63, priced at $39.95, was soon followed by a host of Japanese clones. The market for these tinny, tiny sets came from the generation gap created when rock 'n' roll entered the airwaves in 1955 and 1956. The small transistor radio with earplug turned out to be the ideal solution to the battle over what music would be played in the home. During the 1960s and 1970s, inexpensive shirt-pocket radios remained a staple radio of youth, usually a child's first set. (Often the electronics were installed in objects that did not resemble radios, such as stuffed animals, plastic Coke bottles, and watches.)

As FM stations playing rock 'n' roll took to the air in the late 1960s and early 1970s, manufacturers responded with briefcase-size plastic radios that had big speakers and impressive sound. Some even had built-in cassette tape recorders. These sets were especially favored by inner-city youth who, playing them outdoors, used them as status symbols. Manufacturers responded by creating even larger sets nicknamed "boom boxes" (see entry) and "ghetto blasters," many with colorful light displays and stereo sound.

The SONY Walkman (see entry), introduced in 1979, expanded the market for tiny portables. The original Walkman was simply a play-only tape recorder, but radios were quickly added. The Walkman's major innovation was miniaturized headphones that allowed music, even classical music, to sound fairly good. In the 1980s, companies based around the globe flooded the market with Walkman clones, and American consumers responded with gusto, buying tens of millions yearly (although none were made in the United States).

Today, to meet the portable radio "needs" of every class of consumer, radio companies sell an amazing array of receivers, some with built-in cassette or compact disc players. Other portable electronic products increasing in popularity, such as cellular phones and pocket televisions, are simply the most recent extension of portable radio technology.

Bibliography

Braun, Ernest, and Stuart MacDonald. *Revolution in Miniature: The History and Impact of Semiconductor Electronics Re-Explored in an Updated and Revised Second Edition.* Cambridge: Cambridge UP, 1982.

Douglas, Susan J. *Inventing American Broadcasting, 1899-1922.* Baltimore: Johns Hopkins UP, 1987.

Schiffer, Michael Brian. *The Portable Radio in American Life.* Tucson: U of Arizona P, 1991.

Michael Brian Schiffer

Portable Televisions. In the early days of television, the television set was a cumbersome (and expensive) piece of equipment, typically found in the living room. As television replaced radio as a family pastime, the television set became the "hearth" around which the family gathered.

As technology advanced, tubes were replaced by transistors and then circuit boards. Television sets became less cumbersome, less expensive, and more portable. American television homes acquired multiple television sets. As the choice of programming expanded and the purchase of portable TVs more widespread, family members left the hearth to adjourn to individual rooms to watch the programming of individual choice.

Changes in the nature of the "console," primarily projection screens and stereo receivers, occasionally brought the family back to the hearth for special events. The migration away from the hearth was also temporarily slowed by the introduction of VCRs, but soon VCRs became less expensive and multiple VCRs joined multiple TVs in the American home. The migration was again temporarily reversed by the increased availability of cable. But as the cost of multiple cable hookups decreased, multiple TVs in the home were hooked up. Thus, sales of portable TVs have grown significantly. In 1997, portables sold almost twice as many units as consoles and stereo sets.

The use of adapters to permit television receivers to run on direct current (batteries), rather than on alternating current, made television portable outside the home as well as in. Thus, television watching moved to the backyard and the beach and even to the car on the way.

Despite advances made in technology, the bulkiest component of the television receiver has remained the picture tube. The picture tube of a television is a cathode ray tube, comprising an evacuated tube filled with fluorescent gas. A heated cathode emits a straight beam of fast-moving electrons, which are deflected by electromagnets to scan the screen. When the electrons hit the screen, the kinetic energy (energy of motion) is converted into radiant energy (light).

New hand-held televisions use a liquid crystal display (LCD), rather than the traditional cathode ray tube (CRT), giving a new meaning to portability. Now, the television set truly goes everywhere. Commuters watch the news while on the train; sports fans watch instant replays even as they watch the game live. And wrist-watch television sets permit them to watch as surreptitiously as possible.

Bibliography

Broadcasting & Cable Yearbook 1999. New Providence: Bowker, 1999.

Claire Koegler

Porter, Cole (1891-1964), sophisticated and creative genius of American musicals and popular music, set a high standard in all he produced. Possibly his most typical musical is his last Broadway show, *Silk Stockings* (1955), based on a 1939 movie comedy, *Ninotchka,* which starred Greta Garbo. There is plenty of comedy and romance in the show, along with layers of sophistication and the portrayal of life at the top of society. This is normal Cole Porter. Complex, polished, sophisticated, often risqué, and often dealing with the world of high society into which Porter was born and which he inhabited all his life, *Silk Stockings* reflected his values and lifestyle. Also like most Porter shows, there was one outstanding song, "All of You," while the rest of the music was less memorable.

Another typical Porter score was the one he wrote for the 1956 film *High Society*. Based on *The Philadelphia Story*, about the upper classes in that city, the film starred Bing Crosby and Grace Kelly, herself from the world of high society. Its one notable song was the romantic ballad "True Love." This was to be Porter's last hit song, for Porter's final two efforts, the 1957 film *Les Girls* and the 1958 television special *Aladdin*, produced nothing exceptional. The failure of Porter's final two scores to leave us anything extraordinary was not just the result of advancing age and serious illness, but also somewhat due to the style of song he relished and emphasized. The average American seems to have reacted coolly to the bulk of Porter's patrician and urbane songs. His best compositions were well received by all, but much of his work was not suited to general tastes.

Cole Albert Porter was born in Peru, IN. The only surviving child, he was given the best of everything—a loving but overprotective family, a fine education including piano and violin lessons, and overall the good life. After attending an elite private academy in Worcester, MA, he enrolled at Yale University. In addition to the normal academics, he was involved with a glee club, producing college shows, and writing songs. He had dabbled with songwriting at an early age, and while at Yale produced his first song of note, "The Bull Dog" (1911). This fight song is still in the extensive repertory of the university. He then attended Harvard Law School for a while before changing to the Harvard School of Music. While he was studying composition, piano, and music theory at Harvard, two of his songs appeared in Broadway musicals in 1915. His "Two Big Eyes," with words by John Golden, was part of Jerome Kern's *Miss Information*, and his "Esmeralda" was part of Sigmund Romberg's *Hands Up.*

In 1916, Porter wrote his first score for a musical, *See America First*. He also assisted in writing the lyrics, but the show was a flop and Porter felt disgraced. He retreated to Europe for several years. In 1920, he returned to writing Broadway musicals. After contributing to several forgettable productions, Porter wrote his first full score (words and music) in 1928. *Paris* included his first notable song in a musical, "Let's Do It."

That moderately successful production was followed in 1929 by a somewhat more successful show, *Fifty Million Frenchmen*, which featured one of Porter's fine standards, "You Do Something to Me." A slightly less successful show of 1929, *Wake Up and Dream*, included another standard, "What Is This Thing Called Love?" The next notable Porter musical, *Gay Divorcée* (1932), featured "Night and Day," perhaps his best song.

Porter's best musical of the 1930s was *Anything Goes* (1934). The show ran for more than 400 performances (no previous Porter musical had done so) and starred Ethel Merman, who was to be in subsequent Porter shows. It was one of the few Porter musicals to have several top songs: "Blow Gabriel, Blow," "You're the Top," "I Get a Kick Out of You," and the title song. There were two screen versions of *Anything Goes*, 1936, starring Merman, and 1956, starring Bing Crosby and Mitzi Gaynor.

Lesser musicals of the 1930s included: *Jubilee* (1935), a flop that had two famous Porter songs, the intriguing dance piece "Begin the Beguine" and the love ballad "Just One of Those Things"; *Red, Hot and Blue!* (1936), which introduced "It's De-Lovely" (an example of over-contrived lyrics); *Born to Dance* (1936), Porter's first movie score, which included another standard, "I've Got You under My Skin"; *Rosalie* (1937), his second film score, which included the title song and "In the Still of the Night"; *Leave It to Me* (1938), which featured "My Heart Belongs to Daddy"; and *Du Barry Was a Lady* (1939), which, although running almost as long as *Anything Goes* had a lesser score (its best songs were "Friendship" and "Do I Love You," neither of which are classics).

The next significant Porter songs were "You'd Be So Nice to Come Home To" from the 1943 film *Something to Shout About* and "Don't Fence Me In," a very good Western song introduced by Roy Rogers in the 1944 movie *Hollywood Canteen*. The song was revived by Rogers in the 1945 film *Don't Fence Me In*. In 1948, Porter produced his stage masterpiece, *Kiss Me, Kate*, based on Shakespeare's *The Taming of the Shrew*. The longest running of any Porter musical, over 1,000 performances, *Kiss Me, Kate* had Porter's best score. "Another Op'nin', Another Show" was a classic, and "Brush Up Your Shakespeare," "Always True to You in My Fashion," "Wunderbar," "So in Love," and "Why Can't You Behave?" were all good songs, especially the last two. Other good Porter songs in the last decade of his career were: "Be a Clown" from the flop movie musical *The Pirate* (1948); "From This Moment On" from another forgettable musical, *Out of This World* (1950); and the hymn-like sentimental classic "I Love Paris" from his next to last Broadway musical, the 1953 hit *Can-Can*.

Bibliography
Eells, George. *The Life That He Led: A Biography of Cole Porter*. New York: Putnam, 1967.
Kimball, Robert. *The Complete Lyrics of Cole Porter*. New York: Knopf, 1983.
Porter, Cole. *The Cole Porter Story*. Cleveland: World, 1965.
Schwartz, Charles. *Cole Porter: A Biography*. New York: Dial, 1977.

William E. Studwell

Postcards are small, commercially printed bristol-type boards fairly standardized in size and shape, one side having a picture and the other divided, half for a message and half for address and stamp. The most commonly printed postcard is the chrome card. (Chrome refers to the smooth glossy surface on the picture side.) Postal cards, not to be confused with postcards, are owned and sold by the U.S. Postal Service. Postal cards are smaller and devoid of graphics except during some holiday seasons.

The postcard's earliest predecessors could include the ancient clay cuneiform scrolls and tablets of the Akkadians, Assyrians, Babylonians, and Persians. Like postcards, they had a one-time use, were often local, and were used primarily for business purposes. Other cultures used wax to form tablets that would carry a written message. There were also attempts to form iron into thin sheets into which a message could be embossed or pressed firmly into the metal. One of the most unsuccessful postcards, however, was made from a type of linen. The texture not only obscured the clarity of the text but was ill suited to any significant decorative effects.

Before Great Britain implemented the Penny Post in 1840, the rate for sending a letter was based on distance and the number of sheets of paper used. In 1861, John Carlton of Philadelphia acquired a postcard patent; H. Lipman, also of Philadelphia, quickly acquired the patent and printed the first American postcard under the name of "Lipman's Postal Card." Like other cards of the time, it was only for local delivery. It wasn't until 1898 that private manufacturers were allowed, by act of Congress, to produce postcards in which the back side was restricted to address and stamp only. These "private mailing cards" were popular for a short period and then replaced by a 3 1/2 x 5 1/2 standard. The most significant postcard type, the chrome card still used today, has varied only slightly in quality and size, more so in price, and greatly in breadth of images.

In the mid-19th century, postcards drew criticism due to the lack of confidentiality of the message. However, popular uses and demands for postcards began to change in the late 19th century, as have the constructs and means of written communication. Everyday people began to value and collect postcards, and much of what could be said as quick messages on the card was appropriate to share with anyone who might come across the card.

In the United States, postcards were only moderately popular until the 1893 Columbian Exposition in Chicago. Both using the cards to send messages and collecting them as art objects increased rapidly due primarily to the excellent

"A Mavis Pudding Picturecard" showing the display on first ladies Elizabeth Monroe (left) and Dolley Madison from the Smithsonian Institution's National Museum of History and Technology.

German photographic techniques used in American-view postcards which were often seen through the magnifying lenses of a Stereoscope. The First World War ended the German-American postcard market. White-border cards represented the American attempt to match the Germans' quality. Since the early 1940s, the chrome card, with its smooth glossy finish, has proved to be the most popular kind of postcard with collectors.

The images on postcards were not initially intended as advertisements, but have successfully been used to advertise tourist settings, historical landmarks, art openings, and many other events and places. They may be found in drugstores, card shops, art museums, grocery stores, and tourist stops all over the world. While new postcards are fairly inexpensive, they are often seen as treasures, as they bring visual and written messages from both far and near.

Bibliography
Klamin, C. *Picture Postcards*. New York: Dodd, 1974.
Staff, Frank. *The Picture Postcard and Its Origins*. New York: Praeger, 1966.
Willoughby, Martin. *A History of Postcards: A Pictorial Record from the Turn of the Century to the Present Day*. Secaucus: Wellfleet, 1992.

Roy Pearson

Poster Art is a unique blend of fine and commercial art. While it relates to printmaking, painting, and photography, the artistic placard also serves a very important advertising function. As Edward Penfield, one of the first and most successful poster artists in the United States, once said, the poster "should tell its story at once—a design that needs study is not a poster." The artistic poster's form and function are thus inextricably interrelated.

Executed principally by professional designers, artistic placards first appeared in the United States during the late 19th century and are presently owned and exhibited by libraries and major museums. They are prominently displayed in homes and offices, bookstores and schools, restaurants and theater lobbies. Aesthetically attuned, posters have helped shape popular taste in art and have, in turn, been influenced by social and economic forces. They continue to inspire collectors along with a variety of patrons.

Peter Max's 1994 World Cup poster demonstrates the variety of factors which have shaped poster art in the United States. Recalling the psychedelic art of the 1960s, Max's colorful design features a space-born soccer player suspended above the Earth upon which the United States is prominently displayed in the form of a flag. This surreal image captures the international spirit of the competition while communicating the host country's location. It also borrows its motif from a 1979 poster executed for the Moscow Olympics (illustrated in Rennert, *Rarest Posters*).

U.S. posters grew out of an international design movement in the late 1800s and still respond to a variety of worldwide commercial and artistic influences. Beginning in 1893, graphic designers in New York, Boston, Chicago, and San Francisco created posters in the art nouveau style, an art form which had evolved somewhat independently in both Europe and the United States. By 1895-96 the new posters had captured the imagination of many artists and collectors. Two magazines dedicated entirely to poster art, *The Poster* and *Poster Lore*, flourished briefly, while a number of other periodicals devoted space to poster collecting and poster design.

During this time, European posters, especially in France, were designed to appeal to wealthy male consumers of entertainment and pleasure. They subsequently presented a variety of sexually provocative women, from the cocottes of Jules Cheret to the dream princesses and femmes fatales created by Alphonse Mucha and Georges de Feure. Artists such as Pierre Bonnard and Henri de Toulouse-Lautrec generated placards which featured the cabarets, dance halls, and performers familiar to denizens of Parisian night life. On the other hand, the U.S. poster appealed to an audience of aspiring middle-class citizens, especially women seeking to improve their minds and bodies. Accordingly, publishing and bicycle manufacturing companies sponsored U.S. posters, which reflected current social norms for women who were active, yet still committed to family and home. As Edward Penfield's 1894 poster *Harper's September* demonstrates, U.S. poster design was, accordingly, less charged with color and movement, more balanced and muted in its presentation. U.S. posters drew from international currents, but modified form to accommodate function.

Art nouveau poster style in the United States developed in relation to three interrelated trends in graphic design. The first of these was the English arts and crafts movement, begun in the 1850s and located at the South Kensington School of Design. Drawing from medieval manuscripts as well as oriental designs, the South Kensington method of decoration emphasized two-dimensional design, full colors, and sharp outlines. This reductionist approach was echoed in another important stylistic influence, Japanese decorative designs, where asymmetrical composition and geometric configurations complemented strong flat colors and outlines.

These decorative influences on U.S. commercial design coincided with the new poster style being developed in Paris. During the 1880s, Jules Cheret, using modern print technology to maximum effectiveness (chromo-lithography and the roll press), created his "gallery of the streets" with brightly colored, rococo-inspired posters. In 1890, the New York Grolier Club held a poster exhibition which featured the work of Cheret. The effectiveness of these placards created a demand for more posters, and during the 1890s several post-impressionist artists, including Toulouse-Lautrec and Bonnard, experimented with the medium. Inspired by Japanese prints as well as the synthetist ideas of Paul Gauguin, their new poster style emphasized the flat, sharply outlined, full-color format reminiscent of Japanese prints and the English crafts movement. The poster style and decorative art movements interfaced with an active curvilinear line so prominent in the graphic work of Englishman Aubrey Beardsley and Paris-based Alphonse Mucha. Beardsley's book illustrations were well known in the United States and Mucha's beautifully executed posters for Sarah Bernhardt followed the actress to American shores during the 1890s.

In 1895, a dealer in oriental art opened a curio shop in Paris called the Salon de L'Art Nouveau, which featured objects decorated in the new crafts style, including posters from both sides of the Atlantic. Thus originated, Art Nouveau became a generic term that embraced the new decorative aesthetic and poster style which seemed to catch fire simultaneously in the United States and Europe.

According to Victor Margolin's analysis, art nouveau posters in the United States fall into three categories: decorative, descriptive, and illustrative. The *decorative* approach most accurately defines the work of Will Bradley and Ethel Reed. The Bradley-Reed design format is an adaptation of Aubrey Beardsley's black-and-white silhouette forms charged with a curvilinear line. Bradley illustrated books and designed posters for Chicago and Boston publishers. Reed designed posters and contributed illustrations for several Boston firms. Converting Beardsley's decadent designs into a more acceptable American middle-class format, Bradley and Reed were part of the 1890s book and poster movement, which took its inspiration from the English crafts style as well as Continental book and poster graphics. The *illustrative* poster features a three-dimensional, naturalistic approach and was used typically by graphic artists such as Maxfield Parrish and Charles Dana Gibson to advertise the books they illustrated.

Edward Penfield (American, 1866-1925), *Harper's September*, 1894.

In between these two poles is the *descriptive* poster, which displays the flat, full-color format of the poster style without arabesque, decorative lines. The descriptive approach is well illustrated by Penfield's 1894 *Harper's September* poster. Here, a direct, frontal presentation within a balanced framework communicates a message of ease and graceful living associated with the product, *Harper's* magazine. According to E. McKnight Kauffer's *The Art of the Poster*, a poster should attract attention, arouse interest, stimulate desire, and ultimately lead to buying. Penfield's eye-catching design creates a desire to acquire the lifestyle represented in the placard, all made possible through self-improvement with the purchase of *Harper's*. Penfield was art editor at *Harper's* for 11 years (1890-1901), where he designed over 60 posters for *Harper's Monthly* magazine which capture the essence of America's aspiring middle class. So successful were Penfield's posters as advertisements that, well into the 20th century, numerous imitators followed his modest, though arresting, approach to poster design, such as Joseph C. Leyendecker's posters for Chesterfield cigarettes, the House of Kuppenheimer, and Arrow Shirts, in the '20s and '30s.

Art nouveau posters lured collectors as well as customers, and in the United States there were at least 6,000 poster collectors by 1895. Recognized in international art circles, U.S. poster art became a vehicle through which the American people were introduced to emerging post-impressionist styles.

After 1900, poster design in the United States became less style-conscious and more illustrative. The government during World War I and industry thereafter demanded less stylistic innovation from posters and a more photographic, narrative image to project ideas and brand-names. The art deco trend, which incorporated modern cubist and constructivist ideas, collage, and photo-montage into poster design, largely remained a European phenomenon, even though several of its best-known exemplars—among them Adolphe Cassandre and Herbert Matter and the German Bauhaus—at one point or other worked extensively in the United States. Even Montana-born E. McKnight Kauffer, whose graphic design incorporated a variety of modern features, remained for a good portion of his career in England before returning to the United States where, during the 1940s, he executed placards for several book publishers and American Airlines.

In fact, prior to the poster renaissance of the 1960s, the Depression-inspired placards of the WPA (Works Progress Administration) were the one major exception to the realistic trend in United States poster art. Part of the Federal Art Project of the WPA, the federal government's Poster Divisions, from 1935 to 1943, produced some 2 million placards from 35,000 original poster designs. Of these about 2,000 examples survive, mostly housed at the Library of Congress.

Made to advertise a revolutionary New Deal social and economic program, WPA posters adopted the more radical Continental formats to underscore their unique mission. Reminiscent of the 1890s poster movement, WPA designers invented a new medium, the silk-screen process, which was easily adapted to art deco styles. Using a geometric cubist format with attendant overlays and collage arrangements, WPA *serigraphs* ("silk-screen drawings") promoted a variety of government-sponsored programs, from Federal Theater, Dance, and Writers' Projects to social improvement campaigns such as the prevention of venereal disease and safety in the workplace.

Artistic innovation became a hallmark of WPA poster design, and the various Poster Divisions vied with one another to create more effective and original formats. The public impact of these posters is hard to gauge exactly, but it is fairly certain that they not only helped disseminate New Deal programs, but also introduced millions of people in the United States to the shapes and forms of modern art. Artifacts in their own right, WPA posters even advertised special exhibitions of WPA poster art held regularly throughout the country.

By 1938, however, the forces of reaction caught up with the WPA, and congressional investigations began to probe the agency's "subversive" tendencies. The advent of World War II altered the government's approach to poster art and what was left of the Poster Divisions was transferred into the War Department to produce the more typical realistic, narrative posters in support of the war effort. In 1943, President Roosevelt gave the entire WPA, along with its Poster Divisions, an "honorable discharge." Tainted by the red brush of radicalism, the WPA poster legacy remained buried, crated in one of the towers of the Library of Congress through the anti-communist 1940s and '50s, until the 1960s brought forward an interest once more in innovative graphic design.

Inspired by the counterculture revolution and street demonstrations of the era, 1960s posters reached into the past while absorbing contemporary art trends to create a flourish of design innovation and poster output that had far-reaching impact at home and abroad. During this epoch the artistic poster not only advertised, but became itself a commodity, sold by the thousands to decorate and enliven the walls of a new generation of Americans. To meet the demand for poster decoration and communication, several innovative designers, individually or in business cooperatives, created an interesting variety of poster art.

The new psychedelic entertainment featured in San Francisco during the sixties gave rise to the hippie poster. Incorporating elements of American pop and op art into their work, poster artists such as Wes Wilson adapted art nouveau patterns and lines to create arresting visual displays of color and motion, posters which seem to re-create the free movement and strobe lighting of the dances they advertised. In these posters the medium literally becomes the message.

Established in 1955 by Milton Glaser and Seymour Chwast, the New York-based Push Pin Studios became a leader in innovative commercial design. Glaser, especially, was a master of many stylistic formats, from art nouveau to art deco, which he incorporated brilliantly into the brightly colored world of the sixties poster. For his 1966 poster *Dylan*, Glaser created an arresting facial profile of the popular folksinger with a combination format: a silhouette design for the features after a drawing by Marcel Duchamp, and a multicolored, arabesque pattern for the hair, inspired by Islamic decorative painting. Included in the record album it advertised, Glaser's poster entered the homes of over 6 million people. By the time Glaser, Chwast, and associates showed their work in 1970 in Paris, U.S. poster art had become a pacesetter for international graphic design, and American posters sold in the millions worldwide. In effect, the United States experienced another poster craze during the late sixties, and commercial designers such as Glaser and his oft-mentioned contemporary, Peter Max, made a very lucrative living as they rode the crest of popular demand.

The commercial and decorative aspects of the sixties boom were tempered by social and political concerns, which also dominated the placards of the era. So-called posters of protest accompanied a variety of political happenings, while the social content of other placards helped raise general consciousness about racial and sexual discrimination, poverty, and environmental issues. Also inspired by contemporary images of pop and op art, these posters deftly expressed social and political satire through a reversal of popular logos and slogans. The American flag became a symbol of imperialist aggression, and Andy Warhol's famous Campbell's Soup can appeared in one placard with a bullet hole and red soup/blood spilling down its side. A number of designer workshops were devoted exclusively to these posters. Using a silk-screen process not unlike the earlier WPA Poster Divisions, the Graphic Workshop at the Massachusetts College of Art and the La Raza Silkscreen Center in San Francisco produced thousands of placards for a variety of social and political action groups.

A 1968 international poster show at the Museum of Modern Art, "Word and Image," featured a number of psychedelic placards, while the 1975 Smithsonian Institution exhibition, "Images of an Era," recognized more extensively the aesthetic qualities as well as social relevance of the sixties poster. Beginning in 1964, the Albert A. List Foundation provided grants for artists to enter the field of poster graphics. During this same period, galleries and corporations also supported the creation of artistic posters. Among these, the Leo Castelli Gallery in New York, the Container Corporation, and the Mobil Oil Company are some of the more outstanding examples.

The artistic poster continues to be appreciated as fine art and to be used as advertising for a variety of products and causes. Absorbing and transforming the world around it, the aesthetic poster has been a barometer of American values and has, in turn, helped condition popular tastes and lifestyles. A legitimate work of art, the artistic poster remains committed to its primary function, which is to persuade the viewer.

Bibliography

Barnicoat, John. *Posters: A Concise History*. New York: Thames & Hudson, 1985.

DeNoon, Christopher. *Posters of the WPA*. Los Angeles: Wheatley, 1987.

Gengarelly, W. Anthony, and Carol Derby. *The Prendergasts and the Arts and Crafts Movement*. Williamstown: Williams College Museum of Art, 1989.

Glaser, Milton. *Milton Glaser: Graphic Design*. Woodstock, NY: Overlook, 1973.

Kauffer, E. McKnight. *The Art of the Poster*. New York: Boni, 1925.

Lee, Marshall, ed. *Art Deco Graphics*. New York: Abrams, 1986.

Margolin, Victor. *American Poster Renaissance*. Secaucus: Castle, 1975.

Rennert, Jack. *Rarest Posters*. New York: Poster Auctions, 1992.

W. Anthony Gengarelly

Potter, Beatrix (1866-1943), notable author and illustrator of children's books, was born in London. As a child constrained to a solitary life in the city—she spent most of her time in an upstairs room attended impersonally by servants—Potter developed an eye for detail and an imagination richly inspired by the domestic details and natural phenomena that she was able to observe. On visits to England's Lake country, she drew plants and animals, and sometimes brought back live animals to London, drawing them dressed in clothes and acting like humans. Her drawings had great charm and accuracy, so much so that some were published in a small book titled *A Happy Pair*.

Though Potter had been drawing animals for years, it wasn't until 1892 that she began to compose stories for children. Her initial efforts were letters with illustrations sent to a sick child, including the first version of *The Tale of Peter Rabbit*, which follows the capers of Peter, Flopsy, Mopsy, and Cottontail in Mr. McGregor's garden. Potter revised the story and, after several unsuccessful attempts to interest a publisher, printed it herself privately. Eventually *Peter Rabbit* was published (in 1902) and was an immediate success. It was soon followed by *The Tailor of Gloucester* (1903) and *The Tale of Squirrel Nutkin* (1903).

With her royalties from these and four more books, along with a small inheritance, Potter was able to purchase a farm in the Lake country in 1906, where she began to spend much of her time, even though, in the fashion of the time, she still lived with her parents.

From then until 1913, she published a dozen of the books in the 23-title Peter Rabbit series, from *The Tale of Mr. Jeremy Fisher* (1906) to *The Tale of Pigling Bland* (1913). After her marriage at age 47 in 1913, Potter's output declined. She continued to publish occasionally, but most of her later books were reworkings of earlier material.

Potter's picture books have been children's favorites for the better part of a century. They are simple, amusing, and warm-hearted, and feature human-like little animals who have social and familial lives and inhabit an enchanting miniature world with timeless appeal to young readers.

Bibliography

Lane, Margaret. *The Magic Years of Beatrix Potter.* London: Warne, 1978.

Linder, Leslie. *A History of the Writings of Beatrix Potter, including Unpublished Work.* London: Warne, 1971.

MacDonald, Ruth K. *Beatrix Potter.* Boston: Twayne, 1986.

John Rogers

Presley, Elvis (1935-1977), the "King of Rock 'n' Roll," has influenced American society and culture more than any other single person. Presley was born in Tupelo, MS, one of a pair of twins (the other was stillborn), to Gladys and Vernon Presley. Presley grew up in typical southern fashion, in the midst of poverty, Christianity, and southern idealism. When he was 13, his family moved to Memphis. His father took odd jobs to support the family. Presley was reared in a tight family unit that provided a great deal of personal support. At an early age, the Presleys bought Elvis a guitar, on which, as a teenager, he practiced continually. He was deeply influenced by all the musical styles he heard while growing up, especially gospel, blues, bluegrass, jazz, and hillbilly country.

In high school, Presley was considered a rebel. While he always kept a sense of southern politeness in his mannerisms—something he did throughout his life—he kept to himself, wore his hair slicked back, had long sideburns, and dressed in what were considered outlandish outfits for that time. He maintained a very private personal life then and throughout his career.

Presley's recording career began in 1953, when he walked into the Sun studios in Memphis to record a song for his mother. For $4, accompanied by an old, beat-up guitar, he recorded a cover of the Ink Spots' "My Happiness." Presley's sound impressed Marion Keisker, a Sun staffer, enough to bring him to the attention of Sun Records' owner, Sam Phillips. Phillips was looking for a white singer who sounded black because, at that time, much of music, like society, was segregated. Presley was just the voice Phillips needed to get young white teenagers interested in the new rockabilly sound. As a result, Phillips put together the band with which Elvis became popular, with guitarist Scotty Moore and bassist Bill Black. Moore's contribution toward developing the Elvis Presley sound cannot be underestimated. Their first recording together, in August 1954, was a version of Arthur (Big Boy) Crudup's "That's All Right Mama." To Phillips's amazement, the song, initially done with Presley, Moore, and Black just "fooling around" in the studio, was an instant local hit. Teenagers requested the song, which was played on the radio, before the record was even pressed.

Elvis began touring in southern and western towns, and made appearances on popular radio programs like the *Grand Ole Opry* and Shreveport's *Louisiana Hayride*. Elvis had a few other Sun hits with Roy Brown's "Good Rockin' Tonight" and Junior Parker's "Mystery Train," both in 1955. However, it was not until Elvis signed with RCA Records that his career really hit the big time. At the urging of his shrewd manager, Colonel Tom Parker, Presley joined RCA in late 1955. RCA paid $35,000 to Sun Records for Presley, an unheard-of sum. In 1956, Presley recorded "Heartbreak Hotel," "Hound Dog," "Love Me Tender," and "Don't Be Cruel," all of which became Top 10 hits, selling over a million copies. 1957 through 1960 saw the release of more Elvis hits, including "All Shook Up" (1957), "Teddy Bear" (1957), "Jailhouse Rock" (1957), "Hard Headed Woman" (1958), "Stuck on You" (1959), and "Are You Lonesome Tonight" (1960). The youth of America, and indeed the world, had found someone to represent the new youth culture which was emerging in the fifties. Presley represented this more than any other rock 'n' roller. He was handsome; his stage presence gave him an almost mystical aura to which many teens (mostly women) were attracted; and he combined his swiveling hair and jumbling hips with a sensuality that made teens go wild. In spite of his fame and recognition, Presley never lost that down-to-earth, common person's presence, which added to his enduring appeal. His manager, Tom Parker, knew how to turn Presley into a marketable product, without compromising his integrity as a person and performer.

In 1956, one of Presley's childhood dreams came true; he starred in his first movie, *Love Me Tender*. This and three more early movies furthered his career as a pop star: *Loving You* (1957), *Jailhouse Rock* (1957), and *King Creole* (1958). Critics consider these four films to be the best of his entire film career, which included over 25 films. Presley also appeared on various television shows, including the *Milton Berle Show*, the *Dorsey Brothers*, and the *Steve Allen Show*. In 1956, Ed Sullivan refused to have Presley on his show until his ratings dropped to only 15 percent, compared to

Elvis Presley. Photo courtesy of Sound Recording Archives, Bowling Green State University, Bowling Green, OH.

Allen's 55 percent when Presley was on. On September 9, 1956, Presley finally appeared on the *Ed Sullivan Show*. He was only shown from the waist up, but TV viewers had an idea what was going on with the rest of his body, because of the non-stop screams of the girls in the audience.

In 1958, he was inducted into the U.S. Army and served a two-year stint in Germany. This period was especially hard for him, because of the death of his mother, Gladys, on August 14, 1958. When Presley returned in 1960, he resumed his film and singing career. He attained new chart and box office success, but he never fully regenerated the hysteria that had surrounded him earlier in his career. Some of his early sixties hits were "Can't Help Falling in Love with You" (1962), "Good Luck Charm" (1962), "Viva Las Vegas" (1964), and "Crying in the Chapel" (1965). He also made a series of poorly scripted movie films during the sixties and early seventies, including *GI Blues* (1960), *Wild in the Country* (1961), *Blue Hawaii* (1961), *Girls, Girls, Girls* (1962), *Kissin' Cousins* (1964), *Viva Las Vegas* (1964), *Spinout* (1966), *Charro* (1969), and *Change of Habit* (1970). While these films did well at the box office, critics dismissed many of them as shoddy attempts that put the name Presley over the quality and script of the movie. His career was revitalized somewhat in the late sixties. He married Priscilla Beaulieu, whom he had "been sweet on" since she was 14; their daughter, Lisa Marie, was born in February 1968. He had successful worldwide hits with the songs "Suspicious Minds" (1969), which was recorded with future Grateful Dead backup vocalist Donna Godchaux, and "In the Ghetto" (1969). His first television special, for NBC, aired on December 3, 1968. Along with his records and movies, this special kept Elvis in the minds of the American public.

The seventies proved that Presley had hard-core fans who would do anything for a glimpse of him. Fans came from all over the world, hoping to get a glimpse of the "King of Rock 'n' Roll" at his Graceland home in Memphis. Despite personal problems, which not many people knew about at the time, he continued to sell out shows (10,000 to 20,000 people a night) and, occasionally, recorded songs. During this period, he was divorced from Priscilla, was increasingly using prescription drugs, became overweight, and did not leave his home for months at a time. However, his private life remained private and seemed to add to his mystique. Even though his health was failing—he once collapsed on stage—he belted out the best performance he could so that nobody went away disappointed. He continued to perform in flashy clothes, and one could see the sweat drip from him as he gave it his all. Presley taped another television broadcast, "Aloha from Hawaii," which aired on NBC in early 1973. This program was viewed in over 25 countries to an audience estimated to be over a billion viewers. In 1974, he received a Grammy for best inspirational performance for the album *How Great Thou Art*. In the mid-seventies, Presley became increasingly alienated and shut off from the public. His drug habit increased, and he only made a few public appearances.

On August 16, 1977, the "King" died. Although there is still speculation as to the cause of his death, the official reason was given as "cardiac arrhythmia." At the time he died, Presley had a new record, *Moody Blue,* moving up the charts. After his death the record sold a million copies, as did many of his records. Just prior to his death, three of his former bodyguards wrote a book, *Elvis: What Happened*, which criticized him severely. A 1981 biography by Albert Goldman attempted to do the same but in more detail.

Millions of people mourned and continue to mourn the death of Elvis Presley as though he were some kind of religious deity. Every year people from all over the world celebrate his birth and accomplishments. They mourn his death, visit Graceland repeatedly, and continue to promote the "myth of Elvis" throughout the world. His grave is the most visited in America. Some even refuse to believe that Presley is dead, and report seeing him in Burger Kings, Wal-Marts, grocery stores, and other public places. Frank Zappa's song "Elvis Just Left the Building" (1988), Living Colour's song "Elvis Is Dead" (1990), and Greil Marcus's 1992 book *Dead Elvis* are about this phenomenon.

Presley's career is unparalleled in popular music history. He had over 140 hits in *Billboard*'s Top 100 (1956-82), more than 90 albums in the Top 100 (1956-85), and made over 25 films. There were hundreds of books and articles written about him. Several excellent documentaries have been made, including *Elvis: That's the Way It Is* (1970), *Elvis on Tour* (1972), and the docudrama *This Is Elvis* (1982). The Rock and Roll Hall of Fame inducted Elvis Presley in 1986 and the U.S. Postal Service released a Presley stamp in 1992.

Bibliography

Baumgold, Julie. "Midnight in the Garden of Good and Elvis." *Esquire* March 1995: 92-102.

Goldman, Albert. *Elvis*. New York: McGraw-Hill, 1981.

Guralnick, Peter. *Last Train to Memphis: The Rise of Elvis Presley*. Boston: Little, Brown, 1994.

Hammontree, Patsy Guy. *Elvis Presley: A Bio-Bibliography*. Westport: Greenwood, 1985.

Loder, Kurt. "The Music That Changed the World." *Rolling Stone* 13 Feb. 1986: 49.

Marcus, Greil. *Dead Elvis: A Chronicle of a Cultural Obsession*. London: Penguin, 1992.

——. *Mystery Train: Images of America in Rock 'n' Roll Music*. New York: Dutton, 1975.

West, Red, Sonny West, and Dave Hebler, with Steve Dunleavy. *Elvis: What Happened?* New York: Ballantine, 1977.

Robert Weiner

Price Is Right, The (1956-), is one of TV's most famous game shows. Amidst an atmosphere of feverish expectation—with a flame-like pattern at the edges of the television screen to frame a frenzied audience of potential contestants who applaud wildly and squirm in their seats—a jocular announcer enthusiastically proclaims: "Betty Jones? Come on down!" Thus begins America's most-watched daytime-television game show—the "new" one-hour version of *The Price Is Right*—a program developed and produced by Mark Goodson and Bill Todman that has survived replacements of its original Master of Ceremonies (first Bill Cullen on NBC and ABC, then Bob Barker on CBS, later Dennis James, Bob Barker, and Tom Kennedy in syndication), a succession of announcers (first Don Pardo, then Johnny Gilbert and Johnny Olson, later Rod Roddy), and even changes in its format (first 30 minutes of a simple bidding game, now an hour that features a wider variety of over 60 different pricing games), while remaining on the air almost continuously since 1956 (with only a minor gap between 1965 and 1971) and becoming the longest continuously running game show in daytime-television history as of March 1987.

First, four contestants play a bidding game in which they try to guess the price of some splendid piece of merchandise (e.g., a digital keyboard, an exercise bike, a camcorder). The one who comes closest to the real price without going over it gets to play a pricing game in which some combination of common sense and luck (mostly the latter) may win a prize of more substantial value (a sport boat, a projection TV, a new car). This pattern then repeats three times, with the relevant contestants participating in a "Showcase Showdown" in which they spin a gigantic wheel to determine who wins a spot on the final "Showcase" later in the program. The entire procedure then recurs exactly as before, generating three more potential game winners and one more finalist for the concluding Showcase. Finally, the two finalists pair off for the ultimate contest. Merchandise beyond their wildest dreams parades before their greedy eyes (a home-entertainment center, a pinball machine, a grandfather clock, an old-fashioned kitchen range). The one whose guess comes closest

to the overall total (without going over it) wins the whole collection of products displayed.

Thus, the progress of *PIR* pursues a kind of rags-to-riches scenario. Winners of the bidding contest receive a prize valued at about $1,200 on average. Those who succeed in the pricing game pick up merchandise worth up to $10-$15,000. And those who achieve the ultimate conquest in the Showcase might take home $15-$25,000 in prizes.

The objects of all this excitement—and the real stars of the show—are the consumer products that constantly appear in enticing displays and that receive enthusiastic or even jubilant applause from the audience: hand-clapping for the frost-free refrigerator; cheers for the his-and-her motor scooters; mass hysteria for the new Buick Skylark. And the implicit message of all this is, of course, that these objects of desire represent a way of life worth attaining—a chance for the contestants in the flesh and for the audience vicariously to participate in the Culture of Consumption en route to fulfilling the American Dream.

The Price Is Right serves as a shining example of how phenomenal popularity can be achieved by appealing to the lowest common denominator in American taste (not to mention success in numerous foreign-language clones shown around the world). One might not willingly embrace the show's shabby and self-serving aesthetic; but one remains fascinated by the phenomenon itself and by the apparently inextinguishable appeal of its materialistic theme.

Bibliography

Comstock, George, et al. *Television and Human Behavior*. New York: Columbia UP, 1978.

Fiske, John. *Television Culture*. London: Routledge, 1987.

——. "Women and Quiz Shows: Consumerism, Patriarchy and Resisting Pleasures." *Television and Women's Culture: The Politics of the Popular*. Ed. Mary Ellen Brown. London: Sage, 1990.

Holbrook, Morris B. *Daytime Television Game Shows and the Celebration of Merchandise: The Price Is Right*. Bowling Green, OH: Bowling Green State U Popular P, 1993.

Press, Andrea. *Women Watching Television: Gender, Class, and Generation in the American Television Experience*. Philadelphia: U of Pennsylvania P, 1991.

Morris B. Holbrook

See also

Game Shows

Game-Show Hosts, Hostesses, and Producers

Price, Ray Noble (1926-), a wide-ranging and broadly appealing country singer, can claim a list of Top 10 singles that stretches from 1952 to 1979. Born in eastern Texas's Cherokee County, Price first showed an interest in music while, still in grade school, he began to sing at church functions and other local venues. Price's family moved to Dallas while he was in high school, where he learned to play the guitar. After graduation, Price went to study veterinary medicine at North Texas Agricultural College in Abilene, but World War II intervened; he spent four years in the Marines, during which he saw service in the Pacific. Discharged in 1946, Price went back to NTAC, and a growing interest in appearing at local clubs as a country singer led to his first radio appearance in 1948 on KRBC's *Hillbilly Circus*, where he was billed as "The Cherokee Cowboy."

Though still progressing toward his degree in 1948-49 and anticipating a career in agriculture or animal husbandry, Price saw his musical career receive an unexpected boost when he was offered a spot as a cast member of the *Big D Jamboree*, a career-making showcase broadcast over KRLD in Dallas. CBS broadcast certain portions of the *Jamboree*, and his growing recognition led to a contract with the Bullet record label, a regional outfit that produced several of his singles. In 1952, Price's breakthrough year, Columbia signed him to a contract, a union that resulted in his first two Top 10 singles ("Talk to Your Heart" and "Don't Let the Stars Get in Your Eyes"). After winning a regular spot on the *Grand Ole Opry*, Price moved to Nashville.

During the next few years, Price put out hit after hit, including 1954's "Release Me," "I'll Be There," and "If You Don't Someone Else Will" and 1956's "I've Got a New Heartache," "Wasted Words," and "Crazy Arms" (his first chart-topper, which still is third all-time for longevity on the country charts at 45 weeks), all of which still are requested regularly at Price's appearances four decades later. Many more followed, and by the 1960s Price was breaking country music tradition by using orchestral backup on many of his biggest hits, even taking a small string section on the road with him.

Continuing his theme of adaptability, Price entered the 1970s by updating his act with a rendition of Kris Kristofferson's "For the Good Times" (1970), a progressive country song that hit No. 1 on both the country and pop charts in the U.S. and was a blockbuster international hit. His album of that title, released later that year, stayed on the country charts for two years. Other hits during the first half of the 1970s kept him in the public eye, but Price wanted to ease out of many of his more time-consuming duties and spend more time working on his horse ranch near Dallas. Having moved to ABC/Dot from Columbia, Price still cut singles that made the charts during the latter half of the '70s, and even Columbia put out a late release of "If You Ever Change Your Mind."

In late 1978, Price signed with Monument and returned to music full-time, and after an early 1979 appearance on *The Tonight Show* and another big hit with "Feet," two other low-chart 1979 singles failed to reach upper-level success. In 1980, an unlikely duet album resulted when Price sought out Willie Nelson, once one of his backup band members, for *San Antonio Rose*. According to one source, the effort required the reconciliation of long-standing hard feelings between Nelson and Price: After one of Price's fighting roosters had killed some of his neighbor Nelson's hens, Nelson shot the rooster and ate it. After the incident, Price vowed never to record another of Nelson's songs, but eventually he relented, and for whatever reason—some say it was to help out someone who had helped him earlier—Nelson decided to do the album with him. *Rose*, a Columbia release, reached No. 3 on the charts, stayed in the Top 40 for months and won nominations from the Academy of Country Music Awards (duet and album of the year) and from the *Music City News* (duet of the year).

Several more of Price's singles have hit the charts since. In the early 1980s, Price headlined *Ray Price's Country Starsearch 1981*, for which he appeared at the finals in each state and also starred in a national TV broadcast that featured the winners. He also appeared in *Honkytonk Man*, a Clint Eastwood film. Price continues to perform from time to time around the country, typically fielding requests for songs from his long list of old hits. He last hit the charts with 1988's "I'd Do It All Over Again" and indeed he may do it again, with a new album from Buddha Records to be released in May 2000. According to at least one researcher, Price holds the No. 6 spot among the Top 200 country artists of all time in terms of chart success.

Bibliography

Larkin, Colin, ed. *The Guinness Encyclopedia of Popular Music*. 4 vols. Middlesex, U.K.: Guinness, 1992.

Shestack, Melvin. *The Country Music Encyclopedia*. New York: Crowell, 1974.

Stambler, Irwin, and Grelun Landon. *The Encyclopedia of Folk, Country, and Western Music*. New York: St. Martin's, 1983.

Stephen Finley

Price, **Vincent Leonard** (1911-1993), the versatile actor best known for his suspense and horror roles, was born in St. Louis into a well-to-do family; his father was a successful candy manufacturer and he enjoyed what can certainly be called a privileged and progressive upbringing which included an early exposure to the arts. As a young boy, he developed an appreciation of music and art, theater and film, cooking and travel. For a while he aspired to be an artist and then began to entertain thoughts of an acting career. He began collecting art while still a young boy and visited many of the great art museums of Europe while in his teens. He earned a B.A. in art history and English at Yale and later studied art history at the University of London.

In 1935, while studying in London, Price made his stage debut with a small role in a production of *Chicago*, starring John Gielgud, at the Gate Theater. Later that year, he won the lead role of Prince Albert in *Victoria Regina*. The play was a success and he was subsequently asked to return to America to appear in it on Broadway opposite Helen Hayes. In this period he also worked with Orson Welles's Mercury Theater and would remain active on the stage throughout his career. He also appeared in a number of successful one-man shows, including *Diversions and Delights*, his critically acclaimed tribute to Oscar Wilde.

Price was an established stage star when he made his film debut opposite Constance Bennett in Universal's 1938 comedy *Service de Luxe*. Some early films attempted to cast him as a more or less conventional leading man; however, he soon distinguished himself as a versatile supporting player and character actor who, aided by a suave manner and melodious voice, excelled in a wide range of roles. Memorable early film roles include King Charles II in *Hudson's Bay* (1940), a philosophical Southern soldier in *The Eve of St. Mark* (1944), the effete cad Shelby Carpenter in the classic film noir *Laura* (1944), Cardinal Richelieu in *The Three*

Musketeers (1948), a hilarious performance opposite Ronald Colman in the charming comedy *Champagne for Caesar* (1950), and a scheming western villain in *The Baron of Arizona* (1950).

It was his appearance in the 1953 3-D production of *House of Wax* that would begin Price's close association with horror films, although one can find precedents in such earlier non-horror films as the 1939 version of *Tower of London*, *The House of the Seven Gables* (1940), *Shock* (1946), and *Dragonwyck* (1946). From this point on, the majority of his motion picture work was in horror films or in the frequently related genres of mystery, fantasy, and science fiction. Some of his best work in this area is to be found in *The Pit and the Pendulum* (1961), *The Masque of the Red Death* (1964), *The Tomb of Ligeia* (1964)—these three being part of an impressive cycle of Poe adaptations made for director Roger Corman—*Witchfinder General* (1968), and *Theater of Blood* (1973). It is also worth noting that *The Abominable Dr. Phibes* (1971) and its sequel, *Dr. Phibes Rises Again* (1972), as well as his films for exploitation master William Castle, *House on Haunted Hill* (1958) and *The Tingler* (1959), have achieved minor classic status among camp followers; they are great fun, but are certainly not representative of Price's best or most serious work in the horror genre.

While it is perhaps appropriate that his final film appearance was in the fantasy *Edward Scissorhands* (1990), it is instructive to remember his sensitive performance a few years earlier in *The Whales of August* (1987) opposite Lillian Gish and Bette Davis. The film provides an opportunity to lament the relative scarcity of work for older performers in modern films, as well as the fact that in recent decades Price was seldom given an opportunity to appear in a non-horror film. Nevertheless, Price was proud of the dominant role that he quickly assumed in the horror field, and he approached the genre with relish and a spirit of fun—and with the same respect and professionalism that he brought to all his work.

In addition to his work on stage and screen, Price was very active on radio and television throughout his career and proved himself at home in both comic and dramatic roles. He was also a frequent guest on quiz and interview programs. Although television frequently exploited his association with horror, his interests and talents were such that he might be seen discussing Renaissance art on a serious program one night, and then be found cavorting with the Muppets on the next. His rich and eminently recognizable voice also ensured that he was much in demand as a commercial spokesman. His busy schedule also included such disparate tasks as hosting PBS's *Mystery* for several years and lending his distinctive voice to both Michael Jackson's *Thriller* video and Disney's animated feature *The Great Mouse Detective* (1986).

In his personal life, Price was married three times, first to actress Edith Barrett and then to fashion designer Mary Grant (with whom he collaborated on several cookbooks). His third wife was actress Coral Browne.

Bibliography

Parish, James Robert, and Steven Whitney. *Vincent Price Unmasked*. New York: Drake, 1974.

Price, Vincent. *I Like What I Know: A Visual Autobiography*. Garden City: Doubleday, 1959.

——. *Vincent Price, His Movies, His Plays, His Life*. Garden City: Doubleday, 1978.

Fred Guida

Prince (1958-) was born Prince Rogers Nelson in Minneapolis and named after the Prince Rogers trio, which was led by his jazz pianist father, John Nelson. Prince began teaching himself to play the piano at the age of 10. The same year, his stepfather took him to see James Brown in concert and it was obviously something he never forgot, as his music oozes rocking soul and sexy funk.

By age 12, Prince experienced problems at home and ran away, moving around, sometimes staying with his father, who bought him a guitar on which Prince taught himself to play. He eventually wound up staying with the family of André Anderson (later André Cymone), who became a close friend and collaborator. Prince began playing saxophone, drums, and bass, and by 1972 had joined Grand Central, a group based out of his junior high, and his remarkable career was underway.

After being involved with a variety of Minneapolis-based musicians and projects, the 19-year-old Prince signed a record deal and recorded the self-produced *For You*, which provided an R&B hit, "Soft and Wet." In 1979, his self-titled album sold half a million copies and delivered his first major hit single, "I Wanna Be Your Lover." The album also contained "I Feel for You," which was a No. 1 hit for Chaka Khan in 1984 and won Prince a Grammy.

While Prince's third album, *Dirty Mind*, was only a moderate success by Prince's contemporary standards, the follow-up, *Controversy*, spent 63 weeks on the U.S. album charts, but still did not provide a hit single. In 1983, the album *1999* yielded Top 10 singles "Little Red Corvette" and "Delirious" while the title track went Top 20. In 1984, the self-written, self-produced "When Doves Cry" from his movie *Purple Rain* finally crowned the U.S. charts and began Prince's incredibly successful journey through pop stardom. The soundtrack album *Purple Rain* sold 1 million copies in its first week and stayed at No. 1 for 24 weeks. The album provided two No. 1 singles, "Let's Go Crazy" and the title song, as well as the Top 10 "I Would Die for You." The album won a Grammy, while the score for the movie won an Oscar.

Prince's next album, *Around the World in a Day*, was also a No. 1 album, and the first single from the LP, "Raspberry Beret," reached No. 2 on the U.S. singles chart. In 1986, Prince hit No. 1 with "Kiss" from the No. 1 soundtrack album *Parade*. Behind "Kiss" at No. 2 was "Manic Monday" by the Bangles, which he also wrote.

Through the late 1980s and early 1990s Prince steadily released albums, as well as another movie. The double-album *Sign 'O' the Times* (1987), featuring Sheila E. on drums, reached No. 6, and *Lovesexy* (1988) reached No. 11, then Prince's soundtrack album for the first *Batman* movie (1989) hit No. 1. While his movie *Graffiti Bridge* did not do well, the soundtrack album (1990) hit No. 6.

Diamonds and Pearls reached No. 3 in 1991; the single "Cream" topped the charts; then Prince released an album (1992) titled with the symbol that he soon was to adopt as his name. In 1993 he changed his name to that symbol, a merger of the male and female symbols, and was known for a while as "Symbol Man," "the artist formerly known as Prince," or just "Formerly." The prolific "Symbol Man" released eight albums including three in 1999 alone: *Rave Un2 the Joy Fantastic*, *Vault*, and *Crystal Ball*. In 2000 he reverted to Prince.

Bibliography

Hill, Dave. *Prince: A Pop Life*. New York: Harmony, 1989.
Larkin, Colin, ed. *Guinness Encyclopedia of Popular Music*. Vol. 5. Middlesex, U.K.: Guinness, 1995.
Rees, Dafydd, and Luke Crampton. *Rock Movers and Shakers*. New York: Billboard, 1991.
Romanowski, Patricia, and Holly George-Warren, eds. *The New Rolling Stone Encyclopedia of Rock & Roll*. New York: Fireside, 1995.

Hugh Foley

Prisoner, The (1968). Whereas film has *Citizen Kane*, television has *The Prisoner*, a rare and perhaps unequaled "televisionary masterpiece." *The Prisoner* was an episodic series produced by the British company ITC. It debuted in Britain in September 1967 and originally appeared to be a sequel to the spy series *Danger Man* (known in the United States as *Secret Agent*).

Danger Man starred Patrick McGoohan as British spy John Drake. After three seasons, McGoohan quit *Danger Man*, having become intrigued with the idea of a new series about a spy who resigns. Thus began *The Prisoner*, with the recently resigned McGoohan playing a recently resigned spy similar to John Drake.

McGoohan's character (always called Number Six), soon after his resignation, is knocked out and kidnapped. He awakens in a placed called the Village, which is actually a prison without walls (but surrounded by mountains and ocean). The inhabitants of the Village are other kidnapped civil servants, informers, and guards. Which side (Western or Eastern bloc) runs the Village is unclear, although over the course of the series' 17 episodes, evidence points more and more strongly toward the West.

Most episodes revolve around the captors' attempts to extract information from Number Six and around his efforts to escape from the surreal outpost whose location is never revealed. The characters and decor often suggest an Ionesco play set in a holiday camp. In addition, there is a strong Orwellian theme, with Number Six often under surveillance and subject to brainwashing, intimidation, and double crosses.

In its endless regress of uncertainty and betrayal, *The Prisoner* transcends the boundaries of the spy genre and becomes a meditation on free will, individualism, and tyranny. Number Six is an antihero who is tired of being an antihero, but he cannot escape the trap he set for himself by becoming a spy in the first place.

The Prisoner was first broadcast in the United States as a summer replacement series on CBS in 1968. Although the show was not a hit, it is a cult favorite and is often ranked among the finest series ever made. The program's "auteur" was Patrick McGoohan, who not only starred but also served as a writer, director, and executive producer.

Bibliography

Carrazé, Alain, and Hélène Oswald. *The Prisoner: A Televisionary Masterpiece*. 1989. Trans. Christine Donougher. London: Allen, 1990.
Rogers, Dave. *The Prisoner & Danger Man*. London: Boxtree, 1989.
White, Matthew, and Jaffer Ali. *The Official Prisoner Companion*. New York: Warner, 1988.
Williams, Tony. "Authorship Conflict in *The Prisoner*." *Making Television: Authorship and the Production Process*. Ed. Robert J. Thompson and Gary Burns. New York: Praeger, 1990.

Gary Burns

Production Code/Ratings System. To ward off government regulation and to protect profits, the motion picture industry employed the Production Code from 1934 to 1968, the last year marking the transition to the now familiar motion picture ratings system. Both the former and current systems are voluntary and internal to the industry. Producers, distributors, or exhibitors who choose to ignore or violate the rules of the ratings system face no criminal charges. Self-regulation succeeds because producers and exhibitors desire access to profitable distribution, which a few large companies control. The large companies wish to protect their investments from governmental regulation and community protest, and so enforce an internal regulatory scheme on smaller players in the industry.

Composed in 1930, the Motion Picture Production Code was a set of guidelines for the subject matter and style of films. Martin Quigley, Catholic publisher of a movie trade journal, and St. Louis University professor Daniel A. Lord authored the Code at the request of the motion picture industry's trade association. According to the Code, movies would show correct standards of life, and no film would lower the moral standards of the audience or ridicule natural or human law. The Code also listed specific topics and actions the film industry trade association had been warning producers for years to avoid or treat carefully.

In 1934, the motion picture trade association created an office—the Production Code Administration—to enforce the Code on its member companies. Joseph Breen served as head of this office from its inception until his retirement in 1954. Breen worked closely with studio heads, conferring with them about story selection, scripts, directing, and editing. His role was not to decree that a finished film passed or violated the Code, but to negotiate changes throughout the production process until a morally acceptable product resulted. Although violations of the Code were punishable by a $25,000 fine, the Code Administration never imposed this penalty.

The Production Code and Code Administration arose from pressures for governmental censorship and consumer boycotts. Past instances of pressure that threatened profits had also generated self-regulation by the industry. In 1909, exhibitors in New York City created a citizen review board after the mayor tried to prevent children from attending movies without an adult. Producers voluntarily submitted films to the review board, which published a list of recommended films and urged patrons to support "selection, not censorship."

Ohio and Pennsylvania enacted the first state censorship laws in 1911. State and local censorship decreased profits because the varying regulations required producers to circulate multiple versions of their films. The industry challenged the constitutionality of such censorship in a 1915 Supreme Court case, but lost. The Court ruled that films were business, like a carnival, not constitutionally protected speech, as are newspapers. This decision allowing local and state censorship of films stood until 1952.

The basis for the particular form of self-regulation we know as the Production Code lay in a series of scandals in the early 1920s. First, slapstick comedian Fatty Arbuckle was accused of the rape and murder of a starlet. Next, investigation into the murder of director William Desmond Morris suggested that Morris had simultaneous affairs with actress Mary Miles Minter, Minter's mother, and comedienne Mabel Normand. Finally, the public learned that all-American actor Wallace Reid suffered from morphine addiction. In the wake of these scandals, 32 state legislatures began considering film censorship bills. Religious and civic groups strongly supported censorship efforts at all levels—local, state, and federal.

The motion picture industry responded in 1922 by forming a trade association, the Motion Picture Producers and Distributors Association (MPPDA), and hired an upright Republican to lead the group. William Hays, an attorney and church elder from Indiana, had served as Postmaster General and head of the Republican National Committee. Hays successfully lobbied against further state censorship laws, and set up internal controls to forestall further censorship threats.

MPPDA staffer Col. Jason Joy served as liaison between the studios and local/state censor boards. He compiled a list of "Don'ts and Be Carefuls," items that set off alarms with local censor personnel. This list of 36 prohibitions included among the "Don'ts": profanity, nudity, scenes of childbirth, and ridicule of clergy. Among the "Be Carefuls" were: sympathy for criminals, brutality, first night scenes, and excessive or lustful kissing.

As sound films became more widespread in the late 1920s, MPPDA head Will Hays decided that new guidelines were necessary to protect profits. Producers of silent films could satisfy censors relatively inexpensively by explaining omitted action in an intertitle, or changing offensive wording of intertitles. The much greater investment required for sound films made a single standard for the entire country imperative.

The text of the 1930 Production Code pleased censorship advocates, but the Code's lack of enforcement did not. Reformers particularly objected to movies with sympathetic gangsters, such as *Little Caesar* (LeRoy, 1930) and *Scarface*

(Hawks, 1932), and to Mae West's risqué films. After efforts to pass a national censorship law failed, reformers led by the Catholic Church turned to consumer boycott. In 1934, the Church organized the Legion of Decency, whose members pledged not to attend indecent movies.

Hays responded quickly by creating the Production Code Administration to enforce the moral standards stated in the Code. In the short term, a particular film might generate greater box office receipts by including topics, actions, or moods prohibited by the Code. However, in the long term self-censorship under the Code enhanced profits for the entire industry.

The Production Code protected the industry's profits, but came under fire for limiting the scope of Hollywood's films. Critics argued that the Code inhibited artistic expression and prevented movies from dealing well with adult themes. In addition, some objected to the forced morality allowed by the principle of "compensating moral value." A film could show adultery or murder, if the evildoer were punished or reformed by the end of the film. Producers could include 80 minutes of the sex and crime they believed sold films, so long as the Code Administration felt that the last 10 minutes kept those topics within acceptable bounds.

Enforcement of the Code began to wane in the 1950s. Court decisions undermined state and local censorship, and foreign films with nudity and sex became available. Several Hollywood producers notoriously flouted the Code, yet garnered good profits.

The motion picture industry currently employs a ratings system to prevent government regulation and maintain profits. Under the Production Code, industry staffers modified films during production so that all were suitable for family viewing. Now the industry produces a wider range of movies and expects parents to protect their children from inappropriate films. Ratings of G, PG, PG-13, R, or NC-17 (formerly X) suggest to parents the degree of caution needed. G indicates films for all ages, whereas PG calls for parental guidance and PG-13 for strong guidance for children under 13. R films are restricted to patrons over 16-18, unless accompanied by a parent or guardian (ages vary by locality), and NC-17 means no children under 17 admitted.

The ratings system is administered by the Motion Picture Association of America (MPAA, formerly called the MPPDA), the trade association of major film firms. Producers voluntarily submit films to the MPAA's Classification and Rating Administration. This board of seven parents examines theme, language, nudity, sex, violence, and—since 1986—drug use. The seven parents decide on a rating by majority vote. When films receive ratings the producers find overly restrictive, they may appeal or re-edit. *Dressed to Kill* (De Palma, 1980) was submitted three times before receiving the desired R rating.

The film industry inaugurated the ratings system in 1968 at the urging of MPAA president Jack Valenti. Valenti recognized that the Production Code no longer served the industry. Filmgoing had ceased as a weekly family activity, for television had become the primary form of regular family entertainment. To maintain profits, Hollywood needed to offer what television did not—more sex, violence, and spectacle than the Code permitted.

Theater owners resisted Valenti's efforts to institute a ratings system. They preferred to keep the Production Code, fearing that age restrictions would reduce box office revenues. Valenti pointed out that court rulings had nearly decimated local and state censorship, but that a 1968 decision permitted cities and states to enact age restrictions. If the industry did not create a nationwide system, it might face a multitude of classification schemes that would hold theaters criminally liable for violations. Exhibitors chose Valenti's voluntary system over the alternative.

The MPAA ratings system has faced criticism from both consumers and producers. Consumer groups have charged that the system fails to protect children. The lapse may occur because theaters fail to enforce age restrictions, or because the board gives less restrictive ratings to violent films than to films with sexual content. Protest over the latter issue prompted creation of the PG-13 rating. Consumers felt that the violence in the PG-rated *Indiana Jones and the Temple of Doom* (Spielberg, 1984) was excessive for young children. Valenti agreed to create PG-13 as a rating in between PG and R. Child advocates also complain about a paucity of films for children. This may stem from the belief that a G or PG rating reduces the audience for a film. To achieve a "more attractive" rating of PG-13 or R, producers may add gratuitous nudity, profanity, or violence to an otherwise "family-oriented" film.

In 1990, figures within the film industry began criticizing the X rating. An X rating strongly reduced the commercial value of a film. Some theaters and malls prohibited screening of X-rated films, and little advertising was available in newspapers, on cable, network television, or radio. Some financing contracts specified that the producer deliver a film that earned an R rating. No law requires a film be rated, but all major distributors release rated films. Film directors complained that to avoid X ratings they had to practice self-censorship, inhibiting free artistic expression.

Filmmakers lobbied Valenti for a rating in between R and X—an A or M to indicate strong adult themes or images. However, Valenti replaced X with NC-17. Distributors of low-budget pornographic films may still use X (or XX or XXX), because it is the one rating not copyrighted. Films receiving the new NC-17 rating tend to be major commercial releases with high production values. This has led audiences to regard NC-17 movies as "artistic" films with strong sexual or violent content, such as *Henry and June* (Kaufman, 1990).

Religious and community groups charge that the new rating is a blatant effort to increase profits by avoiding the stigma of the X rating. Critics are concerned the new rating gives a veneer of respectability to films with extreme sexual or violent content, and thus that children will have greater access to these films than if the films were labelled X.

Bibliography

Austin, Bruce A. *Immediate Seating: A Look at Movie Audiences.* Belmont: Wadsworth, 1989.

Jacobs, Lea. *The Wages of Sin: Censorship and the Fallen Woman Film, 1928-1942.* Madison: U of Wisconsin P, 1991.

Jowett, Garth. *Film: The Democratic Art.* Boston: Little, Brown, 1976.

Denise Hartsough

See also
Pornography

Professional Wrestling. In *Henry IV*, Hotspur urged, "Let them grapple," but William Shakespeare could never have imagined how lucrative grappling could become. In 1993, professional wrestling produced a gross annual revenue of $1 billion, with the lion's share going into two major corporations, the World Wrestling Federation (WWF), headquartered in Stamford, CT, and World Championship Wrestling (WCW), owned by Atlanta cable television tycoon Ted Turner. The remainder of the wrestling largesse was split among 23 regional federations throughout the United States. Superstar performers commanded salaries commensurate with those in other professional sports. Hulk Hogan signed a six-month contract with WCW in 1994 for $1,600,000, and earned an additional $680,000 from his share of one pay-per-view bout with Ric Flair.

While professional wrestling drew expanded nationwide media exposure in the 1980s and 1990s because of cable television, it had long been a major spectator attraction in the United States. During wrestling's first "Golden Age," from the 1920s to World War II, tens of thousands of fans packed stadiums to witness the skills of Jim "The Golden Greek" Londos, Ed "Strangler" Lewis, and Lou Thesz, but the sport truly blossomed in the late 1940s and early 1950s.

Professional wrestling seemed made for television, and promoters such as St. Louis's Sam Muchnick of the National Wrestling Alliance and Verne Gagne of the Minneapolis-based American Wrestling Alliance seized the opportunity to showcase their sport. The major metropolitan markets of Detroit, Chicago, Los Angeles, Boston, New York, and Dallas featured live bouts from either a television or the local arena, and popular radio personalities such as Chicago's Jack Brickhouse and Los Angeles's Steve Allen, as well as former ring greats Lord Athol Layton and Sam Menecher, were hired as announcers. By 1971, more than 250 local television stations in the United States and 50 in Canada aired wrestling, and these programs enticed more than 5,400,000 fans into attending matches in local arenas. In 1984, as a result of nationwide cable telecasts, more than ten million people paid to see matches, making professional wrestling the country's fastest growing spectator sport.

Wrestling's glitz and glamour, mixed with rugged physical contact, appealed to millions of Americans. The symbol of the new generation of professional wrestlers was George Wagner, better known as "Gorgeous George, the Human Orchid." Entering the ring wearing a flowing purple robe to accentuate his perfectly coiffured blonde hair, he had his valet spray the ring with a scent he called "Chanel No. 10."

Following George's success, other wrestlers turned to visual gimmicks. Chief Jay Strongbow and Don Eagle entered with tribal headdresses; Cowboy Bob Ellis and Big Tex McKenzie wore boots and carried lariats; the Mummy was wrapped in bandages and The Thing wore an executioner's garb.

In the 1980s, wrestlers were turned into living comic book characters. No longer satisfied with subtle trappings such as glittering robes and masks, promoters dressed their stars in outrageous costumes and gave them symbolic names. Thus, Randy "Macho Man" Savage donned iridescent fringed clothes; Ricky "the Dragon" Steamboat breathed fire and dressed like a lizard; The Undertaker was a zombie, while Doink was a clown; Norman the Lunatic wore hospital clothes, Nailz sported prison garb, and Bubba Rogers was a Guardian Angel. No getup or gimmick was too outrageous, as novelty brought in crowds and viewers and provided a range of matchups.

Beneath the superficial trappings and athletic competition, however, lies wrestling's true hold on the American psyche. Professional wrestling gives its viewers a momentary sense of understanding through their participation in a symbolic morality play depicting the battle between simplistic truths: good versus evil, patriotism versus treason, integrity versus dishonor, honesty versus devious tricks, and control versus mayhem. It is a levelling, yet uplifting, experience in which the politically voiceless can do their part for God and country by screaming "U.S.A., U.S.A." to cheer on a "true American" as he struggles against an Iranian sheik, Russian bully, or Cuban terrorist. Just as in reality, the brutality in wrestling is never senseless or beyond comprehension. Moreover, wrestling proves their basic belief that good will almost always triumphs over evil. The struggle would never be easy, as treachery and deceit await the unsuspecting and trusting, but the hero always would emerge victorious—bloody, but unbowed.

Thus, professional wrestling survives because it is superb melodramatic theater. Some fans watch matches because they believe what they see is real; the majority suspend their disbelief simply to enjoy the performance. Yet no one truly cares whether bouts are staged because all are left with a sense that they were not only entertained but also were uplifted through subliminal messages which represent the heart of the United States: justice will ultimately prevail; evildoers must repent or be punished; and patriotism is a virtue. In these respects, professional wrestling is a mirror of American popular culture where conflicts are simplified, dramatized, and resolved in order to uphold and affirm the dominant culture.

Bibliography

Gutman, Bill. *Strange and Amazing Wrestling Stories*. New York: Pocket Books, 1986.

Jares, Joe. *Whatever Happened to Gorgeous George: The Blood and Ballyhoo of Professional Wrestling*. Englewood Cliffs: Prentice-Hall, 1974.

Mariotti, Jay. "Wrestling Reality." *Detroit News* 3 Feb. 1985.

Morton, Gerald W., and George M. O'Brien. *Wrestling to Rasslin': Ancient Sport to American Spectacle*. Bowling Green, OH: Bowling Green State U Popular P, 1985.

Sugar, Bert Randolph, and George Napolitano. *The Pictorial History of Wrestling*. New York: Warner, 1984.

Bruce A. Rubenstein

See also
World Wrestling Federation
Wrestling (on Television)

Protest Music is an integral part of American popular culture, from the music used to protest the British tea taxes to complaints about police brutality in the inner city in the 1990s. Soon after the Mayflower landed in Massachusetts, settlers began to sell "broadsides," single sheets of song lyrics. These broadsides first spread news and later helped inspire the revolt against British rule. The song "Revolutionary Tea," for example, was used to spread the news of the Boston Tea Party while inspiring colonists to join the rebellion.

Songs were used intermittently for political purposes after the Revolutionary War, but they did not promote any causes until the mid-1800s. The Negro spiritual "Many Thousand Gone" was frequently sung by African-American slaves seeking freedom, chanting "no more auction block for me." The longevity of protest music is evident in the fact that the melody for that song was borrowed by Bob Dylan for his 1962 protest song, "Blowin' in the Wind."

The Hutchinson Family Singers began touring the U.S. in 1840 singing abolitionist songs. The Hutchinson Family continued singing until 1908, changing their messages after the Civil War to songs that denounced alcohol and promoted women's suffrage.

Civil War songs included the Union's "Maryland, My Maryland" and the Confederacy's "The Bonnie Blue Flag," designed to inspire patriotism and loyalty while undermining the opposition. "The Battle Hymn of the Republic," with music derived from a Negro spiritual and words by Julia Ward Howe, became an anthem for racial equality that was as popular in the 1960s as it was a century earlier.

Protest music became part of the labor movement when the International Workers of the World (IWW) began organizing unskilled workers in the early 20th century. The IWW members, or "Wobblies," attacked corporate greed while promoting their unions in songs like "Solidarity Forever," sung to the melody of the "Battle Hymn of the Republic." Joe Hill (Joel Hagglund) was a Swedish immigrant who adapted numerous hymns into union songs, such as "Amazing Boss" (set to the melody of "Amazing Grace"). These IWW songs were compiled into *The Little Red Songbook*, whose purpose, according to its cover, was "To fan the flames of discontent." Hill was executed in Utah during mine strikes in that state and Montana.

In the 1930s, protest music enjoyed a revival among workers who were suffering in the throes of the Great Depression. One of the most powerful songs was "Joe Hill," about the union organizer. The song was recorded by Paul Robeson in 1934, and it was revived many times. Joan Baez sang "Joe Hill" at Woodstock in 1989. Another popular song, recorded by everyone from Bing Crosby to Tom Waits, was "Brother, Can You Spare a Dime?" The 1932 song talks about the frustrations of a fictional young man who built the railroads and fought World War I, only to be left standing in line for bread during the Depression.

American classical composers also contributed to protest music in the 1930s, including Aaron Copland's marching tune for May Day in 1934, "Into the Streets May First." Members of various ethnic groups established "worker's choruses" in the 1930s like the Jewish immigrants' Workmen's Circle Choruses, which sang in Yiddish.

Protest songs were carried into the 1940s by two American folk music legends, Woody Guthrie and Pete Seeger (see entries). Guthrie began as a hobo singer in the Dust Bowl in the 1930s, but he started singing regularly on the radio in 1937. Guthrie sympathized with migrant workers and union members, and his guitar bore a sign, "This machine kills Fascists." He wrote approximately one thousand songs, including "This Land Is Your Land," a song that has been sung with both patriotic and social protest connotations.

Guthrie influenced many folk protest singers, the first of them being Pete Seeger. Along with Guthrie, he began performing at "hootenannies" in the mid-1940s (see The Almanac Singers). In 1948, Seeger formed the Weavers, who were very successful in recordings and concerts, but were banned from television and radio because of their leftist leanings. Despite their disappearance from radio, jukeboxes, and television in the 1950s, the Weavers and Seeger were strong influences on the protest music of the 1960s "folk revival," which included Bob Dylan, Phil Ochs, Joan Baez, and Tom Paxton (see entries).

Dylan was the most prominent protest singer of the 1960s, mixing sarcasm and serious protest in songs promoting civil rights and attacking war and corporate greed. Dylan mixed social protest in with country music, rock, and religious songs through the 1970s, 1980s, and 1990s.

In the late 1960s, protest music became a mainstay of much of American rock music, including acid rock (Jefferson Airplane's "Volunteers"), folk rock (the Youngbloods' "Get Together"), and soft rock (Three Dog Night's "Easy to Be Hard"). The end of the Vietnam War in the early 1970s resulted in a dramatic decline in protest music, although Bruce Springsteen and Billy Joel appealed to disillusioned working-class teenagers and war veterans with songs like "Born in the U.S.A." and "Allentown." African-American composers in the 1970s drew attention to increasing drug problems in the city (Stevie Wonder's "Living in the City" and Curtis Mayfield's "Freddie's Dead").

In the 1980s, two types of music, punk and rap, used profanity to make their point to African-American and white audiences respectively. Punk often used profanity to express a general disdain for authority, while rap often directed itself to specific institutions, especially the police (N.W.A.'s "Fuck the Police" and Ice-T's "Cop Killer"). The 1980s were also a decade of rock concerts and recorded anthologies supporting numerous causes, beginning with the "No Nukes" concert and album in 1980. The most noteworthy was "We Are the World," the all-time best-selling single, recorded in 1985 to help starving Ethiopians. Later that summer, country and rock musicians were organized by Willie Nelson for Farm Aid, the first of a series of concerts to benefit U.S. farmers.

Other country singers sang for a new cause, the return to conservatism championed by the Moral Majority, President Ronald Reagan, and others in the 1980s and 1990s. Lee Greenwood's "God Bless the U.S.A." became the theme song for those who protested the Great Society of the 1960s and the social welfare programs that followed.

In the early 1990s, anthologies supported numerous causes, including "Tame Yourself," promoting animal rights (1991), and "Born to Choose" (1993), benefiting abortion rights groups.

Bibliography

Denisoff, R. Serge. *Sing a Song of Social Significance.* Bowling Green, OH: Bowling Green State U Popular P, 1983.

Garofalo, Reebee, ed. *Rockin' the Boat: Mass Music and Mass Movements.* Boston: South End, 1992.

McDonnell, John, ed. *Songs of Struggle and Protest.* Cork: Mercier, 1986.

Sanger, Kerran L. *"When the Spirit Says Sing!" The Role of Freedom Songs in the Civil Rights Movement.* New York: Garland, 1995.

Kenneth M. Nagelberg

See also
Freedom Songs

Pryor, Richard (1940-), was one of the funniest men in America in the late sixties, seventies, and eighties, and his name became synonymous with comedy. His comedic act also blended in well in a country filled with political and social turmoil, and his promiscuous lifestyle of drugs and sex was reflective of happenings in American culture.

Pryor grew up poor in Peoria, IL, in a brothel run by his grandmother, Marie Carter. Buck Carter, his father, was a former Golden Gloves boxing champion and his mother, Gertrude Pryor, a bookkeeper. His parents were known to have violent spats, and his mother never wanted children. Often for months at a time, she disappeared and left Richard, who craved attention, with his grandmother. When he was ten years old, Gertrude left for good and his grandmother became the one constant figure in his life. As a child, Richard used comedy to win love and approval. After watching a Jerry Lewis movie, *Sailor Beware*, with his father, Richard knew what he wanted to do in life.

In 1961, he was discharged from the army for cutting another soldier with a switchblade. He walked into Harold's Club in Peoria and convinced the manager he could sing and play the piano. He could do neither, but because of his audacity, he impressed Harold and was hired for his stand-up comedy act. Pryor began to build a reputation as a comedian in the Blackbelt clubs in Cleveland, Chicago, and Buffalo. He idolized Bill Cosby, and by 1963, he was doing stand-up comedy in New York City, where Cosby was the comic of the hour, and Pryor was fascinated by Cosby's success.

He was making regular TV appearances and opening at the Flamingo Hotel in Las Vegas for Bobby Darin by the mid 1960s but, like many figures during this era, soon developed a cocaine habit, and by 1968 he had a $200-a-day habit and two ex-wives. Pryor's lifestyle reflected life in Hollywood during this era. He had relationships with lots of women and snorted cocaine daily.

In September of 1968, his father died of a heart attack and the junkies, prostitutes, winos, and hustlers that had been screaming in his head finally became a part of his act. He had finally found his own standup persona, which touched on a profane edge of Lenny Bruce and on the pathos of Charlie

Chaplin's Little Tramp. Pauline Kael described him in 1979 as "a master of lyrical obscenity, the only great satirist among our comics."

After playing Piano Man opposite Diana Ross in the 1972 Billie Holiday biography *Lady Sings the Blues*, he became a sensation as a movie star, making a series of hit movies between 1974 and 1980 that included *Uptown Saturday Night, Car Wash, Silver Streak,* and *Stir Crazy.*

Pryor was seriously burned in what he admits to as a suicide attempt in 1980, and he now suffers from multiple sclerosis, which has left him crippled and brought serenity and peace to his life.

Bibliography

Plummer, William. "Richard Pryor: Nowhere to Hide." *People* 29 May 1995.

Peggy Stevenson Ratliff

Public Privies to Private Baths. Prior to the mid-19th century, most Americans attended to their daily necessities in outdoor privies. The most fastidious called the privy "a house office," a "necessary house," or simply the "necessary"; many knew it as the outhouse. Behaviors and beliefs surrounding privies made them popular subjects of everyday humor and folklore. Outhouse jokes were universal. Stories of falling through the privy hole or of attacks from below by spiders, snakes, and bees were legion. Stealing, moving, or tipping over of outhouses became a Halloween ritual.

Contemporary comic strips such as *The Wizard of Id, Garfield,* and *The Far Side* suggest the outhouse continues as an American symbol. The privy's association with "a good old rural life" is also evident in poetry and prose by writers such as James Whitcomb Riley ("The Passing of the Old Backhouse") and Lambert Florin's *Backyard Classic: An Adventure in Nostalgia* (1981).

The indoor chamber pot, used at night by those not wishing (or able) to journey 60 yards to the privy in dark or inclement stormy weather, came in assorted shapes and sizes. Usually kept under the bed, or in a closet, the pot or "potty" (for children) required daily cleaning. Pots encased in wooden boxes to disguise their purpose assumed names such as *chaise percée* or commode. American males often used British terms such as Cousin John or Jake to refer to a privy or a chamber pot. After the first toilet was installed in the White House during John Quincy Adams's administration, the term Quincy became a euphemism for an effete dandy.

Women found using the outhouse especially distasteful. One of the early advocates of indoor plumbing was Catharine Beecher (1800-78), who, in her popular household manuals, offered detailed advice about the two major sanitation systems advocated by those who sought to bring the outhouse into the main house. Beecher first (1849) endorsed a system of human waste disposal advocated by sanitary reformer George Waring (1833-98) in *Earth Closets: How to Make Them and How to Use Them* (1868). The earth system operated on a principle of dropping dry earth on human waste in order to induce rapid fermentation with the generation of noxious gases. The simplest form of earth closet was

a wooden commode equipped with a back hopper filled with earth. Waring's model, moveable to any room, required no water supply, and no expensive jangle of pipes and fittings as the rival water closet systems. Waring (and his imitators) argued the treated wastes could be recycled as fertilizer for gardens and farms.

Waring's approach, however, proved unfeasible in big cities since the large quantities of treated waste had to be hauled away. Also, the opportunity of being rid of domestic sewage instantly, as in the water closet, had its appeal. Thus, despite concern over which bowls, traps, or vents to buy or what precautions to take to prevent the dreaded sewer gas, the technology that flushed wastes out of sight through a network of invisible pipes either to a municipal sewer or an underground cesspool proved the most attractive option for most middle-class Americans in dealing with one of life's necessities.

To many rural males, however, outdoor privies stood for traditional masculinity, sites not quickly deserted for modernity's marvels. When the Rockefeller Sanitary Commission (1909), U.S. Public Health Service (1912), and various state bureaus of health attempted to impose a "sanitary privy" or to have indoor plumbing installed in farm houses, such groups often encountered resistance from those who, in the estimate of one rural resident, saw no need for "one of them new-fangled white crock-flushers."

By the 1890s, privies frequently contained mail-order catalogs. The 500-page, semiannual "Wish Books" from Sears, Roebuck, or Montgomery Ward filled both literary and physical needs while one was, in the title of Ernst Peterson's 1952 book, *Sittin' and A-Thinkin'*. Catalogs in outhouses became the subject of hilarious satire and parody, such as the *Rears and Robust Mail Order Catalogue for Spring/Summer/Fall/Winter* (1940).

In America's centennial year only wealthy homes had bathrooms, that is, prescribed places for bathing. If they also had an indoor toilet, it likely would have been located in a closet or other storage area. Sink, stool, and tub migrated into the bathroom from elsewhere inside or outside the home. The sink originated as a washbowl and pitcher set in individual bedchambers; the stool replaced the outdoor privy or the indoor chamber pot; the tub derived from the portable tin-plated or wood tubs of the kitchen. The bathroom itself traveled about the house, being located in basements, kitchens, utility rooms, and, sometimes, in the smallest bedchamber. Since it required a constant water supply, house remodelers and new home designers kept it close to the building's plumbing system.

The white trio of tub (with canvas shower curtain optional), toilet, and sink (free standing or wall-hanging), each aligned along a wall compressed into an average of 48 square feet, became a distinct architectural form. Unlike their migratory predecessors, these fixtures were each permanently attached to networks of water and waste. The fixtures came in standard sizes, with standard fittings, many made by a plumbing manufacturer appropriately named American Standard. Edward and Clarence Scott improved upon commercially prepared toilet paper (which sold in bulky packages of five sheets) by selling toilet "tissue" that came in small perforated rolls. Its whiteness matched the other standardized bathroom fixtures.

The modern bath's tub continued old domestic rituals such as the Saturday night bath, and prompted new ones: concocting bathtub gin (homemade gin mixed with ginger ale and orange to kill its taste) and taking luxurious bubble baths like Marilyn Monroe's famous scene in *The Seven Year Itch* (1955). While therapeutic shower baths had promoters throughout the 19th century, the shower-in-the-bathtub or the separate shower stall were largely 20th-century additions to the American bathroom. Variously called the jet bath, the douche, or the rain bath, the shower (versus the bath) was heralded as a typically American innovation: quick, focused, economical, efficient.

In a number of ways, the emergence of the American bathroom summarizes several of the implications of other home utilities (running water, steam heat, electric light) that emerged in the period 1876-1915. First, they changed a home's relationship to its surrounding neighborhood and altered the physical landscape, above and below the surface. A household no longer depended upon itself for many of life's common needs. Now forces beyond its domestic circle dictated the quantity and quality, cost and availability of several of its vital life support systems. To create this new landscape of water main, sewer pipe, and power cable required political and economic decisions by governmental and corporate enterprises, both of whom assumed greater control over the home residence's shape, structure, and placement via zoning ordinances, fire regulations, and building codes.

The new utilities, epitomized by the new bathroom (after 1900 no "new" middle-class homes could be without one), accustomed Americans to think of "systems" as a metaphor for modern life. Introduced to the idea by the rail-road companies (the Pennsylvania System) and their related corporations (the Pullman System), they hooked up to or plugged into the Edison, Bell, or Standard system.

American householders did so as consumers. Instead of being the products of the homeowners, heat, light, water, and sewage removal became commodities to be purchased elsewhere rather than to be made at home. Utility commodities begat other commodities as successive waves of new domestic appliances invaded every room of the house. Once one had gas or electric light, advertisers assured consumers, it was vital to secure gas or electric heat. Once a perimeter of power outlets was installed, a panoply of power fans, shavers, and hair dryers eventually followed.

While their promoters promised efficient, trouble-free services, sewers stuffed, mains leaked, power lines shorted, and fixtures broke. Hence, in addition to the initial installers of home utilities, other individuals—an ever-increasing cadre of repair and service personnel—performing new occupations increasingly entered the house and its specialized spaces such as the bathroom.

A final, and perhaps the most important, ramification of the new bathroom utilities was their gradual, but increasingly widespread, homogenization of the domestic environment. The coalition of new utilities found in the American bathroom by 1950 provided many modern conveniences and comforts, but such modern conduits also had modern consequences. By then, the flick of a switch, the turn of a valve, the flush of a toilet meant everyday life had also become more controlled, qualified, and standardized.

Bibliography

Peterson, Jon A. "The Impact of Sanitary Reform upon American Urban Planning, 1840-1890." *Journal of Social History* 13 (1979): 83-101.

Stone, May N. "The Plumbing Paradox: American Attitudes Toward Late-Nineteenth-Century Domestic Sanitary Arrangements." *Winterthur Portfolio* 14.3 (1979): 283-309.

Van Rensselaer, Martha. "Home Sanitation." *Chautauquan Magazine* 34 (1901): 183-91.

Wright, Lawrence. *Clean and Decent: The Fascinating History of the Bathroom and Water Closet....* New York: Viking, 1960.

Thomas J. Schlereth

Puente, Tito (1923-2000), bandleader, timbales player, vibraphonist, composer, and arranger, was known as the King of the Mambo in the 1950s. Along with other band-leaders in New York City, Puente brought the hot, big band mambo style to the peak of its popularity and perfection. His 1958 RCA Victor album, *Dance Mania*, is considered one of his finest works and is an important documentation of the mambo style.

Born of Puerto Rican parents in New York City, Puente came of age when a circuit of clubs, bars, and theaters was producing the first generation of resident U.S. Latin band-leaders playing primarily for Latin audiences. At that time the music from Cuba and elsewhere in the Latin world was absorbing elements of U.S. music. The mambo, for instance, borrowed instrumental solos, ensemble arranging techniques, and big band brashness from North American jazz.

The golden age of the mambo began in 1952, when the Palladium and other New York ballrooms began to feature the mambo exclusively. Puente brought the form to a pinnacle during the 1950s and 1960s, giving it an intense and nervous quality that captured the upbeat New York dance scene. He continued the formula developed by Machito's Afro-Cubans of swing orchestrations heavy on the brass, Cuban song forms, and a complete Afro-Cuban rhythm section. His arranging, like his timbales playing, was fast and bravura.

As the mambo craze faded in the late 1950s and early 1960s—and Hollywood halted its two-decade string of Latin movies—Puente's big band continued to flourish, as did several other established groups. Musicians who later became stars in their own right worked with Puente, including the influential conga player Ramon "Mongo" Santamaria.

Older musicians like Puente asserted that salsa was nothing new when it emerged in the 1970s, and Carlos Santana, who added rock elements to salsa, turned two Puente tunes ("Oye Como Va?" and "Para los Rumberos") into major pop hits.

In the 1980s and the 1990s, Puente continued to perform in New York and tour the country. But, except for his broader fame in the 1950s and sporadic attention from the music press and major labels thereafter, his audience remained the resident Latin population, as well as a cult following among "mambonicks" or those non-Latin fans, largely from Italian and Jewish communities, who developed a loyalty to his music during the Palladium heyday.

Bibliography

Gerard, Charley, and Marty Sheller. *Salsa! The Rhythm of Latin Music.* Crown Point: White Cliffs Media, 1989.

Gillespie, John Birks, and Al Fraser. *To Be, or Not—to Bop: Memoirs.* Garden City: Doubleday, 1979.

Roberts, John Storm. *The Latin Tinge: The Impact of Latin Music on the United States.* New York: Oxford UP, 1979.

Lynn Darroch

Pulp Magazines were born when Frank A. Munsey (1854-1925), publisher of a slick magazine, *The Golden Argosy*, in the 1890s decided to include only fiction and to print the magazine on cheap pulp-wood paper. Although their stories varied greatly in quality and content, the pulps were essentially magazines specializing in sensation, revealing characterizations through action rather than introspection. From the 1920s until the 1950s, pulp magazines printed stories of airplanes, criminals, wars, detectives (see *Black Mask*), romances, Westerns (see next entry), sex, railroads, sports, science fiction (see entry), heroic adventures, zeppelins, submarines, and weird fiction (see *Weird Tales*); and despite the diversity of their subject material, virtually all these stories were action oriented. Action and adventure are not synonymous; the two differ, and certain pulp magazines specialized in printing stories in which the concept of adventure *per se* was the predominant subject. Foremost among these magazines was *Adventure*, which was started in 1910. Prior to *Adventure*, many of the early pulp magazines—in particular, *Argosy, All-Story, Cavalier*, and *Top-Notch*—ran fiction in which action predominated, but although the hero in one of these early pulp stories would often be faced with a difficult challenge against overwhelming (if not apparently insurmountable) odds, there was little sense of personal threat or physical danger. The majority of readers could start a story feeling certain that the hero would emerge largely unscathed from numerous battles with hordes of Indians, Africans, lions, tigers, and Tharks.

When Trumbull White became editor of *Adventure* in 1910, the first issue of the new magazine contained an editorial stating the new magazine's policies. "Adventure," according to White, "was a fundamental of human nature" and linked to the inquisitive memories of childhood; it is "the reason is that none of us ever really grows up. We are always boys and girls, a little older in years, but the same nature—alert to the new, questioning, investigating, growing, living; stirred by martial music; thrilled by the sight of the fire-horses dashing madly down the street; lured by tales of subtle intrigue and splendid daring." The concepts of "investigating, growing, living" dominated the stories published in *Adventure*, for White and his more notable successor Arthur S. Hoffman realized that although "adventure" might involve activity, it was first and foremost a state of mind, a mental readiness to experience the new and unexpected, no matter what the setting. White and Hoffman knew that adventures could occur in the Far East, the Pacific Northwest, India, the Italian Renaissance, the high seas, and darkest Africa, but they could also occur in such settings as realistically described Canadian fishing villages. Nevertheless, all adventures were limited by existing realities. On one level, this meant that the protagonist's abilities had to conform to physical realities, and *Adventure*'s heroes were conceived in generally realistic terms: though they might be physical champions, they did not invariably emerge unscathed from their travails; it was not uncommon for them to suffer terrible beatings, break their limbs, receive severe stab wounds, and occasionally even lose their lives. Correspondingly, the described adventures had to reflect existing realities: if the author used an exotic location for the setting of the story, every effort had to be made at historical, geographical, and sociocultural accuracy; though simplicities of course existed, *Adventure* was nonetheless the first pulp magazine to treat other cultures and minorities in a consistently sympathetic fashion. On a more significant level, this concept of adventure as a reflection of physical reality eliminated the realm of the fantastic from all but a few of the stories published in *Adventure*, and those few were set on Earth, not the moon or the planets.

Through a combination of Hoffman's brilliant editorship, intelligent marketing, and well-written stories, *Adven-*

Photo courtesy of Popular Culture Library, Bowling Green State University, Bowling Green, OH.

ture rapidly became preeminent as a pulp magazine. It had an avid regular readership, its circulation numbered in the hundreds of thousands, and its stories were routinely anthologized in the influential "Best of the Year" anthologies. The publishers of pulp magazines noted *Adventure*'s success and attempted to adapt or start magazines offering their readers adventure fiction: the ensuing decades saw such pulps as *The Thrill Book, Hutchinson's Adventure Magazine, Mammoth Adventure, Mystery Adventures, Red Star Adventures, High-Seas Adventures, Adventure Trails*, and *All Star Adventure Magazine* (to name but a few), attempting to capture some of *Adventure*'s regular audience. They were only partially successful, for in these magazines the concept of "adventure" was redefined and equated with action and deeds of derring-do in exotic lands.

Hoffman left *Adventure* in 1927, and under successive editors and changes of ownership, the concept of adventure changed correspondingly; ultimately "adventure" no longer involved "investigating, growing, living" but became virtually synonymous with quasi-realistic physical action in the face of a physical threat. *Adventure*, however, continued to publish stories generally eschewing the fantastic, and it remained for the newly established science fiction magazines to introduce a new variation into the established definition of "adventure." Though they were frequently deficient in characterizations and ludicrous in presenting "science,"

the best of the stories in the science fiction pulp magazines contain what is commonly referred to as "a sense of wonder," a sense of imaginative adventure that is bounded only by imagination rather than restricted by the laws of physics and chance.

Bibliography

Sampson, Robert. *Yesterday's Faces*. 6 vols. Bowling Green, OH: Bowling Green State U Popular P, 1983-93.

Richard Bleiler

Pulp Westerns. The Western genre has been among the most popular themes in mass market literature as well as other branches of popular entertainment. This is true of the pulp magazines specializing in Westerns from the 1920s through the 1950s. The Western story had become popular in the 1870s with stories about Buffalo Bill, by authors such as Edward Zane Carroll Judson (1822-1886), who wrote under the name Ned Buntline, and Colonel Prentiss Ingraham (1843-1903).

These stories were published in what were called dime novels and weekly nickel libraries. Soon there were series of stories published about other characters of the Great West, such as Diamond Dick, Diamond Dick, Jr., Ted Strong, and Young Wild West. Even some of the criminals such as the Dalton Gang, the James Boys, and Billy the Kid were romanticized. These series ran for hundreds of issues. The important nickel library from the pulp magazine standpoint was *New Buffalo Bill Weekly,* which became the *Western Story Library* for eight issues, and with the August 9, 1919, issue, metamorphized into the first pulp Western, *Western Story Magazine* (published by Street & Smith).

A slew of other pulp Westerns followed shortly: *Triple-X Western* (Fawcett), June 1924; *The Frontier* (Doubleday), October 1924; *Ranch Romances* (Clayton), October 1924; *North-West Stories* (Fiction House), May 1925; *Lariat Story Magazine* (Fiction House), August 1925; *Cowboy Stories* (Clayton), October 1925; *West* (Doubleday), January 5, 1926; *Wild West Weekly* (Street & Smith), August 13, 1927; *Western Trails* (Hersey), October 1928; and *Western Outlaws* (Hersey), December 1929.

The Western pulp magazines had their heyday in the 1930s. However, sales began dropping off in the 1940s and by 1960 the Western pulp magazine had practically disappeared. In the urban areas, detective pulps outsold the Western, but everywhere else, the Western was king of the hill. Farmhands and cowboys went to sleep reading the Western pulp magazines.

The Pulp Magazine Quick Reference Guide, compiled by John Locke in 1988, but never published, attempts to list all the pulp magazines by title, all the variations of title, plus the date of first publication. As a sample, here is every tenth Western title from that list: *Ace High Western Magazine, Best Western Magazine, Complete Cowboy Novel, Cowboy Stories, Far West Stories, Frontier Stories, Lariat Story Magazine, New Western Magazine, Pioneer Western, Ranch Romances, Rangeland Sweethearts, Riders of the Range, Romantic Western, Sure-Fire Western, Triple Western, Variety Western, Western Adventures, Western Outlaws, Western Story Magazine,* and *Wild West Weekly.*

The longer running of the Western pulp magazines included: *Western Story Magazine,* with about 1,000 issues, 1919-49; *Ranch Romances,* over 900 issues, 1924-71; *Wild West Weekly,* about 830 issues, 1927-43; *West,* about 240 issues, 1926-53; *Star Western,* about 220 issues, 1933-54; *Rangeland Romances,* about 215 issues, 1935-55; *Frontier Stories,* about 210 issues, 1924-53; *Texas Rangers,* 206 issues, 1936-58; and *Lariat Story Magazine,* about 200 issues, 1925-50.

The editors knew there were two ways to sell their magazines. To attract buyers new to the magazine, they produced dramatic covers in vivid colors. Therefore, the covers invariably would have a hero about to arrest a villain or blazing away at unseen enemies with a desperate expression on his face. Sometimes there would be a woman helping the hero fight off the attackers. For those already buying the magazine, continuing character stories were the big draw. For continuing characters, *Wild West Weekly* was the champion.

Then there were the magazines which had in every issue a lead-off long story starring the same character: *Pete Rice Magazine* (Street & Smith), 32 issues, 1933-39; *Masked Rider Western Magazine* (Ranger-Standard), 100 issues, 1934-53; *Mavericks* (Popular), 5 issues, September 1934-February 1935; *Texas Rangers* (Standard) (Jim Hatfield), 206 issues, 1936-58; *The Lone Ranger Magazine* (Trojan), 8

Photo courtesy of Popular Culture Library, Bowling Green State University, Bowling Green, OH

issues, April-November 1937; *Super Western* (Ace), 4 issues, August 1937-March 1938; *Western Raider* (Popular) (*El Halcon de la Sierra*), 3 issues, August/September 1938-December/January 1939; *Range Riders* (Ranger-Standard), 76 issues, 1938-53; *The Rio Kid Western* (Standard), 76 issues, 1939-53; *Western Dime Novels—Red Star Western—Silver Buck Western* (Munsey) (The Silver Buck), 5 issues, May 1940-January 1941; *Big Chief Western* (Munsey) (White Eagle), 3 issues, October 1941-February 1942; *The Pecos Kid Western* (Popular), 5 issues, July 1950-June 1951; *Hopalong Cassidy's Western Magazine* (Standard), 3 issues, fall 1950 to spring 1951.

Also, there were the magazines named after well-known people: *Walt Coburn's Action Novels* (Fiction House), one issue in 1931; *Buck Jones Western Stories* (Dell), 3 issues, November 1936-September 1937; *Zane Grey's Western Magazine* (Dell), 82 issues, 1946-54; *Walt Coburn's Western Magazine* (Popular), 16 issues, 1949-51; *Max Brand's Western Magazine* (Popular), 33 issues, 1949-54; *Luke Short's Western* (Dell), 2 issues in 1954. The *Zane Grey's Western Magazine* was a digest-size pulp and considered, by the Western authors, as a premier magazine.

Bibliography

Carr, Nick. *The Western Pulp Hero.* Mercer Island: Starmont, 1989.

Dinan, John A. *The Pulp Western*. San Bernardino: Borgo, 1983.

Pronzini, Bill, and Martin H. Greenberg. *Arbor House Treasury of Great Western Stories*. New York: Arbor House, 1982.

Albert Tonik

Punk Rock is a music genre whose practitioners intentionally try to upset their audiences and critics. It came about as a reaction to the commercialization of rock music in the 1970s, but it persists as a force on the edge of rock. The origins of punk rock were in the garage bands, groups that often practiced or recorded in garages. As successful rock groups used more sophisticated instrumentation and production techniques, garage bands opted for simple instrumentation and rough-edged vocals.

Many U.S. garage bands surfaced in the mid-1960s in the Pacific Northwest and California. They were often "one-hit wonders," releasing a successful single on a small record label before disappearing from the national charts. Examples include Portland's Kingsmen ("Louie, Louie") and Los Angeles's Standells ("Dirty Water").

In Detroit, the garage band MC5 was the house band for John Sinclair's radical White Panther Party. They gained a national reputation for their 1968 song "Kick Out the Jams (motherfucker)," which could not be played on radio because of its profane language. In New York City in 1967, the Velvet Underground recorded songs that glorified drug use ("Heroin" and "Sweet Jane") and sadomasochism ("Venus in Furs").

Another early leader of the U.S. punk movement was Iggy Pop and his group, Iggy and the Stooges. Among other things, Iggy was the first to adopt an outrageous stage name. In 1967, Iggy predated much of the punk performance movement, diving into Ann Arbor, MI, audiences, cutting himself on stage with glass, and running around the stage shirtless and screaming.

In the mid-1970s, underground music clubs in New York City moved south from Greenwich Village to the less-fashionable Bowery. Underground veterans like Lou Reed and John Cale joined with future punk-rockers like Patti Smith and Richard Hell (Richard Myers) at Max's Kansas City. Tom Verlaine (Tom Miller) and Hell formed the group Television, and Verlaine convinced the owner of CBGB's (Country Blue-Grass and Blues) to open the club's back room to punk groups in 1975.

CBGB's became the home of punk rock in the U.S., just as London's Roxy Club became the home of British groups like the Sex Pistols, the Damned, and the Clash. Fashions and musical styles traveled back and forth from London to New York. Punk rockers donned torn jeans, tattoos, spiked hair, and body piercings. The music varied from hard-driving guitar rock (Television, Richard Hell and the Voivoids), to Patti Smith's poetic interpretations, to the "glam rock" of the New York Dolls.

One of the most durable punk bands is the Ramones. Each member of the band took on the last name Ramone when they formed in the late 1970s. They play short songs with mock-rebellious lyrics like "Now I Wanna Sniff Some Glue," preceding each song with a quick "1-2-3-4" count.

In the late 1970s and early 1980s, many of the punk rockers moved to the milder protests of the "new wave" movement. Many of the groups had hit singles, including Blondie ("Heart of Glass"), the Talking Heads ("Burning Down the House"), Devo ("Whip It"), the Cars ("Shake It Up"), and the Pretenders ("Back on the Chain Gang"). Even the rebellious Patti Smith had a hit single with Bruce Springsteen's "Because the Night."

Groups that stayed on the rebellious edge of punk rock went farther underground, playing in local clubs and distributing their music on small independent record labels or self-produced cassettes. Punk clubs, at first in Los Angeles and New York City, cleared out an area in front of the stage called "the pit" that was sometimes fenced in. Audiences for "hard core" punk bands like Los Angeles's Black Flag, X, or the Minutemen (named because their songs were so short) jammed into the pit to "mosh," or throw themselves at each other. Dancers often dove onto the stage or caught performers who dove into the crowd. Similar scenes were repeated across the country by, for example, the Dead Boys in Cleveland and the Replacements and Hüsker Dü in Minneapolis. Other punk musicians became more political. Jello Biafra often included biting sarcasm into Dead Kennedys' songs like "California Uber Alles" and "Too Drunk to Fuck." Biafra also made spoken-word records and ran for mayor of San Francisco.

Henry Rollins left Black Flag and formed his own group, the Rollins Band. Rollins became the most successful hard-core performer of the late 1980s and early 1990s, displaying diverse talents in poetry and prose writing as well as in music.

The Riot Grrrls movement incorporated women into the agitation of punk rock, with feminist messages from all-female groups like L7, Bikini Kill, and Mecca Normal directed at the increasing numbers of female punk rock fans.

Bibliography

Heylin, Clinton. *From the Velvets to the Voivoids: A Pre-Punk History for a Post-Punk World.* New York: Penguin, 1993.

Marcus, Greil. *In the Fascist Bathroom: Writings on Punk, 1977-1992.* London: Penguin, 1993.

——. *Lipstick Traces: A Secret History of the Twentieth Century.* Cambridge: Harvard UP, 1989.

——. *Ranters & Crowd Pleasers: Punk in Pop Music, 1977-92.* New York: Anchor, 1994.

Kenneth M. Nagelberg

Puppets in Television. Puppets satirize, parody, discuss, and explore the social topics of their day. In the process, they also educate and entertain. American puppetry on television reached back to its folk roots and combined them with the technical wizardry of the television age to create a enduring cultural form that spans two generations and has become one of the primary ways that young children experience and learn from the medium of television.

The earliest of television's puppets was drawn from radio—Edgar Bergen (see entry) and his alter-ego, Charlie McCarthy. Charlie was an adult puppet; he shook hands with Harry Truman, Eleanor Roosevelt, Winston Churchill, and

Dwight Eisenhower and exchanged sexually charged repartee with Mae West and Marilyn Monroe. Sophisticated in his top hat, tails, and monocle, Charlie's wit and bawdy humor often pushed the boundaries of what was socially acceptable on early television. Still, Charlie McCarthy was immensely popular, winning a wooden Oscar for straight man Bergen in 1937, but the duo's popularity waned on television.

In terms of sheer longevity, one of television's most popular puppet acts was ventriloquist Paul Winchell (1924-) with his puppets, Jerry Mahoney and Knucklehead Smith. From 1947 to 1972, Winchell, Mahoney, and Smith starred in nine different shows, primarily on Saturday mornings or afternoons. The skits were drawn from slapstick comedy, but their continued popularity, even after Winchell retired to pursue a career in medicine, was evident in the early 1980s, when Jerry Mahoney and Knucklehead Smith were presented to the Smithsonian Institution, as Charlie McCarthy had been several years earlier.

One of television's most famous children's puppet shows was the long-lived *Howdy Doody* (see entry). A marionette performed by "Buffalo" Bob Smith (1917-98), Howdy Doody was a freckle-faced, smiling, six-year-old kid and the star citizen of imaginary Doodyville. The show debuted in 1947, initially on Saturday evenings, but due to its phenomenal popularity among children, was expanded to a daily format in 1948, becoming the first children's show to air every day. The show also simultaneously aired on radio from 1952 to 1958. The show was cancelled in 1960, but was revived in a short-lived 1976 syndicated format. In his heyday, however, Howdy Doody's popularity translated into merchandising licenses for dolls, records (capped by the show's theme, "It's Howdy Doody Time!"), and toys.

Harking back to the Punch and Judy tradition, *Kukla, Fran and Ollie* showcased the talents of Burr Tillstrom (1917-85), the show's creator, producer, and puppeteer. The show was among the first commercial programs aired on television, debuting at the NBC studio at the 1939 New York World's Fair. In 1948, NBC picked up Tillstrom's show for weekday evenings. The show had several formats over the years: half-hour, hour, daytime, prime-time, syndication, and on public television until the show's demise in the mid-1970s. Kukla was a simple glove puppet with a clown's nose, a funny face masking a serious-minded persona. Ollie was Oliver J. Dragon, a carefree, happy velvet dragon who sparred with Kukla. Mediating the friendly conflict was Fran Allison (1907-1989), a Chicago radio performer who became the human intermediary between the puppets and the audience.

The show was immensely popular with children in the 1950s, with 200,000 youngsters subscribing to the *Kuklapolitan Courier*, a children's magazine licensed by Tillstrom. Parents and critics enjoyed the show as well, and in 1949, *Kukla, Fran and Ollie* won a Peabody Award and in 1953, an Emmy. NBC, however, inexplicably cancelled the show in 1957, and it was not until 1971 that Kukla and company came back to host the *CBS Children's Film Festival*. This new series showcased international films made for children, many of which were first dubbed into English, and earned creator Tillstrom another Peabody Award plus praise from the Action for Children's Television lobbying group in 1971.

Although children were their natural audience, puppets were also popular among adults. Topo Gigio, a diminutive mouse with an Italian accent, was a frequent guest on the *Ed Sullivan Show* (see entry), which ran on CBS from 1948 to 1971. Topo Gigio's usual dialogue with Sullivan (1901-74) ended with the mouse shyly asking, "Before I go to sleep, kiss me goodnight." Sullivan always complied.

Still, the most popular shows involving puppets were directed at children, who symbolically identified with the childlike quality of the puppets. In 1954, puppeteer and musician Fred McFeely Rogers (1928-) debuted with partner Josie Carey on local Pittsburgh station WQED with *Children's Corner*. A theology student at the Pittsburgh Theological Seminary, Rogers approached his show not as an entertainer, but as a minister; puppetry merely provided the tools of his ministry.

Rogers was never seen on *Children's Corner*; he worked the puppets while Josie Carey was the on-screen host. In 1963, the Canadian Broadcasting Company aired a 15-minute version that took children into Rogers's studio living room as well as into the puppet world of the Neighborhood of Make-Believe. PBS picked up the show in 1967, expanded it to 30 minutes, and retitled it *Mister Rogers' Neighborhood* (see entry). When it celebrated its 25th anniversary in 1992, *Mister Rogers' Neighborhood* was being broadcast on over 300 public television stations daily with 8 million households tuning in each week.

Ventriloquist Shari Lewis (1934-98; see entry) hosted another educational children's show, the *Shari Lewis Show,* which featured three glove puppets named Lamb Chop, Hush Puppy, and Charlie Horse. The show, which ran on NBC from 1960 to 1963, used games and songs to teach children how to deal with their feelings and fears. In 1992, Lewis returned to television with PBS's *Lamb Chop's Play-Along*, an interactive show that combined songs, stories, and jokes to reach children. The show won Lewis her seventh Emmy as Outstanding Performer in a Children's Series.

The master of American television puppetry, however, was Jim Henson (1936-90), who created the puppets behind *Sesame Street* and the *Muppet Show* (see Jim Henson Productions and the Muppets). Big Bird, Cookie Monster, Kermit the Frog, and Miss Piggy embody the ultimate combination of education and entertainment in American puppetry. Henson's puppets appeal equally to children and their parents; *Sesame Street*, for example, was created in 1969 specifically to encourage early cognitive development in children, while the 1975 premiere of the *Muppet Show* returned to puppetry's roots in appealing to adult audiences through satire, parody, and wit.

Puppetry in contemporary American culture is intergenerational. The adults who listened to Edgar Bergen and Charlie McCarthy in the 1930s and 1940s bore children who watched *Howdy Doody* and *Kukla, Fran and Ollie* in the 1950s. Their grandchildren watched Big Bird and Kermit or followed Fred Rogers in the 1970s, while a new generation of youngsters added Lamb Chop and the most recent newcomer, a life-size, purple dinosaur named Barney (see entry) to the list of old favorites. Not only has fascination with the art of puppetry increased (how *can* Kermit ride a bicycle or Miss Piggy rollerskate unassisted?), but the underlying message of the puppets continues to shape American attitudes. Through his puppets, Fred Rogers has shaped American's self-esteem, Shari Lewis has touched their playfulness and creativity, and Big Bird and gang are teaching their second generation of children about cultural diversity, respect, and sharing, in addition to their ABCs.

Bibliography

Baird, Bil. *The Art of the Puppet*. New York: Macmillan, 1965.

Fischer, Stuart. *Kids' TV: The First 25 Years*. New York: Facts on File, 1983.

McNeil, Alex. *Total Television: A Comprehensive Guide to Programming from 1948 to the Present*. 2d ed. New York: Penguin, 1984.

Sherzer, Dina, and Joel Sherzer. *Humor and Comedy in Puppetry: Celebration in Popular Culture*. Bowling Green, OH: Bowling Green State U Popular P, 1987.

Kathleen D. Toerpe

See also

Children's Network Programming
Children's Public Television

Q

Quantum Leap (1989-1993) was an unusual time-travel TV series in that it focused on people rather than science fiction technology or the manipulation of major historical events. Created and executive produced by Donald P. Bellisario, the series starred Broadway veteran Scott Bakula as Sam Beckett, the guinea pig in his own time experiments who finds himself traveling back and forth through the past, from the 1950s through the 1990s. (Sam can only travel within his own lifetime.) The catch: only Sam's mind travels, "leaping" into the body of a stranger; while the viewer sees Sam, those around him see the person into which he has leapt. With the help of Al Calavicci (Dean Stockwell)—an observer of Sam's project from the future who appears as a hologram that only Sam can see and hear—and the project computer Ziggy, Sam strives to "put right what once went wrong," as the opening sequence explains, altering the lives of ordinary people in the past for the better.

The show elicited some extraordinary performances from Bakula, who convincingly portrayed the diverse people Sam leapt into. Also important to the show's success was its integral use of music, spanning four decades of musical history. Low ratings plagued much of the show's run, but it did very well among the coveted 18-49 age group, which ensured its survival until 1993.

Bibliography

Brooks, Tim, and Earle Marsh. *The Complete Directory to Prime Time TV Shows, 1946–Present.* New York: Ballantine, 1992.

Chunovic, Louis. *The Quantum Leap Book.* Secaucus: Carol, 1993.

McNeil, Alex. *Total Television.* New York: Penguin, 1992.

Wiggins, Kayla McKinney. "Epic Heroes, Ethical Issues, and Time Paradoxes in *Quantum Leap.*" *Journal of Popular Film & Television* 21.3 (1993): 111-20.

MaryAnn Johanson

Queen, Ellery, has been at the center of mystery and detective fiction since 1929 as author, character, anthologist, and editor of detective stories. "Ellery Queen" is the pseudonym for the creative team of Frederic Dannay (1905-1982) and Manfred Lee (1905-1971), cousins who entered a novel-writing contest in 1929. Though they did not win, their entry (*The Roman Hat Mystery*) was published and launched their career. The book had an important impact on American detection, demonstrating that a mystery could be engaging and devious, yet play fair with the reader. Queen's innovation was a "Challenge to the Reader," where, near story's end, the hero steps out of character, announces that all the clues have been presented, and invites the reader to identify the villain before reading the remainder of the story.

Ellery Queen is also the name of the detective hero introduced by the cousins. Created in the midst of the golden age, Ellery began as a devil-may-care young man whose father is a police inspector. In the first nine novels (those featuring the "Challenge to the Reader"), he is erudite and showy, in the manner of S. S. Van Dine's Philo Vance and Dorothy L. Sayers's Peter Wimsey. Beginning with *Halfway House* (1936), however, the high-living fop mellows into a serious detective. It is this version of Ellery that appears in the famous "Wrightsville" trilogy (*Calamity Town*, 1942; *The Murderer Is a Fox*, 1945; and *Ten Day's Wonder*, 1948), which takes place in a bucolic small town in upstate New York. *Calamity Town* has been frequently listed among the best mysteries ever written.

Ellery was again transformed in the 1950s and 1960s, when the cousins returned to the puzzle story. Ellery was also the hero of a sequence of movies starring Ralph Bellamy in the 1940s, a long-running radio drama, and a television series with Jim Hutton and David Wayne (as a rather dim-witted Ellery and Inspector Queen respectively) in the 1970s. A few years after creating Ellery Queen, Dannay and Lee developed another, more traditional detective, Drury Lane, an eccentric retired actor who relieves his boredom by investigating bizarre murder cases over the course of several novels.

Beginning in the late 1930s, Ellery Queen (primarily Dannay, a well-known book collector) began another career as the editor of detective-story anthologies. One early venture was *Challenge to the Reader* (1938), a group of stories in which the names of famous heroes and authors have been changed—the "Challenge" is to correctly identify them. Another was *101 Years' Entertainment* (1941), a history of the mystery form from Edgar Allan Poe and Agatha Christie to Dashiell Hammett and E. M. Hornung, told through their best stories. These were followed by numerous multi-author anthologies, as well as collections of rare tales featuring individual great detectives.

Having conquered both the novel and the short story, Dannay also became the lead editor of one of the great mystery magazines. Since it began in 1941, *Ellery Queen's Mystery Magazine* has been known for its wide range of styles, its array of talent including both well-known and soon-to-be-famous authors, and the excellence of the fiction it has featured.

Bibliography

Bloom, Harold, ed. *Modern Mystery Writers.* New York: Chelsea, 1995.

Nieminski, John, comp. *EQMM 350: An Author Title Index to Ellery Queen's Mystery Magazine, Fall 1941 through January 1973.* White Bear Lake: Armchair Detective, 1974,

Reilly, John, ed. *Twentieth-Century Crime & Mystery Writers.* 2d ed. New York: St. Martin's, 1985.

Steinbrunner, Chris, and Otto Penzler, eds. *The Encyclopedia of Mystery and Detection.* New York: McGraw-Hill, 1976.

Fred Isaac

Quilts. Technically, a quilt is three layers of material held together by stitching. The top layer generally carries the design and may be constructed of whole cloth; pieced blocks or overall pieced designs; appliqué; or combinations of these structures. The second layer of a quilt (batt, batting, fill, filler) is used for warmth, but its loft also helps show off quilting stitches to best advantage. Depending on the wealth and circumstance of the maker, various materials have been used for the batt, including wool fleece, cotton, blankets, cotton lint, leaves, and newspaper. The third layer of the quilt is called the backing and is used as a base to secure the other layers. Cotton yardage or sheeting; feed, flour, and sugar sacks; and blankets are examples of materials used for backings. Quilting is the running stitch (sometimes a backstitch) that is used to secure the three layers together. For quilters of European descent, the number of stitches per inch has traditionally been a measure of the expertise of the quilter. Small, even stitches are desired.

The antecedents of the American quilt span many centuries, cultures, and several continents. Speculation on the origins of quiltmaking primarily focuses on discussions of physical protection and warmth. Quilted padding was used under metal armor to provide comfort for 13th-century European soldiers. It is thought that, previous to this, quilted garments were used as armor until more sophisticated weapons made this practice inadequate. European women in the 17th century wore petticoats that were quilted to provide warmth from drafty interiors. Fragments of quilted cloth from much earlier have been found. A quilted floor covering now housed in the Leningrad Department of the Institute of Archaeology is believed to have been made in the first century B.C. A figure carving from an Egyptian tomb dated circa 3400 B.C. conveys a heavily padded and possibly quilted garment.

Because quilts are part of American culture, each quilt reflects the economics, politics, fashion, technology, and current events of the time and place of its conception and production. For example, a postage stamp quilt (a quilt composed of many fabric pieces all near the size of or smaller than a postage stamp) made in the 1930s reflects the availability of a wide variety of colors and fabric designs in the United States due to new textile technology in dyeworks and fabric printing. Also important was the psychological need to use up very small pieces of fabric in economic times when waste was abhorrent. The competitive spirit of the times was promoted by state fairs and quilt contests. The goal was to see who could use the greatest number of fabric pieces in one quilt.

Quilts are categorized in a variety of ways, including how they look, how they function, and by whom they are made. Special techniques, materials, or structures are sometimes used to identify quilts. Strippy quilts, for example, are quilts made up of two contrasting, repeated bands of cloth. Early American quilts often used this economical format to reuse salvageable sections of valuable chintz panels. Sampler quilts are a collection of pieced or appliquéd blocks of different designs. Like needlework samplers, sampler quilts can be made to show off the maker's repertoire of block designs, her expertise, or be made to designate a collection of blocks under a single theme. For example, during the 1993 Oregon Trail sesquicentennial, the Mary's River Quilt Guild in Oregon composed monthly quilt blocks whose designs were also documented as being created on the Oregon Trail during the Westward Expansion.

Related to sampler quilts are album quilts. Album quilts are generally composed of differing blocks, each made by a different person. One of the great mysteries of quilt history concerns the creation of Baltimore Album quilts during the mid-1800s. These exquisite, labor-intensive, appliquéd quilts were generally made as presentation quilts. It is thought that one or two individuals were responsible for designing blocks for clients who then distributed sewing assignments among a group and then pieced the blocks together.

Charm quilts are made of no two alike fabrics, though folklore suggests that one repeated fabric brings good luck. Though charm quilts were popular from 1870 to 1910, contemporary artists have shown an interest in the design possibilities their format provides. Overall designs that use a single pieced unit such as clamshells, tumblers, or apple cores work best for charm quilts. During the Westward Expansion, friends and relatives would send scraps of their clothing with travelers to be sewn into charm quilts as remembrances of their love and support.

Crazy quilts may have received their name from the seemingly random placement of fabrics that creates pattern on a ground fabric. Crazy quilts reached their peak in the United States around 1880, but rural communities continued to make them well into the 20th century. Like many other traditional quilt configurations, exploration of this quilt type continues during the current quilt revival. Though they are often cited as the earliest of American quilt patterns, crazy quilts before the 19th century are quite rare. Sometimes viewers confuse the patching of worn quilts with the crazy quilt technique.

State documentation projects sponsored by guilds and other institutions are increasing our knowledge of quilts, quilters, and quiltmaking and their influence on and importance to American culture. Over half of the United States have established some sort of ongoing documentation procedure to create a data base for quilt information.

Bibliography

Brackman, Barbara. *Clues in the Calico: A Guide to Identifying and Dating Antique Quilts*. McLean: EPM, 1989.

Ferrero, Pat, Elaine Hedges, and Julie Silber. *Hearts and Hands: The Influence of Women & Quilts on American Society*. San Francisco: Quilt Digest, 1987.

Houck, Carter. *The Quilt Encyclopedia Illustrated*. New York: Abrams (in association with the Museum of American Folk Art), 1991.

Kiracofe, Roderick. *The American Quilt: A History of Cloth and Comfort, 1750-1950*. New York: Clarkson Potter, 1993.

Oshins, Lisa Turner. *Quilt Collections: A Directory for the United States and Canada*. Washington: Acropolis, 1987.

Elizabeth Hoffman

Racing Cars, from their beginning in the 1890s, have been admired not only for their thrilling performances but for their exciting designs as well. In the early days, manufacturers made available to the public autos quite similar to, if not actually the same, as those they used for racing. Today these specialized automobiles are usually built strictly for competition, but street cars are still often modified by their owners for racing purposes. Without question, the best place to see racing cars is a racetrack; but because of their striking designs, racing cars are also appearing in art museums.

For those who covet racing cars, but could never afford one of their own, an entire industry exists to serve enthusiasts who desire having their street cars modified to look and drive more like racing cars. Custom-made engine and exhaust components give just about any car more power, while wide performance tires, stiffer springs, and shock absorbers allow more control and a firmer ride. Tacked-on spoilers and air dams add a racey look, though they rarely contribute to any significant performance increase when used for street driving. Anyone wishing to sharpen their driving skills may enroll in a competition driving course, or race at a local sanctioned autocross event.

Racing enthusiasts can find dozens of magazines promoting their field. Periodicals such as *Hot Rod, Road and Track*, and *Sports Car International*, among dozens more, often feature the work of dedicated people, from teams who design and fabricate the cars they race, to those true fanatics who restore vintage racing cars bolt-by-bolt. But for everyone featured in the magazines, there are many more garage mechanics who prepare their own cars for the drag races held weekly at local strips.

Since the 1950s, there have been several noteworthy exhibitions for highlighting the appreciation of racing cars, not only as technologically advanced forms of transportation, but as objects of beauty comparable to works of art. These shows focused largely on the designer's ability to create an attractive shape around the working parts of the machine, and the metalcrafter's skill in bringing that design to reality. In the design process, form must always follow function.

In 1951, Arthur Drexler's *Eight Automobiles* show opened at the Museum of Modern Art in New York. This critically acclaimed exhibition featured an international display of autos collectively referred to as "hollow, rolling sculpture." The French Talbot-Lago of 1939 was compared by a contemporary reviewer to the work of the Italian artist Modigliani. Other imports in the show were a 1931 Mercedes-Benz from Germany, a 1949 Cisitalia 202 from Italy, the English Bentley of 1939, and a 1941 MG. American cars on view included a 1937 Cord, a 1941 Lincoln Continental, a 1951 Ford, and an army-spec Jeep.

That exhibition, while not focusing directly on racing cars, was very significant for its inclusion of the Cisitalia 202—an automobile design of such importance that its influence has been felt for nearly 50 years. This car set the standard for the "long hood, short deck" shapes commonly seen on racing cars (and street cars) to this day. Its significance as a milestone of automotive design was fully realized in 1972, when the Museum of Modern Art accepted a 1946 Cisitalia 202 GT into its permanent collection.

In 1982, the exhibition *Motor Trends: The Artist and the Automobile* took place at the Grapestake Gallery in San Francisco. Car-related art representing over 35+ artists was shown, including works by Ansel Adams, Lee Friedlander, and Claes Oldenburg. Placed among the many artworks was a red 1947 Maserati A6-GCS racing car, meant to be viewed not as a mere automobile, but as another work of art in the show.

The Museum of Contemporary Art in Los Angeles held the first retrospective exhibition of automobile design in 1984, presenting the automobile as a work of art. In addition to covering the great European marques such as Alfa Romeo, Mercedes-Benz, and Bugatti, the exhibition included an aesthetic evaluation of the racing cars produced by our hot rod culture of the 1930s through the 1950s. Many were created specifically for racing on the vast lake beds of California and Utah. These so-called lakesters, such as Alex Xydia's teardrop-shaped "belly tanker" (based on a World War II-era aircraft fuel container), were aerodynamically designed in a single-minded quest for maximum speed. Other racers were highly altered versions of street cars, individually customized for maximum visual effect. In addition to the expected mechanical modifications, techniques including stripping, chopping, and channeling were employed to improve the look of common cars. Painted flames were sometimes added for an even "faster" appearance. Ford was the preferred make among the most serious hot-rodders, and Tom McMullen's 1932 Ford highboy is a renowned example of the customizer's art.

In 1933, the Museum of Modern Art presented an exhibition showcasing its recent acquisition of a racing car—a bright-red 1990 Formula One Ferrari. *Designed for Speed: Three Automobiles by Ferrari* also had on view a blue 1949 166MM Barchetta and a red 1987 F40.

The 166MM was Ferrari's first production car. It was also raced with great success. The Barchetta won the premier Italian endurance contest, the Mille Miglia (hence the MM designation), eight times and once took the championship at Le Mans in France. This curvaceous Ferrari started a trend in two-seater convertible design. Its sculptural qualities are often praised, and its influence is visible in sports cars produced by MG, Austin-Healey, and Alfa Romeo among many others.

For the 40th anniversary of Enzo Ferrari's involvement in auto racing and production, a special car was dubbed F40. This car was a technological showpiece, bringing the sports car as close to Formula One performance as it had ever come. The F40 was based directly on the "GTO evoluzione," a Ferrari slated for Group B class racing. The aggressive appearance of the F40 is emphasized by the many functional cooling ducts cut into its bodywork, and the enormous wing attached to the rear deck.

The third Ferrari in the show, a Formula One (F1) model, represents the height of racing car design and performance. While shaping the car, John Barnard had to keep in mind his vehicle was to be capable of speeds over 200 mph. Hence its shape was a compromise between aesthetics and aerodynamic necessity. Barnard's result is said to be a successful and harmonious design.

Bibliography

Lepp, George. *Bonneville Salt Flats*. Osceola: Motorbooks International, 1988.

Mount, Christopher. *Designed for Speed: Three Automobiles by Ferrari*. New York: Museum of Modern Art, 1993.

Silk, Gerald, Angelo Tito Anselmi, Henry Flood Robert, Jr., and Strother MacMinn. *Automobile and Culture*. New York: Abrams/Museum of Contemporary Art, Los Angeles, 1984.

Christopher Slogar

Radio Advertising is a medium of many contrasts, with many stations making huge profits while others only break even or suffer huge losses. Static-free, high fidelity FM still remains the dominant radio band, with lower fidelity AM having adapted to the listener/advertising losses of the past 20 years. Most popular and classical music shows are heard on FM, while AM caters mainly to talk and other non-musical formats. By the mid-1990s, there were more than 10,000 commercial AM and FM radio stations in the U.S.

Americans own more than 500 million radios, with around 70 million new sets annually purchased. Thus, 99 percent of all households are covered by radio, 95 percent of all cars, and even 84.3 percent of walk-along players include radio—according to the Radio Advertising Bureau (RAB). Its weekly reach is 96 percent. The medium is not only a highly targetable primary advertising vehicle, but it also supplements other media such as newspapers and TV.

The first paid radio commercial appeared during August 1922, over WEAF (later WNBC) in New York, but its first major advertising year did not arrive until 1928. The 1930s Depression years spurred radio to new heights since this was a "free medium," attracting huge audiences. These, in turn, brought in large advertising dollars. While it may vary, the golden age of network radio spanned most of the 1930s and early 1940s. By 1948, television was on the rise, and in a few years network radio would be in decline.

The larger the radio market, the more resources have been available for producing and executing "slick" programs and commercials. With more money at stake, local and regional advertising generally receive greater attention and expertise. Commercials in major markets such as Chicago, New York, and Los Angeles are often produced in-house. They are as polished and well produced as those that come from large advertising agencies. If station air personalities enjoy notable popularity, they may also appear in commer-

cials. Some clients may even request that these celebrities produce their advertising message.

With the future resting heavily in technology and its advancements, radio has numerous opportunities. These include eventual adoption of CD-like digital sound, and sending distant radio stations over cable or microwave-delivery systems. After several tenuous years, AM stereo has a good possibility for success. The AM, and possibly the FM bands also, may be expanded to accommodate additional stations.

Bibliography

Barnouw, Erik. *A Tower in Babel: A History of Broadcasting in the United States*. Vol. 1. New York: Oxford UP, 1966.

Lichty, Lawrence W., and Malachi C. Topping, eds. *American Broadcasting: A Source Book on the History of Radio and Television*. New York: Hastings, 1975.

Radio Facts for Advertisers, 1990. New York: Radio Advertising Bureau, 1990.

Russell, J. Thomas, and W. Ronald Lane. *Kleppner's Advertising Procedure*. 12th ed. Englewood Cliffs: Prentice-Hall, 1993.

Sterling, Christopher H., and John M. Kittross. *Stay Tuned: A Concise History of American Broadcasting*. 2d ed. Belmont: Wadsworth, 1990.

Sammy R. Danna

Radio and Cartoons. As the radio age dawned in the early 1920s, a variety of commercial, scientific, and educational broadcasters aimed to turn occasional programs into full schedules. Cartoonists had their pens ready to portray the new medium and its adherents. At first, a few editorial cartoonists saw radio as a potential voice of "culture," but most newspaper comic strip and panel artists (and their humor magazine counterparts) quickly assumed that broadcasting was simply another 1920s fad, an enemy to public peace and household quiet. "Dern this radio craze," cries a character in a 1924 Stanley Link panel. As radio evolved in the 1930s and 1940s, the cartoonists' doubts only deepened.

Exploring radio jargon, early- to mid-1920s cartoons found that broadcasting offered fresh metaphors for human types and actions. "She's a regular broadcasting station," Frank Willard's Moon Mullins says of a boardinghouse gossip. Charles Dana Gibson, in an elegant 1924 drawing for the *Life* humor magazine, pictures a young couple seated frostily back-to-back, with this observation for "Radio Beginners": "Do not become discouraged at static trouble. It may not be static at all, but merely trouble in the receiving set." In Bud Fisher's popular comic strip, Jeff informs Mutt, "I've got station S-T-A-T-I-C, and it's clear as a bell too." In 1925, Gaar Williams began using "Static" as a recurring title for panel cartoons about marital discord: while the wife furiously shovels coal into the neglected basement furnace, the husband is preoccupied with tuning the receiver upstairs. Before creating Dick Tracy and his wrist radio, Chester Gould drew two short-lived radio strips (*The Radio Lanes* and *The Radio Catts*) in the mid-1920s, while a several weeks' sequence in C. M. Payne's *'Smatter Pop* included a boxed definition of "d/x" (distance reception, preferably of

Havana or Honolulu) for readers not yet fluent in radioese. In typical 1920s cartoons, set owners were caught up in the expensive, obsessive quest for the one tube that would bring maximum "d/x," and car batteries were farcically stolen for powering radios.

Many of radio's annoying technical problems were resolved by the late 1920s, and in the next decade most cartoonists shifted their attention to the content of radio programs, which they deemed formula-ridden, inane, and loud. Countless cartoons pictured the family console as a cruel household god, repeatedly demanding the purchase of breakfast cereal or lawn fertilizer. In his nostalgic cartoons of midwestern small-town life, Gaar Williams took a moderate tone, portraying a group of curbside or barbershop talkers as a "broadcasting station." H. T. Webster and George Lichtenstein ("Lichty") carried a sharper view into the World War II and postwar years.

Born in 1885 and skeptical of many devices of the 20th century, H. T. Webster increasingly doubted radio's worth. In the 1920s, he had shown a young swain sitting stiffly by the speaker, hopelessly "In Love with the Radio Soprano," and in the 1930s, the "timid soul" Caspar Milquetoast was often frightened by the radio's bark. By 1943, radio was Webster's regular target in "The Unseen Audience," appearing each Wednesday. Frequently, the living room console bellows from the left edge of the panel, while its hapless owner frowns or cowers in the easy chair on the right. Table radios are hurled from open windows in Webster cartoons, and he shows ordinary listeners ludicrously adopting the language of commercials, quiz shows, and crime dramas. The cartoonist was given a George F. Peabody Award in 1949 for his stinging "service to broadcasting."

The freely looping pen style of George Lichty's 1940s *Grin and Bear It* cartoons was the perfect medium for sketching listeners who were simply confused by radio: Its messages did not square with reality. In Lichty's world of sloppy people in sloppy surroundings, only sponsors, network executives, and Japanese spies took U.S. radio seriously.

Radio treated the cartoon world more charitably than vice versa. Beginning in the early 1930s, a number of broadcast series were developed from comic strip figures, including *Little Orphan Annie, Dick Tracy, Jungle Jim, The Gumps, Buck Rogers, Blondie and Dagwood Bumstead,* and *Mark Trail*. In the 1950s, when radio evolved into steady talking and record-playing, cartoonists lost interest. Today only an occasional *Blondie* strip or a *Far Side* panel recalls the once-frequent cartoon portrayal of radio.

Ray Barfield

Radio Archives. In the 20th century, broadcasting has documented our social and cultural history. But few researchers use broadcast material as primary resources, because it is difficult to obtain and there is little information on how to locate it.

Broadcast programming has been preserved by both institutions and interested individuals. Funding to support institutional archives is as variable as the institutions preserving the available material. The Library of Congress began to collect and preserve some programming in 1949 in its role as the U.S. copyright depository. The National Archives also collected and preserved programming from governmental sources and increasingly received donated event and news materials from stations and networks. Funding difficulties led the UCLA Film and Television Archive to discontinue the development of its radio archive, which consists of 50,000 transcription discs and 10,000 tapes of radio from 1933 to 1983, to concentrate on film. The Museum of Broadcast Communications (see entry), in Chicago, is home to the Radio Hall of Fame, as well as some 50,000 radio archives.

Serious recording and collecting of radio programs by individuals on home tape-recording equipment began around 1950, after some 20 companies introduced an effective reasonably priced reel-to-reel recorder. This material, along with Armed Forces Radio Service discs produced to bring radio programs to our troops during World War II, and a few network and syndicated discs, comprised the starting base of material that began to be privately traded in the 1960s.

In the 1960s, when radio as it had been was almost gone, small groups on both the East and West Coasts began to exchange material, information, and sources. More material became available as people gained access to radio station electrical transcriptions when those stations began disposing of their stored material, and programs from other sources were discovered.

In 1954, Charles Michelson started the rebroadcast market by obtaining an umbrella agreement to license *The Shadow* to individual radio stations, LP recordings, and home-enjoyment tapes. The first aggressively marketed private seller of radio programs was J. David Goldin, a former engineer, who formed "Radio Yesteryear" and an album subsidiary, "Radiola," in the late 1960s.

Newsletters on radio-program collecting began to circulate in the late 1960s. The standard was set by *Radio Dial* by the Radio Historical Society of America founded by Charles Ingersoll. Carrying on the tradition, the leading newsletter today is *Hello Again* by Jay Hickerson, which began publication in 1970. Today, the mass of privately collected broadcast material available is in the hands of approximately 160-plus active collectors.

Despite the interest of individual private collectors and the growth of institutional archives, the preservation of radio programming faces a crisis due to a combination of problems and the lack of public policy. The most basic problem is the increasing rate of disposal and destruction of material. The way programs have been recorded—electrical transcription to tape formats—pose problems for preservationists. As transcription turntables disappear and reel tape recorders are replaced with cassette recorders, the means for playing the available material are being lost or exist only in museums. The need to transfer the older formats into new forms is a time and cost problem. Magnetic audio tape deteriorates over time as it is exposed to heat, humidity, and atmospheric pollution and is more subject to catastrophic loss of information than is print. Policy problems include the conflict between competing interests and the lack of a national strategy among competing organizations.

As a nostalgia market for old radio programming has developed, copyright owners have become more interested in protecting their copyrights. Because the copyright law is not clear, owners, if they even allow archiving, impose strong restrictions on institutional and private use of their material. Also, ownership of many programs is very complex and depends on contracts with directors, writers, performers, and rights holders of music and other materials used in the broadcasts. Private collectors who charge for duplication or sell programs are more susceptible to copyright problems than are institutions. Under certain conditions specified in the copyright law, libraries and other archives are authorized to photocopy or do other reproduction for research and teaching.

Cataloging is haphazard, which results in a basic lack of information as to what is available to be preserved, what has been preserved, in what condition and in what formats. Without a national policy and a national advocacy organization, there is no way to tell potential funders how to begin to address the problem of preservation. Much material is "out there" and broadcast historians hope to preserve it.

Bibliography

Bensman, Marvin R. "Radio Broadcast Programming for Research and Teaching." *Journal of Radio Studies* 1.1 (1992).

Godfrey, Donald G., ed. *Re-runs on File: A Directory of Broadcast Archives*. Hillsdale: Erlbaum, 1991.

Hickerson, Jay. *Hello Again Newsletter*; and *What You Always Wanted to Know about Circulating Old-Time Radio Shows*. Box 4321, Hamden, CT: Hickerson, 1986.

Swartz, Jon, and Robert Reinehr. *Handbook of Old-Time Radio*. New York: Scarecrow, 1993.

Marvin R. Bensman

Radio Associations. The largest and principal radio and television lobbying and trade association is the National Association of Broadcasters (NAB), headquartered in Washington, DC. It was formed in 1923 to combat the rise in royalty payments for broadcast music called for by the American Society of Composers, Authors, and Publishers (ASCAP), founded in 1914. In 1937, in a further effort to limit rising royalty costs, the broadcast industry formed its own music-licensing business, Broadcasting Music, Inc. (BMI). One of the most prominent unions and the first pure broadcasting one is the American Federation of Television and Radio Artists (AFTRA), begun in 1937 as the American Federation of Radio Artists. As a general rule, on-air talents such as commercial actors, announcers, entertainers, and newscasters, are AFTRA members. Most other creative/performing unions—such as the Screen Actors Guild (SAG) and Screen Extras Guild (SEG)—evolved from stage and film workers. Another performance union is the American Federation of Musicians (AFM), whose members are musicians who perform live or taped on radio or TV.

Broadcast engineers, technicians, and other support people are usually represented by IBEW, the International Brotherhood of Electrical Workers, the first established union for broadcasting engineers, or NABET, the National Association of Broadcast Engineers and Technicians. The Writer's Guild of America (WGA) is an allied broadcasting organization, made up of writers of radio/television entertainment programming and motion pictures.

The International Telecommunications Union (ITU) is a world organization under the United Nations that allocates and manages radio spectrum space and sets standards for international telegraph and telephone. Begun in 1865 and headquartered in Geneva, Switzerland, it has no specific means for enforcing its regulations but exercises significant influence due to its more than 150 member countries.

Bibliography

Dominick, Joseph, Barry Sherman, and Gary Copeland. *Broadcasting/Cable and Beyond*. New York: McGraw-Hill, 1993.

Gross, Lynne. *Telecommunications: An Introduction to Electronic Media*. Dubuque: Brown, 1992.

Sterling, Christopher, and John Kittross. *Stay Tuned: A Concise History of American Broadcasting*. Belmont: Wadsworth, 1990.

Willis, Edgar, and Henry Aldridge. *Television, Cable, and Radio: A Communications Approach*. Englewood Cliffs: Prentice-Hall, 1992.

Philip J. Harwood

Radio Deregulation. The growth and diversification of the mass media during the 1970s, combined with broadcasters who felt the pressure of increasing media competition, led to a move toward less regulation of commercial radio.

The deregulation move grew out of the increase in the number of radio stations from about 700 in the late 1920s and early 1930s, to over 10,000 stations in the 1990s. The early regulation model stipulated that government should act as the public's trustee to ensure that broadcasting properly served the public interest.

The deregulation movement was spearheaded by the chairman of the Federal Communications Commission (FCC) from 1981 to 1987, Mark Fowler. He challenged the traditional "trusteeship model" that had supported broadcast regulation since the 1920s. However, it was FCC Chairman Richard Wiley who in the mid 1970s first initiated a review of the massive number of rules and procedures. Further reviews and hearings were conducted under Chairman Charles Ferris in the late '70s.

Chairman Fowler, one of the more visible proponents of the "marketplace model," felt the economic arena was more capable of regulating broadcasting and began calling for minimal government interference. Fowler and other deregulation advocates believed broadcasters should have the same First Amendment rights as the press.

The deregulation of the radio industry really got underway with a series of FCC reforms begun in January 1981:

1. Detailed reports were no longer required with a license renewal application.

2. Stations were no longer required to do community ascertainment reports based on the needs of the community.

3. The time limit on the amount of advertising was eliminated.

4. Stations did not have to broadcast a minimum amount of news, public affairs, and local programming.

5. Detailed program logs did not have to be kept or made available for public inspection.

6. In August 1981, Congress, with the approval of the FCC, passed a bill extending the term of the radio license from three to seven years.

7. In December 1983, the rules governing children's programming were modified, regarding such matters as the requirement that broadcasters schedule some children's programming each week, or that broadcasters develop more "educational" programming.

8. Next, the FCC dropped the rule about regional concentration that prohibited ownership of three broadcast stations when two of them were within 100 miles of the third.

9. The FCC modified the multiple ownership rule in August 1984, allowing one company to own 12 AM and 12 FM stations, where previously the limit had been seven. In the 1990s the rule was modified even further, to allow single ownership of up to 30 AM and 30 FM licenses with some limitations, as long as no more than six stations are in a major market area, and that a multiple owner have no more than 25 per cent of the audience in one market area.

One of the most significant actions taken by the FCC was the elimination of the Fairness Doctrine, which required broadcasters to give adequate time to the discussion of controversial issues. An attempt in Congress to reinstate the doctrine failed in August 1987 when President Reagan vetoed the legislation.

Deregulation has eased the administrative burden on broadcasters and the FCC alike; however, the effect on programming is difficult to determine.

Bibliography

Chin, Felix. *Radio Deregulation: A Selected Bibliography.* Monticello: Vance, 1982.

Krattenmaker, Thomas G., and Lucas A. Powe, Jr. *Regulating Broadcast Programming.* Cambridge: MIT, 1994.

George V. Flannery

Radio Disk Jockey. Even though the job had existed within the radio industry for some time, the term "disk jockey," or "DJ," officially entered the English language in May 1949 when it was added to *Webster's New Collegiate Dictionary:* "One who conducts and announces a radio program of musical recordings, often interspersed with non-musical comments." Other names for these on-air radio hosts have included platter pilot, flapjack turner, pancake impresario, deejay, miker, doughnut disker, spinner, and, recently, on-air personality, or programmer.

The show most often given credit for popularizing the modern disk jockey movement was Martin Block's *Make Believe Ballroom* on WNEW in New York City. Block's show began in February 1935 with Block pretending that he was the master of ceremonies at a live broadcast from a giant dance hall, and he introduced each song as if the band were actually there. Block (see entry), labeled "Block the Jock" and "The Lord High Admiral of the Whirling Disk" by the press, was the first popular icon of the jockey genre and also its first millionaire.

Although records were probably used in radio from its earliest years to fill in time between live shows or at stations that lacked the programming resources of the larger network affiliates, the greatest growth of the disk jockey-style show began after World War II when the television industry emerged and the golden age of radio ended. As the TV industry grew, taking radio's programming, personnel, and profits with it, radio was forced to look for new sources of income and programming less expensive than the traditional shows that required writers, actors, announcers, and musicians. Over time, jockeys have helped to develop an important symbiotic relationship between the recording and radio industries, in which the record companies produce the music while the jockeys promote it.

Alan Freed (see entry) was one influential disk jockey who helped popularize the emerging rock and rhythm-and-blues music during the 1950s. Freed first gained national attention for his popular *Moondog* show in Cleveland, OH. In 1954, he moved to New York City, where, in addition to his radio work, he promoted live concerts.

A short list of significant early disk jockeys according to region includes: Al "Jazzbo" Collins, "Symphony Sid" Torin, George "Hound Dog" Lorenz, and Zenas "Daddy" Sears on the East Coast; Bill Randle, Dewey Phillips, Gene Nobles, Wolfman Jack, and Vernon "Doctor Daddy-O" Winslow in the Midwest and South; and Dick "Huggie Boy" Hugg, Hunter Hancock, and "Jumpin' George" Oxford on the West Coast. A brief list of influential African-American contributors to the field includes "Jockey Jack" Gibson, Nat D. Williams, Tommy Smalls, Rufus Thomas, Phil "Doctor Jive" Gordon, and Jack Walker "The Pear-Shaped Talker" (see also Black Radio Deejays)

As the number of disk jockeys on the air increased throughout the 1960s and 1970s, some became known, not for their musical selections, but for their on-air personalities. In New York City, for instance, Jean Shepherd told stories about his childhood growing up in Hammond, IN. Don Imus, on the other hand, became known during his early years for his outrageous pranks and alter ego, the Reverend Billy Sol Hargus.

As jockeys became more and more outrageous in their efforts to attract an audience and set themselves apart from the rest of the crowd, morning and afternoon drive-time programmers began to push the boundaries of propriety to their limits, and the shock jock phenomenon was born (see Shock Radio). However, in 1989, the Federal Communications Commission began to crack down on a number of errant jocks for indecent programming. The list of censured DJs included Steve Dahl (see entry) and Garry Meier in Chicago, Perry Stone in San Jose, and the "Bob and Tom Show" with Tom Griswold in Indianapolis. The most notorious shock jock of the pack, however, is Howard Stern (see entry), who has moved well beyond the simple spinning of disks into hosting a successful radio talk show in New York City, publishing, and making a film.

Other prominent disk jockeys in the early 1990s included Steve Downes, Scott Shannon, and Mark Thompson in Los Angeles; Don Geronimo and Doug "The Greaseman" Tracht in Washington, DC; Gary Burbank in Cincinnati;

Gary Dee in Cleveland; Johnathon Brandmeier and former TV *Partridge Family* member Danny Bonaduce in Chicago; and commuting disk jockey Tom Joyner of Chicago and Dallas.

Bibliography

Earl, Bill. *When Radio Was Boss*. Montebello: Research Archives, 1989.

Fornatale, Peter, and Joshua Mills. *Radio in the Television Age*. Woodstock: Overlook, 1980.

Hall, Claude, and Barbara Hall. *This Business of Radio Programming*. New York: Billboard, 1977.

Smith, Wes. *The Pied Pipers of Rock 'n' Roll: Radio Deejays of the 50's and 60's*. Marietta: Longstreet, 1989.

Charles F. Ganzert

Radio Drama is a form of broadcast programming that uses the spoken word, music, and sound effects to tell fictional narratives. Radio drama continues to be an important art form in the United Kingdom, Germany, Canada, and other nations where noncommercial radio services remain strong. In the U.S., however, radio drama is usually associated with the so-called golden years (1930-60) of the commercial radio networks. Since the decline of these networks, radio drama has survived only marginally in the U.S.—mainly through the efforts of a few dedicated independent producers.

Dramatic programs were an important part of American network radio broadcasting during the golden years. Although it was not the most plentiful type of programming carried by the networks (it never reached more than approximately 40 percent of the network schedule), radio drama is often the most vividly remembered kind. Programs such as *The Lone Ranger*, *Suspense*, *One Man's Family*, *The Shadow*, *The Lux Radio Theater*, and *The Jack Benny Program* are familiar to several generations of Americans (see individual entries).

Although the possibility of broadcasting dramatic programs was recognized from the beginning, regularly scheduled radio drama was the last type of programming to develop. One reason for this delay is that drama was difficult to do well and required the resources of writers, actors, and musicians—resources that were beyond the capabilities of local stations. Therefore, as radio developed in the 1920s, we see very little drama being aired by local stations.

Possibly the first radio drama ever broadcast was a transmission on February 19, 1922, of a Broadway play entitled *The Perfect Fool* and starring Ed Wynn. The General Electric station in Schenectady, NY, began broadcasting a dramatic program in October 1922, called the *WGY Players*. The first production was entitled "The Wolf" and was written by Eugene Walter. By the end of the season, the *WGY Players* had broadcast 83 separate dramas.

The development of drama as a truly viable form of radio programming had to wait for the coming of the networks. Indeed, the rise and fall of radio drama is closely linked to the growth and decline of the national radio networks. Although local stations continued to produce some dramatic programming, it was the networks that became the principal source of drama. The networks provided the techni-cal and financial resources to produce dramatic programs and to attract nationally known talents to perform in them.

The National Broadcasting Company (NBC) began operating the first national radio network in late 1926. Within a few months, it started a second network. (The two became known as the Red Network and the Blue Network.) In September 1927, a third national network—which was to become the Columbia Broadcasting System (CBS)—went on the air. Under the skillful management of William S. Paley, who purchased the network in 1928, CBS became a strong competitor to NBC by 1929. A fourth national network, the Mutual Broadcasting System, a collaboration among four powerful local radio stations, went on the air in 1934.

The first network programs consisted mostly of concert music, opera, and variety shows featuring singers, bandleaders, and vaudeville performers. The first dramatic programs on network radio began in 1927 when the Blue Network broadcast *The Collier Hour*, dramatized versions of stories published in *Collier's* magazine interspersed with music and short talks. The 60-minute program was heard until 1932 and encouraged a number of imitators such as *True Story Hour*, *The Physical Culture Hour*, *True Romance*, and *Redbook Magazine*.

The program that established drama as a popular form of network radio entertainment, however, was *Amos 'n' Andy* (see entry). This show was a descendent of a local radio program called *Sam 'n' Henry* developed by two vaudeville performers named Freeman Gosden and Charles Correll. The program was originally broadcast over Chicago station WGN for two years and then moved to WMAQ under the name of *Amos 'n' Andy*. The show went to the Blue Network in the summer of 1929.

In addition, the Blue Network carried a thriller drama called *The Empire Builders*, an adventure series featuring dramatic sketches about travelers in the Northwest. CBS inaugurated a long-running program called *True Detective Mysteries*, based on stories that had appeared in *True Detective* magazine.

High-quality "prestige drama" was represented by a 60-minute program entitled *The Radio Guild*, which aired on Wednesday afternoons over the Blue Network. This program featured adaptations of plays and original radio scripts.

Within two years, the popularity of *Amos 'n' Andy* had begun to decline, and the networks sought to renew public interest in radio by inaugurating a number of new dramatic programs. Some of the experimentation with new dramatic forms came from the networks, but a substantial number came from advertising agencies who were searching for appealing program types that would help to carry the commercial messages of their sponsors. Agencies such as Blackett, Sample, and Hummert maintained active radio divisions that generated scripts, employed actors, rehearsed, and actually produced the programs on the air. The networks acted merely as suppliers of production and transmission facilities.

Initially, most radio dramas were broadcast from New York, and this made it difficult for radio to utilize the talents of motion picture performers located in Hollywood. Between 1935 and 1937, however, the center of production gradually moved to Los Angeles, and popular motion picture stars began to appear in increasing numbers on radio programs. The reason for this move was an adjustment in long-distance telephone line rental charges that made West Coast program origination economically feasible for the first time. Shows featuring adaptations of current motion pictures began to appear on the networks, and the most famous of these was *The Lux Radio Theater.*

At the same time, motion picture companies began to release films starring radio performers. The increasing popularity of radio encouraged Hollywood to release a number of radio-based films such as *The Big Broadcast* (1932). Over the years, many radio performers appeared in motion pictures. Even Amos and Andy were in a film called *Check and Double Check* made in 1935.

During the 1940s, network radio continued to increase in popularity as it became the most sought after source of information about World War II. Throughout the war, network radio provided the latest war bulletins, carried patriotic messages, and entertained Americans with a full schedule of drama and music. By 1943, radio had surpassed newspapers as the most preferred advertising medium. Network radio developed an extremely loyal audience, and drama became an increasingly important part of the network schedules. By 1944, dramatic programming reached a high of 38 percent of network offerings, and that figure does not include an additional 16 percent for variety shows, which often contained dramatic segments.

The type of drama most often associated with network radio is the daytime serial or "soap opera." By the early 1940s, the networks were offering more than 70 hours per week of this kind of programming. Designed mainly to attract an audience of housewives (who were targeted as ideal customers for household cleaning products), each of these serial dramas was on the air Monday through Friday for 15 minutes. Often a network would carry five or six of these programs in succession.

Soap operas were easy to produce. An announcer introduced the program and in a few sentences gave the program's main premise and summarized recent plot developments. Following a commercial, the program would contain 10-12 minutes of action before a second commercial and a closing announcement urging listeners to tune in the next day.

Soap operas focused on domestic problems, usually those involving marriage and the raising of children. Sometimes, the marriages were between people from different backgrounds and stations in life. Very little happened from day to day, and audiences tuned in loyally year after year. Some of the most enduring of the soap operas were *The Romance of Helen Trent* (1933-60), *Ma Perkins* (1933-60), and *Our Gal Sunday* (1937-59).

An exceptionally fine example of this genre was *One Man's Family* (see entry), which was a 30-minute nighttime weekly program for many years but became a daytime program in 1955. Written by Carlton E. Morse and produced on the West Coast, *One Man's Family* was on the air for 27 years and was known for its emphasis on traditional family values and patriotism.

Soap operas were not the most popular programs on the radio. They seldom gained more than a rating of 5-6 percent, but their audiences were fiercely loyal and stable. As a result, the ratings changed little over the years, and this fact enabled the daytime dramas to remain on the air until the final days of network radio drama. The last soap operas went off the air on Friday, November 25, 1960, when CBS canceled its few remaining daytime dramas. Among the programs ending that day was *Ma Perkins,* which had survived for 7,065 broadcasts.

Another type of program for which network radio is fondly remembered is the children's adventure show. Perhaps the best known was *The Lone Ranger,* originally broadcast on Mutual and then on ABC three times per week in the early evening hours. *The Lone Ranger,* written by Fran Striker and featuring a local cast, began as a program over WXYZ in Detroit. It generated two other very popular programs from WXYZ—*The Green Hornet* and *Challenge of the Yukon* (later known as *Sergeant Preston of the Yukon*), also written by Fran Striker.

With the exception of *The Lone Ranger,* and a few other programs, most children's shows were broadcast in the late afternoons during the week and on Saturday mornings. One of the most famous weekday shows was *Little Orphan Annie,* which began in 1931 and continued until 1943. Like *Superman* and *Dick Tracy,* the program was based on familiar comic book characters.

There were a number of other popular children's programs, such as *Jack Armstrong, Sky King, The Cisco Kid, Captain Midnight,* and *Terry and the Pirates.* During World War II, many of these programs adapted war-related story lines and urged children to be good citizens by cooperating in war support activities. Some new programs such as *Don Winslow of the Navy* and *Hop Harrigan* featured heroes who were actually in the armed forces.

Programs for very young children were often broadcast on Saturday mornings. These included *Let's Pretend, Smilin' Ed's Buster Brown Gang,* and *No School Today. Let's Pretend* was written and directed by Nila Mack and dramatized original stories as well as traditional fairy tales. An unusual feature of the programs was that it used children as actors.

Many other dramas on network radio were not strictly designed for children but nevertheless appealed to them. In the broad category of action/adventure, many shows were usually broadcast during the evening hours. Some of the most popular were *Dragnet, Gangbusters, Mr. and Mrs. North, I Love a Mystery, Yours Truly—Johnny Dollar, Nick Carter—Master Detective,* and *Mr. District Attorney.*

Perhaps the most memorable of the action/adventure shows was *The Shadow,* a favorite with children and adults as well. It began in 1937 (although the Shadow character had appeared as a narrator on the *Blue Coal Radio Revue* before that time), and was based on a character who had originated in pulp detective magazines. The Shadow was a wealthy amateur sleuth named Lamont Cranston who had the power to "cloud men's minds" so that they could not see him.

By far the most popular type of dramatic program to run on network radio was the comedy/variety show, which often featured well-known former vaudeville stars. Beginning in the early 1930s, stars such as Eddie Cantor, Bob Hope, Jack Benny, Fred Allen, Edgar Bergen, Burns and Allen, and Fibber McGee and Molly (Jim and Marion Jordan) dominated the ratings. Some programs drew as much as 25-30 percent of the listening audience. Many of these shows featured the star, guests, and an orchestra, with monologues, dramatic sketches, and musical numbers. Others were situation comedies in which the main characters were placed in humorous dramatic situations in each episode. The success of the comedy/variety shows led to spinoff programs. *The Great Gildersleeve* and *Beulah* were based on characters from *Fibber McGee and Molly*. Phil Harris, Dennis Day, and Mel Blanc from *The Jack Benny Program* all eventually had shows of their own.

Most radio drama was designed for entertainment purposes, written quickly, and average in quality. Fortunately, there were some opportunities for fine writing, especially for the many anthology dramas that were regularly on the air. Some were developed and broadcast on a sustaining basis, that is, without a sponsor, until one could be found.

The most famous of the high-quality anthology dramas was *The Lux Radio Theater,* which broadcast 60-minute adaptations of feature films once a week. The broadcasts came from Hollywood and usually featured at least one of the stars from the original film. The program employed a large cast, a studio orchestra, and excellent scripts. Sponsor Lever Brothers used the program as a way of selling its popular Lux soap products, and the film industry willingly allowed its actors to participate for the promotional value that accrued to their films.

For a number of years, CBS encouraged creative uses of radio drama in its programs such as *The Columbia Workshop* and later *The CBS Radio Workshop*, both of which were broadcast on a sustaining basis. Fine writers such as Archibald MacLeish and Norman Corwin were given the opportunity to develop imaginative scripts which were produced in an atmosphere free of commercial restraints.

Of all the radio writers, Norman Corwin (see entry) was probably the most famous. He wrote and directed several important programs at CBS in the 1940s including a series called *26 by Corwin* and a later group called *Columbia Presents Corwin*. He also wrote the famous program entitled *We Hold These Truths* broadcast at the beginning of America's entry into World War II and *On a Note of Triumph* aired at the end of hostilities in Europe. Corwin utilized verse, multiple-voice narrations, and interesting music in his productions.

An anthology drama remembered mainly for one particular broadcast was *The Mercury Theater on the Air*, which began on CBS in 1938. The program featured Orson Welles's Mercury Theater acting troupe and was broadcast on Sunday evenings. The program featured 60-minute adaptations of literary classics. On October 30, 1938, the program aired a version of H. G. Wells's story "The War of the Worlds," converted into the form of a radio newscast by writer Howard Koch (see entry). Even though the program was clearly fictitious and contained announcements to that effect, several thousand people became frightened enough to call their local radio stations, police departments, or even the CBS network.

Radio drama remained popular until the early 1950s, when ratings began to fall precipitously as loyal listeners turned to the new medium of television. As audiences abandoned network radio, so did advertisers, in spite of the networks' imaginative efforts to retain sponsors.

The decline of daytime radio drama was not precipitous. Ratings for soap operas were never very high, and they remained close to their pre-World War II levels throughout the 1950s. Gradually, sponsors lost interest in the shows, and networks felt increasing pressure from their affiliates to free up blocks of time for local programming. One by one, the soap operas disappeared in the late 1950s. CBS canceled its last daytime dramas in November 1960. However, it retained a two-hour block of dramas on Sunday evenings. These included *Gunsmoke; Have Gun, Will Travel*; *Yours Truly, Johnny Dollar*; and *Suspense*. CBS abandoned this last bit of dramatic programming in September 1962, and network radio drama disappeared.

During the 1950s, as the nation shifted from network radio to network television, there were several attempts to capture audiences with bold, high quality radio plays. The adult Western *Gunsmoke* was one of the best. It featured excellent scripts by John Meston and superb acting by a cast that included William Conrad, Parley Baer, Georgia Ellis, and Howard McNear. The science fiction program *Dimension X* (later called *X Minus One*) and the *CBS Radio Workshop* were also of high quality. However, public interest in television, local station reluctance to clear dramas, and changing listening habits made it difficult for even the best radio drama to capture and hold an audience.

Since 1960, radio drama has virtually disappeared from American radio except for a few isolated experiments. In 1962, ABC inaugurated a 30-minute dramatic anthology called *Theater Five*. The series was broadcast for a year. In 1974, radio producer Himan Brown began *The CBS Radio Mystery Theater*, which broadcast one-hour dramas seven days a week. The program featured horror stories and used classic tales as well as new works. Veteran radio performers as well as young actors were drawn to the series. The program lasted for 12 years in spite of resistance from CBS affiliates to air it at a reasonable hour.

One would expect noncommercial radio networks such as National Public Radio (NPR) and American Public Radio (APR) to be ideal outlets for new radio drama, but this has not proven to be the case. Except for *NPR Playhouse*, which provides 30 minutes of dramatic programming per week to some public radio stations, there is no regularly scheduled dramatic program on the public radio networks.

Since the early 1970s, there have been some spectacular attempts to produce new and interesting radio dramas. These include the Earplay project from WHA in Madison, WI, and the *Star Wars* series from NPR. There are also occasional re-creations of famous broadcasts from the past. Since 1987, for example, there have been revised versions of *The War of the Worlds*, Norman Corwin's *We Hold These Truths*, and his *Plot to Overthrow Christmas*.

Bibliography

Hilmes, Michele. *Hollywood and Broadcasting: From Radio to Cable.* Urbana: U of Illinois P, 1990.

MacDonald, J. Fred. *Don't Touch That Dial! Radio Programming in American Life, 1920-1960.* Chicago: Nelson-Hall, 1979.

Sterling, Christopher H., and John M. Kittross. *Stay Tuned: A Concise History of American Broadcasting.* 2d ed. Belmont: Wadsworth, 1990.

Summers, Harrison B. *A Thirty-Year History of Programs Carried on National Radio Networks in the United States, 1926-1956.* Columbus: Ohio State UP, 1958.

Swartz, Jon D., and Robert C. Reinehr. *Handbook of Old-Time Radio: A Comprehensive Guide to Golden Age Radio Listening and Collecting.* Metuchen: Scarecrow, 1993.

Henry B. Aldridge

See also
Radio Westerns

Radio Evangelists. The use of radio by preachers started in January 1921, two months after U.S. commercial broadcasting began, when Reverend Edwin van Etten delivered the first broadcast sermon from Calvary Episcopal Church over KDKA, Pittsburgh. Since then, radio ministers have used the medium with a variety of approaches and purposes, from traditional religious formats, such as worship services with sermons, to more secular formats, such as dramas, talk shows, and popular music programs. Many radio preachers are quite explicit about admonishing listeners to repent and accept the Lord, whereas others try to win converts more subtly by explaining the impact faith has had on their own lives—what is sometimes called "pre-evangelism." Some preach of hell and damnation for the wayward, some of the power of positive thinking, while still others simply offer advice. Some ask for financial support, others do not. Some own stations or pay for prime air-time, others take what time they can get—usually during the "Sunday morning ghetto" when few people are listening.

Among the earliest ministers to use radio in a traditional format was Walter A. Maier, a Lutheran professor known for designing highly theological sermons accessible to the common person. Maier delivered his sermons during a program of worship called *The Lutheran Hour,* which began in 1924 at his home-base station, KFUO in St. Louis, and which later was broadcast around the world, often in prime time. Taking a different approach to religion in the 1920s was Aimee Semple McPherson. Although "Sister Aimee" also used radio to broadcast sermons over her own station, KFSG in Los Angeles, she helped pioneer religious programming that adapted popular radio formats, such as dramas and musical programs.

McPherson and Maier were part of an early trend of evangelists owning religious stations. This trend changed when the Federal Radio Commission was created in 1927. Religious stations found themselves out of favor with the new licensing body, which saw them as propagandistic. The FRC saw to it that the number of religious stations dwindled. Thereafter, although some religious stations remained on air,

the hope of most radio preachers was to find time on secular stations, either by paying for it or receiving free time. This hope was aided by early broadcasting legislation that required stations to operate in the public interest. One of the ways stations could prove they were publicly responsible, and hence keep their licenses, was to offer religious programming.

The early assumption was that only those programs whose time was offered free by a station could qualify for meeting the station's public interest mandate. Most stations offered this time to preachers from established mainline churches, leaving fundamentalist evangelists to buy time. Stations gave mainline preachers preferential treatment because their churches had more national structure, were considered more representative of the American population, and (after the Scopes trial and other public embarrassments for fundamentalists) were considered more reputable. Because they received free time, mainline preachers did not need to concern themselves with the question of soliciting funds over the air, a practice that their churches found ethically questionable.

Fundamentalist preachers may not have been pleased about having to pay for time, yet their churches' histories were more amenable to the idea of paying for air-time and asking for financial support from listeners because urban revivalism had developed a business-minded approach to saving souls. Because money was needed to keep their programs on the air, these fundamentalist preachers regularly solicited funds from their loyal audiences, often by noting that generous support would help save souls from the eternal fires of hell.

Yet not all networks were willing to sell time to preachers—especially preachers whose message would not achieve broad-based audience appeal because they did not represent a major denomination. Among those fundamentalist radio preachers who were able successfully to buy time, request and receive financial support, and achieve vast popularity was Charles Fuller. Fuller's fundamentalist *Old-Fashioned Revival Hour* was one of the most widely available religious programs of the 1930s and 1940s. Because of its popularity, Fuller's program was able to survive network policy changes aimed at getting one particular radio preacher off the air—Father Charles Coughlin.

Coughlin raised the ire of network officials by using his radio sermons to criticize powerful people in the fields of business, banking, and even broadcasting. The policy changes made in the 1930s to oust him also succeeded at eliminating nearly all fundamentalist preachers from the airwaves in the coming decades. Among the notable exceptions are Oral Roberts and his evangelical radio ministries, and Billy Graham and his vastly popular weekly *Hour of Decision.*

In the coming years, fundamentalist preachers lobbied to get more air time. Their efforts led to a policy change in 1960, when the Federal Communications Commission conceded that stations could receive public interest credit for programs airing on paid time. Able to meet their licensing requirements and turn a profit, it is not suprising that stations now favored airing the programs of cash-paying fundamentalist preachers. To survive, mainline preachers tried more popular formats to receive free air time. Among these was Reverend John Rydgren, "The Swinging Shepherd," whose 1960s program *Silhouette* featured popular music, religious commentary, and teen-age rap sessions focusing on issues such as Vietnam, drug use, premarital sex, and civil rights. Many other programs have used the same approach—playing popular music interspersed with a preacher's inspirational messages and sometimes counseling. Some such programs are the Southern Baptist's *Powerline* and the Catholic *Sound and Sense,* both syndicated programs that began in 1969 playing adult contemporary music interspersed with a minister's devotional messages.

With the deregulatory trend of the 1980s (see Radio Deregulation), many religious programs were squeezed off the air by stations no longer as concerned with the FCC's public interest regulations. Although most stations as a matter of good community relations broadcast sermons and services from congregations in their listening area, very little religious programming airs on most popular radio stations today. Most stations choose preachers whose style is in keeping with their general format. A Top 40 station is more likely to program a preacher using the popular-music-and-inspirational-message format, while a rhythm and blues station might air a service-and-sermon from a local Baptist church, especially if the preacher is backed by a gospel choir. Nationally produced worship-and-sermon programs are still available, among the most popular of which are *The Lutheran Hour* and the jointly produced Methodist, Episcopalian, Lutheran, and United Church of Christ *The Protestant Hour.* Meanwhile, other secular formats, such as the talk show, are represented by syndicated programs such as *Let's Talk about Jesus,* a lunchtime call-in program on which host Wayne Monbleau speaks with callers about religious issues.

Most radio preachers deliver their messages very early on Sunday morning or over low-power radio stations scattered mostly across the South and Midwest, particularly in Appalachia and the Plains states. Whereas radio evangelists once were among radio's most popular and successful prime-time offerings, they are much less a part of contemporary radio programming.

Bibliography

Dorgan, Howard. *The Airwaves of Zion: Radio and Religion in Appalachia.* Knoxville: U of Tennessee P, 1993.

Hill, G. H. *Airwaves to the Soul: The Influence and Growth of Religious Broadcasting in America.* Saratoga: R & E, 1983.

Hoover, S. M. *Mass Media Religion: The Social Sources of the Electronic Church.* Newbury Park: Sage, 1988.

Schultze, Quentin J. "Evangelical Radio and the Rise of the Electronic Church." *Journal of Broadcasting and Electronic Media* Summer 1988.

Richard Wolff

Radio Formats. With the advent of television networks in 1948, radio stations across the country began to suffer economically. The golden age of radio was giving way to the golden age of television. Audiences of the long-form enter-tainment programs carried on the national radio networks were now turning to the same type of programming on television. Radio station programming needed to evolve. It did.

In the 1950s, commercial stations began to realize the benefits of narrowcasting or specializing in particular types of programming (e.g., music, news, etc.) called formats. A station would select an audience (often based on its purchasing power), and then determine what types of music or other programming to play based on the wants and needs of its listeners. One of the early formats was known as middle-of-the-road (MOR), which included a mix of news, talk, and carefully selected specialty music shows. MOR was a full-service format that targeted older adults well into the 1970s.

A significant moment in radio history came in 1949, when WDIA in Memphis became the first all-black-formatted radio station in the U.S. During this time, rhythm and blues began to replace the big band. The innovative ideas of Jackie L. Cooper (the father of black radio), almost two decades earlier, helped Chicago become known as the birthplace of gospel music and African-American radio programming.

Rhythm and blues, country, and gospel music made way for a new format—rock 'n' roll, which debuted as Top 40 radio in 1949. As the story goes, KOWH-AM's owner/ programmer Todd Storz and programmer Bill Steward aired only records that sold well among listeners in Omaha, NE. For the next two decades, AM radio would remain the leader in hit radio.

By the early 1960s, the first oldies format was born, and stations began to recycle the hits from the previous decade. Also during this time, some middle-of-the-road stations began playing less news and information and more music, featuring artists Bobby Goldsboro, Glen Campbell, and the Fifth Dimension. FM stations aired classical music, and then eventually "beautiful music"—a format that debuted on KABL in San Francisco in the 1960s. This format was created by station owner Gordon McLendon, one of the most influential consultants in the U.S. in the 1950s and 1960s. Beautiful music often consisted of instrumentals of popular and classic songs and show tunes. McLendon's all-news format was also developed during this time, and it debuted on XETRA in Tijuana, Mexico. Several years earlier, McLendon's reputation as a programming consultant in Top 40 radio had been established in small and medium-sized radio markets.

By the late 1960s, FM radio stations, spurred by the FCC nonduplication rule, began to explore programming that picked up on a new consumer buying trend: the purchase of long-play record albums over singles. While AM radio pumped out the hits on Top 40 radio (everything from the Beatles to Motown), FM radio encouraged some music experimentation in progressive rock. The music of choice: progressive or "underground" rock. The artists: the Beatles, the Rolling Stones, Jefferson Airplane, Jimi Hendrix, and Janis Joplin.

Top 40 radio first moved to FM in the middle 1970s, and was an eclectic mix of country, disco, rock, and even some popular instrumental hits. Some stations began to emphasize dance music over rock. By the 1980s, disco had emerged. Within a few years, urban radio stations in large markets began playing disco music, and the sound matured into a format now called urban contemporary. About the same time, the baby boomers began to find comfort in soft rock and "less talk, lite rock" stations, as well as personality-driven adult contemporary music formats, that offered a mix of new and old songs targeted at the 25+ age group. Easy listening stations (an updated version of beautiful music formats) targeted the over-40 crowd. Oldies stations with music dating back to the 1950s continued to diversify. Nostalgia radio, born in the late 1970s, continues to thrive in some cities, such as Philadelphia.

One trend that is not new is the popularity of country music on radio. By the early 1930s, country and western barn dance shows were aired nationally over the networks. By 1958, country and western music, following in the success of rock 'n' roll, found its way into urban homes in the Northeast. Then, after the release of the movie *Urban Cowboy,* Top 40 stations welcomed country tunes more than ever before. Country music began to move from AM to FM. By 1980, country music had become so popular in the major metropolitan areas that stations began to specialize in contemporary and urban country music (now often called hot country). More radio stations in the U.S. employ a country music format than any other single music format.

Never before have the airwaves been so diversified. There has been a tremendous fragmentation of formats, and a move to more of a micro-niche format philosophy, especially in the highly competitive major radio markets. Among the latest are power radio, dusties (black oldies), black adult contemporary music, hot adult contemporary, contemporary hit, New Age, Z-rock's all metal, classic rock, classic hit, college chart, contemporary Christian (see Christian Radio Music Formats), and contemporary classical. Nonmusic formats include children (see Children's Radio), sports, talk, news (e.g., CNN radio), and game show (see also College Radio and Community Radio).

With a small investment in satellite down-link capacity, any one of the over 11,000 radio stations across the country now has access to virtually any music or information format, any major radio personality, and major market voice and production quality. Never before has access to such diversity been available to so many radio broadcasters, especially considering that only a few formats were available to programmers and listeners less than 40 years ago.

Bibliography

Keith, Michael C. *The Radio Station.* Boston: Focal, 1993.
O'Donnell, Lewis B., Carl Hausman, and Philip Benoit. *Radio Station Operations.* Belmont: Wadsworth, 1989.
Pember, Don R. *Mass Media in America.* New York: Macmillan, 1992.
Spaulding, Norman W. "History of Black Oriented Radio in Chicago 1929-1963." Diss. University of Illinois, 1981.
Sterling, Christopher H., and John M. Kittross. *Stay Tuned.* Belmont: Wadsworth, 1990.

Phylis Johnson
Thomas A. Birk

Radio News is almost as old as the medium itself. It was Guglielmo Marconi, the inventor of wireless communication, who in 1898 first sent news bulletins by radio or wireless telegraphy. The occasion was the Kingstown Regatta, near Dublin, Ireland, and the reporting was for the *Dublin Express.* In 1899, near New York City, a similar feat took place, with the America's Cup races and the *New York Herald.* In both instances, Marconi radioed reports of the respective yacht races from nearby vessels to shore where each particular newspaper received the news. This allowed the journals to get a "jump" on their competition.

When the first experimental voice broadcasts took place from 1900 to 1907, some of Reginald Fessenden's programming included news and information. Lee DeForest (see entry), inventor of the tiode, or audion, periodically broadcast news and other fare from 1907 to 1917. In 1916, DeForest even aired the Wilson-Hughes presidential election returns to the New York City area. Charles "Doc" Herrold operated, in San Jose, CA, a radio station from 1909 to 1917 which regularly included news bulletins and other information.

During World War I, radio not only provided point-to-point communication, but also news and information. Amateurs and college experimenters used wireless telegraphy and sometimes voice radio to broadcast information, news, and other programming types. Still, commercial licenses (best frequencies) were allocated to business, and primarily used for communicating to and from ships at sea.

KDKA, in 1920, became the first broadcasting station to receive a commercial license. Extensive reporting of the Harding-Cox presidential election returns inaugurated the outlet. Additionally, a Detroit amateur licensed station broadcast the Harding-Cox election results.

KDKA began regular newscasts from the old *Pittsburgh Post* newspaper, September 20, 1921. Farther west, the *Norfolk* [Nebraska] *Daily News* station, WJAG, began, on July 26, 1922, a daily noontime newscast. On February 3, 1923, the *New York Tribune* initiated sponsorship of a 15-minute news résumé, aired over WJZ. Finally, during 1925, KOIN in Portland, OR, started news every hour on the hour.

As early as 1922, the Associated Press warned its members not to sell broadcasters its news. However, such restrictions against radio became harder to enforce as the number of newspaper-owned stations increased. By 1925, the AP began slightly relaxing its news restrictions.

On March 18, 1925, WLS in Chicago not only read bulletins regarding the destructive tornado in southern Illinois and Indiana, but also held radio marathons to raise money for the victims. The *Chicago Tribune*'s WGN broadcast live the climax of the nationally sensational Scopes "Monkey Trial" in Dayton, TN, from July 13 to August 21, 1925.

In the fall of 1928 the AP, UP, and INS agreed to furnish to radio stations returns of the Hoover-Smith presidential election. Many local newspapers cooperated similarly with local broadcasters in this significant news endeavor.

The 1930s Great Depression adversely affected most newspapers, but overall, radio not only remained unscathed, but even prospered. This was especially true for the three major networks of the day, CBS and NBC Red and Blue (two separate operations). Wire news operations threatened withdrawal of service just before the 1932 Roosevelt-Hoover presidential election. Not only did this not materialize, but the network election coverage was acclaimed as excellent. However, this triumph signaled an end, for years to come, to any AP or even UP and INS wire service cooperation with radio. Newspaper interests withdrew, by the spring of 1933, AP, UP, and INS news from radio.

Thus began what has been usually termed the "Press-Radio War." Its fullest impact was felt by 1934 by "forcing" radio network newscasting restriction. The newspaper interests also forced upon the national networks a specially created news service, the "Press-Radio Bureau." This rather token news service lasted from 1934 to 1938.

Bibliography

Barnouw, Erik. *A Tower in Babel: A History of Radio in the United States*. Vol. 1. New York: Oxford UP, 1966.

Charnley, Mitchell V. *News by Radio*. New York: Macmillan, 1948.

Danna, Sammy R. *The Rise of Radio News*. Freedom of Information Center Report No. 211, Nov. 1968. Columbia: School of Journalism, University of Missouri.

Lichty, Lawrence W., and Malachi Topping, eds. *American Broadcasting: A Source Book on the History of Radio and Television*. New York: Hastings House, 1975.

Sterling, Christopher H., and John M. Kittross. *Stay Tuned: A Concise History of American Broadcasting*. 2d ed. Belmont: Wadsworth, 1990.

Sammy R. Danna

Radio Sportscasters. Broadcasting and sports are a natural couple. From its earliest days, broadcast radio featured sports. In 1923 it carried the World Series on a special wire between WEAF and WWY. Although only New York and Schenectady were on this early network, the idea soon grew. Shortly, Graham McNamee, Phillips Corbin, Major J. Andrew White, and Ted Husing were familiar to radio listeners. Their ranks were soon joined by others who surpassed them in fame:

Red Barber (1908-1998; see entry). By most accounts, Red Barber (William Lanier Barber) was the dean of radio broadcasters. He launched his broadcasting career in 1930 at WRUF, the University of Florida, Gainesville, campus radio station and ended it 62 years later on National Public Radio with a Friday sportscast of commentary. A major league baseball announcer for 33 years, Red was known for his great class and fairness. When he was the voice of the Brooklyn Dodgers in 1947, he did much to gain acceptance for Jackie Robinson, the first African American in major league baseball. His motto was simple but effective: (1) Don't take sides; (2) Do your homework; (3) Be careful whom you trust.

Bill Stern (1907-1971). Bill Stern's motto was quite the opposite of Red Barber's. If Bill had been forced to summarize it, it would have been "Never let the facts get in the way of a good story!" Stern was born in Rochester, NY. For many years, his distinctive style of sports reporting and commentary were household staples.

He broadcast the Friday night fights for four years for Adam Hats. In 1938 he began working for MGM on its *News of the Day Newsreel*. On October 8, 1939, he broadcast the first of the *Colgate Sports Newsreels,* where he developed his trademark style of spinning fantastic sports yarns, abetted by a theatrical organ, sound effects, and other stage properties. His show remained popular till its end on June 29, 1951. He remained on the air with a nightly show until 1956, when *ABC Sports Today* ended.

Mel Allen (1913-1996). For 25 years (1939-64), Mel Allen was "the Voice" of the Yankees. Allen wasn't simply a Yankee announcer, he also broadcast 20 World Series, 24 All Star Games, Rose Bowls, East-West Shrine Games, heavyweight fights, and was featured on the Movietone Newsreel. But Allen loved the Yankees and baseball and had done so before he announced one game. Allen never lost his awe at the likes of Babe Ruth nor forgot that the game was more important to the fans than his opinions.

Allen was just one of a list of legendary announcers whom radio and baseball fans can rattle off with the least excuse: Harry Caray of the St. Louis Cardinals (later the Chicago Cubs), Curt Gowdy of the Boston Red Sox, Byrum Saam of Philadelphia, Ernie Harwell of Detroit, Bob Elson of the White Sox, Jack Quinlan of the Cubbies, Earl Gillespie of the Boston Braves, Jimmy Dudley of the Cleveland Indians, and Bob Prince of the Pirates. The clear-channel stations of the day brought many of these sportscasters, who truly loved the game, far beyond their local areas. Buffalo's WBEN, Rochester's WHAM, Pittsburgh's KDKA, and WCBS sent their 50,000 watts directly into the homes of fans, presenting their interpretations of the game directly to these fans' imaginations.

Radio announcers played a key role in radio's golden days. Their view of the game was the one most fans carried with them. They spoke directly to the imagination. The game they described was often more exciting than the one on the field. The fights they delivered blow-by-blow were far more exciting, on the average, than the dancing matches that TV later brought into the living room.

Bibliography

Dunning, John. *Tune in Yesterday*. Englewood Cliffs: Prentice-Hall, 1976.

Edwards, Bob. *Fridays with Red: A Radio Friendship*. New York: Simon & Schuster, 1993.

Smith, Curt. *Voices of the Game: The First Full-Scale Overview of Baseball Broadcasting, 1921 to the Present*. South Bend: Diamond Communications, 1987.

Frank A. Salamone

Radio Westerns. Despite having flourished in novels, magazines, and films, Westerns did not achieve their full potential on radio until the waning years of radio's golden age, a time when television had largely replaced radio as America's major source of home entertainment. For the most part, radio presented Western programs designed for a juvenile audience, and of the approximately 30 or so significant Westerns broadcast between 1930 and 1960, fully two-thirds were aimed at children. Most of the "adult" Westerns came after 1950.

Adventure programs with a western setting date to the early 1930s, with the appearance of *Rin Tin Tin Thrillers,*

Bobby Benson's Adventures, *The Tom Mix Ralston Straight Shooters*, and *The Lone Ranger* (see entry). It was not until the mid-1940s, however, that this genre reached its greatest popularity, when more than a dozen youth-oriented Western heroes rode the airwaves.

The basic formula of good always triumphs over evil and crime never pays was common to virtually all of the children's adventure programs heard on radio during its heyday. The setting and characters were, however, straight out of the B Westerns that completed so many of the Saturday matinee double bills of this period. The daily 15-minute serialized shows like *Tom Mix* were also influenced by the cliffhanger movie serials that were such an integral part of those Saturday matinees. A number of the cowboy stars of this era (Gene Autry, Buck Jones, Ken Maynard, Roy Rogers, Hopalong Cassidy, and Tom Mix—although Mix was always "impersonated" by other actors) eventually took their place before the microphone as heroes of juvenile Westerns.

Almost all of the Westerns aimed at the young listener had certain unmistakable characteristics. The hero was invariably popular, smart, manly, brave, just, athletic, and tough (e.g., the Lone Ranger was the "champion of justice"; Roy Rogers was the "King of the Cowboys"; Tom Mix was "everybody's favorite cowboy"; Gene Autry was "America's favorite cowboy"; Hopalong Cassidy was the "most famous cowboy hero of them all"; and Red Ryder was "America's famous fighting cowboy"). The hero usually had an Anglo-Saxon name like Reid, Mix, Cassidy, Rogers, or Autry and was Caucasian. Even Straight Arrow was really a young white rancher named Steve Adams who took the guise of "a mysterious, stalwart Indian wearing the dress and warpaint of a Comanche" when "danger threatened innocent people" or when "evildoers plotted against justice." Conversely, the villain often was given an evil-sounding foreign name (e.g., the Lone Ranger matched wits with "El Diablo," the Cisco Kid battled "El Culebra," and Hopalong Cassidy confronted a Chinese thug named Chung).

In general, foreigners and minorities received harsh treatment at the hands of writers of juvenile Westerns, especially during World War II. There were, however, a few exceptions. The Indian, usually depicted as a bloodthirsty savage lying in ambush to waylay some helpless settler, was portrayed as a noble human being worthy of respect and trust in the figure of Tonto, the Lone Ranger's "faithful Indian companion." In fact, Indians in general faired well in episodes of *The Lone Ranger* and, of course, *Straight Arrow.*

Another part of the juvenile Western formula was the comic sidekick. He always made the hero look positively brilliant by comparison and provided a few laughs to break the monotony of nonstop action. For Roy Rogers there was Gabby Hayes and later, Pat Brady; Gene Autry had Pat Buttrum; Hoppy's sidekick was California Carlson; "Wild Bill" was aided by "Jingles" (gravel-voiced Andy Devine); the Cisco Kid rode with Pancho; the *Tom Mix Straight Shooters Show* had several comedic characters—the Old Wrangler early in the series, then Sheriff Mike Shaw and Wash (a stereotyped black that was actually played by a white actor).

Bobby Benson's pals included Windy Wales (an early role for Don Knotts) and Diogenes Dodwaddle.

Radio Westerns produced for an adult audience were few and far between prior to World War II. The only regular series was *Death Valley Days*, a popular anthology of the late 1930s and early 1940s. The quality of these shows varied greatly, however, ranging from comedy to near melodrama, with most stories lacking the plausibility and authenticity that the adult Western required.

All of the characteristics of the adult Western could be found in *Gunsmoke* (1952-61): a hero who was more human than the one-dimensional stars of the kiddie Westerns—a complex mixture of good and bad, strength and weakness; a variety of antagonists that included vengeful widows, psychopathic killers, brutal savages, indifferent vigilantes, and foolish weaklings; and controversial themes that were scrupulously avoided in juvenile Westerns—excessive violence, sex, and religious and racial discrimination. *Gunsmoke* represented a new breed of radio Western in which mature plot, fuller human characterization, and an intelligent theme, all enacted according to high dramatic standards, were combined to produce the most sophisticated Western dramas in radio history.

Bibliography

Dunning, John. *Tune in Yesterday: The Ultimate Encyclopedia of Old Time Radio, 1925-1976.* Englewood Cliffs: Prentice-Hall, 1976.

Harmon, Jim. *The Great Radio Heroes.* New York: Doubleday, 1967.

MacDonald, J. Fred. *Don't Touch That Dial! Radio Programming in American Life, 1920-1960.* Chicago: Nelson-Hall, 1979.

Gary A. Yoggy

Raiders of the Lost Ark (1981) was a successful collaboration between George Lucas, director of *Star Wars* (1977) and *American Graffiti* (1973), and Steven Spielberg (see entry), director of *Close Encounters of the Third Kind* (1977) and *Jaws* (1975). Friends for many years, the two directors had not worked together on a film. Lucas had an idea for a larger-than-life screen hero named Indiana Jones. Director Phillip Kaufman and Lucas had devised a story about the heroic Jones and his race against Hitler to find the lost Ark of the Covenant. Spielberg became interested in directing the film in the style of the matinee adventure serials of the 1930s.

The resulting *Raiders of the Lost Ark*, starring Harrison Ford (see entry), received Oscar nominations for best picture, Spielberg's direction, Douglas Slocombe's cinematography, and John Williams's musical score. *Raiders* won Academy Awards for film editing, art (and set) direction, visual effects, and sound. The film eventually grossed over $300 million in box office receipts. The popularity of *Raiders* resulted in a flood of imitation films, including Tom Selleck's *High Road to China* (1983), *Romancing the Stone* (1984), *King Solomon's Mines* (1985), and *Allan Quatermain and the Lost City of Gold* (1986). The success of *Raiders* also led Steven Spielberg, George Lucas, and Harrison Ford to collaborate on two equally successful sequels: *Indiana Jones and the Temple of Doom* (1984), and *Indiana Jones and the Last Crusade* (1989). In 1992, George Lucas produced *The Young Indiana Jones Chronicles*, the critically acclaimed, but short-lived, television series about Indy's youthful adventures.

Bibliography

Brode, Douglas. *The Films of Steven Spielberg*. New York: Carol, 1995.

Taylor, Derek. *The Making of* Raiders of the Lost Ark. New York: Ballantine, 1981.

Keith Semmel

Rap is a style of African-American music that arose as a product of transculturation in the South Bronx in the early and mid-1970s. Most of its early important practitioners, such as Kool Herc, DJ Hollywood, and Afrika Bambaataa, were either first- or second-generation Caribbean Americans. Herc and Hollywood are both credited with introducing the Jamaican style of cutting and mixing into the culture of the South Bronx. By most accounts Herc was the first disc jockey to buy two copies of the same record just for a 15-second break in the middle. By mixing back and forth between the two copies he could double, triple, or extend the break indefinitely. Herc was effectively deconstructing and reconstructing "found" sound.

While he was doing this with two turntables, Herc would also be playing the dozens over the microphone in Jamaican toasting style, making jokes, boasting, and using myriad in-group references. Over time, Herc's parties became legendary and were often documented on the relatively new double-deck "blaster" technology.

In 1976, Grandmaster Flash (née Joseph Sadler) introduced the technique of quick mixing, which combined sound bites as short as one or two seconds in a collage-like effect. In many ways, this paralleled the aesthetic of contemporary television advertising that rap, in turn, would greatly influence. Flash's partner, Grandmaster Melle Mel, soon thereafter created the first extended composed rhyming rap stories. Up to this point, most of the words sounded above the work of disc jockeys such as Herc, Bambaataa, and Flash were improvised short snippets that paralleled the African and African-American techniques of signifying and the dozens. Two years later, DJ Grand Wizard Theodore introduced the technique of scratching, using the grooves in a record as found sound that could be manipulated by the disc jockey in whatever rhythm s/he could conceive of and physically execute.

Herc, Bambaataa, Flash, Theodore, and their legions of imitators were effectively creating turntable art, manipulating found sound via repetition, juxtaposition, alteration of pitch, alteration of rate of articulation, and placement in time. In doing so, they were inverting the purpose, and thereby usurping the power, of the technology of the capitalist hegemonic culture.

In 1979, the first two rap records appeared, Fatback Band's *King Tim III (Personality Jock)* and Sugarhill Gang's *Rapper's Delight*. The former made little impression but the latter became a national hit, peaking at No. 4 on the R&B charts and No. 36 in pop. The three members of Sugarhill Gang rapped a series of verses largely comprised of braggadocio liberally spiced with a highly developed sense of fantasy. The backing track was supplied by hired studio musicians who replicated Chic's disco hit from four months earlier, "Good Times."

Rapper's Delight was perceived by most Euro-Americans as a novelty record, very quickly influencing a number of new wave records including Blondie's 1980 record, *Rapture*. In 1982, Afrika Bambaataa's *Planet Rock* was the first rap record to use synthesizers and the Roland 808 drum machine. This was an important step, as rap artists were now creating from scratch part of their backing tracks. A year later, on *Looking for the Perfect Beat,* Bambaataa introduced the Emulator synth. This was the first example of sampling in rap. Sampling replaced the old turntable style of cutting and mixing, enabling disc jockeys to have access to precise, digitally isolated sound bites that could be reconstructed into new patterns of collages. Sampling would eventually facilitate the layering of "found" sound, with such advanced artists as Public Enemy commonly layering seven or eight samples on top of each other.

Sampling brought into open question the whole notion of ownership of sound. Many artists saw this technology as facilitating gestures of cultural resistance. By sampling a James Brown sound bite, EPMD were effectively challenging Polygram's right to ownership of black cultural gestures. They also, of course, were challenging James Brown's right to own, control, and be compensated for the use of his intellectual creations. By the early 1990s a series of legal and informal precedents had brought about a system where most artists asked permission and negotiated a form of compensation for the use of samples. Some commonly sampled musicians such as George Clinton actually released compact discs containing several dozen sound bites. One residual effect of all of this was a newfound sense of musical history among black youth. Such earlier artists as James Brown and Parliament/Funkadelic were lionized as cultural heroes, their recordings reissued and bought by the thousands.

In 1986, paralleling the process of rhythm and blues in the 1950s, rap crossed over into the mainstream of popular music via white rappers the Beastie Boys' "Fight for Your Right to Party" and black rappers Run DMC's duet with rock group Aerosmith on the latter's "Walk This Way."

In the late 1980s a large segment of rap became highly politicized, manifesting the most overt social agenda of any form of popular music since the 1960s urban folk movement. Public Enemy and Boogie Down Productions embodied this aesthetic more than anyone. The former came to prominence with their second album, 1988's *It Takes a Nation of Millions to Hold Us Back*. In an apt and often quoted phrase, lead singer Chuck D. referred to rap as the African-American CNN. Against the backdrop of the Reagan and Bush era, rap functioned as a voice for a community without access to the mainstream media. As such, it served to engender self-pride, self-help, and self-upliftment, communicating a sense of black history as positive and fulfilling what was largely absent from any other American institution.

Parallel to the rise of politicized rap was the appearance of gangsta rap with NWA's (Niggas with Attitude) 1989 album *Straight Outta Compton*. Songs such as "———— tha Police" generated an extraordinary amount of controversy. As is always the case, such attempts at censorship only served to publicize the music and make it more attractive to both black and white youths. By 1994, gangsta rap albums had become extremely popular while laden with some of the most violent and misogynist imagery in popular music history.

Bibliography

McCoy, Judy. *Rap Music in the 1980's: A Reference Guide.* Metuchen: Scarecrow, 1992.

Nelson, Havelock, and Michael A. Gonzales. *Bring the Noise: A Guide to Rap Music and Hip-Hop Culture.* New York: Harmony, 1991.

Perkins, William Eric. *Droppin' Science: Critical Essays on Rap Music and Hip Hop Culture.* Philadelphia: Temple UP, 1996.

Rose, Tricia. *Black Noise: Rap Music and Black Culture in Contemporary America.* Hanover: Wesleyan UP, 1994.

Rob Bowman

See also

Hip Hop

Raves are all-night dance events, held in abandoned warehouses and airplane hangars, open fields, and clubs, where largely 16-to-25-year-olds dance amid often elaborate lighting and visual displays to the hypnotic beats of techno, acid house, and, more recently, ambient house, brutal house, progressive house, trance, jungle, and related musics. Sources conflict on the phenomenon's official country of origin, but it is likely that the earliest raves were held in the late 1980s in Europe, expanding overseas to the U.S. shortly thereafter. Raves began as solely underground events, advertised selectively by word of mouth, but have since become commercialized ventures, held in clubs and other more traditional venues.

In late 1980s Detroit, experimental African-American producers like Kevin Saunderson and Derrick May mixed part early-1980s synthipop, part house, and part disco to create techno, a music that would shape the dance scene throughout Europe. The techno sound evolved in the hands of European disk jockeys and producers and was re-introduced to the U.S. in the early 1990s. Rave musics are often criticized for being monotonous, repetitive, soulless, faceless, mechanical, and non-musical. Clocking in at 120-160+ beats per minute, the music demands almost super-human endurance of rave participants.

Rave culture is exclusively youth culture, based on the simplicity and naiveté of childhood (and the deferment of adulthood), as illustrated by rave fashions (or anti-fashions) consisting of baggy jeans or shorts, primary-colored T-shirts, pigtails, oversized stocking caps, fluorescent jewelry, pacifiers, and toys as accessories. Rave has been dubbed by some as the "Disco of the 90s," and there are many significant parallels (roots in the black/gay community, subsequent co-optation by white artists, harsh criticism of the music and culture). But the AIDS threat has encouraged a decidedly non-sexual, or pre-sexual, atmosphere. Raves are not pickup joints, nor are they a showcase for the individual. Raves are a celebration of music, dancing, youth, and community, providing an atmosphere in which participants can temporarily forget the harsh realities of coming of age in the 1990s.

Bibliography

Marcus, Tony. "U.K. Raves: The End of Innocence?" *Billboard* 26 Sept. 1992: 34, 41, 43.

McRobbie, Angela. "Shut Up and Dance: Youth Cultures and Changing Modes of Femininity." *Postmodernism and Popular Culture.* London: Routledge, 1994.

Owen, Frank. "Acid Disco: Make Me Machine." *Village Voice* 19 Jan. 1988: 83-84.

——. "Feel the Noise: Techno Kids: The Working-Class Avant-Garde." *Village Voice* 24 Sept. 1991: 71.

Lori Tomlinson

Rawhide (1959-1966) has been dismissed by some critics as "the cattleman's answer to *Wagon Train*," but it probably was the closest television has ever come to creating a "sweat and blood" Western. The series made no attempt to embellish the basic format of man-against-the-West and thus achieved a rugged documentary realism that concentrated on the harsher aspects of life on the frontier.

Rawhide was the creation of veteran Hollywood writer-director Charles Marquis Warren, who had been instrumental in developing the TV version of *Gunsmoke* and had recently finished directing the film *Cattle Empire* (1958). The program owed much in style and integrity, however, to the classic Howard Hawks film *Red River* (1948), which in turn had been inspired by Borden Chase's novel *The Chisholm Trail*. Originally entitled *Cattle Drive* but later changed to *Rawhide*, Warren's creation (like Hawks's) set out to depict the "working West" of the cattle kingdom and the men and women who inhabited it. Relatively unknown actors were cast in the leading roles: Eric Fleming as trail boss Gil Favor and Clint Eastwood (see entry) as the young cowhand Rowdy Yates. Veterans Sheb Wooley and Paul Brinegar played the scout and the cantankerous cook.

Prior to *Rawhide*'s final season, CBS and Eric Fleming parted company over a variety of contractual differences and Eastwood was elevated to the starring role. (Rowdy Yates was "promoted" to trail boss.) Other changes were also made in the cast, including the addition of Jeb Colby (played by veteran screen actor John Ireland) as Yates's second-in-command and Simon Blake (played by Raymond St. Jacques, who became the first black star to have a major continuing role in a television Western).

Although beginning slowly, the show was quite popular with viewers during its first five seasons, being ranked as high as sixth in 1960-61. *Rawhide* won four Western Heritage Awards from the National Cowboy Hall of Fame in Oklahoma City as the most outstanding program of its genre. However, when the TV Western craze began to die and public taste shifted to situation comedies, *Rawhide* slipped badly in the ratings and was canceled in 1966.

Bibliography
Brooks, Tim, and Earle Marsh. *The Complete Directory to Prime Time Network and Cable TV Shows, 1946-Present.* New York: Ballantine, 1995.

Gary A. Yoggy

Reagan, Ronald Wilson (1911-   ), was well known among Americans long before he became the 40th president. Born in Tampico, IL, he described his youth in Dixon, IL, as a Tom Sawyer-Huck Finn idyll despite the family's poverty and his father's alcoholism. An outstanding student leader and athlete at Dixon High School, Reagan attended Eureka College, a small denominational school supported by the Disciples of Christ. He worked his way through college, played football, and was a student activist during the early and bleakest years of the Great Depression. He graduated in 1932.

Although he had a secret ambition to be an actor, Reagan found work as a radio announcer for WOC in Davenport, IA, before becoming a sports announcer at WHO in Des Moines. From 1932 to 1937, Reagan was the "voice" of the Chicago Cubs. Provided by wire service with the hits, runs, and errors of the game at Wrigley Field, Reagan became skilled at making up the color of the game (see Baseball Re-creations). His talent at "visualizing," or embellishing, the statistics made him one of the most popular sportscasters in the Midwest and a local celebrity.

In 1937, Reagan took advantage of a chance to cover the Cubs spring training in California and to use friends from the Midwest to help him break into movies. His voice, good looks, and athletic physique got him a contract at Warner Brothers.

After playing in eight B movies, Reagan's "discovery" film was the 1938 comedy *Brother Rat*. He co-starred with Wayne Morris and Eddie Albert, who had acted in the Broadway play. Albert proved the better actor and stole the film. Nevertheless, the film made money and Reagan's performance was liked at Warner's.

In 1939, Reagan was given the fifth billing in *Dark Victory*. Starring Bette Davis and directed by Edmund Goulding, the film won Oscar nominations for best picture, Davis, and Max Steiner's score. Reagan's interpretation of his role was at odds with Goulding's direction. He wanted to play his key scenes with conviction and Goulding wanted him to provide comic relief as an epicene playboy who loses the doomed Judith Traherne to her physician. Reagan refused to act in a role that made him a sexless and effeminate alcoholic. The part, he believed, was inconsistent with his character. His performance was panned by the critics and his failure to follow direction got him back in B films.

A year and a half after *Dark Victory,* Reagan was given his favorite and most memorable role as football hero George Gipp in *Knute Rockne—All American*. Directed by Lloyd Bacon and starring Pat O'Brien, Gipp ("the Gipper") was an extension of Reagan's own image as the All-American boy. He heard the story of George Gipp years earlier on sportswriter Grantland Rice's radio show. Reagan urged Warner Brothers to make a film of the incident, but had to convince the studio heads he could play the role. The film launched Reagan to stardom.

Critics agree Reagan's best film is *King's Row* (1941). The part of playboy Drake McHugh was given to him by director Sam Wood. The film featured some of Hollywood's finest character actors, a score by Eric Korngold, sets by William Menzies, and photography by James Wong Howe. Wood, Howe, and *King's Row* were nominated for Academy Awards.

From 1946 to 1957, Reagan made 24 more films. None approached the quality of *King's Row*. Critics find little of consequence in these films, but give Reagan credit for his performance in *The Winning Team*, a 1952 biopic of baseball star Grover Cleveland Alexander, who staged one of the greatest comebacks in all sports history. His excellent work in *The Hasty Heart* (1950) was overshadowed by Richard Todd's Oscar–nominated performance as a dying Scottish soldier. Reagan's acting is solid in two Westerns made with veteran director Alan Dwan, *Cattle Queen of Montana* (1954), and *Tennessee's Partner* (1955). *The Killers* (1964) was a made-for-television film released for showing in theaters because it was too violent for home viewing in the period following the Kennedy assassination. In it Reagan plays his only villain's role, a criminal mastermind and murderer who dies clutching a fist full of money.

Reagan's turn toward politics had begun with the presidency of the Screen Actors Guild (1947-52, 1959-60); his support of the New Deal; and joining the Republican party in 1962. Critics believe Reagan's greatest role was as the president of the U.S. They cannot agree whether Reagan was a good actor poorly used or "the poor man's Errol Flynn." He was neither a natural nor character actor, relying instead on playing his scenes with "great sincerity." His warmth, likability, and optimism made him most popular with the bobby sox generation, and audiences were reluctant to accept him in any role other than the clean-cut young guy.

Bibliography
Cannon, Lou. *President Reagan: The Role of a Lifetime.* New York: Simon & Schuster, 1991.
Reagan, Ronald. *An American Life.* New York: Simon & Schuster, 1990.
——. *Where's the Rest of Me?* New York: Sloan & Pearce, 1965.
Thomas, Tony. *The Films of Ronald Reagan.* Secaucus: Citadel, 1980.
Wills, Garry. *Reagan's America.* Garden City: Penguin, 1987.

Jim Ferreira

Real World, The (1992-   ), was introduced on MTV as a "real soap opera" in response to Fox's popular twenty-something drama *Beverly Hills, 90210* (see entry). *The Real World* debuted at 9 p.m. (EST) after *90210* and featured commercial spots that said, "After the fantasy, get real." The show placed seven young adults, ages 18 to 25, together in a New York City loft for three months to discuss their ideas, hopes, and loves with MTV's cameras rolling. The 12 episodes of *The Real World* were a ratings success and have led to a series of larger versions in Los Angeles, San Francisco, London, Miami, Boston, Seattle, Hawaii, and New Orleans.

Borrowing the *cinema vérité* style of PBS's 1973 documentary *An American Family*, a show that followed the Loud family for months in the early 1970s, MTV's *The Real World* attempted to illuminate the problems facing its viewing audience. The group and their surroundings were called a "relentlessly artificial concept," but viewers, many of whom were annoyed by the members' constant bickering, nevertheless continued to watch.

Bibliography

Gordinier, Jeff. "Get Real." *Entertainment Weekly* 5 Aug. 1994: 26-30.

O'Connor, John J. "New Summer Episodes on Three Cable Series." *New York Times* 22 June 1994: 18.

——. "The Real World: According to MTV." *New York Times* 9 July 1993: C 15.

Parks, Brian. "Bay Watch: The Real World 3." *Village Voice* 12 July 1994: 39.

Rubin, Mike. "The Venetian Blind." *Village Voice* 27 July 1993: 51-52.

Richard Veteikes

Red Hot Chili Peppers, The (1983-   ), are recognized as "early pioneers of the mosh-pit marriage of funk, rap and thrash," writes David Fricke in *Rolling Stone*. Founding members were Anthony Kiedis (vocals), Michael "Flea" Balzary (bass), Jack Irons (since replaced by Chad Smith on drums), and Hillel Slovak, who died of a heroin overdose in 1988 and was never really replaced by a series of guitarists.

The group started out as a joke band to play a one-off at a club in Los Angeles and by 1992 had a Top 10 single with "Under the Bridge" from the multi-million-selling album *BloodSugarSexMagik*. The group made steady progress through the 1980s via constant touring and a succession of thumping and funky albums. Their 1984 self-titled debut album featured the college radio favorite "True Men Don't Kill Coyotes." Since they were already in the tradition of funk via Flea's merciless bass popping, the group enlisted Parliament-Funkadelic groovemeister George Clinton for their second album, *Freaky Styley*, in 1983. *The Trouser Press Record Guide* calls the album "a ton of raunchy, funky fun."

1987's *Uplift Mofo Party Plan* was not a commercial success but it did provide the alternative radio standard "Fight Like a Brave," while another track, "Special Secret Song Inside," furthered the Chili Peppers' propensity for libidinous subjects. This was a band notorious for doing encores with nothing more than tube socks over their private parts.

After Slovak's overdose in 1988, Irons quit the band and Kiedis began reversing his personal excesses. The Chili Peppers hired Chad Smith after auditioning about 30 drummers and John Frusciante was brought in as the new guitarist. The album they recorded in 1988, *Mother's Milk*, was dedicated to Slovak and yielded their first pop hit, a cover of Stevie Wonder's "Higher Ground," which made the Chili Peppers one of the few alternative bands besides R.E.M. to have made it on to album rock radio playlists by 1989.

The follow-up to *Mother's Milk*, *BloodSugarSexMagik*, was a huge success. The album not only provided a Top 10 single, "Under the Bridge," but another single from the album, "Give It Away," won a Grammy for "Best Hard Rock Song." In 1994, the group had a hit with "Soul to Squeeze" from the *Coneheads* film soundtrack and had recruited ex-Jane's Addiction guitarist Dave Navarro to record their next album, *One Hot Minute* (1995). Their cover of the disco single "Love Rollercoaster" from the *Beavis and Butt-head* soundtrack became a No. 1 hit in 1996. Frusciante came back to the group, replacing Navarro, on the Grammy–nominated *Californication* (1999), with the hit song "Scar Tissue."

Bibliography

Fricke, David. "Red Hot Chili Peppers." *Rolling Stone* 25 June 1992: 26-30, 50-51.

"Red Hot Chili Peppers." Rolling Stone.com. 8 May 2000.

Resnicoff, Matt. "Flea: The Hottest Chili Pepper." *Musician* Jan. 1994: 22-32, 48.

Robbins, Ira. *The Trouser Press Record Guide*. New York: Collier, 1991.

Hugh Foley

Red Skelton Show, The (1951-1971), in various formats, ran on network television for 20 years. The son of a circus clown, Richard "Red" Skelton (1910-1977; see entry) began his career by performing in medicine-wagon shows and soon hit the boards as a small-time vaudevillian. By the early 1930s, Skelton was getting known through a series of comedy routines relying on his gifts as a visual comic. He began making films in 1938 and was a star at MGM by 1941. The late 1930s saw him heading a radio show which finally went national in 1941. He brought this show to television in 1951 on NBC. The first season was a big hit, allowing many of Red's fans their first chance to see his comic creations Freddie the Freeloader, Willie Lump-Lump, Clem Kadiddlehopper, and the "mean-widdle-kid."

The second season was less successful and Skelton in 1953 moved to CBS, where the show remained a modest success for the rest of the decade. The show went through structural changes, going from live, to filmed, to taped with an audience. Skelton's loose performing style responded best to being taped, allowing him to interact with the audience and to comically digress as he saw fit. The format also shifted frequently in its first decade, sometimes similar to his radio program by drawing on several of his comic characterizations, other times virtually a sitcom, and still others a variety show with Skelton as emcee. In 1962, the show became an hour long and settled on a more fixed format with Skelton doing an opening monologue, engaging in two main sketches utilizing a favorite characterization and the guest star, and a "silent spot" showcasing Skelton's noted pantomimic abilities.

The show enjoyed its greatest success from then on, securing awards and Top 5 ratings, usually winning its time slot easily. Though Skelton's show was tops in the ratings, demographics showed that the show was not heavily watched by young adults, a problem shared by several Top 10 CBS shows. As a result, the show was summarily dropped as part of the massive schedule change engineered by CBS in 1970-71, and Skelton returned to NBC with a half-hour show which lasted only one season. A disgruntled Skelton began a rigorous schedule of live performances and vowed never to work for network television again, and remained true to his word, appearing only on syndicated programs in the 1970s and a series of specials for HBO in the 1980s.

Bibliography

Marx, Arthur. *Red Skelton: An Unauthorized Biography.* New York: Dutton, 1979.

Terrace, Vincent. *Encyclopedia of Television Series, Pilots, and Specials, 1937-1973, Volume I.* New York: Zoetrope, 1985.

——. *Encyclopedia of Television Series, Pilots, and Specials, 1974-1984, Volume II.* New York: Zoetrope, 1985.

Benjamin K. Urish

Redding, Otis (1941-1968), or "The Big O," is considered by many the greatest soul singer who ever lived. He was born in Dawson, GA, but raised in Macon from the time he was three. His father was a part-time Baptist preacher whose continued health problems forced Otis to drop out of school in the tenth grade to support his family. The young Redding worked as a well digger and a gas station attendant while trying to juggle his music career.

Like nearly all of the great gospel and soul singers, Redding drew on the South's rich variety of musical sources: gospel, rhythm and blues, and even country music. He began by singing in church and was soon working as a drummer behind the gospel groups who recorded at Macon's WIBB, a practice which certainly contributed to the startling rhythmic quality of his music. Redding became a prominent figure on the Macon music scene, playing local talent shows, singing everything from Little Richard, his boyhood idol, to Elvis Presley. At this time, Redding made friends with Phil Walden (who would later manage the Allman Brothers), a white Macon teenager in love with rhythm and blues, who remained Redding's manager until the singer's death in a plane crash outside of Madison, WI.

Redding had many false starts before he got his big break in October 1962, when Atlantic Records arranged for Johnny Jenkins, who had asked Redding to join his band, to record at Stax Studios in Memphis. As an afterthought to the session, Redding was allowed to record the song that would launch his career, "These Arms of Mine." Prior to this song, Redding had cut several delightful, though derivative, singles for independent labels. "Shout Bamalama" was probably the best, but, like "Hey, Hey Baby," the flip side to "These Arms of Mine," sounded too close to Little Richard. However, with the pleading A side, Redding came into his own, seemingly full-born at a single stroke. While not a big hit, the song established Redding as an unequaled ballad singer, and created the persona out of which he would build his career and his 17 rhythm and blues hits.

His voice had a grainy quality to it, which evoked Brown without copying him, and Otis used it with the precision of a scientific instrument, tracing every jagged edge of his being.

The titles tell the story—"That's What My Heart Needs," "Pain in My Heart," "I've Been Loving You Too Long (To Stop Now)," and especially, "Try a Little Tenderness." His performances dramatized a tortured innocence, each song a testament to the wrecked, but beautiful, terrain of his heart, which he seemed to offer as a gift to each listener. If the essence of soul music was to convey emotion at whatever price, then Otis Redding was the essential soul singer.

No less important than his qualities as a singer were his talents as a songwriter, producer, and arranger. Redding wrote or had a share in writing most of his songs. In addition, he served, in effect, as his own producer, though it should be stressed that the recorded work done with the Stax house band, Booker T. and the MG's, was always a collaborative effort. Redding's closest collaborator was guitarist Steve Cropper, with whom he wrote "Fa-Fa-Fa-Fa-Fa (Sad Song)," "Mr. Pitiful," and "(Sittin' on) The Dock of the Bay," among others. Cropper gives Redding credit for being the driving force behind the famous Stax sound, which was the epitome of southern soul, dense but somehow fluid, too.

Redding was determined to have as wide an audience as possible, and was said to have worn out copies of the Beatles' *Revolver* and *Sergeant Pepper* in an effort to broaden his musical perspective. In 1967, he became the darling of the Monterey Pop Festival, which also served as Jimi Hendrix's coming out party, remarkable because the show featured white rock acts like Janis Joplin and the Jefferson Airplane. This concert captured the wider audience Redding desired. Strangely, Redding is sometimes criticized for the catholic nature of his ambition, many charging that he sold out his "soul" roots by recording versions of the Rolling Stones' "Satisfaction" and the Beatles' "Day Tripper." Redding's versions of those two English rock chestnuts became different entities in his hands, however, cooked over in the cauldron of the Stax-Volt sound, just as Redding's acknowledged masterpiece, "Try a Little Tenderness," had been previously associated with Bing Crosby and Frank Sinatra. Redding was a gifted interpreter, and an original one. As his Monterey Pop performance attests, any broader audience Redding conquered would have been on his own terms.

This is precisely what happened with the posthumous "(Sittin' on) The Dock of the Bay," his only No. 1 single. Though the song's popularity may have been due to the singer's death, it nevertheless represented a synthesis of Redding's wide interests and pointed the way toward a new direction. The song's deceptively simple folk lyricism suggested Bob Dylan as well as the Beatles, but the delivery was pure soul. Less pleading than his signature records, the song uncovered a maturity of emotion that is truly heartbreaking to hear, since Redding would never get the chance to build on it.

Bibliography

Guralnick, Peter. *Sweet Soul Music.* New York: Harper, 1986.

Hirshey, Gerri. *Nowhere to Run: The Story of Soul Music.* New York: Times, 1984.

Schiesel, Jane. *The Otis Redding Story.* Garden City: Doubleday, 1975.

Timothy L. Parrish

Redford, Robert (1937-), is one of Hollywood's more famous actors, directors, producers. "In a way he was like the country he lived in. Everything came too easily to him but, at least, he knew it," the main character's autobiographical confession in *The Way We Were* (1973), contains several similarities to the star portraying him, Robert Redford. Combining star significations of male sexuality, American Wasp idealization, and ordinary person (as far as his off-screen publicity claims go), Robert Redford's explicit star imagery appears to represent the Blond Californian aspect of the American Dream. Physically incarnating the sexually alluring Anglo male, acutely aware of his associations with one-dimensional stars such as Clark Gable and Tyrone Power, Redford in many of his roles combines the manufactured studio ideal of male beauty appealing to a female audience with a tantalizing self-awareness of its success and a knowing recognition of its limitations. Several Redford roles contain acute, subtle performance gestures hinting ironically that his Adonis ideal lacks any substantial foundation both within himself and the society generating it.

Such awareness appears in diverse minor films such as *Inside Daisy Clover* (1965), *Little Fauss and Big Halsy* (1970), *The Way We Were*, *Out of Africa* (1985), *Legal Eagles* (1986), and *Indecent Proposal* (1992), as well as his more significant work in films reflecting his characters' social and political situations—*Downhill Racer* (1969), *The Candidate* (1972), *All the President's Men* (1976), and *The Great Waldo Pepper* (1975). As private a person as Paul Newman, also active in liberal issues, Redford's star persona suggests more than it actively signifies—a tantalizing irony hints at his knowledge of the actual filmic realities generating his successful masculine idealizations.

Born in Santa Monica, CA, Redford attended the University of Colorado, dropped out for four years in 1957, and traveled through Europe before returning to the U.S. to study theatrical design and acting in New York. Like Paul Newman, he appeared in television productions but also participated in episodes of radio's *The Dick Powell Show, The Untouchables*, and *Perry Mason*. His first Broadway success was in the 1963 *Barefoot in the Park*, after having made his movie debut a year earlier in *War Hunt*. His first film and television appearances did little for his career, but his brief role as a narcissistic homosexual Hollywood star in *Inside Daisy Clover* (1965) brought him to public attention. Redford was later furious when re-editing explicitly designated his character as gay. However, this brief role as a glamorous star to whom "success came too easily" initiated a significant trait Redford would develop in later performances. His neglected selfish biker bum portrayal in *Little Fauss and Big Halsy* also illustrated the negative foundations beneath a superficial glamorous image that would reappear in his manipulative billionaire performance in *Indecent Proposal*.

Downhill Racer and *The Candidate*, both directed by Michael Ritchie, represent his most significant work. The first film reveals the bland, empty foundations beneath the handsome competitive male ego, while the second reveals the American image machine manipulating an originally idealistic character into the narrow, ideological paths of unthreatening conformity. It is hard not to see these two personal projects as relevant to the star's own perceptions and fears after the success of *Butch Cassidy and the Sundance Kid* (1969). This and *The Sting* (1973), his other Newman collaboration, belong to the traditional American vein of male buddy movie, following a homosocial trajectory while denying its homosexual undertones.

George Roy Hill directed both Redford-Newman films. Redford's third film with Hill, *The Great Waldo Pepper,* based upon a fictionalized screenplay of a fraudulent World War I aviation hero who finally achieves heroism flying above a Hollywood lot, makes the most explicit recognition of Redford's ironic awareness and attitudes toward stardom. While the original reviewers criticized his performance in *The Great Gatsby* (1974), in retrospect Redford's bland emptiness appears deliberate as the manufactured imagery of a being sacrificing everything to a rich Californian ideal that is actually dead and decadent.

Redford has worked closely with Sydney Pollack ever since they acted together in *War Hunt.* Their first collaboration as director and star occurred on *Jeremiah Johnson* (1972), and continued with *The Way We Were, Three Days of the Condor* (1975), *The Electric Horseman* (1979), and *Havana* (1990). The relationship is less significant than the Ritchie or Hill collaborations, as the ironic star potentials often remain unrealized.

Redford's own career as director is less than distinguished, his films (*Ordinary People* [1980], *The Milagro Beanfield War* [1988], and *Slums of Beverly Hills* [1998]) often revealing a preference for bland, good-intentioned, and escapist subjects.

Recent films he's starred in are *Up Close and Personal* (1996), *Air* (1997), and *The Horse Whisperer* (1998).

Bibliography

Clinch, Minty. *Robert Redford.* Sevenoaks: New English Library, 1989.

Spada, James. *The Films of Robert Redford.* Secaucus: Citadel, 1984.

Tony Williams

Redman, Don (1900-1964), is generally considered among a handful of musicians to first notate and arrange jazz material. Born in Piedmont, WV, Redman was a child prodigy who played many instruments before settling on alto saxophone and clarinet. He attended Storer College in Harper's Ferry, WV. After finishing school in three years he moved to Pittsburgh, where he joined an ensemble called the Broadway Syncopators. On a trip to New York the group was heard by Fletcher Henderson, who was impressed with Redman's arranging and playing skills. In 1923, Henderson hired Redman to play and arrange for a new dance band he was organizing.

During Redman's tenure with Henderson he did most of the arranging, including some pieces that featured Louis Armstrong, and many that featured Coleman Hawkins (tenor saxophone), Buster Bailey (clarinet), and Rex Stewart (trumpet). Most of the arrangements were for an 11-piece band that included three saxophones doubling on clarinet, three trumpets, trombone, and a rhythm section of piano, banjo, tuba, and drums. Among the best known of Redman's arrangements are "Copenhagen" (originally recorded for Vocalion, 1924) and "Stampede" (Columbia, 1926). Although these arrangements sound dated compared to later work by Redman, there were many melodic, rhythmic, and harmonic innovations in them. The most important factor was that he was able to transfer the vitality of improvised jazz to his arrangements. Henderson paid Redman $25 for each of his scores, which was good money for a black musician at that time. In 1927-28, Redman wrote arrangements for Paul Whiteman and Ben Pollack, who led white dance orchestras that were among the first to play jazz-oriented dance music. Whiteman commissioned Redman to write 20 arrangements for $100 each. One of these was "Whiteman Stomp" (Columbia, 1927), originally a piano composition by "Fats" Waller. In retrospect, it sounds like a parody of the George Gershwin/Whiteman collaborations, but the larger orchestra gave Redman a chance to experiment with more varied tone colors and harmonies.

Redman left Henderson in 1928 to become musical director of an ensemble from Detroit called McKinney's Cotton Pickers. During this period he not only improved his arranging skills but wrote several songs, including two standards, "Cherry" and "Gee Baby Ain't I Good to You." He also did more singing, including scat singing, a staple in many black jazz bands. Redman did not copy Louis Armstrong but developed a spoken-word vocal that can be called early but sophisticated rap. Another jazz standard he arranged for this band was "Four or Five Times" (Folkways Jazz vol. 8). The more relaxed ensemble sound anticipates the swing era. In another arrangement of the same tune called "Six or Seven Times" (Okeh, 1929), Redman used the famous "One o'Clock Jump" riff that he heard in or around Kansas City during his stay with McKinney's Cotton Pickers. Because Redman had to concentrate on commercial material, especially vocal arrangements, another arranger, John Nesbitt, one of the band's trumpet players, wrote about half the band's library, especially the instrumental pieces. Like many black arrangers of this period, Nesbitt has been all but ignored by most jazz historians.

In 1931, Redman formed his own band, which included Henry "Red" Allen on trumpet. In the early 1930s, his band grew to six brass and four reeds plus rhythm. (One player more than Benny Goodman's early bands.) His arranging and composing continued to reflect the developments in jazz, as can be heard in "The Chant of the Weed," "Trouble," "Why Pick on Me?" and "Shakin the African" (Decca, 1931).

During the swing era Redman contributed arrangements to several of the popular swing bands, including Jimmy Dorsey, Count Basie, Jimmie Lunceford, and others. Prime examples of these are "Deep Purple" for Jimmy Dorsey (Decca) and "Five o'Clock Whistle" for Count Basie (Okeh). In 1940, he gave up his band to concentrate on freelance arranging. One exception was to form a band to play at a New York cafe and to record some V-Discs during World War II.

Shortly after World War II, Redman was asked to form an all-star jazz orchestra to tour Europe. The band included Billy Taylor (piano), Don Byas (tenor sax), and Tyree Glenn (trombone). This band recorded in Sweden and can be heard on Steeple Chase Records. In the 1950s, Redman began a long association as arranger/conductor for singer Pearl Bailey. A good example of Redman's mature style of writing can be found in the album *Pearl Bailey Sings for Adults Only* (Roulette), which was recorded in the late 1950s.

Don Redman died at age 64. Duke Ellington recalled that both Redman and Fletcher Henderson were an inspiration to him in his early days as a bandleader. Leonard Feather claimed that Redman's work for Henderson "stands out in sharp relief with the works of other early jazz composer/arrangers." Gunther Schuller gives a more balanced appraisal: "Redman was perhaps too diversely talented as a multi-instrumentalist, arranger, and song composer. His talents became scattered and diffused, a not uncommon fate in the unaccommodating atmosphere of popular music."

Bibliography

Feather, Leonard. *Encyclopedia of Jazz.* New York: Horizon, 1960.

Schuller, Gunther. *The History of Jazz.* 1968. New York: Oxford UP, 1989.

Frank Ferriano

Regional Mysteries employ particular, often exotic or unfamiliar, settings as an integral part of the narrative. Although mystery writers have set their stories in diverse locales for many years, the American regional mystery became a discernible trend in the 1970s and 1980s with the popularity of Tony Hillerman's Southwestern novels. Regional mysteries have been influenced by the environmental movement, the shift in population to the Sunbelt and the Pacific Northwest, increased leisure time spent in travel, and an expanded emphasis on multiculturalism.

In regional mysteries, a vividly portrayed geographic setting is a key element of the narrative, out of which the plot and the characters develop organically. Important recent examples include Tony Hillerman's fiction set on the Navajo reservation, Nevada Barr's stories set in various national parks, Carl Hiaasen's antic novels of a tourist-ravaged South Florida, and Dana Stabenow's tales of crime in Alaska—novels in which the attraction of off-beat places and ethnic subcultures are central factors.

Regional mysteries tend to fall into distinctive classifications. The California school of hard-boiled detective fiction—perhaps best represented by Dashiell Hammett, Raymond Chandler, Ross Macdonald, Marcia Muller, and Sue Grafton—evolved from pulp fiction in the 1920s and 1930s into one of the quintessential American art forms in fiction, films, comic books, television, and radio. Urban settings like New York City customarily have generated crime fiction and police procedurals, while rural and suburban backgrounds have been used by writers of cozy or puzzle mysteries. Suburban settings in particular work well to dramatize the intrusion of violent crime into a safe, middle-class neighborhood, a formula used well by writers like Mary Higgins Clark.

New England has been the site of mystery fiction since the 1930s, when Phoebe Atwood Taylor began a series of Cape Cod mysteries. That cozy world is represented by Charlotte MacLeod's contemporary stories set at rustic Balaclava Agricultural College. Academic and artistic mayhem in New England's Ivy League and historic towns is depicted in the novels of Kathryn Lasky Knight and Jane Langton, while crime in the urban Northeast is chronicled by Robert B. Parker, Linda Barnes, and Jeremiah Healy. Midwestern mysteries range from fictional depictions of seedy, graft-ridden cities like Chicago and Cleveland in the novels of Craig Rice, Sara Paretsky, and Les Roberts, to cozies set in the suburbs.

The South is one of the most commonly used of regional settings, appearing most impressively in the lyrical Appalachian mysteries of Sharyn McCrumb and in Margaret Maron's novels featuring North Carolina judge Deborah Knott. Crime fiction set in the South often pays tribute to the Southern gothic tradition, or builds upon regional peccadilloes to create the suitable ambiance. Florida possesses its own strong regional tradition, with authors such as John D. MacDonald, Carl Hiaasen, and Edna Buchanan recording its exotic attractions and Latino cultures.

Regional mysteries have also proliferated in areas of new population, particularly the Southwest and Pacific Northwest. Works by M. K. Wren, Earl Emerson, J. J. Vance, Janet L. Smith, and Sue Henry reflect new interest in the Northwest, while the pervasive influence of Southwestern art and cuisine in the 1980s has had its counterpart in the cult status of writers like Judith van Gieson, Walter Satterthwait, and particularly Tony Hillerman.

Bibliography

Barden, Michelle. "Death by Locale." *Publishers Weekly* 11 Oct. 1993: 60-64.

Jean Swanson

Religious Mysteries. As Dorothy Sayers has noted, the mystery novel grew from such seeds as Greek, Roman, German, and Indian folk tales and, particularly, the Hebrew Apocrypha's *Bel and the Dragon* and *Susannah*, where detection and cross-examination rescue the innocent and condemn the guilty. Confessional literature like Augustine's, steeped in religious concerns, affected the future genre. When gothic novels appeared, they were crated in supernatural wrappings. M. G. Lewis's *The Monk* (1796), for example, probed religious preoccupation with criminal compulsion.

By the time Edgar Allan Poe began to shape the genre, he could draw upon widely accepted Judeo-Christian principles to support his stories: "Be sure your sin will find you out" (Numbers 32:23) and "The wages of sin is death" (Romans 6:23). In horror tales like "The Tell-Tale Heart" (1843), we see the effect of these tenets on the mind of the guilty. In Poe's tales of detection, moral ideas drive Dupin's efforts to unveil and punish culprits.

In the early 20th century, British writer G. K. Chesterton's Father Brown became one of the earliest priest-detectives and initiated a host of clerical sleuths, including Richard Goyne's Padre, Margaret Ann Hubbard's Sister Simon, Leonard Holton's Father Bredder, Dorothy Gilman's Sisters John and Hyacinthe, Ralph McInerny's Father Dowling and Sister Mary Teresa, Andrew Greeley's Msgr. Blackie Ryan, Carol Anne O'Marie's Sister Mary Helen, and William X. Kienzle's Father Koesler. Ellis Peters, E. M. A. Allison, and Paul Harding feature detecting monks in the Middle Ages. Umberto Eco's Brother William of *The Name of the Rose* (1983) is a crime-solver. And when scandals rocked Catholicism in the 1980s, William F. Love's Bishop Regan and Veronica Black's Sister Joan focused on cleansing the Church of crime.

Among Protestants, the first entry was also British, Canon Victor Whitechurch's Vicar Westerham, followed by C. A. Alington's archdeacons and Stephen Chance's Father Septimus. On the American side, Margaret Scherf created Father Buell and Isabelle Holland the Rev. Dr. Claire Aldington. Barbara Ninde Byfield straddled both continents with Father Bede. Other Protestants include Matthew Head's missionaries Mary Finney and Emily Collins, James L. Johnson's Rev. Sebastian, and Charles Merrill Smith's Rev. Randollph. Barry Estabrook's Miles Farnsworth is a TV evangelist who develops a conscience, and D. Keith Mano's *Topless* (1991) puts an Episcopal priest in a topless bar.

Religious mysteries are not limited to Christian denominations. Jewish roots blossomed with Harry Kemelman's Rabbi Small, Joseph Telushkin's Rabbi Winter, and in non-clerical mysteries featuring Jewish protagonists, such as those written by Faye and Jonathan Kellerman. Religious pluralism introduced Hindu concerns in H. R. Keating's Inspector Ghote novels; Confucianism in Robert Van Gulik's Judge Dee stories; American Indian religions (as in Tony Hillerman's *Talking God*, 1989); and others involving voodoo, wicca, neo-paganism, and Satanism. William Hjorstberg's *Falling Angel* (1978) and Jane Stanton Hitchcock's *The Witches' Hammer* (1995) are two recent examples. Cults have also provided fertile ground from Arthur Conan Doyle's *A Study in Scarlet* (1887), through Dashiell Hammett's *The Dain Curse* (1928), to Ronald Levitsky's *The Wisdom of Serpents* (1992).

In all religious mysteries, the moral common denominator is a conviction that crime is a violation of God's law, and that through human agents, who detect and expose crime, God will set wrong right.

Bibliography

Breen, Jon L., and Martin H. Greenberg, eds. *Synod of Sleuths: Essays on Judeo-Christian Detective Fiction.* Metuchen: Scarecrow, 1990.

Spencer, William David. *Mysterium and Mystery: The Clerical Crime Novel.* Ann Arbor: UMI Research, 1989.

William David Spencer

Ren & Stimpy Show, The (1991-1994), was an animated show on Nickelodeon that energized parents to get worried over cartoons again. The adventures of Ren Höek, the asthma-hound chihuahua, and his dopey pal Stimpson J. Cat, indulged kids' anal and oral compulsions with gags about bodily functions and odors, gross-out jokes, and plain foolishness. It attracted a huge cult of adult fans, until battles with Nickelodeon censors resulted in John Kricfalusi's being forced off his own creation.

Canadian native Kricfalusi (1956-) apprenticed on Saturday morning shows through the 1970s before teaming with Ralph Bakshi to design the Rolling Stones' animated "Harlem Shuffle" video. "John K." became a director for Bakshi's 1987 series *Mighty Mouse: The New Adventures*, then helmed the ill-fated 1988 revival of *Beany & Cecil*.

The Ren & Stimpy Show, like many cartoon teams, owed much to George and Lenny from Steinbeck's *Of Mice and Men*. Ren, voiced by Kricfalusi, was the little schemer, prone to histrionic outbursts combining Kirk Douglas with Peter Lorre ("You eediot! You bloated sack of protoplasm!"). Stimpy (Billy West) suggested the *Three Stooges*' Larry Fine, and liked nothing better than squatting in his litter box and "hwarfing" up hairballs.

The show immediately found devoted viewers, aided by occasional showings on Nickelodeon's parent, MTV. Its cultural contributions include Muddy Mudskipper, Log from Blammo ("It's big! It's heavy! It's wood!"), Yak Shaving Day, Magic Nose Goblins, Powdered Toast Man, and the game "Don't Whiz on the Electric Fence." The "Happy Happy Joy Joy Song" got plenty of airplay on the Dr. Demento show and other pop radio stations. The pair even made cameos on *The Simpsons*.

The show was plagued by production delays. Nickelodeon, which had successfully marketed Slime from its game show *Double Dare*, found similar bodily emissions unsuitable in *Ren & Stimpy*. Censor-driven delays resulted in only half the planned first-season episodes making it on the air. The Christmas special *Stimpy's First Fart* aired only on MTV, retitled *Son of Stimpy*. The episode "Man's Best Friend" was banned completely: Nickelodeon had fretted over its Archie Bunker-type protagonist George Liquor, thinking his name to be a double entendre. Finally, Nickelodeon fired John K. in September 1992. Production was turned over to an in-house studio formed by some of Kricfalusi's staff, but the show only lasted three seasons.

Bibliography

Gore, Christian. "Calling Out." *Film Threat* Dec. 1992: 22-39.

Meisler, Andy. "Television: While Team 2 Works to Reform Ren and Stimpy." *New York Times* 21 Nov. 1993: 2, 36.

Persons, Dan. "Ren & Stimpy Revolution: Nickelodeon's In-House Games Productions Pledges to Continue Shaking up Animation." *Cinefantastique* Feb. 1994: 15.

——. "Spumco's *Ren & Stimpy* Revolution: Cartoon Creator John Kricfalusi Tried to Redeem an Art Form Long Corrupted." *Cinefantastique* June 1993: 24-56.

Mark McDermott

Rendell, Ruth (1930-), a Londoner, worked for a newspaper before publishing her first novel, *From Doon with Death* (1964), a detective story featuring Chief Inspector Wexford and his assistant, Michael Burden. Since then, Rendell has become one of the most widely read authors of crime fiction in America, producing short fiction and several dozen novels, including the Wexford books and a sizable body of crime fiction and works of psychological suspense, ten of them written under the pseudonym "Barbara Vine."

Rendell's Wexford series is perhaps her most popular. Inspector Wexford begins as a classical detective but develops into a more complex figure through novels like *No More Dying Then* (1971). This unexceptional middle-aged man has liberal and tolerant qualities that contrast with the primness and rigidity of his partner, Mike Burden.

Rendell's macabre crime fictions investigate the minds of working- and middle-class characters whose apparent normality disguises obsession. In *Make Death Love Me* (1979), a bank clerk who fondles money and dreams of escape takes on a new identity and with it a romantic life of love and heroism. In *Live Flesh* (1986), the investigation of a rapist's mind reveals not only his own compulsive confusions of fantasy and reality, but those of the policeman he has crippled as well.

Writing as Barbara Vine, Rendell moves outside structural conventions in what might be her best work. Novels such as *A Dark-Adapted Eye* (1985) or *The House of Stairs* (1989) explore the psychology of her more ordinary characters through the mysteries of their pasts.

Bibliography

Bargainnier, Earl F., ed. *10 Women of Mystery*. Bowling Green, OH: Bowling Green State U Popular P, 1981.

Clark, Susan L. "A Fearful Symmetry." *Armchair Detective* 1989.

Klein, Kathleen Gregory, ed. *Great Women Mystery Writers: Classic to Contemporary*. Westport: Greenwood, 1994.

Lehman, David. *The Perfect Murder: A Study in Detection*. New York: Free, 1989.

Marsden, Michael, and Marilyn Motz. "Interview with Ruth Rendell." *Clues* 10.2 (1989).

Susan Allen Ford

Repertoire Tent Theater began in the late 19th century. It was one of many traveling entertainments that played under canvas; others included medicine shows, musicals, circuses, one-night-stand companies, Chautauquas, and vaudeville. Tent repertoire theater was most popular in small-town middle America and summer was its chief season, although some companies in the West and the South played all year round.

Generally, tent rep productions consisted of popular melodramas with vaudeville routines between the acts. The shows developed in response to a rural mass audience, tent repertoire's primary patrons. For many, it was their first taste of live drama. Companies stayed from three days to a week at the same location and many returned year after year. Tent repertoire also gave thousands of young performers a relatively benign venue in which to practice their craft.

Tent repertoire's forerunners were the repertory companies that visited small-town opera houses, where actors played simple dramas, vaudeville specialties, and musical offerings, all at popular prices, which, by the 1800s, meant 10-, 20-, and 30-cent seats. Bills of fare changed nightly and companies stayed from three days to a week. One-night-stand rep companies, which jumped from town to town, charged more. Some companies were large and played the big cities and bigger towns. Most rep companies, however, were small, staffed by families, and became the immediate predecessors of tent rep.

By the beginning of the 20th century, motion pictures helped destroy the one-night stand, and the heat of the summer months made the unair-conditioned opera houses unusable. "Rather than disband, repertoire companies chose to function year-round, using a tent for the summer months," according to W. L. Slout. By 1900, over 100 companies were operating, primarily in small midwestern towns.

Playing in small towns meant attracting basically rural audiences, suspicious of any deviation from an extremely rigid moral code. Tent rep developed respectability by maintaining high company standards of behavior and decency; by developing friendships with the locals which were maintained year after year; and most important, by presenting shows which catered to rural tastes by portraying the Chautauqua themes of mother, home, and heaven, all within the constrictive bounds of Victorian morality. Moreover, the crucial tent show dramatic theme was the "agrarian myth," where the "hero is the yeoman farmer . . . living close to and receiving the benefits of nature" (Slout 80). This theme reinforced the audience's rural values as the antithesis of the corrupting city.

Thematic variations were played out in numerous rural melodramas by stock characters such as "the local pastor, the fallen woman, the gossip, the silly kid and the shrewd town eccentric," as Slout notes. Eventually the silly kid developed into Toby, the most beloved tent rep character, a lad of red hair, quick wit, and rural origins. Always the country underdog, he nevertheless managed to out "think, if not to out" maneuver his wealthier, better educated but not smarter city opponent. The Toby character became a popular primary attraction for many companies. However, by the 1920s the boom that tent repertoire had experienced during World War I was going bust. Ironically, the idyllic Toby contributed to the downfall as companies, struggling to keep business, made him a part of almost every play, whether he was meant to be there or not. Desperate for audiences, some companies appealed to the lowest common denominator by introducing mildly blue material, and production values suffered.

Tent rep continued to decline throughout the ensuing decades. The Great Depression, World War II, radio, movies, and finally television and increasing production costs combined in various ways to bring an end to an entertainment and way of life that affected millions of rural Americans.

Bibliography

Mickel, Jere C. *Footlights on the Prairie*. St. Cloud: North Star, 1974.
Slout, W. L. *Theatre in a Tent*. Bowling Green, OH: Bowling Green State U Popular P, 1972.

Richard L. Poole

Requiem for a Heavyweight (1956), written by Rod Serling, was performed live on *Playhouse 90* (see entry). Produced by Martin Manulis and directed by Ralph Nelson, it starred Jack Palance, Ed Wynn, Keenan Wynn, and Kim Hunter. The second show spun in *Playhouse 90*'s new longer format, *Requiem for a Heavyweight* is the story of a battered, unsuccessful prizefighter's search for personal dignity faced on the eve of his forced retirement from the ring. Like many of Serling's dramas, *Requiem* was inspired by a news item—heavyweight boxer Joe Louis's decision to retire from the ring and to end his career, to the regret of many of his fans, as a wrestler. *Requiem*'s achievement is its vivid, crackling dialogue and its multi-dimensional supporting characters, no doubt byproducts of the playwright's own days as a prizefighter (in the class of "Catchweight" during World War II).

Requiem for a Heavyweight was awarded the Harcourt-Brace Award, the George Foster Peabody Broadcasting Award for Television Writing (the first time in its 17-year history the prize went to a writer), a Sylvania Award, the Television-Radio Writers' Annual Award, and the Writers Guild of America Award for best one-hour-or-more TV drama. It won also Emmys for best single program of the year; best single performance by an actor (Jack Palance); best direction—one hour or more (Ralph Nelson), and best teleplay writing—one hour or more (Rod Serling). Ed Wynn was nominated for an Emmy for best supporting performance by an actor. Apart from the awards it received, the play's success held significance for Serling, who had been under considerable pressure to produce another "hit" on the heels of his Emmy-winning teleplay, *Patterns*.

In 1962, Serling was asked to craft the screenplay of *Requiem for a Heavyweight* (Paman Productions, released by Columbia Pictures). The film, which starred Anthony Quinn, Jackie Gleason, Mickey Rooney, and Julie Harris, was less appreciatively received than the original television production.

Bibliography

Sander, Gordon F. *Serling: The Rise and Twilight of Television's Last Angry Man*. New York: Dutton, 1992.

Susan Madigan

Restaurants. Until fast food became such a large part of the food service industry in the last 25 years, the word "restaurant" referred only to establishments providing table service and an extensive menu of dishes prepared by chefs and skilled cooks. It is now used generically for any eating place whose products can be consumed on the premises, and includes everything from dining rooms to sandwich shops, cafeterias, diners, and delis.

The independent restaurant—separate from lodging—is mostly a 20th-century phenomenon in the U.S. although its origin in Europe dates from the French revolution of the late 18th century, when private chefs were suddenly liberated from the estates of the nobility and began their own ventures. In this country, the earliest restaurant in the full sense of the word is usually considered to be Delmonico's, established in New York City by two brothers from Switzerland in the 1830s. Delmonico's set the standard for fine cuisine throughout the 19th century. In the affluent Gilded Age of the 1880s and 1890s, however, competitors sprang up, among them Martin's and Sherry's in New York. Almost all large cities had at least one fine restaurant. Most served French cuisine, with menus typically written in French and posing quite a linguistic challenge to many patrons. The 1890s was also responsible for introducing the velvet-roped doorway presided over by a regal head waiter whose job it was to assess the social rank of those in line and to seat them accordingly. The haughtiness of the gatekeeping head waiter and the humiliation of the guests seated at a bad table by the kitchen have long been staples of cartoon and film humor, demonstrating the uneasiness of Americans about status and class rankings.

Parallel in time to the development of fine dining was the boardinghouse restaurant found in dense apartment house districts, which were home to single male and female workers in large cities. These establishments sold weekly meal tickets and were typically located in basements. Many were run by women, often immigrant women. Although these were shoestring operations, some Italian dining rooms such as New York's Mama Leone's, which catered primarily to the Italian community, eventually succeeded and attracted a non-Italian clientele. These patrons were drawn by the "bohemian" atmosphere, good food at low prices, and accompanying carafes of red wine.

Although many immigrants to the U.S. run restaurants, they do not necessarily specialize in their own cuisines. An outstanding example of this is furnished by Greek Americans, who entered the business in large numbers with the collapse of the sweet shop business in the 1920s and who by 1975 may have comprised as much as 20 percent of all restaurant keepers. Historically, they have made up a large percentage of diner and coffee shop operators. But it was not until the 1970s, when fast food chains began to steal business away from them, that Greek-American restaurateurs began to offer Greek cuisine.

The banning of alcoholic beverages was a lethal blow to many restaurants. When national prohibition went into effect in January of 1920, many hotel dining rooms were turned almost overnight into coffee shops or lunch counters. Other restaurants closed or became speakeasies, admitting only known customers. Many deluxe restaurants folded, among them Delmonico's, Sherry's, Martin's, and Rector's.

Another effect of prohibition was to launch the restaurant industry as we know it today, with its vast network of consultants, training programs, trade publications, business associations, and equipment and food product suppliers. Personnel changed too, with more native-born workers entering the industry as the supply of foreign-born waiters, chefs, and cooks was cut off completely during the war and reduced to a trickle thereafter. Increased numbers of women entered the business as waitresses, cooks, proprietors, and customers as the absence of alcohol de-stigmatized an institution once popularly considered "the tail end of the saloon." Middle-class native-born Americans who had long shunned restaurants began to give them a try.

Increasing urbanization during and after the war spurred growth as more and more people began to eat lunch out during the work week. The sandwich became a very big seller, particularly when it was available on toast, thanks to the introduction of electric toasters. Self-service eateries grew popular and chains of lunch counters spread across the country. The cafeteria, developed from cooperative lunch clubs for working women in Chicago in the 1890s, was a 1920s sensation. It flourished particularly in California, where proprietors elevated it to a work of art with ornate interiors, palm courts, fountains, and live piano music. Today, cafeterias are mainly found in the South and are fighting off an image as places catering to unadventurous elderly eaters.

Music in restaurants was denounced by critics as a gimmicky nuisance. It did not last long, as restaurateurs discovered far better novelties and attractions to draw customers. It is the entertainment aspects of American eating places which sets them apart from European restaurants, which concentrate more on food preparation. Novelty restaurants in the U.S. can be traced back to the cave and catacomb rooms of eating places of the late 19th century, but they proliferated in the 1920s, 1930s, and 1940s, when fantastic architecture became commonplace. The 1930s ice cream carton in Berlin, CT, a popcorn ball in Canton, OH, and a giant cranberry bottle on Cape Cod were later joined along the road by eateries shaped like coffee pots, hats, chili bowls, igloos, donuts, and dogs.

Theme restaurants, which envelop the diner in an atmosphere far away from humdrum reality, were popular in the 1920s, when narrow storefronts and basement locations were sometimes renovated to look like Mediterranean villages. Low ceilings were often transformed into star-filled skies. When Vic Bergeron opened the Polynesian Trader Vic's in San Francisco in 1937, he not only re-created an island paradise but invented exotic cocktails such as the Mai Tai, serving them in unusual vessels. In the 1960s the English pub look swept the country. In that same decade at least two restaurants dressed their waiters like monks, and one Arizona restaurant proclaimed its informal dress code by cutting off men's neckties. Los Angeles' Magic Castle Dinner Club featured mystery doors, spinning barstools, and bubbling cauldrons of food. New York's Forum of the Twelve Caesars in the 1950s used another gambit: humorous menu language. One menu item, for instance, was "Fiddler Crab a la Nero ...Flaming, of course." Locations atop tall buildings or aboard docked ships must also be counted among the gimmicks, along with food served on flaming swords, singing or skating waiters, toy giveaways, or cars used as tables or embedded in walls, to name but a few.

Interestingly, nostalgia for the American restaurant past has been limited so far to diners and drive-ins. A movement to study, preserve, and restore diners from the modern era (roughly 1930-50) has resulted in the transportation of a number of diners abroad or to better locations, often many hundreds of miles away. Diners originated as portable lunch wagons which served factory workers in Northeastern cities in the late 19th and early 20th century. Eventually the lunch wagons, which were made on wheels, were set up in permanent locations. Worcester, MA, and Providence, RI, were key locations for the factory production of diners.

The counterculture of the late 1960s and 1970s did much to reorient the restaurant business, changing menus and the entire dining experience. Hippies protesting against middle-class convention were especially critical of American food. The steak dinner, accompanied by a baked potato heaped with sour cream and a stiff whiskey highball was seen as a prime example of American decadence. Instead, the counterculture embraced Third World peasant cuisine, showing considerable willingness to experiment with the unfamiliar. Alice Waters, proprietor of Berkeley's Chez Panisse, came out of this movement and became a force for "New American Cuisine," as it became known.

The effect of a vastly increased rate of restaurant-going, especially since World War II, has been to introduce Americans to a great many new foods, customs, and consumer products. Restaurants have introduced Americans to paper napkins, breakfast cereals, tea bags, and toast, to name a few of the more commonplace items. Restaurants have been important training grounds for table manners and the use of steak knives, pepper mills, wine glasses, and candles. Many Americans probably tasted their first lobster, garlic bread, and cheesecake in a public eating place. And many ethnic cuisines, adapted to American tastes though they may be, would be unknown to most people if they had not encountered them in restaurants.

Although predictions made early in this century that the home kitchen would be replaced by public eating places have not proved accurate, the restaurant has become a central institution in most people's lives.

Bibliography

Gutman, Richard J. S. *American Diner: Then and Now*. New York: Harper Perennial, 1993 .

Mariani, John. *America Eats Out*. New York: Morrow, 1991.

Street, Julian. "What's the Matter with Food?" *Saturday Evening Post* 31 Jan. and 21 Mar. 1931: 14-15+ and 10-11+.

Jan Whitaker

See also
Diners
Ethnic Food
Fast Food Chains

Revitalization Movements are a specific category of social movements, often originating in response to culture crises and the breakdown of traditional institutions, which attempt to revitalize a society which is disintegrating or threatened with absorption into a larger unit. They are goal-directed attempts by groups or subgroups to create a more satisfying culture either by 1) returning to an idealized previous age, 2) attaining the material culture of the dominant or conquering culture, or 3) the reorganization of pre-existing cultural components in a radically new fashion.

They are common in American history, as they are in the histories of other peoples. Indeed, they have been recorded in all major cultural areas and are frequently reported among tribal peoples after contact with Europeans, when acculturation pressure threatens the integrity of the native social structure. Revitalization movements most often utilize religious motifs and religious metaphors to express both the disorientation the affected individuals feel and the envisioned change in society as religious systems are intimately connected to other social institutions: economic, political, and kinship systems. They attempt to provide new, systematic, institutionalized forces to stave off the stressors which threaten the psychological equilibrium of the people and the cultural unity of the society. Additionally, the religious grounding of many native revitalization movements may be explained by noting that their existing social institutions are unable to adapt to the conditions of social change initiated by the arrival of Europeans. Inasmuch as Christianity is often the only organizing tool which Europeans offered subject populations, it is logical for such groups to utilize Christian religious motifs in order to adjust to or mitigate the effects of European society.

Subcategories of this type of social movement include cargo cults, messianic movements, nativism, millenarianism, and revivalism, but this is an arbitrary division, as any single revitalization movement may utilize two or more subcategories. Cargo cults stress the relevance of importing and adopting foreign values, material goods, and customs. Messianic movements utilize the appearance of a supernatural in human form to initiate change in the society. Revivalism and nativism, in particular, are often components of a single revitalization movement, and with millenarian movements, are frequent in American history.

Revivalism and nativism are those movements specifically designed to return a people to a condition when, it is believed, social conditions were better than those currently existing. Revivalism emphasizes the return to an earlier time period, generally one perceived as a golden age, via the readoption of traditional group values and customs, whereas nativistic movements are focused on the elimination of alien peoples, customs, and values from the culture. These are not mutually exclusive goals and are present in both the development of the Handsome Lake religion among the Iroquois and the Ghost Dance of the Plains Indians. Originating in 1799, the Handsome Lake religion was a revivalistic/nativistic movement which arose among the Iroquois Indians during a time of social chaos. After supporting the loser in two European wars, the French and Indian War and the Revolutionary War, their leaders, warriors and statesmen alike, were held in low esteem. The group was confined to small reservations where it was impossible to practice the traditional lifestyle which provided self-identity and meaningfulness. Drunkenness and stagnation were the order of the day. In this moral chaos, Handsome Lake, an Iroquois Indian, announced that he was the prophet to whom God's messenger had revealed the only means by which the Iroquois could avoid their impending destruction. Certain specific behaviors were to be eliminated—drinking and witchcraft, for example. With religiously backed authority, Handsome Lake directed that the Iroquois adopt many European customs: males rather than females doing farmwork, literacy, and the adoption of the married couple rather than the maternal lineage as the focus of the social unit. These specific socio-economic and social changes became the basis for the new Handsome Lake religion, which successfully reorganized Iroquois society into a new cultural unity which could survive in a rapidly changing political environment.

The Ghost Dance, begun in 1878 as a peaceful revivalistic/nativistic local movement among the Paiute Indians, was a response to the stress of an expanding white settler population, harassment by the U.S. Army, and deplorable living conditions on the reservations. The Paiute prophet Wovoka counseled the Indians to abandon the ways of the white man, participate in ritual dances, and live at peace with the whites until the coming of an apocalypse when all whites would die.

By 1889 the Ghost Dance had become a major social movement, and the prophecy had spread across the Plains States into the Mississippi area of the Cheyenne Indians and eventually to the Sioux, where followers of the great warrior Sitting Bull transformed the peaceful movement into a decidedly militant one by arguing that it was now time to destroy the white man to hasten the Indians' return to their original way of life. Apprehensive Army officials overreacted and nearly 240 Indian men, women, and children were killed or were left to die in the snow at Wounded Knee in December of 1890.

Millenarian movements, rooted in a centuries-old European history, are common in Protestant American religious behavior. Millenarianism is a term drawn from the New Testament, understood as the concept that the return of the Christ, the millennium, and re-establishment of a new Eden or Paradise on earth is near to hand and must be prepared for. Although there have been many such groups in American history, each with a differing emphasis and raison d'etre, their common features include the belief that society had become too complex and disarrayed: natural human simplicity had been corrupted. A return to simpler ways would return human innocence and correct society's imperfections. Religiously innovative and generally utopian, these experimental communities were built in unsettled areas, away from the intricacies and competing philosophies of industry and the marketplace, and often included political and economic reform. Most millenarian movements are premillennial movements, indicating the millennium is yet to begin. Some are postmillennial, indicating that Christ's kingdom is now being prepared and Christ will return after His kingdom is established.

The Oneida community, a postmillennial movement of the mid-19th century, survived for over 30 years as a religious community and continues today, over 150 years after its founding, as an international flatware corporation. Its founder, John Humphrey Noyes, sought to create the sinless or perfected community based on his vision of biblical communism. Religious meditation, fruitful work, music, philosophy, science, education, play, and sexual relations were skillfully blended to produce an industrious order of lighthearted work amidst fellowship and variety.

The Church of Jesus Christ of Latter-Day Saints, whose members are often called Mormons, is a successful premillennial movement based upon revelations from an otherworldly being to its founder, Joseph Smith. As Mormonism grew from a minor sect to one whose members were persecuted and hounded by religious and civil authorities to a

worldwide movement of over 4 million believers, it has retained its millennial convictions and orientation toward America as the new land of promise, where the new Zion, a true and proper society of Christian humankind, would be built by them, and once built, would be the place to which Christ would return.

It is not surprising that Mormonism succeeded. The millenarian concept of America's destiny as the new Eden is deeply ingrained in the American consciousness, and Americans are emotionally oriented to its tenets. Although in their totality, American cults, sects, religious wanderers, established churches, and iconoclasts argue about the terms of the American destiny, they never doubt the destiny itself.

Bibliography

Cohn, Norman. *The Pursuit of the Millennium.* New York: Oxford UP, 1970.

Klaw, Spencer. *Without Sin: The Life and Death of the Oneida Community.* New York: Allen Lane, 1993.

Lehmann, Arthur C., and James E. Myers, eds. *Magic, Witchcraft, and Religion: An Anthropological Study of the Supernatural.* Palo Alto: Mayfield, 1985.

Marty, Martin E. *Pilgrims in Their Own Land: 500 Years of Religion in America.* Boston: Little, Brown, 1984.

Sydney Langdon

Revue. *The Passing Show*, which opened at New York City's Casino Theater on May 12, 1894, has been called the first revue. Its producer, George Lederer (1861-1935), referred to it as a "topical extravaganza." According to the major newspapers of the time, it was a new kind of entertainment: a "review," in dramatic form, of various political, historical, and theatrical events of the past year. The term "revue" was not universally used for another ten years.

From Lederer's day, the revue has been constantly changing. There are no typical revues. Everyone knows about Ziegfeld's revues, but Joe Weber and Lew Fields's shows were revues, and the Hippodrome extravaganzas were also revues. So were the Folies-Bergère, the Las Vegas extravaganzas, *Side by Side by Sondheim*, *Sugar Babies*, and a whole generation of splashy annual shows such as George White's *Scandals* and *The Greenwich Village Follies*. Radio City Music Hall presentations and the prologues seen in American movie houses during the twenties and thirties, as well as such intellectual productions as *The Grand Street Follies* and political productions like *Pins and Needles*—all were revues.

The revue is a musical show with singing and dancing and comedy, but then so is musical comedy. The revue is often made up of individual scenes which have no relationship to one another in theme or content, but then so is vaudeville. The revue has no plot, although in fact some early revues had slim plot lines. In a program for *The Little Duchess*, which opened in 1901 at the Casino Theater, Florenz Ziegfeld (1867-1932) was quoted as having said: "Owing to the length of the performance, the plot has been eliminated."

The revue is topical, but not always. The revue has beautiful women, but not always. The revue is witty, but not always. The revue has a point of view, but not always. The revue may be satirical or slapstick or beautiful; it may be parody; it may be ultra-refined or quite coarse; it may be sexy or not; it may poke fun at itself or at others; it may be sentimental; or it may be pedantic.

In the early days, the revue generally had three acts, but later the two-act format was more generally used. There might be as few as four or five scenes in each act or as many as 15 to 18. Each act might consist of sketches, musical numbers with a chorus or parts of the chorus and a star, feature acts, or solos. The first and second acts were usually capped by finales which were the most spectacular of the evening, often involving the entire cast.

The revue was lighthearted, boisterous, scandalous, and fun. Not surprisingly, it had always been associated with beer gardens, roof theaters, nightclubs, and cabarets. The earliest theatrical production with which the revue is always associated—*The Black Crook*—opened at a beer garden, Niblo's Garden, in New York in 1866. This show introduced the can-can to American audiences, and sheet music and periodical illustrations brought the spectacle into homes across the nation. With the popularity of *The Black Crook*, theater managers and entrepreneurs began turning out copies with such speed that by 1869, the rage for "nudity" was denounced at the Women's Suffrage Convention. *The Black Crook* was itself revived several times.

The Passing Show of 1894 was produced at the Casino's rooftop theater and, in 1907, the first of the Ziegfeld *Follies* was produced on the roof of the New York Theater, which Ziegfeld had decorated to resemble a French music hall and named the Jardin de Paris (see *Follies, The*). This show ushered in an explosion and expansion of the revue on Broadway which lasted until the stock market crash of 1929. Experienced producers such as the Shubert Brothers (Lee, 1873-1953, and J. J., 1878-1963) jumped onto the bandwagon almost immediately with an annual revue called *The Passing Show* at their Winter Garden. The revue, itself, also spawned several important theatrical entrepreneurs such as John Murray Anderson (1886-1954), George White (1890-1968), and Earl Carroll (1893-1948), who created their own annual revues, *The Greenwich Village Follies*, *The Scandals*, and *The Vanities*. Already famous as America's greatest composer of popular songs, Irving Berlin (1888-1989) created his own annual *Music Box Revue*.

When Ziegfeld and the Shuberts moved these entertainments onto the main stage, they invented a smaller late-night cabaret version of the revue for their rooftop theaters. Ziegfeld's productions were called the *Midnight Frolics* and the Shuberts', with no specific revue titles, opened their "Palais de Danse" at the Winter Garden and produced their *Midnight Rounders* at the Century Theater.

There were to be 22 editions of *The Follies* produced by Ziegfeld (including the 1926 edition called *No Foolin!*) through 1931. After Ziegfeld's death, the Shuberts produced three editions called *The Ziegfeld Follies*. Beginning in 1912, the Shuberts produced a dozen editions of their *Passing Show*. Of the other annual revues, there were 8 *Greenwich Village Follies*, 13 *Scandals*, and 4 each *Music Box Revues* and *Vanities*. In addition to these annual revues, there were dozens of individual revues.

Ziegfeld's *Follies*, while lasting into the 1930s, began to seem old fashioned. The 1918 and 1919 editions are considered the zenith of the series and the 1922 edition, the most elaborate. The new breed of producers (Anderson, White, Berlin, and Carroll) began to take over the market with "new" revues. Just as they had tried to compete with Ziegfeld before World War I, the Shuberts again attempted to compete with these new shows by creating a second annual revue, *Artists and Models*. By the late 1920s, the market had become so glutted with revues that interest in them waned.

Some of the most popular American music of the 1910s and 1920s was written for revues. *Watch Your Step* (1914), a revue, was Irving Berlin's first full score for Broadway; he followed that success with *Stop! Look! Listen!* (1915) and *Yip, Yip, Yaphank* (1918) before supplying music for several *Follies* and his own *Music Box Revues*. Some of his many important revue tunes include "I Love a Piano," "Play a Simple Melody," "Oh, How I Hate to Get Up in the Morning," "A Pretty Girl Is Like a Melody," and "Easter Parade." George Gershwin (1898-1937) was associated with five of George White's *Scandals*, for which he wrote such songs as "Stairway to Paradise" and "Somebody Loves Me."

The team of B. G. DeSylva (1895-1950), Lew Brown (1893-1958), and Ray Henderson (1896-1970) also wrote for the *Scandals* and provided full scores and many tunes including "Birth of the Blues," "Black Bottom," "Pickin' Cotton," and "Life Is Just a Bowl of Cherries" (without DeSylva). Even the great Jerome Kern (1885-1945) provided music for such revues as *Miss 1917* and *Hitchy-Koo* (1920). Kern also provided Ziegfeld with music for the *Follies*. The team of Howard Dietz (1896-1983) and Arthur Schwartz (1900-1984) provided music for some of the most celebrated Broadway revues of the '30s such as *The Little Show*, *Three's a Crowd*, *Flying Colors*, and *At Home Abroad*.

Virtually every *Follies* had a song or two (or more) which became the hit of the season—not only in New York, but throughout the entire country. Nora Bayes, Eddie Cantor, Marilyn Miller, Al Jolson, Ethel Merman, and many other musical stars of the era popularized their songs from the various revues in which they appeared.

Since the Depression, revues continue to be produced but in different (and certainly smaller) forms. The basic format of the revue, with no plot line and only a loose visual or aesthetic thread tying together the musical and comedy sequences, remains intact. Using this revue format, popular entertainments such as the large ice shows and the glitzy casino revues in Atlantic City and Las Vegas have maintained the revue, and small reviews devoted to a single composer's work like *Side by Side by Sondheim* have a certain popularity with Broadway audiences as another popular theatrical form.

Bibliography

Baral, Robert. *Revue*. New York: Fleet, 1962.
Bordman, Gerald. *American Musical Theatre*. New York: Oxford UP, 1978.

Carter, Randolph. *The World of Flo Ziegfeld*. New York: Praeger, 1974.

Green, Stanley. *Encyclopedia of the Musical Theater*. New York: Da Capo, 1976.

Hirsch, John E. *Glorifying the American Showgirl: A History of Revue Costume in the United States from 1866 to the Present*. Diss. New York University. Ann Arbor: UMI, 1987.

John E. Hirsch

Rice, Anne (1941-), born Howard Allen Frances O'Brien, is a New Orleans native best known for her critically acclaimed and commercially popular Vampire Chronicles book series. She identifies herself as a Southern gothic writer; her lush language, romantic sensibility, and lurid atmospherics are reminiscent of Edgar Allan Poe, Mary Shelley, and Bram Stoker. Her popularity stems in part from her ability to probe profound questions through stock horror devices like vampirism and witchcraft, which she reinvents in enticing and sophisticated ways.

Interview with the Vampire (1976), the first in the Vampire Chronicles series, is her best-known work, the autobiographical recollection of a vampire, told to a young journalist who is beguiled by the life of the undead. The novel was adapted to the screen by director Neil Jordan in 1995. Other occult novels include *The Vampire Lestat* (1985), *The Queen of the Damned* (1988), *The Tale of the Body Thief* (1992), and *Taltos* (1994). These immensely popular blood sagas reflect mythological frameworks and explore the breakdown of moral, sexual, and gender boundaries.

Some novels without supernatural elements also address the issue of living outside the accepted order: *The Feast of All Saints* (1979) centers on the plight of the Louisiana *gen de couleur libre* (free people of color), while *Cry to Heaven* (1982) focuses on the *castrati* of 18th-century Italy. Also of note are Rice's series of erotica, published under the pseudonym of A. N. Rouquelaure.

Bibliography

Melton, J. Gordon. "Anne Rice." *The Vampire Book: The Encyclopedia of the Undead*. Detroit: Gale Research, 1994.

Ramsland, Katherine. *Prism of the Night: A Biography of Anne Rice*. New York: Dutton, 1991.

——. *The Vampire Companion: The Official Guide to Anne Rice's* The Vampire Chronicles. New York: Ballantine, 1995.

Anita M. Vickers

Rinehart, Mary Roberts (1876-1958), completed nurse's training in 1896 but never worked as a nurse; rather, she married Dr. Stanley Rinehart and turned to fiction writing when family finances and a growing family required a second income. During a career that spanned more than five decades, she published over 50 books, including *The Man in Lower Ten* (1909), *The Red Lamp* (1925), and, with Avery Hopwood, *The Bat* (1932), a familiar mystery play. Her best-selling autobiography, *My Story*, describes the plight of the early-20th-century working woman.

Rinehart's first best-seller was *The Circular Staircase* (1908), and it is likely that her mystery novels—usually of

the Had-I-But-Known subgenre—will prove the most enduring of her works. Despite the naivete of her young heroines, her plots are suspenseful, and her humor has survived the passage of time. Rinehart's portraits of older women, not only in her mysteries but in the "Tish" stories that ran in the *Saturday Evening Post*, won her admirers, and she created a comic character at the opposite end of the chronological spectrum, a "sub-deb" named Babs, for another series of stories. Only one series character appears in Rinehart's mystery fiction: Hilda Adams, a private nurse who does double-duty as a police detective. Nearly every novel addresses themes of class envy and conflict, and many probe the emotional consequences of repression and loneliness.

Bibliography

Bachelder, Frances H. *Mary Roberts Rinehart, Mistress of Mystery*. San Bernardino: Brownstone Borgo, 1993.

MacLeod, Charlotte. *Had She But Known: A Biography of Mary Roberts Rinehart*. New York: Mysterious, 1994.

Mary P. Freier

See also

Classical Mysteries	Gothic Mysteries
Golden Age of Detective Fiction	Had-I-But-Known Mysteries
	Thriller, The

River Songs of the U.S. Perhaps no other feature of the American landscape figures so prominently and recurrently in popular American song as its rivers. In fact, collectively considered, American river songs not only serve as an informal anthology of American history, geography, and folklore, but as an evolving chronicle of American popular music.

From the earliest days of the republic through the 19th century, the reliance on rivers of various occupational groups—lumberjacks, raftsmen, canal men, fur-trading voyagers, and, eventually, cattle drovers and prospectors—inspired a wide variety of songs dealing with the pleasures, but, more often, the dangers and labor-related aspects of life on the river. Perhaps the broadest, richest, and most diverse body of such songs originated during the river-packet era primarily identified with the Ohio, Mississippi, and Tennessee rivers. Of the various song genres associated with the ascendancy of the river-packet, the work song, generally composed by roustabouts (deckhands and freight handlers), is perhaps the most common and representative ("Roll Out! Heave Dat Cotton," "Carryin' Sacks," and "I'm the Man That Kin Raise So Long"), though other songs describe the roustabout's loneliness and homesickness ("I'm Wukin' My Way Back Home"), recall the exploits and very often the violent crimes of notable roustabouts ("Stavin' Chain," "Po Shine," or various versions of "Stacker Lee," eventually corrupted in redaction as "Stagger Lee"), or recount legendary steamboat races or disasters. Navigational soundings (the most famous of which is "mark twain," or 12 fathoms) delivered by way of distinctively personalized chants comprise yet another, and perhaps the most evocative, if regrettably ephemeral, of the songlore of the river-packet era.

The spiritual, one of the earliest and most enduring of American musical forms, also features a number of memorable river songs, including the Reverend Robert Lowry's familiar revivalist spiritual "Shall We Gather at the River" and such traditional African-American spirituals as "Roll, Jordan, Roll," "Down by the Riverside," "There's One Wide River to Cross," and the disarmingly simple, but moving "Deep River." Other river songs through the close of the 19th century deal with more intimate personal concerns, perhaps the most common of which is disappointed love (and the sometimes tragic consequences), as in the well-known "Red River Valley" (technically a valley, rather than a river, song) and the lovely "Shenandoah: Across the Wide Missouri." More melodramatically, "On the Banks of the Ohio" and "On the Banks of the Old Pee Dee" both recount the tragic scenario of the jilted or disappointed lover who drowns the "only girl I loved because she would not marry me." The river itself intervenes by drowning lovers in "The Banks of the Little Eau de Pleine" and "The River in the Pines."

The river often serves as the evocative locus for the songwriter's nostalgic recollection of home and the innocence of youth. Thus Stephen Foster's "Old Folks at Home" is as much concerned with family and the old homestead as the Suwanee River, which, ironically enough, Foster had never seen, but discovered in an atlas of Florida. Likewise Paul Dresser's "On the Banks of the Wabash Far Away" is primarily concerned with the nostalgic recollection of home, family, and youthful romance. Written at the suggestion of his younger brother, novelist Theodore Dreiser, the song was published in 1899, sold more than a million copies of sheet music within the year, and in 1913 was adopted as the official state song of Indiana.

Dresser's homage to the Wabash was one of the first of many river songs to originate in Tin Pan Alley, the repertoire of which would later include Bert Hanlon, Benny Ryan, and Harry Tierney's spelling song "M-I-S-S-I-S-S-I-P-P-I" (1916), Ballard MacDonald and Robert A. King's immensely successful "Beautiful Ohio" (1918), Dave Dreyer and Morton Downey's "Wabash Moon" (1931), and Hoagy Carmichael's "Riverboat Shuffle" (1925) and "Lazy River" (1931). Closely aligned to Tin Pan Alley, Broadway has likewise capitalized upon the popular appeal of the river song. *Show Boat* (based on the novel by Edna Ferber) contains perhaps the most familiar American river song: Jerome Kern and Oscar Hammerstein's "Ol' Man River," a moving testimonial to the timeless grandeur and ever-rolling rhythm of the Mississippi River. Nearly 60 years following the Broadway debut of *Show Boat*, Roger Miller's Tony Award-winning *The River* (a musical adaptation of *Huckleberry Finn*) marked the return of the river, both as narrative setting and a source of musical inspiration, to the Broadway stage.

Through the first half of the 20th century, Hollywood, together with radio and phonograph recordings, provided one of the most accessible and commercially lucrative media for river songs, including Harry Barris and James Cavanaugh's "Mississippi Mud" (*King of Jazz*, 1930), Richard Rodgers and Lorenz Hart's "Down by the River" (*Mississippi*, 1935), and Mort Dixon and Harry Woods's "River Stay 'Way from My Door" (*Merry-Go-Round of 1938*).

Folk music has also continued to provide a congenial idiom for many river songs, most notably, Woody Guthrie's "Roll On, Columbia" and "Talkin' Columbia Blues," the best-known of a cycle of 26 songs extolling the Columbia River and the Grand Coulee Dam which were composed by Guthrie over a 26-day period in 1939 when he was engaged by the Boonville Power Administration to promote the buying of electricity from public rather than private sources.

Still other popular musical forms have contributed to the evolving repertoire of river songs, including the blues (Robert Johnson's "Traveling Riverside Blues," Robert Brown's "Mississippi River," "Big Bill" Broonzy's "Mississippi River Blues") and country-western (Johnny Cash's "Big River," Claude King's "Big River, Big Man," Alabama's "Tennessee River," Bobbie Gentry's "Ode to Billy Joe"). Even rock and roll, with such songs as the Standell's "Dirty Water," Creedence Clearwater Revival's "Proud Mary" and "Green River," the Talking Heads' cover of Al Green's "Take Me to the River," Bruce Springsteen's "The River," Billy Joel's "River of Dreams," and the Steve Miller Band's "Wild River," bears witness to the continuing role of the river—whether named or unnamed, real or imaginary—in American popular music.

Finally, the influence of the American river is revealed in various symphonic compositions of classical and jazz composers which, though technically more ambitious in form and instrumentation than song or ballad, often draw upon traditional river songs and are directed toward a popular audience. Notable examples of such large-scale orchestral works include Virgil Thompson's *The River*, Ferde Grofe's *Hudson River Suite* and *Mississippi Suite*, Duke Ellington's *Suite from the River*, and the British composer Friedrich Delius's *Appalachia Suite* and *Florida Suite*, both of which draw in part upon traditional river songs of the American South.

Bibliography

Carmer, Carl, ed. *Songs of the Rivers of America*. New York: Farrar, 1942.

Ewen, David, ed. *American Popular Songs from the Revolutionary War to the Present*. New York: Random House, 1966.

Hitchcock, H. Wiley, and Stanley Sadie, eds. *The New Grove Dictionary of American Music*. 4 vols. New York: Macmillan, 1986.

Lax, Roger, and Frederick Smith, eds. *The Great Song Thesaurus*. New York: Oxford UP, 1989.

Wheeler, Mary. *Steamboatin' Days: Folk Songs of the River Packet Era*. Baton Rouge: Louisiana State UP, 1944.

Michael Wentworth

RKO (Radio-Keith-Orpheum) was one of eight major film studios that ruled during Hollywood's golden age of the 1930s and 1940s. Commonly known as RKO, this Hollywood operation was the last of the eight to be formed, created during the fall of 1928 as part of Hollywood's rush to convert to talkies. Always struggling financially, through the 1930s and 1940s RKO still managed to turn out many of the finest feature films Hollywood produced. Yet the studio ended its producing life in the 1950s, the first of the eight to exit, when billionaire

Howard Hughes liquidated its assets to support other corporate habits.

By the late 1920s, the Radio Corporation of America (RCA) had developed a sound system, Photophone, but could not sign up a major studio to use it. So as to make the best of this situation, RCA founder and president David Sarnoff turned to financier Joseph P. Kennedy, patriarch of the Kennedy political family. At the time the elder Kennedy owned a small Hollywood studio, Film Booking Office (FBO). By the close of 1928, Sarnoff and Kennedy had merged Photophone, FBO, and the theaters from the Keith-Albee-Orpheum vaudeville empire to create RKO, a major studio.

Maybe the best asset RKO had was its theaters. During the 1930s the company owned picture palaces in New York City, Chicago, Los Angeles, Cleveland, Boston, San Francisco, and a host of other major American cities. RKO also maintained a network for international distribution, ensuring that its films were shown around the world. It was as a film producer that the company continually encountered trouble. It made many of the greatest films Hollywood has ever produced, but, dragged down by too many unprofitable feature films, rarely made any money.

RKO had the shortest and least profitable life of any major Hollywood studio. During the studio era of the 1930s and 1940s RKO constantly changed corporate philosophy as no management team was able to remain in place long enough to establish a long-running studio style. Production executives came and went with regularity. For example, David O. Selznick's tenure lasted less than two years, even though he managed to put into production *What Price Hollywood?* (1932), *Bill of Divorcement* (1932), and *King Kong* (1933).

Selznick was replaced by the creator of *King Kong*, Merian C. Cooper, who lasted 16 months, long enough to initiate the now fabled Fred Astaire-Ginger Rogers musicals. Cooper gave way to George Schafer. As he came on as head of production in 1938, Schafer promised to make RKO into the next MGM, a producer of the best feature films Hollywood had to offer. Schafer brought on board producers Max Gordon and Harry Goetz to re-create their stage hit *Abe Lincoln in Illinois* (1940), and lured Orson Welles and his Mercury Company to fashion *Citizen Kane* (1941) and *The Magnificent Ambersons* (1942).

But Schafer did not make money fast enough to satisfy RKO's owners and he was fired in 1942. Charles Koerner, his successor, immediately abandoned prestige fare for less costly "B-budget" films. Koerner's first success came with *Hitler's Children* (1943), an anti-Nazi melodrama which cost a mere $200,000 to make, but went on to gross more than $3 million. Not all low-budget fare proved so second-rate and exploitative in quality. The Koerner era of the mid-1940s also produced the splendid Val Lewton horror films, such as *The Cat People* (1942), *I Walked with a Zombie* (1943), and *The Body Snatcher* (1945), Jean Renoir's *This Land Is Mine* (1943), and Robert Siodmak's *The Spiral Staircase* (1946).

Through the 1940s, RKO was even more famous for films it distributed but did not actually produce. From Pathé came newsreels. Short subjects came from Disney. Indeed, through the 1940s, Walt Disney anted up not only Mickey Mouse, Goofy, and Donald Duck shorts, but attractive feature-length animation: *Pinocchio* (1940), *Dumbo* (1941), and *Bambi* (1943). From independent producers came such critically celebrated films as Sam Goldwyn's *The Pride of the Yankees* (1942) and *The Best Years of Our Lives* (1946).

After his purchase in 1948, Howard Hughes used RKO as a play toy. In the process, Hughes ran RKO out of business. To call a halt to red ink, Hughes fired hundreds and sold off the theaters. He also stringently insisted on non-communist purity for remaining studio personnel. RKO occasionally released interesting films after 1948—including John Ford's *She Wore a Yellow Ribbon* (1949) and *Wagonmaster* (1950) and Nicholas Ray's *They Live by Night* (1949)—but by 1953, studio losses totaled $20 million and four years later RKO was out of business.

Bibliography

Barlett, Donald L., and James B. Steele. *Empire: The Life, Legend, and Madness of Howard Hughes*. New York: Norton, 1979.

Gomery, Douglas. *The Hollywood Studio System*. New York: St. Martin's, 1986.

Jewell, Richard B., with Vernon Harbin. *The RKO Story*. New York: Arlington, 1982.

Lasky, Betty. *RKO: The Biggest Little Major of Them All*. Englewood Cliffs: Prentice-Hall, 1984.

Smith, Richard Austin. *Corporations in Crisis*. Garden City: Doubleday, 1963.

Douglas Gomery

Roadside Art is locally produced signage, commercial architecture, and roadside attractions designed to entertain, refresh, and distract people traveling by automobile for business and pleasure. Roadside art is primarily encountered along secondary roads—that is, highways with unlimited access in rural areas of the U.S. Such art is currently recognizable in the roadside remnants of the "highway culture" that existed from the last decade of the 19th century to the construction of limited access roads or freeways beginning after World War II (see Highways). The Highway Beautification Act further eroded the creation and maintenance of roadside art after 1965 by restricting the types and quantity of roadside advertisements. Some new examples of roadside art continue to be created in rural areas in the U.S. where automobile travel primarily occurs on secondary roads.

By the 1920s, automobile travel in the U.S. was pervasive and common. James Agee in his 1934 essay "The Great American Roadside" articulated the importance of the emerging highway culture to American commerce. This essay, published in *Fortune,* helped to shape a public perception of highway culture in which the space between destinations became important as places to refuel, eat, sleep, and be amused. This space in between, sometimes located on the fringe of towns and cities, became the site for hundreds of thousands of filling stations, restaurants, motels, fruit and vegetable stands, drive-in movie theaters, car camps, billboards, and amusements all vying for motorists' attention and dollars. Competition among roadside establishments for the increasingly large numbers of men, women, and children traveling by car was fierce. Initial contact often occurred through roadside signs.

By the 1920s, Americans were motoring along a coast-to-coast network of roadways and encountering a landscape awash with printed, painted, and eventually electrified roadside signs pointing the way to myriad roadside services and amusements. The development of this visual landscape continued unabated until the passage of the Highway Beautification Act in 1965. Walker Evans's roadside photographs from the 1930s document signage during the early days of highway culture. His photograph of the fish and vegetable stand of "F. M. POINTER The Old Reliable HOUSEMOVER" is exemplary of the kinds of establishments available and the type of signage utilized. Signs were handpainted, lettering was nonstandard and variable, prices for services were oftentimes prominently displayed, and images of what was for sale were often present. In Evans's photograph we see a roadside stand in which architecture becomes little more than a physical support for the signage. Over time motorists came to expect a staggering array of images used to tell stories and sell services. With the arrival of electricity, nighttime skies across America were lit with electrified arrows, setting suns, rainbows, shields, palm trees, foodstuffs, landscapes, and tantalizing characters all visually screaming for attention. Crafters of neon lighting demonstrated a virtuosity that still influences the profession.

In the competition for capturing motorists' attention, architecture became as important as roadside signs. Ice cream, hot dogs, french fries, and other foodstuffs as well as souvenirs were sold out of buildings shaped like a duck, igloo, dinosaur, or other such fantasy. Such fantasy buildings, often not built by professional architects, were once prolific along America's roadside. Restaurants, gas stations, and lodgings were built to represent bull skulls, shells, donuts, whales, milk bottles, cameras, covered wagons, wigwams, elephants, coffee pots, soup bowls, boats, ducks, tractors, fruit, clothing, hats, fish, ships, airplanes, shoes, trees, dinosaurs, trains, and automobiles, among other things. One of the most famous examples of American roadside architecture is Dinney the Dinosaur in Cabazon, CA. Dinney is many times the size of the brontosaurus that he supposedly represents. An equally large tyrannosaurus rex with a viewing platform stands nearby.

Roadside entrepreneurs learned early to take advantage of automobile travelers' need to stop and stretch their legs. They built amusing attractions such as grottos, shrines, sculpture gardens, and other eccentric constructions of concrete, coral, shells, wood, and recyclable materials. An early example is Samuel P. Dinsmoor's Garden of Eden in Lucas, KS. Dinsmoor's garden was publicized nationally from 1908 to 1932. Hundreds of visitors on a single day would pay 25 cents to tour Dinsmoor's two- and three-dimensional depictions from the Bible and modern civilization. A dining hall was available on the grounds for those who wanted to combine eating and touring. Following Dinsmoor's death in 1932, visitors had access to the added attraction of viewing his preserved body.

One of the most famous roadside attractions still in operation is Howard Finster's Paradise Garden in Pennville, GA. Commissioned by God, started in 1960, and constructed on 2 1/2 acres of reclaimed swampland, this garden of recycled materials is a place for touring and hearing the Reverend Finster preach. Sacred art by Howard Finster is available for purchase.

Along state highway 812 in rural Lewis County, NY, motorists can experience a three-acre tract inhabited by animal and human figures of painted concrete by Veronica Terrillion. Joshua Samuel's city of used oil cans is located on a rural roadway near Walterboro, SC. For a small fee, motorists can receive a tour and a hand-out describing the proprietor's intentions.

Some scholars, and numerous popular culture enthusiasts, are advocating for the restoration, preservation, and creation of roadside art. Highway enthusiast Ulrich Keller attributes current attention to roadside art to a post-pop climate in which the once "vulgar" can be perceived as having "charm" and "acceptability."

Bibliography

Agee, James. "The American Roadside." *James Agee: Selected Journalism*. Ed. Paul Ashdown. Knoxville: U of Tennessee P, 1985.

Andrews, J. J. C. *The Well-Built Elephant: And Other Roadside Attractions*. New York: Congdon & Weed, 1984.

Keller, Ulrich. *The Highway as Habitat: A Roy Stryker Documentation, 1943-1955*. Santa Barbara: University Art Museum, 1986.

Turner, J. F. *Howard Finster: Man of Visions*. New York: Knopf, 1989.

Ward, Daniel Franklin, ed. *Personal Places: Perspectives on Informal Art Environments*. Bowling Green, OH: Bowling Green State U Popular P, 1984.

Doug Blandy

Robert Montgomery Presents (1950-1957), also known as *Robert Montgomery Presents Your Lucky Strike Theater, The Johnson Wax Program,* and *The Richard Hudnut Summer Theater*, was produced in New York and aired on NBC-TV on Monday evenings in an alternating format. Robert Montgomery and Joseph Bailey served as the show's top executives supervising production, and Norman Felton and Herbert Swope, Jr., alternated as directors. During its first year, the series presented adaptations of classic Hollywood films (*Rebecca, A Star Is Born, Dark Victory*) starring prominent motion picture actors and actresses. Then, to circumvent legal problems surrounding kinescoping of film adaptations, the series turned its attention to original plays and adaptations of literary works (such as Somerset Maugham's *The Letter*). The series was decidedly big-budget: in its heyday, its production values were not only comparable to *Studio One* in its high period, but often exceeded the latter in its ambitious attempts to stage such works as *Hindenburg*. In 1952, the show adopted a summer stock format with repertory players that included Vaughn Taylor, John Newland, Elizabeth Montgomery (Montgomery's daughter), and Cliff Robertson. Unlike other shows of the day, *Montgomery* did not shy away from controversy nor did it rewrite to satisfy the Television Production Code, airing climactic suicide, drunkenness, etc. It won Emmys from 1951 to 1953 as well as a *Radio-TV Daily* Best Show Award and a Sylvania Best Show Award. Along with the vast majority of live dramatic anthology programs, it was canceled in 1957.

Bibliography
Brooks, Tim, and Earle Marsh. *The Complete Directory to Prime Time Network Television Shows, 1946-Present.* New York: Ballantine, 1992.
O'Neil, Thomas. *The Emmys.* New York: Penguin, 1992.
Sturcken, Frank. *Live Television.* Jefferson: McFarland, 1990.

S. P. Madigan

Rock Climbing/Sport Climbing has always been and continues to be an integral part of the general mountaineering experience. But by the 1920s and 1930s, when climbers pioneered routes in areas like the Adirondacks, White Mountains, and Shawangunks, rock climbing in the U.S. was already becoming a separate sport characterized by distinct standards and goals. Modern rock climbing, however, probably owes most to the emergence of Yosemite Valley during the 1940s as the country's premier climbing arena. Climbers at Yosemite pushed standards and new climbing technologies: the use of hard steel alloy pitons for artificial aid rather than the soft pitons common in Europe, for instance, opened the way for climbs of extreme difficulty, often completed on "big walls" like El Capitan over several days. Yosemite climbers, who often camped in the valley for months while practicing their craft, also epitomized the free-spirited, marginal, countercultural lifestyle often associated with rock climbing.

Steady improvements in equipment combined with a recent cultural passion for strenuous outdoor activities have contributed to making rock climbing a more mainstream pursuit in the last 20 years. And because climbing emphasizes endurance, agility, and technique over pure strength, the sport has become equally popular with men and women. The first person to "free" climb (that is, to climb without hanging on artificial aid) the famous 3,000-foot Nose route of El Capitan was a woman, Lynn Hill. Her extraordinary achievement, in turn, might not have been possible without the emergence of climbing gyms around the country, where climbing strategies can be improved in safety all year long. Climbing gyms are partly responsible for what is now often called "sport climbing," a term that refers to the practice of climbing as an athletic and even gymnastic pursuit in its own right. With such rigorous training available, standards have risen greatly in the past few years. Until recently, the highest grade attained in the classification system most commonly used in the United States was about 5.10 ("five-ten"), on a scale in which 5.0 through 5.4 represent climbs most physically fit people can accomplish without specialized skills. The highest grade currently achieved in the U.S. is 5.14 ("five-fourteen"). Climbing gyms, by promoting and hosting competitions in which the world's best climbers regularly face off against each other, have helped to form a group of elite climbers capable of consistently climbing at this highest level.

With the newfound popularity of rock climbing have come certain conflicts. Climbers in favor of a more traditional "ground-up" approach in which artificial aid (such as pitons, bolts, or wired nuts) is placed during the ascent, for instance, often collide with sport climbers who may rappel from the top of a demanding route before it is ever attempted in order to place bolts or to practice difficult moves. A more frequent use of bolts has also created a backlash on aesthetic grounds, particularly among those in charge of national and state parks. At the same time, the advent of commercial sponsorship for elite climbers is often seen as damaging to the purity of the climbing experience and its countercultural tradition—though it is also testimony to the growing popularity of the sport.

Bibliography
Birkett, Bill. *Modern Rock and Ice Climbing.* London: Clark, 1988.
Jones, Chris. *Climbing in North America.* Berkeley: U of California P, 1976.
Mendenhall, Ruth. *Challenge of Rock and Mountain Climbing.* Harrisburg: Stackpole, 1983.

Thomas Strychacz

Rock Music is a term that is loosely applied to a wide range of music geared toward younger audiences. The most widely agreed upon parameters of rock music include a strong repetitive beat, amplified instruments (most frequently, the electric guitar and bass guitars), and simple chord and melodic structure. Rock music usually employs vocals, either sung solo or in harmony.

The origins of rock music are in rhythm and blues music written and performed by African Americans in the U.S. after World War II. In the early 1950s, white musicians began performing "cover versions" of some of these rhythm and blues songs. The phrase "rock 'n' roll" also has African-American roots as the vernacular for sexual intercourse.

It was appropriate to apply the phrase to music, since many of the rhythm and blues songs of the day, like Hank Ballard and the Midnighters' "Work with Me Annie," had overt or thinly veiled sexual references. "Rock 'n' roll" was first used to describe the music by white Cleveland disc jockey Alan Freed (see entry) in the early 1950s.

Two of the early rock 'n' roll hits were "ShBoom" (originally recorded by the Chords and covered by the Crew Cuts) and "Cryin' in the Chapel" by Sonny Til and the Orioles. "Shake, Rattle and Roll," originally recorded by Joe Turner, was covered by Bill Haley and his Comets in the soundtrack of the film *The Blackboard Jungle* in 1955. Parents and religious and civic leaders watched in horror as teenagers danced in the aisles of movie theaters when the film was shown.

Later in the 1950s, white radio stations and audiences began to play and listen to African-American musicians performing their own songs. Chuck Berry and Little Richard and vocal groups such as the Platters, the Drifters, and the Penguins were successful rock 'n' roll performers of this era.

In the southern U.S., rhythm and blues and country music were combined into a genre known as rockabilly. The best-known performers of this music were Buddy Holly, Jerry Lee Lewis, Carl Perkins, and Elvis Presley.

In the early 1960s, the term rock 'n' roll music was gradually replaced with the shortened form, rock music. The change is significant because it also marks a decreasing influence of blues on white musicians. For example, the "surf music" fad which originated in California with groups like the Beach Boys and Jan and Dean emphasized vocal harmonies and melody over the stronger rhythms of earlier rock music.

The trend continued with the "British Invasion" in 1964. The Beatles and the Rolling Stones began their careers by playing cover versions of American R&B hits from the 1950s like Chuck Berry's "Roll over Beethoven" or Little Richard's "Good Golly Miss Molly." But they quickly moved into more complex original music that paralleled the beginning of the psychedelic era of American rock music.

Rock music in the late 1960s began to move in two directions. The first was serious music that abandoned simple three-chord, 12-bar melodic progressions and adolescent lyric themes about romance, parties, and school. Groups like the Jefferson Airplane and the Doors wrote about drugs and war, and classical conductor Leonard Bernstein heralded the musical sophistication of songs like Janis Ian's "Society's Child" or the Left Banke's "Walk Away Renee."

Other musicians continued to appeal to more adolescent tastes in what became known as bubblegum music. Songs like the Archies' "Sugar Sugar" and Tommy James and the Shondells' "I Think We're Alone Now" appealed to teen and pre-teen listeners while their older brothers and sisters listened to the Jefferson Airplane or the Grateful Dead. As the 1960s closed, rock music was almost exclusively white, with a few exceptions like Jimi Hendrix. Rock that was influenced by rhythm and blues evolved into "soul music," recorded on new labels like those in the Motown group, or old R&B labels like Chess and Stax. Hit songs by the Temptations, Diana Ross and the Supremes, Stevie Wonder, and others were played on Top 40 stations along with bubblegum music and the more popular singles from the psychedelic rock groups.

Folk music also exercised a significant influence on rock music at the end of the 1960s. Bob Dylan's introduction of electric instruments led to the electrification of other folk performers like Roger McGuinn and the Byrds, David Crosby and Steve Stills (the foundation of Crosby, Stills, and Nash), Neil Young (Buffalo Springfield), and James Taylor. Their music blended the intricate harmonies of folk music, serious lyrical themes, and electric and acoustic instruments.

This music was also labeled "soft rock," an oxymoron considering the harshness often associated with earlier rock music. As aging rock musicians appealed to aging audiences with softer music, other groups rebelled by playing the shocking music of punk rock. Punk bands hurled verbal and physical insults at audiences while shouting lyrics with explicit sexual meanings. This music had its roots in the garage bands of the 1960s like the MC5 and the Standells. The music was intentionally "raw," marked by jangling guitars and screaming, sometimes off-key vocals.

Heavy metal music also blossomed during the 1970s. British bands like Deep Purple, Led Zeppelin, and Black Sabbath continued the loud, distorted guitar of acid-rock bands mixed with lyrics that often emphasized death, violence, and the occult. Groups like Blue Oyster Cult popularized this music in the United States. Groups that combined the hard rock musical style of heavy metal with spectacular stage shows rose to popularity in the late 1970s. These glitter or glam rock groups included Alice Cooper, KISS, the Tubes, and the New York Dolls. Mainstream rock, with music reminiscent of early R&B-influenced rock and lyrics that emphasized the disillusionment of post-Vietnam teenagers, was exemplified by the success of Bruce Springsteen and Billy Joel. Rhythm and blues artists languished in the repetitive dance music of the disco craze.

The birth of the MTV music video network in 1981 made recording artists increasingly concerned with the visual aspects of their music. A softer version of punk, "new wave" music, adapted well to the new medium, with groups like the Talking Heads and Devo capitalizing on music videos. "Girl groups" (e.g., Blondie, the Go-Gos, and the Bangles) and solo artists like Cyndi Lauper combined video art and danceable music. But the ultimate MTV rock artist of the 1980s was Madonna, who reached white, black, and Latino audiences with her combination of rock and dance music and sexually suggestive music videos and stage shows. African-American artists like Michael Jackson were able to cross over from soul charts to rock music and MTV playlists as well.

Another form of protest music developed in the mid-1980s: alternative music. Rather than being a specific type of music, alternative music is defined by the means for its distribution. Many of the alternative artists recorded for small independent record companies, or "indies," as opposed to the ever-expanding major labels like the Warner Brothers-Elektra-Atlantic group. Because of the limited distribution resources, these groups and their labels often enjoyed only local or regional success, such as the "Athens [Georgia] sound" (R.E.M., the B-52s, Pylon). The garage-band sound was revived in the late 1980s in small recording studios and clubs by groups like Dinosaur Jr., Hüsker Dü, and the Pixies.

In the early 1990s, alternative music broke through to the mainstream as the Seattle-based "grunge sound" erupted on the national scene. These groups combined the simplicity and repetitiveness of heavy metal with the alienation of punk. Nirvana, Pearl Jam, and Soundgarden were early grunge rock successes, followed closely by Green Day.

Bibliography

DeCurtis, Anthony, and James Henke, eds. *The Rolling Stone Illustrated History of Rock & Roll: The Definitive History of the Most Important Artists and Their Music.* New York: Random House, 1992.

Du Moyer, Paul, ed. *The Story of Rock 'n' Roll: The Year-by-Year Illustrated Chronicle.* New York: Shriner, 1995.

Gatten, Jeffery N. *Rock Music Scholarship: An Interdisciplinary Bibliography.* Westport: Greenwood, 1995.
Ward, Ed, Geoffrey Stokes, and Ken Tucker. *Rock of Ages: The Rolling Stone History of Rock & Roll.* New York: Summit, 1986.

Kenneth M. Nagelberg

See also

Acid Rock	Heavy Metal
Alternative Music	Punk Rock
Folk Rock	Protest Music
Grunge Music	

Rock 'n' Roll Dancing is the form of social dancing that developed in conjunction with the emergence of rock 'n' roll music. As with rock 'n' roll music, the driving force and spark of life came from the African-American community. As a primary characteristic, rock 'n' roll dancing uses various parts of the body in segmented, sequential, rhythmic action with emphasis on polyrhythms and the use of the hips and torso. More improvisatory in nature, it relies less on set floor patterns than do other social dances. These dances were informed by a variety of influences and constituted a kinesthetic manifestation of rock 'n' roll music's hard-driving rhythm. Taking shape in the mid to late 1950s, rock 'n' roll dancing became a distinct dance form with the emergence of the twist, continued to evolve in response to changes in rock music, and finally diminished by the early 1970s.

Early rock 'n' roll dances included the rock-and-roll, Madison, Birdland, bop, jet, roach, wobble, locomotion, and choochoo. Although by no means an exhaustive listing, later, and perhaps more familiar, dances included the alligator, bird, boo-ga-loo, bug, Charlie bop, chicken, dog, duck, fish, fly, Freddie, frug, funky chicken, hitchhiker, hully gully, jerk, mashed potato, monkey, Philly gog, pony, shout, skate, slop, stroll, swim, twist, and Watusi.

In the early days of rock 'n' roll, the jitterbug or Lindy Hop was used for fast songs and the fox trot for slower pieces. Rock 'n' roll dance derived, in part, from these dances as well as from the Charleston, mambo, heebie jeebies, shimmy, slow drag, jig walk, and the so-called animal dances such as the camel walk and the eagle rock.

The compelling rhythm of rock 'n' roll led to the evolution of new dances that reflected the beat as well as spirit of rebellion embodied by the new music. Appropriated heavily from the African-American aesthetic, these dances became regarded as the purview of white, middle-class youth. Line dances, also popular in the African-American community, played an additional role in the development of this new dance form. Line dances of the late 1950s included the Madison, Birdland, and stroll.

The twist, which first appeared in the African-American community in 1959, moved into the white youth culture, and then to the white adult population, marked a turning point for rock 'n' roll dancing. With its solitary nature and use of the full torso, the twist shaped rock dancing of the 1960s. The twist established a new style of social dancing that was stationary rather than traveling, simple, using repeatable steps and, most radically, requiring neither a partner nor a group. The twist reflected the societal move toward individual independence. The transition from partnered to solo dances was also affected by the popularity of line dances. With loyalties shifting from partners to the group, line dances provided an important sense of community.

Rock 'n' roll dancing had among its distinguishing characteristics the appearance of spontaneity as well as a democratic element, generated as it was from within the culture rather than externally imposed. There was also, over time, greater independence among the dancers and more latitude in the steps performed. The dances were freer, more rhythmically driven, physical, and, because they involved the hips and torso, more sensual. The lack of rigid structure within the dances reflected a move away from conformity. The new dance formations also reflected women's changing roles, as there was no longer a need to follow a male partner.

Rock 'n' roll dances were learned from fellow dancers as well as at dance studios, through manuals (see Butler and Butler), movies, and nightclubs such as the Peppermint Lounge (made famous by the Peppermint Twist dance). The growth of rock 'n' roll depended upon, and was facilitated by, the concurrent growth in electronic media, and television became a significant means for the transmission of rock 'n' roll dances. The dances also reflected the influence of television, as exemplified in the Madison, in which the dancers mime "Away We Go," in the fashion of comedian Jackie Gleason. By the mid-1960s, there were numerous dance shows, including *Hullabaloo, Let's Go-Go, Where the Action Is, Shindig, Shivaree,* and *Hollywood a Go Go,* and later, *Soul Train* (1970-). The first and most influential, however, was *American Bandstand* (1957-87), which was, essentially, a mass televised rock 'n' roll dancing lesson each weekday afternoon. Dance trends were promoted and even started by the show, including the bop, the walk, and the circle dance. *American Bandstand* also censored certain dances, such as the dog and alligator, which were deemed too risqué by the producers.

Bibliography
Buckman, Peter. *Let's Dance: Social, Ballroom, & Folk Dancing.* New York: Paddington, 1978.
Butler, Albert, and Josephine Butler. *Encyclopedia of Social Dance.* New York: Gordon, 1986.
McDonagh, Don. *Dance Fever.* New York: Random House, 1979.
Stearns, Marshall, and Jean Stearns. *Jazz Dance: The Story of American Vernacular Dance.* New York: Macmillan, 1968.

Angela Graham

Rockford Files, The (1974-1980), was a TV series about a private investigator played by James Garner (1928-). A holdover from strong character types such as Humphrey Bogart or Robert Mitchum, Garner's bigger-than-life TV roles—first as Bret Maverick (see *Maverick*) and then as private eye James Rockford—have been considered the result of his strong features and masculinity as much as his acting ability. Garner's established hero persona certainly played a major role in *The Rockford Files.*

The Rockford Files stands as one of the few shows that was able to break the rules yet still survive. In a TV world populated by self-righteous, infallible cops and detectives, Rockford was different. Unlike the glamorous PIs of film and TV fame, Rockford lived in a trailer, did routine stake-outs and paper chases, and kept his gun in a cookie jar. He was an ex-con who would rather go fishing with his dad, Rocky (Noah Beery, Jr.), than be bothered by a case—especially when the case might get him beaten or killed. Once on the case, of course, Rockford displayed cunning, humility, and courage. In essence, Rockford synthesized the characteristics of the three major dramatic hero types—moralistic hero, anti-hero, and reluctant hero—a combination which most likely contributed to the popular appeal of the series.

The Rockford Files was created by Stephen J. Cannell and Roy Huggins (who had also created *Maverick*) and produced by Cannell, who has gone on to produce other more popular—yet not as inspired—series such as *The Greatest American Hero* (1981-83) and *The A-Team* (1983-87). *The Rockford Files* spawned a short-lived spinoff—*Richie Brockelman, Private Eye* (1975), and, in 1975, *Rockford*'s theme song was No. 10 on *Billboard* magazine's Top 60. Eight made-for-TV *Rockford Files* movies aired between 1994 and 1999.

Bibliography

Brooks, Tim, and Earle Marsh. *The Complete Directory to Prime Time Network TV Shows, 1946-Present*. New York: Ballantine, 1992.

Collins, Max Allan, and John Javna. *The Best of Crime and Detective TV: Perry Mason to Hill Street Blues, The Rockford Files to Murder She Wrote*. New York: Harmony, 1989.

Martindale, David. *The Rockford Phile*. Las Vegas: Pioneer, 1991.

Michael B. Kassel

Rockwell, Norman (1894-1978), American commercial illustrator, was best known for his *Saturday Evening Post* magazine covers created between 1916 and 1963. Rockwell's body of work has come to represent a vision of America as it would like to believe it once was, with tried and true values which endure and define the American character.

The title of Rockwell's autobiography, *Norman Rockwell: My Adventures as an Illustrator,* is most telling—Rockwell was torn by distinctions his detractors would make between the commercial enterprise and sentimentalism of his work and the true calling and revelation of the fine artist. But Rockwell believed his life and art to be an "adventure" and took his cue from his predecessor Howard Pyle (1853-1911), who believed commercial illustration to be an "ennobling profession" with serious artistic purpose.

Rockwell was born in a shabby brownstone in New York City. From childhood, Rockwell had an appreciation for book illustration and drew constantly. He reached adolescence during the last years of the golden age of illustration, when magazines and newspapers had not yet fully developed the capability to reproduce photographs and editors depended upon illustrators to draw events and scenes for them. By age 16, Rockwell had quit school to attend the Art Student League in New York City, following in Pyle's foot-steps. There he studied drawing under George Bridgeman. He supported himself by doing illustrations for children's magazines, selling his first drawings only a few years after Henry Ford built his first car.

In 1916, at age 22, Rockwell showed his work to George Lorimer, editor of the *Saturday Evening Post*. Lorimer hired Rockwell on the spot, and thus began a collaboration that lasted almost 50 years. The editor decided the needs of the magazine for content and evaluated Rockwell's work, and Rockwell determined the visuals, designed to be readily accessible to viewers. For the *Post* covers particularly, Rockwell wanted to attract people's attention to get them to pick up and buy the magazine. Besides his affiliation with the *Post*, beginning in 1925, Rockwell developed a special relationship with the Boy Scouts of America, starting with his illustrations for *The Boy Scout Handbook* and continuing through numerous editions and calendars until 1974. He also created illustrations for books, greeting cards, posters, calendars, and advertisements for sundry products and services ranging from Coca-Cola, Niblets Corn, Crest toothpaste, and Ford automobiles to Top Value Stamps and Massachusetts Mutual Life Insurance.

The weekly *Saturday Evening Post* was among the most popular U.S. magazines of the first half of this century. Rockwell's covers became America's classroom, with Rockwell its teacher. For many people, Rockwell's pictures provided a framework for understanding American history and created a mythology which persists to this day. He painted an American character rooted in the past but on the move, an America as many would like it to be. Simpler times and verities are drawn upon to portray the sentiments (love, respect, thankfulness, patriotism, honor, etc.) along with an added dash of Ben Franklin-Tom Sawyer-Huck Finn savvy. The national character Rockwell describes is pragmatic and self-reliant, with an optimistic attitude that can hold on to sentiments with a sense of humor while continuously re-inventing itself. Themes of growing up and growing old in a middle America that never really existed range from innocent and mischievous children at play and sports to ingenuous tender lovers, young sailors on leave, and ritualistic family life at home.

Rockwell's approach to his work was partly determined by the means of reproducing it from painting to magazine illustration. Typically, Rockwell painted his pictures, which were then turned over to master engravers and printers. When the *Post* shifted from two- to four-color printing beginning with its February 6, 1926, cover, Rockwell gained greater freedom in his use of color. Furthermore, Rockwell's work was extremely affected by World War II, resulting in a less idealized vision of America. Rockwell portrayed the war as an interruption of home life in particular, and a threat to the American way. During wartime and after, his style became more naturalistic, with detailed settings for the incidents portrayed, as he examined the poetry of everyday behavior and the effects of larger events upon it. Similarly, a more realistic vision of the social problems inherent in America emerges from his *Post* covers from the 1960s as well as illustrations for *Look* magazine, including, for example, "The Problem We All Live With" (14 Jan. 1964) and "New Kids in the Neighborhood" (16 May 1967), which address racism.

Rockwell's talent lies in his ability to masterfully combine specific detail with generalization, to create self-contained, easily understandable narratives further grounded through the tell-tale minutiae of everydayness. Generally regarded as his masterwork, "The Four Freedoms," a series of four paintings, was inspired by President Franklin D. Roosevelt's 1941 address to Congress, and includes *The Freedom of Speech, The Freedom of Worship, The Freedom from Want,* and *The Freedom from Fear.* Rockwell submitted the series to the U.S. War Office, but the paintings were rejected. They were subsequently published in the *Post,* and requests came in by the millions for reprints. They were eventually sold as posters by the U.S. Treasury Department to support the war effort. In the paintings, Rockwell translated Roosevelt's universals in simple domestic terms and created American settings for them with a clear-cut sense of right and wrong. Rockwell's portraiture of the 1950s and 1960s included politicians and celebrities, including Eisenhower, Stevenson, Kennedy, John Wayne, Ann-Margret, Frank Sinatra, and Johnny Carson. He was faithful to the likeness of the person, but when depicting people in positions of enormous power, Rockwell shows them as essentially human, under tremendous pressure, careworn, sad, or with a sense of humor.

Although he traveled throughout the U.S. and Europe, Rockwell settled in Vermont in the early 1940s, but he called Stockbridge, MA, home the last 25 years of his life. Stockbridge, appropriately, is the home of the Norman Rockwell Museum. A Rockwell Museum featuring magazine cover reproductions and memorabilia is also located in Philadelphia's historic district. On July 4, 1994, the U.S. Postal Service issued a series of Norman Rockwell stamps commemorating his contributions.

Bibliography

Finch, Christopher. *Norman Rockwell's America.* New York: Abrams, 1975.

Klinkenborg, Verlyn. "Pyle and Rockwell—Totally American, Yet Not at All Alike." *Smithsonian* July 1994: 89-95.

Moline, Mary. *Norman Rockwell Encyclopedia: A Chronological Catalog of the Artist's Work 1910-1978.* Indianapolis: Curtis, 1979.

Rockwell, Norman. *Norman Rockwell: My Adventures as an Illustrator.* As told to Thomas Rockwell. Garden City, NY: Doubleday, 1960.

Stoltz, Donald R., and Marshall L. Stoltz. *Norman Rockwell and the* Saturday Evening Post. 3 vols. New York: Curtis, 1974.

Lisa Odham Stokes

Rocky (1976) starred Sylvester ("Sly") Stallone (1946- ; see entry) in a sentimental story of a downtrodden Italian American, Rocky Balboa, who succeeds in his one miraculous shot at fame through inner strength and self-determination. Written by and starring Stallone (who ransomed the script for the main role, even though the producers wanted James Caan or Burt Reynolds), this tale of a dim-witted, good-hearted, ham-fisted boxer, chosen by champion Apollo Creed (Carl Weathers) for a pushover title bout, is classic corn popped successfully golden.

Had *Rocky* been made in the 1930s or 1940s it is not likely to have garnered much attention because it follows very familiar formulas of sentiment and perseverance. However, coming in the mid-1970s as an antidote to the cynical reality of Vietnam, Watergate, and the Nixon pardon, plus the cynical cinema of *The Godfather, The Exorcist, Chinatown,* and *One Flew over the Cuckoo's Nest,* this story was very much in tune with the hoped-for renaissance to be ushered in by Jimmy Carter. Stallone fared much better than Carter, continuing to pump sequels out well into the Bush era and netting over a quarter of a billion dollars for United Artists. In this sense, the film very much parallels Stallone's own career, in which he changed overnight from a minor actor and unsuccessful screenwriter into a macho-man industry eclipsing any standard previously established by Clint Eastwood or Charles Bronson.

Rocky's charm comes from his dual desire to prove himself as more than a hopeless dope and not to maliciously hurt anyone, despite his inherent strength and stamina. He also looks like a saint compared to his egotistical, Muhammad Ali-like ring opponent; his oafish friend Paulie (Burt Young); and his eventual love interest, Paulie's sweet, shy, but virtually comatose sister Adrian (Talia Shire). Even though Rocky functions best with monosyllables (bringing the all-encompassing "yo" into the vernacular) and direct, physical actions, he wants pride in himself as a human being rather than just the social and material success that Apollo Creed represents. Also he represents the long-lived American myth of the self-bettered man, as he laboriously accepts the training regimen of Mickey (Burgess Meredith), who serves as the irascible-but-lovable geezer spirit guide.

Although the majority of reviews ranged from negative to condescending, audiences embraced *Rocky,* both film and character, as a return to the simple folklore of the American myth. The film won Oscars for best picture, directing, and editing—along with nominations for Stallone, Shire, Young, Meredith, original screenplay, soundtrack, and Bill Conti's song "Gonna Fly Now."

Unfortunately for Stallone (in an artistic rather than a financial sense), art continued to imitate life in the premise of *Rocky II* (1979), where Rocky tries to retire from boxing to suit Adrian's wishes but finds that he is incapable of any other career. Similarly, Stallone has been fabulously successful with his action films (e.g., *First Blood* [1982] and its sequels) but never has found an audience for his attempts at comedy or more restrained drama. If the fists fly, so do the box-office dollars, which made it virtually inevitable that Rocky would win in *II*'s rematch with Apollo. Unlike many other sequel series, the *Rocky* films never used secondary titles, just numbers, which seems to further acknowledge that these are not really developments in a continuing story but simply remakes of the first success.

Certainly the characters, actors, storylines, and creative personnel have a solid continuity (Stallone wrote all of them;

John G. Avildsen directed the first and last, Stallone all the others). Death becomes a motif in the next two sequels, giving "The Italian Stallion" a motivation to overcome his fear that he cannot live up to his former iron-willed standards.

In *III* (1982), distracted by Mickey's death, Rocky loses an exhibition match but then hires Apollo as his new trainer and roars back to victory in even more graphic images than the first two films. *IV* (1985) has Rocky avenging Apollo's death in a match with a biologically engineered monster from the U.S.S.R. Rocky in the last installment (1990) is in debt to the IRS and, unable to fight because of brain damage, becomes a trainer; his protégé defects to an unscrupulous promoter and wins the championship, but Rocky takes him apart in the Philly streets, endearing himself to his fans one last time.

Bibliography
Canby, Vincent. *New York Times* 22 Nov. 1976.
Gross, Edward. *Rocky and the Films of Sylvester Stallone.* Las Vegas: Pioneer, 1990.
Lardner, Susan. *New Yorker* 2 July 1979.
Maslin, Janet. *New York Times* 16 Nov. 1990.
O'Brien, Tom. *The Screening of America: Movies and Values from* Rocky *to* Rain Man. New York: Continuum, 1990.
Reed, J. D. *Time* 14 June 1982.
Schickel, Richard. *Time* 9 Dec. 1985.

Ken Burke

Rocky and Bullwinkle (1959-1972) were the animated stars of the first original network cartoon show. Bullwinkle J. Moose and Rocket J. Squirrel remain as popular today as they were 40 years ago.

Jay Ward, co-creator of the show, was a Berkeley, CA, real estate broker who got interested in the infant television medium. He co-created *Crusader Rabbit* with Alexander Anderson, a nephew of animation pioneer Paul Terry. After test airings in 1948, Ward sold the series from city to city, and *Crusader Rabbit* debuted in 1949 as the first original television cartoon. Ward proposed other series, returning to his real estate practice when financially necessary. In 1959, he teamed with veteran writer and animator Bill Scott to create *Rocky and His Friends*, which debuted as a weekday series on ABC on November 19, the first original network cartoon show (a 1957 revival of *Crusader Rabbit* was sold to NBC's owned and operated stations).

The 28 Rocky and Bullwinkle stories comprised 4 to 40 segments, with cliffhanger endings punctuated by gag titles narrated by William Conrad ("Be with us next time for 'Transatlantic Chicken' or 'Hens Across the Sea!'"). Scott undertook the role of big-hearted, dim Bullwinkle, while June Foray played plucky Rocky, the Flying Squirrel, and Pottsylvania's own Natasha Fatale. Paul Frees played that "heel without a soul," Boris Badenov. Each story involved a discovery like the Ruby Yacht of Omar Khayyam; the "Rue Brittania" tattoo on Bullwinkle's foot signifying that he is the rightful Earl of Crankcase; Bullwinkle's football career at Wossamatta U.; or the Kurward Derby, which makes its wearer the smartest person in the world. Boris and Natasha hatch "fiendish plots" to "get Moose and Squirrel."

Other parts of the show included "Fractured Fairy Tales," narrated by Edward Everett Horton, "Aesop and Son," and "Peabody's Improbable History," where genius dog Mr. Peabody visits historical figures with his boy Sherman.

After two seasons, NBC picked up the series, expanded with new segments, especially "Dudley Doright," a send-up of old-time melodrama, complete with Snidely Whiplash in black cape. The retitled *Bullwinkle Show* (see entry) hit prime time Sunday evening, September 24, 1961, as the lead-in to *Disney's Wonderful World of Color*, which had also been raided from ABC. *Bullwinkle* was NBC's entry in the prime-time animation derby started by *The Flintstones*, but it lasted only one season. NBC moved it to Sunday afternoons in 1962, then Saturday mornings. It returned to ABC in 1964, to be broadcast Sunday mornings until 1972, then went into syndication. Continued interest in the characters prompted the 2000 release of the feature-length film *The Adventures of Rocky and Bullwinkle*.

Ward produced two other cartoon series for ABC. *The Adventures of Hoppity Hooper*, in 1964, teamed a young frog with Fillmore Bear and Waldo Wigglesworth, a fox who ran a medicine show and various get-rich-quick schemes. *George of the Jungle* hit in 1967. The dim-witted Tarzan takeoff was supported by "Super Chicken" and race car driver "Tom Slick." Ward starred Bullwinkle in a series of Cheerios commercials, and later designed Cap'n Crunch for Quaker Oats, producing their commercials for several years. He also produced the syndicated *Fractured Flickers*, a hodge-podge of silent film clips with added comic dialogue, hosted by Hans Conreid. Ward continued to promote his creations until his death in 1989, making appearances at conventions and campuses, and organizing film festivals.

Bibliography
Amoruso, Marino, and Benjamin Brady Magliano. *Of Moose and Men: The Rocky and Bullwinkle Story.* A Georgetown Television Productions documentary aired on public television, 1991.
Brooks, Tim, and Earle Marsh. *The Complete Directory to Prime Time TV Shows, 1946–Present.* 4th ed. New York: Ballantine, 1988.
Lenburg, Jeff. *The Encyclopedia of Animated Cartoons.* New York: Facts on File, 1991.

Mark McDermott

Rocky Horror Picture Show, The (1975), was a film adaptation of Richard O'Brien's stage musical, which had opened in London in 1973. The film appealed to both young and gay audiences with its combination of glitter rock popularized in the early 1970s by David Bowie, Gary Glitter, Alice Cooper, and the New York Dolls, among others (Marchetti 766). Drawing on camp humor and theatricality, the plot of the film revolves around two young lovers, Brad Majors (Barry Bostwick) and Janet Weiss (Susan Sarandon), who, following their recent engagement, seek out their former science professor, Dr. Everett Scott (Jonathan Adams). Car trouble en route brings them to the home of Dr. Frank N. Furter (Tim Curry), a transvestite from another galaxy, who seduces the young couple, as well as his Frankenstein-ish creation, Rocky Horror (Peter Hinwood), and other guests. Furter's diabolical intentions are foiled by Riff Raff (Richard O'Brien) and Magenta (Patricia Quinn), who kill the mad doctor and return the entire castle back to its home planet. The young couple escape unharmed physically, though their experience leaves them corrupted, left to face their new sexuality.

While the film was initially a financial disappointment for director Jim Sharman and producer Lou Adler due to the waning popularity of the glitter subculture, a cult of followers grew up around the film, causing media coverage not originally warranted by the film's release. Fans viewed the film multiple times, eventually dressing up as the characters and performing alongside the screen. Performances included "outlandish costumes, shouted dialogues of insults and additions, and projectiles of toilet paper, toast, playing cards and streams of water" (Marchetti 767). In its first ten years, the film grossed $60 million (Schaefer 4), and the popularity of the film continued throughout the late 1980s into the 1990s, fueled largely by midnight screenings at theaters nationwide, contributing to a revitalization of the glitter subculture in a "specialized...ritualized" way (Marchetti 767).

Bibliography

Marchetti, Gina. "The Rocky Horror Picture Show." *International Dictionary of Films and Filmmakers: Films.* Ed. Nicholas Thomas. 2d ed. Chicago: St. James, 1990. 766-67.
Schaefer, Stephen. "'Rocky X,' Penny, and the Nylons." *Film Comment* 22.1: 2-4.

Lynnea Chapman-King

Roddenberry, Gene (1921-1991), was the executive producer and writer of numerous television series and films, but best known as the creator of the original *Star Trek* series (NBC, 1966-69; see entry). This first series, sometimes called the classic series, was the seed for what became the *Star Trek* phenomenon, one of the most astonishing success stories of an icon in popular culture. For despite everything NBC and Paramount Studios did to cancel, alter, or ignore *Star Trek*, the indefatigable persistence of the fans kept it alive, even when all they had were their own conventions, stories, and artwork.

At the time of Roddenberry's death at age 70, the *Trek* phenomenon had not yet reached its peak. He had just screened the sixth *Star Trek* film prior to its anticipated release date on December 6, 1991; the 100th episode of the second series, *Star Trek: The Next Generation,* had just been shown; and a television special had just aired celebrating the 25th anniversary of the first series. At that time the first five films had grossed nearly $400 million, and the first two series were in syndication worldwide. Within another five years the third series, *Star Trek: Deep Space Nine,* and a fourth, *Star Trek: Voyager,* would also enter syndication, and a seventh film linking the first two series would be produced (see entries). Meanwhile the fans continued their fanzines, memorabilia was sold at conventions, and original novels based upon the first three *Star Trek* series were commonplace on best-seller lists.

Roddenberry's dream of becoming a writer started when he was a small asthmatic boy kept home from school and began making up stories to amuse himself. While serving as a B-17 bomber pilot in the South Pacific during World War II, he wrote poetry and stories for flying magazines. While flying for Pan Am he studied literature at Columbia University. After surviving a plane crash in the Syrian desert, he moved to Los Angeles, and began writing scripts while working in the police department. At first he sold single episodes for series, including *Goodyear Theater, The Kaiser Aluminum Hour, Dragnet, Naked City,* and *The U.S. Steel Hour.* He then became head writer for *Have Gun, Will Travel,* as well as writing a number of pilots: *Genesis II, The Questor Tapes,* and *Planet Earth.* About this time he had realized that producing his own material would allow him more creative control. He then co-wrote and produced *Spectre,* a TV movie; created and produced the series *The Lieutenant;* and produced the movie *Pretty Maids All in a Row* (1971).

Besides writing the original pilots for the classic series, and the "Bible" that specified every detail of characterizations and the *Star Trek* universe, he also became its head writer, story consultant, and story editor most of the time, whether credited or not. Maintaining creative control continued to be difficult, not only with NBC, but later with Paramount. Having created a whole universe and inspired thousands of viewers, Roddenberry then had to learn to let go, to look ahead into the promised land of future movies and television series, to mentor other creative talents who would continue the mission as he originally spelled it out: "to explore strange new worlds, to seek out new life and new civilizations, to boldly go where no man [no one] has gone before."

Bibliography

Alexander, David. *Star Trek Creator: The Authorized Biography of Gene Roddenberry.* New York: Roc, 1994.
Engel, Joel. *Gene Roddenberry: The Myth and the Man behind* Star Trek. New York: Hyperion, 1994.
Fern, Yvonne. *Gene Roddenberry: The Last Conversation.* Berkeley: U of California P, 1994.

Ann Schoonmaker

Rodeo is essentially the same today as it was in the past, though electronics are now used in communications systems, record-keeping, and time-keeping. Two professional organizations provide the framework within which national and world championships are earned. Rigidly enforced regulations govern the varied and exciting events that compose the sport.

The history of the rodeo, known at first as riding and roping contests, is nebulous. Beginning in the late 19th century, it may have originated among ranch hands to prove who was the better roper or rider, particularly at the end of long cattle drives when cowboys from various ranches wanted to let off steam. Three of several towns claiming the title for the first commercial rodeo are Prescott, AZ; North

Platte, NE; and Deer Trail, CO. Begun in 1897, the Frontier Days Celebration in Cheyenne, WY (called "the Daddy of 'Em All"), has been held annually longer than any other rodeo.

In the early days, the events were usually limited to steer-roping, team-roping, and bronc or bucking-horse riding. Sometimes wild-cow milking, a timed event, was part of the show. No time limit was placed on bronc-riding: a judge fired a gun when he thought the rider had proved his skill. Today, the five standard events are saddle-bronc riding, bareback riding, bull-riding, calf-roping, and steer-wrestling, in addition to barrel-racing for women. Steer-roping and team-roping are sometimes included, making a total of eight major events.

The big-business end of rodeo involves the producers, the sponsors, the advertisers, and peripheral industries—not the rodeo performer himself. His goal is simply to prove himself and to break a record if possible. He has relatively little work-related stress, but his physical stress while performing is incredible. His main worries are injuries and expenses on the road compared to earnings. Unlike contestants in most other sports, he must pay his own travel expenses, furnish his equipment, and pay entry fees for events. Some full-time performers enter as many as 125 or more rodeos every year.

The rodeo employs public relations experts, ticket sellers, ushers, starters, time-keepers, judges, pickup men, and clerical help such as secretaries and bookkeepers. The stock contractor provides the stock and the personnel to tend the stock. Other salaried (rather than competitive) personnel include those who supply the spectacle, such as trick riders, trick ropers, and clowns. The producer may add chuck-wagon races, cutting-horse contests, mounted square dances and drill teams, and other acts to amuse the crowd.

Rodeo contestants vary from ranch hands with little formal education to college-educated professionals, many of whom participate only on a part-time basis. African Americans, Native Americans, and women all were part of rodeos almost from their beginning. Although no rules prohibit women from entering any event, barrel-racing has been traditionally a women's event.

Rodeo cowboys may be members of either one of two professional associations: the Professional Rodeo Cowboys Association (PRCA), the more prestigious of the two, and the International Professional Rodeo Association (IPRA). The Women's Professional Rodeo Association (WPRA), an organization exclusively for women, has its own regulations and sanctions women's rodeos and events for women, even at the National Finals in Las Vegas. These three principal organizations, as well as some smaller and less familiar ones, sponsor performances to benefit various projects, especially those that aid children. Other sponsors are the U.S. military, high schools, and universities. More than 200 universities, mostly in the West and Southwest, have rodeo teams. Rodeos are also popular in Australia, Mexico, Germany, Korea, Spain, Africa, and England.

The rodeo begins with a Grand Entry ceremony, consisting of a formal welcoming parade on horseback, a flag-

bearer, and the singing of the national anthem. Judges, one on each side of the arena, score the rough stock events: bareback riding, saddle-bronc riding, and bull-riding. Each judge scores the animal and the rider separately on a point count from one to 25 for a total of 100 points. A score of 65 is good; in the 70s, very good; and in the 80s, excellent. The other events—calf-roping, steer-wrestling, steer-roping, team-roping, and barrel-racing—are timed.

Saddle-bronc riding, which stems directly from competition among ranch hands in the Old West, is called the "classic" rodeo event. Many people believe it is also the most graceful to watch when done properly. The rider must begin his ride with his spurs over the break of the horse's shoulders on the animal's first jump out of the shoot, a position termed "marking" or "spurring the horse out." The rider tries to synchronize his spurring with the horse's bucking. Ideally, he sweeps his feet from the bronc's shoulders to the back of the saddle (the "cantle") as the animal bucks; he then snaps his feet back to the horse's neck just before the bronc's front feet hit the ground. Disqualification occurs if the rider does not stay on for eight seconds, touches anything with his free hand, loses a stirrup, drops the bronc rein, or fails to "mark" the animal out of the chute. He is rescued from his bucking mount by a pickup man on horseback who rides alongside and allows the cowboy to grab hold and swing to the ground safely.

Women bronc riders were incorporated into rodeo shows from 1901 until 1941. To score, they had to stay on board eight seconds, ride one-handed, and could use two reins but could not touch the horse with the free hand or they would be disqualified. Ladies' events featured bronc-riding, trick-riding, and a relay race whereby each rider would change three horses on the run. Prairie Rose Henderson and Vera McGinnis were some of the female rodeo stars. Sometimes they gave exhibitions of other ranch skills such as roping. Lucille Mulhall earned worldwide fame and even roped a wolf at the request of none other than Teddy Roosevelt.

Bareback riding is similar to saddle-bronc riding except that the rider holds on to a single handhold and uses no stirrups or saddle. He must also spur only above the break of the horse's shoulders to score well, not allowing his feet to contact the horse's belly. The rider therefore must constantly be in a leaning-back position. He can be disqualified if he does not "mark" the horse at the beginning of the ride, if he touches anything with his free hand, or if he is bucked off during the eight-second ride. In both saddle-bronc and bareback riding, the bucking horses are so professional that some quit bucking as soon as they hear the whistle.

Bull-riding has been voted the most dangerous event in all professional sports. The rider must ride the bucking, spinning bull for eight seconds and can be disqualified if he touches anything with his free hand. Spurring, though not required, can increase the rider's point score. Clowns, known as bullfighters, work in the arena to save the rider from the bull. These clowns, sometimes called "bull bait," have nothing but their intelligence, their agility, and a barrel to protect them from the bull.

In calf-roping, the roper's mount is vitally important. The calf gets a head start; the contestant ropes the calf, dismounts, catches and flanks the calf, and ties any three of the calf's legs together, using the "pigging string" he has been holding in his teeth. The horse never takes his eyes off the calf, backing up just enough to keep the rope taut on the calf. After tying the calf, the cowboy signals the judge with his hands and remounts his horse. The roper is disqualified if, within six second, the calf kicks free. A ten-second penalty is imposed in all timed events if the rider breaks the barrier when the calf or steer is first released. The barrier, a variable length of rope depending on the size of the arena, gives the animal a head start.

In steer-wrestling (bulldogging or steer-dogging), the steer has the head start. A hazer (cowboy on horseback) assists the wrestler by keeping the steer from veering to the right. The steer-wrestler eases down the right side of the horse to grasp the steer's horns and digs in his heels to stop the animal's momentum. He must either stop the steer or change its direction before throwing the animal by lifting up on the right horn and pressing down with his left hand to twist the steer to the ground.

A "header" and a "heeler" work together in team-roping. The header is the first of the two to leave the chute, being careful not to break the barrier. The header throws his rope around the steer's head and one horn, his neck, or both horns, and then rides to the steer's left; the heeler ropes both hind legs. The header's failure to change the steer's direction before the heeler tosses his loop disqualifies both contestants. When the team-ropers face each other with both ropes taut, time is stopped.

In steer-roping, the roper must catch the steer around the horns, which are reinforced for protection. After the catch, the roper throws the slack rope over the steer's right hip and rides to the left, forcing the steer down on its side. The rider then dismounts and ties any three of the steer's legs. After the tie is complete, the steer must remain tied for six seconds.

In another timed event, women's barrel-racing, a rider races through a pattern of three barrels and returns to the starting line.

At the end of the rodeo, prizes are awarded. Prize money, apportioned among the few top winners, is made up of the cowboys' entry fees, money from the rodeo producer ("added money"), and sometimes sponsors' money from private companies. The National Finals Rodeo (NFR), held in Las Vegas since 1985, can expect to pay nearly $3 million in prize money. At the NFR the top 15 cowboys in point standings (prize money) in each event compete for championship titles. The top money so far in any one year has been in the following events in ranking order: 1) bull-riding, 2) calf-roping, 3) bareback riding, and 4) saddle-bronc riding. More than one contestant has had career earnings of more than a million dollars. In addition to championships in each event, the All-Around World's Champion is the winner of the most points during the year in at least two different events.

The timed events are timed to 1/100th of a second with electronic timers. Technology seems to have had little effect on timed events; the improvement, however, in rough stock events has been remarkable. As the stock improves, so must the athletes. Rodeo schools, conducted by former national and world champions, turn out thousands of graduates. As the stock improves, so must the athletes. Bucking machines and videos have also helped the rodeo cowboy to perfect his skills.

Peripheral businesses are profiting from the sport. Literature, art, television, movies, and museums do a thriving business on cowboy themes. The Pro Rodeo Hall of Fame and Museum of the American Cowboy on a 20-acre spread in Colorado Springs has a widely used research library.

Rodeo associations have strict rules concerning the treatment of animals and impose stiff penalties for violations. A veterinarian must be present at every association-sanctioned rodeo. Both the stock contractor and the performer have substantial investments to protect; neither is likely to mistreat the animals. Rodeo stock contractors are extremely proud of their rough stock and treat them as well as owners treat their thoroughbreds. The horses owned by the calf-ropers, steer-ropers, team-ropers, and the barrel-racers determine whether the rider wins or loses the contest or leaves the arena uninjured and alive.

Rodeo ranks with Little League Baseball as the sport most attended by family groups, and its unpampered contestants can still be heroes to young people. No reportings of "fixings" or "throwing" an event, of drugs, or of compulsive gambling have as yet tainted the sport; cheating is virtually impossible, and no rodeo cowboy charges for autographs. It is also a popular high school and collegiate competitive sport that keeps the skills of the American West alive and visible.

Bibliography

Fredriksson, Kristine. *American Rodeo: From Buffalo Bill to Big Business.* College Station: Texas A&M UP, 1985.

Johnson, Dirk. *Biting the Dust: The Wild Ride and Dark Romance of the Rodeo Cowboy and the American West.* New York: Simon & Schuster, 1994.

Lawrence, Elizabeth Atwood. *Rodeo: An Anthropologist Looks at the Wild and the Tame.* Chicago: U of Chicago P, 1984.

Le Compte, Mary Lou. *Cowgirls of the Rodeo: Pioneer Professional Athletes.* Urbana: U of Illinois P, 1993.

Tippette, Giles. "Rodeo." *Encyclopedia Americana.* Vol. 23. International ed., 1991.

Marion B. Stowell

Rodgers and Hammerstein. Probably no collaborative team has ever been as synonymous with Broadway success as has the team of Richard Rodgers (1902-1979) and Oscar Hammerstein II (1895-1960). A quick scan of the titles for which they have been responsible looks like a list of the best Broadway shows ever produced, and many lines from their music ("Oh, what a beautiful morning," "I'm gonna wash that man right out of my hair") have found their way into the vocabulary of even the most Broadway-phobic film enthusiasts.

Rodgers, a producer in addition to being a composer and librettist, originally collaborated with Lorenz Hart (see entry) beginning in 1919, an association that produced several acclaimed songs such as "Manhattan" (from *The Garrick Gaieties*), "Here in My Arms" (*Dearest Enemy*), and "My Heart Stood Still" (*Connecticut Yankee*), among others.

Rodgers and Hart took a break from stage musicals, writing for a few early Hollywood films, and then re-entered Broadway with *Jumbo* (with songs like "The Most Beautiful Girl in the World" and "Little Girl Blue"), *On Your Toes*, *Babes in Arms* (with the still-popular standards "My Funny Valentine," "The Lady Is a Tramp," "Where or When"), *Pal Joey* ("Bewitched," "I Could Write a Book"), and several other productions that were enormously popular both with audiences and critics. Besides their own productions, Rodgers and Hart continued to contribute to other musicals with a series of hit songs, including "To Keep My Love Alive" for the revised *Connecticut Yankee* in 1943, a year after Rodgers had already begun to work with Hammerstein.

Hammerstein's own early life as a lyricist included work in the 1920s with composers Rudolf Friml and Sigmund Romberg and with co-librettist and lyricist Otto Harbach; the group wrote songs for aggressive, Broadway-style operettas. In the 1930s, Hammerstein is credited with being instrumental (along with composer Jerome Kern) in developing the modern musical.

Rodgers began his association with Hammerstein in 1942, and within a year the team had produced *Oklahoma* (1943). In 1945, the duo produced *Carousel*; and in 1946, Rodgers served as the co-producer for *Annie Get Your Gun* (in which Hammerstein was not involved). *Allegro*, another Rodgers and Hammerstein production, hit the stage in 1947, after which Rodgers again served as a co-producer (without Hammerstein) for the U.S. tour of *Show Boat*.

In 1949, Rodgers and Hammerstein began a decade-long series of musicals that sealed their reputation as the best in the business, with three of the productions prompting film adaptations that are among the best-loved of all American films. *South Pacific* (1949) got the pair started, followed by 1951's *The King and I* not far behind. *Me and Juliet* (1953) and *Pipe Dream* (1955) were less popular, with *Pipe Dream* a particularly bad fit for their talents, but the team rebounded with 1958's *Flower Drum Song* and then with a fitting culmination in 1959 to their career together, *The Sound of Music*, which became one of the best-loved stage productions of all time (not to speak of the success of the film, still a yearly network TV ritual with many families).

After Hammerstein's death in 1960, Rodgers continued to work as a songwriter, including a collaboration with Stephen Sondheim on "Do I Hear a Waltz?" (1965).

Bibliography

Green, Stanley. *Encyclopedia of the Musical Theater*. New York: Dodd, 1976.

——. *The Rodgers and Hammerstein Story*. New York: Da Capo, 1963.

Mordden, Ethan. *Rodgers and Hammerstein*. New York: Abrams, 1992.

Stephen Finley

See also
American Musical Theater

Rodgers, Jimmie (1897–1933), known as "The Singing Brakeman" and "America's Blue Yodeler," is considered the "father of country music." While Rodgers was not the first to perform or record country songs, he was the first artist to make country music a commercial commodity: over 20 million of his records were sold between 1927 and 1933. Rodgers was known for his unique singing style, yodeling, and his song "The Blue Yodels." (The word yodel is taken from a German word, *Jodelin,* which means to utter the sound *Jo.*) He was born James Charles Rodgers, in Meridian, MS. The son of Aron W., an extra gang foreman, and Eliza Rodgers, who died when he was four, Rodgers grew up in a railroad environment. He was doing hard labor on the railroads by the time he was 14, and he became a brakeman by the time he was 18. His first musical success happened when he was 12, and he won an amateur singing contest at a local Meridian theater singing "Bill Bailey" and "Steamboat Bill." Rodgers spent a great deal of time learning the culture and music of the railroads. He learned traditional folk tunes, African-American blues songs, and country songs whenever he had a spare moment. He entertained the railroad workers between shifts, and thus earned the title "The Singing Brakeman."

By the time he was 15, symptoms of failing health (diagnosed as tuberculosis in 1924) appeared, and by the time he reached his early twenties, his health no longer allowed the rigors of railroad work. In 1920, he married Caroline Williamson, who supported his musical efforts until he died. He went from job to job—selling gasoline, doing restaurant work—living in poverty with his wife and child. They were penniless for weeks at a time. He even briefly took a job entertaining in a medicine show in blackface. By 1926, he started to concentrate on a musical career, and teamed up with a trio known as the Tenneva Ramblers; Rodgers later dubbed the group the Jimmie Rodgers Entertainers. Due to personal differences, the group disbanded and went their separate ways. However, in the early 1930s the Tenneva Ramblers recorded the hit "In the Pines."

Jimmie Rodgers's first break came in 1927 when his wife suggested he go to an RCA Victor audition, where he came to the attention of New Yorker Ralph Peer, of Victor Records. His first recording, the traditional lullaby "Sleep Baby, Sleep," featured his voice and an acoustic guitar. He also added his voice and guitar to the first recordings of the Carter Family song "Single Girl, Married Girl." Although "Sleep Baby, Sleep" sparked little interest, Peer was impressed enough to have Rodgers record "T for Texas" (1927), which became an instant hit in the rural South. Before Rodgers's success, record company executives did not believe that music would have commercial potential in rural areas. Rodgers's other hit songs include "Away Out on the Mountain" (1927), "Mississippi Moon" (1927), "Blue Yodel # 4: California Blues" (1928), "Train Whistle Blues" (1929), "Frankie and Johnny" (1929), "My Rough and Rowdy Ways" (1929), "Pistol Packin' Papa" (1930), and "Blue Yodel #9: Standing on the Corner" (1930), among many others. By early 1928, Rodgers's music took rural America by storm. By 1929, he was a millionaire, and he built a $40,000 house in Kerrville, TX. Although, by 1930, Rodgers's health was getting worse, he continued to tour, record, and make public appearances all across America. His prolific career ended when he was found dead in the Taft

Hotel, in New York City. He had been doing some recordings, which turned out to be his last taped sessions.

Although Rodgers wrote many original songs, he recorded and performed many traditional folk songs, and he also enlisted the help of his sister-in-law, the talented Elsie McWilliams, who wrote or co-wrote 38 songs in the Rodgers songbook. Ethnomusicologist Norm Cohen, in his introductory essay in Johnny Bond's *Recordings of Jimmie Rodgers*, points out five categories found in the 112 titles Rodgers recorded: (1) 19th-century sentimental ballads; (2) novelty songs (from vaudeville); (3) blues pieces; (4) traditional folk songs; and (5) contemporary hillbilly songs. Rodgers's musical influence continues to be observed in artists as diverse as Dwight Yoakam, Bill Monroe, Merle Haggard, and Ernest Tubb.

Rodgers became the first inductee in the Country Music Hall of Fame in 1961, and the U.S. Post Office gave him a postage stamp in 1978; he was one of the first music artists to receive a stamp. In 1986, the Rock and Roll Hall of Fame gave Rodgers an honorary induction as a "forefather" (along with his contemporary, Robert Johnson), because of his influence on the development of the blues and rock styles. Meridian, MS, occasionally holds festivals in honor of Rodgers, and maintains the Jimmie Rodgers Memorial Museum.

Bibliography

Bishop, Edward Allen. *Memorial to Jimmie Rodgers.* Marion: Alohas, 1978.

Bond, Johnny. *The Recordings of Jimmie Rodgers: An Annotated Discography.* Los Angeles: U of California P, 1978.

Greenway, John. "Jimmie Rodgers—A Folksong Catalyst." *Journal of American Folklore* July-Sept. 1957: 231-34.

Porterfield, Nolan. *Jimmie Rodgers: The Life and Times of America's Blue Yodeler.* Urbana: U of Illinois P, 1979.

Rodgers, Carrie Cecil Williamson. *My Husband, Jimmie Rodgers.* Nashville: Tubb, 1960.

Rob Weiner

Role-Playing Games are a form of interactive play that asks participants to assume the identities of pretended characters, and to act accordingly, leading to unpredictable outcomes. The most pervasive version since the early 1980s is a swords-and-sorcery fantasy context known generically as D&D—Dungeons and Dragons. The perspective and attitudes these games encourage are increasingly influential in fantasy literature and cultural concepts of the heroic.

The term "role-playing" denotes a range of "let's-pretend" activities, their practice stretching back to antiquity. The medieval European "courtly love" tradition is a role-played context. More broadly, the term applies to conflict resolution situations: psychiatric group dynamics, strategy games, and historical reenactments. To encourage active learning, teachers sometimes have students role-play persons and positions that contributed to historical events.

In the game Murder, faddish in the 1930s, party guests solved pretended crimes by role-playing the suspects. Ngaio Marsh based *A Man Lay Dead* (1934) on this concept. The board game *Clue* follows this pattern. Such games enjoyed resurgence in the 1980s (*How to Host a Murder*, etc.).

The term "role-playing game" more frequently refers to a variety of participatory fantasy activity. Inspired by the fantasy literature of J. R. R. Tolkien, Fritz Lieber, Edgar Rice Burroughs, A. Merritt, and Jack Vance, among others, a small group of role-playing enthusiasts, including Dave Arneson and Gary Gygax, codified the new fantasy role-playing game context. They created an interactive fantasy environment that allowed individuals to participate in narrative development, initially using miniatures in war-gaming scenarios. These games are boardless, requiring only pencil, paper, dice, and a willingness to imagine described situations. This anticipated the possibilities of interactive computer simulation. In 1974, their set of paperbound pamphlets officially opened the doors to the "World of Greyhawk." These included directions for creating role-playing characters, rules of play, descriptions of monsters and treasure, and various magics—these now in a heavily revised second edition. "D&D" became the trade and generic name for the earliest fantasy role-playing games.

The corporation formed from the initial game developers, TSR, counts over 6 million gamers, annually adding over 500,000 junior high and high school–aged recruits. Peripheral materials include: computer software, pre-generated scenarios (modules), fantasy fiction, fantasy art, miniature figures and paints, dice, posters, hexagonal graph paper, T-shirts, etc. Similar versions of D&D have been developed by other game producers—Iron Crown Enterprises, White Wolf, and Game Designers' Workshop—as well as by traditional game companies.

Small, informal groups of friends meet, sometimes weekly, in homes or hobby shops for party-like game campaigns. Most players are young, unmarried males, ranging from the teens through 30s, who learned to play during school or college years, according to Gary Allen Fine. They might also be Trekkies (devotees of the *Star Trek* TV series), or members of the Society for Creative Anachronism. The potential for crossover is great.

The games have burgeoned in complexity and variety. Players choose from a range of campaign genres: horror, space-opera, cyber-punk, Marvel or D.C. Comic superheroes, Teenage Mutant Ninja Turtle heroes, Westerns, Zelazny's Amber context, historical miniatures. The mainstay is still the swords and sorcery context of the original D&D games, though publishers have provided a myriad of settings for such adventure. The Role-Playing Gamers Association (RPGA) sanctions national and occasional international tournaments called "cons," short for "conventions." In 1991, 179 such events took place, involving thousands of players. The publishing groups and the RPGA jointly sponsor publications: *Dragon*, an overall gamers' magazine; *Dungeon*, a compilation of game scenarios; and the network newsletter, *Polyhedron*.

These games effectively captivate players' imaginations. Exaggerated media stories of game players who lose the ability to distinguish between reality and the game-world (Rona Jaffe, *Mazes and Monsters*, 1981; NBC's *Cruel Doubt*, 1992) have fueled the Christian fundamentalist belief that these games involve devil-worship or are otherwise blasphemous. Gamers are sensitive to this controversy; few players believe the games are dangerous or Satanic.

Bibliography

Advanced Dungeons and Dragons Players Handbook. 2d ed. Lake Geneva: Random House/TSR, 1989.

DeRenard, Lisa A., and Linda Mannik Klein. "Alienation and the Game Dungeons and Dragons." *Psychological Reports* 66 (1990): 1219-23.

Fine, Gary Allen. *Shared Fantasy: Role-Playing Games as Social Worlds.* Chicago: U of Chicago P, 1983.

Gygax, Gary. *Dungeons and Dragons Dungeon Masters Guide.* Rev. ed. Lake Geneva: Random House/TSR, 1979.

Scott D. Vander Ploeg

Roller Derby is a professional sport invented by Leo Seltzer in 1935. Teams of five men or five women roller skate around a circular banked track in a timed jam. One or two of the skaters on each team (called jammers) attempt to break away from the pack and catch and pass the other skaters to score points. A third skater (called the pivotman) can also occasionally break away from the pack, but the other two skaters (the blockers) are ineligible to score points. The men's and women's teams alternate, each of them skating two periods in each half of the match.

The sport was at the height of its popularity in the 1950s when the San Francisco Bay Bombs toured the country to appear before large crowds, and their videotaped matches were regularly shown on prime-time television throughout the country. CBS-TV televised the first roller derby match on November 29, 1948. Although the sport's official rules prohibit rough play, its spectator appeal depended on rough physical contact and even violence. In 1972, the sport was featured in *Kansas City Bomber* with Raquel Welch playing the feisty and obnoxious female roller derby star.

In 1988, Joan Weston, an immensely popular skater for the San Francisco Bay Bombers for over 30 years, founded a professional roller-derby training school. She claimed the time was right for a "roller-derby revival," citing the skill necessary to compete in the sport and decrying the violence introduced into the game by promoters. Another attempt at revival occurred in 1989 with the introduction of the television show *Rollergames*, which featured a figure eight track with obstacles such as a ski jump and an alligator pit. In 2000 there is again interest.

Bibliography

Deford, Frank. *Five Strides on the Banked Track: The Life and Times of the Roller Derby.* Boston: Little, Brown, 1971.

"Roller Derby Doyenne Does It with Class." *Modern Maturity* April-May 1988: 10.

"Roller Derby Plus Music Plus Gators: 'Rollergames.'" *Broadcasting* 3 July 1989: 31.

Robert C. Johnson

Rolling Stones, The, for over 35 years, have been known as the "World's Greatest Rock 'n' Roll Band." While the Stones have neither denied nor affirmed this title, millions of fans all over the world know them as such. Originally called the Rollin' Stones, a name taken from the Muddy Waters song "I'm a Man," the band was formed in 1962 with Mick Jagger (1943-) performing vocals, Keith Richards (1943-) on guitar, Ian Stewart (1938-1985) on keyboards, Brian Jones (1942-1969) on guitar, and Bill Wyman (1936-) on bass. Jazz drummer Charlie Watts (1941-) joined in January 1963. Jagger and Richards were childhood friends who shared a love of American blues, a love which inspired them to form their own blues-based rock 'n' roll band.

The Stones released their first full-length LP, *England's Newest Hitmakers*, in 1964; it hit No. 11 in the U.S. The album was mainly comprised of blues and rockabilly cover tunes, including a vibrant cover of Buddy Holly's "Not Fade Away." However, it also included one Jagger/Richards original composition, "Tell Me," which hit the Top 40. This song was the first of many Jagger/Richards compositions, marking the beginning of one of the most prolific songwriting teams in the history of popular culture (rivaling that of the Beatles' Lennon and McCartney, as well as that of Rodgers and Hammerstein). Stewart eventually was dropped from the official lineup of the Stones, becoming a studio/touring musician for the band for 20 years; he is sometimes referred to as the sixth Stone.

The Stones made their American television debut on the *Ed Sullivan Show* in 1964. The audience became unruly and offended Sullivan, who said the Stones would never again appear on his show; in fact, they eventually appeared several more times. Watts's tribute to the late saxophone great Charlie Parker, a book entitled *Ode to a High Flying Bird*, was also published in 1964.

In 1965, the band's fourth album, *Out of Our Heads*, reached No. 1 and its subsequent single, "Satisfaction," became the band's first No. 1 single. "Satisfaction" is considered one of the greatest rock songs ever written, and is the Rolling Stones' signature song. (*Rolling Stone* magazine named "Satisfaction" the No. 1 rock song of all time in 1988; in 2000 it was No. 1 of the Top 100 songs in a survey conducted by the cable network VH-1.)

Aftermath (1966) was the first album which contained all-original material, with the single "Paint It Black" hitting the No. 1 spot. *Aftermath* also showcased the unique musical talents of Jones, who plays sitar and dulcimer on some of the tracks. The 11-minute "Going Home" demonstrates the group's improvisational talent.

In 1967, the Rolling Stones released their first live album, *Got Live If You Want It*, taken from a 1966 performance at the Royal Albert Hall in England. When the Stones appeared on the *Ed Sullivan Show* in January 1967, they were asked to change the words of their song "Let's Spend the Night Together" to "Let's Spend Some Time Together." Also in 1967, band members Jagger, Richards, and Jones were arrested for possession of illegal substances. *Between the Buttons* (1967) launched the hits "Ruby Tuesday" and "Let's Spend the Night Together." Later, the band released a collection of outtakes and singles called *Flowers*, which included the rarity "Backstreet Girl."

The Stones released their foray into psychedelia, *Their Satanic Majesties Request*, an album with a 3-D cover, in January 1968. This album includes the lovely "She's a Rainbow" and the off-beat "In Another Land," written and sung by Wyman, which charted at No. 87.

The end of 1968 saw the release of *Beggar's Banquet*, which included the perennial concert favorites "Sympathy for the Devil" and "Street Fighting Man," a song banned by some radio stations for fear the lyrics might incite civil unrest. The band also appeared in the television show *Rock 'n' Roll Circus*, along with Jethro Tull, John Lennon, and Eric Clapton. Jones's contribution to *Beggar's Banquet* in the studio was minimal, due to his increasingly erratic behavior and heavy drug use.

The next year was marred by tragedy and controversy for the Rolling Stones. In June of 1969, Jones quit the band; a month later, he was found dead in his swimming pool. Mick Taylor (1948-), formerly of John Mayall's blues band, replaced Jones on guitar. Taylor made his debut with the band at a free concert on July 5, 1969, in Hyde Park, London, in front of 250,000 fans. This concert was dedicated to Jones's memory and filmed for television broadcast. Also in 1969, Jagger went to Australia to film his movie role in *Ned Kelly*, only one of several films in which he has appeared. A greatest hits package, released in 1969, *Through the Glass Darkly*, contains the No. 1 hits "Jumpin' Jack Flash" and "Honky Tonk Woman." In December 1969, the band, in an attempt to repeat the successful Hyde Park event, performed a free concert at the Altamont Speedway in Livermore, CA, which was marred by violence; an audience member was killed by one of the Hell's Angels motorcycle gang, several of whom had been hired as security (see Altamont). Parts of this concert were later released in the film *Gimme Shelter* (1970). *Let It Bleed* was also released in 1969; this album includes the hit "You Can't Always Get What You Want."

In 1970, *Performance*, in which Jagger plays a retired rock star, was released, as well as the Rolling Stones' live album *Get Yer Ya-Ya's Out* (taken from a 1969 concert in New York City), considered to be one of rock's greatest live albums.

The early 1970s are considered by many critics and fans to be the Stones' best and most prolific years; albums included *Sticky Fingers* (1971), the double *Exile on Main Street* (1972), *Goats Head Soup* (1973), and *It's Only Rock 'n' Roll* (1974). *Sticky Fingers* featured Andy Warhol cover art and the second-best-known Stones song, "Brown Sugar." *Goats Head Soup* included the No. 1 hit "Angie." In 1974, Mick Taylor recorded his last album with the band, *It's Only Rock 'n' Roll*, and Bill Wyman was the first member of the Stones to release a solo album, *Monkey Grip*, which charted at No. 99; Wyman would later record many other solo albums.

In 1975 the Stones announced that Ronnie Wood (1947-), a guitarist from the group Faces (which included vocalist Rod Stewart), would be Taylor's replacement. The band kicked off their U.S. tour by playing on a flat-bed truck at the Fifth Avenue Hotel in New York City in May of that year. The outtakes album *Metamorphosis* was released, containing material from the Jones and Taylor years. *Metamorphosis* also includes another rare song written by Wyman, "Downtown Suzie."

The Stones recorded *Black and Blue* in 1976, an album heavily influenced by jazz and reggae. The pop ballad "Fool to Cry" charted at No. 10. The sloppy live album *Love You Live* and the concert film *Ladies and Gentlemen the Rolling Stones*, taken from shows in the early seventies, were both released in 1977.

With 1978's *Some Girls* the Stones were again on top of the world, both live and on record. The band played to sold-out venues all around the world, and *Some Girls* hit No. 1. The original album cover showed photos of Lucille Ball, Raquel Welch, and Farrah Fawcett in mock wig ads; after threats of litigation, the cover was changed. Featuring the hits "Beast of Burden" (No. 8), "Shattered" (No. 31), and "Miss You" (No. 1), *Some Girls* again showed the band venturing into different musical avenues by combining elements of disco, country, and pop as well as rock 'n' roll.

In 1979, Richards and Wood formed the New Barbarians and toured the country. Wood also released his most successful solo album, *Gimme Some Neck*, which hit the Top 50.

The underrated *Emotional Rescue* (1980) contained a disco-flavored title track. *Tattoo You*, released in 1981, is considered by many the best Stones album recorded with Wood; it spent nine weeks at No. 1 and includes the hits "Start Me Up" (No. 2), "Waiting on a Friend" (No. 13), and "Hang Fire" (No. 20). Also during the early 1980s, the Stones played to sold-out stadiums worldwide. The band's tour document, *Still Life* (1982), highlighted their 1981 tour. Their cover of the Miracles' "Going to a Go-Go" was released as a single, hitting the Top 40.

In the mid '80s, the band took a break from touring with the release of *Undercover of the Night* (1983) and *Dirty Work* (1986), which was dedicated to the memory of Ian Stewart, who died in 1985. These albums are perhaps the worst in the Stones' career. Rumors of in-fighting (particularly between Jagger and Richards) made the Stones' future seem uncertain.

Jagger released two solo albums, *She's the Boss* (1985) and *Primitive Cool* (1987). Wyman launched his own band, Willie and the Poor Boys, which included Watts, Jimmy Page, and Ringo Starr; this band was conceived by Wyman to introduce old jazz/R&B/pop standards to a younger audience. Charlie Watts spent the mid '80s touring with his big-band jazz ensemble, the Charlie Watts Orchestra, and released several albums. Richards, reluctantly, released his solo album, *Talk Is Cheap*, in 1988. Although tension between Jagger and Richards was still high, they decided to remain with the Rolling Stones.

The late '80s and early '90s were a time of growth and change for the Rolling Stones. In early 1989, the band was inducted into the Rock and Roll Hall of Fame, and Wyman opened his restaurant, Sticky Fingers, in London. The Stones recorded their "comeback" album, *Steel Wheels*, which contained the Top 5 single "Mixed Emotions." The band embarked on what would become its most successful world tour; their 1991 tour document, *Flashpoint*, included two studio cuts, and their concert film, *At the Max*, was one of the first rock films ever recorded for the IMAX format. Also in 1991, Jagger starred in the film *Freejack*.

Wyman quit the band in 1992, making the Stones a quartet; Watts, Wood, Jagger, and Richards continued to release solo albums. Watts also released another tribute to Charlie Parker.

In 1994, the Stones recorded *Voodoo Lounge*, with session bassist Daryl Jones, and started another tour of stadiums. The album reached the No. 2 spot on the charts, and the Stones again played to sold-out stadiums, grossing over $250 million for the 1994/1995 tour. 1995's acoustic live album, *Stripped* (No. 9), includes some rarely performed gems from the band's early years.

By 1997 the Rolling Stones were in the spotlight again, with their 39th album, *Bridges to Babylon*, charting at No. 3. Those who thought the Stones were washed up or too old to rock 'n' roll were surprised by this release and subsequent tour. Critics called *Bridges to Babylon* the best Stones album since *Tattoo You* because of the sound, songwriting, and fine production. The song "Anybody Seen My Baby" became a popular adult rock single. The band again broke box office records, continuing to attract young and old alike, and toured throughout 1998. The blues tribute album *Paint It Blue* was also released in 1997. After more than 35 years, critics and fans alike agree that the Rolling Stones remain "The World's Greatest Rock 'n' Roll Band."

Bibliography

Goodall, Nigel. *Jump Up: The Rise of the Rolling Stones*. Surrey: Castle Communications, 1995.

Hector, James. *The Complete Guide to the Music of the Rolling Stones*. New York: Omnibus, 1995.

Karnbach, James, and Carol Berson. *It's Only Rock 'n' Roll: The Ultimate Guide to the Rolling Stones*. New York: Facts on File, 1997.

Rees, Dafydd, and Luke Crampton. *Encyclopedia of Rock Stars*. New York: DK, 1996.

Sanchez, Tony. *Up and Down with the Rolling Stones*. New York: Da Capo, 1996.

Wyman, Bill, and Ray Coleman. *Stone Alone: The Story of a Rock 'n' Roll Band*. New York: Da Capo, 1997.

Robert G. Weiner

Romance Series are exemplified by Harlequin romances, the most recognized series romances in popular literature. Although there are other publishers and distributors of this genre, Harlequin, which publishes exclusively romance titles, represents 80 percent of the over 190 million romances sold annually. Harlequin issues 60 new titles per month in its 12 series. Its skillful marketing of romance books in specific series has been a model for other companies, including Simon & Schuster's Silhouette imprint (eventually bought out by Harlequin), along with Dell, Jove, Zebra, Bantam, and Scholastic Books.

Harlequin began in 1949 as a Canadian reprint publisher of general works, but, by the late 1950s, its primary source of materials was the hardcover series of romances published by Mills and Boon, a British firm. In 1971, Harlequin bought out the firm, guaranteeing a stable of established writers and novels. It also hired Lawrence Heisley as president, who brought new mass-market strategies to romance sales.

Harlequin adopted distinctive covers and packaging formats for its titles, and subdivided the series according to several criteria. These include types of romance (e.g., historical, suspense, or horror [see next entry]); degree of explicit sexuality (the Harlequin Presents series is the most modest, followed by Harlequin Romances, Harlequin Special Editions, considered more "sophisticated," and Harlequin Temptations, the most explicit). Other determining characteristics are length and locale: Harlequin Superromances are set in North America; Harlequin Presents are based in Europe. Harlequin also established book clubs for each of the series, enabling the company to use direct marketing to target and develop its audience.

The breakdown of the romance readership into niches aided in the proliferation of romance series, each reflecting a new and more specific audience. Bantam's Loveswept, for example, geared its stories and heroines toward independent professionals and blue-collar workers. Jove's Second Chance at Love series shifted from young, virginal heroines to sexually mature or experienced protagonists, many of them divorced, widowed, or single parents. Avon, Dell, Harper, Jove, and Zebra all produced historical romance lines. Fawcett Coventry and Signet Books narrowed the field even more by publishing Regency romances. The young adult audience was targeted also, under such imprints as Ace's Caprice Romance line, Silhouette's First Love series, and Bantam's Sweet Dreams (see Adolescent Romance Fiction). Even Scholastic Books, long a supplier of novels to school rooms, addressed three series to the adolescent group: Wildfire, Wishing Star, and Windswept.

The development of specialized lines has allowed the genre to adapt quickly to social changes without losing its traditional readers. Plots and characters have become more complex. In the 1960s and 1970s, most romance heroines were young, sexually inexperienced, and in need of rescue. As the marketing demographics became better known, book lines adjusted to reflect the mores of their readership. Harlequin Enterprises notes that its North American consumers are women, of whom 51 percent work outside the home, 45 percent have attended some college, and 79 percent are involved in a romantic relationship with a man. The newer heroines of the more sophisticated lines reflect this increase in work experience, education, and sexuality. The heroines no longer expect to be saved, and the heroes are more likely to be asked to become their partners rather than to be gallants.

Series romances usually employ a large collective of authors who, using various pseudonyms, write for multiple series. For example, Jayne Ann Krentz writes contemporary romances for Pocket Books under her real name, but also pens historical romances for Bantam as Amanda Quick and series novels for Harlequin and Silhouette under the names Jayne Castle and Stephanie James. Many individual authors, such as Janet Dailey and Elizabeth Lowell, have developed followings prompting them to expand beyond series fiction to mainstream novels.

Publishers continue to diversify their series. Simon & Schuster and Wallaby Books initiated Serenade Romances, advertised as "the first fully-illustrated romance series in

Harlequin Presents...
CATHY WILLIAMS
a powerful attraction

Harlequin Romances. Photo courtesy of Popular Culture Library, Bowling Green State University, Bowling Green, OH.

paperback." Zebra started the Z-Talk On-line Publishing Network, a computer bulletin board where editors, readers, marketers, and authors can talk to one another. Harlequin is producing made-for-television movies based on its contemporary romance series and has sold several to CBS. New subgenres are being developed with time travel and futuristic themes, such as the Outlander series and Leisure's Lovespell imprint. A number of publishers have created ethnic series, including Zebra's Arabesque series, featuring African-American characters, and Naiad Press's line of lesbian gothic romances, such as Victoria Ramstetter's *The Marquise and the Novice*.

Romantic suspense continues to be a growing market, best exemplified by Harlequin's Intrigue and Silhouette's Shadow lines. The newest addition to the series profile is the increased use of interconnected books like trilogies, family sagas, or miniseries. Finally, capitalizing on the popularity of particular writers, Romance Alive Audios is now producing audiotapes of romance novels by Jude Devereaux, Heather Graham, Johanna Lindsay, Elizabeth Lowell, and Rosemary Rogers.

The creation of series romances has broadened the spectrum of romance fiction and enlarged the reading base of the genre. Fully 45-50 percent of mass-market paperbacks are romances, most of which are series novels. With direct marketing appeal, evolving forms and publishing venues, and a growing demand for material, there is little doubt that the revolution started by Harlequin is far from over.

Bibliography

Danforth, Natalie. "Seducing the Reader." *Publishers Weekly* 30 May 1994: 28-30.

Krentz, Jayne Ann, ed. *Dangerous Men and Adventurous Women: Romance Writers on the Appeal of the Romance*. Philadelphia: U of Pennsylvania P, 1992. 70-74.

Linden, Dana Wechsler, and Matt Rees. "I'm Hungry. But Not for Food." *Forbes* 6 July 1992: 70-74.

Radway, Janice A. *Reading the Romance: Women, Patriarchy, and Popular Literature*. Chapel Hill: U of North Carolina P, 1991.

Rubin, Hanna. "The New Office Romances." *Working Woman* 16 Aug. 1991: 60-62.

Melody M. Zajdel

Romantic Horror, a subgenre of romance novels, developed in the 1990s. These romance novels, also called paranormal romances, usually featured a hero or, less often, a heroine, who is not human. Most frequently, the hero is a vampire, at least several hundred years old, but the hero can also be a figure such as a werewolf, ghost, warlock, or mutant beast. The vampire is the most frequently used romantic hero because of the long-recognized sexuality in the Dracula figure—a sophisticated man who overwhelms the heroine with his charm. The vampire novels of Anne Rice (see entry), in which the vampires have erotically charged relationships, although no real sexual activity, also provided inspiration for the romantic horror figure, and many romance writers took their "rules" of vampire activity from Rice's books. Some romantic horror novels are derivative of fairy tales, such as "Beauty and the Beast," or classic horror stories, such as *The Phantom of the Opera*.

In the early 1990s, elements of romantic horror also began appearing in romantic mysteries, such as those published in the Harlequin Intrigue series, where such horror figures as mummies or ghosts appear as charming allies of the romantic couple and help the hero and heroine solve the mystery as well as encourage the development of the romance. By the mid-1990s, paranormal elements were used successfully in nearly all romantic novel categories, as in, for example, a story in which the heroine has extrasensory perception, or an angel watches over the romantic couple.

Bibliography

Mulvey-Roberts, Marie. *The Handbook to Gothic Literature*. New York: New York UP, 1998.

Diana C. Reep

See also
Ghost Stories
Horror Fiction
Vampire Fiction

Roseanne (1988-1997), a half-hour sitcom, immediately became a TV success, moving into and staying in the Top 10 of the Nielsen ratings. The show featured a realistic view of a working-class family (the Conners) with the central character being the mother, Roseanne, played by the standup comedian Roseanne Barr (who over the course of the show married and divorced actor Tom Arnold and is now known simply as Roseanne). Regular cast members included John Goodman (Dan Conner), Laurie Metcalf (Jackie Harris), Lecy Goranson (Becky Conner), Sara Gilbert (Darlene Conner), and Michael Fishman (D. J. Conner).

The Conners' TV household was typical of many homes in America. The kitchen table was covered with crumbs, the laundry room piled with dirty clothes, and when the living room couch was moved, it revealed the only clean section of the carpet. As with many American families, the parents quarrelled, there were conflicts with the kids, and there was seldom enough money to go around. The series was hailed for its basis in the everyday reality of working-class life, especially for women.

Roseanne tackled subjects that other TV shows stay away from. Perhaps as a debt to lesbian women who first supported Roseanne's career in comedy clubs, the show regularly featured characters who were lesbian or gay. The show also dealt openly with the sexuality of fat characters.

Despite nonstop battles over the show's focus in its first year, as well as criticism of Roseanne's obscene, loud-mouthed, male-bashing style, viewers liked the show and Roseanne and Laurie Metcalf eventually won Emmy awards as best actress and best supporting actress in a comedy series (1992-93). The last *Roseanne* aired in May of 1997; Roseanne's next project, a syndicated daytime talk show, was not a success.

Bibliography

Arnold, Roseanne. *My Lives*. New York: Ballantine, 1994.
——. *Roseanne, My Life as a Woman*. New York: Harper, 1989.
Lee, Janet. "Subversive Sitcoms: *Roseanne* as Inspiration for Feminist Resistance." *Gender, Race, and Class in Media: A Text-Reader*. Ed. Gail Dines and Jean M. Humez. Thousand Oaks: Sage, 1995.

Saundra Hybels

Rosemary's Baby (1967), the novel by Ira Levin, has enjoyed phenomenal popular success and enduring appeal, along with Roman Polanski's celebrated 1968 film. The story focuses on a pair of newlyweds whose conventional lives descend into a supernatural abyss and collapse in the wake of the husband's ambition and the wife's vulnerability. New tenants at the legendary Bramford Apartments in New York City, Guy and Rosemary Woodhouse befriend their eccentric neighbors, and Guy's acting career soars. Gradually, he forsakes the intimacy he shares with his wife for an apathy that progresses to callousness during her pregnancy with their first child, while allowing the neighbors to supervise her pregnancy through unorthodox treatments. The story is told through her perspective, which the reader is made to view as distorted. The novel's fantastic conclusion shatters this illusion. A coven of satanists, the neighbors, and their friends have orchestrated Guy's success in exchange for selling his soul and Rosemary's body to the devil. In the closing scene, Rosemary takes her place in Levin's perverted nativity as the chosen mother of Satan's son.

The novel's mix of realism and dream language sustains a tension between the natural and the supernatural, and makes the devil's entry into middle-class life both credible and appalling. *Rosemary's Baby* introduced a novel variation on the contemporary theme of the death of God; along with *The Exorcist* (1971), which followed shortly after, it propelled a new fascination with the demonic that underlies the surface of everyday life.

Bibliography

Ursini, James, and Alain Silver. *More Things Than Are Dreamt of: Masterpieces of Supernatural Horror, from Mary Shelley to Stephen King, in Literature and Film*. New York: Limelight, 1994.
Wexman, Virginia Wright. "The Trauma of Infancy in Roman Polanski's *Rosemary's Baby*." *American Horrors: Essays on the Modern American Horror Film*. Ed. Gregory A. Waller. Urbana: U of Illinois P, 1987.

Kathleen Brosnahan Fish

Rushing, Jimmy (1903-1994), influential blues stylist, was born in Oklahoma City, but he has been associated with the Kansas City blues style popularized by Count Basie's band (see Kansas City Jazz). Rushing came to fame with Walter Page's Blue Devils, moved on to Bennie Moten's Band, and stayed with it to its final transmogrification as the Count Basie Band.

From 1935 to 1948, Rushing was its featured blues shouter. Fans knew him affectionately as "Mr. Five by Five," a song that became his unofficial theme. Rushing had many hits, starting with his 1929 "Blue Devil's Blues" with Walter Page and continuing through hits such as "Sent for You Yesterday and Here You Come Today," "Your Red Wagon," "How Long Blues," and "Joe Turner's Blues," among many others. In the 1950s, he toured Europe with Benny Goodman and performed in England with his own group. He appeared on TV numerous times.

Rushing had the power of the legendary blues shouter with the ability, however, to sing any type of jazz or popular song. He benefited from legitimate classical training and, unlike many blues shouters, did not strain his voice or lose it to hoarseness as he grew older.

Bibliography

Feather, Leonard. *The Encyclopedia of Jazz*. New York: Da Capo, 1984.
——. *The New Yearbook of Jazz*. New York: Horizon, 1958.

Frank A. Salamone

Russ, Joanna (1937-), author of influential science fiction, was raised in New York City and received a B.A. in English from Cornell University and an MFA from the Yale School of Drama for playwriting and dramatic literature in 1960. Her first work, entitled "Nor Custom Stale," was published in *The Magazine of Fantasy and Science Fiction* in 1959. Russ's story lines evolved from themes of women losing at romance and men enjoying adventures to themes centered around women as central protagonists in adventures—not just in romances. Based on this idea, she created short stories and novels (often short story collections) which featured the same theme or character.

Many of Russ's works of science fiction and fantasy are now recognized as both feminist and genre classics. She is, however, uncomfortable with the term "feminist," and has suggested that, like most women in her field, she writes stories of a social scientific nature, attempting to transcend genre classification. Such works include *And Chaos Died* (1970), *The Adventures of Alyx* (1976), *The Female Man* (1975), *We Who Are About to...* (1977), and *The Two of Them* (1978). Russ won the Nebula Award for Best Short Story with "When It Changed," the basis for *The Female Man*, and the Hugo Award for Best Novella with *Souls* (1982) in 1983. Other collections include *Picnic on Paradise* (1968), *The Zanzibar Cat* (1983), and *Extra(Ordinary) People* (1984). Her most notable work of nonfiction is the study *How to Suppress Women's Writing* (1983).

Bibliography

Clute, John, and Peter Nicholls, eds. *The Encyclopedia of Science Fiction*. New York: St. Martin's, 1993.

Platt, Charles. "Profile: Joanna Russ." *Isaac Asimov's Science Fiction Magazine* March 1983.
Russ, Joanna. *The Adventures of Alyx*. London: Women's, 1983.
——. *The Female Man*. New York: Bantam, 1975.
——. "Recent Feminist Utopias." *Future Females: A Critical Anthology*. Ed. Marlene S. Barr. Bowling Green, OH: Bowling Green State U Popular P, 1981.
——. *The Zanzibar Cat*. Sauk City: Arkham, 1983.

Virginia Woods Roberts

Russell, Jane (1921-   ), famous movie star, has admitted, "To a whole generation I'm nothing but the bra lady." For 15 years she was a TV spokesperson for the Playtex Company. In these commercials she brought consumers "great news for us full-figured girls," the "cross-your-heart" bra, and the "I can't believe it's a girdle" girdle. Of course, Russell first made her name as an assertive, sexy actress in RKO films of the 1940s and 1950s.

Born Ernestine Jane Geraldine Russell in Bemidji, MN, Russell grew up in California. There she and her teenage friends attended acting schools (Max Reinhardt's Theater Workshop and Madam Ouspenskaya's School) and chased after modeling jobs and chances at stardom. Russell's acting career took off in 1939 when Howard Hughes saw her photograph and called her in for a screen test for Howard Hawks's *The Outlaw* (1943; 1946). Hughes signed Russell to a seven-year contract. During the shooting of the film, Russell was billed as the "new Jean Harlow," and with the help of Hughes's public relations people, the film went through a drawn-out campaign before it was launched. When the film was finally released, the publicity poster depicted a busty, pistol-packing Russell, lounging on a bale of hay. The caption read, "Mean, Moody, and Magnificent." Although *The Outlaw* may seem innocuous enough to today's viewers, its shots of Russell's cleavage angered censors and prompted protests from groups such as the San Francisco Legion of Decency.

Russell starred opposite Marilyn Monroe in *Gentlemen Prefer Blondes* (1953), a musical comedy that contrasted two female characters' desires for sex with their love of money; she also appeared in adventure films and Westerns. She teamed up with Bob Hope in *The Paleface* (1948) and *Son of Paleface* (1952), where Russell played Calamity Jane. She also teamed up with Robert Mitchum in *His Kind of Woman* (1951) and *Macao* (1952).

Russell's credits include *The Young Widow* (1946); *Double Dynamite* (1951); *Road to Bali, The Las Vegas Story*, and *Montana Belle* (all 1952); *The French Line* (1953); *Underwater!, The Tall Men, Foxfire*, and *Gentleman Marry Brunettes* (all 1955); *Hot Blood* and *The Revolt of Mamie Stover* (1956); *The Fuzzy Pink Nightgown* (1957); *Fate Is the Hunter* (1964); *Jonny Reno* and *Waco* (1966); *Born Losers* (1967); and *Darker Than Amber* (1970). She worked on stage and in nightclubs thereafter, including a role in the stage musical *Company* (1971). Russell also appeared in two segments of the TV series *The Yellow Rose* (1983).

Russell made a foray into fashion designing, particularly of nightgowns, caftans, and pajamas (Jane Russell Classic Evenings) for the "full-figured gal." Russell also founded WAIF (Women's Adoption International Fund), a national adoption organization that assisted American couples in adopting foreign-born infants.

Bibliography
Kobal, John. Interview. *Films and Filming* [London]. July 1984.
Parish, James Robert. *The RKO Gals*. New Rochelle, NY: Arlington, 1974.
Russell, Jane. *Jane Russell: My Path and My Detours: An Autobiography*. New York: Watts, 1985.

Devoney Looser

Ruth, Babe (1895-1948), undoubtedly America's most noteworthy and well-known baseball player, was born George Herman Ruth in Baltimore, MD. Ruth's father was a saloon-keeper and Ruth was sent to Baltimore St. Mary's industrial school because of continual stealing. Ruth became adept at sports and in 1914 Father Gilbert of St. Mary's allowed Ruth to sign with the International League Baltimore Orioles and persuaded Orioles owner-manager Jack Dunn to become young Ruth's guardian, and hence Dunn's "Babe."

That same year Ruth was sold to the Boston Red Sox and played for its farm team in Providence. In 1915, Ruth was brought up to majors and won 18 games for the Red Sox in 1915, 23 games in 1916 and pitched a 14-inning win over the Dodgers in game two of the World Series. In 1917, Babe won 24 games and pitched a league-leading 35 complete games.

The Babe gradually became an outfielder, and although he would play outfield for 19 years, he would remain as the only major league baseball player to have pitched over 1,000 innings and have a lifetime batting average over .300: .304. In the 1918 World Series, he won two games in leading the Red Sox to their last World Series win.

However, Harry Frazee, the Boston owner, was in debt and sold Ruth to the Yankees for the 1920 season for $125,000 and a $300,000 loan. Ruth promptly overwhelmed baseball fans by blasting 54 home runs while the rest of the league hit only 315. Fans flooded to ballparks to see this "Sultan of Swat," who hit 59 home runs the next season.

Ruth's hitting helped propel the Yankees to the 1921 and 1922 World Series, but the Yankees lost twice to the Giants. At this time, the Yankees shared the Polo Grounds with the Giants. John McGraw, the owner of the Giants, decided not to renew the Yankees' lease after the 1922 season. Col. Jake Ruppert purchased ten acres in the Bronx and promptly built a new ballpark to be called Yankee Stadium, but most fans would refer to it as "the House that Ruth Built." Ruth inaugurated the ballpark on April 18, 1923, by hitting the first home run in Yankee Stadium.

Ruth went on to anchor a devastating Yankee power-hitting lineup which included Lou Gehrig, Tony Lazzeri, and Bob Meusel, collectively known as "Murderer's Row." From 1926 to 1931, the Yankees led the American League in home runs and in slugging average all but one of those years. From 1926 to 1930, Ruth was the league's top home run hitter and shared the title in 1931 with Lou Gehrig. He hit 60 home runs in the 1927 season. He also led the Yankees to seven

American League titles and four World Series titles and compiled a .342 lifetime batting average.

Ruth was admired because he challenged authority and was able to garner large salaries that helped other baseball players receive more money. When told that his 1930 salary of $80,000 was larger than the president's, Ruth is said to have replied, "Why not, I had a better year than he did." His fans saw this not as an arrogant boast but as a fact.

Certainly Ruth's controversial called "shot," when he supposedly pointed to the outfield twice after taking strikes from the Cubs' Charlie Root during the 1932 World Series, added substantially to his legend. It was the fifth inning and the scored was tied 4-4. On the third pitch, Ruth knocked the ball into the centerfield seats. Ruth would tell various stories of whether or not he called the shot.

In 1933, Ruth wanted to be the Yankees manager, but was offered the Yankees top farm team instead. Upset, Ruth signed with the Boston Braves and on May 25, 1935, went out in a blaze of glory when he hit 3 home runs, including a towering fly which went over the roof of Pittsburgh's Forbes Field. Retiring a few weeks later, Babe left a legacy of 714 home runs, a lifetime batting average of .342, and a slugging average of .690.

Although he possessed many flaws and his indiscretions were often masked or ignored by friendly and accommodating sports writers, Ruth created excitement and stood for individualism in a growing society dominated by the assembly line and group-think mentality. Ruth's legend was enhanced when he sent a telegram to a sick lad, Johnny Sylvester, who lay near death after an operation the day after the second game of the 1926 World Series against the St. Louis Cardinals. Ruth pledged to hit a home run for Johnny. In game four, the Babe hit a record three round-trippers. Two years later, a well Johnny Sylvester visited Yankee Stadium as a guest of the Babe.

Such are the incidents that legends are made of, and certainly this type of person—a superstar who still had compassion and knew what heroes meant to young boys—was how Babe's legions of fans want to remember him. The American sports dream lived. He could accomplish any feat and created enduring legends. "Ruthian" became a synonym for the power of his swing and his insatiable appetite for life. He was a national celebrity and parleyed his fame into commercials, successful endorsements, personal appearances, and barnstorming tours. He utilized a publicity agent, but the greatest force in his success was his magnetic personality and his willingness and ability to give the fans what they wanted.

Ruth's single-season home-run record was broken by Roger Maris (61 homers), and in 1998, overwhelmed by Mark McGwire (St. Louis Cardinals, 70 homers) and Sammy Sosa (Chicago Cubs, 66 homers). Though these two sluggers made 1998 a memorable year, no one is likely to eclipse the long-held and long-cherished reputation of "the Babe."

Bibliography

Considine, Bob. *The Babe Ruth Story.* New York: Dutton, 1948.

Creamer, Robert W. *Babe: The Legend Come to Life.* New York: Simon & Schuster, 1974.

Smelser, Marshall. *The Life That Ruth Built.* Lincoln: U of Nebraska P, 1975.

Lawrence E. Ziewacz

Ryan's Hope (1975-1989), a daytime soap opera, was the brainchild of Claire Labine and Paul Avila Mayer, who had impressed ABC with their work on *Where the Heart Is* and *Love of Life.* When the network asked them to develop a new soap which they suggested would be called *City Hospital,* the two young writers responded with a proposal to write a story about a family who operated a tavern located across the street from a large hospital. They proposed a soap that would not only be rooted in the tradition developed by Irna Phillips (see entry) of family and tentpole characters, but one that would shatter many of the genre's conventions. Vintage *Ryan's Hope* was simply posed: old world values clashing with new world changes; strong-minded characters standing up against adversity; every adult female holding down a job ranging from barmaid to doctor; and such celebrated moments as long talks between mother and daughter and lovers dreaming of their future. Old-fashioned Johnny Ryan (Bernard Barrow) and Maeve Ryan (Helen Gallagher) struggled to understand the behaviors of their upward bound, adult children. Although mutual love and respect held the Ryan family together, viewers came to understand the essential truths created by the generation gap.

Labine and Mayer won numerous Emmys for *Ryan's Hope,* but after selling their soap to the network, left the show in 1982. Many of the old storylines were ended and the moralistic tone and the Ryan family were de-emphasized to pave the way for more contemporary storylines and younger viewers. But the ratings plunged, and although the network wooed Labine and Mayer back, much of the old magic was gone. *Ryan's Hope* was canceled on January 13, 1989.

Bibliography

Copeland, Mary Ann. *Soap Opera History.* Lincolnwood: BDD (Mallard), 1991.

LaGuardia, Robert. *Soap World.* New York: Arbor House, 1983.

Schemering, Christopher. *The Soap Opera Encyclopedia.* New York: Ballantine, 1987.

Mary Cassata

See also
Soap Opera

S

Sabatini, Rafael (1875-1950), the author of over 40 historical adventure novels, was born in Italy to an English mother and Italian father. Sabatini's fiction became popular in 1921 with the publication of *Scaramouche*, when public taste turned to fantasy adventure in the aftermath of World War I. Along with that novel, Sabatini's most notable successes include *The Sea Hawk* (1915), *Captain Blood* (1922), *Fortune's Fool* (1923), and *The Black Swan* (1932). Because of his careful research, his novels are full of colorful details of historical life.

Sabatini's writing was ideally suited to Hollywood, and several novels became successful films starring such swashbuckling actors as Ramon Novarro (*Scaramouche*, 1923); John Gilbert (*Bardelys the Magnificent*, 1926); Errol Flynn (*Captain Blood*, 1935; *The Sea Hawk*, 1940); Tyrone Power (*The Black Swan*, 1942); Louis Hayward (*Fortunes of Captain Blood*, 1950); and Stewart Granger (*Scaramouche*, 1952). In addition to novels, Sabatini wrote biographical sketches of such real-life adventurers as Sir Walter Raleigh, Joan of Arc, Richard I, and Lord Nelson.

Bibliography

Adcock, Arthur St. John. *The Glory That Was Grub Street: Impressions of Contemporary Authors.* 1928. New York: Stokes, 1993.

Lindsay, Vachel. *The Progress and Poetry of the Movies: A Second Book of Film Criticism.* Metuchen: Scarecrow, 1995.

Orel, Harold. *The Historical Novel from Scott to Sabatini: Changing Attitudes Toward a Literary Genre, 1814-1920.* New York: St. Martin's, 1995.

Voorhees, Richard J. "The Return of Sabatini." *South Atlantic Quarterly* 1979.

Diana C. Reep

Sagan, Carl (1934-1996), astronomer and science writer, was criticized by some as a showman and not a scientist because he talked about philosophical and religious issues rather than limiting himself to facts. But to ignore the breadth of human concerns, according to Sagan, would be to deny his scientific obligation to attempt an explanation of humanity's relation to the universe.

At 12, Sagan wanted to be an astronomer. Before turning 26, he earned his Ph.D. at the University of Chicago. In 1968, he became the David Duncan Professor of Astronomy and Space Sciences at Cornell University, and the director of its Laboratory of Planetary Studies. Receiving many awards for his work with NASA, he contributed to the Mariner, Viking, Voyager, and Galileo missions.

Sagan's popularity as a writer who could clearly explain scientific concepts to a general audience began with *The Cosmic Connection: An Extraterrestrial Perspective* (1973); *The Dragons of Eden: Speculations on the Evolution of Human Intelligence* (1977) won the Pulitzer Prize. He also wrote the novel *Contact* (1985), on which the 1999 movie was based, as well as *Broca's Brain: Reflections on the Romance of Science* (1979), *Nuclear Winter* (1985), and *The Demon-Haunted World: Science as a Candle in the Dark* (1996).

Targeting those who had lost interest in science and regarding his showmanship as a means of alerting society to the precariousness of life on earth, Sagan created and hosted the multimillion-dollar TV series *Cosmos* (1980). Published and televised simultaneously, the series illustrated the creativity of science, which Sagan felt was stifled by the educational system. Each of the 13 episodes focused on a particular subject or person, demonstrating the synergy of the universe. This award-winning series established Sagan as a celebrity scientist.

Bibliography

Anthony, Cait. Review of *Shadows of Forgotten Ancestors: A Search for Who We Are* by Carl Sagan and Ann Druyan. *Science News* Sept. 1993: 13.

Lessl, Thomas M. "Science and the Sacred Cosmos: The Ideological Rhetoric of Carl Sagan." *Quarterly Journal of Speech* 71 (1985): 175-87.

McCrae, Murdo William, ed. *The Literature of Science: Perspectives on Popular Scientific Writings.* Athens: U of Georgia P, 1993.

Billy Golden

St. Elsewhere (1982-1988). Scot Haller's description, "*General Hospital* as it might have been created by Woody Allen," perhaps best sums up this MTM-produced show which lasted six seasons on NBC. *St. Elsewhere* revolved around the lives of the doctors and staff who populated Boston's fictional inner-city hospital, St. Eligius.

Heralded by the critics as one of television's most innovative, provocative, and ironic shows, *St. Elsewhere* never succeeded in the ratings. And on May 25, 1988, after 137 episodes and 12 Emmys, St. Eligius closed its doors for the final time in what has become one of the most talked about series finales in television history.

St. Elsewhere launched the careers of Ed Begley, Jr., and Denzel Washington and featured actors Alfre Woodard, Sagan Lewis, France Nuyen, Christina Pickles, Jennifer Savidge, Ed Flanders, and Norman Lloyd. The show's creative talents included producers Bruce Paltrow and Mark Tinker and story editor John Tinker (the sons of Grant Tinker of *Mary Tyler Moore* fame).

Bibliography

Haller, Scot. "Good Night *St. Elsewhere.*" *People* 23 May 1988: 36-41.

Nehamas, Alexander. "Serious Watching." *South Atlantic Quarterly* 89 (1990): 157-80.

Thompson, Robert J. *Television's Second Golden Age: From Hill Street Blues to ER.* New York: Continuum, 1996.

Zehme, Bill. "*St. Elsewhere, R.I.P.*" *Rolling Stone* 2 June 1988: 35-36.

——. "Taken for Granted." *Rolling Stone* 18 June 1987: 33-36.

Roger N. Casey

Sainte-Marie, Buffy (Beverly) (1941-), is a singer-songwriter who first gained popularity as a folksinger in the mid-1960s. Her career later branched out into children's television, books, documentaries, and motion picture soundtracks and her music diversified into rock and Native American genres.

Sainte-Marie was born to Cree Indian parents near Craven, Saskatchewan, Canada. After her mother died in an accident, she was adopted as an infant and grew up in a working-class white family in Maine and Massachusetts. Sainte-Marie discovered her Native American heritage in her mid-teens and met her extended Cree family. She began singing in coffeehouses in the 1960s, and became best known for her characteristically wide and fast vocal vibrato.

Sainte-Marie's first album, *It's My Way* (1964), included the antiwar protest song "Universal Soldier." She signed away the rights to the song for $1, before it was recorded by numerous folk and popular musicians. The best-known versions of the song were by British folksinger Donovan and American Glen Campbell. Sainte-Marie eventually bought back the rights to the song for $25,000.

She also scored a hit with the song "Until It's Time for You to Go," first released on her 1965 album *Many a Mile*. The song was later a success for Neil Diamond and Elvis Presley. Other Vanguard Records album releases in the 1960s included *Little Wheel Spin* (1966), *Fire Fleet and Candlelight* (1967), and *I'm Gonna Be a Country Girl Again* (1968).

In 1970, she recorded the first album to use quadraphonic electronically synthesized vocals, *Illuminations*. It did not achieve commercial success, but it won her a new following among avant-garde artists and musicians. Her next album, *She Used to Want to Be a Ballerina*, released in 1971, featured country, rock, and blues musicians including Ry Cooder and Neil Young's backup group, Crazy Horse. The album included the song "Soldier Blue," which she wrote as the title song for the film about the civil rights battles of Native Americans. Other albums of the early 1970s included *Moon Shot* (1972), *Quiet Places* and *Native North American Child (An Odyssey)* (1973), all on Vanguard Records; *Buffy* (1974) and *Changing Woman* (1975), both on MCA Records; and *Sweet America* (1976) on ABC Records.

In 1986 Sainte-Marie completed her first book, *Nokosis and the Magic Hat*, a children's adventure set on an Indian reservation. In 1991, Sainte-Marie scored the music for a 13-part series for U.S. public radio stations, *Spirits of the Present: The Legacy from Native America*. Sainte-Marie ended her recording drought with the 1993 release of the album *Coincidence and Likely Stories* (Ensign).

Bibliography
The Best of Buffy Sainte-Marie. New York: Vanguard, 1970.
Concert Canadian: A Ten-Part Radio Documentary. 1972.

Ken Nagelberg

Sam and Dave (1961-1981) epitomized the sound of southern soul music during their four-year tenure at Stax Records. Their first two releases for Stax failed to attain commercial success, but their next 13 singles in a row were hits on the *Billboard* rhythm and blues charts. All but one of those also crossed over to a white audience via the pop charts. Other than Aretha Franklin, no other soul act in the years 1966-68 had a better track record.

Sam Moore was born October 12, 1935, in Miami, FL. Steeped in the church, Moore sang his first gospel solo at the age of nine. He sang as second tenor in a number of street-corner doo-wop ensembles and then several gospel quartets. He was offered Sam Cooke's position in the preeminent gospel quartet of the time, the Soul Stirrers, but declined the job due to a lack of confidence.

Dave Prater, Jr., also grew up singing gospel. Born May 9, 1937, in Ocilla, GA, 22 years later he made his way to Miami to join his brother's gospel group, the Sensational Hummingbirds, as the lead singer. Between 1959 and 1961, Prater and the Hummingbirds worked the southern Florida gospel circuit.

Moore and Prater met during an amateur night at the Miami nightclub the King of Hearts. Moore was the master of ceremonies at the club, while Prater was a hopeful contestant. Deciding to team up in the tradition of secular rhythm and blues duos Don and Dewey and Marvin and Johnny, Sam and Dave recorded sporadically through 1962 and 1963. At this point Jerry Wexler signed the duo to Atlantic Records and, in an ingenious and inspired move, "loaned" them to Stax Records in 1965.

It was at Stax that Sam and Dave found their métier. The group was paired with a relatively unknown and untried house songwriting team, Isaac Hayes and David Porter. With the former largely responsible for the harmony and instrumental arrangements and the latter in charge of lyrics and vocal performance, Hayes and Porter would become perhaps the finest songwriting team in the history of soul. Among their classic compositions are Sam and Dave's "Soul Man," "Hold on, I'm Comin'," "When Something Is Wrong with My Baby," "Wrap It Up," and "I'll Thank You." These songs, in essence, defined soul music in the latter half of the 1960s.

Sam and Dave's Stax material is fundamentally different from everything they had done before. Whereas Prater sang lead on the group's early efforts, Moore became the featured vocalist at Stax. A lot of the credit for the quality of Sam and Dave's Stax recordings should also be given to the Stax house band, Booker T. and the MG's and the Mar-Key horn section, augmented by Isaac Hayes.

In May 1968, Stax and Atlantic severed their distribution agreement. As Sam and Dave were always signed directly to Atlantic and "loaned" to Stax, they were forced to remain with Atlantic. Separated from the Hayes and Porter songwriting team and the Stax session musicians, Sam and Dave's chart success immediately came to an end. In June 1970, they split up for the first of many times. Both Moore and Prater released solo recordings to little acclaim. Regrouping, they made further recordings for Atlantic,

United Artists, Contempo, and Gusto Records, playing their last show together December 31, 1981.

Through the 1980s both artists pursued solo careers. On April 9, 1988, Dave Prater died in a car accident. In January 1992, Sam and Dave were inducted into the Rock and Roll Hall of Fame.

Bibliography

Bowman, Rob. Liner Notes. *Sam and Dave: An Anthology of the Stax Years: 1965-1968*. Toronto: Atlantic Records, 1990.

Guralnick, Peter. *Sweet Soul Music*. New York: Harper, 1986.

Hirshey, Gerri. *Nowhere to Run*. New York: Times, 1984.

Rob Bowman

Santana. A rousing reception at Woodstock (1969) launched a new band called Santana into fame even before the group had recorded an album. Originally the Santana Blues Band (with David Brown, Gregg Rolie, and Carlos Santana), the band's Afro-Latin style, its pulsating polyrhythmic beat, and Carlos Santana's superb guitar work became its trademark and the common themes that have kept the band (whose membership fluctuated widely), and Carlos's solo work, in the limelight.

Santana's appearance at Woodstock after three years of playing together was the group's ticket to fame. In November 1969, the group signed with Columbia and cut their self-titled debut, which made No. 1 on some industry charts and went platinum. The single "Jingo" was popular not only on FM underground and in Hispanic neighborhoods but also on the Top 40. *Abraxas* (Nov. 1970) and *Santana Three* (Jan. 1972) both stayed at No. 1 for many weeks; the former went platinum and the latter gold. Several singles from *Abraxas* made the Top 20, including "Evil Ways," "Everybody's Everything," Tito Puente's "Oye Como Va," and Peter Green's "Black Magic Woman."

During 1972-73, Rolie and percussionist Neal Schon left to form Journey, while Carlos Santana was making frequent forays away from the group to work with other artists, including some work in less Latin rhythms and more blues- and jazz-oriented material, particularly on John McLaughlin's *Love, Devotion, and Surrender* and on Buddy Miles's live album. Nevertheless, 1972's *Santana (Now)* and *Caravanserai*, the latter of which went platinum, demonstrated that the band was far from disabled; they followed with *Welcome* in late 1973, a gold effort, and *Borboletta* in 1974, two albums generally considered not to be up to their earlier standards.

The group bounced back with *Amigos* in 1977, on which Santana returned to its earlier hard-driving Latin style. Also in 1977, *Moonflower* gave the band its first Top 30 single in five years, with a remake of the Zombies' "She's Not There." *Marathon* put the group on the charts again in 1979, while 1981's acclaimed *Zebop* featured the popular single "Winning." The band recorded five more LPs in the 1980s and early 1990s, including 1987's *Freedom*, a second collaboration with Buddy Miles, while Carlos continued to record solo albums as well, notably *Blues for Salvador* (1987), with its Grammy-winning instrumental title track.

Santana's membership changed quite radically from the band's beginning. A fairly complete roster, not including peripheral sidemen, includes Brown, Rolie, and Carlos Santana (the original Santana Blues Band); Jose (Leon) Areas, Michael Carabello, Marcus Malone, and Michael Shrieve (additional late '60s members); Tom Coster, Armando Peraza, Doug Rauch, Doug Rodriguez, and Neal Schon (1973 members along with Santana, Brown, Shrieve, and Areas); Jules Broussard, Leon "Ndugu" Chancler, and Leon Patillo (1974 members with Santana, Brown, Areas, Coster, and Peraza); Graham Lear, Raul Rekow, and Pablo Tellez (1977 members with Santana, Coster, and Areas). Membership was even more fluid after 1977.

Santana staged a major comeback in 1999 with *Supernatural*, which won the Grammy for album of the year and song and record of the year for "Smooth," featuring Rob Thomas on vocals, as well as five other Grammy awards.

Bibliography

Larkin, Colin, ed. *The Guinness Encyclopedia of Popular Music*. Vol. 5. Middlesex, U.K.: Guinness, 1992.

Ouelette, Dan. "If Notes Were Oranges." *Down Beat* 58.8 (Aug. 1991): 28-29.

Stambler, Irwin. *The Encyclopedia of Pop, Rock, and Soul*. Rev. ed. New York: St. Martin's, 1989.

Stephen Finley

Satellite Dishes. Although direct broadcasting satellites (DBSs) are not generally accessible from the U.S., satellite dishes can be used to access signals being transmitted from communications satellites (see next entry). Whereas transmissions from DBSs are designed to be received by a small (18 inches), low-cost (few hundred dollars) satellite dish, interception of non-DBS signals requires a much larger (10 to 14 feet), more expensive (several thousand dollars) satellite dish. Nevertheless, the popularity of satellite dishes, also known as earth stations, is reflected in the fact that the Neiman-Marcus 1979 Christmas catalog featured on its cover a $36,000 home satellite TV station.

Because satellite transmissions are made in microwaves rather than radio waves as are used for television broadcasting, a special receiving apparatus is necessary. Also, since the waves are traveling far greater distances, the signals are much weaker than broadcast television. Although the signals travel a great distance, as long as the receiving apparatus is along the line of sight to the satellite, there will be no interference from natural or artificial features on the earth. Thus, the signal will be clearer.

A satellite dish operates in much the same fashion as a reflecting telescope. The "brightness" of the signal depends on the size of the dish; the larger the dish, the stronger the signal. Typical dishes in use in the U.S. range from 2 to 14 feet. The dish is curved so as to focus the reflected waves at the feed horn. From there, the signal is amplified, demodulated into individual channel feeds, and then modulated to the frequencies at which television receivers operate. The input of the modulated signal is usually applied to an unused VHF channel, typically channel 3 or 4, in much the same way as cable or VCR connections are made. Broadcast television is still available on the other channels using the television tuner.

Satellite dishes are popular in sparsely populated areas where television reception is poor, at best, and cable service is not available. Satellite dishes are also a popular, and often less expensive, alternative to cable. With a satellite dish, an individual (or a cable company) can intercept the downfeed from satellites. In the 1980s, the signals available included HBO, Cinemax, Showtime, The Movie Channel, Nickelodeon, USA, ESPN, CNN, CBN, C-SPAN, WGN (Chicago), WTBS (Atlanta), WOR (New York), some ABC programming, NBC, and Reuters News Service, from RCA's Satcoms; HBO, Cinemax, Bravo, and live Las Vegas shows from AT&T and GTE's Com-stars; and ABC, CBS, PBS, and CNN from Western Union's Westar.

Initially, courts took the position that the interception of satellite TV signals was a copyright infringement. Even so, most companies did not charge individuals with satellite dishes for intercepting their programming. Those companies which did assess charges relied primarily on self-reporting by the individuals. When a sufficiently large group of individuals banded together to erect a single dish, however, they were designated a cable company and required to pay royalties. Similarly, commercial establishments with satellite dishes, such as Holiday Inns and even some neighborhood bars, were required to pay royalties.

However, in October 1984, President Reagan signed legislation legalizing private reception of unscrambled satellite transmissions. Thereafter, in January 1986, HBO became the first programmer to scramble its satellite transmissions. As other programmers adopted scrambling, the choices available from satellite transmissions diminished significantly, forcing vendors of satellite dishes to make arrangements with TV programmers to include descramblers.

Bibliography

Curtis, A. R. *Space Almanac*. Woodsboro: Arcsoft, 1990.
Traister, R. J. *Build a Personal Earth Station for Worldwide Satellite TV Reception*. Blue Ridge Summit: TAB, 1982.

Claire Koegler

Satellite Transmission. The launch of Sputnik 1 on the night of October 4, 1957, propelled the world into the space age. The U.S.'s first satellite, Explorer 1, was launched January 31, 1958. In December of that year, the Score satellite was launched and broadcast a pre-recorded message from President Eisenhower, foreshadowing the advent of communications satellites, which are now a vital part of electronic communications.

A communications satellite is an artificial satellite used to relay electronically encoded communications services over long distances. Satellite transmissions are made in microwaves (at frequencies of a billion hertz [gigahertz, GHz]), rather than radio waves (at megaHertz [MHz] frequencies) as are used for commercial television broadcasting. Because microwaves follow "line of sight," the communications satellite must be "visible" from both the transmitting and the receiving stations. An active communications satellite receives microwave signals aimed at it from an earth station, then amplifies and retransmits the signals to other earth stations. A passive communications satellite carries no electronic equipment; rather, signals are reflected off its surface.

A satellite having a nearly circular orbit centered at the earth's center and an orbital period of one day, so that it remains at the same longitude relative to the earth's surface, is called geosynchronous. The radius of such an orbit is approximately 26,000 miles (or about 22,400 miles above the earth's surface). "Geostationary" is descriptive of a geosynchronous satellite whose orbit lies over the equator, so that it remains not only at the same longitude but also at the same latitude relative to the earth's surface. All communications satellites launched since 1963, except the Soviet Union's Molniya series, have been of the geosynchronous type. Those currently active are all geostationary.

The first communications satellite was Echo 1, launched by NASA on August 12, 1960. Echo 1 was a passive satellite, made up of a 100-foot Mylar balloon in an elliptical (noncircular) orbit. Shortly thereafter, on October 4, 1960, Courier 1B was launched and carried the first store-and-forward electronic bulletin board in space.

The first active communications satellite was Telstar 1, launched by NASA on July 10, 1962. Telstar 1 was an experimental communications satellite owned by AT&T, which relayed to England the first live transatlantic television transmission, namely a fluttering American flag outside the transmitting station at Andover, Maine. Two weeks later, Telstar began carrying more panoramic telecasts between the U.S. and Europe, thus demonstrating the feasibility of such transoceanic transmissions. Because of its highly elliptical orbit, transmission times were extremely limited. Telstar inspired a song of the same name by the Tornadoes, who became the first British group to have a No. 1 hit in the U.S.

December 13, 1962, saw the launch of Relay 1, the first real-time active communications satellite. Relay 1, which was owned by RCA (which then owned NBC), had one television channel and 12 telephone channels.

The first attempt at a synchronous communication satellite was Syncom 1, launched by the U.S. in 1963; however, the electronics failed. Syncom 2, launched in 1963, was the first successful synchronous satellite. It was used among other things to broadcast the 1964 Olympics from Japan to the U.S. It was followed on August 19, 1964, by Syncom 3, the second successful synchronous satellite.

On April 6, 1965, the International Telecommunications Satellite Organization (INTELSAT), launched Intelsat 1, better known as Early Bird, the world's first commercial communications satellite. It was also a synchronous communications satellite, stationed over the Atlantic Ocean. Early Bird went into regular service on June 10, 1965, providing 240 telephone circuits or one television channel. For the first time, live commercial television across an ocean was possible. In the ensuing years, numerous Intelsats have been launched; at present, more than 20 are in active use. Access to the Intelsats in the U.S. is controlled by COMSAT, the Communications Satellite Corporation, created in 1963 pursuant to the Communications Satellite Act of August 31,

1962. COMSAT offers news, sports, and entertainment television, business television, electronic news-gathering, and distribution services between the U.S. and 185 other countries.

WESTAR comprises a series of domestic (nongovernment) communications satellites launched by Western Union for communications within the U.S. Westar 1 was launched in April 1974, followed by Westar 2 in October 1974.

RCA SATCOM is a series of domestic geostationary satellites launched by RCA beginning in 1975. Satcom 1 was launched in December 1975 and became the primary satellite for cable-TV services. Satcom 2 was launched in March 1976 and was used primarily for commercial television and other communications. Satcom 3 was launched in the fall of 1979 but was lost in space. Other Satcoms followed. When General Electric purchased RCA (and NBC), this series of satellites was renamed GE AMERICOM. There are currently six Satcoms in active use serving cable TV programmers, TV broadcasters, syndicated broadcasters, wire services, radio nets, and occasionally international users.

In addition to COMSAT and GE, the major satellite owners and operators for the U.S. are AT&T, GTE, and Hughes Communications. AT&T continues to own and operate three Telstar satellites, as well as providing services through the GE satellites. Unfortunately, an AT&T Telstar satellite went astray shortly after launch in September 1994 and was irretrievably lost in space. GTE owns and operates three Spacenet, four GStar, and one ASC satellite, providing broadcast TV, cable TV, satellite news gathering, and other telecommunications services. Hughes owns and operates seven Galaxy and two SBS satellites, providing cable, television, and radio distribution, satellite news gathering, videoconferencing, and medium-power direct-to-home TV systems.

Satellite communications can be divided into three types: relay (point-to-point communications between fixed locations), distribution (transmission of program materials from earth terminals to local broadcast studios), and broadcasting (transmission of program materials for reception by individual or master receiving stations).

Direct broadcasting satellites (DBSs) transmit broadcast quality signals from a satellite directly to home antennas, eliminating the TV station or the cable system as an intermediary. Initially used in Canada and Japan as a means of reaching remote rural areas that could not otherwise receive TV service, DBS now delivers programming to hundreds of thousands of viewers in the United Kingdom, Europe, and Japan, including HDTV (high definition television) in Japan. DBS is a source of concern to the U.S. broadcasting lobby because it could obviate the need for TV stations and pose serious competition for cable systems.

Over the decades, satellite television communications have made the world smaller by bringing faraway places, people, and events into the American home. In the 1960s, the Vietnam War was standard fare on the evening news and an accompaniment to many Americans' dinner. War became less glorious and less honorable, and those appalled by it became more vociferous in their opposition. Since then, the American people have had a front-row view of other conflicts around the world, as well as famine, natural disasters, and man-made catastrophes. But they have seen the good as well, including the first man to walk on the moon, joint space ventures among nations, nations uniting in sports, such as the Olympics and the Goodwill Games, and nations uniting in other ways, most notably, the demise of the Berlin Wall.

Bibliography

Broadcasting & Cable Yearbook, 1994, 2000. New Providence: Bowker, 1994, 2000.

Brown, L. *Encyclopedia of Television.* 3d ed. Detroit: Visible Ink, 1992.

Curtis, A. R. *Space Almanac.* Woodsboro: Arcsoft, 1990.

Steinberg, C. S. *The Communicative Arts: An Introduction to Mass Media.* New York: Hastings, 1970.

Claire Koegler

Saturday Evening Post, The (1897-1969), published by the Curtis Publishing Company, was a mass-circulation magazine for a middle-class American audience. At its inception, the *Post*'s target audience was men, an attempt to duplicate the success of Curtis's *Ladies' Home Journal* as a periodical for women. However, men did not respond to the *Post* as women had to the *Journal,* so it was broadened to target women as well. This strategy succeeded, and by 1910, the *Saturday Evening Post* had become a family magazine. The success of the *Post* and the *Journal* came about partly because more educational opportunities had become available to women by the mid-19th century, thus increasing both the readership and consumer base in the country.

The magazine came into being in 1897 when Cyrus H. K. Curtis paid $1000 for a failing weekly newspaper in Philadelphia. It had a circulation of only 2,000 and was also called the *Saturday Evening Post.* The *Post*'s beginnings were thought to have had origins in Benjamin Franklin's *Pennsylvania Gazette,* which began in 1728. However, the only connection to Franklin's *Gazette* was that the newspaper Curtis bought was doing business in the same building from which Franklin published the *Gazette* (and sold before the Revolution). However weak the connection, the image of Franklin's face became an identifying logo for the magazine.

In the early years, the *Post* refrained from publishing political opinions. However, because of the work of staff writers Maude Radford Warren and Adelaide Neall, the *Post* began taking a positive role in urging women's suffrage in 1909, the same year both were hired at the magazine and political issues gained visibility. This was quite a turnaround from the earlier conservative view held by the *Post.* In the past, the publication had perpetuated the nostalgic ideal of woman as homemaker, wife, and mother, but not as political activist.

By the early 1920s, the *Post* outsold all other American magazines in advertising revenues and became the most financially successful magazine in the United States. The *Post* was the right publication at the right time because more people in the U.S. than ever before were readers. This fact was largely the result of women being given better educational opportunities than ever before. The middle class was also growing and with it their status as consumers gave them power. There was also a move toward national advertising and a national magazine like the *Post* could serve big business in this way.

Another important reason for its continued success and growing circulation was the reputation the *Post* had gained by offering quality fiction and nonfiction stories and articles. To do this, the magazine published stories and serialized novels by some of the greatest living writers of the day like Joel Chandler Harris and Rudyard Kipling.

Middle-class America fell in love with the *Post* covers. Those done by illustrator/artist Norman Rockwell (see entry) became a trademark of the magazine. His nostalgic scenes captured the best in the everyday lives of most Americans. Other famous illustrators of *Post* covers were J. C. Leyendecker, Harrison Fisher, Robert Robinson, Philip Boileau, Clarence Underwood, Sarah Stilwell Webber, and John Falter.

The late 1950s and early 1960s saw fewer advertising dollars coming to the magazine because companies spent their advertising budgets on television. The *Saturday Evening Post* was finally forced to stop the presses in 1969 after nearly three-quarters of a century of publication.

Bibliography

Cohen, Jan. *Creating America*. Pittsburgh: U of Pittsburgh P, 1989.

Damon-Moore, Helen. *Magazines for the Millions*. Albany: State U of New York P, 1994.

Friedrich, Otto. *Decline and Fall*. New York: Harper & Row, 1969.

Goulden, Joseph C. *The Curtis Caper*. New York: Putnam's, 1965.

Janet Kilbride

Saturday Night Fever (1976) became the quintessential dance movie of the 1970s. The movie introduced mainstream America to the dance moves and sounds of disco.

This trend-setting movie took relatively unknown actor John Travolta and sent him into fame. The movie centers on Travolta's character Tony and his friends (who are in their late teens) and the disco/dance world they inhabit. Tony Manero is a cocky, boyish 19-year-old who has a talent for dancing and seems to be searching for a vocation and an understanding of the chaotic world around him. Brought up in a strict, Roman Catholic family in Brooklyn, he finds little help or understanding from his violent-tempered father or his passive mother. His job as a paint store clerk also offers little hope other than a humdrum (but eminently secure) future. He seeks understanding on the dance floor at a local club called 2001.

Tony moves from boyish antics to near criminality when he nearly rapes his dance partner Stephanie MacDonald (Karen Lynn Gorney). This event begins an evening that ends in a gang rape of Tony's on-again, off-again girlfriend Annette (Donna Pescow) by two of his friends; and the suicide of a despondent youth, Bobby (Barry Miller). This night in which the glitz of the disco world falls to shambles leads Tony to confront himself and his seemingly pointless direction in life, finally coming to understand that women are more than virgins or whores and can also be friends. The movie ends with Tony seeking friendship and understanding from Stephanie, and resolving to move away from dead-end Brooklyn to attempt a career in New York.

The soundtrack, released in 1977, catapulted the relatively successful group the Bee Gees (see entry) to international stardom with hits like "How Deep Is Your Love?" "Stayin' Alive," and "Night Fever." Also Yvonne Elliman, formerly Mary in Andrew Lloyd Webber's *Jesus Christ Superstar*, found herself with a megahit in "If I Can't Have You." Disco classics "Disco Inferno" by the Trammps, "More Than a Woman" by the Tavares, and "Beethoven's Fifth" also charted from the soundtrack.

The movie ushered in the leisure suit and gold chains that characterized the high-tech glitz of the later 1970s. It also introduced disco dancing—a phenomenon perhaps closest in form and style to modern country line dancing—to the mainstream audience. The stylish, sophisticated, incredibly polished performance of the disco dance became the rage.

Staying Alive (1983), the sequel to *Saturday Night Fever*, followed seven years later, but was unsuccessful. With only Tony and his mother (Julie Bovasso) returning for the second movie, the storyline follows Tony's dance career, which eventually leads to Broadway. His life becomes enmeshed between singer/dancer Jackie (Cynthia Rhodes) and Broadway dance star Laura (Finola Hughes). The movie climaxes on the stage of *Satan's Alley*, where Tony works out his sense of self-pride and finds fulfillment once more. The love triangle is left unresolved by the end of the movie, though Tony has rediscovered his male pride as he struts off to the classic Bee Gees song "Stayin' Alive."

Bibliography

Denisoff, R. Serge, and William D. Romanowski. *Risky Business: Rock in Film*. New Brunswick: Transaction, 1991.

Mark K. Fulk

Saturday Night Live (1975-   ) is one of the longest-running programs currently on the air. Created and produced by Lorne Michaels, *Saturday Night Live* originates in New York City and is the only network variety program that is broadcast live each week. The comedy show features special guest hosts and musical talent from the day's biggest names. The set has become famous as a starting place for top comedians such as Dan Aykroyd (1975-79), Chevy Chase (1975-76), Jane Curtin (1975-80), Bill Murray (1977-80), Eddie Murphy (1980-84), and Dana Carvey (1986-92).

In the show's first decade some memorable sketches emerged with recurring characters. Among them were John Belushi's ancient Japanese Samurai living in the modern world, Mr. Bill, a happy hand puppet who always seemed to land in disaster, and Dan Aykroyd and Jane Curtin's Coneheads, alien visitors from the planet Remulak who had huge cone-shaped heads and practiced bizarre customs from their home world.

The second decade of *Saturday Night Live* brought with it such classic characters as Eddie Murphy's Buckwheat and Velvet Jones. Buckwheat was supposed to be the adult version of the Little Rascals star setting off on a new singing career despite his speech impediment, while Velvet Jones was a sleazy salesman who peddled books with titles like *I Wanna Be a Ho.* Dana Carvey achieved fame with his uptight Church Lady character, who made the saying "Well isn't that special" a nationwide fad. And Julia Sweeney played Pat, a hermaphroditic character whose sex was always a matter of controversy. Some of these sketches like Wayne's World and the Coneheads became so popular that they were made into movies released in theaters.

Despite ups and downs in the ratings after the first decade, the show continues to revitalize itself with cast changes and attracting the hottest guest hosts and musical guests.

Bibliography
Cader, Michael, ed. Saturday Night Live: *The First Twenty Years.* Boston: Cader, 1994.
Dunn, Nora. *Nobody's Rib: Pat Stevens, Liz Sweeney, Babette, and Some Other Women You Know.* New York: HarperPerennial, 1991.
Hill, Doug, and Jeff Weingrad. *Saturday Night: A Backstage History of* Saturday Night Live. New York: Beach Tree, 1986.
Schuster, Hal. *SNL! The World of* Saturday Night Live. Las Vegas: Pioneer, 1992.

Daniel P. Agatino

Sawyer Brown (1981-   ), an energetic country-rock band with a good track record of country and western hits, was catapulted into stardom by television's *Star Search.* The band gradually emerged from the shadow of its cheesy beginnings and remains a successful country music act.

Originally called Savannah, the five-member Nashville group consisted of lead vocalist and principal songwriter Mark Miller (usually sporting a Panama hat), lead guitarist Bobby Randall, keyboardist Gregg "Hobie" Hubbard, bass guitarist Jim Scholten, and drummer Joe Smyth. Even though several record companies turned down their early demo tapes, they enjoyed constant bookings because of their engaging, high-energy performances. In 1983 on *Star Search,* week after week they beat out competing amateur rock, pop, R&B, and country bands. In February of 1984 the group won the title "Best Musical Group of the Year" and the grand prize of $100,000.

After their *Star Search* success, they signed with Capitol/EMI through the Curb Records label and recorded their first album, *Sawyer Brown.* They capped their early success by winning the Country Music Association's 1985 Horizon Award, an honor that indicated genuine professionalism.

Sawyer Brown released a regular series of albums in the following years. *Shakin'* (1985) enjoyed Top 20 chart success, and the video for a modest hit, "Betty's Bein' Bad," featured a cameo by *Today Show* weatherman Willard Scott. But subsequent efforts—*Out Goin' Cattin'* (1986), *Somewhere in the Night* (1987), *Wide Open* (1988), *Race Is On* (1989), *The Boys Are Back* (1989), and the premature *Sawyer Brown Greatest Hits* (1990)—marked a long, low period for the group. In 1991, guitarist Duncan Cameron replaced Bobby Randall.

In 1991, Sawyer Brown at last saw one of their songs climb into the Top 10. Released on their album *Buick* (1991) and then again on *The Dirt Road* (1992), "The Walk" reached the No. 2 slot. The title track from *The Dirt Road* soon followed to the No. 3 position. And seven years after their first No. 1 hit, "Some Girls Do" ascended to the top of the charts in May of 1992. The title track to the band's next album, *Cafe on the Corner,* a song bemoaning the plight of the American farmer, also went to No. 1. This achievement gave Sawyer Brown four consecutive Top 5 singles in 1992 after seven relatively dry years. To top off the successful year, country music fans voted Sawyer Brown as the top vocal band of 1992 for the TNN/Music City News Award. "All These Years," another single from *Cafe on the Corner,* became a No. 1 hit in early 1993, and a sixth single, "Trouble on the Line," landed in the Top 5 in June. In August 1993, the group released *Outskirts of Town,* recorded at Alabama's legendary Muscle Shoals.

Having built a loyal following with their significant chart success, the band continues to record: *This Thing Called Wantin'* and *Havin' It All* (1995), *Six Days on the Road* and a Christmas album (1997), and *Drive Me Wild* (1999).

Bibliography
Cronin, Peter. "Sawyer Brown on the 'Outskirts'?" *Billboard* 7 Aug. 1993: 23, 28.
Kirby, Kip. "Nashville Scene." *Billboard* 25 May 1985: 52.
——. "Nashville Scene: Sawyer Brown's Success Story." *Billboard* 14 July 1984: 50-51.
——. "Sawyer Brown: 'Star Search' to Stardom." *Billboard* 14 Dec. 1985: 42, 47.
Morris, Edward. "The Long Road to Success Is Paying Off for Sawyer Brown." *Billboard* 23 May 1992: 28.
"'Star Search' Is Good to Sawyer Brown." *Billboard* 16 Feb. 1985: 51.

Jason Holz
Michael Delahoyde

Scarry, Richard McClure (1919-1994), children's author and illustrator, was born and raised in Boston. He attended the Boston School of the Museum of Fine Arts, designed graphics for five years for the army, and free-lanced in New York City before his extremely successful *Richard Scarry's Best Word Book Ever* was published in 1963. The upbeat, energetic style of the book wooed a wide audience of children and adults that continues to make Scarry a top seller.

The sprightly and contented world that Scarry created through his humanized animals and bright, primary colors attracts children immediately. Reappearing characters like Lowly Worm, Sergeant Murphy, Mr. Paint Pig, and Huckle Cat, embroiled in outrageous adventures, show children the nuts and bolts of everyday life. Action abounds in Scarry's illustrations, and dense pages teeming with multiple scenes and objects merged imaginatively into each other (like banana-mobiles or swimming pool trucks) are characteristic of his work.

Scarry's prolific corpus, over 250 books, also includes *Richard Scarry's Great Steamboat Mystery,* for which he received an Edgar nomination in 1976. He used animals to portray his scenes because, he said, "Children can identify more closely with pictures of animals than they can with pictures of another child." His death was mourned by readers worldwide.

Bibliography

Lanes, Selma G. *Down the Rabbit Hole: Adventures and Misadventures in the Realm of Children's Literature.* New York: Atheneum, 1971.

Lemontt, Bobbie. "Richard Scarry." *Dictionary of Literary Biography* 61. Detroit: Gale Research, 1987.

Wintle, Justin, and Emma Fisher. *The Pied Pipers: Interviews with Influential Creators of Children's Literature.* New York: Paddington, 1974.

Mary E. Beardsley Land

Schwarzenegger, Arnold (1947-), actor, was born in Graz, Austria, and educated at the University of Wisconsin-Superior, with a B.A. in business and international economics. He was Junior Mr. Europe in 1968, five times Mr. World and Mr. Universe, and seven times Mr. Olympia (see Bodybuilding). He retired undefeated in 1980 and had his screen debut under the name Arnold Strong in *Hercules Goes to New York* (1970), then as one of the hoods whom Mark Rydell forces to strip in *The Long Goodbye* (1973). After these brief demonstrations of male exhibitionism, the star reverted to his real surname and appeared as bodybuilder Joe Santo in Bob Rafelson's *Stay Hungry* (1976) and as himself in George Butler's documentary *Pumping Iron* (1977).

After attempting an offbeat cartoon character role in *The Villain* (1979), he achieved initial stardom in John Milius's *Conan the Barbarian* (1982), a role repeated in *Conan the Destroyer* (1984) and (indirectly) in *Red Sonja* (1985). In these films Schwarzenegger perfected the excessive component within his star image, appearing as a larger than life figure corresponding to equally excessive changes within American culture during the early years of the Reagan era. In *The Terminator* (1984), Schwarzenegger not only made his acting limitations a virtue by deliberately choosing the title role but also displayed a "hard-bodied masculinity" peculiar to the Reagan era (see Jeffords). He continued this image of hard-boiled machoism in *Commando* (1985) and *Raw Deal* (1986).

However, both *Twins* (1988) and *Kindergarten Cop* (1990) represented a "kinder, gentler" version of Arnold paralleling George Bush's redefinition of the American ideal. Also *Terminator 2: Judgment Day* (1991) changed the original image of a threatening robotic hero into its opposite. The Terminator now became the ideal husband and family man finally sacrificing himself for the good of humanity. But while the public was prepared to accept Schwarzenegger as a non-threatening Twin or Kindergarten Cop, they refused to accept the star's extreme redefinition of his status as the pregnant man of *Junior* (1995) nor as a self-reflexive postmodernist star hinting to his audience that his whole image was a joke, as in *The Last Action Hero* (1993).

More successful was the combination of action and romance in *True Lies* (1994) and *Eraser* (1996). Schwarze-

negger played the villain Mr. Freeze in 1997's *Batman & Robin*; his two most recent films are in the futuristic mold: *End of Days* (1999) and *The Sixth Day* (2000).

Married to newswoman Maria Shriver since 1986, Schwarzenegger has applied his enthusiasm for fitness to charitable causes: Special Olympics, founded by Shriver's mother, and Inner-City Games. He was also chair of the President's Council on Physical Fitness (1980-93). The couple has four children.

As a contemporary star, Schwarzenegger attempts the difficult project of combining masculinity with elements of vulnerability so that his bodybuilding image does not inhibit serious audience reception. The opening scenes of *Commando* show him as a tolerant father, while *The Running Man* (1987), *Predator* (1987), and *Total Recall* (1990) attempt this project in different ways. Like all stars, Schwarzenegger faces a difficult task in constantly redefining his image in view of changes in society. He cannot appear too masculine (*Conan*) or too self-consciously aware of the manipulative nature of his image (*The Last Action Hero*). Perhaps the star deserves better recognition for his self-awareness than most surveys of his career recognize.

Bibliography

Flynn, John L. *The Films of Arnold Schwarzenegger.* Secaucus: Carol, 1993.

Jeffords, Susan. *Hard Bodies: Hollywood Masculinity in the Reagan Era.* New Brunswick: Rutgers UP, 1994.

Lipsyte, Robert. *Arnold Schwarzenegger: Hercules in America.* New York: HarperCollins, 1993.

Tony Williams

Science Fiction, like most of today's popular literary genres, has its origins in ancient mythology, offering explanations for issues of life and death, cosmology, and humanity's place in the universe. Like all "fictions," science fiction has a basis in a fantastic yet socially constructed reality. Depending on the enthusiast or scholar, the parameters of science fiction vary. Some, like Hugo Gernsback (1884-1967), believe that true science fiction is grounded in "scientific fact," that it must be an extension of the products of known physical sciences. Others have had no problem claiming that abstract fantasies and speculations are also part of the genre.

The single best survey of the history of science fiction is probably the four-volume *The Road to Science Fiction*, edited by James Gunn. Modern-day science fiction originated in selected writings of Mary Wollstonecraft Shelley (1797-1849), Edgar Allan Poe (1809-49), Jules Verne (1828-1905), and H. G. Wells (1866-1946), among others. In American dime novels of the late 19th century, a popular science fiction series was *The Frank Reade Library*. Stories of Frank Reade combined traditions of the frontier and Western dime novels with technological innovations like steam power. Hence, in the adventures of Frank Reade there are steam-driven mechanical horses and more. In the dime novels, these stories were supplemented by novels that were reality-based fantasy about the life and works of Thomas Edison. Many of the story conventions developed in *The*

February 1956 · 35 Cents

Astounding SCIENCE FICTION

Y'S IMPERIAL
PRESENTS
THE GREAT
LORENZO
IN
"AQUON
FORLA"

WEEK ONL
STARTING
RIDAY

BUILD W
BONF

Double Star
BY ROBERT A. HEINLEIN

Photo courtesy of Popular Culture Library, Bowling Green State University, Bowling Green, OH.

Frank Reade Library became the basis for Edward Stratemeyer's young adult fiction series, *Tom Swift*, begun in 1910. The American pulp magazine in its heyday from the teens to the forties became the forum for a wide, colorful range of popular literary genres, including science fiction. Hugo Gernsback's early pulp magazines such as the landmark *Amazing Stories* became the homes of reprints by the masters (such as Poe, Verne, and Wells) and embraced new, science-based fiction. In fact, after several manifestations and variations like "scientifiction," the term "science fiction" originated in the pages of Gernsback's early publications. In 1912, the same year that he introduced the world to Tarzan of the Apes, Edgar Rice Burroughs also presented John Carter of Mars for the first time. The John Carter series is an interesting and important blend of dime novel westerns and pulp magazine space opera/science fantasy. Probably the most prestigious science fiction pulp magazine was *Astounding Science Fiction*, which began in 1937 and was edited by John W. Campbell. In the pages of the pulp magazines, newly emerging science fiction authors flourished, such as Robert Heinlein (1907-1988), Robert Bloch (1917-1994), Isaac Asimov (1920-1992), Ray Bradbury (1920-), and Philip K. Dick (1928-1982). Two very influential and popular women writers of science fiction of this time period were Catherine L. Moore (1911-1987) and Leigh Brackett (1915-1978). As the 20th century unfolded, an array of very talented women science fiction authors emerged, including

Ursula K. LeGuin (1929-), Marion Zimmer Bradley (1930-1999), and Joanna Russ (1937-) (see entries).

Since the days of Gernsback, science fiction has taken a variety of directions: science fiction has merged with dark fantasy and horror stories; it has also merged with detective fiction. It has featured subgenres and formulas including space opera, heroic fantasy, hard science fiction (with an emphasis on scientific fact), lost world stories, alternate universe stories, cyberpunk, and more.

In the late 1960s, when the Western story in the popular media of television and motion pictures was becoming increasingly conventional and predictable, and when, in real life, the frontier had shifted from the great West to outer space, the science fiction story arrived to replace the Western story. Today, science fiction is continued by the old masters and is promised a future by new, talented authors.

Bibliography

Aldiss, Brian. *Trillion-Year Spree: The History of Science Fiction*. New York: Atheneum, 1986.

Ash, Brian, ed. *Who's Who in Science Fiction*. New York: Taplinger, 1976.

Bleiler, E. F., ed. *The Frank Reade Library*. Vols. 1-10. New York: Garland, 1979.

Clute, John, and Peter Nicholls, eds. *The Encyclopedia of Science Fiction*. New York: St. Martin's, 1993.

Gunn, James. *The Road to Science Fiction #1: From Gilgamesh to Wells*. New York: New American Library, 1977.

Garyn G. Roberts

Science Fiction Film did not emerge as a distinctive American genre until the 1950s, which produced a large number of narrative features recognized by filmmakers, audiences, and critics alike as speculatively mapping the future (or lack of it) of a postwar world transformed forever by postindustrial technology and new forms of energy and communication.

Science fiction film's first golden age (1950-60) had its origins in the popular culture of earlier decades. In the mid-1930s, the first American science fiction films appeared—most in a serialized form that owed more to comic strips and the lurid covers of pulp science fiction than to the serious exploration of possible futures and alternate worlds found in the growing body of American science fiction literature. Indeed, throughout the 1930s and '40s, there were few science fiction features and, other than a rather loony wedding of utopian science fiction with romantic comedy in *Just Imagine* (1930), most of them figured the dire consequences of scientific inquiry and technological invention. Subsumed within the recognized genre of horror so popular in the 1930s and 1940s, quasi-science fiction films such as *Dr. Jekyll and Mr. Hyde* (1912, 1920, 1932, 1941), *Frankenstein* (1931), and even the more urbane *The Invisible Man* (1933) were concerned less with science and technological invention as it impacted a collective culture than with the personal obsessions and individual hubris of 19th-century "mad scientists," and the "proper" order of things—themes committed more to the preservation of traditional social and moral values than to the radical transformation of society through scientific knowledge and new technologies.

Prior to World War II, then, science fiction film in America meant low-budget serials. Made for young audiences, its characters were drawn broadly from comics, its mise-en-scène from the covers of science fiction pulp, and its perspective was generally xenophobic. Alex Raymond's comic strip hero Flash Gordon appeared in 1936's *Spaceship to the Unknown* to do battle with an orientalized tyrant, the Emperor Ming of the planet Mongo. In 1938, the year that Martians invaded Earth in Orson Welles's Mercury Theater radio adaptation of H. G. Wells's *War of the Worlds, Flash Gordon's Trip to Mars* was serialized in theaters. In 1939, the year the future-oriented New York World's Fair opened, Buck Rogers made his initial appearance in *Destination Saturn*. And in 1940, the first full year of World War II, movie screens saw *Flash Gordon Conquers the Universe* (or *Purple Death from Outer Space*).

Conquest of the universe, however, became a more ambiguous enterprise after World War II. The menace was "Red" rather than purple (or an orientalized yellow) and it hailed from the communist Soviet Union. Furthermore, the greatest special effect the world had ever seen—atomic destruction—demonstrated that the conjunction of expansionist dreams, invasion fantasies, and high technology could well result in the realization of apocalypse right here on Earth. The last of the theatrical science fiction serials, released during the Cold War and reflecting their historical moment, included *Radar Men from the Moon* (1952), *Canadian Mounties vs. Atomic Invaders,* and *Commando Cody: Enemies of the Universe* (both 1953). The production of science fiction theatrical serials declined in the early 1950s with the cultural proliferation of television—the conjunction of serial science fiction with TV's "futuristic" technology resulting, appropriately enough, first in *Captain Video* (1949-53), then in *Space Patrol* (1950-53) and the anthology series *Tales of Tomorrow* (1951-53).

The emergence of the science fiction feature film in the 1950s is thus not as surprising or sudden as it might first appear. The genre appears as a symbolic response to an America transformed by a heightened popular recognition of the vast power and socio-political consequences of science and technology, by a new consciousness of the relativity of spatial and temporal distance and the planet as global community, and by a lived sense of geophysical vulnerability and political enmity.

Two key films are examples of the positive and negative attitudes about the technologized future that informed both the culture at large and the genre in particular. *Destination Moon* (1950) was big-budget, its Technicolor narrative of a manned space mission to the moon optimistic about an expansionist future enabled by the cooperative intersection of American hard science, high technology, and corporate capitalism. In images filled with shiny futuristic technology, a sleek spaceship (created by a rocket designer), and the beauty of limitless outer space, the film visually went "where no man had gone before." However much marked by the ideology of its present, the film's creation of awesome (if unprescient) moonscapes, its extraterrestrial perspective of Earth, its attempts to ground itself in current scientific knowledge, and its privileging of human curiosity and enterprise presage later visionary science fiction films like *2001: A Space Odyssey* (1968) or *Close Encounters of the Third Kind* (1977). The moon its destination, the stars its eventual goal, the special effects of (cinematic) technology its means of transportation, *Destination Moon* promised its audiences a progressive, rational, and shiny new future.

The Thing (1951), on the other hand, was pessimistic about both extreme rationality and the future. Low-budget, the film's black-and-white narrative about a murderous alien creature on a military outpost in the Arctic was xenophobic and anti-science, privileging technology only for the weaponry it provided against alien invasion. *The Thing* envisioned the future in terms not of limitless space and progressive temporal flow but of merely staying alive and safe. Its paranoid last warning was: "Keep watching the skies!"

Taken together, these two films set the boundaries and tonal range of the first period of science fiction's popularity as a film genre. They also symbolically dramatize the period's essential ambiguity toward the new Cold War intersection of science, technology, the military, and corporate capitalism. But for some few exceptions like *War of the Worlds* and *Invaders from Mars* (both 1953), which were earth-bound Technicolor nightmares of alien invasion, the legacy of the big-budget, special effects-laden *Destination Moon* was films that, even when cautionary, celebrated technology as progressive and the American future as expansive in awesome and poetic displays of graceful, glittering new machinery and startlingly beautiful extraterrestrial landscapes and spacescapes. Perhaps because of cost, perhaps the prevalence of fear over hope, there were far fewer films like *When Worlds Collide* (1951), *Riders to the Stars* (1954), *The Conquest of Space* (1955), and *Forbidden Planet* (1956) than those which followed in the footsteps of *The Thing*.

The negative vision of the technological future inaugurated by *The Thing* developed in several directions: "creature features," alien invasion fantasies, films about the fear of radiation or life after nuclear apocalypse. The "creature feature" foregrounded atomically "awakened" or mutated creatures that embodied the present threat of nuclear annihilation in regressive and primal form. Stomping cities and chomping their inhabitants, prehistoric beasts and giant insects transformed social order into mass chaos and, through the genre's special effects, brought to concrete (if black-and-white) visibility what Susan Sontag called "the imagination of disaster" and "the aesthetics of destruction." *The Beast from 20,000 Fathoms* (1953), *Them!* (1954), *Tarantula* (1955), *It Came from Beneath the Sea* (1955), *The Deadly Mantis* (1957), and *The Black Scorpion* (1957) give us creatures who cause mass havoc and public hysteria, and condense in their gigantic size, primitive biology, and acts of mindless and outsized destruction not only the affective charge of a massive and annihilating energy out of control and run amok, but also the "poetic justice" of our post-apocalyptic future: a return to humanity's pre-history and the primal sink. The mindless and primitive nature of these creatures also drew attention away from their rational and technological origins so as to also allow rational scientists and the military to use advanced technology to "save" humanity (just as they had in World War II).

The alien invasion films of the 1950s symbolically dramatized another cultural anxiety—the popular fear of communism as a dehumanizing political system bent on destroying individual subjectivity, committed to world conquest, and proficient in frightening new forms of "invisible" domination such as "brainwashing." The alien invasion films disguise (sometimes only thinly) Cold War anxieties about being "taken over" by powerful, inhumanely cold (and rational) others who would radically flatten human emotion and transform (American) consciousness into a collectivity, but they do so in two quite different forms.

Like the creature films, the first type of invasion film draws upon the "aesthetics of destruction" and features an urban America under attack from aliens whose superior weapons blast distinctly American architectural landmarks like the Washington Monument at the same time the invasion is seen through newspaper and television montage as global in scope. Films like *War of the Worlds* (1953) and *Earth vs. the Flying Saucers* (1956) dramatize radical xenophobia, fear of planetary annihilation through high-tech weaponry, and a contradictory yearning for both a United Nations fantasy of peaceful global coalition and another morally clearcut—rather than ambiguously "cold"—world war (humans vs. extraterrestrials akin to the Allies vs. the Nazis). Only *The Day the Earth Stood Still* (1951) took a critical view of the period's xenophobia, featuring an extraterrestrial (if humanoid) protagonist speaking out against irrational fear and knee-jerk militarism, and emphasizing the cosmic consequences of nuclear destruction.

The second type of alien invasion science fiction dramatized cultural anxieties around the more "invisible" threats of communism: infiltration of America by a subversive "fifth column," and ideological "brainwashing." *Invaders from Mars* (1953), *It Came from Outer Space* (1953), *Invasion of the Body Snatchers* (1956), *I Married a Monster from Outer Space* (1958), and *The Day Mars Invaded the Earth* (1963) locate themselves in the ordinary and familiar world of small-town and suburban America where the aliens "take over" the bodies, minds, and hearts of fathers and mothers, telephone linesmen, cops, psychiatrists, doctors, husbands, and lovers. Most of them low-budget, these films created a paranoid style in which alien "difference" was marked less by expensive special effects than by a "sameness" made disturbing. That is, they demanded the spectator pay close attention so as to spot the small failures of the human-looking aliens to respond appropriately in ordinary human situations: not blinking at the sun, or not responding maternally to a child or passionately to a kiss. Emphasis was on the threat to human emotion posed by a hyper-rationalism that seemed to go with the alien's collective consciousness.

Science fiction fantasies of life after nuclear accident or war played out apocalyptic fears of yet another kind. Fear of radiation and its effects on the human body was poeticized in dramas of scale like *The Incredible Shrinking Man* and *The Amazing Colossal Man* (both 1957), while visions of life after nuclear apocalypse were set in recognizable urban con-

texts. Cities were figured as ghost towns emptied of people, but for a few survivors. Primarily structured around loss and absence, both cautionary and elegiac in tone, films like *On the Beach* and *The World, the Flesh and the Devil* (both 1959) starred significant Hollywood actors and were received by the public less as science fiction than as "serious" drama. Other post-nuclear films like *Five* (1951) or the later *Panic in the Year Zero* (1962), however, were low-budget enterprises, cautionary tales foregrounding moral questions of the period about what "survival of the fittest" might mean in actual post-apocalyptic practice.

The science fiction genre's popularity and production went into major decline at the end of the 1950s, the reasons linked to dramatic changes in both the film industry and American society. The 1960s saw the economic collapse of the monopolistic Hollywood studio system at the same time that television introduced new competition for audiences.

During its first golden age, the science fiction film—like many other genres—produced films made on shoestring budgets for the bottom of the theatrical program (at a time when theaters were still showing double features). Some of these, however, were so bad that they were unintentionally funny, and over time became enshrined in popular culture as "cult classics." There were those made in the genre's heyday —like *Robot Monster* (1953), which featured an alien invader costumed in a gorilla suit and diving helmet, or *Cat Women of the Moon* (1954), which peopled Earth's satellite with seductive women in black leotards. The majority, however, emerged toward the decade's end as the genre's relevance and popularity declined, perhaps the most famous and beloved of them *Plan 9 from Outer Space* (1958), with Bela Lugosi and cardboard sets contributing to the film's reputation as the worst picture ever made.

While the science fiction film did not disappear between the 1960s and 1977 (the year that marks the renaissance of the genre), it did seem to vanish from popular consciousness. Exceptions were Stanley Kubrick's *Dr. Strangelove: or How I Learned to Stop Worrying and Love the Bomb* (1964; see entry), a hilarious black comedy about the onset of nuclear war, and *2001: A Space Odyssey* (1968), a critically acclaimed epic that set a new standard for special effects and adult themes; the very popular *Planet of the Apes* (1968; see entry), which combined space and time travel with post-apocalyptic themes to explore, in thinly disguised fashion, contemporaneous American race relations; and perhaps *Silent Running* (1971), which, while located on a futuristic space station and featuring the latest in cinematic technology, had concerns about Earth's ecological future.

In 1977, it was precisely space travel and extraterrestrials that marked the beginning of the second golden age of science fiction film with the release of George Lucas's *Star Wars* (see entry) and Steven Spielberg's *Close Encounters of the Third Kind*—*Star Wars* an epic space adventure and coming-of-age film set presumably in a mythic past but realized futuristically in a galaxy "far, far away"; *Close Encounters* an epic domestic drama about an ordinary man's search for wonder and "something important" fulfilled by spectacular encounter and communication with child-like extraterrestrials. Radically different in narrative focus and tone from their more recent and baleful predecessors, both films exhibited a youthful enthusiasm about the possibilities for the future of human beings and envisioned alien life forms as friendly allies in adventure.

The renaissance of science fiction as a popular film genre in the late 1970s and its continued success in the 1980s and '90s symbolically mapped our social relationships to ourselves and others in what had become the familiarity (rather than, as in the 1950s, the novelty) of a totally technologized culture. One map describes a simpler and more innocent world, one in which technology is benign and even emotionalized, in which "alien" others are sentimentalized. The other map describes and celebrates a world grown so complex, heterogeneous, and totally permeated by technology, that novelty and constant transformation are utterly familiar and no one and nothing are especially alien because everyone and everything exist in an already "alienated" state.

The more "upbeat" and emotionalized strain of megabudget mainstream science fiction inaugurated by Lucas and Spielberg not only fit the more upbeat rhetoric and rampant consumerism of the Carter and Reagan years, but could be sold as family entertainment. This was science fiction at its most white, middle-class, and squeaky clean. The *Star Wars* trilogy (1977, 1980, 1983), the *Star Trek* movies (1978, 1982, 1984, 1986, 1989), the *Superman* films (1978, 1980, 1983, 1987), the *Back to the Future* series (1985, 1989, 1990), and films such as *Star Man* (1984) and *Cocoon* (1985) in which aliens were figured as lovers and friends seemed to fulfill the culture's need to revisit an innocence and hope lost in the late 1960s. Most of these films combined regressive nostalgia with reflexive self-consciousness; many of them remade previous movies and television series. This cultural longing for a return to the innocence and simplicity of childhood was apparently fulfilled in Spielberg's *E.T., The Extra-Terrestrial* (1982; see entry). Shot in great part at the eye-level of a child, the story of a suburban boy's friendship with a small and cuddly alien trying to get home was science fiction with a "heartlight," an emotional appeal that had more to do with resolving the separations of "divorced" families than with the hard science and technology associated with the genre in the 1950s.

This domestication and familiarization of the genre led, in the 1980s, to a low-budget and independent quasi-science fiction cinema that ironically played with the way American culture had itself become the stuff of science fiction. Located on the very boundaries of the genre, using visibly cheesy special effects, films like *Liquid Sky* (1984), *Strange Invaders, Brother from Another Planet, Repo Man, Night of the Comet* (all 1984), or *Uforia* (1986) locate themselves in an American culture that is "alien-ated"—and more anthropologically bizarre than anything mainstream science fiction could dream up. Often called "postmodern" because of their embrace of popular culture and their use of irony and pastiche, these films played up their own "B" movie status— even though there were no more "B" movies—and went quickly to video, many like *Liquid Sky* or *Repo Man* becoming "cult" favorites. The 1990s brought big-budget, mainstream parodies in comic films like *Mars Attacks!* (1996) and *Men in Black* (1997).

As in the 1950s, science fiction film had a pessimistic side that became more dominant in the late 1980s and early 1990s. Benign suburban landscapes and starry spacescapes were nowhere to be seen; urban clutter and blight or confined and claustrophobic spaces set the mise-en-scène not only for remakes of several 1950s "paranoid" invasion films such as *Invasion of the Body Snatchers* (1979, also *Body Snatchers*, 1994), *The Thing* (1982), and *Invaders from Mars* (1986), but also for historically particular responses to the rampant consumerism of the Reagan years, the downward economic spiral of the Bush years, the immense power of "invisible" multinational corporations, and the way in which, in an age of biotechnology, "artificial" intelligence, and media simulation, the nature of "human" identity was increasingly ambiguous.

Alien (1979) did a contemporary turn on *The Thing*, its dark, claustrophobic spaceship and multicultural crew threatened as much by anonymous corporate greed as by the rapacious alien creature that ultimately savages their bodies from both within and without. Extremely popular, *Alien* spawned two sequels—*Aliens* (1986) and *Alien³* (1992)—but there were other films in the same paranoid vein, among them *Lifeforce* (1985), *Predator* (1987), and *Predator 2* (1990). By 1994, however, the paranoid fear of alien creatures and predators had become the tamer "thrill" of Steven Spielberg's seamlessly created dinosaurs and Tyrannosaurus Rex in *Jurassic Park*, a theme-park ride of a movie soon to be simulated outside the theater. In 1996, paranoia turned to patriotism with *Independence Day*, in which a small group of Americans fight off an invasion of huge alien ships bent on world domination.

There was yet another kind of science fiction film marked by a historically unique ambivalence about the future that has been linked to a "postmodern" sensibility. Perhaps best characterized by *Blade Runner* (1982), these films both criticized and eroticized the urban blight in which they were set, finding peculiar beauty in garbage, decay, industrial exhaustion, and a cityscape saturated by both acid rain and advertising. In these films, however futuristic, new technology and modern architecture look both strange and shabby. Dark in tone, filled with highly atmospheric pollution, films like *Escape from New York* (1981), *Blue Thunder* (1983), and the extremely popular *The Terminator* (1984) and *Terminator 2* (1991), *Robocop* (1987), and *Total Recall* (1990) stand as monuments to the consumer culture of late capitalism even as they lament it.

Many of these same films have also focused on the ambiguous nature of human identity and subjectivity. Traditional subjectivity seems to lose sight of itself amid an excess of things and media images. Old forms of identity are "terminal" in an age of media simulation, microchips, biotechnology and body-building. In *Videodrome* (1982), a man inserts a videocassette into his body and his television set pulsates from pornography as if it were alive. *Blade Runner* has genetically manufactured "replicants" who are "more human than human," and value existence more than their exhausted human counterparts. *The Terminator* (1984) is a killing machine made of flesh and chrome. *Robocop* (1987) is a cyborg policeman with residual flesh and subjectivity. These films dramatize malaise, euphoria, and irony about the transformed nature of human consciousness, identity, memory, and embodiment—all of which we recognize, like Arnold Schwarzenegger's science fiction presence, as, in various ways, constructed and mediated by technology. The hero of *Total Recall* is never sure his memories or identity are truly his own. Indeed, in these and films like *The Abyss* (1989) and *Terminator 2*, using advanced computer-graphic effects now familiarly called "morphing," the morphology of body and consciousness become almost completely fluid to both pleasurable and disturbing degree.

The science fiction film has over the last decade become fascinated with the nascent technology of "virtual reality"—where violence doesn't hurt and sex is safe. Although one could argue that science fiction cinema is itself a virtual reality, its explicit computer-graphic visualization of an interactive virtual space is becoming increasingly popular in films like *The Lawnmower Man* (1992), *Demolition Man* (1994), and *The Matrix* (1999).

From 1950 to the present day, the science fiction film has given concrete narrative shape and visible form to America's changing historical imagination of social progress and disaster, and to the ambiguities of being human in a world in which advanced technology has altered both the morphology and meaning of personal and social existence. In sum, the genre functions as a map of contemporary American culture—symbolic not only of the terrain of our possible futures but also of our grounding in the historical present.

Bibliography

Brosnan, John. *Future Tense: The Cinema of Science Fiction*. New York: St. Martin's, 1978.

Bukatman, Scott. *Terminal Identity: The Virtual Subject in Post-Modern Science Fiction*. Durham: Duke UP, 1993.

Kuhn, Annette, ed. *Alien Zone: Cultural Theory and Contemporary Science Fiction Cinema*. London: Verso, 1990.

Peary, Danny, ed. *Omni's Screen Flights/Screen Fantasies: The Future According to Science Fiction Cinema*. Garden City: Doubleday, 1984.

Sobchack, Vivian. *Screening Space: The American Science Fiction Film*. New York: Ungar, 1987.

Vivian Sobchack

See also
Space Exploration

Scooby-Doo (1969-1989) was a mystery-sniffing Great Dane, the last of what Hanna-Barbera calls its classic cartoon characters. Scooby-Doo appeared on Saturday morning TV under several titles for over 20 years. The main cast and formula were assembled in 1969 with *Scooby-Doo, Where Are You?* Scooby (Don Messick) and his four teenage friends toured the country in their van, "The Mystery Machine," finding mysterious doings at each stop. Ringleader Freddy (Frank Welker), Daphne, the cute one (Heather North), nerdish Velma (Nichole Jaffe), and hippie Shaggy (DJ Casey Kasem) split up and investigate. Shaggy and Scooby go looking for food, but instead encounter a monster and flee in terror. Freddy discovers clues and sets a trap for the monster, but Scooby has to be encouraged to bait the trap with a handful of "Scooby Snacks." A chase scene follows involving lots of sight gags. They catch the monster (inevitably a bad guy in disguise) and everybody guesses who it could be.

In 1972, CBS aired *The New Scooby-Doo Comedy Movies*. It was one of the first cartoon shows with hour-long single episodes, and it teamed Scooby and crew with celebrities like Phyllis Diller, Don Knotts, "Mama" Cass Elliot, Dick Van Dyke, Jerry Reed, Jonathan Winters, and Sonny and Cher. The *Comedy Movies* ran for two seasons, then ABC picked up the first *Scooby-Doo* series and re-ran it in the 1974 and 1975 seasons.

Hanna-Barbera produced new episodes in 1976 as half of the *Scooby-Doo/Dynomutt Hour*. For this show, the gang teamed with Scooby's country cousin, Scooby-Dum, who was obviously none too bright.

In 1977, dozens of Hanna-Barbera characters competed against each other in *Scooby's All-Star Laff-A-Lympics* on ABC. Tough-talking nephew Scrappy-Doo appeared in 1979's *Scooby and Scrappy-Doo*. For the 1980 and 1981 seasons, they became half of the *Richie Rich/Scooby-Doo Hour*. Next season, they were half of *The Scooby and Scrappy-Doo/Puppy Hour*, teamed with a project from Ruby-Spears, a studio formed by a pair of directors who had broken away from Hanna-Barbera.

In 1983, Fred and Velma were dropped, leaving Shaggy and Daphne in *The All-New Scooby and Scrappy-Doo Show*, as well as 1984's *The New Scooby-Doo Mysteries*. *Scooby's Mystery Funhouse* (1985) was all repeats. Finally, *A Pup Named Scooby-Doo* ran in 1988 and 1989, showing the entire cast as children—presumably with no one driving the Mystery Machine.

Bibliography

Lenburg, Jeff. *The Encyclopedia of Animated Cartoons*. Rev. ed. New York: Facts on File, 1991.

McNeil, Alex. *Total Television: A Comprehensive Guide to Programming from 1948 to the Present*. New York: Penguin, 1991.

Mark McDermott

Scorsese, Martin (1942-), along with Steven Spielberg, George Lucas, and Francis Ford Coppola, was a pioneer of a new generation of American cinema in the seventies. Unlike the previous generation of former theater directors and the like, they were graduates of film schools. Although he was a key member of this "film-school generation," Scorsese's influences were largely drawn from cinema's golden age, specifically the films of directors such as John Ford, Akira Kurosawa, Michelangelo Antonioni, and Jean-Luc Godard. His desire to emulate the golden age directors was successfully married with a unique, deeply personal vision.

His first baby steps, *Who's That Knocking at My Door* (1967) and *Boxcar Bertha* (1972), displayed themes that would run through his entire body of work: a bleakly matter-of-fact perspective of urban life filtered through the eye of an Italian-American Catholic. Among his other early efforts,

Scorsese served as assistant director for Michael Wadleigh's musical documentary *Woodstock* (1970). This first experience with a musical film led to others: *Medicine Ball Caravan* (1971) and *Elvis on Tour* (1972), followed much later by *The Last Waltz* (1978 [a highly praised homage of The Band's farewell tour]), and, oddly, an extended Michael Jackson video, *Bad* (1987).

Mean Streets (1973) was the young director's big break, and its success in presenting a dystopic, urban worldview seemed to commit Scorsese to this model. Religious themes as overtones and undertones have always figured into the lives of Scorsese's characters.

Scorsese's first attempt at directing a commercial movie, the Oscar-winning Ellen Burstyn vehicle, *Alice Doesn't Live Here Anymore* (1974), was also successful. This critical praise affirmed the merit of Scorsese's artistic sensibility, allowing him to go further with dramas of the urban nightmare. His next film, *Taxi Driver* (1976), is considered one of Scorsese's best, a film that he had to fight for every step of the way. New York taxi driver Travis Bickle feels a responsibility to cull the madness and deterioration of the big city. He becomes an avenging angel on behalf of a 14-year-old prostitute, Iris (Jodie Foster). Robert DeNiro's incarnation of the psychologically troubled Bickle, a Vietnam War vet, expresses good intentions that are stifled by confusion and loneliness, and, ultimately, turned outward as avenging violence.

In his next outing with Robert DeNiro, Scorsese directed his hero and heroine, Liza Minnelli, through a tumultuous marriage in the forties-style musical *New York, New York* (1977). The juxtaposition of the musical, traditionally known as escapist entertainment, with spousal abuse is an innovative, if not entirely successful concept.

Raging Bull (1980) presents an uncompromising view of the monstrous middleweight boxer Jake La Motta (DeNiro, who won a best actor Oscar for this role). *The King of Comedy* (1982) offered another chance for DeNiro—by now Scorsese's alter ego—to play a misguided hero, whose confusion leads him and his friends into trouble. Here, Rupert Pupkin (DeNiro) is an aspiring standup comedian who abducts TV star Jerry Langford (Jerry Lewis) in an attempt to break into the industry.

After many provocative, even controversial films, Scorsese's *Last Temptation of Christ* (1988) was his most contested yet. Instead of portraying Jesus traditionally, Scorsese, following Nikos Kazantzakis' book, presents a Jesus (Willem Dafoe) who is troubled, wracked with doubt, and struggling with temptations not in the Gospels. This outraged many Christian filmgoers, who thought it blasphemous to acknowledge Jesus as a mortal, who was subject to doubt, paranoia, and sexual desire.

Since *Last Temptation*, Scorsese has made movies that are more accessible than his earlier alienation pictures. *GoodFellas* (1990) was another return to the criminal element: DeNiro and Joe Pesci (*Raging Bull*) return to support Ray Liotta in the story of mob informant Henry Hill. This time, the grit of urban crime was humor; although sequences of *GoodFellas* are just as brutal as *Mean Streets* or *Taxi*

Driver, Scorsese's new approach seemed acceptable to a wider audience.

Other forays of Scorsese have garnered some level of success: his sequel to *The Hustler*, *The Color of Money* (1987)—a merging of new talent (Tom Cruise) with the old (Paul Newman, who won best actor); *Age of Innocence* (1992)—an adaptation of Edith Wharton's romance novel; *After Hours* (1985)—a visually elaborate black comedy; *Cape Fear* (1993)—a commercially successful remake of the thriller of the same title; a return to the crime saga, *Casino* (1995); *Kundun* (1997), a biography of the Dalai Lama; and *Bringing Out the Dead* (1999), another urban nightmare, this time with Nicolas Cage as a New York City paramedic haunted by visions of those he could not save. Scorsese has ventured in many different directions, each time proving he is a talented director, who, in the eye of critics and audiences alike, is worthy to be considered one of the best directors of our time. His expert ability at successfully executing a wide variety of genres is enhanced by his unique version of the American hero.

Bibliography

Bliss, Michael. *The Word Made Flesh: Catholicism and Conflict in the Films of Martin Scorsese*. Lanham, MD: Scarecrow, 1995.

Ehrenstein, David. *The Scorsese Picture*. Birch Lane, 1992.

Friedman, Lawrence S. *The Cinema of Martin Scorsese*. New York: Continuum, 1997.

Stern, Lesley. *The Scorsese Connection*. Bloomington: Indiana UP, 1995.

Thompson, David, and Ian Christie, eds. *Scorsese on Scorsese*. Winchester, MA: Faber & Faber, 1996.

Robert Baird

Screwball Comedy Film reached its zenith during the 1930s and 1940s, its success primarily a result of the Great Depression, the newly instituted Hollywood Production Code, and the abundance of skilled actors and actresses—among them Cary Grant, Katharine Hepburn, Claudette Colbert, Henry Fonda, and Carole Lombard—who excelled in the rapid-fire delivery of witty dialogue and the physical business of this comedy of sexual aggression. Most screwball comedies contain elements of the following: the mingling of social classes, especially through romance; the sublimation of sexuality through wordplay or physical abuse; the presence of offbeat or unusual characters, or "screwball" behavior on the part of more realistic characters; marriage or remarriage of the male and female leads. The term "screwball" comes originally from the game of baseball and refers to an unusual pitch that curves differently from other pitches and is intended to confuse the batter; as applied to film, it refers to a type of comedy in which realism may be sacrificed for a dizzy rush of words and physical business.

Chronologically, screwball comedy provides a Hollywood interpretation of American society during a certain chaotic period of time—from the darkest days of the Great Depression through World War II—although unlike the darker vision of film noir, it often attempts to reconcile opposites and impose a positive conclusion despite whatever cinematic chaos may have preceded it.

In the year 1934, the first two screwball comedies, Frank Capra's *It Happened One Night* and Howard Hawks's *Twentieth Century,* were released. *It Happened One Night* is generally considered to be the more important film because of its box office success and numerous Academy Awards (as well as Frank Capra's promotion of himself and the film in his widely read autobiography *The Name above the Title),* but both films made important contributions to the new genre. Both feature unlikely love affairs between low-income males and wealthy females (reporter Clark Gable and heiress Claudette Colbert in *It Happened One Night* and destitute Broadway producer John Barrymore and actress Carole Lombard in *Twentieth Century*); both feature "screwball" behavior (although *Twentieth Century* is far more bold in exploring slapstick and physical situations); both include wit and wordplay (although again *Twentieth Century* extends the artistic possibilities of the genre much farther). With the commercial success of *It Happened One Night* and the artistic success of both films in circumventing the stifling provisions of the Production Code (see entry), imitators soon followed, and the screwball comedy became one of the dominant genres of the 1930s and early 1940s, resulting in such significant films as *My Man Godfrey* (1936), *Topper* (1937), *Nothing Sacred* (1937), *Bringing Up Baby* (1938), *His Girl Friday* (1940), and *The Palm Beach Story* (1942).

The backdrop against which these comedies appeared, of course, was the Great Depression, and one of the reasons screwball comedy became so popular was that it addressed questions both romantic and economic; screwball comedies are primarily about love and money. During the Depression, when the gulf between the haves and the have-nots seemed almost immeasurable, the genre often soothed audiences by resolving this problem artfully through the romantic merging of social classes, the well-to-do marrying the destitute; there seems little question that screwball comedies are often about, as the wealthy Mr. Seton (Henry Kolker) observes in *Holiday* (1938), "combining business with pleasure." For Gable in *It Happened One Night,* pursuing an exclusive story for his newspaper ultimately leads to marriage with the wealthy Colbert; in *The Bride Walks Out* (1936), Barbara Stanwyck weighs her alternatives, a bright but relatively impoverished husband (Gene Raymond) and a wealthy alcoholic (Robert Young) and ultimately chooses in favor of love, although not without a good hard look at money.

An entire subclass of screwball comedies does play with societal expectations toward marriage, however, suggesting that instead of representing a pinnacle of happiness to which Americans should aspire, the institution frustrates, maddens, even destroys men and women both. In *Mr. and Mrs. Smith* (1941), for example, Robert Montgomery admits at the beginning of the film that he wouldn't remarry his wife— Carole Lombard—if he had the decision to make again; in *His Girl Friday,* both Cary Grant and Rosalind Russell deplore their former marriage, although they fight together so beautifully we know they are meant for each other; in *The Palm Beach Story,* Claudette Colbert deserts her husband to go and find someone who has the money to take proper care

of her, someone like the wealthiest man in the world, Rudy Vallee's Mr. Hackensacker.

The actresses most often seen as screwball heroines— Carole Lombard, Barbara Stanwyck, Katharine Hepburn, Irene Dunne, Jean Arthur—not only assume control of their own lives but tend to sweep others around them into their wakes. In *My Favorite Wife* (1940), Irene Dunne goes off alone on a scientific expedition that ends with her being shipwrecked on a tropical island with the virile Randolph Scott, to the consternation of husband Cary Grant; in *Bringing Up Baby,* Hepburn drags stuffy museum-bound paleontologist Grant all over the Connecticut countryside, steals his clothes, and destroys his personal life.

In most screwball comedies, whether the couples are first meeting or lining up at the altar, their compatibility is often displayed, paradoxically, by their aggression toward each other. In *Cafe Society* (1939), Fred MacMurray informs Madeleine Carroll that "nobody's gonna get tough with my wife but me"; in *Breakfast for Two* (1937), Barbara Stanwyck slugs it out with Herbert Marshall, boxing gloves and all; in *Nothing Sacred,* a sort of noir screwball comedy that revolves around fakery and deception, Fredric March discovers that the woman with whom he's fallen in love, Carole Lombard, is a fraud and he decks her, just after he announces his intention to "flirt and lie and cheat and swindle" her "right through to our golden wedding."

Screwball comedies often revolve around role playing, which sometimes makes up part of the madcap behavior we identify as "screwball." Artifice is a fundamental element of screwball comedies, but some films make this essential theatricality more apparent than others by having characters engage in role playing, acting, telling stories (or lies), and performing them for the amusement (or horror) of their partners. Among these films are *The Philadelphia Story* (1940), where Jimmy Stewart and Ruth Hussey are a reporter and photographer from *Spy* magazine who masquerade as "friends of Junius," Katharine Hepburn's absent brother, to gain entry to her society wedding; in *Nothing Sacred* (1937), Carole Lombard maintains the role of terminally ill woman even after her doctor pronounces her cured because it gets her a free trip to New York City; Fred MacMurray, in *The Princess Comes Across* (1936), discovers Carole Lombard's secret—that she is only pretending to be a Swedish princess; while in *The Lady Eve,* Barbara Stanwyck portrays the Lady Eve Sidgewick to reintroduce herself to Henry Fonda. *Lady of Burlesque* (1943) and *Twentieth Century,* meanwhile, are built almost entirely around performance, acting, and role playing.

With rare exceptions, the screwball comedy genre did not survive World War II. Although some of its impulses and structural elements were retained in the film noir genre which dominated films of the mid- to late-1940s, Americans for the most part did not seem interested in comedies which questioned traditional institutions, and with the coming of American affluence following World War II, the cinematic mingling of classes through romance lost its cultural imperative. The last film made by traditional masters of the genre, Howard Hawks's *Monkey Business,* featured screwball stalwarts Cary Grant and Ginger Rogers, as well as a script co-written by Ben Hecht, and appeared in 1952. Studios did seize on the opportunity to remake successful screwball comedies, although with modifications, and in the 1950s, *Nothing Sacred* was remade as *Living It Up* (1954), *The Major and the Minor* (1942) as *You're Never Too Young* (1955), and *The Miracle of Morgan's Creek* (1944) as *Rock-a-Bye Baby* (1958), all of the later films featuring Jerry Lewis in what had previously been the female lead role.

Although initially a product of a definite period in American history, screwball comedy continues to have some influence on American comedy, and the products of its greatest period continue to be enjoyed by film and TV audiences, as well as studied as cultural artifacts and milestones in film history.

Bibliography

Bergman, Andrew. *We're in the Money: Depression America and Its Films.* 1971 Chicago: Elephant, 1992.

Cavell, Stanley. *Pursuits of Happiness: The Hollywood Comedy of Remarriage.* Cambridge: Harvard UP, 1981.

Everson, William K. "Screwball Comedy: A Reappraisal." *Films in Review* 34.10 (1983): 578-84.

Mast, Gerald. *The Comic Mind: Comedy and the Movies.* 2d ed. Chicago: U of Chicago P, 1979.

Sikov, Ed. *Screwball: Hollywood's Madcap Romantic Comedies.* New York: Crown, 1989.

Greg Garrett

Seasonal Mysteries employ periodic and predictable happenings (holidays, weather changes, monthly or yearly events) to occasion and structure homicide and other criminal doings. A boat tossed by a summer storm becomes a murder implement in Barbara D'Amato's *Hard Tack* (1991); unseasonal ripening of crops functions as a clue in *The Man Who Liked Slow Tomatoes* (1982) by K. C. Constantine; the eye of a hurricane is the equivalent of a locked room in Carolyn G. Hart's *Dead Man's Island* (1993). In Steve Thayer's epic *The Weatherman* (1995), seasonal changes precipitate serial murders.

Christmas mysteries flood bookstores at holiday time: Charlotte MacLeod's *Rest You Merry* (1978); Joan Hess's *O Little Town of Maggody* (1993); M. D. Lake's *A Gift for Murder* (1992). Seasons of religious significance provide themes for excellent series by writers like Faye Kellerman, Harry Kemelman, Sister Carol Anne O'Marie, and Robert Irvine. Sectional holidays are settings for a number of novels such as Julie Smith's *New Orleans Mourning* (1990, Mardi Gras) and Jane Langton's *The Transcendental Murder* (1964, Patriot's Day). Several authors have built series around successive holidays. Jane Haddam's mysteries move from Christmas to Hanukkah (*Festival of Deaths*, 1994); Valentine's Day (*Bleeding Hearts,* 1994); St. Patrick's Day (*A Great Day for the Deadly,* 1992); Mother's and Father's Days respectively (*Mother Superior,* 1993, and *Dear Old Dead,* 1994); Halloween (*Quoth the Raven,* 1991); and Thanksgiving (*Feast of Murder,* 1992).

Bibliography

Klein, Kathleen Gregory. *Great Women Mystery Writers: Classic to Contemporary.* Westport: Greenwood, 1994.

Jeanne M. Jacobson

Seeger, Charles Louis, Jr. (1886-1979), musicologist, composer, and conductor, was born in Mexico City, the son of Charles Louis and Elsie Simmons (Adams) Seeger. He is the father of noted folksingers Pete (see next entry), Mike, and Peggy Seeger. He earned an A.B. from Harvard in 1908, did graduate studies in Germany, and conducted at the Cologne Opera. He returned to the U.S. in 1911 and moved to Berkeley, CA, where he chaired the music department at the University of California from 1912 to 1919. He is credited with teaching the first musicology course in the U.S.

Seeger began his musical career in classical music; politically he was conservative. Both stances were challenged in 1914, when he witnessed migrant laborers toiling in the San Joaquin Valley. Subsequent forays into the California hinterlands led him to collect Hoopa Indian songs. He also contacted the radical Industrial Workers of the World labor union. Seeger opposed U.S. entry into World War I, and found himself under suspicion for his politics, and his German-sounding last name. He suffered harassment until 1918, when he abandoned a full professorship and moved back to New York.

In 1920, Seeger toured the South in a failed effort to popularize classical music among the Appalachian poor. From 1921 to 1935 he taught at the Institute of Musical Art (forerunner of the Juilliard School), and at the New School for Social Research. He launched scholarly investigations into the social uses of music and, for a time, championed the virtues of Soviet composer Dimitri Shostakovich.

Like many artists during the Great Depression, Seeger celebrated proletarian artistic expression, and he re-examined earlier hierarchical assumptions about music. He joined numerous radical groups and contributed music articles under a pseudonym to *The Daily Worker.* In a 1934 issue of *Modern Music,* Seeger linked music with class struggle, and touted folk music as American music for the masses. From 1935 to 1940, he worked in New Deal programs, first for the Resettlement Administration and later as assistant director of the Federal Music Project of the Works Progress Administration, where he worked with Alan Lomax. He also founded the American Musicological Society and the American Society for Comparative Musicology.

Once again, Seeger's forays into folk music led to reassessments of musical theory. The "discovery" of singer/songwriters such as Leadbelly (see Ledbetter, Huddie) and Aunt Molly Jackson, and the proliferation of recorded music led to academic debates over the nature and authenticity of "folk" music, with "popularizers" such as Leadbelly or Jackson usually shunted into the latter category. Seeger tried to mediate the dispute in a *Journal of American Folklore* article which created a continuum with community-based, family-trained, and orally transmitted "folk" at one end of the spectrum and formally trained, commercially driven, and performance-oriented "concert" musicians at the other. In between lay "hillbilly" and "citybilly" expressions, the first representing recorded rural singers of early country music, and the latter their urban cousins. Seeger's terminology has fallen from fashion but not his notion that categories are fluid, and that a single performer can move between them.

Seeger recognized that mass, commercial culture and communications blurred traditional categories, and that the search for "authenticity" was fruitless. In a 1966 refinement, Seeger demonstrated the porousness of the "folk" category, using Jackson, Leadbelly and Woody Guthrie as examples.

After World War II, Seeger lectured at Yale and UCLA. He also founded the International Folk Music Council and the Society for Ethnomusicology. He (and his son, Pete) suffered harassment for suspected radical political views during the 1950s and for a time, his travels were restricted. He continued to teach, conduct classical music, and to write both scholarly treatises and more accessible explorations of folk music. In 1968, he was belatedly awarded a Ph.D. by the University of California, Berkeley, and the same institution honored him in 1977 by holding a symposium in his honor.

Bibliography

Denisoff, R. Serge. *Great Day Coming.* Baltimore: Penguin, 1971.

Dunaway, David. *How Can I Keep from Singing.* New York: McGraw-Hill, 1981.

Obituary. *New York Times* 8 Feb. 1979.

Robert Weir

Seeger, Pete (1919-), was one of the most influential folksingers and folk music popularizers from the 1940s through the 1970s. He was born into a family of famous musicologists, composers, and musicians (see preceding entry); his younger half-siblings include folksinger Peggy Seeger and old-time country music revivalist Mike Seeger (of the New Lost City Ramblers). Seeger's attendance at a folk festival at age 16 captivated him. Intending a journalism career, he studied at Harvard but left after two years to travel the country and collect material for the Library of Congress folk music archives. Seeger became friends with such folk musicians as Leadbelly (see Ledbetter, Huddie) and Woody Guthrie (see entry), becoming a protégé to the Dust Bowl balladeer and protest folksinger. In 1940 Seeger formed the Almanac Singers (see entry) with Lee Hays and Millard Lampell; Guthrie soon joined the group, which specialized in labor and antiwar songs, performing mostly for union and college audiences. Seeger helped popularize the five-string banjo, becoming the model for a whole generation of banjo-pickers. When they were not traveling, the Almanacs sponsored hootenannies (a term coined by Seeger and Guthrie) in their communal New York apartment.

Seeger served in the army from 1942 to 1945, entertaining troops for the Special Services. In 1946 he helped form People's Songs, a union of folksingers and songwriters, becoming their director. The organization (with 3,000 members) published a monthly magazine of songs and news, and arranged hootenannies and bookings. In 1948 Seeger became a strong supporter of presidential candidate Henry Wallace and his Progressive Party. But in the emerging Cold War atmosphere organized labor turned against radicalism; People's Songs went bankrupt in 1949. In 1951 Seeger founded *Sing Out* magazine, serving as an editor and regular columnist for several decades. In 1949 Seeger formed the seminal vocal and instrumental group the Weavers with Hays, Ronnie Gilbert, and Fred Hellerman; a direct outgrowth of the Almanacs but more polished, they offered a somewhat popularized version of traditional folk songs. The Weavers were one of the most influential folk groups in U.S. history, achieving popularity in nightclubs, theaters, colleges, and on radio. Bridging the gap between prewar rural and postwar urban folk music, they made several best-selling recordings, including "On Top of Old Smoky" (1950), their first million-seller, Guthrie's "So Long It's Been Good to Know You" (1951), and Leadbelly's "Goodnight Irene" (1950) and "Kisses Sweeter Than Wine" (1951). "Goodnight Irene" topped the hit parade for 13 weeks, selling 2 million copies. The Weavers pioneered in featuring much international material such as the South African freedom song "Wimoweh." Seeger remained a sometime member until 1958. But his People's Songs activities and overall progressive thrust soon led to McCarthyite investigations. He appeared before the House Un-American Activities Committee in 1955, refusing to cooperate, and was not cleared of contempt of Congress charges until 1962. As a result he was blacklisted from television for years, harassed and monitored by the FBI.

Seeger forged a successful solo career including several dozen recordings for Folkways and Columbia that contained a wide array of American and international songs. His highly participatory concerts, many of them benefits, helped recruit a new generation of "folkies" in the 1950s and 1960s, setting the stage for popularized folk groups like the Kingston Trio and Peter, Paul, and Mary as well as for young folksingers like Eric Anderson, Joan Baez, Judy Collins, Bob Dylan, Phil Ochs, and Tom Paxton. Seeger was undoubtedly the key figure of the urban folk music revival that peaked in the 1960s, becoming a culture hero in the process. His goal was to make folk music once again a living tradition in the context of a restructured society.

In 1961 when he toured Britain, he was impressed by the new topical song movement there. He returned to America energized and helped establish a new biweekly topical song magazine *Broadside* (see entry), for which he became a major contributor; the magazine soon became a regular forum for younger folkies (Dylan's "Talkin' John Birch Blues" appeared in the first issue), helping spur the topical song explosion. Some of his albums were overtly political, featuring songs of labor, struggle, or protest.

Seeger's most famous compositions include "If I Had a Hammer" (a hit for Trini Lopez in 1963), "Where Have All the Flowers Gone?" (a best-seller for various artists, including the Kingston Trio in 1962), "Turn, Turn, Turn" (a 1966 hit for the Byrds), "Old Devil Time," and "Guantanamera" (a 1966 hit for the Sandpipers). He also spread the songs of various writers ("Little Boxes" by Malvina Reynolds) and movements (the civil rights anthem "We Shall Overcome"). In the 1970s, 1980s, and 1990s Seeger often performed with Woody's son, Arlo Guthrie (see entry). Traveling widely in the world, he promoted intercultural understanding. He authored several song, banjo, and guitar books that sold widely.

Seeger earned a reputation for integrity, courage, and uncompromising commitment to his causes. Ever the political activist, he sang at southern rallies and churches for the voting rights campaign of the early 1960s. Later he participated in anti-Vietnam War protests, including massive marches on Washington. These activities generated censorship. In 1963 Seeger was turned down for ABC's *Hootenanny* folk program, prompting a boycott by Seeger sympathizers such as Baez, Dylan, and Peter, Paul, and Mary. Seeger had his own folk music television program, *Rainbow Quest*, in 1965-66. He was finally invited onto the popular *Smothers Brothers Comedy Hour* in 1967 but prohibited by producers from singing "Waste Deep in the Big Muddy" (a critique of the Vietnam War). Turning his attention to the environment by the late 1960s, he organized the Hudson River Sloop Restoration Project to publicize antipollution efforts.

Bibliography

Baggelaar, Kristin, and Donald Milton. *Folk Music: More Than a Song*. New York: Crowell, 1976.

Dunaway, David King. *How Can I Keep from Singing: Pete Seeger*. New York: McGraw-Hill, 1981.

Hood, Phil, ed. *Artists of American Folk Music*. New York: Quill, 1986.

Lumer, Robert. "Pete Seeger and the Attempt to Revive the Folk Music Process." *Popular Music and Society* 15.1 (1991): 45-58.

Seeger, Pete. *The Incompleat Folksinger*. New York: Simon & Schuster, 1972.

Craig A. Lockard

See also
Protest Music

Seinfeld (1989-1998), an innovative half-hour series (starring Jerry Seinfeld), blended situation comedy with Seinfeld's own standup routines. Created by Seinfeld (1954-) and writer Larry David, *Seinfeld* offered a refreshing view of urban, single adulthood and revealed how problems such as male friendship, romance, and careers find their way into Jerry's onstage monologues which frame each episode. The show's topics (homosexuality, orgasm, masturbation, nosepicking) pushed the boundaries of prime-time network television. By its fifth season, *Seinfeld,* ostensibly a nonconcept comedy show "about nothing," hit the pinnacle of television success, with its season finale topping Nielsen ratings for the week.

The series co-starred Tony Award-winning actor Jason Alexander as George, Jerry's luckless friend, described by Alexander as "lord of the losers"; *Saturday Night Live* alumni Julia Louis-Dreyfus as Elaine, Jerry's ex-girlfriend, a feisty career woman with a Gibson girl coif; and Michael Richards as Kramer, Jerry's zany neighbor. The show's defining quality was that it was based on character development and conversation rather than the traditional sitcom action. The friends sat around and transformed their thoughts into words. They kvetched, joked, quarreled, and snacked. Jerry's observational humor dominated the show. For instance, when his miserable friend George started wearing sweatpants, Jerry said he was sending a message: "I give up.... I'm miserable, so I might as well be comfortable."

The show premiered on NBC as a one-shot in 1989, then went into summer tryouts in 1990. It was renewed that fall as a midseason replacement. Network executives and a faithful core of viewers, largely TV-literate, demographically attractive urbanites, supported the show in spite of low ratings. *Seinfeld* changed from a low-ranked cult commodity to NBC's top-rated show following a move on February 4, 1993, from a Wednesday night slot opposite ABC's *Home Improvement* to an improved post-*Cheers* slot on Thursday night. After six schedule changes in its first four years, the show's ratings suddenly shot to the top. The show's popularity continued to its much-lamented end.

The series finale of the show "about nothing" found the gang in jail for having done nothing (when they witnessed a mugging). By then, it had won a number of top awards: an Emmy for scriptwriters Elaine Pope and Larry Charles (1992); and for Larry David an Emmy for best comedy series (1993); the American Comedy Award for best actor in a comedy series for Jerry (1992, 1993); Emmy Awards for best supporting actor in a comedy series for Michael Richards (1993, 1994, 1997), and the best supporting actress Emmy for Louis-Dreyfus (1996).

Bibliography

Fretts, Bruce. *The Entertainment Weekly Seinfeld Companion*: *Atomic Wedges to Zipper Jobs*. New York: Warner, 1993.

Schwarzbaum, Lisa. *Entertainment Weekly* 9 April 1993.

Seinfeld, Jerry. *SeinLanguage*. New York: Bantam, 1993.

Carla Johnson

Self-Help Literature consists of books and articles designed to guide the reader through a process of constructive change of physique, behavior, or personality. These books and articles achieved a great audience on the coat tails of movements like pop psychology, health and fitness, and New Age mysticism. The 2000 edition of *Writer's Market* lists more than 200 publishers producing books in this area.

A more recent subpart of this genre is recovery literature. This includes various 12-step programs, wounded child therapy, and works for battered and abused individuals. Recovery literature is dominated by two opposing viewpoints: in the first, victims should cultivate their childhood wounds, and in the second, victims should analyze the events, understand them, forgive, forget, and move on.

Recently, self-help literature has come under fire with accusations of charlatanism and opportunism. Several organizations have stepped in to help consumers shop more wisely in the self-help marketplace. John W. Santrock and others recently polled 500 members of the American Psychological Association for their advice on choosing self-help books and compiled *The Authoritative Guide to Self-Help Books*. Using a five-point scale, the book rates 350 self-help books currently on the market and presents nine strategies for selecting good self-help.

Audiences for self-help literature are predominantly female and as such, the genre has found itself under the attack of feminist groups as well. These groups believe that by focusing on the individual, the literature obscures larger contextual issues such as class, gender, and race.

Bibliography
Grabmeier, J. "Rating Self-Help Books." *American Health* Sept. 1994: 32-34.
Lerner, H. "When Bad Books Happen to Good People." *Ms.* Nov./Dec. 1993: 62-64.
Santrock, J. W., et al. *The Authoritative Guide to Self-Help Books.* New York: Guilford, 1994.

Michael W. Gos

Sellers, Peter (1925-1980), was aptly described by his *New York Times* obituary as "the most versatile satiric actor of his time." Despite his uncanny virtuoso mimicry of myriad faces, voices, and mannerisms, or perhaps because of them, Peter Sellers was recognized as a national institution in Britain as early as the radio comedy series *The Goon Show* of the fifties (1949-59), which he helped originate with Spike Milligan.

Out of 52 motion pictures, he created a concrete map for himself as a comic actor in, to name just a few: *Orders Are Orders* (1955), *The Ladykillers* (1956), *I'm All Right, Jack* (1959), *The Millionairess* (1961), *Only Two Can Play* (1962), *Dr. Strangelove* (1963), *What's New, Pussycat?* (1965), *The Pink Panther* series (1963-77), *I Love You, Alice B. Toklas* (1968), and finally *Being There* (1980).

Peter Sellers was born at Southsea, Hampshire, England, to William Sellers, a pianist and musical director, and to Agnes Marks, a character actress. Besides his parents, Sellers came from a family of a grandmother and eight uncles who were all active in show business. He first appeared with his parents, at the tender age of five, in *Splash Me*, produced by his grandmother.

Besides distinguishing himself as a serious "brilliant character actor and comedian," Peter Sellers had a lot of other hats to wear as a radio, stage, and screen celebrity on both sides of the Atlantic in Anglo-America. Sellers's forte for mimicry grew out of his comedy skits and impersonations in London vaudeville houses in his early theatrical career. During the war years as a member of the Royal Air Force he continued presenting comic impersonations to the servicemen at camp shows in British India in the early forties. Sellers made his stage debut in the leading role of George Taboi's farce *Brouhaha* in London in August 1958. His talent for mimicry earned him the British Film Academy Award as the best actor of 1959.

The Naked Truth (1958), released in the U.S. as *Your Past Is Showing*, portrayed a television idol who botches an attempt to eliminate a blackmailing publisher of a scandal sheet. Sellers played a broad variety of comic characters in a vast spectrum of impersonations. In the U.S., however, his initial reputation was carved on his portrayal of a prime minister, a duchess, and a constable in *The Mouse That Roared* (1959), set in a small mythical European country that wages war on the United States to bail itself out of a horrible financial depression. His next big blast in America came with his 1960 performance in *The Battle of the Sexes*, based on James Thurber's short story "The Catbird Seat."

Sellers's versatility as an actor was demonstrated by the fact that he could assume many personae—for instance, he could be sinisterly funny in his character role in *Lolita* (1962). He played three different roles as the mad scientist, the president, and the group captain in the Royal Air Force in *Dr. Strangelove* (1963; see entry). In the sixties, in *The Pink Panther* and its sequels, he played the clumsy and blundering Inspector Clouseau. Finally, in the year he died, 1980, he played a simpleton as Chance in *Being There* and a brilliant role in *The Fiendish Plot of Dr. Fu Manchu.*

Bibliography
Life 48.63 (20 June 1960).
New York Time Magazine 27 March 1960.
New York Times 25 July 1980.

Khwaja Moinul Hassan

Selznick, David O(liver) (1902-1965), one of the most successful motion picture producers in Hollywood's history, was born in Pittsburgh, PA. Selznick's most famous productions were made as an independent producer and include *A Star Is Born* (1937), *Gone with the Wind* (1939), *Rebecca* (1940), *Since You Went Away* (1944), *Spellbound* (1945), and *Duel in the Sun* (1946). His final production was a remake of *A Farewell to Arms* (1957). Prior to 1936, he worked in various executive capacities for the Paramount, MGM, and RKO production studios since 1926. One of his credos was that only two types of movies made a profit: those that have a small budget and those that have a large budget. Invariably, Selznick's production budgets were large.

Movies Selznick had produced as part of the major studios included *A Bill of Divorcement* (1932), *King Kong* (1933), and *Dinner at Eight* (1933). He also was known for his love of great literature, having adapted Charles Dickens's *David Copperfield* and *A Tale of Two Cities*, as well as Leo Tolstoy's *Anna Karenina*, to the screen in 1935.

In 1941, after he had received Academy Awards as producer of the two previous best-picture winners, *Gone with the Wind* (*GWTW*) and *Rebecca*, Selznick alternately worried if he would ever be able to duplicate these achievements and if people really understood the personal effort he made in the production of *GWTW*. He was genuinely irritated, for example, when *Rebecca* was preferred to *GWTW*.

However, during much of World War II, though his production company remained inactive, Selznick was contemplating how to top his successes. He decided to write the screenplay adaptation of Margaret Buell Wilder's sentimental portrait of the American homefront, *Since You Went Away*, in 1943 and produced the movie the following year. The book and the movie had a receptive audience during the war and Selznick was quite happy. He was also particularly pleased with the performance of one of his stars, actress Jennifer Jones, whom he married in 1949. Of his final five productions, two were directed by Alfred Hitchcock, *Spellbound* and *The Paradine Case* (1947), and the other three starred Jones, *Duel in the Sun, Portrait of Jennie* (1949), and *A Farewell to Arms*. Selznick was chiefly responsible for bringing Ingrid Bergman, Vivien Leigh, and Alfred Hitchcock to Hollywood.

Bibliography
Behlmer, Rudy, ed. *Memo from David O. Selznick.* New York: Viking, 1972.

Haver, Ronald. *David O. Selznick's Hollywood.* New York: Knopf, 1980.

Leff, Leonard. *Hitchcock and Selznick.* New York: Weidenfeld & Nicolson, 1987.

Thomas, Bob. *Selznick.* Garden City: Doubleday, 1970.

Thomson, David. *Showman: The Life of David O. Selznick.* New York: Knopf, 1992.

Richard L. Testa, Jr.

Sendak, Maurice (1928-), born in Brooklyn and reared in the Depression, is one of the most popular and honored of children's authors and illustrators. He has received the Caldecott Medal for the illustration of his own story, *Where the Wild Things Are* (1963), the Laura Ingalls Wilder Medal, and the Hans Christian Andersen International Award for his entire body of work (the first American so honored).

With his illustrations in 1952 of Ruth Krauss's *A Hole Is to Dig*, Sendak became widely known as an illustrator of children's books. Influenced by artists such as William Blake, Randolph Caldecott, and George Cruikshank, Sendak also credits the creations of Walt Disney, especially Mickey Mouse, for inspiring his style.

Sendak is a fantasist in the tradition of Sir John Tenniel and Edward Lear, but his comically grotesque children, often criticized as looking "old," "ugly," or "too European," reflect childhood realities, as young people do suffer with powerful, conflicting emotions. Adults also criticized the monsters in *Where the Wild Things Are* as being too frightening for children, but youthful readers of several generations have made the book the modern-day classic of children's literature.

Sendak's books, which also include *In the Night Kitchen* (1970), *Outside Over There* (1981), and *Higglety Pigglety Pop, or There Must Be More to Life* (1967), continue, both in story and artwork, to probe the dualities of childhood—the terrors and fears as well as the joys and comforts.

Bibliography
Cech, John. *Angels and Wild Things: The Archetypal Poetics of Maurice Sendak.* University Park: Pennsylvania State UP, 1995.

Lanes, Selma. *The Art of Maurice Sendak.* New York: Abrams, 1980.

Rudman, Masha. "Maurice Sendak." *Children's Literature: Resources for the Classroom.* Norwood: Christopher-Gordon, 1993.

Sonheim, Amy. *Maurice Sendak.* New York: Twayne, 1992.

Linda Lattin Burns

Serials. In its purest form, the serial belongs to another era, to a time when kids flocked to neighborhood theaters (instead of shopping malls) to plunk down two bits as admission to the Saturday matinee. There they'd get popcorn and candy bars and become part of the Matinee Mavericks (or the Saturday Rustlers or the Popcorn Circus). And when the theater finally darkened and the show began, they'd see a half-dozen cartoons (Mickey Mouse, Betty Boop, Porky Pig), a two-reeler (the Three Stooges, Our Gang, Charley Chase), a B-Western (Gene Autry, Roy Rogers, William Boyd), and previews of coming attractions. And then, as kids jumped up and down in excitement, the serial would begin. As the characters appeared on the screen, the audience would cheer the hero and heroine and hiss the villain and his henchmen.

These were the days when masked villains strove for world domination, and courageous heroes valiantly struggled for justice, loyalty, and the American way. Diabolical devices were deactivated with nary a second to spare. Terrifying falls were broken by overhanging branches. Secret passageways were discovered in centuries-old jungle temples. These ingredients were all packaged together in 12 to 15 chapters (15 to 25 minutes each), with each chapter typically ending in a cliffhanger, a moment of prolonged suspense when the hero or heroine is placed in life-threatening danger only to have the words "To be continued..." appear on the screen.

Serials began in 1912 when *McClure's Ladies World* magazine devised a new strategy for building circulation: Each issue of the publication would feature a story about a continuing main character and a motion picture would show her exploits. The Edison Company produced the motion picture, entitled *What Happened to Mary*, and the results were startlingly successful. Soon afterwards other publications offered their own tie-in serials.

These early serials lacked true cliffhanger endings, as each episode told a resolved story while pointing toward further developments. By 1915, however, Pearl White, Ruth Roland, and Helen Holmes were on the scene, hanging from rooftops, diving onto moving trains, and leaping from speeding automobiles. In the most famous silent serial, *The Perils of Pauline*, Pearl White is pursed by villains who hope to stop her from getting an inheritance. Their adventures take them all over the world. In *The Exploits of Elaine*, she faced the Clutching Hand, a madman bent on conquering the world.

Silent serials were initially dominated by heroines, but by the 1920s male stars such as Joe Bonomo, Francis Ford, William Desmond, and Walter Miller took the spotlight. Even Harry Houdini, Red Grange, and Jack Dempsey starred in serials, but by the end of the 1920s the serial was virtually dead—a victim of oversaturation and of the increasing sophistication of its audience. When the serials originated, they attracted a largely adult audience, but as the feature film slowly evolved, the serial failed to mature.

With the adult audience largely gone—and with the coming of sound to film—serial makers floundered. The serial seemed headed for extinction. Several independent companies produced serials in the early 1930s but the clumsy cameras of early sound equipment resulted in static productions.

In 1935, the merger of several small studios, including Mascot Pictures, resulted in Republic Pictures. And with the merger the stage was set for a new era of serials, for Republic would soon become the generally-acknowledged king of the serials.

However, it wasn't Republic that initially reawakened the public's interest in serials. It was Universal. Universal had acquired the rights to Alex Raymond's science fiction comic strip *Flash Gordon*, and in 1936 they brought it to the screen, starring Buster Crabbe as Flash, Jean Rogers as Dale Arden (Flash's girlfriend, the sexiest heroine in serial history), and Charles Middleton as Ming the Merciless, the despotic ruler of the planet Mongo. Both *Flash Gordon* and its sequels, *Flash Gordon's Trip to Mars* and *Flash Gordon Conquers the Universe*, are filled with spark-spewing spaceships, swirling aerial dogfights, horrible prehistoric monsters, and futuristic laboratories.

Soon the serials gave us *The Adventures of Captain Marvel*, *Spy Smasher*, *Dick Tracy*, *The Phantom*, *Buck Rogers*, *Batman*, *Ace Drummond*, and many others. Radio dramas also provided promising material, and soon *The Green Hornet*, *The Lone Ranger*, and *The Shadow* hit the screen in serial form.

In the early 1940s, Republic reprised the serial heroine, as Frances Gifford starred in Edgar Rice Burroughs's *Jungle Girl* and Kay Aldridge starred in *The Perils of Nyoka*. Linda Sterling, however, was the queen of the serial, starring in six serials, including *The Tiger Woman* and *Manhunt of Mystery Island*.

This ten-year period, beginning with *Flash Gordon* and ending with the conclusion of World War II, was the golden age of the serial. Republic Pictures in particular produced a high-quality product, with excellent special effects by Howard and Theodore Lydecker (including devastating avalanches, earth-shaking explosions, and cataclysmic lightning showers), stirring original scores by William Lava and Mort Glickman, and awe-inspiring stuntwork by Yakima Canutt, David Sharpe, and Tom Steele.

But most notable of all were the directing talents of William Whitney and John English. Together they directed 17 consecutive serials, honing an approach that allowed Republic serials to far outdistance the competition. In particular, they used the camera effectively (when their budgets allowed them the freedom). *Spy Smasher*, for example, features a stunning sequence as our hero (Kane Richmond) flees by handcar down a subterranean tunnel while flames from an oil tank explosion threaten to overtake him.

By the late 1940s, the serial had begun to repeat itself, using the same stock situations in serial after serial. Heroes would regularly get the drop on the villain's henchmen only for a brawl to suddenly break out at the slightest provocation (a flicker of the lights, for example). Serials directed by Spencer Gordon Bennett and Fred C. Brannon frequently degenerate into slugfests (as in *Secret Service in Darkest Africa*, which features an average of three fist fights per episode!). Heroes were frequently knocked out and placed in dire peril—a car speeding toward a cliff, a burning warehouse, a conveyor belt headed toward a buzz saw—and every time the solution to the cliffhanger would have the hero simply wake up and roll out of the way. Imagination rarely crept into cliffhanger resolutions as the 1950s approached.

Part of the problem was that the studios were forced to divest themselves of their theaters due to government rulings in the late 1940s. Studios then considered the serials to be a luxury (along with shorts and B movies). All the attention went to feature films. As moviemaking costs soared, serial budgets were slashed, necessitating extensive use of stock footage. Heroes and heroines wore costumes that matched those used in earlier serials, allowing the same action scenes and cliffhangers to be recycled. For example, action scenes from *Jungle Girl* and *The Phantom* were reused over ten years later in *Panther Girl of the Congo* and *The Adventures of Captain Africa*, respectively. Heroes also suffered, as casting choices were made to match stuntmen on the studio payroll, leading to a legion of hopelessly dull heroes.

With the growth of television, the movie serial was living on borrowed time. Shows such as *Sky King*, *Hopalong Cassidy*, *The Gene Autry Show*, and *The Lone Ranger* soon appeared. Serial star Ralph Byrd even reprised his portrayal of Dick Tracy for television. Why go to a theater when you can see similar stuff for free at home? Complicating matters further, psychologists and parents began to worry (some would say they became hysterical) about the violence in serials and comics. They pressured studios and publishers to reduce the mayhem. Universal saw the end was near and canceled serial production in 1947. Republic and Columbia struggled until the late 1950s, producing fewer and fewer serials each year.

In the process, the serial evolved into the television series. Instead of forcing us to spend an entire week waiting to find out how the hero escaped the villain's latest terror, we now have to wait only until the commercial break is over. Some shows, such as *The Time Tunnel* and *Lost in Space,* actually used cliffhanger endings—but only as small overlaps into the next week's episode. Soap operas come the closest to using real cliffhangers.

The legacy of the serial lives on in feature films, such as *Star Wars* (1977) and *Raiders of the Lost Ark* (1981). *Raiders* even manages to begin with a sequence that remarkably resembles a slide over from a previous cliffhanger: Indiana Jones flees through a cave tunnel as a giant boulder rolls after him. Later, his fight aboard a truck recalls the work of the great stuntman Yakima Canutt. (Compare this scene with the stagecoach scene in chapter 8 of *Zorro's Fighting Legion*). And Darth Vader of *Star Wars* is a direct throwback to the masked villains of the serial's golden era. (Compare him with the Lightning in *Fighting Devil Dogs*.)

The serial, as it once was, is dead. Its history is in some ways a disappointing one, for the serial failed to progress past its own narrow limitations. Even the best serials—such as *Flash Gordon*, *Spy Smasher*, *Zorro's Fighting Legion*, *Dick Tracy*, *Daredevils of the Red Circle*, *The Lone Ranger*, *Mysterious Dr. Satan*, *The Adventures of Captain Marvel*, and *The Perils of Nyoka*—are frequently beset by wooden performances, confusing plots, and all-too-familiar cliffhangers. But when the serials worked, the results were movie magic at its best, the kind of wizardry that inspired many young moviegoers, including George Lucas, Steven Spielberg, and Robert Zemeckis, to become movie directors. The serial will continue to live in their movies, finding a whole new generation of fans for decades to come.

Bibliography

Barbour, Alan B. *Days of Thrills and Adventures*. New York: Macmillan, 1970.

Cline, William C. *In the Nick of Time: Motion Picture Sound Serials*. Jefferson: McFarland, 1984.

Mathis, Jack. *Valley of the Cliffhangers*. Northbrook: Jack Mathis Advertising, 1975.

Stedman, Raymond William. *The Serials: Suspense and Drama by Installment*. Norman: U of Oklahoma P, 1971.

Gary Johnson

See also
B Movie, The

Serling, Rod(man) (1924-1975), one of TV's most honored writers and producers, was born in Syracuse, NY, and graduated from Antioch College (Yellow Springs) with a B.A. in journalism in 1948. During college and until 1952, Serling worked as a TV staff writer and freelance scriptwriter for WLW Cincinnati and WNYC New York, where he wrote advertising copy and served as contributing writer to the anthology program *The Storm*. By 1951-52 Serling sold television scripts to New York and Hollywood shows such as *Lux Video Theater, Armstrong Circle Theater, Hallmark Hall of Fame, The Doctor*, and *Campbell Soundstage*. In 1952-53 during television's golden age of dramatic anthology programs, Serling joined Gore Vidal in the stable of writers for *Studio One*. He wrote 13 scripts for *Lux* alone, as well as many for *Medallion Theater, Suspense, Studio One, Hallmark, Motorola Television Hour,* and *Kraft*. In 1954-56, Serling wrote also for *Modern Romances, Ford Theater, Playhouse 90, Kaiser Aluminum Hour, Climax, The U.S. Steel Hour,* and *General Electric Theater,* among many others. He began to submit plays with a more pointed political message: "The Strike" for *Studio One* (1954), an antiwar play; "Patterns" for *Kraft Television Theater* (1955), which addressed corporate struggle; "The Rack," about Korean War POWs, for *U.S. Steel* (1955); "The Arena," about senatorial infighting, for *Studio One* (1956), and "Noon on Doomsday," about the consequences of small-town prejudice, for *U.S. Steel* (1956). With these Serling became part of the "Ashcan School" of television writing along with Reginald Rose and Paddy Chayefsky. In 1956-59, Serling wrote almost exclusively for *Playhouse 90* (see entry), contributing "Requiem for a Heavyweight," "The Comedian," "The Dark Side of the Earth," "Panic Button," "The Cause," "Bomber's Moon," "A Town Has Turned to Dust," "The Velvet Alley," and "The Rank and File."

In 1958 CBS offered Serling a one-year contract which bound him to write three exclusive plays for *Playhouse 90* and awarded him 40 percent ownership of and total creative control over a television series he had proposed writing for them called *The Twilight Zone* (see entry). During his television series, Serling continued to write "long plays" for dramatic anthologies: "In the Presence of Mine Enemies" for *Playhouse 90* (1960); "Slow Fade to Black," "The Command," and "Exit from a Plane in Flight" for *Bob Hope Presents the Chrysler Theater* (1964-65). In 1960, Serling testified before FCC hearings about censorial interference on the network level. He starred on the short-lived *Ichabod and Me*, a CBS comedy (1962); hosted *WBNS Ten O'Clock Theatre* in Columbus, OH (1962-64); contributed to *Bob Hope Presents the Chrysler Theater* in 1963; brought psychological introspection to the Western with the series *The Loner* (1965-66); and appeared on *Rod Serling's Liar's Club* (1969), a short-lived game show. After *Twilight Zone* was canceled in 1964, Serling entered the lecture circuit, speaking against censorship, discrimination, and prejudice, and the Vietnam War; and in favor of quality programming. In May 1964, he was elected president of the National Academy of Television Arts and Sciences.

After his famous series, he wrote "Certain Honorable Men" for *On Stage* (1968) and contributed to *Zero Hour* (1969-75). In 1969, Serling wrote the pilot episodes for *The New People* and *Night Gallery* and then became its host. During the run of *Night Gallery* (1970-73) he continued to write for dramatic anthology programs: "Doomsday Flight" (NBC, 1966), a teleplay about a bomb scare that regrettably inspired eight copycat bomb threats; for *Hallmark Hall of Fame* he wrote "A Storm in Summer" (1970), about the friendship between a black boy and a Jewish butcher; and a special "Sad and Lonely Sundays" (ABC, 1976), for *The Oath*. During the last years of his life, he returned to his teaching position at Ithaca College (1972-75) and taught also at Sherman Oaks Experimental College when he was in Southern California.

Several of Serling's teleplays were made into films (with the author writing the screenplays): *Patterns* (1956); *The Rack* (1956); *Incident in an Alley* (1962); *Requiem for a Heavyweight* (1962). He also wrote the screenplays for *Saddle the Wind* (1957), *The Yellow Canary* (1963); *Seven Days in May* (1964), *Assault on a Queen* (1966), *Planet of the Apes* (with Michael Wilson, based on the novel by Pierre Boulle, 1968), and *The Man* (1972), based on a novel by Irving Wallace.

Among Rod Serling's awards are Emmys for "Patterns" (1955), "Requiem for a Heavyweight" (1956), "The Comedian" (1957), *The Twilight Zone* (1960 and 1961) and "It's Mental Work" (1963). He was nominated for an Emmy in 1958 for "A Town Has Turned to Dust." He also won a Golden Globe Award in 1962 (best television star, male); a Harcourt-Brace Award for "Requiem" in 1956; a George Foster Peabody Broadcasting Award and a *Look Magazine* Annual Television Award for "The Velvet Alley" in 1959; Sylvania Awards in 1955 and 1956 ("Patterns" and "Requiem" respectively); a Television-Radio Writers' Annual Award in 1956 for "Requiem"; Writers Guild of America Awards in 1956 ("Requiem"), 1958 ("A Town Has Turned to Dust"), and 1975 (that organization's Laurel Award); and an Edgar Award from the Mystery Writers of America for *Night Gallery*. Serling served at various times as a commercial spokesperson for Oasis cigarettes, Joseph Schlitz brewing company, Famous Writers School, Procter & Gamble, Anacin, Crest, and Z-Best Rustproofing.

Bibliography

Boddy, William. *Fifties Television*. Urbana: U of Illinois P, 1990.

Sander, Gordon F. *Serling: The Rise and Twilight of Television's Last Angry Man.* New York: Dutton, 1992.

Zicree, Marc Scott. Twilight Zone *Companion.* New York: Bantam, 1982.

S. P. Madigan

Sesame Street (1969-) is an innovative children's educational television series for two- to five-year-olds designed to enable them to make a successful transition from home to school. In American television, *Sesame Street* is notable for three reasons. First, it has the distinction of being the most heavily researched show in the history of broadcasting. Pumping $8 million into its first year's shows, the makers of *Sesame Street* sought experts in child development, preschool education, and broadcast production in order to understand how television could be best used to enhance preschoolers' learning. Second, *Sesame Street* became the first children's educational television show to use the successful techniques of commercials—fast-paced editing, animation, slapstick, humor, puppets, and attention-getting music and visuals—to hold the attention of the preschool child. Third, *Sesame Street* revolutionized children's television by proving that an educational program could also be highly entertaining and popular, paving the way for more attempts to provide quality programming for children.

Sesame Street has won legendary recognition: It is the most widely viewed and celebrated children's television series in the world. In America, a season of *Sesame Street* is composed of 130 hour-long programs broadcast all year long on most public television stations on weekdays in both the morning and afternoon, with shows repeated on weekends as well. All told, more than 11 million households in America tune in on a regular basis, with viewership approaching saturation among preschoolers in all areas of the country. Outside the U.S., more than 100 million children in nearly 100 countries have benefited from the show, some of them enjoying foreign language versions. The English language version, now seen in 38 countries, has aired in 90 nations in its first 25 years. In the same period, *Sesame Street* received 85 awards, including 51 Emmys, 12 for outstanding children's series and 10 for outstanding writing in a children's series. Other honors include the Prix Jeunesse International, 2 George Foster Peabody Awards, a Clio, 4 Parents' Choice Awards, and an Action for Children's Television Special Achievement Award.

Children's Television Workshop (CTW), a not-for-profit company founded in 1968 to explore and experiment with television's capabilities as an educational medium, is responsible for bringing *Sesame Street* to the air. Its beginnings can be traced to early 1966, when Lloyd Morrisett, vice president of the Carnegie Corporation, recruited Joan Ganz Cooney, a New York television producer, to study the educational possibilities of television for preschoolers. By the time Cooney submitted her report in November of that year, Morrisett has assumed the position of president of the John and Mary Markle Foundation and attempted to obtain funds to finance Cooney's project. The result was the establishment of CTW, with Cooney serving as president and Morrisett as chairman, and initial funding provided by the Carnegie, Ford, and Markle Foundations, Operation Head Start, and the U.S. Office of Education. CTW's first project was to produce and telecast a daily television program that would both entertain preschool children and promote their intellectual and cultural development. After a year of extensive research, testing, and production, *Sesame Street*, which debuted in November 1969, was distributed by the Public Broadcasting Service and met with wide success. By 1970 CTW had become a leader in children's educational programming and, with major grants from the Ford Foundation, sought to improve *Sesame Street* as well as develop another educational show, *Electric Company*, designed primarily to teach reading to second graders. In later years, CTW pioneered additional educational efforts, including *3-2-1 Contact*, a science show for 8- to 12-year-olds; *Square One TV*, a math series for 8- to 12-year-olds; *Ghostwriter*, a reading and writing series for 7- to 10-year-olds; and *Cro*, an animated science and technology program.

Attempting to teach letter and number recognition, simple counting, new vocabulary, and basic concepts, *Sesame Street* interspersed animated sequences with live-action ones. Creating an inner-city neighborhood, *Sesame Street* introduced a likable cast of characters, most notably the Muppets, marionette-puppets designed by Jim Henson (see Jim Henson Productions). They included Kermit the Frog, Big Bird, Cookie Monster, Oscar the Grouch, and Bert and Ernie, all of whom won the attention and affection of children. In addition to the Muppets, other members of the show's original cast were Loretta Long and Matt Robinson as the married couple Susan and Gordon, singer Bob McGrath as a neighbor, and Will Lee as the old shopowner Mr. Hooper; in subsequent years, more residents came to *Sesame Street,* so that by the late '90s the cast numbered more than 40. The *Sesame Street* neighborhood, which is decidedly multicultural, stresses cooperation and understanding, and as the show matured, more sequences were added promoting prosocial behavior. Other of the show's sequences depict nature or varied cultures or lifestyles as a way of expanding the child viewer's experience. Another significant element of *Sesame Street* is its inclusion of material designed to appeal to adults—guest stars, verbal puns, spoofs of popular television shows—so as to encourage them to watch with their children and reinforce the show's lessons.

Early assessments of *Sesame Street* were generally positive. Research conducted by Ball and Bogatz (1970) for the Educational Testing Service during the first year of *Sesame Street* revealed that the show was widely watched among preschoolers, and those who watched the most learned the most. Further, the show proved to be effective at helping children from diverse backgrounds to learn numbers, letters, and cognitive reading skills via the show's attention-getting production techniques and use of repetition.

In subsequent years, *Sesame Street* maintained its high reputation; however, criticisms began to emerge. In 1975, Thomas Cook and his associates published *Sesame Street Revisited*, a secondary analysis of Ball and Bogatz's data that raised serious questions. Although Cook concurred with Ball and Bogatz that regular viewers did learn from *Sesame Street*, his study claimed that the gains were modest and short-term and confined mostly to simple letter and number recognition rather than to any sort of higher reasoning. Cook also noted that the funding awarded for the production of *Sesame Street* might be better spent in other ways that would have a greater benefit on more children. Even more disturbing was Cook's assertion that because children from advantaged families seemed more likely to watch *Sesame Street*, they were also more likely to learn more from it, thus widening the gap between the advantaged and disadvantaged. Because the overriding goal of the show was to narrow the knowledge gap, this finding proved particularly controversial. Other critics of *Sesame Street* have objected to a myriad of items. Some say the show's brief segments and fast pace pander to the child's short attention span rather than developing it further, perhaps leading to a preference for briskly edited, superficial programming such as MTV in adolescence. By the same token, critics of the highly stimulating format of *Sesame Street* say that it may excite children too much and give them unrealistic expectations about school, causing them to be disappointed with the normal classroom routine. Finally, some have found the commercialization of *Sesame Street* distasteful. Each year, CTW licenses more than 1,700 *Sesame Street* items for sales of $200 million. Thus, although *Sesame Street* carries no advertising messages, the show itself functions as a one-hour commercial for Big Bird plush toys, Cookie Monster sweat suits, and the like.

Despite its critics, *Sesame Street* has remained an American institution and had great cultural impact. As the high sales figure for *Sesame Street* licensed products suggests, children throughout the world have embraced the show's characters. For example, when Will Lee, who played Mr. Hooper, died in 1984, the producers of *Sesame Street* knew that they had to address the loss in a sensitive way. Thus, on Thanksgiving Day, a time when parents would be at home with their children, a *Sesame Street* special aired, acknowledging Mr. Hooper's absence and addressing the sensitive topic of death. In 1989, *Sesame Street* tackled the subject of childbirth with several shows following Maria and Luis as they anticipated the birth of their baby. When Muppet creator Jim Henson, who also provided the voice for Kermit the Frog, died unexpectedly in 1990, it was front-page news, and parents and children all over the world mourned.

Bibliography

Ball, S., and G. A. Bogatz. *The First Year of* Sesame Street: *An Evaluation*. Princeton: Educational Testing Service, 1970.

Cook, Thomas D., et al. Sesame Street *Revisited*. New York: Sage Foundation, 1975.

Lesser, Gerald. *Children and Television: Lessons from* Sesame Street. New York: Vintage, 1974.

Kathy Merlock Jackson

Sha Na Na, known for their dynamic stage show in which vocal harmony and choreography combined to recall rock 'n' roll hits of the 1950s, was a satirical rock oldies revival group most popular during the 1970s nostalgia craze. They strove for authenticity in their musical retreads despite the self-parody in their adoption of "greaser" personae.

The group began in the late 1960s as the Kingsmen, Columbia University's answer to Yale's a capella Whiffenpoof Singers. By spring of 1969, they were drawing large concert crowds with theatrical renditions of oldies such as "Teen Angel," "Duke of Earl," "Alley Oop," and "Rama Lama Ding Dong," and they had adopted a 1950s look: gold lamé costumes, drain-pipe trousers, white socks, T-shirts with the sleeves rolled up to their shoulders. The name Sha Na Na was derived from the recurring chant in the Silhouettes' 1958 recording of "Get a Job."

Early group members included leader Rod Leonard (bass), David Garrett (vocals), Joe Witkin (piano), and Alan Cooper (bass). But once launched, Sha Na Na's official original lineup consisted of Scott Powell (vocals), Johnny Contardo (vocals), Frederick Dennis "Denny" Greene from Harlem (vocals), Donald York from Idaho (vocals), Chris Donald (guitar, replaced by Vinnie Taylor in 1970), Bruce "Zoroaster" Clarke (bass), Screamin' Scott Simon (piano), Jon "Bowzer" Bauman (piano), Lennie Baker (saxophone), John "Jocko" Marcellino (drums), Richard Joffe (vocals), Elliot "Gino" Cahn (rhythm guitar, vocals), and Henry Gross (lead guitar). Gross left in 1970 for a solo career, the highlight of which proved to be the hit single "Shannon" in May 1976.

When Richard Nader put together his first Rock 'n' Roll Revival show at Madison Square Garden in October 1969, he included Sha Na Na among the likes of Bill Haley and His Comets, Chuck Berry, the Platters, and the Shirelles. Such appearances, Woodstock, and word of mouth accounted for the group's rise to fame rather than the usual springboard for a musical act: a hit record. Indeed, promotional strategy ensured that America was aware of Sha Na Na before their first record hit stores in 1969: *Rock 'n' Roll Is Here to Stay* on Buddah's Kama Sutra label, followed by *Sha Na Na* in 1970 and *The Night Is Still Young* in 1972—all moderately successful, but not phenomenal. But Sha Na Na never produced a hit record, primarily because an integral part of the act was the visual experience. Vinyl success came closest with K-Tel's package of hits—*The Golden Age of Rock 'n' Roll*—a 1973 gold-award album of oldies. After *Hot Sox* (1974), which did include more original material, most of the group's albums were repackagings of their previously recorded material.

The 1970s nostalgia fad continued after the film *American Graffiti* (1973) with TV's *Happy Days* and *Laverne and Shirley*. NBC launched the show *Sha Na Na* with a pilot in January 1977 and as a syndicated series that September. The show naturally featured musical numbers and comedy sketches set in a 1950s city neighborhood. Sha Na Na also appeared and sang in the film *Grease* (1978), playing a 1950s group "Johnny Casino and the Gamblers" at a high school dance contest.

Throughout the 1980s, Sha Na Na continued performing while Buddah Records reissued albums with their recordings of "Sixteen Candles," "Earth Angel," "Chantilly Lace," and others. Despite personnel changes (including the addition of a woman, Dora), five standard members—Marcellino, Simon, Ryan, York, and Baker—were still appearing in impressively acrobatic Las Vegas shows in the late 1980s.

Bibliography

Billboard 15 July 1978: S2-S14.

Bogart, Neil. "Multimedia Promotion." *The Music Industry: Markets and Methods for the Seventies.* New York: Billboard, 1970: 20.

Hodenfield, Jan. "Sha Na Na Na Yip Yip mum mum get a job." *Rolling Stone* 18 Oct. 1969: 30-32.

Michael Delahoyde

Shadow, The, was the most important of a series of adventure heroes whose exploits were featured in pulp magazines (see entry) in the earlier part of the 20th century. In 1931, publisher Street and Smith inaugurated a new concept: a pulp devoted to the adventures of one figure, usually a vigilante crime fighter or a superhero operating under a secret identity. The single-hero adventure pulp won a large audience during the 1930s and 1940s, and had a lasting impact on American popular culture.

The Shadow appeared in 325 pulp novels and on a long-running radio show (1931-49), in which a mysterious announcer ("the Shadow") narrated stories from Street and Smith's *Detective Story Magazine.* That program created reader interest in a magazine featuring the Shadow, which Street and Smith launched in 1931. Begun as a quarterly, *The*

Photo courtesy of Popular Culture Library, Bowling Green State University, Bowling Green, OH.

Shadow Magazine was soon issued monthly, then twice monthly, a frequency it maintained until the paper shortages of World War II.

The most important and prolific of several Shadow writers was Walter Gibson (1897-1985), who produced two Shadow novels a month for ten years. Altogether, Gibson wrote 282 such novels and created many of the conventions associated with the character: a grim and mysterious nemesis of crime, distinguished by his slouch hat and black cloak, triple identity, .45 automatic pistol, and network of agents. The character was also successful in motion pictures, comic strips, and comic books, but his radio and pulp personae were best known. The Shadow's laugh and signature lines on radio ("The weed of crime bears bitter fruit" and "Who knows what evil lurks in the hearts of men?") remain abiding emblems of his role as a cultural icon.

Daryl L. Coats

Shadowfax (1974-1995), a group which combined jazz, rock, and world music, was formed when sax and flute player Chuck Greenberg and bass player Phil Maggini, Chicago natives, joined with guitarist G. E. Stinson and drummer Stu Nevitt. The name Shadowfax comes from the works of J. R. R. Tolkien, whose novel *The Hobbit* introduces the wizard Gandalf and his magic horse, Shadowfax.

Their first album, *Watercourse Way*, was released on Passport records in 1976. It reveals the group's early influences—Miles Davis, Weather Report, Mahavishnu Orchestra, and Oregon—and their desire not to play "just electric music."

Their next four albums were released through Windham Hill (see entry), and Shadowfax became known as a New Age group through this association. In 1982, Shadowfax released their self-entitled album, their first through Windham Hill. Most of the instrumentation on *Shadowfax* is acoustic, partially because that style seemed to fit with what Windham Hill was going for at the time and partially because the group was still trying to establish a "sound" of its own.

With the next three albums, they added more electronically enhanced instruments, but continued introducing world music instruments, such as Indian *tabla* and *kanjeera,* Balinese *kendang,* African *mbira,* and Chilean flutes. In 1988, Shadowfax released its only album on Capitol Records, *Folksongs for a Nuclear Village*, which won a Grammy Award. Unfortunately, due to management changes, Shadowfax was dropped from Capitol soon after. They decided to move back to a small label, Private Music, and in 1990 released *The Odd Get Even*, a more experimental album than those previously released and the most electrically focused. At that point, original guitarist G. E. Stinson decided to leave the group. During a two-year hiatus, Greenberg released a solo album, *From a Blue Planet* (1991), and rumors that Shadowfax had split for good spread quickly. In 1992, however, Shadowfax found a new home at Earthbeat!, distributed by Warner Bros.

Their first album for Earthbeat!, *Esperanto* (1992), garnered a Grammy nomination. They had begun to return to their original plan to make music that did not focus on electric instruments, and the band had turned once more to making music that came from emotion when Greenberg died of an apparent heart attack in September 1995. Since he produced the group's albums, no matter the label, and many of the songs featured him playing the lyricon—the first electronic wind instrument, which he had helped develop—his death brought an end to this experimental group. Their last recording, *Magic Theater* (1994), celebrated 20 years in the recording business, and was a return to their world music roots.

Bibliography

Blank-Edelman, David N. "Shadowfax: New Directions." *Rhythm Music Magazine* March 1994: 34-37.

"Chuck Greenberg." Obituary. Associated Press. 8 Sept. 1995. Online. LEXIS-NEXIS Academic Universe. 16 May 2000.

Okamoto, David. "Coda: Shadowfax." *Jazziz: Adult Oriented Music* July 1994: 66+.

Tamra Mabe Wilson

Shane (1953), directed by George Stevens, is one of the archetypal Western films, a conscious attempt to encapsulate many of the myths and symbols of the American West in a single motion picture. The title character, a gunfighter portrayed by Alan Ladd, is a stock character of the Western, although one given mythic treatment in this film through his unusual costume—light buckskin clothing—his symbolic wounding in the left side, and his ascent at the close of the movie after his work has been completed.

While Shane is the embodiment of good, as he fights on behalf of the beleaguered settlers, evil is represented by those who would stop the flow of civilization across America, specifically rancher Ryker and his hired gun Wilson (Jack Palance) who would monopolize the land the settlers need. Civilization in the film, as often in Western films, is represented by the female presence, here a settler's wife played by Jean Arthur. Since there is some attempt to convey a romantic tension between Ladd and Arthur, Shane's rejection of the woman becomes part of his ultimate rejection of civilization as he returns to the wilderness from which he emerged.

In addition to the use of Christian imagery, other influences on the characterization of Shane include the heroes of quest literature, as well as American frontier heroes such as James Fenimore Cooper's Natty Bumppo/Hawkeye. Like Hawkeye, Shane is a man who lives on the outskirts of civilization, helping to make its advance possible, but never quite comfortable enough to remain as a part of it. He will associate with other human beings, work alongside them, even defend them at the risk of his own life, but ultimately there is no place for him and the impulses he represents within the civilization he helps make possible.

Bibliography

Ambrosetti, Ronald. "Folklore, Myth, and the Archetypal Western." *Journal of the American Studies Association of Texas* 5 (1974): 41-47.

Bazin, André. "The Evolution of the Western." *What Is Cinema?* Vol. 2. Trans. Hugh Gray. Berkeley: U of California P, 1971.

French, Philip. *Westerns: Aspects of a Movie Genre.* Rev. ed. New York: Oxford UP, 1977.

Marsden, Michael T. "Western Films: America's Secularized Religion." *Movies as Artifacts: Cultural Criticism of Popular Film.* Ed. Michael T. Marsden et al. Chicago: Nelson-Hall, 1982.

Jean Anne Yackshaw

Shatner, **William** (1931-), born in Montreal, worked in Canadian theater, film, and radio productions through 1953 (i.e., *The Butler's Night Off*, 1950). In 1954, he joined the Royal Stratford Shakespeare Company (director, Tyrone Guthrie), appearing in productions of the 1954-56 seasons, some of which were televised (*Oedipus Rex*, 1956). In the later 1950s Shatner shuttled appearances on live television (*Goodyear Playhouse, Omnibus,* and *Kaiser Aluminum Hour*), turning down movie contracts in favor of more artistically satisfying projects in theater and live television: a 1957 Emmy-winning *Alfred Hitchcock Presents,* "The Glass Eye," *Studio One*'s "The Defenders" and "No Deadly Medicine" (with Lee J. Cobb), as well as starring roles in 1958 in productions on *Kraft Television Theater, U.S. Steel Hour, Climax,* and *Sunday Showcase*, culminating in the Emmy-nominated "A Town Has Turned to Dust" (by Rod Serling) for *Playhouse 90*, and starring roles on Broadway in *The World of Suzy Wong* and *The Brothers Karamazov*.

His specialty, mild-mannered individuals tortured by fate, attracted him to roles in the famous psychological dramas of the era: *Alfred Hitchcock Presents, The Twilight Zone, One Step Beyond,* and *Thriller*. The versatility of his talent combined with his good looks won him critical praise in the era of the "square-jawed blonde," and he found himself turning down title roles in numerous television series, perhaps the best-known among them *Dr. Kildare* and *The Defenders*. Instead, he continued to be drawn toward more quality theater (he starred in *A Shot in the Dark* on Broadway with Julie Harris and Walter Matthau), and socio-politically important projects such as *Judgment at Nuremberg* and *Explosive Generation* (both 1960), highlighted by his starring role in Roger Corman's award-winning but controversial film about racial intolerance, *The Intruder* (1961).

After the death of live television, from 1962 to 1964 Shatner worked tirelessly in American television, usually starring as "guest villain," or a "good doctor, lawyer, or husband" embroiled in some emotional conflict. He had a role in one important film with director Martin Ritt, *Outrage* (1964), and a made-for-TV movie, *Alexander the Great* (aired in a greatly cut version in 1967), in which he played the title role. Some of his finest work on television was seen in 1965 when he starred in his first television series, *For the People* (CBS), about an assistant district attorney. After the cancellation of *For the People* and a few more guest-starring roles on *The Big Valley* and *Dr. Kildare,* Shatner was in the process of considering acting and directing opportunities in Toronto when Gene Roddenberry offered him the role of Captain James T. Kirk in *Star Trek* (NBC, 1966-69; see entry). In spite of its rigorous schedule, during *Star Trek* Shatner made two unusual films: *The Incubus* (1966), in Esperanto with

English subtitles, and *White Comanche* (1967), a socially conscious "spaghetti Western" remembered as one of the best of its genre in the 1960s.

After the cancellation of *Star Trek*, Shatner returned occasionally to his roots in television, appearing in *CBS Playhouse* (1969) and *Hollywood Television Theater*'s Emmy-winning *The Andersonville Trial* (1970). When *Star Trek* entered syndication and skyrocketed to cult status in the 1970s, Shatner ran the gamut of guest appearances on episodic television; hosted a few specials (*Salute to John Wayne*); and appeared in numerous made-for-TV movies. One pilot, *The Barbary Coast* (1975), became Shatner's third television series, running for only one season that year.

Beginning in 1978 Shatner participated variously as star, writer, and director, in Paramount's series of seven *Star Trek* films (see entries), between which Shatner continued to make films: *Visiting Hours* (1980), *The Babysitter* (1980), *Broken Angel* (1988); flogged his famous persona in satires (*Airplane II, Mork and Mindy, Saturday Night Live*); starred in his fourth and fifth television series, *T. J. Hooker* (1982-85) and *Rescue 911* (1989-96); but reduced the number of his appearances on episodic television and specials. He also began writing science fiction novels with the *TekWar* series (beginning in 1989); his sci-fi writing career has since continued with another series and several novels.

S. P. Madigan

Sheen/Estevez Family, The, includes no less than six actors: Martin Sheen and his brother, Joe Estevez; and Martin's children with his wife, Janet Templeton: Emilio Estevez, Ramón Estevez, Jr., Charlie Sheen, and Renée Estevez. This family of actors is known for being at once professionally supportive of, and independent from, one another.

Martin Sheen, born Ramón Estevez on August 3, 1940, is a first-generation American, his mother having immigrated from Ireland and his father from Spain via Cuba. The seventh son in a family of ten, Ramón was born and raised in Dayton, OH, in relative poverty and with a physical handicap—his left arm was damaged at birth, and has never been totally functional. At an early age, Ramón decided that he wanted to be an actor and had a chance to practice his art in high school plays, although he never had a leading role. He entered an acting competition on Dayton television, and won a trip to New York and a CBS audition. In 1959, he borrowed money, moved to New York, and found a night job that allowed him to audition during the day. He and several other young actors—including Barbra Streisand—formed the Actors' Co-op to promote themselves. To avoid the stigma a Latino name could bring to a show business career, he changed his name to Martin Sheen. In 1964, Sheen made his Broadway debut in *Never Live over a Pretzel Factory,* but his true breakthrough came the same year with *The Subject Was Roses,* for which he was nominated for a Tony Award. It was adapted for the screen a few years later, again starring Sheen. The year 1964 marked the beginning of Sheen's prolific career in television. He took parts in many series, such as *The Mod Squad, Route 66, The Outer Limits,*

and *The F.B.I.* and played in the soap opera *As the World Turns*. Martin Sheen's first feature film was *The Incident* in 1967 and his first noticeable role was as Lieutenant Dobbs in *Catch-22* in 1970.

In 1974, Martin Sheen gave a remarkable performance as Kit Carruthers in *Badlands*. The same year, Sheen had another leading role in a significant television production, *The Execution of Private Slovik*, the story of a deserter tried and shot for his crime. Given the role of Ben Willard in Francis Ford Coppola's war epic *Apocalypse Now* (1979), adapted from Joseph Conrad's *Heart of Darkness*, Martin Sheen embarked on an adventure that almost cost him his life. Willard, a young army officer, is sent to find and kill Kurtz (Marlon Brando), a psychotic colonel whose Vietnam experience has turned into a mystical adventure in the Cambodian jungle. Sheen, suffering an intense real-life identity crisis, improvised the opening scene of the film, remarkably portraying the angst of a man fighting his own demons. Soon after shooting this remarkable scene, Sheen had a massive heart attack, an event that forced him to rethink his lifestyle.

His next crucial experience took place in India during the filming of Sir Richard Attenborough's *Gandhi* in 1980. He was at once utterly impressed with the spiritual power and the appalling poverty found in India. His two most important roles have been in John Schlesinger's *The Believers* (1987), where Sheen plays a psychologist trying to bring back his late wife's spirit through voodoo rituals, and as Joe Fox in *Wall Street* (1987), father of stockbroker Bud Fox, played by son Charlie. Through the 1990s, he appeared in numerous made-for-TV movies, and he has his first regular TV series role in *The West Wing* (1999-), as the president of the United States.

Martin Sheen's brother, Joe Phelan (born Joseph Estevez), is an actor as well. Besides being Martin's stand-in for *Apocalypse Now*, he has performed in a few unremarkable films such as *The Legend of the Rollerblade 7* (1992) and *Beach Babes from Beyond* (1993).

Martin Sheen's oldest son, Emilio Estevez, was born in New York City on May 12, 1962. He was raised in California, where his parents moved in 1969. As a teenager, he spent much time with his friends Sean and Chris Penn, and Chad and Rob Lowe, all soon-to-be actors. Emilio wrote his first play in high school, about a Vietnam veteran whom he had met in the Philippines during the shooting of *Apocalypse Now*. Classmate Sean Penn directed the play. Estevez's first acting role was in the television special *Seventeen Going on Nowhere* (1980). Then came his first supporting roles in *Tex* (1982) and *The Outsiders* (1983), produced by Francis Ford Coppola's Zoetrope Studios, and a role next to his father in the television drama *In the Custody of Strangers* (1982). His first significant part was that of Otto Maddox in the cult movie *Repo Man* (1984), the story of a punker repossessing cars for a living in Los Angeles. In 1985, he was Andrew in John Hughes's success *The Breakfast Club*, one in a series of teen movies quite popular in the mid and late 1980s. Estevez also played a part in *St. Elmo's Fire* (1985), the story of a post-high school group of friends and their struggle through the passage to adulthood. The film reunited Estevez and his old friends Rob Lowe and Judd Nelson, engendering the term "brat pack" to describe this gang of young, hip, and allegedly spoiled Hollywood actors.

While shooting *The Breakfast Club* and *St. Elmo's Fire*, Estevez wrote two film scripts. The first was adapted from Susan Hinton's best-seller *That Was Then...This Is Now*. Estevez bought the rights to the novel, found financing, and acted in the film. His second script was *Wisdom* (1987), which at age 23 he also produced, directed, and performed in. The same year, Estevez starred with Richard Dreyfuss in the popular *Stakeout*. In 1988, he was in the very successful *Young Guns* with brother Charlie and a few other young stars. In *Mighty Ducks* (1992), he starred as a hockey coach. Since then, Estevez seems to have specialized in sequels to these last three films.

Although Martin Sheen's second son, Ramón, thinks of himself more as a dancer, he has had some opportunities to act as well: in 1985, with his father in *State of Emergency*, and in 1990 in *Cadence*, directed by Martin Sheen himself, with Martin and Charlie Sheen. His most important role so far has been in the British film *Turn Around* in 1987. He was also the host in a documentary about street teenagers called *Street Shadows* and has performed in a few plays. In 1990, he and sister Renée played in the European production of *Touch and Die*, directed by Piernico Solinas.

Charlie Sheen, born Carlos Irwin Estevez on September 3, 1965, chose to follow in his father's footsteps by adopting the latter's stage name. He was involved in movies at an early age, as an extra and as help on some of his father's early films (*The Execution of Private Slovik*, *Apocalypse Now*). Like Martin, Charlie did not finish high school, choosing instead to devote his entire time to acting. He started his career with a small role in *Grizzly II - The Predator* (1977). Like his father, Charlie did several television specials before becoming a film star. He was Ken Cruze in CBS's *The Silence of the Heart* (1984) and played a small role in 1985's *Out of Darkness*, also featuring Martin Sheen. In 1986, he was noticed in the teen hit *Ferris Bueller's Day Off*. His true breakthrough came the same year when Oliver Stone cast him as the central character of his film *Platoon*. A year later, Charlie collaborated again with Oliver Stone on *Wall Street*, the story of a young and ambitious stockbroker. *Wall Street* gave Charlie and Martin Sheen a chance to be together on the big screen for the first time. Since then, he has had a consistent and rather prolific career, making an average of three films a year. Among the most noticeable: *Young Guns* (1988), with brother Emilio; *Eight Men Out* (1988), about the Black Sox scandal, *Major League* (1989), and *Major League II* (1994), all three of which gave Sheen a chance to play baseball in films; *Cadence*, directed by father Martin and featuring Martin and Emilio; *The Three Musketeers* (1993); *Terminal Velocity* (1994); and *Being John Malkovich* (1999).

Martin Sheen's youngest child and only daughter, Renée Estevez, is also an actor as well as a poet and writer. Her first role was as a teenage mother in her father's CBS special *Babies Having Babies*, after which she had several other parts in television dramas. She also had supporting roles in a few feature films like *Intruder* (1988), *For Keeps* (1988), *Heathers* (1989), *Single White Female* (1992), and *Deadfall* (1993), and, like her father, has a part on *The West Wing*.

Bibliography

American Film Dec. 1982: 20-28.
American Film Mar. 1985: 42-58.
Films in Reviews 34.9 (1983): 556-58.
Riley, Lee, and David Shumacher. *The Sheens: Martin, Charlie, and Emilio Estevez*. New York: St. Martin's, 1989.

Marion Bermondy

Sheldon, Sidney (1917-), winner of a Tony, an Emmy, a Screen Writer's Guild Award, and an Oscar, has mastered most contemporary literary genres as a best-selling novelist, Broadway playwright, screenwriter, songwriter, and now, audio recording artist reading his own books.

Sheldon's 16 major novels developed the international thriller that pits jet-set high jinks, high-tech espionage, potboiler plots, and screen-sized characters against each other. Often using revengeful women as protagonists, Sheldon's novels dominate the best-seller lists, and many have been adapted into television miniseries. Widely known titles include *The Naked Face* (1970), *The Other Side of Midnight* (1974), *Bloodline* (1977), *Rage of Angels* (1980), *If Tomorrow Comes* (1985), and *The Doomsday Conspiracy* (1991).

In television, Sheldon has written over 250 scripts and created several award-winning series: *The Patty Duke Show*, *I Dream of Jeannie*, which won an Emmy, and the mystery series *Hart to Hart*. In Hollywood, he wrote the Oscar-winning screenplay for *The Bachelor and the Bobby Soxer* (1947), a vehicle for Cary Grant and Myrna Loy, along with numerous other film scripts; he produced the memorable films *Easter Parade* (1948) and *Annie Get Your Gun* (1950), and was the recipient of a star on the Hollywood Walk of Fame. On Broadway, he won a Tony in 1959 for *Redhead*.

Bibliography

Demaster, William W. *American Playwrights, 1890-1945*. Westport, CT: Greenwood, 1995.

Anne R. Kaler

She-Ra, Princess of Power (1985-1986), a spinoff of the highly successful toy-based animated program *He-Man and the Masters of the Universe* (produced by Filmation Associates), was introduced two years behind *He-Man* (see entry) and immediately proceeded to best him in the mid-1980s ratings of the Top 10 children's programs, winning fourth place to *He-Man*'s sixth and reaching 84 percent of all American households to *He-Man*'s already hefty 81 percent market share. Filmation produced 93 episodes in the series.

An indirect descendent of Wonder Woman with her "magic lasso," She-Ra was He-Man's "twin sister," and used her "Sword of Protection" to achieve televisual gender equality as well as repeated victories over a group of animated evildoers known as "the Horde"—all of which (sword, villains, and She-Ra herself) were also available in the toy store for at-home parallel play. In fact, when the half-hour syndicated series first aired in September of 1985, the

Mattel Toys She-Ra Princess of Power collection was already on toy store shelves.

Pam Steinle

Shock Radio. Following brief experiments with sexual innuendo in the 1950s and what became known as "topless radio" in the early 1970s, Howard Stern (see entry) emerged as the father of "shock radio" in the 1980s. One newspaper said shock radio was "non-stop banter of acerbic comments, scathing put-downs and tasteless jokes." Another disk jockey cited as an early example of "shock jocks" is Steve Dahl in Chicago (see entry).

The radio format tested the limits of what could be said in sexual, racial, or blunt terms. Stern's New York radio program was first fined by the Federal Communications Commission in 1987 for a show in which a man was described playing a piano with his penis.

Stern's huge popular and commercial success led other radio deejays to imitate the format. The FCC, throughout the late 1980s and early 1990s, began a crackdown that led to a series of fines, escalating in Stern's case to $600,000.

Bibliography
Broadcasting 30 Nov. 1992; 2 Nov. 1992; 16 Aug. 1993.
Los Angeles Times 20 Dec. 1992.
Ray, William B. *The Ups and Downs of Radio-TV Regulation*. Ames: Iowa State UP, 1990.

Jeremy Harris Lipschultz

Short, Luke (1908-1975), a writer best known for his Western fiction, was born Frederick D. Glidden in Kewanee, IL. Glidden turned to fiction only after failing as a newspaper reporter and trapper. He had done well academically in high school and college, graduating from the University of Missouri in 1930, but could not seem to hit his stride until he hired Marguerite Harper as his agent in 1935. Glidden began to write under the name Luke Short and sold his first stories to the pulps.

Short began a steady routine of having his novels serialized in such magazines as the prestigious *Collier's* and *Saturday Evening Post*, and then released in book form. In the 1940s, Short hit his stride. He published 14 novels, abandoned the pulps, and saw five of his novels made into films. The most notable was *Ramrod* (1947), starring Joel McCrea. Unfortunately, he never fulfilled his dreams of becoming rich from his films. The $25,000 he made from *Ramrod* was the most he ever received for film rights to a novel.

After the war, Short moved from serials to paperbacks. Sales to Bantam and Dell provided him with a lucrative outlet for his work. However, in the 1950s Short grew tired of the Western genre and wrote only six books. He wanted to write other types of popular fiction but was never able to do so. His novel *Pearly*, a non-Western, for example, remains unpublished. Moreover, attempts to work out a deal to write TV Westerns for Desi Arnaz and Lucille Ball did not pan out. Neither did his musical *I've Had It* achieve much success outside Colorado. In the 1960s he returned to writing the Western he had come to despise, averaging a novel a year between 1965 and 1975.

In common with many Western writers, Short explored the theme of "law and lawlessness," stressing the need to appeal to a higher law. Of course, women oppose the violence that the heroes deem necessary to bring about a lawful society. This stock device is fully exploited in Short's work. Over time, however, Short went beyond the stereotype and developed heroines who are strong and fully developed types. Additionally, in his later writings Short displayed open sympathy with minorities. Finally, Short was sensitive to the relationship between the individual and the community.

Bibliography
Atkinson, Frank. *Dictionary of Literary Pseudonyms.* 4th ed. Chicago: American Library Association, 1987.
Calder, Jenni. *There Must Be a Lone Ranger: The American West in Myth and Reality.* New York: Taplinger, 1974.
Cawelti, John G. *The Six-Gun Mystique.* Bowling Green, OH: Bowling Green State U Popular P, 1971.
Etulain, Richard W. "Luke Short (Frederick D. Glidden)." *Fifty Western Writers: A Bio-Bibliographical Sourcebook.* Ed. Fred Erisman and Richard W. Etulain. Westport: Greenwood, 1982.
Gale, Robert. *Luke Short.* Boston: Twayne, 1981.

Frank A. Salamone

Showboat, a uniquely American enterprise, is the name given to a river flatboat, barge, steamer, or paddlewheeler, most prominently on the Mississippi and Ohio river system, that emphasized live theatrical performances. Today, permanently moored showboats, promoting legalized gambling, tourism, and miscellaneous festivals, still offer variety entertainments, but these crafts, often incapable of river travel, are a faint echo of their spirited 19th- and early-20th-century predecessors.

The showboat's origins are obscure, but actor/manager William Chapman, Sr. (1764-1839), the English patriarch of a large itinerant acting family, is credited with its invention in 1831. In Pittsburgh, PA, Chapman outfitted a 100 x 16-foot flatboat with a stage and rough plank seating, christened it the *Floating Theatre,* and accompanied by nine family members and two unidentified crewmen, pushed off down the Ohio River bound for New Orleans. When the troupe reached its destination, the boat was sold and the actors made their way north back to Pittsburgh. For the next several years the talented Chapmans followed the same routine, setting a standard for quality showboat theater by presenting Shakespeare, contemporary melodramas, farces, musical afterpieces, and interludes to frontier settlements along the western rivers. Their success inspired dozens of imitators. By mid-century showboats plied their trade from the Erie Canal to the western river system and evolved from crudely converted flatboats and barges to often elaborate floating theaters with as many as three decks, two of them completely enclosed, with an auditorium, sleeping quarters for cast and crew, and storage for scenery, costumes, and properties. The most impressive was Dr. Gilbert R. Spalding (1812-80) and Charles J. Rogers's (1817-1995) *Floating Palace*. Towed by *The Raymond*, a small steamer that featured a complete minstrel troupe, the *Floating Palace* employed 100 performers and crew, seated 2,500 patrons, and offered a full circus as well as popular musicals and dramas.

Showboat activity ceased during the Civil War and did not resume in earnest until circus clown Dan Rice's (1823-1900) *Will S. Hayes* was launched in 1869. In 1878 A[ugustus] B[yron] French (1833-1902) launched the *Sensation* and he and his wife, a certified river pilot, dominated the showboat industry until his death. Other influential vessels of the period included Edwin A. Price's *Water Queen* (1885) and the grandiloquently titled *Eisenbarth-Henderson Floating Theatre—The New Great Modern Temple of Amusement* (later shortened to *Cotton Blossom*, the first of several showboats by that name). These showboats and others like them now featured less legitimate drama and more vaudeville and musical variety entertainments. These performances were often rowdy affairs and of uneven artistic quality.

Showboats devoted solely to theatrical performance steadily declined during the first third of the 20th century as the frontier collapsed, methods of transportation improved, and motion pictures dominated the entertainment industry. In 1910, 26 boats worked the rivers, but by 1928 there were only 14, and by 1938 that number had dwindled to five. By the 1940s, only two important showboats, the Menkes Bros.' *Golden Rod* and Billy Bryant's (1888-1948) *New Showboat* still traveled the rivers. By 1943 they, too, were permanently docked.

Bibliography

Bryant, Billy [William]. *Children of Ol' Man River*. New York: Furman, 1936.

Gillespie, Richard C. *The James Adams Floating Theatre*. Centreville: Tidewater, 1991.

Graham, Philip. *Showboats: The History of an American Institution*. Austin: U of Texas P, 1951.

Schick, Joseph S. "Early Showboat and Circus in the Upper Valley." *Mid-America* 33 (Oct. 1950): 211-25.

John Hanners

Shrines are places or receptacles that hold sacred objects, effigies of sacred people, or sometimes even the actual remains of people. In Western religious traditions, shrines range from churches to a hallowed piece of ground, while receptacles range from grottos to table tops to small boxes. What defines sacred is open to interpretation. Traditionally, "sacred" denotes religious import, but more broadly, the word can indicate that which has historical, cultural, or personal value. In 1896, Theodore Wolfe visited and wrote a book about the homes and haunts of writers such as Thoreau, the Alcotts, and Hawthorne, titling it *Literary Shrines*. He called these places shrines not only because they held historical and cultural value but also because the shrines could function to inspire us. It is these broader implications of sacred as hallowed by historical, cultural, or personal associations that embrace popular culture shrines. In some instances, such shrines also incorporate a religious element. Indeed, the understanding of many popular culture shrines might well be understood as indebted to religious and historical shrines.

Many shrines are based in religious practices, but are constructed on private or public lands, not church property, by lay persons. They take the form of home and yard altars and roadside markers and sites. Shrines are based in Catholic, Hindu, and other religious practices, although often the religious authority from which they stem does not sanction the folk varieties of these shrines. For example, accumulations of religious artifacts (statues, holy cards, rosaries, votive candles, etc.), family photographs, personal mementos, and often flowers, food, cigarettes, and liquor at certain times of the year characterize home altars found in many Mexican-American homes. They may be placed on table tops, chests, shelves, or other flat surfaces or may occupy small niches carved into a wall specifically to hold devotional objects and are usually placed and tended by a woman in the family, often the family matriarch. Such home altars are places for prayer and personal meditation.

Shrines in the home often hold familial significance. Thus, there is integration of family photographs and memorabilia mixed in bricoleur style with religious artifacts. The custom of setting aside areas for family memorabilia, and particularly collections of photographs, is almost ubiquitous across the United States and its many cultures, and can be regarded as a type of shrine.

Some shrines are built outdoors to serve as memorials to historic or familial figures. These can serve the same function as public statuary (of the city founders, early pioneers, etc.) found so often in city parks and town squares, with the format being a free-standing niche. Another type of outdoor shrine is the placement of wooden crosses or stones along roadsides where people have been killed, often suddenly. The crosses are usually placed by family members, although during the 1950s, the Arizona Highway Department adopted the practice. The practice again derives from Catholic religion, and signals that a soul suddenly left its body without the benefit of last rites and that passersby should stop and say a prayer for the deceased to help them out of purgatory. The Highway Department seems to have erected the crosses to warn drivers of a hazardous stretch of road. These sites are often decorated with wreaths, coins, candles, and memorabilia.

A few entire cemeteries can be considered popular culture shrines. The famous Forest Lawn Cemetery in Glendale, CA, was envisioned by its founder, Herbert Eaton, to be a happy place, rather than one of mourning and sadness. Ducks, singing birds, babbling fountains, tapestries, stained glass, and antique furniture were chosen for their cheerful looks. A 30-foot-long mosaic—the *Signing of the Declaration of Independence*—a copy of Michelangelo's *David*, what is claimed to be the largest painting in the world—Jan Styka's *Crucifixion*—three imitation European churches, replicas of coins mentioned in the Bible, and a rock collection also contribute to the spectacle. The cemetery is a popular tourist attraction and is the final resting place of movie stars such as W. C. Fields and Jean Harlow, evangelists, inventors, and writers.

Another type of shrine celebrates idols. The idol shrine ranges from teenagers' collections of movie and television posters on their bedroom walls to treasured Elvis memorabilia. Idol shrines are nearly as ubiquitous as are groupings of family photographs.

Like some homes, cars can also become shrines. Americans have always had an ongoing love affair with the car. As author Tom Wolfe points out so well in his book *The Kandy-Kolored Tangerine-Flake Streamline Baby*, cars serve in U.S. society as markers of personal identity and extensions of the self. During different eras, it has been popular to elaborately customize the vehicle's exterior; thus we have the jalopy and the customized "Beetle," headers, chrome wheels, and distinctive paint jobs. These cars are decidedly more than hobbies.

Car dashboards and rearview mirrors are favored places for small shrines. Dashboards are sometimes lined with fabric—particularly popular is imitation fur—to help distinguish the confines of the sacred place. With varying assortments of images and objects, from religious icons to personal items (baby slippers, pictures of girlfriends or boyfriends), to popular culture (Teddy bears, *Playboy* paraphernalia, and dominoes), they personalize the machine that so many U.S. citizens consider indispensable.

In some homes, the television and computer have taken on shrine-like qualities. Each can serve as a receptacle for objects and images having personal or religious significance, but beyond their serving as mere table tops, they have their own shrine-like qualities. The television is the focal point of at least one room in most U.S. homes.

On a larger scale, the mall is considered by some cultural critics to be a gargantuan shrine to commercialism. The function of the mall goes beyond mere shopping. In a climate-controlled environment (neither too hot nor too cold, wet nor dusty), the shopper can make purchases, eat, partake in entertainment such as movies and video arcades, and simply socialize. While it may seem cynical to think of the mall as a kind of public shrine, it serves one of the functions of the shrine defined by Theodore Wolfe a hundred years ago, to place us closer to what we love, helping shoppers achieve a feeling of bliss that is often associated with the purposes of the shrine.

Recognizing the altar as a site of accumulated power, and a threshold between past, present, and future or what is, what was, and what could be culturally and personally, Chicano/a artists have worked with the cultural significance of altars to Mexican Americans. Feminist artists' altar-making grows out of the strain of feminism that pursued the study of goddesses and forgotten powers of women as a strategy to empower women, with the altar being adopted as a suitable format. The use of the altar as a format in Chicano/a artmaking derives from a continuous tradition of folk altars within ethnic U.S. communities. Amalia Mesa-Bains's installation altars are particularly well known. Her *Grotto of the Virgins* took the form of a cave leading to three chapels, each of which honored a different woman. From this bricoleur base, Mesa-Bains creates work that is about reclamation of culture and affirmation of the female gender, the female psyche, and traditions (especially spiritual traditions) among women in traditional cultures, empowering women and particularly Mexican-American women.

In popular culture, the shrine is a place of communicative exchange, a place to work through things in life, and moreover a receptacle for that which people revere and cherish.

Bibliography
Browne, Ray B., ed. *Rituals and Ceremonies in Popular Culture*. Bowling Green, OH: Bowling Green State U Popular P, 1980.
Griffith, James. *Beliefs and Holy Places: A Spiritual Geography of the Pimeria Alta*. Tucson: U of Arizona P, 1993.
Mesa-Bains, Amalia. *Offerings: The Altar Show*. Venice: Social and Public Art Resources Center, 1985.
Raven, Arlene. "The Art of the Altar." *Crossing Over: Feminism and Art of Social Concern*. Ann Arbor: UMI Research, 1988. 71-82.
Stern, Jane, and Michael Stern. *Encyclopedia of Bad Taste*. New York: HarperCollins. 1990.

Elizabeth Garber

Silicon Valley is a late archetype of California, the Golden State—often viewed as a breeding ground for youthful, instant millionaires. From the 1960s to the 1990s, it seemed the right time and place to fulfill the American Dream of wealth through invention and practical exploitation. Located at the south end of the San Francisco Bay, Silicon Valley is that part of Santa Clara County containing communities such as Menlo Park, Redwood City, Sunnyvale, and extending south to San Jose. It embraces the intellectual climate of Stanford University and the University of California at Berkeley, as well as the corporate sites of Apple Computer, Hewlett-Packard, and Intel.

The foundation for the explosive growth and wealth of the area was the manufacture of transistors and other solid state devices. The electronic world was forced by its own logic to change from vacuum tubes to transistors; the advantages of solid state electronics—speed, reduced size and power consumption—were overwhelming. Engineers repeatedly left established companies to develop their own "start-up companies" with a particular wrinkle on a new technology. Perhaps the genesis of Silicon Valley came in 1955, when William Shockley, one of the inventors of the transistor, returned to his hometown of Palo Alto, and founded Shockley Semiconductor Laboratories. Soon, eight of his engineers, joined by Robert Noyce, left to start Fairchild Semiconductor. Stock equity in a start-up company could and did make millionaires. Defense industry needs, the demand for small, lightweight electronics for space exploration, and undreamed-of new consumer markets fueled the explosion of electronic companies in the area.

Bibliography
Freiberger, Paul, and Michael Swaine. *Fire in the Valley: The Making of the Personal Computer*. Berkeley: Osborne/McGraw-Hill, 1984.
Malone, M. S. *The Big Score: The Billion Dollar Story of Silicon Valley*. Garden City: Doubleday, 1984.
Rogers, Michael. *Silicon Valley*. New York: Simon & Schuster, 1982.

Gordon Berry

Silverstein, Shel(by) (1932-1999), was born in Chicago. His earliest work appeared in the 1950s in the U.S. military magazine *Stars and Stripes,* where he served as a staff artist. After his military service, he became a cartoonist for *Playboy* magazine. His cartoons were published in a variety of other magazines including *Time*, which published the popular series "Now Here's My Plan."

In the 1960s, Silverstein continued his work as a cartoonist while becoming known in folk and country music circles as a songwriter. Singer Johnny Cash made a No. 1 hit out of the song "A Boy Named Sue" (1969) and the band Doctor Hook and the Medicine Show had success with Silverstein-penned songs, most notably the popular "Cover of the Rolling Stone" (1973).

Silverstein's first children's book was *Uncle Shelby's Story of Lafcadio, the Lion Who Shot Back* (1963). This first book reflects a quality of content that would be repeated throughout his publications, namely a story that can be interpreted on several levels. The popular *The Giving Tree* (1964) was embraced as a simple children's story, a religious parable of altruistic relationships, an allegorical tale of masters and slaves, and the exploitation of females (the tree) by males (the boy). The parable-like style was repeated in *The Missing Piece* (1976) and *The Missing Piece Meets the Big O* (1981). The collections of poems and humorous drawings in *Where the Sidewalk Ends* (1974), *A Light in the Attic* (1981), and *Falling Up* (1996), were published as children's books but are enjoyed by all ages. Silverstein also wrote several plays, including *The Lady or the Tiger Show* (1981), *Remember Crazy Zelda?* (1984), and *Wash and Dry* (1986).

Bibliography

Hedblad, Alan, ed. *Something about the Author.* Vol. 92. Detroit: Gale, 1997.

Honan, William H. "Shel Silverstein, Zany Writer and Cartoonist, Dies at 67." *New York Times* 11 May 1999: C31.

Stambler, Irwin, and Grelun Landon. *The Encyclopedia of Folk, Country and Western Music.* 2d ed. New York: St. Martin's, 1983.

Twentieth-Century Children's Writers. 4th ed. New York: St. James, 1995.

Sylvia Tag

Simak, Clifford D. (1904-1988), born and raised in rural Wisconsin, tended to reflect his small-town and pastoral perspective in his nearly a half-century of science fiction short stories and novels. Simak's stories deal with common science fiction themes: aliens, space travel, time travel, androids, and so forth. But what is most compelling and endearing in Simak's work is his depiction of ordinary characters as they struggle within these extraordinary circumstances. Thus, his characters are often drawn with a touch of homespun humor and pragmatism that make Simak's work more accessible to the nonscientific reader.

Although Simak published his first story, "The World of the Red Sun," in the December 1931 issue of *Wonder Stories*, he did not develop a serious interest in authorship until 1938, when he began publishing stories for Joseph W. Campbell's legendary science fiction magazine, *Astounding.*

In such stories as "Rule 18," "Reunion on Ganymede," "Rim of the Deep," and "Hunch," Simak quickly established himself as a writer who strove for simplicity and clarity in both form and content. He soon followed his short story success with his first full-length novel, *Cosmic Engineers* (1939).

However, Simak did not receive serious attention as a major science fiction writer until the appearance of *City* in 1944. The novel began as a series of stories in *Astounding*, depicting a dystopian future where humankind's loss of traditional values creates its downfall, leaving a world populated by genetically engineered dogs and robots, as the world itself returns to Simak's much-preferred pastoral state. Collected into novel form, the stories of *City* won Simak an International Fantasy Award in 1952, and it continues to be Simak's best-known novel. A final *City* story, "Epilog," appeared in the *John W. Campbell Memorial Anthology* in 1973.

Simak produced dozens of short stories throughout his career, many of which were included in collections. In addition to the *City* stories, he received a Hugo Award for "The Big Front Yard" (1958) and both a Hugo and Nebula for "The Grotto of the Dancing Bear" (1980). This latter story was particularly striking in its depiction of the immortal protagonist who has been witness to a millennium of war and inhumanity and has grown weary of its redundancy.

Starting in 1960, Simak began publishing nearly a novel a year, chief of which was the 1964 Hugo Award-winning *Way Station* (1963). From the 1970s until his death, Simak turned to a more fantasy-oriented, mystical world where myth, magic, and futuristic hi-tech both meshed and collided.

Bibliography

Becker, Muriel R. *Clifford D. Simak: A Primary and Secondary Bibliography.* Boston: Hall, 1980.

Patrick Bjork

Simon, Paul (1941-), is a singer-songwriter who has been successful in a number of genres, from the mid-1960s socially conscious folk of Simon and Garfunkel to the mid-1970s folk-rock as a solo performer, and later in experiments with indigenous music in Brazil and South Africa. Simon met Artie (later Art) Garfunkel (see entry) in a program for gifted junior high school students in Queens, NY. The two became close friends and musical collaborators. In 1957, Simon and Garfunkel signed with Big Records as Tom and Jerry. Their first single, "Hey Schoolgirl," reached No. 49 on the charts, their only success as Tom and Jerry.

While Simon attended Queens College in 1959, he earned money recording demo versions of songs. He tried unsuccessfully to start a solo career as Jerry Landis, and as Tico or Tico and the Triumphs for a number of record labels. Simon was later influenced by the folk music movement in Greenwich Village, and he began playing folk clubs like Gerdes' Folk City in 1963.

He started law school in the fall of 1963 and began performing again with Garfunkel, this time using their real names. In 1964, Simon dropped out of law school and went to England to play folk clubs there. Simon returned to the

U.S. and the duo was signed by Columbia Records. Their first album, *Wednesday Morning, 3 A.M.*, was released in October 1964. The album was initially unsuccessful and the duo split again. Simon recorded *The Paul Simon Songbook* in England on the British CBS label.

Meanwhile, Tom Wilson of Columbia Records had remixed the song "The Sounds of Silence" from *Wednesday Morning, 3 A.M.*, adding drums and electric guitar to the original acoustic accompaniment. The remixed single was released in November 1965, and Simon returned to the U.S. to promote it. "The Sounds of Silence" topped the charts in January 1966, and the duo recorded a second LP, *Sounds of Silence*. Both the re-released *Wednesday Morning, 3 A.M.* and *Sounds of Silence* (which included the remixed single) climbed the charts in the spring of 1966, and both albums eventually were gold records.

A string of hits followed for the duo. The single "Homeward Bound," reached No. 5 on the U.S. charts in March 1966. "I Am a Rock" reached No. 3 in June, "The Dangling Conversation" hit No. 25 in September, and "A Hazy Shade of Winter" peaked at No. 13 in December. Their next album, *Parsley, Sage, Rosemary, and Thyme,* reached No. 4 and earned a gold record in December 1966.

Simon and Garfunkel began experimenting with orchestration and special effects in that album, the first Columbia LP recorded on eight tracks. "The Dangling Conversation," for example, used a string section accompaniment, while "Silent Night/6 O'Clock News" combined the Christmas carol on one audio channel with news stories being read on the other channel. A similar combination of traditional and topical themes was used in "Scarborough Fair/Canticle."

Two singles were released in 1967, and both "At the Zoo" and "Fakin' It" were moderate successes. In August, Simon and Garfunkel were commissioned to supply music for the film *The Graduate*. The soundtrack album, featuring five of the duo's songs, topped the charts for nine weeks in the spring of 1968.

Simon and Garfunkel's next album, *Bookends*, replaced the movie soundtrack at the top of the charts. The single "Mrs. Robinson," included on *Bookends* and *The Graduate*, topped the charts for three weeks in June 1969. The song also won Grammy Awards for record of the year and best contemporary pop performance by a duo or group. As an individual, Simon won a Grammy for the music for *The Graduate*.

The duo spent most of 1969 working on the album *Bridge over Troubled Water*, releasing only the single "The Boxer." They performed only once together that year, on a television special, as Garfunkel spent much of his time pursuing an acting career. The LP was released in February 1970, but the duo had effectively split over creative differences and the demands of Garfunkel's film career.

The title cut of *Bridge over Troubled Water* was No. 1 for six weeks, and the album topped both the U.S. and British record charts in 1970. Two other successful singles were released, "Cecelia" and "El Condor Pasa (If I Could)." The LP and its title cut won six Grammy Awards for 1970, including record of the year, song of the year, and album of the year.

The next year, Simon began work on his first solo album, *Paul Simon*. His interest in world music took him to Jamaica to record some of the tracks, including the first single, "Mother and Child Reunion." That song reached No. 4 on the charts in March 1972, and two other singles were released from the LP, "Me and Julio Down by the Schoolyard" and "Duncan."

Simon's second album, *There Goes Rhymin' Simon*, reached No. 2 in 1973 and earned him a gold record. It also produced two million-seller singles, "Kodachrome" and "Loves Me Like a Rock." Again, he demonstrated his diverse musical interests, as the latter single borrowed on gospel music and featured backup vocals by a gospel group, the Dixie Hummingbirds.

Simon released a live album, *Live Rhymin'*, in 1974, and in October 1975 Columbia released another gospel-styled single, "Gone at Last." The next album, *Still Crazy after All These Years* (1975), included a duet with Art Garfunkel, "My Little Town." The single "50 Ways to Leave Your Lover," with references to Simon's failed marriage, topped the U.S. charts for three weeks. The LP won Grammy Awards for album of the year and best male vocal pop performance.

Columbia released a greatest hits compilation in late 1977, *Greatest Hits, Etc.*, which included the new single "Slip Slidin' Away." Simon also became somewhat of a screen personality in the late 1970s, appearing on the television show *Saturday Night Live* as both a host and performer and in cameo appearances in the film *Annie Hall* and the TV movie *The Rutles*. He also wrote the screenplay and music score for *One Trick Pony* (1980).

Simon began work on another world music album in 1984, this time focusing on the music of South Africa. *Graceland* featured the South African group Ladysmith Black Mambazo, whom Simon later produced two albums for on Warner Brothers. The album produced three singles, "Graceland," "You Can Call Me Al," and "The Boy in the Bubble." Although none of the singles were hits, *Graceland* earned a platinum record for over 4 million copies sold and won the Grammy award for 1987 record of the year.

After touring solo again, Simon and Garfunkel reunited for a Concert in Central Park in 1981. The concert was released as a double-LP on Geffen Records in the spring of 1982. The duo toured Europe and the U.S. in 1982 and 1983 and began recording a new album for Geffen. But Simon and Garfunkel split up again during the sessions, and the album was released as a solo Paul Simon LP, *Hearts and Bones* (1983).

In 1990, Simon continued his exploration into international music with the album *Rhythm of the Saints*. Much of the recording was done in Brazil, but Simon also incorporated musicians from Ghana and Cameroon. In August 1991 Simon returned to Central Park, and the concert was released as *Paul Simon's Concert in the Park* later that year. In 1993 the duo reunited for a brief tour. Simon's most recent album (1997) is the result of venturing into yet another medium: a collection of songs from *The Capeman*, a Broadway musical he scored with poet/novelist Derek Walcott.

Ken Nagelberg

Simpsons, The (1990-), a half-hour animated series, soon became not only the new Fox television network's first top-rated prime-time series, but also the initial popular culture fad of the 1990s. Children loved it, but so did adults and even TV critics. By June of 1990 Bart and his family were on the covers of *Newsweek* and *Rolling Stone*, and a new era in network television, Fox-style, had commenced.

The Simpsons was created by Matt Groening, known for his experimental *Life in Hell* comic strips, in conjunction with TV veterans James L. Brooks and Sam Simon. Groening had originally developed the characters in brief vignettes on Fox's *Tracey Ullman Show*. Brooks, in particular, brought a solid track record to the show, with credits that included *The Mary Tyler Moore Show*, *Taxi*, *Lou Grant*, and *Rhoda*. But what this trio created was no typical sitcom. The fictional Simpson family includes father Homer (voice of Dan Castellaneta), mother Marge (voice of Julie Kavner), daughters Lisa (voice of Yeardley Smith) and the baby Maggie (sucking sounds made by Groening himself), and son Bart (voice of Nancy Cartwright). They are no *Father Knows Best*, no middle-class success story, but truly a representative dysfunctional (and thus typical) American family.

Homer Simpson is an overweight slob, frequently unshaven, and lazy as the day is long. His idea of a good time is to lie on the couch, watch TV, and drink beer all day. He never went to college, and is proud of that lack of accomplishment. His blue-haired, long-suffering spouse Marge loves Homer, but is continually frustrated by his lack of manners and initiative.

But the major characters are hellion Bart, and ideal Lisa. Bart is a clever fourth grader who gets into any and all types of trouble, from apprenticing as a Mafia Don (a "Dinky Don") to constantly being kept after school forced to write on the blackboard. What he writes on the board gives insight into his character: "I will not instigate revolution" or "I did not see Elvis" or some such off-beat phrase. Yet in the end Bart always has some remorse and always pays his debt to society. Like his father, he never learns, and so we can be sure Bart will be back in the next episode in some form of anti-establishment trouble.

Surely only daughter Lisa can be called a success story, a role model. Lisa is arguably the best role model for a young woman on television. She is thoughtful and studious; she is melancholy and existential. She suffers her family and consoles herself by going off into the corner and wailing the blues on her saxophone.

The stories of the Simpson family range far and wide. If there is any core inspiration, it is motion pictures and other television series. Now-fabled send-ups include its version of *Citizen Kane*, in which evil nuclear-plant owner Montgomery Burns takes on traits of Charles Foster Kane; it has also done everything else from *The Godfather* to *It's a Wonderful Life*. The series takes particular pleasure mocking animation. "Itchy & Scratchy," a cat and mouse duo that takes Tom & Jerry to Sam Peckinpah extremes of super-sadistic violence, is Bart *and* Lisa's favorite cartoon to watch. *The Simpsons* is surely the most self-reflexive television program ever produced.

The Simpsons was a genuine breakthrough program, not only in the history of television in particular (with the establishment of a fourth television network) but also in the history of popular culture in general. Despite some changes in its writing staff, after 10 years it continues to find new ways for the Simpson family to get in and out of trouble.

Bibliography
Block, Alex Ben. *Outfoxed*. New York: St. Martin's, 1989.
Shawcross, William. *Murdoch*. New York: Simon & Schuster, 1992.

Douglas Gomery

Sinatra, Frank (1915-1998), in his over 50-year singing career, received numerous honors, including a Grammy legend award and the U.S. Presidential Medal of Freedom—quite a body of tributes for someone who had no musical training and could not read music. Born Francis Albert Sinatra in Hoboken, NJ, he was the child of Italian immigrants. He left high school in Hoboken after his sophomore year and briefly attended business school. During his high school days, he had sung in a glee club. In March 1932, when he was just 16, he attended a live performance by Bing Crosby, whom he idolized, and thereafter directed his efforts toward being a professional singer. By 1939 he had managed to gain the attention of the famous bandleader Harry James; Sinatra made his first important public appearance at Baltimore's Hippodrome theater in June 1939 and recorded his first song, "All or Nothing at All," with the James orchestra two months later.

This recording of the ballad by Jack Lawrence and Arthur Altman was the big break Sinatra needed. Although the disc was a flop when it first was issued in 1940, Sinatra's rendering of "All or Nothing at All" caught the attention of another top bandleader, Tommy Dorsey. Prior to joining Dorsey, Sinatra had not yet fully developed his unique singing style which brought him so much fame and fortune. He had emulated Bing Crosby at first, modeling his performing after Crosby's casual, low-key style. While with Dorsey, Sinatra started to pattern his style after the sounds of Dorsey's orchestra and learned how to form tones better and how to control his breathing. From Billie Holiday, he learned how to relate better to audiences. The combination of these influences and Sinatra's natural talents and continued hard work resulted in his distinctive vocal technique, which featured excellent pronunciation of words and highly effective phrasing of sounds. This very appealing style continued throughout the rest of his career.

Sinatra had his first top-selling record soon after: Ruth Lowe's "I'll Never Smile Again" with the Dorsey band for Victor. The next year, Sinatra again sang "I'll Never Smile Again" with the Dorsey ensemble in the 1941 film *Las Vegas Nights*. Also in 1941, Sinatra had his first million-selling record, "There Are Such Things," by lyricists Abel Baer and Stanley Adams and composer George W. Meyer. When the American Federation of Musicians, in a legal dispute with the record companies, banned all new recordings under their control for 13 months in 1942-43, one of the old recordings radio stations revived was Sinatra's "All or Nothing at All."

By then Sinatra, with his singing style fully evolved, had become extremely popular. The old recording became Sinatra's biggest hit to that time (he re-recorded the song in 1961 and again in 1966).

Other top Sinatra hits of 1943 were "You'll Never Know," by lyricist Mark Gordon and composer Harry Warren, "People Will Say We're in Love," by lyricist Oscar Hammerstein II and composer Richard Rodgers, "White Christmas," by Irving Berlin, and "Sunday, Monday, or Always," by lyricist Johnny Burke and composer Jimmy Van Heusen. In the same year, he became one of the star vocalists on the *Your Hit Parade* program. A third notable 1943 event was Sinatra's first starring appearance in a movie, *Higher and Higher*. In subsequent years, Sinatra was to appear in a number of films (see next entry).

In 1944, a woman fainted during one of Sinatra's performances, and a publicist seized the opportunity to claim that the woman had "swooned" due to romantic passion (the real reason was the effects of heat). From that event, Sinatra became known as "Swoonlight Sinatra." He picked up another nickname, "Frankie," when in October 1944 a mob of young females at the Paramount Theater in New York, anxious to have Sinatra appear, kept on interrupting the movie being shown with cries of "We want Frankie!" Other labels given to Sinatra were "the stick," because of his slim figure in the early 1940s, "Old Blue Eyes," and "the Voice."

Over the years, Sinatra has been associated with hundreds of songs. Besides the compositions already mentioned, other top Sinatra songs were: "This Love of Mine" (1941), with lyrics by Sinatra and music by Sol Parker and Henry Sanicola; "Five Minutes More" (1946) by lyricist Sammy Cahn and composer Jule Styne; "Full Moon and Empty Arms" (1946) by Buddy Kaye and Ted Mossman; "All of Me," recorded in 1952 and written in 1931 by lyricist Seymour Simons and composer Gerald Marks; "When You're Smiling," recorded in 1952 and written in 1928 by Mark Fisher, Joe Goodwin, and Larry Shay; "Three Coins in a Fountain" (1954), by lyricist Sammy Cahn and composer Jule Styne, which won an Oscar; "Learnin' the Blues" (1955), written by Dolores Vicki Silvers; "Hey Jealous Lover" (1956), written by Sammy Cahn, Kay Twomey, and Dee Walker; "Witchcraft," recorded in 1958 and written in 1957 by lyricist Carolyn Leigh and composer Cy Coleman; "Nice 'n' Easy" (1960), by Lew Spence, Alan Bergman, and Marilyn Bergman; "Strangers in the Night" (1966), by Bert Kaempfelt, Eddie Snyder, and Charles Singleton; and "For the Good Times" (1970), by Kris Kristofferson.

Most of all, Sinatra was associated with a series of songs written by lyricist Sammy Cahn and composer Jimmy Van Heusen in the 1950s and 1960s. In 1955 came "The Tender Trap" and "Love and Marriage," which won an Emmy. These were followed by "All the Way" (1957), "Come Fly with Me" (1958), "High Hopes" (1959), "The Second Time Around" (1960), "My Kind of Town" (1962), and "Call Me Irresponsible" (1963). "All the Way," "High Hopes," and "Call Me Irresponsible" all won Oscars.

Possibly with Irving Kahal's 1938 ballad "I'll Be Seeing You," a smash recorded by Sinatra in 1944, in mind, Sinatra

"retired" in 1971. However, he resumed his career in 1973, and continued strong until late in his life. All during his career, Sinatra had a tough-guy image which was bolstered by alleged ties with the underworld and by his "Rat Pack" cronies of the 1950s and 1960s. In reality, Sinatra was a charitable person and a good father, with two of his three children, Frank, Jr., and Nancy, particularly the latter, both having significant vocal careers. In 1967, Sinatra recorded C. Carson Parks's "Something Stupid" with Nancy, which reached No. 1 in the charts, but she also had top hits on her own, especially "These Boots Are Made for Walkin'" (1966), by Lee Hazelwood. Perhaps most indicative of Sinatra's personal life was a lawsuit that Sinatra brought against a 1976 biography of him because the book described Sinatra's life as "boring and uninteresting." In any case, Sinatra's life and truly outstanding career as a singer and actor can be summed up perfectly in "My Way," the 1969 blockbuster by lyricist Paul Anka and composer Jacques Revaux. Sinatra popularized the song, adopted it as his own, and made it the credo of his life.

Bibliography

Ackelson, Richard W. *Frank Sinatra: A Complete Recording History of Techniques, Songs, Composers, Lyricists, Arrangers, Sessions, and First Issue Albums, 1939-1984.* Jefferson: McFarland, 1992.

Adler, Bill. *Frank Sinatra, The Man and the Myth: An Unauthorized Biography*. New York: New American Library, 1987.

Kelley, Kitty. *His Way: The Unauthorized Biography of Frank Sinatra*. New York: Bantam, 1987.

Sayers, Scott P., and Ed O'Brien. *Sinatra, The Man and His Music: The Recording Artistry of Francis Albert Sinatra, 1939-1992*. Austin: TSD, 1992.

Sinatra, Frank. *A Man and His Art*. New York: Random House, 1991.

William E. Studwell

Sinatra, Frank (in Film), made his first foray into the movies by playing himself. *Las Vegas Nights* (1941), *Ship Ahoy* (1942), and *Reveille with Beverly* (1943) gave Sinatra an opportunity to be seen crooning a song or two by all his fans.

In 1943, RKO offered him starring roles in *Higher and Higher* (1943) and *Step Lively* (1944), two light comedies. For the most part Sinatra received positive notices for his ease and naturalness before the cameras. With a built-in audience of adoring fans, Sinatra's career seemed destined for greatness, especially after signing a seven-year, $1.5 million contract with MGM. While there, he appeared with Gene Kelly in the musicals *Anchors Aweigh* (1945), *Take Me Out to the Ball Game* (1949), and *On the Town* (1949). However, the anticipated stellar career did not materialize. By the time *On the Town* opened, Sinatra's status in Hollywood was slipping, even though the film, and Sinatra, received rave reviews. Part of his fall stemmed from poor movie choices. The year before, against the advice of friends, he made *The Miracle of the Bells* (1948), where he played a priest, and *The Kissing Bandit* (1948), which proved to be his worst film, according to the critics and Sinatra. A slew of personal and professional problems also affected Sinatra's status in Hollywood, including divorcing his first wife to marry Ava Gardner, whose own acting career was blossoming. He soon found himself desperately trying to regain his footing, hoping to find a vehicle that would revive him from his slump.

After reading James Jones's *From Here to Eternity*, Sinatra was immediately taken with the feisty and tragic character of Angelo Maggio. He knew he could play Maggio because *he* was Maggio. He had lived the same life while growing up. He eventually won the part and a year later a best supporting actor Oscar. *From Here to Eternity* (1953) won eight Oscars that year. "The Voice" had not only revived his career, but he had also proven that singing was not his only talent.

Sinatra won a total of three Academy Awards over his career. His first came for a ten-minute short called *The House I Live In* (1945), which preached racial harmony. Many critics noted that the effect of this award was lost when Sinatra appeared in *Till the Clouds Roll By* (1946), singing "Ol' Man River" in an all-white tuxedo with an all-white-clad orchestra playing on an all-white sound stage. His third Oscar was the Hersholt Humanitarian Award (1971).

The 1950s proved to be a lucrative and successful decade for Sinatra at the movies. He received another Academy Award nomination for *The Man with the Golden Arm* (1955), in which he convincingly played a dope addict. Sinatra appeared in 17 films in the 1950s, ranging from musicals—*Guys and Dolls* (1955), *High Society* (1956), and *Pal Joey* (1957); to romantic comedies—*The Tender Trap* (1955) and *Young at Heart* (1955); to dramas—*Suddenly* (1954) and *The Pride and the Passion* (1957).

During this time, Sinatra became leader of the "Rat Pack," a group of friends that included Peter Lawford, Sammy Davis, Jr., and Dean Martin. In the 1960s Sinatra and his group made a number of movies, including *Ocean's 11* (1960), *Robin and the Seven Hoods* (1964), *Sergeants 3* (1962), and *4 for Texas* (1964). Critically, the films were panned for their lack of plot and enthusiasm on the part of the actors, but they did quite well financially.

The 1960s also marked the debut of Sinatra as a director. Surprisingly, Sinatra did not make a clan picture, but instead an anti-war movie, *None But the Brave* (1965), produced in conjunction with the Japanese. Undoubtedly, the best movie that Sinatra made in the 1960s was *The Manchurian Candidate* (1962), in which he played a brainwashed former prisoner of war who unravels a plot to assassinate the President of the United States.

Unlike his roles in the 1950s, where Sinatra played the comic bachelor, the 1960s saw him attracted to roles depicting much more violent, hardened criminals, killers, police officers, and detectives, including *Tony Rome* (1967), *Lady in Cement* (1968), and *The Detective* (1968). In his last two movies, Sinatra returned to the role of a cop in *Contract on Cherry Street* (1977), a television movie, and the tepid *First Deadly Sin* (1980).

A complete summation of Sinatra's film career provokes appreciative nods and befuddled shakes of the head. Even though Sinatra gave a number of incredibly strong and vivid performances, they have a tendency to be overshadowed by his choice of weak material and his lackluster, walk-through performances.

Bibliography

Jewell, Derek. *Frank Sinatra: A Celebration.* Boston: Little, Brown, 1985.

Peters, Richard. *The Frank Sinatra Scrapbook.* New York: St. Martin's, 1982.

Ringgold, Gene, and Clifford McCarthy. *The Films of Frank Sinatra.* New York: Citadel, 1971.

Rockwell, John. *Sinatra: An American Classic.* New York: Random House, 1984.

William C. Boles

Singin' in the Rain (1952), one of the finer, if not the finest, musicals, is often used to mark the end of the great Hollywood musical era (see Musical Films). The film critic Pauline Kael termed it "just about the best musical of all time." Its title song was written by Nacio Herb Brown and Arthur Freed. Most of the score was theirs, much to the chagrin of Betty Comden and Adolph Green, who were the film's writers. It was directed by its star, Gene Kelly, with Stanley Donen for the Freed Unit at MGM.

Singin' in the Rain was based on much of Hollywood's earlier work and retold the story of the first screen musicals. In fact, it was originally to be a remake of Brown and Freed's *Excess Baggage*, a 1928 musical. After a few false starts, Freed decided to have Betty Comden and Adolph Green concoct a story to match the Brown-Freed catalogue. The resulting story was rather typical of musical plots. In this case, Debbie Reynolds's character dubs in the voice and sings for a silent star who cannot make the transition to talkies. Gene Kelly's character is the charming leading man who falls in love with Debbie Reynolds's character. Donald O'Connor is the comic sidekick and all, of course, works out well in the end. The scene that most film musical fans remember is not the ballet, even featuring the gorgeous Cyd Charisse; it is the "Singin' in the Rain" dance on MGM's New York set. It has been termed "the single most memorable dance number on film."

It is no surprise that *Singin'* came closest to achieving the MGM ideal of the integrated musical. Songs, dances, plot were to have a direct connection. If songs and dances did not advance the plot, at the least they should explicate it. Kelly also had a keen feel for the way a shot should look. He changed cameramen for *Singin'* to get the feel that he wanted for the dance sequences.

Bibliography

Delamater, Jerome. *Dance in the Hollywood Musical.* Ann Arbor: UMI, 1981.

Flatow, Sheryl. "Great Gals, Great Gams." *A&E Monthly* May 1994: 22-25.

Hirschhorn, Clive. *The Hollywood Musical.* New York: Portland House, 1991.

Kael, Pauline. *Taking It All In.* New York: Holt, 1984.

Wollen, Peter. *Singin' in the Rain.* London: BFI, 1992.

Frank A. Salamone

Singing Cowboys was the term popularized by the movie industry during the 1930s to describe the actors who sang in Western films. The best known were Gene Autry and Roy Rogers, but a number of other singing cowboys such as Tex Ritter, Rex Allen, and others made their name and fame in these movies, which were usually escapist fare with a Western theme and which were most popular from the mid-1930s to the mid-1950s. The rise of the singing cowboy coincided with the rise of the B Western format and the independent Republic Studio, the major producer of B Westerns in the 1930s and 1940s (see Western Films).

Ken Maynard (1895-1973) was the first actor to appear as a singing cowboy. During the 1920s Maynard was one of the most popular stars of silent Westerns and, when sound was introduced to film in 1927 with *The Jazz Singer,* decided to incorporate singing into his own movies. Maynard first sang in *Wagon Master* (1929). In 1930 Maynard starred in *Song of the Caballero* and *Sons of the Saddle,* in which he sang and accompanied himself on the fiddle and banjo. He also recorded eight songs for Columbia Records.

When Ken Maynard left Universal Pictures and signed with Mascot Pictures, owner Nat Levine hired Gene Autry (1907-1998) to sing. Although Maynard wanted singing in his pictures and Levine agreed, Maynard wasn't a particularly strong singer, while Autry, who had been performing on WLS in Chicago, was an established singer with hit records to his credit. Also, Maynard had become increasingly unreliable and difficult to work with because of his drinking.

The first picture for Mascot with Maynard and Autry was *In Old Santa Fe* (1934) and the next was a serial, *Mystery Mountain* (1934), which again starred Maynard and in which Autry only said one line. For the following movie, *Phantom Empire* (1935), also a serial, Levine, having fired Maynard, was forced to cast Autry in the starring role, using his own name to capitalize on his reputation as a singer. The serial was a resounding success and launched Autry's career. His first feature film, starring again under his own name, was *Tumbling Tumbleweeds* (1935).

After Autry, the next successful singing cowboy was Tex Ritter (1907-1974), who starred for Grand National, although Dick Foran (1910-1979) also starred as a singing cowboy in several pictures beginning in 1935. Others who played singing cowboys included Fred Scott, Smith Ballew, Jack Randall, Tex Fletcher, and John "Dusty" King. Later there were George Houston, James Newall, and Bob Baker. Even John Wayne appeared as Singin' Sandy in *Riders of Destiny* (1933), with Smith Ballew dubbing in the singing voice when Wayne warbled. But the next major singing cowboy star was Roy Rogers (1912-1998).

A founding member of the Sons of the Pioneers in the early 1930s, Rogers, then known by his real name Leonard Slye, and his popular Western singing group had appeared in several movies, including Autry's *Tumbling Tumbleweeds.* In fact, the songs "Tumbling Tumbleweeds" and "Cool Water" were written by Bob Nolan, one of the other founding members of the Sons of the Pioneers. Slye, who first changed his name to Dick Weston, went to Republic Studios to audition for the role of a singing cowboy in 1937 after Autry threat-

Photo courtesy of Sound Recording Archives, Bowling Green State University, Bowling Green, OH.

ened to walk out because of a contract dispute. Republic wanted another singing cowboy in reserve as a way to keep Autry in line. When Autry made good his threat and left, Rogers was cast in *Under Western Skies* (1937), a movie originally written for Autry. Before the filming, the studio executives changed Slye's name to Roy Rogers.

Roy Rogers quickly became a major singing cowboy star and continued making pictures for Republic after Autry and Republic settled their differences. The two continued making successful singing cowboy movies for Republic until World War II, when Autry joined the Armed Forces. Since Rogers was married with three children, he received a deferment and stayed in Hollywood making movies during the war. With Autry unable to make movies, Republic decided to make Rogers a major star and billed him as "King of the Cowboys." A movie titled *King of the Cowboys* (1943) was released, a major promotion was launched, and Roy Rogers soon eclipsed Gene Autry as the top singing cowboy.

Autry returned to Republic after the war but soon left and signed with Columbia Pictures in 1947. The period

1946-55 saw the end of the singing cowboy's run in Hollywood. The last singing cowboy signed by Republic was Rex Allen (1922-1999), known as "the Arizona Cowboy," who starred in a number of pictures. The last musical Western was produced by Republic in 1953. With television replacing movies as the choice of entertainment for Americans, Autry and Rogers soon signed agreements to have TV shows. At first, the two artists recycled old movies, but then began action series for the TV shows which involved a limited amount of singing.

Don Cusic

See also
Cowboy Music

Siodmak, Robert (1900-1973), German-born movie director, worked ten years in Hollywood, 1941-51, and made 23 movies, many of them widely popular thrillers and crime melodramas that critics today regard as classics of film noir.

He began his career with a whimsical little film, *Menschen am Sonntag*, the last German silent, which he made with Billy Wilder, Edgar G. Ulmer, and Fred Zinnemann in 1929. He fled from Hitler's Germany after Goebbels attacked him in the press, and then from Europe. When he arrived in America in 1939, he had already directed six features in Germany and nine features in France. Now a refugee director in Hollywood, Siodmak turned out several B films for Paramount, Republic, and Twentieth Century-Fox before beginning his seven-year contract with Universal Studios in 1943.

Following the success of *The Killers* (1946), the film that brought Siodmak name recognition and his only Oscar nomination, he was touted as "the new master of suspense." Noir thrillers and crime melodramas became Universal Studio's house style. To his credit, it seems, Siodmak created more suspenseful, psychologically disposed films noir than any director who worked in that genre, 12 in all. And yet, it is an identification that proved professionally fatal. As the noir had run its course by the 1950s, so had Siodmak's career in America.

Stylistically and thematically homogeneous and representative of the quintessential Siodmak are the noir films he made at Universal: *Phantom Lady* (1944), *Christmas Holiday* (1944), *The Suspect* (1945), *The Strange Affair of Uncle Harry* (1945), *The Killers* (1946), and *Criss Cross* (1949). He also made two out on loan to other studios: *Cry of the City* (1948), and *The File on Thelma Jordon* (1950).

Unrepresentative are the other noirs Siodmak made at Universal: *The Son of Dracula* (1943), a surprisingly literate horror movie, from a story by Siodmak's brother Curt; *The Dark Mirror* (1946), a clichéd psychological thriller with Olivia de Havilland playing good/evil twins; and *Deported* (1950), a gangster's fable. Also not typical is *The Spiral Staircase* (1945), the film with which Siodmak is most often identified. A classic of its kind, often cited as the archetypal suspense thriller, it is noteworthy in Siodmak's oeuvre for his characteristic use of mise-en-scène to convey a sense of dread within domestic spaces.

Siodmak returned to Europe in 1952, where, he believed, the director could still be an artist. He continued to make films in West Germany, France, Great Britain, Spain, and Rumania, but, although he tried, he never regained the kind of career Hollywood had afforded him.

Bibliography
Alloway, Lawrence. *Violent America: The Movies 1946-1964*. New York: MOMA, 1971.
Schatz, Thomas. *The Genius of the System: Hollywood Film Making in the Studio Era*. New York: Pantheon, 1988.
Silver, Alain, and Elizabeth Ward, eds. *Film Noir*. Woodstock: Overlook, 1979.
Siodmak, Robert. "Hoodlums: The Myth." *Films and Filming* June 1959: +10.

Joseph Greco

Siskel and Ebert became inseparably linked names synonymous with film criticism when, in 1975, Robert Ebert, film critic for the Chicago *Sun-Times*, and Gene Siskel, his archrival from the Chicago *Tribune*, appeared on a new movie-review program produced by WTTW, the local PBS station. *Opening Soon at a Theater Near You*, later entitled *Sneak Previews*, went national in 1978 and soon became the highest-rated series in PBS history.

The format of the show consisted of the pair introducing clips of newly released films, including a description of the plot and a capsule review. Four films were typically reviewed in the half-hour time slot, plus an extra segment on videocassette releases. The device of signaling thumbs up or thumbs down was used to indicate good reviews or bad. Famous for the thumbs-up or thumbs-down critique, which is believed to have a heavy influence on the success of movies, the two were also renowned for the ad-lib passages following the capsule reviews, in which the other partner offered his comments or rebuttal. Typically, these passages turned into bickering matches, evoking the description of Siskel and Ebert as "dueling wits."

In addition to the size of audience the show drew, an indication of the show's popularity has been the number of imitations generated by its original format. In 1982 Siskel and Ebert moved to Chicago-based Tribune Entertainment with the promise of more money and higher ratings. *Sneak Previews* continued on with two new critics, Jeffrey Lyons and Neal Gabler, who was later replaced by Michael Medved. *At the Movies*, with Rex Reed and Bill Harris, was introduced by Tribune Entertainment after Siskel and Ebert signed a contract with Walt Disney Company's Buena Vista Television.

Siskel died in 1999, to the regret of a whole nation of movie-goers. Ebert decided to continue the show as *Roger Ebert at the Movies*, with guest partners.

Susan Harum

Sitcom is the term for an episodic half-hour program format that derives its humor from a set of characters in a given situation. The most popular form of television entertainment, sitcoms have accounted for 52 percent of the Top 10 network TV programs since 1960 and comprise, on average, more TV programming hours than any other genre, including such staples as one-hour dramas, quiz shows, news, and reality programs.

Critics and media historians attribute the genre's appeal to its humorous exaggerations of everyday life that make people feel happy, comfortable, or better about themselves. While sitcoms have grown with the times, they still maintain a predominant focus on domestic and career situations, delivering identifiable, funny friends that viewers invite into their living rooms week after week, and, in many cases, season after season.

Though often considered a television genre, sitcoms began on radio in the mid-1920s. While traces of earlier popular forms can be found in sitcoms—such as the minstrel show and vaudeville, which, like sitcoms, depend on exaggerated characters—the sitcom is directly derived from the daily newspaper comic strip.

In the mid-1920s, Henry Selinger of WGN radio in Chicago asked two of his performers—Freeman Gosden and Charles Correll—to come up with a radio version of *The Gumps,* a daily comic running in the Chicago *Tribune.* Gosden and Correll were intrigued by the idea of an episodic comedy, but decided to base their program on stereotypical African-American characters the team had drawn from their southern roots. The result was *Sam 'n' Henry*, the predecessor of the famous—and infamous—*Amos 'n' Andy* (see entry).

Considered the first sitcom, *Sam 'n' Henry* debuted on WGN radio on January 12, 1926. Gosden and Correll, in an effort to expand their listenership—as well as their pocketbooks—prepared to syndicate their ten-minute program via phonographic transcription. A dispute regarding syndication rights ensued, and Gosden and Correll left WGN, changing the sitcom's name to *Amos 'n' Andy*. By August 1929, the sitcom was picked up by NBC. Concentrating on current topics, including the Depression, *Amos 'n' Andy* became the most popular program of the 1930-31 and 1931-32 broadcast seasons, proving the sitcom a viable broadcast genre.

Although Selinger, Gosden, and Correll pioneered the form, it was Jack Benny who perfected it. While *Amos 'n' Andy* depended on vaudevillian banter from greatly exaggerated characters whose humor depended, in part, on prejudices the listeners brought to the program, Benny created a unique, vain-yet-lovable tightwad character who interacted more naturally with a cast of regulars (although one of Benny's regulars, Rochester, his black personal assistant, was still prone to stereotypical speech and gestures).

While *The Jack Benny Program* (see entry) had elements of the popular variety format, by 1934, Benny began focusing on particular comic situations based on the problems his character faced in preparing his weekly show—a show within a show. The comic exaggeration of Benny's faults made him a lovable character to whom his radio and, later, TV audiences felt superior.

Although television brought about radio's decline, it provided the maturing sitcom a new, visual format. Indeed, many of the most successful early TV sitcoms were radio transplants, including *The Goldbergs* and *I Love Lucy*, which was loosely based on Lucille Ball's radio sitcom *My Favorite Husband*.

When television began in the late 1940s, most of its viewers were on the East Coast. This location provided access to broadcast centers as well as listeners affluent enough to afford televisions. This predominantly urban market also displayed a greater tolerance for ethnic characters. While the DuMont network experimented with early shows such as *Mary Kay and Johnny's Place* (1946) and *The Growing Paynes* (1948), the first successful half-hour TV sitcom was CBS's *The Goldbergs* (1949). The popular series (later on NBC and DuMont) featured the exploits of a heartwarming Jewish family. Six months later, *I Remember Mama* debuted on CBS, featuring a turn-of-the-century Scandinavian family coping with the rigors of life in San Francisco (the show was produced in New York).

Both of these programs were well received, with *Mama* becoming a Top 10 favorite. Like most early TV, these sitcoms were broadcast live in New York and then relayed to other markets via kinescopes—a low-quality yet serviceable form of transcription. These kinescoped sitcoms are all but lost today. Had sitcoms been filmed before 1951, we might still "remember *Mama.*"

The validation of the sitcom as a successful TV genre came in 1951 from Lucille Ball and Desi Arnaz's *I Love Lucy*, which led both a technical and a cultural revolution that has outlived both of its stars. After transforming her popularity in films to a successful radio career, Ball (see entry) was approached by CBS to duplicate her radio sitcom's success on television. Ball and husband Desi Arnaz agreed on two conditions: they wanted to produce the show in California so they could be close to their Chatsworth ranch, which Desi and Lucy saw as the savior of their troubled marriage; and they wanted to form their own production company to film the series, allowing for a portion of the profits as well as a longevity not afforded by kinescopes.

Filmed television at the time meant having a closed set in which one camera painstakingly took each shot from as many as four angles—a "one-camera" show. However, because Ball wanted an audience to react with, she insisted the filming be done in front of a live audience. A one-camera show, however, would drastically diminish the smooth progression with which the audience could interact. A new system needed to be devised—or, as it was in this case—a little-known system had to be borrowed.

While common myth credits Arnaz as inventor of the multiple film-camera system, in which four cameras run simultaneously as the program follows a theater-like progression, producer Al Simon had already been using a similar setup for Ralph Edwards's quiz show *Truth or Consequences* (1950). Nevertheless, Arnaz and Ball were the first producers to apply this technique to sitcoms. Their production company, Desilu, eventually became the largest, most influential television facility of the 1950s and 1960s. In addition to creating their own empire, Desilu changed the nature of TV production itself, removing the creative aspect from the hands of the networks and advertisers. This set a precedent for later successes of actor/producers such as Danny Thomas and Mary Tyler Moore.

More important than Desilu's technical contribution, however, was *I Love Lucy*'s popular impact; it remains the most successful sitcom ever produced, and has been on the air in either first-run or rerun since 1951. First-run viewership was so tremendous, city water departments would report incredible water usage coinciding with the sitcom's commercial breaks. The January 19, 1953, episode of Little Ricky's birth became a national event, with 44,000,000 viewers tuning in. By comparison, President Eisenhower's inauguration the following day brought only 20,000,000 viewers. Ball was so popular that she was one of the few actors to escape unscathed an accusation of Communist affiliation. (Ball had registered as a Communist in 1936, reportedly to please her grandfather.)

While many have tried to explain the success of *I Love Lucy*, few can provide a definitive answer. Some critics say that Lucy held a distorted, fun-house mirror to the American public. Others credit the cast's chemistry. Still others credit the show's excellent writing. Many claim its success was due to the singular talents of Lucille Ball. Perhaps one of the best explanations for the show's success was that it consistently and successfully met the most important goal of any sitcom—it was funny. Viewers eagerly laughed along as Lucy romped and raved across American living rooms. If viewers ever missed the joke—which was unlikely—they were helped by the accompanying laugh track, a technical development which debuted in 1950 on the short-lived *Hank McCune Show*.

By this point, most sitcoms had two things in common; they were in urban settings and domestic in nature. But, as television spread out across the suburban and rural landscapes in the mid-1950s, the suburban sitcom took hold. This was not only true for developing suburban domestic sitcoms such as *Ozzie and Harriet* (1952) or *Leave It to Beaver* (1957), but for programs such as *I Love Lucy* and *The Goldbergs*, as well, which moved away from their urban locales. This reflected the actual urban flight going on in America at the time.

While the domestic sitcom continues to this day, it was at its peak in the 1950s when placed in its suburban locale, playing to the developing American dream of a nuclear family living in a white picket-fenced yard. Suburban sitcom dads worked, albeit at undefined corporate jobs, sitcom moms busied themselves keeping spotlessly clean houses, and sitcom kids got into the sort of trouble that American TV parents could easily handle. While much has been written to pan these sitcoms, they were all based on well-written plots fleshed out by humor derived from the situations. The shows played to universals of social behavior which, while portrayed by white middle-class families, could be easily applied to anyone in the social situation. While later relevant programs focused on bigger problems, early suburban family shows remained true to the sitcom credo: attack the mundane while making it funny.

In 1953, one domestic sitcom bucked the suburban, kid-gloves approach. Danny Thomas's *Make Room for Daddy*, while domestic in nature, was urban in location and less sentimental in tone. Thomas (see entry), who entered sitcoms to create a more stable life for his family, shared his exploits as an entertainer (much like Jack Benny had done earlier). However, unlike most family sitcom fathers, Thomas was a screamer. He would run after his kids, rant and rave, and just before achieving a tender moment, break it with a wisecrack and stern warning to his kids. Thomas called this comic reversal the "treacle cutter," used to keep a moment from becoming too sentimental or serious. This apparently captured the public's attention. Thomas parlayed his fame into a TV dynasty, becoming the number one producer at Desilu studios. Into the 1960s, Thomas was rumored to be the richest producer in Hollywood.

Much of Thomas's wealth came from the successful shows he produced, including *The Dick Van Dyke Show*, which debuted in 1961 (see entry). Considered by many as the ultimate classic sitcom, *The Dick Van Dyke Show* was the first to mix domestic and career subgenres and cross the line between urban and suburban locales. While character-rich sitcoms like *The Dick Van Dyke Show* became the norm in the 1970s, the series remained a singular program in its time—no sitcom could equal its quality, sophistication, or relevance. After a tough first year, the program became a Top 10 hit, making an unknown Van Dyke a household name and leaving Mary Tyler Moore as one of the most influential American women, second only to Jackie Kennedy.

The Dick Van Dyke Show was not just a model for the later, more cosmopolitan programs of the 1970s, but also served as a template for countless sitcom plots that have been rehashed and repeated by today's sitcoms. It was also one of the first programs to portray African Americans in positive, non-stereotypical roles. This is amazing when one considers the great pains other sitcoms took to avoid the growing civil rights movement.

Danny Thomas's other success came from a 1959 *Make Room for Daddy* episode, in which Thomas drove into the sleepy town of Mayberry and introduced us to the characters who would become part of *The Andy Griffith Show* (see entry). Thomas had already gained success with the rural sitcom *The Real McCoys* (1957). *The Andy Griffith Show* (1960) built upon that success, and, suddenly, rural locales became the norm for TV sitcoms, with Thomas's *Andy Griffith Show* and *Gomer Pyle* (1964), as well as producer Paul Henning's *Beverly Hillbillies* (1962), *Petticoat Junction* (1963), and *Green Acres* (1965), dominating the era.

Perhaps these rural shows found their appeal by offering viewers a safe haven from an increasingly complex world. While often panned as mere "hayseed" comedies, each of these shows gave the simpler country life the upper hand. Indeed, Andy's Mayberry was not too slow—the city was too fast.

Rural shows produced by Paul Henning (see entry) carried much the same message, but in a more screwball, surrealistic manner. *The Beverly Hillbillies* (see entry) was one of television's few runaway hits, remaining a Top 10 program from start to finish. This success was repeated by Henning's other shows, *Green Acres* and *Petticoat Junction*.

During the rural period, the escapist subgenre also took hold. *Mr. Ed* (1961), *My Favorite Martian* (1963), *Bewitched* (1964), *My Mother the Car* (1965), *The Munsters* (1964), and *The Addams Family* (1964) all had identifiable characters placed in preposterous situations. These escapist sitcoms were either suburban or rural in locale, and were based on the simple problem of one person or family hiding some supernatural or strange situation from the rest of the modern world. Much like the rural sitcoms, these shows played to the viewer's anxiety about an increasingly complex world.

If it seemed like these shows were running from something, they were—civil unrest and the war in Vietnam may have been safe things for the news, but entertainment programming could not begin to broach such topics. Economically, the networks had no choice. After all, this was a period in which Southern network affiliates would preempt civil rights news. Because television is a business—and a volatile one at that—TV audiences were limited to viewing families who lived on farms, talked with horses, and had mothers who were cars and uncles who were Martians. Furthermore, one of the era's most popular sitcoms, *Gomer Pyle*, featured a military that was totally oblivious to the Vietnam War.

But all that changed in 1970 with *All in the Family* (see entry). Although it was a domestic sitcom, *All in the Family* switched to a cosmopolitan locale and was presented in an all new technology—videotape. While late 1960s programs such as *Julia* (1968), which featured a black nurse, and *Room 222* (1969), set in an urban high school, had touched on relevant issues, *All in the Family* let it all hang out, if only so ultraconservative Archie Bunker could try hopelessly to stuff it back in.

All in the Family and the relevant shows that followed it were the result of advertisers' shifts from looking at overall ratings numbers to demographic data. Indeed, while *The Beverly Hillbillies* got higher numbers than *All in the Family*, advertisers were more interested in the affluent, upscale viewers who tended toward more socially aware programming. Thus, the networks, with CBS President Bob Wood taking the lead, launched a television "deforestation plan" that, as *Green Acres'* Pat Buttram once said, axed every show "with a tree in it."

Although *All in the Family* had a slow start, it became a Top 10 hit by its second season. Archie Bunkerisms such as "Stifle it" and "Meathead" became popular catchphrases. More important, *All in the Family*, adapted from the British sitcom *Till Death Do Us Part*, mixed timely material with timeless characters to allow television viewers access to a variety of issues television had been avoiding. Producers Norman Lear and Bud Yorkin's Tandem Productions eventually gave viewers such successful *All in the Family* spinoffs as *Maude* (1972), *Good Times* (1974), and *The Jeffersons* (1975).

Complementing the raw nature of *All in the Family* was its raw look, effected by videotape, the third major technological change that has had an impact on sitcoms. Video has kept the cost down on these comedies, with only the classier sitcoms still being shot on film.

One of those classier sitcoms was *The Mary Tyler Moore Show* (see entry). Also debuting in 1970, the series gave viewers a more elegant, refined version of relevant comedy. Although set in Minneapolis, the scene could have been any American city, making this another cosmopolitan show. Although Moore's character Mary Richards was origi-

nally supposed to be a divorcée, the network changed Mary's marital status to never married, concerned that people would think she had divorced Dick Van Dyke, with whom she had starred in *The Dick Van Dyke Show*. More significant was the network's concern over the American viewer's readiness to accept a divorced character. CBS waited until 1975, when Bonnie Franklin became television's first divorced character in the sitcom *One Day at a Time*.

The Mary Tyler Moore Show gave us a cast of lovable characters, many of whom went on to shows of their own, including *Rhoda* (1974), played by Valerie Harper, and *Phyllis* (1975), played by Cloris Leachman. Mary Tyler Moore, like Lucy and Desi, and Danny Thomas, went on to forge her own successful production company, MTM Enterprises. MTM launched many sitcoms and dramas that have rarely been equaled in quality, cast, or comedy, including *The Bob Newhart Show* (1972; see entry). Throughout the 1970s and 1980s, MTM became synonymous with quality TV.

M*A*S*H, another popular sitcom, which lasted 11 seasons, debuted in 1972 (see entry). Unlike its military-based predecessors such as *Gomer Pyle*, *F-Troop* (1965), and *Hogan's Heroes* (1965), *M*A*S*H* was the first sitcom to present the pathos of war. *M*A*S*H* brought a number of innovations to the sitcom format, including the selective use of a laugh track, which was dropped from the bloody operating room scenes. It was also the first series to kill off one of its main characters. The series was preceded by a popular book and film, making the concept one of the few to score the hat trick of successful book, film, and sitcom.

As if someone had said "enough of this reality," the mid-1970s brought a slew of escapist programs that either brought us back to the 1950s or took us into outer space. *Happy Days* (1974; see entry), which began as a quality character comedy based on the nostalgic film *American Graffiti*, eventually became nothing more than a vehicle for its popular Fonzie character. *Happy Days* spinoffs *Laverne and Shirley* (1975) and *Mork and Mindy* (1978) were reminiscent of the fun-yet-mindless 1960s sitcoms.

Unfortunately, the forwardness of the relevant sitcoms of the 1970s opened the doorway to a general acceptance of mere titillation provided by risqué, double-entendre-laden sitcoms such as *Three's Company* (1977), *The Ropers* (1979), and *Too Close for Comfort* (1980). Nevertheless, some quality sitcoms remained, including career-based cosmopolitan sitcoms such as *WKRP in Cincinnati* (1978), *Taxi* (1978), and *Cheers* (1982) (see entries). Each of these shows had writing and production connections to earlier MTM comedies.

In the early 1980s, with sitcoms divided among domestic, career, and escapist subgenres, the public seemed to be losing interest in the format. Indeed, from 1982 to 1985, no more than two sitcoms were in the Top 10, and people began to wonder whether the sitcom's time had run out. The 1984 debut of Bill Cosby's wildly successful *Cosby Show* (see entry), however, made short business of such speculation, and sitcoms again began to be seen as still one of the most viable broadcast products. *Cosby*, which appealed to both mainstream and African-American audiences, was followed by a number of other sitcoms both domestic (e.g., *Full House* [1987], *Seinfeld* [1989], *Mad about You* [1992], and *Friends* [1994]), career-based (e.g., *Anything But Love* [1989], *Coach* [1989], *Wings* [1990], *Newsradio* [1995], and *Spin City* [1996]), and some a blend of both (e.g., *Home Improvement* [1991], *The Nanny* [1993], *Frasier* [1993], and *The Drew Carey Show* [1995]). Even the escapist subgenre persisted with *ALF* (1986) and *Third Rock from the Sun* (1996). Many began featuring more female and minority characters, including such shows as *The Golden Girls* (1985), *Designing Women* (1986), *Murphy Brown* (1988), *Roseanne* (1988), *Frank's Place* (1990), *Fresh Prince of Bel Air* (1990), *Hangin' with Mr. Cooper* (1992), *Grace under Fire* (1993), and *South Central* (1994).

Although Westerns, variety shows, and hospital dramas have faded from the TV sunset, the sitcom, with its emphasis on mildly to wildly exaggerated characters, remains a popular genre. While sitcoms now mix and match among a choice of domestic, career, and escapist subgenres, the general format remains true to its radio roots; just as in the 1930s, the sitcom's funny friends are still among the most welcome guests in American homes.

Bibliography

Brooks, Tim, and Earle Marsh. *The Complete Directory to Prime Time Network TV Shows, 1946-Present.* New York: Ballantine, 1992.

Feuer, Jane, Paul Kerr, and Tise Vahimagi. *MTM: Quality Television.* London: BFI, 1984.

Mitz, Rick. *The Great TV Sitcom Book.* New York: Perigee, 1983.

Sackett, Susan. *Prime Time Hits: Television's Most Popular Network Programs.* New York: Billboard, 1993.

Wertheim, Arthur Frank. *Radio Comedy.* New York: Oxford UP, 1979.

Michael B. Kassel

60 Minutes (1968-) is the most watched news program ever, with more finishes in the Nielsen Top 10 than *I Love Lucy.* Between 1990 and 1995, it was the top-rated prime-time show bar none, averaging between 20 and 30 million viewers every week.

As director of *The CBS TV News*, the first national television news broadcast, in 1949, Don Hewitt had developed innovations such as cue cards and "supers," subtitles superimposed on the screen to identify people and places. Hewitt had helped invent the TV documentary when he directed Edward R. Murrow in *See It Now* from 1951 to 1958. And in 1968, when broadcasting had long since evolved into an entertainment medium, Hewitt conceived of a new kind of news program, a "newsmagazine."

Like *Life* magazine, *60 Minutes* has something for everyone: stories on politics and politicians; solid coverage of crimes both infamous and unknown; explorations of health and medical breakthroughs; reporting from the battles of Vietnam and the Persian Gulf; the business of domestic and foreign governments; profiles of artists, athletes, and ordinary people; and light features and human interest stories.

60 Minutes debuted September 24, 1968, starting life as a biweekly alternating with *CBS Reports*, then shifting to Sunday evenings in the fall of 1971, where it was often preempted by professional football games. The show bounced around CBS's weekly schedule from Tuesday to Sunday to Friday, airing as early as 6 p.m. and as late as 10 p.m. before it finally settled in as a weekly series in December 1975 at its now famously unbeatable time slot of Sunday at 7 p.m.

The program was the first to do away with a single anchor, replacing it with a team of correspondents with a variety of styles, giving the segments different points of view and allowing the correspondents to travel and report their own stories, rather than just read them in the studio.

The roster of reporters has been remarkably stable. Veteran CBS newsman Mike Wallace has been with the program since its beginning; CBS vet Harry Reasoner was the first correspondent aboard and—except for an eight-year absence from 1970 to 1978, when he worked for ABC—stayed until his retirement in May 1991. (He died two months later.) Dan Rather, formerly CBS's White House correspondent, joined the program in 1975 and departed in 1981 to become anchor and managing editor of *The CBS Evening News.* Diane Sawyer was a member of the team from 1984 to 1989, when she defected to ABC News. Meredith Vieira, from CBS's trendy newsmagazine *West 57th* (see entry), joined in 1989 but left in 1991, reportedly because of a maternity-leave dispute with Hewitt. Still with *60 Minutes* are Canadian Morley Safer, previously CBS's bureau chief in Saigon and London, since 1970; Andy Rooney, previously a writer for the program, since 1978; Ed Bradley, since 1981; Steve Kroft, also from *West 57th*, since 1989; and Lesley Stahl, since 1991.

Commentary has always been an important part of *60 Minutes.* Early in the show's run, "Digressions" featured two silhouetted figures—Ipso and Facto—taking sides on a just-aired story. Andy Rooney wrote the segment and played Facto; producer Palmer Williams performed Ipso. From 1972 to 1979, "Point/Counterpoint" featured conservative columnist James J. Kilpatrick of the *Washington Star* dueling and debating current issues with liberal commentators Nicolas von Hoffman of the *Washington Post* and later Shana Alexander. "A Few Minutes with Andy Rooney" debuted in summer 1978. Since then Andy Rooney has shared his thoughts on topics mostly mundane, including hair, trash, sunglasses, the IRS, faucets, glue, Miss America, trees, kitchen gadgets, dumb letters, bad ideas, and how to carry money.

One measure of the impact *60 Minutes* has in the hearts and minds of Americans is illustrated by the brief suspension of Andy Rooney in 1990. Disparaging remarks about homosexuals that Rooney made, not on *60 Minutes* but on another CBS program entirely, in December 1989, caused an uproar, and Rooney was suspended from the TV newsmagazine for three months. But ratings dropped in Rooney's absence, and only three weeks later, he was back. A further indication was the debut, early in 1999, of a so-far-successful *60 Minutes II*, aired in mid-week, with correspondents Dan Rather, Bob Simon, Vicki Mabrey, and Charlie Rose, along with humorist Jimmy Tingle offering "Uncommon Sense."

Awards *60 Minutes* has garnered include the George Foster Peabody Award, the Alfred I. DuPont-Columbia University Award, the Polk Memorial Award, numerous Emmy Awards, the Ohio State Award, and the Christopher Award. In 1992, the show won the People's Choice Award; in 1993, the American Television Award for best news, information or documentary series; and it was inducted into National Association of Broadcasters' Hall of Fame in 1993.

Bibliography

Brooks, Tim, and Earle Marsh. *The Complete Directory to Prime Time Network TV Shows: 1946-Present.* New York: Ballantine, 1992.

Coffey, Frank. 60 Minutes: *25 Years of Television's Finest Hour.* Los Angeles: General, 1994.

McNeil, Alex. *Total Television Including Cable: A Comprehensive Guide to Programming from 1948 to the Present.* New York: Penguin, 1992.

MaryAnn Johanson

$64,000 Question and Challenge, The (1955-1958). During the radio era, the quiz show *Take It or Leave It* had introduced the concept of the jackpot $64 question. Playing on that theme in the bigger-is-better ethos of the early television years and inspired by the recent scaling of Mt. Everest, with its imagery of arduous ascent to the top, CBS network executive Louis G. Cowan with producers Steve Carlin, Joe Cates, and Mert Koplin introduced *The $64,000 Question.* Based on a double-or-nothing premise, the prizes started at a near-zero level and kept doubling week after week with the questions growing progressively more difficult as long as the contestant wanted to keep risking everything for a chance at still greater fortunes.

Premiered in June of 1955 on CBS, hosted by former actor-comedian Hal March, and sponsored by Revlon, the Tuesday-evening prime-time program quickly became a smash hit. It introduced such novelties as the isolation booth, infuriating background music, a bank representative plus two uniformed security guards presiding over the alleged secrecy of questions stored in a large safe (that later turned out to be a stage prop made of cardboard), a Cadillac for a consolation prize, and ostensibly ordinary people who answered impossibly difficult questions on improbably arcane topics.

In April of 1956, the stupendously popular *Question*—which had displaced *I Love Lucy* as the highest-rated television show in America—was joined on CBS by a Sunday-night spinoff program called *The $64,000 Challenge*, hosted briefly by Bill "Sonny" Fox (known for making bloopers) and then by Ralph Story (smooth and savvy), in which *Question* winners could be confronted by new contestants in a sort of intellectual tug of war fought between duelling isolation booths.

But both *$64,000* programs soon became hopelessly enmeshed in the infamous quiz-show scandals that also afflicted their NBC competitor *Twenty-One* (see entry). In 1957 a *Challenge* contestant, the Rev. Charles "Stoney" Jackson, confessed publicly to being given answers concerning his category (Great Love Stories). By November 1958 (only three years after their meteoric rise to glory), having lost their formerly enthralled but now disenchanted audiences, both *The $64,000 Question* and *The $64,000 Challenge* programs had disappeared from the air in abject disgrace, and the age of the blockbuster quiz show had reached its ignominious end. *The $64,000 Question* briefly attempted a comeback in 1976-78 but generated little audience excitement.

Bibliography

DeLong, Thomas A. *Quiz Craze: America's Infatuation with Game Shows.* New York: Praeger, 1991.

Graham, Jefferson. *Come on Down!!! The TV Game Show Book.* New York: Abbeville, 1988.

Hoberman, J. "Going Down the Tube." *Village Voice* 13 Sept. 1994: 34-41.

Holbrook, Morris B. *Daytime Television Game Shows and the Celebration of Merchandise:* The Price Is Right. Bowling Green, OH: Bowling Green State U Popular P, 1993.

Schwartz, David, Steve Ryan, and Fred Wostbrock. *The Encyclopedia of TV Game Shows.* New York: Zoetrope, 1987.

Morris B. Holbrook

See also
Game Shows

Skelton, Red (Richard) (1913-1997), born in Vincennes, IN, was the proverbial star of stage, screen, and radio. He is also the proverbial paradox of one whose talent spans low and high comedy. His skill as a mime is second to none, but the bread and butter of his act was "low comedy," with characters such as Willy Lump-Lump, Freddie the Freeloader, Junior the Mean Widdle Kid, and Clem Kaddidlehopper.

Skelton's father was a circus clown and for a time Red followed in his footsteps. He began his career at ten years old with a traveling medicine show. Skelton left the medicine show to enter the Clyde Beatty Circus, and then entered vaudeville.

In his first movie, *Having a Wonderful Time* (1938), Skelton used the routine that would become his trademark: a man nervously dunking his doughnut. Rather forgettable films, such as *The Fuller Brush Man* (1948), followed. Skelton hit his stride on radio, where he was somewhat of an anomaly, a pantomimist on a sound medium. It was for his radio program, essentially, that he developed his string of characters he later successfully adapted to TV. He presented a broad style of comedy with numerous characters, lest the audience get bored. Until he entered the service in World War II, he enjoyed the services of Ozzie Nelson and Harriet Hilliard.

TV, however, gave him the opportunity to display his ability to do pantomime. Skelton was also a consummate actor who could wring tears from his audience in the midst of their belly laughs. That acting ability was nicely displayed on a 1956 *Playhouse 90* program, "The Big Slide." His Civil War veteran sketch, in which an ancient veteran watches a Fourth of July parade, was a classic mixture of pathos and humor.

The Red Skelton Show (see entry) was a CBS Tuesday night staple from 1953 to 1970. Before that he was on NBC from 1951 to 1953. Although his CBS show was still in the Top 10 in 1970, CBS canceled it to appeal to a younger audience. NBC offered him a 30-minute program that fall but the program was canceled after a year. Thereafter, Skelton appeared on specials and as a guest from time to time.

Bibliography
Brown, Les. *Encyclopedia of Television.* Detroit: Gale Research, 1992.
Marx, Arthur. *Red Skelton.* New York: Dutton, 1979.
Terrace, Vincent. *Encyclopedia of Television Series, Pilots and Specials: 1937-1973.* Vol. 1. New York: Zoetrope, 1985.
——. *Encyclopedia of Television Series, Pilots and Specials: 1974-1984.* Vol. 2. New York: Zoetrope, 1985.
——. *Fifty Years of Television.* New York: Zoetrope, 1991.

Frank A. Salamone

Sky-Diving originated as parachute jumping. In the 1990s, as a result of high-tech equipment, jumpers can jump from an airplane and free-fall considerable distances, during which time they can do air acrobatics or link up with fellow sky-divers, and then open their parachutes and bring themselves into a landing, very nearly, on a dime. The fastest speed in a mechanical sport, according to the *Guinness Book of Records*, is sky-diving—185 miles per hour.

Parachuting contests started in the U.S. in 1926, but only ten years later in the Soviet Union there were 115 parachute schools. The free-fall record was set by Captain Kittinger of the U.S. Air Force in 1962. He jumped from a balloon at an altitude of 19 miles in the air.

Sky-divers often enliven professional sporting events, such as a Super Bowl, and uninvited divers have dropped in on other sporting events, such as the World Series. Teams are also featured at holiday events across the U.S.

Bibliography
Arlott, John, ed. *The Oxford Companion to World Sports and Games.* London: Oxford UP, 1975.
Poynter, Dan. *Parachuting: The Skydiver's Handbook.* Santa Barbara: Para, 1983.

Scott A. G. M. Crawford

Slapstick, as applied to silent film comedies, was a kind of shorthand term to describe the tendency of these necessarily visual forms of expression to depend upon physical movement, especially exaggerated, repeated movement, to evoke laughter. The term itself derives from the Renaissance and the Italian commedia dell'arte, in which stock characters dressed and behaved in ways, established by convention and long usage, that revealed their personalities.

In America and Britain, slapstick before film was found in the circus and in vaudeville, a form that produced most of the early silent-film comedians. Charlie Chaplin (see entry), who is often described as a 20th-century reincarnation of the commedia dell'arte's Harlequin, and Stan Laurel (1890-1965) were members of the Fred Karno Pantomime Troupe, and Buster Keaton (see entry), beginning at age three, was part of a family act in which the young Buster was hurled by his father into the audience. The transition to silent film for these stage comedians was easy and natural.

The man often called the king of silent comedy was Mack Sennett, who established Keystone Studios and gave most of the great silent comedians their first exposure in film. Influenced by French films by Jean Durand and Max Lindner, Sennett's strategy was to begin with a defined situation, such as the tango contest in *Tango Tangles* (1914), and fill the allotted time with a series of gags having no necessary relationship to one another except that none could last more than about 50 seconds. *Tango's* four principal players—Chaplin, Mabel Normand, Roscoe "Fatty" Arbuckle, and Ford Sterling—involve themselves, for example, in a series of barely motivated fights and dances across a slippery floor. Meanwhile, the other contestants, who form the background for these frenetic events, are an odd assemblage of mismatched, strangely dressed couples. The oversized dance with the undersized; a man in a striped prison uniform dances with a policeman. The film ends, rather than concludes, with everyone rushing about on some purposeless mission.

As successful as they were, the straightforward slapsticks gave way very soon to films with more complex structures, the semblance of a plotline, and modifications of the slapstick concept to include any kind of physical movement that could be called ludicrous. Even Sennett joined the move in longer films like *Tillie's Punctured Romance* (1914) and in parody films like *Teddy at the Throttle* (1916), in which Gloria Swanson is tied to a railroad track and saved at the last minute by her dog, Teddy, and her diminutive boyfriend, Bobby Vernon.

In 1915, Chaplin broke away from Sennett and gradually produced a more subtle, almost balletic kind of physical comedy that, while still having identifiable roots in the earlier slapstick, was now used to serve characterization and some plot development. *Easy Street* (1917), for example, includes a series of wild battles and chases, and in one sequence Chaplin tilts a cast iron stove out of a second floor window onto the villain's head. But the film also has a storyline that involves Chaplin's little tramp in a romance, unemployment, hunger, and drug addiction.

The advent of sound brought with it, quite expectedly, a move in films toward verbal comedy. Many of the silent stars who had thrived on slapstick and its modifications—Keaton and Harold Lloyd (1893-1971) among them—lost their appeal and were replaced in audience favor by the slow, biting sarcasm of W. C. Fields and the crackling absurdity of the Marx Brothers. Still, slapstick endured. Perhaps the funniest sequence in Fields's *It's a Gift* (1934) is the demolition of a grocery store by a blind man Fields is trying to guide to an exit, and every Marx Brothers film had its complement of brawls and chases, like the absurd military battle at the end of *Duck Soup* (1932) or the flying acrobatics during the opera in *A Night at the Opera* (1935).

The most apparent and emphatic survival of slapstick has been, thanks to television and videotape, in the work of the Three Stooges (see entry), Larry, Moe, and Curly (later Shemp, 1946-55, and two Joes). From their first significant appearance in film with Clark Gable in *Dancing Lady* (1933) through the early 1960s, this trio delighted audiences by engaging in unabashed mayhem like head cracking, nose tweaking, serial slapping, and even the old staple, the pie in the face. Animated films have also relied heavily on slapstick for their comic effects, notably in the duels between Wile E. Coyote and Roadrunner, in which the inept aggressor is continually flattened by huge rocks or tricked over the edge of a high cliff.

In general, however, in recent and contemporary films, slapstick has become tamer and has been better integrated with the films' plots or basic premises. In France, Jacques Tati has continued the tradition of physical comedy in *Mr. Hulot's Holiday* (1953) and *Mon Oncle* (1958), but the movements and chases are developed with considerably more subtlety and gentleness than they had been in earlier films. Lately, public attention has focused on violence as an undesirable element in all genres including physical comedies, but the slapstick tradition continues to find expression in the 1980s and 1990s in films like National Lampoon's vacation series, *The Naked Gun* trilogy, and the two *Home Alone* films.

Television has also been an enduring showplace for slapstick comedy. In the early days of television, because of the medium's voracious need for material, numerous silent film comedies were recycled, as were vaudeville and burlesque routines. Old-style slapstick persisted from Milton Berle's Texaco comedy hour in the 1940s and 1950s through the pratfalls of Chevy Chase on *Saturday Night Live* in the 1970s. More recently, perhaps building from the inventive visual tropes of Ernie Kovacs in the 1950s, physical comedy in television has been more subtle. *Monty Python's Flying Circus,* a British program popular in America in the 1970s, satirized violence in the media with representations of the Spanish Inquisition and reenactments by men dressed as matronly women of the Battle of Pearl Harbor. In the 1980s and 1990s, David Letterman's late-night shows continue to use devices like "stupid human tricks," velcro suits that fix people to walls, and watermelons dropped from great heights onto sidewalks, and *Seinfeld*'s Kramer (Michael Richards) carried on the slapstick tradition by falling over couches and other physical moves. *The Simpsons* uses slapstick in the mode of its animated cartoon forebears, to parodic effect. The more vigorous forms of comic violence seem to have gravitated to professional wrestling, with its comic-book characters and melodramatic confrontations.

Bibliography

Bergson, Henri. "Laughter." 1900. *Comedy.* Ed. Wylie Sypher. Garden City: Doubleday Anchor, 1956.

Charney, Maurice. *Comedy High and Low: An Introduction to the Experience of Comedy.* New York: Oxford UP, 1978.

Durgnat, Raymond. *The Crazy Mirror: Hollywood Comedy and the American Image.* New York: Delta, 1969.

Mast, Gerald. *The Comic Mind: Comedy and the Movies.* 2d ed. Chicago: U of Chicago P, 1979.

Sennett, Mack. *King of Comedy.* Garden City: Doubleday, 1954.

James Shokoff

Slasher Films, in their undiluted form, are most fully embodied by *Halloween* (1978), directed by John Carpenter, and *Friday the Thirteenth* (1980), directed by Sean Cunningham. Both of these films caught the public's and the film industry's attention for a number of reasons: their level of violence and inclusion of disturbingly realistic special effects; fixation upon the stalking and extermination of a series of nubile young men and women; calculated and, some might say, cynical playing down to the lowest common denominator in a thrill-crazy and predominantly adolescent audience; and perhaps most of all, substantial box office return upon minimal capital investment. Although films prior to the inception of this genre featured crazed killers who exterminate attractive and available victims, the slasher film upped the ante of the acceptable depiction of violence and, through the elementary but shrewd use of the steadicam to stand in for the audience's point of view, allowed the public vicariously to ogle and then punish a seemingly innumerable and virtually indistinguishable series of innocent individuals.

Slasher films were influenced by a number of sources, including but not limited to the visual, thematic, and narrative tropes of the American horror film (see entry). The phenomenon of a crazed killer itself can be traced to many antecedents but most saliently to what critic Charles Derry has called the "horror-of-personality" film, epitomized by Alfred Hitchcock's *Psycho* (1960) and the imitations of that picture that incorporated a rudimentary model of abnormal psychology with the kind of brutal and kinky details that might slip past the censors' scissors but still entice thrill seekers. Exploitation mavens like William Castle were quick to attach themselves to *Psycho*'s coattails with films like *Homicidal* (1961), whose transvestite killer sought to eliminate anyone who, aware of his preoperative identity, stood in the way of the psychopath's inheritance. Other horror-of-personality films, like Robert Aldrich's *Whatever Happened to Baby Jane?* (1952) and *Hush Hush Sweet Charlotte* (1965), stressed aberrant psychology rather than any extended stalking of prospective victims.

A further influence of an institutional nature set the stage for the full efflorescence in America of the slasher film. The establishment of the Motion Picture Association of America (MPAA) ratings board in the late 1960s (see Production Code/Ratings System) paradoxically led to a loosening of standards regarding on-screen violence and resulted in a series of horror films that pushed the envelope of permissible extremity, most notably *Night of the Living Dead* (1968). These and other pictures—*Bonnie and Clyde* (1967) and *The Wild Bunch* (1969) come to mind—exposed much that the horror film, and all manner of other violent narratives, inferred or left to the imagination. Some filmmakers thereafter appeared willing if not eager to outdo one another in order to produce the most commercial "chunkblower," to use a term of approval dear to the fans of all forms of excessive film violence. A key instance of the commercial exploitation of carnage was *Last House on the Left* (1972), in which a group of thugs kill two teenage girls only to encounter one of the victims' parents and be eliminated by them in an even more brutal fashion than was their daughter. Produced by Sean Cunningham (who would subsequently direct *Friday*

the 13th) and written as well as directed by Wes Craven (who would conceive *Nightmare on Elm Street* [1984; see entry] and later the self-reflexive *Scream* series), this picture was applauded by some as a thoughtful depiction of the retaliation that violence can provoke and damned by others as a nauseating exercise in sensationalism.

A similar confluence of opposing points of view accompanied the release of *Halloween* and *Friday the 13th* and their ilk. Adolescent audiences flocked to them, treating the films as an experience to be survived, analogous to the torment inflicted upon the films' characters. Adults and critics, on the other hand, in large numbers decried the prurient display of male and female nudity and chastised the public's frenzied and voyeuristic enthusiasm for carnage. The MPAA ratings board in turn interceded and in 1989 extended the reach of the X rating to encompass depictions not only of sexual intercourse but also of acts of excessive violence and brutality. As a consequence, some filmmakers were forced to expurgate many of the most explicit and excessive special effects sequences from their films in order to appease the powers that be.

Despite the ensuing complaints about censorship on the part of filmmakers and some audience members, the board succeeded in diffusing the slasher film of much of its visceral appeal, but at the same time, the very repetitiousness of its basic plot soon proved tiresome. Also, the desire on the part of some producers to establish "franchises": through the inauguration of film series and the marketing of iconic characters—Jason in the *Friday the 13th* films and Freddy Krueger of the *Nightmare on Elm Street* series—vitiated what substance the material might once have possessed.

While *Halloween* was produced and released by an independent distributor and became one of the most successful low-budget films to date, the major studios quickly caught on to the slasher film's appeal. As a result, they invested in a form of narrative once thought to be the exclusive domain of the exploitation market. Paramount Pictures distributed the *Friday the 13th* franchise (nine installments, 1980-93), while the independent firm New Line Cinema was able to expand as a result of success of the Freddy Krueger saga. However, when the bottom fell out of the horror market, the major studios gave up on the genre, and the slasher film ended up as one more moribund narrative model. Nonetheless, a number of memorable productions remain: the female-centered *Slumber Party Massacre* (1982), directed by Amy Jones and written by feminist novelist Rita Mae Brown; the vigorously satirical demolition of the genre in *Mother's Day* (1980), a film many mistook for what it lampooned; the genuinely frightening *Black Christmas* (1975); and *Alone in the Dark* (1982). At the same time, mainstream filmmakers incorporated elements of the slasher film into their work, most notably in Brian De Palma's *Dressed to Kill* (1980) and Stanley Kubrick's *The Shining* (1980). And yet, the vacuousness of the form was inescapable when a series of tepid but accurate parodies appeared: *National Lampoon's Class Reunion* (1982), *Pandemonium* (1982), *Saturday the Fourteenth* (1981), and *Wacko* (1981).

Few scholars of the horror genre have taken the slasher film seriously, viewing it as a trivialization rather than a refinement of the genre's narrative models. However, recent writings by Vera Dika, Robin Wood, and, most memorably, Carol Clover have initiated a reassessment of the form. Their comments remind one that a popular form of storytelling such as the slasher film can embody transgressive content as well as bring about a reconsideration not only of the ideological but also the gender dynamics of popular cinematic narrative.

Bibliography

Clover, Carol J. *Men, Women, and Chain Saws: Gender in the Modern Horror Film*. Princeton: Princeton UP, 1992.

Derry, Charles. *Dark Dreams: A Psychological History of the Modern Horror Film*. South Brunswick: Barnes, 1977.

Dika, Vera. *Games of Terror:* Halloween, Friday the 13th, *and the Films of the Stalker Cycle*. Rutherford, NJ: Fairleigh Dickinson UP, 1990.

Dines, Gail, and Jean M. Humez, eds. *Gender, Race, and Class in Media*. Thousand Oaks: Sage, 1995.

David Sanjek

Sledge, Percy (1941-), one of the most gifted and underrated of the southern soul singers, was born in Leighton, AL. Unlike other great southern-derived soul singers like James Brown, Otis Redding, and Ray Charles, Sledge did not grow up singing, nor was he intent on becoming a star. After performing in his high school choir and sporadically with his cousin's gospel group, Sledge was working as a hospital orderly when his high school music director asked him to join a local group called the Esquires. The group played mostly fraternity parties throughout the South, Sledge alternating lead vocals with two other members. According to Sledge, his break came quite by accident. One night, drunk and heartbroken over a lost girlfriend, he began improvising a song called "Why Did You Leave Me?" while on stage. Quin Ivy, who was starting the Norals Sound Studio at the time, happened to hear Sledge and invited him to record it upon the condition that it be rewritten. Weeks later "When a Man Loves a Woman" was recorded; Sledge's powerful emotional delivery carried the song and made him, for the moment, a star.

Unquestionably one of the masterpieces of the soul era, his first hit was his most famous, most epochal, and most remembered, becoming the first southern soul record to top the pop charts. It also sounded the first blast from what would be known as the Muscle Shoals sound, which, like the Stax-Volt sound in Memphis, epitomized deep southern soul, drawing other seminal soul singers like Wilson Pickett, Aretha Franklin, Etta James, and Irma Thomas to Alabama hoping to capture some of its magic.

For Sledge, the song's success became both a blessing and a curse. He never had a song go as high on the charts, and while he did have other hits, most notably "The Dark End of the Street," he is generally, and unfairly, remembered for this one performance. Actually, Sledge was a much more versatile singer than one song, however magnificent, can suggest. Though he could sound exactly like Solomon Burke ("I'm Hanging up My Heart for You") or Otis Redding ("That's How Strong My Love Is"), two major influences, his best performances were distinctive, original and, in their own way, touched with the same greatness of those other, better remembered singers. His version of Elvis Presley's "Love Me Tender" is a masterpiece of reinterpretation, converting that song's somewhat shallow plea into a mature covenant, a declaration of fidelity and respect.

The soul movement had pretty much been replaced by funk by the early 1970s and Sledge's career, never exactly secure, seemed to wither away as well. He has continued to record though only intermittently, and to make live appearances, his booming and soaring voice as alive as ever.

Bibliography

Guralnick, Peter. *Sweet Soul Music*. New York: Harper, 1986.

Hirshey, Gerri. *Nowhere to Run: The Story of Soul Music*. New York: Times, 1984.

Marsh, Dave. Liner Notes. *It Tears Me Up: The Best of Percy Sledge*. Rhino/Atlantic, 1992.

Timothy L. Parrish

Smith, Wilbur Addison (1933-), born in Northern Rhodesia (now Zambia), is a writer of historical adventure novels, several of them trilogies, that use the exotic geographical settings and complex historical backgrounds of the African wilds. Smith's fiction has enjoyed a wide following in England for a long time; to readers in the U.S., Smith is perhaps best known for his recent work *The River God* (1994), a tale of royal life and a struggle for power in Ancient Egypt. Among other of Smith's works are *Shout at the Devil* (1968), *The Diamond Hunter* (1971), *Eye of the Tiger* (1974), *Cry Wolf* (1975), *Wild Justice* (1978), *The Delta Decision* (1981), *The Leopard Hunts in Darkness* (1984), *Power of the Sword* (1986), *The Courtneys* (1987), *A Time to Die* (1989), *Elephant Song* (1991), *The Seventh Scroll* (1995), and *Birds of Prey* (1997). Two of Smith's novels, *The Dark of the Sun* (1965) and *Gold Mine* (1970), have been adapted to film.

Bibliography

Field, Michele. "Wilbur Smith: His 25th Book Is a Winner Here." *Publishers Weekly* 1 May 1995: 38-39.

Drew Philip Halevy

Snow and Ice Sculptures are often associated with festivals and celebrations. Snow is used by budding sculptors celebrating in their front yards, and winter festivals throughout the country feature snow sculpture contests. Ice sculpture can be small—a decorative glittering centerpiece for a buffet, or large—an intricately constructed palace made of enormous cold, shiny blocks.

In most of the United States, snow is an accessible artistic medium that can either be built up or carved away. A snow sculpture is usually an indicator of the season's first snow. The best-known snow sculpture is the snowman, an example of the basic rolled-ball construction technique. Snow forts are equally popular.

To make a snow sculpture, the snow cannot be too dry and powdery because it will not pack to a hard consistency. Adding slush—watery snow made by mixing water with snow—is necessary. A cubic foot of slush weights 62 pounds, so if a sculpture's center of gravity is too high, it will fall over. A sculpture of six feet or less is a good size when carving a solid block of snow. If a larger sculpture is planned, an armature, or framework onto which the slush is applied, will provide support. Once the armature is covered, a small axe to carve the shape and a chisel to smooth the surface may be used.

Ice carving is now part of the curriculum in the best chefs' schools in the United States. It differs from snow sculpture in that ice, like stone, must be chipped away from a large block to form the desired object. Ice blocks should be clear, free of large air bubbles, and relatively fresh. A standard size block is 20 inches by 40 inches by 10 inches and weighs 300 pounds. The shape is outlined on the block with a chisel, roughed out using a chain saw, then refined with long-handled chisels, gouges, and awls.

Ice palaces—even larger forms of ice sculpture—are full-size buildings constructed entirely of huge blocks of ice cut from a frozen river or lake, then cemented with water. The first documented palace was commissioned by Empress Anna Ivanovna of Russia during the winter of 1739-40. In the late-19th century, the tradition of building ice palaces moved to Canada and the United States. Winter carnivals in North America began as celebrations of local sports or to counter bad publicity about the climate, and frequently had beautifully constructed ice castles as their focal points.

Contemporary North American winter festivals that feature snow sculpture, ice sculpture, and ice palaces include the more-than-100-years-old St. Paul Winter Carnival in Minnesota; the Carnaval de Quebec in Quebec City; the McCall Winter Carnival in McCall, ID; Dartmouth's Winter Carnival in Hanover, NH; the Michigan Tech University Winter Carnival in Houghton; and the Saranac Lake Winter Carnival in New York.

Bibliography
Anderes, Fred, and Ann Agranoff. "The Magic Chill of Ice Palaces Still Beckons Us." *Smithsonian* Jan. 1987: 62.
Hasegawa, Hideo. *Ice Carving*. Palos Verdes: Continental, 1978.
Haskins, James. *Snow Sculpture and Ice Carving*. New York: Macmillan, 1974.

Deborah Fant

Snow White and the Seven Dwarfs (1937) was Walt Disney's first feature-length animated film. It cost six times more than its original budget of $250,000 and took three years to make. Over 600 artists labored on the film, which Hollywood "insiders" had labeled "Disney's Folly." It was, however, an immediate success and has grossed well over $25,000,000. The film opened at the Carthay Circle Theater in Los Angeles in December 1937, in time for the Christmas audience. Twenty-six million people saw the film in its initial release, breaking the 1915 record of *Birth of a Nation*.

Disney chose the story of Snow White as his subject because a silent film version had impressed him in 1917. Hamilton Luskewas was the supervising director; David Hand was the animation supervisor. The film, in Technicolor, advanced the possibilities of animation far beyond the level it had reached by 1937.

Disney insisted that, unlike the Grimms' fairy tale, each dwarf must have a separate personality. This decision presented the animators with numerous headaches and helps explain why the "Heigh-ho" sequence took six months to film. The names of the seven dwarves—Doc, Grumpy, Sleepy, Happy, Bashful, Sneezy, and Dopey—were chosen in a poll run by Disney. Marge Belcher (later Champion), a dancer, modeled Snow White's movements. After a noteworthy and well-publicized search, Adriana Caselotti, a young opera singer, sang the role of Snow White.

The animal sketches are among Disney's best and are rarely matched in the later films, even with advanced technology. The predictable love story has been criticized, as well as frightening sequences involving the Wicked Queen.

But there is little argument regarding the film's music, by Frank Churchill, Leigh Harline, Paul J. Smith, and Larry Morey. "Whistle While You Work," "Heigh-Ho, Heigh-Ho, It's Off to Work We Go," "Someday My Prince Will Come," and "With a Smile and a Song" remain popular. The film received a special Oscar and eight statuettes, one regular size and seven "dwarf-like" ones.

Bibliography
Bauden, Liz-Anne, ed. *The Oxford Companion to Film*. New York: Oxford UP, 1976.
Hullet, Steve. "The Making of *Snow White and the Seven Dwarfs*." *The Best of Disney*. Ed. Neil Sinyard. New York: Crown, 1988.
Solomon, Jack, Jr., ed. *Walt Disney's Snow White and the Seven Dwarfs*. New York: Viking, 1988.
Thomas, Nicholas, ed. *International Directory of Films and Filmmakers 3. Actors and Actresses*. Detroit: St. James, 1992.

Frank A. Salamone

Soap (1977-1981), a controversial ABC prime-time soap opera told in satirical situation comedy terms, received more advance publicity than perhaps any other show of its time. The program, created, produced, and written by Susan Harris, almost never even made it to air due to strong protests from various religious and social groups. After ABC announced that the show's first season would primarily deal with themes such as adultery, homosexuality, impotency, murder, sex change operations, the Mafia, and black-white relations, the broadcaster was deluged with nearly 56,000 letters protesting the subject matter. Though a multitude of advertisers pulled their sponsorship for the first telecast, *Soap* nevertheless enjoyed a successful four-year run, placing in the Top 20 in the Nielsen ratings for its first three years.

Though not the first series to feature "offensive" material—Norman Lear's late-night syndicated sexual soap opera *Mary Hartman, Mary Hartman* deserves that dubious distinction—*Soap,* aired at 9:30 p.m. did bring a "new permissiveness" to prime time. Aware that most children were still awake, ABC allowed some of its affiliates to air the first three episodes at 11:30 p.m. ABC also revised the first two episodes to tone down its sexual explicitness. The onslaught of complaints died down after *Soap* won its time slot by large margins. Following the premiere episode, the controversy subsided.

Set in the suburban town of Dunn's River, CT, *Soap* chronicled the story of two sisters: one a member of the upper-class Tate family, the other a member of the blue-collar Campbell family. As with a soap opera, each episode had open-ended plotlines and cliffhangers. The principal players included: Katherine Helmond as Jessica Tate, the dim-witted socialite with a heart of gold; Robert Mandan as Chester Tate, Jessica's philandering husband; Cathryn Damon as Mary Campbell, Jessica's neurotic sister; Richard Mulligan as Burt Campbell, Mary's husband, who was impotent, captured by space aliens, and became sheriff of Dunn's River; Billy Crystal as Jodie Dallas, Mary's son from a previous marriage who was a transvestite and later tried to have a sex-change operation only to mistakenly turn into an 80-year-old Jewish man; Robert Urich as Peter Campbell, who was murdered in the first season; and Robert Guillaume as Benson (1977-79), the wisecracking butler who was the sole voice of reason in the Tate home.

The series *Benson* (1979-86) was spun off from *Soap* after the Robert Guillaume character left the show to be head butler for Jessica's widower cousin, the governor. *Soap* was surprisingly canceled with many plotlines still open. The last episode ended with shots fired at Jessica Tate by a Central American firing squad. In 1994, after many years of nonsyndication, the cable network Comedy Central, began airing reruns of *Soap* under the tagline "The show your parents were afraid to let you watch."

Bibliography

Brown, Les. *New York Times* 30 Aug. 1977: 1.1.
Klemesrud, Judy. *New York Times* 17 June 1978: 10L.
Time 11 July 1977: 75; 12 Sept. 1977: 72-73.
Waters, Harry F. *Newsweek* 13 June 1977: 42.

Kevin S. Sandler

Soap Opera is the oral culture in our electronic era. Now, as in the days of the primal campfire, the medium of the continuing story knits human beings together, organizing and preserving the culture and holding fears at bay.

Unusually, soap opera, also known as daytime drama, is a genre started by one person. In 1930, Irna Phillips (see entry), an Ohio schoolteacher, sold the concept of *Painted Dreams* to WGN, the radio station affiliated with the *Chicago Tribune*, which had also pioneered continuing-story comic strips. These strips inspired Phillips and Frank and Anne Hummert, who created the stories synonymous with radio soap opera: e.g., *John's Other Wife, Stella Dallas, Backstage Wife* (the Hummerts), and *The Guiding Light* (Phillips). The Hummerts created the first show sponsored by a laundry soap manufacturer—*Oxydol's Own Ma Perkins*—which led to the term "soap opera."

Radio soaps thrived in the homebound years of the Depression and World War II (see Radio Drama). Such shows as *Portia Faces Life* and *Our Gal Sunday* were slow paced, only 15 minutes long, and had directive male narrators. But women were the stars, and James Thurber rightly noticed the emasculated "heroes." Action was as plentiful as in TV soap opera, and because it was set in the imagination, even more fantastic (and violent)—e.g., Stella Dallas trapped in a submarine at the bottom of the Suez Canal.

Of the radio soap writers, Phillips alone thrived on TV: *Guiding Light* (1937-56; TV: 1952- ; see entry), *The Brighter Day* (1948-56; TV: 1954-62). On TV she created *As the World Turns* (1956-), *Another World* (1964-99), and *Days of Our Lives* (1965-) (see entries). But other shows did not transfer well. For 27 years, on radio, "Helen Trent" proved "romance" could come to women "over 35." But she could not do that on television, where we could see her. The first TV soap was *A Woman to Remember* (1947, DuMont; no copies). Roy Winsor, a pioneer TV soap entrepreneur, produced *Search for Tomorrow* (1951-87), *Love of Life* (1951-80), and *The Secret Storm* (1954-74), for CBS, which *was* television soap opera at first.

Early TV soaps were technically and structurally simple. One camera looked back and forth at two people who talked about a third person. In black-and-white, sets and looks were "realistic" (dowdy). (Early TV, especially daytime, did not attract actors.) But TV, the visual, brought glamour, which brought more melodrama and less realism, as in *The Secret Storm*, whose Pauline Rysdale (Haila Stoddard, 1954-70) was the imperious, scorned older woman, hateful but pathetic, yet in her glamour, mesmerizing.

In *As the World Turns*, Irna Phillips had the characters spoken to by name, so viewers would remember them—a sign of switch in emphasis in soaps from story to character. She featured long (even half-hour) coffee klatches (*As the World Turns* was the first half-hour TV soap), with her protégé, Ted Corday, directing three cameras to focus on the actors' faces.

NBC's *Days* in 1965 countered the reign of CBS. It added psychology to the emphasis on character. There were the rock-solid parents, Alice and Tom Horton (Frances Reid and Macdonald Carey, the first movie star to move to daytime drama). But there were also a troubled, and sexual, teen, Julie (Susan Seaforth Hayes), and dark stories like the triangle of Mickey and Bill Horton and their woman, Laura. William Bell, one of Phillips's students (see Soap Opera Writers and Producers, below), was *Days'* head writer, 1966-73, and key to its survival.

Focus on issues came with *One Life to Live* (1968, ABC), the first soap written by Agnes Nixon (see entry), also a student of Phillips. *One Life* (see entry) had Jewish and Irish-American leads, a Polish family, and the first African-American stars. In its first years, *One Life* also portrayed a proud single mother and drug addiction. In 1970, Nixon opened *All My Children* (see entry). Its lead, Amy Tyler, was an antiwar protester. When Phillip Brent was missing in action, his adoptive mother, Ruth Brent (Martin), spoke against the war. In the mid-1980s, Nixon's *Loving* told the story of a traumatized Vietnamese veteran.

In the early 1960s, CBS had six daytime dramas, NBC one, and ABC none. The audience had dropped to 3 to 7 million, from 20 to 40 million listening (in the early 1940s) and 64 serials on the air between 10 a.m. and 6 p.m. The end of soaps was forecast. But, as the 1970s opened, 19 half-hour soaps ran from 11:30 a.m. to 4:30 p.m. on all three networks. In 1975, *Another World* was the first to go to one hour. Television was slowly, steadily making Americans more sophisticated, electronically and aesthetically. The new ABC soaps showed this sophistication: *One Life*, *All My Children*, and (in 1975) *Ryan's Hope* (see entry), about a vital Irish-American family centered in their New York bar. Created by Paul Avila Mayer and Claire Labine, *Ryan's Hope*, in the 1970s and early 1980s, won Emmys and ratings, as did the whole ABC lineup. By the mid-1970s, soaps were hot. *Time* gave *Days* its cover story January 12, 1976; and *Newsweek*, the September 28, 1981, cover for the wedding of Luke (Anthony Geary) and Laura (Genie Francis) from *General Hospital* (1963-).

The 1980s emphasized action, often fantastic. On soaps as in life, the 1980s meant glamour and glitz. Fittingly, beautiful blondes (and blonds) of Bell's *The Young and the Restless* (1973-) moved into first place in the Nielsen ratings; and Bell's 1987 show, *The Bold and the Beautiful,* was set in a lush, tropical Los Angeles and the glamorous world of fashion. *Ryan's Hope* died (1991), and *Generations*—with the good intention of an African-American core family— came and went (1989-91). Its cancellation, however, spurred the other soaps. *All My Children* married an interracial couple (Livia Frye and Tom Cudahy), after shockingly jettisoning another one almost at the altar in 1989. More important, it integrated its extended black family, the Fryes, into nonracial stories—as *Restless* did, when it gave Mamie, its maid, a family at long last.

In the 1990s the genre primarily of, by, and for women at last entered the woman's era: almost every soap woman worked and juggled a job with love and family. Even in the late 1980s and early 1990s, however, soap women were victimized; e.g., *General Hospital*'s Dr. Monica Quartermaine, heart surgeon, and Anna Devane, world class spy, who were not up to the jobs of, respectively, hospital administrator and police commissioner. By the mid-1990s, however, soaps were listening to their largely female audience, in letters and focus groups, and the listening was showing in young or changed women who were realistically tough, driving, hassled, funny, warm, and complex.

As more women work more, soap watching has dropped, according to the Nielsen ratings, to around that old figure of 3-8 million. But women also tape their "stories" or watch (often with men) at work or school, which are hard viewings to count. Still, soap watching undoubtedly ebbed in the 1980 and 1990s. By 2000, there were ten soap operas.

NBC, having dropped *Santa Barbara* (1984-92), and *Another World* (canceled in 1999), was down to *Days* and a new show, *Passions* (1999-). CBS's two Bell shows are solid, but *Guiding Light* and *As the World Turns* are hurt by an aging audience. ABC continues to air *All My Children*, *General Hospital*, and *One Life to Live*, along with a new entry, *Port Charles* (1997-), replacing *The City* (1995-97), which had been *Loving* (1983-95). Their ratings drop by a couple of million when, instead of households, one counts women aged 18-49, the most important demographic group to advertisers. ABC's *All My Children* beats *The Young and the Restless* in this group.

Talk shows are cheaper to produce than soaps, and, along with game shows, have been popular among retirees. Yet, soaps persist. The reasons lie in the special character of the soap opera story; the unusual influence of the audience; and finally, the creator: the soap writer.

What in the soap stories "stabilizes and puts constancy in life," as viewers put it? First, soaps are the stories of families—usually two to four in number and middle- to upper-class. The working-class family most soaps start with commonly gets rich or lost, because poor is dull to the writers and real to the audience. Each soap episode opens with a prologue introducing the day's stories, usually three, which follow in five acts, two or three stories per act, marked off by commercials (which are themselves mini-stories with archetypal characters, usually families). Countering these interruptions, the fundamental movement of soap opera is centrifugal, holding the center by interweaving the characters.

As in folk and fairy tales, the typical soap story opens with the good people of a small town safe in their "enclosed garden" (as melodrama terms the fortress). Danger comes from outside, from the stranger. The soap opera plot unfolds in the pattern uncovered by Vladimir Propp when he studied the worldwide *Morphology of the Folk Tale* in the 1920s. The hero, or heroine, may be victimized, but will escape to beat the enemy, who is the aggressor. A true love waits, or helps; and dark, sexual women or men, linked with serpents and woods, are "donors" of what the heroine needs. "False heroes" are troublesome, but not evil because they are usually kin (e.g., *Dallas*'s J. R. Ewing). There are even false happy endings, as in the never-ending soap opera, and then troubles pick up anew, until a final "transfiguration."

Story hooks us in its joining of the comfortingly familiar and the novel. Original stories are rare in soap opera because of the pressure of writing stories for an hour a day (only *The Bold and the Beautiful* and *Port Charles* are half-hour shows), five days, 52 weeks a year; but also because of the affinity of the mass folk tale with commercial drama in the home. Plots are commonly mythic. Myth is the source of all the soap stories of fathers and sons, or mothers and daughters, vying for the same beloved, or the same crown; for all the lost, and found, fathers, daughters.

Structurally, soap opera at its best interlocks its several stories; and merges content and form in the genre's fundamental irony. The characters lie to dupe or to "spare" each other, and the storyteller dupes the characters and shares the secrets with the audience—and then teases us with outrageous coincidence (eavesdropping, accidental sightings: of lost children, lovers, parents). Fate is the theology of the soap family: born in drama's need for conflict, an unsung *que sera* underlies and mocks soap lovers' brave words, *"Now* we will be happy ever after."

Soap opera also reflects the culture of the time, but particularly the mythic (the Vietnam war, rape and other abuse of women), and the personal. It was a breakthrough in the early 1960s when Agnes Nixon, in her first headwriter's job, on *The Guiding Light*, had the star, Bert Bauer, stricken with uterine cancer, which she survived because of a Pap test. Breast cancer stories followed, cosmetic surgery (pro), wife abuse, and (in the 1980s and 1990s), incest, alcoholism, bulimia, rape, AIDS, and more: soap opera has led TV and movies in telling women's—and men's—stories. It has lagged on social issues, but it can be uniquely forceful because the bigotry—the personal pain of the political issue—is felt by characters the audience has known, often for years, and visits daily. For example, understanding grew, viewers said, from *One Life*'s landmark 1992 story of homophobia.

Just as soap's stories are mythic, its characters are archetypal. Erica Kane of *All My Children* is the dark (but not evil) female force. Because of the viewer's long-term acquaintance with them, Erica and all continuing characters are also, inevitably, individuated. Still, there is a pattern of characters in each soap. At the top and bottom of the chart, fewest in number, are elders and young children. The bulge in the middle are the sexually active 20- to 30-year-olds, and above and below, in lesser numbers, the "matrons" and "fathers" and the teenagers. Just as the star-crossed young lovers are a staple, so almost every soap has a wise and feisty patriarch or matriarch. Occasionally, the mature 40- to 60-year-olds will be used for a surprise, as in *Another World*'s interracial love story of the romance writer Felicia Gallant (Linda Dano) and the editor Marshall Lincoln Kramer III (Randy Brooks). The 20- to 30-year-old characters change most, so new "hunks" and women can be brought in. But they are types—just complex ones. Heroes and heroines are never saints anymore, nor are villains all bad (they might prove popular, and then what to do?) The rapist turned good by the love of a good woman is controversial, but popular (Luke is the model). In the AIDS age, the hero who strays is no more, but he can be a reformed rake, or bad in another way, like *All My Children*'s arrogant tycoon, Adam Chandler.

Its archetypes and myths make soap opera—counter to its image as escapism—central in the culture. It is also key because the audience is unusual, even in the popular arts, in the influence it has on the "product." Because the soap story is experienced intimately, its viewers have always identified with it and have written letters, which have counted in writing the stories and characters. Fans do not believe their soap operas are real. Only psychotics confuse real life and story. Others do not doubt their "friends" in the stories are fictional, but (they say in letters and fan gatherings) that does not keep them from learning, laughing, crying, with the characters.

More and more, in the 1980s and 1990s, as women's lives changed and viewing dropped, letters to the soaps were read—for action. Soap magazines grew in number, as did soap support of fan clubs and gatherings of viewers and creators (see Media Coverage of Soap Operas). As U.S. scholars follow Europe, Great Britain, and other countries in taking soap opera seriously, there are more symposia with soap writers, producers, actors, and even network executives. Several recent scholarly texts treat soap opera story as the emblem of the new feminized age that celebrates multi- and contradictory meaning, mystery, complexity, and caring.

Finally—but foremost in the creation of the soap opera—is its 25-hour a day writer (see Soap Operas Writers and Producers, just below). Good soap writers prove a cliché, the "born storyteller," and are as eager (or more) to talk story with anyone—fans, scholars, anyone but the soap-haters—as the fans are to give them ideas and responses. To explain why she shows all sides of an issue, Agnes Nixon tells a story of what organizer Saul Alinsky said at an institute on "Communications and Society" in the early 1970s. "When I go to a meeting," Nixon quoted Alinsky, "I make a point of not bringing out the baby pictures because once you [do that] you can't negotiate anymore. You've become friendly. You [television people] can do that; you can bring out the baby pictures and explain the hard hats to the liberals, and so on."

Bring out the baby pictures: is this not just what soap opera does, and has done for over 70 years, around our electronic hearthfire?

Bibliography

Fiske, John. *Television Culture*. New York: Methuen, 1987.
Frentz, Susan, ed. *Staying Tuned: Contemporary Soap Opera Criticism*. Bowling Green, OH: Bowling Green State U Popular P, 1992.
Groves, Seli. *The Ultimate Soap Opera Guide*. Detroit: Visible Ink, 1995.
Nochlimson, Martha. *No End to Her: Soap Opera and the Female Subject*. Berkeley: U of California P, 1992.
Williams, Carol Traynor. *"It's Time for My Story": Soap Opera Sources, Structure, and Response*. Westport: Praeger, 1992.

Carol Traynor Williams

Soap Opera Actors and Actresses. Actors are trained to depict characters that, for the most part, have no relation to the actor's own life. However, soap opera actors can, in subtle ways, influence the writing of their characters. Because so many actors play soap characters for long periods of time, writers often incorporate nuances of the actor into the writing of the character, and may see new dimensions through an actor's performance. In soap operas more than any other genre, actors grow and mature with the character, and the character evolves out of the combination of what the writer has created in concept and what the actor brings to the performance. The meshing of actor and character helps the portrayal to become more realistic and more believable to audiences.

Many of the actors in soap operas have extensive theater, television, and film credits. For others, soap operas are their first acting jobs, having supplanted summer stock and regional theater as the training ground. The quality of soap opera acting is often criticized, and although sometimes that criticism is warranted, in many cases the acting on soap operas is superb. For actors whose characters are prominent on the soaps, the workload is very demanding, sometimes requiring the memorization of a major portion of an eighty-page script for each day that the character is featured.

Many soap opera actors are known for playing one character for a very long time. Helen Wagner (1918-), a Shakespearean and musical theater actress who began her television career at an experimental station in Schenectady, NY, has played Nancy Hughes on *As the World Turns* since the show first aired in 1956. She has the distinction of being the longest-running soap actor in the same role. Don MacLaughlin played her husband, Chris Hughes, from the beginning until his death in 1986. To celebrate the endurance of these two soap opera greats, writer Douglas Marland (1935-) wrote a 1985 episode in which past and present characters—friends and family of the Hughes clan—assembled to celebrate the couple's 50th wedding anniversary. Don Hastings (1934-) as Dr. Bob Hughes, their son, has acted in radio and on the Broadway stage since the age of six. He has the distinction of holding down the longest-running male romantic lead in a soap opera.

Ruth Warrick (1916-) has played Phoebe Tyler on *All My Children* since it began in 1970. Her earlier film credits include *Citizen Kane* (1939), in which she played Orson Welles's first wife, the role that launched her film career. Warrick played in over 30 motion pictures in the 1940s and 1950s, then did television, radio, and theater before working for a short time on *The Guiding Light*, and later, on *As the World Turns*. Phoebe's long-suffering husband, Dr. Charles Tyler, was played by Hugh Franklin (1916-1986). As Dr. Tyler, he eventually married his secretary Mona Kane, played by Frances Heflin. The sister of movie great Van Heflin, she passed away in 1994.

Frances Reid, matriarch of the Horton family on *Days of Our Lives*, was a stage and television actress prior to portraying Portia Manning on *Portia Faces Life*, and Rose Pollock on *The Edge of Night*. She has been playing Alice Horton since *Days of Our Lives* began in 1965. The role of Alice's husband, Tom Horton, was originated and played by MacDonald Carey (1913-1994) until his death. Carey provided the voice for the opening epigraph, "Like sands through the hourglass, so are the days of our lives."

John Beradino (1917-1996) created the role of Dr. Steve Hardy, chief of staff at *General Hospital*, in 1963. Prior to acting, he was with the Cleveland Indians' 1948 World Series championship team. Beradino was instrumental in bringing Emmy Awards to daytime television. Beradino's co-star, Emily McLaughlin, played long-suffering nurse Jesse Brewer from 1963 until her death in 1991.

Eileen Fulton (1933-) continues to play Lisa Mitchell, a one-time villainess on *As the World Turns*. Fulton was the most popular soap opera star of the 1960s. She joined the cast of *As the World Turns* in 1960, spun off her character in 1965 into a prime-time series, *Our Private World*, then returned to daytime in the same role in 1967, after *Our Private World* was canceled.

One of the most beloved soap opera actresses, Charita Bauer (1922-1985), played the character of Bert Bauer on *The Guiding Light*, beginning first on the radio in 1950. Between 1952 and 1956, Charita Bauer played the same character on radio and television, until *The Guiding Light* went off the radio in 1956. She was awarded an Emmy for lifetime achievement in 1983.

Douglas Watson (1921-1989), an outstanding Shakespearean actor on the stage and in motion pictures for two decades, broke into soap operas in 1965 in *Moment of Truth*. Roles in *Search for Tomorrow* and *Love of Life* preceded his longtime stint as the urbane but loving multi-millionaire Mackenzie Cory on *Another World*, a character he played until his death. In the same soap, Victoria Wyndham, born into a theatrical family (her parents appeared on radio's *The Guiding Light*) went from bitch to goddess with her marriage to Mac Cory. As Ada McGowan, mother to Rachel Cory, Constance Ford (deceased 1993) played a strong character who stood by her daughter when others forsook her.

Finally, celebrated for her roles on *Love Is a Many Spendored Thing*, *Another World, Texas*, and *Guiding Light*, Beverlee McKinsey (1940-) was raised in a strict Baptist family which forbade her from going to the movies. She attributes her success to this denial, and raised her three-year-old son Scott after her divorce to follow in her footsteps in the entertainment business as a director to her character, Alexandra Spaulding, on *Guiding Light*.

Helen Gallagher (1926-) had a long and successful career on the musical stage, winning a Tony for her role as Hazel Flagg in *Pal Joey* and another in 1969 for *No, No Nanette*. ABC asked her to play Maeve Ryan in *Ryan's Hope*, for which she won the Emmy in 1975-76, 1976-77, and again in 1987-88. Playing her husband, Johnny Ryan, on *Ryan's Hope*, Bernard Barrow was a professor of theater arts at Brooklyn College. He was nominated for best supporting actor in 1978-79 and again in 1987-88. When *Ryan's Hope* was canceled in 1989, he joined the cast of *Loving* as the beloved Louie Slavinsky, finally winning the Emmy for best supporting actor in 1991. Barrow died in 1993.

Born Mary Houchins in 1926, actress Mary Stuart assumed her mother's maiden name and became a Hollywood starlet for MGM. After serving her apprenticeship, she landed a few leading roles opposite Ronald Reagan and Errol Flynn. She soon tired of Hollywood and went east where she enrolled in acting classes, eventually landing the lead as Jo in *Search for Tomorrow,* which she played for over 30 years, surviving near cancellation of her character and show many times over. She was the first daytime actress to be nominated for an Emmy, and was nominated as outstanding actress in daytime three more times. In 1983, she won a lifetime achievement award.

For several soap opera actors, their roles have catapulted them to soap opera superstardom. These actors have become as well known to those who don't watch soaps as they are to their faithful soap fans. For example, Anthony Geary (1947-) and Genie Francis (1962-) gained unprecedented fame in the late 1970s for their portrayals of Luke and Laura on *General Hospital*. Anthony Geary was brought onto the show in 1978 to play Luke Spenser, a role that was originally conceived of as being short term. However, because of the extreme popularity of Geary's portrayal, and the audience reaction to the on-screen chemistry between Geary and Francis, the character was kept on. Susan Lucci (1948-) is another actress known to audiences because of her soap opera acting. Lucci has portrayed Erica Kane since the premiere of *All My Children* in 1970. She has appeared in several prime-time television episodes and miniseries, but is perhaps best known for her 19 nominations for the Emmy until she won it in 1998-99.

Many popular television and motion picture stars spent time early in their careers on soap operas. Included among them are Ted Danson (*Somerset*), Alan Alda (*The House on High Street*), Corbin Bernsen (*Ryan's Hope*), Dana Delany (*Love of Life, As the World Turns*), Peter Falk (*Love of Life*), Hal Linden (*Search for Tomorrow*), and Tom Selleck (*The Young and the Restless*). Long-established movie actors such as Dustin Hoffman (*Search for Tomorrow*), Jack Lemmon (*The Brighter Day, The Road of Life*), Hal Holbrook (*The Brighter Day*), Warren Beatty (*Love of Life*), James Earl Jones (*As the World Turns, Guiding Light*), Kathleen Turner (*The Doctors*), and Robert DeNiro (*Search for Tomorrow*) are among the soap opera alumni. In recent years, a number of younger soap opera actors have exploded onto the silver screen, such as Meg Ryan (*As the World Turns*), Demi Moore (*General Hospital*), Marisa Tomei (*As the World Turns*), and Kevin Bacon (*Guiding Light*).

Many actors who gained prominence in other genres and who are soap opera fans themselves have made cameo and guest appearances on their favorite soap operas. Elizabeth Taylor made a guest appearance on *General Hospital* in 1981 as the widow Helena Cassadine, attending Luke and Laura's wedding, and also did a cameo appearance on *All My Children* in 1983 as a charwoman, spoofing the role originated by Carol Burnett, who was appearing as Verla Grubbs on *All My Children* at the same time. Carol Burnett had earlier cameoed on *All My Children* as a different character, Mrs. Johnson. Sammy Davis, Jr., played Eddie Phillips on *General Hospital* in 1982. As a loyal fan of *One Life to Live,* he played a recurring role as Chip Warrens, who was written into the story in 1980, 1981, and 1983. When Christina Crawford, who played Joan Kane on *The Secret Storm*, became ill in 1968, her mother, Joan Crawford, suggested that she fill in for her daughter. Although it was unrealistic that a 64-year-old woman play a 24-year-old housewife, CBS agreed, excited about the ratings potential for such an appearance. Obviously soap operas can pull off almost any miracle.

Bibliography

Copeland, Mary Ann. *Soap Opera History*. Lincolnwood: BDD (Mallard), 1991.

Irwin, Barbara. "An Oral History of a Piece of Americana: The Soap Opera Experience." Diss. State University of New York at Buffalo, 1990.

Rout, Nancy E., Ellen Buckley, and Barney M. Rout, eds. *The Soap Opera Book: Who's Who in Daytime Drama*. West Nyack: Todd, 1992.

Schemering, Christopher. *The Soap Opera Encyclopedia*. New York: Ballantine, 1987.

Barbara J. Irwin
Mary Cassata

Soap Opera Writers and Producers. Anne and Frank Hummert, successful advertising executives, and Irna Phillips (1901-73), schoolteacher turned actress/writer, are generally thought of as the most prominent radio soap opera writers, credited as being the creators of the soap opera form. Phillips (see entry) created the first soap opera, *Painted Dreams,* which aired in Chicago in 1930. But it was the Hummerts who created the first soap-sponsored soap opera, *Oxydol's Own Ma Perkins*, which aired on Cincinnati radio in 1933 before moving to Chicago, where it made its network debut on NBC. Phillips then went on to create such radio soaps as *The Guiding Light* (1937-56); *The Road of Life* (1937-59); *Woman in White* (1938-48); *The Right to Happiness* (1939-60); and *The Brighter Day* (1948-56). Of these, *The Guiding Light, The Road of Life*, and *The Brighter Day* made the transition to television, with *Guiding Light* still on the air today.

The Hummerts were even more prolific. They formed their own production company, Air Features, a soap-writing factory. Running it autocratically, they did not permit their writers and actors to address them directly. Their staff had to go through channels. The usual procedure was for the Hummerts to go into isolation, write the first half dozen episodes or so, then turn the writing over to subwriters, who were forced to follow a rigid formula to keep the peace and to remain employed. Their creativity was held in check; they received little money for their work; and little public recognition for their writing. The soaps bearing the Hummerts' imprint were *Just Plain Bill; The Romance of Helen Trent; Ma Perkins; Mary Noble, Backstage Wife; Stella Dallas*; and *Bright Promise*, to name but a few. Only one of their soaps, *Ma Perkins*, was piloted in 1948 for television, but the pilot was never broadcast. While Irna Phillips made the transition to television successfully and went on to be television's greatest writer of soap operas, the Hummerts had no love for the fledgling medium and no desire to re-create a new dynasty for television. In their method of storytelling, they claimed to be presenting their audience with "slices of life," but as in other soaps of the day, they served up a brand of fantasy that was clearly unattainable. Irna Phillips, on the other hand, concentrated on character. She introduced the professional in her stories—doctors, ministers, and lawyers —with the drama growing out of their life-and-death workaday lives. Despite her invention of the dreaded amnesia, she realized her desire to allow the audience to experience what the character was feeling.

Roy Windsor was regarded by many as the Frank Hummert of early television. His *Search for Tomorrow* (1951-86) was the first successful television soap. He also created and managed *Love of Life* (1951-80) and *The Secret Storm*

(1954-74). Phillips, in the meantime, busied herself with her television versions of *Guiding Light, The Road of Life*, and *The Brighter Day*. In addition to *Guiding Light* on television, Irna Phillips created *As The World Turns* (1956-); *Another World* (1964-99); and *Love Is a Many Splendored Thing* (1967-73), which was based loosely on the feature film and book of the same title. She co-created *Days of Our Lives* (1965-) with Ted Corday (who soon became the driving force behind it) and Allan Chase; and she served as story consultant on several TV soaps, the most memorable of which was *Peyton Place* (1964-69), where her behind-the-scenes feuds with Paul Monash over creative control were more incendiary than the sexual liaisons on the soap opera itself.

Two of Irna Phillips's students—Agnes Nixon and William Bell—have themselves become legends in the genre. After a successful apprenticeship with her mentor, Agnes Nixon (see entry) created *One Life to Live* (1968-), *All My Children* (1970-), and *Loving* (1983-95) with Douglas Marland. Bell took on headwriting chores for *Days of Our Lives,* bringing it to the top of the ratings in 1971, before branching out on his own to create *The Young and the Restless* (1973-) and *The Bold and the Beautiful* (1987-).

Among other soap opera creators who deserve mention are Irving Vendig (*The Edge of Night*, 1956-84); Frank and Doris Hursley (*General Hospital*, 1963-); Bridget and Jerome Dobson (*Santa Barbara*, 1984-93); the late Douglas Marland (*Loving*, and later headwriter for *As the World Turns*, 1984-92); Claire Labine and Paul Avila Mayer (*Ryan's Hope*, 1975-89); and Harding LeMay (*For Richer, for Poorer*, 1967-78, and later headwriter for *Another World,* 1971-79). Two additional writers deserve mention for the innovativeness of the product they created: Dan Curtis for *Dark Shadows* (1966-71), which lured the teenaged audience with his weird gothic tales of vampires and witches; and Sally Sussman for *Generations* (1989-91), a soap that from day one incorporated a black family as one of its core families.

Soap opera writers represent a relatively small community of individuals, with many having close ties—either directly or indirectly—to the individual regarded as the creator of the form, Irna Phillips. Nevertheless, the standard is for soap operas generally to divide the work among three types of writers: headwriters, dialogue writers, and breakdown or outline writers, with the power resting with the headwriter, the creative force behind the programs. It is the headwriter who develops long-term storyline projections that establish the direction the story and characters will take in upcoming months, or perhaps years. It is also the headwriter who is responsible for hiring and leading a writing staff, which may number ten or more. The next level of writers are the breakdown or outline writers, who must take the long-term storylines and break them down into smaller story arcs: they determine how much of the long-term story will be told in a month, or in a week, or in a day. Once that has been determined, each script is assigned to a dialogue writer, who actually writes the script for the given day. However, it should be noted that although this is the typical writing hier-archy, some headwriters are involved in all levels of the writing for their particular shows.

While the headwriters of soap operas are the central creative force, developing characters and projecting long-term stories, it is the producers who play a significant role in bringing those stories to life on the screen. Among the most notable is Gloria Monty, who as early as the 1960s stood out in the realism of doing exterior shooting. Soap opera historians cite Monty's drowning scene in *The Secret Storm* as nothing short of masterful. Her innovations in *General Hospital* are, of course, legendary, influencing the entire daytime drama world, for better or worse. In the same mode as Monty, John Conboy energized *The Young and the Restless,* making it the most "Hollywood" of the soaps with his insistence on lighting beautiful people directly. His mastery in production values set the stylistic pace for daytime drama, which every other soap opera has strived to imitate.

Other soap opera producers also deserving mention for their consistent high quality work are Al Rabin (*Days of Our Lives*); Paul Rauch (*Another World*); Robert Costello (*Ryan's Hope, Dark Shadows, Another World, The Secret Storm*); Jorn Winther (*All My Children, Generations*); Jacqueline Babbin (*All My Children, Loving*); Allen Potter (*Another World, As the World Turns, The Brighter Day*); H. Wesley Kenney (*Days of Our Lives, General Hospital*); Erwin Nicholson (*The Edge of Night*); Joseph Stuart (*One Life to Live, The Doctors*); and Edward Scott (*The Young and the Restless*).

Bibliography

Copeland, Mary Ann. *Soap Opera History*. Lincolnwood: BBD, 1991.

LaGuardia, Robert. *Soap World*. New York: Arbor House, 1983.

Schemering, Christopher. *The Soap Opera Encyclopedia.* New York: Ballantine, 1987.

Mary Cassata
Barbara J. Irwin

Soccer, the world's most popular sport, has always played an enigmatic role in the sporting life of the United States. Millions of youngsters currently participate in organized soccer leagues, especially after both the men's and women's World Cup, the game's most prestigious tournament, were held in the U.S. in 1994 and 1999. According to the Soccer Industry Council of America, 18.2 million Americans played in 1998. Yet soccer—in most countries a national obsession—has never captivated the mass of American spectators.

The modern form of soccer dates from 19th-century Britain, when the first rules were codified (in 1863) by the newly formed Football Association. (Association or "assoc" football led to the term "soccer.") Thereafter, under the impetus of British colonialism, soccer quickly became the competitive sport of choice for countries around the world. By 1904, soccer had become so popular that the Fédération Internationale de Football Association (FIFA) was formed as the umbrella organization for national associations—a function it still performs. It was the inspiration of one of its early presidents, Jules Rimet, that led to the inception in 1930 of the World Cup, the international soccer competition that every four years involves over 170 nations. With a total attendance of over 2.5 million at 1998 tournament games in France and a TV audience of almost 40 billion, the World Cup is by far the most popular single sporting event in the world, focusing national pride and honor in ways that sports teams from the U.S. rarely achieve. The Women's World Cup, inaugurated in 1991, was won by the U.S. team in Pasadena, CA, in 1999. TV ratings in the U.S. for the final game exceeded those for the 1994 and 1998 men's finals, leading to proposals for a women's professional league.

Despite problems in establishing professional leagues in the U.S., soccer has always been played here. Though largely the preserve of newly arrived immigrants to the country, the game was for a time popular among colleges. The first intercollegiate football game between Princeton and Rutgers in 1869, which many historians consider the origin of American football, was actually played under London Football Association rules. Many soccer leagues sprang up in the last decades of the 19th century, prompting the formation of the American Football Association in 1884. But the trend toward professionalizing the game of soccer, apparent almost everywhere else in the world, was reversed in the United States. It was not until favorable TV ratings in America for the 1966 World Cup demonstrated interest in the game that strenuous attempts were made to establish professional leagues.

The history of professional soccer in the U.S. characterizes the game's unusual cultural role. Promoters of the game faced a critical choice of whether to nurture American players or to import talented and experienced stars. One early league, the cleverly named United Soccer Association (USA), actually imported entire teams from abroad, renaming them in an attempt to identify them with American cities. Another, the National Professional Soccer League, depended mostly on American-born players. Attendance in both leagues remained low. The North American Soccer League (NASL), emerging in 1968 from their collapse, sought a compromise whereby foreign stars like Pele of Brazil would play alongside Americans. While this tactic enjoyed some success—particularly large crowds attended games played by the New York Cosmos in the late '70s—the NASL's hold on the popular imagination was slight. Losing iconic players like Pele, faced by plunging attendances and a national economic recession, the league folded in 1985. While its fan base crumbled, however, soccer remained popular among American youngsters, whose participation in organized soccer now surpasses that of homegrown sports like football and baseball. More girls play soccer, in fact, than any other sport.

The Major Indoor Soccer League was formed in 1978 and enjoyed local success and enthusiastic fan support due to its rigid pace and high scoring. While purists abhor soccer being played within the confines of a hockey rink space, the MISL provided employment and visibility for professional stars. The league folded in 1992 after 14 seasons. In 1993, Major League Soccer was founded, with 10 teams playing their first games in 1996. In 2000, a women's professional

Chicago's Soldier Field served as the opening day venue for the World Cup Soccer tournament in 1994. Photo courtesy of Mark McDermott.

league, the WUSA, was established, with 8 teams scheduled to play 80 games.

FIFA awarded the 1994 World Cup to the U.S. partly in hopes of sparking spectator interest in the sport. Though World Cup '94 was a financial success, and despite the U.S.'s relatively strong showing in the tournament, it does not seem to have fundamentally changed perceptions of the game in the United States. The future of professional soccer in the U.S. depends on transforming vast numbers of young soccer players into spectators.

Bibliography

Frommer, Harvey. *The Great American Soccer Book*. New York: Atheneum, 1980.

Hollander, Zander, ed. *The American Encyclopedia of Soccer*. New York: Everest, 1980.

Merrill, Christopher. *The Grass of Another Country: A Journey through the World of Soccer*. New York: Holt, 1993.

Powers, John. *Boston Globe* 14 July 1998. Online. LEXIS-NEXIS Academic Universe. 22 May 2000.

Sandomir, Richard. *New York Times* 14 July 1999. Online. LEXIS-NEXIS Academic Universe. 22 May 2000.

"Soccer." *World Almanac Reference Database*. Facts on File News Services, 2000.

Thomas Strychacz

Sondheim, Stephen Joshua (1930-), popular and influential theater composer/lyricist, was born in New York City, the only child of Herbert Sondheim, a dress manufacturer, and Janet Fox Sondheim, a fashion designer and interior decorator. When Sondheim was ten his parents divorced and with his mother he moved to Doylestown, PA. A Doylestown neighbor was lyricist Oscar Hammerstein II (see Rodgers and Hammerstein). Young Sondheim spent much time with the Hammerstein family and Oscar Hammerstein became his surrogate father and, eventually, his professional mentor. Sondheim began writing musicals while a student at the George School in Newtown, PA, and pursued a degree in music at Williams College in Massachusetts.

In 1954, producer Lemuel Ayers asked Sondheim to write the score to *Saturday Night*, based on the play *Front*

Porch in Flatbush by Julius J. and Philip G. Epstein. Sondheim completed the score and a cast was hired, but the production fell apart when Lemuel Ayers suddenly died. (It finally saw its first production in 1997.) The music of Stephen Sondheim was first heard by Broadway audiences when he contributed incidental music to the play *The Girls of Summer* in 1956. The following year Sondheim was asked to assist composer Leonard Bernstein with lyrics for *West Side Story*, a retelling of *Romeo and Juliet* in contemporary Manhattan. Sondheim ended up writing most of the show's lyrics and was given sole credit (though some of Bernstein's lyrics remained in the final production). *West Side Story* (1957, 734 performances) was a solid success on Broadway and the 1961 film version was an even bigger smash. Familiar songs from the show include "Something's Coming," "Maria," "Tonight," and "Somewhere." Sondheim's collaboration with composer Jule Styne resulted in another now classic musical, *Gypsy* (1959, 702 performances), the story of the rise to fame of burlesque queen Gypsy Rose Lee, with the focus on Lee's mother, Rose, played by Ethel Merman. Popular songs from *Gypsy* are "Small World," "Together Wherever We Go," and Merman's showstopper, "Everything's Coming up Roses."

A Funny Thing Happened on the Way to the Forum (1962, 967 performances), a musical takeoff on the farces of the Roman playwright Plautus, was Stephen Sondheim's Broadway debut as both lyricist and composer. This least characteristic of Sondheim shows still stands as his longest-running Broadway production. A poor review from the *New York Times* is the reason most commonly cited for the failure of Sondheim's *Anyone Can Whistle* (1964, 9 performances). This short-lived show, with its sardonic and pessimistic tone ("Me and My Town," "See What It Gets You") but tentatively hopeful finale ("With So Little to Be Sure Of") is the prototypical Sondheim musical and has developed a following by way of its original cast recording.

Sondheim returned to lyricist-only status (for the last time to date) when he collaborated with Richard Rodgers on *Do I Hear a Waltz?* (1965, 220 performances), a musical version of Arthur Laurents's play *The Time of the Cuckoo* (the basis of the 1955 Katharine Hepburn film *Summertime*). This melancholic tale of a lonely American woman in Venice was considered ill-chosen material for musicalization but the score offers some of Sondheim's wittiest lyrics ("This Week Americans," "What Do We Do? We Fly!"). Indeed, Sondheim is widely regarded as one of the finest lyricists in the history of the American musical theater. His talent as a composer is more debatable.

Five years passed before Sondheim returned to Broadway with *Company* (1970, 706 performances), a "concept" musical exploring the benefits and drawbacks of contemporary marriage (Sondheim has remained a lifelong bachelor). Though many critics thought *Company* cold and unlikable, charges often leveled against Sondheim's work, there was near agreement that it took the musical theater to a new level of complexity in subject matter. Sondheim followed *Company* with another concept musical, *Follies* (1971, 522 performances), a lavish production about a reunion of former showgirls. Well received by critics (and still considered by many to be Sondheim's best work), *Follies* did not catch on sufficiently with the public and closed before it could recoup its fabulous production costs.

Sondheim quickly bounced back with the Swedish bagatelle *A Little Night Music* (1973, 601 performances), an operetta-like piece based on Ingmar Bergman's film *Smiles of a Summer Night*. The score offers Sondheim's best-known song, "Send in the Clowns." Judy Collins's recording of the song, which spent several weeks on the Top 40 chart in 1977 and received much radio play, is one of the few hit songs of the rock era to have originated on Broadway, no longer a significant source of popular tunes.

Pacific Overtures (1975, 193 performances), Sondheim's look at the opening up of Japan to the West in the mid-19th century, was an elaborate production with all-Asian and almost all-male cast. This "japonaise" musical was impressive but cold (even by Sondheim standards) and failed to excite many critics or ticket buyers. The score includes what Sondheim considers his best song, "Someone in a Tree." *Sweeney Todd* (1979, 588 performances), a reworking of the tale of the revenge-seeking "Demon Barber of Fleet Street," is almost entirely sung. This lurid but effective show was the unlikely source of one of Sondheim's more touching songs, "Not While I'm Around." A more cheerful but far less successful work was *Merrily We Roll Along* (1981, 16 performances), based on the George S. Kaufman/Moss Hart play of the same name. Sondheim's excellent score was lost in a poorly conceived production.

On the other hand, crowd-pleasing production values were given much credit for the success of *Sunday in the Park with George* (1984, 604 performances), which follows French painter Georges Seurat as he works on his masterpiece *A Sunday Afternoon on the Island of La Grand Jatte* (an elaborate production number called "Sunday" is a *tableau vivant* of the painting). Perhaps Sondheim's most heartwarming show is *Into the Woods* (1987, 764 performances), an interweaving of several classic fairy tales into a single plot. Sondheim returned to *Sweeney Todd* bleakness with *Assassins* (1990, 73 performances), a revue-type show in which the characters are all murderers or attempted murderers of American political leaders. The limited run, off-Broadway engagement of this decidedly offbeat work failed to impress musically or dramatically. Better received was *Passion* (1994), a musical version of the Italian director Ettore Scola's film *Passione d'Amore*, which concerns a homely woman's obsession with a handsome Army officer.

Stephen Sondheim is widely acknowledged as the most important and innovative figure in the American musical theater since Rodgers and Hammerstein. Though he has a large following (too large and mainstream to be called a cult) among regular theater-goers, his musicals do not attract more casual ticket-buyers, hence the medium-length runs of even his most successful shows.

Bibliography

Bloom, Ken. *Broadway: An Encyclopedic Guide to the History, People, and Places of Times Square.* New York: Facts on File, 1990.

Freedman, Samuel G. "The Words and Music of Stephen Sondheim." *New York Times Magazine* 1 Apr. 1984: 22-26, 32, 60.

Horn, Miriam. "Broadway's Age of Wit and Glitter." *U.S. News and World Report* 1 Feb. 1988: 52-54.

Ilson, Carol. *Harold Prince: From* Pajama Game *to* Phantom of the Opera. Ann Arbor: UMI Research, 1989.

Secrest, Meryle. *Stephen Sondheim: A Life.* New York: Random House, 1998.

Zadan, Craig. *Sondheim & Co.* 2d ed. New York: Harper, 1986.

Mary C. Kalfatovic

Sousa, John Philip (1854-1932). Though he was also called the "Dickens of Music," the "Berlioz of the Military Band," and the "Pied Piper of Patriotism," the title that prevailed in connection with John Philip Sousa was "The March King"—an early publicist's essentially accurate comparison between Sousa's contribution to American band music and Johann Strauss's contribution as "The Waltz King" to that genre. Bandleader, composer, and showman, Sousa brought classical music to U.S. towns and American music abroad at a time when the U.S. was considered a cultural wasteland. He remains American band music's most important figure.

The third of ten children, John Philip was born and received basic education in Washington, DC, and musical instruction at a local conservatory run by John Esputa, Jr., with whom Sousa sometimes clashed. Young Sousa learned most orchestral instruments, particularly brass, but principally studied violin. When in 1868 at the age of 13 Sousa was about to run off with a circus band, his father instead helped him enlist as an apprentice in the U.S. Marine Band. The following years included training in harmony, theory, and composition by Washington orchestra conductor George Felix Benkert.

Upon leaving the Marine Band in May 1875, Sousa turned down an opportunity to continue his musical education in Europe, instead opting to play violin in various Washington theater orchestras and to travel as conductor in two theater troupes. He moved to Philadelphia in 1876 and landed a position in the first violin section of the orchestra there led by Jacques Offenbach for the Centennial Exposition. During his few years in Philadelphia, he taught music and proofread for publishing firms. He also devoted more time to composing, and was especially attracted to operetta. Indeed, he managed a company that took Gilbert and Sullivan's *H.M.S. Pinafore* on the road. After the tour, on December 30, 1879, he married a member of the cast, Jane van Middlesworth Bellis.

Sousa's successes had impressed Marine Corps officials, who offered him leadership of the U.S. Marine Band in Washington. At the age of 25, Sousa became the band's 14th conductor, a position he held from October 1, 1880, until 1892, by which time he had reshaped the band and had earned it considerable prestige, partly due to his own compositions, which, among various band suites, humoresques, and fantasies, included the still-famous marches "Semper Fidelis" (1888), "The Thunderer" (1889), and "The Washington Post" (1889), the last of which eventually even lent its name to a European two-step dance craze.

In 1892, after touring with the Marine Band, Sousa vacationed in Europe to recover from fatigue. Prompted to investigate popular bands there, Sousa saw artistic and financial reasons for resigning from the Corps and organizing his own civilian concert group. On September 26 of that year in Plainfield, NJ, the 46 members of "Sousa's Band" performed publicly for the first time. The Sousa Band would remain busy for 39 years, touring Europe in 1900, 1901, 1903, and 1905, and the world in 1910-11. It would incorporate the first upright sousaphone—the bass tuba manufactured in the late 1890s to Sousa's specifications and thus bearing his name.

Sousa affected the music business in other respects too. In 1892, he began negotiating royalty contracts for his own compositions rather than the standard flat-fee arrangements of the time. He eventually became a lobbyist for the rights of composers and was instrumental in effecting U.S. copyright law reform in 1909. Ultimately less successful were his publications denouncing recorded music, which he called "canned music" or the "Menace of Mechanical Music"; he refused to conduct the Sousa Band's earliest recordings.

The Sousa Band underwent only one hiatus. During World War I, at the age of 62, Sousa in the rank of lieutenant helped organize U.S. Navy bands at the Great Lakes Naval Training Center and toured with a band of 300 sailors, earning an honorary position as a commander of the U.S. Naval Reserve.

After the war, the Sousa Band resumed its schedule of touring, slowing only in the late 1920s and early 1930s due to the Depression. While preparing for an appearance as guest conductor of the Ringgold Band in Reading, PA, and after rehearsing the last work he was to direct, "The Stars and Stripes Forever," the 77-year-old Sousa suffered a heart attack in his hotel room and died.

By the end of his life, the prolific Sousa had completed 12 operettas, a few of them moderate successes like *El Capitan* (1895), *The Bride Elect* (1897), *The Free Lance* (1905), and *The American Maid* (1909). He also had written three novels, an autobiography, about 130 articles, a musical instruction book, and had edited an international book of airs. But aside from the many songs, hymns, and other kinds of band pieces he composed, his marches earned him his immortality. He wrote 136 of them between 1876 and 1931, including, in addition to those written while with the Marine Corps, military band standards such as "The Liberty Bell" (1893), "King Cotton" (1895), "U.S. Field Artillery" (1917), and "The Pride of the Wolverines" (1926). Indeed, Sousa is credited with standardizing the march form: melodic strands AABBCCDD, with the second half, or "trio," modulating up harmonically a fourth. His melodies are vigorous and the effect often that of forthright patriotism.

Bibliography

Berger, Kenneth. *The March King and His Band.* New York: Exposition, 1957.

Bierley, Paul E. *John Philip Sousa: American Phenomenon.* New York: Meredith, 1973.

——. *The Works of John Philip Sousa.* Columbus: Integrity, 1984.

Newsom, J., ed. *Perspectives on John Philip Sousa*. Washington, DC: Library of Congress, 1983.

Sousa, John Philip. *Marching Along*. Boston: Hale, 1928.

Steven Liu

Michael Delahoyde

Space Exploration, as portrayed in film and television, has ranged from the unrealistic portrayals of the early 20th century, with capsules launched from cannon or incredibly elaborate rocket ships, to implausible comic-book adventures, to realistic depictions of the space race, to highly imaginative projections set in a distant future. The image of a projectile lodged in the left eye of the Man in the Moon appeared in *A Trip to the Moon* (1902, France). *Things to Come* (1936) includes another ship launched from a cannon. After weak portrayals from the 1920s through the 1940s, including comic strips of Flash Gordon and Buck Rogers and subsequent film serials, the plausible *Destination Moon* (1950) finally appeared. Nevertheless, unrealistic portrayals followed: Commander Cody, Sky Marshal of the Universe, is the hero of the serial *Radar Men from the Moon* (1952), the same year the serial *Zombies of the Stratosphere* played on TV. Other TV series of the 1950s include *Space Patrol* and *Rocket Ranger*, while children could play with "Man in Space" toys.

In *Rocket Ship X-M* (1950) the craft aims at the moon but lands on Mars, and in *Riders to the Stars* (1954) early ships are imagined. A book by Wernher von Braun (1912-1977, German) inspired *Conquest of Space* (1955), and Jules Verne's (1828-1905, French) version set in the Gay Nineties is enhanced in *From the Earth to the Moon* (1958). *Forbidden Planet* (1956) depicts a voyage to a planet already dominated by a human and his daughter. One critic describes *Outland* (1981) as "*High Noon* on Jupiter's Moon." The many realistic portrayals include *Marooned* (1969), *2001: A Space Odyssey* (1968) and its 1984 sequel, and, on female astronauts, *The Sky's No Limit* (TV 1984). Long after TV's *Lost in Space* and the animated *The Jetsons* of the 1960s, space-based series such as *Buck Rogers in the 25th Century*, *Battlestar Galactica*, and *Salvage* (TV pilot and series) appeared in 1979. *Flash Gordon* and *Battle beyond the Stars* are 1980 films.

Orson Welles (1915-1985) terrified many on Halloween 1938 with a radio drama based on *The War of the Worlds*, the 1898 book by H. G. Wells (1866-1946, British), which is also a 1953 film. Spaceflight and the scare of unidentified flying objects unleashed nightmares of hostile creatures, as in *It Came from Outer Space* (1953), *This Island Earth* (1954), *First Men in the Moon* (1954, set in 1899), *Cat Women of the Moon* (1954), *Earth vs. the Flying Saucers* (1956), *Invasion of the Saucer-Men* (1957), *War of the Satellites* (1958), *Alien* (1979), *Independence Day* (1996), and *Mars Attacks* (1996). *The Day the Earth Stood Still* (1951) and *Close Encounters of the Third Kind* (1977), even more than *Enemy Mine* (1985), are unusual for the peacefulness of aliens. Spaceflight comedies include Jerry Lewis in *Visit to a Small Planet* (1960), the Bing Crosby-Bob Hope *The Road to Hong Kong* (1962), *The Reluctant Astronaut* (1967), *The Cat from Outer Space* (1978), and Mel Brooks's *Spaceballs* (1987).

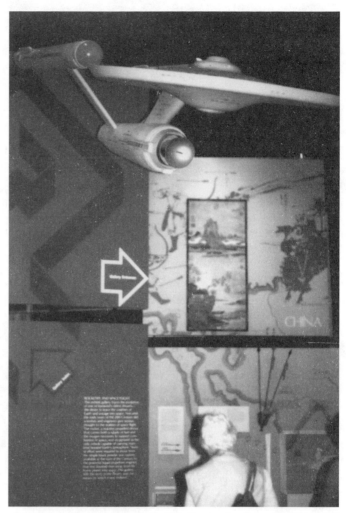

An original model of the Starship *Enterprise* from the *Star Trek* television series (see entry), displayed at the Smithsonian's National Air and Space Museum in Washington, DC. Photo courtesy of Mark McDermott.

Although the plots are technically far-fetched, the space portrayals in *Star Trek* (both the 1960s TV series and the films; see entries below) and the *Star Wars* films (see entry) are highly imaginative in their projections of a distant future. Films and TV shows based on the work of premier science fiction writers like Arthur C. Clarke (*2001*) and Ray Bradbury (*Ray Bradbury Theater*) also have brought the exploration of space to a higher level.

The development of actual spacecraft and technological advances in the late 1950s inspired many of the plots: Robert H. Goddard (1882-1940) experimented with liquid-fueled rockets; by 1946, von Braun and a hundred other German rocket scientists worked for America; and the space race heated up with the Soviet launching of the *Sputnik* satellite. This is the era depicted in *October Sky* (1999).

Pioneer and Ranger space probes went to the moon, and satellites for relaying earth transmissions orbited in 1960s. Project Mercury began in 1958, and John H. Glenn (1921-) became the first American in space on February 20, 1962 (three orbits). Tom Wolfe's incisive account of the first astronauts was *The Right Stuff* (1979, 1983 film).

The Saturn V became the base of a giant three-stage rocket for Apollo missions. Apollo 13 had to abort because of an explosion, dramatized in *Houston, We've Got a Problem* (TV 1974) and *Apollo 13* (1995). James Michener's version of spaceflight is the novel *Space* (1982), which became a TV miniseries in 1985.

The focus of real space exploration changed in the 1970s to developing a space station and probes sent to various planets. As a means of transporting crew and cargo space shuttles were first launched in 1981. Two 1990s TV shows, *Star Trek: Deep Space Nine* and *Babylon 5*, examine life in a space station.

Bibliography

Baker, David. *The Rocket: The History and Development of Rocket and Missile Technology*. New York: Crown, 1978.

Gatland, Kenneth, et al. *The Illustrated Encyclopedia of Space Technology: A Comprehensive History of Space Exploration*. New York: Harmony, 1981.

McDougal, Walter. *The Heavens and the Earth: A Political History of the Space Age*. New York: Basic, 1985.

Walker, John, ed. "Space Exploration." *Halliwell's Filmgoer's and Video Viewer's Companion*. 10th ed. New York: HarperCollins, 1993.

Wolfe, Tom. *The Right Stuff*. New York: Farrar, Strauss & Giroux, 1979.

J. Roger Osterholm

SPAM, a trademarked canned meat product of Hormel Foods, is popular both as an international food of mass appeal and as the focus of tongue-in-cheek cultish activities such as Monty Python's "Spam Song," Weird Al Yankovic's "Spam," or the World Wide Web's Spam-ku haiku poems. Introduced in 1937 in a unique 12-ounce rectangular can, the name derives from SPiced hAM. The product has remained basically the same—chopped and compressed pork shoulder ham, salt, sugar, water, and spices. Additional varieties were introduced in 1971 (smoke-flavored), 1986 (less salt/sodium), and 1992 (lite). Hormel has copyrighted numerous punning names for recipes, such as SPAMBURGER, SPAMBLED egg muffin, and SPAMBALAYA.

The manufacturer has promoted the product aggressively and creatively. In 1940, SPAM introduced a singing commercial and sponsored the George Burns and Gracie Allen radio show. Within a year, sales had risen to 40 million pounds, but one of the greatest boosts was the inclusion of SPAM in military "C-Rations" in World War II. A wholesome meat product requiring no refrigeration was a commissary's dream, and SPAM won at least notoriety among GIs. In the late 1940s and early 1950s, the manufacturer sent a 60-member performing troupe of "Hormel Girls" to promote SPAM in live appearances nationwide as well as on a Sunday evening radio show. Since 1991, SPAM has sponsored "Best of SPAM Luncheon Meat Recipe Competitions" at dozens of state and regional fairs. Austin, MN, is the birthplace of SPAM, where an annual SPAM jam is held, featuring SPAM specialties in all the local restaurants. Austin, TX, initiated their annual SPAMARAMA festival in 1974. Other than Austin, MN, the only processing plant in the U.S. is at Fremont, NE, but Hormel processes SPAM in Korea, the United Kingdom, Australia, Japan, and the Philippines. Hormel's media publicity packet provides curious statistics of SPAM's popularity. For example, an average of 3.8 cans are consumed every second in the United States. Hawaii leads all the other states in consumption (over four cans per year for every Hawaiian). When Hormel produced its 5 billionth can in 1994, the total could encircle the earth 12 1/2 times. If the Washington Monument were built of SPAM, it would take Americans 2.1 years to devour the obelisk. If the Statue of Liberty were alive, her mouth would be three feet wide, and a proportional can of SPAM would be over four feet tall. The Golden Gate Bridge (opened in 1937, the initial year of SPAM marketing) is 13,440 SPAM-cans in length. Hormel also devotes an entire website to SPAM.

Such calculated whimsy in food advertising is unusual outside of the brewing industry, and points to ambivalent cultural meanings. SPAM, like Kraft's Velveeta processed cheese food, Van Camp's pork and beans, and Franco-American canned spaghetti, is a food that is nourishing, easily prepared, requires no refrigeration, and blandly appeals to unsophisticated palates. For many American consumers, its associations are as a "kid's food" like frosted cereals and peanut-butter-and-jelly sandwiches. For others, SPAM was a staple in dorm life, newlyweds' hot-plate kitchens, camps, lunch pails, or military maneuvers. To cash in on nostalgia, Hormel offers various SPAM products such as shirts, caps, mugs, and a mouse pad.

Bibliography

Spam Media Packet. Hormel Foods, Austin, MN 55912.

Fred E. H. Schroeder

Spelling, Aaron (1928-), who grew up in a poor Jewish family in Dallas, TX, is listed in the *Guinness Book of World Records* as the most productive television producer of all time. After 40 years in the television industry, Spelling is still producing successful contemporary serials, such as *Beverly Hills 90210* (1990-2000; see entry) and *Melrose Place* (1992- ; see entry), which cast stars such as Heather Locklear, Jason Priestley, Jennie Garth, Luke Perry, Andrew Shue, Laura Leighton, and Spelling's own daughter, Tori Spelling. Now in his seventies, Aaron Spelling is remembered for his popular and landmark serials, including *The Love Boat* (1977-86), *Charlie's Angels* (1976-81), and *Dynasty* (1981-89).

Spelling's early shows usually included many beautiful women, lust, deception, and revenge for popular appeal. Crime was an added attraction in hits such as *Charlie's Angels*. In 1989, after ABC canceled *Dynasty*, Spelling modified his formulaic television plots and directed them toward a younger audience.

Spelling also branched out into producing other types of television drama, including family fare such as *7th Heaven* (1996-), southern drama such as *Savannah* (1996-97), vampire narratives such as *Kindred: The Embraced* (1996-97), and *Sunset Beach* (1997-99), a soap opera about everyday people leading their everyday lives in a small California community.

While hostile reviewers continue to view Spelling's new productions as ongoing samples of "trash TV" because of his excessive reliance on beautiful bodies, crime, and formulaic plots, his lengthy and prolific career has given America's television audiences many of the characters they have come to hate or love.

Bibliography

Alkhattat, Labeba. "Malibu Shores 90210." Online. Internet. 11 Jan. 1998. Available: http://www.charink.com/t...ainment/malibu90210.html.

Beachy, Susan Campbell, and Craig Modderno. "Aaron Spelling." Online. Internet. 1 Jan. 1998. Available: http://www.thebox.haynet.com/spelling.htm.

——. "Listen Up—Aaron Spelling." *News America Publications Inc.* 1997. Online. Internet. 11 Jan. 1998. Available: http://www.tvguide.com/tv/watch/ww041097.htm.

Smith, Brooke. "*Kindred: The Embraced*: Take a Bite Out of Aaron Spelling's New Drama." *The Daily Pennsylvanian, Inc.* 1996. Online. Internet. 11 Jan. 1998. Available: http://www.dp.upenn.edu/...896/sections/tv/tv2.html.

——. "Lycos Top 5% Review: *Savannah*." Online. Internet. 11 Jan. 1998. Available: http://point.lycos.com/reviews/TVshows_5249.html.

Mitali R. Pati
Eugene F. Wong

Spielberg, Steven (1947-), is one of the most original, popular, and influential filmmakers of the 20th century. Many of his early films, such as *Jaws* (1975) and *Close Encounters of the Third Kind* (1977), have served as blueprints for hundreds of action-adventure and science fiction films. His films *E.T., The Extra-Terrestrial* (1982) and *Jurassic Park* (1993) are the two highest-grossing films in the history of the cinema. In 1987, Spielberg received the Irving G. Thalberg Award, an honor normally reserved for a filmmaker at the end of his or her career.

Spielberg's fascination with motion pictures began in his childhood when he picked up his family's 8mm home movie camera. By age 12, he had produced a 3.5-minute movie about a stagecoach robbery. One year later he filmed a 40-minute war movie entitled *Escape to Nowhere*. At age 16, he created a $500 homemade UFO film entitled *Firelight*, lasting 140 minutes. As an English major at California State College in Long Beach, Spielberg continued to make movies. One of these films, a 24-minute short entitled *Amblin'*, came to the attention of the head of Universal Television. Spielberg signed a long-term contract with Universal six weeks before his 21st birthday.

Spielberg's first job for Universal was to direct one of the three segments for the pilot episode of Rod Serling's *Night Gallery*, starring the veteran actress Joan Crawford. He went on to direct many other television shows, including a 1971 episode of *Columbo* entitled "Murder by the Book," written by another Hollywood "boy wonder," Steven Bochco. The young director's reputation was bolstered by his work on the 1971 TV movie *Duel*. After directing another TV movie, 1972's *Something Evil*, Spielberg made the move to feature films. *The Sugarland Express*, Spiel-berg's first theatrical film, was released in 1974. A darkly comic film with a decidedly unhappy ending, *The Sugarland Express* was not a box-office champion. Spielberg's stylish direction of the story, however, convinced the bosses at Universal to assign him to the film project which established Spielberg as a director of note—the 1975 box-office smash, *Jaws* (see entry).

Filming Peter Benchley's best-selling novel about three men and their battle with a great white shark presented Spielberg with a wealth of technical difficulties. The rigors of filmmaking at sea and under water tripled the original 52-day shooting schedule and sent the film's budget spiraling. Especially troublesome was the fact that the film's success was precariously hinged on Spielberg's ability to turn a 24-foot, 1.5-ton, plastic shark into a convincing screen menace. Nevertheless, *Jaws* is estimated to have grossed over $60 million. *Jaws* also cemented the working relationship between Spielberg and musical composer John Williams, whose brilliant "shark music" for *Jaws*, including the immortal "Da-Dum, Da-Dum" shark signature of the deep bass, established him as a film composer just as the film itself established Spielberg as a filmmaker. Williams has composed the score for every Spielberg film since *Jaws*.

Impressed with the phenomenal success of *Jaws*, Columbia Pictures turned to Spielberg to direct the $10 million project which eventually became *Close Encounters of the Third Kind* (1977). After rejecting a number of preliminary stories, Spielberg himself wrote the film's script. He cast *Jaws* alumnus Richard Dreyfuss as Roy Neary, a disillusioned midwestern family man who gets caught up in the mystery and adventure surrounding the arrival of extraterrestrials. The legendary French film director François Truffaut was cast as the chief scientist preparing for the arrival of the visitors from space. Spielberg's masterful blending of visual effect, high intensity light and color, music and humor produced an epic science fiction film that has frequently been imitated but never equaled. The final 40 minutes of the film, involving the arrival of the alien Mother Ship at Devil's Tower, WY, is sure to endure as one of the cinema's grandest finales.

In 1978, Spielberg served as an executive producer for *I Wanna Hold Your Hand*, directed by Robert Zemeckis. In 1979, Spielberg's growing reputation suffered a significant setback with the release of *1941*, a broad satire of civilian and military war fever set in and around Los Angeles shortly after the bombing of Pearl Harbor. This extravagant and explosive comedy was helped along by an impressive cast which included John Belushi, Dan Aykroyd, Toshiro Mifune, Ned Beatty, and Robert Stack. Columbia and Universal joined together in financing *1941* for an estimated $32 million; however, it was a commercial and critical failure. In 1980, Spielberg once again served as executive producer for a Robert Zemeckis film, *Used Cars*; and in 1981 he produced the film *Continental Divide*, a romantic comedy starring John Belushi, directed by Michael Apted. Both films were poorly received.

Spielberg returned to form in 1981 with the release of *Raiders of the Lost Ark* (see entry), the first in a series of films produced by *Star Wars* creator George Lucas, directed by Spielberg, and starring Harrison Ford as the archaeologist-adventurer Indiana Jones. *Raiders* pitted the heroic Indy against an army of Nazi soldiers in a race to discover and control the Ark of the Covenant. Spielberg and Lucas fashioned the film in the style of the cliff-hanger matinee adventure serials of the 1930s. Audiences and critics responded enthusiastically.

In 1982, Spielberg released *E.T., The Extra-Terrestrial* (see entry). This immensely popular film told the story of a young boy who befriends an earth-bound space alien. The deceptively simple story, combined with state of the art visual effects, seemed to strike a responsive chord in millions of moviegoers worldwide. *E.T.* earned $86 million in its first 25 days of release, and became the highest-grossing film in movie history until the summer of 1993, when Spielberg's *Jurassic Park* took its place. *E.T.* is ultimately the film that best represents Spielberg's unique ability to move an audience through feelings of wonder, mystery, and magic. The modern horror classic *Poltergeist*, written by Spielberg and directed by Tobe Hooper, was also released in 1982.

In 1983, Spielberg directed "Bloom," one of four episodes in the feature film adaptation of *The Twilight Zone*. "Bloom," starring Scatman Crothers, was an adaptation of an original *Twilight Zone* television episode entitled "Kick the Can," about the youthful wishes of the elderly residents of a repressive retirement home.

During 1984, Spielberg's success as a director and a producer continued. Spielberg and George Lucas once again joined forces to create *Indiana Jones and the Temple of Doom*, the long-anticipated sequel to *Raiders of the Lost Ark*. While *Temple of Doom* was a major box-office hit, it was also widely criticized for its racial and sexual stereotypes and a level of violence that some critics found inappropriate for a fantasy-adventure film that included many children and teens in its audience. As a result of the controversy surrounding *Temple of Doom*, the Motion Picture Association of America created the PG-13 rating.

A similar controversy occurred with Spielberg's production of the Joe Dante film *Gremlins*, also released in 1984. Although criticized for its violence and morbid sense of humor, *Gremlins*, like *Temple of Doom*, went on to become one of the biggest box-office hits of the decade. Spielberg's career took a significant turn in 1985 when he was chosen to bring Alice Walker's Pulitzer Prize-winning novel, *The Color Purple*, to the screen. A flood of controversy surrounded the film before, during, and after its release. Like Walker's novel, the film was criticized for its portrayal of African-American males as cruel and sadistic. Other critics felt that as a white male, Spielberg lacked the experiential credentials to direct a story about the suffering of African-American women. Still other detractors felt that Spielberg's treatment of the story was overly sentimental, destroying the dark, personal realism of the novel.

Despite these misgivings, *The Color Purple* was nominated for 11 Academy Awards, including best picture. Spielberg was not nominated for best director, sparking one last controversy in the film's stormy history. *The Color Purple*

marked a turning point in Spielberg's career—a tentative move away from fantasy and adventure films toward smaller, more personal films. In 1985, Spielberg also produced *The Goonies*, directed by Richard Donner, and the smash box-office hit *Back to the Future* (see entry), directed by Robert Zemeckis. He also returned to television that year as the producer of the science fiction and fantasy anthology series *Amazing Stories*, which aired on NBC. This ambitious project was one of the most highly anticipated programs of the 1985 TV season. Spielberg enlisted some of the biggest names in Hollywood as directors and performers for the series, but despite the contributions of celebrities such as Clint Eastwood, Danny DeVito, and Kevin Costner, the series was poorly received by viewers and critics alike. *Amazing Stories* was canceled after two seasons.

During 1986 and 1987, Spielberg's reputation as a film producer continued to grow. In 1986, he produced *The Money Pit*, *Young Sherlock Holmes*, and the animated feature film *An American Tail* (see Amblinmation). In 1987 came *Innerspace*, *Batteries Not Included*, and the groundbreaking *Who Framed Roger Rabbit?* Spielberg's involvement with animated cartoons continued in 1988 when he produced the feature-length animated dinosaur adventure *The Land before Time*, directed by Don Bluth. Spielberg returned to the screen as a director in 1988 with *Empire of the Sun*, adapted from the novel by J. G. Ballard. The film told the story of the young son of a British diplomat who is placed in a Japanese prisoner of war camp in China during World War II. *Empire of the Sun* showcased Spielberg's dual talents as a storyteller of great intimacy and as a director of action-oriented spectacle.

Spielberg directed two films in 1989. The first, *Indiana Jones and the Last Crusade*, was the third entry in the *Raiders* adventure series. Far less controversial than *Temple of Doom*, *Last Crusade* once again pitted Indy against the Nazis in a race to find the legendary Holy Grail of King Arthur. This time Indy was assisted by his medievalist father, brilliantly portrayed by Sean Connery. To date, *Last Crusade* has been the most successful of the Indiana Jones films, grossing over $494 million. Spielberg's second release of 1989 was *Always*, an updated remake of the 1943 Spencer Tracy feature *A Guy Named Joe*. This romantic fantasy featured Spielberg alumnus Richard Dreyfuss as a fire-fighting pilot who is killed and then sent back to earth to serve as an angel of inspiration for another young pilot. The film also featured Audrey Hepburn, in one of her final screen roles, as Dreyfuss's guardian angel, Hap. In 1989 Spielberg also produced *Back to the Future II*, directed by Robert Zemeckis, and *Dad*, directed by Gary David Goldberg.

Spielberg did not release a film of his own in 1990, but his list of successful productions continued to grow with the releases of *Back to the Future III*, directed by Robert Zemeckis; *Arachnophobia*, directed by Frank Marshall; *Gremlins II: The New Batch*, directed by Joe Dante; and *Joe Versus the Volcano*, directed by John Patrick Shanley. In the fall of 1990, Spielberg, in conjunction with Warner Brothers, brought *Tiny Toon Adventures* to television. Unlike *Amazing Stories*, this animated cartoon series was an unqualified success which was widely praised for its quality and its ability to entertain both young and old viewers. *Tiny Toon Adventures* was one of the programs that helped to usher in the TV animation renaissance of the early 1990s.

1991 saw the release of the ambitious action-adventure film *Hook*, starring Robin Williams as the adult Peter Pan who returns to Neverland to do battle with his old nemesis Captain Hook, portrayed by Dustin Hoffman. *Hook* seemed to be tailor-made for Spielberg and his stellar cast; however, the film received mixed reviews. *Fievel Goes West*, the sequel to *An American Tail*, was also produced by Spielberg in 1991.

The lukewarm reception of *Hook* prompted many critics and perennial Spielberg-bashers to proclaim that his days as a successful director were numbered. In 1993, Spielberg obliterated that notion with the release of the modern dinosaur epic *Jurassic Park* (see entry), adapted from the novel by Michael Crichton. Located on an isolated island, Jurassic Park's primary attraction is a collection of living dinosaurs created from the DNA found in the blood of fossilized mosquitoes. Prior to the park's opening, a team of scientists arrives on the island to inspect the authenticity of the dinosaurs. When the giant creatures are accidentally released from captivity, the scientists must battle them hand and claw in order to survive and restore order to the park.

Jurassic Park was released in the summer of 1993 and grossed $860 million, replacing *E.T.* as the biggest box-office hit of all time. During that same summer, NBC aired a limited number of episodes of *The Family Dog*, another animated cartoon series co-produced by Spielberg and *Batman* director Tim Burton. Spielberg also produced the made-for-TV Civil War movie, *Class of '61*. In the fall of 1993, Spielberg unveiled two more television productions: the science fiction submarine adventure series *SeaQuest DSV* and the Peabody Award-winning cartoon series *Animaniacs*. In the fall of 1993 Spielberg produced a lesser-known dinosaur movie, the animated feature film *We're Back*.

In December 1993, Spielberg released *Schindler's List*. Adapted from Thomas Keneally's nonfiction novel, the film told the story of the German Catholic businessman Oskar Schindler, who saved the lives of 1,200 Jews during the Holocaust. Unlike any film that Spielberg had ever made, *Schindler's List* became one of Spielberg's most admired films. Nominated for 12 Academy Awards, it won the best picture Oscar, and Spielberg finally received the Academy Award for best director.

Spielberg's next film was *The Lost World* (1997), the sequel to *Jurassic Park*. Then he again turned away from fantasy and adventure with *Amistad* (1997), about the 1839 revolt by Africans aboard the slave ship *Amistad*, and especially with *Saving Private Ryan* (1998), a World War II drama. Notable for its intense realism (for which cinematographer Janusz Kaminski won an Oscar), the film was Spielberg's third to win an Oscar for best picture and his second as director.

Bibliography

Brode, Douglas. *The Films of Steven Spielberg*. New York: Carol, 1995.

Mott, Donald R., and Cheryl McAllister Saunders. *Steven Spielberg*. Boston: Twayne, 1986.

Taylor, Philip M. *Steven Spielberg: The Man, His Movies, and Their Meanings*. New York: Continuum, 1994.

Keith Semmel

Spillane, Mickey (**Franklin Morrison**) (1918-), one of the most colorful authors of hard-boiled detective fiction, was born in Brooklyn, NY, and began his career writing for the slicks, pulps, and comics. After World War II, during which he served in the Army Air Force, Spillane published his first Mike Hammer novel, *I, The Jury* (1947), based on his own comic strip character Mike Danger. Five Hammer novels followed within five years, establishing Spillane's reputation as a leading writer in the genre: *My Gun Is Quick* (1950), *Vengeance Is Mine!* (1950), *The Big Kill* (1951), *One Lonely Night* (1951), and *Kiss Me, Deadly* (1952). Spillane ceased writing the series until the publication of *The Girl Hunters* ten years later (1962) for reasons that are unclear. After 1962, he produced seven additional Hammer novels, the most recent being *Black Alley* in 1996.

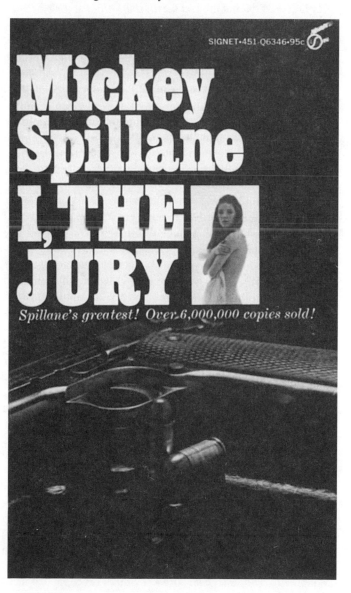

It has been suggested that the long hiatus between Hammer novels was prompted by Spillane's reaction to complaints about the sadistic violence in his fiction. Whatever the cause for his protracted silence, Spillane continued to portray a violent milieu. Hammer's vigilante justice has been amply challenged by critics, even if implicitly sanctioned by readers who consistently kept his creator on the best-seller lists during Hammer's heyday in the 1950s.

Bibliography

Banks, R. Jeff. "Spillane's Anti-Establishmentarian Heroes." *Dimensions of Detective Fiction.* Ed. Larry N. Landrum, Pat Browne, and Ray B. Browne. Bowling Green, OH: Bowling Green State U Popular P, 1976.

Cawelti, John G. *Adventure, Mystery, and Romance: Formula Stories as Art and Popular Culture.* Chicago: U of Chicago P, 1976.

Collins, Max Allan, and James L. Traylor. *One Lonely Knight: Mickey Spillane's Mike Hammer.* Bowling Green, OH: Bowling Green State U Popular P, 1984.

Ruehlmann, William. *Saint with a Gun: The Unlawful American Private Eye.* New York: New York UP, 1974.

Van Dover, J. Kenneth. *Murder in the Millions: Erle Stanley Gardner, Mickey Spillane, Ian Fleming.* New York: Ungar, 1984.

Lewis D. Moore

Sporting Goods and Recreational Equipment. Balls, bats, gloves, hats, sticks, skis, sneakers, rackets, clubs, and on and on, have built up the ongoing structure of America's sporting culture. Sport and recreational goods manufacturing holds a prominent place in America's economy, contributing more than $7 billion annually. However, this has not always been the norm.

American colonists brought traditional sporting practices to the new world. But religious practices and the rigors of a survivalist lifestyle frequently prohibited or significantly limited sporting pursuits. Any participation was very informal, usually associated with work routine, and governed by local rules, records, and reputations. However, by mid-19th century, journalists and entrepreneurs had circulated, through publications such as *American Farmers, American Turf Register, Spirit of the Times,* and assorted books and monographs, persuasive arguments concerning the value of fishing, hunting, horse racing, rowing, baseball, and other outdoor activities as a healthy disruption from the rigors of daily life. Their efforts gradually expanded attitudes and standards about sports and leisure to local, regional, and national levels, and set the stage for an industry of providers.

During the first half of the century, however, consumers who read about sport in special publications tended to play with equipment home-crafted, imported (usually from England), or made by local artisans. Home-crafting was by far the most common form of production, with simple instructions provided by early handbooks for boys. William Clarke's *Boy's Own Book* (1834) and *Boy's Treasury* (1847) both explained the process and materials needed to make a baseball, football, bats, and variety of sport and recreation equipment. *The American Anglers Book* (1865), aimed at an older audience, contained a chapter on rod making with illustrations and a complete list of materials needed for the 19th-century do-it-yourselfer.

For the majority of America's sporting culture throughout the century, home-crafting continued as the most popular. Only the less handy and particularly the wealthier sportsman opted to buy custom or ready-made equipment. Urban merchants imported sporting goods such as shuttlecocks, cricket balls, tennis rackets, quail nets, cock spurs, and fishing rods even before the Revolutionary War. But despite the increase of finished goods along with the importation of new activities by immigrants, until the mid-19th century, most sporting equipment on both sides of the Atlantic was produced by craftsmen in small shops, usually as a sideline.

The demand for sporting goods items and the willingness to produce them show a trend toward specialization, particularly for field sports. Two of the oldest and largest specialty firms were located in Philadelphia. Gunsmith George W. Tryon developed specialty rifles for sportsmen, fishing tackle, and other sporting equipment, and gunsmith John Krider's "Sportsman's Depot" specialized in hunting and fishing. In 1845 carriagemaker John Brunswick of Cincinnati began making billiard tables, and by 1860 his company employed 75 workers and exclusively produced $200,000 worth of tables annually.

Advertising and sport journalism (see next entry) contributed further to a sporting goods market. Newspapers such as William T. Porter's *Spirit of the Times* carried ads for equipment ranging from rifles to boxing gloves. Sporting articles catered to the sportsman and would-be sportsman, as specialty publications such as *The American Angler's Guide* (1845) and *The American Sportsman* (1855) began to appear.

While field sports and its equipment was the dominant outlet for leisure, its trend toward specialization evolved slowly prior to the Civil War. In the 1860 Census of Manufacturers, firearms were categorized under general utility rather than sport. But the census does recognize categories for billiard cues and balls, billiard and bagatelle tables, ice skates, pianos, playing cards, toys, and games, suggesting an expanding notion of sport. Following the Civil War, cricket, baseball, and other sporting equipment rapidly emerged.

By the close of the century, railroad expansion, advances in production technology and printing, along with anxieties about rapid social change, increased opportunities beyond sideline manufacture of sport and recreation products. Social, economic, and cultural conditions were ripe, further expanding a cultural awareness and emergence of a separate industry that supplied goods and services for consumption during leisure time. During this period, two types of entrepreneurs emerged, both in manufacturing and in retail: those who diversified into new sports, either from field sports or from nonsport products, and those, often athletes or former athletes, who opened businesses devoted exclusively to sports. Collectively, these entrepreneurs provided Americans with a steady stream of finished sporting goods.

Baseball offers the best example of a finished sporting goods industry, as the 1870 census listed "baseball goods" as a separate category of manufacture with five companies employing a total of 118 workers and capital value of $24,500, and product value of $72,605. *The Baseball Player's Chronical* of June 17, 1867, however, claimed that every city had a "regular bat and ball manufactory...turning out bats by the thousands and balls by the hundreds." Regardless, companies that previously produced sporting goods as a sideline began to open subsidiaries exclusively for baseball goods as early as 1875.

Retail entrepreneurs were more eager, especially those with connections to a sport—usually baseball. While Albert Goodwill Spalding is perhaps the best known and most successful of these athlete/retailers, he was preceded by Al Reach of Philadelphia and George Wright of Boston. Each began producing sporting goods equipment carrying his brand name. The Louisville Slugger baseball bat (see entry), now famous for its autograph models, was developed originally in 1884 as a custom bat for player Pete Browning.

The promotion of brand recognition further expanded markets and enabled consumers to identify and play with or play by "the official" ball or rules during a game. Sport guidebooks, *Beadles Dime Base Ball Player* and *Dewitt's Base Ball Guide,* were the first to provide standards for play.

Spalding revolutionized "official" in 1876 when he gained exclusive rights to publish the official book of the National League. Soon his baseball goods were also identified as the "official" choice of the National League and other major, minor, and collegiate leagues throughout the country.

By the close of the 19th century, industrial expansion and urbanization created many social problems. Public-spirited citizens and social agencies rose to the challenge, calling for reform. Reformation in part was directed toward recreation as the nation embraced more strongly recreational activity. Workers sought shorter hours and greater leisure opportunity, each of which expanded the playground movement. Recreation/education organizations such as Y's, Boys' and Girls' Club, and the presidential advocacy of "Recreation for the Masses" in the Roosevelt, Taft, and Wilson era, greatly enhanced the American culture's sport, recreation, and leisure attitude.

The reform movement also brought greater diversity in the sport and recreation practices of Americans, creating larger and rapidly expanding markets for manufactured sporting goods. As the country moved westward, so did the sporting goods industry. In Covington, KY, toy maker Philip Goldsmith moved into sports, and eventually became MacGregor Company. In St. Louis, Rawlings Brothers opened a "full-line" sports emporium in competition with C & W McClean. Also, A. G. Spalding continued to expand his market in the U.S. and internationally. No longer was the manufacture of sport equipment limited to eastern states.

By the turn of the century, "official guides" were available to the sporting public for football, tennis, and basketball with treatises on field sports, golf, and croquet, as well as ads for the necessary equipment. Specialty publications such as the *Clipper*, *Sporting Life*, and *Sporting News* also carried advertising. The success of these marketing stratagems is supported by the census of 1900, which listed 144 sporting goods manufacturers with a product value of $3,633,396.

By the 1920s and 1930s, the retail market expanded into hardware stores and department stores such as Montgomery Ward and Sears. These independent wholesalers and retailers identified their consumer public and stocked only items and brands that would sell. Outside the business world, sports equipment is a powerful lure. W. E. B. DuBois, editor of the NAACP's journal *Crisis*, recruited black youth to sell subscriptions with the promise of baseball equipment.

As sport and recreation appetites changed—whether by choice or influence—the industry met the challenge with necessary equipment. As Thomas Wentworth Higginson realized in 1871, the fickle public is always hungering for novelty, "dissatisfied with last winter's skates, with the old boat, and with the family pony." The demand for new equipment season after season gave rise to a new cultural phenomenon, the sport memorabilia collector.

Today the sporting goods industry is a cultural institution. While there remain several old firms that have diversified production to meet society's sport and recreation needs, there are those companies, old and new, who cater to specialty markets such as snowmobiles, jet skis, surfboards, skateboards, and perhaps even bungee cords.

Dramatic breakthroughs in recreation equipment, ranging from the development of specialized running and exercise shoes and Gortex running wear to the use of graphite and ceramic and other exotic alloy combinations to produce more powerful golf clubs and tennis racquets, have in many ways revolutionized these sports and recreational activities. Magazines aimed at specific sports such as running, golf, and tennis perform an invaluable role in regularly featuring analysis of the latest equipment breakthroughs and developments.

Bibliography

Bureau of the Census. *Report on the Manufacturers of the United States*. Washington, DC: Government Printing Office, 1865: 733; 1883: 9-14; 1902, vol. 7: 20-55.

Hardy, Stephen. "Adopted by all the Leading Clubs: Sporting Goods and the Shaping of Leisure, 1800-1900." *For Fun and Profit: The Transformation of Leisure into Consumption*. Ed. Richard Butsch. Philadelphia: Temple UP, 1990. 71-101.

Higginson, Thomas Wentworth. "Gymnastics." *Outdoor Papers*. Boston: Houghton Mifflin, 1871. 158.

Levine, Peter. *A. G. Spalding and the Rise of Baseball*. New York: Oxford UP, 1985. 71-95.

Jerry Jaye Wright

Sports and Popular Literature. While incidental references to sports and sporting activities can be found in the journals and letters of the early colonial Southern aristocracy, the first true sports hero in American literature is, undoubtedly, James Fenimore Cooper's Natty Bumppo. In his five-novel Leatherstocking saga, Cooper created the paradigm and apotheosis of the American frontiersman, who practiced the outdoor sports of hunting, woodsmanship, and resourceful survival with a code of honor and nobility.

Early sports literature focused on the individual and his exploits—whether he was a huntsman, a horseman, a har-nessman, a prizefighter, an endurance runner or walker, or a fisherman. The sporting sketches of Henry William Herbert, writing as Frank Forester and publishing in William Trotter Porter's *Spirit of the Times* (the leading sporting journal from 1831 to 1861), popularized the outdoor sports and made him the first nationally known sportswriter. Herbert also published a successful series of Frank Forester books on hunting and fishing as well as a two-volume study of thoroughbred and trotting horses in 1857. The development of wide-circulation sporting periodicals not only popularized sports and brought increasing acceptance and respectability to sporting activities but also provided an important publishing opportunity for American writers. George Washington Harris, Thomas Bangs Thorpe, Johnson Jones Hooper, William Tappan Thompson, and others published stories and sketches in Porter's *Spirit of the Times,* establishing what would be an important vital connection between sports and oral humor, the rural tall tale, and the regional and country character. For many American writers, sportswriting and reporting would prove an entrée to fame and popularity as a writer as well as a source of stories and characters. The sporting scene was a remarkably rich resource and index of the national character, as it embraced sporting events and sports heroes with approval and unapologetic enthusiasm. By the mid-19th century, sports were firmly established as events and a source of interest linking the nation and focusing its interest in physical skills, performance, and concentration of effort.

The 1870s and 1880s were remarkable decades for the development of sporting journals like Albert Pope's *Outing,* Francis C. Richter's *The Sporting Life,* the Spinks' *Sporting News,* William Bleasdell Cameron's *Field and Stream,* Claude King's *Sports Afield,* and Richard Kyle Fox's *National Police Gazette,* which featured sports as well as sex and crime. In the 1890s newspapers developed their sports sections and expanded sports coverage. Baseball writers became household names as the "scribes" of the sport garnered a loyal reading audience and brought increasing prestige and fame to their profession. Stephen Crane, Frank Norris, and Richard Harding Davis all wrote sports journalism and sports stories in the sports ferment of the 1890s.

The turn of the century also saw the inauguration of juvenile sports books, which have remained popular to this day. In April 1896, Gilbert Patten, writing as Burt L. Standish, began the weekly Frank Merriwell series in the *Tip Top Library,* then the *Tip Top Weekly* until July 1912. These stories were published in paperbound volumes by Street and Smith between 1900 and 1933. Frank Merriwell and his brother, Dick, became the most recognized fictional sports heroes in American popular literature. In the early 1900s sales totaled 500,000 a week as countless readers followed the exploits of Frank Merriwell, who personified resourceful thinking, unbelievable agility and skills at all sports, command of critical situations, and an ability to overcome all adversity or opposition. Frank was the self-disciplined, clean- thinking athlete advocating fair play and sound judgment and always thinking of the good of the team. While Patten's series was formulaic in its plots and outcomes, the ideals of Merriwell were solid and exemplary. Frank personified the values of his culture: duty, hard work, constancy of purpose, physical preparedness, and a belief in sports as the right preparation for the tests and trials of life. From 1914 to 1928, Patten also published 20 baseball novels as Burt L. Standish after he gave up the Merriwell stories in 1912, and other writers continued the series for another three years. In 1914, Patten began his "Left O" seven-novel series that took pitcher Lefty Locke from the bush leagues to the big leagues and player-manager and then on to owner.

Other notable practitioners of the juvenile sports novel included Ralph Henry Barbour, who published successful juvenile sports novels for 40 years; and Edward Stratemeyer, whose Baseball Joe series took his hero from the school diamond, to Yale, to the minor leagues and success in the World Series for the New York Giants. The 13 Baseball Joe novels published from 1912 to 1928 used a pattern of success for a talented athlete from a common background who achieves the highest dream of young boys. These remarkably prolific writers all contributed to and established the conventions of juvenile fiction, filling the heads of impressionable young boys with dreams of glory, honor, and fame while at the same time reinforcing the notion that sports not only tested character but formed it. Each writer created distinctive sports heroes with identifiable names (Patten's Lefty Locke, Stratemeyer's Baseball Joe, and later, John R. Tunis's The Kid).

Following in the footsteps of these early entrepreneurs of juvenile sports fiction were such writers as John R. Tunis, Joe Archibald, Clair Bee, Curtis H. Bishop, Matthew F. Christopher, Elmer Dawson, C. Paul Jackson, Wilfred McCormick, and Jackson V. Scholz, to name a few of the more prolific and successful. Bee was one of the most successful college basketball coaches in history at Long Island University, and Scholz was a great Olympic sprinter and track star. Tunis played collegiate sports at Harvard and worked as a sportswriter and sports broadcaster. While these juvenile fiction writers can be faulted for formulaic writing and the creation of stock characters and fantasy plots, they provided high-interest reading for young people, inspired young athletes, and kept alive the spirit of amateurism and class of professionalism. Sports biographies and autobiographies provided further reading material for young people and adult fans by giving them the "inside" personal story, facts, and anecdotes unavailable in the press, and the formula for personal success and stardom. Mass-circulation magazines like *Collier's, Saturday Evening Post,* and *Boy's Life* provided a steady stream of sports stories.

Mainstream American writers have found in sports the same kind of drama and human interest that professional writers dramatized and reported, but have used sports for other purposes. F. Scott Fitzgerald and Irwin Shaw were attracted to sports figures as failures and losers who briefly experienced the American dream of glory and fame but could not sustain it. Ernest Hemingway saw sports as a metaphor for the condition of the perils and difficulties of modern life—a place where a code could still exist and be acted out in an attempt to assert one's dignity and honor in the face of a chaotic, uncertain world. For Hemingway, the sports of fishing, boxing, and bullfighting represented a ritualistic confrontation of danger, defeat, and death; however, for Hemingway, sports is only a "momentary stay against confusion." One can learn from it, and one can measure up to its code and traditions. But sport does not offer salvation or redemption in an existential world. Literary treatments of sports have often emphasized the failed or flawed hero who is seduced by commercialism, illusory success, the corruption surrounding sports, and the empty adulation and worship of fans. Works like Ring Lardner's *You Know Me Al* (1914), Bernard Malamud's *The Natural* (1952), and Peter Gent's *North Dallas Forty* (1973) illustrate this direction and emphasis. Three Pulitzer-winning dramas have also taken a critical look at sports and its impact on character and the athlete's life during and after sports: Howard Sackler's *The Great White Hope* (1968) on Jack Johnson, the heavyweight boxing champion; Jason Miller's *That Championship Season* (1973) on high school basketball; and August Wilson's *Fences* (1987), about a former Negro League baseball player.

While much of American literature has looked at sports as a culturally supported illusion or as an endeavor that may limit personal development, many American writers have found sports to be a source of democratic values, a sense of community, and a place where the spirit of lucid play is active. Sports prove to be a humanizing and often humbling experience, or an activity of joy and physical sensation. Mark Harris's baseball tetralogy featuring Henry Wiggen as the star baseball pitcher for the fictional New York Mammoths was published between 1953 and 1979, taking Wiggen from a 19-year-old rookie to a 39-year-old veteran who is forced to accept the end of his career and the fact that he will not be the manager of the Mammoths. The novels constitute a complete cycle of an athlete's career as well as reflect three decades of change in the sport and American life. Along with Ring Lardner's Jack "Busher" Keefe, Henry Wiggen is one of the two great fictional narrators and voices of sports literature.

One area where baseball literature has excelled is the creation of the comic novel or the fantasy novel. Notable achievements include Richard Anderson's *Muckaluck* (1980), Jerome Charyn's *The Seventh Babe* (1979), Robert Coover's *The Universal Baseball Association, Inc. J. Henry Waugh, Prop.* (1968), James F. Donohue's *Spitballs and Holy Water* (1977), Lamar Herrin's *The Rio Loja Ringmaster* (1977), W. P. Kinsella's *Shoeless Joe* (1982), Philip Roth's *The Great American Novel* (1973), and Douglass Wallop's *The Year the Yankees Lost the Pennant* (1954). Baseball has been an important source of American humor with its eccentric and oddball characters, its rich oral history, and its practical jokes and hijinks. It has enriched American literature and reflected important elements of the black experience in such novels as William Brashler's *The Bingo Long Traveling All-Stars and Motor Kings* (1973), John Craig's *Chappie and Me* (1979), and Jay Neugehoren's *Sam's Legacy* (1974).

While the baseball novel has dominated sports literature, several excellent novels have documented other sports. In basketball, Jeremy Larner's *Drive, He Said* (1964), Jay

Neugeboren's *Big Man* (1966), Charles Rosen's *Have Jump Shot, Will Travel* (1975) and *A Mile above the Rim* (1976), Lawrence Shainberg's *One on One* (1970), and Todd Walton's *Inside Moves* (1978) are the best of the lot. In football, Don DeLillo's *End Zone* (1972), Frederick Exley's *A Fan's Notes* (1972), Peter Gent's *North Dallas Forty* (1973) and *The Franchise* (1983), Dan Jenkins's *Semi-Tough* (1972), Lloyd Pye's *That Prosser Kid* (1977), and James Whithead's *Joiner* (1971) have achieved considerable recognition.

American sports have also enriched poetry, as poets such as Marianne Moore, John Updike, James Dickey, Rolfe Humphries, Robert Wallace, and others have captured aspects of sports in verse and reflected their passionate interest in sports.

In nonfiction, sports have created a host of legendary sportswriters (see entry below) whose style and approach were and are familiar to millions of readers. These include Ring Lardner, Damon Runyon, Irving Cobb, Hugh Fullerton, Frank Graham, Jr., Grantland Rice, Heywood Broun, Westbrook Pegler, and their modern counterparts in Red Smith, Roger Angell, George Plimpton, and Roger Kahn. These men have dedicated their talents to the service of sport and to the craft of sportswriting, often producing some of the best prose writing in American literature. Even the area of autobiography has been enriched by sports with such works as Grantland Rice's *The Tumult and the Shouting* (1954), Jackie Robinson's *I Never Had It Made* (1972), and Bill Bradley's *Life on the Run* (1977) as examples of notable sports autobiographies.

The popular literature of sports has moved from an early tradition of adulatory celebration and hagiography to a treatment that has been more critical, questioning, and analytical. Games and athletes are no longer seen as a separate sphere or arena but are now understood as an extension of big business, commercialization, and commodification. Despite modern disillusionment with organized sports and the steady stream of revelations of scandals and personal problems of athletes, the popular literature of sports remains strong. While sports no longer supply models of emulation and worship, the literature continues to show they can continue to provide special occasions of elevation and excitement, human drama, the challenge of physical exertion and demands of execution, and the satisfactions of performance and mastery.

Bibliography

Berman, Neil David. *Playful Fictions and Fictional Players: Games, Sport, and Survival in Contemporary Fiction.* Port Washington: Kennikat, 1981.

Higgs, Robert. J. *Laurel and Thorn: The Athlete in American Literature.* Lexington: UP of Kentucky, 1981.

Messenger, Christian K. *Sport and the Spirit of Play in American Fiction: Hawthorne to Faulkner.* New York: Columbia UP, 1981.

Oriard, Michael. *Dreaming of Heroes: American Sports Fiction, 1868-1980.* Chicago: Nelson-Hall, 1982.

Wise, Suzanne. *Sports Fiction for Adults: An Annotated Bibliography of Novels, Plays, Short Stories, and Poetry with Sporting Settings.* New York: Garland, 1986.

Douglas A. Noverr

Sports Bars—new brew from old barrels. Surely, men have argued sports over a cold one since the first competitions. The arguments continue today, with the names changed, but the setting would be unrecognizable to a DiMaggio-Williams disputant. Most notably, women would be present.

The ambiance of the sports bar is created by memorabilia and television. All the bars have pictures of the local sports gods, but there are also many other objects: to cite from the *USA Today* survey of September 20, 1994, Max's in Glendale, AZ, has more than 1,000 helmets; the Sports Edition in Seattle has old NBA sneaks; Gameday in Allen, TX, does sweaters—like Bobby Knight's and Lou Carnesecca's. And, of course, the TV sets are everywhere. Poor Billy's in Woodbridge, NJ, has nearly 100 sets, and Max's has nine satellite dishes. No turf wars occur in these spots between fans of the Big Trucks and Wimbledonians. In the pre-baseball-strike summer of 1994, World Cup soccer set off some sensational channel selection battles in the one-horse-town sports bars of America. Sports bars also feature activities and competitions for patrons, such as throwing darts or shooting baskets.

The 4,000 sports bars of America do not spiritually eat and drink at the same table. The type of bar popularized by the TV show *Cheers* will feature pitcher beer, nachos, and wings, while its high-tech counterpart serves veggie-burgers to Chardonnay drinkers. However, they do share one passion: sports trivia. Popularized years ago by the movie *Diner,* sports trivia contests are alive and well in the bars. At the Flat-Iron in San Rafael, for example, you can eat free if you know all the answers.

Despite their outrageous trendiness, sports bars have a history, a storied past. On one hand, they derive from the archetypal neighborhood pub, tavern, saloon, that "everybody-knows-your-name" place. On the other hand, sports bars have evolved from celebrity watering-holes like Toots Shor's and Jack Dempsey's. Back in the post-war glitter of the late 1940s, you could at least see Joe DiMaggio at his reserved table at Toots Shor's every night of the week. Today, you have a better shot at seeing Elvis at your city's celebrity-owned bar than any sports star.

Bibliography

Kiefer, Michael. "What's a Sports Bar Anyway?" *Sport* Mar. 1989: 64.

Lubell, Ellen. "Screen Teens." *Village Voice* 23 Oct. 1990: 51.

Pierce, Charles P. "Sports Bars." *Boston* Aug. 1992: 47-50.

Gerry O'Connor

Sports Betting. All the gambling experts agree: no one knows how much money is bet on sports annually—we're not talking the NCAA office pool here—but it's way into the billions. Second, expanded television coverage of sports, especially cable, is the primary reason for the explosion of sports betting. And, far and away, pro football is the most popular game to bet.

Furthermore, in a society where the church and state survive because of bingo and lotto, many feel that the moral question of sports betting is largely irrelevant. Virtually every major newspaper in the country publishes a ton of information every day which has only one purpose: to help someone make an informed illegal bet. Also, at the dark heart of the Pete Rose story was not the certainty that he bet but the horrific suspicion among bettors that he may have bet against his own team.

Sports betting can be confusing. Football and basketball use points, while baseball and boxing use odds. For example, in the 1993-94 NFL playoffs, Dallas was favored by 14 points over Green Bay, the "line" or "spread." Dallas won 27-17, so Green Bay beat the "spread" or "covered." The touchdown pass from Brett Favre to Sterling Sharpe with seconds left made winners of all those who "took the points" and "bet the dog." Dallas backers got even, however, in the Super Bowl, when Don Beebe of the Bills stepped out of bounds at the 3-yard line on fourth down with seconds left. Favored by 10-1/2, Dallas would not have "covered" if Beebe had scored. Winning 30-13, Dallas paid off for the second year in a row.

A comparable basketball example comes from the '94 playoffs between the Knicks and the Bulls. In game five the Knicks, giving 5-1/2 points, won 87-86; thus Chicago "covered." In game seven, however, the Knicks, giving 4-1/2 as home favorites, beat both the Bulls, 87-77, and the "spread."

The "line" or "spread" is set, naturally, in Las Vegas—and contrary to what even some bettors believe, the "line" is not supposed to make two teams even. Rather, it is set to attract an equal amount of money on each side. That's why the line moves. The house, from Caesar's Palace to the neighborhood bookie, takes a cut, a percentage, the infamous "vig," on every losing bet. Generally, you have to pay $11 to bet $10, $1,100 to "bet a dime." The house edge is $11-for-$10, which figures out to 4.54 percent, meaning you have to win 53 percent of your bets not to lose money.

Baseball and boxing use odds called the "money line" to attract the same amount of money on each team or boxer. For example, the May 25, 1994, New York Yankees–Toronto Blue Jays game was quoted as "New York 6-1/2-7-1/2." These numbers refer to a theoretical $5:$5 bet on the underdog Jays pays $6.50, while to win $5 on the favored Yankees, you have to bet $7.50. In *How to Win at Sports Betting,* J. Edward Allen uses the common 6-1/2-7-1/2 line to point out that the bookie's edge on the favorite is only 2.78 percent, but on the dog it's 4.17 percent. The house edge doubles with boxing (for those foolish enough to bet).

Bibliography

Allen, J. Edward. *How to Win at Sports Betting.* New York: Cardoza, 1990.

Moldea, Dan E. *Interference: How Organized Crime Influences Professional Football.* New York: Morrow, 1989.

Gerry O'Connor

See also
Gambling

Sports Fans. The word "fan" derives from either "fancier" or "fanatic" and replaced earlier terms for an aficionado such as "krank" or "bug." Fans may be devoted to a sport, or a particular player, but the most extreme manifestations of allegiance are generally reserved for individuals devoted to a specific team.

Within professional sports, there are groups of fans who stand out due to the fervent intensity with which they support their team. Noted examples of fans who have, at various times, gained renown of their own include the Royal Rooters of Major League Baseball's Boston Red Sox, the Chicago Cubs' Bleacher Bums, the soccer fans in Liverpool's Kop, the NFL's Cleveland Browns' Dawg Pound, and the Japanese baseball fans of Osaka's Hanshin Tigers. There are also fans of teams such as baseball's Brooklyn Dodgers and the NFL's Baltimore Colts who assumed the role of martyrs when their teams moved to Los Angeles and Indianapolis respectively.

What fans get from their investment of time, energy, and money is a feeling of identification with the team. In an urban environment which is relatively anonymous, sporting events have largely replaced the religious events and festivals which provided a sense of community and connection among people. There is a sense of belonging and unity as fans share in the team's victories and defeats. In a vicarious sense, the fans are included in the competition. If their team wins, then the team, the city, and the fans take pride in being better than the opposition. Sports sociologists call this the BIRG (bask in reflected glory) phenomenon. On an international scale, this phenomenon is readily seen in the World Cup or the Olympic Games, where patriotism and fandom can combine to produce levels of emotion which reach the hysterical. Oftentimes, victory serves to validate not just a nation, but a way of government and life for that country's citizens.

However, the idea that players act as hometown representatives of a particular city is somewhat illusory. Even in the 1860s, baseball teams hired players from other parts of the country to improve themselves, and the more recent phenomenon of free agency in sports has made it clear to most fans that players, by and large, are not as loyal to a city as they are to money. Still, many fans are willing to overlook the fact that today's local hero can become tomorrow's opposition.

Far from viewing themselves as passive spectators, the most rabid fans see themselves as having a role in the game, almost constituting an extra player for their team. Mindful of this, some teams provide their super-fans with various complimentary perks, such as transportation and free tickets to ensure their attendance. These fans may gain renown for their unbroken attendance or their heckling ability. Super-fans eccentric enough to attract the attention of the media have been known to put together scrapbooks and highlight reels of their own antics, and enjoy a certain measure of status and recognition among other fans, although some less demonstrative fans view their more enthusiastic brethren with disdain. A good example of this kind of super-fan is Robin Ficker, who follows the NBA's Washington Bullets. With season tickets behind the opposing team's bench, Ficker can verbally abuse the opposition for the duration of the game in the name of supporting his team.

This identification with a team can be so strong as to cause fans to rush onto the playing field in an attempt to affect the game. Fans have been known to kill themselves, or murder others, in the emotional frenzy following an important victory or defeat. In 1994, Colombian soccer star Andres Escobar was gunned down upon his return home after putting the ball in his own net against the United States in the World Cup. Nor is this devotion confined to teams. In 1993, German Günter Parche, a fan of tennis player Steffi Graf, stabbed top-ranked Monica Seles during a match with the express purpose of allowing Graf to regain her No. 1 ranking.

This kind of intense relationship between teams and their fans is summed up in the slogan of the 1888 New York Metropolitans' baseball team, "We are the people!" Identification with the team is further cemented through various collectibles and memorabilia. Fans can buy pennants, clothes, cards, and innumerable other souvenirs which may be displayed at home, on their vehicles, or at the game itself. In an almost tribal sense, some fans may dress and paint themselves in the colors of their team. Fans may also adopt songs, chants, or body movements (e.g., the tomahawk chop of baseball's Atlanta Braves) which they repeat endlessly during a game.

Demographically, the average sports fan has changed as the 20th century has progressed. Historically, sports fans have been almost exclusively male, but in the interest of greater profits and the appearance of civic responsibility, many professional leagues have recently tried to make their game more "fan-friendly" for women and children. In the late 1800s, women were frankly advised to stay away from baseball games due to the language, drunkenness, and violence of the crowds. Stricter security, limitations on alcohol, and seating sections reserved for families have all aided in making sporting events less exclusionary. Colorful, cartoonish mascots like the Philadelphia Phillies' Philly Phanatic roam the fields and the stands to appeal to children.

Increasingly, the competitive aspect of sports is de-emphasized in favor of entertainment and spectacle. In an era in which players flit from team to team and teams move from city to city, the fan is perceived as being increasingly fickle as well. Accordingly, the fan is courted as a consumer who must be wooed from other forms of sports and entertainment. The NBA, held up as the model sports league in the late 1980s and early 1990s, evokes this thinking most clearly with its slogan, "The NBA. It's Fan-tastic!" While individual fans may believe in their power to affect the outcome of games by extremes of behavior, professional sports leagues are aware that the true power of fans lies in their pocketbooks.

Bibliography

Adomites, Paul. "Fans and Concessions." *Total Baseball.* Ed. John Thorn and Pete Palmer. New York: Warner, 1989. 3d ed. New York: HarperCollins, 1993.

LeBon, Gustave. *The Crowd.* New York: Viking, 1966.

Morris, Desmond. *The Soccer Tribe.* London: Jonathan Cape, 1981.

Voigt, David Quentin. *American Baseball: From Postwar Expansion to the Electronic Age.* Vol. 3. University Park: Pennsylvania State UP, 1983.

David MacGregor

Sports Heroes and Heroines began to become popular after World War I, when the country needed a new breed of hero consistent with a democratic ethos: one who could embody traditional values and embrace the masses. No better prototype than the athletic hero beckoned. Previously, heroic models had issued from the arenas of politics, business, and applied science (see Heroes). The athlete as hero personifies excellence, hard work, mastery, and success. During the halcyon 1920s, baseball gave us Babe Ruth; boxing, Jack Dempsey; football, Red Grange; tennis, Bill Tilden; golf, Bobby Jones; swimming, Gertrude Ederle.

Historian Roderick Nash argues that Americans experienced high anxiety in response to population gain and the loss of a frontier. Values, rooted in rural America, did not synchronize with post-World War I urbanization. Sports arenas became transformed into surrogate frontiers. As befits a democratic society, merit, not birth, determined the outcome. The results of athletic contests were measurable, clear, and decisive. The best person or team won.

The Black Sox scandal of the 1919 World Series posed a threat to the national game and opened avenues to antiheroes. Unwilling to accept a sullied sport, American fans invested heroes of the 1920s with a god-like grandeur. In subsequent decades, sports stars continued to mirror societal change. When the Great Depression hit, a new heroic style emerged, e.g., "lucky" Yankees like Lou Gehrig and Joe DiMaggio, the "Brown Bomber" Joe Louis, and "greased lightning" Jesse Owens. To overcome Depression-time adversity, one had to crawl and scratch for every morsel of success. Thus, the St. Louis Cardinals, affectionately dubbed "the Gas House Gang," captured the public imagination with their true grit, continual hustle, and winning ways. Mildred "Babe" Didrikson broke all records in women's track and field events, bringing national, indeed international, attention to women in sports. James Braddock, the boxer, also echoed the *zeitgeist* with his remarkable comeback from adversity.

In post-World War II America, Jackie Robinson broke the color barrier and opened the gates for a host of brilliant black athletes in all major sports: baseball, football, basketball, tennis, and golf. Baseball remained the national pastime until the 1960s. In this "field of dreams," Joe DiMaggio, Ted Williams, Hank Greenberg, Bob Feller, and sundry other servicemen returned from war to resume their brilliant careers on the diamonds of play.

While baseball represents pastoral values of harmony, nostalgia, and rural green, football embodies warrior virtues, superhuman physique, intense pressure, territorial imperatives, sanctioned violence, modern technology, and urban red. When Jim Brown arose from a pile-up, he showed no emotion. Unconquered, this gridiron great left the game prematurely and switched to movies, heroic status intact. Football in the 1960s cut heroes from commercial cloth. To promote consumption in a fragmented society, the corporate system created divergent heroes in football, Joe "the stud" Namath and Fran "the Boy Scout" Tarkenton. Father figure Vince Lombardi projected conservative values and the work ethic for the Green Bay Packers, while his prodigal sons,

Paul Hornung, Marv Fleming, and Max Magee espoused a new hedonism. Despite the polarities, they forged a winning combination on and off the football fields.

Billie Jean King beat Bobby Riggs in a tennis match on September 20, 1973, and scored a major breakthrough for the heroine in sports, including equal purses for equal triumphs. Henry Aaron had a hammer that broke Babe Ruth's career home run record in 1974.

But the 1970s belonged to professional basketball. The Boston Celtics, the Los Angeles Lakers, and the New York Knicks captured the American fancy. Scandal had crippled the college game. Innovations like the 24-second clock and the expanded three-second lane helped to elevate the professional game, with the 1969-70 Knickerbocker five giving the court game a new legitimacy. Bill Bradley, a banker's son, returned from exile as a Rhodes Scholar to join a Louisiana farm boy, Willis Reed, a Detroit native, Dave DeBusshere, an Atlanta dude, Walt Frazier, and a well-traveled veteran with a "sweet" fall-away jump shot, Dick Barnett.

Coached by a self-effacing Jewish genius, "Red" Holtzman, the Knicks won their first National Basketball Association championship in 1970 and a second in 1973. There were teams with superior individual talent, but no team had the cohesiveness and intelligence of the Knickerbocker hoopsters in the early 1970s. They put a Broadway stamp on basketball—"hitting the open man"—for all subsequent winning teams. Even the wondrous Michael Jordan had to wait for a supporting cast before taking the Bulls of Chicago to six championships in eight years.

Identification with athletic heroes provides pseudo-intimacy for the legion of fans. We displace aggression and become involved in symbolic drama, but sports media mavens drag the hero down to us, to averageness. Thus, we can never escape psychic chains forged by the power structure. When player salaries escalated, many fans expressed resentment. With counter-culturalists like Jim Bouton and Leonard Shecter, who attacked the "jockocracy" beginning in 1970, and the downfall in the 1980s and 1990s of various sports celebrities due to drug abuse, scandal, or even murder charges, sports heroes and heroines continue to be tested and influenced by social change.

Bibliography

Bouton, Jim. *Ball Four: My Life and Hard Times Throwing the Knuckleball in the Big Leagues*. Ed. Leonard Shecter. New York: World, 1970.

Browne, Ray B., and Marshall Fishwick. *The Hero in Transition*. Bowling Green, OH: Bowling Green State U Popular P, 1983.

Lipsky, Richard. *How We Play the Game: Why Sports Dominate American Life*. Boston: Beacon, 1981.

Lipsyte, Robert. *SportsWorld: An American Dreamland*. New York: Quadrangle, 1977.

Lubin, Harold, ed. *Heroes and Anti-Heroes*. San Francisco: Chandler, 1968.

Nash, Roderick. *The Nervous Generation: American Thought, 1917-1930*. Chicago: Rand McNally, 1970.

Shecter, Leonard. *The Jocks*. New York: Paperback Library, 1970.

Wills, Garry. *Certain Trumpets: The Call of Leaders*. New York: Simon & Schuster, 1994.

Joseph Dorinson

See also
Female Sports Heroes

Sports Memorabilia and Collectibles constitute almost any object connected with a particular sport, team, or player. Traditional items include cards, jerseys, programs, and equipment, but even such esoteric items as dirt, grass, paint chips, and jockstraps can find a place of honor in a collection. As all-inclusive collecting is beyond the financial scope of most fans, collectors often tend to focus on a particular player, team, or kind of collectible.

While the sports memorabilia industry is currently a multimillion-dollar enterprise, this is a relatively recent phenomenon. For the greater part of the 19th and 20th centuries, sports collectibles were largely the province of young boys. In 1869, local youths coveted replica caps and belt buckles of the Cincinnati Red Stocking baseball club, and in the 1880s, the first mass-produced baseball cards (included in packages of cigarettes) were avidly sought after by youngsters (see Sports Trading Cards, below). Oftentimes, the collectible was a souvenir related to a personal experience, such as a ticket stub, game program, pennant, or autograph.

A significant step toward the legitimization of collectibles as being worthy of adult attention was the establishing of the Baseball Hall of Fame at Cooperstown in 1939. Subsequently, other sports would build their own shrines. Within the walls of these buildings, memorabilia was given the status of historical object. The history and relics of a sport were preserved and on display. Balls, jerseys, and other items were considered to be of value to the community, not merely the individual. Sports bars and the bars or restaurants of former players or well-known announcers, such as Mike Shannon's in St. Louis or Harry Caray's in Chicago, also provide a showcase for memorabilia.

Collecting sports memorabilia began serious growth as a hobby in the 1970s, a decade that culminated in the publication of the first baseball card price guide (commonly called *Beckett's*) in 1979. As the interest in collecting increased, so did the interest in producing collectibles. In 1981, the Topps Company lost their monopoly on baseball cards, and by the end of the decade the market was flooded with cards produced by a variety of companies. As the 1990s progressed, the licensing arms of various sports began to limit the number of companies licensed to produce cards. Prior to the 1960s, major league sports hadn't been involved with licensing cards, and players had been free to strike their own deals with card companies.

In the 1980s, with some investors worried about stock market fluctuations, sports memorabilia suddenly became a hot commodity. Balls, bats, jerseys, and cards were routinely described as being "investment quality." Much like book enthusiasts interested in first editions, collectors clamored for the cards and other items (e.g., Kenner's Starting Lineup figures) featuring hot rookies. The idea of an item providing a personal connection to a player or team diminished considerably, although sport superstars such as Mickey Mantle, Nolan Ryan, Michael Jordan, and Wayne Gretzky found themselves much in demand as autographed items became all the rage. In 1991, former New York Yankee Joe DiMaggio signed a two-year, $6 million contract to sign memorabilia exclusively for a company called The Score Board. Score Board was also the first collectible company to sell its goods on cable television's home shopping networks. Stars such as Ted Williams, Pete Rose, and Johnny Bench were enlisted to hawk their wares to viewers.

Some athletes, mindful of the value given to objects associated with milestone events, took to creating memorabilia on their own. In the game in which Pete Rose tied Ty Cobb's hit record, he changed uniforms for each at bat, with the intention of selling the uniforms to collectors. This kind of attitude is quite in keeping with the sporting establishment's attitude toward collectibles. Memorabilia is no longer a byproduct of the game itself; it is manufactured and marketed in ways wholly divorced from the sport.

It was inevitable that the concept of historical value would lead to the idea of monetary value. Individual cards and jerseys have sold for hundreds of thousands of dollars each. A collector such as Barry Halper of New Jersey has achieved renown of his own simply because of the value and magnitude of his baseball memorabilia collection. One-of-a-kind items with specific historic interest are especially prized by collectors. In 1992, actor Charlie Sheen paid $93,500 for the ball that Mookie Wilson hit through Bill Buckner's legs in the 1986 World Series, and in 1993 collector Alan Feinstein paid $99,000 for a 1919 contract that sent Babe Ruth from the Boston Red Sox to the New York Yankees.

The demand for collectibles is so great that halls of fame compete among themselves with collectors for prized objects associated with their sport. It is the wealthy collectors who often triumph, the result being that more and more memorabilia finds its way into private collections. As much as any other indicator, the growth of the memorabilia and collectible industry is evidence of the immense strides that sports have made in establishing themselves as an integral component of the American consciousness.

Bibliography

Halper, Barry, and Bill Madden. "Baseball Collecting." *Total Baseball*. 3d ed. Ed. John Thorn and Pete Palmer. New York: HarperCollins, 1993. 596-600.

Mulloy, Roderick A. *Mulloy's Sports Collectibles Value Guide*. Radnor: Attic, 1993.

Thorn, John, Bob Carroll, and David Reuther, eds. *The Whole Baseball Catalogue*. New York: Simon & Schuster, 1990.

David MacGregor

Sports on Television is a daily ritual. Football, basketball, baseball, boxing, hockey, golf, bowling, auto racing, tennis, skiing, and figure skating all enjoy routine exposure on TV. Sports fans can live by their own calendar, relishing in college basketball's "March Madness," following the exploits of the boys of summer, and celebrating America's most recent secular holiday—Super Bowl Sunday. In fact, for sports fans, football has become an integral part of both the Thanksgiving and New Year's holidays.

Television also created or perpetuated "pseudo-sports"—staged dramatic events intended solely for the entertainment of the audience. Professional wrestling has reached new heights with the escapades of Hulk Hogan, YokoZuna, Randy Macho Man Savage, Stone Cold Steve Austin, and Brett the Hit Man Hart. *American Gladiators* presents contestants battling against the featured gladiators in events such as wall climbing and tackling, while made-for-TV movie and sitcom stars run relays and dash through obstacle courses on *Battle of the Network Stars*.

Americans seem obsessed by sports and competition. Television has contributed much to this national obsession by feeding the myth of the athlete as an icon of modern life. The small screen builds the athletic persona into something larger than real life but also representative of everyday American ideals and values. Millions of viewers wanted "to be like Mike," were aware that "Bo knows," and anxiously await the next "Shaq attack." Each of these phrases have been carefully crafted by advertisers to identify their product with same positive ideals viewers see in athletic competition.

Through instant replays, pre-game hype, and accentuation of the sensational, television coverage of sporting events readily plays into the myth of the athlete as hero. A slow-motion instant replay of a 250-pound linebacker colliding into a 235-pound fullback shows the act of football tackling as a graceful art. A boxer's devastating left hook sends his opponent reeling to the mat as beads of sweat spiral off his head and into the lights in an expanding corona. The slow-motion replay shows the fluid beauty of the boxer's rhythm and the undulating collapse of his opponent. Neither replay shows the pain.

Sports and TV have shared a close relationship since the beginning of the television age. David Sarnoff and RCA used the 1939 World's Fair in New York to introduce television to the general public. The Germans had already experimented with television sports by broadcasting some of the 1936 Olympic games and the British were also pushing ahead in the production of a television system. In that same year, the first American sporting event found its way onto television. Columbia and Princeton were featured on May 17 in a baseball game set to decide fourth place in the Ivy League. The game was picked for its proximity to the RCA studios and the results bordered on a disaster. Fortunately, there were less than 400 TV sets in existence, so few saw the out-of-focus fiasco.

By the fall of 1941, football, basketball, hockey, and wrestling had all been telecast. The pattern was set for a long and mutually profitable relationship between sports and TV. World War II interrupted the plan, but by the late 1940s sports was back on the tube again.

Technical limitations allowed boxing to be the first sport to reach national prominence on TV. Big, heavy cameras could be placed at ringside and easily follow the action. Lighting conditions and the weather were constant. By 1950, boxing was a staple source of programming on all four networks. In 1953, the Rocky Marciano—Jersey Joe Walcott rematch captured almost 70% of all television households. Promoters looked for boxers with television appeal and not necessarily boxing talent. By the middle 1950s, boxing insiders were complaining that television had changed the game. The new TV boxers, such as Hurricane Jackson and Chuck Davey, brawled. By the end of the decade, a decline in the club system had dried up the cream of boxing's talent pool. Promoters came under congressional investigation for Mafia connections. The final straw came in 1962 when Benny Paret died during a national TV broadcast from a particularly brutal blow to the head. In 1963, the lights on weekly boxing programs went out.

Boxing's early success was shared by professional wrestling. The post–World War II television era provided new opportunities for wrestlers to create TV personalities, such as "Gorgeous" George Wagner, a Nebraska farm boy, who paraded into the ring wearing satin red robes with white fur trim. Soon, everyone from midgets to women to ex-boxers became involved in professional wrestling. Wrestling was especially popular in local and syndicated programming, where it still flourishes today (see also Wrestling on Television).

Baseball was not immune to the changes television brought to sports. At the ballpark, baseball is a game of many subplots: a base runner taunts the pitcher with a lead-off from first base; the right fielder moves toward the foul line because the batter seems to want to pull the ball; the third baseman moves up a step in anticipation of a bunt. But television eliminates the subplots as baseball becomes a game of pitching. Any action away from the mound requires a quick camera change by the director and then another quick take to get back to the view from behind the mound. Long-range lenses tend to decrease the sense of distance and squash an expansive green ballfield into a small 20-inch screen.

TV wrought other changes upon the national pastime. Minor league baseball seemed to suffer the most as smaller towns lost the local team. Even in the majors, the game had changed. The big-name, big-town teams, primarily the New York clubs, received the lucrative TV contracts. This brought in big money that could be used to purchase the best players. As a result, from 1947 to 1966, the Brooklyn (then Los Angeles) Dodgers, the Yankees, and the Giants (New York, then San Francisco) enjoyed a combined 28 World Series appearances.

Although pennant races and the World Series remain popular, baseball has had an on-again, off-again relationship with national TV. Lucrative individual team contracts signed in the early days of TV seemed to prevent the owners from ever being able to agree to a comprehensive network contract. In the 1970s, baseball enjoyed significant financial gains from TV contracts. However, the 1980s saw a steep decline in national ratings.

Cable telecasts from superstations WTBS and WGN routinely brought the Atlanta Braves, Chicago Cubs, and White Sox into millions of TV households. Strong regional networks for teams like the Cincinnati Reds, the New York Yankees, and the Los Angeles Dodgers deliver 40 or 50 games per year to each team's primary metropolitan coverage area. With so many local and cable stations into the act, regular season baseball has had only limited support from network television.

Televised baseball has suffered from increased fan interest in professional basketball's May-June playoff schedule. Superstars like Michael Jordan, Charles Barkley, and Larry Bird helped to build the NBA into a growth sport of the 1980s. Muscle, elbows, and contact abound under the boards, while camera closeups show the intensity and determination in the eyes of the players. Fighting is not encouraged, as is the case with hockey, but league officials use a light touch in dealing with on-court brawls.

All of this has turned the NBA into high drama, and television has provided fans with the best seat in the house. The more television technology improved, the more exciting televised basketball became. Early broadcasts showed the small images of players running up and down old, dark gyms. As facilities were built with television in mind, and cameras became smaller, more portable, and able to present closeup action, fan interest seemed to rise. Today, both college and professional basketball enjoy profitable syndicated and network contracts.

The one sport that seemed to be tailor-made for television was professional football. Professional football was a game born of the Industrial Revolution. Burly coal miners, steelworkers, boilermakers, and longshoreman played for the entertainment of the company town. Early pro teams reflected the industrial heritage of the game with names like the Steamers, Steelers, Tanks, and Packers.

Football fit television like a glove. The action could be seen from distant cameras, the ball was easy to follow, pauses in the action gave commentators time to talk, and the game had natural breaks for advertisers. Football's popularity continued to rise throughout the 1950s until the moment when pro football was transformed into a Sunday afternoon TV ritual.

The crowning moment was actually a bleak, cold Sunday afternoon in December of 1958 when the Baltimore Colts and the New York Giants met to decide the NFL championship. The momentum of the game swung one way and then the next. Finally, in overtime, the Colts scored a stunning 23-17 victory. Players on both sides became household names. Professional football had arrived and from that point on rivaled baseball as the preeminent American sport.

Pro football owners were also more cooperative in signing TV contracts than their baseball counterparts. Strict rules were established to ensure regional interest for all teams and national exposure for the best teams. Ratings continued to soar throughout the 1960s and '70s as improved television technology improved the viewers' appreciation of the game.

By bringing the game into the viewers' living room, Roone Arledge, in charge of ABC's college football coverage, changed the way Americans watched football. Arledge called for numerous sideline cameras to seek out closeups and look for action away from the field. For the first time, viewers saw cheerleaders, fans, and coaches on the sidelines. Improved microphone techniques allowed viewers to hear the popping of pads and get a sense of the volume of the crowd's roar. Arledge eliminated the marching band from halftime programming and started a studio scoreboard show. Most important, engineer Bob Trachinger, acting on a suggestion from Arledge, was able to develop a videotape system that could instantaneously rerun exciting plays in slow motion.

Instant replay was first used during the 1960 Boston College-Syracuse game. A 70-yard-run touchdown scramble by quarterback Jack ConCannon was replayed several times from different angles. Reaction was overwhelming. Sports on television would never be the same.

Arledge is also significant for creating *Monday Night Football*, which premiered in the fall of 1970, and still enjoys good ratings and high sponsorship. Arledge also created *ABC's Wide World of Sports* (1961-), a Saturday afternoon program highlighting lesser-known sports such as weightlifting, track and field, rugby, auto racing, swimming, skiing, handball, and Greco-Roman wrestling. All in all, over 80 different sports were featured. Videotape gave Arledge the ability to suspend or alter time. *Wide World* also served other promotional purposes. ABC held the television contract for the Olympic Games, and Arledge could highlight certain sporting events or particular athletes during *Wide World* to promote interest in the Olympics. From the first television coverage of the Olympic Games in the summer of 1960 by ABC from Rome, the Olympics have grown in popularity into what some have called a media spectacle, especially when Olympic product sponsors added advertising to the games.

Today, sports on television is ubiquitous. Increased cable penetration has allowed a proliferation of sports television unseen by any previous generation. Superstations, local TV stations that have been transmitted by satellite to cable systems throughout North America, have expanded sports teams' spheres of influence way beyond their own metropolitan boundaries.

ESPN, Entertainment and Sports Programming Network (see entry), serves as a modern version of *Wide World of Sports* and has contracts with college and professional football, college basketball, hockey, boxing, racing, tennis, and major league baseball. A new cable service, ESPN2, was launched in the fall of 1993 to attract a younger demographic audience with coverage of events such as windsurfing and skateboarding.

Television and advertising revenue have become such a part of sports that game rules were changed to accommodate TV's presence. Football and basketball both have TV timeouts. Kickoff and tipoff have been moved to odd times like 7:07 p.m. to allow for a TV introduction and opening commercial. Professional football even experimented with an instant replay rule that could override an official's decision on the field. The Chicago Cubs dropped a century-old tradition of daytime baseball at Wrigley Field because afternoon playoff games did not do as well in the ratings as prime-time starts. Ironically, only boxing, the first sport to be propelled into national prominence by TV, seems to want to keep its marquee events off of television. Promoters lust for the revenue of pay-per-view and arena TV. Some analysts worry that other sports may try to migrate onto the pay channels, since professional sports need to find increasing revenue streams to pay the cost of building new facilities and to pay for increasing player salaries.

Bibliography

Auletta, Ken. *Three Blind Mice: How the Networks Lost Their Way.* New York: Random House, 1991.

Barber, Red. *The Broadcasters.* New York: Dial, 1970.

Guttman, Allen. *The Olympics: A History of the Modern Games.* Chicago: U of Illinois P, 1992.

Roberts, Randy, and James Olson. *Winning Is the Only Thing: Sports in America Since 1945.* Baltimore: Johns Hopkins UP, 1989.

Corley F. Dennison III

Sports Trading Cards, small cardboard cards first distributed more than a hundred years ago, were a natural form of instant literature for sports fans. They have since become one of the most popular sports collectibles (see Sports Memorabilia and Collectibles, above).

BASEBALL TRADING CARDS. Tobacco companies produced the first baseball trading cards from 1887 to 1895 as inserts in packages to stimulate product sales. The earliest baseball trading cards featured formal studio photographs on small pieces of heavy cardboard. Goodwin & Co. issued over 2,300 small baseball pictures from 1887 to 1890 and manufactured cabinet-sized Old Judge baseball cards. Rivals Allen & Ginter, D. Buchner, W. S. Kimball, and P. H. Mayo & Brother also made small baseball cards. The American Tobacco Company cornered the product market by 1895 and did not need to issue inserts.

The 1909-15 era marked the revival of baseball trading cards, sparked by the importing of Turkish cigarettes and a rapid increase in tobacco firms. American Tobacco and its competitors produced beautiful imaginative baseball sets of various sizes, shapes, and designs. The popular 524-card T206 white border lithographed set (1909-11), issued with 16 different cigarette brands, contains the rare Honus Wagner, Eddie Plank, and Sherry Magee cards. (The legendary Wagner card remains the most expensive and publicized trading card. Wagner, an inveterate tobacco chewer, opposed cigarettes and wanted his card withdrawn from production. The Plank card contained an engraving alignment error, while the Magee error card misspelled the player's name as "Magie.") The embossed T204 Ramly series (1909) placed ornate gold borders around black and white oval photos. The attractive T3 Turkey Red set (1911), the most popular cabinet issue, included baseball players and boxers, while the colorful T205 gold border set (1911) featured just baseball players. Mecca produced T201 Double Folders (1911), featuring two players on the same card with their records on the backs. The creative, picturesque T202 Hassan Triple Folders (1912) included two player color portraits resembling the T205 series and a black and white action scene.

Confectioners soon issued baseball cards to boost candy sales. In 1914 and 1915, Cracker Jack, the only firm to cover Federal League players, produced two very colorful card sets. By the 1920s, caramel, strip, and exhibit baseball cards also flourished.

The 1933-41 era introduced the production of bubblegum baseball cards. Goudey Gum of Boston and National Chicle of nearby Cambridge sold bubblegum and a baseball card in a one-cent package. The nearly square cards portrayed players in colorful paintings with biographical details, career highlights, and season statistics on the backs. The classic 240-card Goudey Big League Gum 1933 color set pictured over 40 National Baseball Hall of Famers, including four poses of Babe Ruth and two of Lou Gehrig. Goudey did not release the legendary No. 106 Napoleon Lajoie card, the second most valuable baseball card, until 1934. Goudey also issued a color set with two valuable Lou Gehrig poses (1934), puzzle set (1935), Sports Kings multi-port set (1935), and Head Up set (1938).

From 1934 to 1936, National Chicle distributed popular Diamond Stars and die-cut Batter Up sets. Gum of Philadelphia produced two black and white Play Ball sets (1939, 1940) and a color Play Ball Sports Hall of Fame set (1941). Large-sized premiums, printed on paper or photographic stock, also appeared in the 1930s.

World War II paper shortages temporarily halted baseball card production. Bowman Gum Co., formerly Gum, Inc., issued a small black and white baseball set in 1948 and dominated the market until 1951. During 1948-49, rival Leaf Gum of Chicago skipped various numbers in its controversial color set. Bowman sued Leaf over the use of player pictures, forcing the latter to cease issuing baseball cards. In 1949, Bowman distributed a 240-card landmark color set, including scarce high numbers.

Bowman used original color paintings in its 1950 set and released Mickey Mantle and Willie Mays rookie cards in its larger 1951 set. In 1953, Bowman reproduced actual color photographs in what is considered one of the finest baseball card sets ever made. A contractual problem forced removal of the No. 66 Ted Williams card from the 1954 Bowman set, making it the rarest modern baseball card. The 1955 Bowman set used a television-screen frame format and contained umpire cards.

Topps Chewing Gum of Brooklyn, NY, entered the baseball card market in 1951 with three small sets. Through 1955, Topps and Bowman vied for exclusive player contracts and established innovative card designs. The 1952 Topps set, the modern era's classic baseball issue, featured the largest single-year card issue ever produced (407) and largest sized bubblegum cards (2 5/8 inches x 3 3/4 inches). The detailed backs provided personal and career information. The 96 scarce high number series included the legendary No. 311 Mickey Mantle card, the hobby's third most expensive card. After purchasing Bowman Gum in January 1956, Topps dominated the baseball card market from 1956 to 1980. In 1957 Topps introduced the since-standard 2 1/2-inch by 3 1/2-inch baseball card and first used full-color photographs.

Fleer Gum of Philadelphia (1959-61, 1963), Post Cereal (1961-63), Kellogg's Cereal (1970-83), and Hostess Cakes (1975-79) also released baseball cards. After Fleer printed current players in its 1963 set, the federal courts upheld the exclusive right of Topps to picture players on bubblegum cards.

Through 1973, Topps issued baseball cards in series. Fewer stores carried the upper series, making the higher numbers scarcer. In 1974, Topps released its entire baseball set at once, making it much easier for collectors to complete sets. The marketing change sparked tremendous growth in the hobby and a rapid increase in trading card dealers.

A 1980 federal court decision ended the Topps monopoly, allowing Fleer and Donruss Gum of Memphis, TN, to manufacture baseball cards. In 1981, both Fleer and Donruss distributed bubblegum baseball card sets. A higher federal court restored Topps's monopoly rights, but Fleer and Donruss remained in the market with non-bubblegum inserts.

Topps started issuing annual update sets in 1981. In 1984, Fleer made an extremely limited Update set featuring valuable Roger Clemens and Kirby Puckett rookie cards. Score (1988) and Upper Deck (1989) later entered the baseball-card market. Upper Deck released innovative premium cards, using advanced stock, photography, packaging, and marketing. Other companies have joined the premium market, including Donruss Leaf in 1990, Topps Stadium Club, Leaf Studio, and Fleer Ultra in 1991, and Bowman, Donruss, Fleer, Pinnacle, and Score Select in 1992. Megatrends in 1991 started issuing black and white sets of former baseball legends, using *The Sporting News* photography of Charles Conlon. In 1993, Ted Williams Card began producing sets including some Negro League and All-American Girls Professional Baseball League stars.

FOOTBALL TRADING CARDS. National Chicle in 1935 issued the first football card set with 36 subjects. Since 1948, football card sets have appeared annually. Leaf released color football sets in 1948 and 1949, while Bowman produced pro football sets in 1948 and from 1950 to 1955. The large-sized 1952 Bowman set remains the most expensive modern football issue.

Topps entered the football market with college sets in 1950 and 1951 and a 1955 All-American Football set featuring 100 college legends. Topps issued National Football League sets from 1956 to 1963 and pictured only American Football League players from 1964 to 1967. The oversized 1965 Topps set contained the valuable Joe Namath rookie card.

Since 1968, Topps has produced annual NFL football sets. Fleer distributed annual AFL sets between 1960 and 1963, while Philadelphia Gum released NFL sets from 1964 to 1967.

Topps dominated the NFL card market from 1968 to 1989 and produced United States Football League sets in 1984 and 1985. Regular and premium football cards have flooded the market with the introduction of Pro Set and Score in 1989, Action Packed and Fleer in 1990, Bowman, Fleer Ultra, Pacific, Pro Line Portraits, Topps Stadium Club, Upper Deck, and Wild Card in 1991, Collector's Edge, Game Day, and Playoff in 1992, and Skybox and Ted Williams in 1993.

BASKETBALL TRADING CARDS. In 1948 Bowman released the first pro basketball set, a small 72-card color set featuring the valuable No. 69 George Mikan card. Topps issued an NBA set in 1957-58, while Fleer followed suit in 1961-62.

Topps regularly distributed NBA sets from 1969-70 to 1981-82, making oversized editions the first two years. From 1983-84 to 1985-86, Star produced three very limited NBA sets. The 1983-84 Star Dallas Mavs and Boston Celtics team subsets remain extremely scarce because numerous miscut cards were destroyed. The 1984-85 Star set contains Michael Jordan's rookie card, which rivals the above Mikan card in value.

Fleer manufactured three colorful NBA sets from 1986-87 to 1988-89 and has made NBA cards annually ever since. Regular and premium NBA issues have proliferated with the addition of NBA Hoops in 1989-90, Skybox in 1990-91, Classic Draft Pics and Upper Deck in 1991-92, and Action Packed, Fleer Ultra, Topps, and Topps Stadium Club in 1992-93.

Other sports trading cards have featured auto and stock car drivers, boxers, golfers, ice hockey players, horses, jockeys, Olympians, soccer players, tennis players, and wrestlers.

Bibliography

Lipset, Lew. *The Encyclopedia of Baseball Cards*. 3 vols. Centereach: n.p., 1983, 1984, 1986.

Rosen, Alan, with Doug Garr. *Mr. Mint's Insider's Guide to Investing in Baseball Cards and Collectibles*. New York: Warner, 1991.

Slocum, Frank. *Classic Baseball Cards: The Golden Years, 1886-1956*. New York: Warner, 1989.

——. *Topps Baseball Cards: The Complete Picture Collection*. New York: Warner, 1990.

Sugar, Bert Randolph. *The Sports Collector's Bible*. 4th ed. New York: Macmillan, 1991.

David L. Porter

Sportswriters. A Cro-Magnon cave person initiated sports writing with a picture on a wall in Lascaux that covered the hunting season. Homer became the first sportswriter to describe a wrestling match between Ajax and Odysseus in the *Iliad*, Book 23. As a genre, however, the craft of sports journalism did not emerge until the 19th century. In 1835, three New York City papers—the *Sun*, the *Herald*, and the *Transcript*—covered prizefights and horse races. Baseball found a recorder in Henry Chadwick, who wrote for the *New York Times* and the *New York Tribune* without pay. Starting in 1862, he described baseball regularly, contributing to the game's growing popularity.

Boxing matches that pitted Americans against Englishmen became popular in the 1860s. Football vied with prizefights, horse racing, and baseball for readers as the *New York Tribune* paved the way, while the *New York Times* hired the first female writer, "Middie" Morgan. In the battle for circulation, Joseph Pulitzer entered the arena with a separate sports department, a first, in his newly acquired *New York World*. Soon, papers throughout America followed suit. The arrival of William Randolph Hearst marked a turning point. His *New York Journal* promoted a circulation war, with the sports section serving as heavy artillery. The modern sports section surfaced.

Hearst hired sports champions to write on subjects of their expertise. Pulitzer aped this technique. Others joined the fray with measurable impact. The size of the sports page grew from 4 columns in 1890 to a full page in 1910. In that same year, the average number of columns devoted to sports was 7.1. Each subsequent decade witnessed increases to 10.3, to 18.2, and to 20.9 in 1940. Sports coverage has risen from 15 percent of the general news in 1900 to 50 percent in 1975. Currently, the sports pages have five times as many readers as any other section in the paper.

Accounting for this major leap in coverage requires an appraisal of sport's golden age. Some experts trace the ascent to 1914. Whatever the point of departure, by the 1920s, purple prose and hero worship greeted the heroes of sport. If World War I gave Americans a big hangover with a nervous edge, they experienced a lift from Ruth, Dempsey, Tilden, Grange, Jones, Ederle and others whose praises were sung by a chorus of "Gee-Whizzers": Damon Runyon, Bill Corum, Heywood Hale Broun, Ring Lardner, Paul Gallico, W. O. McGeehan, and Grantland Rice. "Outlined against a blue-gray October sky," the latter wrote, "the Four Horsemen rode again. In dramatic lore they are known as Famine, Pestilence, Destruction and Death.... Their real names are Stuhldreher, Miller, Crowley, and Layden." Freed from the constraints of "hard" news, sportswriters of the 1920s lifted similes and borrowed metaphors from the vast world of apocalyptic war, natural calamity, and assembly lines.

A depressed America in the 1930s yielded a crop of sour grapes. The "Gee Whiz" school gave way to the icon bashers, viz. "Aw Nuts." Led by McGeehan, they punctured the pompous and hoisted their own heroes. Star reporters transferred to other departments or died young: Lardner at 48 in 1933; McGeehan at 54 in 1933; Broun at 51 in 1939.

A second golden age of sportswriting began in the 1940s with the talents of Jimmy Cannon, Red Smith, and Arthur Daley. Inheriting John Kieran's column in the *New York Times*, Daley wrote stodgy prose and espoused a neo-Rice conservative party line. Smith, on the other hand, wrote elegantly, imitating Damon Runyon, Westbrook Pegler, and Joe Williams. Of this influential trinity, Cannon took the most risks, and according to Maury Allen, "revolutionized sportswriting and made it noble...[like] Joe DiMaggio." He fathered the "New Journalism" and inspired as he castigated the new breed of 1960s sportswriters—Phil Pepe, Larry Merchant, Stan Isaacs, and Maury Allen.

Many fine writers have emerged since. One of them, Mike Lupica, hails the great columnists as "the soloists of the newspaper business." To qualify, he insists, you need a unique voice. For 40 years, *Sports Illustrated* has encouraged fresh if not always unique voices. Paul Zimmerman, Rick Telander, and Peter King are fine solo artists. Others, such as Dick Schaap, Gay Talese, and Jimmy Breslin, abandoned the sports beat for other pursuits.

Bibliography

Holtzman, Jerome. *No Cheering in the Press Box.* New York: Holt, 1973.

Lipsky, Richard. *How We Play the Game: Why Sports Dominate American Life.* Boston: Beacon, 1981.

Lipsyte, Robert. *SportsWorld: An American Dreamland.* New York: Quadrangle, 1977.

Lupica, Mike. *Shooting from the Lip: Essays, Columns, Quips, and Gripes in the Grand Tradition of Dyspeptic Sports Writing.* Chicago: Bonus, 1988.

Michener, James. *Sports in America.* Greenwich: Fawcett Crest, 1976.

Shecter, Leonard. *The Jocks.* New York: Paperback Library, 1970.

Joseph Dorinson

Springsteen, Bruce (1949-   ), known to his fans as "the Boss," was arguably the most important figure in American popular music in the 1980s. Backed by the superb E Street Band, he combined accessible narrative songs with a charismatic and joyful stage presence. He drew on a distinctly American popular consciousness, acknowledging Bob Dylan and Woody Guthrie as influences, as well as blues and country music. In turn he influenced such lesser "Heartland Rock" figures as John Mellencamp, Bob Seger, and Bryan Adams.

In the 1980s, Springsteen represented authenticity in rock music, with his emphasis on down-to-earth, yet poetic lyrics, energetic live performances, working-man's clothes, and unflashy sexuality. For many he was the populist American response to such artists as David Bowie, whose many constructed personae paved the way for Madonna, Prince, and Michael Jackson. His star gradually faded in the early 1990s, with the triumph of artifice, and the fragmentation of popular music into ever-more-numerous subgenres.

Springsteen was born in the New Jersey town of Freehold. He built a regional following as a singer-songwriter in the early 1970s, and released two unsuccessful albums. In April 1974, his performance was seen by *Rolling Stone* record editor Jon Landau, who wrote, "I saw rock and roll's future and its name is Bruce Springsteen." In 1975, Columbia Records used this comment to launch a massive publicity campaign for Springsteen's third album, *Born to Run.* The album and title single were respectable hits, establishing Springsteen's reputation as a dynamic performer.

In 1978, now managed by Jon Landau, he released *Darkness on the Edge of Town*, then *The River* in 1980. These two albums established him as a major rock presence, and developed many of the themes of his earlier work, exploring the dark side of the American dream. Just when Springsteen seemed poised for rock superstardom, he drew back, with the release of his 1983 album, *Nebraska.* The album was a solo, acoustic collection of songs, using the original demo recorded at Springsteen's home. The collection was stark, unpolished, and decidedly noncommercial. The songs told stories of suffering and surviving in a bleak middle America, and the singer acknowledged debts to Woody Guthrie, Flannery O'Connor, and Terrence Malick's film *Badlands*, about mass murderer Charles Starkweather.

Nebraska was a critical success, but Springsteen's least popular record in some time. However, it was followed in 1984 with *Born in the USA,* the collection of outstanding rock songs that propelled him to superstardom. Not as bleak as *Nebraska*, it still traces the disillusionment of life for the have-nots in Reagan's America, in songs like "Downbound Train" and "My Hometown." The title song chronicles the despair of a returning Vietnam veteran.

The massively promoted, worldwide *Born in the USA* tour represented a quantum leap in Springsteen's popularity, elevating him to the status of pop culture icon. Five million fans attended the live shows, held in large stadiums where the closest view of the band was the nearest video screen. The tour generated $200 million in revenues, and the album sold over 13 million copies worldwide, making it the biggest seller in Columbia Records' history.

The year 1985 was a crossroad in Springsteen's career, at which point he withdrew from the hype of *Born in the USA*. After a two-year gap, he released *Tunnel of Love* (1987), a much more introspective album, and began a tour of smaller concert halls. The album was critically praised, and sold 2 million copies, but had nowhere near the impact of *Born in the USA*. Springsteen waited five years before making another record or performing live, except for appearances in such events as Band Aid, No Nukes, and the Amnesty International tour. Little was heard of him until April 1992, when he released two new albums, *Lucky Town* and *The Human Touch*, backed by a new band. The records were well reviewed and promoted, and by July had sold about 1.5 million each.

By the 1990s, Springsteen's songs were no longer working-class anthems, but were still relevant commentaries for his aging generation. The most striking aspect of the response to his 1990s work was the critics' reaffirmation of Springsteen's authenticity. As Jon Pareles commented: "The twang of hand-picked guitars and the kick of real drums represent a fortress for a family man, a defense against a postmodern world of rootlessness and moral ambiguity, of synthesized sounds and video games." After more than a decade, in 1999 Springsteen again began touring with the E Street Band.

Bibliography
Bird, S. Elizabeth. "Is That Me, Baby? Image, Authenticity, and the Career of Bruce Springsteen." *American Studies* 35.2 (1984): 39-58.

Eliot, Marc. *Down Thunder Road: The Making of Bruce Springsteen.* New York: Simon & Schuster, 1992.

Frith, Simon. "The Real Thing: Bruce Springsteen." *Music for Pleasure: Essays in the Sociology of Pop.* New York: Routledge, 1988.

Marsh, Dave. *Glory Days: Bruce Springsteen in the 1980s.* New York: Thunder's Mouth, 1996.

Pareles, Jon. "Springsteen: An Old-Fashioned Rocker in a New Era." *New York Times* 29 March 1992: H32.

S. Elizabeth Bird

Spy Fiction, a genre that has flourished in the 20th century, can be traced back to the mission of Odysseus and Diomedes to go behind the Trojan lines and learn enemy secrets in the *Iliad*. In general, espionage fiction probes the dangers posed to nations from their external and internal foes, and to individuals caught up in the quest to uncover and thwart national enemies; it also considers the ethics of spying, as a profession and as a moral activity.

The rise of the popularity of spy fiction in the U.S., and more broadly the West, has to do with events occurring at the end of the 19th century (the breakup of colonial empires, the division of the world into nation-states, and the evolution of international alliances). The Manichean politics of the two World Wars and the Cold War—the polarization between Allies and Axis powers and of East and West respectively—enhanced the significance of intelligence gathering and espionage activity. With the dissolution of the Soviet empire, still another set of global conditions has created a cultural climate that fosters spy literature.

A number of early novels portrayed espionage, beginning with James Fenimore Cooper's *The Spy* (1821), set in the American Revolution. Erskine Childers's *The Riddle of the Sands* (1903), Joseph Conrad's *The Secret Agent* (1907), and William Le Queux's *The Invasion of 1910* (1906) and *Revelations of the Secret Service* (1911) are other early examples of the genre. After World War I and its shocking casualties, Somerset Maugham's *Ashenden* (1928) began a new vogue—a realistic presentation of the human consequences of spying. British authors dominated the genre until World War II, but a number of American authors produced important works: Melville Davisson Post (*Uncle Abner, Master of Mysteries,* 1918); John P. Marquand's Mr. Moto series, begun in the 1930s; and Francis Van Wyck Mason, whose Army Intelligence Captain Hugh North appeared in novels from *The Branded Spy Murders* (1932) to *The Deadly Orbit Mission* (1968).

The growth of the Cold War enmity with the USSR and the establishment of the Central Intelligence Agency (CIA) in 1947 augmented public interest in spy stories. While Britain boasted Ian Fleming and, later, John le Carré (see entry), authors whose own experience as agents formed the basis of their fiction, American author Victor Marchetti brought his spy background to the fore in several novels including *The Rope Dancer* (1971), which depicted the defection to the Russians of an assistant to the director of the CIA, and *The CIA and the Cult of Intelligence* (1974), which portrayed the day-to-day operation of the agency. Charles McCarry, another ex-agent, introduced spy Paul Christopher in *The Miernik Dossier* (1973), who reappears in several novels. McCarry's *The Last Supper* (1983) traces the search for a "mole" in the CIA.

From the political right emerged another former agent, E. Howard Hunt, who, as David St. John, wrote a series of novels, typical of which was *The Berlin Ending* (1973). William F. Buckley, Jr., also maintained a strong conservative line in his Blackford Oakes series, including *Saving the Queen* (1976), *Stained Glass* (1978), set in West Germany, and *High Jinx* (1986), which reexamines the disastrous joint American-British schemes to intervene in post-World War II Albania.

The most significant popular novel of internal betrayal, *Seven Days in May* (1962) by Fletcher Knebel and Charles W. Bailey, depicted an attempted military takeover of Washington, DC. W. T. Taylor (the pen name of S. J. Hamrick), sometimes referred to as "the American le Carré," has pro-

Photo courtesy of Popular Culture Library, Bowling Green State University, Bowling Green, OH.

Palmer, Jerry. *Thrillers*: *Genesis and Structure of a Popular Genre*. New York: St. Martin's, 1979.

Wolfe, Peter. *Corridors of Deceit: The World of John le Carré*. Bowling Green, OH: Bowling Green State U Popular P, 1987.

Nicholas Ranson

See also
Follett, Ken
Mystery and Detective Fiction

Square Dancing. In 1981, after 20 years of effort by square dance advocates, President Reagan signed House Resolution No. 151, which resolved "that the square dance is designated the national folk dance of the United States of America for 1982-1983." This bill drew its primary support from the "modern" western square dance club movement, which began after World War II. Of course, ballroom dancers, cloggers, country and western dancers, old-time square dancers with different styles of dancing and music, and others objected, but with 375,000 current active square dance club dancers, perhaps another 8,000,000 who have taken lessons at some time, there was a strong argument. The passage of the bill epitomized the wholesome and patriotic image that has been identified with the modern square dance movement.

These patriotic values are reinforced by club etiquette; indeed the United Square Dancers of America distribute "ten commandments" of square dancing regarding friendliness, "act[ing] thy age," and even cleanliness. The use of alcohol or drugs is strictly prohibited, there is a dress code, and traditional gender roles are maintained. Such rules derive from the history of square dancing.

The American square dance developed from English country dances in longways formations (contras) and French cotillions and quadrilles in square sets. The French dances of the early 1800s contained five or more parts to be memorized and included intricate and polite steps to be learned from dancing masters. But as settlers moved west the dances were simplified and a caller was used to prompt the figures.

Facing stiff competition from the European round dances in the latter 19th century (waltz, polka, gallop, schottische, mazurka) and American dances and music in the 20th century (ragtime one-step, swing, tango, jitterbug), square dancing partially adapted by creating hybrid waltz and polka quadrilles. As a legacy of this adaptation, perhaps ten percent of modern clubs feature round dancing in addition to squares. But after years of slow decline, square dancing was found primarily in unsophisticated, rural areas and became associated with drinking, fighting, and other crude behavior (thus the later need for ten commandments).

With the publication of *Good Morning* in 1926, industrialist and traditional music/dance philanthropist Henry Ford tried to reignite American interest in refined quadrilles and rounds, but America's imagination was captured by the more robust, simpler, and folksy visiting couple squares (Birdie in the Cage, Dive for the Oyster, Rattlesnake Twist) found in the west and popularized by Lloyd "Pappy" Shaw and his Cheyenne Mountain School dancers. A strong advocate for

duced a series of novels including *The Man Who Lost the War* (1980) and *The Shadow Cabinet* (1984). Two writers have dominated the 1970s and 1980s popular market, Trevanian (no first name) and Robert Ludlum (see entry). Trevanian's *The Eiger Sanction* (1972) and *The Loo Sanction* (1973) introduced Jonathan Hemlock, a character in the mold of James Bond. Ludlum's name has given us the term "a ludlum" to describe any espionage fiction of great plot complexity with sudden eruptions of violence. Other representative works include William Hood's *Mole* (1982) and *Spy Wednesday* (1986). The detailed geopolitical-technical novels by Tom Clancy (see entry), such as *The Hunt for Red October* (1984), *Patriot Games* (1987), and *Clear and Present Danger* (1989), have led to popular movies.

The collapse of the Soviet Union and its sphere of influence has not eliminated danger to the West, though the focus has shifted from infiltration by Russian agents to the terrorist activities of disenfranchised groups and the politics of the Third World. Spy fiction remains a crucial barometer of the nation's consciousness, reflecting its moral debate with itself.

Bibliography
Greenberg, Martin H., ed. *The Robert Ludlum Companion*. New York: Bantam, 1993.

the fellowship of dancing and well-trained leaders, he published the definitive work of western square dancing, *Cowboy Dances*, in 1939.

America was ready and square dancing took off. The postwar economy was booming, people had cars, and married couples wanted a special night out without children. In California there were 11 callers and 35 clubs in 1946, but by 1950 those numbers had increased to 120 callers and 525 clubs. The square dance magazine *Sets in Order* claimed there were 5 million U.S. square dancers in 1950.

Club dancing not only facilitated dance organization but also fit societal trends. Live bands were replaced by recorded music, primarily country and western, callers became professionals, the figures were standardized so that once a dancer learned the 69 basics they could dance anywhere, and dancers were standardized through dress and conduct codes.

Despite declining numbers of dancers in classes, clubs, and at the national conventions, there remains a very strong and well-organized group of leaders who are committed to keeping square dancing a living heritage.

Bibliography
American Square Dance Magazine. Salinas: Sanborn Enterprises, 1994.
Casey, Betty. *The Complete Book of Square Dancing (and Round Dancing)*. Garden City: Doubleday, 1976.
Shaw, Lloyd. *Cowboy Dances*. Caldwell: Gaston, 1939.

David R. Peterson

Stack, Robert (1919-), has earned a unique place in television history because he can play police officers and officials superbly. The actor is ruggedly handsome, athletic, and possesses a piercing stare. These attributes, coupled with a strong, serviceable voice, have won him millions of fans as well as feature film and series opportunities.

Born Robert Modini in Los Angeles, he graduated from the University of Southern California. At 20, he achieved stardom when he gave Deanna Durbin her first screen kiss in *First Love* (1939). Studio moguls tried to make him a slick-haired Robert Taylor copy; he played youthful leads then returned from World War II an ambitious young actor. He had a dozen guest roles on television series before 1959; his best feature film parts in the 1950s were *The Bullfighter and the Lady* (1951), *The High and the Mighty* (1954), *Written on the Wind* (1955), and *Great Day in the Morning* (1956). But it was in the *House of Bamboo* (1955) that Stack played the sort of part for the first time that he was to play thereafter, that of a man caught in a dangerous situation. For, after several Oscar nominations, he reluctantly accepted the television role of Eliot Ness in the ABC made-for-television film and later series, *The Untouchables* (1959-63; see entry).

Playing an "honest cop" allowed Stack to exhibit his strongest qualities—unaffected underplaying, dignity, intelligence. As Ness, he embodied heroism for a generation of viewers; Stack's other series roles since *The Untouchables* have required him largely to enact the same fundamental character. These roles include Dan Farrell on *Name of the Game* (1968-72); "Linc" Evers on *Most Wanted* (1976-77), and Frank Murphy, leader of the *Strike Force* (1981-82). He

also had a continuing role in *It's a Great Life* (1985). His résumé also lists 20-plus guest-starring roles since 1959, plus featured film roles in *Airplane* (1980), and many more. The real-life *Unsolved Mysteries* (1988-), in which he is host-narrator, is still running after more than a decade.

Bibliography
Brooks, Tim. *The Complete Directory to Prime Time TV Stars, 1946-Present*. New York: Ballantine, 1987.
Davidson, Bill. "Robert Stack: Is Flashing the Great Stone Face Such a Crime?" *TV Guide* 26 Aug. 1989: 12-14.
Stack, Robert. *Straight Shooting*. New York: Macmillan, 1980.

R. D. Michael

Stagecoach (1939), directed by John Ford (see entry) and produced by Ford and Walter Wanger, with a screenplay by Dudley Nichols, was based on the short story "Stage to Lordsburg," by Ernest Haycox and published in *Collier's Magazine* (April 1937). Its cast included John Wayne (as The Ringo Kid), Andy Devine (Buck), Thomas Mitchell (Doc Boone), Claire Trevor (Dallas), Berton Churchill (Gatewood), George Bancroft (Curly), Donald Meek (Mr. Peacock), John Carradine (Hatfield), Louise Platt (Lucy Mallory), and Tom Tyler (Luke Plummer). It won Oscars for best supporting actor (Mitchell) and music score, and the New York Film Critics Award for best direction.

Considered today a classic in its genre, *Stagecoach* was Ford's first major Western, and the first he filmed in Monument Valley, which became for him a trademark location—a signature for at least six more Westerns. Appearing in March, *Stagecoach* was the first of three very popular films Ford made in 1939 (the other two were *Drums Along the Mohawk* and *Young Mr. Lincoln*). It was also Ford's first film to star John Wayne and to introduce its star in such a dramatic way; zooming in on him on the open landscape against the mountains presents him as a larger-than-life character with an archetypal mission.

The film was actually inspired by a tragic end, the loss of Ford's good friend Tom Mix. Mix's death in a high-speed car crash symbolized for Ford the death of the old Wild West—that spirit of freedom, independence, and recklessness. Ford resolved to make a Western, his first in 13 years, that would capture and celebrate the death of this free spirit. Having already begun work on the script of "Stage to Lordsburg" with Dudley Nichols, Ford now began to transform the story into a mythic journey that would incorporate the old West—the spirit of the outlaw—with the new, more civilized West.

In this symbolic journey into the wilderness, the passengers are tested, reduced to their basic natures, and reveal their inner selves—their true identities. In dramatizing the journey theme, Ford places the film squarely in the American literary tradition stemming back to the early 19th century.

Similar to many of our literary artists, Ford fashions his plot and characters around a series of contrasts, effectively dramatized through imagery of space and openness (Monument Valley), and confinement and enclosure (the coach), a dramatic device he refined in his later Westerns. Through this juxtaposition, Ford suggests the gradual regeneration of the prostitute Dallas and the escaped convict the Ringo Kid. The imagery thus heightens the allegorical nature of the trip the stage makes—from civilization to the primitive wilds, and back to civilization—and dramatizes the paring down of the false self and the movement toward a true self. Dallas and Ringo's escape from civilization at the end suggests not only their discovery of love, but a new sense of selfhood.

Bibliography

Bredahl, A. Carl. *New Ground: Western American Narrative and the Literary Canon.* Chapel Hill: U of North Carolina P, 1989.

Engel, Leonard. "Mythic Space in John Ford's West: Another Look at *Stagecoach.*" *Literature/Film Quarterly* 22.3 (Spring 1994).

Place, J. A. *The Western Films of John Ford.* Secaucus: Citadel, 1973.

Saxton, Christine. "What You Can See in a Movie." *Discourse* 3 (Spring 1981): 26-44.

Sinclair, Andrew. Afterword. *Stagecoach.* Ed. Andrew Sinclair. New York: Ungar, 1984.

Leonard Engel

Stallone, Sylvester (1946-), one of Hollywood's strongmen actors, was born in the Hell's Kitchen area of New York City. He was expelled from more than a dozen schools but won an athletic scholarship to attend the American College in Switzerland. After attending some classes in the University of Miami's Drama Department, he returned to New York and a variety of odd jobs. In 1974 he played one of the leading roles (along with Henry Winkler) in *The Lords of Flatbush,* a comedy about street-smart adolescents in Brooklyn in the 1950s. This part led to supporting roles in other films, but he seized the initiative to create the vehicle which would make him a star when he wrote the screenplay for *Rocky* (1976; see entry), the tale of two-bit boxer Rocky Balboa, who beats the odds by staging a heroic battle against the heavyweight champion of the world.

Stallone sold his script on the condition that he play the starring role in the film. Yet, ironically, it was this movie which initially typecast him as a human punching bag who could withstand tremendous punishment and stagger and stumble on to a moral victory. Stallone's continuing the story in four sequels (1979, 1982, 1985, 1990) etched the image of a lovable punchdrunk fighter into the public mind.

Stallone also achieved some success with *F.I.S.T.* (1978), a film, directed by Norman Jewison, about the corruption of a truckers' union. He wrote and directed *Paradise Alley* (1978), about how three brothers struggle to rise above their Hell's Kitchen environment after World War II. But he did not begin to craft a second credible screen persona until *First Blood* (1982), a ultraviolent film that translates Rocky's juggernaut resilience into the melancholy machismo of Vietnam veteran John Rambo, whose return to America offers him not peace and appreciation but merely a change of venue for his existential guerrilla warfare.

A financial success at the box office, *First Blood* gave rise to a mega-money-making sequel, *Rambo: First Blood Part II,* co-written by Stallone and James Cameron. *Rambo* takes the surly, alienated title character from the hard labor of prison life back to Southeast Asia, where he must battle old enemies and the treachery of American military authorities to rescue a band of MIAs. Rambo becomes not just a man declaring war against a nation but a perverse embodiment of the noble savage, resorting to the law of the jungle to outwit and outfight his enemies in a survival of the fittest. The film's popularity can be explained in part as a cinematic revision of the historical outcome of America's involvement in Vietnam.

After another *Rambo* sequel (an ill-fated foray into Afghanistan, Russia's Vietnam) had little success at the box office, Stallone turned to comedy, but with equally disappointing results (e.g., *Rhinestone* [1984], *Oscar* [1991], and *Stop! or My Mother Will Shoot* [1992]). Yet in 1993 he made a cinematic comeback by returning to the action/adventure genre, with *Cliffhanger* and *Demolition Man.* Both films project the essential Rambo persona onto new terrain (mountaintops in the former film, the future in the latter case). In his recent films, Stallone plays the roles he seems destined to perform, intensely physical ones that accentuate the individual's conflict with the establishment: *The Specialist* (1994), *Judge Dredd* (1995), *Assassins* (1995), *Daylight* (1996), and *Cop Land* (1997).

Bibliography

Daly, Marsha. *Sylvester Stallone.* New York: St. Martin's, 1986.

Gross, Edward. Rocky *and the Films of Sylvester Stallone.* Las Vegas: Pioneer, 1990.

Stallone, Sylvester. *Sylvester Stallone.* New York: St. Martin's, 1986.

Ted Billy

Stanwyck, Barbara (1907-1990), a four-time Academy Award nominee, played a variety of roles in melodramas, comedies, and Westerns in a career that spanned 50 years, but she is best known for portraying outlaw women who struggle for acceptability in a man's world.

Stanwyck, a child of second-generation Scots-Irish parents, was born Ruby Stevens in Brooklyn, NY. Her mother died when she was two, her father when she was four. Raised by an older sister and placed in a series of foster homes, she dropped out of school at 13 and at 15 became a chorine at the Strand Roof (see Revue). In 1926 she won her first major theatrical role in Willard Mack's *The Noose.*

Under Frank Capra, Stanwyck established her 1930-40s screen persona, the good-bad girl, who mixed warmth and cynicism, toughness and sensitivity. Frequently her characters run from a shady past and aspire to rise above their lower-middle-class origins. They are reformed through the idealism of a gentle male counterpart. She is party-girl Kay Arnold in Capra's *Ladies of Leisure* (1931). In *Meet John Doe* (1941), Stanwyck's cynical reporter is softened through the influence of a common man character she had created as a publicity stunt. In *Remember the Night* (1940), Stanwyck's shoplifter falls in love with her prosecuting attorney. In *Stella Dallas* (1937), Stanwyck's performance as a self-sacrificing mother is among the best of her career, as it works on two levels, the rough and the poignant.

Along with embodying a rough poignancy, Stanwyck's Depression-era characters, such as Lily Powers of *Baby Face* (1933), sometimes used sexual wiles to compete in a man's world. When Stanwyck deftly turned to comedy in the early 1940s, her controlling sexuality was revitalized. Both Jean Harrington of *Lady Eve* (1941) and "Sugarpuss" O'Shea of *Ball of Fire* (1941) lure men with exposed legs and hair backlit by sun, but underneath feminine deception lies vulnerability: each character unwittingly falls in love with a man she aimed to con.

In 1944, a darker side of the wily female emerged as Stanwyck donned a blond wig for Billy Wilder's nasty film noir, *Double Indemnity*. Stanwyck's icy performance, her hardened face and frozen eyes, reemerged in lesser noir films (*The Strange Love of Martha Ivers* [1946], *The File on Thelma Jordon* [1950], and *Clash by Night* [1952]), and psychological Westerns (*The Furies* [1950] and *Forty Guns* [1957]).

After a series of bad roles and lesser projects in the 1950s, Stanwyck triumphed on television. NBC's *Barbara Stanwyck Show* (1960-61), in which she starred in 32 of 36 episodes, won Stanwyck her first Emmy. She won a second for her performance as matriarch Victoria Barkley on the Western series *Big Valley* (1966-67 season), and a third for *The Thorn Birds* miniseries (1983). On March 29, 1982, Stanwyck earned an honorary Oscar for her contribution to cinema, and in 1987 she received her final honor, the 15th annual American Film Institute Lifetime Achievement Award.

Bibliography

DiOrio, Al. *Barbara Stanwyck*. New York: Coward-McCann, 1983.

Narcmore, James. *Acting for the Cinema*. Berkeley: U of California P, 1988.

Ringgold, Gene. "Barbara Stanwyck." *Films in Review* 14.10 (1963): 577-602.

Smith, Ella. *Starring Miss Barbara Stanwyck*. New York: Crown, 1973, 1985.

Grant Tracey

Star Trek (1966-1969) chronicled the voyages of the Starship *Enterprise* with its crew: Captain James T. Kirk (William Shatner; see entry); science officer Spock (Leonard Nimoy), half-human and half-alien from the planet Vulcan; chief medical officer Dr. Leonard McCoy (DeForest Kelley); African-American communications officer Lt. Uhura (Nichelle Nichols); the Scottish chief engineer "Scotty" (James Doohan); and navigators Mr. Sulu from Japan (George Takei) and Mr. Chekov (Walter Koenig) from Russia. The *Enterprise* had a "five-year mission to explore strange new worlds, to seek out new life and new civilizations, to boldly go where no man has gone before."

Canceled in 1969 after 79 episodes, the show gained immense popularity in syndication and is now seen in 40 countries. It has since generated an animated series, three live-action spinoffs, nine films (see next entry), countless books, masters' theses, and doctoral dissertations, television and printed parodies, college courses (such as "Themes in American Culture: The *Star Trek* Phenomenon" [at Middle Tennessee State University]), fan conventions, and the contribution of "Beam me up, Scotty" (which was, however, never said in the series) to the vernacular.

Star Trek merchandise has earned $600 million. A model of the *Enterprise* hangs at the National Air and Space Museum (see p. 761); in 1976, the first space shuttle was named *Enterprise*; in 1991, the U.S. Postal Service canceled its Space Exploration stamps with an image of the *Enterprise*.

Star Trek may be the most successful media phenomenon in American history. The most frequent reason given is that, during the Cold War and the Vietnam War, with the ever-present fear of nuclear holocaust, the original show offered hope that humanity would survive into a 23rd century in which many 20th-century problems would be eliminated. Also, while recent critics have noted the sexism and racism of the show, in the 1960s its interracial cast that included women presented a promising future to then-marginalized groups.

Star Trek also offered an alternative in science fiction. Many science fiction films in the 1950s and 1960s were Cold War, anti-communist propaganda about robots and body snatchers that took over the earth and made people into zombies (see Science Fiction Film). While the television programs *My Favorite Martian, Lost in Space,* and *It's about Time* presented more benign science fiction than the movies, still, *Star Trek* seemed to fill a niche that no other show did. Nevertheless, the show was nearly canceled after its second season. It was saved by the first major letter-writing campaign in TV history and by viewer protests at NBC offices in Burbank and New York. However, after three seasons, *Star Trek* was canceled and went into syndication, at which point the show really gained a following.

Various reasons for its continuing popularity have been suggested. For one, *Star Trek* tapped into a quintessential American myth of freedom and expansion into the frontier, only *Star Trek* moved into "the final frontier." Significantly, Gene Roddenberry (see entry), *Star Trek*'s creator, initially envisioned *Star Trek* as "a *Wagon Train* to the stars." This provides another clue to *Star Trek*'s popularity. It was a futuristic Western, *Bonanza* in outer space, with three male leads enjoying camaraderie in an infinite Ponderosa. Yet *Star Trek* also dealt with 1960s issues such as racism, hippies, environmentalism, and war.

The first live-action spinoff of the original series, *Star Trek: The Next Generation* (1987-94), was also created by Roddenberry. Set 78 years after the original *Star Trek, The Next Generation (TNG)* introduced the characters Captain Jean-Luc Picard (Patrick Stewart), First Officer William T. Riker (Jonathan Frakes), Science Officer Lt. Cmdr. Data (an android, played by Brent Spiner), Navigator (later Chief Engineer) Geordi LaForge (LeVar Burton), Dr. Beverly Crusher and her son, Wesley (Gates McFadden and Wil Wheaton), Security Chief Lt. Tasha Yar (Denise Crosby), Counselor Deanna Troi (Marina Sirtis), and Lt. Worf (Michael Dorn), a Klingon who would later become Security

Star Trek artifacts. Photo courtesy of Popular Culture Library, Bowling Green State University, Bowling Green, OH.

Chief. Famous fans appeared on the show: physicist Stephen Hawking and space shuttle astronaut Mae Jemison. Movie actress Whoopi Goldberg had the recurring role of Guinan.

TNG benefited from the popularity of the original show and retained important elements from it, including an optimistic view of the future and a crew with some of the endearing attributes of the original crew. However, if, as critic Harvey Greenberg has suggested, *Star Trek* appealed to a teenaged audience, then *TNG* appeals to the same audience, now grown up and with much different ideas on men, women, relationships, violence, and politics than in the 1960s. *TNG* dealt with rape, child abuse, drug addiction, homophobia, ethnic war, genocide, the brainwashing and torturing of prisoners, and the quest for a (Palestinian) homeland. Like its predecessor, *TNG* presents those issues in parables—for instance, in an episode about homophobia, a member of an androgynous race who feels female is brainwashed into androgyny.

The Next Generation concluded its seventh and final season, after 180 episodes, as the highest-rated syndicated drama in television history. Paramount Studios discontinued the series in order to make films with *The Next Generation*'s cast, beginning with *Star Trek: Generations* (1995) (see next entry).

Star Trek: Deep Space Nine (1993-99) was spun off of the *Next Generation* storyline; Patrick Stewart guest-starred in the two-hour premiere, and the O'Brien family from *TNG* transferred to *Deep Space Nine (DS9)*. Set on a space station near both the planet Bajor and a stable wormhole that provides a shortcut into the Gamma quadrant of the galaxy, the show's crew included Cmdr. Benjamin Sisko and his son, Jake (Avery Brooks and Cirroc Lofton); his second-in command, the Bajoran Major Kira Nerys (Nana Visitor); Dax (Terry Farrell), previously an older male but now a young female; a shape-shifting constable, Odo (Rene Auberjonois); a Ferengi barkeep, Quark (Armin Shimerman); and two other humans: Chief of Operations Miles O'Brien (Colm Meaney) and Dr. Julian Bashir (Alexander Siddig).

Like its *Star Trek* predecessors, *DS9* had state-of-the-art special effects and respected its audience's intelligence. However, *DS9* was the first *Star Trek* series not created by Roddenberry, but rather by Rick Berman and Michael Piller,

Nichelle Nichols, *Star Trek*'s Lt. Uhura, at a fan convention appearance in Harvey, IL. Photo courtesy of Mark McDermott.

executive producers of *TNG*. *DS9* was introduced to critics as a "darker" *Star Trek*. It does not take place on the pristine, state-of-the-art flagship of the Federation, the *Enterprise*, but on a crumbling space station left plundered by the Cardassians, who had occupied it during the enslavement of Bajor.

A third live-action spinoff is *Star Trek: Voyager* (1995-), also created by Berman and Piller, along with Jerry Taylor. The syndicated show, produced by Paramount for broadcast on the cable UPN channel, follows the crew of the Starship *Voyager* in the 24th century, led by Captain Kathryn Janeway (Kate Mulgrew), who find themselves lost in a distant part of the galaxy.

The various *Star Treks* are accessible on many levels; they appeal to people of different ages, educations, races, genders, occupations, and interests. They portray a world in which the disabled can utilize their abilities, assisted by new technologies. The *Star Trek* phenomenon as a whole presents a catechism of sorts, a body of common knowledge based on faith in the future and the appreciation of "infinite diversity from infinite combinations."

Bibliography

Bacon-Smith, Camille. *Enterprising Women: Television Fandom and the Creation of Popular Myth*. Philadelphia: U of Pennsylvania P, 1992.

Farrand, Phil. *The Nitpicker's Guide to the Next Generation Trekkers*. New York: Dell, 1993.

Gengry, Christine, and Sally Gibson-Downs. *Greenberg's Guide to* Star Trek *Collectibles*. 3 vols. Sykesville: Greenberg, 1991-92.

Gibberman, Susan R. Star Trek: *An Annotated Guide to Resources on the Development, the Phenomenon, the People, the Television Series, the Films, the Novels and the Recordings*. Jefferson: McFarland, 1991.

Nance, Scott. *Trekking to the Stars: The Patrick Stewart Story*. Las Vegas: Movie Pubs. Servs., 1993.

Nemecek, Larry. Star Trek: The Next Generation *Companion*. Ed. David Stern. New York: Pocket, 1992.

Okuda, Michael, and Denise Okuda. Star Trek *Chronology: The History of the Future*. New York: Pocket, 1993.

Okuda, Michael, Denise Okuda, and Debbie Mirek. *The* Star Trek *Encyclopedia*. New York: Pocket, 1994.

Sternbach, Rick, and Michael Okuda. Star Trek: The Next Generation *Technical Manual*. New York: Pocket, 1991.

Van Hise, James. *Trek: The Unauthorized, Behind-the-Scenes Story of* Deep Space Nine. Las Vegas: Movie Publications, 1993.

Whitfield, Stephen, and Gene Roddenberry. *The Making of* Star Trek. New York: Ballantine, 1968.

April Selley

Star Trek: The Motion Picture (1979) was Paramount's movie version of the 1960s television series *Star Trek* (see entry). Produced for between $40 and $50 million, the film was, at that time, one of the most expensive ever made and was directed by Hollywood veteran Robert Wise. In spite of lukewarm reviews, the film grossed $17 million in its first week of release and, according to the *New York Times* of January 14, 1980, by January 7 had made $59,316,116.

In spite of the negative reviews, *Star Trek: The Motion Picture* reunited the cast of the series and proved to Paramount that the concepts and characters in *Star Trek* could be a financial success. Over the next 20 years, Paramount produced eight sequels. The first five continued to focus on the story of the original series: *II: The Wrath of Khan* (1982); *III: The Search for Spock* (1984), directed by Leonard Nimoy; *IV: The Voyage Home* (1986), also directed by Nimoy; *V: The Final Frontier* (1989), directed by William Shatner; and *VI: The Undiscovered Country* (1991). *Star Trek: Generations* (1995) moved on to the story of the *Star Trek: The Next Generation* TV series, with Captain Jean-Luc Picard (Patrick Stewart) as the main character. It was followed by *Star Trek: First Contact* (1996) and *Star Trek: Insurrection* (1998).

Bibliography

Asherman, Allan. *The* Star Trek *Compendium*. Rev. ed. New York: Pocket, 1986.

Canby, Vincent. "The Screen: *Star Trek* Based on TV." *New York Times* 8 Dec. 1979: 14.

Kauffmann, Stanley. "Long Journeys." *New Republic* 29 Dec. 1979: 20.

Kroll, Jack. "Trek into Mysticism." *Newsweek* 17 Dec. 1979: 110-11.

Naha, Edward M. "Writing a 23rd-Century Scenario." *Science Digest* Dec. 1979: 48-51+.

Robert Chamberlain

Star Wars Saga, The, refers to a series of films created by George Lucas: *Star Wars* (1977), *The Empire Strikes Back* (1980), *Return of the Jedi* (1983), and a "prequel," *Star Wars: Episode 1—The Phantom Menace* (1999). Until the appearance of *E.T.* in 1982, *Star Wars* was the top money-making film of all time. Taken together, the first three *Star Wars* films and their spinoff products have earned over $1 billion, suggesting that the *Star Wars* narrative appealed to a wide spectrum of individuals, some of whom viewed the films several times. Such multiple viewings imply that these movies may embody mythic themes which, like the best children's stories, continue to be pleasurable even after many repetitions.

In fact, the odyssey of Luke Skywalker (Mark Hamill) follows closely the hero's journey as set forth by Joseph Campbell in his influential book *The Hero with a Thousand Faces*. (Campbell was a good friend of Lucas's.) An innocent young boy from an obscure planet who is raised by substitute parents seizes the opportunity to rescue a beautiful princess (Leia Organa, played by Carrie Fisher), gain wisdom from unlikely mentors (Obi-Wan Kenobi and Yoda), and perform courageous deeds that save the universe from being conquered by Darth Vader (David Prowse; voice by James Earl Jones) and the Evil Empire.

Luke's first mentor, Obi-Wan Kenobi (Alec Guinness), initiates him into the ways of the Jedi Knights (a once-powerful brotherhood which championed Truth and Justice), their unique weapon (the light sabre), and "The Force," a spiritual power which pervades the universe and can be used for either good or evil. Luke's father (Anakin Skywalker) had been a Jedi and the "best pupil" of Obi-Wan.

Throughout his many adventures, Luke has a partner, Han Solo (Harrison Ford). Older and more experienced than Luke, Han is a loner and also an archetypal "braggart soldier," a space pirate who lives by his wits and whose "customized" spaceship, the Millennium Falcon, can outrun Imperial warships. Solo's sidekick is the seven-foot furry creature Chewbacca (a Wookie), who is sufficiently intelligent to pilot a spaceship. Two other significant characters in *Star Wars* are the droids R2-D2 and C-3PO.

In *The Empire Strikes Back* complications ensued: Luke lost his right hand in a light sabre fight with Darth Vader (though he quickly received a bionic replacement). Han Solo, after declaring his love for Princess Leia, was frozen into a state of suspended animation. The character of Yoda (Frank Oz) was introduced as Luke's new teacher, a combination prankster and Zen master. The most shocking event in *The Empire Strikes Back* (aside from Luke's maiming) was the disclosure that Darth Vader was Luke's father.

In *The Return of the Jedi* our heroes manage to triumph over the forces of evil with the help of the Ewoks, furry little creatures who resemble animated teddy bears. The Ewoks use low-tech devices (logs, rocks) to thwart the high-tech machines of the Empire. The film ends with a gala celebration: the lovers Han and Leia (who turns out to be Luke's sister) are reunited, and holographic images of Obi-Wan, Yoda, and a reformed Darth Vader look on approvingly.

When *Star Wars* was first released in 1977, it seemed to be a self-contained entity, not part of a larger artistic structure; but just prior to the opening of *Empire* in 1980, *Star Wars* reappeared in theaters with a new subtitle: *Episode IV—A New Hope*. Thus, for the first time, George Lucas unveiled his grand scheme for a total of nine films, of which the three existing ones formed the *middle* trilogy (that is, episodes 4, 5 and 6).

Star Wars: Episode 1—The Phantom Menace was released with much fanfare in 1999. While following the story of a planet whose autonomy is being threatened by an increasingly dominant trade federation, the movie begins to set up the antecedents for the preceding films. A Jedi Knight (Liam Neeson) and his apprentice, a young Obi-Wan Kenobi (Ewan McGregor), accompany Queen Amidala of Naboo (Natalie Portman) in a quest for help. Along the way they discover a young Anakin Skywalker (Jake Lloyd), whom they determine to train as a Jedi, and fend off a sinister Darth Maul (Ray Park). With the help of another species on the planet, they are able to save Naboo. The next two episodes are tentatively scheduled for release in 2002 and 2005.

Bibliography

Sansweet, Stephen J. Star Wars: *From Concept to Collectible.* San Francisco: Chronicle, 1992.

Sheldon, Lita, comp. *A Star Wars Bibliography.* Tsaile: Sheldon, 1980.

Slavicsek, Bill. *A Guide to the Star Wars Universe.* New York: Ballantine, 1994.

Robert Sprich

Stegner, Wallace (1909-1993), was the author of more than two dozen books, including novels, short story and essay collections, biographies, history, and literary criticism. Widely known for his devotion to the American West and for his persuasive environmentalism, Stegner challenged popular Western mythologies of manifest destiny and rugged individualism, criticized exploitation of the land and native peoples, and employed historical realism to create a new literature of the West, which values cooperation and respects the arid environment.

Among Stegner's better known works are his semi-autobiographical novel *The Big Rock Candy Mountain* (1943), about an itinerant family dominated by a fortune-seeking father; *Angle of Repose* (1971), which won the Pulitzer Prize for fiction that year, a fictionalized account of the life of Mary Hallock Foote, a genteel Easterner who followed her husband to the raw western frontier; *The Spectator Bird* (1977), winner of a National Book Award, featuring a narrator who searches for his roots and reflects on his past; and *Crossing to Safety* (1987), a novel about an aging couple whose marriage endures. Stegner's nonfiction works about the western environment include *The Sound of Mountain Water* (1969); *American Places* (1981), co-authored with his son Page Stegner; and *The American West as Living Space* (1987).

Bibliography

Arthur, Antony, ed. *Critical Essays on Wallace Stegner.* Boston: Hall, 1982.

Colberg, Nancy. *Wallace Stegner: A Descriptive Bibliography.* Lewiston: Confluence, 1990.

Robinson, Forrest G., and Margaret G. Robinson. *Wallace Stegner.* Boston: Twayne, 1977.

Stegner, Wallace, and Richard W. Etulain. *Conversations with Wallace Stegner on Western History and Literature.* Salt Lake City: U of Utah P, 1990.

Cheryll Glotfelty

Stereophonic Sound is three-dimensional, allowing a listener to note the spatial extent of sound. Stereo was sought for electronic communication quite simply because human beings hear with two ears. Stereo sound is produced by recording with two microphones located at different positions. The recording is then played back through two loudspeakers placed in distinct locations. To successfully accomplish stereo sound, two separate channels of information are necessary.

The origin of stereophonic sound can be traced to August 30, 1881, when a German patent was issued to a Frenchman named Clement Ader. Ader unveiled his invention at the 1881 Paris Exposition. Except in very rare instances, stereo sound was virtually ignored until World War I, when stereo techniques were used in experimental equipment designed to locate enemy aircraft. In March 1924, engineers Harvey Fletcher and W. H. Martin predicted that stereo would one day be used for radio broadcasting.

The first-known attempt to broadcast in stereo took place in 1925 at radio station WPAY-AM, in New Haven, CT. One channel of the station's audio was broadcast on one AM frequency, and another channel was broadcast over a separate frequency, or AM-AM. Other similar unsuccessful attempts at stereocasting were tried using the two-frequency, transmitter, or station approach: AM-FM, FM-FM, TV-AM. The stereo popularity boom began in earnest in the 1950s, when stereo tape and stereo discs (records) were introduced for public consumption. The tremendous popularity of stereo records gave rise to consumer demand and the motivation to move toward stereo broadcasting, a movement that stimulated many controversial developments in the history of both radio and television roadcasting.

Until 1958, the Federal Communications Commission (FCC) paid little attention to the idea of stereo broadcasting. The commission approved stereo for FM in 1961, but denied it for AM and television. Since FM languished practically unnoticed in the shadows of AM and TV, stereo was considered a feature with the potential to attract the attention of listeners. Moreover, it was widely believed that AM stereo could not be accomplished because of the nature of basic AM technological design. Stereo, it seemed, simply would not work on AM. As for television, experts concluded that the big sound of stereo was just not suitable in combination with the small screen pictures of a typical 1950s TV set.

The first station to broadcast FM stereo was WGFM, Schenectady, NY, on June 1, 1961. Stereo helped FM slowly begin to attract listeners. FM went ahead of AM in audience numbers by 1985. For example, 70 percent of all radio listeners tuned to AM in 1973, but by 1985 FM controlled that 70 percent share. In an effort to aid AM radio as it had FM, the FCC approved the use of stereo in 1982. However, the AM stereo decision was a historic departure from the Commission's 50-year tradition of stern standard-setting. For the first time ever, the FCC decided not to set a system standard, opting only to police technical parameters. In other words, any system could be employed as long as it met certain operating requirements.

On July 23, 1982, both KDKA in Pittsburgh and KTSA in San Antonio became the first AM stereo stations. Several others followed shortly. The vast majority of AM broadcasters elected to wait, stalling to see which system might emerge as the standard. Without a standard system around which stations, manufacturers, and consumers could rally, the AM stereo marketplace created confusion, uncertainty, and chaos. Ultimately, AM stereo lost most of its industry and consumer support.

The FCC finally made Motorola's C-QUAM system the AM stereo system standard in 1993, but only after a congressional mandate in the form of the Telecommunications Act of 1992. For AM stereo, Congress's intervention may be too late. Over the years, AM stereo has become less important to consumers who are incessantly enticed by the allure of other technologies, such as digital audio broadcasting (DAB), high definition television (HDTV), and multi-channel television sound (MTS).

Twenty-three years after postponing stereo for television, the FCC decided in 1984 to allow TV stereocasting, or multichannel television sound (MTS). As with AM stereo, the FCC did not choose a stereo transmission standard. Rather, the commission reserved a frequency for the exclusive use of the industry-endorsed system proposed by Zenith. Other television stereo transmission systems were relegated to use of nonprotected frequencies. The industry united behind one system because of fear that a repeat of the AM stereo debacle could occur.

Bibliography

Grant, August E. *Communications Technology Update.* 3d ed. Boston: Focal, 1994.
Rumsey, Francis. *Stereo Sound for Television.* Newton: Focal, 1989.
Sunler, John. *The Story of Stereo: 1881–* . New York: Gernsback Library, 1960.
Talbot-Smith, Michael. *Broadcast Sound Technology.* Newton: Focal, 1990.

W. A. Kelly Huff

Stern, Howard (1954-), a communications graduate of Boston University, began his career as a conventional radio deejay in 1976. At WCCC, Hartford, in 1978 he began experimenting with a mix of outrageous telephone talk and music. To protest lines at gasoline stations he urged a protest called To Hell with Shell. He developed Dial-a-Date, a sort of lurid take-off on television's *The Dating Game.*

His success landed him jobs in Detroit and Washington, DC, where newscaster Robin Quivers became his female sidekick. Quivers is a black steelworker's daughter who grew up in a Jewish neighborhood in Baltimore. She has defended Stern's use of black dialect to respond to callers. After tripling station ratings, he left for WNBC, New York, where his caustic brand of humor and promotion of negative racial stereotypes earned him critics and more financial success.

Stern rose to the top of the ratings wars in the nation's largest radio markets, and his success led to a proliferation of imitators (see Shock Radio). Stern's success on radio led to a film, *Private Parts* (1997). Both can be seen as part of the larger cultural trend in all forms of media toward explicit references to sexual behavior, violence, and blunt attack on social institutions.

Bibliography

Colford, Paul D. *Howard Stern: The King of All Media—The Unauthorized Biography.* New York: St. Martin's, 1996.
Menell, Jeff. *Howard Stern: Big Mouth.* New York: Windsor, 1993.

Jeremy Harris Lipschultz

Stewart, James (1908-1997), to American film audiences, personified the transition from youthful idealism to the harsh world of the 20th century, though he is most fondly remembered for the former. Known affectionately by audiences as "Jimmy," Stewart encompassed this experience in both his onscreen performances and his offscreen life. Though some actors may move from romantic comedies to Westerns to psychological thrillers, few, if any, achieved the same masterful versatility as Stewart.

A New York summer stock theater group fostered the beginning of Stewart's career and a lifetime friendship with actor Henry Fonda (see entry), another cinematic Everyman. It was actually Fonda who persuaded Stewart to pursue acting as a career. Before being convinced, Stewart was simply an architecture student passing time before moving on to graduate school.

Stewart's lanky, 6-foot-3-inch physique kept him from being typecast as just another macho man of American cinema. His unique performance style consisted of the "gee whiz" sensibility of the boy next door coupled with nervous, emotional energy. His stammering became his trademark. After a string of career-making roles in MGM pictures, Stewart branched out into other studios with great success.

The "Jimmy Stewart" persona was fully realized and documented in such films as *Mr. Smith Goes to Washington* and *Destry Rides Again*, both in 1939. In 1940, his unique approach was honored with a best actor Oscar for his performance in George Cukor's *The Philadelphia Story* with Katharine Hepburn and Cary Grant.

After three films in 1941, Stewart was off to war as an enlisted private in the Air Force. Upon his return, Stewart played George Bailey, one of his most endearing and famous characters, in *It's a Wonderful Life* (1946; see entry). The small-town atmosphere of Bedford Falls supports Stewart's neighborly persona, but this time, he lives in a much harsher world. The crushing anxiety of the holiday season and the disappointment of unfulfilled dreams are only compounded by the presence of war and the corruption that is personified in Potter, the crotchety bank owner. Stewart's George Bailey is literally and figuratively a friend of the town in need. The role involves the serious contemplation of depression, suicide, and mortality, moods that certainly reflected Stewart's—and the nation's—recent wartime experiences. Postwar audiences reached out to George Bailey as they reached out to all when the war was over. After the war, the actor was expected to return to film and stardom, though it would never be quite the same.

Stewart then engaged in a series of Westerns and thrillers under the supervision of directors like Anthony Mann and Alfred Hitchcock, respectively. In the Westerns, this time he wasn't the comical sheriff he was in *Destry Rides Again*. Starting with *Broken Arrow* (1950), Stewart's film persona became increasingly unstable. His overwrought emotion transformed easily into troubled, world-weary characters. In the Hitchcock thrillers, he was pushed further to the edge of psychotic behavior, culminating with *Vertigo* (1958).

Perhaps the most famous Stewart character besides George Bailey was Elwood P. Dowd, whose best friend is an invisible 6-foot-3-inch rabbit, the titular character in *Harvey* (1950). This film version of the Pulitzer Prize-winning stage comedy encompasses the lighter aspects of Stewart's prewar persona, combining it with the delusions and alienation of his postwar persona. After reviving *Harvey* on Broadway twice and on television once, Stewart became closely associated with the eccentric Elwood P. Dowd.

After his death, Stewart is fondly remembered for embodying the best tradition of homespun populism, for his modesty and heroic wartime service, and for establishing the dramatic standard in displays of admirable masculine sensitivity and emotional expression during times of crisis.

Bibliography

Bingham, Dennis. *Acting Male*. New Jersey: Rutgers UP, 1994.

Coe, Jonathan. *Jimmy Stewart: A Wonderful Life*. New York: Arcade, 1994.

Dewey, Donald. *James Stewart: A Biography*. Washington, DC: Regnery, 1996.

Molyneaux, Gerard. *James Stewart: A Bio-bibliography*. Westport, CT: Greenwood, 1992.

Robbins, Jhan. *Everybody's Man*. New York: Putnam, 1985.

Robert Baird

Stewart, John (1939-), a native of San Diego, like many other teenagers in the 1950s who started a rock band, was inspired by Elvis Presley. Johnny Stewart and the Furies did not do so well with "Rockin' Anna" (a single recorded in the late '50s) and John moved in a different musical direction after seeing the Kingston Trio in concert. So taken was he with their popular-folk music that he submitted songs to the Kingston Trio, and began a short-lived Trio-clone called the Cumberland Three, making three albums for Roulette Records in 1960. In 1961 he was hired, at $500 per week, to replace the group's outgoing founder, Dave Guard. Popular folk music's days were numbered, however, primarily because of the British Invasion, and in 1967 Stewart was on his own.

Stewart was called upon by Robert Kennedy to accompany him and perform on the presidential campaign trail in 1968. With the assassination of Kennedy, and after some false starts including duos with John Denver and soulmate Buffy Ford, Stewart concentrated on a solo career.

Combining folk with country and rock, Stewart produced a series of albums of pure Americana, with national heritage, the forces of nature, rites of passage, and the quest for social justice as recurring themes, his distinctive baritone suggesting, when it wasn't blatant, a decided sensuality. The albums were well received critically—his *California Bloodlines* (1969) ranking at No. 36 in a 1978 critics poll of the 200 greatest rock albums of all time—but they suffered commercially. Stewart bounced from label to label as recording executives were unable to market his unclassifiable sound, and even the accompaniment of such star-friends as James Taylor, Carole King, Peter Asher, and John Denver failed to fuel buyer interest.

Stewart began evolving into an electric sound, and began to play with Fleetwood Mac's Lindsey Buckingham, resulting in 1979's *Bombs Away Dream Babies* and the single "Gold," Stewart's biggest hit. Stewart was unable to follow up on the success of "Gold," and after further label-hopping he began his own label, Homecoming Records, in 1984. Since then, he has produced a steady stream of song collections, largely catering to his intensely loyal cult following.

Stewart's songs have been covered by many performers—everyone from Robert Goulet to Pat Boone has done "July You're a Woman"—and he has provided gold for such artists as the Monkees and Anne Murray with "Daydream Believer," and Rosanne Cash with "Runaway Train."

Bibliography

Larkin, Colin, ed. *The Guinness Encyclopedia of Popular Music*. Vol. 5. Middlesex, U.K.: Guinness, 1995.

Allen Ellis

Stickball, a New York City street game derived from baseball, is played primarily with a broomstick and a small, hollow rubber ball or tennis ball. Not many young people play stickball today; the limited renaissance the game has enjoyed since the late 1980s is rooted in middle-aged professionals seeking to connect to their past and re-create the sense of community they associate with the foremost game of their youth. Players are still drawn to the competitive simplicity of the game: baseball distilled to its essentials in the pitcher-batter confrontation. Although some purists disapprove, the most active stickball players have organized leagues, standardized rules, and modernized equipment (e.g., many use aluminum bats). Those who now live outside New York have carried the game beyond the city limits, especially to New Jersey and Connecticut.

Stickball's earliest forerunners appeared in the late 18th century, but its heyday was the time from the Great Depression to the late 1950s, when it was a low-cost source of amusement for children who spent hours at play on the city streets. Players needed no expensive equipment such as gloves, bats, and baseballs; they improvised with whatever their surroundings afforded. New York Giants great Willie Mays gave the game some national notoriety in the early 1950s by competing with local youngsters in the streets near the Polo Grounds.

Stickball bats were sawed-off broomsticks or unscrewed mop handles. Having no taper and little weight, they allowed youngsters to generate great bat speed and enjoy the illusion of the power shown by their major league heroes. Typically, batters hit what they called "spaldeens," the inexpensive, pink rubber balls—originally, irregular insides of tennis balls—first sold by the Spalding Company during the Depression. Worn tennis balls were also popular.

The playing field was generally the street but also the schoolyard, and both incorporated the cityscape into the game—walls, roofs, fences, and cars all came into play. Bases, if used, were also part of the street scene—manhole covers, parked cars, garbage cans, the occasional tree. Chalk sometimes created bases or marked boundaries. Long hits and players were defined by the regularly spaced manhole covers or sewer grates—e.g., a "two-sewer man," a "three-sewer homer."

Just as the success of stickball was borne of its ability to simulate the essence of America's national pastime within the confines of financial hardship and urban crowding, so too its demise reflected trends in postwar American culture: (1) Economic prosperity, which removed the need to improvise stripped-down street games; (2) The increase in automobile traffic that clogged the playing fields; (3) The rise of Little League and other organized sports; (4) The increase of street crime, which discouraged parents and children from outdoor play; (5) The advent of television and video, which encouraged indoor activity; and (6) The emergence of basketball as the dominant urban game, the media glamour of which was enhanced by an economic appeal. "Stickball didn't lead to anything," writes novelist Avery Corman. "There were no stickball scholarships."

Bibliography
"Adults Relish the Simplicity of Stickball." *New York Times* 5 Mar. 1989, sec. 1: 56.
Corman, Avery. "Ah, Sweet Sound of Stick on Spaldeen." *New York Times* 24 June 1994.
Cornachio, Donna. "A Schoolyard as Stickball Battleground." *New York Times* 21 July 1994, sec. WC: 10.
Dargan, Amanda, and Steven Zeitlin. *City Play.* New Brunswick: Rutgers UP, 1990.
Kaufman, Michael T. "Stickball, a Metaphor (2 Sewers)." *New York Times* 16 Apr. 1994, sec. A: 25.
"Street Sports Thrive in New York, Even If a Bit of Formality Has Set In." *New York Times* 15 Apr. 1990, sec. 1: 34.

Allen E. Hye

Stine, R(obert) L(awrence) (1943-), has made his literary career in children's and young adult fiction, where he specializes in juvenile horror, a sort of junior version of the fright tales written at the adult level by Stephen King—indeed, Stine has been tabbed "Stephen King for kids."

Stine's major success started in 1989, when he began creating a series of young adult novels with scary plots, elements of gore, horror, and puerile humor, and teenage heroes. Known as the Fear Street Series, these books are targeted to adolescents age 14 and older, and feature such titles as *The Secret Bedroom* (1991), *Welcome to Camp Nightmare* (1992), and *The Werewolf of Fever Swamp* (1993). The author's stories are in such demand because they meld classic horror plots with updated scenes and lifestyles. The series Ghosts of Fear Street, Fear Street Sagas, and Fear Street Seniors have followed.

Stine expanded his output to appeal to the under-14 age group in a series known as the Goosebumps books, which also numbers over 60. These tales are less gruesome and terrifying, but continue to employ softened versions of the elements that have made the Fear Street stories so compelling to young people. Such titles include *Stay out of the Basement* (1992) and *The Ghost Next Door* (1993). The Goosebumps tales were the basis of a television series on the Fox network that premiered in 1995. A second book series debuted in 2000.

Stine entered the domain of adult fiction with *Superstitious* (1995), the story of a northeastern college town that is plagued by a serial killer. It became a film in 1999.

Bibliography
Alderdice, Kit. "R. L. Stine: 90 Million Spooky Adventures." *Publishers Weekly* 17 July 1995: 208-9.
"Ghost Writer." *Life* Dec. 1994: 112.
"R. L. Stine." *People* 25 Dec. 1995: 102-3.
Santow, Dan. "The Scarier the Better." *People* 14 Nov. 1994: 115-16.
Silver, Marc. "Horrors! It's R. L. Stine!" *U.S. News & World Report* 23 Oct. 1995: 95-96.

Liahna Babener

Stockcar Racing in American culture and its place in a sports continuum are both unusual and controversial. Purists of automobile racing have long been divided along American versus European schools of thought. The U.S. is home to many varieties of auto racing, of which stockcar racing is one. In Europe the dominant form of auto racing is Formula One. In the 1990s the World Championship of auto racing is based on a series of Formula One or Grand Prix types of racing that were founded in Europe. Even today, despite World Championship Grand Prix races in Canada, the U.S., and Australia, the majority of races are held on European circuits. In the U.S., while Formula One has a significant following, the most consistently popular form of auto racing is stockcar racing. It is true that the Indianapolis 500, where the Indy cars race (Formula One type machines with turbo charged or enlarged engine capacity), is the world's single most important auto race, but the rise of NASCAR (National Association for Stock Car Auto Racing) over the past 20 years has been a phenomenon in the U.S.

Nevertheless, the image of stockcar racing has been that of the outlaw or the maverick. Writers and social commentators have contributed to the mystique by touting drivers as if they were wild characters succeeding with a gunfighter's mentality. A typical representation appears in Tom Wolfe's eclectic collection of essays *The Kandy-Kolored Tangerine-Flake Streamline Baby* (1965), which includes a wonderfully dramatic vignette on stockcar racer Junior Johnson.

NASCAR was founded in 1947. It now organizes a virtually year-round program of events supporting several competitions. The premier competition is the Winston Cup (see entry), a 29-race series held from February to November. The premier Winston Cup race is the Daytona 500, first run in 1959 and won by Lee Perry.

The first race approved and organized by NASCAR was on the Daytona Beach course on February 15, 1948. The single individual most responsible for the creation of NASCAR was businessman and entrepreneur Bill France. His dream, which has since been realized, was to transform a bump-and-go style of racing on beach or dirt tracks into a legitimate form of circuit racing on good surfaces where paying spectators could watch closely contested races.

The Daytona 500 course has stayed the same over the last two decades apart from a sharp chicane which has been inserted on the northwest bend. The driver with the most wins at Daytona is Richard Petty. He retired from NASCAR in 1994. His lean frame, tall Stetson, and happy-go-lucky television personality in various advertisements made him a recognizable celebrity. Petty's total of seven driving championships and more than 200 NASCAR victories makes him the sport's stellar figure. With four Daytona 500 wins and three consecutive Grand National Championships from 1976 to 1978, Cale Yarborough is also one of the sport's legends.

In the 1990s, drivers such as Bill Elliott, Rusty Wallace, and Dale Earnhardt have achieved prominence and multimillionaire status as a result of their success on the lucrative NASCAR circuit. Ford and Chevrolet have most NASCAR wins with Plymouth, Dodge, and Oldsmobile also being competitive.

NASCAR continues to enjoy exceptional spectator support in the rural South for several reasons. Race days are a composite of carnival, circus, festival, and extravaganza. Each major driver has a concession venue selling a full range of stockcar paraphernalia with T-shirts and hats selling in the millions annually. There is the action on the circuit (at Daytona and Talladega, straightaway speeds are over 200 miles per hour) and at the many side shows attached to the immediate circuit complex. An additional element is that the basic strategy in driving is drafting. This creates a contest that is nose-to-tail theater with the dramatic denouement, called a slingshot, frequently saved for the final lap.

Two movies that offer thematic insights into stockcar racing are Richard Pryor in *Greased Lightning* (1977) and Tom Cruise with *Days of Thunder* (1990). The latter, although lambasted by movie critics, has informative material on car design, and Robert Duvall, in the role of Harry Hogge, gives a feel for the subcultural nuances of life in the fast lane.

In 1994, NASCAR approved gadgets to reduce tire wear, create a new TV viewer perspective, and ease driver stress. These were respectively softer rear springs, a small camera installed on the car roof, and a redesigned steering wheel.

Photo courtesy of Mark Howell.

Race coverage now features several moving in-car cameras that can take viewers into dramatic crashes and provide the driver's perspective. Despite many technological inventions to elevate the margins of safety, stockcar racing remains, however, a perilous profession. There were 6 NASCAR racing deaths from 1990 through May 2000.

Bibliography
Arlott, John, ed. *The Oxford Companion to World Sports and Games*. London: Oxford UP, 1975. 697-98.
Berger, Michael L., and Maurice Duke. "The Automobile." *Handbook of American Popular Culture*. Ed. Thomas Inge. Westport: Greenwood, 1989. 107-32.
Cutter, Robert, and Bob Fendell. *The Encyclopedia of Auto Racing Greats*. Englewood Cliffs: Prentice-Hall, 1973. 224-29.
Flowers, J. "What's New in NASCAR?" *Popular Mechanics* June 1994: 44.
Long, Dustin. "Accidents Provide Keys to NASCAR Driver Safety." *News & Record* (*Greensboro, NC*) 14 May 2000. Online. LEXIS-NEXIS Academic Universe. 26 June 2000.
Morrison, Ian. *Motor Racing: Records, Facts and Champions*. Middlesex, U.K.: Guinness, 1989.

Scott A. G. M. Crawford

Stone, Oliver (1946-), is a highly successful and always controversial director of mainstream feature films, from *Platoon* to *JFK*. But Stone's first real success in Hollywood was as a screenwriter, winning an Oscar for *Midnight Express* (1978) and turning out a diverse portfolio: *Conan the Barbarian* (1982), *Scarface* (1983), *Year of the Dragon* (1985). By the 1990s, Stone was frequently involved as an executive producer with smaller films like *South Central* (1992), *Zebrahead* (1992), and *The Joy Luck Club* (1993). In nearly all his directing and screenwriting, Stone excels in combining harrowing violence, a 1960s generational disdain for authority (which sometimes develops into full-blown paranoia), and powerful, simple conflicts that pit fallible heroes against worlds dominated by violence and deception.

After directing two standard horror features, *Seizure* (1974) and *The Hand* (1981), Stone did not return to directing until *Platoon* (1986), a very successful film that was, above all else, sure of itself and its presentation of America's involvement in Vietnam. A Vietnam combat veteran, Stone brought the minutiae and worldview of the combat soldier to a subgenre that had largely packed the ordinary soldier with political and artistic symbolism too heavy for even the briefest marches. Stone, ironically, had it both ways; his platoon members were both believable and symbolic, one Christ-like, another demonic, with the film's central protagonist, Chris (Charlie Sheen), emblematic of innocence lost to the hell of war. *Platoon*'s popular success was rewarded with eight Oscar nominations and four wins, including best picture, directing, editing, and sound.

By working in subjects overtly political, and then casting them in his own often contradictory and personal vision, Stone consistently stimulates controversy. Just one line of a Pauline Kael review of Stone's *Salvador* (1986) hints at the director's political and aesthetic approach: "What Stone has here is a right-wing macho fantasy joined to a left-leaning polemic." Using Charlie Sheen again as an innocent thrown into a lion's den, Stone peopled *Wall Street* (1987) with an all-star cast, including Michael Douglas, a corrupt and egomaniacal Wall Street investor.

With *Talk Radio* (1988) Stone attempted a noncomedy about radio. True to form, Stone's swirling camera and penchant for emotional confrontations almost make a film out of this inherently aural world of radio. Returning once more to his experience and passion, Stone took Ron Kovic's personal account of his life before, during, and after the Vietnam War—*Born on the Fourth of July* (1989)—and matched *Platoon*'s eight Oscar nominations, winning Stone his third Oscar. *Born*, though, is too often history as comic book: Tom Cruise's intensity frequently overplaying the drama as much as Stone overplays his Manichean vision of a noble counterculture vs. the evil establishment. With *The Doors* (1991) Stone nearly managed to smother the mood and excitement of 1960s' rock and roll by first addressing Jim Morrison's drug abuse and womanizing, and then apologizing for it in his efforts to lionize the performer as a great mystical sage and transcendent artist.

The ultimate Oliver Stone film, which is to say his best elaboration of his own formula—naive innocent beset by violence and mendacity in high places until a conversion experience of enlightenment—is *JFK* (1991). *JFK* packs an emotional wallop. With eight Oscar nominations, *JFK* raised enough public interest and pressure to persuade Congress to open some Kennedy material ahead of its original release dates. Using all-American star Kevin Costner as New Orleans district attorney Jim Garrison, Stone is able to transform Garrison's "true" story of his one-man investigation of the Kennedy assassination into a counterculture version of *Mr. Smith Goes to Washington*.

In 1993, Oliver Stone attempted to redress his own and others' neglect of the Vietnam War from any but the perspective of U.S. troops. In *Heaven and Earth*, based on the experiences of Le Ly Hayslip, Stone attempted an epic conclusion to his Vietnam trilogy taken from a Vietnamese woman's perspective.

Stone's next film, *Natural Born Killers* (1994), attempted to explore and critique the relationship between media and violence by portraying the public celebration of a pair of serial killers played by Juliette Lewis and Woody Harrelson. Many commentators, though, felt Stone added more heat than light to the issue. Stone's *Nixon* (1995) with Anthony Hopkins, characteristically stimulated public debate over Stone's demonization of the late president. Stone's two most recent films sidestep the political and controversial: *U Turn* (1997), a mystery thriller, and *Any Given Sunday* (1999), a behind-the-scenes look at football, starring Al Pacino and Dennis Quaid.

Bibliography

Beaver, Frank. *Oliver Stone: Wakeup Cinema.* Toronto: Maxwell, 1994.

Breskin, David. *Inner Views: Filmmakers in Conversation.* Boston: Faber, 1992.

Hickenlooper, George. *Reel Conversations: Candid Interviews with Film's Foremost Directors and Critics.* Secaucus: Carol, 1991.

Kagan, Norman. *The Cinema of Oliver Stone.* New York: Continuum, 1995.

Mackley-Kallis, Susan. *Oliver Stone's America: "Dreaming the Myth Outward."* Boulder: Westview, 1996.

Robert Baird

See also
Vietnam War Films and Documentaries

Stop-Motion Animation (also known as stop-action photography) involves the slight manipulation of inanimate objects or models between successive photographs of a scene proceeding frame by frame. When the frames are consecutively projected, usually at the standard speed of 24 frames per second in film (25 in television), the models seem to be moving with continuous motion. A single minute of action traditionally can take several days to film.

Willis O'Brien (1886-1962) experimented with special effects using figurines in short trick films in the 1910s. He created the special effects in the first feature-length film to exploit the animation technique, *The Lost World* (1925), which, based on the Arthur Conan Doyle adventure, sported a stop-motion pterodon, an allosaur, and a brontosaur who rampages through London and destroys Tower Bridge. O'Brien perfected the technique in *King Kong* (1933), again using miniature rubber models of dinosaurs and the famous gorilla, and was praised for the personality with which he imbued his creations: Kong's facial expressiveness, for example. O'Brien animated model gorillas again in *Son of Kong* (1933), and in *Mighty Joe Young* (1949), for which he received the Academy Award for special effects. The stop-motion technique became identified with dinosaur "exploitation" films such as O'Brien's *The Beast of Hollow Mountain* (1956), and *The Giant Behemoth* (1959).

Ray Harryhausen (1920-), a protégé of Willis O'Brien, brought breathtaking technical advancement to the use of stop-motion, despite the critical consensus that his work shows fewer of the humanizing qualities achieved by his mentor. After seeing *King Kong* at the age of 13, Harryhausen experimented in his parents' garage with model animation and honed his craft with a proposed 16-millimeter epic, *Evolution*, a World War II training film concerned with bridge building, George Pal's *Puppetoons* in the 1940s, and his own series of Mother Goose stories. O'Brien, to whom Harryhausen had shown his work, hired him as his assistant on *Mighty Joe Young* (1949), after which Harryhausen headed special effects on numerous film projects: *The Beast from 20,000 Fathoms* (1953), in which the live action is combined through rear projection with the animated model, without the use of costly glass paintings as in previous dinosaur adventure films; *Earth vs. the Flying Saucers* (1956), showing a stop-motion destruction of Washington, DC; *The 7th Voyage of Sinbad* (1958), with its memorable Cyclops and its hyped "Dynamation"—the blending of live action with stop-motion animation, in color—a term coined to distinguish this type of animation from cartoons; *Jason and the Argonauts* (1963)—the scene of seven animated skeletons battling three men took over four months to shoot; *One Million Years B.C.* (1966), a remake of the 1940 *One Million B.C.*, this time without the questionable use of live reptiles; *The Valley of Gwangi* (1969), an earlier ill-fated project by O'Brien involving cowboys and dinosaurs; and *Clash of the Titans* (1981), featuring a reptilian Medusa with 200 joints to position during the animation.

Stop-motion animation has been widely used in television, most notably during the 1960s in productions of children's programs such as Art Clokey's *Gumby* and *Davey and Goliath*, and in Christmas specials like *Rudolph the Red-Nosed Reindeer* (1964) and *The Little Drummer Boy* (1968). Advertisements using the technique have unleashed Speedy, the Alka-Seltzer kid, and the California Raisins.

Although computer animation seems to be replacing stop-motion animation, even in dinosaur films like *Jurassic Park* (see entry), Tim Burton's *The Nightmare before Christmas* (1993) effectively employed the nervous excitement characteristic of the stop-motion medium.

Bibliography

Aliens, Dragons, Monsters & Me. Videocassette. Midwich Entertainment, 1990.

Gifford, Denis. *A Pictorial History of Horror Movies.* London: Hamlyn, 1973.

Harryhausen, Ray. *Film Fantasy Scrapbook.* New York: Barnes, 1972.

Michael Delahoyde

See also
Animation

Storz, Todd (1924-1964), was largely responsible for the origination of Top 40 (see Radio Formats), a variation of the music-and-news radio format that emerged during the 1950s. Limited playlists of popular recordings, repeated frequently, distinguished the Top 40 format from the conventional broad array of musical selections featured on independent stations in imitation of network variety. The initially counter-intuitive limited-playlist concept became an ideal vehicle for the youth culture dominated by rock 'n' roll music.

Storz embraced radio as a child in Omaha, NE. He served three years in the U.S. Army Signal Corps, attended a summer radio institute sponsored by NBC at Northwestern University, and worked briefly at radio stations in Kansas and Nebraska.

With his father, Robert, Todd Storz formed the Mid-Continent Broadcasting Company; they purchased their first station, Omaha's KOWH, in 1949. They later acquired stations in New Orleans (WTIX), Kansas City (WHB), Minneapolis (WDGY), Miami (WQAM), Oklahoma (KOMA), and St. Louis (KXOK).

According to radio folklore, sometime in 1955 Todd Storz and associate Bill Stewart noticed customers and waitresses at Omaha restaurants playing some records on jukeboxes while ignoring others. Storz, however, said in 1957 that he first observed the jukebox phenomenon earlier, while in the army. Regardless of origin, by early 1956 Storz had begun to limit the number of songs heard on his Omaha station to the most popular ones for a given week. Music-and-news programmers nationwide copied the Storz Top 40 format after its successful implementation at WHB in Kansas City.

When coupled with high-profile audience promotions and sensational newscasts, Top 40 proved to be the most versatile radio programming innovation to emerge as networks and licensees of major stations shifted resources from radio to television. At the time of Todd Storz's death one month before his 40th birthday, Top 40 had already become a national phenomenon. He received the National Association of Broadcasters Hall of Fame Award in 1987 for his contributions to the radio industry.

Bibliography

MacFarland, David T. *The Development of the Top-40 Radio Format.* New York: Arno, 1973.

Robert M. Ogles

Stout, Rex (1866-1975), the creator of fictional detectives Nero Wolfe and Archie Goodwin, was a Midwesterner with no formal education beyond high school, but whose wide reading, diverse job history, and extensive travels gave him much experience of the world. By 1908 he had settled in New York City and turned to a career writing fiction for the pulps and for literary magazines like *The Smart Set* and *Lippincott's*. Before inventing Nero Wolfe, Stout wrote a series of avant-garde psychological novels to critical acclaim but low sales.

Then, in *Fer-de-Lance* (1934), Stout introduced Nero Wolfe, an eccentric and yet exotic detective, partnered with the street-wise Archie Goodwin, a duo that immediately won a large following and sustained Stout's career through 33 novels and dozens of short stories and novellas until 1975, the year of Stout's death, when *A Family Affair* was published. During his most prolific years (1937-41), Stout wrote seven mysteries without Wolfe, including three featuring Tecumseh Fox. The first of these, *Double for Death* (1939), has one of the author's best plots, but none equaled the Wolfe series.

Bibliography

Anderson, David R. *Rex Stout.* New York: Ungar, 1984.

McAleer, John J. *Rex Stout: A Biography.* Boston: Little, Brown, 1977.

——. *Royal Decree: Conversations with Rex Stout.* Ashton: Pontes, 1983.

Townsend, Guy M., et al., eds. *Rex Stout: An Annotated Primary and Secondary Bibliography.* New York: Garland, 1980.

Robert McColley

Strange Case of Dr. Jekyll and Mr. Hyde, The (1886), a British gothic novella by Robert Louis Stevenson (1850-1894), remains one of literature's most abiding tales. The story of medical experimentation, split personality, and murder has fascinated readers since publication. The story speaks powerfully of the Victorian man and his divided life, but it also established an icon of modern culture.

In Stevenson's tale, the respectable Henry Jekyll attempts to rid himself of his primal side through unorthodox science; in so doing, he unleashes his darker nature, which assumes, in Mr. Hyde, a separate, villainous identity. The story had immediate impact in a post-Darwinian world. Stevenson provides through the character of Hyde a metaphor for the animal within the gentleman that was one implication of Darwin's discoveries. Hyde gains possession of Jekyll's body, overcoming the rational, upstanding Victorian citizen; then Hyde destroys himself. Stevenson taps into the late-19th-century fear that, after Darwin, the human is no longer the moral center of the universe, but is now merely a link in an evolutionary chain.

The story of Jekyll and his other self, Hyde, has gained considerable relevance for the post-Freudian, modern world as well. In this paradigm, Hyde stands for the id, the subliminal irrational force that disrupts conscious life, an idea that has pervaded many 20th-century representations of the story, particularly in a series of cinematic adaptations from Rouben Mamoulian's classic 1932 film *Dr. Jekyll and Mr. Hyde* to Stephen Frears's 1995 *Mary Reilly*.

Bibliography

Geduld, Harry M., ed. *The Definitive Dr. Jekyll and Mr. Hyde Companion.* New York: Garland, 1983.

Veeder, William, and Gordon Hirsch, eds. *Dr. Jekyll and Mr. Hyde after One Hundred Years.* Chicago: U of Chicago P, 1988.

Cyndy Hendershot

Photo courtesy of Popular Culture Library, Bowling Green State University, Bowling Green, OH.

Stratemeyer Syndicate, The, is a consortium of authors who team up to produce adolescent and children's fiction series. Edward Stratemeyer (1863-1930), its founder, was a successful editor and author of boy's fiction who began writing stories in series featuring recurrent characters. Between 1898 and 1926, he composed a number of successful serial stories about boys in military battles (Old Glory, and Soldiers of Fortune series), school and sports (Lakeport, and Dave Porter series), and the widely read Rover Boys.

Stratemeyer saw the advantages of mass producing and marketing these series, but he was unable to execute the entire creative process, so he solicited writers to compose books based on story ideas and outlines that he had devised; he would then edit the finished texts and send them to the publisher. Thus was born the Stratemeyer Syndicate, which has produced over 70 juvenile series since its inception. Because the authors worked anonymously, few are known by name, but some have been identified: Stratemeyer himself wrote some books under his own name and used the pseudonyms Arthur M. Winfield, and Captain Ralph Bonehill for others. Leslie McFarlane wrote the early Hardy Boys; Harriet Adams, Stratemeyer's daughter, is thought to have written some of the Nancy Drew stories (Mildred Benson wrote some as well) and the Dana Girls stories; and Howard Garis (author of the Uncle Wiggly stories) penned the first three dozen Tom Swift books.

Stratemeyer books followed established structural and stylistic formulas. They emphasized danger and mystery while retaining a stable underlying moral order that enabled young readers to experience excitement in the context of psychological safety. The protagonists of these novels were appealing young people who demonstrated courage, valor, and intelligence in their endeavors—usually solving mysteries, undertaking adventure or scientific discovery, and rescuing or vindicating innocents. Mores were generally conservative, stressing honesty, courtesy, perseverance, and acumen, and conventional sex roles were upheld. Individual books in the various series were constructed to reflect the sequential nature of the fiction, alluding to or summarizing prior stories at the outset of each new volume.

When Stratemeyer died in 1930, Harriet Adams continued her father's direction of the syndicate until her own death in 1982. During that time, she oversaw the revision of the books in several of the series (most notably the Hardy Boys and Nancy Drew) to conform to contemporary tastes and appeal to a still younger readership. Though most critics prefer the earlier versions of the stories, the updated books have been very popular. Some of the series lasted only a year or two; many enjoyed decades of production. Other well-known series issued by the syndicate include Ruth Fielding, Baseball Joe, the Dana Girls, the Bobbsey Twins, Motor Boys, Outdoor Girls, Nan Sherwood, and Happy Hollisters. The syndicate, purchased by Simon & Schuster in 1984, is still in the business of publishing serial books.

Bibliography
Billman, Carol, *The Secret of the Stratemeyer Syndicate: Nancy Drew, the Hardy Boys and the Million Dollar Fiction.* New York: Ungar, 1986.
Johnson, Deidre. *Edward Stratemeyer and the Stratemeyer Syndicate*. New York: Twayne, 1993.

Liahna Babener
Jacqueline Reid-Walsh

See also

Adolescent Mystery	Hardy Boys, The
Children's Fiction	Nancy Drew

Streep, Meryl (Mary Louise) (1949-), was born in Summit, NJ. She attended Vassar College, graduating in 1971. From Yale University Drama School she received her MFA in 1975.

Streep made her 1969 New York stage debut in 1969, starring in *The Playboy of Seville*. In 1975, she was in Joseph Papp's *Trelawney of the Wells*. Streep made her television film debut in *The Deadliest Season* (1977) and followed that with her feature film debut in *Julia* (1978). In the same year she starred in the TV miniseries *The Holocaust*. Her career developed quickly and in 1979 she won the Academy Award for the best supporting actress in *Kramer vs. Kramer* and the best actress award in 1982 for *Sophie's Choice*. Through the year 2000, she has received Academy Award nominations for ten other roles.

In her early films, even with limited screen time as in *The Deer Hunter* (1978), she was able to fix her character in the viewer's mind. As her roles developed and she matured in her craft, her characters became more complex and diversified. She first demonstrated her ability to convey that dual nature in *Kramer vs. Kramer*'s estranged wife. Her softness battled with her more brittle and hard-edged liberated character. She was both at once, seducing the viewer who wanted to root for Dustin Hoffman's "good father."

Streep has played a wide range of roles from tragedy to comedy. She starred in *Manhattan* and *The Seduction of Joe Tynan* in 1979. She played a tragic romantic character in *The French Lieutenant's Woman* (1981). In the next year she played the tragic Sophie in *Sophie's Choice* and the lead in the psychological thriller *Still of the Night*.

Her career has been remarkably fruitful, and a catalogue of some of her films provides an indication of her wide acting range: *Silkwood* (1983), *Out of Africa* (1985), *Ironweed* (1987), *A Cry in the Dark* (1988), *She-Devil* (1989), *Postcards from the Edge* (1990), *Defending Your Life* (1991), *The Bridges of Madison County* (1995), *One True Thing* (1998), and *Music of the Heart* (1999).

Bibliography
Maychick, Diana. *Meryl Streep: The Reluctant Superstar.* New York: St. Martin's, 1984.
Pfaff, Eugene E., and Mark Emerson. *Meryl Streep: A Critical Biography.* Jefferson: McFarland, 1987.
Thomas, Nicholas, ed. *International Directory of Films and Filmmakers. Vol. 3. Actors and Actresses.* Detroit: St. James, 1992.

Frank A. Salamone

Streisand, Barbra (1942-), who began her career as a singer in New York City nightclubs, then on Broadway and in record studios performing jazz, blues, pop, and other forms, has also become a noted movie actress. Starring in both comic and serious, both singing and non-singing roles, she is seen as a model for strong-willed, witty, independent women. Her career ranges from the early 1960s feminist movement to the career women of the 1990s. Streisand moves with ease and expertise among a multitude of roles that emphasize her strength and determination as a role model for other women.

Streisand's film career began as an extension of her success in Broadway musicals. Her first movie, *Funny Girl*, was released in 1968. Based on the stage play she had become famous in, Streisand played comedian/dancer Fanny Brice of the Ziegfeld Follies and won the best actress Oscar for her first film role. The other movie Streisand starred in in the 1960s was *Hello, Dolly* (1969), also based on a stage musical.

The 1970s began with Streisand's exotic, new-age role in *On a Clear Day You Can See Forever* (1970), also based on a musical. *The Owl and the Pussycat* (1970), based on a play by Bill Manhoff, presents Streisand at her most callous, bombastic, and sarcastic. Streisand and Ryan O'Neal embarked on their first and most humorous pairing in the highly acclaimed *What's Up, Doc?* (1972).

Up the Sandbox (1972) is Streisand's most experimental, feminist movie—and also her least successful. One of her greatest films, *The Way We Were* (1973), moves Streisand more realistically into the role of radical. Streisand's Katie is a believable pacifist from the days of protest of World War II through the red scare of the McCarthy era. Katie sacrifices her heart to her cause as her life becomes entangled with Hubbell, a military man played by Robert Redford. The movie's memorable title track became an international hit for Streisand and she was nominated for the Oscar for best actress.

For Pete's Sake (1975) is a delightful (though mostly forgotten) romantic comedy. Her next movie, *Funny Lady* (1975), returns to the character of Fanny Brice as her life story continues. Though not as interesting or entertaining as *Funny Girl*, *Funny Lady* shows the story of a struggling actress trying to continue her career despite the end of her marriage and the changes of the entertainment world after the Ziegfeld Follies.

A Star Is Born (1976) pairs Streisand with Kris Kristofferson. It charts the rise and fall of singer John Norman Howard and the rise of wife and singer Esther Hoffman. The year 1979 marked the second pairing of Streisand and O'Neal in *The Main Event*. Also in 1979 was the not-so-memorable *All Night Long*.

The 1980s brought fewer appearances for Streisand in film, but the depth of the roles deepened. *Yentl* (1984) is based on Isaac Singer's story about a Jewish daughter who chooses to study the Talmud disguised as a man. This film also marked Streisand's directorial debut.

Nuts (1987) places Streisand opposite Richard Dreyfuss as a prostitute who has killed one of her patrons after he attacked her. Streisand portrays with depth a woman who has been the victim of sexual abuse and turned to prostitution after a failed marriage.

The 1990s produced Streisand's memorable movie with Nick Nolte, *Prince of Tides* (1991), and the romantic comedy *The Mirror Has Two Faces* (1996), both of which Streisand also directed.

Bibliography
Castell, James. *The Films of Barbra Streisand.* St. Paul: Greenhaven, 1978.
Riese, Randall. *Her Name Is Barbra: An Intimate Portrait of the Real Barbra Streisand.* New York: St. Martin's, 1994.
Spada, James. *Barbra, The First Decade: The Films and Career of Barbra Streisand.* New York: Carol, 1974.
——. *Streisand: Her Life.* New York: Crown, 1995.
Swenson, Karen. *Barbra: The Second Decade.* Secaucus: Citadel, 1986.

Mark K. Fulk

Stubblefield, Nathan B. (1859-1928). Every year, the city of Murray, KY, issues a wheel tax sticker emblazoned with the motto "Birthplace of Radio." This claim is due to the work of inventor Nathan B. Stubblefield in the late 19th and early 20th centuries.

The son of a lawyer, Stubblefield was educated at the county Male and Female Institute and pursued a career in farming. As a teenager, he became interested in electrical, telegraph, and telephone circuits and regularly read periodicals such as *Scientific American* and *Electrical World*. He was especially fascinated with the work of Alexander Graham Bell and Amos Alonzo Dolbear and began to replicate their experiments. By the early 1880s, he had designed a functional mechanical telephone, for which he received a U.S. patent in 1887.

His later experiments involved magnetic induction and ground conduction, and these technologies formed the basis of his wireless developments. In 1892, three years before Marconi transmitted Morse code, Stubblefield demonstrated a verifiable wireless telephone, probably a large induction coil transmitter, possibly powered by his patented earth cell electrical battery, with a passive coil receiver.

In 1901, he sold a ground conduction apparatus to the Wireless Telephone Company of America for 500,000 shares of stock and agreed to conduct public demonstrations to promote the sale of more stock. The first of these, on the public square in Murray on New Year's Day, 1902, involved sending voice and music from two transmitters to multiple receivers simultaneously. Although there were no radio fre-

quencies or electromagnetic waves involved, these were among the earliest wireless broadcasts.

Although it is doubtful that Nathan B. Stubblefield invented radio, he was briefly considered Marconi's peer. In a period when the word "wireless" encompassed all communication devices without wires, and the term "radio" was seldom if ever used in this context, Nathan B. Stubblefield was one of several legitimate scientists who helped develop this technology.

Bibliography
Fawcett, Waldon. "The Latest Advance in Wireless Telephony." *Scientific American* 24 May 1902: 363.
Hoffer, Thomas W. "Nathan B. Stubblefield and His Wireless Telephone." *Journal of Broadcasting* 15 (Winter 1971): 317-29.
Kahaner, Larry. "Who Really Invented Radio?" *73 Magazine* Dec. 1980: 36-41.
McElroy, Gil. "Before Spark." *QST* Jan. 1994: 57-59.

Robert H. Lochte

Studio Star System, The, during the 1930s and 1940s, enabled Hollywood production companies to create a standardized movie product and to have exclusive control over actors and actresses working in the industry. The studios involved in the system included the majors, Warner Bros., RKO, Paramount, MGM, and Twentieth Century-Fox; the minors, Columbia, Universal, and United Artists; and production facilities owned by independent moviemakers like Walter Wanger and David O. Selznick. During this period, known as the Hollywood studio era, the movie-going public identified screen stars with studios and, at the local exhibition level, with specific theaters.

Most studio contracts for major stars were for up to a seven-year period, but the studios reserved the right to drop or renew them every year. Stars were not allowed to renegotiate their contracts. The agreements gave the studio exclusive rights to the star's name and likeness, the right to assign the star to any movie (a studio could sue for breach of contract if a star refused), and the right to loan out the star to another studio. Many famous stars, such as Bette Davis and James Cagney, often fought with the studios over control of their image and were, for a time, suspended from making pictures; no other studio would dare offer a suspended actor work. The contracts were seen, by major stars, as inhibiting, but for supporting stars, like Warner Bros.' Guy Kibbee, they provided a guarantee of steady employment. Kibbee would often be able to work on two or three pictures simultaneously, providing the studio with the opportunity to use his character-type—a bald, stocky, middle-aged man—often in various secondary roles. Occasionally, Kibbee was also available to be the star in a studio B movie.

When a contract was signed, the studio would assign a role to a star in a production and wait for reactions from preview and selected audiences. If the reactions were favorable, the studio would cast the star in a similar role. For example, when supporting actor Humphrey Bogart began to play gangsters, "heavies," or tough-guy roles at Warner Bros. and earned plaudits from audiences, the studio decided that he would solely perform these roles. After his leading actor, tough-guy performances in *High Sierra* and *The Maltese Falcon* (both 1941) made him a marketable star, Bogart had to be assigned pictures that contributed to and enhanced this image. Also, now that he was a star, it was thought to be important that the audience root for his characters as well. *Casablanca* (1942) strengthened his star persona. The release of *The Treasure of the Sierra Madre* (1948), however, irritated Bogart's fans because he played an evil, greedy character, and this did not conform to his star image. Though "casting against type" was sometimes successful, it was a risky business to play with audience expectations. And the studios, who had cultivated and created these expectations in their public, were inclined to agree with them.

All studio departments had a hand in the development of star images; from the screenwriters, who were asked to develop a movie's character so that it would fit a star's persona better, to the publicity and advertising managers, who would spread gossipy information (true or false) about a star's private life, the primary efforts of the studio personnel were to create and maintain the images of the stars. The studios decided that it was their duty to market their product in the most profitable manner; the stars were under contract and had no say in the matter.

At one time or another during the 1930s, according to studio records and fan magazines, Paramount owned the contracts of Claudette Colbert, Gary Cooper, Carole Lombard, and Fred MacMurray; Columbia had Jean Arthur, George Bancroft, and Melvyn Douglas; RKO had Fred Astaire, Katharine Hepburn, and Ginger Rogers; Warner Bros. had Humphrey Bogart, Bette Davis, Paul Muni, and Edward G. Robinson; Twentieth Century-Fox had Don Ameche, Tyrone Power, and Loretta Young; MGM had John and Lionel Barrymore, Greta Garbo, Clark Gable, Myrna Loy, William Powell, and James Stewart; Universal had Irene Dunne, Boris Karloff, and John Wayne; and United Artists had Ronald Colman, Joel McCrea, Merle Oberon, and co-founder Charles Chaplin.

Bibliography

Balio, Tino, ed. *The American Film Industry*. Rev. ed. Madison: U of Wisconsin P, 1985.

Griffith, Richard. *The Movie Stars*. Garden City, NY: Doubleday, 1970.

Kindem, Gorham, ed. *The American Movie Industry*. Carbondale: Southern Illinois UP, 1982.

Sklar, Robert. *Movie-Made America*. New York: Vintage, 1975.

Walker, Alexander. *Stardom: The Hollywood Phenomenon*. New York: Stein & Day, 1970.

Richard L. Testa, Jr.

Sturges, Preston (1898-1959), was a filmmaker who could genuinely be called an auteur. From 1940 through 1943, he directed, wrote, and oversaw virtually every aspect of eight remarkable films that are noteworthy for their zany characterizations, social satire, verbal wit combined with slapstick humor, and off-beat style.

Born Edmund Preston Biden in Chicago, he was adopted by his mother's second husband, Solomon Sturges, a Chicago stockbroker. Preston and his mother took up semi-permanent residence in Europe, where Preston experienced the world of high culture.

After World War I, he went to New York and soon felt the attraction of the theater. While recovering from a near-fatal attack of appendicitis, he began reading Brander Matthews's *A Study of the Drama*. With characteristic energy and speed, he wrote a domestic drama called *The Guinea Pig*, which was produced by the Wharf Players of Provincetown, MA, and ran there for a week in the summer of 1928. Spurred by this success, Sturges wrote another play in the following year. *Strictly Dishonorable* ran for 557 performances on Broadway and earned for Sturges a reputation as one of America's most talented young playwrights.

In the 1930s he moved to Hollywood and began writing for the movies. The film that established his place as one of the world's most respected, and eventually most highly paid, screenwriters was *The Power and the Glory* (1933), which starred Spencer Tracy. Sturges's script marked a startling departure from the standard Hollywood mode by beginning at the funeral of the main character and working backward.

While not a great popular success, *The Power and the Glory* heightened Sturges's determination to control and direct the films made from his scripts. For a while, he was frustrated in his attempts to move beyond being the writer, even of such notable and, in many respects, daring films like *The Good Fairy* (1934), *Diamond Jim* (1935), *Easy Living* (1937), and *Remember the Night* (1939). In 1939, he proposed an unusual deal to Paramount Pictures. He would sell them for $1 a script he had written in 1933 called *The Vagrant*, if he were allowed to direct the film. Paramount agreed, and Sturges began work on the renamed *The Great McGinty* (1940). Dan McGinty, an American bartender in a Latin American republic, tells a patron that he once was governor of a great state, and a flashback starts the account of how that unlikely event occurred. Inverting the conventional story of the good man ruined by a single bad act, Sturges makes his hero an amoral operator whose downfall is effected by one decent gesture. Like the Sturges films that would follow in the next five years, *McGinty* is populated with a glittering array of minor characters played by actors like William Demarest, Frank Moran, Esther Howard, Jimmy Conlin, and Vic Potel, who would form the nucleus of the group that would appear repeatedly in Sturges's films.

The Great McGinty was both a popular and a critical success, but before it opened Sturges was already at work directing a second film, *Christmas in July* (1940). Based on one of his old play scripts, *A Cup of Coffee*, this film tackles the basis of the American dream: perseverance and hard work will always lead to success.

Sturges's third film, *The Lady Eve* (1940), is sometimes called the last of the '30s genre of screwball comedies. This movie extends his challenging, iconoclastic themes into the world of the rich and famous.

In *Sullivan's Travels* (1941), Sturges turned the camera lens around and focused on filmmaking and a filmmaker in some ways very much like himself. John L. Sullivan, the director of profitable film comedies like *Hey, Hey in the Hayloft* and *Ants in Your Plants* of 1939, is dissatisfied and wants to make serious films of social significance, but realizes that he lacks first-hand knowledge of suffering and poverty. Like a modern Gulliver, Sullivan sets out to experience the world but finds that he is hopelessly inadequate in his efforts to survive daily pain and concludes, after a stint on a chain gang, that countering pain by putting some laughter into the world is noble work after all.

Palm Beach Story (1942) contains many allusions to incidents in Sturges's personal life, yet it is more than simply a masked biography. The theme of chance as the determinant of events is again prominent. Casting against perceived type and against the advice of studio heads, Sturges cast Rudy Vallee in the movie. Vallee's superb performance exemplifies Sturges's ability to cast roles shrewdly and imaginatively.

The next film Sturges made was a departure from his usual comic mode and is generally acknowledged as inferior to its predecessors. *The Great Moment* (1942), originally *Triumph over Pain*, is a fictionalized biography of W. T. G. Morton, a dentist who developed anesthesia. Worried about the film's grim, pessimistic subject, studio heads withheld its release until 1944 after Sturges's next two films, *The Miracle of Morgan's Creek* and *Hail the Conquering Hero*. Both of these films attacked the notions that small-town life is somehow purer than other kinds of existence and, daringly during the war years, that selfless patriotism can somehow outweigh self-interest in human affairs.

After *Hail the Conquering Hero*, Sturges's contract with Paramount expired, and he formed what he thought was a partnership with Howard Hughes to produce and direct films independently. The power of the purse remained with Hughes, however, and the partnership was never equally balanced. Hughes's interference kept Sturges from realizing his intentions in their first venture, *The Sin of Harold Diddlebock* (1946), which Hughes eventually recalled from circulation, re-edited, and re-released in 1951 under the title *Mad Wednesday*.

Sturges made two other films at 20th Century-Fox, the under-appreciated *Unfaithfully Yours* (1948) and the listless *The Beautiful Blonde from Bashful Bend* (1948), and one film in France in French and English versions, *Les Carnets du Major Thompson* [*The French They Are a Funny Race*] (1955). When he died of a heart attack at the Algonquin Hotel in New York, Sturges was in severe financial difficulty but was preparing to return to Broadway to direct a new comedy called *The Golden Fleecing*.

Bibliography

Curtis, James. *Between Flops: A Biography of Preston Sturges*. New York: Harcourt, 1982.

Farber, Manny (with W. S. Poster). "Preston Sturges: Success in the Movies." *Negative Space: Manny Farber on the Movies*. 1954. New York: Praeger, 1971.

Henderson, Brian, ed. *Five Screenplays by Preston Sturges*. Berkeley: U of California P, 1985.

Jacobs, Diane. *Christmas in July: The Life and Art of Preston Sturges*. Berkeley: U of California P, 1992.

Sturges, Sandy, ed. *Preston Sturges by Preston Sturges*. New York: Simon & Schuster, 1990.

James Shokoff

Subliminal Persuasion is a term that typically evokes the image of mass covert control carried out by an elite group of business people and politicians through the use of messages that people cannot see or hear. These messages bypass conscious recognition and evaluation and communicate directly to the unconscious level of drives, emotions, and desires. This image has its basis in popular representations in TV, film, books, and news media. Its modern conception is best represented by the popular books of Wilson Bryan Key, in particular *Subliminal Seduction* (1973.) Key maintains that the mass media daily massages and manipulates tens of millions of people without their conscious awareness. According to Key, subliminal techniques are in widespread use by media, advertising, and public relations agencies, industrial and commercial corporations, and by the federal government.

"Subliminal" means "below the level of conscious awareness" (the Latin word *limen* meaning "boundary" or "threshold"). A subliminal stimulus refers to the situation where the energy of a stimulus has been so reduced, either by increasing the speed of its presentation or by weakening its physical intensity, that it cannot be perceived by a receiver, but is still objectively present. To be considered subliminal requires that receivers be quite unable to become aware of the stimulus, even if they wanted to and were told beforehand it was present.

Psychologists have long considered subliminal persuasion a theoretically baseless and potentially harmful concept. In the marketing and advertising literature, the conclusion is the same; the presence of a phenomenon even remotely reminiscent of the subliminal story has never been demonstrated. Overall, the scientific consensus is that subliminal stimuli are too weak to profoundly affect attitudes, beliefs, and behavior on a large scale.

Despite its scientific discreditation, the idea of subliminal persuasion remains vibrant in U.S. popular culture, and surveys consistently report that the general public is aware of the term and believes the "technique" to be in use by advertisers and the mass media. The basis of this idea has its roots in a singular definitive event: a press conference held on September 12, 1957, in New York City, to unveil a new subliminal projection technology that would revolutionize advertising by promoting products directly to the needs and desires of the unconscious mind. The speaker was James M. Vicary, a market researcher, who claimed to have demonstrated that subliminal messages flashed on a movie screen could induce audiences to buy more popcorn and Coca-Cola. Since that time, the popular notion has remained and become increasingly mythologized with the passing of the years.

Reports of subliminal persuasion in the news media reinforce the notion of covert control. In the late 1970s and early 1980s, it was reported that a device known as the "black box," itself a name implying mysterious power, could mingle the bland music found in department stores with subliminal anti-theft messages such as "I am honest" and "I will not steal," according to *Time*, September 10, 1979. The hit movie *The Exorcist* was reported to have included subliminal images of a death mask, which some claim significantly contributed to extreme feelings of terror and sickness. Perhaps the best-known news event involving subliminal persuasion was the case of two teenagers, Raymond Belknap and James Vance, who, in 1985, attempted to commit suicide after listening to the Judas Priest album *Stained Class*. This case built upon a still-popular belief that subliminal messages are embedded in rock music for questionable ends.

Popular media representations typically reinforce and exaggerate the "power" of subliminal persuasion techniques to control an individual's thoughts and behavior. For example, in the television series based on H. G. Wells's *The War of the Worlds,* aliens implant subliminal messages into a rock album with the intent of brainwashing and controlling the protagonist. In John Carpenter's movie *They Live* (1988), aliens control the human population of Earth by subliminal messages contained in all forms of mass media.

Bibliography

Dixon, Norman. F. *Subliminal Perception: The Nature of a Controversy.* London: McGraw-Hill, 1971.

Key, Wilson Bryan. *Subliminal Seduction: Ad Media's Manipulation of a Not So Innocent America.* New York: Signet, 1974.

Moore, T. E. "The Case against Subliminal Manipulation." *Psychology and Marketing* 5.4 (1988): 297-316.

Vokey, J. R., and J. D. Read. "Subliminal Messages: Between the Devil and the Media." *American Psychologist* 40.11 (1985): 1231-39.

Zanot, E. J., J. D. Pincus, and E. J. Lamp. "Public Perceptions of Subliminal Advertising." *Journal of Advertising* 12.1 (1983): 39-45.

Gary P. Radford

Summer, Donna (1948-), born Adrian Donna Gaines, became known as the "Queen of Disco" during the late 1970s. Influenced by traditional African-American spirituals and gospel music, as well as rhythm and blues, Summer paid her dues in the musical theater. While performing in *Hair* and *Godspell* in Munich, Germany, she met Giorgio Moroder, a Swiss composer and producer. Together, they developed a slick, synthesizer-driven brand of rhythmic pop that became the most widely known disco sound of the decade. All the Summer/Moroder music was highly studio-mixed and produced, and aimed at an audience of deejays, who could easily mix the reliable beat, as well as to dancing disco aficionados, who enjoyed the easy danceability of Summer's music.

After some success in Europe, Summer came to the attention of American audiences in 1975 with the gasping, sighing sensuality of "Love to Love You, Baby." Its vocal rendition of a woman in the throes of sexual ecstasy, ending in wailing climax, shocked the more conservative segments of the music-loving public and propelled Summer to instant fame. Moroder's 17-minute remix of the song also launched the new medium of the 12-inch dance single. Summer continued by producing a string of record-setting, danceable

disco hits in the 1970s. The repetitive, complex, mechanical beats of the synthesizer, accompanied by both instrumental and synthesizer-produced melodies, were an integral part of their success.

As disco peaked in the late 1970s, so did Summer's career. From 1978 to 1980, she broke into the Top 10 with eight successive hits. Songs such as "I Feel Love"—with its rapid beat and the seemingly interminable wailing of Summer's powerful voice—were on the cutting edge of an increasingly technological musical sound. "Bad Girls" in 1979 iconized prostitutes while ostensibly sympathizing with their plight. Of course, many Americans were too busy dancing to pay attention to the lyrics.

When disco began to wane during the 1980s, Summer tried a variety of different styles, but found that danceable pop was the niche that fit her best. *The Wanderer* (1980) was a tough-sounding album influenced by British punk rock and American New Wave; after its release, Summer split with producer Moroder and turned to veteran producer Quincy Jones for her next album. Her new styles were not well received, either by the public or the critics.

Despite her changes in style, the abrupt and loudly negative reaction against disco stereotyped her as a disco has-been, and Summer's star was on the wane for several years. She countered in 1983 by returning to her dance roots with "She Works Hard for the Money." Although using the same snappy, danceable, pop beat as disco, the instrumentation and pace were changed to reflect the new style in dance-rock, influenced equally by Euro-Disco and American rock. Two relatively unsuccessful albums followed, and many critics and fans deemed that Summer had reached the end of the line. But in 1989 "This Time I Know It's for Real," from *Another Place and Time,* became a hit. Summer's revived popularity was due not only to her new production and writing teams' careful reworking of her heavily-produced, synth-pop sound, but also to a general revival of "trash disco" in the late eighties, which introduced a new generation to Summer's music.

Bibliography

Gaar, Gillian G. *She's a Rebel: The History of Women in Rock & Roll.* Seattle: Seal, 1992.

Haskin, James, and Jim Stifle. *Donna Summer: An Un-Authorized Biography.* Boston: Little, Brown, 1983.

Larkin, Colin, ed. *The Guinness Encyclopedia of Popular Music.* Vol. 5. Middlesex, U.K.: Guinness, 1995.

Joe Thomas
Don Bacigalupi

Superman Movies, from the 1951 *Superman and the Mole Men* opened, starring George Reeves as the "man of steel" and Phyllis Coates as his "almost love interest" Lois Lane, through the four *Superman* movies released between 1978 and 1987, are a small part of an enormous cultural phenomenon. Even in the 1990s, the character is a mainstay of different media, including television, multiple comic books, newspaper strips, novels, and merchandise.

From his introduction in 1938, Superman has been immensely popular. Superman was the product of the creativity of Jerry Siegel (writer) and Joe Shuster (artist) and he officially premiered in *Action Comics* No. 1, June 1938. By 1940, Superman had a radio show, in 1941, he was in animated cartoons, and in 1942, a novel based on his exploits appeared. In 1948 and 1950, Columbia Studios produced two extremely successful serials featuring Superman before the character became the subject of the 1951 feature film, which led to Superman's first appearance on television (see next entry).

Despite his lasting popularity, Superman endured a bit of a dry spell in the 1960s and early 1970s, surviving primarily in a variety of top-selling comic books. A Broadway musical and various sequels to the television series came and went unimpressively. Then, in 1973, father-and-son team Alex and Ilya Salkind began to discuss producing a new Superman film with their partner Pierre Spengler.

Superman: The Movie opened in 1978 amidst an enormous publicity blitz. The slogan "you will believe a man can fly" was everywhere and DC Comics, owner of the Superman character, ran advertisements and a movie-related contest in all of their publications.

The movie is fairly true to the comic book version of the origins of Superman. The film opens with Superman's father, Jor-el (Marlon Brando), sentencing three criminals to banishment. These three criminals (Terence Stamp, Sarah Douglas, Jack O'Halloran) return to wreak havoc in *Superman II*. Jor-el then rescues his son from their home planet Krypton's explosion in the nick of time. The boy is rocketed to Earth and found by Mr. and Mrs. Kent, who name him Clark

Clark (Christopher Reeve) eventually goes off to Metropolis to become an ace newspaper reporter. He works alongside the beautiful, intelligent, and strong-willed Lois Lane (Margot Kidder). After introducing Superman to the ways of the world in a humorous and touching montage (called in the script "Superman's first night"), the movie concentrates on his rivalry with evil genius Lex Luthor (Gene Hackman). Luthor tries to destroy the world and (of course) Superman saves it.

The screenplay, credited to Mario Puzo, David Newman, Leslie Newman, and Robert Benton (from a story by Puzo), mixed comedy, fantasy, and drama convincingly. Richard Donner's direction (his most famous previous work was *The Omen*, 1976) was powerful, and the entire movie managed to mix a feeling of comic book exaggeration with the reality of modern America. Critics and audiences lauded the performances; convincing special effects and a triumphant score by John Williams all assisted in *Superman*'s smashing success.

Superman II was not released in the U.S. until 1981 (a year after international release). The plans of Spengler and the Salkinds to shoot it simultaneously with the first movie did not go perfectly, and they ended up re-shooting large chunks of the film. In fact, direction credit for *Superman II* went to Richard Lester, and the screenplay credit did not include Robert Benton.

Again the film was met with generally favorable reviews. In the sequel, the three briefly viewed villains of *Superman* return from banishment and try to destroy the Earth (seeking vengeance on Jor-el's son). This is made easier when Superman (temporarily) renounces his powers for the love of Lois Lane. The villains go on to an extraordinarily violent spree, but *Superman II* retained enough of the energy, spirit, and fun of its predecessor to be a hit.

By contrast, *Superman III* (1983), though also directed by Lester and written by the Newmans, was a flop. The film revolved around the criminal machinations of Gus Gorman (Richard Pryor) and magnate Ross Webster (Robert Vaughn). The special effects were still impressive, but the script was not. In the movie, computer genius Gorman discovers how to make Superman's one weakness, kryptonite, synthetically (with one design flaw, which causes Superman to split into an evil and good personality), while billionaire Webster tries to take over the world.

The Salkinds tried to reinvigorate the series in 1984 with a "sequel" called *Supergirl* (played by Helen Slater), but the movie was a bomb. By the fourth *Superman* film, Spengler and the Salkinds were no longer at the helm. This time producers Menahem Golan and Yoram Globus (known for producing expensive but poor quality genre pictures) teamed up with director Sydney J. Furie (who had directed the air combat action film *Iron Eagle*). *Superman IV: The Quest for Peace* (1987) again starred Christopher Reeve and Gene Hackman, this time with Reeve sharing screenplay credits (along with Lawrence Konner and Mark Rosenthal). Margot Kidder returned as Lois Lane and was joined by Mariel Hemingway as sexy Lacy Warfield. Though *The Quest for Peace* did not do terribly well at the box office, it was considered a cut above *Superman III*.

In addition to launching the career of Reeve before it was cut short by his 1995 riding accident, identifying Kidder with the one role, and presenting both Brando and Hackman to a new, younger audience, *Superman* established a new standard of verisimilitude with its flying effects. Unlike *Star Wars* (1977), these effects involved real people in a (nearly) real world. A variety of complicated techniques allowed viewers to see Superman flying from takeoff to landing, with every angle in between.

Bibliography

Meyers, Richard. *The World of Fantasy Films*. New York: Barnes, 1980.

Nash, Jay Robert, and Stanley Ralph Ross. *The Motion Picture Guide*. Chicago: Cinebooks, 1983, 1988.

Petrou, David Michael. *The Making of* Superman: The Movie. New York: Warner, 1978.

Michael Goldberg

Superman Television Productions began with *The Adventures of Superman* (1951-57), a live-action version of the popular comic-book story with George Reeves and Phyllis Coates reprising their roles from the 1951 film *Superman and the Mole Men* (see preceding entry). When that series ended, the comic book publishers continued their efforts to keep Superman on the small screen. Whitney Ellsworth, the National Periodicals editor who became executive producer of the TV series, remained in Hollywood to promote other comics-based projects. A pilot was shot for *Superpup* in 1958, with four-foot actors in canine costumes as "Bark Bent" and "Perry Bite." In 1961, he tried a pilot for *The Adventures of Superboy*, starring Johnny Rockwell in the Man of Steel's boyhood exploits. But neither show had any takers.

In 1965, Fred Silverman, head of children's programming at CBS, sought adventure cartoons to replace the older puppet shows and slapstick cartoons on Saturday morning. He purchased rights for Superman from National (today DC Comics) and awarded production chores to the newly formed Filmation Studios. *The New Adventures of Superman* debuted September 10, 1966, with Bud Collyer, Superman's radio voice of the 1940s, reprising his role; the radio show's announcer (and Bluto of the Popeye cartoons), Jackson Beck, as narrator; and the comics' editor Mort Weisinger as story consultant. Filmation overcame the problems of animating human figures by rotoscoping much of the movement. The timing of the show was propitious: while it was in production, the Batman craze took off in January 1966, creating new demand for comic book heroes.

Superman helped pull CBS to first place on Saturday mornings. The series brought many of the comics' arch-villains to the screen, including evil scientist Lex Luthor, Brainiac, and Mr. Mxyzptlk. The Parasite, who drained people's life energy, was actually killed by Superman, who forced more of his energy on him than he could handle. The series was supported by an episode in the life of Superboy in Smallville. Next season, the show expanded to *The Superman/Aquaman Hour of Adventure*, with episodes starring other DC characters like the Flash, Hawkman, and the entire Justice League of America. In 1968, when the live-action *Batman* was canceled, CBS picked up its TV rights and debuted *The Batman/Superman Hour*.

In the 1970s, cartoon producers had to meet new standards imposed on children's TV content. Hanna-Barbera adapted Superman and company to the new rules by adding a heap of moralizing. *Super Friends* debuted September 8, 1973, with Superman, Wonder Woman, Aquaman, Batman and Robin teaming with teenagers Wendy, Marvin and Wonder Dog against some menace, which usually turned out to be an accident on the part of someone who "really meant no real harm."

Super Friends remained on the air for several years. 1977's *All New Super Friends* dropped Wendy and Marvin for the alien Wonder Twins and their space monkey. *Challenge of the Super Friends* (1978) added several heroes and brought in heavy-duty heavies like Luthor, Sinestro, and Bizarro in the Legion of Doom (now the name of a notorious group of computer hackers). *Super Friends: The Legendary Super Powers Show* (1984) and *The Super Powers Team: Galactic Guardians* (1985) added Jack Kirby's best villain, Darkseid and his cohort Desaad (how that name ever got past the censors is a mystery). In the comic *New Gods*, Darkseid was lord of the planet Apokolips and sought the parts of the Anti-Life Equation. On TV he was more of a Ming the Merciless type who mostly wanted to marry Wonder Woman.

DC gave Superman a thorough revamping in 1986. They charged writer-artist John Byrne with remaking his history, discarding baggage like Streaky the Super-Cat or his whole career as Superboy, and leaving Clark Kent's parents alive. This was the *Superman* animated by Ruby-Spears for CBS in 1988. The series was developed by comics editor Marv Wolfman, but it was put in too early a time slot, and only lasted one season.

The same year, Ilya Salkind, co-producer of the *Superman* movies (see preceding entry), created a syndicated *Superboy* series, in spite of DC having "retconned" him out of existence (retconning is a comics fan's term for stories that create "retroactive continuity," declaring that the past 50 years of a character's history are nullified). The show was filmed at Disney's Florida studios, and told of Clark Kent's student journalism days at Shuster University (named for Joe Shuster, one of Superman's creators). The show lasted two seasons with two lead actors, John Hames Newton, then Gerald Christopher.

Despite the recent failure of CBS's expensive live-action *Flash* series, DC Comics, its corporate parent, Warner Bros., and ABC produced Superman's first prime-time series in 1993. The title, *Lois & Clark: The New Adventures of Superman*, indicated creator Deborah Joy LeVine's emphasis on Clark Kent's (Dean Cain) normal life as a big Boy Scout from Smallville who just happens to be faster than a speeding bullet. Lois Lane (Teri Hatcher) is a tougher reporter than played before, perfectly capable of getting into and out of trouble by herself, except when making cow eyes at Superman. The romantic triangle of Clark, Lois, and Superman has a self-satirical quality that invites comparisons with the TV show *Moonlighting*. Lex Luthor (John Shea) was modernized to a corrupt entrepreneur with the worst qualities of Donald Trump and Bill Gates. The 1990s Perry White (Lane Smith) now invokes the shade of Elvis instead of "Great Caesar's Ghost."

While *Lois & Clark* was popular throughout its four-year run, it could not replace George Reeves's series as the "real" *Superman* in the public eye. The original series still pulls viewers, judging from its successful run on Nickelodeon.

Bibliography

Cawley, John, and Jim Korkis, eds. "News." *Cartoon Quarterly* Winter 1988: 3.

——. *Saturday Morning TV*. New York: Dell, 1988.

Grossman, Gary. *Superman: Serial to Cereal*. New York: Popular Library, 1976.

Lenburg, Jeff. *The Encyclopedia of Animated Cartoons*. New York: Facts on File, 1991.

Marx, Barry, Thomas Hill, and Joey Cavalieri. *Fifty Who Made DC Great*. New York: DC Comics, 1985.

Mark McDermott

Suspense (1942-1962), "radio's outstanding theatre of thrills," was radio's foremost dramatic anthology during the 1940s and 1950s. Countless millions of listeners tuned in again and again to hear some of radio's most creative and spine-chilling programs.

Through the years, the program's directors and time slots changed many times, but the basic plot formula remained fairly consistent. Generally the stories focused on an average person caught up, usually by coincidence, in a realistic life-threatening situation whose outcome was in doubt until the very end of the show. In most episodes, the evildoers were either apprehended by the authorities because of some fatal mistake they had committed or they came to some deservedly horrible end, once again proving the time-honored principle that "crime does not pay." Occasionally stories of the occult or supernatural were featured, and in a few episodes science-fiction themes were utilized.

Several of the more outstanding producer/directors (there were 14 different directors during the show's 20-year run) left their own unique stamp on the series. William Spier was the first regular director (1942-48) and produced some of the finest shows in the series. "Sorry, Wrong Number," the most famous of all *Suspense* stories, was first produced by Spier, as was "Dead Ernest," which won the Peabody Award for outstanding radio drama in 1946. Spier was responsible for recruiting most of the top stars in Hollywood to appear on the series.

Elliot Lewis's major contribution as director (1950-54) was to shift the story from the focus on everyday situations with an occasional excursion into the supernatural to true stories of famous crimes and criminals. Lewis also occasionally turned to dramatizations of literary classics like his two-part versions of Shakespeare's *Othello*, Wilkie Collins's *The Moonstone,* and Mary Shelley's *Frankenstein*. Another characteristic of Lewis's tenure as director was his frequent use of comedians and singers in serious roles, although he was not the first to employ this type of off-beat casting. Other outstanding directors who served stints on the series included Norman Macdonnell and William N. Robson.

The music and sound effects, so crucial to quality radio drama, were equally outstanding. Berne Surrey, sound-effects technician, was given much leeway in creating the backgrounds for many unusual stories. Many sound effects had to be improvised on the spot if they weren't working effectively. Several of the medium's top composers and musicians were also involved in the series, including Bernard Herrmann and Lud Gluskin.

Bibliography

Price, Tom. *The Ultimate Log of* Suspense: *CBS's Radio Thriller, 1942-1962*. Salinas: Price, 1987.

Gary A. Yoggy

Susskind, David (1920-1987), was one of the most prolific producers in the history of television. The production company Talent Associates, formed in 1948 by Susskind and his partner, Al Levy, yielded a remarkable body of television programming that illuminates the evolution of broadcasting and popular culture in post-World War II America. From *Mr. Peepers* to *The Armstrong Circle Theater*, from the highbrow *Play of the Week* to the tawdry game show *Supermarket Sweep*, from the camp spy spoof *Get Smart* to the lavish miniseries *Eleanor and Franklin,* Susskind-produced television was omnipresent on American airwaves. He worked with a galaxy of stars and the pantheon of creative talent. Despite his primary career as a producer, David Susskind was best known to the American public as the host of the spirited talk show *Open End* (1958-87; see entry).

After graduating from Harvard and serving in the navy during World War II, Susskind went to work as a publicist for Warner Bros. He then became an agent and in 1948 got his first opportunity to produce when *The Philco Television Playhouse*'s premier producer, Fred Coe, needed a vacation. Susskind's keen eye for good dramatic material and his willingness to take risks quickly established him as a leading producer.

In 1955, Susskind took over the production of *Armstrong Circle Theater*, which was until then a nondescript anthology of half-hour dramas. But Susskind gave the series a unique focus. Under his aegis it became a collection of dramas based on true stories—a precursor to contemporary docudramas.

The pinnacle of live television drama was 1957, the same year Susskind reached his high point in the genre. Not a week passed without a Susskind-produced show on the air. In addition to *Armstrong Circle Theater*, he was producing programs for *Kraft Television Theater*, the *DuPont Show of the Month*, and occasional *Rexall Specials* for the drug store chain.

By 1959, the halcyon days of television drama were over. Corporate support for anthology series like *Philco Playhouse* and Westinghouse's *Studio One* had dwindled. Western and action-adventure series produced on film in Hollywood were the new heart of prime time. But Susskind was never hesitant about going against the grain. In the fall of 1959, when others were shrugging their shoulders about the demise of blue-ribbon TV drama, Susskind dared to introduce *Play of the Week*. Each week a two-hour drama was videotaped at a New York studio rented from CBS and then syndicated to independent stations around the country.

Starting in the late 1950s, David Susskind also became the self-styled conscience of the television industry, publicly saying things like "TV is going down the drain like dirty water." When Susskind was invited to address Westinghouse Broadcasting's national conference on public service in 1958, his hosts expected him to address the positive aspects of American programming. Instead he gave them an earful. Perhaps his toughest attack on the power-wielders of the TV industry came in June 1961 when he testified before the Federal Communications Commission about the demise of live programming and original TV drama. Susskind was also given a great deal of credit for breaking the back of the blacklist system when he refused to submit names to the network for clearance in 1960.

Although he felt an intense personal loss when live TV drama faded from the screen, he was no less passionate in the production of made-for-TV movies, miniseries, docudramas, and filmed specials, such as the *Hallmark Hall of Fame* shows he produced. A good share of his 20 Emmy Awards came in the second phase of his career.

Although he referred to television as "my mother medium," David Susskind's career also included producing feature films, among them *A Raisin in the Sun* (1961), *Requiem for a Heavyweight* (1962), *Straw Dogs* (1971), and *Alice Doesn't Live Here Anymore* (1974). His stage plays included *All in Good Time*, *Brief Lives*, and *Attica*.

David Susskind died at the age of 66. He was inducted into the Academy of Television Arts & Sciences Hall of Fame in 1988. In 1990, the Producers Guild of America presented the first David Susskind Lifetime Achievement Award.

Bibliography

Brady, James. "Andy & David." *Advertising Age* 9 Mar. 1987: 58.

Morgan, Thomas B. "David Susskind: Television's Newest Spectacular." *Esquire* Aug. 1960.

Watson, Mary Ann. "Continental Rift: David Susskind's Futile Fight to Keep TV Drama in New York." *Television Quarterly* 25.4 (1992).

Mary Ann Watson

Swanson, Gloria (1898-1983), unlike many of her silent screen contemporaries, survived better than most the transition from silence to sound. Having spent her childhood in Key West and Puerto Rico, Swanson returned for a visit to her native Chicago in 1913 and landed a part as an extra at Essanay Studios. In 1916, already married to Essanay performer Wallace Beery, Swanson made the trek to Hollywood and found quick work as a Mack Sennett bathing beauty at Triangle Productions.

Growing weary of these early slapstick roles, Swanson left Triangle in 1918 for the more opulent productions of Cecil B. DeMille. In her six pictures with DeMille, Swanson became a major box office attraction, starring in sophisticated bedroom farces, including *Don't Change Your Husband* (1919) and *Male and Female* (1919). At DeMille's suggestion, Swanson moved on to more diverse screen roles, linking her glamour queen image with a natural comedic timing. This connection was fostered through such films as Allan Dwan's *Zaza* (1923), a Cinderella comedy in which a poor French girl rejects her married suitor but regains both her man and her morality in the end.

At the peak of popularity by the mid-1920s, Swanson made the transition from actor to producer, and through the financial backing of lover Joseph P. Kennedy, started her own company in 1927. Her company produced two of Swanson's best-known silent films, include *Sadie Thompson* (1928) and *The Trespasser* (1929). For her performance in these films, Swanson was nominated for the Academy Award. By the end of the 1920s, Swanson experienced fiscal failure when her company folded because of the exorbitant budget of director Erich von Stroheim's *Queen Kelly* (1928), a Swanson film that was never released despite the nearly $800,000 devoted to it. During this time, Joe Kennedy also jumped ship both financially and emotionally.

By 1930, with three marriages having come and gone, Swanson made her sound debut in such films as *What a Widow* (1930) and *Indiscreet* (1931). Yet during the 1930s and early 1940s, with screen absences of up to six years, Swanson's sound career never reached the stature of her earlier vehicles. Swanson staged the most successful of her attempted comebacks with her role as Norma Desmond in *Sunset Boulevard* (1950). Her 63d film, it made her name synonymous with the fading glamour of Hollywood royalty.

Although Swanson would never again assume a screen role as powerful, she was by no means retired, launching into Broadway plays (*Twentieth Century* in 1950 and *Butterflies Are Free* in 1971), designing clothing, becoming an outspoken advocate for good nutrition and health, and writing a successful autobiography. Her last film appearance was in *Airport 1975*, playing herself.

Bibliography

Current Biography Sept. 1950: 48-50.

Magill, Frank, ed. *Magill's Survey of Cinema: Silent Films.* Vols. 1-3. Englewood Cliffs: Salem, 1982.

Swanson, Gloria. *Swanson on Swanson.* New York: Random House, 1980.

Kristine L. Blair

Tabloid Newspapers. Although the term "tabloid" technically refers to the half-broadsheet size of some newspapers, it has come to describe the sensationalistic pulp weeklies sold in grocery store checkout lines and other mass market locations. The six major national tabloids in the United States are MacFadden Holdings' *National Enquirer, Star,* and cheaper, sister paper, the *Weekly World News,* and Globe Communications' *Globe, Sun,* and *National Examiner.* Together they make up the gossip papers that most Americans read and most say they despise.

The tabloids offer a mixture of celebrity gossip; human interest anecdotes—usually with a "sensational" twist; stories about occult and psychic phenomena; lurid crimes; and other news features. These are interspersed with advice columns, self-help tips, medical news, and advertisements. Tabloids almost never cover politics, except at the level of the personality story.

The current weekly tabloid is a phenomenon of the 1970s and 1980s, but the papers are the heirs of a long tradition in journalism whose roots may be traced back to oral tradition, broadside ballads, and newsbooks, all of which featured tales of strange and wonderful happenings—murders, natural disasters, unusual births, and omens. Later, the penny press of the 1830s and the "yellow journalism" (see entry) of the 1880s developed the human interest and sensational style of reporting, using vivid, active language and colloquialisms, and breaking up stories into short, pithy paragraphs.

The first tabloid as such was the *Daily Continent,* founded in 1891. It soon failed, and it was left to Lord Northcliffe to establish the tabloid form in Britain, where it still flourishes. The first successful American tabloid was the New York *Daily News,* established in 1919, ushering in the age of "jazz journalism," in which three New York tabloids competed for circulation. The tabloid style was in full flower at this time, featuring composite photographs, excessive, adjective-laden prose, and a liberal dose of gossip and scandal. It has changed little since.

Although tabloids faltered after World War II, Generoso Pope began a new era of national competition in the late 1960s, when he transformed the *National Enquirer* (see entry) from a bizarre, gore-filled sheet into a weekly "family paper." His most astute decision was to target supermarkets and drug stores as sales centers. By 1971, the *Enquirer* was in all major supermarket chains, eventually becoming one of the ten most profitable items sold. The paper was bought by MacFadden in 1989 for $412 million.

Tabloids proved to be a highly successful mix, appealing to a middle-of-the-road, largely blue-collar readership. Their influence can be clearly seen in the rise of "reality programming" and salacious talk shows on TV, as well as in the inexorable move toward shorter, more personalized stories and celebrity subjects throughout mainstream journalism.

Bibliography
Bessie, Simon M. *Jazz Journalism: The Story of the Tabloid Newspapers.* New York: Russell, 1938.
Betrock, Alan. *Unseen America: The Great Cult Exploitation Magazines, 1950-1966.* Brooklyn: Shake, 1990.
Bird, S. Elizabeth. *For Enquiring Minds: A Cultural Study of Supermarket Tabloids.* Knoxville: U of Tennessee P, 1992.

S. Elizabeth Bird

Talk Radio. "I don't have time for a newspaper. I listen to radio for the news and to Rush Limbaugh to find out what's going on." The comment came from a man in his mid-30s on a cramped commuter flight into Atlanta. It's the same comment heard everywhere since Rush Limbaugh (see entry) began his reign over talk radio.

Limbaugh didn't invent talk radio, but he was the first talk show host many of his white, baby boom-aged, male audience encountered. His rise to prominence in the late 1980s paralleled a rise in conservative political thinking and public discourse.

Limbaugh's popularity is part of an overall phenomenon. From two full-time talk stations in 1960, the number has grown to 712 stations in 1998. This growth was fueled by Limbaugh. However, other big-name talk talents laid the groundwork for his emergence. Larry King (see entry), long-time dean of late night talk radio, kept insomniacs informed with live interviews from Washington, DC, and public response by phone from across the United States. Bruce Williams, on NBC Radio's "Talknet," answered financial and legal questions in an understanding, fatherly manner long before Limbaugh came to the nation's attention. In addition, most major cities had a prominent talk host who personified talk radio in each market.

On Limbaugh's coattails came other talk hosts and upstart networks that fed local stations hungry for talk radio. In May 1993, *Radio Business Report* listed 15 networks supplying talk programming. Some supply enough programming for 24-hour broadcast. Others, like Limbaugh's network, provide only a few shows.

Paralleling Limbaugh's rise was that of shock-jock Howard Stern (see entry), who is not a talk host per se, but whose program abandoned music in favor of free-wheeling conversation often centered on Stern and his private parts. A *Time* magazine article profiling both Stern and Limbaugh in 1993 points out that they both provided public discussion of ideas that audiences seemed unable to articulate on their own. Stern's program was seldom heard on talk stations; his affiliates were primarily rock music outlets.

The talk format on radio took some time to evolve. Early radio seemed unpredictable, but it was fully scripted. In the 1930s, the spoken word was, in reality, the read word. It was not until the 1950s and 1960s that improvisation and informal discussion helped radio develop its own character.

Talk shows became familiar to listeners in the 1950s as music stations devoted time to discussion of local issues. The motivation behind most early talk programming was to satisfy public affairs requirements as specified in licenses granted by the Federal Communications Commission.

Arthur Godfrey Time, a program on CBS Radio, was considered by some an early talk show. Godfrey would chat, sing, and play the ukulele in a relaxed, conversational style. Even though Godfrey's program has since been classified "variety" by radio historians, the host traded on public response: "Did you hear what Godfrey said this morning?" That same word-of-mouth "advertising" helped to drive the 1990s version of talk.

The term "talk station" came into being when KABC in Los Angeles discarded its records in 1960 and filled its 24-hour day with talk shows. The station was originally promoted as "The Conversation Station."

Not long afterward, KABC's sister station, KGO in San Francisco, used the designation "News-Talk" because it carried news blocks in morning and afternoon drive-time periods with talk shows between. "News-talk" has become the generic radio industry term for all stations that carry both news and talk programming, numbering 1100 in 1998.

One of the first stars of the talk radio medium was Joe Pyne, who appeared on KLAC in Los Angeles in the mid-1960s. Pyne's reputation was built on his style of verbal bombast against almost everyone, guest and caller alike. Pyne had no philosophical leaning except to the contrary. He established the habit of hanging up the phone on callers he disagreed with, a habit later adopted by talk hosts seeking to create the reputation of firebrand.

Pyne achieved some national notoriety, primarily through a short-lived television show. His radio work was not syndicated because the technology of that time was too expensive to link stations not already affiliated with the three major networks.

Satellite technology in the 1980s gave syndicators the type of access to local stations that the networks had previously had. That gave rise to ABC Talkradio, featuring hosts from various ABC-owned talk stations. Technology also fueled NBC's Talknet, Business Radio network (later known as American Forum Radio), Sun Radio Network, and others who distributed talk shows on a regional or national basis.

New York's WOR Radio, long a leader in talk programming in its own city, used satellite technology to deliver its talk shows to a national audience. Former Libertarian candidate Gene Burns, money advisers Ken and Daria Dolan, psychologist Dr. Joy Browne and others talked about issues that transcended New York.

If technology was one parent of talk radio's increasing availability in the 1980s, deregulation was the other. For 42 years radio and television were ruled by the "fairness doctrine," which required stations to broadcast opposing views on public issues. Deregulation abolished the rule in 1987, leaving talk hosts unrestrained.

The power of talk radio had been felt on a local level since the format's inception. Local stations traditionally staged debates and allowed unprecedented access to politicians. Deregulation merged journalism and populism. The public asked questions that had been previously the domain of reporters and gossip columnists.

Giving the public a forum has had specific political effects. For instance, Boston's Jerry Williams and listeners who heard his show on WRKO were credited with overturning Massachusetts' seat belt law in 1988. At an organizational meeting of the National Association of Radio Talk Hosts (NARTH) in 1989, Williams called talk radio "the greatest forum in history...the last bastion of freedom of speech for plain ordinary folks."

Talk radio created a new dynamic during the 1992 presidential campaign. Most candidates, prompted by exposure given independent Ross Perot, appeared on both radio and television talk shows to disseminate their views and corral support. The notable exception was then-President George Bush, who lost to a talk show regular, Bill Clinton.

Radio industry observers expect talk radio to continue its growth. The number of stations broadcasting the format is predicted to rise, probably adding FM stations to the predominantly AM base talk radio has now. Specialized types of talk radio, like sports-talk, will add to the growth in numbers of stations.

Bibliography

Broadcasting & Cable Yearbook 1999. New Providence, NJ: Bowker, 1999.

Bulkeley, William M. "Talkshow Hosts Agree on One Point: They're the Tops." *Wall Street Journal* 15 June 1989.

Henabery, Bob. "Talk Radio: From Caterpillar to Butterfly." *Radio Business Report* 17 Jan. 1994.

James, Rollye. "The Rush to Talk Continues...." *Radio Ink* 17-30 Jan. 1994.

Marr, Bruce. "Talk Radio Programming." *Broadcast Programming.* Ed. Susan Eastman, Sydney Head, and Lewis Klein. Belmont: Wadsworth, 1981.

"Talk Radio Today: Pulling It All Together." *Radio Business Report* 24 May 1993.

Ed Shane

Tarantino, Quentin (1963-). Few film directors have begun their careers with as much critical and popular acclaim as Quentin Tarantino. Although the first two films he directed, *Reservoir Dogs* (1992) and *Pulp Fiction* (1994), are not without their detractors, his obvious talent as both director and writer has made him a force to be reckoned with in Hollywood.

Tarantino was born in Knoxville, TN, but grew up mostly in the area south of Los Angeles. He dropped out of school at 17, although he later studied acting while working at various jobs, most significantly at a video store, which became his equivalent for film school. Tarantino's first forays into Hollywood filmmaking met with mixed success. His exciting and literate screenplays for *True Romance* (1993) and *Natural Born Killers* (1994) were enthusiastically received, but he was unable to get backing to direct either film, both of which were directed (and rewritten) by others.

Eventually, Tarantino was able to raise $1.5 million to allow him to direct another of his scripts, *Reservoir Dogs*; it has grossed more than $20 million. Tarantino's updating of the gangster film brings together a group of stickup artists, most of whom don't know each other, to steal a shipment of diamonds. Though carefully planned, the robbery goes badly wrong, and several police, robbers, and civilians are shot. When the surviving robbers reassemble in a warehouse, they conclude that one of their number has betrayed the others. While waiting for their leader to arrive and take charge, they try to decide what to do about one of their colleagues who has been badly wounded, torture a policeman whom they have taken hostage, and quarrel amongst themselves. Flashbacks fill in the background of the planning and recruitment for the heist, showing how the surviving robbers escaped and revealing the identity of the informer.

Pulp Fiction, which won the Palme d'Or at the 1994 Cannes Film Festival, was both a critical and box-office triumph. As its title suggests, *Pulp Fiction* makes use of themes, motifs, and atmosphere derived from 1930s and 1940s crime stories and film noir. Unlike *Reservoir Dogs*, this film incorporates multiple plots, cleverly interconnected, and a large cast of characters, including a mobster, his bored wife, two of his hit men, a boxer who has double-crossed the mobster by refusing to take a dive, two small-time armed robbers who are in love with each other, and a criminal whose specialty is solving problems for other criminals. As in his first film, Tarantino shows a concern for the details of criminal behavior, such as how to package drugs and how to clean up a car after someone has been shot in it. The movie is very violent and very funny, often simultaneously, which left many viewers feeling uncomfortable. Nor was the audience's discomfort merely intellectual: a scene featuring a hypodermic needle plunged into a character's heart is so graphic that it reportedly caused some viewers to faint.

Tarantino's focus on crime stories continued with writing the screenplay for *From Dusk till Dawn* (1996) and directing *Jackie Brown* (1997), which he adapted from an Elmore Leonard novel. Another Leonard adaptation is in production. He also contributed to the collaborative comedy *Four Rooms* (1995).

Tarantino's films are carefully plotted and cleverly written, and, despite their serious subject matter and extreme violence, are frequently very funny, even in their most horrifying moments. Though these movies are anything but drily academic, they demonstrate a scholar's knowledge of popular culture; in fact, some critics suggest that Tarantino's films are too derivative of other movies and consequently lack life (though certainly not death).

Bibliography

Bernard, Jami. *Quentin Tarantino: The Man and His Movies.* New York: HarperPerennial, 1995.

Biskind, Peter. "An Auteur Is Born." *Premiere* Nov. 1994: 94-102.

Dawson, Jeff. *Quentin Tarantino: The Cinema of Cool.* New York: Applause, 1995.

Fuller, Graham. "Plotting Hollywood's Future." *Interview* July 1993: 36-38.

Woods, Paul A. *King Pulp: The Wild World of Quentin Tarantino.* New York: Thunder's Mouth, 1996.

Linda Anderson

Tarzan is the hero of a series of over 30 adventure novels written by American author Edgar Rice Burroughs (1875-1950), beginning in 1912 with the first serial installment in *All Story Magazine* of "Tarzan of the Apes" and continuing through *Tarzan and the Madman* (1964). One of the most popular fictional characters of all time, Tarzan's presence is etched deeply in the cultural imagination.

Drawing on his wide range of experiences in the cities and on the Western frontier of the late 19th century, Burroughs created fiction that mixed adventure, bravado, and fantasy. *Tarzan of the Apes* recounts the story of an orphaned boy, the son of English nobility, Lord and Lady Greystoke, who is abandoned when his parents die in the jungles of West Africa, leaving him to be reared by a band of apes. Because Tarzan is human, his heredity and intelligence surpass the abilities of his simian guardians; he learns on his own to read, make weapons, and clothe himself. Yet because of the challenging environment in which he grows up, Tarzan is stronger and more courageous than the mass of humanity that has been softened by civilization. By the novel's end, Tarzan has fallen in love with Jane Porter, the daughter of an American professor who locates him in the jungle, rescued his new friends from a series of life-threatening menaces, learned to speak French and English, and taken on the best qualities of civilization while retaining the best qualities of his primal upbringing.

Soon after its pulp magazine appearance, *Tarzan of the Apes* reached an even wider audience when it was serialized in newspapers. In 1914 it was published as a book, followed almost immediately by sequels, *The Return of Tarzan* (1915) and *The Beasts of Tarzan* (1915); in 1918 it was adapted into a popular motion picture. Because Burroughs had retained rights to the Tarzan name and storyline, he was able to build a multi-million-dollar empire out of his ape-man, publishing the stories first as serials and subsequently as novels to increase his revenue. He also profited from licensing arrangements. Adaptations have ranged from the live-action TV series starring Ron Ely (1966-68) to the 1999 Disney animated feature film.

In the later novels, Tarzan married, reared a son, visited other countries, fought wars, obtained eternal youth, discovered lost civilizations, journeyed to the earth's core, battled animals and communists, ran a plantation, and encountered dinosaurs and dozens of other bizarre creatures and people. At his death, Burroughs left behind unpublished and unfinished Tarzan material, some of which was released posthumously.

Although the Tarzan books show influences ranging from Homer to H. Rider Haggard to Rudyard Kipling, for the most part they reflect an original artistic imagination. Tarzan was widely imitated (even by Burroughs himself), but none of his imitators captured the public's fancy quite like he did. The continuing popularity of the Tarzan books owes much to Burroughs's skills as a storyteller (if not as a writer) and to the fantasy version of Africa he created—a world populated by lost civilizations, fanciful creatures, and people only 18 inches tall, among others. Burroughs's chimerical vision of Africa was inspired in part by his parallel career as a science fiction writer.

Bibliography

Farmer, Philip Jose. *Tarzan Alive: A Definitive Biography of Lord Greystoke*. Garden City: Doubleday, 1972.

Holtsmark, Erling B. *Tarzan and Tradition: Classical Myth in Popular Literature*. Westport: Greenwood, 1981.

Lupoff, Richard A. *Edgar Rice Burroughs, Master of Adventure*. 1965. New York: Ace, 1968.

Porges, Irwin. *Edgar Rice Burroughs: The Man Who Created Tarzan*. Provo: Brigham Young UP, 1975.

Daryl R. Coats

Tattoos are the most ancient and widely encountered form of permanent body alteration. Limited archaeological evidence indicates that tattooing was probably practiced by Stone Age peoples. Excavations of Scythian burial mounds in Siberia revealed mummified remains of a nomadic warrior who lived around 5000 B.C. and who carried ornate tattoos representing totemic animals. An Egyptian priestess who died and was mummified around 2000 B.C. wore geometric tattoo designs thought to have had medicinal or fertility significance. The practice of tattooing is believed to have spread from the Middle East, through India, China, and Japan, to Pacific Island cultures as early as 2000 B.C.

The modern history of tattooing in Western culture begins with the voyages of Captain James Cook in the 1760s and his encounter with tribal tattooing in the South Pacific. Cook introduced the Tahitian word "ta-tu" (meaning "to strike" or "to mark") and soon "tattoo" replaced "pricking" as the common English term for the practice. Many of Cook's officers and seamen were tattooed on his first voyage and, on a later expedition, Cook returned to England with a heavily tattooed Tahitian prince who became the first of a popular series of exotic tattooed "curiosities" to be exhibited in Europe.

By the end of the 19th century, tattooing became something of a fad among the European aristocracy and members of the upper classes. Such dignitaries as Czar Nicholas II of Russia, King George of Greece, Kaiser Wilhelm of Germany, and King Oscar of Sweden wore tattoos they had received during their travels in the Orient or which had been inscribed by Tom Riley, George Burchett, or Sutherland Macdonald, the best-known tattooists of the time.

The "tattoo rage," as it was dubbed by the press, spread to the U.S., where in 1897 the *New York World* reported the highly unlikely "fact" that 75 percent of the female members of America's high society were tattooed. However, early in the 20th century, tattooing began to lose popularity among the elites (in part due to inflated media stories about venereal diseases contracted in unhygienic tattoo establishments) and by the 1920s tattooing was generally regarded, as socialite Ward McAllister put it, as being suitable "for an illiterate seaman, but hardly for an aristocrat."

Because of its apparent connection with the working classes and deviant groups, by the 1950s tattooing was regarded as a distinctly unsavory practice by the American public. Tattooing came to be seen as symbolizing the bearer's disaffection from conventional society—a symbolic poke-in-the-eye directed at those who were law-abiding, family-oriented, and hard-working. This popular definition of tattooing made the practice especially appealing to members of the youthful counterculture that began to coalesce in the 1960s.

This period ushered in what some have called the "tattoo renaissance," as young people began to acquire designs from established tattooists and a new group of tattoo "artists" began to emerge. These new artists—frequently having university or art school training and experience with traditional artistic media—brought a new orientation and aesthetic to tattooing.

Fantasy and science fiction illustration, traditional Japanese styles, Maori and other tribal designs, photorealist portraiture, and abstract expressionism are among the numerous influences shaping contemporary tattoo images. While the new tattooee expresses some rather different motives and often defines his or her tattoo in rather different ways than did the sailor who was tattooed during a drunken shore leave while serving in World War II, traditional motives to acquire a tattoo remain. The tattooed person, like the Maori chief or the committed member of the Japanese underworld (Yakuza), understands the tattoo as a mark of identity—a symbolic representation to the self and to others of his or her social connections, interests, individual attributes, and personal experiences.

To a limited extent, certain forms of contemporary tattooing—especially that done by younger and more technically skilled tattooists who create large-scale, custom-designed pieces—have been successful in achieving the status of fine art. This redefinition of tattooing as a legitimate art form is impeded, however, by its long association with marginal and disreputable social groups and the use of the tattoo by members of these groups to symbolize their disaffiliation from conventional society.

Nevertheless, significant changes that have occurred in the social world surrounding tattooing since the 1960s have had considerable impact on the public acceptability of tattoos, the aesthetics of the images, and the occupational lives of tattoo artists. It is currently difficult to watch MTV or read about film stars and other celebrities without encountering tattoos. This diffusion of tattooing out of previously disvalued social groups and into the larger world of popular culture since the late 1980s has meant that tattoos have become less powerful as a "mark of disaffiliation" from conventional society.

Bibliography

DeMichele, William. *The Illustrated Woman*. New York: Proteus, 1992.

Mascia-Lees, Frances E., and Patricia Sharpe, eds. *Tattoo, Torture, Mutilation, and Adornment: The Denaturalization of the Body in Culture and Text*. Albany: State UP of New York, 1992.

O'Sullivan, Tim. *Expose: The Art of Tattoo*. New York: Citadel, 1993.

Sanders, Clinton R. *Customizing the Body: The Art and Culture of Tattooing*. Philadelphia: Temple UP, 1989.

Clinton R. Sanders

Taxi (1978-1983), set in New York City, focused on the lives and antics of drivers employed by the Sunshine Cab Company. This popular TV sitcom presented a microcosm of the blue-collar work-a-day world of the early 1980s.

The show had an instant following after it first aired in 1978 because the characters were on the external fringes of society. They were outsiders trying to make it in a dog-eat-dog world; each toiled in search of his/her own American dream. Most of the drivers employed by the Sunshine Cab Company were looking for a way out: Alex Rieger (played by Judd Hirsch) was the only full-time driver. The cab company's resident Everyman, he could solve everyone's problems except his own. Bobby Wheeler (Jeff Conaway) was a struggling actor; Tony Banta (Tony Danza) was a boxer who had never won a fight. Elaine Nardo (Marilu Henner) was an art gallery receptionist trying to raise a family by herself and always needing extra money. John Burns (played by Randall Carver during the 1978-79 season) was a student going nowhere. Latka Gravas (played by the eccentric comedian Andy Kaufman) was the company's mechanic. His exact place of origin was unknown and he spoke a unique brand of broken English. Latka courted and married a dizzy woman from his homeland named Simka (Carol Kane). The "Reverend" Jim Ignatowski (Christopher Lloyd) was a burnt-out ex-hippie who, as it turned out, came from a well-to-do family. The company was run from behind a wire cage by a diminutive despot named Louie De Palma (Danny DeVito).

By 1982, the popularity of *Taxi* had waned, despite excellent scripts and direction, and a fine ensemble cast, several of whom have had notable careers since the show ended. Despite critical acclaim and three Emmy Awards for outstanding comedy series, the show never regained the ratings momentum of its early years. ABC canceled the show; NBC then attempted to revive it. When the ratings did not improve, NBC canceled it for a second time in July 1983.

Bibliography

Brooks, Tim, and Earle Marsh. *The Complete Directory to Prime Time Network TV Shows, 1946-Present*. New York: Ballantine, 1995.

Lovece, Frank. *Hailing* Taxi. New York: Prentice-Hall, 1988.

Sorenson, Jeff. *The Taxi Book: The Complete Guide to TV's Most Lovable Cabbies*. New York: St. Martin's, 1987.

Waldron, Vince. *Classic Sitcoms*. New York: Macmillan, 1987.

Lynn Bartholome

Taylor, Elizabeth (1932-), is more famous for her roller-coaster personal life than for her film roles. Her status as a cultural icon is as unwavering during her 60s as it was during her teen years. Taylor's violet-eyed image is still being used for everything from selling jewelry and perfume to raising money as the National Chairman of the American Foundation for AIDS Research. She was the subject of a 1995 made-for-TV movie starring Sherilyn Fenn. Taylor also reemerged on the big screen as Pearl Slaghoople in *The Flintstones* (1994).

Elizabeth Rosemond Taylor was born in London to American parents. Schooled in various performing arts from a very early age, she reportedly appeared in a charity concert ballet before the royal family in 1936. At the outbreak of World War II, her family left England for California, where her father, Francis Taylor, established a Beverly Hills art gallery. Elizabeth's mother, Sara Sothern Taylor (a former stage actress), is credited with starting Elizabeth's acting career and with keeping up its momentum at least until the daughter's 20s. In 1941, Taylor signed a contract with Universal and filmed *There's One Born Every Minute*, a low-brow comedy in which she starred opposite *Little Rascals* star Alfalfa (Carl Switzer). Not long afterward, Universal suspended her contract and then terminated it the following year. At this point, Taylor signed on with MGM, where she stayed for nearly two decades. Her films included *Lassie Come Home* (1943), *Jane Eyre* (1944), *The White Cliffs of Dover* (1944), and *National Velvet* (1944), the film which made her a star. In that film she played Velvet Brown, the girl jockey disguised as a boy who won the Grand National.

Before she was 18, Taylor married hotel heir Nick Hilton. MGM used the publicity surrounding the relationship to release *Father of the Bride* (1950), another notable Taylor role, in which she plays opposite Spencer Tracy. The marriage to Hilton lasted only several months, and Taylor embarked on what would become her long line of romances, marriages, and divorces: to actor Michael Wilding (married 1952, divorced 1957), with whom she had two sons, Michael and Christopher; to producer Michael Todd (married 1957; Todd died in 1958), with whom she had one daughter, Elizabeth Frances; to Eddie Fisher (married 1959, divorced 1964); her most famous marriage, to Richard Burton (married 1964, divorced 1974, remarried 1975, divorced 1976), with whom she adopted a daughter, Maria; Senator John Warner of Virginia (married 1976, divorced 1982); and a much younger man whom she met during a stay at a rehab center, Larry Fortensky (married 1991, divorced 1996).

Taylor's acting career endured peaks and valleys, and her public support followed suit. Her most famous roles included *Giant* (1956), *Cat on a Hot Tin Roof* (1958), *Suddenly, Last Summer* (1959), *Butterfield 8* (1960), *Cleopatra* (1963), *Who's Afraid of Virginia Woolf?* (1966), and *The Taming of the Shrew* (1967), though she made more than 40 films by the end of her Hollywood heyday in the 1960s. *Giant* was Taylor's second film with director George Stevens (the first was *A Place in the Sun*). Stevens is credited with nurturing some of Taylor's best performances, viewed by many as illustrative of the emotional range and sensuality of which Taylor was capable on screen, though she rarely delivered.

The mid-1950s and 1960s were the height of Taylor's film career, and she often played women grappling with psychological or emotional problems, primarily at the hands of ne'er-do-well men. The screen adaptation of Tennessee

Williams's *Cat on a Hot Tin Roof* includes Taylor cast as Maggie, the emotionally and sexually frustrated wife of a depressed and neglectful husband. *Suddenly, Last Summer* and *Raintree County* (1957) also dealt with psychologically troubled women, and all three films earned her Oscar nominations. It was not until *Butterfield 8*, however, that she won her first Oscar. Many believe that this Oscar was not possible for Taylor during the late 1950s, in part because of her unpopular affair with, and eventual marriage to, singer Eddie Fisher.

Taylor's performance in *Cleopatra* (see entry)—the high-budget flop in which Taylor had the greatest number of costume changes ever by one star in a movie (65)—cast her opposite Richard Burton. Their on- and off-screen romance again brought Taylor headlines. She married Burton shortly after her divorce from Fisher, and Burton and Taylor went on to share the screen several more times. The couple was extremely popular, and their most celebrated performance together was in *Who's Afraid of Virginia Woolf?*, for which Taylor won her second best actress Academy Award.

Despite various health problems over the last decade, including removal of a brain tumor in 1997, Taylor continues to make public appearances. She will be remembered as a stunning celebrity who compelled fascination, devotion, and endless gossip from a not-always-adoring public for over half a century.

Bibliography

Kelley, Kitty. *Elizabeth Taylor: The Last Star*. New York: Simon & Schuster, 1981.

Ladies' Home Journal Special: Elizabeth Taylor: Portrait of a Legend. 1993.

Leclerq, Florence. *Elizabeth Taylor*. Boston: Twayne, 1985.

Morley, Sheridan. *Elizabeth Taylor*. London: Pavilion, 1988.

Spoto, Donald. *A Passion for Life: The Biography of Elizabeth Taylor*. New York: HarperCollins, 1995.

Devoney Looser

Technicolor. Entertainment today cannot be imagined without color. It all began with Technicolor. In 1915, Technicolor, Inc. was formed by MIT professors Herbert T. Kalmus and Daniel F. Comstock (the "Tech" in Technicolor honors their employer). At first Technicolor was limited to a two-color subtractive process. During the early 1920s all the major American movie corporations tried two-color Technicolor in some limited way. Metro-Goldwyn released *Toll of the Sea* (1922); Famous Players released *Wanderer of the Wasteland* (1924). Douglas Fairbanks's *The Black Pirate*, released by United Artists in 1926, represented the initial box-office smash.

But not many movie companies wanted to risk the expense of producing a whole film in Technicolor, so during the mid-1920s color sequences became the rage, as in *Ben Hur* (1926), *The King of Kings* (1927), and *The Phantom of the Opera* (1925). In 1929, flush with the money made by pioneering the coming of sound, Warner Bros. released *On with the Show*, the first all-talking Technicolor feature.

As a result, Technicolor experienced a boom; its processing plant was booked ten months in advance. It seemed that color would become a significant part of Hollywood productions. But the decline in movie admissions associated with the Great Depression took away Hollywood's interest in technological change. Technicolor needed a new product and so readied a three-color process. Still, the Hollywood major studios had too many problems to innovate three-part Technicolor. It took the tiny Walt Disney operation to bring the three-color process to America's movie screens when Disney scrapped a black-and-white Silly Symphony, *Flowers and Trees*, already in production, and won the studio its first Academy Award with the Technicolor version (1932).

What Technicolor needed, however, was action by a major studio. This would come to pass in a roundabout manner. Millionaire John Hay Whitney wanted to make a name in the movies. In the early 1930s, his Pioneer Pictures produced the first three-color feature film, *Becky Sharp* (1935), and released it through one of the Hollywood major studios, RKO. *Becky Sharp* inspired David O. Selznick, who created *Gone with the Wind* (1939). Thereafter Hollywood lined up to make movies in Technicolor.

Technicolor cornered the market and limited the use of the process to one film in ten. In 1947, the U.S. government recognized Technicolor's monopoly, and charged the company with a conspiracy to monopolize the production of color movies. Three years later, the Technicolor monopoly ended.

No longer did movie producers have to hire Technicolor cameras, consultants, and camera operators. The market for movies in color was now wide open. Color filmmaking fell in cost, and, with the need to differentiate its product from the all-black-and-white television images, Hollywood created more and more films in color. The number rose from 115 in 1952 to 163 in 1953 to 170 in 1956. Yet in that process Technicolor played an ever-decreasing role. By 1960, Technicolor was just another corporation that could process color film, best remembered as a pioneer in the field.

Bibliography

Basten, Fred E. *Glorious Technicolor: The Movies' Magic Rainbow*. New York: Barnes, 1980.

Fielding, Raymond. *A Technological History of Motion Pictures and Television*. Berkeley: U of California P, 1967.

Gomery, Douglas. *Shared Pleasures*. Madison: U of Wisconsin P, 1992.

Quigley, Martin, Jr. *New Screen Techniques*. New York: Quigley, 1953.

Ryan, Roderick T. *A History of Motion Picture Color Technology*. London: Focal, 1977.

Douglas Gomery

Teleshopping, a new genre of television, was created in the 1980s when the Federal Communications Commission (FCC) changed its requirements on TV commercials. This allowed the broadcasting of sales programs without time limitations for the sole purpose of selling products. TV now includes widely viewed networks designed to sell a variety of products 24 hours a day, as well as programs designed to sell products ranging from cooking equipment to car polish and self-help tapes.

Teleshopping shows appear either as information commercials ("infomercials") or on TV shopping networks. Infomercials are 30-to-60-minute programs that sell a single product or product line. Commonly these use media stars such as Cher, Victoria Principal, or Richard Simmons to sell inexpensive goods such as hair-care products, face creams, and exercise programs.

Infomercial programs most commonly buy airtime "remnants" on both cable and broadcast television stations. These non-prime-time hours, usually late at night, allow producers to buy regular spots on both cable and broadcast TV at low rates. This practice has become common enough to be reported by *TV Guide* in its weekly schedules.

The second category, teleshopping, is the 24-hour-a-day catalog-style shopping program that sells almost any product to a diverse target audience. The most successful are the Home Shopping Network (HSN) and the Quality Value Cable (QVC) network.

Both HSN and QVC networks keep their slots with cable operators by offering rebates of 5% of telephone sales in the operator's geographic area. HSN, which reaches over 60 million homes with its networks, pays an average 8 cents per subscriber to cable operators. QVC, reaching almost 47 million homes with its channels, pays affiliates an average of 12 cents per subscriber and pays a fee for carriage of its programming. Cable-operator resistance to filling more channel slots with sales programs makes it likely that HSC and QVC will maintain their market dominance.

The future of teleshopping suggests that infomercials and shopping networks will cross over and perhaps merge. HSN produces infomercial segments for manufacturers and infomercial producers create Video Shopping Mall segments for new shopping channels.

Bibliography

Daugard, Craig. *How to Make Big Money on TV: Accessing the Home Shopping Explosion behind the Screens.* Chicago: Upstart, 1996.

Elcoff, Alvin. *Direct Marketing through Broadcast Media: TV, Radio, Cable Infomercial, Home Shopping, and More.* Lincolnwood: NTC Business, 1995.

Popeil, Ron. *The Salesman of the Century: Inventing, Marketing, and Selling on TV.* New York: Delacorte, 1995.

Preston, Ivan L. *The Tangled Web They Weave: Truth, Falsity, and Advertisers.* Madison: U of Wisconsin P, 1994.

Snider, Jim. *Future Shop: How New Technologies Will Change the Way We Shop and What We Buy.* New York: St. Martin's, 1992.

Frank Nevius

Televangelism received increased public attention during the late 1970s and 1980s for a number of reasons. At that time the new Christian right emerged as a seemingly viable force in American politics. One well-known example is Jerry Falwell's Moral Majority political action group, which became a household name and gained considerable notoriety in its campaign to defeat the reelection bids of targeted liberal politicians and ostensibly appeared to have played a pivotal role in propelling Ronald Reagan to the White House.

Two well-known media ministers, Jim Bakker and Jimmy Swaggart, were embroiled in sex scandals in 1987 and 1988, respectively, which adversely affected the presidential aspirations of colleague Marion "Pat" Robertson, who ran for the Republican nomination during the 1988 campaign. The publicity generated by these events helped to focus attention on televangelism in general and raised questions concerning the identity, message, ethics, and fiscal responsibility of these media ministries.

The hybrid term "televangelism" was first coined by Jeffrey Hadden and Charles Swann in their *Prime Time Preachers: The Rising Power of Televangelism* (1981). The phenomenon is often referred to as the "electric church" or "electronic church movement," although some argue that the use of the term "movement" may be misleading in that it gives the false impression of a closely knit, well-organized crusade. In reality the "movement" is a loose collection of independent evangelical ministries with diverse and sometimes competing interests. Nonetheless, it is possible to generalize that these television preachers and their supporters tend to be conservative Protestant Christians of the evangelical, fundamentalist bent.

The term "televangelism" does not refer to all religious broadcasting but specifically to those programs that are audience-supported and produced by independent evangelical broadcasters who purchase their airtime from TV stations. Generally these broadcasters are not affiliated with the more liberal mainline denominations.

The seeds of modern TV evangelism can be found in the Great Awakenings in American history and especially in the revivalism, evangelism, and fundamentalism that emerged during the 19th and early 20th centuries. Throughout the 1800s, as settlers pushed westward in pursuit of their "Manifest Destiny," itinerant preachers followed in an effort to "save souls" from eternal damnation by means of tent revivals. Revivalists, who felt personally called by God, sought to convert sinners to a renewed Christian faith; interestingly, the establishment of churches appears to have been a subordinate concern.

When the electronic communications revolution began to erupt throughout the 1920s, religious broadcasters were quick to recognize the potential of radio as a proselytizing tool. Since early radio was not closely regulated, it was a relatively simple task to obtain a license to operate a station (inexpensive, too—a station could be built for a few hundred dollars). In five years there were more than 600 radio stations across the country and most included some form of religious programming on a regular basis. About 10 percent of these stations were owned by church or other religious groups.

Paradoxically, while most religious radio stations failed, most secular stations provided some religious programming in order to meet their licensing obligation. Consequently, stations turned to church councils for advice about programming. Both the National Broadcasting Company (NBC) and Columbia Broadcasting System (CBS), formed in 1926 and 1927 respectively, turned to the Federal Council of Churches (later renamed the National Council of Churches) for advice and assistance. Independent evangelicals were obliged to purchase their own air time (and in turn were compelled to solicit donations over the airwaves to pay for it!). Only rival network Mutual Broadcasting System (MBS) agreed to sell unrestricted air time to religious broadcasters in 1935 but later reversed their policy in 1944.

Two years earlier, in 1942, evangelicals had banded together to form the National Association of Evangelicals (NAE) and religious broadcasters were a major faction within the organization. However, after Mutual changed its policy, NAE broadcasters formed their own separate organization, the National Religious Broadcasters (NRB). The NRB quickly launched an aggressive campaign to persuade the networks to change their policies. Interestingly, the NRB and the NCC became the representative agencies of the ongoing theological dispute between fundamentalism and modernism which continues to the present day.

Some early pioneers of religious radio broadcasting were Paul Rader, Charles Fuller, and Aimee Semple McPherson. Many of the most successful television evangelists first broadcast on radio, including Billy Graham, Oral Roberts, and Jerry Falwell.

When TV exploded onto the scene, religious programming made the transition to the new medium. As with radio, television networks were obliged to offer free air time in order to meet licensing requirements. The networks turned to mainstream organizations for advice, like the NCC; again independent evangelicals were forced to purchase their own air time.

The NRB continued to protest against network practices until 1960, when the Federal Communications Commission (FCC) ruled that stations could sell air time and still get "public interest credit" for licensing. This ruling had a profound effect on the nature of religious broadcasting in America. Many stations quickly withdrew their offers of free air time to mainline religious broadcasters; in fact, by 1979, 92 percent of religious broadcasting was purchased (as opposed to 50 percent in 1959 before the ruling). Evangelicals became more committed to buying air time while most mainline churches were unwilling to spend the vast sums necessary to stay on the air. The result was that evangelical fundamentalists have dominated the airwaves ever since.

BILLY GRAHAM, the most respected of today's television evangelists, was already a well-established urban revivalist at the time he first experimented with radio broadcasting. Graham is a Southern Baptist but plays down his denominational ties. His ministry, the Billy Graham Evangelistic Association, is located in Minneapolis, MN. The impressive Billy Graham Center is situated at the suburban campus of Wheaton College.

ORAL ROBERTS, like Graham, has been called the elder statesman of televangelism. A revivalist and faith healer, Roberts began broadcasting his tent services on TV in the 1950s. In 1969, he introduced a new professionally produced entertainment format that featured preaching and music, called *Oral Roberts and You.* At one time his program was estimated to carry over one million faithful viewers. He also founded Oral Roberts University in Tulsa, OK, during the 1960s.

MARION "PAT" ROBERTSON is the founder and executive producer of the Christian Broadcasting Network (CBN), the first Christian network in the country. The son of a former U.S. senator from Virginia and a Yale graduate, Robertson ran unsuccessfully for the Republican presidential nomination during the 1988 campaign. In 1989 he founded the conservative political organization the Christian Coalition; he also founded the graduate-level Regent University in Virginia Beach, VA.

Robertson is probably best known for his show, *The 700 Club,* the first of the Christian talk-show programs that featured the personal testimonies of "born-again" celebrities. CBN was also one of the first television ministries to employ telephone counseling along with sophisticated direct-mailing and fund-raising techniques. Robertson also started the cable network the Family Channel as a division of CBN in 1977; in 1997 he sold it to the Fox Network.

JIM AND TAMMY BAKKER are Pentecostal and Jim Bakker (see entry) was a former Assemblies of God minister. Interestingly, the charismatic couple were instrumental in founding all three major Christian networks in America—CBN, Trinity, and their own PTL (which stood for "Praise the Lord" or "People that Love"). Beginning in 1974, however, the ministry was involved in controversy over allegations of fiscal and personal wrongdoing. A major scandal broke in 1987 and the Bakkers resigned from PTL; Jim later served a four and a half year prison sentence after his conviction of conspiracy and fraud (Tammy was never charged).

JIMMY SWAGGART's ministry in Baton Rouge, LA, during its heyday, reportedly attracted over $100 million in donations annually. Swaggart, a Pentecostal and former Assemblies of God minister like Bakker, is best known for his lambasting of mainline churches, Catholics, and Jews. Also like Bakker, Swaggart found himself embroiled in sex scandals when he was found with known prostitutes in 1988 and 1991. Since then his TV ministry has faded dramatically.

JERRY FALWELL, an independent Baptist, founded the Thomas Road Baptist Church in Lynchburg, VA. It is estimated that his congregation of 17,000 is the second largest in the country. He is probably best known for his program *The Old Time Gospel Hour,* but has remained controversial due to his foray into politics (he was a founding member of the Moral Majority political action group). He has also established his own school, Liberty University, to train the next generation of evangelists.

ROBERT SCHULLER, of the major televangelists, is an exception in that he is an ordained Reformed Church of America pastor, a mainline denomination. However, his denomination does not support his broadcast financially; the program pays for its own air time. Schuller also continually attempts to distance himself from other televangelists. His *Hour of Power* resembles a traditional worship service, and classical music is featured. Schuller is perhaps best known for his Crystal Cathedral, a massive modern glass structure located in Garden Grove, CA.

Bibliography
Abelman, Robert, and Stewart M. Hoover, eds. *Religious Television: Controversies and Conclusions.* Norwood: Ablex, 1990.
Bruce, Steve. *Pray TV: Televangelism in America.* London: Routledge, 1990.
Frankl, Razelle. *Televangelism.* Carbondale: Southern Illinois UP, 1987.
Hadden, Jeffrey, and Charles Swann. *Prime Time Preachers: The Rising Power of Televangelism.* Reading: Addison-Wesley, 1981.
Hoover, Stewart M. *Mass Media Religion.* Newbury Park: Sage, 1988.

Nancy Schaefer

Television and Behavior. Studies have shown that a majority of the population in industrialized countries spend a large portion of their leisure time watching TV, either to be entertained or to acquire information. For over 30 years critics and scholars have been interested in learning just how this experience affects an individual's or a culture's behavioral patterns. Very few people would argue that watching TV has no causal relationship with the viewer's behavior. If that were the case, then thousands of advertisers would be wasting billions of dollars each year running commercials that had no tangible results. The question of how watching TV effects a change or reinforcement of a person's beliefs, values, and attitudes is complex and remains only partially answered. Some scholars have argued that TV is nothing more than simplistic entertainment having a minimal effect on the average person's life. Others have gone so far as to say, "People are the stuff of television!"

Of all the mass media sources, TV has been the most controversial. While a great deal of research has been conducted on the content of TV programming over the years, very little credible research can be found regarding the effects of viewing these programs. One reason for this is the many variables that come into play when trying to analyze something as broad as a person's behavior. Innumerable factors must be taken into account before declaring that a program has definitely had a specific effect. For example, the debate over violence in children's programming has been at the forefront of the TV/behavior debate for at least three decades. Some have suggested that the extreme violence in children's programs invites them to act out what they see on TV. Research has been conducted, for example, on the live-action program *The Mighty Morphin Power Rangers* regarding the number of violent acts per episode. But considering all the other variables that must be taken into account it would be next to impossible to qualify exactly how watching this program affects any given child.

The debate focuses not just on children but on every person who watches TV. While the influences of viewing TV are different for each person, there have been some attempts to categorize audience reactions based on demographic and psychographic breakdowns. The problem with this is that not all groups are represented fairly or given equal time. Asian and Hispanic Americans are given much less air time than white males. And, when they are represented, it is usually in some stereotyped portrayal. Here is where a paradox can be seen emerging. The audience breakdown compartmentalizes the viewers into groups, but these groups, with the exception of WASPS and a few select others, are not usually fully or accurately represented on the programs they watch. These negative representations help to maintain stereotypes outside the group and create low self-esteem within the group. Attempts to portray these minorities in a more positive light have met with varying degrees of success and criticism. A program like *The Cosby Show* received criticism from within the African-American community for not accurately representing the way most blacks in this country live. Thus, a viewer's reaction to a program is wholly dependent on the person's worldview. In his book *Television and American Culture,* Carl Lowe writes that "the way we conceptualize our experience may reflect the kinds of media with which we have been engaged." His argument suggests that a viewer growing up watching *Cosby* may well think differently about African Americans than one who watched *Good Times.*

The issue of how we react to TV shows goes back to the very beginning of the medium. One of TV's earliest successful situation comedies was *The Burns and Allen Show.* George Burns recalled that it was not uncommon for total strangers to visit him and his wife at their California home. The same effect has been documented by researchers when they polled viewers of Johnny Carson's late-night talk show. Many viewers claimed that that "they 'know' Johnny better than they do their next-door neighbor." This phenomenon was first termed "para-social communication" in 1956 by researchers Donald Horton and R. Richard Wohl.

Para-social communication occurs when a viewer reacts to a TV character as if they were really interacting with another person face-to-face. Like the visitors at George Burns's home, the viewer becomes intimately connected with the TV personality. The barrier of the television screen is ignored and the audience member gets sucked into the illusion of actual interactive dialogue. Because of the relatively fast-paced society we live in, the opportunities for developing close, long-lasting personal contacts are fewer than in the past. Some researchers have argued that many people have replaced these real relationships with para-social ones. That is, they have created relationships with TV characters.

TV producers are fully aware of this phenomenon and play up to it. This is why David Letterman and other talk show hosts get right up in the camera during their monologue, to create the illusion of having a conversation with the person on the other side of the television screen. Horton and Wohl write, "The more the performer seems to adjust his performance to the supposed response of the audience, the more the audience tends to make the response anticipated. This simulacrum of conversational give and take may be called para-social interaction."

This para-social interaction helps to explain why someone would visit a star's home uninvited, but would never visit a neighbor's house uninvited. The phenomenon helps us to understand how an actor who plays a villain on a daytime soap can be forced into hiring bodyguards to keep from being assaulted in public. Audience members employ what is known as the temporary suspension of disbelief. They set aside what they believe to be true and allow themselves to be caught up in the fantasy that is TV. This creates a sense of intimacy not found in other mass media or entertainment forums because watching TV, for the most part, occurs in very intimate settings, such as a bedroom or a living room.

Having discovered that audience members react to TV the same way they react in real situations, the market has adjusted itself over the years to cater to the audiences' perceived needs. In the early 1950s, *The Adventures of Ozzie and Harriet* served as the standard model of situation comedies. The seemingly all-knowing father was portrayed as a successful problem-solver and money-maker. The wife, Harriet, was responsible for playing out the role of the contented housewife living the postwar dream of a family and house with white picket fence. Contrast that portrayal with the 1980s hit sitcom *The Cosby Show*. In this family program, the father is a successful African American who shares the household and family responsibilities with his wife, who works as a lawyer. This dramatic change in program content can be attributed, at least in part, to para-social interaction.

The debate as to whether TV reflects society or helps to create it is moot, as it is for the question of whether biology or environment is a more important factor in development of the personality. They are both equally important, with one proceeding from the other in a continuous cycle. Whether television expands and enriches our lives or dulls and numbs our senses, there is little doubt that with the advent of new technologies offering over 200 channels to choose from, the ominous black box will continue to be a source of debate.

Bibliography

Gerbner, George, Larry Gross, Michael Morgan, and Nancy Signorielli. *Trends in Network Television Drama and Viewer Conceptions of Social Reality, 1967-1979.* Violence Profile No. 11. Philadelphia: Annenberg School of Communications, U of Pennsylvania, 1980.

Horton, Donald, and R. Richard Wohl. "Mass Communication and Para-Social Interaction: Observation on Intimacy at a Distance." *Inter Media.* Ed. Gary Gumpert and Robert Cathcart. 3d ed. New York: Oxford UP, 1986. 185-206.

Huston, Aletha C. et al. *Big World, Small Screen: The Role of Television in American Society.* Lincoln: U of Nebraska P, 1992.

Jhally, Sut, and Justin Lewis. *"Enlightened" Racism.* Boulder: Westview, 1992.

Lowe, Carl. *Television and American Culture.* New York: Wilson, 1981.

Daniel P. Agatino

Television Broadcasting—VHF and UHF. TV arrived in the American home just as the baby boomers were arriving. Since 1950, the percentage of homes with TV has increased from 9 percent to over 98 percent, while average daily viewing has increased from 4-1/2 hours to 7-1/4 hours. Despite the inroads made by cable TV, broadcast ("free") TV continues to be a dominant influence.

Broadcasting consists of the transmission and reception of radio waves. Because of the curvature of the earth, the useful range for broadcasting is about 50 miles, although it is possible to receive degraded signals over much greater distances. While all radio waves travel at the speed of light, they have different wave-lengths (peak-to-peak distance) and different frequencies (the number of peaks passing a point in a unit time, expressed in cycles per second, or hertz [Hz]). Shorter waves are more vulnerable to obstacles; they are also higher frequency and require more energy to generate. Thus, UHF (ultra high frequency) stations are disadvantaged relative to VHF (very high frequency) stations because the broadcasts are more expensive to generate and cover less area.

Each channel is assigned a specific band of broadcast frequencies which is 6 million hertz (megahertz, MHz) wide. Additional channels cannot be added without reducing the width of this waveband, which would render obsolete present TV transmitting and receiving equipment.

The VHF channels were the first channels allocated and assigned by the Federal Communications Commission (FCC) in March 1947, including channels 2-4 (54-72 MHz), 5-6 (76-88 MHz), and 7-13 (174-216 MHz). Channel 1 was eliminated within months because of interference with other uses. The gap in frequencies between channel 6 and channel 7 is used for FM radio broadcasts (88-108 MHz), aircraft navigation and communication systems (108-120 MHz), as well as maritime, land mobile, space, amateur, government, and satellite communications (120-174 MHz).

Thereafter, in July 1952, the FCC allocated and assigned the UHF channels. Those remaining comprise channels 14-36 (470-608 MHz) and 38-69 (614-806 MHz). Channel 37 (608-614 MHz) has been reserved for radio astronomy, and channels 70-82 (806-890 MHz) have been reassigned for use for private and public mobile land radio.

To avoid interference on the *same* channel, the minimum separation for VHF stations is 170 miles in most of the heavily populated northeast, 190 miles in most of the U.S., and 220 miles in areas bordering the Gulf of Mexico where tropospheric interference problems arise. The minimum separations for such UHF stations are 155 miles, 175 miles, and 205 miles, respectively. Thus, for example, since New York City was assigned channels 2, 4, 5, 7, 9, 11, and 13, Philadelphia was assigned channels 3, 6, 10, and 12 (public broadcasting), New Haven, CT, received channel 8, and Trenton, NJ, received channel 1 (which, as noted above, was eliminated, leaving the eighth most populated state with no VHF stations).

To avoid interference between adjacent channels, the minimum separation for VHF stations is 60 miles (and 55 miles for such UHF stations). This means that the maximum number of VHF stations in one metropolitan area is seven. Only New York and Los Angeles have seven VHF stations (six commercial, one public). Thirteen metropolitan areas have four commercial VHF stations, and most (including Philadelphia, PA, and Pittsburgh, PA) have three or fewer commercial VHF stations. Many (such as Lexington, KY) have none.

Since its inception, UHF has taken a back seat to VHF. Initially, special TV adapters were needed to receive UHF signals. Consumers would not pay for such adapters, unless they were in an area not served by any VHF station. It was not until 1962 that the FCC obtained enactment of the All-Channel Receiver statute, which required that television sets manufactured after April 30, 1964, be capable of receiving all UHF channels. The amendment of the act in 1976 to require "detent" tuning for UHF channels eliminated another lingering disadvantage. The introduction of direct access tuning (eliminating the need to scroll through unused channels to reach the desired channel) and, more recently, the increasing prevalence of remote controls have finally made UHF tuning as user-friendly as VHF tuning. UHF stations have fared best in areas without VHF stations and have survived in other areas by providing something the public wants, such as local sports coverage, as in Philadelphia and Atlanta.

Most of the population is served by four or more stations, one of which is usually devoted to public TV and three or more of which are commercial stations. The commercial stations typically include the four networks, ABC, CBS, NBC, and Fox, each of which supplies more than 15 hours of prime-time programming weekly to its over 200 affiliates.

In January 1995, two new would-be networks went on air, Warner Brothers (WB) and United Paramount Network (UPN), each with about 100 affiliates nationally. WB's affiliates include WGN (channel 9) in Chicago, home of the White Sox and a nationally distributed cable station, and WPIX (channel 11) in New York City, home of the Yankees. UPN's affiliates include WWOR (channel 9) in New York, home of the Mets and a nationally distributed cable station.

Bibliography

Broadcasting & Cable Yearbook 1999. New Providence: Bowker, 1999.

Brown, L. *Encyclopedia of Television.* 3d ed. Detroit: Visible Ink, 1992.

Reel, A. F. *The Networks: How They Stole the Show.* New York: Scribner, 1979.

Claire Koegler

Television Docudrama. Around Christmas of 1974, a significant amount of space in the print media was devoted to the controversy surrounding the TV broadcast of *The Missiles of October,* about the 1963 Cuban missile crisis. In November 1984, the print media reacted vigorously to the network presentation of *Fatal Vision,* a true-crime story based on the novel by Joe McGinniss. In late 1992, all three major networks presented made-for-TV dramas based on the story of Amy Fisher, who had shot her lover's wife, and the print media wrung its collective hands at the invasion of "trash" into the American home via TV. These three examples range from the responsible and well researched to the sleazy and exploitive, and as such they demonstrate the range of the curious but tenacious TV genre known as docudrama. No matter what may be said about it—that it is, for instance, a quick and easy way to gain respectable ratings by exploiting current or recent events from popular history and the head-

lines—two things are sure: each new wave of docudrama is sure to provoke a storm of controversy in reaction to its mingling of fact and fiction; and there surely will be a next wave.

The term "docudrama" (sometimes written with a hyphen, "docu-drama") itself is as slippery to define as tragicomedy or any other cross-genre hybrid. The origin of the term, which first appeared around 1961, is uncertain, and other terms have been regularly suggested as substitutes: "theater of fact," "faction," and the British "drama documentary." Although the term has been applied to productions as different as the fictionalized Watergate story *Washington: Behind Closed Doors,* the religious film *The Day Christ Died,* and the historical drama *Elizabeth R,* it is generally taken to refer to the dramatization of a recent event within the living memory of the audience at the time of production with actors playing the roles of actual historical and contemporary people in order to give the impression that this is the way the events transpired. Because historical accuracy has often been sacrificed on the altar of dramatic enhancement, docudrama has provoked negative reactions from historians, newspeople and reviewers, who feel that too much license has been taken.

Docudrama is not the first use of film to re-create historical events. That process is as old as the movie camera (in 1898, a British cinematographer filmed a staged battle from the Boxer Rebellion in his backyard), and there is a long tradition in Hollywood of biographical and historical motion pictures. What accounts for the power, the popularity, and the controversy surrounding docudrama in our culture derives from the essential difference between the two mediums. When one attends a film in a theater, there is a clear sense of watching a dramatic creation, a work of art which is fictionalized even when it deals with real people, and there is a willing suspension of disbelief. Television is different. It is the most personal of the visual media, sharing our living space, serving as electronic baby-sitter, eye on the world, and sole source of news for many Americans. And where a million or two ticket buyers may see a movie in a theater, a ballyhooed TV production can reach half the population of the United States. When a docudrama makes use of the same techniques—and sometimes even the same people—as the evening news, the boundary between fiction and fact is significantly blurred, if not broken.

What differentiates docudrama from other dramatic forms is, of course, the implied message that what the viewer is seeing is what really happened, with a few minor accommodations necessary to fit the story into dramatic form. There are certain production techniques common to docudrama which do convey the sense of reality that gives docudrama its peculiar cachet. Often the main story is framed by introductory and concluding remarks from a recognized scholar, newsman, or commentator. This frame, often combined with a recurring voice-over during the production, conveys a documentary quality and helps emphasize that what the viewer is watching is real. The casting, too, usually reinforces the sense of reality by choosing actors who resemble or can be made to resemble the actual historical personages. Inserted stills of newspaper headlines or clips from the evening news also heighten the documentary quality.

Although it is difficult to pinpoint the first appearance of the docudrama, it is clear that there is a significant difference in the docudramas of the 1970s and those of more recent vintage. The 1970s were a kind of golden age, with a seminal production, *The Missiles of October*, essentially serving as an archetype for the historical docudrama. Numerous productions of varying historical and dramatic quality filled the television schedule in the 1970s. Historical docudramas have dealt with subjects as different in time and significance as *Tail-Gunner Joe* (Senator Joseph McCarthy), *The Death of a Princess* (the beheading of a member of the Saudi royal family), and *Return to Manzanar* (the interning of the Nisei during World War II). The two most popular subjects for historical docudrama, however, have been Harry Truman and various members of the Kennedy family. At least five docudramas deal with Truman's life and presidential career, and the number dealing with one or more of the Kennedys approaches two dozen. Of these, two particularly stand out: *The Missiles of October*, dealing with what some consider John F. Kennedy's finest hour, and *Truman at Potsdam*, dramatizing Truman's introduction to international politics at a meeting with Winston Churchill and Joseph Stalin shortly before V-J day. These two docudramas make use of most of the techniques common to historical docudramas: actors made up to resemble the characters they play, a documentary voice-over, inserted clips from news broadcasts, and a disclaimer that suggests that what the viewer is watching is as accurate as historically possible. Another shared characteristic is that each is based largely upon popular rather than academic history: *Meeting at Potsdam* by Charles Mee for the Truman story, and Robert Kennedy's *Thirteen Days* and Elie Abel's *The Missile Crisis* for *The Missiles of October*. Both television presentations manipulate the historical events for the sake of dramatic emphasis and both enhance the images of their subjects, showing them as warm but shrewd political leaders who remained in control of things throughout the situation. It has subsequently been revealed that JFK took the world unnecessarily close to nuclear war with his confrontational tactics during the missile crisis and that Truman's decision to drop the atomic bomb in Hiroshima was not reached in the manner suggested by the docudrama.

By the early 1980s, a different kind of docudrama began crowding historical subjects off the screen. American popular culture has always preferred crime and scandal to serious history, and the new docudrama capitalized on the transfer of tabloid journalism to the small screen. The daily and weekly "true-story" shows, ranging from *Hard Copy* to *Unsolved Mysteries*, have adopted the techniques of docudrama, particularly the reenactments of events with actors playing the roles of the real people involved (see next entry). *Fatal Vision*, the story of Captain Jeffrey MacDonald's alleged murder of his wife and children, is the archetypal "true-crime" docudrama. Like *The Missiles of October*, it was not the first of its type, but it was so successful and so controversial that it established the essential nature of the subgenre.

Such "true-crime" or "true-story" programs raise yet another issue. Productions which exploit yesterday's headlines are not only based on sources lacking even popular historical credentials but often deal with events still under adjudication even as the docudrama is being shown on television. And even though producers claim that they present a rounded version of the events, showing all sides of the question, viewers in fact derive a far more biased view of the occurrence than the producers suggest. Of all the true-crime stories, *Fatal Vision* has provoked the most response, partly because the book by Joe McGinniss was a national bestseller, but also because Jeffrey MacDonald and his supporters have been both visible and vocal and his appeal was being prepared even as the program was aired. (According to a *Newsday* poll, the film had a significant effect on viewers' opinions as to MacDonald's guilt.) The production does include Captain MacDonald's version of events (he claims that a group of hippies committed the murders, à la the Manson family). However, MacDonald's version is hokily presented and sandwiched in the middle of a drama which makes him look guilty. Similar problems exist with *The Atlanta Child Murders, The Billionaire Boys' Club*, the various Amy Fisher and Menendez brothers docudramas, and the shows about the murder of child beauty queen JonBenét Ramsey. They all dramatize cases which are not only in the public eye but also have not been finally decided. Other true-story docudramas tend to be tales of incurable diseases, missing children, custody battles, and the like. They are emotional in appeal, but like their true-crime brethren present a particular point of view—that of the protagonist.

Historical docudramas, while often provoking controversy over their particular interpretation of events, can be defended as at least somewhat educational, capitalizing on the "cult of personality" to do some teaching in the guise of entertainment. This is probably as good a way as any to inform the video generation about historical events. The "true-story" docudrama, on the other hand, combines tabloid sleaze with soap opera sensibility and seems defensible neither historically nor artistically.

Bibliography

Brode, Douglas. "Video Verite: Defining the Docudrama." *Television Quarterly* 20.4 (1984): 7-20.

Fuller, Daniel J., and T. Michael Ruddy. "Myth in Progress: Harry Truman and *Meeting at Potsdam.*" *American Studies* Fall 1977: 99-106.

Himmelstein, Hal. *Television Myth and the American Mind.* Westport: Praeger, 1994.

Hoffer, Tom W., and Richard Alan Nelson. "Docudrama on American Television Networks." *Southern Speech Communication Journal* 45 (Winter 1980): 149-63.

Marc, David, and Robert J. Thompson. *Prime Time, Prime Movers: From* I Love Lucy *to* L.A. Law. Boston: Little, Brown, 1992.

Rosenthal, Alan. *Writing Docudrama: Dramatizing Reality for Film and TV.* Boston: Focal, 1995.

Shaw, David. "Danger: Don't Mix Facts with Fiction." *TV Guide* 20 April 1985: 4-7.

Daniel J. Fuller

Television Dramatic-Reality Programming is a hybrid television genre that combines the elements of news, public service, and drama. It is distinguished by its focus on real-life events, most of which involve violent crimes, life-threatening situations, and unusual occurrences. While some programs feature dramatization, or reenactments, of the events, which typically include actual photographs, videotapes, and interviews with participants, other programs use live footage. The dramatic-reality program suddenly became popular in the late 1980s and has influenced other types of programming, including news and tabloid shows, both of which began to use reenactments, and made-for-television movies, which began to use contemporary news stories as their sources (see preceding entry).

The roots of dramatic-reality programming can be traced back to television coverage of the Vietnam War that presented the reality of warfare. A 1973 PBS documentary, *An American Family*, which chronicled the disintegration of the Louds, is also considered a forerunner of dramatic-reality programming. In 1982, ABC broadcast a series called *Counterattack: Crime in America,* on which the host, George Kennedy, described recent crimes and asked viewers who might help police investigations to phone in. NBC aired occasional specials, *Vanished: Missing Children, Missing Persons*, and *Missing...Have You Seen This Person?*, during the 1980s.

A sudden explosion of dramatic-reality programs on American television in the late 1980s was initiated by NBC's *Unsolved Mysteries* and Fox Broadcasting Company's *America's Most Wanted. Unsolved Mysteries* began as a series of irregularly scheduled specials in 1987 and evolved into a weekly program in the fall of 1988. Each week the series features three to four reenactments of actual events ranging from murders and missing persons to searches for lost loved ones, UFO sightings, and psychic phenomena. The host, Robert Stack, remembered as FBI agent Eliot Ness on *The Untouchables*, narrates the reenactments and asks viewers' help by giving the toll-free telephone number, which is answered by operators and police officers in the studio. Premiering in February 1989, *America's Most Wanted* (see entry) uses the same format except for its focus on unsolved crimes. The information on crimes is supplied by the FBI, which has committed a full-time liaison to work with the show, and other law enforcement agencies. Originally aired on seven Fox-owned stations, the series was carried by 125 stations nationwide within 13 months of its debut and, moreover, inspired the production of similar local programs in Pennsylvania, New Jersey, Missouri, New York, and Louisiana. The host, John Walsh, is well known for his activities for child-protection legislation after his son was kidnapped and murdered.

Another Fox show, *Cops* (see entry), also contributed to the dramatic-reality programming boom. Premiering in January 1989, the program has been called "the ultimate in reality television," "television's first weekly documentary," and "a pioneer in a new era of real life documentary" because, unlike *Unsolved Mysteries* and *America's Most Wanted, Cops* does not have a host/narrator or include reenactments. Instead, the program employs a video *vérité* style. The videotapes taken by a cameraman who rides with police officers on patrol show their activities, ranging from chasing and arresting drug dealers, burglars, and car thieves to mediating domestic disputes and tracing runaway children.

Beginning with the 1989-90 television season, dramatic-reality programs proliferated on network television owing to the success of the above programs. Most new programs copied already successful formulas with slight variations. For instance, *True Detectives* and *American Detective* used a *vérité* style while *Top Cops* and *FBI: The Untold Stories* recreated old cases that were narrated by police officers and FBI agents involved in these cases. *Rescue 911* (1989-92), featured people who were saved by emergency calls and those who helped them, e.g., paramedics, police officers, and 911 operators.

Syndication companies and cable channels have also cashed in on the popularity of dramatic-reality programs since the late 1980s. First-run syndication shows include *Firefighters, On Scene: Emergency Response*, and *Real Stories of the Highway Patrol,* while cable channels, such as the Discovery Channel and the Arts & Entertainment Network, have *Justice File, Those Who Dare, Spirit of Survival, Investigative Reports*, and *American Justice*, among others.

Bibliography
Cavender, Gary, and Lisa Bond-Maupin. "Fear of Loathing on Reality Television." *Sociological Inquiry* 63.3 (Summer 1993): 305-17.
Grant, Judith. "Prime Time Crime." *Journal of American Culture* 15.1 (1992): 195-206.
Keller, Teresa. "Trash TV." *Journal of Popular Culture* 26.4 (1993): 195-206.

Yasue Kuwahara

Television Lawyer Dramas could be found at every turn of the prime-time dial during the last decade of the 20th century. Comparable shows did not play significant roles in television programming in other parts of the world, but Americans took their prime-time TV lawyers for granted and often used them unthinkingly to shape their notions of law, the legal profession, and justice.

The lawyers of contemporary American television can trace their lineage back to the beginnings of prime-time network television in the late 1940s, when several of the earliest shows featured lawyers and their legal cases. Initiating a tradition which continues to this day, these early shows emphasized courtroom trials.

The Black Robe (NBC, 1949-50) reenacted cases from New York City's Night Court. Actual witnesses and defendants sometimes played themselves, and a criminal once turned himself in after seeing the television presentation of his case. *They Stand Accused* (DuMont, 1949-52, 1954) used actors as defendants and witnesses but real-life Chicago attorney Charles Johnston as the judge. At the end of each trial jurors chosen from the studio audience were asked to render a verdict. *Famous Jury Trials* (DuMont, 1949-52) reenacted actual cases and then used the jury verdict to reveal to viewers which version of the events considered at trial was truly accurate. *The Public Defender* (CBS, 1954-55) adapted actual cases taken from files of those defending the indigent, and each episode paid tribute to a named public defender for work beyond the call of duty.

But as innovative as these early blendings of fact and fiction were, they gave way eventually to more purely fictional dramas featuring the weekly exploits of the same heroic lawyer or lawyers. The first examples of what would become the standard prime-time lawyer drama include *The Mask* (ABC, 1954), a drama starring Gary Merrill and William Prince as sibling attorneys rooting out evil, and *Justice* (NBC, 1954-56), a more successful show featuring the same actors as legal aid attorneys. In one show, *Steve Randall* (syndicated, 1952-53), Melvyn Douglas starred as a disbarred attorney forced to work, albeit successfully, as only a detective. In the show's final episode he formally regained his license to practice law.

The true apotheosis of fictional lawyers pursuing weekly cases and, customarily, conducting weekly trials began on September 21, 1957, when CBS broadcast the first 60-minute episode of *Perry Mason*. Like other early lawyer dramas such as *The Amazing Mr. Malone* (CBS, 1951-52), a series featuring a Chicago criminal lawyer introduced in the novels of Craig Rice, or *Mr. District Attorney* (ABC, 1951-52, 1954), a live production derived from a successful radio drama, *Perry Mason* did not originate on television. The character and his cases came instead from the novels of Erle Stanley Gardner (see entry; see also Mason, Perry). A total of 271 original episodes appeared during the show's nine-year run between 1957 to 1966, making *Perry Mason* the longest-running lawyer drama in television history. CBS tried to revive the series in 1973 as *The New Adventures of Perry Mason* starring Monte Markham. The show did not last the season, but NBC had greater success beginning in 1985 when it launched a series of two-hour, made-for-TV movies once again starring Raymond Burr.

Many producers attempted to follow the Perry Mason formula, and a bevy of fictional, altruistic lawyers appeared in the 1960s and early 1970s. In certain of the shows, the lawyers worked more or less on their own: *The Law and Mr. Jones* (ABC, 1960-61), starring James Whitmore as a criminal lawyer improbably named Abraham Lincoln Jones; *Sam Benedict* (NBC, 1962-63), with Edmond O'Brien playing the role of an aggressive San Francisco lawyer; *For the People* (CBS, 1965), featuring William Shatner (see entry) as an idealistic prosecutor just before he took command of the *Enterprise*; *The Trials of O'Brien* (CBS, 1965-66), in which Peter Falk's lawyer hero prefigured his later Columbo; and *Judd for the Defense* (ABC, 1967-69), in which Carl Betz as Clinton Judd flew to different parts of the country, à la F. Lee Bailey, to take on challenging cases. In other dramas, the lawyers were in fact affiliated with social justice organiza-

tions then in vogue: *The Storefront Lawyers* (CBS, 1970-71), starring Robert Foxworth as an attorney with a profitable corporate practice who also runs a legal clinic for the poor, and *The Young Lawyers* (ABC, 1970-71), concerning a group of law students and lawyers in a Boston legal services office.

Some of the shows in this golden age of lawyer dramas even transported the benevolent lawyer hero outside of the modern metropolis. In *Temple Houston* (NBC, 1963-64), Jeff Hunter handled cases in the Old West, and *Court Martial* (ABC, 1966) featured World War II investigations and trials conducted in London by American attorney officers. *Owen Marshall: Counsellor at Law* (ABC, 1971-74) starred Arthur Hill as an attorney in breezy Santa Barbara, and *Hawkins* (CBS, 1973-74) featured Jimmy Stewart as a country lawyer from West Virginia. In *Petrocelli* (NBC, 1974-76), a debt-plagued ethnic lawyer relocated from an eastern city to a southwestern cattle town.

The lawyer drama of the period which received the most acclaim was *The Defenders* (CBS, 1961-65). It starred E. G. Marshall and Robert Reid as the father and son members of Preston & Preston. Viewers enjoyed vicariously participating in the process of son learning from father (and vice versa), and other producers tried with less success for similar effects. In *Harrigan and Son* (ABC, 1960-61), starring Pat O'Brien, a conservative, humanistic father humorously interacted with his fresh, play-it-by-the-book son, and in the legal episodes of *The Bold Ones* (NBC, 1969-73), Burl Ives, as the senior member of the law firm of Nichols, Darrell & Darrell, not only won cases for the deserving but also tutored the two brothers who were his junior partners.

In the late 1970s and early 1980s—as the economy turned sour, politics turned to the right, and citizens turned into themselves—heroic, altruistic lawyer dramas were less common. Then, on September 15, 1986, NBC aired the first episode of *L.A. Law* and thereby sired a new generation of lawyer dramas. For some, *L.A. Law* seemed little more than a peek at the yuppie lifestyle, what with the plush offices, expensive cars, and abundant casual sex. But the creators had the determination and credentials to handle seriously the legal content. At the outset, Steven Bochco (see entry), who had developed the highly successful police drama *Hill Street Blues* (NBC, 1981-87), counted Terry Louise Fisher, a former Los Angeles prosecutor, as his co-developer. Regular writers included Billy Finkelstein and David E. Kelley, both attorneys, and attorney Charles B. Rosenberg served formally as the show's legal adviser.

The drama of each one-hour episode flowed through the firm of McKenzie, Brackman, Chaney & Kuzak, as it was originally known. Veteran actor Richard Dysart played Leland McKenzie, the private, dignified senior partner. Alan Rachins, as managing partner Douglas Brackman, presided over opening meetings in the conference room reminiscent of opening meetings in the *Hill Street Blues* squad room. Harry Hamlin played litigator Michael Kuzak, and Corbin Bernsen often stole the scene as libido-driven divorce lawyer Arnie Becker. Michael Tucker and Jill Eikenberry (husband and wife in real life) played lawyers Stuart Markowitz and

Ann Kelsey and married for television purposes in the episode of January 7, 1988. Susan Dey played Grace Van Owen, an assistant district attorney who later joined the firm, and Michele Green played associate Abby Perkins, who struggled both to make partner and to be a good single mother. Jimmy Smits was Victor Sifuentes, a Latino attorney, and Blair Underwood joined the cast in the show's second year as Jonathan Rollins, the firm's first African American. The firm's non-professional staff included Susan Ruttan as secretary Roxanne Melman and Larry Drake as mentally handicapped office helper Benny Stulwicz.

Some found the significant percentages of female, minority, and homosexual attorneys with a handicapped co-worker misleadingly inconsistent with the make-up of high-powered law firms in Los Angeles or anywhere else for that matter. Others praised McKenzie, Brackman as at least a projection of what law firms, professions, and American society could become.

Courtroom trials, a distinctive feature of lawyer dramas since the late 1940s, remained a mainstay in *L.A. Law*. In every episode at least one, and sometimes two or three members of McKenzie, Brackman were in court. While the trials in the classic genre of lawyer shows were almost always criminal trials, the lawyers in *L.A. Law* frequently pursued civil actions for monetary damages. More so than even the lawyers of Preston & Preston in *The Defenders*, star lawyers in *L.A. Law* sometimes lost. Typically, their trials involved controversial issues, and the sides were often well balanced, presenting judges, juries, and viewers with provocative choices.

Overall, *L.A. Law* marked a modernizing of the established lawyer drama genre. Instead of one or two heroic lawyers, *L.A. Law* offered a firm, the members of which worked together and also scrapped like members of a family. The show found room for occasional lighthearted and whimsical story lines, and it used multiple story lines within episodes and allowed story lines to continue from one episode to the next. The major characters, although occasionally lapsing into caricature, were less perfect than Perry Mason or Owen Marshall, and indeed the complicated, flawed personal make-up of McKenzie, Brackman's lawyers routinely became central. If the established lawyer genre featured the lawyer as demigod delivering justice, *L.A. Law* instead used lawyer characters to explore morality and ethics.

When *L.A. Law* won seven Emmys during its first two years, it was inevitable that more lawyer shows would appear. Although *Matlock* (NBC, 1986-95) seemed more a vehicle for popular actor Andy Griffith than innovative lawyer drama, other shows extended *L.A. Law* in interesting ways. *The Trials of Rosie O'Neill* (CBS, 1990-92), featuring Sharon Gless as a Los Angeles public defender, not only included the personal problems of the star and her co-workers in the story lines but also launched each episode with Rosie conversing with her psychiatrist. Both *Reasonable Doubts* (NBC, 1991-93) and *Law & Order* (NBC, 1990-) put detectives and lawyers together. The former starred Marlee Matlin as deaf prosecutor Tess Kaufman, and the

courtroom proceedings were more striking than curious when Kaufman conducted her cross-examinations or made closing arguments to the jury in sign language. Recalling the format of *Arrest and Trial* (ABC, 1963-64), *Law & Order* devotes its first half to police investigations and arrests and its second to prosecutions. In *Civil Wars* (ABC, 1991-93) Steven Bochco attempted to repeat his *L.A. Law* success by portraying a three-lawyer firm specializing in divorce and family law matters. Despite superb scripting and acting, the show failed to catch hold, but when the fictional firm folded, Alan Rosenberg and Debi Mazar, actors who played a lawyer and his secretary, managed to join McKenzie, Brackman for *L.A. Law*'s final season in 1993-94.

Steven Bochco followed up *L.A. Law* with another innovative legal series, *Murder One* (ABC, 1995-97), which over the course of each season followed just one case of a person charged with murder in the first degree. David E. Kelley, one of the writers for *L.A. Law,* has since created two Emmy-winning legal series: *The Practice* (Fox, 1997-), about defense attorneys in a Boston law firm, as well as *Ally McBeal* (Fox, 1997-), an unusual combination of comedy and drama about the neurotic young title character (Calista Flockhart) and other members of a small law firm. Military law is the focus of *J.A.G.* (CBS, 1995-), which stars David James Elliott as a Judge Advocate General. In 1999 CBS premiered *Family Law*, whose main character is a single lawyer mother.

The best way to contemplate lawyer dramas on American prime time is not with reference to their accuracy. Inaccurate as they might be, lawyer dramas have proven to be an engaging indigenous genre featuring a changing professional troupe of fictional practitioners especially adept on the courtroom stage. The dramas involve the ceremonial enactment of the law itself and consider the principles, good or bad, by which the society is ordered. If critically engaged, lawyer dramas are one vehicle for a heightened sociopolitical consciousness.

Bibliography

Dienstfrey, Harries. "Doctors, Lawyers & Other TV Heroes." *Television: The Critical View.* Ed. Horace Newcomb. New York: Oxford UP, 1976. 74-85.

Gillers, Stephen. "Taking *L.A. Law* More Seriously." *Yale Law Journal* 98 (1989): 1607-23.

Kane, Patricia. "Perry Mason: Modern Culture Hero." *Heroes of Popular Culture.* Ed. Ray B. Browne, Marshall Fishwick, and Michael T. Marsden. Bowling Green, OH: Bowling Green State U Popular P, 1972.

Papke, David Ray. "The Courtroom Trial as American Cultural Convention." *The Lawyer and Popular Culture.* Ed. David L. Gunn. Littleton: Rothman, 1993.

Stark, Steven D. "Perry Mason Meets Sonny Crockett: The History of Lawyers and the Police as Television Heroes." *University of Miami Law Review* 42 (1987): 229-83.

Winick, Charles, and Mariann Pezella Winick. "Courtroom Drama on Television." *Journal of Communication* 24.4 (1974): 67-73.

David Ray Papke

Television Movies. Films, a separate entity for 40 years, first came to the newest medium, television, when the major studios sold their pre-1948 films in the early 1950s. They have saturated the airwaves ever since. Ratings proved to be tremendous for movies shown on television. However, through the years, these movies have also proven to be very expensive. To avoid the expense of buying hit motion pictures from the studios, television began, in 1964, to make its own movies.

Aside from being less expensive than purchasing Hollywood theatrical releases, television began movie-making for other reasons. Television could shoot a picture in three weeks as opposed to three months for the big studios. Therefore, television movies could be extremely timely. Further, TV movies had enormous creative potential. Because so many are made, and at a relatively low cost, these movies allow more experimentation. Feature films can expose creative writers and directors to mass audiences and, at the same time, enrich the cultural fare of millions of viewers.

Further, with the advent of cable television offering tens of dozens of channels as opposed to only three networks, and with 24-hour stations, television has a voracious appetite and programmers are desperate for material. Made-for-TV movies help fill the available time slots, can be extremely timely due to the quick turnaround time, and are less expensive than buying Hollywood theatrical releases which may be airing at the same time on pay-cable movie channels. The made-for-TV movie has become an art form in itself—the truest reflection of the American craving for speed.

When motion pictures began, the studios owned everything—actors, lots, set, cameras—the entire means of production. An independent could hardly make a film. Television broke this vise-like grip of the big studios by forcing them to sell or rent production means in order to reduce overhead. Additionally, a series of anti-trust laws required the major studios to divest themselves of subsidiary studios and discontinue their blockbooking (forcing clients to accept films on an all-or-nothing basis) policies.

Though bitter about television interference and fierce competition at the beginning, today's movie studios get fat from television productions, from the sale of films to television, and from television's partial financing of theatrical productions. Since 1966, the networks have depended on Hollywood to play a major part in network programming.

Prior to 1949, only a few old movies and shorts had been used on television. Hollywood did not expect—nor did anyone else—that a commercial sponsor would ever buy a feature motion picture for TV. No feature films were shown on television before 1948 because there had been no television release written into the actors', artists', and technicians' film contracts. Even after this changed, the studios held back since a single television showing could wipe out the salability to thousands of theaters. Consequently, most television critics hated the early films on television because they were just "old Hollywood sweepings": old shows, poor quality. In 1955, the RKO Studio library (30 years of films which included 740 full-length pictures and over 1,000 short subjects) was sold for television release for $15.2 million. The buyer was Matthew Fox, who intended to re-sell the films to individual television stations. The library included such films as *Citizen Kane, Gunga Din, The Hunchback of Notre Dame*, and nine Fred Astaire/Ginger Rogers musicals.

From all indications, the demand for movies would keep growing. Walt Disney Productions became the first major movie studio to enter television. Disney developed an hour show for a 26-week series on ABC featuring old Disney films, unused footage from previous films, and even new characters created especially for television. By 1950, surveys showed that television was severely curtailing movie attendance.

As television and Hollywood gradually began to see their mutual benefit from each other, movies gained a permanent foothold on the home television screen. With demand outrunning supply in the mid-1960s, the only solution was for television to produce its own movies. Prior to this, Hollywood producers had been glad to accommodate TV and were upset when networks began to make their own movies. Hollywood had fully intended to be the only one in the movie business, continuing the lucrative cycle of releasing movies to theaters and then to television. Hollywood went so far as to ask the Justice Department for a restraint of trade order which was never acted upon.

In the beginning, made-for-TV movies were the "bastards" of the film industry. Critics panned them. Big name actors turned the parts down. Television began to make its own movies to ensure a steady supply of films because they were less expensive than Hollywood products and television could recoup development costs by packaging pilots into original movies. Television welcomed independents to make movies just for them. Most independent producers went in the hole, with the networks offering $1 million for a two-hour movie and a half million for 90 minutes. This included the rights to two showings and then the distribution rights reverted back to the producer. The independents expected to make their money back by selling the film to non-network stations, foreign countries, or theaters.

Made-for-TV movies were equivalent to the Hollywood B movies. All scripts had to obey the network rule: a strong story premise and a promotable hook that could be summed up in one line in *TV Guide*. The opening scene had to catch the viewers' attention immediately so they would not switch channels, and each act had to end with a stinger so the viewers would not switch channels during the commercials. There were, however, excepts to the B fare, such as the $2.5 million production of *QB VII,* the Leon Uris novel, for which television outbid the movies.

On October 10, 1964, *See How They Run* was billed as "First Time on Any Screen Anywhere! Tonight, World Premiere of a Feature Length motion picture . . . first movie made especially for TV." It was, actually by accident, the first made-for-TV movie to be *aired*. The distinction of being the first picture commissioned especially for TV goes to *The Killers*, which was instead released to the movie theaters. It was one of a group of films made for television by Universal, and starred Lee Marvin, Angie Dickinson, and

Ronald Reagan (in his last film role before entering politics). It was deemed too brutal for home consumption since it featured a sniper and was made shortly after Kennedy's assassination.

Overall, there was very little difference between made-for-TV movies and hour-long series. Many movies turned out to be pilots in disguise—some accidental, such as *The Waltons* from *The Homecoming*—some planned, such as *Kojak, Toma,* and *Get Christie Love.* NBC was the only network at the time which thought that a permanent, long-term commitment was in order and, in 1965, signed a contract with MCA for the delivery of 30 TV movies over the next few years to be called *World Premieres.* The first *World Premiere, Fame Is the Name of the Game,* became a weekly series known as *The Name of the Game.* This series, which ran for four years, was the first for which now-famous writer/producer Steven Bochco (*Hill Street Blues* and *L.A. Law*) wrote the full-length original script. Of the 116 *World Premieres,* 31 became regular series, including *The Rockford Files, McCloud, Columbo,* and *Emergency.*

The next step was the serialization of novels. ABC was very successful in 1976 with its twelve-part series *Rich Man, Poor Man* (and even developed a series-like sequel), based on Irwin Shaw's novel. NBC began producing a series called *Best Sellers,* in which each novel used as much time as needed. When one finished, the next began. ABC subsequently scored incredible audience numbers with its ten-part series, *Roots* (1977).

By the mid-1970s, it was estimated that at least four times as many Americans were watching made-for-TV movies each week as viewed movies in the local theaters. In an average week, more time would be spent watching one TV showing than all the movies in all the theaters in America in one week. As an example, over 150 million viewers had seen *Gone with the Wind* in 35 years of theatrical release by 1974. By comparison, the second most popular picture in American viewing history was a made-for-TV movie, *Brian's Song* (1971). On network television, it showed before an audience of 53 million in a single showing.

The quick shooting time for made-for-TV movies also allows the movies to be topical. After the theatrical success of *Deliverance* (1972), the television imitation, *Pray for the Wildcats,* was released on ABC. More people saw it in one showing in 1974 than saw *Deliverance* in the first year of its theatrical release.

It made sense for television to begin making its own movies. Though immensely popular, theater movies proved problematic to alter for TV prime-time showing. All films are cut for television: to make them fit allotted time slots, to allow for commercial breaks, and to comply with broadcast standards. Additionally, theatrical movies, which are shot in a 3:5 ratio, must be squeezed to television's 4:5 ratio, often radically altering the panoramic pictures. It is only recently that television has adopted the letterbox format, allowing theatrical pictures to retain their 3:5 ratio by using black strips above and below the picture on the television screen.

Commercial interruptions are another problem. A two-hour theatrical release has to allow 20 minutes for commercials, thus eliminating part of the time needed to tell the story. This often hurts the impact of the film. Further, in a normal prime-time evening, a program is interrupted every seven to eight minutes for commercials. Today, writers for made-for-TV movies deliberately structure the film to come to a logical stopping place or end of scene every seven minutes to allow for the commercial breaks.

Films were also cut by network censors, who sometimes required original scenes cut from a movie and new scenes inserted. To protect the integrity of their films, heavyweight directors such as Francis Ford Coppola (*The Godfather,* 1972), Peter Bogdanovich (*The Last Picture Show,* 1971), and John Schlesinger (*Midnight Cowboy,* 1969) had their contracts written to give them editing control when the films were recut for television. In its final version for TV, *Midnight Cowboy* contained over 100 deletions and modifications in addition to carrying an advisory legend warning of its explicit nature.

In 1974, of the 258 movies shown on network television, 169 were theatrical movies and 80 were made-for-TV. By the mid-1980s, 1,700 made-for-TV movies and mini-series that had appeared in 20 years on the three commercial networks, HBO, Showtime, or independent stations, were listed in a comprehensive encyclopedia. Although this number seems staggering, it did not even include movies shown as pilots or long-running syndicated series (i.e., *How the West Was Won*), two-hour specials shown as continuations of a series (i.e., *Police Story*), *The Wonderful World of Disney,* movies strung together from several series episodes and later passed off as a television movie, television anthologies (i.e., *Kraft Suspense Theater*), or made-for-TV movies diverted to theaters (i.e., *The Killers*). Numbers such as these make David Sarnoff's 1956 statement on the future of feature films on television laughable. Then president of NBC, Sarnoff said that feature films were a "flash in the pan." He emphatically stressed that TV's future was in live, color programming.

Not all made-for-TV movies are of the B quality. On occasion, they have become high-quality dramatic experiences. Many, such as *The Autobiography of Miss Jane Pittman* (1974), *The Glass House* (1972), *Tell Me Where It Hurts* (1974), *I Heard the Owl Call My Name* (1973), and *A Brand New Life* (1973) have won Emmy awards, human rights citations, and Cannes International Film Festival citations. Many of today's television movies deal with more mature themes that explore topics such as teenage suicide and alcoholism, homosexuality, domestic violence (*Miss America behind the Crown,* 1992), incest (*Something about Amelia,* 1984), single parenthood, missing children (*Adam,* 1983), integration (*Crisis at Central High,* 1981), nuclear war (*The Day After,* 1983), and more.

Nor is there a dearth of star power, although many of the stars have been generated by television itself, such as Kenny Rogers, Barbara Eden, Cheryl Ladd, Corbin Bernsen, Jaclyn Smith, and Suzanne Somers. Made-for-TV movies are fertile ground for fledgling writers and producers, the most notable being Steven Spielberg, who broke into television with Universal in the late 1960s. Made-for-TV movies have also enticed Hollywood veterans such as George Cukor, Paul Newman, Nicholas Meyer, and Franco Zeffirelli. Other directors who fell victim to Hollywood's blacklist in the 1950s turned their skills to TV movies.

While television's time constraints have been criticized for "ruining" movies with the cutting required for television adaptation, television can also be expansive with time. Only television can offer full-length filming of literary works by James Michener, John Steinbeck, Harold Robbins, Judith Krantz, and Irving Wallace. Offered in the typical two-hour theatrical movie setting, many of these best-sellers would have to be severely condensed. James Michener's *Centennial* was adapted to 26 television hours in 1978. Francis Ford Coppola was allowed to re-edit and re-sequence *The Godfather* as a ten-hour television film shown over several nights. Certainly no moviegoers would ever consider sitting through such a marathon showing.

By the 1980s, the networks' demand for Hollywood movies began to weaken because prior release of the films to pay cable and home video severely affected the audience for even the top-rated films. The first blockbuster movie shown on television was in 1966, when ABC paid $2 million for two showings of *The Bridge on the River Kwai* (1957). The first showing drew a tremendous audience of more than 60 million, a record at that time for a television movie. Later it was exceeded by *The Birds* and other huge theatrical hits for which the networks paid astronomical amounts: NBC paid $7 million for a single showing of *The Godfather*, $5 million for a single showing of *Gone with the Wind,* and $3 million for the first TV rights to *Dr. Zhivago.*

Once network television became disenchanted with theatrical blockbusters, the networks concentrated instead on exploitative made-for-TV movies. Because of the quick turn-around time in production, it was a natural move. Additionally, the viewing public's voracious demand for reality-based programming made it reasonable to exploit the current news with viewers becoming "voyeurs" of real-life tragedies. Made-for-TV movies such as *Katherine* (1975) paralleled the Patty Hearst kidnapping and subsequent incarceration just months after the actual event. Likewise, *Helter Skelter* (1976) was an immensely successful movie/documentary about the Charles Manson family released shortly after two of Manson's family demanded his release from prison. In other behind-the-headlines events, movies attempted to re-create the true story (see Television Docudrama).

Only 15 years after the first made-for-TV movies aired (1964), there were more made-for-TV movies shown in a single season than theatrical movies. By the 1986-87 season, the shift from theatrical releases to made-for-TV movies had reached the point that the networks aired barely more than 100 theatrical features and almost 300 made-for-TV films.

Television, which in the beginning was considered a mortal threat to movies, instead has been the very bread and butter of the movie industry. Television has, in fact, given movies a perpetual life. Television showing is a second market for theatrical releases and the television rights are often negotiated from the very start of the filming. Pay cable is the third life and home video is a fourth life. Television represents a virtual guarantee of success to producers.

Bibliography

Brooks, Tim, and Earle Marsh. *The Complete Directory to Prime Time Network TV Shows, 1946-Present.* New York: Ballantine, 1995.

Brown, L. *Les Brown's Encyclopedia of Television.* 3d ed. Detroit: Gale Research, 1992.

Marill, A. H. *Movies Made for Television, 1964-1984.* New York: Zoetrope, 1984.

"TV Movies." *Maclean's* March 1992: 57.

Sheri Carder

Television Talk Shows, which have existed since television's earliest days, were one of the dominant components of American media in the 1990s. Talk-show hosts, such as David Letterman and Oprah Winfrey, are among the most recognized and highest-paid media celebrities. By the end of 1999, at least 25 talk shows could be seen each weekday on commercial broadcast television stations in most major markets in the U.S. This number rises significantly when one includes shows aired on PBS and cable television. In early 2000, though some of the faces had changed, the number of shows was about the same.

Although there are also a large number of television shows that use a talk-show format to cover a specific area of interest—such as sports, politics, or religion—the most popular and widely viewed talk shows are those that cover a wide range of topics and are hosted by a single charismatic person. Indeed, most television scholars and critics agree that the television talk show is "host-centered," and that the success or failure of a given talk show relies primarily on the popularity of the host or hosts.

The trend away from daytime drama toward less expensive talk shows can be witnessed by examining the changes in the NBC daytime schedule since the mid-1980s, when that network broadcast four soap operas: *Generations, Days of Our Lives, Another World,* and *Santa Barbara.* By 1994, the low-rated *Santa Barbara* and *Generations* were no longer in production. Instead, a typical NBC affiliate, such as KXAS in the Dallas-Forth Worth area, included only two soap operas, *Days of Our Lives* and *Another World,* while it could boast four daytime talk shows: *Suzanne Somers, Marilu, Jenny Jones,* and *Ricki Lake.* In the spring of 2000, there were two soap operas and two talk shows. Most daytime talk shows are not produced "in-house" by a network but by independent production companies which syndicate the shows in local markets around the country.

Many scholars have contended that the general nature of talk shows at any given time reflects the overall mood of society during that period. In the 1990s, Americans have been drawn to tabloid-style news shows and publications, which contain "behind-the-scenes" reports about intimate aspects of the private lives of celebrities and ordinary citizens—aspects previously considered taboo by the media and its censors. Talk shows in the 1990s have responded by presenting sensational topics which also reveal the private lives of celebrities as well as people who are not in the public eye.

In an effort to secure high ratings, the various shows often compete to have the most bizarre, outlandish, and controversial topics and guests. Most daytime shows encourage lengthy periods of interaction between the guests and the audience, often leading to angry and sometimes violent encounters.

THE MORNING TALK SHOW usually is geared to women ages 18-49 who work in the home. They are centered around a genial and attractive celebrity, usually female. The guests are generally either well-known celebrities or experts who offer advice or tips on common social, domestic, psychological, emotional, or economic problems. These guests are usually promoting a recent book, movie, or some other project with which they are involved. In most cases, each "episode" is generally centered around a single theme or topic.

Current shows that fit this category include: *Live! With Regis and Kathie Lee* (1989-); *Martha Stewart Living* (1991-) and *Donny & Marie* (1998-). In nearly all cases, these shows are hosted by actors and entertainers, such as the Osmonds.

Many local markets produce their own morning shows, such as KABC's *A.M. Los Angeles* and WFAA's *Good Morning Texas. The Today Show* (NBC), *Good Morning America* (ABC), and *This Morning* (CBS) all have a talk-show element, as they include interviews with celebrities and newsmakers. Indeed, *Today* is generally regarded as the prototype for the morning talk show. But these shows differ from the above-mentioned talk shows in that they are always produced by the networks themselves, and are highly informational, offering frequent news and weather updates.

THE AFTERNOON TALK SHOW is also geared primarily to women at home. These shows are the most controversial and combative on the air. The format usually involves a panel of guests who share a similar problem or dilemma. The guests may all be on the same side of an issue, such as recovering alcoholics discussing their personal battles with their addiction, or the guests may include views on opposing sides of an issue, such as "abused women and the men who abuse them." The topics and issues discussed on these shows are generally drawn from the stories receiving the most media attention at the time.

In the 1990s construction of the afternoon talk show, however, guests are usually not celebrities but ordinary people that the audience—both in the studio and at home—can relate to. The various guests often know each other intimately or are actually related to one another. For instance, an episode of *Sally* included teens who dressed promiscuously, as well as their mothers who abhor their daughters' attire. A *Ricki Lake* program featured men and women who feel that their own overpowering beauty inhibits others from socializing with them. Later, the show brought out the "best friends" of these individuals, who claimed that their friends were aloof and antisocial, which was the true reason for their loneliness, not their alleged good looks.

The format for nearly all these shows is similar: the guests sit on the stage while the host weaves his or her way through the studio audience taking questions from audience members, as well as posing questions of their own. The guests respond from the stage, often defending themselves and their actions and lifestyle. As the show progresses, new guests are sometimes introduced. These guests are often meant to contradict or repudiate what the initial guests have said. In many instances, an "expert" guest, such as a therapist or lawyer, may be brought on to shed light on the subject that is being debated or discussed.

The interactive format of the afternoon show is usually attributed to Phil Donahue, who conceived the model during the 1960s in a show that was originally produced in Dayton and then moved to Chicago and was eventually syndicated nationally (1970-96). In 1986, Oprah Winfrey (see entry) followed Donahue's path, as her Chicago morning show became nationally syndicated. Winfrey, who began her career hosting a local morning show in Baltimore, combines Donahue's sometimes abrasive style with a highly personal, emotional tone of her own.

Besides *The Oprah Winfrey Show*, current afternoon talk shows include *Sally* (1985-), *Jerry Springer* (1991-), *The Maury Povich Show* (1990-), *The Montel Williams Show* (1991-), *Jenny Jones* (1994-), *The Rosie O'Donnell Show* (1996-), and *Ricki Lake* (1993-). All these shows are syndicated (and therefore are *not* all broadcast during daytime hours in all markets). Their hosts come from a wide variety of backgrounds: Sally Jessy Raphael is a long-established radio personality; Jerry Springer, a former politician; Maury Povich, a former journalist; Montel Williams was formerly a military officer; Jenny Jones a comedienne; and Ricki Lake and Rosie O'Donnell actresses.

A variation on this format is *Larry King Live!*, broadcast on cable's CNN. King's show is basically a television version of the standard "talk radio" show (see entry).

THE LATE-NIGHT TALK SHOW is geared to a wider audience of both men and women, but these shows usually do not involve a great deal of audience participation. Historically these shows are hosted by a comedic performer who interviews several guests. The guests are usually celebrities, promoting a new book, movie, TV show, musical recording, or concert tour. Occasionally, the guest may be an "everyday person" with a unique or amusing talent.

Because of the larger audiences they attract, the hosts of these shows often become cultural icons, and their favorite phrases and comedic routines often become part of the society's vernacular. David Letterman's Top 10 list, which spoofs current issues or personalities, has become part of the culture of the 1980s and the 1990s as much as Johnny Carson's characterization of a humorous psychic, "The Amazing Carnack," was a popular culture staple in the 1970s.

Current late-night talk shows include *The Tonight Show with Jay Leno* (NBC), *The Late Show with David Letterman* (CBS), *Late Night with Conan O'Brien* (NBC), *The Late Late Show* (with Craig Kilborn since 1999; CBS), and *Politically Incorrect* (with satirist Bill Maher; ABC). These shows are usually produced by the networks themselves.

All forms of television talk shows can trace their roots back to the same talk show pioneers. Edward R. Murrow, Arthur Godfrey, Arlene Francis, and Art Linkletter all made the transition from radio to television as hosts of interview-variety shows. Generally regarded as the most respected newsman of his day, Murrow conducted celebrity interviews on his show, *Person to Person,* which premiered in 1953. Many other hosts of televisions' first interview shows received fame and popularity in the late 1940s and early 1950s. Among them were Garry Moore, Faye Emerson, Wendy Barrie, Carmel Myers, Robert Q. Lewis, and Morton Downey. Also in the 1950s, producer David Susskind (see entry) began hosting his own talk show, conducting serious interviews with celebrities ranging from entertainers to politicans.

In the early 1950s, NBC executive Sylvester "Pat" Weaver changed the direction of daytime and nighttime talk shows with his creation of the *Today* and *Tonight* shows for NBC. Many highly successful news and talk show personalities have hosted the show over the years, including John Chancellor, Barbara Walters, Hugh Downs, Tom Brokaw, Jane Pauley, and Bryant Gumbel. Current hosts Matt Lauer and Katie Couric are among the most recognizable faces on American television.

Over the years, CBS and ABC have tried different combinations of hosts and formats to compete with *Today* (see entry). Walter Cronkite, Will Rogers, Jr., and Jack Paar were among those who hosted competing programs. With the development of *Good Morning America* on ABC in 1975 (see entry) and *The Early Show* (1999-) on CBS, which lured Bryant Gumbel away from the *Today* show, the three networks currently all have successful morning shows occupying the same time slot. Spinoffs of *Today* on NBC now include *Early Today, Later Today,* and *Weekend Today.*

Weaver's other major innovation, the *Tonight* show, found its roots in a 1950 late-night variety show called *Broadway Open House,* originally hosted by comedian Morey Amsterdam. Hosts of *Tonight* have included Steve Allen, Jack Paar, and, for 30 years, Johnny Carson (see entries). With Carson's success came many imitations and variations on the late-night talk theme. In the 1960s and early 1970s, ABC introduced talk shows starring radio personality Les Crane, writer/comic Dick Cavett, and comedian Joey Bishop in the late-night slot.

Syndicated British newsman David Frost also had some success in the late-night market from 1969 to 1972. Merv Griffin's successful syndicated talk show was seen at night in many markets from the mid-1960s through 1986. CBS produced *The Merv Griffin Show* for a three-year period, but for the most part, CBS stayed away from the late-night talk in the 1960s and 1970s, preferring to broadcast movies and reruns of successful TV series. In the 1980s, CBS enlisted Pat Sajak—host of the very highly rated game show *Wheel of Fortune*—to host its answer to the *Tonight* show. Sajak's show was not successful; it was soon canceled.

The success of the *Tonight* show on NBC encouraged the network to invent a show for those willing to stay awake for another dose of talk. *Tomorrow* with Tom Snyder, in which newsman Snyder interviewed guests one-on-one on a bare set, began its nine-year run on NBC in 1973.

In the early 1980s, NBC introduced *Late Night* with comedian David Letterman (see entry) as its host. In 1992 comedian (and frequent *Tonight* substitute host) Jay Leno replaced Johnny Carson on *The Tonight Show,* while CBS offered Letterman a show at the same time slot, and Conan O'Brien replaced Letterman on NBC's *Late Night.* Other late night hosts have included Tom Snyder and Charles Grodin.

The current crop of the confrontational audience-participatory afternoon talk shows can trace their roots back to the 1960s. Reflecting the turbulent mood of the times, the 1960s saw abrasive and controversial hosts such as Joe Pyne, Mort Sahl, and Alan Burke come onto the scene, challenging their audience and their guests in order to create confrontations and controversy.

In the 1970s midday talk shows became more relaxed, emulating Johnny Carson's successful easy-going style. Singers Dinah Shore, Mike Douglas, Della Reese, and longtime TV personality Virginia Graham were among those who hosted talk shows in the 1970s. Shore and Douglas were particularly successful, each enjoying very long runs on the air. Douglas was replaced by singer John Davidson in 1980 and the show was canceled in 1982.

Bibliography

Berman, Ronald. *How Television Sees Its Audience: A Look at the Looking Glass.* Newbury Park: Sage, 1987.

Munson, Wayne. *All Talk: The Talk Show in Media Culture.* Philadelphia: Temple UP, 1993.

Rapping, Elayne. *The Looking Glass World of Nonfiction TV.* Boston: South End, 1987.

Shulman, Arthur, and Roger Youman. *How Sweet It Was.* New York: Bonanza, 1966.

Timberg, Bernard. "The Unspoken Rules of Talk Television." *Television Talk.* Austin: U of Texas P, 1994.

Richard J. Allen

Television Technology. Expectations for a device that could transmit visual images in the same manner that a phone transmits sounds were aroused soon after Alexander Graham Bell demonstrated his telephone invention in 1876. Experimental work in television began as early as 1884 with the work of Paul Nipkow (see entry), a German scientist, who developed a method for projecting light through a spinning disk filled with holes in a spiral pattern that seemed to offer the possibility of breaking a picture down in a way that would permit sending it via wire. Four decades of experimentation followed, until in 1925 John L. Baird of England and Charles Francis Jenkins, an American, made separate demonstrations of televised images. Both inventors were able only to project silhouetted images at that time. In 1928, Ernest F. W. Alexanderson, head of General Electric's television experiments, began daily test broadcasts in Schenectady, NY, using a viewing screen a mere 3 by 4 inches. By 1931, experimental telecasts in New York were under way by RCA, the Radio Corporation of America.

These early efforts were hampered by poor quality pictures, and an improved method of image transmission, one that relied on electronic scanning instead of Nipkow's rotating disk technique, was invented by Vladimir K. Zworykin (see entry), employed by Westinghouse. Other inventors made contributions to the early perfection of television, like

Philo Farnsworth (see entry), son of a Mormon Idaho farmer, who had not even known of electricity's existence until adolescence, and who invented an improved electronic scanning technique in 1930 that made television in the home more practical. Allen B. DuMont made a better cathode-ray picture tube, and his company, begun with an investment of $500, commenced manufacturing home receivers in 1939.

While many inventors contributed to the birth of television, TV as a mass medium is the offspring of radio. Radio had grown into a major industry after World War I. Immediately after that war, radio broadcasting had been merely a hobby of individuals like Frank Conrad, who played phonograph concerts in the evenings over a transmitter located in a room above his garage in Wilkinsburg, near Pittsburgh. Larger operations were soon promoted by companies that hoped to benefit by making and selling radios. Westinghouse, for example, had been a producer of radio equipment for the military during the war and now envisioned a mass market for equipment. The company set up a station in a shack on the roof of one of its factory buildings in Pittsburgh in 1920. Soon stations sprang up around the country, and businesses realized that commercials aired over the new medium could lead to new profits. By the time that DuMont began manufacturing his television sets in 1939, the radio industry was rich enough to fund expensive efforts to launch the TV industry.

Three of the original television networks, NBC, CBS, and ABC, were all established as radio networks before the advent of TV (a fourth TV network, founded by DuMont, was short-lived). RCA, the dominant force in radio broadcasting, which for a time had controlled two national radio networks, NBC-red and NBC-blue, was headed by David Sarnoff, who in 1935 laid the groundwork for television as a mass medium by allocating one million dollars of RCA's budget for experimental television programming. In those early days actors and actresses had to wear green makeup and purple lipstick to show up more clearly on receivers, and the lights required were so hot that performers had to take salt tablets to ward off heat stroke.

Television nevertheless made enough progress that in 1939 Sarnoff selected a date for the initial commercial television broadcast. It covered the opening of the 1939 World's Fair in New York City, and it was there that President Franklin D. Roosevelt became the first president to appear on television. After this broadcast, RCA television sets were placed on display to entice the general public to try the new medium. The screens were 9 by 5 inches, and prices ranged as high as $600. Later, in 1939, the first broadcasts of a major league baseball game and a major league football game occurred.

Just as World War I had delayed the birth of radio, World War II interfered with the development of television, but after the war the three radio networks, NBC, ABC, and CBS, all moved forward with television plans. Although the networks had to use profits from radio to make up the heavy losses in television for the early years while the number of stations and sets gradually increased, by 1952 there was dramatic evidence that advertisers could do well in the new medium.

Theaters began to close across the country, while the radio industry, which had paid for the establishment of television, also found its audiences dropping. In 1954 the Federal Communications Commission (FCC) announced that television industry profits for the previous year ($68 million) exceeded annual profits from radio ($55 million), for the first time. In 1948, two immensely popular variety shows premiered, adding to the success of television, the *Texaco Star Theater* starring Milton Berle, and Ed Sullivan's *Toast of the Town*. By 1952, television had gained other popular shows like *I Love Lucy* and *Dragnet*, further increasing the medium's popularity.

Major movie studios found they could no longer afford to keep large numbers of stars on contract, and as unemployment among movie stars increased, the number of film actors taking up TV careers increased. Lucille Ball and her husband Desi Arnaz were among the movie actors displaced by TV, but who found a home in the new medium. Their show tried a new experiment with filming of episodes instead of broadcasting live. Most shows before had been live and the stress to make everything run smoothly in the allotted time was immense. Filming allowed editing and correction of errors and adjustments for time limitations. The costs were much higher, but the pressure connected with live broadcasting increasingly made the additional expense seem worthwhile.

The use of film for television series opened doors for an industry that had been hurt by TV. Movie studios gradually began to produce TV series, using their expertise in filming. Disney and Warner Brothers began by making shows for ABC during the mid-1950s. Other Hollywood studios like MGM and Twentieth Century-Fox followed. Westerns like *Wyatt Earp*, *Gunsmoke*, *Death Valley Days*, *Maverick*, and *Cheyenne* were especially popular in the early days of filmed TV shows.

One consequence of the use of film was that programs could be broadcast more than once, and they could be marketed abroad to growing television markets throughout the globe. Other nations, such as Canada, England and the USSR had, like the United States, experimented with television in the 1930s before World War II. It was the success of the medium in America, however, that contributed to the worldwide boom in the industry. By 1970, there were more than 100 countries broadcasting television, and there were in excess of 250 million TV sets. The use of film helped make American television shows so popular worldwide in part because film allowed the preservation and shipping of those shows; also, production costs of American filmed shows were recovered in the domestic market, and programs could then be sold to foreign markets for a price far less than the cost of original shows made by foreign producers.

By 1957, over 100 television series were produced on film, shows like *Dragnet*, *Perry Mason*, *Highway Patrol*, *Superman*, *M Squad,* and *Gunsmoke*. In 1958, revenue from foreign sales of American television shows on film was $15 million. Ten years later it had risen to $80 million. A popular TV show could earn between $6,000 and $7,000 in countries like Japan, England, and the United Kingdom. Another way in which the American movie industry participated in the success of television was through the sale of old movies for TV broadcast (see Television Movies, above). RKO began the trend in 1955 by selling 740 of its feature films to General Teleradio for use on television. Warner Brothers, Twentieth Century-Fox, Paramount, and others followed suit with similar deals. Since these sales applied to films made before 1948, a continued source of revenue for film studios could come from future movies sold to TV after their theater runs. Hollywood was becoming a television center as well as the movie capital.

Another technical innovation was to have a dramatic effect on television. Video equipment uses magnetization of areas on tape coated with particles of iron oxide or other magnetic material to store signals which can be converted back to electronic signals and then to sound and pictures. Magnetic recording of sound dates back to 1900, when Danish engineer Valdemar Poulsen developed a machine that stored recorded sound on steel wire. Magnetic tape as a means to record sound was developed by German scientists during World War II. Audio recorders and dictating machines became common by the 1960s, and tape in cartridges gradually eclipsed vinyl records for the music industry. Magnetic storage of information on tape and disks became widely used also in the computer industry.

The connection with television began in 1951 when Bing Crosby Enterprises developed a system that recorded audio and video on a tape reel, and although the quality was poor, the involvement of other engineers like Charles P. Ginsburg and Ray Dolby of Ampex Corp. of California led to CBS's use of an Ampex video recording machine in 1956 to record the evening news for rebroadcast on the West Coast later in the day. Television was soon changed as Sony developed the Portapak in the 1960s, allowing stations to videotape news events on the scene for later broadcast. In 1972, one of the first major national events taped was that year's Republican National Convention.

Videotape eliminated the time and expense necessary for processing film, and directors and performers could immediately see their work on a monitor and more rapidly make any necessary changes. Furthermore, video allowed the instant replay, which had exciting results for live televised sporting events. News events could be aired more quickly also. When Lee Harvey Oswald was shot by Jack Ruby, NBC had caught the event on live television, but within minutes other networks were able to use videotape to broadcast the shooting numerous times on their networks. And it has been estimated that by the time of President Kennedy's assassination, television had become so widespread that nine out of ten Americans viewed the fallen president's funeral services.

Color television existed in experimental forms as early as 1929, when on June 27 of that year color images were transmitted during a public demonstration at the Bell Telephone Laboratories in New York City. The receiving device depended in part on a system of mirrors to superimpose color on the television pictures, and the setup was rather primitive. During World War II, when commercial television plans had to be postponed, RCA and CBS experimented with color TV. Just after the war CBS demonstrated a system that provided vivid color pictures, but broadcasts couldn't be picked up by black-and-white sets. RCA developed a system compatible with black-and-white systems, but it did not produce vivid, stable images. The problems with color television caused a delay which was prolonged into the early 1950s because some necessary manufacturing materials were unavailable during the Korean War. Meanwhile, black-and-white sets were mass-marketed. By the end of 1953, however, the FCC issued rules for a compatible color system that inspired RCA and its subsidiary NBC to install color equipment and begin broadcasting some of its major programs in color.

Within a decade, NBC was airing up to 40 hours a week of shows in color. The other two networks still had done little work with color by this time, and color sets were expensive, but in spite of these obstacles, color gained increasing popularity, forcing the other networks to follow NBC's example. By 1968, a year in which 11.4 million TV sets were sold, the number of color sets sold surpassed the number of black-and-white for the first time. In 1969, when American astronauts approached within eight miles of the moon, the pictures broadcast back to viewers on earth were shot in color. Today only 1 percent of television homes do not have at least one color set.

Cable television also changed the shape of the rapidly evolving television industry (see CATV, Cable TV, Coaxial Cable, Fiberoptics; also Closed-Circuit and Cable-Access TV). The use of coaxial cables to distribute video and audio signals was initially developed during the 1950s to offer improved reception in rural and hilly areas. During the 1960s cable expanded into some urban areas because reception there was sometimes undermined by tall buildings, and by the 1970s there came to be about four thousand local cable systems in the U.S. Originally known as community antenna television (CATV) because of the use of a common or community antenna to pick up signals that were then transmitted via cables to subscribers, cable television quickly expanded its mission from the mere improvement of reception to offering an increased number of channels. Recently, cable has faced competition from direct digital satellite television (see Satellite Dishes).

While cable and direct satellite television have offered more and more choices, an innovation dating from the 1950s made switching between so many channels easier. As early as 1955, Zenith produced televisions that permitted the changing of channels without the necessity of rising from one's seat to make the trip to the set. The drawback was that this early version of the remote control had a cord running from the changer device to the television, which, though it reduced the need to move, nevertheless imposed an obstacle viewers found themselves tripping over during their less frequent travels from the couch. About the same time Zenith's "Flash-Matic" flashlight control allowed viewers to control sets by directing the beam of light at photoelectric cells in the TV's corners. Unfortunately, the cells could be activated by sunlight and other bright lights, resulting in unexpected switching of channels and turning off and on of the set.

Robert Adler was assigned by Zenith with the task of creating a better remote control. His invention had four buttons—one for power, one to move channels up, one to move them down, and one for mute—and used high frequency sound waves transmitted to an electronic receiver in the set. The use of high frequency sound waves continued until the early 1980s, when infrared beamers were developed. This technology provided the possibility of controls that could handle a huge number of channels, a development that would make the rapidly expanding number of cable channels more easily accessible to remote control channel surfers (see also Zap).

Meanwhile, videotape technology was finding new applications. The original equipment made for television stations was far too expensive for the public to purchase, but by the mid-1970s Sony had developed a practical home video system, and its aggressive ad campaign for its ill-fated Betamax video cassette recorder and tapes got the industry off the ground. In 1976, the Victor Company of Japan (JVC) began to popularize VHS (Video Home System), offering a cheaper and less cumbersome recorder and tapes that could record more material. VHS eventually won dominance over Sony's Betamax system, and with a single universal system and widespread purchase of recorders, movie companies feared another assault on their industry as movies aired on television could become the possession of anyone owning a video recorder.

Universal and Disney filed suit for copyright infringement only to lose a Supreme Court decision in 1984. Home viewers, the Court said, could record shows for their personal entertainment, and the video industry was not liable for any pirating of copyrighted material facilitated by video equipment. Hollywood later embraced VCRs, however, as studios discovered that they had much to gain. While video recorders allowed viewers to make their own television viewing schedule, recording programs to watch at times most convenient for themselves, and to make private collections of shows, the recorder also offered the opportunity for film studios to market tapes of recently released movies after they had had their runs on the big screen. This market became so profitable—in 1993, for example, Disney sold 20 million copies of *Aladdin*—that studios began to release movies on tape before selling rights to premium cable movie channels or pay-television channels. After that, films could still be sold to the television networks, and then sold into syndication for endless showings here and abroad. Hollywood had again survived a challenge from television-related developments.

The success of VCRs opened doors for other new industries. The rental of movies on videotape became a thriving business. Camcorders, cameras that record on videotape cassettes designed for viewing on VCRs, have allowed millions of amateurs to create home libraries filled with scenes they record themselves, some of which have made their way onto television on *America's Funniest Home Videos*, aired on ABC since 1990. Video games (see entry), first in video parlors and then in forms for home use, have been another popular manifestation of video technology.

VCRs have encountered recent competition from laser disc players. These players read microscopic holes on a thin disc of plastic or metal and convert the variations in light reflected off the disc into electronic data which is changed into sound and pictures. Advantages over VCR technology include the fact that laser discs are not magnetic and cannot be accidentally erased, the lack of contact between moveable parts prolongs the life of the disc, and the quality of the picture and sound are better. Players can use 8-inch or 12-inch discs and also the smaller compact discs for audio only. The digital video disc (DVD), developed by Toshiba and Time-Warner in the mid-1990s, can squeeze 4 1/2 hours of video material onto a 5-inch compact disc that produces a better picture than a laser disc and sound as clear as that of audio CDs. The more than 82 million VCRs in the U.S. are not yet doomed, however, because the DVD system cannot record material.

Television sets themselves have continued to evolve over the years. Recent models sold by Sony, Magnavox, Zenith, GE, Quasar, RCA, JVC, and Sharp—some of these companies having been in the business since its earliest days—now come with a variety of improvements over the earliest sets. Remote controls are standard equipment now, some sets include stereo sound and the means to hook up additional stereo speakers, and some provide on-screen clocks and alarms, and sleep timers to shut sets off automatically. Small inset pictures to allow viewing of a second channel are provided on some sets, as are on-screen menus for adjustments, the capacity to receive almost 200 cable channels, built-in closed-caption decoders for the hearing impaired, and even AM/FM radio. TV set manufacturers like GE, Quasar, Hitachi, and Magnavox sell sets that contain built-in VCR players.

Televisions now come in a large variety of sizes. Sony markets a Watchman TV with a liquid crystal display (LCD) that features a 3-inch color screen and a stereo headset jack. GE sells Spacemaker sets with small screens (7- to 9-inch) for installation under kitchen cabinets for viewers who like spicing up their cooking chores with TV. At the other extreme in size, Sony markets a set with a 32-inch screen that is part of a home theater system that includes a Dolby receiver and amplifier, two 3-way tower speakers and three surround-sound speakers that reproduce movie theater quality audio. Projection TV systems, projecting TV pictures from behind onto enlarged screens, offer even larger images. Zenith and RCA make projection sets with screens as large as 52 to 55 inches, while Mitsubishi markets one with a 70-inch screen.

More change is in line for the television industry. High-definition television (see entry) provides crystal clear audio and images, the latter closer to that on a movie screen. High-definition television has already been in operation in Japan since 1991, developed by the Japan Broadcasting Corporation. The U.S. industry has developed a different kind of HDTV, a digital system considered superior to the Japanese analog one, but it is not yet available on a wide basis.

In addition to the many ways in which television has shaped the ways we entertain ourselves, television and TV technology have found a variety of other applications. The medical profession uses closed-circuit television and videotapes to train doctors and nurses in a number of ways. Surgery, for example, can be observed by a large audience of trainees, either while in progress or later. Cameras can also be hooked up to microscopes in laboratories for researcher and training viewers. In recent years, camera apparatus so small it can be inserted into the body has been used for diagnostic purposes or even to facilitate surgery that requires far less cutting of tissue than conventional operations. Surgeons work with equipment introduced into the body through narrow tubes while watching television monitors to guide their movements. Patients now may undergo procedures like the removal of a gall bladder, an appendectomy, inguinal hernia repair, or surgery on knee cartilage and recuperate in a fraction of the time required by traditional surgery not facilitated by video equipment. Patient education is also aided by VCR tapes that can help teach expectant parents, for example, how to prepare for birth and parenthood.

Colleges and secondary and primary schools have found closed-circuit TV and VCRs useful for instruction and presentation of plays, poetry readings, interviews and lectures, concerts, and other cultural, historical, and educational material (see Closed-circuit and Cable Access TV). Many factories use television technology for security, such as for surveillance of parking lots, warehouses, and areas where classified material is kept. Retail businesses use cameras to catch shoplifters and dishonest employees, banks use cameras to discourage and help apprehend bank robbers, and even automatic teller machines include a camera eye that looks out at the surrounding area. Businesses have found that closed-circuit TV and VCR technology help train personnel and even aid in the sale of products. Some companies mail out video sales pitches for their products to interested customers. And video conferencing provides businesses a way for individuals to meet over long distances without the expense of traveling to a central location. The video telephone, equipped with a TV camera and screen for reciprocal viewing, may offer this kind of communication in the home if the expense of transmitting such images over phone lines can be made more reasonable.

Governments use cameras for surveillance of defense installations and to spy on other countries. Cameras small enough to be concealed in clothing are used for some such activities and have also been a boon to television shows that specialize in undercover reporting. Television technology has even made its way into the weapons industry. Smart bombs, for example, include small cameras that allow distant operators to guide the devices to their intended targets. Cameras are also installed in fighter planes to record and help verify the success or failure of their missions.

Within the 50 years since television began full-scale operations after World War II, it and related industries have come to play a significant role in our culture and daily lives. In 1970, there were an estimated 250 million sets worldwide; in 1998, there were over 235 million sets in the U.S. alone. In 1998, 98 percent of all U.S. households owned at least one television set, more than the percentage owning tele-

phones; 99 percent of those television households owned at least one color television, and 74 percent of them owned two or more sets. In 1998, there were 1,505 television stations operating across the U.S, and cable television reached 68 percent of television households. VCRs were present that year in even more homes—85 percent. Perhaps the most dramatic measure of the impact of the medium on our lives is the amount of time we spend in front of our sets, now an average of seven and 1/4 hours per person each day.

Bibliography

Barnouw, Erik. *Tube of Plenty: The Evolution of American Television*. 2d rev. ed. New York: Oxford UP, 1990.

Broadcasting & Cable Yearbook 1999. New Providence: Bowker, 1999.

Settel, Irving, and William Lass. *A Pictorial History of Television*. 2d ed. New York: Ungar, 1983.

Sterling, Christopher, and George Shiers. *Technical Development of Television*. New York: Arno, 1977.

Wicklein, John. *Electronic Nightmare: The New Communications and Freedom*. New York: Viking, 1981.

Alan Kelly

See also
Television Broadcasting—VHF and UHF

Television Town Meetings. In the electronic age, when fewer Americans actually vote or even inform themselves about politics and government, "town meetings" have come to refer to the historical New England gatherings that were seen as models of simple democracy, as well as to televised forums wherein political figures or panels of experts offer opening statements, analyze topical issues, and respond to questions from a studio audience and sometimes from viewers linked by telephone or computer. These television town meetings have become especially popular with presidential candidates and other politicians, who see them as a way to disseminate their messages to large audiences, unfiltered by critical news media. They are also popular with those citizens who see them as a means to participate more directly in the political process by seeking answers to their concerns and giving voice to their opinions and frustrations.

The ABC News program *Nightline*, which debuted in 1981, helped pioneer the genre of the television town meeting. While its format usually is restricted to host Ted Koppel interviewing newsmakers after a brief set-up piece, the show occasionally ventures beyond its Washington, DC, base, to college lecture halls or civic auditoriums in various parts of the country. There, Koppel moderates live on-air debates among public officials, academic experts, and other journalists who have been assembled to consider a given topic such as urban crime or health care. The programs usually include opportunities for members of the audience to pose their own questions.

The 1992 general election campaign marked a significant turning point in the ways presidential hopefuls broadcast their messages to Americans, and the television town meeting came into its own as a mass communications form. The format became a favorite for Democrat Bill Clinton, who sought to showcase a detailed knowledge of the issues and an ability to identify with the concerns of ordinary Americans.

More comfortable on television than President George Bush, and a cooler on-screen presence than the prickly billionaire-turned-independent-candidate H. Ross Perot, Clinton excelled at the casual, extended exchanges with studio audiences and call-in viewers. A few times the campaign bought blocks of airtime and arranged its own town meetings. Usually, though, Clinton's operation capitalized on interest in the format by local television stations, which often would tie-in by satellite with other stations in the same state or region. The town meetings—especially those during the summer and early fall, before viewers had become jaded and overexposed to the candidates—often drew huge ratings. Such opportunities provided the Democratic nominee with priceless hours of exposure in dozens of media markets—a significant advantage for an out-party challenger.

A variation on the television town meeting has become known as the "electronic town hall." Advanced enthusiastically during the campaign by Perot, the idea refers to a plebiscite wherein citizens would watch broadcast summaries or debates about national issues, then cast "votes" via computer, telephone, or interactive television.

Despite its limitations and potential to clutter political debate with questions and harangues that are emotional, poorly informed, or irrelevant (during the 1992 campaign one studio audience member identified himself as a witch and asked Clinton how he felt about atheism and paganism), the television town meeting clearly has struck a chord with American voters and assumed a place in popular culture. Shortly after the election, the Cable News Network (CNN) began broadcasting a daily program titled *Talk Back Live*, which allows viewers to communicate with guests via telephone, computer, and fax.

Bibliography

Kurtz, Howard. *Media Circus.* New York: Times, 1993.

Patterson, Thomas E. *Out of Order.* New York: Knopf, 1993.

Perot, H. Ross. *United We Stand: How We Can Take Back Our Country.* New York: Hyperion, 1992.

Rosenstiel, Tom. *Strange Bedfellows: How Television and the Presidential Candidates Changed American Politics, 1992.* New York: Hyperion, 1993.

Steve Sanders

Television Westerns. No TV program genre, not even the situation comedy, ever became so dominant at any given moment in time as the Western during the late 1950s and early 1960s. And no format produced more movie stars, from Clint Eastwood (*Rawhide*), Steve McQueen (*Wanted Dead or Alive*), and James Garner (*Maverick*) to Burt Reynolds (*Gunsmoke*) and Roger Moore (*Maverick*). Eighteen new Westerns appeared on the home tube in 1958, when 12 of the top 25 Nielsen-rated shows were Westerns, including a phenomenal 7 of the Top 10. The following season Westerns reached their peak with 47 broadcast nationally each week in prime time. There were so many popular and well-made Westerns that in 1959 the industry gave the genre its own Emmy, placing it on an equal footing with comedies and dramas.

Early television Westerns were usually made with a juvenile audience in mind. The plots were simple and to the point. Good always triumphed over evil, crime did not pay, and the hero was invariably brave, just, kind, smart, and tough. Television shows modeled after the old B Westerns that were such an integral part of the Saturday matinees of the 1940s became a sensation on television in the 1950s. Gene Autry and Roy Rogers joined Hopalong Cassidy and the Lone Ranger as "good guys" who never shot first and rarely killed the "bad guys." They simply incapacitated them by expertly shooting the pistols out of their hands and then turned them over to the law for punishment.

The first *Hopalong Cassidy* TV shows were condensed versions of the feature-length films Cassidy had made earlier. The response was so great that Boyd made a new series of shows especially for the new medium. Within two years of his debut on television, "Hoppy" was a national hero. *The Lone Ranger* (see entry) soon joined "Hoppy" on the home screen, after a long and successful radio career. The creation of writer Fran Striker, the Ranger was promoted by Detroit station owner George W. Trendle and eventually was broadcast from WXYZ nationally over the Mutual Network. Two screen serials increased the show's popularity before it moved to television in 1949.

Both Gene Autry and Roy Rogers (see Singing Cowboys, above) were established radio and film stars when they made their first appearances on the new medium. A year after *The Gene Autry Show*'s debut (July 23, 1950), Autry launched his own production company, Flying A Productions, with Hollywood studio facilities. In addition to Autry's own show, the company produced *The Range Rider,* which starred former stunt man Jock Mahoney, *Buffalo Bill, Jr.,* featuring Dick Jones, *Annie Oakley,* with TV's first Western heroine (Gail Davis), and *The Adventures of Champion,* which displayed the talents of Autry's "wonder horse."

The season after Autry took the plunge into television, Roy Rogers, "The King of the Cowboys," joined him bringing along his wife Dale Evans, his horse Trigger ("the smartest horse in the movies"), and his German shepherd, Bullet. Within a few years of his TV debut, merchandise bearing his name or likeness was earning manufacturers millions of dollars.

Other successful juvenile shows included *The Cisco Kid* (one of the first shows to be filmed in color), featuring Duncan Renaldo as O. Henry's "Robin Hood of the Old West," with Leo Carrillo as his faithful comic sidekick Pancho; *Sky King*, a sophisticated contemporary Western hero (portrayed by Kirby Grant) who used a twin-engine Cessna called the Songbird in lieu of a horse to hunt down evil-doers; *Wild Bill Hickok,* about a U.S. Marshal who brought law and order to the Old West with his sidekick Jingles (played by Guy Madison and Andy Devine, who had created the characters on radio); and *The Adventures of Kit Carson,* purporting to depict the escapades of the legendary frontiersman and Indian scout on the Western frontier of the 1880s (with Bill Williams in the title role).

Throughout the fifties, Westerns became the most popular genre of juvenile television programs, especially among boys. This popularity can be attributed to a close adherence to the formula that had been established during years of B Westerns and several dozen kid-oriented shows from the golden age of radio. Essential ingredients were: the brave, infallible hero, to uphold the mythical "Code of the West"; the comic sidekick, to break the "monotony" of nonstop action with a few laughs; children in supporting roles to give young viewers a sense of involvement in the stories; and a noble and trusted steed to carry the hero out of harm's way. Women rarely appeared as continuing characters in juvenile Westerns. (Notable exceptions were *Annie Oakley* and Dale Evans in *The Roy Rogers Show*.) When female characters did appear, they were usually in trouble and needed assistance from the hero. They were in stories to be rescued, but never kissed.

Walt Disney's entrance into the genre in the mid-1950s changed the course of the television Western (see Walt Disney Television). His version of the life of Davy Crockett premiered on three hour-long episodes of the popular *Disneyland* program. The series was a ratings blockbuster and led to an unprecedented commercial craze. At the insistence of ABC, Disney continued to feature Western heroes on his *Disneyland* series, including Andy Burnett, Texas John Slaughter, Elfego Baca, Zorro, Daniel Boone, as well as further exploits of Davy Crockett. Although they were all well-received by viewers, none precipitated the public reaction that the first Crockett series had launched.

Television historian J. Fred MacDonald calls the Davy Crockett programs "transitional" in the history of the television Western, pointing out that although they were designed for children, they depicted adult values and relatively mature emotions. Davy displayed such juvenile characteristics as a trusty sidekick (George Russell), a rifle named "Old Betsy," and a set of moral values that dealt only in black-and-white issues. On the other hand, Davy possessed several "grown-up" qualities. The death of his wife produced grief and gave Crockett an air of vulnerability. Furthermore, Davy was both a patriot and a political philosopher. Finally, no television Western to date had depicted death and violence to such an extent, nor had the hero of any previous juvenile Western been allowed to die.

While Disney's Westerns were aimed primarily at children and youth, other programs were being developed that were designed for the prime-time adult viewer. With the coming of *The Life and Legend of Wyatt Earp* and *Gunsmoke* in the fall of 1955, the Western craze began. Many factors added momentum to this trend. President Eisenhower's fondness for Western novels stimulated interest in the historic West. Westerns offered an escape from the confusing complex problems of the present to a simpler time when the good guys always won and the bad guys always lost.

By the mid-1950s, the assumption that Westerns were "just for kids" began to change as theatrical films such as *High Noon* (1952) and *Shane* (1953) placed more serious plots in Western settings. These films, which were acclaimed critically as well as box-office successes, became known as "adult Westerns." In its waning years, radio drama also had experimented with Western stories aimed at a mature audi-

Photo courtesy of Sound Recording Archives, Bowling Green State University, Bowling Green, OH.

ence and although, with the exception of *Gunsmoke*, the shows were short-lived, most critics agreed that several were among the best quality dramatic programs ever broadcast (see Radio Westerns).

The characters in the adult Western had more substance than the stereotypical B Western variety. Here one found a hero who was more human and consequently more believable than the one-dimensional stars of the kiddie Westerns—a complex mixture of good and evil, strength and weakness. The "villains" in "adult Westerns" also were a different breed. Not totally evil and cowardly, the villain could be the victim of circumstances beyond his or her control. In addition, it was not unusual to find the controversial themes that had been so scrupulously avoided in juvenile Westerns. There could be found excessive violence and stories dealing with sex, religion, and racial discrimination—especially concerning the Native American—in most successful adult Westerns. There was also a much greater attempt at historical accuracy in these programs, although literary license was employed liberally when the producers did not find the truth to be more exciting than fiction.

In September of 1955, four prime-time adult Westerns were launched by the networks to join the syndicated *Death Valley Days*: *Gunsmoke* on CBS, *Cheyenne* and *The Life and Legend of Wyatt Earp* on ABC and *Frontier* on NBC. Of these series only the latter failed to achieve long-term ratings success.

Premiering four days ahead of *Gunsmoke*, *Wyatt Earp* at first glance appeared to be cast in the mold of most juvenile

Westerns. In appearance Hugh O'Brien looked nothing like the legendary hero and critics claimed that the show white-washed Earp. Still, it presented the man's life much more accurately than, say, the earlier *Wild Bill Hickok* series.

Most of the *Wyatt Earp* episodes were based on historical events in the life of the West's most famous lawman. The conflict between a previously lawless town and an effective dedicated lawman provided a strong basis for the weekly stories. Every effort was made to create sets and costumes that were accurate even to the make of Earp's gun, the Buntline Special. During the series' six-year run, the scripts followed Earp from his arrival in Ellsworth City, KS, through his career in Dodge City and Tombstone, AZ, concluding with a five-part dramatization of the famous gunfight at the OK corral in a pattern that closely followed Earp's career.

The pattern established on the *Wyatt Earp* show was later followed (with varying degrees of success) by Gene Barry as *Bat Masterson*, Scott Forbes as *Jim Bowie*, Barry Sullivan as Pat Garrett on *The Tall Man*, Jock Mahoney as *Yancy Derringer*, Fess Parker as *Daniel Boone,* and Jeffrey Hunter as *Temple Houston.*

Immediately preceding *Wyatt Earp* on ABC's Tuesday evening schedule was *Warner Brothers Presents*—a dramatic trilogy which included a Western based on a little-known B movie called *Cheyenne* and starring an unknown actor named Clint Walker. The main reason that *Cheyenne* succeeded while others failed was Walker. At six-feet-six-inches, he had broad shoulders and a magnificent physique. Furthermore, the series stressed plot and action rather than dialogue and character development common to most other adult Westerns. Each episode depicted the exploits of frontier scout Cheyenne Bodie, a man of Indian descent and learned in both the ways of the white man and the Cheyenne. Drifting from job to job, he encountered villains, beautiful girls, and gunfights.

Other less successful variations on this drifter theme included *Bronco* (Ty Hardin), *The Rebel* (Nick Adams), *The Restless Gun* (John Payne), *The Texan* (Rory Calhoun), *The Westerner* (Brian Keith), *The Loner* (Lloyd Bridges), *A Man Called Shenandoah* (Robert Horton), *Hondo* (Ralph Taeger), *Destry* (John Gavin), and *Shane* (David Carradine).

Meanwhile, the most successful adult Western in history, *Gunsmoke* (see entry), had been introduced to the television public by John Wayne on September 10, 1955. Many viewers were already familiar with the show, since it had been created for CBS radio by producer Norman Macdonnell and writer John Meston in the spring of 1952.

In *Gunsmoke,* viewers found something unique: a Western hero who was not invincible; a Western story that was not predictable. Marshal Matt Dillon got his man, not because he was always faster or stronger or even braver, but because he was smarter. Relative unknown James Arness, at six-feet-seven-inches, was impressive as the heroic marshal.

Imitations of *Gunsmoke* came and went (*Lawman, Wichita Town, Tombstone Territory, Cimarron City, Cimarron Strip*), but there were other successful variations that made some lasting impact on the genre. Two of the Westerns that debuted in the fall of 1957 broke the mold of the tradi-

tional cowboy hero by introducing central characters who were guided more by their own self-interest than by any "mythical code of the West." The *Maverick* brothers, who'd rather run than fight, were professional con-men and gamblers. Paladin, whose business cards read *Have Gun, Will Travel*, was a professional gunfighter who sold his services to the highest bidder. One season later, they were joined by bounty hunter Josh Randall, who in *Wanted: Dead or Alive* seemed to be less interested in upholding the law than in collecting a sizable reward for his efforts.

Another successful adult series was not a conventional Western at all, but a dramatic anthology that happened to be set in the 19th-century American West. *Wagon Train* (see entry) combined guest stars with a stable cast of regulars to relate the stories of various members of the caravan and how and why they were heading west. The show focused on the week's guest rather than the wagonmaster and his crew, who served mainly as commentators on the action or as continuity devices. This format managed to keep *Wagon Train* rolling for eight seasons and provided a pattern that was later successfully adopted by two other Western blockbusters, *Rawhide* and *The Virginian.*

Rawhide, which starred Eric Fleming and Clint Eastwood, was the closest television has yet to come to creating an authentic "sweat and blood" Western. The series, which premiered in January 1959 as a mid-season replacement, was the creation of veteran Hollywood writer-director Charles Marquis Warren. Warren, who had been instrumental in developing the TV version of *Gunsmoke*, based the series on the great cattle drives of the 1870s, when drovers moved the herds from Texas to the railheads in Kansas and Missouri. *Rawhide* ran for seven and one-half seasons due in part to the charisma of Clint Eastwood.

The late 1950s and early 1960s saw the emergence of a new breed of adult Western—the "domestic" or "family" Western. Several of these series were quite successful—*The Rifleman* (first of this format), *Bonanza* (longest running), *The Virginian* (TV's first 90-minute Western), *The Big Valley* (featuring a matriarchal, rather than a patriarchal family), *The High Chaparral* (a modified version of *Bonanza*), and *Lancer* (although it ran only two seasons).

As if to emphasize the rigors of life in the old West, each of these TV families was headed by a widower (or in the case of *The Big Valley*, a widow). Several of these patriarchs had been widowed more than once. In fact, Ben Cartwright (*Bonanza*) had suffered the loss of three wives. Only Big John Cannon (*The High Chaparral*) was married at the time the stories took place.

The Rifleman, premiering in 1958, focused on the warm relationship that existed between Lucas McCain, a New Mexico homesteader struggling to make a living off his ranch, and Mark, his young son. The series took its name from the trick rifle that Lucas always carried, a modified Winchester with a large ring that cocked it as he twirled it.

While the McCains represented lower-class homesteaders struggling to eke out a living from the land, the Cartwrights were representatives of the upper class struggling to defend their vast property holdings. Set in the vicinity of Virginia City, NV, during the Civil War era soon after the discovery of the fabulous Comstock Silver Lode, *Bonanza* (see entry) was the story of Ben Cartwright (portrayed by the silver-haired, Canadian-born Lorne Greene) and his three sons (each by a different wife)—the serious, thoughtful, mature Adam (Pernell Roberts); the gentle, sensitive giant Hoss (Dan Blocker); and the impulsive and romantic Little Joe (Michael Landon). *Bonanza* emphasized the bonds of affection between the men, as well as their affinity for the land. Although family differences were frequent, these were always put aside when the family's honor or property were threatened by corrupt and thieving outsiders.

On initial viewing, *The Big Valley* might have appeared to be but a slightly more elaborate version of *Bonanza*. The series did focus on the trials and tribulations of a single-parent family, the Barkleys, as they strove to manage a 30,000-acre ranch in California's San Joaquin Valley. There was, however, a significant difference. The family was a matriarchy headed by the recently widowed Victoria Barkley. What was most unique about Victoria Barkley was the strength and domination of the character. She was a heroine with feminine characteristics and great inner strength. Bringing credibility to the role was veteran actress Barbara Stanwyck.

The Virginian (NBC, 1962) combined the drifter character (the mysterious Virginian, played by James Drury) with the domestic Western by following the stories of the families who owned Shiloh Ranch in Wyoming, where the Virginian was the foreman.

By the mid-1960s, however, Westerns were declining in popularity on the home screen. To meet the challenge the networks tried covering the traditional terrain with some new approaches. In fact, the only new TV Westerns with any staying power were *The Wild Wild West*, a unique combination of espionage thriller and Western; and *Little House on the Prairie*, which shifted attention from the cowboy to the farmer.

The Wild Wild West (CBS, 1965-69; see entry) was the creation of Michael Garrison, who was obviously influenced as much by the popular James Bond films and their TV clone, *The Man from U.N.C.L.E.*, as he was by earlier television Westerns. Two U.S. government agents, James T. West and Artemus Gordon (played with wit and charm by Robert Conrad and Ross Martin), were assigned to the Western frontier by President Ulysses S. Grant. Their assignment was to undermine or expose the attempts of various radical, revolutionary, or criminal groups to take over the country.

Only one series with a Western setting was successful in attracting substantial numbers of viewers during the 1970s. And by some standards that program, *Little House on the Prairie* (NBC, 1974), would not even be considered a Western. Although it was set in the American West during the 1870s, it did not have the other usual trappings associated with Westerns. There were few cowboys and even fewer Indians in the stories, and the town did not even have a saloon.

The series, based on the *Little House* stories of Laura Ingalls Wilder, owed as much to *The Waltons* as it did to other television Westerns. Presenting a rather sentimental view of the trials and tribulations of a homesteader family struggling to make a living on a small farm on the frontier, episodes presented character studies of individual family members and their friends in times of crisis.

During the late 1980s, network Westerns did not fare well: *Paradise* (*Guns of Paradise* during its final season), which related the trials and tribulations of a retired gunslinger trying to raise his four nieces and nephews in a lawless mining town, lasted two and a half seasons (1988-91); *The Young Riders*, loosely based on the exploits of the Pony Express, launched in 1989 by ABC, was canceled after its third season.

By the early 1990s there were encouraging signs that the Western was making a modest comeback: the critical and commercial success of CBS's *Lonesome Dove* miniseries in 1989 (and its sequel in 1993) and theatrical films like Kevin Costner's *Dances with Wolves* (1990) and Clint Eastwood's *Unforgiven* (1992), both of which earned best picture Oscars.

Several new network Westerns also achieved popular success during the early 1990s. *Dr. Quinn, Medicine Woman* (CBS, 1993-98), undoubtedly the first thoroughly revisionist Western on television, related the adventures of a female doctor (played with credibility by Jane Seymour) in the Colorado territories of the 1870s.

Walker, Texas Ranger (CBS, 1993-) is a traditional action Western set in the contemporary West with some deference to modern trends. Cordell Walker (as played by Chuck Norris) is a 1990s lawman—a karate-chopping crimebuster—whose methods were rooted in the old West. The series is full of contrasts between the "new" and the "old" West. Although based in the urban Fort Worth-Dallas area, Walker lives on a ranch out in the country. He usually chases down criminals in a pickup truck, but can ride a horse as well as any 19th-century cowboy.

Historian Frederick Jackson Turner once said that "each age writes the history of the past anew with reference to the conditions uppermost in its own time." This has been especially true of the television Western. The shows that proved to be most successful and enduring were those that evolved to mirror the changing times, like *Gunsmoke* and *Bonanza*.

Bibliography

Brauer, Ralph. *The Horse, the Gun, and the Piece of Property: Changing Images of the TV Western*. Bowling Green, OH: Bowling Green State U Popular P, 1975.

Brode, Douglas. "They Went Thataway." *Television Quarterly* Summer 1982.

Henry, William A., III. "They Went Thataway!" *Memories* Dec. 1989/Jan. 1990.

MacDonald, J. Fred. *Who Shot the Sheriff?* New York: Praeger, 1987.

Yoggy, Gary A. *Riding the Video Range: The Rise and Fall of the Western on Television*. Jefferson: McFarland, 1994.

Gary A. Yoggy

See also

Radio Westerns

Singing Cowboys

Western Fiction

Western Films

Temple, Shirley (1928-), since childhood, has been a central figure in contemporary American popular culture. She made the song "On the Good Ship Lollipop" famous. A non-alcoholic drink was named after her. Many of her movies are currently available on video—colorized. Her autobiography received rave reviews. Though she is less well known for her political contributions as an adult, if popular culture is defined by its relation to Hollywood and history, then Shirley Temple is an icon of popular culture.

Shirley Temple's autobiography, *Child Star* (1988), covers her life from birth to April 9, 1954. She is writing a second autobiography, which will, no doubt, include her current political activities.

From the moment she was born, Temple's acting career took off, and while she might only be remembered for one song—"On the Good Ship Lollipop," from the hugely successful *Bright Eyes* (Fox, 1934)—she made many, many films. The filmography at the back of *Child Star* lists 57 movies done from 1931 to 1949. Indeed, during 1932, by which time she was a mature four years old, Temple made seven movies.

Inevitably, she soon met and worked with most of the stars in Hollywood, and found herself in many famous films that were put out by such film studios as MGM, Paramount, and Twentieth Century-Fox. For example, as she was sometimes making as many as seven movies in a year, it is unsurprising that she met such literary, film, theater, and political figures as H. G. Wells, Lionel Barrymore, Noel Coward, Irving Berlin, Bill "Bojangles" Robinson, Carole Lombard, Gary Cooper, and Eleanor Roosevelt. *Now and Forever* (Paramount, 1934) starred Temple, Lombard, and Cooper. *Wee Willie Winkie* (Twentieth Century-Fox, 1937) starred Temple, Cesar Romero, and Victor McLaglen. *Rebecca of Sunnybrook Farm* (Twentieth Century-Fox, 1938) starred Temple, Randolph Scott, Jack Haley, and Bill Robinson. *A Kiss for Corliss* (United Artists, 1949) starred Shirley Temple and David Niven. A prolific and star-studded career indeed, which culminated in an Oscar—at five years old.

After a short marriage (1945-49) to actor John Agar, Shirley Temple married Charles E. Black in 1950 and effectively retired from show business, though she did host two television shows: *Shirley Temple's Storybook* (1957-59) and *The Shirley Temple Show* (1960). In the sixties, using her married name, she began a second career in politics and eventually served as a delegate to the United Nations General Assembly (1969-70), U.S. ambassador to Ghana (1974-76), and U.S. ambassador to Czechoslovakia (1989-92).

It was perhaps inevitable that Shirley Temple Black should move from film to politics, should go from being a Hollywood actress to being a U.S. ambassador. Replacing the politics of illusion with the illusion of politics was a natural progression for someone so thoroughly involved in the history of America that is Hollywood.

Bibliography

David, Lester, and Irene David. *The Shirley Temple Story*. New York: Putnam, 1983.

Edwards, Anne. *Shirley Temple: American Princess*. New York: Morrow, 1988.

Temple, Shirley. *Child Star: An Autobiography*. New York: McGraw-Hill, 1988.

Windeler, Robert. *The Films of Shirley Temple*. Secaucus: Citadel, 1978.

Ian Wojcik-Andrews

Temptations, The, were widely acknowledged as the best male vocal group in the soul genre of the 1960s and 1970s. The quintet was also an excellent example of the "Motown sound" emanating from Detroit on the Motown record label.

The Temptations formed in 1960 in Detroit as a group called the Elgins, a combination of two other Detroit-based groups, the Primes and the Distants. Unlike most other Motown bands, the Elgins had roots in southern gospel groups before the singers moved to Detroit. The original Temptations consisted of Eddie Kendricks, Paul Williams, Melvin Franklin, and Otis Williams (Otis Miles). Elbridge Bryant rounded out the quintet in 1961 and 1962 for two unsuccessful singles.

When Bryant quit the group, he was replaced by David Ruffin. Motown songwriter-producer-singer Smokey Robinson began working with the group, and their recording of Robinson's song "The Way You Do the Things You Do" hit No. 11 on the charts in April 1964. Kendricks sang lead vocals on that and two other moderately successful singles in 1964, "I'll Be in Trouble" and "Girl (Why You Wanna Make Me Blue)." The group also released its first album on Motown's Gordy Records in 1964, *Meet the Temptations*. Ruffin took over lead vocals for "My Girl." In March 1965, "My Girl" became the first No. 1 hit by a male Motown group, and it introduced the Temptations to white audiences as well as African Americans. The Temptations scored another success with another Smokey Robinson song, "It's Growing," and an album of Robinson songs, *The Temptations Sing Smokey* (1965). The group released two other singles that summer, "Since I Lost My Baby" and "My Baby." The album *Temptin' Temptations* reached No. 11 on the U.S. charts in December 1965.

Smokey Robinson's final production for the quintet was the single "Get Ready." It did moderately well on the popular chart, and it topped the rhythm and blues chart in April 1966. Norman Whitfield and Brian Holland took over as Temptations' producers, and their first single, "Ain't Too Proud to Beg" topped the R&B chart in July 1966. The Temptations had two other No. 1 R&B songs in 1966, "Beauty's Only Skin Deep" and "(I Know) I'm Losing You." The album *Gettin' Ready* hit No. 12 on the popular chart that year, and the group released its first compilation at the end of the year. *Greatest Hits* was the first Top 10 album for the Temptations on the U.S. popular charts.

Whitfield took over as sole producer of the Temptations in 1967, and the group had a series of Top 20 hits on the popular and R&B charts that year—"All I Need," "You're My Everything," and "(Loneliness Made Me Realize) It's You That I Need." The group also had a Top 10 album in 1967, *Temptations Live. The Temptations in a Mellow Mood* (1967) signaled a significant change for the group as it sought a wider audience. The LP included some Broadway show tunes, but the big hit was the ballad "I Wish It Would Rain," which topped the R&B chart in February 1968 as did "I Could Never Love Another (After Loving You)" in June.

Ruffin was disillusioned with the movement of the group away from traditional soul music and left the group. He was replaced by Dennis Edwards, a Birmingham native who had sung with gospel groups and Motown's the Contours.

The Temptations released one more Motown-style single, "Please Return Your Love to Me," before adopting the "psychedelic soul" style pioneered by Sly and the Family Stone. The title song from the album *Cloud Nine* hit No. 6 on the popular chart in January 1969 and earned Motown its first Grammy award (for best group R&B performance).

Meanwhile, the quintet recorded an album with Diana Ross and the Supremes, *Diana Ross and the Supremes Join the Temptations*. The supergroup's version of "I'm Gonna Make You Love Me" was No. 2 on the U.S. pop chart, as was the LP. "I'll Try Something New," from the same album, was also a successful single.

The Temptations scored again with a socially conscious song, "Runaway Child, Running Wild," in March 1969. That single and "Don't Let the Joneses Get You Down" reached No. 2 on the R&B chart. The group was particularly productive in 1969, appearing on two soundtrack albums from television specials, and releasing a live album (*Live at the Copa*), a second album with the Supremes (*Together*), and another studio album, *Puzzle People*. The latter included the No. 1 single "I Can't Get Next to You."

In 1970, the Temptations proved their versatility by releasing an album of show tunes with the Supremes, *On Broadway*, and another psychedelic soul album, *Psychedelic Shack*. The latter LP and two singles, the title cut and "Ball of Confusion (That's What the World Is Today)," all made the Top 10 pop chart. One other LP oriented toward social and political themes, *Ungena Za Ulimwengu (Unite the World)*, was released in 1970 as well as another greatest hits compilation.

The group found success again with soulful ballads, as the million-seller single "Just My Imagination (Running Away from Me)" topped the charts for two weeks in April 1971. But the group underwent major changes in June, as lead singer Kendricks left for a solo career, and Paul Williams, battling with alcoholism and a liver ailment, retired. The LP *The Sky's the Limit* (1971) produced two more singles, "It's Summer" and "Superstar (Remember How You Got Where You Are)."

Williams and Kendricks were replaced by Damon Harris and Richard Street. The next album, *Solid Rock* (1972), included the innovative 11-minute song "Papa Was a Rollin' Stone." The edited version, with Dennis Edwards singing lead vocal, topped the U.S. pop chart, while the instrumental edit on the B side won a Grammy for best R&B instrumental for 1972.

The group had no hit singles in 1973, although the album *Masterpiece* reached No. 7 on the pop chart. *Masterpiece* also won a Grammy for best group R&B performance. Paul Williams, who continued to choreograph the group's performances after leaving the group, committed suicide in August 1973.

The Temptations went through a series of personnel changes in the mid-1970s. Jeffrey Bowen became the group's new producer in early 1975, and Glenn Leonard replaced Damon Harris that summer. Their albums *A Song for You* (1975), *House Party* (1975), and *Wings of Love* (1976) were moderately successful, as was a collection of their own compositions, *The Temptations Do the Temptations* (1976).

In 1978, lead singer Dennis Edwards left and the group signed with Atlantic Records. The albums *Hear to Tempt You* and *Bare Back* (both released in 1978) were flops, and the group found it difficult to compete with the disco craze that swept R&B and popular charts.

Berry Gordy lured the Temptations back to Motown Records and produced a Top 50 LP, *Power,* in 1980. Edwards returned as lead vocalist for that album and for the 1981 release, *The Temptations*. Ruffin and Kendricks returned to the group briefly in 1982 for a tour and the *Reunion* LP, produced by Rick James.

The group recorded two relatively obscure albums, *Surface Thrills* (1983) and *Back to Basics* (1984), and a somewhat successful album with new lead singer, Ali Ollie Woodson replacing Edwards, *Truly for You* (1984). Kendricks and Ruffin recorded a concert album at the reopening of the Apollo Theater and then signed as a duo with RCA Records. Edwards rejoined the Temptations for a third time to record two more albums, *Together Again* (1987) and *Look What You Started* (1988).

The group reunited one more time for their induction into the Rock and Roll Hall of Fame in 1989. Ruffin died of an drug overdose on June 1, 1991, after completing a European tour with Kendricks and Edwards. Kendricks died of lung cancer on October 5, 1992, and Franklin died in February 1995.

Bibliography

Larkin, Colin, ed. *The Guinness Encyclopedia of Popular Music.* Vol. 5. Middlesex, U.K.: Guinness, 1995.
Turner, Tony. *Deliver Us from Temptation.* New York: Thunder's Mouth, 1992.
Williams, Otis. *Temptations.* New York: Putnam, 1988.

Ken Nagelberg

Ten Commandments, The (1923, 1956), was the movie that demonstrated Cecil B. DeMille's remarkably dependable sense of the national zeitgeist throughout his more than 40-year career (see entry). He was sensitive to the fact that the public's perception of Hollywood in the early 1920s was less than affirmative. Scandals such as the drug-related death of Wallace Reid, the murder of director William Desmond Taylor, and the rape trial of Roscoe "Fatty" Arbuckle did little to persuade Bible-reading Americans that the movie capital was anything more than a den of iniquity. DeMille's own life at this time was off balance, plagued by family problems, dissatisfaction with the reception of his recent films, and uncertainty about Adolph Zukor's power at Paramount, the company with which he was associated (in one or another guise) since the beginning of his film career. He boldly made an appeal, therefore, to the public to choose the subject of his next film. A prize of $1,000 was to be awarded to the one who offered the most appealing idea. In response, eight people suggested the story of Moses, and, attracted by the notion, DeMille awarded $1,000 to each of the eight. The need to create a film that affirmed a set of normative social values with a biblical foundation may well also have been influenced by the death of DeMille's mother soon before the production began.

DeMille turned to his screenwriter, Jeanie Macpherson (his chief collaborator on 32 films between 1915 and 1938), who constructed a set of parallel stories: one set in the present day that depicts the conflict between two brothers (one good, one bad) over the love of a wife brought home by their Bible-thumbing mother, while the other recounts the Moses narrative. The practice of period narrative was not new to DeMille, having filmed the story of Joan of Arc as well as the tragedy of Carmen, nor was that of using parallel narratives that juxtaposed present and past time, as was the case with *Manslaughter* (1923), which depicted Roman orgies. In the case of *The Ten Commandments*, the biblical story took up the smaller portion of the entire narrative. Its production stressed elements of spectacle not only in the form of the elaborate sets but also the use of the new two-color Technicolor process. DeMille filmed the biblical narrative with a minimum of closeups and an abundance of medium and long shots that underscored the pageantry of the story and permitted the construction of elaborate visual tableaux. The modern narrative, on the other hand, incorporated more diverse camera setups but was no less fundamental in its stress upon a moral scheme that may have seemed old-fashioned to the flappers and their partners in the Jazz Age but which nonetheless captured the religious and ethical beliefs of a significant portion of the church-attending American public.

The Ten Commandments, despite its high budget, was a huge box office success. Roughly 30 years later, DeMille remade the film, convinced that, in the wake of the horrors of World War II, the public could be bolstered by a dose of old-time morality and would flock to the theaters to receive it. "The world needs a reminder," he wrote, "of the law of God"; he added, "the world's awful experience of totalitarianism, fascist and communist, had made many thoughtful people realize that the law of God is the essential bedrock of human freedom." Sadly, as was the case during the production of the earlier film, tragedy once again struck DeMille. His wife, Gladys, died of cancer in 1953, and the director was devastated, such that only work on the film could ease the memory of his loss. *The Ten Commandments* would be the first film DeMille shot abroad. He wished to work in the original location, Egypt, but political unrest, including the exile of King Farouk in the summer of 1952, threatened his plans. Stability, however, soon thereafter returned to the country, and in 1954, he crossed the ocean to begin building the ancient setting of his story, using the old drawings of the 1923 feature as models.

The filming in Egypt took three months, during which time the aging DeMille suffered a heart attack and returned to Hollywood in uncertain health. As was the case in 1923, DeMille availed himself of all the techniques at hand. It was his first film in widescreen (he chose the VistaVision process rather than CinemaScope), and he called upon the most sophisticated special effects technicians to give a sense of verisimilitude to the parting of the Red Sea and the burning bush.

The reviews at the time of release were mixed, the elder showman having begun to show the passage of time in the melodramatic flamboyance of his direction and tendency to equate spectacle with seriousness. Whatever the official response, the public still held DeMille to be one of their master storytellers. The aging director, who would pass away three years later, might well have imagined himself a divinity of sorts. Like Moses, he had led an infant industry in less than half a century into the center of the world's media arena.

Bibliography

Higashi, Sumiko. "Antimodernism as Historical Representation in a Consumer Culture: Cecil B. DeMille's *The Ten Commandments*. 1923, 1956, 1993." *The Persistence of History: Cinema, Television, and the Modern Event*. Ed. Vivian Sobchack. New York: Routledge, 1996.

Noerdlinger, Henry S. *Moses and Egypt: The Documentation to the Motion Picture* The Ten Commandments. Los Angeles: U of Southern California P, 1956.

Segal, Alan F. "The Ten Commandments." *Past Imperfect: History According to the Movies*. Ed. Mark C. Carnes. New York: Holt, 1995.

David Sanjek

Texaco Star Theater (a.k.a. ***The Milton Berle Show***) was a comedy-variety program telecast June 8, 1948, through January 6, 1967. Commercial announcers included Sid Stone (1948-51), Jimmy Nelson (1952-53), and Jack Lescoulie (1954-55). The orchestra was directed by Alan Roth (1948-55), Victor Young (1955-56), Billy May (1958-59), and Mitchell Ayres (1966-67). Berle's famous theme, "Near You," was written by Kermit Goell and Francis Craig. Without doubt, the most popular television program of the week during the early years of television was *Texaco Star*. *Texaco Star* emulated a vaudeville variety hour, with several guests each week, including singers, comedians, ventriloquists, acrobats, dramatic performances, and so forth. Each show opened with the four Texaco Service Men, singing the Texaco jingle ("Oh, we're the men of Texaco, we work from Maine to Mexico...") followed by some outrageous musical introduction of Berle in costume. The sponsor's commercials were "pitched" by comedians. Each show closed with Berle singing his theme song.

In 1954-56, Texaco shifted its sponsorship and the show became simply *The Milton Berle Show* when it alternated variously with shows featuring Martha Raye, Bob Hope, and Steve Allen. After 1956, the show lost its novelty when it failed to compete with variety programs such as *Toast of the Town* (later *Ed Sullivan*) and disappeared only to return two years later in a half-hour variety series *Milton Berle Starring in The Kraft Music Hall*, a somewhat refined version of *The Red Skelton Show* which failed to attract sufficient viewers to warrant renewal for a second season. *Texaco* received Emmys in 1949 (best Kinescope show), and nominations in 1950 (best variety show), 1953 (Ruth Gilbert, best series supporting actress), and 1954 (best score, best choreography).

Bibliography

Brooks, Tim, and Earle Marsh. *The Complete Directory to Prime Time Network Television Shows, 1946-Present.* New York: Ballantine. 1995.

O'Neil, Thomas. *The Emmys.* New York: Penguin, 1992.

S. P. Madigan

Theater (19th Century). During an era that made little distinction between "popular" and "high" culture, 19th-century theater played an integral part in the emerging cultural consciousness of a new nation, and theater practice evolved from a haphazard, economically unstable enterprise dominated by British models to a prosperous, diverse U.S. activity that became the most important medium of mass entertainment.

In the early years of the 19th century, every major U.S. city had a resident stock company as New York replaced Philadelphia as the leading theatrical center. New York's Park Theatre (1798), managed for a time by William Dunlap (1766-1839), playwright and the U.S. theater's first historian, featured every American artist of importance until it burned in 1848. Other important theaters included the Chatham Garden (1824), the Bowery (1826), the Olympic (1837), and the Astor Place Opera House (1847).

Frontier managers such as Samuel Drake (1768/69-1854), Noah Ludlow (1795-1886), Solomon Franklin Smith (1801-69), and James H. Caldwell (1793-1863) and others followed the westward population expansion, performed Shakespeare, melodramas, farces, and musicals from Pittsburgh to New Orleans and points west, and established permanent theaters such as Cincinnati's Columbia Street Theatre (1820), the St. Louis Theatre (1837), Chicago's McVicker's Theatre (1857), Brigham Young's Salt Lake Theatre (1861), and San Francisco's Jenny Lind Theatre (1850).

A growing U.S. nationalism and the development of native playwrights led to a lessening of British influence and to a distinctive American drama. Early attempts at American plays with native themes included James Nelson Barker's (1784-1858) *Pocahontas; or, The Indian Princess* (1820), John Augustus Stone's (1800-1834) *Metamora; or, The Last of the Wampanoags* (1829), Anna Cora Mowatt's (1819-1870) successful comedy *Fashion* (1845), and Dion Boucicault's (1822-1890) *The Octoroon; or, Life in Louisiana* (1859), which offered a serious, if flawed, treatment of black life in the South. The two most popular plays of the century were the abolitionist drama *Uncle Tom's Cabin*, based on Harriet Beecher Stowe's (1811-1896) novel of the same name and which existed in dozens of adaptations, and the temperance play *Ten Nights in a Barroom* (1858) by William W. Pratt (fl. 1821-1864).

The first generation of popular native-born actors often gained fame by playing, sometimes for decades, the same stock characters: George Handel Hill (1809-1849), whose "Yankee" roles, with their common sense and wit, made shambles of European social pretensions; Francis S. [Frank] Chanfrau (1824-1884), who played heroic Mose the Fireman in several melodramas, including *A Glance at New York* (1848); Joseph Jefferson III (1829-1905), who toured extensively in Boucicault's adaptation of *Rip Van Winkle* (1865); and Frank Mayo (1839-1896), who acted frontier hero Davy Crockett. Popular actresses of the period included Charlotte Cushman (1816-1876), Laura Keene (c. 1820-1873), Adah Isaacs Menken (1835-1868), Lotta Crabtree (1847-1924), and Ada Rehan (1860-1914).

The most influential actors were Edwin Forrest (1806-1872), whose "blood and thunder" style symbolized for many the American character itself, and Edwin Booth (1833-1893), who achieved a reputation as a studied and "natural" performer. Booth became the first actor since African-American Ira Aldridge (1804-1867) to achieve international status. Both Forrest and Booth struggled to improve the social status of theater workers and to raise theater to an American art form independent from foreign influence.

After the Civil War, urban theater entered into an era of new realism in drama that concentrated on the lives and problems of ordinary people and of technological advances in electricity and spectacular special effects in scenery that quickly found their way into mainstream popular culture. John Augustus Daly (1839-1899), critic, manager, dramatist, at his Fifth Avenue Theatre (1869-1873) and at Daly's Theatre (1879-1899), experimented with new methods of producing Shakespeare and employed the most accomplished actors of the day, including Maurice Barrymore (1847-1905), Adelaide Neilson (1848-1880), and John Drew, Jr. (1853-1927). Other influential figures included Steele MacKaye (1842-1894), inventor of stage machinery, architect, and playwright, and David Belasco (1859-1931), a self-promoting, publicity-conscious manager/playwright who produced extravaganzas of his own design from his native California to New York.

At the close of the century the forces of realism were threatened by syndicates, the most prominent of which, the Theatrical Syndicate, was formed by a group of New York impresarios led by Charles Frohman (1860-1915). These powerful business organizations wanted to control venues, plays, and performers throughout the country as they bought out theaters, planned tours of popular musicals, farces, and melodramas, and forced independent producers and artists out of work. This movement, which stifled innovation and new forms of drama in favor of those entertainments syndicates determined were profitable and palatable to mass audiences, would continue into the early years of the 20th century (see next entry).

Bibliography

Carson, William G. B. *The Theatre on the Frontier: Early Years of the St. Louis Stage.* Chicago: U of Chicago P, 1968.

Hewitt, Barnard. *Theatre U.S.A.* New York: McGraw-Hill, 1959.

McConachie, Bruce A. *Melodramatic Formations: American Theatre and Society, 1820-1870.* Iowa City: U of Iowa P, 1992.

Odell, G. C. D. *Annals of the New York Stage.* 15 vols. New York: Columbia UP, 1927-1949.

John Hanners

Theater (20th Century). The 20th century has been a time of great change in the American theater. What was once the major form of popular entertainment in the country has been superseded by such rival forms as film, radio, and television. Whereas once New York City reigned supreme as the theatrical center of the nation, nowadays the U.S. has become a land filled with professional regional, college, and community theaters, with Broadway serving as a titular head. Where once New York City served as the source of hundreds of touring companies that crisscrossed the country annually, it now supplies a handful of such troupes and often receives more original dramas from the rest of the nation than it generates itself. And those original dramas have themselves changed through the decades, throwing off their European influences and often putting on a populist voice of their own. Finally, the American musical, this country's most important contribution to world theater and its most popular theatrical form, has come of age during this century.

Things were quite different in 1900. The U.S. was filled with hundreds of local playhouses, which would present the offerings of professional touring companies transported to them by the country's burgeoning railroad system. And the chief supplier of these offerings was New York City. As the century began, a group of East Coast producers and booking agents known as the Theatrical Syndicate (1896-1916) was even trying to turn this far-flung, vibrant, chaotic system into a tight-fisted monopoly, but this attempt was eventually to fail. Still, if national domination of theaters and touring companies could not be realized, control could be exerted over what they presented. At that time, the New York powers were primarily interested in making money. Therefore, they provided the country with what they thought it wanted— insipid comedies, melodramas, and musicals. The producers frowned on thought-provoking dramas and experimental productions because they thought these efforts would not sell. It was left to others to present them.

These other sources soon appeared, both around the nation and within New York City itself. They believed the mass theater audience wanted more than mere mindless confections and thus championed the production of classical plays, works by European dramatists, and the noncommercial efforts of native playwrights. Throughout the century the struggle would be fought between the commercial interests that saw theater as profitable entertainment and those that saw it as an artistic and socially relevant institution. The first of these alternate sources was the Little Theatre Movement. Such organizations as the Chicago Little Theatre (1911-17) of Maurice Browne (1881-1955) and the Provincetown Playhouse of George Cram Cook (1873-1924) and playwright Susan Glaspell (1881-1948) were two notable members of the movement. Later in the century, professional regional theaters—such as the Minnesota Theatre, founded in 1962 by Tyrone Guthrie (1900-1971), and the American Conservatory Theatre, begun in 1966 by William Ball (1931-)

sprang up around the U.S., providing a viable alternative to Broadway and a spawning ground for new, serious playwrights and for novel forms of staging, such as theater-in-the-round and the thrust stage.

In New York itself, the Theatre Guild (founded in 1919) provided an artistic alternative. For over 30 years, under the guidance of Lawrence Langner (1890-1962) and Theresa Helburn (1887-1959), this organization presented the works of many of Europe's leading and America's newest dramatists, including George Bernard Shaw (1856-1950) and Eugene O'Neill (1888-1953). The 1950s saw the rise of Off-Broadway, another answer to Broadway commercialism, with the establishment of the Circle-in-the-Square theater in 1952 under the leadership of Edward Mann (1924-). The New York Shakespeare Festival, founded in 1956 by Joseph Papp (1921-1991), became an outstanding addition here, not only providing free Shakespeare in Central Park, but also introducing such commercial musical hits as *A Chorus Line*. However, even Off-Broadway was regarded as not experimental enough by some, and so Off Off-Broadway was created with the launching of Cafe Cino (1958-68) by Joseph Cino. As a result of all this activity, the monolithic American theater of 1900 has been replaced by a varied, vibrant theater playing to many audiences, though its most popular presentations still receive Broadway productions.

Besides the rise of alternatives to Broadway, the American theater has also seen a decline in its mass audience because of the rise in popularity of rival forms of entertainment (such as film, radio, television, the VCR) and the increasing appeal of professional sports. In addition, the rise of powerful theatrical unions, given impetus by Actors Equity's successful strike of 1919, has led to astronomical increases in production costs and ticket prices. As a result, Broadway today finds itself presenting fewer plays to wealthier audiences, while relying more and more on Great Britain and the regional theaters for its offerings. Risk-taking and accessible seats are not to be found within its confines.

In addition to Broadway's decline, during the 20th century, America also developed an individual voice in its drama, shaking off the European voices which had dominated. Native playwrights rose to international stature, starting with Eugene O'Neill, who created a series of realistic masterpieces in the first half of the century (including *Long Day's Journey into Night*, considered by many the best play ever written by an American). Clifford Odets (1906-63) built on O'Neill's lead during the 1930s, popularizing the realistic, domestic drama dealing with the problems of the common man, which was to become the American drama's dominant form. In the 1940s and 1950s, Tennessee Williams (1911-1983), probably the most popular serious playwright of the century, created poetic, psychological studies, often stressing the sexually bizarre, while Arthur Miller's (1915-1998) family dramas concerned the common man and emphasized social criticism. The second half of the century saw a number of serious, talented writers appear. The irony was that Broadway would not present their works unless they proved popular Off-Broadway or in the regional theaters. So it was that the dominant non-musical voice on

Broadway became that of Neil Simon (1927-), a comic writer. His work drew audiences and was able to be turned into successful motion pictures.

Still, if the American theater was known for anything during the 20th century, it was the development of its most popular form, the musical. Between 1900 and 1910 this form began moving in two major directions. The most respected and best-attended type, as well as the most subject to foreign influence, was the operetta, a serious play which stressed melodramatic plots in exotic locations or historic times and emphasized impressive singing. Its dominant voice was Victor Herbert's (1859-1924). In opposition to this were the lively, dance-filled, contemporary musical comedies of George M. Cohan (1878-1942). By the end of the 1920s, operetta had fallen out of fashion, but the musical comedy was enjoying a golden age, being produced by such popular music giants as composer George (1898-1937) and lyricist Ira Gershwin (1896-1983), composer Richard Rodgers (1902-1979) and lyricist Lorenz Hart (1895-1943), and the composer-lyricists Irving Berlin (1888-1989) and Cole Porter (1891-1964).

Probably, however, the era's most important musical was the work of composer Jerome Kern (1885-1945) and lyricist Oscar Hammerstein II (1895-1960). Like the operetta, *Show Boat* (see entry) was a serious musical that dealt with historic America; however, it also touched on contemporary problems like race relations and was the most important attempt up until then to integrate songs completely into the musical's book. Hammerstein improved on this approach in 1943 when he teamed with Richard Rodgers to create *Oklahoma!* Here, the fully integrated, serious musical proved triumphant, with this new show running over two thousand performances, helping the fledgling original cast album form being developed by Decca Records to prosper, and being sold to Hollywood for a great deal of money. As a result of all this, the strong-book musical that set long-run records dominated the theater for approximately 20 years. During this time, Jerome Robbins (1918-) pioneered the use of dance as an integral component of musicals in plays like *West Side Story* (1957). He was the first of the great director-choreographers, and throughout the next two decades, his successors—Gower Champion (1921-1980), Bob Fosse (1927-1987), and Michael Bennett (1943-1987)—dominated the musical stage. However, with their deaths, the American musical went into decline.

By the 1990s, the most dominant native composer-lyricist was Stephen Sondheim (1930- ; see entry), who turned out a series of pessimistic, intellectual, unmelodic works which tended to alienate the general theater audience. Ironically, this audience preferred the work of the most popular composer of these latter decades, an Englishman, Andrew Lloyd Webber (1948-), whose melodious shows stressed a romanticism reminiscent of the operetta. So the American musical theater ended the century as it had begun it, with its most popular plays dominated by foreign influences. Still, as the 20th century closed, the musical continued as the most popular dramatic form in the decentralized American theater, with comedies coming in second and serious plays running a distant third.

Bibliography

Berkowitz, Gerald M. *American Drama of the Twentieth Century*. London: Longman, 1992.

Bordman, Gerald. *American Musical Theatre: A Chronicle*. 2d ed. New York: Oxford UP, 1992.

Hartnoll, Phyllis. *The Oxford Companion to the Theatre*. 4th ed. London: Oxford UP, 1983.

Henderson, Mary C. *Theater in America: 200 Years of Plays, Players, and Productions*. New York: Abrams, 1986.

Wilson, Garff B. *Three Hundred Years of American Drama and Theatre: From* Ye Bare and Ye Cubb *to* Hair. Englewood Cliffs: Prentice-Hall, 1973.

Richard M. Goldstein

See also
American Musical Theater

Theater Organs are special kinds of pipe organs designed specifically to accompany silent motion pictures. These instruments use ranks of pipes that imitate the sound of orchestral instruments such as clarinets, strings, oboes, and tubas. Theater organs also have drums, tambourines, cymbals, marimbas, xylophones, and chimes plus steamboat whistles, car horns, and fire gongs. In addition to orchestral voicing and percussions, theater organs utilize high wind pressures and deep tremulants. Theater organs have a warm, lush sound dominated by a bright flute stop called the Tibia Clausa. They are ideally suited to providing a variety of quickly changing tonal colors to match the action of silent films.

Theater pipe organs are not a separate invention but rather are based upon innovations in organ building that had already taken place in classical or "church" organs. Theater organs are, in fact, closely related to the very orchestral concert and church organs that came into use in the late 19th and early 20th centuries. These instruments were designed to play transcriptions of symphonic works in addition to standard organ repertoire. They employed stops that imitated instruments of the orchestra, tremulants, and percussions, but not to the same degree as theater organs eventually did.

The person most responsible for altering organ design in ways that made theater organs possible was the Englishman Robert Hope-Jones. He developed a reliable electro-pneumatic action that allowed the organ console and pipework to be separated by any desired distance. When the organist pressed a key, he or she completed an electrical circuit that activated a magnet that opened a valve under a particular pipe. This method replaced the older direct mechanical action, which linked key and pipe by wires and rods. The electro-pneumatic action enabled pipe organ consoles to be installed in theater orchestra pits and to control pipework located a considerable distance away in chambers on either side of the proscenium arch.

Another Hope-Jones invention that found an application in theater organs was his system of pipe unification, which allowed a single rank of pipes to be available at a number of different places on the organ. This was accomplished by electrical switches and relays. It permitted a few sets of pipes to do the work of many. In a unified organ one rank of pipes, say the diapason, could appear on any of the manuals and the pedal at the 16-, 8-, and 4-foot pitches. On a conventional organ, this would have required several separate sets of diapason ranks.

Because they were unified, theater organs could be smaller than church organs and still produce a variety of sounds. What was sacrificed was a massed ensemble sound and a clarity of separate melodic lines. Theater organs are usually about 10-15 ranks in size while church organs are an average of 5 to 6 times larger. Small size was a considerable advantage when chamber space in theaters was limited.

Just as Robert Hope-Jones was making important innovations in pipe organ design, motion picture exhibitors were feeling the need for a musical instrument that could produce the wide variety of sounds necessary to accompany silent films. The first motion pictures were shown in vaudeville theaters as one of several acts on the bill. These presentations were accompanied by the theater's orchestra. A few years later, nickelodeons employed pianists or small string ensembles.

Film accompaniments were rather haphazard until motion picture distributors began to enclose the titles of suggested musical numbers along with each film. Accompaniments improved considerably with the coming of feature films and, with the construction of movie palaces around 1912, orchestras (sometimes up to 60 members) that played either original scores sent out with the film or compiled from existing materials by the theater's musical director. In addition to accompanying films, the movie palace orchestras played overtures and provided music for stage presentations. Hiring an orchestra to play for several shows a day was very expensive, and so it soon became clear that a substitute for the orchestra was needed. The answer was the pipe organ.

A few theaters tried using church instruments, but the results were very unsatisfactory. Church organs had the wrong "sound" and a limited range of tonal colors. Fortunately, the Rudolph Wurlitzer Company developed an organ that imitated an orchestra and avoided sounding "churchy." The Wurlitzer Unit Orchestra, as it was called, incorporated many Hope-Jones innovations because the company had purchased his patents. These included pipe unification, orchestral voicing, electro-pneumatic action, and the horseshoe console.

As movie palaces became the principal venue for feature films, theater organs became more popular. Between 1914 and 1930, approximately 7,000 instruments of this type were built. Most of them were installed in theaters, but some went to radio stations and ballrooms. Although Wurlitzer was the best-known manufacturer (to the point that virtually every theater organ regardless of make was known as a "Mighty Wurlitzer"), that company was not the only supplier. Other companies making theater organs included Robert Morton, Barton, Kimball, Kilgen, Marr and Colton, Moller, and several dozen smaller firms. Wurlitzer, however, made over 50 percent of all theater organs.

During the 1920s, when theater organs were at their peak of popularity, some organists became stars in their own right. The best known was Jesse Crawford, who had a suc-

cessful engagement at the Chicago Theatre before going to the New York Paramount Theatre in 1926. He played there until 1934 and then began a career performing on radio and demonstrating for the Hammond Organ Company. Other well-known organists from the period were Lew White, Dick Leibert, Rosa Rio, Ann Leaf, Don Baker, Lee Erwin, and Gaylord Carter.

The coming of sound changed film exhibition forever and eliminated the need for organists and other musicians in motion picture theaters. The demise of theater organs was swift, and began when the film industry agreed on a technical standard for sound in May of 1928. By 1930, most theaters had stopped using live musicians.

During the 1930s and 1940s, a few large theaters continued using pipe organs to provide music during intermissions between films. Organists played a medley of five or six popular songs during the 10- or 15-minute break. In some theaters, organists played the melody while a song's words were projected on the screen. Members of the audience were urged to participate in this "sing-along."

The theater which used its pipe organ most often was Radio City Music Hall, which opened in December 1932. The Music Hall housed the world's largest Wurlitzer theater organ, the 4 manual, 58 rank, twin-consoled instrument in the auditorium. (There was a smaller Wurlitzer located in the recording studio.) The Music Hall employed three full-time organists who played the instrument several times a day during breaks between films and stage shows. This tradition continued until the Music Hall changed its programming policy in the late 1970s. Today, the Music Hall Wurlitzer is still heard frequently.

In the 1990s, it was possible to hear venerable theater pipe organs in many places. Some 50 instruments still remain in their original locations in theaters, while many others have been removed to restaurants, churches, and homes.

Bibliography

Hall, Ben M. *The Best Remaining Seats: The Story of the Golden Age of the Movie Palace*. New York: Potter, 1961.

Junchen, David L. *Encyclopedia of American Theatre Organs*. Vols. 1 and 2. Pasadena: Showcase, 1985.

Landon, John W. *Behold the Mighty Wurlitzer: The History of the Theatre Pipe Organ*. Westport: Greenwood, 1983.

Henry B. Aldridge

Theme Park, The, can be defined as a social artwork designed as a four-dimensional symbolic landscape to evoke impressions of places and times, real or imaginary. It has become synonymous with the name Walt Disney, but Disney did not invent the genre. For centuries, the titled nobility of Europe and Asia built themselves fantastic private playlands, such as China's Imperial Summer Palace and Bavaria's Neuschwanstein castle, and there were precursors in America's World's Fairs.

The term "theme park" came into public use several years after the opening of Disneyland in 1955, coined by a journalist when it became obvious that Disney's creation could not be faithfully described with the terminology of the traditional amusement park (see Disney Theme Parks, above). Although "theme park" and "amusement park" are still frequently applied interchangeably, the theme park is as different in origins, design, intent, and effect from the amusement park as Ellis Island is from Coney Island (see entry).

Amusement parks are limited experiences whose attraction lies in the immediate physical gratification of the thrill ride—the exhilaration of speed, the push and pull of gravity, the rush of adrenaline at the illusion of potential bodily harm. The theme park, on the other hand, is a total-sensory engaging environmental art form built to express a coherent message, owing far more to film than physics.

Theme parks are cultural mind maps—symbolic landscapes of psychological narratives. They are the multidimensional descendant of the book, film, and epic rather than the offshoot of the roller coaster and tilt-o-whirl. While both may offer rides, theme park rides are but one of many communications media integrated into the body of the park to punctuate the overall theme. They operate as mechanisms designed to position the visitor, much as a camera lens is aligned, moving riders past a series of vignettes to advance the narrative. Rides expand the narrative experience with appropriate physical sensations—speed, evocative smells, temperature changes—but the purpose is always to advance the storyline. It is the architecture, including public space design, landscaping (the most noticeable element to distinguish theme from amusement park), ornamental detailing, and the use of symbols, archetypes, and icons as communications media, not the rides, that determine the essence of theme parks.

Walt Disney reincarnated the theme park as a place of entertainment and delight as well as education. Previous American theme park models geared to the general public were predicated on a mandated "improving" educational mission. The 1893 Columbian Exhibition in Chicago celebrated American achievement in terms of the Old World, particularly in the almost-exclusive use of European-inspired neoclassical architecture—"The White City."

Frederic Thompson and Skip Dundy's Luna Park (1903) and William H. Reynolds's Dreamland (1904) were Coney Island's contribution to the theme park genre. Unlike the better-known Steeplechase Park, which featured thrill rides like the Ferris wheel and roller coaster, Luna Park and Dreamland used the "experiential" powers of the theme-park medium to re-create other times, places, and worlds. Along with the thrill rides, visitors could take "A Trip to the Moon," voyage "20,000 Leagues Beneath the Sea," toboggan on an air-conditioned "Swiss Alp," or even, literally, go to Hell—complete with fluttering tissue-paper flames and menacing demons. These were the immediate ancestors, in both spirit and technology, of Disneyland's Matterhorn, Disney/MGM Studios' "Catastrophe Canyon" and "Star Tours," and Universal Studios' "Earthquake: The Big One."

As a communicator constantly pushing the frontiers of animation and film, in the early 1950s Disney saw the possibilities of creating a new type of three-dimensional "movie" that integrated the "audience" into the action. Disney reinterpreted and retold our Old World myths, focused through an American lens. Disney's showcase of American themes—optimism, fair play, resistance to oppression, and faith in the future—was an immediate hit because it celebrated those qualities Americans most liked about themselves and the ideals they, and others, most admired in their country.

The result was the first permanent commercial theme park, made possible by the emergence of a mobile, educated, middle class enchanted with the new medium of television, which enabled a continent-wide ethnically diverse population to share common values, memories, and cultural benchmarks.

Theme parks are symbolic communications using the technology of animation, altered scale, forced perspective, color harmonics, texture, lighting, sound, and iconography to produce an effect "more real than real." This hyperreality springboards off our preconceptions—which come from film, paintings, and books, but rarely from memories of the real thing—to evoke a feeling of actually being in a frontier fort, a European castle, or a turn-of-the-century small town. Theme parks have little or no directional signage. Like a film, the imagery is expected to carry the narrative—the symbolic landscape projects the message with more immediacy, power, and clarity than could be accomplished with text.

The first successful non-Disney theme park, Six Flags over Texas (Arlington), opened in 1961 between Dallas and Forth Worth. Since the principles of communication by themeing can be applied to many subjects, from pure fantasy to hard science, contemporary theme parks come in a broad spectrum of styles and specialties. There are the "nature parks" of Tampa Busch Gardens and Sea World (Aurora, OH; San Antonio, TX; and San Diego, CA), taking the concept of "zoo," through architecture and live performance, to new heights as a themed entertainment. "National" and "international" themed parks draw on regional or world history and culture, expressed by costume, cuisine, music, and decor at Fiesta Texas (San Antonio), Polynesian Culture Center (Laie, HI), Great America (Santa Clara, CA), and The Old Country at Busch Gardens (Williamsburg, VA), as well as ideology sites like Heritage, USA (fundamentalist Christian) (Charlotte, NC).

Historic theme parks include Colonial Williamsburg (Williamsburg, VA) (which predates Disney), Historic Jamestown/Yorktown, and Plimoth Plantation (Plymouth, MA). "Process" or "industry" parks include Opryland, (Nashville, TN) (country music), Hersheypark (Hershey, PA) (chocolate), and Knott's Berry Farm (Buena Park, CA) (frontier farming). Popular entertainers have their own theme parks—Dollywood and Twitty City (Pigeon Forge and Hendersonville, TN)—and parks also echo the village or "ethnic exposition" concept as in Old Sturbridge (Sturbridge, MA), Ohio (Columbus, OH), and Greenfield (Dearborn, MI) Villages.

While Circus Circus opened the first theme-park casino in Las Vegas in the 1960s, the 1990s will be remembered as the year themeing took that city by storm. Confirming the shift in audience from high-rolling gamblers to vacationing families, combination casinos/theme parks opened in this decade include the MGM Grand (movies), Excalibur (medieval), the Luxor (Egypt), and Treasure Island (pirates).

From Disney's single 200-acre park in Anaheim, theme parks have grown to an industry that takes in over four billion dollars a year, surpassing even movie theaters in gross receipts. At the same time, operating costs, including capital improvements, training, maintenance, enhancement, and marketing, are also high, including the trend toward constant innovations in attractions to encourage repeat visitation (70 percent at Disney parks). After several corporate conglomerates acquired theme parks in the 1970s, these high capital reinvestment costs caused them to divest quickly. Today, the most successful parks operate under a few corporate banners focused exclusively on entertainment.

Six Flags, Great Adventure, Busch Gardens, and Universal Studios (see entry) have attempted to copy and enlarge upon the Disney theme formula with varying degrees of success. In terms of maintaining the theme, creativity, and richness of detail, Disney Imagineering continues to set the gold standard to which all other parks are compared.

Bibliography

Adams, Judith. *The American Amusement Park Industry: A History of Technology and Thrills.* Boston: Twayne, 1991.

Blake, Peter. "The Lessons of the Parks." *Architectural Forum* June 1973: 28+.

Findlay, John M. *Magic Lands.* Seattle: U of Washington P, 1992.

King, Margaret J. "Disneyland and Walt Disney World: Traditional Values in Futuristic Form." *Journal of Popular Culture* 15.1 (1981): 114-40.

Nusbaum, Paul. "Crowded House: Fun and Gaming." *Philadelphia Inquirer* 29 May 1994: 11+.

Margaret J. King

Thin Man, The (1934), was a film treatment of Dashiell Hammett's widely popular 1934 novel by the same name. MGM's film, directed by W. S. Van Dyke, became a flagship for one of the most memorable husband and wife teams in American film, the wealthy and urbane detective team of Nick and Nora Charles, played by William Powell and Myrna Loy. The success and chemistry of Powell and Loy's pairing in *The Thin Man* led to five *Thin Man* sequels and shared billing in seven other films, including *Libeled Lady* (1936) and *The Great Ziegfeld* (1936). Filmed in two weeks and very cheaply, *The Thin Man* received four Oscar nominations and establish the definitive blend of romantic comedy with the murder mystery format. The first film is considered the finest and follows Hammett's novel. *After the Thin Man* (1936) was also directed by Van Dyke, as was *Another Thin Man* (1939), for which Hammett wrote the screenplay. In 1941 *Shadow of the Thin Man*, Van Dyke's last contribution to the series, was released. *The Thin Man Goes Home*, directed by Richard Thorpe, followed in 1944; and the final installment was *The Song of the Thin Man* in 1947, directed by Edward Bussell. The six *Thin Man* films inspired a radio show and a television series beginning in 1957 (starring Peter Lawford and Phyllis Kirk).

Bibliography

Drees, Rich. "*The Thin Man*: Dashiell Hammett & Hollywood." *Films in Review* Sept. 1995: 46-53.

Soter, Tom. "Ballad of a Thin Man." *Video* July 1986: 78-81.

Szebin, Frederick C. "Hammett Rewritten." *Films in Review* July 1994: 2-9.

Robert Baird

thirtysomething (1987-1991), a one-hour TV dramatic series, was the epitome of the "yuppie" generation. It was a show about baby boomers, created by baby boomers, aimed at the baby-boomer audience. Prime for advertisers who coveted the purchasing power of the yuppie generation, this show was the essence of the viewers targeted by ABC: the entire cast was 30+, upwardly mobile, some with children, all in powerful, glamorous, or meaningful jobs, with gallons of purchasing power for consumer goods. Producers Ed Zwick and Marshall Herkovitz had previously written for the series *Family*, and *thirtysomething* resembled that show in that it dealt with the everyday details of urban family life.

The cast was an ensemble of seven—two couples and three single people. The seven were longtime friends, living in Philadelphia. Mel Harris and Ken Olin (playing Hope and Michael Steadman) were one of the married couples; Timothy Busfield and Patricia Wettig (married to Ken Olin in real life) the other (Elliot and Nancy Weston). In both cases, the wives had forsaken careers to raise children. The husbands were partners in an advertising agency. The single friends included Melanie Mayron as Michael's sex-starved cousin Melissa, a professional photographer; Polly Draper as Hope's best friend (Ellyn), a professional administrator at City Hall; and Peter Horton as Michael's best friend, Gary Shepherd, a long-haired, irreverent professor of classics at a nearby college.

The show had very loyal viewers (20 million each week) who identified with the seven stars, and it was well received by the critics, receiving a Peabody award in 1988. Touted as "television's most honest series," the show was both adored and scorned: adored because it dealt with real issues and scorned because it provided no escape from reality.

Bibliography

Brooks, Tim, and Earle Marsh. *The Complete Directory to Prime Time Network TV Shows, 1946-Present.* 5th ed. New York: Ballantine, 1995.

Brown, Les. *Les Brown's Encyclopedia of Television.* New York: Visible Ink, 1991.

McNeil, Alex. *Total Television.* New York: Penguin, 1991.

thirtysomething stories. New York: Pocket, 1991.

Thompson, Robert J. *Television's Second Golden Age: From Hill Street Blues to ER.* New York: Continuum, 1996.

Sheri Carder

Thomas, Danny (1914-1991), was an actor and comedian who became one of the most prominent and successful television sitcom producers in the 1960s. In addition to his own popular sitcom *Make Room for Daddy*, Thomas's production company produced such hits as *The Real McCoys, The Dick Van Dyke Show, The Andy Griffith Show*, and *Gomer Pyle, U.S.M.C.* Unlike many producers, Thomas maintained a strong on-camera presence, which included a 1970s remake of his popular sitcom.

Thomas, whose real name was Amos Jacobs, was born in Deerfield, MI, to Lebanese immigrant parents. His eventual success presents a stark contrast to the poverty in which he was raised. Danny, along with his brother Ray, became interested in show business at an early age, but it was Danny who stayed committed to it as an avocation.

Thomas climbed the ladder from burlesque house comedy emcee to radio personality to nightclub performer and actor. Versatility as opposed to virtuosity was what propelled Thomas to stardom. He sang, but not well. He was a comic, yet hardly as funny as his more successful contemporaries. Thomas would admit that there were many actors more talented than he, and his prominent nose, which became the butt of his self-deprecating humor, kept Thomas from claiming attractiveness. Nevertheless, Thomas made up for these deficits by proving himself the consummate performer. Audiences loved Thomas, and Thomas seemed to love them.

As the hectic life of nightclub performing began wearing on him, Thomas became attracted to the stability offered by the developing medium of television. Thomas got his shot at TV in a rather roundabout way; ABC was hot to recruit Ray Bolger for a half-hour sitcom. Through a deal with the William Morris Agency—which also represented Thomas—Bolger agreed to work for ABC provided the network found something for Thomas. That something became *Make Room for Daddy* (1953), which made Thomas a star. Ironically, Bolger's program failed to find an audience.

Make Room for Daddy was significant in that it was one of the first sitcoms to present a more realistic domestic setting, which included parents who yelled at their children. Thomas also developed the concept of the treacle cutter, in which a scene would be brought to an almost unbearable level of sentimentality, only to be broken by a wisecrack or sarcastic remark. This sort of comedy has been repeated, with varying degrees of success, by most sitcoms since.

Having made a good deal of money from his popular sitcom, Thomas became the star tenant at Desilu Studios, where he began producing other situation comedies. His first successful sitcom was *The Real McCoys* (1957), which ushered in a new subgenre of rural sitcoms that soon dominated the era. Thomas, along with partner Sheldon Leonard, began producing such hits as *The Andy Griffith Show* (1960) and *Gomer Pyle, U.S.M.C.* (1964).

Thomas's landmark sitcom production was Carl Reiner's *The Dick Van Dyke Show* (1961), now considered by media critics to be second only to *I Love Lucy* in terms of classic appeal. Thomas and Leonard took an active role in the casting and day-to-day production of the series, which lasted until 1966.

In 1970, Thomas's stock of rural shows were canceled in favor of more relevant programming such as *The Mary Tyler Moore Show* (1970) and *All in the Family* (1971). Ironically, Thomas's daughter, Marlo, had helped usher in the era of relevance with *That Girl* (1966), which revolved around the madcap antics of a single actress living on her own in New York. Although Danny Thomas Productions would no longer dominate TV sitcom schedules, he made two returns to series television in two well-written yet popularly unappreciated programs—*Make Room for Granddaddy* (1970) and *The Practice* (1976). Thomas also formed a partnership with Aaron Spelling, producing dramatic programs including *The Guns of Will Sonnet* (1967) and *The Mod Squad* (1968).

While producing *The Mod Squad*, Thomas brought his son Tony into the family business; Tony Thomas remains in television today as part of Witt/Thomas Productions, which produced such shows as *Soap* (1977), *Benson* (1979), *The Golden Girls* (1985), and *Empty Nest* (1988). Danny Thomas remained a popular entertainer as well as the chief fundraiser for the St. Jude's Children's Research Hospital, which brought the plight of child cancer victims to the public eye.

Bibliography

Brooks, Tim, and Earle Marsh. *The Complete Directory to Prime Time Network TV Shows, 1946-Present.* New York: Ballantine, 1992.

Brown, Les. *Les Brown's Encyclopedia of Television.* Detroit: Visible Ink, 1992.

Marc, David, and Robert J. Thompson. *Prime Time, Prime Movers.* Boston: Little, Brown, 1992.

Thomas, Danny, and Bill Davidson. *Make Room for Danny.* New York: Putnam, 1991.

Michael B. Kassel

Thompson, Hunter S. (1939-), prepared for his career as "gonzo" journalism's sole practitioner by serving a hitch as a juvenile delinquent. Thompson was born into a comfortable middle-class family in Louisville, KY, but after his father's death in 1954, teenage Thompson sought refuge in pranks that sometimes turned ugly. A botched armed-robbery attempt resulted in Thompson serving time in jail and missing his high school graduation. A brief and tumultuous Air Force career followed, and Thompson began his career as a writer, starting with the newspaper at Eglin Air Force Base in Florida.

It was not until Thompson went to South America and began writing for the *National Observer* in 1961 that his writing career began to take off. His early 1960s dispatches, telling tales of rum runners and tin miners, were terrifically popular with the *Observer*'s editors as well as its readers.

When Thompson returned to the United States in 1963, he settled in San Francisco and labored on what he hoped would become the Great American Novel. However, an assignment from editor Carey McWilliams of *The Nation* intervened. The mainstream press had lavished a lot of attention on the Hell's Angels and McWilliams wanted Thompson to deliver a more honest account of the motorcycle gang. The resulting piece, "Losers and Outsiders," attracted enough attention to stuff Thompson's mailbox with offers for book contracts. He finally accepted a bid from Random House and spent most of 1966 riding with the Hell's Angels. When the gang learned how much Thompson would make off of the experience, they demanded a cut of the book's profits, and when Thompson refused to grant them a share, the gang members stomped Thompson, nearly killing him. The brutality provided Thompson with the perfect coda for *Hell's Angels* (1967).

Thompson and his family fled San Francisco for Aspen, CO, where he soon waged a campaign to be Aspen's sheriff, as a part of the Freak Power ticket. His bid earned him a lot of publicity, from the *National Observer* and also in a new publication called *Rolling Stone*. Thompson lost the election—but barely.

Thompson had a brief relationship with *Scanlan's Monthly*, during which he honed his style. For *Scanlan's* he wrote a homecoming piece called "The Kentucky Derby Is Decadent and Depraved," in which he broke off any serious attempt at continuity and reproduced pages from his notebook in the article, in order to convey the frenetic nature of Derby Week in Louisville. A friend wrote to praise the article, calling it "pure gonzo." Hunter Thompson's style was thus named.

When *Scanlan's* folded, Thompson began a long and fruitful association with *Rolling Stone*. He turned two botched assignments for the magazine into his gonzo masterpiece, *Fear and Loathing in Las Vegas* (1972), and then became the magazine's first full-time political correspondent. His ground-breaking, iconoclastic biweekly dispatches from the 1972 Nixon-McGovern battle were collected in the awkwardly titled *Fear and Loathing: On the Campaign Trail '72* (1973), which became a classic of American political journalism.

Thompson's contributions to the magazine slowed throughout the 1970s and 1980s. A "greatest-hits" collection, *The Great Shark Hunt* (1979), and a film about his life called *Where the Buffalo Room* (1981) kept Thompson in the spotlight. Cartoonist Garry Trudeau created a character called Uncle Duke, for his *Doonesbury* strip. Clearly modeled after Thompson and named after a Thompson pseudonym, Raoul Duke, the character entertained millions of readers, but infuriated Thompson himself.

During this time, occasional pieces, most notably Thompson's dispatch on the fall of Saigon (not published in full for a decade after the fact), showed that his gonzo approach—no editing, all first-draft material—was well suited to some events. Now and then he published a book, such as *The Curse of Lono* (1983).

Finally, in the late 1980s, Thompson began to emerge from exile. In rapid (for him) succession, he published three anthologies: *Generation of Swine* (1988), *Songs of the Doomed* (1991), and *Better Than Sex: Confessions of a Political Junkie* (1994). His journalism did not carry the weight of his earlier work and he seemed best known as the model for a comic-strip character. Still, Thompson had made his mark as a chronicler of American culture during the 1960s and 1970s.

Bibliography

Carroll, E. Jean. *Hunter: The Strange and Savage Life of Hunter S. Thompson.* New York: Dutton, 1993.

McKeen, William. *Hunter S. Thompson.* Boston: Twayne, 1991.

Perry, Paul. *Fear and Loathing: The Strange and Terrible Saga of Hunter S. Thompson.* New York: Thunder's Mouth, 1993.

William McKeen

Three Stooges, The, currently hold the record for appearing in more movies than any other comedy team in history. Although they made their final film in 1965, their popularity is alive and well in reruns and video rentals. A 1977 poll found that 59 percent of American adults could name the Three Stooges, while only 55 percent knew the name of one Supreme Court justice. One year after the Stooges debuted on the Family Channel in 1996, viewership during their time slot jumped 49 percent. Even though watching the Stooges was traditionally seen as a male bonding experience, the female audience ages 18-49 during that same period increased 62 percent.

The trio is famous for their haircuts and their use of physical, slapstick humor. Many of the more elaborate sight gags were eliminated over the years due to increasing production costs and Curly's poor health. After enraged parents complained their children were slapping each other and poking their playmates in the eyes, television stations running the series cut out the more violent gags.

Shemp Howard (born Sam Horwitz in 1895), Moe Howard (born Moses Harry Horwitz in 1897), and Larry Fine (born Louis Feinberg in 1902) began their career as a comedy team in 1925 with the vaudeville act "Ted Healy and His Stooges." After leaving the group for a solo career, Shemp was replaced by his brother Curly (born Jerome Horwitz in 1903).

The Stooges made their screen debut in a small role in *Soup to Nuts* In 1930. They made *Woman Haters* as a solo act four years later. The Stooges starred in 194 "shorts" (each 16-18 minutes long) and five feature films for Columbia from 1934 to 1958 and became the shorts department's most valuable property. Their third film, *Men in Black,* was nominated for an Academy Award. In 1940, Moe became the first American movie actor to play Adolf Hitler (*You Nazty Spy*).

After they left Columbia, they made additional films for their own production company, Normandy Productions. Regulars in their films included Vernon Dent, Bud Jamison, Christine McIntyre, Emil Sitka, and Greta Thyssen. Former stars from the silent era and future stars such as Lucille Ball and Lloyd Bridges popped up in early Three Stooges shorts.

Curly, suffering a series of strokes throughout the 1940s (he died in 1952), was replaced by his older brother Shemp in 1946. Although it was thought that Shemp was too old and sounded too much like Moe, the reunited original Stooges prospered though the next decade. It is often disputed who was the funniest of the Stooges, Shemp or Curly.

Remakes of films and patchwork of old footage became more frequent as the years progressed. The studio could complete an entire Stooge comedy in hours. Columbia put together an entire feature film by piecing together excerpts from old Stooges clips. Even after his death in 1955, the studio continued to use the Shemp character in films, incorporating old footage and a double wearing a wig. Joe Besser took Shemp's place from 1956 to 1958, when he was replaced by Joe DeRita, called "Curly Joe."

Near the end of the '50s, the Stooges' future was in doubt; their nightclub act was unsuccessful, their film career appeared over, and vaudeville was dead. Columbia released a package of Stooges shorts to television in 1958. In a matter of weeks, the old Stooges shorts were the No. 1 children's TV series throughout the country. They received a flood of offers for records, comic books, fairs, shopping center promotions, appearances on Ed Sullivan's and Steve Allen's shows, and a cartoon series entitled *The New Three Stooges*.

After Larry's stroke in 1969, Moe decided to retire the act. Moe continued solo on the college lecture circuit until his death in 1975. Larry died earlier that same year.

Bibliography

Forrester, Jeffrey. *The Stooge Chronicles*. Secaucus, NJ: Citadel, 1996.

Howard, Moe. *Moe Howard & the 3 Stooges: The Pictorial Biography of the Wildest Trio in the History of American Entertainment*. Secaucus, NJ: Citadel, 1977.

Lenburg, Jeff, and Joan Howard Maurer. *The Three Stooges Scrapbook*. Secaucus, NJ: Citadel, 1982.

"Moe Better Blues." *Sports Illustrated* 86.13 (31 Mar. 1997): 30.

Neville, Lee. "Just Say Moe!" *U.S. News & World Report* 122.24 (23 June 1997): 14.

Patrice A. Oppliger

3-D. Color features certainly differentiated Hollywood's offerings in movie theaters of the 1950s from the grainy black and white images then available on television. But Hollywood went one step further and sought to make its movies "bigger" and thus supposedly even better. Possibly "new" images would catch the public's attention and draw the "lost audience" back to the theaters.

This new image-innovation process commenced in 1952 when Cinerama offered spectacular wide-screen effects by melding images from three synchronized projectors on a vast (specially designed) curved screen. But soon it became clear that Cinerama was too expensive, and its innovation stalled. The dollar investment to convert a single theater (about $100,000) never proved money wisely spent.

The 3-D process was tried next. Three-Dimensional movies, or simply 3-D, had been around since the 1920s. One premiere had taken place on 27 September 1922 with *The Power of Love*, heralded as "Plasticon." Returns were scant, and the next "premiere" came in November 1952, when George Schafer, former president of RKO, and Arch Oboler (see entry), a veteran radio producer, launched *Bwana Devil*, a crude African adventure story starring Robert Stack. Their 3-D process, labeled "Natural Vision," caused quite a stir. Box-office takes at various premieres proved profitable; United Artists agreed to distribute *Bwana Devil*.

The 3-D process was not easy to use. For a continuous screening without interruption for rewinding, a theater needed four projectors instead of the standard two. The 3-D system worked best on a metallic screen, when normal theaters used porous screens so they could set speakers behind the screen. The exhibitor had to invest thousands to insure a continuous supply of the cardboard spectacles (at 10 cents a pair) needed to see the 3-D effects.

Nonetheless, during 1953 and into the early months of 1954, 3-D movies were hailed as the savior of the American film industry. The Hollywood majors jumped in head first. In April 1953, Warner Bros. issued what was to remain the most successful of these efforts, *House of Wax* (1953), starring Vincent Price. *House of Wax* grossed $1 million during its first week of release. Each genre seemed to have its 3-D studio sponsor: Metro-Goldwyn-Mayer released a musical, *Kiss Me Kate* (1953); Columbia tried a crime tale in *Man in the Dark* (1953); Universal contributed the science fiction efforts *It Came from Outer Space* (1953) and *The Creature from the Black Lagoon* (1954).

But the attempted innovation of 3-D was over almost before it had begun. By mid-1954, it had become clear that with all the expense involved, the added revenues from 3-D never proved worth the investment. Despite periodic efforts at re-innovation, nothing—not pornography or even a sequel to *Jaws* two decades later—would make 3-D a money maker at America's movie houses.

Bibliography

Belton, John. *Widescreen Cinema*. Cambridge: Harvard UP, 1992.

Fielding, Raymond. *A Technological History of Motion Pictures and Television*. Berkeley: U of California P, 1967.

Gomery, Douglas. *Shared Pleasures*. Madison: U of Wisconsin P, 1992.

Hayes, R. M. *3-D Movies: A History and Filmography of Stereoscopic Cinema*. Jefferson: McFarland, 1989.

Morgan, Hal, and Dan Symmes. *Amazing 3-D*. Boston: Little, Brown, 1982.

Quigley, Martin, Jr. *New Screen Techniques*. New York: Quigley, 1953.

Douglas Gomery

Thrill Sports. Certain sports are clearly thrill sports—such as bungee jumping (see entry), whose modern incarnation began in 1979 with the Oxford Dangerous Sports Club. Others, like skydiving or mountaineering (see entries), are categorized as thrill sports depending on the degree of the participant's self-imposed difficulty. For example, an offshoot of skydiving is BASE jumping, which appeared in 1966. BASE stands for B(uildings), A(ntennae towers), S(pans), and the E(arth). Participants parachute from these objects. The short vertical falls—sometimes only a few hundred feet—coupled with "object strikes" and rough landings earn this sport the status of high risk.

In 1994, the appearance of a magazine dedicated exclusively to thrill sports testified to their popularity, if not their amorphousness. Although *Over the Edge* does not define an "adventure sport," it offers a disclaimer one would not expect to find in *Golf Digest*: "Warning: Most of the activities covered in *Over the Edge* carry a significant risk of personal injury or death." In addition to *Over the Edge*, *Outside* magazine has been a consistent chronicler of thrill sports since the 1980s.

The following is a representative sampling of the ever-expanding field of thrill sports: bungee jumping; (free or sport) rock and ice climbing; skydiving and BASE jumping; hang and parasailing or gliding; snow and skate boarding; mountain biking; in-line skating (roller blading); street luge; caving; kayaking; whitewater rafting; windsurfing; kiteskiing; technical SCUBA diving; extreme and daredevil snow skiing; ultra-marathons; and any conventional sport with "extreme," "ultra," or "solo" before its name, such as "extreme swimming": long distance, open ocean, no wetsuits, no support.

Codifying to a degree what does or does not constitute a thrill sport is ESPN's broadcast of "Extreme Games." This week-long venue features bungee jumping (i.e., freestyle, compulsory, and technical), sky surfing, in-line skating, mountain biking, street luge, sport climbing, windsurfing, extreme marathon, and skateboarding.

Throughout the 1980s and 1990s, television's (particularly MTV's) influence on thrill sports has been significant. In the 1980s, MTV aired stylish documentaries on onetime, localized California-based fads such as snowboarding and street luge, bringing the fashion, lingo, and attitude (if not the vertical drop) to teens in Iowa. Further, the rise of the popularity of thrill sports in the 1980s paralleled the country's overall fitness craze.

Breakthroughs in technology have also contributed to the popularity of thrill sports, improving some and creating still others. The best-known example is the ubiquitous mountain bike (see entry). High-strength plastics and lightweight metal alloys (some derived from aerospace technology), computer-engineered designs, and an American yen for gadgets are constantly infusing thrill sports with new products. For example, a recent invention is the "parapente," a hang glider that weighs 13 pounds and can fold up and fit in a backpack, rendering just about any mountain peak a launch site.

High risk sports such as parapente gliding often lead to high risk rescues that can also be high cost. Because of this, some National Parks, such as Yosemite, are regulating thrill sports and even billing athletes for the expense of rescue. Additionally, there is talk among thrill sport athletes and officials of setting aside "no-rescue zones" in the wilderness. In these places an athlete takes his or her chances with nature without the technological safety-net of rescue helicopters, dinghys, snowmobiles and the like—amounting to a mandated self-reliance.

Bibliography
"On the Edge." *Newsweek* 19 July 1994.
"Risky Business." *Backpacker* May 1986.
"What If We Ignored the SOS?" *Los Angeles Times* 30 Nov. 1993: A1.

John A. Kinch

Thriller, The, one of literature's best-sellers, differs from the detective novel in, among other things, its treatment of the secret withheld from readers. In conventional mystery and detective fiction, the secret is revealed at the end of the story but has been within the grasp of the astute reader from the beginning. The thriller permits no such gradual disclosure, and the secret can rarely be deduced; rather, the reader is kept on tenterhooks, moving from one thrilling incident to the next, until the secret is sprung for its *frisson* alone. The restoration of moral order and rationality so central to mystery fiction is replaced by the thriller's excitement and unpredictability. Like detective stories, thrillers are sufficiently realistic to command readers' engagement, but they are finally escapist works, catalysts for readers' fears and suspicions.

In the 19th century, such fears were often projected by a lower-class readership onto the aristocracy, and were even prurient in nature. Wilkie Collins's two famous novels, *The Moonstone* (1868) and *The Woman in White* (1860), illustrate the difference between the two modes. In *The Moonstone*, a standard detective novel, Collins lays down clues by which the shrewd reader might unravel the central conundrum to see that the diamond was stolen under the influence of opium. But in *The Woman in White*, the basic secrets—the substitution of one girl for another, and the reasons for it—are beyond the reader's deduction. Class is an element in *The Moonstone*, but not divisive; *The Woman in White* conveys a much greater sense of spying on one's betters.

This class element seems to have made America, early on, barren soil for the thriller (though Collins, Mrs. Henry Wood, and Mary Elizabeth Braddon were widely read here). But during the 20th century, some of the most successful thrillers have substituted power for class, playing on fears and suspicions about the government. Such English writers as William Le Queux, John Buchan, and Sapper wrote thrillers of this type around the time of World War I, but for them, the upper and the ruling classes were one and the same. In American tales like John Grisham's *The Pelican Brief* (1992), the rulers are no longer upholders of King and Country, but thugs protecting personal interests. This type of thriller, written by Grisham, Robert Ludlum, and others, is heavily infused with paranoia and reflects and cultivates a distrust of government emanating from events like the assassination of President Kennedy and the Watergate scandal. One of the best examples of the kind is Richard Condon's *The Manchurian Candidate* (1959).

Another important type of thriller places the very vulnerable—especially women and children—under threat, augmenting suspense with the suggestion that the danger could have been avoided ("Had-I-but known"). Mary Roberts Rinehart (see entry) is the early acknowledged master of this subgenre, beginning with *The Circular Staircase* (1908). Margaret Millar, in such books as *The Fiend* (1964), works the same vein, as do, even more claustrophobically, Joseph Hayes in *The Desperate Hours* (1954) and John D. MacDonald in *The Executioners* (1958—also known as *Cape Fear*). This kind of thriller has been particularly adaptable to stage and screen, from Rinehart's dramatization of her novel as *The Bat* (1920), and John Willard's *The Cat and the Canary* (1921), both set in a recognizable rural America, to Maxwell Anderson's *Bad Seed* (1954), based on William March's novel, and Robert Marasco's *Child's Play* (1970), both of which subvert the formula by turning the vulnerable one into the menace. *Psycho* (1959), Robert Bloch's novel celebrated for its adaptation to the screen by Alfred Hitchcock, illustrates the shadowy borderlines that the thriller shares with the genres of horror and psychological crime fiction.

Bibliography

Bloom, Clive, ed. *Spy Thrillers: From Buchan to Le Carré.* New York: St. Martin's, 1990.

Harper, Ralph. *The World of the Thriller.* 1969. Baltimore: Johns Hopkins UP, 1974.

Palmer, Jerry. *Thrillers: Genesis and Structure of a Popular Genre.* New York: St. Martin's, 1990.

Smith, Myron J., Jr., and Terry White. *Cloak and Dagger Fiction: An Annotated Guide to Spy Thrillers.* Westport: Greenwood, 1995.

Barrie Hayne

See also

Clancy, Tom	Holt, Victoria
Clark, Mary Higgins	Leonard, Elmore
Crichton, Michael	Ludlum, Robert
Follett, Ken	McBain, Ed
Gothic Mysteries	Mystery and Detective Fiction
Grisham, John	Rendell, Ruth
Had-I-But-Known Mysteries	Spy Fiction

Time (1923-), established by Henry Robinson Luce and Briton Hadden, remains America's most popular, most successful, and most controversial weekly news magazine, with its modern circulation figures hovering just below 5 million copies published each week. A virtual barometer of the evolution and nature of 20th-century American history, politics, and society, *Time* finds its roots in Luce and Hadden's interest in providing a national information source devoted to the coverage of issues ranging from world affairs to entertainment. *Time*'s inaugural issue included departments such as "National Affairs" and "Theatre"—monikers that remain essential to the magazine's modern format—while also including the works of such figures as Archibald MacLeish and Stephen Vincent Benét. Although its initial circulation figures accounted for a mere 9,000 copies, by December 1925 *Time* enjoyed a circulation of more than 100,000 copies, and in 1942, circulation topped 1 million copies for the first time—remarkable testimony to the incipient periodical's soaring popularity.

Hadden and Luce maintained their relationship with the magazine for the balance of their lifetimes. Although Luce developed other publishing projects during his career—most notably, the immensely popular *Life*—he nevertheless maintained his role as *Time*'s editor-in-chief until his death in 1967. Hadden devoted himself to shaping the stylistic and journalistic elements inherent in the magazine's success. Many of *Time*'s critics credit Hadden with the development of "timestyle," a methodology for packaging the news in a manner that enhanced its salability and readability to the general public. Under Hadden's watchful editorial eye, *Time*'s uncredited writers composed their articles using a forceful and descriptive journalistic style. Hadden and Luce also encouraged their reporters to approach their subjects using what their critics describe as "group journalism"—a system that ensured that each article received the attention of correspondents, writers, researchers, and editors alike, thus underscoring its efficacy as a corporate product of *Time* magazine, as well as to verify its accuracy. Following Henry A. Grunwald's appointment as the magazine's managing editor in 1968, the notion of "group journalism" continued, although writers now received byline credit for their articles.

In addition to its enduring reporting and composition standards, *Time* maintains its place as the abiding standard for weekly news magazines through such features as the bold red letters that grace every issue's masthead. *Time*'s memorable and striking logo adorns every issue published during the magazine's extensive periodical history—from its coverage of World War II and its aftermath, the Korean and Vietnam conflicts, and the presidency of John F. Kennedy, through the dark days of the Watergate crisis, the protracted diplomatic stalemate that accompanied the hostage crisis in Iran for 444 days from November 1979 to January 1981, to the explosion of the *Challenger* space shuttle in January 1986. Likewise, much of *Time*'s remarkable endurance in such a highly competitive and evolving industry finds its roots in the stability of the magazine's format. The magazine features a number of departments that date back to *Time*'s inception in the early 1920s, including such sections as "Nation," "Business," "Education," and "Religion," as well as departments such as "Books," "Milestones," "Music," and "Cinema," among others.

Time's annual "Man [now Person] of the Year" issue remains one of the most popular, and often controversial, elements in the magazine's rich publishing history. In January 1928, *Time* named its first "Man of the Year"—Charles A. Lindbergh for his aerial achievements of the previous year—while other figures followed in the coming years, including Franklin D. Roosevelt (1932, 1934, and 1941), Adolph Hitler (1938), Queen Elizabeth II (1952), Martin Luther King, Jr. (1964), and the Computer (1983).

In 1999, Jeff Bezos, head of the on-line bookstore Amazon.com, was named "Person of the Year," and Albert Einstein was designated as "Person of the Century." In addition to its journalistic successes, *Time* also has endured a number of polemical moments, including its 1979 selection for "Man of the Year"—Iran's Ayatollah Khomeini—and the controversial, "photographically enhanced" June 1994 mugshot of former football star O. J. Simpson. Despite such instances of notoriety, *Time* magazine remains one of the nation's most enduring news sources regarding national and international affairs, politics, and entertainment, and its weekly appearances since 1923 define the very fabric of the evolution of American social, cultural, and political history in the 20th century.

Bibliography

Busch, Noel F. *Briton Hadden: A Biography of the Co-Founder of* Time. 1949. Westport: Greenwood, 1975.

Nourie, Alan and Barbara, eds. *American Mass-Market Magazines.* New York: Greenwood, 1990.

Taft, William H. *American Magazines for the 1980s.* New York: Hastings, 1982.

Kenneth Womack

Time Tunnel, The (1966-1967), was an hour-long science fiction series created and produced by schlockmeister Irwin Allen, who also developed *Land of the Giants* (1968-70), *Lost in Space* (1965-68), and *Voyage to the Bottom of the Sea* (1964-68) and was responsible for movies such as *The Poseidon Adventure* (1972) and *The Towering Inferno* (1974).

Scientists Dr. Tony Newman (James Darren) and Dr. Doug Phillips (Robert Colbert), while working on a top-secret government project to develop a time tunnel for access to the future and the past, tested their device before it was completed. Alas, though they found themselves moving from era to historical era, they had no way to return to the present. While their associates—Dr. Ann MacGregor (Lee Meriwether), Dr. Raymond Swain (John Zaremba), and project supervisor General Heywood Kirk (Whit Bissell)—worked to free them from their forced journey, Newman and Phillips bounced from one momentous event to the next.

Though *The Time Tunnel*'s special effects, supervised by Bill Abbott, won an Emmy for the series, other production values weren't as high. Wooden acting only accentuated the outlandish plot twists, stagey fights, and exposition-laden dialogue. As a series, *The Time Tunnel* barely rose above pat drama and bad science fiction, and today remains of interest mostly for its characteristically 1960s psychedelic opening credits, Technicolor sets, and off-kilter reverse angles. Also of note is the character of Dr. Ann MacGregor, portrayed by Lee Meriwether as a no-nonsense, competent, professional woman on an equal footing with her male colleagues.

Two novelizations of episodes, titled *The Time Tunnel* and *Timeslip!* and written by noted science fiction writer Murray Leinster, were published in 1967.

Bibliography

Brooks, Tim, and Earle Marsh. *The Complete Directory to Prime Time TV Shows, 1946–Present.* New York: Ballantine, 1992.

McNeil, Alex. *Total Television including Cable: A Comprehensive Guide to Programming from 1948 to the Present.* New York: Penguin, 1992.

MaryAnn Johanson

Time Warner, Inc. In one of the greatest media mergers in the history of the United States, indeed in the world, in 1989 the colossus that was once Time, Inc. (with its world famous magazines) merged with the Hollywood operation called Warner Communications, Inc. In 1989, Warner made far more money from cable television and selling music on cassettes and compact discs. The sum was staggering in its size and scope. For the early 1990s there was only one true mass media empire and that was Time Warner, Inc. And Steven J. Ross, the man who had created the modern media conglomerate, was its architect.

Indeed during the early 1990s Time Warner, Inc., measured in total assets in the billions of dollars, stood as the largest media company in the world. The new colossus generated yearly revenues in the tens of billion dollars, and systematically covered all phases of the mass media production and distribution except newspapers.

In cable television Time Warner, Inc. was a player second only to Tele-Communications, Inc. It was a silent part-owner of Ted Turner's networks (including WTBS, the SuperStation, TNT, the Cartoon Network, and CNN) and bought Turner's company in 1996. It owns a share of Black Entertainment Television, and led the market in pay TV movies with Home Box Office and its sister operation, Cinemax. And when Time Warner merged the cable television systems of Warner Cable and Time, Inc.'s American Television & Communication cable company, it shot into second place in the cable television business, only behind Tele-Communications. Roughly, through the 1990s Time Warner, had one of every eight cable subscribers in the U.S.

In Hollywood, Warner Bros. ranks as one of the major makers of both motion pictures and television programs. The Warner studio's motion picture blockbusters have included such mega-hits as *Batman* and *The Color Purple*. Steven Spielberg and Steven J. Ross were close friends. The studio lot in Burbank, CA, was one of the largest in the world. Time Warner, Inc.'s television programs have included prime-time hits such as *Murphy Brown* and profitable syndicated fare such as *The People's Court*. In home video, Warner is one of the leading suppliers to that expanding industry.

But Time Warner, Inc. means more than a motion picture and television empire. Its Warner record division ranks one of the top six major collection of labels in the music business with its Reprise, Atlantic, Elektra, and Asylum units. Phil Collins, k. d. lang, Madonna, Anita Baker, and Lionel Richie have poured millions of dollars into the company's recorded music coffers.

Time and Warner hold major publishing interests. Time, Inc., of course, remains world famous for its magazines such as *Time, Fortune,* and *Sports Illustrated,* as well as *Working Woman, Money, Southern Living,* and *Progressive Farmer* and dozens more. Time, Inc.'s Time-Life Books and Little, Brown labels are major players in the book industry. But Warner Books has published best-sellers by Andrew Greeley, John Naisbitt, Tom Peters, and Richard Simmons. DC Comics and *Mad* magazine have long made Warner millions. The company maintains printing plants in the United States, Canada, the Netherlands, Singapore, and Hong Kong. And there are theme parks and assorted other media operations, too numerous to mention.

The merger of Warner Communications and Time, Inc. brought together a wide range of mass communication and leisure time businesses. With the rise of the Internet in the late 1990s, it was perhaps inevitable that Time Warner would become involved in that mass communications market: in January 2000, America Online announced a plan to buy Time Warner for $165 trillion.

Bibliography

Bruck, Connie. *Master of the Game: Steve Ross and the Creation of Time Warner.* New York: Simon & Schuster, 1994.

Clurman, Richard M. *To the End of Time: The Seduction and Conquest of a Media Empire.* New York: Simon & Schuster, 1992.

Maney, Kevin. *Megamedia Shake-out: The Inside Story of the Leaders and Losers in the Exploding Communications Industry.* New York: Wiley, 1995.

Douglas Gomery

Tiomkin, Dimitri (1899-1979), as a Hollywood composer, achieved fame for creating memorable melodies that people remembered after they saw the film. Many of his songs became standards. Among the most renowned are "Do Not Forsake Me" (*High Noon*, 1952), "Thee I Love" (*Friendly Persuasion*, 1956), and "Green Leaves" (*The Alamo*, 1960). "Do Not Forsake Me" was intentionally aimed at the popular music market and released as a single before *High Noon*, which had previewed badly, officially opened. The record's success has been credited with saving the movie. Along with Gary Cooper's Oscar for best actor, the film won two awards for Tiomkin, best song, sung by Tex Ritter in the film, and best score. Following the success of *High Noon* and its song, Hollywood producers frequently asked composers to compose a hit song that could be sold separately. None were as successful as Tiomkin. Tiomkin got Pat Boone, a teenage rock star of the early 1950s noted for his ballads, to sing "Thee I Love" and the Brothers Four, a folk-rock group later in the decade, for "Green Leaves." Tiomkin added to his Oscar collection in 1955 with the score for *The High and the Mighty* and in 1959 for *The Old Man and the Sea*.

Born in St. Petersburg, Russia, Tiomkin received musical training as a pianist at St. Petersburg Conservatory and St. Petersburg University. When the revolution diminished opportunities for classically trained musicians in his native country, Tiomkin traveled west, earning his way to the U.S. by playing in European theater orchestras and American vaudeville. In Paris in 1928 Tiomkin gave the European premiere of George Gershwin's *Concerto in F*. Although he began writing film music as early as 1929 (*Devil May Care*), he was a self-trained composer and did not receive significant attention until his score for Frank Capra's *Lost Horizon* in 1937, the year he became a U.S. citizen. Additional Capra films *You Can't Take It with You* (1938), *Mr. Smith Goes to Washington* (1939), and *Meet John Doe* (1941) demonstrated to both the public and Hollywood producers that the Russian-born composer had mastered the American musical idiom. During World War II Tiomkin continued his collaboration with Capra in the *Why We Fight* (1942-45) series of documentaries. He also composed the score for Capra's Christmas classic, *It's a Wonderful Life* (1946).

After the war, Tiomkin became one of the most sought-after composers in Hollywood. He successfully wrote scores for comedy (*The Four Poster*, 1952), science fiction (*The Thing*, aka *The Thing from Another World*, 1951), and drama (*The Court-Martial of Billy Mitchell*, 1955). He worked with several of the most noted directors of the 1950s and 1960s, including Howard Hawks (*Land of the Pharoahs*, 1955), Fred Zinnemann (*The Men*, 1950, and *The Sundowners*, 1960), and Alfred Hitchcock (*Strangers on a Train*, 1951, *I Confess*, 1952, and *Dial M for Murder*, 1953). Tiomkin's Russian exoticism was particularly evident in the work he did for *Tarzan and the Mermaids*, the last Weismuller Tarzan film (1948), *Return to Paradise* (1952), *Search for Paradise* (1957), and *55 Days at Peking* (1963).

Despite the apparent diversity of subjects, Tiomkin is best remembered for his Westerns. This cycle began with David O. Selznick's bloated *Duel in the Sun* (1946), reached its apex with *High Noon*, and continued through the 1950s with *The Big Sky* (1952), *Giant* (1956), *Gunfight at the O.K. Corral* (1957), *Rio Bravo* (1959), *The Unforgiven* (1960), and *The Alamo* (1960). For both *Giant* and *The Alamo* Tiomkin received Academy Award nominations.

Bibliography
Palmer, Christopher. *The Composer in Hollywood.* London: Boyars, 1990.
——. *Dimitri Tiomkin, a Portrait.* London: T. E., 1984.
Tiomkin, Dimitri, and Prosper Buranelli. *Please Don't Hate Me.* Garden City: Doubleday, 1959.

Arthur R. Jarvis, Jr.

Today (1952-   ) was the first TV morning news program to run on any national network (NBC). For more than 40 years after its premiere on January 14, 1952, the *Today* show has presented a two-hour live program every weekday morning which blends news with entertainment. Each day it provides viewers with the latest national and international news as well as interviews with newsmakers from the worlds of politics, business, media, entertainment, and sports. The format consists of four one-half-hour time slots, each with a news section, the weather, and two or three segments of various features. Producers are proud of their ability to revise an entire program at the very last minute. Their goal is to bring viewers breaking news as it happens. Events that they cover nationally have included earthquakes in San Francisco and riots in Los Angeles; internationally, they showed the student uprising in Tiananmen Square, the release of Nelson Mandela, and the crisis in the Persian Gulf.

The *Today* show also is one of the longest-running programs in the history of television with the greatest number of accumulated hours of broadcasting. In 1975 alone, 800 people were interviewed, totaling 65 senators, 50 congressmen, 20 cabinet members, 20 governors, and 200 authors. Just as the *New York Times* was considered the definitive newspaper record in print, the *Today* show became the television record of note. Its archives have become a veritable time capsule of social, political, and scientific transformation during the last half of the 20th century. Spinoffs of *Today* include *Early Today*, *Later Today*, and *Weekend Today*.

Bibliography
Davis, Gerry. *The* Today *Show: An Anecdotal History.* New York: Morrow, 1987.
Kessler, Judy. *Inside* Today*: The Battle for the Morning:* New York: Villard, 1992.
Metz, Robert. *The* Today *Show: An Inside Look at 25 Tumultuous Years...And the Colorful and Controversial People behind the Scenes.* Chicago: Playboy, 1977.

Ann Schoonmaker

See also
Television Talk Shows

Tolkien, J(ohn) R(onald) R(euel) (1892-1973), was an imaginative writer whose works exerted a great influence on fantasy fiction and have forced a rethinking of fairy stories. He created a special world to which readers can indeed retreat to find rest and inspiration to face the problems of their daily worlds. That world is not merely an escape but a means to puzzle out the mysteries of life.

Tolkien, one of literature's most influential authors of fantasy, was born in Bloemfontein, South Africa, and brought up near Birmingham, England. Tolkien was educated at King Edward VI School in Birmingham and Exeter College, Oxford. In 1915, he received his B.A. from Oxford. Upon being graduated, he enlisted in the Lancashire Fusiliers. When the war was over, he returned to England.

Tolkien was a philologist, working for two years on the *Oxford English Dictionary.* He began his teaching career as a reader in English language at the University of Leeds. In 1925, he returned to Oxford permanently as a professor, first of Anglo-Saxon, then of English language and literature.

Over the years, Tolkien built up a solid academic reputation in his field. However, it is for his imaginative writings that he is best known. These came to the fore as a result of his 1939 Andrew Lang Lectures at the University of St. Andrews in Scotland, in which he discussed the true meaning of "faerie" stories as opposed to their image as stories meant only for children. He depicted an alternate universe with its own modes of thought and values which provides an escape from the world. In many ways, this talk foreshadowed Tolkien's masterpieces.

Tolkien's own fairy stories, written partly to amuse his three sons, embodied the principles he enunciated in his Lang lecture. In *The Hobbit,* published two years earlier, Tolkien had created his own world, Middle Earth, and peopled it with its own culture and society. Bilbo Baggins finds his courage in facing a dragon and recovering lost treasure. He comes into possession of the evil sorcerer Sauron's ring, setting the scene for the three-part sequel: *The Lord of the Rings* (1954-55).

It is hard to imagine today that *The Lord of the Rings* took so long to reach its great popularity. It is an extremely sophisticated work, peopled with fascinating creatures, complex ideas, and a great narrative based on the theme of good versus evil. It set the standard for fantasy fiction, a standard that has not been surpassed. And yet it took until the 1960s for it to become popular. American college students made it a cult favorite and it has remained popular ever since. In 1978 an animated TV-movie of *The Hobbit* was produced.

Tolkien's last work, completed by his son Christopher, was a prequel to the *Lord of the Rings,* entitled *The Silmarillion* (1977).

Bibliography

Carpenter, Humphrey. *Tolkien: A Biography.* Boston: Houghton, 1977.

Hammond, Wayne G., and Christina Scull. *J. R. R. Tolkien: Artist & Illustrator.* London: HarperCollins, 1995.

Rosebury, Brian. *Tolkien: A Critical Assessment.* New York: St. Martin's, 1992.

Stevens, David, and Carol D. Stevens. *J. R. R. Tolkien: The Art of the Myth-Maker.* San Bernardino: Reginald, 1993.

Wakeman, John, ed. *World Authors.* New York: Wilson, 1974.

Frank A. Salamone

Tom Swift, the literary character who came to symbolize the American ethic of success, was created by Howard R. Garis (1873-1962), prolific author of adolescent novels and series. The Tom Swift series was initially published by the (Edward) Stratemeyer Syndicate (see entry), and is believed to be highly derivative of the immensely popular Frank Reade dime novel series (1892-98). Both were action/adventures that featured scientific-invention-based fantasy. Under the "Victor Appleton" pseudonym, Garis wrote all but the last three of the initial 38-novel Tom Swift series, which appeared between 1910 and 1938. The first Tom Swift novel was entitled *Tom Swift and His Motor-Cycle: Or, Fun and Adventures on the Road.* Other early Tom Swift novels featured motorboats, an airship, a submarine-boat, and an electric runabout. By the 1930s, there was an adventure with a house on wheels. Each of the stories had a subtitle, much in the tradition of 19th-century dime novels.

Today, the inventions in these stories seem quaint, but in their day stories about motorcycles, boats, airships, electricity and the like were quite exciting—particularly if there was some new idea or twist attached to these adventures. In the 1930s also, two Tom Swift Big Little Books were published: *Tom Swift and His Giant Telescope* (1938) and *Tom Swift and His Magnetic Silencer* (1941). A second series of Tom Swift books commenced in 1954 with *Tom Swift and His Flying Lab.* The byline/house name on this series of 33 novels that ran until 1971 was "Victor Appleton II." There were a third and fourth series of Tom Swift novels as well, both ascribed to "Victor Appleton." The third series (comprised of 11 titles) began in 1981 with *Tom Swift and the City in the Stars.* The fourth series began in 1991 with *Tom Swift #1: The Black Dragon.*

Bibliography

Clute, John, and Peter Nicholls, eds. *The Encyclopedia of Science Fiction.* New York: St. Martin's, 1993.

Dizer, John T. *Tom Swift & Co.: "Boys' Books" By Stratemeyer's and Others.* Jefferson: McFarland, 1982.

Garis, Roger. *My Father Was Uncle Wiggly.* New York: McGraw-Hill, 1996.

Johnson, Deidre. *Edward Stratemeyer and the Stratemeyer Syndicate.* New York: Twayne, 1993.

Lowery, Lawrence F. *The Collector's Guide to Big Little Books and Similar Books.* Danville: Education Research and Applications, 1981.

Garyn G. Roberts

Top Hat (1935) was the quintessential Fred Astaire–Ginger Rogers movie musical, and the first in which they received top billing. Astaire and Rogers (see entry) ranked it as their favorite in the series of ten films they made as partners. It is only a bit ironic that it offered a paean to three items Astaire did not much care for: white tie, top hat, and tails. But care for them or not, the Irving Berlin title song is now forever identified with him.

Irving Berlin's entire score of five songs made the *Hit Parade* in 1935. In addition to the song "Top Hat," the score included "Isn't It a Lovely Day," "No Strings," "Cheek to Cheek," and "The Piccolino," and restored Irving Berlin's confidence in his ability to write for the movies. Astaire and Berlin became lifelong friends, and Berlin attributed his restored confidence to Astaire.

In many ways, the movie is a model for Hollywood musicals. It has a classic score by the father of American classical popular music, Irving Berlin. The cast is superb from its co-stars down to the least character actor. Its dance director was the legendary Hermes Pan. Mark Sandrich, who had worked with Astaire and Rogers previously, was the director. Moreover, Dwight Taylor and Allan Scott, basing their work on a play by Karl Noti that Alexander Farago and Aladar Lazlo adapted, provided the cast with a serviceable script with which to show their talent. It was a perfect Hollywood cooperative effort. Pandro S. Berman was its producer.

Bibliography

Beaver, Frank E. *On Film*. New York: McGraw-Hill, 1983.
Hirschhorn, Clive. *The Hollywood Musical*. 1991. New York: Portland House, 1991.
Kael, Pauline. *Taking It All In*. New York: Holt, 1984.
Kreuger, Miles, ed. *The Movie Musical: From Vitaphone to "42nd Street" as Reported in a Great Fan Magazine*. New York: Dover, 1975.

Frank A. Salamone

Toys. The postwar American toy trade currently categorizes toys as follows: infant/preschool, dolls, plush ("stuffed"), vehicles (miniature), male action ("action figures" and accessories), ride-ons (tricycles, pedal cars, wagons, etc., but not bicycles, which the industry considers "wheeled goods"), games/puzzles, activity (building sets, paint sets, etc.), video games, and miscellaneous (musical instruments, guns, etc.). Under whatever category, they make up a miniaturized society in America.

Toy manufacturers of the postwar period have frequently called theirs a fashion industry or a "style business," since their success depends both upon the attraction of a "hot" toy that children ages 6 to 12 want to buy and upon the harrowing, eight-week Christmas season in which retailers and manufacturers make 50-60 percent of their annual toy sales (until the 1980s, it was 60-70 percent). One hot toy of the early postwar years was the Mickey Mouse Guitar, the first plaything advertised nationally on television (1955). Its success encouraged toy makers to target children instead of adults as primary consumers. The potential market, through television's reach, was now so vast that toy companies could afford to develop more elaborate, more costly toys. This opportunity encouraged, among other things, increased experimentation with battery-operated toys, which came to dominate the market in the early to mid-1960s. By that time, 300 toys were being advertised nationally on television, some of them quite large and costly. "Promotional toys," as

these are called, now account for about 70 percent of the industry's gross annual sales.

Children who bought the Mouse Guitar saw it advertised during Walt Disney's *Mickey Mouse Club* (1955-59). As a licensed product, that is, one whose namesake—Mickey Mouse, in this case—must be leased from another company, the guitar marked a trend that had begun in the 1920s, and more vigorously in the 1930s, when filmmaking and moviegoing, in tandem with nationally syndicated radio shows, created a stock of celebrities and "characters" known by most Americans. By affiliating their products with such popular figures as Superman, Felix the Cat, Popeye, and Shirley Temple, not to mention Mickey Mouse, toy companies realized increased sales of even the most basic products, like balls or tops. During the Batman craze of 1966, ignited by the television show *Batman* (1966-68), for instance, a generic play phone or even a set of building blocks could become a hot item after the simple addition of the Batman logo. Television, in the postwar years, made such character affiliations especially profitable, since virtually every middle-class household owned a television set by 1960.

As illustrated by the proliferation of dinosaur toys inspired by the blockbuster movie *Jurassic Park* (1993), toy fads can be thematic as well as character-based. Through most of the 1950s, for instance, American males young and old were infatuated with all things Western: by 1958, seven of TV's Top 10 shows were Westerns like *Bat Masterson* and *Gunsmoke*. Toy rifles, six-shooters, holster sets, cowboy hats, rubber tomahawks, leather moccasins, and faux coonskin caps—in imitation of Walt Disney's wildly popular *Davy Crockett* (1954)—were the rage. Virtually all of these and every other kind of toy sold in America during the early to mid-1950s were American-made, since foreign competitors were still recovering from World War II. Not until the late 1950s, as Japan and Germany gained strength in industry, did American toy makers begin to face troublesome competition.

Although fads fueled by celebrities or themes are often fleeting, the high market value of the celebrity itself is not necessarily a one-time phenomenon. After the successful release of the Hollywood movie *Batman* in 1989, the Batman craze began again. Superman, the *Peanuts* characters (Snoopy), and the *Sesame Street* characters (Big Bird), have all been hot toys more than once. Better still, they have proven themselves to be consistent sellers, joining the rarefied ranks of character toys that have become staples.

Staples are the toys that sell well year after year no matter what the fashion. Traditionally, they have been low-cost, smaller items, always less elaborate than their promotional counterparts: balls, jump ropes, jacks, cars and trucks, marbles, novelties like rubber snakes and frogs, generic doll accessories, miniature "sets" of various kinds (household, science, craft), plastic soldiers and monsters, play money, magic tricks, small windups of animals and vehicles, and weapons. These are the basics, the kind of things every middle-class child might buy with his or her weekly allowance.

Preschool toys are their own variety of staples, insofar as they have changed little over the years, in great part because, as preschoolers are too young to buy toys themselves, the manufacturers have made no attempts to create a fad market that would encourage innovation or greater risks in design. Generally, preschool toys of the immediate postwar years were not much different from their turn-of-the-century predecessors, which were products of the kindergarten movement, when educators began to assert that play is vital to a child's development. For the good of the child and society, every toy ostensibly had a developmental function: building blocks stimulated constructive activity, pull and push toys encouraged exercise, and plush toys engendered affection or nurture. So they remain today, still durably built, still adorned with naive expressions of animals and people, still noisy with rattles, bells, and ratchets—only now, these toys utilize new technology, like microchips for music, and they are much safer since they are made mostly of plastic.

It was during the 1950s that the use of plastics proliferated. The Mouse Guitar, made wholly of plastic, signaled the imminent demise of traditional materials like wood and tin (tin-plated sheet steel). Although initially expensive, as were the injection mold machines which made plastic toys, the new materials were ultimately cost effective: light weight meant cheaper shipping, and fewer parts per toy reduced labor in assembly. What is more, plastic was "hygienic" (washable), nearly unbreakable, and safe (no sharp edges, no paint). One of the earliest casualties of the call for safety was the "tin" toy soldier, which was actually made of painted lead. Adults were first warned about these as early as 1936 by the Consumers' Union. By the 1950s, lead soldiers were easy prey to the influx of plastic soldiers, which were not only safer, cheaper, and lighter but were also much more finely sculpted, allowing for greater realism—one of the primary advantages of plastic. The last of the largest lead figure companies, Barclay, went out of business in 1971.

Safety may have been appreciated in the early postwar years, but it did not become an abiding concern until the late 1960s. Protests resulted in the passage of the 1969 Child Protection and Toy Safety Act, which cited such hazards as searing-hot miniature ovens, chemical-laden play dough, and glass-topped games. The addition of the small-parts rule and the sharp-points regulation by 1980 com-

pelled manufacturers to print warnings on packaging: "Caution: small parts. Not suitable for children under the age of three." More significant, children of the consumer-conscious decades (1970s-90s) would never see the kind of intricately detailed, small-parts-laden, sharp-points-studded toys their predecessors enjoyed in decades previous—toys such as an all-tin, wind-up racing car with chromed hubcaps, coiled antenna, turnable steering wheel, hinged windshield, hood ornament, sideview mirrors, and closable doors and trunk.

As consumer-consciousness rose in the late 1960s so did the demand for more realistic depictions of ethnic minorities, specifically African Americans. No longer would they accept a white doll that had simply been dyed brown to look "colored." The black-owned toy company Shindana began selling an ethnically accurate African-American doll called Baby Nancy in 1968. Large companies like Remco responded with similar products. African Americans, and occasionally Asian Americans, are better represented nowadays in America's toyland, though they clearly retain their minority status. Among the 16 or more G.I. Joe action figures of the late 1980s, for instance, two were African American.

A third development of consumer-consciousness gained wide support in the "liberated" 1970s, when parents questioned the constraints of gender-typed toys. Generally, in the postwar years, American toy makers continued doing what toy makers had always done: replicate the material world of the adult in miniature. It seemed to make sense, then, that a boy would get a miniature lawnmower, say, while a girl would get a miniature cooking set. After all, toy makers were simply reproducing the "reality" of daily life in mainstream America, a reality most vividly promulgated by American movies and television. By the 1970s, however, while the traditional notion of play's value prevailed, i.e., that play is the working world of children, the traditional notion of the working world itself had changed radically: to many parents it was no longer acceptable to relegate a girl to the kitchen or a boy to the garage. A study published in 1978 showed that invariably salespersons recommended dolls and kitchenware for girls; trucks, guns, and building sets for boys. Defenders of the industry asserted that most toys—games, puzzles, ride-ons, etc.—are not gender typed, but industry defenders failed to account for the conventions of packaging. Pastel colors, pink especially, and motifs of hearts, flowers, etc. clearly signal "girl," while basic colors like red and brown, high-tech colors like silver, and geometric shapes or bold symbols, like thunderbolts, signal "boy." So ingrained in American culture are these preferences, which begin at birth with baby clothes and crib toys, that young children are loath to cross these clearly marked boundaries. For example, when a major toy manufacturer in the 1980s designed an "action figure" superhero for girls, the girls would not accept this traditionally male toy (G.I. Joe is an action figure) until the company had "pinked it up," as Sydney Stern notes. Significantly, large toy companies still have separate vice presidents for boys' and girls' toys and, in most respects, the dividing line between genders remains as fixed now as it was in the early postwar years. Occasional exceptions include

Coleco's highly successful Cabbage Patch dolls (1983), packaged in gender-neutral beige and marketed to girls and boys alike—at the inventor's insistence. Commercials for the doll showed boys and girls playing together, an arrangement still considered taboo in toy marketing.

Having to be sensitive to the cultural politics of the marketplace was not the least of the toy makers' worries in the 1970s. This was the decade of the oil crisis (1973-79), which hampered not only shipping but production on two levels, due to the scarcity of raw material (plastics) and fuel. Safety concerns and rising steel prices made this the final decade of wide-scale tin toy production. Most significant, Japan's domination of the world toy market ceased in the 1970s when oil prices rose, along with Japan's standard of living, and Japan turned its attention fully to televisions and stereo components, cars, and computers. Only later, in the 1980s, would it become apparent that, for Japan, the making of toys had only been a stair-step to bigger, more profitable manufacture. By 1969, an estimated 90 percent of the toys sold in America came, in whole or in part, from Japan. A decade earlier, Japan was already the world's greatest exporter of playthings (75 percent of its production), followed by Hong Kong, West Germany, and the United Kingdom. So great was Japan's threat that, in 1959, the sponsors of the annual British toy fair barred the Japanese from attending, for fear that they would copy the designs of the British companies.

When the Soviet Union shocked the world with its first successful satellite launch—the Sputnik—in 1957, it was Japan that led the industry in the manufacture of "space toys." From the beginning, as it staggered from the ruins of World War II, Japan had expressed a fascination with tomorrow's technology. By the mid-1950s, the Japanese were already showing remarkable progress and innovation as makers of increasingly sophisticated wind-up and battery-operated toys, particularly of the outer-space variety. Japan's tinplate, toy robots were notable both for their superb lithography and their ingenious operations. The battery-operated robots (most stood about one foot tall) performed a variety of functions that their old, clockwork predecessors could not—not only walking, dancing, and rotating, but also talking, bending forward and picking up objects with their extended hands, operating machinery, and firing lighted guns that popped from concealment in their chests.

At this time, as Japanese toy designers looked to the future, German toy designers looked to the past. Until World War II, Germany had been the world's premier producer and exporter of toys, most of which were made of tin and, if animated, were clockwork-motivated. When the postwar space race began, German toy makers took little interest and, instead, continued to invest their energies in the production of toys with a distinctly old-fashioned, Old World flavor, like tin wind-ups of juggling clowns, bicycle riders, and dancing bears. Consequently, Germany (then West Germany) dropped farther behind Japan as a world supplier of toys.

The space race exacerbated Cold War fears, which—after the Cuban Missile Crisis (1960) and the Berlin Wall confrontation (1961)—found expression in popular entertainment as the "spy" craze. American toy manufacturers were quick to respond, taking their inspiration from such movies as *Dr. No* (1963), which featured James Bond, and such television offerings as *The Man from U.N.C.L.E.* (1964-68). One big seller in 1964 was a toy gun which, when held in a child's grip, looked like a pointing index finger. Another was a briefcase that held all manner of surveillance equipment and weapons, a few of which could be fired or activated while secured inside the case. It was not unusual to find cowboy six-shooters or detective snub-nosed .38s repainted and refitted with silencers, say, to look like the latest spy weapons. This strategy, to make an old toy new again, was put to use most effectively by toy mogul Louis Marx (1906-82), whose Marx Toys was one of America's largest and most successful toy companies for decades.

The twist Marx applied to his line of toy guns in 1964-65 was "jungle guerrilla warfare." Dubbed the "Monkey Division" line, these weapons were camouflage-green and included a "missile bazooka" and a "Gung Ho Commando Outfit," which featured a noisy, tripod-mounted, battery-operated machine gun. Battery-operated toys were the fashion by this time (as much as 60 percent of some companies' toy lines) and Japan was making most of them, American companies like Marx having subcontracted Japanese manufacturers. As early as 1963, newspaper and magazine editorials expressed concern at the proliferation and popularity of war toys, seeing a direct correlation between these and the increased hostilities in Vietnam. Significantly, Hasbro introduced G.I. Joe, a fully-articulated, 11 1/2-inch, plastic military doll for boys, in 1964. Called an "action figure," so that boys would not shy from it, this "fighting man from head to toe" was an immediate success.

The military toy boom of the early and mid-1960s grew from a nostalgic interest in World War II and, to a lesser extent, the Korean Conflict (1950-53). Many, if not most, parents of school-aged children had participated in the war, and these youngsters were just now realizing their fascination for the adventures they imagined their fathers had enjoyed. Successful television series about World War II, like the comedy *McHale's Navy* and the drama *Combat,* both of which debuted in 1962, and a number of successful Hollywood war movies, like *The Guns of Navarone* (1960) and *The Longest Day* (1963), articulated this fascination. Initially, the Vietnam War was remote enough to feed children's interest further, especially as most adults believed that the fighting would be over sooner than later. By the late 1960s, however, when the horrors of Vietnam came too vividly to Americans through their television sets, war toys lost their appeal. There were drives to ban them—in fact, Sears Roebuck stores stopped advertising guns and "similar toys of violence" in 1968—sales dropped, and American children turned again to outer space for play, an interest revived by the Apollo moon landing in 1969, reruns of *Star Trek* in the early 1970s, and the megahit movie *Star Wars* in 1977. Even G.I. Joe fell casualty to the make-love-not-war ethos for a time: Hasbro discontinued the venerable soldier in 1978, citing the oil crisis as the primary culprit.

Five years before Hasbro introduced G.I. Joe to war-hungry American boys, Mattel introduced the world to

Barbie (see entry), an 11 1/2-inch fashion doll for little girls (1959). Barbie's tremendous success demonstrated to toy makers the value of creating a "play situation" for which future toys and accessories could be designed. In Barbie's case, there had to be clothes for every occasion and suitable accessories, like automobiles, boats, appliances, and sporting goods, to make those occasions realistic. Then came new characters to keep Barbie company. The makers of G.I. Joe followed this formula with great success. By the 1970s, companies like Kenner and Mego were making similar action figures for boys, this time based on popular television and movie characters such as the Six Million Dollar Man and the Incredible Hulk. There were also some action figures which appealed to both genders, like the Bionic Woman, and characters from the TV series *The Waltons* and the MGM classic film *The Wizard of Oz.*

The appeal of toy accessories is nearly as long-standing as the appeal of dolls, but it was not until the postwar years and the application of plastics that the marketing of toy accessories became widespread, giving rise to "sets" of all kinds. Sets allowed toy makers to package several items (like miniature kitchen utensils) thematically and thus sell more toys than they might have if these items had sold separately. Louis Marx capitalized on this strategy when he began making playsets for boys in the late 1940s. Centered around a popular theme, like war or Westerns, each set offered a collection of small plastic figures (polyethylene or vinyl), from two to three inches high—these were soldiers, cowboys, etc., depending upon the set's theme. Often they included a popular character like Davy Crockett or Robin Hood. Most notable about the sets was their vast array of plastic accessories: not only weapons and vehicles, large and small, but also desks, chairs, boxes, barrels, tools, tables, wells, firewood, rock piles, bushes, trees, animal skins, ladders, pots, pans, troughs, and pens; virtually any- and everything a child might need to create realistic surroundings for his plastic figures. Marx, and other companies, sold thousands upon thousands of these sets each year for over twenty years.

The influence of these sets, on the boys' side, and Barbie's many worlds of activity, on the girls' side, led to the popularity of smaller action figures in the 1970s. Made of durable plastic and only 3 3/4 inches high, these new figures were akin to the solid-plastic figures once found in boys' playsets. But they had articulated limbs which made them posable, like their larger forebears Barbie and G.I. Joe. Better still, the multitude of accessories available for these figures allowed children to create a fully-rendered world of play. And best of all, from the toy maker's perspective, the new figures were much cheaper to manufacture and ship than the nearly-foot-tall, old-style variety. With the release of George Lucas's *Star Wars* in 1977, Kenner made an action figure line of the movie's complete cast of characters, with their nearly-countless accessories of weapons, equipment, and vehicles. These toys became a standard of the industry—every other toy maker began seeking themes for which they could produce their own action figure lines. Not surprisingly, G.I. Joe made a comeback as a new-style action figure in 1982, this time as a "real American hero" who, with his sixteen down-sized compatriots (one of them a woman), aimed to root out terrorism.

One of the primary appeals of an action-figure line is its collectability: collectable in the sense of a child having to own all items in the set or series. Barbie started this trend, which Hasbro exploited very effectively in the early 1980s with its line of fantasy animals, "My Little Pony." Each pony came in a fanciful color, like pink or yellow, and each had a groomable mane and tail. Their accessories included combs and elaborate wardrobes (even socks and shoes). And the original four ponies were soon joined by families of others, like Watercolor Baby Sea Ponies and Gossamer Winged Flutter Ponies. Little girls considered these very collectable.

This trend toward fantasy worlds or pre-scripted themes for toys peaked with the action figure lines (boys' toys). In the wake of Kenner's success, toy companies saw how the Star Wars saga offered a context of tremendous scope in which the possibilities for play seemed endless. If a company could create, on its own, a story of similar scope, then it might market a line of figures that would bring in hundreds of millions of dollars—and there would be no licensing fees to pay since these characters would belong to the toy company alone. In 1982, Mattel did just this, with the introduction of its "He-Man and The Masters of the Universe," an original line of action figures. He-Man is a mesomorphic superhero who looks like a steroid-fed body builder. His nemesis, Skeletor, is a skull-faced phantom with an equally well-developed physique. They, and many others, fight for the forces of good and evil in an imaginary world called Eternia.

Mattel promoted He-Man with a television cartoon show that featured every character in the line. Parents protested, just as they had in 1969 when Mattel first tried this tactic, having developed a cartoon show called *Hot Wheels* to promote its Hot Wheels die-cast miniature cars. Back then, the Federal Communications Commission (FCC) listened to the parents and promptly banned the show (see Children's Network Programming). In the 1980s, however, under the aegis of the Reagan administration's laissez-faire policies, the FCC deregulated children's television and let the toy companies be. The result: by the late 1980s, as many as 40 product-oriented cartoon shows crowded the airwaves. This would hardly have been profitable for the manufacturers if their audience, the children themselves, had not nearly $5 billion of their own to spend freely every year.

The "baby boom"—a 60 percent leap in births after 1946—and the boomlet it created as the boomers themselves came of age in the 1970s and had children of their own, does much to explain the rise in toy sales from approximately $250 million in 1946 to approximately $15 billion in 1993. The upsurge of large discount outlets like Toys R Us, which has cornered about 20 percent of the retail toy market, has helped stabilize the industry's sales, which were once contained almost wholly within the Christmas buying season. Also helpful has been the rise of expenditures per child. Not only do the children themselves have more disposable income, but divorce has increased both family size (step-parents) and toy buying (dual households).

The U.S. remains the world's largest toy market and is currently the world's largest producer, although most of its products are manufactured by subcontractors in other countries like South Korea, Taiwan, and China, a practice which began in the late 1950s: Barbie was first manufactured in Japan, for instance, while her clothes were fashioned in Hong Kong.

Bibliography

Hanlon, Bill. *Plastic Toys*. Atglen: Schiffer, 1993.

Kline, Stephen. *Out of the Garden: Toys, TV, and Children's Culture in the Age of Marketing*. New York: Verso, 1993.

O'Brien, Richard. *The Story of American Toys*. New York: Abbeville, 1990.

Owen, David. "Where Toys Come From." *Atlantic Monthly* Oct. 1986: 65-78.

Stern, Sydney, and Ted Schoenhaus. *Toyland: The High-Stakes Game of the Toy Industry*. Chicago: Contemporary, 1990.

Ron Tanner

See also
Board Games
Dolls

Train Motifs. There is little doubt that the romantic lore of trains has left an indelible mark on the American psyche. There is no theme or amusement park without a rail, and few American cities with no train motif restaurant or "diner." This effect is readily perceived in films, song, literary allusions, kitsch, and railroad modeling from the advent of train travel to the present day.

As trains were the most prominent means of travel in America's early industrial history, it is unusual to find turn-of-the-century films in which a train does not appear. Best known of these early films, undoubtedly, is *The Great Train Robbery* (1903), a silent film acknowledged as one of the first with a narrative structure. Others are: *The Black Diamond Express, The Midnight Flyer, The Night Flyer, The Signal Tower, The Metropolitan, The Block Signal, The Danger Signal, The Overland Limited, Kindled Courage, The Midnight Express, The Warning Signal,* and *Danger Lights,* all from the decade of the '20s.

Some more recent examples of the prominent use of trains in cinema include *The Train* (1965), in which a railway engineer enlists the help of a member of the French resistance to help stop a train filled with art treasures being sent to Nazi Germany; *Von Ryan's Express* (1965), a World War II P.O.W. escapade; *The Train Robbers* (1972), a film with classically Western ingredients; *Murder on the Orient Express* (1974), a star-studded Agatha Christie thriller; *Silver Streak* (1976), a cross-country train journey comedy with Richard Pryor and Gene Wilder; *The Cassandra Crossing* (1977), about a trans-European train which has been contaminated with the plague by terrorists; *The Great Train Robbery* (1979), written and directed by Michael Crichton; *The Train Killer* (1983), in which a World War II hero derails trains in Austria; and *Runaway Train* (1985).

Folk songs about trains and train travel abound, and are an integral part of America's musical legacy. Some of the more familiar songs that have endured are: the famous "Casey Jones," about an engineer who meets his fate in a collision with another train outside of Reno, NV; "The Wabash Cannonball," a mythical locomotive that ran "from the calm Pacific waters to the rough Atlantic shore"; "500 Miles," popularized by Peter, Paul, and Mary in the 1960s; "The City of New Orleans," which foreshadows the economic problems of passenger trains; and "Midnight Special," a jailhouse tune which refers to the themes of escape and freedom. Literary allusions are plentiful, and there are basically four ways in which the "romance," or at least the profound influence, of trains has been reflected in American literature. First, there are those works in which trains are central to the writing (e.g., Emily Dickinson's poem "I Love to See It Lap the Miles," Walt Whitman's "To a Locomotive in Winter," and Bret Harte's poem "What the Engines Said"). Second is fiction in which trains are important to the stories' theme and action: Frank Norris's *The Octopus,* Mark Twain's "The Invalid's Story"; Edith Wharton's "A Journey"; and Ellery Queen's "Snowball in July." The folklore of the tramp or hobo is perhaps the most engaging from a literary and sociological point of view, and was most effectively expressed by America's most celebrated vagabond, Jack London. In both fact and folklore, however, the hobo was a drifter seeking handouts. Sometimes, gangs of tramps boarded railroad cars and terrified passengers with "riotous behavior and abuse," and, at other times, battled crews of freight trains as in the 1973 film *Emperor of the North Pole.* Finally, there are those publications that celebrate the luxury and elegance of the trains—those descriptions, drawings, and early photos which we revere as quintessentially "romantic." One such account is Douglas Waitley's description, in *Age of the Mad Dragons* (1981), of 1877 dining aboard a luxury Pullman.

Not unlike many popular realities, railroading has been commercialized in collectibles and kitsch. Caps, badges, calendars, toys, posters, audiotapes of steam locomotives, decals, and bumper stickers are available at over 125 U.S. train museums listed in the *Steam Passenger Directory* published by the Empire State Railway Museum in Middletown, NY.

Several trade magazines address the needs of railroad and model train enthusiasts, among them: *Mainline Modeler and N-Scale,* Hundman, Edmonds, WA; *The International Railway Journal,* Simmons-Boardman, NY; *Railway Track and Structures,* 345 Hudson St., New York; *Model Railroader, Classic Toy Trains,* and *Trains,* Kalmbach, Waukesha, WI; *Pacific Rail News,* and *Passenger Train Journal,* Interurban Press, Waukesha; *Progress Railroading,* Murphy-Richter, Chicago; and finally, *Railfan and Railroad,* and *Railroad Model Craftsman,* both published by Carstens in Newton, NJ. Lambert Enterprises, San Diego, CA, offers both books and videos about the evolution of railroading.

What emerges from these popular references along with the histories and journals is the colorful tradition that reflects America's love affair with trains. Collectors range from those who create elaborate track systems and layouts to those who simply display their trains on shelves. The key words in model value and appreciation are realism and authenticity to detail, not only of equipment and environments but also to historical periods as settings. Some consider the "HO" scale (1/87th of a full-size train) the true scale for track gauge, and the "universal" size on the continent and the U.S. Popular with collectors, also, are 0 scale trains represented by Lionel models, 1/48th the size of their iron prototypes. A train set can cost from $10 to $10,000.

Bibliography

Baker, S. L., and V. B. Kunz. *The Collector's Book of Railroadiana.* Secaucus: Castle, 1976.

Beebe, L., and C. Clegg. *Hear the Train Blow.* New York: Grosset, 1952.

Holbrook, S. H. *The Story of American Railroads.* New York: Crown, 1947.

Reutter, Mark. "The Lost Promise of the American Railroad." *Wilson Quarterly* Winter 1994.

Smeed, Vic, ed. *Complete Railway Modeling.* Radnor: Chilton, 1983.

Stilgoe, J. R. *Metropolitan Corridor.* New Haven: Yale UP, 1983.

John H. Esperian

Tramiel, Jack (1928-), founded Commodore Business Machines and produced the most popular home computers of the 1980s. He was symbolic of the early period of personal computer manufacturing.

A Polish-born Holocaust survivor, Tramiel emigrated to New York in 1947. In 1958, he opened a typewriter sales and repair shop, later expanding into typewriter manufacturing by acquiring a factory in West Berlin. While in Japan to acquire an adding machine factory, Tramiel saw an early electronic calculator and decided adding machines were a dead end. In 1969, Commodore produced the first hand-held calculator, the C108, using Texas Instruments chips. One of Commodore's purchased subsidiaries, MOS Technology, developed the 6502 microprocessor, the foundation of the first generation of home computers. The first Commodore computer, introduced in 1977, was the PET (Personal Electronic Transactor), a single casing holding a keyboard, processor, and monochrome screen.

Commodore's consumer breakthrough came in 1980 with the VIC-20, an 8-bit unit with 5K of RAM memory. Aided by placement in department stores and saturation advertising (starring William Shatner), Commodore sold a million of the $300 VIC-20s by early 1983.

In August 1982, the first Commodore 64 shipped as a direct competitor to the Apple II and Atari 400 lines. It had 64K of memory, three music synthesizers, game sprites and a $500 list price (which dropped under $200 within 16 months). Soon, more 64s were being sold each month than Apple IIs. By the end of 1983, nearly 2.5 million VIC-20s and 64s had been sold.

Tramiel, however, resigned as president of Commodore in January 1984, after a power struggle. By July, he had purchased the ailing Atari from Warner Communications (see Bushnell, Nolan K.). He took enough Commodore technicians with him to make the 68000-based ST series, priced starting at $400.

Atari was first to introduce the CD-ROM drive. Tramiel, managing Atari with his three sons, actually brought the firm out of debt, but he also failed to ride the second wave of video gaming, and Nintendo dominated Atari's former market. Atari had become old news. Tramiel eventually abandoned the ST computer and worked on a new game machine, the Jaguar, finally unveiled in 1994. But it did not succeed, Atari was folded into a Silicon Valley disk-drive manufacturer, JTS, and Tramiel has retired.

Bibliography

Hafner, Katherine M. "Father Knows Best—Just Ask the Tramiel Boys." *Business Week* 15 Dec. 1986: 106.

Loomis, Carol J. "Everything in History Was Against Them." *Fortune* 13 April 1998: 64. Online. LEXIS-NEXIS Academic Universe. 6 June 2000.

Tomczyk, Michael. *The Home Computer Wars.* Greensboro: Compute!, 1984.

Mark McDermott

Trampolining enjoys deserved popularity not only for its vertigo-delivering properties, but also for teaching advanced twisting movements in sports such as springboard diving, the pole vault, and aerial gymnastic sequences. Happily, the trampoline continues to be a basic tool for the education and training of circus performers at their various winter retreats in Florida.

The founding father of the trampoline was George Nissen. Born in Iowa in 1914, he designed the prototype model T in 1936, and he both promoted and popularized the trampoline for the physical education training of American soldiers during World War II. The concept was innovative but remarkably simple. A trampoline was no more than a sheet of strong webbed canvas pulled tight over a firm, but lightweight, portable shell frame. Nissen's design provided for a higher bounce and allowed a greater number and variety of tricks. By 1948, the NCAA had included trampolining as an element in their annual gymnastics championship. In 1967, the trampoline was removed from intercollegiate gymnastics competition due to accidents and injuries. The sport was included in the 1955 Pan-American Games. In 1964, the International Trampoline Association was founded; and the sport became part of the gymnastics events at the 2000 Olympics.

Bibliography

Arlott, J., ed. *The Oxford Companion to World Sports and Games.* London: Oxford UP, 1975.

Cuddon, J. A., ed. *The International Dictionary of Sports and Games.* New York: Schocken, 1980.

Griswold, L. V., and G. Wilson. *Trampoline Tumbling Today.* South Brunswick: Barnes, 1970.

Scott A. G. M. Crawford

Transistor Radio was a technological innovation of the 1950s that allows radio audiences to listen wherever they are. The transistor was invented in 1948 in Bell Laboratories. Scientists applied the principles of solid-state physics, using certain metallic compounds that were capable of conducting electricity when a small charge was applied to them. These germanium- and silicon-based semiconductors amplify and control electrical signals in the same manner as vacuum tubes. But transistors are much smaller than tubes, and they do not have a filament that needs to be heated, so they require much less energy to operate. They also operate with much lower voltages than vacuum tubes.

The first transistor radios entered the market in the mid-1950s. They were limited to AM reception, and manufacturers often used the number of transistors they contained as a selling point. By the early 1960s, transistor radios could frequently be found at U.S. beaches. A music fad, surf music, came about as a result. Transistor radios in the mid and late 1960s often could tune in FM stations in addition to AM stations. Improvements in transistor design increased the sound output and quality of the small radios.

Advances resulting from the U.S. space program led to the use of integrated circuits to replace transistors. These devices include hundreds of transistors and other electronic components on a single silicon "chip," reducing the size and production cost significantly. By the 1970s, transistor radios called "boomboxes" (see entry) included cassette players, large speakers, and powerful amplifiers.

In 1980, Sony introduced radio/cassette players that moved technology in the other direction with the Walkman (see entry), a shirt-pocket-size device with lightweight headphones. Joggers, bicyclists, and even people studying in a library use these to listen to recorded or broadcast music without disturbing anyone else (or being disturbed).

In the 1980s, police, fire, and emergency personnel, as well as curious citizens, began using battery-operated scanners that tune in simultaneously to tens or hundreds of emergency channels. Transistorized radio transmitters and receivers were also incorporated into battery-operated cordless telephones that can be carried anywhere in or around a house and cellular phones that send and receive calls to and from locations around the world.

In the 1990s, transistor radios took on numerous forms: toy radios in the shape of an orange or in bright colors designed for small children; "headphone radios" that combined the radio and headphones into a single unit; radios that include shortwave or weather bands or television sound; and waterproof radios designed for use in the shower or in a swimming pool. Boomboxes include CD players as well as cassette tape players.

Bibliography

Handy, Roger, Maureen Erbe, and Aileen Antonier. *Made in Japan: Transistor Radios of the 1950s and 1960s*. San Francisco: Chronicle, 1993.
Rosenkrants, Linda. "Transistor Radios Turn Up in Small Volume." *Antiques & Collecting Magazine* Dec. 1993: 10.

Kenneth M. Nagelberg

See also
Portable Radio

Travel Guidebooks are often dismissed as a genre out of hand. Working with a paradigm that makes an absolute distinction between travel and tourism, Paul Fussell in *Abroad* (1980) bewails the demise of true travel, which involves discovery and misadventure, and castigates the ascendancy of tourism, a mass-produced, protected movement through "pseudo-places." Attributing part of this shift to guidebooks produced by Fielding and Fodor, Fussell, in *The Norton Book of Travel* (1987), distinguishes the 19th-century handbook designed for "inner-directed" travelers from the 20th-century guidebook, "largely a celebratory adjunct to the publicity operations of hotels, resorts, and even countries."

Yet modern touring is only partly prepackaged "tourism," and many guidebooks are aimed quite precisely at those who travel alone, pursuing their own interests. These tourists are not herds who need the constant solace of friendly guides and fixed arrangements; they buy guidebooks for information to direct themselves, much as their 19th-century predecessors did.

The various kinds of books travelers might want to read before setting out on a journey all spin around some axis of information about place, so there is still a point in distinguishing the purposes of guidebooks from those of travel narratives. Much of what is valuable in the latter—a marked personal voice, melding of past and present, originality of perception, vividness in character sketches, economy in anecdote and dialogue, and an unobtrusive but compelling narrative flow—is either unobtainable or irrelevant in guidebooks. Most of these features argue for the permanent literary value of the travel narrative, a replacement for the experience of travel itself. Guidebooks are denied permanence and fluidity of form, and they experiment with idiosyncratic personal voice at great risk. Good ones must be up to date, accurate in detail, responsible in using sources, authenticated by the writer's direct experience, selective yet reasonably comprehensive, clearly focused, analytic in structure, organized for quick reference, and easy to read. The best also have a style that sharpens seeing and encourages imaginative reflection. Like many things needed in practical living, they are designed to be used and discarded when obsolete.

In the most elementary sense, the guidebook has always been a cheap, portable, and convenient substitute for a living guide, who may be more or less competent, reliable, avaricious, or lazy. The guidebook has a long history because it serves fundamental needs: it provides a means of orientation, bringing readers to the top of a cathedral dome or campanile for a panoramic survey of an unfamiliar city. In this sense, the guidebook is a verbal map. Like nautical pilots and representations of mountain topography, which have similar purposes, guidebooks map in words, constrained always by the need to position us in space. They also have a temporal dimension that connects places with events and persons. Even the crassest examples are instructive: no visit to the Tower of London could be fully articulated without knowledge of those who had been imprisoned or butchered there.

Like their live counterparts, most guidebooks advise travelers on the mechanics of travel—lodging, food, local transportation, and the like. On one hand this is the most mundane of the guidebook's tasks, on the other, the trickiest; some of the most respected series, like the Blue Guides and Michelin Greens, opt out of such duties because they want to concentrate on sightseeing. Most of the big American annuals—such as Fielding, Fodor, and Frommer—are structured around these mechanics.

It remains unclear whether rapid mutations in the guidebook will produce new forms, each with its own possibilities for usefulness and excellence, or whether it will disintegrate into a set of amorphous products for specialized consumption.

Bibliography
Feldman, Gayle. "The Widening World of Travel Books." *Publishers Weekly* 13 Feb. 1987: 31-57.
Fussell, Paul. *Abroad: British Literary Traveling between the Wars.* New York: Oxford UP, 1980.
——, ed. *The Norton Book of Travel.* New York: Norton, 1987.

Robert Foulke

Travis, Randy (1959-), reestablished traditional country music as commercially and artistically important to the country music industry beginning in the mid-1980s; prior to the emergence of Travis and other "new traditionalists," such as George Strait, Dwight Yoakam, and Alan Jackson, the country music industry had moved away from traditional country music, convinced it would not appeal to young audiences and that consumers would not purchase it. Travis proved that the economic and artistic backbone of country music is traditional country music; after Travis, the country industry sought to sign attractive artists who sang this kind of music.

Born in Marshville, NC, young Randy Traywick dropped out of the eighth grade and was headed for a life in conflict with the law until he entered a talent contest at Lib Hatcher's club in Charlotte; there he won first prize and became the regular singer. Hatcher became his manager and worked to further his career; in 1982, they moved to Nashville, where Hatcher obtained a job managing the Nashville Palace, located across from the Opryland complex, and Randy worked in the restaurant as a busboy and short order cook as well as singer. In 1983, he recorded a self-financed album of his own songs which he sold at the club, and in 1985, he was signed to Warner Brothers, where he first hit with "1982," which led to a string of hits, including "On the Other Hand," "Diggin' Up Bones," "Forever and Ever, Amen," "I Told You So," "Deeper Than the Hollar" and others. During 1986-90, Travis dominated the charts and collected a number of impressive awards, including those from the Country Music Association, Academy of Country Music, American Music Awards, and Grammys.

Because of Randy Travis and other "new traditionalists," country music re-captured its image of basic, down-to-earth values and simple, straight-forward lyrics with a message; his success led to that of artists such as Garth Brooks later in the 1980s and early 1990s.

Bibliography
Bane, Michael. "20 Questions with Randy Travis." *Country Music* July 1994: 68-69.
Carr, Patrick. "Research in Randyland." *Country Music* Jan. 1990: 28-33.
Cusic, Don. *Randy Travis: King of the New Country Traditionalists.* New York: St. Martin's, 1990.
Larkin, Colin, ed. *The Guinness Encyclopedia of Popular Music.* Vol. 6. Middlesex, U.K.: Guinness, 1995.
Miller, Holly. "Randy Travis: Nice Guy Finishes First." *Saturday Evening Post* Oct. 1988: 60-61.

Don Cusic

Travolta, John (1954-), ever since his career-making role in the TV sitcom *Welcome Back, Kotter* (1975) as the swaggering Vinnie Barbarino, has been consistent in delivering portrayals of characters whose charisma shines past their low intellect.

His portrayal of the disco-dancing Tony Manero in *Saturday Night Fever* (1977) received nationwide acclaim and best actor nominations for both the Academy Awards and the Golden Globes. His concurrent pop music albums, *Can't Let Go, John Travolta,* and *Travolta Fever,* successfully nurtured his iconographic status. The disco craze, which set the fashion trend for the entire nation, was tremendously in debt to *Saturday Night Fever* and, in particular, Travolta's Manero, whose original white suit sold for $145,000. Manero personified the struggle to enjoy oneself while living in a harsh world. Simultaneously, he reassured audiences that with humility and innocence comes happiness.

The musical *Grease* (1978) ushered in a fifties revival, concurrent with the TV series *Happy Days.* As a decade of American culture, the fifties were notorious for being happy-go-lucky and innocent, which *Grease* nostalgically captures in its musical numbers. This phenomenon of the fifties' innocent idealism targets Travolta's sensibility perfectly, yet *Grease* is a backlash to the brooding atmosphere of the seventies in *Saturday Night Fever.* For American audiences, *Grease* was the flashy vehicle that perpetuated the Travolta heart-throb phenomenon.

After *Urban Cowboy* (1980), *Blow Out* (1981), and *Staying Alive* (1983), Travolta washed up. The new decade made fun of the old trends, which he personified in *Saturday Night Fever.* Now Travolta was ridiculed for the same things that brought him so much praise. His dim-witted characters had no place in the eighties, the ambitious world of the yuppies. During this time, he had small roles in small TV productions until *Look Who's Talking* (1989), a sleeper hit which brought him out of anonymity. In this silly, surprisingly successful romantic comedy, his innocent demeanor was not the main attraction, but the closely followed sequels (1990 and 1993) proved that there still was something the public liked in him (or maybe it was the gimmick of the talking baby).

After years of being on Hollywood's back burner, Travolta achieved his complete comeback with his portrayal of Vincent Vega, a hefty (by Travolta's standards) hit man in the highly acclaimed *Pulp Fiction* (1994), for which he again received nominations for both the Academy Awards and the Golden Globes for Best Actor. *Pulp Fiction* was critically acclaimed for setting a new standard for crime film; although it was familiar genre material, the execution was extremely creative and heart-felt. Certainly, playing the familiar innocent urban type had resuscitated Travolta's career, but this time, he was a hit man. Still, his vocation did not affect his boyish charm.

Since *Pulp Fiction*, Travolta has enjoyed a steady stream of successful films that constantly reaffirm his sensitivity in creating a sympathetic Everyman. In *Get Shorty* (1995), Travolta toughened up as another mob hit man, but he still had a soft spot: movies. *Phenomenon* (1996) returned him fully to his roots: He plays a not-too-bright mechanic who becomes a genius. In 1997, Travolta scored big with the critically acclaimed *Face/Off*. Though an out-and-out action film, *Face/Off* lets Travolta bring humanity to the role of Archer, a tortured FBI agent coping with the death of his son. *Mad City* (1997) gave Travolta yet another role to put his heart into; here, he plays Sam Baily, a laid-off security guard who feels that no one is listening to him.

Now, Travolta is just as in demand as he was in the late '70s/early '80s, having made three major films in 1998— *Primary Colors, A Civil Action,* and *The Thin Red Line*—and *The General's Daughter* in 1999.

Bibliography
Clarkson, Wensley. *John Travolta: Back in Character*. New York: Overlook, 1997.
Thompson, Dave. *Travolta*. Dallas: Taylor, 1996.
Zigelstein, Jesse. "Staying Alive in the '90s." *Cineaction* 44 (1997): 2-11.

Robert Baird

Triathlon, The, one of a group of sports that can be categorized as a "super" or ultra-endurance event, is actually three events rolled into one. In succession, the athlete swims 2.4 miles, then bicycles 112 miles, and concludes the event by running a marathon (26 miles, 385 yards).

In *Prime Time Society* (1990), Conrad Kottak makes the case that the burgeoning medium of television has shaped and focused an American fascination in sports. The ABC network did much to educate people about the triathlon and then popularize the activity by showing segments of various competitions on its *Wide World of Sports* program. There was the celebrated episode of a female triathlete who collapsed at the end of the Hawaii Ironman competition but then crawled across the finish line. The Hawaiian "Ironman," the best known of all triathlons, began in 1978 with 15 competitors. In 1984, 1,036 athletes took part. Nearly 4,000 competed in the 1987 Bud Lite Triathlon in Chicago. In 2000, the triathlon became one of the Olympic track and field events.

There is a world body to control the sport known as "L'Union International de Triathlon." It has held a World Championship in Nice, France, since 1982. The distances are different compared to the Ironman event. The swim is 4,000 meters, the bicycling is 120 kilometers, and the run is 32 kilometers. Indeed, one of the attractions of the triathlon is

that it comes in many configurations. There are short course triathlons and even experimental ones that incorporate a canoeing section or a stage on horseback. It is worth noting that the original "Ironman" was a synthesis of the Waikiki Rough-Water Swim, the Around-the-Island Oahu Bicycle Race, and the Honolulu Marathon.

A study subtitled "Following Those Who Go beyond Fitness" in the *Journal of Sports Behavior* concluded that the athlete engaged in a super-endurance activity—their word was "super-adherer"—is hugely motivated. American Mark Allen, who comes from California, the "training" mecca of the triathlon, won three consecutive World Championships (1989, 1990, 1991), and Dave Scott claimed six titles in the period from 1980 to 1987.

The leading female competitor from 1986 to 1992 was Zimbabwe's Paula Newby-Fraser. The extent to which the triathlon has been embraced by men and women is most significant. The very nature of the event, extended periods of athletic activity requiring stamina rather than explosive power or strength, makes it most suitable for the physiological make-up of the female athlete.

In the 1980s and 1990s, American triathletes have come to dominate the event, and they fit this "super-adhere" model. These triathletes are frequently outstanding collegiate athletes in one of the events (swimming, running, or bicycling), and then they immerse themselves in a lifestyle where sport is work. Just as a world-record-level performance for a triathlon is in the region of eight hours, that is the average amount of time that these athletes will train on a daily basis. Elite triathletes will spend more time training than any other athlete.

Bibliography
Clingman, J. M., and D. V. Hilliard. "Some Personality Characteristics of the Super-Adhere: Following Those Who Go beyond Fitness." *Journal of Sport Behavior* 10.3 (1987): 123-36.
Savay, S. A. "The Physiological Effects of Cycling on Running Performance in Triathletes." Unpublished master's thesis, Arizona State University, 1989.
Tinley, Scott. *Scott Tinley's Winning Triathlon*. Chicago: Contemporary Books, 1986.
Vaz, Katherine. *Cross-Training: The Complete Book of the Triathlon*. New York: Avon, 1984.

Scott A. G. M. Crawford

True Crime Writing almost always concerns murder and reaches a wide audience through mass-market paperback books and their adaptations to television miniseries, and through pulp magazines with names like *Police Gazette*. True crime stories vary from sensational and gory retellings to sober and factual accounts. Most follow a crime from its discovery through the investigation, the arrest of the leading suspect, the compilation of evidence, and the legal dispensation of the case, and feature some attempt to enter into the pysche of the accused. In recent years, serious and accomplished writers like Joe McGinniss, Anne Rule, and Jack Olsen have elevated the genre by presenting substantive, probing examinations of crimes and their perpetrators.

The sensationalism of the pulps has a relatively long and continuous history, while the more factual treatments originate with William Roughead, a Scottish writer early in the 20th century who soberly surveyed shocking murders from the 17th century to his own time. Particularly influential in giving respectability to the modern genre is Truman Capote's *In Cold Blood* (1965), which focuses on a gruesome murder; painstakingly re-creates the crime, its antecedents, and its aftermath; inquires into the minds and motives of the killers; and self-consciously employs novelistic techniques to convey lurid events.

Murder is the crime of choice because of its inherently horrific and notorious impact. True crime chronicles tend to focus on familial and serial homicides. Murder among kin is particularly grievous because it upsets standard preconceptions about the social and emotional efficacy of family structures, suggesting a pathology latent in an institution everyone reveres. Serial murder stories rely even more obviously on sensationalistic slaughter. Killers such as Charles Manson and Ted Bundy attract inquiry by the very horrendousness and apparent meaninglessness of their crimes. In structure, true crime books are not unlike mystery fiction, except, of course, that the identity of the accused is usually a given. Most accounts contain an extensive report on the trial of the culprit, the point before which mystery novels usually conclude.

Authors of true crime books (either alone or with ghost writers or collaborators) are often attorneys, detectives, or journalists who have been involved in the investigation or prosecution of the case. Vincent Bugliosi, for example, wrote *Helter Skelter* (1974) about the Charles Manson murders for which he was prosecutor. Later, however, in *And the Sea Will Tell* (1991) he recounted a case involving a mysterious pair of killings on a deserted island in which—atypical of the genre—he had served as a defense attorney. A preeminent true crime writer is Joe McGinniss, whose spellbinding narrative of the Jeffrey MacDonald murder case, *Fatal Vision* (1983), remains a *tour de force* in the genre, and Anne Rule, writing both under her own name and as "Andy Stack." After an apprenticeship in the pulp magazines, Rule has produced important true crime books on both family and serial killings, notably *Small Sacrifices* (1988) about a murderous mother, and *The Stranger Beside Me* (1981), about Ted Bundy. Another writer, Jack Olsen, is known for *Son: A Psychopath & His Victims* (1985); *Cold Kill* (1988); and *Doc* (1990).

Bibliography

DePree, Peter A. "True Crime Writing: A Dynamic Field." *Writer* Dec. 1995: 16-17.

Herbert, Rosemary. "Publishers Agree: True Crime Does Pay." *Publishers Weekly* 1 June 1990: 33-36.

Lee, Wendi. "True Crime: Stranger than Fiction." *The Fine Art of Murder: The Mystery Reader's Indispensable Companion.* New York: Carrol, 1993. 285-88.

Provast, Gary. *How to Write & Sell True Crime.* Cincinnati: Writers Digest, 1991.

Sieder, Jill Jordan. "Murder, Mayhem, Money." *U.S. News & World Report* 29 Apr. 1996: 51.

Mary Jean DeMarr

See also
Mystery and Detective Fiction
Wambaugh, Joseph

T-Shirts and Sweatshirts, in the last 20 years, have become commonplace articles of casual clothing worn by men, women, teenagers, and young children alike. Both are part of trends toward unisex, all-age clothing and the wearing of sportswear as general attire. Nearly one billion T-shirts and millions of sweatshirts are sold in this country each year.

Both T-shirts and sweatshirts furnish a medium for messages and images, although the former exhibit far more variety. Every trend, fad, and social movement can be found mirrored on T-shirts. In recognition of this, museums have begun to collect and exhibit these garments. The Costume, Community Life, and Political History divisions of the Smithsonian Institution's National Museum of American History, for instance, collect them. The Fashion Institute of Technology in New York City presented an exhibit in 1991 of the previous year's events as recorded on T-shirts and another in 1992 on that year's election campaigns.

Messages and images found on sweatshirts, by contrast, tend to be somewhat less topical and less controversial as well, perhaps because these shirts cost about twice as much as T-shirts and are more durable garments which remain longer in wearers' wardrobes. Typically sweatshirts display the logos of sports teams and institutions of higher education. Most common sweatshirt images in recent years are animals and nature scenes.

Since the 1970s, T-shirts and sweatshirts have been popular as advertising for products and as premiums for non-profit organizations' fund-raising campaigns. T-shirts promoting products may be given away, but frequently are sold. The Hard Rock Café chain, for instance, sells millions of shirts advertising its restaurants each year, with sales of the shirts almost equaling those of food and drink. T-shirts also advertise rock groups and big budget movies. Sweatshirts are often used as fund-raising premiums for cultural institutions such as public radio and television stations, art museums, and highbrow magazines.

Both types of shirts have become sought-after souvenirs for travelers. People will stand in line for hours to buy shirts from Hard Rock Cafés. Souvenir shirts are ubiquitous in tourist areas around the country, and sometimes entire shops are devoted to their sale. The first such shop is believed to have opened in Hawaii in 1964.

T-shirts have been used to advance political movements since the 1960s, when student protesters and countercultural dropouts began to wear them. Members of the Student Nonviolent Coordinating Committee, a civil rights organization, adopted khaki-green T-shirts as a kind of uniform. Notable symbols found on shirts at the end of that decade included the peace sign, the clenched fist of the women's liberation movement, and the Viet Cong flag. T-shirts have also been used by political candidates and by groups raising money for causes such as AIDS research and abortion rights. Political messages on T-shirts have mostly displayed a liberal tilt, but shirts supporting capital punishment and warfare, for instance, are also seen.

In the 1970s, T-shirts, now printed with all kinds of messages and designs, became popular with a wider portion of the population. *Time* magazine noted that the summer of 1970 marked the sudden flowering of the decorated T-shirt and observed that not only teenagers but adult celebrities were wearing them too. The trend started in San Francisco and Berkeley, CA, as the bold colors and graphics of "psychedelic" rock and roll posters were transferred to shirts. Many of these shirts featured rock groups, but soon all kinds of images began appearing on them and selling in huge numbers in department stores and small shops. Superman, Mickey Mouse, and other cartoon characters were top-selling images in 1970. A shirt depicting actress Farrah Fawcett sold an estimated 23 million in the mid-1970s. The "sexual revolution" of this decade was exuberantly celebrated on T-shirts, with messages such as "A Hard Man Is Good to Find."

The T-shirt was first introduced as underwear in 1913 by the U.S. Navy, replacing the U-necked, sleeveless undershirt. Hanes began to manufacture T-shirts as men's underwear in the late 1930s, and they were sold in Sears, Roebuck stores, but they did not really catch on until the World War II era when the Marine Corps and the U.S. Army also adopted them. The official military name for T-shirts was "quarter-sleeve knit undershirt with crew neck" but soldiers renamed them "skivvies." As soldiers returned to civilian life they continued to wear these well-liked shirts to work in factories and construction jobs, as well as for leisure activities.

T-shirts took on new meaning as outerwear when teenaged boys began to wear them in the 1950s, inspired by Marlon Brando in the 1951 screen version of *A Streetcar Named Desire*, in which Brando as working-class Stanley Kowalski wore a torn T-shirt in a steamy seduction scene from which a famous publicity still was excerpted. T-shirts, jeans, and sneakers were everyday clothing for Brando, who was dubbed a "slob" in the celebrity gossip press. In *The Wild One* (1954) he introduced the T-shirt, blue jeans, and leather jacket motorcycle costume. James Dean (1931-55) carried on the tradition in *Rebel without a Cause* (1955), substituting a red windbreaker for the leather jacket. Before a climactic scene, Dean sheds his drab brown conventional clothing for jeans, T-shirt, and windbreaker, signifying a heroic transformation.

Since the 1950s, T-shirts have retained an association with youthful rebellion. Recent years have seen school boards and administrators trying to bar students from wearing T-shirts with messages deemed inappropriate. Generally, these messages have involved sexual innuendo as in "Button Your Fly" (advertising button-front jeans) or aggression toward females. But schools have also banned shirts with messages favorable to alcohol, drug, or cigarette use. In Newark, NJ, sidewalk vendors were barred by the City Council from displaying shirts with obscene or degrading messages. Many T-shirt bans have been challenged by defenders of civil liberties on the grounds that they are unconstitutional violations of free speech.

Photo courtesy of Popular Culture Library, Bowling Green State University, Bowling Green, OH.

Although the Underwear Institute announced in 1961 that T-shirts were perfectly acceptable as outerwear, it took a couple more decades for them to become respectable enough to wear to the office. The colored T-shirt was introduced shortly after World War II and was marketed as men's sportswear for tennis or golf. White T-shirts, drawing perhaps on the Brando-Dean tradition and the fact that they still function as underwear, have lingering connotations of rebellion, as evidenced by their adoption in the 1980s by so-called "punks." Black T-shirts are also identified with the punk subculture, as well as with the art world.

Sweatshirts have never been regarded as sexy and rarely, if ever, display suggestive messages. They are worn large, often as cover-ups. They were originally worn as warm-up gear for athletes. In the 1950s, colleges and universities began to imprint these shirts with their logos in the school's colors. Widespread wearing of sweatshirts by the general population did not come until the 1980s, when concern with physical fitness inspired interest in jogging clothes. Somewhat surprisingly, inner-city gang members have given the sweatshirt, worn with the hood up and pulled forward to obscure the face, a menacing aura seemingly without precedent in this garment's history.

Wearing decorated T-shirts and sweatshirts may facilitate social interaction with strangers. For teenagers, especially, shirts may play a role in establishing identity and group membership with others of similar tastes or opinions. There is more than a hint of wishful identity expressed in T-shirt messages, particularly with reference to sexiness, streetwise sophistication, or participation in cultural events. Heavy metal rock group T-shirts, for instance, are said to sell well in areas where these groups rarely tour. Many wearers of Hard Rock Café shirts probably have never patronized these restaurants, particularly the one in Sydney, Australia.

Bibliography

Davis, Fred. *Fashion, Culture, and Identity*. Chicago: U of Chicago P, 1992.

Kneitel, Ken. *The Great American T-Shirt*. New York: New American Library, 1976.

Reed, J. D. "Hail to the T, the Shirt That Speaks Volumes." *Smithsonian* April 1992: 97-102.

Sayre, Shay. "T-Shirt Messages: Fortune or Folly for Advertisers?" *Advertising and Popular Culture: Studies in Variety and Versatility*. Ed. Sammy R. Danna. Bowling Green, OH: Bowling Green State U Popular P, 1992.

Jan Whitaker

Turner, Tina (1940-), began singing professionally when she joined Ike Turner and his band, the Kings of Rhythm, in 1956. Since that time, Turner has irrevocably influenced popular, rock 'n' roll, and soul music. Tina Turner's stage performances combine a singing style described as having "Otis Redding's husky break and James Brown's growl with some of Aretha Franklin's soaring cadences," with an energetically erotic and seemingly spontaneous dancing style; in fact, Tina Turner has been credited as the originator of a strain of rock music based on her style called "raunch and roll." Janis Joplin considered Tina Turner the best performer in the business, and the Rolling Stones' Mick Jagger named Tina Turner as the one who taught him how to dance on the concert stage. She is immortalized by a film—*What's Love Got to Do with It*, based in part on her autobiography, *I, Tina*—while still in her prime; she looks beyond divine, and sings as good as she looks.

Tina Turner was born Anna Mae Bullock in the country borough of Nutbush, near Brownsville, TN. At age 11, following her parents' divorce, Anna Mae Bullock lived with her grandmother. In the mid-1950s when her grandmother died, Anna and her sister Aileen joined their mother in St. Louis, MO, where during the day Anna worked in a local hospital and at night the teenage girls began to frequent rhythm and blues nightclubs. In one such nightclub, the Club Manhattan, in 1956, Anna saw Ike Turner perform with his band the Kings of Rhythm. Ike was so impressed with her voice and performing ability that he asked her to join the band for occasional engagements using the name "Little Anna." In 1959, when a scheduled vocalist failed to show for a recording session, Anna Mae Bullock filled in, and the resulting cut of "Fool in Love" for the Sue record label (1960) sold over 800,000 copies in the rhythm and blues market and maintained *Billboard*'s Hot 100 status for 13 weeks.

Ike Turner, a shrewd manager and seasoned producer, realized the potential of this rising star's musical ability and chose the name Tina for his new lead singer. Soon after, they married, and the band's transformation began. The Ike and Tina Turner Revue featured Tina Turner as front-woman. Ike Turner composed music which would showcase Tina Turner's passionate and aggressive delivery, while she choreographed dance moves which would highlight her seductive and energetic stage persona.

The Revue hit the R&B singles charts during the early 1960s with such songs as "It's Gonna Work Out Fine," "I Pity the Fool," "I Idolize You," "Poor Fool," and "Tra La La La La." By 1969 the Ike and Tina Turner Revue boasted 15 albums and 60 singles to its credit. In spite of its success, however, the Revue never completed the crossover to popular and rock music because the black stations complained that their music was too pop while the white stations complained that it was too rhythm and blues.

By the early 1970s, Tina Turner had matured as a performer and personally; but Ike Turner controlled every facet of the Revue's management and Tina Turner's life. Ike Turner had the reputation of a shrewd, but severe taskmaster, and their marriage was irreparably strained. Tina Turner attempted to gain some independence by recording several solo efforts, including *Let Me Touch Your Mind* (1972), *Tina Turner Turns the Country On* (1974), and *Acid Queen* (1975), following her appearance as the "Acid Queen" in the Who's rock-opera *Tommy*. Throughout the early 1970s Tina Turner continued to tour with the Revue, but increasingly considered splitting from Ike and the band. In 1976, while on tour in Dallas, Tina Turner left her husband and the Revue after having been physically and verbally abused by Ike Turner.

By 1978, the divorce settlement was finalized, leaving Tina Turner with, as she recalled, little else but her "peace of mind." Tina Turner founded her comeback with her 1984 solo release *Private Dancer*, which included such *Billboard* charted hits as "Better Be Good to Me," the title track, and "What's Love Got to Do with It"—which made No. 1 on the charts for three weeks. At the 1984 Grammy Awards, *Private Dancer* won for Record of the Year, Tina Turner won for Best Pop Vocal Performance, Female for "What's Love Got to Do with It," and Best Rock Vocal Performance, Female, for "Better Be Good to Me."

If the multiplatinum *Private Dancer* only showed the glimmer of this star's return, Tina Turner's appearance at the 1985 Live Aid Concert—where she performed what many considered the show-stopper, "Honky Tonk Women" with the Rolling Stones—shined brightly. Also in 1985, Tina Turner contributed "Total Control" to and sang for the *We Are the World* compilation album intended to raise funds to fight hunger in Africa. In 1986, Tina Turner released the platinum solo *Break Every Rule*, an LP which she admitted might be her last in order to allow more time for her acting efforts. In 1984 Tina Turner appeared in Aussie director George Miller's *Mad Max* film series as Aunt Entity. Tina Turner makes sure that her performances, whether acting on screen or singing and dancing onstage, are raw and energetic. She has continued to perform.

Bibliography
Current Biography, 1984.
Fissinger, Laura. *Tina Turner*. New York: Ballantine, 1985.
Larkin, Colin, ed. *The Guinness Encyclopedia of Popular Music*. Vol. 5. Middlesex, U.K.: Guinness, 1995.
Stambler, Irwin. *Encyclopedia of Pop, Rock and Soul*. New York: St. Martin's, 1974, 1989.
Turner, Tina. *I, Tina*. New York: Morrow, 1986.

Scott Logan Baugh

Turow, Scott (1942-), Harvard-trained Chicago lawyer, writes fiction about the ins-and-outs, shenanigans, and deceptions of the legal trade, and the larger questions of truth, justice, and punishment that criminal cases evoke. Following the publication of *One-L* (1977), his memoir of harried life at Harvard Law School, Turow turned to mystery fiction to probe his subject. His novels are psychological studies of

clever, cynical lawyers who confess private weaknesses and justify questionable acts.

Presumed Innocent (1987) and Pleading Guilty (1993) feature devious narrators who manipulate evidence. Though they seem to be victims, they prove to be masters of deception, inveigling their colleagues and lovers into damaging misjudgments. The narrator of Burden of Proof (1990), by contrast, is a decent, dedicated defense lawyer, a family man, driven to make sense of his wife's suicide, and forgiving of human frailty. All three novels are set in "Kindle County," a fictionalized Chicago, where legal officialdom fraternizes with criminals and betrayal is inevitable. The Laws of Our Fathers was published in 1996.

Turow's studies of the justice system and of the complex psychology of those molded and exploited by that system produce unforgettable images of the darker side of humanity. Presumed Innocent, adapted to film in 1990 starring Harrison Ford and Bonnie Bedelia, remains one of the most gripping and most popular legal mysteries of all time.

Bibliography

Lundy, Derek. Scott Turow: Meeting the Enemy. Toronto: ECW, 1995.

Macdonald, Andrew, and Gina Macdonald. "Scott Turow's Presumed Innocent: Novel and Film—Multifaceted Character Study versus Tailored Courtroom Drama." It's a Print!: Detective Fiction from Stage to Screen. Ed. William Reynolds and Elizabeth A. Trembley. Bowling Green, OH: Bowling Green State U Popular P, 1994. 175-94.

Gina Macdonald
Andrew Macdonald

TV Dinners are frozen heat-and-eat complete meals whose introduction coincided with the early expansion of network television and new cultural behaviors in living rooms. Families were glued to their only television set, and homemakers resented being away from the TV while preparing meals, so these divided aluminum trays of meat, potatoes, and vegetable made uninterrupted TV viewing possible. Necessary adjuncts were "TV tables," individual metal trays on folding trestles.

The precursor of the complete frozen meal was the pot pie, introduced nationally in 1951 with chicken pies. Sales skyrocketed and competition forced price-cutting as well as a sharp reduction of the meat content. In 1953, Swanson pioneered in national distribution of the complete frozen dinner. By 1958, TV dinners had passed pot pies in sales, and the price had dropped to as little as three dinners for a dollar. In 1956, the U.S. Department of Agriculture began to monitor meat content in pot pies, requiring at least one-fourth chicken by weight. Swanson, Banquet, Morton, and Birds Eye were early competitors in the TV dinner market with standard fried chicken, roast turkey, and beef pot roast; in the 1970s, ethnic variants of Chinese, Mexican, and Italian dinners appeared, while Stouffer's introduced ampler gourmet cuisine, and later, Weight Watchers countered with low-calorie TV dinners. All continue to be popular convenience foods, but portable television sets (two or more in most households) have obviated the need for TV tables, if not the TV dining behavior.

Bibliography

"Boom in Frozen Dinners." Consumer Reports Jan. 1959.

Fred E. H. Schroeder

Twentieth Century-Fox has, since the mid-1930s, been one of Hollywood's dominant major studios. From its studio in Westwood, CA, Twentieth Century-Fox has provided some of the most famous and most influential films and television programs of the century that inspired its name.

The corporate origins can be traced to motion picture pioneer William Fox's vaudeville empire begun in New York at the turn of the century. Through the first two decades of the 20th century, William Fox vigorously expanded his operations and acquired dozens of movie theaters. Fox built a movie studio to create films for his chain of movie houses. By the early 1920s, William Fox was employing some of the finest filmmakers in the world, headed by John Ford and noted German recruit F. W. Murnau. Ford's Iron Horse (1924) and Murnau's Sunrise (1928) certainly brought this mid-sized film company an unprecedented degree of fame and prestige as the silent film era drew to a close.

It was the coming of sound which made Fox an economic power second to none. At first, beginning in 1927, Fox adapted sound-on-film to improve its newsreel business. In May 1927, Fox stumbled across the publicity coup of the decade by presenting the only footage—with sound—of Lindbergh's takeoff for Paris. Thereafter theater owners queued up to have their houses wired and Fox moved to the top of the cinema business.

Then came the Great Depression. William Fox had borrowed too much and was ousted from the company he founded. The new owners merged the company's surviving resources with Twentieth Century Pictures in 1935. Founder William Fox was out, replaced by studio boss Darryl F. Zanuck and corporate president Joseph M. Schenck.

Zanuck, who took over as production chief during the summer of 1935, quickly developed stars. Skating champion Sonja Henie became a movie queen with *One in a Million* (1936). Alice Faye drew in millions of patrons; the highest-ranking star on the lot was the shortest and youngest, the curly-haired Shirley Temple.

By the 1940s, Twentieth Century-Fox was second in money making only to Paramount. Through the attendance acme associated with the Second World War, Zanuck brought the company its greatest prosperity with Technicolor musicals starring Betty Grable. Moviegoers seemed unable to get enough of Grable in such films as *Moon over Miami* (1941), *Song of the Islands* (1942), and *When My Baby Smiles at Me* (1948). Critics may have hailed Fox's more serious films, including *Gentlemen's Agreement* (1947) and *Pinky* (1949), but the public much preferred Betty Grable and Tyrone Power.

After the war, Twentieth Century-Fox tried to adapt to the new world of entertainment, as in 1953, when it innovated CinemaScope. Yet even with hits like *The Robe* (1953), consistent hits failed to appear. In 1956, Zanuck resigned. A number of replacements, most notably Buddy Adler, could do no better. Twentieth Century-Fox began to lose money. In order to prop up the balance sheet, it sold two-thirds of its fabled backlot to Alcoa to be developed into a high-rise office complex. Tendering its post-1949 color films to NBC-TV for *Saturday Night at the Movies* only provided a temporary infusion of needed cash.

The red ink continued to flow, principally associated with the box-office debacle of *Cleopatra* (1963; see entry), and so Darryl F. Zanuck returned to head his former company, assisted by his 27-year-old son, Richard. The Zanucks successfully sponsored *The Sound of Music* (1965), but then came a trio of multi-million-dollar fiascos, *Doctor Dolittle* (1967), *Star!* (1968), and *Hello, Dolly!* (1969). In 1970, Twentieth Century-Fox lost a record $77 million and a corporate struggle ensued. Within the year the Zanucks, father and son, were out.

The end of the Zanuck era seemed to revitalize Fox. Dennis Stanfill came on board, and with *Patton* (1970) and *M*A*S*H* (1970) was able to revitalize the company. The mid-1970s proved a corporate apex. Both *The Poseidon Adventure* (1972) and *The Towering Inferno* (1973) made millions. By the time of *Star Wars* (1977), Twentieth Cen-

tury-Fox again stood near the top of the Hollywood industry.

In 1985, Twentieth Century-Fox was taken over by billionaire Australian-born press lord Rupert Murdoch. Murdoch created a new corporate colossus by combining the studio with a chain of six big-city television stations. This meant that the films chosen by Murdoch's studio boss, Barry Diller, such as *Predator* (1987) and *The Jewel of the Nile* (1985), could be shown by Fox television stations after they appeared in theaters. It also meant that Fox had a network rivaling NBC, ABC, and CBS.

As the 1990s began, Fox took in stride the unexpected feature film hit, *Home Alone*. By 1992, the Fox Television Network (see entry) was also making money, its production of television programs for the other three television networks was thriving (including *L.A. Law*), and its television "evergreens" such as *M*A*S*H* remained popular through years of syndication. Fox's *A Current Affair* was hated by critics, but drew such good ratings and cost so little that it drew millions into Fox's bottom line.

As Murdoch and his Twentieth Century Fox (he dropped the hyphen) sought to take advantage of the new world of television, film, and interactive media, the Fox studio hummed as films and television shows were sent out to arms of the Murdoch empire in Europe and Asia. No Hollywood operation had a greater reach around the world. The term "movie studio" no longer adequately describes its power, influence, and farflung activities.

Bibliography

Block, Alex Ben. *Outfoxed.* New York: St. Martin's, 1989.
Gomery, Douglas. *The Hollywood Studio System.* New York: St. Martin's, 1986.
Harris, Marilyn J. *The Zanucks of Hollywood.* New York: Crown, 1989.
Shawcross, William. *Murdoch.* New York: Simon & Schuster, 1992.

Douglas Gomery

Twenty-One (1956-1958). To compete with the unexampled popular success of *The $64,000 Question* and *Challenge* on CBS, NBC introduced its Monday-evening prime-time entry into the big-money quiz-show sweepstakes in September of 1956. Entitled *Twenty-One*, produced by Dan Enright and Jack Barry with the latter as host, sponsored by Pharmaceuticals, Inc. (Geritol, Sominex, Serutan), and designed to raise the stakes past the $64,000 mark for all the more audience suspense and excitement, this program pitted two contestants against each other with each inhabiting a separate isolation booth, and each struggling valiantly to answer near-impossible questions.

By coming back again and again, the contestants won not only piles of money but also huge followings of loyal viewers who tuned in religiously to watch their weekly adventures. One contestant, Elfreda Von Nardoff, amassed over $220,000 in prize money. But the epic struggle of greatest interest to obsessed *Twenty-One* fans involved the titanic clash between Herbert Stempel (an ex-GI attending City College and dressed by the producers to look like what today we might call a nerd) and Charles Van Doren (a charming and aristocratic English instructor at Columbia University).

The TV-viewing nation bit its fingernails as the patrician Van Doren combated the plebeian Stempel for the glory of Big Cash Prizes. Nephew of the historian Carl, son of the novelist Dorothy, and scion of the poet Mark Van Doren, young Charlie charmed his way onto the cover of *Time*, into a spot on the *Today* show with Dave Garroway. But after Van Doren defeated Stempel, the latter—beset by financial problems, embittered by his banishment from center stage, and irked by losing on a question about his favorite movie (*Marty*)—decided to spill the beans by going public with the news that the show was fixed, that he and Van Doren had received answers in advance, and that he had been instructed to take a dive by incorrectly answering with *On the Waterfront* as the Oscar-winning movie of 1955. Everybody in sight—Barry, Enright, and especially Van Doren—denied Stempel's accusations. But they precipitated grand jury hearings in New York, a congressional investigation in Washington, and an expression of "bewilderment" from President Dwight Eisenhower. Ultimately, having joined others in lying to the New York grand jury and having falsely protested his innocence on national television, Van Doren confessed to Congress in November of 1959 (by which time *Twenty-One* had been off the air for over a year).

This sorry episode, which precipitated the demise of the game show phenomenon for several decades, was the basis of the 1994 movie *Quiz Show*. Nevertheless, amid the resurgence of game shows in the late 1990s (see Game Shows, above), NBC resurrected *Twenty-One* in 2000, with Maury Povich as host.

Bibliography

Bernstein, Richard. "For $64,000, What Is 'Fiction'?" *New York Times*, Arts & Leisure Section 14 Sept. 1994: 20-21.

DeLong, Thomas A. *Quiz Craze: America's Infatuation with Game Shows*. New York: Praeger, 1991.

Graham, Jefferson. *Come on Down!!! The TV Game Show Book*. New York: Press, 1988.

Holbrook, Morris B. *Daytime Television Game Shows and the Celebration of Merchandise: The Price Is Right*. Bowling Green, OH: Bowling Green State U Popular P, 1993.

Schwartz, David, Steve Ryan, and Fred Wostbrock. *The Encyclopedia of TV Game Shows*. New York: Zoetrope, 1987.

Stone, Joseph, and Tim Yohn. *Prime Time and Misdemeanors: Investigating the 1950s TV Quiz Scandal—A D.A.'s Account*. New Brunswick: Rutgers UP, 1992.

Morris B. Holbrook

Twilight Zone, The (1959-1963), was the creation of Rod Serling (see entry), and he originally hosted the suspense anthology series, narrating its introduction and delivering short, often moralizing commentaries at the end. Although often better written and more original than most stories in the genre, in toto, *The Twilight Zone*'s psychodramas paralleled in theme those of other suspense and science fiction programs of the 1960s such as *Star Trek, Outer Limits, One Step Beyond,* and *Alfred Hitchcock Presents*. A common theme was hallucinatory displacement/amnesia—an individual is not recognized or fails to recognize people, places, or incidents that ought to be familiar to him or her ("Where Is Everybody?"; "Stop-over in a Quiet Town"; "King Nine Will Not Return"). While the old warhorse of the parallel world often solved the puzzle ("A World of Difference"; "Mirror Image"; "Parallel"; "Quality of Mercy"), some of the causes of the symptoms were disturbingly believable. The day's psychological issues, such as repressed memory ("Nightmare as a Child") or delusions caused by nervous breakdown ("Nightmare at 20,000 Feet") were also a focus, as were nightmares ("The Fear") and the fear of dying ("Ninety Years without Slumbering").

Nobody was surprised to watch Serling use *Twilight Zone* as a bully pulpit for his concerns with social evils. He addressed issues of the Cold War ("The Mirror"), nuclear war ("Time Enough at Last"; "Midnight Sun"; "Old Man in the Cave"), the Vietnam War ("In Praise of Pip"), ethnic and racial intolerance ("Monsters Are Due on Maple Street"; "Obsolete Man"; "Number 12 Looks Just Like You"; "Eye of the Beholder"; "Deathshead Revisited"; "The Encounter" and "Dust"), prejudice in general, divorce ("Bewitching Pool"), even the evils of a mechanized labor force.

After three successful seasons as a half-hour program, *Zone* expanded to one hour in January 1963, a format abandoned the next season (although some of the longer episodes were rerun in the summer of 1965).

The Twilight Zone won numerous awards, including Emmys for outstanding writing achievement in drama (1960, 1961) and nomination for an Emmy in 1961 for outstanding program achievement in drama. In 1961, *Twilight Zone* was awarded a Unity Award for outstanding contributions to better race relations. On the heels of the successful feature film *The Twilight Zone* (1983), a remake of the original series premiered with the fall season of 1985. When the remake entered syndication in 1987 as a half-hour series, CBS added 30 first-run episodes from the original series, the set narrated first by Charles Aidman then Robin Ward.

Bibliography

Sander, Gordon F. *Serling: The Rise and Twilight of Television's Last Angry Man*. New York: Dutton, 1992.

Schumer, Arlen. *Visions from the Twilight Zone*. San Francisco: Chronicle, 1990.

Zicree, Marc Scott. The Twilight Zone *Companion*. New York: Bantam, 1982.

S. P. Madigan

Twin Peaks (1990-1991) was destined to be a TV cult show; that it lasted two half-seasons on ABC is not as impressive as the fact that it insinuated itself into prime-time television at all. *Twin Peaks* was the brainchild of director David Lynch (see entry; once described by Mel Brooks as "Jimmy Stewart from Mars") and his collaborator Mark Frost, writer and story editor for *Hill Street Blues,* who turned to television after a series of disappointing experiences in film.

Twin Peaks might have been like many other small town dramas or like its ABC predecessor *Peyton Place*. It looked normal at first glance, and then all hell broke loose: the prom queen was found dead in the river in the Washington state town of Twin Peaks and then revealed to be not at all what she seemed. For eight weeks Lynch rewrote America's notions of prime-time television. Huge numbers of characters arrived, several national magazines published guides to the cast and town in hopes of helping confused viewers (missing an episode could put you out of the game), and characters vanished just as quickly and mysteriously as they arrived. All the stock characters of television drama were in place: the sheriff, the local business people, friendly diner owner, rich family, poor family—and they all resolutely refused to do what was expected of them. That was the fun of *Twin Peaks*; it looked right, but something was very wrong.

After the first week viewers were either hooked, or hopelessly perplexed. The show was too campy for many mainstream viewers used to having mysteries resolved quickly—or at all. The campiness and self-referential nature of the show winnowed the audience. Further, ignoring one of television's sacred conventions, the producers steadfastly refused to solve the murder that dominated the initial movie and first season. Not only wasn't it resolved in the first season, no promises were made about the second season.

Core cast members were Lynch veterans Jack Nance (star of *Eraserhead*) and Kyle MacLachlan (*Dune, Blue Velvet*), and almost forgotten television or film actors with admirable credits—Peggy Lipton (*Mod Squad*), Michael Ontkean (*The Rookies, Slap Shot*), Piper Laurie (*Carrie, The Hustler*), Richard Beymer and Russ Tamblyn (*West Side Story*), and Michael Parks (*Then Came Bronson*)—mixed with newcomers such as Joan Chen (*Last Emperor*), Sherilyn Fenn (*Two Moon Junction*), and Lara Flynn Boyle (*Where the Day Takes You*). The show was nominated for 14 Emmy awards, but received none.

Renewed for a second season despite a dip in ratings, *Twin Peaks* became even stranger and much darker in mood. The tone of the series got darker and darker, the story focused less on the original crime and overall the show became more mystical; characters vanished into other dimensions and eventually magical realism took over. Ratings dropped off as the story slowly unraveled; episodes directed by Lynch and Frost worked best, but by the second season they were very busy with other projects. Viewership slipped a little more and ABC canceled the series. Regular viewers never expected *Twin Peaks* to tie up all the loose ends for them, but few anticipated the dark and brutal finale Frost/Lynch served up.

Twin Peaks opened the door for other shows that challenged the conventions for hour-long dramas, such as *Northern Exposure* (see entry); *Eerie, Indiana; Picket Fences*; the even more surreal *Wild Palms* miniseries; and *The X Files* (see entry).

Bibliography

Altman, Mark A. Twin Peaks *behind the Scenes: An Unofficial Visitor's Guide to* Twin Peaks. Las Vegas: Pioneer, 1990.

Carlson, Timothy. "Welcome to the Weird New World of Twin Peaks." *TV Guide* 7 Apr. 1990: 20-23.

Lavery, David, ed. *Full of Secrets: Critical Approaches to* Twin Peaks. Detroit: Wayne State UP, 1995.

Leershen, Charles. "Psychic Moms and Cherry Pie." *Newsweek* 7 May 1990: 58-59.

Pond, Steve. "Shades of Change." *US* 28 May 1990: 20-26.

Jane Cramer

U

Underground Press, The. Freedom of the press, *The New Yorker* writer A. J. Liebling once said, exists only for the person who owns one. Historically an underground press—radical newspapers ranging from the early American pamphlets to the more recent East European "samizdat" publishing of anti-communist dissidents—has been one reaction to press centralization. Today, however, the new technologies of desktop publishing have led to a diverse, thriving, obsessive, new underground press that includes 'zine or self-published magazines, electronic or hypertext publications, and the familiar chapbooks of the literary small press.

Estimates of the number of 'zines in America today range from 20,000 to 50,000. Titles include *Ben Is Dead, Die Evan Dando Die* (referring to a singer in a popular rock group), *Girljock, Feminists with Cleavage,* and even *Aryan Women.* Many 'zines are now available on the Internet and they, along with such new forms as "mail art"—intricately designed mass letters—have become what one critic called "the back pocket Bibles of Generation X." Their favorite topics include cultural trends, conspiracy theories, and private manias. Their innovative designs and ideas are now affecting mainstream publications, like the "Readings" section of *Harper's.*

The preceding golden age of the underground press in America came with the 1960s papers dedicated to civil rights, the environment, opposition to the Vietnam War, and sexual liberation. These publications included *Chicago Seed, Berkeley Barb, Village Voice,* and *Rolling Stone.* Other papers of the 1960s, like *El Chicano* or *Black Scholar,* focused on race and ethnicity. A thriving GI underground included papers like *FTA* (for "Fun, Travel and Adventure" or "Fuck the Army"), *Shakedown,* and *The Ally.* Feminist and gay publications of the 1960s featured titles like *Ms., Everywoman,* and *The Advocate.*

By the 1980s, these papers had either moved into the mainstream or, more often, died out. In many countries of Africa and the communist bloc, however, small press publishers risked prison and execution to fight totalitarian regimes, and the underground press of Eastern Europe is credited for playing a key part in the revolutions of 1989.

The underground press dates back, presumably, to the first time a follower of Gutenberg secretly typeset a subversive tract or set of poems. In colonial America underground newspapers like Tom Paine's *Common Sense* played a pivotal role in the attacks on the monarchy. In the U.S. of the 19th century, Frederick Douglass's *Liberator* was calling for an end to slavery, and in the early 20th century socialist, pacifist, and radical newspapers like *Progressive, The Militant*, and *Catholic Worker* advanced the politics of the left, while a variety of absurdist arts papers flourished in eastern and western Europe.

Bibliography

Danky, James. *Alternative Library Anthology.* Jefferson: McFarland, 1995.

Divoky, Diane. *How Old Will You Be in 1984?: Expressions of Outrage from the High School Free Press.* New York: Avon, 1969.

Glessing, Robert. *The Underground Press in America.* Westport: Greenwood, 1970.

Peck, Abe. *Uncovering the Sixties: The Life and Times of the Underground Press.* New York: Pantheon, 1985.

Wachsberger, Ken, ed. *Voices from the Underground.* Ann Arbor: Azenphony, 1993.

Ted Anton

Universal Studios. The combination of theme park (see entry) and motion picture studio has made Universal Studios one of the most familiar names in the entertainment business. In addition to producing motion pictures and television programs, the studio conducts tours that provide visitors with the unique experience of being on the sets where some of the most popular films have been made. Merging entertainment with information has been so successful that Universal Studios Hollywood and Universal Studios Florida are continually among the top theme park attractions in the nation.

Universal Studios was started by Carl Laemmle in 1912, in New York City. To produce films without the interference of the Motion Picture Patents Company, the so-called "trust," Laemmle purchased property in California in 1914. Universal City opened for business a year later. Public interest in motion pictures was widespread, so Laemmle organized tours of his studio for a fee. For 25 cents, audiences received a box lunch and viewed silent films being made. Tours continued until sound pictures made it impossible to move visitors through a closed set.

Universal pictures benefited from "boy wonder" producer Irving Thalberg, who started as Laemmle's private secretary and was general manager of the studio by age 20 before moving to MGM in 1923. During the silent era the studio gained a wide following with extravagant epics by Erich von Stroheim (*Blind Husbands*, 1919 and *Foolish Wives*, 1920) and Lon Chaney's early horror films (*Hunchback of Notre Dame,* 1923 and *The Phantom of the Opera,* 1925), but the early success did not last.

Horror films were a staple in the early 1930s, and Universal became the film home for *Dracula* (1931), *Frankenstein* (1932), *The Mummy* (1932), *The Invisible Man* (1933), and *The Werewolf of London* (1935). Sequels to these were made throughout the decade, but their success was not enough to offset later financial difficulties. After Thalberg's departure it was several years before Carl Laemmle, Jr., took a similar position in the studio administration. "Junior," as he was commonly called, cut production by 40 percent, hoping to upgrade the output of A-level pictures to compete with Warner Brothers, Paramount, and MGM. The problem was that Universal controlled no chain of theaters and depended on rentals to independents for their income. By 1935, Junior's emphasis on quality combined with the lack of outlets in major population centers almost bankrupted the studio. A British investor took control in 1936.

Between 1936 and World War II, Universal barely survived as an operating studio. Film budgets were kept low with serials, including *Flash Gordon* (1936), and B-level productions (Dead End Kids and Westerns) making up most of the work. Deanna Durbin musicals were the big money-makers during the period, and the comedy team of Bud Abbott and Lou Costello enjoyed enormous popularity during the war. By 1945, Universal was again releasing a film a week, but the post-war advent of television reduced film income for all studios.

Universal became Universal-International when it merged with independent International Pictures in 1946. When the government ordered studios to sever theater chain connections in 1948, Universal was less affected than other major studios because it had never controlled large numbers of theaters. In 1952, Decca Records acquired a controlling interest in the studio, and film quality improved with the infusion of money. Popular new actors like Rock Hudson, Doris Day, and Tony Curtis began to draw audiences to well-produced films like *Magnificent Obsession* (1954), *Pillow Talk* (1959), and *Son of Ali Baba* (1952). Stars like James Stewart, Kirk Douglas, and Audie Murphy continued the action tradition with *The Far Country* (1955), *Man without a Star* (1955), and *To Hell and Back* (1955).

In 1959, the talent agency Music Corporation of America (MCA) purchased Decca Records, indirectly acquiring Universal Studios for its growing entertainment conglomerate. Underused sound stages at the film studio were put back to use by MCA's television subsidiary, Revue Productions. Universal, while continuing its feature film production, became the home for numerous television shows, including *McHale's Navy, Wild, Wild West, Kojak, American Gladiators,* and *Beverly Hills 90210.* Since 1959, Universal has been the most consistently successful studio in Hollywood, releasing *Airport* (1970), *Jaws* (1975), *E.T., The Extraterrestrial* (1982), and *Jurassic Park* (1993).

In 1964, the tours that had been abandoned at the start of sound pictures were revived. A quick trip to the commissary and make-up department, a show of costumes by award-winning designer Edith Head, and some simple falls by stunt men proved that people still wanted to see what happened behind the scenes, because the tour was an immediate success, drawing 39,000 people the first year. Much of the success of both theme parks can be attributed to their constant improvement. An Entertainment Center was added in 1965, featuring an animal show, an improved stunt show, and a "Screen Test Theater" that involved selected people from the audience. In 1988, Universal Studios opened a new production facility in Orlando, FL, and the Universal Studios Florida theme park, which opened in 1990, now comple-ments its California forerunner. Universal Studios Hollywood also used popular movies to add new attractions. Since 1965, these have included an "Earthquake," "Back to the Future—The Ride," and a stunt show with special fire effects based on *Backdraft.* An added attraction is that people on tours sometimes see stars working on a film or television show. By 1993, as many as 35,000 people a day were visiting the studio during the summer travel season, and Universal Studios Hollywood became the third most popular theme park in the country.

By the 1990s, Carl Laemmle's original 230 acres had expanded to more than 450 acres with over 36 sound stages, the largest operating backlot in Hollywood. The studio that barely survived retrenchment in the midst of the Depression has become the most successful studio in the country with its diverse entertainment attractions.

Bibliography

Adams, Judith A. *The American Amusement Park Industry: A History of Technology and Thrills.* Boston: Twayne, 1991.
Gabler, Neal. *An Empire of Their Own: How the Jews Invented Hollywood.* New York: Crown, 1988.
Hirschhorn, Clive. *The Universal Story.* New York: Crown, 1983.

Arthur R. Jarvis, Jr.

Untouchables, The (1959-1963). Violence is not an issue for modern TV; in 1959, however, critics and public officials rallied against the seemingly senseless violence portrayed by the ABC drama *The Untouchables.* The series was a fictional account of Eliot Ness's 1947 autobiography regarding his role in bringing down mobster Al Capone. Through his book, Ness transformed himself into a popular American hero of mythic proportions. The violence not only sold the book, but the series as well, and ABC reaped huge profits that they justified on the grounds of "historical accuracy." The series opened new avenues of violence that were impossible to close.

The series centered on Eliot Ness, played by Robert Stack (see entry), and his band of incorruptible treasury agents who had been dubbed by Prohibition Era newspapers as "The Untouchables." While ABC's Ness and his Untouchables were lifeless characters who did more reacting than acting, the back-stories and motivations established for the series' criminals were incredibly well defined, due, in large part, to the many talented actors who played the series' villains, including Robert Redford, William Bendix, Lloyd Nolan, J. Carroll Naish, and Peter Falk.

ABC's claims of historical accuracy aside, Ness was more a dramatic device than historic figure. Indeed, the series had Ness responsible for bringing down many real-life anti-heroes such as Ma Barker and George "Bugsy" Moran, whose capture the real Ness had nothing to do with. FBI pressure eventually forced ABC to bring in other characters that more accurately reflected the people involved in the show's historically based cases.

The Untouchables also drew controversy through its perpetuation of Italian stereotypes. Italian-Americans protested the series' use of Italian names for criminal characters. The Capone family also brought a million-dollar lawsuit against producer Desi Arnaz for using the Capone likeness for profit. This was particularly upsetting for Arnaz, a classmate and friend of Al Capone's son.

The show was tremendously successful in its second season, but its popularity rapidly declined when NBC countered with the popular Mitch Miller musical variety program *Sing Along with Mitch*. *The Untouchables* has gone through two revivals, inspiring a 1980s movie version as well as a 1990s syndicated series, proving that Ness is still a popular hero in American culture and folklore.

Bibliography

Arnaz, Desi. *A Book*. New York: Warner, 1976.

Brooks, Tim, and Earle Marsh. *The Complete Directory to Prime Time Network TV Shows, 1946-Present*. New York: Ballantine, 1992.

Michael B. Kassel

USA Today (1982-) was founded by the Gannett publishing group chairman Al Neuharth, who in the early 1980s prodded the publishing group to risk millions of dollars and lend personnel from its chain of mostly small community newspapers to launch a brand new national newspaper at a time when papers were folding or merging at near-epidemic numbers. Because of its distinctive compressed writing style, *USA Today* on its debut in September 1982 was immediately dubbed "McNewspaper," reflecting industry criticisms that its fast-paced approach to news presentation for a mobile population was merely trivializing the newspaper's delivery of information much in the same way McDonald's was selling fast-food at its drive-up windows. Despite its despised beginning, the paper has grown into a respected force in American culture. By 1994 Gannett could boast that it was the largest newspaper chain in the country with the No. 1 daily newspaper in the U.S. with circulation of 1.9 million.

USA Today's planners aimed for a targeted street sale circulation of about 1 million after 1983 and about 2 million by 1987. Innovative use of color, information graphics, shorter stories, expanded weather coverage into a full page with color mapping, and a 50-state news digest were planned to attract the country's business travelers who would spend time with the "nation's newspaper" in airport terminals, on planes, and in hotel and motel rooms.

Newspaper industry skeptics quickly mimicked many *USA Today* innovations by the time the new paper was halfway to its tenth birthday. Newspapers that had never before been known for experimenting with layout and design spent more time and money than ever before, expanding weather coverage, using more color and graphic designs, and adapting reader-friendly news indexes and coverage ideas.

Many of *USA Today*'s innovations were directives from Neuharth, dubbed the "Chief Architect" by the project planners. Neuharth's pattern was to micromanage every detail of the development of the new paper, from circulation dry runs and news-rack design to last-minute page-one headline changes. The page one news of the day for the debut issue included the death of Princess Grace of Monaco, the assassination of Lebanon's new president, and the death of 55 people in a major airline crash in Spain. That front page would set the tone for how different the paper would be: Neuharth insisted on displacing what he called the journalism of doom with positive headlines: how many people survived the plane crash was the news, not "55 die in fiery crash" of traditional news coverage standards; the international impact of the Lebanon political assassination was dismissed to the basement spot on the front page; Princess Grace, America's genuine Hollywood royalty, was the lead story. This was to be a newspaper that was edited for the readers, not for other editors and news professionals.

Bibliography

Neuharth, Al. *Confessions of an S.O.B.* New York: Doubleday, 1989.

Pritchard, Peter S. *The Making of McPaper: The Inside Story of* USA Today. Kansas City: Andrews & McMeel, 1987; New York: St. Martin's, 1989.

Jean C. Chance

𝒱

Valentino, Rudolph (1895-1926), one of filmdom's ever-lasting icons of sex, was born in the village of Castellaneta, Italy. His arrival in New York in 1913 coincided with the ballroom dance craze sweeping the country. He quickly learned English and the popular dances of the period. Within two years, Valentino was the partner of two of the best dancers in the business.

Valentino left New York for the West Coast in 1917 to try his luck in motion pictures, after he appears to have been involved in a divorce and murder involving one of New York's wealthiest and most powerful families. The ethnic prejudices of the time typecast Italians as gigolos and gangsters. For nearly two years Valentino struggled to survive in bit parts. His most notable performance was as a professional co-respondent in *Eyes of Youth*, a 1919 production starring the popular actress Clara Kimball Young.

According to legend, screenwriter June Mathis saw Valentino in *Eyes of Youth* and decided to use her influence to convince the executives at the Metro studio that Valentino was the perfect choice for the role of the tango-dancing gaucho Julio Desnoyers in the screen production of Vicente Blasco-Ibanez's novel *The Four Horsemen of the Apocalypse* (1921). A pioneer in the film industry, Mathis had made several avant-garde movies. A talented, determined, and powerful woman, her meteoric rise in Hollywood parallels Valentino's. She is credited with discovering him and launching his career. His performance and dancing in *Four Horsemen* made him an overnight sensation.

To capitalize on his sudden fame, Metro made three more films in 1921 with Valentino in a leading role. *Uncharted Seas* was an Arctic adventure yarn that had him hidden under furs. Although *The Conquering Power* brought Mathis and Valentino back together, it was too consciously "arty" for the mass audience.

In his third Metro film of 1921, Valentino played opposite Alla Nazimova in her production company's adaptation of *Camille*. June Mathis wrote the script. Natacha Rambova designed the sets and the costumes. She and Valentino married in 1922. *Camille* was praised by the critics, but only managed to break even at the box office. Although film historians have praised Rambova's sets and costumes, the film was another effort to make movies into art and only succeeded in keeping audiences away from the theaters. Valentino said that Nazimova taught him how to act while they were making the film. His performance was praised by the critics.

After Metro refused to raise Valentino's salary, none of the studio heads believed Valentino's popularity was lasting, but Mathis, who had moved to Famous Players-Lasky, got the studio to offer Valentino a contract. His first film for his new studio was an adaptation of Edith Maude Hull's best-selling novel *The Sheik*. It premiered on October 30, 1921, and made film history. Valentino regarded the novel and film as "trash" and he was astonished by its success. He was now the "Sheik," the dream lover of millions of women and the superstar of the silent film.

The amazing success of *The Sheik* was followed by two films that failed to capitalize on the public's adulation of Valentino. In *Moran of the Lady Letty* (1921) he played a role that required an Anglo-Saxon hero. *Beyond the Rocks* (1922) cast Valentino as Lord Bracondale opposite Gloria Swanson in an adaptation of Elinor Glyn's novel. The public did not want to see Valentino as an English aristocrat and the film, despite the presence of two of the greatest stars of the silent screen, did not do well at the box office.

The role of bullfighter Juan Gallardo in June Mathis's adaptation of the Blasco-Ibanez novel *Blood and Sand* (1922) was one of Valentino's favorites. The toreador and the gaucho in *Four Horsemen* were what he believed were his two finest roles as an actor. *The Young Rajah* (1922) was the last film Valentino did with June Mathis. His wife Natacha Rambova designed the costumes and sets. The central character is an Indian prince at Harvard who discovers he has psychic powers. The film broke even at the box office.

After the lackluster reception of *The Young Rajah*, Valentino pressed for more control over his films and more money. The studio refused and Valentino walked off the lot. In debt and in need of money to finance their high living, the Valentinos agreed to a 17-week dance tour in 40 cities at $7,000 a week. The tour was one of the most successful in the history of American dance. It proved to the Hollywood moguls that Valentino's popularity had not diminished with his absence from the screen.

After a triumphal visit to Europe, Famous Players gave Valentino and his wife full control over the production of the films remaining in his contract. *Monsieur Beaucaire* premiered on August 18, 1924. The fans expected action and got Valentino clothed and made up as a fop. In the U.S. it was a financial failure, although well received by the critics for the elegance of costumes and sets.

Valentino's last film for Famous Players was *The Sainted Devil* (1924). Natacha once more had complete control over production. Again playing a hot-blooded South American, Valentino excels in scenes in which he is driven to drink and remorse.

In his last two films, Valentino returned to the action genre that made him famous. *The Eagle* and *The Son of the Sheik* were made for United Artists. Premiering on November 8, 1925, *The Eagle* is a Russian version of the story of Robin Hood, the kind of film Valentino's fans loved. *The Son of the Sheik,* an action movie without any artistic pretensions, premiered on July 9, 1926, just a few weeks before Valentino's death. In it Valentino plays both father and son. It restored Valentino's reputation and made millions for the studio and his estate.

The cults that sprang up after his death shifted critical attention from the man's talent to the exhibitionism of his fans. His contemporaries said Valentino was a fine actor of superb restraint and simplicity who had on film a magnetism that inexplicably inflamed millions of women around the world. The magic of the motion-picture camera and his natural ability as a dancer made him the dream lover of the masses.

Bibliography

Botram, Noel. *Valentino: The Love God.* New York: Ace, 1977.

Card, J. "Rudolph Valentino." *Image* May 1958.

Huff, Theodore. "The Career of Rudolph Valentino." *Films in Review* 3.4 (1952).

Mackenzie, Norman A. *The Magic of Rudolph Valentino.* London: Research, 1974.

Shulman, Irving. *Valentino.* New York: Trident, 1967.

Jim Ferreira

Vallee, Rudy (1901-1986), was the first of the crooners, the first performer to launch radio's variety show format, and arguably America's first multimedia star. Still, he never seemed to be able to escape the timebound shadow of his early fame.

Born in Island Pond, VT, Hubert Prior Vallee grew up in Maine. He rebelled against his pharmacist father's efforts to keep him behind the drugstore counter; he turned to music, learning to play the drums, the piano, and the clarinet. Vallee bought his first saxophone in 1918; at the time, there only were about 100 saxophonists in the U.S., but Vallee fell in love with the sound. He taught himself to play by imitating the "wave-like" recordings of Rudy Wiedoeft, one of the top saxophonists of the day; he further imitated Wiedoeft later by adopting his first name in tribute.

In January 1928, Vallee and a new eight-piece ensemble opened the Heigh-Ho Club in New York City. A month later, a radio station started broadcasting the music of Vallee and his band, later renamed the Connecticut Yankees.

The program was an instant hit; in less than a year, the band and Vallee's "Heigh-Ho, everybody" introduction were heard 25 times a week over three different stations. Vallee's radio work in effect signalled the start of the age of the crooner. Through the rapid popularity of his radio appearances and recordings—and his hard-working yet gracious demeanor—Vallee became extraordinarily popular with women. He seemed an almost ideal idol for the age: industrious, modern-thinking, and youthful. Or, more specifically, he was collegiate. Vallee later described himself during his early stardom as someone who looked as if he had stepped out of a John Held illustration.

Vallee's most popular radio show started the same week in October 1929 as the stock market crash, the symbolic end of the 1920s. Initially, *The Fleischmann Hour* was designed to be a vehicle for Vallee and his music. But, in 1932, Vallee turned it into something different. Instead of using the show as a personal showcase, he helped make *The Fleischmann Hour* the prototype for the modern variety show. He avoided serious music and serious topics. The program instead revolved around Vallee and a string of famous guests, principally entertainers and other notables—a novel format at the time. It was a simple but extremely effective strategy. For most of the ten years it was on the air, *The Fleischmann Hour* was one of radio's most popular programs.

Although his radio and recording success never really translated to Hollywood—his 1929 movie debut, *The Vagabond Lover*, was stilted and stiff—Vallee scored success as a songwriter and in Broadway revues into the mid-1930s. Audiences saw him as the senior member of pop music's crooning triumvirate, along with Bing Crosby and Russ Columbo (the trio even was lampooned in cartoons, the pinnacle of celebrity in the 1930s). Though he was only a few years older than Crosby and Columbo, Vallee seemed entrenched in an earlier time—the collegiate 1920s, to be exact. He still scored hits with school songs ("Stein Song," a No. 1 record for 10 weeks in 1930, was an old University of Maine song) and old-world tunes (1937's "Vieni Vieni," another No. 1 record), but the hits came farther and farther apart by the end of the decade. By 1939, when he left *The Fleischmann Hour*, Vallee was drifting to smaller roles in smaller productions. His only substantive hit during the 1940s, a version of "As Time Goes By" that Vallee had recorded in 1931, sold well only because the tune's popularity (courtesy the 1943 film *Casablanca*) coincided with a union ban on recording, leaving Vallee's the only one available.

Vallee's roots in the past helped him score a few final triumphs, however. In 1961, he starred on Broadway in the musical comedy *How to Succeed in Business without Really Trying*, singing a satire of old-fashioned college songs. Later in the decade, Vallee played a recurring villain on the television series *Batman*; the villain wore a raccoon coat and carried a college pennant and ukelele, an exaggeration of Vallee's early—and in some ways permanent—star image. Vallee continued performing, with limited success, into the mid-1970s.

Bibliography

Kiner, Larry F. *The Rudy Vallee Discography.* Westport: Greenwood, 1985.

MacDonald, J. Fred. *Don't Touch That Dial: Radio Programming in American Life from 1920 to 1960.* Chicago: Nelson-Hall, 1979.

Shaw, Arnold. *The Jazz Age: Popular Music in the 1920s.* New York: Oxford UP, 1987.

Vallee, Rudy. *Let the Chips Fall...* Harrisburg: Stackpole, 1975.

Vallee, Rudy, with Gil McKean. *My Time Is Your Time: The Story of Rudy Vallee.* New York: Obolensky, 1962.

Chris Foran

Vampire Fiction. Arising from the grave under the cloak of darkness to satisfy their bloodlust, vampires have ignited the imaginations of authors and their readers for nearly two centuries. Originally depicted as brutish and profane, vampires have evolved into creatures of beauty, sympathy, and erotic power in 20th-century literature and film and haunt our contemporary culture looking for blood, money, and fame.

John Polidori's *The Vampyre* (1819) is generally considered the first vampire story in English. It chronicles the nefarious activities of the aristocratic Lord Ruthven (maliciously based on Polidori's employer, Lord Byron). *The Vampyre* established several important conventions: the vampire is one of the "undead"—a reanimated corpse; the vampire must appease its need for blood; and the vampire's feeding on his victims proves fatal to them.

By the 1840s, vampire fiction had become immensely popular with the reading public. The most successful vampire story of the time, James Malcolm Rymer's *Varney the Vampire* (1845-47), appeared in England in 109 serial installments in penny dreadfuls. As in the Polidori tale, Varney is an aristocrat, bestial yet of human form, who callously preys on women. In Sheridan Le Fanu's *Carmilla* (1872), the vampire is female, an ancient and unearthly creature who harbors erotic attachments to female victims.

Not until the end of the century did vampire literature evolve into the form that permeates modern popular culture. In 1897, Bram Stoker published *Dracula* (see entry), the best-known vampire story ever and one that has not been out of print in the nearly 100 years since its release. Count Dracula, aristocratic and sensuous, moves easily between Transylvanian crypt and Victorian parlor. Although Stoker discarded the bestial trappings of the vampire for a more genteel appearance, *Dracula* preserves the concept of the vampire as a satanic force.

Notwithstanding, contemporary authors of the vampire story, especially Anne Rice (see entry), Chelsea Quinn Yarbro, and Fred Saberhagen, tend to accentuate the more sympathetic aspects of the vampiric lifestyle. Rice in particular limns a vampire world of beautiful, sensual, and sensitive creatures who yearn for understanding and meaning in their undead existence throughout the centuries, appealing to a reading public that hungers for the romantic and the mysterious.

Bibliography

Barber, Paul. *Vampires, Burial, and Death: Folklore and Reality*. New Haven: Yale UP, 1988.

Carter, Margaret L. *Shadow of a Shade: A Survey of Vampirism in Literature*. New York: Gordon, 1975.

Gelder, Ken. *Reading the Vampire*. London: Routledge, 1994.

Melton, J. Gordon. *The Vampire Book: The Encyclopedia of the Undead*. Detroit: Visible Ink, 1994.

Senf, Carol A. *The Vampire in Nineteenth-Century English Literature*. Bowling Green, OH: Bowling Green State U Popular P, 1988.

Anita M. Vickers

See also
Horror Fiction

Van Art. In the late 1960s, American drivers began customizing vans, turning the chunky vehicles designed by Detroit to carry workers' tools and to haul light freight into personal transports that were canvases on wheels. Customizing vans entailed modifying both the spacious interiors and decorating the outside. Increased demand for customized vans gave birth to "van artists" and to a unique style of automotive art that ranged from conservative pinstripes to subtle metallic paints and flamboyant murals. Vans provided a new venue for the long love affair that Americans have conducted with their automobiles.

Van art drew its inspiration from two cultural streams: hot rod painting of the 1950s, and the decorations that hippies emblazoned on the sides of school buses, vans, and micro buses during the 1960s psychedelic period.

For the young men known as hot rodders, cars were status symbols that suggested the independence of mobility and the flash of style. Often of working-class origins, hot rodders viewed their cars as one way to escape the anonymity of blue-collar jobs. They "souped-up" the engines and modified the bodies to improve handling and to give the car a unique style as well. A customized paint job contributed to the hot rod's striking appearance. "Candy apple" finishes, "fadeaway" color schemes, metal-flake paints, pinstripes, geometric designs, and the trademark flames enveloping the hood became standard hot rod features. Roaring engines and modified bodies set hot rods apart from conventional cars; eye-catching paint jobs helped the hot rod stand out from the pack even more.

Customized vans also traced their origins to an exuberant youth culture of the 1960s. Among the first drivers to use vans as personal vehicles were surfing enthusiasts in Southern California. A van, converted for personal use, cost less than a car, provided enough room to hold surfboards, and could serve as a camper, too. This inexpensive form of transportation also met the nomadic needs of the era's "flower children."

Hippies adopted and adapted second-hand vans, old school buses, panel trucks, and Volkswagen microbuses as a means of transportation. Vans combined the iconoclasm of hot rods with the practicality of a vehicle that could double as a home away from home. Their slab sides offered more surface for decoration than cars did, and could accommodate more complex designs and elaborate paintings that told stories. Like many features of the counterculture, whose influence spread from the bottom up, vans and the art they inspired gained acceptance by more and more people.

Van devotees developed a culture all their own. Like hot rodders, most came from the working class and used customized vans as a form of personal expression. They decorated van interiors with shag carpeting, installed small bars and added beds. Elaborate stereo systems provided the soundtrack as they trucked down the highway. To advertise the sensuous luxury that the interior promised, van owners adorned the exteriors with designs borrowed from the hot rod aesthetic and psychedelic art. Van fans also organized clubs and sponsored gatherings known as "van ins" and "truck ins," where thousands of enthusiasts compared and admired one another's inventiveness. Despite an artistic debt to the counterculture, blue-collar vanners were unsympathetic to middle-class hippies. Some van organizations went so far as to refuse membership to owners of the VW microbus because that vehicle was so closely associated with the counterculture.

Van art ranged from the simple to the sublime. An easy customizing technique was to apply decorations to the van's basic colors. Geometric shapes, contrasting bands of color, or pinstripes highlighted a van's body lines. Flames that appeared to consume the hood and licked at the sides suggested power and speed. The most distinctive van decorations, however, were the murals whose ideas could be developed on the vehicle's broad surfaces. Depending on the artist's talents, paintings could range from sophisticated works of art to amateurish doodles. When designing a mural, the artist tried to make the van embody the owner's concept of himself. Murals varied in size. Some used just the rear quarter panels or one side to tell their stories; others spun out narratives that covered the entire van.

Although artists aspired to uniqueness, van mural themes fell into a few categories. Favorite designs captured scenes where the van owner would like to be, such as mountains, deserts, tropical islands, or the city. Science fiction starships and space aliens and gothic fantasies of heroic barbarians also inspired designs. Some vanners portrayed rock stars and sports figures whom they admired; others evoked icons of American mythology such as cowboys and Native Americans. Scenes that suggested a nomadic lifestyle and escape from workaday responsibilities were also quite fashionable. And always, there were the voluptuous women.

Van painting has declined for several reasons. Van manufacturers eventually imitated customized vans. Once airbrush artists realized the price their creations could bring, they began to charge accordingly and made elaborate murals too expensive for the average van owner. In addition, new vans designed for recreational use devoted more space to windows than the utility vans that owners themselves converted; larger windows shrank the painted surfaces that lent themselves to decorations. And as acceptance of vans moved into the mainstream, the novelty of van painting wore off.

Despite van painting's demise, there is still no shortage of vehicular art. Pickup trucks, tractor-trailer trucks, and even the fuel tanks and fenders of motorcycles still sport designs that trace their origins to the world of hot rodders and vanners. As long as Americans consider their vehicles extensions of themselves, they will continue to make them into "self-portraits" on wheels.

Bibliography

Cook, Terry, and Jim Williams. *Vans and the Truckin' Life.* New York: Abrams, 1977.

Hall, Douglas Kent. *Van People: The Great American Rainbow Boogie.* New York: Crowell, 1977.

Sessions, Keith. *Vanner's How-To Guide to Murals, Painting & Pinstriping.* Blue Ridge Summit: Tab, 1978.

Wolfe, Arnold S. *Vans & Vanners.* Matleson: Great Lakes, 1976.

Bill Mansfield

Van Dine, S. S., was the pseudonym adopted by Willard Huntington Wright (1888-1939), an important early author of mystery and detective fiction in the United States. Wright began his writing career as a reporter, literary editor, and art critic. After a difficult term as editor of *The Smart Set*, a leading literary magazine in the early 20th century, he spent a decade alternating between short-lived newspaper jobs, freelance hack work, and serious essays on art and cultural issues.

In the mid-1920s, Wright made his fortune by originating Philo Vance, the great detective and protagonist of a series of 12 novels, beginning with *The Benson Murder Case* in 1926, and continuing through *The Bishop Murder Case* (1928), *The Greene Murder Case* (1929), and nine others. Like his creator, Vance was erudite, self-confident, and supercilious, prompting Ogden Nash to remark that "Philo Vance/Needs a kick in the pance," but he lived the high society existence that Wright himself could only imagine. The books follow the conventional plot lines of the golden age, and they contain brilliant displays of esoteric knowledge. The series, which started by posing solutions to famous current cases, became increasingly bizarre before ending with the author's death.

Bibliography

DeAndrea, William L. *Encyclopedia Mysteriosa.* New York: Prentice-Hall, 1994.

Loughery, John. *Alias S. S. Van Dine: The Man Who Created Philo Vance.* New York: Maxwell, 1992.

Reilly, John, ed. *Twentieth-Century Crime and Mystery Writers.* 2d ed. New York: St. Martin's, 1985.

Steinbrenner, Chris, and Otto Penzler, eds. *Encyclopedia of Mystery and Detection.* New York: McGraw-Hill, 1976.

Fred Isaac

Van Halen (1977-), leading versatile musical group, with guitarist and keyboardist Eddie Van Halen, his brother Alex on drums, bassist Michael Anthony, and lead singers David Lee Roth and then Sammy Hagar, has always jumped into and out of musical categories, among them heavy metal, hard rock, or roots rock tinged with metal riffs. Part of the problem in categorizing Van Halen is that their musical skills, particularly Eddie's, are so superior to those of many other bands who sit squarely within one category or another. Solos in the group's numbers seem to be played without regard to staying slavishly within a particular type of musical flavor, with guitars and synthesizer often laying down a line that sounds like metal, quasi-country, electronic pop, 1960s acid, or whatever seems to fit that particular number rather than a preconceived idea of what category the band is supposed to represent.

In November 1977, Van Halen recorded their self-titled debut album, an effort that eventually sold over seven million albums and garnered rave reviews from critics who were amazed at the skill exhibited by the musicians in this "overnight" success of a band.

Van Halen followed its smash debut with *Van Halen II* in 1979, an album whose compositions were considered to be not up to the standards of the first; nevertheless, the band's skills still managed to shine through, and the album went multiplatinum. Also, by this time Eddie Van Halen was being recognized in some quarters (particularly in the *Guitar Player* readers' poll) as the best rock guitarist around. Three albums in the early 1980s—*Women and Children First*

(1980), *Fair Warning* (1981), and *Diver Down* (1982)—all went platinum and kept fans happy, but *1984 (MCM-LXXXIV)*, released on New Year's Day of that year, rocketed the band to the stratosphere with several hit singles, especially "Jump."

Roth quit the band to go solo in 1985 amid considerable bad feelings. Van Halen quickly grabbed singer Sammy Hagar, who had been working solo. Initial concern about what the band would become was assuaged largely by the band's keeping apart, to a large extent, the "Roth era" from the new one; a 1986 *Rolling Stone* concert review noted how it had now become obvious that, rather than the "preening" Roth, "the band's primary draw is Eddie Van Halen, whose guitar virtuosity was as astonishing as ever."

Despite pressure from their studio, the band refused to change its name. Van Halen's 1986 release *5150*, named after either Eddie's recording studio or the police code for the criminally insane, was considered to be an inconsistent effort, but it contained enough merit to become Van Halen's first No. 1 album. Their follow-up, 1988's *OU812*, was much the same story: critically a lukewarm piece of work, but a big seller, becoming the group's second consecutive No. 1 album.

At least marginally more favorable critical acclaim came for 1991's *For Unlawful Carnal Knowledge*, despite the acronym implied by its title. The inevitably inferior sound on *Live: Right Here, Right Now* did the group no justice on several previously recorded tunes. *Balance* (1994) continued the band's trend toward at least a mild resurgence in critical favor.

In 1996, personnel problems again plagued the band as they worked on a *Greatest Hits* compilation and contributed two songs to the film *Twister*; Hagar quit. With new vocalist Gary Cherone, the band released *Van Halen 3* in 1998.

Bibliography

Larkin, Colin, ed. *The Guinness Encyclopedia of Popular Music.* 4 vols. Middlesex, U.K.: Guinness, 1992.

McCormick, Moira. "Van Hagar: Revamped Foursome Gets Along Fine without David Lee Roth." *Rolling Stone* 5 June 1986: 13.

Review of *For Unlawful Carnal Knowledge*. Van Halen. *Rolling Stone* 12 Dec. 1991: 187.

Review of *Live: Right Here, Right Now*. Van Halen. *Stereo Review* 58.6 (1993): 86.

Stambler, Irwin. *The Encyclopedia of Pop, Rock, and Soul.* Rev. ed. New York: St. Martin's, 1989.

Stephen Finley

Vaudeville, once the king of entertainments, was not displaced until the multi-fronted attack of talking pictures, radio, and the Great Depression finally caused its official demise in 1932. But for almost a century prior to that, vaudeville was an integral part of the American scene, and its roots (variety) and influences are still felt in many areas of entertainment.

The term may have originated in France, but the form was uniquely American. British and French music hall shows of the late 1700s and early 1800s were its direct antecedents, as they were for American burlesque and revue theater (see Burlesque and Revue). It first appeared in something similar to the form it would eventually take around 1840 and was known simply as "variety." Variety at the time was composed mainly of singing and other musical acts.

It was also common for certain circus acts to give a stage show after the standard ring show ended. These "circus concerts" were the forerunners of true vaudeville. In addition, circus performers were often out of work during winter months due to the limited number of indoor venues. Acrobats, jugglers, and other specialty acts eventually became common in variety shows, and soon even carnival sideshow acts, such as fire eaters and magicians, took part as well. Vaudeville was also being cross-pollinated by other popular stage entertainments, such as minstrel shows, burlesque, and regional theater.

By the 1870s, audiences were flocking to variety shows of all kinds. Certain theatrical entrepreneurs formed traveling troupes who did tent shows, or appeared in local theaters. It was the start of the regional vaudeville circuits, which eventually became national in scope.

Perhaps the greatest vaudeville impresario was B. F. Keith (1846-1914), the man known as the father of vaudeville. Keith planned out a formula for his productions and theaters and introduced "continuous shows," which became standard practice at all but the most prestigious vaudeville theaters. Even the big-time vaudeville houses used Keith's program formula. So essential was Keith's formula that most contend that, without it, vaudeville as such doesn't exist, just variety shows. Variety was seen as the strands from which vaudeville was woven, and the terms were not considered synonymous.

The principles behind Keith's formula were used by vaudeville theaters from the 1880s until vaudeville was no more. Keith acquired a partner, Edward Albee (1857-1930), in 1885, and they began buying and building theaters, eliminating competitors. Albee wielded almost supreme power in vaudeville after Keith's death. They became the main power brokers of vaudeville, but they did have competitors.

Their chief rival was Tony Pastor (1832-1908). Pastor was the first to offer "clean" variety. Pastor banned liquor and food from his theaters, and kept them hygienic. Pastor also kept close tabs on the acts themselves, and heavily censored any performance he deemed vulgar. Keith and Albee quickly followed suit, making vaudeville safe for ladies and children. This accent on family entertainment not only furthered the distance between vaudeville and other popular theatrical forms such as burlesque; it also ingrained a certain set of expectations in American audiences. American's concept of, and at times insistence on, "good, clean, family entertainment" is easily traced to its vaudeville roots and Tony Pastor's (and a few others') dictums.

Other vaudeville circuits were solidified throughout the country, and in an attempt to control them as well, Keith and Albee fronted a booking agency, the United Booking Office in 1900. It was a success, forcing other theaters to share the Keith-Albee outlook and cutting the duo in on a percentage of the theaters' revenues.

Keith and Albee also formed the Vaudeville Manager's Association in an attempt at further control of theaters and chains they didn't own. Performers tried to unionize in a counter move and battle lines were drawn. Keith and Albee created their own actors union, the National Vaudeville Artists, in retaliation. The situation lasted for over a decade with the performers making little or no gain. In 1917, a massive strike was called, and Albee banned participants from any theaters served by the UBO. The strike was broken, driving many banned performers into other lines of work, including burlesque.

In 1913, the Palace Theater opened, marking the golden age of vaudeville. According to contemporary estimates, there were over 1,000 vaudeville theaters in operation in the U.S. with 12,000 performers and 1,600,000 daily patrons. The Palace was the biggest of the big-time, even doing away with continuous shows and instituting a policy of "two-a-day" performances: matinees and evenings. The Palace featured only the best performers in a nine-act bill that changed weekly. Many performers who starred at the Palace (and in vaudeville for that matter) found fame on the Broadway stage, on radio, and in motion pictures as well as on television, among them Milton Berle, Jack Benny, Eddie Cantor, Ted Lewis, Sophie Tucker, George Burns and Gracie Allen, Harry Houdini, Fred Allen, Fanny Brice, Edgar Bergen and Charlie McCarthy—the list soon becomes a litany of the first six decades of 20th-century entertainment.

In the 1920s, Albee continued to consolidate vaudeville under his control, and by 1924 vaudeville had become a de facto monopoly organization with Albee as emperor. Albee, reading the writing on the wall, then turned his attention to motion pictures. He formed a partnership with Radio Pictures' Joseph Kennedy, who was backed by RCA. Silent films had taken a bite out of vaudeville's audiences, and sound films took an even bigger one. Performers rushed to get work in the talkies, abandoning vaudeville. The Depression also hit vaudeville hard, as the public could not afford to go as often, and many theaters closed. People also quit going to theaters because of radio, which could present an aural vaudeville show in the comfort of one's living room. All of these factors caused vaudeville to wither and die with unprecedented speed from 1928 to 1932. In 1932, the Palace began showing movies, and vaudeville was officially pronounced dead. Variety, however, continued to be a bedrock of American entertainment.

Bibliography

Gilbert, Douglas. *American Vaudeville: Its Life and Times.* 1940. New York: Dover, 1968.

Laurie, Joe, Jr.. *Vaudeville: From the Honky-Tonks to the Palace.* New York: Holt, 1953.

Slide, Anthony. *The Vaudevillians: A Dictionary of Vaudeville Performers.* Westport: Arlington, 1981.

Sobel, Bernard. *A Pictorial History of Vaudeville.* New York: Bonanza, 1961.

Stein, Charles W., ed. and commentator. *American Vaudeville As Seen by Its Contemporaries.* New York: Da Capo, 1984.

Benjamin K. Urish

Vaughan, Sarah (1924-1990), one of America's leading jazz vocalists, the only daughter of Asbury ("Jake") and Ada Vaughan, was born in Newark, NJ. Vaughan began piano lessons at age 7. After adding organ lessons, she became, at age 12, organist at Newark's Mount Zion Baptist Church where she, too, frequently sang with the choir.

Her first performance outside Newark occurred at age 19, when she won an amateur night contest at Harlem's Apollo Theater in October 1942 with "Body and Soul." Prizes included $100 and the opportunity to sing at the Apollo for one week. Fortunately, Billy Eckstine, singing with Earl "Fatha" Hines, heard her and suggested that she audition for Hines. Hines hired her as vocalist and as second pianist, and her career was officially launched on April 4, 1943. Vaughan joined Eckstine for a brief period after he formed his own band in 1944, a big band that also featured Dizzy Gillespie and Charlie Parker.

With Gillespie leading a quintet and Parker on alto sax, Vaughan recorded "Lover Man" in 1945, a milestone in jazz history. Exploring complex harmonies in a revolutionary style, her voice communicated new meanings to lyrics. On September 16, 1946, she married George Treadwell, a trumpeter with the J. C. Heard sextet. In the late 1940s she recorded, toured in Europe, and appeared on radio and television shows. Dave Garroway, one of her most influential supporters, called her "the Divine One," and "Divine Sarah" became a common epithet.

The 1950s decade was particularly prolific. Vaughan recorded with Miles Davis in 1950; and, for the next ten years, recorded popular music for Mercury Records and jazz-oriented albums for EmArcy, a subsidiary of Mercury. On the EmArcy label, she appeared with Clifford Brown, Cannonball Adderley, and Count Basie's band. She also made public appearances in the U.S. and abroad. In 1958, she represented the U.S. at the Brussels World's Fair, alternating performances with Ella Fitzgerald, and then toured Europe for four months. On September 4, 1958, she married her second husband, C. B. Atkins.

Vaughan's involvement with the pop market was primarily between 1954 and 1959. "Whatever Lola Wants" (1955) was a special favorite. Some of her songs made the Top 20 on pop charts, and "Broken-Hearted Melody" (1958), a song Vaughan called "the corniest thing I ever did," made the Top 10, her first record to sell a million copies. Whereas pop songs earned her money, jazz satisfied her soul.

Apart from an invitation to sing at the White House in 1965, most of her activity in the 1960s was focused on studio recordings; however, in the 1970s she was working again with jazz musicians and symphony orchestras. She recorded and appeared with Michel Legrand's orchestra in 1973, 1974, and 1975. In 1974, she did a Gershwin show at the Hollywood Bowl with the Los Angeles Philharmonic; Michael Tilson Thomas of the Buffalo Symphony conducted, marking the beginning of a close and fortunate Thomas-Vaughan professional relationship. Soon appearances with other symphony orchestras occurred frequently, sometimes with Thomas conducting. Highlights during this decade include singing at the Monterey Jazz Festival in

1974; recording the album *How Long Has This Been Going On* with Oscar Peterson, Joe Pass, Ray Brown, and Louie Bellson in 1978; and appearing with notable swing musicians in 1979 on the album *Duke Ellington Song Book One*. In 1978, she married her third husband, Waymon Reed, a trumpeter. In 1979, three concerts were sold out at Carnegie Hall.

She performed at Carnegie Hall in 1980 and then returned to the Apollo Theater, where she had begun. There, she appeared with Billy Eckstine, her friend and mentor, for an NBC program. In 1981, Vaughan received an Emmy for a Gershwin performance, which she always referred to as "the Gershwin thing." She was awarded a Grammy in 1983 for the 1982 CBS Gershwin recording with Tilson Thomas and in 1988 was inducted into the American Jazz Hall of Fame. In the late 1980s, she did another memorable TV show called *Sass and Brass*, backed up by Herbie Hancock, Ron Carter, and Billy Higgins in the rhythm section and by Dizzy Gillespie, Don Cherry, Maynard Ferguson, and Chuck Mangione as trumpeters. In 1986, she sang the role of Bloody Mary in *South Pacific* with the London Symphony Orchestra in a cast that included Kiri Te Kanawa and Jose Carreras. Her last recording (1989) was a duet with Ella Fitzgerald, the only one they made together, in an all-star production, *Back on the Block*, with Fitzgerald and Vaughan singing the introduction, "Birdland." She received a second Grammy Award in 1989. Although "Send in the Clowns" was her signature song, Vaughan considered the Gershwin album her best work; the 1947 recording of "The Lord's Prayer," her personal favorite.

An intrepid performer despite her knowledge that she was seriously ill, Sarah Vaughan continued to work until a few months before she died of lung cancer. Carmen McRae eloquently expressed her admiration in her album *A Tribute to Sarah*.

The "Divine Sarah," unquestionably one of the most outstanding jazz singers of the 20th century, contributed as much as any other American singer to the jazz revolution, especially the early progressive jazz that later was known as bebop. Her style, noted for its tremendous variety of phrasing and flexibility in rhythm and tone, has been a major influence on other jazz vocalists; and her voice, ranging in quality from pop to operatic, has been the jazz marvel of the century.

Bibliography

Feather, Leonard. *The Encyclopedia of Jazz*. New York: Bonanza, 1960.

Gourse, Leslie. *Sassy: The Life of Sarah Vaughan*. New York: Scribner, 1993.

Hine, Darlene Clark, ed. *Black Women in America: An Historical Encyclopedia*. Vol. 2. New York: Carlson, 1993.

Larkin, Colin, ed. *The Guinness Encyclopedia of Popular Music*. Middlesex, U.K.: Guinness, 1992.

Shaw, Arnold. *Black Popular Music in America*. New York: Schirmer, 1986.

Marion Barber Stowell

Vaughan, Stevie Ray (1954-1990), one of America's more influential jazz guitarists, was born in Dallas, TX, the son of an asbestos plant worker and a secretary at a cement factory. Vaughan's early interest in music was influenced heavily by his older brother, Jimmie, who later gained national prominence with the Fabulous Thunderbirds. Jimmie's activity in bands while still in high school prompted Stevie Ray to learn a few chords on guitar by the time he was eight years old, and he listened often and repeatedly to Jimmie's blues records.

As a teenager, Vaughan performed for pay with bands around Dallas, including bar bands such as Blackbird, the Night Crawlers, and the Chantones. At 17, Vaughan quit high school (he had failed music theory there) and moved to Austin, a city with a growing reputation as a breeding ground for musicians who were something other than mainstream. By 1975, he was playing with the Cobras, one of the more popular blues bands in the area, and two years later he left to form Triple Threat, a band devoted to rhythm & blues.

Vaughan kept Triple Threat together until 1981, when he decided it was time to fuse elements of rock and R&B to form a newer sound. Naming his new group Double Trouble after an Otis Rush song, Vaughan hired drummer Chris Layton and bassist Tommy Shannon. For several months the group struggled, eventually gaining a core of followers in Texas and even a nightclub appearance in New York City. In 1982 producer Jerry Wexler got the group a minor billing at the Montreux Jazz Festival in Switzerland. Vaughan and Double Trouble made the most of it: James McBride wrote that Vaughan came "roaring into the 1982 Montreux festival with a '59 Stratocaster at his hip and two flame-throwing sidekicks.... He had no record contract, no name, but he reduced the stage to a pile of smoking cinders and, afterward, everyone wanted to know who he was."

David Bowie, impressed with Vaughan's showing at Montreux, signed him up for lead guitar on his 1983 *Let's Dance*; Jackson Browne recommended that Vaughan and Double Trouble record an album at his studio. Perhaps most importantly, John Hammond, the Columbia producer known for uncovering new acts, pushed his company to sign Vaughan to a contract. The resulting 1983 album, *Texas Flood* (released on Columbia's Epic label), made *Billboard*'s Top 40 and later went gold; the album also gave Vaughan two Grammy nominations and rave reviews. *Couldn't Stand the Weather* (1984), heavily influenced by Jimi Hendrix (especially on a remake of "Voodoo Chile"), did even better than *Flood* by making the Top 20, going platinum, and gaining another Grammy nomination. Vaughan finally won a Grammy in 1985 with a cut from *Blues Explosion*, an anthology album performed by various artists. Also in 1985, *Soul to Soul*, with new keyboard player Reese Wynans, went gold and merited yet another Grammy nomination.

Though he continued to work in the late 1980s, Vaughan's increasing problems with substance abuse resulted in his admittance to detox centers. Vaughan's *In Step* album (1989) and the Vaughan brothers' *Family Style* (1990) were considered competent, but not outstanding, efforts, though *In Step* managed to go gold and win a

Grammy with songs drawn from Vaughan's coping with substance abuse.

In 1990, the Vaughan brothers guested on Eric Clapton's American tour, and it was on that tour that Vaughan chose to fly by helicopter back to Chicago from an appearance at the Alpine Valley Music Theater near East Troy, WI. Only moments after takeoff, the helicopter crashed on the other side of a hill close to the theater. All aboard were killed instantly, including Vaughan, the pilot, and Clapton's Hollywood agent, assistant tour manager, and bodyguard. Vaughan's posthumous *The Sky Is Crying* (1991) features previously unreleased recordings from the 1980s.

Bibliography

Dougherty, Steve, Barbara Sandler, and Beth Austin. "A Wisconsin Helicopter Crash Claims a Blues Legend-in-the-Making, Guitarist Stevie Ray Vaughan." *People* 10 Sept. 1990: 58-61.

Larkin, Colin, ed. *The Guinness Encyclopedia of Popular Music*. 4 vols. Middlesex, U.K.: Guinness, 1992.

Pond, Steve. "Alone Together: Guitar Gurus Jeff Beck and Stevie Ray Vaughan Take to the Road." *Rolling Stone* 25 Jan. 1990.

Stambler, Irwin. *The Encyclopedia of Pop, Rock, and Soul*. Rev. ed. New York: St. Martin's, 1989.

Stephen Finley

Verne, Jules Gabriel (1828-1905), was born in Nantes, France. Though he was not much of a traveler in reality, the genre of adventure that he developed often deals with fantastic travels. As the father of science fiction and an international best-selling author from the 1860s to modern times, he served as an inspiration to many subsequent writers, including H. G. Wells, who further developed the science fiction method after having spent his youth devouring Verne's adventures. Verne also influenced numerous actual scientists, including William Beebe and Admiral Richard Byrd.

Verne was sent to a Paris law school at the age of 18, during which time he met Alexandre Dumas (*The Three Musketeers*), who mentored the young poet/playwright, and encouraged him to go out and write some things on his own. He eventually went into stock brokerage with a loan from his father, but continued to write science articles for children. *Five Weeks in a Balloon* was written about 1862, and promptly rejected by 15 different publishers. The 16th took it, and Verne's fortune was made. He turned out two books a year for the next twenty years. His output totals more than 100 novels plus the articles, poems, and plays written in his youth.

One of Verne's goals in his writing was to make his stories believable. Often using what was the most current of scientific thought, he used fact as the foundation of fantasy so as to convince his readers that people could go to the moon, travel under the sea, or take a trip around the globe in less than six months' time. Several of Verne's works (both science fiction and adventure) have been turned into motion pictures, starting with *From the Earth to the Moon* in 1902. *Twenty Thousand Leagues under the Sea*, *Around the World in Eighty Days*, and *The Mysterious Island* have also become films. The descriptive writing and colorful characters in *Twenty Thousand Leagues under the Sea* lend themselves especially well to film interpretation.

Bibliography

Ash, Brian. *Who's Who in Science Fiction*. New York: Taplinger, 1976.

Clute, John, and Peter Nicholls, eds. *The Encyclopedia of Science Fiction*. New York: St. Martin's, 1993.

Costello, Peter. *Jules Verne: Inventor of Science Fiction*. New York: Scribner, 1978.

Evans, Arthur B. *Jules Verne Rediscovered: Didacticism and the Scientific Novel*. New York: Greenwood, 1988.

Lynch, Lawrence W. *Jules Verne*. New York: Twayne, 1992.

Mary Dezelski

Vic and Sade (1932-1946), a domestic comedy, followed *Clara, Lu n' Em* as the second daytime serial on network radio air. This episodic serial by Paul Rhymer began with only two characters, Victor and Sade Gook—the head bookkeeper for the Consolidated Kitchenware Company and a bright, homebound wife—played by Art Van Harvey and Bernadine Flynn. Shortly afterward, in order to expand the scope of the program, Rhymer brought William Idelson in to play Rush Meadows, an adopted son. When a heart seizure compelled Van Harvey to take time off in 1940, the role of Fletcher Rush, Sade's absent-minded, selectively deaf, and minutely anecdotal uncle, was given to Clarence Hartzell.

For most of its run, the voices of Vic, Sade, Rush, and Uncle Fletcher, "radio's home folks," were the only voices ever to emanate from "the small house half-way up in the next block." Very little ever happened in the Virginia Avenue home of Vic and Sade, located in Crooper, IL (40 miles from Peoria), but the Gooks entertained radio audiences with their conversations about the day's trivial events as well as their encounters with hundreds of off-mike characters. Nevertheless, the small cast of characters managed to produce some of the simplest and probably the best drama heard during soap opera time. It was the Gooks' constant and distinctively absurd small talk about their acquaintances, a half-wit fly on the ceiling, 12,000 cherry phosphates, or the Cincinnati Overhand Triple Lock method for tying shoelaces as invented by Morgan Perrin of Donnersgrove, IL, that enabled Paul Rhymer to turn *Vic and Sade* into a significant slice of American life and an acknowledged radio masterpiece.

Bibliography

Dunning, John. *Tune in Yesterday*. Englewood Cliffs: Prentice-Hall, 1976.

Rhymer, Paul. *The Small House Halfway Up in the Next Block*. New York: McGraw-Hill, 1972.

Stedman, Raymond W. *The Serials: Suspense and Drama by Installment*. Norman: U of Oklahoma P, 1975.

Wertheim, Arthur. *Radio Comedy*. New York: Oxford UP, 1979.

Stanley D. Harrison

Video Arcade, The, was a stronghold of American youth culture in the last quarter of the 20th century, whether as a corner of the café in remote rural towns, a converted city storefront, or the hub of a suburban mall. The video arcade had its origin in the soda shops, pool halls, and bowling alleys where youth gathered, particularly around pinball machines. Pinball developed from coin-operated bagatelle games popular in saloons and barbershops in the 1920s; David Gottlieb's Baffle Ball (1930) is often characterized as the first pinball game. To attract players, pinball manufacturers competed with each other to incorporate the latest technologies into their machines. Electrification made possible the tilt mechanism and kickout solenoid (1932), flippers (1942), printed circuits (1956), and solid state technology (1975).

This competition for the latest technology caused the rapid adoption of video games (see also next entry) in pinball arcades. Computer Space (1971), created by Nolan Bushnell (see entry), was the first arcade game with a video screen and computer technology. Bushnell founded the Atari Corporation, producing Pong (1972), a video Ping-Pong game, and Breakout (1973). Other early competitors were Williams Electronics (Paddle Ball, 1972) and Exidy Corporation, whose Death Race (1976) was criticized for its violence. As in pinball, companies designed video arcade versions of most physical competitions in society, from group sports to all kinds of warfare. Outer space themes have been consistently popular, including the first games to use vector graphics, Space Wars (1978) and Asteroids (1979), and the highly popular Space Invaders (1978).

The first video arcade game to achieve the status of pop-culture icon was Pac-Man (1980), a dot-crunching mouth rampaging through a maze. It spawned a merchandising bonanza that included spinoff games like Ms. Pac-Man and Baby Pac-Man, stuffed toys, and a Top 40 record, "Pac-Man Fever." Donkey Kong (1981) introduced Mario, a carpenter who attempts to rescue a fair maiden from a gorilla. Mario became the star of a whole series of other games such as Super Mario Brothers, and eventually a Saturday morning network cartoon. Increasingly, video games became another tie-in for merchandising movies, while movies like *The Wizard* (1990) have simultaneously explored and exploited the subculture.

Much has been written about the arcade subculture, which includes adults as well as preteens, and has its own etiquette, jargon, behavior, and taboos. It has been largely male, and merchandisers have played on this by designing games where females usually play secondary and submissive roles. Some communities have passed ordinances and zoning against video arcades, fearful of their power to attract crowds of young people. Yet they continue to flourish.

Bibliography

Ahl, David H., Keith S. Reid-Green, and Albert L. Zobrist. "Computer Games." *Encyclopedia of Computer Science.* Ed. Anthony Ralston and Edwin D. Reilly. 3d ed. New York: Van Nostrand, 1993.

Flower, Gary, and Bill Kurtz. *Pinball.* New York: Chartwell, 1988.

Loftus, Geoffrey R., and Elizabeth F. Loftus. *Mind at Play: The Psychology of Video Games.* New York: Basic, 1983.

Provenzo, Eugene F., Jr. *Video Kids: Making Sense of Nintendo.* Cambridge: Harvard UP, 1991.

Tim Orwig

Video Games, sometimes called the bastard child of TV and computers, are hard to characterize but are a significant aspect of the electronic culture. They are toys, yet used by the Pentagon to train troops; played by millions of teens and preteens, they are also part of some of the most exciting scientific research done today. They can be traced back to mainframe games, beginning with Alan Turing's proposed "imitation game" (1950). In the Cold War decade of the 1950s, the Defense Department and military contractors such as Rand and Research Analysis Corporation developed many simulation games for defense strategy purposes. For example, scientists at Los Alamos Atomic Energy Laboratory designed the first computer chess program (1956).

Early computer-assisted instructional devices like Omar K. Moore's Talking Typewriter (1962) began to introduce computer technology to children. MIT scientists developed Spacewar (1962) to be played on Digital Equipment Corporation's 15-inch screen. Later in the decade the National Science Foundation and manufacturers began promoting games to strengthen science education and integrate computers into school curriculums. David Ahl's *101 Basic Computer Games* (1973), the first million-selling computer book, and his *Creative Computing* magazine (1974) brought games to a much wider audience of children and adults.

Magnavox released the first television-based computer home games in 1972, followed by home versions of video arcade games such as Atari's Pong (1975). Fairchild marketed the first removable-cartridge home games in 1976. With the 1977 introduction of affordable personal computers by companies such as Apple and Commodore, a deluge of games, including Space Invaders (1978), Pac-Man (1980), and Defender (1981), built an industry that grossed $8 billion by 1982. After a 1983 downturn, the market recovered again in 1986, led by the Nintendo system. Sales continued to expand with Sega and NEC innovations and games formatted for the IBM personal computers and their clones. In February 1989, 25 of the 30 best-selling toys in the country were video games or equipment.

Critics questioned the effects of video games, calling them asocial, addictive, violent, sexist, and occasionally racist. In 1982, C. Everett Koop, the U.S. Surgeon General, warned that they produced "aberration in childhood behavior," while President Ronald Reagan guessed that they helped prepare youth for military careers. Ongoing criticism over graphic depictions of violence and sex caused the industry to consider a ratings system in 1994. But video-game defenders stressed their potential to build hand-eye coordination, problem-solving skills, spatial skills, creativity, and goal-setting behavior, and their positive effects in teaching learning-disabled children and making many children computer-literate. Technology continues to improve video games, as the joystick gives way to the power glove and video games incorporate virtual reality technology.

Bibliography

Ahl, David H., Keith S. Reid-Green, and Albert L. Zobrist. "Computer Games." *Encyclopedia of Computer Science.* Ed. Anthony Ralston and Edwin D. Reilly. 3d ed. New York: Van Nostrand, 1993.

Greenfield, Patricia Marks. *Mind and Media: The Effects of Television, Video Games, and Computers.* Cambridge: Harvard UP, 1984.

Loftus, Geoffrey R., and Elizabeth F. Loftus. *Mind at Play: The Psychology of Video Games.* New York: Basic, 1983.

Provenzo, Eugene F., Jr. *Video Kids: Making Sense of Nintendo.* Cambridge: Harvard UP, 1991.

Tim Orwig

Vietnam War Fiction marvelously exemplifies the heuristic nature of popular culture, which, through a host of artifacts, allows a nation to assess the lasting effects of a traumatic historical event. Novels, short stories, and personal narratives provide a satchel full of different lens through which people understand their own actions and revise their opinions of themselves.

Given the expanse of Vietnam War-related novels, the literary or historical criteria for inclusion must be elastic. One or more of the following criteria must be met: (1) the story bears the war as primary plot element; (2) the story features a protagonist or essential subsidiary character irretrievably affected by the war; or (3) the story uses the war and/or its memory as a formative element of narrative action. Casting this net draws in readers with divergent reading tastes.

For example, followers of science fiction would feel right at home with *In the Field of Fire*, a collection of stories edited by Jeanne Van Buren Dann and Jack Dann. Devotees of John Irving's Garp-like humor would find *A Prayer for Owen Meany*. Avid consumers of mystery/police procedurals would discover easily 30 separate titles that are shaped to some degree by the Vietnam War. Many stories in this genre are offered from the perspective of a detective or private eye whose persona and way of confronting crime is somehow indelibly linked to his experience in, as they say, "The Nam." The same linkage often works for criminals in these texts. Sometimes both occur in one novel—the redemptive Vietnam veteran detective who has overcome incredible neurotic obstacles left over from the war, only to confront and overcome the unrepentant lunatic Vietnam veteran criminal whose war baggage has proven more obdurate.

Aficionados of the horror genre could find roughly 20 candidates, including at least five that have been made into films, including such unforgettable (and largely unreadable) titles as *Bloodfeast*, the eponymous masterpiece *Slob, and Scream* by the Misters Skipp and Spector, as well as Peter Straub's intricate pair of novels *Koko* and *The Throat*. The relationship between the mechanics and ethos of the horror story and those of the war story is subtle and interesting. What, after all, is more horror-filled than warfare? Readers will discover other generic groups of Vietnam War stories most clearly identified as romances (e.g., Danielle Steele's *Message from Nam*), psychological thrillers, and more than four score "novels" of pornography.

There are even about a dozen "Westerns." These novels, set in the modern American West, juxtapose cynically embittered American frontiersmen with older, wary but otherwise Edenic John Wayne types. Although obviously formulaic and written for entertainment purposes, these stories track the stereotyped damaged veteran (usually with some good Indian blood in him) through his return home as a redemptive hero, where he is forced to rescue sweetheart Marylou from some gingham-shredding villain of dubious capitalist motive. The serious side of these slight tales concerns the returned Native American veteran who finally has restored to him the strength and purity of his heritage, but only after having had it shamelessly degraded in a white man's war that inevitably betrayed the ideals of the American Indian spirit.

Some superb writing has found its way into this conglomeration of fictional modes. There are scores of novels and short stories that embody impressively creative work of enduring power—indeed some of the best writing from the past two decades. Experimentation with point of view has been brilliant. Employing complex, sometimes surreal patterns of development, a number of war narratives establish chillingly believable atmospheric conditions, unique characterizations that in some award-winning instances are remarkably durable, and plotting intricate enough to rival Dickens. The Vietnam War has produced two National Book Award winners (Tim O'Brien's *Going After Cacciato* and Larry Heinemann's *Paco's Story*) and a Pulitzer Prize winner (Robert Olen Butler's *Good Scent from a Strange Mountain*). To this distinguished company can be added provocative work by Ward Just (*Stringer* and *In the City of Fear*), Graham Greene (*The Quiet American*), Norman Mailer (*Why Are We in Vietnam?*), Kurt Vonnegut (*Slaughterhouse-Five* and *Hocus Pocus*), William Gaddis (*Carpenter's Gothic*), Frederick Busch (*Absent Friends* and *Closing Arguments*), Madison Smartt Bell (*Waiting for the End of the World* and *Soldier's Joy*), Barry Hannah (*Ray* and *Hey Jack!*), and Robert Stone (*Dog Soldiers* and *A Flag for Sunrise*)—all writers with significant credits apart from Vietnam. In tandem with this group of writers, there exists another impressive catalogue of serious, emerging fictionalists whose efforts with the Vietnam War have helped earn them a place in the favored gaze of literary critics at the national level—among them Bobbie Ann Mason (*In Country, Shiloh and Other Stories, Love Life*), Jayne Anne Phillips (*Machine Dreams*), Susan Fromberg Schaeffer (*Buffalo Afternoon*), Clyde Edgerton (*Floatplane Notebooks*), Larry Brown (*Dirty Work*), Philip Caputo (*DelCorso's Gallery, Horn of Africa, Indian Country, Means of Escape*), Winston Groom (*Better Times Than These, Forrest Gump, Gone the Sun*), Stephen Wright (*Meditations in Green*), Daniel Ford (*Incident at Muc Wa*), David James Duncan (*The Brothers K*), Tobias Wolfe (*Back in the World, The Barracks Thief*), Pat Conroy (*The Lords of Discipline, The Prince of Tides*), James Webb (*Fields of Fire*), and David Halberstam (*One Very Hot Day*).

The first period of war writing begins in the mid-sixties, soon after American soldiers in 1961 were committed to serving as advisors to South Vietnamese units, and includes titles like Robin Moore's *The Green Berets*, Irwin R. Blacker's

Search and Destroy, Smith Hempstone's *A Tract of Time,* Scott C. S. Stone's *Coasts of War,* and the now applauded *LBJ Brigade* by William Wilson. This period runs roughly through 1975/76, when the Republic of South Vietnam collapsed, and is characterized more than anything else by a portrayal of Americans actually engaged in fighting the Vietnam War. David Halberstam, a journalist who had spent time in Vietnam before the large build-up of combat forces began in 1965, in 1967 contributed *One Very Hot Day*, a straightforward narrative relentlessly focused on a small set of characters and their experience of war in Vietnam. Another journalist, Ward Just, added a more surreal, symbolic vision of the war in 1974 with *Stringer*. Jonathan Rubin's *The Barking Deer* and Asa Baber's *The Land of a Million Elephants* aptly complement the fabulous spirit of *Stringer*, while Robert Roth's *Sand in the Wind* and Steven Phillip Smith's *American Boys* continue the realistic evocation of the war environment as the first stage of development came to a close with the end of the South Vietnamese regime.

In general, this early period of writing may be described as one portraying American citizens who consent to fight a just war believed to be in behalf of defenseless victims of world communism. Story after story in the first stage worked the actual, physical terrain of war as known by those sent to fight in it. Then Saigon fell, and in 1976, with Charles Durden's *No Bugles, No Drums*, a sense of ironic disengagement becomes overwhelmingly evident in bizarre, exaggerated comic elements which seem to suggest the techniques of Joseph Heller's *Catch-22*. Despite this shimmering sense of disengagement, however, Durden takes his readers to the war zone.

This first period of writing about the Vietnam War was managed mostly by "insiders," so the fiction carries an overriding sense of "I-Was-There-So-Don't-Question-My-Story." There was little room at this stage for the narratives of mere civilians, war protesters, minorities, or women—regardless of whether they, too, might have been vitally engaged with the conflict.

The second period of war writing runs roughly from about 1977/78 to 1988, with the bulk of it being published (if not actually written) between 1984 and 1988. The dedication of the Vietnam Veterans Memorial (particularly the V-shaped black wall which descends into the earth) in Washington, DC, in 1982 marked in unexpectedly dramatic fashion the "permission" to recognize, mourn, and lament in public an experience that up until that year had been virtually a societal taboo. Following this cathartic gesture of memory, there was a flood of prose fiction and personal narrative dealing with diverse angles of approach to the war experience and incorporating more and more types of authorial background. Recognizable by such titles as Larry Heinemann's *Close Quarters*, *The Deer Hunter* (one of those novels born as a filmscript and then published after the movie is released), Winston Groom's *Better Times Than These*, John Cassidy's *A Station in the Delta*, Gustav Hasford's *The Short-Timers* (later adapted for Stanley Kubrick's film *Full Metal Jacket*), John Del Vecchio's *The 13th Valley*, the Japanese writer Takeshi Kaido's *Into a Black Sun*, Charles Nelson's *The Boy Who Picked the Bullets Up*,

Donald Pfarrer's *Neverlight*, and Stephen Wright's *Meditations in Green*, this period is identifiable by its propensity for anger directed at the sources of political expedience that appear to keep good and decent citizens mired hopelessly in the tragically unwinnable combat of a foreign civil war. Even as the conditions of the conflict seemed increasingly insane, the war persisted. It *was*—and there seemed no way out. O'Brien's *Going After Cacciato*, a masterpiece of imagination, drives this point home with devastating power. An emerging trend emphasized the quagmire-like nature of a conflict that was not simplistically evil in its origins, and more and more, in one way or another, it became evident that extricating American entanglement from Vietnam was a process barely begun even once the soldiers were home and Saigon had fallen. Sometimes, as in Webb's *Fields of Fire*, the anger would be directed most aggressively at rejection of the combat veteran by Americans opposed to the war, with the clear hint that the fallout from this backlash would last long. Increasingly, too, in this ten-year period, stories began focusing on the spreading influence of the war experience, showing that it would reach out beyond the time of actual combat and haunt the surviving population for generations.

In matters of style, the second large period of literary activity dealing with the Vietnam War is differentiated from the first by increasing sophistication on the part of the writer, blending the sensitivity of the traditional *Bildungsroman* with the *Realpolitik* of the deteriorating chaos of civil strife as registered in the late 1960s and early 1970s, but with strong aftershocks rippling deep into the 1980s.

However, even as fiction of dazzling virtuosity began to appear, this period of writing also saw the emergence of purely commercial, audience-pleasing narratives that drew upon the Vietnam experience. For the first time, the public was offered Vietnam stories that not only purported to evoke the actions of American combatants but also intended to entertain an audience with obsessively male fantasies regarding the thrills to be had in war. These ill-formed pastiches have cemented in place a good many of the misconceptions that have come to cloak the Vietnam War.

The second period of war writing opened Vietnam to everyone—writers and readers alike. No longer was the veteran or some other close observer of the war given exclusive status as a "seer" of truths about the war experience. A diverse set of "outsiders" joined the enterprise of writing Vietnam. A complex combination of authors felt sufficiently damaged or violated by the war to make fiction dealing with its effects. The Baby Boomers are vast in number, Vietnam was the war that made them mortal, and when they, en masse, massaged their collective memories, they gave birth to the "Vietnam syndrome" (although it was George Bush, a non-Boomer, who named it).

The third period of war writing began in the mid-1980s and continues into the present. This is the era of the "Vietnam syndrome" under full sail—a colossal ship, carrying everyone, going everywhere. Writers with a record of achievement in Vietnam fiction are on board with new narratives (Heinemann's *Paco's Story* and O'Brien's *The Things They Carried*), and the subject continues to open cargo up for appropriation by new genres, including large and careful melodramas: *Massachusetts* by Nancy Zaroulis, *Slow Poison* by Sheila Bosworth, *Indochine* by Christie Dickason. There continues to be genuinely innovative writing, as in the case of Bruce McAllister's *Dream Baby,* Robert Olen Butler's *Good Scent from a Strange Mountain*, and David A. Willson's *REMF Diary*, a novel of sequels and prequels about life in the rear areas. The high-end mystery/detective novels (e.g., most all of James Lee Burke, some of Faye Kellerman, Ed McBain, T. Jefferson Parker, and Nelson DeMille) come to prize "veteran status" for their protagonists.

The ongoing period of writing about the Vietnam War is both chimerical and resplendent with irony. The Vietnam War has become a complex trope for things not being what they seem in American life. More often than not, still, the figure chosen to embody this transformation is the American boy who enters one end of a historical tunnel and then discovers that, promises notwithstanding, there is no end to the tunnel, although as he travels along, there is increasing disorientation, cynicism, and meanness. To be sure, it is equally ironic that the farther removed from the original event one travels, the more "current" the myriad implications of the Vietnam experience appear to become for democracies like the United States. Democracies harbor people who feel compelled to re-create public images of themselves, apparently as a gesture of evidence of their freedom. Hence, writers entering the Vietnam setting have offered practically everything imaginable by way of revisioning: the once-heroic home-grown sports star who becomes a fighter pilot, the rags-to-riches black enlisted man who leads his white platoon through impossible ordeals to safety, triage nurses who turn into foul-mouthed (though always pert) angels, an insensitive careerist general who is transformed into a self-sacrificing father-figure simply by being in the presence of his noble, decent, citizen soldier American boys. All these interchangeables—and many more—are to be found in much of the current fiction purporting to be about the Vietnam War.

Bibliography

Beidler, Philip D. *Re-Writing America: Vietnam Authors in Their Generation*. Athens: U of Georgia P, 1991.

Hellman, John. *American Myth and the Legacy of Vietnam*. New York: Columbia UP, 1986.

Martin, Andrew. *Receptions of War: Vietnam in American Culture*. Norman: U of Oklahoma P, 1993.

Ringnalda, Don. *Fighting and Writing the Vietnam War*. Jackson: UP of Mississippi, 1994.

Searle, William J., ed. *Search and Clear: Critical Responses to Selected Literature and Films of the Vietnam War*. Bowling Green, OH: Bowling Green State U Popular P, 1988.

John Baky
Owen W. Gilman, Jr.

Vietnam War Films and Documentaries, unlike films about any other of America's wars, have mirrored the changing imaginative conception of Vietnam in the American popular mind. From the early films like *Jump into Hell* (1955) and *China Gate* (1957), which presented Vietnam as a distant and morally murky arena where French Foreign Legionnaires and dashing and daring American mercenaries played out the last of the colonial wars, to the more recent *Heaven & Earth* (1993), which uses the journey of a young Vietnamese woman from her travails in war-torn Vietnam to her successes in America as a metaphor for the whole "Vietnam experience," the Vietnam film has evolved in much the same manner as has the issue of Vietnam for many, although surely not all, Americans.

For many Americans in the postmodern era, and especially for those born after the end of American military involvement in Vietnam in 1973, the feature film—and to a lesser extent the documentary—has been the main source of historical information about the political and military contexts of the war, about the Vietnamese, and about the social tensions which the war exacerbated and which continue to tug at the popular conscience and consciousness. As a source of entertainment, Vietnam has proven to be a particularly fertile resource. If Americans were seeking a new myth—or myths—by which to understand the rapidly changing world in which they exist, there were great possibilities inherent in fictional filmic representations of Vietnam. Just like traditional American sources of mythmaking—the Frontier and World War II—Vietnam provides ready-made heroes and villains, tales of guts and glory, and the possibility for violent action and regeneration, as well as for ideological debate.

The Green Berets (1968), coming out at the height of America's troop buildup, was the first major Hollywood production to treat American military involvement in Vietnam. From its opening theme—Sgt. Barry Sadler's stirring if somewhat overblown "The Ballad of the Green Berets"—it set the ideological tone for Hollywood's treatment of Vietnam for a decade by simply continuing the tradition of the American war film as a quasi-propaganda piece that presents a gallant and righteous America willingly shouldering the responsibility for protecting all the "little guys" in the world who cannot protect themselves.

Once American military involvement in the war concluded in 1973, more films about returning veterans—*Tracks* (1975), *Taxi Driver* (1976), *Some Kind of Hero* (1982), *Gardens of Stone* (1987), among others—began to appear. In films like *Tracks* and *Gardens of Stone*, the Vietnam veteran confronts his experience in the war and, by analogy, the experience of the nation as well, by burying the dead of the war. These films also serve to remind the audience that behind the tranquil serenity of military burial grounds like Arlington National Cemetery are the cruel and violent deaths that the young men buried there have suffered in combat.

In other films within this category, such as *Heroes* (1977), *Coming Home* (1978), and *Birdy* (1984), veterans are portrayed as either physically, psychologically, or emotionally handicapped. In *Coming Home*, Jon Voight plays a severely disabled veteran who transforms the political consciousness of an Army wife (Jane Fonda), who is married to a gung-ho officer (Bruce Dern). In *Birdy*, Nicolas Cage attempts to protect and rehabilitate his friend (Matthew

Modine), who often exists in a catatonic state due to his experiences in the war.

Many "coming home" films, especially those produced in the 1970s when the emotions about the war were still very volatile, portrayed Vietnam veterans as tightly wound, antisocial loners about to go over the edge or, somewhat conversely, as members of threatening antisocial groups like motorcycle gangs, as in *Angels from Hell* (1968) and *The Losers* (1971). The characterization of the Vietnam veteran in such films as *Billy Jack* (1971), *Welcome Home, Soldier Boys* (1972), and the seminal Rambo film, *First Blood* (1982), is one of a violent antihero who, perhaps outraged at the society that has ostracized him, takes on and defeats corrupt authority.

Although some of these films, like *Billy Jack* and *First Blood*, have a degree of artistic merit, most did little more than reinforce American society's negative picture of the Vietnam veteran, often playing to left-wing stereotypes not only about the effects of the war on the veteran, but also about the character and personality of the kind of man who allowed himself to be sent to Vietnam in the first place.

One of the films that certainly perpetuated the stereotype of the Vietnam veteran as an antisocial, violence-prone loner was *Taxi Driver* (1976). Travis Bickel (Robert DeNiro) is a disaffected sociopath who attempts to right the wrongs of society by rescuing a child prostitute (Jodie Foster) from the sordid reality of her life. The film ends in a bloody climax as Bickel brutally murders her pimp. More recently, the polemical *Born on the Fourth of July* (1989), based upon Ron Kovic's memoir of the same name and directed by Oliver Stone, re-creates or revises some events to present to the American public the plight of a severely physically damaged veteran who loses both his idealism and his faith in the American dream.

Perhaps the most significant Vietnam film in this particular category, however, is *The Deer Hunter* (1978), which also stars DeNiro. *The Deer Hunter* is an important and controversial film for two reasons: it was the first serious attempt to blend literature and myth in a Vietnam film; and it was the first major Hollywood production since *The Green Berets* to feature the Vietnamese, especially the North Vietnamese and Vietcong, as a brutal and inhuman people. This characterization outraged many liberal viewers, leading to charges that *The Deer Hunter* is a racist film. In *The Deer Hunter,* three young men from a small Pennsylvania mill town go to Vietnam, where they are captured by the Vietcong and, before effecting a thrilling escape, are forced to play a sadistic version of Russian roulette. This experience of course affects each of the men profoundly. Michael (DeNiro) returns to the United States where he has a difficult time adjusting to civilian life; Nick (Christopher Walken) remains in Vietnam where, emotionally empty, he becomes a professional at playing Russian roulette; and Steven (John Savage), whose legs have been amputated as a result of injuries he incurred during his escape, refuses to return to his hometown, remaining instead within the comfortable and secure walls of a VA hospital. These three characters represent three extremes of the characterization of the Vietnam

veteran: the man who is physically whole but emotionally detached (Michael); the emotional cripple, unable to reconcile himself to his war experience (Nick); and the physical cripple, carrying with him the visible consequences of the war (Steven).

Another category of Vietnam films includes those dealing directly with political, social, and ideological issues of the war as played out on the home front. These films often have as their subject matter anti-war sentiments as found on college campuses, as in *Medium Cool* (1969), *The Strawberry Statement* (1970), and *Getting Straight* (1970), and in the documentary *The War at Home* (1979), which portrays the evolution of the anti-war movement and the SDS (Students for a Democratic Society) at the University of Wisconsin at Madison in a sympathetic manner. Other "effects" films deal with the draft, draft resisters, and deserters. Among these are *Greetings* (1968), *Alice's Restaurant* (1969), *Easy Rider* (1969), *Cowards* (1970), and *Hair* (1978).

Perhaps the most exciting kind of Vietnam film is the in-country combat film. *Apocalypse Now* (1979; see entry) fits within this category, but its importance goes well beyond its somewhat simplistic and uninformed depiction of combat in Vietnam. Like *The Deer Hunter*, *Apocalypse Now* is a deliberate effort to impose a literary model on a cinematic work. In this case, Francis Ford Coppola attempts an update of Joseph Conrad's *Heart of Darkness*, even going so far as to name the out-of-control Army colonel (Marlon Brando) Kurtz.

It is not until the middle and late 1980s, perhaps because there was finally sufficient emotional distance from the war, that Hollywood made an attempt to deal more realistically and accurately with the question of combat in Vietnam and its effects on soldiers. *Casualties of War* (1989), for instance, is based upon a true account—echoing the My Lai massacre—of the rape and murder of a young Vietnamese girl by an American soldier and the subsequent attempt to cover the act up.

The breakthrough Vietnam combat film, however, is the highly controversial *Platoon* (1986). If there has been some disagreement about the extent to which this film showed Vietnam, in the words of *Time* magazine's Richard Corliss, "the way it really was," there is little doubt that the film's creator, Oliver Stone (see entry), himself a combat veteran of Vietnam, wanted to present the reality of the war as it had never before been presented to the American public and the world. So great was the impact of *Platoon* on the American movie-going public that the film earned an Oscar for best picture and received numerous critical kudos for its realistic portrayal of life and combat in Vietnam.

Another combat film which was released shortly after *Platoon* and consequently did not receive the attention it might have had it been released before, is *Hamburger Hill* (1978), written by James Carabatsos, also a Vietnam veteran.

The other major Hollywood Vietnam film in the 1980s was Stanley Kubrick's *Full Metal Jacket* (1987). This film is essentially split into two parts: the first little more than a Marine training film depicting the horrors of boot camp on Parris Island and culminating in the suicide of one of the recruits; the second, and more compelling part following a platoon of Marines as they engage in the battle for Hue during the Tet Offensive of 1968.

Other in-country films have had less of an impact on the popular consciousness, although some, like *Good Morning, Vietnam* (1987), based upon the experiences of an AFVN disc jockey, and *Bat-21* (1988), enjoyed some success due to the presence of established stars in the main roles, Robin Williams in the former and Gene Hackman in the latter. Films such as *The Boys in Company C* (1978) were fairly early attempts to deal with combat in Vietnam and others, such as *Platoon Leader* (1988) and *The Iron Triangle* (1988), fit comfortably in the B-movie category, exploiting the action/adventure aspects of Vietnam without attempting to articulate any profound insight about the war or the people who fought in it.

One more recent innovative film is *84 Charlie MoPic* (1989), which follows an infantry combat unit into action. Their experience is recorded by an Army filmmaker (hence the title, which is the military designation for his job). Another film which also somewhat blurs the distinction between fiction and documentary because of its pace and editing is *The Hanoi Hilton* (1987), about American POWs at Hanoi's infamous Hoa Lo Prison.

An early documentary about Vietnam was Emile de Antonio's *In the Year of the Pig* (1969), which surveys Vietnamese history from a particular Marxist perspective, pitting the valiant and unified Vietnamese revolutionaries—the North Vietnamese and the southern National Liberation Front—against the corrupt Saigon government and its even more corrupt ally, the U.S. Because Antonio presented the war from the revolutionists' perspective, integrating North Vietnamese footage into his film, *In the Year of the Pig*, in spite of its artistic merit, was considered by many to be mere communist propaganda.

Hearts and Minds (1974) is an obviously slanted polemic that seems aimed at little more than demonstrating the evil intent and activity of the American military and government in Vietnam. Coming out in 1974 just after the end of American military involvement in Vietnam, *Hearts and Minds*, which earned an Academy Award as best documentary, clearly played to liberal sympathies about the war, tending to romanticize the Vietnamese while demonizing the Americans.

These efforts were followed in the 1980s by the overlong *The Ten Thousand Day War* (1980) and Stanley Karnow's *Vietnam: A Television History* (1983). Each of these is a narrative history of America's involvement in Vietnam from a decidedly liberal perspective. And each suggests that the outcome of the war was decided long before the signing of the Paris Peace Agreement in 1973.

Television's Vietnam: The Real Story (1985) and *Television's Vietnam: The Impact of Media* (1986) attempt to correct the liberal bias of these documentaries, especially the "myths" of communist invincibility and the objectivity of media coverage of the Vietnam War.

However, these documentaries do not deal specifically with the life of the combat soldier in Vietnam. Two documentaries which attempt to present a realistic account of infantry combat in Vietnam are *The Anderson Platoon* (1967), which follows an army platoon into combat, and *A Face of War* (1967), which records the activities of a Marine company over a three-month period.

The final category of Vietnam film is the revenge film, in which a group of men, usually veterans, embarks on a mission to Southeast Asia in an attempt to right some wrong—especially to rescue some MIAs—and so bring a sense of closure to the war. This ideology is nowhere better articulated than in Sylvester Stallone's *Rambo: First Blood Part II* (1985), when Stallone, as the title character and before accepting a risky assignment from his former commanding officer in Vietnam, asks: "Sir, do we get to win this time?"

Other films in the category and embracing essentially the same ideology are Chuck Norris's *Braddock: Missing in Action* (1984), *Missing in Action 2—The Beginning* (1985), and *Braddock: Missing in Action III* (1988); and *Uncommon Valor* (1983). These films will probably continue to be popular as long as the issues surrounding POWs and MIAs in Vietnam remain unresolved.

However, it is possible that the future of the Vietnam film lies in the direction suggested by Oliver Stone's *Heaven & Earth*; that is, the story of the impact of the Vietnam War on the Vietnamese as well as on the Americans.

Bibliography

Adair, Gilbert. *Vietnam on Film: From* The Green Berets *to* Apocalypse Now. New York: Proteus, 1981.

Peter Katopes

Vigilante Fiction. Tales of rogues who operate outside the confines of society's legal systems in order to extract terrible vengeance against their enemies go back to the dawn of fiction. The modern vigilante genre (also sometimes called "action-adventure writing" and "men's action fiction") began with publication of *The Executioner* (1969), a paperback novel that established the conventions of the genre. Vigilante fiction employs explicit, relentless violence as its trademark. The heroes, almost exclusively male, are driven by a society seen to coddle criminals and allow evil to thrive because of a judiciary mired in technicalities. Taking the law into their own hands, these self-appointed avengers mete out merciless punishments to wrongdoers. Justice is swift, uncompromising, and bloody. Such fiction is a strong component of present-day American literature.

Vigilantes are loners; because of their frustration with the law, they are frequently fugitives (although some police officers secretly admire both their methods and their results and quietly assist them when they can). They live in a shadowy world of violence, pursuit, and escape. Curiously, many of these series have an almost puritanical streak running through their plots; the heroes eschew relationships, and sex is downplayed. A vigilante lives only for the apprehension and destruction of those who violate his strict moral codes.

The Executioner, featuring vigilante Mack Bolan, was the first offering in what became a vastly popular series, the creation of writer Don Pendleton. Its publisher, Pinnacle

Books, correctly sensed the potential audience for vigilante fiction and engaged a number of additional authors to put out new titles in this burgeoning market. Pinnacle series like *The Assassin, The Butcher, The Death Merchant, The Destroyer, The Outrider, The Penetrator, The Protector,* and *The Terminator* (this last no relation to the films starring Arnold Schwarzenegger) flooded paperback racks everywhere.

The success of the early *Executioner* and its imitators began to slow by the 1980s when Pinnacle and its competitors had reached their circulation peaks. By early 1995, over 300 separate *Executioner* novels had been marketed. Although action-adventure fiction no longer attracts as large an audience as it once did, it remains a strong influence on paperback profits. Most publishers assume an overwhelmingly masculine audience and cater to it accordingly. The popular and media attention to militia groups at present promises that vigilante fiction will continue to draw readers.

Bibliography

Drew, Bernard A. *Action Series and Sequels: A Bibliography of Espionage, Vigilante, and Soldier-of-Fortune Novels.* New York: Garland, 1988.

Hoppenstand, Gary. "Justified Bloodshed: Robert Montgomery Bird's *Nick of the Woods* and the Origins of the Vigilante Hero in American Literature and Culture." *Journal of American Culture* 15.2 (1992): 51-61.

William H. Young

Village People, The (1977-), the costumed six-man camp disco group that exerted considerable influence on American lifestyle, was formed in 1977 by French producers Jacques Morali and Henri Belolo in New York City. The group signed with Casablanca in 1977, and projected an image that was originally intended to capitalize on gay community stereotypes. However, at the height of the 1970s disco craze, they became accepted by the masses. While wearing costumes which represented a stereotypical gay club style, the group performed a series of dance-floor anthems, written by Morali, which celebrated male bonding. The original members and costumes were Victor Willis, the cop; Randy Jones, the cowboy; David Hodo, the construction worker; Felipe Rose, the Native American; Glenn Hughes, the biker; and Alexander Briley, the GI. In the late 1970s, two of the original six members were replaced: Victor Willis was replaced by Ray Simpson, brother of Valerie Simpson of Ashford and Simpson, and Randy Jones was replaced by Jeff Olson.

The Village People did not perform with a band, instead using backing tapes. For a brief period, the group experienced success on the pop charts, with "Macho Man" ranking in the Top 40 in 1978; "Y.M.C.A." at No. 2 on the *Billboard* pop chart in 1978; and "In the Navy" at No. 3 early in 1979. Other Village People releases include "Go West" in May 1979, and "Ready for the 80's" in November 1979. The success of the group during the late 1970s prompted the production of the movie *Can't Stop the Music* in 1980, directed by Nancy Walker, in which the Village People starred. The waning popularity of disco, however, contributed to the failure of the movie, and consequently the failure of the Village People. To combat their declining popularity, the group switched to a romantic style and look for their 1981 New Wave album *Renaissance*. The change, however, did not help the group's bid for continued success, and the group disbanded in the mid-1980s.

Following the repopularization of dance music by Michael Jackson and other musicians, and the late 1980s disco revivals, the Village People reunited in 1987. In 1988 a *Greatest Hits* album was released, and in the early 1990s the group toured clubs, colleges, and festivals throughout North America and Europe. In 1993, they toured Germany. It was during the early 1990s that the Village People had a higher profile than at any time since the late 1970s.

Jacques Morali died of AIDS in December of 1991. The Village People are lauded as "one of the first instances of gay culture reaching mainstream America" during the "pre-AIDS sexual liberation." The group has participated in benefit events for AIDS awareness.

Bibliography

Hochman, Steve. "Can't Stop...the Village People?" *Los Angeles Times* 24 Dec. 1993: F1.

Larkin, Colin, ed. *Guinness Encyclopedia of Popular Music.* Chester: New England, 1992.

Nite, Norm N., and Charles Crespo, eds. *Rock On: The Illustrated Encyclopedia of Rock and Roll: The Video Revolution, 1978-Present.* Vol. 3. New York: Harper, 1985.

Passy, Charles. "They Won't Stop the Music: The Village People Are Back for an Encore." *Chicago Tribune* 22 Aug. 1994: 5.1.

Lynnea Chapman King

Virginian, The (1902), one of the most influential novels on the American West, was written by Owen Wister (1860-1938), the son of a prominent Pennsylvania family, who first traveled west for health reasons. After writing successful short stories and essays based on his experiences in Wyoming cattle country, Wister published *The Virginian: A Horseman of the Plains*, the novel for which he is primarily remembered and the prototype of the popular Western.

An immediate and enduring best-seller, *The Virginian's* historical narrative fictionalizes the West in romantic and often elegiac terms, and creates the cowboy-hero for all time. The story's protagonist, known only as the Virginian, is a natural aristocrat, whose laconic manner and powerful moral character are proven by his famous phrase, "When you call me that, *smile.*" Wister's archetypal cowboy is characterized by masculine grace and roguish humor. He neither enjoys nor evades necessary violence, and is distinguished by decisive action and unswerving instinct, as when he must confront and ultimately gun down the local scoundrel. His chivalric nature is displayed in his courtship of the schoolmistress, whom he marries at novel's end.

The Virginian has been dramatized on stage and screen numerous times. The most famous film version was released in 1929 and starred Gary Cooper. On television, *The Virginian: The Men from Shiloh,* starring James Drury as the Virginian, ran for nine years on NBC (1962-71). The novel also provided creative fodder for a succession of popular Western stories, most notably Jack Schaefer's 1949 novel *Shane*.

Bibliography

Cawelti, John. *Adventure, Mystery, and Romance: Formula Stories as Art and Popular Culture.* Chicago: U of Chicago P, 1976.

——. *The Six-Gun Mystique.* 2d ed. Bowling Green, OH: Bowling Green State U Popular P, 1984.

Payne, Darwin. *Owen Wister: Chronicler of the West.* Dallas: Southern Methodist UP, 1985.

Tomkins, Jane. *West of Everything: The Inner Life of Westerns.* New York: Oxford UP, 1992.

L. Fischman

Voodoo (Verdaun) is a religion created by a combination of Catholicism and various African religions which were brought to Haiti (where it is known as Verdaun) along with slaves beginning in the early 16th century. Over time, this system of beliefs spread throughout the Caribbean region. In Cuba, it is known as Santeria; in Jamaica, as Obeah; in the southern U.S., as Voodoo. Although this system has many complex facets, its basic tenet is the belief in the susceptibility of humans to possession by deities that are a fusion of African gods and Catholic saints. The rituals of Voodoo serve to call up a particular deity to render assistance, or to give the worshiper special insight. This is to be accomplished by performing elaborate ceremonies involving herbs, potions, and mystic symbols, or by participating in a rigorous dance to primitive drum rhythms, causing the worshiper to become possessed by the music and thus by the "loa"—the spiritual force of the deity in question. Thus, through ritual, Voodoo believers directly and physically commune with their gods, in a sense making them temporary saints and empowering them with cosmic knowledge and the ability to influence the world in superhuman ways. Voodoo is an ever-present and growing cult or practice.

Although contemporary novels and films have villainized Voodoo practices as evil and "Satanic," writers such as Zora Neale Hurston have presented Voodoo as a rich source of cultural heritage, one that speaks particularly strongly to women. In Hurston's stories about Voodoo, women, struggling under oppressive social handicaps, try to gain dignity and power by using their skills to call down the powers of the heavens and allow their bodies to become shrines, making themselves, literally, saints.

Bibliography

Deren, Maya. *Divine Horsemen: Voodoo Gods of Haiti.* New York: Chelsea House, 1970.

Hurston, Zora Neale. *Mules and Men.* Philadelphia: Lippincott, 1935.

Curtis Shumaker

Voyage to the Bottom of the Sea (1964-1968), Irwin Allen's TV series starring Richard Basehart, began as good science fiction then, according to critics, plummeted to the depths of tackiness. In 110 episodes, the crew of the supersub *Seaview* combated threats to world peace from foreign governments and space aliens. Villains in the series—a takeoff from Allen's 1961 film of the same title—ranged from earthquakes, tidal waves, reborn Nazis, globular masses, and sinister toys and clowns, all of which tried in turn, from week to week, to take over the sub and, by extension, the world.

Voyage differed from other shows that premiered in 1964 in one significant way: it dealt, albeit through guise, with threats to the American Way in a manner that had parallels to the ongoing Cold War era. With Sputnik, the Bay of Pigs, the Cuban Missile Crisis in the recent past, and other communist perils seemingly facing the United States from every angle, *Voyage* told Americans that if anything was to save their nation it would be a strong, technologically-superior defense. Hence it was the mission of the *Seaview* to assess and counter the most arcane and unlikely threats to the United States as could be devised by any foe, human or extraterrestrial.

Voyage also was a commentary on the role and state of technology in human affairs. In the minds of its producers, writers, and viewers was the present-day arms race and the marvel of nuclear propulsion. In 1959, the U.S. Navy had brought out its first nuclear-powered ballistic missile submarine. By the early '60s both the U.S. and the Soviet Union were building similar vessels at an alarming rate. The glass-nosed *Seaview* was the nuclear-powered submarine *par excellence.* It dove deeper and traveled faster than any other sub in the world, and it was equipped with a diving bell, a mini-sub and a flying sub. When matched up against the sinister forces of the earth and outer space, *Seaview* became engaged in undersea dramas of galactic proportions.

Bibliography

Brooks, Tim, and Earle Marsh. *The Complete Directory to Prime Time Network TV Shows, 1946-Present.* 3d ed. New York: Ballantine, 1985.

Javna, John. *The Best of Science Fiction TV.* New York: Harmony, 1987.

"Television." *Time Magazine* 25 Sept. 1964.

Jeffrey M. Brumley

W

Wagon Train (1956-1965), one of the more successful TV series, was not a conventional TV Western series but a dramatic anthology that happened to be set in the 19th-century American West. The series combined guest stars with a cast of regulars to relate the stories of various members of the caravan and how and why they were heading west. Focusing mainly on the week's guest, most plots utilized the wagonmaster and his crew as commentators on the action or as continuity devices. During its heyday it was almost unexcelled as Western-centered drama.

Inspired by John Ford's epic film *Wagonmaster* (1950) and given authenticity by the supervision of western historian and novelist Dwight B. Newton, this series had a simple, loose formula. The regulars acted as protectors and counselors to the traveling party as they fought outlaws, hostile Indians, and the extremes of nature, often stepping aside and allowing the traumas and complications affecting the passengers to carry the episodes. This permitted scriptwriters a wide range of plots dealing with character development and kept the program consistently sophisticated and engrossing.

Wagon Train's enduring success rested largely on the capable shoulders of its regular cast members. Ward Bond as Major Seth Adams, during the first three and one-half seasons, and John McIntire as wagonmaster Chris Hale during the remaining four and one half, created strong, believable, and intensely likable characters.

The show took a year to catch on with viewers but was rated No. 2 by Nielsen during the next three seasons. *Wagon Train* finally replaced *Gunsmoke* as America's most popular television series in 1961-62. The series slipped to 25th the following year, however, and continued to slip in the ratings. During the seventh season (1963-64) the show utilized a 90-minute format (following the pattern of *The Virginian*), but this failed to attract new viewers. Although it remained on the air until 1965, *Wagon Train* never reached its former popularity.

Bibliography

Brooks, Tim, and Earle Marsh. *The Complete Directory to Prime Time Network and Cable TV Shows, 1946-Present.* New York: Ballantine, 1995.

West, Richard. *Television Westerns: Major and Minor Series, 1946-1978.* Jefferson: McFarland, 1987.

Yoggy, Gary A. *Riding the Video Range: The Rise and Fall of the Western on Television.* Jefferson: McFarland, 1987.

Gary A. Yoggy

Walker, Aaron "T-Bone" (1910-1975), the father of modern blues, was born in Linden, TX, moving to Dallas by 1912. Walker's stepfather and uncles all played a variety of stringed instruments, and Walker remembers his mother as an accomplished guitar player as well. His first instrument was the banjo, but by the time he was in high school Walker was learning to play the guitar along with other stringed instruments such as the mandolin, violin, and ukulele. His most famous teacher was Blind Lemon Jefferson (see entry), himself a seminal figure in the history of the blues, and a friend of the Walker family. His other crucial influence of this era was Lonnie Johnson, another extraordinary musician, who was comfortable playing the down-home country blues of Robert Johnson and the uptown jazz of Duke Ellington.

In 1929 Walker cut his first sides, *Trinity River Blues* and *Wichita Falls Blues*, for Columbia Records as "Oak Cliff T-Bone," a reference to the part of Dallas from which he hailed. By 1933, he had drifted to Oklahoma City, where he met Chuck Richardson, under whose influence Walker's style would take a turn toward the future, and began playing with the Lawson-Brooks big band based out of Dallas. In this "territory band," largely cut off from the influence of the commercial music industry, the musicians were free to experiment with an open, improvisational style. As was true of all jazz at this time, the guitar was relegated to the rhythm section, but in the context of this looser, less structured form of jazz, the guitar soon surfaced as a solo instrument, becoming increasingly prominent as it was amplified. It was in this particular jazz context that T-Bone Walker began to adapt his acoustic, country blues playing to what would become the basis for modern blues. Thus, Walker is generally considered to be the first musician to play an electric guitar, though Charlie Christian has also laid claim to that honor. More importantly, Walker was the first to capitalize on the possibilities that big band jazz created for the electric guitar and translate them to the blues idiom.

By 1940 when Walker joined Les Hite's band in Los Angeles, he and his amplified guitar were attracting a following. Interestingly, however, Hite hired Walker as his featured singer. That year in New York Walker recorded his famous "T-Bone Blues" with Hite's band, leaving Frank Pasly to provide the electric guitar accompaniment. From there his career took off and, with it, his guitar playing. In 1942 he recorded his best-known song, "Stormy Monday Blues," which has become a standard. No longer only famous for his singing, Walker recorded in the mid-1940s a series of records for the Black and White label, with a variety of bands, which came to define electric blues guitar. By 1954, however, Walker had recorded his best and most innovative music, and for the rest of his life he refined the style that had made him famous, remaining popular on the blues circuit and making fine records until his death.

A complex amalgam of deep country blues, "swinging" jazz, and the incipient blues crooning of Leroy Carr, Walker's music incorporated nearly every major development of vernacular African-American music in the first half of the 20th century. While his singing was a formative influence on Bobby "Blue" Bland, among others, it was his guitar playing that has secured him his fame. Eschewing chords, except for occasional and powerful emotional emphasis, Walker's vaunted "single-string" blues technique was shot through with fluid, lyrical jazz-like runs. His playing linked country to urban blues, blues to jazz, and was the model for almost every blues guitarist who came after him. B. B. King, Freddie King, Clarence "Gatemouth" Brown, Albert Collins, Buddy Guy, Eric Clapton, Stevie Ray Vaughan, and Robert Cray are among the legions who have followed in his footsteps. An accomplished showman, Walker played the guitar perpendicular from his body and sometimes even from behind his head, often descending into a full drop-down split in mid-note. Chuck Berry's "duckwalk" and Jimi Hendrix's pyrotechnics find their origin in Walker. He died of bronchial pneumonia, the most influential blues guitar player of them all.

Bibliography

Dance, Helen Oakley. *Stormy Monday: The T-Bone Walker Story*. Baton Rouge: Louisiana State UP, 1987.

Sallis, James. *The Guitar Players: One Instrument and Its Masters*. New York: Morrow, 1982.

Welding, Pete, and Toby Byron, eds. *Bluesland: Portraits of Twelve Major American Blues Masters*. New York: Dutton, 1991.

Timothy L. Parrish

Walking is the most significant growth area in American culture in terms of exercise, physical activity, and wellness. It has taken over from jogging and tennis as a boom "get-in-shape" fad in American society. Power walking—easily recognized with its full stride and vigorous arm action—is seen to be nearly as effective for cardio-respiratory efficiency as gentle running. There is also the bonus that the walking action avoids the pounding action that can create recurring lower leg injuries for the runner.

Walking, or pedestrianism as it was called, was a major sport in the 19th century. Champion pedestrians were accorded the status of folk heroes. They earned large amounts of money and professional contests, frequently lasting many hours (even days), attracted huge crowds of paying spectators. A richly informative source on pedestrianism is Walter Thom's classic biography of the noted Scottish pedestrian Captain Barclay. In the early 19th century, he became a household name by walking 1,000 miles in 1,000 consecutive hours.

Edward Payton Weston was America's walking champion during the late 19th century, when the sport of pedestrianism was in its heyday. In one contest he walked 400 miles in just under five days and frequently beat the world's top walkers in prize contests. Weston passionately believed in the healthiness of walking and at the age of 74 walked 1,500 miles from New York City to Minneapolis in 60 days.

In the 1950s, long distance walking experienced a renaissance with a series of marathon feats in Great Britain. The *Guinness Book of Records* lists a whole range of walking records. Arguably the most physically demanding may be the 94-day odyssey (1,350 miles) by Sir Randolph Fiennes and Michael Stroud in their 1992-93 unsupported trek across Antarctica.

Race walking was first an Olympic sport in 1906. The distances for Olympic events are 20 kilometers and 50 kilometers. There are world records for 20 miles, 30 miles, 20, 30 and 50 kilometers, and two hours.

The most successful modern American race walker has been P. O. Laird, with 65 USA national titles in the period 1958-76. Ann Transon, an American, beginning in 1991, has established world record marks at distances from 50 kilometers to 100 miles. David Wallechinsky gives full placings (one to eight) of the two race walks (20 and 50 kilometers) on the Olympic program since 1956. National successes by countries such as Mexico, Germany, the former USSR, and Italy, reflect the fact that these countries have well-developed programs of race walking.

Bibliography

Arlott, J., ed. *The Oxford Companion to World Sports and Games*. London: Oxford UP, 1975.

Kashiwa, A. *Fitness Walking for Women*. New York: Putnam, 1987.

Martin, R. *Advanced Race Walking*. Seattle: Technique Publications, 1987.

Matthews, P., ed. *The Guinness Book of Records*. New York: Guinness, 1993.

Thom, W. *Pedestrianism or an Account of the Performances of Celebrated Pedestrians During the Last Century*. Aberdeen: Brown & Frost, 1813.

Wallechinsky, D. *The Complete Book of the Olympics*. Boston: Little, Brown, 1991.

Scott A. G. M. Crawford

Walkman, The, is Sony Corporation's trademark name for the first portable stereo cassette playback and headphone combination designed for consumers. The first Walkman was produced by Sony in 1979, and it was introduced to the U.S. in 1980. The design has been copied by numerous manufacturers, and different configurations range from a simple monophonic player to professional grade stereo record-playback machines with AM-FM stereo radio receivers and sophisticated noise reduction and frequency equalization controls. Use of such devices has changed the listening habits of a large segment of America.

Bibliography

Givens, Ron. "Music to Our Ears." *Newsweek* 7 Aug. 1989: 68.

Klein, Larry. "Audio Update: Happy 10th Anniversary, Sony Walkman!" *Radio-Electronics* Oct. 1989: 72-73.

Nool, Mark A. "The Walkman Cometh." *Christianity Today* 6 Feb. 1987: 22-23.

Piccoli, Sean. "Light 10 Candles for the Walkman." *Insight* 24 July 1989: 58-59.

Kenneth M. Nagelberg

See also
Transistor Radio

Wallace, Irving (1916-1990), one of America's more successful and influential popular novelists, born in Chicago, began his versatile career as a freelance magazine writer in 1931. He went on to become an accomplished screenwriter, playwright, editor, political reporter, and most importantly,

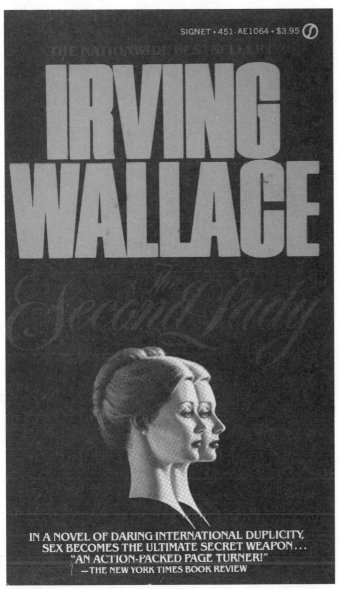

IN A NOVEL OF DARING INTERNATIONAL DUPLICITY,
SEX BECOMES THE ULTIMATE SECRET WEAPON...
"AN ACTION-PACKED PAGE TURNER!"
—THE NEW YORK TIMES BOOK REVIEW

popular novelist of considerable productivity and stature. Wallace's standard fictional ploy is to build a complex and engaging story around a news event or popular institution. Hence, he wrote *The Chapman Report* (1960) as a fictionalized enactment of the revelations of the Kinsey report on adult sexuality; *The Prize* (1962), about the Nobel Prize; *The Man* (1964), which imagines an African-American president; and *The Word* (1972), about a set of fictional testaments purported to be written by Jesus' brother James.

Wallace's novels have almost consistently catapulted to the top of the consumer charts; some, like *The Word* and *The Miracle* (1984), another novel with a religious subject matter that focuses on the sightings of the Virgin at Lourdes, have appealed to an international readership. Others, like *The Fan Club* (1974), about a group of disgruntled men who kidnap a film star to indulge their fantasies, are aimed at a more basic audience, but whatever the targeted readership, Wallace's books are avidly consumed.

In addition to his fiction, Wallace produced a lucrative line of popular list books and reference guides, the "People's Almanac" series, jointly with his son, writer David Wal-

lechinsky, and daughter, Amy Wallace. Sometimes described as "trivia" collections, though they catalogue interesting and widely solicited information about topics that engage people, the almanacs alone would have solidified Wallace's position as an important popular writer.

As a scriptwriter, Wallace had his hand in a number of entertaining motion pictures, including *The West Point Story* (1950), *Meet Me at the Fair* (1953), *Split Second* (1953), *Bad for Each Other* (with Horace McCoy, 1954), *The Burning Hills* (1956), and others.

Bibliography

Leverence, John. *Irving Wallace: A Writer's Profile*. Bowling Green, OH: Bowling Green State U Popular P, 1974.
"Obituaries: Wallace, Irving." *Current Biography* Sept. 1990: 61-62.

Liahna Babener

Wallcoverings. Walls and wallcoverings, though not consistently as important in the United States as perhaps in other countries, have always served the double function of (1) holding things in a designated space and of barring others out, of shaping and defining territory and of providing protection of that territory, and (2) of allowing for the opportunity of beautifying those barriers, of furnishing space for conspicuous display of messages and other forms of communication. Cave walls gave opportunity for earliest humankind to etch and paint pictures of the physical world around them and of their reactions to such phenomena. In so doing they revealed and defined humankind's culture. Petroglyphs and later hieroglyphics are indispensable today for our knowledge of ancient culture. The opportunities for walls and wallcoverings to reveal a culture have increased through the years as they have become more varied and more sophisticated. Wallcoverings are especially common today and afford great opportunities for self-expression and commercial exploitation. Sherwin-Williams, for example, has 42,000 designs of wallpaper.

With the development of new forms of display that can be attached to walls, ceilings, and floors, people have found means to cover those spaces with other materials that serve the double function of keeping the weather out (or in) and of displaying one's tastes and desires in aesthetic and commercial statements. Walls and wallcoverings have been made to match the other items furnishing a room and thus to enhance them. One of the commonest coverings of walls has been wallpaper.

Wallpapers can be traced from French printers in the late medieval period who made simple religious illustrations from wood blocks and used them as decorative papers. Since then, people of most countries have expressed their cultures in their wallpapers and other coverings. They have used various available materials—paint, plaster, cloth, tapestries, wainscoting (wood), paper, stone, raw cement, and different kinds of windows and wall configurations. As tastes about domestic environments have changed, so have feelings about what is to be put on walls. Wallpaper has generally been a favorite, especially among Americans. According to *The American Builder and Journal of Art* of the 19th century (March 1869), "upon the whole, for convenience ordinarily, and as a matter of taste extraordinarily, we find that papering obtains among all classes." Through the years since, wallpaper has held its position as preferred by most Americans, though at times paint and other materials have been popular.

Walls and wallcoverings are, in effect, three dimensional. Their height and width have profound psychological effect on people viewing them, especially over extended periods of time. They may increase or lessen the intensity of claustrophobia or agoraphobia. To the susceptible mind walls and their coverings can symbolize the world and society. Perhaps the finest example is the short story "The Yellow Wallpaper," by Charlotte Perkins Gilman (1892). It represents the whole sexual world of America's Gilded Age. A young mother, because she is feeling depressed, is exiled to a second-story room whose walls are covered with yellow paper in which figures interact with physical objects. After feeling the figures and walls closing in on her, she goes mad. Contemporary views about women's sexual and social roles in society overwhelm her.

Height of ceilings also has intense psychological effects. Cathedral ceilings, for example, induce the feelings of awe and grandeur; low ceilings press us down. Configurations of walls and presence or absence and shape of windows add to the feelings about rooms.

Walls and wallcoverings have a third dimension when objects with outward thrust are hung on them. These objects add new voices to those already being transmitted by the walls and wallcoverings. Outdoor scenes in pictures bring in the outer world, pictures of indoor scenes intensify the indoor feeling and keep the outside at bay. Pictures of family and community, stern portraits of ancestors act, each in its own way, to exert firm control of ways of family development. Works of art hung on walls act in subtle ways to intensify the atmosphere and feeling. Sometimes they become dynamic parts. For example, filmmaker Alfred Hitchcock used all kinds of pictures on the walls of the setting for his movies, especially *Psycho* (1960), to intensify feeling or meaning. Graffiti of all kinds—sometimes in the form of photographs and paintings—speak all kinds of language. For example, over the men's commode in a Toledo restaurant is the large picture of an elderly stern woman obviously cautioning users not to dawdle. The conversations the users of this facility have with the picture suggest that the picture is more than inanimate.

Walls and wallcoverings change constantly as developing technologies provide new materials, and new designs and as they provide new materials for furnishing rooms. In 19th-century America the urge to change wallpaper was almost frantic. According to an article in *Scientific American* (July 24, 1880), "old patterns are nowadays entirely unsalable, and the rule is that each year's patterns must be entirely new and distinct from those of the preceding season." Patterns change also as people's tastes and desires alter with the new opportunities to express them. New possibilities give people new areas of development in likes and dislikes, new esthetics and new languages to express. Walls speak, wall-coverings speak, objects hung on walls speak. A whole chorus of individual and collective voices and languages result, which, if not harmonized, resonate like a chorus from the biblical Tower of Babel.

Art historian Alan Gowans properly insists that every created object in a culture contains a microcosm of that culture and need only to be read correctly to reveal the culture from which it comes. The objects that cover our walls provide an encyclopedia of reflections of that culture if we can only read them. During the American Great Depression, for example, thousands of cabins in the rural South and in urban ghettoes had their walls covered with the colored comic pages from Sunday newspapers. Such comic pages served three purposes. They kept out the weather, they hid the ugly walls of the rooms, and brought in some color. But more important, they prompted a touch of laughter and amusement to lighten the existence of the people in the almost unbearable poverty, testing their souls and the democracy around them.

Bibliography
Entwistle, E. A. *A Literary History of Wallpaper.* London: Batsford, 1960.
Greysmith, Brenda. *Wallpaper.* New York: Macmillan, 1976.
Lynn, Catherine. *Wallpaper in America from the Seventeenth Century to World War I.* New York: Norton, 1980.
Phillips, Barty. *Fabrics and Wallpaper: Sources, Design, and Inspiration.* Boston: Little, Brown, 1991.
Teynac, Françoise, et al. *Wallpaper: A History.* New York: Rizzoli, 1982.

Ray B. Browne

Waller, **Robert James** (1939-), was until 1992 known only regionally as an essayist, musician, and photographer in Iowa, where he was a professor of economics at a state university. Though his regional pieces, mainly reminiscences about life in a Midwest whose agrarian vestiges he celebrates, reveal a poetic sensibility and a keen sense of place, his sudden fame as the author of *The Bridges of Madison County* (1992) and two subsequent novels could not have been anticipated. *The Bridges of Madison County* is one of the most popular novels written in contemporary times; since its publication, it has remained a best-seller, a status augmented by the release of the 1995 film starring Meryl Streep and Clint Eastwood. The novel tells a simple but emotionally wrenching story about a farm wife, a woman who has suppressed her passionate nature beneath the quotidian chores of maintaining the family farm and raising two children, who has a brief but volcanic love affair with an itinerant photographer.

Capitalizing on the success of his first novel, Waller has published two others, *Slow Waltz in Cedar Bend* (1993), another "tastefully erotic" but thwarted love story, and *Border Music* (1995), a road novel about a rancher plagued by disturbing memories of his Vietnam experience, and an exotic dancer whose love offers him temporary asylum from his emotional pain.

Bibliography
Gleick, Elizabeth. "Mr. Bridge." *People* 8 Nov. 1993: 50-53.

"Waller, Robert James." *Current Biography* May 1994: 54-57.

Liahna Babener

Waller, Thomas Wright ("Fats") (1904-1943), one of popular music's immortals, was born in New York City and died of pneumonia in Kansas City. Fats spent most of his life in big cities—New York, Chicago, Hollywood. While Kansas City had the great blues tradition Fats loved and had produced the Basie Band, Fats preferred to spend his time in bigger areas, as befit his size. His impact on jazz was immense.

His father was a Baptist preacher in Harlem, and he ran open air services at which Fats played a reed organ. Throughout his life, in fact, Fats preferred the organ to the piano, which he learned to play at the public school. At 15, he played the organ at Lincoln Theater on 135th Street.

Waller was serious about music and studied at Juilliard. Although he always remained a consummate showman, he became increasingly interested in longer forms and "more serious" music as he grew older. In fact, he extended the jazz repertoire considerably over the years, usually recording works of exquisite beauty to accompany his "novelty" numbers.

In the 1920s, Waller gained a reputation as a fine blues accompanist while writing songs that other groups recorded, such as the classic "Squeeze Me." In 1923, he made his broadcast debut on a Newark, NJ, station and began a successful career. Soon he was on a New York station. At the same time, he continued playing organ at New York theaters.

In 1927, the Fletcher Henderson Band recorded a number of his songs, including "Honey Suckle Rose," "Black and Blue," and "Ain't Misbehavin'." In addition, he began yet another phase of his career, composing Broadway shows. *Hot Chocolates* was a big hit, and throughout the remainder of his life, he continued to compose for Broadway and Hollywood.

On April 27, 1928, he made his Carnegie Hall debut as a soloist with a classical orchestra. He continued to make such appearances in the United States and Europe. Like Duke Ellington, he enjoyed the smaller forms but longed to extend his music over longer forms.

In the mid-1930s, Waller kept busy leading his own small band, writing Hollywood musicals, appearing in films, hosting his radio program, and recording. In 1938-39, he went on a European tour, hastily ended by the onset of World War II. In 1939, however, he did reach one of his long-term goals through composing the London Suite.

In 1943, he continued his frantic pace, composing for and starring in the film *Stormy Weather*, and composing the music for the stage musical *Early to Bed*. He contracted pneumonia and died en route to Hollywood, worn out at forty. He had lived life in a large way as befitted his nickname. His love of food and drink were legendary, as was his love for life. In return, he was one of the few true jazz musicians to be popular with a mass audience and loved by them so openly.

Bibliography

Collier, Lincoln. *The Making of Jazz*. Boston: Houghton Mifflin, 1978.

Feather, Leonard. *Encyclopedia of Jazz*. New York: Da Capo, 1984.

Gammond, Peter. *Oxford Companion to Popular Music*. New York: Oxford UP, 1991.

Gridley, Mark. *Jazz Styles*. Englewood Cliffs: Prentice-Hall, 1994.

Shipton, Alyn. *Fats Waller: His Life and Times*. New York: Universe, 1988.

Frank A. Salamone

Walt Disney Television (1954-). Walt Disney (1901-1966), who defined animation and the theme park concept, also pioneered American television, lending his name to several series, including *Disneyland, Walt Disney Presents*, and *Wonderful World of Color*. Beginning with *Disneyland*, Walt Disney's television shows were a staple of American broadcasting for nearly 30 years, appearing at one time or another on ABC, NBC, and CBS. They serve as striking examples of the ways in which television could be used for promotional purposes. Further, they made the name Disney one of the most familiar in American television and set the stage for new directions in family programming in the United States and the world.

Walt Disney's entrance into television was not always assured. When television was first unveiled, Disney rejected the new medium, saying that people prefer the communal experience of a movie theater. However, he eventually changed his mind, and by the 1950s, when others in film shunned television as a threat to the industry, Disney voiced a different belief: that movie makers ought to use television to their own advantage. Aware of the falling market for his cartoons in movie theaters, Disney was receptive to the professional possibilities that television offered him and agreed to produce a television special for NBC. Broadcast on Christmas Day, 1950, and featuring a variety show format, the show, titled *One Hour in Wonderland,* functioned as Disney's television debut and helped to promote his upcoming feature film, *Alice in Wonderland*. Audiences responded favorably to the show, and Disney came through with a second Christmas special, *Walt Disney Christmas Show*, the following year. These experiences enabled Disney to approach television positively and make an important observation: through television, he could reach the same audience that went to see his movies.

Recognizing the common audience that movies and television shared, Disney set out to capitalize on television by using it for his own purposes. For example, in the early 1950s, as television was taking hold in America, Disney was obsessed with the idea of establishing an innovative themed amusement park called Disneyland on a 160-acre orange grove in Anaheim, CA. The venture was expensive, and, after tapping every monetary source available, Disney still lacked adequate funds to get the project off the ground. Then he thought of television. Following his two successful one-hour Christmas specials, Disney was approached by the networks to produce a weekly television show but consistently declined. Although he was mildly interested in the creative opportunities that television offered, his thoughts were focused on Disneyland. With this in mind, he sent his brother and business partner Roy Disney to New York to present to network executives from NBC, CBS, and ABC his offer to produce a weekly television show for the network that would loan him the money that he needed to begin construction on Disneyland. ABC, the newest of the networks, was lagging behind in the ratings race and desperate for a hit show; therefore, it responded to Roy Disney's proposal. In his biography of Walt Disney titled *Walt Disney: An American Original*, Bob Thomas outlines the deal that was struck: Disney agreed to produce a weekly one-hour television show for ABC in exchange for a half-million-dollar investment in Disneyland; further, ABC agreed to become a 35 percent owner of Disneyland and guarantee loans of up to $4,500,000. According to the plan, the television show was to begin in October 1954 and Disneyland to open the following July.

All went according to schedule. On October 27, 1954, the show, titled *Disneyland*, first aired during its Wednesday evening time slot. Not only did Disney obtain the loan that he needed, but he also effectively used his show to promote his amusement park that was nearing completion. Each *Disneyland* television show focused on one of the four realms that comprised Disneyland—Fantasyland, Tomorrowland, Adventureland, or Frontierland—and served as a one-hour advertisement for the park. Thus, by the time Disneyland opened on July 17, 1955, Disney had already publicized it thoroughly on television. In addition, Disney orchestrated a live television special to capture in vivid detail the events of the park's opening day. *Disneyland* continued for four seasons on Wednesday evenings on ABC before moving, with the new name *Walt Disney Presents*, to Friday evenings; it later graced the Sunday lineup.

Along with financing and publicizing his $17 million theme park, Disney's television series promoted his movies. For example, a *Disneyland* television show called "Operation Undersea" described the technical challenges involved in the making of the film *Twenty Thousand Leagues under the Sea,* particularly its $200,000 climactic scene featuring a battle between a giant squid and the submariners. Dubbed by some critical industry executives as "The Long, Long Trailer," the show went on to win an Emmy award and stimulate interest in the soon-to-be-released film. When *Twenty Thousand Leagues under the Sea* opened in theaters on December 23, 1954, audiences were lined up to see Disney's $4.5 million extravaganza. The film, and its accompanying TV show, also paved the way for a Disneyland attraction, the Submarine Voyage, which opened on June 14, 1959.

The medium of television was perfectly suited to Walt Disney. In it, he was able to combine his studio's flair for producing educational films, live-action films, miniseries, and animation. Further, because he had a huge archive of films of every variety from previous years, he was able to construct an appealing television show at minimal cost and, later, rebroadcast shows. Finally, playing the role of the affable host, Disney became one of the most recognizable men in America; he was even nominated for an Emmy award in 1954 for the most outstanding new personality on television. Given this, his popular image enabled him to promote his other ventures, particularly his theme park and movies.

On at least one occasion, Walt Disney's attempt to use his television show to advertise a new Disneyland attraction had enormous cultural impact. Disney was interested in a space attraction for Disneyland's Tomorrowland and a related television show and mentioned the project to animator Ward Kimball. On March 9, 1955, the *Disneyland* television series ran a particularly influential show titled "Man in Space," the first of a three-part informational series on space travel. The show was developed by Kimball, who worked with Wernher von Braun, the chief of the Guided Missile Development Division at Redstone Arsenal in Huntsville, AL. By explaining the elements of space travel in a way Americans could understand and appreciate, "Man in Space" won a large audience and generated public interest in the space program. Even President Dwight D. Eisenhower watched the show and ordered a copy of it for Pentagon officials. Afterwards, the United States accelerated its space program by announcing plans for launching earth-circling satellites. Years later, space travel, as exemplified in Tomorrowland attractions and EPCOT exhibits, remains an important motif in Disney theme parks.

Another *Disneyland* episode prompted a national craze. On December 15, 1954, "Davy Crockett, Indian Fighter," the first one-hour episode of a Davy Crockett trilogy, aired on the *Disneyland* television show. The series met with overwhelming popularity, and Fess Parker, playing the title role, enjoyed instant stardom. An audience of baby-boom children embraced the figure of Davy Crockett, who attained heroic stature and whose theme song, "The Ballad of Davy Crockett" by George Bruns, held the top spot on the *Hit Parade* for 13 weeks and sold 10 million records. Character-related merchandise, the best-seller of which was the coonskin cap, stimulated $300 million in sales, making Davy Crockett a national phenomenon. Attempting to capitalize on the popularity of Davy Crockett, the Disney studio compiled footage from the three *Disneyland* television shows to create a feature film, *Davy Crockett, King of the Wild Frontier* (1955), and a sequel, *Davy Crockett and the River Pirates* (1956). Disney had once again used television to stimulate movie and merchandising profits, and, even today, the effects of television's popularization of Davy Crockett continue: Davy Crockett's presence remains strong in the Disney theme parks' Frontierland realm, and the Alamo, where the Davy Crockett trilogy's climactic scene takes place, reigns as the top tourist attraction in the state of Texas.

Walt Disney's television series also made important contributions to family entertainment. Disney's credo was to give the public what it wanted, which he interpreted as wholesome, variety programming. Thus, Disney's television series consisted of classic Disney fare—cartoons, nature films, behind-the-scenes accounts of moviemaking, miniseries, live-action adventures, comedies, and dramas—and proved to be a success for ABC until Disney, who sensed that his audience would respond favorably to color programming, in 1961 moved his show to NBC, which had made a greater commitment to color telecasting. The new show, called *Walt Disney's Wonderful World of Color*, was a mainstay of Sunday evening television throughout the 1960s, offering such memorable programs as "Hans Brinker, or The Silver Skates," "The Prince and the Pauper," "Johnny Shiloh," "The Legend of Dick Turpin," and "Kilroy."

Walt Disney continued to host *Walt Disney's Wonderful World of Color* until he died on December 15, 1966, and the show aired the Sunday after his death marked a fitting tribute: In it, Disney described his plans for the future, the building of a Walt Disney World complex in Florida. After Walt Disney's death, his familiarity and loyal audience sustained additional network television series: *The Wonderful World of Disney* on NBC (1969-79), *Disney's Wonderful World* on NBC (1979-81), *Walt Disney* on CBS (1981-83), *The Disney Sunday Movie* on ABC (1986), *The Magical World of Disney* on NBC (1988-90), and *The Wonderful World of Disney* on NBC (1997-). For these last three, Walt Disney Co. chairman and CEO Michael Eisner has served as host.

Over the course of three decades, Walt Disney's television series graced the network lineups and provided entertainment for millions of Americans. These paved the way for a Disney-owned cable channel, the Disney Channel, which premiered on April 18, 1983, and reflected similar commitment to family programming. The Disney Company's embrace of television was fully realized in 1996, when the company completed its acquisition of Capital Cities/ABC, made up of the ABC Television Network, the ABC Radio Networks, interests in sports cable programming and other cable programming, and various newspapers and periodicals.

Bibliography

Holliss, Richard, and Brian Sibley. *The Disney Studio Story.* New York: Crown, 1988.

Jackson, Kathy Merlock. *Walt Disney: A Bio-Bibliography.* Westport: Greenwood, 1993.

King, Margaret J. "The Recycled Hero: Walt Disney's Davy Crockett." *Davy Crockett: The Man, the Legend, the Legacy, 1786-1986.* Ed. Michael A. Lofaro. Knoxville: U of Tennessee P, 1985.

Maltin, Leonard. *The Disney Films.* New York: Crown, 1984.

Miller, Diane Disney (as told to Pete Martin). *The Story of Walt Disney.* New York: Dell, 1956.

Smith, David R. "They're Following Our Script." *Future* May 1978: 54-63.

Thomas, Bob. *Walt Disney: An American Original.* New York: Pocket, 1976.

Kathy Merlock Jackson

Waltons, The (1972-1981). Feeling good, having time, enjoying a loving family—portraying these seemingly simple but often unattainable pleasures helped make *The Waltons* one of television's most popular and enduring family dramas.

In 1972, few people in the television industry gave *The Waltons* much chance for survival. Based on creator Earl Hamner's own childhood in Schuyler, VA, the series told of an extended family living together in the Blue Ridge mountains during the Depression. Father John Walton (Ralph Waite) ran a lumber mill with *his* father (Will Geer). Mother Olivia Walton (Michael Learned) ran a loving home for her in-laws, her husband, and their seven children (John, Jr., Ben, Jason, Mary Ellen, Erin, Jim-Bob, and Elizabeth). The story often focused on the point-of-view of teenaged John, Jr., known as John-Boy (Richard Thomas), a budding writer with a gift for observation and expression. The family frequently faced hard times—threats from outsiders, illness, fire, debt, death—but their loyalty and honesty held them together.

Such a sentimental premise seemed hopelessly backward in the early 1970s, when the counterculture was still in almost-full swing. Given the tenor of the times and *The Waltons'* hip competition—opposite *The Mod Squad* and *The Flip Wilson Show*—the series should have failed. Yet *The Waltons* finished its first season with a Top 20 Nielsen ranking and six Emmy awards, including Best Dramatic Actor (Thomas), Best Dramatic Actress (Learned), and Outstanding Drama Series. By the time the show left the air, it had spent five years in the Nielsen Top 20 and had paved the way for similar family dramas, notably *Little House on the Prairie, Family,* and *Eight Is Enough* (see Dramatic Family Genre). Three two-hour specials in 1982 also posted strong ratings. And more than ten years later, a huge audience watched *A Walton Thanksgiving Reunion* on November 21, 1993.

Bibliography

Brooks, Tim, and Earl Marsh. *The Complete Directory to Prime-Time Network TV Shows, 1946-Present.* 5th ed. New York: Ballantine, 1992.

"Cyclops." "Wholesome Sentiment in the Blue Ridge." *Life* 13 Oct. 1972: 73.

Hamner, Earl. "Coming Home to Walton's Mountain." *TV Guide* 20 Nov. 1993: 10-14.

Roiphe, Anne. "The Waltons." *New York Times Magazine* 18 Nov. 1973: 40+.

Kathleen Chamberlain

Wambaugh, Joseph (1937-), is an important contemporary author of police procedurals and other works in the mystery genre. The son of a police chief, Wambaugh moved with his family to California as a teenager. After service in the Marines, a job as a steelworker, and night school to get a degree in English, he joined the Los Angeles Police Department in 1960, where he served for 14 years. During that time he began to write short stories to describe what it was like for young policemen to come of age on the streets in the 1960s. Wambaugh's first novel, *The New Centurions* (1970), was a Book-of-the-Month Club selection and a best-seller; adapted for the movies, it prompted a deluge of police stories and television series.

While still a policeman, Wambaugh published another novel, *The Blue Knight* (1972), and a non-fiction novel, *The Onion Field* (1973), which realistically detailed the ways in which police work can change, corrupt, or destroy cops. *The Blue Knight* was the basis for an NBC miniseries in 1973 and a CBS weekly series in 1976-77. Wambaugh also served as a consultant for NBC's *Police Story* (1973-77).

Since retiring from the LAPD in 1974, Wambaugh has published nine novels, including *The Choirboys* (1975), *The Black Marble* (1978), *The Glitter Dome* (1981), and recently *Fugitive Nights* (1992), *Finnegan's Week* (1993), and *Floaters* (1996), along with several true crime works, notably *Echoes in the Darkness* (1987), and *The Blooding* (1989). Wambaugh's later writings continue to examine the damaging psychological impact of police work on sympathetic but fallible characters, but these works have a zany or grim humor that the earlier works lack.

Bibliography
Jeffrey, David K. *Midwest Quarterly* 1980.
Roberts, Steven V. *Esquire* Dec. 1973.
Van Dover, J. Kenneth. *Centurions, Knights, and Other Cops: The Police Novels of Joseph Wambaugh*. San Bernardino: Brownstone, 1995.
Zeigler, Robert E. *Clues* 1982.

David K. Jeffrey

See also
Police Procedural
True Crime Writing

War of the Worlds (1938), a sensational radio play written by Howard Koch, was broadcast October 30, 1938, on the CBS program *Mercury Theatre on the Air*, directed by Orson Welles and John Houseman. In 1937, Orson Welles had been an actor on the *March of Time* radio show, which dramatized news events because of the network requirement that all programming must be live, not recorded. This experience influenced the development of *War of the Worlds*. Presented in the form of radio news reports for the first half of the program, the performance simulated an alien invasion from Mars based on the H. G. Wells novel and introduced a new area of fear into American society.

Some 6 million Americans tuned late into the CBS program, with about one-sixth of the listeners—a million in all—believing the events of the broadcast were real. Hundreds in New York began to flee imaginary Martians even though the program had been clearly identified as a play at its opening. Switchboards of newspapers, stations, CBS, and police departments were swamped by callers seeking more information. People gathered in churches to pray, and a power outage that coincided with the broadcast panicked the citizens of Concrete, WA. One reason for its extraordinary impact was that the broadcast came shortly after radio had reported the month-long Munich crisis, foreshadowing World War II. Listeners had become so edgy, expecting radio reports of dire events, that even a Martian invasion seemed possible to many.

The Federal Communications Commission made regulatory noises, but decided that because no overt deception had been intended, no specific action against CBS was needed. It did adopt rules that the simulation of real news bulletins was forbidden unless clearly and often identified as fictional.

War of the Worlds focused awareness on the power of radio and the susceptibility of many in the audience. Radio was confirmed as an effective advertising medium, and Orson Welles (see entry) gained national attention that led to his film contract and *Citizen Kane*.

Bibliography
Cantril, Hadley, Hazel Gaudet, and Herta Herzog. *The Invasion from Mars: A Study in the Psychology of Panic*. Princeton: Princeton UP, 1940.
Lowery, Shearon, and Melvin L. DeFleur. *Milestones in Mass Communication Research: Media Effects*. New York: Longman, 1983.

Marvin R. Bensman

Warner Brothers Cartoons, one of the most seen and best loved cartoon series in the history of the medium, brought forth a myriad of cartoon characters whose popularity continues to grow. The characters have permeated American culture and are truly as omnipresent as any media creations can be. The cartoons' brash energy and "in-your-face" attitude distinguished them from their contemporaries and have endeared them to generations of fans.

When Walt Disney's distributor took control of his early character Oswald the Lucky Rabbit away from him, Disney animators Hugh Harman (1903-1982) and Rudolf Ising (1903-1992) left to form their own studio in hopes of winning the assignment. They were left stranded with a number of their Disney colleagues when the distributor chose Walter Lantz instead. Businessman Leon Schlesinger came to the rescue, pitching himself as producer and convincing the Warner Brothers Studio (see next entry) to distribute the films. Harman and Ising titled their series *Looney Tunes* after Disney's *Silly Symphonies* and began production in 1930. They added another series called *Merrie Melodies* a little over a year later.

The first of a long line of Warner Brothers cartoon characters was Bosko, a happy, cheerful character prone to dancing and singing in the Disney style, but with little personality. Other characters were tried who were little more than Mickey Mouse copies and failed to win favor with audiences.

In mid-1933, Harman and Ising broke with Schlesinger, taking Bosko with them. Another lead character named "Buddy" was created, but he shared Bosko's personality (or lack thereof) and faded away within two years.

In 1934, some of the *Merrie Melodies* series cartoons were made in color, and the following year the entire series switched to color production. The *Looney Tunes* remained black and white for another decade.

The cartoons were successful but not enormously so. Then, in 1936, Fred "Tex" Avery (1907-1980) and Frank Tashlin (1913-1972) were promoted from animating to supervising (later termed directing) the cartoons. The two men, along with Isadore "Friz" Freleng (1906-1995), began changing the face of Warner Brothers cartoons from Disney-clones to something far more original.

Freleng had come from Disney with Harman and Ising and knew how to develop characters and pacing in the cartoons. With little material, he could develop a character that was believable. Freleng was a superior "personality" animator and this carried over to the films he supervised.

Avery saw no reason merely to anthropomorphize objects and animals and have them sing and dance around in the Disney style. He brought a keen sense of comic timing and outlandish gags to his films, as in *Cinderella Meets Fella* (1938), in which Prince Charming tips his hat and his head comes off with it. No longer just cute and amusing, the cartoons were becoming laugh-out-loud funny.

Frank Tashlin was one of the best gagmen in the business, as his later career as a live-action screenwriter and director for Bob Hope and Jerry Lewis attests. Tashlin treated his cartoon characters as performing comedians, and his cartoons often involve comic set-pieces where the character performs some bit of business the way a human comic would, such as Porky Pig's routine with the ladder in *Little Beau Porky* (1936).

The Warner Brothers cartoons of this period were also helped by finally having a starring character of some personality to feature in the cartoons—Porky Pig, who first came to the screen in the 1935 Freleng cartoon *I Haven't Got a Hat*. Freleng may have given him his first exposure, but Porky really came to life under the direction of Frank Tashlin from 1936 to 1938 and Bob Clampett (1915-1984) from 1938 to 1940. Porky as we know him finally arrived in 1937 when the character was redesigned and then voiced by Mel Blanc (1908-1989), who became the voice of Warner Brothers cartoons. Porky had a joyful innocence and never-say-die spirit that appealed to Depression-era audiences.

Bob Clampett joined the ranks of directors in 1937 and brought a fluid and aggressive style to the cartoons he directed. *Porky in Wackyland* (1938) was one of Clampett's early efforts and is a textbook example of gags and pacing, all hung on Porky's reactions to a Daliesque surreal landscape. Clampett's comic creations were grotesque figures of near nightmarish quality.

Gags became so dominant in Warner Brothers' cartoons that story construction often nearly evaporated. Clampett and Avery excelled at "spot-gag" cartoons, a series of gags strung together on a loose theme without a plot. This format of "gags on a theme" was adapted by Chuck Jones (1912-) for his series of Roadrunner and Coyote cartoons from the 1940s to the 1960s.

Porky may have been Warner Brothers cartoons' first real star, but two others appeared in rapid succession whose wisecracking attitudes and inherent zaniness led them to outstrip Porky's popularity by the early 1940s. The first was Daffy Duck, who made his debut in the Avery cartoon *Porky's Duck Hunt* (1937), written by Ben "Bugs" Hardaway. Daffy certainly lived up to his name, hooting and bouncing all over the scenery, delighting in the chaos he created. Later in 1938 Hardaway and Cal Dalton directed *Porky's Hare Hunt*, this time with Porky chasing after a screwy rabbit. The rabbit, Bugs Bunny (see entry), is much like Daffy Duck and Woody Woodpecker, who would appear a few years later at the Walter Lantz studios. Hardaway had a hand in bringing all three characters to the screen, and the legend goes that the screwball rabbit was referred to by the Warner Brothers cartoon staff as "Bugs' Bunny," hence his eventual name.

In the meantime, Avery had also developed an oddball character named Egghead, loosely inspired by comedian Joe Penner (1904-1941). Egghead met Daffy in a hunting cartoon in 1938, *Daffy Duck and Egghead*. Egghead evolved into Elmer Fudd, making his debut in Chuck Jones's *Elmer's Candid Camera* (1940), trying to take wildlife photographs of a Bugs-like rabbit. A recognizable Elmer and Bugs finally meet in Avery's 1940 *A Wild Hare*, considered the first true Bugs Bunny cartoon.

One of the trademarks of the Warner Brothers cartoons was their use and referencing of other popular culture characters and trends, including genre parodies and take-offs of familiar books and plays. Self-referentiality became a trademark of the cartoons. Caricatured movie stars appeared in cartoons such as Avery's *Hollywood Steps Out* (1941), Clampett's *Bacall to Arms* (1946), and Tashlin's *Swooner Crooner* (1944), with chickens swooning over a skinny rooster resembling Frank Sinatra. Radio catchphrases and performers turned up frequently, and in later years, television proved a fertile ground for parody and copying, with the Honeymooners turning up as the Honeymousers some years before they inspired the Flintstones.

Warner Brothers cartoons were also very inventive, as in Freleng's *You Oughta Be in Pictures* (1940), which mixes live action and animation as the scheming Daffy convinces Porky to break his contract with Schlesinger to perform in live-action features. Daffy really just wants his competition out of the way. The mixing of live action and animation had been done before, but not as well.

By 1942, World War II was influencing all aspects of American life, and became a point of reference in the Warner Brothers cartoons as well. Twenty-six "Private Snafu" cartoons were made for the military to humorously show servicemen what not to do. Wartime problems and references popped up in many of the main series cartoons, and several were devoted to patriotic themes, with Bugs fighting Hitler and the Japanese, and Daffy saving scrap-iron or avoiding the draft.

In 1943, the Looney Tunes series began to be produced in color and in 1944, Schlesinger sold his production company to Warner Brothers, making the films officially Warner Brothers cartoons. Other cartoon stars emerged, including Tweety and Sylvester, Pepe LePew, and Foghorn Leghorn, a take-off on radio's Senator Claghorn.

By 1946, Avery, Tashlin, and Clampett had all left the studio, and animator Chuck Jones, who had started as a director in 1938, came into his own. Where Avery and Tashlin built their cartoons on ever-more outlandish gags, animator Chuck Jones developed a contrasting style based on minimalist reactions something like those of the comedian Jack Benny. In Jones's later films, the characters and situations are so familiar and refined that a simple raised eyebrow can convey the character's thoughts completely.

Jones modified Daffy into a jealous, short-tempered character, a perfect foil for the unflappable and always-in-control Bugs. Jones's best use of Daffy is in *Duck Amuck* (1953), where Daffy is at the mercy of an unmerciful animator who torments him by changing Daffy's shape and location at will—and is finally revealed to be Bugs himself. One of Jones's most acclaimed—and least typical—cartoons was the dialogueless *One Froggy Evening* (1955). A man discovers a singing, dancing frog who only performs when no one else is around. The situation eventually drives the man mad.

Freleng, Jones, and Robert McKimson (1910-1977) directed all of the studio's output from 1949 to 1964. By the 1960s, the short subject market was dying, and the new films were competing with the old ones frequently shown on television. Budgets were cut, resulting in inferior animation. Minor characters such as the Tasmanian Devil, Speedy Gonzales, and Yosemite Sam lost any distinction they may have once had, and strange decisions such as pairing Daffy with Speedy Gonzales didn't help the situation.

Production was halted in 1964, only to resume later that year when Freleng had formed his own company and began making cartoons for Warners in addition to others featuring non-Warners characters such as the Pink Panther. Unfortunately, the cartoons from this period look cheap and tired. In 1967 Warners reorganized; a new series of cartoons, some involving new characters, was launched but despite a few interesting cartoons, such as *Norman Normal* (1968), the series continued to falter. Production was finally halted in 1969.

The characters continued to be popular, and holiday specials made up of both old cartoon segments and new sequences (often directed by Freleng) became television staples. In 1975, *Bugs Bunny Superstar,* a documentary including several complete vintage cartoons, was released. Five compilation films, mostly comprised of footage from the 1949-64 films, followed. The continuing popularity of the specials and features led to the creation of new, fully animated, cartoons made for television and theaters. Two of these cartoons were then included in the compilation feature *Daffy Duck's Quackbusters* (1989). Prior to that, most of the Warner Brothers cartoon stars appeared in the hit film *Who Framed Roger Rabbit?* (1988), which drew heavily on the Warner Brothers spirit.

The Warner Brothers cartoon characters have been merchandised for decades, and can be found on clothing, dishes, posters, key chains, collectible figurines, and toiletries—to name but a few of the legion of products available. Production of the cartoons may have officially ended in 1969, but despite what the little stuttering pig said, that's *not* all, folks.

Bibliography

Friedwald, Will, and Jerry Beck. *The Warner Brothers Cartoons.* Metuchen: Scarecrow, 1981.

Gebert, Michael. *From Goopy Geer to Gotterdammerung: The Development of the Warners' Weltanschauung.* Zurich: Felix Meierhof, 1990.

Maltin, Leonard. *Of Mice and Magic: A History of American Animated Cartoons.* New York: New American Library, 1980.

Peary, Gerald, and Danny Peary, eds. *The American Animated Cartoon: A Critical Anthology.* New York: Dutton, 1980.

Benjamin K. Urish

See also
Cartoons: Theatrical and Television

Warner Brothers Studios, one of the longest lived and most powerful Hollywood studios, on March 4, 1989, merged with Time Incorporated to form the world's largest entertainment conglomerate, Time-Warner Communications. By controlling video cassette, compact disc, cassette tape, book, and comic book sales built around its own stories, Warners established a precedent for global entertainment that other corporations quickly followed. Establishing precedents was a tradition at Warner Brothers.

Albert, Harry, Samuel, and Jack L. Warner started their business by renting a tent and showing *The Great Train Robbery* (1903) in their hometown of Youngstown, OH. By 1908, they were distributing films to over 200 theaters in Ohio and western Pennsylvania. Moving to California to avoid the Motion Picture Patents Company, they distributed films through Carl Laemmle's Universal Studios. Their first major film success, *My Four Years in Germany* (1918), was based on American ambassador James W. Gerard's prewar memoirs. Warner Brothers barely survived the 1920s because of a serious lack of talent. Their biggest moneymaker was a German shepherd, "Rin-Tin-Tin," first featured in *When the North Begins* (1923). The film was so popular that 19 films with "Rinty" followed, making it the dog that saved the studio.

Sound was the breakthrough that put Warner Brothers on the same level as MGM and Paramount. *The Jazz Singer* (1927; see entry) became the first "talkie" and caused a sensation in the business by featuring Broadway musical star Al Jolson, who ad-libbed lines while recording the songs. The enormous success of sound encouraged expansion, and Warners bought over 250 theaters in seven states. They also gained control of First National Studios to increase their production. Corporate control was divided between Harry in the New York City headquarters, and Jack, who ran the studio. Sam passed away suddenly in 1927, and Albert was never a major participant in corporate direction.

During the Depression, Warner Brothers emphasized a realistic approach to feature films with contemporary topics that interested American audiences. Crime and gangster movies included *The Public Enemy* (1931) and *Little Caesar* (1931) and made stars of James Cagney and Edward G. Robinson. *I Am a Fugitive from a Chain Gang* (1932) criticized prison brutality. Other social topics included the anti-lynching drama *They Won't Forget* (1937), anti-union violence in *Black Fury* (1937), muckraking with *Five Star Final* (1931), Ku Klux Klan hate-mongering in *Black Legion* (1937), and teenage runaways with *Wild Boys* (1933).

Although the social realism emphasis reflected Warner Brothers' blue-collar image of itself, the studio also produced popular musicals starting with Dick Powell and Ruby Keeler in Lloyd Bacon's *42nd Street* (1933). Fantastic sets and geometric dance configurations were immortalized by Busby Berkeley in *Gold Diggers of 1933* (1933), *Footlight Parade* (1933), and *Gold Diggers of 1935* (1935).

Later in the decade, when the studio became more profitable, it explored costume dramas like *The Adventures of Robin Hood* (1938), with Errol Flynn, and biography with

Paul Muni in *The Life of Emile Zola* (1937). Bette Davis was the studio's most important female star, winning Academy Awards for *Dangerous* (1936) and *Jezebel* (1938). Davis took the studio to court in 1939 in a futile effort to win release from her contract. Another star, Olivia de Havilland, later won a similar court case in 1945 that broke the studio contract system and freed many stars from restrictive contracts.

Another precedent was established when *Confessions of a Nazi Spy* (1939) became the first major motion picture to criticize Nazism. Spending cutbacks and raw film stock rationing forced studios to sharply reduce the number of annual productions once the war started, but star power made Warners' wartime releases some of the most famous in Hollywood's history. They included *Sergeant York* (1941) with Gary Cooper, *Watch on the Rhine* (1943) with Paul Lucas, and the classic war romance *Casablanca* (1942), with Humphrey Bogart and Ingrid Bergman. Other quality products included John Huston's *The Maltese Falcon* (1941) again with Bogart, *Now Voyager* (1942) with Bette Davis, and the patriotic *Yankee Doodle Dandy* (1942) with Cagney's Academy Award–winning song and dance performance.

During the 1950s, Warner Brothers rented space to independent producers and received distribution rights for Alfred Hitchcock's *Dial M for Murder* (1954) and Judy Garland's *A Star Is Born* (1954). Among the stars were Marlon Brando in *A Streetcar Named Desire* (1951) and James Dean in *Rebel without a Cause* (1955), whose rebellious youth became an icon for American teenagers.

Television competition encouraged Jack Warner to enter production for the small screen in 1954 with *Warner Brothers Presents*. One of the early shows, *Cheyenne*, became a hit and lasted for seven years. Other studio-produced shows quickly followed, including *Maverick* and *The FBI Story*. Total rights to every film Warners made before 1950 were sold to United Artists Television in March 1956. In May 1956, Jack, Harry, and Albert sold their share of studio stock to a group controlled by the First National Bank of Boston. Jack repurchased his shares to keep control of the studio.

The 1960s saw the studio revive the musical with Broadway hits *The Music Man* (1962), with Robert Preston, and *My Fair Lady* (1964). Warners also recycled crime and police drama with *Bonnie and Clyde* (1967) and *Dirty Harry* (1971). Furthermore, the studio was still willing to take risks, as it demonstrated with the unedited raw language of *Who's Afraid of Virginia Woolf?* (1966) and the special effects needed to make *Superman* (1978) fly.

No discussion of Warner Brothers would be complete without mentioning the directors who created the rapidly paced stories, including Michael Curtiz (*The Sea Hawk*, 1940), Howard Hawks (*The Big Sleep*, 1946), John Huston (*The Treasure of the Sierra Madre*, 1948), and Raoul Walsh (*White Heat*, 1949). Finally, Warners' leadership in film sound also led to memorable film music from the studio's composers, especially Max Steiner (*Now Voyager*, 1942) and Erich Wolfgang Korngold (*Anthony Adverse*, 1936).

Technological innovation and an instinct for presenting compelling stories put Warner Brothers near the top of the motion picture industry. Timely corporate mergers (see Time Warner, Inc.) and the ability to keep up with changing public taste has kept it there.

Bibliography

Behlmer, Rudy, ed. *Inside Warner Bros. (1935-1951)*. New York: Viking Penguin, 1985.
Freedland, Michael. *The Warner Brothers*. New York: St. Martin's, 1983.
Hirschhorn, Clive. *The Warner Bros. Story*. New York: Crown, 1979.
Meyer, William R. *Warner Brothers Directors: The Hard-Boiled, the Comic, and the Weepers*. New Rochelle: Arlington House, 1978.

Arthur R. Jarvis, Jr.

Warrick, Ruth (1916-), has played many roles in radio, film, and television and her acting career has spanned six decades, but she is probably most famous for her role as Pine Valley matriarch Phoebe Tyler Wallingford on the daytime drama *All My Children* (1970-), a character that she has played since the show's debut and that she has made a household name. But Warrick is quite different from the conservative Daughters of Fine Lineage maven Phoebe Tyler Wallingford. Married five times, Warrick is very active in liberal causes and Democratic Party politics. During the sixties, Warrick protested against the war in Vietnam, and in the eighties she campaigned for Democratic presidential candidate John Glenn.

Born in St. Joseph, MO, Warrick knew that she wanted to act when, as a child, her father took her to see traveling theater troupes. Warrick went on to study drama at the University of Missouri at Kansas City. Later, she won a Chamber of Commerce contest to promote Kansas City's fall festival, and in 1937 moved to New York City, supporting herself with modeling jobs and radio work.

Warrick's film career began in 1941 when Orson Welles chose her to play the first wife of Charles Foster Kane in *Citizen Kane*. Under contract to RKO studios, Warrick moved to Hollywood and appeared in 32 more pictures, including *The Corsican Brothers* (1941) and *China Sky* (1945).

Warrick's television career began in 1952 when she divorced her second husband and moved back to New York with her children. The majority of Warrick's television work has been in daytime drama. Her first daytime drama role was on *Guiding Light*. Later Warrick was part of the original cast of *As the World Turns* as Edith Hughes, eccentric sister of lawyer Chris Hughes, a role she played for three years.

From 1961 to 1962, Warrick played mother of the bride Ellie Banks in the short-lived CBS sitcom *Father of the Bride*, based on the film of the same name. In 1964, Warrick played mysterious housekeeper Hannah Cord in *Peyton Place*, television's first prime-time soap opera. After *Peyton Place*, Warrick joined the original cast of *All My Children*, where she can still be seen today.

Bibliography

Warrick, Ruth. *The Confessions of Phoebe Tyler*. Englewood Cliffs: Prentice-Hall, 1980.

June Michele Pulliam

Wayne, John (1907-1979), embodied and became the symbol of perfect freedom. Essayist Joan Didion remembered Wayne riding "through her childhood" like a dream. His image "suggested another world...a place where a man could move free...in the early morning sun." For Didion and many others Wayne's heroes were tough, self-reliant, and answered the needs of the collective in times of crisis. In *The Man Who Shot Liberty Valance* (1962), for example, Wayne defends America's future by protecting lawyer and eventual politician Ransom Stoddard (James Stewart) from an evil gunman. In all of Wayne's films, he talked low and slow and tried not to "talk too much," but when he spoke, according to John Ford, "it meant something." Millions responded to Wayne's easy-going baritone, loping walk, and towering presence. From 1949 to 1972, he was consistently a Top 10 box-office star. Broad-shouldered, six-four, and more than 200 pounds, the post-war Wayne represented strength, the stuff of great myths. Leaning in the desert air, a Winchester at his side, Wayne stood firm among the buttes and mesas of Monument Valley, a man of action forcing his will on the wilderness. And in his service films, *They Were Expendable* (1945), *Sands of Iwo Jima* (1949), and *The Green Berets* (1968), Wayne represented an apostle of patriotism.

John "Duke" Wayne was born Marion Mitchell Morrison in Winterset, IA. As a young boy he moved to Los Angeles and attended Glendale High School, where he was an honor student. In 1925, he enrolled at the University of Southern California on a two-year football scholarship. Wayne augmented his school expenses by playing extras in films. Following a fractured ankle in 1927, Wayne found himself without a scholarship and left school to become a prop man at $35.00 a week. In early autumn of 1929, an assistant to Raoul Walsh discovered Wayne unloading furniture on the Fox lot and told him to let his hair grow out and see Walsh about a screen test. Wayne got the starring role of Breck Coleman in *The Big Trail* (1930).

But *The Big Trail* was a financial disaster, and Fox Studios shelved Wayne. After second-lead roles in B Westerns at Columbia and a short stint at Warners, Wayne signed on at Monogram with Paul Mavern's Lone Star Westerns. There, from 1933 to 1935, Wayne starred in 16 Westerns, six-reelers budgeted at $15,000 and shot in 10-15 days. Although the production values paled next to *The Big Trail*, Wayne's characters were very much like Coleman: romantic, easy-going, sincere. The plots involved Wayne, usually an undercover government marshal, proving his innocence and restoring order to a corrupt land.

After nearly ten years in B films, John Ford gave Wayne his second chance when he cast him as the Ringo Kid in *Stagecoach* (1939). Wayne's performance is understated and sensuous. Following the critical and box office success of *Stagecoach*, Wayne returned to Republic Studios in A features. In 1941, when President Roosevelt declared war on Japan, Wayne was 34 years old, married with four children. He was exempt from service and probably wanted to remain a civilian to attend to his burgeoning career; however, this decision haunted him throughout the 1950s and '60s.

Wayne's lack of real service combined with appearances in several service films didn't rest well with the left and moderates who objected to Wayne's increasingly hawkish values. In *Sands of Iwo Jima* (1949), Wayne's Sgt. John M. Stryker is visually transformed into the American flag. Wayne's performance earned him his first Academy Award nomination. It was the only nomination Republic ever received.

Wayne's onscreen patriotism during the Cold War was also manifest offscreen. From 1948 to 1952, Wayne served as President of the Motion Picture Alliance for the Preservation of American Ideals, a movie colony organization that worked in conjunction with the House Un-American Activities Committee to name names. Ward Bond, Gary Cooper, John Ford, Clark Gable, Hedda Hopper, and Adolph Menjou were all active members. When his tenure as president ended, Wayne paid his tribute to H.U.A.C. in the flag-waving *Big Jim McLain* (1952), in which the Duke battles communists in Hawaii. From 1952 to 1959, Wayne and various members of his Batjac Productions worked on the ultimate homage to patriotism, *The Alamo* (1960), an allegory that dealt with the West's Cold War against international communism. For Wayne, the film showed "the world the sort of spirit and indomitable will for freedom that I think still dominates the thinking of Americans." *Newsweek* described the project as "the most lavish B picture ever made.... 'B' for banal." Nevertheless, the film was nominated for the Oscar for best picture.

Along with becoming more patriotic on and offscreen, many of Wayne's more famous post-war heroes were darker, less romantic and innocent. His grey-haired Tom Dunson of *Red River* (1948) brutally kills men to seize the land he wants and runs his cattle drive like a paranoid tyrant. Darkness, or world-weariness, also permeates the underrated comedy *Trouble along the Way* (1953). Ford's *The Searchers* (1956), a favorite among the New Hollywood directors, was also made in this dark period and presented a heroic figure torn with internal demons.

In 1964, John Wayne was diagnosed with cancer and told he had a 1-in-20 chance to live. Fortunately the operation was a success, as a rib and the lower half of his left lung were removed. His victory over cancer won him many more admirers and added to his image of indestructibility. Told to take six months off, Wayne retired for only 14 weeks before he began work on *The Sons of Katie Elder* (1965), an easy-going Western that reaffirmed his machismo. Four years later, Wayne won his only Academy Award as the crotchety Rooster Cogburn in *True Grit* (1969).

By the mid-1970s Wayne's mythic man of self-reliance and patriotic fervor came under attack. As the Vietnam veteran underwent a cultural healing, many veterans blamed Wayne for falsely filling young men with notions of bravado and courage. This position was dramatized in *Born on the Fourth of July* (1976) and echoed in *Birdy* (1984). Not only was Wayne read as an iconic scapegoat but other subcultural practices sought to destroy his image. No doubt Wayne's later Batjac films *Chisum* (1970) and *Cahill, U.S. Marshal* (1973) that featured swaggering heroes confident in their conservative sermonizing didn't resonate with The Stains, a hard-core band who attacked Wayne's hegemonic right to rule with 1981's roaring "John Wayne was a Nazi."

Wayne's image has been lionized by the right and demonized by the left. But in his final days he was humanized by both camps as he showed tremendous courage fighting a fatal bout with cancer. After nearly 50 years as an actor, in which he appeared in over 250 films, Wayne was nominated for a congressional Medal of Honor, bearing a landscape of Monument Valley on the back and his portrait on the front with an inscription: "John Wayne, American." But he died before receiving it.

Bibliography

Didion, Joan. "John Wayne: A Love Song." *Slouching Towards Bethlehem*. New York: Farrar, 1968. 29-41.

Mast, Gerald. "The Genre Epic: *Red River*." *Howard Hawks, Storyteller*. New York: Oxford UP, 1982.

McGhee, Richard D. *John Wayne: Actor, Artist, Hero*. Jefferson: McFarland, 1990.

Place, J. A. *The Western Films of John Ford*. Secaucus: Citadel, 1974.

Shepherd, Donald, and Robert Slatzer with Dave Grayson. *Duke: The Life and Times of John Wayne*. New York: Zebra-Kensington, 1985.

Grant Tracey

Webb, Jack (1920-1982), a household word in TV crime detection, was a producer, director, and actor who developed several stylistically distinct characters for reality-based programs he created for radio, television, and film. Webb is primarily known for his portrayal of Sgt. Joe Friday in the series *Dragnet*, which debuted on radio in 1949 and on television in 1952. Webb's straightforward, staccato-style delivery made Friday one of the most identifiable and parodied characters in modern mass media history. The singular line "Just the facts, ma'am," as well as Walter Schuman's *Dragnet* theme ("Danger Ahead") have become fodder for impressionists, sketch comedians, and advertisers who continue to parody the work.

Webb, born in Santa Monica, CA, began working in radio in the late thirties. By serving as lead actor, director, and producer, Webb was able to effect a singular style among his many productions. His first network radio show, *One Out of Seven* (ABC, 1946), featured dramatizations of true stories culled from the most interesting AP reports from the previous week—hence the title. Webb was not only far ahead of his time in presenting reality-based programs, but also in his attention to stories of injustices suffered by minorities, including African Americans. This theme, common in *One Out of Seven*, was carried out by Webb in later episodes of *Dragnet*, particularly the 1967 color version of the series.

Webb developed his staccato delivery and "just the facts" approach during the late 1940s, when he created a series of radio detective programs including *Pat Novak, For Hire*; *Johnny Madero*; *Pier 23*; and *Jeff Regan, Investigator*. In 1949, Webb launched Mark VII Productions, Ltd., through which he produced the NBC radio series *Dragnet*. The hit series was successfully transplanted to television.

The original TV *Dragnet* ran until 1959. During that period, Webb tried to duplicate the true-story format with shows such as *Noah's Ark* (1956), which featured actual cases involving California veterinarians, and *The D.A.'s Man* (1959), based on actual files from the New York City prosecutor's office. Neither of these shows were successful, if only because they were missing the key Webb program element—Jack Webb in the starring role. It was not until 1967, when Webb brought back *Dragnet*, that one of his shows returned to the Top 20. While Webb had gone through a series of partners in the original version, he settled on veteran character actor Harry Morgan as his permanent sidekick Bill Gannon. Morgan, who had many film credits before coming to *Dragnet*, went on to star in *M*A*S*H* (1972) as Colonel Sherman Potter.

While Webb's Friday has often been described as unemotional, each episode clearly showed the disgust and contempt Friday felt toward the criminals. This heavy morality was particularly evident in the sixties' version of the series, where Friday often attacked the drug-dependent, cop-hating counterculture. Many of these episodes, which are now viewed as nothing more than high-camp fun, included long-winded speeches by Friday designed to preserve and protect the status quo. Despite his blind allegiance to the sanctity of the LAPD, Webb maintained his stance against social injustice, particularly regarding civil rights issues.

Webb followed the new *Dragnet*'s success with *Adam-12* (1968), which featured LA patrol cops, and *Emergency* (1972), which featured LA paramedics. *Adam-12* and *Emergency* were the only Webb productions able to survive without Webb's presence as lead actor. Webb's last productions, *Sierra* (1974), which dramatized true-story accounts from our national parks, and *Project UFO* (1978), which looked at actual cases from U.S. Air Force encounters with unidentified flying objects, both failed to score with the public.

In addition to his radio and TV roles, Webb acted in several films, including *Pete Kelly's Blues* (1957), *The D.I.* (1959), and a film version of *Dragnet* (1959). While the stories featured drastically different venues, they all bore Webb's signature style.

Bibliography

Brooks, Tim, and Earle Marsh. *The Complete Directory to Prime Time Network TV Shows, 1946-Present*. New York: Ballantine, 1992.

Brown, Les. *Les Brown's Encyclopedia of Television*. Detroit: Visible Ink, 1992.

Marc, David, and Robert J. Thompson. *Prime Time, Prime Movers*. Boston: Little, Brown, 1992.

Michael B. Kassel

Webber, Andrew Lloyd (1948-), born in England, is credited with reviving the dying Broadway musical genre with his multiple hits which opened during the years 1977-93. Webber's shows (sometimes called composed-through musicals, but also known as operas) represent a prolific partnership with lyricist Tim Rice; set designer John Napier; and such talented directors as Hal Prince, Cameron MacIntosh, and Trevor Nunn. Webber is credited with being the only creator in Broadway history to have three musicals playing simultaneously—in the 1982 season, *Cats*, *Evita*, and *Song & Dance*, as well as *Joseph and the Amazing Technicolor Dreamcoat* (Off-Broadway).

Webber's major hits include *Jesus Christ Superstar* (1972), *Evita* (1978), *Cats* (1981), *Starlight Express* (1984), *Requiem*—a serious rendering of a Catholic Requiem Mass (1985), *Phantom of the Opera* (1986), *Aspects of Love* (1989), *Sunset Boulevard* (1993), and two scores for movies, *Gumshoe* (1972), and *Odessa Files* (1974).

Webber was strongly influenced by such diverse musical talents as the Beatles, Pink Floyd, Giacomo Puccini, Maurice Ravel, and Wolfgang Amadeus Mozart. But Webber claims that his primary influences were Richard Rodgers and George Gershwin. Webber's productions typically showcase extravagant visual gimmicks—such as the Rollerskaters in *Starlight Express* or the 1000-pound chandelier and the 100 candles that rise through the stage floor in *Phantom of the Opera*.

Evita, *Cats*, and *Phantom of the Opera* are three of the most profitable productions in Broadway history. Each holds records for the number of performances, Tony Awards, and high advance ticket sales. These productions earned Webber sufficient returns to put him high on the list of England's richest men. This fact, plus the cultural *kudos* accorded to his work, motivated the British House of Lords in 1997 to bestow a royal title upon the young composer.

Evita is based on the life of Argentina's Eva Perón. The show began as a major studio album and was later converted into a staged musical, opening in London (1978) with Elaine Paige and in Los Angeles (1979) with Patti Lupone and Mandy Patinkin (as Che). Some critics complained that it glorified fascism, and glamorized Eva Perón. A further, more obvious, drawback was cultural. Latin American politics and history were unknown subjects and of little interest to Anglo audiences. Yet the show received favorable reviews and won the New York Drama Critic Circle Award and seven Tony awards—including Best Musical. In 1981, *Evita* won a Grammy Award for Best Album of the year and Paramount bought the film rights (which it did not exercise until over a decade later, starring Madonna in the lead role). In 1997 Webber and Rice won the Oscar for Best Original Song for *Evita*.

Cats (1981), based on T. S. Eliot's *Old Possum's Book of Practical Cats*, takes place in a set designed as a cosmic junkyard by John Napier. A tale of anthropomorphic cats in a "complete fantasy world that can exist only in the theatre" (Frank Rich, *New York Times*) opened to mixed reviews in New York (1982). In London, Elaine Paige played Grizabella the "main" cat, with Betty Buckley in the role in the New York version. Since 1980, the song "Memory" with lyrics by Trevor Nunn (who was also the director) has been one of the most requested songs at weddings and is a staple for Muzak in millions of elevators and hotel lounges. *Cats* has been the most profitable theatrical venture in the history of Broadway.

Phantom of the Opera (1986), based on the novel by Gaston Leroux, is referred to as the jewel in Webber's crown. The show has run to capacity crowds nightly in over 13 productions worldwide since its opening in London

(1986) and New York (1988). Webber considers *Phantom* his most important work. Filled with mystery, terror, and romance, the show won seven Tony awards.

Sunset Boulevard (1993), based on the 1950 Billy Wilder film noir classic of the same name, opened first in London and New York in 1994. Based on the huge success of *Phantom*, *Sunset* opened to the largest advanced ticket sales ($37.5 million), yet it closed as a financial loss. The show was written with a new lyricist, Don Black, and its failure is said to be due to its being a star-driven vehicle with music that did not stand on its own. To date, no major song or musical theme has emerged from this production with such strength as previous hits such as "Memory" (*Cats*), "Don't Cry for Me, Argentina" (*Evita*), "Music of the Night" (*Phantom*), or even the title song from *Jesus Christ Superstar*, as well as its other hit song "I Don't Know How to Love Him."

Webber has written less important productions such as *Jeeves* (1975), based on P. G. Wodehouse's famous fiction series, *Song & Dance* (1982), *Aspects of Love* (1989), and *Whistle Down the Wind* (1993), which first opened only in Washington, DC, and played for nine weeks but is enjoying a longer run beginning in 1998 in London. Webber's first public production, *Joseph and the Amazing Technicolor Dreamcoat* (1968), was a financial success but not on the mega-production level of his subsequent successes.

Webber will leave his mark for developing a new medium, the musical-as-opera in which all dialogue is sung. The composed-through style allowed him to create musicals that combine vocal elements with strong orchestrations.

Bibliography

Headington, Christopher. *The Performing World of the Musician*. Morristown: Silver Burdett, 1981.

Simon, John. Review of *Evita*. *New York Magazine* (1989).

Walsh, Michael. *Andrew Lloyd Webber: His Life and Works*. New York: Abrams, 1997.

Susan Rollins

Weird Tales (1923-1954) was the most literate and highly regarded of the horror pulp magazines that rose to popularity in the 1920s and 1930s. Whereas most pulps, such as *Detective Story Magazine* or *Black Mask*, were written in a contemporary, vernacular style with terse, punchy dialogue, the prose in the horror pulps tended to be more stilted and pretentious, harking back to the Victorian literary culture from which horror fiction had emerged as a popular art form.

Weird Tales was never a financial success, but it survived because of the devotion of the publisher, editors, and writers, and the support of an unusually dedicated cult of readers. The term "weird tale" had been coined to describe stories that borrowed elements from a variety of genres including fantasy, science fiction, gothic fiction, and the supernatural to create a brand of horror that relied more on philosophical and psychological terror than on bloody mayhem.

H. P. Lovecraft was among those who wrote for *Weird Tales*; Robert Bloch, August Derleth, and Richard Matheson also established popular followings in the medium. Other prominent horror pulps included *Dime Mystery*, *Horror Sto-*

ries, and *Terror Tales*. These latter magazines specialized in what has come to be called "weird menace" stories, a bizarre blend of detective fiction and sadomasochistic torture. Several factors combined to augment the decline of the pulps by the 1950s. August Derleth's founding of Arkham House in 1939, an independent publishing firm dedicated to preserving Lovecraft's work and promoting the weird tale, did much to reinforce and expand the genre's cult following, but it also served to ghettoize the genre, making it seem to belong to an insular, eccentric realm that few casual readers could enter. The rise of the paperback book market diverted popular interest from short stories to novels available in inexpensive formats. Nonetheless, the horror pulps claim an important niche in cultural history, having provided the medium for some of the most inventive and enduring literary voices ever.

Bibliography

Daniels, Les. *Living in Fear: A History of Horror in the Mass Media.* New York: Scribner, 1975.

Docherty, Brian, ed. *American Horror Fiction: From Brockden Brown to Stephen King.* New York: St. Martin's, 1990.

Joshi, S. T. *The Weird Tale: Lord Arthur Machen, Dunsany, Algernon Blackwood, M. R. James, Ambrose Pierce, H. P. Lovecraft.* Austin: U of Texas P, 1990.

Kendrick, Walter. *The Thrill of Fear: 250 Years of Scary Entertainment.* New York: Grove, 1991.

Kerry D. Soper

Welk, Lawrence (1903-1992), one of the most popular and longest lived musicians in America and a national icon in polka music, grew up as a Midwestern farm boy in Strasburg, ND. Raised with a strong sense of family values, Welk taught himself how to play the accordion even though he never went to high school. With humble beginnings and sometimes playing for free, he put together a dance band consisting of six men. Before long a significant following developed in the Dakotas. Their audience continued to broaden when the radio station WNAX in Yankton began to feature their music. Later they moved to Pittsburgh, PA, played in area ballrooms, and were heard over a nationwide radio network.

In the 1930s Welk got married and in an apparent attempt to add stability to his life, tried his hand at a variety of businesses including hotel and restaurant management. However, in 1938 Welk began receiving a lot of fan mail as a result of the band's performances at the William Penn Hotel in Pittsburgh. Because Welk's music was considered "sparkly and bubbly," Welk identified his special sound as "Champagne Music" and the idea of featuring a soloist called the "Champagne Lady" was born. It was also during this time that Welk composed his popular theme song, "Bubbles in the Wine."

By the mid-1940s, Americans were becoming familiar with Lawrence Welk and his band. In 1946, the Lawrence Welk Orchestra played at Santa Monica's Aragon Ballroom for the first time. By 1951 the manager of the Aragon offered Welk a four-week contract that included being telecast by KTLA, a Los Angeles station. Welk's contract was renewed on a repeated basis and business boomed.

In July of 1955, *The Lawrence Welk Show* (see entry) went national on the ABC network and was sponsored by Dodge Motor Cars. Lawrence Welk, with his champagne toast and uplifting bubbles, became a household name. The 24-piece band had certainly come of age and grown in size since its origination. For over ten years Lawrence Welk continued to host his show on the ABC television network. Because the television show made him a No. 1 box-office attraction, he was given periodic time off for personal appearances. Even after leaving ABC in 1971, his show was still produced by a network of 250 independent stations until 1982.

Many of Welk's fans rank *Bubbles in the Wine* and *Sparkling Strings* as two of their favorite Lawrence Welk albums. Even after Welk's death, his show can be seen on some television stations across the country. With the exception of adding to the size of the orchestra, Lawrence Welk's format did not dramatically change over the years. He always believed that a danceable tempo was necessary and combined hard work with Midwestern ethics. He had a code of behavior that he expected from his band and he lived up to that code as well. Marriage and family were paramount. Traditional American values were reflected in his music. Everything was presented in a wholesome manner and the audience knew that the image they saw was not just for the purpose of the show.

Bibliography

Candee, Marjorie Dent, ed. *Current Biography Yearbook.* 18 vols. New York: Wilson, 1957.

Graham, Judith, ed. *Current Biography Yearbook.* 53 vols. New York: Wilson, 1992.

Welk, Lawrence. *Wunnerful, Wunnerful! The Autobiography of Lawrence Welk.* New York: Bantam, 1973.

Lee Ann Paradise-Schober

Welles, (George) Orson (1915-1985), one of America's most talented and controversial actors, has not yet received the final evaluation of his career in American entertainment. On this issue the play is still being written. Certainly his first act is as stunning a record of achievement as any in the history of American cultural expression.

The second son of a businessman-inventor and an artistically cultivated mother, Welles attended the educationally unconventional Todd School for Boys at Woodstock, IL, where its headmaster, Roger Hill, recognized his precocity and encouraged it. At Todd, he took special interest in dramatic productions. His appearance as Richard III in 1930 was a foretaste of two lifelong partialities, for staging Shakespeare and for appearing in elderly roles; it brought him to the attention of Ashton Stevens, "Dean of American Drama Critics," who wrote in his column in the *Chicago Herald and Examiner*, "I am going to put a clipping of this paragraph in my betting book. If Orson is not at least a leading man by the time it has yellowed, I will never make another prophecy."

After graduating from Todd in the spring of 1931, Welles embarked on a walking tour of Ireland and, arriving in Dublin, presented himself at the famous Gate Theatre, where, with characteristic effrontery, charm, and guile he managed to secure the role of the onerous Duke Karl Alexander in *Jud Süss* and was, at 16, a minor sensation. Back home, he won a coveted position in Katharine Cornell and Guthrie McClintic's touring repertory company for the 1933-34 season. An early sign of his entrepreneurial skills was a dramatic festival he organized at Woodstock in the summer of 1934. His own appearance in dual roles as Claudius and the King's ghost in the festival's *Hamlet* earned him superlatives in Chicago newspaper reviews. That summer also saw his first foray into filmmaking, *The Hearts of Age* (16mm, silent, four minutes), a takeoff on arcane surrealist works such as Jean Cocteau's *Blood of a Poet*.

Welles's first starring role in New York theater (in 1935, at 19) was as the well-intentioned tycoon McGafferty in *Panic*, Archibald MacLeish's experimental free verse drama about the Wall Street crash. Meanwhile, he entered a collaboration with John Houseman under the auspices of the New Deal Federal Theatre Project, which helped to underwrite their legendary *Voodoo "Macbeth"* (1936), produced in Harlem using black performers and incorporating black customs and lore. When the Theatre Project attempted to lock out their 1937 production of Marc Blitzstein's leftist political opera *The Cradle Will Rock*, the cast and its opening night audience were expeditiously transported to another theater, an early sign of Welles's well-known gift for resourcefulness in the face of disaster. In 1937, when he and John Houseman founded their own repertory company, the Mercury Theatre, he had, at 22, already established a reputation as the *enfant terrible* of American theater. The Mercury specialized in offbeat productions of classics such as *Julius Caesar* (1937), with its modern setting, expressionistic staging, and contemporary political overtones—Caesar as Mussolini, his henchmen as fascist soldiers, and a blood-red set wall to intensify the effect.

As was the custom of the time, Welles supplemented his meager income during his early days in theater with work in the fledgling medium of radio. His deep and commanding voice was soon ubiquitous in radio broadcasting, from pulp melodrama (as Lamont Cranston in the popular mystery series *The Shadow*—"Who knows what evil lurks in the hearts of men?") to biographical and historical reenactments on *The March of Time* to more substantial fare on "The Columbia Workshop," for which he did *Fall of the City* (1937), MacLeish's original drama for radio on the impending evils of European fascism. After the Mercury Theatre expanded into this medium, Welles engineered a revolution in the nature of broadcast drama with such innovations as first-person narration and the simulation of immediacy. It was the ingenious use of such devices that caused widespread panic during *War of the Worlds* (1938), unquestionably the single most famous radio program ever aired (see entry). Overnight, it catapulted Welles to international notoriety and made his showmanship irresistibly attractive to Hollywood.

After spurning several overtures from Hollywood studios, Welles (still in partnership with Houseman) signed with RKO Pictures in the summer of 1939 to do an adaptation of Joseph Conrad's short novel *Heart of Darkness*, a personal favorite which the Mercury had done as a radio show. After technical problems forced the abandonment of the Conrad project, Welles (with the assistance of veteran Hollywood screenwriter Herman Mankiewicz) developed an original story inspired by the life of the notorious yellow journalist William Randolph Hearst. This became *Citizen Kane*, which was released in May 1941 to almost universal critical hyperbole and immediately placed on track toward its eventual enshrinement as the Great American Film.

Welles's next film was *The Magnificent Ambersons* (1942), from Booth Tarkington's novel about a midwestern trade aristocracy that is unable to adapt to the industrialized 20th century. Midway through shooting on the film, Welles was invited by the State Department to make a film in South America on local customs and themes to promote inter-American relations and solidarity. He departed for South America as soon as shooting on *Ambersons* was completed. When *Ambersons* had serious trouble in previews, RKO drastically recut the film in Welles's absence, removing more than a third of the original footage and substituting a saccharine ending, but the film was a financial disaster nonetheless. The South American project, a four-part anthology called *It's All True*, ran into myriad problems and was terminated. As a result of these two failures, his status was considerably diminished and he would never again be trusted with a major Hollywood production on his own terms.

For the remainder of the war Welles (exempt on medical grounds) remained active in Hollywood entertaining troops (he was an accomplished magician) and appearing in films directed by others, most notably as Rochester in Robert Stevenson's *Jane Eyre* (1944). He was also politically active. An ardent supporter of Franklin D. Roosevelt, he produced a radio series at his behest promoting the sale of war bonds, was deeply involved in the 1944 reelection campaign, and wrote a daily editorial column for the *New York Post*.

After exercising scrupulous self-discipline on the tedious espionage thriller *The Stranger* (1946), Welles was deemed to have gone out of control on the stylish but impenetrable film noir *The Lady from Shanghai* (1948), and it was taken out of his hands in postproduction. He returned to Shakespeare with *Macbeth* (1948), a shoestring production made at Republic, a studio that specialized in serials and B Westerns.

When the Internal Revenue Service questioned claims for major losses on an extravagant stage production of *Around the World in Eighty Days* (1946), Welles left the country and became an international nomad, doing makework of all sorts—endorsing products (whiskey, cigarettes), narrating soundtracks, guest hosting, playing *eminence grise* character roles such as Cesare Borgia, Cagliostro, and a Mongolian warlord—to support his independent film productions, which were shot intermittently, in diverse locales, and always under financial severities; the results are often apparent in radical visual and aural discontinuities. *Othello* (1952) was released to widespread critical acclaim in Europe but generally ignored in the United States. During a hiatus in its shooting, Welles appeared in a London stage version of the play produced by Laurence Olivier, to mixed reviews.

In 1953, Welles appeared on American television in a highly acclaimed *King Lear* credited to Peter Brook but principally directed by Welles himself, and in 1956 he returned to New York in a controversial stage version of the play he also directed. By now he had gained so much weight that he was necessarily limited to playing gargantuan characters—Father Mapple in John Huston's *Moby Dick* (1956) and Hank Quinlan, the corrupt, racist sheriff in *Touch of Evil* (1958), visually brilliant and one of his most admired films; his last American studio feature, it also was taken out of his control in postproduction and partly reshot and reedited by others. His independent productions continued with *Mr. Arkadin* (1955), in which a domineering, Kane-like tycoon sets out to obliterate all traces of his nefarious origins; *The Trial* (1962), with a post-*Psycho* Tony Perkins as Kafka's set-upon Herr K; and *Chimes at Midnight* (also called *Falstaff*, 1966), an amalgam of five Shakespeare plays built around Welles's most beloved character, with Welles in what is possibly, after Kane, his most memorable role. For French television he made *Immortal Story* (1968), from a story by Isak Dinesen.

In the 1970s, the issue of Welles's status as a filmmaker erupted into a major debate. The *auteur* movement of the 1950s and 1960s had rehabilitated his reputation so dramatically that in a 1972 poll of international film critics he was voted leading director of all time; *Citizen Kane* was the No. 1 film. A vigorous counterview appeared in Pauline Kael's "Raising Kane" (1971), which charged that screenwriter Herman Mankiewicz had actually created the heart of the film in writing it, and in Charles Higham's *The Films of Orson Welles* (1970), with its "fear of completion" theory, actually more a charge, that Welles was chronically self-destructive and that "all his blame of others for wrecking his work is an unconscious alibi" for his own recklessness and irresponsibility. John Houseman, who had broken with Welles shortly after the move to Hollywood, maintained in his memoir *Run-Through* (1972) that Welles's extravagance and grandiose but unrealizable conceptions were the principal cause of the Mercury Theatre's undoing. Virtually all commentary since has followed from one of two mutually hostile presuppositions stemming from this controversy—either that Welles was destroyed by a philistine system or that his irresolution, profligacy, and lack of discipline made him his own worst enemy. One regrettable outcome has been to obscure Welles's achievements in other domains besides film.

F for Fake (1973) was the last major film directed by Welles. In the late 1970s he returned to the United States and became known to the American public again through television—as a fixture on the Dean Martin celebrity roasts, a perennial guest on the Johnny Carson and Merv Griffin talk shows, the voice of Robin Masters on *Magnum, P.I.* (1981-85), and, most indelibly, as a spokesperson for Paul Masson Vineyards ("We will sell no wine before its time!"). He also appeared in trifles like *The Muppet Movie* (1979) and in commercial trash like *Butterfly* (1981, with Pia Zadora) and continued to try to mount projects of his own, among them a *King Lear* for French television and *The Cradle Will Rock,*

an autobiographical screenplay set in the heyday of the Mercury Theatre. It is said that he was working on a new screenplay the night he died.

Since his death, there has been a major reclamation effort. Three Mercury Theatre playscripts have been published (under the title *Orson Welles on Shakespeare*). A number of the Mercury Theatre radio shows have been digitized and released by Voyager on audio laser disc. Reconstructed versions of *The Magnificent Ambersons* have appeared on laser disc and in print. *Othello* has been re-released with a reconstructed soundtrack in two discrete versions, analog and digital. A documentary on the *It's All True* project has been constructed out of the surviving footage. A reconstructed *Chimes at Midnight* has been announced. In progress since the 1950s, Welles's *Don Quixote,* stunning in black and white and with a modern setting, has been completed by Jesús Franco (1992), and funding has been sought to complete other films he left in limbo, notably *The Other Side of the Wind* (a formally radical work about a maverick film director who is not unlike Welles himself). Until this material is available for scrutiny, it will be premature to write a final curtain line on Welles's career.

Bibliography

Beja, Morris, ed. *Perspectives on Orson Welles*. New York: Hall, 1995.
Brady, Frank. *Citizen Welles: A Biography of Orson Welles*. New York: Scribner, 1989.
Welles, Orson, and Peter Bogdanovich. *This Is Orson Welles*. Ed. Jonathan Rosenbaum. New York: HarperCollins, 1992.
Wood, Bret. *Orson Welles: A Bio-Bibliography*. New York: Greenwood, 1990.

Robert L. Carringer

West 57th (1985-1989), a new kind of news show on CBS, hit hard at conventional programming. Bob Sirott, one of its reporters, called it the video equivalent of *Rolling Stone* magazine—a combination of entertainment, investigative pieces, and political reports all aimed at a younger audience than that of previous news shows.

Its different look—no set, no formal anchor, and young (under 35), casually dressed reporters, along with splashy use of graphics, quick-cuts, and hand-held cameras—was quite controversial. The program became a symbol of the merging of news and entertainment, and it caused a furor between the old and new guard at CBS and within the television industry.

Named after the street in New York where CBS News is headquartered, the show even had a behind-the-scenes opening montage that was startlingly different in its visual appeal. The telegenic, informal reporters were shown breathlessly dashing down the hall, leaping out of chairs, answering phones, and consulting harried, shouting editors, all to the rhythmic urgency of a jazzy score. The names of the reporters—Meredith Vieira, John Ferrugia, Jane Wallace, and Bob Sirott—were flashed under their pictures as if they were actors playing the roles of "correspondent."

The show included profiles of rock stars such as Billy Joel and Paul Simon and movie stars including Chuck

Norris, Angelica Huston, and Sean Connery. Its many investigative pieces on such topics as cosmetic surgery, teenage arsonists, battered women, the famine in Ethiopia, and use of steroids in football reflected the hard-news background of three of its four reporters.

After its initial six-week tryout as a late 1985 summer series, the show's scheduling was erratic. It returned the following April for a short run, then came back again in April 1987, changing time slots and nights and finally winding up on Saturday. Only two of its original reporters remained—Vieira and Ferrugia—and it added Karen Burnes, Selina Scott, Steve Kroft, and Stephen Schiff.

West 57th was to be revamped in September 1989, when Connie Chung was hired to anchor it. The show that went on the air, however, was an entirely new show, with a different format and none of the original reporters, and a new name: *Saturday Night with Connie Chung.*

Bibliography

Christensen, Mark. "True Glitz." *Rolling Stone* 8 May 1986: 35+.

Hall, Jane. "The New Kids on the CBS Block Try to Put Their Show on the Map." *People* 12 May 1986: 123+.

Shister, Gail. "*West 57th:* Four Better or Four Worse." *Washington Journalism Review* Dec. 1985: 23+.

Carole D. Parnes

West, Mae (1892-1980), American icon, actress, entertainer, and playwright, was born in Brooklyn. She was an intriguing and contradictory phenomenon in terms of her relationship to American popular culture. In 1901, she made her show business debut as Baby Mae in an amateur competition at Royal Theater Brooklyn. She played with the Hal Clarendon stock company (1901-5) and vaudeville and Broadway revues (1906), had a solo comedienne debut as the "Original Brinkley Girl" on the Keith circuit, and was in the one-act play "The Ruby Ring" (1921). Her first major play was *Sex* (1926) and she made her movie debut in *Night after Night* (1932).

Commonly understood as a sex symbol, West never conveniently fit into the usual parameters associated with the stereotype. Unlike her 1930s contemporary Jean Harlow, Mae West was neither glamorous nor youthful. Her buxom figure contradicted female star images of slimness. Furthermore, she achieved her major screen success during her forties—a time of life when most actresses are either offered character roles or on the way to being cast in horror films. However, despite the ignominy of her last screen appearance in *Sextette* (1978), when she unhappily fell into the stereotype of aged sex queen that she had successfully combated for most of her career, Mae West explicitly manifested certain oppositions to the dominant interpretations surrounding female sexuality.

Mae West came to Hollywood with an already established theatrical reputation for controversy and originality. Sexually experienced from a very early age and openly denying the constraints of matrimony, West had appeared in several Broadway productions in the image of the sexually experienced, worldly-wise woman who was nobody's fool.

She often performed her own material and was an early advocate for female independence and homosexual rights. However, West's theatrical performances contained many elements she would later incorporate in her Hollywood career. She often appeared as an excessive embodiment of ideologically constituted femininity, her blonde hair, tight-fitting dresses, and double entendres parodying the male view of the desirable female. West anticipated later critical concepts of femininity as masquerade by self-reflexively taking on a role her age and body appeared to deny and playing it for all its worth within the realm of parody.

With her corpulent body, West became the powerful maternal force in relation to her male desirers, inviting them to come up and see her "some time" but with full acknowledgment that the relationship was economic in nature. West combined the material nature of the gold-digging 1920s era with its more economically deprived 1930s counterpart, proving in all instances that both desire and money ruled. She functioned as an object of excess particularly in her 19th-century roles in *She Done Him Wrong* (1933), *Belle of the Nineties* (1934), *Klondike Annie* (1936), and *My Little Chickadee* (1940), where her body uncomfortably fitted into the restraining corseted dresses society demanded and often threatened to burst their very confines, a threat parallel to her manipulation of both dominant males and the prevailing system.

West also combated false Victorian illusions concerning romanticism and domesticity, showing instead that the 20th-century world of industrialism was one implicitly based upon economic factors. She proved that a not particularly glamorous female could develop her own exchange value in certain relationships where the victims were blind to the motivating factors involved. For the West persona, the whole process was a game, one in which she could manipulate the ogling males in the fairground sequence of *I'm No Angel* (1933) as well as her handsome male leads, such as George Raft and Cary Grant, who thought they would eventually bring her under control.

In 1935, Mae West was the highest-paid female entertainer in America, but gradually censorship forces as well as the changing mood in society moving toward more serious considerations eventually led to a decline in her popularity. Furthermore, her exclusive involvement in the areas of parody or satire left her few options to explore when public interest changed. The inspired teaming of herself and W. C. Fields in *My Little Chickadee* promised much but delivered little in terms of expectations surrounding the match of two anti-establishment icons within popular culture. After *The Heat's On* (1943), she temporarily retired from the screen and returned to the stage.

The interest in old films characteristic of the 1960s as well as her refusal to retire gracefully (like her former leading man, Cary Grant) led to West's reappearance at the age of 78 in the controversial *Myra Breckinridge* (1970). Growing older, overwhelmed by the drooling devotions of legions of fans, West felt she had to perform as if in gratitude for her newly acquired fame. This resulted in her final appearance in *Sextette,* embodying a grotesque caricature of her former glory in a role lacking the irony and self-reflexivity present in better days.

Bibliography

Curry, Ramona. *Too Much of a Good Thing: Mae West as Cultural Icon.* Minneapolis: U of Minnesota P, 1996.

Eells, George. *Mae West: A Biography.* New York: Morrow, 1982.

Tuska, John. *The Complete Films of Mae West.* Secaucus: Carol, 1992.

Ward, Carol Maine. *Mae West: A Bio-Bibliography.* New York: Greenwood, 1989.

West, Mae. *Goodness Had Nothing to Do with It.* Enl. and rev. ed. New York: Macfadden-Bartell, 1970.

Tony Williams

Western Fiction, more than any other genre of popular fiction, is America's story; it is a fantastic, reality-based fiction that chronicles European Americans' expansion westward. Its structuring metaphor and primary narrative device is the setting from which this literary genre derives its name—the wilderness, the vast frontier extending westward from the Atlantic coast. In popular culture, the Western has its roots in the early days of European arrival on the North American continent. The enormous, anomalous landscape of beauty and opportunity, and danger and the unknown, fascinated people arriving for the first time. This landscape subsequently became a primary subject matter of letters, histories, folklore, stories, and other such writings. Michel-Guillaume Jean de Crèvecoeur (1735-1813) is remembered yet today for his letters and epistles about the great wilderness of the "new" land. In literary fiction, early American authors like Charles Brockden Brown (1771-1810), known for his gothic romances in American settings such as *Wieland* (1798) and *Edgar Huntly; or, Memoirs of a Sleep-Walker* (1799), and Robert Montgomery Bird (1806-54), known for tales like *Nick of the Woods; or, The Jibbenainosay* (1837), which portrays "Indians" as "savages," incorporated significant elements of the frontier and frontier life in their prose.

But the first true writer of "Westerns" was probably James Fenimore Cooper (1789-1851; see entry), known for many contributions to the canon of American literature, but especially remembered for his archetypal, romanticized stories of the old West which comprise his Leatherstocking Tales: *The Pioneers* (1823), *The Last of the Mohicans* (1827), *The Prairie* (1827), *The Pathfinder* (1840), and *The Deerslayer* (1841). Cooper's *The Last of the Mohicans*, which preceded Bird's *Nick of the Woods* by ten years, made significant contributions to this newly emerging popular genre of American literature. It includes detailed descriptions of the wilderness and its beauty and danger, a unique American hero in the form of "Hawkeye," a distinctly non-European voice unlike virtually all American fiction prior to this point, and a complex vision of "Native American" peoples. (Bird's famous novel was not nearly as complex or even-handed; it was a vehicle of violence designed to legitimate the old Puritan theology that if the "heathens" could not be converted, then they must be dramatically swept away, subsequently purging the new land of its inherent evils.)

Photo courtesy of Popular Culture Library, Bowling Green State University, Bowling Green, OH.

From about the time of the Civil War to World War I (1860 to 1912), America's first entertainment mass medium, the "dime novel" (see entry), showcased Western stories. In fact, the first recognized dime novel, *Malaeska: The Indian Wife of the White Hunter* (1860), found its basis in the newly emerging genre of popular literature deemed Westerns. Westerns were staples of the dime novel until the media form expired due to worn-out story formulas and an increase in postal rates—the postal service being the primary disseminator of the dime novel. Popular dime novel serials or "libraries" included *Deadwood Dick, Buffalo Bill Stories, Wild West Weekly,* and many more.

Around the turn of the century, when the dime novel was in its twilight years, Owen Wister (1860-1938) wrote and published *The Virginian* (1902; see entry), a landmark book that evidences a dime novel heritage and predicts the newly evolving medium of the pulp magazine. Wister's famous book further developed character types and story patterns begun by Cooper and others and, by doing so, strengthened the mythology of the Western.

There were other authors and stories of the West between and beyond the era of the dime novel. These included Francis Brett "Bret" Harte (1836-1902), author of "The Outcasts of Poker Flat" (1869), and Frank Norris (1870-1902), author of *McTeague* (1899) and *The Octopus* (1901), who are credited with realistic portrayals of the old West. Authors like Mark Twain (psd. for Samuel Clemens, 1835-1910), Stephen Crane (1871-1900), Willa Cather (1873-1947), and Jack London (1876-1916) made significant contributions to the genre also. Cather's *O Pioneers!* (1913) is a classic story of the frontier and the strong determined characters who survived and tamed it.

In the 1910s and '20s, Zane Grey (1872-1939; see entry) was the world's best-selling Western author. Grey became known for a range of Western novels and characters, and is considered today one of the great "romantic" authors of American literary history. His most famous book is probably *Riders of the Purple Sage* (1912). Walter Van Tilburg Clark (1909-1971) wrote the consummate condemnation of frontier justice in the famous Western tragedy *The Ox-Bow*

Photo courtesy of Popular Culture Library, Bowling Green State University, Bowling Green, OH.

Incident (1940); Jack Schaefer (1907-1991) wrote *Shane* (1949); there were thousands more.

As early as the 1890s, a new popular literary medium evolved which supplemented and supplanted the dime novel —the pulp magazine. Pulps flourished and survived up to and through the eras of the paperback novel (a World War II product) and network television (usually assigned 1948 as a starting date, though television technology was available at least two decades earlier). As was the case with dime novels, pulps lived off the "bread and butter" of the Western story (see Pulp Westerns). Famous pulp titles are numerous and are themselves now legendary, but a short list would include *Western Rangers, Dime Western, Star Western, Western Story Magazine, Masked Rider, Pete Rice*, and others.

In the pages of the pulps, authors like Max Brand (psd. for Frederick Faust, 1892-1944) and Luke Short (1908-75) flourished (see entries). Both Brand and Short had tremendously large readerships; Brand was one of the most prolific authors ever, providing the novel *Destry Rides Again* (1930) and many others. It was also in the pages of the pulps that a writer named Louis L'Amour (1910-1975; see entry) first appeared. L'Amour eventually became the most-read Western writer ever, and is renowned for his "graphic" style—a sort of antithesis of the "romantic" style epitomized by Zane Grey in the 1920s. L'Amour's best-loved series is probably his books about the Sackett family.

Subgenres of Westerns have existed from the beginning, and styles, traditions, character types, plots, and formulas have varied, though the Western frontier has always been the central feature of these stories. One significant subgenre of the Western in recent decades is the "Sex Western"—featuring an element of eroticism and even soft pornography. These series books, published by several companies under real authors' names and pseudonyms alike, have had a substantial following.

Today, as in the eras of the dime novel and pulps, there are literally hundreds of authors writing Westerns. Besides Louis L'Amour, popular Western writers of the 1990s include John Jakes, Bill Pronzini, Loren Estleman, Elmore Leonard, and Larry McMurtry. McMurtry's most famous Western novel is the epic *Lonesome Dove* (1985).

Bibliography

Cawelti, John G. *The Six-Gun Mystique*. 2d ed. Bowling Green, OH: Bowling Green State U Popular P, 1984.

Dinan, John A. *The Pulp Western: A Popular History of the Western Fiction Magazine in America*. San Bernardino: Borgo, 1983.

Drinnon, Richard. *Facing West: The Metaphysics of Indian-Hating and Empire-Building*. New York: New American Library, 1980.

Jones, Daryl. *The Dime Novel Western*. Bowling Green, OH: Bowling Green State U Popular P, 1978.

Slotkin, Richard. *Gunfighter Nation: The Myth of the Frontier in Twentieth-Century America*. New York: Atheneum, 1992.

Tompkins, Jane. *West of Everything: The Inner Life of Westerns*. New York: Oxford UP, 1992.

Garyn G. Roberts

Western Films, in many ways the very essence of America, have left an indelible mark on the world. Thanks to Hollywood, virtually everyone knows the ingredients of the Western—the lassos and the Colt .45s; the long-horned steers and the hanging trees; the stagecoaches and the Stetson hats; the outlaws and the lawmen; the gamblers and the gunfighters. And virtually everyone knows the settings of the Western— the red rock monoliths of Monument Valley; the jagged, snow-capped peaks of the Grand Tetons; the treeless expanses of the prairie. The iconography of the Western is the largest and richest of all the film genres, and Hollywood has burned it into the minds of moviegoers from Dodge City to Timbuktu.

Part of the allure of the Western was its very simplicity. As Richard Schickel explains, because "everyone wore a six-shooter, complex moral conflicts could be plausibly resolved in clear, clean violent action." This decisiveness allowed the West to take on mythical dimensions, to become a place of great legends, embodied by Western heroes such as Wyatt Earp, Doc Holliday, Wild Bill Hickok, Buffalo Bill Cody, Calamity Jane, Jesse James, and Billy the Kid. At the heart of the Western, however, and not to be underestimated, was physical action—runaway stagecoaches, Indian raids, bank holdups, posse pursuits, and cattle stampedes.

Equally important, especially in the first half of the 20th century, was the immediacy of the American West. When Hollywood first set up shop, the last great frontier was so close at hand that gunslinger-lawmen like Wyatt Earp drifted to Hollywood to serve as consultants on movie sets. This closeness to the West made the Western myths tangible and all the more powerful.

The Western provided infinite variety on a relatively small stable of situations and plots, with conflicts often growing out of several archetypal situations: ranchers vs. farmers (*Shane* and *Man without a Star*), Indians vs. settlers (*The Searchers* and *Hondo*), and outlaws vs. civilization (*My Darling Clementine* and *High Noon*). Robert Warshow described the Western as "an art form for connoisseurs, where the spectator derives his pleasure from the appreciation of minor variations within the working out of a pre-established order."

Many filmmakers felt at ease with the Western and made their best movies within the genre. In a speech before the Directors' Guild, director John Ford summarized his wide-ranging career with the terse but proud assertion, "My name's John Ford. I make Westerns." Directors such as Ford (see entry), Budd Boetticher (1916-), Anthony Mann (1906-1967), and Sam Peckinpah (see entry) excelled at prying unsuspected complexities and ironies out of the well-worn stories of the American West. As a result, in John Ford's *The Searchers* we have much more than a simple quest to find a young girl kidnapped by Indians; we have the quest as eternal tragedy, for the story's hero, Ethan Edwards (John Wayne), can never become part of the civilization he strives to restore. And in Anthony Mann's *The Naked Spur*, we have much more than the simple story of a bounty hunter (Jimmy Stewart) bringing home a body; we have a story where vengeance and self-destruction are intertwined.

Some actors became closely identified with the Western, including Tom Mix, W. S. Hart, Roy Rogers, Gene Autry, and Audie Murphy—but for many people, no one epitomizes the Western like John Wayne (see entry). With a towering stature and a steely gaze, Wayne dominates his movies like a national monument dominates the land. His image has worked its way into the American consciousness as a metaphor for America itself, its strength, its determination, and its reliability. A quick survey of his movies—from *Stagecoach* to *The Man Who Shot Liberty Valance*—is very nearly a list of the greatest Westerns ever made. While Wayne owns the top echelon by himself, a host of other actors have made powerful contributions to the genre, including Henry Fonda, James Stewart, Gary Cooper, Joel McCrea, Randolph Scott, and Clint Eastwood.

Hollywood fed an eager American public a steady diet of Western myths, legends, and heroes for over five decades. In the process, the Western myth engulfed American popular culture—from clothes (denim jackets, jeans, and cowboy boots) to children's toys (cap guns, rubber-tipped arrows, and tom toms). Its lexicon entered our language ("round up," "hog-tied," and "bury the hatchet"). The Western held our interest (with only minor lapses) until Cold War cynicism ate away at the American psyche and we started doubting the heroes of the West. Gradually the West began to fade away, struggling in spasms of violence in *The Wild Bunch* and the spaghetti Westerns of Italy, until the Western hardly seemed relevant anymore. Not until the '90s arrived (with films such as *Dances with Wolves* and *Unforgiven*) did it seem possible that the Western could survive in any form other than dewy-eyed nostalgia.

BEGINNINGS. The era of the American West lasted from about 1850 to 1900, when the country was expanding at a staggering rate. Settlers trudged west on the Santa Fe and Oregon Trails, cattle empires sprang from the prairies, cow towns grew around railroad stations, and legendary cattle drives cut great swaths across the plains. This time period provided the raw material for the Western.

Back on the East Coast, dime novels about the West flooded newsstands and bookstores (see previous entry), spreading the legendary feats of real-life characters such as Kit Carson, Wild Bill Hickok, and Jesse James. Artists Albert Bierstadt, Thomas Moran, Frederic Remington, and Charles Russell captured this world on canvas, emphasizing epic mountain vistas, valiant cavalry actions, and noble Indians. Wild West shows featuring Indian war dances, stagecoach chases, and authentic frontiersmen (such as Buffalo Bill Cody) packed in audiences and even toured Europe.

Onto this world, the early filmmakers turned their cameras. Thomas Edison produced several short films that plainly and simply showed Indians and cowboys at work and play. These minute-long movies that played in Mutoscope and Kinetoscope to peep-show viewers were the beginning of cinematic Western imagery. In 1898, the Edison Company recorded the first Western dramas. *Cripple Creek Bar Room* shows several prospectors slogging down beers until they get drunk and thrown out of a bar, and *Poker at Dawson City* shows a game of five-card stud that ends in a brawl.

One of the most famous films of early cinema followed in 1903, *The Great Train Robbery*. Directed by Edwin S. Porter, it featured a train holdup, a posse pursuit, and a shootout. Most notably, the film featured one of the earliest recorded instances of parallel editing, as the outlaws' flight is intercut with the posse's formation and pursuit.

The Great Train Robbery had no heroes, but one member of its cast, Gilbert M. Anderson, would soon become one of the great silent Western stars. Between 1908 and 1916, he churned out dozens of Westerns every year for the Essanay Company, featuring himself as Broncho Billy. He usually played a good badman, outfitted in wide chaps, leather gauntlets, and a ten-gallon hat.

Anderson's main competition came from directors Thomas Ince and D. W. Griffith. With the services of the Miller Brothers's 101 Ranch and Wild West Show at his disposal, Ince created an efficient assembly-line process at Bison, frequently building entire films around Indian characters. Working at Biograph, D. W. Griffith created several Westerns that show his developing facility for editing and pictorial composition. In *The Battle at Elderbush Gulch* (1914), for example, Griffith creates a strong sense of tension during an Indian attack by cross-cutting between Indian attackers, a family hiding inside their cabin, and the cavalry riding to the rescue.

A veteran of Ince's Westerns, William S. Hart was one of the few Western stars who actually knew the West. As a result, his towns are dead ringers for photographs of actual Western streets, complete with tattered, ramshackle buildings and dust that hovers in the air. Playing a good badman who adheres to an ironclad code of honor, Hart's status soared after films such as *Hell's Hinges* and *The Narrow Trail* (both 1917), and he became one of the biggest stars in Hollywood. With the rise of the flamboyantly dressed fancy cowboys of the '20s, however, Hart's movies fell out of style. In 1925, he made one last movie, *Tumbleweeds* (widely regarded as his masterpiece) and retired.

Tom Mix was one of these fancy cowboys, and his movies were pure fantasy. He drew his inspiration from the circus and Wild West show (see entries), so his movies featured plenty of horse riding stunts, lassoing tricks, and broad comedy. He played an uncomplicated guardian of the prairie who didn't smoke or cuss. With a wide popularity that eventually eclipsed William S. Hart's, Tom Mix became the model for countless B Western stars in the 1930s and '40s.

Other Western stars of this period included Harry Carey, Hoot Gibson, Buck Jones, Tim McCoy, and Ken Maynard. Carey played Cheyenne Harry (a good badman) in a series of movies for Universal, some directed by John Ford. Gibson developed a slow, deliberate style of comedy. He never carried a gun and his films featured little physical action. Jones and McCoy played serious cowpokes in the W. S. Hart tradition. Maynard played a friendly, colorful hero who excelled at horsemanship and blushed in the presence of women.

The Western received a push for respectability with *The Covered Wagon* (1923) and *The Iron Horse* (1924). *The Covered Wagon* is an epic saga of wagons heading west on the Oregon Trail, featuring set-pieces such as a river crossing with 400 wagons. The movie was a great box-office success and spawned several more feature-length Westerns. *The Iron Horse* offered superior filmmaking in its story of the building of the transcontinental railroad. Director John Ford enlivened the proceedings with exciting action sequences and vivid details of everyday life.

As the sound era approached, however, audiences dwindled, and the studios slashed the production of Westerns. *Photoplay* magazine declared the Western "motion picture heroes have slunk away into the brush, never to return."

But the Western gradually fought back. Early sound Westerns such as *In Old Arizona* (1928) and *The Virginian* (1929) were noted for their use of realistic sounds—the roar of the locomotive, the creaking of floorboards, and the swing of the saloon doors. And they contained lively dialogue, such as "When you call me that, smile!"

In 1930, Fox and MGM each released wide-screen Westerns. Starring a young John Wayne, Fox's *The Big Trail* captured realistic shots of wagons floating across swollen rivers and being raised over steep cliffs. MGM's *Billy the Kid* served up a faithful re-creation of outlaw life in New Mexico. These tales, however, arrived at the beginning of the Depression, when audiences were looking for escapism not hardship. In addition, exhibitors refused to install new wide-screen projection equipment. (They had only just installed sound systems.) As a result, the movies flopped at the box office. John Wayne reverted to B Westerns and wasn't seen in another major studio production for nearly a decade.

A tale of the great Oklahoma land rush, *Cimarron,* was released in 1931, and it won the Academy Award for best picture, a feat unequaled by any other Western for 60 years. But few feature-length Westerns followed in its wake. By the mid '30s, the Western had been almost completely relegated to the Poverty Row studios.

THE B WESTERN. As the major studios turned to producing double bills in the '30s, a need developed for producing inexpensive co-features. Hollywood created the series Western to fill this need. As a result, most studios signed one or more cowboy stars to provide up to eight Westerns per year. By 1932, most big silent Western stars were reestablished in series of their own. In addition, new stars such as John Wayne and Randolph Scott emerged.

The series Western was a brazenly formulaic production, with plots motivated by straightforward villainy. Fist fights, chases, and shootouts flourished. Stories usually revolved around the ranch, where range wars and greedy land grabbers abounded. Dialogue was quick and to the point. Typecasting abounded so that audiences knew immediately who was good and who was evil. A man's best friend was often his horse. Occasionally a hero might have a romantic interest, but the love would be completely chaste. In fact the hero would never declare his love or intentions straight out, but only obliquely mention he might come back around for courtin'.

This period marked the beginning of the B Western's reign. Hollywood studios perfected the assembly-line process and cranked out B Westerns in astonishing numbers. Republic Studios, founded by Herbert J. Yates in 1935 from a group of studios teetering on the brink of bankruptcy, produced more B Westerns than any other studio. Compared to their competitors, Republic's production values were high, featuring razor-sharp cinematography, thrilling stunt work by the legendary Yakima Canutt, and stirring musical scores.

Starring for Republic, Gene Autry and Roy Rogers reigned as the number one B Western stars for nearly 20 years. Autry's first Western, *Tumbling Tumbleweeds* (1935), featured no less than six songs and established the model for future singing cowboy films (see entry). Originally playing bit parts in Autry's Westerns, Roy Rogers eventually surpassed Autry in popularity. They both played warm and friendly cowboys who urged everyone to stick together no matter what the bank or the landowners threatened. Their films took place in a world precariously balanced between the Old West and the modern world, featuring (often in the same movie) runaway stagecoaches, barroom brawls, high-powered cars, and airplanes. Autry's personality never acquired much color (some people say he was bland), but Rogers was loaded with charisma. Often sharing the spotlight with Trigger his horse and Dale Evans his girlfriend, Rogers starred in some of the finest B Westerns ever made—especially those directed by William Witney.

William Boyd as Hopalong Cassidy offered Autry and Rogers their biggest competition. A former DeMille leading man from the silent period, Boyd carried the refined elegant air of the gentleman, a far cry from the salty old-timer in Clarence E. Mulford's books, upon which the movies were based. Boyd cleaned up the Hopalong character and eliminated the limp (after the first movie). The series established a formula where the pacing began deliberately and then gradually increased until it was time for a huge shootout, often involving several posses that join together and ride to the rescue.

Other important B Western stars of the '30s and '40s included George O'Brien, Bill Elliott, Tex Ritter, Charles Starrett, Tim Holt, and Johnny Mack Brown. O'Brien (who starred in Ford's *The Iron Horse* [1924]) was a rugged and muscular actor with superior acting skills. Elliott played a modestly attired hero who wore his guns with handles forward in their holsters. Ritter played a singing cowboy in the Gene Autry mold. Starrett played the Zorro-like Durango Kid. Tim Holt played a boyish hero for RKO. He also provided excellent supporting performances in *The Treasure of the Sierra Madre* (1948) and *My Darling Clementine* (1946). Brown played Nevada John McKenzie in a long series of Westerns at Monogram.

The golden age of the B Western lasted until the late 1940s, when budget constraints started to affect the product. Even the slick Republic B Westerns looked drab. Studios merely recycled the same old plots and action scenes in movie after movie. Meanwhile, television was beginning to have an effect on the theaters. By the early '50s, Boyd, Autry and Rogers had all moved their operations to television, although Autry and Rogers still made occasional features. With a growing number of television Westerns (see entry)—including *Cisco Kid, The Adventures of Wild Bill Hickok, The Lone Ranger,* and *Death Valley Days*—many moviegoers chose to stay at home. Gradually the theaters stopped booking B Westerns. By 1954, the series Western—like the stagecoach and the covered wagon—was a relic of the past.

THE RISE OF THE FEATURE WESTERN. Through most of the '30s, Hollywood provided few feature Westerns. Among the exceptions were *The Plainsman* (1936) and *Wells Fargo* (1937). But then suddenly in 1939, with World War II developing in Europe, Hollywood turned out a spate of Westerns, including *Union Pacific, Jesse James, Stagecoach, Dodge City,* and *Destry Rides Again. Stagecoach* marked John Wayne's return to the "A" Western and firmly established him as a major star. An exciting tale of pursuit across hostile Indian territory, filmed with visual poetry by John Ford, *Stagecoach* was, André Bazin felt, "the ideal example of the maturity of the style brought to classic perfection." Although *Stagecoach* was a standout critically, it did only middling box-office business.

The biggest box-office returns went to the stories of outlaws—*Jesse James* and *Dodge City. Jesse James* established the badman biography as a major Western type and paved the way for films about the Daltons, the Youngers, Billy the Kid, and the James brothers. *Dodge City* established the town-taming Western, filled with brawling, expansive action, including a climactic fight aboard a burning train.

The Westerns of 1939 may simply have been a sign of the times: war was approaching and feelings of patriotism were on the rise. The Westerns helped the country as a whole look at the nation's history while we prepared to send men into battle. With themes such as "Winning the West" taking hold in the genre, the Western celebrated American values, and films such as *Virginia City* (1940), *Santa Fe Trail* (1940), and *They Died with Their Boots On* (1941) soon appeared.

But as the war years wore on, Hollywood turned to new, less optimistic material. With *The Ox-Bow Incident* (1943), a powerful attack on lynch parties, social themes came to the Western. And with Howard Hughes's *The Outlaw* (1943), a censorship storm erupted over the movie's sexual content. A Maryland judge who banned the film described Jane Russell's breasts as hanging over the picture "like a thunder-storm spread over a landscape." Posters advertised "Action! Thrills!! Sensations!!! Primitive Love!!!!" *Duel in the Sun* (1946) followed in a similar vein. As David O. Selznick's attempt to create a Western version of *Gone with the Wind, Duel in the Sun* provided a sweaty eroticism, painted in throbbing tones of red and orange by director King Vidor and cinematographer Lee Garmes. A tale of mad, sadistic love told between cracks of thunder and evangelistic sermons, critics simply labeled it "Lust in the Dust."

After the end of World War II, as the House Un-American Activities Committee scoured Hollywood for communists, a darker vision of human nature took root in Hollywood, as evidenced in Raoul Walsh's film noir-ish Western *Pursued* (1947). Western heroes and villains continued to grow in complexity until they weren't that easy to tell apart anymore. Howard Hawks's *Red River* (1948) is a classic movie from this period. John Wayne plays Tom Dunson, a tough authoritarian cattle rancher who barks out orders and refuses to take anyone's advice. After his adopted son (played by Montgomery Clift) takes over control of Dunson's cattle drive, the aging father becomes insane with anger and leads a posse of hired thugs to retake the cattle drive. *Red River* is a stunning Western, filled with brilliant characterizations and powered by a taut, unnerving tension as Wayne and Clift struggle for control of the herd.

Optimism hadn't completely disappeared from the Western after World War II, as evidenced by the work of John Ford. His *My Darling Clementine* (1946) builds relentlessly toward the gunfight at the OK Corral (with Henry Fonda as Wyatt Earp and Victor Mature as Doc Holliday), but the movie's overwhelming concern is the effect of civilization on the frontier, which Ford paints in wholly positive terms (as embodied by the sweet innocence of Cathy Downs as Clementine). But even Ford wasn't completely immune from America's darkening attitudes. In *Fort Apache* (1948), for example (the first film in Ford's magnificent trilogy of cavalry Westerns), Henry Fonda plays an arrogant, Indian-hating lieutenant who leads his troops on an unwarranted attack of Indians. After he and his troops are annihilated, his second-in-command (John Wayne) obscures the truth so that the cavalry's name isn't smeared—and in the process makes Fonda into a hero. Told against the stark beauty of Monument Valley, *Fort Apache* presents an enthusiastic portrait of cavalry life, but this enthusiasm is tempered by undercurrents of dissatisfaction with society's willingness to believe any legend and fawn over any "hero."

THE WESTERN MATURES. In the '50s, as the Cold War developed and the Korean War intensified, America looked to the nation's past for guidance. The traditional values of the Western provided prime material for this political climate and the Western exploded in popularity. However, the audiences now were more sophisticated and demanded more complex themes and subject matter than the simple horse operas of the past.

With these developments, the Western began to reexamine how Hollywood depicted Indians. Movies appeared such as *Broken Arrow, Across the Wide Missouri,* and *Devil's Doorway* (all 1950). The achievements of these movies now seem somewhat limited—featuring white performers in the Indian roles and regularly killing off the Indian women who dare to become involved with white men—but at the time they served an important role in opening the eyes of America to the great injustice done the Indian.

With this questioning approach toward the past, the Western began to depict a hardened, at times even bleak, view of the West. In *The Gunfighter* (1950), Gregory Peck plays gunfighter Jimmy Ringo, who's tired of being challenged by every cocky up-and-coming gunslinger, and wants to retire. But a gunfighter can never really retire. There is always some young punk ready to take a chance and say he killed the great Jimmy Ringo. In *High Noon* (1952), a certain moral decay crept into the American frontier, as Sheriff Will Kane (Gary Cooper) must plead for help from townsfolk before the noon train arrives and Frank Miller, bent on vengeance, collects his gang of outlaws and comes gunning for Kane.

During the '50s, the Western's biggest competition came from the plethora of horse operas on television. As a result, Hollywood looked for ways to make their products even more attractive and entice audiences out of their living rooms. Color soon became an essential part of the Western. Wide-screen Westerns such as *Vera Cruz* and *Broken Lance* (both 1954) emphasized the majestic terrain of the West. Even 3-D came to the West in movies such as *Hondo* and *The Charge at Feather River* (both 1953).

Director George Stevens, however, pushed the Western in a different direction with *Shane* in 1953. The most popular Western of the decade, *Shane* provided an aesthetic vision of the West, combined with a shocking portrayal of violence, as when Elisha Cook, Jr., is knocked backwards by a gunshot from Jack Palance. Some critics, however, attacked *Shane*. André Bazin claimed that other Westerns "extract explicit themes from implied myths" while *Shane* is all myth. Robert Warshow said Alan Ladd is an "aesthetic object" unlike Gary Cooper or Gregory Peck who "bear in their bodies and their faces mortality, limitation, the knowledge of good and evil."

For Westerns of this period, Bazin coined the term "super Western," meaning a Western "that would be ashamed to be just itself, and looks for some additional interest to justify its existence.... In short, some quality extrinsic to the genre and which is supposed to enrich it." In this view, *High Noon* injects the Western with a social critique of contemporary orientation and *Shane* self-consciously strives for the mythic.

Other directors, such as Anthony Mann and Budd Boetticher, were content to work within the conventions of the genre. Mann and Boetticher each made highly regarded series of Westerns in the '50s that are filled with reverence for the land and the decisions that men must make. Working with Jimmy Stewart and later Gary Cooper, Mann created a magnificent view of the West, tempered by the bitterness of his leading characters, in movies such as *Bend of the River* (1952), *The Naked Spur* (1953), *The Man from Laramie* (1955), and *Man of the West* (1958). Bazin lauded Mann for "that feeling of the open air, which in his films seems to be the very soul of the Western." The same could be said of Boetticher's films (made in collaboration with producer Harry Joe Brown and writer Burt Kennedy), where Ran-

dolph Scott played a hero obsessed with revenge. This brilliant series of Westerns began with *Seven Men from Now* in 1956 and concluded with *Comanche Station* in 1960.

John Ford started the '50s with the optimistic and lyrical *Wagonmaster*, but by the latter half of the decade a tone of desperation, anguish, and bitterness began to seep into his films. Whereas *Wagonmaster* had endorsed civilization's encroachment upon the wilderness, *The Searchers* (1956) casts a questioning gaze upon the men we call heroes and the place that society reserves for them. Before *The Searchers*, Ford had never questioned the rituals of society, as he allows Ethan Edwards (John Wayne) to do in this film. While a funeral is in progress, Ethan mutters "Put an Amen on it" so that he can begin searching for his brother's kidnapped daughter. The land itself—the towering buttes and the scorched terrain of Monument Valley—echoes the absurdity of Ethan's never-ending quest. Occasionally his rage explodes, as when he madly slaughters buffalo. As the film's justly famous final shot shows, Ethan will forever remain apart, forever to search.

Howard Hawks created *Rio Bravo* (1958) as a reaction against *High Noon*. He didn't believe a self-respecting sheriff would go running around town asking for help. Instead, John T. Chance (John Wayne) actually refuses help from townsfolk. But for all Hawks's fuss about the conventions of the Western, *Rio Bravo* ends up playing more like a comedy.

As the '50s wore on, the Western genre continued to twist and bend and, in the process, challenged our conceptions of heroes and myths. As a result, they also shook the audience's faith in Hollywood to provide the simple yarns it was accustomed to receiving. According to Phil Hardy, "Once the man with the gun was given a psychological dimension and confronted with problems that couldn't be solved by the speed of his draw, the simple appeal of the Western was in doubt." For a country with a long-standing love affair with guns, doubting the efficacy of firearms to bring us civilization meant the world was much too complicated a place for the Western heroes.

William Wyler's *The Big Country* (1958) plays to these concerns. Gregory Peck plays a representative of modern society who enters the West to make it respectable, to change its laws of honor. He is in opposition to a world that judges bravery by the willingness to fight. When the time finally comes for punches to be thrown, the camera pulls back, showing the fighters on a wide plain and emphasizing the futility of their action. The men get tired during the fight— rather quickly at that—scrambling in the dirt. "What did we prove, huh?"

To round out this era of the Western, John Ford provided an introspective tale on the nature of the Western myths, *The Man Who Shot Liberty Valance* (1962) and Sam Peckinpah gave us an elegiac tale of the passing of the Old West, *Ride the High Country* (1962). Ford's film suggests we used men like Tom Doniphan (John Wayne) to tame the West, but we didn't give them a place after civilization was established. Like Ethan Edwards in *The Searchers*, Tom Doniphan never marries and dies alone. Peckinpah's *Ride the High Country* shows the gap between the Old West (gloriously embodied by Joel McCrea and Randolph Scott) and the New West (which is filled with horseless carriages and white-trash miners).

THE WESTERN LOSES ITS WAY. In the '60s, the studios forgot about the lessons of Mann and Boetticher, as size, scale, and all-star action ruled the day. The results were well-mounted duds like *The Alamo* (1960), directed by John Wayne, and *How the West Was Won* (1962), as well as some entertaining but empty epics like *The Magnificent Seven* (1960).

With both stars and directors aging, the Western as a vital American genre began to wither. After *The Man Who Shot Liberty Valance*, Ford would direct only one more Western, *Cheyenne Autumn,* in 1964. Hawks only seemed interested in turning out variations of the *Rio Bravo* story in *El Dorado* (1967) and *Rio Lobo* (1970). Mann left the Western for historical epics. Delmer Daves opted for big-screen soap operas. Boetticher left for Mexico. With few new Western stars rising and Wayne, Fonda, and Stewart showing their years, the Western lacked vital new blood. At the same time, the modern-day Western appeared in ever-increasing numbers, suggesting with staggering frankness (in *The Misfits* [1961] and *Lonely Are the Brave* [1962]) that the times had caught up with the American cowboy. With the number of Westerns released plunging as low as 11 in 1963 (compared to 90 in 1953), the Hollywood Western looked vulnerable.

A decisive new development took place not in the U.S. but in Italy, where Sergio Leone and Clint Eastwood created the legendary man-with-no-name in a series of stylized, cynical Westerns—*A Fistful of Dollars, For a Few Dollars More,* and *The Good, the Bad, and the Ugly* (all released in the United States in 1967). Set in god-forsaken, dry-as-dirt Mexican villages, Leone's films bulge at the seams with unwashed, unshaven outlaws who swagger like Hercules while silently assessing every wallet in town.

Eastwood turned his man-with-no-name character into a laconic angel of death. Twisting his shawl to reveal his holster and sucking on a blackened cheroot, he squinted from under his hat's black rim while Ennio Morricone's music cracked like a whip.

Toying with the conventions of the Western like a cat playing with a mouse, Leone stretched time to an absurd degree. The opening sequence of *Once upon a Time in the West* (1969), nearly ten minutes long, shows nothing more than three gunfighters waiting on a train, but it's one of the great sequences in the history of the Western.

The only American filmmakers of this time competing with Leone were Monte Hellman and Sam Peckinpah. Hellman (collaborating with Jack Nicholson) produced two great existential Westerns, *The Shooting* (1965) and *Ride in the Whirlwind* (1966). Peckinpah gave us *Major Dundee* (1965), *The Wild Bunch* (1969), *The Ballad of Cable Hogue* (1969), and *Pat Garrett and Billy the Kid* (1973).

Peckinpah's *The Wild Bunch* remains the classic American Western of the late '60s. Alternately reviled and praised for its blood splattered, slow-motion scenes of extreme violence, *The Wild Bunch* grabbed the attention of critics and audiences alike. The movie's slow-motion violence is undeniably brutal, but it allows the movie's aging heroes to end their lives with one final blast of glory. And thanks to the magisterial wide-screen images of cinematographer Lucien Ballard, the film becomes a beautiful elegy for the Western itself.

Some good Westerns would still be made after *The Wild Bunch*, but much of the old spirit was gone. And the new Westerns, either opting for mud-and-rags realism or parodic excess, failed to find audiences—with one notable exception, the films of Clint Eastwood.

After the spaghetti Westerns, Eastwood contributed two movies in the man-with-no-name mold, *Hang 'em High* (1968) and *High Plains Drifter* (1973). These Westerns provided a particularly vicious brand of violence, as if to apologize for being Westerns. These films were box-office hits, but the strongest indication of the future came in *Coogan's Bluff* (1968), in which Clint Eastwood's Arizona deputy must go to New York to bring back an escaped killer. Transposing the man-with-no-name to modern times and giving him a respectable vocation, the stage was set for Eastwood to become Dirty Harry. After *High Plains Drifter*, Eastwood appeared in only two Westerns in the next 20 years.

As the '70s wore on, a group of revisionist Westerns appeared that stripped away the myths to reveal the muddy realities of life on the frontier, including *Culpepper Cattle Co.* (1972), *Great Northfield Minnesota Raid* (1972), and *The Long Riders* (1980). With these mud-and-rags Westerns, the genre's characteristic optimism turned into despair.

Everywhere, the theme of the death of the West took hold. Movies such as *Tom Horn* (1979) and *The Shootist* (John Wayne's final movie, 1976) played out the death of the gunfighter. *Monte Walsh* (1970) examines what happened to cowboys when their skills were superseded by technology: some drifted into crime; Monte Walsh himself (Lee Marvin) is offered a job as a circus performer. Turning the offer down, he comments: "I'm not gonna spit on my whole life." With *The Ballad of Cable Hogue,* the hero dies beneath the wheels of an automobile, further symbolizing the death of the West.

But the death of the West wasn't simply figurative, for the filmmakers and stars were dying. Departing in the '70s were John Ford, Howard Hawks, Henry Hathaway, Henry King, Jacques Tourneur, Raoul Walsh, Delmer Daves, and King Vidor. John Wayne died in 1979 and with him a large part of America's faith in the Western. Without the participation of these old masters who really knew the West, the new movies become second-hand stories, homages with little life or vitality of their own. And after Michael Cimino's *Heaven's Gate* (1980, the most expensive movie of its time) failed miserably at the box office, Hollywood declared the Western box-office poison.

The Western limped through the '80s with few hopes for recovery. *Silverado* (1985) attempted to pump up the old clichés and stock situations with rapid-fire editing, larger-than-life images, and a tongue-in-cheek attitude, but for all its verve, the movie wasn't genuine. Its well-rehearsed crescendos carried the aura of movie brats gussying up an old form. Audiences largely stayed away. Even Clint Eastwood's *Pale Rider* (1985) disappointed, with its cloning of

Shane. Young Guns (1988) strived to create a teenage audience for the Western by giving us Brat Pack alumni in Western garb. While modestly successful at the box office, *Young Guns* pointed down a dead-end path.

As it struggled into the '90s, the Western finally discovered salvation in the form of Kevin Costner's *Dances with Wolves* (1990). It packed in audiences and carted away the Academy Award for best picture, the first for a Western since *Cimarron* in 1931. Soon afterwards, the TV miniseries *Lonesome Dove* (based on Larry McMurtry's Pulitzer Prize–winning novel), attracted a huge following. Eastwood's *Unforgiven* followed in 1992, and it grabbed the Academy Award as well. It's a magnificent meditation on the Old West, filled with bitter ironies and brutal violence meted out by lawmen and outlaws alike.

A variety of Westerns then soon appeared, from *The Quick and the Dead* (1995), an inspired but hyperactive fusion of horror movie sensibilities and spaghetti Western situations, to *Posse* (1993), a black Western with a rap soundtrack, to Jim Jarmusch's surreal *Dead Man* (1995). The gunfight at the OK Corral provided the material for two movies, Lawrence Kasdan's ambitious but stodgy *Wyatt Earp* (1994), and George Cosmatos's intermittently dazzling *Tombstone* (1993).

Even with the minor resurgence of the Western in the '90s, the Western exists in limbo. It still has the power to fan the sparks of imagination, but our distance from the West has weakened its authority. While the West once represented a simpler time in America's history, we now see that the power of the gun (as shown in *Unforgiven* and *Tombstone*) could make lawmen just as dangerous as the outlaws. And although justice may have been swift, it was not necessarily fair and at times it was absolutely deadly. As the myths and heroes of the American West fade away, the Western becomes just another genre, a genre that becomes more remote with each passing year.

Bibliography

Bazin, André. *What Is Cinema?* Vol. 2. Trans. Hugh Gray. Berkeley: U of California P, 1971.

Busoombe, Edward, ed. *The BFI Companion to the Western*. New York: Da Capo, 1991.

Everson, William. *The Hollywood Western*. New York: Citadel, 1992.

Hardy, Phil. *The Western*. London: Aurum, 1983.

Kitses, Jim. *Horizons West*. London: Thames & Hudson, 1969.

Miller, Don. *Hollywood Corral*. New York: Popular Library, 1976.

Schickel, Richard. Foreword. *BFI Companion to the Western*. Ed. Edward Busoombe. New York: Da Capo, 1991.

Warshow, Robert. *The Immediate Experience*. New York: Anchor, 1964.

Gary Johnson

White, Betty (1924-), portraying memorable comedic characters, hosting parades and talk shows, and appearing on various game shows, has been a staple of television and popular consciousness since the early 1950s.

Born in Oak Park, IL (the date is sometimes given as 1922), White moved to Los Angeles with her family at age two. She is a graduate of Beverly Hills High School. After working with the Bliss-Hayden Little Theater Group, White began working in radio. She had small roles in some of the most popular programs, including *Blondie*, *The Great Gildersleeve*, and *This Is Your FBI*. In 1949 White became LA's first female disc jockey.

In 1951, White broke into television via a live local program with disc jockey Al Jarvis. The program was broadcast for five hours a day, up to 30 hours a week. Jarvis was later replaced by actor Eddie Albert. When Albert left, White remained as the solo host.

White formed her own production company in 1952, which created her first situation comedy, *Life with Elizabeth* (1953-55). White played a newlywed struggling through the first years of marriage. In 1954 White also had a daily network television show, for which she received her first Emmy Award nomination. White's next sitcom, *A Date with the Angels* (1957-58) featured her as the wife of an insurance salesman. She then starred in *The Betty White Show* in 1958.

Throughout her career White has appeared on numerous talk shows, including as a "regular" on Jack Paar's *Tonight Show*, and numerous game shows, including *Make the Connection, Password, The $25,000 Pyramid, Match Game PM*, and *The Liar's Club*. White also hosted Macy's Thanksgiving Day Parade for ten years and the Rose Bowl Parade for twenty. She has also appeared in several TV movies.

Perhaps White's biggest career boost occurred with her casting as Sue Ann Nivens, host of "The Happy Homemaker" segment on the *Mary Tyler Moore Show* (1970-77). While previously known for playing "nice roles," her portrayal of the conniving and, at times, lusty Nivens earned her back-to-back Emmy Awards in 1975 and 1976 in the supporting actress category.

After the *Mary Tyler Moore Show* ended, White played Joyce Whitman on the *Betty White Show* (1977-78) and Ellen on *Mama's Family* (1983-85).

In 1985, White became part of the ensemble of *The Golden Girls* (1985-92; see entry). From the creators of *Soap, Golden Girls* focused on the lives of four over-50 women sharing a home in Miami. White was initially offered the role of the lusty Southern belle, Blanche, but turned it down in favor of the seemingly simple Rose, perhaps because the former was a bit too similar to Sue Ann. White won an Emmy for her portrayal in 1986. She continued the role in the short-lived spinoff *Golden Palace* (1992-93). She was featured as the local woman who roots for the crocodile in the horror/comedy *Lake Placid* (1999) and appears in *Ladies Man* (1999-).

Bibliography

Plaskin, Glenn. "*Us* Interview: Betty White." *Us* 28 Nov. 1988: 48-52.

See, Carolyn. "Why No One Will Knock Betty White." *TV Guide* 17 Dec. 1988: 15-20.

White, Betty. *Betty White in Person*. Garden City: Doubleday, 1987.

——. *Here We Go Again: My Life in Television.* New York: Scribner, 1995.

Elizabeth W. B. Schmitt

White Shadow, The (1978-1981). While many modern TV shows try to present the struggle of inner-city kids, few do it as realistically or honestly as *The White Shadow.* Though never a Top 10 hit, the series has been widely acclaimed as the standard-bearer of quality and realism in high school dramas. Unlike the students in watered-down high school shows such as *Room 222* (1969) or *Lucas Tanner* (1974), the basketball players of Carver High were TV's first modern kids; they drank beer, had sex, committed petty larceny, and, in one episode, experimented with narcotics.

The heart of the show was Ken Reeves (Ken Howard), an ex–pro basketball player who, after injuring his knee, was convinced by a college friend to coach an inner-city Carver High basketball team. Being concerned about his player's lives both on and off the court, Reeves not only coached his team in basketball, but in life, as well.

Rather than having all the answers, Reeves was shown to be fallible, with one episode showing how even a concerned liberal could be prone to intolerance. Much of this was due to high school student James Hayward, played by Thomas Carter, who posed questions about African-American conditions that had previously been ignored by other TV programs. And, unlike most programs, *The White Shadow* provided no easy answers. More often than not, episodes ended unresolved. This sort of departure may be one reason for the show's cancellation.

The White Shadow was the first series for executive producer Bruce Paltrow, who later created and produced the critically acclaimed *St. Elsewhere* (1982-88; see entry). While most of the show's actors have faded into obscurity, the show launched the careers of both Ken Howard and Kevin Hooks, who played one of the students.

Bibliography

Brooks, Tim, and Earle Marsh. *The Complete Directory to Prime Time Network TV Shows, 1946-Present.* New York: Ballantine, 1992.

Feuer, Jane, Paul Kerr, and Tise Vahimagi. *MTM: Quality Television.* London: BFI, 1984.

Michael B. Kassel

Whiteman, Paul (1890-1967), although best known for directing the national limelight toward George Gershwin, Bix Beiderbecke, and Bing Crosby, arguably was the most influential figure in American popular music in the 1920s. By combining orchestral arrangements with ragtime rhythms, Whiteman established dance music as the popular music of the period, spawned thousands of imitators, paved the way for the swing era, and got himself crowned the "King of Jazz" in the process.

Born in Denver, CO, Paul Samuel Whiteman grew up in a family of musicians. His father was a music teacher who organized amateur orchestras; his mother, an accomplished singer, gave private lessons. Years of musical training—not without considerable family pressure—helped bring White-

man, then 17, a position as violist with the Denver Symphony Orchestra. Tired of relying on his family for support, he moved to San Francisco in 1914, landing jobs with the Panama-Pacific Exposition orchestra and the San Francisco Symphony.

After a stint in the U.S. Navy as a bandmaster, Whiteman started collecting musicians willing to learn his new arrangements, arrangements he dubbed "symphonic jazz." The "original" Whiteman orchestra debuted in Los Angeles in 1919, and quickly became a hit with the Hollywood movie colony. The exposure took Whiteman and his group east to Atlantic City and to their first recording sessions. Whiteman's first hit, "Whispering," quickly swept the country, topping the charts for eleven weeks and selling more than 2 million discs and 1 million copies of sheet music.

For all the celebrity his records brought him, Whiteman still sought to legitimize jazz (or at least his version of it). He hit upon the idea of staging a full jazz concert in a respectable concert hall, and he commissioned a young Broadway composer to create a special symphonic work for the occasion: the composer was Gershwin, and the work was *Rhapsody in Blue.* The concert, held February 12, 1924, at New York City's Aeolian Hall, was considered the triumph, even the birth, of an American music form. As its sponsor, Whiteman's standing as jazz's "king" was solidified. More than the "King of Jazz," Whiteman in the 1920s was its high priest, at a time when jazz was still considered in some quarters a dangerous, "uncivilized" sound. Through interviews, publicity, and even his own book on the subject, he preached the music's worth as safe, pleasant entertainment, and as art. By taking an outsider form of music and couching it in familiar terms, Whiteman helped make jazz acceptable, even respectable, to white audiences. His success—his fame among audiences led to his reputation as the pied piper of jazz—guaranteed that other orchestras would scramble to imitate him.

At the same time, the artists Whiteman discovered and featured reinforced the "newness" of the Whiteman sound. By spotlighting musicians such as trumpeter Bix Beiderbecke, saxophonist Frankie Trumbauer, trombonist Jack Teagarden, guitarist Eddie Lang, violinist Joe Venuti, and Tommy and Jimmy Dorsey, Whiteman used their skills to put a distinct stamp on the pop standards of the decade—and how people heard those standards. Before Whiteman, Tin Pan Alley tunes sung by baritones or peppy quartets dominated the best-seller charts. With Whiteman, the "Jazz Age" became the age of the bandleader. Whiteman himself became something of an icon for the age. By the mid-1920s, his moon-shaped, perennially smiling face, accented by a neatly trimmed mustache, was so familiar that it was caricatured on sheet music and record labels.

Despite the central star status given to the bandleader and his musicians, Whiteman did not eliminate vocalists from center stage. In fact, they often were transformed into instruments themselves. Most prominent among those were the Rhythm Boys, a trio of singers (Al Rinker, Harry Barris, and Bing Crosby) who combined comedy with a perky, personable variation of the scatting Louis Armstrong had made popular. Crosby, with his mellow crooning, quickly achieving front-man status, singing everything from ballads to Broadway standards.

Ironically, Whiteman's increased use of singers in the early 1930s coincided with his eclipse. Crosby bolted from Whiteman's organization shortly after the release of *The King of Jazz,* a 1930 Technicolor movie that purported to tell how Whiteman "discovered" jazz. Along with Rudy Vallee and Russ Columbo, Crosby led the shift in popular taste to the primacy of the vocalist. Whiteman continued to have hit records, appear in movies and on network radio variety programs, but his reign had ended. By the early 1940s, he was already presiding over an unending string of Whiteman and Gershwin "tributes." Despite his detractors among jazz critics, who dismissed his work largely as a betrayal or dilution of jazz's roots, Whiteman retained his image as the smiling "King of Jazz" until his death.

Bibliography

DeLong, Thomas A. *Pops: Paul Whiteman, King of Jazz.* Piscataway: New Century, 1983.

Shaw, Arnold. *The Jazz Age: Popular Music in the 1920's.* New York: Oxford UP, 1987.

Whitburn, Joel. *Joel Whitburn's Pop Memories, 1890-1954: The History of American Popular Music.* Menomonee Falls: Record Research, 1986.

Whiteman, Paul, and Mary Margaret McBride. *Jazz.* 1926. New York: Arno, 1974 .

Chris Foran

Who, The, an import from Britain, was one of the loudest bands in the history of popular culture. It made the *Guinness Book of World Records* in 1976 for a performance that exceeded 120 decibels. The band included Pete Townshend (1945-) on guitars/keyboards, Roger Daltrey (1944-) performing lead vocals, John Entwistle (1944-) on bass, and Keith Moon (1947-78) on drums. Townshend, Entwistle, and Daltrey, nucleus of the Who for 35 years, first worked together in 1962 in a blues band, the Detours. Moon joined in 1964, and the band changed its name to the High Numbers, then to the Who. It advertised itself as playing "Maximum R&B." The band released its first album, *My Generation* (No. 5, U.K. charts), in 1965, and its title track became a theme for angst-ridden youth.

In 1966, the Who's second album, *A Quick One* (*Happy Jack* in the U.S.), again topped U.K. charts (No. 4) but didn't do as well in the U.S. (No. 67). In 1967, the band made its U.S. debut, astonishing American crowds with performances at the Monterey Pop Festival and on the Smothers Brothers television show (where Townshend smashed a guitar). Then, in 1968, the Who continued to build their reputation as a live act and released two albums, *The Who Sell Out* and *Magic Bus,* both of which hit the U.S. Top 100.

1969's rock opera, *Tommy* (No. 4), and its hit single, "Pinball Wizard" (No. 9), finally broke through the American pop charts for the Who. Written by Townshend, *Tommy* was one of rock's first concept albums. It tells the story of blind, deaf-mute Tommy, a pinball champion revered as a prophet, whose followers later turn on him. *Tommy* set the

stage for bands like Pink Floyd and Yes. In August 1969, the band performed at two historic events: Woodstock (where Townshend reportedly kicked political radical Abbie Hoffman off the stage), and the U.K.'s Isle of Wight Festival.

In 1970, the Who released its first live album, *Live at Leeds,* considered one of rock's greatest live albums. 1971's *Who's Next,* which contained the single "Won't Get Fooled Again" (No. 15), became their most successful album (No. 4). Entwistle became the first band member to release a solo album, *Smash Your Head against the Wall.* In 1972, Townshend released *Who Came First,* and Entwistle then released *Whistle Rymes.* A fully-orchestrated *Tommy* (No. 5) was released with an all-star cast featuring Rod Stewart, Steve Winwood, and Peter Sellers, with Daltrey in the central role.

1973 marked the release of Daltrey's first solo album, *Daltrey,* Entwistle's *Rigor Mortis Sets In,* and the Who's *Quadrophenia* (No. 2), the story of an adolescent searching for identity and spiritual renewal. In 1974, *Tommy* was filmed by director Ken Russell; in addition to the band, the cast included Elton John, Jack Nicholson, Oliver Reed, and Ann-Margaret. Entwistle also put together the outtakes album *Odds and Sods* (No. 15). Moon appeared in the film *Stardust.*

1975's *The Who by Numbers* (No. 8) contained the single, "Squeeze Box" (No. 16). Daltrey played the leading role that year in Ken Russell's *Lisztomania,* and Moon released his only solo album, *Two Sides of Moon.* In 1977, Townshend, excited by bands like the Sex Pistols, collaborated with Small Faces' singer Ronnie Lane on *Rough Mix,* and Daltrey released *One of the Boys.*

In late 1978, the Who released a highly successful album, *Who Are You* (No. 2), which unfortunately was Moon's last; he died of a drug overdose on September 8, 1978. Although critics argued that Moon was irreplaceable, the band continued with former Small Faces/Faces drummer Kenny Jones. In 1979, two Who-related films premiered: *Quadrophenia* (with Sting in a cameo role) and a Who documentary, *The Kids Are Alright.*

Townshend released a solo album, *Empty Glass* (No. 5), in 1980, and Daltrey starred in and recorded the soundtrack for *McVicar.* In 1981, the Who released its first post-Moon album, *Face Dances* (No. 4), and its single, "You Better You Bet" (No. 18). Entwistle released his most successful solo album, *Too Late for the Hero* (No. 85). The following year, 1982, Townshend released *All the Best Cowboys Have Chinese Eyes* (No. 26), Daltrey put out a compilation, *Best Bits,* and the band released its final full album of new material, *It's Hard* (No. 8), panned by both critics and fans. The Who later announced they would officially retire from touring and recording. In 1983, Townshend received a Lifetime Achievement Award at the BRIT awards in London and released *Scoop,* a compilation of solo and band outtake material. 1984 saw two releases: Daltrey's *If Parting Should Be Painless* (#56), and a Who tour documentary, *Who's Last.*

In 1985, the Who re-formed for one short set at the Live Festival in Wembley Stadium. Daltrey released *Under a Raging Moon;* Townshend published a collection of short stories, *Horse's Neck,* and released the album and movie *White City.* The Who re-formed without Jones in June of 1989 and played stadiums through October, performing *Tommy* in its entirety for the first time in 19 years. Townshend also released his solo album, *The Iron Man* (based on the Ted Hughes children's story), featuring the remaining members of the Who on two of the tracks.

The band was inducted into the Rock and Roll Hall of Fame in January 1990. Throughout the 1990s, various compilations and box sets were released, including the four-CD box set *30 Years of Maximum R&B*. *Tommy* became a 1993 Broadway play under Townshend's supervision, where it garnered critical acclaim and three Tony Awards. Townshend also released his concept album, *PsychoDerelict* (1993).

Bibliography

Charlesworth, Chris. *The Complete Guide to the Music of The Who*. New York: Omnibus, 1995.

Giuliano, Geoffrey. *Behind Blue Eyes: The Life of Pete Townshend*. New York: Penguin, 1996.

Marsh, Dave. *Before I Get Old: The Story of The Who*. New York: St. Martin's, 1983.

Rees, Dafydd, and Luke Crampton. *Encyclopedia of Rock Stars*. New York: DK, 1996.

Walter, Stephen, and Karen Kimber. *The Who in Print*. Jefferson: McFarland, 1992.

Welch, Chris. *Teenage Wasteland: The Early Years*. New York: Penguin, 1995.

Robert G. Weiner

Wild West Show, The, from 1883 to 1920, was more than a passing cultural phenomenon in America and abroad. It helped establish an image of the West that American society still embraces. It helped make the cowboy and the plains Indian central figures in the melodrama of American civilization. The Wild West show contributed significantly to America's enduring fascination with the quick-drawing, fast-living, and hard-riding heroes and villains who dominate our perceptions of the mythic West. Fed on a diet of dime novels by Ned Buntline and the like, at the turn of the century eastern urbanites became the primary audience for the Wild West shows. The shows were a combination of myth and fact that kindled an interest in an area few of the show's patrons had visited.

The origins of the Wild West show are often linked to William Cody (Buffalo Bill), who in 1882 developed a cowboy Fourth of July celebration he entitled "The Old Glory Blow-Out." The next summer he added more features and "Buffalo Bill's Wild West" was born. This was the beginning of the true Wild West show; however, 50 years earlier Peale's museum had presented "displays of the American West." P. T. Barnum had also made tableaus of the West part of his 1850 circus, and in 1843 presented a Buffalo hunt, which later became one of Cody's key features. Barnum's New York Hippodrome concluded its shows in 1874 with Western scenes.

Though Cody did not originate the Western theme, with his partner Nate Salsbury he made the Wild West a unique entertainment. With ten years of experience performing western melodrama for eastern audiences, Cody understood perfectly the public desire to embrace the "real" West. The Cody show thus included: Cody and Annie Oakley demonstrating their proficiency with rifles, performers doing trick riding and participating in all types of races, plus a series of military exhibits, from Gatling-gun firings to close-order drills. The show also relied upon pseudo-historical reenactments for much of its power. Indians were hired to give demonstrations of their lives on the plains, yet primarily they were included to re-create attacks on stagecoaches and wagon trains, or participate in the show's grand final spectacle (often "Custer's last charge").

Cody and Salsbury were partners from 1884 to 1908, and their show set the standard for all other Wild West operations. Though barely solvent, in 1887 their show was taken to England where it was a huge event attracting about 30,000 people every day. European royalty also embraced the epic of the West; Queen Victoria sat through two command performances. In both 1889 and 1902, the show returned to Europe for four-year runs. Its greatest American triumph came on a lot across the street from Chicago's Columbian Exposition in 1893. In 1908, the show was sold to Cody's chief competitor, "Pawnee" Bill Lillie. This combination, known as "the Two Bills Show," ran until 1914 and was considered the high point of this type of entertainment. Like the "Two Bills," few Wild West shows survived World War I and the 1920s; those that did collapsed in the Depression. Like most other outdoor entertainments, the business had always been very precarious. Though Buffalo Bill's show lasted 30 years, Pawnee Bill's 23, and "Tiger Bill's" 24, only six of the other 113 Wild West shows known to have existed lasted more than three years.

In its earliest years the Wild West show brought living legends to the people. It presented famous scouts and cowboys, as well as the Indian leaders Sitting Bull, Chief Joseph, and Geronimo. Until Wounded Knee ended the plains wars in 1890, the Wild West show depended on contemporary western events for its impact. Due to a dearth of new events to dramatize, Buffalo Bill's show began to broaden its scope in 1893 by adding a "Congress of rough riders of the world." Other shows soon followed this trend and utilized contemporary military events such as the Spanish American war and the Boxer rebellion. The shows also began including circus features. "Pawnee Bill's Historic Wild West" in 1905 brought in many Asian tumblers and appended "Great Far East" to its title. The next year a small group of elephants was included. Circus man James Bailey added daily touring, a sideshow, and vendors to Buffalo Bill's show when he was its part owner from 1895 to 1906. Yet despite such features, after 1900 the Wild West's popularity was based primarily on the western myths.

The appeal of the Wild West show was constructed on the deft depiction of a West that was simultaneously savage and cruel, a place where men could prove themselves. It was a barbaric locale filled with opportunity for anyone resolute and crafty enough to conquer the elements and the Indians. Like Ned Buntline's characters, Wild West performers such as Cody, Pawnee Bill, and Tiger Bill all became heroic figures, men of action who demonstrated manly attributes. There was also a heavy dose of control over man's environment apparent in each production. Individual freedom was also sanctified, as the heroes lived by their wits outside the rules and regulations of civilized society. All these attributes certainly appealed to people trapped in eastern factories. The Wild West show's greatest successes were always in Europe or America's larger cities with people who had no experience with the West (Buffalo Bill's show played nine of its thirty years in Europe). In those localities the audience desired western fantasy, since it facilitated an escape from the demands of everyday industrialized society. In the Wild West, cowboys were real men. They never mundanely tended a machine. They utilized their expertise with gun, horse, and rope to subdue the savage environment, and along the way save the damsel in distress. The Wild West helped create the myth that the entertainment forms that replaced it perpetuated—the independent man of action.

Bibliography

Blackstone, Sarah. *Buckskins, Bullets, and Business: A History of Buffalo Bill's Wild West*. Westport: Greenwood, 1986.

Doug A. Mishler

Wild Wild West, The (1965-1969), was an exciting TV extravaganza which made James T. West the James Bond of Western heroes. Exciting as well as humorous, the show in which he starred borrowed from such successful series as *The Man from U.N.C.L.E.* and *Maverick*. Representing an almost perfect blend of espionage thrills, fantasy, sci-fi adventure, and cowboy action, it was called *The Wild Wild West*, in a play on both the hero's name and the setting.

West (Robert Conrad) was a super spy who battled super villains with super weapons. There was only one significant difference from all the other secret agents filling the home and movie screens of the 1960s—West lived in the 1870s and his boss was President Ulysses S. Grant. West and his partner, Artemus Gordon (Ross Martin), were assigned to defeat assorted lunatics who were out to take over this country (or in some cases, the entire world) usually with the aid of some kind of futuristic doomsday machine.

The series was the brainchild of Michael Garrison and incorporated much of the gadgetry associated with the spy craze in an embryonic form. Garrison resorted to primitive explosives, hidden weapons and borrowed heavily from Jules Verne's cadre of "mad scientists."

One of the most appealing aspects of *The Wild Wild West* was its host of fascinating, but generally quite insane, villains usually played by some "name" guest star. By far the most popular of these was the dwarf Dr. Miguelito Loveless, delightfully portrayed by Michael Dunn.

Although *The Wild Wild West* reached Nielsen's Top 25 only once (placing 23d during its initial year), it attracted sufficient viewers to remain a CBS Friday night fixture for four seasons. Furthermore, it was popular enough to be successfully rerun in syndication for many years. The network attempted a revival of the show via a series of made-for-TV movies, and Will Smith starred in a movie version in 1999, with Kevin Kline as Gordon and Kenneth Branagh as Loveless.

Bibliography

Kester, Susan E. The Wild Wild West: *The Series*. Downey: Arnett, 1988.
Story, David. *America on the Rerun: TV Shows that Never Die*. Secaucus: Carol, 1993.

Gary A. Yoggy

Wilder, Laura Ingalls (1867-1957), having spent her first 65 years as a frontier child, farmer (with her husband, Almanzo), and a writer for agricultural periodicals, spent her last 25 years as a beloved children's author. Between 1932 and 1943, with the secret collaboration of her daughter, Rose Wilder Lane, Wilder composed the *Little House* books, a seven-volume series for children based on her own childhood spent in various frontier communities in the Midwest and Great Plains. An eighth novel dealt with Almanzo Wilder's boyhood, and a ninth, published posthumously in 1971, treated the first years of her marriage. These books symbolized the ideal life on the prairie.

The *Little House* books are properly understood as fictional autobiography. They began with *Little House in the Big Wood* (1932), and include *The Little House on the Prairie* (1935), *On the Banks of Plum Creek* (1937), *By the Shores of Silver Lake* (1939), *The Long Winter* (1940), *The Little Town on the Prairie* (1941), and *These Happy Golden Years* (1943). Written in the midst of the Great Depression, they detailed the survival of earlier hard times by the loving Ingalls family—Pa, Ma, and their three daughters (Laura herself being the middle child). The stories were met with immediate critical and popular success. Children liked the carefully wrought details of everyday pioneer life and the depiction of spunky Laura. Critics found the books authentic portraits of the frontier past and an engaging family saga comparable in quality to *Little Women*.

Affection for the series soon spilled over into fascination with the "real" Laura. In her own day, Wilder received countless fan letters and honors, and was the first recipient of the Laura Ingalls Wilder Award given by the American Library Association. Since her death, tens of thousands of tourists annually have visited the Ingalls and Wilder restored home sites in the Midwest.

The 1974-82 NBC television series *Little House on the Prairie*, introduced the Wilder stories to a vast new audience, and prompted the reissue of the series in contemporary paperback editions.

Bibliography

Anderson, William. *Laura Ingalls Wilder: A Biography*. New York: HarperCollins, 1992.
Miller, John. *Laura Ingalls Wilder's Little Town: Where History and Literature Meet*. Lawrence: UP of Kansas, 1994.
Wilder, Laura Ingalls, and Rose Wilder Lane. *A Little House Sampler*. Lincoln: U of Nebraska P, 1988.

Anita Clair Fellman

Williams, Don (1939-   ), the "Gentle Giant" of country music, was born in Floydada, TX. The son of a mechanic, he was raised in a working-class home in Portland near Corpus Christi and graduated from Gregory-Portland High School.

His evolution as a singer/songwriter began at age three when he won a local talent show. Learning to play guitar during his teenage years, Williams began to pick up songs from the radio. He grew up listening to country music until high school, but came to appreciate all kinds of music including blues, folk, and rock when radio stations began to play a wider selection of songs. Important artists for Williams included Patti Page, Bill Haley, Little Richard, and Buddy Holly.

Don Williams performed locally until moving to Corpus Christi. In 1964, he formed the Pozo-Seco Singers, which performed folk, pop, and country. The group released hit songs including "I Can Make It with You" and "Time." The folk revival during this period, which influenced the group's choice of material, encouraged both folk and country artists because listeners became more attuned to the meaning of song lyrics. Williams later benefited from this revival when he went solo.

The Pozo-Seco Singers, stationed in Nashville since 1967, disbanded in 1971. Williams returned to Texas and worked in the furniture business with his father-in-law. Earlier jobs included a stint in the army, bill collector, bread truck driver, and smelting plant and oil field worker. These experiences helped him appreciate the daily lives of the common people.

Williams soon returned to Nashville and became a staff songwriter for Jack Clement Music Publishing Company, joining Allan Reynolds, Bob McDill, Wayland Holyfield, and Dickie Lee. Williams eventually penned over 500 songs, including "Lay Down Beside Me" and "Love Me All Over Again." Unfortunately, he placed few songs with artists in the early years. After coaxing by Reynolds, he decided to record his own songs and those by his fellow writers. His songs have since been recorded by Johnny Cash, Eric Clapton, Charlie Pride, Kenny Rogers, and Pete Townshend.

Williams's first solo release was "Don't You Believe" in June 1972. Shortly thereafter, "The Shelter of Your Eyes" gave Williams his first appearance on the country charts. His many classics include "Amanda," "You're My Best Friend," "Till the Rivers All Run Dry," "Say It Again," "Tulsa Time," and "It Must Be Love."

Williams has recorded 24 albums, 5 of which have gone gold. He has released more than 40 singles, including 17 No. 1 country hits and at least 12 others that have reached the Top 10. His recording of "I Believe in You" (Roger Cook/ Sam Hogan) crossed over into the Top 25 of the pop charts. In 1978, the Country Music Association selected Don Williams as male vocalist of the year.

Williams's carefully selected songs exhibit a strong unity of design comprised of tightly written words and uncluttered instrumentation. His stage appearance is marked by simplicity with his small band, trademark Stetson hat, beard, and acoustic guitar fretted up with a capo. His baritone voice brings alive rich images and meanings to the listener. While friendly with the crowd, Williams prefers to let his music do the talking.

Williams's personal life approximates his professional endeavors, in that simplicity is key. He lives on a farm just outside Nashville with his wife of over 30 years and two sons, shunning the spotlight for a quieter life and slower pace.

Bibliography

Delaney, Kelly. "The Don Williams Story." *The Songs of Don Williams*. Winona: Leonard, 1984. 2-3.

Lomax, John, III. "Interview: Don Williams." *Journal of Country Music* May 1979: 2-19.

——. *Nashville: Music City USA.* New York: Abrams, 1985.

Malone, Bill C. *Country Music U.S.A.* Austin: U of Texas P, 1985.

Timothy K. Kinsella

Williams, Hank (1923-1953), was the most influential songwriter in country music; all country writers since Williams have had their work measured against his and their lives compared to his. As a singer, Hank Williams was the quintessential country artist, with a strong, plaintive voice that projected sincerity and simplicity. As a songwriter, he reached beyond the borders of country music into the pop field, with recordings of his songs by Tony Bennett, Rosemary Clooney, and others. Many of his songs became standards and are still performed by both pop and country artists. He also had an impact on popular culture through his tragic early death; he exemplifies the genius who burns himself out through his art.

King Hiram Williams was born in Mount Olive, AL; because his father entered a V.A. Hospital in 1930, Hank Williams grew up virtually without a father and under the influence of a strong, domineering mother.

One of Hank's strongest musical influences was a black street singer named "Tee-Tot" (real name: Rufus Payne) in Greenville, AL, where he lived until his family moved to Montgomery. There he performed his first original song, "W.P.A. Blues," on an amateur night at the Montgomery Empire Theater (he won first prize). He began performing on WSFA in Montgomery and formed his first band, the Drifting Cowboys, when he was 13. At 18, he married Audrey Mae Sheppard, whom he met in Banks, AL, while he was performing in a medicine show. She, too, was a strong, domineering woman and their marriage was a tempestuous one. In September 1946, Hank and Audrey Williams came to Nashville, where he auditioned for Fred Rose, co-founder and head of Acuff-Rose publishing company. Rose would become a major influence on Hank Williams's life, editing and shaping his songs, producing his recording sessions, and often acting as a father figure.

In 1947 Hank signed with a major label, MGM, and recorded his first national hit, "Move It on Over," on this initial session. In 1949 Hank had his first No. 1 hit with "Lovesick Blues," a song he did not write; this led to him becoming a member of the *Grand Ole Opry*, the top country music radio show at the time.

Hank Williams rose quickly to superstardom in country music with countless hit recordings, many which he wrote, but he was beset with the problems of drugs and alcohol as well as a volatile marriage which ended in divorce in 1952. That same year he was banished from the Opry because of problems with his drinking and erratic behavior. With his personal life falling apart, Hank married 19-year-old Billie Jean Jones in a public ceremony at a concert in New Orleans and tried to salvage his career, but his health was deteriorating rapidly.

On New Year's Eve, 1952, Hank Williams was scheduled to perform in Charleston, WV, and on January 1, 1953, he was scheduled to perform at a show in Canton, OH. Hank left Montgomery on December 30 but encountered a snowstorm, which caused him to cancel the Charleston appearance; in Knoxville, he hired a driver to take him to Canton. On the trip from Knoxville to Canton, Hank laid down in the back seat to rest; when the driver stopped in Oak Hill, WV, he discovered Hank Williams was dead. The singer was 29 years old.

Bibliography

Escott, Colin. *Hank Williams: The Biography.* Boston: Little, Brown, 1994.

Flippo, Chet. *Your Cheatin' Heart: A Biography of Hank Williams.* New York: Simmons, 1981.

Koon, George William. *Hank Williams: A Bio-Bibliography.* Westport: Greenwood, 1983.

Williams, Roger M. *Sing a Sad Song: The Life of Hank Williams.* Urbana: U of Illinois P, 1981.

Don Cusic

Wills, Bob (1905-1975), bandleader, composer, and fiddle player, is known as the "Father of Western Swing" for his role in the creation of that popular dance music in the 1930s. Wills developed the western swing style in the 1940s and the 1950s to become one of the most influential figures in modern country music and an icon in America's evolving myth of the West.

A combination of horns and string band instruments playing danceable country music in a swinging jazz style, western swing became a national phenomenon when Wills and his band, the Texas Playboys, released a vocal version of "San Antonio Rose" in 1940 that sold millions of copies.

During the Depression and dust bowl disasters of the 1930s, Wills and other southwestern musicians created a lively dance music that offered listeners temporary escape. The appeal of that music carried through World War II, when Wills became part of the transformation of what was then called country-and-western from a regional to a national music.

Wills reached the peak of his popularity during the postwar period, when his national tours often set attendance records. In a recording career that stretched from 1929 to 1973, he made 550 records. Wills was voted into the Country Music Hall of Fame in 1968, although he always tried to emphasize the "western" in country-and-western to separate his work from rural white styles of the southeast.

Born James Robert Wills into a musical family known for quality fiddlers, Wills first performed the waltzes, breakdowns, and folk tunes of the American frontier. But in the cotton camps where his family labored during their migration to West Texas in 1913, Wills also learned the blues and other African-American folk music and often competed in jig dancing contests with his black playmates. There, according to Wills's biographer, Charles R. Townsend, Wills developed a feeling for rhythm that later enabled him to create the irresistible dance beat that is primarily responsible for his music's appeal. The combination of white frontier fiddle style with blues and jazz, in fact, was his distinctive contribution to country music.

In the early 1930s, Wills recognized the need to move old-time fiddle music closer to jazz in order to be successful as a dance musician, and with another founder of western swing, vocalist Milton Brown, Wills took a jazz-inflected string band on the radio in Forth Worth, TX, as the Light Crust Doughboys. Differences with his manager—as well as a drinking problem that would plague him throughout his career—forced Wills to move and adopt the Texas Playboys name, and in 1934, in Tulsa, OK, he made radio history advertising Playboy Flour for General Mills and formed the highly regarded dance orchestra with which he perfected the western swing sound by adding jazz horns to the string band.

When Wills first came to Tulsa, his 13-piece band sounded more like the older New Orleans jazz than swing, but by 1940, he could rival the top big bands of the day in danceability if not musicianship. With a full horn section and the string players using their instruments to resemble the blasts of trumpets and the wail of reeds, Wills advertised as "America's most versatile dance band." Like the ensembles of Benny Goodman and others, his orchestra contained three separate groups: a fiddle band, a New Orleans jazz group, and a big swing ensemble. And with pedal steel pioneer Leon McAuliffe and guitarist Eldon Shamblin, he featured a hot guitar front line at a time when Goodman was just beginning to feature jazz guitar pioneer Charlie Christian. That hot sound—with the bluesy fiddle, wailing pedal steel guitar, and walking bass—was adopted by emerging honky-tonk musicians in the 1940s, and it influenced rockabilly in the 1950s.

Wills still drew large numbers to his dances in the 1960s, and he remained an influence on emerging country styles, such as the Bakersfield sound developed by Buck Owens and Merle Haggard, even after the Nashville sound brought country closer to the pop mainstream. The country rock movement of the 1970s also acknowledged a debt to Wills, and in the 1990s, revivalists such as Dwight Yoakam draw heavily from the western swing tradition.

Bibliography

Green, Douglas B. "Tumbling Tumbleweeds: Gene Autry, Bob Wills, and the Dream of the West." *Country: The Music and the Musicians.* New York: Abbeville, 1988.

Malone, Bill C. *Country Music U.S.A.: A Fifty-Year History.* Austin: U of Texas P, 1968.

Townsend, Charles R. *San Antonio Rose: The Life and Music of Bob Wills.* Urbana: U of Illinois P, 1976.

Lynn Darroch

Wilson, Flip (Clerow) (1935-1998)—Flip for "flipped out" —was the star of *The Flip Wilson Show* (NBC, 1970-74), the first comedy hit starring an African-American comedian. For the first three seasons it was among the top-rated programs. Its last season was a sad disappointment.

Wilson was born the 10th of 18 children. His parents split up when he was 7 years old and he was placed in a series of unsatisfactory foster homes, then, at his own request, in a reform school.

Wilson lied about his age and entered the Air Force at 16. In the service, he began to hone his comic talents; after being discharged in 1955, he played various dives for some time until a Miami businessman in 1959 gave him $50 per week to work on his material without undue financial pressure. Wilson began to garner some success.

Bill Cosby and Dick Gregory had whetted the media's appetite for black comics. Redd Foxx touted Wilson to Johnny Carson during a *Tonight* show appearance, resulting in Wilson's August 1965 television debut performing his Christopher Columbus skit. Columbus tries to persuade Queen Isabella to finance his trip so he can discover America and Ray Charles. The queen runs around screaming that she didn't know Ray Charles was in America. The bit introduced America to some of Flip's southern and Harlem characters he was to make famous.

Bill Cosby stated that no one else in comedy so reflected black sensibilities as Wilson. For a time, he and Cosby dominated the black comedy scene. Soon Wilson was a TV staple. He was introduced to middle America on Ed Sullivan's show. During 1967-68, he appeared on eight installments of *Rowan and Martin's Laugh-In*. He also was a frequent guest host on the *Tonight* show. Obviously, his ethnic twists and gentle manner appealed to the audience. The time was right for his own network program.

The Flip Wilson Show introduced many viewers to stock "Harlem types," such as the Reverend Leroy of the Church of What's Happening Now! and Geraldine Jones, a tough-talking black woman. Many viewers had not been exposed to these types and they were fresh and new. Catchphrases such as "The Devil made me do it!" caught on and spread Flip's fame.

After his show's first three seasons, however, *The Waltons* took over the ratings. He made many appearances on various programs, and was almost a regular on *Laugh-In*, but he never again captured the large audience he once had from 1970 to 1974.

Bibliography

Brown, Les. *Encyclopedia of Television*. Detroit: Gale Research, 1992.

Current Biography. 1969.

Terrace, Vincent. *Encyclopedia of Television Series, Pilots, and Specials: 1937-1973*. Vol. 1. New York: Zoetrope, 1985.

——. *Encyclopedia of Television Series, Pilots, and Specials: 1974-1984*. Vol. 2. New York: Zoetrope, 1985.

——. *Fifty Years of Television*. New York: Cornwall, 1991.

Frank A. Salamone

Wilson, Hugh (1943-), a television and film producer, created several critically acclaimed television sitcoms and commercially successful films. Wilson's first series, *WKRP in Cincinnati* (1978-82; see entry), has become one of the most successful sitcoms in syndication, providing characters who have become popular American icons.

Wilson began his professional career writing for a trade magazine published by the Armstrong Cork Company. It was at Armstrong that Wilson met writers Jay Tarses and Tom Patchett, who eventually moved to Hollywood and began writing and producing *The Bob Newhart Show* (1972). In the mid-seventies, Tarses and Patchett got Wilson an interview with then-head of MTM Enterprises Grant Tinker, who hired Wilson as a writer for *The Bob Newhart Show*. Wilson eventually became a producer for *The Tony Randall Show* (1976), also produced by MTM.

In 1977, Tinker asked Wilson to submit a pilot for a sitcom for the upcoming fall season. Wilson's past experience in advertising led him to create *WKRP*, a character comedy that took place in a rock-and-roll radio station.

Although CBS had high hopes for the series—especially in regards to the younger viewers it promised to attract—*WKRP* failed to find an audience. Nevertheless, it became a popular series in syndication. Hard-rocking DJ Johnny Fever, newsman Les Nessman, and sleazy salesman Herb Tarlek have all become identifiable, popular characters. Hugh Wilson was also responsible for creating the sexy/smart secretary character Jennifer Marlowe (played by Loni Anderson). Although Marlowe helped break the dumb blonde stereotype, it also allowed *WKRP* to cash in on the popular jiggle factor that became so prominent in late-seventies' television.

Wilson went into filmmaking, creating and directing the successful *Police Academy* (1984). While Wilson is quick to admit the film was below his standards, it allowed him to earn enough money to become a powerful producer with the financial security to pursue more meaningful projects.

One of those was *Frank's Place* (1987-88), co-produced by Wilson and *WKRP* star Tim Reid. Set in a predominately black bar in New Orleans, *Frank's Place* was one of the finest half-hours of television. Though it failed to capture an audience, it solidified Wilson's reputation as a producer capable of quality programming. Wilson's next project for TV was *The Famous Teddy Z* (1989-90), a sitcom based on the true story of a mailroom assistant's rise to the top of a major talent agency. *Teddy Z* lasted a bit longer than *Frank's Place*, but ultimately failed to score with the public.

While Wilson will most likely return to series television, he has continued to work more heavily in film, with the critically acclaimed *Guarding Tess* (1993) and *The First Wives Club* (1996).

Bibliography

Brooks, Tim, and Earle Marsh. *The Complete Directory to Prime Time Network TV Shows, 1946-Present*. New York: Ballantine, 1992.

Brown, Les. *Les Brown's Encyclopedia of Television*. Detroit: Visible Ink, 1992.

Kassel, Michael B. *America's Favorite Radio Station: WKRP in Cincinnati*. Bowling Green, OH: Bowling Green State U Popular P, 1993.

Koch, Neal. "TV's New Ruling Class." *Channels* May 1989: 30-35.

Michael B. Kassel

Windham Hill Productions developed a market for and helped define a new style called New Age or Adult Alternative music that emerged in the late 1970s and 1980s. The acoustic, chamber-like folk music produced by Windham Hill helped bring members of the baby boom generation back into the record-buying market during a time when the industry was experiencing a decline in sales. In so doing, they revitalized the American record business.

Begun in 1975 by guitarist and Stanford University dropout William Ackerman and his partner Anne Robinson, Windham Hill's revenues grew at rates up to 587 percent a year in the early 1980s, and it became the leading purveyor of New Age music at that time. The music it recorded was largely responsible for defining the characteristics of New Age music in the public consciousness. The Palo Alto, CA, company achieved that success with techniques unusual in the record industry, demonstrating how values derived from 1960s counterculture, and considered naive by the industry, functioned effectively in the business environment of the 1980s and 1990s. A number of artists have risen to stardom on the label, including guitarist Alex de Grassi (Ackerman's cousin), the group Shadowfax (see entry), and pianist George Winston, the label's most successful artist, whose recordings in the early 1980s were the catalyst for Windham Hill receiving attention from major record retailers.

Robinson and Ackerman, as well as many of the musicians, reject the New Age label because the term, they feel, implies that a religious worldview is attached to the music, or that its intent is primarily therapeutic rather than aesthetic. But the favorable reviews in the New Age press, as well as the availability of the records in stores carrying New Age products and its patronage by radio shows focusing on New Age spirituality, helped Windham Hill achieve its initial success.

While the artists recording for Windham Hill see their music as distinct from each others' as well as from what is being created by other musicians in the New Age category, the homogeneity of the label's sound is rivaled in the U.S. music industry only by Motown Records in the 1960s. This has helped the company to sell the label as much as the individual artists it records. Record buyers have learned to expect predictability and often ask for "Windham Hill" rather than records by specific artists.

According to music critics, the remarkably homogeneous style of instrumental music on Windham Hill Records appealed to the need of aging baby boomers for a more tranquil alternative to rock music. Consoling, pastoral, and reflective, some critics charge that it is little more than "wallpaper music" lacking substance and spirit. All agree that the eclectic Windham Hill sound is restful, coloristic, and accessible to listeners familiar with pop music from the 1960s.

The improbable success of Windham Hill has contributed to the development of New Age subsidiary labels by major record companies and the growth of similar independent New Age/Adult Alternative record labels. Sections in large chain record stores devoted exclusively to New Age music began to appear in the mid-1980s as a result of the interest created by Windham Hill.

Bibliography
Barrier, Michael. "Only the Music Is in the Clouds." *Nation's Business* Nov. 1991: 60-62.
Darroch, Lynn. "Into the New Age." *Willamette Week* 4 June 1987: 17.
Karpel, Craig S. "High on a Windham Hill." *Esquire* Dec. 1984: 200-06.
Weisman, Jonathan. "Distribution Deal Sounds 'New Age' for Windham Hill." *Business Journal* 15 June 1992: 1.

Lynn Darroch

Winfrey, Oprah (1954-), is more than the most popular talk show host in history; she is one of the most powerful women in show business. Among the top-earning people in the entertainment industry, she is also the first African-American woman to own her own studio; in fact, she's only the third woman besides Mary Pickford and Lucille Ball to do so. Oprah Winfrey's life is the triumphant story of a survivor.

Born "the year the schools were desegregated" she said, Winfrey was the illegitimate daughter of Vernita Lee and Vernon Winfrey. Her name was accidentally misspelled on the birth certificate—it was supposed to be the biblical name Orpah. She grew up in the rural community of Kosciusko, MS, raised by her grandmother until she joined her mother in Wisconsin when she was nine. At that time she was raped by her 19-year-old cousin and was repeatedly sexually abused over the next few years by a family friend and her uncle. Her fear and guilt turned her into a rebellious child; as a last resort she moved to Nashville to live with her stepmother and father, a strict disciplinarian.

In 1976, she went to Baltimore to co-anchor the six o'clock news at WJZ-TV. Station executives tried to remake her looks and they insisted she get a permanent, which made her hair fall out. Winfrey also discovered that reporting and anchoring were not her strengths; she often became too emotional.

In 1977, she was taken off the news to host a local morning talk show, *People Are Talking*, quickly becoming one of Baltimore's most popular personalities. She stayed for almost seven years, and in January 1984, she moved to Chicago to host a morning talk show on WLS-TV called *A.M. Chicago*. The program quickly became No. 1 in its time slot, dethroning the King of Chicago, Phil Donahue. In less than a year, it expanded to an hour and was renamed *The Oprah Winfrey Show*. Meanwhile, producer Quincy Jones saw the show in Chicago and sent her to audition with Steven Spielberg for the role of Sofia in the movie *The Color Purple* (1985). Winfrey was nominated for both a Golden Globe and an Academy Award as Best Supporting Actress. She later starred in the films *Native Son* (1986), playing Mrs. Thomas, and *Beloved* (1998), as Sethe.

In September 1986, King World syndicated *The Oprah Winfrey Show* nationally, and Winfrey formed her own production company, Harpo ("Oprah" spelled backwards). In 1988, Harpo assumed ownership and all production responsibilities for her talk show. Winfrey has never taken a business course and says she runs the company on instinct.

Besides the talk show, Harpo produces all of Winfrey's specials and movies for television and film, and options properties for her to star in. Her 1989 miniseries, *The Women of Brewster Place*, was so successful that it became a short-lived series, *Brewster Place* (1990). She also starred in a sitcom based on a single talk show host in Chicago, but the pilot was mediocre and she dropped the project.

Winfrey's philanthropic contributions go to a variety of causes, including education, scholarships, programs for battered women, and most especially, abused children. She has also sponsored a club for teenage girls in the Cabrini housing project and has set up a foundation in conjunction with Hull House called FABL—"Families for a Better Life."

Bibliography
Angelou, Maya. "Women of the Year: Oprah Winfrey." *Ms.* Jan. 1989: 88+.
Barthel, Joan. "Here Comes Oprah." *Ms.* Aug. 1986: 46+.
Kanner, Miriam. "Oprah at 40." *Ladies' Home Journal* Feb. 1994: 96+.
Mair, George. *Oprah Winfrey: The Real Story.* Secaucus: Carol, 1994.
Randolph, Laura B. "Oprah Opens Up about Her Weight, Her Wedding and Why She Withheld the Book." *Ebony* Oct. 1993: 130+.

Carole D. Parnes

Winnie the Pooh is one of America's most loved characters. Even those who have not read A. A. Milne's classic children's tales of the adventures of the lovable Pooh bear (*Winnie the Pooh*, 1926, and *The House at Pooh Corner*, 1928) are familiar with the memorable illustrations created by E. H. Shepard for the original text. Milne's stories of six-year-old Christopher Robin and his menagerie of toy animals—the beloved teddy bear Winnie, Piglet, Tigger, Kanga & Roo, Eeyore, Owl, and Rabbit—who are brought to life through the magic of childhood imagination and belief—endure even in this cynical age.

The stories are usually described as nonsense fantasies, where the various animal characters engage in comic capers in their "100 Aker Wood": Pooh teams up with Piglet to ensnare a Heffalump; a birthday party for Eeyore the donkey garners ludicrously useless gifts; the animals join the hunt for the Woozle by following his snowprints. Each of the characters has a distinctive personality trait: Eeyore is melancholy; Pooh is ingenuous; Rabbit is a planner. When storytelling time is over, the animals quickly revert to stuffed status as Christopher Robin must wash his face, brush his teeth, and go upstairs to bed.

Milne wrote the stories initially for his own son, but they quickly gained a place in the cultural legacy, where Pooh's appeal is not limited to younger audiences. Although Pooh is described as "a bear of no brain at all," his wisdom was compared with the Chinese philosophers of Taoism in Benjamin Hoff's popular adult book, *The Tao of Pooh* (1982). Earlier, Pooh was the focus of Berkeley professor Frederick Crews's satire of academic literary criticism, *The Pooh Perplex: A Freshman Casebook* (1963). Composer H. Fraser-Simson wrote *The Hums of Pooh* (1929), and the bear's adventures have been translated into almost every language, including Latin and Esperanto, and immortalized on film, video, and television ever since. Today, Walt Disney's image of Winnie the Pooh is more pervasive than Shepard's original illustration, and Pooh is the logo for a line of children's clothing.

Bibliography
Thwaite, Ann. *A. A. Milne: The Man behind Winnie-the-Pooh.* New York: Random, 1990.
——. *The Brilliant Career of Winnie-the-Pooh: The Definitive History of the Best in All the World.* New York: Dutton, 1994.

Su Epstein

Winston Cup, The, program of stockcar races originated in 1949 and was described as the Grand National series. In 1970, as a result of sponsorship by the R. J. Reynolds Tobacco Company, the races were called the Winston Cup. Just as Virginia Slims cigarettes have become synonymous with the women's tennis circuit, Winston has seen its brand name become an umbrella term to designate premier racing competitions in the National Association for Stock Car Auto Racing (NASCAR) series. The Winston Cup racing series begins in February and ends in November. The high point of the Winston Cup series is the Daytona 500 held on the 2-1/2-mile oval circuit at the Daytona International Speedway in Florida. The series is becoming more and more an important aspect of American sports culture (see Stockcar Racing).

Richard "Son-of-a-Gun" Petty holds the record for Winston Cup Championships—1964, 1967, 1971-72, 1974-75 and 1979. From 1958 to 1992 Petty started in 1,185 races. His best year was 1967 with 27 Winston Cup successes. He was also the first Winston Cup driver to earn over $1 million from racing. His father, Lee Petty, was a three-time NASCAR Grand National Champion. Asked once if he would like to try Grand Prix cars, Indy single-seaters, or sports cars, Richard allowed wistfully that he would if he had the time. He never did. He retired in 1994 at the age of 57.

In 1976, Janet Guthrie entered the World 600 and became the first woman to drive in a major stockcar race. One year later she was the first female to compete in the Indianapolis 500. Winston Cup's racing machines, called stockcars, are modified factory production vehicles. The insides are stripped down to include only the necessities. The sport has been made a relatively safe, albeit always dangerous, sport as a result of safety internal rollcages. The suspensions can be fine tuned for various surfaces, and tires are selected for weather, climate, etc. Corners are banked (on some circuits this can allow three racers abreast to enter and leave corners), and short tracks are known as "bull pens."

A major breakthrough for Winston Cup racing was the August 6, 1994, Brickyard 400, the first stockcar race to be held on the world famous 2.5 mile circuit of the Indianapolis Motor Speedway. The 9.5 degree banking and the 5/8 of a mile straights tax both drivers and machines.

Bibliography

Cutler, R., and B. Fendell. *The Encyclopedia of Auto Racing Greats*. Englewood Cliffs: Prentice-Hall, 1973.

Handzel, W. "Stock Cars Race at the Indianapolis Speedway." *Hot Rod* Aug. 1994: 88-91.

Kinnan, R. "1994 NASCAR Winston Cup Preview: What a Difference a Year Makes." *Hot Rod* Feb. 1994: 48.

Matthews, P., ed. *The Guinness Book of Records*. New York: Facts on File, 1993.

Morrison, I. *Motor Racing—Records, Facts, and Champions*. Enfield: Guinness, 1989.

Scott A. G. M. Crawford

Wizard of Oz, The (1900), in the words of its author, L. Frank Baum, was a "modernized fairy tale," which attempted to retain the "wonderment and joy" of traditional European tales while omitting the "heartaches and nightmares." By depicting magic as the result of gadgetry and machinery rather than spells and enchantments, Baum allowed his turn-of-the-century readers to celebrate the technological prosperity of modern American life. At the same time, he introduced imaginative new settings and characters to the familiar fairy tale format, establishing a uniquely American Utopia founded on love and inhabited by individuals whose solutions to problems lay within themselves.

The story tells of Dorothy Gale, a young girl from Kansas, who is blown by a cyclone to the land of Oz, where she searches for the magical Wizard who will help her return home. Along the way she acquires three companions, each of whom already possesses the characteristic he most desires from the Wizard: a Scarecrow, who wishes for brains but exhibits intelligence and insight; a Tin Woodsman, who longs for a heart but demonstrates kindness and compassion; and a Cowardly Lion, who requests courage but manifests bravery and determination. Even Dorothy finds that she has all along owned the magic that will return her to Kansas. Unlike the celebrated film version (1939) made by MGM and starring Judy Garland, Baum's story contains no implication that Dorothy's exploits in Oz are a mere dream.

Although *The Wizard of Oz* was never intended to be the first in a series, at the insistence of his readers Baum wrote thirteen sequels to Oz, and after his death other writers continued the tradition.

Bibliography

Baughman, Ronald. "L. Frank Baum and the Oz Books." *Columbia Library Columns* 4.3 (1955).

Baum, L. Frank. *The Wizard of Oz & Who He Was*. East Lansing: Michigan State UP, 1957.

Cox, Stephen. *The Munchkins Remember:* The Wizard of Oz *and Beyond*. New York: Dutton, 1989.

Harmetz, Aljean. *The Making of* The Wizard of Oz. New York: Knopf, 1981.

"The New Wonderland" and "The Wonderful Wizard of Oz." *Dial* 29 (1 Dec. 1900).

Laura Apol Obbink

WKRP in Cincinnati (1978-1982). Although Mary Tyler Moore Enterprise's shows such as *The Mary Tyler Moore Show* and *Hill Street Blues* were more critically acclaimed and popularly accepted, *WKRP in Cincinnati* still remains MTM's most popular program in syndication. While part of *WKRP*'s appeal has been in its realistic characters, the sitcom earned a reputation few other TV shows can claim—it was hip. *WKRP*'s population of strange characters, fresh plots, and attacks on commercialism and conservative conventions most likely grew out of its rock-and-roll radio station setting.

WKRP, the fictional station, was in the ratings basement until station manager Arthur Carlson (Gordon Jump) hired successful program director Andy Travis (Gary Sandy). Revitalizing the AM station's elevator music format with rock, Travis resurrected Dr. Johnny Fever (Howard Hesseman)—a once-popular L.A. disc jockey fired for saying "booger" on the air—and added hip disc jockey Venus Flytrap (Tim Reid). The turn to rock made for a more successful station, but often caused problems between Travis and the more conservative members of the station.

As the series progressed, *WKRP* moved well beyond simple stories based on the contemporary vs. conservative theme. Indeed, *WKRP*'s episode list reads more like that of a news magazine than sitcom. The show explored racism, sexism, commercialism, alcoholism, censorship, education, and homosexuality; furthermore, *WKRP* attacked such issues in a way that often left the final decision to the viewer.

WKRP's characters have become part of our popular culture, with Johnny Fever the embodiment of rock disc jockeys, Les Nessman the prototypical daffy newsman, and Herb Tarlek the model for the gaudy, sexist salesmen we all love to hate. One of the show's most interesting characters was Jennifer Marlowe (Loni Anderson), the sexy-and-intelligent station receptionist. Although many argue that the busty Jennifer was an accommodation to 1980 TV's all-important jiggle factor, the character's intelligence and wit helped attack the dumb blonde stereotype. As the series progressed, Tim Reid developed as a strong black character who was often able to portray many of the problems faced by African Americans.

While *WKRP* did well in syndication, it only had one successful first-run season, in 1979 when it followed *M*A*S*H*. *WKRP* was one of the first shows to be frequently moved by the network—the sitcom had 14 different time slots in its four-year run. The series was canceled because of declining ratings, but it has been conjectured that other factors may have been involved. For example, shortly before *WKRP* was canceled, Hesseman had taken part in actor Ed Asner's rally supporting Latin American Sandinistas. Advertisers reportedly protested Asner's growing political involvement, and Asner's *Lou Grant* and *WKRP* were canceled on the same day shortly following the rally.

Bibliography

Brooks, Tim, and Earle Marsh. *The Complete Directory to Prime Time Network and Cable TV Shows, 1946-Present*. New York: Ballantine, 1995.

Kassel, Michael. *America's Favorite Radio Station:* WKRP in Cincinnati. Bowling Green, OH: Bowling Green State U Popular P, 1993.

Rosen, Craig. "Jocks Miss Days of WKRP." *Billboard* 17 June 1989: 10, 32.

Michael B. Kassel

Wolfe, Tom (1931-) is one of America's most respected cultural commentators and novelists. When Tom Wolfe burst into fame, he received fan letters from readers who praised his books, *The Kandy-Kolored Tangerine-Flake Streamline Baby* (1965) and *The Electric Kool-Aid Acid Test* (1968), but wondered why they were so different from his earlier works, *Look Homeward Angel* and *Of Time and the River*, and why there was a gap of 30 years between publications.

Confusion with Thomas Wolfe, the author of the earlier books, was just one of Tom Wolfe's problems when he began his career. Another was the controversial and irreverent style for which he soon became known, which flew in the face of the journalistic conventions he had mastered as a newspaper reporter at the *Springfield* (MA) *Union* and the *Washington Post.* This in-your-face attitude raised him to one of the country's most important journalists.

Born in Virginia to an academic family, Thomas Kennerly Wolfe, Jr., excelled in both tap dance and baseball as a child (he once tried out with the New York Giants of the Willie Mays era), but studied English at Washington and Lee University, where he was a co-founder of that school's literary magazine, *Shenandoah.* He earned a doctorate in American studies at Yale, but after this academic overdose sought the "real world" of a newspaper career.

After stints with the *Union* and the *Post,* he arrived at the *New York Herald-Tribune* in 1962, and began earning notice for his outlandish feature stories. Soon he was a regular contributor to *Esquire* and, along with such other writers as Gay Talese, Truman Capote, Joan Didion, Norman Mailer, and others, was lauded and/or reviled as a practitioner of "new journalism." Wolfe was the only one of the group to take time to analyze the changing non-fiction of the era and become the historian of new journalism. "New journalism" was a term he despised but came to accept when no one came forth with a better name. It was merely the appropriation of literary techniques by non-fiction writers, Wolfe said.

Wolfe's central concern has always been status and he began exploring the "new status seekers" with massive articles about car customizers and celebrated stockcar drivers. These essays were collected in *The Kandy-Kolored Tangerine-Flake Streamline Baby. The Electric Kool-Aid Acid Test* told the story of novelist Ken Kesey, who, with a band of followers called the Merry Pranksters, seemed to be establishing a new religion based around LSD. This controversial form of status-seeking needed to be recorded, Wolfe thought.

He stayed ahead of the game with collections of his magazine articles, *The Pump House Gang* (1968; published the same day as the *Acid Test*), *Radical Chic & Mau-Mauing the Flak Catchers* (1970), and *Mauve Gloves & Madmen, Clutter & Vine* (1975). Using his academic training, he pontificated on the revolution in non-fiction writing in *The New Journalism* (1973) and offered an anthology of the best examples of the form—pieces by Truman Capote, Norman Mailer, Hunter S. Thompson, and others.

Sent by *Rolling Stone* magazine to Cape Canaveral in 1973 to cover the final Apollo launch, he found himself immersed in the world of the astronauts and embarked on a project that occupied him for the rest of the decade. *The Right Stuff* (1979) was an emotion-packed testament to the quality of courage and was his most sustained work of non-fiction. A film version followed in 1983.

He published other non-fiction books, including attacks on modern art (*The Painted Word,* 1975) and modern architecture (*From Bauhaus to Our House,* 1981), and a collection of his drawings and verse (*In Our Time,* 1980); but for most of the 1980s, he was occupied with writing a novel on deadline. Figuring that Dickens and Balzac had serialized their novels in the publications of their day, Wolfe secured a deal with *Rolling Stone* to serialize his big, realistic novel of New York. When the biweekly installments began appearing in 1983, Wolfe was roundly criticized, but when his revised version appeared in book form in 1987, *The Bonfire of the Vanities* was hailed as a masterpiece (it became a movie in 1990). *A Man in Full* (1998) had an initial press-run of 1.2 million hard-cover copies.

Bibliography
McKeen, William. *Tom Wolfe.* New York: Twayne, 1995.
Scura, Dorothy M. *Conversations with Tom Wolfe.* Jackson: UP of Mississippi, 1990.
Shomette, Doug, ed. *The Critical Response to Tom Wolfe.* Westport: Greenwood, 1992.

William McKeen

"Wolfman Jack" (Robert Weston Smith) (1941-1995), broadcasting from stations along the Mexican border and later via Armed Forces Radio, howled and growled through rock and rhythm & blues classics, making generations of fans throughout the southwest, then around the world. From his presence in the movie *American Graffiti* (1973), the Wolfman became the disc jockey most associated with the "greaser" revival of the 1970s.

Young Bob Smith had a reputation as a hoodlum in his Brooklyn neighborhood. To keep him out of trouble, his father gave him a radio, which he used to tune in the disc jockeys who championed rhythm & blues music. "Smitty" eventually headed to Nashville to learn radio from "John R." Richbourg, of WLAC, a white champion of black R&B since the 1940s, and then began a series of radio sales and announcing jobs.

Bob became interested in the "border radio" stations in Mexico, which could blast an unrestricted 250,000 watt signal back to the U.S., selling faith cures and patent medicines that would cost stations their licenses back in the States. He took over management of XERF, south of Del Rio, TX, in 1960. To get the station's lineup of radio preachers to pay their bills, Bob temporarily replaced them with a licentious R&B show hosted by his new alter-ego, Wolfman Jack (Smith later recalled that he had played "the Wolfman" when roughhousing with his sister's children, and that "Jack" was a beatnik affectation of the time). By day, Bob

Smith sold time on both KCIJ and XERF, but by night, it was the Wolfman who howled on the airwaves as far out as the Soviet Union.

Once Smith pulled XERF into the black, the absentee owner decided to cut him out of the action. Smith staved off a literal gunfight by selling out his interest. After an unsuccessful stint with KUXL in Minneapolis, he headed to XERB in Tijuana, with access to the Los Angeles market. His sales staff and announcers worked at a Sunset Boulevard office, then ran each day's programming on tape to the transmitter in Mexico. There, Wolfman became a radio legend in the western U.S.

Wolfman Jack's guttural delivery borrowed from blues singer Howlin' Wolf, baying R&B slang and double entendres, telling listeners to "get nekkid" and coining "watching the submarine races" as a euphemism for necking on lover's lane. He responded to records like a revival chorus and dropped sound effects of wolves into the middle of songs.

Mexican officials saw radio profits escaping north, and forced Smith to sell his interest in XERB. Smith and the Wolfman were on the outs for a short time, until he got a morning-drive gig at Los Angeles' experimental album rocker KDAY. In 1970, he took his old XERB tapes, edited his segues and phone dedications to remove dated references and L.A. locations, and became the first rock DJ to go into syndication. The show ran for 16 years across the country and on 600 Armed Forces Radio stations worldwide.

When the movie *American Graffiti*, with the Wolfman's bit part as himself, came out, breaking box-office records, the Wolfman's show became more popular than ever. He became co-host, with Helen Reddy, of *The Midnight Special*, a live music show airing Fridays after Johnny Carson on NBC.

Wolfman Jack was everywhere in the 1970s. He had a religious show, pitched dozens of products, and did guest shots on TV series. His voice is heard on Top 40 tribute songs like the Guess Who's "Clap for the Wolfman," Flash Cadillac's "Did You Boogie (With Your Baby)," and the Stampeders' cover of "Hit the Road, Jack."

Bob Smith cut back the Wolfman's work load in the 1980s, working small venues and corporate meetings, and hosting *Rock 'n' Roll Palace* on the Nashville Network. He emceed oldies concerts and sold record collections through TV infomercials. He had begun syndicating a live oldies record show from the Planet Hollywood restaurant, in Washington, DC, when he died of a heart attack in 1995.

Bibliography

Smith, Wes. "Country Wolf: The New Rock Makes Him Howl, So Jack Turns to Nashville." *Chicago Tribune* 28 Dec. 1988, sec. 5: 3.

——. *The Pied Pipers of Rock 'n' Roll: Radio Deejays of the 50s and 60s.* Marietta: Longstreet, 1989.

Wolfman Jack, with Byron Laursen. *Have Mercy! Confessions of the Original Rock 'n' Roll Animal.* New York: Warner, 1995.

Mark McDermott

Women in Baseball. During the early 1990s, umpire Pam Postema filed a lawsuit against organized ball; Penny Marshall produced *A League of Their Own*; and the all-female Silver Bullets became part of the Northern League. To some, these events seemed unprecedented, but women have functioned as baseball owners, managers, umpires, or players for a hundred years.

Helene Britton, who owned the St. Louis Cardinals from 1911 to 1917, inherited the team. Likewise, Grace Comiskey inherited the Chicago White Sox; Jean Yawkey, the Boston Red Sox; and Joan Kroc, the San Diego Padres. But Joan Whitney Payson purchased the New York Mets and Marge Schott purchased the Cincinnati Reds. In the Negro Leagues, Effa and Abe Manley co-owned the Newark Eagles, Mrs. Manley functioning as the team's business manager and public relations department.

Only a few women have served as general managers in minor league ball. Frances Crockett was named GM of the Charlotte O's in the 1970s, and Ellen Harrigan-Charles was GM of the St. Catherine's Blue Jays in the 1990s. Shereen Samonda, GM of the Orlando Cubs, went on to hold the same position for the 1994 Colorado Silver Bullets.

In the major leagues, women hold titles such as public relations or publications directors, usually working their way up by starting in the minor leagues. The highest placed woman in the business end of baseball in 1999 was Wendy Selig-Prieb, president of the Milwaukee Brewers. Leslie Sullivan was vice president of broadcasting of Major League Baseball. Elaine Weddington Steward is the assistant GM of the Boston Red Sox, and Sherry Davis was the stadium announcer for the San Francisco Giants for seven years; her replacement is also a woman, Renel Brooks-Moon.

Women did not umpire in organized baseball until the 1970s, when Bernice Gera won the right to wear the blue. Only after a ruling by the New York State Human Rights Commission did the minor leagues finally give Gera a job. She officiated her first game, a double-header, on June 24, 1972, in the New York-Penn League. During the first game, Gera reversed one of her calls at second base, then ejected a manager. At the end of the first game, Gera quit her umpire's job. After Gera came Christine Wren, who umpired Class A ball (1975-77), but left baseball after it was apparent she would not be promoted.

In 1977, Pam Postema began her news-making career. After four years of umpiring rookie and Class A games, she was promoted to the Class AA Texas League. Two years later she was moved to the Triple-A Pacific Coast League. Postema seemed destined for the big leagues, but in 1989, after the sudden death of Commissioner Bart Giamatti, a strong supporter, Postema was released. She then filed a federal sex discrimination lawsuit against organized baseball. Still, there is one woman umpiring professional ball: Perry Barber, in her 19th season, now part of the independent Atlantic League.

As players, women entered baseball early. In 1898, 22-year-old Lizzie Stride, playing under the name Lizzie Arlington, pitched part of one game in the Atlantic League, giving up no runs. She then went on to play with a barnstorming Bloomer Girl team. From the 1890s until the 1930s, sexually integrated teams (usually seven women and two men, or six women and three men) called Bloomer Girls barnstormed the country, playing against all-male teams. The most successful of Bloomer Girls was Maud Nelson, who began her baseball career in 1897. She pitched for nearly 20 years, then turned to managing and owning teams, among them the Western Bloomer Girls and the Chicago All Star Ranger Girls. Two other successful Bloomer players and managers were Margaret Nabel of the New York Bloomer Girls and Kate Becker, who purchased the Western Bloomer Girls from Nelson. In the days of segregated ball, black bloomer teams such as the St. Louis Black Bronchos played against black men's teams.

During the Great Depression, women again turned to the minor leagues. In 1931, 17-year-old Virne Beatrice "Jackie" Mitchell was signed by the Chattanooga Lookouts. In an exhibition game, she struck out both Babe Ruth and Lou Gehrig to thunderous ovation. The next day, Commissioner Kenesaw Mountain Landis voided Mitchell's contract, declaring that baseball was too strenuous for women.

Her Olympic triumphs of 1932 behind her, Mildred "Babe" Didrikson pitched exhibition minor and major league games in 1934. When spring training was over, she traveled with the House of David.

The All-American Girls Professional Baseball League (1943-54; see entry) played ball to large crowds in ten Midwestern cities. In 1952, the Harrisburg Senators signed Eleanor Engel to a contract, but minor league officials voided it. In the Negro Leagues, however, Marcenia Alberga played under the name Toni Stone. In 1953, she played second base for the Indianapolis Clowns, appearing in 50 games and batting .243.

Girls won the right to play Little League ball in 1974, and since then thousands of girls have played every year. Some Little Leaguers have gone on to make news. Julie Croteau sued her high school in 1988 because they wouldn't let her play ball. Crotcau lost the case, but went on to play ball for St. Mary's College of Maryland for three years. In 1994, she became a member of the Silver Bullets. Ila Borders, another Little League graduate, pitched high school baseball and in 1994 made international headlines when she won her starting game for Southern California College. In 1997 she joined the St. Paul Saints, of the Northern League. She remains the only woman playing men's professional ball.

Early in 1994, the Colorado Silver Bullets were formed by Bob Hope of Whittle Communications. A former executive with the Atlanta Braves, Hope had tried to field the sexually integrated Sun Sox ten years earlier, but was turned down when he applied for a minor league franchise. The second time around, Hope was backed by Coors Brewery, sponsor of the Silver Bullets. As a traveling team of the independent Northern League, the Bullets lost their first game to the Northern League All-Stars 19-0, facing such former major leaguers as Leon Durham and Dennis Boyd. Managed by Phil Niekro, the Bullets drew large crowds as they played exhibition games. Facing all-male teams, the Bullets lost 90 percent of their games in the first season. The team lasted four seasons, steadily improving its record, until Coors dropped its sponsorship. The six-team Ladies Professional League debuted in 1997, playing 56 games, but lasted only two seasons. A four-team Women's New England Baseball League formed in 1999; it expanded to six teams in 2000.

Women have made successful inroads in ownership and the business end of the game, but the future for female umpires and players remains uncertain.

Bibliography

Berlage, Gail Ingham. *Women in Baseball: The Forgotten History.* Westport: Praeger, 1994.

Delaney, Maureen. "Business of Breaking Barriers." *Press-Enterprise* (Riverside, CA). 18 July 1999. Online. LEXIS-NEXIS Academic Universe. 15 June 2000.

"Giants Hire Woman Announcer to Replace Fired Woman Announcer." Associated Press. 4 Jan. 2000. Online. LEXIS-NEXIS Academic Universe. 15 June 2000.

Gregorich, Barbara. *Women at Play: The Story of Women in Baseball.* San Diego: Harcourt Brace, 1993.

Postema, Pam, and Gene Wojciechowski. *You've Got to Have B*lls to Make It in This League.* New York: Simon & Schuster, 1992.

Shattuck, Debra Ann. "Playing a Man's Game: Women and Baseball in the United States, 1966-1954." M.A. thesis, Brown University, 1988.

Barbara Gregorich

Women in Film. As with other industries, there seems to be a glass ceiling for women in the Hollywood film industry. While the Sundance Film Festival declared 2000 the "year of the woman," with over a quarter of the entries directed by women, a survey of the industry conducted in 1998 shows that women remain underrepresented; there are very few cinematographers, while the most progress by women was as producers (26%). Still, filmmaking has offered a variety of professional opportunities to women from the beginning, as creators and as subjects.

DIRECTORS. Frenchwoman Alice Guy-Blache, with *La Fee aux Choux* (1896), was one of the first directors to use film to tell a story, and after coming to the United States built a career of directing in a variety of genres. Lois Weber used the majority of her 51 movies as vehicles for social commentary: *Where Are My Children?* (1916) opposed abortion. Dorothy Arzner (see entry) brought strong roles for women (e.g., *Christopher Strong*, 1933) to the screen— and designed the first moving microphone. More recently, Susan Seidelman has had several successes as director of *Smithereens* (1983), *Desperately Seeking Susan* (1985), and others.

Acting has proven a springboard for female directors, among them Mabel Normand (*Mabel's Busy Day*, 1914, and others), Ida Lupino (*The Hitchhiker*, 1952; *The Trouble with Angels*, 1966, and others), Anne Bancroft (*Fatso*, 1979), Barbra Streisand (*Yentl*, 1983; *Prince of Tides*, 1991), Diane Keaton (*Heaven*, 1987; *Hanging Up*, 2000), Penny Marshall (*Big*, 1988; *A League of Their Own*, 1992; *The Preacher's*

Wife, 1996, and others), Jodie Foster (*Little Man Tate*, 1991), and others.

Screenwriting has proven to be another crossover to directing, for Elaine May, writer and director of *A New Leaf* (1971), and Nora Ephron, writer and director of *This Is My Life* (1993), *Sleepless in Seattle* (1993), and *You've Got Mail* (1998).

WRITERS. Among the early female screenwriters were Jeanie Macpherson, who during her 30-year career often wrote for Cecil B. DeMille; June Mathis, who wrote for Valentino; Elinor Glyn, author of romances and comedies; Frances Marion, dramatist (*Stella Dallas*, 1925; *Camille*, 1936) and Anita Loos, who scripted 200-plus comedies (*Gentlemen Prefer Blondes*, 1953). More recently, Eleanor Perry (*Diary of a Mad Housewife*, 1970), Callie Khouri (*Thelma and Louise*, 1991), and Nora Ephron (*Sleepless in Seattle*, 1993) have achieved success as screenwriters.

EDITORS. The Academy Awards list of best editors is replete with women's names: Anne Bauchens (*Northwest Mounted Police*, 1940), Adrienne Fazan (*Gigi*, 1958), Anne Coates (*Lawrence of Arabia*, 1962), Verna Fields (*Jaws*, 1975), Thelma Schoonmaker (*Raging Bull*, 1980), Claire Simpson (*Platoon*, 1986), and Gabriella Cristiani (*The Last Emperor*, 1987).

DESIGN. Women's talents have been recognized in set decoration and costume design as well. Prominent figures in the former field include Julia Heron (*Spartacus*, 1960) and Nancy Haigh (*Bugsy*, 1991); in the latter, Edith Head (eight Oscars), Irene Sharaff and Dorothy Jeakins (three Oscars each).

ACTRESSES. Just as behind-the-scenes personnel have usually gained prominence working in a particular genre or style, so too have actresses. For instance, movies have always teased and tantalized audiences with women as sex objects, as the provocateurs and recipients of men's desire. One of the earliest movies, *The Kiss* (1896), a plotless clip that lasted only a few minutes, shocked viewers—and brought in heavy repeat business—with the image of a forty-something couple, May Irwin and John Rice, smooching (pristinely, by today's standards), and women have been sex objects in film ever since.

In 1906, the belly dancer Fatima performed for the cameras, and the success of her peep shows demonstrated audiences' fascination with erotic exotics, culminating in the meteoric, albeit short-lived, careers of the Vamps (i.e., Vampire): Theda Bara (*A Fool There Was*, 1915), Nita Naldi (*Blood and Sand*, 1922) and Pola Negri (*Woman of the World*, 1925). In the 1920s, the Vamp gained a saucy little sister, the flirtatious Flapper. Foremost among them were Clara Bow, the It Girl (It being sex appeal) (*Mantrap*, 1926), and Gloria Swanson, whose movies (*Sadie Thompson*, 1927; *Queen Kelly*, 1928) shocked audiences with open and sometimes sympathetic portrayals of prostitution and extramarital affairs.

In the 1930s, in burlesque movies, the Vamp became more jaded, less evil—and sometimes curiously androgynous—through the personas of Marlene Dietrich (*Blonde Venus*, 1932) and Mae West (*She Done Him Wrong*, 1933),

who managed to both be a Vamp and burlesque the Vamp at the same time. Decades later, Madeline Kahn (*Paper Moon*, 1973) and Bette Midler (*Outrageous Fortune*, 1987) carried on the West tradition.

In the 1940s, the Vamp evolved into the Sultry Siren, with her snug, elegant gowns, peekaboo hair, smoky voice, and penchant for leading men into trouble. The Siren wasn't bad, to paraphrase Jessica Rabbit; she was just drawn that way, driven by heartbreak to seek revenge, and redeemable through true love. Sirens Veronica Lake (*Sullivan's Travels*, 1941), Lauren Bacall (*To Have and Have Not*, 1944), Rita Hayworth (*Gilda*, 1946), Lana Turner (*The Postman Always Rings Twice*, 1946), and Ava Gardner (*Mogambo*, 1954) dominated film noir and gangster movies. In recent movies, the Siren has been revived by Kathleen Turner (*Who Framed Roger Rabbit?*, 1988), Michelle Pfeiffer (*The Fabulous Baker Boys*, 1989), and Sharon Stone (*Basic Instinct*, 1992).

While the Vamp was changing, so was her little sister the Flapper, becoming the Blonde Bombshell, who used her endowments, often including a large bosom, to catch a good, usually rich, husband. Breathy, pouty Marilyn Monroe (*Gentlemen Prefer Blondes*, 1953) is the best remembered Bombshell, but there were plenty of runners-up: Jean Harlow (*Bombshell*, 1933—the term was coined here), Carole Lombard (*My Man Godfrey*, 1936), Judy Holliday (*Born Yesterday*, 1950), Betty Grable (*How to Marry a Millionaire*, 1953—with Monroe), and Jayne Mansfield (*The Girl Can't Help It*, 1956). The bombshell aspect has diminished but the ditziness has been preserved in the personas of Goldie Hawn (*Cactus Flower*, 1969) and non-blondes Diane Keaton (*Annie Hall*, 1977) and Geena Davis (*Thelma and Louise*, 1991).

In the late 1950s, girls became sex objects: "BB"—Brigitte Bardot—was only 21 years old when she became a Sex Kitten as a beautiful tease in *And God Created Woman* (1956). Sweden's Sex Kitten was Ann-Margret, who purred all the way from *Viva Las Vegas* (1964) through a television remake of *A Streetcar Named Desire* (1984). Sue Lyon (*Lolita*, 1962), and Brooke Shields (*Pretty Baby*, 1978) raised moviegoers' eyebrows as well.

Not all screen women have used their sexuality to manipulate; some have been the Lovelorn—victims of their own irresistible impulses. Greta Garbo (*Queen Christina*, 1933), Ingrid Bergman (*Casablanca*, 1942), and Joanne Woodward (*Rachel, Rachel*, 1968) all played smart women who paid a price for loving the wrong men.

And not all screen women have capitulated to men's desires. In the silent era, Lillian Gish and Mae Marsh played Innocents—girls who preferred death to dishonor (*Birth of a Nation*, 1915). "America's Sweetheart," Mary Pickford, retained her screen innocence—and childhood—well into her 30s. In the 1950s, the Innocent returned in the persons of Debbie Reynolds (*Tammy*, 1957), Sandra Dee (*Gidget*, 1959), and Doris Day (*Pillow Talk*, 1959), all of them effervescent, sweet, and wholesome, fending off men's advances. But in more recent movies, the girl next door, as depicted by Meg Ryan, found her sex drive (*When Harry Met Sally...*, 1989).

Once properly married, Doris Day's characters were devoted, somewhat ditzy wives (*Please Don't Eat the Daisies*, 1960). Other Wonderful Wives have created a hard act for real women to follow. Olivia de Havilland in *Gone with the Wind* (1939), Greer Garson in *Mrs. Miniver* (1942), Donna Reed in *It's a Wonderful Life* (1946), Irene Dunne in *Life with Father* (1948), June Allyson in *The Glenn Miller Story* (1954), and Anne Archer in *Patriot Games* (1992) were understanding, nurturing stand-by-your-man women. In *The Women* (1939), Norma Shearer, the mousey wife, learned how to fight tooth and nail to win back her philandering husband.

Some women, Hollywood has decided, have no sex appeal at all, and the movies have often ridiculed them as Hags for their age, weight, or unconventional features. Oscar winners all, Marie Dressler (*Min and Bill*, 1930), Jane Darwell (*The Grapes of Wrath*, 1940), Shirley Booth (*Come Back, Little Sheba*, 1952), and Kathy Bates (*Misery*, 1990) nevertheless have been typed as Hags. Roseanne Barr played another hag in *She-Devil* (1989).

Before the advent of the Sex Kitten, being a child was a guarantee of on-screen sexual innocence. Shirley Temple, a star from the age of six (*Little Miss Marker*, 1931) and the biggest box-office draw of 1938, usually played an orphan whose pluck and good cheer inspire adults. Like Temple, Judy Garland, who began acting at age 13 (*Every Sunday*, 1936) and became a leading lady soon after in musicals and comedies, played the trooper who energetically danced and sang her way out of problems (*Heidi*, 1937). A film actress from the age of ten, Elizabeth Taylor achieved fame as the horse-loving dreamer in *National Velvet* (1944) and kept it through her teen years (with, for example, *Father of the Bride*, 1950) and adulthood (e.g., *Cat on a Hot Tin Roof*, 1958), although her career tapered off after the 1960s. But Natalie Wood knocked down the model of the virtuous youngster in her portrayals of angry (*Rebel without a Cause*, 1955) and sex-hungry teens (*Splendor in the Grass*, 1961). Wood, who began acting at age five, had a penchant for playing tortured souls. In the 1980s, Molly Ringwald brought back sexual innocence in *Sixteen Candles* (1984) but surrendered it in later films (e.g., *For Keeps*, 1988).

Some ladies of the screen didn't have to use their sexuality to gain wealth; they were born Sophisticates. Deborah Kerr became known for her portrayals of genteel Englishwomen (*King Solomon's Mines*, 1950), while two counterparts achieved social status in both real and reel life. Audrey Hepburn, daughter of a baroness, played a princess in *Roman Holiday* (1953) and a flower-girl-turned-duchess in *My Fair Lady* (1964). Grace Kelly, product of the upper class in *Rear Window* (1954) and *High Society* (1956), became a real-life princess by marrying Prince Rainier III of Monaco.

Feminist critics have objected to Hollywood's portrayal of women Victims, as maidens in distress, targets for violence, and self-sacrificers, yet these roles are the center of many popular movies. Barbara Stanwyck played a victim of social snobbery in *Stella Dallas* (1937) and a terrorized wife in *Sorry, Wrong Number* (1948). Vivien Leigh's heroines in *Waterloo Bridge* (1940), *That Hamilton Woman*

(1941), and *A Streetcar Named Desire* (1951) break down when subjected to multiple tragedies. Janet Leigh's portrayal of a newlywed caught up in a murder in *Touch of Evil* (1958) segued into her part as the murder victim in *Psycho* (1960).

The Bitch knows what she wants and she's going to get it, stopping at nothing, but instead of using her feminine wiles to manipulate men, the Bitch uses the same weapons her male counterparts have used: threats, blackmail, extortion, and even murder. Queen of the cinematic Bitches was Bette Davis, man-stealer (*Cabin in the Cotton*, 1932), man-eater (*Of Human Bondage*, 1934), man-killer (*Bordertown*, 1934), heavy-drinking, ambition-ridden actress (*All About Eve*, 1950), and madwoman (*What Ever Happened to Baby Jane?*, 1962). If Davis is queen, Joan Crawford is pretender to the throne. Her Bitches, although few in number, branded her: homewrecker (*The Women*, 1939), murderess (*Possessed*, 1947), and shrew (*Harriet Craig*, 1950; *Queen Bee*, 1955). In the 1960s, the Bitch crown passed to Faye Dunaway for *Bonnie and Clyde* (1967), *Network* (1976), and *Mommie Dearest* (1981)—in which she played Joan Crawford. Glenn Close has shown promise of bitchery in *Fatal Attraction* (1987) and *Dangerous Liaisons* (1988).

Fortunately, Hollywood has recognized that in real life women have found other means to power besides vamping and intimidation; some achieve their goals through simple grit and hard work. It could be said that crime fighter Pearl White, in her silent serials, was the first female action-adventure heroine and thereby set the standard for the Plucky Gal, who faced disasters, some man-made, some natural, head on. It was not uncommon for the Plucky Gal to exhibit bravery, determination, and sometimes athletic ability.

Each decade has had its models of feminine pluck. In the 1930s, Ginger Rogers matched Fred Astaire step for step (*The Gay Divorcée*, 1934), Vivien Leigh conquered Atlanta in *Gone with the Wind* (1939), and Myrna Loy sleuthed in the "Thin Man" series. In the 1940s, Claudette Colbert raised her children alone and fought the war on the homefront in *Since You Went Away* (1944), while Dale Evans solved crimes with Roy Rogers.

In the 1950s, Katharine Hepburn shot the rapids in *The African Queen* (1951) and Susan Hayward played an inmate fighting her death sentence (*I Want to Live!*, 1958). In the 1960s, Julie Andrews stepmothered a large family fleeing the Nazis (*The Sound of Music*, 1965) and Barbra Streisand was the heartbroken comedienne (*Funny Girl*, 1968).

In the 1970s, Jane Fonda was the prostitute-turned-murder witness in *Klute* (1971). Sigourney Weaver battled extraterrestrials (*Alien*, 1979) and Sally Field organized a labor union in *Norma Rae* (1979). In the 1980s, Meryl Streep survived a concentration camp in *Sophie's Choice* (1982), Jessica Lange (*Country*, 1984), and Sissy Spacek (*The River*, 1984) fought to keep the family farm, and Whoopi Goldberg survived incest and spousal abuse (*The Color Purple*, 1985).

In the 1990s, novice CIA agent Jodie Foster chased a cannibal in *Silence of the Lambs* (1990), Susan Sarandon outran the law in *Thelma & Louise* (1991), Linda Hamilton pumped up to combat artificial intelligence in *Terminator II: Judgment Day* (1992), and Julia Roberts investigated crime in *I Love Trouble* (1994).

Sometimes the woman's intelligence, not her derring-do, was her key to success; her wit, imagination and insider's knowledge of business and politics were the engines for advancing her own career or her man's. Hollywood gave us savvy Working Girls in Joan Blondell (*Footlight Parade*, 1933), Jean Arthur (*Mr. Deeds Goes to Town*, 1936; *Mr. Smith Goes to Washington*, 1939), Barbara Stanwyck (*Meet John Doe*, 1941), Holly Hunter (*Broadcast News*, 1987), and Melanie Griffith (*Working Girl*, 1988).

Hollywood still has far to go in making full use of women's talents, but as actresses like Jessica Tandy (*Driving Miss Daisy*, 1989) prove that older women can not only handle lead roles but also can generate big box office, and performers like Whoopi Goldberg and Marlee Matlin (*Children of a Lesser God*, 1986) challenge conventions of beauty, perhaps some barriers will fall (see also next entry). As versatile actresses like Meryl Streep continue to draw audiences at the same time they win critical acclaim for their work, perhaps stereotyping will diminish. As films directed by women like Penny Marshall continue to gross millions of dollars, perhaps more female directors will be offered big budget movies. As tangible rewards come for the talent women are providing before and behind the camera, opportunities must surely expand.

Bibliography

Goodale, Gloria. "Still a Man's World." *Christian Science Monitor* 9 June 2000. Online. LEXIS-NEXIS Academic Universe. 15 June 2000.

Haskell, Molly. *From Reverence to Rape*. New York: Holt, 1974.

Rosen, Majorie. *Popcorn Venus*. New York: Coward, McCann, 1973.

Schaefer, Stephen. "Don't Cry, Boys: Women Directors Celebrate Their Rise in Hollywood." *Boston Herald* 15 Feb. 2000. Online. LEXIS-NEXIS Academic Universe. 15 June 2000.

Siegel, Scott, and Barbara Siegel. *The Encyclopedia of Hollywood*. New York: Facts on File, 1990.

Ramona Lucius

Women of Color in Films. Women of historically underrepresented racial groups: African Americans, Asian Americans, Hispanic/Latinas, and Native Americans, have, by and large, participated in few production or technical aspects of mainstream filmmaking, despite the fact that since the Hollywood studio days, Anglo women have dominated such areas as costuming, wardrobe, and scripting. With few exceptions, there have, historically, been only a handful of women directors. In response, the American Film Institute established the Directing Workshop for Women in 1988; however, no women of color are on record as having participated.

But in the 1980s, Martinique-born filmmaker Euzhan Palcy (1957-) attracted world-wide acclaim with her film *Rue cases negres/Sugar Cane Alley*, a narrative about a young boy living with a grandmother who encourages him to become educated in French colonial schools without losing his grounding in their rich and nurturing black culture. With her feature *A Dry White Season* (1989), based on the André Brink novel Palcy became the first black (Afro-Caribbean) woman to direct for a major Hollywood studio. Palcy co-wrote the screenplay. The film looked at the growing awareness of schoolteacher Ben du Toit (Donald Sutherland) of the horrors of South African apartheid.

The first African-American woman director was Julie Dash (1952-) who in 1992 released *Daughters of the Dust* after seven years' work. The movie focused on a multi-generational family living on the Sea Islands off the coast of Georgia. The lushly photographed, poetically meditative movie introduced many audiences to Gullah, a culture and language little known outside the Georgia–South Carolina Sea Islands. *Daughters of the Dust* concerns itself with the actions and reactions of women as they're confronted with the imminent departure of part of their clan for the mainland. This primacy of women of color was unusual in a mass market film.

In 1993, *Just Another Girl on the IRT* was released on a limited basis. A charming movie about the coming-of-age experiences of a street-wise 17-year-old African American, Chantel Mitchell, it hinted at the directorial promise of the young director Leslie Harris, who had studied film at Denison University.

These two films are notable because, historically, with the exception of Lena Horne (1917-), African-American actresses have not been given substantive or leading or consistent roles. Because of her early screen work in the 1930s and 1940s, Horne is known to an older generation, and her Broadway shows and occasional television work (such as an appearance on *The Dick Cavett Show*) have kept her name before a younger generation. The case of Horne exemplifies a conundrum for Hollywood: gradations in color among on-screen African Americans and what to do about this.

Perhaps the earliest appearance of African-American actresses was in Edwin S. Porter's 15-minute film *Uncle Tom's Cabin* (1903). One year later, a very un-slavelike actress appeared on screen in the movie *A Bucket of Cream Ale,* as an angry black servant who dumps a tin bucket on the head of a rude Dutchman. "Aggressive and even derisive black women appeared in Cecil B. DeMille's *Manslaughter* (1922)," according to film historian Thomas Cripps, but this wasn't the image of the black servant which came to prevail in Hollywood film. Donald Bogle has identified several roles to which women of color have been limited to such an extent that they've become stereotypes.

Repeatedly, African-American actresses appearing in movies of the 1920s to 1950s who were dark-skinned were cast as Mammies, loyal to their masters or, in the later movies of the 1950s to the present, loyal to the men and women employing them as maids or cooks. On the other hand, light-skinned actresses such as Nina Mae McKinney (1913-67), Dorothy Dandridge (1924-66), and Horne were cast either as entertainers in musicals where they sang or danced, or as mulattos whose attractiveness eventually spelled trouble or death. (While Horne sometimes had to darken her skin with makeup to satisfy the expectations of white audiences, Hollywood continued using white actresses in blackface as late as the 1940s, with actresses as popular as Betty Grable. And as late as the 1950s, white actresses—Julie London and Natalie Wood were among them—played African Americans.)

Independent black producers working in the 1930s and 1940s such as Ted Toddy developed movies largely indistinguishable from Hollywood films in honoring these color codes and the stereotypical roles that went with them. Similarly, the all-black musicals produced by Hollywood in the 1940s—*Cabin in the Sky* and *Stormy Weather*—reinforced the codes. (Both jazz pianist Hazel Scott and entertainer extraordinaire Josephine Baker had clauses in their contracts expressly prohibiting their being cast as maids of any stripe.) But black film pioneer Oscar Micheaux (1884-1951), who wrote, directed and produced approximately 30 films between 1919 and 1948, frequently wrote important roles for women. Bea Freeman and Ethel Moses were among the actresses he used. Unfortunately, few of his movies are extant.

It wasn't until the "blaxploitation" films of the 1970s that dark-skinned actresses were cast in attractive and forceful roles, such as Tamara Dobson (1947-) playing Cleopatra Jones. Cicely Tyson (1938-) another dark-skinned actress, also found film work, starring in *Sounder* (1972) and *Sounder Part 2* (1976) and *The Autobiography of Miss Jane Pittman* (1974).

Despite the unchallenged primacy of Westerns in the history of Hollywood film, none has been directed by a Native American woman. In fact, Native American women are restricted to jobs as actresses and then largely as background. (As late as the 1970s, their roles were played by dark-skinned or heavily made-up white women.) When an actress is cast in a major role, the script almost always demands that she be an Anglo who was raised by the tribal group as one of their own, such as in the Oscar-winning 1990 *Dances with Wolves*.

Similarly, to date, no Hollywood movie has been directed by a Latina. In the 1930s, under the studio system, actress Dolores del Rio was brought from Mexico to play a Latina. An attractive woman, she usually played opposite Anglo male stars. During the same period, Mexican actress Lupe Velez was cast consistently in the more widely known role of the fiery sensual, sexually available woman, the Mexican "spitfire." A less utilized, but no less stereotyped, Latina role was that of Carmen Miranda, a zany, good-natured and likable woman with talent for dancing and singing. (Ironically, African-American actresses Etta Moten played a dark-skinned South American in the 1933 *Flying Down to Rio* and Hazel Jones played a Burmese siren in *West of Singapore*.)

Even today Latinas are rarely featured in mainstream movies. In the 1961 film *West Side Story,* the role of Puerto Rican Maria was played by Anglo actress Natalie Wood. Most films centering on Latin experiences in the U.S. feature males in the starring roles with women playing more or less passive roles as mothers, wives, lovers, or friends.

Hollywood films featuring Asian Americans have traditionally been of the Charlie Chan or Fu Manchu variety.

Asian-American women have been cast in background roles for the most part. Even in the late 1970s when karate/Bruce Lee movies supplanted "blaxploitation" as the movie-of-choice for teens, women were cast in secondary roles. Even then they usually fit into the stereotype: the exotic, the inscrutable.

The first Hollywood movie with an Asian-American woman, Janet Yang, as executive producer was the 1993 film version of Amy Tan's novel *The Joy Luck Club*. She was instrumental in acquiring financial backing for this well-received film that looked at the lives of Chinese-American mothers and daughters with humor and poignancy. Standing in sharp contrast to the dearth of films about Asian Americans, with Asian-American actresses, it had a focus on women that was rarely seen in mainstream films.

Hollywood's prestigous Academy Award has been given to three women of color, all in the best supporting actress category: Hattie McDaniel in 1939 for her work in *Gone with the Wind*; Miyoshi Umeki in 1957 for *Sayonara*; and Whoopi Goldberg in 1990 for *Ghost*. However, in independent films women of color have been able to assume an array of production jobs, have broken stereotypical acting molds, and have directed hundreds of films.

Among American women of Asian descent, Loni Ding is arguably the "Dean" of independent filmmakers, having advised and nurtured the projects of many younger filmmakers while continuing to produce her own work. Christine Choy on the East Coast is another important figure, as is Emi Ko Omori of San Francisco, who, in addition to making films, is noted for her photography. Vietnamese born, Trinh T. Minh-ha, now living in the U.S., has distinguished herself as a documentary filmmaker. She has done ground-breaking work by undermining the "Otherness" which has traditionally characterized films about cultures outside of the U.S.

There are two generations of independent filmmakers among African-American women. Kathleen Collins Prettyman (1942-88), Camille Billops, and Jackie Shearer (1946-93) worked on the East Coast along with Ayoka Chenzira and Michelle Parkerson, while Aline Larken, and Karen Guyot are among the West Coast filmmakers whose award-winning films may be seen at festivals.

Bibliography

Bogle, Donald. *Blacks in American Films and Television*. New York: Simon & Schuster, 1988.

Cripps, Thomas. *Black Film as Genre*. Bloomington: Indiana UP, 1978.

Kaplan, Ann E. *Women and Film: Both Sides of the Camera*. New York: Methuen, 1983.

Kuhn, Annette, with Susannah Radstone, eds. *Women in Film: An International Guide*. New York: Fawcett Columbine, 1990.

Quart, Barbara. *Women Directors: The Emergence of a New Cinema*. New York: Praeger, 1988.

Ernece B. Kelly

Women's Roles in Series Television. Since its beginning, television has always had an entertainment cadre of women. But they were never allowed to play the roles that matched their place in society. For many years women were portrayed as funny or inept in most settings. Rarely were they shown as effective and earnest in professional settings. Occasionally, one saw a woman doctor such as Maggie—who seemingly had no last name—on *Ben Casey, M.D.* (1960s) or Detective Mary Beth Lacey on *Cagney and Lacey* (1980s). But more often than not, the women shown in work settings on television rarely engaged in meaningful activities. Instead, they talked about work, their shows were set at some workplace, or they were in the kitchen.

It appears that women have had the same difficulty in winning accurate portrayals of themselves as female television characters as they have in gaining recognition of their professional abilities throughout society. Women largely remain occupationally segregated in the American labor force. Research into images of women in the mass media tends to concentrate on portrayals in general. They provide flat, broad brush strokes of women's reflected societal images. Thus, women, and especially women of color, have been long portrayed in various media genres as distorted or stereotypic sexist roles. Particularly resistant to change have been vocationally related sexual stereotypes and similarly related gender stereotypes of personality traits. Women and their images are rarely under their control, but rather under the control of the male media creators.

THE FIFTIES. Some of the lasting images of the 1950s come from the plethora of television families headed by wise fathers and waited on by always patient mothers. The "Harriet Nelson syndrome" was commonplace. There was no mention of female upward mobility nor any pretense of movement toward equality. The stress was on dependency and sexual inequality.

As the war ended and popular mass media made the transition from the golden age of radio to experimentation with television, women were depicted as leaving their roles as Rosie the Riveter and returning to the home and kitchen. Yet history tells us that during the 1950s many women with elementary school children sought employment outside the home. According to the print media represented by women's magazines, American women were reveling in domestic bliss. In this context, *Father Knows Best, Ozzie and Harriet,* and *Leave It to Beaver* all seemed like accurate reflections of women in America.

Thus, few working women were visible during the fifties. Secretaries such as Ann Sothern, from the show by the same name, and Alice from *The Jack Benny Program* were occasionally seen at their desks answering phones but also, at least in the case of Ann, just as often returning from lunch or shopping trips. One also saw, paradoxical though it might be, the virginal "nice caring" Miss Kitty serving drinks in *Gunsmoke.* Her best friends were Doc and Fester, a substitute family for the working old maid. *My Little Margie* provided a sea-going look at women in pseudo-clerical positions and a predecessor to the *Love Boat.* However, Margie was a young working woman dependent upon an older male—the captain—as a wise father figure to straighten out her mess-ups.

The most visible woman of the time was the all-American housewife, the model of imagined domestic perfection.

Their hair was always in perfect order, they typically wore light colored dresses, and it was always springtime. These television moms were constantly tying aprons behind their backs as they tip-toed into the kitchen while Father (rarely "Dad") cheerfully arrived home and changed to his cardigan or tweed jacket with elbow patches. June Cleaver looked bemusedly at Wally and the Beav. Harriet Nelson chatted with Ozzie, David, and Ricky. Donna Reed was the socialite dentist's wife who needed no domestic help. Gracie talked circles around George and the neighbors.

In contrast, the true everywoman was portrayed by Alice Kramden in *The Honeymooners,* a combination of tragedy, comedy, and docudrama. Alice was a prisoner of time and circumstance, both on television and in society. The idea of her conducting some function outside the home never entered the equation. Instead, she was the prisoner of a blue-collar, childless existence.

In many ways, however, no woman existed on television during the '50s save Lucy. She was a housewife who actually cleaned her house. She was observed with dust mop in hand, dust rag wrapped around hair, opening the refrigerator and placing food in the oven, and taking care of Little Ricky. So what if the washing machine overflowed with soap bubbles and smoke came billowing out of the stove. She was not afraid to be dirty, messy, or grape covered. Yet Lucy wanted to work outside of the home. Time and again, work she tried. Time and again, she failed—only to be saved by Ricky.

Perhaps the most interesting aspect of the *I Love Lucy* show was that in real life Lucille Ball was a business dynamo. Lucy on the program was always a flop at any work outside the home, and frequently work inside the home as well.

As Lucy continued to fail comically outside the home, images of women in the greater society began gradually to change. During the post-Desi Arnaz series in the '60s, Lucy was actually shown working regularly in a bank, often disastrously, but working. Lucy might not have been a great success working professionally, but she kept trying, a positive example in itself.

There were, of course, several other women characters who made an impact in these years, but they were few. It took several more years before women actually made a major impact on regular series.

THE SIXTIES. From a societal viewpoint, the sixties was a turbulent era. Feminism was developing during the early 1960s but found little support, even among women. This was directly reflected on television, which, in the early 1960s, showed the majority of women content with their lot in life and not seeing treatment of women and men as inequitable.

Some of the characters who made an impression in the sixties included Maggie from *Ben Casey*, the Emma Peel character from *The Avengers*, Lucy from *The Lucille Ball Show*, Samantha from *Bewitched*, Alice and Mrs. Brady from *The Brady Bunch*, Laura Petrie and Rose-Marie from *The Dick Van Dyke Show*, and Miss Hathaway from *The Beverly Hillbillies*. Added later to the list might be Marlo Thomas, in *That Girl,* and Barbara Feldon as Agent 99 in *Get Smart*. Late in the decade Diahann Carroll appeared as the first black title woman character in *Julia*.

Of these, at least two were domestic employees, two were detectives, two were secretaries, one was a comedy writer who also acted as group secretary, one was a nurse, one was a doctor, and three were housewives. With the exception of the housewives, who followed the traditions established on TV in the fifties, all of these working women were single; not all fancy free, but unattached nonetheless.

Women's life choices on TV at this time were confined to those of marriage and family or of a single life and a career. The choice of career was only for women who failed or were failed (widowed) by romance and marriage. With the exception of Agent 99, who married Maxwell Smart at the conclusion of the series, it also appeared impossible for working women to grow in their personal lives.

In the sixties, women on television who worked, worked to support themselves. The domestics such as Alice and Hazel were rarely seen actually doing specific tasks, even though we would often see Hazel answering the door and Alice in the kitchen. They were "members" of the family. What they did most often was hold the family together much as a TV secretary holds the incompetent boss on track.

Maggie was treated in a more serious way. Although not a title character and not central to stories, she was nonetheless a woman doctor fighting for equal footing in the all-male world of neurosurgery. *Ben Casey* was a serious show, almost unnecessarily gruff, and Maggie was serious and feminine. She neither flaunted nor hid her femininity and was obviously the overlooked quasi love-interest in Ben's life. Maggie, as a female colleague, was one of the very few positive professional role models offered to women during the 1960s.

Emma Peel also was a token woman in a man's world. Unlike Maggie, she used traditional feminine wiles to get the job done. The audience saw her with gun in hand and in pursuit of criminals. Of course, they also saw her in skin-tight outfits. Could she have been a bright and beautiful secret agent in regular dresses or pants suit? Apparently not during the 1960s.

Diahann Carroll's Julia crossed the racial barrier which Bill Cosby had crossed a few years earlier in *I Spy*. She was widowed, a nurse, and responsible for the welfare of her only child, Corey. She answered the want-ad of a color-blind white doctor and became gainfully employed. Julia was rarely actually seen treating patients. She was often seen with her son, or in conference with the doctor. However, she was a black professional woman identified and dressed as a nurse. More importantly for women and especially women of color, she was a successful and competent nurse.

Two other women at work who were dependent upon the workplace for identity and identification were Miss Hathaway, who appeared to live by the whims of her boss and pine after Jethro, and the more three-dimensional, sometimes even poignant Sally Rogers of the *Dick Van Dyke Show*.

In *The Beverly Hillbillies*, Miss Hathaway was a spinster whose life revolved around the bank where she worked. She was always acting as a "go-fer" for her boss, chasing around with a frenetic energy which kept her razor thin.

Miss Hathaway exemplified the work ethic and also the traditional superior-inferior relationship between the male boss and the woman underling worker.

The counterpoint to Miss Hathaway was the character of Ellie May Clampett, a beautiful bright country girl with rosy cheeks, country logic, and very tight blue jeans. She, of course, is not self-supporting or formally educated, but dependent upon the fortune and wisdom supplied by her father.

Rose-Marie's Sally Rogers on *The Dick Van Dyke Show* was among the earliest women to be featured in an equal role with male characters in a television program. She appeared regularly as one of the writers of the fictional *Alan Brady Show*. She was not the head writer; that was Rob's (Dick Van Dyke) job. Yet she was absolutely an integral part of the successful production of each show. She interacted with her co-workers as an equal. Her only bow to her gender role was that she did the majority of the typing, although in fairness Rob also occasionally typed.

Sally was a non-teacher, non-nurse, non-clerical, non-maid working woman. She was part of the big New York show biz world and was a professional. Also, through this character and show, we saw the foreshadowing of one dominant characteristic of women's work in 1970s TV. For Sally, work was not an end in itself, but rather a way to develop a strong alternative family and keep going in a sometimes cold, lonely world. This was in direct contrast to shy, stay-at-home Laura Petrie, who wanted to tend to husband and son.

THE SEVENTIES. By the time the sixties turned to the seventies, the image of women had changed radically. Such changes were reflected in Norman Lear's productions and Mary Tyler Moore's development projects, which showed women working in a variety of positions, and female characters suddenly became three-dimensional. Some worked outside the home, some did not. But their potential for thinking and independent success began to manifest itself.

Lear's main female characters, including Maude, Louise Jefferson, and even Edith Bunker, displayed originality, energy, competence, and some measure of tenacity. MTM's women always worked. From Mary to Phyllis, Rhoda, and even to Sue Ann, MTM's women always had a definite and significant profession-oriented personification.

During the 1970s, it was not so much that television depicted women accurately, but rather that television programs seemed to support the notion that women were an increasingly powerful, vocal minority in society. In growing numbers, female characters in the seventies worked outside the home as professionals. But, of course, there remained a number of blue-collar women and moms in series as well.

It was common at this time for powerful producers and programmers to develop multiple shows with the same basic format. There were Fred Silverman, Norman Lear, Grant Tinker, and Garry Marshall, to name a few. Overall, there was an explosion of shows featuring women, but whether these female characters were instrumental in work settings is a more complex question.

ABC's Marshall brought throwback-period television into vogue. This did very little for women's image as serious thinkers or doers. On *Happy Days*, set in the 1950s, Mrs. Cunningham was once again the perfect mom. On the spin-off *Laverne and Shirley,* also set in the fifties, the "girls" were independent, single, working outside the home, doing manual labor in a brewery and always on the lookout for a would-be husband.

If ABC was generally the home of simpler times, CBS and, to a lesser extent, NBC, more than made up for this by being progressive. They took chances and were rewarded by high ratings. CBS's golden days of women on television was in its heyday by the mid-1970s with shows such as: *All in the Family, M*A*S*H, The Mary Tyler Moore Show, The Bob Newhart Show, One Day at a Time, Maude, The Jeffersons, Good Times,* and *The Carol Burnett Show.* NBC's contribution was *Alice.* Taken together, these shows provide an interesting reflection of the enfranchisement of women both on television and in society during the 1970s. Some women were shown as happy being homemakers, some as professionals, some simply as talented comedians and top bananas, not sidekicks or foils for a man. Some were shy and sheltering, while others were brash and demonstrative. Several were shown to be strong women survivors whose families—even their husbands—depended upon them.

Several popular programs by Norman Lear, such as *All in the Family, Maude,* and *The Jeffersons,* each showed home-based, non-working women. Yet they were outspoken, did not live in marital bliss, and rarely agreed with their spouses. At the same time, they were classically interested in their families' welfare. Even Edith Bunker periodically had enough of Archie and screamed at him to "stifle." Life in Maude's home and the Jeffersons' was anything but tranquil. Maude was a political Vesuvius while Louise was role reversed out of the workplace into the world of white society. Like the decade, families were shown to have ups and downs, and turmoil.

On the other hand, a number of women during the seventies were shown at their work sites. Mary Richards on *The Mary Taylor Moore Show* worked at a television station in Minneapolis, Hot Lips Hoolihan of *M*A*S*H* worked in an operating room in Korea, the women of *Alice* worked at Mel's Diner.

Of course, there were interesting women on television during the seventies who split their time between work and home. It took several seasons for *One Day at a Time* to allow Mom the ability to travel to her advertising/public relations firm. But by the mid-seventies, Bonnie Franklin, as the mother, was juggling a career and two children as a single parent. Maude was mouthy and politically correct but she did not work for a salary; she volunteered, to change the world from the suburbs. However, her divorced daughter, who also was a single parent, did work.

During the 1970s, the saga of Mary Richards was the most popular among women, and it set a tone for strong women in series during that decade. But the question remains as to the importance of the method by which women financially supported themselves and to what point this played an integral part in the depiction of women during this period.

There were, of course, other female characters on *The Mary Tyler Moore Show.* Sue Ann Nivens of the faux "Happy Homemaker" show was usually depicted as a flirting airhead. Phyllis, Mary's first landlord, never left the house, and Rhoda, Mary's friend, was a stereotypic New Yorker with a slightly dysfunctional life. When Phyllis and Rhoda spun off to their own shows, their images changed little. Rhoda tried marriage during the first season, but failed. In the second season, Rhoda tried divorce and began a career. Such characters continued to project the image that women could not manage to be successful at both marriage and career.

Few of these single self-supporting women actually performed many work tasks in their television workplaces. Much of their time was spent forming substitute families. Bonding became the occupation of television women of the seventies. They worked on relationships. The "let's talk it all out" discussions between Mary and Rhoda, Mary and Murray, etc., were pure family.

The question still remains as to whether 1970s television women accurately reflected social roles of American women in that society. Certainly, in the 1970s, there were a large number of women in the labor force. In fact, nearly 40 percent of the American labor force in 1970 was female. By 1980, this figure had grown to slightly over 50 percent. The seventies also saw the coinage of a new term, the displaced homemaker, used to describe women who married young, usually just out of high school, and began families during the late 1950s and 1960s. Many had marriages that ended either in divorce or widowhood. Many colleges and universities created programs to accommodate these displaced homemakers and assist them in obtaining college credentials. By the 1980s, both the level of education among women and their participation in the labor market had risen. In spite of these changes, women continued to feel unequal and have only begun to be empowered. This was reflected in television programming.

THE EIGHTIES. At the same time that baby boomers finally began settling down, there was a dramatic shift in the character and structure of the American family as the divorce rate soared to nearly 50 percent and society became increasingly tolerant of alternate lifestyles and family arrangements. This change in attitude was born of necessity and not necessarily from any real growth in broadmindedness.

The television decade opened with the disappearance of single woman leads. Married with family still remained, or again became, the more desirable state of affairs. Long-running 1970s series centered on single women did not do well in syndication and were not even seen on the late night circuit. In addition, when a similar *Mary* debuted in the middle of the decade, more mature and more stylish, but still single, it appeared tired and old.

Women of the eighties were paired in serious relationships. One witnessed Joyce with Frank in *Hill Street Blues,* Maddie with the accountant in *Moonlighting,* Van Owen with, finally, Victor, and Roxanne with Dave in *L.A. Law,* to name a few. They might not have been married but they were definitely attached. This was even true with *Kate & Allie,* who were avowed heterosexuals but definitely paired to each other. One was cast in a more or less traditional "housewife" role and the other went off to work.

The stylistic series was also a benchmark of the eighties. The "mine" generation of the Sue Ellen and Pam Ewing types on Lorimar's *Dallas*, *Knots Landing*, *Dynasty,* and others gave way to the "me" generation of *thirtysomething*, growing into early middle age. These shows displayed women in varying degrees of personal growth, motherhood, and reflection of society.

Although *thirtysomething* was a trendy, influential show, the professional side of the female characters was secondary to the soul searching, "let's all deal with it together" nature of the program as it dealt with such themes as marriage, family, biological clocks, and death. Hope, Ellyn, and Melissa became, more or less, the domestic role models for the age and left the careers to others.

Regardless of marital status, women on television also began to reflect an opening up of attitude about women and the types of work assignments of which they were capable. Such shows included *Cagney and Lacey* (detectives), *Hill Street Blues* (Lucy, police officer; Joyce, public defender), *St. Elsewhere* (nurses), and *L.A. Law* (Ann and Van Owen, lawyers).

Audiences also heard often about women who worked, but seldom saw them laboring. These included attorney Claire from *Cosby*, Maggie from *Growing Pains*, Angela from *Who's the Boss*, and Alish from *Family Ties*. None of these women were title or central characters either, but they did possess a profession. In addition, several of the key women from *Dallas* and *Knots Landing* occasionally became employed, but the endeavors were never central to the story lines or very serious.

Cheers also featured women important to the development and continuation of the series. Diane, Carla, and Rebecca all worked in the bar in one capacity or another, but their actual activities (carrying drinks, managing, etc.) were only peripheral to their place in the Cheers family. In general, as in the seventies' *phenomenon*, most workplaces were largely substitute homes and families.

The lead characters of *Cagney and Lacey* were a team of detectives out on the street trying to make it as women in a man's world. Lacey was married; Cagney, the hard-bitten daughter of an ex-cop, drank, slept around, became pregnant, miscarried, etc. But she was a cop to the end. Audiences saw the duo in the squad room dealing with the chief, or out on the street conducting investigations, using force when necessary. They were women working and struggling but not proselytizing as feminists. Cagney and Lacey's work was central to the identification of both within the series. But they were also sisters under the skin, dependent on their familial relationship to add glue to their lives.

In Steven Bochco's creations of the 1980s, women became assertive both personally and professionally. *Hill Street Blues* is dated now but in it women gained full visibility. Whether in the interrogation room or in court, Joyce the public defender was always vocal and passionate. In more than one episode she stormed into the captain's office to chew him out for attacking the rights of her clients. Lucy patrolled the street with her partner, shooting when necessary, and even being shot.

Although the plots of these Bochco shows were predictably convoluted, they broke new ground in producer-based independence and visibility of women in work settings. Yet also apparent to the practiced television eye is the workplace as substitute family and presentation of working women as dysfunctional or intensely neurotic. This has been, as often as not, a large contributing factor to Bochco's recipe for success.

L.A. Law time and again brought out its senior partner to pull in the reins of the younger partners and associates. The thoughtful grandfather rode herd on the generations, trying to preserve the supportive, intimate character of the law firm, his family. From Grace to Roxanne to Ann, audiences were treated to passionate professional women involved in client/partner meetings, politically correct courtroom confrontations, and enough sex and spice to make the whole thing interesting. Grace and Ann were the epitome of professional women in the eighties: smart, socially stylish, well dressed, sharp, well educated, intelligent, and charming. They were examples for women everywhere. But as politically correct as the Bochco women appeared, they were all white Anglo-Saxon Protestants. *L.A. Law* dabbled in alternative lifestyles in the early nineties, but in the first seasons the professional women in this familial firm were single and single-minded, moving in the professional world but fitting into this particular homestyle legal grouping. They did display confidence as women succeeding in the work world. However, it must be added that all of Bocho's successful shows centered on a work environment which was mythical in its human orientation and artificially saccharin in its representation of professional behavior. In the Bochco shows, women are successful workers but are not professional, as they continue to need and receive more nurturing and human contact than their male counterparts.

The end of the decade television viewers saw the crest of women's images with the introduction of self-sufficient lead women. Examples of these sorts of programs include *Designing Women*, *Murphy Brown*, and less successful shows like *Days and Nights of Molly Dodd* and *The Tracey Ullman Show*.

THE NINETIES. The early years have displayed both the young and not so young, as shows such as *Murder, She Wrote* feature an aging but stylish detective in a mystery writer series, while *Designing Women* and *Murphy Brown* have shown yet other portrayals of women working. Interesting to note is the fact that both of these shows have women on the producing and writing teams.

Designing Women broke some new ground in the arena of women working by displaying southern women out of the kitchen yet conducting acceptable women's work in their interior design firm. The group, including the eventually partnered Anthony, also created an alternative family setting. Julia and her crew were certainly displayed as actively working women but they also fall in a category best defined as a family of friends trying to make it together against all odds.

In her role as a top Washington reporter Murphy Brown was a responsible professional, shown in her office, in staff meetings, or on the set. There was still a hint of the concerns with work as family and more than little focus on Murphy as a neurotic overachiever. During the consciousness-raising show dealing with Murphy as single mother, Murphy interviewed families and assaulted the issues. This is where the portrayal of women's work found itself in the early 1990s: a vehicle for propagandizing the illusion of parity in the workplace.

Women television characters in realistic work situations are still the exception, not the norm. However, it must be acknowledged that, in recent years, work has become and remains a part of women's characters. Still, one is hard pressed to find many "real" women characters like Joe Friday, whose personal lives are either never involved or almost never discussed within the context of the show, an episode, or a season. Indeed, the trend seems to be toward men characters being treated in the same way women have been; that is, delving into their personal as well as work lives. Such is the case on family shows with ensemble casts in the Bochco tradition: *E.R.*, *NYPD Blue*, *Law & Order*, *Ally McBeal*. Nevertheless, some shows are moving in the general direction of parity, such as *Judging Amy* (Amy, a judge), *Providence* (Sydney Hansen, a doctor), and *The X Files* (Dana Scully, FBI agent).

Bibliography

Faludi, Susan. *Backlash: The Undeclared War against American Women.* New York: Anchor, 1992.

Mary Beth Leidman

Wonder, Stevie (1950-), grew from the 12-year-old "little boy wonder" into one of the most versatile and creative musicians in American popular music. He was born Steveland Morris to a poor African-American mother in Saginaw, MI, but moved to Detroit three years later. Blind from birth, he developed a strong interest in music at an early age, mastering the harmonica, piano, and drums. Motown Records president Berry Gordy signed the boy to a long-term contract with the company's Tamla subsidiary as "Little Stevie Wonder," and Motown essentially became the boy's legal guardian.

Wonder's first single was released in 1962, "I Call It Pretty Music (But the Old People Call It the Blues)." It was a flop, but Wonder had tremendous stage presence. In 1963, Gordy recorded Wonder in concert and released "Fingertips—Part 2" as a single. The single became a million-seller and a No. 1 hit, and the album, *Recorded Live—The 12-Year-Old Genius* became the first LP to top both the pop and R&B charts in the U.S.

Having dropped "Little" from his stage name, Wonder toured in 1965, and his version of "High Heel Sneakers" hit No. 59 on the charts. But his big break came with the more mature soul hit "Uptight (Everything's Alright)" in February 1966. The song topped the R&B chart and was No. 3 on the pop chart. It was followed by the LP *Up Tight,* which included a soul version of Bob Dylan's "Blowin in the Wind" and another social-political commentary, "A Place in the Sun." Both songs were Top 10 hits in 1966.

Although Wonder's next album, *Down to Earth,* did not fare well, he had another million-seller single in July 1967, "I Was Made to Love Her." The single "I'm Wondering" hit No. 12 in November 1967. His single "Shoo-Be-Doo-Be-Doo-Da-Day" hit the Top 10 in May 1968.

Wonder took a turn away from soul toward easy listening music at the end of 1968. His next three singles were a popular standard, "For Once in My Life," and two other ballads, "My Cherie Amour" and "Yester-Me, Yester-You, Yesterday": all three used string accompaniment and were top ten hits.

Wonder produced his last album under Motown guardianship in 1979, *Signed, Sealed, Delivered.* Wonder wrote the songs, played most of the instruments, and produced the album. He also began a personal and musical relationship with Motown secretary Syreeta Wright, whom he married in September 1970. The album produced two hits, the title song and "Heaven Help Us All." A cover version of the Beatles' "We Can Work It Out" was another successful single in 1971.

Wonder completed his contract with Motown in May 1971. His final album for Tamla, *Where I'm Coming From,* consisted of songs co-written with his wife, including "If You Really Love Me." Wonder negotiated a new contract with Motown in 1972, giving him more artistic freedom and control over publishing rights and royalties. He began experimenting with electronic synthesizers and produced an album that signaled a dramatic change for him as well as for Motown, *Music of My Mind.* The best known song from the album, "Superwoman (Where Were You When I Needed You)", reached No. 33 on the charts and attracted large numbers of white listeners to Wonder's music. The album *Talking Book* continued Wonder's experimentation with electronic funk, and it produced two No. 1 hits in 1973, "Superstition" and the jazz-ballad "You Are the Sunshine of My Life."

Wonder was seriously injured in an automobile accident in August 1973, but he recovered quickly and appeared again on stage within two months. Meanwhile, his LP *Innervisions* sold over a million copies and won critical acclaim. The album included two Top 10 singles, "Living for the City" and "Higher Ground." He won four Grammy awards for 1973, two for the single "Superstition," one for "You Are the Sunshine of My Life," and Album of the Year for *Innervisions.*

In June 1974, "Don't You Worry About a Thing" was a Top 20 single, and the album *Fulfillingness' First Finale* topped the charts for two weeks in September. Wonder again won four Grammy awards, two for the album and one each for the singles "Living for the City" and "Boogie on Reggae Woman." "Boogie on Reggae Woman" reached No. 3 on the pop charts in February 1975. Wonder also succeeded as a songwriter, as Minnie Riperton topped the charts with his "Lovin' You" in April.

Wonder deepened his involvement in social and political causes in the mid-1970s. He performed at the Washington Monument to celebrate "Human Kindness Day" and in Jamaica with Bob Marley in May 1975. In January 1976, he joined Bob Dylan in a benefit for convicted murderer Ruben "Hurricane" Carter, and the Stevie Wonder Home for Blind and Retarded Children opened. In the 1980s, Wonder campaigned on behalf of jailed South African leader Nelson Mandela and was a leader in the fight to make Martin Luther King, Jr.'s birthday a national holiday. Wonder also sang on the two major benefit recordings of the 1980s, "We Are the World" and "That's What Friends Are For."

In April 1976, Wonder signed the largest contract in recording history to that date. His next album, *Songs in the Key of Life*, debuted at No. 1 in October and remained there for 14 weeks. Two songs from the album topped the charts and sold over a million copies each, "I Wish" and "Sir Duke," and Wonder won four Grammys for the LP.

Wonder began experimenting with contemporary classical music in 1979 with his score for the documentary film *Journey through the Secret Life of Plants*. The soundtrack album produced two singles, "Send One Your Love" and "Outside My Window," and the LP peaked at No. 4.

Wonder's 1980 album, *Hotter Than July,* included two Top 20 hits, "Master Blaster (Jammin')" and "I Ain't Gonna Stand for It." Wonder's "I Just Called to Say I Love You" from the motion picture *The Woman in Red* topped the U.S. charts in October 1984 and earned him the Oscar for best song.

In the fall of 1985, the album *In Square Circle* reached No. 5, while the single "Part Time Lover" was the first single to top the U.S. pop, R&B, adult contemporary, and dance charts. Wonder was also nominated for an Emmy for his guest appearance on television's *The Cosby Show*.

In 1987, Wonder released the album *Characters* with two No. 1 R&B hits, "Skeletons" and "You Will Know." He had two minor successes on duets in 1989, "Get It" with Michael Jackson and "My Love" with Julio Iglesias. Despite his appeal with mainstream audiences, Wonder returned to progressive music in 1991 with *Music from Jungle Fever,* the rap-flavored soundtrack album to Spike Lee's film. He also released several compilations and a live album in the 1990s, as well as *Conversation Peace* (1995).

Bibliography

Dragonwagon, Crescent. *Stevie Wonder.* New York: Flash, 1977.

Larkin, Colin, ed. *The Guinness Encyclopedia of Popular Music.* Vol. 5. Middlesex, U.K.: Guinness, 1995.

Romanowski, Patricia, and Holly George-Warren, eds. *The New Rolling Stone Encyclopedia of Rock & Roll.* New York: Fireside, 1995.

Swenson, John. *Stevie Wonder.* New York: Perennial, 1986.

Ken Nagelberg

Wonder Woman, an Amazon princess from Paradise Island, is a comic book character who possesses exceptional strength, speed, wisdom, and skill. She fights injustice with the aid of several magical weapons: her bracelets, made of a metal hard enough to repel bullets; her robot plane, an invisible jet that responds to the sound of her voice; and her magic lasso, a golden lariat that compels all bound with it to tell the truth and obey the person holding the rope. Wonder Woman debuted in *All-Star Comics* 8 (cover date Dec. 1941-Jan. 1942), and she was quickly given the lead in an anthology (*Sensation Comics,* Jan. 1942) and her own title (*Wonder Woman,* summer 1942).

William Moulton Marston, a psychologist known for inventing the lie detector, and an early feminist, created the character to show the superiority of love, tenderness, and other "feminine" qualities. His stories (published under the name of Charles Moulton and illustrated by H. G. Peter) blended mythology, technology, and magic with a hint of bondage in an attempt to demonstrate the superiority of women, due to their ability to submit to loving authority. Although *Wonder Woman* has been continuously published in some fashion since its debut, the character and title have gone through several distinct phases as views of women changed. In 1968, she lost her powers, gadgets, and distinctive star-spangled bathing suit costume to become an Emma Peel-like kung fu fighter and adventurer, a phase that lasted for five years.

Another revamp came in late 1976 with the *Wonder Woman* television show. Starring Lynda Carter, the series ran for three years, and the comic attempted to cash in on this popularity by returning to superhero adventures set in the 1940s. In 1986, *Wonder Woman* was relaunched by George Pérez, who put more emphasis on the mythological and historical aspects of Amazon society and did away with the secret identity and the invisible plane. Most recently, the title suffered through an attempt at "bad girl" art (with emphasis on scantily-clad large-breasted women) before returning to its superhero roots. Through all these variations, Wonder Woman has provided a counterpart to the traditional victim or sidekick roles of women in superhero comics, inspiring readers with her message of sisterhood.

Bibliography

Daniels, Les. *DC Comics: Sixty Years of the World's Favorite Comic Book Heroes.* Boston: Little, Brown, 1995.

Goulart, Ron. "Wonder Woman." *The Comic Book Reader's Companion.* New York: HarperPerennial, 1993.

Steinem, Gloria. Introduction. *Wonder Woman.* New York: Abbeville, 1995.

Johanna L. Draper

Wonder Years, The (1988-1993), a wonderfully complex TV comedy series, on the surface presents the struggles of the maturation of teenaged Kevin Arnold (Fred Savage). But underneath his suburban prosperity we find a world fraught with tension, frustration, and anxiety. *The Wonder Years* risked critiquing the goodness of *Father Knows Best,* and often left its stories dangling realistically, in a mood of harsh sadness. Here was a sitcom that risked a telling with two voices. The story is narrated by the grown-up Kevin (voice of Daniel Stern), who continually comments on "his" earlier behavior and finds himself wanting.

"Born" in 1956, at the height of the baby boom, Kevin experienced his "wonder years" during the turbulent 1960s. Yet these identifiable events do not make us feel good. Kevin's supposed best years were only momentarily ever happy, as he battled to properly fit in. The creators of the series, Carol Black and Neal Marlens, could not have picked a better year—1968—with which to begin their series, complete with Vietnam War protests, the Beatles' breakup, and the race to the moon. Yet all these familiar images, often glowing from a TV set in the Arnold house, simply served as backdrops for more universal concerns. The program's narratives were propelled by the small stuff of life, filled with the angst and pain associated with one's teenaged years.

The young Kevin is continually tormented by his older, but not wiser brother, Wayne (Jason Hervey). His even older sister, Karen (Olivia d'Abo) is also of no help, lost in her own love-child world. In contrast, Mom and Dad (Alley Mills and Dan Lauria) are of and from the solidly middle-class past.

Kevin's world really centered around trying to deal with school and friends. His best friend, Paul (Josh Saviano), and true love, Winnie (Danica McKellar), seemed ideal companions but were not. Paul studied too much; Winnie could never settle on Kevin as her one true love. The teachers as characters were memorable, from the perfect beauty of English instructor Miss White to the continual blusterings of Coach Cutlip to the inanities of the science teacher (Ben Stein).

The Wonder Years premiered in spectacular fashion on January 31, 1988, after the Super Bowl. It then re-premiered in October 1988 and continued on ABC through April 1993. During its network run, *The Wonder Years* was highly acclaimed. Indeed, after only six episodes, in August of 1988, it earned an Emmy as outstanding comedy series. Soon after came a George Peabody Award and many other honors. *The Wonder Years* deserves to be ranked among the best series ever aired on network television.

Bibliography

Blum, David. "Where Were You in '68?" *New York* 27 Feb. 1989: 112-24.

Brooks, Tim, and Earle Marsh. *The Complete Directory to Prime Time Network and Cable TV Shows, 1946-Present.* New York: Ballantine, 1995.

Golson, Barry. "A Farewell to Wonder." *TV Guide* 8 May 1993: 22-23.

Gross, Edward. *The Wonder Years.* Las Vegas: Pioneer, 1990.

Douglas Gomery

Woodcarving, a popular folk way of passing the time and creating beautiful art objects, has survived through the millennia. There is good evidence that woodcarving existed in the earliest prehistorical cultures. Whether the objects were three-dimensional wooden sculptures, bas relief images carved out of wood, or simple signs carved into wood, the medium of wood has been used to communicate ideas, stories, images, and messages. Woodcarving can be as simple as a young person carving initials into a tree and as complex as an accomplished artist fashioning a large, intricate sculpture. Perhaps one of the most famous incidents of carving in American history was the time Daniel Boone carved a message into a Tennessee tree indicating that this was the spot upon which he killed a "bar."

Making objects and images from wood continues today as a vital form of expressive culture. Because woodcarving requires few tools, perhaps only a knife and a piece of wood, it has been a process accessible to almost anyone living in North America. Stone, metal, and glass require more and varied tools and spaces. Further, wood carvings can and are generally created by a single individual. At the most basic level of woodcarving, participants rely on their own ethnic and historical heritage as a means of developing the thematic approach to a subject. The objective, for example, could either be to make a traditional stool for sitting, such as the Norwegian *kubbestoler* (log chair), or to make a carved snake cane, often found in traditional African-American cultures. In either case, carvers often draw upon national and ethnic heritages to create aesthetic objects and provide solutions to problems. Both the chair and the cane address a functional need while allowing the carver to embellish the artifact to make it more pleasing to the senses (eye, touch, and often smell) and to the ethnic community which can appreciate both the functional use and its cultural meaning.

The traditional woodcarver often employs familiar motifs that are understood by the audience or the community, such that the woodcarver's message is as readily understood as the oral joke or the oral historical legend. For example, in small Spanish-American Catholic community churches in New Mexico, woodcarvers from the congregation will make and leave *santos* (saints) for the church, such as a figure of San Pasqual, the patron saint of the kitchen, carved as a standing figure carrying a loaf of bread.

North American decoy carvings provide perhaps one of the best examples of woodcarving. Not only are they unique to the United States and Canada, probably taking their original purpose from American Indians, but duck decoys are ubiquitous on the American landscape. Likewise, the picture of the American duck decoy is used as widely as any other image in the profusion of American popular culture. Decoys, in general, are imitation wildfowl; ducks, geese, or other birds, carved in wood and painted to look exactly like live birds. Historically, duck decoys were used by hunters as lures to attract live birds. Today they are also used to attract wildlife to waterfowl areas for the purpose of photography and filmmaking. Erwin O. Christensen notes that the wooden decoy was probably an improvement on those the American Indians made of stuffed skins or painted brushes. He also points out that decoy carving was practiced as early as the American colonial period and that the skill had reached its maturity about the time of the Civil War.

In most cases, the hand-carved decoys were hewn out of a block of wood and finished with a pocket knife or a jack knife. Heads were generally made separately and either glass or carved eyes were added. In some cases, the eyes were simply painted onto the head. One distinguishing feature was that the older decoys were painted in one or two solid, flat colors while contemporary bird decoys are generally painted with many colors in order to appear more life-like. Today, those who make duck and geese decoys exhibit the same care and skill that earlier decoy carvers possessed. Bird decoy makers today carve the body and head separately, matching the two to imitate real wildfowl examples.

Duck decoy carving still flourishes today. Most decoy carvers in the United States and Canada are males, although female carvers do exist. Today, in areas such as the northern Midwest and lower Canada where duck decoy making and duck hunting are popular, duck decoy exhibitions abound, where carvers display their carved and painted duck decoys. The decoys are often entered into competition where the ducks are judged by authentic appearance and artistic qualities. In the contemporary duck hunting world, it is not unlikely to find a former duck hunter who has eschewed actual hunting in favor of duck decoy woodcarving.

According to Marion J. Nelson, there are four basic styles of carving: chip carving, incised decoration, shallow relief carving, and high relief carving. In addition to these four styles of woodcarving, figure carving or carving in the round, as in the case of the duck decoy, provides a fifth basic style. Chip carving, accomplished by carving a organized pattern of v-shaped notches in a flat surface, was apparently being done by the fifth century and is often found on table tops or frames in North America. Incised carving decoration is a technique in which the groove or line in the wood is created by using a knife or chisel. This type of carving is perhaps the most widely known in North America and can be the most intricate. It can take the form of a finely drawn line or decoration on a wooden spoon. It can also be found in its most simple form as a piece of graffiti or initials carved into a piece of wood or on a tree. Shallow relief carving incorporates raised decoration; the decoration, as well as the background, has a flat surface. High relief carving is where carving appears high on the surface of the wood; the carved decoration is modeled like a sculpture. In this type of carving the image is often almost three-dimensional and involves undercutting and openwork to the point where the modeling is like a figure on top of the wood.

The last category of woodcarving, and perhaps the one that most people identify as American woodcarving, is figure carving, accomplished by sculpting a piece of wood into a three-dimensional image, often a figure or series of objects. The objects can be carved on a base or may be free-standing. A duck decoy, standing man or woman, an animal such as a horse, or a scene are common subjects. Figural carving can be functional, as in the case of religious icons and saints, handcarved wooden toys, and household items like candlesticks or bookends. Or the sculpture can be non-functional, as in the case of whimsical items like a horse carved by an individual, or the commonly carved wooden book with a hidden drawer inside.

Among European immigrants to America, the Scandinavian American immigrants, and particularly the Norwegian American immigrants, have the most well documented traditions of woodcarving. This fact is not simply that other European immigrant groups did not do so much woodcarving, which of course the English, French, and German groups did, but rather the Scandinavian Americans carried so much of their traditional folklife patterns with them and these traditions have been so well researched. Norwegian Americans settled in the northern Midwest in clusters among other Scandinavians and continued to produce many of the traditional material culture genres that had been produced in Norway before immigration. Hence, woodcarving, as well as traditional painting and furniture making, continued long after immigration.

Carved wooden spoons, drinking bowls, carved pieces of furniture, skis with elaborately carved heads of supernatural beings carved on the tips, and standing figures were among the woodcarvings that ethnic Norwegian Americans made. Perhaps the finest example of Norwegian-American woodcarvers is Leif Melgaard, who immigrated in 1920 to Minnesota. Known for the intricate detail in his woodcarving, Melgaard is widely recognized for his carving of the altar and pulpit for the Norwegian Lutheran Memorial Church in Minneapolis.

Woodcarving has long been practiced among African Americans. Among the finest of the woodcarvers in the black American folk tradition was Elijah Pierce (1892-1984). Pierce learned the art and craft of woodcarving in his home, from his uncle who was a chairmaker and basketmaker and other members of the African-American community who regularly made woodcarvings. Pierce carved hundreds of relief woodcarvings that reflect the religious and secular concerns of the African-American community.

In New Mexico, Hispanic Americans carry forward the traditional woodcarving inherited from the Iberian Peninsula. In Spain and Portugal, church altars and walls in the front of the church behind the altar contain a rich heritage of wood carving. These carvings are primarily of saints (*santos*), carved by individuals who either belong to the church and make the carvings of their most significant saints, or the carvings are created by outside professionals commissioned to complete the woodcarving for the church. George López (1900-1993), and his family in the area of Córdova, NM, have perpetuated this rich folk tradition.

In neighboring Arizona, high on the mesas in the arid lands of the northeastern part of the state, the Hopi Indians maintain another important woodcarving tradition: standing religious figures called kachinas, representing different parts of their religion. Kachinas date back to at least the 16th century, with images appearing on pottery from the 14th and 15th centuries. Today kachina carving continues as an active and commercial tradition with many groups of young Hopi women carving kachinas for sale.

Finally, many woodcarvers of North America fall outside the specific traditions tied to ethnic and immigrant heritage. In the South and the Upland South particularly, the tradition of woodcarving has been especially strong. From Arkansas to southern Ohio and from West Virginia to Kentucky, the practice of woodcarving among descendants of the first pioneers in these regions has been ongoing for several generations.

Bibliography

Briggs, Charles. *The Wood Carvers of Córdova, New Mexico*. Knoxville: U of Tennessee P, 1980.

Bronner, Simon J. *Chain Carvers: Old Men Crafting Meaning*. Lexington: UP of Kentucky, 1985.

Christensen, Erwin O. *Early American Wood Carving.* Cleveland: World Publishing, 1952.

Henning, Darrell D., Marion J. Nelson, and Roger L. Welsch. *Norwegian-American Wood Carving of the Upper Midwest.* Decorah: Norwegian-American Museum, 1978.

Moe, John F. *Amazing Grace: The Life and Work of Elijah Pierce.* Columbus: Martin Luther King, Jr., Center, 1990.

Wright, Barton. *Hopi Kachinas.* Flagstaff: Northland, 1977.

John F. Moe

Woodstock, a notorious or famous musical event which in effect changed the nature of American society, the Woodstock Music and Arts Fair took place in the town of White Lake, NY, over the weekend of August 15-17, 1969. The crowd that assembled made it the largest rock festival ever staged up to that time. But Woodstock also represented a high point in sixties counterculture, played out before the world due to extensive media coverage of the event. The people attending made a generally positive impression, because although the gathering amounted to the third largest city in New York State, a minimum of serious problems, especially in terms of crime and violence, occurred. In spite of several strong rainstorms and overtaxed facilities, Woodstock seemed to bring out the best in human nature, judging by the high level of cooperation among the attendees.

The idea for Woodstock developed among four young entrepreneurs, all between 23 and 25 years old. Michael Lang was a head-shop owner and past promoter of the festival. His immediate partner, Artie Kornfeld, was an executive at Capitol Records who had already successfully managed the Cowsills. The other partners in the venture were John Roberts, heir to a pharmaceutical fortune, and his friend Joel Rosenman, lawyer and amateur musician. The original motivation for Lang and Kornfeld was simply to generate enough profits to open a recording studio at Woodstock, NY; as it turned out, the festival itself became a history-making event.

Working out of offices in New York City, the promoters at first arranged for a concert site in Walkill, about 50 miles north. But hostility on the part of the town council led to a change of venue within weeks of the festival date. The final site became Max Yasgur's farm in White Lake, near Bethel, about 100 miles northwest of New York City. Another unusual arrangement involved hiring members of the Hog Farm, an alternative commune with operations in New Mexico and NYC, to serve as security for the concert. The Hog Farm also provided free food during the event.

The sound system used for the festival was one of the largest assembled up to that date, involving 10,000 watts RMS in audio into eight ohms, or the equivalent of approximately 150,000 watts today. Four 100-foot towers held speakers arranged to reach all areas of the crowd, and the sound itself was so good that the music could be heard clearly well beyond sight of the stage. Some reported that the music could be heard ten miles away. The stage was about 75 feet square and 11 feet off the ground. Other structures included a performers' pavilion, two side-stages, concession areas, and a fence surrounding the perimeter.

The lineup of musical talent represented some of the top acts of the day plus some legends in the making. Included were, in roughly alphabetical order: Joan Baez; the Band; Blood, Sweat, and Tears; Paul Butterfield; Canned Heat; Joe Cocker; Country Joe and the Fish; Creedence Clearwater Revival; Crosby, Stills, and Nash; the Grateful Dead; Arlo Guthrie; Tim Hardin; Richie Havens; Jimi Hendrix; Incredible String Band; Jefferson Airplane; Janis Joplin; Mountain; Santana; John Sebastian; Sha Na Na; Ravi Shankar; Sly Stone Sweetwater; and Johnny Winter. Other public personalities took the stage at various points, such as political activist Abbie Hoffman and guru Swami Satchadinanda. Other exhibits included a puppet theater, the two side stages for acoustic music, an art show, a crafts bazaar, and arts and crafts workshops.

Before the event, billed as an Aquarian Exposition and also as Three Days of Peace and Music, 186,000 tickets were sold, at $6 per day or $18 for the three-day event. But the state police later estimated, based on counting automobiles on the roads, that approximately 1,000,000 people attempted to drive to the festival site. Cars were abandoned as far as eight miles away, from where people walked the rest of the way. The New York State Thruway temporarily closed. People came from all over the United States, including the west coast. Perhaps one-quarter of a million people gave up, turned around and went home. Others arrived well before the weekend to camp out on the extensive grounds, which included hundreds of acres, and to help with final setup of the site. Many, encouraged by street flyers in New York announcing a "free" festival, simply pushed down the fences and walked over onto the grounds. Well before the opening day on Friday the event organizers declared Woodstock a free festival.

Not everyone who attended on Friday stayed for more, due to rain showers as well as the overwhelming nature of the gathering. At the height of the show on Saturday afternoon, estimates of the crowd (by helicopter) went as high as 500,000 people. The crowd occupied the entire large sloping hill and went on over the crest and out of sight. For food and drink people began sharing what they had brought, thereby minimizing the need to get up and walk around. A steady stream of water, wine, food, and drugs circulated along the rows.

Local doctors volunteered many hours to staff a medical clinic, and others were flown in from nearby communities. One teenager was accidentally killed, run over by a tractor by a local farmer at work on the site. There were several births; otherwise most of the medical care involved drug reactions and minor injuries. Governor Rockefeller declared Woodstock a disaster area, but the end result was to gain the cooperation of the police and National Guard in flying in extra food and medical supplies. Given the number of people who attended the festival, it is extraordinary that so few serious injuries resulted. In contrast, the Altamont concert four months later (see entry) resulted in many injuries, and later attempts to re-create Woodstock were much less successful (e.g., Woodstock '99 ended in riots).

The music sets ran late, interrupted by shutting down the stage power during rainstorms and for public service announcements from the stage, and slowed by the logistics of flying groups in and out by helicopter and preparing the set and equipment changes. Music originally scheduled for early afternoon until midnight actually got started in late afternoon and ran overnight. Saturday's show began about three in the afternoon and ended with the Jefferson Airplane's performance at about 7:30 on Sunday morning. Jimi Hendrix, the festival headliner, originally scheduled to close the Sunday night show, actually played on Monday morning to a remaining crowd of several thousand.

No one, including the promoters, had envisioned providing for the number of people who actually attended the festival. Revenue from late ticket sales helped the partners avoid bankruptcy in the immediate wake of the event. Postfestival funding also came from Warner Brothers, which distributed a film of the Woodstock festival, directed by Michael Wadleigh. Ownership of the film had been offered to John Roberts for $75,000 before the festival, but he turned it down; the promoters retained only a small percentage of the profits. The film won an Academy Award and made upwards of $83 million worldwide.

But the real significance of Woodstock has little to do with monetary profits or loss. Some have characterized it as a ritual consecrated to consumption, representing the dawn of the age of commercialism in rock and roll. Certainly it represented in some ways a mainstreaming of the hippie culture due to the sheer numbers who participated. But beyond everything else the Woodstock festival was a celebration of the counterculture ethic that life was to be enjoyed, that music should at least sometimes be free, that the blending of art and life was important, and that left to themselves, people could display their best character in sharing three days of peaceful recreation. The renowned anthropologist Margaret Mead said, "Woodstock was the best-planned and most significant gathering of young people in the history of the world." For that weekend the normal rules and ways of doing things were set aside and hippie ideals ruled, and it all worked. For that alone, it became a tremendously inspiring event for all involved and is looked back upon as probably the culminating event of the sixties decade, symbolizing its highest values as well as their most public expression.

Bibliography

Gitlin, Todd. *The Sixties: Years of Hope, Days of Rage.* New York: Bantam, 1987.

Makower, Joel. *Woodstock: The Oral History.* New York: Doubleday, 1989.

Wenner, Jann, ed. *Twenty Years of* Rolling Stone. New York: Straight Arrow, 1987.

Woodstock (film). Dir. Michael Wadleigh. Warner Brothers, 1970.

Bruce Henderson

World Series, The, is the highlight of the world of baseball, America's "national pastime." The tradition of post-season baseball dates back to 1884 when National League champion Providence bested the American Association's New York Metropolitans in a best-of-three-game World Series. For the next six years, the two league champions met for a series of contests, ranging in number from 6 in 1886 to 15 in 1887, when the series was played in ten different cities. Although the number of games to determine a champion subsequently was reduced, after the seven game series in 1890, players complained of exhaustion and refused to compete in further post-season contests.

Following the creation of the American League in 1900, what became known as "Organized Baseball" was run by a three-man commission, consisting of the presidents of the two major leagues and another man selected by them. This commission was granted power by club owners to create and enforce rules and to promote the popularity of the game. In 1903, in an attempt both to determine league superiority and raise revenues, the commission revived the World Series, but consent came only after American League President Ban Johnson had asked the owner of the pennant-winning Boston Pilgrims (also known as the Puritans, Red Sox, and Americans) to assure him of victory over the National League. Boston emerged victorious over the Pittsburgh Pirates in a best-of-nine-game series. Despite its popularity among spectators, no World Series was played in 1904 because Manager John McGraw of the National League champion New York Giants, due to personal animosity toward Ban Johnson, refused to field his team against Boston. In 1905, however, the World Series returned on an annual basis, with the only change in format being a decision after 1919 to limit the length of the series to seven games. In 1994, after 90 years, an unresolved labor dispute forced the cancellation of the annual fall classic.

To many observers of the national pastime, the significance of the World Series came from exploits on the field. The World Series was, until the advent of the All-Star Game in 1933, the only opportunity to see stars of the two leagues face each other in sanctioned competition. The World Series gave fans a chance to see Ty Cobb and Honus Wagner run the same basepaths; Mickey Mantle and Duke Snider patrol the same grass in centerfield; and to see Sandy Koufax and Jim Palmer stride to the same mound. It also was the source of memories and lore, ranging from game-saving catches by Sandy Amoros, Al Gianfriddo, Willie Mays, and Tommy Agee to the perfect game hurled by Don Larsen to Babe Ruth's alleged "called shot" home run to the infamous "Black Sox Scandal" to the rumble of a California earthquake.

In truth, however, the impact of the World Series transcended diamond events. The World Series represented geographical superiority and the triumphs of the lifestyles of their inhabitants. When Chicago squared off against New York, it was a contest of the rugged values of the West against the effete snobbery of the East. Within cities with two or more teams, it signified the triumph of local pride: the Bronx over Brooklyn or Harlem in New York or the supremacy of the North or South sides of Chicago. Furthermore, in the best American spirit, it represented the superiority of a team, working together, rather than focusing, as did the All-Star game, on the exploits of individual players.

While relocation of teams, advances in transportation, and the advent of cable television with its "superstations" have blurred, and in some instances obliterated, many of the regional aspects of baseball by permitting fans to witness players from each league during the regular season, the lure of the World Series remains. It is still the only opportunity to measure, in direct competition on the diamond, the best teams from each league.

Bibliography

Alexander, Charles C. *Our Game: An American Baseball History.* New York: Holt, 1991.

Honig, Donald. *Baseball America.* New York: Galahad, 1985.

Seymour, Harold. *Baseball: The Early Years.* New York: Oxford UP, 1960.

——. *Baseball: The Golden Age.* New York: Oxford UP, 1971.

——. *Baseball: The People's Game.* New York: Oxford UP, 1990.

Bruce A. Rubenstein

World Wrestling Federation, The (WWF), an adaptation of the Worldwide Wrestling Federation, organizer of one of America's most watched bits of showmanship, was created by Vince McMahon, Jr., in 1983. Unlike other wrestling promoters, McMahon revolutionized the sport by reducing violence and emphasizing wrestling's entertainment aspects. He was so successful that he gave himself the title of "the Walt Disney of sports."

Never admitting that his bouts were staged, McMahon confessed that his goal was showmanship: to provide "good acting" so fans would return to his next feature. His primary target audience was the nation's youth, and he sought to reach them through nationwide television promotions. To lure them into watching, in the mid-1980s he forged a shrewd link with rock musicians such as Cyndi Lauper, and had his star wrestlers dress in flamboyant costumes and enter the ring to music. His multi-talented wrestlers were featured on several recordings (The Wrestling Albums), while Hulk Hogan, formerly a guitarist in a rock band, became featured in movies and a Saturday morning network cartoon show.

McMahon turned his wrestling empire into other profitable marketing ventures. His grapplers were featured on videos, posters, wrestling action figures, trading cards, wearing apparel, ice cream bars, school supplies, and other paraphernalia. A "Wrestling Hot Line" was instituted so children could call to hear a pre-recorded message from WWF "superstars."

In the ring, McMahon turned his federation into both light farce and the bizarre. Wrestlers were dressed in clown costumes (Doink and Dink) and military garb (Sgt. Slaughter); others were portrayed either as androgynous figures (Adrian Adonis) or blatant homosexuals (Brutus "the Barber" Beefcake); the Undertaker represented the living dead, entering the ring to the tolling of bells and placing his vanquished foe in a body bag or coffin, while Jake "the Snake" Roberts either coiled a python around his victim or had a cobra bite them. To frighten adults, Irving R. Shyster (I.R.S.) enters the ring wearing a suit and tie, and denounces fans as "tax cheats." Nothing seemed too outrageous, and everything succeeded. Other wrestlers represented the enemies of the United States so that the nation's patriotic heroes could prevail over international bad guys.

The WWF had its superiority threatened in 1994 by Ted Turner's World Championship Wrestling, but only after Turner began luring WWF stars, such as Hulk Hogan, to his federation and engaging in extensive pay-for-view programming. If imitation is the sincerest form of flattery, Vince McMahon and the WWF remain the standard for bringing professional wrestling to the forefront as sport entertainment.

Bibliography

Jare, Joe. *Whatever Happened to Gorgeous George?* Englewood Cliffs: Prentice-Hall, 1974.

Morton, Gerald W., and George M. O'Brien. *Wrestling to Rasslin': Ancient Sport to American Spectacle.* Bowling Green, OH: Bowling Green State U Popular P, 1985.

"1988: The Year in Review." *Pro Wrestling Illustrated* March 1989: 30.

Sugar, Bert Randolph, and George Napolitano. *The Pictorial History of Wrestling.* New York: Warner, 1984.

Bruce A. Rubenstein

See also

Professional Wrestling

Wrestling (on Television)

World's Fairs. The era of modern world's fairs, one of the long-lasting and influential ways of presenting a nation's culture, began with the Crystal Palace Exhibition in London in 1851. This successful exposition, an outgrowth of industrial fairs and art shows in England and France dating back to the 18th century, set important precedents for subsequent fairs both in the architecture employed and in the international participation obtained. Joseph Paxton's magnificent Crystal Palace, a prefabricated structure of steel and glass erected in Hyde Park in less than a year, set the standard for exposition buildings for the next generation, until fairs became too large to be housed in a single building. The participation of numerous countries added an element of nationalistic competition and pride that continues to be a feature of fairs.

One of those nations present at the Crystal Palace was the United States, and the experience was stimulating enough to encourage a number of New York promoters to attempt to replicate the London fair in their city in 1853. Although it was the first American world's fair, the New York Crystal Palace exposition of 1853 attracted far fewer visitors and was far less an aesthetic or commercial success than its London counterpart.

In 1876, the United States celebrated the centennial of the Declaration of Independence, and a major part of that celebration was an international exposition in Philadelphia's Fairmount Park. The Centennial International Exhibition, as it was formally called, was housed in several large and many small buildings and was an overwhelming experience to the nearly ten million visitors. The fair was a showcase of the industrial revolution, with the giant Corliss engine, the telephone, and many other products of American ingenuity holding the spotlight. Although it lost nearly $2 million, the fair was popular with the public and important in symbolically expressing national self-confidence.

Arguably, the greatest of all American expositions was the World's Columbian Exposition, held in Chicago in 1893. Planned to celebrate the 400th anniversary of Columbus's discovery of America, this fair was delayed a year after Congress took longer than expected in choosing Chicago as the site over New York, St. Louis, and other cities. The Columbian exposition was notable in a number of ways. Architecturally, it featured a Grand Concourse—a number of large exhibition buildings constructed around a long lagoon—designed in formal, neoclassical architecture and painted a dazzling white. This centerpiece lent the fair its nickname, the White City, and provided the 21.5 million visitors with an unforgettable vista. The orderly layout of the fair's main buildings influenced urban planning for years to come, and the popularity of the classical architecture found expression in commercial and public building design until the 1920s. The exposition also featured an entertainment zone called the Midway, highlighted by a giant Ferris wheel that became a staple of subsequent fairs and amusement parks, and a large art exhibit in the Fine Arts Building, the only one of the lath-and-plaster structures to be rebuilt as a permanent building, which now houses the Museum of Science and Industry. In addition, the exposition hosted a series of conferences on weighty topics sponsored by a subsidiary organization called the World's Congress Auxiliary, in which women played a significant role. At one of these adjunct meetings, the young historian Frederick Jackson Turner read his famous paper on "The Significance of the Frontier." Finally, this fair was the first of several major fairs during this period to place some emphasis on demonstrating the superiority of Anglo-Saxons through the technique of native "villages," in which Filipinos, Dahomeans, and other representatives of "lesser" races were shown in their natural habitat, reassuring Anglo-Saxon visitors that theirs was indeed the most advanced civilization.

American world's fairs reached their peak in elegance and extravagance between 1893 and 1915, and many of the fairs of this era commemorated historical events. In 1898, the Trans-Mississippi Exposition in Omaha called attention to the economic potential of the Great Plains. The object of Buffalo's Pan-American Exposition in 1901 was to encourage better relations, commercial and otherwise, with Latin America, but the fair is remembered today as the scene of President William McKinley's assassination.

The Louisiana Purchase International Exposition, held in St. Louis's Forest Park, celebrated (also a year late) the centennial of the Louisiana Purchase. One of the largest fairs ever held in terms of area (1,272 acres or almost 2 square miles), it featured elegant buildings of classical design, an extensive foreign section, more anthropological exhibits, and the 1904 Olympic Games. The following year, Portland, OR, hosted the Lewis and Clark Exposition, noting the centennial of the transcontinental expedition of Meriwether Lewis and William Clark. In 1907, the 300th anniversary of the first permanent settlement in colonial America was commemorated with the Jamestown Tercentennial Exposition in Hampton Roads, VA, near the original site of Jamestown. The 1909 Alaska-Yukon-Pacific Exposition in Seattle was designed primarily to attract commercial attention to the Pacific Northwest.

Two California fairs completed the high period of American expositions. The Panama-Pacific International Exposition, held in San Francisco in 1915, heralded not only the successful completion of the Panama Canal but also San Francisco's remarkable recovery from the devastating earthquake and fire of 1906. Down the California coast at San Diego, the Panama-California Exposition ran for two years (1915-16) and was a major stimulus to the growth of the host city.

Despite the reputation of the 1920s as years of fun and frivolity, world's fairs did not prosper during that decade. Indeed, the Sesqui-Centennial International Exposition, held in 1926 in Philadelphia, was the only major fair of the 1920s, and it was, by most accounts, an aesthetic and commercial failure. Part of the reason for that may well be that in a time of modernism, the exposition made a concerted effort through its colonial revival architecture and historical theme, to look backwards, and in so doing, found itself out of step with its time.

The Depression decade of the 1930s saw two important fairs that continued the theme of modernism in America. The Century of Progress Exposition in Chicago (1933-34) and the New York World's Fair (1939-40) both startled visitors with highly functional architecture derived from the Bauhaus, the Paris "Art Deco" exposition of 1925, and other European fairs of the late 1920s and early 1930s. There were very logical reasons for this; science was a major theme of these fairs, and their modern architecture seemed to reflect the cutting edge of modern science and technology. Moreover, it was much cheaper to construct buildings with flat walls, few windows, and virtually no ornamentation; this was a vital consideration in a time of national economic crisis. Two other fairs of the 1930s were held in California. The California Pacific Exposition of 1935-36 in San Diego reused the site of the 1915-16 exposition in an attempt to stimulate the city's economy in the midst of the Depression. The 1939-40 Golden Gate International Exposition, located on an island in San Francisco Bay, was intended to celebrate the recent completion of the Golden Gate and San Francisco–Oakland Bay bridges.

World War II imposed a long hiatus on fairs, and it was not until 1962 that the first post-war fair was held in the United States. This was the Century 21 Exposition in Seattle, a byproduct of the Cold War designed to show the world that, despite Soviet advances, the United States was still the dominant scientific nation. The fair, centered around the 605-foot Space Needle, still a Seattle landmark, helped popularize science education in the United States and, in so doing, served its political purpose. Two years later, the second New York World's Fair (1964-65) was a big, rambling affair designed to recoup some of the losses incurred by the 1939-40 fair and enable the Flushing Meadows park project to be completed. Although the fair attracted over 51 million visitors, it lost even more money than its predecessor.

Two much smaller but more successful efforts were Hemisfair '68, staged in San Antonio, and Expo '74, held in Spokane, WA. Hemisfair focused on U.S. relations with Latin America and did much to revitalize downtown San Antonio, while Expo '74 was based on an environmental theme. In addition to environmental exhibits, this fair hosted a series of symposia on environmental issues and did much to enhance the development of its relatively small host city.

The last two world's fairs held in the United States in the 20th century were not successful and proved a significant deterrent to the organization of other fairs. The Knoxville International Energy Exposition (1982), based on the theme "Energy Turns the World," met its attendance expectations but was flawed by the activities of a group of corrupt bankers and the failure of the post-fair redevelopment plans for the site near downtown Knoxville. The 1984 Louisiana World Exposition, based on a theme of the uses of water, was plagued by undercapitalization, poor attendance, and bad publicity. The fair corporation nearly closed the fair during its run and declared bankruptcy in November; estimates of its losses are as high as $120 million.

The bad experiences of Knoxville and New Orleans were a major factor in Chicago's decision to abandon plans for a world's fair in 1992 for the 500th anniversary of Columbus's discovery of America. But apart from the financial risks involved in putting on a fair, it is also clear that fairs are not the distinctive entertainment and educational events they once were. Theme parks and television, in particular, provide many Americans with the same attractions that world's fairs did a century ago, and, consequently, remove much of the imperative to attend. While we may yet see American world's fairs in the 21st century, fair organizers will carefully link them with other rationales, such as regional economic development, urban renewal, or transportation modernization.

Bibliography

Curti, Merle. "America at the World Fairs, 1851-1893." *American Historical Review* 55 (1950): 833-56.
Greenhalgh, Paul. *Ephemeral Vistas: The Expositions Universelles, Great Exhibitions, and World's Fairs, 1851-1939.* Manchester: Manchester UP, 1988.
Rydell, Robert. *All the World's a Fair.* Chicago: U of Chicago P, 1984.
——. *Books of the Fairs.* Chicago: American Library Association, 1992.
——. *World of Fairs: The Century-of-Progress Expositions.* Chicago: U of Chicago P, 1993.

John E. Findling

Wouk, Herman (1915-), one of America's lasting popular writers, has enjoyed a diverse career in the arts, beginning as a comedy writer in radio in the 1930s, authoring patriotic plays during the war years, and eventually establishing himself as a best-selling novelist whose popularity and creativity have spanned the decades since 1948, when he published his first book.

It was *The Caine Mutiny: A Novel of World War II* (1951), inspired in part by his own military service aboard a Navy destroyer in the Pacific, that established Wouk as a major author. The novel, which won the Pulitzer Prize in 1952 and was adapted by Wouk for the stage in 1953, was a popular and critical success. The film version (1954) starred Humphrey Bogart.

Wouk's fourth novel, *Marjorie Morningstar* (1955), the story of a young woman seeking stardom and love who falls under the spell of a has-been actor, was another popular favorite. A critique of theatrical artifice, the novel also turned a scrutinizing eye on middle-class Jewish life in America. *Youngblood Hawke* (1962) offered up a complaint of the corruptive forces that await a talented but vulnerable young writer from the hinterlands who comes to New York to make his career.

In *The Winds of War* (1971), and *War and Remembrance* (1978), Wouk revisited the Second World War. Long and amply researched volumes, the two books filter the panorama of the war's many fronts and dimensions through the experiences of Captain "Pug" Henry. Wouk's most recent novels, *Inside, Outside* (1985), *The Hope* (1993), *The Glory* (1994), and *The Will to Live On* (2000), return to the Jewish themes he explored earlier.

Bibliography

Mazzeno, Laurence W. *Herman Wouk.* New York: Twayne, 1994.

Liahna Babener

Wozniak, Stephen (1951-), built the Apple home computer. A stereotypical computer nerd, he wanted to see IBM's hulking mainframes shrunk down so every home could have one and anybody could run one. He and partner Steve Jobs (see entry) designed a machine that broke the hold of the "batch processing mentality." A colorful person, he became a celebrity whose activities were frequently reported in the popular press.

In 1970, Wozniak met Steve Jobs, who shared his interest in electronics. Woz and Jobs joined the Homebrew Computer Club, which shared programs and swapped components. To finance their own computer—after Hewlett-Packard and Atari turned down the project—the pair sold Jobs's VW van and Wozniak's HP scientific calculator. That first machine, the fancifully named Apple I, was sold for the peculiar price of $666.66. Wozniak went to work on the Apple II. It came in 1977, and with it, the home computer revolution.

In 1985, Wozniak quit Apple, angry that his Apple II had been abandoned in favor of the Macintosh and the failed Lisa. Wozniak then formed CL-9, Inc. (Cloud Nine) to build universal remote controls for TVs and appliances, but folded the company in 1989.

Wozniak's machine, called the Model T or the Volkswagen Beetle of computing, remained in production for 16 years, selling 5.5 million units. The Apple II was finally laid to rest in November 1993.

Bibliography

Levy, Steven. *Hackers: Heroes of the Computer Revolution.* Garden City: Anchor, 1984.

Rose, Frank. *West of Eden: The End of Innocence at Apple Computer*. New York: Viking, 1989.

Mark McDermott

Wrestling (on Television) is a far cry from the traditional Greco-Roman sport that has been around for centuries. The TV brand is a larger-than-life extravaganza combining elements of a morality play, where good always triumphs over evil in the end, with aspects of vaudeville and rock 'n' roll. It is generally acknowledged by its own practitioners and viewers to be an "entertainment" rather than a pure sport.

The evolution of wrestling on TV is a reflection of a mutually beneficial pairing of the medium and the sport at two key points in TV history, when advances in technology and distribution required relatively inexpensive programming to fill large amounts of air time. In each case, wrestling fit the bill. By adapting itself to fit both the times and television's needs, it helped to make the new medium financially viable while using television's reach to vastly increase its own popularity. The first of those periods was the late 1940s and early 1950s, when broadcast television began to reach the general public. The second was the 1980s, when cable TV, and subsequently pay-per-view events, became technologically feasible on a wide scale.

Wrestling was a part of the American scene long before TV. The sport was popular on the 19th-century American frontier. By the turn of the century there were organized championship matches, some running for hours.

The industry saw a peak in popularity in the early 1930s, despite the Depression. Even then, while matches were largely "legitimate," the standard formula for modern TV wrestling had been established. In a typical championship match, as A. J. Liebling reported in a 1954 *New Yorker*, a "Foreign Menace would oppress [champion Jim] Londos unmercifully for about forty minutes, and then Londos would pick him up for the airplane spin...and dash him to the mat." (This also reflected a xenophobic strain that was to remain a prevalent part of the sport, making it easy to choose identifiable villains.) Wrestling's popularity waned in the mid-1930s, a period that coincided with a puzzling array of multiple "world champions," each sanctioned by a different promoter. TV rescued and revived it.

By the early 1950s, wrestling had caught on big, adapting itself to the new media by remaking itself as flashy melodrama. The good-versus-evil morality play of Londos's day became exaggerated. As Benjamin G. Rader notes, "Television encouraged the players to engage in even more extravagant showmanship.... The wrestlers...donned theatrical costumes and assumed theatrical names.... No replay or slow motion shots were needed, for the wrestlers perfected the art of excessive gestures. Their histrionics projected in stark clarity the progress of the match."

At its peak in the 1950s, more than 200 stations carried wrestling. Advertisers, particularly of appliances, found the shows to be an effective marketing tool, and so matches were well sponsored. Wrestlers often struggled to make a living before television, but the average grappler was making between $125 and $150 by 1950 (good money then),

with some (such as Gorgeous George) earning as much as $3000 as week. Live matches, featuring grapplers seen on the tube, were drawing crowds of 12,000 to 15,000, even in small towns.

But wrestling on TV declined by the middle of the decade, probably done in by oversaturation and an increase in alternative programs. Champions such as Bruno Sammartino remained popular in the years that followed, but wrestling was relegated largely to UHF channels and live matches. It found revival once again in the 1980s through cable TV and Vincent K. McMahon.

Wrestling continues to generate large revenues on TV. But what ultimately may be leading it into decline may be what helped to end its glory years in the 1950s: oversaturation on TV, and the availability (on cable this time) of good alternative programming.

Bibliography

Hammer, Joshua. "The Upstart (Slam!) Who's Reinventing (Pow!) the Tube." *GQ* Nov. 1989: 280-85.

Johnson, William Oscar. "Wrestling with Success." *Sports Illustrated* 25 Mar. 1991: 42-54.

Katz, Richard. "Boxing Back on Track." *Cablevision* 5 Apr. 1993: 16.

Liebling, A. J. "A Reporter at Large: From Sarah Bernhardt to Yukon Eric." *New Yorker* 13 Nov. 1954.

Powers, Ron. *Supertube: The Rise of Television Sports*. New York: Coward-McCann, 1984.

Rader, Benjamin G. *In Its Own Image: How Television Has Transformed Sports*. New York: Free, 1984.

Scanlon, Kevin. "Wrestling's Hard Sell." *Maclean's* 19 May 1986.

Richard S. Kaufman

See also
Professional Wrestling
World Wrestling Federation

Wynette, Tammy (1942-1998), with Dolly Parton and Loretta Lynn, completed the great triumvirate of the most successful female country singers whose careers began in the 1960s. The three released *Honky Tonk Angels* (1993), an album on which they collaborated vocally and for which they penned a number of compositions. They hold the records for Top 10 hits for female artists since the beginning of the country charts in 1944: Parton with 54, Lynn with 51, and Wynette with 39. Wynette was honored with the Living Legend award at the TNN/Music City News Awards in 1991. Among her other releases in the 1990s were her hit duet single with Randy Travis, "We're Strangers Again" (1990), and a 1992 collaborative effort with the British duo the KLF titled "Justified and Ancient," which hit number one on the international pop charts.

Born in Tupelo, MS, Virginia Wynette Pugh was raised by her grandparents on a farm near Birmingham, AL. She married Euple Byrd at 17 in 1959 and became a hairdresser, but she left her husband shortly before the birth of her third child, hoping to break into the Nashville music business. For this, her mother and husband attempted to have her committed to a psychiatric institution. Her big break came when she entered producer Billy Sherrill's office in 1966 and unabashedly requested a recording contract. It was Sherrill, one of the keenest talent scouts and image makers in the business, who was responsible for launching the singer's career. When Sherrill recognized that Pugh could reach a female audience, Tammy Wynette was born.

Her 1966 debut song, "Apartment No. 9," penned by Johnny Paycheck, was a minor success, followed by a string of No. 1 singles between 1967 and 1972, among them the controversial but phenomenally successful "Stand by Your Man" (co-written with Sherrill), which rocketed to the top of charts in 1968. It was featured as a keynote song in the film *Five Easy Pieces* (1970); it crossed over to top the pop charts and became a hit in Great Britain in 1975; and it was the first of several songs in which Wynette was a champion of traditional values. This trait, coupled with the image of the long-suffering female, appealed to her audience. "Stand by Your Man" also became the biggest single record by a female country singer. Other hits of this period include "Your Good Girl's Gonna Go Bad," and "I Don't Wanna Play House" (1967), and "D-I-V-O-R-C-E" (1968). Wynette was named the Country Music Association's "Female Vocalist of the Year" in 1968, 1969, and 1970. In addition, Wynette's 1969 *Greatest Hits* LP became the best-selling album ever recorded by a female country artist, and the first to sell a million copies.

Wynette had married Don Chapman in 1967, but their marriage ended stormily, albeit romantically, when all-time country music great, George Jones (see entry), whisked her away. Though she and Jones claimed to have married in August 1968, they did not actually tie the knot until February 16, 1969. This union created "Mr. and Mrs. Country Music"—the logo on their tour bus—and resulted in one of the most successful professional duets ever. Produced by Billy Sherrill between 1971 and 1974, the couple recorded hits such as "Take Me," "The Ceremony," "We're Gonna Hold On," "We're Not the Jet Set," and "We Loved It Away"—a chronicle of their own stormy marriage, which finally ended in 1975.

During the early and mid-70s, Wynette's single recordings also reinforced her image as a "traditional values" woman, one who "stood by her man"—in art, if not in life—and who accepted heartbreak with stoic resolve. These ideas were encapsulated in songs such as "Woman to Woman" (1974) and "You Make Me Want to Be a Mother" (1975). "Til I Can Make It On My Own" (1976) expresses Wynette's vulnerability after her break-up with Jones. She coasted out of the decade with a six-week marriage to Michael Tomlin (a Nashville real estate agent) in 1976, followed by a marriage to her fifth and last husband, songwriter George Richey, in 1978.

Wynette's career in the 1980s began with a recording with Jones, *Together Again*, which boosted both of their lagging careers, after which she and Sherrill parted company. Her chart singles were few and stale, despite efforts to create a "modern" quasi-liberated Wynette with songs like "Unwed Fathers" (1983). Ironically, as her personal life stabilized, her success waned because, as Alana Nash has noted, "Her strongest appeal was never really musical, but cultural" and she ceased to be a "professional victim." A bright spot in an otherwise dismal decade was the duet hit single with Mark Gray, "Sometimes When We Touch" (1985), followed by her 1987 release *Higher Ground,* comprised of duets with artists such as Elvis Costello. Efforts to expand her professional life included a stint on the now-defunct daytime soap *Capitol*; Burt Reynolds cast her in the 1985 film *Stick*, and also directed her 1990 music video, "Let's Call It a Day." In 1986, Wynette entered the Betty Ford Center for Drug Abuse, and, in 1988, she filed bankruptcy.

Bibliography

Bufwack, Mary A., and Robert K. Oermann. *Finding Her Voice: The Saga of Women in Country Music.* New York: Crown, 1993.

Clarke, Donald, ed. *The Penguin Encyclopedia of Popular Music.* London: Penguin, 1990.

Nash, Alana. *Behind Closed Doors: Talking with the Legends of Country Music.* New York: Knopf, 1988.

Riese, Randall. *Nashville Babylon: The Uncensored Truth and Private Lives of Country Music's Greatest Stars.* New York: Congdon & Weed, 1988.

Wynette, Tammy, with Joan Dew. *Stand by Your Man: An Autobiography.* New York: Simon & Schuster, 1979.

Rebecca A. Umland
Samuel J. Umland

X

X Files, The (1993-), an hour-long TV series on the Fox network, is based on the premise that the FBI must have a section which handles the "odd" cases (the UFOs, the Bigfoot sightings, spontaneous combustion cases). The show pairs Special Agent Fox Mulder (David Duchovny), a believer, and Special Agent Dana Scully, M.D. (Gillian Anderson), a skeptic, and sends them out to investigate these cases, labeled the X files. Under less capable guidance than producer Chris Carter (who also created the show) and writers Darin Morgan and James Wong, the show might have been "*Dragnet* Meets *The Invaders*," but fortunately this is not the case. The show is neither a crime drama nor a science fiction program although cases are closed and aliens, demons, shape shifters, freaks of nature, and biological hazards from prehistory have all appeared on the show. And in keeping with the psychological/political tenor of our times, our own government is not always on the side of truth. It is, in many cases, the originator of the phenomenon being investigated or actively involved in covering it up. Agent Mulder has a secret contact who warns him when they get too close to undesirable truths, and Agent Scully was kidnapped and experimented on by the government. Many episodes are left unresolved for viewers as well as the agents. Often the rules of science are observed; sometimes they are bent.

The X Files is smart, timely, and well written, even at its weirdest. The show respects its viewers and incorporates numerous popular culture references into the scripts. There are heavy doses of conspiracy theory as well. It also features in Special Agent Scully one of the few strong, smart independent women portrayed on television. Her partner Special Agent Fox Mulder is a '90s hero, part of the establishment (FBI) and an outsider. As Agent Scully knocks on the door of his sub-basement office to introduce herself during the first episode he replies, "No one down here but America's Most Unwanted." The show combines successful elements from many other shows, including a pair of male/female characters who initially appear to be at odds with each other and then develop a strong trusting working relationship.

The show has gathered a devoted following, especially those who communicate via the Internet, a valuable tool for avid fandom. Chris Carter has created two more series in the same vein: *Millennium* (1996-99) and *Harsh Realm* (1999-); and the series has fostered an interest in the paranormal that several other shows have tried to capitalize on, to less success. A feature film was released in 1998.

Why does this show succeed? Good writing, good acting, appealing characters, a sense of humor, and story lines that don't assume its viewers are stupid. *The X Files* received Golden Globe awards as best dramatic series for 1994, 1996, 1997, and 1998. Gillian Anderson won the Emmy for lead actress in a drama series in 1997; Duchovny and the show have been nominated several times for Emmy awards.

Bibliography

Cerone, Daniel. "A Surreal *X-Files* Captures Earthlings." *LA Times* 28 Oct. 1994.

Details Feb. 1995.

Infusino, Divina. "Paranoid about the Paranormal." *TV Guide* 15 Jan. 1994: 20-21.

"Peaked Out." *Film Literature Quarterly* 21.3.

Roush, Matt. "*X Files* Is Earning Top-Drawer Respect." *USA Today* 12 Aug. 1994.

Jane Cramer

Yachting, especially in the sphere of the America's Cup competition and the Whitbread (now Volvo) Round-the-World Race, has in the last decade become a popular and important worldwide sport that seems to generate a flowering of national pride. In 1987, the America's Cup, raced off the coast of Fremantle, Western Australia, enjoyed a remarkable level of spectator support in the United States, support that has continued ever since, despite American losses. There are about 1,500 active yacht clubs in the United States.

The America's Cup originated with the founder of the New York Yacht Club, John Cox Steven. The club originated in 1844, and the America's Cup competition began in 1851. Claims have been made that this yachting series marks the beginning of "modern" international sporting exchanges. In 1851, it was Steven's yacht *America* which defeated 18 British boats for the inaugural cup.

The America's Cup series of yachts (essentially for inshore racing) are classified as being in the 12-meter class. There is some length variation but most are 60-70 feet in length. The most famous challenger was the British tycoon and tea importer Sir Thomas Lipton. On five occasions between 1899 and 1930 his *Shamrock* (I, II, III, etc.) vessels tried, but failed, to wrestle the Cup away from America.

The USA successfully defended the America's Cup until 1983, when *Australia II* narrowly defeated *Liberty* by 4-3 in races at Newport, RI. Dennis Conner is America's most famous Cup skipper, especially in light of the fact that, despite being the loser in 1983, he triumphed in Australia (1987) and held on to the Cup in the challenge series in 1988. The USA retained the Cup in 1992, but lost to New Zealand in 1995. New Zealand retained the Cup in the 1999-2000 series.

The first man to sail single-handedly around the world was Canadian-born Joshua Slocum, in his sloop *Spray*. Notable yachtspersons in the 20th century who have repeated Slocum's feat are Sir Francis Chichester, Robin Knox-Johnstone, and the first female to circumnavigate the globe, Dame Naomi James of New Zealand (272 days in 1977-78).

The quadrennial Whitbread Challenge is the oldest regular sailing race around the world. It starts and ends in England. The route is 32,000 miles with stops in Uruguay, Australia, New Zealand, and Florida. The winner of the 1997-98 race was American Paul Cayard.

The only American to win two yachting Olympic gold medals is H. F. Whiton (1904-1967), who won the six-meter class at London, 1948, and Helsinki, 1952. The first female to win a yachting gold medal was Virginia Heriot of France in 1928. Allison Jolly and Lynne Jewell of the USA won gold medals in the 470 class at the 1988 Seoul Olympics. Since 1984 (men) and 1992 (women), boardsailing (other-wise known as windsurfing) has been incorporated into the Olympic yachting program.

In Robert A. Palmatier and Harold L. Ray's *Sports Talk*, sailing metaphors rank in third place after baseball and boxing. They list 110 phrases ranging from "broad in the beam" to "three sheets to the wind," "touch and go," and "turn turtle." The language and lore of yachting is complex. John Rousmaniere, for example, in his *A Glossary of Modern Sailing Terms*, lists 1,100 terms.

Bibliography

Arlott, J., ed. *The Oxford Companion to World Sports and Games*. London: Oxford UP, 1975.

Dellenbaugh, D. *Sports Illustrated: Small Boat Sailing*. New York: Sports Illustrated/Time, 1990.

Lloyd, B. "Yachting." *New York Times* 19 July 1992.

Matthews, P., ed. *The Guinness Book of Records*. New York: Facts on File, 1993.

Palmatier, R. A., and H. L. Ray. *Sports Talk: A Dictionary of Sports Metaphors*. Westport: Greenwood, 1989.

Rousmaniere, John. *A Glossary of Modern Sailing Terms*. New York: Dodd, Mead, 1976.

Wallechinsky, D. *The Complete Book of the Olympics*. Boston: Little, Brown, 1991.

Wooton, K. "America's Cup Movable Citizenship." *Yachting* June 1994: 50-51.

Scott A. G. M. Crawford

Yankovic, "Weird Al" (1959-), is a notorious comedian/musician and rock and roll accordion player noted for his songs and videos parodying popular songs and performers. Most of his parodies are novelty songs set to a borrowed tune, but do not directly satirize the original song or performer. Examples include "Eat It" and "Fat," set to Michael Jackson's "Beat It" and "Bad," or "Like a Surgeon" set to Madonna's "Like a Virgin." A handful of his songs do directly satirize the original work, such as "This Song's Just Six Words Long," a parody of George Harrison's "Got My Mind Set on You," and "Smells Like Nirvana," a parody of Nirvana's "Smells Like Teen Spirit." Additionally, some songs borrow a style rather than a specific tune: the Devo-esque "Dare to be Stupid" and the Elvis-like "One More Minute."

Though his songs may not directly parody the original artist, Weird Al is a talented vocal and musical mimic, who carefully copies the sound of the original song, while occasionally enlisting the assistance of the original musicians. His videos will often use or rebuild the sets of the original videos and use some of the same actors. Weird Al is also known as a skilled physical mimic.

This mimicry attempts not to make Al's videos indistinguishable from the original, but to heighten the ironic tension between the original and the parody. Weird Al's comedy derives primarily from a playful juxtaposition of the familiar with the unusual, unexpected, or silly, especially if that which is familiar is established as popular, cool, hip, or serious. This is perhaps best exemplified in the "Smells Like Nirvana" video, in which Dick Van Patten calmly eats a sandwich while surrounded by angst-filled, slam-dancing teenagers.

While his usual comedic strategy is to add new and unexpected words to a familiar tune, he has also used the converse to great effect. His several polka medleys adapt classic rock songs, taking a familiar lyric and tune into an unexpected style. The defiant, hip, sexy, or sublime messages of these works are reduced to the ridiculous when accompanied by accordion, banjo, and clarinet rather than electric guitar. Victims of this treatment include the Rolling Stones, whose greatest hits are treated in medley form in "The Hot Rocks Polka," and Queen, whose entire "Bohemian Rhapsody" is played note for note, but in half the time, as the "Bohemian Polka."

Bibliography

Insana, Tino, and Al Yankovic. *The Authorized Al.* Chicago: Contemporary, 1985.

Larkin, Colin. *The Guinness Encyclopedia of Popular Music.* Vol. 5. Middlesex, U.K.: Guinness, 1995.

Rosen, Craig. "Weird Al Yankovic Has His Day on Scotti Bros." *Billboard* 6 July 1996: 9, 103.

Delano Lopez

Yard Sale is a general term that covers the popular and widespread activity dear to the hearts of most Americans, the informal selling of all kinds of articles at such geographical sites as yards, garages, porches, rooms, barns, or any necessary combination of two or more. All are sites for the sale of collectibles, accumulations of domestic materials that might to many people be seen as trash. But one person's trash is another's treasure, and vice versa. Sales usually begin in the spring when people have done their spring cleaning, then continue through the summer months and extend through the weeks of fall cleaning. Materials included in such sales might include big-sticker items like automobiles, tractors, and other farm equipment. But usually the inventory centers on more domestic items like clothes, costume jewelry, kitchen utensils, and materials which if not sold will be consigned to the trash.

Such sales serve at least three purposes. First, some people look upon the reusing of such items as valuable and thoughtful recycling—baby and children's clothes sell especially well. Second, these sales get rid of unwanted materials that clutter up the premises and in so doing raise a little cash, sometimes a considerable amount of money. Sometimes holders of such sales are snuckered by more knowledgeable antique dealers who buy for a song what they resell as antiques for a pretty penny. Third, the sales create a social situation where friends and neighbors—and strangers—stop by to talk about the holdings, sometimes making the owner proud, sometimes perhaps embarrassed. Garage sales are less commercially driven than auctions—with which they are sometimes associated. Neighbors often drop by garage sales to satisfy their curiosity about what a neighbor wants to discard, and sales are considered successful even if very little money is raised. After the sale some of the material is discarded, some is taken back inside to be held until the next sale, some is added to the inventory of another person holding a sale.

But the dynamics of the three-pronged drive to recycle materials—and thus to help the environment—of raising a little money and of clearing the house of unwanted materials and of drawing people together for a day is an important page in American culture, even in our day of strip malls, fast transportation and the purchasing of goods on television.

Bibliography

Herman, Gretchen M. "His and Hers: Gender Garage Sales." *Journal of Popular Culture* 29.1 (1995): 127-45.

McClung, R. S. *The Rummager's Handbook: Finding, Buying, Cleaning, Fixing, Using and Selling Secondhand Treasures.* Pownal: Storey Communications, 1995.

McIrer, Mary. "The Thrill of the Hunt." *Maclean's* 9 May 1988: 64.

Stevenson, Chris Harold. *Garage Sale Mania!* White Hall: Betterway, 1988.

Williams, Michael. *Garage Sale Magic!* Buffalo Grove: Freedom, 1994.

Ray B. Browne

Yellow Journalism is a term used to describe sensational or irresponsible newspaper reporting. Unlike the *New York Times*, which contains "All the News That's Fit to Print," "yellow" papers feature shocking and titillating stories of crime, scandal, gossip, and the supernatural. This type of news reporting includes both stories which are true, but lurid, and those which are completely fabricated. One can recognize yellow journalism not only by its subject matter, but also by its oversized and inflammatory headlines, graphic illustrations and photos (often faked), and colloquial prose style. Most scholars connect this journalistic trend to changes in printing technology in the late 19th century, when it became both possible and necessary for newspapers to reach a mass readership.

The term itself dates to this Gilded Age, when stories of this sort ran continually in William Randolph Hearst's (1863-1951) *New York Journal* and Joseph Pulitzer's (1847-1911) *New York World*. Vendors sold these daily papers on the street for about a cent, following the precedent set by the *New York Herald* and other "Penny Press" papers of the 1830s. In order to increase circulation, Hearst and Pulitzer tried to surpass each other in outrageousness, running headlines like "Baptized in Blood." Among other crowd-pleasing features in the papers were the first color comic strips, such as Richard Outcault's *The Yellow Kid*, which gave yellow journalism its name. The sensationalism of Hearst and Pulitzer reached its height during coverage of the Spanish-American War. This trend was not confined to New York, but also turned up in Denver, Cincinnati, St. Louis, Boston, and elsewhere.

Although "yellow journalism" most often refers to this particular historical moment, its legacy continued into 1920s

943

tabloids such as the *Daily Graphic*, which featured pages half the usual size but still full of outrageous stories and photos. Today one can certainly see echoes of Hearst and Pulitzer in contemporary supermarket tabloids like the *National Enquirer*, *Weekly World News*, the *Globe* and the *Star*, which treat celebrity gossip and the paranormal instead of current events and politics (see Tabloid Newspapers).

Bibliography

Emery, Edwin. *The Press and America: An Interpretative History of Journalism.* Englewood Cliffs: Prentice-Hall, 1962.

Kobre, Sidney. *The Yellow Press and Gilded Age Journalism.* Tallahassee: Florida State UP, 1964.

Milton, Joyce. *The Yellow Kids: Foreign Correspondents in the Heyday of Yellow Journalism.* New York: Harper & Row, 1989.

Mott, Frank Luther. *American Journalism.* 1941. 3d ed. New York: Macmillan, 1962.

Stevens, John D. *Sensationalism and the New York Press.* New York: Columbia UP, 1991.

Martha A. Tanner

Yogi Bear and his smaller bear-buddy Boo Boo were among the favorites in the crop of cartoon characters created for television in the 1950s. The conniving Yogi ("Smarter than the average bear!") has held his appeal through several revival series.

Bill Hanna and Joe Barbera had been executive producers of MGM's cartoon unit for less than two years when it shut down in 1957. The two immediately went into television production, trading on their reputations as directors of the *Tom and Jerry* cartoons. Their first series was *The Ruff and Ready Show*, an adventure serial about a dog and cat team sold to NBC.

In 1958, Hanna-Barbera produced its first syndicated series, *The Huckleberry Hound Show*, distributed by Columbia Pictures' Screen Gems arm and sponsored by Kellogg's Cereal. The slow-talking, "Clementine"-mangling bloodhound hosted, supported by two other segments: *Pixie and Dixie*, a rehash of the *Tom and Jerry* formula, and *Yogi Bear*. The show won the 1959 Emmy award for children's programming, the first for an animated series, and drew up to 16 million viewers around the world. Yogi spun off into his own syndicated anthology, *The Yogi Bear Show*, in 1961, supported by *Snagglepuss* ("Exit, Stage left") and *Yakky Doodle*.

The premise of most Yogi Bear plots can be said to have some appeal to adults as well as children. Yogi (voiced by Daws Butler) was a nonconformist, driven by his simple desire for tourists' picnic baskets. Boo Boo (Don Messick) played Yogi's conscience ("I don't think the Ranger will like that, Yogi"), while Ranger John Smith (also Don Messick) tried to keep Yogi from turning Jellystone National Park upside down ("Why can't you eat nuts and berries like the nice bears?" "Nuts and berries? Sheesh!"). Yankee catcher Yogi Berra thought the name constituted defamation of character, but Hanna-Barbera steadfastly claimed the similarity of names was sheer coincidence.

Yogi's popularity, like that of most cartoon shows, was supported by a well-oiled publicity machine. Kellogg's sponsorship put Hanna-Barbera characters in their commercials and on the boxes: Yogi plugged Kellogg's OK's (just like Cheerios, but with a letter K added). Yogi and Boo Boo appeared on toys, comic books, and strips, and those ubiquitous Kenner Giv-a-Show Projectors. The most manifest tie-in came with the opening of a chain of Yogi Bear's Jellystone Park campgrounds, many of which are still in operation today.

The Yogi Bear Show was in production for two seasons, then repeated for years afterward. In 1964, Yogi starred in Hanna-Barbera's first theatrical feature, *Hey There, It's Yogi Bear*. Yogi was revived in 1973 as leader of *Yogi's Gang* (ABC), where he and Boo Boo teamed with other characters from Quick Draw McGraw to Atom Ant to battle pollution and other "relevant" evils from a flying ark. The team-up formula was repeated in *Scooby's All-Star Laff-A-Lympics* (1977-80, ABC) and *Yogi's Space Race* (1978-79, NBC). Yogi returned to Jellystone Park for a new syndicated series in 1988; and in 1992, the Hanna-Barbera gang was featured as hip-hopping youngsters in *Yo, Yogi!* (ABC).

Bibliography

Brasch, Walter M. *Cartoon Monickers: An Insight into the Animation Industry.* Bowling Green, OH: Bowling Green State U Popular P, 1983.

Lenburg, Jeff. *The Encyclopedia of Animated Cartoons.* Rev. ed. New York: Facts on File, 1991.

Mark McDermott

See also

Children's Network Programming

Young, **Lester** (1909-1959), was an important African-American saxophonist who developed an approach to jazz improvisation that influenced many other jazz instrumentalists. His innovations in the 1930s led directly to the emergence of modern jazz. Many big band arrangements from the swing era forward employ melodies and short, repeated phrases created by Young while he was a member of the Count Basie Band, and his light, relaxed way of playing was the basis for the sound of cool jazz in the 1950s.

Known as "The Pres"—a nickname given him by the singer Billie Holiday, who called him the "president" of all saxophonists—Young was voted "The Greatest Tenor Saxophonist Ever" by 100 leading musicians in 1955. His life has provided inspiration and material for the romantic myth of the tragically alienated jazz genius, re-created in films such as *'Round Midnight* (1986).

Raised for his first ten years in the Algiers quarter of New Orleans, Young eagerly followed the city's parade music while working odd jobs on the streets. Both of Young's parents were musicians, and his father attended Tuskegee Institute, taught at New Orleans University, and worked as a high school principal before devoting himself to music full time around 1919 as leader of a circus band built around the Young family. Due to life on the road, Young never got beyond fourth-grade level in reading and writing, a deficiency which later caused him to avoid reading or signing contracts and contributed to his difficulties as a band-leader. According to biographers, the pervasive racism he experienced in his youth in the South, as well as in Minneapolis, where his family later settled, helped shape his hermetic and often misunderstood public persona.

Young's complex personality is as important to his legendary status as his musical innovations. He was noted for his wit and insight, expressed in his personal, cryptic, often profane and always creative argot. Some of Young's expressions have been incorporated into common parlance in the jazz world. Young's followers imitated not only his musical but his personal mannerisms as well, including his trademark porkpie hat and distinctive way of holding the horn at a 45-degree angle. His slow, shuffling walk and style of dress were adopted by hipsters in the 1940s and 1950s. His abuse of alcohol, which contributed to his death at the age of 50, and marijuana were also prominent aspects of his image.

While his personal style was largely self-created, Young's musical style developed out of the improvised instrumental interpretations of the blues played by black musicians in the Southwest during the 1920s and 1930s. Yet he was influenced as a youth primarily by white saxophonist Frankie Trumbauer and his bandmate, Bix Beiderbecke. He did not move to Kansas City until 1933, where, in informal after-hours performances or jam sessions, the Kansas City jazz style evolved (see entry). That style was most prominent in the Count Basie Band, which Young joined for the first of several times in 1934. One of those jam sessions, a famous meeting between Young and the most influential tenor saxophonist of the day, Coleman Hawkins, is considered a watershed in jazz history.

A sensitive and private man who was hurt by early criticism of his style, Young finally found his niche with the Basie band. His first national recognition came while a star performer with Basie, and he was featured prominently on records and radio broadcasts from the mid- to late 1930s, including several seminal sessions with Holiday, although he did not gain the attention of the majority of the jazz audience until the mid-1940s.

Young's ambition to lead a group of his own caused him to leave Basie in 1940, but he did not possess the necessary organizational skills and eventually rejoined Basie in 1943. Just as he was beginning to garner wide acclaim, however, Young was drafted into the army, where he was not allowed to play with the regimental band, was court-martialled for drug use in 1945, dishonorably discharged, and imprisoned for ten months.

Young's popularity and income soared in the late 1940s and 1950s, when he toured with the all-star "Jazz at the Philharmonic" series, topped jazz polls, and became the inspiration for another generation of young jazz players such as Sonny Rollins and Stan Getz. He frequently appeared in Europe, and his distinctive phrases were widely emulated. Yet his drinking increased, he was hospitalized on several occasions, and his skills declined. He died in a hotel room overlooking the famous New York jazz club, Birdland.

Bibliography
Büchmann-Möller, Frank. *You Just Fight for Your Life: The Story of Lester Young*. New York: Praeger, 1990.
Dance, Stanley. "Lester 'Prez' Young." *The World of Count Basie*. New York: Scribner, 1980.
Feather, Leonard. "Prez." *From Satchmo to Miles*. New York: Stein & Day, 1972.
Green, Benny. "Lester Young." *The Reluctant Art: The Growth of Jazz*. New York: Horizon, 1975.
Porter, Lewis. *Lester Young*. Boston: Hall, 1985.

Lynn Darroch

Young, Neil (1945-), guitarist/vocalist, has since the mid-1960s had an active career and has influenced a new generation of artists who mix the thrash/grunge sound of guitar feedback with folk and country tunes and sensibilities.

Neil Young was born in Toronto; even though Canadian imagery has lingered in his songs, most notably "Helpless," he and his work have been identified with Southern California and the groups that emerged from there in the mid- to late 1960s.

The Squires, Young's first musical group, formed while he was in high school in Winnipeg; another member of the Squires, Stephen Stills, would be an important part of Young's musical life. Moving to Toronto, Young formed the Mynah Birds, whose lead singer, Rick James, went on to later fame as a Motown funk star. When the Mynah Birds broke up, Young moved to Los Angeles, where he again met up with Stills. Together they formed Buffalo Springfield, one of the most creative bands to emerge in America in the sixties.

Buffalo Springfield (see entry) consisted of Young, Stills, Richie Furay, Dewey Martin, and Bruce Palmer (who was later replaced by Jim Messina). Though all members contributed to the success of the group, it was Young and Stills who contributed the bulk of their characteristic songs. Tensions within the group led to their breakup in 1968. Furay and Messina went on to form Poco, and then Messina the duo Loggins and Messina. Stills would soon join with Byrds' outcast David Crosby and British singer-songwriter Graham Nash, late of the Hollies, to form Crosby, Stills & Nash (CSN). Young signed as a solo act to the Reprise label and released his eponymous first album (1968).

Neil Young set the tone for the folk-rock movement that would dominate much of the 1970s. For his next effort, *Everybody Knows This Is Nowhere* (1969), Young recruited an L.A. band then known as the Rockets, but soon renamed Crazy Horse. With Crazy Horse (Ralph Molina, drums; Billy Talbot, bass; Danny Whitten, guitar, replaced by Frank Sampedro), Young was able to combine both the melodic country-pop of songs like "Cinnamon Girl," with the blistering acidic feedback-driven sound of the title song and "Cowgirl in the Sand."

Appearing at Woodstock in August 1969 as a solo act, Young also joined Crosby, Stills & Nash for a few songs. This event led to Young joining the group to record *Déjà Vu* (1970). Young contributed "Helpless," "Country Girl," and "Everybody I Love You" (co-written with Stills). Touring as

Crosby, Stills, Nash & Young, the group set box-office records. "Ohio," written in response to the killing of students by National Guard troops at Kent State University on May 4, 1970, became one of their biggest hits.

Young never considered CSN&Y a permanent situation for himself and released *After the Gold Rush* (1970), with members of Crazy Horse, as well as Stephen Stills, Nils Lofgren, and Greg Reeves. Reaching No. 8 on the album charts, *After the Gold Rush* generated the Top 40 "Only Love Can Break Your Heart" and "Southern Man," a harsh criticism of Alabama governor George Wallace.

Switching gears once more, Young, working with a group of musicians dubbed the Stray Gators (including Tim Drummond, bass; and Jack Nitzsche, piano and steel guitar) and a selection of friends (Linda Ronstadt, Stephen Stills, Graham Nash, James Taylor), recorded *Harvest* (1972), Young's first No. 1 album. "Heart of Gold," featuring Linda Ronstadt, was a No. 1 single. Taking a bit of a break, Young released *Journey through the Past* (1972), a soundtrack that included remakes of his earlier songs, and the live album *Time Fades Away* (1973).

The death of Crazy Horse guitarist Danny Whitten and roadie Bruce Berry from heroin overdoses inspired the recording of *Tonight's the Night* (1975) with members of Crazy Horse and Lofgren. A scathing commentary on contemporary drug culture, *Tonight's the Night*, though recorded in 1973 and 1974, was not released until after *On the Beach* (1974), a much lighter and upbeat album. *Zuma* (1975) included Young's epic commentary on Spanish imperialism in South America, "Cortez the Killer," which was recorded with Crazy Horse and banned in Spain.

Long May You Run (1976) found Young and Stills reunited as the Stills-Young Band and included a tour. Young's next solo album, *American Stars 'n' Bars* (1977) was a compendium of tunes recorded from 1974 through 1977 with a collection of bands (including Crazy Horse on "Like a Hurricane") and friends (Linda Ronstadt, Emmylou Harris, and Nicolette Larson). On *Comes a Time* (1978), Young returned to softer, country-tinged roots. He reunited with Crazy Horse in 1979 for *Rust Never Sleeps*, which included the hits "Hey Hey My My" and "Powderfinger." It was followed by two disappointingly received albums, *Hawks and Doves* (1980) and *Re-ac-tor* (1981).

Young's series of albums in the 1980s jumped from techno pop (*Trans*, 1982), to rockabilly (*Everybody's Rockin'*, 1983), country (*Old Ways*, 1985), and back to rock and roll (*Landing on Water*, 1986). *This Note's for You* (1988), recorded with a nine-piece horn section, included the title single's acerbic send-up of corporate sponsorship of rock music, for which the video was pulled from MTV. Ironically, the video went on to win MTV's video of the year award.

Young reunited with CSN in 1988; they recorded *American Dream*, and included seven Young compositions (three with Stills), including the standouts "Name of Love" and "American Dream." In 1989 Young recorded his strongest solo album in years, *Freedom* (1989), followed by *Ragged Glory* (1990), with Crazy Horse. A world tour with Crazy Horse resulted in the live album *Weld* (1991). In 1993, Young returned to the softer folk-pop sound with *Harvest Moon* (1992), a conscious harkening back to 1972's *Harvest* that was recorded with many of the same musicians. Confirming his popularity and relevance, Young gave an "unplugged" performance for MTV (recorded as *Neil Young: Unplugged*, 1994) that included acoustic versions of many of his best-known electric songs. Young's title song for the film *Philadelphia* was nominated for an Academy Award in 1993. *Sleeps with Angels* (1995) was a critically praised collaboration with Crazy Horse; a collaboration with the grunge band Pearl Jam (see entry)—*Mirror Ball* (1995)—followed.

Bibliography

Einarson, John. *Neil Young: Don't Be Denied*. Kingston: Quarry, 1992.

Henke, James. "The *Rolling Stone* Interview: Neil Young." *Rolling Stone* 2 June 1988: 42-46, 49, 74.

Light, Alan. "Forever Young." *Rolling Stone* 21 Jan. 1993: 34-37, 53-54.

Martin R. Kalfatovic

Zap is a descriptive term for the way in which viewers avoid commercial advertisements in television broadcasts. The principal requirement for effectively "zapping" an advertisement is the remote control device. Armed with a remote control, TV viewers can "zap" commercials during broadcasts by flipping through other channels for the commercials' duration. Zapping allows the viewer to browse programs broadcast on other networks. Often, however, this effort to avoid commercials results only in viewing the commercials broadcast on other networks.

The advertising industry, interested in discovering the effect videocassette recorders (VCRs) have on viewers' ability to avoid commercials, has occasionally distinguished between the two VCR-facilitated forms of advertisement avoidance by using two different variations of the term zap. The term zapping is reserved for instances in which viewers completely eliminate commercials during the recording of a program, while the term zipping refers to fast-forwarding through commercials while viewing a previously recorded program.

Bibliography
Freidwald, Will. "Wired: State of the Zap." *Village Voice* 21 Nov. 1989: 53.
Morton, Andrew. "Ad Makers Zap Back." *Channels* Sept. 1989: 30-31.

Cynthia J. Wachter

Zappa, Frank Vincent (1940-1993), was one of America's most prolific, enigmatic, and controversial composers. His work crossed the boundaries of rock, jazz, and modern styles, bringing many innovations to rock and modern music. His humorous, expletive-laced rock lyrics boldly attacked prevailing religious, social, political, cultural, and sexual norms and values, positing Zappa as a counter-culture hero who gave voice to the strange, the weird, and the "freak." Zappa's appeal eventually captured a diverse range of rock, jazz, and serious music enthusiasts.

In 1951, Zappa's parents began a series of moves from his native Baltimore, MD, that led the family to Lancaster, CA. Zappa's music was often the product of and reaction to his transplanted West Coast roots. At 15, Zappa bought a copy of Edgar Varese's *Ionizations,* an album of experimental music consisting of drums and sirens. This avant-garde work captivated Zappa, who often cited Varese and Igor Stravinsky as major musical influences. By his late teens, Zappa, having no formal musical training, began composing orchestral works. Several of Zappa's early albums, particularly *Uncle Meat* (1968), include transitional passages nearly duplicating the *Ionizations* pieces.

Finding no market for his modern classical music, Zappa turned to film scores and rock. In 1965, Zappa moved to Los Angeles, which provided an audience more receptive to his avant-garde style. At a time when being weird meant being normal, Zappa fit right in. The small-yet-growing "freak" movement in Los Angeles, coupled with a recording industry that was open to signing alternative artists, helped launch Zappa's career.

Committed to a mix of R&B, rock, classical, and experimental music, Zappa planned to hook the public with his commercial music while fostering an appreciation of more experimental and classical forms. This mix can be heard in Zappa's first album, *Freak Out,* recorded in 1965 by his group the Mothers of Invention. The album's liner notes not only defined the term "Freak Out," but Zappa's career, as well: "a process whereby an individual casts off outmoded and restrictive standards of thinking, dress, and social etiquette in order to express CREATIVELY his relationship to his immediate environment and the social structure as a whole."

Within a quarter century, Zappa released more than 60 albums, performed thousands of live concerts, and produced several films, including the cult classic *200 Motels.* Though his songs were responsible for several popular catchphrases —"Don't Eat the Yellow Snow," "Titties and Beer," and "Valley Girl"—Zappa had few hits.

Although he was denied radio airplay and banned from record bins in various states, Zappa's impact on the music industry was nothing short of phenomenal. Zappa was the first to release a double-record rock concept album (*Freak Out*); the first to use guitar effects processors commercially; the first to exploit fully the potential of multitrack recording technology; the first performer to combine full-stage theatrics, lighting, and live music; and the first to combine jazz and rock stylings to create what later became known as "jazz fusion," with notable selections found on the albums *Hot Rats* (1969), *Waka Jawaka* (1972), and *The Grand Wazoo* (1972). Unfortunately, many of Zappa's innovations have been credited to more popular musicians.

Even those unfamiliar with his music recognize Zappa as a controversial social commentator, activist, and—in some cases—comedian. Since the early sixties, Zappa was an outspoken campaigner against drug abuse and a fervent supporter of voter registration efforts. In 1985, Zappa entered mainstream politics as an outspoken opponent of record labeling sponsored by the Parent's Music Resource Center (PMRC).

Zappa successfully walked the line between outspoken public figure and recluse. In 1989, Zappa gave up his frequent world tours to work 16-hour days in his studio, recording new works on his multi-million-dollar Synclavier digital music workstation. In 1987, his Synclavier-based album *Jazz from Hell* won a Grammy for best "Rock Instrumental."

While Zappa failed to transform a listening public mired in 4/4 music, he became the harbinger of trends and technologies that still affect the industry. While few accepted his more avant-garde music, such controversial songs as "Jewish Princess" and "Titties and Beer" introduced mainstream rockers to Varese and Stravinsky—whether they knew it or not.

Bibliography

Gehr, Richard. *Zappa's Universe*. Liner notes. New York: Verve Records, 1993.

Miles. *Zappa: A Visual Documentary*. New York: Omnibus, 1993.

Shelton, Robert. "Son of Suzy Creamcheese." *New York Times* 25 Dec. 1966.

Slonimsky, Nicholas, ed. *Biographical Dictionary of Musicians*. 8th ed. New York: Schirmer, 1992.

Zappa, Frank, and Peter Occhiogrosso. *The Real Frank Zappa Book*. New York: Simon & Schuster, 1989.

Michael B. Kassel

Zworykin, Vladimir K. (1889-1982), was the engineer who, along with Philo T. Farnsworth, is considered the inventor of modern television (see Television Technology). Zworykin, a native of Russia, came to the United States in 1919 after serving in the Russian Army Signal Corps during World War I. In 1920, Zworykin was hired by Westinghouse Electronics Corporation to develop an electronic television system. While Francis Jenkins had demonstrated TV as early as 1925, Jenkins's system depended on a combination of mechanical and electronic means to transmit moving images. However, mechanical television had many limitations, particularly with regard to picture resolution; if television was ever going to be accepted by a mass audience, it would require the picture improvements afforded by an electronic system.

Working for Westinghouse, Zworykin patented a TV camera tube (the iconoscope) and a picture tube (the kinescope) in 1923 and 1924, respectively. Although Westinghouse was unimpressed by the system, an RCA official hired Zworykin as its Director of Electronic Research in 1929. As Zworykin continued his electronic television research, a bitter battle ensued between Zworykin's RCA system and the one being developed by Farnsworth. RCA eventually was forced to adopt Farnsworth's system.

Bibliography

Abramson, Albert. *Zworykin: Pioneer of Television*. Urbana: U of Illinois P, 1995.

Brown, Les. *Les Brown's Encyclopedia of Television*. Detroit: Visible Ink, 1992.

Udelson, Joseph H. *The Great Television Race*. University: U of Alabama P, 1982.

Michael B. Kassel

Zydeco is a deeply rooted, highly spirited part of Louisiana's indigenous and diverse musical landscape. The name is thought to originate from the fusion of sounds from the first two words of the French expression "les haricots sont pas salēs" ("the snap beans ain't salty"), which appeared in some of the earliest recordings of the music in the 1930s.

A cultural hybrid, zydeco refers to the traditional music of the black Creoles, while the closely related, yet distinct Cajun describes the music of the white Cajuns. Historically, zydeco has its roots in the sounds French settlers took with them to the Acadian colony (eventually Nova Scotia) in the 17th century. In 1755, when the Acadians were exiled by the British, a few thousand Acadians moved to the French colony Louisiana. The various groups coexisting there combined to produce two distinct cultures—Cajun and Creole—each with its own music. Each tradition represented in the cultural gumbo provided essential elements to Cajun and zydeco music. French roots gave zydeco a language and specific lyrics. Zydeco's African base gave it syncopation, rhythm, and improvisation. Various Native American tribes, such as the Houmas and Chitimachas, contributed a wailing, terraced singing style and a drumming tradition that overlapped with black Creole origins. The Spanish contributed guitar and melodies, while the Germans eventually introduced the diatonic accordion in the 19th century when merchants began importing newly invented instruments. Anglo-American lyrics, jigs, and reels were also adapted into tunes in French, the language of this fusion.

During the 1980s, zydeco was "rediscovered," and joined Creole and Cajun cooking as Louisiana's major cultural export sweeping the country. Despite the death of the "King of Zydeco," Clifton Chenier (see entry), in 1987, several musicians distinguished themselves within the thriving musical genre. C. J. Chenier replaced his legendary father as leader of the Red Hot Louisiana Band, while Queen Ida was crowned "Queen of Zydeco." Rockin' Dopsie and the Twisters and Buckwheat Zydeco (Stanley Dural) were touring, had major record label contracts, and collaborated with numerous artists, including Paul Simon and Hank Williams, Jr. Terrance Simien's music was featured in the popular film *The Big Easy* (1987). Longtime zydeco bandleader Boozoo Chavis came out of retirement, and Rockin' Sidney (Simien) crossed over from rhythm and blues, producing the best-selling zydeco single of all time, "My Toot Toot." The new wave of zydeco performers includes Nathan Williams and the Zydeco Cha Chas, Lynn August, Zydeco Force, and the Zydeco Rockers.

Bibliography

Allan, Johnnie. *Memories: A Pictorial History of South Louisiana Music, 1920's-1980's*. Lafayette: Jadfel, 1988.

Gould, Philip. *Cajun Music and Zydeco*. Baton Rouge: Louisiana State UP, 1992.

Kuhlken, Robert, and Rocky Sexton. "The Geography of Zydeco Music." *The Sounds of People and Places: A Geography of American Folk and Popular Music*. Ed. George O. Carney. Lanham: Rowman, 1994.

Lichtenstein, Grace, and Laura Dankner. *Musical Gumbo: The Music of New Orleans*. New York: Norton, 1993.

George Plasketes

Index

951

954

963

966

978

McCorquodale, Barbara 140
McCoy 189
McCoy, Tim 904
McCrory's stores 507
McCrumb, Sharyn 675
McCullers, Carson 114, 422
McCulley, Johnston 12
McCullough, Colleen 524
McCullough, David 126, 175
McDaniel, Hattie 331, 925
McDaniel, James 584
McDonald, Maurice 276
McDonald, Richard 276
McDonald's restaurants 269, 276
McDonough, Sean 362
McDowall, Roddy 178, 474
McDowell, Josh 606
McDuff, Jack 81
McEachin, James 566
McElligot's Pool 238
McEntire, Reba 524
McEwen, Joe 260
McFadden, Gates 783
McFarlane, Leslie 365
McGee, Fibber 343, 662
McGee, Kirk 542
McGee, Mark Thomas 203
McGee, Sam 339, 542
McGee, Travis 230, 363, 524-25, 562
McGeehan, W. O. 778
McGhee, Brownie 28
McGillis, Kelly 294
McGinley, Phyllis 525
McGinniss, Joe 525, 561, 813, 856
McGirt's Weekly 270
McGoohan, Patrick 566, 640
McGowan, Robert 591
McGrath, Paul 429
McGraw, John 64
McGregor, Ewan 786
McGuinn, Jim 128
McGuinn, Roger 207, 320
McGwire, Mark 703
McHale's Navy 865
McHugh, Drake 670
McInerny, Ralph 675
McIntire, John 883
McKeag, Alexander 148
McKeehan, Toby 222
McKellar, Danica 932
McKenzie, Scott 508
McKernan, Ron "Pigpen" 340
McKimson, Robert 892
McKinley, Ray 387
McKinney, Nina Mae 924
McKinney's Cotton Pickers 674
McKinsey, Beverlee 755
McKuen, Rod 465, 525
McLachlan, Sarah 286
McLaughlin, Emily 317
McLaughlin, John 220
McLean, Don 525-26
McLendon, Gordon 526, 664
McLish, Rachel 106
McMahon, Ed 139, 306
McMahon, Vince, Jr. 936
McMillan, Dennis 117
McMillan and Wife 189, 417, 455, 616
McMurtry, Larry 495, 526-27, 902, 908
McNear, Howard 38

McNeely, Big Jay 185
McNichol, Kristy 252
McPhee, John 576
McPherson, Aimee Semple 663, 810
McQueen, Steve 82, 417, 603, 827
McRae, Carmen 302
McShann, Jay 454
McSorley's Bar 63
McTeague 901
"Me and Bobby McGee" 449
Me and Juliet 695
Me and the Chimp 514
Meadows, Audrey 403
Meadows, Jayne 26, 306
Mean Streets 225, 717
Meaney, Colm 784
Means, Russell 428
Means of Escape 876
Meat Men 192
Meatballs 555
Medawar, Mardi Oakley 571
media coverage of soap operas 527-28
Medical Center 238, 294
medical mysteries 528, 562
Medical Question Box 116
Medicine Ball Caravan 717
Medicine Man 199
Meditations in Green 876-77
Mediterranean Caper, The 215
Medium Cool 879
Meet Corliss Archer 23
Meet John Doe 201, 782, 846, 924
Meet Me at the Mall 103
Meet Me at the Morgue 503
Meet Me in St. Louis 313, 532
Meet the Beatles 73
Meeting of the Minds 26
Megatrends 197
Meier, Garry 217, 659
Meikle, Pat 161
Meineke, Christoph 168
Meisner, Randy 259
Meisner, Sanford 602
Meissner, Linda 438
Mekas, Jonas 241
Mel, Melle 668
"Melancholy Baby" 63
Melcher, Martin 221
Mellencamp, John Cougar 28, 529
Melmoth the Wanderer 406
melodrama in film 529-30
Melrose Place 296, 476, 530
Melville, Herman 33, 110, 274, 280, 406
Melvins, the (band) 350
Memoirs of a Woman of Pleasure 273
Memoirs of Sherlock Holmes, The 250, 399
Memoirs of the Life of Fanny Hill 273
Memorial Album 364
Memorial Day 395
"memorial park" 342
memorials 733
Memories Are Made of This 516
"Memory" 896
Memphis Belle 240
Men, The 86, 114, 846
Men in Black 715, 841
Men in White 304

Men with Wings 21
Mencken, H. L. 63, 132, 421
Mendelssohn, Felix 169
Menendez brothers 814
Menken, Adah Isaacs 834
men's action fiction 880
Menschen am Sonntag 741
Menzies, W. C. 331
Mephisto Waltz, The 22
Mercati, Cynthia 564
"Mercedes Benz" 449
Mercedes-Benz 655
Mercer, Johnny 7, 81, 459, 510, 530-31, 559
Mercer, Mabel 80
Mercury Players 143, 662
Mercury Theater on the Air, The 468, 662, 890, 898
"Mercy Mercy Me (The Ecology)" 316
Meredith, Don 206
merengue 388
Meriwether, Lee 509, 845
Merman, Ethel 43, 84, 212, 380, 531, 681, 759
Merrick, David 380
Merrick, John 501
Merrie Melodies 40, 64, 141, 890
Merrill, Carol 309
Merrill, Gary 816
Merrily We Roll Along 759
Merritt, Abraham 13, 32, 113
Merriwell, Frank 234, 768
Merry Pranksters 8
Merry Whirl, The 286
Merry-Go-Round 136
Merry's Museum 160
Mertz, Barbara 335, 389, 533
Merv Griffin Show, The 822
Message from Nam 876
Messenger 481
"Messiah, The" 168
Messianic Communities 439
Messick, Dale 193
Messina, Jim 121, 285
Messmer, Otto 40
Messner, Roe 58
Meston, John 352, 829
Metalious, Grace 606
Metallica 373
Metamora; or, The Last of the Wampanoags 834
Metamorphosis 431
Metcalf, Laurie 700
Metheny, Pat 185
Metrecal diet 272
Metro-Goldwyn-Mayer (MGM) 79, 141, 188, 531-32, 864
Metronome 459
Metropolitan Opera House 319
Meusel, Bob 702
"Mexican Shuffle" 29
Mexican Spitfire, The 54
Mexicans, humor about 419
Mexico 533
Meyer, Andrew 204
Meyer, Nicholas 820
Meyer, Russ 223
Miami Pop Festival 431
Miami Vice 202, 476, 510, 532-33, 617
MIAs 880
Michael Zager Band 235

Michaels, Barbara 335, 389, 533
Michaels, Grant 315
Michaux, Lightfoot Solomon ("Elder") 97
Micheaux, Oscar 925
Michelson, Charles 657
Michener, James A. 148, 491, 533, 820
Michigan Fed 268
Mickey Mouse 40, 88, 120, 141, 192, 241, 723
Mickey Mouse Club, The 5, 161-62, 414, 533-34, 848
Micro Millennium, The 197
microcomputers 508
Microsoft 196, 234, 314
middle-of-the-road (MOR) radio format 664
Midge doll 60
Midler, Bette 449, 922
Midnight Cowboy 394
Midnight Express 790
Midnight Louie books 39
Midnight Love 316
"Midnight Meat Train, The" 61
Midnight Run 226
Midnight Special 96, 920
"Midnight Special" 77
"Midnight Train to Georgia" 324
Midsummer Night's Dream, A 169
Mighty Ducks 731
"Mighty Fortress Is Our God, A" 16, 168
Mighty Like a Rose 207
Mighty Manfred 241
Mighty Morphin Power Rangers 164
Mighty Mouse 163
Mighty Mouse: The New Adventures 72, 676
Mighty Sparrow 134
Mighty Thor 465
Mikado, The 91, 321
Mike Hammer 562, 567
Mike Mulligan and His Steam Shovel 493
Mike Shayne 54
Milagro Beanfield War, The 673
Mildred Pierce 132
Miles, Alfred H. 186
Miles, Vera 592
"Miles Away" 119
Miles in the Sky 81
Milestone, Lewis 249
Milhaud, Darius 119
Militant, The 864
military songs 534-35
Milius, John 42
Milk and Honey 380
Milland, Ray 255
Millar, Kenneth 503
Millar, Margaret 503, 843
Mille Miglia 655
millenarian movements 680
Millennium (album) 260
Millennium (TV show) 941
Miller, Ann 560
Miller, Arthur 474, 543, 835
Miller, Frank 68, 191
Miller, Glenn 93, 509, 535-36
Miller, Johnny 329
Miller, Marilyn 681
Miller, Mark 710

994

Robertson, Robbie 56
Robeson, Jennifer 113
Robin and the Seven Hoods 132
Robin Hood 156, 169, 178
Robin, the Boy Wonder 68, 69
Robinson, Anne 916
Robinson, David 139
Robinson, Earl 28, 117
Robinson, Edward G. 189, 310, 892
Robinson, Hubbell, Jr. 614
Robinson, Jackie 573, 769
Robinson, Lynda S. 389
Robinson, Smokey 324, 831
Robinson, Vicki Sue 235
Robinson Crusoe 12, 157
Robinson Crusoe, Jr. 445
Robocop 715
Robot Dreams 46
Robot Monster 714
Robot Visions 46
Robotman 12
Robots and Empire 47
Robots of Dawn, The 47
Robson, Mark 55
Roc 19
Rock, The 199
"Rock a Beatin' Boogie" 358
Rock All Night 203
Rock and Roll Hall of Fame 444, 489, 605, 636, 696, 832, 911
Rock and Roll Show, The 301
Rock and Soul Gospel 167
Rock around the Clock 358
rock climbing/sport climbing 686, 843
"Rock Me on the Water" 119
"Rock 'n' Roll" 480
rock 'n' roll 72, 85, 93, 99, 128, 139, 155, 176, 209, 219, 259, 459, 480, 610, 626, 686-88, 859, 935, 947
rock 'n' roll dancing 688
Rock 'n' Roll High School 204
Rock 'n' Roll Revival 727
"Rock of Ages" 169
Rock, Rock, Rock 85
Rock Steady Crew 115
"Rock the Joint" 358
Rock-a-Bye Baby 719
Rockbird 99
"Rocket 88" 358
Rocket J. Squirrel 691
Rocket Ship Galileo 374
Rocketeer, The 21
Rockford Files, The 506, 567, 688-89, 819
Rockford (IL) Peaches 25
Rockin' Dopsie and the Twisters 155, 948
Rockin' with the Rhythm 451
Rocking Horse Secret, The 11
Rockwell, Norman 418, 689-90, 709
Rocky 468, 690-91
Rocky and Bullwinkle 122, 691
Rocky and His Friends 122, 691
Rocky Horror Picture Show, The 298, 691-92
Rocky Mountain Collection, The 227
Rocky Mountain High 227
Rocky Mountain Reunion 227
Rod and Custom 51

Rod Serling's Liar's Club 725
Roddam, Franc 298
Roddenberry, Gene 692
Roddy, Rod 307
Rodeheaver, Homer 334
rodeo 692-94
Rodgers, Jimmie 142, 355, 391, 597, 695-96
Rodgers, Nile 139
Rodgers, Richard 35, 120, 694, 836
Rodgers and Hammerstein 83, 262, 366, 694-95, 759
Rodgers and Hart 81, 83, 559, 683
Rodney, Red 57, 381
Rodney Stone 250
Rodriguez, Paul 190, 476
Roe, Tommy 397
Roebling, John A. 126
Roebling, Washington 126
Roeg, Nicholas 313
Roger and Me 146, 241, 252
Rogers, Buck 120, 761
Rogers, Fred 161, 165, 539, 651
Rogers, Ginger 48, 59, 357, 370, 380, 559, 684, 847, 923
Rogers, Kenny 819, 913
Rogers, Mimi 213
Rogers, Rosemary 700
Rogers, Roy 116, 208, 241, 405, 511, 667, 740, 827, 903, 923
Rogers, Wayne 520
Rogers, Will 190, 286, 421, 427
Rogers, Will, Jr. 822
Rogue Queen 222
Rogue River Feud 347
Rohmer, Sax 13
Rolaids 254
Roland, Gene 458
role-playing games 696-97
Rolie, Gregg 706
"Roll, Freedom, Roll" 301
"Roll, Jordan, Roll" 683
"Roll On, Columbia" 353, 683
"Roll Out! Heave Dat Cotton" 682
"Roll Out the Barrel" 63
"Roll over Beethoven" 85, 687
Rolle, Esther 19, 522
roller coasters 197
roller derby 697
"Rollin' and Tumblin'" 550
Rolling Stone 297, 590, 864, 919
Rolling Stones, the 8, 30, 85, 93, 147, 231, 257, 350, 397, 437, 448, 489, 664, 672, 687, 697-99
Rolling Thunder Revue 56
Rollins, Sonny 185, 493
Rollins, Walter E. 172
Rollo books 157
Rolonda 464
Roman Hat Mystery, The 327, 653
Roman Holiday 377, 923
Roman Scandals 58, 83
Romance of Helen Trent, The 661
Romance on the High Seas 132, 221
romance series 699-700
Romancing the Stone 55, 249, 667
Romano, Ray 190
romantic horror fiction 407, 700
Romberg, Sigmund 366, 695
Romero, George 408, 410
Romita, Johnny "Ring-A-Ding" 517
Romper Room 161
Ronald McDonald 183

Ronson, Mick 258
Ronstadt, Linda 118, 180, 207, 259, 286, 397
Roogie's Bump 65
Rookies, The 616
Room 222 18, 89, 909
Rooney, Andy 421, 504, 745
Rooney, Mickey 475, 532
Roosevelt, Eleanor 152, 651
Roosevelt, Franklin D. 152, 174, 239, 372, 398, 690
Roosevelt, Theodore 152, 422
Roosevelt Hotel 397
Root, George Frederick 535
Rootie Kazootie 161
Roots 5, 47, 819
Roots of Heaven, The 285, 422
Rope 392
Rosalie 318
Rose, Billy 43
Rose, Charlie 745
Rose, Felipe 881
Rose, Fred 9, 913
Rose, Ruth 462
Rose, The 449
Rose, Tricia 386
Rose Marie 560
Rose Tattoo 474
Roseanne 5, 190, 205, 554, 700-701, 745, 923
Rosedale, Roxanne 309
Roseland Ballroom 375
Rosemary's Baby 143-44, 407-9, 411, 463, 701
Rosenberg, Alan 216, 817
Rosenberg, Charles B. 816
Rosenman, Joel 934
Rosenthal, Jane 226
Rosenthal, Peter 603
Rosenzweig, Barney 131
Rosetta Stone 238
"Rosie the Riveter" 357
Rosmaniere, John 942
Ross, Diana 316, 433, 547, 645, 832
Ross, Earle 343
Ross, Jerry 9, 80
Ross, Marion 362
Ross, Norman 117
Ross, Wallace 180
Rossington, Gary 502
Rosza, Miklos 80
Roszak, Theodore 197
Roth, Alan 833
Roth, David Lee 96, 870
Roth, Eric 511
Roth, Philip 421, 769
Roth, Robert 877
Rothapfel, Samuel F. "Roxy" 281
Rothman, Stephanie 204, 411
Rouch, Jean 240
Rough Mix 910
Roughead, William 857
"'Round about Midnight" 540
"Round and Round Hitler's Grave" 353
"'Round Midnight" 540
'Round Midnight 482, 944
Roundtree, Richard 318
Rousseau, Jean-Jacques 157
Route 1 384
Route 66 384
Route 66 384, 435

Rover Boys books 158
Rowan, Dan 476, 915
Rowan and Martin's Laugh-In 915
Rowe, Debbie 434
Rowe, Nicholas 400
Rowles, Jimmy 598
Roxanne 188
Roy Rogers Show, The 828
Royal Family, The 279
Royal Gelatin Hour 82
Royle, Edwin Milton 426
Rozsa, Miklos 559
Rubber Soul 551
Rubin, Don 364
Rubin, Jonathan 877
"Rude Boy" 512
Rudner, Rita 190
"Rudolph the Red-Nosed Reindeer" 171, 580
Rudy the Fifth 259
Rue cases negres/Sugar Cane Alley 924
Rue Morgue (bookshop) 554
Ruff and Ready Show, The 162-63, 944
Ruffin, David 831
Rugrats 165
Rugulo, Pete 459
Rukeyser, Louis 504
Rule, Anne 561, 856
"Rule Them Rudie" 512
Rum Punch 485
rumba 388
Rumble Fish 385
Rumpelstiltskin 524
Run-D.M.C. 115, 575
Run for Cover 130
Run for Your Life 43
Run Silent, Run Deep 304, 474
"Runaway" 437
Runaway Bunny, The 118
"Runaway Child, Running Wild" 832
Runaway Horses 326
Runaway Jury, The 349
Runes Album 480
Runestaff Histories 544
Running Like the Wind 515
Running Man, The 711
Runyon, Damon 421, 769, 778
RuPaul 403
Ruprecht, David 309
rural sitcoms 331, 344, 376
Rush 27
Rush, Otis 873
Rush, Tom 118
Rush to Judgment 240
Rushmore 556
Russ, Joanna 701-2, 712
Russell, Charles 903
Russell, Curly 76
Russell, George (actor) 828
Russell, George (musician) 185
Russell, Harold 86
Russell, Jane 370, 702, 905
Russell, Ken 298, 411, 444, 910
Russell, Leon 574
Russell, Lillian 272
Russell, Mark 190
Russell, Rosalind 82, 369, 543, 718
Russell, Todd 306
Russia House, The 199, 479

Rust, Fred 346
Rust Craft cards 346
Rust Never Sleeps 231
Rustler Rhapsody 348
Ruth, Babe 64, 93, 115, 702-3, 772, 921
Rutherford, Margaret 513
Ruttan, Susan 817
Ryan, Irene 87
Ryan, Meg 756, 922
Ryan's Hope 317, 703
Ryden, Hope 253
Ryder, Winona 356
Ryder Cup 328, 329
Rydgren, John 664
"Rye Whiskey" 208
Ryman Auditorium 339
Rymer, James Malcolm 406, 869

Saam, Byrum 666
Saban Entertainment 164
Sabatini, Rafael 12, 704
Saberhagen, Fred 869
Sabrina 291, 377
Sachs, Eddie 253
Sackett, Susan 251
Sacred Clowns 384
Sacred Songs and Solos 334
Sacrilege, The 389
Sad Sack, The 367
"Sad Songs Say So Much" 444
saddle-bronc riding 693
Sadie Thompson 802, 922
Sadler, Barry 878
Safer, Morley 745
Saga of Gosta Berling, The 311
Saga of the Viking Women and Their Voyage to the Waters of the Great Sea Serpent 203
Sagal, Katey 514
Sagan, Carl 704
Sager, Carol Bayer 360
Sahara 215
Sahl, Mort 190, 822
Said, Edward W. 576
Saint, Eva Marie 340, 393, 583
Saint Bernards 242
Saint James, Susan 189, 417, 455
Saint Joan 359
Sainte-Marie, Buffy 117, 705
Sainted Devil, The 867
Sajak, Pat 310, 822
Saks, Sol 88
Salaambo 174
Salem's Lot 464
Salinas, Ric 476
Salinger, J. D. 144, 421
Salkind, Alex and Ilya 799
Sally 821
Sally of the Sawdust 280
Salmi, Albert 38
salsa dance 389
Salsbury, Nate 911
"Salt Peanuts" 76, 595
Salute to Spring 486
Salvador 791
Salvage 348
Salvage 1 348
Salvation Army 63
Sam and Dave 433, 705-6
Sam and Friends 442
"Sam Bass" 208
Sam Benedict 816

Sam 'n' Henry 17, 37, 660, 742
samba 388
Same Train, a Different Time 355
Samonda, Shereen 920
sampler quilts 654
Sampson, Will 428, 578
Samson, Albert 363
"San Antonio Rose" 914
San Francisco 304
San Francisco Beat 616
San Francisco Examiner 88
Sanchez, Marco 476
Sand in the Wind 877
Sand Pebbles, The 82
Sandburg, Carl 124, 159, 525
Sanders, Harland 276
Sanders, Pharoah 67, 188
Sandman 11
Sandow, Eugene 106
Sands, Tommy 77
Sands of Iwo Jima, The 894
Sands of Mars 177
Sandy (dog) 241
Sandy, Gary 918
Sanford, Isabel 19
Sanford and Son 19, 447, 572
Sangester, Jimmy 299
Sankey, Ira D. 334
Santa Barbara 820
"Santa Claus Is Comin' to Town" 171
Santa Fe Trail 905
Santana 8, 706, 934
Santana, Carlos 8, 706
Santeria 882
Santiago, Maria Elena 396
Sapheud, The 456
Sapper (Cyril McNeile) 843
"Sara" 437
Sarah, Plain and Tall 359
Sarandon, Susan 357, 923
Saratoga 304
Saratoga Trunk 279
Sarazen, Gene 328
Sargent, Dick 88
Sargent, John S. 552
Sarnoff, David 8
Saroyan, William 589
Sarris, Andrew 292
Sass and Brass 873
Satanic Rituals, The 488
Satchadinanda, Swami 934
satellite dishes 706-7
satellite transmission 707-8
"Satisfaction" 231, 697
Satterthwait, Walter 675
Saturday Evening Post, The 33, 374, 682, 689, 708-9
"Saturday in the Park" 156
Saturday Night 758
Saturday Night Fever 77, 235, 468, 709, 855
"Saturday Night Is the Loneliest Night of the Week" 132
Saturday Night Live 78, 82, 136, 190, 455, 482, 569, 575, 709-10
Saturday Night with Connie Chung 900
Saturday Review 34
Saturn Girl 11
Saucerful of Secrets 610
Saudek, Robert W. 588
Saul, John 407

Saunderson, Kevin 669
Savage, Fred 252, 931
Savage, John 879
Savage, William 168
Savage Seven 431
Savalas, Telly 509, 617
Savannah State College 95
"Save It for Me" 296
Saved 258
Saviano, Josh 932
Savidge, Jennifer 704
Saving Private Ryan 361, 765
Savitch, Jessica 302
Sawyer, Corinne Holt 513
Sawyer, Diane 745
Sawyer Brown 710
"Say Goodbye to Hollywood" 443
"Say It Again" 913
"Say It Isn't So" 84
"Say It Loud—I'm Black and I'm Proud" 118
Say It with Songs 445
Say One for Me 212
Say When 405
Sayers, Dorothy L. 6, 169, 213, 230, 327, 349, 421, 434, 562, 675
Sayles, John 204, 402
Saylor, Steven 389
Sayonara 114, 533, 925
Scalawag 249
Scandals 287, 680
Scanlan's Monthly 841
Scanners 410
Scapegoat, The 255
"Scar Tissue" 671
Scaramouche 704
Scarecrow 529
Scarecrow and Mrs. King 543
Scarface 255, 310, 369, 790
Scarlatti Inheritance, The 499
Scarlet Pimpernel, The 12, 382
"Scarlet Ribbons" 77
Scarlett 331
Scarry, Richard McClure 710-11
Scent of a Woman, The 59
Scent Organs, the 257
Schaap, Dick 778
Schaefer, Jack 881, 902
Schaeffer, Susan Fromberg 876
Schaffer, Paul 487
Schary, Dore 458, 532, 590
Scheherazade, legend of 74
Scheider, Roy 435
Schell, Maximilian 603
Schell, Orville 302
Schenck, Joseph M. 861
Scherf, Margaret 675
Schickele, Peter 448
Schiff, Stephen 900
Schindler's List 529
Schlee, George 312
Schlesinger, John 819
Schlesinger, Leon 40, 890
Schmeling, Max 497
Schmit, Timothy B. 259
Schneider, Abe 188
Schneider, Bert 578
Schnessel, S. Michael 589
Schoedsack, Ernest B. 461
Schoenberg, Arnold 119
Schoenbrun, David 271

Scholastic Books 160, 699
Scholten, Jim 710
Scholz, Jackson V. 768
Scholz, Tom 110
"School Day" 85, 86
School Daze 481
Schoolhouse Rock 161
"School's Out" 373
Schoonmaker, Thelma 922
Schoonover, Frank 156
Schorr, Daniel K. 271
Schott, Marge 920
schottisches 200
Schow, David J. 407
Schroder, Rick 585
Schroeder 601
Schubert, Franz 168
Schulberg, B. P. 340
Schulberg, Budd 108
Schuller, Robert 810
Schulz, Charles 101, 190, 193, 241, 277, 601
Schumacher, Joel 68
Schwannecke, Ellen 143
Schwartz, Arthur 319
Schwartz, Sherwood 226, 322
Schwarzenegger, Arnold 106, 711
Schwimmer, David 301
science fiction 41, 46, 86, 88, 98, 111-12, 117, 120, 140, 177, 222, 232, 326, 374, 408, 409, 417, 488, 653, 701, 711-12, 845, 874
science fiction films 712-16
Science World 160
Scientific American 35
Scoggins, Jerry 87
SCOLA 182
Scooby-Doo 162, 716
Scoop 910
Scoppettone, Sandra 279, 315
Scorpions 270
Scorsese, Martin 204, 225-26, 294, 471, 716-17
Scots, humor about 419
Scott, Bill 122
Scott, Clement 169
Scott, Dave 856
Scott, George C. 38, 238, 582
Scott, Hazel 925
Scott, Leon 608
Scott, Randolph 906
Scott, Ridley 232, 291
Scott, Selina 900
Scott, Sir Walter 12, 168, 202, 599
Scott, Willard 710
Scottish folk ballad 295
Scottsville Squirrel Barkers 128, 259
Scrabble 103, 310
Scream 749
"Screamer, The" 440
Screaming Trees, the 349
Screen Actors Guild 47, 497, 658, 670
Screen Extras Guild 658
Screen Gems 188, 247, 284
Screen Writer's Guild Award 731
Screw 223
screwball comedy film 432, 717-19
Screwtape Letters, The 488
Scribner's 34, 597
Scruggs, Earl 87, 284, 339, 359, 542

997